SPARTAN SPORTS

ENCYCLOPEDIA

A History of the Michigan State Men's Athletic Program

JACK SEIBOLD

www.SportsPublishingLLC.com

Director of production: Susan M. Moyer
Project manager: Tracy Gaudreau
Interior design: Jennifer Polson
Dust jacket design: Christine Mohrbacher
Developmental editor: Mark E. Zulauf
Copy editors: Cynthia L. McNew and Holly Birch

ISBN: 1-58261-219-6

Photographs in *Spartan Sports Encyclopedia* are courtesy of the Michigan State University Sports Information Department, the University's Department of Archives and Historical Collection, H. Frank Beeman and the school's annual *Wolverine* from which photos were copied.

Dust Cover (front):

Through the years, Michigan State University has supported men's varsity intercollegiate teams in 15 different sports. Through uniform, apparatus or equipment, each is represented in the collage on the front of this book's dust cover. Those sports, the year of their introduction at MAC-MSC-MSU and the representative items in the collage are as follows:

Baseball (1884): jersey (away), hat, baseball bat, gloves, and batting helmet.
Track and Field (1886): MSC sweatshirt (lower left), trophies (far left and far right), shoes (leaning on the trophy at the right).
Football (1896): helmet, retro helmet (circa 1920, left of batting helmet), two balls (Rose Bowl and one used in 1913 win over Michigan), jersey (worn only one year—2002).
Basketball (1899): ball, net, jersey (1979 vintage), Michigan Aggies pullover.
Cross Country (1910): jersey (between MAC pennant basketball jersey).
Tennis (1913): racquet and balls.
Hockey (1922): stick, puck and skates.
Swimming and Diving (1922): 1945 national championship trophy (above boxing gloves), kick board, goggles and suit (behind lacrosse stick).
Wrestling (1922): headpiece (barely visible to left of boxing gloves).
Fencing (1926): helmet and sabre weapon.
Golf (1928): clubs and ball.
Boxing (1934): mounted gloves (trophy of 1951 NCAA championship team).
Gymnastics (1948): rings (yellow, below football helmet).
Soccer (1956): ball (far left) and jersey (upper right with block "S").
Lacrosse (1970): stick.

Photographs

Find the following Spartan heroes pictured on the dust cover collage: Jim Cotter in action (BS 77-79C), undefeated 1951 football team, 1963 Big Ten championship fencing team, Joe Selinger (HO 57, 58, 59), Charlie Wedemeyer (FB 66, 68), Greg Kelser (BK 76, 77, 78 CoC, 79 CoC), Stan Drobac (TE 52, 53), 1956-1957 basketball team, 1951 boxing champions Chuck Spieser and Jed Black with coach George Makris and All-American Don Mason (FB 47, 48, 49).

Also in the picture is a marching band hat with plume (far left, center), Jack Heppinstall's trainer bag (lower far left), MAC blanket (senior varsity award), 1988 Rose Bowl ticket, miniatures of Beaumont Tower, Spartan statue and Spartan Stadium.

Dust Cover (back):

Spartans pictured on back of the dust cover are (from the top and clockwise) Clarence "Biggie" Munn, Mateen Cleaves, Earvin "Magic" Johnson, Ron Mason, Charles "Bubba" Smith, Jud Heathcote, Kirk Gibson and Robin Roberts.

Printed in Canada

Sports Publishing L.L.C.
www.sportspublishingllc.com

During 2001-2002 as workmen completed their task of thoroughly renovating Jenison Gymnasium-Fieldhouse, memories of athletes who toiled there in the 1940s and 1950s were rekindled. This was "home" for members of all sports that comprised the Michigan State intercollegiate program of the time. While sharing Jenison's common facilities, a fraternal linkage and loyalty transcended team to team. It is to these men this publication, *Spartan Sports Encyclopedia*, is dedicated.

From the words of Joe DiBello, who wrestled for Fendley Collins from 1949-1951, one gleans the sense of camaraderie that has prevailed among the Spartans, both past and present:

Remember when:

• The wrestling room was on the top floor of the Jenison gymnasium across from the boxing practice room. We would occasionally sneak over to watch someone else take it on the chin for a change.

• On the gymnasium floor down below, gymnasts were swinging, bouncing and generally doing all those impossible stunts with the urging of George Szypula.

• Not far from there, the fencing practice room was filled with the noble athletes of thrust and parry, charge and retreat, all under the watchful eye of Coach Schmitter. What a friendly, considerate man Charley was. A real friend to all athletes.

• An occasional slip into the warm pool area was a good way to keep a sweat going and watch the swimmers suffer for a change. When it comes to practice, misery loves company, and Coach McCaffree managed to extract his measure of sweat and toil from the swimmers.

• Later, our after-practice road work around the fieldhouse basketball court reminded us that the glory boys of the hoop world were also paying their dues with practice, practice, practice!

• And finally, those friendly and smiling faces of Robby and Jack, the best and most caring trainers ever to staff a training room—anywhere!

CONTENTS

Foreword vii
Acknowledgments ix
Introduction xi

Michigan Agricultural College

1884-1893 1
1893-1899 7
1899-1904 13
1904-1909 19
1909-1910 27
1910-1911 33
1911-1912 39
1912-1913 45
1913-1914 51
1914-1915 59
1915-1916 65
1916-1917 71
1917-1918 77
1918-1919 83
1919-1920 89
1920-1921 95
1921-1922 101
1922-1923 107
1923-1924 113
1924-1925 119

Michigan State College

1925-1926 125
1926-1927 133
1927-1928 139
1928-1929 145
1929-1930 151
1930-1931 157
1931-1932 165
1932-1933 171
1933-1934 177
1934-1935 185
1935-1936 193
1936-1937 201
1937-1938 209
1938-1939 217
1939-1940 223

1940-1941 231
1941-1942 239
1942-1943 247
1943-1944 253
1944-1945 255
1945-1946 261
1946-1947 269
1947-1948 277
1948-1949 285
1949-1950 295
1950-1951 303
1951-1952 313
1952-1953 325
1953-1954 335

Michigan State University

1954-1955 345
1955-1956 353
1956-1957 363
1957-1958 373
1958-1959 381
1959-1960 391
1960-1961 399
1961-1962 409
1962-1963 417
1963-1964 425
1964-1965 433
1965-1966 441
1966-1967 451
1967-1968 461
1968-1969 469
1969-1970 479
1970-1971 489
1971-1972 499
1972-1973 509
1973-1974 517
1974-1975 525
1975-1976 533
1976-1977 541
1977-1978 549
1978-1979 559
1979-1980 569
1980-1981 579
1981-1982 589
1982-1983 601
1983-1984 611

1984-1985 621
1985-1986 631
1986-1987 643
1987-1988 653
1988-1989 665
1989-1990 677
1990-1991 689
1991-1992 701
1992-1993 717
1993-1994 729
1994-1995 743
1995-1996 755
1996-1997 767
1997-1998 779
1998-1999 791
1999-2000 803
2000-2001 817
2001-2002 831
2002-2003 845

Athletic Venues 859
Athletic Directors 872
Glossary 874

Statistics

Baseball 877
Basketball 901
Boxing 921
Cross Country 923
Fencing 932
Football 939
Golf 960
Gymnastics 967
Hockey 973
Lacrosse 988
Soccer 992
Swimming and Diving 998
Tennis 1009
Track and Field 1020
Wrestling 1034
Letterwinners 1045

Bibliography 1075

FOREWORD

Nick Vista

THE MOST EXHAUSTIVE RESEARCH EVER UNDERTAKEN on Michigan State University men's athletics has resulted in the publishing of *Spartan Sports Encyclopedia,* authored by Jack D. Seibold, a Spartan varsity swimming letterman, and later a long-time member of the university's admissions office.

THIS GIGANTIC PROJECT TRACKS MORE THAN 7,000 FORMER ATHLETES and coaches who have represented Michigan State over three centuries in 15 different varsity sports and includes such Spartan luminaries as Magic Johnson, Kirk Gibson, Robin Roberts, Biggie Munn and Duffy Daugherty.

SECTIONS OF "GREAT STATE DATES" CHRONICLE MORE THAN 1,200, GAMES, MEETS AND MATCHES in which Michigan Agricultural College, Michigan State College and Michigan State University competed and won. Supplementing these facts and figures are first-hand accounts of the action of more than 30 familiar heroes, including former school presidents Frank Kedzie and John Hannah.

SEIBOLD USED AS HIS LAUNCHING PAD THE PUBLICATION *Spartan Saga,* a brief history of State athletics published in 1971 by retired MSU athletic business manager and 10-time Spartan letterwinner Lyman L. Frimodig, and veteran MSU sports information director Fred W. Stabley Sr.

JACK TOOK OFF FROM THERE, SPENDING THOUSANDS OF HOURS for many years digging through records in the MSU sports information office and in the MSU archives, as well as reading clips from *The Lansing State Journal* and *The State News,* MSU's student daily, and several MSU history books.

FROM THE 19TH CENTURY BASEBALL TEAMS of MAC to MSU's championship basketball teams of the 21st century, these and numerous other surprising particulars are "Spartlited" throughout the pages.

ALSO INCLUDED ARE INCREDIBLY THOROUGH APPENDICES that contain all the statistics one person can handle— letterwinners, coaching records, season and career statistics by sport, and much more.

READERS CAN EASILY FIND DETAILS ON NATIONAL CHAMPIONSHIPS earned by State teams in football, cross country, soccer, basketball, boxing, swimming and diving, gymnastics, hockey and wrestling, as well as records of team titles earned in the Big Ten since State entered the conference in 1950.

SEIBOLD, ONE OF THREE BROTHERS FROM JACKSON, MICHIGAN, who earned varsity letters in swimming, has kept a close watch on the Spartan athletic scene since his undergraduate days. Over the years he served the swimming team as the starter at home dual meets. He has also made outstanding contributions to the Varsity Alumni "S" Club, organization of alumni letterwinners, including stints as president and editor of the club's publication.

IT TOOK MASSIVE EFFORTS TO PUT TOGETHER THIS ENCYCLOPEDIA. Jack has made his publication a most interesting and enlightening one and has created "must" reading for genuine Spartan fans young and old. It is a splendid production that one can keep elbow's length away for years to come. Those in the Spartan world will hail Jack Seibold for his dedication.

Nick Vista
MSC Class of 1954
MSU Sports Information, 1955-1988

"I have always thought that a sound athletic program was good for a university. It is good for the athletes, if they are full-time bona fide students who must maintain satisfactory standards of scholarship and performance. Athletics unify a university probably more than any other feature of the institution. They merge the enthusiasm of students, alumni, faculty, friends and supporters of the university, and all to the university's good."

John Hannah
From his book, *A Memoir*
Michigan State University Press, 1980

ACKNOWLEDGMENTS

Fred Stabley, who served MSC-MSU as sports information director from 1948 to 1980, had his *Spartan Saga* published in 1971. Co-authored with Lyman Frimodig, this 264-page book was the first definitive written history of Michigan State athletics. Copies of the *Saga* likely remain today on bookshelves of countless media people across the state.

Shortly after his retirement from the University, Fred replaced former swim coach Charles McCaffree in the roll of executive secretary for the Michigan State Varsity Alumni "S" Club, a position Stabley would hold before "retiring again" in 1992. It was during those years I served in various capacities for the "S" Club (board member, secretary and president) and consequently worked with Fred on various projects. It was sometime in 1991 he introduced the idea to me of undertaking the assignment of writing an updated version of his 1971 *Saga*. Although flattered by his suggestion, I deferred a positive decision until after my own retirement from the University later in that same year of 1992. Facetiously, I suggested it was finally time to put my 1950 MSC degree into action (BA from the School of Journalism with a minor in history). Soon thereafter, research was underway for *Spartan Sports Encyclopedia,* the eventual sequel to *Spartan Saga*. It was never envisioned to be an *11-year* on-again off-again project; yet that's exactly what it became. Regrettably, Fred Stabley will never see this completed product. He died on December 8, 1996.

Of the many stories about MAC-MSC-MSU sports that remain untold, none are more conspicuous by their absence from *Spartan Sports Encyclopedia* than those pertaining to the Spartan women. Meanwhile, we have documented a period of more than 120 years represented by nearly 7,000 male athletes within more than 1,000 pages of copy—and even keeping the material close to this prescribed limitation has proven to be a nearly impossible task. Many features had to be streamlined or eliminated and an early decision was made to refrain from including the story of women's sports. For now, I apologize to the ladies in Green and their coaches. An equivalent publication awaits.

Grandson Jeremy Lantz could be defined as a co-author, a driving force and certainly a technical genius in the strange world (to me) of personal computers. During latter years of this project, his support has been all of the above and more. Production could have stretched beyond 11 years had he not been the incessant taskmaster.

Next, I wish to recognize Mike Pearson, former assistant sports information director at MSU and past SID at the University of Illinois. Mike continually extended encouragement and advice to me during the ongoing years of preparing this publication. I admire his writing skills and extensive knowledge of the collegiate sports scene.

No one could successfully proceed on a writing project such as this without the support of the given school's Sports Information Department. John Lewandowski, assistant athletic director for media relations, and his staff continually welcomed me and provided the necessary assistance while sharing information and services of their office. Particularly helpful have been Becky Olsen, sport information director and office assistant Paulette Martis both have proven to be excellent ambassadors for their office and MSU.

Individually, a pair of young men came aboard for short stints in 2002 to assist in writing some stories of the 1980s and 1990s. They were Ben Phlager, who was with the Sports Information Department at the time and Eric McKinney, a member of *The State News* writing staff. Thanks to both.

Two additional university departments provided support, the Archives and Historical Collections along with the microfilm staff at the library. Likewise, the microfilm services of the State of Michigan Library afforded valuable information.

Thanks to the following who assisted in assembling and staging the collage which highlights the dust cover of the book: Jim Cotter, Glen Brough, Rick Atkinson, Bob Knickerbacker, Dave Pruder, Ted Mahan, Tom Minkel, Richard Bader, Joe Baum, Rich Kimball, Matt Gianiodis, Tom Magee, Fred Freiheit, Val Berryman and Mike Vollmar.

Orchestrated by grandson Jeremy, the proofreading team was a family affair. Included were his parents Carol and Lee Lantz, along with brother Jason and sisters Michelle and Heather. Also, imported from Muncie, IN, came daughter, Laura Caudill-Seibold and her son Ritchie. From Adrian, MI, another daughter, Jill Forman and her son Tyler, an MSU student, joined the team.

The list of Spartans who provided stories and story material for this book is too lengthy to single them out as individuals. Thanks to one and all.

Finally, to Dianne, my patient and understanding wife. Somehow she had envisioned that "retired life" would unfold a bit differently. Month after month, year after year, all too often she found that existing as a writer's "widow" could be extremely lonely. Dianne was pleased to experience "fini" as she joined the family proofreading team. An apology and many thanks are extended to Dianne.

Go Green!
Jack Seibold
JDSeibold@aol.com

INTRODUCTION

On Wednesday, May 13, 1857, the Agriculture College of the State of Michigan was dedicated with proper ceremony, and on the next morning, 63 young men filed from their dormitory, Saints Rest, and reported for classes in College Hall.

It had not been an easy birth. Even in mid-19th century, the shadow of "big brother" in Ann Arbor was ever present. While debate raged in the state legislature over the establishment of the new agricultural school, Henry P. Tappan, president of the University of Michigan, actually traveled to Lansing and lobbied in opposition. He explained that he would resist the location of the school anywhere except in Ann Arbor. Fortunately, for sundry reasons, Tappan was not popular among legislatures, and as a result, his resisting words ultimately fell upon deafened ears. On February 12, 1855, governor Kingsley S. Bingham signed the bill that authorized the new school.

From that day and over a lengthy period of 14 years, this new experiment in higher education continually faced an issue of survival. The school's leaders, out of necessity, focused on overcoming a seemingly endless list of unforeseen roadblocks: ongoing financial hardships, mass student enlistment into the Union army, a malaria outbreak, and a diphtheria epidemic that took five lives in 1862. Three years earlier, in 1859 and amidst one of the frequent fiscal emergencies, a bill was actually introduced in the legislature that would have closed the school, auctioned its assets, and created a department of agriculture science at the U of M. Although this measure was defeated by a vote of 50 to 21, the idea would not vanish. In the biennial legislative sessions of 1867 and 1869, similar bills to transfer operations of the college to Ann Arbor enjoyed substantial support.

Finally, in March of 1869, the opposition crumbled when the legislature approved not only that year's appropriations but also a grant of $30,000 for a new dormitory. The Agriculture College of the State of Michigan was finally secure. The editor of the *Lansing Semi-Weekly Republican* (a precursor to the *Lansing State Journal*) wrote: "This is the fifth battle for the college that we have had a hand in. We rejoice in the victory."

―――――――――――――――――――

At the time of founding the school, there were virtually no organized sports in the USA as we now know them. Then, from the end of the Civil War until the turn of the century, the gaslight era saw the greatest surge of sports in this country's history. It would remain for the academicians of the time to evaluate whether or not to welcome these new symbols of Americana onto their individual campuses. As for the Agriculture College, there was no significant support for the proponents of sports and, in fact, there were two unique realities that worked heavily against such thinking.

First, the philosophy of the Agriculture College was to combine 15 hours a week in class with 15 to 20 hours in manual labor, which often consisted of clearing land and planting fields. With such wholesome exercise built-in, a question prevailed whenever debate of organized sports would arise: why waste time kicking a football or batting a baseball when a shovel or rake can be picked up and productively put to use?

Though during those forerunner years a portion of the students likely disapproved of toiling in the fields, they did in fact receive monetary earnings. An hourly rate that began at five cents was inflated to seven and one-half cents by 1874 and prior to classes of the ensuing year, the scale had jumped to 10 cents per hour.

It was theorized that the practice of joining farming with classroom science would result in scientific agriculture. Whether or not this 19th century equivalency of co-operative education was instrumental in proving this supposition, the policy remained in place until 1896.

Also in place through the first four decades of the school's existence was yet another reality of the time, the school's unique three-term academic year running from the final week of February until late November. Upon altering the three terms to the more traditional September to June, also in 1896, the calendar became more harmonious with those of sister institutions; consequently, ultimate scheduling of athletic contests would become more harmonious.

With this pair of policies removed, the work program and the unique calendar, campus adherents of organized athletics had reason to celebrate.

―――――――――――――――――――

From student diaries and letters it seems that typical informal athletic activities took place on the campus from its conception. One student, C.J. Monroe, recorded such activities as hop-step-jump, running races, pom-pom pullaway, tag, leap frog, along with "one" and "two"-cat ball games (baseball, using only one or two bases.). Other references were made to quoits, wicket ball, and football (soccer). It was also chronicled that a trapeze and swinging rings were suspended from campus trees. A reference in the *1896 Heliostat*, an early yearbook, alludes to "the open-air gymnasium that developed our early athletes." As for swimming, it takes little imagination to visualize one or more fatigued student-laborers at day's end scurrying for a dip in the cool waters of the Red Cedar River.

Young men of the 1800s were likely no different from those of contemporary times. Regardless of studies or work schedule, they presumably sought ways of unleashing energy and enjoying themselves in leisure time. As a result, semi-organized team activities eventually evolved with perhaps soccer and baseball—the sports to gain early attention. Also, in the 1870s, rugby appeared and croquet and lawn tennis became popular.

The early weekly publication, *The M.A.C. Record*, carried stories of three letters from graduates on consecutive Tuesdays in May of 1916. Each gave testimony to memories of early baseball on campus with C.M. Thayer (class of 1868) of Flushing reaching back the furthest to 1865. He reported that back then not much was known of athletics, but there happened to be one student in their midst, Monroe Diver of Marshall, who had seen a baseball game on a visit to Detroit. Meeting with a group of interested students in the chapel of College Hall, Diver described the game as best as he could recall. Subsequently, a team was organized with this "father" of MAC athletics, Monroe Diver, being chosen as the pitcher while C.M. Thayer, the storyteller, was selected team captain. Practices began on the site of Williams Hall (current location of the museum).

As confirmed in Madison Kuhn's book, *Michigan State, the First Hundred Years*, that team of 1865 called itself the Star Base Ball Club. They wore red caps with long visors and shiny black belts with white stars and the initials B.B.C. for Base Ball Club. (The word baseball was often reported as two words.) Their first game was a 34-27 win over the Capital Club of Lansing, a game that utilized two scorers to account for all of the tallies.

In September of the next year, that Star Club accompanied by four fans, traveled to Mason aboard the newly opened Jackson-Lansing-Saginaw Railroad. This has therefore been recorded as the first rail trip for a Michigan State athletic team.

During that same month, the team was one of four clubs that formed the Central Michigan Baseball Association to stage a tournament at the Central Michigan Fair in Lansing. In the opening round the Stars this time lost to the Capital Club by a score of 65 to 48. The ultimate tournament winner, the Monitor Club of St. Johns, defeated the Farmers Club of Okemos.

S.M. Tracy (class of 1868), yet another who chronicled those early years, recalled the sport of baseball flourishing when he entered MAC in 1866. There were so few students (only about 100) that some faculty members were recruited to be members of the team. Included was standout pitcher Dr. Daniells, assistant in chemistry. Also recalled were Prentiss of botany and Cook of entomology, the latter playing second base until he broke his ankle sliding into home. Tracy reported losing to the University of Michigan in 1868 by a score of 2-1, declaring the small score as a "world record" for the time.

Frank S. Kedzie (class of 1877 and college president from 1915 to 1921) recalled baseball teams from his youth, having come to Agricultural College (the actual name of the community at that time) in 1863 at the age of six. He suggested there were games against teams from the University of Michigan even earlier than 1884, the year generally accepted as the first between the two schools.

The majority of the games played in those early years were against town teams that were springing up in neighboring communities. Even as collegiate games against the U of M and Olivet would mark the year 1884 as the first "official" MAC baseball team, matches against nines from neighboring villages and cities would remain on the schedule into the early 1890s. Included were Cass, Ionia, Owosso, Greenville, Battle Creek, Charlotte, Jackson, Northville, Sparta, and Flint.

There is the story of yet another MAC team that in 1871 traveled to Detroit to play one of that city's top sandlot teams. The game was rained out and thus negated the game receipts that had been earmarked for payment of the return rail fare. Although there is no record of how long it took them to return home, they eventually hitchhiked rides on horse-drawn buggies.

In the 1870s, the *Semi-Weekly Republican* now and then printed a column entitled Agricultural College News. It featured stories ranging from bee keeping to an occasional baseball game, such as:

—Friday, June 25, 1875: A match game of ball players last Saturday between a nine from Lansing and a college nine resulted in a score of 33 to 22 in favor of the college.
—Friday, June 21, 1877: The sophomore class base ball club played at Bath Saturday, June 16, with a score of 25 to 24 in their favor.
—Tuesday, May 22, 1877: A match game of base ball between the Nine-Spots of the junior class and a picked nine from the college resulted in favor of the college nine with a score of 16 to 9.

Then this story, where the reporter found an accident during the game more newsworthy than the contest's results:

Tuesday, June 8, 1875: Quite a serious accident happened to one of the students during a game of base ball last Saturday. The club slipped from the hands of the striker, hitting one of the students in the face and smashing his nose.

The most renowned of these early baseball clubs was the Nine Spots, organized by the class of '78 and mentioned in the preceding news story of May 22, 1877. W.K. Prudden, a member of that team was the third alumnus to write his baseball memoirs for *The MAC Record* in 1916. During the break between summer and fall terms of 1877, the Nine Spots played in Jackson, Charlotte, Hastings, Grand Rapids, Owosso, and Flint, traveling between points by train and winning four of the six games. There were 10 men on the team with the one substitute serving as water boy and infrequently filling in at one of the positions. Tiring of menial duties and inactivity, the 10th man periodically resigned to be replaced by some other hopeful.

The Nine Spots owned 10 brown-trimmed white flannel uniforms, bats, balls, and little more. Catcher Prudden used neither mask nor chest protector and caught with a common buckskin work glove from which the fingers had been removed.

The pitcher depended on varying speeds, either a swift ball or a slow ball delivered with his hand below the waist. Yet the man at the plate somewhat controlled his own destiny. The rules provided that the hitter could designate the desired location of the pitch, either a high ball (between the shoulder and waist) or a low ball (between the waist and knees). To be called a strike, the ball had to be delivered within the requested range. Initially there was no curve ball, but by 1877 members of the team had heard of it and collected $10 to get a player from Detroit to demonstrate. As Prudden reported:

The $10 was easy to get, as some of the subscribers expected a return of their money. The curver having agreed to perform gratis in case he did not curve the ball.

In addition to Prudden, who later became a prominent Lansing philanthropist and industrialist (Prudden Wheel Co., later the Motor Wheel Co.), team members included: Jay Monroe, pitcher; Satterlee Trowbridge, first base; Charles Shilling, second base; Ed Rawson, shortstop; James Lewis, third base; Ollie Foote, left field; E.H. Hunt, center field; and F.E. Skeels, right field.

Obviously, upon graduation of the class of 1878, the Nine Spots folded. With them went the brown-trimmed white flannel uniforms and the balls and bats that comprised their equipment.

As noted earlier, it is conceded that students of the 1860s, 1870s, and 1880s likely engaged in additional sports, even if in an unstructured way. During his comments in 1916, Prudden recalled, "There was no football as the game is now played, simply old style rugby [soccer], in which the hand played no part in the game."

There is ample indication that during this period a growing number of students favored institutional support for intercollegiate sports. This was evident from *The Speculum* of April 1882, in which the editor stated the following position:

Why can we not form a College athletic association? The matter has been discussed for some time. Now that the season for sports and out of door work is opened, why can we not agitate the question? It is safe to say that every College of equal prominence with ours has such an association and that the students derive both pleasure and profit from it. Why should we be behind other Colleges in this respect? At present our sports are confined to an occasional scrub game of baseball or to a miscellaneous kicking of the football. Why cannot the energy displayed in these games be organized and improved?

Apparently there were no converts.

Four years later, in August of 1886, the editor of that same student publication (by now a monthly at 75 cents a year or 10 cents a copy) wrote a lengthy commentary as follows:

We hope it will not be long before the athletics of the college are as well organized as are the other departments. The value of systematic physical training in college is too well established to need comment here. Anyone who has observed the tireless energy of the strong physique and compared it with the weaker efforts of the enfeebled prodigy of learning cannot hesitate as to which is the wise course for students to follow.

He then pointed out: True, our labor afternoons has (sic) lessened the need of athletics, but when laboratory work partially takes the place of field labor, as it should and doubtless will do as the number of students increases, there will be need for better means of athletic exercises.

Perhaps it was "pressure from the press," but whatever the factor, this time someone was listening. In October of 1886, the management of athletics was consolidated as a student-run athletic association with the popular mathematics professor, Rolla Carpenter, as manager. Under the advice and consent of the still reluctant faculty, this organization was to have control of all college athletics. Until that time, all engagements on the play field had been entered into with no administrative sanction.

The 1884 August issue of The College Speculum praised that spring's baseball team (the school's *first* official athletic team) and credited its success to "awakening some interest in other athletic sports, enough so to give birth to our first field day, which was held on the grounds June 14." Indeed, the annual field days would eventually provide the opportunity to promote a variety of sports at the Agricultural College. As the program developed over the years, competition would include track and field, baseball, football, gymnastics, tug-of-war, bicycling, fencing, tennis, wrestling, and boxing.

In that same issue of the *Speculum,* a summary of results revealed the events that were contested on June 14: wrestling, throwing a 35-pound weight, running jump (triple jump), 100-yard dash, high kick, broad jump, a tug-of-war between the classes of '86 and '87, a football game between the college 11 and a "picked 11," and a baseball game against the University of Michigan. This latter game was a lopsided 13-3 loss, thanks to 11 unearned runs via 14 errors by the "farmers."

There is no written evidence of who introduced or carried out the idea of that original intramural field day or how the idea would later spread to the campuses of Olivet and Albion. Regardless, in the spring of 1886, representatives from these three schools joined together in reaching an accord to engage in two weekends of athletic competition. The first would take place at the Agricultural College on May 14-15, while Albion College would host the encore on June 4-5. What was initially an intramural event had now become a full-fledged intercollegiate activity.

On June 4, 64 MAC men boarded a special Lake Shore and Michigan Southern railroad train for a two-hour trip to Albion and the second field day of 1886. For no explainable reason, the Olivet men had chosen not to compete in this follow-up weekend of events. Consequently, it was simply MAC vs. Albion. The MAC men carried away prizes in 10 of the 17 events contested.

By the next year, 1887, the idea of field days was solidly in place with three Friday-Saturday dates scheduled. Activities would take place at a trio of sites, Olivet, Albion, and finally on June 3-4 back on the grounds of the Agricultural College. It was at this third field day that Hillsdale College entered a squad of 30 men to become the fourth school in the spring competition. They not only performed well in their first try (two boxing titles and the champion of the 100-yard dash), the men of Hillsdale would contribute significantly to the planning and growth of the annual get-togethers.

Even more momentous was the increased display of acceptance of athletics by the MAC faculty. At the Friday evening reception of June 3, the respected Dr. Robert Kedzie gave the welcome address while professor Liberty Hyde Bailey acted as toastmaster. Furthermore, the turnout of fans was impressive. On that same Friday evening about 600 fans were squeezed into the botanical laboratory for refreshments.

Soon after concluding the field days of 1887, James Heckman of Hillsdale College submitted a proposal to the joint representatives. His plan was to focus on a *single* weekend of field day activities, saving both time and money. Rather than a host school absorbing the primary expenses which might range somewhere between $100 and $300, he suggested that each participating school could annually share the outlay upon payment of a $75 team entry.

The "Heckman" proposal was kept alive over the next eight months and a conference of delegates was called to meet in Jackson on St. Patrick's Day of 1888 to further explore the idea. A number of schools were invited to send representatives, including the University of Michigan. Only four elected to do so: Albion, Hillsdale, Olivet, and Michigan Agricultural College. It was at this initial meeting that the idea of organizing a formal athletic conference first surfaced. Those in attendance were instructed to study the idea and reconvene one week later on Thursday, March 24, at a location in Albion. On that date a constitution was drawn up and the MIAA (Michigan Intercollegiate Athletic Association), under its original name, the Inter-Collegiate Athletic Association, became a reality. It was reputed to be "the *first* athletic conference west of the Allegheny Mountains."

At subsequent annual spring meetings, the field day directors would decide on the prizes for the upcoming events. There was no apparent consistency. One year a winner might be awarded a gold medal, another year a silver medal, yet another an entirely different memento. Occasionally, a more practical prize would be on the line. As examples: in 1888 a racquet and racquet case were accorded the winner in tennis singles; in 1890 the winner of the 400-yard bicycle race was to receive a "fancy" bicycle.

The Brackett Cup, donated by R.E. Brackett, a Lansing jeweler and sports enthusiast, was awarded to the winning baseball team each year. A school could periodically retire a cup after three consecutive championship years. Kalamazoo was able to do it in 1899 and Albion followed three years later.

Points were tallied for individual events (5-3-1 for first, second, and third) with banners being bestowed the school with the highest point total for the indoor events as well as the outdoor events. A special cup and pennant would be the prize for winning the mile relay.

One event introduced in 1889 would attempt to identify the "best all-around" athlete. The winner's award was described as a crescent-shaped badge of gold with diamond set valued at $40. Much like a decathlon, competitors qualified by achieving at least the identified minimal standard in seven of the following 10 events:

hammer throw	70'
running high jump	4' 8"
shot put	25'
hop, step and jump	35'
440-yard run	1 minute
standing broad jump	9' 4"
pole vault	7' 6"
running broad jump	18' 6"
100-yard dash	11.5 seconds
120-yard hurdles	20.0

Of the 10 "best all-around" titles during the years, MAC men carried off seven of the diamond awards: Leander Burnett in 1889, 1890, and 1892, Frank Poss in 1894, George Wells in 1897 and 1898, with Bill Russell the winner in 1899. The event was not held at the rain-shortened 1893 program in Jackson and the event was dropped for good in 1900.

At the first four MIAA field days, only the charter schools (Albion, Hillsdale, Olivet, and Michigan Agricultural College) entered the competition. Michigan Normal (Eastern Michigan) joined the Association and fielded a squad for the first time in 1892. Kalamazoo College joined four years later in 1896, while Alma College was admitted to the Association in 1902. Although Adrian College would not officially become an MIAA member until 1908, they did enter a field day team in 1900.

The MIAA board of directors met twice each year, once in the fall and a second time in the spring, often on the Monday following Field Day. In the process, the assembled delegates would elect officers, resolve disputes, act on new membership, adopt rules, ratify a budget, and approve events for the next year

While the school's administration provided no direct financial support for these field days, the usual tax on students and contributions of up to five dollars each from MAC professors were used for routine expenses. Other ingenious methods were tried.

The baseball team manager, L. Whitney Watkins, was determined to raise money to hire the trainer (coach) from the Detroit Athletic Club (DAC) in preparations for the 1893 field day. With the local baseball grounds lacking a fence it was impossible to generate revenue through gate receipts, so Watkins promoted the sale of 10-cent souvenir tickets among the crowd. The idea was a financial success as nearly everyone purchased the mementos. The DAC trainer was hired.

Fans of the 19th century certainly knew how to exalt in victory. Following success in the championship baseball game of the 1892 field day, more than 200 steadfast MAC rooters rejoiced by throwing hats, canes, umbrellas, chairs—anything they could get hold of—into the air. They then swarmed onto the playing field, swept up their heroes, and paraded around the grounds while yelling, blowing horns, and waving green flags and ribbons. When the crowd had finally quelled, a hat was passed into which $25 was willingly collected from the excited students. With this fund a band of musicians was engaged which led a Saturday night parade into Lansing and, as reported in—*The Speculum*, "The city was painted 'green' by the victors and a general overflow and inflow of good 'spirits' was indulged in."

The field day team of 1897 was particularly applauded. Following an atypical year in 1896 in which the Farmers had slipped all the way to fifth place, the '97 squad had once again reached the pinnacle. Upon their return by rail from Hillsdale, supporters greeted team members, as described in *The M.A.C. Record*:

> When our special train pulled into the depot at Lansing we were reminded of the old days in '90, '91, '92 and '93, the days of Burnett and Boss, when MAC used to return with the lion's share of glory. The whole College was there to greet our victorious representatives, whom they mounted upon their shoulders and, amid blare of tin horns and the glare of fireworks, carried up and down the streets until fairly exhausted. Then taking trolley cars for the College, the overjoyed students kept up their celebration until after midnight.

From that year until 1907, when Michigan Agricultural College would conclude its MIAA competition, they would outscore all other teams in 10 straight field days. In only one year was a team within 20 points of the Farmers. As for that final season, 1907, MAC's total of 67 points would be only one shy of the aggregate for all other schools.

In the late 19th century there was no national governing body to oversee operations pertaining to eligibility for competition, (the NCAA, with the original title, Intercollegiate Athletic Association, was not born until 1906). As a result, individual schools began to invoke their own standards. Such was the case at MAC when in the spring of 1895 a resolution was adopted by the faculty and approved by the Board of Agriculture. It was decreed, commencing that next fall, students who participated in intercollegiate athletic competition would have to meet the following conditions:

(a) He must have been in regular attendance for at least the term preceding the term of competition and shall have taken in that term the equivalent of three studies.

(b) He must have "an average standing of eight or more on the scale of ten [the apparent grading system of the time]."

(c) He must have received a statement, in writing, from the secretary of the faculty certifying his eligibility under these rules.

The significant enrollment growth of the Michigan Agricultural College and its ultimate dominance on the MIAA athletic field would eventually lead to its separation from the association. By 1907, MIAA schools were becoming weary of lopsided loses to MAC, not only in track and field, but other sports as well such as baseball, football, and basketball.

Perhaps a telegram from Albion officials at 7:00 a.m. on the morning of Saturday, November 9, 1907, should have been an indicator of things to come. It was only at that moment MAC athletic director/coach Chester Brewer was informed that Albion College would not be fulfilling its scheduled football game commitment for *that very afternoon.* An immediate telephone call did not result in a reasonable explanation, but local supporters drew their own conclusion—Albion was a weak team and was unwilling to face another humiliating loss. After all, twice that autumn they had been defeated by high school teams, and most recently had suffered a 73-0 loss at Olivet.

The matter chilled into the winter months. Then on Saturday, February 1, 1908, members of the MIAA board of directors (minus uninvited MAC) quietly stole into Lansing and went into secluded executive session at the Hotel Downey. Eight men gathered at 7:30 p.m. and continued deliberation until 4:00 a.m. Sunday morning. Rumor had become reality. Although the attending delegates immediately denied it, MAC had been voted out of the MIAA and Adrian had been taken in.

Even though the issue was handled poorly and MAC officials were irritated over the "cold shoulder," the decision was accepted with no rebuke. The philosophical position was, "We are now free to make an independent schedule, a position which we have looked forward to for several seasons."

To assist in explaining MAC's presence in and departure from the MIAA, the following enrollment figures are offered of the four charter schools in the founding year (1888) and in MAC's final year with the MIAA (1907):

	1888	1907
Albion	460	460
Hillsdale	447	345
Olivet	277	283
MAC	312	1,191

As can readily be seen, by comparative size, the Michigan Agricultural College was appropriately included when conference delegates first met. Conversely, it seemed fitting 19 years later for the MIAA Board of Directors to excuse MAC from future competition as, by then, it had nearly quadrupled in enrollment while the others schools, by design, had remained proportionally the same.

Michigan Agricultural College had outgrown the very conference it had helped organize in 1888 and in which it had competed throughout the ensuing 20 years. Other than limited competition offered by the Central Collegiate Conference (track and field, cross country, and later swimming and diving), for the next 41 years MAC-MSC would compete as an independent.

MAC
1884-1893

TALES TO TELL

N.S. Mayo, class of 1888, reported to *The MSC Record* in March of 1927 an interesting account that likely described the first time MAC followers wore green as a school color. It was during the 1887 Field Day at Olivet.

As a group of student rooters headed west aboard the Grand Trunk train out of the Trowbridge station (East Lansing), Mayo and J.N. Easterbrook decided to do what rooters from other MIAA schools had been doing, adopt an identifying color. They arbitrarily decided upon green, a color that none of the other MIAA schools had. The train made a stop in Lansing where the students jumped off and succeeded in buying some bronze green (olive) ribbon along with some miniature iron rakes, hoes and spades. These trinkets were tied to the purchased ribbon and worn that afternoon to identify the students as MAC fans.

By 1891, with Olivet again hosting the Field Day, the idea had stuck. On that occasion it was reported: "a special train of four coaches left Lansing, filled with wearers of the MAC green of every conceivable shade."

The neutral color of white was likely later adopted as a companion color, much like other schools that were initially identified with a single color had done: Harvard crimson (crimson and white), Yale blue (blue and white), Columbia blue (blue and white), and Dartmouth green (green and white).

TEAM OF THE YEARS

In what would be the school's most impressive baseball season of the decade, the 1888 team won six and lost only one game. Two of those victories came in a feature event of the first organized MIAA Field Days. A four-team playoff. The Farmers first defeated Olivet 12-2 and then edged Albion in the championship contest, 10-8. It would be the first of four Field Day titles MAC would capture over a five-year span.

HEADLINES

1884: Mark Twain publishes the classic *The Adventures of Huckleberry Finn*.
1886: The Statue of Liberty, a gift of the French people, is dedicated in New York harbor.
1888: George Eastman perfects the Kodak hand camera, making possible the first amateur photography.
1889: Electric sewing machines are marketed by Singer, and in New York City the Otis Brothers install the first electric elevator.

SCOREBOARD

	W	L	T	Avg.
Baseball (1884-93)	43	32	0	.573
Track (1886-91)	0	0	1	.500

MAKING HISTORY

The birth of the Michigan State intercollegiate athletic program has been identified with the baseball team that played six games in the spring of 1884. Opening with a 20-9 defeat of Olivet on May 19, the Farmers would finish with a 4-2 season record.

Oscar Clute, who served as the school's president for a short span (1889-1893) was a visionary and a man of action. During his watch, off-campus courses were first offered, agricultural research was encouraged through experimental stations, the library was expanded, a curriculum in mechanical engineering was launched, and the school's athletic program took root.

Also, in 1891 Clute initiated the unique idea of providing the campus facilities and faculty for ongoing study to the secondary school teachers of Michigan during the summer. These special semesters, running from June through August, furnished opportunities for expanded and revised study in various disciplines. Instruction was offered in agriculture, botany, horticulture, chemistry, zoology, physics, English, mathematics, languages, economics, mechanical drawing and engineering. The only hang-up was the lack of housing for these "new students." No facilities had yet become available on campus for ladies, and space for men was limited. Similar to the post-World War II days when row upon row of bunks were set up on the gymnasium floor of Jenison to accommodate the increase in enrollment, the Armory floor was temporarily put to use each summer as a "giant" dormitory for men.

It seems that MAC-MSC-MSU officials have always found it difficult to remain out of the microscopic eye of the legislatures at the capital. On April 21, 1893, it was announced that the management of the Agricultural College would be investigated. The following concurrent resolution was adopted by the state legislative body:

"The criticisms both in private and through the public press upon the conduct and general usefulness of the Agricultural College are such that it is due to both the management of the College and those who criticize it that a thorough investigation be made thereof and a full report of the same be made at as early a date as is practicable."

The summation was that an investigation would include the policy, course of study, conduct and general management of the college. Once more, MAC had to justify its very existence.

The baseball game played against Michigan on June 14, 1884, has always been considered the first recorded competition against the U of M. A re-

Team of the Years. The MAC baseball team posed shortly after that final game in 1888. In the back row, far right, is Rollo Carpenter, identified as the school's first baseball coach. The team's star player was Leander Burnett (middle, second row).

GAME OF JUNE 14, 1884

Lansing Nine

Name	POS	AB	R	IB	TB	PO	A	E
Vance	p.	5	0	0	0	1	15	2
Welch	1 b.	5	0	0	0	13	0	4
Hinebauch	3 b.	4	0	1	1	4	0	4
Sage	c.	4	1	1	1	9	3	2
Lawson	c.f.	4	2	3	3	0	0	1
Ross	s.s.	4	0	0	0	0	4	0
Gammon	2 b.	3	0	1	1	0	1	0
Mathews	r.f.	4	0	0	0	0	0	1
McColloch	l.f.	4	0	0	0	0	0	0
Totals		37	3	6	6	27	23	14

University Nine

Name	POS	AB	R	IB	TB	PO	A	E
Walker	3 b.	5	4	4	5	4	2	2
Weatherwax	2 b.	5	1	2	3	1	2	2
McMillan	s.s.	5	1	0	0	1	1	0
Condon	l.f.	5	1	1	1	0	0	0
Hibbard	p.	5	1	0	0	2	8	2
Payne	r.f.	5	0	1	1	0	0	0
Palmer	1 b.	5	0	0	0	14	1	1
Bast	c.f.	4	2	1	1	0	1	0
Smith	c.	5	3	2	2	4	6	1
Totals		44	13	11	13	26	21	8

Earned Runs—University 2; College 1. First base on errors—U. 9; C. 6. First base on called balls—U. 2; C. 1. Total called balls—U. 44; C. 83. Struck out—U. 9; C. 5. Total strikes—U. 36; C. 56. Left on bases—U. 4; C. 6. Two base hits—U. 2; C. 0. Double plays—U. 1; C. 1. Passed balls—U. 1. Wild pitches—U. 1; C. 2. Flies caught—U. 2; C. 1. Fouls caught—U. 2; C. 1. Time of game, two hours and fifteen minutes. Welch out on being hit with batted ball.

cently uncovered article written by George Alderton for the July, 1937, issue of *The MSC Record* has revised this historic perspective. The revealing story fixed on the personal recollections of C. Fred Schneider, MAC class of 1885, who visited with Alderton during the MSC-Nebraska baseball game of June 12, 1937. It seems there was a meeting of the MAC-Michigan teams preceding that June 14 game in 1884. Schneider, who identified himself as manager of the 1884 baseball team, recalled:

"We had only about 125 students in the college, and we had quite a time getting a ball team together. But we had a lot of spirit. We coaxed the boys at Ann

Arbor a long while before they agreed to come to East Lansing for a game. I remember we had to pay them $2 each for expenses to get them here. And then we licked them, 4-3. They howled for a return game, which we grudgingly granted and met defeat [see above]."

GREAT STATE DATES

Baseball—April 29 and June 11, 1887 (A): Two of the 11 baseball victories in 1887 were over the University of Michigan, both games at Ann Arbor. In the season opener, the Aggies pushed across two runs in the top half of the ninth inning for a 10-8 margin and then du-

plicated the winning effort six weeks later by an 11-9 score with four of the runs unearned. Going four-for-four in the first game, Art Cordley was the hitting star. Birkley Canfield accounted for three of the 15 hits in the June game. Captain Don Yerkes, winner of both games, pitched all 18 innings.

Baseball—September 17, 1887 (H): Playing an abbreviated *fall* baseball schedule is not new: MAC played two games in September of 1887. In the first game, against a team from the village of Aurelius, they hammered out 20 base hits, accompanied by 14 errors, en route to an easy 24-8 win. The Aggies were nearly as generous, muffing 11 chances in the field. The Aurelius team was a family affair with four Edgars in the starting line-up.

Baseball—September 23, 1887 (H): Alumnus Don Yerkes, who had been the top hitter and number 1 pitcher of the 1887 team, returned in the fall with two brothers and six others from his hometown of Northville. One can only imagine the friendly chatter from across the infield during the contest. The Aggies, playing well without Yerkes, opened with six runs in the first, built an 11-run lead, and then went on to a 17-6 victory.

Baseball—July 4, 1888 (H): Scoring at least once in each of the nine innings, the Farmers built up the fifth highest run total ever achieved by an MAC team, downing the Owosso city team, 22-3. Likely no Aggie or Spartan has ever equaled or bettered Leander Burnett's hitting performance of that day. Playing third base and acting as the leadoff hitter, he had a perfect day at the plate, going six-for-six, including a three-base hit.

Baseball—June 11, 1889 (A): Of the four baseball victories in 1889, three were won in the final inning of play. Included was the 12-10 win over Michigan, when the Aggies scored four runs in their last time at bat. The Wolverine defense was generous, as they committed 11 errors while their pitcher uncorked five wild pitches.

Baseball—June 4, 1892 (H): The final game of the 1892 Field Day tournament between MAC and Olivet was a true pitchers' duel. Just as the game seemed destined for extra innings, the Aggies' William Bernart was perched on third in the bottom of the eighth. Leander Burnett then displayed why he was recognized as MAC's premier athlete of the time by slashing out what proved to be the game-winning RBI single. *The Lansing Republican* reported the postgame jubilee:

"Hats, canes, umbrellas, chairs, anything that could be got hold of were thrown in the air. The first man caught was Bernart, then came Burnett, the telling scorer, and then every man on the team was carried around on the one-fifth-mile track, followed by two hundred students yelling, blowing tin horns, floating green flags and ribbons and yelling for kill."

Baseball—April 29, 1893 (H): It seems the scheduled baseball game with Olivet was more than just a baseball game. The story printed in the *Lansing Republican* reported:

"The first event of the afternoon was the running broad jump, which was won by Beese. The 100-yard dash was also won by Beese. The shot put was won by Rittinger, the running hop, step and jump by Beauvias, the standing broad jump by Partridge, the one-mile bicycle race by J. Clark, one-half-mile run by Petty and the pole vault by Allen."

When the ball game finally got underway it must have been exciting to watch. After seven innings, the Comets held what seemed to be a commanding lead, 9-2. The Farmers then scored three in the eighth, four in the ninth to tie the score and then pushed across the winning run in the 10th for the 10-9 victory.

ATHLETE OF THE YEARS

Leander Burnett (baseball 1889-1892 and track and field 1888-1892) was, as Fred Stabley described him, "Michigan State's first bona fide athletic hero." He was born of an Ottawa Indian mother on December 14, 1868 in Little Traverse (now Harbor Springs), Mich. Following his graduation from Harbor Springs High School in 1887, he entered Michigan Agricultural College to study agriculture. At the time MAC was a charter member of the MIAA along with Olivet, Hillsdale and Albion. It was in this competitive atmosphere Leander excelled as a baseball player (pitcher, third baseman, outfielder) and shined as a track and field star in the annual MIAA spring Field Days. These were the only two sports available at the time. Although many of his Field Day gold medals were in unheralded events such as the backward broad jump, the fact is he won 37 events in a span of five years.

Leander Burnett

His feat of June 6, 1890 is particularly noteworthy. Of the 20 events contested that afternoon, Burnett competed in 12, winning 10, while placing second in the other two.

IN THE SPARTLITE

Baseball: The MAC baseball team defeated the Lansing Capital City team, 53-0, on June 10, 1886. This established a team scoring record that likely will remain forever. A total of 36 errors by the losers (another possible record) obviously aided in the lopsided margin. Riddle: How did MAC score the solitary run in the 9-1 loss of June 27, 1891, against the Sparta (Mich.) city team if no *Aggie* ever crossed home plate? Here is how it happened. When the game promptly began at 2:30 P.M., the Farmers had only eight players available. To complete their line-up, the host city team loaned the college boys a player by the name of Ganzell. It was Mr. Ganzell who tripled in the first inning and later scored to register the only run of the game for the Agricultural College. By the second inning, Charlie Weideman, the tardy player,

had arrived from East Lansing, whereupon he was immediately inserted into the lineup, replacing the "loaner." Consequently, no MAC player scored in that game at Sparta.

Boxing: Michigan State boxing champions were first crowned during the MIAA Field Days of 1888-1892. Contests were held in four competing weights: featherweight (120 pounds and under), lightweight (120 to 140 pounds), middleweight (140 to 160 pounds), and heavyweight (160 pounds and over). Winning five championships between 1890-1892, Edward Polhamus was the most successful pugilist of those early field days. Although not a "legitimate" heavyweight, he was a three-time champion in that division, as well as an earner of "double" titles, at 140 pounds in 1890 and 160 pounds in 1892. His success in the ring was accompanied by respect from fellow students whom he trained in boxing and physical culture. Prior to the Field Day of 1893, MIAA delegates met in Jackson and voted to streamline the two-day program of activities. Boxing was one of the events eliminated; thus it would become dormant as an intercollegiate sport in East Lansing for 43 years.

Football: As early as the fall of 1890 there was evidence of football activities on the MAC campus. On April 17 of that following spring, the Olivet College team met the Farmers at the baseball park in Lansing and won with ease, 72 to 0. In a return game at Olivet two weeks later it was a near carbon copy, with the Comets scoring another effortless win, this time 78 to 0. Members of the Aggie team learned their lesson well. Instead of fulfilling a scheduled third consecutive contest at the field days in June, they forfeited and settled for an exhibition game of two teams drawn from the combined squads.

The inter-class game on Columbus Day of 1892 was thoroughly documented in *The College Speculum* of November 10. The game, a 22-6 win by the juniors over the sophomores, was played on the parade grounds with Professors Vedder and Woodworth officiating. The student writer's concluding paragraph in *The Speculum* left a positive tone:

> "The scene during the game as viewed from the eastside of the grounds was like some which we see pictured in the illustrated weeklies, but know little about here. The players in the foreground, the enthusiastic and noisy students along the side lines, the bright costume and eager faces of the fair spectators

in the carriages or on the benches, the afternoon sun of the autumn day, all formed a most pleasant picture. It is to be hoped that the friendly contest did much to awaken our interest and dissipate our prejudice against this—the greatest of college sports."

Track and Field: The MIAA Field Days of 1888 through 1907 seemed to provide the primary forum for the runners and jumpers of the day to display their special talents. Meanwhile, the school's first "official" track and field meet was a home triangular affair held on May 14-15, 1886. Five team points were awarded for *only* first place (four points in ties). Host MAC was the winner with 19 points, followed by Albion with 14 points while Alma went scoreless. Accounting for the Aggie total were: Donald Yerkes in the standing broad jump, William Kinnan in the running high-kick, Henry Avery in the standing high-kick, and Charles Hemphill, who tied in the 100-yard dash. Three weeks later the team traveled to Albion where, on June 4, the Aggies settled for a 25-25 tie in what is historically noted as the school's first dual track meet. Taking the firsts were Yerkes in the shot put and standing broad jump, Sanson in the sledge throw, Kinnan in the hitch and kick, and Avery in the running high-kick. One can only attempt to visualize how the hitch and kick and running high-kick events were con-

ducted and measured. It is noted that Avery, the Aggie star, competed 90 times in the running high kick event and was never defeated. His record leap was 21 inches above his head. At Sarnia, Ontario, in the summer of 1885, he defeated the Canadian champion, Henry Zimmerman.

In the 220-yard dash of the 1891 Field Day at Olivet College, Lagrande G. Rickerd of Albion battled down the stretch against Ralph Haskin of MAC. As Rickerd, the winner, broke the tape the timers checked their watches and were unbelieving. Following some discussion, the word was passed to the track announcer, who raised the megaphone to his lips and bellowed to those assembled in the grandstand: "The winner of the 220 yard dash...Rickerd of Albion...the time, twenty-one and two-fifths seconds...A NEW WORLD'S RECORD!" As noted in the *Lansing Republican*: "cheers upon cheers broke out when the time was announced, followed by calls of incredulity."

Shortly thereafter, a suspicious track marshal called for a surveyor's measuring tape. Ecstasy became reality. Upon re-measure, it was determined that Lagrande Rickerd had established a "world's record" for the *203 yard dash* and not the 220.

The MAC 1892 Field Day team

TALES TO TELL

Perhaps based on a more complete schedule of games (four), the team of 1896 has been declared the school's first official football team.

The MAC Record confirms that season's opener in a detailed eight-paragraph story that opens with:

> "MAC and Lansing high school opened the football season at Elton Park last Saturday afternoon. An element of uncertainty as to the outcome, from the fact that six of the MAC boys were new men, and that Cole, Judson, and Rork, three old MAC men, were to play with the high school team gave interest to the game and brought out a good-sized crowd."

The Lansing Republic covered the story in a more concise manner:

> "The M.A.C. Juniors and the Lansing High School football club played a hot game at Elton Park today. The college boys won by a score of 10 to 0."

City maps of the period do not identify the existence of Elton Park. Subsequent research has yet to uncover its exact location.

TEAM OF THE YEARS

With a record of 1-2-1, the football team of 1896 did not leave an impressive record. It was, however, MAC's pioneer edition, and therefore designated as the team of

This team picture was taken on the lawn south of the library (today's Linton Hall).

HEADLINES

1894: Sunday comics first appear in newspapers.
1895: Sears Roebuck Company opens a mail-order business.
1896: The ancient Olympic Games are revived in Athens, Greece.
1898: The U.S. battleship *Maine* is blown up in the Havana, Cuba harbor, initiating the Spanish-American War.

SCOREBOARD	W	L	T	Avg.
Baseball (1893-99)	28	33	1	.452
Track (1898)	2	0	1	.750
Football (1896-99)	11	11	3	.440
Basketball (1898-99)	0	2	0	.000

the years 1893-1899. Without a coach, the team captain, Wilfred R. Vanderhoef, likely arranged for practices and the scheduling of games.

MAKING HISTORY

Michigan Agricultural College witnessed the introduction of no less than nine sports into its athletic program during the latter portion of the 19th century. Baseball's first year in East Lansing was in 1884, track and field in 1886, football in 1896 and basketball in 1899. Additionally, through MIAA Field Day competition from 1888-1899, fencing, boxing, tennis, gymnastics and wrestling were contested for the first time by Aggie student-athletes. Performing before what *The MAC Record* described as a "large and enthusiastic crowd," the first-ever MAC indoor track meet was held on February 5, 1898. The opponent was a team from the Lansing High School and the site was the city's new armory. Events of the day were the 25-yard dash, shot put, both standing and running high jump, and wrestling in four weight classes. The feature of the program was a bag-punching exhibition by William Pool of Detroit. The Aggies hosted a rematch on March 12.

GREAT STATE DATES

Football—November 17, 1894 (H): *The Speculum* reported on "one of the most interesting and exciting games of football that the college has had the pleasure of witnessing for a long while." The contest was against Albion College, and the Aggies scored in the final three minutes to gain a 6-4 victory. One minor note is needed: Albion had fielded their second team that day.

Baseball—May 3, 1897 (H): In the 37-5 defeat of Hillsdale, the Aggies recorded the school's second highest-ever output of runs during a regular game. Scoring came as follows: four in the first, eight in the third, eight in the fourth and 17 in the fifth.

Football—November 6, 1897 (H): It appears the Michigan Agricultural team of 1897 was too much for Alma to handle. With the rule in place that the team scored upon had to kick off back to the team that just scored, the Aggies seemed to be on the offense throughout the opening 25-minute half. By intermission they led 22-0 on four touchdowns (four points each) and three successful conversions (two points each). MAC began the second half rather listlessly, and the Scots scored their only touchdown, but the Farmers responded with three more TDs. The final score ballooned to 38-4.

Track and Field—May 13, 1898 (N): The one outdoor dual meet of 1898 was against Olivet at Charlotte, presumably at the county fairgrounds. Not only was the chosen site a convenient midpoint between the two schools, but the town's citizens demonstrated generous hospitality. For each event, the Charlotte merchants offered first, second and third place prizes which ranged from a smoking jacket valued at $6.50 to an ordinary $0.10 shave. The events of the day were as follows: 100-yard dash, half-mile run, 220-yard hurdles, hammer throw, pole vault, quarter-mile run, running broad jump, running high jump, 120-yard hurdles, one-mile run, shot put, one-mile relay and the mile walk. Also, there were two bicycle races at half-mile and one-mile distances. The mile walk was the only event won by an Olivet team member. Bill Russell, Chandler Tompkins, George Wells and Byron Holdsworth accounted for 13 of the 16 blue ribbons won by the Farmers. With the addition of nine second places and 11 thirds, MAC defeated the Comets, 77-24.

Baseball—May 20, 1898 (H): The game against Albion must have been a thriller to watch. MAC opened with six runs in the first inning, yet, upon the conclusion of five innings, they trailed the Britons, 9-8. The Aggies regained command, 10-9, on a two-run homer by Charley Adams in the seventh. But the visitors wouldn't quit. By the time the Farmers reached the bottom of the ninth, once more they trailed, 12-10. With the bases loaded, Ellis Ranney blasted a ball that came down in the tops of the evergreens in front of the Armory for a home run. By the time he reached home plate, a howling mob was there to greet him, whereupon he was mounted their shoulders and carried away.

Football—October 8, 1898 (A): In the season-opening 11-6 football victory at Ypsilanti against Normal, a free-for-all nearly resulted when someone in the crowd struck MAC star Bill Russell in the back following an Ypsi touchdown. Someone else attacked Coach Keep, who was doubling as the game's referee (a common practice for the time). Quick action on the part of the home team averted further trouble. It was pleasing to find that, according to *The MAC Record,* the Normal students were in no way responsible, the trouble being caused by the rowdy element in the city.

Basketball—February 27, 1899 (H): The article below from the March 7 issue of *The MAC Record,* an alumni publication, describes the first-ever basketball game by an Aggie team, which the Aggies lost, 6-7:

> "An exceedingly interesting game of basket-ball was played in the Armory, on Monday afternoon of last week, between M.A.C. and Olivet. The teams were so evenly matched that at the end of two 20-minute bouts the score was a tie. In the third bout—10 minutes—Olivet scored after eight minutes of hard playing, on a free trial at goal for a foul. The game was hard and fast from start to finish but was characterized by entirely too many fouls that were not noticed by the referees. Interference with the ball when it was clearly in the hands of an opponent was of too frequent occurrence. The most brilliant play in the game was a long goal from field by Ranney."

Baseball—May 1, 1899 (A): The Albion game of 1899 was a thriller. In the top of the ninth, with the score tied 6-6, the Aggie's Art Decker beat out a bunt, Alex Krental was safe on an error, Roy Norton and Fred Murphy singled, and then Sam Kennedy hit a long double, clearing the bases. The final score: MAC 10, Albion 6.

ATHLETE OF THE YEARS

Ellis Ranney of Belding, Mich., is recognized as the first MAC football hero, as he played three years at quarterback from 1897-1899. In addition, Ranney, a good baseball hitter, played second base on the 1897-1900 teams and was also a starter on the first two Michigan Agricultural College basketball teams (1899 and 1900). He was selected as captain in his final two years of football and in his junior year of baseball.

Ellis Ranney

IN THE SPARTLITE

Baseball: A *Speculum* reporter included a sideline observation in his story of the home opener at the Parade Grounds on April 15, 1893:

> "A pleasing feature was the large attendance from Lansing. The attendance of the fair sex was especially large, and their cheers and bright faces were among the principal features of the ball game. Up to the eighth inning most of the student onlookers found them of more interest than the affairs of the diamond."

In true editorial style, an 1894 issue of *The Speculum* lashed out at the seemingly non-supporting fans who were attending games at the Parade Grounds:

"A feature played here by the regular team has been the sale of score cards. These little mementos of the game placed in the hands of hustling students are a source of revenue that is pleasing. The last two named games very nearly paid expenses, more than that we do not ask for. [program sales for note: exact revenues from those games were, Albion $11.95 and Olivet $16.70]. Lansing visitors come out in quite large numbers and are reported by the 'hustlers' as mighty poor pay. College students never expect, never get any thing free in the city in the way of entertainment and are righteously indignant when cigaretted dandies, men of more sober estate, and street gamins in troops come out to sponge an afternoon at the college."

The 4-1 loss to Hillsdale in 1896 must have been a frustrating afternoon for both teams. In total, they hammered out 25 hits (12 by MAC) and managed *only* five runs, of which three were earned. *The MAC Record* detailed a triple play, highlighting the 2-0 loss to Albion in the Field Day championship game of 1897:

"It was an excellent game and presented one feature not often seen and not seen in the M.I.A.A. for at least eight years, viz: a triple play. Albion had filled the bases, with no men out. A hard drive was sent to Ranney at second, who caught it about four inches from the ground. All base runners had started at the crack of the bat. Ranney stepped on second, retiring the runner between second and third, then threw to first in time to catch the runner who had left that base."

Unlike football, the annual financial statement for baseball listed *both* receipts and expenses:

Receipts:

Donations	$135.00
Tickets sold	$30.35
TOTAL	$165.35

Expenses:

Two dozen balls	$24.00
Ten bats	$7.50
Mask	$2.50
One dozen caps	$9.00
Mitts	$6.00
Gum	$2.75
Witch hazel	$0.75
TOTAL	$52.50

The Aggies took to the road for an unusual morning-afternoon doubleheader on May 14, 1898. The morning contest, opposite Michigan Normal in Ypsilanti, was to be followed by an afternoon game in Ann Arbor facing the U of M. In the opener, a 20-8 win for the Farmers, MAC's captain Frank Warren injured his knee. Regardless, he fulfilled his scheduled afternoon start on the mound against the Wolverines, only to have the injury force him to the sidelines after four innings, trailing 10-0. In a strange gesture by today's standards, he was replaced by Ikey Clark, the Michigan coach. The home team must have equally relished their mentor's offerings as they scored another 10 runs, eventually winning the abbreviated eight-inning game, 20-1.

On April 14, 1899, the general agent for Spalding Sporting Goods Company measured members of the team for yet another new uniform. That edition included a white shirt, green pantaloons and green cap (identified as the Boston pattern). In what is likely a team record, Roy Norton committed four errors in the opening inning of the Kalamazoo game of May 20, 1899, helping pave the way for an 11-run outburst. Also contributing to the eventual 16-11 loss was the pregame resignation of team captain, Ellis Ranney. His departure was to avoid further trouble stemming from a protest lodged by the Albion team. It seemed that during the previous summer Ranney had played for one of the northern resort teams for which he received board, an apparent break of MIAA rules. As it turned out, the protest was not sustained, probably because every college in the association played men with similar experience. Ranney would later return to the team.

Basketball: It is not known who introduced the game of basketball to the student-athletes at MAC in 1899. Ironically, Charles Bemies, who had learned directly about the sport from Dr. James Naismith in Springfield, Mass., and thus became one of the sport's pioneering proponents, would not become MAC's first director of physical culture until the following fall. A variation of the game of basketball, the "cage game" was played at the turn of the century. The chief distinction of the cage game was the feature of a cage immediately surrounding the

area of play, the cage being a heavy wire net of fencing that prohibited the ball from going out of bounds unless it went over the top. Play was continuous. The name "cagers" remains in the lexicon of veteran sportswriters when making reference to today's game.

Football: Football activities of 1893 centered on a team fielded by the Class of 1896. The records reveal that those sophomores played and were victorious in a pair of November games. First was a 40-4 win at the campus over Lansing High School and a victory one week later in Lansing from a team identified as the State Auditor General's Office. Both games apparently drew a substantial number of curious spectators, and, in a visionary perspective, *The College Speculum* noted that many other schools were apparently finding the game of football a source of revenue. That day of "revenue" seemed a long way off for MAC. The football financial statement of that year reported only expenses:

Expenses:

Railroad fare	$79.84
Bus fare	$5.70
Meals	$4.75
Coach	$11.50
TOTAL	**$101.79**

Colleges commonly played high school teams in the 1800s. MAC was no exception. Although *The College Speculum* of Nov. 10, 1894 does not report the final score of a game in Detroit, the story hints at the result:

> "Our first 11 went to Detroit October 20 to play the Detroit high school. This game demonstrated once more the fact that a team can not put up a good game unless they play together. The team must play as a unit, not as a number of individuals. Before the second rush was made, Captain Vanderhoef was ruled off the field for "slugging." This weakened the team very materially, as it left it without a leader."

In those early years, the football team was allowed to use the parade grounds for practice only two days each week, and a typical afternoon workout was described as "forty-five minutes of practice followed by a mile run and a rub down." On the other three days players ran wind sprints on the grounds near the president's home. Further complicating organized workouts, some students were released from classes at 4:00 P.M. while others were not available until after 5:00 P.M. Finally in October of 1899 arrangements were reached for all members of the team to be available for practice before sundown and at the same hour.

The Notre Dame team of 1897 was a frightening opponent to face. Their line averaged 190 pounds and featured a center weighing in at 246, huge for players of those early years. Notwithstanding the size differential, MAC played them with great inspiration that fall. Early in the second half, George Wells broke into the clear but was hauled down at the five-yard line. On the next play, Hugh Baker carried the ball into the end zone and Bill Russell kicked the goal. As for scoring, that was it for the Aggies. At game's end the scoreboard in South Bend read: Home Team 34, Visitors 6.

Games were frequently played on plots of flat ground circumscribed by a restraining rope stretched from post to post. Fan comfort was minimal or nonexistent, and spectators would frequently burst through the restricting lines and stand halfway across the field to view the game.

Track and Field: In the 100-yard dash of the 1894 MIAA "all-around" competition the judges had declared that Cadwallder of Olivet finished ahead of Jim Petley of Michigan Agricultural. A camera fanatic was on hand in the person of Mr. Nellist, MAC class of 1896 football manager. He snapped a very clear picture showing Petley ahead of Cadwallder by some distance and thus the original call was protested.

The quarter-mile run of the 1895 MIAA field day competition centered on Shipp of Albion and Patridge of MAC. As the pair raced side-by-side to the finish line, an over-enthusiastic Albion man darted out and "coached" Shipp over the line with a first-place time of 54.3 seconds. The unaided Patridge was a close second. According to the rules governing such cases, no attendant could accompany a competitor, and on this ground the race was declared illegal. In what now seems like a ludicrous method for resolving the issue, the judges decided to have the race re-run at Eaton Rapids on Saturday, June 15.

There is no disclosure of exactly where the race was re-run, perhaps on a school ground. Yet the result is well documented. Patridge took an early lead and hung on for a ten-foot victory as Shipp narrowed the gap with a strong sprint over the final 220 yards. The time was a slow 57.0.

SPARTAN SCRAPBOOK

─── BASEBALL ───

First baseball team (1884)

MAC
1899-1904

TALES TO TELL

A season-ending summary report published in the Dec. 10, 1901, edition of *The MAC Record* focused on two problems for football: practice time and finances. As for practice on the parade grounds, football competed with military drill and was limited to one hour, from 4:00 to 5:00 P.M. By the time the men were in their gear and on the field it was 4:30 P.M., giving them only 30 minutes to work out. Team costs were yet another problem. Lacking a fence, the field did not provide the opportunity to charge an admission fee for games. Costs were partially absorbed by a voluntary student athletic association fee of 50 cents per term. Of the 800 enrolled students, only 448 joined the association, with 94 of that number unpaid. Thus, funds were limited.

At the conclusion of the undefeated 1903 basketball season, overtures were made to host a postseason game against the highly successful University of Minnesota team. It was suggested this proposed game would be for the "championship of the United States." Plans hinged on raising guarantee money and the Gopher team gaining school approval for the trip. The $125 guarantee money was raised by MAC, but a March 19 telegram from the Minnesota team manager burst the bubble. It read: *"Sorry, basketball team is unable to go east."* Thus, lost was the opportunity to play for the first ever "national championship" title. Instead, the *Encyclopedia of Basketball* notes that Columbia University claimed the first national championship after defeating Minnesota 27-15 and Wisconsin 21-15 in regular season play of 1905.

HEADLINES

1900: Johann Waaler, a Norwegian inventor based in Germany, patents a tiny device made of bent wire: it is soon called the paper clip.

1901: King C. Gillette begins manufacturing the modern safety razor with disposable blades.

1903: At Kitty Hawk, N.C., Orville and Wilbur Wright, Ohio bicycle makers, launch the world's first successful manned flight in a motorized airplane.

1904: Henry Ford sets a new land speed record of 91.37 mph in his motor car "999" on frozen Lake St. Clair, near Detroit.

SCOREBOARD

	W	L	T	Avg.
Baseball (1900-04)	26	30	0	.464
Track (1902-04)	5	0	0	1.000
Football (1899-1903)	16	17	3	.444
Basketball (1899-1904)	21	7	0	.750

TEAM OF THE YEARS

The 1903 basketball team posted a 6-0 record and completed MAC's third consecutive undefeated season. They totally dominated the opposition, as noted by the composite point totals of 225 versus 36.

The five starters (who frequently played the entire game), were John Schaffer, seated in front, along with Foley Tuttle, Edward Balbach, captain Joseph Haftencamp and Ray Tower, seated left to right in the middle row. The manager (back row, middle) was Wilson Millar, who often refereed home games. Millar lettered in football and baseball. He is flanked by (left) Bauld and (right) Morgan.

MAKING HISTORY

On April 18, 1902, the baseball team played its first game on the new diamond across the river at Old College Field (Kobs Field). Furthermore, they played the game in new green-and-gray uniforms. Unfortunately, the visiting Michigan Wolverines were not impressed, easily winning, 20-2. Reflecting the poor defensive play, 17 of the winners' 20 runs were unearned.

The early football rules could inspire lopsided scores. The scored-upon team was required to immediately surrender the ball by kicking off to the team that just scored. Conceivably, the weaker team might go for extended periods of time without ever putting the ball into play offensively. A 1903 rule change modified all of that by providing the scored-upon team the option of kicking *or* receiving the ball.

Ed Pinnance, star of the 1903 baseball team, struck out nine as he faced only 29 Alma batters in pitching the first-ever Aggie no-hit, no-run game. Only two Scots reached base, one on an error and another by drawing a walk. Following that season, Pinnance left school to become MAC's first ever major leaguer, as he signed a contract with Connie Mack's Philadelphia Athletics. He met his new team in Cleveland and eventually saw action in two games, pitching a total of seven innings. Credited with one save, his ERA was 2.57. That was Ed Pinnance's total major league career.

GREAT STATE DATES

Basketball—February 1, 1902 (H): During this period of paltry scoring, it is difficult to conceive the Farmers topping Alma by a team-record differential score of 102-3, but it happened. James Cooper led the scoring parade with 27 points. Ed Balbach, Joe Haftencamp and Ray Tower chipped in 24 points each, as Charles Blanchard rounded out the scoring with three points. The astronomical score was somewhat attributed to 1902 rules that provided for *all* field goals to be credited with *three* points.

Basketball—**February 15, 1902 (A):** As an obvious enticement for female attendance, the admission charge for the Governor's Guard game at the Lansing Armory was 25 cents for gentlemen and 15 cents for ladies. It is noted that a large and enthusiastic crowd witnessed the contest and enjoyed the music rendered by the MAC band. Winning with ease, 19-0, this would be the only shutout ever posted by a State basketball team.

Basketball—**March 15, 1902 (A):** This game at Hillsdale must have been interesting. Similar to the "cage" game noted in the 1893-1899 section, it was played with no out-of-bounds and with the ball in constant play. From *The MAC Record*: "This fact caused considerable tussling for the ball, but made it a very lively contest." It was indeed a "lively contest." One Hillsdale player left the game in the second half with a dislocated shoulder. The final score was MAC 36, Hillsdale 17.

Track and Field—**May 24, 1902 (N):** Perhaps it was a compromise of travel to meet midway at Ithaca, for that is where the dual track meet with Alma was held. Considering facilities, it was not likely a good choice. *The MAC Record* suggested that Harry Moon, the freshman sprinter, would have run the 100 yards faster than 10.4 seconds if "the track had not been covered with grass and sand." Furthermore, that afternoon the inside lanes were so wet and muddy that longer races were run at least 10 feet from the pole lane. In accumulating the winning total of 114 points, the Farmers won 16 of the 20 events with Moon accounting for three firsts and three seconds. In addition to the familiar events of today, the program included the standing broad jump and three bicycle races competed at one-quarter-mile, one-mile and five-mile distances.

Basketball—**January 26, 1903 (H):** The ease in defeating the Detroit YMCA (score: 43-8) came as a complete surprise. They were held to just one point in the second half of this season opener. Regardless, the Detroiters were respected as a worthy opponent, and throughout the ensuing 15 years they would never again be so dominated by MAC as they were in 1903.

Basketball—**January 29, 1903 (H):** Perhaps the jump-ball situations (after each made basket) were officiated a little differently in 1903. *The MAC Record* reported in the story of the 49-2 win over Hillsdale that "Balbach (the MAC center), to keep the interest up, would jump and seize the ball with both hands when it was put in play (with a jump ball)." The Aggie apparently gained confidence as the game progressed. It was noted that,

"Tuttle would leave his opponent and visit with the other players."

Baseball—**April 18, 1903 (H):** With College Field under water from spring floods, the baseball team was back at the familiar Parade Grounds for the Michigan game. Seats from the Armory were placed along the foul lines and approximately 1,000 fans were in attendance at game time. The pitching and hitting star proved to be 23-year-old Ed Pinnance of Walpole Island, Ontario. With the score tied 9-9 in the bottom of the ninth, Pinnace, a right-handed pitcher but left-handed hitter, smashed a line drive over first base which scored the winning run. The crowd swarmed onto the field and carried the players off on their shoulders. Continuing their celebration, a procession of 600 rooters, accompanied by the band, paraded through the streets of Lansing throughout the evening.

Football—**November 14, 1903 (H):** The Albion game was for the MIAA championship of 1903. Scoring late in the game (five points for a touchdown), the Aggies successfully converted the point-after for a tie score of 6-6. The Albion team strongly disputed MAC's point-after-touchdown, claiming it had been an illegal play. Following postgame debate, it was agreed to take the dispute to a three-man panel consisting of the U of M Coach Yost, Keene Fitzpatrick (Michigan's trainer) and Arthur Curtis, the Wisconsin coach, who was in Ann Arbor for a game. The trio listened to both sides and finally agreed the Aggie play was legal. Thus, MAC tied Albion for the conference title.

Baseball—**May 20, 1904 (H):** The University of Wisconsin, leading the Western Conference and just having split a pair of games with Michigan, came to town for a single contest. The game started late because the Badgers had difficulty locating the campus. After three innings the score was knotted at 2-2, and over the next 11 innings no runner crossed the plate. Finally, to the delight of the local fans, the Aggies managed to break the tie, scoring the winning run in the bottom of the 15th. Bert Ellsworth scored on an infield out after singling and working his way to third on a sacrifice and fielder's choice. Carl Hyde pitched the entire game for MAC and surrendered only five hits. This was the first-ever game against a Western Conference opponent, other than the University of Michigan.

Baseball—**May 30, 1904 (H):** Memorial Day began damp and rainy, enough that the scheduled baseball game with Michigan Normal was canceled. Then, as the

morning brightened, a game was quickly arranged with the Oldsmobile team, a semi-professional aggregation from Lansing. Word spread, and eventually 1,700 fans made their way to College Field. Among them, sideline betters were wagering that the "college boys" wouldn't even score a run. One can only imagine the surprise when the Aggies squeezed out a 3-2 win over their more experienced opponents. Lansing merchants seized the opportunity of the day to honor the Aggie second baseman and Lansingite, Russ Canfield. Upon his initial appearance at the plate, time was called, and he was presented with a gold watch.

Baseball—June 4, 1904 (H): In the Field Day championship game, before 3,000 spectators, the Aggies defeated the favored Albion nine, 2-1. Trailing 1-0, Andy Armstrong opened the seventh by reaching first on an error. He then stole second, took third on a sacrifice, and scored on Russ Canfield's single. Canfield then stole second, stole third and scored the ultimate winning run on the catcher's overthrow of the third baseman. The Britons had captured the title over the preceding four years, and MAC had not won the championship since 1892.

Football—October 29, 1904 (H): By defeating Hillsdale, 104-0, in the fifth game on the schedule, the Farmers reached a score that remains the second highest total in school history. The Chargers were held to a scant two first downs and total of 17 yards gained from scrimmage. MAC reeled off 1,511 yards for the day while scoring 16 touchdowns. The attack was led by Wilbert Holdsworth and Oscar Kratz with four touchdowns each. Frank Kratz scored three times with Walt Small, Steve Doty, Amos Ashley, Harvey Hahn and Bob Bell each registering one TD.

ATHLETE OF THE YEARS

Harry Moon, a four-year track and field star from 1902-1905, won nine MIAA Field Day titles. In 1904 his 10.0 in the 100-yard dash set a meet record that would not be bettered until 1937, one-third of a century later. On that same afternoon in 1904, Moon ran the anchor leg of the winning mile relay. He was 25 yards behind the leader when he took the baton and then, 440 yards later, broke the tape 40 yards in front of the competition. In June of that year Harry was runner-up in both the 100- and 220-yard dashes at the World's Collegiate Championships, held as a pre-Olympic meet at St. Louis.

Those finishes would garner MAC a third-place tie with Illinois in the team standings. Although he did *not* compete in the Olympic Games held later that summer in St. Louis, Moon has historically been erroneously identified with the USA team.

Harry Moon

IN THE SPARTLITE

Baseball: Beginning in 1902 and continuing through 1906, the team opened the season with an exhibition game against a local high school.

MAC concluded the 1903 season on Memorial Day when their star pitcher, Ed Pinnance, defeated a team from his hometown, the Walpole Indian School of Canada, 10-4. The 12-man squad displayed some wonderful and classic Chippewa Indian names: Kewadek, Pontiac, Mahjeyahssing, Hiawatha, Penaces, Pashku, Kuhbakeshegud, Tecumseh and Auhyahkaosa.

On April 30, 1904, the Farmers headed for Detroit and a game with Detroit College. The day was rainy, and no field had been arranged for the game, so a grassy park was located and a diamond laid out. As could be expected, the assigned umpire couldn't locate the impromptu game site and never showed up. It was agreed the Detroit coach's son, a young lad by the name of Doyle, would fill the role as arbitrator. The game ran smoothly until the bottom of the ninth with MAC leading, 4-1. *The MAC Record*

suggested that young Doyle "lost his eyesight" during the home team's final time at bat. The first three batters received walks, the next two hit safely, and suddenly the game was over, 5-4 in favor of the Detroiters.

Basketball: MAC trailed at halftime in the Olivet game of Feb. 3, 1900, 8-1. While the Aggies held the Comets scoreless in the second half, they managed five points to finish just short, 8-6. With two points each, Tom Agnew, Eugene Brewer and Leavitt were in a three-way tie for the Farmer's high point man. At $0.15, it was a bargain night for the fans, as a second game was played in which the Aggie women defeated Lansing High School, 16-4.

Eleven days following the 1901 team's organizational meeting, a practice game was played against a faculty team which included Coach Bemies. The varsity team of Ed Balbach, Charles Blanchard, Joe Haftencamp, James Cooper and Johnson defeated the teachers, 8-4. This game was preceded by a women's game against a team from Ypsilanti Normal. Shut out by the Huron women, 26-0, there was no high-point person for the Aggies.

The basketball team opened the 1903 season in new uniforms. Without detailed description, *The MAC Record* noted, "The contrast in color between the suits of the home team and the (Detroit) YMCA made the game particularly interesting from the spectators' point of view."

The financial balance sheet for the four home games of 1904 reveal receipts of $55.00 and expenses of $120.75. It would seem the sport was not yet a "money maker."

Attesting to the primitive facilities of the time, during the 1904 game at Alma, a host player received severe burns on his hand from the exposed steam pipes on the wall behind the basket.

Without revealing its dimensions, the gymnasium at the Grand Rapids YMCA was depicted as "very narrow" and difficult "to do good team work." Regardless, it was likely no smaller than the basketball floor at Hope College that measured 30 feet from end to end. Conceivably, a full-court press and a zone defense could have likely been employed simultaneously.

Football: Team facilities improved when the bathroom in the basement of Abbot Hall (site of the current Music Practice Building) was turned over to the athletic director in 1900. After affixing a dressing room to the lavatory, the football team members had accommodations heretofore unavailable. Prior to this, each player would change in and out of his uniform back in his dormitory room.

Three home games were played during the 1900 season. At least one of the contests (Albion) was scheduled at the Lansing race track.

The rules called for two 35-minute halves; but, if appropriate excuses (darkness, or permitting a team to catch a train) existed, the length of playing time could be shortened by mutual consent of the two captains. A story pertaining to the 1901 game at Kalamazoo confirmed a devious method for shortening a contest when it seemed prudent to do so. Leading MAC by a score of 15-5, the host team, "K" College, was permitted excessive time-outs by the local referee each time MAC moved the ball offensively. The end result was a game prematurely concluded on account of darkness after only ten minutes of play in the second half. The 10-point Kalamazoo lead held up.

Transferring from one school to another was apparently commonplace. Listed among the "new" MAC men of 1902 were Wesley Cortright from Hillsdale College, Thomas Agnew from Albion College and Watson from Alma College. It was not novel or inappropriate to see the famed Michigan coach, Fielding H. Yost, "scouting" other collegiate campuses for athletes to add to his talent-rich squad.

There is evidence the 119-0 loss to Michigan in 1902 was a "practice game;" nevertheless, the result remains in the records as the school's most humiliating loss. In his book, *The Spartans*, Fred Stabley reveals the following anecdote. Just before the game concluded, the same U of M coach, Fielding Yost, spotted an MAC player passing behind the Michigan bench en route to the dressing room and inquired, "The game's not over yet, son. Where are you going?" The totally exhausted Aggie responded, "Mr. Yost, they told us up home we were coming down here for experience, and for me, I've had mine."

Track and Field: In 1901 Harry Schultz would capture the 100- and 220-yard dashes, running broad jump, hop-step and jump, pole vault, high jump, plus finish second in the standing broad jump and third in the 220-yard hurdles. He was comfortably leading in that hurdle race until he lost a shoe while negotiating the fourth barrier. Keene Fitzpatrick, meet referee and director of athletics at the U of M, acknowledged that Schultz was the best all-around athlete he had ever seen.

Although the 50-38 victory over Alma in 1904 is historically recorded as a "track and field" win, some of the contested events that afternoon made it sound more like a carnival: the high dive (head-first high jump), club swinging, parallel bars and wrestling in six weight classes.

SPARTAN SCRAPBOOK
—— BASEBALL COACHES (1884-2003) ——

Max Beutner (1899)

Charles Bemies (1900-01)

George Denman (1902-03)

Chester Brewer (1904-10, '18-20)

John Macklin (1911-15)

John Morrissey (1916-17, '22)

George "Potsy" Clark (1921)

Fred Walker (1923-24)

John Kobs (1925-63)

Danny Litwhiler (1964-82)

Tom Smith (1983-95)

Ted Mahan (1996-)

Note: No coach, 1884-98

1904-1909

TALES TO TELL

Here's the answer to a trivia question that will surprise many Spartans fans. Question: In what year was a Michigan State athlete first credited with winning an individual Western Conference (Big Ten) championship? Realizing that Michigan State was not voted into the conference until Dec. 12, 1948, it seems obvious the answer would be sometime thereafter . . . wrong! The answer is the year *1908* when Ralph J. Carr captured the outdoor Big Ten two-mile race held at Marshall Field in Chicago. From 1901 until 1926 the annual conference track meet was an open meet with teams as far away as California invited and entered. In addition to 1908, MAC teams of 1909, 1921 and 1925 also scored points.

The *Chicago Record-Herald* vividly reported Carr's exciting victory:

"In a sensational finish, Carr of Michigan Agricultural, a thoroughbred 'dark horse,' won the two-mile run from a classy field of long-distance stars with Waggoner of Ames, second, and Maundrell of Stanford third. Carr's time was 9:56.2.

Maundrell was the foremost figure in the race for more than three-fourths of the way. He led for seven laps with a listless-looking lot of long-distance runners tagging after him. The last lap was superlatively eventful. Smith of Wisconsin drew up even with Maundrell at the start of the lap. He started up the back stretch, with Drew of Wisconsin third and Carr and Waggoner in the rear. At the last turn Waggoner forged to the lead and seemed to have the race in his pocket, when Carr shot up from the bunch in a sensational burst of speed, passed Waggoner like a flash and won by four yards. Maundrell came in third and the Wisconsin contenders finished out."

MAC's total of 8 points was bettered by only six schools: Chicago, 22 2/3; Wisconsin, 20; Illinois, 18; Stanford, 17 2/3; Grinnell, 9 2/3; and Purdue, 9.

In 1909, the year following Ralph Carr's dramatic victory, Fred Tillotson duplicated the effort in the same event. *The Holcad* described the race:

"'Tillie' drew 11th place in the starting, but had hardly run 20 yards before he had worked his way

1905: New York Central Railroad's "20th Century Limited" travels between New York City and Chicago in 18 hours.

1908: The 47-story Singer Building in New York City becomes America's first skyscraper.

1909: The Lincoln penny, issued by the Philadelphia Mint, replaced the Indian-head penny, which had been in circulation for 50 years.

1909: Arctic explorer Robert Peary, his aide Matthew Henson, and four Eskimos are the first to reach the North Pole.

SCOREBOARD

	W	L	T	Avg.
Baseball (1905-09)	42	28	1	.592
Track (1905-09)	13	2	0	.867
Football (1904-08)	34	7	5	.739
Basketball (1905-09)	55	17	0	.764
Tennis (1909 only)	1	0	0	1.000

over to the pole with but six men in front of him. Holding this position, he ran about the fifth lap when he worked ahead again to third place. Stophlet had set the pace at the start, and at the end of the first mile, still led with a great lead, going at a 440 clip.

As the runners went up the back stretch of the sixth lap, Tillotson jumped into second place and closed up directly behind Stophlet, where he stayed until coming into the stretch of the eighth lap. Nearly every athlete on the field by this time was calling and yelling to "Tillie" to "beat him up," and a terrific sprint up the straight away put Tillotson in first place.

Tillotson was given a great ovation as he finished the race, both by the men on the track and the four or five thousand spectators."

Tillotson's victory gave the Aggies five points and a tie with Colorado for seventh place behind Illinois, 36; Stanford, 28; Chicago, 21; Wisconsin, 12; and Minnesota and Purdue, six each.

TEAM OF THE YEARS

The 1908 football team posted a record of 6-0-2 with both ties in scoreless games (Michigan and DePaul). In fact, the Aggies were unscored upon until the sixth contest of the season, a 46-2 victory over Olivet. During the course of the eight-game schedule, MAC outscored its opposition 205-22.

MAKING HISTORY

A football rule change in 1906 called for the playing field to be marked off in checkerboard fashion with five-

1908 football team

Pictured above are (first row, left to right) Cogsdill, W. Frazer*, B. Shedd (captain), M. Lee, C. Moore. (second row, left to right) R. Wheeler, F. Stone, C. Ballard, I. Cortright, A. Campbell, P. McKenna, Sorensen. (back row, left to right) Coach C. Brewer, G. Allen, L. Exelby, J. Campbell, C. Burroughs, Maleski, B. Patterson, unknown.

* William Frazer would later become an Olympian in the pistol event.

yard lines paralleling the sidelines over the entire field. This layout, in place through the 1909 season, was designed to assist officials in requiring the first player receiving the ball to go five yards to the left or right of the snapper before crossing the line of scrimmage. This applied to both the passer and the runner. The rule, stricken from the books in 1910, was initiated in hopes of neutralizing the brutality which seemed to be characterizing play at the center of the scrimmage line.

Ed Krehl was the basketball team's go-to guy in 1905. Scoring 22 points in the second half of the Jackson "Y" game on February 4, he finished the afternoon with 29 of the Aggies' 47 winning points. In the 94-4 rout of the Battle Creek YMCA three weeks later, Krehl scored a remarkable 42 points and set a team scoring record that would hold, incredibly, for 50 years.

On May 5, 1905, the Aggie track team defeated Notre Dame, 75-56. It was the first MAC victory of any kind over the Irish.

Fourteen years after the sport of basketball was introduced at the YMCA in Springfield, Mass., terminology was still being contrived. In a 1905 game summary, *The MAC Record* alluded to "baskets thrown," and not field goals. Also, those playing the guard positions were often referred to as "backs."

With the first hint of a college football poll, *The Chicago Tribune, The Grand Rapids Press,* and *The Chicago Record-Herald* each named Notre Dame as Western Champions for 1909. MAC, Minnesota, Missouri, Marquette and Michigan were all mentioned among the next strongest teams.

Eleven years after MAC completed its first basketball season, the University of Michigan began competition. The two teams met for the first time on Jan. 9, 1909. In its publication of January 12, *The MAC Record* reported the results:

"In the first basket ball game of the season M.A.C. easily defeated the Michigan five in a game at the Michigan Gymnasium Saturday night by a final score of 24-16. This is the first year that Michigan has tried the game, and it was her first inter-collegiate contest. On the other hand the M.A.C. team, though having had little time to round into shape, was composed of stars of last year's championship team and had but little difficulty in putting up team work which told against the playing of the individual stars which composed the University team.

Both teams showed lack of training, and a total of 32 fouls were called, of which MAC was guilty of 15 and Michigan 17. Dickson, who has played for three seasons, proved a star at throwing field baskets, getting three during the game. Farquar, of Michigan, threw eight baskets out of 13 chances from fouls and McKenna threw eight out of 17 for M.A.C."

The return game at the Armory would be an even easier victory, 45-23. Nine years would pass before the U of M would again appear on the Farmers's schedule.

GREAT STATE DATES

Football—**November 11, 1905 (H):** The most spectacular touchdown of the year was scored in the 46-10 MIAA title-winning game over Albion. Just as a Brit runner was crossing into the end zone, he fumbled, and before the 600-plus spectators (the largest crowd ever in East Lansing) knew what had happened, the Aggies' Jesse Boyle, the 152-pound right end, had scooped up the elusive ball and sprinted 107 yards the other way for a score. The MAC fans rose en masse and, as *The Lansing Daily Journal* reported, "nine rahs after nine rahs were accorded Boyle."

Basketball—**February 10, 1906 (A):** The undefeated Aggies opened the season with their fifth straight victory, a convincing 25-20 win at the Grand Rapids YMCA. It was the first loss in three years for Grand Rapids on their home court. Scoring for MAC were Ed Krehl, 11; Roy Vondette, eight; and Dickson, Waterman and Hannish, two points apiece.

Baseball—**May 2, 1906 (A):** The most zestful game of 1906 was a 1-0 Aggie victory at Hillsdale. With the game scoreless, Andy Armstrong led off the ninth with a perfect bunt single down the third baseline. Jesse "Guinea" Boyle was sent up to sacrifice but was forced to square away after fouling off the first two pitches. The next pitch was high, one of Boyle's favorites, and the reliable catcher smashed it out over second base and by the outfielder. Armstrong raced all the way home with what would prove to be the game's only run.

Track and Field—**May 26, 1906 (H):** Winning 10 of 15 events in a triangular meet, MAC defeated Kalamazoo 71-43, while Mt. Pleasant Normal scored only eight points. Accepting the fact that the track was heavy from recent rains, the following times and distances were

recorded: Small (120-yard high hurdles) 17.8; Graham (100-yard dash) 10.4; Pearsall (220-yard dash) 24.2; Pearsall (220-yard low hurdles) 29.2; Small (broad jump) 19' 9 1/2"; Allen (1/2 mile) 2:15.0; Waite (mile) 5:00.0; Carr (2 mile) 11:01.0; Burroughs (discus) 105' 7 1/2"; Verran, Bignell, Waite, Allen (mile relay) 3:40.8.

Basketball—**March 2, 1907 (H):** The 1907 Aggies saved their highest output for the last as they closed their 14-2 season with a 72-13 pasting of the visiting Michigan Normal team from Ypsilanti. Scoring for the Farmers were Roy Vondette, 32; captain Ed Krehl, 18; Parnell McKenna, 12; Claude Hannish, eight; and Leslie Westerman, two.

Baseball—**May 15, 1907 (H):** The excitement of the 15-0 victory at Hillsdale centered on Eric Nies who had held the Crusaders hitless over the first eight innings. By the time he took the mound in the ninth, spectators were aware of the pitching gem and responded with accompanying cheers on every pitch thrown by the Aggie ace. Suddenly two men had been retired and Nies faced the last hitter in the batting order. Perhaps it was nerves or fatigue, but Nies yielded his first base on balls of the afternoon. Then the leadoff man, a first baseman by the name of Watkins, cracked a single through the infield, and that was it. The final batter grounded to shortstop and Eric Nies settled for a one-hitter.

Football—**October 26, 1907 (H):** The "kickable" pudgy ball used during the early years also led to frequent fumbles. Perhaps this is why field position seemed more significant than ball control. The following excerpt from *The Lansing Journal's* report of the 15-6 win over Wabash seems unrealistic:

> "At the beginning of the second half, Wabash kicked to MAC, and McKenna returned the kick fifteen yards. On the first down Vaughn punted and Wabash followed suit. On the exchange of kicks the Farmers gained about twenty yards. Wabash punted again and Vaughn again lifted the leather for fifty yards. Hargraves fumbled the ball on the Hoosiers' five-yard line, but recovered. Standing behind the goal, he attempted to punt (for a third straight time), but Shedd broke through the line, blocked the kick, and fell on it as the ball rolled over the Wabash goal line giving MAC their first touchdown."

Basketball—**February 17, 1908 (H):** The traveling Haskell Indians out of Lawrence, Kan., coached by the legendary Phog Allen came to town for a game. After Bob Dickson opened the affair with three straight baskets in the first five minutes, the Haskell players became aware they were up against a formidable opponent. They suddenly began to resort to their well-known "roughhouse" style of play. Shortly thereafter, Claude Hannish retired with a wrenched knee and Ed Krehl received a badly bruised hip. Offensively, the Indians had difficulty locating the target as many long shots hit the Armory's infamous ceiling girders and dropped to the floor. In the second half of play they did not convert a single field goal. MAC was the winner, 33-18.

Baseball—**April 23, 1908 (A):** The DePaul game at Chicago concluded in dramatic style. Entering the bottom of the ninth, MAC led 6-1. With one run already across, the Blue Demons loaded the bases with two outs. The next batter smashed a bases-clearing hit beyond the outfielders. Carrying the potential tying run, he circled the diamond as the ball was being tracked down and relayed to the plate. The final exchange was just in time, as Chase Crissey, the catcher, put the tag on to preserve a 6-5 Aggie victory.

Football—**October 3, 1908 (H):** The Michigan game, played in East Lansing for the first time, ended in a scoreless tie. Although many years later Duffy Daugherty would compare a tie with "kissing your sister," the 6,000 hometown spectators responded quite differently that October afternoon in 1908. At game's end, they "made the air black with hats and pennants," the *State Journal* reported. Players were carried from the field across the wooden bridge into the locker room of the Armory. Then, approximately 600 students, dressed in their nightshirts, took streetcars to Lansing and snake-danced through the town. They climaxed their celebration with a big bonfire at Washington and Michigan Avenues. As for the game, the Aggies dominated play. Three-quarters of the plays were in Wolverine territory. Only four times did the U of M make first downs, while the host did so eight times. MAC's goal was in danger but once, while six different occasions the Farmers worked the ball to within the shadows of their opponent's goal posts. First Parnell McKenna and then Ion Cortwright missed drop-kick field goal tries.

Football—**October 10, 1908 (H):** Two MAC players gained particular adulation in the 35-0 defeat of the Western Michigan Normals. Parnell McKenna dodged

and side-stepped the entire team of defenders when he returned one kickoff 100 yards for a touchdown. Another of his sensational runs came on the final play of the half when he returned yet another kickoff, this time being stopped at the visitors' 25-yard line. Leon Exelby was cited for his bursts into the line as it was reported he made from 15 to 40 yards on every carry.

Baseball—April 17, 1909 (H): *The MAC Record* erroneously labeled the season home opener as "slow and devoid of sensational features." Actually, it was a superb pitchers' affair of rare vintage. Pat Peterson surrendered only one hit in the nine innings, as his opponent, Sanford of Olivet, was even more miserly, throwing a no-hitter. Regardless, void of any hits, the Aggies had registered what proved to be a game-winning unearned run in the very first inning.

ATHLETE OF THE YEARS

Parnell McKenna, from Quinnesac in the upper peninsula, had followed his brother to East Lansing. Edward starred at MAC from 1903-1906 in both football and track. Parnell was a member of the football, basketball, and track teams, and earned a total of nine letters. He captained both the basketball and football teams of

Parnell McKenna

1909. In football, McKenna was a mainstay of four Aggie teams that lost a total of only five games. He played a vital role in holding the Wolverines to a scoreless tie in 1908.

IN THE SPARTLITE

Baseball: It seems strange by today's standards: On May 30, 1905, the Aggies played the Detroit Business University (DBU). The Detroit team was composed of professional players who were hired to represent the school in an advertising way. Not one of them was a student.

The cost of attending home games likely varied over those early years. In 1906, for $1.50, a season ticket could be purchased to cover all home games. In the following year, 1907, admission to individual games was set at 35 cents, with ladies admitted to the grandstand at no charge.

For the first time in the school's history, a doubleheader was scheduled, and it was on opening day, 1906, against Olivet. The Congregationalists won the first game 7-4, and MAC returned the favor, 5-2, in the nightcap.

A star of the 1906 and 1907 teams was Forrest "Parrot" Akers. This was the same Forrest Akers who would become a generous benefactor and have his name affixed to the university forever (Forrest Akers Golf Course). It could be suggested that as MAC pitcher, Akers ran into some bad luck. Two of his five losses in 1906 were games in which MAC was held scoreless. In 1907 he threw a two-hitter against the undefeated Irish at South Bend, only to come up the loser, 1-0.

The 1909 season opened with athletic director Brewer engaging John Morrissey, manager of the professional Lansing Senators of the Southern Michigan League, to train the squad through the preseason and early portion of the schedule. Seven years later, Morrissey would officially become the Aggies' head coach for two seasons, 1916 and 1917.

Basketball: The layout in the Armory held a truly "home court" advantage. The baskets and backboards were attached flush to the brick walls and the overhead steel girders were so low that visiting marksmen were baffled at shooting through or around the obstacles. Accustomed to these obstructions, clever MAC players became adept at arching long shots between the beams. Robert "Red" Dickson, (BK 06-09) also perfected a trick shot that was the joy of the home crowd and a headache for the enemy. As reported in *The M.S.C. Record,* he overcame his lack of stature by being able to scramble up the

steam pipes, beneath the basket at each end, and dump the ball into the basket. Dickson could therefore be considered the school's first "dunk-shot" artist.

There seemed to be extreme flexibility in scheduling basketball games. Within a week of a Jan. 26, 1906, encounter with the Flint YMCA, word came that the Y-men would not be fulfilling their commitment. Hurriedly, three days before game day, a substitute opponent was found in Albion College. The Brits then quickly sent word they couldn't make it after all. Finally, Coach Brewer turned to Owosso, where the YMCA team accepted the challenge, an eventual ignominious 76-12 shellacking from the Farmers.

Poor rail connections accounted for the late arrival of the Albion College team on March 3, 1906. As a result, it was agreed to shorten the two periods of play to 15 minutes. At intermission, MAC led 15-4, and it was a runaway after that as the Aggies wrapped it up, 59-8. Sophomore Roy Vondette was the leading scorer with 28 points.

What a disappointment on Februrary 19, 1907, for a crowd reported to be the largest-ever at the Armory: By a score of 23-17, the Detroit YMCA handed MAC its second loss of the 1907 season and what would be the only setback at home. The Aggies failed to convert one field goal during the first half of play. Both losses of the 14-2 season were at the hands of the Detroit "Y."

The 1908 home opener, an eventual 46-21 victory over Oberlin, was delayed when something went wrong at the power plant, and the entire building was left in darkness. As reported in *The Lansing State Journal*, the large crowd sang "Oberlin poor Oberlin" and "gave the locomotive and nine rahs for the team until the lights came on and the game began."

When the Detroit YMCA agreed to a pair of games in 1909, home and away, it was also settled that the game at the "Y" on February 11 would be played under YMCA regulations, while intercollegiate rules would control play one month later in East Lansing. As it turned out, when the Detroiters arrived at MAC on March 11 they reneged and insisted on again using the YMCA rulebook. The Aggie captain, Parnell McKenna, reluctantly yielded. Regardless, the Aggies proceeded to defeat the "Y" men, 33-28. The primary difference in the two sets of regulations was that the collegiate rules provided few restrictions on fouling and fewer time-outs.

Football: Players of the early 1900s must have mended quickly from their bumps and bruises. Twice during the schedule of 1905 two games were played within the same week. On Saturday, October 7, four days after the Notre Dame game at South Bend, Michigan Agricultural defeated Port Huron YMCA, 43-0. Two weeks later it was another "double dose." On Saturday Olivet succumbed, 30-0, and after only one day's rest, the Aggies blanked Hillsdale, 18-0, in a rare Monday afternoon contest.

Affirming the diminutive size of players during the period, the listed weights of the 1905 starters were as follows: Jesse Boyle, 152; Walter Small, 135; H.B. McDermid, 174; Ed McKenna, 157; George Boomsliter, 175; Oscar Kratz, 159; Charles Burroughs, 190; Steve Doty, 160; James Fisk, 174; Bert Shedd, 168; and Wilbert Holdsworth, 142.

In summarizing the successful season of 1908 (6-0-2), *The MAC Record* spoke critically of the student support:

> "The most noticeable defect of the season was the woeful lack of student spirit. At times when every person connected with the college should have been down on the bleachers, many of the students could be found at the roller rink or other down town places of amusement."

During halftime at the 1907 Wabash game, a new team mascot was introduced when a student paraded out a large white rooster with wings that had been painted green. The bird was eventually placed in the middle of the field with the pretense of guarding the game ball. The painted cock was featured in two additional seasons. Yet another mascot came on the scene in September of 1909 when a little brown bear was shipped to the football team from Montana. The gesture was perpetrated by a group of MAC forestry students who were working in the west during the summer. The forest creature, quickly embraced and given the name "Monty," was freed from his cage behind the Armory and dragged to College Field for display at home games that fall. Eventually, at season's end, arrangements were made for the young bear to be adopted by a zoo, the John Ball Park in Grand Rapids.

It seems that sometimes coach Chester Brewer also served as ticket manager. *The MAC Record* of Nov. 24, 1908, reminded readers to contact Brewer if they needed tickets for that season's finale, the Thanksgiving Day game in Detroit against the Athletic Club.

The Holcad reported total gate receipts for the 1909 season at $4,568.85.

Hockey: On Saturday, Feb. 10, 1906, playing 20-minute halves, the MAC hockey team met defeat at the hands of the Lansing High School team, 2-1. The game was played in Lansing at the Piatt's dam. The team lined up as follows: R. Edwards at goal, Hopson at left wing, C. Edwards at center, Hughes at right wing, Frazer at point, O'Gara at cover point and Boss, the team captain, at rover.

The MAC Record had particular praise for O'Gara:

"O'Gara played a game such as is seldom witnessed outside the professional teams of the International League. His posing, checking and shooting were excellent, he being credited with securing the only goal registered by MAC."

One week later, the seven-man Aggie team once more headed downtown to skate against the "high schoolers." This time they returned home as winners, 3-1. The game was reported as "faster and cleaner hockey." Again, O'Gara was singled out by *The Record*:

"O'Gara's rushes were the feature of the game, he repeatedly skated through the entire Lansing team, and being prevented from scoring more goals only by the fact that the Lansing spectators crowded around the Lansing goal to such an extent that the goal was hardly visible. His defense work was also good, as he broke up the High School's combinations as fast as they were formed."

The Farmers also had followers at the dam, all 50 of them. How imprudent it would have been for any of those early hockey rooters to suggest that more than 70,000 would someday gather to watch the school's hockey team in action.

The 1904 MAC band

SPARTAN SCRAPBOOK
———— TRACK and FIELD ————

1900 Field Day track and field team

MAC
1909-1910

TALES TO TELL

For State fans who become frustrated by the lack of attention afforded the Spartans by the Detroit media, the provocation is not new. Consider *The Detroit Free Press* Sunday edition of Nov. 14, 1909. The first page of the sports section carried an eight-column composite football picture featuring the 12-6 Michigan defeat of the University of Pennsylvania in Philadelphia. This was accompanied by three separate stories on that big U of M win. Also tucked onto the page were stories of three other games: Minnesota-Wisconsin, Chicago-Cornell and Yale-Princeton. Where was the report of the MAC-Marquette game, played in East Lansing that Saturday? It took some searching to locate and finally detect, eight pages into the section, beyond two full-page ads for the Crowley-Milner department store and a page featuring the local bowling scores. There it was, an 11-inch story in the middle of the seventh column next to a near equally long story of a U of M freshman game. Gaining the attention of the Detroit media always has been a struggle for the green and white.

Not bothered by the lack of media attention, the first MAC cross country team brought home the Hope College Invitational team title in 1910.

HEADLINES of 1910

- Spokane, Wash., becomes the first city to celebrate Father's Day.
- Boy Scouts of America and the Camp Fire Girls are established.
- Electric washing machines are introduced and production of a practical electric cooking range begins.
- A French chemist, Georges Claude, invents the neon light.

SCOREBOARD

	W	L	T	Avg.
Baseball	8	6	0	.571
Track and Field	1	0	0	1.000
Football	8	1	0	.889
Basketball	10	5	0	.667
Tennis	1	1	1	.500
Cross Country	no dual meets			

TEAM OF THE YEAR

For an unknown reason, MAC did not meet Michigan on the gridiron in the fall of 1909. Completing a season record of 8-1, the only defeat was a 17-0 loss to Notre Dame. In the eight wins, the Aggie defense proved impenetrable, as all opponents were held scoreless.

1909 football team. Shown below (front row, left to right) C. Ballard, F. Davis; (second row, left to right) E. Horst, W. Barnett, L. Exelby, I. Cortright, G. Wooley, R. Montford; (third row, left to right) Coach C. Brewer, A. Campbell, C. Lemmon, captain P. McKenna, C. Moore, B. Shedd, manager L. Johnson; (back row, left to right) W. Riblet, L. Hill, J. Campbell, J. McWilliams, B. Patterson, F. McDermid, F. Stone, O. Carey.

MAKING HISTORY

For the seventh year in a row the Aggies would complete their home football schedule without a loss. The last setback at home had been in the closing game of the 1902 season. The impressive streak would continue through the 1910 season and the opening game of 1911. On the next Saturday, Oct. 14, 1911, the University of Michigan came to town and defeated MAC, 15-3, to end the remarkable run at 44 straight victories (including two ties).

In what is recorded as the first Michigan State cross country team, an Aggie sextet was among the five teams and 30 individual entries that toed the line at the Hope College Invitational on Saturday, April 9. Just as with today's scoring, the team's point total was based on the finish of the first five members of each team. A harbinger of great future performances for Michigan State, the neophyte Aggies of that day took both the individual honors and the team title. Fred Tillotson won the race in a time of 21:15 over the course of approximately four miles. Other Aggie team members finished as follows: Charles Perkins, fourth; Arthur Warner, ninth; Robert Rosen, 11th; and Horace Geib, 14th. MAC's winning team total was 39 points, followed by 58 for Olivet, 71 for the Grand Rapids YMCA, 80 for Hope, and 89 for Muskegon High School. The handsome hammered-brass shield, shown with the 1910 team, was to be contested for 10 years with the school having the most wins keeping it.

GREAT STATE DATES

Football—**October 16, 1909 (H):** The 28-0 defeat of Wabash had to be an exciting game for the spectators. It included some unusual plays. The opening two points came from a safety when a visiting defender was tackled in his own end zone after unwisely attempting to run out an intercepted pass. Within five minutes of the safety, Parnell McKenna secured the ball on a triple pass and dodged through the entire defense for a 45-yard touchdown run. In the second half "Ex" Exelby broke through the line and raced 75 yards for a TD. Employing the on-side kick on the ensuing kickoff, a reserve by the name of Woodley managed to gather in the elusive ball and ramble into the end zone for yet another score.

Football—**November 25, 1909 (A):** The Aggies closed out the season on Thanksgiving Day with a fairly easy 34-0 defeat of the Detroit Athletic Club. Reflecting on the "mud bath" playing conditions of the day, *The Detroit Free Press* reported:

> "Five minutes after the beginning of hostilities not a man on the field would have been able to recognize his own image in a mirror. Faces, hands and clothing were coated with mud an inch thick."

The MAC band and what was described as a "handful" of rooters made the journey to the big city in support of their team. An interesting story lay in who didn't play for the Athletic Club rather than those who did. Again, quoting from the *Free Press*: "The University of Michigan men who were expected to play with the DAC team failed to put in an appearance." This is the way it was in those early years, "guns for hire."

Basketball—**February 7, 1910 (H):** For a team averaging only 31 points for the season, registering 84 points against the Bay City YMCA was a true anomaly. Upon reporting the story, the *Bay City Times* boldly stated the 84 points rung up by the Aggies was a national scoring record—who could challenge such a claim? Top scorers in that win were Bill Barnett and Fred Busch with 28 and 26 points, respectively.

Basketball—**February 19, 1910 (H):** For the first time ever, the Aggies defeated Notre Dame twice within a basketball season. The second victory, in the Armory, was a fairly easy 43-23 decision. MAC starters that evening were Fred Busch and Bill Barnett at forward, Art Campbell at center, and guards captain Claude Hannish and Parnell McKenna, in his fifth season. With no recorded explanation, the Irish were off the Aggie schedule for the next two years.

Track and Field—**February 26, 1910 (H):** Visualizing the limitations of the Armory floor (60' x 90'), it is understandable why it was extremely difficult to conduct an indoor track meet there. Notwithstanding this fact, the Ypsilanti Normal School came to town for such a competition and would later leave on the short end of the score 43-28. The program of events that Friday evening included a relay, 30-yard dash, high dive, standing high jump, running high jump, shot put, standing broad jump and the pole vault. The take-off runway for that latter event could not have been more than 40 feet in length.

Basketball—**March 7, 1910 (A):** Upon defeating the Detroit YMCA, 27-24, the biased *MAC Record* claimed a "state basketball championship" for the year. The vanquished "Y" team had been the holder of the title over the preceding two seasons.

Baseball—**May 14, 1910 (H):** *The Lansing Journal* described this MAC-Western State game as a "weird exhibition of the National game." After six innings the visitors led 4-0. At this juncture, inexplicably, the Normal coach relieved his starting pitcher who had been mystifying the Aggie batters. The new twirler was wild and was immediately worked for a series of walks and hits. Before the home half of the seventh was concluded, the Aggies had registered nine runs. They continued the assault in the eighth with three more tallies. When the dust had settled, what seemed destined a certain loss became a 12-7 win.

Baseball—**May 21, 1910 (H):** It would be no exaggeration to suggest pitcher Ben "Pat" Pattison had control trouble in the 3-1 win over Alma. In the shortened six-inning Saturday morning contest he walked six batters, uncorked three wild pitches and hit one batter with the bases loaded to force across the only run for the visitors. The game, which lasted only one hour and 15 minutes, was terminated after the sixth, enabling the Scots to catch a train north.

Track and Field—**May 21, 1910 (H):** Scoring a total of 77 points, the Aggies completely dominated the annual triangular meet with Olivet, 12 points, and Alma, seven points. *The Holcad* highlighted the work of George Shaw to whom they attributed two new state intercolle-

giate records: a 26.4 in the 220-yard low hurdles and a winning height of 11' 3" in the pole vault. They further boasted that Rupert Giddings equaled a state record with his 10 seconds flat in the 100-yard dash.

Baseball—**June 4, 1910 (H):** Herb Mills, the team's only four-year veteran, closed out the home schedule in memorable style against Michigan Normal. In his final at-bat, in the eighth inning, the second baseman slashed out a long drive that skipped past the outfielders. Utilizing his speed, he circled the bases as the defense chased the drive (no fences) and then avoided the embarrassment of a putout by sliding headfirst into the plate. It was only the team's second home run of the season. Mills shared the spotlight with pitcher Ben Pattison who yielded only three hits in the 5-1 win.

ATHLETE OF THE YEAR

Leon Exelby, the five-foot-nine, 190-pound fullback, along with teammate Ernest Baldwin (170-pound left guard), became the first Aggies to be honored by *The Chicago Tribune* as members of Walter Eckersall's All-Western football team. G. Patterson of *Collier's Weekly* wrote of "Ex":

"Another splendid fullback in the West this year is Exelby of the Michigan Aggies College, a man who would have forced more attention if he had been on a prominent team."

Upon graduation in 1912, Exelby became the head coach at the University of Wyoming.

IN THE SPARTLITE

Baseball: The decade opened with new uniforms of medium gray with dark blue trimmings and the classic interlocking MAC logo adorning the left breast. Caps and stockings were of the same color and the warmup coats were reverse colors, blue with gray trimming.

With the bleacher section along the first base line completed for use, admission for home baseball games was 25 cents with season tickets at $1.75 or $1.25 for those who held membership in the school's booster group.

In the third inning of the 12-1 drubbing of Ohio Wesleyan on April 29, the Aggies pushed across seven runs. The highlight of that inning was the unusual hitting of two triples by one player, Herb Mills.

During the two-game home series against Wabash College on May 28 and 30, the local fans cheered the efforts of Ash, a one-armed outfielder for the visitors. Originally enrolled at MAC but unable to make the squad, he transferred to the Indiana school and earned a spot as a starter.

Leon Exelby

Basketball: From January 25 to 30, the team was on an extended five-game trip. Beginning with a 27-18 win at the Jackson YMCA, the seven-man squad caught the Lake Shore Railroad into Indiana for the remaining four games against Purdue, Rose Poly, Wabash and Notre Dame. Facilities were described as an enormous floor in a magnificent new gymnasium with plate glass "back stops" (Purdue); a box-like floor (Wabash); and an immense court, 100 feet long with a dirt floor (Notre Dame).

With a limited number of schools fielding teams in the early years of the century, MAC continued to engage YMCA affiliates through the 1920 season. Also, from 1909-1914 the Aggies scheduled Detroit club teams such as Spalding (Dick Jackson's Sport Shop), Rayls Sport Shop, and the team sponsored by the Burroughs Adding Machine Co.

For the first time, the basketball expense report for the year revealed a profit of $89.66. Income totaled $813.06 ($519.05 from home games and $294.01 from away games). Expenses totaled $723.40.

Cross Country: The annual intramural cross country run took place before the Olivet baseball game on April 16 and was completed on a new course of nearly four miles. The winner, Ralph Chamberlain, was timed in 21:56.2. He, along with the second-and third-place finishers, Robert Rosen and Arthur Warner, received the traditional awards, the cross country jerseys.

Football: By strange scheduling quirks, three games were played in mid week. The season opened with two games at home and only two days apart, Thursday, October 7 against Detroit College and Saturday, October 9 against Alma. Later, in November, Marquette and Olivet were faced, back-to-back on a Wednesday and a Saturday. The other non-Saturday game was the Detroit Athletic Club game on Thanksgiving Day.

There are no statistics available to accurately evaluate the impact of the passing game in the season-opening 27-0 victory over Detroit College. In its story, *The Detroit Free Press* does hint at the success:

"Only twice did the state college err in working the forward pass, and many of the large gains were made by that route. McKenna and Cortright worked this play to great advantage, and all of the scores but one were indirectly due to 40 or 50-yard gains by passes."

Perhaps the 1909 Michigan Agricultural College team could be historically perceived as at least one of the pioneers of the forward pass. That recognition has always been credited to the Notre Dame team that upset Army four years later, in 1913.

A story in the Wednesday, October 13 edition of *The Lansing Journal* covered the issue of automobile parking at football games, at apparently no charge. The problem of parking, an issue that would multiply in intensity with each succeeding season, was in its infancy in 1909:

"One feature this year will be the parking of automobiles at the entrance to the field. Any person wishing to leave his auto outside the grounds may do so, and it will be looked after by a competent attendant. Space has also been reserved for autos on the east side of the field."

Tennis: The combined men and women's team competed in three matches during the spring, winning one, losing one and tying yet another.

Track and Field: The team finished second in the annual triangular meet with Notre Dame and Armour Tech. The host Irish scored 72, MAC 43 and Armour 11.

That spring some of the college boys had a little fun which paid off. It had been rumored that MAC would not be permitted to enter a squad in an invitational track meet sponsored by the Grand Rapids YMCA, due to the objections by some other teams. Instead, with tongue in cheek, an eight-man team was entered under the "colors" of the fictitious "Okemos Athletic Club." To the surprise of the self-appointed "club president and physical director," L.L. Jones of Napoleon, the entries were accepted and eight badges were mailed back that gave competitors access to the track and field. The "team" eventually succeeded in winning a large number of points, including a victory in the mile relay.

The 1910 tennis team consisted of (left to right) Arao Itano of Japan, Marjorie Kedzie of East Lansing, Harry Taft of East Lansing, and Lucy Armer of Traverse City. Seated at the far right is the team manager. Tennis was contested with a combined men-women's squad until 1917 when the women began competing as a separate team.

MAC
1910-1911

TALES TO TELL

In replacing the departed Chester Brewer, president Snyder selected the coach from the University of Arkansas, 27-year-old Hugo Bezdek. As it turned out, there proved to be one slight problem, Bezdek could not be released from his contract at Arkansas. He later became head coach at Penn State from 1918 to 1929. In a rather unique role, he doubled as baseball manager of the professional Pittsburgh Pirates in 1918 and 1919.

The next candidate to be offered the Aggie job was Jesse Harper, the Wabash College coach; however, the State Board of Agriculture would not approve the deal. The proposed annual salary of $2,200 ($200 over Brewer's final year) apparently seemed exorbitant. Instead, Harper signed on with Notre Dame in the following year.

With Brewer gone and the post unfilled at calendar year's end, the president invoked a temporary measure by appointing a student-athlete, the basketball team captain Fred Busch, as interim head coach and athletic di-

rector, a bizarre move by today's standards. Somewhat desperate, yet determined to fill the Brewer position with the best man, Snyder packed his suitcase and headed east. He sought the advice of a friend who was one of the top coaches of the day, Mike Murphy of the University of Pennsylvania. Murphy, the three-time U.S. Olympic track and field coach, handed Snyder the name of only one man. With it, the president's next stop was Pawling, N.Y.

On Jan. 11, 1911, the news was released. Returning from the three-day eastern sojourn, President Snyder announced he had secured the services of John F. Macklin, a star of football, baseball and track at Penn in 1906 and 1907. Since graduation, Macklin had spent three years developing teams at Pawling Prep School. To the delight of all, John Macklin was available for immediate service, and, with baggage in hand, he arrived on campus Tuesday, January 17. Thus, he relieved the student-administrator Fred Busch, who had held the duties for a mere 17 days. With the title of professor of physical culture and athletic director, Macklin would be paid $2,000 per year.

HEADLINES of 1911

- Calbraith Rodgers makes the first cross-country airplane flight in 82 hours, four minutes.
- The will of journalist Joseph Pulitzer calls for the establishment of the now-coveted Pulitzer Prizes.
- Norwegian explorer Roald Amundsen becomes the first to reach the South Pole.
- Willis Carrier publishes his basic Rational Psychometric Formula, which still stands as the basis of all fundamental calculations in the air conditioning industry.

SCOREBOARD

	W	L	T	Avg.
Baseball	11	5	0	.688
Track and Field	0	0	0	.000
Football	6	1	0	.857
Basketball	5	9	0	.455
Tennis	2	2	0	.500
Cross Country	1	0	0	1.000

TEAM OF THE YEAR

The 1911 baseball team won 11 of 16 games. Three of the men came through the season sporting batting averages above .300, as John Dawson led the trio with an even .400 mark. Norm Spencer and Ben Pattison were a formidable duo on the pitching mound.

the most dramatic of the four coming from Hill on the opening play of the second half. Taking the kickoff at the two-yard line (the playing field, goal line to goal line, was 110 yards long until a rule change in 1912 shortened it to 100 yards), he fell in behind excellent interference and raced the full length of the field. This 108-yard touchdown run of a kickoff return should be listed as a school record. However, because the MSU record book includes only those statistics of the "modern era," the record is listed at an even 100 yards.

In 1910, a collegiate policy was adopted requiring freshman to sit out of varsity competition. Lacking an enforcement body such as the NCAA, the policy was obviously voluntary, as MAC first-year men continued to compete on varsity teams. The school eventually conformed to the policy in 1917.

Beginning with the 1910 football season, playing time for collegiate football games was changed from two 30-minute halves to the format of today, four quarters of 15 minutes each with the teams changing goals at the beginning of the second and fourth periods. Under the

Pictured with Coach Macklin is the 12-man baseball team of 1911 (one player is missing from the picture). Only four members of the team are identifiable. Front row: first from left, R. Dodge (P); second from left, N. Spencer (P); fourth from left, captain I. Cortright (2B) and fifth from left, E. Gorenflo (RF). Other Members of the team included: B. Harvey (CF), M. Griggs (1B), R. McCarthy (C), J. Dawson (LF), H. Rogge (3B), F. Busch (SS), H. Baker (RF) and N. Mogge (LF).

MAKING HISTORY

Halfback Leon "Bubbles" Hill and fullback Leon "Ex" Exelby provided Coach Brewer with an impressive offensive pair that played a significant role during the seasons of 1909 and 1910, which included 14 wins and only two defeats. In the victory over Lake Forest in 1910 each of the stars was credited with a pair of touchdowns,

prior rule, teams changed goals after each touchdown. This new playing time format provided for a substitution rule. Previously, once a player left the game, he could not re-enter. A player could now withdraw from the game and return at the beginning of a subsequent period.

GREAT STATE DATES

Football—**October 6, 1910 (H):** Opening their schedule against Detroit A.C. on a rare Thursday afternoon, it took Coach Brewer's boys just one-and-a-half minutes to score the season's first touchdown. Detroit kicked off. "Bubbles" Hill returned the ball 10 yards and added 15 more on a run around left end. Clint Ballard gained ten yards through the right side, and then a successful Bill Riblet-to-Fred Stone pass put the ball within the five-yard line. Roy Montford, filling in for Leon Exelby at fullback, plunged over for the touchdown. He would score two more times in the easy 35-0 victory. Only 500 spectators were in attendance.

Football—**October 8, 1910 (H):** It was a scheduling phenomenon unheard of by today's standards. Checking the date above, October 6, it is readily noted the Aggies played *two* varsity games in *three* days. This second game, against a scrappy team from Alma, also ended up in the MAC win column, this time by a more modest score, 12-0. Leon "Bubbles" Hill scored all of the winners' points, two touchdowns (10 points) and two conversions (four points). His first TD came early in the opening quarter and his second was scored in the third quarter.

Football—**October 29, 1910 (H):** While MAC appeared to control every facet of the game, Notre Dame seemed bent on self-destruction (fumbles, penalties, poor punting and dropped passes). Taking full advantage, the Aggies upset the Irish, 17-0, to hand them their only loss of the season. The first touchdown (five points) came on a blocked punt, and the second was setup by a 30-yard Leon Exelby burst off tackle. Two 30-yard field goals by "Bubbles" Hill completed the scoring. Strange tactics by today's standards, both sides frequently punted on third, second and even on first down. The extraordinary victory sustained Chester Brewer's eight-year-old coaching record of never being defeated on friendly College Field. The losing coach, Frank "Shorty" Longman, complimented the Aggies:

"We were simply outclassed. MAC is vastly underrated. There is no team in the West that can defeat the Farmers on their own field. We were licked, and the sting of defeat is allayed by the fact that we lost to such a sportsmanlike bunch of men."

Football—**November 5, 1910 (A):** The sub-headline in the November 7 issue of *The Holcad* read: "Hill's Toe and MAC's Wonderful Defense Prove Too Much for the Strong Marquette Team." This was perhaps an appropriate summary of a 3-2 victory. The winner's score came in the second quarter as "Bubbles" Hill split the uprights with a 40-yard field goal into the face of a strong wind. Shortly thereafter, Hill had his punt from the 3-yard line blocked by a surging lineman, resulting in a Marquette safety. Thereafter, much of the excitement came from scores that were not made. During the third period, a Hilltopper pass receiver was stopped six inches from the goal line. In that same quarter Fred Stone was likewise stopped inches from the opposite goal line. This was Marquette's first loss of the year.

Football—**November 19, 1910 (H):** With the preseason announcement of Coach Brewer's resignation, the season-ending 62-0 defeat of Olivet was to be his final as MAC's head coach. Seven different Aggies scored touchdowns: Leon Exelby, Jim McWilliams, Elmer Gorenflo, Bill Riblett with Jim Cambell, Ion Cortright and "Bubbles" Hill each crossing the goal line twice. The stubborn MAC defense forced the play into the Comet end of the field for nearly the entire game, as the visitors gained only four first downs.

MAC vs. Notre Dame

Basketball—**January 18, 1911 (A):** This game at the Light Guard Armory in Detroit, a re-match with the Detroit Spaldings, was the first for new coach John Macklin. He had arrived in East Lansing the day before. The Spaldings had handed the Aggies a rare home loss, 21-9, in the season opener just nine evenings earlier. MAC came into the game with a 0-3 record, but they were buoyed by the opportunity to show the new mentor they were really winners. Fred Busch, a team captain who had filled in as interim coach, was the evening's top scorer with 13 points. The contest remained close until the final 10 minutes when the Farmers built a sufficient lead to win by seven points, 25-18. Only two others scored for the winners; Herb Duthie and Bob Goss were each credited with six points. It was an auspicious beginning for the new coach.

Basketball—**January 21, 1911 (H):** In defeating Armour Institute, 51-11, MAC won its most one-sided verdict of the season. Fred Busch led the way in the opening half, scoring 16 of his team's 18 points. Thereafter, he was continually harassed, held, tripped and, as reported in *The Lansing Republican*, the Armour players tried everything from "dirty play to intimidating the officials." In the process, two of the Chicagoans were sent to the sidelines for illegal play. Somewhat ignored in the second half, teammate Ralph Chamberlain took up the offensive role, netting 14 points. Fred Busch was ultimately the game's leading scorer with 23 points.

Basketball—**January 30, 1911 (A):** Much like the Aggies had experienced at Purdue in the preceding year, glass backboards had been installed in the gymnasium of the Detroit YMCA. A writer for the *Detroit Free Press* offered them as an excuse for MAC's 22-11 loss: "In defense of the Farmers it must be said that they appeared lost on the strange floor and up in the air shooting against the baskets with the glass backs."

Basketball—**March 3, 1911 (H):** In only the fourth home game of the season, MAC closed out the year by defeating Hope College, 36-24, with Ralph Chamberlain's 16 points leading the way. In a fairly common practice, Coach DeKruif of Hope acted as referee. The record at home would end 3-1 and the road record 2-8. A quick summary suggests the Aggies should have scheduled more games at the Armory. The problem was that more and more opponents had become reluctant to accept the built-in challenge of the "home" court.

Baseball—**April 28, 1911 (H):** Norm "Baldy" Spencer relinquished two hits in the opening inning and then proceeded to shut the door on Western Reserve to gain a 5-0 victory. Featuring doubles by Elmer Gorenflo, Mark Griggs, Bill McCarthy and Ion Cortright, all of the Aggie runs were scored in the second inning. It was the second year in row MAC shut out the Clevelanders.

Baseball—**May 5, 1911 (H):** Michigan Agriculture College, 6, Ohio State, 1. It was the fulfillment of the time-honored formula for winning baseball games: strong pitching, solid defense and robust hitting. "Pat" Pattison was on the mound for the full nine innings and surrendered just two hits. Although booting two balls, the fielders were impressive when it counted, and 14 hits were lashed out with Bill McCarthy and Freddie Busch collecting three apiece.

Baseball—**May 12, 1911 (H):** After losing to the Syracuse Orangemen in 1908 and 1910, John Macklin's 1911 crew finally defeated the visiting Easterners, 6-4. More than 900 loyal fans watched the Farmers open with three runs in the first, score two in the fourth, and one in the sixth. Norm "Baldy" Spencer pitched effectively, scattering eight hits and yielding no walks.

Baseball—**May 13, 1911 (H):** Ralph Dodge pitched his first game as an Aggie, yielding only five hits to defeat the Alma Scots, 6-2. The Jackson, Mich., freshman also excelled at the plate, managing a pair of hits, including a three-bagger to highlight the four-run second inning.

Track and Field—**May 20, 1911 (H):** For the second straight year, MAC captured the triangular meet against Olivet and Alma. Two of the five individual winners for the Aggies claimed College Field records: Bill Blue, who tossed the discus 114' 2", and the three-year veteran Horace Geib, who posted a 4:42.8 in the mile. The other first-place finishers were "Tillie" Tillotson in the two-mile run, Art Day in the shot put and Charles Lord in the high jump.

Baseball—**May 25, 1911 (H):** Lake Forest opened with one run in the first inning, but the game dragged until the ninth before the Aggies managed to score the equalizer, forcing extra innings. In the tenth inning, Freddie Busch smashed a long drive over the center fielder's head and to the river scoring "Baldy" Spencer for the 2-1 victory. The rules of the period provided that an extended game ended the minute the winning run scored. Otherwise, the final tally would have likely read

4-1. Added base runner Bill McCarthy was right behind Spencer, and Busch could have easily circled the bases on his long drive. Spencer pitched the entire game, allowing only three base hits.

ATHLETE OF THE YEAR

Ion Cortright was a scholastic star at nearby Mason High School. At MAC from 1908-1911 he was a nine-letter man in track, baseball and football, captaining both baseball and football in his senior year. Ion joined the MAC coaching staff in the fall of 1911 and served various positions prior to leaving in the summer of 1914 to become head coach for athletic teams at the University of South Dakota. In the fall of 1916 he would move on to the University of Cincinnati, where he assumed a similar coaching position.

Ion Cortright

IN THE SPARTLITE:

Baseball: As early as mid-February, Coach Macklin had summoned the pitchers and catchers to workouts in the Armory.

In an April issue of *The Holcad,* fans were reminded that season tickets were available at $2.75 or $2.25 for members of the athletic association, the school's booster group. As stated: "The tickets can be had of Andy at the barber shop or any member of the athletic board of control." Could Andy be considered the school's first ticket manager?

The school contracted the services of the Michigan Central Railroad for transporting fans to Ann Arbor for the Michigan baseball game May 30. At a cost of $1.30 round trip, reservations were made available for 250 local fans. They were accompanied by team members and the cadet band. They should have stayed home. The final score read U of M 8, MAC 2.

Basketball: Upon arrival on January 17, the Aggies' new coach, John Macklin, directed his team to three straight wins before he was hit with his first loss, a 22-11 defeat at the Detroit YMCA. But, what could he expect? That evening his team was able to score only two field goals during the 40 minutes of action.

As years went by, it became more difficult to entice teams to play in the Armory with its challenging low beams. Listed are the home-away numbers for 1909, 1910, and 1911: 10-5, 5-10 and 4-10.

Football: Chester Brewer would complete the football schedule as a "lame duck" coach. One week prior to the start of the season he announced his resignation, effective January 1. The popular coach had accepted a position as director of physical training at the University of Missouri.

At a round trip fare of $1.25, Aggie fans were able to catch the rail to Ann Arbor for that fall's clash with the University of Michigan. By any and all means of travel, 1,200 rooters for the Green were on hand for this fifth meeting of the two intrastate rivals. Admission to the game was 50 cents. Begrudgingly, by the narrow margin of 6-3, it was another loss to the Wolverines. The outstanding MAC halfback Leon "Bubbles" Hill kicked a field goal early to put the Aggies in front 3-0. Later in the first half, Hill ran back a Michigan punt 70 yards for what would have been a game-winning touchdown. The U of M coach, Fielding H. Yost, intervened, came onto the field, and persuaded officials to nullify the score for a claimed holding call far behind the play. After the game, the Michigan player who allegedly had been fouled admitted he was not within 15 yards of the place the foul supposedly ocurred. Such was the influence of the reputed Fielding H. Yost. Rather than complain about the incident, in a postgame interview Coach Brewer spoke proudly of his team:

"I never in my life saw better defensive playing than our team put up, and their tackling took Michigan off their feet. Ralph Hoagland, the referee, told me that MAC played the gamiest and best defensive ball that he ever saw. Our men fought to the last ditch. They were on the job every minute, and every MAC rooter was proud of them."

Although the game drew a good crowd, U of M officials saw fit to pay MAC officials only $200 for their share of the receipts.

Entering the Lake Forest game on October 22, Coach Brewer instructed his players to "use straight foot-ball tactics and reserve the new plays for the bigger games." He was convinced that Notre Dame and Marquette "spies" would be in the stands watching and taking notes.

The season ended prematurely with the 62-0 defeat of Olivet. The Thanksgiving Day game with Wabash was canceled after the Crawfordsville, Ind., school disbanded their team following the death of a player in an October 22 game at St. Louis.

Track and Field: At the season's end, only six team members were recipients of the monogram sweater. They were: Bill Blue, Horace Geib, Art Day, Ed Friar, Leon "Bubbles" Hill and Charles Lord.

Captain Ion Cortright (holding ball) led the 1910 MAC football team to a 6-1 record.

MAC
1911-1912

TALES TO TELL

As part of their introduction to life at MAC, freshmen were quickly schooled in memorizing the sundry cheers led by the Aggie yell master. The man who held this prestigious position of yell master did so by way of an annual campus-wide student election. Below are five classic cheers circa the 1910s:

Rat-a-to-thrat! To-thrat! To-thrat!
Terrors to lick! To lick! To lick!
Kick-a-ba-ba! Kick-a-ba-ba!
M.A.C.! M.A.C.!
R-r-rah!

Osky-wow-wow, Skinny-wow-wow,
Skinny-wow-wow, wow-wow-wow-wow.

Down before the Farmers,
Down before the Farmers,
Down before the Farmers
Michigan goes!
Boom! Rah! Aggies!

Um-m-m-m-m! Ah-h-h-h!
You can't fool the Farmers! By heck!

Rah! Rah! Rah!
Uz, Uz, Uz,
M.A.C.
Tiger!

For the first time in the rivalry, the Michigan football game was played in East Lansing. A special song, to the tune of "Alexander's Ragtime Band" was composed and distributed for singing that afternoon:

HEADLINES of 1912

- New Mexico and Arizona become the 47th and 48th states respectively, while Alaska becomes recognized as an organized U.S. territory.
- Captain Albert Berry becomes the first American to make a parachute jump from an airplane.
- Perhaps the best all-around athlete in history, Native American track and field star Jim Thorpe, dominates the Olympic games in Stockholm by winning both the decathlon and the pentathlon events.
- The steamship *Titanic* collides with an iceberg in the Atlantic and sinks with a loss of more than 1,500 lives.

SCOREBOARD

	W	L	T	Avg.
Baseball	10	3	0	.769
Track and Field	0	1	0	.000
Football	5	1	0	.833
Basketball	12	3	0	.800
Tennis	record not available			
Cross Country	0	0	0	.000

*Come on and cheer; come on and cheer
for the Farmers' football team,
Come on and cheer; come on and cheer;
they are the best we've ever seen.
They can pull a forward pass like you
never saw before,
So nat-u-ral that it makes another score,
Rah! Rah! for the good old olive green, M.A.C.*

*Come on and cheer, come on and cheer
for the Farmers' football team,
Come on and cheer, come on and cheer
for the Farmers all the time.
Oh look a' here, look a' here, how they're
smashing up the line.
And if you want to see those Aggies make
another touchdown,
Come on and cheer, come on and cheer,
for the Farmers all the time.*

TEAM OF THE YEAR

With an overall record of 10 wins against three losses, the baseball team posted the school's best winning percentage in 20 years. Especially gratifying were the three victories over Michigan. In each of these games, second-year man Ralph Dodge played a vital role. In the first contest he scored the winning run and was then the winning pitcher in both the second and third game against the Wolverines. Over the 13-game season, third baseman Charles Bradley was the leading hitter as he achieved an impressive .546 average. Right fielder Norton Mogge was the top defender, finishing the season without having committed an error. Norm Spencer, along with Dodge, presented an impressive and successful mound duo.

1912 baseball team. All members of the team are not identifiable; those that are include (front row, left to right) R. Dodge (P), second from left, B. Harvey (CF), fourth from left, M. Griggs (1B), N. Spencer (P), A. Bibbins (C); (back row, left to right, beginning fourth from left) N. Mogge (RF), E. Gorenflo (2B), Coach Macklin. Other members of team are J. Dawson (LF), H. Rogge (SS), C. Bradley (3B) and P. Dancer (RF).

MAKING HISTORY

The 1911 football season included only six games. This was a result of two cancellations, the first being the October 21 game with Buchtel (University of Akron) and the second, which had been rescheduled with Ohio Northern for Friday, November 17. The Buchtel athletic manager gave notice in late September, providing ample time for MAC officials to make adjustments. They did so with a triple-header. A varsity-reserve game was scheduled and meshed between two other pairings, the senior class versus the sophomore class and MAC freshmen against Mt. Pleasant Normal (Central Michigan). As for the second cancellation, it was an unusual twist along with rainy weather conditions that led to rubbing out the scheduled game with Ohio Northern. Originally, the game was to have been played on Saturday, November 18. At the request of Coach Macklin, it was moved back one day, enabling the Aggie mentor to accept an invitation for he and members of his team to be guests at the Michigan-Pennsylvania contest in Ann Arbor that Saturday (Macklin was a Penn alumnus). As fate would have it, an unrelenting downpour on Friday made conditions of the home field impossible for play. Pocketing their guarantee money, the Ohio Northern contingent returned to Ada, Ohio, without even soiling their uniforms. The embarrassed Macklin could only return to the practice field on the following Monday and prepare for the season closer against Wabash on Thanksgiving Day. Oh yes, in that game in Ann Arbor, Michigan defeated Pennsylvania 11-9.

GREAT STATE DATES

Football—**November 11, 1911 (H):** Accounting for three field goals, three touchdowns (five points each), and two PATs, "Bubbles" Hill was credited with every point in the 26-6 victory over Mt. Union. His longest field goal that afternoon was from the 45-yard line and his most impressive TD was a 65-yard return of an intercepted pass.

Football—**November 30, 1911 (H):** The Wabash College team came to town touted as the best edition of football in the school's history. Moreover, they were seeking atonement for three straight losses to MAC in 1907, 1908 and 1909. The Aggies, closing out their first season

under John Macklin, read the script differently for this Thanksgiving morning contest. They would cross the goal three times and, by a score of 17-6, make it four in a row over the Little Giants. Carp Julian had a busy holiday. He blocked a punt to account for the second TD and then put the game away in the final minute with a pass interception touchdown.

Basketball—**February 10, 1912 (H):** In one of the more lopsided games ever turned in by a MAC team, the Winona College quinter was easy prey, 67-4. It could easily be suggested the visitors found that shooting through the Armory ceiling beams was an unrewarding experience. Three weeks earlier they had battled the Aggies before succumbing, 37-21. In the return victory, George Gauthier and Ralph Chamberlain each tossed in 22 points to share scoring honors.

Basketball—**February 21, 1912 (H):** Have you ever heard of going to the "Big Dance" and *not* playing basketball? It happened at MAC in 1912. Valiant but unsuccessful efforts were made to reschedule the home basketball game against Hope College as it was the same night of the all-important J-Hop. Junior starters Norman "Baldy" Spencer and Ralph Chamberlain had to make a choice, go dancing or play basketball. A shocker by today's thinking, the pair opted to go dancing. They were replaced in the line-up by Ralph Dodge and Rod Mathieson. Even playing with substitutes for the dancers, the Aggies won the contest with apparent ease, 55-23.

Basketball—**March 4, 1912 (A) :** In the season finale at Detroit, the Aggies had battled the "Y" men scoreless for seven minutes when Ralph Chamberlain broke away for a field goal. George Gauthier and Abe Vatz followed with baskets, and by intermission MAC led, 14-8. The second half also began slowly as six-and-one-half minutes were gone before Vatz registered on a long shot. From there the hosts began to outshoot MAC and narrowed the differential to one point during the closing minute of the game. Just before the clock ran out, Bob Goss tossed in a long shot to make the final score read 20-17. With that victory and a 12-3 overall season, as in 1910, MAC boosters again proclaimed the "unofficial" title of state champions.

Baseball—**April 13, 1912 (H):** Norm Spencer was called upon to pitch the season opener against Alma, and he responded with a two-hit, 3-0 victory. He fanned eight men in the abbreviated six-inning contest. First baseman Mark Griggs, who had transferred from Alma one year

earlier, was the hitting star with two hits, including a two-run homer in the fourth inning. Charles Bradley also connected for a pair of hits.

Baseball—**May 4, 1912 (H):** In the first game of the season's series against Michigan, the Wolverines led 6-5 after eight innings and the tail end of the MAC batting order stood ready in the ninth. Art Bibbins, the number eight hitter, singled to center field. Pinch-hitter Ralph Dodge and then Charles Bradley followed with hits to load the bases. Norton Mogge, the next batter, was instructed to lay down a bunt and produce the tying run using the old squeeze play. With the runners quickly on the move, Mogge's bunt was so perfectly placed that *both* Bibbins and Dodge raced home with the tying and the winning runs.

Baseball—**May 10, 1912 (H):** As in the previous four seasons, Syracuse again came to Michigan for weekend games in East Lansing and with the U of M at Ann Arbor. The Aggie-Orange contest of 1912 was decided in the tenth inning. With the score knotted at 1-1 and MAC runners at the corners, the Syracuse catcher, without calling timeout, strolled to the mound for a conference with his pitcher. An alert Mark Griggs, the runner perched on third, seized the opportunity and raced to the unprotected home plate with the winning run.

Baseball—**May 18, 1912 (A):** Game number two of the three-game season series with the U of M shifted to Ann Arbor where Ralph Dodge, the Jackson sophomore, was again supreme. He granted the Michigan batters a scant three hits and was never in trouble in a 5-1 victory. The Aggies packed most of their offense into the third inning. With one down, both Art Bibbins and Dodge reached base on an error. Charles Bradley singled, scoring Bibbins, and Elmer Gorenflo doubled, scoring Dodge. Norton Mogge singled, scoring Bradley, and when the Wolverine catcher threw wild to second, Gorenflo came home with the fourth run of the inning.

Baseball—**May 30, 1912 (A):** Accompanied by 100 rooters properly dressed as true Michigan State Aggies in farmer straw hats and red bandanas, Coach Macklin and his squad returned to Ann Arbor for the third game of the spring against the Wolverines. Although the U of M managed to score three times, once more Ralph Dodge baffled their hitters, yielding only four hits in nine innings. Meanwhile, the MAC offense featured 15 hits, including a triple by Mark Griggs and doubles from the bats of Charles Bradley, Burwell Harvey and Dodge, leading to a comfortable 8-3 victory.

Track and Field—**May 25, 1912 (H):** In what was becoming a spring tradition, Michigan Agricultural hosted Alma and Olivet in a triangular track meet at College Field and scored 61 points to win. The Comets managed 39 points and the Scots 35. To the Aggies this was an important meet since the athletic department policy dictated a major monogram would go to each MAC man who captured a first place. Earning the honor this afternoon were Howard Beatty, Robert Brown, Charles Lord and Horace Geib, the latter becoming a four-time letterwinner in the process. Beatty, the talented freshman, won both the high hurdle event (17.0) and the low hurdles (28.0), along with a second in the broad jump and third-place finish in the pole vault. Brown took the 440 in 53.8 and Lord leaped 5'5" the high jump. Captain Geib led the field in his specialty, the two-mile run, with a clocking of 10:23.0.

ATHLETE OF THE YEAR

Leon "Bubbles" Hill of Benton Harbor was a three-year member of the football team (1909-1911) and lettered twice (1910-1911) as a member of the track and field squad. At five foot nine and 153 pounds, Hill was not an imposing figure, but he was a standout halfback during a span in which Aggie teams posted an impressive composite record of 19-3.

Leon "Bubbles" Hill

IN THE SPARTLITE

Baseball: In the first competition of any kind against Ohio State, the Buckeyes came to town on Monday, April 22 and won a high-scoring 11-8 verdict in a game played for the most part in a drizzling rain.

Travel during this period is exemplified by the baseball team itinerary to Ohio on March 21-23, 1912. The squad departed from Lansing by rail at 7:05 P.M., pulling into Detroit at 9:10 P.M. At 10:30 P.M. they were aboard a sleeper car headed for Delaware, Ohio, arriving at 6:35 A.M., in ample time for the 3:30 P.M. game against Ohio Wesleyan. On the next morning they headed north, reaching Cleveland at 11:00 A.M., five hours prior to the scheduled 4:00 game against Western Reserve. That evening they boarded a D&C boat for the Thursday trip across Lake Erie to Detroit. From there, the westbound 10:58 P.M. train took the tired players back to Lansing, dropping them sometime after midnight. Such was travel in the early 20th century.

As for that season finale home game against Normal, the star was pitcher Ralph Dodge. The steady junior struck out 16 batters while throwing a one-hitter in the 8-0 victory. Also featured were the free-wheeling Aggie runners who stole 12 bases on the visitors' pitchers.

Basketball: Only seven men made up the traveling team for the January 12-13 games against Armour Institute in Chicago and Northwestern College at Naperville, Ill. Such small squads were common, as starters frequently played the entire game. On this trip, however, there was need for a replacement as Ralph Chamberlain fouled out of the Northwestern game.

During this era of the two-handed set shot, it seemed strange to read in the Jan. 16, 1912, issue of *The Holcad:* "all baskets made by Alma were one-handed shots." Was it possible the Scots' coach was decades ahead of his time?

The road game at Holland against Hope proved to be the most exciting game of the year, even if it ended up in the loss column. After playing a second overtime period, the Dutchmen prevailed, 41-40. In the final few seconds, Macklin's five once more had an opportunity to tie the game but missed a free-throw attempt.

Compared with the preceding season, the 1912 team was a virtual scoring machine. Over the 14-game 1911 season, the Aggies averaged 24.0 points per game. One year later they opened the schedule by pouring in 72 points to defeat Central State and then went on to average 43.4 in 15 games.

Cross Country: In 1911 the team returned to Holland, Mich., for defense of their Hope Invitational title. Although Tillotson and Geib ran one-two, the Aggies fell short in their quest, being outscored by runners from the Grand Rapids YMCA. The team totals were: Grand Rapids "Y" 28, MAC 39, Muskegon 54 and Hope College 100.

Football: Statistics of the 17 men who comprised the varsity team of 1911 show they averaged 165 pounds and stood five foot 10. The heaviest player was center James McWilliams who, at 208, was the only player over 200 pounds. Back-up quarterback Earl Shuttleworth was the smallest team member, and he tipped the scales at 122 pounds and was five foot six.

For the second time in the six-year series, Fielding Yost and his Michigan aggregation were lured to East Lansing for what had now become an annual intra-state rivalry. Approximately 6,000 fans, by far the largest home turnout to ever assemble for an athletic event in East Lansing, watched as the courageous Farmers finally yielded to the larger and stronger team from Ann Arbor, 15-3. However, it didn't come easily for the Wolverines. Not only had the Macklin men held them scoreless, but they had outplayed them over the opening 30 minutes of action. In the third quarter the Aggies scored first on a "Bubbles" Hill field goal from the 35 yard line. Shortly thereafter that score was matched and the third period ended 3-3. In the final quarter, the weight and endurance of the visitors began to tell as some successful passes, punt returns and untimely penalties resulted in the pair of Wolverine touchdowns.

It seems the friendly press frequently tried to put a positive spin on a season. Upon closing the 5-1 schedule with a 17-6 defeat of Wabash (Ind.), *The MAC Record* claimed the Aggies were "*minor* college champions of the West."

Track and Field: Coach Macklin accompanied a team of 14 to Detroit on February 15, when they engaged the "Y" team in the only indoor track meet of the year, a 40-37 loss. The absence of the injured Captain Horace Geib was the difference. Aggies winners were Charles Lord, high jump, five foot nine; Howard Beatty, pole vault, 10' 3"; Robert Brown, 880-yard dash, 2:05.6; Art Day, shot put, 44' 3"; Warren, Beebe, Sanford, Servis, relay (18 laps, 50 yards each), 1:16.0.

SPARTAN SCRAPBOOK
—— TRACK and FIELD COACHES (1898-2003) ——

Henry Keep (1898)

Ion Cartright (1914)

George Gauthier (1915-19)

Arthur N. Smith (1920-21)

Albert Barron (1922-23)

Ralph H. Young (1924-40)

Karl Schlademan (1941-58)

Francis Dittrich (1959-75)

Jim Bibbs (1976-95)

Darroll Gatson (1996-)

Pictured elsewhere: George Denman 1902-03[BS]; Chester Brewer 1904-10[BS]; John Macklin 1911-13[BS]

[BS] see baseball coaches

MAC
1912-1913

TALES TO TELL

As noted earlier, travel during these times could be a real adventure. Take, for example, the basketball team's four-game swing (February 26-March 2) by rail into Ohio. On Wednesday, the squad left aboard the noon train for Toledo and an evening game on the slippery dance floor at St. John's College. MAC was victorious 39-24. An early departure the next morning took them to Akron, via Cleveland, for a Thursday night defeat by Buchtel College (Akron College), 35-30. On the next morning it was necessary to rise early, catching a 5:00 A.M. train for Centerville. There they boarded the Toledo & Ohio Central connection for Granville where they were to play an 8:00 P.M. game against Denison College. That Centerville-Granville link-up proved to be aboard the caboose of a freight train. All was going smoothly for approximately ten miles when the locomotive was disconnected and headed forward to assist in clearing a wreck from the tracks. Following two hours of standing still, a southbound passenger came through on a parallel track and picked up the athletes. After a short distance they too were upon the wreckage scene where they experienced an additional two and one-half hour delay. The long day finally concluded when the train pulled into Granville at about 8:30 P.M. The patiently waiting Denison College team agreed to a belated 9:00 P.M. game start. After a full day of travel and little to eat, the outcome seemed inevitable: Denison 44, MAC 18. Following this third game, the team traveled a short distance to Newark for a midnight supper and much needed rest. The next stretch of travel was on Saturday morning from Newark to Dayton and the week's final game, a last-minute loss to St. Mary's, 28-26. On the next day the team had to wait around until 8:00 in the evening before catching a train north for the return trip to Michigan.

TEAM OF THE YEAR

Discounting the embarrassing 55-7 loss to Michigan, the Aggies completed a 7-1 football season topped by the Thanksgiving Day upset of Ohio State, 35-20. In those seven wins, Macklin's crew posted four shutouts and offensively generated 290 points for an impressive average of 41 per game.

HEADLINES of 1913

- Grand Central Station opens in New York City.
- Through passage of the 16th amendment to the Constitution, the federal income tax becomes law.
- The Ford Motor Company sets up the first moving assembly line and soon produces 1,000 Model T's per day.

SCOREBOARD

	W	L	T	Avg.
Baseball	11	7	0	.611
Track and Field	1	3	0	.250
Football	7	1	0	.875
Basketball	8	5	0	.615
Tennis	1	1	1	.500
Cross Country	1	0	0	1.000

1912 football team. All members of the team are not identifiable. Those that are include (front row, far left) C. Gifford, G. Gauthier, third from left, (middle row) R. Chamberlain, far left, E. Gorenflo, B. Miller, W. Riblet, G. Julian; (back row) J. DaPrato, second from left, Coach Macklin, L. Campbell. Other members of the team are F. Chaddock, R. McCurdy, C. Dendal and L. Service.

MAKING HISTORY

As per a 1912 rule change, the football playing field was significantly altered. From goal line to goal line, the length of the playing field was reduced from 110 yards to 100 yards. At the same time, two 10-yard end zones became a part of the playing field; thus, the field as we know it today was in place. As a byproduct of this new grid, a kickoff would hereafter be booted from the 40-yard line rather than the 55-yard line, as was previously the case.

Another rule change added an additional down (from three to four) for advancing the ball the necessary 10 yards to gain a new set of downs.

Prior to 1913, a basketball goal was only scored when, as stated by the rule, "it remained in the basket." Although various devices were invented to release the ball quickly from its suspended position within the enclosed hoop, it was always rather a nuisance to do so. Beginning in 1913, today's configuration was achieved. The hoop was opened with a net hung from the bottom to momentarily check the flight of the ball to confirm it passed through. This prompted the rule change to read that a goal counted if the ball "passed through" the net.

GREAT STATE DATES

Football— **October 26, 1912 (H):** Prior to a rule change in 1903, the team scored upon was required to immediately kick the ball back to the team that had just scored. The new rule, as it has remained thereafter, provided the scored-upon team the choice of kicking or receiving. As one would expect, today the choice is a given…the team that scores kicks off. Not so in 1912 if you were the coach of DePauw University. After each of the Aggie's nine touchdowns, with no reason or explanation, the Little Giants opted to kick the ball back to the "red hot" Macklin men. If the visitors' strategy was to depend on their defense, it wasn't working. Quarter by quarter the MAC scoring unfolded as follows: 0-14-12-32, for a final of 58-0. As the gun signaled the end of the contest, the local heroes were poised for yet another score. Playing before a crowd of 1,200, Blake Miller had led the parade of scoring with four TDs.

Football— **November 16, 1912 (H):** By a convincing 24-0 score, MAC defeated Wabash for their sixth win of the season and their fifth in a row over the Indiana school. It was the visitors' first setback after six straight victories. Although the game was slowed by the wet field, it did not discourage the Aggies from opening up a startling passing game. Captain Bill Riblet succeeded with frequent completions to George Gauthier, Elmer Gorenflo and Blake Miller. Carp Julian scored the first touchdown. Gauthier scored twice and Miller once. It brought the fall's overall record to an impressive 6-1 with one game remaining on the schedule.

Football— **November 28, 1912 (A):** In a Thanksgiving Day game, the Aggies pulled off one of the school's most satisfying wins in 17 years of competition. Trailing Ohio State 20-14 after three quarters of play, the Aggies came roaring back with three touchdowns to defeat the favored Buckeyes, 35-20. Aided by two turnovers, the MAC fourth-quarter blitz was led by little George Gauthier, who hit Blake Miller with a short pass for one touchdown and following a pass interception plunged for another. Bill Riblet scored the final TD after Ralph Chamberlain had recovered a Buck fumble at the OSU 25-yard line. The marching band and 200 fans made the 500-mile round trip ($3.88 fare) to Columbus and thus witnessed the first-ever football win over a Western Conference opponent. *The MAC Record* labeled it, "The most significant victory in the history of football in Michigan."

Upon returning to the city at 4:30 A.M. the next day, the exuberant fans made a noisy tour of the campus. In further celebration, classes were dismissed after the first two hours of that Monday morning, whereupon students piled into several trolley cars and headed for the Lansing train station. There they greeted the 11:00 A.M. train bearing their gridiron heroes whom they escorted back to the campus.

Basketball— **January 11, 1913 (H):** In what would prove to be both the largest score of the season as well as the widest point spread, MAC opened the schedule by defeating Winona College of Minnesota, 75-14. Expecting a winning carryover from that fall's 7-1 football record, Aggie followers turned out in great numbers to cheer on a team that included gridiron stars George Gauthier and the Miller brothers, Blake and Hewett. Not only did all squad members see action on January 11 but nine were on the scoring sheet. Captain Bob Goss led the way with 19 points. The visitors managed only three field goals for the entire evening and were never in the contest.

Basketball— **January 27, 1913 (H):** At intermission MAC trailed Alma by two points, 24-22; thereafter, a likely passionate halftime plea by Coach Macklin led to a complete turn around. The Aggies stormed back to outscore the visitors 26-0 and gain an easy 48-24 victory in the process.

Basketball— **February 13, 1913 (H):** The greatly proclaimed Notre Dame team had come to town holding an impressive 11-1 season record and local interest was eminently aroused. Fans were further tweaked with memories of how the Irish had avoided MAC since their double-loss during the 1910 season. The Armory was filled to capacity and latecomers were milling around outside foolishly hoping to somehow gain a glimpse of the action. Others clustered around the windows to sneak a limited view. One can only visualize the spectator enthusiasm as the contest became one-sided and ended anticlimactically, 40-7, in favor of the Farmers. The Aggies elevated their season mark to 5-2. The sub headline of the next day's game story on the sports page of *The Detroit Free Press* read, "Notre Dame Is Almost Too Easy To Be Interesting In Basketball Encounter." The article told of Ralph Chamberlain's 14-point performance and of his strong defensive performance along with Norm "Baldy" Spencer. The Detroit paper further suggested the score may well have been higher had not Coach Macklin freely used substitutions in the second half after leading 20-4

at the intermission. Other scorers that evening were Abe Vatz with eight, Hewett Miller six, Spencer six, Bob Goss four, and George Gauthier two.

Basketball— **March 8, 1913 (H):** The MAC-Detroit YMCA match-ups had been ongoing since 1903 and often during those years the annual winner could justifiably proclaim a state championship. Although there was no such title at stake in 1913, the Aggies were determined to end the season on a winning note, especially against a team that held an 8-5 series advantage. As a further incentive, one month earlier in Detroit the "Y" men had squeaked out a 23-22 victory tainted by an official's questionable call. The Farmers would need no help from the referee in this rematch. As *The State Journal* put it, leading 18-8 at the intermission, "they (MAC) succeeded in registering a point every minute during the second half." This translated to a 38-9 final score as the visitors managed one solitary point in the final 20 minutes of play. With 12 points, Blake Miller was the game's leading scorer. It was the final collegiate game for the two seniors, Ralph Chamberlain and Norm Spencer.

*Track and Field—***May 5, 1913 (H):** With a scoring system that rewarded only the top two finishers (five points for first and three points for second) MAC defeated Western Reserve at home, 71-46. First-place finishers were LeRoy Alderman in the two sprints, Robert Rosen in the mile run, Charles Herr in the two mile, Robert Brown in the 880, Clarence Loveland in both pole vault and high jump, E.G. Baxter in the 120-yard high hurdles, H.V. Kittle in the hammer event and the relay team of Warner, Lewis, Bishop, and Alderman.

Baseball— **May 9, 1913 (H):** MAC took advantage of eight stolen bases, including two double steals, and five Syracuse errors to upset the traveling Orangemen, 5-1. Only one run of the winning total was earned. Meanwhile, Carl "Pete" Peterson, the Aggie pitcher, was touched for only three hits in the first seven innings. Dreams of a shutout were dashed in the ninth when Pete tired, yielded the one run on a walk and pair of singles.

Baseball— **June 6, 1913 (H):** Defeating a Western Conference team, even the cellar-dwelling Ohio State Buckeyes, was gratifying. Even more exhilarating was how it was accomplished. The Buckeyes looked like the inevitable winners as they led 4-1 after seven innings. In the eighth the Farmers closed the gap by scoring twice, but approaching the ninth they needed one run to tie or two to win. Catcher Art Bibbins opened with his third single

of the afternoon. Harold Clark, hitting for the pitcher, flew out to center field. Paul Dancer revived hope by singling sharply to left. Bibbins reached second but was later tagged at third on Abe Vatz's fielder's choice. Then with two out, Norton Mogge laced a hard smash to right field. Dancer scored the tying run as Vatz scampered to third. In the continuation of action, Mogge headed for second on the play at the plate and the alert Vatz raced home with the winning run. Blake Miller, pitching before a home crowd for the first time, struck out 13 batters, walked only one, and scattered eight hits.

ATHLETE OF THE YEAR

George Gauthier first stole the hearts of Aggie football fans when he became a primary factor in the 1912 upset of Ohio State. One year later the Detroit native would become an all-time Aggie hero as he engineered the huge 12-7 defeat of Michigan. He quarterbacked teams in 1912 and 1913 that would win 14 games against only one loss. "Gooch" was also a frequent starter on the basketball court from 1911-1914, being selected captain his senior year. The Detroit native stayed in East Lansing following graduation, assuming different MAC coaching roles until departing in 1920. In the fall of 1921 he accepted the position of coach and athletic director at Ohio Wesleyan and for 35 years would serve that Dover, Ohio, school.

George Gauthier

IN THE SPARTLITE

Baseball: Traveling to Ada, Ohio, on May 23, the Aggies found a brutal way to lose a baseball game, 3-2. After struggling to score one run in each of their final two at-bats, they faced the Ohio Northern lineup in the bottom of the ninth with the game tied 2-2. With two men out and extra innings ominous, the Polar Bears' center fielder gained first base on a fielding error by shortstop Walter Thomas (the only MAC boot of the afternoon) and soon afterwards, he stole second base to set up the nightmare finish. The next hitter followed with a high pop fly over the infield sending the runner on his way. Both second baseman Charles Trowbridge and pitcher Carl Peterson circled under the impending third out only to pull the Alphonse and Gaston stunt as the ball dropped safely between them. By the time a desperate throw had reached the catcher, the winning run had crossed home plate and the game was over.

Basketball: The new blanket tax made it possible for students to attend basketball games without any additional fee. This was a "student friendly" gesture that turned sour. The promise of free admission meant a larger number of students were in line for the same limited number of spectator seats. Ultimately, more and more fans were turned away at the door, leading to a broader base of malcontents.

The 1913 basketball season saw more players in game action than during previous years when the starting five often played the entire game. As an example, 11 names were listed in the summary of the 58-25 victory over Hope.

Football: When you lose 55-7 (vs. Michigan, October 12, 1912) and have nothing to cheer about, you boast of your band (*The MAC Record,* October 15, 1912):

"Those who went to Ann Arbor Saturday realized that M.A.C. was represented there by two organizations—the football team and the band.

The band, 51 men strong, arrived in Ann Arbor with the team and rooters at 11:15 A.M., and from that time until the special left in the evening they were busy cheering the team on and advertising our college.

Expressions of surprise and praise were heard on every side as the band, filling the street from curb to curb, marched the mile and a half from the hotel to the field. Between halves, the band marched around the field and were heartily cheered by the thousands in the bleachers, both Michigan and M.A.C. All through the game, whenever opportunity offered, songs were led by the band and finally, after the last whistle had been blown, they led the entire M.A.C. section in a verse of Alma Mater.

From the field back to the hotel, the fellows worked with just as much vim as though we had won. And we had won; for the band was admitted by the Michigan students to be in a class by itself as compared to the university band, and the team had put up a good fight against heavy odds."

In summarizing the 46-0 defeat of Ohio Wesleyan, *The MAC Record* reported "the right shift formation was responsible for the long gains at various times." One can only guess at to what "the right shift formation" was.

Tennis: In his 1971 *Spartan Saga,* Fred Stabley identifies the 1913 tennis team as the school's first. This ignores the fact that MAC entered co-ed teams in the annual MIAA Field Days (1896-1907). Furthermore, although no complete record has ever been uncovered, accounts of matches from 1909-1912 were sporadically reported in the local newspaper and *The MAC Record.* As for the team members in those first dozen years, the same Harry G. Taft, winner of the 1907 MIAA title, had an extended Aggie career, competing until graduation in 1912. Hailing from East Lansing, Harry was the son of MAC staff member Levi Taft, the superintendent of Farmers' Institutes. A sister, Ethel, competed in 1913 and 1914. Marjorie Kedzie, a sibling of the respected chemistry professor, Frank Kedzie, was a standout player from 1909-1911. Other standouts were: Lucy Arner of Traverse City; Paul "Cal" Calrow from Winnetka, Ill.; and Arao Itano from Okayamaken, Japan.

Track and Field: Capturing nine of the 14 events, the track men defeated Western Reserve 71-46. A high wind that swept across the field blew directly against the dash men and also hindered the achievements in the field events. With the exception of a mark of 7.8 seconds in the 100-yard dash, all running events were far from speedy. That impressive sprint was turned in by "Clipper," assistant coach Ian Cortright's beautiful hound. The dog had responded to the starter's gun for the sprint and then proceeded to lead LeRoy Alderman and the others down the straightaway to the tape.

SPARTAN SCRAPBOOK
─────── FOOTBALL ───────

1884 Field Day football team was organized, but never played one game.

MAC
1913-1914

TALES TO TELL

Following the historic victory over Michigan on the gridiron (see Extra! page 56), Edgar Guest, the whimsical poet of Detroit, had the following published in the Oct. 13, 1913 issue of the *Free Press* entitled *The M.A.C. Grad*:

I met him on the street this morn;
His smile was good to see;
He walked about with chest puffed out
As proud as he could be
What means this stride, this look of pride?
I asked; thus answered he:

I've never bragged this way before, when others
* gave their college yells.*
I gave no raucous cheers for mine, I blew no
horns and rang no bells.
I wore no badge upon my coat to show where
in my youth I'd been,
What alma mater mothered me when I

was very young and green;
But now hip, hip, hooray! And wow! At last
the day has come for me,
We've got a team that beats them all.
I studied at the M.A.C.

They used to mop the earth with us;
they used to break our favorites backs;
Our full back always used to look as
though he'd been against an ax.
The called us rubes and farmers, too,
because we studied seeds and soil,
And so I never bragged about where
I had burned the midnight oil.
I've had no chance to yip before of where
I captured my degree,
But now I want the world to know
I studied at the M.A.C.

In silence I have gone for years,
in patience silence I have borne,
The cheers of others in my ears and

HEADLINES of 1914

- The Ford Motor Company raises basic wage rates from $2.40 for a nine-hour day to $5.00 for an eight-hour day.
- Germany declares war on France. England declares war on Germany and World War I begins.
- The last-known passenger pigeon dies in the Cincinnati zoo.
- Edgar Rice Burroughs, novelist, publishes *Tarzan of the Apes*, the first of many books about an infant abandoned in the jungles and reared by apes.
- The Panama Canal is completed.

SCOREBOARD

	W	L	T	Avg.
Baseball	12	5	0	.667
Track and Field	1	1	0	.500
Football	7	0	0	1.000
Basketball	8	4	0	.667
Tennis	1	1	1	.333
Cross Country		no team		

I have heard men speak in scorn.
Of my dear alma mater, but at last
we've come into our own
We've got the coach, we've got the team,
we've got the muscle, brain and bone!
Hip, hip, hooray! A tiger too! In me I
want the world to see.
A proud and happy student of that
grand and glorious M.A.C.

TEAM OF THE YEAR

As the undefeated football team posted its 7-0 record, offensively they averaged 25.7 points per game and defensively held opponents to a total of only 28 points, including three shutouts.

MAKING HISTORY

Upon concluding the undefeated 1913 football season, many attractive offers for postseason games were received by the school. Notre Dame, Chicago and Nebraska were undefeated teams desiring to meet the Green and White. The best offer came from the U of M (6-1-0). Desirous of a return game, they were willing to pay $5,000 or a split of the gate receipts. Although the financial offers were tempting, Coach Macklin stuck to his position of no postseason games.

The Chicago Evening Post selected Blake Miller to its postseason All-Western eleven, with Carp Julian and Gideon Smith gaining second-team recognition. Without identifying the publication, *The Holcad* reported that one eastern daily listed "Dutch" Lenardson as an All-American.

In addition to the intercollegiate and YMCA rules, basketball games could be conducted under yet another version, the AAU rules. The latter rendition called for no personal fouls, encouraging much rougher play. Such was the case in the 26-25 loss to the Toledo Buckeye Paint team in 1914. Blake Miller sprained his ankle badly and Jerry DaPrato suffered a cut over his eye that required several stitches. One year later, in 1915, the colleges, AAU and YMCA combined to form the Joint Rules Committee to govern the game.

1913 football team

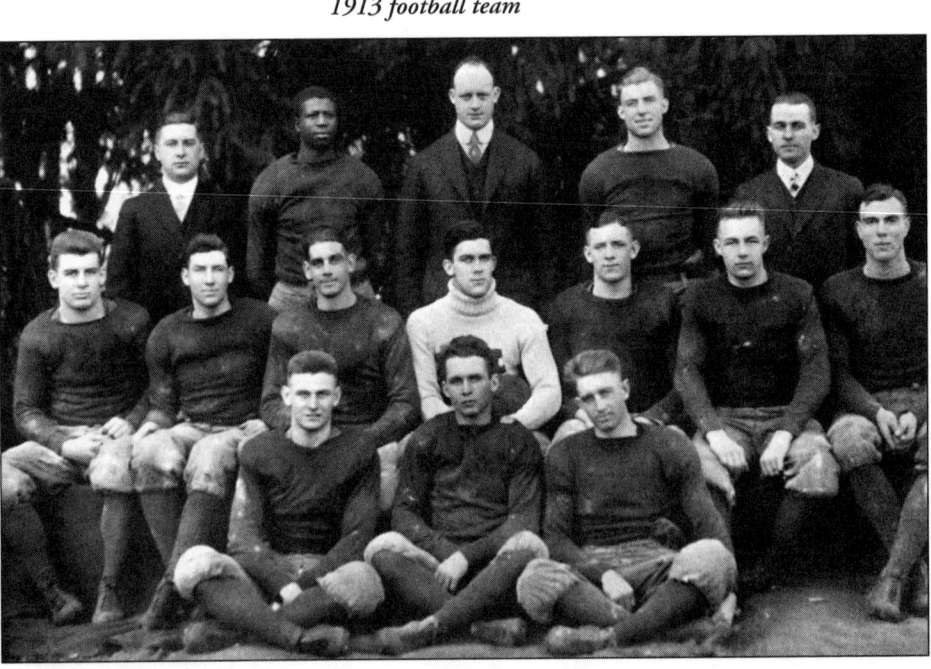

(Front row, left to right) Oscar "Dutch" Miller, George Gauthier, Hewett Miller. (Second row, left to right) Larry Vaughn, Hugh Blacklock, Blake Miller, Chester Gifford, George "Carp" Julian, Ralph Henning and Nemo Jerry DaPrato. (Back row, left to right) Manager Frank "Sun" Yuhse, Gideon Smith, coach John Macklin, Faunt "Dutch" Leonardson and assistant coach Ion Cortright. (Missing from picture) Russell McCurdy and Herb Straight.

GREAT STATE DATES

Football—**October 25, 1913 (A):** If MAC's defeat of Michigan opened the eyes of the fans and sports writers, the 12-7 defeat of Wisconsin on the following Saturday at Madison made them believers. The Badgers, defending Western Conference champions, entered the game undefeated, untied, and as the prohibitive favorites. Whereas in the Michigan game it was the passing of quarterback George Gauthier, this time the Farmers featured their running game of Blake Miller (recovered from the injury sustained at Ann Arbor), Hugh Blacklock and "Carp" Julian. The Wisconsin coach was particularly impressed with Julian, praising him as the "greatest fullback" he had ever seen. The green front line, although outweighed 15 pounds to the man, completely outplayed the Badgers with the defense gaining credit for the clinching touchdown. Captain Chester Gifford blocked a punt, and left end H. Schultz retrieved the ball and carried it in for the score. Schultz was really Oscar "Dutch" Miller of Saginaw who hid behind the pseudonym because his parents were opposed to football. Gurd Hayes, the *State Journal* writer, extended particular plaudits to the sophomore left tackle, Gideon Smith, whom he described as a "star of the first magnitude":

> "Playing against Wisconsin's Butler, the All-American tackle of last year, Smith made his heavier opponent look like a dirty duece in a new deck. He stopped the mighty rushes of Cummings, Tormey, and VanGhent and his tackling was sure and low. He broke up many of (Coach) Juneau's best plays and on one occasion intercepted one of Bellows' forward passes and raced down the field 15 yards before being downed."

Basketball—**January 16, 1914 (H):** Opening the season by defeating the Ohio Buckeye team of Toledo was a pleasant surprise. The favored Ohioans, playing their third game of the season, had already defeated the University of Chicago and Ohio State. The Farmers led 23-8 at halftime and were never in trouble thereafter. The margin of victory (40-24) was an even greater surprise than the win itself. As usual, the hindrance of the low girders in the Armory seemed to affect the visitors' performance. The big crowd, which was packed to the doors and overflowed outside, was compelled to view the game while standing. There was no reported explanation, but

Gideon Smith, "a star of the first magnitude"

the arena was lacking its customary bleacher seats. The starting line-up had Bob Goss and "Dutch" Miller at the guard positions, Lyman Frimodig at center and George Gauthier and Hewett Miller in the forward positions.

Basketball—**January 30, 1914 (H):** The 29-22 win over Detroit Burroughs was obviously played under AAU rules and not the college rules, in which a player was disqualified upon committing his fourth personal foul. Of the 29 fouls called on the Aggies, Hewett Miller was whistled 13 times. The Detroiters made a game of it at the charity line, netting 20 of the 29 attempts while connecting on only one field goal over the course of the entire contest.

Baseball—**April 18, 1914 (H):** With two innings remaining in the season opener, MAC trailed Olivet 3-12. Only the real diehards had hope. Then in the eighth, everything seemed to go the Aggies' way and before they would be retired, 11 runs had crossed the plate. They then hung on to defeat the visitors, 14-12. It was probably the most impressive comeback in school history.

Baseball—**April 24, 1914 (H):** Featuring 16 hits registered by the first five in the batting order, Macklin's men easily defeated Western Reserve of Cleveland, 13-3. Both Ralph Dodge and Elmer Chilton were credited with

With Gideon Smith far left (wearing primitive nose guard), Blake Miller breaks loose against Wisconsin.

four hits in six at-bats. The team's total of 19 singles might well be a school record.

Baseball—**May 8, 1914 (H):** For the fourth straight year, the Farmers defeated the traveling Syracuse Orangemen. Trailing 4-3 after seven innings, the Aggies managed two unearned runs in the eighth inning for a 5-4 victory. The "unscored" runs leading up to the eighth seemed unreal as 13 men were stranded on the bases. In back-to-back innings, the Aggies had runners perched on second and third with only one out but failed to cash in. Then in the fourth inning, the team was aided by three bases on balls, two stolen bases, and a base hit, yet not one runner crossed home plate. Two MAC defensive gems were featured. One was a beautiful throw by Ralph Dodge, playing right field, which nailed a runner attempting to score following a fly out. The other was a bases-loaded double play, catcher Bibbins to first baseman Mark Griggs, ending a late-inning threat.

Track and Field—**May 9, 1914 (H):** In winning all but four events, Coach Ion Cortright's trackmen garnered 87 points to outscore Alma (25 points) and Olivet (19 points) in the annual triangular meet on College Field. Howard Beatty captured three firsts: the 120-yard high hurdles in 17.6, the 220-yard low hurdles in 26.6, and the broad jump with a leap of 19' 10". Other winners for MAC were LeRoy Alderman in both the 100-and 220-yard dashes with times of 10.8 and 22.6, Frank Stewart in the mile, Clayton Barnett in the two mile, Clarence Loveland in the pole vault and "Carp" Julian in the shot put.

Baseball—**May 30, 1914 (A):** After dropping the Friday afternoon game to Michigan, 10-3, the Aggies, featuring the four-hit pitching of Ralph Dodge, reversed form on the next day, 8-1, to split the two-game weekend series. MAC gathered a total of 13 hits, including four by Elmer Chilton and three by Charles Hood. All but two of the winners' runs were unearned. Dodge was in supreme control and fanned 15 hitters, including the great George Sisler twice.

ATHLETE OF THE YEAR

George "Carp" Julian competed four years in football (1911-1914) and two years in track and field (13-14). He was selected as captain of both teams in his final year of competition. In the 75-6 romp over Akron on Oct. 31, 1914, Julian scored seven touchdowns. Although not included with modern-day records, no State player has ever equaled or bettered his effort that afternoon. Carp was severely injured in a postcollege accident and spent many years in convalesence.

George "Carp" Julian

IN THE SPARTLITE

Baseball: During a scheduled trip into Ohio in late May, MAC won games on three consecutive days. Blake Miller threw a four-hitter in the 4-2 opener against Oberlin, with Mark Griggs's home run highlighting the offense. Traveling into Cleveland on the next afternoon, the Aggies found the Western Reserve nine not very competitive. Led by Ralph Dodge's three singles and a double, they hammered out a total of 17 hits and, aided by five host errors, registered a comfortable 13-3 victory. This was followed by a train ride to Columbus for a Thursday afternoon game against Ohio State. The feature of this concluding game of the trip was the mound work of the preceding day's hitting star, Ralph Dodge. Before relinquishing the chores to Blake Miller because of a strained side muscle, the star of the pitching staff had permitted only one run and was eventually credited with the 5-3 win.

In the season-closing 12-4 loss to Notre Dame, Ralph Dodge's pitching was totally off-form as he yielded 11 runs before giving way to Blake Miller in the eighth. Likewise, Dodge played below par defensively, registering errors on three successive plays in the seventh inning.

The top hitters over the 18-game season were Miller .470, Dodge .400, Elmer Chilton .348, and Merrill "Chief" Fuller .309.

Basketball: Anticipating an excessive turnout of spectators for the Notre Dame game, additional courtside bleachers were installed along the west side of the Armory. On game night, during a preliminary contest between teams from the junior and sophomore classes, the expanded seating collapsed. Considering the fact that they were loaded with spectators at the time, it was a miracle no one was seriously injured. The displaced fans were accommodated as best as possible for the feature game, which the Farmers won with surprising ease, 45-22.

The scorekeeper at the 1914 Detroit Burroughs game of January 30 must have had a headache before it was all over, for it was truly "Miller time." Starters for MAC were Hewett Miller and Oscar Miller (no relation) with Blake Miller coming off the bench. The opening five for Detroit included Joy Miller and Jack Miller.

By 1914, basketball had proven an attraction to the students. They were often found hanging from the rafters overlooking the Armory floor. The following commentary was included in the *Holcad* report of the January 30 victory over the Detroit Burroughs team:

"As usual, the beams were well populated, those occupying these advantageous but hardly comfortable points of observation being compelled to wipe the dust of ages from their resting places before letting themselves gingerly down upon them."

Football: For many years the school supported class football on an intramural basis with four teams competing: freshmen, sophomores, juniors and seniors. In November, it was announced that following the 1913 season the school would no longer maintain the program. Class teams in both basketball and baseball would continue under the direction of the school's student council.

For the first time in the school's history, the football team of 1913 had an off-campus preseason training period. Coach Macklin had prevailed upon C.P. Downey, of Downey's Hotel in Lansing, for the use of his large cottage at Pine Lake (Lake Lansing). Downey also consented to throw in the services of his chef, with the Automobile Club of Michigan providing food for the team. That early in the season, the squad consisted of only 15 men, consequently; the cost of feeding the men was not prohibitive.

The Ivy League schools were still the measuring stick for collegiate football supremacy. With the connecting links of MAC's 12-7 win over the U of M and the 45-7 Michigan victory over Syracuse, *The Detroit Free Press* compared select game scores and contrived the following fanaticized conclusions: MAC 35, Princeton 7; MAC 45, Harvard 7; and MAC 79, Yale 7.

Plans evolved early in the fall for transporting 125 fans to Madison for the University of Wisconsin game. The itinerary included leaving the campus on Friday evening at 5:00 P.M. aboard the interurban connection to St. Johns. From there a Grand Trunk train would take the rooters to Grand Haven for a night boat ride across Lake Michigan to Milwaukee. In relay fashion, another special train would meet the travelers on Saturday and carry them into Madison. The round trip fare for each of the 125 fans was set at $9.29.

Tennis: In summarizing the 1914 tennis season, the 1915 Wolverine yearbook noted that the upkeep of the courts, instead of being a responsibility of the societies as in the past, would henceforth be undertaken by the Athletic Department.

Continuing as a co-ed team, the four varsity spots were ably handled by captain Paul Calrow, L.C. Moskowitz, Haidee Judson and Ethel Taft.

Track and Field: Garnering the most points during the limited three-meet outdoor season was Abe Alderman, who excelled in the sprint events. Howard Beatty was a top performer as a hurdler and Clarence Loveland vaulted 11' 6" to better the school record he had established in 1913. In addition, six others earned varsity monograms: Charles Herr, Ralph Dinan, "Carp" Julian, Fred Jones, David Peppard and Clayton Barnett.

In the February 16 edition of *The Holcad*, a writer portrayed how the limitations of the Armory handicapped the indoor track team:

> "Imagine a man training for the mile event in an armory barely twenty-five yards long with no track, and no banks at the turns. Or picture a runner fitting himself for the hundred yard on a dance floor, where the longest possible straight away is barely thirty-five yards, from corner to corner. For these reasons, the mid-winter track training has been given up, and no meet can therefore be arranged with the Detroit "Y" or other towns."

Regardless, an interclass meet was conducted on March 18 with the following events contested: 25-yard dash, 25-yard low hurdles, 25-yard high hurdles, one-half mile, high jump, quarter mile, high dive, shot put, mile and relay.

Although failing to score, three members of the team were entered in the 14th Annual Western Conference meet conducted on June 6 in Chicago. MAC was one of the record number of 21 teams that competed in the championships that year.

EXTRA!

October 18, 1913—MAC's First Football Win Over Michigan: According to Fred Stabley, in his book, *The Spartans*, published in 1988 by Strode Publishers of Texas, this eighth game of the great State–Michigan intrastate rivalry was a bone-crunching physical battle in which the Farmers finally prevailed, 12-7. It was the first-ever MAC victory over the U of M on the gridiron. The only other previous moment of glory came five years earlier when a Chester Brewer team had held the Wolverines to a 0-0 standoff.

In this game Coach Macklin's squad suffered a setback when ace sophomore end and sometimes halfback, Blake Miller, was carried from the field unconscious near the end of the first half. He had made eight yards on a fake punt, and was tackled by Paterson, the Wolverine captain. Then, Tommy Hughitt, the Michigan quarterback, playing well out in mid-field, made a special effort to run some 20 yards to where Miller lay, near the sideline, and jumped on his neck with both knees. Miller would regain consciousness three hours later in an Ann Arbor hospital. Supposedly, the U of M would later "blackball" the game official who apparently observed the infraction and did not take appropriate action.

One of the MAC touchdowns was scored by Carp Julian on a three-yard carry up the middle in the opening quarter and the second was credited to Hewitt Miller, who had replaced his injured brother. Hewitt's score came

Quarterback George Gauthier drops back for one of his 19 pass attempts against Michigan.

early in the second half when he scooped up a U of M fumble and raced untouched 46 yards into the end zone, giving the Aggies a 12-0 lead. From there they hung on.

Throughout the afternoon, quarterback George Gauthier connected on 7-of-19 passes good for 100 yards, a phenomenal performance with the fat ball of the time. Nine of the MAC starters played the entire game without substitution. In the postgame celebration, hundreds of reveling students poured onto the field and lifted the 20 members of the squad onto their shoulders. The conquering heroes were carried in triumph to the dressing room. The jubilant rooters then returned to the field where the celebration continued for another 30 minutes. Then, led by the 62-piece ROTC Cadet Band, the scene shifted to the streets of the city where the band struck up a familiar tune, Michigan's own *The Victors*, for it would

be 1916 before Irving Lankey's *MAC Fight Song* would be available. Back in Lansing it was the inevitable bonfire and snake dance in front of the state capitol building, free admission to the Bijou Theater and a day off from classes on the following Monday.

That Sunday a fire leveled the barn of Addison Makepeace Brown, secretary of the state Board of Agriculture. It stood near the site of the current Student Union Building and had been considered pretty much an eyesore by most of the community. Although the cause of destruction was listed as "defective wiring" the suspicion always prevailed that one or more celebrants may have torched the structure. The issue was never resolved.

With mere seconds remaining in the game, 1,500 MAC fans sense a big victory over Michigan.

SPARTAN SCRAPBOOK
—— FOOTBALL COACHES (1900-2003) ——

Frank Sommer (1916)

Henry Kipke (1928)

James H. Crowley (1929-32)

Charles W. Bachman (1933-46)

Clarence "Biggie" Munn (1947-53)

Hugh "Duffy" Daugherty (1954-72)

Dennis E. Stolz 1973-75)

Darrell Rogers (1976-79)

Frank "Muddy" Waters (1980-82)

George Perles (1983-94)

Nick Saban (1995-99)

Bobby Williams (2000-02)

Pictured elsewhere: Henry Keep 1897-98_{TR}; Charles Bemies 1899-00_{BS}; George Denman 1901-02_{BS}; Chester Brewer 1903-10, 17, 19_{BS}; John Macklin 1911-15_{BS}; George Gauthier 1918_{TR}; George "Potsy" Clark 1920_{BS}; Albert Barron 1921-22; Ralph Young 1923-27_{TR}

_{TR} see track and field coaches

_{BS} see baseball coaches

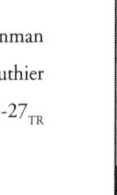

John L. Smith (2003-)

MAC
1914-1915

TALES TO TELL

The following excerpt from a letter to a relative, from Clarence Oviatt (FB '14, '15), describes the 6-3 football victory at Penn State on November 13:

"Their field is open, with a windbreak to the west, but the wind did blow. There was a continuous stream of hats and leaves coming across and down the field. This wind made it almost impossible to play our open game and each side had to be extremely careful of fumbling. Punting against the wind was almost impossible. One time our man punted and the ball returned to within 5 yards of where he stood.

The game was one of the best I ever witnessed. There were only two penalties given out which indicates how clean it was. At one point in the second quarter Penn State had moved to a first down on our four yard line, but our boys held for downs with the ball only one foot from our goal line. Our six points came in that same quarter. Hewett Miller made 40 yards around end behind perfect interference and nearly broke loose for a touchdown. Julian added five yards and Miller shoved it for seven more and Julian made it first down with about eight yards to go for a touchdown. Following three plunges we were still six yards away and finally Julian carried it over. Penn State scored their three points on a third quarter field goal and had a chance to tie us by repeating with another field goal but their man got nervous and our ends had him before he had the ball placed. Along the end of the game the Penn State coach sent in a new man for every play to tell the quarterback what to call. In all he used 22 substitutes but it helped him not, for the Green and White won, 6-3.

After the game we went to their training quarters for supper. They surely treated us like kings. In the evening the band made things lively around town and I never saw such a good bunch of losers. They cheered us off as if we were their own team."

HEADLINES of 1915

- The taxi industry begins when automobile owners discover that people will pay for a short automobile ride.
- William Fox founds the Fox Film Corporation which eventually evolves into Twentieth Century Fox.
- Alexander Graham Bell in New York and Thomas Watson in San Francisco complete the first transcontinental telephone call.
- The British ship *Lusitania* is sunk by a German submarine. Among others, 128 American passengers are lost.

SCOREBOARD

	W	L	T	Avg.
Baseball	8	6	0	.571
Track and Field	1	1	0	.500
Football	5	2	0	.714
Basketball	7	9	0	.438
Tennis	5	0	0	1.000
Cross Country	no team			

1915 tennis leaders L.C. Moskowitz and Haidee Judson

TEAM OF THE YEAR

Continuing the format adopted from the MIAA Field Days (1896-1907), tennis was competed as a co-ed sport through the 1916 season. Thereafter, the women began competing within their own schedule. The undefeated 1915 squad (5-0) was led by captain L.C. Moskowitz and Haidee Judson. Other contributors were Rusty Crozier, Otto Vergeson and Van Cleve Taggart along with Ethel Taft and Ruby Clinton. The five-meet season included victories over Olivet, Alma, Ypsi Normal, the Detroit Law School and the U of M freshmen. Such competition may not have seemed impressive, but the margins were decisive, winning 28 matches and losing only five.

MAKING HISTORY

Before an apparently "less than full house," "Carp" Julian scored seven touchdowns in MAC's 75-6 romp over Akron. Although not included with "modern day" records, no State player has ever equaled or bettered Julian's efforts of that afternoon.

In the season-closing game at Penn State the Aggies were compelled to conform to a rule of the Eastern schools which required numbers be worn on the backs of the jerseys. Thus, for this one game, numbers were quickly painted on the game-day jerseys. This idea stuck, and beginning the next season large white numbers were more permanently stenciled on. Numbers would not appear on the front of Spartan jerseys until 1931. The collegiate rules committee listed the numbering policy as a recommendation in 1916, but it was not mandated until 1937.

Jack Heppinstall, the school's first full-time trainer, arrived in the fall of 1914. He would remain for 45 years until his retirement in 1959.

On Feb. 10, 1915, it was disclosed the college had come into possession of 325 acres south of the Red Cedar River known as the Woodbury farm. This would prove to be a significant acquisition, as the plot included the land where Spartan Stadium stands today.

Carp Julian scores one of his record-setting seven touchdowns against Akron.

A group of lettermen gathered on Monday evening, April 26, 1915, with the purpose of organizing a campus varsity club with all current junior and senior varsity men identified as charter members. "Carp" Julian was elected president, Les Cobb became vice-president, Art Bibbins was recording secretary, Jerry DaPrato was corresponding secretary and Clarence Loveland was treasurer.

GREAT STATE DATES

Football—**November 7, 1914 (H):** In what proved to be the most exciting game on the schedule, MAC came from behind to defeat Mt. Union 21-14. Aided by a 20-yard penalty, fullback "Carp" Julian scored the Aggies' first touchdown in the second quarter, climaxing a 40-yard five-play drive. Trailing at intermission 14-7, the Aggies used a pair of third-period pass interceptions to first tie the game and then score the winning TD. Gideon Smith's interception led to a six-play 18-yard drive with Captain Julian scoring again. The winning score came on a pass batted down by Ralph Henning and then picked off by Frank Chaddock who raced 40 yards into the end zone. The Raiders attempted 31 forward passes and completed eight for a total gain of 56 yards and the Farmers completed four of 17 passes netting only 25 yards.

Basketball—**January 13, 1915 (H):** In its story of the 56-20 defeat of Hope College *The Holcad* expounds on the talent of Lyman Frimodig who scored 30 points:

> "He easily upheld the reputation gained last year of being the best center seen here in some time, as his efforts scored more than half of his team's points, no less than fifteen baskets being credited to him. He shot from every conceivable angle, and with a certainty which brought the crowd to their feet again and again."

Along with Frimodig, the starting five included Blake Miller, Hewett Miller, Oscar Miller and Jerry DaPrato. In a preliminary contest, East Lansing High School defeated Lansing High School, 27-8.

Basketball—**January 23, 1915 (H):** Even though the final score of the victory over Defiance College was 54-12, Coach Macklin did attempt to show mercy on the Ohio school. Only one starter, Lyman Frimodig, played any portion of the second half. The reserve five of Charles Hood, Fred Ricker, Dave Peppard, Art Sheffield and Al McClelland performed more than adequately as they outscored the visitors over the final 20 minutes of play, 20-6.

Basketball—**February 2, 1915 (H):** The Fighting Irish of Notre Dame attracted yet another record turn-out in the Armory. As had become familiar, the beams above the floor were occupied with rows of fans, clinging

to their precarious positions. With two regulars, Lyman Frimodig and Blake Miller, out of the line-up with injuries and the visitors leading 11-5 at intermission, it looked bleak for MAC. Upon opening the second half, the score began to change favorably for the home team and the crowd was on its feet (except those on the beam) from the outset where they remained until the final gun. A deafening clamor followed the basket which tied the score 11-11. Then, following ten minutes of scoreless play, Hewitt Miller wrestled the ball from a ND player and tossed it over his shoulder to Dave Peppard, who went in for two points and the lead. With the crowd still roaring its approval and with less than one minute remaining in the contest, the Irish scored their only field goal of the half to again knot the score. Hewitt Miller became the ultimate hero as he netted the game-winning point from the free-throw line with seconds remaining. The final score read 14-13. Two weeks following that game, Hewitt Miller quit the team. His departure followed an impassable disagreement with Coach Macklin. "Dutch" Miller (no relation) replaced Hewitt as team captain.

Baseball—**April 23, 1915 (H):** Being only the third game of the young season, Coach Macklin had Blake Miller and Harold "Brownie" Springer shared the mound duties as they teamed to defeat Western Reserve, 6-1. Both Aggies pitched as if in midseason form. In five innings Miller gave up three hits and struck out 11 of the 17 men he faced. Springer yielded one hit and fanned seven over the final four innings. Accounting for the six MAC runs with RBI hits were Walter Thomas, "Chief" Fuller, "China" Clark, Miller and two from the bat of Art Brown. The solitary run from the losers was unearned.

Track and Field—**May 1, 1915 (H):** The 1915 MAC-Alma-Olivet triangular meet would be the fifth and final edition. The hosts scored 90 points to the Scots' 27 and the Comets' 14. With the Aggie margin of victory having grown from 15 to 63 points over the years, the two MIAA schools likely felt it was time to break off the relationship. Three Aggies were credited with double wins. Howard Beatty took the high hurdles in 16.6 and the lows in 27.0. Earl Sheldon raced to firsts in the half-mile with a 2:09.0 and the mile in 4:46.8. Bill Blue was tops in tossing the shot put 39' 2" and the discus 123' 4". Other winners for the Green and White were Brusselbach with a 10.4 in the 100-yard dash, LeRoy Alderman's 23.0 in the 220, Clayton Barnett's 10:27.0 in the two-mile, Hugh Blacklock's 103' 3" hammer throw, and Clarence

Loveland's vault of 10'. In addition, the mile relay team of Frazier, Hammill, Jewett and Bussellbach finished the afternoon in a winning time of 3:36.8.

Baseball—**May 12, 1915 (A):** The combination of errorless defense and solid pitching featured the 3-1 victory of the University of Michigan. Again, the Blake Miller and "Brownie" Springer duo controlled the game from the mound, Miller relinquishing three hits in six innings and Springer facing only nine batters in the final three frames. The MAC offensive production was limited to the third inning when they combined three hits, two errors and a passed ball for the three runs. Leading the attack with two hits each were Dean Williams, Bob McWilliams and "Frim" Frimodig.

Baseball—**May 29, 1915 (H):** Once more the Farmers defeated the U of M, this time 4-2, to take the 1915 series two games to one. The scoring opened with one run in the fifth, and the Aggies then broke the game open with a three-run surge in the sixth. With two outs, Art Brown and Art Bibbins singled and Maurice Weeder and Hilmar Fick followed with walks, the latter forcing in one run. Walter Thomas then hit to third, whereupon the third baseman threw wildly to first, permitting Bibbins and Weeder to score. Weeder, relieved by "Brownie" Springer in the eighth, held the Wolverines in check with two runs on eight scattered hits.

Tennis—**May 14, 1915 (A) & May 15, 1915 (H):** The tennis team opened the season with a weekend pair of 5-1 victories. On Friday they were in Olivet where both doubles teams, Ethel Taft-Ruby Clinton and L.C. Moskowitz-Otto Vergeson gained points along with single wins from Haidee Judson, Clinton, Moskowitz and Rusty Crozier. Returning home for a Saturday meet with Alma, Moskowitz was the only loser when he dropped a third set in an 11-9 marathon.

ATHLETE OF THE YEAR

Blake Miller was a nine-letter star, excelling in football (1912-1915), basketball (1913 & 1915) and baseball (1913-1915). Following the 1913 football season, Miller was included in the All-Western team as selected by *The Chicago Evening Post* and then the same honors were extended in 1915 by Eckersall. Blake twice served his alma mater as an assistant coach, serving a short stint as coach at Central Michigan in between.

Blake Miller

IN THE SPARTLITE

Baseball: Upon defeating the University of Michigan on May 15, 1915, for the second time, team captain Arthur Bibbins boasted:

"The 1915 baseball season at MAC was a success because we beat Michigan. Regardless of the results of other games, the college must remember that we won from the university two out of three, and decisively showed that MAC possessed the best team of any school in the state."

These were bold words on behalf of a team that had managed an undistinguished 8-6 season record.

Basketball: Bob Goss and George Gauthier, team captains in 1913 and 1914 respectively, stayed on to become assistant coaches during the 1915 season. In the following year, Oscar Miller replaced Goss for a one-year stint.

A *Holcad* story of February 1915 suggested, "Gentlemen who attend games should remove their hats; and rooters should be led in some real MAC yells rather than those borrowed from Michigan and elsewhere."

School officials made a politically prudent decision on February 2, the evening of the Notre Dame game. As many as 50 state legislators were escorted to seats of honor in the first row of the bleachers where the captive audience heard pre-game speeches in support of a new gymnasium. Delivering the message were assistant coach George Gauthier and three student-athletes, including "Carp" Julian. Also, a petition directed to the governor and in support of a new facility was passed into the stands for signatures.

Even with a less-than-impressive record of 6-8, the Aggies hoped to close the season by defeating Hope College and the Detroit YMCA to legitimately claim the title of "state champions." The Dutchmen cooperated, falling 46-28, but the "Y" men would have no part in the drama as the Detroiters embarrassed the guys in Green, 21-9. Lyman Frimodig netted the only MAC field goal of the evening.

Playing in 10 of the 16 games before quitting the squad, Hewitt Miller completed the season holding the best scoring average at 11.9 per game and Lyman Frimodig scored the most points at 126.

Football: In expectation of the large crowd for the Michigan game of October 17, a new bleacher section to accommodate 1,400 was constructed on the east side of the field. In addition, temporary seats were added to the north and south ends to bring the total seating capacity to nearly 7,000. There must have been many fans in the "standing room only" category, because allegedly 10,000 fans witnessed this third U of M visit to College Field. As it turned out, it was a heartbreaking loss for Aggie followers. Jerry DaPrato missed two field goal chances in the opening 30 minutes of play. Also, another Aggie drive ended on the Michigan five-yard line as the scoreless first half ended. Still with no points on the scoreboard and time running out, Michigan completed a late-game desperation pass to set-up a successful drop kick from the 15-yard line. That was it, 3-0. Even as the Farmers outrushed the Wolverines, 253 yards to 109 yards, the final score sadly read U of M- 3, MAC-0.

Purdue University was on the 1914 schedule for a game at West Lafayette on November 7. Belatedly the Boilers cancelled the game with the reasoning they did

not approve of Aggie freshmen playing on the varsity squad. Strangely, the Purdue people were well aware of MAC's policy when the contract was originally negotiated. It would be another 24 years before the two land-grant schools would first hook-up on the football field.

Originally, Coach Macklin's staff consisted of backfield coach Ion Cortright and line coach Chester Gifford. Before the season was underway, Cortright left to become head coach at the University of South Dakota. George Gauthier replaced him.

During a three-night stand, January 11-13, a motion picture of the MAC-Penn State game (a 6-3 Aggie win) was shown at the Bijou Theater along with the regularly scheduled feature film. A ticket for the double feature sold for 25 cents with the school band profiting 10 percent on tickets sold by band members.

Hockey: Discussions for developing an outdoor ice rink and plans for supporting an intercollegiate hockey program took place on the campus in January. The initial idea was to create an ice surface on the parade grounds west of the Armory. Owing to the long distance from a water source (Red Cedar River), and other insurmountable difficulties, this site had to be abandoned. Strategy shifted to the river itself immediately above the Farm Lane

Bridge where the span was approximately 60 feet. It was here a rink was developed on eight inches of ice. A gasoline engine and pump were moved there, with which the surface could be flooded whenever necessary to keep it smooth and in good playing condition. A team of horses was made available to pull a scraper for clearing the ice of snow when needed. By late January, hockey goal cages had been delivered, an intramural schedule developed and Coach Macklin himself was available for refereeing the first games. Hockey had arrived to the campus, albeit short of intercollegiate competition.

Tennis: Most frequently, four single matches (two men and two women) and two doubles matches (one men and one women) constituted a meet. It was agreed to include two additional men's singles matches when they squared off against Ypsi Normal, a 7-2 win. Detroit School of Law did not have a women's team; consequently, that was a 3-0 score for the Aggies.

Track and Field: Original plans were to send the relay quartet of Bill Harvie, LeRoy Alderman, Howard Beatty and Bill Blue to the Penn relays in Philadelphia. The plans were aborted when Blue became injured and unable to compete.

After the football team completed a big win, MAC students would parade en masse to the state capitol.

TALES TO TELL

On October 23, nearly 3,000 Aggie football followers traveled to Ann Arbor to witness the annual struggle with the University of Michigan's eleven. Three different railroad lines promoted special trains. The Michigan United Traction Company ran special cars at 5:30 A.M. and 7:15 A.M., with roundtrip tickets priced at $2.15. The Pere Marquette Railroad, carrying the team and band, departed from behind the Engineering Building at 8:30 A.M. Space was offered for a roundtrip ticket price of $2.50. Also leaving at 8:30 that morning, from their depot in Lansing, the Michigan Central Railroad was prepared to handle 1,000 fans for a fare of $2.46. That afternoon, another 2,000 curious fans lined in front of the *State Journal* Building in Lansing to hear a public address play-by-play report which emanated off the teletype machine and was broadcast onto the street. There were many opportunities for the Aggie fans to cheer, as the 24-0 football victory over the U of M was convincing. It was the third most decisive loss in 24 years for the Wolverines, as the Macklin men proved superior in every facet of the game. The sports writer for the *Detroit Times* summarized the results as follows:

"What was the score? Just coming to that. It read 24-0 on the official blackboard, and the men who possessed the two dozen points were the Aggies. Michigan claimed ownership of the zero, and if there had been any numeral lower than that to hang up on the scoreboard they would have been forced to display it to indicate the Wolverines' accomplishments."

There were stars aplenty: Blake Miller and his brother Hewett, Hugh Blacklock, Charley Butler, Howard Beatty, and the ever-present Lansingite Gideon Smith, who was credited with over half of the tackles during the afternoon. Yet most scintillating of all was Jerry DaPrato. With three touchdowns, three PATs, and a field goal, the fullback from Iron Mountain scored all 24 of his team's points. He gained 153 yards from scrimmage and had several other impressive runs called back for penalties. The Farmers were opportunists as well. The field goal came after a fumble recovery; the first TD was set up by a blocked punt; and the second touchdown came following a pass interception. The "take home" earning from the Michigan game was $5,268. This was immense when compared to the $164 profit for the Alma game two weeks previous on College Field.

HEADLINES of 1916

- The first Professional Golfers Association tournament is held at Bronxville, N.Y.
- The National Park Service is established as part of the U.S. Department of the Interior.
- Mexican revolutionary Pancho Villa leads guerrilla raids into New Mexico and Texas.
- Illustrator Norman Rockwell begins creating covers for *The Saturday Evening Post*, continuing until 1963.

SCOREBOARD

	W	L	T	Avg.
Baseball	11	4	0	.733
Track and Field	1	1	0	.500
Football	5	1	0	.833
Basketball	8	8	0	.500
Tennis	8	2	1	.727
Cross Country-dual meets	0	0	0	.000

TEAM OF THE YEAR

The 1915 football season concluded the collegiate grid careers for some great Aggie performers: Howard Beatty, Blake Miller, Hewitt Miller, Jerry DaPrato and Gideon Smith. During the span of their four years (1912-1915), MAC posted an impressive composite record of 24-4 for a winning percentage of .857. Granted, by 1917 there would be extenuating intervening variables, but even the most pessimistic MAC fan would have never envisioned a winless season just two years hence.

MAKING HISTORY

Following the 1915 football season, Coach Macklin was granted a leave of absence to return to Pennsylvania to investigate the coal mining business owned and operated by his father-in-law. As it turned out, mining bituminous was to Macklin's liking. On April 19, he sent a letter to President Kedzie saying he had been compelled to give up hopes of returning in September. Thus, his leave of absence officially became a resignation. Macklin's collegiate coaching career ended as abruptly as it began five years earlier.

From a tryout list of 80 candidates, professor Clark, the school's band director, selected 50 men to fill the spots that would make up the 1915-1916 edition of the MAC military marching band. The size of the band was slightly diminished from previous years with the expressed intention of providing better quality rather than quantity. In addition to performing for frequently scheduled events on campus, twice during the fall the Aggie band was recruited by the Wolverine Pavedway Association of Lansing to accompany a caravan of automobiles and other musical organizations that traveled through cities east and west out of the Capital City. The association organized these tours with the intent to promote the completion of a proposed *paved* road that would stretch across the state from Detroit to Grand Haven.

Students desiring to be managers and assistant managers of the various athletic teams had to be "politicians" as well as hard workers. Each spring candidates would campaign and gain their positions through a campuswide student election.

The 5-1 football team of 1915: (front row, left to right) C. Oviatt, H. Springer, B. Huebel, H. Fick; (middle row, left to right) H. Beatty, C. Butler, L. Frimodig, B. Miller, R. Henning, J. DaPrato, and D. Vandervoort; (back row, left to right) assistant G. Gauthier, H. Straight, G. Smith, coach J. Macklin, H. Blacklock, H. Miller, and manager M. "Chief" Fuller.

The 1916 starting (and finishing) five (left to right) Charles Hood, Cyril Rigby, William Wood, Lyman Frimodig and Fred Ricker.

GREAT STATE DATES

Football—**October 9, 1915 (H):** Mounting the second-highest point total ever accorded an MAC team, the Alma Scots were humbled, 77-12. At the close of the opening quarter, the advantage was only 19-12, and the eventual lopsided victory was not foreseen. That was as close as it would get. The Farmers' scoring machine suddenly came alive with 21 points in the second quarter, 17 points in the third and 20 more points in the final stanza. Eight players joined in the TD parade, with Hugh Blacklock scoring three times and Jerry DaPrato twice. DePrato also added to the winning total with a 35-yard drop kick.

Football—**November 6, 1915 (H):** The hometown fans must have enjoyed this one. Blake Miller gathered in the opening kickoff and raced the ball back to the Marquette 25-yard line. Three plays later and in less than one minute, Jerry DaPrato scored the game's first touchdown. Before that quarter ended, the Aggies had managed four more touchdowns, and the scoreboard read Michigan Agriculture, 34, Marquette, 0. The rout was on. By halftime it was 47-0, and by the time the clock

had run down in the final session, MAC was in total command by a score of 68-6. DaPrato accounted for four of the touchdowns, and Gideon Smith, who regularly played at left tackle, moved to the backfield long enough to score three TDs.

Basketball—**January 12, 1916 (H):** In what would prove to be their highest scoring total of the season, the Aggies defeated Western Michigan in the season opener, 51-21. The Broncos were competitive through the opening half, as they trailed by only five points, 20-15, at intermission. Thereafter it was no contest, as MAC outscored the visitors, 31-6. Fred Ricker led all scorers with 17 points, followed by Art Brown and Lyman Frimodig with 10 points each.

Basketball—**February 4, 1916 (A):** The Aggies defeated Hope College 21-18 to redeem a 20-14 loss three weeks earlier in the Armory. It was the fourth game in a row in which Coach Macklin started the quintet of Charles Hood, Cyril Rigby, William Wood, Lyman Frimodig and Fred Ricker. The 40-minute game was played with neither team making a substitution.

Basketball—**February 12, 1916 (H):** Of the eight victories over the season, the 27-23 defeat of the Detroit YMCA was particularly satisfying. The Detroit team had been undefeated during the season. Contrary to the usual Aggie offense of playing for the short shots in close, many of the field goals (four apiece by Fred Ricker and Charles Hood, and three by Lyman Frimodig) were from long range.

Baseball—**May 12 & May 13, 1916 (H):** The Wabash Little Giants came to town for a two-game series and found the Aggies' star pitching duo of Art "Lefty" Brown and Ray "Frenchy" DeMond in rare form. In the 4-1 MAC victory on Friday, Brown, the Hastings southpaw, surrendered only four hits and permitted no bases on balls while striking out nine batters. After five scoreless innings, the Aggies sandwiched two hits between two errors to produce three runs in the sixth. Harold "China" Clark knocked in two and then scored the third run on a mishandled bouncer off the bat of Merrill "Chief" Fuller. The final MAC run came in the eighth inning when Clark singled home Robert Huebel who had tripled. On the next afternoon's 6-1 win, DeMond nearly equaled Brown's performance as he yielded five hits, permitted no walks and put eight batters down via the strike out. As in the Friday game, a sixth inning outburst spelled doom for the visitors. "Chi" Fick's single and Fuller's double were followed by two base on balls and a pair of costly errors. Lyman Frimodig concluded the two-out rally by doubling home the fifth run.

Baseball—**June 1, 1916 (H):** Following seven losses to Notre Dame, spanning 10 years, the first ever win over the Irish was registered at home by a score of 5-2. Arthur "Lefty" Brown was the winning pitcher, relinquishing only five hits over the nine innings. The hitting star was Hilmar Fick, who had a hand in all five runs for the winners. He tripled home three runs in the second inning and later in the game scored the remaining two tallies.

Baseball—**June 3, 1916 (H):** In the most impressively pitched game of the season, Ray "Frenchy" DeMond closed out the 1916 schedule by throwing a two-hitter while striking out 12 Michigan Normal hitters in a 9-1 victory. In the fifth inning the Aggies chalked up four unearned runs on a single by Walter Thomas, three bases on balls and five errors.

ATHLETE OF THE YEAR

Jerry DaPrato (FB '12, '14, '15 and BK '15) was the school's first football player to gain All-American consideration, being recognized by both *The Detroit Times* and the International News Service. His accomplishment of scoring all of his team's points in the 24-0 victory over Michigan opened the eyes of many from the media. Like Lyman Frimodig, another star of the period, DaPrato was a "UP-er," hailing from Iron Mountain.

Jerry DaPrato

IN THE SPARTLITE

Baseball: One week prior to opening the schedule against Olivet, Charlie Hood, the starting third baseman, was taken to Sparrow Hospital for an appendicitis operation and was eventually lost for the season.

Another loss to Notre Dame, 2-0, might have been more appropriately reported as an Aggie defeat of themselves. The hitters managed only five hits, and in the field the defense committed seven errors, including miscues that accounted for both Irish runs.

The quality of umpiring remained in question during this decade. Returning from a three-game eastern swing in 1916, players were convinced the one loss at Syracuse was "stolen." The umpire supposedly called one Aggie out after only two strikes, and one MAC inning was ruled complete after only two men had been retired.

Basketball: The mystique of playing "through" the low rafters of the Armory did not prove as advantageous in 1916 as in previous seasons. The Aggies were only able to win six of 11 games played on the home court.

In late January, the Aggies made a three-game trip to South Bend, Ind., Naperville, Ill., and Chicago, where they suffered defeats at the hands of Notre Dame, Northwestern College and Illinois A.C. The 50-18 win by the "Y" team (their 16th straight win of the season) was particularly humbling. It was the second-highest margin of loss ever inflicted on an Aggie team.

The 24-23 home loss to the Irish two weeks later was highlighted by the fact that a Notre Dame player by the name of Fitzgerald scored 22 of the winners' 24 points.

Cross Country: On November 6, in what was billed as the first-ever state intercollegiate cross country championship, 23 runners raced across a five-and-a-half mile course that began and ended on College Field. Counting the top three finishers from each school, the University of Michigan won the trophy with men placing second, fourth and fifth for a team score of 11. An Albion runner won the gold medal in a time of 29:33.0, and with teammates crossing in the sixth and eighth spots, they scored a runner-up team total of 15 points. The MAC trio of Sheldon, Harris, and Warren finished in the third, seventh and 15th slots for a team score of 25. A U of M freshman trio placed fourth in the competition and the MAC freshman trio wound up fifth.

Also that fall, MAC began entering runners in the annual Detroit YMCA Thanksgiving Day race on Belle Isle.

Football: Two years earlier, the undefeated team of 1913 began with their preseason conditioning program at Pine Lake (Lake Lansing). Not wanting to break this pattern of success, the three-week encampment continued in 1915 with assistant coach George Gauthier in charge. A total of 28 men checked into the "tent city" on September 9 for the two-a-day sessions.

A football rule from 1898 remained in force which provided for a game to be shortened by mutual agreement between the captains of the contesting teams. Such

was the case in the season opener against Olivet, when the first and third quarters were shortened to 10 minutes and the second and fourth to eight minutes. Regardless, the Aggies had ample time to score five touchdowns and gain a comfortable 34-0 victory.

The 1915 team was the school's first "scoring machine." During the six-game season, the offense averaged 43.2 points per contest.

A total of 67 men, an astonishing number, were included in the squad picture featured on the first page of the November 1 issue of the *The Holcad.*

Tennis: This is how one recruited in 1916. An article in the April 10 issue of *The Holcad* solicited both men and women candidates for the college tennis team. Interested parties were instructed to submit their names to "Dutch" Oviatt as soon as possible so that a tournament might be bracketed to identify the most qualified players for intercollegiate competition. Ultimately, the six varsity players (four men and two women) chosen completed an impressive 8-2-1 season.

Track and Field: With George Gauthier taking over the coaching reins, two dual meets were held in the spring, both resulting in identical scores. One was a 90-41 loss to Notre Dame and the other was a 90-41 victory over the U of M freshman squad.

On April 29, the first State Intercollegiate Track and Field meet was held at College Field. Team scoring was as follows: MAC, 54 1/2; Hillsdale, 43; Western State, 16; Olivet, 10; Hope, 6; and Michigan Normal at Ypsilanti, 1 1/2. Others competing but not scoring were: Kalamazoo, Albion, Detroit Junior College and Alma. With the exception of the cancellation in 1944 because of World War II, the State meet was conducted annually through 1945 with MAC-MSC winning 17 team titles and 151 individual championships.

Original plans were to send four or five men to the Western Conference championships in Evanston (the conference did not begin to use the closed meet format until 1925). When distance star Earl Sheldon was stricken by an illness and unavailable to compete, the idea was withdrawn.

SPARTAN SCRAPBOOK

—— BASKETBALL ——

Pioneer basketball team (1906)

MAC
1916-1917

TALES TO TELL

George Alderton passed along the story of an incredible weekend in 1916 for Hugh Blacklock, the football star from Grand Rapids. Following the exhausting season-ending loss to Notre Dame at home on Saturday, November 18, Hugh took the interurban train to Detroit, where he fought a 10-round boxing bout on Saturday evening. He then continued to Dayton, Ohio, where he played a professional football game on Sunday (frowned upon in the collegiate world, but a common practice). Upon returning to campus, Blacklock prevailed upon Jack Heppinstall to powder and camouflage his facial bruises so that he would look presentable for the team picture that Monday. How good a job did Heppinstall do? You be the judge from the picture on the right.

Soccer at MAC in 1917? The following excerpt is from the December 5, 1916, edition of *The Holcad:*

"During the past month or so the first efforts towards establishing soccer at MAC have been made. Under the able direction of Jack Heppinstall, who played the game in England with several championship teams, a considerable number of the fellows have

been working out this fall on the drill grounds. While the game is new to the most of them they have made a great deal of progress and Jack promised a crack team next year."

There was no evidence of a "crack team" being fielded in the spring of 1917.

Hugh Blacklock's 1916 team photo

HEADLINES of 1917

- The U.S. officially enters World War I on April 6.
- The U.S. purchases the Virgin Islands from Denmark for $25 million.
- Puerto Rico becomes a U.S. territory and its inhabitants become U.S. citizens.
- For the first time, radios are used for ground-to-air and air-to-air communication.

SCOREBOARD

	W	L	T	Avg.
Baseball	6	5	0	.545
Track and Field	0	1	0	.000
Football	4	2	1	.643
Basketball	11	5	0	.688
Tennis		no team		
Cross Country	0	0	0	.000

TEAM OF THE YEAR

The 1916-1917 edition of MAC basketball would play the final full season in the "friendly" Armory. The 11-5 record was registered in streaks, winning the first nine games on the schedule before losing four in a row and concluding with two added victories before bowing to the Detroit YMCA quintet. All five losses were road games. Although four other men played minor roles during the season, the six-man rotation (shown below) carried the load over the 16-game season.

MAKING HISTORY

A preseason football feature story in the *Holcad* boasts that the 1916 Aggie forward wall was the largest in the school's history. The starters and their reported weights were, from left end to right end: Larry Archer, 185; Sherm Coryell, 190; Herb Straight, 192; Lyman Frimodig, 187; Adelbert Vandervoort, 196; Hugh Blacklock, 192; and Ralph Henning, 175.

The original version of the school's fight song was written by cheerleader F.I. Lankey. It should be noted that in the opening stanza of his original piece, lyrics read:

On the banks of the Red Cedar,
There's a school that's known to all.
Its specialty is farming,
And those farmers play football.

Also, by 1916 the school had adopted an alma mater which held, with slight ongoing alterations, until the introduction and adoption of *MSU Shadows* in 1949. The lyrics to the original alma mater were sung to the tune of Cornell University's song:

Close beside the winding Cedar,
Sloping banks of green,
Spreads the campus Alma Mater,
Fairest ever seen.

First of all thy race, fond mother,
Thus we greet thee now,
While with loving hands the laurel,
Twin we o'er thy brow.

(chorus)
Swell the chorus, let in echo,
Over hill and dale
Hail to thee, our loving mother,
M.A.C. all hail.

1917 basketball team. (Front row left to right) Art Sheffield, captain Al McClelland and Paul Vevia. (Back row, left to right) Lyman Frimodig, coach George Gauthier, David Peppard and Byron Murray.

MAC engaged in another sport during the winter of 1916-1917. It was bowling, taken up as an intercollegiate activity. The team consisted of seven men, and the organization was called the Inter-Society League. They did not meet their opponents in actual competition but bowled on home alleys and telegraphed the results to their respective opponents. The league consisted of Yale, Princeton, Lehigh, Colby and Stevens in the eastern division, and Syracuse, Cornell, Michigan, Illinois and MAC in the western division. Of 12 games rolled, the Aggies won five. There is no record of the competition continuing beyond that 1917 season.

GREAT STATE DATES

Football—**September 30, 1916 (H):** Before a home crowd of more than 2,000, MAC easily dispensed of Olivet, 40-0. It was an auspicious debut for the first-year coach, Frank Sommers. Captain Ralph Henning, right end, likely ran from the backfield position as well. He was credited with three of the six touchdowns, with only one of the three scores made from a pass reception. Quarterback Bob Huebel scored once, as did two new backfield starters, Charles Butler and Fred Jacks.

Football—**October 28, 1916 (H):** The MAC-North Dakota varsity contest was preceded by two games. The first was between the junior and senior class teams and the second was the annual freshman game, MAC versus Michigan. Local interest for the second game was so whetted that the bleachers were packed with fans before either yearling team took the field. With 30 seconds of playing time remaining and the Aggies trailing 7-6, the Wolverine rookies unwisely attempted a pass near midfield. A MAC reserve tackle by the name of Allen broke through the line, deflected the aerial attempt and intercepted the ball in midair. To the howling delight of the local fans, he then rambled 50 yards for the winning marker as time ran out. This exciting finish left the afternoon's feature game, a 30-0 varsity victory over the Dakota team, an anti-climactic affair.

Basketball—**January 12, 1917 (H):** Seldom does one man dominate a team's scoring the way center David Peppard did in the 41-22 season-opening victory over West Virginian Wesleyan. The East Lansing native connected on 14 field goals and three free throws for 31 points. Paul Vevia contributed the remaining 10 points from his forward position.

Basketball—**January 26, 1917 (H):** With the reputation of having sustained only two losses in seven years, the Illinois Athletic Club team trotted onto the Armory floor exuding confidence. Although during warm-ups those same IAC players began to express concern over the necessity to shoot through the infamous low girders, they remained undaunted. The visitors were so confident that two regular starters sat on the bench during the opening half of play as the Aggies maintained an 11-9 advantage. By the time the Chicago coach decided to play his full complement, it was too late. Gauthier's fivesome continued their dominance to win fairly easily, 39-27.

Basketball—**February 1, 1917 (H):** Perhaps the University of Buffalo team was not aggressive enough. Over the entire game against MAC they were *never* called for a personal foul. At the same time, they were never in the game, losing 36-17. The New Yorkers could have been travel weary. They had opted to come to East Lansing via automobiles. Considering those early vehicles, the crude roads of the time, and the distance of approximately 400 miles, they could have been on the road for as much as 10 hours. The game start was delayed two hours awaiting their arrival.

Basketball—**February 10, 1917 (H):** Lyman Frimodig later confirmed the 20-19 victory over Wabash as his greatest thrill during four years of MAC athletics. Lyman scored 12 of the winners' 20 points. It was the ninth straight victory for the undefeated Aggies.

Basketball—**March 8, 1917 (H):** With construction progressing on the gymnasium building across the street, Aggie followers were convinced the Marietta College game would be the final varsity game on the beloved Armory floor. Those who crammed into the 31-year-old building that night were also saying farewell to the senior five of Lyman Frimodig, Al McClelland, Dave Peppard, Art Sheffield and Paul Vevia. The game proved exciting as the visitors built a 16-12 halftime lead before the Aggies could respond with a stirring comeback, outscoring the Pioneers 18-4 in the final 20 minutes. The chalkboard in the corner displayed the final score: MAC 30, Marietta 20. The Armory would continue to host MAC basketball through nearly all of the following season.

Baseball—**April 21, 1917 (H):** The second of the weekend's two-game series against Marshall was truly a pitchers' battle. Ray DeMond was sent to the mound by Coach Morrissey, and he responded with an impressive pitching performance. Regardless, it took an extra inning

before the Aggies could push across an unearned run for the victory. Both teams opened with a first-inning marker, and the 1-1 game held until the tenth inning when Lyman Frimodig was walked. A subsequent out, an infield error, and a wild pitch saw the big first baseman ramble home with the deciding run.

Track and Field—May 12, 1917 (H): Although only three teams were entered, MAC captured the running of the Second Annual Michigan Intercollegiate track meet at College Field. The Aggies accounted for 53 points followed by Hillsdale, 45; Michigan Normal, 18; and the MAC freshmen, 10. Winners for the varsity were Ernest Carlson in the 100-and 220-yard sprints, Clark Barrell in both the high and low hurdles, David Peppard in the 440-yard run and Art Atkin in the discus, as well as a second place in the shot put.

ATHLETE OF THE YEAR

No Aggie-Spartan athlete has ever equaled or bettered Lyman Frimodig's exploit of having earned a total of 10 varsity awards during his MAC career (four in basketball, four in baseball and two in football). By that measure alone, through the years many have considered "Frim" the greatest to have ever worn the Green and White. Originally from Calumet, Mich., Frimodig returned to the UP upon graduation, where he coached and was principal of Escanaba High School until entering the armed forces in 1918. One year later he was hired as the freshman coach by his alma mater, and he never left the scene, serving 30 years at different times as assistant athletic director, varsity basketball coach and professor of health and physical education. In 1949 Frimodig assumed the position of ticket sales manager in the department, a position he held until retirement in 1960.

IN THE SPARTLITE

Baseball: As the United States declared war on Germany on April 6, 1917, the college's academic term was shortened to expedite the process for young men to enlist in the armed forces. The clouds of war also impacted the athletic scene. A planned trip to play West Virginia, Virginia Wesleyan, Washington and Jefferson, Pittsburgh and Carnegie Tech was canceled. Also, no games were played against the U of M. Michigan had canceled all of their athletic events for the remainder of the academic year. A total of 11 MAC games from the original 17-game schedule were played.

To help fill the scheduling void, a team labeled "Campus All-Stars" was quickly organized. Borrowing "Frenchy" DeMond as their pitcher, they took on the remaining varsity squad. To the embarrassment of the varsity, the All-Stars prevailed in the shortened six-inning contest, 7-6.

In a two-game series at College Field against Notre Dame, Ray "Frenchy" DeMond nearly pulled off a remarkable pitching feat. In the first game, he shut the Irish out on two hits as the Aggies scored five times on 11 hits and played errorless ball in the field for a 5-0 victory. On

Lyman Frimodig

the very next afternoon, Coach Morrissey again called upon DeMond. The big right-hander responded by continuing to hold the Irish scoreless for seven more innings. Leading 2-0 going into the eighth, "Frenchy" finally tired. Yet, it was a misjudged fly by Bob McWilliams that led to the scoring of Notre Dame's first three runs and the lead. They scored once more in the ninth and squeezed out a 4-2 win.

Basketball: Twice during the nine-game winning streak that opened the schedule, the Aggies held their opponent to less than 10 points. Alma was a 47-7 victim on January 20, and three weeks later Ohio Northern fell 53-9 when the MAC five scored their highest total of the season.

Season-ending totals reveal that of 11 men who were on the composite scoring sheet, four were, by far, the top contributors: Dave Peppard, 190; Paul Vevia, 105; Lyman Frimodig, 72; and Byron Murray, 64. The remaining five contributed a total of only 33 points.

Cross Country: On November 18, the morning of the Notre Dame football game, an invitational meet was run over the three-mile course through the campus. Of the nine schools invited to compete, only two accepted, Albion and the U of M. The team totals in order of finish were as follows: Michigan, 8; Albion, 16; MAC, 32; Michigan freshmen, 52; and MAC freshmen, 58. The three varsity Aggies who figured in the scoring were Longnecker, fifth, Warren, 13th, and Allen, 14th.

Football: The freedom to alter playing time of a game remained in the rule book. The season opener with Olivet was played in 10-minute quarters, and then one week later, the quarters of the Carroll game were extended to the customary 15-minute periods.

The Aggie team that entered the South Dakota game as a three-touchdown favorite on November 4 had to settle for a 3-3 tie in a game played at Vermillion. The interpretation of one particular play could have led to a more pleasant result. As reported in *The Holcad*:

> "In the third quarter the team did score a touchdown, that is everyone thought so, but Referee Elseman, after blowing his whistle when the ball was across the line, permitted the Coyotes to shove Huebel back. When the mass of players was untangled, the ball was seen lying six inches from the line. That was the only chance the Michigan boys ever had to score a touchdown, and Huebel's drop kick, just before the game ended, staved off defeat."

After defeating Michigan twice in three years (1913 and 1915), local fans were becoming overconfident that their heroes could frequently duplicate the effort. Thus, the 0-9 defeat on October 21 and the 0-14 loss to Notre Dame three weeks later were deeply disappointing. Even with a respectable 4-2-1 season record, backing for Coach Sommers rapidly deteriorated. On the Saturday of the final game (against the Irish with Charley Bachman starting at left guard) the headline of a *State Journal* article read: "Believe Sommers Will Not Coach Ags Again." Supposedly fans had taken a disliking to him because of his method of "bawling out" players in front of the grandstand. Also, it was suggested he was not able to marshal his men into a team-like unit for the big games and, furthermore, there appeared to be friction between the coach and his players. Regardless, some of those players spoke out in favor of their coach with one being quoted as saying: "Every member of the football squad believes that Coach Sommers has delivered the goods and we think he ought to be asked back next fall." In a final gesture, Sommers went before the State Board of Agriculture and made a personal appeal. It was all for naught. Frank Sommers would return to Pennsylvania and MAC would again be looking for a football coach.

Financially, the Athletic Association had an on-hand balance November 30 of $4,004.54 against $6,325.30, the previous year's balance. Coach Gauthier explained that the smaller balance was due to outfitting a larger than normal freshman team of 50 men ($2,240.66), plus the increase in coaches' salaries which, along with other labor expenses, totaled $2,261.65.

Following the 1916 season, officials of the Lansing Automobile Club met with school administrators to outline a plan of jointly engaging in the recruitment efforts by providing summer job opportunities for student athletes. Unrestrained at that time by any NCAA policy, the idea gained support.

Track and Field: The entire season of 1917 took place on College Field within three days. First was the 83 2/3 to 42 1/3 loss to Notre Dame on Thursday, May 10. This was followed by the state intercollegiate meet two days later. In that loss to Notre Dame, only two Aggies earned clear-cut first-place finishes: Dave Peppard won the 440-yard run, and Clark Barrell captured the 120-yard high hurdle event. A total of 14 men were awarded varsity letters.

SPARTAN SCRAPBOOK

BASKETBALL COACHES (1900-2003)

Lyman Frimodig (1921-22)

Alton Kircher (1950)

Peter F. Newell (1951-54)

Forrest A. Anderson (1955-65)

John E. Bennington (1966-69)

Gus G. Ganakas (1970-76)

Pictured elsewhere: Charles Bemies 1900-01$_{BS}$; George Denman 1902-03$_{BS}$; Chester Brewer 1904-10$_{BS}$; John Macklin 1911-15$_{BS}$; George Gauthier 1917-20$_{TR}$; Fred Walker 1922-24$_{BS}$; John Kobs 1925-26$_{BS}$; Ben VanAlstyne 1927-49$_{GO}$

$_{BS}$ see baseball coaches
$_{TR}$ see track and field coaches
$_{GO}$ see golf coaches

George "Jud" Heathcote (1977-95)

Tom Izzo (1996-)

MAC
1917-1918

TALES TO TELL

In 1917, Chester Brewer was lured back to East Lansing after spending seven successful years as combined athletic director and coach at the University of Missouri in Columbia, Mo. Perhaps the popular Brewer should have been advised that "you can never go back." His original eight years at MAC (1903-1910) were memorable and auspicious. Then came the fall of 1917 at MAC. Struggling through a 0-9 football record, Coach Brewer would be forever linked to the school's only winless grid season. Perhaps the demise was attributable to a more challenging schedule with Detroit, Northwestern, Syracuse and Camp MacArthur (Texas), the latter loaded with ex-college stars replacing Olivet, Carroll, North Dakota and South Dakota. It also might be claimed that the Aggies' downfall could be ascribed to the departure of experienced manpower into the armed forces. Regardless of any reasoning or rationale, one fact remained: following the winless season of 1917, the Brewer record at Michigan Agriculture would forever be tarnished.

Led by Yellmaster T.C. Dee, two additional cheers were added to the list reported in 1911-1912:

Rat-a-to-thrat! to-thrat! to-thrat!
Terrors-to-lick! to-lick! to-lick!
Kick-a-ba-ba! Kick-a-ba-ba!
M.A.C.- M.A.C.- Rah! Rah! Rah!

R-r-r-r-r-r-r-r-r-r-r-r-h Varsity, Rah!
R-r-r-r-r-r-r-r-r-r-r-r-h Varsity, Rah!
R-r-r-r-r-r-r-r-r-r-r-r-h Varsity, Rah!

On February 23 the athletic office proudly released the names of 49 former Aggies athletes who were serving in the United States Armed Forces. The list included many of the bright stars of past MAC teams. Among them were: Art Bibbins, Hugh Blacklock, Ralph Chamberlain, Ion Cortright, Jerry DaPrato, Hilmar Fick, Elmer Gorenflo, Parnell McKenna, Blake Miller, Hewett Miller, Oscar Miller, Dave Peppard, Fred Stone and Adelbert Vandervoort.

HEADLINES of 1918

- World War I ends on November 11.
- For the first time, daylight-saving time goes into effect.
- Robert Leroy Ripley, cartoonist, begins his syndicated "Believe It or Not" series of strange and unusual facts.
- First scheduled air-mail service begins between New York City and Washington, D.C. Stamps initially cost $0.24, later reduced to six cents.

SCOREBOARD

	W	L	T	Avg.
Baseball	7	5	0	.583
Track and Field	0	1	0	.000
Football	0	9	0	.000
Basketball	6	10	0	.375
Tennis	1	0	1	.750
Cross Country	no dual meets			

TEAM OF THE YEAR

Having little to choose from, with their record of 7-5, the baseball team has been identified as the outstanding team of the year for 1917-1918. Of those seven victories, the 4-0 shutout of Notre Dame was the feature game of the spring.

1918 baseball team. (Left to right) H. Peters, P. Donnelly, S. Johnston, J. Hammes, I. Snider, G. Hayes, manager Borgman, captain R. DeMond, coach C. Brewer, W. Collinson, H. Andrews, G. Mills, O. Kellogg and H. Doscher.

MAKING HISTORY

Originally, the new Gymnasium Building (Circle IM) was to have been available for the basketball schedule of 1917. Compounded by the inability to secure certain building materials during the war years and the reality of an untimely labor strike, it would not be available until Thursday, Feb. 21, 1918 when the first official function, the junior prom, was held. The inaugural athletic event would take place two evenings later when approximately 1,000 fans cheered the Aggies to a 35-20 basketball win over Oberlin. Leading the way for MAC were Byron Murray with 13 points, Charles Higbie, 10, and Irving "Shorty" Snider, 8. Formal dedication of the new facility took place on the evening of May 22, 1918, three days short of a one-year delay from the contracted date for completion. The ceremony was simple as Robert H. Graham, president of the state Board of Agriculture, made a presentation speech and passed the keys of the building to President Kedzie. In turn, Kedzie handed them over to Chester Brewer, who by then held the title of director of athletics. Among the hundreds who sauntered through the building that evening were approximately 30 varsity alumni who were invited as guests of honor. These men were given seats on the platform, and during the course of the evening were presented with certificates of their athletic achievements as souvenirs of the dedication exercises. The gymnasium building would provide the im-

petus to usher three additional intercollegiate sports onto the scene: fencing, swimming and wrestling. Also, women would take a more active role with an extensive intramural program to include basketball, tennis, field hockey, track and field, swimming and rifle shooting. A separate shower room, dressing room and lounging room had been included for the needs of the co-eds.

GREAT STATE DATES

Cross Country—**November 3, 1917 (H):** Placing first, fourth and eighth for 13 points, the MAC runners captured the third running of the state intercollegiate championships. The U of M, winners of the first two meets, settled for second place with 17 points, followed by Albion with 27. The Aggies' Louis Geiermann was the winner over the three-and-a-half-mile run mile run in a comparatively slow time of 19:29.4. The course was described as follows: the start was from in front of the gymnasium. The trail immediately crossed over the College Field Bridge and then followed the river east to the Pinetum Road (Hagadorn). The course then went north to Grand River Road and west along the road, reentering the campus at the orchard (northeast corner), wandering back via the current west circle drive to the finish line at the gymnasium.

Basketball—**January 19, 1918 (H):** After opening the season with six straight losses (five on the road), MAC gained their first victory of the season, 24-20, against the Ft. Custer Officers of Battle Creek. Leading at halftime 8-8, the Aggies outscored the soldiers 16-12 in the final 20 minutes. The starting five played the entire game: George Garrett, Charles Higbie, Larry Kurtz, Hobert Brigham and Byron Murray. Captain Murray led all scorers with nine points.

Basketball—**February 1, 1918 (H):** Even as the cries from the vanquished bewailed how the low rafters of the Armory acted as a "sixth man" for the hometown Farmers, the decisive 27-12 victory over Notre Dame was nevertheless a satisfying win. Granted, more than a share of the Irish field goal attempts were tangled in the ceiling structure; regardless, the MAC defense was persistent, holding the visitors to a total of four points in the opening half and only three field goals over the entire 40 minutes of "action." MAC's winning 27 points were divided as follows: Charles Higbie, eight; Hobert Brigham, seven; Byron Murray, six; and Larry Kurtz, six.

Basketball—**March 9, 1918 (H):** In the third game played in the new gymnasium, the Aggies closed out the season in winning style with a 23-16 victory over the Detroit YMCA. They led 8-4 at intermission and then with Charlie Higbie and Larry Kurtz warming up in the second half, the Farmers outscored the Y-men 15-12. This would be the last time Michigan Agriculture would match up against the Y team. Over the 15 years of friendly competition, MAC had won only 12 of the 27 games played. In a preliminary game earlier in the evening, the freshmen team defeated the Detroit Junior College. Also, in an apparent opportunity to display the extended facilities of the new gymnasium, during half time of the varsity game, a relay was run on the upper-level track between the varsity and freshman track teams.

Baseball—**May 9 and 10, 1918 (A):** Although Kalamazoo College managed an unusual six runs on eight hits off of Ray DeMond, the outcome of the game was never in doubt as MAC posted five runs in the opening two innings and never trailed, 10-6. With three hits, left fielder Herm Doscher was the star at the plate. On the next afternoon the Aggies moved down the street and easily defeated Western State, 10-3. George Mills pitched scoreless ball in seven innings of relief to gain the decision.

Baseball—**May 11, 1918 (A):** "Frenchy" DeMond pitched the best game of his collegiate career when he permitted Notre Dame but one scratch hit in a 4-0 victory. It was the first loss of the season for the Irish and only their third loss at home in a span of seven years. Also of historic note, it was MAC's first-ever win at South Bend and helped to soothe the loss one week earlier in East Lansing. In back-to-back innings the Aggies scored a pair of runs. In the fourth "Shorty" Snider drove home George Hayes and William Collinson, who had both singled. In the fifth Ward Andrews and DeMond scored, following successive base hits.

ATHLETE OF THE YEAR

Although he participated in but one sport, pitcher Ray "Frenchy" DeMond is recognized as the Athlete of the Year. He was MAC's outstanding baseball player in both the 1917 and 1918 seasons. Not only was DeMond the ace pitcher in 1918, but the season statistics reveal he was also the team's leading hitter. From the May 20, 1918, issue of *The Holcad*:

Ray "Frenchy" DeMond

"Frenchy DeMond was our mainstay in the box and led in hitting. Frenchy gets a gold baseball in recognition of the services he has given the team, both as a pitcher and as an all-around player."

Later, in the 1940s, his son John would star as a member of the varsity swimming team.

IN THE SPARTLITE

Baseball: In the first inning of the season-closing 5-2 loss at Ann Arbor, the Farmers registered a triple play with the left fielder Herm Doscher, shortstop Howard Peters and catcher William Collinson being credited with putouts. The defense for the remainder of the game was not so splendid. A total of 13 errors were committed by the Aggies, including three by that same "triple-play" shortstop, Howard Peters.

Batting averages for the season were: Ray DeMond, .372; Ward Andrews, .333; Stan Johnston, .300; John Hammes, .279; George Hayes, .257; Irving "Shorty" Snider, .256; Herm Doscher, .238; Orson Kellogg, .210; William Collinson, .172; and Howard Peters, .111.

Jimmy Hasselman, the school's first equivalent of a sports information director, doubled as the freshmen baseball coach during the 1918 season.

Basketball: For this final year of varsity basketball in the Armory, a notable change was made in the layout of the court. A reconfiguration had the baskets in the east and west ends of the arena rather than north and south as previously. Thus, the infamous low girders ran across the floor layout rather lengthwise. This provided short shots from the side at greater angles than before.

Cross Country: One week before hosting the state intercollegiate championships on November 3, the all-college meet was conducted with 12 men entered.

MAC took second place in the Thanksgiving Day run held in Detroit under the auspices of the Detroit YMCA. The course was not run on the Belle Isle course, as in former years, but on Woodward Avenue from Grand Boulevard to Grand Circus Park on an unfamiliar hard surface and over a distance of two-and-a-half miles. The five-man Aggie team was headed by Tony Brendel and finished third about 80 yards behind the winner from the Y team. Other finishers for the Green and White were Longnecker fifth, Allen 11th, Geiermann 16th and Sturm 18th. Louis Geiermann led the field during practically the entire race before being compelled to drop back because of a hobbled knee.

Honoring a nation at war in Europe, the 1917 Aggie green jerseys were replete with a version of "Old Glory" large enough to cover the entire front.

Football: While posting a sorrowful 0-9 record, it was a season of "might have beens." The closest the 1917 team came to winning a game was in the 7-3 home loss to Kalamazoo on the second Saturday of the season. On six separate instances that afternoon the Aggies found themselves within five yards of the goal yet unable to register a touchdown. Specifically, on one of those occasions the ball rested on the one-yard line and with two downs the offense couldn't push the ball over. John Hammes successfully executed a field goal in the third period but a second attempt in the fourth quarter hit the goal post and failed. Yet, with four minutes to play and possessing a 3-0 lead, MAC was on the verge of a win when Orson Kellogg fumbled a punt that had been kicked out of danger from inside the 10-yard line. The ball was scooped up by a "K" College player who raced 40 yards for the winning score.

Struggling for any positive sign amidst the winless season, *The Holcad* reported the 21-7 homecoming loss to Syracuse should have been a 7-7 tie. MAC scored first on a Larry Archer to C.F. Ramsey pass midway through the opening quarter. Shortly thereafter the Orange had knotted the score on a 60-yard run through center. Syra-

cuse put the game away on two third-quarter TDs, both from Aggie miscues, first on a 50-yard run of a fumble recovery and then on a 30-yard run following a pass interception.

Original plans were for the Syracuse game on November 24 to close out the season. Belatedly, a Thanksgiving Day game was added on November 29 against the Camp MacArthur team of Waco, Texas, with its roster of experienced college players. Although the Farmers held the army team scoreless over the first half of play, the talented soldiers took charge after intermission and eventually had their way, 20-0.

Illustrating the futility of the season, throughout the course of the nine games Brewer's squad was outscored by a composite margin of 179 to 23. They were shut out five times.

Swimming: Upon opening of the new Gymnasium Building and its 30-yard pool, there was no immediate action to initiate a competitive swimming team. The tank was filled for the first time in preparation for a "formal christening" on Saturday, May 4, 1918. At that time swimmers from MAC and a group of seven from the Detroit YMCA were featured in an aquatic exhibition. From the *MAC Record*:

"Fred Jorn of the Detroit "Y" will give an exhibition and incidentally will try for a record plunge in the new 90 foot tank. Several students reputed to be veritable "water dogs" will put on some fancy swimming acts and some excitement will be injected with contests in water basketball and polo. The christening will start at 8 o'clock."

Tennis: There is no record of how many tennis meets were originally scheduled or how many were cancelled by weather conditions, but only two were apparently conducted in the spring of 1918. They were two meetings against Michigan Normal, away and home. The results were a 4-2 victory at Ypsilanti and a 3-3 tie in East Lansing. Julie Rigterink and Ruth Schuppert were the co-ed representatives with George Wible and Santiago "Sammy" Iledan representing the men. Sammy, a student from the Philippines, stood barely four feet in height.

On March 2, 1918 the MAC basketball team plays its second game in the new gymnasium. The U of M team was the featured opponent and the Blue prevailed, 33-25.

Track and Field: With the war still raging in Europe, a reflection of military training was embraced in the Michigan intercollegiate championships of 1918 when the javelin throw was replaced on the program by the hand grenade throw. Accuracy was the prime requisite for the event as the missile was tossed 150 feet toward a series of concentric circles and, oh yes, the grenades were *not* loaded. The final team scoring for the meet was as follows: MAC 48 1/2, Western State 38 1/2, MAC Freshmen 30 1/2, Kalamazoo College 14 1/2, Michigan State Normal 14, Detroit Junior College 12 and Hillsdale 7 1/2.

A total of 11 men were available to represent MAC in the only dual meet of the spring, an 85-35 loss to Notre Dame at South Bend. Larry Kurtz and W.H. Sturm took first and second respectively in the quarter-mile, Lou Geiermann was second in the half-mile, A.J. Mitchell second in the mile, and Tony Brendel second in the two-mile run. Second places were also garnered by W.V. Taylor in the high hurdles, C.M. Hatland in the low hurdles, Robinson in the high jump and Titkens in both the shot put and discus. Walter Simmons placed third in both the 100- and 220-yard dashes.

George Wible (left) and Santiago "Sammy" Iledan of the Philippines who stood just four feet in height.

MAC
1918-1919

TALES TO TELL

From March 1918 until November of 1919 the United States endured the nation's worst single epidemic when the outbreak of Spanish influenza killed more than 500,000 people. It was this scourge that penetrated into the football scene that fall, wreaking havoc on the scheduling of games. After opening the season with easy wins over Albion and Hillsdale, the Aggies were to face Michigan and Northwestern on consecutive Saturdays, October 19 and October 26. Even though the flu quarantine would have made it difficult for students to get away, by midweek of the scheduled U of M game, it was announced that special interurban trains would be transporting rooters to Ann Arbor. Coach Gauthier continued team practices in seclusion, attempting to add a surprise twist to his game plan. Then on Thursday, literally hours before kickoff time in Ann Arbor, the game was called off because of the epidemic. The decision was made following a late-hour meeting on Wednesday night involving governor Albert Sleeper and Dr. H.M. Olin, secretary of the state board of health. Members of the team had not been immune from the disease. During

that week of October 13-19 Dean Ferris, Herb Dunphy, Harry Graves and "Shorty" Snider had been in and out of the college infirmary. Regardless, by the following Monday all of the stricken, although weakened, were at practice, but by then Coach Gauthier had been sidelined and assistant Ion Cortright was in charge. As that week progressed in preparation for the game at Evanston, it appeared that only two men would miss the contest, Phil Bailey and Snider. Then on Thursday, as the week before, it was announced there would be no game. The Illinois health authorities had intervened and made the decision. By now, school officials were becoming anxious. Athletic department expenses were continuing to mount but revenues were nil. Just the cost for assorted football equipment added up to something more than $2,500 for the season and the anticipated revenue from the Northwestern game, now unrecoverable, was expected to have been somewhere between $3,000 and $5,000. But the "bleeding" would stop. The season resumed at home on the following Saturday, November 2, against Western State, and the remainder of the schedule was played out without subsequent interruption. Furthermore, the University of Michigan did manage to

HEADLINES of 1919

- Jack Dempsey becomes the world heavyweight boxing champion when he defeats Jess Willard in Toledo, Ohio.
- The world's oldest airline, KLM, is founded.
- Radio Corporation of America (RCA) is established.
- Allied nations and Germany sign the Treaty of Versailles ending World War I.

SCOREBOARD

	W	L	T	Avg.
Baseball	4	9	0	.308
Track and Field	1	1	0	.500
Football	4	3	0	..571
Basketball	9	9	0	.500
Tennis	3	2	1	.583
Cross Country	no team			

TEAM OF THE YEAR

The football season of 1918 produced one of MAC's best squads ever, yet it was a team that could win only one out of four major games (Notre Dame). As seen by the game scores, the Aggies were competitive even in those three losses (14-6 versus Purdue, 21-6 versus Michigan and 7-6 versus Wisconsin).

1918 football team. (Front row) J. Brady, D. Ferris, W. Simmons. (Middle row) J. Bos, J. Schwei, R. VanOrden, I. Snider, H. Dunphy, H. Graves, E. Young and P. Bailey. (Back row) Trainer J. Heppinstall, J.E. Johns, H. Franson, captain L. Archer, C.W. Anderson, H. Wilson and coach G. Gauthier.

MAKING HISTORY

open a slot on their calendar and the 1918 MAC—U of M game was played after all, on November 23, five weeks later than originally scheduled.

In April, Chester Brewer released a new set of guidelines for acquiring the varsity monogram in the six sports. The coach-athletic director summarized the new criteria as being the same as all Western Conference schools. He further noted: "The new system will raise standards of athletic work at MAC and add to honor of the coveted varsity insignia." With such definition it seemed obvious that earning the varsity sweater would not become *easier*.

On November 11, the German army capitulated to the Allies thus ending World War I. In reaction, state government officials planned a celebration in conjunction with MAC's game against Notre Dame, the home finale on the following Saturday. The Irish came to town led by a first-year head coach named Knute Rockne. In the Notre Dame line up was the heralded George Gipp and a teammate who would later become famous as coach of the Green Bay Packers, Curly Lambeau. With only one tie on its season record and having dominated the series with MAC, 10-1, since 1897, ND was highly favored. On the morning of game day, amidst tempera-

tures in the low 60s, a steady rain began which quickly turned into a torrential downpour that continued, uninterrupted, through the afternoon. It rained so hard that all planned activities related to the Armistice were canceled. By game time the field could have been considered unplayable, but as is the tradition in football, the game would go on.

When interviewed at his home in West Yarmouth, Mass., during the summer of 1995, Herb Dunphy (FB 18), a starting halfback that afternoon, recalled that in many spots on the field, rainwater was so deep that it seeped over the tops of the players' hightop shoes. The *Lansing State Journal* reported the game results in its Monday edition:

> "The Michigan Aggies cruised their way through a sea of mud Saturday to a 13-7 victory over the University of Notre Dame. It was a victory won without flukes or horseshoes, under conditions which made the playing of real football well-nigh impossible."

Although this singular win was cherished, it did not make a season. The Aggies were 4-3 overall. Meanwhile, it was the only loss for Notre Dame that season and, furthermore, it would be the only setback that Coach Knute Rockne's teams would sustain in the three-year period 1918-1920.

The athletic department seized the opportunity of the Annual Farmer's Week to show off the facilities of the new gymnasium building to the rural gentry of the state. On the evening of February 6 nearly 3,000 guests roamed through the facility and were entertained with exhibition swimming by representatives from the Detroit Athletic Club, wrestling matches, boxing bouts and most intriguing, a demonstrating of ju jitsu by a talented international student from Japan.

GREAT STATE DATES

Football—**October 12, 1918 (H):** At halftime, with MAC leading Hillsdale 27-0, Coach Gauthier made a decision to turn the game over to his second unit. After the reserves had been outscored 7-0 in that third period, the Aggie starters returned to the field and once more took command. Scoring four more times, the final count read: MAC 66, Hillsdale 6. Of the numerous men who saw action against the Chargers, Dean Ferris and Harry Graves stood out. Ferris demonstrated impressive field generalship at quarterback and fullback Graves, who scored two touchdowns, roared along with impressive gains every time he carried the ball. Regardless, more threatening competition lay ahead: Michigan, Northwestern, Purdue, Notre Dame and Wisconsin.

Basketball—**January 15, 1919 (H):** Over all other games during the season the Aggies averaged 21 points and then on this evening, against Kalamazoo College, they doubled their output, winning 42-20. *The State Journal* offered some explanation: "The MAC team played a well-regulated game last night with increased speed in all departments and with more cleverness in handling the ball."

The Journal also reported they developed "an entirely new defensive play" but gave no details as to what that meant. Larry Kurtz was forced from the game after twisting his knee. It was an injury that would nag him through most of the season.

Basketball—**February 1, 1919 (A):** MAC concluded a three-day trip through Indiana with a 32-28 victory over Notre Dame in a game played on the dirt floor of the Irish fieldhouse. The stop in South Bend was preceded by games at Wabash and DePauw. The team scoring was distributed among the five starters: Wayne Palm 14, Larry Kurtz 6, "Shorty" Snider 6, Walt Foster 4 and George Garratt 2. Of the two reserves who made the trip (Franson and Coleman) only Coleman played briefly as a substitute for Snider.

Basketball—**February 7, 1919 (H):** Taking the sting out of the Wabash loss one week earlier at Crawfordsville, Ind., the Farmers defeated the Little Giants, 37-26 for their eighth win of the year. Perhaps the Aggies became complacent after leading 25-10 at the intermission. The Indiana boys were not going to go away as they returned to the floor and proceeded to outscore the Green 13-4 over the opening portion of the final 20 minutes. Over the final four minutes of play, the Aggies once more found their touch and put the game out of danger. Leading 35-26 and the clock ticking down, Walt Foster let one go from well beyond mid-court and it rattled through just as the gun sounded at the end of the game.

Basketball—**February 28, 1919 (A):** On three successive opening game possessions against Michigan, sophomore center Walt Foster won the center jump to one of his guards who passed the ball to accurate-shooting sophomore forward Wayne Palm and suddenly the

score was 6-0. The Wolverines never recovered from that initial surge and the Aggies led at halftime 20-9 and won with apparent ease, 33-24. Palm was credited with 17 of his team's points. *The Holcad* noted that "the MAC five-man defense was working to its best advantage" and further described that the U of M players "gave up hope of getting close to the basket and contented themselves with attempting long shots." Was the student writer really describing the current day "zone defense?"

Baseball—**April 30, 1919 (A):** In a well-played game at South Bend, MAC edged Notre Dame 2-1, ending the Irish six-game winning streak. Sophomore pitcher Herb Hartwig yielded a single run in the first inning and then "shut the door" on the Irish over the final eight innings of play. Meanwhile, the Aggies scored two runs on four straight hits in the third inning from the bats of "Shorty" Snider, Nels Carr, John Hammes and Bill Johnston. That was it: MAC 2, ND 1.

Baseball—**June 7, 1919 (A):** Fans in Kalamazoo turned out expecting a real offensive outburst. After all, MAC had won the first game against Western State one month earlier in East Lansing by a football-sounding score of 20-12. As this one turned out, it was an antithesis, a four-hit 2-0 shutout pitched by Paul "Lefty" Donnelly. The game was scoreless until the seventh inning when "Shorty" Snider led off with a successful bunt down the third base line. He was sacrificed to third where he scored on Johnny Hammes's base hit. The second run was scored in similar fashion in the ninth when Ward Andrews walked, made it to second and third on successive outs and scored on a double off the bat of "Siwash" Franson.

Track and Field—**May 24, 1919 (H):** MAC ran away with the fourth annual Michigan Intercollegiate track and field meet held at College Field. The team scoring was as follows: MAC 57, Kalamazoo 30, Albion 23, MAC Freshmen 20, Western State 10, Detroit Junior College 9, Michigan Normal 6, Hillsdale 3. During the afternoon seven meet records were bettered, including three by Aggies. Fred Spiedel pole vaulted 11', adding six inches to the previous mark. In the mile, Tony Brendel ran a 4:40.6 to better by 12 seconds the time posted by Earl Sheldon in 1916. Running for the freshman team, DeGay Ernst established himself as a future great MAC athlete by defeating the varsity's Larry Kurtz in the quarter-mile in a new meet record time of 52.0. Other varsity winners were Walt Simmons with a 10.2 in the 100-yard dash, William Harvie who nosed our Simmons in the 220 with a 23.8 and captain Art Atkin who tossed the shot put, 38' 6".

ATHLETE OF THE YEAR

John Schwei of Iron Mountain was a three-sport star for the Aggies, lettering in football three years (1918-1920), wrestling as the team's heavyweight and lettering four times in track and field (1919-1922). He earned a starting position at end in his very first varsity football season and then was switched to right halfback in 1919 when he scored eight of his team's 17 touchdowns before being sidelined with an injury. To utilize John's husky frame, in 1920 new coach "Potsy" Clark switched the senior to the fullback position from where he managed five TDs as the team's "battering ram." As a weight man with the track and field team, Schwei often placed behind teammate Clarence Fessenden in the shot and discus, but he was most proficient in the javelin where he held the varsity record.

John Schwei

IN THE SPARTLITE

Baseball: The team had visions of complementing their spring schedule with an April 29 game against the National University of Cuba team. The idea fell through when the Cubans opted to limit their visit to schools of the south.

Four men finished the season with a batting average above .325. Pitcher Paul Donnelly led the quartet with a .363 average. "Shorty" Snider, Johnny Hammes and catcher Stanley Johnston each hit for identical .327 averages.

Although there were a few high-scoring games during the decade, pitching seemed to dominate the period. Starring on the mound for the Farmers during the 1910s were Ben Pattirson, Norm "Baldy" Spencer, Ralph Dodge, Al LaFever, Blake Miller, Carl "Swede" Peterson, Art "Lefty" Brown, Ray "Frenchy" DeMond and Harold "Brownie" Springer.

Basketball: From 1899 through the 1918 season the Aggies had posted an impressive composite record of 92 wins against 21 losses on the floor of the Armory. With the entire 1919 varsity basketball home season played in the new Gymnasium Building, the friendly environs of the Armory were gone forever. Future Spartans would no longer gain the home court advantage of perfecting field goal attempts through low-hanging girders.

Perhaps the series against the U of M never recorded a more evenly matched game than that played in the Gymnasium on February 15. There were never more than two or three points separating the teams at any time during the contest. The first half ended with the count 9-9. The third period also ended with the game all even. At the end of regulation the tally-sheet showed the score to be 16-16. During the first five-minute overtime each team managed one free throw and the score read 17-17. Finally, and unfortunately, in the second extra session the Wolverines hit a long field goal that could not be matched and the Aggies went down to defeat 19-17.

Football: The 1918 14-6 home loss to Purdue could be included on the list of historic setbacks administered by the Boilermakers. Second-quarter miscues by the Aggies led to both of the visitors' scores. From his own 40-yard line, Harry Graves attempted a pass to Dean Ferris. The ball was instead gathered in by a PU defender who returned it untouched for the score. Thirty seconds before the finish of that period, the Boilermakers failed to make a first down and punted from their own 40-yard line to Ferris, who was waiting on his own 25-yard line. He fumbled the ball, and an on-charging lineman fell on it at the three-yard line. One play later the score was 14-0. A lone Aggie TD also came on a Purdue error. An attempted punt from their end zone in the third quarter was jointly blocked by Larry Archer and Harry Franson. Archer fell on it for the touchdown. In the final quarter, the Farmers marched the ball to the shadows of the visitors' goal line three times only to lose the ball by mishaps or fumbles.

The 7-6 loss to Wisconsin on Thanksgiving Day was also a big disappointment as the Badgers scored the tying touchdown and ultimate winning PAT during the final 30 seconds of the contest. The real merit of the two teams was hidden thanks to the atrocious playing conditions in Madison. With a couple inches of slush making a quagmire of the playing field, nearly every attempt to circle the end resulted in loss of yardage. The passing game was nonexistent. Compounding the condition, snow driven by a fast wind that swept down the field led to numerous fumbles. MAC scored in the opening quarter when Larry Archer broke through the line and blocked an attempted punt from midfield. He scooped up the ball and raced to the one-yard line before being dropped. Dean Ferris bucked over on the next play for the score but Archer's conversion attempt failed, due largely to the soggy condition of the ball.

Track and Field: On May 10 the Spartans ran up a team-high 101 points as they won all but two events while slamming three (first, second and third in the 100-yard dash, shot put and discus). This was an impressive road victory, but there was one catch—they had not defeated Michigan or Notre Dame but rather Detroit Junior College (Wayne).

Tennis: Beginning with the spring of 1919 the varsity tennis team would no longer be comprised of both men and women. The co-eds would compete within their own schedule until 1928 when women's sports was absorbed into the Women's Athletic Association (WAA), which represented an intramural approach to all athletics, encompassing 13 different sports.

Central State at Mt. Pleasant carried off the honors at the First Annual Men's State Intercollegiate tennis championships held in East Lansing in conjunction with the State Intercollegiate track and field championships. MAC had no finalists.

SPARTAN SCRAPBOOK
— TENNIS —

First tennis team (1913)

MAC
1919-1920

TALES TO TELL

The November 11 issue of *The Holcad* described the pageantry and football halftime humor displayed during homecoming 1919:

"At 1:40 the band arrived on the field followed by the students and the alumni, in order of classes. Fifteen minutes later the South Dakota players and the Green and White team came on the field amid the cheers of the crowd from the stands.

The team was followed by a jazz band of international type which led on the field the football teams from Morrill and Wells Hall. The game which was held during the intermission between halves results in a victory for the girls. One young lady in a bright red dress was clever in line plunges and recovering fumbles, another with red silk hose starred in the aerial type of play and scored a touchdown in the last minute of play. The head linesman had a difficult task but was equal to the situation."

In the "real" game, the Aggies scored two touchdowns in the first half and sent the alumni and local fans home with memories of a hard-fought 13-0 victory.

Raising ticket prices and then having to explain it away is not new. From *The Holcad* of Jan. 27, 1920:

"Many students have been asking the reason for the extra charge for the reserved seats at basketball games, Director Brewer in answer to this question made the following statement:

'The Coach wishes it distinctly understood that the student athletic fee does not nearly cover the cost of the actual return secured by the individual student and that, also, the extra reserve seat fee barely pays for the cost of placing and removing the chairs along the sidelines and other incidental expenses incurred.

The reserved seat fee is charged merely to hold seats for downtown followers of the cage sport or persons not having the time to rush to the gym an hour before the game is to begin. Director Brewer

HEADLINES of 1920

- KDKA, America's first commercial radio station, begins operation in Pittsburgh, Pa.
- The 19th Amendment to the U.S. Constitution is ratified, granting voting rights to women.
- Prices of the time included: bread 12 cents/loaf, milk 67 cents/gallon and gasoline 13 cents/gallon. A new automobile could be purchased for $525 and the average annual income was $2,160.
- Robert Goddard, the "Father of American Rocketry," suggests using rockets to reach the moon.

SCOREBOARD

	W	L	T	Avg.
Baseball	6	9	0	.400
Track and Field	2	4	0	.334
Football	4	4	1	.500
Basketball	21	15	0	.583
Tennis	4	0	1	.900
Cross Country	no dual meets			

styles the large following of outsiders—non-college folk—as the financial lifeblood of the athletic department. The seats must be held for these Aggie enthusiasts, hence the cause of the nominal extra fee.

Sideline seats at all western conference games cost one dollar per seat. At Aggie games the charge is seventy-five cents while students gain admission to the same game at about ten cents per game without reserved seat or twenty-five cents with a reserved chair.'"

Football-baseball player Harold "Brownie" Springer contributed the following story to Fred Stabley's book *The Spartans:*

"The only help I got from MAC was a job at the gym and meals at training table during baseball and football seasons. I believe I got 40 cents an hour. Jack Heppinstall kept track of the hours I worked and I must say he was quite generous.

Many of the (football) players played on Sundays on other teams to get extra money, I myself included. The Heralds of Detroit, the Ft. Wayne Friars and the team coached by Jimmy King, the former Harvard fullback. It was called the Pine Village Chargers. I played for them after the Purdue game (Nov. 1, 1919). We played at Des Moines, Iowa. I got $150 and expenses. Later in 1920 I played for the Friars on Sunday."

TEAM OF THE YEAR

The *Wolverine* yearbook hails the 1919-1920 basketball team as "the fastest and smoothest working outfit ever seen in Aggie uniforms." Their 21 victories included wins over Creighton, Notre Dame and twice over Michigan. They finished the season with a unique seven-game, one-week tour into northern Michigan with stops in Alpena, Munising, Marquette, Ishpeming, Gwinn, Lake Linden and, for the first time, games against Northern Michigan and Michigan College of Mines (Michigan Tech). The trip was a success. With six wins in seven games, the overall season record jumped from 15-14 to 21-15.

Harold "Brownie" Springer, in a 1920 MAC football uniform

1920 basketball team. (Front row, left to right) W. Palm, captain G. Garrett and E. Gilkey. (Middle row, left to right) L. Heasley, J. Hammes, W. Foster, C. Higbie, L. Kurtz and R. Robinson. (Back row, left to right) Athletic director Brewer, Coach Gauthier, Trainer Heppinstall.

MAKING HISTORY

A new football rule provided that the ball for the point-after-touchdown try could be placed *anywhere* along the five-yard line. Prior to 1920 the ball was put in play on the five-yard line at the spot *directly out* from where the ball crossed the goal on the touchdown.

The first-ever intercollegiate track meet in the new gymnasium was a close 47-42 loss to Western State Normal on Wednesday evening, February 25. Four of the gymnasium records that had been established in an inter-class meet earlier in the year were broken by the varsity runner and jumpers. Howard Wilson bettered both the high jump and the pole vault marks with new standards of 5' 7" and 10' 5 1/2". New course records for the track were set by Howard Hoffman with a 2:31.1 half-mile and DeGay Ernst's 56.3 in the quarter-mile. Bleach-ers were conveniently arranged in the middle of the floor so spectators could view activities on both the gymnasium floor and the track above. Regardless, the turnout of spectators was much lower than had been expected.

Reported annual salaries for the coaches were Chester Brewer, $4,500; George Gauthier, $2,200; and Lyman Frimodig, $1,800. As the 1919-1920 freshman coach for football, basketball and baseball, "Frim" would begin his 41-year coaching-administrative career at his alma mater. Meanwhile, that spring George Gauthier would conclude his ties with MAC. Since his graduation in 1914 "Gauthie" had served in numerous capacities, filling in as either head or assistant coach in football, basketball and track. In April of 1920 he departed to take up the position of physical training and recreational supervisor in the Bay City community. He would later move on to a long and successful career as coach and athletic director at Ohio Wesleyan.

GREAT STATE DATES

Football—**October 25, 1919 (H):** Jack Schwei gained at will through the DePauw defense and scored three touchdowns before being replaced in the second quarter because of injuries. "Shorty" Snider scored the final TD by running 50 yards after taking a forward pass from Harold Springer in the fourth quarter. The final score read MAC 27 and DePauw 0.

Basketball—**January 2, 1920 (A):** Apparently back in the early years, guards were supposed to "guard." In reporting the 36-8 defeat of Oberlin, *The State Journal* article noted the defensive play of Larry Kurtz and George Garrett (the starting guards) in holding the Yeomen to only two baskets from the floor.

Basketball—**January 24, 1920 (A):** Early in the first half the Aggies managed a two-point advantage over Knute Rockne's Notre Dame squad and, although several times the margin was cut to one point, they never relinquished the lead and went on for a 23-20 victory. Midway in that first half difficulties in the college's electrical powerhouse left the gym in total darkness and for ten minutes the two teams and the spectators were forced to mark time. For their inconvenience, Notre Dame was given a free throw when the game was resumed.

Lloyd Heasley, in a 1920 MAC basketball uniform

Basketball—**January 30, 1920 (A):** The first half of the MAC-Michigan game ended 6-5 in favor of the Aggies. Was it combined poor offense or solid defense? One can only submit conjecture because newspaper accounts do not offer much explanation. It is noted, however, that MAC outscored the Maize and Blue 17-8 in the final 20 minutes and won going away, 23-13. Ed Gilkey led the team in scoring with 11 points before fouling out.

Basketball—**February 6, 1920 (H):** With the clock showing four minutes of time remaining, a successful long shot by a Wabash player locked the score at 27 all. During the next three minutes and 20 seconds neither team could gain the advantage, and then with 40 seconds remaining Lloyd Heasley, Aggie sophomore forward, received a short pass, dribbled a few feet and swished in a basket to secure the win for MAC, 29-27. With 12 points total, Heasley led the team in scoring.

Basketball—**February 28, 1920 (H):** MAC jumped to an early 6-0 lead over the University of Michigan and, although the contest was tied on two occasions, the Aggies never trailed in an impressive 34-27 victory. Chuck Higbie, the junior from Napoleon, Mich., led all scorers with six field goals while adding four-for-four as the designated free-throw shooter. Eddie Gilkey contributed 10 points, and Larry Kurtz, playing his usual impressive defensive game, added six and Larry Foster two. Captain George Garrett, the fifth starter (there were no substitutions), fulfilled the role of "designated goal defender." The Green and White led at halftime, 16-15. To accommodate a record turnout of 3,000 spectators, several hundred additional chairs and temporary rows of bleachers were brought into the gymnasium.

Track and Field—**March 5, 1920 (A):** Losing only two events, the shot put and the 40-yard low hurdles, the Aggies easily defeated Kalamazoo College, 79-25. Both Howard Wilson and DeGay Ernst displayed their versatility. Wilson won both the high jump and the pole vault while Ernst captured a pair of firsts, the 40-yard dash and then the 440-yard dash.

Baseball—**May 1, 1920 (A):** "Lefty" Brown started his first game in an Aggie uniform in two seasons and while he was touched for five hits in five innings, he held the Normal Teachers (Eastern Michigan) at bay and eventually earned a 5-1 victory. Coach Brewer chose to pitch George Mills over the final four innings and the senior threw even more effectively than Brown. He disposed of

John Hammes

all 12 batters that he faced, six by the strike-out route. The MAC runs came early, two in the third and three in the fourth. Karl Hendershot, led the nine-hit attack with three singles.

Tennis—**May 15, 1920 (H):** With a meet consisting of four points, MAC defeated Kalamazoo College 3-1 by taking two out of three singles and the only doubles match to be played. In the first set the diminutive "Sammy" Iledan came back for a 7-9, 6-3, 6-1 victory. George Wible gained the second point 4-6, 6-4, 6-4 and the pair of Wible and H.A. Goss gained the decisive third point 7-5, 8-6.

ATHLETE OF THE YEAR

At the end of the 1919 football season, "Big" John Hammes, fullback, was picked by Walter Eckersall for his mythical All-Western second team. In addition to three years of football (1917, 1919, 1920), the big guy from Newberry was a two-year contributor in basketball (1918, 1920) and a three-year letter winner in baseball (1917-

1919). Overall he earned eight varsity awards, an accomplishment only topped by nine other athletes who wore the Green.

IN THE SPARTLITE

Baseball: The team headed East on April 11 for a scheduled five-game trip into New York, Pennsylvania and Ohio. After opening with a 7-0 shutout of Rochester the Aggies were defeated by Penn State 14-5 in a snowstorm. The lingering winter weather was a prognosis of things to come as scheduled games with Washington and Jefferson, Marietta and Akron were all cancelled and Coach Brewer returned home with his squad.

New MAC uniforms in 1920 were white, trimmed in green with "Michigan Aggies" in block letters across the jersey front. The stockings were green and the hat was white.

It had to be a record of some sort. Right fielder Irving "Shorty" Snider had only four chances to make putouts during the 12-11 loss to Notre Dame on May 25. Instead he recorded four errors as errant balls bounced from his glove and off his shins.

Basketball: On the weekend of December 19-20 the Aggies opened the season by dividing the squad into two teams. The group of John Hammes, Jack Foster, Eddie Gilkey, Lloyd "Doc" Heasley, John Bos, David Robinson and Ed Matson went east for games against the Detroit Athletic Club and DevVilbis College in Toledo. Another seven-man squad, George Garrett, Larry Kurtz, Wayne Palm, Hutchings, Wilson, Miller and Gustafson headed west to matchup against the Ft. Custer Officers and the Muskegon YMCA. Among the spectators for the 58-3 lopsided victory at Ft. Custer was General George Pershing, a hero of the recent war in Europe.

In a preliminary basketball game to the regular home opener (a 32-25 loss to the University of Chicago) an East Lansing High School girls' team played a team from Perry High School. General admission for the "doubleheader" was $0.75, with students paying $0.10 or $0.25, depending on the seat location.

If the current ever-popular AP or ESPN team-rankings had been in place during the 1920s, Creighton University would have certainly been among the elite. Yet, in 1920 MAC defeated the highly successful Nebraska school twice, 18-15 in Omaha and two weeks later

in East Lansing, 31-24. That 18-15 game was the first Creighton setback at home in three years.

The first-ever game against the University of Indiana was a 20-19 loss at home. A Hoosier forward connected with the winning field goal from mid-court just as the pistol cracked to end the game.

Football: Balancing football income (including a guarantee of $5,000 from the game in Ann Arbor) against expenses ($12,402), an approximate profit of $3,000 was recorded for the year.

With the return of servicemen to campus, the 1919 football team was well-stocked with experienced players, included a plethora of former captains: Del Vandervoort, captain-elect for the 1917 team before entering the army; Sherm Coryell, who was named to fill Vandervoort's shoes, but who also wound up in France; Irish Ramsey, who finally captained the 1917 team; Larry Archer, captain of the 1918 team; and Harry "Siwash" Franson, captain-elect of the 1919 squad. Also returning from military service was Blake Miller. The former star joined the staff as an assistant coach. Blake had coached Mt. Pleasant Normal in 1916. While in the service he played one season with the Camp Custer officer's team.

In the second meeting in two years against Purdue University (the Boilers won in 1918, 14-6) MAC dropped another close one, this time 13-7. All three touchdowns were the result of blocked punts. Larry Archer, the Aggie kicker, was twice victimized and then, when on the defensive side of the line, he broke through to block a Purdue kick that captain Harry Franson fell on for the lone Farmers' score.

Tennis: Prior to the tie-breaker, tennis matches could sometimes be lengthy. As an example, in the May 20 match against Albion, the doubles team of Wible and Iledan went 22 games before winning the opening set 12-10.

In the spring, three courts were added to the tennis layout behind the Women's Building (Morrill Hall), bringing the total to 10. Also, getting a jump on the season, in April a net was strung in the gymnasium for preseason play.

Track and Field: Before the outdoor season of 1920 was well underway, three stars had been sidelined. Lloyd Thurston suffered a badly sprained ankle while engaged in cavalry drills; Ernst had pulled a ligament in his left leg; and captain Howard Hoffman suddenly took ill and was lost for the entire season. These misfortunes obviously impacted MAC's overall season record. As an example, comparing performances in the 50-27 loss to Notre Dame, DeGay Ernst would have won three races and Thurston would have been good for several more points. One performance did stand out that afternoon. Clarence Fessenden established a new school record of 120' 9" in the discus throw.

Bub Kuhn, in the new 1920 MAC baseball uniform

MAC
1920-1921

TALES TO TELL

The sub-headline to a story in the April 15, 1922 issue of *The Holcad* could have been preserved and re-used over and over through the years. It read "Athletics Hampered Through Lack of Funds." The article went on:

"In order to meet the vast increase in railroad rates, hotel expenses, and cost of equipment, the State Board of Agriculture authorized the Athletic Department to raise the student athletic fees fifty cents for this term. This is not permanent, however, for the students themselves will be given the opportunity later to express their sentiments on a definite fee to care for these expenses.

That there may be a clearer understanding of why the raise was necessary, a brief explanation may be of value. During the last ten years with a fee of $2.00 it has been possible to carry on athletics with institutions of which we as a college take much pride in meeting, but now with the great increase in the expenses involved and left to choose between raising the fee and continuing with our high standard in athletics or taking smaller and less important institutions on our schedule.

Before the war it was possible to send a team to Ann Arbor at the rate of $1.25 per man round trip. It now costs $3.98 or more than double. In order to get other colleges to come here for the games and track meets, the costs have more than doubled. The University of Iowa asked a minimum of $200 to send her baseball team here this spring. The University of Michigan and Notre Dame each need $150 to cover their teams' expenses."

Doing "triple-duty" in February and March, Coach "Potsy" Clark handled the daily freshman basketball practices, worked indoors with the baseball squad, and conducted unprecedented twice-a-week classroom sessions with the football team. Perhaps the workload was too much. At the spring sports banquet in June, Clark announced his resignation; whereupon he accepted a position as head coach at the University of Kansas. Bert Barron would sign a three-year contract as his successor.

HEADLINES of 1921

- The first *Reader's Digest* magazine is published.
- The first Miss America pageant is won by Margaret Gorman, Miss Washington, D.C.
- Insulin is first isolated, providing a treatment for diabetes.
- Hermann Rorschach, Swiss psychiatrist, introduces his famous inkblot test for study of personality.

SCOREBOARD

	W	L	T	Avg.
Baseball	6	8	0	.429
Track and Field	3	1	0	.750
Football	4	6	0	.400
Basketball	13	8	0	.619
Tennis	3	4	0	.429
Cross Country	1	0	0	1.000

TEAM OF THE YEAR

In his first year as head basketball coach, Lyman Frimodig saw his squad open the season by winning its first five games in a row, and eventually managed to put 13 in the "W" column including victories over Creighton and Notre Dame.

MAKING HISTORY

Emerging from World War I in 1918, the American public faced the realization that many of its young men had been physically unprepared for the rigors of active military service. Physical preparedness and conditioning became topics of concern. In response, during the fall of 1920 MAC added Jimmy Devers of Jackson, Mich., to its staff as an assistant instructor in physical training with the title of coach of combative sports. As a former contender for the world's lightweight boxing championship and more recently a coach at numerous athletic clubs and YMCAs, he held the proper credentials. Although wrestling would not dawn as an intercollegiate sport at MAC until the following year and boxing would not be endorsed by the school until 1935, Devers had been working with a large number of men throughout the fall and winter of 1920-1921 instructing them in the finer points of the martial arts. Some of his students had performed at halftime of basketball games that winter, but then an entire evening of boxing and wrestling took place on Monday, Feb. 28, 1921. A raised ring had been constructed on the gymnasium floor and 400 chairs were

1921 basketball team. (Front row, left to right) E. Gilkey, E. Matson, L. Heasley, captain W. Foster, C. Higbie, C. Fessenden and J. Barr. (Middle row, left to right) W. Palm, Gustafson, S. Pacynski, manager F. Zimmerman, H. Swanson and A. Brown. (Back row, left to right) Voorheis, trainer J. Heppinstall, Coach Frimodig, F. Wilcox.

arranged for spectators to view six three-round boxing bouts and four eight-minute wrestling matches.

In the spring of 1921 the first NCAA outdoor track and field championships were hosted by the University of Chicago.

GREAT STATE DATES

Football—**October 30, 1920 (H):** How does a team manage to score 16 touchdowns for a total of 109 points while holding the opposition scoreless? There is and always has been a trustworthy factor to the formula. It helps to schedule a team that is far less talented. Such was the case when poor little Alma came to town in the fall of 1920. MAC had "grown up" since the turn of the century when the Scots won three in a row from 1900-1902. Since that time the Aggies had prevailed against Alma with only one loss in 17 years. Accounting for the TDs in this most lopsided game in school history were: Jacob Brady, five; John Schwei, three; Ubold Noblett, two; Murray Jacklin, two; Johnny Hammes, two; Fred Wilcox, one; and Roy MacMillian, one.

Cross Country—**November 12, 1920 (H):** When the state intercollegiate cross country meet was introduced in 1915, it was pronounced that the initial cup would be retired to the first school registering three championship victories. As runners lined up for the sixth running of the event, it seemed obvious one of the two favorites, MAC or Michigan, would be taking permanent possession of the silver trophy. Both schools were eligible to do so, having already claimed a pair of wins in previous seasons. To the delight of Aggie fans, the local team would carry the day by amassing 26 team points to 31 for the U of M. Trailing behind were Hope 48, Albion 61 and Kalamazoo 65. Lloyd Thurston finished first for Coach Smith, Tony Brendel was second, Allen placed fifth, Fred Adolph sixth and G.W. Nesman 12th.

Cross Country—**November 25, 1920 (H):** On Thanksgiving Day the cross country team defeated Notre Dame with a perfect score of 15-40. The four and a half mile race began on the track during the break between the first and second periods of the football game with the Irish. Completing the prescribed course, the runners concluded the race in front of the grandstands at half time. To the delight of Aggie fans, all five of the MAC men were on the home stretch of the running track before any of the Irish were in sight.

Basketball—**January 8, 1921 (H):** MAC opened the season against Central State of Mt. Pleasant and led at halftime 13-5. Returning to the court after intermission, "Frimodig's Five" saw their advantage slowly melt away until the five-minute mark, when they trailed by a point. Regaining the lead, the Aggies scored the final six points to end the game at 26-21 and run their all-time record with the Chippewas to 8-0.

Basketball—**February 1, 1921 (H):** Filling every available seat, every inch of standing room and even places on the iron beams above the playing floor, approximately 4,000 people, the largest crowd to ever witness a basketball game in East Lansing, saw MAC defeat Notre Dame 37-25. The final score was somewhat deceiving. A determined Irish team battled back from the 24-13 halftime deficit to come within four points before the Aggies regrouped and pulled away to the delight of the partisan throng. Eddie Gilkey, the little forward from Lansing, led the way with 21 points on six field goals and nine of 10 from the free-throw line. Halftime extravaganzas are not new. From *The State Journal* of February 2:

> "Between the halves of the game, two girls, Misses Lillian Lewton and Marita McClane, who are enrolled as freshmen in the division of agriculture at the college, entertained the crowd with a Scottish folk dance in costume."

Basketball—**March 2, 1921 (H):** Lacking video tapes or national media exposure often meant facing an unknown opponent with no knowledge of its prowess. Such was the case when the Bethany College team came to town for the first-ever meeting between the two schools. It was anticipated the little West Virginia college would challenge the Aggies who were closing out their schedule with an 11-8 record. The game had not progressed more than a couple of minutes before it was obvious any concern was unwarranted. The halftime score favored the Aggies 24-9 and even with Coach Frimodig clearing his bench, the final count reached a score of 41-18. When the teams next met, in 1930, the Bison would return the favor.

Tennis—**May 3, 1921 (A):** Harry Young, the new volunteer coach, took seven men to Pontiac for matches against members of that city's local club. From that experience, along with the all-college tournament which followed, the following nucleus for the varsity team emerged:

Wayne Palm, Henry Goss, Herb Freeman, Clato Coe, Dick Beal, Burwell Cummings and Jack Croll. Coe and Beal would finish the season as the top players.

Baseball—May 20, 1921 (H): In an unusual fourth-inning scoring binge against Oberlin, MAC managed 10 runs, their entire production of the afternoon, leading to a 10-2 victory. Aided by three bases on balls and two errors, the entire double-digit inning almost miraculously occurred on only four hits.

Track and Field—May 28, 1921 (H): Capturing nine firsts out of a possible 15, the Aggies rolled up 59 points to regain their supremacy in the state intercollegiate track meet. Trailing the Aggies were Kalamazoo 33, Western State 24 1/2, Detroit Junior College 23, MAC Freshmen 11, Hillsdale 8 1/2, Olivet 5, Michigan Normal 1, and Highland Park Junior College 1. Eight titles were garnered by MAC men, all with record performances. DeGay Ernst led the parade with three firsts: 15.8 in the high hurdles, 24.6 in the 220 low hurdles, and 50.4 in the 440. Tony Brendel captured the 880 in a time of 2:01.8; Fred Adolph's 4:33.2 led the milers; Hazen Atkins raised his high jump record to 5' 9"; Clarence Fessenden tossed the discus 131' 1/12", and John Schwei's 157' 2" throw won the javelin.

Jack Foster

ATHLETE OF THE YEAR

Walter "Jack" Foster excelled as a basketball prep star in East Lansing before enrolling at MAC where he competed as a member of the 1918 freshman team. Then, not uncommon for the time, he lettered in four years (1919-1922) and was captain of the 1921 team. Foster's height and speed made him a starter at the pivot position from his very first year of varsity competition. In an era of the center jump ball after each field goal, he consistently out-jumped players he faced.

IN THE SPARTLITE

Baseball: The May 11 game against Michigan was a disappointing 11-inning affair with the Wolverines prevailing 7-6. The Aggies continually left men on the bases, three in the third, two in the fifth and two in the sixth. Finally, in the bottom of the ninth and trailing 6-3, the MAC bats came alive. MacMillan singled, Fuller tripled and Brown doubled to chase the starter. After two outs, Oas blopped one into left center field to score Brown and send the contest into extra innings. Yielding only five hits, it was a difficult game for pitcher Bub Kuhn to lose. Five of the U of M runs were scored on errors made at crucial moments.

Third baseman Roy MacMillan, the Detroit sophomore, led the offense with a lusty batting average of .376. He was followed by first baseman Al Brown's 359, Walt Willman and "Chief" Fuller tied at .333, Bill Johnson 309, Stan Pacynski .280 and Reggie "Swede" Oas at .273. No other player batted more than .200.

Basketball: The season opened with added seating in the gymnasium, raising the capacity to more than 2,500. Five rows of bleachers were installed on each side of the floor, replacing the four-row configuration and two rows of bleachers were set up on the running track above the floor. Concurrently, a new plan for spectator seating was announced. Seats on the south side were for juniors and seniors and any accompanying ladies. The bleachers on the west side and on the running track were similarly reserved for first- and second-year men. The east bleachers were for co-eds and the 300 seats on the north side were set aside for faculty, alumni and outsiders at a fee of $1.00 per game.

Until 1921, starting fives often played the entire game, primarily because the rules stated that once a player left the game he could not return. A change that season provided for a player who had left the game to re-enter one time.

Boxing: Although they did not have a team, Michigan Agricultural College joined with a group of other schools in 1921 to become charter members of the Intercollegiate Boxing Association of America. This organization's primary purpose was to promote boxing as an intercollegiate sport while determining rules for weight categories, length of rounds and glove weight. It would be 1924 before the organization conducted its first championship. Weight classifications in that first national meet, won by Penn State, were: 115, 125, 135, 145, 155, 165, 175 and heavyweight. Fourteen years would pass before the sport would be officially recognized at the intercollegiate level in East Lansing.

Cross Country: The MAC cross country team competed, as an at-large entry, in the Western Conference Championships over the new five-mile course at the University of Illinois. The Aggies finished eighth in the field of 14 teams.

Fencing: The athletic department invited members of the legislature, state officers and Lansing businessmen to the gymnasium for a demonstration of various athletic skills on the evening of February 8. Included was an exhibition of fencing tactics performed by a class voluntarily taught by professor O.M. Lebel, an instructor in French. It was likely the first public showing of the sport before Lansing-area people. By the spring of 1925 Lebel had initiated a team that eventually competed in one match, an 8-1 loss to Michigan in Ann Arbor. By that fall, fencing had been adopted as an official intercollegiate sport at MSC. Perhaps the professor could well be considered the school's "Father of Fencing."

Football: In another scheduling aberration, the 1920 Aggies played three games within seven days: Albion on Saturday, October 2, Alma the following Wednesday, and Wisconsin at Madison on the next Saturday. Fortunately, the Wednesday game was an easy 48-0 win, enabling Coach Clark to rest his starters.

Undefeated in 1918 and 1919, little Marietta (Ohio) College, located along the Ohio River near Parkersburg, W.Va., was a respected power. They came to East Lansing on October 23 with the national reputation of having perfected the passing game. The Farmers joined in. The final statistics revealed that a combined total of 57 passes were attempted that afternoon. Obviously, the Ohioans were more successful at the art as they left town with a fairly easy 23-7 victory. Their coach was Earle "Greasy" Neale, who would gain greater fame as an NFL coach and be enshrined into the NFL Hall of Fame at Canton, Ohio.

Three of the year's four victories (Alma, Olivet and the Chicago YMCA) were by a composite score of 238-0. The 109-0 demolition of the Alma Scots still remains a team record.

Tennis: At a preseason meeting in April, Wayne Palm was elected captain and team manager. Also, at that time it was disclosed that three of the college courts would be reserved for varsity players from 4:00 until 7:00 P.M, two for the men's team and one for the women.

In the singles competition of the state intercollegiate championships, Herb Freeman lost in the second round, while Jack Croll reached the finals before bowing out. Team scores were as follows: MAC 7, Kalamazoo 6, Central State Normal 4, Detroit Junior College and Hillsdale 1 each, Albion and Western State Normal, no score. As a reward for the championship and for the first time, letter sweaters with small monograms were awarded to Palm, Goss, Freeman, Croll, Coe and Beal.

Track and Field: Clarence Fessenden and DeGay Ernst represented MAC in the season-ending Big Ten meet at Stagg Field in Chicago. Fessenden was eliminated in the trials of both the shot put and the discus. Meanwhile, Ernst placed first in his trial heat of the 440-yard run despite having another runner knock him to the cinders at the finish line. In the finals the next afternoon, he ran to a third-place finish.

EXTRA! MICHIGAN STATE RELAYS
1921—The Inaugural Year

The Michigan Aggie Indoor Track Carnival was first run on March 12, 1921 as a forerunner to the Michigan State Relays. It was quite accurately predicted that "this meet will be continued annually." Indeed, finally settling on early February for future dates, the Relays flourished for nearly seven decades.

Until moving into Jenison Fieldhouse in 1939, competition was conducted in the Gymnasium and, other than a couple of appearances by a Marquette University squad, those early meets included only trackmen from Michigan schools. On the gym surface they competed in the 40-yard hurdle event, 40-yard dash, along with the pole vault, high jump, and shot put. Relay events and longer races from 300-yards to the two-mile were run on the embanked one-16th mile oval encircling one-story above the basketball floor. Aggie winners in that inaugural meet were sprinters DeGay Ernst and Mark Herdell, while the half mile relay trophy went to the MAC quartet of Pollock, Carl Perry, Art Atkins, and Ernst. Team results of that initial meet were: MAC 24, Michigan 20, Western State 13, with Kalamazoo, Detroit Junior College and MAC freshmen scoreless.

By 1923 the team scoring idea was aborted and it was never again reinstated. Also, in that third year, The featured event in that third year was the two-mile relay in which a U of M quartet was matched against John

Killoran, Leonard Klasse, Paul Hartsuch, and Keith Baguley of the host Aggies. One can only visualize the spectators peering up to the narrow track from their vantage points below to follow the progress of the race. Killoran and Klasse trailed on their opening half-mile legs (eight laps each) and then Hartsuch followed his man closely and finished with a sprint to hand Baguley a slight lead for the anchor leg. The Tawas (Mich.) junior held on as long as he could, but the fourth man for Michigan finally crowded ahead at the finish to gain the victory. One year later, Clarence Ripper and John Killoran teamed with the returning Baguley and Hartsuch to gain sweet revenge. The outcome of that 1924 rematch was once more in doubt until the final leg. Paul Hartsuch, this time running in the fourth spot, fought neck and neck with the Wolverine anchorman for more than a lap. He finally took command and finished several yards ahead.

In 1926 and 1927, with the emergence of the sprinting twosome of Fred Alderman and Bohn Grim, the Michigan State Track Carnival enjoyed record-shattered performances and burgeoning attendance. Also, to showcase the school's talented athletes, Coach Ralph Young was entering collegiate relay meets at: Butler, Armour (Chicago), Illinois, West Virginia, Ohio, Rice, Texas, Kansas, as well as the prestigious Drake and Penn Relays. It began even earlier than 1926. At the Drake Relays of 1922 the team of Tony Brendel, Bob Houston, Keith Baguley, and Paul Hartsuch won the two-mile college relay in a record time of 8:16.4. In that same meet, DeGay Ernst captured the gold medal in the 440-yard hurdle event. Clocked at 54.8, his time was within a second of the world record and more than three second faster than the winning time posted at the more prestigious Penn Relays, competed on that same weekend.

Relay events and longer races conducted in the gymnasium were run on the oval track that hung above the basketball court.

MAC
1921-1922

TALES TO TELL

Carl Moore, a member of the school's first official hockey team, was interviewed at his home in the summer of 1994, just prior to his 91st birthday celebration:

"Practically all of us were from the UP: DeLisle, McDonald, Noblet, Wallace and Haupti. Also, there were Taylor, Keller and Frank Doherty who came down from the Soo with me. Therefore, we knew each other pretty well. We were just regular guys who had played hockey all of our lives, from kids on up. There was no one person who could be credited with organizing the team at school (MAC), we just wanted to play.

We got some help from the school. They assigned us lockers in the gymnasium [Circle IM] and we would run from there to the rink. As far as equipment goes, they provided us with gloves. The jerseys were borrowed from football and the goalie used a baseball chest protector. Some guys wore kneepads, but there were no shoulder pads or helmets back then. We provided our own skates but the school would get them sharpened for us.

In the first two years, 1922 and 1923, we played on the Red Cedar River, just above the dam. We would get paid 40 cents an hour to flood the river ice in order to create a good skating surface. There was no team the next year and then in 1925 we had an unusually mild winter. After a game in January at Ann Arbor, the remainder of the schedule against Notre Dame, Minnesota and the U of M had to be cancelled. We had no ice to play or practice on. In my final year we were playing on the flooded tennis courts along Grand River behind the Women's Building (Morrill Hall). Facilities were rather basic back then, although I do recall the rink up at the Soo. It was within a corrugated metal building and there were bleachers for the spectators. The building was not heated and between periods people would walk around in the building to keep warm.

Local people came out to watch, mostly out of curiosity. They were not that familiar with the game. There were no seats or bleachers, they just stood around the edge of the rink and watched us play.

Rules were entirely different back then, and as a result the game was much slower. It seems they patterned the game after the basketball rules of the time.

HEADLINES of 1922

- The Lincoln Memorial is dedicated in Washington, D.C.
- A British watchmaker invents the self-winding watch.
- C.K. Nelson of Onawa, Iowa, is awarded a patent for the first ice cream bar, named the Eskimo Pie.
- The songs "Toot Toot Tootsie," "Chicago" and "Way Down Yonder in New Orleans" are introduced.

SCOREBOARD

	W	L	T	Avg.
Baseball	8	9	0	.471
Track and Field	4	1	0	.800
Football	3	5	0	.375
Basketball	11	13	0	.458
Tennis	3	2	2	.571
Cross Country	1	0	0	1.000
Swimming and Diving	0	5	0	.000
Wrestling	1	3	0	.250
Hockey	0	3	0	.000

We played four quarters instead of three periods and the substitutions were again like basketball, you were permitted to leave the game and return only once during a quarter. Actually, some of us would play the entire game without a rest. Also, there were no blue lines or red lines, so each member of the team had to be on side all of the time. Therefore, you would have to always be skating behind the puck and as a result there were no forward passes. I don't think that style of play would go over very well today."

Carl Moore was honored at Munn Arena prior to the Bowling Green game of Nov. 20, 1994. Greeted before a standing ovation, he received a varsity jacket, a personalized team jersey and a framed picture of the 1926 team. Less than two years later, on June 14, 1996, Carl Moore died.

TEAM OF THE YEAR

The track and field team of 1922 ran off four straight victories (two indoor and two outdoor) before dropping their final dual meet of the spring to Ohio State 68-58. At the Drake relays in Des Moines the Aggies turned some heads. The quartet of Brendel, Baguley, Hartsuch and Houston won the two-mile relay in a time of 8:16.4 and DeGay Ernst captured first place in the 440-yard hurdles in 54.4, only two-tenths slower than the world record. MAC concluded the season by racking up 60 points and easily defending their state title.

1922 track and field team. (Front row, left to right) H. Shannon, K. Baguley, R. Houston, M. Herdell and P. Hartsuch. (Middle row, left to right) F. Carver, F. Adolph, H. Atkins, D. Ernst, A. Brendel, J. Schwei and L. Thurston. (Back row, left to right) trainer J. Heppinstall, P.F. Temple, C. Fessenden, coach A. Barron, H. Wilson, P. Weamer and manager T. Willoughby.

MAKING HISTORY

Three sports were "officially" introduced into the school's athletic program in 1921-1922: hockey, swimming and diving and wrestling. An organizational meeting for hockey was held on Tuesday evening, Jan. 10, 1922. From this gathering a group of interested students was selected to represent the college in a game against the U of M at Ann Arbor on the very next afternoon. It seems unbelievable that those "volunteers" would only lose that first game by a score of 5-1. Carl Moore gives credit to another student from the UP, Jack Vernon, for assembling those pioneer skaters. Vernon, whose father was a big lumber man back at the Soo, could well be identified as Michigan State's ice hockey founder. Plans were set in motion for the first swimming and diving team to begin competition in January of 1921. There was one slight problem: there was no one on campus who possessed an aquatics background and the plan was necessarily put "on hold." Then, in the fall of 1921 Southard Flynn enrolled as a graduate student in entomology. He had once served as a YMCA swimming instructor in Berkeley, Calif., and had competed three years as a member of the varsity team at the University of California. Flynn held the necessary credentials. He was approached and accepted the assignment as MAC's first swimming and diving coach. This opened the way for assembling the first team which was defeated in its inaugural meet against Detroit Junior College at the Gymnasium pool on Jan. 29, 1922.

In reporting the story of the Western State Normal basketball game of Jan. 10, 1922, *The Holcad* noted a new wrinkle, the practice of introducing the players before the game:

> "Mark Small introduced each player on the opposing team and then the MAC man that was to play against him. The students responded with yells, thus showing that they approved the idea."

GREAT STATE DATES

Football—**October 22, 1921 (H):** The Western State Normal football game could have been scripted by a Hollywood writer. Playing with a patched-up lineup due to injuries, MAC trailed at half time, 14-7. Included among the missing that day was the fullback Harry Graves of Pratt, Kan., who had been hospitalized with acute indigestion. Discharged from the infirmary that morning, he sat through the first half as a spectator. It seemed the sight of the second Normal touchdown was too much. He bolted from the bleachers and during the intermission dressed for action under the stands. Immediately inserted into the fray to open the second half, Graves carried the ball on almost every other down as the varsity marched down the field to tie the score. He would later provide the margin of victory, 17-14, with a successful 33-yard drop kick.

Cross Country—**November 24, 1921 (A):** In the only dual meet of the fall, the harriers, as in 1920, shutout Notre Dame, 15-40, by running 1-2-3-4-5. Lloyd Thurston was the first across the finish line having completed the three and a half mile course in 19:25. He was followed to the tape by Fred Adolph, Bob Houston and Tony Brendel and Keith Baguley. The race was coordinated to be completed at half time of the football game with the Irish.

Basketball—**January 3, 1922 (H):** In the fourth game of the basketball season, an obviously out-manned squad from the Detroit School of Law should have thrown itself onto the "mercy of the court." Never able to penetrate the Aggie defense for a field goal, the Detroiters had to settle for a total of three free throws in a humiliating 56-3 defeat. For a continuous 10 minutes of the first half (center jump after each made basket) the ball was in the hands of the MAC players and the halftime score read 29-0. In final statistics, Ed Gilkey led the scoring with 21 points, followed by captain Lloyd Heasley with 16.

Wrestling—**February 25, 1922 (A):** In the official first year of the sport, Jimmy Devers's squad upset the University of Michigan, 24-20. Leading the team were 125-pound Homer Hansen, who won by a decision in overtime; Zera Foster, dominating his opponent in the 135-pound division; 145-pound Harold Koopman, on top of his opponent for nine minutes; and heavyweight John Schwei, who won by a decision. The U of M coach, Richard Thom, could not have been accused of being unprepared. Four weeks earlier he had seen the Aggies "up close" as he refereed the MAC-Indiana matches. Thom had been quoted as saying the Aggies represented the greatest bunch of wrestling novices he had ever seen and predicted unusual success for them.

Baseball—**April 28, 1922 (A):** The baseball team topped Armour Tech of Chicago by a score of 31-7. It remains the second-highest run total ever recorded by a State team (May 3, 1897, 37-5 over Hillsdale). Outfielder Stan Pacynski led the way with seven hits. Later selected to captain the 1923 team, Pacynski would never play in that senior year. In the 12th inning of an 8-7 loss to Bethany College (W.Va.) on June 16 he broke his leg sliding into third. The fracture was severe enough to terminate his college career.

Track and Field—**April 22-23, 1922 (A):** At the Drake relays the team of Tony Brendel, Bob Houston, Keith Baguley and Paul Hartsuch won the two-mile college relay in a record time of 8:16.4. In that same meet, DeGay Ernst captured the gold medal in the 440-yard hurdle event. Clocked at 54.8, his time was within a second of the world record and more than three seconds faster than the winning time posted at the Penn relays, competed on that same weekend.

Tennis—**May 12 and 13, 1922 (A):** In a tournament that combined results of both the men's and women's scores, the Aggies captured the team trophy at the Kalamazoo College state invitational tennis meet. On the men's side, Croll won the singles title and then teamed with Coe to take the doubles championship. Although the ladies did not capture one of the titles, Hester Hedrick, Mary Ranney and Ruth Palmer won enough matches to earn four points toward the joint winning team total of 12. Other competing schools that weekend included Michigan Normal, Western State, Central Michigan Normal, Albion, Detroit School of Law and host Kalamazoo.

Track and Field—**May 30, 1922 (A):** Even without two of their stars, DeGay Ernst and Clarence Fessenden, a squad of 11 men amassed a total of 67 1/2 points to capture the trophy in an invitational Memorial Day meet hosted by DePaul University and conducted on the Northwestern track in Evanston, Ill. On that weekend Ernest and Fessenden had opted to compete in the Big Ten Championships. The pair should have stayed with their teammates. Neither was able to place in the conference meet at Iowa City, Iowa.

ATHLETE OF THE YEAR

The *Wolverine* yearbook described DeGay Ernst (TR 20-21C-22C) as having a remarkable stride and natural track instincts. He was an immediate success as a standout on the freshmen track and field team and continuing through an illustrious varsity career. As a winner of three state intercollegiate track championships (high hurdles, low hurdles and quarter mile) and holder of four team records (both hurdle events, the quarter mile and the 100-yard dash), his versatility continually made him a top point-getter during his Aggie career. Ernst captained both the 1921 and 1922 track and field teams.

DeGay Ernst

IN THE SPARTLITE

Baseball: For only the second time since 1908, MAC did not meet the University of Michigan on the baseball diamond. Rain-soaked field conditions resulted in cancellation of game on May 2 in East Lansing and two weeks later at Ann Arbor.

Basketball: Prior to a rule change for 1922, running with the ball (steps) was considered a foul leading to a free throw. Hereafter, the violation simply resulted in a turnover.

After losing in overtime at Ann Arbor, 27-26, hope ran high for the return U of M game at home. In what was reported as the most exciting encounter of the year, this time it took the Wolverines two overtimes. With ten seconds remaining in regulation and MAC trailing 15-13, a photographer snapped a picture of the Michigan team. The players and spectators mistook the noisy and glaring flash system for that of the timekeeper's gun signaling the end of the game and fans poured onto the floor. The referee, with assistance from others, finally cleared the playing surface and inexplicably gave the players another whole minute to play. Wayne Palm took advantage by netting a long shot and sending the game into an extra frame. During the added five-minute period the teams traded two-pointers raising the score to 17-17, necessitating yet another OT. In the final overtime, the Aggies had numerous opportunities but could not match a solitary Wolverine field goal. The final score read Michigan 19, MAC 17.

Cross Country: Hosting the state intercollegiate meet, the Aggies placed second behind Michigan, 29-38. Finishing for the MAC varsity were Thurston second, Adolph third, Brendel fifth, Houston sixth, and Hartsuch 22nd. Had coach Floyd Rowe selected Don Clark to run with the varsity quintet rather than Paul Hartsuch that afternoon, the Aggies would have nosed out the Wolverines, 28-29. Running for the reserve team, Clark had been the 12th runner to complete the distance.

With his wife hospitalized, Coach Rowe was unable to accompany the team to Bloomington, Ind., for the Big Ten championships. He did, however, make arrangements for the squad to travel with the U of M team under the guidance of their coach Steve Farrell. Also lending his valuable assistance was the team manager, Ted Willoughby. Running for the Aggies were Fred Adolph, Tony Brendel, Bob Houston, Lloyd Thurston and D.E. Clark. They managed to score as the seventh-place team, landing ahead of Minnesota, Iowa, Northwestern and Indiana.

Football: For a sum of $7.05, fans were offered a game ticket and round-trip rail fare to South Bend for the Thanksgiving Day game against Notre Dame. As it turned out, the game was no fun. Absorbing a 48-0 loss to the once-beaten Irish, the Aggies never gained a first down all afternoon. This would terminate the State-ND gridiron relationship for 27 years. The two schools would not hook-up again until 1948, the second year of the Biggie Munn era. One week prior to that varsity game of 1921, the MAC freshmen hosted and defeated the Notre Dame yearlings, 10-6. Those Irish freshmen included the future-fabled Four Horsemen.

Hockey: To accommodate the two home games of 1922 (3-1 loss to Notre Dame on January 18 and the 9-0 loss to Michigan on January 23) arrangements were made with the athletic department to prepare a rink on the river above the dam at the very same site as in 1914. Sideboards were installed, nets were put in place and a pump was engaged for flooding the sheet each night.

Swimming and Diving: Swimming and diving for the Aggies in the first year of competition were captain Murray Jacklin of Fremont, Frank Niederstadt from Saginaw, Leonard "Dutch" Van Noppen from Niles, Edwin Brown of Oshtemo, Mich., Arno Johnson from Jacksonville, Fla., Ed Copperton of New York City, Jack Bailey from Lakewood, Ohio, and Bert Gilbert. The team also included a pair of football stars: Maurice Taylor of East Cleveland, Ohio, and John Bos of Grand Rapids.

Tennis: The schedule of 1922, with 12 dual matches as first announced, was the most ambitious ever for the sport at MAC. Due to rainouts and cancellations, including two matches against the University of Michigan, only seven were eventually contested.

The line-up throughout the spring included John Croll of Beaverton, Burwell Cummings of Butler, Penn., Clato Coe from Moose Jaw, Saskatchewan, and J.R. deFrance in the singles with the two doubles teams of Coe and Croll along with Cummings and Dudley Pritchard of Allegan.

Track and Field: By 1922 the program of events for indoor meets included the 40-yard dash, 40-yard high hurdles, 40-yard low hurdles, 440-yard dash, one-half mile, mile run, high jump, pole vault, shot put and relay.

Three indoor and four outdoor track records were established during the 1922 season. New indoor marks were Fred Adolph's 10:26.6 in the two-mile run, and Bob

Houston's 2:09.8 in the 880 and 4:43.6 in the mile. The new outdoor standards included a 100-yard mark of 10 seconds flat, a time shared by Mark Herdell and DeGay Ernst; Tony Brendel's 1:59.8 clocking in the half-mile; and an additional pair by the talented team captain, Ernst: 15.6 seconds in the 120-yard high hurdles and 50.2 in the 440-yard run.

In the loss to Ohio State, Ernst captured two firsts, a second and a third with his top performance in the low hurdles where he easily defeated McCreary, the Big Ten champion.

Wrestling: Matches were held in the center of the basketball floor within the gymnasium building. Seating arrangements were the same as for basketball games. As the local team gained more success through the years, interest in the sport expanded and often more than 1,000 spectators, often excessively vocal, would cheer their favorites on.

Weight classes during the 1920s were as follows: 115 pounds (bantamweight), 125 pounds (featherweight), 135 pounds (lightweight), 145 pounds (welterweight), 158 pounds (middleweight), 175 pounds (light heavyweight), and more than 175 pounds (heavyweight).

The position of Aggie Yellmaster was won through the annual popular vote of the student body.

MAC
1922-1923

TALES TO TELL

The school authorized the installation of a private wire to the Armory Building in order that the returns from the five out-of-town football games could be heard directly. The procedure, through Western Union, required a man at the game site to telegraph the ongoing game to a second person stationed in the Armory. A third person would verbally report the game's progress to the assembled fans. By October 28, for the second road game of the fall, against Indiana, the band and cheerleaders had been added to offer the proper atmosphere.

TEAM OF THE YEAR

After being hammered by Michigan 16-2 on May 2, 1923, the overall win-loss baseball record stood at 5-4. This was the wake-up call for Coach Walker's crew, and they finished the season by winning nine straight games. That string of Ws and the season total of 14 victories were both school records.

1923 baseball team. (Front row, left to right) Stephens, J. Brady, W. Johnson, B. Kuhn, L. Ross, W. Daley and R. MacMillan. (Middle row, left to right) Trainer J. Heppinstall, J. Sepaneck, F. Williams, H. Gasser, S. Higgins, G. Wenner, Passage, A. Beckley and coach F. Walker. (Back row, left to right) Assistant manager C. Williams, Farley, Wallis, Cutler, Mason, Ubele, C. Baynes and manager M. Ralston.

HEADLINES of 1923

- Colonel Jacob Schick receives a patent for the first electric shaver.
- The DuPont Company acquires the rights to manufacture cellophane.
- The bulldozer is invented.
- *Time* magazine begins publication, providing the news in a flavorful, succinct manner.

SCOREBOARD

	W	L	T	Avg.
Baseball	14	4	0	.778
Track and Field	1	3	0	.250
Football	3	5	2	.400
Basketball	10	9	0	.526
Tennis	2	6	1	.278
Cross Country	1	1	0	.500
Swimming and Diving	1	3	0	.250
Wrestling	1	3	0	.250
Hockey	2	4	0	.333

MAKING HISTORY

The plunge was one of eight events conducted in intercollegiate dual and championship swimming and diving meets until dropped from the program in 1926. As described in the NCAA rules, the event was conducted as follows:

"A plunge shall be a standing dive made, head first, from a firm take-off, free from spring, and no more than 18 inches above the water. The event shall terminate at the expiration of 60 seconds if the competitor has not already raised his face above the surface of the water. The duration of the event shall begin when the competitor's feet leave the take-off. If a contestant touches the side of the pool he shall be compelled to stop and his distance taken. The distance of the plunge is measured to the farthest point reached by any portion of the competitor's body. Each competitor shall be permitted two plunges. At the expiration of 30 seconds, the plunger shall be notified of his distance covered and his direction by the referee. The chief timer shall notify each contestant at the expiration of 60 seconds by the report of a pistol."

It was in this event that Miss Dorothy McWood, a Detroit freshman, excelled. In 1923 she successfully defended her national title at the Detroit YMCA by coasting a distance of 54 feet. She thus became the school's first national champion of any sport, man or woman.

GREAT STATE DATES

Football—October 21, 1922 (H): For the third straight meeting, during a four-year period, South Dakota failed to score on the MAC defense. Consequently, the Aggies needed only one touchdown to defeat the Coyotes, 7-0. The low score could *not* be attributed to ignoring the passing game. During the contest both teams attempted a composite of 55 aerials with the Aggies connecting on 12 of 31. Jake Brady, playing in his first game of the season, was the primary ball carrier during the afternoon. Yet, a teammate, simply referred in the newspapers as "fulback Burris," accounted for all of the scoring. He bucked over for the touchdown in the first half and dropkicked the conversion. "Fullback Burris" had not been heard from before, nor was he heard from thereafter. As part of a doubleheader, before a crowd of 3,000, the freshmen opened the day's activities with a surprising 18-6 defeat of the Grand Rapids Junior College. Given the manner in which *The Lansing State Journal* detailed the pregame activities, it may well have been the first-ever flag-raising ceremony:

"Following the game between the Aggie All-Fresh and Grand Rapids Junior college, the big Aggie band marched onto the field and took up its position in front of the flag pole erected behind the north goal post. While the band played 'The Star-Spangled Banner,' a large American flag was raised to the top of the pole. After this, and while the band played Alma Mater, a Michigan Aggie banner was raised to a position directly under the flag."

Cross Country—October 28, 1922 (H): In the third straight win over Notre Dame, 21-36, sophomore Keith Baguley led all runners on the five-mile course with a winning time of 25:59.0. The course was described as beginning at the athletic field and following east along the south side of the Red Cedar River to Pinetum (Hagadorn Road) and returning to Farm Lane. From there the course ran south to the Grand Trunk railroad tracks, then west along the tracks to a spot just south of the athletic field and by a crooked route back to the field.

Cross Country—November 30, 1922 (A): At the annual YMCA Thanksgiving Day morning run around the Belle Isle course in Detroit, Keith Baguley led the way in a time of 23:42.2. Bill Willard of the Aggies finished third, Glen Nesman fourth, Leonard Klaase sixth,

Don Clark seventh and John Van Arman eighth. With 21 points, the Aggies captured the team title as well. Overall, 37 individuals competed, including runners from Michigan Normal, Western State and Kalamazoo College.

Cross Country—**December 9, 1922 (A):** The final meet of the season was in the second annual run sponsored by the Saginaw YMCA. Following their win of 1921, the Aggies maintained possession of the silver cup which, as prescribed, would be permanently retained by the first team to gain three victories. Keith Baguley returned to top form as he led all Aggie runners to the finish line with his second-place finish.

Basketball—**January 13, 1923 (H):** The excitement of the MAC-Eastern Michigan game was packed into the final minutes of play, bringing the crowd to its feet. The score was tied at 11 points each when Ypsi broke away for a four-point lead. This was partially cut down when Roy McMillan scored on two free throws and the count was evened again when "Mac" hit a field goal. Viv Hultman then sent the Aggies into the lead with a basket, which was quickly matched by the visitors. With seconds remaining, it was McMillan who again broke through the defense, this time sinking the winning basket for a 19-17 victory.

Swimming and Diving—**January 19, 1923 (H):** Capturing five of the eight events and finishing as runners-up six times, the Farmers opened the season on January 19 with a 45-23 win over the Grand Rapids YMCA. It is historically noted as the school's first victory in swimming and diving.

Wrestling—**February 2, 1923 (H):** Featuring three falls, Coach Devers's men topped the Chicago YMCA College squad, 18-13, for the only victory of the season. The team suffered a severe blow when Homer Hansen, a consistent winner in 1922, was thrown and dislocated his elbow in his featherweight bout. He was lost for the remainder of the season.

Basketball—**February 28, 1923 (A):** The 40-15 season-opening loss to Notre Dame was later avenged at South Bend. With 30 seconds remaining in that second game and the Irish leading 21-20, Wes "Red" Eva grabbed a pass in front of the Irish goal and tossed in the winning basket. The records do not reveal the exact site of this game in South Bend. On some occasions the Irish played in the gymnasium at the local YMCA, while other times they scheduled games for the dirt floor of their fieldhouse.

Baseball—**April 13, 1923 (H):** The Michigan Normal game was tied 5-5 in the bottom of the ninth with Aggie runners on second and third. A bizarre finish would ensue. The Normal coach came to the plate to protest that the game should be called because of darkness. While the verbal exchange proceeded, Jake Brady, the Aggie runner on third, slyly slipped home from third with the winning run. The umpire had neglected to call time out.

Baseball—**April 28, 1923 (H):** In the 13-1 win over Albion, pitcher Bernard "Bub" Kuhn missed recording a no-hit, no-run game on an eighth inning "no call" by the umpire. An Albion batter bunted the ball toward first base and accidentally kicked the ball as he raced down the baseline. The umpire later confessed not seeing the incident, which should have been an automatic out, ending the inning. Instead, that bunt (Albion's only hit) had scored the solitary Briton run.

Baseball—**May 4, 1923 (H):** The home win over Notre Dame was of the come-from-behind variety. Lagging 5-4 in the final inning, Bub Kuhn walked and was replaced on the bases by Arthur Beckley. The pinch runner then advanced to second on a declared balk. Bill Daley, the next batter, bunted on the second pitch. The pitcher fielded the ball and, in attempting to cut down Beckley at third, sailed an overthrow so deep into left field that both runners scored and MAC was the winner, 6-5.

Track and Field—**May 12, 1923 (A):** One week following their overwhelming loss to Ohio State in Columbus, 91-34, the Aggies battled a cold and drizzling rain at Oberlin to gain their only victory of the year. In premeet chatter, Coach Barron predicted a one-point victory for the Farmers and, sure enough, the final score read 66-65. As is often the case in close meets, it was the result of a late-finishing event from the infield that marked the winning margin. This time it was the javelin event in which Phil Weamer outdistanced the Yeomen rivals with a throw of 154' 9".

ATHLETE OF THE YEAR

Roy MacMillan earned seven varsity monograms in three sports while at MAC. His collegiate career was interrupted in 1921-1922 when he was forced to drop out of school for one academic year. The native of Mt. Clemens, Mich., lettered twice in football as a backup quarterback and two times in basketball (1923 and 1925) as a starting forward and steady scorer in his final year. He was a three-year starter as the third baseman and lead-off hitter in his primary sport of baseball (1921, 1923, 1924).

Roy MacMillan

IN THE SPARTLITE

Baseball: For the first time in the memory of the MAC faithful, not a single contest in the entire season was postponed or canceled because of bad weather or wet grounds.

Basketball: The new coach, Fred Walker, seemed to have a difficult time deciding on his starting five. He began the season with forwards Roy MacMillan and Matt Nuttila, guards Clarence Fessenden and Wes Eva, and Ellwood Mason in the pivot. Before the schedule had concluded, 14 other Aggies had started or played in one or more games: Ray Kipke, Bob Bilkey, Art Beckley, Vic Hultman, Rollie Richards, Jim Kidman, Merle Ralston, Bub Kuhn, Hugo Swanson, Chet Archbold, Lambertus "L.E." Beeuwkes, Bill Cutler, Bill Johnson and Hugh Robinson.

Of the first 16 games on the schedule, *15* were played on the home court. The final three contests, against Notre Dame, St. Ignatius of Cleveland and Oberlin, were all on the road.

As fear of a scarlet fever epidemic swirled, schedule changes were mandated. February dates for both Alma and Orchard Lake St. Mary's were moved forward nearly one week.

Cross Country: Floyd Rowe, a former U of M runner and local resident, coached the MAC harriers for only one year (1921). Although the records list football mentor Al Barron "doubling" as cross country coach in 1922, a preseason story in *The Holcad* notes, "Athletic Director Barron will render his service as well as several other coaches on the athletic staff."

The five-mile course for the 1922 Big Ten meet at West Lafayette was described as a hard-finished road with brick pavement. Race day conditions included a cold wind that confronted the runners. The Aggie team comprised of Dayton "Bill" Willard, Don Clark, Leonard Klaase, Glen Nesman, and John Van Arman placed sixth in a field of ten, beating out Minnesota, Purdue, Indiana and Iowa. In the individual race to the tape, Willard was the sixth runner to cross the finish line and thus earned a varsity "S" sweater.

Football: The Oct. 31, 1922, issue of *The Holcad* listed the means by which Aggie fans could reach Ann Arbor for the November 4 football game:

"The team and band and any interested fans will go on the Pierre Marquette train, leaving from the College switch behind Wells Hall at 8:00 Saturday morning. The round trip fare will be $3.50, arriving in Ann Arbor at 10:00-10:30 a.m. Returning, the train will leave at 7:00 and arrive here at about 9:30 or probably sooner.

Those wishing to go by interurban may do so, leaving from the station at the Bank at 6:30 and as often as there is a load or in time to get to Ann Arbor for the game. The round trip-ticket is $3.15. Return trips from Ann Arbor will be anytime Saturday night or Sunday.

A number of men are going in the usual fashion in tin cans [automobiles]. If you wish to brave the weather you can do the round trip in one of Bret Neller's trucks for $1.50 round trip or $1.00 one way. Trucks will leave about 8:30 and arrive about 11:30."

Coach George Gauthier, former MAC star, brought his Ohio Wesleyan team to East Lansing and edged the Aggies 9-6 on three successful field goals. At halftime of the game, Coach Gauthier was presented with a floral display by the MAC Varsity Club.

In defeating Massachusetts State, 45-0, in the final home game of the season, the Aggies scored only 21 fewer points than they would total in all the other nine games on the 1922 schedule.

Playing away on Thanksgiving Day, the Farmers opposed St. Louis University at Sportsman Park, the home of baseball's St. Louis Browns. It was a contest played in a sea of mud, and although such conditions should have favored the heavier Billikens, the game ended in a 7-7 tie.

Swimming and Diving: An annoying incident came during the 52-16 loss at Indiana University. In order to create a little interest in the meet, a male student dressed like a lady was to surprisingly fall into the pool before the final event. Unfortunately, he chose to make his splash prematurely, amidst the running of the 100-yard freestyle event. The comic intruder landed right into Dutch VonNoppen's lane as he was negotiating his final turn. There was no compensation from meet officials. All in all, it was a long, tiring and unrewarding 23-hour trip for Coach Rauch and his eight-man team.

In two dual meets against the University of Michigan, the Aggies ended up on the short end by identical scores of 48-20. The only noteworthy Aggie performances came from Rollin Kiefaber, who twice won the "fancy diving" event, and VonNoppen, who, while swimming the 100-yard freestyle in the meet at East Lansing, was once again interfered with. This time the trespasser was a competitor who had swum out of his lane and locked arms with "Dutch," bringing him to a dead stop. Appropriately, the end result was a disqualification of the U of M competitor, giving the victory to VonNoppen who finished with a time of 1:03.4.

Tennis: The chemistry professor, Charles Ball, returned to his spot as head coach in 1923, replacing Harry Young. He would serve in the capacity for the next 23 years. In preparation for the 1923 season, Coach Ball held Thursday evening lectures during the winter weeks. Also, every night from 6:30-9:00 P.M. indoor practices were conducted in the Armory, which was now referred to as the gymnasium handball room.

Winning the doubles title, Jack Croll and C.R. Coe led the Farmers to a tie with Western State Normal in the state invitational tournament championship. Having won the tournament outright in 1922, MAC retained custody of the trophy.

The season concluded with a team of three (Burwell Cummings, Clato Coe and Jack Croll) on the road representing MAC in matches against Oberlin, Penn State (Coach Ball's alma mater), Pittsburgh and Allegheny College. To keep the locals appraised, results of those matches were wired back to Ivery's Drug Store, where they were posted in the window.

In recognition of his undefeated season, Croll was awarded a major letter sweater, as opposed to the usual *minor* award extended to tennis players.

Track and Field: Although the Aggies did not score a point, three members of the team competed in the Big Ten outdoor championships at Ann Arbor. Mark Herdell ran the sprints, Phil Weramer threw the javelin, and Clarence Fessenden entered both the shot put and the discus.

Wrestling: Rules called for a match to be 12 minutes in length unless there was a fall. A decision was given if the opponents had wrestled for 12 minutes and one man had been on top for seven or more minutes. If no decision could be resolved during regulation, two three-minute overtime periods would ensue with hopes of breaking the tie. A fall counted six points for the team's scoring total and a decision received five points.

SPARTAN SCRAPBOOK
—TENNIS COACHES (1913-2003)—

Harry C. Young (1921-22)

Charles Ball (1923-46)

Gordon A. Dahlgren (1947)

*H. Frank Beeman
(1948-50, '53-57)*

Thomas Martin (1951)

John A. Friedrich (1952)

Stan Drobac (1958-89)

Jim Frederick (1990-91)

Gene Orlando (1991-)

Note: no coach 1913-20

MAC
1923-1924

TALES TO TELL

The 1924 basketball games against Central Michigan (January 29) and the University of Michigan (February 6) were sent out play-by-play over WKAR radio. It is believed the game against Mt. Pleasant was the nation's first-ever basketball game to be broadcast live. As in football, Jimmy Hasselman, the school public relations man, was at the microphone. Mailed responses confirmed listeners from the Atlantic and Gulf coasts to Alberta, Canada in the north and Nebraska in the west. This somewhat authenticated the station's boast of possessing apparatus for broadcasting up to 2,000 miles under favorable conditions. Many respondents identified themselves as having never seen a basketball game or understood it, but they became interested from listening to Hasselman. By 1926, all home games would be broadcast, part by Lansing station WREO and part by WKAR.

TEAM OF THE YEAR

In terms of successful seasons, 1923-1924 was not a great year for MAC athletics. It is noted the basketball team with 10 wins and 10 losses posted the most impressive record of the eight varsity squads. Victories over the likes of John Carroll and Valparaiso may not seen impressive today, but these were highly successful teams of the day.

HEADLINES of 1924

- The motion picture industry is in "motion." Marcus Loew, Samuel Goldwyn and Louis B. Mayer form Metro-Goldwyn-Mayer, and Harry Cohn founds Columbia Pictures.
- The *Little Orphan Annie* comic strip is created by Harold Gray.
- J. Edgar Hoover becomes director of the Bureau of Investigation (renamed Federal Bureau of Investigation in 1935).
- After a sensational trial, Nathan Leopold and Richard Loeb are sentenced to life imprisonment for the kidnapping and murder of Bobby Franks.

SCOREBOARD

	W	L	T	Avg.
Baseball	6	7	0	.462
Track and Field	2	3	0	.400
Football	3	5	0	.375
Basketball	10	10	0	.500
Tennis	1	2	0	.333
Cross Country	0	2	0	.000
Swimming and Diving	3	4	0	.429
Wrestling	0	3	0	.000

MAKING HISTORY

Beginning with the 1923-1924 basketball season, each player had to shoot his own free throws upon being fouled. Previously, each team usually designated one player to toss all free throws.

The January 11 basketball game in Ann Arbor was the inaugural in the U of M's Yost Fieldhouse. The thought of playing on a portable floor concerned Coach Walker enough that he took his squad to Ann Arbor a day early to practice under the conditions. Tied 13-13 at the intermission, the Aggies connected on four free throws but only one field goal in the second half. The Wolverines were pleased to open their new facility with a win, 23-19.

The first NCAA swimming and diving championships were held at the U.S. Naval Academy in Annapolis, Md.

GREAT STATE DATES

Football—**October 6, 1923 (H):** Playing for the first time in the new stadium and before 8,000 spectators, the Aggies scored early and hung on to defeat Lake Forest, 21-6. A Roland Richards to Ray Kipke pass off of a faked field goal attempt opened the scoring in the first quarter. On the very next possession, Verne Schmyser scored and Elton Neller's PAT made it 14-0. The third MAC touchdown was the result of back-to-back 25-yard

1924 basketball team. (Front row, left to right) M. Nuttila, M. Ralston, R. Bilkey, W. Eva, C. Kitto, R. Richards and J. Kidman. (Middle row, left to right) B.H. Marx, P. Hackett, V. Hultman, L. Smith, E. Mason, Brinkert and coach F. Walker. (Back row, left to right) Manager H. Newman, Green, W.N. Kidman, H. Robinson, Starrett and trainer J. Heppinstall.

pass plays with the Richards-Kipke connection accounting for the score. Led by Eddie Eckert's rush, the MAC defense continually harassed the Foresters' attempts to counter with passes. Of their 19 attempts, only four were complete and another four were intercepted. Ticket prices for games in the new stadium were set at $1, with seats in the two center sections going for $2.

Football—**November 17, 1923 (A):** In the season-closer against the U of D, the Titan punter saw an errant center snap go sailing over his head and into the end zone. As quickly as he could, he raced back to retrieve the ball. Quickly behind him was the Aggies' Don Haskins, a sophomore tackle from Grand Rapids. Haskins dropped the would-be punter in the end zone for a safety. That was the extent of the scoring for the afternoon, as the two points held up for an Aggie win, 2-0.

Basketball—**January 18, 1924 (H):** Things do change over time. Today it seems strange to have competed against a school as small as John Carroll. Stranger still is to read that a 24-17 victory over them was an upset. Yet during the preceding season (1923), the Aggies twice lost to the Cleveland school when it still carried the name St. Ignatius. In this 1924 encounter, MAC led 14-10 after the first half and then held a five-point lead throughout most of the second half before Matt Nuttila put the game away with two late field goals. It was John Carroll's second loss of the campaign and only their sixth setback in the span of three seasons.

Swimming and Diving—**February 13, 1924 (A):** Combining men's and women's swimming meets is not a recent innovation. It happened nearly 80 years ago when both men and women Aggie teams traveled to Ypsilanti for a double-dual affair against Michigan Normal College. The races alternated, men-women, through the eight-event program, with the men winning, 38-30, and the women coming up short, 39-11.

Basketball—**March 6, 1924 (H):** In their most impressive victory of the season, Fred Walker's five defeated a highly successful Valparaiso team, 22-12. It was only the second loss of the season for the Crusaders. MAC led

at halftime 12-9 and never trailed thereafter. Merle Ralston was the leading scorer with 10 points.

Swimming and Diving—**March 10, 1924 (H):** Avenging the 42-25 loss two weeks earlier, the Aggies topped Grand Rapids Y in the rematch, 36-32. Ernest Richmond was credited with a pair of firsts: springboard diving and the 50-yard backstroke (35.5). Other firsts came from Briggs in the 100-yard freestyle (64.5) and Eckerman in the 50-yard breaststroke (41.0).

Baseball—**April 29, 1924 (H):** In his first appearance as an Aggie, an 8-0 shutout of St. Mary's College of Orchard Lake, Harry Wakefield pitched a nearly perfect game. In nine innings the big right-hander from Kinde, Mich., struck out 17 batters and allowed only one hit. The visitors assisted the MAC cause by booting 11 chances in the field.

Baseball—**May 30, 1924 (H):** With the Wisconsin game tied at 4-4, Fred Ranney, Jack Sepanek and Roy MacMillan opened the bottom of the seventh with consecutive base hits. Coupled with a sacrifice fly and a perfectly executed squeeze play, three runs were scored and the Aggies held on for a 7-4 victory. The game featured three circus catches. Twice Rollie Richards made spectacular grabs of low liners into center field, and second baseman Harold Kiebler raced into right field for a diving somersault catch in the eighth inning.

Track and Field—**May 3, 1924 (H):** The running of the first event in the opening meet of the outdoor season, against Detroit City College, was delayed two hours by a drenching rainstorm. Although Mark Herdell would contribute three firsts and 15 team points, his failure in the broad jump nearly led to an MAC loss. Usually dependable, on this afternoon Herdell never registered a legitimate leap as he fouled on every attempt. Meanwhile, the burden of winning that final event then fell on the shoulders of the team's number two man, Lloyd Kurtz. The Kalamazoo sophomore responded with a jump of 20' 4 1/2", good enough for first place, five points and a 67-64 victory.

ATHLETE OF THE YEAR

Roland Richards of Lansing earned six varsity awards in three sports. He lettered three times in football (1922-1924), and was the starting quarterback in his final two seasons. Richards twice earned monograms in basketball (1924-1925) and earned one in baseball as the regular center fielder in 1924, switching to the shortstop position in 1925 when he served as team captain. "Rollie" performed an unexcelled feat in the 8-4 win over Butler on May 31, 1924. Twice, he reached first base (base hit and base on balls) and proceeded to steal second base, then third base and finally home.

Roland Richards

IN THE SPARTLITE

Basketball: Athletic director Ralph Young was concerned about the way local supporters were shouting and yelling when opposing players were at the free-throw line. In early February he began instructing game officials to call a foul on MAC if fans persisted in such unsportsmanlike behavior.

The first half of the Lombard College (Galesburg, Ill.) game February 1 ended with MAC trailing, 10-8. At the opening of the second half, the visitors' intentions were immediately detectable. Nursing their two-point lead and playing the old "freeze" game, they held the ball for ten straight minutes. Over the remaining time, the frustrated Aggies did create a few scoring chances, but the undefeated Lombard five had accomplished their mission, emerging as the 13-12 winners. This slowdown style of play was not greeted favorably by the majority of the local spectators. As reported in the *MAC Record*:

> "The tactics of the winners met with the general disapproval of the crowd, and some of the remarks addressed to the Lombard players were not of the nature which is generally believed to characterize a college crowd."

At the conclusion of the 1924 schedule, Ralph Young announced that 15,532 fans had attended the 16 home games, but he also pointed to a fiscal deficit of $524.11. Regardless of this deficiency, the season was declared a financial success, because the shortage was half the loss of the preceding year.

Cross Country: Trainer-groundskeeper Jack Heppinstall was recruited to double as coach of the cross country team for the 1922 season. In attempting to fulfill this secondary assignment, he would often call upon the team manager to conduct the team workouts. Perhaps it was lack of talent, or perchance lack of attention led to the winless season for the MAC runners.

In the Big Ten conference championship meet at Columbus, Ohio, the at-large MAC quintet finished ahead of Indiana and Chicago, in the eighth spot. The 25-year-old Doc Willard was the top finisher for the Aggies, negotiating the course in 27:26.0 for 16th place out of 60 entrants. Captain Keith Baguley finished in 26th place, C.E. Ripper in 44th, Paul Hartsuch in 45th and Floyd Harper in the 49th spot.

Football: As noted earlier, radio broadcasts of basketball games were first aired during the 1924 season. Although the signal was not relayed to the Lansing area, the September 29 football opener against Chicago was broadcast direct from the sidelines to radio listeners throughout the Chicago area. Back home, fans in theater-style seating followed the game's progress in the gymnasium via "grid-graph." This was an 8'x14' board of glass and lights used in following progress of the game as telegraphed from the site. The center of the display area simulated the playing field while lights on the board's perimeter highlighted lineups, game clock, score, and type of play.

Hockey: At its December meeting in 1923, the Athletic Board of Control authorized the construction of a hockey rink on the lighted area at the rear of College Field's west stands. Members of the team had presented a petition stating they would personally undertake the construction of the necessary sideboards without expense to the college. For undisclosed reasons the project was delayed and the team never arranged a schedule.

Swimming and Diving: In the 50-18 home loss to Michigan, MAC continued to dominate the diving event as L.A. Bordeaux and Ernest Richmond finished one-two. Richmond, team captain, became the first MAC swimmer-diver to earn a major letter.

The recorded times and achievements of the early swimmers and divers pale in comparison to today's performances. Nevertheless, fan support was impressive. As an example, in 1924 a total of 1,191 paid to attend the five home meets at the gymnasium pool.

Tennis: In early spring, it was announced that grading and landscaping around the recently completed Home Economics Building would be discontinued until June 1. This action was necessary to provide temporary use of the clay tennis courts that lay amidst the new construction. In revealing the decision, Herman H. Halladay, the Secretary of the Board reported the old courts would be put back in first class condition and that new courts were under construction east of the old ones.

Jack Croll completed his MAC career by capturing the state intercollegiate singles title, but the defeat of Croll-Lawrence in the doubles final led to a share of the team trophy with Western State Normal.

Track and Field: Competing before more than 5,000 spectators at the prestigious Illinois relays, Paul Hartsuch placed second in the 1,000-yard run. The field of 15 runners represented many of the big colleges and universities of the Midwest. Five other Aggies entrants failed to place in their respective specialties.

On May 10 the squad was in Ames, Iowa, for a dual meet with Iowa State. The talent-rich Cyclones, coached by Art Smith, the former Aggie mentor, laid the greatest loss ever on a Spartan track team, 102-29. Actually, there were a few highlights. Mark Herdell tied the team record with a 10.0 clocking in the 100-yard dash; captain Keith Baguley ran his personal best in the mile by 11 seconds; Bill Willard clipped 20 seconds from his best two-mile performance; Paul Hartsuch ran his best 880 of the year and Maurice Elliott raised a personal best shot put mark by more than a foot. Yet none of these achievements could earn a first-place finish against Art Smith's crew.

Competing with the freshman team, Fred Alderman of Lansing and Bohn Grim of Sturgis stole the show in the eighth running of the State Intercollegiate meet. The pair ran one-two in the 220-yard dash as Alderman bettered the meet record with a time of 21.7 seconds. He also came within a half inch of the broad jump record with a winning leap of 22' 2".

On the weekend of May 30-31, Alderman and Grim, along with varsity runners Paul Hartsuch, "Red" Baguley and Mark Herdell, competed in the sectional Olympic Trials at Ann Arbor. Although all five Aggies performed well, only Alderman, with two third-place finishes, qualified to advance to the final Olympic Trials, held at Harvard Stadium, June 13-14. There he missed making the USA team by a matter of inches in the final qualifying race of the 100-yard dash. The Lansing native had to wait four more years before wearing the red, white, and blue colors of his country at the IX Olympiad in Amsterdam.

Wrestling: The wrestling team traveled to Ann Arbor fully confident they could gain their first win of the season. It almost happened. With one match remaining and the team scoring tied at 9-9, the heavyweights would decide the meet. The ensuing battle was furiously fought, and at one moment in the scuffle, MAC's Eddie Eckert and his opponent broke through the ropes that surrounded the mat and came crashing down over the scoring table. Following the final whistle, the Michigan grappler was declared the winner via a riding time advantage of three minutes and 29 seconds. The Aggies went winless in 1924.

SPARTAN SCRAPBOOK

─── CROSS COUNTRY ───

First cross country team (1910)

MAC
1924-1925

TALES TO TELL

The current football rule following the scoring of a safety provides that the team scored upon must put the ball in play by a free kick from its own 20-yard line. Prior to 1926, the rule maintained that the team yielding the safety would continue possession by putting the ball in play with a first down from scrimmage at its own 30-yard line. That is exactly what happened in MAC's game in Evanston, Ill., October 25. Leading 13-7 with less than a minute to play, Northwestern had possession with fourth down on their own 10-yard line. The would-be punter took the snap from center and immediately raced back into the end zone, surrendering a safety to yield two points. With the score now 13-9, the Wildcats took possession at their own 30-yard line and ran out the remainder of playing time to ensure the victory. From this game result, the rules committee saw the interpretation flaw and changed the rule, commencing in 1926.

The original college land-grant philosophy called for instruction in agriculture and applied mechanics. By 1924, MAC had embraced other facets of higher education, including engineering, home economics, applied science and liberal arts. It was considered by many that an institution with such diverse offerings was described incompletely or inappropriately when it carried the title of Michigan Agricultural College. A campaign to change the name gained momentum, and in March of 1924, at the urging of acting-president Robert Shaw, a poll was conducted among students. The survey revealed a ratio of seven-to-one in favor of a name change. Although the name Michigan State College was the most popular alternative, other names surfaced such as Wolverine State University and University of the Great Lakes. Those in support of the agricultural heritage were defiantly opposed to the removal of that word from the school's name. In a conciliatory mood, the State Legislature proposed a change in name to Michigan State College of Agriculture and Applied Science. This proved acceptable to all concerned, as the bill was approved unanimously by the Senate and passed in the House by a substantial margin. The new name became official on May 13, 1925.

HEADLINES of 1925

- The *WSM Barn Dance*, later renamed the *Grand Ole Opry* in 1928, premieres.
- *The New Yorker* magazine is founded.
- The popular dance step, the Charleston, bounces into dance halls across America.
- The Rivoli and the Rialto, in New York City, become the world's first air-conditioned theaters.

SCOREBOARD

	W	L	T	Avg.
Baseball	9	5	1	.633
Track and Field	1	3	0	.250
Football	5	3	0	.625
Basketball	6	13	0	.316
Tennis	4	3	0	.571
Cross Country	1	2	0	.333
Swimming and Diving	2	4	0	.333
Wrestling	2	4	0	.333
Hockey	0	1	0	.000
Fencing	0	1	0	.000

TEAM OF THE YEAR

John Kobs's first baseball team in East Lansing was the 1925 outfit that won nine of 15 games. Two of the biggest wins were at home over Minnesota and Notre Dame.

MAKING HISTORY

The Michigan game of Oct. 10, 1924, would be marked as the first MAC home football game broadcast over the radio with play-by-play. As in basketball, Jimmy Hasselman, the school's public relations man, was at the WKAR microphone. He attempted to eliminate the crowd noise by broadcasting from inside a telephone booth, and he did the same the following year from Ferry Field in Ann Arbor. While broadcasting that 1925 game, Hasselman likely appreciated the fact that the Spartans wore white jerseys for the first time to distinguish themselves from the home team Wolverines with dark jerseys. By 1927, games were being carried from the open press box. It was concluded that crowd noise would add to the interest of the game for the listeners. The first-ever baseball game against the University of Minnesota was played on May 14 and was also the initial appearance of a Michigan State College athletic team. The new name had been officially adopted on the very day before. While leading the Gophers 5-2 in the ninth inning, pitching ace Harry Wakefield hurriedly replaced starter George Kuhn, who left the bases loaded with only one out. Wakefield succeeded by striking out a pinch hitter and getting the final batter on a weak infield grounder. By the season of 1926, uniforms reflected the name change as "Michigan State" replaced "Michigan Aggies" on the shirt fronts.

1925 baseball team. (Front row, left to right): H. Wakefield, R. Spiekerman, G. Kuhn, C. Fisher and D. Zimmerman. (Middle row, left to right) R. Davis, Spotts, H. Kiebler, D. Fleser and P. Fremont. (Back row, left to right) trainer J. Heppinstall, Gauss, coach J. Kobs, G. Rowley and manager M. Burlingame. Missing from the picture: captain Roland Richards.

Cross country, swimming and diving, hockey, tennis and baseball were surprisingly all listed, along with football and basketball, as "money makers" for the year. Below were the receipts and disbursements for all varsity teams:

Sport	Receipts	Disbursements
Baseball	5,417.94	4,927.89
Track and Field	4,065.23	4,187.50
Football	47,834.98	27,940.19
Basketball	7,215.66	5,335.91
Tennis	844.33	799.02
Cross Country	1,304.72	1.109.19
Swimming/Diving	1,524.57	1,402.22
Wrestling	1,791.66	2,237.56
Hockey	492.74	360.57

John Kobs's 1924-1926 multi-coaching obligations are best described as simply unbelievable. Upon wrapping up his responsibility as freshman football coach in the fall, he moved onto the gymnasium floor as head basketball coach. In addition, during the winter season he doubled as hockey coach. All of this was in prelude to his responsibility as baseball coach in the spring.

GREAT STATE DATES

Football—**November 15, 1924 (H):** With 11 men playing their final game for MAC, the stage was set for a thrilling season-closing game against South Dakota State. The Aggies played up to the occasion and by a score of 9-0, defeated a team that had tied for the lead of the North Central Intercollegiate Association. The Dakota team came to town as masters of the passing game, but Coach Young had his defenders prepared for the attack. Pressure from the front wall of Eckert, Hultman, Eckerman, Hackett, Haskins and Robinson continually forced premature and unsuccessful tosses. Meanwhile, "Stub" Kipke, playing his final game for the Green, set up the only touchdown of the game when he fell on a muffed punt attempt at the visitors' 15-yard line. Three plays later and on the first play of the second period, quarterback Verne Schmyser bolted over from the one-yard line. Elton Neller, who had been the top ground-gainer all afternoon, provided the needed insurance with a 45-yard drop kick in

the middle of the third quarter. It was only the second successful field goal attempt by MAC in four years.

Wrestling—**January 17, 1925 (H):** Coach Burhans's squad opened the season with a convincing 20-6 victory over Michigan. Garnering the points for the Green and White were 125-pound F. H. Williamson, who won in overtime; Captain Hansen, who threw his opponent in the 135-pound division; A.W. Bergquist (145-pounds) and J.A. Murray (175-pounds), both of whom won on pins.

Basketball—**February 11, 1925 (H):** Three of the six victories of the season were of the overtime variety. Such was the case in the University of Detroit game. Paul Hackett hit a field goal with three seconds remaining in regulation to tie the score 22-22. During the extra five-minute period, Roland Richards swished through one free throw, and that was it. This time, to the delight of the home crowd, the Spartans resorted to stalling tactics to preserve their 23-22 winning advantage.

Basketball—**February 28, 1925 (H):** State administered Oberlin College its only loss of the season, 29-27 in overtime. With only 30 seconds of regulation remaining and trailing by two points, Rollie Richards intercepted an Oberlin pass and tossed it to Hugh Robinson, who sunk a one-handed jump shot to knot the score 23-23 as time ran out. Roy MacMillan scored four of the points in overtime as State sealed the victory.

Baseball—**April 16, 1925 (A):** What a way for John Kobs to begin his illustrious 39-year career as the school's head coach. In the season-opening 9-0 victory over Armour Tech in Chicago, Harry Wakefield pitched a no-hit, no-run game, striking out nine. He forced 18 other Armour batters to either pop easy flies to the infield or dribble weak ground balls. With his teammates playing errorless ball behind him, Harry missed a perfect game by walking two men. Hitting stars for MAC were Rollie Richards, who homered and doubled, and Roy Spiekerman, who punched out three timely singles in four trips to the plate.

Baseball—**May 14, 1925 (H):** Rushed to the relief of George Kuhn in the ninth inning, Harry Wakefield pitched the Spartans out of a tough spot and salvaged a 5-2 victory over the University of Minnesota. With but one man out and the bases loaded, Wakefield fanned the first man he faced, a pinch hitter. The next batter hit a feeble grounder to Spiekerman at first, who stepped on the bag to end an exciting battle.

Baseball—**June 6, 1925 (H):** Coach John Kobs's first Spartan team closed out its regular-season schedule with an exciting 5-4 victory over Notre Dame. Although he permitted nine hits, two of them for extra bases, Harry Wakefield, the State moundsman, deserved a big share of the credit for the win. He struck out 10 batters, often in crucial times, as the Irish left 10 men stranded on the bases. Captain Roland Richards played his best game of the year at shortstop as he handled eight chances, many of them difficult. He turned in three singles in four appearances at the plate. The only MSC extra base hit was off the bat of Don Fleser, who hit a ground-rule double into the protruding bleachers of right center field. By the following season that structure would be burned to the ground by pranksters celebrating the defeat of Michigan.

ATHLETE OF THE YEAR

The records support a claim that Don Fleser was the most effective hitter in the school's baseball history. He stroked a lusty .589 average in his sophomore season of 1925, the second-highest hitting record ever achieved by an Aggie-Spartan batter. The highest average ever achieved by a player who wore the Green came in the very next year, 1926, and it was the same Mr. Fleser who this time posted a remarkable .667 average. He closed out his collegiate career as captain in 1927, a season in which he recorded a more human-like .404 average. In 1959, 32 years later, his son, John Fleser, would lead the Spartans in batting with a .347 average.

Don Fleser

IN THE SPARTLITE

Basketball: Two weeks before the 1925 season opened against Adrian, a story in the *Lansing State Journal* reported: "The basketball schedule will not be announced for several days yet. Unexpected developments in the booking of one or two games have delayed the announcement." As it eventually turned out and as strange as it seems, the first official announcement of the schedule was not released until one day following that game with Adrian. So much for preseason ticket sales.

The 28-16 loss to little Franklin (Ind.) College was no surprise. The "Little Wonder Five," as they were called, had defeated MAC three weeks earlier back in Indiana. This second game was broadcast by WKAR, and to the amazement of Franklin fans with radios, they were clearly able to hear a play-by-play account of the action more than 200 miles away. The Franklin story is part of a Hoosier basketball legend in which a quintet of grammar school-age boys organized a Sunday school team under the guidance of their teacher, Mr. "Griz" Wagner. He continued as the boys' high school coach in Franklin, and they responded with two state championships. Then, when some of those same boys headed for the local college, "Griz" was once more persuaded to be their coach. During three years of collegiate competition, the "Little Wonder Five" suffered only two defeats.

Fencing: By 1924, Professor Lebel had begun a fencing club for which he acted as a volunteer coach. He started with a group of ten men, and by the spring of 1925, five remained as regulars. That May, this group journeyed to Ann Arbor for the school's first fencing match since the MIAA Field Day of 1895. Lebel's squad was routed that afternoon by the U of M team, 8-1.

Football: Even though the entire four-game home schedule of 1923 had been played in the new stadium, the dedication of the facility was delayed until Oct. 10, 1924, when Michigan came to town for only the third time in the 19-year-old history of the series. In the early part of the contest, the Aggies had two opportunities to get on the scoreboard, only to have a pair of field-goal attempts sail wide of the mark. With three minutes remaining and a scoreless tie seemingly imminent, a dismal conclusion was to unfold. With the U of M in possession near midfield, they tried a long pass that Herb Steger, the U of M captain, gathered in and carried over the goal line—so much for the scoreless tie. The final

count: Michigan 7, MSC 0. Prior to that Michigan game and as a part of the stadium dedication, a memorial stone was unveiled that remains today near the stadium's tunnel entrance. The bronze plaque reads: "In memory of MAC varsity athletes who gave their lives in the World War. Olen Hinkle, E.E. Peterson, F.I. Lankey."

The Aggies of 1924 may not have won often (5-3), but when they did, they usually won big: 59-0 over Northwestern at Naperville, Ill., a 54-3 defeat of Olivet, a 34-3 victory over the Chicago YMCA College, and 42-13 over Lake Forest.

Hockey: Due to warm weather, the hockey team was unable to complete its schedule that had included outdoor home games against Michigan, Notre Dame and Minnesota. The only game played was a 6-3 road loss to the U of M. Goals that afternoon came unassisted from both Robin Hancock and Carl Moore. The third goal was also from Moore, assisted by Cliff Hauptli.

Swimming and Diving: Team practice was conducted nightly for one hour from 5:00 until 6:00 P.M. The 1925 season was to have opened at home against Northwestern, one of the nation's top squads which featured two members of the 1924 USA Olympic team. One week before the scheduled meet, Wildcat officials notified Lyman Frimodig, assistant director of athletics, that they would not be fulfilling their commitment. It seems that a conflicting meet on the west coast was more enticing.

Following is a sampling of some of the better times recorded during the season by Aggie swimmers: 50-yard freestyle (27.2), 100-yard freestyle (62.0), 100-yard breaststroke (1:25.0) and the 100-yard backstroke (1:17.4).

Track and Field: The season of 1925 marked the beginning of the varsity sprint careers of Fred Alderman and Bohn Grim. In the first outdoor meet of the spring, a 70-61 loss to Detroit City College, Alderman posted winning times of 10.0 and 21.0 seconds in the 100- and 220-yard dashes. Although it was never submitted for recognition, the later time for the furlong was better than the listed world record. That afternoon Fred also placed first in the broad jump and javelin throw. In that same meet, Grim took the 440 in 51.1 seconds. Fred achieved his top century time three weeks later in the State Intercollegiate meet. His 9.7 seconds nearly equaled Charles Paddock's world record. The Lansing sophomore also captured the 220 (21.2) and the broad jump (23' 3/8").

The 1925 Big Ten championship was the final meet open to non-conference schools. The closed-meet format was in place thereafter. In that 1925 meet at Columbus, Alderman won the 220 in 21.1 seconds, the top "official" time in the USA for the year. Perhaps it was first-year jitters or fatigue from a long season, but in the NCAAs at Chicago, Alderman settled for a disappointing third in the 220. The winner's time of 21.9 seconds was considerably slower than Fred had been running all spring.

Wrestling: After easily winning the first two meets of the year, 20-6 over Michigan and 15-2 over Northwestern, false hope emerged that Coach Burhans had collected a team of national caliber. Reality rapidly set in. Those early victories were met by the following losses in the ensuing weekends: Indiana 29-0, Ohio State 13-7, Iowa State 17-3 and Purdue 11-9. By season's end, two facts had been proven: (1) The MAC team was average and (2) the Michigan and Northwestern teams were below average.

SPARTAN SCRAPBOOK
──── CROSS COUNTRY COACHES (1910-2003) ────

Howard Beatty (1916-17)

Floyd A. Rowe (1921)

John G. Heppinstall (1923)

Morton Mason (1925-30)

Lauren P. Brown (1931-46)

Jim Gibbard (1968-83)

Jim Stintzi (1984-)

Note: no team 1913-14, 1918

Pictured elsewhere: Chester Brewer 1910$_{BS}$; John Macklin 1911-12$_{BS}$; George Gauthier 1915, 1919$_{TR}$; Arthur N. Smith 1920$_{TR}$; Bert Barron 1922$_{TR}$; Ralph Young 1924$_{TR}$; Karl Schlademan 1947-58$_{TR}$; Francis Dittrich 1959-67$_{TR}$

$_{BS}$ see baseball coaches

$_{TR}$ see track and field coaches

TALES TO TELL

On April 3, 1926, the name "Spartans" was first identified with Michigan State. The creator was, of course, George Alderton, then the sports director with *The Lansing State Journal*. During an interview in November 1993 at his home in Traverse City, he related the following:

"I had come there [Lansing] in February of 1923, and they were still calling them the Aggies. They had been Michigan Agriculture College originally, and then when they changed to Michigan State College there was a feeling they wanted a name other than the Aggies. Jim Hasselman was a one-man-band in the way of publicity for Michigan State. I came to know Jim really well. He spearheaded an idea that spring [1926] for the campus [students] to submit a batch of names from which the new name would be chosen. Of all things, it was eventually announced they were going to be called 'Staters'—and that didn't ring right with me at all. In fact, I never did use the name 'Staters.'

It was April, and the baseball team was preparing for their trip down south. Because I was not going with the team, I asked Perry Fremont [one of the players] every time they played a game if he would send me a night press rate collect with his abbreviated story about the game they had just played. He agreed to do it. Well, he sent me the story that first night [against Ft. Benning] and I had it on my desk that next morning when I got to the paper. It [Fremont's story] was just in conversational language, of course, and I had to rewrite the thing. When I was rewriting it and went back to read the copy, I noticed that Perry had used the name Aggies. Right then I thought, we have to have a better name than that. I got a hold of Hasselman [by telephone] and asked if he still had all of the entries in the contest. He said, 'Oh yeah, they're here, but they're in the waste basket. If you want to see them, come on out [to the campus].' And so I went out and looked through them and came across the name Spartans—instantly it rang with me. That was a good one. There were no other Spartans that I knew of in this part of the coun-

---

HEADLINES of 1926

- Miniature golf is introduced in Lookout Mountain, Tenn., and from there it expands to more than 40,000 courses within three years.
- Gertrude Ederle, at 19, is the first woman to swim the English Channel.
- Book-of-the-Month Club, the first mail-order book program, begins enrolling members.
- RCA organizes the National Broadcasting Company (NBC), the first nationwide entertainment radio broadcasting network.

SCOREBOARD

	W	L	T	Avg.
Baseball	13	7	0	.650
Track and Field	2	3	0	.400
Football	3	5	0	.375
Basketball	5	13	0	.278
Tennis	9	5	0	.643
Cross Country	1	2	0	.333
Swimming and Diving	2	4	0	.333
Wrestling	0	5	0	.000
Hockey	0	4	0	.000
Fencing	1	0	0	1.000

try. So I inserted the name Spartans in the baseball story and I spelled it just as I had come to know it, with an—O—Sparton—like the radio made in Jackson at the time. I spelled it that way and used it in the paper for two days. Then a history professor at Michigan State called me and told me, 'You are spelling that word wrong, there are two As in it.' So I changed it immediately and the rest of the way it was Spartans. I didn't have anybody call me up and protest or even talk about it. I thought, well, maybe it's going to work. The next day the student newspaper used the name Spartan—and the baby was born."

That story in *The State Journal* read as follows:

"Fort Benning, Ga., April 3—The Michigan State College baseball team hopped a rattler here last night for Macon, Georgia, where the northerners stack up against the Mercer University nine in their third game Saturday afternoon. The Fort Benning Officers heaved a sigh of relief when Coach John Kobs bundled his rampaging Spartons aboard the train, for during the afternoon, they had mauled another army pitcher and came through to a 4 to 1 victory over the Officers."

TEAM OF THE YEAR

The *Wolverine Yearbook* bluntly opens their commentary with: "The 1926 baseball squad was the most successful in the history of the college." It could also be said that it was the first Aggie-Spartan team to open the season with a Southern trip. Their 13 Ws during the season included victories over Bradley, Michigan, Notre Dame and Western Michigan.

1926 baseball team. (Front row, left to right): D. Haskins, G. Kuhn, captain H. Kiebler, H. Wakefield, P. Fremont, R. Spiekerman. (Second row, left to right) F. Rinehart, C. Baynes, A. Tolles, D. Fleser, G. Rowley, D. Zimmerman. (Back row, left to right) Manager G. Brown, coach J. Kobs, trainer J. Heppinstall.

MAKING HISTORY

Some team uniforms of 1925-1926 reflected the change in the school name from Michigan Agriculture College to Michigan State College. The lettering on both the basketball and baseball uniforms changed from Michigan Aggies to Michigan State. Whereas the 1925 cross country shirts displayed a small block "S," track and field replaced the classic intertwined MAC with a large, full front block "S" on the singlet. The swimming and diving tank suits had the stenciled MSC letters on the front with the athlete's number.

The date of Feb. 27, 1926, can be placed next to Feb. 12, 1972, as another significant date in Michigan State track and field history. On both of these Saturdays a pair of sprint stars registered world-record times. In 1926 it was Fred Alderman and Bohn Grim, and 46 years later it would be Herb Washington and Marshall Dill. The story of 1926 comes from the Illinois relays at Champaign-Urbana. First, Bohn Grim was clocked in at 7.6 seconds for the 75-yard sprint to tie a mark that had originally been set in 1891. Then in the 300-yard dash, Fred Alderman defeated Roland Locke of the University of Nebraska in a world record-tying time of 31.2. That spring, Locke would capture NCAA titles in both the 100- and 220-yard dashes.

College Field was first put in use in 1902. At what point in history did College Field become *Old* College Field? Would it have been as early as 1926? In a May 26 story for his paper, *The State Journal*, George Alderton came close while referring to the site as *historic* College Field.

GREAT STATE DATES

Football—**October 17, 1925 (H):** Coach Young secretly whisked his players to Pine Lake on the Thursday evening before the Centre game. Without distractions, the team ran through light signal drills on the dance floor at Joe Palmer's roadhouse on the north end of the lake. Following a light lunch on Saturday, the team motored directly to the stadium. Perhaps the idea of isolating the team was effective. With little time remaining in what was billed as the first big intersectional game in the new stadium, sophomore Paul Smith from Saginaw suc-

cessfully booted a game-winning 58-yard drop-kick field goal to defeat the Bo McMillan-coached "Praying Colonels" of Centre College, 15-13. Starting in 1920, this small school, located in Danville, Ky., had gained national recognition by taking measure of everyone in its path. Their defeat of Harvard was a particular eye-opener to the nation. Coach McMillan would later return to East Lansing in 1933 as head coach of Kansas State and again in 1939 in a similar capacity with Indiana University. He would conclude his coaching career as head man of the Detroit Lions.

Football—**November 7, 1925 (H):** Playing amidst a torrent of rain and before a handful of spectators, Michigan State defeated Toledo on a mismatch, 58-0. Scoring three touchdowns during their first four possessions, they led 20-0 by halftime and then broke the game wide open with four TDs in the third quarter and twom more in the final period. The solitary flaw in the MSC attack was the lack of consistency in conversion attempts, making only four-of-nine attempts at dropkicking the soggy ball. As coach Young freely substituted, quarterback Richard Lyman led the way with three touchdowns while Roy Spiekerman, Jim McCosh, Bohn Grim, Les Fouts, Paul Smith and Perry Fremont were credited with one score apiece. This would be the only time the two schools would face on the gridiron.

Basketball—**December 19, 1925 (A):** The undefeated MAC team won its third straight in a come-from-behind victory over the University of Chicago 28-21. After being outscored 16-8 in the opening 20 minutes, the young Spartans, with four sophomores as starters, began playing like veterans. By the time the game clock had reached five minutes to play, they had finally gained the lead and were never threatened thereafter.

Basketball—**February 19, 1926 (H):** John Kobs's crew snapped out of an extended nine-game losing streak by defeating Carnegie Tech, but it didn't come easily. They trailed 14-8 at intermission, and it would have been more depressing if John Kelly had not been inserted into the contest just prior to the break. The Grand Haven sophomore hit two quick field goals to double the MAC output. Returning from the locker room, the Aggies whittled away at the Tartans' lead and by the end of the third quarter were within one point. For the first time in five weeks the local fans found an opportunity to become excited, as the guys in Green came alive. Ken Drew hit a pair of field goals as did Ollie Hood. Captain Paul "Snoopy"

Hackett contributed a two-pointer, and suddenly the Tech players seemed demoralized. The turn-around was complete, and when the gun sounded the end of the game, the scoreboard read MSC 27, visitors 22.

Track and Field—**February 20, 1926 (H):** The Aggies closed out their home indoor season with a 47 1/2-38 1/2 defeat of Western State. The meet went down to the closing relay. Had the Teachers won the race, they would have logged a one-point victory. The MSC quartet of Russell Lord, Horace Farley, Bohn Grim and Fred Alderman took care of that by combining for an easy win, as anchorman Alderman crossed the finish line 30 feet in front.

Baseball—**April 3, 1926 (A):** During the school's first-ever southern trip, Harry Wakefield tossed a beautifully-pitched 1-0 shutout of Mercer College in Macon, Ga. Three of the six hits he surrendered that afternoon came in succession to open the third inning. Calling upon his experience and talent, he forced the clean-up hitter to pop-up and then proceeded to strike out the next two men to end the Bears' only threat of the afternoon.

Baseball—**April 17, 1926 (H):** The Spartans averaged three runs per inning in the first five innings and then tacked on three more in the eighth to down Bradley Poly, 18-3. Don Fleser, en route to his school record .667 batting average, went five-for-five and managed four stolen bases.

Baseball—**April 29, 1926 (H):** Harry Wakefield was touched for three unearned runs in the opening two innings on one hit, two bases on balls and two errors. He then settled down and permitted only two more hits and one walk over the remaining seven innings, as State topped Syracuse, 4-3. Of the Aggies' 12 hits, Del Zimmerman, Carl Baynes, and Harold Kiebler each slashed out three-baggers.

Baseball—**May 1, 1926 (H):** Featuring a team-record 17-run third inning in which the State hitters batted around three times, the Lake Forest Foresters were humiliated 26-5. In only seven of 18 basketball games that winter did the cagers ellipse that point total. The game concluded sometime after 6:00 P.M. and the scorekeepers remained well after that hour to compute the results and verify the final statistics. Of the 22 MSC hits, Don Fleser and Perry Fremont were each credited with three.

Track and Field—**May 1, 1926 (H):** In the first outdoor meet of the season and the inaugural meet at the stadium oval, Ralph Young's crew outscored City College of Detroit (Wayne), 74 1/2 to 56 1/2. Particularly busy were Fred Alderman, Paul Smith and Bohn Grim. Alderman copped four firsts, winning the 100-yard dash, 220-yard dash, javelin and broad jump. Entered in six events, Smith scored first place in the pole vault, and second in the shot put, discus and javelin. Grim placed second in the 100, third in the 220, and set a new school record with a 50.0 in the quarter mile. His time was two-tenths of a second better than the former standard set by DeGay Ernst in 1922.

Tennis—**May 4, 1926 (H):** Victory in four singles matches was all that was needed for State to upset Notre Dame in a Friday afternoon match at the college's clay courts, 4-3. The biggest surprise was Dean Lawrence defeated ND's Donovan in the number-one position, 6-1, 3-6, 6-4. Other winners were D. Stouffer 9-7, 6-1; E.A. Pierson 6-1, 6-2; and Ted Hendershott 6-4, 8-6.

Baseball—**May 24, 1926 (H):** Featuring Del Zimmerman's home-run blast into the Red Cedar River, outstanding defense by Don Haskins and Don Fleser, and clutch pitching by George Kuhn, State defeated the University of Michigan, 8-5. It was the first win in any sport over the archrival in 11 years. A celebration that lasted far into the night included the torching of the abandoned football bleachers that protruded into center field and were an impediment to baseball play. From an interview at his home in Vero Beach, Fla., during the summer of 1995, back up catcher, John Carusuo (BS 27-28) tells of the postgame celebration:

> "A huge postgame celebration started at the Union Building. A band was playing and there was dancing in the street. All of the businesses closed down. The lieutenant governor of the state happened to be driving through on a return trip from Detroit. He joined in, bought all the pies at the local restaurant bakery, and handed them out to the students. Later we all got out on the baseball field and suddenly the old football stands in center field were ablaze. Arm in arm, students were swinging around in a chain of people, and I was on the very end. Being whipped around, I was actually off of my feet, and I recall floating directly over that fire from the bleachers."

Baseball—**June 5, 1926 (H):** Although allowing nine hits to the Notre Dame batsmen, George Kuhn was miserly in the pinch, and his teammates combined four hits with a generous nine Irish errors for a 5-3 victory. As it turned out, the Spartans only needed the first inning, when they chased across four runs.

ATHLETE OF THE YEAR

Sprinter Bohn Grim of Sturgis unfortunately or fortunately (depending on a point of view) came upon the East Lansing scene at the same time (1924-1927) as Fred Alderman. Unfortunately, it was Alderman who was most frequently a step quicker and thus stole the headlines. Fortunately, Bohn was able to team with Fred, and in 1927, along with H.L. Henson and Forrest Lang, they became a near unbeatable foursome as they dashed to victory at the Rice, Texas, Ohio and Pennsylvania relays.

Bohn Grim

Grim, captain his junior year, lettered three years in track (1925-1927) and twice in football (1925-1926).

IN THE SPARTLITE

Baseball: Weather permitting, full houses were expected at College Field during the baseball season.

Basketball: Coach John Kobs began the 1925-1926 season with four outstanding recruits, including three members of the Jackson High School championship team Leroy "Tot" Russo, and George and Roy Jagnow. In addition, one of the greatest centers ever developed in the Lansing area, Torrance Johnson, came to MSC. The expectation of success was short lived. Johnson and George Jagnow were declared academically ineligible shortly before the season opened. Then the second blow hit. As the winter term rolled around, Roy Jagnow and Russo were also lost to scholastics. Coach Kobs could only wonder what might have been.

The season opened with three straight wins in December over Olivet, Adrian and the University of Chicago. Never would even the least optimistic fan ever have considered the possibility that MSC would register only two more victories in the remaining 15-game schedule.

The less-than-impressive 5-13 season record was punctuated by the fact that only six team members would earn varsity awards. They were captain Paul Hackett, Clarence Cole, Ken Drew, Charles Fredericks, Oliver Hood and Louis Smith.

On June 3, 1926, it was disclosed that Benjamin Francis VanAlstyne had been hired from Ohio Wesleyan to succeed John Kobs who would now devote his time totally to hockey and baseball. As had been the situation with Kobs, VanAlstyne's responsibilities would include coaching freshman football. John Kobs could now focus on his "love"—baseball. He would patrol the Spartan dugout for 38 more seasons.

Cross Country: Along with two other outsiders (Notre Dame and Marquette), MSC entered the 16th running of the Western Conference meet, hosted by the University of Michigan on November 21. The Aggies finished in a tie with Northwestern for the tenth and final spot. It would be 25 years before Michigan State, upon gaining conference membership, would again vie for Big Ten honors in cross country.

Fencing: Under the supervision of captain Ross E. Larson of the Military Science department, an all-col-

lege fencing tournament was held on Jan. 16, 1926. The top three finishers were Max Goodwin, Gordon Jarman and T.E. Carbine. Then in May, an announcement was released by the athletic department officially recognizing the sport of fencing as the latest minor sport at MAC and that yet another all-college tournament was called for. Again, Max Goodwin emerged as the top swordsman and was chosen captain of the team that would face Michigan in the gymnasium on May 29. Josef Waffa, a graduate student from Egypt, volunteered to act as coach. The incredible neophytes defeated the Wolverines, 10-6.

Football: Don Haskins, tackle and captain of the 1925 team, missed the 58-0 win over Toledo University. In an unusual ploy, Coach Young had sent Haskins, his captain, to Iowa City, Iowa, on a mission of scouting the season-ending opponent, the University of Wisconsin. There is no recorded evidence as to the impact of Haskin's report, but the final outcome read 21-10 in favor of the Badgers. The Wisconsin athletic director, George Little, came into the State dressing room after the game and told the visitors; "I want to congratulate you on your fight and tell you that we regard you as real rivals and a team of conference caliber." Also traveling to Madison was MSC's 60-piece ROTC military band. Upon concluding their halftime maneuvers, the band received a standing ovation from the assembled crowd.

Hockey: Athletic director Ralph Young returned from the December Western Conference meeting of coaches with details of a proposed hockey league. Teams projected into the plan were Minnesota, Wisconsin, Michigan, Notre Dame, St. Thomas, Carlton, Hamlin and Michigan State.

Although the idea of a league never reached fruition, the board in control of athletics did seize the opportunity to authorize that an outdoor rink be built immediately east of the tennis courts behind the Women's Building (Morrill Hall). The rink would be 200'x100' and surrounded by boards four feet high, electrically lighted (six 2,000-watt bulbs), and later furnished with a warming house. By mid-January the project was completed and the rink was in full use.

Establishing a season record of 0-4, there was little to get excited about. Yet the performance in the season finale, a 2-0 loss to Minnesota, was most impressive. The game was scoreless entering the final stanza as George DeLisle, the Aggie goalie, kicked out 13 shots in the first two periods. The Gophers did manage to score twice in the final period for the win. As was typical of the time, MAC used a total of only four spares during the contest. Between periods, Coach Iverson of Minnesota, a member of the 1912 U.S. Olympic figure skating team, gave an exhibition of his talents.

Swimming and Diving: Among the freshman group of 1926 was Joe Katsunuma from Hawaii. His father, a U.S. government official, had sent his son off to attend the University of Michigan. Katsunuma caught the wrong train out of Chicago and ended up in Lansing rather than Ann Arbor. He enrolled at MAC and quickly displayed his aquatic prowess on the freshman swimming team. Unfortunately, he became lonesome. Learning that a fairly large conclave of Pacific-rim students was enrolled at the University of Kansas, he transferred there prior to his sophomore year.

Tennis: Grand Rapids Junior College was a surprise winner in the state intercollegiates held on the new MAC courts. The Aggies settled for the third spot behind Grand Rapids and Western State Normal. In a positive look to the future, the Michigan Agriculture College freshman team placed fifth among the record number of entries, which included representatives from the University of Detroit, Detroit City College, Albion, Adrian, Michigan Normal, Olivet, Central Normal of Mt. Pleasant, Highland Park Junior College, Kalamazoo College and Battle Creek College.

Track and Field: Michigan State turned some heads at the Ohio relays in Columbus when the quartet of Horace Farley, D.M. Van Noppen, Fred Alderman and Bohn Grim sprinted to first in the quarter-mile relay. The half-mile team captured second, the medley relay foursome was third and the two-mile quartet was fourth.

The result of the MSC-Iowa State meet run on the new stadium oval was undecided until the final event, the mile relay. Running the third and fourth legs, Alderman and Grim could not close the gap of 75 yards, and the Cyclones won the race and the meet, 67-64. Alderman's anchor lap of 48.4 was one second off the world record and swifter than the 48.7 which won that year's NCAA championships. Fred had concluded a busy afternoon after finishing first in the 100, 220 and broad jump. It would be the final time the two schools would go head-to-head in track and field.

Although featuring such stars as Alderman, Grim and distance ace Henry Wylie, Ralph Young's squad was not deep in talent. This was exemplified in the 11th An-

nual state intercollegiate meet held in the new stadium on May 22. While capturing six first places the Spartans failed to score in high hurdles, high jump, low hurdles, shot put and javelin. Team scoring placed MSC in third position: Michigan Normal 48 2/3, Detroit City College 44 2/3 and Michigan State 42 1/3.

With the Western Conference now a closed meet, the Central Intercollegiate Conference was created and conducted its first outdoor meet at Milwaukee. Victorious in the broad jump (22' 9-1/4") and both the 100- and 220-yard dashes (10.2 and 22.4), Alderman was easily the star of the meet. Ivan Tillotson won the discus event with a toss of 133' 7-3/4". Team scoring totals were as follows: Notre Dame 72 1/2, MSC 47, Marquette 36 1/2 and Butler 10.

Alderman, Grim, Wylie, and Ivan Tillotson represented State at the NCAA Championships in Chicago. Alderman was the only one to place. The Lansing native flashed brilliant form to take fourth in the 100 behind Locke of Nebraska, Hester of Michigan and Sharkey of Miami. He finished third in the 220, following Locke and Sharkey. Within a few days after the meet, Alderman was in the hospital undergoing an operation for a hernia.

Wrestling: One of the matches in the February 6 loss to Cornell College (Iowa) became the highlight of an ignominious season. That afternoon Ken Landsburg of Deckerville faced the 1924 USA Olympian who was billed as the world's amateur middleweight champion. To the delight of the home fans, the 158-pound Aggie managed to stay off his back and actually lost in points only by the narrowest of margins. Landsburg's twin brother was the team's back-up competitor in the 145-pound class.

Posting an unimpressive overall three-year record of 2-12, wrestling coach Brick Burhans decided it was time to step aside following the 1926 season. In 1935 he would resurface to become the school's first boxing coach and then, following a seven-year stint in that capacity, would complete his Spartan years solely in the role of assistant professor within the department of physical education.

1920s baseball action at College Field.

SPARTAN SCRAPBOOK
—— HOCKEY COACHES (1925-2003) ——

1922 hockey team

Amo Bessone (1951-79)

Rick Comley (2003-)

Harold Paulson (1950-51)

Ron Mason (1980-2002)

Pictured elsewhere: John Kobs 1925-31 BS

BS see baseball coaches

TALES TO TELL

Upon his entry into the university's Athletic Hall of Fame in 1993, Fred Alderman responded to the question of his most memorable moment as a Spartan:

"I consider my best performance was winning the 100-yard and 220-yard sprints in the 1927 NCAA championships at Chicago's Soldier Field. In the 100, both Anderson of the University of Washington and Hermanson of Northwestern were both ahead of me with only five yards remaining. Coach Young was sitting in the stands at about that point along the course and he was convinced I would be settling for third. Fortunately, they both straightened up at the tape while I leaned in to get the win. My teammate Bohn Grim was a close fourth. The competition in the 220 was not quite as challenging. I coasted the last 50 yards and finished in 21.1 seconds.

Perhaps my best indoor race was the 300-yard dash at the Illinois relays in February of 1926. It was

Fred Alderman (center) takes first place and Bohn Grim (far right) places fourth in the 1927 NCAA 100-yard dash.

my best effort for two reasons. First, in the process I defeated Roland Locke of Nebraska, who would win both sprints at the NCAA championships that spring. Secondly, my time of 31.1 tied the world's indoor record. In recognition, coach Ralph Young later presented me with a miniature gold track shoe with a diamond in the toe. I prize it next to my Olympic gold medal (1,600-meter relay).

HEADLINES of 1927

- Charles Lindbergh, in his airplane the "Spirit of St. Louis," becomes the first pilot to fly the Atlantic solo.
- In the motion picture business, The "Age of the Talkies" arrives with Warner Brothers' release of *The Jazz Singer*, starring Al Jolson.
- Babe Ruth sets the home-run record when he hits 60 for the season.
- The Holland Tunnel, linking New York and New Jersey, is opened to vehicular traffic.

SCOREBOARD

	W	L	T	Avg.
Baseball	13	8	0	.619
Track and Field	4	0	0	1.000
Football	3	4	1	.438
Basketball	7	11	0	.389
Tennis	2	7	1	.250
Cross Country	0	3	0	.000
Swimming and Diving	4	3	0	.571
Wrestling	4	3	0	.571
Hockey	1	3	0	.250
Fencing	2	2	0	.500

TEAM OF THE YEAR

By the spring of 1927 coach Ralph Young had assembled one of the most talented groups of track and field athletes ever to represent Michigan State. It was a squad particularly endowed with sprinters: seniors Fred Alderman and Bohn Grim of Sturgis, and sophomores Lyle Henson of Lansing, Forrest Lang of Beaverton, and Bill Kroll of Detroit. The undefeated team was composed of more than sprinters. Harold McAtee of Dundee was a splendid pole vaulter; Ivan Tillotson from Petosky and Paul Smith of Saginaw added points in the weight events; and the veteran Henry Wylie from Sparta teamed with newcomers Roy Severance of Decker and Meredith Clark from Vicksburg to form an intimidating distance trio.

MAKING HISTORY

By the fall of 1926 MSC had assembled its most complete athletic staff to date. New additions were Ralph Leonard and Sterry Brown, both of whom had come to East Lansing that September. Leonard, who had most recently coached at Brooklyn Polytechnical Institute, was hired as varsity and freshman coach for wrestling with added responsibilities of reviving boxing and initiating the sports of soccer and lacrosse. Brown, coming from the University of Illinois, would become the new varsity-freshman coach for swimming and diving. The two augmented the staff of Athletic Director Ralph Young (football and track), who was ably assisted by "Mike" Casteel and Barney Traynor, John Kobs (baseball and hockey), Ben VanAlstyne (basketball) and Morton Mason (cross country and assistant in track and field).

1927 track and field team. (Front row, left to right) Williams, W. Kroll, H. Wylie. R. Severance, F. Alderman, B. Grim, F. Lang, L. Henson and T. Willmarth. (Midddle row, left to right) P. Smith, H. McAtee, V. Rossman, C. Passink, M. Clark, R. Lord, E. Wareham and R. Olsen. (Back row, left to right) Trainer J. Heppinstall, coach R. Young, I. Tillotson, J. Joachim, D. Davis, B. Diller, A. McCabe, assistant coach Casteel and manager W. Sparling.

In his annual report of 1926 Ralph Young wrote:

"Lacrosse, a game which is causing so much favorable comment today and which is highly developed among the colleges of the East and Canada, will be introduced at Michigan State during the spring term. Lacrosse is a combination of basketball and football, and is often said to be the fastest of all team games. If sufficient interest is shown, a game to be played during commencement week will be scheduled with some Canadian team. This will enable the students and alumni to see a real game, and it is predicted lacrosse will win a place in the hearts of all."

It would be 43 years before hearts would find a place for lacrosse.

GREAT STATE DATES

Football—**October 2, 1926 (H):** Using an all-sophomore line over a great portion of the game, State struggled a bit before putting the Kalamazoo Hornets aside, 9-0. As for the scoring, it was all Paul Smith, the Saginaw junior. The Spartans' lone touchdown came in the opening quarter when Smith grabbed a short pass from Rudy Boehringer. He then baffled the defense with his side-stepping and change of pace as he dodged 50 yards into the end zone. Then, in the third period, Paul concluded the day's scoring with a successful field goal after the Spartans failed to score a TD with possession on the Kazoo four-yard line.

Basketball—**January 8, 1927 (H):** Following three straight road losses (Michigan, Chicago and Northwestern), the Spartans returned home for a thrilling win over Marquette. It was the first match-up within the newly formed Central Intercollegiate Conference (Marquette, Notre Dame, Butler and Michigan State). With the Hilltoppers leading 30-28, Monty Hood dribbled the length of the floor and tossed in the tying basket with two seconds remaining. Then, within the five-minute overtime, VanAlstyne's men outscored the visitors 5-3, for the 35-33 victory.

Basketball—**January 15, 1927 (A):** Following the loss to Butler on the night before, the Spartans traveled to Ft. Wayne, where they took the floor against the Maroon and White of Concordia College. The final score, 45-25, would end up being the second highest point to-

tal and largest MSC victory margin of the year. Verne Dickeson, with 13, and Carl "Red" Colvin, with 10, were the scoring leaders.

Wrestling—**February 11, 1927 (H):** Led by falls from Foster Mohrhard (125 pounds), Billy Haskins (135 pounds) and Allerd Berquist (145 pounds), Coach Leonard's men completed a rare shutout, 36-0 over Notre Dame. It would be another 59 years before the two schools would again meet on the wrestling mat.

Wrestling—**February 26, 1927 (H):** From the time the husky Ohio University crew walked onto the gymnasium floor until the final bout, the record crowd of 1,300 was kept on edge. The excitement of the evening began with the opening match when Frank Gibbs, the MSC flyweight, gained a time advantage victory over his opponent to finish the dual-meet season undefeated. MSC then won three of the next five matches to lead 14-10. Only the heavyweights remained. The Ohio Conference champions needed only a pin for a one-point victory. Fortunately, Fred Barratt, State's "heavy," proved to be more powerful than his opponent, and although it took overtime, he gained a decision and State won the meet, 17-10. Jimmy Hasselman had broadcast the entire festivities on WKAR.

Swimming and Diving—**March 4, 1927 (H):** The 1927 squad was applauded as the school's most successful swimming and diving team to date, winning four of seven dual meets. The featured home meet was the season-closing 45-24 victory over Wooster College, in which three varsity records were lowered: the 240-yard freestyle relay, the 180-yard medley relay, and the 100-yard freestyle. The highly staged event was apparently intimidating to the visitors. Years later, a member of that Wooster team shared a memory with his friend, MSC's Al Ellinger, a member of the MSC team:

"Our team had endured a 12-hour train ride to get to Lansing only to find a huge tank., 90'x40', with a crowd of some 500 fans in the stands. The MSC athletic department even had cameras in action taking movies of the swimmers for training purposes. Our lads were very used to a very small pool and rarely did the students come to the meets. I had no idea why we were swimming against a power like Michigan State, but there we were, and a swimming lesson we got."

Fencing—**March 19, 1927 (H):** The final meet of the season, against Michigan, was somewhat of an extravaganza. Both the varsity and freshmen were in competition. Also, interesting side attractions to the afternoon were several exhibition bouts by members of the Detroit Fencing Club. In addition, the college band was on hand to provide music at appropriate times. It all proved to be a fitting close to the season, as both the MSC varsity and freshman teams won their matches by identical scores, 5-4.

Baseball—**May 7, 1927 (A):** Yielding only four hits, Albert "Lefty" Tolles handed Notre Dame only its fourth loss of the season, 4-1. Reporting on the pitching performance, *The Lansing State Journal* writer suggested the "bespectacled Tolles may suffer from astigmatism, but has a very well defined location of the home plate." Forrest Rinehart scored the game's first run in the seventh after connecting on a terrific triple to deep right. Earlier the partisan South Bend crowd applauded the junior left fielder in the sixth when he raced to the foul line and speared a sinking fly ball with one hand.

Baseball—**June 1, 1927 (H):** Riding the solid performance of their ace pitcher, "Lefty" Tolles, the Spartans topped the University of Michigan, 4-1. The largest home crowd of the spring cheered loudly when third baseman Gail Rowley opened the scoring in the third inning with a two-run homer into the far reaches of center field. Nebelung, the losing pitcher for the U of M, had been a member of the Spartan freshman team before transferring.

Fred Alderman

backed down. He earned points when needed in races ranging from 100 to 440 yards, plus the broad jump or javelin field events.

ATHLETE OF THE YEAR

While in attendance at MSC from 1924-1927, Fred Alderman, a Lansing native, gained national attention as he sprinted to victory in major track and field meets from Texas to New York. He reached the pinnacle of his Spartan career in 1927 when he finished first in both the 100-yard and 220-yard dashes at the NCAA championships in Chicago. In doing so he became the school's first national collegiate champion in any sport. One year after graduation, in 1928, Alderman became Michigan State's first Olympian as a member of the gold medal 1,600-meter relay team that established a world's record at Amsterdam. He was a fearless competitor who never

IN THE SPARTLITE

Baseball: In summarizing the season, the 1927 team averaged more than eight runs per game, while the opposition made little more than three. The leading hitters were Del Zimmerman .545, Don Fleser .404, Carl Baynes .363, Gail Rowley .310 and Forrest Rinehart .348. A statistic of note: the outfield went through the entire season without committing an error.

Basketball: Upon defeating MSC 53-16, Butler University administered the most humiliating loss ever on a State basketball team. Although this 1927 edition of Butler basketball was not one of their best, on this evening it seemed that every shot tossed up found its mark.

Cross Country: Not one member of the 1926 varsity team had competitive experience prior to enrolling at MSC; thus the 0-3 dual-meet season was not unexpected. Yet, that same crew combined for a surprising victory in the inaugural Central Intercollegiate Conference meet. Headed by captain Roy Severance, MSC scored 37 points. They were followed by Marquette 47, Notre Dame 55 and Butler.

The most excitement generated that fall came from the freshmen team headed by Detroiters Lauren Brown and Ted Willmarth. "Brownie" romped to an easy first-place victory at the state intercollegiates, finishing a full quarter-mile ahead of the field.

Fencing: A graduate student from Egypt, Josef Waffa, continued as the volunteer coach for four seasons, 1926-1929. Additionally, in September of 1927, he began teaching fencing classes, open to both men and women. A total of 18 co-eds signed up that fall term. The end result was the formation of the Spartan Fencing Club, an organization including both genders that was chartered to promote greater interest in the sport. A series of exhibitions was held in East Lansing People's Church during the winter term.

Football: In March of 1926, assistant coach "Tarz" Taylor had "officially" been granted a leave of absence. In reality, Ralph Young had become disenchanted with his assistant, feeling that he fraternized too closely with the players. Taylor did not return to MSC but eventually ended up as a line coach at Marquette. Barney Traynor, former Colgate star of the early 20s and, more recently, line coach at Wisconsin, was hired to replace Taylor. He took immediate control and began by assuming the responsibilities of supervising spring practices.

Team captain-elect Martin Rummell would sustain injuries from an automobile accident in the summer of 1926 and be lost for the entire season.

President Kenyon Butterfield was a special guest among the 10,000 spectators for the Cornell-MSC game at Ithaca, N.Y. on October 16. He likely watched the 24-14 loss with mixed emotions. The star of the game was the Big Red quarterback who, on that afternoon, gained more yardage rushing than the entire State offense. That young man was Vic Butterfield, the MSC president's son.

Hockey: In a January 28 *State News* story, a sports writer predicted a bright future for the emerging sport of ice hockey. Little did he know how intuitive he would be:

"Hockey has been coming to the fore with unheard of rapidity, and the experts agree that it is only a question of time until every town in the northern part of the country will boast a team. The puck-chasing game is without a doubt the fastest of any game."

Swimming and Diving: One star of 1927 was Al Ellinger, who became the first Aggie to swim the 100-yard freestyle in less than one minute. Other standouts were Reinold Thomas, winner of the most thrilling race of the season when he defeated the Notre Dame captain and star Jerry Rhodes in the 200-yard breaststroke, and Edward "Red" Cook, who was not graded below a seven in any dive during the dual-meet season.

Although neither Thomas nor Cook reached the finals, they became the first to represent the school at the NCAA championship meet. "Red" literally fell from contention during the preliminaries when he slipped from the board during one dive.

A sample of team records established through 1927 included 50-yard freestyle 26.4, 100-yard freestyle 59.8, 100-yard breaststroke 1:25.1, 200-yard breaststroke 3:02.6 and the 150-yard backstroke 1:56.7.

Tennis: Following a not-too-successful dual meet season (2-7-1), the Spartans hosted the State Intercollegiate tournament. With more than 100 players representing every tennis college in the state except Michigan, three days were needed to complete the pairings. In a major surprise, Merwyn Farleman and captain Ted Hendershott captured the doubles competition for MSC.

Track and Field: Michigan State emerged from the Illinois Relay Carnival, which attracted entries from 69 schools, as a bona fide contender for Midwest honors. The Spartans captured two first places, tied for another, captured a second in the 1,500-meter run and took a close third in a fast mile relay. Fredy Alderman won the 300-yard crown for the second consecutive year, taking an easy first in 31.6, four-tenths slower than his own world record. Bohn Grim won the 75-yard dash in 7.7 seconds. Harold McAtee, an outstanding sophomore, surprised by tying for first in the pole vault at 12'6".

Lyle Henson and Forrest Lang, joined seniors Alderton and Grim to form a speedy half-mile relay team. With Bill Kroll as an alternate, no group of Spartan trackmen had ever collected more honors, as they dashed to victories at the Rice, Texas, Ohio and Pennsylvania relays. In addition, these speedsters won the quarter-mile

trophy at the Rice and Texas relays. They were second in the mile relay at Ohio, and won the college division of that four-lap event in the Penn Relays. They gathered more than 30 gold and silver wristwatches, in addition to an impressive array of trophies, medals and ribbons.

Captain Alderman added to his laurels in the IC4A meet at Philadelphia when he displayed his versatility with a brilliant victory in the quarter-mile race. Although it was his first intercollegiate appearance at that distance, his time of 48.3 would prove to be two-tenths faster than the winning time of that spring's NCAA championship meet.

In addition to smashing school standards in the 440-yard relay, the 880-yard relay and the mile relay, six other individual records were bettered by the 1927 track and field team. Alderman graduated with new records in the 100 (9.6), 220 (20.5) and 440 (48.3). McAtee raised the pole vault mark to 13' 3-5/8". Smith bettered the shot put record with a heave of 43' 10-3/8", and Joe Joachim established a new mark in the javelin at 161' 6-5/8".

Wrestling: By padding the walls with protective mats, the room in the gymnasium formerly known as the visiting team room was turned over to the varsity. Lockers were in place and a series of pulley ropes, designed by the new coach, Ralph Leonard, were installed for strengthening back muscles. The former varsity wrestling room was made available for the freshmen.

From left to right, Michigan State track stars Bill Kroll, Fred Alderman, Bohn Grim, Lyle Henson, and Forrest Lang pose with their many honors.

MSC
1927-1928

TALES TO TELL

John Caruso (BS 27,28), from an interview at his home in Vero Beach, Fla., during the summer of 1995:

"Back then we played because we loved to play the game of baseball. We had no vision of getting into the big leagues. It was an honor to win a letter. That was the important thing, winning a letter. We proudly wore our 'S' sweaters around campus, and we also wore hats with an 'S' on them.

As far as financial assistance, it would be in the form of a job someplace. I recall working on field trips for the agricultural department and also working for Jack Heppinstall in the training room.

We began our practices in February with workouts in the livestock arena [located south of the International Center and razed in 1997]. The lighting was bad there, and of course we gained no experience handling balls hit into the air. In the second game of the 1928 southern trip, we were at Ft. Benning, and I was having all sorts of problems judging some high pop ups (as the catcher). After about the third one, our pitcher, Lefty Tolles, comes off of the mound and says, 'Wait a minute, let me get you an umbrella before you kill yourself.'"

TEAM OF THE YEAR

All members of the undefeated cross country team of 1927 were awarded major varsity "S" letters. This was unprecedented. In the past, only occasional outstanding individuals of minor sports would be singled out for the honor. Led by Lauren Brown and Elmer Roossien, the squads of 1928 and 1929 also went undefeated.

HEADLINES of 1928

- Sir Alexander Fleming, an English bacteriologist, discovers penicillin.
- The public first meets Mickey Mouse in Walt Disney's cartoon, "Steamboat Willie," the first animated film to use sound.
- Jerome Kern and Oscar Hammerstein write the score for *Showboat*, which includes the song "Ol' Man River."
- The first coast-to-coast bus service is offered by the Yellow Bus Line. The trip from Los Angeles to New York City takes five days and 14 hours.

SCOREBOARD

	W	L	T	Avg.
Baseball	11	7	0	.611
Track and Field	2	2	0	.500
Football	4	5	0	.444
Basketball	11	4	0	.733
Tennis	5	2	0	.714
Cross Country	3	0	0	1.000
Swimming and Diving no team, pool unavailable				
Wrestling	4	2	0	.667
Hockey	3	3	0	.500
Fencing	2	3	0	.400
Golf	6	2	0	.750

MAKING HISTORY

The football goalposts, which had previously been on the goal line, were moved ten yards onto the back line of the end zone where they have remained ever since.

For the first time, a postseason basketball honor team was chosen. The Central Intercollegiate Conference (Notre Dame, Marquette, Butler and MSC) first team selections included Verne Dickeson at left forward. Carl Felt was selected as the second team center with Ken Drew gaining honorable mention.

Marking a new era in intercollegiate wrestling, the first NCAA championships were conducted on March 30-31, 1928, at Iowa State College in Ames. Although individuals were crowned in seven weight classes, no team title would be awarded until 1929.

1927 cross country team. (Below, left to right) Coach M. Mason, I. Crow, F. Roberts, captain H. Wylie, E. Roossien, T. Willmarth, L. Brown and manager A. Carlson. L. Dowd is missing from the photo.

GREAT STATE DAYS

Football—October 1, 1927 (H): Coach Young was in an experimental mood when the Spartans engaged Ohio University in the second game of the season. He started three first-year men in the backfield along with captain Paul Smith. Henry Schau was at fullback, Harold Wilson at one halfback position and Verne Dickeson at the other. This foursome's performance was impressive, as they accounted for three touchdowns in the opening quarter and a fourth in the third period. It took only three minutes to score the first time as Schau went over from the one-yard line. Although Smith was credited with the second touchdown, Wilson contributed most of the yardage leading to the score. The third and fourth TDs were the result of Schau-to-Dickeson passes. One telling statistic confirms the futility of the Bobcat offense. They connected on only 14-of-40 passes with eight being intercepted.

Cross Country—November 5, 1927 (A): Led by the 1-2 finish of Lauren Brown and Elmer Roossien, the Spartans topped the favored U of M, 20-35. "Brownie's" winning time of 25:31.7 was the year's fastest time over five miles and it broke the Ann Arbor course record of 25:59.7 established by Phelps of Iowa in winning the 1924 conference run. Brown finished 150 yards ahead of his teammate, Roossien, who in turn was a safe margin over the fastest Michigan finisher. Other MSC finishers were Ted Willmarth (fifth), Henry Wylie (sixth), Floyd Roberts (seventh) and Irvin Crow (eighth).

Football—November 11, 1927 (H): Michigan State joined 44 other schools across the nation to host a Friday afternoon game to commemorate Armistice Day, acknowledging the cessation of hostilities in World War I, 1918. Perhaps the idea was to secure another day for a traditional annual game such as Thanksgiving Day or New Year's Day, but the idea never really stuck. By 1928, State was back to primarily Saturday-only games. In that 1927 contest, the Aggies trailed Albion 6-0 at the half but bounced back after intermission. Verne Dickeson climaxed an early third-quarter drive with a seven-yard plunge into the end zone. The score was tied 6-6 following three periods. "Duke" Schau, the husky sophomore fullback, was used repeatedly in a 55-yard drive that culminated with the winning touchdown. On their very next possession the Spartans drove to the Britons' 31-yard line, from where Ernest Deacon sprinted off right tackle into the end zone for the final score: MSC 20, Albion 6.

Wrestling—January 14, 1928 (H): By a score of 36-0, the wrestlers opened the season with a shutout of Lawrence College from Appleton, Wis. Excluding the 115-pound win by forfeit, all other matches, except the 175 class, were won by a fall or throwing of the opponent. The Vikings were obviously at a disadvantage. This was the school's first collegiate meet. Prior to this season, wrestling had only been an intramural sport. Furthermore, the team had no coach and consequently supervised its own workouts and negotiated its own schedule and travel.

Basketball—January 30, 1928 (H): The impressive finish in the defeat of Hope College was a highlight of the 1927-1928 season. Entering the final eight minutes of play, MSC was leading by the narrowest of margins, 22-21. Thereafter, the Spartans hit for 14 straight points and held the Dutchmen scoreless. In that stretch run, Dickeson, who was the game's leading scorer with 16 points, netted five field goals, while Carl Felt and Fred DenHerder each hit for one bucket.

Hockey—February 1, 1928 (H): The Spartans pulled off the school's first-ever win over the University of Michigan, 2-1. The Wolverines were recognized as better skaters, but they were unable to break through the airtight defense massed around Plaunt, the winning goalie, who made 23 stops on the afternoon. Jones, his counterpart from the U of M, was called upon to make only 10 saves. Burris and Hancock, the MSC defenders, not only checked the Wolverine attack in splendid style, but were significant factors in the few offensive drives marshaled by the State skaters. Within a minute following Michigan's only score at the 17-minute mark of the opening period, Burris carried the puck down the right side, through the defense, and sent it into the net to even the score. *The Lansing State Journal* story described the winning marker at the 8:35 mark of the second period:

> "At the outset of the second period, State took the advantage of a strong wind and launched several drives at the Michigan goal. About the middle of the stanza, three Spartans skated in on Jones, and Harris passed to Hancock who beat the Wolverine captain with a pretty shot."

Basketball—February 3, 1928 (H): The 26-16 victory over Notre Dame was a particularly cherished win, as the team had suffered a 29-25 triple-overtime loss at South Bend one week earlier. The Irish entered this sec-

ond game with only one loss and had numbered among its victims Minnesota, Iowa, Northwestern, Wisconsin, Princeton and Pennsylvania. To the delight of nearly 3,000 fans who packed the gymnasium, State outscored the Irish 11-1 in the final 13 minutes, and that was the game. It was the first win over ND since 1923.

Basketball—**January 13 (H) and February 17 (H) 1928:** MSC managed to top the University of Detroit twice, with both wins coming in overtime under similar circumstances, 27-23 and 17-13. Trailing in the January game, 23-22, with ten seconds remaining, Carl Felt was fouled and calmly dropped in the tying point, forcing overtime. In the return match at East Lansing, it was Felt who again sank a free throw to send the game into OT, this time at 13-13. In both overtime sessions the Spartans outscored the U of D 4-0. In the February game, a rare technical foul was charged to the *visitors* for abusive fan conduct.

Basketball—**February 25, 1928 (H):** Closing out the 1928 schedule with a 30-25 victory over Marquette, State finished the home season undefeated while posting an outstanding 11-4 overall record. It was a game won at the free-throw strip, where the Spartans outscored the visitors 14-7.

Golf—**May 9, 1928 (A):** *The Michigan State News* carried only one story all spring long pertaining to the fledgling sport of golf. It covered the season's first match, a 3-0 win:

> "The newly formed Michigan State College golf team golfed its way to victory over the Flint Junior College outfit at Flint on Wednesday. The Spartans won all three matches played. Today the Spartan team will go to Grand Rapids to play the Grand Rapids Junior College team.
>
> The team is managed by John Kelly, and much enthusiasm is being shown by the candidates for the team. In the Flint match, Minier, Connelan and Jack DeLair defeated their opponents in fine shape. In the Grand Rapids meet four matches will be played. Bredlow, Campbell, and Cook are among those who are out for the team."

Tennis—**May 12, 1928 (H):** State defeated Notre Dame, 4-3, for their third win of the spring. Paul Kane of Owosso opened the afternoon with a hard-fought victory, 6-4, 4-6, 6-4. Don Swan of Detroit and Ralph Bentley, also of Owosso, following with team points from

the fourth and fifth singles positions. The Kane and Merwyn Farleman doubles victory, 7-5, 3-6, 6-1, cinched the meet for State.

Baseball—**May 15, 1928 (H):** In the Bradley Tech game, the Spartans led 5-4 with two outs in the top of the ninth. Suddenly Braves hitters managed a single and triple off "Lefty" Tolles to tie the score. In the tenth, Bradley kept rolling, as they scored twice and took the lead, 7-5. Then it was State's turn, as two singles and a walk filled the bases. Max Crall knocked in a pair to knot the score, and then Marv Eggert slashed out a game-winning base hit scoring pinch hitter Stan Weed.

Baseball—**June 16, 1928 (H):** Before a commencement week crowd of more than 5,000, the Spartans gained revenge for a heartbreaking extra-inning loss to Michigan on the preceding afternoon. Gerald Byrne moved from his outfield position to the mound, where he outpitched the U of M ace for a 9-4 victory. Byrne, a sophomore from Lowell, aided his own cause with his second homer of the series, this time with two men on base. Having wrapped up the Western Conference title, it was only the third loss of the season for the Wolverines.

Verne Dickeson

ATHLETE OF THE YEAR

Verne "Dick" Dickeson, from Highland Park, was a six-letterman, earning three monograms in football and three in basketball during the seasons of 1927-1929. He was a starting halfback in football during both his junior and senior years, serving as team co-captain in that final season. In basketball, Dickeson was the team's scoring leader both in 1927 and 1928. In 1927, the year he served as captain, Verne scored a total of 162 points. This represented 32 percent of the team's 18-game aggregate of 503. In the following year he scored an even 100 points, which was 21 percent of the 1928 Spartans' total of 473.

IN THE SPARTLITE

Baseball: Albert "Lefty" Tolles, designated captain of the 1928 baseball team, did not remain with the team during his senior year. He had been suspended by Coach Kobs for personal reasons. Tolles signed a professional contract with the St. Lous Cardinals while Forrest Rinehart assumed the responsibilities of team captain.

Basketball: State opened the season with a 5-1 record followed by three losses in a row. VanAlstyne's crew then closed out the season with six straight Ws, including "pay backs" over Notre Dame and Marquette. The overall record of 11-4 was the most impressive season since the 1912 team went 12-3.

Cross Country: At the Central Intercollegiate Conference (CIC) meet, Lauren Brown gained ample revenge for his only loss of the season when he led Pfleiger, the Marquette star, to the finish line by several hundred yards, while setting a new five-mile course record of 25:45.7. "Brownie's" teammates followed along: Theodore Willmarth (sixth), Elmer Roossien of Grand Haven (seventh), Irvin Crowe of Alpena (eighth), and Henry Wylie of Sparta (ninth). The Aggies easily defended their CIC team title.

Fencing: One of the stars of the 1928 varsity team was a co-ed, Miss Audrey Glenn of West Branch, Mich., who was able to out-duel most of her opponents. Though only decorated with a "minor" letter sweater, she became the first woman to be so honored at Michigan State. By the final meet of the season, another woman, Miss Leah Turner, was also competing for the varsity.

Football: The 1927 game at Ann Arbor was played, for the first time, in the Wolverines' new stadium designed to hold 84,401 fans. A total of 27,864 were on hand for the intrastate battle, won by the U of M, 21-0.

The 25-0 win over Butler was particularly satisfying. The Indianapolis team was coached by George "Potsy" Clark, the man who had left East Lansing following one year (1920) as the Aggie head coach.

The final game of the 1927 schedule was played in Raleigh, N.C., against North Carolina State. It was scheduled so late in the season that the *Wolverine* yearbook referred to it as a postseason game. If team members had envisioned an escape to the more favorable climate of the sunny south, a constant downpour of rain on game day dashed such thoughts. The predictable by-product of lousy weather were the fumbles, and that was exactly the Spartans' undoing in the 19-0 loss.

With a five-year acumulative record of 18-22-1, coach Ralph Young was hearing the murmur of disgruntled fans. The North Carolina State game would be his last as he wisely stepped aside as head football coach.

Golf: Playing without a coach and not "officially" recognized as an MSC varsity sport until 1930, six men ventured into an eight-match schedule, practicing and playing at the Lansing Country Club.

Against the likes of Grand Rapids Junior College and the Detroit School of Law, it could be suggested the team played a "patsy" schedule, but it was a beginning.

Hockey: With the widening of Grand River Avenue, the tennis courts, and thus the ice rink, were removed. A new rink was set up on the parade grounds near the Armory.

The team's first two scheduled home games, Michigan on January 10 and Minnesota on January 16, were cancelled because warm weather had thawed the ice surface. The game with Minnesota was never rescheduled. However, the U of M eventually came to town on February 1.

Swimming and Diving: In what would be considered a recruiting coup by today's standards, a pair of standout swimmers from Detroit Northwestern High School enrolled at State in 1928. They were Horace Craig, a national interscholastic backstroke champion, and John Tate, the Detroit city champion in the freestyle.

The school was forced to abandon intercollegiate swimming during the winter of 1928. Apparently a defective filtering system led state health authorities to rule that only a limited number of swimmers could use the pool each day. As a result, the aquatic classes took precedence; thus, the competitive program was placed in dry dock for the season.

Tennis: In the fall of 1927, the third-ranked player in the nation, George Lott Jr. of Chicago, enrolled at MSC. Before he could play one match as a collegian he opted to leave school in the spring term to compete for a spot on the American Davis Cup team. Sure enough, on May 19, 1928, it was announced that Lott had been selected as a member of the prestigious four-man team. Unfortunately, the Chicago native's Davis Cup experience was not too glorious. In 1929 and 1930, playing in the number-two position behind Bill Tilden, Lott lost all four matches to the French, who won the coveted trophy both years. Lott returned to the college scene as a student-athlete at the University of Chicago, where he won the Big Ten title in 1929. He later went on to gain world acclaim as a doubles player, winning three Wimbledon championships from 1931 to 1934 and eight U. S. doubles and mixed doubles titles from 1928 to 1934.

Track and Field: Although Fred Alderman had graduated in 1927, he continued to compete as a member of the Illinois Athletic Club team. His efforts were rewarded, as he became MSC's first Olympian in 1928. Following those Olympic Games in Amsterdam, Alderman helped the USA team win the International Track and Field Meet at Cologne, Germany. There he placed fourth in the 200 meters and competed as a winning member of the 400-meter sprint relay, an event not included in the Olympic Games program of the time.

Oh, the advantage of having the coach also be the athletic director! Ralph Young unilaterally made a decision to move basketball practices from the gymnasium (Circle IM) to the auxiliary gymnasium of the newly opened Demonstration Hall. This enabled his track team to take over the gymnasium for their winter workouts.

MSC hosted the Michigan AAU indoor championships and repeated as victors, as they managed 40 points to outscore 13 other teams. The outstanding performer of the meet was MSC pole vaulter Harold McAtee who sailed over the bar at 13 1/2 feet to better his meet record

of 12 feet. Two other Spartans captured first places, Lyle Henson in the 40-yard dash and Lauren Brown in the two-mile run.

In outdoor action, Notre Dame edged the Spartans 64-62 in one of the most exciting meets in the school's history. The outcome of the meet remained in doubt until the final event, when Abbott of Notre Dame edged Lewis Hackney by six inches in the half mile. Jim Hayden set a new college record in the javelin with a heave of 182' 1-1/4".

Piling up 53 16/21 points, the Spartans retained their state intercollegiate title. Gold medalists were Henson in both sprints, Brown in the two-mile run and McAtee, who tied for first place in the pole vault.

At the IC4A meet in Harvard Stadium, Henry Wylie and Meredith Clark finished third and fourth in the mile; Brown was third in the two mile; and Henson captured fourth place in the 220-yard dash. The efforts of the four tied MSC with Princeton for eighth spot in the final team standings.

At the NCAA championships in Chicago, Lyle Henson placed third in the 220, while Harold McAtee tied for fourth place in the pole vault. Their performances enabled MSC to finish ahead of Wisconsin, Minnesota, Indiana, Purdue, Indiana, Notre Dame and 49 other colleges and universities.

Three school records were broken during the season: Wylie in the mile (4:22.2), Brown in the two mile (9:37.5), and Hayden with a javelin heave of 182' 1-1/2".

Wylie and Brown achieved All-American recognition. Such honors were extended to the top five collegians in each of the track and field events.

Wrestling: Although the Spartans were able to win only one match in the 22-5 loss to Michigan, it was a particularly satisfying victory. Norman Stoner, the talented 135-pounder, pinned Dulude in less than five minutes. Dulude had been a Spartan prior to transferring to Ann Arbor.

MSC hosted the State AAU-Olympic Regional tournament and walked off with the trophy. The Spartans scored 18 points to runner-up Michigan's 15. Crowned as champions were George Ferrari of Bessemer, at 191 pounds, and freshman Lyle Shader of Grand Rapids, at 115 pounds.

MSC
1928-1929

TALES TO TELL

When 28-year-old rookie football coach Harry Kipke opened the 1928 season with his team walloping the Kalamazoo College Hornets 103-0, controversy arose. Had his Spartans unnecessarily poured it on hapless "K" College? There was evidence he may have. After finishing the first half with reserves in the game and having built a 39-0 lead, the third quarter opened with the starters reinserted. Six touchdowns later State led 76-0. Some critically spoke out, such as sports editor Roscoe Bennett of the *Grand Rapids Press*. The tenor of his column was that Michigan State overstepped the bounds of good sportsmanship in beating up the visitors from Kalamazoo. He suggested that Coach Kipke did not exercise his best judgment and that he was a bit unethical in letting his team continue the massacre. Others like George Alderton of *The Lansing State Journal* wrote in support of Coach Kipke:

"Wonder if there lives a coach who would risk reversing himself by telling his athletes to quit playing so hard, that they had the other fellow down and there wasn't any use rubbing it in. Perhaps that can be done in the boxing ring, but we haven't heard of a football coach telling his men to quit trying. What a fine fix a coach would find himself in if he told his boys to hit 'em hard one minute and bawl them out the next for doing it."

One fact is clear: it would be the final time the two schools would meet on the football field. Also, the Kipke "bashers" were likely content one week following that 103-0 game when the new Spartan coach would have settled for just three of those points served up to Kalamazoo. The final score, in an upset, Albion 2, MSC 0.

SCOREBOARD

	W	L	T	Avg.
Baseball	12	11	1	.521
Track and Field	2	2	0	.500
Football	3	4	1	.438
Basketball	11	5	0	.688
Tennis	3	3	0	.500
Cross Country	3	0	0	1.000
Swimming and Diving	3	3	0	.500
Wrestling	1	3	0	.250
Hockey	3	3	1	.500
Fencing	4	3	0	.571
Golf	4	1	0	.800

TEAM OF THE YEAR

The annual yearbook, *The Wolverine*, boldly began the summary of the 1929 basketball season with: "Featuring one of the fastest offenses in the entire country, the 1928-29 Michigan State College basketball team was rightfully regarded as the greatest in the history of the school."

Their 11-5 record was highlighted by a season-opening 31-24 victory over the University of Michigan in a game played at Ann Arbor. The win column also included a pair of gratifying defeats of Eastern invaders, Penn State and Cornell, plus a pair of wins over archrival Marquette.

MAKING HISTORY

Saturday, Nov. 12, 1928, could officially be listed as the date of Michigan State's first-ever soccoer game. On that date, a neophyte MSC team met defeat 3-2 by the Lansing Soccer Club, champions of the Central Michigan Soccer League. The idea of a team was initiated by Ralph Leonard, the wrestling coach, who put out a call when students had first arrived in September. A total of 35 men initially reported, most out of curiousity. This game against the Lansing team had not been scheduled until the very day before the contest, consequently only about 100 rooters turned out at College Field to witness the event.

1929 basketball team. (Front row, left to right) A. Haga, J. VanZylen, captain C. Felt, F. DenHerder and R. Grove. (Middle row, left to right) D. Grove, L. Russo, E. Totten and E. Scott. (Back row, left to right) Manager V. Anderson, coach B. VanAlstyne, trainer J. Heppinstall.

At the November meeting of the athletic council, it was announced the department concluded the preceding academic year with a profit of $4,000.

A $75,000 gift was bestowed upon the school for funding construction of the memorial tower which would commemorate the site of the school's first classroom building, College Hall. The benefactors of the generous gift were Mr. and Mrs. John W. Beaumont of Detroit. One month later, the previously unnamed structure was auspiciously named Beaumont Memorial Tower.

GREAT STATE DATES

Cross Country—**November 3, 1928 (A):** The opening meet of the season was the closest of the season, a 27-28 margin over Notre Dame. With his magnificent closing sprint, Lauren Brown broke the tape 150 yards ahead of the Irish top runner, also named Brown. His winning time of 25:58 set a new record for the South Bend course which measured five miles plus 200 yards. Ted Willmarth placed third, finishing just behind W.J. Brown. Previously, the Irish had been undefeated with victories over Illinois, Wisconsin and Marquette. A mainstay of the MSC team, Irvin Crow, severely injured his ankle during the race and was lost for the season.

Cross Country—**November 17, 1928 (A):** The 23-32 win over the U of M featured a spirited race between Monroe, the Michigan ace, and Lauren Brown, who had to surmount a running error. One and one-half miles from the finish line the Spartan captain wandered from the course for approximately 40 yards before he realized his mistaken wrong turn. Once back on the prescribed trail, Brown soon overtook Monroe and eventually won the five-mile race by 75 yards.

Football—**November 24, 1928 (H):** State closed the 1928 season with a 7-0 victory over North Carolina State. As was typical of the time, most of the players were on the field for the full 60 minutes. A total of 13 Spartans played while only 12 visitors saw action during the afternoon. Filling in for the injured fullback, Henry Schau, Fred Danzinger scored the solitary touchdown in a third-quarter, fourth-and-three plunge off right tackle. The Detroit junior had two defenders hanging on as he crossed the goal line. Also a common strategy of the period, both teams often punted on third down. Sophomore Roger Grove was the featured kicker for the Spartans as he continually booted the ball far down the field.

On one occasion, kicking from the end zone, he lofted the ball out of bounds at the Wolf Pack 43-yard line. This would be Coachg Kipke's final game as MSC's head coach as he would leave East Lansing after one year to take the reins of the program at his alma mater, the University of Michigan.

Basketball—**December 7, 1928 (A):** State opened the 1928-1929 season on the road with a 31-24 victory over Michigan, the eventual conference co-champions. Playing without their injured center, Carl Felt, MSC initially fell behind 12-1, but the Spartans fought back, connecting on 11 of 16 field goals and outscoring the Wolverines 21-10 in the second half. It was State's first win over the U of M since 1920.

Basketball—**January 3, 1929 (H):** One day following MSC's 16-14 win over Penn State, the Cornell basketball team came to town. Trailing 7-5 at the 10-minute mark, Coach VanAlstyne sent in an entirely new team of Jim VanZylen, Don Grove, Fred DenHerder, Ed Scott and Art Haga. After acquiring a feel for the floor, the replacements outscored the Big Red 15-6 to gain a 20-13 advantage at the intermission. Having proven their merit, the substitute five started and played the entire second half, outscoring the visitors 18-11 for a 38-24 victory.

Swimming and Diving—**February 2, 1929 (H):** After a one-year hiatus as a result of the pool closure, the Spartans returned to competition with an easy 38-20 win over the Grand Rapids YMCA. The top performance was a pool record-shattering swim of 1:14.1 by the 120-yard freestyle relay team of Charles Scheid from Kalamazoo, and the Detroit trio of John Tate, Horace Craig and captain Al Ellinger.

Swimming and Diving—**February 9, 1929 (A):** The following winning times were swum by Spartans in the 20-yard tank at Michigan Normal: 1:19.8 by Paul Freeland in the 100-yard breaststroke; Tate with a 27.6 in the 50-yard freestyle; 1:15.2 by Craig in the 100-yard backstroke; Ellinger at 1:06.9 in the 100-yard freestyle; and Freeland with a pool and varsity record 2:42.1 in the 220-yard freestyle.

Basketball—**February 15, 1929 (H):** For the second time in the season, MSC defeated the University of Detroit, this time by a convincing 40-15 score. The Titans were held to one field goal in the opening half and a total of five for the entire contest. Before it was over, Coach VanAlstyne had used his entire squad of 14 men, 10 of whom joined in the scoring.

Hockey—**February 2, 1929 (H) & February 15, 1929 (H):** Two of the season's three hockey victories were over the University of Detroit and both by identical 8-0 scores. In the second game of that pair, the Titan skaters were held to a miserly four shots on the net. Meanwhile, Art Harper, State's speedy defenseman, led the offensive surge with five goals. Such an offensive outburst, five goals by one man, is impressive until one recalls that starters often played the entire game.

Baseball—**May 21, 1929 (H):** In a repeat of 1928, Gerry Byrne was again the master on the mound against the U of M, as he surrendered only five hits in a 4-3 ten-inning victory. Trailing 3-1 after six frames, the Spartans tied the contest in the seventh as Bob McCauley doubled down the first base line to score two. Then in the 10th, Eddie Gibbs singled home the winning run.

ATHLETE OF THE YEAR

Lauren Brown entered Michigan State from Detroit as a freshman in 1926 and he never left. Excelling as a distance runner, "Brownie" began winning races and setting new cross country marks from that very first year. In

Lauren Brown

Lauren's three seasons of varsity competition (1927-1929) the Spartans were undefeated. In his senior year, for the first time, State entered a full team in the celebrated IC4A meet in New York City and, led by his third-place finish, the team placed in the runner-up spot. Appointed head coach in 1931, five times in a row (1933-1937) his teams would capture that coveted IC4A title. His 1939 squad would capture the school's first-ever NCAA team championship in any sport. In 1947, after 16 years, "Brownie" would leave the coaching ranks to work full time as director of the school's Mimeograph Department (later University Printing). He retired from the University in 1970.

IN THE SPARTLITE

Baseball: After splitting the annual pair of baseball games with Michigan in 1926, 1927 and 1928, the two coaches agreed that, commencing with the 1929 season, a third game would be played to establish a two out of three champion. Inauspiciously, the U of M would be the first to win the extended series, two games to one.

Basketball: Before an overflow and vocal crowd at the gymnasium, the Spartans carried the Fighting Irish through two overtime periods prior to coming up short, 28-27. It was the accuracy of one player that dealt the fate as Bobby Donovan of the Irish three times looped in longer-than-usual shots. The first tied the game 24-24. The next one matched Ed Totten's field goal in the first OT. The third proved one point better than Verne Dickeson's free throw in the final five-minute period.

Cross Country: Scoring 29 points to runner-up Butler's 36, MSC won a third straight Central Intercollegiate Conference championship over a muddy and windswept home course. Joe Sivak of Butler nosed out Lauren Brown for individual honors. The two ran side-by-side until the final half-mile when, on this occasion, the Spartan captain was out-sprinted to the finish line. The winner's time of 26:13.0 was short of "Brownie's" course record 25:47.7.

The Spartans were to have entered the IC4A meet as a team in 1928, but at the last minute it was decided that only Lauren Brown would make the trip to New York. As an individual entrant, he finished second in the prestigious season-ending meet.

Fencing: With only senior Ed Gruettner returning, Coach Waffa built his 1929 team around five sophomores who had been introduced to the sport as freshmen: George Bauer of Hastings, William Kershaw from Wyandotte, Karl Voightlander of Jackson, Gorden Evans from Detroit and L.B. Haight of Lansing. Of these, Bauer was the standout as he became the school's first star in the sport and would become Waffa's successor as the MSC coach.

Two tournaments were held on campus. The first, conducted in the gymnasium building on March 23, drew 44 entries from across the state. The second, held on Saturday, June 1, was under the auspices of the Spartan Fencers Club and an entry fee of $1.50 per weapon helped defray the expenses of the gold, silver and bronze medals awarded the top three contestants in sabre and epee. The matches were held in front of the old Armory.

Football: For the first time in 13 years, the University of Michigan failed to score a touchdown against the State defense. Regardless, the Wolverines did manage the only score of the afternoon, a field goal from the 12-yard line in the second period. It was a frustrating afternoon for the Spartan faithful among the 28,067 rain-soaked spectators. Twice during the opening quarter the Spartans drove deep into U of M territory only to run out of downs. They first surrendered the ball at the 10-yard line and later at the eight-yard line. MSC had one final opportunity during the second half. With little time remaining and fourth down at the 14-yard line, Coach Kipke opted for a tie. It just wasn't meant to be. Marian Joslin's field goal attempt was low and missed the crossbar.

The Spartans again concluded the football season against North Carolina State, this time at home. Played in snow flurries, the teams battled on even terms until the final period when Fred Danziger crashed over from the 14-yard line and a 7-0 MSC victory. This would be Harry Kipke's final game as the head coach. At season's end he successfully opted out of his three-year contract and accepted the head coaching position with his alma mater, the U of M. Many fans who initially cheered his hiring at Michigan State suddenly felt betrayed.

Golf: It apparently came with the territory. Upon accepting the position as head football coach, there was an expectation that Harry Kipke would spend his springs working with the golfers. Consequently, he is listed as the school's first coach in the sport.

Paying their own green fees, all varsity candidates reported for the initial team tryout at Lansing's Municipal Groesbeck Golf Course on Saturday, April 27. Thereafter, through his connections, Coach Kipke made arrangements for free use of the Lansing Country Club links.

The varsity five of Howard Minier, Sam Disentis, Chuck Hower, Larry Pace and Max Doerr completed a respectable 4-1 record.

Hockey: The season opener was a 1-0 loss at Battle Creek against the Civic Club. The low score was understandable. The entire game, at home on the Red Cedar River, was played amidst snow flurries which hampered the game throughout.

A January 17 home contest scheduled against the University of Minnesota was cancelled for lack of ice.

Only seven men were awarded their minor letters with another seven earning "service" awards (sweater with no letter). Letterwinners were Donald Clark, Don Jones, J. Parks Pinson, Elwood Harris, defensemen John Hawkins and Art Harper and goalie Willard Kennedy.

Swimming and Diving: On March 9 Northwestern came to town for the final swimming meet of the season and easily defeated the Spartans, 52-15. Featuring two national record holders, the Wildcats bettered every pool record except the 100-yard freestyle. Yet the real crowd-pleaser of the afternoon was Northwestern's Walter Colbath, NCAA diving champion and member of the USA Olympic team. Colbath performed several exhibition dives for the benefit of the appreciative crowd.

Four new varsity records were set during the 1929 season. New standards were set for both relays along with individual record performances by Paul Freeland in the 220-yard freestyle and Horace Craig in the 150-yard backstroke. Although swimming and diving was still listed as a minor sport, Freeland and Craig received major "S" sweaters.

Tennis: Following season-opening tennis victories over Detroit City College and Albion, the rain-saturated clay courts made play impossible for the scheduled double-header against Colgate and Michigan on May 4. Neither game was ever rescheduled; consequently, it would be one of few years State would not meet Michigan.

Track and Field: For the third straight year, MSC hosted and won the state outdoor intercollegiate championships.

To illustrate the caliber of competition at the IC4A meet in Cambridge, Mass., Lauren Brown placed sixth in the two-mile event with a time of 9:28.0. This clocking was nearly 10 seconds under "Brownie's" previous best and five seconds faster than the winning time at that spring's Big Ten championships in Evanston, Ill.

Winning the third consecutive Michigan Intercollegiate track title, a balanced Spartan team piled up 44 points to outscore 14 other schools. Western State was runner-up with 38 1/2 points. In the process, the Spartans captured only two individual titles both with new meet marks. Lauren Brown won the two mile in 9:41.3 and Harold McAtee captured the pole vault with 12' 9 1/2".

Wrestling: With State leading Ohio University, 16-13, heavyweight Marion Joslin needed only a draw to ensure a Spartan victory. The two contenders struggled though the 12-minute regulation time and, according to the referee and meet officials, no decision had been reached and an overtime period was in order. Coach Riches vehemently protested the decision, claiming that Joslyn had been on top for at least seven minutes of the match and consequently should have been awarded the decision. The protest was never considered and, as fate would have it, the MSC "big man" was thrown in the first overtime and the Bobcats gained five points and an 18-16 win.

A physical education class inside the Gymnasium.

MSC
1929-1930

TALES TO TELL

The pinnacle of the undefeated cross country season was the perfect score (15-40) registered against Michigan on November 2. The race was completed in the stadium during half time of the MSC-Case football game. The first three runners, Lauren Brown, Ted Willmarth and Clark Chamberlain finished well ahead of the remainder of the pack.

Willmarth, team captain, shares this story:

"Prior to the Michigan meet Coach Mason suggested that if we (Brown, Chamberlain and myself) had the expected commanding lead at the end of the race, the three of us hold hands at the finish line and produce a three-way tie for first place. We agreed to the idea. Upon entering the football stadium (for the final one-quarter mile of the race) the plan was put in place as we were 300 or more yards ahead of the next runner. We came down to the finish line in a solid front. About three yards short of our goal, I changed my mind, thinking that Lauren was deserving of the honor. He had led the race and after all this was his final home appearance. Just before we crossed the line I gave Brown a slight bump putting him in first place as Clark and I finished tied for second.

To my amazement and surprise, Lauren whirled around and denounced me for what had happened. 'It was a dirty trick' he shouted. 'You didn't keep your word.' I tried to explain but he wouldn't listen. More than a week went by before the silence was broken. All the while I worried how this event might effect our team spirit in the forthcoming IC4A run in New York. I should have realized that Brown was not the person to carry a long-lasting grudge. We once again became close friends, a friendship that lasted for many years until his death."

HEADLINES of 1930

- The first supermarket opens in Queens, N.Y., offering lower prices and a huge selection. It achieves tremendous success overnight.
- Prices at the time included: bread nine cents/loaf, milk 56 cents/gallon and gasoline 10 cents/gallon. A new automobile could be purchased for $610 and the average annual income was $1,973.
- Chic Young, cartoonist, develops the popular newspaper comic strip "Blondie."
- America's first planetarium, Adler Planetarium, opens in Chicago.

SCOREBOARD

	W	L	T	Avg.
Baseball	16	6	0	.727
Track and Field	2	3	0	.400
Football	5	3	0	.625
Basketball	12	4	0	.750
Tennis	2	9	0	.182
Cross Country	3	0	0	1.000
Swimming and Diving	4	3	0	.571
Wrestling	3	3	0	.500
Hockey	1	4	0	.200
Fencing	2	3	0	.400
Golf	7	2	0	.777

TEAM OF THE YEAR

Based on the overall record of 8-1 against teams in the state of Michigan, Spartan baseball supporters claimed the mythical state collegiate championship. The total record for the season (16-6) included victories over Syracuse, Cincinnati and two defeats of both Michigan and Notre Dame. Eddie Gibbs was the team's top hitter with an average of .454 as sophomore pitcher Charley Griffin posted a record of 9-1 on the mound.

MAKING HISTORY

Marion Joslin, Merrill Marshall and Norm Stoner were entered in the 1930 NCAA wrestling championships held at Penn State. Both Joslin and Marshall, who dropped weight to the 145-pound class, lost opening bouts. Stoner threw his initial opponent to garner one team point for State's first-ever scoring in the championships. He would later lose in a bout for third place.

The 1930 baseball season opened with the inauguration of a College Field "first," an electrically operated scoreboard. Located in right field, the board was illuminated from instructions by telephone from behind home plate with electric lights indicating balls, strikes, outs and inning by inning score.

1930 baseball team. (First row, left to right) J. Hayden, M. Crall, A. Sachs, C. Pevic, P. Bullach. (Middle row, left to right) Macauley, J. Barnard, W. Knisel, H. Kahl, K. Byrne and capt. E. Gibbs. (Back row, left to right) Coach J. Kobs, C. Cuthbertson, J. Madonna, C. Griffin, trainer J. Heppinstall, manager L. Brown.

GREAT STATE DATES

Football—**October 26, 1929 (H):** The 1929 homecoming was celebrated with a surprisingly easy 40-6 defeat of North Carolina State. As the Spartans racked up 436 yards and 12 first downs, Max Crall scored on the longest scamper of the day, a 71-yard end run. Four other TDs were from runs of 20 yards or more, two by Carl Nordberg and a pair by Gerald Breen.

Football—**November 9, 1929 (A):** Featuring the passing of Roger Grove and the running of Verne Dickeson, who scored four touchdowns, State topped Mississippi A&M, 33-19. This ended a six-year jinx of not having won an away game. The last previous road win was the 2-0 shutout of the University of Detroit on Nov. 17, 1923.

Basketball—**January 1, 1930 (H):** It was a festive occasion. First, it was New Year's Day; second, it was the opening game of the basketball season; and finally, it was the inaugural game in Demonstration Hall. Unfortunately, the Syracuse University team was not in a cooperative mood as they came from behind to snatch the victory, 21-19. There was certainly no "home court" advantage. An unexpected condensation on the surface of the new portable floor caused numerous spills of the "fast-breaking" Spartans. With one minute of time remaining and State leading 19-17, a substitute center entered the game for the Orange. He immediately became their hero by scoring twice, first the tying and then the winning basket. Although the formal dedication of the facility would be delayed until Michigan came to town six weeks later, more than 3,000 curious townspeople turned out for this "first ever" game at Dem Hall.

Wrestling—**January 18, 1930 (A):** After losing to a strong University of Chicago team on Friday, the wrestlers came back on Saturday night to dominate a Northwestern team that was considered the favorite, 25-3. The only loss came at 175 pounds where Charles Slaght was defeated by the ace of the Wildcat team.

Basketball—**January 22, 1930 (H):** A local record crowd of more than 4,000 howled in delight as State defeated Notre Dame, 28-21. It was only the second win over the Irish within a ten-year span. In a significant move for Coach VanAlstyne, the longtime exponent of the zone defense switched overnight to the man-to-man defense. Perhaps it was simply an element of surprise, but it did frustrate the high-scoring stars from South Bend. With 12 points, MSC's Don Grove, the 121-pound forward, was scoring leader for the game. Only six men saw service for the Spartans: Don and Roger Grove, Fred DenHerder, Art Haga, Ed Scott and Harold Haun.

Basketball—**January 31, 1930 (H):** Trailing Marquette University 17-16 in the waning minutes of the game, Don Grove broke through the zone defense for a lay-up to give State their first lead of the evening, 18-17. On their next possession the Spartans withdrew to a stall, whereupon Fred DenHerder, Ed Scott and Grove played catch for nearly a minute. This tactic forced the Hilltoppers from their zone. Grove responded by quickly busting through for a lay-up and a three-point advantage. With the visitors growing desperate as the clock ticked down, both Scott and Grove slipped by their coverage for uncontested baskets. The final score read 24-17.

Swimming and Diving—**February 1, 1930 (H):** Matched against the Grand Rapids YMCA, a non-collegiate team, Coach Daubert was provided the opportunity to combine his freshmen and varsity squads. The meet was a thriller from start to finish as the Spartans secured the 38-37 win with a victory in the final event, the 180-yard medley relay. New team records were hung up that afternoon: the 240-yard freestyle relay (2:11.4) and the meet-winning medley relay (1:55.9).

Hockey—**February 6, 1930 (H):** Putting the puck into the net twice in the final period against the University of Detroit, MSC won its only game of the season, 2-0. Clark produced both scores. He beat the U of D goalie with a corner shot early in the third period and later picked up a loose puck and sailed in the insurance goal at 13:40. Charles Pevic gained the shutout in net for State. Coach Kobs inserted only four substitutes onto the ice during the game.

Swimming and Diving—**February 8, 1930 (H):** An additional four school records were established in a triangular meet with Case Tech and Western Reserve. New standards were set by Ray Schaubel in the 50-yard freestyle (26.0) and Horace Craig in the 100-yard backstroke (1:08.8), while Charles Scheid lowered the 220-yard freestyle record from 2:42.1 to 2:40.7; and with a time of 1:54.1, the team of Craig, Dale Vaughn and Schaubel once more bettered the school record in the medley relay event.

Basketball—**February 15, 1930 (H):** Two weeks prior to the 1930 Michigan game, a Detroit newspaper published a story claiming the Wolverines' head coach had requested coach Ben VanAlstyne to refrain from using his highly successful zone defense in the upcoming square-off. Van denied the allegation by stating, "The University of Michigan has never asked Michigan State to use any particular style of play whatsoever." This game was preceded by formal dedication services for the new facility and 5,847 fans packed into Demonstration Hall, topping the record-setting turnout three weeks earlier against Notre Dame. At the outset, State led, but trailed at half time, 17-13. In the final five minutes of play the crowd stood amidst the excitement as the lead changed hands seven times. With less than 30 seconds to play, Michigan scored to take command, 26-25. On the ensuing jump ball (which the rule still required after every made basket) Roger Grove gained possession, wheeled in his tracks, and let the ball fly. It dropped through the mesh, and 15 seconds later the gun cracked to signify the end of the game: MSC 27, Michigan 26.

Baseball—**April 12, 1930 (H):** State celebrated the opening of the 1930 season with a convincing 12-4 victory over the University of Chicago. Leading the 15-hit attack was center fielder Eddie Gibbs who went four-for-four with a single, double and two home runs. The game was tied 4-4 until the fifth when the Spartans exploded with a five-run barrage. Harry Kahl, the veteran right-hander, yielded only six hits as he pitched the entire nine innings.

Track and Field—**April 19, 1930 (H):** In defeating Detroit City School, 78 2/3 to 52 1/3, the Spartans demonstrated the value of team depth. Although Detroit captured eight first places to MSC's seven, Green and White team strength was supreme as they slammed (first, second, third) five of the 15 events. Headed by Clark Chamberlain's demanding double-win in the mile and the two-mile, State gathered all available points in those races along with the two hurdle events and the discus.

Golf—**May 2 and 3, 1930 (H):** Following only two formal practices, the golfers opened at home with a pair of wins over Grand Rapids Junior College and St. John's of Toledo. The best round that weekend was the 77 shot by Howard Minier in the 13 1/2-4 1/2 victory of St. John's.

Baseball—**May 3, 1930 (H):** Charley Griffin pitched a remarkable game, permitting only four hits in defeating Notre Dame 3-2. The sophomore southpaw let up momentarily in the third inning and it nearly cost him the game as the Irish wove together a base on balls and a pair of hits to score their two runs. All three MSC runs, two in the second and one in the fourth, were assisted by Irish misplays or miscues.

Baseball—**May 26, 1930 (A):** In the spring rematch against Notre Dame, Charley Griffin was breezing along with a 1-0 lead until the seventh when his mates scored one more time and the game seemed sewed up. The Irish would have none of that. In the bottom of the eighth they put three hits and a throwing error together to tie the score at 2-2. The Spartans answered back with a three-run ninth inning highlighted by Max Crall's two-RBI triple. Once more ND came back, but their one run in the ninth only made the final score close, MSC 5, Notre Dame 3.

Baseball—**May 30, 1930 (H):** The Spartans opened against Michigan with Eddie Gibbs's first-inning home run followed by a pair of runs in the second. Those three tallies were more than enough for State's pitching sensation, Charley "Chip" Griffin, who was touched for only two hits and one unearned run in the ninth.

Baseball—**June 21, 1930 (H):** With the 8-4 defeat of the Wolverines in the season finale, Charley "Chip" Griffin, the crafty southpaw from Shelby, Mich., shared the limelight with Wendell "Windy" Knisel, who played a part in all eight runs. With four hits, the junior right fielder batted in six, engineered a double steal that led to the go-ahead run, and later came home on a perfectly executed squeeze play for the final run.

ATHLETE OF THE YEAR

Roger Grove, a two-sport star, lettered three years in football (1928-30) and three years in basketball (1929-31). At six foot one and 185 pounds the Sturgis, Mich., native was an imposing athlete. He was the starting quarterback in his final two years on the gridiron. Excelling as a punter, Roger often forced opponents to begin their offensive drives from deep in their own territory. He led the basketball team in scoring in both his junior (91 points) and senior (135 points) years. When asked about his most memorable thrill as a Spartan, Grove recalled his senior year when he caught a midair fumble and raced 36 yards for the first touchdown in the 14-7 upset of Colgate.

Roger Grove

IN THE SPARTLITE

Baseball: Coach Kobs had a trio of talented pitchers he could send to the mound. Charley "Chip" Griffin, a sophomore sensation, was particularly impressive as he won nine and lost only one. Two of those victories were over Notre Dame, 3-2 and 5-3, and two were over the University of Michigan, 3-1 and 8-4. The other two pitching mainstays of the spring were Pete Bulloch who went 3-0 and Harris "Jumbo" Kahl who was 5-4.

Basketball: The feature of the 1930 season was the installation of the new portable floor and the ensuing move of the varsity schedule into Demonstration Hall. In the joint-use agreement with the ROTC Department, the portable floor in Demonstration Hall was in place only during the first six weeks of winter term (January 1-February 15). Consequently, any game scheduled prior to the first of the year was played at the Boys Vocational School (Johnson Fieldhouse) in Lansing and, with few exceptions, the team "hit the road" for any contests after mid-February. The move to Dem Hall proved to be a financial success. Setting a season's attendance record in 1930 of more than 22,000 fans, the gate receipts for the ten home games ($8,254.50) nearly doubled the revenue

of the ten home contests of the preceding year in the Gymnasium ($4,321.50). Athletic Director Young announced that for the first time in the school's history, basketball had become a moneymaker. Regardless, because of the restrictive use of the facility there was continued push for a "Jenison-like" facility.

Cross Country: For the first time, MSC entered a full team in the IC4A meet at Cortlandt Park in New York City. The Spartans placed second behind a strong team from the University of Maine. The Spartans placed as follows: Lauren Brown third, Clark Chamberlain fourth, Ted Willmarth eighth, Elmer Roossien 29th and Robert O'Conner 37th.

Football: Perhaps understandably, the writers for the *Michigan State News* were likely disappointed with having to report a loss to Michigan for the 14th year in a row. Offering few details of the 17-0 defeat, the edition buried the six-paragraph story on the back page. Strangely, an accompanying story detailing Michigan's upcoming game with Purdue drew more space.

Golf: This was the year that golf became acknowledged as an "official" minor sport at MSC. To gain a perspective of the talent, the following individual scores are reported from the 17-1 loss to the U of M at Ann Arbor: Howard "Hez" Minier, 76-76; Arnold Duffield, 76-79; Charles Huwer, 82-82; and Larry Pace, 90-82. This foursome, along with newcomer Bill Kane, became the first MSC golfers to be awarded (minor) letters.

Negotiations were solidified for the team to play all home matches at the Walnut Hills Golf Club, a new 18-hole layout.

Like Harry Kipke in 1928, coach Jim Crowley would be required to divide his time between the golf team and the spring football practices.

With some exceptions, meets conducted from 1930-1943 would include four competitors per team, each playing either 18 or 36 holes of medal play against an opponent. Each one-on-one match-up would vie for three team points with one point being awarded each of the follows: lowest score for the first nine or 18 holes; lowest score for the second nine or 18 holes; and one point for the lowest total score for the round(s). During those same rounds a two-man best ball score would be recorded with three team points awarded exactly the same as the one-on-one matches. The six matches (four singles and two best ball) would be played for a total of 18 points.

Swimming and Diving: The decade of the '30s opened under the leadership of new coach Russell Daubert. Even as strides were made in the program during his dozen years at the helm, lacking a conference affiliation was a severe handicap.

The training schedule for the season, begun in November, was sculptured around the availability of Coach Daubert, who held other assignments within the department. Workouts were held on Tuesday and Thursday from 4:00-6:00 p.m. and Wednesday and Friday from 5:00-6:00 p.m.

Although the likes of captain Ed Cook, Horace Craig, Charles Scheid and Ray Schaubel were talented athletes, losses in 1930 to Michigan and Northwestern were predictable. Those two institutions were the giants of intercollegiate swimming in the Midwest. Comparing some MSC team records with NCAA records of 1930 disclose how the Spartans were millenniums from getting into the swim of things:

	MSC	NCAA
100-yard freestyle	57.1	52.8
220-yard freestyle	2:39.8	2:16.6
300-yard medley relay	3:39.5	3:09.0

Tennis: The 8-1 loss to Notre Dame was played at the municipal courts on Michigan Avenue. Paul Kane, team captain and a consistent winner all season, accounted for that solitary Spartan team point of the afternoon match.

The Spartans are stopped for a slight loss on an end run, but go on to defeat Mississippi A&M, 33-19.

Track and Field: At the Indoor Central Intercollegiates hosted by Notre Dame, MSC was credited with two firsts, Bob Olsen in the pole vault and Lauren Brown in the two-mile with a time of 9:39.2, establishing both a varsity and ND fieldhouse record. In the same event two weeks later Brown would set a Chicago University gymnasium record during the 46 1/2-39 1/2 dual meet loss.

Moving outdoors, "Brownie" would begin sharing the spotlight with a rising Spartan star, sophomore Clark Chamberlain. Regardless, the senior captain had moments of stardom. At the Penn Relays Lauren ran a 9:54.4 to win the 3,000-meter steeplechase by 70 yards over a field of the best from the East. In the final home meet of his MSC career, the State Intercollegiates, he won the two-mile in 9:34.8 to better the meet, varsity and stadium record. Meanwhile, Chamberlain was gaining most attention as a miler but moved up to the two-mile in the season-ending Central Collegiates where he outlasted Brown for the title.

Other Spartans standouts were pole vaulter Bob Olsen along with hurdles Walt Russow, Bob Russell, Stan Oswalt and Central Collegiate champion Ken Yarger.

Wrestling: At the age of 27 Fendley Collins joined the staff, and would begin his 33-year career as Michigan State's head wrestling coach. Fendley's first Spartan team lined up as follows with their season's record noted in parentheses: Hubert Miller (1-5) at 115, Addison Wilbur (2-4) 125; Norm Stoner (4-2) 135; Richard Tompkins (5-1) 145; Merrill Marshall (5-1) 155; Paul Shepard (3-3) 165; Charles Slaght (3-3) 175; and heavyweight Marion Joslin (5-1).

MSC
1930-1931

Russell B. Daubert

TALES TO TELL

On Friday afternoon, May 15, 1931, approximately 400 people crowded into the spectator balcony of the gymnasium pool to get a firsthand look at Johnny Weissmuller, who would display the speed and ability that had made him the world's greatest swimmer. His visit had been sponsored by the F.N. Arbaugh Co., the Lansing department store. As Weissmuller stood ready to enter the water from the end of the pool, MSC coach Russell B. Daubert (a personal friend of Weissmuller) announced the famous swimmer would swim an exhibition 50-yard freestyle. Daubert pulled out his stopwatch and prepared to give Weissmuller the starting signal. The tall, muscular Olympic champion paused a moment and then turned to the Spartan coach and asked what the local record was for the event. Being informed the varsity record was 25.3 seconds, Johnny responded, "Well, I'll do it in 24." Almost nonchalantly he plunged into the pool and without apparent effort negotiated the 50 yards. Coach Daubert looked at his timepiece and announced, "time, 23.1." At the NCAA championships that year, Scherer of Princeton won the 50-yard freestyle in a time of 24.6.

Johnny Weissmuller

HEADLINES of 1931

- "The Star-Spangled Banner" is officially named the U.S. national anthem.
- Cartoonist Chester Gould introduces *Dick Tracy* into the comic strips. It first appears in The *Chicago Tribune*.
- An architectural landmark of New York City, The 102-story Empire State Building, is opened.
- Ernest Lawrence, physicist, invents the cyclotron, a particle accelerator popularly known as an "atom smasher."

SCOREBOARD

	W	L	T	Avg.
Baseball	13	9	1	.587
Track and Field	5	0	0	1.000
Football	5	1	2	.750
Basketball	16	1	0	.941
Tennis	2	6	1	.278
Cross Country	1	2	0	.333
Swimming and Diving	4	1	0	.800
Wrestling	3	1	0	.750
Hockey	no games due to weather			
Fencing	1	3	0	.250
Golf	6	4	0	.600

TEAM OF THE YEAR

Although their basketball schedule was not loaded with national "powers," within their victory column the Spartans did include Cincinnati, Brigham Young, Marquette, Xavier (Ohio), Colgate and Detroit. The solitary loss of the season, to Michigan, came in the second game of the season. Thereafter, the Spartans ran off a string of 15 straight. Of those 16 wins, the average margin of victory was nearly 12 points per game. If, as today, a national ranking system had been in place, State would have likely been a top-20 team.

MAKING HISTORY

The following fiscal report demonstrated how football, by 1930, had become the primary financial source for the entire athletic program:

	Income	Expenses
Football	$63,168.04	$38,816.91
Basketball	$ 9,863.95	$ 7,595.83
Track	$ 731.47	$ 9,245.47
Cross Country	$ 3.50	$ 1,503.17
Swimming	$ 415.20	$ 1,581.53
Wrestling	$ 375.00	$ 1,617.02
Hockey	$ 50.00	$ 574.49
Fencing	$ 20.00	$ 233.78
Tennis	$ 105.00	$ 1,125.49
Baseball	$ 3,926.00	$ 6,186.63
TOTALS	**$78,658.16**	**$68,480.32**

1931 basketball team. (Front row, left to right) W. Scott, A. Haga, R. Boeskool, J. McCaslin, R. Grove and D. Pinneo. (Second row, left to right) W. Vondette, Wykes, A. Duffield, M. Holcomb and A. Kircher. (Third row, left to right) J. Gafner, manager R. Carruthers, coach B. VanAlstyne and trainer J. Heppinstall.

The three-meter springboard diving event was introduced into the NCAA swimming and diving championship meet.

The basketball season ended on Saturday, February 28, with a 24-21 overtime road victory over Marquette. Of historical note, the team traveled to Milwaukee by air, becoming the first MSC athletic team of any kind to travel that way. The small aircraft in which they flew was capable of seating only six passengers; consequently, the 12-man entourage made the 80-minute flight from Grand Rapids to Milwaukee in two separate groups. They departed on Friday and returned Sunday, following the Saturday night game. The first group (see photo) took off at 11:40 A.M. The second group of Monte Holcomb, Gerry McCaslin, Bill Vondette, Al Kircher, John Gafner and team manager, Bob Carruthers waited until 3:10 P.M. to catch the second flight.

A 27-year-old Fendley Collins joined the staff and would begin his 33-year career as Michigan State's head wrestling coach.

cluding one on a 55-yard run in the opening minute of the second half. Other TDs were credited to Roger Grove, Monnett and reserve fullback Joe "Butch" Kowatch, the "Ionia Steam Roller." One of the features of the afternoon was the punting of Grove. In the third period he booted a 65-yarder that went out of bounds at the 5-yard line and eventually set up the fourth Spartan score.

Football—**October 18, 1930 (H):** Bobby Monnett was the star in the homecoming game against the champions of the East, undefeated Colgate. With the score tied 7-7 and only two minutes remaining, Monnett picked his way through a hole in the right side of the big line, side-stepped and dodged his way 62 yards for the winning touchdown. This was the first defeat of a nationally prominent team since the Aggies conquered Notre Dame 12 years before.

Cross Country—**October 25, 1930 (A):** The season's only dual-meet win, 25-30 over Butler University, was concluded during half time of the Case football game. Clark Chamberlain led the pack by one-half mile

The first MSC athletes to travel by plane, (from left to right) Dee Pinneo, Art Haga, Randy Boeskool, Coach Van Alstyne, Edward Scott, and Roger Grove.

GREAT STATE DATES

Football—**October 11, 1930 (A):** Led by brilliant play from a pair of sophomores, fullback Abe Eliowitz and halfback Bobby Monnett, State easily handled Cincinnati, 32-0. Abe scored two of the touchdowns, in-

as he sprinted into the stadium for the final 440 yards. His 22:48.3 time for the four-mile course bettered Lauren Brown's previous record of 22:56.0.

Football—**November 8, 1930 (H):** Bobby Monnett intercepted three forward passes in the 19-11 win over North Dakota State. With the Spartans trailing 11-6 in

the second half, he snatched his third aerial and returned the ball 65 yards for what would become the winning score.

Basketball—**December 5, 1930 (H):** In the 22-8 triumph over Cincinnati, all eight Bearcat points were from the free-throw line. During the entire game they were never able to penetrate the Spartan defense for one field goal.

Basketball—**December 29, 1930 (H):** MSC led the highly respected Brigham Young five 15-13 at intermission but the Cougars temporarily took command in the second half and built a 26-21 advantage. Randy Boeskool, the 6'4" center from Grand Rapids, then managed to score on three successive possessions to regain the lead 27-26. With three minutes remaining and after the visitors had tied the game on a free throw, Roger Grove won the game with a tip-in of a Dee Pinneo missed free throw. The final score favored the Spartans, 29-28.

Basketball—**January 9, 1931 (H):** State defeated the highly regarded quintet from Marquette University, 19-16. There was reasonable explanation why the Spartan team that would eventually average 30 points over the season, could score no more than 19 against the Hilltoppers. Leading 17-16 midway through the second half, Coach VanAlstyne called for the stall tactic. The "freeze" lasted for about nine minutes before the Marquette coach aborted the zone defense and chased the MSC ball handlers. It was too late. State hit one more field goal to seal the victory.

Basketball—**January 16 and 17 1931 (A):** The squad of 11 took the train to Hamilton, N.Y., for a unique Friday-Saturday "doubleheader" against Ben VanAlstyne's alma mater, Colgate University. What a gratifying weekend it must have been for the coach, as the Spartans captured both games, 41-31 and 50-30. Roger Grove was the offensive leader, scoring a two-game total of 26 points.

Basketball—**January 30, 1931 (A):** Leading at halftime 18-10, it appeared MSC would have little trouble winning their ninth in a row, but the Western Reserve quintet would not go down easily. Upon returning to the floor from intermission, the Red Cats quickly outscored the MSC five 10-2 to tie the count 20-20. Both teams then found trouble finding the range, but by the time the clock had reached the one-minute mark the Clevelanders had secured the lead, 24-23. It was then that Dee Pinneo, the pint-sized Spartan, sank a long shot to secure the final score, 25-24. The closing moments

were tense when a Cat was fouled and stood at the line with a chance to tie or win the game with three seconds remaining. To the relief of Coach VanAlstyne and his squad, both free throws missed the mark and their win streak was intact.

Basketball—**February 6, 1931 (H):** It was a game that was never in doubt. Led by Roger Grove's 12 points, the Spartans took command early, built a 25-5 halftime lead and then turned the Alma five over to the reserves. The visitors proved more than equal to the MSC second team, outscoring them 9-6 during the first 12 minutes of the second half. The starters, Dee Pinneo, Randy Boeskool, Art Haga, Ed Scott and Grove returned to the contest to close it out with 11 points and a 42-20 verdict.

Track and Field—**February 7, 1931 (H):** Considered a mild upset, State topped the University of Chicago, 58 2/3 to 36 1/3, for the school's first track and field victory over a Big Ten opponent. In what had become expected, Clark Chamberlain led the team with victories in both the mile and two-mile. The team captain first traveled the 16 laps of the oval in 4:26.8 to lower his own varsity and gymnasium record by four seconds. One hour later he lapped the entire field in the two-mile to again register his rigorous "double." Norman Smith, a sophomore, bettered another varsity record as he captured the high jump event with a leap of 5' 9-1/2".

Swimming and Diving—**February 20, 1931 (A):** With two exceptions, State captured all other possible places (firsts and seconds) in downing Wooster College, 57-18. Two varsity records went by the boards. Gordon Snyder broke his own 100-yard breaststroke mark by swimming the race in 1:18.7. The medley relay trio composed of Horace Craig, Snyder and Howard Clark lowered the 180-yard time, turning it in 1:52.6.

Wrestling—**February 27 and February 28, 1931 (A):** The team traveled into New York where they finished the dual-meet season with wins over Mechanics Institute in Rochester, 22-10, and Alfred College, 25-5. In the opener against Mechanics, the Spartans lost only the matches at 145 and 175 pounds. On the next afternoon at Alfred, Tom Roberts, at 125 pounds, was the sole loser.

Fencing—**March 6, 1931 (H):** Led by player-coach George Bauer, R.W. Bristol and K.A. Krentel, MSC would register the only win of the season as they surprised the Northwestern Wildcats in a payback victory, 9-8.

Baseball—**April 18, 1931 (H):** The home opener of the 1931 baseball season was a thrilling 3-2 victory over Michigan Normal. The game was tied 2-2 entering the bottom of the ninth and extra innings seemed assured when both "Chip" Griffin and Abe Eliowitz went down swinging. Hopes were ignited as John "Jabber" Barnard, the senior catcher, slashed a double into center field. Coach Kobs then played a hunch and called upon sophomore John Gafner of Escanaba as a pinch-hitter. Gafner responded with an opposite field line drive into right, easily scoring Barnard with the winning run.

Baseball—**May 2, 1931 (H):** Charley "Chip" Griffin shaded the ace of the Western State pitching staff, 2-1, in a battle of southpaws. "Chip" allowed only four scattered hits while he and his teammates managed six. The Spartan runs came in the sixth inning on two singles, an error and a passed ball. The Teachers scored their sole run in the eighth on a single and an error.

Baseball—**May 23, 1931 (H):** The Spartans scored five runs in the opening two innings to build a cushion the University of Michigan could never overcome. The Wolverines did come to life in the sixth when, aided by two errors and a walk, they did touch, Charley Griffin for four runs. During the next two innings the State offense generated four more markers to put the game away, 8-4. Harold Cuthbertson led the 10-hit attack with three safeties. Al Kircher and Eddie Gibbs chipped in with two each.

Baseball—**June 1, 1931 (A):** Eddie Gibbs collected only one hit, but regardless was a hero in the 11-inning victory over Indiana. Trailing 9-8 into the bottom of the ninth he found life on an error, stole second base and scored on a single by John Barnard to send the game into extra innings. In the 11th inning the senior captain singled, once more pilfered second base and continued to third when the Hoosier shortstop booted the attempt to make the putout. The ball was retrieved by the second baseman who heaved it far over the third baseman's head and Eddie raced home with the winning run, 10-9.

Baseball—**June 20, 1931 (H):** The Spartans closed out the season by topping the Wolverines of Michigan 5-0 and thus gave claim to the mythical college baseball title of the state. Junior "Chip" Griffin, the winning pitcher, had perfect support in the field and held the U of M batters to six scattered hits. The game was put out of reach in the fourth inning when Griffin aided his own cause by driving a home run ball into Red Cedar River with two mates aboard. The next hitter, Abe Eliowicz,

followed suit with another four-bagger. Eddie Gibbs, senior outfielder, singled in the eighth and eventually scored the fifth MSC run. By nightfall Gibbs had signed a professional contract with the Detroit Tigers and was on his way to join the Evansville team of the Three-I League.

ATHLETE OF THE YEAR

In addition to being the 1930 IC4A cross country champion, Clark S. Chamberlain was an imposing performer for the undefeated 1931 track and field team. During the indoor season he set school records in his two specialties, 4:26.8 in the mile and 9:44.4 in the two mile. Going outdoors, as the team's lone entry in the two-mile at the Drake Relays he would hit the finish line 150 yards ahead of the pack in a meet record-setting time of 9:23.1. He then ran the nation's fastest mile (4:16.8) at the State Intercollegiates and two weeks later the nation's fastest two-mile (9:18.7) at the Central Intercollegiate Conference meet at Milwaukee. He topped his Spartan career by winning the NCAA two-mile title. A true "walk-on" by today's lexicon, Chamberlain had absolutely no high school athletic experience of any kind. Furthermore, he was frail and exhibited ludicrous form as he ran nearly flat-footed, and at full speed there was little change in his style.

Clark Chamberlain

IN THE SPARTLITE

Baseball: MSC hosted Hosei University, the national collegiate baseball champions of Japan, for a pair of games, May 11 and 13. Averaging 5' 6" in height, yet 22 years of age, the visitors from the orient were diminutive, but experienced. Combining near-errorless defense with clever pitching and timely hitting, they managed to twice defeat the Spartans, 5-3 and 4-1. Journalists covering the game were challenged with such names as Nagasawa, Wakabayashi and Nishigaki.

Basketball: Much like that fall's football team, the 16-1 basketball team excelled on the defensive end of play. Over the complete season they yielded an average of less than 20 points per game.

The team co-captains, Roger Grove and Art Haga, were the top scorers over the season, Grove netted 135 points and Haga 120. Dee Pinneo ranked third in the season-ending statistics with 102 total points. Also, Haga was recipient of the Athletic Council award honoring the overall senior athlete who, over four years, distinguished himself in both athletics and academics.

Cross Country: Small in stature but huge at heart, Clark Chamberlain concluded his undefeated cross country season with a first-place finish at the IC4A Championship run in New York. As MSC's sole entry, he paced the six-mile course in 30:19, 40 yards in front of the runner-up. At one point in the race Clark ran off the course for 140 yards. Had he not done so, he would have likely set a record for the event.

Fencing: The six-man team of Bauer, Ken Stonex, Ralph Bristol, Arthur Cash, Jim Wells, and K.A. Krentel journeyed into Illinois for weekend matches with Northwestern and the University of Chicago. Although they returned from the Windy City with two losses, there was a moral victory in the narrow 11-9 setback to the skilled thrusts from the Maroon of Chicago. They had been Big Ten runners-up in 1930.

Upon completion of graduate studies in the spring of 1929, Joseph Waffa, the venerable pioneer of Michigan State fencing, returned to the country of his citizenship, Egypt. His replacement, 31-year-old player-coach George Bauer, would be the most effective competitor in a less-than-impressive season for the team. He won 18 out of 21 jousts with opponents from Big Ten schools. His total record over three years included 64 victories while losing only 21. In recognition, the Hastings senior was awarded a major letter, thus becoming the first-ever fencer to be so honored at MSC.

Football: In his second year at the helm, coach Jim Crowley abandoned the old green jersey with the leather side pieces in favor of a white jersey with a pair of green bands around the sleeve and green numbers on the back. Matching white hose, green satin pants and a green helmet completed the uniform. This was the Spartan look until the next coaching change took place in 1933.

For the second time in the 25-year rivalry, the MAC-U of M game ended in a scoreless tie. Although the Wolverines would capture the battle of statistics, 289 total yards and 13 first downs to 118 total yards and four first

Bobby Monnett (number 33) charges into the line during a 0-0 game at Michigan.

downs, the State defense would win the day. Time after time Crowley's courageous crew would stave off a Wolverine goal-line drive.

Captain-elect Harold Smead, who had lost his leg in a motorcycle accident during the summer in the East, was an emotional incentive that afternoon in Ann Arbor as he made a surprise sideline visit to the team in his wheelchair.

Over the entire eight-game schedule of 1930 the Spartans yielded only 32 points for an average of merely four per contest.

The only loss of the football season was at the hands of Georgetown in the Spartans' first-ever night game, played at Griffith Stadium, the home of major league baseball's Washington Senators. Fans were offered a special $37.28 rail rate aboard the team train from Lansing to the nation's capital. Before 15,000 spectators, the Hoyas led from a pair of scores on long runs, one of 47 yards and the other an 85-yard return of the second-half kickoff. Twice during the first half the Georgetown defense stopped the Spartans on goal-line stands, once on the two-yard line and the second inside the one-yard line. The game's conclusion could have been interesting if the current two-point conversion had been in place along with the tiebreaker. Trailing 14-6, the Spartans blocked a punt and following a short series of plays, Jacob Fase grabbed a Roger Grove TD pass on the final play of the contest. The conversion kick, the lone available PAT option at the time, only made the final count close, 14-13.

An idea surfaced to move the date of the U of D football game from Saturday, November 22 to Thanksgiving Day and the site from East Lansing to the University of Michigan Stadium in Ann Arbor. Upon presenta-

tion to the Athletic Council, the idea was totally rejected. The game ended in a frustrating 0-0 tie, the second scoreless game of the fall.

Golf: Following appropriate team try-outs, the 1931 team was selected and included returning lettermen captain Arnold Duffield and Howard Minier, along with three newcomers: Harold Mayne, Sam Disantis and Don Jones.

In the 15-3 loss to Michigan, Minier shot a 74 to gain all of his team's points.

The 15 1/2-2 1/2 home win over the U of D would be the most convincing victory over the Titans until a shutout administered by the 1962 Spartans. That 1931 match-up was played back at the Lansing Country Club.

Hockey: Preseason planning called for an impressive schedule from January 17 through February 16 to include games against Michigan Tech, Detroit City College, Michigan, Marquette and U of D. For sundry reasons, not one of those scheduled games would be played. Michigan Tech cancelled with little notice and Haley AC, leader of the Detroit Municipal Hockey League, filled the date and defeated State, 4-1. It was then learned that the next opponent, the City College, had suddenly disbanded its team. A spell of mild weather took care of the remainder of the schedule. As Coach Kobs astutely put it, "If you don't have ice, you can't have a team." The season of 1931 had ended. Few would have ventured a guess that it would be 19 years before Spartans would again lace on skates.

Swimming and Diving: In winning four of five dual meets and one triangular meet, the swimming team established six varsity records. It was the most successful season since the sport's introduction in 1922.

The last Michigan State hockey team until the return of the sport in 1950.

Tennis: Led by Hilding Olson and Dee Pinneo, Coach Ball's squad struggled to a record of 1-6-1.

Track and Field: Clark Chamberlain captured the two-mile event at the NCAA championships held on Stagg Field at the University of Chicago. Although a soggy track from a daylong rain and accompanying strong windy conditions altered his performance, his 9:23.0 time was the second fastest ever recorded in the ten year history of the meet. Also, Ken Yarger placed fourth in the 120-yard high hurdles. Garnering 14 points, MSC finished in a tie with Oregon for 10th place.

Later that spring at the *Chicago Herald-Examiner* AAU meet, Yarger and Ed Bath ran one-two in the high hurdles; Cliff Liberty was second in the 220 low hurdles; freshman Charles Warren captured the 440; and Robert Olsen won the pole vault.

Wrestling: Richard Tompkins replaced Norm Stoner as captain of the 1931 team. Stoner had opted to sit out the 1930-1931 season (State's first red shirt?). Tompkins proved to be the team leader in more ways than one, as he was undefeated through the season. In the dual meet with Michigan he hurled his opponent to the mat with such force that he was knocked unconscious.

Coach Collins entered Stan Ball and Harry Byam in the NCAA championships held at Providence, R.I. Both men reached the semifinal round before bowing out. Byam went on to capture his consolation match for the third spot in the lightweight division.

Coach Collins entered three men in the National Amateur Wrestling tournament held in Grand Rapids. Merrill Marshall, star from the 1930 squad, advanced to the finals of the 165-pound division before bowing to the NCAA champion from Oklahoma A&M. Harry Byam lost in his 135-pound semifinal match and freshman heavyweight Gordon Reaveley dropped his opening square-off to the eventual meet runner-up.

EXTRA!
MICHIGAN STATE RELAYS (1930s)

During the decade of the 1930s, the Michigan State Relay Carnival continued to gain in prestige; yet, the cramped facilities of the Gymnasium hampered the expansion of competition beyond the colleges of Michigan. As an example, in 1933, 150 entries jammed the five-hour program while representing 12 schools: Western State Normal, Detroit City College, Highland Park JC, Flint JC, Grand Rapids JC, Michigan Normal, University of Detroit, Albion, Detroit Tech, Adrian, Hillsdale and host Michigan State. In this 13th running of the meet the Spartans won the high hurdles, quarter mile, the two-mile relay, and the 880 relay. Other MSC finishes were second in the two-mile run and thirds in four events: the shot put, pole vault, high jump, and 300-yard run.

MSC 1931-1932

TALES TO TELL

Arthur Buss (FB 31-33 and TR 32-34) recalls what he describes as his first big game, the 20-7 loss to Army played at West Point:

"The Army game of 1931 was my first big game as a starter. Although we lost the game, we outplayed them and stopped their running game cold. Two late Cadet passes spelled the difference, 20-7. Meanwhile, both Bobby Monnett and Abe Eliowitz had great days, as usual.

Coach Jimmy Crowley had set up an effective defense against the great Army offense. Their tackles and ends would pull from the line and lead the interference with runs to the opposite side. Ralph Brunette and I, as tackles, were instructed to immediately follow right behind that pair of blockers and clog up the backfield. Most frequently we would arrive during the exchange from the quarterback to the halfback. They didn't adjust which resulted in Brunette and I having a field day. Being totally exhausted late in the game, I fell to the ground and became our only player to be substituted for. I lost 11 pounds during the afternoon."

Arthur Buss was a terror on defense against Army at West Point.

HEADLINES of 1932

- Radio City Music Hall opens in New York City.
- Erskine Caldwell, author, publishes his book, *Tobacco Road*, telling of life in the "dust bowl" of the southwest.
- Aviator Amelia Earhart becomes the first woman to fly alone across the Atlantic. Five years later she disappears on a flight across the Pacific Ocean.
- The nationwide depression reaches a low as monthly wages are about 60 percent of those in 1929.

SCOREBOARD

	W	L	T	Avg.
Baseball	10	12	2	.458
Track and Field	4	1	0	.800
Football	5	3	1	.611
Basketball	12	5	0	.706
Tennis	9	2	0	.818
Cross Country	2	1	0	.667
Swimming and Diving	1	3	0	.250
Wrestling	4	1	0	.800
Fencing	5	4	0	.556
Golf	5	4	0	.556

TEAM OF THE YEAR

The 1932 wrestling team went 4-1, including shutouts of Toronto College and Mechanics Institute of New York. The biggest win was the 14 1/2-13 1/2 squeaker over Michigan. Four Spartans, Stanley Ball, Norm Stoner, Gordon Reaveley and Lee Marza, were entered in the Fifth Annual NCAA championships hosted by Indiana University. Of the four, Ball was the only one to place, taking third in the 123-pound division.

MAKING HISTORY

Swimming and diving coach Russ Daubert was the inventive type. In the spring of 1932 he was busy perfecting a devise to be used in training divers. The apparatus was a belt that fastened around the athlete's waist and was controlled by a rope and pulley attached to the ceiling and manipulated by a partner. The object was to provide divers an opportunity to experiment on new dives without fear of injury. The idea stuck. Similar riggings are used today by diving coaches. Five years later Daubert was tinkering with yet another device. An article in the October 26, 1937 *State News* revealed:

"He has developed a diving board with the novel feature of a movable fulcrum, which can change the stiffness of the board in proportion of the diver's weight. Those who have tried it find it highly successful."

Again, this idea stuck, and today movable fulcrums are standard equipment.

1932 wrestling team. (Front row, left to right) Stanley Ball, captain Harry Byam, Norm Stoner and Floyd Austin. (Back row, left to right) Coach Fendley Collins, Paul Murdock, Gordon Reaveley, Olin Lepard and Paul Jensen.

GREAT STATE DATES

Football—**October 24, 1931 (H):** The Spartans set their sights on gaining revenge for 1930s disappointing 14-13 loss at Georgetown. Before a slim crowd of 10,000, they achieved their goal with the game's only score in the opening quarter. Taking advantage of an ineffective punt that sailed out of bounds at the Hoya 25-yard line and a subsequent penalty, Abe Eliowitz culminated an abbreviated drive, scoring from less than a foot out. That's all it would take with MSC the winner, 6-0.

Cross Country—**October 24, 1931 (A):** In the season's first meet, a 19-36 victory over Butler, Clark Chamberlain picked up where he left off in 1930. Running a course-record 16:00.4, the Spartan star led the second-place runner by 40 seconds.

Cross Country—**October 30, 1931 (H):** Coach Brown achieved what no previous State cross country coach could claim, a first-year defeat of Michigan. "Brownie's" runners splashed through mud and a cold drizzling rain on their home three and a half mile course to defeat the Wolverines, 24-31. Spartans and their finishing positions were Clark Chamberlain first, Otto Pongrace third, Wes Hurd fourth, Walt Wissner seventh, and Robert O'Conner ninth.

Football—**November 7, 1931 (H):** Little Ripon College of Wisconsin was the victim of a 100-0 slaughter at Macklin Field that saw Crowley's men rack up 823 yards on the ground. Although playing only the first and third quarters, Bobby Monnett would amass 32 points on four TDs and eight extra points. Through that 1931 schedule of nine games, the 170-pound halfback would score 127 points, a team record that has not been surpassed by the "modern day" players. Abe Eliowitz would also score four touchdowns in that Ripon game.

Wrestling—**January 15, 1932 (H):** Of the four victories of the year, none was more cherished than the 14 1/2 to 13 1/2 win over Michigan, the first over the Wolverines since 1925. Before a capacity crowd in the gymnasium, the Spartans won only three of the eight bouts, but both Stan Ball and Norm Stoner pinned their opponents, and thus each gained five team points rather than the customary three points. Floyd Austin won on a decision and Olin Lepard was awarded a tie following completion of two overtime periods.

Basketball—**January 29 (H) and January 30 (H), 1932:** With winning scores of 30-21 and 29-28, State repeated its 1930-1931 back-to-back double win over Colgate. Following the rather easy win on Friday night, the Maroon proved far more competitive in the second game. Leading 18-17 at half time, the visitors maintained a margin in the second session that at one juncture grew to seven points. The dogged Spartans kept battling away, and their efforts were finally rewarded. Seldom in the spotlight, Alton Kircher became an instant hero. The Gladstone (Mich.) junior scored with less than 10 seconds remaining in regulation to tie the game and then duplicated the effort in overtime for the win.

Basketball—**February 13, 1932 (H):** Playing before a packed-in crowd of more than 5,000 in Dem Hall, the game with the University of Michigan was knotted at 11-11 at the conclusion of regulation. It would then take two overtimes before MSC could gain the winning margin. Once more Al Kircher proved to be the star, sealing the victory 14-13 on a free throw with virtually no time remaining in the second OT.

Baseball—**April 21, 1932 (H):** In their biggest offensive outburst of the spring, MSC made quick work of Central State Teachers, scoring seven runs in the opening inning and going on for a convincing 19-2 victory. Aiding in the 17-hit State attack was a generous Central defense, committing seven errors, yielding two passed balls and a pair of wild pitches. Coach Kobs seized the opportunity to work 20 players into the lineup.

Track and Field—**May 7, 1932 (H):** Notre Dame entered the 1932 dual meet as the top-heavy favorite. After all, they had won 16 of the previous 18 match-ups in a series that began in 1905, and this 1932 team had already scored victories over Illinois, Wisconsin and Iowa. As the meet progressed, the team score seemed to change hands with the conclusion of each event. Cliff Liberty, who had taken a first and a second in the two hurdle events, would finish the day at the broad jump pit. It was there, in the final event of the afternoon, that Cliff would leap to a third-place spot. Sometimes even a third place is important. The Spartans won the meet by the slimmest of margins, 65 3/4 to 65 1/4.

Baseball—**May 14, 1932 (H):** Charley Griffin, ace of the MSC team, yielded only five hits that led to a 5-2 victory over Notre Dame. It was the southpaw's third straight defeat of the Irish over his three-year Spartan career. The game was really decided in the fifth inning when "River" Morse drove in three runs with a base-clearing double.

Tennis—May 16, 1932 (N): The 6-3 win over Michigan Normal, played on the U of M courts, was achieved despite Stan Weitz and Rex Norris being upset in both singles and doubles. Guy Stonebraker, Don Link, Bill Loose and Dee Pinneo carried the load for State.

Tennis—May 21, 1932 (H): Including four straight-set victories in the singles and one straight set win in the doubles, State defeated Notre Dame, 7-2. Winners were Stan Weitz, 6-2, 6-0; Rex Norris, 6-1, 6-2; Don Link 6-2, 6-1; Bill Loose 6-1, 6-1; and captain Hilding Olson 6-1, 4-6, 6-1. Winners in the pairs were Weitz and Norris, 6-3, 2-6, 6-2 and Loose with Guy Stonebraker, 6-2, 6-2. One week later at South Bend they would repeat the win, this time by an 8-1 score.

Golf—May 27 and 28, 1932 (A): Coach VanAlstyne's squad made the weekend trip to Detroit profitable as his men matched their double sweep of Detroit City college and the U of D achieved in East Lansing two weeks earlier. The winning four-man combination consisted of Arnold Duffield, Don Jones, Carl Mitchell and Bob Mueller.

Baseball—May 30, 1932 (H): Charley "Chip" Griffin closed out the 1932 home schedule in style. A Hollywood screenwriter could not have scripted the finale any better. With two outs in the bottom of the ninth, State trailed the University of Chicago, 6-5. Jerry McCaslin was perched on first base with the potential tying run. Griffin, in his concluding home appearance, stood at the plate with a full 3-2 count. With the game on the line, he took a vicious cut at the next pitch and caught the ball solidly, sending it deep into right center. While local fans roared and the Maroon outfielders ran the ball down, "Chip" circled the bases behind McCaslin and eventually beat the throw to home plate. Griffin had won his own ball game, 7-6 on a two-run homer.

ATHLETE OF THE YEAR

Abe Eliowitz was a two-sport star, excelling in both football and baseball. The Governor of Michigan Award, presented annually to the football player voted as the most valuable by teammates, was introduced in 1931. Eliowitz was the first to be so honored. In baseball, his three-base hit total of 10 from 1931-1933 remains among the Spartan career records, the oldest standing statistic.

IN THE SPARTLITE

Baseball: The Michigan game at Ann Arbor ended in a rare tie. Abe Eliowitz sent the game into extra frames when he knotted the score 3-3 on a ninth-inning home run. The game was eventually called because of darkness after 16 innings.

Charley "Chip" Griffin was a pitching star during a three-year Spartan career, 1930-1932. His sophomore year record of 7-1 included two victories against Notre Dame and a pair of wins over Michigan. Griffin continued his mastery over the U of M during his junior year with two additional victories, the second being a six-hit 5-0 shutout.

Basketball: In what could likely be a record, for a span of six games from January 30 to February 20, the basketball team engaged in five overtime games. They defeated Colgate, Michigan, Marquette and Detroit, before losing to Xavier.

In the 27-5 basketball loss to Michigan, MSC managed their second-lowest point total ever. Surprisingly, during the first half of that game, State was in control of

Abe Eliowitz

the ball 75 percent of the time and had 15 shots to the Wolverines' one. Yet it took nine minutes and 10 seconds before State would score its first and what would prove to be its final field goal.

Cross Country: In the final dual meet of the fall, Clark Chamberlain posted a course record time of 24:01.3 over the four and a half mile layout at Notre Dame. He broke the tape nearly one minute ahead of the field. Unfortunately, his teammates came up one spot short, resulting in a 27-28 Irish win.

Fencing: Among competitors who faced MSC as members of the Cadillac A.C. in Detroit was the future Spartan coach, Charlie Schmitter.

Football: The U of M game was the next to the last game of the season, and for the second straight year the battle ended in a scoreless tie. Representing the largest crowd to have experienced this annual tussle, 51,000 fans sat through less-than-favorable weather conditions. Played in an afternoon-long rain shower, both teams had scoring chances aborted by the elements. Monnett once broke into the open with an intercepted pass but slipped and fell. Eliowitz returned the second-half kickoff to midfield and may have gone all the way, only to lose his footing. Statistically, the game was close. Michigan made five first downs and 131 net yards, and State managed four first downs and 120 yards.

Golf: It was finally realized that sharing coaching time between spring football and golf was not a good idea. Jim Crowley relinquished the golf position after only two years in the dual capacity. Basketball coach Ben VanAlstyne assumed the post and would remain for 28 seasons, 18 as head coach for both sports.

Swimming and Diving: With the graduation losses of Horace Craig, Ray Schaubel and Howard Clark, Coach Daubert was justifiably apprehensive upon opening the 1932 season. Just two weeks prior to the season opener against Grand Rapids Junior College, Coach Daubert was still looking for help. A piece in the January 8 issue of the *Michigan State News* read as follows: "Men who have had experience on swimming teams should report to Coach Daubert any night during the week at five o'clock."

Tennis: Up from the freshman team, the trio of Don Link of Owosso, Rex Norris from Lansing and Stan Weitz, the Grand Rapids city champion, would instill a winning attitude into the Spartan varsity program. During the seasons of 1932-1934, MSC would register an impressive composite team record of 32-3.

Track and Field: For the third year in succession MSC placed second behind Michigan Normal for supremacy in the State Intercollegiate meet. Three Spartans won titles. Otto Pongrace, with a time of 1:56.5, captured the 880-yard run. Roger Keast took the quarter-mile in 49.3 seconds and Ralph Small led the way in the two-mile with a 9:47.

Competing in the Central Intercollegiate meet at Milwaukee, the Spartans placed fifth out of a field of 17 Midwestern schools. The fine work of three men, Pongrace, Ken Lafayette and Keast, left nothing to be desired. Pongrace continued a series of wins by taking the 880 with a varsity record time of 1:56.3. Lafayette turned in the best performances of his college career, placing third in the 100- and 220-yard dashes behind Ralph Metcalf, the winner and three-time NCAA champion in both sprints. Quarter-miler Keast, who would eventually place fifth at the NCAA championships in Chicago, settled for a third place.

At the Olympic team trials in Palo Alto, Calif., two Spartans earned their way onto the U.S. squad, Ernest Crosbie in the 50,000-meter walk and Tom Ottey in the 10,000-meter run. Clark Chamberlain, also competing in the 10,000-meter run trials, placed fourth, one spot removed from making the team. At the Games in Los Angeles, Crosbie finished eighth and Ottey ninth in their respective events, both top spots for the USA.

Wrestling: Fendley Collins's 1932 team finished with a record of four wins against one loss. That one setback was to Indiana University, the Big Ten champions. The pair of sophomore additions, 118-pound Floyd Austin and heavyweight Gordon "Buck" Reaveley, had won both Michigan AAU titles as freshmen. Austin, from Lansing and a graduate of the Michigan School for the Blind, had a serious handicap of defective vision.

Stan Ball, Norm Stoner, Lee Marza and Buck Reavely competed in the NCAA championships held at Indiana University. Being an Olympic year, the seven official Olympic weights (123, 134, 145, 158, 174, 191 and more than 191 pounds) were substituted for the regular NCAA program. Stan Ball placed third in the 123-pound division as Norm Stoner and Lee Marza reached the second round before elimination.

SPARTAN SCRAPBOOK
—— SWIMMING and DIVING ——

First swimming and diving team (1922)

MSC
1932-1933

TALES TO TELL

MSC's heavyweight wrestler of 1932, Buck Reaveley, missed the 1933 season due to an undiagnosed illness that kept him hospitalized for two weeks in a weakened condition. Olin Lepard filled the spot admirably. With his patented scissor hold, Lepard became a home crowd favorite. When he clamped his long limbs about an opponent's midriff, the crowd would let out a roar and then settle back to watch Olin's opponent try to escape. Among his victories in 1933 was a win over Robert Jones, the NCAA runner-up from the University of Indiana. In correspondence, Lepard reveals a deeply guarded secret:

"I entered Michigan State in the fall of 1929 and graduated in the spring of 1933. I had never seen a wrestling match until I got to MSC. Fendley Collins worked out with me a good deal of the time as he taught me how to use my legs during competition.

My weight was about 190 pounds. I could make the 175-pound class if needed, but most frequently wrestled as the heavyweight. I was able to win about one-half of my matches as a freshman and most of them thereafter.

In the summer between my junior and senior years I secured a job with Oakland Dairy Farms about two miles out of Ann Arbor. My job was to assist in transporting and exhibiting a herd of show cattle to various state fairs including Wisconsin, Minnesota, Missouri and North Dakota. I eventually hooked up with a side show that accompanied those fairs wherein I would come forward and challenge anyone in the audience to stay in the ring with me for five minutes without being pinned. If they could do so they would get $25. The challenge was no problem as I could have pinned most of them in less than five minutes. This was not allowed as it would have spoiled the act. I made an extra $150 to $175 that way.

I have never told this story before for fear of jeopardizing my amateur status. Now, after 68 years, I feel safe in doing so."

HEADLINES of 1933

- The Tennessee Valley Authority (TVA) becomes an independent government agency to conserve area resources.
- Among the songs introduced during the year are "Stormy Weather," "Smoke Gets in Your Eyes," "Heat Wave," and "Easter Parade."
- The American League topped the National League, 4-2, in baseball's first All-Star game, and the Chicago Bears defeated the New York Giants, 23-21, in the NFL's first championship game.
- The first drive-in theater opens in Camden, N.J., accommodating 400 automobiles.

SCOREBOARD

	W	L	T	Avg.
Baseball	13	7	0	.650
Track and Field	3	0	0	1.000
Football	7	1	0	.875
Basketball	10	7	0	.588
Tennis	11	1	0	.917
Cross Country	3	0	0	1.000
Swimming and Diving	3	4	0	.429
Wrestling	3	2	0	.600
Fencing	4	3	0	.571
Golf	5	4	1	.550

MAKING HISTORY

A basketball rule was introduced in 1933 and has remained a part of the men's game ever since: a team must move the ball beyond the mid-court line within ten seconds after gaining possession.

GREAT STATE DATES

Football—**October 22, 1932 (A):** In their fifth game of the season, the Spartans played the previously unbeaten and unscored-upon Fordham Rams at New York City's Polo Grounds. Bobby Monnett's opening play, an 80-yard touchdown dash, furnished the winning inspiration for his teammates in what would be a 19-13 upset victory. In an unimaginable maneuver by today's standards, Coach Crowley used only 16 players during that entire afternoon. The visit to New York City would prove costly. Enamored by Crowley's style, Fordham officials began a relentless and ultimately successful campaign of luring the popular coach to the Bronx school.

TEAM OF THE YEAR

Led by the running of co-captains Bobby Monnett and Abe Eliowitz, the 1932 varsity football squad (pictured below) reveals a 20-man squad that averaged 172 pounds in weight and five feet, 10 1/2 inches in height. Compare this to the 2002 Spartan squad of 102 players who averaged 225 pounds and six foot two in height.

1932 football team. (Front row, left to right) Terlaak, Klewicki, Kircher, Monnett, Eliowitz, Meiers, Vandermeer and Kowatch. (Second row, left to right) Squier, Armstrong, Brunette, Handy, Jones, Lay and Keast. (Third row, left to right) Manager Morrison, Reaveley, Butler, Buss, McNutt and Ferrari. (Back row, left to right) Coaches Casteel, Crowley and Carberry, trainer Heppinstall.

Football—**October 29, 1932 (A):** For the second Saturday in a row, MSC met an Eastern power and once again emerged the winner, State 27, Syracuse 13. Ed Klewicki paved the way for the first TD when he blocked an Orange punt at the 28-yard line in the second quarter. Four plays later Bernie McNutt crashed over right tackle for nine yards and the score. An Al Kircher-to-Bobby Monnett, 38-yard pass play made the score 14-0, and a sustained drive of 60 yards netted the third score with Abe Eliowitz going in from the 18-yard line. After the Orangemen had crossed the goal line twice, they again turned the ball over; this time "Red" Vandermeer recovered a fumble on the Syracuse 21-yard line. Two plays later McNutt once again carried the ball for the score.

Cross Country—**October 29, 1932 (A):** In his first varsity meet, Tom Ottey led the pack over the three and a half mile course at Ann Arbor in a record-setting time of 17:25. With a score of 26-31, the State squad outran the Wolverines for the fifth time in six years. Following the new Spartan star to the finish line were Otto Pongrace fourth, Walt Wissner sixth, Ralph Small seventh, John Hammer eighth, and Loring Fullerton ninth.

Basketball—**January 17, 1933 (A):** Concluding a five-game series in three years against Colgate University, the Spartans were once again victorious. In this final encounter of the senses, the Spartans scored their second-highest point total of the year in a relatively easy 40-26 win. Reserve center Arnold VanFaasen scored 20 and was therefore responsible for half of the team total.

Basketball—**January 28, 1933 (H):** Before one of the year's largest home crowds, the Spartan cagers swamped the touring team from Meiji University of Japan, 63-15. The diminutive Meiji players were at a distinct disadvantage with the jump ball after each made a basket. The tallest player on the Japanese squad stood five foot nine.

Wrestling—**February 4, 1933 (H):** The Ohio State match proved to be the most exciting of the season. Trailing in the team scoring 11-6, Lee Marza, wrestling at the 165-pound weight division, pinned his opponent. Bobby Monnett followed with a win at 175 and heavyweight Olin Lepard held on for a tie to gain the margin of victory, 15 1/2-12 1/2.

Basketball—**February 15, 1933 (A):** State edged the U of D in the final home game of the season, 30-28. Leading 18-10 at half-time, VanAlstyne's men were outscored 18-12 during the final 20 minutes but hung on in a game described by the *Wolverine* yearbook as "almost degenerating into a free-for-all." A two-team total of 36 personal fouls were called as four Titans were whistled with four game-ejecting infractions.

Track and Field—**March 3, 1933 (H):** Fresh from triumphs over Notre Dame and Wisconsin, Marquette came to town with their Olympic sprinter, Ralph Metcalf, who would win six NCAA championships from 1932 to 1934. Although the Hilltopper ace won his specialties, the 40-yard and 220-yard dashes, the Spartans defeated the visitors, 61-3/5 to 47-2/5. Juniors Otto Pongrace and Tom Ottey, who returned from a lengthy injury, led the Spartans. Pongrace won the half-mile in 2:02.6, while Ottey established a new gymnasium record with his 9:39.7 two-mile victory.

Fencing—**March 4, 1933 (H):** Two of the year's four victories were over the Detroit Turnverein team to which Charles Schmitter had changed affiliation from the Cadillac A.C. The second match was particularly exciting as Bauer's squad came back, 9-8, after trailing 6-3.

Baseball—**April 13, 1933 (H):** Returning from the annual southern trip with a record of 2-3, Coach Kobs called upon his left-hander Berwyn Pemberton to pitch the first game of the regular season against the Iowa Hawkeyes. The Imlay City senior came through with a two-hit 4-0 shutout. State banged out 12 base hits, nine of them in the last three innings when they scored all four runs. With three hits, Al Kircher was the offensive star of the day. Floyd Morse, Art Rouse and Pemberton each accounted for a pair of hits.

Baseball—**April 29, 1933 (A):** Jerry McCaslin pitched a masterful game in downing the University of Michigan, 5-1. He never permitted more than one hit per inning, yielding a total of seven. It was the first MSC win at Ann Arbor since 1914.

Baseball—**May 3, 1933 (H):** For five innings State trailed Notre Dame 2-1. They then scored four runs over the remaining three frames to defeat the Irish 5-3. It was the Spartans' sixth straight win since returning from the southern trip. The game was tied 3-3 in the bottom of the eighth when Al Kircher bounced a single through the middle scoring the lead runs.

Track and Field—**May 6, 1933 (A):** In MSC's only dual meet of the spring, Ralph Young's squad registered a rare win at South Bend, 67-64. Wes Hurd provided an impetus for the team's performance. Disgusted at losing the opening event, the mile run, Hurd successfully badgered his coach into letting him enter the two-mile race,

Wes Hurd demonstrates his "never-say-die" attitude.

an event for which he had never trained. The result was melodramatic as the day's hero won the eight-lap event and, in so doing, awakened a winning spirit within his teammates. As could be expected, the final meet result was in doubt until the last event when the relay quartet of Roger Keast, Otto Pongrace, Charles Warren and Frank Hoff beat the Irish to the tape.

Golf—**May 20, 1933 (A):** It what would be their most decisive win of the spring. State topped the University of Detroit over their Clinton Valley course, 13 1/2-4 1/2. Playing in rain and mud, Russ Turrill led the way by carding a two-over-par 74.

Baseball—**June 3, 1933 (A):** The State bats accounted for 16 hits, including home runs by Abe Eliowitz and Al Kircher, to hand Notre Dame a 14-5 defeat, the most decisive win ever over the Irish. Garold McCaslin, relieved by Berwyn Pemberton, gained the pitching victory. The pair gave up only six hits.

Tennis—**June 3, 1933 (N):** The Spartans of Michigan State were crowned state collegiate champions after winning both the singles and the doubles titles from Michigan Normal players on the Western State courts. Stan Weitz, while concluding his junior year as the number-one man, was matched against Lou Carson of Ypsi,

the defending champion. Weitz lost his first set of the year in the opener, 4-6, and then reversed form to tie it up, 6-3. Long, drawn-out points in the third set had the large crowd of fans gasping with amazement. Both men held serve for 12 games before Weitz broke through and followed with a service win for the 8-6 victory. Stan then teamed with Rex Norris for an easy 6-2, 6-0 doubles championship. Team points were: MSC eight, Michigan Normal and Western State tied with six each, and Kalamazoo two.

ATHLETE OF THE YEAR

In a personal interview just before his death, George Alderton identified Bobby Monnett, the happy-go-lucky running back from Bucyrus, Ohio, as the greatest Spartan football player he ever recalled. Monnett would frequently make the clutch offensive play to win the given game, and in both 1931 and 1932 he led the nation in scoring. He was the recipient of the 1932 Governor of Michigan Award, given annually to the player voted as the most valuable by teammates. In addition to his gridiron heroics, in 1933 Monnett lettered as the wrestling team's 165-pound entrant. Following his Spartan days, Bobby played professionally for the Green Bay Packers from 1933-1938.

Bobby Monnett

IN THE SPARTLITE

Baseball: For non-conference affiliate Michigan State, defeating a Big Ten school was particularly gratifying. This they managed to do five times in 1933: shutting out Iowa 4-0, defeating Michigan 5-1 and Chicago 9-2 and topping Northwestern twice, 5-4 and 7-3.

Shadows of the Great Depression caused many schools of the North to abort their traditional Dixie spring training trip. Although the financial crunch was real, Coach Kobs found adequate funds to leave the chill of Michigan in late March for a five-game set in North Carolina via a true "economy plan." The team traveled in personal automobiles driven by Kobs, and, in exchange for gasoline and oil, by assistant team manager Dave Ireland and Ken Wood, another student. Head manager Robert M. Pratt drove his light coupe pulling a trailer carrying the luggage and team equipment. Playing against Elom College, Wake Forest and North Carolina University, the travelers slept in makeshift accommodations within the host's athletic facilities while dining at school boarding clubs.

Basketball: Ten men received their varsity awards: Co-captain Alton Kircher, Gladstone senior; Co-captain Garol McCaslin, Saginaw senior; Arnold VanFaasen, Holland sophomore; James Dekker, Muskegon junior; Robert Herrick, Eaton Rapids sophomore; Charles Muth, Kalamazoo sophomore; Wendall Patchett, Adrian junor; Edward Riorden, Lansing sophomore; Nick VanderRoest, Kalamazoo junior; and William Vondette, Saginaw senior.

Cross Country: Tom Ottey of Philadelphia followed Clark Chamberlain as State's next distance running star. He had come to know Clark from various meets and decided to follow the diminutive star's path to East Lansing. Ottey had been a member of the 1932 USA Olympic team as an entrant in the 10,000-meter run; consequently, much was expected of him in his first varsity season. He fulfilled those expectations by capturing first place in all three dual meets and leading the team to an undefeated season.

The date of the Michigan intercollegiate championships occasionally conflicted with the running of the more prestigious IC4A. Consequently, the New York City meet often took preference over the state title. No Spartan team was entered for that state championship of 1930, a partial "A" team placed third in 1931, and a "B" team likewise placed third in 1932.

Fencing: Seven of the nine places in the 1933 National Junior Championships were captured by current or former Spartans. Jack Murphy, 1933 team captain, won second in the foil and third in the sabre matches. K.A. Krental and Art Cash finished first and third in the epee. Ralph Bristol, who had originally been elected captain of the 1933 team but failed to return to school, was the star of the tournament as he won both foil and sabre, while placing second in epee.

Football: At a team banquet following the 7-1 season, Coach Crowley recognized his senior co-captains Bobby Monnett and Abe Eliowitz with the following comments:

> "In all my years of coaching I have never run across a finer pair of football players and men than Bob Monnett and Abe Eliowitz. They are two of the most unselfish, loyal, hardworking boys I have ever had the pleasure to work with. In all their games they worked for each other, the team, and the school. They played hard and fair. They are real men."

In February "Sleepy Jim" Crowley and his two assistants, Glen "Judge" Carberry and Frank Leahy, departed for Fordham. One month later, Charlie Bachman began a 13-year stint as MSC's 12th head coach. For his staff, he retained the likable Mike Casteel and added Tom King, a Notre Dame teammate who had been serving as director of athletics at the University of Louisville.

Golf: Again seeking a "home" for his team, Coach VanAlstyne secured time at the Lansing Country Club for practice on Monday and Friday afternoons.

The 1933 team was built around returnees Russ Turrill, Bob Mueller and Bill Mitchell, along with Robert Clark, Robert Herrick and Bob Malloy.

Based on points earned for the team over the season, the top four Spartans were Turrill 23, Mueller 22, Clark 18 1/2 and Mitchell 12 1/2.

Swimming and Diving: Of the 50 swimming and diving hopefuls who responded to Coach Daubert's call for tryouts, 11 would eventually comprise the core of the varsity team. Leonard Montgomery, a junior from Detroit, would be the season's top scorer with 47 points.

Tennis: The outstanding player in the 5-4 loss to Michigan was MSC's Stan Weitz. Playing in the number-one position, he won a brilliantly played three-set victory over Colby Ryan, the star of the U of M team. Weitz continued his winning ways in the summer of 1933

by capturing the state title at Grand Rapids while also gaining the 12th position in the official Midwest rankings with Rex Norris close behind in 13th place. Although not a State starter in 1933, Don Sexton played surprisingly well that summer and captured the Illinois Open crown at Olympic Fields near Chicago.

Track and Field: The mile medley relay team of Charles Warren, Andrew Cobb, Frank Hoff and Otto Pongrace set a new American Intercollegiate record of 3:37.4 at the West Virginia Relay Carnival.

At the IC4A meet, Pongrace finished third in the 800-meter run with Ted Bath taking a third place in the high hurdles.

During the summer of 1933 Tom Ottey trained by pulling a rickshaw at the Chicago World's Fair.

Wrestling: On a whim, Bobby Monnett, the football star, showed up in the wrestling room and suddenly became the team's entry at the 165-pound class.

Stan Ball and Olin Lepard finished the 1933 dual-meet season undefeated; however, due to lack of funds, both men were prevented from representing the team in the NCAAs at Lehigh University in Bethlehem, Pa.

Joe Kowatch (31) on the move against Michigan.

MSC
1933-1934

TALES TO TELL

Correspondence from Theron Fager (BS 33 35) recalls the game played against the Cleveland Indians of the American League on June 4, 1934. It was the only time, before or since, that a Spartan team would take the field against a major league opponent:

"Sixty years ago, John Kobs's Spartan baseball team played an exhibition game with the American League leading Cleveland Indians on Old College Field. Pitching for Cleveland was manager Walter Johnson, considered by many as the greatest right hander of all time. Although his regular pitching days were over, he could still throw that high hard one with accuracy. In 1936, he was elected to the Hall of Fame with the inaugural class which included Ty Cobb, Honus Wagner, Babe Ruth and Christy Mathewson. We were thrilled to get a chance to hit against this great hurler who would eventually pitch the entire nine-inning game. Charlie Brown had an experience he likely never forgot. In the very first inning he parked one of Johnson's offerings into the Red Ce-

dar River for a grand-slam home run. For the remainder of the afternoon the veteran pitching ace had the Spartans flying out, although Arnold Parker, our center fielder, did manage two hits. Meanwhile, the Indian regulars bombarded the Spartan trio of John Berg, George Hopkins and Allan Kronbach for 19 hits and 14 runs, as Earl Averill (another member of baseball's Hall of Fame) and Hal Trosky led the way with three hits apiece. To somewhat ease the pain of a one-sided game, our infield of Eddie Fiedler, Art Rouse, 'Buzz' Bartling and myself turned three double plays. Other starters that afternoon were Berg, Brown, Freddie Ziegel, 'River' Morse and Bill McCann.

The following day many of us went to Detroit to see the Tigers in a double header against the Indians. Detroit won the first game with the second ending in a tie due to darkness (no lights at Navin Field). The Tiger victory put them in first place, which they held to win the pennant of 1934. We always said that we had a part in Detroit's success as we softened Cleveland up the day before."

HEADLINES of 1934

- The bank robber and murderer John Dillinger, public enemy number one, is shot and killed by the FBI.
- Al Capp, cartoonist, introduces the comic strip "Li'l Abner."
- Clarinetist Benny Goodman, the "King of Swing," organized one of the first swing bands to popularize jazz dance music.
- The Dionne quintuplets, five girls born in Ontario, Canada, are the first known quintuplets to survive.

SCOREBOARD

	W	L	T	Avg.
Baseball	10	11	1	.477
Track and Field	1	2	0	.333
Football	4	2	2	.625
Basketball	12	5	0	.706
Tennis	12	0	0	1.000
Cross Country	3	0	0	1.000
Swimming and Diving	1	4	0	.200
Wrestling	2	4	0	.333
Fencing	5	1	0	.833
Golf	2	8	0	.200

TEAM OF THE YEAR

The Stan Weitz, Rex Norris-led tennis team would complete an undefeated season with 12 victories and no defeats. Included among their victims were the University of Chicago, and both Michigan and Ohio State twice. These three teams finished first-second-third respectively in that year's Big Ten championships. By this measure alone, it could be argued the 1934 team was the best ever at State.

MAKING HISTORY

The pinnacle performance of the undefeated 1933 cross country season was run at Van Cortlandt Park in New York City when the Spartans finally captured the coveted IC4A title. Tom Ottey led a field of 124 runners to the tape as he edged the star of the East, Joe Mangan of Cornell, by five seconds. Rounding out the winning team total of 54 points were Otto Pongrace in ninth, Ed Becktold 14th, John Hammer 18th and Walt Hertzler 20th. Bob Gardner, although not counted in the team score, captured the 35th spot. Following MSC in the final team scoring were Manhattan with 84, Yale 100, Cornell 113, Syracuse 118 and Maine 177. Rhode Island, Harvard, Pittsburgh and Penn State also placed in the team scoring. The *Michigan State News* unfurled a front-page story with the headlines reading: "State X-Country Team Now Ranks First In Nation." With the inaugural NCAA title run still four years away, such boasting was undisputable.

1934 tennis team. (Front row, left to right) Stan Weitz and Rex Norris. (Back row, left to right) Coach Charles Ball, Don Sexton, Will Klunzinger, Bill Loose, Dick O'Dell, Marshall Goodwin, Don Link and Sawyer, the manager.

GREAT STATE DATES

Football—**October 21, 1933 (A):** Because of the adverse playing conditions, George Alderton remembered the Marquette game in Milwaukee as the "strangest" he had ever witnessed. It was a day of an unceasing downpour of rain, and by game time there were three to four inches of water covering the entire field. Under such hopeless conditions, both coaches engaged in the same game plan of punting and waiting for the opposition to fumble the wet and slippery ball. Sure enough, it was a first-quarter Marquette fumble on their own 10-yard line that led to the only score of the game. From Alderton's story in *The Lansing State Journal*:

> "The first play following the fumble sent McNutt whirling and spinning through left tackle on a reverse play to the weak side of the line. McNutt skidded over the goal line half the length of his body when tackled. This was the only thrill that the 5,000 or so spectators, who sat through the pouring rain, had to cheer them."

George further reported:

> "The game was drab. Now and then there was a laugh or a thrill as the players, pulling and plowing, they could not be accused of running, through the mud put on a little tumbling and high diving act."

During the afternoon, State ran the ball only 10 times for a total of 21 yards (there were no passes), while they punted the soggy ball 20 times, averaging 33.2 yards.

Football—**October 28, 1933 (H):** With a score of 27-3, State upset the previously undefeated Syracuse Orange for their fourth win of the season. State had trailed 3-0 at the half when an Al Kircher to Ed Klewicki pass opened the scoring for the Green in the third quarter. The Spartans then put the game away with three touchdowns in the final period, two by sophomore Kurt Warmbein of St. Joe, one of which was an impressive 70-yard scamper. Not one to bask in his success, after the game, Warmbein showered, dressed and hurried over to the college infirmary to scrub floors in fulfillment of responsibilities for his campus job.

Cross Country—**October 28, 1933 (A):** The highlight of the second straight undefeated dual-meet season was a near-perfect 17-40 win over the U of M at Ann Arbor. Tom Ottey, Ed Becktold, John Hammer and Otto Pongrace had completed the course before the first Wolverine crossed the finish line. With Michigan temporarily dropping the sport, the two schools would not meet again until 1952.

Basketball—**December 9, 1933 (A):** In only his second varsity game, sophomore Maurice Buysse was a significant contributor in the see-saw win at Ann Arbor. Yet, it was another sophomore and Lansing product, Danny Reck from Central High School, who scored the winning basket. With State holding a 21-16 lead late in the game, the Wolverines rallied to forge ahead, 22-21. After exchanging scores and with precious time remaining, Reck broke through two Michigan defenders and unleashed a field goal that rolled around the edge of the rim dramatically before dropping through for a final score of 26-25.

Basketball—**February 5, 1934 (A):** A big road win was registered at Madison, Wis., when VanAlstyne's men edged the Badgers, 23-22. With only seconds remaining in the game, Nick VanderRoest took a pass in the corner, faked around his defender, dribbled under the hoop, and easily dropped in the game winner. The margin of victory was revealed in the game statistics: while the teams both made eight field goals, the Spartans converted a perfect seven-of-seven free throws while the host Badgers sank six-of-nine attempts.

Basketball—**February 10, 1934 (H):** In follow up to the win at Ann Arbor in December, the Spartans again topped the Wolverines, this time more easily, 33-26. It was the first double win over the U of M since the season of 1920. Scoring 13 and 11 points respectively, Maurice Buysse and Arnold VanFaasen would account for 24 of the team's winning total.

Tennis—**April 27, 1934 (A):** The season opened at Ann Arbor, where the Spartans edged the Wolverines 5-4. With the team score tied 4-4, the doubles team of Bill Loose and Don Link took the court for the final pairing of the afternoon. In the first set, the Michigan pair grabbed the lead, but they went to deuce twice before the MSC duo took charge for a 6-4 win. After dropping the second set, 7-5, the Spartan seniors played superb tennis for a 6-4 third set win, match, and meet victory.

Track and Field—**May 5, 1934 (H):** For the third time in four years, State easily defeated the U of D, this time by a convincing score of 95-34. This was enough

for the Titan coach. Never again would Detroit engage the Spartans in a dual meet. Al Jackson completed a rare "triple" as he won the high jump, broad jump, and 120-yard high hurdle event.

Baseball—May 9 (H) and June 2 (A), 1934: As in 1933, the Spartans pulled off a rare double win over Notre Dame, 8-1 at home, and three weeks later 13-9 in South Bend. In the game on College Field, State struck early, combining three hits with three Irish errors to produce a five-run cushion in the very first inning. This proved a comfortable margin for lanky John Berg, as he scattered six hits over nine innings. Art Rouse was the hitting star, going three-for-three. The follow up game was somewhat similar. State struck early (five runs in the first three innings) and the ND defense was generous (seven errors over nine innings). "River" Morse connected for three hits in four at-bats.

Tennis—May 12 (H) and May 19 (A), 1934: It is difficult to believe, but State topped Notre Dame twice without using their number-one player Stan Weitz on either occasion. There is no record of why the star from Grand Rapids sat out the two matches. In the 7-2 victory at home Rex Norris, Will Klunzinger, Don Link and Bill Loose won easily in straight sets, as did the doubles teams of Link-Loose and Marshall Goodwin-Klunzinger. One week later on the courts at South Bend, it was a similar scenario with Coach Ball's squad scoring a 6-3 team victory. The Loose-Don Sexton doubles team played the most exciting match in their 6-4, 5-7, 9-7 win.

Baseball—May 19, 1934 (H): After dropping a 14-inning Friday afternoon game to Ohio State, 6-4, the Spartans came back with a vengeance on the next afternoon, lashing out 18 hits, including three home runs and five triples, to roast the Buckeyes, 13-4. The four-baggers came from the bats of "River" Morse, Charlie Brown and Theron Fager. Sophomore first baseman Irving Bartling led the offense with four hits in five appearances. Adding to the MSC offense, two double steals were successfully executed.

Tennis—May 25, 1934 (H): For the first time ever, the Spartans defeated the University of Michigan twice in one spring. After handling the Wolverines 5-4 in the season opener at Ann Arbor, they topped them on the return match at East Lansing 7-2. By capturing the first five matches, the repeat team win was assured early. Number-one player Stan Weitz and number-two Rex Norris led the way with straight-set victories and then teamed up in doubles for a satisfying 6-1, 4-6, 6-2 conclusion to the afternoon.

Tennis—May 28, 1934 (H): Everybody loves a winner. As the undefeated 1934 season closed down, the *Michigan State News* was publishing full-column tennis stories. Also, without reporting exact numbers, the paper of May 29 did suggest increased spectator interest for the match against the Big Ten champions from Chicago University:

> "One of the largest tennis galleries in the history of the school turned out for the Chicago match Monday afternoon, and was rewarded by a great exhibition of tennis put on by Stanley Weitz and Max Davidson, Western Conference champions.
>
> Weitz's blistering, unorthodox two-handed forehand and crisp backhand shots drew the plaudits of the gallery continuously. The Spartan co-captain harried the little Chicagoan with a tantalizing chop stroke that he intermingled with his drives."

To the delight of the assembled partisans, Weitz, now in his senior year, eventually subdued the Big Ten champion, 7-5, 5-7, 6-1 and the team topped the Maroons, 5-1. A few fans were able to park their automobiles nearby and watch the action "live" while listening to "Blondie" Farleman's courtside report over WKAR radio.

ATHLETE OF THE YEAR

Stan Weitz was a winner and a leader on and off the tennis courts. In the three years prior to his appearance on the scene, MSC teams had established a composite dual-meet record of 7-18-1. In the three years the Grand Rapids native patrolled the courts as a Spartan (1932-1934), the team won-loss record jumped to an impressive 32-3. In addition to his outstanding singles play, Weitz teamed with Rex Norris to form a doubles combo that continually conquered the pick of collegiate netters in the Midwest. Stepping out of the college scene in the summer of 1933, Stan won the singles state amateur championship.

Stan Weitz

IN THE SPARTLITE

Baseball: Bill McCann (BS '32, '34) recalls the final two home games of the 1934 baseball schedule, against the University of Iowa:

"There was nothing unusual about the games, we won both, 6-0 and 6-1. The unusual thing was that they were the first baseball games to be broadcast by WKAR radio (140 kilocycles). George Alderton was at the microphone. The college station had broadcast basketball games in the mid-20s with the athletic publicity director Jim Hasselman, giving the play-by-play from a telephone booth that overlooked the gym floor. However, those games of June 8 and 9 were the first to be broadcast from Old College Field."

Listeners beyond a 50-mile radius of East Lansing were asked to send responses regarding the reception. This feedback would assist college officials in reaching a decision on a proposal to broadcast football games in the fall.

Basketball: Sophomore Maurice Buysse (pronounced "bushy"), a six foot three graduate of Lansing St. Mary's High School, earned the starting pivot position during the 1933-1934 season and would become the team's leading scorer. Playing the pivot with his back to the basket, his patented move was a sweeping left-handed hook shot, as described in an interview with teammate Howard Kraft:

"He would start at the key (paint area) and drive straight toward the corner, and a step or two from the corner he would wing that ball and it wouldn't get much higher than the basket and . . . swoosh. He put so much English on it that the ball would just drive itself into the basket."

Maurice dropped out of school during the next academic year and then returned to reclaim a starting position for his senior year, 1935-1936. It was in that season that the three-second rule was introduced to college basketball, and the impact was immediate, especially for Buysse who loved to "camp" underneath. An example of the new rule's presence was demonstrated in the statistics of the second game of the season, a 26-21 loss at Madison, Wis. Neither Buysse nor his Badger counterpart ac-

counted for a single field goal that evening. Compared to his season scoring total of 126 in 1933-1934, his senior year total reached only 71 as play underneath the offensive basket was significantly altered forever. The Maurice Buysse story met a tragic end on February 27, 1937, when he was killed in an automobile accident north of Jackson.

The *Wolverine* yearbook described the January 6 triple overtime loss to Notre Dame as "the most spectacular game ever seen on this campus." The contest was tied 11 times, including a 13-13 score at halftime. By the time the deciding third OT was underway, three Spartans starters, Buysse, Danny Reck and Bob Herrick, had fouled out. With less than a minute remaining in that final overtime, "Moose" Krause of ND, All-American center and later athletic director at his alma mater, put the game on ice with a pair of short jump shots to overcome State's three-point lead. The final score read 34-33, the 20th win in a row for the Irish.

Fencing: After dropping out of school in 1933, Ralph Bristol returned and, along with Captain Morris Glass, starred during the 1934 season with five wins and one loss. Fencing with all three weapons, the pair won 86 percent of their bouts and in foil competition dropped only one bout all year.

On two consecutive weekends (February 2-3 and February 9-10) the team was on the road for five of the season's six matches. A trip into Ohio resulted in the season's one loss, to OSU, followed by a pair of wins, 11-6 over Wittenberg and then north to Ada for a 15-2 defeat of Nothern Ohio. *The State News* noted that the final saber bout against Wittenberg was forfeited when it was felt one of their men was "performing a bit rougher than necessary." On the following weekend, State gained easy victories against Notre Dame and Purdue as Bristol and Glass accounted for 15 of the 22 bouts credited to State.

Just two days prior to the scheduled Michigan-MSC meet in Ann Arbor, Fielding H. Yost, the U of M athletic director, informed Ralph Young their team had "folded" due to financial problems. With the Wolverines sheathing their weapons and aborting the sport, it would be 50 years before the two schools would again cross swords.

Football: In the scoreless Carnegie Tech game of 1933, Spartan punter Bob Armstrong launched an 85-yard punt that carried from his own 15-yard line into the visitors' end zone. As could be expected, his boot was aided by gale force winds blowing directly north to south through the stadium.

Golf: With the loss of two stalwarts (Bill Mitchell was academically ineligible and Bob Herrick was not enrolled spring term), the Spartans suffered their first losing season on the links (2-8).

After being shut out for the first time ever (against Michigan 27-0) and embarrassed by Grand Rapids Junior College, 15-3, VanAlstyne's men easily handled the U of D Titans, 14 1/2-3 1/2. Ed Riordan, playing in the number-two position, won medal honors with a score of 79. Carl Nosal, a sophomore, handed in the second lowest card with an 83.

The five mainstays of the team all received major letters. They were Riordan, Nosal, Bob Mueller, Bob Malloy and Mott Heath.

In an intrasquad tournament held that fall, Neal Taylor, a freshman from Louisville, Ky., stamped himself as a candidate for the 1935 varsity team when he shot a 78 over the Groesbeck course. In doing so he edged both Riordan and Nosal, who tied for second place with 79s.

Swimming and Diving: The 1934 team was in the pool only three hours a week, Tuesdays, Wednesdays, and Fridays from 4:00-5:00 p.m. Innovative for the time, that spring Coach Daubert called for a postseason workout schedule that emphasized stroke work and conditioning.

Perhaps the varsity schedule was a bit too ambitious. Three of the four losses were at the hands of Big Ten foes, Michigan, Iowa, and Ohio State. The Wolverines and Hawkeyes would later finish one-two in the conference meet at Iowa City. In the 51-33 loss to the Buckeyes, Don Trapp established a new varsity record for the 220-yard freestyle with a clocking of 2:40.2.

Sophomore Tom Morris competed in the 11th Annual NCAA swimming and diving championships at Columbus, Ohio. As one of 14 entrants in the 150-yard backstroke event, he finished fifth in the first heat of the qualifying rounds but failed to make the finals.

Tennis: With the clay courts unplayable due to wet conditions in early April, the squad opened practice at Demonstration Hall, and when weather permitted, they boarded the street car and headed for the city concrete courts located between Lansing and East Lansing.

As a boost to the sport in the Lansing area, on May 5 more than 4,000 fans turned out at the Boys' Vocational Fieldhouse (Johnson Fieldhouse) to watch a group of touring professionals in a featured exhibition match

between two former U.S. Open champions, Bill Tilden and Elsworth Vines.

MSC won the state intercollegiate title for the second successive year. Led by their two stars, Stanley Weitz and Rex Norris, the Spartans, who had been undefeated in 20 dual meets over two seasons, rolled up enough points in the quarterfinal and semifinal rounds on Friday to clinch the victory. It was a championship in which all competitors were bracketed into one tournament. As a result, teammates Weitz and Norris locked up in the finals with Rex emerged as the upset winner. The pair then teamed to easily capture the doubles crown. The team scoring had Michigan Sate with 13, Western State eight, and Michigan Normal one.

In late June, Stan Weitz and Rex Norris were in Philadelphia for the NCAA championships where both met similar fortunes, 6-3, 6-3 eliminations in the second round. By the luck of the draw, Weitz had been paired against the 1933 champion from Cal-Berkeley.

Track and Field: The Spartans performed well in the 40th Annual Penn Relays at Philadelphia. Al Jackson out leaped all others in the hop, step, jump event; Rex Steele finished fourth in the 400-meter hurdles; and John Hammer was third in the steeplechase. Two relays, the medley and the four mile, finished in runner-up positions.

State competed in two other preseason outdoor relay carnivals. At the Texas relays in Austin, Texas, the Spartans registered 18 points to tie Kansas State for team honors. At the 30th Annual Kansas Relays, Charles Dennis, Nelson Gardner, Tom Ottey and Wes Hurd ran a combined 17:42.0 to win the four-mile relay.

Coach Ralph Young's squad captured the State Intercollegiate title for the first time since 1929. Although winning only five firsts, MSC gathered points in all other events except the high jump. The five winners were William Hart, who posted a 10.0 in the 100-yard dash, Captain Otto Pongrace with a 1:56.4 that captured the half-mile crown for the third straight year, Wesley Hurd with a 4:33.7 time in the mile run, Fran Dittrich who leaped to a title in the broad jump and Cleo Beaumont who won his specialty, the javelin.

At the IC4A outdoor championship meet at Franklin Field in Philadelphia, four Spartans finished in scoring positions and earned a team total of nine points. Wesley Hurd finished third in the 1,500, Otto Pongrace was third in the 3,000 meters; Tom Ottey fourth in the 800-meter race and Cleo Beaumont finished fifth in the javelin.

The ace MSC distance runners were the point gatherers at the NCAA meet held at the Olympic Coliseum in Los Angeles. Tom Ottey ran seventh in the two-mile race and captain Otto Pongrace and Wes Hurd placed fifth and seventh respectively in the mile run.

Wrestling: Heavyweight Buck Reaveley had difficulty finding bulky workout partners. He eventually convinced the football star, Howard Zindel, into action as a practice companion. Maybe Howard never wrestled on the varsity, but he would later have two sons who did: Bruce (WR 70) and Jack (WR 68, 69, 70).

The season reached a disappointing and rapid conclusion at the NCAA championships held in Ann Arbor. All three entrants, Floyd Austin, Walt Jacobs and Reaveley, were eliminated in the first round of action.

Michigan State runners lead the way at the 1934 State Intercollegiate meet.

SPARTAN SCRAPBOOK
—— SWIMMING and DIVING COACHES (1922-2003) ——

Southard Flynn (1922)

Richard Rauch (1923)

Wright B. Jones (1924-25)

Rollin D. Keifaber (1926)

W. Stery Brown (1927)

Frank Hoercher (1929)

Russell "Jake" Daubert (1930-41)

Charles McCaffree Jr. (1942-69)

Richard B. Fetters (1970-87)

William Wadley (1987-89)

Richard Bader (1989-2000)

Jim Lutz (2000-)

Note: no team, 1928

MSC
1934-1935

TALES TO TELL

For the first time since 1915, the Spartans defeated the U of M on the gridiron. Unfortunately, this was not the top sports story around the state on Saturday, October 6. For the first time since 1909, the Detroit Tigers were in the World Series. Being upstaged by the World Series did not dampen the spirits of the Spartan fans who had traveled to Ann Arbor with hopes and expectations. They were not denied. Leading 3-0 in the fourth quarter on Steve Sebo's field goal, Kurt Warmbein took the ball on the U of M 28-yard line and started around right end. Aided by great blocking up front, he cut back across the field and plunged over the goal line for the first touchdown. Warmbein would intercept a pass and set up his second score of the afternoon, a 13-yard run over right tackle. MSC fans gleefully returned home with a 16-0 victory and long sought-after bragging rights.

Assistant football coach Henry Johnson (second from left) watches as Coach Bachman draws up a play.

HEADLINES of 1935

- George and Ira Gershwin's opera *Porgy and Bess* opens at Boston's Colonial Theater.
- The passage of the Social Security Act provides a federal program of unemployment compensation and old-age retirement insurance.
- The first night baseball game in the major leagues is played in Cincinnati between the Reds and the Phillies.
- Pan American Airways begins the first trans-Pacific air service from San Francisco to Manila.

SCOREBOARD

	W	L	T	Avg.
Baseball	11	9	1	.575
Track and Field	0	2	0	.000
Football	8	1	0	.889
Basketball	14	4	0	.778
Tennis	4	5	1	.450
Cross Country	3	0	0	1.000
Swimming and Diving	4	3	1	.563
Wrestling	4	4	0	.500
Fencing	6	2	0	.750
Golf	5	4	1	.550
Boxing	0	1	0	.000

Henry Johnson was on the football squad from 1931 to 1933, and from 1934-1937 he served as an assistant coach under Charlie Bachman. Johnson left East Lansing in the spring of 1938 to pursue a master's degree and serve as an assistant coach at Springfield College in Massachusetts. In a letter, he reminisces about life as an MSC substitute in the '30s:

"The number of men on the squad would average 33 at the start of the season. The prevailing NCAA substitution rule permitted a player to enter a game only one time each half. This rule was later altered to permit a player to enter the contest once each quarter. Consequently, men played both ways, offensively and defensively, and they seldom left the game un-less seriously injured. Players like me, who lined up behind three men who were bigger, better and stronger, spent more time warming up than actually playing. To earn a varsity letter you had to play a minimum number of minutes in major games. To record playing time, a manager kept track of the substitutions and, using a stopwatch, recorded the number of minutes each player was on the field. Although I never qualified for a varsity award, I received three 'service awards.' These were sweaters without monograms. Concluding my final season, I was given a silver plaque inscribed: 'For four years of exceptional loyalty and service to football at MSC.' I would have swapped it for an 'S' sweater."

TEAM OF THE YEAR

With an 8-1 record, the 1934 football team completed the most impressive season since the undefeated team of 1913.

The only loss was at Syracuse, while the list of the vanquished included Carnegie Tech, Kansas, Texas A&M and Michigan. The victory over the Wolverines would begin a four-year stretch in which State would dominate the intra-state rivalry.

1934 football team. (Front row, left to right): B. Demarest, R. Armstrong, E. Klewicki, R. Reynolds, J. McCrary, A. Brandstatter, A. Baker. (Row two, left to right) D. Wiseman, K. Warmbein, R. Colina, G. Dahlgren, S. Wagner, L. Zarza, J. Brakeman. (Row three, left to right) Buzolits, H. Zindel, H. Williamson, S. Sebo, R. Edwards, M. Wilson, J. Sleder. (Row four, left to right) Ross, A. Agett, F. Ziegel, V. Vanderburg, H. Kutchins, R. Allman. (Back row, left to right) Trainer J. Heppinstall, assistant coach T. King, head coach C. Bachman, assistant coach M. Casteel, manager E. Slater.

MAKING HISTORY

At their monthly meeting on Dec. 15, 1934, the school's athletic council tentatively sanctioned boxing as MSC's 12th sport. (The tentative sport gained full acceptance four years later, in 1938.) Two positive facts likely influenced this favorable decision. First, it was disclosed that volunteer coach Leon "Brick" Burhans of the PE staff had a total of 30 eager candidates already working out in the gymnasium. Secondly, athletic director Ralph Young disclosed an enticing offer from University of Wisconsin officials volunteering to pay all travel expenses for a Spartan squad to engage the Badgers in a dual meet at Madison on March 8.

An all-college tournament set the team for the Wisconsin matches: Wendell Genson (115 lbs.), Roosevelt Barnes (125 lbs.), Loren Farrell (135 lbs.), Bill Frutig (145 lbs.), Fred Lindenfield (155 lbs.), Lou Zarza, the future coach, (165 lbs.), Jack Vecoerelle (175 lbs.) and Frank Gaines (heavyweight). More than 5,000 faithful Wisconsin Badger fans found their way to the University Armory through a traffic-crippling sleet storm. All of the Spartans performed admirably, but only Genson, also a varsity wrestler, and Vecoerelle, the AAU champion from the state of New York, emerged as winners. Michigan State's first season of boxing competition began and ended that Friday night in Madison.

GREAT STATE DATES

Football—**October 13, 1934 (H):** Playing a highly respected Carnegie Tech in the third game on the schedule, the Spartans were sluggish in the opening half that ended in a scoreless tie. Early in the third quarter Dick Colina recovered a fumble just inside the Tech territory. On the very first play, Coach Bachman called for a little razzle-dazzle. Colina handed the ball to Ed Klewicki who, in turn, lateraled to Russ Reynolds. The captain from Flint took it the rest of the way and MSC was finally on the scoreboard, 7-0. The remainder of the points came from a pair of short field goals, making the final score 13-0.

Cross Country—**October 27, 1934 (A):** Duplicating the performance of 1929 when the Spartan harriers blanked Michigan, for the second time in the school's cross country history, MSC finished 1-2-3-4-5 and registered a perfect 15-point total, this time against Notre Dame. Tom Ottey led all runners to the line, followed by Eddie Becktold, Nelson Gardner, John Hammer and Chuck Dennis. Paul Holton, yet another Spartan, was the seventh runner to finish, pushing the Irish back one spot further in the team scoring to a total of 44. The course was laid out around the shores of beautiful St. Mary's Lake on the South Bend campus, providing a pretty setting for the race. Several Spartans were leading going into a forest area. Upon emerging from the wood lot, to the surprise of the green-clad bunch, two Irish harriers had "discovered" a shorter route and were suddenly leading the pack. Perhaps it was an inspiration, as five Spartan runners overcame the "short-cutters."

Football—**November 3, 1934 (H):** A Marquette touchdown pass in the opening moments of the game acted as a wake-up call for the undefeated Spartans. An ensuing interception by Russ Reynolds breathed life into the sluggish "S" offense. Jim McCrary followed with a run to the Hilltopper 10-yard line. Next, to the delight of the partisan locals, Steve Sebo raced around and into the end zone. The cheers were somewhat muted when the conversion attempt was kicked wide and Marquette remained in the lead 7-6. Finally, after intermission, Reynolds tossed a 38-yard pass to big Ed Klewicki who was standing on the goal line. This time the PAT was good. The State defense dug in, and the final score read 13-7.

Cross Country—**November 3, 1934 (H):** Through the 1930s, Indiana was the strength of the Big Ten Conference, and it was a team of this caliber that stood between MSC and a third straight undefeated dual-meet season. The race began and ended in the stadium during the homecoming football game. Thus it was the largest crowd to ever see a cross country meet in East Lansing. Captain Tom Ottey lost the first-place battle to the Hoosiers' star, Don Lash, who overcame a 30-yard deficit during the final mile and broke the tape 80 yards ahead in a course-record time of 23:40.4. The remaining head-to-head battles were won by Spartans Eddie Becktold, Nelson Gardner, John Hammer and Chuck Dennis. When the scores were totaled 2-3-5-7-9 defeated 1-4-6-8-10. Coupled with an exciting 13-7 victory on the gridiron, it was a happy ending to a great day in East Lansing.

Football—**November 17, 1934 (H):** Richard Edwards booted the opening kickoff to the Detroit 25-yard line. Inexplicably, the Titan players stood by and watched the ball roll along the ground. The alert Sid Wagner raced down the field, fell on the free ball, and State was immediately in business. On the second play from scrimmage, Kurt Warmbein circled right end, and aided by stellar blocking led by Russ Reynolds, scored standing up. Art Brandstatter's extra-point try was successful and the Spartans had completed their scoring for the afternoon. A few plays later, a fumbled Michigan State punt return set the U of D up for their only marker. The conversion attempt failed and that was the difference, 7-6.

Cross Country—**November 20, 1934 (A):** In 1934, Lauren Brown's squad was again in New York City toeing the line against the best in the east. When the places were recorded, the Spartans' 77 points were good enough for their second IC4A championship. Tom Ottey again led the field to the tape, as he became a back-to-back titleholder. Equally impressive was the performance of sophomore Nelson Gardner who finished in the third spot. The remainder of the winning five were Johnny Hammer, 22nd; Eddie Becktold, 28th; and Charley Dennis, 31st. It should be noted that when determining team scores, the names of finishers who are not competing as a team are eliminated and the names and places of "team" runners are moved up to fill those slots.

Basketball—**December 27, 1934 (H):** State played the touring Stanford Indians under Pacific Coast Conference rules. Rather than a center circle jump ball after each score possession was awarded out of bounds to the team scored upon. Thus, Michigan State was one of first Midwest schools to compete under this interpretation, which was endorsed nationally three years later. The Spartans must have liked it. The final score read Michigan State 25, Stanford 18.

Wrestling—**January 12, 1935 (H):** With one bout remaining in the season-opener at East Lansing, State led the U of M, 15-14, and the stage was set for the heavyweights to determine the match. Tussling with caution, neither Buck Reaveley nor the Wolverines' sophomore challenger, Harry Wright, could muster a point in regulation. Finally, at 1:48 in overtime, Reaveley managed to throw his less experienced adversary and gain five points for MSC, resulting in a 20-14 final score.

Basketball—**January 17, 1935 (H):** Arny VanFaasen was the hero in the 30-29 triumph over Marquette. It was his one-handed pivot shot, with less than half a minute to play, that spelled defeat for the Milwaukee squad. Overall, State connected on 10 of 48 shots (.208 percentage) from the field, an accuracy level that seemed acceptable for the time.

Fencing—**January 26, 1935 (N):** Never able to defeat Ohio State in eight previous seasons, the mission was finally accomplished with a convincing 12-5 margin in a meet held at Detroit. Led by Ted Szymke, Milt Stoker and Phil Bombenek, MSC built a commanding lead as they dominated the foil bouts, 6-2. While acting as a judge that afternoon, captain Lutz received a scare when poked in the eye by a foil tip. Fortunately, no serious damage was done, and he went on to compete in the epee event.

Swimming and Diving—**February 2, 1935 (H):** While defeating Wayne, 57-27, in the home opener, the Spartan swimmers bettered two varsity records. Jim Harryman lowered his own record in the 440-yard freestyle, clocking in at 5:44.6, and the medley relay of Tom Morris, Art Herner and Fred Ziegel finished in 1:50.8.

Fencing—**February 8, 1935:** The fourth win of the season, 9 1/2-7 1/2, was against the Salle de Tuscan Club of Detroit, considered the best fencing school in the state. It was headed by Bela de Tuscan, the former national sabre champion. Among the club's best known fencers was Joanna de Tuscan, captain of the American women's foil team in the 1936 Olympics.

Basketball—**February 9, 1935 (H):** As could be expected in the close 30-28 win over Michigan, fans in Demonstration Hall were in a constant uproar all through the game. While the lead frequently changed hands during the evening, the noise became so intense that at times the players could not hear the official's whistle.

Wrestling—**February 9, 1935 (A):** In the MSC-Michigan rematch, the Spartans jumped to an early 10-0 lead as both Wendell Genson and Gus Taske registered pins. Walter Jacobs accounted for three points with a decision at 160 pounds. The Wolverines scored the next 12 points. As in the January meet at East Lansing, the heavyweights would determine the outcome. As before, the more experienced Buck Reaveley matched against the 235-pound Wolverine. In the first eight minutes of action neither man dominated, then Reaveley methodically worked the younger opponent to his back and the Spartans were credited with their third fall of the afternoon.

By a final score of 18-12 and for the first time ever, MSC had defeated the U of M twice in one season.

Basketball—**February 13, 1935 (H):** Although there were no modern-day media polls to fall upon, sports writers seemed to be in concordance that Adolph Rupp's Kentucky team of 1935 was the nation's number-one team in 1935. Consequently, the 32-26 Spartan victory was rightfully acknowledged as a major upset. With four minutes remaining in the contest and the score knotted 26-26, the Spartans connected for six more points as they held the Wildcats scoreless. Ron Garlock (BK 35-37C) recalls:

"Adolph Rupp, coach of the University of Kentucky, came into East Lansing on a 26-game winning streak. We were not given much of a chance of handling them. After one or two minutes of the first half, our Arnie VanFaasen had three fouls trying to guard the biggest and fastest guy I had ever seen in a basketball game. This was LeRoy Edwards who quit in his sophomore year to go to the pros. Then it came time for me to guard him. The only answer I could see was to hold onto his pants and step on his shoes. Before long, I too had three fouls. But we did the job. The final score was 32 to 26, which was quite an upset. I also recall Mr. Rupp screaming at the official, Dwight Rich, who would later become superintendent of schools for the city of Lansing."

Baseball—**April 13 and April 20, 1935 (H):** The opening two games of the 1935 regular season were both come-from-behind thrillers. In the opener, against Hillsdale, the visitors scored eight runs in the third inning to go ahead 8-4. State came back to win it 9-8. On the following Saturday, Northwestern also jumped to an early big lead, blasting two State pitchers, Arnold Parker and Allan Kronback, for seven runs in the second inning. Once more the Spartans came from behind to salvage a win, 8-7.

Baseball—**April 25 and April 26, 1935 (H):** On only one other prior occasion, back in 1904, had the University of Wisconsin stopped for a game against MSC prior to heading for Ann Arbor. This time it was a two-day stand, a gesture to be repeated the next three seasons. In the first game, as they seemingly had been do-

ing all season, State came from behind for a 4-3 win. On the next afternoon the Spartans jumped to a 7-0 lead and then hung on for a 7-6 victory. In that second game, sophomore Milt Lehnhardt led the eight-hit attack with a two-run homer.

Baseball—**May 2, 1935 (H):** For the fourth time in five outings the Spartans won a game by the slimmest of margins, defeating Notre Dame, 5-4. Allan Kronbach, who heretofore had been used in relief, started on the mound and was impressive for six innings. He tired in the late innings, yielding a total of eight hits and four runs before George Hill rescued him in the ninth. It was the fifth straight win over the Irish.

Tennis—**May 11, 1935 (A):** The most gratifying win of 1935 was the 5-3 victory in South Bend over Notre Dame. That afternoon the six single matches were split 3-3 with Bob Rosa, Hock Scholtz and Dick O'Dell gaining victories. The Spartans came alive with doubles wins by Rosa-Will Klunzinger and Scholtz-Don Sexton. Leading 5-3 and team victory assured, captain Will Klunzinger agreed to call the third doubles match a draw when a Notre Dame player turned his ankle and had to retire.

Baseball—**May 30, 1935 (H):** After the double-header scheduled for Ann Arbor was rained out, the 1935 series with the U of M would be a one-game showdown on College Field. That day belonged to the Spartan battery of pitcher George "Dodo" Hill and catcher Steve "Stubby" Sebo. Hill, the South Haven sophomore, gave up only seven hits and left 12 Michigan runners stranded, while his batterymate was the hitting star, driving in three runs in the 4-1 victory.

The opening tip-off in State's 30-29 win over Marquette.

Tom Ottey

ATHLETE OF THE YEAR

One year prior to enrolling at MSC, Tom Ottey had been a member of the 1932 USA Olympic team and finished ninth in the 10,000-meter run at the Games in Los Angeles. Focusing on cross country while at MSC, the Philadelphian captured three state intercollegiate titles, two IC4A individual championships and a pair of Central Collegiate crowns. He captained both the 1933 and the 1934 Spartan teams, each of which went undefeated in dual-meet competition. Clark Chamberlain, Spartan star of immediately preceding years, came to know Ottey from national competition and was influential in recruiting the distance star.

IN THE SPARTLITE

Baseball: The 1935 team played an inordinate number of one-run games. During the regular phase of the season, 10 of the 15 games were decided by that narrowest of margins, with eight of the ten ending up in the Spartan win column.

Basketball: Much like current scheduling, State opened the 1934-1935 season with a November 23 exhibition game, as they defeated a team from Grand Rapids sponsored by the Universal Car Loaders. In the 31-25 loss at the U of M on December 15 the Spartans were hampered by illness and injury. Big Arnie VanFaasen was sidelined by influenza, Ron Garlock was out with an injured shoulder, Bob Herrick played but was hampered by a swollen ankle and reserve Curtis White was out with an infected foot.

It was not a joyous New Year's Eve for the Spartans, who traveled to Madison, Wis., and suffered an overtime heartbreaking loss on December 31, 23-21. State led at halftime, 13-9, and maintained the advantage until the final minute of play, when a Badger stole the ball and dribbled in to tie the game, 20-20. State was outscored in OT, 3-1.

Cross Country: The Spartans competed in the National AAU championships conducted on the 10,000-meter course at the University of Iowa. Indiana's Don Lash defeated Tom Ottey by the slimmest of margins, 32:17.2 to 32:17.5, and the team settled for second place behind the Millrose Athletic Club of New York City.

Nelson Gardner, a member of the 1934-1936 teams, shares a memory:

"On Monday nights we always ran six miles. We ran as a team group encouraging the slower ones to keep up as long as possible. 'Brownie' (Coach Brown) would come by in his car encouraging and threatening us with 'pick it up.' The team members threatened to buy him a black top hat, black mustache, and buggy whip to go along with his Simon Legree tendencies."

Fencing: With an unblemished record standing at 5-0, the Spartans concluded the season with a three-match

trip into Illinois. The first stop was at Champaign-Urbana where the Illini jolted the Spartans with their first loss of the year. Traveling up to the Windy City for Friday and Saturday matches, the State swordsmen managed to defeat Northwestern before suffering their second loss of the season against an experienced University of Chicago team. The pair of losses was predictable, as the University of Illinois had been a dominant force in the Big Ten with conference titles from 1928-1932. The Chicago Maroon had picked up the championship in 1933 and 1934. The strength of the sport at these two schools was built in because all male students were required to enroll in a fencing class as a physical education requirement. Thus, each year 300 to 500 men became possible candidates for the varsity teams at these schools.

Football: On October 20, State defeated Manhattan College at Ebbets Field, home of the Brooklyn Dodgers. This made the fourth major league baseball park in which the Spartans had performed. They had played St. Louis University in Sportsman Park (field for both the Cardinals and Browns) in 1924, Georgetown at Griffith Stadium (home for the Washington Senators) in 1930, and Fordham University at the Polo Grounds (home of the New York Giants) in 1932.

Suffering only the 10-0 loss at Syracuse, Bachman's gang posted an 8-1 record, the best since the undefeated team of 1913. After the final game the men took their bows and turned in their uniforms. Such was college football in the '30s. A similar season today would be glorified by poll-watching and extension of the season with a bowl bid.

Golf: In the second match of the season, the quartet of Ed Riordan, Bob Herrick, Neal Taylor and Cliff Hamlin defeated Wayne State (formerly Detroit Junior College) 12 1/2 to 5 1/2 on Detroit's Western Golf and Country Club course. Two days later, at the Lansing Country Club, the revamped line-up of Carl Nosal, Lee Hendrickson, Taylor and Herrick defeated Grand Rapids Junior College by the slimmest of margins, 9 1/2-8 1/2. Gaining two and a half points for GRJC that afternoon was Ed Flowers. Ed would transfer to MSC and earn varsity awards in 1937 and 1938.

In a rematch at Grand Rapids four days later, the JCs reversed the outcome, 11-7. It would be the final time State would compete against a junior college.

Swimming and Diving: Weakened by a flu epidemic that reached members of the team, the Spartans settled for a rare tie, 42-42, against Western Reserve. Trailing early in the meet, divers Arthur Herner and Fred Blackmore finished one-two to lead MSC back into contention. James Harryman again put his name on the team record board by lowering the standard in the 220-yard freestyle a full eight seconds to a new mark of 2:40.2.

Although soundly defeated 54-30 by Iowa State, the meet at Ames against the Big Six Conference champions drew particular interest. Coach Daubert was matched against his father, who coached the Cyclone squad. Adding yet another family touch, Jake's brother was the referee for the meet.

Track and Field: The outdoor season of 1935 was a busy one with entries in the Texas relays, Kansas relays, 41st Annual Penn relays, state intercollegiate meet, 59th annual IC4A meet, 10th annual Central Intercollegiate, Western Michigan AAU meet, 14th annual NCAA championships, Michigan AAU meet and the National AAU championship meet. Impressive performances were turned in by Fran Dittrich in the broad jump, pole vaulter Bill Uckele, Jim Wright in the 880 and sprinter Carl Mueller. The distance quartet of Charles Dennis, Nelson Gardner, Tom Ottey and Wes Hurd combined for numerous relays, including a four-mile championship at Kansas. In the NCAAs in Berkeley, Calif., Ottey was second in the two-mile run, Wright placed sixth in the half-mile run, and Gardner finished eighth in the mile run.

Wrestling: As with the other so-called "minor" sports, only exceptional performers were acknowledged with a varsity major "S" award. Such was the case at the conclusion of the 1935 season when three men were singled out: Walter Jacobs, Wendell Genson and Gordon Reaveley.

SPARTAN SCRAPBOOK
─────── WRESTLING ───────

First wrestling team (1922)

TALES TO TELL

One of the more memorable games of the 6-2 football season was against Temple University. The Owls took the field with a 15-game undefeated string (nine games in 1934 and six in 1935). Art Brandstatter Sr., (FB 34, 35, 36) reminisces about that afternoon in Philadelphia:

"Emotion has also been a factor in athletics, often affecting an individual or team's performance. One such personal experience took place in 1935 at Philadelphia against Temple. The Owls, coached by the legendary Glenn Scobey 'Pop' Warner, had a string of victories that extended from the year before, and they were considered the best team in the east. We played them in our sixth game of the season and they had not lost or tied a game.

Neither team dominated during the first 30 minutes, but Temple led at halftime, 7-6, thanks to a fumble I had committed. Since Coach Bachman platooned his teams every other quarter, I had plenty of

Art Brandstatter's prowess as a fullback eventually led to his induction into the MSU Athletic Hall of Fame.

HEADLINES of 1936

- The highest dam in the world, Boulder (Hoover) Dam on the Colorado River in Nevada and Arizona, is completed.
- *Life* magazine, a weekly photographic news and feature magazine, is first published.
- Margaret Mitchell, author, publishes her only book, *Gone With the Wind*.
- Edward the VIII becomes King of England, but then abdicates because of opposition to his marriage to a divorcee and commoner. George VI, his brother, replaces him on the throne.

SCOREBOARD

	W	L	T	Avg.
Baseball	13	7	0	.650
Track and Field	1	1	0	.500
Football	6	2	0	.750
Basketball	8	9	0	.471
Tennis	12	2	0	.857
Cross Country	2	1	0	.667
Swimming and Diving	5	2	0	.714
Wrestling	0	6	0	.000
Fencing	8	4	0	.667
Golf	6	4	0	.600
Boxing	0	1	0	.000

time on the sideline to agonize over my error and work myself into a lather awaiting re-entry into the game. I was highly emotional during play that next quarter and was given several opportunities to carry the ball. We dominated that portion of the game, and my teammates later told me that I was virtually unstoppable. I did not remember too much of this, but when we got down inside Temple's five-yard line, their defense was set up to stop me. Countering, we called an end-around play with Frank Gaines scoring the winning touchdown. The final score was MSC 12, Temple 7. Emotions had overtaken me and I had made amends for my earlier error."

TEAM OF THE YEAR

The 1935 cross country team followed a 2-1 dual meet season with an impressive championship run which included three titles: the state intercollegiate, the Central Intercollegiate (CIC), in a perfect winning score of 15, and the team's third straight victory in the Intercollegiate Amateur Athletic Association of American (IC4A) meet at Van Cortlandt Park in New York City. Eddie Bechtold finished ahead of the pack of 140 starting runners at that IC4A meet, followed by teammates Ken Waite (third), John Nelson Gardner (sixth), Gerard Boss (ninth) and Art Green (11th) for a winning score of 30 to runner-up Manhattan's 93. In addition, Harold Sparks and Jim Wright were the 14th and 15th over the finish line.

1935 cross country team. (Front row, left to right) Boss, Waite, Green, Bechtold, Sparks, Gardner, Wright and Hills; (middle row, left to right) Bath, Smith, Hinz, Dennis and Grantham; (back row, left to right) Coach Brown and Manager Brundage.

MAKING HISTORY

On November 9, John Macklin, the successful coach from 1911-1915, returned to campus on a special train with his family and many friends from Philadelphia. It was a big day for the Macklin clan. School officials had agreed to name the enlarged football stadium "Macklin Field" in honor of the old coach. Speaking through a public address system from the center of the gridiron at halftime of the Marquette game, Macklin commented: "It means that my name will be connected with this grand, old institution and written upon the annals of her history for all time to come." Not exactly true, coach! It seems that from the beginning, school officials secretively held an ulterior motive. John Macklin was married to the daughter of one of the big coal barons of Pennsylvania. When he left the Aggie coaching ranks in 1915, he became an executive in that business. Now, 20 years later, Macklin had amassed a sizable fortune in the company reputedly valued at $60 million. There was greedy hope that one day he would fondly remember those MAC ties in a monetary way. Following his death on Oct. 10, 1949, it soon became obvious such expectations would not be realized. With the upper deck in place and the final stadium expansion completed in 1957, Macklin Field became Spartan Stadium.

Walter Jacobs, a 158-pounder from Manchester, Mich., would become MSC's first NCAA wrestling champion in 1936. Ironically, he would do so during the only season in which the Spartans would be winless as a team. Following graduation, Jacobs would become a three-time AAU as well as a three-time YMCA champion (1937-1939). A true disciple of his coach, the champion competed with great use of his legs and was hence defined as a "scissors man."

GREAT STATE DATES

Football—**October 5, 1935 (A):** With the Detroit Tigers' return to the World Series, the annual game at Ann Arbor once again competed for the attention of the press. From the Spartan side this was a pity, for the game ended up being a lopsided 25-6 victory, dispelling any skeptics who considered the 1934 win a one-year anomaly. State scored on the eighth play of the game, following a drive of 59 yards. A 23-yard pass from Kurt Warmbein

to Steve Sebo ended at the seven-yard line, from where Art Brandstatter scored on the next play. Midway in the second period Dick Colina fielded a punt on the MSC 40-yard line. Behind effective blocking, he skirted the sideline for 60 yards and the TD. Following intermission, Warmbein connected with Colina on a 22-yard pass play, making it 19-6. Al Agett, filling in for Warmbein, completed the scoring with his 47-yard sprint in the fourth period. Sid Wagner was among the linemen receiving praise that afternoon, and at season's end he would gain All-American status.

Cross Country—**October 26, 1935 (H):** MSC defeated Notre Dame and, for the second year in a row, did so with a perfect score, 15-44. Ed Becktold was the winner with a time of 17:39 over the three and a half mile course. He was followed in order by Ken Waite, John Nelson Gardner, Jim Wright and Harold Sparks.

Football—**November 16, 1935 (A):** Before a crowd of 12,000 at Gilmore Stadium in Los Angeles, MSC closed the season with a convincing 27-0 victory over Loyola of California. The Spartans scored touchdowns in the second and third quarters and two in the fourth. Howard Zindel blocked a punt and Joe Bucolits, the center, picked up the ball and ran ten yards for the first score. Don Wiseman plunged over in the next quarter. Lou Zarza and Fred Schroeder tallied in the fourth.

Basketball—**December 30, 1935 (H):** In an exciting overtime game, MSC topped West Virginia, 25-24, before the smallest home crowd of the season. With 30 seconds remaining in regulation, Joe Smith managed to hit a free throw to tie the game at 20-20. Maurice Buysse became the ultimate hero, as he scored the game-winning field goal in the final minute of OT.

Basketball—**January 18, 1936 (H):** As a result of unusual scheduling, State played Marquette three times in 1936. The first two games were played back-to-back at home. After losing the Friday night opener, 21-20, the Spartans came back for an exciting win on the next evening, 35-31. Play was rough, as four players (three Marquette and one MSC) were ejected on fouls. MSC's center, Dorian "Moose" Wilkinson, was decked by a blow to the groin; two players engaged in fisticuffs; and Joe Smith was lost with a dislocated ankle.

Basketball—**February 22, 1936 (A):** The third Spartan-Hilltopper meeting, a 29-28 MSC win in the season-closer at Milwaukee, was also foul-riddled. Marquette was whistled 17 times and State called for 12

personal fouls. Curtis White and Hock Scholtz were starters for the first time. Ron Garlock and Maurice Buysse shared scoring honors with seven points each. The three Hilltopper-Spartan match-ups had been decided by a total of six points.

Track and Field—**February 29, 1936 (A):** The underdog Spartans pinned Marquette with their first home defeat in a decade, 55 1/2 to 53 1/2. The result of the meet was not decided until the final event, the one-mile relay. With 2,500 home fans standing and screaming, Al Agett, the football halfback, led off and managed a slight lead as he passed the baton to Carl Mueller. Mueller and the number-three man, Clare McDurmon, increased the advantage to eight yards. Anchorman Bob Adcock left little doubt as he pulled away and broke the tape with a full 10-yard lead. The 2,500 fans were no longer screaming.

Swimming and Diving—**March 6, 1936 (A):** The University of Wisconsin was not a swimming power in the 1930s; notwithstanding, any victory over a Big Ten school was revered. Such was the case when MSC topped the Badgers, 53-31, in the 20-yard mini-pool on the Wisconsin campus. In reporting the meet results, The *State News* story of March 10 discloses an interesting revelation:

> "Al Black was the hero of the meet when he saved the medley relay for State after Grudzina had put Wisconsin into the lead as he beat Tom Morris by a pool length on the first leg of the race. Black swimming the tiring butterfly stroke, overtook his opponent and went into the lead by a yard, and Bill Bell increased this in the final leg of the race to give State a winning time of 2:32.3."

In the 1930s the breaststroke was in transition with swimmers opting to recover their stroke under water as we know it today or recover the stroke out-of-water a la the emerging butterfly, yet with the familiar frog kick in either rendition. Finally, by the 1940s, the overarm recovery had proven to be more efficient, and consequently became the norm throughout competition. In 1956, the rules accepted the dolphin kick and with it the evolution of two strokes for competition: the breaststroke and the butterfly.

Tennis—**April 18, 1936 (H):** The Spartans displayed their team depth with a 12-3 season opening win

over Kalamazoo College on the home clay courts. The extended meet consisted of ten singles and five doubles matches. Individual winners for MSC were Willard Klunzinger, Bob Rosa, Hock Scholtz, Louis Stonebraker, Walter Eissler, George Hyatt, Ward VanAtta, Duffy Arntz and Robert Perrin. Doubles that won team points were Rosa-Stonebraker, Klunzinger-Scholtz and Eissler-Hyatt.

Baseball—**April 18, 1936 (H):** After going unbeaten in their trip south, State opened the regular schedule at home with a 7-0 win over Toledo. A few hundred fans braved the chilly weather to witness the undefeated Spartans' fifth straight victory. Donning one of the green caps, which were a part of the new uniform, President Robert Shaw opened the season officially by pitching the first ball to Clark Brody, a member of the Board of Agriculture.

Baseball—**May 9, 1936 (A):** Following eight straight losses over four years to Western State, the Spartans finally managed to top the Teachers with a convincing 11-0 score. It was the first Spartan shutout of Western since 1919. Pitcher George Hill allowed only five hits while "Red" Randall, a promising sophomore infielder, led the MSC offense with four hits.

Baseball—**May 14, 1936 (A):** An eastern trip was hampered by rainy weather and, as a result, all but one game was cancelled. The lone contest was a 7-2 win over Cornell University, as the Spartans were never in trouble after breaking out to an early 6-2 lead. Warren "Lefty" Walters was the pitching star as he struck out 10 men and allowed only seven scattered hits. Shortstop Clyde "Red" Randall, who was starting only his third game, laced out three hits to again lead the offense. Over a three-game span, the Detroit sophomore, had connected for 10 hits in 14 plate appearances for a remarkable .714 average.

Tennis—**May 14, 1936 (H):** The 5-4 victory over Kentucky ended a 10-meet consecutive winning string of the Wildcats. In a featured singles match at the number-five slot, Walter Eissler dropped the opener 4-6 and then came back to take a marathon 11-9 set and the clinching third, 6-4. Other winners were number one Will Klunzinger, number three Hock Scholtz, number four Lou Stonebreaker and the number three doubles team of Walter Eissler and George Hyatt.

Tennis—**May 15, 1936 (A):** The Spartans easily smothered Michigan, 8-1, by sweeping the six single matches, marked by Hock Scholtz's prolonged struggle,

6-4, 12-14, 6-3, and three-set matches won by Will Klunzinger, 1-6, 6-2, 6-2, and Walt Eissler 6-4, 6-0, 6-2. Captain Robert Rosa and Lou Stonebraker, after dropping the first set in the doubles, 0-6, came back to win 7-5, 6-0. State had also defeated the Wolverines, 6-3, three weeks earlier in East Lansing.

Baseball—**May 22, 1936 (H):** Catcher Steve Sebo broke a 1-1 tie in the fifth inning of the Ohio State game with a home run drive that sailed far into left center field with Merle Stemm aboard. With no outfield fence in place, Sebo, of course, had to beat the throw to the plate. The Spartans hung on, behind the pitching of George Hill, for a satisfying 6-5 win, their fifth in a row.

Golf—**May 23, 1936 (A):** In the first-ever meeting with Ohio State, all four Spartans turned in cards of the seventies and, in the process, defeated the Buckeyes, 9-3. Both sophomore Tom Brand, who led the field with a 73, and Hank Zimmerman, with a 76, swept their opponents to each gain three team points. Hal Richardson, playing in only his second varsity match, earned two points, and Neal "Scotty" Taylor scored a 76 to capture one of the three points against his opponent.

Baseball—**June 4 and 5, 1936 (H):** State won both ends of a two-game series against the University of Iowa, 4-3 and 3-0. In the Thursday game, pitcher Blaine Henkel allowed only six hits but survived a loosely played ninth inning in which the Hawkeyes threatened to tie it up. On the next afternoon, behind a more solid defense, "Lefty" Walters also threw a six-hitter to earn the team's sixth shutout of the spring. In that second game Milt Lehnhardt smashed a four-bagger into the trees in right center that traveled a good 450 feet on the fly. Coach John Kobs later said it was the longest drive he had ever seen hit on the home field.

ATHLETE OF THE YEAR

Sid Wagner was the first Spartan football player to break prominently onto the All-American lists. Light, aggressive, a superb blocker and deadly tackler, he was selected as a guard on the 1935 All-American teams of the United Press, *New York Sun*, and Liberty All-Players. Perhaps Wagner's most memorable game was against Boston College in 1935 when he was credited with 23 tackles.

Sid Wagner

IN THE SPARTLITE

Baseball: For the first time since inaugurating the spring trip in 1925, the team returned with an unblemished record. Wins were posted over Clemson, Newberry, North Carolina State and Wake Forest, with three games being rained out. Warren "Lefty" Walters was the pitching star. The sophomore yielded a scant five hits to shut out Newberry, 5-0, and then threw a six- hit 4-1 win over Wake Forest.

Boxing: The team, student body and community awaited the first-ever home matches at the Gymnasium Building on Friday, March 13, 1936, against Loyola of Chicago. Unfortunately, a telegram was received the day before informing athletic director Young that the trip to East Lansing had been cancelled because a flu epidemic had decimated the Ramblers' squad. As in 1935, the Spartans' meet at Madison, Wis., would constitute "the season."

Student writer George Maskin, who would later spend a lengthy career with the *The Detroit Free Press,* wrote an article for *The Michigan State News* on January 14. In it he suggested that boxing as an intercollegiate sport at MSC would remain in peril as long as so few Midwest schools supported teams. Maskin was on target, as this became a primary factor for the discontinuation of the sport 22 years later.

Cross Country: In again capturing the IC4A title at Van Cortlandt Park, the 1935 Spartans equaled a meet record established by Cornell runners 10 years previous when they also won three team titles in a row. More surprising was the individual title captured by Captain Eddie Bechtold, who led the pack of 140 starters up and down the six-mile course in an impressive time of 26:13. Teammates who followed were Ken Waite (third), John Nelson Gardner (sixth), Gerard Boss (ninth), and Art Green (11th). Although not included in the winning team total, Harold Sparks and Jim Wright finished impressively in 14th and 15th places.

The Central Intercollegiate Conference run of 1935 was particularly memorable. The star of the Michigan Normal team, Bill Zapp, captured individual honors with MSC Ed Becktold in second. Because the Hurons did not enter a complete team, Bechtold's finish was interpreted as a first place when the team results were tabulated. The scoring of all other runners moved up one spot and as a result, the Spartans registered a perfect score

of 15: Eddie Becktold (first), Ken Waite (second), Bob Hills (third), Gerard Boss (fourth) and Jim Wright (fifth). Notre Dame completed the run with 61 points, good for second place.

Fencing: During the 1936 season, the team's outstanding performer was the one-armed captain Theodore Szymke of Hamtrmck. During the tournament held on March 7 in Detroit by the State Amateur Fencing League Association, he placed second in foil and then received the medal for first place in the epee competition.

A new trophy was introduced by John Osis of Lawrence Institution of Technology to be awarded the winning team in Michigan Intercollegiate fencing competition. By remaining undefeated in matches with Michigan schools, George Bauer's squad was the initial recipient.

Football: Inaugurated by the *Chicago Tribune's* sports editor, Arch Ward, the College All-Star game was a popular preseason highlight during the 1930s and 1940s. The players and coaches were selected from a nationwide ballot conducted by the paper. The chosen squad would then do battle with the NFL's defending champions in a September night game at Soldier Field. In 1935 a well-organized and successful campaign was waged across the state on behalf of Coach Bachman. When the final tally was recorded, the Spartan mentor had garnered enough votes to place second and become the top assistant behind Frank Thomas, coach of the Rose Bowl champion Alabama Tide. Joining Bachman as players were two graduate seniors, Ed Klewicki and Russ Reynolds. Across the line that evening was big Art Buss (FB 31-33) who claimed the honor of being the best lineman on the field as the Bears' left tackle. The 1935 game was played in a driving rainstorm with the Chicago Bears earning a 5-0 victory.

Golf: Even as some practice rounds were played at Walnut Hills for the sixth year in a row, the varsity competitive matches were held at the Lansing Country Club.

The ten candidates who would contend for the varsity were Tom Brand, who had won the West Virginia State Amateur tournament in 1935, Lee Hendrickson, Neal "Scotty" Taylor, Carl Nosal, Hank Zimmerman, Lewis Richardson, Ed Flowers, Jim Reasoner, Howard Silcox and R.E. Lefferle.

In the Western State meet at Kalamazoo, Hank Zimmerman had halved the team point for the front nine and played his opponent on even terms all the way to the final hole. Stroking a hopeful final putt to tie his oppo-

nent for the back nine (1/2 point), and the overall match (1/2 point), Hank's ball stopped short at the lip of the cup. With it, Western gained the 6 1/2-5 1/2 victory. Zimmerman and his teammates left little doubt when the teams squared off six days later in Lansing. The final score that afternoon was MSC 10 1/2, Western State 1 1/2.

Brand became the first Spartan golfer to be awarded a major "S" sweater.

Swimming and Diving: For the third year in a row, State opened its season against Michigan, this time before an overflow crowd at home. The eventual outcome of the dual meet was never in doubt; after all, the Wolverines were the defending Big Ten champions. Regardless, the real hero of the evening would be MSC's sophomore star Bill "Whitey" Bell, who captured the 100-yard freestyle event in a varsity record-setting and respectable time of 56.4. Although back in 1923 Dutch VonNoppen was credited with winning the same event against the U of M, it was tainted by the disqualification of an opponent who had actually touched first. Thus, this win of Bell's might be registered as the first "legitimate" swimming victory over Michigan.

A home meet scheduled with the University of Texas on Friday evening, February 27, never took place. As the Spartans waited at pool side, the Longhorns never showed-up.

"Whitey" Bell was to have entered the NCAA championship meet in New Haven, Conn. Official meet results do not confirm this indeed happened.

Tennis: The Western State match at Kalamazoo might well have been the longest dual meet in NCAA history. It began on Friday, May 1, and concluded on Saturday, May 30. Here was the scenario. Weather permitted only the six singles matches to be played on May 1 before showers concluded competition for the afternoon with the Broncos leading 4-2. It was agreed the doubles competition in the rematch of May 30 would also serve to close the scoring in this postponed meet. Although the Spartans would be victorious in that second meeting, 6-3, they did drop one of the three doubles matches thus finalizing the score of the May 1 meet as a 5-4 loss.

Track and Field: A highlight of the indoor season took place on Saturday, February 1, when a quartet of Spartan runners competed at the Melrose Games in New York's Madison Square Garden. Before a capacity crowd of more than 16,000 spectators, the two-mile relay team of Russell Bath, Charles Dennis, Jim Wright and Ken Waite, raced to third place behind Manhattan and Boston College. Ohio State finished fourth. Running on boards for the first time, the foursome performed admirably, bettering the winning time of 1934 by more than two seconds.

At the Kansas relays, Fran Dittrich captured a second in the broad jump with a leap of 23' 7-3/4" and placed third in the hop-step-and-jump. The four-mile relay team placed third with the following splits: Art Green (4:20), Ken Waite (4:26), Bob Hills (4:31) and co-captain Charley Dennis (4:29). One week later at the historic Penn Relays, Dittrich was runner-up in the hop-step-jump event.

Training outdoors was hampered by having no home track to practice on. The old oval at Macklin Field had been torn away to make room for stadium improvements and the new track layout was still under construction. The state intercollegiate meet was transferred to Ferry Field in Ann Arbor, and two home freshmen meets were conducted at Pattengill Field in Lansing.

In the NCAA championships at Stagg Field, Chicago, it was Kenny Waite's turn to star. He placed third in the metric mile, while Dittrich captured fifth in the hop-step-jump.

Three members of the team, Bob Hill, Jim Wright and Fran Dittrich, entered the Midwest regional Olympic tryouts held in Milwaukee. Although none of the men advanced beyond that, Dittrich would be in Berlin that summer after all. He had been chosen as one of the 27 physical education students to represent the USA in the International Physical Education Congress that was being held in conjunction with the XI Olympic Games.

Ernest Crosbie, State grad and employee at Oldsmobile, did, however, earn a slot on the USA Olympic team by winning the National AAU 50,000-meter walking event at Cincinnati in a time of five hours, 16 minutes and 16 seconds.

Wrestling: For the only time in Fendley Collins's 31-year career as head coach, his team went winless, losing to Ohio State, Washington & Lee, Cornell College, the Big Ten champions from Indiana and twice to Michigan.

SPARTAN SCRAPBOOK
── WRESTLING COACHES (1922-2003) ──

James Devers (1922-23)

Leon Burhans (1924-26)

Ralph Leonard (1927-28)

Glenn Ricks (1929)

Fendley Collins (1930-62)

Phil Parker (1987-91)

Tom Minkel (1992-)

Grady Peninger (1963-86)

TALES TO TELL

Frank Gaines Jr. (FB 35-37) talked about the 1936 football season:

"The most memorable part of my MSC football days is to have played on teams that beat the University of Michigan four years in a row. Those seniors who played on our Orange Bowl team of Jan. 1, 1938 can say that they never heard the 'Victors' while they played at Michigan State.

The game of football was played differently back then. In our days the quarterback called the plays and blocked for the two halfbacks and the fullback. There were no messages or signals from the bench. It was our team policy that only the two ends were permitted to talk to the quarterback in the huddle (I played left end). Other players relayed weaknesses they saw in the opponent to the ends, who in turn could talk to the quarterback. I participated in two specific plays which were the result of this method of communication.

I scored the first touchdown against Michigan in 1936 on a 40-yard end-around play that was called because Chuck Halbert, our quarterback, saw the secondary move to the left whenever we ran a reverse play with the handoff to the fullback, Art Brandstatter. Bob Terlaak, the right guard, said, 'The end will be crashing, so don't try inside, I'll take him in.' It worked exactly as planned. I took the ball, went around end, and everybody in the Michigan secondary was looking for the fullback reverse. I never saw anyone on the way to the touchdown.

The other play that occurred in much the same way was during the Kansas game in 1936. I noted that the left side linebacker would jump into the line whenever we shifted to the right side, and he anticipated the same fullback reverse play. I suggested a fake reverse and a quick pass over the center to the left end in the vacancy left by the linebacker. We ran that play for 15 minutes and scored two touchdowns. I ran 156 yards and was so tired I had to come out of the game to rest.

As I said at the beginning, the game of football was played differently back then. All of the play calling was done on the field and not by the coaches on the sidelines."

HEADLINES of 1937

- Dow Chemical begins manufacturing polystyrene plastic products.
- The Golden Gate Bridge, the longest span bridge up to this time, is completed.
- The dirigible *Hindenburg* explodes near mooring at Lakehurst, N.J., killing most passengers and crew.
- Walt Disney produces the first feature-length cartoon film, *Snow White and the Seven Dwarfs*.

SCOREBOARD

	W	L	T	Avg.
Baseball	16	11	0	.593
Track and Field	5	1	0	.833
Football	6	1	2	.778
Basketball	5	12	0	.294
Tennis	11	1	0	.917
Cross Country	2	1	0	.667
Swimming and Diving	7	2	0	.778
Wrestling	1	6	0	.143
Fencing	2	7	0	.222
Golf	5	4	0	.556
Boxing	2	0	1	.833

TEAM OF THE YEAR

The 1937 tennis team posted an impressive 11-1 record that included victories over Wisconsin, Ohio State, Indiana and Kentucky, as well as 9-0 shutouts of Marquette, Cincinnati and Kalamazoo. The lone loss was to Northwestern, the defending Big Ten champions.

Hock Scholtz, team captain, reminisces about that season:

"Tennis during my time was played on white clay courts located just north of Morrill Hall. My 'scholarship' in those days consisted of a job paying 30 cents per hour. During the tennis season I sprinkled, brushed, rolled and lined the courts. Off season I worked for Albert Amiss in the stadium and on the grounds. Tennis attire was very 'Spartan,' consisting of T-shirts and 'white duck' pants supplied by the school. We furnished our own rackets (one), but were given one restringing job each season. We used private cars for all of our away matches and Coach Ball did not always go with us on the trips as he was a chemistry professor and had classes to teach. The 1937 season was one of the most successful seasons in the history of the school, winning 11 matches, and losing only one. An interesting sidelight of that year was playing my older brother, Wilbert, in singles, and losing to him in a bitter three-set match. He played for Ypsilanti Normal. That spring our team went to the National Intercollegiate Tennis Tournament at Haverford, Pa. (near Philadelphia), held at the Merion Cricket Club on grass courts. It was my first and last experience on grass courts, as we were all soundly beaten in the first round."

1937 tennis team. (Kneeling, left to right) Gibbs, Kositcheck. (Back row, left to right) Coach Ball, Hyatt, Stonebraker, Scholtz, Ross, Burgdorfer and manager Stable.

MAKING HISTORY

New rules in basketball specified that no member of the offensive team could remain in the foul lane more than three seconds. Also, the number of timeouts allotted a team was increased from three to four.

The first-ever home boxing meet and first-ever team victory came with a 6 1/2-1 1/2 win over Toledo University on February 26. The evening featured a pair of Spartan TKOs that came from both ends of the line-up, bantamweight Max Wilcox, who had never before fought a bout, and the heavyweight veteran, Frank Gaines. Wilcox had been the only entrant in the college tournament, and consequently earned his varsity spot uncontested.

The first NCAA boxing championships were hosted by the University of California, Davis.

The University of Chicago track and field meet of April 17 (an 88-43 victory) was selected as the date for dedicating the new layout, later named Ralph Young Field.

GREAT STATE DATES

Football—October 3, 1936 (A): The Michigan game at Ann Arbor was viewed by 55,000 spectators, setting yet another attendance record for the classic encounter. The game had been tied at halftime, 7-7. Still substituting his teams every other quarter, the daring and audacious Charlie Bachman started the second half with a trio of inexperienced sophomores in the backfield: John Pingel, George Kovacich and Jack Coolidge. The threesome responded with a ball-control drive that featured a pair of dashes by Pingel, one of 30 yards and the other a 12-yard cut-back run through the middle and into the end zone. Leading 14-7, the yearlings returned the game to the veterans, Art Brandstatter, Al Agett, Steve Sebo and Charley Halbert for the final quarter. Agett, from Kingsport, Tenn., iced the game when he jaunted, untouched, for 82 sensational yards and the third touchdown of the afternoon. The final score read 21-7, and the Spartans had registered three in a row over the Wolverines.

Football—October 17, 1936 (H): In the 13-0 homecoming victory before 15,000 fans, the University of Missouri fumbled the ball nine times, five of which were recovered by the Spartans, with two of them leading to the game's only touchdowns. The first came on Tom Gortat's recovery at the Tiger 18-yard line, setting-up a TD pass from Steve Sebo to Milt Lehnhardt. The clinching touchdown, scored by Art Brandstatter in the fourth quarter, followed a fumble recovery by Sam Ketchman at the Mizzou 17-yard line.

Cross Country—October 17, 1936 (H): For the seventh year in a row, "Brownie's" men opened with a comfortable win over Butler College, 17-38. Finishing in the scoring spots for State were: Kenny Waite (first), Art Green (second), Harry Butler (third), Bob Hills (fifth), and Captain Nelson Gardner (sixth). Butler, the sophomore, came from New York City, where he had captured the citywide interscholastic title as a high school senior.

Cross Country—October 24, 1936 (A): Notre Dame had been on the schedule for the 16th year in a row, but in the spring of '36, the Irish dropped the sport. The open date was filled, as the Pittsburgh Panthers hosted a dual meet over their challenging four and a half mile course. Ken Waite would eventually lead the way to a fairly easy 18-37 victory. Bob Hills relates an incident during the race:

> "We were about halfway into the race when teammate Ken Waite, running next to me, introduced me to John Woodruff of the Pittsburgh team, who had won the gold medal at the Berlin Olympics that summer. We shook hands and kept running."

Basketball—January 9, 1937 (A): In the 42-41 victory at Beaver Falls, Pa., over Geneva College, Leonard Oesterink scored an impressive 21 points, which accounted for exactly half of MSC's winning score. His season-end total of 112 would lead the team for the year.

Basketball—January 14, 1937 (H): Two weeks following the 28-21 loss to Kentucky in Lexington, the Spartans entertained a rematch with the Wildcats in Dem Hall. Nearly 3,500 exuberant fans saw the visitors build an early 11-5 lead during the first 17 minutes of the game. The Spartans took charge early in the second half and led 23-15 with eight minutes remaining. KU came back, closed within one, missed two final shots, and State hung on for a 24-23 upset. Howard Kraft converted a free throw that proved to be the winning margin.

Fencing—February 27, 1937 (A): With the season record at 0-6, the Spartans finally broke into the victory column with a convincing 11-6 win at Lawrence Tech.

Six points were earned in foil, three in epee and a surprising two in the sabre, an event in which State had been woefully weak all year. Scoring one of the epee points was a late-season newcomer, Tony Smirniotis, the drum major for the marching band.

Swimming and Diving—**March 6, 1937 (H):** Five new varsity records were established in the Ohio Wesleyan meet. In addition to new standards in both relays, Ed McNamara bettered the 100-yard freestyle mark with a 56.2, Harry Carr posted a 1:49.6 in the 150-yard backstroke and Al Brightman finished a few feet ahead of teammate Al Black with a new mark of 2:49.0 in the 200-yard breaststroke event.

Golf—**April 30, 1937 (A):** The Spartans opened the season by shutting out the Marquette Hilltoppers 18-0 in a match in Milwaukee. They played in fog and a steady drizzle that frequently prevented the players from seeing the ball after it left the club head. Roy Nelson, a sophomore who had captured the all-college crown in 1936, led all scorers with a 73.

Track and Field—**May 21, 1937 (H):** After scoring a meager 20 3/4 points in a 1936 triangular meet against Notre Dame and Ohio State, MSC managed a 66 1/2 to 64 1/2 victory over the Irish one year later. On a track covered with mud, Wilbur Greer, the Spartan speedster, was a double winner, as he negotiated the 100-yard dash in 9.7 and later turned in an impressive 20.9 for the 220. The outcome of the meet was in question until Wesley Orr accounted for the winning margin with a second-place finish in the discus event.

Baseball—**May 26, 1937 (A):** It was fitting that Eugene Ciolek was the hitting star in this 10-3 victory over Notre Dame. His home was in Michigan City, Ind., just 35 miles west of South Bend. Gene blasted out two home runs to lead a nine-hit attack. It was reported that the pair of circuit-clouts were two of the hardest hit drives seen on Cartier Field in several seasons.

Baseball—**May 29, 1937 (H):** This 4-1 Spartan victory over the U of M was well pitched by George Hill, who seemed to be in complete control all afternoon. State scored three of their four runs in the fifth when Gene Ciolek tripled home Milt Lehnhardt and Johnny Kuk and then scored on Hill's base hit. It was Kuk's fielding that won the applause of the sun-baked crowd as he tracked down nine fly balls, many after long runs.

Baseball—**June 5, 1937 (H):** In one of the more lopsided games on the books, State completely dominated Michigan Normal, 18-0. A four-run splurge in the opening inning was ample enough to win the game, but the Spartans continued with six runs in the second, two in the fourth, and six more in the seventh. There were some hefty extra-base hits. Johnny Kuk, Milt Lehnhardt and Steve Sebo hit home runs as Merle Stemm and George Kovacich both tripled. Using a rotating pitching plan, Coach Kobs called upon Art Libbers, Kaz Nevulis and Pete Dalponte, who combined for the shutout. A doubleheader had been scheduled, but with State leading 6-4 in the fifth inning of that second game, a torrential cloudburst terminated action. It was not a complete game; consequently it has not been included in the record book.

Baseball—**June 12, 1937 (H):** As his team scored four runs in the opening three innings of this season finale against Nebraska, Coach John Kobs felt confident enough that he began substituting and switching men in positions to the extent that 16 men saw action in the eventual 6-0 victory. He even split the pitching assignment with seniors Blaine Henkel and George Hill sharing in the shutout. Henkel relinquished two hits in the opening five innings, and Hill held the Cornhuskers hitless thereafter.

ATHLETE OF THE YEAR

Steve Sebo, from Battle Creek, was a two-sport star, lettering in football (1934, 1935, 1936) and baseball (1935, 1936, 1937). He was the starting right halfback for three years during which State accumulated a 20-4-2 record, including three victories over Michigan. Each spring Steve turned to the diamond where he was the starting catcher for three seasons, being selected team captain in his senior year. He was the team-leading hitter in both his junior year (.342) and senior year (.402).

Steve Sebo

IN THE SPARTLITE

Baseball: The unpredictable weather of early spring has always impacted the home schedule. The 1937 season was no exception. The opener against Toledo was set for Thursday, April 15. Instead, the community awakened to a surprise snowfall of seven inches. The season eventually opened one week later against Wisconsin.

Bob Pratt, student manager of the team in 1934, personally initiated a trophy which was to be annually presented to the leading hitter among the Spartan regulars. With a season average of .327, Milt Lehnhardt earned the prize in the first year.

From correspondence with Blaine Henkel (BS 36, 37), one absorbs the persona of coach John Kobs:

"Several things I remember about those great days concerning coach John Kobs, who was one of the most gruff, yet most caring men I've ever known. I may have been one of his best pitchers in 1937, yet I could never talk him out of a scholarship. He did see that I got a job cleaning the English building at the huge salary of 25 cents per hour.

John also arranged for a summer job for me in 1936 with the Lansing Motor Wheel Corporation, which needed a pitcher for its city league entry. I was assigned to an oil burner stove assembly line where I was responsible for installing the stove nameplate and inserting the burner base. About midmorning I let three consecutive units get by without name plates and the foreman fired me on the spot. I went back to see the employment manager, who happened to be the company's baseball coach. He sent me back to a different assembly line on the same floor. The only difference was that my pay was raised five cents to around 80 cents per hour. I didn't goof off again, made some great friends, ate salt tablets for the first time, and the ball team won the city championship.

John Kobs also suggested I participate in a tryout with the St. Louis Browns [currently the Baltimore Orioles], which resulted in a job with the Class D Mayfield [Ky.] Clothiers of the Kitty League and a $75 per month salary for the three months of 1937 I played there. Thanks to a lot of hitting and fielding support, I did well at Mayfield, which won the league championship, and I was offered $150 a month to play Class B at Meridian [Miss.] in 1938. After my summer with Mayfield, Kobs had a job waiting for me with the United Press news service. When the next spring rolled around John recommended that I accept the Meridian offer only if they would guarantee me a full no-cut season. They declined, and I was formally declared a holdout. While serving in the war my contract was twice traded, to Minneapolis and then to Toledo. After the war I returned to everybody's good graces when the American League, at my request, declared me reinstated and retired."

Basketball: In the *Michigan State News* of January 15, the following column piece was headed by the question "Do you smoke?":

"Coach Ralph Young, director of athletics, requested last night that the attention of spectators be called to the 'No Smoking' rule in Demonstration Hall. During the last half of the Kentucky game the air over the court was clouded with smoke, putting the players under a decided handicap.

Out of respect to the players and for the benefit of other spectators, it is asked that the no smoking rule be observed rigidly at all future games in Demonstration Hall."

Coach VanAlstyne, unsatisfied with a 4-4 season start, juggled his lineup for the year's fifth home game, a 36-30 victory over Syracuse. He supplanted Ole Nelson and Ben Dargush with Dorian Wilkinson and Eddie Rolen. The new pair was immediately assigned the chore of double-teaming the visitors' chief scoring threat, center Ed Sonderman. It worked. The pair held him to one field goal and three free throws. Meanwhile, Len Oesterink and Ron Garlock were the scoring leaders with 13 points each. It would be the final W of 1936-1937, as the Spartans would plunge into an eight-game losing streak to end the season.

The touring Hawaiian All-Stars not only caught the fancy of the local fans, but in the process also managed to edge the Spartans, 25-24. The visitors' lineup of Moraguchi, Ching, Akau, Pang and Wong proved that size isn't everything as they performed sleight-of-hand passing and darting maneuvers. With the ball described as being whizzed around at a dizzy pace and coming at unexpected angles, one conjures a Globetrotter-like exhibition. The MSC crowd turned traitor as they shouted and cheered every basket the Stars made and booed offi-

cials for calls against them. The Hawaiians were so adept at intercepting passes and harassing shooters that State scored only one field goal in the second half.

Boxing: The season closed at home with a 4-4 draw against St. Norbert's of DePere, Wis., before a packed gymnasium of 1,600 spectators. The quartet of Spartan winners were Roosevelt Barnes, Nick Novosel, Don Rossi, and Bill Adamson. The charm of the previously undefeated pair, Max Wilcox, the little neophyte, and the likable heavyweight, Frank Gaines of Lansing, ran out. They both lost matches by decision.

Cross Country: For the fourth year in a row, State's harriers of 1936 led the field to the individual and team titles at the annual IC4A run in New York City. Setting a new course and meet record over the hilly five-mile course, Kenny Waite paced the field. In so doing, he became the fourth straight Spartan to wear the crown. The 140-pound distance ace sprinted to a long lead in the first mile and finished the windswept course in 26:26.3, more than 100 yards ahead of the second-place finisher. Contributing to the team's winning total of 46 points against runner-up Manhattan College's 66 were Harry Butler in sixth, Nelson Gardner in ninth, Gerard Boss in 16th and Art Green in 18th. Also finishing were Harold Sparks in 25th, and George Grantham in 29th. In addition, Dick Frey, the sensational first-year man, started the day by winning the featured preliminary three-mile race for freshmen.

Football: In a night game at Philadelphia, Art Brandstatter again proved to be an antagonist for Pop Warner and the Temple Owls. Trailing 7-0, "Brandy" raced to the Owls' 41-yard line. Four plays later, with the ball resting on the 15, the big fullback barreled in for the score to assure a 7-7 tie. Leaving the field after the game, Coach Warner supposedly asked an assistant, "Is that Brandstatter a senior?" The response was affirmative, whereupon the legendary coach said, "Thank goodness!"

Vince Vanderburg, the original starting center, was lost for the 1936 season when he wrenched his knee in the Michigan game. His replacement, Sam Ketchman, not a previous letter-winner, became the only Spartan to work with both of the two teams that Coach Bachman alternated during the games. As a result, the Battle Creek senior turned in a record 328 minutes of playing time, which resulted in his selection for the team's "Iron Man Award." Sam was also recognized as the team's MVP, and thus became the recipient of the Governor's Award.

Golf: Ed Flowers, Tom Brand, Roy Nelson and Scotty Taylor were the nucleus of the 1937 team, with Flowers the most frequent team medalist. Both Flowers and Brand played in the U.S. Open qualifying round held on the famed Oakland Hills course in Birmingham. Of the two, Flowers came closest to reaching the goal. With one hole remaining he only needed to shoot a par five on the acclaimed 18th. The task seemed surmountable; after all he had birdied this closing hole in the three preceding rounds. Fate stepped in and seven shots later the Spartan's number one man was motoring back to East Lansing still wondering what happened.

For the first time, MSC would be represented at the NCAA championships. Flowers, Brand, Taylor and Stan Minor were selected to represent the Green and White at the Oakmont course near Pittsburgh.

Swimming and Diving: Following four meets on the road, the Spartans finally opened their home schedule with disappointingly close losses to Western Reserve and the University of Wisconsin on February 27 and March 1. The Monday match-up against the Badgers was particularly exciting, as the outcome was in doubt until the final event, the medley relay. Anchorman "Whitey" Bell closed a five-foot deficit only to be touched out at the finish, guaranteeing a 42-39 win for the visitors. Both the Western Reserve and Wisconsin matches were broadcast live over WKAR radio with Al Theiler, the *Michigan State News* sports editor, at the microphone. It marked the first time swimming meets had ever been broadcast by the college station.

The season closed with MSC recording a perfect 70-14 score against hapless DePauw.

Tennis: The season opened on six new concrete courts that were installed and opened north of the clay courts adjacent to Macklin Field and on the site of the current IM West Building.

Although occasionally preempted by broadcasts of baseball games and track meets, WKAR radio covered numerous home tennis matches during the spring of 1937.

As in baseball, weather conditions of early spring continually hampered play. Matches against Kalamazoo College and the U of M were cancelled and the season-opener against Wisconsin was moved inside Dem Hall and limited to six singles matches. Two weeks later, rain showers at Evanston forced the meet with Northwestern to be moved into McGaw Hall, the Wildcats' fieldhouse.

The 1930s saw two brother acts. Louis Stonebraker, 1936-1937, was the younger brother of Guy, who played in the number six position for the undefeated 1934 team. Chester Olson, who lettered in 1938-1940 was the brother of Hilding Olson, captain of the 1932 team.

The foursome of number one Bob Ross, number two Hock Scholtz, number three Louis Stonebraker, and number four George Hyatt contributed to a team record of 23 wins and only three losses over their final two seasons of competing for MSC, 1936 and 1937.

Track and Field: Darwin Dudley established a new varsity record in the 440 with a clocking of 55.3 against Marquette in the final indoor meet of the season.

Distance ace Dick Frey had an impressive sophomore year highlighted by a first place in the mile at the Texas relays and a third in the two-mile race at the NCAAs in Berkeley, Calif.

Wrestling: Had it not been for a scheduling change, 1937 may well have been another winless season. Original plans called for a match in Oxford, Ohio, against Miami University. When it was discovered the Redskins were using freshmen in their line-up, MSC reneged and scheduled Wheaton College as a replacement. The Crusaders proved to be a fairly weak wrestling school as State handled them rather easily, 17-9.

Michigan State Cheerleaders of the mid '30s

SPARTAN SCRAPBOOK

——— FENCING ———

First fencing team (1926)

MSC
1937-1938

TALES TO TELL

Having defeated Michigan three years in a row, those in the Spartan football camp were feeling rather confident. Varsity basketball-track athlete Bill Carpenter and some fraternity brothers decided that one of the goalposts at the stadium in Ann Arbor should be prepared ahead of time to facilitate its demise following the expected victory on October 2. He described the incident:

"At about 10:30 P.M. on the Wednesday night before the big game, eight of us (two carloads) left East Lansing, arriving in Ann Arbor at about midnight. We climbed over the high-wire fence, which had three strands of barbed wire at the top. Lookouts were posted at the ends and sides. Armed with a sharp pipe cutter, some crack filler, two shelter halves and some flashlights, the 'cutting crew' began the task of cutting through the two uprights about halfway. Detection was avoided by placing the two shelter halves over and around the upright being cut.
We finished at about 12:45 A.M., signaled in the lookouts, climbed back over the fence, got in our cars, and took off for East Lansing.

"Following the victory on Saturday, MSC fans poured out of the stands and attacked the weakened goal post. To our amazement, it would not budge. Talk about a frustrated legion of ecstatic fans! A couple of days later we learned from a U of M student and friend that, on Friday, during their team's place kicking practice, a football struck the crossbar so solidly that the two uprights wobbled violently, causing immediate and thorough investigation and subsequent installation of a new goal post. All our work was for naught, somewhat dampening MSC's fourth in a row."

As for that 19-14 Spartan victory, here is an excerpt from the story by Arch Ward, the venerable sports editor of the *Chicago Tribune:*

"This was State's fourth-straight triumph over Michigan, the first time the Wolverines have lost four in a row to any opponent since the turn of the century. Considering the tenderness of the season, the Spartans played brilliant football. Their timing was right, their blocking effective. Their machine-like precision at times was almost too mechanical. When they re-

HEADLINES of 1938

- Superman, the mighty hero from the planet Krypton, makes his debut in Action Comics.
- Lajos Biro of Hungary invents the ballpoint pen.
- Germany begins its European conquests by invading Austria.
- The radio play "War of the Worlds" is broadcast by Orson Wells, causing widespread panic among listeners who believe its story of an invasion from Martians is true.

SCOREBOARD

	W	L	T	Avg.
Baseball	15	9	0	.625
Track and Field	5	3	0	.625
Football	8	2	0	.800
Basketball	9	8	0	.529
Tennis	7	4	0	.636
Cross Country	1	1	0	.500
Swimming and Diving	6	3	0	.667
Wrestling	5	4	0	.555
Fencing	5	2	1	.688
Golf	7	1	0	.875
Boxing	0	3	0	.000

"In the fourth quarter Michigan scored and made it 14-13 in their favor. In our huddle before receiving the next kick-off, our captain Harry Speelman asked for ideas. Ole Nelson, our rangy 6'3" left end, spoke up and suggested, 'Throw me the ball, that Renda is lost in the grass.' Hercules Renda, the U of M defensive back, was no more than five-feet, eight inches tall and, oh yes, the grass in the Michigan stadium was long, as usual.

Following the kick off and two running plays, we had the ball at our 42-yard line. On third down I completed a pass to Nelson over the middle in front of Renda for a 15-yard gain. Now at their 43-yard-line and just over a minute to play, we hooked up again, this time in the left middle. Ole grabbed the ball over Renda's head and carried it into the end zone for the touchdown and the game, 19-14. What a game it was! Renda sure was 'lost in the grass.'"

ally turned on the power, the Wolverines were a lot of disorganized kids trying to stop the flywheel of a powerhouse with bare hands and belting bodies."

In correspondence, star halfback John Pingel, coincidentally Bill Carpenter's roommate, recalled that afternoon:

TEAM OF THE YEAR

In the 11th year as a varsity sport, the 1938 golf team would post a 7-1 record, including victories over Northwestern, Notre Dame and twice over Michigan. Ed Flowers established himself as one of the favorites at

1938 golf team. (Left to right) Roy Nelson, captain Ed Flowers, coach Ben VanAlstyne, Tom Brand and Warren Tansey.

the NCAA championships in Lexington, Ky., when he carded a 150 for the fourth best score in the 36-hole qualifying rounds. Unfortunately, his exit came earlier than hoped as he was eliminated in the second round of match play. Flowers' three teammates failed to survive the NCAA qualifying rounds: Brand and Nelson scored 157s, while Tansey recorded a 163. In the team standing, the composite score of 627 placed the Spartans in 12th place. Although still considered a minor sport, the four varsity team members were awarded a major "S" for their outstanding record.

MAKING HISTORY

The football season of 1937 marked the first time girl cheerleaders were on the Green and White sideline. The three co-eds brightening Saturdays that fall were Violet McComb of St. Joseph, Betty Blackburn of Houston, Texas, and Eunice Chamberlain of Watervliet.

In Naismith's original basketball rules of 1891, no mention was made for the process of starting the game or putting the ball in play following a goal. The only rule that approximated this situation is that on a disputed out-of-bounds ball the umpire threw the ball "straight into the field." Two years later, in 1893, the center jump was initiated to begin play and to be repeated following every score. Such was the play over a span of 44 years. In 1931, the southern division of the Pacific Coast Conference agreed to adopt a three-year experiment in which the team scored upon took the ball out of bounds from the end line immediately after a score. Hosting and defeating the Stanford Indians, 25-18, on Dec. 27, 1934, the Spartans were one of the first Midwest schools to play under this rule interpretation. In 1937, the Big Ten Conference and then the National Basketball Coaches Association joined the Pacific Coast Conference by voting to abolish the center jump after each successful field goal and successful free throw. The game of basketball was drastically changed forever. In the season of 1937-1938, the first under the new rule, scores increased dramatically and the game seemingly became more appealing to spectators. The two-team total-score average for MSC games vaulted from 56 points to 76 points in the intervening year.

GREAT STATE DATES

Cross Country—**October 16, 1937:** Prompted by the success of recent years, a record number of runners were vying for the coveted spots on the varsity team. Consequently, Coach Brown felt obligated to permit as many as 14 men to run the course in the opening meet against Butler University. Entered as the varsity team were Captain Ken Waite, Dick Frey, Jerry Boss, Dick Granthum, Harry Butler, Arthur Green and Harold Sparks. Also lined up for the three and a half mile grind were Willard Fager, Bob Hills, Bill Mansfield, George Keller, William Beek, Phil Hartman and Harvey Seeley. Boss, a three-year veteran, led the way over the three and a half mile course in a meet record time of 17:48.3. State's complete dominance of the meet was shown by the fact that all seven members of the "official" team crossed the line before one Butler harrier had finished.

Football—**November 27, 1937 (A):** The regular season concluded with a 14-0 win over San Francisco University at Kezar Stadium. The game was scoreless into the third period, when Pingel put MSC on the board with a run that began at his own 25-yard line. He slipped through left tackle, shook off pursuing tacklers, raced into the clear, and bolted across the goal line for the first score. Later in the fourth stanza, the junior from Mt. Clemens was loose again. Starting from the San Francisco 34-yard line, he found an opening at left tackle, swerved to the sideline and crossed the goal at the extreme corner. The Spartans had closed their season with an impressive 8-1 record. On their scenic tourist-like return train trip from San Francisco, Coach Bachman was summoned from the train at a scheduled stop in Spokane, Wash. He responded to a telephone call from Orange Bowl officials extending an invitation for Michigan State to participate in the fourth annual game, scheduled for Miami on Jan. 1, 1938. Approval was immediate. Their foe would be the Auburn Tigers.

Basketball—**January 8, 1938 (H):** The 43-38 victory over Kentucky was meaningful in that it was the first defeat of the season for the Wildcats. Sharing the scoring load for the Spartans with a combined total of 30 points was the sophomore trio of George Falkowski, Marty Hutt and Frank Shidler. During the entire game, only six Spartans saw action.

Basketball—**January 28, 1938 (H):** Against Butler, Coach VanAlstyne adopted a defensive ball-control style of play which proved effective in a 21-15 first-ever victory over the Indianapolis school. At the same time, the game was described as the dullest game of the year. With the score tied 2-2 at the ten-minute mark, the starting five went to the bench and never returned. The reserves, led by Leo Callahan and Marty Hutt, gained an 8-6 halftime advantage and outscored the visitors 13-9 in the final half.

Basketball—**February 12, 1938 (H):** After suffering five straight losses to Michigan, the local heroes turned the tide in the final home game of the 1938 season. Marty Hutt, the splendid sophomore, scored 17 to enjoy his best night of the season. Although, the Spartans held a short lead at most stages of the contest, the outcome remained in doubt until Ben Dargush hit a field goal to ice the win 41-35 as time ran out.

Swimming and Diving—**February 12, 1938 (H):** As in 1937, WKAR radio was back at poolside for a stroke-by-stroke live broadcast of the University of Cincinnati meet. It proved to be the most lopsided Spartan win ever, 64-10.

Track and Field—**March 30 (A) & April 1 (A), 1938:** During spring break the squad packed their bags and headed east. After edging Pittsburgh for top honors at the West Virginia relays, it was on to a decisive win over the University of Maryland, with Herb Woodstra, Wilbur Greer and Arthur Jenkins all double winners. From there, it was on to a fairly easy 75-51 win over Penn State. Woodstra set field records of 14.9 seconds for the high hurdles and 24.6 seconds for the lows. Other winners were Wilbur Greer, Roy Fehr, Ken Waite, Bob Hills, Art Jenkins, Lodo Habrie and Cy Moore. Notwithstanding, the most memorable moment of that meet against the Nittany Lions was not a leap or a run, but an interruption of activities through an act of nature. During the two-mile race, a limestone cavern below the surface of the field gave way and caused a section of the running oval to disappear from sight.

Tennis—**April 16 (H) & April 23 (A), 1938:** With three wins in a row, Coach Ball's squad opened the season on a positive note. The victories over Kalamazoo College and Ohio State were decided in similar fashion. Each time, with the team score tied at 4-4, the number-three doubles team of Wendell Flotz and Irv Rawitz inherited the task of gaining the deciding point, and both times they succeeded.

Golf—**April 23, 1938 (A):** The Spartans opened the season at Ann Arbor with an 11-6 smashing in their first-ever victory over the U of M, a team that would eventually place third in the Big Ten championships. The quartet of winners for MSC were Ed Flowers, 76; Roy Nelson, 75; Tom Brand, 70, and Warren Tansey, 83. Three weeks later, in a rematch at Walnut Hills, State's foursome topped the Wolverines even more decisively, 14 1/2-3 1/2.

Baseball—**May 7, 1938 (H):** By a score of 5-2, State defeated Notre Dame for the eighth time out of the last 11 games. It was a contest that featured defensive gems, evoking applause from the capacity home crowd of over 5,000. The infield pulled off three fast double plays, and Allen Diebold made a couple of spectacular catches off the screen in right field to close out potential Irish rallies in both the eighth and ninth innings.

Tennis—**May 10, 1938 (H):** In the second State-vs.-Michigan meet of the spring the Spartans dominated with victories in singles by number one Herm Struck, number two Chet Olson, number three Captain Leonard Kositcheck, number five Charles Gibbs, and number six Irv Rawitz, a transfer from the U of M. The doubles pair of Struck and Olson also garnered a point which resulted in a convincing 6-3 winning score.

Baseball—**June 3, 1938 (A):** In shutting out the Ohio State Buckeyes, 2-0, sophomore Glenn Rankin, yielded a mere four hits, fanned nine and permitted only four balls out of the infield. Johnny Kuk, the big center fielder, provided the needed offense, first scoring after tripling in the fourth and then, in the eighth, lashing a home run over the right field screen and into the Red Cedar River.

ATHLETE OF THE YEAR

Allen Diebold was a six-letterman Spartan (FB 36-38C & BS 37-39C) who earned the starting quarterback spot on Charlie Bachman's 1938 team. In the spring, Al turned to the diamond where, for two seasons, he patrolled the outfield and was the team leadoff hitter. He epitomized the role of "quiet leader," yet was not overlooked by those around him; teammates of both the 1938 football squad and the 1939 baseball team selected him their team captain. As was typical of the time, quarterback Diebold engineered the single-wing formation directly from the field with no "sideline" signals from coaches or plays being shuttled in by a substitute. He was one of the baseball team's premier hitters, but more impressive were the Jackson, Mich., native's defensive skills in the field.

Al Diebold

IN THE SPARTLITE

Baseball: In State's most impressive beginning, the 1938 Spartans tuned up for the season with an all-conquering seven-game winning streak through Dixie.

Completing the season with a 15-9 record was impressive when examining the team's credentials. They hit for a paltry .238 and closed with a less-than-impressive .941 fielding average.

Basketball: A new agreement was reached between the ROTC department and the intercollegiate athletic office. The basketball team was now able to open its season in Demonstration Hall rather than playing those early season games at the Boys Vocational School in Lansing.

The February MSC-Kentucky rematch at Lexington was no match, as the Wildcats clawed out a 44-27 margin. Bill Carpenter recalls playing in Lexington, Ky., in both 1937 and 1938:

"Coach Rupp met us at the rail terminal and, acting as a perfect host, escorted us on a walking tour of the horse farms and other attractions. We soon realized this was all part of his connivance as he walked our legs off prior to the game. In spite of this, we did respect the old coach."

Boxing: After three years of struggle, the school's athletic council finally accepted boxing as a full-fledged sport in 1938. This meant that Coach Burhans was immediately elevated to full-time status. Also, for the first time, team members became eligible to earn varsity letter sweaters. On the downside, the sport would have to conform to the NCAA policy of barring freshmen from varsity competition.

The year included another positive note. Bouts would now be staged on a new elevated ring that had been raised four feet off the gymnasium floor. This setting would offer a more professional appearance and also give spectators a better view.

In the home opening 4-3 loss to the University of Florida, Herb Zindler had to forfeit in the 115-pound bout when he weighed in several pounds under the minimum weight for competition. This was balanced when Don Rossi was awarded a forfeit win as his opponent withdrew with an eye injury. In slugging out a winning decision in his 135-pound bout, Clint Braidwood would suffer a fractured bone in the hand, sidelining him for the remainder of the season.

To accommodate the growing local spectator interest, the season finale, against Washington State, was moved to Demonstration Hall with its larger seating capacity. A 50-cent admission charge was introduced.

Cross Country: It had been the plan since the IC4A introduced its trophy in 1914. The first school to win the coveted cup five years in a row would gain permanent possession. State finally completed the sweep (1933-37) in the fall of 1937. Leading the winning quintet in New York City was Waite, the 1936 champion, who placed fifth, some 50 yards behind the winner. Close behind came Dick Frey (sixth), followed by Art Green (15th), Harold Sparks (16th) and Jerry Boss (17th). When the points were totaled Michigan State's 59 was 10 better than runner-up Syracuse.

Fencing: The Spartans completed the season with three wins in a row followed by a season ending 8 1/2-8 1/2 tie against the usually powerful team from Chicago University.

Football: There was an obvious team letdown one week following the win over Michigan, as State dropped a 3-0 encounter to defensive-minded Manhattan College at Ebbets Field, the home for baseball's Brooklyn Dodgers. The Jaspers' winning field goal came in the last minute of the third quarter following recovery of a fumble at the State 25-yard line. Although John Pingel did not have his typical "triple-threat" game, he did display brilliant punting with a 52-yard average for the afternoon.

The 1937 junket to Columbia, Mo., for the Saturday, October 16 game against the University of Missouri spanned portions of five days. Departing Lansing at 4:20 p.m. on Thursday by rail, the 35-man squad would arrive at its destination, via Chicago and St. Louis, at 1:00 p.m. on Friday. The return trip was likewise tedious. Departing Columbia on Saturday evening at 9:45 p.m. (CST), the Green and White entourage arrived back at the Lansing Grand Trunk station at 1:25 a.m. Monday morning. As for the game, the Spartans defeated the Tigers by the smallest possible score, 2-0.

Having won MSC's fifth consecutive IC4A title, the 1937 cross country team admires their prize. (From left to right) Dick Frey, Harold Sparks, Art Green, captain Kenny Waite, Jerry Bosss, Harold Butler and Bob Hills.

Golf: The quartet of Ed Flowers, Roy Nelson, Tommy Brand and Bud Tansey would end up playing the entire seven-meet MSC schedule. There were no substitutions.

The wet spring was particularly difficult on the Lansing Country Club course, making it unplayable through mid-April. Seeking an alternate home, arrangements were made for the Spartans to play at Walnut Hills, for both practice and, for the first time since 1930, the varsity schedule. Perhaps VanAlstyne had an "in" at Walnut Hills. The professional at that local course, Elsworth "Mike" Tansey, was the father of sophomore team member Bud Tansey.

Closely pressed for the first time, State barely edged Northwestern by the narrowest of margins, 9-8. It was a gratifying win over the Big Ten's defending champions. The winners' scores were as follows: Flowers, 74; Brand, 78; Nelson, 77; and Tansey, 79.

Even with a squad including the likes of Walter Hagen Jr., son of the great champion, Notre Dame proved no match for the Spartans of 1938. In the final home contest of the year, State topped the Irish, 11-7.

Later that summer in a match-play championship, Ed Flowers defeated "Chick" Harbert 4-3 to capture the state amateur championship in a tournament held at the Gull Lake Country Club. Harbert would later become a successful PGA touring professional.

Swimming and Diving: On the weekend of February 18-21, the swimming and diving team traveled into Ohio for dual meets on Friday, Saturday and Monday. The results were an easy win over Case Tech, a disappointing loss to Western Reserve at the Cleveland Athletic Club and an exciting 44-31 win over Ohio Wesleyan. In commenting on the trip and the problems of competing in unfamiliar settings, Coach Daubert noted that the ceiling at one of the pools they competed in was so low the divers could touch it when they stood on the board. The Ohio Wesleyan pool was 50' x 20', making it difficult to determine the number of lengths needed to complete a long race such as the 440-yard freestyle. Although standardized competitive pools of 60 and 75 feet were becoming most common, venues like the Wesleyan pool would occasionally be a challenge.

By season's end, Ladd Loomis had established a varsity record of 2:45.5 in the 200-yard breaststroke, while the medley relay team of Ed Ochocinski (Ocean), Allan Black and Herb Dales set a new mark of 2:55.4.

Tennis: At the NCAA championships held in Chicago, Chester Olson, Charley Gibbs and Leonard Kositchek and the doubles teams of Herm Struck-Olson and Gibbs-Kositcheck were all eliminated in qualifying rounds.

Track and Field: At a special 1939 pre-Olympic meet in Chicago, Wilbur Greer won a sprint series of three races at 40, 50 and 60 yards and was awarded a diamond medal. Had the intervention of World War II not caused cancellation of the 1940 Olympic Games, Greer would likely have been a U.S. representative in the sprints. The August 1939 issue of the AAU publication, *Amateur Athlete*, listed the Spartan as the number one 100-yard dash man in the country. Yet, it had always been suggested that Greer was more interested in pursuing his musical talents than being a track and field star. Teammate Clare Graft shares this story:

"I was a good friend of Wilbur Greer. He did not like to practice track and preferred playing the clarinet in the band. He had already proven himself as a great sprinter, but Coach Young wanted Wilbur to try the long jump event. Although he had never before attempted a leap, one day during practice Wilbur reluctantly gave in. He raced down the runway and sailed out impressively for nearly 24 feet. Unfamiliar with the techniques of the event, he landed in the pit on one foot with the spikes on the trailing foot penetrating the shoe of the other. Wilbur picked himself up and said "no more." To the best of my knowledge he never did another jump. The winning leap at that year's NCAA championship meet was 25' 1-1/2"."

Wrestling: The dual-meet season concluded with an extended trip east in late February, which began with a shattering 26 1/2-1 1/2 loss to the talented Franklin and Marshall team of Lancaster, Pa. The next night in Providence, R.I., MSC edged Brown University, 15 1/2-14 1/2. Finally, the trip concluded in Cambridge, Mass., with a 38-0 rout of MIT in which seven Spartans registered falls.

EXTRA! 1938 Orange Bowl

January 1, 1938—Miami, Florida

	1	2	3	4	F
MSC	0	0	0	0	0
Auburn	0	6	0	0	6

Starting line-up:

Ernie Bremer	LE
Harry Speelman (C)	LT
Lyle Rockenbach	LG
Tom McShannock	C
Walt Lueck	RG
Howard Swartz	RT
Frank Gaines	RE
Allen Diebold (C)	QB
John Pingel	LH
Steve Szasz	RH
Usif Haney	FB

With snow covering the campus in early December, the squad of 41 players began preparations for the school's first bowl appearance with daily workouts on the tanbark of Demonstration Hall. Then on December 20, the team boarded a train for Gainesville, Fla., where they would set up a four-day training session at the University of Florida. From there they headed further south to Miami where they continued to tune their game plan on the grounds of Miami High School. By game day it was predicted the new $360,000 facility (Roddy-Burdine Stadium) would be filled to its 23,000 capacity. Consequently, the actual turnout of 18,970 was likely a disappointment to game officials. Nothing seemed to fall into place for State during that New Year's Day game. With their top receiver, Ole Nelson, hobbling with an ankle injury, the passing game was ineffective. The Spartans' offense never became a factor as John Pingel threw an atypical three interceptions and the squad gained only two first downs during the afternoon's 6-0 loss. Meanwhile, Auburn drove within the MSU 30 five times without putting points on the board. Another statistic was even more compelling—the Tigers totaled 278 scrimmage yards (rushing and passing) compared the Spartans' 67 yards. The State fans likely found more entertainment from the halftime show which featured twelve bands and five brilliantly attired drill teams, the prelude to Orange Bowl extravaganzas of the future. The six points scored during the contest still ranks as the lowest-scoring game in Orange Bowl history.

MSC 1938-1939

TALES TO TELL

Upon becoming the country's 32nd president in 1933, Franklin Roosevelt began initiating federal legislation to counterattack the Great Depression, which had had a stranglehold on the economy and society of the nation since 1929. His idea called for the use of funds to construct public works as administered through the Works Progress Administration (WPA), later relabeled the Public Works Administration (PWA). The idea was to put hundreds of thousands of the unemployed back to work. By 1938, MSC's foresighted team of President Robert Shaw and Board Secretary John Hannah would take full advantage of this WPA-PWA plan, which called for the federal government to provide 45 percent of funding for approved buildings erected by public agencies. As a result, in addition to construction of a new Farm Lane bridge, the music building, the auditorium, Campbell Hall and Olin Health Center, the athletic plant was significantly improved. First, the football field was lowered, thus eliminating the running oval. Then appropriations were provided for the replacement track west of the sta-

dium, which opened in 1937. Finally, included in this period of mass construction was the approval of a long-awaited indoor facility (Jenison) that opened in 1940.

TEAM OF THE YEAR

The fencing team is designated as Team of the Year in recognition of it being Charles Schmitter's first team as head coach at MSC. The likeable Schmitter would continue on for a school-record 45 years before retiring following the 1983 season. His 1939 team was marked by outstanding individual and team scores, completing the season with a 7-4 record, including victories over Marquette, Wisconsin and Purdue. Captain Manuel Aretga brought his career to a close by winning 80 percent of his bouts as the number one man in foil. Jerry Richardson was close behind with a 78 percent over the 11 meets. William Hasselback scored 70 percent as the number one sabre man. The number one in epee was Benjamin Bisgeier, who managed a 70 percent record.

HEADLINES of 1939

- Motion picture releases of the year include *Gone With the Wind* and *The Wizard of Oz*.
- At the World's Fair in New York City, thousands ogle an RCA TV featuring a 12-inch screen reflected in a cabinet-lid mirror.
- Hitler's forces invade Poland. Great Britain and France respond by declaring war on Germany.
- Irving Berlin releases the popular patriotic song "God Bless America," sung by Kate Smith.

SCOREBOARD

	W	L	T	Avg.
Baseball	13	10	0	.565
Track and Field	2	5	0	.286
Football	6	3	0	.667
Basketball	9	8	0	.529
Tennis	10	5	0	.667
Cross Country	3	0	0	1.000
Swimming and Diving	3	5	0	.375
Wrestling	5	3	0	.625
Fencing	8	4	0	.667
Golf	5	3	0	.625
Boxing	2	1	1	.625

MAKING HISTORY

In the initial run of 1938 and for 26 consecutive years thereafter, the NCAA cross country title chase was held on the MSC campus. The Indiana Hoosiers, a team that State had defeated in a dual meet one month earlier, captured the first trophy.

Of the four Spartan entrants at the NCAA boxing championships in Madison, Wis., on March 30-31 and April 1, Don Rossi and Clint Braidwood were eliminated with opening round losses, while Carl Thompson reached the second bracket before sustaining his initial loss of the year. Heavyweight Ernie Dunn earned MSC's first-ever championship point upon reaching the semifinals where he was eliminated by the eventual champion.

GREAT STATE DATES

Football—**November 12, 1938 (A):** At Milwaukee, in the eighth game of the season, Marquette jumped to a two-touchdown lead in the opening quarter. In the second period, the Spartans came back to tie the score, 14-14. Later, with only four minutes remaining in the contest, John Pingel booted a 61-yard punt that Dave Diehl downed at the four-yard line. The Hilltoppers were held and forced to turn the ball over, but the return punt came out only to their 39-yard line. On the sixth play following that exchange, Pingel passed to Jack Amon in the end zone. The sophomore from Grand Rapids initially juggled the ball but finally held on for the 20-14 MSC victory. It was Pingel's third scoring pass of the afternoon.

Football—**November 19, 1938 (H):** In the final game of the season, the larger Temple eleven gained more yardage in both running and passing, but they could not chalk up points on the scoreboard. In the second period,

The 1939 fencing team. (Left to right) W. Hasselback, B. Bisgeier, G. Oswald, G. Richardson, W. Hammond, E. Kay, O. Sussman, G. Grenzke, M. Artega and manager H. Chandler; coach C. Schmitter (below).

a flea-flicker pass and lateral from Ed Pearce to Ralph Bennett to Usif Haney put the ball at the Owl 20-yard line. Four plays later, Pearce, the speedster from Flint, dodged two would-be tacklers and went in for a touchdown. Les Bruckner's field goal in the fourth quarter made the final score 10-0.

Basketball—December 28, 1938 (H): The prepublicity for the Penn State game elaborated on the visitors' huge height advantage, further noting the starting five averaged six-foot-two. The "towering" Nittany Lions showed little disposition to make an interesting game of it. They virtually walked through the first half and frequently just held the ball outside the zone defense. By the 14-minute mark their deliberate tactics had yielded a boring 5-3 Spartan lead. In the second half, led by Bob Phillips, Max Hindman and Chet Aubuchon, the Spartans opened the game up with a running offense and a nagging full-court press. The scoreboard soon read 25-7 and Coach VanAlstyne was clearing his bench. The final score: MSC 35, Penn State 21.

Basketball—January 23, 1939 (A): Featuring the floor play of Chet Aubuchon, the scoring of George Falkowski and defensive play of Leo Callahan, MSC pulled out a close 35-31 victory over the University of Tennessee before 1,800 yelling fans in Knoxville. The Spartans were on top at halftime, 19-15, but things heated up during the second period as the lead continually flip-flopped. Finally, with four minutes remaining, State's Frank Shidler dropped in a field goal for a 32-31 advantage. Thereafter, the Volunteers never scored again.

Wrestling—February 10 & 11, 1939 (A): Even if Wisconsin and Northwestern were not Big Ten powers in wrestling, a successful two-win trip to Madison (score 20-8) and Evanston (score 22-8) was the highlight of the MSC 5-3 season. On that weekend, Dale Ball, Lloyd Russell, Benny Riggs, Charlie Hutson and Steve Slezak were all double winners.

Swimming and Diving—February 18, 1939 (H): The sophomore-dominated 1939 team scored a victory over Western Reserve, 42-23. In that meet the quartet of Geoffrey Gough, Gil Ziegenfus, Don Ladd and Barney Slamkowski splashed home with a new team record of 3:25.0 in the 360-yard freestyle relay. This was the home pool version of the 400 yard freestyle relay event. As the 3-5 season concluded, Coach Daubert likely looked longingly to 1940. The crop of 1939 freshmen had collectively smashed all but two of the school's frosh records.

Boxing—March 14, 1939 (H): More than 2,000 fans turned out at Dem Hall for the matches against a talented University of Miami (Fla.) team. The Hurricanes opened with a pair of wins, one by their 1938 NCAA finalist and the second by a member of the 1936 U. S. Olympic team. After that it was all MSC. Because of injuries, the Hurricanes were forced to forfeit the 145-pound bout to Don Wagner and the heavyweight to Ernie Dunn. Meanwhile, Clint Braidwood, Carl Thompson and Joe Cestowski hammered out decisions while Captain Don Rossi scored a technical knockout when his rival suffered a cut forehead in the second round of their light-heavyweight battle.

Fencing—April 6, 1939 (H): In a late-season contest, the Spartans defeated a touring team from Dartmouth College with surprising ease, 11-6. The Big Green from Hanover, N.H., would later tie for second place at the 1939 Eastern Intercollegiate Conference meet.

Track and Field—April 16, 1939 (H): A significant addition to the team was the arrival of multitalented Walt Arrington. In the 76 1/6 to 54 5/6 victory over Purdue, the sophomore contributed a pair of record-breaking performances. First, he established a new field mark of 23' 5-1/2" in winning the broad jump, and then erased the oldest varsity mark in the books by managing 6' 1-3/4" in the high jump. Charles Lord had set the previous team standard of 6'-1/2" in 1912.

Tennis—April 21, 1939 (H): MSC opened at home with an 8-1 victory over the University of Cincinnati. Rain forced play onto the indoor court laid out in Demonstration Hall where matches began at 1:30 p.m. and, one by one, were played uninterrupted until the last doubles game was concluded at 10:30 p.m. From start to finish it was a nine-hour match. The single Cincinnati team point was earned by Billy Talbert who defeated co-captain Herman Struck at the number-one position. Talbert would later become a leading professional player.

Baseball—April 28, 1939 (A): State was outhit by Michigan 11-6, but the Spartans took full advantage of the host's generosity to post a 6-3 victory. The gifts came in the form of seven Wolverine errors, seven bases on balls, and two hit batsmen. Paul Derrickson, a stocky sophomore, pitched the entire game for State, and, except for the shaky first inning when he yielded all three runs, the situation seemed well in hand.

Golf—May 3 (A) & May 22, 1939 (H): Much like the 1938 team, the 1939 version of Spartan golf completed a sweep of Michigan, the runners-up at the Big

Ten championships. In the first match-up, delayed two weeks by weather, Roy Nelson led the way to the 10-8 win with a four-under-par 68, the lowest score ever turned in by an MSC varsity player. Stan Kowal and Art Kerkau managed 76s and Tansey an 80. It was the U of M's first defeat of the season. In the rematch three weeks later at Walnut Hills, balanced scoring led to a more decisive winning score, 11 1/2-6 1/2. Kowal and Kerkau shared medalist honors with 72s. Nelson shot a 73 and Bud Tansey a 77.

Track and Field—**May 15, 1939 (H):** Spartan fans stood and cheered home the winner of the two-mile race, even though he was not wearing the green and white. They were simply expressing appreciation for a record performance. Greg Rice of Notre Dame, with a clocking of 9:06.4, had negotiated the fastest eight-lap race ever run by a collegian. Over the remainder of the afternoon, the Spartans excelled enough for a 70-61 winning score. Rudy Yovonovitz led the way by taking both hurdle races, and, in the final and deciding race of the afternoon, the quartet of Don MacInnes, Roy Fehr, Warren Cooley and co-captain Bob Hills left no doubt with a convincing first place in the mile relay.

Baseball—**May 20, 1939 (H):** In a pregame agreement similar to an earlier era, the contest against the University of Minnesota was called at the end of seven and one-half innings, permitting the Gophers to catch a train home. Even within the abbreviated format, John Kobs's offense managed 11 hits leading to a relatively easy 8-3 win. Collecting two hits each were Allen Diebold, George Stark, Norm Duncan and Sam Nuznov, who belted a pair of triples.

Baseball—**June 10, 1939 (H):** The Spartans closed their season with a 1-0 victory over Western State Teachers College, and in so doing they avenged a 2-1 loss one week earlier in Kalamazoo. The game was errorless and featured a sizzling pitching duel between State's George Monroe and Frank "Stubby" Overmire, who would later perform 10 years in the majors. A couple of hits in the sixth inning were all it took. Shortstop George Owen opened the frame with a single, went to second on Monroe's sacrifice bunt, and scored on Allen Diebold's ringing single to center. It was a fitting climax to Diebold's three-year football-baseball career.

ATHLETE OF THE YEAR

John Pingel was truly a "triple threat" star. With a punting average of 42.6 yards, he led the nation in 1937 and then booted for a 42.6 average in his final season of 1938. Additional statistics from his senior year reflect impressive credentials as a passer and runner: 54 of 101 completions for 571 yards in the air and an average of 5.0 yards gained in 110 carries. John made postseason appearances in the East-West and *Chicago Tribune* College All-Star games. He also gained All-American recognition by many of the selection committees, including the Hearst Syndicate and the Associated Press.

John Pingel

IN THE SPARTLITE

Baseball: The two-day offensive outburst against Ohio Wesleyan and Notre Dame on May 5-6 has seldom been topped over the 100-plus years of Michigan State baseball. In the Friday afternoon game against the Battling Bishops, the MSC batters lashed out 19 hits in a 17-7 lopsided win. Still at home on the next afternoon, an 18-hit attack produced a 14-9 advantage over the Fighting Irish. Ray Dahlstrom, Casey Klewicki and George Stark each collected three hits.

Up from the freshman team, shortstop Norm "Shorty" Duncan would prove to be an instant star, as he won the team batting title with a .341 season average. In a stellar fielding gem of the season, Duncan started a triple play in the 7-5 loss to Wisconsin. With runners on first and second, he snared a sinking line drive at his feet, stepped on second and threw to first for the third out. Observers were convinced he could have easily opted for an unassisted triple play by chasing down the runner who had been caught between first and second base.

Basketball: Optimism reigned prior to the 1938-1939 season. Coach VanAlstyne predicted, "We have the finest material to work with this fall, and (we) should be able to have the greatest quintet in the history of the college." Much of the enthusiasm was generated by the emergence of a sophomore class that included a trio of graduates from Gary (Ind.) Horace Mann High School who would affectionately be referred to as the "Gary Gang." This threesome included the future All-American Chet Aubuchon, Bob Phillips and Max Hindman, a 6' 3" center. Max had played two years with an independent team in Crown Point, Ind., before enrolling at MSC. Even with a roster that included eight letter winners from 1937-1938, on some occasions during the year, the starting line-up would include all three of the "Gary Gang." Conforming to a nationwide trend and differing from VanAlstyne teams of the past, the Spartans of 1938-1939 used a more "racehorse" style of play. As the 17-game season unfolded, game-by-game results demonstrated that an unrealistic expectancy had been placed on this edition of Spartan basketball. Perhaps there were three plausible reasons for the less-than-impressive 9-8 season. First, there were nagging illnesses and injuries that impacted the line-up during the season. Second, of the eight losses absorbed, four were by a margin of two or fewer points, and finally, the 1938-1939 schedule was reflective of far more challenging competition. Teams like Hope, Case and Buffalo had been replaced by the likes of Penn State, Indiana, Tennessee and Temple.

For Indiana University, it would be their first and only trip into East Lansing until 1950. The Spartans put up a lively scrap before yielding to the undefeated Hoosiers, 37-33. At one time in the second half State had pulled to within two points, 25-23. The telling difference was at the free throw line, where Indiana hit on 11 of 14 while MSC managed only 9 of 18.

Boxing: Before a home crowd of over 2,600 fight fans, the Spartans completed the 1939 schedule scoring a 4-4 tie with Penn State. The four Spartan wins were turned in by Don Wagner, Don Rossi, Ernie Dunn and Carl "Fumbles" Thompson, the undefeated sophomore. State had to forfeit a costly point when Clint Braidwood came down ill and was unable to box.

Cross Country: Following five straight IC4A titles (1933-1937), the State runners settled for a runner-up position in 1938. Manhattan accumulated 38 points to MSC's 76.

Fencing: The low point in an otherwise impressive 7-4 season was the double loss to Lawrence. This meant forfeiture of the Lawrence Trophy awarded annually to the top team in Michigan.

Football: On back-to-back Saturdays, State hosted undefeated opponents. With runs of 23 and 28 yards, John Pingel scored a pair of touchdowns and passed to Ole Nelson for the third score, leading to an impressive 19-12 victory over Syracuse. On the following Saturday, Santa Clara came to town with its unblemished record. When Pingel scored on a four-yard end run in the second quarter, it was only the second time the Californians' goal had been crossed all season. Missing the conversion proved costly. Later in the game, playing within the limited substitution rules of the time and with John Pingel on the sideline, Ed Klewicki lined up as the substitute punter. The kick was blocked and a Bronco lineman ran the ball in for the score. The all-important PAT was good, and Santa Clara left Macklin Field still undefeated, 7-6.

Golf: In early April practices, Coach VanAlstyne began the process of finding replacements for Ed Flowers and Tom Brand, the two graduates of 1938. Eventually Stan Kowal of New York Mills, N.Y., and Art Kerkau surfaced as adequate replacements. Their combined average score over the eight-game schedule was 74.0, which compared favorably to the Flowers-Brand 75.6 in the eight-game 1938 season.

State was again represented at the NCAA championships, but Roy Nelson would not be among them. The team captain had a prior commitment, an ROTC summer camp in Wisconsin.

Swimming and Diving: Freestylers Leon Williamson and Don Ladd competed in the NCAA championship meet at Ann Arbor, but neither reached the finals.

Track and Field: In February it was announced that Fran Dittrich, varsity standout (1934-1936), would join the staff as the freshman and assistant varsity track and field coach.

Without the services of their sprinting ace Ernie Greer, the Spartans hosted and lost a close meet to Penn State 74-57. Suffering from a pulled leg muscle, Greer came to the track for a warm-up, but his hobbled condition persisted and he remained unavailable to the team. His absence was costly, as the Lions gained 16 points in slamming both the 100- and 220-yard races, as well as nosing out State's mile relay team. MSC's star of the day was Walt Arrington, the sophomore jumper from Pelham Bay, N.Y. He first won the high jump at a height of 6'-1"

and then, with a leap of 24'-3", he improved the varsity broad jump record for the fourth successive time.

Wrestling: In 1939, Michigan State's wrestling program became recognized as a "major" sport within the athletic department. Until that season, the coach could petition the athletic council for a major "S" on behalf of an individual who may have had a particularly outstanding season.

With seven wins in eight matches, 175-pound Steve Slezak recorded the most impressive dual-meet record of the season.

Coach Collins entered five men in the 1939 Interstate Wrestling Championships held in Cleveland. Bill Martin, Benny Riggs and Steve Slezak emerged as champions and with 20 team points, MSC finished second behind Kent State with 32.

In an effort to encourage high school wrestling in Michigan, where no program was sanctioned, Coach Collins initiated an interscholastic state tournament on the campus. Held in late March, nine schools entered a total of 51 wrestlers.

Coach Schlademan with his gifted star Walter Arrington.

MSC
1939-1940

TALES TO TELL

It was just prior to the six-game trip west that basketball's Chet Aubuchon appropriated an old lantern that eventually became the custody of Everett "Mac" MacDaugal, team manager. "Mac" cleaned up the lantern, gave it a coat of bright red paint, and took it aboard the train. He initially walked into the fieldhouse at Creighton University swinging the glowing kerosene lamp, and the assembled crowd in Omaha went wild. When the team members saw the reaction of those fans they just naturally absorbed a little of the glowing heat and knocked off the Blue Jays, 32-30. That evening a good luck charm was born and, regardless of the nasty odor from the burning kerosene, it held a permanent spot along the team bench for the remainder of the season. Marty Hutt reminisced about that unprecedented two-week rail journey in late December in which the entourage traveled aboard a private car, complete with professors available to monitor academic work. Hutt, the team's co-captain, jokingly admitted that more time was spent at card games than at studies.

Chet Aubuchon (front center) and teammates watch Everett MacDaugal, student manager, fire up the Red Lantern.

HEADLINES of 1940

- As the war in Europe expands, German troops enter Holland, Belgium and Luxembourg, and eventually force the surrender of France.
- Franklin Roosevelt returns as president in an unprecedented third term.
- "Eh, what's up, Doc?" A new star is born as Bugs Bunny makes his first screen appearance in "A Wild Hare."
- Popular radio listening of the period includes "The Shadow," "Gangbusters," "Fibber McGee and Molly," and "The Jack Benny Show."

SCOREBOARD

	W	L	T	Avg.
Baseball	12	8	2	.591
Track and Field	0	5	0	.000
Football	4	4	1	.500
Basketball	14	6	0	.700
Tennis	6	6	1	.500
Cross Country	2	1	0	.667
Swimming and Diving	7	2	0	.778
Wrestling	5	2	1	.688
Fencing	14	1	0	.933
Golf	5	3	1	.611
Boxing	0	3	3	.250

Completing the 1940 boxing season with only one victory was disappointing, but it was not a tragedy. The death of a team member would be a tragedy. At 12:10 a.m. on Saturday, March 2, two days before the final home meet of the season against Temple, heavyweight Ernie Dunn of Saginaw was struck and killed by a hit-and-run driver. After stepping off a city bus at Harrison and Michigan Avenue, Ernie and his roommate were walking south on Harrison Road. The fatal impact took place almost directly in front of the State Police administration building, just blocks from his rooming house on Marigold Avenue. Later that afternoon, the guilty driver, a 45-year-old factory worker from Lansing, surrendered to police. He had been drinking at a local bar prior to the tragedy. Incredibly, there was no apparent thought for canceling the Monday night match with the Owls, which turned out to be a 4-4 tie. It went on as scheduled. Also surprising is that in their reports of the MSC-Temple match, neither *The Lansing State Journal* or *The Michigan State News* made reference to Ernie Dunn's death.

TEAM OF THE YEAR

Lauren Brown's 1939 cross country squad would capture a prestigious prize, the team title at the second running of the NCAA championship, once more conducted on the MSC campus course. Headed by Captain Dick Frey, who placed fifth, they edged the University of Wisconsin by three points to register the school's first-ever National Collegiate title in any sport. The five-man team consisted of Frey, Roy Fehr, who placed 13th, Ed Mills 19th, Al Mangan 20th, and Bill Mansfield 22nd. Non-scorers that afternoon were George Keller, who finished 26th, and Warren Anderson 45th.

The 1939 cross country team. (Front row, left to right) W. Anderson, G. Keller, R. Fehr, D. Frey, W. Mansfield, E. Mills, A. Mangan; (middle row, left to right) assistant manager D. Smith, W. Beardslee, D. Cowden, W. Scales, A. Wetzel, assistant manger G. Campbell; (back row, left to right) coach L. Brown, manager W. Christman, trainer J. Heppinstall.

MAKING HISTORY

A football rule was passed requiring players to wear helmets.

In swimming, rules provided for the official men's competitive suit to be reduced from a full tank suit to trunks.

Upon return from the six-game 1939 Christmas-break basketball trip to California and Oregon, the excitement of opening Jenison Fieldhouse was four days away. Chet Aubuchon recalls hardly having enough time to unpack his bags. The date was Jan. 6, 1940, and the opponent was the University of Tennessee. The playing surface of the new fieldhouse was the same that had been used at Demonstration Hall. The 96-piece floor had been disassembled and moved across the street in December. Although the first-ever PA system for an MSC basketball game was in service for the game, the scoreboards and new glass backboards had yet to be installed. In this fresh environment of Jenison and beginning with that inaugural contest, games began to be orchestrated with more flair. Shortly before tip-off, the fieldhouse was darkened and a spotlight was placed on the flag as the band played the national anthem. The spotlight was then focused on each member of the starting teams as they were individually introduced to the crowd of 6,500. It was an exciting game decided in the final minutes of play with Joe Gerard the hero. With the Vols leading, 19-18, the sophomore connected on two free throws and a field goal, and the Spartans never trailed after that, winning 29-20. That evening, Bob Phillips played with a heavy heart as he learned one hour before tip-off of his father's death.

GREAT STATE DATES

Cross Country—**October 14, 1939 (H):** MSC opened the season at home with a convincing 24-33 triumph over powerful Penn State. The feature was the individual battle between Roy Fehr and Penn State ace Bill Smith for meet honors. The latter set the pace, and Fehr, the Royal Oak veteran, remained one stride behind until hitting the final quarter-mile on the running track. Then, with a burst of speed he drove ahead of the IC4A champion and hung on for the win even as Smith challenged all the way to the tape.

Football—**October 28 (H) & November 4 (A), 1939:** Two weeks in a row, Wyman Davis was MSC's star performer. Tied with Illinois Wesleyan 6-6, with only 36 seconds remaining, the Dundee sophomore zigzagged 23 yards into the end zone with the winning touchdown. One week later in the 14-3 win over Syracuse, Davis was instrumental in both TDs. He first scored on a short pass from Ed Pearce and then was on the throwing end of a 35-yard scoring toss to Bruce Blackburn.

Football—**November 25, 1939 (H):** Led by sophomore Mike Scheib, State wound up the season with a 18-7 win over Temple. The 162-pound speedster from Allegan rattled off runs of 21, 41, 36 and 47 yards with a game total of 180 yards rushing. It was State's third straight win over the Philadelphians, and it would be the renowned "Pop" Warner's final game as head coach of the Owls.

Basketball—**January 8, 1940 (H):** Joe Gerard became an instant hero as he filled in for the absent Bob Phillips. With the game against Syracuse tied 29-29 and seven seconds remaining, the stocky 5' 10" forward dribbled through three Orange players and sunk a spectacular one-handed shot, giving MSC a hard-earned two-point victory to the delight of 4,000 fans.

Wrestling—**January 22, 1940 (H):** Following Spartan losses in the opening two matches of the evening, Lee Merrill, Bill Martin and co-captain Ben Riggs followed with consecutive pins which led to a 23-11 victory over the Northwestern Wildcats. This was the initial wrestling match to be held in the newly opened Jenison Fieldhouse.

Basketball—**January 26, 1940 (A):** In what would be Michigan State's first appearance in the "Big Apple," they took on the powerful Long Island University team coached by the legendary Clair Bee. Co-captain Marty Hutt recalls the experience:

"Probably one of the greatest thrills of my career was playing in the famous Madison Square Garden in New York City. The team attended the hockey game the night before at the Garden and we were introduced to the capacity crowd. To play a game the next night on what was an ice rink the night before was a marvelous accomplishment in those days. We played and suffered a 34-25 loss to the Long Island Blackbirds, at that time one of the best teams in the country."

Basketball—February 3, 1940 (H): Even as VanAlstyne endorsed the "racehorse" style of basketball that had escorted the 1937 center jump rule change, he remained a teacher of the fine art of defense and ball control. As the 1939-1940 season progressed, his short bench was shortened even more with nagging injuries. This led Van to inject his patented "build a lead and stall" tactics. While the Spartans were closing the season with five straight victories, the system was working to perfection. One of the cherished wins in that closing streak was the 48-41 home victory over Wisconsin. The lead bounced back and forth until Max Dalrymple sparked State to a 26-20 halftime edge. The Spartans continued their scoring rally for the opening six minutes of the second half and built a 14-point advantage. That was sufficient as Coach VanAlstyne then called for his stall tactics, and the game ended 48-41 in MSC's favor. This was a talented Badger team. They were one year away from being crowned national champions at the NCAA tournament in Kansas City, Mo.

Swimming and Diving—February 24, 1940 (H): Of the three "payback" wins of 1940 (Purdue, Indiana, and Cincinnati), the victory over Indiana University was the most gratifying. Leading 37-31 entering the final event, the Spartans needed to finish first in the freestyle relay to secure the win. Dale Hansen led off and gained a two-yard advantage that was increased by Huntley Johnson and Don Farmer and maintained by Captain Don Ladd in his anchor-leg position. Gaining seven points, the final score read MSC 44, IU 31.

Basketball—March 1, 1940 (H): State concluded the most impressive season (14-6) since 1935 when they convincingly defeated Temple University, 44-28. With 13 and 12 points respectively, Chet Aubuchon and Joe Gerard led all scorers, while seniors Marty Hutt and Max Dalrymple wrapped up their collegiate careers to the resounding cheers and applause of the 4,000 fans. Hutt marked up four points to increase his three-year scoring total to 404, the largest career total in 20 years of Michigan State basketball.

Swimming and Diving—March 6, 1940 (H): Fred Himmelein, then a sophomore from Sandusky, Ohio, recalls the meet against Kenyon College:

"In one of the final men's varsity swimming meets in the old Gymnasium pool, MSC entertained Kenyon College, a perennial power in college swimming. They were undefeated and had triumphed in 55 of their last 56 meets. With two events remaining we were leading by a score of 33-27, but it was still possible for Kenyon to win if they could capture those final two events, the 440-yard freestyle and the freestyle relay.

Of all the Kenyon swimmers, one was outstanding, their backstroker Bill Griffin, who would finish fourth in that year's NCAA championships. It was to him that the Kenyon coach turned in hopes of a victory in the 440-yard freestyle. This was my event, and to my surprise Griffin would swim all 14 2/3 laps using his specialty, the backstroke [as the name implies, a competitor can swim a freestyle event "freely," in any stroke he desires]. Griffin started out with a fast pace and opened up a lead of one-half length. Fortunately, the distance was too great for him and slowly I drew even, and by the 12th lap I had overtaken him and went to win by nearly a length of the pool."

The undefeated had been defeated. This was the last time Kenyon would schedule Michigan State in swimming.

Baseball—March 27, 1940 (A): Playing against South Carolina in the final game of the 1940 southern trip, State jumped to a 7-0 lead after five innings. Aided by a sloppy Spartan defense, the Gamecocks came storming back and after nine innings the scoreboard read, Michigan State 10, South Carolina 10. In the first extra inning, each team scored one run, and in the 11th MSC pushed three more runs across while the Carolinians' one-run response fell short. The final score read Michigan State 14, South Carolina 12, as State managed 22 hits in the 3 hour, 20 minute "hit parade."

Baseball—April 30, 1940 (A): Coach Kobs was pleased with the 5-4 victory over the U of M, the third straight win in Ann Arbor. Yet, it had been a frustrating afternoon for his Spartans as they stranded 13 base runners while managing 16 hits off of four Wolverine pitchers. Leading 5-1 after eight innings, State had to withstand a three-run Michigan splurge in the ninth as Frank Mekules relieved captain George Monroe on the mound to retire the final two batters.

Baseball—**May 11, 1940 (A):** Trailing 5-0 after seven innings, State seemed destined to lose its second game to Western State in two weeks. Then it all happened in one inning, the eighth, when Norm Duncan, Wil Davis, Steve Jakubowski, Cas Klewicki, George Owen, Paul Starck and Leo Wolkowicz scored consecutively off a parade of three Bronco hurlers. The one-inning surge held up for a 7-5 victory.

Golf—**May 4, 1940 (H):** Shooting a combined school-record low of 297 strokes, State easily defeated Northwestern University, 16-1. Leading the record performance was Ralph Kortge, Midland sophomore, who carded a 73 on the Walnut Hills course. Stan Kowal and Bud Tansey each followed with scores of 74 while Bill Zylstra trailed two strokes back at 76.

Tennis—**May 11, 1940 (H):** Having defeated Kentucky 9-0 three weeks earlier, State posted its second "white washing" of the spring; this time the Indiana Hoosiers were the victims. IU never won a set during the quick two-hour engagement. Winners at singles were Chet Olson 6-1, 6-1; Fred Perkins 6-0, 6-3; Herm Struck 6-0, 6-1; Irving Roberts 6-0, 6-0; Floyd Krause 6-2, 6-3; and Bob Harris 6-1, 6-0.

ATHLETE OF THE YEAR

Chet Aubuchon (BK 1939, 1940, 1942C) came to East Lansing following a brilliant career at Horace Mann High School in Gary, Ind. He would be a three-year starter for the Spartans, with 1940 his most productive season when he led the team in scoring (169 points) during a 14-6 season. Also, in that junior year Chet gained All-American recognition, the first Spartan basketball player to be so honored. During the summer of 1940, Aubuchon was stricken with a blood infection that nearly took his life and forced him to drop from school while he convalesced back home in Gary. Returning in 1942, Aubie assumed a rather unique role, often acting as a player-coach and frequently remaining on the bench during the first portion of the game absorbing the opposition's talent and style of play. Upon entering the game, he would put his suave to work while "quarterbacking" the team through the remainder of the game. Standing only 5' 9" and weighing 140 pounds, he was not big for a basket-

Chet Aubuchon

ball player, even for those days. His primary forte was his ball-handling and dribbling skills that gained him the moniker "Houdini of the Hardwood" from a sportswriter of the time.

IN THE SPARTLITE

Baseball: The top pitcher of the season was Frank Mekules, the Detroit sophomore, who posted a 5-2 record. Norm Duncan, the Mayville, Mich., shortstop, led State hitters for the second straight year, as he pounded out 35 hits in 88 times at bat for an impressive .398 average.

Basketball: An idiotic policy of the time robbed the 1939-1940 team of two seniors, reserve Frank Shidler

and the team's leading scorer of the preceding season, George Falkowski. The two were majoring in police administration, a curriculum that forced students to spend their fourth year (field study) in the State Police barracks. The accompanying school policy stated that anyone stationed in the barracks could not participate in school activities. Thus, there would be no Frank and no George, and a shortage of talented reserves would eventually impact an otherwise impressive 14-6 record.

The season opened with the starting quintet set with the "Gary Gang" of Bob Phillips, Max Hindman and Chet Aubuchon, accompanied by the senior co-captains Marty Hutt and Max Dalrymple.

When the season opened on December 4, the new home court, Jenison Fieldhouse, was not ready for occupancy; consequently, the first two home games were played at the familiar Boys' Vocational Fieldhouse in Lansing.

As the team of 1931 had done, the 1939-1940 squad flew to Milwaukee to play Marquette in the final road game of the schedule. This mode of travel was a welcome relief for the Spartans, who had covered more than 7,100 miles by rail during the season.

Boxing: Don Rossi surrendered his final year of eligibility (1940) and became the assistant coach with primary responsibility to the freshman boxers.

With a dual meet consisting of eight bouts, a tie with four wins and four losses would seem a likely possibility. Sure enough, for the Spartans of 1940 it was more than a possibility, it became a fairly common occurrence. Throughout their six-meet schedule they settled for ties three times: against Syracuse, Bucknell and Temple.

Joe Cestowski reached the semifinals of the NCAA championships before being eliminated. Clint Braidwood, who won four out of five dual-meet bouts, was also entered in those championships but opted to stay home because of a heavy academic schedule.

Cross Country: Led by Roy Fehr, Bill Mansfield, Ed Mills, captain Dick Frey, George Keller and Al Mangan, the Spartans captured both the State Intercollegiate meet over the new MSC four-mile course and the State AAU championships at Kalamazoo.

For the second straight year, State had to settle for the runner-up spot behind Manhattan College in their quest of the IC4A title at Van Cortland Park in New York City. Led by Roy Fehr, the Spartans finished in the eighth, 13th, 14th, 17th, and 18th spots for a team score of 70, significantly short of the winners' 42.

As described earlier, one week following the loss in New York, Brownie's crew bounced back and upset the favored Wisconsin Badgers for the NCAA title. The meet attracted 79 harriers from 22 schools. The top teams and their accumulated scores were MSC 54, Wisconsin 57, Indiana 84, Drake 104, Oklahoma A&M 114, Michigan Normal 129, Alfred 138, Notre Dame 217 and Ohio State 227.

Fencing: Compiling a record of 14-1, second-year coach Charles Schmitter's 1940 squad completed the school's most impressive dual-meet season ever. Initially, little could have been expected as they opened with a 9-8 loss to Lawrence Tech; however, this would be the only setback of the season, and furthermore, they would top LIT twice during the subsequent 14-match win streak.

Coach Schmitter continued his full-time job in Detroit and commuted two times a week to coach his squad. Finally, in 1941 he would receive a full-time appointment and move to the East Lansing area.

The line-up for 1940 included Captain Jerry Richardson and Ben Biegeler in foil and epee, George Grenzke in sabre, Bill Hammond in foil and sabre, and Garth Oswald in epee. George Willis, Francis "Bob" Thalken, and Oscar Sussman were in reserve. High score man for the year was Biegeler, who won 26 out of 31 foil bouts and also ranked near the top in epee competition.

The progress of Garth Oswald epitomizes the value of an experienced teacher-coach like Charlie Schmitter. As a sophomore in 1938 and before Schmitter's arrival, Garth was an inexperienced reserve on the squad. In the following season, Charlie's first at the helm, Oswald took his spot as a regular in the epee competition. In 1940, with more instruction from the master, Oswald opened his senior year by capturing the state novice championship. This was followed by a runner-up finish in the Fencers League of America junior epee tournament in which he was edged out by a member of the 1936 USA Olympic team.

In closing the 1940 season with victories over Wayne and Lawrence Tech, MSC laid claim to the newly named Osis trophy, symbolizing them as the state collegiate fencing champions for the year.

Football: With the score tied 14-14 in the Marquette game, Wy Davis punted from his own goal line and lifted a 30-yard kick. Bill Batchelor, racing down under it, raised his arms as if to catch it. He withdrew his arms and the ball dropped, but officials ruled he had interfered with

the Hilltoppers' opportunity to make a fair catch. Following the penalty step off, the rule interpretation provided the option of putting the ball into play at the line of scrimmage or with a free kick (uncontested by the defense). The visitors selected the latter, and the ensuing 15-yard field goal split the uprights, defeating State 17-14.

Swimming and Diving: Only the 150-yard backstroke event survived the season-long assault on the varsity record list. New standards were established in both relays and in all of the following events: Dale Hansen with a 24.9 and 55.6 in the 50- and 100-yard freestyles; Don Farmer with a 2:24.0 in the 220-yard freestyle; Fred Himmelein with a 5:27.0 in the 440-yard freestyle; and Ladd Loomis with a 2:38.0 200-yard breaststroke.

Farmer, Hansen, Don Ladd and Huntley Johnson were entered in the NCAA championships held at Yale University. The foursome swam the 400-yard freestyle relay in 3:46.2 but were edged for the sixth and final qualifying spot by a University of Texas quartet. In the 220-yard freestyle event, neither Don Farmer nor Don Ladd reached the finals as they finished in the ninth and 12th spots, respectively.

Track and Field: The track squad began practicing in their new facility, Jenison Fieldhouse, on January 15 and the first meet was held there on February 7, a 57 2/3 to 37 1/3 loss to Notre Dame. There were few highlights for MSC that afternoon. Captain Roy Fehr tied for scoring honors, as he opened the evening by winning the mile run with a respectable 4:25.5 and later captured first place in the half-mile. Walt Arrington, State's all-around man and jumping star, established a new varsity record with a leap of 6' 5-1/8" in the high jump. The trio

of Dick Frey, Bill Mansfield and Ed Mills went one-two-three in the two-mile run.

Jenison Fieldhouse was showcased as MSC hosted, back-to-back, the 29th Michigan State Relays and the Central Collegiate indoor championships. The latter event had always been held in South Bend.

Two weeks later at the Illinois relays, Arrington won the seven-event mini-decathlon feature event.

Captain Roy Fehr had an outstanding senior year, never finishing lower than third place in any event during 13 meets. He began the spring season by winning the two-mile event at the Penn Relays and then capped the year by capturing the NCAA two-mile run in a 9:18.9 wire-to-wire performance over a rain-soaked surface at the University of Minnesota. Also at those NCAAs, Walter Arrington, who Ralph Young would publicly recognize as the best all-around athlete he had ever coached, captured sixth place in the broad jump.

Suffering through a six-loss combined indoor-outdoor dual-meet season, Ralph Young decided it was time to relinquish his head coaching responsibilities and devote full time to the position of athletic director. He had been head track and field coach for 17 years.

Wrestling: With eight wins, including five straight pins, sophomore 128-pounder Leland Merrill completed the dual-meet season undefeated.

Because of approaching term-end examinations, only two wrestlers, Charles Hutson and "Wild Willy" Martin, were entered in the annual interstate tournament at Cleveland, Ohio, and only Martin and Benny Riggs competed in the NCAA championship meet in Champaign-Urbana. For sundry reasons, Coach Collins's top trio of Merrill, Hutson and Jack Orr were unavailable.

Jenison Fieldhouse. The track and field team moved into their new facility on January 15, 1940.

SPARTAN SCRAPBOOK

——— FENCING COACHES (1926-1997)———

Josef Waffa (1926-1929)

William Kershaw (1930)

George Bauer (1931-37)

Thomas L. Caniff (1938)

Charles Schmitter (1939-1983)

Fred Freiheit (1984-1997)

MSC
1940-1941

TALES TO TELL

Paul Griffeth recalled the homecoming football game of 1940, a scoreless tie with Santa Clara. Earlier in the season his right knee had been injured with ligament and cartilage damage and it was conceded he would never play again. That's when Jack Heppinstall, the ingenious trainer, stepped in. As described in a letter from Griffeth:

"Because I was the designated captain for the homecoming game, the coaches wanted me dressed and on the field. Knowing this, Jack patched up my knee. First, he shaved my leg from top to bottom. Next, he cut strips of rubber innertube a few inches wide. Then he criss-crossed and taped the strips on each side of the joint and said, 'There, those will serve you as ligaments, maybe Charlie [Coach Bachman] will let you play a few minutes.' When the officials called for the team captains, Bachman sent me out for the coin toss. I thought that was all that I would do for my final home game. But, because I was the captain, Charlie said I should be on the field for the kickoff. I expected to be pulled after the kickoff, but Charlie,

Paul Griffeth, yet another Michigan State athlete brought back to playing form by the talent and ingenuity of trainer Jack Heppinstall.

in his immutable way, forgot all about me. I played the full 60 minutes, holding a powerful Santa Clara team to a 0-0 tie, recovering a fumble, and losing several pounds. Today, Jack Heppinstall couldn't do for me what he did back then. Where would he find innertubes?"

HEADLINES of 1941

- Following the December 7 sneak attack on Pearl Harbor, Congress votes to declare war on Japan, Germany and Italy.
- Prices of the time included: bread eight cents/loaf, milk 54 cents/gallon, and gasoline 12 cents/gallon. A new automobile could be purchased for $850 and the average annual income was $1,777.
- Joe DiMaggio hits safely in 56 consecutive baseball games, a major league record that still stands.
- Begun in 1927, the Mt. Rushmore National Monument in South Dakota is completed.

SCOREBOARD

	W	L	T	Avg.
Baseball	13	10	0	.565
Track and Field	0	6	0	.000
Football	3	4	1	.438
Basketball	11	6	0	.647
Tennis	7	7	0	.500
Cross Country	2	1	0	.667
Swimming and Diving	6	3	0	.667
Wrestling	8	1	0	.889
Fencing	2	7	0	.222
Golf	5	3	0	.625
Boxing	4	2	0	.667

TEAM OF THE YEAR

In their impressive 8-1 season record, the Spartan wrestlers won 52 of 72 individual matches for an imposing .722 percentage. Of those victories, 25 were won by falls. Coach Fendley Collins selected a four-man team to represent MSC at the NCAAs held at Lehigh University in Bethlehem, Pa. The four were Burl "Cut" Jennings, Merle "Bo" Jennings, Bill Maxwell and Charles Hutson. Merle (121 pounds) and his twin brother Burl (128 pounds) captured back-to-back championships. Maxwell (136 pounds) finished in the runner-up spot to the defending champion and Hutson (165 pounds) was the winner in the consolation bracket. The foursome accounted for 26 points, placing MSC in second place behind the Aggies from Oklahoma with 37.

MAKING HISTORY

In a telegram received on Nov. 4, 1940, Robert Kiputh, coach at Yale University and chairman of the NCAA swimming committee, notified Coach Daubert that MSC had been selected as the site for the NCAA championship meet, March 28-29, 1941. This opportunity to showoff the new Jenison facility would significantly provide for the future growth of MSC's swimming program. Advance ticket sales were brisk and eventually all seats were purchased in advance of the meet. Reservations for the entire program sold at $3.30. Individual tickets were 55 cents for one day's preliminaries and $1.10 for one evening's finals. The entry list of 180 individuals from 42 colleges set a championship record, but there were few bright spots for the MSC entrants. The Spartan threesome of John Becker, Chuck Bigelow and Ralph Newton placed sixth in the 300-yard medley relay with a time of 3:05.3. On the second day of competition, the 400-yard freestyle relay team of Don Farmer, Harold

The 1941 varsity wrestling team. (Front row, left to right) B. Jennings, M. Jennings, B. Maxwell, B. Riggs and D. Pletz. (Back row, left to right): Coach F. Collins, M. Dendrinos, L. Merrill and team manager. Missing from picture, Charles Hutson.

Heffernan, Newton and Don Ladd also qualified sixth but could do no better in the finals with their clocking of 3:42.7. Those were the two fleeting opportunities for the host school to break into the scoring column. Unfortunately, only the top five finishers registered team points.

The very first NCAA fencing championships were conducted on March 29, 1941, at Ohio State University, with a total of 19 colleges and universities and 76 individual contestants entered. Co-captain Bob Thalken reached the sabre finals and eventually placed fourth, despite the fact he defeated the eventual champion from Dartmouth in both the preliminaries and finals. As a team, Michigan State placed eighth.

The 1941 NCAA swimming championships were held in MSU's Jenison pool.

GREAT STATE DATES

Football—**October 12, 1940 (H):** Although many recall the great Spartans from Charlevoix, Bob and Bill Carey, few know of their older brother, Chuck. Arriving in the fall of 1939, the elder Carey did not even report for freshman football practice instead he chose to play in the intramural touch football league. It was at this level of competition his passing and running skills caught the eye of Don Rossi, who had just completed his Spartan playing days and had become a football staff assistant.

Rossi successfully persuaded Carey to come out for practice in the spring of 1940, but Chuck failed to get any farther than the scrub team. He remained a scrub in fall practice and then suddenly, in the second game of the year, against Purdue, Coach Bachman named the Charlevoix sophomore as the surprise starter at right halfback. Although he didn't dominate the game, he scored the final touchdown and kicked the PAT in the 20-7 victory. Due to injury and assorted circumstances, that Purdue game would prove to be the only game of his Spartan career. Chuck would return to Macklin Field two years later as a member of the highly favored Great Lakes Navy team.

Cross Country—**October 12, 1940 (A):** The team opened the season at State College, Pa., without Coach Brown. It seems that "Brownie" was detained by his duties as head of the school's mimeograph department. Fran Dittrich, assistant track coach, filled in. The meet was run on a five-mile course between halves of the Penn State-West Virginia football game, Lion star Billy Smith led the field to the tape by nearly a-quarter of a mile. Team balance prevailed as five Spartans claimed the next five spots for a 20-33 win: Bill Scott (27:02), Ralph Monroe (28:37), Al Mangan (28:41), captain Ed Mills (28:58) and Jerry Page (29:04).

Basketball—**January 4, 1941 (A):** In one of the biggest victories in school history, MSC's young team upset previously undefeated Long Island University, 31-26, before 14,437 spectators at Madison Square Garden. In the opening two quarters the Spartans played a control game, primarily attempting shots from the perimeter. These tactics did not produce, as they trailed 14-8 after 20 minutes of play. Immediately taking command at the outset of the third quarter, Joe Gerard, Max Hindman, Bill Burk and Bob Phillips each scored and State led 16-14. LIU twice tied the score after that, but Van's crew hung on for the upset.

Basketball—**January 6, 1941 (A):** As part of a doubleheader at Convention Hall in Philadelphia, the Spartans snapped Temple's six-game winning streak, in overtime, 37-35. With virtually no time remaining in regulation and the Owls leading 34-33, Carl Petroski sank a crucial free throw to extend the contest. Bob Phillips's field goal clinched the victory in OT.

Basketball—**January 13, 1941 (H):** One week following their trip east, MSC again faced the Temple Owls, this time in Jenison, and once more the struggle led to an exciting MSC victory. With the game tied at 22-22 and less than a minute to play, the Spartans held the ball for the final shot. With five seconds remaining, Max Hindman drove to the basket but was forcefully knocked to the floor as the horn sounded the end of the game. The Gary senior stepped to the line and calmly dropped in one free throw good enough for the 23-22 victory.

Wrestling—**January 29, 1941 (H):** With a record wrestling crowd of more than 2,000 on hand in Jenison Fieldhouse, by a margin of 16-14, the Spartans earned the first victory over the U of M since 1935. As was becoming a custom, the Spartan "lightweights" struck early. Merle Jennings opened with an easy 7-1 decision, brother Burl was awarded a win by default, and with only 41 seconds remaining in the 135-pound bout, Leland Merrill pinned his previously undefeated opponent. Billy Maxwell then had the responsibility for maintaining the momentum. With seconds remaining in the third period and trailing 14-9 in points, Billy "shot" for his opponent's legs, took him down, and scored a near fall with a body press. Adding his riding time, he gained a 17-14 verdict to give MSC what proved to be an insurmountable 16-0 lead.

Swimming and Diving—**February 8, 1941 (H):** In taking first and second places in all but one event, the Spartans registered a nearly perfect 58-16 score in their defeat of Ohio Wesleyan. It was MSC's initial victory in Jenison pool. Clocked in 3:09.1, the medley relay team of John Becker, Chuck Bigelow and Don Ladd clipped 6.1 seconds from the former varsity record established in 1939.

Boxing—**February 8 (A) & February 26 (H) 1941:** In a boxing rarity, Coach Burhans scheduled West Virginia in a pair of meets, away-home. A unique collegiate rule interpretation eventually led to the MSC victory in the first meeting played in Morgantown. In the opening round of the 145-pound bout, the Mountaineers' Eastern Collegiate champion cut the eye of State's Bud Davidson. By rule, this led to the referee's stoppage of the fight and the call of a draw—hence, 1/2 point for each team and the eventual score of MSC 4 1/2, West Virginia 3 1/2. In the follow-up match before 2,500 fans in Jenison, the Spartans trailed 3-1 before Joe Cestowski, Glen Menter, and heavyweight Charlie Clark were victors for a 4-3 team win.

Basketball—**February 12, 1941 (H):** Approximately 8,500 fans filled the seats of Jenison and another 500 were turned away at the door. The U of M was in town. Leading 33-32 and with 1:15 of playing time remaining, the Spartans moved into the offensive end with hopes of stalling out the remainder of the clock; however, the Wolverines forced a turnover at the 0:50 mark. The visitors could not score, and MSC gained control and once more initiated their delay tactics. A Michigan foul ensued and Van's boys elected to forsake the free-throw opportunity in favor of taking the ball out of bounds, an option that rules of the time provided. Then with 35 seconds remaining, Bill Burk worked his way free under the basket and managed a final field goal to secure the 35-32 victory. The starting five of Frank Mekules, Joe Gerard, Max Hindman, Bob Phillips and Burk played the entire game without substitution even though they weren't exactly shooting the lights out at 33 percent (11 of 33). The Wolverines were hitting a slightly less impressive 32 percent (12 of 37).

Swimming and Diving—**February 28, 1941 (H):** Punctuated by two record performances, the tankers gained a 47-28 victory over Wisconsin in the final home dual meet of the season. The new varsity standards were by Ralph Newton in the 100-yard freestyle (55.4) and Chuck Bigelow in the 200-yard breaststroke (2:36.7). Coach Daubert wasn't there to see the triumph. He had been called to Ames, Iowa, after the death of his father who formerly coached the swim team at Iowa State.

Basketball—**March 1, 1941 (H):** The Spartans closed the year with their biggest victory of the season, a convincing 44-35 upset of Notre Dame. For one night, VanAlstyne had his gang switch from the slow-working tactics to a "run-and-gun" style of play for the entire 40 minutes. A partisan crowd of more than 7,000 roared their approval. The evening produced another hero, Carl Petroski, a Schenectady, N.Y., sophomore, who scored 11 points.

Tennis—**May 2, 1941 (H):** Winning all singles matches, State easily topped Illinois, 8-1, for only their second win of the season. Gaining the victories were Fred Drilling (6-4, 6-0), Fred Perkins (6-1, 6-3), Billy Maxwell (6-3, 6-4), Frank Beeman (6-0, 6-1), Floyd Krause (6-0, 6-2) and Irving Roberts (6-4, 9-7, 6-4). Points in the doubles came from Drilling-Perkins (6-1, 8-6) and Beeman-Maxwell (6-1, 6-1).

Baseball—**May 10, 1941 (H):** Behind the three-hit pitching of Frank Mekules, State scored seven runs in the first three innings and went on to easily defeat Notre Dame 10-2. Three Irish errors and 12 bases on balls augmented the 10-hit MSC attack. In addition, Spartan runners managed six stolen bases. The leading hitter was left fielder Howard Ladue, who went three-for-three including a sixth-inning triple.

Baseball—**May 23, 1941 (H):** The Spartans handed Western State its first defeat in 18 games, 3-2. A large share of the credit for the victory belonged to Frank Mekules, who pitched over five infield errors. The State batters hit the Bronco star and future Detroit Tiger starter Stubby Overmire hard with six of their seven hits for extra bases. There were four doubles, a triple by Wyman Davis and a home run by Bob Young. Twice MSC had to come from one-run deficits, first in the second inning and then in the fifth, before Davis scored the go-ahead run in the sixth.

Golf—**May 23, 1941 (H):** The Michigan coach was suspect when Ben VanAlstyne moved Bill Zylstra to the number-one spot for the May 23 match at Walnut Hills. The Wolverine mentor countered by sending his top man against Stan Kowal in the number-three position. The U of M's counter strategy failed when Zylstra won his match with a 71 and Kowal was a winner with his 74. Also adding to the 19-8 winning margin were impressive performances by Ralph Kortge who fired a 76, Lee Hutt with a 77 and Jim Funston with a 78.

ATHLETES OF THE YEAR

What a bargain! Wrestling coach Fendley Collins used only one of his athletic scholarships to lure both of the twins, Merle "Cut" Jennings and Burl "Bo" Jennings, from Tulsa, Okla., where they had been state high school champions. Both responded as two-time National Collegiate champions with titles in both 1941 and 1942.

Burl won his championships in the 128-pound division, yet to enhance the team line-up for certain dual meets, he occasionally moved up one weight category. The opportunity for a third individual NCAA crown was dashed when the championships of 1943 were cancelled with the intervention of World War II.

Burl "Bo" Jennings

IN THE SPARTLITE

Baseball: The University of California ended the season with a trip into Michigan for a pair of games with State on June 6-7. Al Jones pitched an impressive 3-0 shutout in the opener, then the Golden Bears hammered out an 8-5 win in the season's final game.

Casey Klewicki, the starting third baseman, opted to leave the team and turn professional following the 1941 season. Sadly, his dream was never realized. On October 3 of that fall, in an accident on the streets of Lansing, Casey was thrown from his vehicle and killed in a two-car collision.

Basketball: Most frequent starters during the season were seniors Max Hindman and Bob Phillips, along with juniors Joe Gerard and 6' 4" Frank Mekules of Detroit. Another Hoosier, 5' 10" Bill Burk, stepped in for the convalescing Chet Aubuchon.

"Iron Man" Max Hindman played 666 out of a possible 680 minutes during the season. He also led the team

in scoring with 144 points, followed by Joe Gerard with 100 total points and Phillips with 90.

Composite home attendance over the 12-game home season was 36,656, a school record.

The Spartans were embarrassed at Ann Arbor, 42-14. A mere four "S" field goals were scored in the first half followed by only one in the final 20 minutes. Completing the evening of futility, a meager four of 16 free throws were converted. It was the worst beating that a VanAlstyne-coached MSC team had ever suffered.

Postseason rumors circulated that the Spartans, sporting an 11-6 record, would receive a bid to compete in the National Invitational Tournament (NIT) at Madison Square Garden. With the proposed tournament schedule in conflict with term-end examinations, college officials appealed for special scheduling consideration. NIT coordinators never responded and an invitation was never delivered

Boxing: Sustained by their successful dual-meet season, Bill Zurakowski and Joe Cestowski were entered in the NCAA championships at State College, Pa. Both were eliminated with opening bout losses.

Cross Country: For the first time, the cross country team took and airplane rather than a train into New York City for the IC4A championships. In what would be described as the biggest upset in the 32-year history of the event, Rhode Island outscored the favored Spartans by ten points, 72 to 82. Al Mangan, of Lowell, Mass., a member of the 1936 Olympic team as a walker, paced the MSC entrants with his 11th-place finish. The other Spartans placed as follows: Ralph Monroe 13th, Ed Mills 17th, Bill Scott 19th, Walter Beardslee 23rd and Jerry Page 28th.

Fencing: Following the first win of the season, 17-10 over Case Tech at Cleveland, the Spartans returned for their only home appearances of the year, against Wisconsin and Notre Dame on February 28 and March 1. The matches, both 14-13 losses, were held in the boxing room of Jenison, the first such competitions in the new building.

Letterwinners were co-captains George Willis and Bob Thalker, George Wlodyga, Lyle Burdy, Loren Tukey and Leonard Herscher.

Football: Michigan may have had Tom Harmon, but Michigan State had Walt Pawlowski. In the U of M game of 1940, Walt, a junior playing in his first college game, caught a pair of touchdown passes from Dick Kieppe. The first score came with only 62 seconds remaining in the first half, while the second came with barely two minutes remaining in the game. The second half score covered 44 yards, as the little 157-pound halfback from Calumet City, Ill., carried a Wolverine defender on his back as he fell across the goal line. Meanwhile, that Harmon fellow was scoring three touchdowns. The Spartans ended up on the short end, 21-14.

Golf: The season opened on the new $800,000, 36-hole championship course at Ohio State. The Spartan foursome of Stan Kowal, Bill Zylstra, Ralph Kortge and Detroit sophomore Jim Funston managed to break even in the morning's best ball matches, but gained only two points in the afternoon matches, resulting in a 13-5 defeat.

Following the opening two meets that spring, the remaining schedule was played in the new six-man format. Sharing the added two spots in the line-up for those final five matches were George Busch of Grand Rapids, Chet Kennedy from Royal Oak and Lee Hutt, brother of basketball star Marty.

As with other sports, rigid guidelines were in place to qualify as a major "S" recipient. Boasting awards in 1941 were Bill Zylstra, Stan Kowal, Jim Funston and George Busch.

Swimming and Diving: Whereas all other major components of the new athletic facility, Jenison Gymnasium-Fieldhouse, were in use during by the 1940 winter season, the pool was not filled with water until later that spring. The inaugural meet was held on Jan. 25, 1941, a 42-33 loss to perennial power Ohio State in front of a crowd of more than 600 loyal spectators.

Tennis: A pair of new and talented players filled the roster in 1941. They were Frank Beeman of Royal Oak, who would later be the varsity coach, and Billy Maxwell, whose primary impact came on the wrestling mat.

Exhibiting team balance, each of the top four players of 1941, captain Fred Perkins, Fred Drilling, Maxwell and Beeman, won seven or more matches during the season. Frank Beeman topped them all as he finished the season with 11 straight victories in singles competition.

Drilling, Beeman and Floyd Krause would conclude the season by competing in the Central Collegiate championships in Chicago. Conflicting year-end exam schedules prevented Perkins and Maxwell from joining the others.

Track and Field: For the second straight year and Karl Schlademan's first as head coach, MSC was winless in dual-meet competition.

Walter Arrington, star jumper of whom much was expected, was unavailable for most of the season, having severely sprained his ankle when, ironically, he stumbled over a two-foot high sign in Beal Garden. By mid-May he was finally 100 percent when he piled up a meet-record 19 1/2 points at the State Intercollegiates with firsts in broad jump, discus, shot put, and a tie with teammate Jim Milne in the high jump. His efforts led to the Spartans' only bright spot of the season, as they edged Michigan Normal 74 to 71 1/2 for the team title. Other team scoring was Western State 40, Wayne 24 1/2, Central State eight, Hillsdale three, Alma two and Albion and Kalamazoo one point each. The outcome of the meet would center on the final event, the one-mile relay, but only after Ted Wonch garnered a first in the pole vault. The four-man relay only had to place ahead of Michigan Normal, and they did, nabbing third place from the Ypsi quartet.

Walt Arrington concluded his collegiate career in the NCAA championships in Palo Alto, Calif. Although clearing only 6' 2-3/8" in the high jump (2-3/4" below his varsity record), Walter managed a seven-way tie for sixth place (along with Don Canham, future University of Michigan athletic director). This put Michigan State on the scoreboard with 1/7 of a point.

Wrestling: Extensively revised rules in 1941 ushered in the point system as administered today (takedown, escape, near fall, etc.). Also, an individual match was divided into three three-minute periods.

The three new stars for Coach Collins, Billy Maxwell and the Jennings twins, boasted of native American heritage. Maxwell was one-sixteenth Apache and Merle and Burl were one-thirty-second Cherokee.

EXTRA! MICHIGAN STATE RELAYS(1940s)

The Spartans moved into their new home (Jenison Fieldhouse) for an initial workout on Monday, January 15, 1940 and for those athletes whose careers straddled both sites, the new venue must have seemed like a palace. Furthermore, there were likely immediate visions of how the Michigan State relays could become an even more stellar attraction in this "massive" facility.

Ypsi Normal dominated the 21st running of the Michigan State relays (1941), yet MSC fans could revel in capturing four of the titles. Starr Keesler won the broad jump with a leap of 22' 3-3/8"; Cleon Smith was a surprise victory in the 300-yard dash; Ted Wonch settled for a tie as he cleared 13' in the pole vault; and the quartet of Dale Kaulitz, Danny Rosenbaum, Bob McCarthy, and George Doran captured the gold medal in the 440-yard sprint relay.

From a contemporary view, it is incredible to find that the Michigan State relays were once held somewhere other than East Lansing and in, of all places, Ann Arbor. Here is the explanation. Learning that the Wolverines were left without an indoor meet in 1945 when the Big Ten schedules were drawn up, generous athletic director Ralph Young offered the U of M the opportunity to host the traditional MSC event. Even more remarkable, Fritz Crisler, the Wolverine AD, accepted the proposal. The February 11, 1945 issue of the *Detroit Free Press* summarized the results, yet never eluded to the event as the "Michigan State relays."

With the relays shut down for two years during World War II, the silver anniversary meet was celebrated in 1947. The event attracted 518 athletes who represented 31 colleges and universities from the Atlantic seaboard to Wyoming and into Texas. A record crowd of 5,439 packed the balcony for the finals thats featured Fred Johnson as a double-winner. The Grandville freshman set a pair of records in winning the broad jump (24' 6-5/8") and the 75-yard low hurdles in 8.5 seconds. Jack Dianetti, running the fourth leg of the distance-medley relay, came from behind to pass Michigan's anchorman and gain the win. Bill Mack of Drake would capture the mile run in a time of 4:20. As a transfer, Mack would compete as a Spartan in 1949 and 1950.

Michigan State was a dominating team in 1949. Johnson once more captured two gold medals (broad jump and the dash) as teammate Horace Smith equaled the effort with championships in both hurdle events. Other Spartan winners were Tom Irmen in the two-mile run and three relays: the medley, two-mile and 240-yard shuttle hurdle.

SPARTAN SCRAPBOOK

——— GOLF COACHES (1928-2003) ———

Pioneer golf team (1930)

Ben VanAlstyne (1932-59)

Bruce Fossum (1966-89)

Ken Horvath (1990-99)

Mark Hankins (1999-)

Pictured elsewhere: Harry G. Kipke 1928₍FB₎;
James Crowley 1930-31₍FB₎; John Brotzmann 1960-65₍BX₎

₍FB₎ see football coaches

₍BX₎ see boxing coaches

TALES TO TELL

On March 27 and 28, just three and one-half months following the December 7 Japanese sneak attack on Pearl Harbor, Michigan State hosted the 15th annual NCAA wrestling championships in Jenison Fieldhouse, which was festooned in a patriotic atmosphere. The awards platform was decorated with flags, flowers, and a six-foot-high fabricated wooden "V" (for victory). Team captain Leland Merrill, who placed third in the 155-pound division, accepted the runners-up team trophy from former Spartan football player Bill Batchelor, who was a marine in full dress uniform. In correspondence, Merrill later added some insight:

"A most interesting side to that NCAA meet of 1942 was that five of the eight champions came from the same high school, Tulsa Central. We had Cut and Bo Jennings, along with Bill Maxwell, while Oklahoma A&M had Buddy Arndt and Vernon Logan. Also, their high school coach, Art Griffith, had moved on to become the Aggies' head coach.

Of the remaining three champions, only 175-pounder Richard DiBattista of Pennsylvania was not from Oklahoma. Of the two other A&M champions, heavyweight Loyd Arms hailed from Sulfur, Okla., and Virgil Smith, at 165-pounds, called Ponca City, Okla., his home.

The U.S. had entered the war three months earlier. This contributed to the fact that the total number of competitors was down to 79 from 129 in 1941. Regardless, Fendley Collins always said that all of the good kids were there, including two boys from San Diego State. They rode a bus all the way to East Lansing. One of them caught the flu, was hospitalized at Olin Health Center, and was never able to compete."

HEADLINES of 1942

- Using a coupon system, wartime rationing of gasoline limits non-essential driving to three gallons a week.
- The Kellogg Company launches a new product, sugar-coated corn flakes staring Tony the Tiger.
- Bell Aircraft builds and tests the first U.S. jet, the XP-59.
- Bing Crosby, the "crooner," releases "White Christmas" from the film *Holiday Inn*, and it becomes the biggest-selling song from a movie in history.

SCOREBOARD

	W	L	T	Avg.
Baseball	13	11	1	.540
Track and Field	3	4	0	.429
Football	5	3	1	.611
Basketball	15	6	0	.714
Tennis	10	5	0	.667
Cross Country	2	1	0	.667
Swimming and Diving	2	3	2	.429
Wrestling	7	1	0	.875
Fencing	5	2	1	.688
Golf	3	4	1	.438
Boxing	3	3	0	.500

TEAM OF THE YEAR

For the second successive year, Fendley Collins's wrestling squad completed the dual-meet season with one loss, again to Oklahoma A&M. Once more at the NCAA title meet they settled for second place behind the Aggies, who corralled their 13th title in 15 years. In the Saturday night finals, the local crowd was ecstatic as State opened with victories by Merle Jennings (121 pounds), Burl Jennings (128 pounds) and Billy Maxwell (136 pounds). Adding Lee Merrill's third-place victory at 155 pounds, MSC had corralled 26 team points but had no other wrestlers in the finals. Slowly the Aggies cut into the lead until they had reached their winning total of 31 points. It would be the last championships to be held before a three-year interruption due to World War II.

MAKING HISTORY

Following the 1942 basketball season, Marshall Dann, *State News* sports writer, asked Coach VanAlstyne to reflect on his 16 years as head coach at Michigan State and identify an all-time Spartan team. Consenting to do so, Van began by selecting Chet Aubuchon (Class of 1942) and Bob Herrick (Class of 1935) as guards. He added forward Joe Gerard (Class of 1942) and center Max Hindman (Class of 1941) and then, unable to make a clear fifth choice, he added two names, Marty Hutt (Class of 1940) and Ron Garlock (Class of 1937).

1942 varsity wrestling team. (Back row, left to right) coach F. Collins, M. Dendrinos, J. Spalink, B. Maxwell. (Front row, left to right) H. Thompson, B. Jennings, L. Merrill, M. Jennings and J. Marr.

GREAT STATE DATES

Football—**October 11, 1941 (H):** With the score of the Marquette game knotted at 7-7 in the final period, Dick Kieppe became an instant hero. He fielded a low punt on his own 47-yard line, streaked toward the east sideline and raced down the field and into the end zone with the winning touchdown. The triumph broke a two-year spell the Hilltoppers had held over State.

Cross Country—**October 11, 1941 (A):** The season opened at home with a 23-34 defeat of Drake on the morning of the first home football game. Walter Mack, a Buffalo, N.Y., sophomore, led the way over the new three-mile course which started and ended at the track. Following Mack were Ralph Monroe (fourth), Bill Scott (fifth), Walt Beardslee (sixth) and Maurice Horski (seventh).

Football—**November 15, 1941 (H):** The Spartans unleashed their most devastating offensive outburst of the season when they shelled and bombarded the highly ranked Temple Owls, 46-0. Little Mike Scheib scored a pair of TDs within two minutes on successive punt returns of 53 and 42 yards. The final result was the largest win margin State had ever established on a major opponent and the worst defeat in Temple grid history.

Football—**November 22, 1941 (H):** As in the Temple game one week earlier, Mike Scheib remained the offensive go-to guy in the 31-7 victory over Ohio Wesleyan. The Allegan senior sparked the 19-point outburst in the second quarter. He first scooped up a bouncing punt on his 35-yard line and ran down the sideline 65 yards for a score. Then, on the final play of the half, he tore around the left end and raced 24 yards into the end zone.

Basketball—**December 27, 1941 (A):** Game officials called a total of 50 fouls in the Spartans' 33-31 win at Syracuse. By the time the contest reached its closing minutes, eight players (four from each team) had fouled out. It was a game in which State led 23-14 at halftime and then hung on as they scored only one field goal in the final period. A potential tying Orange basket rattled off the rim as the game clock expired.

Basketball—**January 6, 1942 (H):** The first big home game of the season was the upset win over the star-studded team representing the Great Lakes Naval Training Station. The sailor starters included former All-Americans Bill Menke, Frank Baumholtz, and the U of D's Bill

Callahan. Overcoming a 19-13 halftime deficit, the Spartans led 33-29 with four minutes remaining. After MSC had successfully stalled for three minutes, Callahan intercepted a pass, scored, and closed the gap to 33-31. Aubuchon, flashing his brilliant skills, dribbled up the floor, in and out of players, and around in circles until the final 60 seconds ticked off the clock.

Wrestling—**January 17, 1942 (A):** Realizing his team was outgunned against the Spartans, coach Cliff Keen of Michigan had two men drop weight to possibly provide a more competitive line-up. The plan almost worked. The determining bout was at 155 pounds, where Leland Merrill defeated the Wolverines' top wrestler, Bill Courtright, who had dropped down from his normal 165-pound division. Only the bell saved the U of M captain from being pinned. John Spalink then assured the State victory by easily handling his 175-pound opponent. Final score: MSC 17, U of M 13.

Basketball—**February 11, 1942 (H):** The 57-34 defeat of Michigan, before 8,300 fans, was the largest margin of victory ever recorded over the in-state rival. Dudley Jones was the offensive star as he scored 25 points to set a new modern-day varsity single-game scoring record. When Jones was double-teamed, Joe Gerard stepped forward and tallied 15 points.

Boxing—**February 11, 1942 (H):** Approximately 7,000 of the basketball fans remained for the second feature of the Wednesday night doubleheader in Jenison, a boxing match against the University of Florida. It was the largest crowd ever to have assembled for boxing at MSC. Even before the first bell rang, MSC had posted one point on the score sheet. The Gators had no heavyweight entry and conceded the normal closing bout to the Spartans. With the team score tied at 3 1/2-3 1/2, light heavyweight Charles Calkins would battle for that deciding single point. To the delight of the record assembly, he managed to out-punch his taller opponent and gain the victory.

Track and Field—**February 21, 1942 (H):** The Spartans edged the Marquette Hilltoppers, 65 1/2-45 1/2, for their first dual-meet victory in three years. New varsity records were established by Jim Milne with a leap of 6' 5-3/8" in the high jump and Dale Kaulitz who ran a 50.4 quarter mile.

Basketball—**February 28, 1942 (H):** The year would close at home and the opportunity presented itself to register the 15th win of the season, the third high-

est total in school history. Playing Notre Dame, a team with an eight-game winning string, Coach VanAlstyne chose to play his starters for the entire game. Fred Stone joined the four seniors, each flashing his unique skills: Joe Gerard, who took the scoring honors; Chet Aubuchon, who displayed his ball wizardry; Mel Peterson, the assist man; and Bill Burk, the defensive stalwart. With three minutes remaining and State leading 46-43, it came time for the noted MSC stall, giving Aubie one final chance to demonstrate the ball-handling skills that had won him All-American honors in 1940. When the game ended the scoreboard still read MSC 46, Notre Dame 43.

Fencing—**March 7, 1942 (H):** Headed by 4-0 performance by the sabre team of Bob Thalken and Al Booth, the dual-meet season ended in Jenison Fieldhouse on a high note with a surprising 10-7 victory over Ohio State. Three weeks later the Buckeyes would be crowned NCAA champions.

Baseball—**April 24-25, 1942 (H):** For the third year in a row, State played a two-game series against the University of Wisconsin, and for the first time they gained a double victory. In the Friday opener the Spartans struck early, scoring eight runs in the first four innings, and then held on for a 9-6 decision. Third baseman Nick Picciuto choked off a potential Badger rally in the fifth with an unassisted double play. Al Jones, junior right-hander, went the distance, but he struggled, giving up 10 hits and walking six men. Three times on the next afternoon, John Kobs's crew overcame Wisconsin leads. Trailing 7-5 going into the bottom of the eighth, Picciuto tripled home both Howard Ladue and Joe Nelson and later scored the eventual winning run on a sacrifice fly. Dick Bernitt picked up the win in relief.

Tennis—**April 25, 1942 (A):** The Spartans completely dominated Ohio State as they blanked the Buckeyes, 9-0. Frank Beeman and Billy Maxwell opened with straight set victories followed by three-set wins from Earl May, Roger Cessna and Bill Heil. Herb Hoover was awarded a team point by default. Doubles winners, all in two sets, were Beeman-May, Maxwell-Hoover and Cessna-Heil.

Baseball—**May 28, 1942 (H):** In one of the biggest innings ever against Michigan, Spartan hitters crossed the plate seven times in the fifth on the way to a 12-1 victory. Hits by Frank Pellerin, Nick Picciuto, Pete Fornari and Wy Davis; two bases on balls; two errors; and a per-

fectly executed squeeze play produced the runs. State managed two runs in the sixth and finished it off with three more in the eighth. The Wolverines' lone score, which came in the first inning, was unearned. Joe Skrocki, Saginaw junior, closed the door the rest of way as he yielded only four hits.

ATHLETES OF THE YEAR

Merle "Cut" Jennings (121 pounds), along with twin brother Burl, captured national collegiate crowns in both 1941 and 1942. When the NCAA abandoned their championships the next year due to a world at war, "Cut," along with six teammates, entered the National AAU tournament in New York City. Working his way through an impressive field of talent, he would emerge with the title in the 134-pound division. Merle was also a two-time recipient (1942 and 1943) of the coveted Walter Jacob Award, annually acknowledging the Spartan wrestler who earns the highest point total for the season.

Merle "Cut" Jennings

IN THE SPARTLITE

Baseball: The bleachers were filled on May 25 to watch the Spartans play an exhibition game against the Great Lakes Naval Training Station team which included a handful of major league players including Mickey Cochrane, former Tiger manager and later Hall of Famer. Frank Pellerin led all Spartan batters with three hits in the 4-3 loss.

Basketball: The initial Spartan starting quintet of 1941-1942 found Joe Gerard and Dudley Jones at forward, with Fred Stone, the 6' 6" sophomore from Chicago, at center, and the guard spots anchored by Bill Burk and the returning captain Chet Aubuchon.

Gerard set a team record of 239 points for a season, outscoring "Aubie" by 110 points.

Boxing: Two Spartans would compete at the NCAAs in Baton Rouge, La. Bill Zurakowski was eliminated in the quarterfinals while Charles Calkins became MSC's first finalist. Although losing that concluding match, Calkins gained three team points leading to a seventh-place tie for Michigan State. Harvey Trombley had also intended to enter those nationals, but he was under imposed travel restrictions as an impending inductee into the U.S. Army.

Cross Country: After opening the season with wins over Drake and Pittsburgh, the Spartans returned home to face their nemesis of the preceding two seasons, Indiana University. The race was run over a revamped four and a half mile course with the concluding half mile traced around the oval of the new track. MSC's top finishers were Ralph Monroe (third), Walter Mack (fourth), Robert Thompson (fifth) and Walter Beardslee (seventh). As it turned out, the meet would be decided further back in the pack, as Maurice Horski was nosed-out by half of a second for what would be the meet-deciding eighth-place finish. The final score read 27-28 for yet another Hoosier victory.

Fencing: Although MSC was represented at the NCAAs held at Washington University in St. Louis, Coach Schmitter's top two performers, George Willis and Bob Thalken, were unavailable. Willis failed to make the trip for personal reasons and Thalken remained home for an army induction medical examination. Regardless, five members of the team scored a total of nine points, good enough for eighth place in the team standings. Accounting for the points were Lyle Burdy with three, George Wiodyga and Al Booth with two each, plus one point each for Chuck Sherman and Morris Shephard.

The co-captains, Willis and Thalken, would be rewarded with major "S" sweaters.

Football: Bachman's assistants beginning with the 1941 season were Al Kawal, Dave Diehl and Ed Pogor. Kawal came from Boston University where he had served as line coach. Diehl co-captain of the 1938 Spartan team, returned to his alma mater after two years of professional football with the Detroit Lions. Pogor was an MSC letter-winner in 1938.

During halftime of the 1941 Michigan game, Ralph Young honored the legendary Fielding H. Yost by awarding him a varsity "S" blanket. The Wolverine athletic director and former coach had announced his retirement after 40 years of service to the U of M.

Opening the season against Michigan, there was an early glitter of hope. Hardly four minutes into the game, Jack Fenton, State's right halfback, broke off tackle and ran 74 yards for a score. The fun didn't last. The Wolverine eleven picked themselves up and posted three unanswered touchdowns for their fourth straight win over the Spartans, 19-7.

Completing a four-year series with Santa Clara on October 18, Charlie Bachman and his entourage once again headed west. State would win the battle of statistics against the Broncos, including nine first downs to four and an advantage in total scrimmage yards gained, 170-103. Unfortunately, when the game ended the scoreboard read 7-0 in favor of the Californians. It wasn't that MSC lacked opportunities. Three times they surrendered the ball on downs within the 10-yard line, on the seven, six and three.

Golf: At one time or another during the year, four different men filled the number-one position in the lineup. Both Joe Watson and Ralph Kortge played from the top spot on three occasions, while George Busch and George Zimmerman each held the honor once.

At the request of the coaches of both Northwestern University and Indiana University, the site of the two scheduled matches were switched to Ann Arbor. This enabled the two teams to become acquainted with the site for that year's Big Ten championships.

At the home meet against Michigan, the coaches agreed upon a format of five one-on-one matches for a total of 15 points (one point each for front nine holes, back nine holes, and 18-hole total). George Zimmerman shot a 78 and garnered three points; Joe Watson carded a 76 and collected two points; George Busch also scored two points with his 78; and Phil Goodrich salvaged 1/2

point while firing an 82. The result was a 7 1/2-7 1/2 tie and a "moral" victory for MSC.

In the NCAA tournament at the Chain-O-Lakes Country Club near South Bend, Ind., MSC golfers placed 11th in the team standings with a total of 625 strokes when totaling the four lowest individual scores over 36 holes. Watson carded a 151, Kortge 155, Busch 157, Goodrich 162, Zimmerman 162 and Bob Billig 163.

Swimming and Diving: Coach Charles "Mac" McCaffree opened his first year in East Lansing and, seeing the need for a season-ending championship meet, gave birth to the Central Collegiate Conference (CCC) for swimmers and divers of non-Big Ten schools in the Midwest. Coaches of teams from Wayne, Detroit Tech and Bowling Green responded with entrants in that first year and a one-day nine-event meet was conducted in the new Jenison pool. The CCC would provide a welcome annual event until Big Ten officials granted MSC conference membership on Dec. 12, 1948.

In the NCAA championship meet held at Harvard, the medley relay team of John Becker, Chuck Bigelow and Ralph Newton was 5.6 seconds from reaching the finals. Even though Newton won his 100-yard freestyle heat in a varsity record-setting time of 54.5, he, like Bigelow in the 200 breaststroke, failed to reach the evening finals.

Tennis: The pictured vehicle, MSC's version of the stretch limo, will look familiar to many athletes of the 1930s and 1940s. Small squads, such as wrestling, boxing and tennis would frequently engage this means of travel.

By 1942 a point system was in place to determine the guidelines for earning a varsity "S." It translated as follows: a man had to earn at least 75 points in major meets. A singles victory in number-one position counted as 12 points; number-two position as nine points; number-three and number-four positions as eight points, and the number-five and number-six positions as seven points. A victory in doubles would count one-half as much as the singles. As a result, weekly challenges to earn the coveted spots were often fierce and highly competitive. Frank Beeman, Floyd May, Bill Maxwell, Roger Cessna and Herb Hoover all reached the required point total.

Track and Field: In the 67-37 defeat by Illinois, Bill Scott ran a 4:19.2 mile to establish a new indoor varsity record.

Michigan State nearly sprang an upset at the 16th Annual Central Collegiate championships held at Jenison on March 7. With only the one-mile relay to contend, MSC and Notre Dame were tied 43-43. Although the Irish stormed to an easy win in that final event, debate raged long after as to the possibility of a disqualification. The ND win held up, and the Spartans settled for second place.

At the Illinois Tech relays, the Spartan quartet of Dale Kaulitz, Hughie Davis, Bob McCarthy and Bill Scott established a new American record of 3:31.6 in the seldom-run sprint medley. The total distance was 1 1/4 miles made up of four legs measuring 880, 220, 220, 880 yards.

Only five men made the trip to the Kansas Relays. Art Dehn, Dale Kaulitz and Bob McCarthy teamed with Bill Scott for a third place in the half-mile relay and then joined with Hughie Davis for a third in the sprint medley.

Of the 14-man squad that competed at the Drake Relays, only three men placed. The vaulting duo of Bob Harris and Ted Wonch were among four others in a tie for fourth place. Kaulitz, in his first-ever effort in the 400-meter hurdles, finished an incredible second behind former Indiana star Roy Cochran of the Great Lakes NTS team, who set a new world record of 52.2.

After clearing only 6' 2" at the Drake Relays and finishing out of the money, Jim Milne was back in form at the Penn State dual meet when he cleared the bar at 6' 4-3/4" to set a new varsity record.

Scoring 103 1/2 points, the highest total ever, Schlademan's crew walked off with the team trophy while hosting the 27th State Intercollegiates. An all-day downpour maintained a couple inches of water on the running track and drastically affected individual achievements. With obviously poor footing, the discus event was cancelled. Other field events were moved inside the fieldhouse, as well as running events that could be accommodated to the 1/8-mile oval.

At the IC4A meet in New York, Wonch cleared 13' in the pole vault, which resulted in a three-way tie for first place.

Two men accompanied Karl Schlademan to the NCAA meet at Lincoln, Neb., high jumper Milne and miler Scott. As it turned out, one was hot and one was not. While Scott did not place in his specialty, Milne ended in a three-way tie for second in the high jump. His six team points placed MSC tied for 20th, ahead of 15

other schools, including Oregon State, Wisconsin, Michigan, Washington, Texas and Missouri.

Wrestling: New additions to the 1942 Spartan lineup were Herb Thompson, a back-up in 1941, and John Spalink of Grand Rapids, up from the freshmen team. John Orr, expected to return to the 175-pound spot following a one-year absence, joined the U.S. Navy during the Christmas break. John Marrs from Bristow, Okla., was another significant addition to the squad as a sophomore. His value stemmed from his willingness to wrestle wherever he was needed, at weights ranging from 145 to 165 pounds.

The talent pipeline from Oklahoma remained open in 1942. The freshman class that year included Pat Sullivan and Bill Ross of Bristow, Wesley Gougler from Tulsa and Burt Boring of Ponca City. Joining these four was another newcomer, Iggy Conrad from Cleveland.

On February 14, nearly 3,000 spectators found their way to Jenison Fieldhouse for the match against the na-tional champions, Oklahoma A&M. After Herb Thompson's opening loss at 121 pounds, Cut Jennings brought the spectators to their feet with a quick 57-second pin of his adversary at 128 pounds. The roaring partisans were convinced brother Bo would equal or better that sub-minute performance in his match at 136 pounds. To the shock of nearly all assembled and by the slimmest of margins (one point), Bo suffered his solitary defeat of the season. To make the loss more wrenching, he was defeated by Sidney Marks, who had originally enrolled at MSC in 1939. Marks had succumbed to homesickness and returned to Oklahoma. As the remaining bouts were being played out, hope rekindled on the Spartan bench when Billy Maxwell and John Spalink both pinned their opponents, turning the Spartans into the lead, 15-11. Unfortunately, Michigan State contenders were no match in the final two upper divisions (175 and heavyweight), and the favored Aggies closed the card out with a pin, a decision and a 19-15 winning score.

Members of the MSC tennis team sit in the school's limousine.

SPARTAN SCRAPBOOK
——— BOXING COACHES (1935-1958) ———

Pioneer boxing team (1937)

Al Kawal (1942-43)

Lou Zarza (1946-47)

John Brotzmann (1956-58)

George Makris (1948-55)

Pictured elsewhere: Leon "Brick" Burhans 1935-41$_{WR}$

$_{WR}$ see wrestling coaches

MSC
1942-1943

TALES TO TELL

Those unfamiliar with how prime athletes were coveted and amassed on the nation's military and naval bases during the war years of 1942-1946 would not have been impressed by opponent names such as Bambridge Navy, Camp Grant or Iowa Naval Pre-Flight. Yet these, and other training centers, often fielded, particularly in football, star-studded aggregations. If a base commander sought recognition through successful sports teams, identifiable talent would be plucked from the normal rigorous trainee routine and placed under the tutelage of the installation's athletic director. In exchange, the pampered stars would experience a more comfortable lifestyle. The 1942 team from the naval station at Great Lakes, Ill., laden with a bevy of proven stars on loan from colleges and professional ranks, epitomized such a squad. On October 23 they were in town as MSC's homecoming opponent. A story in that morning's *Detroit Free Press* predicted the outcome:

"Odds were anchored tight in favor of the Great Lakes Naval Training Station team today as the well-manned sailors and Michigan State College wound up preparation for their battle before a homecoming throng of 12,000 at Macklin Field tomorrow."

Although coach Tony Hinkle brought a comparatively small squad of 33 players, the Blue Jackets' complement bristled with enough talent to send the scoreboard spinning against what probably is its weakest opponent in five starts.

Ed Ripmaster carries the ball in MSU's victory against the Great Lakes team.

HEADLINES of 1943

- Polyethylene plastic is introduced.
- In the Pacific theater of World War II, the U.S. naval and amphibious forces begin island-hopping operations against Japanese-held territory.
- The postal zoning numbering system starts in 178 cities.
- A French oceanographer invents the aqualung, an underwater breathing device that opened a whole new postwar recreational sport of scuba diving.

SCOREBOARD

	W	L	T	Avg.
Baseball	9	7	0	.563
Track and Field	3	2	0	.600
Football	4	3	2	.556
Basketball	2	14	0	.125
Tennis	7	1	0	.875
Cross Country	1	2	0	.333
Swimming and Diving	4	2	0	.667
Wrestling	5	2	1	.688
Fencing	2	4	0	.333
Golf	3	4	1	.438
Boxing	2	3	1	.417

degrees Fahrenheit, as hundreds of students and townspeople lined the banks to watch. "It was worth it," he later said. 'I never thought the Spartans would trip Great Lakes.'"

TEAM OF THE YEAR

With rain forcing the cancellation of three meets, the tennis team completed a compressed 7-1 season for a winning percentage of .875. No other MSC athletic team of 1942-1943 was nearly that successful. Although the season was completed void of matches against the likes of Ohio State, Kentucky, Purdue, Indiana and Illinois, the record did include wins over Michigan and Notre Dame.

Coach Bachman would likely have totally agreed with the journalist's analysis. At a Lansing Rotary Club luncheon on the previous afternoon, he expressed little hope for a victory over the talent-rich team from Illinois. In fact, he said, "I am willing to wade the Red Cedar if we win." Well, the "old coach" would prove to be "all wet," as suggested by the story in the *Detroit Free Press* on October 25, 1942:

"Led by Dancing Dick Kieppe, a shifty sharpshooter from Lansing who missed last week's game because of the flu and was kept away from practice most of the week, Michigan State's Spartans caused one of the upsets of the 1942 football season today by defeating a bigger, more experienced and heavily favored eleven from Great Lakes Naval Training Station, 14 to 0, in a Homecoming Day battle that was witnessed by 11,657.

Charlie Bachman was a man of his word. At high noon of the very next day, he followed through with his promise. Wearing business clothes, a light jacket and swim fins on his feet, the Spartan coach waded across the waist-high river in water registering 40-

The 1943 varsity tennis team. Pictured above (left to right): coach Charles Ball, Mel Ott, Earl May, Frank Beeman, Frank Zieman and Joe Climer (not pictured, Billy Maxwell and Carl Petroski).

MAKING HISTORY

Responding to an ongoing wartime manpower shortage, the NCAA declared that beginning March 1, 1943, current freshmen would be eligible for varsity competition. For Charles "Chuck" Davey, a curly-haired 17-year-old southpaw, the policy change would signal the launching of a incomparable boxing career. At 127 pounds, he joined Bill Zurakowski, Ed Wood and Edo Mencotti to

complete State's entry list for the national collegiate championships in Madison, Wis. This would be Chuck's initial step into stardom, as his presence gave MSC its first impact boxing team. A feature story in the March 28 edition of the *Lansing State Journal* told the story:

"Michigan State College today owned two national boxing titles thanks to a couple of excellent performances turned in here last night by captain Bill Zurakowski and Charles Davey.

Zurakowski, fighting in the finals of the 120-pound class, defeated Jim Demos of Miami (Fla.) University on a three-round decision. After a slow first round where he watched his opponent carefully, Zurakowski went out after Demos in the second to pile up a tremendous advantage. Out-punching him consistently, Zurakowski had Demos reeling at the bell.

Davey, a boxer who is exceptionally tall for his 127-pound weight, held a considerable advantage in reach over John Werren of Wisconsin, his opponent. A left-hander, Davey shot right jabs at Werren that continually caught the Badger off balance. Davey took all three rounds decisively."

Bill Zurakowski remembers preparing for those championships:

"My only loss in 1943 was to Jackie Grey of Penn State. Movies were taken of that bout held back at East Lansing in January. While training for the nationals, I reviewed that film many times. It was found his left jab set up his damaging right cross. As a result of this observation, I trained conscientiously with my twin brother Walt, our trainer Earl Reid, and Chuck Davey. It was found that I was able to block the left jab, counter punch and avoid the right cross. During the semifinals of the national tournament, Jackie was my opponent. All this training was brought to a fruitful climax. I won that bout by a decision and then defeated Jim Demos of Miami in the finals to become, along with Chuck Davey, Michigan State's first national champions."

Ed Wood expressed mixed feelings about those 1943 NCAA matches:

"Our 1943 team produced two national champions, our team captain, senior Bill Zurakowski at 120 pounds, and Chuck Davey at 127 pounds. We also had two others who were undefeated in dual- meet competition, Edo Mencotti at 175 pounds and myself at 135 pounds. As a team, we were runner-up to the University of Wisconsin. The greatest disappointment in my boxing career came at that 1943 NCAA championship meet. Being undefeated, I was entered as one of the favorites at 135 pounds, but an accidental head butt in the bout I was engaged in caused a severe cut in my eyebrow that required several stitches. Occurring in the first round, the officially rendered decision was 'no contest.' However, due to the severity of the injury I was not permitted to continue further in the tournament. Unfortunately, at that time protective head gears were not required as they were to become so at a later date. Had they been in 1943, who knows what might have happened.

GREAT STATE DATES

Cross Country—**October 17, 1942 (A):** Although the score of the dual meet at Des Moines against Drake stands as a 15-40 perfect-score Spartan victory, it should have been more properly registered as a forfeit. The pace set over the four-mile course was so exhausting that only four members of the Bulldog team managed to negotiate the distance; hence, lacking a fifth man, the Drake team did not officially complete the race. Led by sophomore Roy Niemeyer of Arlington Heights, Ill., State's other finishers were Bill Scott, Ralph Monroe, Bill Hershiser, Maurice Horski and Bill Fritz.

Football—**November 14, 1942 (H):** Following a scoreless first half, the Spartans hit for two touchdowns with devastating speed in the first eight minutes of the second half leading to a 19-6 victory over Purdue. Dick "Little Egypt" Kieppe and Morgan Gingrass were the principal ball carriers. Bernard Roskopp was outstanding on defense and credited with many of the 76 yards PU lost in rushing attempts. This was the seventh loss in eight games for the Boilermakers.

Wrestling—**January 18, 1943 (H):** Before a home crowd of 1,200, the Spartans defeated archrival Michigan, 16-14. The meet saw the return to action of Burl

Jennings, who had been recuperating from an abdominal operation. He won by decision, as brother Merle and Bill Maxwell gained the only State pins. In a match between two football players, State's Mike Dendrinos staved off the attempts of John Greene to earn a fall for the U of M that would have led to a tied score.

Basketball—**February 4, 1943 (H):** After only one win (Dearborn Naval Training Station) in 10 starts, the struggling Spartans found another upstart squad they could handle, as they rolled-up a 69-37 count on the team from the Romulus Army Air Force Base. From the moment Ollie White scored his first of nine buckets there was little doubt about the outcome. The Cleveland sophomore racked 19 points, one more than Jack Cawood. This pair continually raced down court and scored ahead of the Flyers' attempt to set up a zone defense.

Swimming and Diving—**February 19 & 20, 1943 (A):** A journey west was scheduled to include one meet against Coach McCaffree's former school, Iowa State, followed by an extended trip to Lincoln, Neb., for a meet with the Nebraska Cornhuskers. Eventually, wartime travel restrictions curtailed the extra mileage into Nebraska, and McCaffree opted to spend a second day in Ames duplicating the easy win over the Cyclones. Capturing every first place in the unique doubleheader, the Spartans returned home with victories of 63-21 and 57-27.

Track and Field—**February 20, 1943 (H):** In defeating the University of Illinois, 62-42, State captured all but four firsts while slamming the 75-yard dash and the high hurdles events. The surprise of the meet was Marv Fraser's win in the 440-yard run. Fraser, a sophomore from Fowlerville, had no running experience at all before enrolling at MSC. Hughie Davis captured scoring honors for the evening when he took first in the broad jump and 75-yard dash for as total of 10 points.

Boxing—**March 6, 1943 (A):** With the mid-season NCAA rule-change permitting freshmen to compete, Coach Kawal opted to use four first-year men: Chuck Davey, Mike Gibbons, Jerry Wingaert and heavyweight Ogostino "Augie" Orlando in the final match of the season, a 5-4 defeat of West Virginia. *The Lansing State Journal* writer wasted few words in describing Davey's winning performance that afternoon: "Charles Davey gave a pretty exhibition of boxing in his bout."

Baseball—**April 24, 1943 (A):** The Spartan hitters came alive in the second game of a two-game set against Ohio State and defeated the Buckeyes, 10-6. Leading the way were Art Maichoss and Howie Ladue, as both collected four base hits in five trips to the plate. Their hitting was also timely as each man batted across four runs during the afternoon. Big George Killmaster, freshman first baseman, accounted for the remaining two runs with a double in the third inning.

Tennis—**April 26, 1943 (H):** The Spartans defeated the University of Michigan 6-3 in the season opener. Frank Beeman won his singles match in straight sets, 6-2, 6-1, as did Earl May, 6-4, 6-3, and Billy Maxwell, 6-3, 7-5. Beeman, paired with Fred Zieman, also won in doubles, as did the team of May-Maxwell. The remaining team point was contributed by newcomer Mel Ott, who won his singles match 6-1, 7-5.

Baseball—**June 5, 1943 (H):** Playing Western Michigan, MSC was scoreless until the bottom of the ninth. By combining a pair of Bronco errors, a base on balls, and a perfectly executed squeeze play by Tom King, the Spartans pulled it out, 2-1.

ATHLETE OF THE YEAR

John William "Billy" Maxwell entered MSC in the fall of 1939 following impressive prep years in Tulsa, Okla. Billy would complete a unique double-sport collegiate career that would earn him three letters in wrestling at 136 pounds (1941-1943) and two in tennis (1942-1943). Maxwell's pursuits on the mat were climaxed with a national collegiate title at 136 pounds in 1942 and the 145-pound crown at the National AAU's the following year when he was additionally honored as the meet's Outstanding Wrestler. Tennis teammate and MSC coach Frank Beeman expounded on the virtues of the talented "Okie" on the courts:

"Maxwell's forte was upper body strength and ambidexterity. He did not use a backhand, rather he chose to play by switching the racquet from one hand to the other. He came with impressive credentials, having been named to the Junior Davis Cup team during his high school career."

John "Billy" Maxwell

IN THE SPARTLITE

Baseball: The baseball team of 1943 played the school's first night games during a two-night stand against the Badgers at Madison, Wis., on May 10-11.

Basketball: After the 1942-1943 schedule was released on November 24, some last-minute changes were put into place. Indiana University officials canceled the December 12 game at Bloomington for no given explanation. Also, a pair of games scheduled with the Iowa Navy Preflight School was scrubbed as they had dropped their basketball program. The latter two dates were filled by teams from Dearborn Naval Training Station (NTS) and Romulus Army Air Force Base. These additions were fortunate, for as it turned out, they were the only two games the Spartans were able to win in the 16-game season.

The 1942-1943 opener, a 36-31 overtime loss to Michigan, was a game that the Spartans actually seemed to have in hand. They led 15-6 at the break and 26-16 with 10 minutes remaining, but the Wolverines slowly crept back to tie the count, 29-29, and force the extra five-minute period.

The home finale, a 45-42 loss to Notre Dame, was the sixth defeat of the season with a margin of five points or less. The teams were tied at halftime 22-22 and the score was 29-29 after seven minutes of the second stanza. The Irish finally worked to a five-point lead and the teams exchanged baskets down the stretch before time ran out with the visitors in command, 45-42. In that morning's issue of the *Michigan State News* it had been predicted that the MSC-ND game might be "the final game for the duration of the war." This prediction proved to be accurate as the fieldhouse lights were dimmed and intercollegiate basketball was put on hold for 22 months.

Cross Country: Lauren Brown was one of the first coaches to feel loss of talent to the armed forces. Gone from 1941 were sophomores Colby Thompson, George Byelick, Earl Cady and Walter Mack.

Fencing: The team included the following six from the 1942 squad: seniors Lyle Burdy, Charles Sherman, and Ted Bourobias, along with juniors Morris Shephard, Ed Popper and Don Krushak. Included on the travel team were sophomores John Wicham, Gordon Hueschen and Bob Stipek.

With only one match scheduled in Jenison, Charley Schmitter's crew opened and closed their home season with a 14-13 verdict over Notre Dame on February 13.

Football: The most spectacular play of the 1942 season was engineered in the final 10 seconds of the first half in the 25-13 loss at Washington State. Dick "Little Egypt" Kieppe gathered in a punt on his own 10-yard line and sprinted to the Spartan 30, where he lateraled to Bob Otting who then headed down the sideline. Cutting back into the center of the field, he raced into the end zone, concluding a 90-yard touchdown play.

In the season finale, a 7-7 tie against the Rose Bowl champions from Oregon State, 11 MSC seniors played their final collegiate game. They were Kieppe, Walt Pawlowski, Ed Ripmaster, Jack Fenton, Bill Milliken, Dick Mangrum, Bob McNeil, Bill Monroe, Mike Miketinac, George Radulescu and Bernard Neubert.

Golf: The clouds of war were closing in. Through graduation, armed forces enlistment and the military draft, only George Zimmerman returned from 1942. Joining him for an eight-match schedule were Clifford Kirtland, Bob Bowen, Jim Davis and Dave Hicks.

To save on travel, two triple-dual meets were scheduled. One at Ann Arbor included Notre Dame and a second was held at South Bend, but the University of Illinois was a no-show.

The season closed on a positive note with a pair of convincing wins over Michigan Normal, 17-1 and 12-6.

Swimming and Diving: Again, MSC hosted and easily won the CCC Championships, which attracted only three challengers: Wayne, Bowling Green and Lawrence College of Appleton, Wis. McCaffree's men rolled up 100 points in taking nine of the 10 events. Setting varsity records were Bob Allwardt, with a 2:21.5 in the 220-yard freestyle; Harry Cooley, who lowered the mark in the 150-yard backstroke to 1:44.5; and Johnny Nichols, who captured the 440-yard freestyle by almost a pool length in 5:20.1.

For the first time in the school's history, the Spartans broke into the scoring at the NCAA championships held at Ohio State. By placing fifth in both relays, McCaffree's men racked up a total of four points. The 400-yard freestyle relay quartet of Allwardt, Harold Heffernan, Jimmy Thomas and Ralph Newton swam a 3:45.7, while the medley relay team of Cooley, Bob Knox and Allwardt finished with a time of 3:09. It seems only fair to note that of the 23 schools represented in the meet, only *five* chose to enter relays.

Tennis: Spring rains caused havoc for the 1943 schedule. Three meets were washed out and four others were rescheduled. With this abbreviated schedule, members of the MSC team were in dire need of points toward earning their varsity "S." As a result, the U of D matches in Detroit, played amidst steady showers, found the Spartan players incessantly coaxing the Titan players to "hang in there" in hopes of continuing play, winning the match and gaining the points. Frank Beeman recalls that, during that afternoon, it proved more productive to target return shots at the ever-growing puddles of rainwater rather than to aim for the lines or corners. As it turned out, only Beeman, Billy Maxwell and Floyd May earned the minimum 75 points to qualify for the coveted major letter.

Track and Field: MSC hosted and was runner up to Notre Dame at the indoor Central Collegiate Conference meet. State won only two firsts: captain Bill Scott with a 4:19.9 in the mile and Ted Wonch, who cleared the pole vault bar at 13' 3-5/8". One week later, high jumper Jim Milne hit his stride for the first time when he leaped 6' 5" to capture first-place honors at the Knights of Columbus relays held in Cleveland. On that same weekend, the bulk of the team was at the Purdue relays, where Hughie Davis won the 60-yard dash in 6.4.

From the end of the indoor season on March 27 to the first outdoor meet on April 17, Coach Schlademan lost a total of 13 of his most consistent performers to various branches of the armed forces.

In the first meet of the spring, against Purdue, the multifaceted Mel Buschman accounted for 16 of the team's 81 winning points. He won both hurdle events and the broad jump, and placed third in the shot put.

John Liggett recalls that year's State AAU Championships held at Kalamazoo, when Coach Schlademan displayed his uncanny coaching ability. Talking to Liggett during warm-ups he suggested:

"John, I don't think you can win the half-mile, but the only one that can beat you in the quarter is Dale [Dale Kaulitz, the team's best quarter-miler]. I believe Dale can win the 220-low hurdles. So, if it's okay with Dale and you we'll run that way."

They did, and the coach was right. Each captured their predicted first places.

For the first time since 1938, three Spartans placed at the National Collegiates. Jerry Page ran an incredible second in the two-mile, while the captain, Bill Scott, wrote "finis" to a great Spartan career with a fourth-place finish in the mile. Although dropping from his second-place finish in 1942, Jim Milne was pleased to finish the year as the fifth best collegiate high jumper.

Wrestling: Wartime conditions began to impact team personnel. Following the first Michigan meet, John Spalink enlisted in the army. On a sad note, two years later, the March 25, 1945, issue of *The State Journal* reported that Spalink died of wounds suffered during the army's invasion of the Japanese-held Luzon Island in the Philippines.

Engulfed by the realities of World War II, the NCAA wrestling committee, headed by Fendley Collins, opted to abandon the championship meet for the duration. Consequently, seniors Merle Jennings, Burl Jennings and Bill Maxwell would be denied the opportunity to defend their titles in 1943. The championships would not resume until 1946.

In lieu of the 1943 NCAA meet, Coach Collins entered a team in the National AAU meet in New York City. Both "Cut" Jennings and Bill Maxwell battled their way through three matches to claim titles, with Maxwell being voted the outstanding wrestler of the meet.

MSC 1943-1944

TALES TO TELL

As the nations of the world engaged in yet another year of global conflict (World War II), indications were bleak for intercollegiate sports at Michigan State.

First, in April of 1943, imposed wartime travel restrictions led to forced cancellation of football games that would have involved movement of personnel over significant distances. For MSC, this meant that scheduled contests against Oregon State and Washington State had to be scuttled.

As to participants, the "call to arms" continued to drain the campus of potential Spartan athletes as enrollments dipped from 6,352 in 1942 to 3,540 in 1943 with women outnumbering the men three to one. Even as the East Lansing campus suddenly became available for training detachments for the Army Air Force (approximately 2,000 men at any one time), not one of these "temporary students" was permitted to compete in intercollegiate athletics. Such was the philosophic stance of the United States Army. Meanwhile, on campuses where specific United States Navy units were being schooled, such as the University of Iowa and the University of Michigan, trainees were not only permitted to compete, but were encour-

aged to do so. It seems that on this matter the philosophy of the two military branches was paradoxical.

By the summer of that year, President John Hannah had seen the "handwriting on the wall" and on August 11, 1943, he announced the suspension of all intercollegiate competition for the "duration." In his statement he noted that with nearly all the able-bodied men of the college having left their studies to serve in the armed forces, remaining talent for legitimate competition just wasn't available. While no one apparently questioned the president's interpretation of the word "duration," his statement noted the college would resume a full varsity athletic program at that time deemed appropriate.

On Sept. 9, 1943, within four weeks following Hannah's announcement to suspend intercollegiate athletics, it was disclosed that a five-team campus football league would be formed. There is no recorded commentary on why such an activity was undertaken, but soon five teams were organized into somewhat of a intramural format while primarily engaging men who were in fields of study where military deferment was in place. The five squads included veterinary medicine students who were coached by John Kobs; the off-campus engineering students coached by Joe Holsinger; the on-campus engineer-

---

HEADLINES of 1944

- The liberation of Europe commences with the landing of Allied troops on the beaches of Normandy, June 6, 1944, D-Day.
- Franklin Roosevelt is re-elected president for an unprecedented fourth term.
- A total of 167 are killed in a fire that destroys the main tent of Ringling Brothers Barnum & Bailey Circus during a performance in Hartford, Conn.
- Howard Aiken invents an automatic calculator that is the forerunner of digital computers.

ing students who were coached by Gordon Dahlgren; the ROTC team with Al Kawal as coach and the civilian team coached by Karl Schlademan. Team practice sessions were limited to one hour, 5 to 6 P.M. daily, Monday through Friday.

The "season" opened on October 23 with a series of Saturday afternoon doubleheaders. The round-robin schedule involved 160 players, some of whom had previously earned major letters at MSC and others who would become varsity players in subsequent years. They included Bill Beardsley, Glenn Johnson, Pete Fornari, Bob Krestel, Fred Aronson, Bob Godfrey, Jack Breslin and Clayton Kowalk (basketball).

As it turned out, John Hannah's "duration" was not all that long-lasting. News came forth of his intentions to resume intercollegiate athletics officially on July 1, 1944. While approval of the plan awaited confirmation from a meeting of the faculty and eventual official announcement on April 7, baseball coach John Kobs "jumped the gun" when, on March 28, he called for all students interested in playing baseball to sign up in the physical education office. Athletic Director Ralph Young emphasized this would be an "informal" team. The only man Kobs could turn to with experience was Jack Breslin, and he became the catcher. Word spread about the pend-

ing team and others indeed "signed up:" Bob Krestel, Meredith Yarling, Fred Meyer, Tom Ashley, Ed Cook, Warren Hennessey, Lee Grunst, Dana Costin, Web McDonald, Ron Reed and Jack MaCris. As the season began, others turned up: Bill Turk, Howie Workman, Jim Grant and Darrell Couey.

In addition to scheduled games with Wayne, U of D, Grosse Ile Navy, Romulus Air Base, Ft. Custer and the Detroit Coast Guard, exhibition games were also played against Reo Motors, Motor Wheel, and even the inmates at Ionia Prison. That "informal" team of 1944 would post a record of 5-4. Consequently, contrary to all previous records, Spartan baseball never really was interrupted during the self imposed intercollegiate sports shutdown of 1943-1944.

There was obviously action from another venue in the spring of 1944, a year of "no intercollegiate sports at Michigan State College." The NCAA archives note the following from the national track and field championships hosted by Marquette University in Milwaukee that spring: "Two Miles: 4. Price (Michigan St.)." It is assumed this was the Robert E. Price who would letter and captain both the 1944 cross country team and the 1945 track and field team.

After wartime travel restrictions forced a cancellation of intercollegiate athletics, MSC formed a five-team campus football league.

MSC
1944-1945

TALES TO TELL

In August of 1944, though the world conflict would rage for another 12 months, the school president sanctioned the restart of Spartan sports. Coach Bachman had returned from his one-year stint at Camp Grant, and MSC football practices were in full swing. With only 500 male students enrolled in school, the turnout of 75 grid candidates was impressive.

A seven-game schedule was quickly mustered, and game tickets went on sale at $1.50 for general admission and $2.25 for reserved seats.

In the fall of 1944 two more Spartan heroes of the past were added to the casualty list of World War II. On November 11 it was reported that captain Olin "Max" Hindman, center on the basketball teams of 1939-1941, had been killed in action while serving with the U.S. Army in Germany. Eleven days later, on November 22, Eddie Pearce, a letter-winning halfback with the football teams of 1937-1939, was reported killed when the Air Force bomber on which he served crashed in North Africa.

TEAM OF THE YEAR

Solely through the efforts of four first-term freshmen, Dave Seibold and John DeMond of Jackson, along with Howard Patterson and Jim Quigley of Saginaw, MSC garnered the National AAU team title in the summer of 1945 at Cuyahoga Falls, Ohio. It remains the only national title ever won by a Michigan State swimming and diving team. Seibold was a double winner, capturing firsts in the 200-meter breaststroke and 300-meter individual medley. Patterson placed second in the 200-meter backstroke and DeMond finished third in the 100-meter freestyle event. Completing the MSC scoring, the trio of Patterson, Seibold and Quigley teamed for a gold medal swim in the 300-yard medley relay. Michigan State's winning total of 26 points was three points better than those of runner-up Great Lakes Naval Training Center.

HEADLINES of 1945

- Yielding to Russian troops from the east and Allied troops from the west, the Germans surrender, ending six years of war in Europe.
- After the death of 130,000 people from two atomic bombs dropped at Hiroshima and Nagasaki, Japan announces its unconditional surrender, bringing closure to World War II.
- The Coca-Cola Company registers "Coke" as a trademark.
- Percy LeBaron Spencer invents the microwave oven in Massachusetts. The idea comes to him after a factory radar power tube melts a chocolate bar in his pocket.

SCOREBOARD

	W	L	T	Avg.
Baseball	12	4	0	.750
Track and Field	2	2	0	.500
Football	6	1	0	.857
Basketball	9	7	0	.563
Tennis	3	1	0	.750
Cross Country	2	2	0	.500
Swimming and Diving	1	2	0	.333
Wrestling	5	0	0	1.000
Fencing	1	1	0	.500
Golf	0	6	0	.000
Boxing	no team			

The 1945 summer swimming and diving team. Pictured above (front row, left to right): John DeMond, Howard Patterson, David Seibold, Jim Quigley, Ralph Mercer and Harland Dodge; (back row, left to right) acting coach Ken Hawk, T. Bolenbaugh, Thomas Barber, B. Stevens, Henry D. Paton Jr.

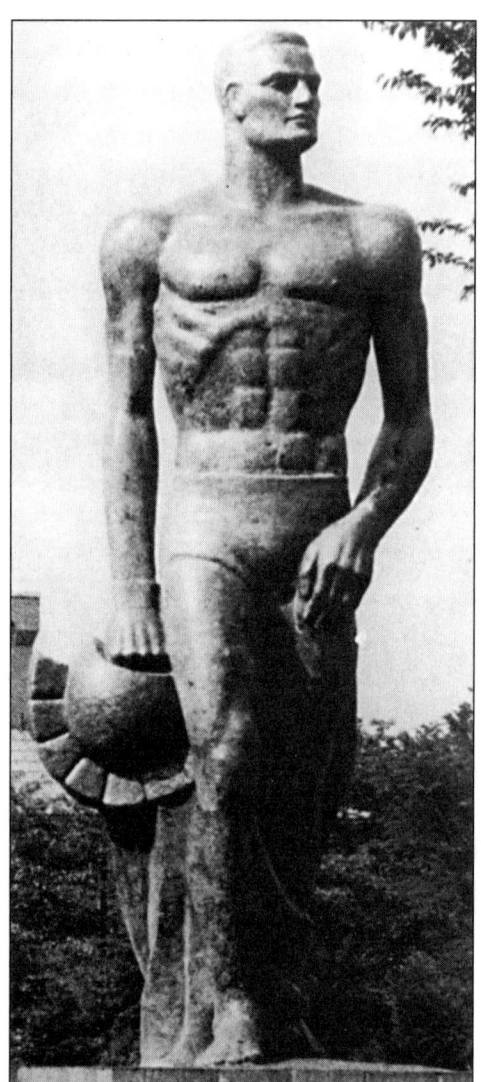

MSC's Spartan statue

MAKING HISTORY

The huge Spartan statue, a creation of Professor Leonard Jungwirth of the MSC Art Department, was unveiled in ceremonies on June 9 during commencement week.

The collegiate basketball world was shocked by news from New York City in early February. It seems that players of the Brooklyn College team had succumbed to bribes from gamblers and "thrown" a game played at a neutral location in Boston. Pundits immediately related the "fix" to competing at off-campus venues. In reaction, MSC president John Hannah announced that in the future, Spartan teams would play games only on their own campus or, when away, at sites commonly used by their opponents as "home" ground. One week earlier VanAlstyne's squad had played Temple in the Buffalo (N.Y.) Coliseum as part of a doubleheader.

GREAT STATE DATES

Football—**October 7, 1944 (A):** For the third time in the school's history, State won a game by the slimmest possible total score. A State scoring drive stalled on the University of Kentucky seven-yard line and the Wildcats elected to immediately punt out of danger. Don Grondzak, a 17-year-old freshman left end from Saginaw, broke through the center of the line and blocked the kick. Robert Brogger, the right end, dropped on the ball in the end zone for the safety. That was it. The final score: MSC 2, Kentucky 0.

Football—**October 20, 1944 (A) & November 11, 1944 (H):** An oddity of the seven-game football schedule that athletic director Ralph Young arranged for 1944 was that it included a unique two-game away-and-home series with the University of Maryland. The first game, a Friday night affair, was played in Washington, D.C., amidst a relentless driving rain that discouraged all but about 800 brave spectators. Jack Breslin accounted for the solitary touchdown when he broke off left tackle for a 12-yard score in the second period. The hosts surrendered a safety in the fourth quarter in make the final count read 8-0. Three weekends later, before 8,000 shivering homecoming fans at Macklin Field, the Spartans closed their abbreviated season, once more defeating the Terrapins, this time by a more impressive score, 33-0. Breslin, in his final Spartan appearance, accounted for three of the team's five touchdowns and 127 of the 253 rushing yards.

Cross Country—**November 25, 1944 (H):** When Wayne University backed out of its November 2 meet due to injuries, it was decided to not reschedule. As a unique alternative, it was agreed that times registered in that fall's NCAAs would be recorded and a dual-meet score determined. Those integrated times eventually favored MSC, 19 to 38.

Basketball—**December 2, 1944 (H):** Following the wartime interruption of varsity competition, the MSC cagers resumed play with a convincing 44-36 victory over Drake University. The Bulldogs were in command until the final six minutes when the Spartans took charge and outscored the visitors, 16-3. Among the 2,000 spectators that evening was U.S. vice president Henry Wallace, who was on campus as guest of school president John Hannah.

Wrestling—**February 2, 1945 (H):** After eight losses to Indiana, reaching back as far back as 1922, the 1945 Spartans defeated the Hoosiers for the first time, 14-12. It was IU's first loss of the season. Each team was credited with four individual wins, but the difference in the team scoring was a pair of pins (Gale Mikles and Don Anderson), as opposed to only one pin for Indiana. Winning a match for the visitors was Carl Nestor of East Chicago, Ill. Carl would later transfer to Michigan State to compete in wrestling as well as letter in football.

Wrestling—**February 3, 1945 (H):** Within 24 hours of their defeat of Indiana, Fendley Collins's squad came back even stronger to top Ohio State, 18-13. By the time Don Anderson had pinned his 165-pound opponent at the 2:32 mark, State had compiled the insurmountable 16 points. That lead was fortuitous, for the Buckeyes finished with a decision at 175 pounds, and their 340-pound heavyweight threw Harold Dachtler at the 27-second mark of the opening period.

Basketball—**February 5, 1945 (A):** Selecting the 1945 game of the year is easy. The repugnant Adolph Rupp brought his Kentucky team to town for the return match of the home-and-home series. State had been dispatched rather easily three weeks earlier, 66-35. By now the Wildcats had posted a 14-2 record for the year with each loss, to Notre Dame and Tennessee, by a single point. With another "slaughter" nearly assured, only 1,600 fans showed up for a rare Monday night encounter. Somehow the typically rangy Kentucky team that took the floor that evening (six-foot-four average) did not intimidate the more diminutive Spartan starting five that would ultimately play the entire game: Sam Fortino, Robin Roberts, Bill Rapchak, Joe Beyer and team captain Nick Hashu. Oddly, the Cats were never in it, as State led 33-22 at the intermission and then outscored the favored UK team, 33-28, in the second half for a shocking 66-50 upset win. Kentucky did come within seven points, 50-43, in the final quarter, but MSC sprinted away again as three Spartans reached double figures: Rapchak with 20, Fortino 19 and Roberts 11.

Fencing—**February 17, 1945 (H):** Following the one-year departure from all sports, Michigan State marked its return to fencing on a winning note by edging Ohio State, 14 1/2-12 1/2. The Buckeyes carried a one-point margin, 5-4, in both the foil and sabre events, but the Spartans' 6 1/2-2 1/2 edge in the epee event was the telling difference. Dick Pinkerton in the foils, Louis Marion in the epee, and Dick Shelly in the sabre were the standouts for Coach Schmitter.

Track and Field—May 19, 1945 (A): Trailing Indiana, 55 1/2-43 1/2, with three events remaining, the Spartans scored first and second in the low hurdles and won the mile relay to tie the score. All attention then focused on the broad jump pit, where Wayne Finkbeiner eventually outleaped the Hoosier entries to earn five points. MSC registered a come-from-behind 61 1/2-60 1/2 victory.

Baseball—May 24, 1945 (A): Keith Steffee, Sturgis pitching ace, pitched a one-hitter to defeat the University of Detroit, 2-0. In the Spartan eighth inning, Jack Breslin scored the first run on a base hit by Marty Hansen, who in turn scored later on an RBI single by Ben Hudenko. State's line-up included Breslin 1B, Dick Mineweaser 2B, Vanar Kostegian 3B, Hansen SS, Rudy Castellani LF, Lee Grant CF, Don Schuler RF and Hudenko C.

ATHLETE OF THE YEAR

In the summer of 1945, David Seibold (1945 and 1947-1950) entered MSC following an impressive prep swimming career at Jackson High School. He was not only the Michigan State High School champion in the breaststroke event, but he had also won the National AAU indoor championship at the New York Athletic Club that same winter. His two individual titles in the summer of 1945, along with contributing to the gold-medal finish in the 300-meter medley relay, cemented the Spartan team victory at the National AAU outdoor championships. That year he was chosen as the state of Michigan's candidate for the coveted Sullivan Award, which denotes the nation's amateur athlete of the year. Following a one-year hitch of military service, Seibold returned to school and placed in four subsequent NCAA championship meets. Initially awarded a varsity "S" for his efforts in the summer of 1945, Seibold would complete his career as the only modern-day Spartan to earn five monograms in one sport.

David Seibold

IN THE SPARTLITE

Baseball: Flood waters kept Old College Field submerged in mid-May. Consequently, the site for the scheduled doubleheader against Ohio University was relocated to Sycamore Park in Lansing, where the team split a doubleheader, losing the first 11-4 and winning the second 8-7. It was one of the few times State played a home game at an off-campus location. It was also a costly day of action. Nick Gregory, second baseman, broke his thumb tagging out a sliding runner, and in other action Dick Mineweaser, third baseman, suffered a fractured finger.

With his perfect pitching record of six wins and no losses, Keith Steffee, the ex-serviceman, won exactly half of his team's victories in 1945.

Basketball: Following three straight losses, Coach VanAlstyne inserted Robin Roberts, an 18-year-old freshman from Springfield, Ill., into the line-up against the University of Cincinnati on January 6. "Robbie" responded as the team's leading scorer with 16 points in a 37-39 loss. He remained a starter for the remainder of the season.

Boxing: Unlike all other sports that emerged from the one-year hibernation due to wartime restrictions, boxing remained non-active for two seasons, 1943-1944 and 1944-1945.

Cross Country: Following the school's self-imposed 1943 wartime ban on intercollegiate athletics, a team was organized for 1944 when a mere six runners reported for the initial workout. The team eventually consisted of Bob Price, Wayne Finkbeiner, Gordon Frost, John Brummer and Harold Schlichting.

Football: Playing before home crowds that averaged approximately 7,000, a surprising 6-1 1944 season was recorded. Until the 13-7 loss to Missouri in the sixth game of the season, the Orange Bowl was actually making overtures. The record was achieved with an all-civilian squad, composed entirely of discharged servicemen, 4-Fs (physically unfit for military service), 17-year-olds, and a few awaiting military service.

Coach Bachman introduced a new type of offense that he felt was suited to his material. While retaining the balanced line of the Notre Dame system, the patented shifting backs and flexing ends were aborted. Instead, the backs lined up in a "Z" formation and started plays without shifting. The innovative formation was appropriately labeled the "flying Z."

Golf: For the first time since the school's initial team of 1928, the Spartans were winless, this time in a six-meet season. Individual cards from the 11 1/2-6 1/2 loss to Wayne offer evidence for the struggling team of 1945: Bob Backus 93, Stu Helliwell 94, Joe Murphy 97 and Paul Cline 100.

Swimming and Diving: Following a one-year wartime suspension, the NCAA championship meet was resumed at Ann Arbor, where the Spartans managed a fourth-place tie with Minnesota, their best showing until that time. Ralph Mercer placed fifth in the 220-yard freestyle, as did Tom Barber in the one-meter diving event. The medley relay of Mercer, Jack McGrath and Joe Mueller finished fourth while the freestyle relay of Mercer, Mueller, Jack Kasten and Richard Chesney managed a third place.

Confident he had the makings of a championship contender, coach Charles "Mac" McCaffree assembled a collection of nine swimmers and one diver in the summer of 1945 with the purpose of vying for that National AAU team title. One thing the likable mentor had not foreseen was that he would not be at poolside when the ten-man team was put to the task on August 9-12. Responding to his nation's call, Mac was on duty in Italy as a postwar civilian physical education consultant with the Armed Service Force of the Special Services Division. Ken Hawk, an instructor in physical education and full-time coach in the Jackson school system, was designated as the acting coach. While McCaffree's team proceeded to capture that coveted title, he was 5,000 miles from the scene.

Tennis: Still responding to wartime travel restrictions, the schedule of 1945 was limited to a pair of weekend series, home-and-away, against Wayne and the University of Detroit. New names emerged on the scene for MSC: Harvey Hunyady, Jack McGrath, Ben Porter, William Coleman and Bob Ballard.

Track and Field: The Spartans defeated Wayne University in an indoor meet, 66-2/3 to 37-1/3, but the Tartars had the star of the meet, Lorenzo Wright, the future Olympian. That evening, he captured four firsts but was nearly matched by State's Wayne Finkbeiner, who won the 880-yard run, was second in the broad jump, tied for first in the pole vault, tied for second in the high jump and ran on the winning relay team.

MSC was never a factor in the Central Collegiate championships held on March 10 at Jenison Fieldhouse. The only bright spot of the evening for State was the gold medal performance of the mile relay team comprised of Finkbeiner, Lee Pickering, Ray Beckord and Herb Speestra.

Competing in three events at the Drake Relays in Des Moines, Iowa, MSC failed to place in the mile relay, but finished fourth in both the sprint medley and half mile events. Representing the Spartans were Pickering, Finkbeiner, Beckford, Frank Cappaert, Bill Maskill, Bob O'Leary and captain Bob Price.

Wrestling: The pair of Tulsa stars, undefeated freshmen Don Anderson and Gail Mikles, capped their 1945 season in Dallas, Texas, at the National AAUs. Leading 7-6 with five seconds remaining in his semifinal bout, Anderson was taken down for his first loss of the year. Meanwhile, the 17-year-old Mikles was crowned the 145-pound champion with a convincing 4-0 shutout in the finals.

Jim Grams's story is one of perseverance. He received his numeral award as a member of the 1935 freshmen team, and then *10 years later*, the married war veteran and father of three children enrolled as a postgraduate student, whereupon he won his varsity letter.

SPARTAN SCRAPBOOK
—GYMNASTICS COACHES (1948-2001)—

First gymnastics team (1948)

George Szypula (1948-88)

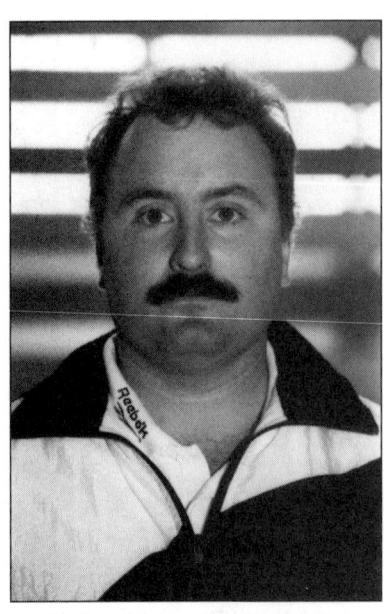

Rick Atkinson (1989-2001)

MSC
1945-1946

TALES TO TELL

With his fast ball and curve working to perfection, Robin Roberts pitched a no-hit, no-run game against the Great Lakes Naval Training Station on May 26, 1946. The next day, *The Chicago Tribune* featured a story of Ben Hogan winning the Western Open golf tournament at St. Louis with its first-place prize of $2,000. Another story told of Ralph Hepburn smashing the Indianapolis 500 qualifying record time with a speed of 133.94 mph. Buried on page three of that edition was the following story:

"Robin Roberts of Michigan State pitched a no-hit game yesterday as the Spartans defeated Great Lakes Naval Training Center, 8 to 0, for their 17th victory against four losses. The sailors committed nine errors, contributing to six Michigan State runs."

Teammate George Rutenbar (BS '46, '49) recalls that no-hitter:

"Basketball season ended and a stocky youth from Springfield, Ill., was honored as the state of Michigan's best collegiate player. Baseball coach John Kobs had a dilemma. The winter call for players to staff the 1946 Spartan squad had such a resounding response that more than 300 hopefuls filled the field. Now he must choose about 24 players, in his estimation the best, to make the spring Southern trip. Two facts should be noted. One is that Kobs must have made a wise choice of players because the team returned from the South with a perfect 9-0 clean sweep. Secondly, while the team was away, the above mentioned basketball player came to Jenison Fieldhouse each day to throw baseballs in order to be ready to be 'batting practice' pitcher for the dream team. Five weeks into the regular season that basketball/baseball player had gone from batting practice pitcher to a regular in the rotation.

When, on May 26, it came time to take the field against the Great Lakes Navy team, loaded with big leaguers, the big question loomed: who would be the 'sacrificial lamb,' the certain losing pitcher? Just before the 2:00 p.m. game time Coach Kobs pointed a menacing finger at our basketball playing teammate and ordered, 'Get cranked up, you're in there.' There was a stunned silence on the bench, but a good deal of relief among the other pitchers.

HEADLINES of 1946

- The ranch-type home becomes popular, as many find the low-slung, single-story home appealing.
- Consumers rush to buy the new 10-inch RCA television set for $375 that ushers in the TV age.
- Winston Churchill makes a speech at Fulton, Mo., warning of Soviet expansionism and coining the phrase the "Iron Curtain."
- Printed circuits are developed.

SCOREBOARD

	W	L	T	Avg.
Baseball	21	5	0	.808
Track and Field	5	1	0	.833
Football	5	3	1	.611
Basketball	12	9	0	.571
Tennis	4	10	0	.286
Cross Country	1	3	0	.250
Swimming and Diving	4	3	0	.571
Wrestling	5	2	1	.688
Fencing	3	5	0	.375
Golf	7	5	0	.583
Boxing	0	3	1	.125

They reasoned: 'At least it won't be me who gets hammered unmercifully.' And that day we all, in utter disbelief, experienced what I remember as my greatest sports experience. For you see, I had the privilege of playing in a no-hit, no-run game pitched and won by the 'Spartan of Spartans.' That lowly batting-practice pitcher never again in his entire career pitched another no-hitter, but went on to be toasted as a Philadelphia Phillies legend and holder of numerous major league pitching records. That man is Robin Roberts. As I climbed aboard the bus to bring us back from Chicago to East Lansing that night I thought, 'A little of sports history was made here today.' And it was, for a hero emerged that day and went on to bring well-deserved honor and notoriety to himself and MSC. Congratulations, Robbie. You are still our hero. You are one in a million."

TEAM OF THE YEAR

Featuring double wins over Ohio State and Wisconsin (the eventual Big Nine champions), the 1946 baseball team established the greatest won-loss percentage record (.808 with 21 wins and only five losses) of any Spartan baseball team before or since. Furthermore, defeating the likes of Georgia, South Carolina, North Carolina, Duke and North Carolina State, this Spartan team emerged from the traditional southern trip with a rare perfect record, 9-0.

The 1946 varsity baseball team. (Back row, left to right) trainer J. Heppinstall, manager D. Arnson, D. Massuch, N. Gregory, B. Page, assistant coach A. Kircher, head coach J. Kobs. (Middle row, left to right) P. Peppler, G. Rutenbar, E. Walsh, R. Roberts, H. Hughes, B. Groves, E. Sobczak. (Front row, left to right) D. Mineweaser, P. Fornari, J. Skrocki, B. Hudenko, F. Guest, J. Breslin, M. Hansen and K. Steffee.

MAKING HISTORY

Floyd Guest (BS 1946) reminisced about the collection of candidates for the 1946 baseball team:

"Weather conditions prevented outside preseason practice for the 1946 MSC baseball season. But there was a large contingent of hopeful players who answered the call to Demonstration Hall for indoor practice. Many players from previous years were again 'out for the team' and so were returning World War II veterans, some of whom had never played for State. Practice uniforms were scarce, so some tried out in their army khakis. However, Coach Kobs saw to it that we all had a chance and it became obvious that the batting cage was the first battleground for would-be Spartan players to prove themselves. It was there Kobs worked with the pitchers and watched batters closely. The fuzzy cheek youngsters and grizzled war veterans tried to catch Kobs's eye and perhaps be rewarded with a practice uniform, with their pitching form, or by smacking the ball through the box."

At the NCAA swimming and diving championships hosted by Yale University, MSC would make its first significant impression on the national scene. With less than a second separating the final six teams in the 400-yard freestyle relay, the quartet of Zigmund Indyke, John DeMond, Jim Quigley and Bob Allwardt prevailed by capturing the school's first NCAA title with a time of 3:27.2. Abel Gilbert placed in three freestyle races; Paul Seibold was fourth in the 200 breaststroke; and the medley relay of Willard Cooley, Seibold and Allwardt also finished fourth. When the team scores were totaled, MSC had accumulated 18 points, placing them third behind Ohio State and Michigan.

GREAT STATE DATES

Football—**October 13, 1945 (A):** Rated the underdog and expected to lose by as many as four TDs, State registered one of the nation's major upsets when they completely outplayed the University of Pittsburgh, 12-7. A 60-yard quick-kick by Jack Breslin set the stage for the first score and his pass interception sent State moving toward the second touchdown. Following the game,

Pitt coach Shaughnessy acknowledged: "Breslin is the best college back I've seen in five years."

Football—**November 3, 1945 (H):** Three weeks following the upset of Pittsburgh, Bachman's crew pulled off another surprise, this time a 14-7 homecoming win over Missouri, the champions of the Big Six Conference. With the score knotted at 7-7 and State at the Missouri 26-yard line early in the final quarter, Russ Reader dropped back to pass. Trapped, he whirled away, eluding the onrushing linemen, raced around right end and down the sideline to score the eventual winning touchdown. The Tigers, who had won four in a row, also lost the battle of statistics: 14 first downs to seven and 251 to 105 in total yards gained.

Cross Country—**November 9, 1945 (H):** Closing the dual-meet season against Wayne, Lauren Brown's crew captured their only victory of the fall, 19-38. Walter Mack, Walt Kalmbach, Don Thaden and Wayne Finkbeiner led the way as they finished one-two-three-four.

Football—**November 17, 1945 (H):** With both Russ Reader and Jack Breslin in the starting backfield, MSC administered their third upset of the fall, this time over heavily favored Penn State. The Nittany Lions, who had previously been defeated only by the powerful Navy squad, never came close, being shut out 33-0. Reader connected on 16 of 30 passes for 270 yards and two touchdowns, both gathered in by Warren Huey, a 17-year-old freshman;, while Breslin, in his final home appearance, also scored twice.

Basketball—**January 7, 1946 (H):** Before the largest Jenison Fieldhouse crowd in five years, State took the measure of Michigan, 49-36. The 8,594 spectators saw a close first half (MSC 19, U of M 18) and then watched the Spartans take command and outscore the Wolverines 30-18 in the final 20 minutes. With Matt Mazza operating skillfully at the pivot and Sam Fortino and Robin Roberts whipping the ball around, Michigan State definitely had the edge during the final period. Defensive play of Don Waldron, freshman guard, stood out.

Swimming and Diving—**January 19, 1946 (H):** In the 48-36 victory over Illinois and before nearly 700 spectators at the Jenison natatorium, Abel Gilbert, the Penn State transfer and Ecuadorian import, established a new varsity record with a 2:17.6 clocking in the 220-yard freestyle. In addition, with a time of 4:41.1, the 400-yard freestyle relay team of Jim Thomas, Bob Allwardt,

Zigmund Indyke and Jim Quigley established yet another team record. Feeling quite at home in the Jenison pool and diving for the Illini that afternoon was Tom Barber, who had captained the Spartans' championship AAU team of the preceding summer. He had transferred to Illinois in successful pursuit of a degree in dentistry.

Wrestling—**January 19, 1946 (A):** With his team leading Illinois by a scant one point, 12-11, freshman heavyweight Bob Maldegan took to the mat knowing the outcome of the meet rested directly on his broad shoulders. Equal to the challenge, he handled the Illini "big man" with seeming ease and a 6-1 decision. The Spartans returned home with a 15-11 victory over the eventual Big Ten Conference champions.

Wrestling—**February 2, 1946 (A):** In what was billed as the first-ever triple-dual meet in college wrestling, Coach Collins took his squad to Evanston, Ill., where they shutout the Wildcats, 28-0, and defeated Minnesota, 23-8. Spartan double-winners were Cliff Fletcher at 121, Bill Covey at 128, 155-pound Gale Mikles, and heavyweight Bob Maldegan.

Basketball—**February 7, 1946 (H):** With 45 seconds remaining and before an exuberant crowd of 4,875 at Jenison, Don "Tony" Waldron let go a long shot that found its mark to put the Spartans within one point of Wayne University. Then, following a pressing defense, Tony picked up a loose ball and dropped it over the rim with only two seconds on the game clock. MSC finished on top, 46-45.

Basketball—**March 1, 1946 (H):** Michigan State concluded the season at home with the second victory in less than a week over the University of Wisconsin. The story of the night produced a new hero, big Dave Lumsden, a 6' 4", 235-pound freshman from Stony Point, N.C. He left the obscurity of the bench to pace the Spartans in scoring with 12 points. Midway into the final period with MSC leading 53-39, the reserves entered. Taking advantage, the Badgers slowly crept back with a 13-0 run. Now leading by just a single point, Coach VanAlstyne quickly rushed his regulars back onto the floor to preserve what remained of the lead. This they did with the final score reading 56-52 for the 12th win of the season.

Baseball—**April 19-20, 1946 (H):** MSC opened the regular portion of the schedule with easy back-to-back victories over Wisconsin, 11-3 and 12-2.

Michigan State hitters were busy as they collected 31 hits over the weekend, building an eight-run lead after four innings on Friday and piling up a nine-run lead after just two innings on Saturday. These would be the 10th and 11th wins in a row for the Spartans. The Badgers would go on to capture the Big Ten championship.

Golf—**April 29, 1946 (H):** The top performer in the 20-4 win over Marquette was Jim Funston who posted a 74 over the Lansing Country Club course. His card was highlighted by a hole-in-one at the 17th hole.

Tennis—**May 4, 1946 (A):** Wet grounds and continual rain forced the Michigan State-Indiana matches indoors onto the basketball floor of Jenison Fieldhouse where, one by one, the Spartans registered a 9-0 shutout of the Hoosiers.

Golf—**May 8, 1946 (H):** Again led by Jim Funston, who battled the strong wind over the Lansing Country Club course for a one-under-par 71, the Spartans captured four of the six singles matches and all three of the best-ball foursomes to down the University of Michigan, 20-7. Other singles winners were Jim Anderson, John Wawzysko and George Teale.

Track and Field—**May 18, 1946 (H):** One of the top performances in the 87-44 victory over Notre Dame came in the mile run when freshman Jim Gibbard sprinted past the leaders in the final 25 yards to break the tape in a time of 4:23.2. Double winners were Harold Mayhew in the hurdles and Bob Schepers in the sprints. Other first places came from Jim Fraser in the quarter-mile, Walter Mack in the half-mile, Ted Wonch in the pole vault and Bruce Drynan in the discus.

Baseball—**May 30, 1946 (H):** Robin Roberts assumed relief roles on the mound to help MSC sweep a Memorial Day doubleheader from Ohio State, 4-3 and 7-3. The ace right-hander hurled three innings in the first game and four in the nightcap. The opener was tied 3-3 entering the ninth when Pete Fornari doubled, Roberts walked, Pat Peppler singled and Floyd Guest lashed a game-winning single into center. In game number two State jumped to a 2-1 lead in the opening inning. Three runs on five hits in the eighth decided the issue.

Baseball—**June 1, 1946 (H):** Keith Steffee pitched a five-hitter while blanking Western Michigan 7-0. Spartan hitters did the damage with only eight hits as the Bronco pitchers and defense unwillingly chipped in. Their starter on the mound hurled three wild pitches and balked in one of the four runs in the fifth. Two bases on balls

and two infield errors helped State to score three more unearned runs in the eighth.

Track and Field—**June 1, 1946 (H):** Winning all but two events and going one-two-three in four events (pole vault, the quarter mile, the 100-yard dash and the high hurdles), the Spartans easily handled Penn State 98 1/2-32 1/2. Double winners were Bob Schepers in both sprints (10.5 in the 100 and 23.1 in the 220) and Harold Mayhew (15.8 in the high hurdles and 25.7 in the low hurdles).

ATHLETE OF THE YEAR

During his years at Michigan State, Robin Roberts (BK 1945-47 and BS 1946-47) was remembered more for his exploits on the basketball floor than on the baseball field. In fact, in later years Robbie would recall a basketball memory, the 1945 defeat of number one-ranked Kentucky, as his most cherished collegiate experience. In addition to being the team's second-highest scorer during his three-year basketball career, his court presence, dribbling skills and ball handling set him apart from other players. Following the 1946 season *The Detroit Free Press* named the six-foot 185-pounder, along with Sam Fortino, to its All-Michigan quintet while tapping Roberts as Player of the Year. The story prevails that in baseball he initially sought an opportunity to earn a spot at first base, whereupon Coach Kobs assured the 19-year-old from Springfield, Ill., that MSC already had a first baseman—Jack Breslin. Kobs then suggested an opportunity might be available as a Spartan pitcher. With that, Roberts took to the mound, and the remainder of the story is history as he became the most renowned baseball player to ever wear the Green and White. Robbie's professional career is legendary. Following his signing, a $25,000 bonus contract (huge for the time) with the Philadelphia Phillies he spent one year in the minor leagues. One season later, in 1948, he joined the parent team to commence a 19-year major league career that would be accentuated by a total of 286 victories and eventual induction into major league baseball's Hall of Fame in 1976.

Robin Roberts

IN THE SPARTLITE

Baseball: Joining the team late following the basketball season, Robin Roberts posted a 4-2 record and a team-leading 1.72 earned run average (ERA). Yet Robbie shared the pitching spotlight with Keith Steffee, who recorded a 7-1 record and 1.85 ERA; Bill Page, who won four games with no setbacks; and Joe Skrocki, who pitched the greatest number of innings, 65, while compiling a 4-2 record.

First baseman Jack Breslin captured the batting title with a .338 average on 26 hits in 77 times at bat.

A postseason honor was achieved by star shortstop Marty Hansen when he was selected as a member of the West team that played the first college All-State game. John Kobs joined him as one of the coaches.

MSU football great Jack Breslin

Basketball: Encouraged by early season victories over Minnesota, Syracuse, Cincinnati and Michigan, there was hope in the Spartan camp for a repeat of the 1945 upset of the Kentucky University. It was not to be. Led by a pair of freshmen and future All-Americans, Ralph Beard, the scorer, and "Wah-Wah" Jones, the rebounder, the visiting Wildcats won with relative ease, 55-44.

Against DePaul and before 19,000 fans in the Chicago Stadium, the Spartans turned in one of their best performances of the year, although it was a 58-52 loss. The game was tied at 52-52 with less than a minute to play when the Blue Demons sank three quick baskets to secure the game. Bill "Shorty" Krall, State's center, likely never forgot this contest as he was matched against the legendary George Miken, who scored 23 points.

With the addition of an end-zone bleacher section, a record crowd of 10,085 turned out for the Notre Dame game on February 20. Students arrived as much as two hours in advance of the tip-off to guarantee the more coveted sideline seats. Holding a halftime lead of 28-27, MSC finally gave way when the Fighting Irish began to hit from seemingly every spot on the floor as they prevailed, 56-54. One year later, that attendance record would be broken when the MSC-ND game attracted 11,187.

At season's end MSC was obliged to decline an invitation to compete in the NIT tournament at Madison Square Garden in New York. Once more the dates conflicted with term-end examinations.

Boxing: The first home meet since 1943 took place in Jenison immediately following the Ohio State basketball game. Gaining decisions by Doug Hooth and John Tierney, a draw by Jim Denigan and a knockout by Lloyd Coon, State managed three and a half points, one short of a victory over Syracuse.

Jack Dempsey, former professional world heavyweight champion, visited the campus on February 6 and worked out for 30 minutes in the boxing room at Jenison. During his stop, the "Manassa Mauler" visited with some of the Spartan boxers and offered coach Lou Zarza some personal tips to pass on to his charges.

The policy to qualify for a major letter in boxing was written as follows: "Men who win a majority of their bouts during a season, providing at least five meets are scheduled, four of which are major meets." With only a four-meet schedule, the Spartan pugilists of 1946 never had a chance to earn the coveted "S" sweater.

Cross Country: A new three-mile cross country trail was inaugurated on October 13 when the Ohio State Buckeyes defeated MSC, 32-23, in the first-ever meeting between the two schools. Walter Mack, top finisher for the Spartans, was back in school following a stint of active duty in World War II. The remainder of Mack's running career would be hampered by a foot wound inflicted during the war. State dropped its second match of the fall at Bloomington, Ind. Mack ran a 19:01 to place second over the three and a half mile Indiana University layout. Other finishers were Kevin Higgins (third), Don Thaden (eighth), Wayne Finkbeiner (ninth) and Dick Zobel(10th).

Fencing: Acceding to meet the University of Wisconsin on January 26, the agreement might have concluded with, "We'll meet you halfway," for the meet was conducted on neutral grounds at the University of Chicago.

Don "Tony" Waldron puts up a shot as teammates Bill "Shorty" Krall (number 22) and Robin Roberts (number 17) look on.

In addition to placing in the NCAA tournament, the policy for earning a major "S" award in fencing was to participate in 80 percent of the meets and win 60 percent of the bouts in the man's main weapon. Apparently no one achieved this formula in 1946. The following fencers qualified for the minor award: Tom Billig, Dearborn sophomore; John Connell, Milwaukee junior; Greg Dean, Detroit sophomore; Louis Marion, Chicago junior; Chris Murphy, Miami, Fla., junior; Richard Shelby, Birmingham sophomore; Chuck Thompson, Bay City sophomore; Alejandro Valiente, El Salvador junior.

Football: Because of a wartime rule waiver, Jack Breslin was permitted to play in the annual East-West Shrine game of 1945 (for seniors only) even though he had a final season of eligibility remaining. Jack also turned down a lavish $2,500-a-year contract to play professionally. Instead he returned to campus for one final year and captained the 1945 team.

Swimming and Diving: Totaling 77 points, MSC dominated the seven-team field of the Central Collegiate Conference meet. Gold-medal winners were Abel Gilbert in the 220-yard and 440-yard freestyles; Howard Patterson, undefeated all season in the backstroke; the medley relay trio of Patterson, Paul Seibold and Jim Quigley, and the 400-yard freestyle relay of Zigmund Indyke, John DeMond, Quigley and Bob Allwardt.

In June, Coach McCaffree again assembled a summer squad with the hopes of achieving the same success as the 1945 championship team. Traveling to Hamilton, Ontario, the 10-man team dominated the Canadian national meet. But a repeat of the USA title was not to be. Only Gilbert managed to score points at the National AAU championship in San Diego, Calif.

Tennis: By 1946, returning servicemen began to fill spots on the squad. Included were Roger Cessna from the Army Air Corps; Dave Phillips, a Naval Air Corps pilot; Carl Frans, an ex-Army Air Force man; and Tom Martin from the U.S. Army. Rounding out the squad were Herb Hoover, Mike Yatchman, Jack McGrath, and Bob Malaga, the Ohio state high school singles champion.

Beginning in mid-February of 1946, evening practices were being conducted by stretching a canvas covering over the Jenison Fieldhouse basketball floor.

In 1946 the first NCAA championships were held. Entered but not scoring any team points in the matches at Evanston, Ill., were Cessna, Malaga, Phillips and Hoover.

Track and Field: The indoor season opened with a surprising 68-50 victory over Ohio State. Ted Wonch, in his first competition since returning from a three-year stretch in the naval air corps, managed a vault of 13' 7-1/4" to break his own varsity and Jenison Fieldhouse record.

MSC won places in all five relays they entered at the Drake Relays, winning two. The quartet of Al Lagrou, Marv Fraser, Jim Tanner and Walt Mack captured the gold with a 3:32.2 in the sprint medley, and the foursome of Richard Zobel, Jim Gibbard, Lagrou and Mack won the university two-mile relay in a time of 7:57.3.

Piling up 21 1/2 points, MSC placed fourth among 33 squads participating at Annapolis in the 70th running of the IC4A track and field meet. Again clearing 13', Ted Wonch led the field of vaulters, and his teammate Bob Vosburg shared second place. Four more points in the field events went to State when Leonard Naab placed second in the javelin with a throw of 187' 1/2". Jim Fraser ran a 48.7 in the quarter mile, the fastest of his career, but was nosed out by the NCAA champion in the 880. Harold Mayhew placed fourth and sixth in the low and high hurdles, and the mile relay team of Lloyd Whetter, Gibbard, Lagrou and Fraser ran a 3:20.9, good enough for third place.

At the NCAAs in Minneapolis, the Spartans managed five points, with Leonard Naab placing fifth in the javelin and Fraser taking sixth in the 440 with a time of 49.0. Jim Gibbard dropped out of the mile with a pulled muscle, and Ted Wonch was forced from the pole vault competition with a knee injury.

Wrestling: Even into the 1940s there were not many officials to referee dual meets. Strange as it seems, Cliff Keen, the University of Michigan coach, often donned the striped shirt to referee MSC home meets.

Prior to the third meet of the 1946 season against Purdue, 175-pound John Orr declared, "Win, lose, or draw, this is my last collegiate match. I've got to concentrate on studies." Leading his Boilermaker opponent 4-1 on points in the second period, Orr was dropped on his side and severely injured. Unable to continue, he forfeited and indeed it was his final match. A man of his word, on the following Monday Orr turned in his equipment.

Gale Mikles was defeated by the U of M's Bill Courtright in the 1946 dual meet. It was his first loss since high school in 1943.

At the NCAAs in Stillwater, Okla., Mikles placed third with Iggy Konrad and Cliff Fletcher each placing fourth.

MSC
1946-1947

TALES TO TELL

The date was May 23, 1947, and the opponent was the University of Michigan. That late Friday afternoon a dual track meet submitted as the most exciting and cherished victory in over 100 years of Michigan State track and field competition took place. The unusual 6:00 P.M. Friday meet was set to accommodate the state high school championships, traditionally held on Saturday. Weatherwise it turned out to be a poor trade-off. Competition was conducted amidst persistent rainfall. As the meet progressed, many events followed form: the U of M strongman, Charley Fonville, threw the shot put to a field record; Fred Johnson outleaped all broad jumpers; and Schlademan's dashman, Bob Schepers, captured both sprints. There was one inspirational effort from the infield, as Jim Zito, on loan from the football team, sailed the discus beyond Fonville's best effort. Four particular running events could have been labeled "too close to call," and three times the tape was broken by a Spartan. Jack Dianetti won the one-half mile first and then took the

mile run as he avenged an earlier indoor loss to Michigan's Herb Barten. Following 13 events, the scorekeeper checked and rechecked his dampened clipboard, and with only one event remaining the score read: Michigan 58 2/3, Michigan State 58 1/3. Coach Karl Schlademan's premeet prediction had come true: "the outcome of the meet should hinge on the final mile relay event." While the steady rain continued, Schepers, the Spartan sprinter, carried the baton on the opening leg and was five yards off the pace when he passed off to Jim Fraser, the second runner. The darkening day seemed even more dreary. Afterall, the meet was resting on Fraser who had placed a disappointing third in the quarter mile earlier. On a hopeful note, the senior, now running his final race on the MSC track, had a chance to atone. With an immediate emotion-packed burst of speed, he gained the lead on the very first turn. Now, could he hold it? Indeed, to the delight of the loyal State fans who had remained, he opened a 10-yard lead by the time it was Hal Mayhew's turn. The hurdler-sprinter doubled the margin on the third leg, and then it was up to the short, but muscular,

HEADLINES of 1947

- Jackie Robinson becomes the first African-American major league baseball player when he signs with the Brooklyn Dodgers.
- The Polaroid Land camera is patented by Dr. Edwin Land, providing prints that develop inside the camera within a minute. It enters the market the following year, selling for $90.
- Secretary of State George C. Marshall proposes the European Recovery Program (The Marshall Plan) to give economic aid to certain war-torn European nations.
- The transistor is developed by Bell Telephone Laboratories, and it becomes one of the most significant advances in consumer electronics, paving the way for miniature TV and radio sets.

SCOREBOARD

	W	L	T	Avg.
Baseball	16	8	0	.667
Track and Field	6	1	0	.857
Football	5	5	0	.500
Basketball	11	10	0	.524
Tennis	11	6	0	.647
Cross Country	1	1	0	.500
Swimming and Diving	8	2	0	.800
Wrestling	7	3	0	.700
Fencing	5	3	0	.625
Golf	4	6	0	.400
Boxing	4	2	0	.667

first-year star from Buffalo, Jack Dianetti. To this day, from his home in Victor, N.Y., Jack would probably never confess to it, but somehow as Herb Barten closed the margin, it seemed that Jack was setting the Wolverines up for an eventual "mud bath." As the pair raced tandem down the backstretch, Dianetti's spikes pelted the challenger with a rat-tat-tat of "here's mud in your eye" from the saturated cinder track. The Wolverine quickly looked more like a mud wrestler than a relay runner. Then, with about a furlong remaining, Dianetti threw it into "sprint gear" and Barten was soon mercifully out of range. Somehow, the instant Jack Dianetti crossed the finish line it would have seemed appropriate for the sun to break through to create a rainbow. It didn't happen. The rain continued, but it failed to dampen the spirits of Schlademan's soaked, but jubilant Spartans. Final score: Michigan State 68 1/3, Michigan 63 2/3.

The 1947 varsity track team. (Front row, left to right) J. Gibbard, B. Vosburg, P. Christenson, H. Mathew, J. Fraser, W. Mack, J. Zito, B. Schepers and J. Dianetti. (Second row, left to right) F. Johnson, M. Bowerman, W. Kalmbach, D. Sorenson, A. Lagrou, G. Shomin, J. Mueller and R. Sewell. (Third row, left to right) Manger John Warner, M. Arndt, J. Vaughn, H. Dawson, B. Fraser, F. Collins and W. Atchinson. (Back row, left to right) assistant coach L. Brown, trainer J. Heppinstall, head coach K. Schlademan and assistant coach F. Dittrich.

TEAM OF THE YEAR

Continuing its postwar rise under coach Karl Schlademan, the 1947 MSC track and field team was recognized as one of the powers of the Midwest. Led by sprinter Bob Schepers, middle-distance runner Jack Dianetti and all-around athlete Fred Johnson, the Spartans posted an overall 6-1 dual meet record and were undefeated outdoors. At the NCAAs in Salt Lake City, a trio of Spartan stars scored in their specialties. Dianetti ran second in the half-mile; Schepers finished a respectable third in the 220-yard dash; and Johnson, far off his previous form, jumped to a sixth-place tie at 23' 9". Totaling 16 team points, MSC finished in ninth place, ahead of such teams as Michigan, Indiana, UCLA, Texas, Rice, Baylor, Kansas and Wisconsin. A record total of 26 men received their varsity awards.

MAKING HISTORY

The first NCAA baseball championship finals were hosted by Western Michigan on June 20-21. The bracket provided for eight teams.

To accommodate the growing number of hopeful athletes within the postwar burgeoning enrollments, Michigan State, among many other schools, introduced junior varsity (JV) competition in 1946-1947. Abbreviated schedules were provided in nearly every sport. Although coaching staffs were somewhat augmented, for the most part, existing staffs took upon the added responsibilities. The 1946 JV football team of over 40 members included future Spartan stars Hal Vogler, John Polonchek, and Howard Adams. Junior Varsity teams continued on the scene until 1950-1951, when once more the NCAA removed freshmen from varsity competition thus returning to the freshman team-varsity team composition.

GREAT STATE DATES

Football—**September 28, 1946 (H):** Before an opening-day record crowd of more than 20,000, the Spartans struck quickly and often in an impressive 42-0 victory over Wayne University. In *The Michigan State News* story an effort was made to assist in pronouncing the name of a new hero: "Sparkled by little George Guerre (pronounced Gary) from Flint, 160 pounds of football dynamite the second stringers went to work on the tired Tartars."

Football—**October 19, 1946 (A):** With the Spartans trailing 14-0 in Happy Valley, George Guerre came off of the bench to lead MSC to a 19-16 victory over the previously undefeated Nittany Lions. Guerre rolled up 152 yards in 14 carries, including a 52-yard touchdown dash and other runs of 46 and 20 yards. He also completed three passes, punted effectively, recovered a fumble, and intercepted a pass. There is no report as to whether or not he drove the bus home.

Cross Country—**October 26, 1946 (H):** In the only home meet of the fall, the Spartans defeated Notre Dame by the slimmest of margins, 27-28. Jack Dianetti, who broke the tape 17 seconds ahead of the leading Irish runner, was followed by teammates in fourth, fifth, eighth, and ninth spots. The meet was in doubt until the final 500 yards when Herb Kebschull, a St. Joseph freshman,

moved up from 11th to eigth place, and Ed Kiezenski, a Sault Ste. Marie sophomore, beat out the ND fifth man for the ninth slot.

Basketball—**December 20, 1946 (H):** State opened the home season with an impressive 57-45 victory over Stanford University. The roster featured the familiar faces of Robin Roberts, Ollie White, Pat Peppler, Don Waldron, Jack Cawood and Matt Mazza. Entering their first year as Spartans were Hugh Dawson, Jack Wulf, Fred Stone and Bob Geahan.

Basketball—**December 31, 1946 (A):** The 61-57 win on New Year's Eve at Syracuse came in overtime after the Orangemen had tied the game 49-49 with 15 seconds remaining in regulation. Robin Roberts paced the offense with 17 points as Ollie White, Don Waldron, and Hugh Dawson carried the load in OT.

Track and Field—**January 25, 1947 (H):** Karl Schlademan would later acknowledge the Ohio State meet as the most dramatic he had ever witnessed in 30 years of coaching. Thanks to multiple ties in the high jump and pole vault, the scorer was dealing in fractions of points, and the meet was on the line as the lead-off men toed their mark for the final event of the evening, the one-mile relay. Then, with victory riding on the legs of anchorman Jack Dianetti, the assembled 1,700 fans came roaring to their feet as they saw the 18-year-old speedster break the tape two yards ahead of the Buckeyes' Mel Whitfield, who would later win the NCAA outdoor title in the 880. The final score read: MSC 66-7/12, OSU 66-5/12.

MSC track coach Karl Schlademan with his co-captains, Jack Dianetti (left) and Horace Smith (right)

Fencing—**February 1, 1947 (H):** Forced from Jenison in favor of the Michigan State Relays, the fencers entertained Notre Dame at the Women's IM Building (Circle IM). Exchanging 5-4 scores in the foil and sabre, the meet was won by MSC in epee. Jacob Venema stretched his consecutive victories to six by sweeping all three matches. Ed Popper also won three times, and Chandler Washburn took two, totaling an 8-1 advantage and the winning composite score, 17-10.

Wrestling—**February 8, 1947 (A):** The fourth meet on the 1947 schedule was a rematch against Purdue. Featuring upsets throughout the card and MSC trailing 12-9, the outcome was to be decided on the final match of the afternoon. Heavyweight Bob Maldegan's scheduled opponent had been declared ineligible earlier in the day due to scholastic deficiencies. So now he was going against the Boilermakers' backup, and Bob needed a pin for a State victory. From the opening whistle Maldegan was in charge. Leading on points with 61 seconds remaining, the Redford sophomore finally turned his opponent on his back, pressed his shoulders to the mat and, by a score of 14-12, State had defeated the eventual conference runners-up for the second time in three weeks.

Swimming and Diving—**February 14, 1947 (H):** Iowa State came to town undefeated and left after being humiliated 58-26 by Charles McCaffree's ever-improving squad that registered its sixth win in a row. During the evening, both Don Paton and George Hoogerhyde lowered their own existing school records: Don with a 22.8 in the 50-yard freestyle, and George with a 4:56.3 440-yard freestyle. It addition to capturing both relays, other individual winners were Will Cooley in the backstroke and Dave Seibold in the breaststroke.

Wrestling—**February 14, 1947 (H):** One week following the close victory at West Lafayette it was déjà vu, as the MSC-Illinois meet also rested with the heavyweights. Needing only a win by decision, Bob Maldegan piled up a 7-0 verdict while totally outclassing his Illini opponent. The result was another 14-12 team victory. Gale Mikles had set the stage earlier when he pinned the Big Ten champion at the 39-second mark of the final period.

Basketball—**February 19, 1947 (H):** With 5,789 fans cheering him on, Bob Geahan fell two points short of tying the 26-point MSC modern-day single game scoring record. Ironically, Sam Fortino, the record-holder, was in the U of D starting line-up that evening. Fortino had

transferred to the Detroit school in pursuit of a degree in dentistry. It must have been a strange experience for Sam, who in the preceding season had been MSC's leading scorer. Geahan, a Lansing native, was himself a transfer, having been the leading point producer for the University of Michigan in 1945. State defeated the Titans with relative ease, 55-48.

Wrestling—**February 28, 1947 (H):** In the 18-8 victory over Michigan, three seniors closed their home careers as winners. They were: captain Iggy Konrad at 128, Don Johnson 145, and Burl Boring at 175 pounds. Coupled with decisions by Gene McDonald and 136-pound Bob Gang, the Spartans built a comfortable early 12-0 lead and eventually lost only two matches during the evening.

Boxing—**March 1, 1947 (H):** With the score tied at 3-3, the outcome of the Penn State match was in the fists of the "heavies." Both 175-pound Bill Richey and heavyweight Art Hughlett responded with knockouts, leading to a 5-3. Even the loyalist of Spartan fans would have wagered against the plucky Hughlett, outweighed by 45 pounds, before he dropped his opponent in the second round. It was the first-ever team victory over the Nittany Lions.

Boxing—**March 14, 1947 (H):** Perhaps it was the change of venue. After suffering seven straight road losses to the Wisconsin Badgers, the scene shifted to Jenison Fieldhouse, and the Spartans finally topped the eventual NCAA champions, 5 1/2-2 1/2. Or was it a question as to whom the opponent had really been? At Madison, Badger Athletic Director Harry Stuhldreher said it was the university's "B" team that had bowed to MSC. Meanwhile, coach Lou Zarza told reporters he understood the Spartan squad was competing in a varsity match. If so, it was the first varsity loss for the Badgers in two years.

Baseball—**April 19, 1947 (H):** Before 3,000 chilled fans in the home opener, Marty Hansen cracked out four hits, and Ed Barbarito three hits to lead the convincing 9-0 win over the University of Detroit. Don Harris, the winning pitcher, was credited with the four-hit shutout.

Baseball—**May 6 (A) & May 27 (H) 1947:** For the first time since 1930, the Spartans swept the two-game series from Michigan, 2-1 and 8-1, as Robin Roberts gained credit for both victories with complete games. In the first game, State scored both tallies in the opening inning. Pat Peppler led off with a three-bagger, Dick Massuch singled and following a wild pitch, Ed Barbarito

scored Massuch with a base hit. Three weeks later the game was iced with a six run fifth inning, featuring a double by Peppler and triples from the bats of Roberts and Marty Hansen.

ATHLETE OF THE YEAR

Gale Mikles (1945-1948C) was described by Wrestling Coach Fendley Collins as one of the most versatile wrestlers he ever developed at Michigan State. He had the speed of a sprinter, the agility and suppleness of a dancer, and the athletic poise of a champion. Gale lost only one match in four years of dual-meet competition while capturing the National AAU 145-pound title as a freshman and the National Collegiate 155-pound crown as a junior in 1947. He settled for the NCAA runner-up spot one year later as a senior. Following graduation, Mikles became the Spartan assistant coach from 1951-1960 and later served for many years as chairman of the MSU Department of Health, Physical Education and Recreation.

Gale Mikles

IN THE SPARTLITE

Baseball: Highlights of the spring trip were: (a) Pat Peppler's five hit performance (including two home runs) in the first Georgia game; (b) Dick Mineweaser's first inning three-run homer leading to victory in the second Georgia game; (c) the offensive outburst of 18 hits off Newberry pitching (the total included two triples and a double by Dick Massuch, and a pair of doubles and a triple by Marty Hansen; and Dirk Dieters pitched a three-hit shutout); (d) the five hit, ten strikeout performance by freshman Don Harris in the first South Carolina game; and (e) Frank Bagdon's game winning pinch hit in the ninth inning of the Duke game. Ed Barbarito and Marty Hansen scored on his single to break a 2-2 tie.

In the season closer, Robin Roberts was matched against the Ohio State star, Pete Perini. Each man allowed only six hits with Roberts having the edge in strikeouts, nine to two. In the end, a run scored from the game's only error, on a ground ball off the bat of Fred Taylor (latter day OSU basketball coach). The Buckeyes prevailed, 2-1.

Basketball: Senior Dan Pjesky, letterwinner and sometimes starter, had his career end abruptly when he slipped on a wet spot on the floor of Jenison and severely twisted his knee during a preseason workout.

The 86-36 humiliation at Lexington, Ky., was the most one-sided defeat in the school's history. This infamous record would stand until the 107-55 replacement-team loss to Indiana on January 4, 1975. State scored first in that UK game, but they did not score another field goal until just before halftime, at which time they trailed 50-11.

Boxing: The 10th annual NCAA tournament was held in the University of Wisconsin fieldhouse on March 27-29, with the Saturday night finals drawing a capacity throng of 15,000. In addition to capturing his second title, the undefeated Chuck Davey was awarded the John S. LaRowe trophy, given to the competitor who best exemplifies boxing ability, sportsmanship, and proper conduct as a participant. Art Hughlett, Ernie Charboneau, Pat Dougherty, Bill Richey, and Dan Hickey all failed to reach the finals. Hickey's elimination was particularly disappointing. He actually won his semi-final bout, but in the process, suffered an eye cut that prevented his continuation in the tournament. The man he defeated went on to take the title. The top scoring teams were: Wiscon-

sin, 24; Idaho, 12; MSC, 8; Penn State, San Jose, and Syracuse, 6 each.

Cross Country: Coach Brown looked to the new season and the emergence of a new star, Jack Dianetti, who had suffered a leg injury and was unable to compete in 1945. As a prep star in East Rochester, N.Y., Dianetti had gained nationwide recognition by capturing the National AAU 1,500-meter title.

The season opened on a 25-31 losing note over the hilly layout at State College, Pa., with the finish at New Beaver Field during halftime of the Michigan State-Penn State football game. The run for first-place honors was a thriller. Trailing Gerry Karver, the leading Lion, by 11 seconds at the four-mile turn, Dianetti slowly closed the gap over the final mile. One can only imagine the roar from the football crowd during the closing quarter-mile in the stadium as the Spartan freshman came up one-tenth of a second short of winning the race.

Dianetti finished fifth among 140 entrants at the annual IC4A meet in New York City.

For the third straight year, the Drake Bulldogs left East Lansing with the NCAA team trophy. Meanwhile, led by Dianetti (14th), Ed Kiezenski (39th), and Jim Gibbard (50th), the Spartans placed sixth in the field of 20 teams vying for the title.

Fencing: The season concluded with the Spartans earning 24 1/2 points and finishing fifth in the NCAA championships held in Chicago. Earning the team points were Ed Popper, 6; Al Kwartler, 6 1/2; Jacob Venema, 5; Bill Lacey, 4; John Connell, 2; and George Custer, 1.

In a traditional post-season display of dominance over his pupils, Coach Schmitter single-handedly defeated the nine-man varsity squad, 18-9. His scores were 7-2 in foil, 7-2 in sabre, and 4-5 in epee.

Football: On the short end of the 39-14 score at Lexington, Ky., Coach Bachman and his team suffered more than a loss to the Wildcats. Russ Reader tore cartilage in his right knee and missed the remainder of the season; Ed Bagdon sustained a shoulder separation; Jim Zito lost several teeth; Pete Fusi reinjured his ankle; Steve Sieradski left the game with bruised ribs; and both Mark Blackman and Rus Gilpin endured banged-up noses.

Golf: Most consistently in the Spartan line-up were Bob Tansey, Brien Charter, Dunc Fisher, Bob Billig, and Jack Gale. Howard Visger, Don Vantine, and Jack Monteer also contributed over the six-win season.

Swimming and Diving: Even though once more defeated by Michigan, the outcome of this annual meet was no longer a given. The meet would eventually hinge on the final event, the 400-yard freestyle relay, in which the Wolverine quartet touched-out the MSC foursome of Jim Duke, Bob Allwardt, Orlin Johnston, and Abel Gilbert, to gain the 45-39 victory.

Thirteen hundred Spartan fans crammed into the seats at Jenison pool to watch Ohio State demonstrate why they were the national collegiate champions, as they handed MSC their second setback of the season, 47-37.

Again hosting the CCC championships, the Spartans racked up a record-shattering 102 points, posting their fifth straight title.

George Hoogerhyde performed impressively at his first NCAA championship meet, held in Seattle. He opened the competition by setting a new freshman record in winning the grueling 1,500-meter freestyle event. Before the weekend was complete, the Grand Rapids ace would place second in the 220-yard freestyle and fourth in the 440-yard event. Rounding out the scoring was a sixth place in the breaststroke by Dave Seibold; a sixth by the medley relay trio of Will Cooley, Paul Seibold, and Jim Duke; and a fourth-place finish by the 400-yard freestyle relay quartet of Gilbert, Johnston, Duke, and Allwardt. The accumulated total of 18 points would garner a fourth-place finish in the team standings.

Tennis: After 24 years as head coach, Professor Charles Ball stepped down and was replaced by a member of the physical education staff, Gordon "Jake" Dahlgren.

With only two lettermen, Bob Malaga and Roger Cessna, returning, the 1947 tennis team was bolstered by three transfers: Jack Shingleton, from Western State; Bob Chuck, all the way from the University of Hawaii; and Al Reynolds, who came from the University of Kentucky. Cessna, the team captain in 1947, recalls his subtle recruitment of Reynolds:

"During 1946 we played Kentucky, and I faced Al Reynolds at the number-one position. During the match Al mentioned that he was thinking of transferring to another school, and I suggested State. As a result we got a fine number one player for the next two years."

The most lop-sided defeat of the season was the 8-1 loss to the College of William & Mary during a spring trip in Virginia. Later that spring, William & Mary would win the coveted team title at the NCAA championship in Los Angeles.

Track and Field: For the first time ever, MSC won both the indoor and the outdoor Central Collegiate conference titles. Jack Dianetti captured both the 440- and 880-yard indoor runs, sharing the spotlight with such future Olympians as Wayne's Lorenzo Wright and Baldwin-Wallace's Harrison Dillard. The only other Spartan first place came in the pole vault, as Bob Vosburg and Francis Bowerman shared in a three-way tie at 13 feet. Outdoors, Bob Schepers was the champion at 220-yards. He then teamed with Bob Fraser, Bill Fraser, and Harold Mayhew to capture the 440-yard relay. Jim Gibbard then replaced Mayhew to form the winning quartet for the one-mile relay.

With a winning time of 3:25.7, Jim Fraser, Schepers, Mayhew, and Dianetti successfully defended MSC's sprint medley title at the Drake Relays. Dianetti, running the half mile anchor leg, was ten yards off the pace in fifth place as he took the baton. The "Rocket" made up the deficit with a brilliant closing lap to win.

Wrestling: Another trio of standout Oklahoma freshmen joined the squad in 1947: 121-pound Gene McDonald and 128-pound Dick Dickenson, both from Tulsa, and Bob Gang of Perry. By now, of the 23-man squad, 10 had come to East Lansing following prep careers in Oklahoma.

At the national championship in Champaign, Ill., MSC scored 11 points and finished in fourth position behind Cornell College 32, Iowa Teachers College 19, and Oklahoma A&M, 15. Heading the Spartan entrants was Gale Mikles, who, with a pin, captured the 155-pound title that had eluded him in 1946. In the consolation bouts for third and fourth places, Don Johnson was a winner at 136 pounds, while both Don Anderson (165 pounds) and Dickenson (128 pounds) met defeat.

Dick Mineweaser crushes a long fly to center field.

SPARTAN SCRAPBOOK
— SOCCER COACHES (1956-2003) —

The idea of an MSC soccer team was initially introduced in 1928 and pictured above with a fledgling lacrosse team.
The venture lasted but one year. It would be another 28 years (1956) before soccer would resurface at MSU.

Gene Kenney (1956-69)

Payton Fuller (1970-73)

Ed Rutherford (1974-76)

Joe Baum (1977-)

MSC
1947-1948

TALES TO TELL

On May 19, it was announced that Bob Brannum, first string center at the University of Kentucky in 1944, would transfer to Michigan State. He had been demoted to the Wildcat second team in the post war 1946-1947 season, and, according to the UK coach, Adolph Rupp, he "wasn't good enough" for the varsity squad. Taking issue with the famed coach, the 6' 5" Brannum packed his bags and headed to East Lansing. Under NCAA policy of the time, he gained immediate eligibility and played one season at MSC (1947-1948). Dr. Robert Jones, the Lansing dentist, had been the "recruiter." Doc had been acquainted with the big Kansan while they were both in the U.S. Army the year before at Camp Hood in Texas. As luck would have it, MSC had scheduled a 1948 home contest against the University of Kentucky, and by game day, January 10, they had recorded a 5-2 record with the undefeated Wildcats coming to town nationally ranked number one. Rightfully expecting a memorable match up, 14,967 fans came through the turnstiles, setting a Jenison attendance record that was never again surpassed.

That evening, Bob Brannum nearly gained total revenge for his "treatment" in Lexington as he led all scorers with 23 points, including a pair of field goals in the final two minutes of play which knotted the score, 43-43. With precious time remaining, Tony Waldron's long field goal was matched by the Cats, and then a pair of UK free throws spelled the difference, 47-45. Dropping a meager four of 17 free throws in the second half had sealed the doom for State. In the post-game interview, Adolph Rupp, the Kentucky coach, never mentioned Bob Brannum. Over the season, the transplanted center averaged 15.6 points per game and gained All-American honors. Choosing to forego one final year of eligibility, in 1949 he entered the professional ranks. In a 1998 telephone interview, Brannum recalled that 1948 MSC-Kentucky game and his obvious satisfaction of having outscoring Lou Groza, his replacement at Kentucky, 23 points to 10. Reminiscing, Brannum was also assuring that in the ensuing years, he and Coach Rupp had an amiable relationship.

HEADLINES of 1948

- Thor Heyendahl, the Norwegian adventurer, along with five companions, sails the Pacific from South America to Polynesia on a raft named Kon-Tiki.
- Oak Ridge (Tenn.) National Laboratory begins to develop peaceful uses for atomic energy.
- Peter Goldmark of Columbia Records develops the 33 1/3 rpm or long-playing (LP) phonograph record.
- In its first year, Ted Mack's *Original Amateur Hour* becomes the most popular show on television. Also, *The Ed Sullivan Show* premieres but initially receives poor viewer response.

SCOREBOARD

	W	L	T	Avg.
Baseball	10	14	1	.420
Track and Field	2	2	1	.500
Football	7	2	0	.777
Basketball	12	10	0	.545
Tennis	13	4	0	.765
Cross Country	2	1	0	.667
Swimming and Diving	8	2	0	.800
Wrestling	9	0	0	1.000
Fencing	6	3	0	.666
Golf	6	6	0	.500
Boxing	4	3	1	.563
Gymnastics	1	5	1	.214

TEAM OF THE YEAR

Their undefeated 9-0 season record endorses the 1948 wrestling team as one of the school's best ever. The dual-meet schedule was no walk in the park, with matches against Cornell College (Iowa), the 1947 NCAA champions; Iowa State Teachers College, the 1947 NCAA runners-up; and both the 1947 and 1948 Big Ten champi-

ons, Illinois and Purdue, respectively. Competing in the NCAA championships at Lehigh University, the Spartans placed men in five of the eight weight classes to roll up a team total of 28 points, five shy of the eventual champions from Oklahoma A&M. Dick Dickenson captured the 136 1/2 pound title, while Gale Mikles at 160 1/2 and heavyweight Bob Maldegan were both runners-up. Placing fourth were Gene McDonald (125 1/2) and Don Anderson (147 1/2). Two other entries, Jack Hancock and Dan Goldsmith, had the ill-luck of drawing eventual tournament finalists in their opening rounds and consequently failed to advance.

MAKING HISTORY

The Olympic Games, interrupted by World War II since 1936, were reinstated in 1948 and held in London, England. Five 1947-1948 Michigan State athletes, two alumni, and an incoming freshman represented Uncle Sam in four different sports that summer. The USA wrestling squad included a pair of Spartans. Heavyweight Bob Maldegan was runner-up at the trials and earned the trip as an alternate, and 160-pound Lee Merrill, captain of the 1942 MSC team, won a position on the team by defeating Gale Mikles on a split decision at the trials. He would later earn a bronze medal in London. Two swim-

The 1948 wrestling team. (Front row, left to right) J. Kreiner, R. Gang, P. Sullivan, D. Anderson, R. Dickenson, G. McDonald and J. Hancock. (Back row, left to right) coach F. Collins, J. Dowell, D. Goldsmith, R. Maldegan, B. Waterman, J. Brentar and G. Mikles.

Bob Maldegan, MSC's heavyweight star, was a member of the USA's 1948 Olympic team.

mers gained spots on the team at the trials held in Detroit. George Hoogerhyde qualified as an alternate on the 800-meter freestyle relay and Howard Patterson made it as one of three entrants in the 100-meter backstroke. Patterson, a Saginaw sophomore, swam a 1:09.9 in the preliminaries, one-tenth of a second shy of advancing to the finals. Others earning spots were boxers Chuck Davey, along with freshman-to-be Chuck Spieser, and two walking specialists, alumnus Ernest Crosby and sophomore Adolph Weinacker. The latter would finish first among America's entrants in the 50,000-meter event at those XII Games.

The year opened with an announcement that Michigan State would commence an intercollegiate team in gymnastics under the tutelage of George Szypula, a three-time NCAA champion at Temple. The community was introduced to the new sport with an exhibition during halftime of the October 18 football game against Iowa State. That initial team was comprised primarily of raw talent gleaned from physical education classes and included Devern Chubb, Pat Carnahan, Peter Zenti, Gordon Thomas, Arnold Nelson, John Robuck, Louie Beechnau, Ivan Towns, George Newcombe, Jack Wyatt, and Jack Parker. Competition was engaged in six events: horizontal bars, parallel bar, tumbling, swinging rings, side horse, and trampoline.

GREAT STATE DATES

Cross Country—**November 1, 1947 (H):** Backed by the performances of Bob Sewell (third), Clark Atcheson (fourth), Tom Ireman (fifth), Jack Dianetti (sixth) and Kevin Higgins (eighth), the Spartans managed to edge the previously undefeated Penn State harriers, 26-31. Avoiding construction on campus, an alternate course had been laid out for the race, and the trail was marked with a white line. On Saturday morning a road scraper used to smooth the road for football traffic erased the line. This caused several runners to make an improper turn and negotiate a detoured route over a short portion of the race.

Football—**November 29, 1947 (A):** The final game of coach Biggie Munn's first Spartan season was an easy 58-19 victory in Honolulu against the University of Hawaii. It was then that Biggie and his staff initiated a long and lasting friendship with Tommy Kaulukukui, who at the time was coach of the Hawaiian team. After leaving collegiate coaching, Kaulukukui would later direct an impressive list of Pacific Islanders toward East Lansing, Including Billy Kaae, Bob Apisa, Dick Kenney, Charles Wedemeyer, Charley Ane, Larry Cundiff, Roger Lopes, Jim Nicholson and Arnold Morgado.

Basketball—**December 18, 1947 (H):** Before 7,633 fans in Jenison, Michigan State opened the season with a satisfying 43-38 victory of the University of Michigan. Assistant Coach Al Kircher handled the team as Ben VanAlstyne was at home convalescing from an appendectomy he had undergone on December 8. Michigan held the lead at halftime, 26-24, and State finally took control four minutes into the third quarter. The 6' 5" Bob Brannum, a transfer from the University of Kentucky, was a standout as he led all scorers with 14 points on five field goals and four free throws.

Basketball—**December 23, 1947 (H):** Not since 1928 had MSC faced a team from Indiana University, but when the occasion was presented 19 years later, the 1947 edition of Michigan State basketball took full advantage before 6,000 spectators. Playing in only his third game for the Green and White, Bob Brannum displayed why local fans would begin filling the remaining bleacher seats of Jenison as the season progressed. He was the heart of the State team, scoring 23 points, followed by Bill Rapchak with 11 and Bob Geahan and Don Waldron with eight each. Though State led 34-30 at halftime, the

Hoosiers came back after intermission, tying the score four times and leading at 50-49, 54-51, and 60-56. Finishing in a flurry over the final two minutes, Brannum and Rapchak scored four points each to secure the 64-60 victory.

Basketball—**December 29, 1947 (H):** Harvard was successfully stalling out the clock while leading 44-40, and many fans were headed for the exits as the fieldhouse clock had turned red indicating less than one minute to play. It was then that Bill Rapchak stole the ball and tossed in a looping field goal from the corner. Another steal ensued with tens seconds remaining in regulation, and Bob Geahan wasted little time as he burst through the defense to tie the count at 44-44. Leon Hess foolishly committed a foul with no time remaining. As the shooter toed the mark, fans shouted and screamed in hopes of distracting him. Sure enough, the ball bounced from the rim and it was overtime. During the five-minute extra period, the Spartans took command and outscored the Ivy Leaguers, 9-3, for a 53-47 victory.

Wrestling—**January 16, 1948 (H):** Trailing 13-5 at the end of five matches, State gained nine points by sweeping the final three bouts to upset Iowa Teachers College, 14-13, in the season opener. Gale Mikles started the comeback when he defeated the NCAA champion at 155-pounds, by a 3-0 score. Gale suffered a sprained ankle on an early take-down but had it taped and continued to gain the decision. John Dowell followed with a 3-2 decision at 175 pounds to close the scoring gap at 13-11. Bob Maldegan answered the call at heavyweight, as he slowly piled up a winning 6-1 score to the delight of the 4,126 spectators at Jenison.

Track and Field—**January 24, 1948 (H):** It would have seemed unlikely to have matched the closeness of the 66-7/12 to 66-5/12 Ohio State-MSC dual meet of 1947; but, the two squads were at it again one year later as once more the Spartans prevailed, this time by a 57-1/6 to 56 5/6 difference. Victory did not come until Jack Dianetti crossed the finish line four yards in front of the Buckeye anchorman to win the final event, the mile relay. Once more, the speedy duo of Horace Smith and Fred Johnson were the primary contributors, each with a pair of firsts. Smith equaled Fieldhouse records in the high hurdles (9.0) and low hurdles (8.3). Johnson captured the 75-yard dash in 7.6 and likewise bettered a Jenison record with his leap of 24' 8-3/4" in the broad jump. Prior to his heroic relay leg, Dianetti captured the

Jack Tierney registered a knockout in the Spartans' 1948 season-opening match.

880 in a time of 1:57.8, and Bob Sewell won the most exciting race of the evening when he raced from 10 yards behind to win the two-mile in 9:46.8

Wrestling—**January 24, 1948 (A):** Taking the decision in every weight class, State shutout Ohio State, 24-0, before a crowd of 1,800 in the Buckeye gymnasium. Winners, from 121 pounds to heavyweight were John Hancock, Gene McDonald, Dick Dickenson, Pat Sullivan, Don Anderson, Glen Waterman , who replaced the injured Gale Mikles, John Dowell and Bob Maldegan.

Boxing—**January 30, 1948 (H):** The largest crowd in Spartan boxing history, some 3,786 fans, watched State open its season with a 6-2 victory over Minnesota. Knockouts were registered by Chuck Davey, a two-time NCAA champion who put his opponent away at 1:40 of the second round, and Jack Tierney, who stopped his 145-pound opponent at 1:20 of the third round. Other Spartan win-

ners were Ernie Charboneau at 125 pounds, John Buda at 165 pounds, light heavyweight George Smith from the football team, and backup heavyweight Art Hughlett.

Wrestling—**February 7, 1948 (A):** Bert Waterman, competing against Illinois at 155 pounds, suffered a broken collar bone when he was thrown to the mat with an attempted hip lock. As the meet wound down and State still trailed 11-9, Bob Maldegan turned the tide with a win in the heavyweight division and a team lead of 12-11. The matches were not over. In a pre-meet agreement, the 165-pound square-off would complete the evening of competition. It seems the Illini wrestler had a conflict with a classroom examination earlier in the evening. Gale Mikles clinched the team's win, 17-11, by pinning his "scholar" opponent at the 5:45 mark of the opening period.

Swimming and Diving—**February 14, 1948 (H):** Dual-meet records were shattered in four events during the easy 63-21 victory over Indiana University. The Spartan 300-yard medley relay of Don Korten, Paul Seibold, and Bob Alwardt established a new mark of 2:59.7; Jim Duke lowered the 100-yard freestyle standard to 53.7; Korten clipped five full seconds from the previous 150-yard backstroke record of 1:43.9; and Dave Seibold set a new mark of 2:26.7 in the 200-yard breaststroke.

Wrestling—**February 23, 1948 (A):** The Spartans topped the University of Michigan, 19-8, for their eighth straight win. It was the most dominant performance ever over the U of M. Winners by decision were Gene McDonald, Dick Dickenson, Don Anderson, Gale Mikles, and John Dowell. Heavyweight Bob Maldegan closed out the evening with a pin.

Basketball—**February 24, 1948 (A):** Trailing Notre Dame at intermission, 28-16, Coach VanAlstyne replaced Hugh Dawson with six-foot-five Jack Wulf. Along with Bob Brannum, also six-foot-five, the pair began to control the boards. In the first eight minutes of the third quarter, State racked up 17 points while limiting ND to three. A basket by Bill Rapchak gave MSC a 33-31 lead, and then the teams traded baskets, with Rapchak and Robert Robbins (not to be confused with Robin Roberts) leading the scoring over the closing minutes. Hanging on for a 54-50 victory, it was the first MSC defeat of Notre Dame at South Bend since 1923.

Tennis—**April 28, 1948 (H):** New coach Frank Beeman, saw his squad open the home season with a 6-3 victory over Michigan. It was MSC's first tennis victory over the U of M since 1943, when Beeman himself captained the State team. Earning points for the Spartans were Jack Shingleton, Bob Chuck, Jim Fleischmann, and Don Waldron in singles matches, plus the doubles teams of Captain Al Reynolds-Shingleton and Bob Malaga-Chuck.

Baseball—**May 4, 1948 (A):** Described as the most exciting game of the season, After eight innings, the Spartans trailed the U of D 5-1 with Titan ace Bob Miller (Philadelphia Phillies, 1949-1958) still on the mound. Then, with RBIs by Frank Bagdon, Ed Barbarito, Joe Bechard, and Ed Zbiciak, State scored four times in the ninth to send the game into extra innings. Finally, in the twelfth, Dan Urbanik opened with a single to right field and moved to third on Jack Dillon's hit and run single. Dillon stole second and Urbanik scored on a fielder's choice. Barbarito then came through with his fourth hit of the afternoon, driving in Dillon. The Titans failed to counter and that was it, MSC 7, U of D 5.

Tennis—**May 7, 1948:** One of the most gratifying encounters of the spring was the 6-2 win over Illinois, the 1947 Big Nine runner-up team. The competition was fierce as Jack Shingleton turned in the only two-set victory. In a match that took longer than three hours to complete, Bob Malaga eventually subdued his Illini opponent at the number-three position, 6-8, 13-11, 8-6.

Golf—**May 8, 1948 (H):** For the first time since 1940, the Spartans defeated Ohio State in a dual meet by a slim 14-13 score. Bob Tansey led the way with a one-under-par 71, taking three points in the process. Ray Newman's 75 and Captain Don Jarrard's 77 also gained team points in the singles competition. Point gathers in the foursomes were the teams of Tansey-Dunc Fisher and Jarrard-Ray Newman.

Baseball—**May 12, 1948 (A):** Unleashing a 10-hit attack that included two base hits by Pat Peppler, Frank Bagdon, and Joe Bechard, State topped the U of M, 7-3. The game, played in a drizzling rain, was shortened by the weather to a seven-inning affair. Lou Bloch, who relieved Dick Dieters in the second, was credited with the win. Twice he had to pitch out of tight spots after the Wolverines had loaded the bases.

Lynn Chandnois

ATHLETE OF THE YEAR

Lynn Chandnois (FB 1946-1949, BK 1947) was a stellar running back during an era in which MSC football basked in the national spotlight. Playing on both sides of the ball (frequently for the full 60 minutes), the Flint Central product was a consensus 1949 All-American pick. Offensively he averaged 6.34 yards per carry during his four-year career. Now, one-half of a century later, the Chandnois name remains atop the team record book with the longest run from scrimmage (90 yards), the season rushing average leader (7.48 yards), career interceptions (20), and career interception yards (384). He is also listed among former Spartans in 12 other statistical categories. Although not a starter, he contributed as a member of the 1947 basketball team. As the Pittsburg Steelers' number-one pick, he played seven years professionally (1950-1956) with that franchise, being named to the All-Pro squad three times. In 1952 Lynn was selected as NFL Player of the Year by the Washington Touchdown Club.

IN THE SPARTLITE

Baseball: The prospects for 1948 looked excellent until the lure of major league bonuses swept the team of key performers. Robin Roberts was lured away by a $25,000 signing bonus from the Phillies. Robby, of course, commenced a 19-year major league career that would end with 286 pitching victories and induction into baseball's Hall of Fame in 1976. Additional losses included shortstop Marty Hansen, also to the Phillies; Rod Morgan to the Yankees; freshman Don Harris to the St. Louis Browns; and first baseman Dick Massuch, to the Dodgers.

Basketball: Twice MSC met defeat by DePaul and their All-American 6' 7" center, George Mikan. The 52-42 road loss was played as part of a doubleheader in the famed Chicago Stadium. Even with Bob Brannum's emergence as the game's top scorer with 19 points, State was never in it after the opening 15 minutes.

Boxing: George Smith, the popular field-goal kicker on the football team, earned a spot on the 1948 boxing squad as a light heavyweight.

Chuck Davey suffered the only blemish in four years of collegiate boxing when he suffered a cut near his eye at the close of the opening round against the University of Virginia. The bout was concluded and recorded as a draw.

The weight divisions for the NCAA championships that year were adjusted to equate to the international metric weight standards that governed Olympic competition.

At the NCAAs, the fast-moving Davey became only the fifth man in the tournament's history to win three titles. Earlier on the card, Ernie Charboneau found the Olympic-year weight classifications to his liking. Engaging a slim field of only seven competitors in the flyweight division (112-pounds), he captured State's fourth ring championship. Teamwise, MSC finished a distant second behind the host Wisconsin Badgers. A total of 49,800 spectators sat through the three days of action, completely shattering the former attendance record of 38,900, established at Madison in 1947.

Cross Country: In 1947, following 16 successful years as head coach, Lauren Brown stepped aside to devote full measure to his job as director of the college mimeograph department. Karl Schlademan, who had been coaching the track and field team since 1941, took charge and became the school's first two-sport coach since 1930 when John Kobs served in a dual capacity for ice hockey and baseball.

Biggie Munn (third from left) with his first coaching staff at Michigan State. (Left to right) Duffy Daugherty, Forest Evashevski, and Kip Taylor.

Led by Jack Dianetti, Tom Irmen, Walt Atcheson, Bob Sewell, and Kevin Higgins, the Spartans finished fifth at the IC4A meet and sixth at the NCAA meet, which was again run over the campus course at MSC.

Fencing: Nick Kerbawy, sports information director from 1944-1948, had a flair for eye-catching news fillers and unique prop-staged photo shots. An example of the former was the following: "George Armstrong Custer III, great grand nephew of the late American Civil War general and Indian fighter, was a 1948 member of Michigan State's varsity fencing team."

At South Bend, Notre Dame rallied in the sabre, the final event of the match, to edge State, 15-12 and keep their record clean. The Irish outscored the Spartans 8-1 in sabre to erase an 11-7 deficit. The Spartans were particularly strong in the epee, in which Chandler Washburne was 3-0, and both Ed Popper and Gerry Payton finished the day at 2-1.

Entering the NCAA tournament, Charlie Schmitter's squad placed seventh in the team standings.

Football: With the arrival from Syracuse of the new head coach Clarence "Biggie" Munn and his staff excitement prevailed in anticipation of the new era.

Biggie jettisoned the black and gold uniforms of the Bachman period and introduced the home and away options that, with slight variation, still prevail. A white winged leather helmet, similar to that of the Bachman uniform (without an "S"), was worn in one game, that fall's 55-0 shellacking in Ann Arbor. Perhaps Biggie was superstitious, as that headgear was never again seen in varsity combat.

One of the two losses of 1947 was particularly costly. In the fifth game, against Kentucky, George "Little Dynamite" Guerre broke his leg as he hurled himself over the goal line for the team's only score. George recalled that "Bear" Bryant, the UK coach, was his first visitor in the hospital after the game.

A student-government sponsored "card section" was introduced during the homecoming game against Iowa State. Approximately 800 students used individually held colored cards to form giant-sized messages visible to those seated across the field.

Gymnastics: Ivan Towns proved to be the first Spartan gymnastics star. In the Western Conference open meet at Chicago, he captured first place in the trampoline.

Hopes of a Spartan gaining a spot on the USA Olympic team were dashed when the talented freshman, Mel Stout, failed the first qualifying test, finishing in one of top eight spots at the National AAUs hosted by Penn State.

Swimming and Diving: The quality of performance in the Central Collegiate Championships was improving. Four of the winning times of the nine swimming titles exceeded the performances posted in the concurrently run Big Ten meet. Included among those bettering the Big Ten performances were Don Paton in the 50

yard freestyle, Abel Gilbert in the 220-yard freestyle, and George Hoogerhyde in the 440-yard freestyle.

The quartet of Abel Gilbert, George Hoogerhyde, Bob Allwardt, and Jimmy Duke combined for a 3:31.0 winning time in the 400-yard freestyle relay at the NCAA meet in Ann Arbor. Other point-gatherers were Don Paton with a third place in the 50-yard freestyle, Don Korten with a sixth place in the 150-yard backstroke, a fourth and fifth by Hoogerhyde and the fourth place medley relay team of Howard Patterson, Paul Seibold, and Duke. Accumulating 21 points, the Spartans finished in third place.

The season concluded at the National AAU championships in New Haven, Conn. Led by two third-place finishes by Hoogerhyde, the Spartans garnered 17 points and fourth place.

Tennis: The 36-year-old coach, Gordon "Jake" Dahlgren, who had been on medical leave since November, succumbed to cancer on February 26, 1948.

A youthful Frank Beeman, Lansing city singles champion and just five years removed from his senior year as an MSC star, took over the head-coaching duties for a squad that would complete an impressive 13-4 season, including victories over Ohio State, Michigan, Purdue, Chicago and Illinois.

In the final meet of the southern trip, North Carolina, led by Vic Seixas, blanked State, 9-0. Seixas would later become U.S. Open, Wimbledon and Davis Cup champion.

Track and Field: Highlighted by sweeping the top three spots in both the 60-yard dash and the low hurdles, MSC held a 52-47 lead over Michigan with one event remaining in their indoor dual meet at Ann Arbor. After watching the team scoring change hands seven times during the evening, the Wolverines managed to win the final event, the mile relay, ending the meet in a 57-57 tie.

In a losing cause to Penn State, 77-54, Jack Dianetti was the star. He set a new course record with a 1:54.5 in the 880-yard run, followed by a winning 48.6 quarter-mile and a come-from behind anchor leg win in the mile relay.

Tom Irmen was discovered by Coach Schlademan during an intramural meet in 1947. In his first year as a varsity runner, Tom cracked the Central Collegiate Conference mile indoor record with a time of 4:21.9. In the spring, he broke the University of Illinois' field record in the two-mile event with a time of 9:21.4.

Waiting one year following his transfer from Drake, Bill Mack competed unattached in various meets during the winter and spring. At the indoor National AAU championships in New York, he placed third in the one-mile run.

Paige Christiansen, a junior from Washington, D.C., copped the IC4A 120-yard high-hurdle title with a time of 14.9 seconds.

Wrestling: Both Gale Mikles and Dick Dickenson completed the dual-meet season undefeated. Mikles scored four falls and won four decisions in eight appearances while Dickenson scored one fall and eight decisions in nine matches. Bob Maldegan and Don Anderson each suffered one setback in nine square-offs. Gene McDonald, who posted a 7-2 won-loss record, and John Dowell, with five victories in six bouts, rounded out Coach Collins' winning line-up.

For the fourth consecutive year, the Walter Jacobs Trophy, awarded annually to the Spartan who scores the most team points, was earned by Mikles who totaled 39 points. Maldegan with 37 points and Dickenson with 36 finished a close second and third.

MSC
1948-1949

TALES TO TELL

The day of acceptance into the Big Ten Conference, December 12, 1948, was a day of rejoicing as this affiliation would have great impact on the school's athletic program, as well as its stature as an educational institution. Yet, there was an immediate negative jolt. It seemed that membership had been offered with an understanding that the Jenison athletic scholarships, deemed improper, must be immediately phased out. These awards had been providing room, board and tuition to a fixed number of Spartan student athletes of the day. With personal sacrifice, men would now be set adrift. Ironically, the "inappropriate Jenison" was a facsimile to the latter date NCAA-approved athletic tender program.

Four Spartan baseball players would soon find that conference jurisdictional powers could even be retroactive. During the summer of 1948, third baseman and captain Danny Urbanik, center fielder Ed Sobczak, catcher Frank Bagdon, and pitcher Charles "Buz" Bowers joined other collegians competing within a Vermont resort league. In lieu of expenses incurred, each player would receive a stipend of $175, a financial arrangement totally acceptable by the NCAA governing body. Prior to that 1948 season and from a unilateral position contrary

to the NCAA, the Big Nine conference banned its member-school players from playing in that Vermont league. By the time the matter of the "Spartan Four" had been brought to the attention of the commissioner's office, it was late May of 1949. Belatedly, their eligibility then became an issue. In shocking disbelief, on June 3, Kenneth "Tug" Wilson, the Big Ten commissioner, ruled against further eligibility for the Spartan quartet. As expressed by coach John Kobs:

> "I can only say that I feel very sorry for the boys and I think an injustice has been done to them. The injustice part comes in this . . . they were charged with some inadvertent circumstance that occurred before we were admitted to the Big Nine, and we were living up to our rules at the time and those of the NCAA. This retroactive aspect is unfair."

Sobczak and Urbanik were seniors and consequently missed only the remaining three games on the 1949 schedule. For the other two, the decision had far reaching implications. Bagdon, a junior, lost his final year eligibility and Bowers was through as a collegian after having played only in that spring of 1949.

HEADLINES of 1949

- Brief bathing suits for women, called "bikinis," are introduced to the American fashion scene.
- The world's first training shoe is launched by the German sportswear manufacturer Adidas.
- The permanent headquarters of the U.N. is dedicated in New York City.
- Johnny Marks, songwriter, writes the popular holiday song, "Rudolph the Red-Nosed Reindeer."

SCOREBOARD

	W	L	T	Avg.
Baseball	19	8	1	.696
Track and Field	5	0	1	.917
Football	6	2	2	.700
Basketball	9	12	0	.429
Tennis	12	6	0	.667
Cross Country	2	0	1	.833
Swimming and Diving	8	1	0	.888
Wrestling	6	1	1	.750
Fencing	3	5	0	.375
Golf	3	5	0	.375
Boxing	4	3	1	.563
Gymnastics	1	5	1	.214

TEAM OF THE YEAR

Newcomers Warren Druetzler, the sophomore sensation, and Bill Mack, the transfer star from Drake University, teamed with the veteran trio of Tom Irmen, Robert Sewell and Jack Dianetti to accomplish the first-ever grand slam in collegiate cross country history. The Spartan quintet captured the IC4A, NCAA and National AAU titles during the fall of 1948. It was the beginning of a dynasty that garnered seven national titles in 12 years.

MAKING HISTORY

In the summer of 1948, Fred W. Stabley, who had served as news editor in MSC's department of public relations, was named MSC's sports editor. He replaced W. Nicholas Kerbawy, who resigned to accept the position of director of public relations for the Detroit Lions football team.

The 1948 cross country team. (Front row, left to right) T. Irmen, W. Mack, R. Sewell, J. Dianetti and W. Druetzler; (Back row, left to right) manager L. Johns, G. Hunt, C. Atchinson and coach K. Schlademan.

Fred Stabley later became Michigan State's sports information director.

GREAT STATE DATES

Football—**October 9, 1948 (H):** Against Hawaii, the Spartans ran up 10 touchdowns for their highest scoring total since 1932, but it was the wild-passing Rainbows who gave the 30,281 East Lansing fans some added entertainment. The visitors' two quarterbacks threw 52 forward passes, completing 23 for 306 yards. Also, the visitors' bare-footed kicker presented a long-range field goal exhibition at half time. The final score read: Michigan State 68, Hawaii 21.

Cross Country—**October 23, 1948 (A):** By a score of 21-36, the Spartans opened the season by defeating Penn State, the defending NCAA champions. Howard Ashenfelter, the ace Lion runner, bettered the 18-year-old course record with a time of 25:03.2. Four Spartans followed the winner: Bill Mack (second), Tom Irmen (third), Warren Druetzler (fourth), Bob Sewell (fifth), and Jack Dianetti in seventh place.

Football—**November 20, 1948 (H):** The Spartans shutout Washington State, 40-0, for their fourth straight victory in which they scored 40 or more points. The first of six touchdowns concluded the opening 80-yard drive with Bud Crane bolting over from the one-yard line. Before the first quarter had run out, two additional TDs had raised the score to 19-0. Lynn Chandnois scored from the 14-yard line following a fumble recovery, and a 5-yard George Guerre to Ed Sobczak pass concluded a 10-play 94-yard drive. The final three scores came in the second half of play, two by Chandnois and the concluding marker on a last quarter 12-yard run by the reserve halfback, sophomore Everett Grandelius George Smith succeeded on four of six conversion attempts.

Basketball—**December 18, 1948 (H):** The 49-43 victory over Iowa was the first win over a Big Nine foe since being invited to join the conference one week earlier. Trailing early, State played cautiously most of the way but finally took the lead at 37-35 and then outscored the Hawks, 12-8, over the final five minutes of action. The contest unveiled a new star in Jim Snodgrass, a 6' 1" sophomore from Pierceton, Ind., who led all MSC scoring with 16 points

Basketball—**December 29, 1948 (H):** In their seventh game of the season, MSC hosted, not Mississippi State, not the University of Mississippi, but Mississippi College of Clinton, Miss. As it turned out, this small college was capable of only a small score as the Spartans notched their fourth win of the schedule, 74-28. The MSC total was the fourth highest in the school's basketball history. Coach VanAlstyne engaged 13 players with forward Bill Rapchak and reserve Bob Stevens each scoring 14 points to nearly equal the total score for the visitors.

Basketball—**January 22, 1949 (A):** When the points of the MSC-Wayne game were totaled, it was reminiscent of the 1930s. At the end of regulation, in a game played before 3,100 fans at the Detroit Fairgrounds Coliseum, the score read 29-29. Thereafter, it took two overtime periods before Bob Geahan dropped in a winning one-handed set shot to give MSC the 37-35 decision. The game statistics revealed "believe it or not" numbers for a winning team: State had hit on 15 of 82 field goal attempts for a paltry shooting percentage of .163.

Wrestling—**February 7, 1949 (H):** For the second year in a row, the Spartans defeated Cornell College of Iowa, the 1947 NCAA champions, by a score of 15-13. The victory came on only two "legitimate" wins during the afternoon, from Bill Buckingham and Bob Maldegan.

Four additional points came on a pair of draws and the remaining five points were awarded in the 145-pound division when Don Anderson's opponent was disqualified for an illegal body slam.

Track and Field—**February 17, 1949 (H):** In the only indoor dual meet of the season, the Spartans more than doubled the score against Ohio State, 79 1/2-34 1/2. Featured performers in the 12-event program included Jack Dianetti, with a new team-record 4:15.8 mile run and Horace Smith, who bettered his own fieldhouse record with a 6.2 in the 75-yard low hurdles. George Alderton of *The Lansing State Journal* suggested that this was the "best track team to ever carry the colors of Michigan State College."

Basketball—**February 19, 1949 (H):** In MSC's sixth win of the season over a major opponent, Bill Rapchak, ace forward, poured in 29 points for a modern Spartan scoring record as he paced his team past the favored University of Virginia, 62-43. The Whiting, Indiana, junior netted 12 field goals and five free throws to eclipse Sam Fortino's record of 26 points made during the 1945-1946 season against Syracuse. The Spartan zone defense gave the Cavaliers plenty of trouble as the UVa star, Joe Noertker, the nation's second leading scorer with a 22-point average, was held to two field goals and a single free throw.

Swimming and Diving—**February 19, 1949 (H):** In defeating Iowa State, 53-28, three varsity records were bettered. Both Don Paton and Dave Seibold bettered their own standards, Paton with a 23.2 in the 50-yard freestyle and Seibold with a 2:23.7 in the 200-yard breaststroke. Howard Patterson swam a 1:37.4 in the 150-yard backstroke to erase the 1:39.7 mark of teammate Don Korten.

Boxing—**February 26, 1949 (H):** The Michigan State boxers pulled a stunning surprise by defeating Penn State's highly favored team, 5-3. Art Hughlett, heavyweight, pulled out the victory when, with the meet all even, he decisioned the Nittony Lion football star, Chuck Drazenovich.

Swimming and Diving—**March 3, 1949 (H):** Coach McCaffree always seemed to have an eye for gaining attention to his swimmers with record-seeking performances in seldomly competed events. Such was the case amidst the easy 50-32 victory over Wayne in the final dual meet of the season. Don Korten, Don Miller, Hal Shoup, Howard Patterson and Rod Quigley teamed to better the listed standards by Yale and Ohio State in

the 600-yard and 750-yard backstroke relays. Similarly, Al Omans, Dave Seibold, Howard Wilson, Jack Seibold, Dick Robie, and Mack Goodwin, joined to erase 1939 performances by Ohio State and Michigan in breaststroke relay races ranging from 800 to 1,200 yards.

Fencing—**March 4, 1949 (A):** Winning their third and final match of the season, Coach Schmitter's squad topped Northwestern 17-10. The Spartans won the epee and foil events by scores of 7-2, and the Wildcats took the saber competition, 6-3. in singles matches. Vern Andrews, John Probert and Bill Lacey each won all three of their matches for State.

Golf—**April 19, 1949 (H):** MSC golfers came from behind to defeat the University of Wisconsin, 18-15, in a match played over the Walnut Hills course. Jim Anderson and Duncan Fisher had the best cards of the day with 76s. Also scoring team points in the foursome and twosome formats were Bob Fairman, Rex Newman, Don Wawzysko, Bill Haynes, Don Perne and Cliff Taylor.

Tennis—**April 25 (H) & April 26 (A), 1949:** Coach Frank Beeman's squad demonstrated their depth as they blanked the U of D 8-0 and Wayne University 9-0 on successive days. Individual winners on Monday were Bob Malaga, Bob Fleischmann, Tom Martin, Mike Yatchman, Jerry Teifer and Dan Perillo. Bruce Brevitz replaced Teifer for the shutout against the Tartars on Tuesday.

Baseball—**May 6 (H) & May 7 (H), 1949:** The pair of victories over Ohio State were of two different varieties, 5-4 and 14-0. The first game was an extra inning affair in which the Bucks scored twice in the eleventh after two were out. State came back with three runs on hits by Jack Kinney, Frank Bagdon, Ted Maupin and Buzz Bower, who had just "put out the fire" in relief. On the next afternoon, Bower, the sophomore from Wayland, Massachusetts, returned to the mound where he continued to baffle the OSU batters, surrendering a trifling four hits. Defensively, Ohio State supplemented the 12 hit Spartan attack with four errors, four wild pitches, and seven bases on ball. First baseman Ted Maupin and shortstop Joe Barta each collected three hits.

Track and Field—**May 7, 1949 (A):** Supplementing the indoor victory over the Buckeyes, Michigan State's power-packed team defeated Ohio State outdoors, 79 1/2-52 1/2, in what was the Bucks' first dual-meet loss in the horseshoe since 1940. MSC had two double winners. Fred Johnson swept to victories in the 100-yard dash (9.9) and broad jump (22' 11 1/2") while Horace Smith copped

both hurdle events (14.3 and 23.4). Other winners for Coach Schlademan were Bob Schepers in the 220 (22.0), Dave Peppard in the 880 (1:56.1), Jack Dianetti in the mile (4:20.1), and Tom Irmen in the two-mile (9:24.7). Fran Bowerman earned a first-place tie with a 13' effort in the pole vault.

Track and Field—**May 14, 1949 (A):** Horace Smith, the IC4A indoor champion, swept both hurdle events in eye-popping times (14.0 and 22.5), as the Spartans routed Penn State 83 1/2-47 1/2 before 5,000 spectators on a rain-soaked track at State College. Once more sharing hero honors with Smith was Fred Johnson who won the 100-yard dash in 9.7 and the broad jump at 24 feet. Other MSC firsts were posted by Zach Skokos in the 440 (49.7); Jack Dianetti in the 880 (1:54.6); Warren Druetzler in the two-mile (9:21.5); John Mueller with a 49'-2/8" in the shot put; Mike Bowerman with a 13 foot vault; and Carl Miller who tossed the discus 141'-11 1/2".

Tennis—**May 18, 1949 (A):** Forced into the fieldhouse to play on indoor courts because of the weather, MSC's tennis forces defeated Purdue 7-2. With wins in the number one and number two single's positions, Bob Malaga and Bob Fleischmann each stretched their season's record to 9-1.

ATHLETE OF THE YEAR

In his sport of boxing, Chuck Davey was something special. Other than having to settle for a draw from a cut eye in one meet during his junior year, Davey won every time he answered the bell over a four-year Spartan career. This would translate to a remarkable fourth NCAA championship in 1949, a feat that was never again equaled. Furthermore, Davey was a three-time recipient of the John S. Larowe Trophy, awarded annually to the athlete "whose sportsmanship, skill and conduct perpetuate the finest attributes in college boxing." No other fighter won that award more than once. After his college years, which included a spot on the 1948 USA Olympic team, Chuck took his talents to the professional level (see story 1952-1953).

IN THE SPARTLITE

Baseball: The 1949 outfield trio was one of the best in the school's history. George Rutenbar, Ed Sobczak and Jack Kinney finished one-two-three in team batting for the year with respective averages of .377, .347 and .344.

Shortstop Frank Bagdon voluntarily moved behind the plate after Hoby Landrith, a glistening sophomore catching prospect, was enticed into signing professionally with the Cincinnati Reds.

Basketball: In a 57-47 losing cause against Minnesota, Bob Geahan, senior co-captain, played one of the best games of his career. He was all over the floor on defense and led the team in scoring with 14 points. In the Gopher line up was Bud Grant, who would later gain fame as a successful head coach for the NFL's Minnesota Vikings.

Against Notre Dame, in his final game as head coach, Ben VanAlstyne saw his squad lead a late charge only to come up short 43-41. At halftime, the veteran Spartan coach of 23 years was honored by friends and former players.

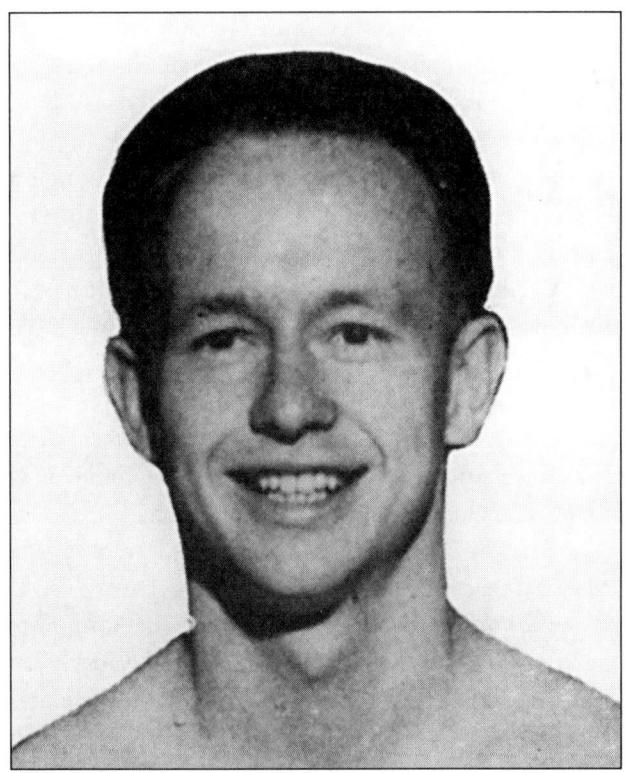

Chuck Davey

Boxing: The seventh meeting between MSC and Wisconsin ended in a 4-4 draw before 6,000 spectators in Jenison Fieldhouse. It was a case of the pupil almost giving the teacher a lesson, as coach George Makris led his squad against his alma mater, headed by the veteran coach, Johnny Walsh. The Badgers, defending NCAA champions, trailed after seven bouts but then managed to win the heavyweight battle to gain the tie.

After working his way into the 1949 starting line-up at the 135-pound spot, Bert Davey, Chuck's bother, was sidelined following a near fatal accident on February 11 when he was struck by an automobile and suffered two broken legs.

MSC hosted and then nearly captured the 12th annual NCAA tournament, April 7-9, drawing close to 7,000 fans to Lansing for the Saturday night championships. With three finalists and a team-leading 13 points, there was reason for Spartan optimism. If at least two of the Spartan finalists (Pat Dougherty, Chuck Davey, and Jim Gemmell) emerged as winners, the team title would go to Michigan State. It wasn't to be. Dougherty lost a split decision in his 135-pound match and Gemmell dropped a unanimous decision at 165 pounds. Chuck Davey, pride of the squad at 145 pounds, was the only MSC champion. He thus concluded a four-year career undefeated as a college boxer in 35 bouts, and stepped forward as the only four-time champion in the history of the NCAA tournament. Also, for the third consecutive year, Davey was awarded the LaRowe trophy as the outstanding boxer in the tournament. The final scoring for the top five schools read: LSU 20, MSC 18, San Jose 17, Idaho 13 and Minnesota 11.

Cross Country: The assignment of Schlademan to the cross country post caught the eye of Bill Mack (no relation to Walter), who had led Drake University to the 1946 NCAA championships with his fourth-place finish. Prompted by the departure of the Drake coach to the University of Kansas, Mack seized the moment to join Schlademan, whom he highly respected. After sitting out 1947, the required one year as a transfer, Bill Mack's impact on the MSC program became extensive.

Football: It apparently took stadium dedications to lure the U of M to East Lansing for football games. That was the occasion on their visit in 1924 and their next visit in 1948. The newly enlarged Macklin Stadium was packed with 51,526 spectators, doubling the biggest home crowd heretofore assembled. Although the Wolverines would pull it out in the final quarter, 13-7, it was obvious another "super power" was emerging in the state.

The most disappointing game of the fall was not a loss, but a 14-14 tie at College Park, Pa. A questionable call by an official left the team angered and disappointed. George "Little Dynamite" Guerre intercepted a Penn State pass in the end zone and raced the length of the field. With the numerous twists and turns it was suggested that Guerre may have run closer to 150 yards on the play. Down and exhausted in the end zone, George looked back to see an official's penalty marker lying on the grass some 70 yards down the field. His dramatic run had been nullified. Days later, upon dissecting the game film the "phantom" clip that had cost the record run and Spartan victory could not be detected.

Other than both being from Flint, George Guerre and his backfield mate, Lynn Chandnois, were a contrasting pair. George (5' 7 1/2", 160) was a "jitterbug" who would stop and bounce in any direction to avoid the grasp of the 200-pound linemen of the day. "Chad" (6' 2", 192) used his smooth, yet high-pumping, stride to circle the ends and break into the open. They were truly a "dynamic duo." During their collegiate careers each ran for more than 100 yards in six games.

Golf: The 1949 team was built around veterans Duncan Fisher and Rex Newman, along with outstanding newcomers Cliff Taylor and Bill Hanes.

Taylor finished the eight-meet season with the team low average of 75.5 with Fisher one stroke back at 76.5.

Gymnastics: Mel Stout, George Szypula's first nationally ranked competitor, was a consistent star all season long. As a one-man team at the NCAA championships in California, he captured the parallel bar crown and was second in the all-around to place MSC sixth in the team standings.

Swimming and Diving: Racking up a record 105 points, State once more hosted and dominated the Central Collegiate Conference meet. George Hoogerhyde led the way with three first places, while Don Paton established a new pool record of 22.8 in winning the 50-yard freestyle.

It seems that Coach McCaffree had his swimmers properly tuned for the NCAAs as they finished in a seventh place tie with Northwestern. Paton moved up one spot from 1948 to take runner-up in the 50-yard freestyle; Breaststroker Dave Seibold finished third behind the gold and silver medalist from the Olympics in London; Don

Korten and Howard Patterson placed fifth and sixth in the backstroke; and Hoogerhyde was fourth and sixth in the 100- and 220-yard freestyle events.

Tennis: In the May 16 loss to Michigan, Bob Malaga was a surprise winner in the number-one position as he defeated Andy Paton, the Western Conference singles champion.

Track: The Spartans swept the three IC4A team titles of 1948-1949. Having won the cross country championship in the fall, the track and field team next scored 35 2/5 points to capture the indoor title before a crowd of 10,000 in Madison Square Garden and later won the outdoor meet at Randall's Island in New York. Broad jumper Fred Johnson and hurdler Horace Smith led the way with gold medal performances in both meets.

One week following the IC4A indoor victory, first-place finishes by Johnson, Smith, and distance ace Bill Mack, the Spartans successfully defended their Central Collegiate title in Jenison Fieldhouse.

In what could be labeled as the greatest dual track meet in Michigan State history, Karl Schlademan and his team flew west on April 15 to engage the eventual NCAA champions from Southern California in a truly East-vs.-West affair at the Los Angeles Coliseum. On paper it was predicted to be an evenly matched affair, and at the conclusion, when the points were totaled, it couldn't have been closer. Each team won seven events. For MSC there was: Bill Mack with the nation's fastest outdoor half-mile of the season in 1:52.2; Fred Johnson, a double-winner in the broad jump (25' 2") and low hurdles (22.9); and Carl Miller in the discus (142' 3-7/8"). In three events MSC "slammed" the Trojans with Mack, Tom Irmen and Warren Druetzler going one-two-three in the mile (pictured at right) and Horace Smith, Paige Chrisiansen and Jesse Thomas sweeping the high hurdles. In the two-mile run, Irmen, Druetzler and Bob Sewell so completely outclassed the Trojan runners that they eased up, locked arms, and finished in a triple dead heat with a time of 9:48. After 13 events MSC had 61 points to USC's 54. The meet rested on the concluding event, the mile relay, and the 12,293 mostly partisan Trojan fans, rose to their feet as USC led all of the way. Although anchorman Jack Dianetti narrowed the 30-yard gap in half, USC had the win and the final score read 61-61.

At the National Collegiate championships in Los Angeles, the Spartans finished in a disappointing fourth place behind Southern California, UCLA, and Stanford.

Leading the way were Johnson with a first-place in the broad jump; Horace Smith with fourth in the 220-yard low hurdles; Paige Christiansen with a fourth-place finish in the high hurdles; and Warren Druetzler, with second in the two-mile run.

Wrestling: Following the undefeated season of 1948, State opened 1949 with a 13-13 tie with Big Nine runner-up Illinois. That afternoon, from 121 pounds to heavyweight, the Spartans lineup as follows: Jack Kreiner,

Tom Irmen (left), Bill Mack (center) and Warren Druetzler finish the mile in the top three places.

Joe DiBello, Dick Dickenson, Don Anderson, Pat Sullivan, John Dowell, Gene Gibbons and Bob Maldegan.

It had never happened before and has not been accomplished since—back-to-back shutouts. First, on January 14 at Manhattan, Kan., the Spartans combined five decisions and three pins for a 32-0 blanking of Kansas State. One week later, at Columbus, they gained decisive wins in all eight classifications to register a 28-0 victory over Ohio State.

Two Spartans managed runner-up spots at the NCAAs in Fort Collins, Colo. Dick Dickenson lost in the final match to relinquish his 136-pound title. Also in the finals, Bob Maldegan led the two-time champion from Oklahoma A&M 3-2 with 30 seconds remaining, but a quick takedown turned the tide for the favored Aggie. Two weeks later Big Bob would compensate for this disappointing loss by capturing the national AAU title.

EXTRA! Joining the Big Ten

The date was Dec. 12, 1948, and on the next day the *Detroit Free Press* headline read: "Michigan State College is Voted Berth in Western Conference." Following four decades of hope and three years of formal requests, the long wait was over.

Michigan State president John Hannah, the architect of the crusade to join the Big Ten

While the Big Nine would be reborn with its former title, Big Ten, Michigan State seized the coveted offer of membership to further authenticate its rocketing sports program of the 1940s. Yet becoming the new "kid sister" wasn't easy. First, it was expected that University of Michigan officials would be non-supportive and that's exactly what President Hannah noted in his book, *A Memoir*, 32 years later:

"We knew from the beginning that there would be no friendly consideration of Michigan State's cause by the Big Ten if the University of Michigan had its way. We anticipated that Ann Arbor would be unfriendly and critical and obstructive, and that is exactly what they were."

Adding to the anxiety of this occasion was the apparent serious competition from the University of Pittsburgh. Navy Captain Tom Hamilton, retired as athletic director at the Annapolis Academy, had recently assumed a similar role with that western Pennsylvania school.

Hamilton was the same officer who had worked closely with the Big Ten commissioner Kenneth "Tug" Wilson in establishing the Navy's pre-flight programs on many of the conference campuses during World War II. Concern prevailed in the Green and White camp…would this be payback time?

Fortunately, the master planner, Michigan State president John A. Hannah, had been patiently orchestrating this dream of a conference berth long before that weekend in Chicago. He had hired a winning football coach in Clarence "Biggie" Munn, expanded the athletic program and waged a cunning, cleverly conceived and perfectly executed campaign conducted at the college president's level.

Even prior to 1946, the year the University of Chicago withdrew from the conference, there was a Midwest consortium of university presidents made up of all the Big Ten presidents, plus the presidents of the University of Kentucky and Michigan State. These twelve gentlemen met regularly in Chicago for a full day at least twice a year to talk over common problems. John Hannah never missed one of those meetings. He once admitted: "I followed the practice that I always followed in new organizations of keeping my eyes and ears open and my mouth shut." If Hannah found another school president interested in athletics, a special point of relationship would immediately be encouraged. The particularly close personal friendship gained with Dr. Louis "Lou" Morrill of the University of Minnesota would eventually pay dividends. It would be Morrill who became Michigan State's most outspoken advocate and its prime campaigner for conference membership. He, in turn, enlisted the aid of president Fred Hovde of Purdue and support followed from the other land-grant institutions: Illinois, Ohio State and Wisconsin.

Looking beyond this, Hannah recognized the need to first persuade the majority of the conference schools that MSC would be an asset as a new member. The fact that Michigan State was a rapidly growing institution seemed convincing enough. Enrollments had tripled from 5,284 in 1945 to a burgeoning 15,208 in 1947. Furthermore, a massive post-war building program had included a stadium addition raising the capacity from 28,000 to 51,000.

Football players Hal Vogler (left) and George Guerre (right) get a lift during the jubilant celebration on Grand River Avenue.

The hard-working and discerning MSC president found it comforting to have been invited earlier to Evanston for a fact-finding session where he spoke to those who would eventually cast the deciding votes: the conference faculty representatives. It seemed clear to Hannah that serious consideration was being given to the possibility of Big Ten membership. Yet it was difficult to erase from his mind the "run-around" the Spartans had been getting in the preceding three years. Regardless, on Dec. 12, 1948, John Hannah, quietly confident, was back at his campus home where students were "cramming" for term-end examinations. In Chicago, akin to expectant fathers, his representatives were pacing the floor beyond closed doors of the meeting room at the University Club.

The conference faculty representatives continued to wrestle with the question of membership for what would total nearly 15 hours.

Finally, at approximately 5:00 P.M., in parliamentary procedure, professor Henry Rottschaefer, the University of Minnesota faculty representative, made a motion for a vote. A second to the motion was provided by Purdue's professor Herman Freeman and the resolution for-or-against Michigan State was at hand. It was later proclaimed to have been a unanimous ballot. One fact was certain, the suspenseful weekend had finally run its course. Committee chairman, professor Frank Richart of Illinois greeted the Spartan delegation of athletic director Ralph Young, football coach "Biggie" Munn and faculty representative dean Lloyd Emmons. Richart had fulfilled his pledge that the Spartans would be given a definite answer following the Sunday meeting. His statement ensued:

"The faculty committee has voted that Michigan State be admitted, the admission to take effect as such time as a committee of the faculty representatives shall have certified to the conference that the rules and regulations and other requirements of the conference are completely enforced."

In festive response, an estimated 5,000 jubilant students poured onto East Lansing's Grand River Avenue, obstructing traffic along that primary artery as they celebrated the event of the day—a great excuse for interrupting studies. The celebration continued beyond midnight and eventually surged over to Cowles House, the residence of John Hannah. The president greeted the students and commented:

"I am sure that we can live up to Western Conference (Big Ten) standards, we are a great university. We needed this to put us ove the hump in the minds of a few remaining skeptics."

As quickly as the campus had erupted, serenity was regained.

Within five months, the on-site review committee had fulfilled its task and formal admission to the conference was announced on May 20, 1949. The episode was not without concessions.

In addition to forfeiting the Jenison Scholarship program, one additional disappointment was soon realized. Although beginning with the 1950-1951 academic year, Michigan State would enter into the Big Ten championship format, it would not become a candidate for the football title until 1953. Ultimately, for those who were patient, the general issue of football scheduling would become a major plus when, along with Michigan, games with Minnesota, Ohio State, Purdue, Indiana, Iowa, Illinois, Wisconsin and Northwestern would soon dot the fall calendar.

MSC 1949-1950

TALES TO TELL

Following an absence of 20 years, an announcement in 1948 heralded the return of ice hockey as MSC's 13th intercollegiate sport beginning in 1949-1950. This time the skaters moved indoors. Plans were put in place to renovate old reliable Dem Hall as an indoor facility, and work soon began on construction of the necessary refrigeration system. As for spectator space, the 3,000 balcony bleacher seats, which served basketball as recently as 10 years earlier, only had to be dusted off. The husky vertical I-beams that obstructed the view of cage fans remained as a reminder for the new breed of Spartan rooters.

Harold Paulsen, a former University of Minnesota star, was hired as coach, and by the time of the first tryout on February 21, 1949, 206 eager hopeful candidates had signed up. These preparatory measures began prior to the renaissance season, which opened nearly one year later, on January 12, 1950, against Michigan Tech, a team coached by a future Spartan coaching hero, Amo Bessone. Coach Paulsen was likely more prophetic than he had

intended to be when, in a January 8 *State Journal* story, he said, "We will be fortunate if we win one match. All I hope is we can make it interesting for the spectators."

Sure enough, MSC was not fortunate, as all 14 games ended up in the loss column with opponents scoring double-digit totals on 10 occasions. As an enticement of attracting spectators to this on-going losing season, those holding ticket stubs were permitted to a free skate following each game until closing time at 10:45 P.M.

TEAM OF THE YEAR

By 1950, in his ninth year at the helm, swimming and diving coach Charles "Mac" McCaffree had positioned MSC as one of the elite programs in the nation. Over an eight-year stretch from 1945-1952, his teams finished in the top four at the NCAA championships six times. The 1950 edition was particularly special. Posting a 10-1 dual meet record, it was the first State team to

HEADLINES of 1950

- Nine men wearing Halloween masks hold up Brink's, Inc., a Boston armed-car service, and escape with $1 million in cash.
- Prices of the time include bread 14 cents/loaf, milk 84 cents/gallon and gasoline 18 cents/gallon. A new automobile could be purchased for $1,511 and the average annual income was $3,216.
- Good Ol' Charlie Brown enters American culture as cartoonist Charles Schulz creates the legendary comic strip "Peanuts."
- The first credit card is introduced through the Diners Club.

SCOREBOARD

	W	L	T	Avg.
Baseball	19	9	0	.679
Track and Field	3	0	0	1.000
Football	6	3	0	.666
Basketball	4	18	0	.182
Tennis	8	10	0	.444
Cross Country	2	0	0	1.000
Hockey	0	14	0	.000
Swimming and Diving	10	1	0	.909
Wrestling	5	5	0	.500
Fencing	7	1	1	.833
Golf	4	6	0	.400
Boxing	6	0	0	1.000
Gymnastics	1	5	1	.214

Williams won both diving events followed by teammate Danny Simpson; Howard Patterson successfully defending his 150-yard backstroke title, and Dave Seibold won an unprecedented third straight championship in the 200-yard breaststroke.

MAKING HISTORY

Running before 40,139 track fans at the Los Angeles Coliseum Relays on May 20, 1950, the two-mile relay team of Bill Mack, Don Makielski, Warren Druetzler and Dave Peppard outdualed a USC quartet and topped the existing world record in the process. The winning time of 7:31.8 bettered the old mark of 7:34.5 set by a University of California team in 1941. Anchor Bill Mack overcame a slight Southern Cal lead on the final lap as he passed and beat the Trojan runner to the tap by two-tenths of a second. Splits for the MSC runners were: Peppard (1:55.7), Druetzler (1:52.0), Makielski (1:52.3), and Mack (1:51.8).

defeat "Mac's" alma mater and perennial power, the University of Michigan. This had been a McCaffree goal since he had come to East Lansing in 1942. The single loss of 1950 was administered by National Collegiate champion Ohio State, 42-38. With Big Ten championship competition beckoning in 1951, the Spartans concluded their string of Central Collegiate Conference titles at eight by scoring 147 points. With the exception of the 100-yard freestyle, MSC captured every title contested. Dave Hoffman was a triple winner in the distance races; Ray

The 1950 swimming and diving team. (Front row, left to right) R. Williams, L. Cull, A. Krajczinski, J. Duke, E. Dzioba, D. Hoffman and D. Simpson. (Middle row, left to right) manager P. Melnitsky, J. Seibold, D. Robie, J. Weitzmann, R. Miller, and coach C. McCaffree. (Back row, left to right) D. Korten, R. Schumacher, C. Scholes, G. Verity, D. Miller, J. Quigley, H. Shoup and H. Patterson.

Michigan State's world record-breaking two-mile relay team of (left to right) Bill Mack, Don Makielski, Warren Dreutzler and Dave Peppard.

GREAT STATE DATES

Cross Country—**October 15, 1949 (A):** Warren Dreutzler paced all runners in setting a new Purdue course record at 21:51. The mark eclipsed the former record by 28 seconds. It was a challenging route of endless uphill and downhill sections over the school's 18-hole golf course. Don Makielski finished third, followed by Bob Sewell, Clark Atcheon, and Bill Mack, who locked arms in a triple tie for fourth. In similar fashion, Jack Dianetti, along with newcomers Francis Carey and "Red" Maloney, completed the race in a three-way tie for seventh as the Spartans scored an easy 19-44 victory.

Football—**October 29, 1949 (H):** Al Kawal, who had served as an assistant at Michigan State as recently as 1946, returned as head coach of Temple University and met a sobering 62-14 defeat. It would have been even more one-sided had Coach Munn not turned the game over to second- and third-stringers early, as a total of 42 squad members saw action. Lynn Chandnois, in his All-American senior season, was particularly impressive, scoring twice before sitting out the entire second half. He first raced 55 yards to score on a punt return and then contributed a 70-yard TD run from scrimmage. Other backs who accounted for scores were Jim Blenkhorn, Bud Crane and Jesse Thomas. The corp of receivers joined in with scoring catches by John Gilman, Bob Carey, Dorne Dibble and Bill Carey from tosses by Al Dorow, Bob

Ciolek and Bud Crane. This would end the Michigan State-Temple football series with State holding a 7-1-2 overall advantage.

Cross Country—**October 29, 1949 (H):** In front from the start, Warren Druetzler led a 22-35 victory over Penn State. The junior from LaGrange, Ill., negotiated the four-mile course in a record time of 20:24 to finish 150 yards ahead of the field. Teammate and captain, Bill Mack, placed third, followed by Jack Dianetti and Don Makielski in a dead heat for fifth and Clark Atchinson completed the scoring in eighth place.

Football—**November 19, 1949 (A):** In shutting out the University of Arizona, 75-0, the Spartans equaled the fourth highest point total ever achieved by a State team. Quarterback Al Dorow scored twice and passed to each of the Carey twins, Bob and Bill, for two more TDs. Captain Hal Vogler, who had been unable to play during the entire season because of a serious neck injury, had his chance in the final seconds of that season finale. He was sent in for one play, holding down the defensive safety position as the clock ran out.

Basketball—**December 29, 1949 (H):** After losing the first seven games on the schedule, State defeated previously unbeaten Cornell University, 61-54. The Spartan victory came in the nightcap of the inaugural Holiday Tournament in Jenison. Leading the scoring with 23 points was Danny Smith, a sophomore from Gary, Ind.

Basketball—**January 13, 1950 (H):** In the 81-64 win over Marquette, Bill Rapchak scored 34 points to smash his own modern-day, single-game scoring record of 29, set in 1949. The senior forward from Whiting, Ind., was nearly unstoppable as he hit the hoop from all sides with his two-handed push shot.

Boxing—**January 28, 1950 (A):** Chuck Spieser, the 175-pound Olympian, began his collegiate career with a resounding victory in the Spartan's 5-3 defeat of Penn State. An overflow crowd of 6,000 sat in awe as the Detroit sophomore took every round by a wide margin. Other MSC winners were Henry Amos, Pat Dougherty, Rae Johnston and Jim Gemmell. Gabby Marek's loss to Chuck Drazenovich, the Nittany Lion football-boxing star, would be the only flaw on his season record until the pair met once more in the NCAA finals.

Fencing—**February 3, 1950 (H):** In the team's most convincing victory of the year, State defeated Buffalo, 22 1/2-4 1/2, with the sabre team of Dwight Patton, Eugene Balogh and John VanDagens scoring a 9-0 slam. Schmitter's squad also had the edge in foils, 7-2, and epee, 6 1/2-2 1/2.

Wrestling—**February 7, 1950 (H):** For the third straight time, Michigan State wrestlers defeated the U of M, but it had never before been done so convincingly. The two teams divided decisions through the first four matches, with 121-pound Bill Buckingham and Bobby Gang at 135 pounds gaining the MSC wins. Beginning at the 155-pound division, the next four Spartans, Orris Bender, brother George Bender, Gene Gibbons and heavyweight Ralph Gill each scored a crisp decision over his opponent. Of all the bouts, 175-pound Gibbons was most convincing, as he demonstrated exceptional skill and strength in a dominating 7-0 victory over the defending Big Ten champion. The final team score read: MSU 18, Michigan 6.

Swimming and Diving—**February 8, 1950 (H):** Since their first meeting back in 1922, State had never defeated the U of M in a dual swimming and diving meet. Finally, 1950 was the year. The Spartans were ahead 38-34 going into the final event, the 400-yard freestyle relay. A Michigan win would have ended the meet at 42-all. The MSC quartet of Don Miller, Gordon Verity, Jim Quigley and Jimmy Duke would have none of that. After his three teammates gained a slight lead, anchorman Duke, the popular senior captain, maintained the advantage, and, accompanied by a deafening roar from a packed gallery of 1,100, finished about four feet in front.

The Spartan team of 1950 had finally done it, defeating the Wolverines 46-38. "I never felt happier in my life," Coach McCaffree said as he climbed out of the Jenison pool, dripping wet after his celebrating team had thrown him in.

Track and Field—**February 18, 1950 (H):** In the only indoor dual meet of the year, the Spartans topped Ohio State, 67-47. Bill Mack won the mile run in an impressive 4:09.6, the second fastest time ever recorded on an American indoor dirt track. The slim senior from Palos Park, Ill., defeated Len Truex by 45 yards after the Buckeye star had led the race over the first half mile.

Gymnastics—**March 2, 1950 (H):** In a triangular meet hosted by the University of Illinois, the Spartans easily handled the University of Wisconsin, 59-35. Mel Stout, the talented junior and future national champion, won three events: the high bar, parallel bars and flying rings. He placed in two additional events on the program to account for nearly half of the Michigan State point total.

Boxing—**March 10, 1950 (A):** Before an estimated crowd of 13,000, the Spartans concluded the dual meet season of 1950 with a narrow 4 1/2-3 1/2 win at Wisconsin. It was the Badgers' first defeat at home since 1933 and a sweet homecoming for Coach George Makris, a U of W alumnus. Following the first five bouts, State trailed 3 1/2-1 1/2. Then Jim Gemmell led the comeback with a decisive win in the 165-pound division. He was followed by the usually dependable duo of Chuck Spieser and Gabby Marek. Spieser was awarded a decision by the narrowest of margins, 29-28. Then it was Marek's turn. Gabby tagged Vito Parisi, the 1948 NCAA champion, early in the second round and sprawled him over the ropes. The Badger was up before the count of 10, but his coach threw in the towel, and with it the Spartans finished the season undefeated.

Baseball—**April 18, 1950 (A):** Imposed by weather induced cancellations of early regular-season games, the Spartans traveled to Ann Arbor for a rare regular-season opener against the Wolverines. Right fielder Jack Kinney smashed out three doubles that led the Spartans into the ninth inning tied, 5-5. In that final frame, shortstop Joe Barta opened with a double and then moved to third on a sacrifice fly ball. Art Ronan followed with a sharp single into left field scoring Barta with the eventual winning run. Lou Bloch, who relieved Chuck Carlson in the third, was credited with the win.

Baseball—**April 21 & 22, 1950 (H):** Under prevailing chilly April conditions, State opened at home with a pair of wins over Purdue, 8-5 and 9-3. In the first game, Jack Kinney was again the hitting star, as he collected three of the team's 11 hits, including a two-run homer that cleared the fence at the 389-foot mark. It was the Owosso senior's sixth circuit clout of the season and gave him an RBI total of 21. Sharing the spotlight was center fielder Vince Magi, who made a diving catch of a line drive with the bases loaded in the seventh inning. In the second game, sophomore Herb Schroeder, Detroit right hander, hurled a three-hit game. He tired in the final inning and lost the shutout while issuing three walks, hitting one batter and committing a balk.

Track and Field—**April 22, 1950 (A):** State opened the outdoor season with the school's first win ever against Ohio State at Columbus. It was a triangular affair with the Spartans scoring 65 1/2 points, followed by OSU with 57 1/2, and Penn State 38. Winning only five of the 14 events, MSC's superiority was traced to strength in the distance events and team depth throughout the program. Those five winners were Jack Dianetti in the 440-yard dash, Dave Peppard in the 880-yard run, Bill Mack in the mile, Warren Druetzler in the two mile, and Jesse Thomas in the broad jump.

Tennis—**May 2, 1950 (H):** Against Notre Dame, Len Brose won an endurance test in his opening set and then held on for a 12-10, 4-6, 6-2 victory. The Spartans added three other singles victories and one doubles win to edge the Irish, 5-4.

Baseball—**May 10, 1950 (H):** State captured another one-run victory over Michigan, 7-6, to take the 1950 season series. Playing in chilly weather and trailing 6-3, the home crowd was resigned to absorbing the season's first loss at Old College Field, but then things began to happen. Dick Blanchard opened the ninth with a double to left field. Art Ronan reached first base on an error and Jack Kinney loaded the bases with a blast that almost knocked the third baseman down. Suddenly the 3,000 hopeful fans were roaring with excitement. With one out, Ted Maupin rammed a clean single into center, scoring two runs. Then Joe Barta, the spectacled infielder, whacked a line-drive triple down the left field foul line that scored Kinney and Maupin with the tying and winning runs. Michigan employed 19 players and MSC 16 during the three hour, 29 minute game.

Golf—**May 27, 1950 (H):** State closed out the season with an 18 1/2-8 1/2 win over the U of Detroit.

Shooting 73s and tying for medalist honors were Rex Newman, Don Perne and Bob Tansey. Cliff Taylor and Arthur "Biff" Hills turned in 75s and Jack Zinn recorded a 77.

Bob Carey

ATHLETE OF THE YEAR

A rarity of modern times, Bob Carey (FB 1949-1951, BK 1950-1952, TR 1950-1952) not only lettered in three sports but was a standout in all three. He excelled as a 1951 consensus All-American end in football, three-year starter at center in basketball, and top-ranked shot putter in track and field (1952 Big Ten champion and NCAA third place finisher). Tied with two other past Spartans, his name still tops all other Michigan State receivers with eight touchdown receptions in one season. Even though his football responsibilities meant he would report late for basketball, he ranked third in team scoring as a junior and second in team scoring as a senior. Entering the professional ranks upon graduation, Carey played six seasons in the National Football League, four with the Los Angeles Rams and two with the Chicago Bears. His twin brother Bill also lettered in football (1949-1951) and basketball (1951-1952), while older brother Chuck lettered as a member of the 1940 football team. The Carey's were from Charlevoix, Mich., where their high school coach was Ray Kipke, a star of the 1923-1924 MAC football teams.

IN THE SPARTLITE

Baseball: Posting a season won-loss record of 19-9, Michigan State was an at-large selection in the NCAA region IV tournament at Madison, Wis. In a one-game elimination format, the Big Ten co-champion Badgers dispensed of the Spartans, 13-6. State was in it until the seventh inning, when Wisconsin struck for four runs on five hits. MSC managed 12 hits, including home runs by Joe Bechard and Bob Ciolek. Yielding nine runs before being relieved, Lou Bloch, the Spartan pitching ace, suffered his first defeat in eight games.

Basketball: Alton Kircher, captain of the 1933 team, became head coach, replacing Ben VanAlstyne, who had stepped aside after 22 seasons on the Spartan bench. One can only imagine Kircher's excitement in assuming the head position at his alma mater and then the disappointment and agony of completing a 4-18 record. Throughout those 18 losses, the scoring differential averaged 14 points. There was likely little hesitation at season's end in Kircher's acceptance of the offer to leave town and head west as a football assistant to Forest Evashevski at Washington State.

Chet Aubuchon, the great Spartan All-American, shared the torment of that losing season of 1949-1950. Leaving his coaching position at Owosso High School, he had returned to his alma mater as an assistant while pursuing a master's degree.

With early season invitational tournaments becoming popular in the 1940s, Michigan State initiated their own Holiday Tournament at Jenison on December 28-29, 1949. However, the idea never seemed to catch the fancy of local fans. In the first three years of the two-night affair, Ivy League schools such as Harvard, Cornell, Princeton and Dartmouth were featured. Even in 1952, when inviting presumably more attractive teams (Kansas State, UCLA and Notre Dame), spectator interest continued to wane, as a mere 2,425 spectators showed up for the championship game. This was enough to discourage the money counters, for it had been estimated that at least 7,500 paying customers were needed to break even. The tournament was shelved following 1952, and it would be 1980, 28 years later, before the idea would resurface as the Oldsmobile Cutlass Classic.

Boxing: During the undefeated six-meet schedule, the 1950 boxing team usually lined up as follows: Ernie Charbonneau (125 pounds), Hank Amos (130 pounds), Jack Tierney (135 pounds), Pat Dougherty (145 pounds),

Rae Johnston (155 pounds), Jim Gemmell (165 pounds), Chuck Spieser (175 pounds) and Gabby Marek (heavyweight). Spieser, the 1948 Olympian, and Marek provided great closing insurance for coach George Makris, as they jointly went 10-1-1 over the season. Gabby was a particular fan favorite, frequently going toe-to-toe as he administered four TKOs among his five dual-meet wins.

The Spartans were conceded as the NCAA tournament favorite, and three of the teams members, Amos, Spieser and Marek, proceeded to earn their way into the finals at State College, Pa. One championship victory would assure MSC of at least a share of the team title. Unfortunately, as in 1949, it didn't happen. They were shutout and State had to settle for a third-place in the team standings.

Cross Country: Running over the familiar campus layout, Karl Schlademan's squad successfully defended the NCAA crown won in 1948. The veteran team included Warren Druetzler, who finished the four-mile course as runner-up, team captain Bill Mack, Bob Sewell, Walter Atcheson and Jack Dianetti. Finishing in the second, sixth, ninth, 15th and 27th slots. The Spartan's team score of 59 was comfortably below the totals of the next three teams: Syracuse 81, Manhattan 86 and Penn State 93.

The 1949 team fell short of the triple-crown edition of 1948. One week following the NCAA title run, they raced to a second-place finish in the National AAU meet run over the six and one-quarter mile course on Detroit's Belle Isle. They lost that title to Syracuse by a single point.

Running on the IC4A five-mile course at VanCortlandt Park in New York City, the Spartans could do no better than third place.

Fencing: The strength of the 1950 team centered on John VanDagens, Bill Pierson, and star foilsman Bill Lacey, who dropped only one of 26 matches during the season. The team's 7-1-1 record was the most impressive year since 1940. The single loss on the schedule came in the opener at South Bend, Ind., when the Irish outscored MSC, 20-7.

In their fifth match of the season, against Illinois, the squads registered a rare tie, 13 1/2-13 1/2. State won both the foil and sabre by identical 6-3 scores, but the Illini took the epee 7 1/2 to 1 1/2. Bill Lacey of Detroit remained undefeated in the foil.

Schmitter's swordsmen finished with four straight road victories, over Chicago, Wisconsin, Wayne, and the University of Detroit. It was the Badgers' first defeat of the season.

Football: It was a major upset at Portland's Multnamah Stadium when Oregon State shocked MSU 25-20 in the seventh game of the season. The winning coach, Kip Taylor, had to have been overjoyed. Until that year he had been Biggie's end coach at MSC. Kip had not departed East Lansing on the greatest of terms with Munn.

Upon conclusion of the 1949 season, backfield coach Forest Evashevski followed Taylor to the Northwest, becoming head man at Washington State for a reported salary in excess of $10,000. He took freshman coach Bob Flora with him as line coach and eventually Al Kircher as backfield coach. Named in mid-February as replacements on Munn's staff were Lowell "Red" Dawson, previous head coach at Tulane and the professional Buffalo Bills, and Steve Sebo, former Spartan football ace, who had been backfield coach at Harvard University. Also filling staff positions one year earlier in 1949 had been Dan Devine and Earle Edwards.

Three seniors of 1949, Don Mason, Ed Bagdon and Lynn Chandnois, were named first team All-Americans by various section committees, and all three played in the post-season East-West Shrine game in San Francisco. In August of the following summer, Chandnois and Bagdon also played in the College All-Star game sponsored by the *Chicago Tribune.*

As the recipient of the Outland Trophy, Ed Bagdon was recognized as the national interior lineman of the year.

Joining the professional ranks, Chandnois signed with the Pittsburgh Steelers and Bagdon with the Chicago Cardinals.

Five graduates of the 1950 team entered the high school head-coaching ranks. Gene Glick went to Saginaw St. Andrews, Jim Blenkhorn was hired at Davison, Frank "Muddy" Waters began his career at Walled Lake, John Gilman started at Otsego, and Carl Cappaert signed on at Aurora, Ill.

Golf: During the 10-meet season of four wins and six losses, Captain Rex Newman scored the low average of 76.1, followed closely by teammate Cliff Taylor with a 76.2 average.

Gymnastics: In just the third season since the sport's introduction to MSC in 1948, George Szypula had put a competitive team on the floor with the 1950 edition posting a 4-4 record.

The 49-47 loss to Minnesota was as close as could be envisioned. The Gophers captured tumbling 12-4, rings 9-7 and the parallel bars 9-7. State took the advantage in two events: 10-6 in trampoline and 11-5 in horizontal bars. The two teams tied 8-all in the pommel horse.

Despite an impressive performance by Mel Stout, the University of Illinois topped MSC in a triangular meet at Champaign, Ill., 52-44. Meanwhile, Stout's three firsts were instrumental in the 59-35 defeat of Wisconsin, the third team in the meet.

Swimming and Diving: Three days following the victory over Michigan, the Spartans easily handled the Purdue Boilermakers, 54-30. Of significance that afternoon was the subtle emergence of a new star, Clarke Scholes. A mid-season addition to the squad, he won the 100-yard freestyle event in 52.8 seconds.

On the day before the Central Collegiate Conference meet, star freestyler and team captain Jim Duke of Erie, Pa., fell on the pool deck and fractured his elbow. He was out of competition for the remainder of the season.

The NCAA championships were held in the Ohio State Natatorium, where Scholes was a surprising winner, capturing the first of his three 100-yard freestyle championships. For the third year in a row, big Don Paton reached the finals in the NCAA 50-yard sprint.

Tennis: Prepared to compete in the Big Ten championships in 1951, the Spartans bowed out of Central Collegiate competition as winners by collecting nine and a half points to overcome runner-up Notre Dame's eight. Len Brose pulled the biggest upset of the tournament when he defeated the tournament's top seed, Bob David of the Irish. Other winners were Dave Mills and Dick Rieger in their respective brackets and the number two doubles team of Doug Curley and Don Perillo.

Len Brose was State's only entrant in the Eastern Collegiate meet at Montclair, N.J. He lost in the second round to a Cornell player who eventually reached the finals. Later, at the NCAAs in Austin, Texas, Brose was eliminated in the second round.

Track and Field: Once more, the Spartans faced the Southern California Trojans in the Los Angeles Coliseum, but the results were a far cry from the 61-61 tie of 1949. Crippled by injuries and ill-preparation due to miserable spring weather in Michigan, the Spartans proved to be no match for USC. This time Yale University joined in to make it a triangular affair, and the final

scoring read: Southern Cal 96, MSC 34 and Yale 32. State runners managed three firsts in the 15-event program. Bill Mack won the mile in 4:13.9, Jack Dianetti took the 440 in 48.6 seconds, and the Spartan mile relay team broke the tape in a time of 3:17.0.

With Big Ten competition one year away, this would be Michigan State's final Central Collegiate Conference indoor championship. Furthermore, with the college suffering a coal shortage, the meet was switched to South Bend where Notre Dame hosted the 23rd annual meet.

At the outdoor IC4A championships in New York, State scored 22 points and settled for third place in the team standings. Horace Smith was the Spartans' top scorer, earning second place in both the 120-yard high hurdles and 220-yard low hurdles and a fifth in the 100-yard dash. Bill Mack and Warren Druetzler finished two-three in the mile. Jesse Thomas was fourth in the high hurdles and big Bob Carey finished fourth in the shot put.

It was a record-setting spring. Bill Mack bettered the varsity mile mark with his 4:12.2; Warren Druetzler smashed the team record with a 9:33.6 in the 3,000-meter steeplechase; and Bob Carey broke the varsity shot put record in his first year of competition.

An unsung hero of 1950 was senior Adolph Weinecker, who won the National AAU championship over the 30-kilometer (18 1/2 miles) walking race conducted in Philadelphia. He defeated his nearest rivals by more than four minutes in his time of 2 hours, 48 minutes.

Wrestling: Gene Gibbons of Cleveland, a future NCAA champion, was the recipient of the Walter Jacob trophy, which acknowledged him as the team member earning the most points over the season.

Horace Smith clears a hurdle at the IC4A championships.

MSC
1950-1951

TALES TO TELL

Rigid translation of NCAA rules cost the Spartans key members of the boxing team, first in 1951 and again in 1952. Following the 1951 season opening 6-2 victory over the Quantico Marines, Gabby Marek found his collegiate career terminated. It seemed his pre-college amateur career was not in compliance with stringent NCAA rules, and he was summarily excluded from further competition. One week prior to that season's collegiate championships, the NCAA eligibility committee was at it again. This time the target was Jed Black, State's crafty 145 pounder. The sports editor of *The Daily Cardinal*, the University of Wisconsin's student paper, had blown the whistle by quoting a rule that eliminates anyone from intercollegiate matches who, after reaching their 18th birthday, engages in competition for any team other than a school team. Although it seemed that Black was guilty by strict interpretation, this time the NCAA eligibility committee recognized extenuating circumstances, and

Gerald "Jed" Black, the Janesville, Wis., welterweight was given a repricve. This favorable decision then became a factor in State's drive for the title during the NCAA championships hosted in Jenison Fieldhouse. When it came down to the final bouts on Saturday, State had two boxers remaining in the competition, Black and Chuck Spieser, the highly favored light heavyweight. Responsing to the cheers from the home crowd of 3,500, Black, the 145 pounder, engaged in a slugfest with his South Carolina opponent and it seemed the Spartan gained the better of the battle as he buckled the southerner's knees with several punishing blows in the second round. Following the three-round battle, the decision was announced in Black's favor. Along with Spieser's easy win at 175 pounds, MSU had won its second NCAA championship in three years. One year later and two weeks prior to the 1952 NCAA championships, Jed Black's eligibility case resurfaced. This time the committee reversed their decision of 1951 and ruled against the defending welterweight champion, shattering the dream of another MSC team title.

HEADLINES of 1951

- With disagreement on the conduct of the war in Korea, president Harry Truman relieves general Douglas MacArthur of his far Eastern command.
- The *I Love Lucy* TV show debuts to tremendous success, creating the mold for TV sitcoms.
- NBC begins the first network coast-to-coast television programming and CBS broadcasts the first commercial-colored television.
- Remington Rand makes the first commercially available computer, the Univac 1.

SCOREBOARD

	W	L	T	Avg.
Baseball	17	9	0	.654
Track and Field	2	4	0	.333
Football	8	1	0	.888
Basketball	10	11	0	.476
Tennis	12	4	0	.750
Cross Country	2	1	0	.666
Swimming and Diving	9	1	0	.900
Wrestling	6	3	0	.667
Hockey	6	11	0	.353
Fencing	7	3	0	.700
Golf	10	3	0	.846
Boxing	2	3	2	.429
Gymnastics	6	3	0	.667

TEAM OF THE YEAR

After recording a less-than-impressive 2-3-2 dual meet record, Michigan State hosted the 14th annual NCAA boxing championships in Jenison Fieldhouse April 5-7. Following two days of keen competition with 46 action-packed bouts, the University of Idaho advanced three men into the finals and carried a one-point lead over MSC in the team scoring, 12-11. Chuck Spieser

and Jed Black remained alive for the Spartans. If just two of Idaho's three finalists captured titles, the Vandals would claim the team trophy. Much like the disappointing final chapter for State in 1950, this time it happened to Idaho, as all three of their entries lost in title bids. Meanwhile, both Spieser and Black had their hands raised in victory, and the John Walsh team trophy was presented to Coach George Makris. Two other Spartans, Hank Amos and Leon Hamilton, reached the semi-finals before elimination. The scoring for the top five teams was as follows: MSC 21, Wisconsin 20, Washington State 17, Idaho 12, and Minnesota 11.

MAKING HISTORY

Led by Captain Len Brose who won the number one singles honors and later teamed with John Sahratian to take the number one doubles title, the 1951 tennis squad was the first Michigan State athletic team to capture a Big Ten team title. This was a successful conclusion to an undefeated 9-0 regular season record.

Jack Shingleton, former varsity player, longtime team supporter and university administrator, reminisced about that championship team:

"Winning State's first Big Ten title had its anxious moments. Len Brose, who won the number one position title by defeating the U of M's Al Hetzek, put

1951 NCAA boxing champions Chuck Spieser (left) and Jed Black (right) with coach George Makris (center)

it this way, 'We really had to sweat it out. Ken Kimble, one of our players came down with the mumps just before a match with Purdue. The highly contagious incubation period was 14 to 16 days, and the 21st day was the day we clinched the championship without anyone else catching the mumps. Had another player come down with the mumps we most likely would have lost the title.'"

However, coach Lt. Frank Beeman and his stand-in, coach Tom Martin, insisted they installed no pickle test or other mumps-detection device in the three-week period. Yet Brose and his five teammates couldn't put mumps out of mind until the championship had been stowed away.

Watson Spolstra, writing in the *Detroit News*, reported that "State's conquest came in the first Big Ten tennis meet it was permitted to enter. Coach Beeman knew he had assembled a powerhouse, but in April, shortly after his return from a southern training tour, the coach received orders reactivating him into the Army."

"I got a break when they assigned me to infantry instruction in the ROTC unit right on our own campus... it could have been Korea or some other far off place," Beeman said.

This appointment enabled Frank to stay within volleying range of Brose and the other boys, while a protege and graduate student, Tom Martin, took over the active coaching. When the squad headed for the championships at Evanston, Ill., Coach Beeman was close behind with a three-day military pass in hand.

As a result, it was a twin-coaching triumph as State swept through a nine-match schedule without a defeat before driving and lobbing to a Big Ten title.

GREAT STATE DATES

Football—**September 30, 1950 (A):** The 1950 team exploded onto the national scene with an 8-1 mark which included a thrilling, closely-fought, 14-7, defeat of Michigan, the first over the Wolverines since 1937. Sonny Grandelius, who would be the top rusher all season, scored both touchdowns. One came on a 68-yard run and the other on one of three pass receptions he made during the

afternoon. Don Coleman, beginning to gain national respect for his remarkable line play, had an impressive afternoon and was named Midwest lineman of the week by the United Press. The lead line in the *Detroit Free Press* story of October 1, 1950, read, "Michigan State hit football's glory road and soared into national prominence as it scored a smashing 14-7 upset victory over the University of Michigan."

It was a gratifying win over a team that would go on to win the Big Ten title and represent the conference in the Rose Bowl. Across the country, Spartan alums enjoyed going to work that following Monday.

As recalled by team captain, LeRoy Crane:

"Although 53 years can cloud the memory, certain events of the 1950 win over Michigan remain as clear as if it was yesterday. On our first touchdown pass from Al Dorow, Sonny Grandelius nearly dropped the ball. It hit him about belt high, he cupped his hands and arms, and then had to crouch down as the ball nearly slipped out of his arms.

Another moment of that game sticks in my mind. I was on the punting team as a blocker on the right side in the backfield. After Al Dorow kicked the ball, I ran as fast as I could down the right sideline for coverage. Their Frank Howell had received the punt and started my way, heading to my left in hopes of circling me and reaching open field. My momentum was enough to catch him, just barely, as he reversed his field. I dove, reached out, caught his foot, and down he went on their four-yard line.

After the game some of us were carried off the field. Was I proud of that team! Four years earlier I had sat in that very stadium in Ann Arbor and watched State take it on the chin from the Wolverines [Biggie's first year at State]. In that lopsided 55-0 loss, the Michigan coach rubbed it in by leaving the starting team in the game during the entire fourth period. This is when I developed a distaste for our archrival."

Cross Country—**October 21, 1950 (H):** Led by Don Makielski's first-place finish and Bob Kepford's third-place position, the Spartans finished 1-3-4-5-7 to defeat Ohio State 37-20.

Boxing—**January 6, 1951 (H):** College boxing was viewed as the "manly art of self defense," and conse-

The 1951 tennis team. The squad includes (left to right): W. Kau, L. Brose, D. Mills, D. Rieger, Keith Kimble, J. Sahration and Ken Kimble.

quently, knocking an opponent unconscious was not the desired goal. Regardless, the spectators that turned out always hopefully anticipated that a local favorite would lay an opponent out. Such was the case in the final two bouts in the 6-2 victory over the Quantico Marines. With the approval of the 1,200 fans in Jenison, light heavyweight Chuck Spieser belted his opponent, the National AAU champion, with vicious lefts and rights from the opening bell. Finally, with his rival sprawled to the floor, Spieser was awarded a TKO at 1:45 of the second round. Not to be outdone, Gabby Marek, the Spartan heavyweight and always a crowd-pleaser, followed by knocking his opponent to the canvas three times before the referee stepped in with one minute remaining in the second round.

Basketball—January 6, 1951 (A): New coach Pete Newell and the Spartans entered the school's first-ever Big Ten title chase at Evanston, Ill., with a well-earned 67-62 victory over Northwestern. Trailing 62-61 with two minutes remaining, consecutive baskets by Bill Bower, Bob Carey, and Leif Carlson sealed the win.

Swimming and Diving—January 15, 1951 (H): The Spartans had an early-season opportunity to feel good about themselves when they completely dominated the University of Michigan team, 55-29, at the Jenison pool. McCaffree observed, "This was one of the greatest examples of a team victory ever displayed by Spartan swimmers." Sprint champion Clarke Scholes and the sophomore distance ace Bert McLachlan were double winners, while both relays managed first-place finishes. In the opening relay, the 300-yard medley, George Hoogerhyde set the tone as he began 10 feet behind as anchorman,

but left the Wolverines in his wake as they came down the final length. McLachlan's time of 4:42.5 in the 440-yard freestyle was the second fastest time recorded by a collegian since 1935. There was no letup as the visitors managed only one first out of the eight races swum.

Basketball—January 20 (A) and February 17 (H) 1951: For the first time since 1934, the Spartans topped the U of M twice in one season, 49-36 in Ann Arbor and 43-32 four weeks later at Jenison Fieldhouse. The rematch in East Lansing was a particularly impressive defensive performance as they held the visitors to a mere seven successful shots out of 43 field goal attempts, a dismal .129 shooting percent. It took the Wolverines 10 minutes to score their first two-pointer, and they netted only one more before intermission. At half time it was 21-11 with State pulling away at a rapid clip. It took the visitors four and a half minutes of the second half to hit their third field goal, and nine minutes elapsed before the fourth. By then the MSC reserves were on the floor.

Basketball—January 25, 1951 (H): Enhanced by a parade of automobiles, a huge bonfire, and an address by Coach Newell, approximately 600 students attended the school's first-ever basketball pep rally prior to the home game against Notre Dame. That evening the team responded with a convincing 60-43 victory as Newell introduced a platoon system. Starting the first and third quarters were Bill Eckstrom, Tom McAuliffe, Jim Snodgrass and the Carey brothers, Bob and Bill. Opening the second and fourth periods was the quintet of Bill Bower, Leif Carlson, Ray Steffen, Gordy Stauffer, and Sonny Means. Again, the defense excelled as the Irish were held to a meager nine field goals.

Wrestling—**February 3, 1951 (A):** Headed by pins from Marty Sherman at 137 pounds and George Bender at 167, State defeated Purdue, the defending Big Ten champions, 18-11. Also contributing to the team's winning total were 157-pound Orris Bender and 177-pound Gene Gibbons, both of whom won by decision, and heavyweight Frank Kapral, who earned a draw.

Track and Field—**February 10, 1951 (H):** Led by Warren Druetzler's victories in the one- and two-mile races, along with Jesse Thomas's win in both hurdle events and second place in the broad jump, MSC defeated Penn State and Northwestern in a triangular meet at Jenison. Other winners for Michigan State were Don Makielski in the 880-yard run and Robert McClelland in the pole vault. A two-way tie for second and three-way tie for fourth in the high jump led to some weird team point totals: Michigan State 66-2/3, Nittany Lions 47-1/2, and the Wildcats 26-5/6.

Hockey—**February 15 & 16, 1951 (H):** The weekend home sweep of Michigan Tech was the highlight of an eventually unimpressive season record of 6-11-0. With the Friday night game tied at 2-2, Bill McCormick scored the winning goal with 6:32 remaining in the second period on an assist from Bill Blair. On the next night, McCormick was even busier, as he accounted for three of the Spartan goals. His third score, at 17:02 of the final period, was the insurance goal following Connie Buck's tiebreaker at 12:45. Although college hockey was making giant strides, it is interesting to note that players were still playing unusually long shifts. State called upon nine spares, and Tech's bench was even shorter with only seven additional skaters.

Gymnastics—**February 17, 1951 (A):** Mel Stout and Bob Feldmeier starred in the double dual meet, downing Wisconsin 64-32 and the University of Illinois-Chicago 67-29. Stout took firsts on the side horse, parallel bars, horizontal bars and flying rings. In addition, he took second on the trampoline and in tumbling. Against the Badgers, Feldmeier took second on the side horse, horizontal bars, and parallel bars, while against Chicago he won first on the side horse and third on both the horizontal and parallel bars.

Gymnastics—**March 5, 1951 (H):** Mel Stout compiled 26 1/2 points with four firsts and a third-place tie to lead Michigan State to the first-ever defeat of Michigan, 56-40. The versatile senior captured the flying rings, parallel bars, high bar and tumbling events. The tie came on the side horse. This being the final regular meet of the season, Stout closed out his career having outscored all opponents in dual-meet competition over his final two years. Bob Feldmeier placed second behind the captain in both the parallel and high bar and scored a fifth on the side horse. Other runner-ups were Arnold Nelson on the side horse, Ken Cook on the flying rings, and Allan Hannas on the trampoline. Additional team members gaining points were George Kuczerepa, John Walker, Jack Rauton, and Don Vest.

Baseball—**April 20, 1951 (H):** MSC 25…Wayne 1….whoa! It was the largest Spartan point total since the 31-7 romp of Armour Tech in 1922. The Spartans lashed out a total of 17 hits, including homers by Bob Ciolek, Vince Magi, Joe Rivich, Herb Schroeter and Darrell Lindley. The pitching chores were shared by Chuck Carlson, Roger Howard, and Chuck Gorman, each yielding one hit in three innings.

Baseball—**April 25 (A) & May 9, 1951 (H):** With 9-1 and 3-2 victories, State swept the two-game Notre Dame series for the third year in a row. Held to only five hits, it took a sacrifice fly to score the winning run in the second game. After the Spartans had scored a pair in the seventh inning, the Irish knotted the score in their very next at-bat. Then in the bottom of the eighth, with Joe Rivich and Vince Magi on base from walks, Bob Ciolek beat out a sacrifice bunt attempt. With the bases loaded and nobody out, Darrell Lindley lofted a ball into right field and Rivich sprinted home with the eventual winning run.

Baseball—**May 4 & May 5, 1951 (H):** Michigan State opened its first-ever Big Ten title run with a two-game sweep of the University of Iowa, 8-5 and 12-9. The Friday opener featured the effective pitching of Chuck Gorman, four double plays on defense and home runs by Bill Bower, Dick Moser and Darrell Lindley. On the next afternoon, both teams hammered the ball, State getting 13 hits and Iowa earning 10. The Hawks took the lead 3-1 with three runs in the second inning, but the Spartans responded with one in the second and then gained the lead with five in the third. After that explosion, the visitors were never able to catch up. Shortstop Joe Rivich hit a three-run homer in the sixth, and Charley Jablonski batted in a pair with a double in the seventh.

Tennis—**May 17, 1951 (H):** The MSC squad, undefeated through the regular-season schedule, easily made the University of Michigan their eighth straight victim, 8-1. Len Brose, Dave Mills, John Sahration, Dick Rieger, and Keith Kimble were all winners at singles, with Kimble working overtime in the second set, 4-6, 12-10, 6-4. Victorious in the doubles competition were Brose-Sahration, Rieger-Kimble, and Mills, who teamed with Wally Kau, the only Spartan to have suffered a loss in the singles competition.

ATHLETE OF THE YEAR

Warren Druetzler of LaGrange, Ill., was one of the greatest long-distance runner in Michigan State history. Over three years of competing in the NCAA cross country run (1948-1950), he finished fifth as a sophomore, tenth as a junior, and was runner-up in his senior year. His placing contributed to team titles in 1948 and 1949 and MSC's second place finish in 1950. As a member of the track team, Warren ran races from 880-yards to the 3,000-meter steeplechase. At the 1948 outdoor national collegiate championships held in Minneapolis, he finished second in the two-mile run. Two springs later, at the 1950 NCAAs, again hosted by the University of Minnesota, Druetzler dropped down to the one-mile run, where he captured first-place honors. His winning time of 4:08.8 was the second fastest ever recorded in the 30 years of NCAA championship competition. Twice selected by the National AAU track committee to represent the USA in overseas competition, in 1949 he was in Ireland, England and several Scandinavian countries, and one summer later he competed in Japan. Maintaining his edge after graduation, Warren earned a spot on the 1952 U.S. Olympic team. He is one of the few Spartan athletes to have been selected as the captain of two teams in his senior year.

Warren Druetzler

IN THE SPARTLITE

Baseball: The overall season record of 17-9 was impressive, but the 4-6 Big Ten record was only good enough for a seventh-place finish.

Offensive stars for 1951 were sophomore Darrell Lindsay, whose overall .418 average was MSC's highest average since 1933, and senior Captain Vince Magi, who set a team record with his 21-game hitting streak.

Basketball: Princeton, defending Ivy League champion and winner of 16 straight in two seasons, added another "W" by defeating State 52-46 in the championship game of the Spartans' Holiday Tournament. Leading the scoring for Princeton was Dave Sisler, son of baseball's Hall-of-Famer, George Sisler.

The 1950-1951 season would not only be Pete Newell's first as MSC's head basketball coach, but it would also be the school's first to be included in the Big Ten Conference title chase. The Spartans opened with four

straight wins to equal the total output of the immediately preceding season of 1949-1950.

With only seconds remaining in the eventual 50-44 win over Minnesota, the visitor's star, Whitey Skoog, was ejected for voicing unsavory comments to an official. His coach, Ozzie Cowles, became so enraged that he purposely did not replace Skoog; opting to finish the contest with only four players on the floor.

Attesting to Coach Newell's success as a defensive strategist, State's opponents over the 21-game schedule averaged only 47.5 points per game, the fourth lowest output among all major colleges. Conversely, this was not a sharp shooting MSC team, as they made only 337 out of 1034 field goals attempts for a trifling .289 percent.

Boxing: Excuses, excuses! A scheduled match with Superior State was canceled when the Lakers reported that five men had been lost to the armed forces and another two had been declared scholastically ineligible.

Cross Country: After being hit hard by graduation, coach Karl Schlademan successfully molded a 1950 squad that included returnees Warren Druetzler and Don Makielski, along with five sophomores, Jim Kepford, Mickey Walter, Wayne Scutt, Jerry Zerbe and Dick Roberts. The new-look Spartans captured the runner-up positions in both the Big Ten and NCAA championship runs. Scoring in the national meet were Druetzler as runner-up, Kepford in 12th, Makielski in 15th, Zerbe in 19th and Roberts in 23rd to finish with 55 points, only two shy of Penn State's winning total.

Fencing: Leading swordsmen for Charles Schmitter were John Van Dagens, who won 25 of his 29 duals in sabre, and Ray Todde, who earned a won-loss record of 23-7 in foil competition.

Football: It seemed that in the eyes of Big Ten officials, Michigan State was neither "fish nor fowl." When accepted into conference membership in December of 1948, it was stipulated that MSC would not be in contention for the football title or Rose Bowl participation until 1953. Yet when it was disclosed in November of 1950 that Cotton Bowl officials were making overtures, the conference commissioner, Kenneth "Tug" Wilson, nixed any thought about the Spartans performing in that New Year's Day game.

Golf: Carrying the load over the 10-3 season were captain Don Perne, Reggie Myles, Arthur "Biff" Hills, Carl Mosack, Jack Zinn, and Dick Bishop.

Firing an aggregate total of 567 strokes, Coach VanAlstyne's squad could finish no better than sixth in MSC's first-ever appearance in a Big Ten championship meet.

Gymnastics: Captain Mel Stout was a one-man scoring machine. At the Big Ten meet he set a conference record with five first places to win the all-around title. This led to MSC's 49 points and second-place showing. At the NCAAs Mel finished third in the all-around after gaining a first in the flying rings, a fifth in the high bar and sixth in the parallel bars. His 16 1/2 points thrust State into a sixth-place finish in team scoring.

Hockey: State opened the season with a 21-goal outburst, accounting for two victories over Ontario Agricultural College, 9-5 and 12-3. It would hold as the highest goal output two-game team record until the 1964-65 team found the Ohio University net for 25 goals. In the 12-3 victory, before 1,464 fans, MSC scored twice in the first period, five times in the second, and added five more during the final 20 minutes. Six of the dozen scores were netted on power plays. In the 11 losses over the season, State was outscored 78-29.

Of the team's top 10 scorers, only Canadian Dick Lord, was not a United States citizen.

Swimming and Diving: This was one of Coach McCaffree's best teams ever. Following a 9-1 dual meet season, the Spartans finished second in the school's inaugural Big Ten conference championship appearance in Minneapolis. It was then on to Austin, Texas where during three days of NCAA competition eight men would contribute to 60 team points and earn a second-place finish behind Yale University with 81. It was the highest Michigan State finish, before or since, at the annual championship meet. Clarke Scholes was a double winner in the 50- and 100-yard freestyle events; Bert McLachlan raced to a second, fourth and fifth in the 1,500-, 220-, and 440-yard freestyle events; Hal Shoup was fourth in the two backstroke events; Al Omans was third in the 200-yard breaststroke, and Dave Patton finished fourth in the 100-breaststroke. The medley relay trio of Shoup, Patton and George Hoogerhyde placed second, and the team of Scholes, Hoogerhyde, Dave Hoffman and Jim Quigley won the 400-yard freestyle relay.

Tennis: It has to be a record of some sort. State opened the regular portion of the season with five straight 9-0 shutouts against Wayne, Wisconsin, Minnesota, Purdue and Notre Dame. In the singles positions num-

ber one through number six were Len Brose, Dave Mills, John Sahration, Keith Kimball, Dick Rieger, and either Wally Kau or Doug Curley. The most consistant doubles teams were Brose-Sahration, Mills-Kimball and Rieger-Kau.

Track and Field: In a race run in the fall, Adolph Weinacker captured the National AAU 40-kilometer walking title over a round-trip course between Springfield and Urbana, Ohio. It was Weinacker's sixth national championship.

The quartet of Jim Kepford, John Walter, Don Makielski and Warren Druetzler, was the surprise of the 42nd annual Drake Relays in Des Moines, Iowa. Projected behind both Washington State and Michigan for the four-mile relay title, the foursome breezed home as winners in the sizzling time of 17:21.2, which clipped more than eight seconds from the 12-year-old relay mark of 17:29.6.

In the first year of competition as a member of the Big Ten, the Spartans of 1951 nearly pulled off a shocker at the outdoor championships in Evanston. Although not considered a real contender for the team title, with four events remaining on the meet schedule, the scoreboard read Michigan State 49, Illinois 33, Michigan 21 among the top three teams. The unhappy fact was that while the Spartans were blanked in the remainder of the program, the Illini collected 22 1/2 additional points and moved to the front with 55 1/2 points to MSC's 49. Indiana was a poor third and favored Michigan a vanishing fourth. Jesse Thomas won top honors for the weekend, with firsts in the 100-yard dash and 220-yard low hurdles, and a second in the 120-yard high hurdles. Don Makielski, an Ann Arbor senior, won the half-mile, while Bob Carey, with a 53-foot toss, was a surprise winner in the shot put.

At the NCAA championships hosted by the University of Washington, the Spartans managed 23 points to place 5th in the field of 42 schools. Leading the team was distance ace Captain Druetzler, who captured the one-mile run in an impressive time of 4:08.8; Thomas, who placed fourth and fifth in the low and high hurdles, and Bob Carey, who took third in the shot put.

Later that summer, Coach Schlademan accompanied Druetzler and Thomas to Japan for competition as members of an AAU-sponsored USA track team. During the numerous meets there, Druetzler consistently defeated the Japanese national champion in the metric mile. Also, in one meet at Yawata, the Spartan distance

ace set a Japanese national record in the 3,000-meter steeplechase. Thomas frequently captured firsts in his specialties: the sprints, hurdle events, and broad jump. Shot putter Bob Carey was also invited to join the tour, but an ROTC summer camp commitment intervened.

Wrestling: Both George Bender (167 pounds) and Gene Gibbons (177 pounds) entered the Big Ten championships undefeated in dual-meet competition and emerged with conference titles.

Although hampered by a sore rib, Gibbons dropped one weight division and captured the 167-pound class at the NCAAs held in Bethlehem, Pa. With his seven points, MSU tied Ohio State and Toledo for sixth place in the team standings.

EXTRA! FOOTBALL 28-GAME WIN STREAK

One of the longest winning streaks in NCAA history was achieved by the Biggie Munn coached teams of 1950-1953. As could be expected, over a stretch of 28 games, there were incredible finishes (Ohio State in 1951, 24-20); one-sided victories (Marquette in 1952, 62-13) and last-second squeakers (Oregon State in 1952, 17-14). After the streak-ending upset at Purdue on October 24, 1953, the Spartans reeled off another four straight wins to finish that season tied for first in the conference with a 5-1 (9-1 overall) record. It was a remarkable and memorable era of Michigan State football.

(#1) October 14, 1950 (H): Initally trailing 7-6, the Spartans eventually racked up a total of 26 first downs and 458 yards to defeat William and Mary, 33-14. Fullback Leroy Crane lead all runners with 91 yards. Everett "Sonny" Grandelius, who entered the game as the nation's fifth leading ball carrier, carried the ball 12 times for 87 yards. Near the end of the opening period and to the delight of the home crowd, Jesse Thomas gathered in a punt at his own 10-yard line, sprinted to the west sideline, and behind blocks by Ray Vogt, Don Coleman, and Doug Weaver, went all the way. The 90-yard punt return still ranks as the third longest in school history.

(#2) October 21, 1950 (H): Leading Marquette 20-6, Coach Munn inserted a new fullback, Dick Panin. The Detroit sophomore responded with a pair of touchdown runs, first from 18 yards followed by a 15-yard run. Grandelius scored on a 34-yard broken field run

and end Dorne Dibble accounted for State's other two touchdowns, catching an Al Dorow pass in the first quarter and another from sohomore Don McAuliffe in the second period. At game's end the Macklin Stadium scoreboard read: MSC 34, Marquette 6.

(#3) October 28, 1950 (A): With each team scoring five touchdowns and three successful PATs, the difference in this 36-33 victory over Notre Dame proved to be a third-period field goal from the toe of Bob Carey. The host Irish scored first and State countered with three quick TDs within the opening quarter. Vince Pisano went in from the 15-yard line; Doug Weaver intercepted a pass and set the offense in business at the ND 25 from where Sonny Grandelius scored three plays later; and then Jimmy King blocked a punt from the end zone with Weaver falling on it for a 20-7 lead. Notre Dame tallied on the first play of the second stanza and the score read 20-13 at intermission. The opening MSC drive of the second half eventually netted the 27-yard Carey field goal and the Irish responded with a pair of scoring passes. Now trailing 26-23, State stormed back to regain the lead on a pair of TDs of their own. First, Grandelius bounced in from the two, capping a 63-yard drive, and then Don McAuliffe scored the clincher following a crucial John Wilson interception. A Fighting Irish touchdown in the waning minutes only made the score close, 36-33. With 124 yards, Vince Pisano was the Spartans' leading carrier in this first-ever victory over Notre Dame in the modern era.

(#4) November 4, 1950 (H): A crowd of 45,237, the largest of the home season, sat through snow showers to watch the vaunted Spartan ground game completely dominate Indiana, 35-0. Sonny Grandelius was credited with 177 of his team's 339 rushing yards, for his fifth 100-plus yardage game of the season. Combined, Leroy Crane and Vince Pisano added another 166 yards. The 34-degree weather, accompanied by a 30 mph north wind, fostered turnovers and the MSC defense took advantage with recovery of six IU fumbles and four pass interceptions. One of the misguided aerials was picked off by Ed Timmerman, sophomore linebacker, who raambled 60 yards down the west sideline for the game's final touchdown. Quaterback Al Dorow attempted only two passes all afternoon.

(#5) November 11, 1950 (H): Overcoming a much larger opponent, MSC demonstrated consistency by tallying in every quarter to win their seventh game of the season, 27-0 over Minnesota. Each member of the starting backfield, Grandelius, Pisano, Crane, and Dorow was

credited with a touchdown. There were other outstanding performers. Defensive ends Jim King and Dorne Dibble continually turned back the Gopher runners and Jesse Thomas returned a punt for 58 yards to set-up the first score. Game statistics confirm the Spartan dominance: 21 first downs to Minnesota's 10 and 371 to 188 in net yardage. Snow-showers that prevailed until kick-off did not impact play, but approximately 3,000 from the sellout crowd of 47,452 were no-shows.

(#6) November 18, 1950 (A): Led by their miserly defense, the Spartans wrapped up the season with a 19-0 victory at Pittsburgh. "Duffy's Tuffys" (an adopted moniker for line coach Daugherty's stalwarts) dropped Panther passers for 17 sacks thus attributing to Pitt's net output of minus 11 yards for the afternoon. Meanwhile, the hosts held Sonny Grandelius to 73 yards in 19 carries, his lowest output of 1950. Regardless, the eventual All-American's season total of 1,023 rushing yards made him only the 17th back in NCAA history to exceed the milestone of 1,000 yards. Beginning the final quarter and the game in hand, Coach Munn paraded many of the reserves from western Pennsylvania into the game.

EXTRA! MICHIGAN STATE RELAYS (1950s)

In a time of 7.7, Jim Bibbs of Eastern Michigan won the 75-yard dash at the Spartan Relays of 1951. He would, of course, later serve as Michigan State's head coach.

The highlight of 1954 was supplied by the Kansas University medley relay team that broke the meet, fieldhouse and American record of 10:04.5 when they raced to victory in 9:51.4. On the anchor leg, Wes Santee ran a 4:02.6, unofficially, the world's fastest-ever indoor mile. The Spartan quartet of Joe Savoldi, Henry Gillis, Harlan Benjamin and John Corbelli captured the only MSC first place with a 29.8 in the 240-yard shuttle hurdle relay.

In the 1957 relays, Glenn Davis of Ohio State, the 1956 Olympic champion in the 400-meter hurdle event at Melbourne, Australia, won both hurdle events and placed fourth in the broad jump. MSU utilized the depth of distance runners to capture two events, the distance medley relay (David Lean, Kcn Defoe, Gay Denslow and Crawford Kennedy) and the two-mile relay (Crawford Kennedy, Henry Kennedy, Selwyn Jones and Dave Lean).

SPARTAN SCRAPBOOK
──── LACROSSE ────

1970 lacrosse team

MSC
1951-1952

TALES TO TELL

Stories abound as to how physical college hockey was in its early years. Dick Lord, who lettered in 1951-1953, relates the followed story:

"For many years Michigan State had a love/hate relationship with Michigan Tech in hockey. This was apparent after 1951, when Amo Bessone changed allegiance by leaving his coaching position at Houghton to begin his illustrious career at Michigan State. When the Tech team came down to East Lansing for two games in late January of 1952, their players were not only convinced they would defeat us, but it was immediately apparent they planned to beat us up physically on the ice at the same time.

During any heavy-hitting game many personal insults would be exchanged to rile the players and provoke penalties. Seeing I was the only black player in the league, several of our opposition would use racial slurs in an attempt to aggravate me, but I always managed to control myself until this particular game against Tech in 1952. I had been taking my share of knocks, as well as chosen names throughout that contest. I certainly resented the abuse but was able to control myself until a final incident when there were only about two minutes to play. I was just leaving the Michigan Tech zone when, from behind my back, someone suggested my mother wasn't married to my father. Immediately spinning around, I grabbed the first person in reach, who happened to be Joe DiBotciano, and a battle royal ensued. In a matter of seconds it seemed as if the entire Tech team was on me. Meanwhile, only one teammate, Steve Raz, had come to my assistance. Fearing that a riot would follow, Amo discouraged any other players from joining in. The melee lasted for nearly five minutes and many of us were, of course, ejected.

Oh, incidentally, we won the game.

As I said at the beginning, it was a love/hate relationship with Michigan Tech. Joe DiBotciano and I would eventually become good friends, but the battles continued. Another royal battle unfolded one year later, in 1953, this time up at Houghton."

HEADLINES of 1952

- An armistice ends the Korean War, and the battle line (the 38th parallel) becomes the boundary between North and South Korea.
- The world's first thermonuclear weapon, a hydrogen bomb, is successfully tested.
- Hollywood develops three-dimensional movies (3-D) which must be viewed through special eyeglasses. After brief success the novelty wears off.
- Reports of unidentified flying objects (UFOs) are first reported flashing across night skies all over the country.

SCOREBOARD

	W	L	T	Avg.
Baseball	18	14	1	.563
Track and Field	4	1	0	.800
Football	9	0	0	1.000
Basketball	13	9	0	.591
Tennis	12	4	0	.750
Cross Country	2	0	0	1.000
Swimming and Diving	8	2	0	.800
Wrestling	5	2	2	.667
Hockey	7	13	0	.350
Fencing	8	1	0	.899
Golf	5	5	0	.500
Boxing	7	1	2	.800
Gymnastics	6	0	0	1.000

TEAM OF THE YEAR

The 1951 football team was the first of two successive undefeated teams, as they went 9-0, including wins over three ranked teams: Michigan, Ohio State and Notre Dame. Regardless, the Spartans could not generate adequate media support and consequently settled for a second-place finish in both the Associated Press (AP) and United Press (UP) season-ending polls behind the also undefeated University of Tennessee. In his fifth season at the helm, Biggie Munn's multiple offense generated 2,645 rushing yards and 40 touchdowns with the tight defense yielding only 986 yards on the ground and a meager 17 touchdowns. Of the richly talented squad shown below, four players gained All-American recognition: quarterback Al Dorow, defensive back Jimmy Ellis, end Bob Carey, and tackle Don Coleman, the latter being distinguished on 13 mythical teams and thus recognized as a unanimous All-American.

The 1951 football team. (First row, left to right) L. Smith, D. Garner, B. Horrell, D. Kuh, A. Dorow, Bob Carey, M. McFadden, Bill Carey, B. Ciolek, D. Coleman and A. Jones. (Second row, left to right) D. McAuliffe, V. Pisano, D. Weaver, D. Panin, E. Timmerman, J. Morgan, R. Vogt, D. Tamburo, W. Benson, F. Kush and G. Serr. (Third row, left to right) L. Bolden, J Ellis, D. Kauth, D. Dohoney, C. Frank, D. Bobo, E. Luke, J. Wilson, P. Decker, L. Boyd, and T. Yewcic. (Fourth row, left to right) asst. coach S. Sebo, trainer J. Heppinstall, backfield coach L. Dawson, head coach B. Munn, J. Klein, equipment manager E. Kapp, line coach D. Daugherty, student manager C. Johnson, L. Fowler, end coach E. Edwards, and E. Slonac.

MAKING HISTORY

On December 14, consensus All-American Don Coleman returned to his hometown of Flint, where a capacity crowd of 400 honored him with a civic luncheon at the Elks Club. Coach Biggie Munn, who accompanied his star tackle, seized the opportunity to announce that Coleman's jersey number 78 would be retired as a Michigan State number. This was the first time a Spartan football player was so honored.

In defeating the Northwestern Wildcat basketball team 82-49 on January 7, State established a Jenison Fieldhouse scoring record. Led by Keith Stackhouse with 17 points, 10 other Spartans contributed to the scoring. The previous mark of 81 points had been turned in by the 1950 team in their win over Marquette.

Ginny Baxter, a Detroit freshman, became a member of the 1952 USA Winter Olympic team as a figure skater. She did not medal but finished fifth in her specialty. Acknowledging her accomplishment, she was later awarded a varsity letter sweater, the first female to be so honored.

Don Coleman's no. 78 was the first Michigan State football jersey number to be retired.

GREAT STATE DATES

Cross Country—**November 10, 1951 (H):** Although Notre Dame's Jack Alexander was a surprise winner, he was followed immediately by a trio of Spartans, Jim Kepford in second, Lyle Garbe in third, and Jim Arnold in fourth. Jack DeLang finished seventh and Doug Boyd ended up 10th to close out the MSC scoring. The final totals had State with the win, 26-29. The victory came with three top runners sidelined with minor injuries: Ron Barr, Wayne Scutt and Jerry Zerbe.

Basketball—**January 2, 1952 (A):** Opening his second season at the helm, Pete Newell saw the 1951-1952 squad rack up a perfect 7-0 pre-conference record. The seventh win was an impressive 66-52 victory over Notre Dame. In doing so, the Spartans snapped an Irish at-home winning streak of 20 games. Following a meager 31-29 halftime lead, Bob Carey headed a third quarter 22-point outburst leading to the final 14-point edge. Four starters hit double figures: Carey 16, Gordy Stauffer 16, Keith Stackhouse 15 and Bill Bower 13.

Hockey—**January 12, 1952 (H):** Following a Friday night loss, State topped North Dakota in the second game of the home stand, 4-3. Trailing 3-0 after one period, MSC came back and eventually tied the score midway through the final stanza on a long shot by Dick Lord. Then, with only 1:08 remaining in regulation, Connie Buck took a pass from Derio Nicoli and slammed home the winner.

Swimming and Diving—**January 12, 1952 (A):** Competing against Iowa State in their cozy 20-yard pool was always a severe challenge, and 1952 was no exception. Even as the Spartans opened the meet with a victory in the 300-yard medley relay and led in the point total throughout the afternoon, the Cyclones stayed close with victories in both sprints, the backstroke, and the breaststroke. MSC countered with distance ace Bert McLachlan taking both the 220- and 440-freestyle races, Bruce Aldrich winning the individual medley, and the diving pair of John Hellwege and Don Morey scoring first and second. The winning freestyle relay of Tom Payette, Charles Baldwin, Bob Schumacher, and Clarke Scholes closed out the meet with the Spartans winning, 54-39.

Boxing—**January 19, 1952 (H):** A crowd of approximately 3,400 cheered their Spartans to a 7-1 victory over the Army team from West Point, New York.

Center of the 1950-51 Michigan State hockey team, Dick Lord.

The 175-pound Chuck Spieser won an easy 30-21 decision, and welterweight Jed Black's verdict was even more decisive at 30-17. Other winners for State were three freshmen: 125-pound Jimmy Evans, 139-pound Herb Odom, and Tom Hickey at 156, along with Norm Adrie at 132 pounds and heavyweight Alex Tsarkiris.

Basketball—**January 26, 1952 (H):** This game was billed as the conference's top offensive team, Purdue (scoring 77 points per game), against the Big Ten's top defensive team, MSC (yielding 50.8 points per game). In posting a 56-47 victory, on at least this day, Michigan State proved that a good defense beats a good offense. The Boilermakers were held to 30 points below their season average.

Wrestling—**January 26, 1952 (H):** MSC won three of the final four matches to score a 16-11 verdict over the defending conference champions from Ohio State. Bob Hoke, a National AAU titlist from 1951, pinned his Buckeye opponent at 157 pounds. Orris Bender, who moved up one weight classification, won a 7-4 decision at 177 pounds, and sophomore Larry Fowler shut out his heavyweight opponent, 5-0.

Fencing—**January 26, 1952 (A):** In a double dual meet, MSC defeated both the University of Detroit 18-9 and Wayne University 15-12. They outscored the Titans on all three weapons, 5-4 in epee, 5-4 in foil, and 8-1 in sabre. The Wayne foil team outscored State 6-3, but lost the epee 7-2 and sabre 5-4.

Wrestling—**February 1, 1952 (H):** The Spartans topped previously unbeaten Purdue, 19-8. The highlight of the meet was 167-pound Orris Bender's pin with one second remaining in the final period. Bob Hoke continued unbeaten in the 157-pound division, with other winners being Bob Gunner at 123 pounds, Ed Casalicchio at 137 pounds, and Larry Fowler at heavyweight. Jim Knotts completed the scoring with his draw at 167.

Fencing—**February 2, 1952 (A):** For the first time since 1947 and by the narrowest of margins, the Spartan swordsmen defeated Notre Dame, 14-13. Leading the way with three wins each were Fred Freiheit in sabre and Dick Berry in epee. Also scoring points for MSC were Ralph Kalmar, Ray Totte, Bob Bristol, Al Walker, Bill Pierson, and Ray Monte.

Basketball—**February 16, 1952 (A):** With Wisconsin leading 55-53 at Madison and the clock running down, Sonny Means hit a jump shot to tie the game. The Spartans immediately stole the ball and with two seconds remaining Leif Carlson hit a push shot from medium range that fell through for the 57-55 verdict. The horn sounded before the Badgers could take the ball out of bounds.

Basketball—**March 1, 1952 (H):** The home schedule closed with an 80-59 victory over Michigan before 8,624 fans. The win assured the Spartans of their most successful season in 10 years and avenged an earlier season loss at Ann Arbor in which State hit only 17 percent of their field goal attempts. The rematch was marred by a total of 63 personal fouls, with five Wolverines being ejected with their fifth infraction. Neither team took particular advantage at the free throw line. Michigan State converted only 20 of 37, while the U of M was only a shade better with 21 of 36. Making their final home appearance were six seniors, all of whom scored: Bob Carey, Bill Bower, Gordy Stauffer, Bill Eckstrom, Leif Carlson and Sonny Means.

Gymnastics—**March 1, 1952 (A):** The gymnasts finished the season undefeated (6-0) with an impressive 57-39 victory over Michigan. It was the school's first unblemished record since the sport was introduced in 1948. As had been the case all season long, sophomore ace Carl Rintz took scoring honors with 19 points. He won the side horse and flying rings, and placed second on the horizontal bars and third on the parallel bars. Highlighted by his first place on the horizontal bars, captain Bob Feldmeier was second in scoring with 14 points. John Walker was the other Spartan winner with a first place on the trampoline.

Baseball—**March 29, March 30, April 1, 1952 (A):** Michigan State, along with Yale University, joined host North Carolina for a pre-season round robin tournament at Chapel Hill, N.C. Behind outstanding pitching, MSC won all four games. First, Don Quale tossed a three-hitter to shut out the Tar Heels, 3-0. On the next afternoon, Roger Howard yielded only one earned run in defeating Yale, 6-3. Dick Moser and second baseman Corky Ghise each hammered out three hits in the contest. In a twin bill the next day, junior right hander Bob Dangl set the Ivy Leaguers down on two hits, as State scored the game's only run in the bottom of the ninth. In the second game of the afternoon, a 6-3 win over Carolina, Don Quayle relieved Gus Carlson in the sixth and put out the fire with the bases loaded. The Spartans garnered all of the tournament prizes. Coach John Kobs was presented the team trophy with individual awards going to Quayle for his mound work, senior shortstop Joe Rivich for defensive play, and sophomore Jack Risch for topping all batters with a .454 average.

Golf—**April 19, 1952 (H):** As usual, battling the weather conditions of early spring was as challenging as facing the opposition. Opening the season on the wet and sloppy Walnut Hills course, State defeated Western Michigan, 23-3. Chuck Davenport was the medal leader with 73.

Baseball—**May 9 (H) & May 10 (A), 1952:** In the annual series against Michigan, State took two out of three. The Friday battle in East Lansing went to the Spartans when they broke a 5-5 tie in the bottom of the ninth. With two out, Corky Ghise and Ray Lane hit back-to-back singles, and Bob Ciolek was hit by the pitcher to load the bases. Then Dick Moser came to the plate. The left fielder had already batted in three runs with a pair of hits. This time he just stood there. The U of M pitcher could not find the plate, and suddenly it was ball four. This forced Ghise home with the winning run, ending the game, 6-5. On the next afternoon in Ann Arbor, pitcher Tom Lawson held the Michigan hitters to just two hits in gaining a 4-0 shutout. Meanwhile, Moser, still swinging the hot bat, collected four base hits, Ray Lane came up with three, and Ghise accounted for the only other MSC hit, a third-inning home run.

Tennis—**May 13, 1952 (H):** Stan Drobac, Tom Belton and John Sahratian led State to the first-ever 9-0 sweep of the U of M. Playing in the number-one spot, Drobac won in straight sets, 7-5, 6-3. Belton scored a 6-1, 6-3 easy win, and Sahratian disposed of his opponent 6-2, 6-2. Other Spartan winners at singles were Keith Kimble, Dick Roberts, and Richard Reiger. Combined with the three victories in the doubles, MSC dropped only two sets all afternoon.

Track and Field—**May 17, 1952 (H):** A slim crowd of shivering fans watched Jim Kepford, John Walter, and John Cook open with a 1-2-3 slam in the mile run. The Spartans continued with victories in nine of the 14 remaining events to outclass the Syracuse Orange, 100-36. Bob Carey concluded his final home appearance by smashing the varsity and field records in the shot put with a toss of 53' 11 1/2". Other winners were Chuck Roland in both sprints, Henry Gillis in the two hurdle events, Lyle Garbe in the 880, Russ Olexa in the broad jump, Rodger Summers in the discus, Arnold Smith in the pole vault and Ray McKay and Jim Vrooman tied for first in the high jump.

Baseball—**May 17, 1952 (H):** MSC swept both games from Indiana University, rallying in the final three innings to grab the opener, 5-3, and then pounding out an 8-2 decision in the nightcap. Tom Lawson and Don Quayle were State's winning pitchers, both going the distance. The highlight of the afternoon was an unusual triple play that came in the sixth inning of the second game. With the bases loaded, the Hoosier third baseman hoisted a sacrifice fly ball to Jack Risch, scoring a run. The center fielder's return throw trapped the IU runner going from second to third, and he was tagged out after a run-down. The runner who had been on first was also trapped and vainly tried to scramble back to the bag but was tagged by right fielder Bob Dilday.

Clarke Scholes

IN THE SPARTLITE

Baseball: The 1952 season opened on a sore note as two regulars from 1951, third baseman Dick Blanchard and outfielder Darrell Lindley, aborted their college careers and signed professional contracts, Blanchard with the Indians and Lindley with the White Sox. Among others who signed professionally, prematurely or upon graduation, during the 1950s were: Tom Yewcic (Tigers), Dick Radatz (Boston), Bob Powell (White Sox), Ron Perranoski (Los Angeles), Larry Foster (Tigers), Dan Brown (Cubs), Dick Idzkowski (White Sox), Jim Sack (Dodgers), Roger Howard (White Sox), Wayne Lawrie (Red Sox), Charlie Gorman (Orioles), Walt Godfrey (Tigers), Chuck Mathews (Orioles), Frank Franchi (Tigers), Al Luplow (Indians), Jack Risch (Tigers), George Smith (Orioles), Dean Look (White Sox), Ed Hobaugh (Senators), Dennis Mendyk (Tigers) and Al Luce (Tigers).

Season-fielding honors went to outfielder-first baseman Dick Moser, a Kalamazoo senior who handled 99 chances without a flaw.

ATHLETE OF THE YEAR

Swimmer Clarke Scholes is the only Spartan to have ever won an Olympic gold medal in an individual event. He did so in winning and setting an Olympic record in the 100-meter freestyle at the 1952 Olympiad in Helsinki, Finland. Three years later, Clarke won the gold medal and set a record in the 100-meter freestyle at the Pan-American Games. Initially a walk-on as a sophomore in 1950, three times he captured the National Collegiate 100-yard freestyle title (1950-1952). He also won the NCAA 1951 50-yard freestyle event and was a member of the championship 400-yard freestyle relay team that same year. Clarke was selected three times as an All-American by the College Swimming Coaches Association and chosen Swimmer of the Year in 1952. Scholes was twice crowned National AAU champion in the 100-yard freestyle (1950 and 1952), and he captured three Big Ten titles (50-yards freestyle in 1951 and 100-yard freesyle in both 1951 and 1952). He was inducted into the International Swimming Hall of Fame in 1980.

Spartan first baseman Dick Moser captured 1952 season fielding honors.

Basketball: After State opened with seven straight wins, including a 66-52 victory over top-rated Notre Dame, the AP weekly poll listed the Spartans in the 20th spot. The streak was the longest since the 1934-1935 season when the Spartans won 10 in a row on the way to an impressive 14-4 record. The early season success was primary attributed to seniors Gordy Stauffer, Bill Bower, Sonny Means and Bob Carey, along with sophomores Hugh McMasters of Hazel Park; Doneal Hartman of Ft. Wayne, Ind.; Rickie Ayala from Brooklyn, N.Y.; and Keith Stackhouse of Bourbon, Ind. MSC returned to earth quickly as they opened the Big Ten season losing four out of five. Injuries contributed to the demise, as six different players were sidelined at one time or another during the season.

Season-end statistics revealed that 18 players, an inordinate number, contributed to the scoring over the 22-game season. Sophomore Keith Stackhouse was the team leader with 236 points for a 11.8 average in 20 games.

Boxing: As in 1951, the dual meet season closed with a 4-4 tie against the University of Wisconsin. State led 4-3 before the Badger heavyweight concluded activities abruptly with a 67-second TKO of Al Tsakiris. MSC winners were Herb Odom, Dick LaForge, Tom Hickey, upon stopping his opponent after only 65 seconds, and Chuck Spieser, who won by forfeit.

Of the seven men entered in the NCAAs, only LaForge at 147 pounds and 178-pound Spicer reached the championship final. LaForge lost in that closing bout, but Spieser completed his undefeated Spartan career by once more being crowned the light heavyweight collegiate champion. Before a sellout crowd of 13,231 in the Wisconsin fieldhouse, the Badgers easily topped State for the team title, outscoring the second place Spartans 27 to 14.

By virtue of winning the district AAU titles in Toledo, Odom and Jed Black joined Spieser as competitors in the 1952 American Olympic trials. Odom bowed out in the semi-finals, Black lost in the finals, while Spieser gained his second Olympic team berth with a TKO during the first minute of action in the final pairing. Later, while in training, Chuck sustained a badly bruised eye and cut lip that prevented him from seeing action at the XI Olympiad in Helsinki.

Cross Country: Failing to place in the top three spots, five Spartan runners were good enough to finish amidst the next group of 13 and amass 49 points to win MSC's first Big Ten title. Scoring for Coach Schlademan were Jim Kepford in fourth place, Ron Barr in fifth, Jim Arnold in ninth, Jerry Zerbe in 15th, and Dick Jarrett right behind in 16th place. It was the first of 11 conference trophies Michigan State runners would collect over a span of 13 years.

Again hosting the NCAA championship run, MSC could do no better than fifth place, with Ron Barr and Wayne Scutt the top finishers at 11th and 13th.

Fencing: Dick Berry, a transfer from Highland Park Junior College, was the standout of the 1952 squad that completed the dual meet season at 8-1, finished second in the Big Ten meet, and ended fifth at the national collegiate championships. He captured the conference epee title and then finished in a tie for second at the NCAAs. Berry was singled out for an additional honor at the national meet in New Haven, Conn., where he was selected recipient of the Illinois Memorial Trophy, awarded annually based on competitor's technical skills and sportsmanship. Also starring for the Spartans in the post-season was Fred Freiheit, who won the Big Ten sabre championship and placed fifth at the NCAA tournament.

Football: A total of 7,605 fans purchased season tickets in 1951.

Discarding their traditional army ROTC colors, the marching band opened the 1951 season in new green-and-white uniforms.

In reporting the 30-26 win over Indiana, sportswriter Tommy Devine of the *Detroit Free Press* wrote of the Spartans: "Champions one week, stumblebums the next!" The paper's sports office was deluged with letters protesting the harsh judgment, and the responses became so intense that the paper had to pull Devine from the East Lansing beat."

Bob Carey was a consensus All-American in 1951, while Al Dorow and Jim Ellis each attained one All-American selection. Topping them all, Don Coleman became the school's first consensus All-American.

During the holidays, ten members of the squad competed in bowl games. Al Dorow quarterbacked his squad to a 15-14 victory in the East-West Shrine game at Kezar Stadium in San Francisco. The East team was coached by Biggie Munn and also included Don Coleman and linebacker Bill Hughes. Guards Dean Garner, tackle Marv McFadden and end Bill Carey played in the Blue-Gray game in Montgomery, Ala., while guard Dick Kuh, center Jim Creamer and Bill Horrell were in Miami for the North-South game.

Golf: Represented by captain Jack Zinn, Joe Albright, Harold Ware, Arthur "Biff" Hills, Charles Davenport, and Carl Mosack, the golf team split 5-5 in the dual meet season but could not escape a last place finish at the Big Ten championships in Champaign, Ill.

Gymnastics: After scoring 85 1/2 points and finishing second at the Big Ten meet at Bloomington, Ind., George Szypula's squad managed a sixth-place finish at the NCAA championships in Boulder, Colo. Bob Feldmeier placed seventh in the horizontal bars, eighth in the side horse, and seventh all-around for a total of 11 points. Carl Rintz matched those 11 points with a sixth in the side horse, eighth in the flying rings and eighth all-around. Senior Al Hannas completed the MSC scoring with a seventh-place finish on the trampoline.

Hockey: The new look of the State squad included not only Amo Bessone in his first season, but 11 first-year players, eight of whom dressed for the opener against Ontario Agricultural College. Also new, State opened the season as a member of the neophyte Midwest Hockey League that included Michigan, Michigan Tech, North Dakota, Minnesota, Colorado, and Denver. Both the eventual league champion and runner-up were pegged to be representatives for the NCAA championships in Colorado Springs, Colo. Encumbered by a strange policy, only the first game of each two-game weekend series would count toward the team standings.

Ticket prices for games in Dem Hall were as follows: reserved seats $1.50, general admission $1.00, and 60¢ for students and school employees.

The season opened at home with a pair of wins against the always accommodating Ontario Agricultural College, 8-2 and 7-4. During seven years of competition from 1950 to 1957, the Spartans would build a 15-0 record over the Ontario team.

Rounding out their winning ledger for the season, the Spartans took four from an unusually weak Michigan Tech Huskie squad.

Season-end statistics revealed that seven of the top eight MSC scorers were freshmen. In leading the team with 29 total points (11 goals and 18 assists), center Johnny Mayes established a new team record. Weldie Olson led with goals scored (13) and was second in total points (19).

Swimming and Diving: After placing second to Ohio State in the Big Ten championship meet, the Spartans garnered 27 points and finished fourth at the NCAA championship meet in Princeton, N.J. In addition to Clarke Scholes's victory in the 100-yard freestyle, Bert McLachlan finished fifth in the 220-yard, 440-yard, and 1,500-meter freestyle events. The 400-yard freestyle quartet of Tom Payette, Bob Schumacher, Chuck Baldwin and Scholes settled for second place after being nosed out 3:25.7 to 3:25.9.

Tennis: Although capturing two doubles titles, Stan Drobac-Tom Belton at number one and Dick Roberts-Jim Pore at number three, State was dethroned by Indiana, 70-56, for the Big Ten team championship.

Track and Field: Totaling only 11 3/5 points, the track and field team dropped to fifth place at the Big Ten indoor championships in Champaign, Ill., after placing third in their inaugural season of 1951. Russell Olexa and Chuck Roland finished third and fifth in the broad jump. Other Spartan scorers were Henry Gillis, third in the high hurdles; Jim Vrooman, third in the high jump; Don Schiesswohl, fifth in the shot put; and Arnold Smith, a five-way tie for fourth in the pole vault.

At the outdoor meet in Ann Arbor, they could do no better, placing fifth with 10.85 points.

Wrestling: Taking to the mat for coach Fendley Collins over the nine-meet season were: Ruben Shehigian at 115 pounds, Bob Gunner at 123, Dick Gunner at 130, Ed Casalicchio at 137, Vito Perrone and Jim Knotts at 147 pounds, Bob Hoke at 157, Orris Bender at 167, Dick Thornton at 177 and heavyweight Larry Fowler.

At the conference championships in Ann Arbor, State managed 19 points for a third-place finish. Bender, the Lakewoood, Ohio, senior, who had gone undefeated through the dual meet season, captured the 167-pound crown that his brother had won in 1951. Adding to the scoring were runner-up finishes by Hoke and Dick Gunner, and fourths by Bob Gunner and Fowler.

EXTRA! FOOTBALL 28-GAME WIN STREAK CONTINUES

One of the longest winning streaks in NCAA history was achieved by the Biggie Munn coached teams of 1950-1953. It was a remarkable and memorable era of Michigan State football.

(#7) September 22, 1951 (H): Upon assuming the head coaching position in 1947, Biggie Munn initiated a tradition of awarding the game ball to a deserving player following each victory. Jimmy Ellis, a defensive back, was so honored following the season-opening 6-0 win over Oregon State at Macklin Field. The fleet sophomore from Saginaw intercepted three passes as well as returning a pair of punts for 30 and 40 yards. The game's only touchdown, which came in the second quarter, was scored from the Beaver one-yard line and generated from a broken play. The center snap, intended for Dick Panin, hit him in the chest and bounced into the air but luckily fell into Al Dorow's hands. The alert quarterback quickly pitched it back to a surprised Don McAuliffe who was running a fake to his right. The burly halfback caught the ball in stride, angled toward the corner of the field from about the eight-yard line, and scored standing up. In the postgame press conference Biggie commented on his number-two ranked Spartans: "It seems the boys believed too many of those newspaper and radio ratings. We have a long way to go to be a football team."

Quarterback Al Dorow and coach Munn plot their "transcontinental pass" play.

(#8) September 29, 1951 (A): In shutting out the Wolverines, 25-0, the Spartans enjoyed the widest-ever margin of victory in this classic intrastate series. Game statistics were even more one-sided: first downs, 21 to 4; rushing yardage 249 opposed to *minus* 23; and passing yardage 58 versus 29. All of this in a game in which State turned the ball over eight times (5 fumbles and 3 pass interceptions). Leading only 6-0 at the intermission, Jim Ellis gathered in the second half kickoff at his own 12-yard line and romped 88 yards for an apparent TD only to have stepped out at the Michigan 14. Four running plays later and a Bob Carey conversion raised the score to 13-0. Coach Munn would later comment on the Ellis run: "It really gave me a thrill. Something like that is bound to give the club a big lift." Indeed it did. State went 91-yards for the third touchdown, the payoff play being a 38-yard run to the one-yard line by Wayne Benson. LeRoy Bolden sprang over for the score. The final scoring drive, in the fourth quarter, covered 46 yards with Vince Pisano bolting into the end zone from the three. Standing out for the defense that held the Rose Bowl champions to minus rushing yardage were Ed Luke, Don Dohoney, Bill Horell, Frank Kush and perhaps the most towering figure of all, linebacker Bill Hughes.

(#9) October 6, 1951 (A): This Ohio State-Michigan State contest will forever by referred to as the "transcontinental pass" game. Trailing 20-10 in the fourth quarter the number-one ranked Spartans concluded a 75-yard drive with a one-yard touchdown pass on fourth down, Al Dorow to Paul Dekker. Bob

Carey converted and the Ohio Stadium scoreboard flashed: OSU 20, MSC 17, with 5:46 remaining. A script writer could not have fashioned a more exciting conclusion. On the second play following the ensuing kickoff, the Buckeye fullback fumbled and Ed Luke, a defensive end, pounced on the arrant ball at the OSU 45-yard line. The Spartans had been handed a golden opportunity. Led by Billy Wells, playing his first varsity game, the Spartans worked the ball to the 27-yard line but were faced with a fourth down and 12 situation. It was time for Biggie to dig deeply into his play book: the "transcontinental pass." Here is how it worked. Sophomore Tom Yewcic, who had just begun playing quarterback during the preceding week, entered the game at left halfback. The snap went to Evan Slonac, sophomore fullback. He faked a line buck and slipped the ball to quarterback Al Dorow who, in turn, threw a backward pass to Yewcic. The quarterback-halfback then ran wide right giving Dorow time to head for the opposite corner. Yewcic stopped and pitched the ball diagonally across the field to Dorow who caught the ball at the 11-yard line, avoided one tackler, and crossed the goal line. Following Carey's conversion, the Ohio Stadium scoreboard read MSC 24, OSU 20, with 2:34 remaining on the clock. The Buckeyes never threatened thereafter.

Tom Yewcic later recalled:

"Biggie and Duffy came up with the transcontinental pass. We worked on it at practice, but not to a big degree. This play would only be used if the situation presented itself. This was a great Ohio State football team, so you have to pull out all of the tricks in the bag. It never entered my mind that it would not succeed, I didn't have time to think about it (maybe 10 seconds), but it was just as well. The only thought in my mind was to get the pass to Dorow and make it work. The thought of losing never entered anybody's mind. When you're young, inexperienced and competitive, you always think positively. We had no losers on that team."

(#10) October 13, 1951 (H): Led by the future "pony backfield" stars, Billy Wells and LeRoy Bolden, number one-ranked MSC came from behind to defeat a stubborn Marquette team, 20-14. Wells opened the MSC scoring with a 69-yard dash in the second quarter and then hooked-up with Al Dorow for a fourth-quarter 46-yard pass reception-run, closing the deficit to 14-13 on Gene Lekenta's PAT. On the very next possession the Spartans went 75 yards. The key play, leading to the winning touchdown, was a 49-yard pass, Dorow to end Paul Dekker. Then, four plays later from the eight-yard line, it was Bolden's turn. Swinging wide around his right end and behind excellent blocking from Dean Garner, Marv McFadden and Frank Kapral, the Flint speedster crossed the goal line untouched.

Fullback Dick Panin shows his heels to a pair of Notre Dame pursuers en route to an 88-yard touchdown run on the second play of the game on Nov. 10, 1951.

(#11) October 20, 1951 (A): Trailing Penn State 14-13 early in the third quarter, the Spartans registered 19 straight points before the Nittany Lions would score again. The final read: Michigan State 32, Penn State 21, as the Green offense was credited with a total of 403 yards rushing and passing. It was a contest of long scoring plays. Don McAuliffe threw a 40-yard touchdown pass; Jim Ellis rambled back a punt for 57 yards and a TD; and LeRoy Bolden, the freshman halfback, scampered 65 yards for the final MSC touchdown. The Spartan de-

fense, led by the linebacking trio Bill Hughes of Lewiston, Pa.; Dick Tamburo of New Kensington, Pa., and Ed Timmerman from Grand Rapids, kept the Lion runners in check all afternoon as they yielded a paltry 67 yards on the ground. Hughes also was credited with three fumble recoveries, a team record still unsurpassed. Don Coleman was a monster on kicks as he accounted for every tackle on punts and kickoffs.

(#12) October 27, 1951 (H): The Spartans again followed their come-from-behind script and scored five second-half touchdowns to overcome Pittsburgh, 53-26, in the Homecoming game. The offense amassed 27 first downs and a staggering total of 637 yards (436 rushing and 201 passing), second only in team history to the 694 against Marquette in 1949. Impressive offense plays included: Dick Panin's 60-yard touchdown run and his 62-yard dash to setup the third TD; a 42-yard pass from Dorow to McAuliffe; a touchdown punt return of 55 yards by Jim Ellis; and Wayne Benson's 24-yard bolt up the middle to account for the final score of the afternoon.

(#13) November 10, 1951 (H): One of the most memorable victories in Michigan State football lore was the 35-0 shutout at home against Notre Dame in 1951, often remembered as the "Dick Panin" game. With barely two and a half minutes of playing time consumed and many fans still headed toward their seats, the junior fullback from Detroit burst through the Irish line and raced 88 yards into the north end zone. It was State's first play from scrimmage. Still in the opening period and featuring runs by Don McAuliffe, Vince Pisano and Panin, the Spartans pieced together a six-play, 68-yard scoring drive. This was followed by an 11-play, 74-yard drive which included a diving catch by Bob Carey at the ND six-yard line and the scoring plunge by McAuliffe. Although the MSC rushing game was dominant, the remaining pair of scores, both in the second half, were short passes from Dorow. The first to Captain Carey and the second to Ellis Duckett. It was the worst defeat of coach Frank Leahy's career and the first time the Irish had been held scoreless since 1946.

Linebacker Bill Hughes recalls:

"Three days before the Notre Dame game of Nov. 10, 1951, Mother Nature dumped over 12 inches of snow on Macklin Field. As MSC's ground crew worked around the clock on snow removal for fear a ground freeze might contribute to poor footing. Biggie worked the team with equal diligence. Maybe it would be better to say he worked us 'super hard.' Most of the drills were held inside Jenison Fieldhouse because of the weather. We knew Biggie wanted an upset over Notre Dame. He wanted it more than anything else, more than any preceding game or likely more than any game he would coach in the future."

The ultimate result made it all worthwhile as the Sunday headline read "Michigan State College 35, Notre Dame 0." Zilch, zip, nada....a day to remember. A football rivalry that was terminated in 1921 had been rekindled in 1948. While the 36-33 Spartan win in the preceding year at South Bend awakened the sports world to the football renaissance in East Lansing, that dominating 35-0 victory of 1951 confirmed it.

(#14) November 17, 1951 (A): On a snowy, blustery afternoon in Bloomington, the Indiana squad gave "Biggie's Boys" all they wanted before bowing, 30-26. The Spartans sprang to a two touchdown lead in the first quarter and then saw IU match it by halftime, 14-14. State scored the next 16 points, including a 30-yard Carey field goal, and then hung on as the Hoosiers closed the gap with a pair of TD's. Billy Wells, of the "pony backfield," accounted for the "go-ahead" third score when he broke away on an 83-yard touchdown run. Surprisingly, Indiana won the statistical battle, 351 to 333 in total yards.

SPARTAN SCRAPBOOK
——LACROSSE COACHES (1970-1996)——

Turf Kauffman (1970)

Ted Swoboda (1971-72)

Bob Stevenson (1973)

Fred Hartman (1974-76)

Nevin Kanner (1977-80)

Boku Henderson (1978-80)
(co-coach with Kanner)

Rich Kimball (1981-96)

MSC
1952-1953

TALES TO TELL

In a letter dated Feb. 14, 1953, from Big Ten commissioner Kenneth "Tug" Wilson, president John Hannah was notified of the conference's intention to slap MSC with a one-year probation for a fund allegedly raised by alumni to financially assist Michigan State athletes. Part of the erring group (The Spartan Foundation) was known as the Century Club. For a $100 contribution, members of that club would gain certain privileges available through the athletic department, such as special ticket allocations and admission to otherwise closed football practices. School officials denied any involvement with the accused foundation, and they vigorously fought the action of the commissioner's office. One week following the Wilson communiqué, faculty representatives of the Big Ten schools met in Chicago to subsequently ratify the probationary action after hearing Michigan State's appeal submitted by deans Lloyd Emmons and Tom King. In his presentation, Emmons included the following:

"We had expected, as a freshman member (of the Big Ten), to be hazed a bit. We knew we would have to dispel rumors, meet charges of violations from time to time, explain why any really good athlete came to us rather than enter any of the other institutions, and that if we should happen to make a real good showing in any one sport, we would be the target for missiles of a wide variety."

As it turned out, the probation only amounted to a severe public censure and had no effect on the athletic schedule or program. By a vote of the faculty representatives, the ordeal was over on Dec. 10, 1953. Facts later revealed that 10 members of the 1951 football team had collectively received postseason loans totaling $3,183 from the implicated Spartan Foundation.

HEADLINES of 1953

- Edmund Hillary of New Zealand and Tenzing Norgay of Nepal are the first to climb 29,028-foot Mt. Everest.
- A new cabinet-level Department of Health, Education and Welfare is created in Washington, D.C.
- Ian Fleming, the English writer, publishes Casino Royale, the first of 13 novels featuring secret agent 007, James Bond.
- Golfer Ben Hogan is king of the links. "Bantam Ben" wins the Masters Tournament, the U.S. Open and the British Open.

SCOREBOARD

	W	L	T	Avg.
Baseball	11	17	0	.393
Track and Field	4	1	0	.800
Football	9	0	0	1.000
Basketball	13	9	0	.591
Tennis	12	4	0	.750
Cross Country	1	1	0	.500
Swimming and Diving	7	1	0	.875
Wrestling	7	2	0	.778
Hockey	5	16	1	.250
Fencing	5	5	0	.500
Golf	5	5	1	.500
Boxing	5	2	0	.714
Gymnastics	2	6	0	.250

Collateral honors were extended to Munn as Coach of the Year, while six players, Ellis Duckett, Tom Yewcic, Dick Tamburo, Don McAuliffe, Frank Kush and Jimmy Ellis, were each listed on two or more of the sundry All-American teams. The Washington Touchdown Club honored McAuliffe with the Walter Camp trophy, recognizing him as back of the year. Most frequently, the starting offense team lined up as follows: number 84 Doug Bobo LE, number 56 Gordy Serr LT, number 55 Ferris Hallmark LG, number 51 Jim Neal C, number 64 Bob Breniff RG, number 70 Larry Fowler RT, number 81 Paul Dekker RE, number 41 Tom Yewcic QB, number 40 Don McAuliffe LHB, number 14 Billy Wells RHB and number 33 Evan Slonac FB. Listed on the defensive side were number 85 Ed Luke LE, number 72 Charlie Frank LT, number 67 Henry Bullough LG, number 60 Frank Kush RG, number 79 Jack Morgan RT, number 80 Don Dohoney RE, number 30 Ed Timmerman LB, number 52 Dick Tamburo LB, number 45 John Wilson DB, number 49 Rex Corless DB and number 11 Jimmy Ellis at safety.

TEAM OF THE YEAR

Sporting an undefeated 9-0 record on the gridiron, including convincing victories over Michigan and Notre Dame, Biggie Munn's sixth Spartan team finished the season as number one in the two primary polls, Associated Press (AP) and United Press (UP), and was thus declared consensus national champions for 1952. Offensively, the team averaged 34.7 points per game, and defensively, the team surrendered fewer than 10 points per contest.

MAKING HISTORY

Upon completing his highly successful collegiate boxing career in 1949, Chuck Davey set out on a meteoric professional career that by 1953 had reached an unblemished 40-0 record. Then on Wednesday evening, February 11, 1953, before 17,000 fight fans at the Chicago Stadium and a nationwide television audience, the popular southpaw entered the ring for a title shot against the welterweight champion of the world, Kid Gavilan

The 1952 football team

of Cuba. Although Davey fought a courageous battle that evening, his dream of becoming the world's champion was not to be. Three times Chuck was dropped to the canvas in the ninth round, and then, bloodied, he was too weakened to answer the bell for the 10th. The Spartan hero had suffered his first loss, a technical knockout (TKO).

GREAT STATE DATES

Cross Country—**October 25, 1952 (H):** Led by Jim Kepford's record-breaking performance, MSC scored an impressive triangular meet victory over Penn State and Michigan. Kepford negotiated the home course in 20:06.6, the fastest four miles ever turned in by a Spartan. Completing the team's winning total of 31 points were Wayne Scutt in fourth place, Jerry Zerbe in sixth, Lyle Garbe in seventh and Mickey Walter in 13th. The Nittany Lions were 10 points back with 41 points, followed by the U of M with 50 points.

Basketball—**January 17 (A) & March 7, 1953 (H):** For the first time since 1933-1934, the Spartans managed to defeat the U of M twice during a season. In the first game at Ann Arbor, with the score tied at 64-64, and only three seconds of time remaining, Deneal Hartman, the Ft. Wayne junior, swished in the game winner from the side of the court. The rematch, before 7,923 fans in Jenison, was likewise a close contest. The Wolverines connected on seven of their first eight field goal attempts and maintained a lead until State went ahead, 47-46, at the beginning of the final 10-minute quarter. When the MSC lead reached 51-48, Coach Peter Newell called a time-out to set up a stall (no 24-second clock), a plan that ultimately worked. The 55-52 victory was won at the free-throw line, where State outshot the visitors 17-8. Al Ferrari, the sparkling sophomore forward, was the scoring leader with 25 points.

Basketball—**January 31, 1953 (H):** Trailing Minnesota 21-12 in the second quarter, the Spartans, led by Keith Stackhouse, suddenly found the range and outscored the Gophers, 14-1. With the game tied 36-36 early in the third period, Al Ferrari hit a field goal to put State ahead for good. Although the visitors came within two points twice, 57-55 and 59-57, MSC hung on for a 64-60 victory. The winning edge came at the free throw line, where State held an 18-14 edge. Eleven of those charity tosses came in the final 10 minutes.

Swimming and Diving—**January 31, 1953 (A):** In a gratifying win, Michigan State defeated Ohio State, the defending NCAA champions and eventual Big Ten champions, in a dual meet, 51-39. This ended an uninterrupted OSU string of 25 straight dual meet victories that began in 1947. Although the Spartan victory cannot be diminished, it was somewhat tainted. First, two of Ohio State's very best, sprinter Dick Cleveland and distance star Ford Konno, were sidelined by a weird policy that made them ineligible for having been absent from the campus while they trained for the Olympics during the preceding year. Secondly, in the opening event, the 300-yard medley relay, the Buckeyes finished first by 10 yards only to be disqualified when the anchorman left the mark prematurely. Led by Bert McLachlan, Frank Reynolds, Tom Payette, and Chuck Baldwin, MSC won four of the next five events and never trailed thereafter.

Hockey—**February 6 (A) & February 20, 1953 (H):** Hockey at Michigan State was in its fourth season of rebirth and Ws were still not coming easily. Finally, following 10 straight 1952-1953 losses, Amo Bessone's squad registered its first Midwest Collegiate Hockey League victory at Houghton, where they edged Michigan Tech, 2-1. Two weeks later, back in Dem Hall, the Spartans again defeated the Huskies, 6-5. The winning goal, scored by Weldon Olson on a pass from Ray Brooks, came at the 57-second mark of a 10-minute sudden death overtime session. The five goals during regulation were credited to Olson, Steve Raz, James Ward, Derio Nicoli (all in the opening period), and Nicoli's tying marker in the third period.

Wrestling—**February 13, 1953 (H):** Losing only two matches, the Spartans completely dominated their Illinois opponents, a squad that one month later would be good enough to finish fourth in the conference championships. Ed Casalicchio at 130 pounds, Vito Perrone at 167 and heavyweight Larry Fowler each posted 6-0 shutout victories. The remaining three winners for State were Jim Knotts at 147 pounds, Bob Hoke at 157 and light heavyweight Ralph Gill.

Track and Field—**February 24, 1953 (A):** In defeating Notre Dame 73 1/3-40 2/3, the Spartans dominated the scoring as the Irish captured only three firsts in the 12-event program. Jim Kepford set the pace for the evening as he smashed the meet record for the mile run in 4:18.0. Other winners for MSC were Louis Vargha in the 440; Dick Jarrett in the 880; co-captain Mickey Walter

in the two-mile, and Henry Gillis in both hurdle events. On the infield, Jack Cunningham won the shot put, Russell Olexa took the broad jump, and Jim Browman and Ray McKay tied for first place in the high jump.

Gymnastics—**February 28, 1953 (H):** MSC ended the dual meet season on a winning note by edging Michigan, 48 1/2-47 1/2. It was the third-straight victory over the Wolverines. Carl Rintz, State's top all-around performer, was the individual star of the meet with three first places and a third to account for 21 of State's winning total. Rintz won the side horse, horizontal bars and flying rings. His achievement on the side horse was nearly flawless as the judges awarded him a composite 278 score out of a perfect 300. John Walker added a first in the trampoline and a win in the final event of the evening, tumbling. The only other Spartan first came from Harry Wilkinson on the parallel bars.

Boxing—**March 28, 1953 (H):** After losing the opening two bouts, State won five of the concluding six match-ups to defeat Maryland 5-3. Sophomore Bill Greenwood, a 156-pounder from Kalamazoo, scored the only knockout of the evening when his bout was stopped after 50 seconds into the second round. Other Spartan winners were 139-pound Bob Hoffman, by a score of 29-28; 147-pound Herb Odom, 30-24; 165-pound Tom Hickey, 30-27; and light heavyweight Al Tsakiris, 30-28.

Baseball—**May 9, 1953 (H):** In the first game of a doubleheader against Michigan, the Spartans trailed 5-2 entering the ninth inning, when they managed to tie the score, sending the contest into extra innings. Then, as leadoff man in the 11th, catcher Tom Yewcic met the first pitch served up to him and sent it over the left field fence to secure a 6-5 Spartan victory. Chuck Gorman, who pitched hitless balls in relief, gained the victory. In the second game of the afternoon, Yewcic broke his finger and was lost for the remainder of the season.

Track and Field—**May 9, 1953 (H):** The Spartan runners exploded with power as they swept eight first places in the track events while taking two field events to defeat Penn State, 89-47. Leading the parade of winning performances was Lou Vargha, who ran the 440-yard run in 48.2, setting a new meet, field, and varsity record. The previous varsity standard had been the oldest in the books, set by the Olympian Fred Alderman in 1927. Vargha wasn't through. He came back to take the 220-yard dash in a time of 21.5 to tie the field record.

Tennis—**May 13, 1953 (A) & May 18, 1953 (H):** In winning its fifth straight dual meet on May 13, State

handed the U of M their first loss of the season, 7-2. State players won the first five singles matches to assure the decision and then followed by winning two of the three doubles matches. In a return square-off five days later in East Lansing, the 7-2 winning margin was duplicated. Scoring victories on both occasions were Stan Drobac, John Sahratian, Dick Roberts, Jim Pore, and the doubles teams of Drobac-Tom Belton and Sahratian-Roberts. In an interesting twist, both of John Sahratian's singles victories came at the expense of Dave Mills, a two-time Spartan player (1950-1951) who had transferred to Ann Arbor in pursuit of a dental degree.

Baseball—**May 15, 1953 (A):** State saved itself the embarrassment of being the first Big Ten team to lose to Indiana in 1953. The Hoosiers were 0-9 in conference play. Trailing 1-0 after six innings, the Spartans finally put together three runs in the seventh and three more in the eighth for the 6-1 victory. Pitcher Bud Erickson struck out eight and allowed the Hoosiers seven scattered hits.

Tennis—**May 16, 1953 (H):** By a respectable margin of victory, State defeated the eventual 1953 conference champions from Indiana University, 6-3. With the victory, the Spartans avenged a 1952 dual-meet defeat at the hands of the Hoosiers, the only conference setback since entering Big Ten competition in 1951. Posting singles wins were Stan Drobac, Tom Belton, Jim Pore and Howard Tier. Rounding out the scoring in doubles competition were Drobac-Belton and Pore-Dave Oakland.

Golf—**May 18, 1953 (A):** Wisconsin dominated the foursome play, 6 1/2-2 1/2, but the Spartans won four of the six singles matches, opening the way to a 15 1/2-11 1/2 team victory. Scores submitted over the Walnut Hills course were: Dave Mancour 74, Bill Albright 74, Don Stevens 74, Hal Ware 76, captain Carl Mosack 79, and Arthur "Biff" Hills 82.

Baseball—**May 30, 1953 (H):** In their Memorial Day game at Old College Field, the Spartans combined good pitching, timely hitting, and errorless fielding for an 8-0 win over the University of Detroit. Dick Idzkowski provided the five-hit performance on the mound. State's 15-hit attack featured three home runs, two by Dan Brown and one from the bat of Wayne Lawrie. Fielding laurels went to the left side of the infield, where shortstop Bill Hopping and third baseman Jack Zeitler flawlessly handled nine of their team's 11 assists.

ATHLETE OF THE YEAR

Carlton Rintz, five foot six and 135 pounds, began his marvelous gymnastics career as a sophomore in 1953, when he copped Big Ten titles in the side horse, horizontal bars and flying rings, and then claimed the side horse title at the NCAAs where he would also place in three other events. Two former Olympic champions acting as judges at that national meet claimed they had never seen a better side horse performance than that executed by Rintz. His impressive season was all the more remarkable given he had undergone knee surgery in early January. His collegiate career continued with three more conference titles in 1954 (flying rings, horizontal bars and all-around) and another three in 1955 (flying rings, side horse and all-around). The Girard, Pa., native topped off that senior season by becoming the only Spartan ever to capture three NCAA titles in one season. This he accomplished on the horizontal bar, parallel bars and side horse.

Carlton Rintz

IN THE SPARTLITE

Baseball: Opening the season with a 1-8 record, the 1953 Spartans posted the poorest southern swing record since first heading south in 1926.

Catcher Tom Yewcic broke a finger in the Michigan series, forcing him to miss the final eight games of the season. As the season progressed into late May, Coach Kobs's line-up card usually included: Jack Zeitler 3B, Stan Turner or Bill Hopping SS, Chuck Mathews 1B, Dan Brown or Bob Powell LF, Captain Bob Dilday RF, Wayne Lawrie 2B, Jack Risch CF, and either Ken Stanick or Dick Edin filling in for the injured Tom Yewcic behind the plate. Bob Dangl, Bud Erickson and Dick Idzkowski rotated the starting spot on the pitching mound.

Mathews and Dilday were awarded positions on the NCAA District Four All-American team.

Basketball: After leading Indiana at half time, 40-34, MSU succumbed to a 22-point third quarter outburst that eventually paved the way for the 69-62 Indiana victory at Jenison. The Spartans had given the eventual NCAA champions all they could handle. The game was actually lost at the charity line, where the Hoosiers outshot State 27 to 12.

Al Ferrari scored 16 points in the final game on the schedule (Wisconsin) to bring his season total to 351 and surpass the team record 344 set by Bob Brannum in 1948. Ferrari's record was short lived, as Julius McCoy totaled 409 points one year later.

Boxing: Herb Odom, Bill Greenway, Tom Hickey, Alex Tsakiris and Jim Evans competed in the NCAA championships at Pocatello, Idaho. Hickey finished the season undefeated as he punched his way by three opponents to eventually capture the 165-pound title on a split decision. He thus became State's sixth NCAA boxing champion. Earning 10 team points, MSC tied with North Carolina A&T and San Jose in fourth behind host Idaho State with 25, Wisconsin 19 and Louisiana State 16.

Cross Country: The team that won the first-ever triple-crown of cross country (conference title, IC4A and NCAA) comprised Ed Townsend, John Cook, John Walter, Jerry Zerbe, and Lyle Garbe, Jim Kepford, Wayne Scutt, and Manager Bill Olson and was led by Coach Schlademan. Running for the winning points in both the Big Ten and IC4A meets was the quintet of Kepford, Zerbe, Walter, Schutt and Cook. Assisting in capturing the NCAA title was Lyle Garbe. Running as an extra, his

29th-place finish counted in the scoring as Jerry Zerbe was forced from the race after developing a pain in his side. Placing for the other four was: Kepford in third, Walter in fourth, Scutt in 12th, and Cook in 13th. When the team totals were tabulated it proved to be a close call. State tallied 65 points, which was three more than the defending champions of Indiana University.

Fencing: Led by Dick Berry, who took first place in the foil event, State compiled 29 points in the Big Ten championships at Columbus, which was good enough for a third-place finish. Dave Chase was runner-up in the epee and Ray Monte ended fourth in sabre. Berry's championship didn't come easily. Initially tied with two other competitors, he was engaged in five fence-offs before he emerged the winner.

Football: Single game tickets at home games sold for $3.60.

A season statistical leader was Billy Wells, who earned 585 net yards rushing for a 4.9 average. Quarterback Tom Yewcic completed 43 percent of his passes for 941 yards and 10 touchdowns. Ellis Duckett was on the receiving end of 10 passes, good for 323 yards and 5 touchdowns. Complemented by 37 PATs, fullback Evan Slonac was the team's scoring leader with 61 points. Next came Don McAuliffe and LeRoy Bolden, each with nine touchdowns good for 54 points.

When in Washington, D.C. to receive the Walter Camp trophy from Vice President Alban Barkley as back of the year, Don McAuliffe met the fabled Red Grange. The former Illinois All-American told him of an experience from over 20 years earlier. In Don's words:

"Grange said that in the 1920s he was making $125,000 per year playing with the Chicago Bears, and his exploits were emblazoned in headlines across the nation. Following one of the immortal's great seasons, an Illinois congressman accompanied Red to Washington to meet president Calvin Coolidge. In the introduction, the congressman said, 'Mr. President, I would like you to meet Red Grange, he's with the Chicago Bears.' President Coolidge greeted Grange with, 'Mr. Grange, it's very nice to meet you. I've always admired animal acts.'"

Not eligible for one of the limited bowl games of 1952-1953, Spartan seniors participated independently in All-Star postseason games. Dick Tamburo, Paul Dekker and Don McAuliffe were members of the Shrine Bowl East team coached by Biggie Munn. Frank Kush, John Wilson and Ed Luke played in the North-South Game; Gordie Serr, Wayne Benson and Ed Timmerman were in the Blue-Gray Game; Kush and McAuliffe were in the Senior Bowl, and Dekker was in Hawaii for the Hula Bowl.

John Wilson, a slender defensive back from Lapeer, Mich., and the first of three Wilson brothers to letter at State, was named to the inaugural Academic All-American football team. John was later selected as a Rhodes Scholar.

Golf: At the Big Ten championships, held in Ann Arbor, Ben VanAlstyne's 1953 squad carded an aggregate of 1586 strokes, which was 77 strokes better than 1952; regardless, once more they failed to escape the tenth place conference position. Over the 72 holes, Don Stevens led the team with a 77.7 average, followed by Bill Albright and Dave Mancour, who tied for second with a 79.2 stroke average, Arthur "Biff" Hills, 79.5, co-captain Carl Mosack, 80.2 and co-captain Hal Ware, 82.5.

Gymnastics: In addition to Carl Rintz's triple victory in the Big Ten championships, three other Spartans earned points toward the team's third-place total of 72. Harry Wilkinson was eighth in the parallel bars and 10th in free exercise, while John Walker and Joe Staser were sixth and 10th respectively in the trampoline event.

Featuring Carl Rintz's first-place finish on the side horse event, MSC tallied 38 points and finished seventh in the NCAA championships held at Syracuse.

Hockey: During the holiday period (December 26-January 3) the Spartans traveled west, where they played a murderous league opening six-game schedule in a nine-day period. The fact that they lost all six games (two each against North Dakota, Denver and Colorado College) is one reality. More devastating was how the games were lost, the first four by one-goal margins: 5-4, 5-4, 2-1 and 5-4. The team never recovered, finishing with an overall record of 5-16-1.

Upon completion of the season, two sophomores were honored. Weldie Olson was acknowledged as the team's MVP, and Jack Mayes, who scored 26 points, took team-scoring honors for the second straight year.

Swimming and Diving: Scoring 48 points, the team finished third at the Big Ten championships and later placed fifth at the NCAAs with 14 points.

Top performers of the year were senior distance man Bert McLachlan, freshman breaststroker John Dudeck, and individual medley specialist Frank Reynolds. McLachlan won the 440-yard freestyle event at the Big Ten meet and placed second in the 1,500-meter freestyle and 200-yard backstroke. He placed third in the 1,500-meter event at the National Collegiates. Dudeck established a new team record in the 200-yard breaststroke (2:20.1) and later won the 100-breaststroke title at the Big Tens, followed by a fifth-place finish in the same event at the national collegiates. During the dual-meet season, Reynolds posted a team record 1:34.6 in the 150-yard individual medley and then swam to a second and fourth in the IM at the conference and national meets, respectively.

Tennis: The Spartans took four titles at the conference championships held in Evanston, Ill. Stan Drobac at number one and Jim Pore at number five claimed singles titles, and then Drobac teamed with Tom Belton to take the number one doubles title with John Sahratian and Dick Roberts scoring an upset victory in the number two doubles position. Compiling a team score of 58 1/2, State fell just shy of Indiana's championship total of 64 1/2.

Completing his collegiate career, Drobac finished the season undefeated and with only one loss over two years.

Track and Field: Jim Vrooman high jumped 6' 4 1/4" to become State's only winner at the Big Ten indoor championships. Totaling 15-5/12 points, the team finished fifth.

Seven men scored points, and the team moved to the third spot at the outdoor conference meet. Miler Jim Kepford upset the defending champion while capturing first place in a time of 4:18.4. Lou Vargha finished second in the 440 and third in the 220, while John Corbelli captured second place in the low hurdles and fourth in the highs. Other scoring came from Russ Olexa's third in the broad jump; Richard Jarrett's fifth-place in the 880; Ray McKay's third place tie in the high jump. Vrooman, the indoor champion, slipped to a fifth-place tie also in the high jump.

One week following his Big Ten championship run, Kepford ran an even faster 4:14.2 mile to defeat all challengers at the Central Collegiate meet in Milwaukee.

Wrestling: After finishing in third place over its first two seasons at the Big Ten championships, State scored 22 points and moved to the runner-up spot at the 1953 meet held in Bloomington, Ind. Two Spartans were crowned champions, Bob Hoke at 157 pounds and Vito Perrone at 167.

Freshman Jim Sinadinos and Dale Thomas, the grad student assistant coach, emerged as champions at the National AAUs held in Toledo, Ohio.

EXTRA! FOOTBALL 28-GAME WIN STREAK CONTINUES

One of the longest winning streaks in NCAA history was achieved by the Biggie Munn-coached teams of 1950-1953. It was a remarkable and memorable era of Michigan State football.

(#16) September 27, 1952 (A): In the season-opener, Michigan scored first with a pair of touchdowns but its vision of an upset quickly vanished as State followed with four scores and won going away, 27-13. On the first play from scrimmage following the second Wolverine TD, McAuliffe broke loose on a 70-yard gallop behind a crushing block by Doug Bobo. That one run covered more yardage than the total of all nine touchdowns which Don scored in 1951. Moments later, on their very next possession, it was time for Tom Yewcic to step forward. The new starting quarterback engineered a four-play touchdown drive that began at the State 31 and included two passes, a 23-yard hookup to LeRoy Bolden and then a 40-yard thriller to Ellis Duckett. Still in the first half, State broke the 13-13 tie on an 86-yard drive following a Jim Ellis interception. Billy Wells ran it in from the 10. Nine plays produced the final touchdown midway into the third quarter. Tommy Devine, *Detroit Free Press* staff writer and past Spartan critic, had to concede: "Michigan State displayed great power, explosive speed, superlative depth, and championship poise."

(#17) October 4, 1952 (A): The opponent was Kip Taylor's Oregon State Beavers and the place was Multnomah Stadium in Portland. The score was knotted at 14-14 with only seconds remaining in the contest. Doug Weaver tells the story from there:

Spartan safety Jim Ellis runs the ball against the Wolverines.

"There are, no doubt, more famous field goals in Spartan football history. However, the field goal kicked by Gene Lekenta, after the apparent end of the game, may have had the greatest ramification— the sine qua non—the kick without which the streak would have ended and a chance for a national championship denied. Other Spartan heroes had emerged during the streak and more would arise. On this Saturday a seldom-used senior from Grand Rapids would rise from certain anonymity to perpetuate the 1952 Spartans' chance at football immortality. I still remember the sidelines (traveling squads were much smaller then) and seeing my teammates. Some were standing, some were kneeling and some praying. The ball was snapped by Jim Neal. The ball was caught and placed by Tom Yewcic. The line blocked ("Biggie's Broad Beams") and there was silence as Gene put his foot into it. Finally, the Green-and-White sideline turned into a madhouse as the kick went straight and true. Time marched on. Memorable games were contested and bigger-name opponents defeated, but here's to you Gene Lekenta, wherever you are."

Note: One additional fact embellishes Doug's story. Lekenta initially *missed* the kick, but Oregon State was offside. After administering the five-yard penalty, it was Gene's second try that split the uprights and landed in the bleachers as time ran out.

(#18) October 11, 1952 (H): Before a near sellout home crowd of 49,123 and a national TV audience, the Spartans racked up 592 total yards, 30 first downs, and seven touchdowns to defeat Texas A&M, 48-6. Over the course of the afternooon, State, second-ranked in the Associated Press poll, poured three left halfbacks, three right halfbacks, four fullbacks, and two quarterbacks into the battle. As the A&M coach said after the game: "It's not Michigan State's first team that gets you. It's their second and their third and their fourth that gets to you." Ellis Duckett, sophomore, end, was credited with two touchdowns, one covering 80 yards just before half time. The remaining five TDs were credited to: Don McAuliffe, LeRoy Bolden, Evan Slonac, Bert Zagers and Herb Raterink.

(#19) October 18, 1952 (H): The Spartans entered the Syracuse game ranked as the nation's number-one team by the AP wire service and then proved it with a one-sided 48-7 shellacking of the Orange. Before five minutes had ticked off the Macklin Field clock, Jim Ellis, the clever safety, gathered in a punt at his own 42 and raced down the east sideline for the first TD. That was only the beginning. It was 27-0 by half time, 41-0 at the conclusion of the third period, and before it was over 61 MSC players had seen playing time. The MSC defense was solid with Frank Kush, Henry Bullough, Don Dohoney, Ed Luke, Jack Morgan, Dick Tamburo, Doug Weaver and Don Kauth who recovered two Syracuse fumbles on the afternoon.

(#20) October 25, 1952 (H): Penn State scored first but MSC, before a Homecoming crowd of 51,162, scored second, third, fourth, fifth and sixth to win their 20th in a row, 34-7. Spartan passers connected on only nine of 21 tosses, but four were for touchdowns: Yewcic to Doug Bobo, Yewcic to Ellis Duckett, and Yewcic to Don McAuliffe. The senior back-up quarterback with a seemingly scripted name, Willie Thrower, tossed the final score to LeRoy Bolden. The only TD made on the ground came on the second posession of the second half when Billy Wells carried the final 20 yards of a nine-play drive. Paul Dekker cleared the path with a smashing block that knocked down, not one, but two Lion defenders.

(#21) November 1, 1952 (A): State scored two first-half touchdowns and then hung on to defeat the Purdue Boilermakers, 14-7, at Ross-Ade Stadium. Pesky Purdue began a potential game-tying drive from its own 20-yard line late in the fourth quarter. As the clock ticked down the Boilers moved relentlessly down the field and with little more than two minutes remaining they had reached the Spartan nine-yard line. On a second down quarterback Dale Samuels, the best forward passer in the conference and 17 of 31 for that afternoon, made his bid with a jump pass over the middle. Linebacker Doug Weaver, the 188-pound senior from nearby Goshen, held his ground and the ball came directly into his hands. "The Weave" calmly clutched the ball and raced back to the "S" 20-yard line before he was brought down. Michigan State had survived for its 21st win in a row.

(#22) November 8, 1952 (A): Playing before a meager 22,000 in Bloomington and amidst intermittent rain showers, State ground out a "seldom in doubt" 41-14 victory over Indiana. Because of the slippery ball, the attack was confined mostly to the ground with halfback Billy Wells and fullback Evan Slonac the primary contributors. Wells carried 24 times for 135 yards and two touchdowns while Slonac rushed 19 times for 104 yards. Other TDs were scored by Don McAuliffe (2), Doug Bobo, and LeRoy Bolden. While Tom Yewcic completed only two passes in four throws, the 61 yards gained gave the Conemaugh, Pa., junior an accumulated season total of 872 yards, thus eclipsing the record previously held by Al Dorow of the 1951 team at 842 yards. The game was marred by "extra curricular" roughness and game officials responded by ejecting six Hoosiers and two Spartans.

(#23) November 15, 1952 (H): The largest crowd ever to pack Macklin Field, 52,472 fans, sat through perfect football weather to see the Spartans defeat Notre Dame for the third straight time, 21-3. All points came in the second half with the Irish scoring first on a 16-yard field goal. State then followed with three touchdowns, two by captain Don McAuliffe in the third quarter, and another by Evan Slonac on a 24-yard end run in the final period. Slonac converted all three PATs. ND held the nation's number one offensive team to an unaccustomed 169 yards, this against State's seven game average of 475 yards. One figure that glared from the game's statistical chart was under "fumbles lost." Seven times the visitors dropped the ball and seven times the alert Spartan defense pounced on it. Dick Tamburo, the outstanding linebacker, fell on three of the turnovers with Gordie Serr, Don Dohoney, Ray Vogt, and Henry Bullough accounted for the remaining four. Two of the recoveries led directly to Michigan State TDs.

(#24) November 22, 1952 (H): In their most one-sided victory since 1949, MSC closed out a second successive undefeated season by overwhelming the Hilltoppers of Marquette, 62-13. It was 28-7 at the intermission and as the points rolled up in the second half Coach Munn cleared his bench with all 60 players seeing action. State's game statistics were impressive, regardless of the fact that a saturating rain fell all morning until kickoff. They netted 601 yards on the day with a rushing total of 454, 11 shy of the team's best ever. They racked up a record 33 first downs of which 25 were by rushing, yet another team record. Fullback and place kicker Evan Slonac, tied the point-after-touchdown record of eight made by George Smith in two 1948 games. Nineteen seniors played their final game as Spartans.

Coach Munn and Gene Lekenta examine the shoe that kicked the winning field goal on Oct. 4, 1952.

MSC
1953-1954

TALES TO TELL

The conference baseball title was decided on the final weekend of Big Ten play when the Spartans edged Ohio State twice, 6-4 and 6-5. Perhaps that entire afternoon hinged on an incident in the opening game as told by the sophomore third baseman, Jim Sack:

"From my vantage point at third base, the following play remains vividly in my mind. My involvement is minimal, but the net effect is considerable. It was the final Saturday of the Big Ten baseball season at home at Old College Field. We needed a double-header win over Ohio State to win the first-ever MSC Big Ten baseball championship. Around the fifth inning of the first game Buckeye shortstop (football All-American halfback) Howard 'Hop-a-Long' Cassady is on first base. Our first baseman was Chuck Mathews, a focused competitor and marvelous hitter as well as a classy fielder. He was a key man in our lineup. The batter in the box lifted a high foul ball near the third base bag. As I stepped across the foul line to make an easy catch, I became aware out of the corner of my eye of some commotion as Cassady scrambled back to first base. He had apparently taken off with the pitch for second on a hit-and-run play. I hoped and prayed my throw to first after the catch would be accurate and in time for the double play. It was, and Chuck put a 'hard tag' on Cassady. 'Hop-a-Long,' also a competitor, came up swinging, and, in the ensuing melee, Chuck sustained a blow to the head, which Doc Feurig said was a slight concussion and said that Chuck was finished playing for the day. Coach Kobs then inserted Bob Williams, a right-handed hitter, into the lineup. We won the first game, and in the second, it was Williams, Mathews' replacement, who hit two homers, including one to dead center field, that helped win the clincher. He was heard to remark as he is crossed home plate after the second home run, 'I'm sure getting into a rut.' That was how Michigan State won its first Big Ten baseball championship . . . perhaps."

SCOREBOARD

	W	L	T	Avg.
Baseball	25	10	1	.708
Track and Field	1	2	0	.333
Football	9	1	0	.900
Basketball	9	13	0	.409
Tennis	9	7	0	.563
Cross Country	1	2	0	.333
Swimming and Diving	6	2	0	.750
Wrestling	6	2	0	.750
Hockey	8	14	1	.370
Fencing	2	9	0	.182
Golf	7	4	0	.636
Boxing	4	1	2	.625
Gymnastics	3	4	0	.429

The Big Ten champion Spartans hosted and defeated Ohio University in a two-out-of-three district playoff series to qualify for MSC's first-ever appearance at the College Worlds Series in Omaha, Neb., June 10-14. The ensuing games were broadcast to mid-Michigan by Bob Shackleton over WKAR radio.

State opened the series in style by mauling the University of Massachusetts, 16-5. The game unraveled in the fourth as UMass fielders committed four errors leading to Tom Yewcic's grand-slam home run. John Matsock connected for a three-run homer in the fifth, and Jack Risch did likewise in the seventh. Ed Hobaugh was the winning pitcher.

Game number two ended in a slim 2-1 victory over the pre-tournament favorites, the University of Arizona. Walt Godfrey opened on the mound but was forced to the bench in the fifth. Reliever Dick Idzkowski pitched brilliantly over the closing four innings, allowing no hits while striking out eight with his blinding fast ball. The game was won in the sixth as pinch hitter Ron Stead of Midland accounted for both runs with a slashing double just inside the third base line.

In game number three, a night affair that ran well past midnight, State met its first loss in the double-elimination tournament. Little Rollins College of Winter Park, Fla., cut through a 4-1 deficit to score once in the sixth and the eighth, and twice in the bottom of the ninth to hand MSC a bitter 5-4 defeat.

The next evening State stayed alive by reversing form on the Rollins team, 3-2. Trailing 2-0, John Polomsky managed to send the game into extra innings with a two-RBI sixth-inning double. In the 10th, Bob Powell scored the eventual winning run on a base hit by Jack Risch.

Playing their fifth game in five days, State bowed out of the tournament, losing to the eventual champions, the University of Missouri, 4-3. With the game tied 3-3 after 8 1/2 innings, the winning run was generated by a base on balls, a passed ball and an RBI single off the bat of the pitcher. Base hits by Bob Brown, Yewcic, and Stead had accounted for two MSC runs in the seventh, and Chuck Mathews scored after leading off the eighth with a triple.

TEAM OF THE YEAR

With a team record 25 wins and an appearance at the NCAA tournament, the 1954 baseball Team of the Year is pictured below.

The 1954 baseball team. (Front row, left to right) G. Smith, W. Hopping, C. Gorman, B. Williams, J. Zeitler, J. Risch, D. Brown, E. Erickson, J. Sack. (Second row, left to right) J. Wenner, E. Morrall, R. Stead, J. Polomsky, D. Idzkowski, W. Godfrey, B. Powell, J. Matsock. (Third row, left to right) mgr. D. Loundy, J. Heppinstall, C. Mathews, R. Collard, W. Mansfield, E. Hobaugh, Coach Kobs, Asst. Coach F. Pellerin.

MAKING HISTORY

Upon gaining Big Ten Conference membership back in 1949, a stipulation was imposed that State's entry into a football title chase would be deferred until 1953. Consequently, that fall's season-opening 21-7 victory over Iowa would have historic significance as MSC's first win as a conference member. The eventual season record of 9-1 was good enough for a first-place tie with Illinois, necessitating a vote of the conference athletic directors to determine the Big Ten representative in the Rose Bowl, the only postseason option at the time. The entire campus waited Sunday, November 22, in eager anticipation. Finally, at 8:30 P.M., to the surprise of most, Michigan State received the favorable selection following five straight tie ballots.

A spring intramural soccer league was put in place by the Spartan Soccer Club in anticipation of the sport gaining full intercollegiate recognition by the university athletic department in the fall of 1954.

GREAT STATE DATES

Cross Country—**October 10, 1953 (H):** Completing the home course in 20:46.8 with seemingly little exertion, captain Lyle Garbe led the defending NCAA champions to a season-opening 23-33 victory over Notre Dame. His nearest competitor, the top Irish runner, was 80 yards behind. Finishing the scoring for State were: John Cook in third, Ron Barnes and Dick Jarrett tied for fifth and Ken Barley in eighth place.

Football—**November 7, 1953 (A):** Following the 6-0 loss to Purdue, the only setback of the season, the Spartans defeated Oregon State 34-6 and then headed for Columbus, Ohio. Entering the final quarter of that game against the Buckeyes, Biggie's crew led 14-13, but OSU was on the MSC 23-yard line. The defense responded, forcing a field goal attempt that was blocked by Jerry Planutis. Taking over on their own 30-yard line, the Spartans drove 70 yards, and LeRoy Bolden negotiated the final 20 yards for his third touchdown of the afternoon. As the crowd was leaving the stadium, MSC scored again, this time on a Tom Yewcic to Ellis Duckett pass with 18 seconds remaining. The final score read: MSC 28, Ohio State 13.

Football—**November 14, 1953 (H):** Playing before 52,324, the second largest crowd in Macklin Stadium history, and another 55 million television viewers as NBC's "Game of the Week," State defeated Michigan, 14-6, for the fifth time in a row. Coupled with Wisconsin's defeat of Illinois, Michigan State was guaranteed a share of the conference title in its first year of Big Ten competition. Both touchdowns were on short passes. Earl Morrall threw five yards to Jim Ellis in the second quarter, while Bert Zagers tossed four yards to Ellis Duckett shortly after the second half started. Evan Slonac kicked both extra points.

Basketball—**December 5, 1953 (H):** With 2:15 to go in the game against Creighton, Jim Schlatter scored one of his two field goals to raise the score to 83-47 and break the record for the most points scored by a State team in Jenison Fieldhouse. Al Ferrari shot 48 percent on the night for a total of 26 points, pacing the Spartans to the 88-51 milestone in front of 6,614 enthusiastic fans. In an effort to keep the score down, coach Pete Newell gave his reserves plenty of playing time, and 13 of his 15 players scored. Defensively, MSC kept Creighton to 21 percent from the field, holding their star center to just one field goal and forcing 27 of their points to come from free throws. Sophomore Julius McCoy added 14 points for the victors, Bob Armstrong scored 12 and sophomore Duane Peterson put in 10.

Wrestling—**January 18, 1954 (A):** By the narrowest of margins, State defeated Iowa, 15-14, in the second dual meet of the season. The Hawkeyes actually won one more match than Fendley Collins's crew (four to three with one tie), but Jim Sinadinos and Ed Casalicchio had back-to-back pins in the 130- and 137-pound divisions to gain the bonus team points accounting for the one-point advantage. Captain Bob Hoke, at 157 pounds, scored a 6-1 decision for the Spartans' only other win.

Swimming and Diving—**January 22 & 23, 1954 (A):** By identical scores of 53-47, the Spartans took back-to-back meets against Iowa State and the University of Iowa. Capturing firsts in both meets were Tom Payette, 50-yard freestyle; John Dudeck, 200-yard breaststroke; Jack Beattie, 440-yard freestyle, and the medley relay team of Frank Paganini, Dudeck and Chuck Baldwin.

Basketball—**January 23, 1954 (H):** Sophomore Julius McCoy, the six-foot-two Farrell, Pa., scoring sensation, led MSC to a 83-76 victory over Ohio State before 7,676 fans at Jenison. The dazzling sophomore

poured in 34 points to tie the team's modern day scoring record established by Bill Rapchak against Marquette University in 1950. The game was much closer than the final count would indicate as the Spartans trailed 63-58 before catching fire and outscoring the Buckeyes, 25-13 over the final eight minutes of play.

Boxing—**January 30, 1954 (A):** Tom Hickey, George Sisinni and Mike Maekawa scored first round knockouts to lead MSC to a 5-3 victory over Penn State. Hickey needed 1:45 minutes and Sisinni's bout lasted 1:50, while Maekawa unleashed a barrage of lefts and rights to finish his opponent in just 37 seconds. Herb Odom's split decision win and draws by Bob Mullins and Jack Reilly completed the Spartan scoring.

Wrestling—**February 5 & 6, 1954 (H):** In a highly gratifying weekend, the grapplers first defeated Purdue, 18-10, and then easily handled an old nemesis, the Iowa State Teachers College, 24-4. The victory on Friday over the eventual Big Ten champions, was paced by Dick Abraham, who upset the Boilermaker's entrant, a Turkish Olympian. Other winners over PU were Jim Sinadinos, Ed Casalicchio and Larry Fowler. On Saturday evening, 157-pound Bob Hoke won the feature match when he easily defeated the Teachers' defending NCAA champion, 9-1.

Gymnastics—**February 11, 1954 (H):** For the second straight meet, Carl Rintz won all four events in which he participated, leading the Szypula crew to an upset 49-47 victory over the strong University of Minnesota squad. With only one event remaining on the program and trailing 43-37, the Gophers were confident their tumbling squad was capable of overtaking the Spartans' margin, but the MSC trio of Ben Gunning, Bud Bronson, and Jerry Gildemeister managed six points to preserve a two-point win.

Fencing—**February 20, 1954 (H):** In a triangular meet, also involving Wisconsin University, Charley Schmitter's squad edged the Iowa Hawkeyes 14-13. Although Jack Moffett led the way by winning six bouts, Ralph Powell was the climactic hero as he managed to win his final match to seal the team's one-point victory.

Basketball—**March 6, 1954 (H):** In the season finale, a 76-61 victory over Michigan, Julius McCoy tossed in seven field goals and 10 free throws to establish a team record season high of 409 points. His mark bettered teammate Al Ferrari's 351 established in 1952-1953. As the final score of the game might indicate, the contest was

never in real doubt. The Spartans jumped in front at the start, raced to an eight-point lead at the quarter, 23-15, and were ahead at halftime 39-29. Maintaining the momentum, State gradually widened the breach and twice led by 20 points. Hitting double-digits along with McCoy's 24 were Duane Peterson with 18 and Bob Devenny 14.

Hockey—**March 6, 1954 (H):** In the most exciting victory of the year (there were only eight), State topped the North Dakota Sioux in overtime, 2-1. Due to injuries, Amo Bessone's squad was so short-handed that defenseman John Thomas played the entire 20 minutes of the opening period and was on the ice almost continually over the final two periods. Recruited to fill in for the injured, Buck Nystrom from the football team played sparingly.

Boxing—**March 8, 1954 (H):** The Spartans boosted their record to 4-0-1 after stopping Idaho State, the 1953 NCAA champions, 6-2. This rematch followed a 4-4 tie between the two teams three weeks earlier in Pocatello, Idaho. Before the bell sounded for the opening round, Michigan State was in a comfortable position, because the Bengals, decimated with injuries, had been forced to forfeit the 119, 165 and 178 pound bouts. Three successive wins put the match away for MSC. Norm Andrie registered a close 29-28 victory at 139 pounds; Bob Mullins followed with a third-round TKO after he himself had been knocked down in the opening round, and Herb Odom, who had moved up one division to 156 pounds, scored a unanimous 30-24 decision.

Track and Field—**May 1, 1954 (H):** State opened the outdoor dual meet season with an impressive 79-62 victory over Notre Dame. Individual winners were Kevin Gosper in the 440, Dick Jarrett in the 880, Don Hillmer in the high jump, Ed Brabham in the broad jump, David Goodell in the shot put and John Corbelli in both hurdle events.

Golf—**May 3, 1954 (H):** Ben VanAlstyne's golfers won their third straight match of the spring by defeating Notre Dame, 15 1/2-11 1/2. After the squads broke even in the morning doubles matches, captain Joe Albright, Ken Rodewald and Bill Diedrich each managed afternoon round victories in the singles competition that earned three points toward the team as winning total.

Baseball—**May 8, 1954 (A):** In the third weekend of Big Ten play, State raised its conference-leading record to 6-1 on Saturday with a double win at Minneapolis, 8-

5 and 6-2. Sophomore Ed Hobaugh and senior Bud Erickson were the pitchers who went the distance for the winners. MSC was never really in trouble in the opener after scoring three times in both the second and third innings. Ray Collard, Tom Yewcic and Bob Powell each smashed a home run. State put the second game away, 6-2, with four runs in the fifth.

Tennis—**May 15, 1954 (H):** With Coach Stan Drobac at the microphone, the 7-1 victory over Wisconsin was the first tennis match to be televised by the college station, WKAR-TV. The abbreviated team score (eight total points, not nine) is attributed to the fact that the number one doubles match, involving MSC's Jim Pore and Dick Menzel, was aborted prematurely to permit the Badger team members to make their rail connections at the Grand Trunk station in Lansing.

ATHLETE OF THE YEAR

No Spartan football player ever broke into the line up in a more auspicious style than Tom Yewcic (FB 1951-1953, BS 1953-1954) in 1951. Trailing Ohio State 20-17, the Conemaugh, Pa., sophomore, entered his first collegiate game with little more than five minutes remain-

Tom Yewcic

ing and immediately threw the illustrious game-winning "transcontinental pass" to Al Dorow. As the starting quarterback over the next two seasons, Yewcic engineered the Spartans to a combined 19-1 record, including the 28-20 Rose Bowl victory over UCLA. Although he played during a "running" era, as part of the famed "Pony Backfield," his passing proficiency was great enough that his name remains in the team's Top Ten list, with 18 career and 10 season touchdown passes. As one of the last triple-threat back to wear the Green and White, Tom remains listed with the team's 11th-best career punting average. Yewcic has the rare distinction of having been selected as an All-American in football (NBC-TV, 1952) and as a catcher in baseball (American Association of College Baseball Coaches, 1954). During that senior baseball season of 1954, when MSC finished third at the College World Series, Tom Yewcic was selected as the tournament's MVP.

IN THE SPARTLITE

Baseball: Chuck Mathews (1B), Jack Risch (CF) and Tom Yewcic (C) ended the season by being selected to the All-Big Ten first team. Second team picks were John Matsock (SS) and Bud Erickson (P).

Basketball: Coach Pete Newell had his entire team back from the 1952-1953 edition that had tied for third place in the conference. Unfortunately, problems set in from the beginning. Academic ineligibility sidelined Rickey Ayala and Walt Godfrey, and injuries hindered Bob Devenny and Jim Schlatter, forcing two high-scoring forwards, Al Ferrari and Keith Stackhouse, to fill unfamiliar spots in the back court.

In a contest that could be labeled as both the most exciting and most disappointing of the season, State was edged by the defending NCAA champions and conference leading Indiana University, 63-61. A rally pulled State from a 15-point deficit in the third quarter to a 61-61 tie with two minutes to play. Then with 1:20 remaining, the visiting Hoosiers grabbed the ball and waited patiently as the clocked ticked down (no shot clock). With one second remaining, a 20-footer caught nothing but net as the horn sounded to end the game. Among the capacity crowd of 10,948 were 80 who had made the trip from Julius McCoy's hometown of Farrell, Pa. He had responded with a game-high 20 points.

Pete Newell's final season at MSC would be 1953-1954, as the popular coach would depart after signing a three-year contract with the University of California at Berkeley effective July 1, 1954.

Boxing: An interesting sequence of events led to the 4-4 draw at Idaho State. First, Coach Makris had planned to move Tom Hickey up to the 178-pound slot, replacing Bill Greenway, who was in the hospital nursing a kidney injury. Then before heading west, it was revealed that Idaho State's only 178-pounder had suffered a broken bone in his hand, thus giving Hickey a forfeit win. With this turn of events, Hickey was returned to his familiar 165-pound slot in the Spartan lineup. Then, during the pre-fight weigh-ins, it was learned the Idaho State 165-pounder had come down with the flu and was unable to compete. Once more, the Chicago junior was awarded a forfeit. He had registered a double-win without lacing on a pair of gloves.

There doesn't seem to be any justice. Consider heavyweight Jack Reilly. It is likely that no one spent more time running, punching the bag, skipping rope or sharpening his skills in the boxing room during the 1954 season. Furthermore, with a personal overall record of 0-6-1, few teammates likely took any more punches over the course of the season. Yet, lacking the required two wins to qualify, Reilly did not earn a varsity award. Little wonder he didn't return in 1955.

Once more, out-of-the-ring factors dashed the hopes for another NCAA team title. When winter term grades were reported just days prior to scheduled departure for the NCAAs at College Station, Pa., both newcomer Choken Maekawa and Tom Hickey, the 1953 champion, were declared academically ineligible. It was a devastating blow. Regardless, Herb Odom, Bill Greenway, George Sisinni, Norm Andrie and little-used 119-pound Shedd Smith took up the cause. Undefeated for the entire season, Odom was the sole survivor as he battled to the welterweight championship on a judge's unanimous decision. The win marked the 11th individual championship secured by a Spartan boxer.

Cross Country: Even with the loss of the top four runners from the championship squad of 1952, Coach Schlademan managed to field a team that successfully defended the Big Ten and IC4A titles. They did fall short of another NCAA championship, finishing in sixth place. At the conference meet in Chicago, State scored 39 points, four better than Indiana, to win their third straight team

title. John Cook was the top Spartan, finishing in second place; Ron Barr was sixth; Lyle Garbe seventh; Dick Jarrett was 10th and Ken Barley was 14th.

At the IC4A in New York City, Garbe was 11th, Cook 18th, Dick Jarrett 19th, Ron Barr 29th, and Ken Barley 31st. The team's score of 82 points barely edged the Pittsburgh quintet that combined for 84 points followed by Penn State, the pre-meet favorite, finishing third with 88. Upon returning to Lansing, 120 loyal Spartan fans were on hand to greet the team at the Capital City Airport.

Fencing: Jack Moffet placed third in the epee event at the conference meet, as the Spartans finished sixth among seven competing teams.

Football: The 1953 football season opened under new NCAA rules that abolished two-platoon football, allowing players to enter the game only once each quarter.

The 1953 team posted a 9-1 record and featured a starting backfield diminutive in size and billed as the "Pony Backfield:" Tom Yewcic (5-11, 172), QB; LeRoy Bolden (5-7, 157), HB; Billy Wells (5-9, 175), HB; and Evan Slonac (5-8, 170), FB. The quartet played hard, but such mettle was necessary against the big linemen they encountered.

The 28-20 Rose Bowl win on January 1, 1954 would be Biggie Munn's final game as head coach. He soon replaced Ralph Young as Director of Athletics.

Golf: Ken Rodewald scored a 81-76-74-76—307 to finish in 11th place at the Big Ten meet, with the team ending up in eighth place.

Gymnastics: Having accumulated 54 points by winning the horizontal bars and all-around titles, Carl Rintz topped all competitors at the Big Ten tournament. He also tied teammate Ken Cook in the flying rings and placed second on both the side horse and parallel bars. Sophomore Ben Gunning added to the team's fourth-place 71 points with a fourth in the parallel bars.

At the NCAAs in Champaign, Ill., Carl Rintz was unable to successfully defend his side-horse title, finishing second. He placed in three other individual events and was fifth in the all-around. With 37 points, State was fifth in the team standings.

Hockey: State opened the season with a flurry of 36 goals leading to victory in four of the first five games. Then, before the season could resume on January 8, the team had lost captain Henry Campanini and high-scor-

ing winger Jack Mayes via the academic eligibility route. The team then lost nine in a row before registering another win.

On February 6, goaltender Ed Schiller made a school-record 73 saves in the 5-4 loss to Denver and a record 123 saves in that weekend's two-game series. Three nights later, for the first time since the 1929 season, State played a 0-0 scoreless tie, this time against the University of Michigan.

Even amidst another losing season, center Weldie Olson continued steady play by winning his third straight team scoring title with 21 goals and 19 assists for a total of 40 points.

Swimming and Diving: Leading the swimmers and divers of 1953-1954 was John Dudeck of Detroit, who broke a Big Ten record with a 59.7 in the 100-yard breaststroke at the conference meet. Also scoring at those championships were Bruce Aldrich, fifth in the 150-yard individual medley; Don Morey and Lewis Michaud, fifth and sixth respectively in the diving; Tom Payette, sixth in the 50-yard freestyle, and Jack Beattie, sixth in the 220-yard freestyle. With a team total of 35 points, State finished in the third spot.

Tennis: The 1954 edition of MSC tennis included a brother combination of number three singles sophomore Dave Brogan and number five singles junior John Brogan. Growing up in the East Lansing area, the pair was encouraged and tutored by former MSC great Rex Norris (1932-1934).

In Champaign, Illinois, Indiana University edged State 64 1/4 to 58 1/4 to win the Big Ten championship. The Spartans did capture two singles and two doubles titles. Captain Stan Drobac, who didn't lose a match all season, emerged as champion in the number-one position while Jim Pore took the number five singles crown. In doubles, Drobac and Tom Belton were champions at number one, and the team of Dick Roberts-John Sahratian took the honors at number two.

Track and Field: The Illinois and Kansas University track and field teams remained in East Lansing following the MSC Relays to engage the Spartans in a Monday night triangular meet at Jenison Fieldhouse. The Illini managed 48 1/2 points to finish first, followed by State with 42 and Kansas 39 1/2. The Jayhawks' Wes Santee

stole the headlines when, in the opening event, the mile run, he broke the tape in 4:04.9 to establish a new world's indoor record.

At the conference indoor championships in Champaign, Ill., State finished in the fifth spot with 19 1/2 points. John Cook was the only Spartan champion, as he posted 1:54.9 in the 880-yard run. Other individual scorers for MSC were Ray Eggleston, Dave Goodell, Joe Savoldi, Lyle Garbe, John Corbelli, Ed Brabham and Travis Buggs.

The foursome of Harlan Benjamin, John Corbelli, Ray Eggelston and Bill Brendel captured the 480-yard shuttle hurdle event at the Drake Relays. The latter two runners were substitutes for the injured Henry Gillis and Joe Savoldi.

As in the Conference Indoor championships, John Cook was the sole Spartan champion at the Big Ten outdoor meet where he ran a 4:14.1 mile.

One week following MSC's third place finish at the Big Tens, an eight-man team captured the Central Collegiates at Milwaukee. Two Spartans emerged as champions, Ed Brabham who ran a 21.9 in the 220-yard dash and Australian Kevin Gosper set a school record with a 47.8 in the 440.

Wrestling: In 1954, the Northwestern Wildcats initiated a quadrangular meet that included Minnesota, Purdue and Michigan State. This four-team format in January would continue for 14 seasons. Going undefeated and leading MSC to victory in that first meet were: captain and 157-pound Bob Hoke, 177-pound Richard Abraham and heavyweight Larry Fowler.

After failing to win a match as a sophomore in 1953, Ted Lennox won his first collegiate match when he shutout the Ohio State captain, 5-0, in MSC's 20-6 victory over the Buckeyes. Lennox, of Lansing, was totally blind.

Bob Hoke, undefeated through the dual meet season, captured his second straight 157-pound Big Ten title in the conference meet held at Jenison Fieldhouse. Jim Sinadinos was beaten in the finals, while Vito Perrone, Ed Casalicchio, and Larry Fowler met defeat in the semifinals. As a team, the Spartans collected 20 points to finish in third place.

State scored only 11 points to finish in sixth place at the NCAAs hosted by the University of Oklahoma.

EXTRA! 1954 Rose Bowl

January 1, 1954—Pasadena, California

	1	2	3	4	F
MSC	0	7	14	7	28
UCLA	7	7	0	6	20

Starting line-up:

Bill Quinlan	LE
Jim Jebb	LT
Ferris Hallmark	LG
Jim Neal	C
Henry Bullough	RG
Larry Fowler	RT
Don Dohoney (C)	RE
Tom Yewcic	QB
LeRoy Bolden	LH
Billy Wells	RH
Evan Slonac	FB

Taking advantage of two Michigan State turnovers, UCLA jumped to a 14-0 lead before the Spartans could work their way back into contention in this, the school's first-ever Rose Bowl appearance. The key to the resurgence came when the speedy defensive end, Ellis Duckett, streaked in from the left flank to block a Bruin punt at the 10-yard line with 4:45 remaining in the first half. The ball hit the ground on UCLA's seven-yard line, bounced back into Duckett's arms and he carried it into the end zone unmolested. With Evan Slonac's PAT the halftime score read 14-7. More significantly, State had gained the momentum. Taking the second half kickoff, they drove 78 yards on 14 running plays with LeRoy Bolden diving in from the one-yard line, and six minutes later Billy Wells capped a 73-yard drive with a two-yard scoring run. The drama persisted as UCLA scored with 12:36 remaining but their kicker missed the point after. Hanging on 21-20 and with 4:51 remaining, Wells put the game away when he gathered in a punt and raced 62 yards for an insurance touchdown. Slonac completed four-of-four conversion attempts. Including a meager 11 yards passing, MSU totaled 206 yards (running and passing) as opposed to 242 for the losing team. As the leading ball carrier, Wells picked up 80 yards on 14 carries.

Ellis Duckett blocked UCLA punter Paul Cameron's attempt in the second quarter and then returned the ball six yards for a touchdown to put the Spartans on the board in the 1954 Rose Bowl.

EXTRA! FOOTBALL 28-GAME WIN STREAK ENDS

One of the longest winning streaks in NCAA history was achieved by the Biggie Munn coached teams of 1950-1953. After the streak-ending 6-0 upset by Purdue on October 24, 1953, the Spartans reeled off another four straight wins to finish that season tied for first in the conference with a 5-1 (9-1 overall) record.

(#25) September 26, 1953 (A): The national champions of 1952 opened their inaugural Big Ten season at Iowa City, Iowa, and emerged with a 21-7 victory over the Hawkeyes. The Spartans were poised and steady as Larry Fowler recovered a first-quarter Iowa fumble which led to the initial touchdown with Billy Wells going in from the 3-yard line. A Jerry Planutis interception led to the second TD, a one-yard score by Jimmy Ellis. The final was a 47-yard pass play, Tom Yewcic to Wells. A new rule of 1953 abolished two-platoon football with players permitted to enter the game only once each quarter. For a deep team like Michigan State this substitution rule had little negative impact. Also, a new Big Ten rule limited traveling squads to 38 players. In this season opener Biggie used 30 of them.

(#26) October 3, 1953 (A): "It was my greatest thrill." Those were the words of coach Biggie Munn after the Spartans had shutout his alma mater, the Golden Gophers, 21-0, at Minneapolis. Headed by a splendid pair of ends, Ellis Duckett and Don Dohoney, the Spartan defenders held Minnesota to a meager 75 total yards. The MSC offense featured a pair of sophomores, quarterback Earl Morrall of Muskegon and fullback Jerry Planutis of Hazelton, Pa., filling in for the injured Tom Yewcic and Evan Slonac. Yet it was little LeRoy Bolden that stole the show. The Flint junior scored all three touchdowns, from 69 yards, nine yards, and 11 yards and accounted for 145 of the team's 297 rushing yards.

(#27) October 10, 1953 (H): With three quarters gone and Texas Christian leading 19-7 at jam-packed Macklin Field, the question prevailed with even the most loyal Spartan fans: "Was this the end of the streak?" Only the offense could respond. First Biggie sent out Bert Zagers at right halfback along with Jerry Planutis (FB), Earl Morrall (QB), and LeRoy Bolden (LH). They answered in 10 plays and State trailed, 19-13. Then the coach called on his "Pony Backfield" of Billy Wells, Bolden, Tommy Yewcic, and Evan Slonac, the latter two

hooking-up on a 35-yard TD screen pass. With a successful conversion State was leading for the first time, 20-19. A concluding touchdown came from five yards out when, on fourth down, reserve halfback Jimmy Ellis caught a Yewcic pass in the end zone. Final score . . . 26-19, and the streak had reached 27.

(#28) October 17, 1953 (H): Held scoreless by Indiana in the opening quarter of the homecoming game, the Spartans tore loose for three touchdowns in the second quarter to lead at halftime 19-6, and then add two more in both the third and fourth periods for a final tally of 47-18. End Ellis Duckett and Billy Wells, scored two touchdowns each with Jimmy Ellis, John "Thunder" Lewis and Gene Lekenta each scoring once. The most spectacular touchdown of the afternoon was by Wells who raced 58 yards with a pass interception. Coach Munn used three separate backfield combinations during the game. Following the "Pony Backfield" came Earl Morrall, Bert Zagers, Jerry Planutis and Jimmy Ellis, a quartet that accounted for the first two TDs. The third foursome of John Matsock, Vic Postula, Gary Lowe, and Lekenta finished the scoring parade with a 40-yard drive following a Wells interception.

October 24, 1953 (A): In his book, *The Spartans,* Fred Stabley recalls exchanging pleasantries with Danny Pobojewski in West Lafayette, Ind., on the Friday before the Spartan-Boilermaker game. Fred knew the native of Grand Rapids when Danny played a little football at Michigan State without lettering. Transferring to Purdue, Pobojewski had assumed a role as reserve fullback on a team that had lost four straight games. With a parting gesture in their brief conversation, Fred offered, "Good luck tomorrow, Danny. Hope you get into the game." Sure enough, Danny did "get into the game." Ironically, it would be that little-known former Spartan who would plunge into the end zone for the game's only score, shattering State's 28-game winning streak. Even then, the Spartans almost pulled it out. Bolden ran back the ensuing kickoff 95 yards for an apparent touchdown, only to have it canceled by a clipping penalty far back down the field.

TALES TO TELL

For the first time since 1912, Michigan State captured all three baseball games in their series with the U of M. The opener on May 13 at Ann Arbor was 0-0 until the seventh, when MSC scored twice on singles by Ray Collard and Bob Powell, a double by pitcher Walt Godfrey, and a sacrifice fly from John Matsock. Godfrey, who struck out four and walked five, needed no other runs than the one he drove in himself, as he recorded the only Spartan shutout of the spring. Powell, who was three-for-four on the afternoon, slammed one over the left field fence in the ninth for the final tally. Back home on the next afternoon, both Ed Hobaugh and Dick Idzkowski pitched complete games in 8-5 and 4-3 victories. Bob Powell continued his hitting heroics with a three-run homer in the fifth, and then, in the seventh, after Michigan had tied it up, he drove a ball into right center field to score George Smith with the winning run.

Powell (BS 1953-1955) recalls that series, particularly that third game—and why not?

"Beating Michigan was always a requirement for having a successful season, so the entire week leading to the Michigan series was one of complete concentration and confidence building. Friday's 3-0 victory in Ann Arbor set the stage for the doubleheader back in East Lansing. We all arrived at the fieldhouse earlier than usual. Everyone wanted to be in the same spirit that we ended Friday's game with, one that allowed the emotional strength to confront anything that might arise. Saturday's activity started with our 8-5 victory in the first game, with the spectators and players all primed for the final encounter. The Spartan team got together in the dugout and reminded ourselves that State had not swept Michigan three games in one season for 60 years, but this season would be the next. The desire and emotions of everyone were sky high, and we were all roaring to go when the second game started. We started the scoring in the fourth inning when I was able to connect for a home run with two runners aboard. The Wolverines then rallied for three runs in the top of the seventh to tie the score. When I came to the plate in the bottom of the seventh (the final inning) with George Smith on second and Ray Collard on first, I was concentrating on the Michigan pitcher, saying to myself, 'It's you against me.' Fortunately, I was able to deliver a base hit that drove in the winning run. The entire Spartan bench swarmed onto the field to celebrate and release emotions that had built up over the preceding week."

HEADLINES of 1955

- Disneyland, the first themed amusement park, opens south of Los Angeles in Anaheim.
- The American Federation of Labor (AFL) and the Congress of Industrial Organizations (CIO) merge.
- Jim Henson creates Kermit the Frog, the first of the Muppets.
- The U.S. Air Force Academy opens in Colorado Springs, Colo.

SCOREBOARD

	W	L	T	Avg.
Baseball	21	11	0	.656
Track and Field	2	1	0	.667
Football	3	6	0	.333
Basketball	13	9	0	.591
Tennis	8	7	0	.533
Cross Country	1	2	0	.333
Swimming and Diving	7	3	0	.700
Wrestling	2	7	0	.222
Hockey	9	17	1	.352
Fencing	3	9	0	.250
Golf	4	7	0	.364
Boxing	4	1	1	.750
Gymnastics	5	1	0	.833

TEAM OF THE YEAR

With the team's impressive season record of 30-11-1 in individual bouts, Coach Makris entered his entire lineup into the NCAA meet hosted by Idaho State in Pocatello on March 31-April 2. The first day of competition was a near Spartan disaster as Choken Maekawa, John Trahan, James Buck, George Sisinni and Andie Ronie all bowed out in opening match losses. At that point, little hope for a team title prevailed. On the second day of bouts, Bill Greenway reached the semi finals before elimination, while three other Spartans punched their way into the finals: John Butler, Herb Odom and the three-time Louisiana state amateur champion, seldom-used 119-pound Bob Boudreaux. At that conclusive stage of the tournament, the ever-persistent Wisconsin Badgers had equaled MSC's success with 12 team points and three finalists; yet, oddly enough, none of the six Michigan State-Wisconsin finalists were scheduled to meet head-to-head in the championship bouts. In an unpredictable conclusion, one-by-one the Spartans and Badgers were failing in their mission. First, MSC's Bob Boudreaux was stopped in his title bid. Next, 132-pound Johnny Butler was vanquished, and things looked bleak

for the Green and White. Wisconsin's 139-pounder failed the test. Finally, 147-pound Herb Odom was a winner as described in the April 3 issue of the *Idaho Sunday Journal*:

> "That left the job squarely up to the slender, sharp-punching Odom. The first round was close, with both boys feeling each other out. But Odom opened up in the second round, flailing Contri with lefts to the body and head and driving the Nevada puncher back. Contri tried to save the fight by attacking in the third, but Odom's masterful boxing and solid countering blows gave him a unanimous decision that boosted the Spartans' team total to 17."

With two more Wisconsin men contending, first at 165 pounds and then at heavyweight, it became a waiting game. To the delight of the Spartan contingent, neither of the Badgers ended up on the victory stand and Odom's five points held up as Michigan State registered their second championship in five years. Scoring for the top five teams was as follows: MSC 17, LSU 13, San Jose State 13, Syracuse 13 and Wisconsin 12.

The 1955 NCAA boxing champions. (Kneeling, left to right) J. Butler, B. Munn, Head Coach G. Makris, asst. coach J. Brotzman. (Standing left to right) J. Buck, C. Trahan, host representative, B. Greenway, H. Odom, A. Ronie, B. Boudreaux, G. Sisinni, C. Maekawa, F. Stabley, J. Heppinstall, unknown.

MAKING HISTORY

Feb. 12, 1955 marked the centennial date for the founding of the Agricultural College of the State of Michigan, and the school began a 10-month-long celebration. During this period, one of the goals of the administration was to see fruition of their ongoing campaign to once more rename the school, this time from Michigan State College to Michigan State University. As it turned out, gaining the needed support of the State Legislature would become a challenge. Reminiscent of 100 years earlier, when advocates of the University of Michigan unsuccessfully lobbied against the agricultural school's creation, it seemed that once again rumblings of disfavor emanated from Ann Arbor. The detractors centered their position on two issues; first, they claimed that the state already had a state university (it was located in Ann Arbor), and secondly they argued that the existence of two state universities would simply be too confusing. Regardless, on March 22, by a vote of 88-14, a name-change bill was approved in the legislature's lower body and forwarded to the Senate. From there, following the necessary protocol of committee review, the bill reached the floor of the chamber for discussion and final resolution on April 13. The overwhelming defeat of substitute measures to rename the school Michigan Agricultural University and then Michigan State Central University provoked reason for optimism. Then it happened. Before a gallery packed with MSC students and alumni, the senate voted overwhelmingly, 23-2, in favor of the name change. At last, the issue had been resolved—Michigan State College would become Michigan University.

GREAT STATE DATES

Football—**October 9, 1954 (A):** Duffy Daugherty earned the first win of his Michigan State coaching career against Indiana University, topping them 21-14. Though it was clearly a strong team effort, John Matsock played one of the best games of his career. He racked up 78 yards rushing, ran back four punts for 104 yards and a touchdown, returned a kickoff for 71 yards, completed

Duffy Daugherty's first staff: (front row, left to right) Burt Smith, Sonny Grandelius, Duffy and Dan Devine; (back row, left to right) Bill Yeoman, Bob Devaney and Don Mason

a 13-yard pass and added an excellent defensive game. The Spartans were the first on the scoreboard when Earl Morrall connected with sophomore Clarence Peaks, who ran 60 yards for a touchdown early in the first quarter. Before the half, however, the Hoosiers took the lead, finding the end zone twice. In the third quarter, Matsock scored his kickoff return TD, and just five plays later, the winning points came as sophomore Pat Wilson ran one in from the one-yard-line.

Cross Country—**October 23, 1954 (H):** Terry Block and Gay Denslow left their competition in the dust to take first and second in the four-mile run and edge out Wisconsin 27-28. Block finished at 20:39.6 and Denslow was just one tenth of a second behind him. The

Badgers managed to sweep the next spots, three through six, and then came the remaining Spartans, Ron Davis in seventh, Dave Hoke in eighth, and John Proctor in ninth to seal a one-point victory.

Football—November 20, 1954 (H): Concluding a season of few bright spots, the Spartans left their fans with an optimistic feeling for 1955 by walloping Marquette, 40-10. Clarence Peaks, the Flint sophomore, ran the ball six times for 150 yards, including carries of 53 and 65 yards. Quarterback Earl Morrall completed three touchdown passes: 62 yards to Jerry Planutis and twice to John "Thunder" Lewis, 59 and 63 yards. Upon leaving the stadium, few fans would have been willing to predict the 3-6 Spartans of 1954 would spawn a 9-1 season in 1955, including a Rose Bowl victory?

Hockey—December 3, 1954 (H): Michigan State opened league play by defeating North Dakota, 6-2. Initially the game was close, as the score read 1-1 following one period but the Spartans busted it open with an unanswered three-goal outburst in the middle stanza and then netted two more in the final 20 minutes. Three of the goals on the evening were made with a Sioux skater in the penalty box. Center Jim Ward and winger Steve Raz each scored twice, and Weldon Olson and Gordie King collected one apiece. Goalie Ed Schiller was called upon to turn back 24 shots.

Hockey—January 1, 1955 (H): Happy New Year! On a rare scheduling date of January first, MSU came from behind twice to defeat Michigan Tech, 5-3. The Huskies opened the scoring with a pair of goals in the first period. Steve Raz, assisted by Jim Ward, and then Ward unassisted evened the count at 2-2 before intermission. Tech regained the lead in the second period, but Dave Hendrickson, on a pass from Derio Nicoli, again deadlocked the score. Finally, Jack Mayes put State ahead for the first time at 15:26 with assists going to Ward and Raz. John Gipp, on a pass from Karl Jackson, turned the light on with an insurance goal in the third period.

Basketball—January 8, 1955 (H): The Spartans defeated Wisconsin, 94-77, bettering the team scoring record of 91 set five weeks earlier against Marquette. After the Badgers had forged into a 25-17 lead, Coach Anderson replaced his starting guards, Bob Devenny and Walt Godfrey, with Jimmy Raymond and Pat Wilson, a late arrival from the football squad. It was the type of move that could make a coach a visionary prophet. With the revised lineup, in slightly more than five minutes State

had outscored the visitors, 17-1, and led 34-26. The Badgers would never come closer.

Gymnastics—January 15, 1955 (H): By an impressive score of 59-37, the Spartans opened the season by defeating Michigan for the fourth time in a five-year span. With four firsts and 24 points, Carl Rintz led the way for George Szypula's squad.

Basketball—January 15, 1955 (H): The largest home crowd in two years, 11,295, witnessed the annual battle with the University of Michigan, a game which turned out to be a see saw affair. With the Wolverines leading 12-2, substitute center Duane Peterson was inserted into the lineup. His presence proved to be the proper catalyst, as the Spartans climbed back to tie it up at 36-36. Al Ferrari then erupted with seven straight points, but the Wolverines burst back for a 60-51 lead in the third quarter. Then it was State's turn, as they outscored the U of M, 15-4, and gained a 66-64 advantage. It continued back and forth down to the wire with MSU eventually hanging on at the buzzer, 84-82. It was the fifth straight victory over Michigan in friendly Jenison Fieldhouse.

Fencing—January 29, 1955 (H): George Thomas won all three of his sabre bouts to pace MSU in its 15-12 defeat of the University of Chicago. Additionally, both Luigi Odorico and Bill Lacey went 2-1 in sabre to give State a commanding 7-2 superiority in the weapon. In epee, Dale Blount and Jim Dooley each won twice and Harry Blount won once for a 5-4 team advantage. While the Spartans lost in foil 6-3, the three points earned there were the difference in the team victory.

Swimming and Diving—February 18, 1955 (H): Tied 40-40 entering the final event, the Spartan 400-yard free style relay team of Tom Wines, Jim Clemens, Frank Parrish, and Tom Payette turned in a winning time of 3:30.8 to seal the victory over the Iowa Hawkeyes, 48-44. The top individual performance of the afternoon came from Lanny Johnson, who established a new varsity record in winning the 150-yard individual medley in 1:34.1. It would be a busy weekend for Don Leas, who won the one-meter diving with a score of 197.4. On the next afternoon he was in the fieldhouse competing in three events for George Szypula's gymnasts against Ohio State.

Wrestling—February 19, 1955 (H): Amidst an atypical 1-5 season, the Spartans were definite underdogs when the Iowa Hawkeyes came to town sporting their impressive 7-1-1 record. Coach Fendley Collins met the

challenge by juggling his lineup. Dick Hoke opened the evening with a 4-1 upset and was followed by Bob Gunner's 1-1 draw of Iowa's 1954 NCAA champion. Norm Gill, who had been moved to the 137-pound spot, came through with a 14-1 win, giving the Spartans an 8-2 lead. Jim Sinadinos, normally the 137-pounder, moved to the 147-pound slot and gained a 6-2 victory. Dick Abraham's 5-0 win at 167 pounds was the determinant as the Spartans upset the Hawks, 14-11.

Boxing—**February 19, 1955 (H):** Featuring two TKOs and four perfect 30 point decisions, Coach Makris's squad defeated the 1954 NCAA champions from the University of Wisconsin, 6-2. Both John Butler at 132 pounds and light heavyweight Bill Greenway put their opponents away in the second round, while Chowen Maekawa at 125 pounds; John Trahan at 139 pounds; Herb Odom at 147 pounds, and 165-pound George Sisinni earned decisive wins. The third man in the ring was the former Spartan great Chuck Davey.

Gymnastics—**February 25, 1955 (A):** Previously undefeated Minnesota was in for a surprise, losing to MSC 55-41. Carl Rintz led the Spartans, scoring 24 points with first place finishes on the side horse, horizontal bar, parallel bars and flying rings. State's other winner was Roland Brown, who took top honors in tumbling. The Gophers left with only one win, on the trampoline.

Basketball—**February 28, 1955 (H):** The 93-77 win from Indiana University was the first over the Hoosiers since State entered the conference. However, the team victory took a back seat to the individual statistics registered by Al Ferrari in his final home appearance. The senior from Brooklyn Tech in New York set three team scoring records on the evening: 21 successful free throws (also a Big Ten record), 35 total points, and a season scoring total that would ultimately reach 442. His three-year career point total of 1,109 would also establish a Spartan record. When he left the game with time remaining on the clock, the applause was the noisiest of the season. Lost in Ferrari's record night was an impressive 30-point performance by the team's center, Duane Peterson.

Basketball—**March 5, 1955 (A):** Performing before a nationally televised audience, State finished the season with a satisfying 83-68 defeat of Michigan in a game at Yost Fieldhouse. Free throws were a-plenty, as officials whistled 41 fouls (24 against Michigan and 17 against MSC). Trailing 46-40 at the break, the Spartans, led by Bob Devenny and Julius McCoy, eventually caught

the Wolverines at 60-60. From there they built a 15-point margin and the "S" reserves finished it out. Scoring 19 points, Devenny, a 5' 10" guard, garnered scoring honors for the winners.

Baseball—**April 22, 1955 (H):** MSU opened defense of its Big Ten title at home with a convincing 21-hit 14-8 thumping of the University of Wisconsin. Chuck Mathews and Lou Costanzo each belted out four hits, with Jim Sack and captain John Matsock collecting three apiece. The game was tied 8-8 after five innings, whereupon State scored twice in the sixth and put it away with four in the seventh.

Baseball—**April 29, 1955 (A):** In defeating Purdue 22-8, State recorded the greatest number of runs the school had ever posted against a Big Ten team. It was a costly victory, however. Second baseman George Smith, the conference's leading hitter, was accidentally spiked on the ankle by teammate Chuck Mathews when the two infielders raced into foul territory after a pop fly. He was sidelined for eight games. The Spartans gained their impressive run total on 17 hits, seven walks, and eight Boilermaker fielding errors. For State, shortstop Earl Morrall collected three hits, as did catcher Al Luce, including a grand-slam home run in the seventh.

Track and Field—**May 6, 1955 (H):** Winning or tying seven of the 14 events and displaying team depth, the Spartans downed the Indiana Hoosiers, 71 1/2-60 1/2, in a Friday afternoon meet at Ralph Young Field. Julius McCoy, Ed Brabham and Kevin Gosper swept the 220-yard dash, while Brabham and McCoy finished one-two in the 100. Dave Hoke and Terry Block finished one-two in the one-mile, as did Gay Denslow and Ron Davis in the two-mile. Joe Savoldi won the shot put, was second in the 120-yard high hurdles, and third in the high jump.

Baseball—**May 7, 1955 (H):** State topped Iowa twice, 9-6 and 2-1, for their first doubleheader win of the spring. Ed Hobaugh pitched more than six Spartan errors for the opening game victory. Being credited with five of those miscues, Earl Morrall ignominiously established a Big Ten record. Wisconsin's Harvey Kuenn, eventually a 15-year major leaguer, held the previous record at four. With each connecting for a home run, Chuck Mathews and Jim Sack led the 10-hit attack in game one. Dick Idzkowski came up with a three-hit mound performance in the second game and scored the eventual winning run in the fifth inning on a base hit by Sack.

Tennis—**May 20, 1955 (A):** Featuring all straight-set victories, Frank Beeman's netters shut out the Minnesota Gophers 9-0 in the final road trip of the spring. Singles winners, number one through number six were Dave Brogan, 6-1, 6-1; Dick Menzel, 6-4, 6-1; John Brogan, 6-3, 6-2; George Stepanovic, 6-2, 6-3; Jim Beachum, 6-3, 6-1; and Fred Levine, 6-1, 8-6. Winners in the doubles were Stepanovic-Menzel, 6-4, 6-1; Ralph Braden and Dave Brogan, 6-4, 6-3; and John Brogan-Beachum, 7-5, 6-3.

Baseball—**May 23, 1955 (A):** In the second of their two-game series, Notre Dame scored twice in the bottom of the eighth to erase the Spartan lead and tie the score at 3-3. Then in the ninth, Earl Morrall and Chuck Mathews hit back-to-back triples to retake the lead and eventually win the game. Having defeated Notre Dame six weeks earlier back in East Lansing, for the third straight season the Spartans swept the two games scheduled with the Irish.

ATHLETE OF THE YEAR

Boxer Herb Odom opened his collegiate career impressively by capturing the National AAU middleweight title during his freshman year of 1952. At 6' 1", the 147-pounder usually possessed an advantageous reach over

Herb Odom

his opponent, and, coupled with impressive quickness, he compiled a four-year personal dual-meet record of 23-3-2. Within that span, George Makris's teams would post a winning record of 20-5-5. Odom, a four-time letter winner (1952-1955), would win back-to-back NCAA titles in 1954 and 1955, becoming the third Spartan to be a repeat winner.

IN THE SPARTLITE

Baseball: With John Kobs recovering from major surgery, assistant coach Frank Pellerin took over the head coaching choirs of the 1955 team on April 29. Kobs attempted to return to the bench for the Michigan doubleheader on May 14 but lasted only five innings. He retreated to his automobile where he listened to the balance of the games on WKAR radio, both MSC victories, 8-5 and 4-3.

The 1955 Spartans were one of the most prolific hitting teams in the school's history. Throughout the Big Ten season, they led the conference with an overall average of .311. In addition, they provided the conference individual batting champion in second baseman George Smith, who hit .495 in 10 games.

Basketball: The 1953-1954 season was the last in which basketball was in the format of four 10-minute quarters. Beginning with 1954-1955 the game was played, as today, within two 20-minute halves.

Forddy Anderson began his 11-year coaching stint at MSU with the 1954-1955 season. In that first year he changed the position of the players' bench from the ends of the floor as in past seasons to the east side of the court. They would remain there until the game moved to Breslin Student Events Center in 1989.

Sonny Means, captain of the 1952 team, joined the staff as an assistant coach. His annual salary was set at $5,000. After four seasons, Sonny left to become head coach at Western Michigan in 1959.

Boxing: In the 4-4 tie against the Quantico Marines, Bill Greenway suffered a loss dictated by a bizarre NCAA ruling. The ring doctor stopped the fight following the second round after the Spartans' 178-pounder had belted his opponent with enough hard rights that his eye was badly bruised and swollen. Strangely, by way of the collegiate standards, it was the battered marine who was awarded the decision because he was leading on points at the time.

Cross Country: Following three championship seasons, 1954 was an off year for MSC cross country. Coach Schlademan would have to settle for the runner-up spot in the conference meet and no better than 10th at the annual NCAA meet in which Gaylord Denslow, who finished in 16th place, was the top Spartan finisher.

Fencing: Paced by George Thomas's sabre title, the Spartans finished third in the Big Ten championships held in Madison, Wis. In other individual performances, fourth-place medals were garnered by Jim Dooley in epee and Luigi Odorico, also with the sabre weapon.

Nearly 100 fencers representing 28 colleges and universities came to Jenison Fieldhouse on March 25-26 for the 11th annual NCAA championships. With no more than one man per school dueling in each of the three weapons, the format called for a complete round-robin with a competitor going against every entrant in a given weapon. In winning 13 of his 22 sabre matches, George Thomas finished in sixth place. Between the two of them, Gerry Breen, in foil, and Jim Dooley, in epee, won 18 matches. That 31-point total placed State 14th in the field of 28 teams.

Football: The 1954 6-0 loss to Wisconsin is a game most long-time Spartans fans will likely never forget. The one TD was a second-quarter 28-yard ramble by Alan "The Horse" Ameche against a *10-man* defense. On the play preceding the touchdown, LeRoy Bolden had been injured along the sideline in front of the home bench. Before a replacement could be inserted, play resumed and Ameche was in the end zone, having raced through Bolden's vacated position. Although game officials were initially blasted for the unfair disadvantage, it was later admitted that the State coaches had the responsibility for immediately inserting the substitute.

Jerry Planutis recalls the October 16 football game on the muddy, rain soaked field at South Bend in which the Irish defeated the Spartans, 20-19:

"I had an opportunity to tie the game on the point after touchdown, but the ball missed to the right by inches. In the locker room after the game, President Hannah put his arm on my shoulder and said, 'Jerry, you will have next year and you will do better.' Sure enough, one year later, in 1955 we defeated Notre Dame, 21-7, and I was later selected back of the week by *Sports Illustrated*. Once more Dr. Hannah appeared in the locker room after the game, again putting his arm on my shoulder this time he said, 'Congratulations Jerry, this was a better year.'"

The large watercolor painting of the 1953 Rose Bowl squad that is located in the Jenison lobby was presented to Biggie Munn and the school on the occasion of the Downtown Coaches Club annual all-sports night banquet on May 10, 1955. Raynord LeNeil was the artist and the donor was anonymous.

Golf: The golf team could do no better than seventh place at the Conference championship on the Purdue University course. In a weekend hampered by rain, the matches were decided in three rounds rather than the customary four. Jim Sullivan, Grand Rapids sophomore, led the Spartan scorers with 82-76-76 to equal 234.

Gymnastics: For the third straight year, Carlton Rintz proved himself to be the top gymnast in the conference, as he captured three individual events (horizontal bar, pommel horse and rings) and his second all-around title at the championships. In addition, he scored a second, a third and a sixth for a 55-point total and indi-

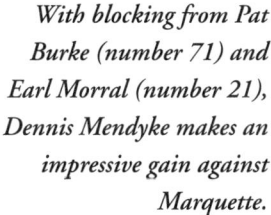

With blocking from Pat Burke (number 71) and Earl Morral (number 21), Dennis Mendyke makes an impressive gain against Marquette.

vidual scoring honors. Others contributing to the 91 1/2 points and second-place finish behind Illinois were Roland Brown, Jim Breeza, Don Leas, Dick O'Brien, Ben Gunning, Dick Phillips, and Herm Junker.

Rintz was also a standout performer at the NCAA championships hosted by UCLA. There he won the parallel bars, the horizontal bar and his second title on the pommel horse. State earned 55 points, good enough for fifth place in the team standings.

Hockey: The team concluded its Western Intercollegiate season at home against the University of Minnesota. Thanks to a hat trick by senior winger Weldie Olson, the Spartans managed a 5-5 tie on Friday night. Then, on Saturday, trailing 7-3 with six and a half minutes remaining in the final period, the team suddenly came alive. For a five-minute stretch, the deficit was closed to 7-6 on goals by Jim Ward, Olson and Derio Nicoli. Then, goalie Ed Shiller was pulled for an added attacker, and the few remaining fans roared with approval as the Spartan offense managed eight quality shots over the final minute and a half only to fall short in the thrilling finish.

Weldie Olson closed out his remarkable collegiate career by becoming the only Spartan to lead the team in scoring goals for four straight seasons.

Swimming and Diving: Scoring 27 1/2 points, MSC earned a fifth place finish at the Big Ten championships held in the Ohio State University natatorium. Top individual finishers were John Dudeck and Tom Payette. Dudeck finished runner-up in both the 200-yard butterfly and the 200-yard breaststroke, while Payette finished third in the 50-yard freestyle and fourth in the 100. Other Spartan finalists were Jack Beattie, Lanny Johnson, Jim Clemens, Frank Parrish, and Frank Paganini.

For the first time since 1944, MSC did not score at the National Collegiate championship meet.

Tennis: At the Big Tens in Evanston, MSC managed 18 1/2 points, which placed them in sixth place. The number three doubles team of captain John Brogan and Jim Beachum was the only Spartan duo to reach the finals. They were defeated in straight sets, 8-6, 6-1.

Track and Field: In a quadrangular meet on February 12 at Jenison, MSC topped Ohio State but finished behind Missouri and Penn State. Joe Savoldi was a busy Spartan that afternoon as he won the high jump, placed second in the high hurdles, and was fourth in three events: the low hurdles, shot put and broad jump.

At the indoor Big Ten championships, also at Jenison, the Spartans finished second in the team standings. The "Big Three" of Ed Brabham, Kevin Gosper, and Joe Savoldi accounted for 35 of the team's 46 1/2 point total. Brabham was high-point man of the meet, winning the 60-yard dash and the broad jump and placing second in the 300-yard dash. Gosper posted victories in the 440- and 600-yard runs and ran the anchor leg of the third place mile relay team. Savoldi finished second in the high hurdles and third in both the shot put and broad jump. Chuck Coykendall's varsity record-setting 13' 9-3/8" was good enough for second place in the pole vault with George Best tying for fourth place. Travis Buggs completed the MSC scoring with a third place finish in the 60-yard dash.

On May 20, before a crowd of 56,000, Australian Kevin Gosper ran an impressive 46.9 440-yard dash to defeat a highly-touted field at the Los Angeles Coliseum Relays. It was the fastest quarter-mile clocking of the year. Gosper, the Spartan captain and British Empire Games champion, later joined with Julius McCoy, Ron Suess and Ed Brabham to finish third in the 880-yard relay.

Although Ed Brabham and Kevin Gosper would each win their specialty at the conference outdoor meet, the broad jump and 440-yard run respectively, the team could manage no more than 19 points for a fifth place finish.

Wrestling: The wrestlers dropped all the way to sixth place at the Big Ten championships, the lowest spot since MSC began conference competition in 1951. Previously unbeaten 137-pound Jim Sinadinos made it to the finals after taking a pair of decisions but was shutout 4-0 in his title bid. Ted Lennox, the veteran blind grappler, settled for a fourth place. Due to injuries and illnesses, Coach Collins entered only six men in the tournament.

TALES TO TELL

During the 1950s, only one Big Ten school was permitted to play in the football postseason and that was, of course, at the Rose Bowl. Furthermore, the conference contract stipulated that no school would make consecutive appearances at Pasadena on New Year's Day. With Ohio State having been the representative for the 1954 season, the scenario on November 19, the final Saturday of the 1955 season, was quite simple. Although that afternoon's non-conference MSU-Marquette game had no bearing on the eventual picture, the annual tussle being played in Ann Arbor did indeed. If Michigan defeated OSU, the Wolverines would be headed west. A Buckeye victory would send Michigan State. As the Spartans headed for an eventual 33-0 win, the 41,484 fans at Macklin Field were riveted to portable radios throughout the stadium. On one occasion during the third quarter of the MSU game, referee Ross Dean had to halt play. It seemed the Hilltoppers' quarterback was unable to make his signals audible above the roar of the throng in approval of news of an Ohio State score transmitted via the radio waves. As both games were winding down and the Bucks were sealing a timely 17-0 victory, students poured

from the stands in East Lansing and surrounded the field of play. It was about then that the PA announcer dangled this offer to the State students: "I am authorized to announce that, if the students restrain themselves in celebration of the anticipated Rose Bowl bid, Thanksgiving recess will begin next Tuesday evening, a day early." The bribe went unheeded, as students tore down the south goal posts before the game finished and the uprights at the north end soon thereafter.

TEAM OF THE YEAR

With memories of the 3-6 record of 1954, little preseason optimism prevailed for Spartan football in the fall of 1955. Dropping a 14-7 game to Michigan in the second game of the schedule did little to build confidence. Yet, as the season progressed, Duffy Daugherty's second as head coach, a winning team emerged to produce a 9-1 overall record including the dramatic 17-14 victory in the Rose Bowl. At the season's end, both of the two major polls, the Associated Press and the United Press ranked State second to undefeated Oklahoma.

HEADLINES of 1956

- Soviet troops brutally suppress an anti-Communist revolution in Hungary.
- The Federal Aid Highway Act authorizes a 13-year interstate highway-building program.
- Don Larsen, New York Yankees right-hander, pitches the first no-hit, no-run game in World Series history.
- Singer Elvis Presley achieves national fame with the song "Heartbreak Hotel." For the next 16 months he has at least one song in the top 10, including "Hound Dog," "Don't Be Cruel" and "Love Me Tender."

SCOREBOARD

	W	L	T	Avg.
Baseball	16	13	0	.552
Track and Field	3	1	0	.750
Football	9	1	0	.900
Basketball	13	9	0	.591
Tennis	12	5	0	.706
Cross Country	2	0	0	1.000
Swimming and Diving	4	3	0	.571
Wrestling	4	4	1	.500
Hockey	5	18	0	.217
Fencing	3	5	0	.375
Golf	4	5	0	.444
Boxing	0	4	1	.100
Gymnastics	3	3	1	.500

The team included four players who were recognized as All-American on one or more polls: QB number 21 Earl Morrall, LT number 57 Norm Masters, RG number 68 captain Carl "Buck" Nystrom and FB number 45 Jerry Planutis. Other starters included LG number 77 Embry Robinson (until an injury in the sixth game on the schedule ended his season and he was replaced by number 55 Dan Currie), RT number 71 Pat Burke or number 75 Leo Haidys, LH number 26 Clarence Peaks and RH number 14 Walt Kowalczyk. Also on that team were RE number 89 Dave Kaiser, C number 56 Joe Badaczewski and LE number 87 John "Thunder" Lewis.

MAKING HISTORY

Ernestine Russell was the first Michigan State co-ed to earn an athletic tender. The vivacious Windsor, Ontario, girl won five consecutive Canadian gymnastics championships (1954-1958) and two United States titles (1955 and 1958). Three times she was named Canada's Outstanding Woman Athlete and was her country's only feminine representative in gymnastics at the 1956 Olympic Games in Melbourne, Australia. Although men's coach George Szypula offered assistance and advice to Ernestine, for the most part she practiced three to four hours daily by herself. Of course, no NCAA-sponsored competition was available.

The 1955 football team. Front Row (left to right): E. Robinson, A. Lee, G. Musetti, G. Lowe, C. Nystrom, head coach D. Daugherty, G. Planutis, E. Morrall, L. Haidys, E. Zalar and N. Bufe. Second row (left to right) J. Lewis, J. Hinesly, R. Jewett, J. Matsko, J. Badaczewski, D. Hollern, C. Alden, N. Masters, R. Gaddini,, D. Berger and G. Eyde. Third row (left to right): L. Rutledge, G. Pepoy, H. Dukes, L. Costanzo, J. Bigelow, W. Kaae, W. Kowalczyk, T. Kolodziej, T. Anderson, F. Nauyokas, L. Bernard, L. Postula and T. Saidock. Fourth row (left to right): J. Carruthers, P. Wilson, J. Fomenko, D. Mendyk, C. Peaks, H. Neeley, J. Jones, M. Panitch, J. Chidester, D. Gilbert, A. Matsos, D. Barker, D. Jeter and E. Roberts. Fifth row (left to right): G. Hecker, D. Kaiser, J. Soave, D. Zysk, G. Burgett, R. Rickens, G. Briggs, W. Cleaver, K. Perryman, P. Burke, A. Aljian, J. Capes, C. LaRose, L. Harding, R. Handloser and J. Wulff. Sixth row (left to right): equip. mgr. K. Early, asst. trainer T. Dielhm, trainer G. Robinson, end coach R. Devaney, line coach L. Agase, R. Popp, D. Currie, P. Sagan, B. Wierbowski, Darwyn Hepler, J. Ninowski, M. Cisco, A. Sieminski, backfield coach E. Grandelius, line coach B. Smith, asst. coach B. Yeoman and asst. coach J. Wilson.

The NCAA Football Rules Committee relented somewhat on the "anti-platoon" substitution rule which had been in affect since the 1953 season. Beginning in 1955, players who started each quarter were eligible to leave and re-enter once during that quarter.

A total of 9,000 new seats were added to Macklin Field, raising the capacity to 60,000.

GREAT STATE DATES

***Football*—September 24, 1955 (A):** Indiana opened the scoring and led 7-0 before the Spartans, headed by the new running back tandem of junior Clarence Peaks and sophomore Walt Kowalczyk, drove 66 yards in nine plays whereupon Earl Morrall tossed a seven-yard TD pass to Bob Jewett. Another sophomore, Jim Wulff, 5'9", 172, put State in the lead for good when he returned a punt 64 yards behind the well-executed blocks of Joe Carruthers and Pat Wilson. The third touchdown, on a one-yard plunge by Jerry Planutis, climaxed an 11-play drive on the first possession of the second half. The final score read 20-13 in favor of MSU. Totally, on the afternoon, the Spartan defense yielded a meager 42 yards rushing.

***Football*—October 8, 1955 (H):** Stanford, a team that had toppled Ohio State on the previous Saturday, succumbed early on this sunny afternoon at Macklin Field. The Green struck early and often, scoring at 4:43, 6:48, and 13:51 of the opening quarter. The game ended with the big board in the stadium reading, 38-14, but there is no telling what it might have been if Duffy had not cleared his bench early.

***Football*—October 15, 1955 (H):** MSU 21, Notre Dame 7. It was only the fourth game on the schedule, but that Sunday's *State Journal* sports page headline prematurely blared: "1955 State Team One of Spartans' Best." This was a good Notre Dame team that came to East Lansing. Led by quarterback Paul Hornung, they sported an 11-game winning streak extended over two seasons. Even on this afternoon ND won the battle of statistics, but the Spartans took advantage of opportunities, exhibited poise, and used a deep bench to gain the advantage. Tied 7-7 at halftime, State took command after the intermission on short yardage scores by Jerry Planutis and Earl Morrall. Planutis, the 25-year-old army veteran, may

Earl Morrall

well have been the difference between the two teams. On defense he was a terror, and on offense he tore into the Irish line for 91 yards on 20 carries.

***Football*—October 22, 1955 (H):** The 21-7 victory over Illinois was a game of big plays. The first Spartan score, in the opening quarter, consumed only two plays, a 60-yard pass-run from Morrall to John "Thunder" Lewis and a 29-yard scoring scamper by Walt Kowalczyk. The second TD came on the first play following the second half kickoff. From his own 40-yard line and running to his right, Morrall stopped and pitched a long pass toward Dave Kaiser, who then raced through the Illinois secondary. The third touchdown, a 21-yard pass, Morrall to Bob Jewett, climaxed an eight-play drive in the third quarter. Jerry Musetti and Dennis Mendyk shared the left halfback position as they filled in for the injured Clarence Peaks.

***Cross Country*—October 22, 1955 (H):** It was predicted that Henry Kennedy would be a standout collegiate runner, and by the second meet of the fall, an easy 18-43 win over Penn State, such prophesying had been confirmed. On that Saturday morning, the Canadian sophomore broke the campus four-mile course record, running a brilliant 19:28.3. Furthermore, it was the fastest four miles ever run by a collegian. Selwyn Jones, the junior captain, finished second behind Kennedy with a personal best time of 20:00.0. Other Spartan scorers were Gay Denslow, who finished third in 20:38; Terry Block

who ended fifth in 21:24.3, and Ed Townsend who took the seventh spot in 21:45. It was the first win over the Nittany Lions since 1948.

Football—**October 29, 1955 (A):** In the first Spartan shutout since 1953, State defeated the Wisconsin Badgers, 27-0. Walt Kowalczyk, the 198-pound halfback from Westfield, Mass., made two touchdowns and rolled up 172 yards on 10 carries. His 72-yard opening score still ranks among the top 20 longest scoring runs in Michigan State history.

Football—**November 5, 1955 (A):** The Purdue game at West Lafayette, a 27-0 Spartan victory, included two odd-scoring plays. The first involved the Boilermakers' Bill Murakowski and Earl Morrall. Charging into the line on a touchdown try, the Purdue fullback was stopped on the seven-yard line. Immediately twisting when hit, he foolishly attempted to lateral the ball. Morrall lunged, made a spectacular one-handed interception on the 10-yard line, and sprinted down the sideline for 90 yards and a touchdown. Oddity number two involved John Matsko Jr., the MSU center and kick-off specialist from St. Michael, Pa. Following the second State score, Matsko booted the ball to the five-yard line, where it was handled cleanly and moved forward to the 20-yard line. At that point, the carrier was hit on a jarring tackle by Jim Hinesly, and the ball popped up and into the hands of the surprised kicker, John Matsko. He kept right on running, down the sideline and into the end zone for his only collegiate touchdown.

Football—**November 12, 1955 (H):** The Spartans concluded their Big Ten schedule at home with an easy 42-14 victory over Minnesota. They wasted little time taking charge with two blocked punts setting up a touchdown and safety. State led after the first quarter, 16-7. A 76-yard eight-play drive netted another score before intermission and then the reserves took over. Daugherty called upon 14 backs and they all saw more than token service. Walt Kowalczyk, the big sophomore, was the most effective ground-gainer. He ran only seven times with the ball but netted 41 yards. Clarence Peaks was the busiest runner with 11 carries.

Hockey—**December 17, 1955 (H):** The Spartans came from behind in the closing minutes of the final period to defeat the favored University of Denver, 4-3. It was the first and, sadly, the only league victory of the season. Trailing 3-1 in the final period, State responded with three unanswered goals. The first was unassisted from Gene Grazia, who intercepted a Pioneer pass and skated in all alone. Art Baker scored at 13:53 on a power play, and the winning marker came from Joe Balai at 16:06 with an assist from Bert Pomerleau.

Basketball—**January 7, 1956 (A):** Trailing the Hawkeyes at Iowa City by 13 points with 10 minutes remaining, coach Forddy Anderson called for a full-court press, a tactic which would symbolize later University of Iowa teams. The pressure tactic resulted in five turnover field goals, cutting the deficit to three points. The Hawks answered by rebuilding their lead, 64-57, but that would be the end of their scoring. The Spartans added eight more points and hung on for a 65-64 victory. It would be the only loss that would blot the Iowa conference record, as they would go on to be runner-up in the NCAA tournament.

Swimming and Diving—**January 21, 1956 (A):** By the narrow margin of 48-45, State defeated the U of M for the first time since 1951 and for the first time ever in Ann Arbor. Larry Ellis was the only double winner, as he finished first in the 50- and 100-yard freestyle races. The outcome of the meet was in doubt until the next to the last event, when MSU garnered the needed points with John Dudeck and Paul Reinke finishing 1-2 in the 200-yard breaststroke.

Basketball—**January 28, 1956 (H):** A total of 12,154 fans showed up at Jenison for the Ohio State game that had been billed as a battle of the Big Ten's best point producers, the visitors' Robin Freeman and Julius McCoy. The fans were not disappointed, as the postscript could have read: "MSU lost the battle but won the war." Freeman scored 46 points, one shy of the Big Ten record, while McCoy swished in 40 toward Michigan State's winning count, 94 to 91. OSU held a commanding half time lead, 60-51 but the Spartans whittled away, and, with just two minutes remaining, McCoy wove through the entire Buckeye defense to lay one in and finally gain the lead, 92-91. From there they hung on. During the evening, the Spartans netted 35 of 79 shots for a .443 percentage, and Ohio State had a slightly better mark of .449 on 31 of 69 attempts.

Wrestling—**February 4, 1956 (H):** In a meet that included an unusual three draws, State defeated Purdue 20-19. MSU's winning margin came on three decisions and one pin (14 points) against one pin, one default and one decision (13 points). The Spartan victories were from Tom Larsen at 115 pounds, Jim Sinadinos at 137 pounds,

Dick Gunner at 157 pounds and the pin by Don Stroud at 123. With State having already achieved the points needed for victory, Brian Harrison's injury and subsequent default in the heavyweight division impacted only the final score and not the outcome.

Gymnastics—**February 4, 1956 (H):** State took the measure of Ohio State and chalked up their first win of the season, 70-42. Capturing every first except the trampoline, individual Spartan winners were Don Leas in both the horizontal bars and flying rings, Cal Girard on the side horse, Richard O'Brien on parallel bars and Roland Brown in the free exercise event. Based on team points earned, the individual scoring honors went to Don Leas with 16, followed by Cal Girard with 12 1/2.

Basketball—**February 6, 1956 (H):** In what Jenison fans had come to expect, Julius McCoy set a torrid scoring pace and led the Spartans to a convincing 86-76 triumph over the University of Michigan. He roamed the floor like a one-man team, netting 14 field goals and cashing in 13 of 15 free throws for a total of 41 points.

Basketball—**February 20, 1956 (H):** The veteran team trainer Jack Heppinstall expressed it this way, "I have been around here 42 years, and this is something new to me. It was a strange, strange sight, I hope I never see it again." He was reacting to the incredibly bizarre behavior displayed by the local rooters during the second half of the Northwestern game. After State had built a seemingly commanding 62-40 lead by intermission, fickle Spartan fans increasingly cheered with approval as the Wildcats began clawing their way back into contention. Reaching a crescendo pitch, perhaps it was the cheer-for-the-underdog syndrome that prevailed. After all, Northwestern had come to town with only one win all season long and a 0-10 conference record. Coupled with MSU turnovers and poor shooting, the Cats rode the support of their new fans to a remarkable 93-92 lead. Now with State trailing, the wayward Jenison crowd suddenly grasped the reality of the situation and returned to the more familiar grounds of supporting their guys in green. With closing baskets by Julius McCoy and Jack Quiggle, State eventually prevailed, 96-93.

Fencing—**February 24 & 25, 1956 (H):** Closing out the schedule with only their second and third wins of the season, Coach Schmitter's crew defeated Buffalo 19-8 on Friday night and then Wayne University 16-11 on Saturday afternoon. It was the first win over the Tartars since 1952. Heading the Spartan victories were George Thomas, Harry Blount, Fred Shulak, Luigi Odorico and Gerald Breen.

Baseball—**April 3 & April 4, 1956 (A):** State returned from the annual southern swing with a 4-5 record, but most importantly, they won the final two games of the trip, both by one run. At Durham, N.C., under a consistent rain, State broke a 3-3 ninth-inning deadlock with Duke when Gary Warner scored on a Jim Sack sacrifice fly. The next afternoon at Chapel Hill, N.C., pitcher Walt Godfrey allowed only three hits in a 2-1 victory over North Carolina. Also a star at the plate, Godfrey knocked in the eventual winning run.

Golf—**May 7, 1956 (A):** MSU rolled over Wisconsin, 20-7, in a tremendous team showing with just two strokes difference from top to bottom in the six-man line up. Ken Rodewald, Otto Schubel, and George Wakulsky led the team, each shooting a 74 in the singles competition. The Spartans picked up most of their points in the best ball doubles play, which they won 12-6, led by Arlin Dell and Schubel.

Track and Field—**May 12, 1956 (A):** Winning eight of the 13 individual events and sharing first in yet another, MSU defeated the University of Wisconsin, 72-60. Ed Brabham, then in his senior season, captured both sprint events, with a 9.9 in the 100 and 21.6 in the 220. Other firsts were turned in by Selwyn Jones, who ran a 4:24.1 mile; Joe Savoldi, who ran a 14.6 in the high hurdles; Henry Kennedy, who ran a 9:48.3 two-mile; and David Hoke, who captured the low hurdles in 25.9. A pair of wins came from the infield, where George Best pole-vaulted 13' and Tom Wagner broad jumped 21' 1/2". The tie came at the high jump pit where Don Hillmer and a Badger both cleared the bar at 6' 5 1/2".

Tennis—**May 12, 1956 (H):** Action had ceased on all but one court and the score was tied, MSU 4, Illinois 4. Strangely, Frank Beeman's squad had reached this dramatic point having won only two matches during the afternoon, Dick Menzel at number two and George Stepanovic at number three. An injury to an Illini player had resulted in forfeiture of points at number six singles and number three doubles, thus the 4-4 score. Attention centered on the number two doubles match that would decide the winner in this final home meet of the year. That Spartan pair of captain Dave Brogan and Stepanovic struggled, losing the opening set 6-2, but they eventually prevailed, winning the next two sets, 6-3, 6-4, taking the match and eventually the meet.

Baseball—**June 2, 1956 (H):** State closed the season at home with their second win of the spring over Western Michigan, this time by a 12-9 score. It was the first time since 1931 that the Spartans had captured the two-game series against the Broncos. Jim Sack collected a pair of hits, including a home run, as he finished the season with a team-leading .393 average. His .419 mark in Big Ten play was good enough for third best in the conference.

ATHLETE OF THE YEAR

In 1956, Julius McCoy was the second Spartan basketball player to be recognized as a collegiate All-American. Also, by a vote among the 12 Associated Press basketball writers who covered Big Ten games, McCoy became the first Michigan State player ever to be chosen as a Big Ten first-team selection. Gathering 11 of the dozen ballots, the mystery was how one scribe had the audacity not to include the six-foot-two Farrell, Pa., forward. McCoy was a prolific scorer. On three occasions during his senior year, Julius accounted for 40 or more points in a single game. Against Notre Dame on December 21, 1955, he scored 45 points to establish a team single-game scoring record that stood for 20 years. His 20 field goals in that same game remain a team record. He concluded the senior season of 1955-1956 with 600 total points and an average of 27.2 ppg, both team records that would hold for 14 years. With 1,377 career points, he ranks 15th on the Spartan list of all-time scorers. McCoy was also a significant contributor to the track and field team, for which he earned two varsity letters as a sprinter.

Julius McCoy

IN THE SPARTLITE

Baseball: The Big Ten opening weekend games on May 12-13 against Purdue and Illinois were played at Post Park in Battle Creek. Old College Field had been flooded from the swollen waters of the Red Cedar river.

The spring flooding conditions prompted Athletic Director Munn to publicly predict that a new baseball field would likely be forthcoming. He identified a location south of Shaw Lane and west of the secret practice field but conceded that any such plan would have to be approved by the school's governing board.

A number of major league scouts were in the stands for the season-closing home game against Western Michigan on June 2, 1956. Particular interest centered upon Jim Sack, Walt Godfrey and Ed Hobaugh. In addition, coach Frankie Albert of the NFL's San Francisco 49ers football team was on hand and that evening signed Earl Morrall to an NFL contract. The MSU quarterback-shortstop had been the 49ers' number one draft choice, but had delayed signing to maintain his amateur status for a final year of baseball.

Basketball: The "go-to" guy of the 1955-1956 squad was, of course, senior Julius McCoy. His incredible 27.2 scoring average throughout the 22-game season was a team record at the time and has been topped only three times since: by Ralph Simpson with 29.0 in 1969-1970; Terry Furlow with 29.4 in 1975-1976; and Scott Skiles with 27.4 in 1985-1986.

In early July, it was announced that assistant coach John Bennington would leave his position to become head coach at Drake University in Des Moines. Freshmen coach Bob Stevens was appointed to fill the vacated position.

Boxing: The 1956 season was frustrating for first-year coach John Brotzmann. Indeed, there were three proven winners available in Choken Maekawa, John Butler and George Sisinni. Beyond that trio, the roster lacked talent and experience. Little wonder that for the first time since 1946 the team was winless over the dual-meet season.

The Spartans managed a fourth-place finish at the 19th annual NCAA championship hosted by the University of Wisconsin. Harvey Lancour and Johnny Butler met opening bout eliminations, while Choken Maekawa and George Sisinni reached the finals, and Maekawa of Hawaii went all the way. Not only did he capture the school's 13th NCAA individual title, but he was also voted

Choken Maekawa in action

recipient of the John S. LaRowe Trophy, acknowledging him as the outstanding boxer of the tournament. He would later win a spot on the 1956 U.S. Olympic team but could not make weight at the official weigh-in and consequently was disqualified from competing in Melbourne, Australia.

Cross Country: Led by 23-year-old Canadian sophomore Henry Kennedy, a native of Glasgow, Scotland, Michigan State returned to the national spotlight in 1955. Although the IC4A team title eluded MSU, Kennedy finished first at the 47th running of this historic race in New York City. One week later he led the way to State's fourth Big Ten Conference title in six tries. Following him across the line were Selwyn Jones in third, Gaylord Denslow in sixth, Terry Block in seventh and Ed Townsend in 19th.

These two meets set up the real test, the NCAA title run on Monday, November 28, over the familiar MSU campus course. With the temperature dipping to 12 degrees Farenheit, Kennedy led the race until the closing strides, when Deacon Jones of Iowa surged past to deny him a "triple crown" in 1955. However, as a team they came through once more for Michigan State's sixth championship. This time Denslow was sixth, Jones was eighth, Block was 11th and Townsend was 46th.

Fencing: The three-man team of George Thomas (sabre), Jerry Breen (foil), and Bill Kester (epee) managed enough wins in the National Collegiate championship meet at the Naval Academy that MSU finished 13th out of 34 competing schools.

Football: For the first time, all players' helmets were equiped with face masks. It was a single metal bar.

The 14-7 loss to Michigan, the season's only setback, was one of the most disappointing in the long rivalry with the U of M. State statistically outplayed the Wolverines, as they gained more first downs (14-7) and more yardage (215-151), but also turned the ball over five times on three fumbles and two pass interceptions. Yet, the most telling error of the afternoon came late in the third quarter with the game tied at 7-7. Earl Morrall's successful punt to the Michigan 14-yard line was nullified by an offside call. His second attempt was blocked, setting up the winning touchdown drive at the MSC 21-yard line. Adding to the frustration of the afternoon, twice State surrendered the ball after driving inside the five-yard line. Coach Daugherty lamented, "They capitalized on their opportunities and we didn't."

Golf: The 1956 team usually consisted of Ken Rodewald, Arlin Dell, James Sullivan, George Wakulsky, Otto Schubel and Robert Nodus.

Rodewald, playing in the number one position, shot

a 297 and placed fourth in the Big Ten championship at Evanston, Ill. As a team, State finished in a tie for sixth place.

Gymnastics: Even with two champions, the Spartans could finish no better than third place at the conference championships in Champaign, Ill. The two gold medalists were Roland Brown in free exercise and Don Leas on the still rings.

Three men managed to score enough team points at the NCAA championships in Chapel Hill, N.C., that MSU finished in sixth place. Brown tied for second in free exerecise and placed fifth in tumbling. Leas took a sixth in still rings and Jim Breza was ninth in tumbling.

Hockey: Thank goodness for Ontario Agricultural College. For six seasons (1951-1956) the Spartans were 13-0 (2-0 in 1956) against the Canadian school. This represented 33 percent of the 40 victories achieved within that same span of time.

In his sophomore season, Joe Selinger's goals against average was 3.40, the lowest in the team's history.

Another sophomore, Ross Parke of Winnipeg, Manitoba, was the team leader in goals, assists and overall points for he season.

Swimming and Diving: The NCAA swimming and diving championships of today include a championship final of the top eight qualifiers and a consolation race featuring qualifiers nine through 16. In 1956, and for another eight years, only six men would place and score points in championship meets. Consequently, the 1956 NCAAs at Yale University had to be a frustrating weekend for Coach McCaffree and his squad. Both Ken Gest and Les Lobaugh just missed the finals with seventh place finishes in their specialties. Likewise, Paul Reinke, Tom Kwasney, Gordon Fornell, Jim Clemens, and Frank Parrish would have earned points had today's system of 16 finalists been in place. Ultimately, MSU failed to score in the championships for the first time since 1944.

Tennis: Including three perfect 9-0 scores, State opened the regular season with eight straight victories in their southern trip. Thereafter, they could do no better than a 5-5 record and a sixth-place finish in the conference championship. At that Big Ten meet in Minneapolis, captain Dave Brogan was the most successful Spartan, advancing to the semifinals before being eliminated. The remaining entrants, Dick Menzel, Bill Bisard, George Stepanovic, Jim Beachum and Charles Dare were eliminated early.

Jim Sinadinos wrestled his way to two national titles as a Spartan.

Track and Field: Amidst cold and rainy conditions, Joe Savoldi headed MSU's 11-man contingent to the Drake Relays by capturing the 120-yard high hurdles in 14.2, one-tenth of a second from the meet record.

The Spartans finished in fourth place both at the indoor and outdoor championships. Capturing indoor titles were Savoldi (75-yard high hurdles) and Ed Brabham (60-yard dash), with Selwyn Jones, Henry Kennedy and Gaylord Denslow finishing 2-3-4 in the two mile. Outdoors, Brabham raced to wins in both sprint events (100 and 220), while Kennedy won the two-mile title.

Paced by the Canadian duo of Kennedy and Jones, MSU placed fourth at the NCAA outdoor championships with a total of 29 points. Both runners captured individual titles with meet record times, Jones in the 10,000-meter and Kennedy in the 3,000-meter steeplechase. In addition, Jones took third in the 5,000-meter run, while Brabham placed fifth in the 200-meter dash and Dave Lean finished sixth in the 400-meter hurdles.

Wrestling: Don Stroud and Jim Sinadinos were the elite Spartan performers of 1956. As the team struggled to a fourth-place finish at the conference championship, sophomore Stroud was winning the 123-pound title while Sinadinos, senior and team captain, was crowned champion at 137 pounds. Two weeks later at the NCAA tournament in Stillwater, Okla., Sinadinos managed to wrestle his way to a national title, while Stroud settled for a fourth-place finish. A total of 20 team points put MSU in an eighth-place tie with Illinois. This was a second national championship for Sinadinos. He had captured the AAU title as a freshman in 1953.

Ken Maidlow, wrestling in the 191-pound division, won the Greco-Roman title at the 1956 National AAU championships.

EXTRA! 1956 Rose Bowl

January 2, 1956—Pasadena, California

	1	2	3	4	F
MSU	0	7	0	10	17
UCLA	7	0	0	7	14

Starting line-up:

John Lewis	LE
Norm Masters	LT
Dan Currie	LG
Joe Badaczewski	C
Carl Nystrom (C)	RG
Leo Haidys	RT
Dave Kaiser	RE
Earl Morrall	QB
Clarence Peaks	LH
Walt Kowalczyk	RH
Gerry Planutis	FB

It was significant that number-two State scored twice on touchdown passes against number-four UCLA: first for 13 yards from quarterback Earl Morrall to halfback Clarence Peaks with 5:52 remaining in the second quarter, then a 67-yard toss-run from Peaks to John "Thunder" Lewis on the third play of the second half. These scores made possible Dave Kaiser's 41-yard game-winning field goal with seven seconds remaining in the game. Dave tells the story years later:

"Through the years I have often wondered when and where the story of the 1956 Rose Bowl actually began. New anecdotes are always popping up. A different story is heard with a new introduction, and with the passage of time, the mind commences to confuse fact with fiction. So knowing all this, maybe this story actually started when a little sixth grade kid started to shag footballs for his older brother during his summer workouts. One will not bore you by telling of the many days of practice I had while in grade and high school.

Leap-froging over these many practice sessions and football games, I now find myself in Ann Arbor on the field in the Michigan Stadium awaiting the referee's whistle to start the second half. During the kick-off, a block was thrown that I was able to avoid, except for a flying heel to the right knee. Considerable swelling occurred over the weekend. Fortunately, even though the knee could no longer take the strain of kicking, it was able to withstand the other rigors of playing football.

By the time the season ended with MSU chosen to represent the Big Ten in the Rose Bowl, the knee had healed. Upon reaching Pasadena, I once again went to work on my kicking game. For some unknown reason, with Earl Morrall holding, we seemed to practice a little more than usual on field-goal kicking. This is where the blurring of time takes its toll. Even though the last several minutes of the game at one moment seemed to last forever, at other times for only seconds, to me it still seems like only yesterday."

UCLA has the ball . . . back five yards for being off sides. On the next play, which was most confusing, an illegal forward pass with loss of down was called, pushing them back another 15 yards. Knox goes back to kick and gets off a beauty, but UCLA is guilty of fair catch interference and we pick up 15 free, easy yards. A running play over the right side nets five to six yards, but we fumble. The ball is just out of my reach, but before a white shirt can fall on the ball, Don Zysk reaches out and 'slams' the ball to his stomach. With no time outs remaining, we rush back to the huddle, and this is what I remember, quarterback Earl Morrall: 'We are going for a field goal, Dave, you kick it.' As we lined up, Rudy Gaddini comes running in with the kicking tee. The clock stops as the officials walk-off a five yard delay of game penalty. We line up again...the official gives the start the clock signal...Earl looks at me...I point to the spot where I want the ball to be spotted...Joe Badaczewski snaps the ball...Earl places the ball on the tee...it's booted...I look up...'My God, it's going to be good,' I said to myself. Now, for some unexplainable reason, I turned, because I wanted to watch the referee throw his arms in the air with the 'it's good' signal. Forty-one yards...seven seconds left... MSU 17-UCLA 14! As I turned back toward the team, all I could see was a wave of smiling faces wearing green shirts running toward me...complete pandemonium followed."

Dave Kaiser's field goal gave the Spartans a 17-14 1956 Rose Bowl victory over UCLA.

MSU
1956-1957

TALES TO TELL

Jim Clemens, swimming and diving team captain, recalls the 1957 season and the culmination of a Big Ten championship team:

"Our dual-meet record was 7-2, impressive but less than perfect. The pair of losses, to Ohio State and Michigan, was predictable; after all, the two had ruled the Big Ten for more than two decades. Immediately following that loss to the U of M, as captain, I called a team meeting to share thoughts about the possibility of winning the team championship at the upcoming meet in Minneapolis. The meeting concluded with a commitment to return to two-a-day workouts as our class schedules permitted. The concept of year-round and multiple daily workouts is universally accepted among top-flight swim coaches today, but in 1957 it was little more than a promising theory that was worth an experiment.

The final dual meet on the schedule was a convincing 70-35 defeat of Wisconsin. Afterwards, the Badger coach volunteered that, in his opinion, we

were the team to beat for the title. As we made final preparations for the big meet, Coach Mac received permission from Athletic Director Munn to take extra swimmers along in hopes that team depth would pay off.

When the meet began, MSU failed to score in the opening event, the 1,500-meter freestyle, but as the weekend progressed it would prove to be the only swimming event in which we would be shut out. In the next race, the 200-yard butterfly, four of the six finalists, Wally Dobler, Les Lobaugh, Tom Kwasney and Roger Harmon, wore green and white. This would typify the remainder of the meet, as Coach McCaffree had envisioned, we had strength in numbers. In the 50-yard freestyle, Don Patterson, Ken Gest, and Larry Ellis finished third, fourth and fifth. We were winning with numbers. Furthermore, with those extra swimmers who came along, we had the largest and loudest cheering section on the pool deck.

The momentum continued. Paul Reinke won the 100-yard breaststroke to become our only individual champion. Don Nichols finished fourth in the 200-yard backstroke. I was third in the 220-yard

HEADLINES of 1957

- The Russians launch Sputnik 1, the first artificial satellite, and one month later Sputnik 2 is launched with a dog aboard.
- The world's longest suspension bridge, the Mackinac Straits Bridge, opens, connecting Michigan's two peninsulas.
- Dr. Seuss, penname of children's writer Theodor Seuss Geisel, publishes *The Cat in the Hat* and *How the Grinch Stole Christmas*.

SCOREBOARD

	W	L	T	Avg.
Baseball	18	13	1	.578
Track and Field	3	2	0	.600
Football	7	2	0	.778
Basketball	16	10	0	.615
Tennis	7	10	0	.412
Cross Country	4	0	0	1.000
Swimming and Diving	7	2	0	.778
Wrestling	7	2	0	.778
Hockey	7	15	0	.318
Fencing	7	3	0	.700
Golf	8	6	0	.571
Boxing	2	3	0	.400
Gymnastics	7	1	0	.875
Soccer	5	0	1	.917

freestyle and our 400-yard freestyle relay finished first. As the evening ended we held a 50-42 edge over second-place Michigan.

The final night was more of the same. Dobler and Harmon in the 100-yard butterfly; Patterson, Parrish and Ellis in the 100-freestyle; Reinke in the 200-yard breaststroke; Nichols in the 100-yard backstroke, and I finished sixth in the 440-yard freestyle. With one event remaining, the 400-yard medley relay, we held a two-point lead over Michigan. Our quartet of Nichols, Reinke, Harmon and Parrish were up to the challenge as they finished ahead of the field to win the event and the team championship.

A wild poolside celebration followed that included the traditional dunking of the coach. Before the jubilation concluded, every Spartan was in the water. We had ended a 21-year domination of Big Ten swimming and diving by Michigan and Ohio State."

TEAM OF THE YEAR

It took Forddy Anderson only three years to recruit and mold a team that would win a share of the Big Ten title. Combining the scoring of Jack Quiggle, Larry Hedden, George Ferguson and Bob Anderegg, along with the rebounding and defensive play of Hedden and Johnny Green, the Spartans posted a 10-4 conference record to tie Indiana for the top spot. They put themselves into the title picture by defeating the Hoosiers, 76-61, in a showdown at Jenison in the final home game of the season. By a favorable vote from the conference representatives, State was selected to be the Big Ten's sole representative (as was the policy in the 16-team NCAA tournament field). At the Midwest Regional in Lexington, Ky., State edged Notre Dame, 85-83, and then overcame the Wildcats' home-court advantage, 80-68, to advance to the final four in Kansas City. The tournament trail ended dramatically when the Spartans dropped a triple-overtime thriller, 74-70, to North Carolina, the eventual champions. How significant had Johnny Green been to the Spartan team of 1956-1957? Consider this. Before "Jumpin' Johnny" became eligible to compete (winter term), State had logged an unimpressive 4-7 record, gained a tie for the conference title and eventually earned a trip to the Final Four.

The 1957 basketball team. (Front row, left to right) J. Quiggle, J. Stouffer, H. Lux, capt. G. Ferguson, P. Wilson, D. Scott and T. Rand. (Back row, left to right) coach F. Anderson, B. Anderegg, T. Markovich, J. Green, G. Siegmeier, C. Bencie, L. Jennings, L. Hedden, J. Reading, asst. coach R. Stevens and trainer G. Robinson.

MAKING HISTORY

The width of basketball's free-throw lane was increased from eight feet to 12 feet.

Rumors had circulated during the entire 1957 season that MSC might abandon boxing as a varsity sport. Confirming the supposition, official disclosure came from the May 1 meeting of the Athletic Council and was later corroborated by the Board of Agriculture, the college's governing board. Athletic director Biggie Munn emphasized that the sport was not being disbanded because of pressures claiming that boxing is a dangerous sport, but purely because of the cost for maintaining the team. Lengthy travel for meets and lessening fan support at home confirmed Munn's rationale. Because schedules had been prearranged through 1958, one more season was anticipated. The decision to drop the sport seemed to be accepted with little dispute. There were no demonstrations in support. No petitions were circulated. More than two weeks passed before the *Michigan State News* reacted with a condescending editorial, noting that the resolution to abort the sport was "a most sensible decision."

GREAT STATE DATES

Football—**October 6, 1956 (A):** In what was billed as the largest paying sports crowd in the state's history, some 101,000 fans sat through occasional pelting rain to watch the Spartans break a 0-0 halftime deadlock and go on for a 9-0 victory over Michigan. The opening score, early in the third quarter, came on a John Matsko 30-yard field goal. He had been called upon in the absence of the injured Dave Kaiser. Following a fumble recovery at the U of M 21-yard line, the "S" offense, running exclusively from the split-T formation, found the end zone on a six-play drive. Leading the defense in the shutout were Emil G. Matsos, Jim Hinesly, Jim Wulff and Joel Jones, the latter setting up the lone touchdown when he tore the ball away from the Michigan fullback.

Soccer—**October 13, 1956 (H):** This was State's first soccer game to be played at the varsity level, even if the season was listed as being on a "trial basis." Varsity games were played on a layout located on the east side of the grounds now identified as football's secret practice field. Matched against Michigan, the Spartans played a

dismal first half and fell behind 1-0. After intermission, they seemed to take control, exerting continual presure on the U of M defense. Santiago Cabal tied the score with a high hard one that just squeezed in under the bar. Karl Snilsberg scored minutes later to take the lead, 2-1, and then Paz Saria followed with goal number three as he booted in his own rebound after hitting the goal post on his first attempt.

Football—**October 20, 1956 (A):** Michigan State 47, Notre Dame 14. It would have seemed the three-hour rain in the morning of the game would have slowed the offensive show. This was not the case as MSU, led by Clarence Peaks, Dennis Mendyk, Pat Wilson, Jim Ninowski, Don Arend, and Don Gilbert scored seven touchdowns and ran up a total score never before achieved against the Irish. It was a game of big plays. Mendyk produced touchdown runs of 62 and 68 yards, and Arend turned the end for a 65-yard scoring jaunt. Peaks also streaked 93 yards for what would have been the longest rushing play in school history, but it was nullified by a penalty. State amassed 369 yards rushing and 125 passing with all scores coming via the ground attack

Football—**November 3, 1956 (H):** Bouncing back from the 20-13 upset in Champaign, Ill., State defeated Wisconsin 33-0. Any lasting recollection of that game against the Badgers does not pertain to the brilliant 67-yard punt return for touchdown by Dennis Mendyk or the great passing afternoon by Pat Wilson or the 123 yards gained by Tony Kolodziej as a receiver. Insead, it was the memory of the "hurry-up huddle" offense inserted by Coach Daugherty in the second half of the game. Although two fumbles and a pass interception halted three promising drives, the perpetual motion of the 11 players gained roaring vocal support from Spartan fans. In his post-game press conference, Coach Dougherty summarized, "That gimmick sure moves the ball doesn't it?"

Cross Country—**November 5, 1956 (A):** State conducted an undefeated dual-meet season with a 19-38 victory over Notre Dame. Henry Kennedy again led the Spartans, running the five-mile course in 25:05.2. Gaylord Denslow finished second, Selwyn Jones third, Don Wheeler sixth and Terry Block seventh.

Football—**November 10, 1956 (H):** With Michigan State leading 12-7 in the final quarter, Purdue was in possession, first-and-10 at the MSU three-yard line. The slim five-point lead was in serious jeopardy. Aided by an illegal procedure call, the line of scrimmage moved back

to the eight-yard line, and from there, the stout defense took over. Featuring Emil Matsos, John Matsko and Joel Jones, three savage running stops ensued, followed by a Jim Ninowski breakup of a fourth-down pass in the end zone. The Boilers were not through. Blanche Martin was trapped in the end zone for a safety, making the score 12-9. Regaining the offense, PU drove to the MSU 44-yard line where they attempted a desperation field goal that fell short with three seconds remaining on the clock. The win was costly as Joel Jones of Weirton, W.Va., a bulwark in the line and a definite All-American candidate, suffered a career-ending knee injury.

Fencing—**January 19, 1957 (H):** Opening his 18th year as head coach, Charley Schmitter's squad edged the always challenging University of Detroit Titans, 14-13. Outdueled in both the epee and foil weapons, the Spartans gained the winning margin when George Thomas, Darold McCalla, and John Kalasky garnered seven of the nine points at stake in the sabre competition.

Basketball—**January 26, 1957 (A):** At Minnesota for their third straight road game, State would begin its ten-game winning streak with the newest Spartan, Johnny Green, in the lineup. The Minnesota players were in awe as Green, in complete control of the backboards, struck for a quick 10 points. Aided by Larry Hedden's game-high 25, State was in front by as many as 20 points during the second half. With a final score of 72-59, it was the first Michigan State victory at Williams Arena in the 14-year history of the series.

Basketball—**January 28, 1957 (H):** The Buckeyes came to town as the 10th-ranked team in the nation and the conference leader with a perfect 6-0 record. Frank Howard, who would later make his name as a professional baseball player, was their scoring star. Led by Jack Quiggle's game-high 21 points, MSU finally put it away, 73-64, after the lead had changed hands nine times during the latter portions of the game. Led by Johnny Green, the Spartans out-rebounded the Bucks, 48-23. The win put Forrdy's team into a sixth-place conference tie with their 2-3 record.

Swimming and Diving—**February 9, 1957 (A):** Indiana University was four years away from dominating the Big Ten swimming and diving scene, but as early as 1957, world-class competitors were already finding their way to Bloomington. Consequently, defeating the Hoosiers 63-42 was a noteworthy victory. In addition to taking both relays, the Spartans managed to win five of the

nine individual events: Larry Ellis and Don Patterson in the 50- and 100-yard freestyle, Don Nichols in the backstroke, Paul Reinke in the breaststroke and Don Morey in the one-meter diving.

Wrestling—**February 9, 1957 (A):** Making a tremendous comeback, which included two pins, the Michigan State wrestling team defeated the small school wrestling power, Iowa State Teachers College, 16-14. After Don Stroud won the opening match for MSU, the Teachers won four straight to build an 11-point advantage. Trailing 14-3, the Spartans had to win the final three match-ups with at least two by pins to pull off a successful comeback. In the 167-pound division Jim Ferguson did everything but put his opponent's shoulders to the mat, as he won by an 11-4 score. The burden then fell on State's final two competitors, both of national caliber, 177-pound LeRoy Fladseth and heavyweight Ken Maidlow, and each responded with the necessary pin to ensure the victory.

Basketball—**February 11, 1957 (A):** Jack Quiggle's long set-shot with eight seconds left climaxed a great MSU comeback and led to an exciting 68-66 victory over Purdue. State trailed by nine points with 9:30 remaining but scored eight unanswered points to cut the deficit to one, 58-57. From there, the two teams battled back and forth, and, with the score at 66-66, Johnny Green saved the day with a phenomenal block of a lay-up attempt. With 20 seconds showing on the game clock, the Spartans hurried the ball up court and set the stage for Quiggle's dramatic one-hander. Larry Hedden led all Spartan players with 17 points. George Ferguson hit for 13, Green 11 and Bob Anderegg scored 10.

Basketball—**February 16, 1957 (H):** Opening the second half of the conference schedule, MSU defeated Iowa, 77-67, for their sixth-straight win. In each of the preceding victories, State had won the battle of the boards, but on this night the Hawkeyes out-rebounded "Jumpin' Johnny" and Co., 42-31. Instead, for the first time Green assumed the spot of leading scorer as he connected for 23 points. Normally confining his game to defense and ball-handling, Pat Wilson suddenly sharpened his shooting eye, as he hit on four of five field goals in the first half. Yet, the most crowd-pleasing shot of the game came in the first half when Jack Quiggle ally-ooped a feed to Johnny Green, who slammed it through the basket.

Wrestling—**February 16, 1957 (A):** With a win by Michigan's 157-pounder, the Wolverines forged to a

lead that held up until the final match. Jim Ferguson began the Spartans' comeback when he held the 167-pound conference champion to a draw. Next, State's LeRoy Fladseth decisioned his 177-pound opponent with ease, 9-3. All attention then fell on the heavyweight division where MSU's Ken Maidlow, a National AAU champion in 1956, disposed of his adversary, 4-2. The final score was as close as it could get: Michigan State 16, Michigan 15.

***Basketball*—February 18, 1957 (A):** With an 89-83 win over the University of Illinois, MSU was nestled into second place behind Indiana in the conference standings and talk was humming about the Spartan-Hoosier match up two weeks hence. The Monday night victory in Champaign was the first time a visiting team had won on the George Huff gymnasium floor in the last 22 tries. The Spartans shot 44 percent from the field compared to Illinois' 35 percent. Commenting on the unusually high 89-point output, coach Forddy Anderson said that preparing for the Illini, the stress turned from defense to offense.

***Track and Field*—February 18, 1957 (A):** Although the Spartans won only six of the 15 events contested, team depth triggered a 74 1/2-66 1/2 dual-meet victory over Ohio State. Twenty of Coach Schlademan's 24 entries scored points. The primary strength was displayed in the distance events in which MSU runners scored 17 out of a possible 18 points. Junior Dave Lean won both the 880-yard and 1,000-yard runs, and other firsts came from Bill Hughes in the 600-yard run, captain Sewell Jones in the mile, Henry Kennedy in the two-mile, and Sam Eliowitz in the shot put. The Ohio State Olympic hurdle champion Glenn Davis had a busy afternoon, taking four firsts, a second, a third-place tie and then a victory as the anchor for the winning relay team.

***Gymnastics*—February 18, 1957 (H):** Trailing Michigan by one point, Coach Szypula put hopes on his three entrants in the closing event, tumbling. When the results were in, Jim Breza had finished first, Roland Brown was third, and George Hopely took fifth. The final point total then read 58.5-53.5 in favor of the Spartans. It was the fifth win over the U of M in a seven-year span since 1951.

***Basketball*—February 23, 1957 (H):** The winning streak had now reached seven in a row, and by the time Minnesota came to town for the next-to-last home game of the season, fans were packing the seats of Jenison. As the game progressed, the Gophers proved to be in no disposition to roll over. Their zone defense and outside shooting found them leading by five points at intermission. Opening the second half, Larry Hedden and Jack Quiggle began hitting from outside the zone and finally, at the five-minute mark, State took the lead, 42-41, on a free throw by Bob Anderegg. The game then seesawed back and forth until a Quiggle lay-up put the Spartans ahead to stay, 50-48, with 7:36 remaining. Johnny Green pulled down 16 caroms to lead State's dominance in rebounding, 45-36. Scoring honors went to Larry Ferguson 19, Hedden 16 and Quiggle 15.

***Gymnastics*—February 23, 1957 (H):** Raising their season record to 6-1, State defeated Wisconsin, 74-36, as five seniors competed in Jenison for the final time: Jim Breza, Roland Brown, Don Leas, Don Marcini and Dick O'Brien. Michigan State performers captured five of the seven events on the program: George Hopely in free exercise, Marcini on the trampoline, Brown in tumbling, Leas on the horizontal bar and Cal Girard on the parallel bars. O'Brien placed second on the horse, while Russ Paul was runner-up on the flying rings.

***Basketball*—February 25, 1957 (A):** Biggie Munn came to the bench at halftime of the Wisconsin game to tell Coach Anderson that Michigan had upset Indiana, 87-86. Suddenly, the results of the Badger contest and the upcoming battle with IU took on added significance. First, it must be realized that in those years only *one* team represented the conference in the NCAA tournament. A meeting of Big Ten faculty representatives two weeks earlier had resolved the issue in the event of a Spartan-Hoosier first-place tie. The plan would give the slot to the team that had been longest out of the coveted national championships. Since MSU had never been in the tournament and Indiana had gone in 1954, the Spartans would automatically be the conference choice. Initially holding the good news from his team about the Indiana loss to the U of M, Anderson found the appropriate moment during a time-out when nursing a slim 55-54 lead. It proved to be a tonic. Over the remaining time, State outscored the Badgers, 23-8, and won with relative ease, 78-62. Displaying team balance, five players scored in double figures: Johnny Green 20, Larry Hedden 17, Bob Anderegg 13, Jack Quiggle 13 and Larry Ferguson 11.

***Basketball*—March 2, 1957 (H):** The fire marshal must have been out-of-town. A total of 13,871 fans found

some place to sit or stand in Jenison, which had a capacity of 12,500. The foe was Indiana University and at stake was a share of the conference title plus that trip to Lexington, Ky., to represent the Big Ten in the NCAA Midwest regional tournament. Ending the first half on top 35-31, State expanded the lead to 10 points during the opening seven minutes of the second half. Thereafter, the Spartans had the game under control. They made a minimum of mistakes, executed sharp passes, and beat the opponent of the evening with their own patented style of play, the fast break. The final score read, MSU 74, Indiana 61. As usual, Johnny Green controlled the backboards with 19 rebounds and pumped in 13 points. Leading the scoring parade were Jack Quiggle with 23 and Larry Hedden with 22.

Hockey—**March 8, 1957 (H):** On the final weekend of the schedule, Amo's squad managed their seventh win of the season, a 4-2 decision over the North Dakota Sioux in the Friday night encounter. Trailing 1-0 at the first intermission, the skaters left the ice after two periods with the score knotted at 2-2 on goals by Ross Parke and Fred DeVuono. Six minutes into the final period, Bill MacKenzie scored the eventual winner on a power play and Parke slapped the insurance goal by the net minder with less than two minutes to play.

Boxing—**March 11, 1957 (H):** Trailing in points 17-20, Fred Pettyjohn came through in the final round of his 165-pound bout to TKO his opponent and give State the necessary fifth team point in their 5-3 victory over the defending NCAA champions, the Wisconsin Badgers. The evening opened on a positive note with wins by Harv Lancour at 125 pounds and Bob Jemilo at 132. John Butler followed with one more team point, this by a forfeit. In a highly entertaining bout, 147-pound Sherald Haynes gathered momentum over the three rounds, even staggering his opponent against the ropes in the final round to eventually earn a 29-28 decision and the fourth MSU point, setting up the dramatic Pettyjohn bout.

Tennis—**April 20, 1957 (A):** Returning from a less-than-impressive 2-5 southern trip, Frank Beeman's squad opened the regular portion of their schedule by easily handling the Ohio State Buckeyes, 8-1. Sweeping to straight set victories in the singles were number one Bill Bisard, number two captain George Stepanovic, number three Mike Zaremba, number four Ron Mescall and number six Foster Hoffman. The Spartans then added to their victorious afternoon by taking all three doubles matches: Bisard-Zaremba, Stepanovic-Luis Vela and Mescall-Hoffman.

Baseball—**April 26, 1957 (A):** Raising his season record to 6-1, Ron Perranoski pitched superlatively with the 4-2 win over Indiana in the conference opener at Bloomington. The southpaw junior struck out 16 batters, just two shy of the conference record set by an Illinois pitcher in 1948. Leading 3-2 going into the ninth, Dean Moore provided an insurance run when he led off with a 350-foot home run over the right-center field fence.

Baseball—**April 30, 1957 (A):** State scored four runs early and hung on to turn back Notre Dame, 4-3. Everything seemed to fall into place for John Kobs's squad. They banged out 12 hits, committed only one error, and the pitching duo of Dick Griffin and Bill Mansfield scattered nine hits. Griffin, starting his first game as a Spartan, pitched scoreless ball for six innings before tiring and needing relief in the eighth.

Golf—**May 13, 1957 (H):** The Spartans played stellar golf over the Lansing Country Club course to easily defeat the University of Michigan, 26 1/2-9 1/2. George Wakulsky led all scores with a two-under-par, 70-72, to give him a 142 score. Other scores were Otto Schubel, 73-74, 147; Ken Rodewald, 71-77, 148; Jim Sullivan, 73-75, 148; Bob Nodus, 75-74, 149; and Arlin Dell, 73-77, 150.

Tennis—**May 18, 1957 (A):** The Spartans closed the dual-meet season at Madison, Wisconsin, with a 5-4 victory over the Badgers. Winning at singles were number two captain George Stepanovic, number three Mike Zaremba and number four Ron Mescall. The outcome of the meet rested in the doubles and both the number one pair of Bill Bisard-Zaremba and number two team of Stepanovic and Luis Vela gained the deciding team points.

ATHLETE OF THE YEAR

Reminiscing in a personal interview on February 20, 1999, during the weekend celebration of Michigan State's basketball centennial, Forddy Anderson related the Johnny Green story. With tongue in cheek, the former coach called it "the recruiting job of the year:"

"He [Green] was in the marines serving in Japan. A friend of mine who was a football coach wrote saying they had a guy in the marines that had never played high school basketball but could jump like

crazy. I said, 'Well, when he is through [with military service] have him come and see me.' We'd need to figure the military forms, the schedule, the books, etc. So, on his own he showed up and enrolled. Upon returning from the Iowa State game [Dec. 1, 1956], we had just lost and I was upset. I said, 'Bob [assistant coach Bob Stevens], you take them [the freshmen players, in their first practice], I've got to practice these guys [the varsity] downstairs [in Jenison Fieldhouse].' Within a half-hour Bob came racing down [from the Jenison gymnasium] and said, 'Have the guys shoot free throws.' I said, 'What for?' Again, he said, 'Have them shoot free throws!' So, he took me up to the freshmen court, and there the other freshmen were standing and watching as Johnny was jumping next to this 12-foot-high room divider, and he was grabbing it [at the top] and grabbing it. I said [to Bob Stevens], 'Find out what this guy needs…RIGHT NOW!' The next day he was with the varsity. He [Green] was ineligible until winter term. I remember the first time I put him in. Some guy took a jump shot from the base line, and Johnny knocked it into the fifth row of the bleachers and after that everything changed."

Appropriately nicknamed "Jumpin'" Johnny Green, the springy-legged ex-GI became an instrumental part of the team during the second half of the 1956-1957 season as well as leading the 1957-1958 edition and the 1958-1959 squad that won an outright Big Ten title. During his two and a half years in the lineup, State's combined record was 49-13 for a winning percentage of .790. In the immediate three years prior to his arrival, MSU had won 35 and lost 31, which equates to a depressed .522 record. Statistics in the three seasons following Green's departure were even less impressive, 25 Ws and 42 losses for a .372 average. Predictably, local fan interest was aroused by the positive spin by "Green and Co." Playing before home crowds of 6,000 to 7,000 in the opening games of 1956-1957, sellouts were being reported during the stretch drive of February and March. By the home closer on March 2 against Indiana, a total of 13,871 fans found some place to sit or stand in a fieldhouse with a capacity of 12,500.

Johnny Green

IN THE SPARTLITE

Baseball: Returning from the Florida spring trip with a modest 6-5-1 record, coach John Kobs may have found answers to previous questions regarding his starting lineup, but other facts were simply confirmed. Catcher Al Luce would be the leader of the team. Frank Palamara would be the most consistent player on the field, and Ron Perranoski would be the most dependable pitcher.

The starting lineup was soon set: John Russell RF, Gary Warner 3B, Frank Palamara 2B, Al Luce C, Dick McKenzie CF, Dean Moore or Ken Warren LF, Roscoe Davis 1B and Jerry Korwek SS. The top three pitchers were Ron Perranoski, Bob Rabias and Bill Mansfield.

Postseason honors included Davis and Luce as first team All-Big Ten, and Palamara and Perranoski were selected to the second team.

Finishing the season with a .358 average, Palamara was the team's hitting leader. In the pitching department, with an impressive 1.48, Mansfield registered the lowest earned run average (ERA), while Perranowski was the strikeout leader with 86.

Basketball: As the only guest team in the Big Seven holiday tournament at Kansas City, State defeated Nebraska, lost to Colorado, and then topped Oklahoma, 76-74 in OT to gain third place in the eight-team field.

Following the 10-game win streak, which assured State of at least a tie for the conference crown, the schedule closed out on the road in Ann Arbor. A win against Michigan would translate to an outright title, but the Wolverines would have none of that as they played the role of spoiler, 81-72.

The polls ranked State eighth upon completion of the regular season.

Boxing: With Harvard Lancour, Bob Jemilo, and Johnny Butler all losing semi-final matches, for the first time since 1941, not a single Spartan reached the finals of the NCAA championships.

Cross Country: In a repeat performance of the 1952 "grand slam" team, the 1956 cross country quintet of Henry Kennedy, Gaylord Denslow, Sewell Jones, Terry Block, and Phil Wheeler raced to titles at the IC4A meet and the Big Ten championships in Chicago. Then, with Ed Townsend filling in for Wheeler, the Spartans topped it off by successfully defending their NCAA title with an impressive score of 28. Over the entire history of the NCAA championship meet, only two teams have ever won in a more impressive style. Scoring positions were as follows: Henry Kennedy, second; Gaylord Denslow, third; Selwyn Jones, fourth; Phil Wheeler, seventh; and Terry Block, 12th.

MSU had gained quite a reputation. The Texas coach's pre-race instructions to his only Longhorn runner, the eventual individual winner, were: "Pick out a green-and-white runner to follow and then pass him before the finish."

Fencing: As unlikely as it seems, it is possible to sustain an injury in the sport of fencing. George Thomas sat out the triangular meet at Madison, Wis., as he remained home nursing an eye injury he'd acquired during "combat."

Later returning to the lineup for the conference meet in Champaign, Ill., Thomas would recapture the Big Ten sabre title that he had won in 1955. The remainder of

Charlie Schmitter's entrants did not fare as well. Ed Kotlar and Warner Johnson in epee, Hal Simonds in foil and Darold McCalla in sabre failed to continue beyond the preliminary round. Ed Hilldebrant did qualify but dropped four straight bouts in the finals.

Football: Early in the 1956 season, Duffy was featured in a fall *Time* magazine cover story that acclaimed him "the master craftsman of the most intricate offense in modern football." The publication could have also described the lovable Irishman as the "master recruiter." The 47-14 win over Notre Dame was an example of the depth of talent with which Duffy continued to surround himself. Six different players shared the touchdown parade: Dennis Mendyk (2), Pat Wilson, Clarence Peaks, Larry Harding, Don Gilbert, and Don Arend. Other ball carriers against the Irish were Jim Ninowski, Walt Kowalczyk, Mike Panitch and Blanche Martin. Defensive standouts included Tony Kolodziej, John Matsko, Dan Currie, Les Rutledge and Joel Jones.

Going into Champaign-Urbana for the fifth game of the season, MSU was ranked number one in the polls and favored by three touchdowns. Leading 13-0 at halftime, it looked like another easy win until Clarence Peaks suffered a severe knee injury and left the game. The Illini then stole the Spartans' script and came from behind to score 20 unanswered points for the upset.

Golf: In the Big Ten Conference tournament at Iowa City, Iowa, MSU golfers finished seventh with a combined total score of 1564, which was 52 strokes from Wisconsin's winning score of 1512.

Gymnastics: Scoring 68 1/2 points, Coach Szypula's squad finished a distant third at the conference championships in Ann Arbor. Don Leas placed third on the flying rings and was also busy placing fourth or better in free exercise, the trampoline and high bar. Russ Paul scored on the flying rings, the high bar, and parallel bars; Roland Brown contributed points in free exercise and tumbling. Others contributing points were Dick O'Brien on the side horse, Jim Cook on flying rings, Cal Girard on the parallel bars and Jim Breza in tumbling.

Hockey: In preseason publicity, it was reported that for the first time in the history of hockey at MSU, the team would rotate three full lines during games of the 1956-1957 season. The season opened with those lines represented by Keith Christofferson, Ross Parke, and Glen MacDonald; Joe Polano, Gene Grazia and Bill MacKenzie along with Fred DeVuono, Dickie Hamilton and Ken

James. By season's end and with only a handful of games in the "W" column, Coach Bessone had shuffled his lines as follows: Parke, Polano and Grazia; Christofferson, DeVuono and Hamilton; plus MacKenzie, James and MacDonald.

In a different twist from current customs, the Green and White game (varsity vs. freshmen in 1957) was played at the conclusion and not prior to the season. The team banquet followed, at which time Bob Jasson received the MVP award and Parke was acknowledged as the team's top scorer. In addition, Christofferson received a gold watch for his outstanding academic record.

This was not a great year for the University of Minnesota. State managed to win only seven games all season long, but three of the victories were at the expense of the Gophers.

Soccer: After toiling as an intramural club sport for four years, Gene Kenney was hired as coach, and soccer emerged as a varsity sport on a "trial" basis in the fall of 1956. Upon concluding a remarkable 5-0-1 season, which opened with a 3-1 victory over Michigan, there was ample reason to confirm that Spartan soccer had successfully emerged from its trial period.

The first-ever varsity team consisted of Al Sasanko, Jordan Tatter, Leo VanderHorst, Bill Malcolm, Ray Burdett, George Sepetys, Santiago Cabal, Al Sarria, Art Southan, Karl Snilsberg, Wally Burger, Neil Butler, Angelos Pilitsis, Morris Russ, Jocko Nevis, Al Lonigro, John Asmah, Dan Clifford, and Aurelio Guzman.

Swimming and Diving: At the NCAA championships in Chapel Hill, N.C., a first-place tie in the 400-yard medley relay, a second-place finish in the 400-yard freestyle and scoring in individual events by Roger Harmon, Don Patterson, Wally Dobler, Paul Reinke and Jim Clemens led to 52 team points, good enough for a third-place finish behind Michigan with 69 and Yale with 61.

Tennis: After finishing the regular portion of the dual-meet schedule with a 7-4 record, the Spartans met with little success in the Big Ten championship meet in Evanston, Ill. Playing in positions number one through number five: Bill Bisard, captain George Stepanovic, Mike Zaremba, Ron Mescall and Luis Vela met early departures from the competition, while number six Foster Hoffman was eliminated at the semi-final stage. The only doubles team to go beyond the opening round was the number one pair of Bisard-Zaremba, and they advanced no further. As a team, Beeman's gang placed sixth in the weekend of matches.

Track and Field: Australian trackmen Dave Lean and Kevin Gosper were the only two MSU athletes to earn medals at the Olympic Games in Melbourne, Australia. Lean, a sophomore, and Gosper, the 1955 team captain, formed one-half of the Aussie's silver-medal winning mile relay team.

Freshman Willie Atterberry of Detroit was the star of stars at the Ohio Relays in Columbus where he completed the fastest 600-yard run ever recorded. His 1:08.5 bettered the previously best time by one full second. Not competed in as a world

The 1957 Big Ten champion Michigan State swimming and diving team

event, the performance was submitted as an American record.

Totaling 27.6 points, the team placed third at the indoor championships but managed only 16 points outdoors, settling for a fifth place tie. Dave Lean, the conference indoor champion in the quarter-mile, moved up to the half-mile at the outdoor meet, where he captured first place in an impressive time of 1:52.9. Other Spartan finalists were Selwyn Jones and Gay Denslow, who finished second and fourth in the two mile; Forddy Kennedy, who was fourth in the mile; Sam Eliowitz, who was fifth in the shot put; and George Best, who tied for fourth in the pole vault.

Wrestling: Only three team members finished in one of the top four spots at the Big Ten championships hosted by Ohio State. Norm Gill placed third in the 137-pound division; LeRoy Fladseth was fourth at 177; and heavyweight Ken Maidlow gained a third place. With a total of 18 points, the team finished in a sixth-place tie with Indiana.

EXTRA! 1957 NCAA BASKETBALL TOURNAMENT

Michigan State placed fourth in the 1957 NCAA tournament. The following are the Spartans' box scores from those games.

MICHIGAN STATE 85–NOTRE DAME 83

	FG-FGA	FT-FTA	REB	PF	TP
Ferguson	8-20	0-0	10	4	16
Hedden	4-16	5-12	11	3	13
Green	8-21	4-7	27	3	20
Quiggle	8-22	2-3	7	3	18
Wilson	0-2	0-0	3	1	0
Scott	1-2	2-4	3	0	4
Anderegg	4-8	6-8	5	2	14
TOTALS	33-91	19-34	66	16	85

Halftime: Michigan State 37-36; **Officials:** Fox, DiGravio; **Attendance:** 11,000.

MICHIGAN STATE 80–KENTUCKY 68

	FG-FGA	FT-FTA	REB	PF	TP
Ferguson	5-15	5-6	12	3	15
Hedden	4-16	2-6	7	2	10
Anderegg	1-4	0-0	1	2	2
Markovich	0-0	0-0	1	1	0
Green	5-11	4-6	18	5	14
Bencie	2-5	1-2	5	1	5
Quiggle	9-22	4-4	4	4	22
Wilson	3-10	0-0	3	0	6
Lux	0-1	0-0	0	0	0
Scott	1-3	4-5	0	0	6
TOTALS	30-87	20-29	51	18	80

Halftime: Kentucky 47-35; **Officials:** Anderson, Mihalik; **Attendance:** not available.

NORTH CAROLINA 74–MICHIGAN STATE 70 (3OT)

	FG-FGA	FT-FTA	REB	PF	TP
Quiggle	6-21	8-10	10	1	20
Green	4-12	3-6	19	2	11
Ferguson	4-8	2-3	1	5	10
Hedden	4-20	6-7	15	5	14
Wilson	0-3	2-2	5	1	2
Anderegg	2-7	3-6	3	2	7
Bencie	1-6	0-0	2	1	2
Scott	2-3	0-2	3	1	4
TOTALS	23-80	24-36	58	18	70

Halftime: 29-29; **Regulation score:** 58-58; **First overtime:** 64-64; **Second overtime:** 66-66; **Officials:** Ogden, Lightner; **Attendance:** not available.

SAN FRANCISCO 67–MICHIGAN STATE 60
(Consolation Game)

	FG-FGA	FT-FTA	REB	PF	TP
Green	4-9	1-1	13	5	9
Ferguson	4-11	6-9	11	2	14
Hedden	4-10	1-2	5	5	9
Wilson	3-6	0-1	0	1	6
Lux	2-2	1-1	3	2	5
Anderegg	2-8	3-4	4	5	7
Scott	2-6	0-1	3	1	4
Bencie	0-5	0-0	4	1	0
Quiggle	2-6	2-2	4	1	6
TOTALS	23-63	14-21	47	23	60

Halftime: San Francisco 33-30; **Officials:** Ogden, Lightner; **Attendance:** not available.

MSU
1957-1958

TALES TO TELL

Upon losing a close decision at the Inter-Mountain boxing tournament in January to Idaho State's Harold Espy, the 1957 NCAA champion, Tom McNeeley immediately spoke of redemption. The opportunity presented itself two months later when Idaho State came to East Lansing for the Spartans' final home appearance, ever. Representing the largest crowd of the season, nearly 1,000 fans began their verbal support of McNeely as the two gladiators entered the ring and eyed each other from their respective corners. The bell rang and the two charged to the center of the ring. McNeely, a good boxer, always seemed to be a better slugger, and he found Espy a willing opponent as the two battered each other toe-to-toe for three full rounds. Although there were no official knockdowns, twice McNeely slammed his opponent through the ropes and in the final round bulled him over the first strand and onto the apron of the ring as the uproar from the crowd reached a crescendo. With both men still whaling lefts and rights beyond the final bell, it took the referee and both coaches to pry the pair apart. It

was a fitting climax to 22 seasons of MSC boxing. As the ring lights dimmed and Spartan boxing supporters filed out of Jenison for the final time, few cared that MSC had lost the meet, 4-3; the lingering memory was how Tom McNeely had avenged his earlier season loss at Pocatello, Idaho.

TEAM OF THE YEAR

As the 1958 gymnastics season unfolded, there was little hint that Michigan State would be in the title hunt when championship time rolled around in April. They had done no better than 7-3 through the dual-meet season, placing third in the Big Tens. Just hosting the 1958 NCAA championship meet in Jenison Fieldhouse seemed rewarding enough for some. However, when the two-day meet opened, coach George Szypula unveiled a "secret weapon," Ted Muzyezko, who had transferred from the University of Illinois-Chicago just two weeks earlier in pursuit of an engineering degree (generous NCAA

HEADLINES of 1958

- Stereo LPs are introduced.
- The first working integrated circuitry is perfected, which revolutionizes the electronic industry.
- The atomic submarine Nautilus makes the first underwater crossing of the North Pole.
- The National Aeronautics and Space Administration (NASA) is established and the U.S. successfully sends unmanned satellites into space.

SCOREBOARD

	W	L	T	Avg.
Baseball	22	12	0	.647
Track and Field	3	3	0	.500
Football	8	1	0	.888
Basketball	16	6	0	.727
Tennis	6	8	0	.428
Cross Country	3	0	0	1.000
Swimming and Diving	8	1	0	.888
Wrestling	3	5	0	.375
Hockey	12	11	0	.522
Fencing	5	5	0	.500
Golf	6	2	1	.722
Boxing	0	2	2	.250
Gymnastics	7	3	0	.700
Soccer	6	0	2	.875

transfer policy of the time). Muzyezko, a talented gymnast, returned immediate dividends, winning the national collegiate title on the parallel bars, placing third on the side horse, seventh on the horizontal bar and second in the all-around. More importantly, his efforts accounted for 32 points toward MSU's composite of 79, which proved ample enough for a share of the team title with the University of Illinois. Also adding to the Spartans'

winning total were Stan Tarshis and Dick Becker, runners-up on the horizontal bar and in the free exercise, respectively. Becker had been a recruit from the cheerleading squad. Another standout was Cal Girard, who finished fourth on the high bar, sixth on the side horse, seventh on the parallel bars and third in the all-around. Jim Cook was eighth on the flying rings and captain Russ Paul was ninth on the parallels. The Illini had trailed State by 20 points entering the final event, but a one-two finish by their tumblers made up the difference and cinched the deadlock.

MAKING HISTORY

With the greatest margin of victory since the 93-0 Alma game of 1932, State opened the 1957 football season with a convincing 54-0 victory over Indiana. The Spartans flirted with some other records that afternoon: (1) engaging more talent than in any previous State game, 67 players, including 30 first-year men (sophomores) played; (2) a total of 21 Spartans carried the ball one or more times; (3) a staggering total of 32 first downs surpassed any previous conference mark; and (4) the 570 total net yards gained was within two yards of the all-time team mark.

Basketball's free-throw bonus rule was initiated in 1957-1958. After a team committed its sixth personal foul in either half, the opponent would be awarded a bonus try for each foul thereafter.

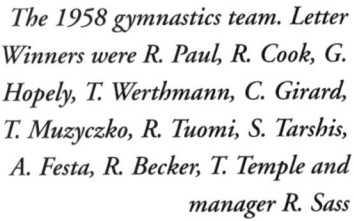

The 1958 gymnastics team. Letter Winners were R. Paul, R. Cook, G. Hopely, T. Werthmann, C. Girard, T. Muzyczko, R. Tuomi, S. Tarshis, A. Festa, R. Becker, T. Temple and manager R. Sass

In swimming, until 1958 there were three competitive strokes: the freestyle, backstroke and breaststroke of the time. The latter was a combination of the arm action from today's butterfly stroke with the frog kick from today's breaststroke. Then, in 1955, the previously illegal butterfly "whip" kick became acceptable, thus evolving today's butterfly stroke. The breaststroke returned to the underwater recovery and, connected with the frog kick, became the fourth competitive stroke beginning at the 1958 collegiate championships.

Although not sanctioned as an official varsity sport by either Michigan State or the NCAA, the MSU Weightlifting Club hosted and proclaimed themselves NCAA champions with a team total of 38 points, 20 better than second place Ohio State. Two Spartans gained titles, Joe Dewland at 132 pounds and Dave Norton at 141.

GREAT STATE DATES

Football—**October 12, 1957 (A):** Scoring the highest point total ever in the intrastate rivalry, the number two-ranked Spartans thoroughly dominated the number six-ranked Wolverines, 35-6, before the usual sellout crowd at Michigan Stadium. State ripped the U of M defense for 376 yards over the ground and 160 on passes. The maize and blue did everything possible to stop the onslaught, but there were just too many angles to content with. If they corralled Walt Kowalczyk, who had a great day (6.6 yard average on 17 tries), there would be Don Gilbert up the middle or Blanche Martin circling the ends. Finally, there was the aerial threat of quarterback Jim Ninowski, who hit eight of 13, including touchdowns to Bob Jewett and Sam Williams. The first half ended with Michigan State leading 8-0. Scoring came on a short plunge by Kowackzyk following a fumble recovery and then a safety via a blocked punt by Sam Williams. In the second half, Ninowski connected for touchdown passes to Bob Jewett and Sam Williams. The remaining touchdowns were made by Mike Panitch and Art Johnson after an exciting 62-yard run.

Cross Country—**November 2, 1957 (A):** With Forddy Kennedy setting a new University of Wisconsin course record in 20:22.5, the harriers shut out the winless Badgers, 15-44. Finishing behind Forddy, second through fifth, were: Ron Wheeler, captain Henry Kennedy, Bob Lake and Dave Lean.

Football—**November 9, 1957 (H):** Before a record crowd of 75,391 in the newly enlarged and renamed Spartan Stadium, State defeated Notre Dame for the third straight year, 34-6. What was becoming a Spartan tradition, the bulk of the points came in the second half, as the quarter-by-quarter scoring read: 0-7-20-7. Notre Dame's lone touchdown did not come until the Spartans had all of their points on the scoreboard. Led by Blanche Martin, Walt Kowalczyk, Art Johnson, and Bob Bercich, 12 runners lugged the ball for Duffy. The most exciting plays were a 41-yard sprint by Kowakczyk, a 50-yard scoring dash by Johnson, and a Jim Ninowski to Sam Williams pass-run in which the big end caught the ball at the ND 48-yardline and carried it to the four-yard line.

Soccer—**November 16, 1957 (A):** The Spartans closed the season with a comfortable 7-0 victory over Indiana. Although seven goals were the top production over the eight-game season, only two players contributed. Al Sarria, who was an All-Midwest selection by the National Soccer Coaches Association, accounted for four of the winning total, raising his season record to nine. Art Southan booted in the remaining three, giving him 11 for the year.

Basketball—**December 21, 1957 (H):** Trailing Notre Dame at the break, 43-35, the Spartans looked like an entirely different team when they returned for action in the second half. Johnny Green took over the job of guarding the Irish sharp shooter, Tom Hawkins, and the big Irish center missed his next 10 shots from the field. Meanwhile, Larry Hedden and Horace Walker were beginning to hit, and soon MSU had pulled abreast at 55-55. They then captured the lead at 57-56 when Green dunked one of his patented rebounds. From there it was a close contest until Hedden and Walker canned a pair of quick baskets to make it 74-66. The final score read 79-72 for Michigan State.

Hockey—**January 8, 1958 (H):** Finally, after eight years of MSU "renaissance" hockey, during which the record against the University of Michigan had grown to 0-28, the spell was broken as the Spartans skated to a 4-2 victory before a capacity crowd of 2,378 in Dem Hall. Mel Christofferson opened the scoring after 16 minutes of play, and Terry Moroney followed with a screen shot from the blue line with only three seconds remaining in the opening period. At 8:56 of the second, Ross Parke, camping right in front of the net, took a Richard Hamilton pass from behind the goal and made it 3-0.

Just as the allegiant faithful were basking in the moment, the Wolverines struck for a pair of goals, one in the second period and another in the third. Suddenly it was 3-2 and thoughts turned to, "Here we go again." But Amo's gang would not be denied. At 15:45 in the final period, Freddie DeVuono blasted a 20-footer past the Michigan goalie, and that was it, 4-2. The game was complete with a wild fracas in the second period that even involved a spectator, who suffered a scalp wound requiring 10 stitches.

Gymnastics—January 10, 1958 (H): Michigan State gymnasts captured only three firsts, but team depth proved instrumental in a close 56 1/2-55 1/2 victory over the Minnesota Golden Gophers. Spartan winners were Stan Tarshis in the horizontal bars, Tom Temple on the trampoline and Dick Becker in the free exercise. George Hopely was high scorer, as he accounted for 11 of the winning 56 1/2 points.

Fencing—February 1, 1958 (H): The fencers swept a triangular meet by defeating Illinois, 15-12, and the University of Chicago, 15-9. Darold McCalla, was the leading Spartan as he completed the afternoon matches undefeated.

Swimming and Diving—February 8, 1958 (A): Surviving disqualification of the winning medley relay in the opening event, the defending conference champions went on to win all but one of the remaining events to defeat Indiana, 59-42. Led by Bill Steuart's double win in the 220- and 440-yard freestyle events, Gordon Fornell, Wally Dobler, Jerry Chadwick, Roger Harmon, Don Patterson and Frank Modine each won his specialty event, and the relay team of Dobler, Jim Lanker, Dean Taylor and Patterson also prevailed. Indiana was emerging as the Big Ten power. This would be State's final victory over the Hoosiers until the 1990 season.

Basketball—February 10, 1958 (H): In a rare offensive output, three Spartans reached 25 or more points in a hard-earned 90-84 home victory over Iowa. Larry Hedden led the trio with 27 points, including 13 field goals. He was followed by Jack Quiggle, who reached his season high with 26, and Johnny Green, who scored 25. Leading by only three points, 85-82, with 3:22 remaining, Bob Anderegg fouled out and was replaced by a relatively untested sophomore, Lance Olson of Green Bay, Wis. Taking advantage of the opportunity, the big newcomer played a furious game; he grabbed three key rebounds, scored three baskets and sank four of four from

the line. The win gave State a 5-3 conference mark, which moved them into a first place tie with Indiana.

Hockey—February 14, (H) & February 15, 1958 (A): On one weekend, the Spartans defeated the U of M twice, 3-1 and 2-1. In Friday's game, Keith Christofferson opened the scoring at 7:16 of the first period, and at 16:22, Fred DeVuono made it 2-0. Michigan beat goalie Joe Sellinger in the second period to make it 2-1 but after Bill MacKenzie's unassisted insurance goal midway through the third period, the Wolverines never threatened again. The rematch on the following evening in Ann Arbor was the thriller of the season. Following a scoreless opening period, DeVuono netted his second marker of the series at 7:20 of the second with assists from Ross Parke and MacKenzie, and that 1-0 score held until one minute of regulation time remained. It was then that Michigan gained the equalizer and, in fact, turned the red light on one more time, with 30 seconds remaining, only to have the referee disallow the apparent second goal. The Spartans were stunned but determined. At 6:33 of overtime, Terry Moroney became the hero as he skated in, faked a shot to the left, moved to his right, and fired it between the goalie's pads.

Basketball—February 15, 1958 (H): In a season that found MSU in and out of the top spot of the conference standings, a poor-shooting University of Illinois team was down 21-1 following the opening eight minutes of action at Jenison. Played before slightly more than 7,000 fans and a regionally televised audience, the outcome of this game was never really in doubt after that. Less than 10 minutes remained in the opening half before the Illini hit their first field goal. It was their 18th attempt. Meanwhile, State built a 39-18 halftime lead. Playing before MSU reserves much of the second half, the visitors came alive with 38 points to make the final outcome look respectable, 69-56.

Wrestling—February 15, 1958 (A): Defeating his 130-pound Illinois opponent by a 5-1 count, Don Stroud remained the only undefeated member of the 1958 team. Other Spartan winners with decisions were Gordon Johnson at 147 pounds and Bob Moser at 157. Meanwhile, both 123-pound Richard Eachert and 177-pound Tim Woodin pinned their opponents. The afternoon closed with a match up of champions. Ken Maidlow, the eventual winner of the NCAA 191-pound crown, lost a close 3-1 decision to Bob Norman, two-time NCAA heavyweight champion. State won the meet, 19-9, but

one month later, the Illini finished runner-up at the conference championships, one notch above Michigan State.

Basketball—**February 17, 1958 (A):** Led by hot-shooting Bob Anderegg's 25 points and a successful zone defense, State defeated Michigan, 79-69, in a Monday night game in Ann Arbor. It gave coach Forddy Anderson a 5-2 record over the U of M since his arrival in 1954. One by one, three different Wolverines were called upon to neutralize Johnny Green underneath the basket. By the time the final buzzer sounded, all three had been strapped with their fourth foul. Seemingly uninterrupted, Johnny continued to control the boards and, in addition, contributed 18 points. Now with a 7-3 record, the Spartans were atop the conference standings.

Tennis—**April 30, 1958 (A):** State opened the spring with a 9-0 sweep over the University of Detroit. Coach Stan Drobac was pleased with the strong showing of his team as they prepared for the rest of the season. Bill Bisard, Bill Hotchkiss, Robert F. Hoffman, Doug Smith, Bob Sassack and Jeff Green all took their singles matches. In doubles, the pairs of Bisard-Hoffman, Smith-Hotchkiss and Sassack-Green each won.

Baseball—**May 3, 1958 (H):** Following a convincing doubleheader sweep over Ohio State, 14-0 and 7-1, MSU vaulted into the conference title picture with nine Big Ten games remaining. As the scores would indicate, lusty hitting was combined with impressive pitching. Dick Radatz was the winner in the opener, as he shut out the Buckeyes on four hits. In the second game, sophomore Larry Foster had given up only two hits until, with two out in the seventh, OSU marshaled three additional hits to account for its only run of the afternoon. Meanwhile, Spartan batters had a field day as they clobbered six Buck hurlers for a grand total of 29 base hits, 16 in game one and 12 in game two. John Fleser, sophomore left fielder, collected five hits, and Dean Look, also a sophomore, connected four times, producing four RBIs.

Track and Field—**May 3, 1958 (H):** Capturing nine events, the Spartans outscored previously undefeated Notre Dame, 75-66. Winners included Brian Castle in the 440, Bob Hughes in the 880, Forddy Kennedy in the two mile and Bill Oswalt in the pole vault. Sam Eliowitz won two weight events, the discus and the shot put, while Willie Atterberry completed a unique double, winning the 220 and the mile run as the injured Dave Lean's replacement. The unbeaten mile relay team of substitute Ken Defoe, Hughes, Castle and Atterberry completed

the afternoon with one more win.

Golf—**May 3, 1958 (H):** Just one week following the 18-6 defeat of Northwestern in the first meet at the newly-opened Forest Akers Golf Course, Michigan State closed their home season in a triangular meet against the University of Detroit and Notre Dame. In team points, MSU topped the Irish, 23-13, and defeated the U of D, 31-5. Medalist for the 36 holes was Otto Schubel, who fired a 70-77—147. Closely back in the second spot with his 76-73—149, was George Wakulsky. Other Spartan scorers were Arlin Dell with 78-78—156; Tom Baldwin 79-78—157; Steve Miller 78-80—158; and Jack Reynolds 82-80—162.

Baseball—**May 16, 1958 (H):** Dick Radatz raised his Big Ten mark to three wins and no losses, as he blanked the University of Illinois, 3-0. Using his side arm fast ball, he limited the Illini to just four hits and struck out 14. John Fleser opened the scoring in the second inning when he hit a fast ball far over the left field fence.

Baseball—**May 17, 1958 (H):** Michigan State was perched atop the Big Ten standings after subduing a pair of stubborn foes, Purdue University and threatening weather. Two complete games, both in the W column, were needed for MSU to maintain its slim conference lead. The Spartans poured out 13 base hits behind the effective pitching of Ron Perranoski to win the opener, 8-5. Then, after Dean Look put State on the scoreboard with an opening inning three-run homer in the second game, the rains came down, resulting in a 15-minute delay. A second cloudburst, heavier than the first, interrupted plays for 20 minutes in the fourth. Luckily, the skies eventually cleared long enough for Larry Foster to finish his five-hitter to chalk up this "must" win, 3-1.

ATHLETE OF THE YEAR

As a sophomore in 1958, Bill Steuart, a South African Olympian from Johannesburg, burst onto the MSU aquatic scene spontaneously and established a varsity record for the 440-yard freestyle in his very first collegiate meet. He remained undefeated through that season and topped it off by winning both the 440- and the 1,500-meter freestyle events, first at the Big Ten meet and one week later at the NCAAs in Ann Arbor. Swimming even

faster in his junior year, Steuart was once more the conference and national collegiate freestyle champion in the 440-yard and 1,500-meter races. Moreover, in that year's Big Ten meet, Steuart added the 220-yard freestyle to his list of titles. Invoking an odd Big Ten rule as it pertained to international athletes with Olympic background, Steuart was forced to sit out the 1960 season. A rescind of that rule in the following year permitted Bill to "get back in the swim," but the one year layoff had taken its toll. Never regaining the competitive edge, by midseason he switched to the butterfly stroke, in which he became a national finalist and, for the third year, a collegiate All-American.

Bill Steuart

IN THE SPARTLITE

Baseball: Michigan's retiring coach, Ray Fisher, on the job for 38 years, declined to accept an "S" blanket by way of a Spartan honor in pregame ceremonies on April 25. Just prior to game time, the U of M's star catcher had been ruled ineligible by the Big Ten office. It seems that John Kobs had been the one to blow the whistle on this particular player's qualification to compete in a fourth year. The fuming Wolverine coach said, "I couldn't accept that blanket because I would be a hypocrite if I did." State won the game, 4-2, behind the four-hit pitching of Ron Perranoski.

Closing the conference season on the road, State defeated Iowa, 5-2, in a Friday game to remain in the title picture. Moving on to Minneapolis, they then needed only a split of the double header to win the Big Ten championship. Instead, the Gophers took hard-fought games and the title, 3-2 and 2-1.

Led by pitching standouts Dick Radatz, Ron Perranoski, and Larry Foster, the 1958 Spartans held their opponents to an average of only 3.35 runs per game, the most impressive such record of the 1950s. The 1956 Big Ten championship team had yielded 5.38 runs per game.

Basketball: Rated sixth nationally in preseason polls and then opening with a 7-1 record, State facilitated illusions in East Lansing of repeating as conference champions and perhaps returning to the NCAA tournament trail. Such optimism was rudely dashed when it was announced on December 21 that David Scott, starting guard, and Horace Walker, an outstanding sophomore addition, were both declared scholastically ineligible beginning with winter term. Regardless, led by Johnny Green, Larry Hedden, Bob Anderegg, Lance Olson, and Jack Quiggle, State built a 9-4 conference record before placing it all on the line in the season closer at Jenison against Indiana. As the two teams battled to the final buzzer, the Hoosiers gained the victory, 75-72, and with it the Big Ten title and NCAA tournament slot (at that time only *one* conference team would qualify). State settled for a second-place tie with Purdue.

In postseason honors, Green repeated as a Big Ten All-Conference first-team selection, and Anderegg was again picked as a second-team choice.

Boxing: During the entire 1958 season, State did not have a competitor in the 125-pound division; consequently, each dual meet opened with a forfeiture. When

reviewing the team scoring over the 0-2-2 season (3-5, 3-5, 4-4 and 4-4), it is easy to understand the significance of always opening with an 0-1 deficit.

John Horne finished the dual-meet season undefeated, having never lost a round. His pattern of success continued into the NCAA championships at Sacramento State on April 3-5, where he captured MSC's 14th individual title. In so doing, John dethroned the 1957 champion from Idaho State. In other NCAA action, Tom McNeeley, Harvey Landcour, Bob Epperson, Sherald Haynes and John Gehan were defeated in early bouts. Gehan caught the attention of those in press row, as he was awarded the trophy for displaying the best sportsmanship. As a team, State finished in seventh place.

An ironic footnote to MSC's final year of a sanctioned team in NCAA competition; John Brotzmann, the man without a team, was elected to the post of president of the National Collegiate Association of Boxing Coaches for 1959.

Cross Country: Karl Schlademan coached his final season of cross country, devoting full attention to track and field.

This was the only year that the Kennedy brothers, Forddy and Henry, competed together. With the added trio of Robert Lake, Ron Wheeler and David Lean, State managed to successfully defend their Big Ten and IC4A titles but were edged by Notre Dame, 121-127, in the 19th running of the national collegiate championships. Forddy captured the individual title in the New York run, the same race his brother Henry had won in 1956.

Fencing: Dave McCalla placed second in the sabre event at the Big Ten championships.

Football: The fourth game of 1957 was at home against Purdue. Had game officials that day rendered a rule properly, the Spartans could have possibly laid claim to a national championship. Sadly, a Walt Kowalczyk touchdown had been erroneously nullified on a penalty sustained after the big halfback had crossed the goal line. The correct ruling should have included another State touchdown with the penalty assessed on the ensuing kick off. The officials blew it, and the "Spoilermakers" from West Lafayette, Indiana, had done it again, this time 20-13. With little solace, the Big Ten office later confirmed and apologized for the inaccurate rule interpretation.

Duffy called the 1957 team the greatest he had coached. After all the returns were in, State wound up third in the polls behind Auburn and Ohio State.

1957 All-American Walt Kowalczyk

Two Spartans earned All-America status, Kowalczyk and Dan Currie, and four others joined that pair for All-Big Ten honors, Jim Ninowski, Pat Burke, Ellison Kelly and Sam Williams. Big Sam would attain the All-American rank in the following season.

Golf: The 1958 golf team of Tim Baldwin, Arlin Dell, Jack Reynolds, Otto Schubel, George Wakulsky and Bob Walsh was the first to play on the university's newly opened course, Forest Akers.

Green fee rates for the new course were set at 75 cents for students, $1.50 for faculty-staff, $2.50 alumni, and $4.00 for the general public.

Gymnastics: Cal Girard was busy at the Big Ten championship meet in Iowa City. He tied for second on the parallel bars, was fifth on the still rings, seventh in free exercise and 10th on the side horse.

Hockey: The 1958 squad featured two sets of brothers, Ed and Bruno Pollesel from Copper Cliff, Ontario, as well as Keith and Mel Christofferson of Maidstone, Saskatchewan. There were no consecutive sellouts to boast of back in 1958. In fact, at times the crowds were so sparse that athletic director Munn frequently declared free admission nights.

With a season record of 12-11-0, the 1957-1958 edition of Michigan State hockey was the first since the rebirth of the sport in 1950 to post a winning record. Of the dozen victories, the 19-0 annihilation of Ohio State

on December 7 remains today as a team scoring record. During the game, which was played in Troy, Ohio, 70 miles west of the Columbus campus, goalie Joe Sellinger and his replacement Eldon VanSpybrook were called upon to make only 10 saves. Meanwhile, except for those two net minders, every skater in green and white was credited with either a goal or an assist. The top line of Fred DeVuono, Dick Hamilton and Ross Parke produced seven goals, with Parke scoring the hat trick. A footnote to the story is that the Buckeyes were without a coach and labored as a club team without varsity status. Lacking a local ice sheet, three nights a week the team would travel roundtrip 140 miles to that rink in Troy for practice. In a second MSU-OSU face-off eight weeks later, the Spartans scored six goals in the opening seven minutes and prevailed by a final score of 17-3.

Soccer: As in the inaugural season of 1956, the 1957 team completed its schedule without a loss. Remarkably, in its infancy as an MSU varsity sport, the two-year record read 11-0-3.

Swimming and Diving: Bob Mowerson, successful prep coach at Battle Creek Central High School, joined the staff as the first full-time assistant coach for swimming and diving.

With an 8-1 dual-meet season, it was a particularly successful year for Charles McCaffree's squad. In the postseason, they finished second in the conference meet and then collected an MSU-record number of five individual titles at the NCAA championships. In the final race at that national meet, the 400-yard medley relay, if a certain placement of teams had occurred it would have been feasible for State to have tied for the championship. It didn't happen, as the Spartan relay in that event placed second, securing a third-place finish with 62 points, 10 shy of the winner's circle. Those individual champions were Don Patterson in the 100-yard freestyle, Frank Modine in both the 100- and 200-yard breaststroke, and Bill Steuart in the 1,500-meter and the 440-yard freestyle events.

Tennis: Replacing Frank Beeman, who moved on as director the school's intramural program, former star Stan Drobac began a 32-year career as MSU's head coach.

The 1958 team would usually line up, number one through number six singles as follows: Bill Bisard, Bill Hotchkiss, Foster Hoffman, Doug Smith, Bob Sassack and John Green, with the doubles pairings of Bisard-Hoffman, Hotchkiss-Smith and Green-Sassack.

Track and Field: In March, the Spartan quartet of Brian Castle, Bob Hughes, Willie Atterberry and Captain Dave Lean struck gold at the *Chicago Daily News* indoor track meet. First they combined for a 3:20 victory over Nebraska and Purdue in the one-mile relay. Later they returned to the boards for another first place with a 7:40.7 clocking in the two-mile relay, this time defeating teams representing Illinois and Indiana. With Bob Lake replacing Hughes, the foursome opened the outdoor season by capturing the two-mile relay at the historic Penn Relays in Philadelphia.

Wrestling: Ken Maidlow won the National AAU title in 1956 but was hampered thereafter by a recurring knee injury. Happily, he concluded his collegiate career by winning the 191-pound crown at the NCAA championships held at Laramie, Wyo. Sophomore Tim Woodin, a Big Ten champion, finished second at 177 pounds and Jim Furgeson ended in third at 167. Gaining 35 team points, State finished fourth, the highest placement since the second-place finish in 1948.

MSU
1958-1959

TALES TO TELL

Following a 2-0-1 start, the 1958 football team fell into a dismal five-game losing streak that left the Spartans in the conference cellar at the season's end. Accompanying this unfortunate demise was an increasingly strained relationship between athletic director Biggie Munn and coach Duffy Daugherty. It seems the fifth loss, 39-12 to the University of Minnesota before many of Biggie's old friends in Minneapolis, had embarrassed the AD. As reported by Fred Stabley in his book *The Spartans,* Munn vented his anger before a gathering of newsmen in a Minneapolis restaurant following the game. A feature story in the next day's *Detroit News* quoted Biggie:

> "I've been in football since I was 14 years-old, and I've never been dumb enough to think that you can win them all. But when you throw the game away like we did today by losing the ball ten times, it's terrible...just terrible. It was the most futile display I've ever seen, utter futility. I've never taken losing so bad, but I cried after this one."

With the rift now made public, school president John Hannah intervened. Following a meeting with Biggie and Duffy, he issued a statement in which he said (again from *The Spartans*):

> "I had a long and profitable discussion with Director Munn and Coach Daugherty and was gratified to have them confirm my belief that reports of differences between them have been greatly exaggerated. There has been no loss of confidence in their ability or their dedication to the best interests of the university. They are united in their determination to restore the fortunes of the Spartans. As far as I am concerned and as far as Mr. Munn and Mr. Daugherty are concerned, this is a closed incident, and there will be no additional comment."

As sports writers continued to overplay the topic, Duffy attempted to clear the air by insisting:

> "I owe a lot to Biggie. He gave me my first real chance to play at Syracuse. We were as close as any two men could be."

HEADLINES of 1959

- Alaska and Hawaii become the 49th and 50th states of the Union.
- The St. Lawrence Seaway is opened.
- Castro's forces topple Batista's government in Cuba.
- Haloid launched Xerox, the first copier able to reproduce documents at the press of a button.

SCOREBOARD

	W	L	T	Avg.
Baseball	21	14	0	.600
Track and Field	1	4	0	.200
Football	3	5	1	.389
Basketball	20	4	0	.833
Tennis	9	7	0	.562
Cross Country	1	1	0	.500
Swimming and Diving	5	3	0	.625
Wrestling	5	3	1	.611
Hockey	17	6	1	.728
Fencing	3	8	0	.273
Golf	11	1	0	.917
Gymnastics	7	2	0	.777
Soccer	8	0	0	1.000

TEAM OF THE YEAR

Playing before sellout crowds at Jenison Fieldhouse, the 1958-1959 Spartans returned to the top of the conference basketball standing with a 12-2 record, an impressive four games better than 8-6 runner-up Michigan. Although the postseason NCAA trail was short-lived with a loss to Louisville in the Mideast Regional finals, the overall season record of 19-4 was the best ever in East Lansing since the 1907 Aggie team went 14-2. At the season's end State was ranked third by UPI and seventh by the Associated Press. Led by Johnny Green, voted the Big Ten's MVP, the Spartans' starting five included forwards Bob Anderegg and Horace Walker, along with guards Lance Olson and Tom Rand. The individual team scoring leader was Anderegg (19.5 ppg), followed closely by Green (18.5 ppg).

Regardless of efforts to smooth the waters, there would be ripples of conflict in the Munn-Daugherty relationship for the remainder of their joint careers at MSU.

The 1959 basketball team. (Front row, left to right) L. Fanning, W. Golis, D. Stouffer, co-captain B. Anderegg, coach F. Anderson, co-captain J. Green, T. Rand, D. Richey and D. Fahs; (back row, left to right) trainer G. Robinson, T. Wilson, H. Turak, H. Walker, L. Olson, T. Wasson, A. Gowens, B. Bechinski, J. Young and student manager J. Ulmer.

HISTORIC MOMENTS

On Feb. 14, 1959, State racked up its first-ever 100-plus basketball score in their series with the University of Michigan. Was it possible that the Wolverines had been psychologically defeated prior to the opening tip-off that afternoon? Consider this, dunking the basketball was just becoming more commonplace in the 1950s. Although seldom used in a game, the Spartans of 1959 included five players that embraced the glamour shot in their repertoire. During pregame warm-ups, Lance Olson, Bob Anderegg, Horace Walker, Johnny Green and Art Gowens lined up in tandem and, one by one, dribbled toward the basket head on and jammed away (unlike today, rules did not prohibit this in the warm ups). Spartan fans learned to arrive early for the show and with each shot respond with screams of delight that echoed from the Jenison rafters. Prior to that game of February 14, as the leaping five executed their crowd-pleasing shots, the U of M players totally stopped their own drills to watch the antics. It seems the visitors had been psyched out long before the opening tip-off. The final score read MSU 103, Michigan 91.

Through the joint campaigning efforts of track and field coaches Karl Schlademan and the U of M's Don Canham, a proposal was approved to add the 440-yard intermediate hurdles, triple jump, hammer throw, 3,000-meter steeplechase and three-mile run to the annual NCAA outdoor track and field championship format beginning in 1959. As these are Olympic events, previously they had been tacked onto the championship program only in Olympic years.

GREAT STATE DATES

Football—**September 27, 1958 (H):** State opened the season with a convincing 32-12 win over California, the second in a row over the Bears and the 11th consecutive over a Pacific Coast conference team. The statistic sheet made the victory even more convincing, as it reflected 502 total yards and 24 first downs for the Spartans. The most impressive scoring drive, the second of the day, consumed 11 plays, covered 93 yards, and concluded with an eight-yard Art Johnson touchdown run. Johnson then followed by scoring the first-ever Michigan State two-point conversion. The 1958 season introduced this new conversion option.

Cross Country—**October 25, 1958 (A):** Forddy Kennedy crossed the finish line 300 yards ahead of his nearest rival and led the Spartans to a 23-32 victory over Penn State. His time of 24:55 bettered a Nittany Lion course record of 25:20, which had been established by his brother Henry in 1956. Following Forddy across the line were Bob Lake and Bill Reynolds in third and fourth, and Jim Horan and Tony Smith in seventh and eighth.

Soccer—**November 15, 1958 (A):** Michigan State reached a new scoring record when they defeated the Indiana Hoosiers 11-3 in the season's final game. Captain Art Southan, the team's top scorer in 1957, connected for four goals, Al Sarria booted in three, Erich Streder scored twice and Bruce Okine and John Asmali were credited with one goal each. State scored three times in the opening quarter and then four times in the second to put the game out of reach. Three weeks earlier the Spartans had set a team record 10 goals against the University of Illinois in Champaign, Ill.

Swimming and Diving—**January 8, 1959 (H):** In the season's opening meet, a 73-23 victory over Iowa State, MSU's three NCAA champions picked up right where they had left off one year before. Frank Modine not only won the 200-yard breaststroke, but he did so in a time of 2:23.5, which bettered the American record of 2:24.3. Coach McCaffree's top sprinter, Don Patterson, cruised to a win in the 100-yard freestyle in 51.0, and the South African distance star, Billy Steuart, captured the 220-yard freestyle in a time of 2:07.7. Other winners for State were Ernest Dewell in the 440, Robert Thomas in the butterfly, Al Coxon in the backstroke, and Jerry Chadwick in diving.

Gymnastics—**January 17, 1959 (H):** Finishing first in five of the seven events and runner-up in three, the State gymnasts earned an adequate number of points to defeat Southern Illinois, 64-48. The Salukis were a talented squad that finished seventh at that year's NCAA meet. Cal Girard did not have too much time for rest during the evening, as he won the side horse event and the parallel bars, was second on the horizontal bar, third on the still rings and fourth in floor exercise. Other Spartan winners were Jack Daniels in the free exercise, Chuck Thompson on the trampoline and Stan Tarshis on his specialty, the horizontal bar.

Basketball—**January 19, 1959 (H):** Horace Walker recalls the 92-77 victory over Ohio State at Jenison. After going through the usual weekly scouting reports in

Horace Walker

the practices prior to game day, it was determined that, on defense, Horace should sag back to clog up the middle and assist Johnny Green. With such a maneuver, the Buckeyes' Joe Roberts would be left alone because, as the scouting report revealed, "He couldn't hit the broadside of a barn beyond 15 feet." Practice was conducted with this concept in mind. In Horace's own words:

"On game day we were fired up in the locker room as Forddy [Anderson] gave his pep talk. We had a great warm up, and then the game began. We were following the plan with me sagging back in the middle, leaving Joe Roberts in the corner about 30 to 35 feet out. Realizing he had minimal coverage, Roberts put up a 35-footer that swished the net. He followed up their next two trips down the court with similar successful 30-foot jumpers. Forddy called time out. In the huddle, I asked the coach, 'Who ever the hell said he [Roberts] couldn't hit the broad side of a barn needs his rear end kicked. He's killing us.' Needless to say, we changed our strategy."

The Spartans eventually took command and defeated the Buckeyes with relative ease, 92-77.

Basketball—**January 24, 1959 (A):** Playing before a noisy Williams Arena crowd numbering 16,187, the Golden Gophers whittled a Michigan State lead of 56-40 to only three points, 71-68, with four and a half min-

utes remaining. It was then that Johnny Green, benched with four fouls, reentered the game to spearhead a Spartan resurgence and an eventual 82-76 winning margin. All five Spartan starters scored in double figures: Bob Anderegg 24, Lance Olson 17, Green 15, Horace Walker 14 and Tom Rand 14.

Hockey—**February 6 (H) & February 7, 1959 (A):** As the weekend series with Michigan opened in Dem Hall, Amo's guys struck early and often to build a 3-0 lead within the first 13 minutes of play. Ed Pollesel started the scoring at 1:18 when his blast from the blue line was deflected past the goalie. Terry Moroney made it 2-0 at 3:26, banging the puck home from a scramble in front of the net. Andre LaCosta scored goal number three at 12:33 with assists to Jack Roberts and Elwood "Butch" Miller. Over the remaining 47:27, the Spartans took a primarily defensive posture, while on the other end, goalie Joe Sellinger was kicking out 37 of 38 shots, making the final score read 3-1. The Saturday night game on Michigan ice was a reversal of form, scoring late not early. Tied at 1-1 after the opening 20 minutes, the Spartans led by a scant 2-1 after two periods and then outscored the Wolverines 3-1 in the final stanza for a convincing 5-2 victory. State's goals were credited to Joe Polano (two), Glenn MacDonald, Tom Mustonen and Moroney. Once more, Sellinger, State's All-American goalie, had to be sharp, as he turned back a total of 43 shots.

Wrestling—**February 20, 1959 (H):** As often happens in wrestling, the outcome of this meet was determined by the heavyweights in the evening's concluding square off. Minnesota led 14-11 after eight matches, meaning that MSU's Tom Woodin needed to earn five points from a pin to gain a 16-14 team verdict. Although his opponent was undefeated and much larger at 220 pounds, Woodin swarmed all over the Gopher and after 2:15 of the opening period had his shoulders on the mat…mission completed. Other winners in this fifth Spartan victory of the season were 130-pound Norm Young, 157-pound Bob Moser and Jim Ferguson, who gained a pin at 167 pounds.

Fencing—**February 28, 1959 (A):** In a quadrangular meet hosted by Wayne State University, the Michigan State swordsmen closed out the season by edging Case Tech of Cleveland, 14-13, and more easily defeating Indiana University, 17-10. Charlie Schmitter Jr. and Stan Arnst were the stars for MSU, Schmitter winning seven of eight matches in foil and Arnst eigth of nine in sabre. Against Case, the Spartans won in foil by a 7-2 count,

just enough to offset losses in epee, 3-6, and sabre, 4-5. The Hoosiers also won in epee, 5-4, but State countered with a 7-2 win in foil and 6-3 win in sabre.

Basketball—**March 1, 1959 (A):** For ample reasons it was an evening to celebrate. Forddy Anderson's team had just defeated the defending Big Ten champions Indiana on their court, 86-82. More importantly, the win guaranteed the 1959 conference title to Michigan State and with it a berth in the NCAA championship field of 32 teams. Trailing 45-44 at halftime, a plan was hatched during intermission to not over-challenge the Hoosiers defensively. The strategy was to back off once the shooters made a commitment. How well the strategy worked is noted from the fact that during an 18-minute stretch, not one foul was called on MSU. Meanwhile, the IU shooting percentage dropped from .529 to .340. During this span, though, the outcome of the game remained in doubt, as at no time did one team gain a significant advantage and six times the score was tied. Finally, State spurted ahead and, with 1:46 remaining, held their largest lead of the contest, 85-77, and from there hung on for the 16th win against three losses. Johnny Green and Bob Anderegg shared the scoring honors with 20 points each. Horace Walker added 16 and Dave Fahs contributed 14.

Basketball—**March 7, 1959 (H):** In the final home appearance of the season, the Spartans avenged one of their four losses of 1958-1959 by defeating Iowa, 84-74. Bob Anderegg, playing his final game before the home fans, hit for 32 points, the highest of his career. The lead switched back and forth during the opening half, with State on top 41-38 at the break. The Hawkeyes tied it 44-44 early in the second period but thereafter, MSU took charge, outscoring the visitors 40-30. In a pregame ceremony, the four seniors, co-captains Anderegg and Johnny Green, Tom Rand and reserve Dave Stouffer were individually introduced and received the traditional standing ovation from the appreciative fans. Following the game, coach Forddy Anderson proudly accepted the Big Ten championship trophy.

Baseball—**April 3, 1959 (N):** When the Spartans arrived in Tallahassee, Florida, for the week of spring training, they recognized some familiar faces. The University of Illinois, Western Michigan and the U of M were also on the Florida State campus for their week in the sun. State completed a record of three victories and four losses. Included with the wins was a 1-0 shutout of Michigan on the final Friday afternoon. John Russell won that game

on a freakish home run. With one out in the first inning, the MSU right fielder hit a high fly into left-center field. Two pursuing defenders collided, and, as they lay dazed on the outfield grass, Russell circled the bases with what would be the only run of the game. The winning pitcher, captain Dick "Moose" Radatz, who scattered nine hits in gaining the shutout victory, shares this memory:

"My entire career at MSU was a series of highlights, playing for the great John Kobs and playing with such outstanding players as Ron Perranowski, John Russell, Ed Hobaugh, and Frank Palamara. In the 1959 spring training trip to Florida State University, I was to pitch against our arch rival, the U of M. The night before the game my good friend and our right fielder, John Russell, said he felt extremely confident about the U of M game and asked me if I was equally 'pumped up.' I told him that I was as ready as I could be, and if he hit a home run that's all that I would need, because I intended to shut them out. Well! He did and I did. We beat them 1-0. It was truly one of my biggest thrills, not only at State, but in the 11 years I played professionally. As the commercial said, 'It doesn't get any better than that.'"

Baseball—**April 24 (A) & April 25 (H) 1959:** The Spartans captured the regular season series with the U of M, two games to one. In the Friday game in Ann Arbor, Coach Kobs once more called upon Dick Radatz, who delivered from both the mound and the plate in a 3-2 win. Leading 2-1 after eight innings, the big pitcher doubled home Bill Schudlich in the ninth for what would prove to be the winning run. Michigan hitters got to Radatz for one run in the bottom of the ninth, but he ended up striking out the final two batters with the tying run perched on third. In the opener of the doubleheader on the next day at Old College Field, the Wolverines grabbed an early three-run lead, but State hitters responded with six runs in the second inning, leading to an eventual 17-12 slugfest win. Al Luplow was the hitting star with a home run and four RBIs. Don Sackett, who was on the mound for the final four innings, was given credit for the victory.

Track and Field—**May 2, 1959 (H):** Two versatile athletes on loan from the football team, made the difference in the 72-59 defeat of the University of Wisconsin. Jason Harness, a sophomore end from St. Joseph, won the high hurdles, tied for first in the high jump, and placed

second in the broad jump. John Sharp, a former Flint Northern athlete, placed second in the 100-yard dash. Between the pair, the winning MSU score was enhanced by 15 points. Following their contribution, it was back to Spartan Stadium for a full-pad scrimmage. The remaining team managed to win six additional events. Mike Kleinhans was a double winner in the pole vault and low hurdles; George Ward won the broad jump; Forddy Kennedy finished first in the two mile, and Bob Lake won the opening event of the afternoon, the one-mile run in a new field record time of 4:12.1. In the closing event, the mile relay team of Don Marsh, Jim Carr, Bob Hughes and Brian Castle ran a winning time of 3:26.4.

Tennis—**May 4, 1959 (H):** The University of Detroit players never had a chance. In being shutout they failed to win a single set, and in nine sets, they failed to win a game. Winners and their scores, number one through number six: Bill Hotchkiss 8-1, 6-0; Doug Smith 6-1, 6-0; Foster Hoffman 6-1, 6-2; Roger Plagenhoef 6-0, 6-0; Bob Sassack 6-1, 6-3; and Ron Mescall 6-1, 6-0. Winners in doubles were Hotchkiss-Smith 6-0, 6-0; Hoffman-Sassack 6-4, 6-1; and Ruzzo-Gobel 6-0, 6-0.

Baseball—**May 13, 1959 (H):** With State trailing Notre Dame 4-2 entering the bottom of the ninth, Al Luplow quickly tied the score with a two-run line-drive home run over the right field fence. John Fleser and Bill Schludlich followed with base hits. It was now up to catcher Bob Monczka, who had entered the game late as Jim Conlin's replacement. Suddenly it was a two-strike count, and on the next pitch, he lifted a fly just out of the reach of the left fielder. Fleser, headed home at the crack of the bat, scored from second, and the Spartans had registered their 14th win of the season.

Golf—**May 16, 1959 (A):** Having announced his retirement at the end of the season, Coach Ben VanAlstyne must have enjoyed those final matches in Detroit. It was a three-way win, 19 1/2-16 1/2 over Michigan, 23-13 over Wisconsin, and 32-4 over the host U of D. The 36-hole gross scores for the Spartans were as follows: Tim Baldwin 152, Ty Caplin 152, C.A. Smith 158, Jack Reynolds 161, Ted Schmidt 165 and Gary Barnett 166.

Baseball—**May 22, 1959 (H):** The 6-4 win over Minnesota came one year too late, but there was some satisfaction in temporarily blocking the Gophers' run for a second straight title. Dick Radatz set the champions down with a well-pitched nine-hit game. Three of the runs he surrendered were unearned as he fanned 12. State

bunched hits very well, collecting three runs in the third to open the scoring. Singles by Bill Schudlich, Radatz, John Russell and John Fleser did the trick. The Spartans then wrapped it up with three runs in the sixth. Fleser doubled, Bob Monczka walked, Bob Golden singled and Radatz again hit safely. It was MSU's 20th victory of the season.

ATHLETE OF THE YEAR

Crawford "Forddy" Kennedy, a Canadian via Glasgow, Scotland, was a three-time (1957-1959) All-American cross country pick. He had been immediately preceded at MSU by his brother Henry, likewise a champion and an All-American. Over three years, Forddy led MSU teams to three Big Ten titles, three IC4A titles, where he finished first each time, and two National Collegiate championships. He won the conference race in his senior year and was the individual champion in the NCAA title run of 1958. In his other two appearances at the national meet, Kennedy was fifth as a sophomore and third as a senior. As a member of the 1959 track team, he won the Big Ten outdoor two mile run.

Crawford "Forddy" Kennedy

IN THE SPARTLITE

Baseball: The Spartans opened the regular portion of the schedule with the following starting lineup: John Russell LF, Dean Look CF, John Fleser RF, Bill Schudlich 1B, Jerry Korwek 2B, Dick Golden SS, George Marcum 3B.

Dick Radatz concluded his MSU career in 1959 as one of the greatest Spartans of all time. His name continues to appear at the top of the school season record book in innings pitched (96.1), and his won-loss record of 10-1. Additionally, his name remains ranked third in strikeouts (106) and earned run average (1.12). At season's end the 6' 5", 235-pound pitcher was honored as a second team All-American selection, and in an endorsement from an unusual source, the editorial page of the student paper, *The State News*. Radatz would, of course, enjoy a successful eight-year major league career, whereupon he would be tagged with a new moniker, "The Monster."

Basketball: The only bump along State's stretch drive to another conference crown came at West Lafayette when the Boilermakers weathered a second half see-saw battle to upset the conference leaders, 85-81. The Spartans were hurt when Johnny Green, who grabbed 18 rebounds and led all scorers with 25 points, fouled out with seven minutes remaining in the game.

In the eighth edition of the annual East-West College All-Star game played in Kansas City, the East was the winner, 102-71. A member of that winning team was MSU's Green, who was the game's leading rebounder with 11.

Bob Stevens, three-year assistant to Forddy Anderson and former MSU varsity player, accepted the position as head coach at the University of South Carolina.

Cross Country: Coach Fran Dittrich's first team, the 1958 edition, won all three major runs: the Big Ten, the IC4A in New York City, and the NCAA championship run contested once more on the MSU campus. For the first time, the race was run over the four-mile layout on Forest Akers West Golf Course.

State maintained its mastery of the Western Conference by taking its third straight team crown and its sixth in seven tries. Forddy Kennedy lost his only race of the season, settling for second place. Teammates and their places of finish were: Billy Reynolds in eighth, followed by Jim Horan, David Lean, and Robert Lake in places 10, 11 and 12.

Forddy Kennedy rebounded from his loss in the Big Ten meet by successfully defending his IC4A title and leading the team to another title. This completed the necessary five team titles to once more gain permanent possession of a trophy, first accomplished in 1933-37.

Racing through a two-inch snowfall that had covered the Forest Akers course during the night, the 140-pound Forddy Kennedy became MSU's first national champion as he led the team to the school's seventh NCAA team championship. Completing the team scoring were Reynolds in sixth, Lake in 14th, Horan in 34th and Lean in 49th.

Fencing: The season opened with the usual crew of eager but inexperienced candidates who would await the crash course in fencing mechanics from the master coach Charlie Schmitter. Struggling through the schedule, the team managed one victory in the first nine contests. They then finished strong with a pair of wins over Case Tech and Indiana. The obviously improved team carried the momentum into the Big Ten championships where they finished in a surprising third spot. Leading the way were Chuck Schmitter, the coach's son, with a third place in epee, Terry Glimn, who finished third in foil and Steve Arnmest, the team captain, who was fourth in sabre.

Football: It was a frustrating October afternoon before a Spartan Stadium record-setting crowd of 76,434, as the underdog Michigan Wolverines scored twice in the first half and then hung on for a 12-12 tie. Both U of M scores came from State miscues, the first on a 42-yard interception of a Mike Panitch lateral, and the second following the recovery of a Panitch fumble. Junior Dean Look led the Spartan comeback with a third period touchdown on a school record setting twisting 92-yard punt return. The final score was followed by a 97-yard sustained drive in the final quarter, which Coach Daugherty would later define as "the most determined march I've ever seen in football." It was not a pleasing afternoon for the place kickers. Any one of the PAT attempts could have spelled victory for one side or the other. They all failed. After missing on their first try, Michigan's option to pass for a two-pointer fell incomplete. State actually had three opportunities to gain the one-point advantage. A penalty gave kicker Sam Williams a repeat try following the second State touchdown. The eventual answer to the place kicking woes, the idea of a soccer-style kicking specialist, was one year away.

Delaying his college career until after a four-year hitch with the U.S. Navy, Sam Williams was physically large (6' 5", 225) and mature. As a two-way player, Williams could dominate a game from either side of the line. Exemplifying his impact, he gained All-American status in 1958 even though the team completed a losing season record of 3-5-1.

Tackle George Perles suffered a career-ending knee injury in the 9-7 loss to Wisconsin.

Golf: With the university declining to support a spring break trip to the south for the golf team, four prospects decided to drive and pay their own way. The foursome were: Ty Caplan, Plymouth junior; Gary Barrett, Owosso sophomore; C.A. Smith, Jackson sophomore, and Bob Walsh, Grand Haven junior. They traveled to Gulfport, Mississippi, where for seven days they played at the Great Southern Golf Course.

Amassing 1,615 strokes over the four rounds, State could do no better than a seventh place finish at the Big Ten championships in Ann Arbor. The four-round total scores were as follows: Tim Baldwin 317, C.A. Smith 323, Ty Caplin 324, Gary Barrett 335 and Jack Reynolds 342.

Gymnastics: Stan Tarshis succeeded in defending his horizontal bar title as the Spartans earned 72 points to finish third in the conference championship meet in Bloomington, Ind. John Daniels placed third in the free exercise and second in tumbling. With 17 points, he, along with Angie Festa, tied as team scoring leader at the meet. Others contributors were Chuck Thompson with 13 points, Tarshis with 11, Cal Girard with 6, Mike Coco with 5 and Hal Shorr with 3.

Tarshis completed an unbeaten season by winning the horizontal bar title at the NCAA championships in Berkeley, Calif. In addition, Daniels tied for fifth in floor exercise; Thompson finished sixth on the trampoline; Festa placed tenth in both the still rings and horizontal bar; and Girard was sixth on the parallel bars, eighth on horizontal bar and eighth in the all-around event. The five Spartans earned a total of 39 team points, placing Michigan State in fourth place behind Penn State, Illinois and the host California Bears.

Hockey: Michigan State boasted of being "Big Ten champions" of hockey, a title endorsed by the conference office. It was strictly bragging rights. Nothing official was ever recorded and no trophy exchanged hands. The claim was based on competition between the only three conference schools engaged in the sport. State finished at 5-2-1, Minnesota was 4-3-1, and Michigan was 2-6.

Goalie Joe Sellinger's statistics for the season were tops for the nation, and, consequently he was appropriately designated as All-American, MSU's first in the sport.

Soccer: In MSU's opening three seasons of varsity soccer competition (1956-1958), the Spartans were undefeated as they compiled a 19-0-3 record. This achievement is likely unparalleled for a pioneer sport at any school.

Prior to 1959, the year in which the NCAA would first endorse a championship playoff for soccer, the National Soccer Coaches Association conducted a ballot to determine the "most outstanding U.S. team." The 1958 vote ranked Michigan State second for the honor.

In that same balloting, Al "Phantom" Sarria became MSU's initial first-team All-American. At that same time Leo Vanderhorst and Bernie Cook were selected as third team designates.

Freshmen Cecil Heron, Gerry Heron and Ed Saunders were invited to the tryouts in St. Louis for the USA Olympic team.

Swimming and Diving: Hosting the Big Ten championship meet in the new IM pool, MSU managed only 53 1/2 points and settled for a fourth place finish. Bill Steuart was the hero for the home crowd, as he won three events: the 220-yard freestyle, the 440-yard freestyle, and the 1,500-meter freestyle. Two weeks later in Ithaca, N.Y., Steuart succeeded in defending the two NCAA titles he garnered at the 1958 championships.

In both cases, his 1959 winning times were faster. He improved the 440-yard freestyle from 4:34.3 to 4:31.9, and in the 1,500-meter freestyle, he improved from 18:45.8 to 18:26.2. Breaststroker Frank Modine surrendered his 1958 titles, finishing third in the 100-yard breaststroke and fifth in the 200. Likewise, Don Patterson dropped from first to third in his specialty, the 100-yard freestyle. Adding to points gained from the relays, State scored 35 for a fifth place finish.

Tennis: Hosting a conference championship does not guarantee success. Such was the case at the 1959 Big Tens held on the MSU courts south of the stadium. State's Ron Mescall at number six, the only Spartan to reach the finals where he met defeat. Collecting a mere 19 1/2 team points, the Spartans finished in fifth position.

Track and Field: Scoring only 13 1/2 total points, State finished the Big Ten indoor championship meet in seventh place, the lowest standing since becoming a conference member. Bob Lake was one shining light for the

Spartans, as he won the mile run in a respectable 4:10.9, the fastest effort all winter in the conference. Other MSU finalists were: captain Forddy Kennedy with a third in the two mile, Jim Carr's fourth in the 660, Terry Smith's fifth in the 1,000 and Bob Hughes's fifth in the 880. Mike Kleinhans tied for fourth in the pole vault and the mile relay placed fifth.

Managing 11 points and an eventual eighth place finish, moving outdoors was even more disappointing. Regardless, there were two conference champions that wore green. As indoors, Bob Lake, a Kalamazoo junior, proved to be king of the mile, as he negotiated the four laps in a conference record time of 4:08.5. Forddy Kennedy won the two mile in 9:15.1.

Wrestling: As a team, MSU could do no better than third place at the conference championships; despite that, three Spartans wrestled to individual titles. Norm Young, a sophomore from Lansing, was the winner at 130 pounds on a 6-5 decision. Jim Ferguson, 167 pounds, shutout his counterpart from the U of M, 4-0, and Tim Woodin, the 1958 champion at 177 pounds, moved up to capture the heavyweight title with a 6-4 decision

Wrestling in the 191 pound class, Woodin placed second at the NCAA championship in Iowa City, Iowa. Ferguson was the only other Spartan to earn team points, as he reached the quarterfinals before losing. In total, the 17 points tied the University of Minnesota for the ninth spot.

Engaging a travel-weary national team from Japan in a postseason exhibition, State won four of nine matches before a slim crowd of 500 at the IM arena.

EXTRA! 1959 NCAA BASKETBALL TOURNAMENT

Michigan State reached the regional finals in the 1959 NCAA tournament. The following are the Spartans' box scores from those games.

MICHIGAN STATE 74–MARQUETTE 69

	FG-FGA	FT-FTA	REB	PF	TP
Anderegg	10-19	3-7	8	1	23
Walker	9-21	2-3	8	2	20
Green	6-18	2-4	18	5	14
Olson	1-7	6-8	4	4	8
Rand	1-5	1-2	5	2	3
Fahs	2-6	0-1	1	0	4
Gowens	1-1	0-0	1	0	2
Team			6		
TOTALS	30-77	14-25	51	14	74

Halftime: Michigan State 38-34; **Officials:** Anderson, DiGravio; **Attendance:** 9,200.

LOUISVILLE 88–MICHIGAN STATE 81

	FG-FGA	FT-FTA	REB	PF	TP
Anderegg	8-21	6-10	3	5	22
Walker	1-9	1-1	9	5	3
Green	11-21	7-12	23	3	29
Olson	6-15	4-4	3	3	16
Rand	1-7	0-0	2	3	2
Fahs	0-5	0-1	1	2	0
Gowens	1-1	1-2	0	0	3
Stouffer	3-5	0-0	1	0	6
Team			7		
TOTALS	31-84	19-30	50	21	81

Halftime: Michigan State 43-40 **Officials:** Miahlik, Anderson; **Attendance:** not available.

EXTRA! 1959 NCAA HOCKEY TOURNAMENT (Finals)

As yet unaffiliated with the WCHA, MSU entered the NCAA tournament in Troy, N.Y., by winning the Big Ten title with a 5-2-1 conference record. They defeated Boston College 4-3 to enter the finals, at which they lost to North Dakota 3-4 in overtime.

March 13, 1959—Troy, N.Y.
MSU 4, Boston College 3
1st Pd.: 1. MSU, Mustonen (LaCoste, Roberts), 3:50; 2. BC, Jangro (Daley), 7:50.
2nd Pd.: 3. MSU, Hamilton (Polano), 3:11; 4. MSU Roberts (Mustonen), 5:33; 5. MSU, Moroney (Polano), 8:10.
3rd Pd.: 6. BC, Daley (Jangro), 5:34; 7. BC, Leonard (Cusack), 11:54.

March 14, 1959—Troy, N.Y.
North Dakota 4, MSU 3 (OT)
1st Pd.: 1. MSU, Pollesel (LaCoste, Mustonen), 14:38.
2nd Pd.: 2. ND, Lyndon (Morelli, Miller), 7:21; 3. ND, Walford (King, Haiey), 8:57; 4. ND, Paschle (Lyndon), 9:37.
3rd Pd.: 5. MSU, LaCoste (Roberts, Norman), 8:05; 6. MSU, Roberts (LaCoste), 16:20.
Overtime: 7. ND, Morelli (Miller, LaFrance), 4:18.

MSU
1959-1960

TALES TO TELL

Who remembers the annual Band Day? That was when a cluster of high school bands would join the MSU band on the field at halftime of an early-season football game and play a selection of prearranged numbers in massed formations. From across the state they would come, arriving in early morning hours aboard their yellow school buses, and unload and hustle to Old College Field for instructions and group rehearsal. From there they would file to Spartan Stadium and march onto the field, unit by unit in two-minute intervals beginning at 11:30 A.M. At halftime, they would leave their bleacher seats in either the southwest corner or the north end zone and move onto the floor of the stadium for an appearance that many of the young people would likely never forget. The Fifth Annual Band Day, the 1959 version, was on September 26, and included 2,600 musicians from a combined 35 aggregations ranging in size from Riverview of Wyandotte with 30 band members to Saginaw High School with 140 (the MSU band included only 120 pieces at that time). The first formation was "25 years-MSBOA" to honor the Michigan School Band and Orchestra Association, at which time the massed group played "Semper Fidelis March" and "Silver Anniversary March." After that, the musicians shifted to the formation of letters "M-S-U" and played the Spartan fight song along with the alma mater "MSU Shadows."

Band Days are now but a memory. As the demand for game tickets grew year after year, it didn't take long for the money crunchers to figure this one out. A total of 2,600 seats at $34.00 (2002 ticket price) could produce enough revenue to budget one or more non-revenue teams.

"So long kids….nice having you with us."

Band Day at Spartan Stadium

HEADLINES of 1960

- A U-2 reconnaissance plane piloted by Francis Gary Powers is shot down over Russian territory.
- The Flintstones debut as prime time's first animated television sitcom.
- Israeli agents capture Adolf Eichmann, German Nazi official, in Argentina. He is tried and hanged for World War II crimes.
- Chubby Checker, singer, causes an international dance craze with his recording of "The Twist."

SCOREBOARD

	W	L	T	Avg.
Baseball	17	13	0	.567
Track and Field	2	1	0	.667
Football	5	4	0	.555
Basketball	10	11	0	.476
Tennis	17	3	0	.850
Cross Country	2	1	0	.667
Swimming and Diving	7	3	0	.700
Wrestling	7	1	1	.833
Hockey	4	18	2	.208
Fencing	2	8	0	.200
Golf	9	1	0	.900
Gymnastics	10	0	1	.955
Soccer	7	2	0	.777

TEAM OF THE YEAR

The 1959 cross country squad ran to Michigan State's third grand slam (Big Ten, ICAA and NCAA) in four years. Although MSU teams would continue to dominate the Big Ten conference for another 12 years, 1959 would conclude an imposing record of seven National Collegiate titles over a span of 12 years.

The first stop on their 1959 victory trail was the conference meet in Chicago, where Forddy Kenndy finally captured the individual title that had eluded him for two years. He negotiated the five-mile course at Chicago's Washington Park in 20:12.3. Kennedy was followed by Bill Reynolds in second with a time of 20:17 and Ed Graydon in third with a 20:24. Jerry Young and Bob Lake finished fifth and sixth to complete the winning total of 17, a Big Ten record score that still stands.

Moving on to New York City three days later, Kennedy ran an impressive 23:51.8 to win a third straight IC4A individual crown. MSU took a fourth straight and 11th overall team title. Running behind team captain Kennedy were Reynolds in sixth, Young in ninth, Graydon in 14th, and Lake in 25th.

By totaling 44 points to runner-up Houston's 120 in the national championship run, this State team was more dominant than any previous team. Forddy Kennedy finished in the third spot with Billy Reynolds two seconds back in fourth. Gerry Young was 11th and teammate Bob Lake finished 20th. Morgan Ward, a sophomore from Long Beach, Calif., completed the scoring with a 25th place finish. As prescribed by NCAA policy, finishing positions of those runners who competed as individuals and not as team members were pared away, leaving the Spartan five contributing the following points: 3-4-9-12-16–44.

The 1959 cross country team. Letter Winners were J. Horan, R. Lake, W. Smith, C. Kennedy, G. Young, W. Reynolds, E. Graydon, M. Ward and manager D. Coombs.

MAKING HISTORY

Even as MSU dropped sponsorship of the sport of boxing in 1958, John Horne completed what Biggie Munn called, "one of the greatest athletic accomplishments I have ever experienced." Even with no dual-meet competition to sharpen him and no regular coach to condition him, Horne successfully defended his NCAA light-heavyweight title in 1959 and again in 1960. A true Spartan warrior, he completed his MSU career undefeated.

At that 1960 national meet held in Madison, Wis., Charles Mohr, the 165-pound competitor for the University of Wisconsin, collapsed during his championship bout. He never regained consciousness and died eight days later. This tragedy proved to be a major setback for the sport. Within a month, the University of Wisconsin's governing board voted to end intercollegiate boxing, terming it "not an appropriate sport." The NCAA ultimately followed suit by withdrawing its support as an approved competitive sport.

Lyman Frimodig, a living legend on the campus for over 40 years, retired from the university on July 1, 1960. He left behind a distinguished career that began as a three-sport star to his final position as business manager in the athletic department. As a proper tribute, he was honored by nearly 500 friends, relatives and associates at a "Friends of Frim" recognition banquet in the Kellogg Center on May 14, 1960.

John Horne, undefeated MSU champion

GREAT STATE DATES

Football—**October 3, 1959 (A):** From the outset, the 1959 version of the annual MSU-Michigan tussle was billed as a mismatch favoring the Spartans. That is exactly how the game unfolded before a record crowd of 103,234. State scored on three of their first four possessions and on Bob Suci's 93-yard touchdown run of a pass interception. Even the final score, 34-8, does not clearly define Michigan State's dominant role. As an example, one drive, a 93-yard march after the second-half kickoff, ended scoreless at the U of M one-yard line on a turnover from a fumble. Although Blanche Martin was the leading ground gainer with 99 yards on nine carries, this was an afternoon in which the glory was divided among many. Two of the scoring drives were engineered by Tom Wilson and two by Dean Look. As for the touchdowns, they were scored by Herb Adderly, Martin, Look, Suci, and Don Stewart, while Art Brandstatter Jr. connected on four PATs. The Wolverines' score came late in the game following a pass interception. Perhaps the losing coach, "Bump" Elliott, summarized it best when he said, "The turning point was the opening kickoff."

Football—**October 17, 1959 (H):** In this, the fourth game of the season, Dean Look would be given the starting quarterback assignment on a full-time basis and the Spartans responded with a 19-0 victory over Notre Dame. There were other new names and new faces. Larry Hudas, a Detroit sophomore with no previous carries, scored the opening touchdown on a four-yard run. This culminated a sustained 71-yard drive in the opening quarter. The second score came in the third period on a Look to Fred Arbanas 52-yard pass play. Yet it was another sophomore listed as the fourth-string fullback, Ron Hatcher of Carnegie, Pa., who scored the final touchdown on a 10-yard carry. Another sophomore runner, Don Stewart of Muskegon, picked up 74 yards on 13 carries as a substitute for the injured Gary Ballman. For additional heroics, this was an afternoon for the defense. On four separate occasions in the final period, the Irish were thwarted after setting up first-and-goal to go inside the two-yard line.

Soccer—**October 24, 1959 (H):** Featuring Cecil Heron's second four-goal game of the season, State defeated Indiana, 5-1. Bruce Okine scored first on a point-blank shot early in the third quarter and Heron took over from there. He first netted a pair in that same period,

one on a head shot conversion of John Southan's corner kick, and then finished the afternoon with a pair of short shots in the final period. Coach Kenney singled out halfbacks Peter McKinnon and George Sepetys for superior defensive play.

Cross Country—**October 30, 1959 (A):** Closing out their abbreviated dual-meet schedule, the cross country team was in South Bend, where they easily outran the Irish, 17-42. Bettering the course record in the process, Forddy Kennedy finished first, followed by teammates Bob Lake and Bill Reynolds in second and third. Rounding out the team scoring were Ed Graydon in fifth and Morgan Ward in sixth.

Soccer—**November 14, 1959 (A):** MSU concluded a 7-2 season with a 2-1 victory over Pittsburgh on a field described as "grassless" and a "sea of mud." After a scoreless first half, Cecil Heron took a pass from Bernie Cook and booted one in from six yards out in the third quarter. After Pitt had converted a corner kick to tie the score in the final period, Erich Streder connected on a penalty kick with four minutes remaining in the game. The free shot had been awarded after a defender had taken Dave Christie down in front of the Panther net.

Basketball—**December 5, 1959 (H):** In a game in which the lead seesawed back and forth with neither team possessing more than a four-point lead during regulation, MSU topped Notre Dame in overtime, 61-56. Art Gowens, the springy-legged 6' 2" center topped all scorers with 28 points on eight field goals and 12 free throws.

Basketball—**January 2, 1960 (A):** The conference schedule opened on the road with a 91-79 victory over the Wisconsin Badgers. This would be the final game for starters Art Gowens and Jim Bechinski, and reserve Bill Pauline. All three were declared academically ineligible following a report of fall term grades. The loss of Gowens was particularly hard felt, as he was averaging 18.6 points a game.

Swimming and Diving—**January 7, 1960 (H):** A sophomore-dominated Spartan squad opened the season with a 77-28 defeat of Iowa State. Although the Men's IM pool had first been used to host the preceding year's conference championship, this meet with the Cyclones was the first dual meet to be held at the new facility. First-year man Dick Brackett was the only double winner, taking the 220- and 440-yard freestyle. Other sophomores to claim victories were Dan Convis in the 50-yard freestyle; Carl Shaar in the butterfly; Ron Gage in the backstroke; Dennis Ruppart in the breaststroke; and diver Ron Welfare. The only upperclassman to capture a first was Larry Jones, who won the 100-yard freestyle. With both relays going to State, the visitors were able to salvage only one first, the 200-yard individual medley.

Basketball—**January 9, 1960 (H):** Even with a re-vamped starting lineup that included Art Schwarm and Dave Scott, who replaced the ineligible Art Gowens and Jim Bechinski, State handled the University of Michigan with ease, 89-58, before a sellout crowd of 12,208. It was the largest Spartan margin of victory in the history of the 73-game series. Led by the dependable front court pair of co-captains Horace Walker, who finished with 24 points, and Lance Olson, who scored 23, State struck early to build a 50-36 lead at halftime. When the margin reached 20 points midway in the second half, Coach Anderson cleared his bench.

Hockey—**January 16, 1960 (H):** Playing before a sellout crowd of 2,275 in Dem Hall, the Spartans snapped a tight 2-2 game with third period goals by Real Turcotte and Andre LaCoste for a 4-2 victory over Michigan. Turcotte's tie-breaker came with only 28 seconds having transpired in the third period as he picked up a loose puck in front of the Wolverine's cage and fired it home. LaCoste put the Spartan fans at ease when he skated in alone, faked to the right, and hit the lower left-hand corner to complete the evening's scoring at 17:23. Defenseman Mel Christofferson and winger Al Checco had scored the first two goals.

Basketball—**January 23, 1960 (H):** Playing before a national television audience, the Spartans defeated Iowa, 90-80, to gain some redemption for a loss at Iowa City 12 days earlier. Lance Olson led the attack with a career-high 35 points, Horace Walker hit for 20, and little Dave Fahs scored 19. Dave Scott and Art Schwarm were singled out as defensive standouts. After State opened with a 49-28 first half lead, the pesky visitors clawed back to within eight points before they were put away. As the conference leader in rebounding percentage, the Spartans dominated the Hawks on the glass, 63-48.

Wrestling—**February 26, 1960 (H):** Coach Fendley Collins had predicted that a victory in the first match of the afternoon was crucial for any chance of an upset over the University of Michigan. 123-pound George Hobbs accepted that challenge and opened the meet with a 7-3 defeat of his previously undefeated opponent. From there, with victories by Norm Young, Duane Wohlfer,

and unbeaten Bob Moser at 157 pounds, State built a 12-3 lead. After losing the 167- and 177-pound matches, the lead diminished to 12-9, and the entire affair rested with the heavyweights. John Baum only needed a draw to close out a 14-11 Michigan State victory, and that's exactly what he delivered, a 3-3 tie, to remain undefeated on the season.

Gymnastics—February 26, 1960 (A): With only a tie with Iowa to mar their record, the gymnasts concluded the dual-meet season undefeated with an impressive come-from-behind 60-52 defeat of Michigan. Trailing with two events remaining, the Spartans took command by finishing 1-2-5 on the still rings and then completely dominating the tumbling event with John Daniels, Chuck Thompson, and Steve Johnson taking the first three spots. Steve Tarshis, the two-time NCAA champion, concluded an undefeated dual meet season on the high bar. Daniels, who also won the free exercise event, was State's only double winner, and Captain Angelo Festa was the high-point man with 16 points.

Fencing—April 13, 1960 (A): In a triple dual meet at Madison, the Spartans won their second meet of the season, squeaking by the Wisconsin squad, 14-13. The foil team of Chuck Schmitter, Doug Lawless, and William McNamara scored a 6-3 win, and the epee trio of Art Dowd, Jim Clary and Doug Jewell out-dueled the Badgers 5-4. Steve Arnest was the individual winner in sabre, but the squad was a 3-6 loser.

Baseball—May 7, 1960 (A): Mickey Sinks, the ace of the 1960 mound corp, yielded a mere five hits in downing the Michigan Wolverines 2-1 in the opener of a doubleheader in Ann Arbor. Both Spartan runs were unearned. Ron Holmes scored on a throwing error in the third inning and Tom Riley reached first base on yet another U of M miscue in the sixth. He later scored the winning run on a deftly executed double steal with Jerry Lumianski.

Tennis—May 7, 1960 (H): State posted its 16th straight dual-meet victory of the spring with an 8-1 defeat of the University of Illinois. Only Roger Plagenhoef in the number four singles position met defeat. Scoring straight set victories were number one Brian Eisner, number two Bill Hotchkiss, number three Doug Smith and number five Ron Mescall. Only Ron Henry needed three sets to gain a team point from the number six position. The doubles teams of Eisner-Smith, Hotchkiss-Plagenhoef, and Mescall-Henry concluded the afternoon with easy wins.

Track and Field—May 14, 1960 (H): With a convincing win in the final event of the afternoon, the mile relay, the Spartans turned a 64-62 deficit into a 72-69 victory over the Notre Dame Irish. Other winners on the oval for MSU were Zach Ford in the 100-yard dash; Atterberry, who set a new Ralph Young Field record with a 47.4 in the 440; Brian Castle in the 880; sophomore Tim Jefferson in the high hurdles, and Billy Reynolds in the two mile. On the infield, Sonny Akpata, the Nigerian star, leaped 23'-5 1/2" to take the broad jump event. New field records were set by Mike Gerhard with a high jump of 6' 4" and Mike Kleinhans with a vault of 14' 6".

Golf—May 16, 1960 (H): The final dual meet of the year was as close as it could get, Michigan State 18 1/2, Notre Dame 17 1/2. Tim Baldwin was the medalist with a 146, followed by Jack Reynolds, who carded a 149. This translated to four team points from Baldwin's game and four and a-half from Reynolds. Tad Schmidt shot a 150 and earned three points. The remaining team points were generated by Ty Caplin with a 151, Don Cochran with a 157 and C.A. Smith with a 158.

ATHLETE OF THE YEAR

Dean Look was one of those natural athletes. As a scholastic star at Lansing Everett High School, he was an All-State selection in basketball and football, as well as a state champion and record-setting pole vaulter with the track and field team. Settling on two sports as a Spartan, Dean earned three varsity awards in football and two in baseball. His versatility was further reflected in football, where, as a halfback in 1958, he was the team's top runner with a 3.6 average per carry. One year later Coach Daugherty summoned the 5' 10", 188-pound Look to lead the team from an unfamiliar spot at quarterback. From that new position he became a true triple threat star (punt-pass-run). He responded by three times being chosen to United Press International's backfield star of the week, as well as being named All-American by several selection committees including *Look Magazine*, for which he was appropriately featured on the publication's cover. In baseball he played centerfield, hit for a lusty .412 average, was named to the All-Conference team, and voted the team's MVP in his sophomore year. In the spring of 1959 Dean was switched to second base, a position he had never played, and batted .298. Forgoing his senior

year on the diamond, in November of 1959, Dean Look signed a $50,000 contract with the Chicago White Sox. He later continued on the football field with a long career as a National Football League official.

Dean Look

IN THE SPARTLITE

Baseball: With an overall record of 17-13, the Spartans completed a seventh straight winning season but the conference record was no better than 4-7, resulting in an eighth place finish.

Mickey Sinks, in his junior year, was the team's top pitcher with a 7-3 won-loss record. Also, in 92.2 innings, he recorded an impressive 1.64 earned run average.

Coming on strong with seven hits in the final three games on the schedule, Bob Ross ended the season with a team-leading hitting average of .389. Rounding out the top batters and their averages were Bob Monczka .283, Don Sackett .278, Pat Sartorius .263, Bill Schudlich .259, captain Dick Golden .238 and John Hendee .236.

Basketball: The most exciting game of the season was played on the Jenison floor, January 30, against Ohio State, a team that would go on to win the 1960 NCAA tournament. Furthermore, a 1999 Gannett News Service poll identified this Buckeye team, featuring All-Americans Jerry Lucas and John Havlicek, as the seventh-best collegiate basketball team of the 20th century. On this afternoon, Forddy Anderson's scrappy crew was up to the challenge. Led by clutch scoring from Horace Walker and Lance Olson, a jam-packed crowd of 12,500 was in a continual roar during the second half when the score was tied six times and MSU led on five occasions. The Bucks did not go ahead to stay, 76-75, until the 4:38 mark of the final period. Exchanging shots in the final moments, three times the Spartans drew within one point but could never again regain the lead. The final score read OSU 84, MSU 83.

Upon dropping the season-closer to Indiana, 86-80, on March 5, the Spartans completed the season with a 10-11 record, the first Anderson-coached MSU team to finish below .500. They did not surrender to the Hoosiers submissively. Behind 44-33 at the half, State bounced back to actually lead 72-70 with 3:52 remaining. Thereafter, eight unanswered Hoosier points ended any hope of a victory.

Hitting for 473 points (22.6 ppg), Horace Walker finished the season with the second highest individual total score in school history. In addition, he set a conference single-season rebound record with 286 and was selected as consensus All-Big Ten and third team All-American.

As a precursor to what would become a traditional senior day farewell, both Lance Olson's and Horace Walker's mothers were in attendance and were introduced to the Jenison crowd of 11,861. It was the first time Mrs. Walker had seen her son play as a collegian.

Cross Country: With the first team practice not scheduled until October 12, no formal squad was entered in the October 3 Michigan AAU race at Western Michigan. Instead, 14 aspiring members of the 1959 team independently traveled to Kalamazoo to run the four-mile course unattached.

State lost its season opener to Western, 27-28. Although it was conceded that the Broncos were a talented squad, at that time there were likely very few who would have projected MSU as a national championship team.

The five-mile course over the Forest Akers West course was laid out and first used in the dual meet against Penn State on Friday, October 23.

Fencing: Posting a 1-7 season record, 1960 proved to be one of the most disappointing years of Charley Schmitter's coaching career. Of the seven losses, five could have gone either way. The team consisted of son Chuck Schmitter, Dick Lawless and Bill McNamara in foil; Steve Arnest, Don Johnson and Neil Brown dueling in sabre; and Jim Clary, Doug Jewell and Art Dowd in the epee.

For the third time, alumnus Allan Kwartler was a member of the USA Olympic team. He had previously earned a spot on the teams that competed in 1952 and 1956 and thus became the only Spartan to have ever competed in three Olympiads.

Of the five teams competing in the conference meet, State tied for fourth.

Football: In 1959 there was no talk of red shirting first-year men. By midseason no less than 16 sophomores (freshmen were not eligible for varsity competition) had earned playing time, some serving major roles in the team's 5-4 record. Working their way into starting spots with the offensive unit were Art Brandstatter Jr., playing end and serving as field goal kicker; Dave Manders at center; and Gary Ballman at halfback. Ron Hatcher, Larry Hudas, Carl Charon, and Bob Suci added depth to the running game. On the defensive side, tackle Pete Kakala, end Jim Corgiat and defensive back Don Stewart had become frequent starters. Other rookies to see action were Ed Ryan, John Sharp, Dick Oxendine, Tony Kumiega, Bob Szwast, and Don Kopach.

Golf: This was John Brotzmann's first year as head golf coach, and the team responded admirably with a 9-1 dual-meet record. On three consecutive Saturdays in May they entertained triple dual meets and managed to defeat Northwestern, Wisconsin, Illinois, Michigan and Iowa, while losing to the eventual conference champions from Purdue.

The Big Ten championships were played on the Forest Akers east course. With the best five-man scoring total over four rounds of 18 holes, State totaled 1,531 strokes, 11 more than the winning Purdue University team. Firing the rounds for State were Tim Baldwin, Ty Caplin, Jack Reynolds, Ted Schmidt, C.A. Smith and Don Cochran.

Gymnastics: Even with due respect for the 1952 squad that was undefeated at 6-0, the 1960 team, that went 10-0-1 was likely the greatest dual-meet team ever assembled at MSU.

At the conference championships, State scored 104 points but finished a disappointing third behind Illinois at 114 1/2 and Minnesota at 105 1/2, two teams they had defeated in the regular season. Stan Tarshis was the only Spartan champion as he captured his third straight high-bar title.

Tarshis would be the only Spartan, in any sport, to win an individual NCAA title in 1959-1960. For the second straight year the Los Angeles native did so on the horizontal bar at the championship meet in University Park, Pa. Failure to win the national title as a sophomore in 1958 was the only blemish over an otherwise all-vic-

Stopping Notre Dame four times inside the two-yard line during the game on October 17, 1959, prompted Coach Duffy to quip, "I wish they would have those goal-line stands in the middle of the field where I could see them better."

torious collegiate career. Other team members to score in those 1960 NCAAs were John Daniels, Gani Browsh, Chuck Thompson, Angie Festa, and Jim Durkee.

Hockey: Playing over major personal losses by graduation, the ice hockey team took a major tumble from the NCAA finalist team of 1958-1959, as they managed only four victories.

Eldon VanSpybook, who replaced the graduated All-American Joe Selinger in goal, was kept busy, stopping a school record 793 shots over the 24-game season.

Weldie Olson and Gene Grazie were members of the famous USA Olympic team of 1960 that won the gold medal and the hearts of the nation with stunning victories over Russia and Czechoslovakia.

Soccer: High-scoring forwards Cecil Heron and Erich Streder were named to first team berths on the 1959 Wheaties All-American soccer team. Heron, the 30-year-old Jamaican, broke the team scoring record with 19 goals and was not shut out in any of State's nine games. Considered the hardest shooter on the squad, Streder tied the old scoring record of 12 goals set by Al Sarria in 1956.

Swimming and Diving: Coach McCafffree's team managed a fourth-place finish at the 50th anniversary of the Big Ten swimming and diving championships, held in Madison, Wis. The breaststroke trio of Dennis Ruppart, Bill Singleton and Frank Modine finished third-fourth-fifth in the 100-yard event with Ruppart, and Modine swam to a fourth and sixth in the 200. Butterflyer Carl Shaar was fourth in the 200 and sixth in the 100. Dick Brackett placed fifth in the 440-yard freestyle and sixth in the 220-yard, and Ron Gage finished sixth in the 100-yard backstroke.

At the NCAA meet State dropped all the way to 16th place from the fifth place finish they enjoyed in 1959. Leading the team were newcomers Brackett, who finished fifth in the 220-yard freestyle, and Shaar, who placed sixth in the 200-yard butterfly.

Tennis: The conference championships, originally scheduled for the outdoor courts at Northwestern University, were forced into the field house at the University of Chicago by unrelenting rain showers. MSU finished third with 27 points. Ron Moscall, who worked his way undefeated through the brackets, emerged as the champion at the number five singles slot. Brian Eisner reached the finals at number one but settled for the runner-up position after meeting defeat, 6-2, 6-3.

Track and Field: Willie Atterberry captured first in the 1,000-meter run at the indoor conference championship in Columbus, Ohio, leading MSU to a third place finish. Other contributors were Zach Ford, fourth in the 300; Brian Castle and Jim Carr, second and fourth in the 600; and captain Bob Lake and Billy Reynolds, second and third in the two-mile. In the field events, Sonny Akpata placed third in the broad jump, Mike Gerhard tied for third in the high jump, and the pole vaulting pair of Mike Klienhans and Gerry Debenau shared the third spot.

In the outdoor Big Tens held at Ralph Young Field, MSU compiled 22 points to finish in fourth place. Klienhans tied for first in the pole vault at 14' 3-5/8"; Atterberry finished second in the 440 and third in 220; Castle was second in the 880; Sonny Akpata, fourth in the broad jump; Bob Lake sixth in the mile; and Bill Reynolds and Jerry Young finished second and third in the two mile.

Kleinhans finished in a four-way tie for first place at the IC4A outdoor championships in Philadelphia, Pa.

At the NCAAs in Berkeley, Calif., Sonny Akpata managed a leap of 47' 1/2" in the triple jump event to put MSU on the scoring sheet with one point. Atterberry and Kleinhans also competed but did not score.

Wrestling: In the 1940s, Fendley Collins stocked his squads from talent-rich Oklahoma and thereafter with top wrestlers from Cleveland, Ohio. Gaining momentum as an interscholastic sport in Michigan, slowly talent was being developed, particularly in the Lansing schools. By 1960, State's squad included eight from the Capital City area: John Baum, Doug Millman, Norm Young, Bob Weber, Duane Wohlfert, Roger Tavenner, Doug Brown and Mike Senzig.

Leading the team to the impressive 8-1 dual-meet season of 1960 were heavyweight Baum with a 13-3-2 won-loss-tie record, 130-pound Young with a 12-5-1 record and 123-pound George Hobbs with an 11-5-2 mark.

The Spartans managed 37 points and a fourth-place finish in the Big Ten championship meet but gained only nine points at the national meet, tying for 18th spot with Michigan and Indiana.

The only Spartan to be crowned a national champion in 1960 was 174-pound Jim Ferguson, who successfully defended his National AAU title. Ferguson had also won a gold medal at the 1959 Pan-Am Games where he represented the USA.

TALES TO TELL

Jack Damson was a member of the tennis squad from 1961-1963, during which the teams collectively won 44 meets and only lost 13. In 1961 he was the Big Ten singles champion in the number four position. He reminisces about his tennis days at MSU:

"Tennis in the early 1960s was a sport in transition in the sense that it was still by-and-large a seasonal sport. Most of the team members were multi-sport athletes in high school and generally concentrated on tennis only in the spring and summer months. For example, Dick Hall, who won a Big Ten championship in 1961 at the number two position, also was the basketball team's leading scorer that year.

A major recruiting weapon for State during that period was the sparkling new IM Building that offered the prospect of indoor tennis on the floor of the arena in what was then considered a state-of-the-art setting. Never mind that the space had to be rotated between PE classes, wrestling and gymnastics meets, to many of us who never had the opportunity to play during the winter months, it was tennis heaven. There were so many lines on the floor for the various sports that one needed a road map and a surveyor's scope to determine what was what.

A concluding benefit of making the team during that time was the opportunity to spend the spring break in the Carolinas. The prospect of leaving cold weather for blooming aromatic dogwood, mild temps and the clay composition tennis courts at Chapel Hill, Davidson, Raleigh and Wake Forest was an incredible perk for a group of young men, many of whom had never ventured out of the Midwest. Nothing created bonding and a sense of team more than spending hours each day traveling in the extended length vans used by MSU for team travel.

Ultimately, I believe most of us as athletes and members of a Spartan team playing against Big Ten competition, have been enriched immeasurably by the experience."

HEADLINES of 1961

- In the Bay of Pigs incident, about 1,500 Cuban exiles trained by the U.S. make an unsuccessful attempt to invade Cuba and overthrow Fidel Castro.
- Soviet cosmonaut Yuri Gagarin becomes the first man in space, and Alan Shepard follows as the first American in space with a 15-minute flight that reached an altitude of 115 miles.
- President John F. Kennedy establishes the Peace Corps to give trained manpower and technical assistance to underdeveloped nations.
- East German communists build a wall dividing East and West Berlin.

SCOREBOARD

	W	L	T	Avg.
Baseball	21	11	1	.652
Track and Field	2	2	0	.500
Football	6	2	1	.722
Basketball	7	17	0	.292
Tennis	16	4	0	.800
Cross Country	1	1	0	.500
Swimming and Diving	8	2	0	.800
Wrestling	8	1	0	.889
Hockey	11	16	0	.407
Fencing	4	5	0	.444
Golf	10	3	1	.750
Gymnastics	8	2	0	.800
Soccer	8	1	0	.888

TEAM OF THE YEAR

Completing the most impressive dual-meet season since the undefeated team of 1948, the 1960-1961 wrestling squad finished with an 8-1 record and then managed to dethrone the University of Michigan for the Big Ten title at the championship held in MSU's IM Arena. State would finish with 69 points and runner-up Michigan with 65. It was Michigan State's first conference wrestling championship since entering Big Ten competition

in 1951. Of the four Spartans who managed to reach the finals, Okla Johnson at 115 pounds and Norman Young at 137 pounds won gold medals, while both George Hobbs at 123 pounds and John McCray at 177 pounds gained second-place team points. Also scoring with fourth-place finishes were Don Hoke at 130 pounds, Duane Wohlfert at 157 and Bob Schluter at 167. Winners in consolation matches were 191-pound Merle Prebel and heavyweight Mike Senzig. Projecting ahead from that point on the message was quite clear. While State was through scoring, Michigan had contenders in both of the final two championship matches, at 191 and heavyweight. If just one of these Wolverines emerged as a champion, the team trophy would have been headed for Ann Arbor. It didn't happen, as in each of those final two matches a Northwestern Wildcat proved superior.

MAKING HISTORY

In planning for the Iowa football game, Coach Daugherty made a decision that would have significant national impact on the future of the game of football. Duffy had been impressed with the booming balls he saw rising from the soccer field located adjacent to the football practice field on Shaw Lane. Gaining soccer coach Gen Kenney's approval, he invited a pair of stars from that team, Reiner "Dutch" Kemeling and Cecil Heron,

The 1961 wrestling team. Letter Winners were N. Young, D. Wohlfert, J. McCray, R. Schluter, M. Senzig, G. Hobbs, D. James, G. King, M. Prebel, O. Johnson and A. Valcanoff.

to try their skills at field goal kicking. Duffy liked what he saw and announced the twosome would join the squad for that Saturday's game against the Hawkeyes. Dutch and Cecil wore their soccer shoes and shorts with football jerseys numbered "0" and "00." As for protective equipment, the football rules specified that only a helmet and kneepads were required, and to that extent the two complied. Although novel, the kicking innovators had little bearing on the game of that afternoon. Kemeling booted two kickoffs in the second half but eventually surrendered the chores to the more orthodox kicker, Art Brandstatter Jr. A future day would await the total repercussions of the soccer-style kickers.

GREAT STATE DATES

Football—**October 1, 1960 (H):** The first half of the annual battle with Michigan was unsettling as the lead went back and forth. Then, when State scored to make it 14-10, the home fans in Spartan Stadium gained confidence. Why worry? After all, the maize and blue had not defeated the favored Spartans since 1955. Then, on the ensuing exchange, the U of M's Dennis Fitzgerald gathered in Art Brandstatter's kickoff and rambled off a team-record 99-yard scoring return. At intermission the scoreboard read Michigan 17, MSU 14. The second half saw two additional scores; fortunately, the home team posted both. First, Brandstatter kicked the fourth field goal of his career to equal the team record established by Bob Carey. The score remained tied 17-17 until 12 minutes had elapsed in the fourth period when a defensive play set the stage for the winning counter. Jim Kanicki and Dave Behrman trapped the Wolverine quarterback at his own three-yard line. A short wobbly punt turned the ball over to State and the offense responded. It took only five plays before Carl Charon crossed the goal line with the winning touchdown.

Football—**November 5, 1960 (A):** In his first six years at the helm, Duffy's teams had compiled only a .500 record against Purdue (3-3); therefore, trailing at halftime, 7-3, in West Lafayette was not a great surprise. Furthermore, the Boilermakers led 13-11 with 2:50 remaining on the clock. It was during those closing minutes that some genuine Spartan heroics unfolded. As the hosts threatened to score once more, George Saimes in-

tercepted a pass at the MSU one-yard line. From there, quarterback Tom Wilson orchestrated a 99-yard seven-play scoring drive that featured his own 46-yard twisting run along with a 47-yarder by the sophomore fullback Saimes. With precious seconds remaining, Wilson carried it over from the one-yard line and State escaped with a 17-13 victory.

Cross Country—**November 5, 1960 (A):** In an unusual appearance beyond the immediate Midwest area, coach Fran Dittrich took his squad to the rarefied air of Colorado for a dual meet against the Air Force Academy. In the closest win since 1954, they defeated the Cadets, 26-29. Billy Reynolds led all runners to the tape in a course record, 20:33.2. Other Spartan scorers were Clayton Ward in second, Gerry Young in fourth, and Don Castle and Roger Humbarger in the ninth and 10th spots.

Soccer—**November 5, 1960 (A):** On a scoring binge that remains a team record, State humiliated the Purdue Boilermakers, 17-0. Leading the team with six goals, Mabricio Ventura tied Cecil Heron's single game record output set in the season-opener against Earlham. Rounding out the impressive offensive display were Heron with four, John Gelmisi and Dave Christie with two each, and Bernie Cook, Jean Lohri and Cesar Dominguez with one goal each.

Football—**November 12, 1960 (A):** Trailing 12-0 at the half, State stormed back in the final 30 minutes to capture the lead from a stubborn Northwestern team, 21-18. Ron Hatcher, a junior fullback, spearheaded the Spartan comeback with scoring romps of 34 and 52 yards. Gary Ballman, another junior, ran 74 yards for his touchdown. Yet, the game really belonged to the field goal kickers. Whereas MSU's left-footed Art Brandstatter split the uprights on all three of his conversion attempts, the Wildcats' Mike Stock, who had been perfect all season, missed on every one of his attempts. Yet, the clawing Cats weren't through. In the waning four minutes of the game they drove 78 yards to State's two-yard line. Unable to score the go-ahead touchdown, coach Ara Parseghian once more called upon Mike Stock, this time for a game-tying field goal. Hampered by a 12-mph headwind, his attempt drifted off-course and MSU's advantage was preserved.

Gymnastics—**January 14, 1961 (A):** George Szypula's gymnasts opened the season in Iowa City, Iowa, with two victories, 77-35 over Iowa and 78-34 over Minnesota in a triple dual meet. Jerry Daniels in free exer-

MSU's sure-footed kicker Art Brandstatter Jr.

cise, Charles Thompson in rebound tumbling, Larry Bassett on the parallel bars and Steve Johnson in tumbling were all double winners. Bob Dendy and Wayne Bergstrom tied for first on the side horse event in both meets.

Basketball—**January 16, 1961 (H):** MSU never trailed, building an early 15-5 lead, making it 44-27 at halftime and finally closing it out 81-69 over the Michigan Wolverines. Altogether, the shooting statistics were not impressive, the Wolverines connected on 25 of 66 field goals for a .380 percentage and State's offense was even less impressive at .350 percent on 27 of 80 attempts. Regardless, four Spartans scored in double figures, with Dick Hall's 25 leading the way. Ted Williams, the rangy center, had a remarkable evening, scoring 16 points while pulling down 25 rebounds. Dave Fahs connected for 12 and Art Schwarm 10. The game was played in Jenison before a less-than-sellout crowd of 8,015 fans.

Track and Field—**January 28, 1961 (A):** Trailing Ohio State in the meet score from the very first event, Jerry Young and Billy Reynolds went 1-3 in the next-to-last event, the two-mile run. This finally put the Spartans ahead by a slim two and two-thirds points with the meet now hinging on the result of the closing race, the mile relay. A bizarre conclusion followed. On the second lap of that relay, Michigan State's leadoff runner, Zack Ford, was fouled on a curve that sent him to the ground and knocked the team out of the race. The consequences also knocked the Buckeyes out of the race, as they were disqualified for the incident. As a result, the final score reverted back to the pre-relay count, which favored MSU, 64 1/3-61 2/3.

Hockey—**February 3, 1961 (H):** With 51 seconds of playing time remaining and a crowd of 2,250 looking on, Captain Andre LaCoste steered in a long shot by Frank Silka to up-end the Michigan Wolverines, 3-2. The game was knotted 1-1 in the final stanza when Ed Ozybko scored at 4:30. "Red" Berenson, the U of M star, evened the count on a power play at 10:22 to set up the dramatic clincher. The Spartan goalie, sophomore John Chandik played brilliantly as he brushed aside 31 shots.

Swimming and Diving—**February 18, 1961 (A):** In a meet at Ohio State that would be decided in the final event, the 400-yard freestyle relay quartet of Doug Rowe, Bill Wood, Larry Jones and Mike Wood swam to a pool record 3:22.9 as the Spartans defeated the Buckeyes, 54 1/2-48 1/2. Mike Wood and Billy Steuart were both double winners, Wood taking firsts in the freestyle sprint events and Steuart capturing the 440-yard freestyle and swimming a 2:07.7 200-yard individual medley to set a pool record. In addition to winning the 200-yard butterfly, Carl Sharr was a member of the winning medley relay team that included Jeff Mattson, Dennis Ruppart and Larry Jones.

Wrestling—**February 18, 1961 (H):** Okla Johnson, a sophomore from Norfolk, Va., opened the Iowa meet with a pin at 5:02 in his 115-pound match. What followed was a barrage of favorable Spartan decisions by George Hobbs, Jerry Hoke, Norm Young, Duane Wohlfert, Bob Schluter, John McCray, Merle Prebel and a forfeiture win by Mike Senzig at heavyweight. The only setback in the 31-3 victory was at 147 pounds.

Fencing—**February 18, 1961 (A):** In a triple dual meet in Columbus, Ohio, the fencing squad won their third meet of the season, 14-13, over Notre Dame. A spectacular performance by Dick Schloemer in his final foil bout secured the team victory. Coming back from a 4-2 deficit, he won the match and eventually the meet when the last touch of the bout was the deciding moment. Don Johnson was MSU's high scorer in sabre, as

he made a clean sweep in all of his bouts. Others securing points for the team victory were Chuck Schmitter, Bill McNamara, Bob Brooks and captain Dick "Tiger" Lawless.

Basketball—**February 20, 1961 (H):** Amidst a struggling 1-10 conference season, any win would be gratifying, and a 90-80 victory over Illinois would be no exception. Once the Spartans built a halftime lead of 46-38, they were reluctant to surrender it. Yet, that's what happened as the Illini made a move in the second half to lead by a single point, 52-51. After State regained the advantage, they did not relinquish it, building the lead to as many as 14 points, 74-60. Art Schwarm, turning in his best game of the year, led the team in scoring with 23 points. Three others scored in double figures: Dick Hall 19, Dave Fahs 18 and John Lamers 13. Although center Ted Williams had a cold night in shooting, 3 for 16, he managed to pull down a game-high 16 rebounds.

Wrestling—**February 20, 1961 (A):** Featuring pins by George Hobbs and Duane Wolfert and Norm Young's 5-2 decision at 137-pounds, State jumped to an early 13-0 lead over the University of Michigan and hung on to win 29-16. It was the second year in a row that the Spartans topped the Wolverines, and it was the U of M's first loss of the 1960-1961 season.

Wrestling—**February 25, 1961 (H):** Aided by forfeiture in four matches and Norm Young's pin at 137-pounds, the Spartans amassed a team-record 40 points in shutting out the University of Minnesota. The Gophers' performance was so inept that they did not register a single point until the sixth match of the afternoon, won by Duane Wohlfert, 9-2. Okla Johnson and George Hobbs had opened the meet with identical 7-0 decisions, and Bob Schluter closed the action with a 10-5 decision at 167 pounds.

Track and Field—**February 24, 1961 (H):** Coach Dittrich's long-distance runners saved the afternoon as MSU edged Central Michigan, 71 1/2-69 1/2. While the Chips took eight of the 14 events and tie in two others, Morgan Ward and Roger Humbarger finished one-two in the mile and Jerry Young, Ward and Bill Reynolds went 1-2-3 in the two mile. The only other clear winners for State were Sonny Akpata in the broad jump, Bill Mann in the high hurdles and Jim Kanicki in the shot put. Adding significantly to the winning point total were eight other runner-up slots gained by the Spartans.

Tennis—**April 15, 1961 (A):** Returning from their southern trip with a 5-2 record, the tennis squad opened the regular portion of the schedule by blanking Ohio State, 9-0. All winners completed their matches in straight sets. In singles positions one through six were Brian Eisner, Dick Hall, Roger Plagenhoef, Jack Damson, Ron Henry, and Bill Lau. In the most interesting match of the afternoon, the number one pair of Eisner-Hall extended the second set to 12-10 before gaining the win.

Golf—**May 1, 1961 (A):** Under a new conference 18-hole format, each member of a six-man team tallied their scores for a team total. With a composite of 962 strokes played over the University of Wisconsin course, State managed to defeat, not only the host team (979 strokes), but also Notre Dame (974 strokes) and Northwestern (988 strokes). Tad Schmidt led the MSU scoring with 156, Buddy Badger (imagine the Wisconsin people watching a Buddy Badger compete against their beloved Badgers) shot 157, Marty Kleva 160, Larry McMillan 162, C.A. Smith 163 and Don Cochran 164.

Baseball—**May 20, 1961 (A):** Yielding only one run in 19 innings, State's pitching led the way to a doubleheader sweep of Purdue, 4-0 and 4-1, in the closing weekend of conference play. The opener, scheduled to go nine innings, was scoreless until the Boilers' pitcher tired in the 12th and loaded the bases on walks. Bob Ross, the Spartans' relief pitcher, followed with a long bases-clearing single and then scored himself on a Wayne Fontes double. In game number two, it was all Ken Avery, as he yielded only two hits in seven innings. Tom Riley, the eventual team batting leader with a .359 average, accounted for two of the winner's runs with a four-bagger and RBI double.

Baseball—**May 24, 1961 (H):** Outfielder Tom Riley, who would complete the season as the team's leading hitter with a .359 average, was the primary run producer in the 5-4 verdict over Notre Dame. The Winnetka, Ill., senior had a run-producing single in the third and a two-run triple in the fifth to account for three of Michigan State's five scores. Over the first six innings starting pitcher Bob Ross yielded six hits and had a seemingly comfortable 5-0 lead, but the Irish were not yet ready for their showers. In the seventh, three singles, a base on balls and a hit batsman brought three runs across the plate and also brought an anxious coach John Kobs out of the dugout. Gary Ronberg replaced Ross and Ken Avery replaced Ronberg before the victory was secured, 5-4, and State had grasped the 21st victory of the season.

ATHLETE OF THE YEAR

Norm Young, one of the many high school champions who prepped under MSC alum Iggy Konrad at Lansing Sexton High School, became Michigan State's 11th NCAA wrestling champion when he captured the 137-pound title at the 1961 nationals in Eugene, Oregon. Tagged as an underdog, he worked his way through the brackets to the gold-medal round, where he was paired against the entry from the host school, Oregon State. Locked into a 3-3 tie with 20 seconds remaining in that final match, Norm shot for the legs and gained a quick takedown and then hung on for a 5-3 verdict.

Young struggled a bit through his sophomore season of 1959, but then peaked in March to win a surprising Big Ten championship at 130 pounds. Missing the top spot in 1960, Norm returned to the conference winner's circle in his senior year two weeks before the national collegiates. That second Big Ten title was instrumental in State's team title. Upon conclusion of the 1961 season, Norm Young was elected as honorary team captain.

Norm Young

IN THE SPARTLITE

Baseball: One of the all-time low points in Michigan State baseball history took place on Saturday, April 29, 1961, when Michigan came to town and left with not one or two, but three wins. The oddity of a tripleheader was set in place when the Friday game in Ann Arbor was rained out. The Michigan coach, sensing he had a contending team for the title, wanted to play as many games as possible and successfully pushed for adding the third game.

Basketball: To the delight of the majority of the 12,147 in attendance at Jenison Fieldhouse, MSU led NCAA defending champion Ohio State, 39-38 at halftime. The scrappy Spartans hung on well into the second half until the center, Ted Williams, picked up his fifth foul. From that point on, OSU had its way and with late scoring built a misleading 83-68 winning margin. The Buckeye All-American Jerry Lucas scored a Big Ten individual scoring record with 48 points.

Two weeks later at West Lafayette, Ind., Purdue's big center, 6' 7" Terry Dischinger, did Lucas four better, scoring 52 points that led to a 85-74 defeat of the Spartans.

Cross Country: Racing over the same Washington Park course in Chicago that had been the challenge of Big Ten runners since 1938, MSU's Gerry Young set a course record of 19:35.3 as the 1960 winner. In doing so he led the Spartans to a sixth straight conference championship with a winning total of 30 points. Iowa was the closest challenger at 61. Completing Michigan State's scoring were Morgan Ward, third; Billy Reynolds, fifth; Frank Weaver, 11th; and Bob Humbarger, 13th.

Penn State snapped MSU's four-year reign as the IC4A champions, and in fact, the Spartans finished third with 130 points behind the Nittany Lions with 70 and Army with 119. Gerry Young in the third spot and Bill Reynolds in fifth were the top finishers for State.

At the 23rd annual NCAA championship run, Gerry Young, in the 18th spot, was the first Spartan to finish. Others that followed were Don Castle 57th, Patrick Stevens 69th, Michael Humbarger 77th and Robert Fulcher 79th. As a team, Michigan State was in ninth place, the school's second lowest finish ever in the national meet.

Fencing: State finished fourth in a field of six teams at the conference championships in Madison, Wis. In fence-offs to determine the individual champions, Don

Johnson emerged as the sabre titlest, while Chuck Schmitter settled for second place.

Dick Schloemer, Johnson and Schmitter represented MSU at the NCAA championships in Princeton, N.J., none of whom scored high enough to win team points.

Football: Does anyone remember Leroy Loudermilk? He came to Michigan State as a highly-recruited quarterback and began his first year as the back-up. When he did not play in the opener against Pittsburgh (many friends from hometown Wilkinsburg, Pa., had traveled to East Lansing for the occasion) Loudermilk was outraged and embarrassed. With little hesitation, he left school and in short order had enrolled at the University of Colorado in Boulder where Sonny Grandelius, former MSU All-American and assistant coach, had taken up the post as head coach.

The third game on the schedule, against the nationally third-ranked and eventual conference co-champion Iowa was a shocker. Trailing 14-0 at the half, MSU came back on a pair of second half 80-yard touchdown drives and a two-point conversion to lead 15-14. With only 2:50 remaining, the Spartans recovered a Hawkeye fumble at the Iowa 33-yard line and set about running out the clock. On the next offensive play, quarterback Tom Wilson took the snap, turned to his right, and shoved the ball into fullback Carl Charon's stomach. As an option of the system, Wilson pulled the ball back. It slipped from his hands, popped into the air and nestled into the outstretched arms of a surprised onrushing Iowa defender. In the silenced stadium, it seemed as if you could hear every step the interloper took over the lonely 67-yard jaunt into the south end zone. But it wasn't over. In the ensuing series, a Spartan pass was intercepted, and two plays later the final score was 27-15. Although it was a devastating loss, State ended the season with a 6-2-1 record and was ranked 13th nationally.

The October 22 game in Bloomington, Ind., was the game in which Indiana University dedicated their new stadium.

With Bob Shackleton and Larry Friymire at the microphone, WKAR radio broadcast the Spartan games to mid-Michigan.

Golf: In a quadrangular match in West Lafayette, Ind., Buddy Badger shot a 147 for 36-holes. His score was two strokes short of medalist honors but was five strokes better than Ohio State's top player, a young man by the name of Jack Nicklaus.

In the conference championships in Bloomington, Ind., State's five-man team finished a close third. The Ohio State squad took 1,527 strokes over the four rounds, Minnesota used 1,536, and the Spartans, 1,539. Individually, finishing sixth in gross score and first for MSU was C.A. Smith with a 305. Gene Hunt and Badger fired 307s to tie for 11th place. That same Jack Nicklaus, as a medalist, finished with a 283, which was 14 strokes better than his nearest challenger.

Gene Hunt, a member of the 1961 team, shares a Nicklaus story:

"In 1961, I reached the 36-hole NCAA semifinals when I met Jack Nicklaus on the Purdue University South Course in a 36-hole match play format. After our 18-hole morning round, I held a 4-up lead. My medal score was 68 to Jack's 72. Following lunch, Nicklaus birdied seven of the first 11 holes we played. It was difficult to come up with a defense for his performance, although I still played well and took the match to the 35th hole before losing 2-1. Jack went on to the finals and won the tournament. That match with Jack Nicklaus was not only the highlight of my golfing career, but also the topic of many conversations since."

Gymnastics: At the Big Tens in Ann Arbor, MSU totaled 91 points for a third-place finish. Leading the way were Larry Bassett, who tied for first on the parallel bars; John Daniels, who finished second in free exercise and seventh in still rings; Steve Johnson who placed second on the trampoline and sixth in tumbling; Charley Thompson who ended third on the trampoline and tied for fourth in tumbling and Wayne Bergstrom, who earned a sixth place on the side horse.

Competing within a field of 29 teams at the NCAA championship in Champaign, Ill., State's gymnasts scored 38 1/2 points to tie Illinois for fifth place. Johnson and Thompson finished first and fourth respectively on the trampoline; Daniels and Gani Browsh were back-to-back third and fourth in free exercise; and Bassett ended up ninth on the parallel bars and eighth in free exercise.

Hockey: State first played Ohio University in 1961. The Spartans overwhelmed the Bobcats in a two-game series on Dem Hall ice, 12-0 and 8-1. It appeared the Ohioans had seen enough to reflect and evaluate. Consequently, they were off the MSU schedule for two years.

In 1964, they tried again and were once more humiliated by State, 11-1 and 7-4. In 1965, it was State 12-0, 13-1. OU had seen enough, and the two schools did not face each other again. In the final game of the season, State dropped a heart-breaker to Michigan, 4-3, in Ann Arbor when Gordon "Red" Berenson scored the winning goal with less than four minutes remaining in the game. The hockey team defeated the University of Denver, 4-3, in overtime of the playoff game, which gave Michigan State third place behind Michigan Tech and Michigan.

Soccer: Cecil Heron's six goals against Earlham set an MSU scoring record.

Setting a team scoring record, Mab Ventura booted in 22 goals during the season.

State's defense featured All-American Reiner "Dutch" Kemeling, All-Midwest Ken Graham and Sam Donnelly, the team's MVP.

Swimming and Diving: Failing to capture one individual title, Coach McCaffree's swimmers and divers managed a fourth-place finish at the Conference Championships for the fourth year in a row. Contributing to the 100 1/2 team points were Bill Steuart, Carl Shaar, Mike Wood, Bill Wood, Bill Singleton, Larry Jones, Juergen Matt, Dennis Ruppart, Jeff Mattson, Doug Rowe, Dick Blazejewski, Dick Brackett, Bill Williams and Ron Syria.

At the NCAA meet in Seattle, Wash., the freestyle relay team of Mattson, Bill Wood, Jones and Mike Wood finished second, and the medley relay foursome of Mattson, Bill Singleton, Shaar and Mike Wood came in third. In individual events, Mattson was third in the 100-yard backstroke and Bill Steuart placed fifth in the 100-butterfly and ninth in the 1,500-yard freestyle.

Tennis: In the 5-4 loss to Indiana, Roger Plagenhoef played a 16-14 marathon third set before losing his number three singles match.

With a Big Ten dual-meet record of seven wins against two losses, MSU's second-place finish at the conference meet is about all that might have been expected. Hosting the matches, State emerged with two singles titles, Dick Hall at number two and number four Jack Damson. Other Spartans who reached the finals before bowing out were number three Plagenhoef, number five Ron Henry and the doubles combinations of number one Brian Eisner-Hall and number three Henry-Bill Lau.

Track and Field: At the indoor conference championships in Champaign, Ill., Michigan State scored 16 points to settle for a sixth-place finish. Gerald Young was MSU's only titlest with his victory in the two-mile run. Other top Spartan finishers were Don Voorheis with a second in the 300-yard dash, Bill Mann with a third in the high hurdles and Solomon Akpata with a third-place finish in the broad jump.

Moving outdoors changed the outcome very little as once more State managed 16 points, good enough for yet another sixth-place finish. Sprinter Zach Ford was second in the 220-yard dash and fourth in 100; Morgan Ward placed second in the mile run; Young was fourth in the two mile; and Akpata improved to second in the broad jump.

At the NCAA outdoor championships, Sonny Akpata failed to place in his specialty, the hop, step and jump, but he did leap 24' 4" to take fourth place in the broad jump. Young in the one mile and Ward in the steeplechase failed to place.

Wrestling: There were circumstances, some directly related and others seemingly unrelated, that punctuated the only loss of the year, 19-8, at Pittsburgh. First, the Panther coach refused to include the 115-pound and 191-pound weight classes in the meet format. These were matches penciled in as sure wins for MSU. The next problem was one of travel. The trip, by bus, was short-circuited by a major snowstorm that crippled travel across Ohio. Retracing their tracks as far back as Detroit, the entourage boarded a train that dropped them in Pittsburgh at 2:30 A.M. on Saturday morning. Later, it seemed obvious that this lack of sleep had negative effects on the athletes' performances.

Garnering 19 team points, State finished in a tie for eighth place at the NCAA meet in Corvallis, Ore. Fourteen of those points came from Norm Young's championship in the 137 pound division. George Hobbs, Jerry Hoke and Duane Wolfert accounted for the remaining five team points.

EXTRA! MICHIGAN STATE RELAYS (1960s)

The entry list of 1961 included 375 athletes from a total of 23 colleges and universities. Among the schools represented were Iowa, Purdue, Ohio State, Kansas State, Colorado, Iowa State, Missouri, Drake, Houston, Wichita, Notre Dame, Bowling Green, Miami (Ohio), and Ohio University. MSU's Sol "Sonny" Akpata, the Nigerian, captured his team's only first with a leap of 23' 6" in the broad jump.

In 1962, some 3,200 track fans, the most to attend the meet in recent years, packed into the best viewing areas, the north and south ends of the balcony, to watch the 275 athletes from 18 schools perform. John Parker won the broad jump, Sherman Lewis finished first in the 300-yard dash while tying the varsity record of 31.2. Overall, it was a "hard luck" meet for MSU. In the opening event of the evening a student helper prematurely stepped onto the track to set-up a knocked down hurdle and in the process interfered with Bill Mann who was attempting to jump his first hurdle. The Spartan shuttle-hurdle relay team was leading at the time. Challenging for first in the final event, the mile relay, anchorman Parker noticeably began limping coming off the next-to-last turn. He had sprained his ankle and limped home in fourth place.

Bobby Moreland established a meet record of 6.1 in winning the 65-yard dash in 1964. He would later combine with Parker, Walker Beverly and Mike Martins to capture the medley relay event in a time of 3:27.5, only one second from the meet record. It was MSU's first relay victory at its own meet since 1957 when the Spartans won both the two-mile and distance-medley events.

Two years later, with 4,018 fans looking on, the Spartans of 1966 collected five titles, two more than any of the other 25 teams competing. Jim Garrett won the long jump with a leap of 23' 7 1/2". The shuttle hurdle relay team of Clint Jones, Bob Steele, Fed McKoy and Gene Washington successfully defended their 1965 title and did so in a meet and fieldhouse record time of 28.8. With a final burst of speed, Jim Summers captured the 60-yard dash and Washington, in his junior year, won both hurdle events. The other Spartan victories were recorded by Washington in the two hurdle events.

In the 1967 Relays, Charles Pollard, MSU's sophomore hurdler, set a meet, fieldhouse and American dirt track records of 8.2 in the preliminaries of the high hurdles

and then, running a slower 8.3 in the finals, defeated his teammate Gene Washington who had won the event in both 1965 and 1966. The evening sellout crowd of 6,500 was attracted by mile world record holder Jim Ryan of the University of Kansas and they were not disappointed. Cheering him on with a standing ovation over the final two laps, the Kansan set a new meet and fieldhouse record of 4:03.7. The Spartan quartet of Pollard, Washington, Bob Steele and Allan Mailback won the shuttle hurdle relay in a time of 28.8, tying the American, meet and fieldhouse records set by Washington, Steele, Clint Jones and Fred McKoy in 1966.

In both 1967 and 1968, Jim Ryan made encore appearances in the mile run while continuing to steal the attention of the assembled crowd. After setting meet and fieldhouse records with a 4:03.7 in 1967, he returned in 1968 to better that mark with a 4:03.4. That performance followed a spectacular 3:57.5 that he had run the night before in New York's Madison Square Garden. Other Spartans also had moments of glory. Roger Merchant defeated the 880 field with a time of 1:53.0 and the team of Bill Wehrwein, Don Crawford, Dick Dunn and Rich Stevens posted a winning time of 3:25.3 in the sprint medley relay.

Even though the University of Kansas captured an unprecedented seven firsts in 1969, State's middle distance star Bill Wehrwein stole the spotlight when he completed the 600-yard dash in a time of 1:09.0, two-tenths of a second faster than the American record set by a Yale runner in 1964. Freshman Herb Washington, one year removed from his first varsity competition, streaked to a 6.2 first place in a special edition of the 60-yard race. Even with these impressive races by Spartans, the majority of the 5,600 fans had really turned out to watch the world's dominating distance runner, Jim Ryan, in his final appearance at Jenison Fieldhouse. The Jayhawk senior easily won his third-straight mile title but the time of 4:06.2 was well below his 1968 record performance of 4:03.4. Regardless, the appreciative fans gave the much-heralded Jayhawk star a standing ovation.

Michigan State attempts to out-duel the University of Detroit in this 1961 fencing meet.

The Spartans' Dick Johnstone scores against North Dakota.

MSU
1961-1962

TALES TO TELL

Each fall during the preseason football practice period, a band of midwest newsmen used to make the rounds of the Big Ten camps for one-day stops. On what was appropriately dubbed "the Skywriters Tour," writers would fly in as a group, talk to coaches, visit practices, interview players and, upon completion, feel versed enough to predict the outcome of the upcoming season.

Duffy Daugherty, sparked by his renowned wit, used to relish the visits, and the media folks looked forward to the stop in East Lansing. During the 1961 tour "Old Duff" was in rare form. In the middle of a picture-taking session at the Kellogg Center, Daugherty suggested to the writers that a good coach could make a star of any kid. To demonstrate his claim, he summoned a husky looking lad that he spotted in the lobby who, dressed in a white coat, appeared to be a waiter from the dining room. After the boy claimed to have only sandlot football experience, the coach "sent him out" for a pass. From down the lobby the "waiter" snared an errant toss one-handed. Six more times the stunt was repeated with one-handed grabs. Duffy had indeed demonstrated that he was a good coach. The grinning Daugherty then identified his accomplice as Ernie Clark of Lockport, N.Y., a varsity starter who was endowed with huge ham-like hands. The coach's final reminder was: "To show you how smart our coaching staff is, this guy is on our *defensive* team."

On March 1, 1988, the Big Ten athletic directors voted to discontinue the Skywriters Tour. Subsequently, an annual August luncheon in downtown Chicago has served as a substitute. A combined attendance of often more than 1,000, includes coaches, select players, school sports information personnel, media folks, conference representatives and invited guests.

HEADLINES of 1962

- The Cuban missile crisis is resolved when Soviet Premier Khrushchev agrees to dismantle the bases.
- John Glenn becomes the first American to orbit the earth in a spacecraft.
- Entertainer Johnny Carson begins to host *The Tonight Show*.
- Century 21 World's Fair opens in Seattle, Wash. The 600-foot Space Needle with revolving restaurant is a popular attraction.

SCOREBOARD

	W	L	T	Avg.
Baseball	17	13	0	.567
Track and Field	2	0	0	1.000
Football	7	2	0	.777
Basketball	8	14	0	.381
Tennis	12	5	0	.706
Cross Country	3	1	0	.750
Swimming and Diving	5	4	0	.555
Wrestling	6	1	2	.778
Hockey	13	11	1	.540
Fencing	6	6	0	.500
Golf	11	2	0	.846
Gymnastics	8	4	0	.667
Soccer	8	1	0	.889

The 1961 football team. (First row, left to right) L. Hudas, B. Suci, C. Charon, J. Corgiat, W, Fontes, M. Biondo, captain E. Ryan, B.B. Szwast, T. Kumiega, M. Newman, D. Stewart, D. Manders, and P. Kakela; (second row, left to right) G. Saimes, E. Clark, G. Azar, J. Sharp, R. Parrott, R. Hatcher, T. Winiecki, J. Kanicki, D. Bergman, T. Jordan, and J. Bobbitt; (third row, left to right) M. Snorton, L. Sanders, P. Smith, M. Currie, E. Budde, D. Proebstle, D. Underwood, E. Lattimer, D. Lincoln and S. Lewis; (fourth row, left to right) S. Mellinger, D. Herman, H. Johnson, C. Brown, R. Lopes, freshman coach B. Smith and R. Rubick; (back row, left to right) assistant coaches G. Serr, H. Bullough, V. Carillot, C. Boisture, B. Yeoman and C. Stoll, head coach D. Daugherty, manager J. Arbury, trainer G. Robinson and equipment manager K. Earley.

TEAM OF THE YEAR

The 1961 football squad has never been listed among the championship Spartan teams. Upon examining the season record of 7-2, this is fully understandable. Yet they fielded an outstanding defensive team, ranking among the top in sundry statistical categories. Yielding only seven touchdowns, no other MSU team has been that stingy. Including all scoring (field goals, PATs, etc.), they surrendered an average of 5.6 points per game, a statistic equaled only by the national championship team of 1965. Only two State teams (1963 and 1965) yielded fewer total yards per game than the 194.5 allowed credited to the 1961 team.

MAKING HISTORY

Historically, Notre Dame should always be respected as a school that lent significant impetus in Michigan State's seemingly precipitous rise to football respectability. Actually, it was a four-step plan, the first of which came on the hiring of Biggie Munn as coach in 1947. Secondly, by the following year, came the stadium enlargement boosted the capacity from 26,000 to 51,000. Next, a sure-fire opponent was needed to periodically draw fans to those new seats. President John Hannah, the brilliant man who orchestrated the entire plan, conferred with Notre Dame officials, and a deal was cut for a long-range football pact beginning at South Bend in 1948. Step four, of course, was becoming a member of the Big Ten that same year. The Irish won the first two encounters of the revitalized series, but, from 1950 through 1961, the Spar-

tans held a commanding 9-1 record. That 1961 game, like all in between, was played before a sellout crowd in Spartan Stadium. By then, seating capacity had risen to 76,000, with the upper deck in place.

The Big Ten enacted a new financial aid rule that eliminated the "need principle," which had previously been a factor in extending a tender to an athlete. Also, minimal high school class rank and nationally standardized test scores were established as the criteria for determining a recruit's eligibility for receiving said financial aid. The inclusion of the 2.0 minimum grade point average was not a factor until 1973.

GREAT STATE DATES

Cross Country—**October 7, 1961 (A):** The team opened the season in Columbus by defeating Ohio University and the host Buckeyes in a triangular meet. Jerry Young, MSU captain and defending Big Ten champion, completed the four-mile course in first place, as the Spartans scored 35 points to the Bobcats' 42 and the Buckeyes' 47. Other finishing positions for Michigan State were Roger Humbarger fifth, Al Duncan seventh, Pat Stevens 10th, Dick Gyde 12th, Bob Fulcher 15th, Don Castle 16th and Rob Berby 18th.

Football—**October 14, 1961 (A):** Although it was only the third game of the season, both Michigan State and Michigan were undefeated and nationally ranked in the top six. Drawing 103,198 fans to Michigan Stadium and millions of viewers to their TV sets, it was hyped as the "Game of the Week." However, it didn't take long for the game to take on a "green glow" with two Spartan touchdowns in the opening quarter. The first came eight plays after Wayne Fontes recovered a fumble at the U of M 31-yard line. The next was set up on a 46-yard Pete Smith to Matt Snorton pass play with George Saimes scoring from the 17-yard line. A second quarter scoring pass from Smith to halfback Carl Charon covering 11 yards raised the total to 21-0. The final TD was on a three-yard run by Sherman Lewis behind Ed Budde's block. Art Brandstatter Jr., converted all PATs, and the game ended 28-0.

Football—**October 21, 1961 (H):** Number one Michigan State came from behind to defeat number six Notre Dame, 17-7, for the sixth straight time. It was a game of two halves, with ND owning the first 30 min-

utes of play and the Spartans finally awakening after intermission. Until halftime, State trailed 11-4 in first downs and 170-12 in rushing yardage, and the score also favored the visitors, 7-0. In the second half MSU gained more first downs, 9-3, and rushed for more yardage, 190-61, and most importantly outscored the visitors, 17-0. If one person had to be singled out, it would be George Saimes. Playing both ways for a total of nearly 50 minutes, the Canton, Ohio, native was a stellar defender and offensively scored from 24 and 25 yards out. Both touchdowns were set up by pass interceptions, the first by Herman Johnson and the second by Carl Charon. Another run by Saimes, this time 28 yards, set up the final score, a 20-yard field goal by Art Brandstatter Jr.

Soccer—**October 21, 1961 (H):** Indiana managed only one shot on goal as MSU totally dominated the Hoosiers, 10-0. It was the fourth shutout in five games for the Spartan goalie, captain Ted Saunders. The Michigan State scoring barrage was distributed as follows: Mabricio Ventura tallied four, Rubens Filizola booted in three, Jerry Heron netted two and Ted Seyfarth contributed one. In the process, Ventura, a 19-year-old from Kingston, Jamaica, established a new team scoring record with 31 career goals and 18 markers for 1961 that tied Cecil Heron's season record established in 1959.

Cross Country—**October 21, 1961 (H):** Again led by Jerry Young, MSU managed a one-point victory over previously undefeated Penn State in a dual-meet run over the Forest Akers layout. Young, the lanky senior from Berkley, crossed the finish line in 20:32.4 with plenty to spare. Roger Humbarger placed in fourth, Pat Stevens in sixth, Don Castle in seventh and Bob Fulcher, Hazel Park sophomore, battled his way by a Nittany Lion runner for the all-important ninth spot to secure the 28-27 win.

Football—**November 25, 1961 (H):** Featuring a pair of Sherman Lewis touchdowns (a 54-yard run and 57-yard pass from Pete Smith), MSU closed the 1961 season with a 34-7 victory over winless Illinois. Sherman's first TD came during a sequence when the offense baffled the Illini by running their plays in a crowd-pleasing no huddles, quick-snap fashion.

Hockey—**January 5-6, 1962 (H):** In the midst of a mini eight-game winning streak, the MSU skaters topped a good University of Minnesota team twice, 5-3 and 5-2. In the opening two minutes of the Friday night game, the Gophers were on a relentless attack when Carl Lackey picked up a loose puck, raced down the left side and fired

home an unassisted goal from 15 feet out at 2:03. Minnesota continued the pressure, but five minutes later the Spartans scored once more on a ten-footer by Art Thomas on a pass from Dick Johnstone. Second period goals by Gus Hendrickson and Jim Jacobson made it 4-0 before the visitors awakened with their first score followed by two power play goals in the opening three minutes of the final period. Nursing their 4-3 lead, Claude Fournel closed the scoring on an open-netter at 19:42. On the next night, a record crowd of 3,416 witnessed a near duplicate game. The first period ended with State leading 3-1 on goals by Johnstone, Fournel and Marty Quirk. Bob Doyle scored in the second and Lackey in the final seconds when Minnesota again opted to pull their goalie.

Basketball—**January 20, 1962 (A):** Guided by a pair of sophomores, Pete Gent and Fred Thomann, the Spartans defeated Michigan, 80-74, for their first conference win of the season. Gent collected 22 points and pulled down 17 rebounds, and Thomann, the big center, scored 21 and gathered in 15 caroms. The Spartans were in front throughout the final three quarters with the largest lead, 61-51, at the 11:16 mark. But this game, like so many, was not completed without a dramatic finish. The Wolverines clawed back to within two with 25 seconds remaining. Captain Art Schwarm was fouled, could not connect on the front end of the one-and-one, but did manage a tie-up on the rebound. Lonnie Sanders snared the ensuing jump ball and passed to Gent, who was likewise fouled and cooly converted both attempts. The 6' 3" forward later rebounded a U of M attempt to score and fed Schwarm for a game-ending lay-up.

Wrestling—**January 20, 1962 (A):** Trailing 11-2 midway through the Iowa meet, Coach Collins could only hope for a complete turnaround. Hap Frey provided a glimmer of hope in a 7-4 decision at 157 pounds, but 167-pound John McCray could do no better than a draw. In the 177-pound class, Alex Valcanoff edged his opponent, 2-1, to bring MSU within three points, 13-10. It was then up to the heavyweights. If John Baum could gain a decision, it would end 13-13. But, the big captain would have none of that. Wrestling as if possessed, he soon had his opponent turned over, and at 2:38, a pin ended it all. The final score: Michigan State 15, Iowa 13.

Swimming and Diving—**January 27, 1962 (H):** McCaffree's men totally dominated the Purdue Boilermakers, running up a score of 77-22, while winning every event except the diving. Spartan winners were Dan Jamieson, Bill Driver, George Brown, and Mike Corrigan with a 3:59.2 in the medley relay; Doug Rowe, with a 2:04.4 in the 220-yard freestyle; Jim White with a 23.3 in the 50-yard freestyle; Bill Wood with a varsity record of 2:05.9 in the 150-yard individual medley; 200-yard butterflyer Carl Shaar with a 2:01.8; Mike Wood with a 49.4 in the 100-yard freestyle; Jeff Mattson, with a 2:08.8 in the backstroke; Neil Watts with a 4:45.6 in the 440-yard freestyle; Dennis Ruppart with a 2:21.6 in the backstroke; and the quartet of Dennis Collins, Juergen Matt, Jim White and Dick Blazejewski with a 3:24.2 in the 400-yard freestyle relay.

Gymnastics—**February 3, 1962 (A):** Winning every event except the parallel bars, State easily outscored the Minnesota Gophers, 71-41. Jim Durkee led the way with a first on the horizontal bar, a second on the still rings, and a third on the trampoline for a total of 13 points. Other firsts came from Jerry George on the side horse; Steve Johnson on the trampoline; Dale Cooper on the still rings; Gani Browsh in the free exercise; and sophomore Dick Gilberto in the tumbling contest. As the team score mounted significantly in favor of MSU, Coach Szypula began making line-up switches to lessen the blow.

Fencing—**February 10, 1962 (A):** Charley Schmitter and his team traveled to Iowa City, Iowa, and returned with two wins, 14-13 over Wisconsin and 16-11 over the host Hawkeyes. The match against the Badgers was at 13-13 and one point to go in the foil competition. Bob Brooks was the hero as he defeated his competitor 5-4 to gain the winning team point. Against Iowa, both the epee and foil teams lost 5-4 decisions. It looked bleak, but fortunately, in Lou Salamone, Phil Slayton and Joe Antonetti, State had a strong sabre team. The trio outscored Iowa 8-1 to turn the final score in favor of the Spartans.

Basketball—**February 24, 1962 (H):** Reaching their highest point total of the conference season, State closed out the home schedule with a 97-85 defeat of Indiana University. Five Spartans scored in double figures: Lonnie Sanders 22, Pete Gent 22, Ted Williams 14, Fred Thomann and Bill Schwarz with 11 each. Two minutes into the second half, State had lost the 47-42 halftime lead and trailed 48-47. Pete Gent then responded with a 20-jumper at 17:52 and MSU never trailed thereafter.

Tennis—**May 5, 1962 (H):** After defeating Indiana University 8-1 on Friday, coach Stan Drobac's squad came back on Saturday for a duplicate 8-1 victory, this

time against the University of Illinois. It took Brian Eisner three sets to subdue his Illini opponent in the number one spot, 11-9, 3-6, 6-2, but after that, Tom Jamieson, Jack Damson, Ron Lickman and Tom Wierman each posted easy two set victories. With those five singles matches in the win column, the Spartans were assured of their ninth win of the season. The doubles teams continued by adding three points to the final score: Eisner-Damson 4-6, 6-3, 6-0; Dick Colby-Wierman 6-1, 6-3; and Jamieson-Bill Lau 6-0, 6-8, 7-5.

Golf—**May 7, 1962 (H):** In defeating Northwestern 22 1/2-13 1/2, the State fivesome raised their record to ten wins in a row. Buddy Badger shot a 71-75—146 to earn medalist honors and gain 5 1/2 team points. Other Spartans, their 36-hole scores and team points were as follows: Dan Townsend 75-72—147 for 6 points; Gary Barrett 77-72—149 for 5 points; Jim Neumann 77-77—154 for 2 points; Jon Overgard 75-81—156 for 2 points and Gary Panks 84-77—161 for 2 points.

Track and Field—**May 12, 1962 (H):** In the only home appearance of the outdoor season, Michigan State garnered 75 1/2 points to outscore both Michigan 65 1/2 and Ohio State 31 1/2. It was only the second time ever that a Spartan track and field team managed to defeat the U of M. The sprinters led the way. In the 100-yard dash Sherman Lewis finished first in 9.8, followed by Zach Ford in second and Ron Watkins in fourth. Ford, Lewis and John Parker ran 1-2-3 in the 220. Moving up to the 440, Parker coasted home with a ten-yard lead in 48.5. Wilmer Johnson cleared 6' 5" to tie for first in the high jump, and Jerry Young and Clayton Ward purposely tied in the two-mile run; as the two locked arms and broke the tape together in 9:27.3. An additional smattering of seconds, thirds, and fourths throughout the entire program of events were instrumental in reaching the winning score. In the final event of the afternoon, the mile relay, MSU needed at least a second-place finish to secure the victory. After the final baton handoff, John Parker found himself in second place, but he wasn't willing to settle for anything but first. With a great burst of speed, he passed the Wolverine anchorman on the backstretch and pulled away to break the tape a good ten yards ahead in an impressive split time of 47.2 and composite time of 3:17.2.

Baseball—**May 16, 1962 (H):** Not wanting to overwork any one pitcher with the final Big Ten weekend two days away, Coach Kobs sent a parade of three, Gary Ronberg, Jack Nutter and Wes Klewicki, to the mound and they jointly responded by shutting out the Notre Dame hitters, 4-0. State scored one unearned run in the second on Jerry Lumianski's single to center. Jerry Sutton's single opened the three-run fourth and, following a sacrifice, scored on Dan Costello's base hit. Lumianski drilled his second hit, a triple to center, and he followed Costello home on a relay overthrow to third base.

ATHLETE OF THE YEAR

Gymnast Dale Cooper came to State from the Los Angeles, Calif., area in 1961 as a specialist in the still ring event. At five foot five and 140 pounds, he was not a large athlete but was extremely strong, as any competitor must be to successfully perform the ring event. His impact on the collegiate scene was immediate. In winning the first of three Big Ten titles (1962-1964), Dale scored a 99.5, the highest score ever awarded to a competitor in conference competition. He continued undefeated through three years, including championship performances at the NCAAs in 1962 and 1963. In his final appearance as a Spartan, at the 1964 national collegiate championships, he came out of one maneuver too soon in the eyes of one judge, and thus failed to win the gold as a senior. His routine was so spectacular that Japanese national officials extensively filmed his movements for training purposes.

Dale Cooper

IN THE SPARTLITE

Baseball: As in the preceding two years, the 1962 spring trip was played completely at military installations where the team could avail itself of the government's generosity of room and board. The stops included Camp LeJeune, Ft. Lee and Ft. Belvoir.

With a season average of .397, Jerry Sutton led the State hitters and was followed by three additional .300 hitters: Joe Porrevecchio at .392, Jeff Abrecht at .351 and Jerry Lumianski at .314. In post season honors, Porrevecchio was selected to the All-Big Ten first team.

The season ended abruptly following the 16-11 loss to the University of Detroit. The game at Notre Dame was rained out and the final doubleheader against Western Michigan was cancelled when the Broncos became an NCAA tournament team and had games scheduled on the same weekend.

Jerry Sutton batted .397 for MSU during the 1962 season.

Basketball: The 1961-1962 Ohio State team completed the regular season undefeated; consequently, they included MSU on their list of vanquished. Yet, the Spartans did not shrivel away in their only encounter with the Bucks, at Jenison on February 17. Playing before a sellout throng of 12,213, the Spartans led by 24-23, 26-25, 32-30, and left at intermission tied 32-32. OSU opened the second half with eight straight points and reality began to settle in. Regardless, Pete Gent, Lonnie Sanders, Bill Berry and crew never let up, climbing as close as 75-70 with 3:11 remaining, but that was as close as it would get. Jerry Lucas, John Havlicek and company prevailed 80-72.

Cross Country: Only once since 1951 had Michigan State failed to win the Big Ten championship. During that span the Spartans also captured five NCAA trophies. In the fall of 1961, the Iowa Hawkeyes broke the spell as their runners came through with finishes that netted 45 points to runner-up MSU's 59. Gerald Young placed second over the four-mile couse at Washington Park in Chicago. Also finishing in the top 15 were Roger Humbarger in 12th and Pat Stevens in 13th.

After losing their IC4A crown in1960, coach Fran Dittrich's squad returned to upset favored Penn State in 1961. Registering 82 points, eight better than the Nittany Lions, Spartan finishers were Gerry Young fourth, Don Castle 12th, Robert Fulcher 15th, Pat Stevens 28th and Ron Berby 39th.

Representing the school's second-lowest finish since the first NCAA meet in 1938, MSU settled for ninth place in the 23rd running of the collegiate championship meet. In the 18th spot, Gerry Young was the first Spartan to finish. Others that followed were Don Castle 57th, Patrick Stevens 69th, Michael Humbarger 77th and Robert Fulcher 79th.

Fencing: Featuring Bob "Clutch" Brooks as champion in epee competition, Charles Schmitter's crew scored 27 points at the Big Ten championship to finish in second place behind Illinois with 35 points. Brooks captured his title with a 5-4 verdict in a fence-off against the top man for the Illini. In foil, Nels Marin and captain Dick Schloemer finished fourth and fifth, and in sabre Joe Antonetti placed fifth.

Football: For the 1961 season, Coach Daugherty elected to move the home team bench to the east sideline, across from the press box.

The Spartans of 1961 embraced a particularly stingy defensive unit. They surrendered a meager seven touchdowns over the entire nine-game schedule.

Only marred by defeats from Duffy's two nemeses, Minnesota and Purdue, the 7-2 Spartans of 1961 wound up third in the conference and eighth in the national ratings.

Fullback George Saimes and guard Dave Behrman, both juniors, gained All-American recognition.

Golf: After completing an impressive 11-2 dual meet record, finishing seventh in the Big Ten championships at Champaign, Ill., was an extremely disappointing conclusion to the season. The 72-hole cards for the five-man team were as follows: Buddy Badger 302, Clint Townsend 303, James Neumann 309, Tom Early 310 and Gary Barrett 317.

Gymnastics: Coach Szypula's squad scored 106 1/2 points to gain the runner-up spot at the 1962 Big Ten championships in Columbus, Ohio. In addition to Dale Cooper's title in the still rings, two other Spartans emerged as champions. Gani Browsh defeated the defending champion to win in free exercise and Steve Johnson edged out two previous Big Ten and NCAA winners in capturing the trampoline event. After qualifying first on the high bar, tragedy hit team captain Jim Durkee. On his dismount in the finals, he hit the bar and fell, dislocating

Cross country captain Jerry Young sets the pace in a one-point victory over Penn State, 28-27.

his elbow. Adding to the team point total were Larry Bassett, Wayne Bergstrom, Dick Giliberto, John Brodeur and Jerry George, who placed in four events.

Cooper and Johnson maintained their winning edge three weeks later as they won NCAA titles at the championships in Albuquerque, N.M. Scoring 52 1/2 team points, State finished in the fifth spot.

Hockey: From the standpoint of the won-loss columns, this was a season of two seasons for MSU hockey. In the first 15 games, the skaters posted a record of 12-2-1 to sit atop the Western Collegiate Hockey Association (WCHA) standings. They then closed out the regular season winless at 0-8-0. Regardless, they ended up qualifying for the WCHA tournament as the fourth and final team. Losing 5-1 to the eventual NCAA champions of Michigan Tech in the opening round, they came back in the consolation game to defeat Denver 4-3 in overtime.

Finishing the season as the top three scorers on the team, Bessone's "French Line" of Claude Fornell, Real Turcotte and Bob Doyle accounted for 87 of the team's 224 point total. At the other end of the ice, goalie John Chandik was selected as the first team All-American.

Soccer: Carrying an unblemished 8-0 record, MSU concluded the schedule by hosting St. Louis University on November 11 with a likely NCAA playoff berth at stake. With a record crowd of 4,500 on hand, the Billikens scored in the closing minutes of the opening period. Fans displayed little concern—after all, the Spartans had averaged nearly six points a game through the season. It was just a matter of time, or was it? This team from Missouri had been a jinx. In nearly six years of competition, State had won 42 games and lost only three with two of those setbacks handed to them by the St. Louis team. Along with balls ricocheting off the cross bar and just outside the posts, State outshot their guests 17-4; but there was no additional scoring this afternoon, the 1-0 score stood. It was a sad close to the second 8-1 season in a row.

Swimming and Diving: Coach McCaffree took advantage of a new NCAA policy that permitted junior college transfer students to become immediately eligible for competition. Doug Rowe had come to East Lansing following a two-year career at Long Beach (Calif.) Junior College, where he had set three national JC records. He teamed with Jeff Mattson, Bill Wood and Mike Wood (no relation) to win the Big Ten and NCAA 400-yard freestyle events, setting a new Ameri-

can record of 3:15.5 in the process. Also, at that year's conference meet in Bloomington, Ind., Mike Wood captured the 220-yard freestyle event to become MSU's only individual winner. Mattson contributed with runner-up appearances in both the 50- and 100-yard freestyle, while five other Spartans placed sixth or higher in individual events. They were butterflyer Carl Shaar, freestyler Jim White, breaststroker Bill Driver, Rowe and Bill Wood. With a total of 96 1/2 points, State ended up in fourth place.

In addition to winning the relay at the national championships, Mike Wood was third in the 220, Mattson was fourth in the 100-yard backstroke and Bill Wood was sixth in the individual medley.

Tennis: For the first time in four years, MSU did not come up with an individual title at the Big Ten championship held in Minneapolis, Minn. The number two doubles team of Dick Colby and Tom Wierman came the closest by winning three matches before losing in the finals. Regardless, State corralled 29 points, good enough for third place.

Track and Field: Amidst a team hobbled with injuries, illnesses and poor performances, sophomore Sherman Lewis accounted for 14 1/2 of State's 28 points at the Big Ten indoor championships held in Jenison Fieldhouse. He was the surprise of the meet, taking the broad jump with his career-best leap of 24' 6" and also running a swift 31.2 for a gold medal in the 300-yard sprint. In addition, the Louisville, Ky., sophomore placed second in the 60-yard dash and led off the mile relay that tied for fifth place. Other members of that relay were Bill Green, Herman Johnson and Ron Horning.

Moving on to Madison Square Garden and the IC4A indoor championships, Lewis easily captured first place in the broad jump with a leap 23' 11".

Compiling 34.4 team points, Michigan State finished the conference outdoor championships in third place. Jerry Young was the only Spartan to capture a title as he negotiated the two-mile run in 9:12.0. Runner-ups and their respective events included: Zach Ford in the 100, Sherman Lewis in the 220, and high hurdler Herman Johnson. Third-place finishers were Jerry Dehenau in the pole vault, high jumper Wilmer Johnson, Lewis in the 100, and Don Castle with a 4:13.4 in the one-mile run.

By winning the 400-meter hurdles in 50.3, Willie Atterberry contributed to the 128-107 USA victory over the Russian national team in a special meet at Stanford, Calif. Atterberry last ran as a Spartan in 1960.

Wrestling: While relinquishing their 1961 team title, MSU tumbled all the way to fifth place at the Big Ten championships in Minneapolis, Minn. State's best showing came in the opening match when George Hobbs placed second in the 123-pound division. Heavyweight John Baum, who had been undefeated all year, lost in the consolation match to the 1961 conference champion from Northwestern. Also scoring team points for the Spartans were Tom Mulder, fourth at 137 pouns; Walt Byington, fourth at 147; and Alex Valcanoff, third at 177 pounds.

Three weeks later in the NCAA championships at Stillwater, Okla., 115-pound Okla Johnson and Baum both took third place as State finished tied for ninth.

MSU
1962-1963

TALES TO TELL

When athletic director Biggie Munn sought a replacement for the veteran John Kobs in 1963, he vowed to find the "best college baseball coach in the country." With that pledge, Biggie brought the obvious question to his good friend, Dr. Robert Jones, "Who is the best baseball coach in the country?" Doc brought the puzzle to his son Robert Jr. (SW 1969-70), and the teenager's answer was relayed back to the AD: "Danny Litwhiler of Florida State."

Munn accepted the answer and telephoned Litwhiler in Tallahassee. Although flattered, Danny initially conceded no interest in the move. With assistant professorial rank and an annual $9,000 salary, he avowed to be content in the Sunshine State. Yet, through the coaching fraternity, Danny had worked with John Kobs and so was familiar with the Big Ten Conference. He had second thoughts. At least a trip to East Lansing seemed appropriate, and in early July of 1963, Danny flew into the Capitol City airport. His visit proved to be a pleasant experience, and he was favorably impressed as President Hannah proposed a full professorship and Biggie offered a salary of $13,500.

Upon returning to Florida, Litwhiler confided in Gordon Blackwell, his school's president, and a counter offer of $11,000 was extended. This was the maximum proposition available at Florida State for faculty members not holding a doctorate. However, the tenacious Munn wasn't through, and he telephoned an improved proposition of $15,000. Litwhiler didn't hesitate—this was an offer he couldn't refuse. The Spartans signed "the best college baseball coach in the country."

Danny Litwhiler replaced John Kobs as the Spartans' head baseball coach in 1963.

HEADLINES of 1963

- Dr. Martin Luther King Jr. leads a massive march on Washington in support of equal rights for blacks and delivers his famous speech, "I have a dream . . ."
- Popular TV series of the time include: *The Twilight Zone, Mr. Ed, Perry Mason, Dr. Kildare, Gunsmoke, Leave it to Beaver, Bonanza, The Beverly Hillbillies,* and *The Dick VanDyke Show.*
- The most expensive motion picture to date ($37 million), *Cleopatra,* opens in theaters nationwide.
- Polaroid introduces color film, and for the first time color TV is relayed via satellite.

SCOREBOARD

	W	L	T	Avg.
Baseball	18	14	1	.561
Track and Field	2	0	0	1.000
Football	5	4	0	.555
Basketball	4	16	0	.200
Tennis	16	5	0	.762
Cross Country	1	2	0	.333
Swimming and Diving	8	4	0	.667
Wrestling	7	3	0	.700
Hockey	11	12	0	.478
Fencing	7	3	0	.700
Golf	8	4	1	.615
Gymnastics	7	3	0	.700
Soccer	9	2	0	.818

TEAM OF THE YEAR

Although finishing the dual-meet season with a less than perfect 7-3 record, the Michigan State fencing squad rose to the occasion when tournament time came along. Hosting the annual Big Ten meet in the IM sports arena and being led by the "S" men, Schloemer, Salamone and Slayton, MSU scored 33 bout victories to win the school's first conference fencing team title. Defending champions Illinois and Wisconsin were both close with 31 each, Ohio State scored 15, Iowa posted 10 and Indiana finished with nine. Lou "Lulu" Salamone and Phil Slayton finished one-two in the sabre competition. The outcome of the meet came down to foilsman Dick Schloemer, an East Lansing senior. He had registered a 4-1 record in the finals and shared the top spot with a member of the Wisconsin team. This necessitated a fence-off. It was the final duel of the day, and the team title rested on the outcome. With all eyes focused on the pair, several off-target actions ensued before Schloemer landed the winning contact to capture the foil title and ensure the Spartan win. He was immediately swamped by his teammates. Other contributors for the Spartans were John Pelletier, fourth in epee, and Nels Marin, fifth in foil. Highlighting his 25th year as head coach, the championship was a fitting reward for Charley Schmitter.

The 1963 fencing team. (Kneeling, left to right) Dick Schloemer and Lou Salamone; (back row, left to right) Nels Marin, Bob Brooks, John Pelletier and Phil Slayton.

MAKING HISTORY

For the first time ever, a Michigan State hockey team swept all four regular season games played against the University of Michigan. The first two wins, 2-1 and 4-3, were played in Ann Arbor and were as closely matched as the scores would indicate. In game number one, State spotted the Wolverines one goal and matched it in the third period before scoring the winner at 2:16 of overtime. On the next night, Michigan scored first once more, but this time Amo's gang countered with four straight goals and then hung on for the season's second win against the arch rival. The third game, three months later back in East Lansing, was never in doubt as the Spartans scored the first four goals and won with ease, 6-2. On Saturday night, the fourth game of the rivalry was a 2-1 win with Doug Roberts scoring both MSU goals, one late in the second period and another early in the third. It seems only fair to note that being entrenched in the cellar of the Western Collegiate Hockey Association, this was not a talented Wolverine team.

In the double dual swimming meet against Northwestern and Bowling Green, Coach McCaffree put together a 400-yard freestyle relay that swam a 3:14.4, which eclipsed the NCAA record of the time. The foursome and their splits were: Jeff Mattson (48.7), Dick Gretzinger (49.4), Bill Wood (48.1), and Mike Wood (48.2).

During game time-outs, basketball coach Forddy Anderson began using canvas camping stools as seats for players. The idea was not ongoing but later was reintroduced by Jud Heathcote. It has since been replicated by many other college coaches.

Beginning with meetings in February of 1963, the Lacrosse Club was first organized with the intent of eventually gaining varsity status. Three games were scheduled for April.

The six-mile run was added to the NCAA track and field championship format.

GREAT STATE DATES

Football—October 13, 1962 (H): Before a record crowd of 77,501, MSU managed four touchdowns to defeat Michigan with a score identical to the year before, 28-0. Seven minutes into the game, Sherm Lewis opened the scoring on a seven-yard pass play from quarterback

Pete Smith off a fake field goal. Three minutes later, back-up quarterback Charlie Migyanka found Lonnie Sanders on a pass-and-run scoring play from the Wolverines' 18-yard line. Twice in the second half, Lewis concluded scoring drives with short carries over the goal. If this final score does not illustrate State's dominance, perhaps these statistics will: (a) in total offense, the U of M managed 112 yards, as opposed to Michigan State's 459; (b) the visitors failed to capitalize on seven turnovers; and (c) the Spartans never punted in the entire 60 minutes of play.

Football—October 20, 1962 (A): An all-day drizzle that contributed to a soggy and slippery playing field in South Bend did not detour the Spartans' powerful ground attack. Rolling up a devastating 411 rushing yards, State topped the Irish 31-7 and thus became the first school to ever defeat Notre Dame seven years in succession. For the second year in a row, George Saimes was the star of the game, as he scored three times, from 54 yards, 15 yards and 49 yards. Yet, the longest scoring run of the afternoon was credited to Sherman Lewis, who sped around and down the sideline for a 72-yard sprint in the opening quarter.

Cross Country—October 27, 1962 (H): Finishing in a cluster from positions three through seven, State outscored Notre Dame, 25-34. Crossing the finish line in that order were Roger Humbarger, Jan Bowen, Don Castle, Bob Fulcher and Mike Kaines. Bowen, a sophomore, might well have been the winner that afternoon. He jumped out early and led by 20 yards at the two-mile marker, but he veered off course and was approximately 100 yards down the wrong path before returning to the race. MSU's Dick Gyde and Pat Stevens were the ninth and 10th finishers which, by the rules of cross country scoring, forced the Irish runners into the 11th and 12th spots for team scoring purposes.

Soccer—November 3, 1962 (A): Sophomore Dennis Checkett and senior Rubens Filizola each scored three goals to lead the Spartans to a 12-0 trouncing of Indiana University. Jean Lohri, Mabricio Ventura, Cezar Dominguez, Reinier "Dutch" Kemeling, Earl Thiele and George Rendon contributed one goal each. The shutout was goalie Bill Onopa's fifth of the season and his third in a row.

Basketball—December 8, 1962 (H): Scoring 17 straight points to break a 29-29 tie, Michigan State went on to defeat the University of Kansas, 81-62. Pete Gent

and Marcus Sanders paced the Spartans with 22 and 20 points. The statistics weighed heavily in favor of the Spartans as they shot 42 percent from the field as opposed to 29 percent for the Jayhawks. Led by Bill Berry with 26, State also out-rebounded KU, 67-52.

Hockey—**December 8, 1962 (H):** As a mid-season graduate, Claude Fornell played his final game for the Spartans in the 6-5 defeat of North Dakota. And what a way to end his career! Trailing 5-4 with 3:42 remaining in the final period, Fornell took a pass from Bob Doyle to tie the score and then 17 seconds later connected with the winning goal on an assist from Real Turcotte, who was also playing his final game for the Spartans.

Basketball—**January 12, 1963 (A):** Desperate for a victory following a 1-5 season start, Coach Anderson installed a slow and deliberate style of offense and a zone defense against the University of Wisconsin, and it worked for a 75-68 victory. Ted Williams, the 6' 7" pivot man, playing his first game of the season, had 14 points and 11 rebounds. Held to three points in the opening half, Pete Gent came back for 16 in the second half and a game-leading total of 19. Including 10 free throws, Bill Berry scored a total of 14, Marcus Sanders had 11, and Jack Lamers finished with nine.

Swimming and Diving—**January 12, 1963 (A):** Opening the season in Iowa City, State captured every event except diving to easily defeat the Hawkeyes, 73-32. Mike Wood was the only double winner, taking both the 100 and 200-yard freestyle events. Other individual firsts were registered by Denny Collins in the 50-yard freestyle, Neil Watts in the 500-yard freestyle, Dick Gretzinger in the individual medley, Chuck Strong in the butterfly, Jeff Mattson in the backstroke and Bill Driver in the breaststroke.

Wrestling—**February 9, 1963 (A):** State wrestlers won the opening four matches against Illinois: Gary Smith with a 5-0 decision at 123 pounds; Cecil Holmes, a 4-3 victor at 130 pounds; Dave James, a 4-1 winner at 134 pounds, and Monty Byington in a close 7-6 decision at 147 pounds. Then it was the Illini's turn, as they gained victories in the next three divisions: at 157 pounds, 167, pounds and 177 pounds. With the score favoring State at 12-9, a tie in the concluding heavyweight match would seal the win, and that's exactly what Homer McClure delivered a 1-1 draw. The final score was 14-11.

Gymnastics—**February 15, 1963 (H):** The MSU winning score of 79-21 would suggest a rather one-sided

win over the University of Illinois. Another clue would be to notice that State's gymnasts finished one-two in six of the seven individual events as follows: Jerry George and Dick Gilberto in floor exercise; John Noble and Jim Gregg on the trampoline; Manuel Turchan and George on side horse; Bob Carman and Turchan on the horizontal bar; George and John Brodeur on the parallel bars; and Dale Cooper and George on the still rings. In tumbling, the only event won by an Illini, Dick Gilberto placed second.

Wrestling—**February 16, 1963 (H):** With one match to go, the score stood at Michigan State 11, Iowa 11, and it was once more up to the heavyweights. Completing a rather lethargic three periods, State's 240-pound Homer McClure earned a 2-1 verdict with the deciding point coming on "riding time." The final score read 14-11 in favor of the Spartans. Earning the other 11 team points were Gary Smith at 123, Monty Byington on a draw at 147, Hap Frey at 157, and Alex Valcanoff in a close 3-2 decision at 177 pounds.

Fencing—**February 16, 1963 (H):** In an unusual split schedule, the fencers defeated Ohio State 15-12 in the morning and then came back to Jenison in the afternoon to defeat Notre Dame 17-10. Led by the co-captains Bob Brooks and John Pelletier, the epeemen turned back both the Bucks 5-4 and the Irish 6-3. Dick Schloemer, and his foil squad lost to OSU 6-3 and then turned that same score around against ND. Featuring Lou Salamone and Phil Slayton, the sabre trio first defeated the Buckeyes 7-2 and then Notre Dame 5-4.

Hockey—**March 2, 1963 (H):** The Spartan skaters finished the season on a high note as they jumped to a 5-1 lead in the opening period and then went on to defeat a highly-favored University of Minnesota team, 6-3. Picking up the offense for the injured and side-lined Doug Roberts and Bob Doyle, Mal Orme and Tony Elliot each scored a pair of goals. Two of the first period goals were scored by Art Thomas and Dick Johnstone, the latter unassisted. State's goalie John Chandik was busy turning back 34 of 37 shots on goal.

Tennis—**April 20, 1963 (A):** The Spartans, playing without captain Jack Damson, who had been hospitalized with a foot infection, earned two team victories during their stop in Champaign, Ill. They first edged the visiting University of Wisconsin team 5-4 and then defeated the host Illini, 6-3. With threatening weather closing in, the opening matches against the Badgers were ex-

peditiously played in a one-set pro format, in which the victor had to win eight games instead of six. Gaining the five team points against Wisconsin were Tom Jamieson, Tom Weirman, Dwight Shelton, Charles Wolff and the doubles team of Jamieson-Tony O'Donnell. Winners against the University of Illinois were Jamieson, O'Donnell, Shelton, Wolff, and Dave Click, along with the number three doubles team of Wolff-Bill Bremer.

Golf—**April 27, 1963 (H):** In an early season triple-dual meet, MSU defeated Northern Illinois 16 1/2-14 1/2 and Notre Dame 21-16. Scores for the Spartans were Bob Meyers, who was medalist with a 74-75—149; Gary Panks 79-73—152; Phil Marston 77-75—154; Tom Gorman 80-79—159 and Doug Swartz 83-81—164. Dennis McDonnell shot a 76 morning round and Shep Richard shot a 76 as his replacement in the afternoon.

Baseball—**May 4, 1963 (H):** Banging out 14 hits, including a pair of home runs, Michigan State batters ruffled four Iowa Hawkeye pitchers for an easy 16-8 victory. The Spartans jumped out early with six runs in the opening inning, including catcher George Azar's bases-loaded home run. Third baseman Joe Porrevecchio accounted for the other four-bagger with a second-inning two-run liner that cleared the fence. The remaining eight runs were amassed over the next three innings.

Baseball—**May 11, 1963 (H):** With both first baseman Jerry Sutton and center fielder Bob Maniere nursing leg injuries, Coach Kobs was forced to face Michigan with a patched-up line-up. However, pitcher Doug Dobrei was in complete control for a well pitched 3-1 victory. He did not allow a hit until the fourth inning as he struck out seven of the first nine men he faced. He weakened a little in the sixth when the Wolverines gained their only run on a walk and two base hits. By then the Spartans had scored their three runs. An error behind singles by Dennis Ketchum and Joe Porrevicchio gave State a run in the first, and a walk and hits by Mal Chiljean, Porreviecchio and Sam Calderone made it 3-0 in the third.

Track and Field—**May 11, 1963 (H):** After completing what seemed to be the final event of the afternoon, the one-mile relay, the Spartans had outscored Notre Dame, 69-61. Then the question arose as to whether the hop-step-jump event, conducted earlier in the day, should have been included in the team scoring. There was disagreement. MSU's Karl Schlademan had considered it an exhibition event and had not even en-

tered competitors. Alex Wilson, the Notre Dame coach, thought otherwise and was insistent that his boys' 1-2-3 finish be included, thus switching the final score to read 70-69 in favor of the Irish. Eventually, a compromise was reached in which State could at least have an entrant. So after nearly everyone had left for home, coach Fran Dittrich retrieved Sherman Lewis from the locker room. Lewis, who had already won the broad jump and placed second in both sprint events, needed only a third place to preserve a Spartan victory. Sherm, the team captain, was better than that, as he proceeded to leap 42 feet and gain second place. That legitimately sealed it for Michigan State, 72-67.

Golf—**May 11, 1963 (A):** In one afternoon at Evanston, Ill., Ben VanAlstyne's golfers won more than half of their season's victories. Completing 36 holes, the five-man MSU team combined for a total of 770 strokes. This bettered Purdue with 775, host Northwestern with 779 and Illinois with 804. Completing a card of 75-75—150, the Spartans' Phil Marston finished with runner-up honors. Also competing for Michigan State were Bob Meyer, John Hunter, Shep Richard, Gary Panks and Dennis McDonnell.

ATHLETE OF THE YEAR

At five-foot-10 and 186 pounds, fullback-linebacker George Saimes was not physically large when compared to the bruising players of more contemporary times. Yet, to even the most casual observer, the Canton, Ohio, native seemed to relish the contact he encountered on both sides of the line as a two-way player. He is remembered as the one who wore five-pound "spats" on each ankle to strengthen his leg muscles during the summer. Fred Stabley notes in his book *The Spartans,* that "Saimes's name appears nowhere among all-time outstanding performances in State's record book." Yet anyone who saw him in action would endorse him as one of the super backs in the school's football history. He had no glittering specialty but was a consummate all-around back, able in blocking, tackling, running, pass receiving, and defense. He rarely made a mistake. George was the team-rushing leader in both 1961 and 1962 and recorded a three-year total of 1,253 yards and 18 touchdowns. Upon concluding his senior season in 1962, Saimes was chosen as an All-American by seven of the more prestigious se-

lection committees of the time, including the Associated Press, United Press, Football Writers Association, and the Football Coaches Association. Although his professional career was short lived, he eventually earned All-Pro honors as a defensive back with the Buffalo Bills.

George Saimes

IN THE SPARTLITE

Baseball: The 1963 team, which compiled a record of 18-14-1, was John Kobs's final as head coach. In 39 years of coaching, his teams won 557 games against 364 losses for a winning average of .605.

Upon completing his final year, Coach Kobs was honored by the National Rockne Club as the Collegiate Baseball Coach of the Year on March 5, 1964 in Kansas City.

First baseman Jerry Sutton and left fielder Joe Porrevecchio were both selected to the 1963 All-Big Ten first team.

Basketball: With a record of 4-16, the 1962-1963 season was the most disappointing since 1949-1950 when Al Kircher's team went 4-18. The schedule concluded with nine straight losses as the opposition averaged 92 points a game.

The Spartans were busy absorbing some records thrown at them in Bloomington, Ind., on February 23. The Hoosiers' hot-shooting Jimmy Rahl unleashed 48 field goal attempts, connected on 23, and scored a total of 56 points, all Big Ten records that have survived.

Jenison Fieldhouse was the site of an NCAA regional tournament that included Loyola of Chicago, Illinois, Bowling Green and Mississippi State. Those Bulldogs from the south had to literally sneak out of town to join the competition. There were factions down there that opposed participating against teams that included black players. Loyola eventually won this regional and was crowned NCAA champion at the Final Four in Louisville, Ky.

Cross Country: For the 10th time in 12 years, the MSU runners captured the conference title. The first four State runners were so closely bunched that only 22 seconds separated them. The scorers were Jan Bowen third, Roger Humbarger fifth, Don Castle seventh, Mike Kaines eighth and Bob Fulcher 16th.

Of the 14 teams entered in the 24th NCAA championship run, Michigan State placed fifth. Spartan finishers and their team placements were: Humbarger 15th, Castle 18th, Bowen 26th, Kaines 35th and Fulcher 53rd. Finishing the conference championship run with 39 points, the Spartans were 25 better than the nearest competitor, the host team from the University of Iowa.

Fencing: Season-ending statistics showed Dick Schloemer the leader with a record of 24-3. He was followed by Lou Solomon at 17-11.

Football: Ranked sixth in preseason, the 1962 team tumbled from the polls early upon losing the season opener to Stanford, 16-13.

As restricted by conference policy at the time, traveling squads were limited to 40 players. That number was later increased to 44 in 1967 and other increment changes through the years until it reached the current limit of 70.

At season's end, guard Earl Lattimer and halfback Sherman Lewis gained All-American recognition.

Golf: State closed the season tied with Illinois for seventh place in the conference championships held in Madison, Wis. The 72-hole scores for each of the Spartans were: Phil Marston 310, Gary Panks 311, Bob Meyer 312, Shep Richards 318, Dennis MacDonell 318 and John Hunter 322.

Gymnastics: Scoring 51 points, State finished fourth in the eight-team field at the conference championships held at Jenison Fieldhouse. This is likely the highest spot that could have been expected. Beyond Dale Cooper, who even had to share the still rings title, this was not a deeply talented gymnastics squad.

Cooper, undefeated in dual-meet competition for two straight years, won his second straight still rings title at the NCAA championships in Pittsburgh. Cooper's performance pushed MSU into a tie with Illinois and Yale for 11th place in the team standings.

Hockey: Although falling short of a .500 season with an 11-12 overall record, the 1962-1963 team was the most successful since the NCAA tournament squad of 1959.

With both Real Turcotte and Claude Fournel graduating at midseason, Coach Bessone lost his top two scorers from 1961-1962 after only nine games of action. The top scorers of the total 23-game 1962-1963 season were two center linemen, Dick Johnstone with 29 points and Bob Doyle with 27. At season's end, writers of the *Denver Post* newspaper selected centerman Johnstone to its first team All-WCHA. Defenseman Carl Lackey and Bob Doyle, another center iceman, were designated with second-team honors.

Soccer: For the second year in a row, Michigan State concluded its soccer season with a loss to St. Louis University. Before a home crowd of 7,500, the Billikens eliminated State from the NCAA tournament, 2-0. The outcome of the game was in doubt until the second goal was scored on a penalty kick in the waning minutes of the final stanza.

Swimming and Diving: A record-setting 2,059 fans packed the IM pool bleachers to watch the undefeated Indiana Hoosiers stretch their dual meet winning streak to 26 in a row with a hard earned 61-44 victory over the Spartans.

The only bright spot of Michigan State's fifth place finish at the Big Ten conference meet was Jeff Mattson's victory in the 100-yard backstroke event, in which he posted an impressive time of 54.6. Two weeks later at the NCAA championships in Raleigh N.C., Mattson swam a 54.0, good enough for second place. Other finalists at those nationals were Bill Wood, sixth in the individual medley, and Bill Driver, sixth in the 100-yard breaststroke. Rounding out the scoring, the freestyle relay team placed fifth in a time of 3:15.1. With 15 points, State tied Princeton for seventh place in the team standings.

Tennis: Michigan State concluded its spring trip by winning the Cherry Blossom tournament held in Washington, D.C. They earned their way to the title by defeating Dartmouth, 7-2, George Washington, 5-4 and Georgetown 5-4.

With 30 1/2 points, State ended up in the fourth spot at the Big Ten conference championships held on the Northwestern University courts. Two Spartans reached the finals but did not survive, number three Jack Damson and number five Dwight Shelton. Finishing third by winning consolation matches were number six Charles Wolff and the number three doubles team of Tom Wierman-Shelton.

Track and Field: Led by Sherman Lewis and Bobby Moreland, Michigan State scored 30 points at the Big Ten indoor meet in Madison to finish in fourth place. Lewis won the broad jump with a leap of 23' 8 1/2" and placed second in the 300-yard dash and fifth in the 60-yard dash. Moreland won that 60-yard dash in a clocking of 6.1, which tied the conference record.

In an impressive performance, State captured three firsts at the historic Penn Relays. The relay team of Moreland, John Parker, Walker Beverly and Sherman Lewis won both the 440-yard and the 880-yard relays, and Moreland mixed in a 9.5 100-yard dash for yet another gold-medal performance.

With 31 points, MSU finished fourth at the outdoor conference championships hosted by the University of Minnesota. Heading the State contingency were Jan Bowen, who won the one-mile run, and Moreland, who was runner-up in both the 100 and 200-yard dashes. Other Spartan finishers were Parker, third in the 440; Jim Mather, fourth in the 660; Mike Kaines, fourth in the mile; Peckham, fourth in the high hurdles; and Bill Berry of the basketball team, third in the high jump.

Wrestling: As wrestling became a more significant interscholastic sport throughout Michigan, Coach Grady Penninger continued to lure talent from Oklahoma. The 1963 squad included six Sooners: Homer McClure, Bob Archer, Hap Fry, David James, Cecil Holmes and Gary Smith.

The eighth-place finish at the conference championships was a big disappointment as not one Spartan reached the finals. The only bright spots came in the consolation brackets, where Happy Fry placed third at 157, Okla Johnson was fourth at 123 and David James finished fourth at 137.

MSU
1963-1964

TALES TO TELL

With a conference mark of 4-0-1 going into the season finale at home against the University of Illinois at 4-1-1, the Big Ten football title and Rose Bowl berth were at stake on Saturday, Nov. 23, 1963. On the day before that showdown game, the nation was stunned by the assassination of president John F. Kennedy in Dallas, Texas. While many Saturday games were immediately canceled, the important Michigan State-Illinois game remained a "go" until a few hours before kickoff. Eventually, responding to public pressure, all Big Ten action for that day was postponed. The title game was rescheduled for the following Thursday, Thanksgiving Day. In the ensuing week of preparation, it seemed the two squads were apparently headed in opposite directions. From Fred Stabley's book, *The Spartans*:

"Illinois coaches were joyful as they took their club back home, they said later. They had felt their team was not emotionally keyed for the game, and this delay looked to them like a reprieve from disaster. Spartan coaches, conversely, felt their club had never been more eager and ready. To let off steam, the team ran through a dummy scrimmage that Saturday afternoon in the indoor baseball arena of the Men's IM building and simply exploded with spirit and ferocity.

But State was flat in practice the following week and never regained the fine competitive edge it had had on Saturday. However the Illinois team—again by the word of its own coaches—started rising and reached an excellent emotional pitch for the game."

Whatever the reason, State was never in the game. The Ilinois defense, with All-American linebacker Dick Butkus as its vanguard, created seven State turnovers on the afternoon, which eventually translated to a 13-0 defeat of the home team. Spartan fans quickly altered their plans for New Year's Day.

HEADLINES of 1964

- Jimmy Hoffa of the Teamsters is convicted of fraud in the misuse of union funds and of jury tampering.
- Beatle-mania spreads throughout the world as the Beatles singing group breaks all existing sales records with such hits as "She Loves You" and "I Want to Hold Your Hand."
- Cassius Clay (later known as Muhammad Ali) wins the heavyweight boxing title from Sonny Liston.
- Broadway musical hits of the year include "Fiddler on the Roof," "Funny Girl" and "Hello Dolly."

SCOREBOARD

	W	L	T	Avg.
Baseball	22	12	0	.647
Track and Field	4	1	0	.800
Football	6	2	1	.722
Basketball	14	10	0	.583
Tennis	14	6	0	.700
Cross Country	2	1	0	.667
Swimming and Diving	6	2	0	.750
Wrestling	5	5	1	.500
Hockey	8	17	1	.327
Fencing	7	4	0	.636
Golf	7	12	0	.368
Gymnastics	5	3	1	.611
Soccer	9	1	0	.900

TEAM OF THE YEAR

Since the inaugural MSU soccer season of 1956 and through 1963, the Spartans had amassed an impressive record of 50-7-3. To this total, the 1963 team contributed a regular season mark of 9-0, good enough to win the Midwest Collegiate Soccer Conference championship. That title was secured by defeating St. Louis University, 4-3, for victory number nine at home before 5,000. The hero was Van Dimitrou, a reserve forward, who was inserted into the game at the outset of the second quarter. Trailing 2-0, Dimitrou erupted for three goals to put State in front 3-2 at the half. Two minutes after St. Louis tied the game in the third period, Clare DeBoer booted home the eventual winning goal. Goalie Charlie Dedich and the defense held on for the cherished victory. Two weeks later, on November 22, the historic day on which President Kennedy was assassinated, St. Louis returned to East Lansing for the opening round of the NCAA tournament. Once more the Billikens were in form and they ended the Spartans' season, 2-0.

Pacing the team with 14 goals and 11 assists, was Bill Schwartz, a member of the basketball team, who belatedly decided to join Coach Kenney's soccer squad for the first time in 1963, his senior year. Also in his first varsity year, sophomore George Janes was second in scoring with 13 goals, 11 assists, and Payton Fuller, yet another sophomore, was third with 11 goals and eight assists.

The 1963 soccer team. Letter Winners were A. Dworken, S. Stelmashenko, S. Donnelly, G. Rendon, C. Checkett, L. Eckhardt, E. Thiele, C. DeBoer, C. Dedich, V. Dimitrou, L. Christoff, T. Enustun, P. Fuller, G. Janes, manager W. Horn.

MAKING HISTORY

The season of 1963-1964 was a prolific scoring season for the MSU basketball team. Over the 24 games (14 wins and 10 losses), the Spartans averaged 92.1 points to rank third nationally behind the University of Detroit with 96.1 and the University of Miami (Fla.) 95.44. State topped the 100 mark on 10 occasions. Including just the 14 games on the winning side of the ledger, the "scoring machine" averaged 99.8 points per game. As could be expected, there was little to boast about on defense. Over the entire schedule, opponents managed 89.8 points per game.

The total combined points (218) in the 118-100 basketball win over Oklahoma on December 21, 1963 remains as a team record. Three other scoring records established in 1963-1964 have since been tied: field goals made (50) against Oklahoma; field goals attempted (101) against Brigham Young; and rebounds (84) versus Iowa on February 15.

While gaining the 61-44 victory over the Ohio State swimming and diving team, Jim MacMillan won the 200-yard freestyle in 1:48.0, which bettered the Big Ten record and established a new pool and varsity record.

The 22 wins by the baseball team tied the regular season team record and a new team record was set with a total of 27 home runs.

GREAT STATE DATES

Cross Country—**October 19, 1963 (H):** Led by the 1-2 finish of sophomores Dick Sharkey and Eric Zemper, the Spartans defeated Penn State, 21-40. It was MSU's most impressive win over the Lions since the 1959 team posted a similar victory margin. Finishing fifth through seventh, Ron Berby, Jan Bowen and Mike Kaines closed out the scoring.

Football—**November 9, 1963 (A):** As usual, this was a football Saturday in which "all precincts had to be accounted for." First, Michigan State had defeated another stubborn Purdue University team, 23-0. Then came news from Champaign, Ill., that Michigan had upset previously unbeaten Illinois, 14-8. This all meant that three teams were in contention for the top spot: MSU at 4-0-1, Ohio State 3-0-1, and Illinois 3-1-1. Furthermore, it was apparent that a big game was brewing two weeks

hence when the Illini were to visit East Lansing. Back to West Lafayette, the obstinate Boilers yielded a mere field goal by halftime. Although the Spartans managed 20 points in the second half, only one score resulted from a sustained drive. The State victory was sealed on one touchdown via a fumble recovery and another with only five seconds of playing time remaining following an intercepted pass. The defense was penurious, yielding a scant 68 yards on the ground and 68 yards passing.

Soccer—**November 9, 1963 (H):** With a 4-3 upset win over St. Louis University, Gene Kenney's squad presented themselves with three reasons to celebrate. It was the first-ever win over the NCAA defending champion Billikens; it gave the Spartans the Midwest Collegiate Soccer Championship; and it ensured State a berth in the NCAA playoffs. Trailing 2-0 after the opening period, it was Van Dimitrious, a recent transfer from the U of M-Dearborn, who sparked the comeback by personally accounting for three straight goals. His go-ahead boot came with only 10 seconds remaining in the first half. Playing like true champions, St. Louis came back with a game-tying goal in the third period. Two minutes later, at 16:15, Clare DeBoer kicked in what would be the winning goal. Led by net-minder Charlie Dedich, the defense held on to seal the verdict in the battle of the two undefeated teams.

Football—**November 16, 1963 (H):** For an unprecedented eighth time in a row, Michigan State defeated Notre Dame, this time by a 12-7 score. On seven occasions during the afternoon, Spartan offensive errors turned the ball over, three times within the 25-yard line. Yet, the only incident on which the Fighting Irish capitalized was early in the first period, following a fumble recovery at the State 15-yard line. Thereafter, the mighty Spartan defense stood strong, as time and again they were forced to thwart an ND attack. Climaxing a 26-yard drive, the initial MSU score came on a three-yard run by Sherman Lewis with 2:52 remaining in the first half. When the two-point conversion attempt failed, the green and white continued to trail. As the score remained at 7-6 late in the third period, consider the emotional roller coaster experienced by the sellout crowd and TV audience. Recovering an errant center snap (one of those seven turnovers) the Irish took over at the State 18-yard line. In a position to put the game away, the visitors were only able to gain five yards before once more yielding position. Two plays later Lewis skirted off right tackle and, aided

by key blocks from Mike Currie and Tom Krezmienski, sprinted 85-yards for the deciding score. The remainder of the contest was a defensive struggle.

Hockey—**December 21, 1963 (A):** Colorado College held a 3-0 lead until Mac Orme finally put MSU on the scoreboard with only seconds remaining in the opening period. Rich Hargreaves scored for State in the second to pull within a point. Early in the final period, Orme, assisted by Doug Roberts, tied the game with his second goal, but at 18:08, the Tigers scored once more, making it 4-3 with 1:32 remaining. Pulling their goalie for another attacker, Don Heaphy, assisted by Orme, found the back of the Colorado net with only 46 seconds to play. In overtime, it took the Orme from Roberts connection only 29 seconds to seal the 5-4 Michigan State victory.

Swimming and Diving—**January 11, 1964 (H):** The Spartans opened the 1964 season by defeating the University of Iowa squad, 79-26, before 1,940 fans at the IM pool. En route to the one-sided victory, State captured 10 of the 11 events, losing only the springboard diving. Five of the eight individual winners were sophomores: Jim MacMillan in the 50-yard freestyle; Bob Sherwood, in the 100-yard freestyle; Darryle Kifer, in the 200-yard freestyle; Dennis Hill in the 200-yard individual medley and Lee Driver, who set a varsity record of 2:19.9 in the 200-yard breaststroke. Other victors were senior Chuck Strong in the 200-yard butterfly; junior Bob Desmond in the 200-yard backstroke; and junior Neil Watts with a varsity record-setting 5:10.8 in the 500-yard freestyle.

Hockey—**January 18, 1964 (A):** MSU completed its most successful weekend of the season, first defeating Ohio State 10-2 and then moving on to Athens, Ohio, for a two-game sweep of Ohio University, 11-1 and 7-4. State trailed in the second period of that final game, 4-1, and then awakened to score four unanswered goals and a 5-4 lead at the intermission. The Spartans continued their barrage with two markers in the final 20 minutes. The scoring was well distributed with Mike Coppa, Jim Jacobson, Doug Roberts, Mac Orme and Rich Hargreaves each netting a goal and captain Carl Lackey finding the mark for a pair of goals. Goaltender Harry Woolf was credited with 28 saves, while his Ohio counterpart stayed busy stopping 52 shots.

Gymnastics—**January 18, 1964 (H):** With five victories in the seven events, MSU defeated Ohio State, 60

1/2-51 1/2, in the second meet of the year. Those winners were Todd Gates on the parallel bars; Dave Price on the horizontal bar; Bill McFillen in tumbling; Ted Wilson, who tied for first on the side horse; and Dale Cooper, who brought his undefeated dual meet record on the still rings to 22 straight. The sport was proving to be dangerous. Bob Beguelin, filling in for the injured Jim Curzi, fell from the horizontal bar and dislocated his elbow.

Basketball—**February 15, 1964 (H):** The Michigan State-University of Iowa game at Jenison Fieldhouse was one of big numbers. The score, MSU 107, Iowa 82 gave State a 25-point victory margin, which was the greatest ever against the Hawkeyes. Six men were in double figures for State. Stan Washington led the way with 28, followed by Bill Schwartz with 14, Bill Berry 13, Marcus Sanders 11 and Pete Gent and Fred Thomann both had 10. A total of 57 fouls were whistled, of which 29 calls were on the home team, with four players, Gent, Sanders, Thomann and Berry, being sent to the bench with five each. Finally, with 84 rebounds, the Spartans equaled a team record established in 1959 against Ohio State.

Wrestling—**February 15, 1964 (A):** By a close 14-11 score, State defeated a solid Indiana University team that ultimately finished in third at the conference championships. Although the Spartans would never trail in the scoring, the final result was in question until Homer McClure closed it out with a 1-1 draw and two team points. Winners for MSU were Al Huckins in the opening square-off at 115-pounds; Joe Ganz, whose opponent at 137 pounds had been undefeated; 147-pound Bob Hansen, who filled in for the ailing Dick Cook; and Terry Leonard, a 2-1 winner at 167-pounds.

Fencing—**February 15, 1964 (H):** In their final home appearance of the season, the fencers defeated Iowa 15-12 and Wisconsin 18-9. Key men in the double victory were Lew Leonard, Nels Martin and Bryan Kurchins in foil; captain Lou Salamone and Mark Haskell in sabre; and epee duelers John Lewis and Joel Serlin.

Basketball—**March 7, 1964 (A):** Michigan State closed the season by defeating Ohio State, 81-80 for the school's first-ever basketball win in Columbus. Furthermore, it was the first home loss for OSU in 55 games and would ultimately cost them their fifth straight conference title. The Buckeyes held a halftime lead of seven points and stretchd it to 11 before MSU began their winning rally. With 2:22 remaining, Pete Gent hit a jumper

to finally put the Spartans in front, 75-74. With the Bucks having regained the lead, 80-79, and just eight seconds remaining, Gent became the ultimate hero as he connected one final time for the victory.

Golf—May 2, 1964 (H): Led by Phil Marston's 73-74—147, the Spartans pulled off a trifecta as they defeated the University of Wisconsin, Northwestern University and highly ranked Michigan all in one day at the Forest Akers Course. Deviating from the norm of six-man teams, agreement was reached with the coaches of the Badgers and Wildcats to use scores of seven players, while the meet with Michigan included cards of nine men. The eventual score against Wisconsin was 912 to 950 while the Wildcats were closer at 912 to 926. The nine-man scores versus Michigan were 1390-1407. Following Marston were Bob Meyer and Dick Marr with identical 77-75—152 scores. Behind them came Shep Richard and Doug Swartz with similar totals of 78-75—153; Ken Benson 74-81—155; Fred Mackey 62-76—158; Dave Miller 82-78—160 and Ron Hartman 79-81—160.

Track and Field—May 9, 1964 (A): Competing against the Notre Dame Irish as well as wind gusts that were recorded as strong as 30 mph, State won the second outdoor meet of the season, 67-55. Winners on the afternoon included Walker Beverly, in both the 100 and 220-yard dashes; Ayo Azikiwe in the intermediate hurdles; Bob Fulcher in the 880; Dave Mutcher in the shot put; Tom Herbert in the discus; Fred McKoy in the high jump; and Eric Zemper in the two-mile run. The final event, the mile relay, also went to the Spartans in a time of 3:19.2.

Tennis—May 9, 1964 (H): Posting their fifth shutout of the spring, State defeated Illinois 9-0 with no match going beyond the required two sets. In singles positions one through six with their winning scores were: Tom Jamieson 6-2, 6-1; Tony O'Donnell 14-12, 6-1; Dwight Shelton 8-6, 6-4; Charlie Wolff 6-3, 6-4; Laird Warner 11-9, 7-5; and Mike Youngs 6-3, 6-4. Winners in doubles were Jamieson-Wolff 6-4, 9-7; O'Donnell-Shelton 6-1, 6-3; and the sophomore pair of Warner and Youngs, 6-4, 7-5.

Baseball—May 18, 1964 (H): The University of Michigan scored two runs in the opening inning off starting pitcher Bill Collins, and after that he settled down allowing only five hits while holding the Wolverines scoreless the rest of the way. The Spartans got back in it during the fourth inning on a Dick Billings single, a Bruce Look double and a fielder's choice. One inning later, in the fifth, Billings stroked another base hit to left field,

this time delivering the eventual winning run for the 3-2 victory.

Baseball—May 26, 1964 (H): Playing amidst intermittent showers, MSU closed their home schedule under the lights of Lansing's Municipal Field with an 8-7 victory over Western Michigan. Three times the Spartans had to come from behind at 2-0, 5-3, and 7-6. That latter deficit was overcome in the bottom of the eight on RBI singles by John Biedenbach and Jerry Sutton. Howie Miller, the third of five State pitchers, threw to one batter in the eighth and was credited with his third win against two losses.

ATHLETE OF THE YEAR

A five-letterman in football and track (FB 1961-1963 and TR 1962-1963), Sherman Lewis was elected as a captain of both squads in 1963. At 152-pounds, he packed a mass of talent into a small frame. On the football field Lewis was regarded as one of the most dangerous breakaway runners in the game, as well as an accomplished receiver and dependable defensive back. Five of his carries during the 1963 season were for touchdowns of 80 yards or more: two on pass receptions, two on running plays and the fifth on a punt runback. During that senior year, Sherm was an All-American pick by the major selection committees: the Associated Press, the United Press, the Central Press and the Football Writers Association. Selected as the team's MVP,

Sherman Lewis

he finished third in the 1963 Heisman Trophy voting. Lewis concluded his Spartan career as number five on the school's rushing list, and number three in touchdowns and in total points scored. Despite the terrific pounding he took on the field, he never missed a minute of play due to injuries. For two years with the track team, Sherman contributed heavily as a sprinter, jumper and relay member. In 1962 he captured Big Ten indoor titles in both the broad jump and the 300-yard dash and repeated as jump champion in the following year.

IN THE SPARTLITE

Baseball: State ran off a string of seven straight wins on their southern trip before coach Danny Litwhiler took the team to Tallahassee, Fla., where his former team, the Florida State Seminoles, were inhospitable, handing the Spartans two setbacks, 10-5 and 7-6.

The 22 wins tied the regular season record and a new team record was set with a total of 27 home runs.

Basketball: It took two to outscore one. Marcus Sanders and Bill Schwarz combined for 49 points to offset a 48-point effort by Ohio State's Gary Bradds when MSU defeated the Bucks on the Jenison floor, 102-99.

Fred Thomann of Taylor Center, Mich., and Pete Gent from Bangor, Mich., shared the title of the team's MVP. Thomann was the team's top rebounder and Gent led the team in scoring with a 21.0 points per game.

Gent was selected by the Baltimore Bullets of the NBA in the 14th round of the draft, but talent scouts of the National Football League were more impressed. Although void of any college football experience, Gent was capriciously signed by the Dallas Cowboys and then proceeded to be a pleasant surprise, enjoying a successful five-year career as a pass receiver.

Cross Country: Cramming five runners into the top 16 slots over the University of Illinois course, State easily captured their second straight conference championship. The Spartans finished as follows: Dick Sharkey second, Jan Bowen 10th, Eric Zemper 11th, Ron Berby 15th and Paul McCollam 16th.

Coach Fran Dittrich's squad duplicated its fifth place NCAA finish of 1962. Placing for State were Dick Sharkey 10th, Jan Bowen 34th, Paul McCollam 48th, Ron Berby 77th and Mike Kaines 82nd.

Fencing: Traveling all the way to Colorado Springs, Colo., the fencing squad returned with a pair of wins, edging the host Air Force Academy, 14-13, and also defeating the University of Wisconsin, 15-12. One week later the two wins were forfeited when it was disclosed that two Spartans were ineligible at the time they competed.

Relinquishing to Illinois the Big Ten team title they had won in 1963, State settled for a second place tie with Iowa. The best performer for the Spartans was Bryan Kutchins, who finished second in the epee weapon. Lou Salamone, the defending sabre champion, dropped to fourth place.

Kutchins, Michigan State's lone entrant in the NCAA championship, failed to finish in the top 20.

Football: Gaining postseason honors, co-captains Sherm Lewis and end Dan Underwood were first-team All-Big Ten selections. Guard Earl Lattimer and fullback Roger Lopes were selected to the second-honor team.

Five Spartans were selected in the annual NFL draft, but none of them experienced an impact professional career. The five were: Matt Snorton by the Lions; Ed Lothamer and Roger Lopes by Baltimore; Herman Johnson by the Rams; and Sherman Lewis, by the Cleveland Browns.

Golf: At the Big Ten golf championships hosted by the University of Minnesota, Coach Brotzmann's team was led by Phil Marston, who fired a four-round total of 298. Other Spartan scorers were Bob Meyer and Ken Benson, both with 305, Shep Richard 310, Doug Swartz 318 and Dick Marr 323.

Gymnastics: The team suffered a crippling blow in the very first meet of the season when on January 11 sophomore sensation Jim Curzi dislocated a shoulder while performing on the horizontal bar. He was sidelined for more than a month, returning on February 22 to spearhead a 56-56 tie with Michigan.

Another intervening factor impacted the narrow 56-55 loss at Minnesota when NCAA champion Dale Cooper would forego the meet to submit to a physical examination for the U.S. naval air corps.

On February 9, in his final home appearance on the still rings, Cooper received a rare 100 from one of the four judges.

Jim Curzi captured the all-around title in the Big Ten Championships in Madison, Wis. The sophomore sensation won the horizontal bar event, and finished third in the long horse vault, fourth in the side horse, and fifth in both the parallel bars and floor exercise. Scoring a 9.75, Dale Cooper successfully defended his still ring title as Michigan State settled for a third-place finish.

Later, at the NCAA championships in Los Angeles, Cooper, a senior, was unsuccessful in an attempt to defend his two-time NCAA title. Suffering a significant flaw in his performance, he dropped all the way to seventh. Todd Fates finished 10th on the horizontal bars, while teammate Curzi gained 19 1/2 of the team's 23 1/2 points with a third on the horizontal bars, seventh on the horse vault, and a third-place finish in the all-around event. In the team standings, MSU finished in eighth place.

Hockey: A Western Intercollegiate Hockey League rule went into effect in June of 1963 that was designed to encourage American players and discourage the use of the older Canadian players. The rule noted that: (a) anyone who has played junior "A" hockey is ineligible and (b) anyone who competes in hockey after his 19th birthday, other than on a secondary or college level, will lose one year of eligibility for each year over 19.

Soccer: Although waiting until his senior year before trying his foot at soccer, Bill Schwarz, a starter on the basketball team, did more than earn a spot on the team. He ended up as the top scorer with 14 goals and 11 assists.

Selected to the postseason Midwest All-Conference team were captain Sam Donnelly at left halfback, Stan Stelmashenko at right fullback and George Janes at inside left.

Swimming and Diving: The dual meet at the University of Minnesota was a thriller. The winner was decided on the final event of the afternoon, the 400-yard freestyle relay. The two teams battled to the end, with the Gopher anchorman just touching out Jim MacMillan with a relay composite time of 3:16.5 compared to MSU's 3:16.7.

Scoring 88 points, State finished fifth in the Big Ten championships. Leading scorers were sophomore MacMillan who finished second, third and fourth in three individual events, and junior Dick Gretzinger, who finished with a third, fourth and sixth. In the final event of the meet, they joined with Bob Sherwood and Darryle Kifer to capture the 400-yard freestyle relay in a varsity record time of 3:13.9.

The only Spartan qualifier in the NCAA meet at Yale University was MacMillan, who placed seventh in the 100-yard freestyle and 11th in the 200-yard freestyle.

Tennis: MSU's only finalist in the season-end Big Ten matches was the number two doubles team of Tony O'Donnell and Dwight Shelton. They bowed out 3-6, 6-8. Tom Jamieson captured the number one singles consolation match, 1-6, 6-0, 6-4, as did the number three State doubles team of Laird Warner and Mike Youngs, 4-6, 6-2, 6-4. The Spartans' 25 1/2 team points placed them in the fourth slot behind Indiana, Michigan and Northwestern.

Track and Field: At the conference indoor championship in Columbus, Ohio, Michigan State finished third. Bob Moreland successfully defended his 60-yard dash crown, while first-year man Mike Martens captured the 1,000-yard run. Jim Garrett gained yet a third MSU championship when he out-leaped all competitors in the broad jump.

Runner-up slots at the Big Ten outdoor meet were filled by Martens in the 880, Garrett in the broad jump, and Ron Horning in the 660. Fred McKoy was the only Spartan to place in two events. The Plainfield N.J., sophomore finished fourth in the high hurdles and fifth in the high jump. Other scorers were Jan Bowen, fifth in the mile; Ayo Azikewe third in the intermediate hurdles; and Eric Zemper, fourth in the two-mile. Totaling 22 team points, as in 1963, State completed the weekend in fourth place.

Wrestling: Only twice has a Michigan State wrestling team ended up in the conference cellar, 1964 was the first time. With the exception of heavyweight Homer McClure, all of MSU's entrants were eliminated in the opening round. McClure won one match to account for the Spartans' single point.

All three of State's competitors in the NCAA championship meet in Ithaca, N.Y., were defeated in the first round. The trio consisted of Emerson Boles at 177-pounds, Jim Maidlow at 191 pounds and heavyweight McClure.

MSU
1964-1965

TALES TO TELL

The *2001-2002 Big Ten Conference Record Book* notes that, in 1965, "Athletic Directors established television production guidelines for coverage of Conference football and basketball based on principles of noninterference with the conduct of the game." The key word is noninterference.

It is no secret that the television industry has taken over complete disposition of how a football or basketball game is conducted. As an example, resumption of play following a prescribed TV commercial timeout during a football game is totally orchestrated by the media production staff. A specially assigned person is stationed on the playing field and attired as a game official in a black and white shirt and with earphones. Until so instructed from the press box, this "unofficial" official curtails further action on the field. Televised games can often last up to 30 minutes longer than non-televised games. These

extended delays, especially during inclement weather, can be exasperating to fans in the stands, coaches, players, and even the "legitimate" game officials.

As for basketball, television has intruded to the extent that games are controlled with the infusion of eight media timeouts. Upon the first stoppage of play after the game clock works its way past the 16-, 12-, 8- and 4-minute marks of each half, the timekeeper alerts the game officials and a media timeout prevails to accommodate commercials, even when games are not being televised. It would be conceivable for a team to use one of its prescribed timeouts when the game clock is at (as an example) 4:02 and then after resumption of play the game clock is stopped for an appropriate reason at 3:58. This would call for a media timeout and result in two major breaks in action within a four-second interval.

The 1965 "television production guidelines for coverage of conference football and basketball" should be expunged from the policy book. It no longer applies.

HEADLINES of 1965

- Edward White is the first American to walk in space when he spends 23 minutes outside the Gemini 4 spacecraft.
- The Astrodome, the first completely covered stadium in the world, opens in Houston, Texas.
- The National Guard restores order following six days of rioting in the Watts section of Los Angeles.
- War in Vietnam intensifies with air raids into North Vietnam and significant buildup of U.S. troops.

SCOREBOARD

	W	L	T	Avg.
Baseball	28	11	0	.718
Track and Field	4	0	0	1.000
Football	4	5	0	.444
Basketball	5	18	0	.217
Tennis	11	6	0	.647
Cross Country	4	1	0	.800
Swimming and Diving	11	1	0	.917
Wrestling	7	3	1	.682
Hockey	17	12	0	.586
Fencing	7	5	0	.583
Golf	5	12	0	.294
Gymnastics	6	4	0	.600
Soccer	10	1	2	.846

TEAM OF THE YEAR

Accumulating 56 points, MSU captured the school's first-ever Big Ten Outdoor Track and Field Championship. This success was predictable. During the winter, the team was barely edged by Wisconsin, 46-45 1/2, for the indoor title, as hurdler Gene Washington, sprinter Daswell Campbell and miler Keith Coats captured firsts. Also, in the first NCAA indoor championships held at Detroit's Cobo Hall in March, a three-man team of Washington (first in the 60-yard hurdles), Jim Garrett (second in the long jump), and Campbell (fifth in 440-yard dash) managed 11 points for a fourth-place tie in the team standings.

Moving outdoors in Iowa City, Iowa, the Spartans displayed an impressive team effort by scoring in 12 of the 15 events. Garrett, from the football team, emerged as the star with firsts in the long jump and 220-yard dash, as well as a second place in the 100. Other winners for State were Coates in the mile, Mike Bowers in the high jump and Washington in the high hurdles along with his second in the intermediate hurdles. Campbell also finished strong in two events, earning a second in the 440 and a third in the 220. Yet another MSU sprinter, Jimmy Summers placed third in the 100 and fourth in the 220. Other contributors were: Clinton Jones, third in the high hurdles; Mike Chains fifth in the mile, and Tom Herbert with a surprising third in the discus.

Bowers, the sophomore high jumper from Litchfield, was State's top performer at the NCAA Championships in Berkeley, Calif. Although his 6' 10" leap tied for second best in the tournament, he had to settle for fourth place because of a greater number of misses along the way. In the high hurdle event, Washington was bumped on the final barrier dropping back to sixth place but then joined Campbell, Clinton Jones and Summers to form a 440-yard sprint relay quartet that finished third. Combining for 11 points in team scoring placed MSU in the 24th spot. Multi-event star Garrett, hobbled by a foot injury, failed to gain the finals in any of his events.

The 1965 track team.

MAKING HISTORY

For the first time in history, the Big Ten athletic directors voted to provide team championship trophies in football, basketball, hockey and baseball.

Spelling "Michigan State" above the numbers on the front of the 1964 football game jersey, MSU became the first school to be identified in such style. Even as other institutions copied this distinguishing fashion, it remained a feature of the Spartan uniform until the radical alterations of 2002.

After hosting the NCAA cross country championship every fall since the inaugural run of 1938, 1964 would be the last on the MSU campus. Beginning in 1965 and thereafter, the race would be run at different host schools.

Enlivening a ho-hum 73-31 dual swimming meet victory over Northwestern, Coach McCaffree assembled a foursome for the final event , the 400-yard freestyle relay. The result was a time of 3:08.1, which tied the existing American record and bettered the NCAA mark of 3:08.7. The splits were as follows: Ken Walsh 46.8, Jim MacMillan 47.2, Darryle Kifer 47.9 and Gary Dilley 46.2.

As per a directive from the NCAA, beginning with the 1965 season the field event historically known as the broad jump would thereafter be known as the long jump.

GREAT STATE DATES

Football—October 3, 1964 (H): Midway through the opening quarter, Dick Kenney, the barefooted kicker from Hawaii, sailed a team record-setting field goal 49 yards through the uprights for a 3-0 lead over Southern Cal. That was the total scoring for the first 30 minutes of play. Following the second-half kickoff, the Trojans were held deep in their territory and forced to punt. The kick only reached their own 45-yard line, and from there the Spartan offense ran up three first downs and a touchdown from the two by Clinton Jones. State led 10-0. There was no time to rest as Southern Cal came right back for an undisturbed 80-yard touchdown drive, making it 10-7. On yet another USC thrust, Don Japinga intercepted a pass and ran it out from the 25-yard line in midfield. That would be the final threat as a pass from halfback Harry Ammon to Gene Washington closed out the scoring for a 17-7 MSU win.

Soccer—October 3, 1964 (A): Led by All-American George Janes, coach Gene Kenney's squad won its second game of the season by rolling up an impressive 15-0 victory over the Purdue Boilermakers. It was the highest total ever scored by a Spartan team, a record that still stands. Janes, the team's second highest scorer in 1963 as a sophomore, tied a Spartan record by booting in six of the goals. Clare DeBoer and Nick Krat scored three times each, and Sydney Alozie, Larry Christoff, and John McLane were credited with one apiece. Scoring 15 times on 41 shots, State shot an impressive .366 percent.

Cross Country—October 10, 1964 (H): When the three-way meet over the re-routed Forest Akers course concluded, MSU had defeated Wisconsin, 22-37, and Indiana, 16-42. State's Jan Bowen and Rick Zemper led throughout the race, with Bowen the winner as he outsprinted his teammate to the tape over the final 100 yards. His time of 20:30.2 established a course record. Zemper finished second, Mike Chains was fifth, Paul McCollam placed sixth, and Jack Amie rounded out the Spartan scoring by finishing ninth.

Cross Country—October 17, 1964 (A): The first dual meet ever against Minnesota proved to be an exciting 27-28 victory for Michigan State. The excitement centered on four individual battles, each won by a Spartan. Eric Zemper captured first by five seconds; Jan Bowen nipped a Gopher by four-tenths of a second for third place; Mike Kaines won the battle for seventh place by 1.6 seconds; and sophomore George Balthrop decided the meet's outcome in what could be considered a photo finish as he slipped into the tenth slot by one-tenth of a second. If any one of these battles had gone the other way, the meet would have gone to the University of Minnesota.

Football—November 7, 1964 (H): Carrying the ball 24 times for 145 yards, Dick Gordon surpassed the 100-yard rushing mark for the third straight Saturday, and also for the third straight week, MSU was victorious, this time topping Purdue, 21-7. After giving up a touchdown in the opening quarter, the Spartan defense clamped down and controlled the visitors' offensive weapons, including their touted quarterback Bob Griese, who was rushed hard and sacked for losses totaling 47 yards. A budding Spartan star, sophomore Clinton Jones gained 56 yards and scored both second-half touchdowns, one on a 15-yard pass from Steve Juday and the other on a three-yard run.

Track and Field—**January 30, 1965 (A):** Led by the sophomore crew that accounted for eight wins, the Spartans easily defeated the Buckeyes of Ohio State, 87-54. Also impressive were the five MSU grand slams. The trio of Gene Washington, Bob Steele and Clinton Jones swept both the high and low hurdles. Jim Summers, breaking the tape with a 6.4 in the 60-yard dash, was followed by Drake Garrett and Norm Sinclair. State's 1-2-3 finish in the mile run was led by Keith Coates in 4:17.0, while Mike Kaines and Eric Zemper trailed. In the next- to-last event of the afternoon, the two mile, George Balthrop finished first, Paul McCollam was second and Jack Amie was third. Dashwell Campbell won the 440, Keith Coates the 880, and Jim Garrett the long jump. The meet closed with Jim Bowers's leap to a varsity high jump record of 6' 8".

Hockey—**February 5 (A) and 6 (H), 1965:** The hockey team completed a gratifying weekend with two decisive wins over the University of Michigan, 7-4 and 6-2. The Spartans broke out early on Friday evening in Ann Arbor with four goals in the opening stanza. Doug Volmar found the target twice, and linemates Tom Mikkola and Doug Roberts were credited with a goal apiece. Second period scores by Mikkola and Gary Goble basicallly put the game to rest, although the Wolverines went down fighting. Sandy McAndrews scored goal number seven in the closing period. Before 3,589 fans in Dem Hall on Saturday night, the drama played out significantly different as the U of M scored twice within the opening three minutes of play. Jack Ford put MSU on the board with a first period score when both teams were short-handed. The second period belonged entirely to State as they controlled play and scored four times. First it was Roberts, who tipped in a Don Heaphy blast from the blue line at 6:13. The next two markers were recorded identically, McAndrews from Mike Jacobson and then Volmar put one away on a faceoff pass from Mike Coppo. Jacobson closed the evening's scoring in the third period on his 23rd goal of the season, tying the all-time Michigan State season goal-scoring record.

Swimming and Diving—**February 13, 1965 (A):** Capturing seven of 11 events and scoring one-two finishes in four, MSU defeated Ohio State, 60-45, for the ninth victory in 10 starts. Jim MacMillan touched out his teammate Ken Walsh in the 200-yard freestyle and then won the 100-yard freestyle in 47.9. Gary Dilley, an Olympian, was also a double winner with triumphs in the 200-yard backstroke and the 50-yard freestyle. In the

latter event, he tied a varsity record with a time of 21.8. Terry Hagan and Dick Gretzinger swam first and second in the 200-yard butterfly, as did Ed Glick and Denny Hill in the 500-yard freestyle. The foursome of Darryle Kifer, Gretzinger, Glick and Dilley closed out the scoring by winning the final event, the 400-yard freestyle relay. The setback was the first of the season for the Buckeyes after they had won five in a row.

Gymnastics—**February 20, 1965 (H):** Taking four events by the identical score of 11-5, State defeated Wisconsin, 63-57, for its fourth win of the season against Big Ten foes. Undaunted by a nagging ankle injury, Jim Curzi was nearly a one-man show as he captured firsts on the horizontal bar and the parallel bars, and then sealed the team victory with a first place on the still rings. Senior Earl Andrews was credited with the remaining Spartan first when he scored a season high 9.45 on the side horse.

Fencing—**February 27, 1965 (H):** Outscoring the Indiana squad in foil, 7-2, and in sabre, 8-1, the fencers closed out the dual meet season with a 19-8 victory. Terry Givens and Bryan Kutchins were winners in foil; Mark Haskell and Mel Laska were both undefeated in sabre; and Don Lund was the highest scorer in the 5-4 epee loss.

Baseball—**May 7, 1965 (H):** The Spartans had been held to just four hits and one run in eight innings and trailed the Iowa Hawkeyes 3-1. Bob Speer led off the bottom of the ninth with a base on balls, but Dick Billings forced him at second. Two pinch hitters were then called upon. Bruce Pettiboune singled and Dick Killbourn, a .268 hitter, followed with a base-clearing triple to deep center field. Jerry Walker popped to second and up came John Krasnan, the pitcher. "Skip" Litwhiler played a hunch and let him bat for himself. The decision was vindicated, as Krasman won his own game with a single to right field that scored Killbourn from third.

Tennis—**May 7 & 8, 1965 (H):** With a sweep of Ohio State, 9-0, and a near sweep of Purdue, 8-1, the tennis squad won the eighth and ninth meets of the spring. Eight of the points earned against the Buckeyes were of the straight-set variety: Dwight Shelton, Charley Wolff, Laurd Warner, Vic Dhooge and Mike Youngs in singles, and Sheldon-Wolff, Tim Phillips-Young and Warner-Youngs in doubles. Phillips was also a winner, but it took a third set to gather the win. On the next afternoon the identical lineup prevailed against the Boil-

ermakers, but Sheldon took a 6-3, 6-2 loss, the only setback of the weekend.

Baseball—May 14 (A) & 15 (H), 1965: Connecting for 15 hits, the Spartans defeated the U of M, 6-3, in Ann Arbor for MSU's first win there since 1960. Then on Saturday, State won the nightcap of a twin bill, 5-4, at Old College Field. John Krasnan, the junior left hander, put the Wolverines down with eight hits on Friday as he struck out five and walked only one to win his third game of the spring. State scored twice in the second inning, twice in the third, and widened the winning margin with single runs in the seventh and ninth. Steve Juday banged out three of the winners' hits. Bob Maniere, Bruce Pettibone, Dick Billings, Jerry Walker, and John Biedenbach each collected two safeties. The Saturday victory was Michigan State's 25th of the season, which broke the regular season record win total of 24 set by the 1954 squad. Billings accounted for what proved to be the winning run when he homered in the sixth. Doug Dohrei received credit as the winning pitcher but received relief help from Fred Devereux in the seventh.

Track and Field—May 15, 1965 (H): Competing in a heavy drizzle, the Spartan runners and jumpers found the weather as much of a challenge as the Notre Dame track and field team. Capturing 11 of the 15 events, Fran Dittrich's squad handled the Irish with ease, 98-43. Jim Garrett paced the Spartans by winning three events: the 100-yard dash in 9.9, the triple jump in 45' 2 1/2" and the long jump in 23' 10". In addition, there were three double winners: Daz Campbell in the 220 and 440; Tom Herbert in the shot put and discus, and Gene Washington in both hurdle events. Jan Bowen opened the meet with a first place in the mile and Mike Bowers would close the afternoon events with a varsity and field record high jump of 6' 7 1/2". Little did he know that two years later as a senior he would obliterate that record with a skyward leap of 7', a team record that would hold for ten years.

Golf—May 15, 1965 (A): In a seven-team match at West Lafayette, Ind., State's five-man squad shot a composite 771 to top Wisconsin 783, Northwestern 784, Minnesota 804 and Illinois 804. Doug Hankey, the 1964 Michigan amateur champion, scored rounds of 75-74—149; Fred Mackey was three shots back with a 74-78—152 card and Ken Benson had a 76-77—153 score.

ATHLETE OF THE YEAR

It was in his genes. Gary Dilley's father was a champion backstroker at Purdue University, and Gary's brother Alan (1970-1973) would follow him to MSU and actually better some of his record-setting times. One might suggest that Gary reached the apex of his career before it began. In the summer of 1964, prior to his first collegiate competition, he became a silver medalist in the 100-meter backstroke event at the XIV Olympiad in Tokyo. Thus, he shouldered stupendous expectations beginning with his sophomore year . . . but he delivered. During his Spartan years from 1965-1967, Gary was undefeated in dual meets and the "king of the backstrokers" nationally. Three times he won both the 100- and 200-yard events at the Big Ten championships. Likewise, he was the double-winner at the NCAA level in 1965 and 1966. Sadly, his unrelenting path of victories met an abrupt end in 1967 when that March he relinquished his titles at the national championships. Ironically, that meet was conducted in his home pool at the IM Building. In addition to being a champion, Gary Dilley was an innovator. Working with assistant coach Dick Fetters he initiated an alternate race start that was soon dubbed the "Dilley start." Whereas other competitors began in the water with their hands on the gutter top and feet firmly against the wall, Gary began above them with his feet on the gutter top and his hands grasping the sides of the starting block on the pool deck.

Gary Dilley

IN THE SPARTLITE

Baseball: The annual spring break training trip to Florida was productive in two ways. First, with a 10-3 record, there was success from the standpoint of wins and losses. The impressive start was a springboard to a 28-11 season, a team record for wins. Secondly, during the two weeks in the sun, Coach Litwhiler discovered a catcher. Dick Kilbourn, a 6-3, 190-pound junior from Mt. Pleasant, had headed south as the third-string back-stop and he returned as the starter. He completed the season with an overall .268 average.

In defeating Notre Dame 8-6, State registered its 26th victory of the season, breaking a team record of 25 that was set in 1954.

Basketball: In the six post-Johnny Green seasons from 1960-1965, Forddy Anderson's teams had estab-lished a composite 48-86 record for a winning percent-age of .358. More relevant in a negative way was the record achieved by the 1964-1965 team that finished 5-18 with a 1-13-conference record. Athletic Director Biggie Munn had seen enough. At the end of the season, John Bennington, former MSU assistant and head coach at St. Louis University replaced Anderson.

Cross Country: The winners of 11 of the preceding 13 Big Ten titles, Michigan State was dethroned as con-ference champion by Minnesota at the meet on the Sa-voy Golf Course in Champaign, Ill.

Fencing: There are not likely too many overweight fencers. As a sophomore, Mark Haskell took a physical education fencing class and fell in love with the sport, but he weighed 225 pounds and realized his handicap. By the time tryouts for 1965 rolled around, he had lost 50 pounds to a svelte 175. The "new" Mark Haskell not only made the varsity squad, but he became one of its stars and later the elected captain of the 1967 team.

Football: Upon conclusion of the 1964 season, the talent was in place for the dramatic years of 1965 and 1966: Steve Juday, Don Japinga, Ron Goovert, Harold Lucas, Bob Apisa, Bob Viney, Clinton Jones, George Webster, Gene Washington, Bubba Smith, Dick Kenney, Pat Gallinagh, Phil Hoag, Jerry Jones, Jimmy Summers, Charley Thornhill and Jerry West.

Golf: For the seventh time in a row, a State golf team settled for the seventh spot in the conference champion-ship matches. Ken Benson was State's top scorer with his four round totals of 70-74-77-80—301. His teammates

scored as follows: Fred Mackey 306, Doug Swartz 309, Sandy McAndrew 311, Doug Hankey 317 and Buck Morrisson 333. Intermittent rain showers impacted the Spartan scores as the meet wore on, first dropping from third to fifth and eventually from fifth to seventh.

Gymnastics: Beginning in 1965, the Big Ten team championship was determined by the dual-meet records of the competing schools, and the Spartans settled for third place. The heretofore championship meet was con-ducted as usual but only to determine the placing for the individual athletes. In that year's meet, two Spartans claimed titles, Jim Curzi on the parallel bars and Tom Hurt on the long horse. Earlier during the weekend, Curzi had relinquished two titles he had won in 1964, the high bar and the all-around.

Performing before over 10,000 spectators who packed the new arena at Southern Illinois in Carbondale, Curzi executed a flawless routine, winning the parallel bars competition at the 1965 NCAA championships. His horizontal bar routine could also be classified as flawless, but he had to share the title with a member of the cham-pionship team from Penn State. In both events he exhib-ited the smoothness and skill that earned him the praise of the assembled coaches, as well as competitors.

Hockey: State opened the season with 13 returning lettermen, including eight of the top nine scorers from 1964. With John Chandik once more in goal and the blue-liners headed by Frank Silka, Bob Kempf, Carl Lackey and Jim Jacobson, Coach Bessone was convinced that the Spartan defense would be vastly improved from 1963-1964. Upon completion of the 29-game schedule the facts indeed revealed an improvement. While the 1964 defense yielded a 5.15 goals against average, the 1965 edition permitted an average of 3.93 goals per game. The overall won-loss record was even more enhanced, from 8-17 to 17-12.

Michigan State split the two Western Collegiate Hockey Association playoff games with North Dakota at Grand Fork, N.D. The Spartans won on Saturday, 6-4, after dropping the Friday game, 7-1. Unfortunately, it was a series determined on total goals; consequently, the Sioux advanced based on an 11-7 differential.

Soccer: Completing the regular season with a 6-0-2 record, Gene Kenney's team opened the NCAA tourna-ment trail with a first-round 1-0 victory over Maryland, followed by an easy 4-0 defeat of overmatched East Stroudsburg (Pa.). Those wins put Michigan State in the

Final Four at Providence, R.I., where in back-to-back games they met the U.S. Military Academy and the U.S. Naval Academy. The Black Knights were a determined squad seeking their spot in a potentially classic Army-Navy final. Tied 2-2 after regulation, Sydney Alozie, a student from Nigeria, settled any such notion as he booted home the winning goal at 3:25 of the sudden-death extra period. It had been an anxious closing period for the Spartans as they closed out that semi-final game with their regular goalie, Charles Dedich, on the sideline. Hampered by a severely sprained ankle, he was replaced in the net by Van Dimitrious, who regularly played as a forward.

As might be expected in New England on the first Saturday of December, weather was an intervening factor when the Spartans and Midshipmen faced-off in the NCAA finals. Chilly winds that followed two days of persistent rain had transformed the pitch into an icy surface, which nullified the passing game and team speed. Instead, the game quickly settled into a defensive struggle, and an eventual Navy goal at 17:38 of the final quarter held up. At the other end of the field, for the first time in 1964, State was being held scoreless. Several opportunities in the opening two quarters had been negated by the conditions, and the green and white suffered the only loss of the year, 1-0. Despite the setback, it was the highest finish ever posted by a Michigan State soccer team.

Swimming and Diving: Led by sophomore Gary Dilley, who won both backstroke races in conference records times and placed second in the 50-yard freestyle, Coach McCaffree's squad managed 273 points and a third-place finish at the Big Ten meet in Madison, Wis. Ken Walsh finished first in the 100-yard freestyle, followed by teammate Jim MacMillan in second. The team of Dilley, Dick Gretzinger, Darryle Kifer and MacMillan also set a new conference record with the winning time of 3:11.54 in the 400-yard freestyle relay.

Two weeks later in Ames, Iowa, Dilley proved himself to be the nation's best backstroker with NCAA winning and record-times of 52.6 in the 100 and 1:56.2 in the 200.

Tennis: Only two Spartan entrants reached the finals of the 1965 Big Ten championships held on the courts at Indiana University. At the number five singles position, Vic Dhooge was eventually defeated 6-2, 7-5, and once more he met defeat, this time going down 8-6, 6-2 as part of the number two doubles pair with Jim Phillips.

Finishing the meet with 82 points, State was just two behind third place Northwestern.

Track and Field: The young Michigan State team proved to be the surprise at the Big Ten indoor championships in Champaign, Ill., but they were just shy of enough points, 46-43 1/2, for overtaking Wisconsin in the battle for the team title. The hurdlers totaled a gaggle of points, with Gene Washington setting a conference record of 7.8 in winning the lows. He was followed by Bob Steele and Clinton Jones in third and fifth. In the highs, Jones and Washington placed third and fourth. Other Spartan winners were Jim Garrett, who successfully defended his long jump title with a leap of 24' 11"; Keith Coates with a 4:09.5 in the mile; and Daswell Campbell, who finished the 300-yard dash in 30.9. Silver medalists included Mike Bowers with a second-place tie in the high jump and Summers, who added a second in the 60-yard dash.

Gene Washington reached the apex of his collegiate track and field career by winning the 60-yard high hurdle event in the inaugural NCAA indoor championships held at Cobo Hall in Detroit. Jim Garrett finished second in the broad jump and Daswell Campbell was fifth in the 440-yard dash. Totaling 10 points, MSU ended in a tie for fourth place with Maryland.

At the NCAA outdoor championships in Berkley, Calif., a five-man MSU team managed 11 points to finish in 24th place, the highest of any Big Ten school. The quartet of Clinton Jones, Jim Summers, Gene Washington and Daz Campbell led the way with a third place finish in the quarter-mile relay. Mike Bowers was fourth in the high jump and Washington was sixth in the high hurdles.

Wrestling: Scoring 38 points and boasting two individual titles, MSU placed second at the conference championships held in Ann Arbor. Don Behm, with an untarnished 11-0 dual-meet record, emerged on the top rung of his 130-pound class, and another sophomore, 230-pound Jeff Richardson, became State's first conference heavyweight champion. Adding to the team's scoring total were 177-pound Emerson Boles, who managed a third-place finish, and Gary Smith, who settled for a fourth place.

Behm finished third at the NCAA meet, thus earning enough points to place Michigan State in a two-way tie for 15th.

MSU 1965-1966

TALES TO TELL

John Spain, the Spartans' ace middle-distance runner, was not a natural athlete. He was not a star performer in high school at Dearborn and certainly not a blue-chip recruit. He went out for the high school track team only in his senior year and competed, not all too successfully, in the 440- and 880-yard runs. John enrolled at MSU and became a member of the freshmen team, where he again did nothing to be projected as a star of the future. John Spain was just another promising sophomore when practice began in 1966. He worked and practiced diligently, but until the Ohio State meet of May 7, he remained just another guy trying to make the team. Against the Buckeyes, he was entered in the 880-yard run. Off at the crack of starter's pistol, he immediately forged to the front. Running in an almost perfect stride, Spain remained in front all by himself, and, to the amazement of his coaches and teammates, the sophomore crossed the finish line 20 yards ahead of the nearest challenger. When the watches were compared it was announced that he had run the half-mile in an unbeliev-able time of 1:49.1, a new varsity record. On the following weekend, he proved it was no fluke when he broke the tape against Notre Dame in a slightly slower 1:49.8. Two weeks following the unknown runner's explosion onto the scene, John Spain was crowned champion at the Big Ten meet in Bloomington, Ind. His winning time of 1:48.0 established a new conference record. By then he had earned the spot of anchorman on the mile relay quartet, again emerging as the hero. Taking the baton for the final leg in the conference meet, John initially slipped back into the pack, but then turned on the speed down the stretch to pass the Minnesota and Iowa runners for the win. John Spain's contributions aided in securing the 52.5 points that led to another conference track and field team title. He concluded his Cinderella season with a seventh place finish at the NCAA championships, also held in Bloomington, Ind.

HEADLINES of 1966

- RCA introduces integrated circuits in its new television sets, and Sony offers the first commercial home-video tape recorder.
- Miniskirts and bell-bottoms come into fashion.
- The New York Central and Pennsylvania railroads combine to create the largest merger in history.
- The truth-in-packaging law requires clear and accurate statements of ingredients and amounts.

SCOREBOARD

	W	L	T	Avg.
Baseball	24	13	1	.645
Track and Field	4	0	0	1.000
Football	10	1	0	.909
Basketball	17	7	0	.708
Tennis	11	7	0	.611
Cross Country	2	3	0	.400
Swimming and Diving	10	2	0	.833
Wrestling	10	2	0	.833
Hockey	16	13	0	.552
Fencing	9	4	0	.692
Golf	6	7	0	.462
Gymnastics	8	0	0	1.000
Soccer	10	2	0	.833

TEAM OF THE YEAR

By losing the first four games on the schedule, the 1965-1966 hockey team had the worst beginning since the winless campaign of 1949. By the end of January, the team had struggled to a 7-10 mark, a record that cer-

tainly would not have engendered expectations of a championship. There was a flicker of excitement when they duplicated the 1965 back-to-back weekend sweeps of both Michigan and Wisconsin in early February. The next step to respectability came when State, the league's sixth-place team, defeated both Michigan and Michigan Tech in the season-ending WCHA playoffs. This earned them a trip to the University of Minnesota's Williams Arena and the NCAA's Final Four, where they shocked the collegiate hockey world with wins over Boston University and then Clarkston.

MAKING HISTORY

In measuring the combined successes of all 13 intercollegiate athletic teams, the 1965-1966 year was arguably the most successful ever for Michigan State varsity sports competition. In the fall, the football team completed the schedule undefeated, winning the Big Ten crown, finishing first in the UPI poll, and earning the trip to the Rose Bowl. The cross country team was runner-up in the Big Ten title run, and Gene Kenney's soccer team reached the NCAA championship final game for the fourth year in a row. During the winter, the indoor track squad and the wrestling team won Big Ten team titles. The gymnastics team, undefeated in dual

The 1966 hockey team. (Front row, left to right) G. Cooley, M. Mulcahy, D. Heaphy, J. Fisher, M. Coppo, T. Purdo, L. Roach; (second row, left to right) trainer C. Stretch, S. McAndrew, T. Mikkola, M. Jacobson, D. Vedejs, R. Roth, D. Volmar, T. Crowley, W. Duffett, coach A. Bessone; (back row, left to right) manager W. Smith, R. Bois, B. Faunt, D. French, N. Cristofoli, R. Fallat, J. Schuster, and manager R. Faust; (not included) R. Brawley.

meets, and the basketball squad at 10-4 was the runner-up in the conference. In fencing, along with swimming and diving, MSU finished third. At the national level, the gymnasts were third, the swimmers and fencers fourth, and the wrestlers sixth. As noted earlier, with a national championship, hockey was the biggest surprise of all. The Spartans of spring were also busy. The tennis team finished second in the Big Ten meet, and both the golf and baseball teams ended in the conference's fourth spot.

At track and field's prestigious Drake Relays, Fred McKoy, Clinton Jones, Gene Washington and Bob Steele formed a shuttle relay that set a new American record of 57.4, edging a Nebraska quartet in the finals.

With its approval as an "official" MSU varsity sport still four years away, the Lacrosse Club continued to impress. On April 9, they crushed the University of Michigan, 12-1.

GREAT STATE DATES

Cross Country—**October 2, 1965 (H):** The Spartans opened the 1965 season with a 15-47 shutout of Indiana. Finishing one through five respectively were Dick Sharkey from Detroit Redford, George Balthrop of Staunton, Va., Art Link also of Detroit Redford, Captain Paul McCollam from Hartford, Conn., and Ralph Stadelman of West Lafayette, Ind. Not scoring, but finishing sixth was Keith Coates from Sarnia, Ontario. Sharkey returned to action after sitting out the 1964 season after knee surgery.

Football—**October 9, 1965 (A):** The 24-7 victory over the University of Michigan was a contest dominated by the "S" defense, spearheaded by Bubba Smith and George Webster. The All-American pair completely controlled the line of scrimmage, as the Wolverines were held to a minus 39 rushing yards. Regardless, the game proved to be much closer than what might have been expected. Playing before a crowd of 103,219, the win wasn't really secured until late in the final quarter when Dick Kenney kicked a 35-yard field goal that gave the Spartans a 18-7 lead. Fullback Bob Apisa would later add a clinching 39-yard touchdown run with two seconds of playing time remaining. Quarterback Steve Juday opened the scoring with a one-yard carry in the first quarter, followed by a second-period Kenney kick, and Clinton Jones's 10-yard score in the third. Gene Washington had a busy afternoon, as he hauled in Juday passes for a total of 71 yards.

Football—**October 16, 1965 (H):** Once more it was the smothering defense that stole the show as Bubba Smith and the "Gang Green" held the Ohio State running game to a minus 22 yards, while the offense outscored the Buckeyes 32-7. On a first quarter cut-back 80-yard touchdown run by Clinton Jones, MSU led at intermission, 7-0. Following a scoreless third quarter, the Spartans added 25 points on a Dick Kenney 35-yard field goal; a safety after Ron Goovert and Buddy Owens corralled the Bucks' quarterback in the end zone; a Steve Juday to Jones 12-yard touchdown pass; and a score by Charles Lowther after the reserves had taken over in the waning minutes. Final statistics showed that the Michigan State offense had piled up 387 yards rushing and 151 passing on 11 of 16 from Juday. Gene Washington had six catches for 83 yards.

Soccer—**October 30, 1965 (A):** Although they only scored twice, State totally dominated this game over the Ohio University Bobcats. Using a packed-in defense designed to keep the score down, OU seldom had control of the ball in the Spartans' end of the field, as they were outshot 37-3. Guy Busch scored the first goal at 9:35 of the second quarter on a pass from behind the net by Gary McBrady. In an unusual ploy, goalie George Janes was called upon to take a free kick with about 10 minutes of playing time remaining, and he connected for the game's only other goal. Janes thus kept his record clean as the team's penalty kicker at three for three.

Football—**November 20, 1965 (A):** By defeating Notre Dame 12-3, Michigan State closed the season with an unblemished 10-0 record. It was not an impressive offensive display that afternoon in South Bend, but it didn't have to be as the stingy Spartan defense was again unpenetrable, holding the Irish to minus 12 yards rushing, three first downs and 24 yards passing. Following a scoreless opening half, Clinton Jones scored on a three-yard touchdown run in the third period. The second score came in the closing quarter on a 19-yard pass from Steve Juday to Dwight Lee. The inability to convert points after touchdown was not a factor on this day, but the entire Spartan family bemoaned a repeat performance 42 days later in Pasadena, Calif.

Wrestling—**January 22, 1966 (H):** A crowd of 1,200 in the IM West Sports Arena roared with delight as MSU swept the final four matches against Minnesota to turn a close meet into a rout, 20-8. Don Behm, at 130-pounds, opened the Spartan scoring with a 5-2 de-

cision, his 11th straight. Sophomore Dale Anderson, in his first match as a Spartan, followed Behm with a convincing 11-2 victory at 137 pounds. The parade of closing winners included Dick Cook at 157 pounds, George Radman and his pin at 167 pounds, a narrow 4-3 win by 177-pound Bill Bradley, and a victory by heavyweight Jeff Richardson in his second win since rejoining the team following the Rose Bowl football game.

Hockey—**February 4 (H) & 5 (A), 1966:** State swept a home-and-away weekend series with Michigan, 8-7 and 4-2. Standouts in the Friday night home game were Doug Vollmar and Tom Mikkola. Vollmar posted a hat trick with all three scores coming in the opening period while Mikkola was the ultimate hero when he slapped a rebounder past the Wolverine goalie for the winning goal with only 20 seconds of regulation time remaining. Bill Faunt, Mike Coppo, Wayne Duffett and Bob Fallat each collect a goal in the Saturday game. Overall, a total of 30 penalties were called during the two games with many precipitated by fights. In addition, each evening a fan was involved. At Dem Hall on Friday, a spectator was ejected after he climbed over the screen to attack a Michigan player who had speared the Spartans' Sandy McAndrew. The next evening, a rambunctious U of M follower found a loose stick and struck McAndrew in the head.

Swimming and Diving—**February 18 & 19, 1966 (A):** State closed out the 1965-1966 dual-meet schedule with a pair of wins on the road, 73-50 over Wisconsin and 77-46 at Minnesota. Noteworthy performers at Madison were freestylers Denny Hill in the 1,000, Ken Walsh in the 200, and Jim MacMillan, who swam the 50 in 21.98. In winning the 200-yard individual medley in 2:02.17, Pete Williams bettered his own varsity record established earlier in the season. After finishing first in the three-meter diving event against the Badgers, Fred Whiteford won both boards the next day at Minneapolis. Coach McCaffree juggled his line-up against the Gophers, yet his swimmers still managed to win all but the final two races of the evening.

Gymnastics—**February 19, 1966 (H):** Dave Thor, working six events, captured three firsts to lead MSU to a 192.45-184.0 victory over the always competitive University of Illinois. He took top honors in floor exercise, with a 9.4 performance; side horse, with a season-high 9.6; and the vault, in which he scored 9.45. Other winners were Larry Goldberg, who was awarded a 9.4 in the ring event, and Jim Curzi, who contributed a season-

high 9.65 in the parallel bars for which he teamed with Thor and Ted Wilson to register an impressive 28.05-23.40 team advantage.

Fencing—**February 19, 1966 (H):** With Sergio Montalvo and Mark Haskell scoring the winning points, the fencing team defeated Ohio State and Notre Dame by identical scores, 14-13. Montalvo gained the team-wining point in the next-to-last foil bout against OSU, and Haskell's concluding win in saber proved the margin over Notre Dame. The saber crew again proved its superiority by winning eight of nine bouts against the Buckeyes and seven against the Irish.

Track and Field—**February 26, 1966 (A):** The scoring sheet read Michigan State 63, Wisconsin 63 and there was but one event remaining, the one-mile relay. Having battled back from an early 37-17 deficit, State was fortunate to have reached this point still in contention, but coach Fran Dittrich was faced with a dilemma. One member of his final relay quartet, Keith Coates, had become ill during the meet and was unavailable. A substitute needed to come forth, and the coach turned to Jim Garrett, the sprinter-jumper who had never before run the 440 in competition. Although he had already competed in three events, winning the long jump, finishing second in the 300 and third in the 60, Garrett tuned in a credible 51.0, as he teamed with Bob Steele, Daz Campbell and Mike Martens to finish in 3:20.8, safely three strides ahead of the Badger team.

Gymnastics—**February 26, 1966 (H):** In a battle of unbeaten Big Ten powers, MSU knocked off Michigan, 190.45-183.5, to close out the school's first undefeated and untied dual meet season. An overflow record crowd of 3,750 in the IM Building gym watched the Spartans in their best effort of the season, winning five of the seven events and totaling 27 points or better in six of them. Jim Curzi scored a 9.35 to win the parallel bars; Dennis Smith took honors in the side horse with a 9.25; Dave Thor's 9.4 was tops in floor exercise; and Ed Gunny was a double winner, as he scored a 9.5 in both the high bars and the rings. The contest was a fitting finale to the careers of five seniors: Captain Curzi, Ted Wilson, Ray Strobel, Bob Cordero and John Rohs.

Fencing—**February 26, 1966 (A):** Charlie Schmitter's squad ended their dual-meet season on a winning note as they defeated both Indiana, 24-3, and the host University of Detroit, 16-11. Captain Mark Haskell, Mel Laske and John Beam were the standouts in saber. Terry Givens, Charlie Baer, Rodger Loutzenhiser and

Warren Lucas headed the foil division, and Bill Siebert, Andre Lee, Carl Gross, Frank Schubert and Don Lund scored in epee. Haskell and Laske were undefeated during the afternoon.

Basketball—**March 7, 1966 (H):** With only one conference team eligible for postseason play, a Michigan State season-ending 86-77 victory over Michigan was for bragging rights only. The Wolverines had already annexed the conference title. Succeeding on their first three attempts of the game, State forged to a 45-36 halftime lead and then took total control after intermission. Hitting an impressive 49 percent of their shots, they built a 19-point margin with 11 minutes of time remaining and never looked back. A tenacious defense that held the Wolverines to a 39 percent shooting night, also produced numerous turnovers. A pair of Spartan seniors led the scoring, Bill Curtis with 26 points and Stan Washington with 23.

Baseball—**March 24, 1965 (A):** In their third game of the annual spring trip, Danny Litwhiler's hitters were in an offensive mode, as they collected 16 hits, including six doubles and a home run to route Miami, 13-3. Leading the attack were Bob Sper, who connected for the four-bagger, and Steve Polisar, who hit a pair of doubles. The seven-run outburst in the second inning proved to be adequate enough, but the production continued with one run in the fourth, four in the sixth, and one in the ninth. Howard Miller pitched four middle innings without allowing a run and gained credit for the victory. It wasn't entirely a hit and run show. The Spartan infield generated five double plays during the nine-inning afternoon affair.

Tennis—**April 30, 1966 (H):** In a triple dual meet on the home courts, State blanked Northwestern and then won all three doubles matches to top Wisconsin 6-3. Winning matches against both the Cats and Badgers were: number three Laird Warner, number five Vic Dhooge, and number six Mike Youngs, as number one Rich Monan, number two Mickey Szilagyi and number four Jim Phillips each gained a win and a loss.

Golf—**April 30, 1966 (H):** New coach Bruce Fossum initiated a one-day 36-hole meet and invited Wisconsin, Western Michigan and Bowling Green. The five-man team totals were as follows: MSU 766, Wisconsin 774, Bowling Green 787 and Western 838. Medalist for the day was Ken Benson, 75-71—146. Other Spartans scores were Sandy McAndrew 78-71—149, Steve Benson 79-78—157, George Buth 77-80—157 and Doug Hankey 81-76—157.

Baseball—**May 16, 1966 (H):** In a rare night game at Lansing's Municipal Park, John Walters and Dick Kilbourn, bench warmers earlier in the season, accounted for all of State's runs in a 7-3 victory over Notre Dame. Walters hit a pair of three-run homers for six runs batted in, and Kilbourn hit a solo shot for the other MSU run. John Krasnan started on the mound and was credited with the win, his second of the year. Jim Goodrich relieved in the sixth and Dick Holmes pitched the ninth. The trio totaled 19 strikeouts during the evening.

ATHLETE OF THE YEAR

Bob Steele (TR 65-67) is the only Spartan trackman to ever win back-to-back NCAA titles. He did so in the 440-yard intermediate hurdle event during his junior and senior years. In Bob's own words:

"The story of back-to-back NCAA track titles (1966 and 1967) is very important to me. As a point of reference, it should be noted that NCAA outdoor track was dominated by the West Coast track powers [UCLA, USC, Oregon, etc.] during my career, as well as in more recent years. The most recent Big Ten track and field athlete to have captured an NCAA title had been the half-mile champion George Kerr of Illinois back in 1960.

In 1966, everything just blossomed for me as I won the 440-yard hurdles in a world-leading time. The year was a dream come true. I later made the American International Team and traveled with Olympic champions of my youth [Ralph Boston, Jim Ryun, Willie Davenport, etc.].

My senior year [1967] was a time of self-imposed pressure...1966 had seemed like a long-ago story. I found myself throwing-up before competition, basically afraid the previous year had been a fluke. The California coaches were telling Jim Gibbard, our assistant coach, that 1966 was an odd happening for the Midwest schools. Amidst it all, I seemed to be finding ways to lose. As the season progressed and the failures mounted, I trained harder and began to find relief that I was once again the 'underdog.'

I approached the NCAAs at Provo, Utah in 1967 with a belief that I could possibly return to the top.

In the preliminaries I felt that old flow and went to the finals with great confidence. Sure enough, running in the finals was a return to the dream, as I repeated my championship of the year before. I won by five yards and again in a world-leading time.

A lesson had been learned: that talent can be suffocated by self-imposed pressure. The next eight years, I ran throughout the world (30 countries) and always went to the starting line with a stoic/relaxed confidence. I often wonder what my track future would have been without that race at Provo in 1967. Also, I often wonder what my track future would have been without teammates Clinton Jones and Gene Washington. For those two were superior in the shorter hurdle event and consequently forced me to the longer race that proved to be more suitable."

A broken leg sustained in a Hamilton, Ontario, track meet prevented Steele from successfully competing for a spot on the 1968 USA Olympic team.

Bob Steele

IN THE SPARTLITE

Baseball: In the major league's June draft of amateur players, four Spartans were selected. Those picked and the teams making the selections were: Jim Blight (Tigers), Dick Holmes (Twins), John Biedenbach (Washington Senators), and sophomore Tom Binkowski (Kansas City Athletics). Binkowski would forego the option and return for two more years as a Spartan.

Biedenbach and Bob Speer were named to the all-Big Ten team as selected by the conference coaches. Biedenbach was a unanimous selection for the third base position, while Speer was tabbed for the leftfield spot.

Basketball: First-year coach John Bennington was quickly considered a miracle worker. He had taken a last place conference team with a 1-13 record (5-18 overall) and, adding only one new significant contributor, Moberly (Mo.) Junior College transfer six-foot-five center Matthew Aitch, rocketed the Spartans to a 17-7 1965-1966 record and a 10-4 runner-up spot in the conference.

Upon conclusion of the season, assistant coach Sonny Means, who had been a Spartan player in 1949-1952, left the team to accept the position of head coach at Western Michigan.

Cross Country: As in 1964, the Spartans found themselves in the unfamiliar runner-up spot at the conference championships in Minneapolis, this time yielding to a surprising Northwestern team, 40 points to 65. Finishing for MSU were Dick Sharkey third, Paul McCollam sixth, George Balthrop eighth, Art Link 11th, and Keith Coates 37th. Three days following the Big Ten run, MSU was once more at VanCortlandt Park in New York for the 57th running of the IC4A race, where they finished 6th in a field of 23 teams. Sharkey was eighth and McCollam 12th.

After 25 consecutive years in East Lansing, the NCAA moved their championship run to Lawrence, Kan. No longer was MSU synonymous with NCAA titles. Led by Dick Sharkey, who was 36th, and Paul McCollam, who finished in the 40th spot, the team of Spartans finished in the 15th spot.

Fencing: It seems difficult to accept that a fencer would sustain an incapacitating injury while in competition, but that's what happened to foil star Terry Givens. While competing in a triple-dual meet at Iowa City, Iowa, on February 13, he severely twisted his ankle and was lost for the remainder of the season.

Seniors Mark Haskell and Mel Laska finished 1-2 in the sabre competition at the Big Ten meet in Iowa City, but the team showed little more, finishing in third place.

Led by Haskell's impressive second place showing in the NCAA sabre competition, Charlie Schmitter's squad finished in the sixth spot at the championship meet hosted by Duke University. Gaining additional team points were Laska in sabre, Steve Vore in foil and Don Lund in epee.

Football: To the chant of "Kill, Bubba (Smith), Kill" from the student section in Spartan Stadium, the 1965 defensive unit permitted an average of just 45.6 yards per game to lead the nation. On the scoreboard this translated to a paltry 6.2 points per game. Against Big Ten foes, the "Gang Green" was even more miserly, as they yielded the puny average of 34.6 yards over seven contests, which today remains a conference record. Along with Bubba Smith, were George Webster, Bob Viney, Ron Goovert, Charlie "Mad Dog" Thornhill, Don Bierowicz, Buddy Owens, Harold Lucas, Jerry Jones, Don Japinga, Don Weatherespoon, Jimmy Summers and Jesse Phillips.

Bubba Smith led the "Gang Green's" smothering defense in 1965.

Duffy Daugherty was selected to coach the East team in the All-American football game held in Atlanta, Ga., on July 29. The "Gang Green" led the nation in rushing defense, permitting an average of just 45.6 yards per game, which included an average of 34.6 in seven Big Ten contests, still a conference record.

By a unanimous vote, Michigan State was selected as recipient of the MacArthur Bowl by the National Football Foundation and Hall of Fame. Thus, MSU was recognized as the nation's number one collegiate team.

Golf: Over the three days of play in the Big Ten championships at Iowa City, Iowa, the Michigan State golfers moved from sixth place to fifth place and finally to fourth place. John Bailey's four round total of 301 (78-75-75-74) finished 13th to lead all Spartans. He was followed by Rick Mackey, who was one shot back at 302. Rounding out the six-man team were Captain Ken Benson at 305, Sandy McAndrew at 308, Doug Campbell at 309 and Steve Benson at 322.

Gymnastics: The conference coaches constructed a new method for determining the season-ending champion. In the past, the conference meet solely determined winners of the various individual events with the dual meet records determining the team championship. Beginning in 1966, the team champion would be decided by a combination of both dual-meet and championship-meet placing. Under this system, Michigan was awarded six points for the best dual-meet record and 16 for finishing first at the championship meet. Meanwhile, MSU claimed seven points for the second-best dual-meet record and 14 points for the second place finish at the championship meet in Bloomington, Ind. Thus, the U of M finished with 22 points and Michigan State ended with 21. Individual championships were a-plenty: Dave Thor finished first in side horse, floor exercise and the all-around event; Jim Curzi placed first in both the horizontal and parallel bars; and Dave Croft was first on still rings.

At the NCAAs in University Park, Pa., State scored a team total 184.75 points to place third behind Southern Illinois (187.80) and California (185.14). Leading the way for the Spartans were Jim Curzi, who successfully defended his parallel bars title and then placed second on the horizontal bar; Ed Gunny, a surprise winner in the still ring competition; and Dave Thor, who, although ill all week with the flu, managed a third place finish in the all-around competition. Coach George Szypula was honored as Coach of the Year and Curzi was

honored as the top senior gymnast by being presented the Nissen Award.

Hockey: Prices for home hockey games were set at $1.50 for reserved seats, $1.00 for general admission and 50 cents for students with proper ID.

Doug Volmar captured the individual scoring title of the Western Collegiate Hockey Association with 41 points on 18 goals and 23 assists in 20 WCHA games.

Soccer: MSU reached the Final Four of soccer by easily defeating the University of Maryland-Baltimore, 7-0, and then squeaking by little East Stroudsburg in overtime, 2-1. Both games were played on the East Lansing home field.

As in the previous season of 1964, MSU faced the Cadets of West Point in an NCAA semi-final match up. Played on a Thursday night in St. Louis before an estimated 7,000 spectators, Gene Kenney's crew was up to the task with a 3-1 win. The first score, in near record time, came on a boot by Rich Nelke at the 44-second mark of the opening period. Army tied the game six minutes later, and the 1-1 count held until the third period when Guy Busch regained the lead with his 23rd goal of the season on a pass from Orhan Enustun. His marker surpassed the season record of 22 goals set by Mabricio Ventura in 1961. Busch drilled home an insurance goal in the opening minutes of the third period. Thereafter, the Spartans played out the game in a successful defensive posture.

In what seemingly had become a bad habit, once more the soccer team failed in its bid for an NCAA title, again losing to an old nemesis, St. Louis University, 1-0, before a record crowd of 7,234 on the Billikens' home field. A disputed penalty shot in the third quarter that eluded senior goalie George Janes resulted in the only score of the game. Unquestionably, there had been contact in front of the Spartan cage, but the referee who whistled the infraction leading to the goal could not reasonably explain his call at the time. Coach Kenney later said, "The call (tripping) was horrible and highly disputable, resulting in a tainted goal. A penalty shot should come from a very obvious foul in a game this important." State did have ample quality opportunities to knot the score. Gary McBrady and Guy Busch both hit the crossbar on driving shots, and Busch missed once more when his shot hooked away from the corner of the net at the last second.

Swimming and Diving: John Narcy became State's first full-time diving coach. Coming from Hinsdale High School in Illinois, he had been an All-American performer at the University of Michigan. Narcy remained as an MSU coach until he retired in 2002.

Flashing team depth never before displayed by a Spartan team, a record number of 16 swimmers and divers contributed to the 273 points and third place finish at the conference meet in Madison, Wis. Leading the way was backstroke champion Gary Dilley, along with Pete Williams, Ken Walsh, Ed Glick, Dennis Hill, Lee Driver, Jim MacMillan, Rolf Groseth, Dan Pangborn, Dan Harner, Bob Wolf, Darryle Kifer, John Musulin and Jack Marsh in addition to divers Fred Whiteford and Ken Genova.

Featuring Gary Dilley's successful defense of his two backstroke titles, State assembled enough points (173) to finish in fourth place at the NCAA championships. Dilley's time in the 100-yard finals, 52.3, established a new American and collegiate record. Lee Driver's third in the 200-yard breaststroke and Pete Williams's fourth in the grueling 400-yard individual medley added important team points, as did the three relays and the top performances by Ed Glick, Dennis Hill, Ken Walsh and diver Fred Whiteford.

Tennis: In an unusual crossover, Mike Youngs, the 1966 team captain, had come to State as a football recruit. An injured shoulder forced him to the sidelines and onto the tennis courts in 1965.

With Big Ten championship action on their home courts, the MSU netters amassed 113 team points, which was good for second place in the tournament. In the process, the Spartans captured three titles. Mickey Szilagyi, the sophomore lefthander from Milwaukee, Wis., disposed of the top two seeds on his way to the championship at number two singles. Meanwhile, Vic Dhooge capped his run to the number five singles title by handing the Michigan entrant his first setback of the season. The third Michigan State title came in the doubles competition, for which Dhooge teamed with Jim Swift to take the number two crown. In doing so, he became the first State player in 13 years to win two championships in one Big Ten championship meet. Coach Stan Drobac had performed the double win when he competed as a Spartan in 1953.

Track and Field: Hosting the conference championships in Jenison, Michigan State managed 50 points, 12 better than Wisconsin, to win the school's first Big Ten indoor track and field title. Leading the way was the hurdling trio of Gene Washington, Clint Jones, and Bob Steele who finished 1-2-3, respectively in both the high and low for a total of 24 points. State had two other champions, Dick Sharkey, who broke the conference and field house records with a 9:01.9 two- mile run, and Jim Garrett, who successfully defended his long jump title.

At the indoor national collegiates in Detroit, Gene Washington, the defending champion in the high hurdles had to settle for fourth place. The only other MSU finalist was Jim Garrett who finished fifth in the long jump.

Although managing only four firsts, the Spartans successfully defended their outdoor Big Ten title, scoring 52 1/2 points to runner-up Iowa's 43. The impressive team effort featured three conference record-setting performances: John Spain, who ran a 1:48.0 in the 880-yard run; Washington, with a 13.8 in the high hurdles; and Steele, who captured the inaugural running of the 440-yard intermediate hurdle event in a time of 50.7. Also scoring were Mike Martens, Jim Garrett, Daz Campbell, Tom Herbert, Fred McKoy, Mike Bowers, Art Link and Dick Sharkey. The outcome of the meet remained in question until the final event, the one-mile relay. Running the first three legs for the winning foursome, Martens, Rick Dunn, and Campbell forged to the front, and then Spain, initially dropping back into the pack, sprinted down the straightaway to pass the Iowa and Minnesota anchormen and seal the team victory.

In addition to Bob Steele's gold medal performance in 440-yard intermediate hurdles at the NCAAs in Provo, Utah, three other Spartans placed in the finals. Gene Washington was fifth in the high hurdles, John Spain was seventh in the half mile, and Dick Sharkey seventh in the three-mile run.

Wrestling: After placing no better than third in the 1966 Big Ten meet, Dick Cook, senior captain, was an amazing winner of the 152-pound title at the NCAA championships in Ames, Iowa. Also scoring for State were 130-pound Dale Anderson, who placed sixth, and heavyweight Jeff Richardson, who was fifth.

Along with coach emeritus Fendley Collins, three former Spartan wrestlers were voted into the Amateur Wrestling Hall of Fame in 1966. They were Burl "Bo" Jennings, Merle "Cut" Jennings, and Billy Martin, who wrestled in unheralded fashion during the 1939-1940 season. Martin's induction to the Hall was not as a competitor but as a successful high school coach in Norfolk, Va. Among the 75 college wrestlers he had developed, three found their way to East Lansing: Okla Johnson, Dale Carr and George Radman.

EXTRA! 1966 Rose Bowl

January 1, 1996—Pasadena, California

	1	2	3	4	F
MSU	0	0	0	12	12
UCLA	0	14	0	0	14

Starting line-up (offense)		Starting line-up (defense)	
Jim Proebstle	LE	Bubba Smith	LE
Jerry West	LT	Buddy Owens	LT
Norm Jenkins	LG	Harold Lucas	MG
Boris Dimitroff	C	Don Bierowicz	RT
John Karpinski	RG	Bob Viney	RE
Joe Przybycki	RT	Ron Goovert	LLB
Gene Washington	RE	Charles Thornhill	RLB
Steve Juday (C)	QB	George Webster	ROV
Dwight Lee	LH	Jim Summers	HB
Clinton Jones	RH	Don Japinga	HB
Eddie Cotton	FB	Jesse Phillips	S

State supporters had legitimate expectations of a victory in this game; after all, their Spartans had completed a 10-game schedule undefeated. Furthermore, the list of vanquished included this same UCLA team, whom the Spartans defeated 13-3 in the season opener. Unfortunately, the Bruins were likely also capitalizing on that first game in order to wreak revenge. As the game progressed, Michigan State committed four first-half turnovers, which, along with a successful on-sides kick put the opposition in position with a 14-0 halftime lead. The Green-and-White defense picked up the slack in the second half to give the team a fighting chance. Unfortunately, the offensive rally did not begin until late in the fourth quarter, when they scored twice in the final 6:13. First, Steve Juday completed a 42-yard pass to Gene Washington to set up Bob Apisa's 38-yard touchdown run. The two-point try was stopped to set the score at

14-6. On their next possession the Bruins could not gain a first down and Bubba Smith partially blocked their punt to give the Spartans the ball on the UCLA 49. Fourteen plays later, Juday was in the end zone on a one-yard sneak with 0:31 remaining. Apisa's running attempt for two points failed and the score was soon final, 14-12. Though they did not take home the win, State did outgain their competition in total yards, 314-212, with Clinton Jones rushing for 113 yards on 20 carries.

EXTRA! 1966 NCAA HOCKEY TOURNAMENT (National Champions)

After a slow start to the season, Amo Bessone's team won 12 of its last 16 games, including four victories over Michigan, and it beat defending champ Michigan Tech to earn a place in the NCAA tournament. There, they rose to the occasion with a 2-1 triumph over Boston University and a 6-1 demolition of Clarkson to bring home State's first national hockey crown. Netminder Gaye Cooley was named the tournament MVP, while Don Heaphy, Mike Coppo and Brian McAndrew were first team all-tournament picks. Bob Brawley and Tom Mikkola were second-team selections. Amo won the Spencer Penrose Award as national coach of the year.

March 18, 1966—Minneapolis, Minn.
MSU 2, Boston University 1
1st Pd.: No Scoring.
2nd Pd.: 1. MSU, French (unasst.), 15:20.
3rd Pd.: 2. MSU, Volmar (Brawley, Faunt), 12:21; 3. BU, McLachlan (O'Connell, Finnie), 19:37.

March 19, 1966—Minneapolis, Minn.
MSU 6, Clarkson 1
1st Pd.: 1. MSU, Coppo (Heaphy), 14:31; 2. CC, Hamilton (McLennan, Hurley), 17:54.
2nd Pd.: 3. MSU Brawley (McAndrew, Heaphy), 14:31.
3rd Pd.: 4. MSU, Coppo (Faunt), 0:17; 5. MSU Fallat (McAndrew), 3:38; 6. MSU, Volmar (Faunt), 12:12; 7. MSU, Faunt (unasst.) 19:32.

EXTRA! SEVEN BIG TEN WRESTLING TITLES IN A ROW

(#1) 1966—Champaign, Ill.: In one of the closest championship meets in Big Ten history, State picked up 71 points to nose out Michigan with 67 and Minnesota 65. Three Spartan sophomores laid claim to conference titles: Dale Anderson (130 pounds) and Dale Carr (137 pounds) with Mike Bradley's victory at 177 pounds particularly significant. Had he lost by a decision to his Minnesota opponent the Gophers would have tied for the title, but the Ypsilanti light heavyweight rose to the occasion and the team trophy was headed for East Lansing. Two 1965 conference champions, both heavyweight Jeff Richardson and 123-pound Don Behm, slipped to a second place finish. Behm was leading in his final match when he was injured and forced to concede the title.

The 1966 Big Ten championship wrestling team. Letter Winners were R. Cook, J. Maidlow, D. Behm, J. Richardson, M. Johnson, F. Larson, D. Campbell, G. Radman, D. Anderson, D. Carr, R. Ott, M. Bradley, and manager M. Gunesch. Individual conference champions included D. Anderson (130 pounds), D. Carr (137 pounds), M. Bradley (177 pounds).

MSU 1966-1967

TALES TO TELL

Just mention the score, 10-10, and veteran Spartan football fans conjure a memory of the 1966 Notre Dame-Michigan State classic when the nation's number one (ND) and number two (MSU) ranked teams met on November 19. It was the game of the year, the game of the decade, the game of the century, or popularly dubbed the "poll bowl," depending on which sports journalist was writing the story. Even the *Wall Street Journal* covered the pregame hype with a front-page story. Twenty-six years later, in 1992, Simon & Schuster, Inc. published *"The Biggest Game of Them All"* by Mike Celizic, whose subject was the 1966 game.

Before a Spartan Stadium record crowd of 80,011 and an estimated 35 million watching on ABC television, the opening quarter that afternoon was scoreless. In the second period, State worked the ball to the four-yard line, from where fullback Regis Cavender scored. Bare-footed Dick Kenney converted. Later in the same quarter, Kenney hit a 47-yard field goal, and the home crowd was ecstatic with the 10-0 lead. It wasn't to last. With four and a half

minutes remaining before intermission, the Irish hit on a 34-yard touchdown pass, closing the margin to three points. The third quarter, like the first, was scoreless, but on the opening play of the final stanza, the Irish tied the game on a 28-yard field goal. That concluded scoring for the afternoon.

Regis Cavender (number 25) scores from the four-yard line in the memorable game of Nov. 19, 1966.

HEADLINES of 1967

- Christian Barnard, a South African surgeon, performs the first human heart transplant.
- The Broadway musical "Hair" emphasizes rock music and features the song "Aquarius."
- The Green Bay Packers defeat the Kansas City Chiefs, 35-10, in professional football's first Super Bowl.
- On Thursday and Friday, January 27-28, a record snowfall paralyzes the Lansing area as 24 inches of the white stuff falls within a 42-hour period. For the first time, MSU classes are cancelled for one day.

SCOREBOARD

	W	L	T	Avg.
Baseball	22	23	1	.489
Track and Field	4	0	0	1.000
Football	9	0	1	.950
Basketball	16	7	0	.696
Tennis	15	4	0	.789
Cross Country	4	1	0	.800
Swimming and Diving	9	1	0	.900
Wrestling	8	1	1	.864
Hockey	16	15	1	.516
Fencing	4	8	0	.334
Golf	5	1	0	.833
Gymnastics	5	3	0	.611
Soccer	10	0	2	.917

The most lasting memory of this contest came in the final 1:24 minutes of the game. Notre Dame had possession on their own 30-yard line, first and ten. Three running plays netted one first down, and as they chose to keep the ball on the ground, it soon became apparent that Coach Parseghian was settling for a tie. A chorus of boos greeted the final two plays as the game ended on the ND 39-yard line. In 1966, the rules did not provide for a tie-breaker.

Sports Illustrated later paraphrased the famous ND fight song with: "tie, tie for old Notre Dame."

The Spartans had a slight edge in the final statistics of the defense-dominated contest. They had 284 yards of net offense, equally split between running and passing. The visitors managed 91 yards rushing and 128 in the air for a total of 219 yards.

From the *Chicago Tribune Magazine's* November 1, 1992 condensed preview of the Mike Celizic book:

"You watch a tape of any game from that year, and you'll see the same attitude. In the Michigan State-Notre Dame game, not one player from either side can be seen gloating over a fallen opponent. The game was filled with monster defensive hits, with great efforts, with tackles for losses, tackles for no gains, passes broken up along with the receivers who were trying to catch them. And after every great play, the athletes picked themselves up and got back into the huddle. That was it. No pointing. No gloating. No woofing. Not even a little leap of triumph. Just business."

That game concluded the MSU schedule for 1966, but Notre Dame finished one week later with a victory over Southern California, a win that garnered enough ballots for the Irish to secure both the Associated Press (AP) and United Press International (UPI) mythical titles for 1966.

TEAM OF THE YEAR

Wrestling coach Grady Peninger put together a squad that posted a 9-1-1 dual-meet record, successfully defended the Big Ten title with a record 92 points, and climaxed the season at Kent State, where they captured the school's only NCAA team wrestling championship by scoring 74 points. That winning total was achieved with two individual championships, a pair of second place finishes, a third, a fourth and a sixth. In his 137-pound title match, Dale Anderson gained a tie with seconds remaining and then won in overtime. George Radman captured the 167-pound title with a fairly easy 17-8 decision. The runner-up slots were credited to Don Behm at 130 and Mike Bradley at 177, while Jack Zindel was third at 191. Jeff Richardson was fourth among the heavyweights and Dale Carr finished sixth in the 145-pound division.

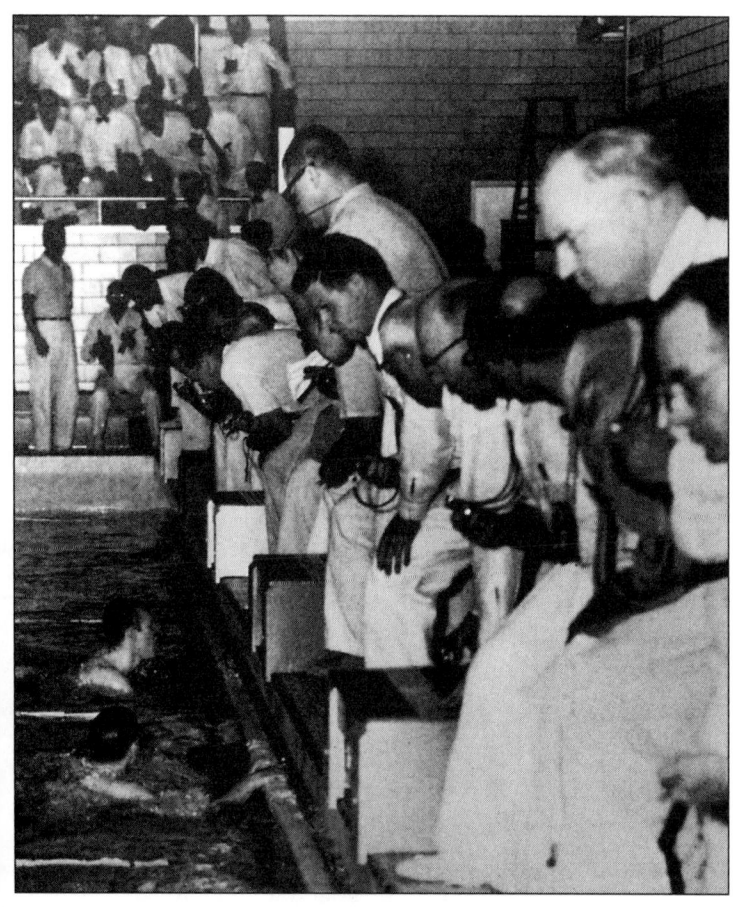

MAKING HISTORY

Following 40 years of service, Leonard Falcone retired as the director of MSU's marching bands in July of 1967. Throughout those four decades he had built the band membership from 65 to 185, and in recent years he had developed "Patterns in Motion" as the band's trademark.

For the first time, an automatic timing device was used in conducting the Big Ten and NCAA swimming and diving championships. Both meets were held in MSU's IM pool, first the conference meet (March 2-4), followed by the national championships (March 23-25).

OPPOSITE PAGE LEFT
The 1967 wrestling team. (Front row, left to right) D. Behm, G. Bissell, D. Anderson, K. Lowrence, D. Campbell, F. Larsen and G. Hody; (row two, left to right) J. Zindel, M. Johnson, M. Gudiness, D. Carr, G. Sinadinos, B. Darche and M. McGilliard; (back row, left right) coach G. Peninger, C. Beatty, G. Radman, D. Cox, M. Johnson, N. Peterson, J. Richardson, J. Schneider and M. Bradley

Although the timing system did not include a large display board as it does today, it did clock races to the 100th of a second and picked places to the 1,000th of a second. A technician had to read the machine's interpretation, which was verbally passed along to another person, who in turn recorded the results on a paper form.

Conforming to the NCAA program of events, the Big Ten added the 440-yard relay, the triple jump, the three-mile run, and the 3,000-meter steeplechase to the championship format.

Until the introduction of the electronic timing and placing devices in 1967, as many as 36 officials would be used to run a swimming meet.

GREAT STATE DATES

Football—**September 17, 1966 (H):** Under the direction of a new signal caller, Jimmy Raye, Michigan State opened the season with a satisfying 28-10 victory over North Carolina State, coached by former MSU assistant Earle Edwards. Raye engineered all four touchdown drives, which covered 60 yards, 80 yards, 22 yards and 74 yards. Some marquee players from the undefeated 1965 team returned for key roles: Clinton Jones, Dwight Lee, Gene Washington, Dick Kenney, Bubba Smith, George Webster, Charlie Thornhill, Jesse Phillips, Jimmy Summers, Drake Garrett, Joe Pryzbycki, Jerry West and Bob Apisa. Unfortunately, Apisa began the season with a debilitating knee injury that negatively affected his performance all season long. The revamped defense yielded a net gain of 27 yards rushing which hinted the 1966 edition could be as stingy as its predecessor.

Football—**October 8, 1966 (H):** A record-setting crowd of 78,833 jammed into Spartan Stadium to watch Coach Daugherty's squad defeat Michigan for the second year in a row, 20-7. Protecting a seven-point lead for three quarters, they secured the insurance of two additonal touchdowns in the final period (Bob Apisa's seven-yard run and a 25-yard Jimmy Raye to Gene Washington pass). The latter score followed a U of M fumble recovery by Charlie Thornhill. The final point spread may well have been greater had State not been forced to overcome seven

penalties totaling 85 yards. Two of these calls nullified touchdowns: (1) Al Brenner's 53-yard punt return; and (2) Clinton Jones's 44-yard dash to paydirt. The MSU defense was once more miserly, holding the Wolverine runners to a net of 47 yards.

Football—**October 15, 1966 (A):** After gaining a safety on an errant center snap for a punt, Ohio State held a 2-0 advantage through the first half of play as a hard-driving rain with accompanying high winds continued to keep the Spartans' powerful running game in check. Sensing that a field goal might win the game, Dick Kenney tried boots of 40, 47 and 49 yards. Missing all three, he finally succeeded with a 27-yarder in the third quarter. This only seemed to rouse the Buckeyes, and on the opening play of the fourth quarter they connected on a 47-yard touchdown pass play. Failing to convert the point after, the Bucks led, 8-3. On the first play following that score, quarterback Jimmy Raye hit receiver Gene Washington for 18 yards. Al Brenner was the target on the next two tosses, good for 14 and then 17 yards. On a third and ten situation, Raye combined with Washington for a first down on the two-yard line. From there it took all four tries before Bob Apisa could negotiate the remaining six inches into the end zone. A successful two-point PAT made the eventual final score read 11-8. That next week, pollsters apparently weren't impressed as Notre Dame replaced State atop both wire service tabulations.

Cross Country—**October 21, 1966 (H):** Finishing 1-2-3, the senior threesome of Dick Sharkey, George Balthrop and Eric Zemper ran away from the pack as MSU defeated Notre Dame, 27-30, and Eastern Michigan, 20-36, in a triangular meet. Sharkey, the Detroit Redford native, raced home in 20:18 to set a meet and varsity record on the Forest Akers course. It was the third meet in a row in which the Spartan captain took individual honors in record time. Sophomores Roger Merchant and Dean Rosenberg completed the scoring by finishing in the 10th and 16th places respectively.

Football—**October 22, 1966 (H):** Duffy turned to the "I" formation for the first time, and the result was an impressive 41-20 win over Purdue University. After State built a 21-0 halftime lead, the two teams traded touchdowns over the final 30 minutes of play. Playing before a regional television audience and an overflow homecoming crowd of 78,014, Jimmy Raye, the junior quarterback, matched the efforts of the Boilermakers' All-American, Bob Griese. Often battling a wind that gusted up to 35 miles per hour, Raye hit on 10 of 17 for 158 yards with one touchdown, a six-yarder to Bob Apisa. Griese was 18 of 30 for 186 yards. Apisa, the senior fullback, scored three times. Dwight Lee and reserve Regis Cavender accounted for the other two tuchdowns.

Soccer—**October 29, 1966 (H):** Featuring a pair of goals from each of the team's top two scorers, Tony Keyes and Tom Kreft, MSU shut out Ohio University, 5-0. Guy Busch, missing opportunities all day, finally scored in the final period on a pass from Barry Tieman, who handed off three assists on the afternoon.

Swimming and Diving—**January 21, 1967 (A):** Although the swimmers lost both relay events, they won five of the nine individual races and surprisingly both diving events to edge Michigan 63-60 for only the fourth time ever. Ken Walsh was a double winner, taking the 100-yard freestyle (47.4) and 200-yard freestyle events (1:46.0). Other winners were Gary Dilley with a pool record 1:58.9 in the 200-yard backstroke; Ed Glick in the 200-yard butterfly (1:58.4); and Pete Williams with a 2:01.6 in the 200-yard individual medley. John Narcy's divers came through with 14 of the possible 18 points. Doug Todd and Fred Whiteford went one-three in the one meter event and Duane Green and Whiteford followed with a one-two slam on the three-meter board.

Wrestling—**January 21, 1967 (A):** In a murderous schedule, the MSU wrestlers took to the road for back-to-back meets against Oklahoma A&M and Oklahoma University. Following a 14-14 tie against the nationally ranked number two Cowboys on Friday night, Grady Peninger and his crew were in Norman, Okla., for a showdown against number one-ranked Oklahoma. Within the opening six matches, State had earned only two verdicts, Don Behm at 130-pounds and Dale Anderson at 137-pounds. Trailing 12-6 at this point, the Spartans faced the unenviable task of needing to close out the evening with three favorable decisions to gain an upset victory. In shocking fashion, that's exactly what happened. Answering the challenge first was George Radman, the eventual NCAA champion at 167. Next to have his arm raised in victory was 177-pound Mike Bradley and finally, Jeff Richadson of Johnstown, Pa., who captured the heavyweight match, to give State the 15-12 win.

Hockey—**February 10 (H) & 11 (A), 1967:** On the scoring of co-captains Tom Mikkola and Mike Jacobson, plus stellar goaltending by Gaye Cooley, State swept a two-game weekend series against archrival Michi-

gan, 4-3 and 5-1. Mikkola scored the winning goal at Dem Hall on Friday night with less than two minutes remaining in the game and then took part in all of MSU's scoring the next night in Ann Arbor with two goals and three assists. Jacobson scored State's first two goals on Friday and had a goal and three assists on Saturday night.

Basketball—**February 13, 1967 (H):** A crowd of 7,127 was at Jenison Fieldhouse to watch State build and then lose a 12-point lead early in the second half prior to rallying for a 86-77 victory over Indiana. Lee Lafayette led the way with 10 rebounds and a personal season-high 24 points. Steve Rymal scored 19, and John Bailey and John Holms, the Lansing sophomore, each had eight. Matt Aitch, the big center, contributed 14 points even though he sat out a good portion of the game after committing four fouls in the opening eight minutes. Leading at halftime 47-39, State never trailed thereafter, but the Hoosiers did pull within one point midway in the second half. Vern Johnson aided in the late resurgence with seven points off the bench.

Gymnastics—**February 15, 1967 (A):** Although lacking depth, the Spartans won every event but the trampoline to edge the Michigan Wolverines, 190.80-190.42. Dave Thor, as usual, had a busy afternoon, featuring firsts in the vault and high bar. Dennis Smith won the side horse, Toby Towson took the floor exercise, and Cliff Diehl won the parallel bars. The meet result hinged on the final event, the rings, in which Ed Gunny and Dave Croft came through, tying for the top spot.

Basketball—**February 18, 1967 (H):** Highlighted by a controversial field goal by Steve Rymal from 45 feet with three seconds of time remaining in the game, State boosted its conference-leading record to 6-2 with a 66-65 victory over Minnesota. Rymal's shot seemed to miss the mark to the right where teammate Lee Lafayette apparently reached up, grabbed the ball and stuffed it through for the winning basket. The officials did not see it that way and gave the goal to Rymal. In protest, the Minnesota coach claimed Lafayette did indeed dunk the original shot, which would have been goatending. Coach Bennington agreed that Lafayette was the scorer but that he did not complete the score from above the cylinder, thus no goal tending. Either position is moot. The game official's interpretation remains today—Steve Rymal scored the winning basket.

Fencing—**February 25, 1967 (A):** For the 10th year in a row, Charlie Schmitter's Spartans defeated the Indi-

ana Hoosiers, this time by a commanding 17-10 score. The State swordsmen were Terry Givens, Serge Montalvo and Roger Loutzennhiser in foil; Charlie Baer, Pete Kahle and Dean Daggett in sabre; and Ken Summerville, Frank Shubert and Bill Kerner in epee.

Track and Field—**May 6, 1967 (H):** It could easily be argued that George Balthrop, Mike Bowers, Keith Coates, Dick Sharkey, Bob Steele, Gene Washington, Dazwell Campbell and Eric Zemper, comprised the best senior class to ever complete in track and field for Michigan State. On this Saturday afternoon, their final home meet, they all contributed in the 115-58 victory over Ohio State. The seniors entered nine individual events and won them all. Running a 9.7 100-yard dash, a 21.6 in the 220, and a 14.3 in the high hurdles, Washington was a triple winner. Sharkey added a double win, the steeplechase in 10:10.3 and the three mile in 14.29.0. Other seniors to break the tape were Steele, who ran a 52.6 in the intermediate hurdles; Campbell, who coasted to an easy 48.6 victory in the 440; and Zemper, who won the mile with a career-best time of 4:10.2. Yet, the superior performance of the afternoon came in the high jump pit, where Mike Bowers cleared the bar at seven feet to set a new varsity and Ralph Young Field mark. Furthermore, it was the best effort ever by a Big Ten jumper.

Baseball—**May 7, 1967 (A):** After being rained out on Saturday, State hung around Champaign, Ill., one extra day and then defeated the Illini in a doubleheader, 7-2 and 5-4. In the opener, State scored once in the first, twice in the third, once in the fourth and three times in the seventh. Tom Hummel, the junior transfer from Southern Methodist, led the offense with three hits, while Mel Behney and Tom Ellis connected for solo home runs. In the second game, State trailed 4-3 with one inning remaining when they linked together a walk, a single and an error to load the bases, whereupon Tom Binkowski doubled to left-center to score the tying, and eventual winning, run. The starting and winning pitcher, Mickey Knight, recovered from a shaky fourth inning to hold the Illini hitless in the final three innings.

Tennis—**May 9, 1967 (H):** It took four hours and 25 minutes to finish all nine matches, but the result was worth it as State edged Michigan 5-4. After losing at the number one, number two and number three singles positions things looked bleak, but the Spartans responded with victories by John Good at number four, Vic Dhoogea at number five and Jim Phillips, who remained unbeaten

at the number six spot. The meet then came down to who could win at least two of the doubles matches. The no. 1 pair of Chuck Brainard-Rich Monan did their part 7-5, 3-6, 6-1. Then, for the first time all season the number three team of Dhooga and Phillips met defeat. Thus, the entire afternoon was left on the rackets of the number two duo, Mickey Szilagy and John Good and after losing the opening set 6-4 they came through 7-5, 6-3. As they shook hands with the victory it was 7:25 p.m.

Golf—**May 12-13, 1967 (H):** Led by Steve Benson's medalist score of 75-74—149, Bruce Fossum's golfers managed to overcome a two-stroke deficit in the final two holes of play to defeat Michigan, 613-617, in the 11-team field of their own Spartan Invitational Tournament. Through 16 holes on the last day, the Wolverines held precariously to a two-stroke lead. Following the 17th, the four-man State team had made up the difference and had actually taken a one-stroke lead. On the final hole they continued to perform like winners, gaining three more strokes to finish with a four-stroke victory. In addition to Benson, John Bailey shot a 154, Sandy McAndrew and Troy Campbell both fired totals of 155. Other teams competing in the university division were Central, Eastern, Northern, Western and Wayne.

ATHLETE OF THE YEAR

Gene Washington (six foot three, 218 pounds) achieved an impressive double as an MSU two-sport star. He was twice selected as an All-American in football (1965 and 1966), and as a track star he ran to the 1965 NCAA indoor title in the 60-yard high hurdles. For three seasons as a Spartan hurdler he also gained six Big Ten championships, indoor and outdoor. Gene's gridiron achievements as a pass receiver are legendary, being listed first with yards per catch in a season (25.0 yards in 1966) in the school record book. Washington's name also remains affixed to seven other team-leader category lists. Following his Michigan State career, he was a first-round draft pick by the NFL's Minnesota Vikings, a team with which he gained all-pro status twice.

IN THE SPARTLITE

Baseball: Summarizing his thoughts following the team's 7-7-1 southern trip, coach Danny Litwhiler quipped, "Our errors came in bunches but our hits didn't."

As the regular season opened, the four starting pitchers were Dick Kenney, Mel Behney, Zana Easton and Mickey Knight.

The team seldom put it all together (hitting, fielding and pitching) on the four-game weekends against Big Ten competition. The final record of 6-8 put the team in fifth place.

Third baseman Bill Steckley injured his left wrist during Christmas break. X-rays proved negative, but as pain persisted during spring training a second x-ray exposed the reality of a broken bone. Rather than miss the season he kept the wrist taped and continued to play. Was his performance affected? By season's end he had compiled a .325 average, the team-leading average.

Gene Washington

Basketball: The Detroit Pistons selected Matthew Aitch in the 13th round of the NBA draft. Two rounds earlier, perhaps as a publicity stunt, the Baltimore Bullets had chosen Bubba Smith of football fame.

Cross Country: For the third straight year, MSU was runner-up in the conference championship run held in Madison, Wis. Totaling 61 points, State was a distant 20 points behind Iowa. Dick Sharkey finished in second place, followed by George Balthrop sixth, Eric Zemper 11th, Roger Merchant 16th and Dean Rosenberg 26th.

Both Dick Sharkey and the MSU team finished 12th at the NCAA Championships run over the hilly six-mile course at Kansas University. He was followed by Eric Zemper 55th, Roger Merchant 68th, Art Link 118th, and Pat Wilson 177th. Competing in unseasonable 70-degree weather affected Don Rosenberg as he blacked out after five and a half miles and did not finish. His absence significantly affected the Spartan's team scoring.

Fencing: In a *State News* story of January 10, 1967 the writer attempts to untangle the mystique of the sport of fencing:

> "In the foil opponents both attack and defend. Players score points by hitting their opponents with the point of the foil from the waist to the neck, not including the arms. The winner is decided when one player has been hit five times.
>
> The sabre differs from the foil not only in weapon but also in where a player may be hit and how. The attacking is done with the point, front edge and back third edge of the sabre. Also, a hit is allowed above the waist, including the arms and head.
>
> The epee is played more electrically, as both players are wired along with the tips of their weapons, and a buzzer sounds a hit. A hit is allowed anywhere on the body."

State collected 25 points to finish behind Wisconsin with 37 and Illinois with 32 at the Big Ten championships. The most productive performer for MSU was senior Frank Shubert, who completed the afternoon second in the epee with an 8-1 mark. Charlie Baer finished in a three-way tie for first but lost in the fence-offs and had to settle for third with his 7-2 record.

Football: In leading the 56-7 romp of Iowa, Clinton Jones completed a Big Ten Conference record-setting afternoon by carrying for 268 yards in 21 carries. Illinois'

Jim Grabowski had been the Big Ten's best (239 yards in 33 rushes against Wisconsin in 1964). Playing before 67,211 fans that sat through 35-degree weather, the Cleveland, Ohio, senior clicked off touchdown runs of 79 and 70 yards. Jones also scored a third touchdown culminating a 72-yard 11-play drive in which he accounted for 69 of the yards on 10 carries.

While sharing the spotlight with Notre Dame, the 1966 Spartans gained recognition as national champions by four major selectors beyond the popular AP and UPI polls, one of which resulted in being awarded the MacArthur Bowl for the second year in a row.

Golf: The golf team came from behind to edge Ohio State by three strokes to finish third in the Big Ten Championships in Ann Arbor. Most importantly, their performance qualified them for the NCAA tournament. Shooting a respectable 310, Ed Murphy was the top Spartan and sixth in the 72-hole tournament. Adding to the team score of 1,583 were John Bailey 314, Steve Benson 317, George Buth 320 and Sandy McAndrew 322.

In the 36-hole NCAA tournament at Shawnee, Pa., the State fivesome shot a respectable composite score of 598 to finish tied for sixth. They were 13 strokes from the winning University of Houston team. It was MSU's first appearance in the national championship since 1961.

Gymnastics: At the Big Ten meet, Dave Thor successfully defended his all-around title but lost the floor exercise and side horse crowns when he unfortunately injured his ankle in warmups and had to withdraw. Sophomore Toby Towson was nearly flawless in his floor exercise routine and earned a 9.5 score to win first place. Dave Croft, defending champion in the ring event, scored a 9.2 and settled for a first place tie this time around. As a team they placed third.

It was just one of those years for Dave Thor. On the day before the NCAA regional qualifying meet in Wheaton, Ill., he was involved in an automobile accident causing personal injury that necessitated his withdrawal from competition. Consequently without his talent, State did not qualify as a team title contender. Five Spartans did, however, qualify to compete as individuals in the NCAA meet in Carbondale, Ill.: Towson, Croft, Ed Gunny, Dan Kinsey and Norm Haynie.

On the following weekend at the national meet, both Towson and Croft were eliminated after experiencing major flaws in their routines. Limited success came with Gunny's fourth place on the rings and sixth on the horizontal, along with Kinsey's fifth place on the rings.

Hockey: The Spartans were defeated by Michigan 5-3 in the finals of the inaugural Great Lakes Invitational held in Detroit.

Although no trophy was ever awarded, the Big Ten office announced that the team with the best record in regular season games between the three hockey schools would be acknowledged as the conference champion. MSU boasted the title in 1967. The Spartans did, however, win some actual hardware, the Michigan Press Trophy, which went annually to the team with the best record between MSU, Michigan Tech and Michigan.

State advanced to the NCAA tournament in Syracuse, N.Y., by defeating Michigan, 4-2 and Michigan Tech, 2-1, but that was the end of the line, as the Spartans lost to Boston University, 4-2, in a semi-final match up. Two nights later, Amo's crew regained some pride with a 6-1 win in the consolation game against North Dakota.

Soccer: Undefeated in eight games, the Spartans took to the road for the season finale against St. Louis University, the defending NCAA champions. In what was promoted as the game of the year, the teams held each other scoreless until late in the third period when Guy Busch put State in front with a header on a pass from Tom Kreft. The Billikens tied the game on an unassisted goal with five minutes to go in the final period. Two five-minute overtimes could not break the tie and Gene Kenney's crew returned home disappointed, yet with their undefeated record still in tact.

After registering victories in the opening rounds of the NCAA tournament (2-0 over Akron and 3-1 over Temple), the Spartans earned their way into the tournament semi-finals against Long Island University. On third-period goals by Barry Tiemann and Guy Bush, the Spartans managed to tie LIU, 2-2, and set the stage for four ensuing scoreless overtime periods. It was then that the Spartans were victimized by a strange method for arbitrating tied games, as the Blackbirds were granted a spot in the NCAA finals on the basis of a 6-5 margin in corner-kicks. On the next day Long Island lost in the title game to San Francisco, 5-2. The MSU team had reached an abrupt ending for a stellar season (10-0-2). During the 12 games they had outscored their opponents 66-6 with the pair of Guy Busch and Tony Keyes, the Jamaican sophomore, accounting for 41 of the goals.

On May 6, the team assembled to take on the USA Olympic Team that included MSU freshman, Ernest Tuchscherer. As could have been expected, the USA team came through with a 4-0 victory.

Swimming and Diving: Hosting the conference championships, State finished third behind Indiana and Michigan primarily on the strength of two seniors, Ken Walsh and Gary Dilley. After finishing second in the 500-yard freestyle, Walsh swam to a pair of freestyle firsts in Big Ten record times, 1:43.45 in the 200 and 46.17 in the 100. His preliminary time of 46.02 bettered the NCAA mark. For the third year in a row, Dilley captured both backstroke events with a conference record swim of 53.1 in the 100 and 1:56.23 in the 200. The two stars also contributed to a Spartan first place in the 400-yard freestyle relay with splits as follows: Walsh 46.4, Gary Langley 48.5, Don Rauch 47.5 and Dilley 46.2.

As the National Collegiate championships were also conducted in the Men's IM pool, Ken Walsh apparently liked the idea of swimming in familiar surroundings. In somewhat of a surprise, the lanky senior not only won the 100-yard freestyle, but he did so in an impressive time of 45.6, tying the American record. At that same meet, two-time champion senior Gary Dilley, who had never lost a backstroke race as a Spartan, finally faltered as he relinquished his titles in both the 100- and the 200-yard races.

Walsh later earned a spot on the 1967 USA Pan-American team that competed in Winnipeg, Canada, in July of 1967. He not only won the 100-meter freestyle race at that meet, but he established a new world's record of 52.58 on the leadoff leg of the 400-yard freestyle relay.

Tennis: Returning from a less than impressive southern trip (4-4), the varsity tennis team proceeded to complete their regular season undefeated (11-0), somewhat mirroring the 1953 schedule 14 years prior when the Spartans were 12-4 overall and undefeated in the regular season (10-0).

Stan Drobac's squad captured two singles titles and all three doubles titles to defeat the University of Michigan by four and a half points at the Big Ten championships held on the U of M courts. Spartan winners in singles were number four John Good, 6-1, 4-6, 6-1, and number six Jim Phillips, 6-3, 6-3. Phillips later teamed with Vic Dhooga to seal the team victory for MSU with a come-from-behind win at number three doubles 5-7, 6-2, 7-5. The other champion pairs for State were no. 1 Chuck Brainard-Rick Monan, 6-3, 6-1 and number two Good and Mickey Szilagyi, 6-3, 6-2. Four of the five

Michigan State titles were gained over Michigan opponents in the finals.

Vic Dhooga was the only member of the Big Ten championship team that decided to compete in the NCAA tournament in Carbondale, Ill. He won his first match before being eliminated.

Track and Field: In the third running of the NCAA indoor championships at Cobo Hall in Detroit, three Spartans reached the finals. Don Crawford placed fourth in the 440, Gene Washington was fifth in the high hurdles, and Pat Wilson finished fifth in the 600-yard run.

Michigan State was unable to successfully defend the indoor and outdoor conference championships of 1966, each time settling for second place. At the indoor meet they were edged by Wisconsin, 56 3/4-53 and outdoors by Iowa 51 1/2-49. At the indoor meet in Madison four Spartans won their events: Dick Sharkey in the two mile; Pat Wilson in the 600-yard run; Mike Bowers in the high jump; and Roland Carter in the pole vault. Six MSU entries took second place in the meet: Sharkey in the mile; Roger Merchant in the 1,000; John Spain in the half-mile; Gene Washington in the high hurdles; and Daz Campbell in both the 300 and broad jump.

Outdoors, in conference-record performances, Carter won the pole vault with a vault 16' 3/4"; Washington won his third consecutive high hurdle championship in 13.7, and Spain finished first in the 660 with a time of 1:16.7 to become the only track man to hold two conference records. He had set the 440-yard record the year before. Earning team points in their specialties were Wilson, Sharkey, Campbell, Bob Steele, and Charley Pollard.

At the NCAA championships in Provo, Utah, Bob Steele successfully defended his 1966 national title. Along with Dick Sharkey's sixth place in the six-mile race, State finished the weekend with 12 points and a 14th-place finish.

Wrestling: Going against Michigan in the final meet of the season, undefeated MSU was leading, 14-8, with their Big Ten champion Mike Bradley up next for the 177-pound match. In a disappointing conclusion, the Ypsilanti light-heavyweight was defeated, 3-2, and heavyweight Jeff Richardson was pinned, and suddenly State had absorbed the first and only loss of the season, 16-14.

EXTRA! 1967 NCAA HOCKEY TOURNAMENT (Third Place)

The Spartans' postseason play looked very similar to that of the year before. At the end of the regular season they had placed only fifth in the conference, but in the WCHA playoffs they defeated Michigan 4-2 and Michigan Tech 2-1 in overtime to again become a surprise participant in the NCAA tournament. There Boston University found its revenge, topping MSU 4-2, but State overcame North Dakota in the consolation game to come home with a third-place finish.

March 17, 1967—Syracuse, N.Y.
Boston University 4, MSU 2
1st Pd.: 1. BU, Bassi (unasst.), 4:18; 2. BU, Quinn (Sobeski, Gilmour), 8:36.
2nd Pd.: 3. MSU, Faunt (Fallat, Anstey), 10:02; 4. BU, Bassi (Quinn, Sobeski), 19:52.
3rd Pd.: 5. MSU, Mikkola (Hathaway), 10:08; 6. BU, Abbott (Gilmour), 14:34.

March 18, 1967—Syracuse, N.Y.
MSU 6, North Dakota 1
1st Pd.: 1. ND, Kartio (Bamburak), 8:00; 2. MSU, Jacobson (Hathaway, Mikkola), 13:25; 3. MSU, McAndrew (Brawley, Cristofoli), 15:06.
2nd Pd.: 4. MSU, Duffett (McAndrew, Cristofoli), 2:08; 5. MSU, Mikkola (Jacobson, McAndrew), 8:14; 6. MSU, Mikkola (Bois), 10:21.
3rd Pd.: 7. MSU, McAndrew (Brawley, Cristofoli), 10:18.

EXTRA! SEVEN BIG TEN WRESTLING TITLES IN A ROW

(#2) 1967—Columbus, Ohio: Grady Peninger's team totally dominated the championship meet of 1967 by collecting a conference-record 92 points on five firsts, two seconds and a third place in the nine weight classifications. Gary Bissell opened the evening with a win in his 123-pound consolation match. This was followed by the crowning of three straight Spartan champions. First, Don Behm finished his undefeated weekend with a high-scoring 15-8 win. Next came Dale Anderson whose path to the finals included two pins, and he became the State's second champion with a 3-0 decision at 137 pounds. Dale Carr's 7-2 victory at 145-pounds sealed the team championship for MSU. David Campbell, the surprise of the meet, made it to the finals before bowing out. Two more Spartans followed with championships, George Radman at 167 and Mike Bradley, who successfully defended his 177 pound title. The evening concluded with heavyweight Jeff Richardson being pinned by Michigan's NCAA champion Dave Porter.

MSU
1967-1968

TALES TO TELL

A memorable Spartan moment took place at a wrestling meet in venerable Jenison Fieldhouse on Saturday evening, February 17, 1968. In a post-meet interview, coach Grady Peninger expressed it this way:

> "This was the highlight of my entire coaching career. It's even more exciting than winning the nationals last year. No one would have ever guessed that this would have ever happened."

Although MSU had won two straight Big Ten championships and the NCAA title in 1967, a Spartan team had not defeated Michigan in a dual meet since 1964. The eventual story that evening was not that the tables had finally been turned, but the story was how the victory unfolded. With the Wolverines leading 14-9, State's 177-pound Mike Bradley, a two-time conference champion, produced a 9-2 verdict, closing the gap to a two-point deficit, 14-12. Next came the heavyweights. In one corner stood the U of M's Dave Porter, a formidable opponent who had been defeated only one time in three

years of college competition and never pinned. A product of Lansing Sexton High School, he had won the national collegiate title in 1966. In the opposite corner was Coach Peninger's newest recruit, Jeff Smith, a junior college champion from Bellflower, Calif., who had given Porter all he could handle at an AAU meet the previous summer. During the recruiting phase of their relationship, Smith had told Grady, "I think I can handle that Porter." Grady was a believer.

Jeff Smith made everyone a believer when he pinned Michigan's Dave Porter.

HEADLINES of 1968

- Dr. Martin Luther King Jr. is assassinated in Memphis and senator Robert Kennedy is assassinated in Los Angeles.
- The Motion Picture Association of America introduces movie ratings. The original classifications are G, M (mature audiences), R and X.
- The naval intelligence ship, U.S.S. Pueblo, is seized by North Koreans in January and finally released in December.
- Congress recommends that the U.S.A. switch to the metric system within 10 years.

SCOREBOARD

	W	L	T	Avg.
Baseball	32	10	1	.756
Track and Field	0	1	0	.000
Football	3	7	0	.300
Basketball	12	12	0	.500
Tennis	11	10	0	.523
Cross Country	1	4	0	.200
Swimming and Diving	8	3	0	.727
Wrestling	9	4	0	.692
Hockey	11	16	2	.414
Fencing	6	8	0	.429
Golf	4	1	0	.800
Gymnastics	6	3	0	.667
Soccer	12	0	2	.929

As the 3,250 fans that packed the bleachers on the east side of the fieldhouse were in one continuous deafening roar, the two went at it. From the beginning it seemed obvious the blonde Californian was out to make good his prophecy. At 1:49 he was awarded two points on a predicament as Porter managed to wriggle off of the mat to avoid the inevitable. Then, at 3:31 the native Lansing-ite once more found himself looking up at the Jenison ceiling, and this time there was no escape . . . it was a pin. Jeff Smith indeed "could handle" Dave Porter.

Of the many treasures that adorned Athletic Director Munn's office, one that hung from the wall was a large picture of that "memorable Spartan moment" at 3:31.

TEAM OF THE YEAR

Topping their 10-0-1 regular season run, Gene Kenney's soccer squad defeated Maryland, 4-1, and Akron, 3-1, in opening NCAA rounds to earn a trip to the Final Four for the fourth straight year. On the concluding weekend in St. Louis, Mo., State defeated Long Island University, 4-0, with goals by Gary McBrady, Alex Skotarek, Ernie Tuschscherer and Guy Busch. The championship game against St. Louis University opened two days later on a pitch described as swamplike. A torrential rain had left the playing field nothing but mud, covered with water and in a dangerously unplayable condition. Regardless, officials opted to begin the games, but halted the proceedings with two minutes remaining in the scoreless opening half. With players slipping and sliding, the game had been more of a sideshow than a soccer championship. The conditions mandated that the two finalists be crowned co-champions for 1967. In his post season interview, Coach Kenney stated, "It's not too bad at all to be co-champion. It's a lot better than being second. There just wasn't anything else to be done. Field conditions were absolutely unbelievable."

Recognized as 1967 All-Americans from that team were Peter Hens, Ernie Tuchscherer, Trevor Harris and Guy Busch.

The 1967 soccer team. (Front row, left to right) assistant coach K. O'Connell, R. Nelke, T. Keyes, J. Baum, O. Enuston, E. Tuchscherer and D. Trace. (Middle row, left to right) Coach G. Kenney, G. McBrady, T. Harris, N. Archer, P. Hens, G. Busch, B. Myerson, T. Kreft, B. Tiemann and Asst. Coach T. Bidiak. (Back row, left to right) J. Zensen, E. Skotarek, A. Skotarek, T. Belloli, B. Jacobsen, D. Boles, K. Hamann and T. Sanders.

MAKING HISTORY

The hockey coaches of the Big Ten schools, Ohio State, Wisconsin, Minnesota, Michigan and Michigan State, initiated a conference tournament to be played during the last week of December. The inaugural effort, in 1967, was hosted by the University of Minnesota. The Spartans lost the opening game to the Gophers, 6-3, but closed out the week by defeating Ohio State, 7-0, and Wisconsin, 4-3, to gain third-place honors. The idea of the tournament never really gathered much support, and by 1970 it had run its course.

Dave Thor was recipient of the Nissen award as the nation's outstanding senior collegiate gymnast. Spartan Jim Curzi had been the first winner of the award in 1966.

With approximately 2,500 track fans cheering him on, pole vaulter Roland Carter needed to clear 16' 3" in the Ohio Relay competition to claim the championship. On his final effort, he propelled himself up and over to set a new meet and MSU outdoor varsity record. At that time Carter was the only 16-foot vaulter in Big Ten history.

GREAT STATE DATES

Soccer—**September 30, 1967 (A):** Responding to the fact that State had scored a total of 17 points in their first two games, the Pittsburgh strategy was obvious—defense. The result was a one-goal game on a score by Trevor Harris at the 20:30 mark in the third quarter. It wasn't that the Spartans lacked other opportunities. There were a total of 24 additional attempts on target, plus numerous other shots that hit a post or sailed over the net. Meanwhile, goal tender Joe Baum at the other end of the field had to make only one save all day long.

Football—**October 7, 1967 (H):** In defeating Wisconsin, 35-7, State won its 15th straight conference game stretching over three seasons. Dwight Lee scored the opening two touchdowns, the first following a six-play 63-yard drive on the opening possession of the game, while the second touchdown finalized a 16-play drive that covered 89 yards. Inserted into the starting lineup for the first time, halfback LaMarr Thomas led an 80-yard 13-play drive for touchdown number three, and he then tossed a 44-yard pass-run to Al Brenner making the scoreboard read 28-7. With 26 seconds remaining in the game, Frankie Waters crossed the goal line for the final

score. Charley Bailey had a stellar game on defense, making 13 tackles and recovering two Badger fumbles.

Football—**October 14, 1967 (A):** Leading Michigan 7-0 following a 90-yard scoring drive in the opening quarter, the Spartans struck for three touchdowns in the closing two and a half minutes of the first half to put the game out of reach. The three-touchdown blitz was orchestrated by Jimmy Raye and included his two-yard scoring plunge and two passes for touchdowns, a 65-yarder to Al Brenner and an eight-yard toss to Frank Foreman. That fourth score was set up on a pass interception by Sterling Armstrong that he returned to the U of M eight-yard line. On his only carry of the afternoon, Dick Berlinski burst over the goal line from the eight-yard-line in the fourth quarter to seal the final score at 34-0.

Cross Country—**October 21, 1967 (H):** Trailing throughout the race, junior Roger Merchant sprinted to the finish line, completing the five-mile Forest Akers course in a winning time of 25:43.5. Sophomore Ken Leonowicz was five seconds back in second place and was followed by captain Dean Rosenberg in fourth place, Bill Bradna in ninth, and Gary Bisbee right behind in 10th. Out of the the team scoring but finishing in the next slots, 11-12-13, were Rich Stevens, Dale Stanley and Pat Wilson. When points were totaled, the Spartans had edged Eastern Michigan, 26-29.

Hockey—**January 6, 1968 (H):** The largest crowd in Michigan State hockey history, 4,139, had hardly settled into their seats when junior center Chuck Phillips scored at the 18 second mark. That was followed by a Nino Cristofoli goal at 4:38, which the University of Michigan matched on a power play before the opening period had concluded. Following a scoreless second period, the Wolverines took command in the third and scored at 3:53 and at 9:17 to take a 3-2 lead, but Amo's guys were not through. With a two-man advantage, Cristofoli found the back of the net one more time on a poke shot following a scramble in front of the goalie. This sent the game into overtime, and after nearly six minutes of the extra session, junior winger Lee Hathaway stole the puck at mid-ice and broke in all alone. Faking the net minder to the left, he put it away on the glove side to gain a 4-3 victory at 6:06.

Gymnastics—**January 6, 1968 (A):** Dave Thor turned in a remarkable one man show, leading MSU to a comfortable 186.10-165.75 victory over Ohio State. He scored 55.4 points, for an average of 9.23 in winning the side horse, vault, parallel bars and horizontal bars, and

earning seconds in floor exercise and still rings. Toby Towson was the winner in floor exercise, while Dan Kinsey was first on the rings. The Buckeyes managed to capture only one event, the trampoline.

Basketball—January 13 (A) & February 3, 1968 (H): For the first time since 1955-1956, MSU defeated the University of Michigan twice in one season, both times by five-point margins. After being behind, 42-37, at half-time of the first game, State roared back for a satisfying 86-81 win. Heywood Edwards and Jim Gibbons came off the bench to lead the resurgence by combining for 25 points. Center Lee Lafayette led the team with 21. Guard John Bailey and forward Bernie Copeland each chipped in 12. In the return game, an 82-77 victory before 13,202 fans in Jenison, Harrison Stepter, a 6' 2" junior from St. Louis, Mo., scored 20 points, including 14 in the second half when the Spartans broke a 39-39 tie. Lafayette and Copeland contributed 21 and 16 points respectively. John Benington's squad never trailed after grabbing a 61-60 lead with 7:26 remaining.

Wrestling—January 13, 1968 (A): With four decisive wins and two ties, MSU managed a 16-13 verdict over Arizona State. Along the way, the meet was tied at 5-5, 8-8, and 10-10, and the final result was in question until 167-pound Rod Ott and 177-pound Mike Bradley won back-to-back decisions.

Wrestling—January 26, 1968 (H): In the most convincing conference win since 1961, the Spartans defeated Purdue, 35-0. The inordinately large score was misleading, as the Boilermakers forfeited three matches and automatically yielded 15 points. A pin by Dale Anderson at 138-pounds followed by legitimate decisions from Keith Lowrance, Dale Carr, Ron Ouellet, Rod Ott and Mike Bradley closed out the scoring.

Fencing—February 9, 1968 (A): Charley Schmitter's crew edged Wisconsin, the Big Ten defending champions, 14-13. Leading the way was the sabre team of undefeated Charlie Baer, Dean Daggett and Pete Kable. Also, the foil pair of Glenn Williams and Don Satchell were significant contributors.

Swimming & Diving—February 17, 1968 (A): The Spartans outscored the Minnesota Gophers, 72-50, concluding the dual meet season with an 8-3 record. Both diver Jim Henderson and freestyle sprinter Don Rauch were double winners. Also finishing first were Chuck Geggie in the 1,000-yard freestyle, Pete Williams in the individual medley, John Muslin in the butterfly and Bruce Richards in the breaststroke.

Basketball—February 24, 1968 (H): The Spartans led the Wisconsin Badgers, 41-29, at intermission and then went on for an 87-77 victory. The story of the game was in the second half when the Spartans hit 18 of 22 field goal attempts for a blistering 82 percent shooting average. Primary sharpshooters during those final 20 minutes were John Bailey, 3 of 4; Lee Lafayette, 5 of 6; and Jim Gibbons, 4 of 5.

Tennis—April 12, 1968 (H): Michigan State, the defending conference champions opened the Big Ten season with a close 5-4 defeat of Illinois. The winning margin came in doubles where the Spartans won two of the three pairings. Singles winners and the scores were: number one Chuck Brainard, 6-3, 6-2; number three Mickey Szilagyi, 7-5, 6-4; and number four John Good, 6-4, 6-4. The winning pairs were number one Rich Monan-Brainard, 5-7, 6-3, 6-2; and Szilagyi-Good, 6-3, 6-3.

Track and Field—April 13, 1968 (A): Bill Wehrwein was busy in Michigan State's first outdoor meet of the season in Champaign, Ill., where he won the 440 in 49.1, took second behind teammate Rick Dunn in the 220, was second in the triple jump, and teamed with Dunn, Ken Little and Don Crawford for a win in the 440-yard relay. It was a triangular affair in which the Spartans totaled 93 points, Illinois took 75 and Northwestern earned 44. Other firsts came from Crawford in the broad jump, Pat Wilson in the 660, Charley Pollard in the high hurdles, and Roland Carter, who erased a Memorial Stadium record by soaring over the pole vault bar at 15' 3/8". The winning mile relay team of Jim Bastian, Dick Elsasser, Rick Stevens and Wilson concluded the afternoon with a time of 3:22.9.

Golf—April 24, 1968 (A) & May 8, 1968 (H): Two matches against Michigan ended the dual-meet format that had been in place since the 1930s. Hereafter the golf season would only include tournament play. The Spartans defeated the University of Michigan on both occasions. In the 619-630 victory in Ann Arbor, Dick Hill was medalist with a 75 score.

Baseball—May 10, 1968 (A): When your pitchers allow a total of only three hits in a doubleheader, good things will likely happen. In this instance, the Northwestern Wildcats were the victims. Mel Behney, junior southpaw from New Jersey, tossed a one-hitter in the opener as his teammates slashed out 10 hits for a 6-0 victory. The offense featured catcher Harry Kendrick, who supplied three hits, and first baseman Tom Binkowski who blasted a three-run 390-foot home run in the fourth.

In the second game, Spartan hitters generated 16 hits, while Dan Bielski was touched for a pair of harmless singles in a ho-hum 12-0 win. Rick Harlow went four-for-four at the plate, and Steve Garvey, sophomore third baseman, duplicated Binkowski's first-game dinger to left center.

Baseball—May 17 & 18, 1968 (H): After a pair of doubleheader victories, coach Danny Litwhiler appropriately commented, "I've been around baseball for a long time, and this is the best pitching staff I've ever had." On Friday, Mel Behney tossed a 9-0 two-hitter against Illinois and Dan Bielski won a four-hitter, 3-2. Both Mickey Knight and Zana Easton picked the next afternoon to pitch one-hit shutouts as the Spartans took two from Purdue, 9-0 and 1-0, and pushed their front-running Big Ten record to 12-2.

ATHLETE OF THE YEAR

Dale Anderson was a high school state wrestling champion from Waterloo, Iowa, who first committed to attend Michigan State but then made a belated switch to stay close to home and enter Iowa State. When expectations in Ames were not immediately realized, once more his thoughts turned to MSU, and in a matter of days he was enrolled as a Spartan. Anderson would further justify the transfer as fulfilling a desire to work with Coach Grady Peninger and his assistant Doug Blubaugh. Described by Peninger as "Mr. Intensity," Dale made an immediate impact. In his sophomore season of 1966, he lost only one match and captured his first of three Big Ten titles (130 pounds). After placing fifth in that year's NCAA championships, he moved on to become the collegiate champion at 137-pounds as a junior and again as a senior. Dale Anderson was a star on the mat as well as in the classroom. He later graduated from the University of Virginia law school and today he is a practicing attorney in Illinois.

Dale Anderson

IN THE SPARTLITE

Baseball: The baseball team won a record-setting 32 games in 1968. Along the way was an unbeaten string of 15 games from April 30 to May 18 that also established an MSU record, a standard that still stands. Seven of those 15 victories were by shutouts.

With MSU boasting a 13-2 conference-leading record and the University of Minnesota at 12-2, it was fitting that the two faced off on the final Big Ten weekend of the season. A split of the doubleheader would have been enough. Although relinquishing only four hits, Mel Behney dropped the opener, 3-2, when the Gophers broke the deadlock in the first extra inning. With a rare display of control problems, Behney had walked the bases full before Mickey Knight, in relief, yielded the run-scoring base hit. The whole season then came down to a winner-take-all second game, and once more Knight was called upon. Through five innings, State trailed 2-1. Then came Minnesota's sixth inning which, before it was over, saw relievers Dan Bielski and Phil Fulton touched for eight runs on five walks and four hits, including a three-run homer. Although the Spartans responded with three runs in the seventh, the lead was insurmountable, and the "dream season" had suddenly come to an end with two crushing losses that unfortunately overshadowed an otherwise remarkable record-setting season.

Basketball: With the 76-71 loss to Iowa in Jenison on January 23, State's home win streak ended at 26 games.

Of the 12 losses over the season, few were close. The average point differential, as many as 28 against Ohio State, was an average of 11.8.

Runner-up for the team scoring leader in 1966-1967, Lee Lafayette was the top Spartan in 1967-1968 with a 16.8 average.

Cross Country: Although the future would hold three more Big Ten titles, 1967 saw the beginning of the decline of the once powerful cross country reign in East Lansing. For the first time since initiating the NCAA championship run in 1938, Michigan State did not qualify a team.

One Spartan runner did, however, run in the championships held that fall in Laramie, Wyo. Roger Merchant, the Sarnia, Ontario, junior, qualified by finishing 11th in the Big Ten meet and 27th at the IC4As in New York. He was out of contention in the subsequent race in Wyoming.

Fencing: Earning 25 points, State fencers finished fifth in a field of six Big Ten teams at the annual championship meet held in Champaign, Ill. Charlie Baer, who entered the meet with an impressive 35-6 record, faltered to a disappointing fourth-place finish. He later finished 12th as MSU's sole entrant at the NCAAs which were held in Detroit. That effort would place MSU 29th in the team standings. Also competing were Bobby Tyler and Dan Satchell, both of whom failed to score.

Football: Former Duffy Daugherty assistant Bill Yeoman brought his Houston Cougars to East Lansing for the season opener and scored an easy 37-7 victory using his newly installed veer offense.

The team rushing leader for the year was Dwight Lee, who ran for 529 yards on 116 carries and seven touchdowns in 10 games.

For the second year in a row, Jimmy Raye tossed for more than 100 passes, but his production dropped significantly from 1966. In the previous year he had completed 62 passes for 1,110 yards and 10 touchdowns. In 1967, he connected on 42 aerials for 580 yards and only four touchdowns.

Golf: In spite of a disastrous second round, the Spartans finished the 72-hole Big Ten tournament in second place with a total of 1,523 strokes, trailing the host and winning Indiana Hoosiers by 12. Only three strokes from the top after the opening round, State soared to 399 on the next 18 and dropped to 19 back. They were unable to card adequate numbers thereafter to generate a significant threat. Sophomore Lynn Janson finished with 74-75-73-78—300, good for seventh place. Other MSU scores were Larry Murphy 310, George Buth 312, Lee Edmundson 313 and John Bailey 314.

Advancing to the NCAA championship at Las Cruces, N.M., MSU finished ninth with a 72-hole total of 1,175—21 strokes behind the winning University of Florida team. Junior Larry Murphy led the State finishers with a 291, followed by Lynn Janson and Lee Edmundson both with 292, Steve Benson with 300, and George Buth with 305.

Gymnastics: Led by two champions, Toby Towson in floor exercise and Dave Thor on the horse vault, State captured first place in the conference meet held in Jenison. However, based on a pre-arranged procedure that factored in dual-meet results, State had to share the Big Ten Champion title with both Michigan and Iowa. Initially, all three teams were thought to be headed for the nationals, but NCAA officials intervened, declaring that only

one team could represent the conference at he championships in Tucson, Ariz. After much anguish, discussion and debate, a three-team playoff was arranged at Williams College in Downers Grove, Ill., where Iowa emerged the winner with 189.80 points. Michigan scored 187.60 and MSU dropped to a disappointing 184.45. Regardless, two Spartans did move on as individual entrants. Dave Thor finished third in the all-around competition and Toby Towson shared the first place title in floor exercise.

Towson later won the free exercise event at the National AAU championships held in Long Beach, Calif. He had captured that same title as a freshman in 1966.

Dave Thor won a spot on the USA 1968 Olympic team.

Hockey: Doug Volmar, a three year member of the Spartan squad (1965-1967) became a member of the USA national team that competed in the 1968 Olympic Games in Grenoble, France.

One of the lines that Amo Bessone put on the ice in 1968 was nicknamed the "pony line" or "peewee line" and consisted of five-foot-seven, 160-pound Pat Russo from the Soo, five-foot-10 Bob Pattullo of Dearborn, and 146-pound Chuck Phillips from Copper Cliff, Ontario.

Soccer: In the 1960s, St. Louis University was the team to beat in college soccer. Unfortunately, Michigan State seldom found the answer. Suffering a 1-8-2 won-loss-tie record with the Billikens since 1959, the whammy prevailed in 1967. Even with two penalty shots in overtime, the Spartans settled for yet another draw, 3-3.

Swimming and Diving: Shutout in their quest for any Big Ten individual titles, State placed in every event to compile 248 points and finish in the third spot for the third year in a row. Scoring for State were John Musulin, Don Rauch, Mike Kalmbach, Rollie Groseth, Greg Brown, Bob Burke, Pete Williams, Bruce Richards, Chuck Geggie, Duane Green, Mark Holdridge, Gary Langley and divers Doug Todd, Duane Green and Jim Henderson.

At the NCAA championship meet hosted by Dartmouth College, the Spartans garnered 38 points and settled for a 13th place finish. Top performers were Williams, who scored in three events; Richards, who placed in two events; and Todd, who was a finalist in both the one-meter and three-meter diving events.

Tennis: When the final pairings were reached at the Big Ten championships in Iowa City, State and Michigan had players matched up against each other in four brackets, three in singles and one in doubles. Both Cap-

tain Rich Monan, at the number-two slot and number five Steve Schafer captured straight set victories, while number three Mickey Szilagyl and the defending champions in number one doubles, Chuck Brainard-Monan, met defeat. Since 1965, the team championship had been decided by combining results of dual-meet competition with points earned in the conference finals. When the calculations were made, MSU totaled 100.5 points for a second-place finish behind the University of Michigan with 148.

Monan, John Good and Schafer competed in the NCAA championships held at San Antonio, Texas. While Good and Schafer did not survive the opening round of singles, Monan reached the second round before being eliminated. The Monan-Good doubles team was also dispensed in round two.

Track and Field: Finishing fourth at the Big Ten indoor meet with 25 points, the only MSU first place came in the final event on the program, the one-mile relay. The foursome of Don Crawford, Rich Stevens, Pat Wilson and Bill Wehrwein was clocked in 3:14.4. In individual events, Wehrwein was second in the 300, Stevens was fourth in the 440, Charles Pollard was second and fifth in the high and low hurdles, and Roland Carter was third in the pole vault.

At the fourth annual NCAA indoor championships held in Cobo Hall in Detroit, State scored eight points, good enough for a ninth-place finish. Carter vaulted 16' 4" for third place, Pollard placed fourth in the high hurdles, and the mile relay team ran second.

State mustered only 21 points at the conference outdoor meet and dropped to seventh place, their lowest slot since 1959. Although the Spartans failed to garner one first place, Wehrwein and Crawford placed second and third in the quarter-mile, Roger Merchant ran third in the 880, Dean Rosenberg and Dale Stanley were fourth and fifth in the mile, and Ken Leonowicz finished fifth in the steeplechase. Three Spartan stars, pole vaulter Carter, sprinter Pollard and middle distance runner Wilson were hobbled by injures that attributed to sub-par performances.

At the NCAA outdoor meet hosted by Washington State, Don Crawford reached the finals of the mile but did not place. He did, however, anchor the mile relay team that placed fifth.

Wrestling: Dale Anderson successfully retained his 137-pound title at the NCAA championships held at University Park, Pa. Dale Carr (145-pounds) finished fourth, John Schneider (191-pounds) was fifth, and Rod Ott (167-pounds) was sixth. Jeff Smith faced Michigan's Dave Porter in the semi-finals, but this time Porter carried the decision, forcing the Spartan heavyweight to settle for third.

The most impressive success story of the 1968 season came from an alumnus, Don Behm. Competing in the XVI Olympiad in Mexico City, the 126-pound Behm was awarded the silver medal. Continuing competitively for another four years, he was a gold medalist at the 1969 Pan-Am Games and served as an alternate for the U.S.A. team at the Munich Olympics in 1972.

Coach Grady Peninger was honored as amateur wrestling's Man of the Year. He was later selected as co-coach of the East team for the annual East-West meet held at Oklahoma State in Stillwater. Members of the team included Anderson and Mike Bradley.

EXTRA! SEVEN BIG TEN WRESTLING TITLES IN A ROW

(#3) 1968—Iowa City, Iowa: After finishing a comparatively unimpressive 9-4 dual-meet season, Grady Peninger's 1968 edition of MSU wrestling captured the Big Ten championship with 74 points followed by Iowa, Michigan and Northwestern all tying with 50 each. Three Spartans departed with gold medals. For both Dale Anderson, at 137 pounds, and 177-pound Mike Bradley it was a third straight title, while heavyweight Jeff Smith denied the U of M's Dave Porter the same honor by defeating the Wolverine 3-2. State's Dale Carr reached the finals at 145 but lost 4-3 to also be denied a third straight title. Rod Ott, at 167 pounds, was also a runner-up. Keith Lowrance won his 130-pound consolation match while 123-pound Mike McGilliard lost his and settled for a fourth-place finish.

Anderson's trip to the top began with a pin of the Wisconsin entrant followed by a decision of Michigan's 137-pounder. Dale had little trouble in the finals as he defeated Northwestern's best, 9-1. Mike Bradley won four matches on the way to his title. He reached the championship match on a pair of decisions and one pin. In his final match Bradley defeated Iowa's last hope on an 8-4 decision.

Although the outcome of the team title chase had been decided long before the heavyweights came to the mat, there was great anticipation. Once more it was Jeff Smith, the rookie challenger, against Michigan's Dave Porter, the defending champion. The Wolverine was out for revenge from his dual meet-deciding loss to Smith two weeks earlier. Even as the referee raised Smith's arm in victory, Porter had consolation that this time he was not pinned.

The 1968 Big Ten championship wrestling team. Letter Winners were D. Anderson, D. Carr, R. Ott, M. Bradley, J. Alsup, D. Cox, R. Byrum, G. Hoddy, M. McGilliard, J. Schneider, J. Smith, P. Karslake, K. Lowrance, R. Ouellet, J. Zindel and manager C. Beatty. Individual conference champions included D. Anderson (137 pounds), M. Bradley (177 pounds), J. Smith (heavyweight).

MSU 1968-1969

TALES TO TELL

Occasionally the execution of a school's athletic program is impacted by decisions made within the boardrooms of the ivy towers. Such was the case as it pertained to the Spartan football schedule of 1968. Over the first 50 years of the annual Michigan State-Michigan fall classic, the Wolverines had agreed to play in East Lansing on only six occasions. Then the upper deck was installed to Spartan Stadium in 1957, thus increasing the seating capacity to 76,000. This provided the leverage, along with pressure from key officials at the State Legislature, for the 1958 game to be played in East Lansing and on every even-number year thereafter. This plan fell into place until the series reverted back to Ann Arbor ten years later in 1968 after the University of Michigan had reportedly requested the schedule switch to coincide with that school's sesquicentennial celebration. At the time, this decision, made at the presidential level, seemed like a downright neighborly deed; but it was later revealed, yet never admitted, that the schedule switch had been a payoff. A bargain had been struck.

It was a known fact that the U of M had resisted the idea of State's pursuit of a four-year degree-granting medical school ever since the notion first surfaced in 1959. Opposition became so intense that President Hannah backed off in 1964, declaring, "The commotion about this medical school is a myth." This only provided a "cooling off" period as the exploratory committee continued the quest. Finally, the myth became a reality when on September 25, 1967, after a deadlock vote one month earlier, the State Board of Education voted in favor of expanding MSU's two-year preparatory medical program to a full four-year degree program.

Back to that bargain that had been struck. It seems the 1968 Michigan football schedule had an unfamiliar look to it, only five games at home with an equal number on the road. Something had to be done. The agreement entered into, never publicly confirmed or denied, was that if State would return to Michigan Stadium one more time back-to-back (1967 and 1968), then the U of M would relent in its pressure to deny MSU the much sought after medical school. Such is life at the top administrative level.

HEADLINES of 1969

- With his famed "It's one small step for man, one giant leap for mankind," Neil Armstrong is the first man on the moon.
- The Boeing 747 Jumbo jet and the Concorde, a French supersonic aircraft, both make their maiden flights.
- Woodstock Art and Music Festival, a three-day rock concert, is held near Bethel, N.Y.
- A car driven by Senator Edward Kennedy plunges off a bridge on Chappaquiddick Island, Martha's Vineyard. Mary Jo Kopechne drowns.

SCOREBOARD

	W	L	T	Avg.
Baseball	24	17	0	.585
Track and Field	1	3	0	.250
Football	5	5	0	.500
Basketball	11	12	0	.478
Tennis	6	12	0	.333
Cross Country	7	0	0	1.000
Swimming and Diving	12	2	0	.857
Wrestling	9	2	0	.818
Hockey	11	16	1	,411
Fencing	6	8	0	.429
Golf	tournament play only			
Gymnastics	7	3	0	.700
Soccer	11	1	3	.833

TEAM OF THE YEAR

Since joining the Big Ten competition in 1951, the Michigan State golf teams most often ended up in the lower tier at the conference championships. There had been few exceptions. The 1960 team finished second and was within 11 strokes of the champion Purdue team, and as recently as 1968, the runner-up Spartans were just 12 shots from the title. As the 1969 season approached there were positive thoughts . . . could this finally be a green-and-white year? After all, the championships would be played on the familiar Forest Akers east course. Furthermore, the "Fossum Six" had left some early clues when, on back-to-back weekends, they had finished first at the Wisconsin Invitational and first at the Purdue Centennial Tournament. As the championship opened with 36-holes on May 16, State propelled to an 11-shot lead, but the Purdue team would not go away. Following opening

rounds on Saturday, the Boilermakers had cut that margin to one stroke. It was then that Lynn Janson, the Michigan amateur champion, provided the needed spark. While teammates seemed to be tiring, he finished strong with a sub-par 71 for that final 18 holes. When all of the cards had been totaled and abstracted, MSU had used 1,501 strokes and the Boilers 1,507. Individual performances were as follows: Janson 78-77-72-71—298; Woulfe 78-72-75-76—301; Edmundson 70-74-80-78—302; Cooke 76-76-78-75—305; Vass 74-75-74-87—310; Murphy 82-74-81-75—312.

Coach Bruce Fossum later recalled that championship season:

"Every player, every team and each tournament through the years could become a story worth telling, but in my career as the golf coach, nothing can compare with our first, and only, Big Ten title in 1969. The victory for MSU completed an athletic sweep, through the years giving us at least one conference championship in every sport. We were elated and, of course, Biggie Munn [athletic director] was ecstatic. He thrived on victory with a capital 'V!' The players that made it happen were [pictured below, left to right] captain and senior Larry Murphy; Graham Cooke, Rick Woulfe, Lynn Janson, Denny Vass and Lee Edmundson. The win took place at Forest Akers, our home turf in front of a very responsive gallery. The tournament consisted of 72 holes, 36 each day over two days. The guys were exhausted and yet totally thrilled at the same time."

The 1969 golf team. (Left to right) R. Woulfe, L. Janson, L. Edmundson, L. Murphy, D. Vass, G. Cooke and coach B. Fossum.

MAKING HISTORY

President Hannah represents one of the three retired football jerseys at MSU. Duffy Daugherty withdrew number 46 on the occasion of John Hannah leaving the university in 1969 after 46 years of service to become director of the Agency for International Development in President Nixon's administration.

Football's Al Brenner was the big man in 1968. He achieved All-American honors as a defensive back, All-Big Ten awards both on offense and defense, and was honored as an academic All-American.

The Big Ten began using three officials in conference basketball games and for non-conference games upon mutual agreement of the coaches.

From the report of a borderline sport, for the third straight year Michigan State won the Big Ten bowling championship. This enabled MSU to retire the team trophy.

GREAT STATE DATES

Football—**September 28, 1968 (H):** On his way to an All-American season, team captain Allen Brenner had an impressive afternoon in the 28-10 defeat of Baylor in the second game of the season. Getting to a jump start with an 83-yard touchdown pass to open the scoring in the first period, the Niles senior connected for 153 yards on six receptions to set a new team record for yards gained on passes. The achievement is still listed among the top performances for Spartan receivers.

Cross Country—**October 12, 1968 (H):** What an inaugural season for first-year coach Jim Gibbard's squad. First, they opened with a 28-29 win in Bloomington over the Big Ten champions, the Indiana Hoosiers. Returning home, one week later the Spartans ran to another one-point victory. This time they topped the University of Wisconsin, 27-28. Junior Ken Leonowicz broke the tape against the Badgers in 24:55.8 to establish a new record over the five-mile course at Forest Akers. Completing the scoring for State were Kim Hartman, who finished third; captain Roger Merchant, who placed fifth; Dan Simeck, ending eighth; and John Mock, who completed the scoring in 10th.

Soccer—**October 12, 1968 (H):** Undefeated State won its seventh straight shutout of the season, defeating once-beaten Air Force, 8-0. Junior Dave Trace scored four goals, Tony Keyes booted in two, and Alex Skotarek and Tom Kreft were credited with one apiece. Trevor Harris notched four assists to tie a Michigan State season record. Senior goalie Joe Baum shared the net minding duties with backup Les Lucas.

Cross Country—**October 19, 1968 (H):** The 27-29 victory over Minnesota was somewhat tainted. The front-running Gopher actually broke the tape as the winner but was disqualified after shortening the distance about 70 yards when he took a wrong turn toward the end of the race. With the disqualification, sophomore Kim Hartman was awarded the win in 24:48.8, which bettered Ken Leonowicz's course record established one week earlier against Wisconsin. In this meet Leonowicz placed second. Roger Merchant finished in 6th, John Mock ended in seventh, and Dan Simeck placed 11th.

Football—**October 26, 1968 (H):** The most gratifying victory of the season was the 21-17 upset of Notre Dame. At that Friday night's press dinner, with a smile on his face, Coach Daugherty suggested he might open the next day's game with an on-side kick-off. His comments elicited the usual chuckles as those close to the scene brushed away the thought as just another "Duffyism." The real story unfolded on the next afternoon. Before a capacity crowd of 77,339 and a nationwide television audience, the Spartans indeed opened the game with an on-side kickoff, and it worked. Kenny Heft recovered at the 42-yard line, and six plays later Tommy Love scored from the 11, putting State ahead, 7-0. The Fighting Irish responded with an 11-play, 67-yard scoring drive to tie the game. MSU would score once more, followed by an ND field goal and a fumble recovery in the end zone for a touchdown. Trailing 17-14, quarterback Bill Triplett calmly engineered the winning 80-yard touchdown drive in the third quarter and Gary Boyce converted his third PAT. However, this was not a game of touchdowns made, but a game of touchdowns not made. Four times the visitors were foiled inside the 12-yard-line. The final threat was stopped at the three-yard line with less that two minutes of time remaining. Those defensive stalwarts for Duffy included Wilt Martin, Bill Dawson, Charley Bailey, Ron Curl, Gary Nowak, Rich Saul, Don Law, Jay Breslin, Frank Waters, Allen Brenner, Cal Fox, Heft, and two-way player Allen Brenner.

Hockey—**January 18, 1969 (A):** Settling for a 2-2 tie following a scoreless overtime period on Friday, the

Spartans and Minnesota Gophers were at it again on Saturday, this time knotted at 1-1 after regulation time. With the clock reading 6:18 in that extra stanza, co-captain Ken Anstey took a pass from Bob DeMarco and put the winning goal behind the Gopher goalie who had previously blocked 31 shots during the evening. State's goal tender, Bob Johnson, had likewise been busy sweeping away 40 shots.

Hockey—**January 24-25, 1969 (H & A):** With a rare double-win over Michigan, the Spartans topped their favorite foe, 7-3 and 5-1. In a wild first period at Dem Hall on Friday, Nelson DeBenedet opened State's scoring at 2:02 on a pass from Gerry DeMarco. Ken Anstey made it 2-0 with an unassisted marker at 7:56. Any jubilation was short-lived. Before the buzzer had ended in that first 20 minutes of play, the U of M had scored three times with their final pair of goals coming within 11 seconds of each other in the final two minutes. Anstey responded with a tying goal in the middle period and Bill Watt regained the lead at 0:35 in the third. Amo's crew was just warming up. DeBenedet found the back of the net for his second goal at 4:44 and Watt banged home his second at 5:52. By then the U of M's All-American goalie had been replaced. Randy Sokoll finished the scoring with goal number seven at 16:07. On Saturday in Ann Arbor, once more State jumped out early, but this time the Wolverines had no answers. At the conclusion of period number one it was 4-0 on two goals by DeMarco and one apiece by Sokoll and Bob Pattullo. The Wolverines' lone goal came at 13:05 of the second period, and four minutes later Randy Sokoll, as on Friday night, finished the scoring for another MSU four-goal differential win.

Fencing—**January 24-25, 1969 (A):** Charlie Schmitter and his squad opened the 1969 season in Minneapolis with an 18-9 defeat of the University of Minnesota on Friday and then an outdueling of Iowa State, 16-11, and St. Thomas, 21-6, on the next afternoon. MSU's top performer was Glenn Williams, who had a perfect 9-0 weekend in foil competition. Other winning performers were Bob Kreitsch (8-1), Don Satchell (7-2), Harry Sorensen (7-2), Larry Norcutt (6-3), Bobby Tyler (5-4), Harry Mamassian (5-4) and Bob Rosenberg (5-4).

Gymnastics—**February 1, 1969 (A):** Michigan State, 179.975, and Illinois, 179.750, how close can a meet get? As one week earlier against Indiana State, MSU trailed with one event remaining. Up stepped horizontal

bar specialist Norm Haynie, who would win the event and gain the needed points for victory. Other firsts came from Toby Towson in the floor exercise, Dennis Smith on the side horse and Mickey Urm, who tied for first on the parallel bars. Although not gaining an individual first in either the rings or trampoline, in each case Szypula's performers outscored their Illini counterparts.

Basketball—**February 8, 1969 (A):** After State led 43-33 at intermission, Michigan came storming back in the second half to make a game of it. Throughout the final seven minutes, the score was knotted four times and then with 16 seconds remaining and nursing a two-point lead, 82-80, Lloyd Ward was at the line in hopes of putting it away. His free-throw attempt was off target, but Tom Lick, a 6' 10" substitute center from Gaylord, went over two Wolverines to grab the rebound and drop it through for a commanding four-point advantage. Michigan quickly scored one more time and Tim Bograkos hit two free throws after time had expired to seal the final score at 86-82. Hitting 10 of 14 shots from outside and finishing with 23 points, Jim Gibbons was the leading scorer.

Wrestling—**February 8, 1969 (H):** State swept the opening five matches and then watched the talented Iowa Hawkeyes win three in a row before bowing, 18-9. Gary Bissell opened with a narrow 4-2 decision at 123 pounds. The next three match-ups were one-sided: Mike Ellis, 13-5, in the 130-pound division; 137-pound Keith Lowrance, 16-5, over a previously unbeaten opponent, and Ron Ouellet, 12-5, at 145 pounds. The meet's most exciting pairing came at 152 pounds, where Spartan sophomore John Abajace, trailing 6-3 in the final period, scored an escape, a take down and then added riding time for a 7-6 win. Three Hawk entries defeated Tom Muir, Pat Karslake and Jack Zindel in succession before Jeff Smith totally dominated his heavyweight opponent, 13-1.

Basketball—**February 15, 1969 (H):** It is often suggested that a strong defense will defeat a strong offense. A Jenison crowd of 7,020, plus a regional TV audience, would have agreed to that wisdom after State upset eighth-ranked Illinois, 75-70. Bouncing back from an opening 10-2 deficit, the Spartans gained a 16-13 advantage with 13:38 remaining in the first half, and they never looked back. Playing man-to-man throughout the full 40 minutes, guards Harrison Stepter and Tim Bograkos totally frustrated their counterparts with stolen passes, forced

turnovers, and a sticky defense that yielded the Illini back court only 14 points. Meanwhile, the Stepter-Bograkos duo was countering with a combined 23 points. Lee Lafayette had a productive afternoon as he accounted for 23 points and out-rebounded his larger opponent in the pivot, 14-3. Jim Gibbons hit nine of 11 shots and totaled 19 points.

***Swimming and Diving*—February 15, 1969 (A):** In pre-meet observations it became immediately clear that the Ohio State swimmers had pointed toward this meet in that they had "tapered and shaved." In lay terms, "tapered" meant that in days immediately preceding the meet they had slackened their daily workouts to rest their bodies. "Shaved" meant exactly what the word implies. Through proven performances over the years it had been shown that swimmers could significantly enhance their performance by shaving the body hair from their torsos and limbs. The "tapered and shaved" Buckeyes were prepared for a win, but it was MSU that clung to a one-point lead, 56-55, with one event remaining, the 400-yard freestyle relay. It was "winner take all." Though all of the attention now rested on the swimmers, it had been John Narcy's divers that had put the Spartans in this favorable position. OSU had always been a proven power at the diving end of the pool (44 previous NCAA titles), but this time around it was Michigan State. Spartans Duane Green and Jim Henderson had finished one-two in the three-meter event, while Tom Cramer and Henderson had been one-three off of the one-meter board. So it came down to that final relay and Coach "Mac" McCaffree had played his cards right. He had four of his best sprinters at the starting block: Don Rauch, Mark Holdridge, Gary Langley and Mike Kalmbach. They won the event with two full seconds to spare and consequently took the meet by five points, 64-59.

***Wrestling*—February 15, 1969 (A):** After dropping a narrow decision in the opening 123-pound match, Spartan wrestlers rebounded with winning performances in the next five matches that eventually led to the 20-9 victory over Michigan. Mike Ellis capped a comeback with a reversal in the closing seconds of his 130-pound bout to gain a 7-6 win. Keith Lowrance totally dominated his 137-pound foe, 15-3; Ron Ouelllet won 6-4 at 145-pounds; John Abajace followed with an easy 8-0 win at 152; and Tom Muir gained a 5-2 decision at 160. Upon losing the next two matches, the score stood at 15-9 for State. With an MSU team victory assured and not wanting to risk injury to his 180-pound heavyweight, the U of M coach decided to forfeit the final bout to the talented Big Ten champion, Jeff Smith.

***Track and Field*—February 22, 1969 (H):** Led by Bill Wehrwein, who ran another record-setting 600-yard race, State defeated Ohio University, 80-69, in the final indoor dual meet of the season. Wehrwein, the Roseville, Mich., junior, had originally set a new American record of 1:09.0 in the MSU relays. His performance against the Bobcats was even more remarkable at 1:08.6. In addition, Bill anchored the mile relay team, which included Bill Bastian, Roger Merchant and Pat Wilson. Other Spartan firsts came from Marion Sims in the 60-yard dash, Wayne Hartwick in both hurdle events, Gordon Bowdell in the high jump, and Kim Hartman, who ran a personal best 4:08.3 in the mile.

***Baseball*—April 19, 1969 (H):** Playing before 1,350 chilled fans at the newly renamed Kobs Field, Michigan State opened the Big Ten schedule with a doubleheader win over the U of M, 5-4 and 18-3. The visitors struck early, and by coupling a shoddy Spartan defense with four hits, they gained a four-run lead in the opening inning. It could accurately be suggested that starting pitcher Mickey Knight settled down thereafter, as the Wolverines were held hitless for the remainder of the seven-inning game. It took the Spartans those full seven innings to muster the needed five runs for the win. Trailing 4-3 into that final frame, Rich Miller dropped a double down the right field line with the infield pulled in to produce the tying run. Tim Bograkos later drew a bases-loaded walk to force home the winning run. In the second game, State picked on four pitchers for nine hits and took advantage of 12 walks to total a record number of 18 runs against a Michigan team. They had previously scored a 17-12 victory in 1959. While producing five runs from three hits, Miller was the hitting star of that nightcap. Dan Bielski cruised through the seven innings to gain the win, his third in five games.

***Tennis*—April 20, 1969 (H):** The outcome of the Sunday matches against Northwestern were not decided until the third set of the number three doubles had been played out. In that match, John Bufe and Wes Ichesco came from behind 1-6, 6-3 and 8-6, to win the decisive point for the 5-4 team victory. The showdown was set up when Tom Gray and John Good came through with a win at number one doubles, 9-7, 3-6, 6-2 to even the team score at 4-4. Gaining the other three points earlier

were Rick Raines at number four singles, Bufe at number five and Dave Mitchell at number six.

Golf—**April 21, 1969 (A):** Bruce Fossum's squad finished atop the four-team field at the Wisconsin Invitational. Rick Woulfe captured medalist honors with a 36-hole score of 67-71—138. He was followed by teammates Lynn Janson and Graham Cooke, who tied for second place with identical cards of 72-73—145. Captain Larry Murphy, Lee Edmundson and Denny Vass all scored 76-80—156. Teams competing, along with the host Badgers, were Northern Illinois and Northwestern.

Golf—**April 26, 1969 (A):** In winning the Purdue Centennial Tournament, the Spartans not only defeated the Boilermakers but also outscored Ohio State, Indiana, Iowa and Illinois. Senior captain Larry Murphy finished second in the competition with a 71-69—140, and Sophomore Denny Vass fired the third lowest score, 70-75—145. Other Spartan scores were Lynn Janson, 72-74—146, Graham Cooke, 73-73—146, and Lee Edmundson, 72-78—150.

ATHLETE OF THE YEAR

Called "the greatest individual performer ever at MSU" by his coach George Szypula, Toby Towson was a combination of power and grace when he competed in his gymnastic specialty, the floor exercise. As a Spartan, he captured four Midwest Open titles, three Big Ten titles, three National AAU titles, and two NCAA championships. In winning the final conference crown in 1969, he was awarded a 9.6, the highest score of any competitor in any event that weekend. Three weeks later at the NCAAs in Seattle, Wash., an appreciative crowd of more than 4,000 gave him a standing ovation upon the completion of his gold-medal performance. On that occasion, Towson scored a meet-high 9.6. In further endorsement from his coach, the native of Blue Mound, Ill., was described in 1969 as being "the epitome of grace and style. The reason he is so great is that his routine contains all of the required elements: flexibility, balance, tumbling and strength, in excess."

IN THE SPARTLITE

Baseball: At their monthly meeting in March, the school's Board of Trustees approved naming the baseball diamond John Kobs Field to honor the longtime coach who retired from the post in 1963 and died on January 26, 1968. The formal dedication took place between the doubleheader games against Wisconsin on May 10.

Call it patience, persistence or perseverance. The George Petroff story could fit all three. Not originally included in the MSU plans for 1969, the Lansing Everett High School product and Lansing Community College transfer paid his own way to be with the team during the spring training trip in March. After playing in four games while in Florida and hitting .333, Petroff opened the regular season at shortstop, filling in for the injured Rich Vary. George's defensive and offensive play were so impressive that he remained a fixture at the infield spot throughout the entire season.

Basketball: John Bennington's team had the thrill of playing in New York City's famous Madison Square Garden but absorbing two losses at the ECAC Holiday Festival Tournament, 61-51 to St. John's, and 75-66 to Villanova, was no thrill.

Toby Towson

As the varsity team struggled through an 11-12 season, often times local fans would gaze into the future by arriving early to watch the preliminary freshmen game featuring the highly touted recruit, Ralph Simpson of Detroit Pershing High School. Playing against an alumni team on January 7, he totaled 50 points. Later, in a 91-90 victory over Michigan at Ann Arbor, Simpson scored 42.

After suffering a heart attack on April 11, Coach John Bennington remained hospitalized at Sparrow Hospital until his release on May 6. A second massive heart attack on September 10 took his life. He was 47 years old.

Cross Country: Under their new coach, Jim Gibbard, the harriers of 1968 completed a fantastic season, going 7-0 in dual meets and edging Minnesota at the Big Ten championship run. Not much had been expected of the Spartans after placing eighth in the conference in 1967. Heading the winning quintet over the rain-soaked five-mile Ohio State course, were sophomore Kim Hartman, junior Ken Leonowicz and Captain Roger Merchant, who finished fourth, fifth and sixth respectively. Sophomores Dan Simeck and John Mock completed the scoring in the 27th and 28th spots.

In back-to-back runs at VanCourtland Park in New York City, State finished fourth out of 33 teams in the IC4A and 13th of 24 teams at the NCAAs.

Fencing: It was a disappointing Big Ten meet for Charlie Schmitter's fencers as they tied Indiana for fourth spot. Not one Spartan made it to the finals of the sabre or epee, while captain Don Satchel placed third and Glenn Williams fifth in foil.

Finishing no higher than 36th at the NCAA meet in Raleigh, N.C., the State fencers did score in each of the three events. Satchell was 27th in foil; Glenn Williams, switching to epee for the first time, finished 29th and Don McGaw placed 37th in sabre.

Football: The cost of watching Michigan State football became more expensive in 1968 as individual game ticket prices jumped from $5.00 to $6.00.

Michigan State's All-American Don Coleman, who had signed on as an assistant coach in 1968, resigned in January of 1969 to assume a position in the school's Office of Student Affairs. Another Spartan All-American, Sherman Lewis, replaced Coleman and commenced a coaching career that continues to flourish in the NFL.

Golf: In the rain-shortened Illinois Invitational, in which State finished fourth in a 13-team field, Lynn Janson was a medalist as he shot a 70-37—107 over 27 holes.

Gymnastics: State opened the season with the unexpected loss of two members from the 1968 squad. Junior Joe Fedorchik was injured in practice and underwent surgery in mid-January to repair a torn biceps tendon. The Belle Vernon, Pa., native had been counted upon heavily after finishing third in the all-around event at the Big Tens in 1968. Cliff Diehl, a versatile senior from Butler, Pa., was also a casualty with a career-ending shoulder injury.

Two Spartans won Big Ten titles as the team settled for a third place tie at the championships in Ann Arbor. As expected, Toby Towson won his third straight floor exercise crown, scoring a meet-high 9.5. Horizontal bar specialist Norm Haynie was the other MSU champion. Along with Towson and Haynie, Craig Kinsey qualified for the NCAA meet in Seattle, Wash., with a third-place finish on the side horse.

At the national collegiate meet Towson repeated as champion in the floor exercise. Haynie entered the horizontal bar finals in first place, but, after brushing his foot against the bar, he suddenly became out of sync and settled for a fourth place finish. Kinsey fell from the side horse during his routine and failed to make the finals.

Hockey: One can only imagine the complexity of running two practices on Dem Hall ice during an afternoon. Such was the case in 1968-1969 as the former MSU goalie, Alex Terpay, coached a freshmen team through a limited three-game schedule. An NCAA policy to make freshmen eligible for varsity competition came into effect one year later in 1969-1970.

Earning a spot in the WCHA four-team playoff, State was eliminated with a 4-2 opening game loss to Michigan Tech. The Spartan goals were scored by co-captain Ken Anstey and sophomore Randy Sokoll.

Net minder Rick Duffet was named All-American for the NCAA west section. His goals against average of 2.4 was lowest in the WCHA.

Soccer: As in 1967, Michigan State entered the NCAA tournament and worked its way through the brackets. They first outscored North Carolina, 5-0, and then edged Akron, 1-0. After going 2-2 against West Chester (Pa.), MSU was declared the winner based on the tie-breaker of being awarded more corner kicks

throughout the game. From there, it was on to the Final Four in Atlanta, Ga., with games played on Grant Field, home of the Georgia Tech football team. In the opener against Brown University, play was scoreless until the final period when State booted home a pair of goals for a 2-0 win. Ernie Tuchscherer scored on an assist from John Zensen, and then Alex Skotarek knocked in a header with an assist from Tom Kreft. For the second consecutive year, State had reached the championship game, this time the opponent was the University of Maryland. Also, for the second consecutive year, the Spartans were destined to be crowned co-champions, this time sharing the title with the University of Maryland. This shared title was not the result of unplayable field conditions, as in 1967, but instead it was a contest in which two overtime sessions could not break a 2-2 tie. MSU's first goal, an equalizer, was booted home in the third period by Tony Keyes, his 28th marker of the season. At 2-1, once more State had to come from behind. Frank Morant responded with his first goal of the season in the final period of regulation. Both teams had ample opportunities in OT, but neither could connect. Coach Kenney later mused: "All I can hope for next year is to improve on this year's performance . . . and that might be quite hard to do." How true, it has been very hard to do. That was 1968, and the goalie of that team, Joe Baum, has continued to pursue the dream as head coach, a position he has held since 1977.

Swimming and Diving: The team returned from the Big Ten championships in Madison, Wis., with two titles and a third-place team finish. In the 400-yard individual medley, Bruce Richards, the versatile junior from Washington, upset the defending champion from Michigan with a winning time of 4:16.09. Once more, Coach McCaffree had assembled a winning 400-yard freestyle relay team, as the foursome of Mike Kalmbach (48.4), Mark Holdridge (48.6), Dick Crittenden (47.8) and Don Rauch (46.2) edged Michigan for first. Jim Henderson finished fifth in both diving events; Bob Burke was third in both the 100- and 200-backstroke, and freestyler Rauch placed sixth in the 50, fifth in the 100 and third in the 200.

Collecting 38 points, the swimmers and divers finished 12th at the NCAA meet held in Bloomington, Ind. Leading the Spartans was Mike Kalmbach, who ended up fourth in the 100-yard freestyle with a 46.89. The Big Ten championship relay team managed to improve their time to 4:10.9 but could do no better than ninth place.

Tennis: Other than hosting the Big Ten championships, Michigan State tennis followers had little to cheer about as the Spartans finished in eighth place with 42 points. Rick Raines won his first two matches at number four before being ousted, and Tom Gray reached the finals at number one, where he lost 7-5, 4-6, 6-1.

Track and Field: Star hurdler Charlie Pollard was forced to forego the indoor season to provide adequate healing time for a foot injury that he had suffered in the spring of 1968 and continued to bother him.

Bill Wehrwein set a conference record of 1:09.4 in winning the 600-yard run at the indoor championships in Champaign, Ill. He also anchored the winning mile relay time that included Jim Bastian, Roger Merchant and Pat Wilson. Their time of 3:13.4 set a new varsity mark.

At the fifth annual NCAA championships run on the boards at Cobo Hall in Detroit, Wehrwein became MSU's first indoor national champion, as he led the field to the finish in his specialty, the 600-yard run. His recorded time of 1:09.8 was a bit slower than his winning performance at the conference meet in the University of Illinois Armory.

Running unattached at the Ohio Relays, freshman Herb Washington began to turn heads as he easily defeated some of the best sprinters in the Midwest. Despite horrible conditions of near-freezing temperatures and driving sleet, he won the 100-yard dash in a respectable clocking of 9.7.

MSU track standout Bill Wehrwein

Once more, just like indoors, Wehrwein led the way, and also like indoors, MSU finished fourth at the conference outdoor championships. Wehrwein won the 440-yard race, later placed third in the 220, and anchored the runner-up mile relay team.

Bill Wehrwein finished his outstanding junior year on the University of Tennessee track in Knoxville, Tenn., where he ran a 45.9 440-yard dash to finish third at the NCAA outdoor championships. He was two-tenths of a second from the gold medal.

Wrestling: Concluding the NCAA meet in fourth pace and void of any individual championships, Coach Grady Peninger concluded, "We didn't wrestle as well as we are capable of in several classes." Jeff Smith lost his first match of the season in the heavyweight finals. Other finishers were Keith Lowrence, third; Tom Muir, fourth; Jack Zindel, sixth; and Don Schneider, third in the 191-pound division. In the annual East-West All-Star meet, Spartans John Schneider and Jeff Smith both won matches for the East team, assisting in a 23-11 team victory.

The 1969 Big Ten championship wrestling team. Letter Winners were G. Bussell, G. Hoody, M. McGilliard, J. Schneider, J. Smith, P. Karslake, K. Lowrance, Ron Ouellet, J. Zindel, M. Ellis, T. Muir, J. Abajace, and manager D. Luckenbill. Individual conference champions included G. Bissell (123 pounds), Keith Lowrance (137 pounds), J. Smith (heavyweight). Individual conference champions included G. Bissell (123 pounds), Keith Lowrance (137 pounds), J. Abajace (152 pounds), Tom Muir (160 pounds), J. Zindel (177 pounds), J. Smith (heavyweight).

EXTRA! SEVEN BIG TEN WRESTLING TITLES IN A ROW

(#4) 1969—East Lansing, Mich.: Before an overflow crowd of 2,600 in the Men's IM Arena, the Spartan wrestlers totally dominated the Big Ten tournament as they accumulated 97 points, nearly doubling runner-up Iowa's 50. In fact, Grady Peninger's crew had earned enough team points through the preliminary matches to prematurely claim the title. That fact did not slow down the "Graplers in Green" on Saturday night as six of the nine eventual titlests were Spartans: Gary Bissell (123 pounds), Keith Lowrence (137 pounds), John Abajace (152 pounds), Tom Muir (160 pounds), Jack Zindel (177 pounds) and Jeff Smith (heavyweight). Bissell won a fairly easy 7-1 decision; Lowrance pinned his opponent in 2:59; a reversal in the final period along with riding time gave Abajace a championship, 4-1; Muir defeated the defending champion, 3-2 and Zindel defeated the number one seed in the semi-finals and the number three seed in the finals. Jeff Smith, voted the meet's outstanding wrestler, won his second-straight conference crown and did so on three pins in an accumulated time of 5:39. The remaining MSU contenders all earned team points. Ron Ouellett (145 pounds) won two matches before being eliminated. Mike Ellis (130 pounds) lost in the finals and Pat Karslake (167 pounds) finished fourth.

TALES TO TELL

With the premature departure to the professional ranks of such Michigan State basketball stars as Earvin "Magic" Johnson in 1979; both Jason Richardson and Zach Randolph in 2001 and Marcus Taylor in 2002, few Spartan fans recall that another budding star had preceded them all with an early departure to the "promised land" of professional basketball back in 1970. After only one year of varsity competition, Ralph Simpson, enticed by a million-dollar proposition, inked his name to a professional contract offer by the Denver Rockets of the American Basketball Association (ABA).

Recruited out of Detroit Pershing High School in 1969 by the new head coach Gus Ganakas, Simpson's first and only year as a Spartan was everything that could have ever been expected. Setting a team scoring record (667 points, 29.0 average), he was named on the All-Big Ten first team and was picked by the Helms Foundation for its All-American team.

In 1970, coming out early was a bit different than today. First, the fledgling ABA (later to merge with the NBA) was new on the scene, and consequently, in a competitive mode with the NBA for talent, was dangling lucrative offers previously unheard of. There was another matter. To keep some harmony with the NCAA on this fragile issue of luring pre-seniors, the professionals agreed to sign those with remaining college eligibility only if they were identified as hardship cases. Although there were no set guidelines on what constituted hardship, the Simpson household back in Detroit was certainly a busy one. Ralph had eight brothers and sisters, all under 16. Also, his father, Ralph Sr., had recently suffered a heart attack.

So, Ralph Simpson, whose name remains near the top of the school's single season record book, aborted a distinguished one-year collegiate career for what would

Ralph Simpson left Spartan fans wondering what might have been when he turned pro after only one season of collegiate play.

HEADLINES of 1970

- National Guard troops fire on 1,000 anti-war protesters at Kent State in Ohio. Four students are killed.
- "Doonesbury," a satirical comic strip created by Garry Trudeau, makes its debut in 30 newspapers.
- Congress creates Amtrak, a federal corporation authorized to operate passenger trains between U.S. cities.
- Postal Service, an independent agency, replaces the U.S. Post Office Department.

SCOREBOARD

	W	L	T	Avg.
Baseball	28	15	2	.644
Track and Field	1	3	0	.250
Football	4	6	0	.400
Basketball	9	15	0	.375
Tennis	11	8	0	.584
Cross Country	5	1	0	.833
Swimming and Diving	10	1	0	.909
Wrestling	16	1	0	.941
Hockey	13	16	0	.413
Fencing	6	7	0	.462
Golf	tournament play only			
Gymnastics	4	7	0	.364
Soccer	7	2	1	.750
Lacrosse	1	11	0	.083

become a successful professional career. As could be expected, Coach Ganakas was gracious with his remarks:

> "We're going to miss him greatly. You can't help but miss a player of his prominence and stature. He accomplished a great deal for MSU and stimulated our basketball program. I just wish Ralph a lot of success."

TEAM OF THE YEAR

The 1969-1970 wrestling team turned in a remarkable 16-1 dual meet record including convincing victories over Oklahoma, the 1969 NCAA runner-up, and seven conference teams. The only setback was a one-point, 17-16, loss to perennial power Oklahoma State. At the conference meet held in Ann Arbor, five Spartans were crowned champions, as the team won an easy fifth straight victory. Piling up 96 points, the nearest competitor was the Iowa Hawkeye squad with 65 points. Those five gold medalists for MSU were Greg Johnson at 118 pounds, Tom Milkovich at 134, Keith Lowrance at 142, Jack Zindel at 190 and heavyweight Jeff Smith.

At the NCAA tournament hosted by Northwestern University, the Iowa State Cyclones successfully defended their crown by gaining 99 points, while the Spartans finished in a close runner-up position with 84. Close behind in the third and fourth slots were Oregon State (80 points) and Oklahoma State (79 points). Six Spartans reached the semi-final round, but only 118-pound Greg Johnson emerged with a title. Jack Zindel and Vic Mittelberg lost overtime decisions, while Tom Milkovich and Gerald Malecek each lost by a single point in the regulation eight minutes. Keith Lowrance was pinned by the ultimate champion in the 142-pound division.

The 1970 wrestling team. Letter Winners were P. Karslake, K. Lowrence, R. Ouellet, Jack Zindel, Bruce Zindel, T. Muir, L. Hicks, G. Malecek, R. Radman, T. Milkovich, G. Johnson, D. Ciolek, B. Lewis, M. Malley and manager David Luchenilll.

MAKING HISTORY

That fall's home football schedule opened on the newly installed artificial surface, Tartan Turf. Including reinstallations in 1974, 1983 and 1994, the synthetic surface remained a fixture in Spartan Stadium for 33 seasons. Finally, in 2002, the full cycle had been reached and once more natural grass returned to the stadium playing field.

In addition to sprinter Herb Washington's record-setting indoor performances, two other Spartans set varsity records in winning Big Ten championships. Bill Wehrwein successfully defended his 600-yard run title and did so in 1:09.3, one-tenth of a second better than his record-setting time in 1969. Football star Eric Allen bettered the triple jump record with a leap of 48' 5 1/2".

Gene Kenney resigned his post as head soccer coach to step into a newly created position as assistant to Biggie Munn, director of athletics.

By slashing out 37 home runs, the 1970 Spartan baseball team established a new season record, elapsing the previous mark of 31 set in 1963.

Former MSU tennis star Rex Norris passed away. Norris played for the Spartans from 1932 through 1934 and captained the team in his senior year.

GREAT STATE DATES

Football—**September 20, 1969 (H):** Featuring the running of Don Highsmith and Eric Allen, MSU won the season opener over the University of Washington, 27-11. State trailed 9-7 after 30 minutes of give-away in which each team turned the ball over three times. Following intermission, the Spartans found the right plays and improved execution to score three unanswered touchdowns. The most exciting of the three was credited to the defense. Linebacker Don Law, a six-foot, 220-pound senior, intercepted a pass at the MSU 30-yard line and rambled down the sideline untouched, escorted by Will Martin and Mike Hogan.

Cross Country—**October 4, 1969 (H):** The Spartans opened the season with a gratifying 21-38 win over the always competitive Hoosiers of Indiana. Kim Hartman, a consistent performer as a sophomore in 1968, led the way over the five-mile Forest Akers layout in a course record time of 24:52.5. Senior Ken Leonowicz, sophomore Dave Dieters, and freshman Warren Krueger finished within three seconds of each other in the third, fourth and fifth spots respectively. Freshman Ralph Zoppa completed the team scoring with an eighth place finish.

Soccer—**October 17, 1969 (H):** Battling a strong wind and a rugged University of Akron defense, the Spartans were scoreless until 15:41 of the third period. It was then that All-American Trevor Harris headed the ball into the far corner of the net on a pass from Alex Skotarek. That one goal held up, as the MSU defense likewise played a strong game. Coach Kenney had particular praise for Buzz Demling and goalie Les Lucas.

Football—**October 18, 1969 (H):** Coach Daugherty topped Bo Schembechler's squad in Bo's first year as the Michigan head coach, 23-12. Behind locked gates, Duffy prepared for the annual tussle by scuttling his veer option attack while installing the power-I. It worked. Led by quarterback Bill Triplett's 143 yards and Don Highsmith's 134 yards, the State runners racked up a season-high 348 yards on the ground.

Basketball—**December 13, 1969 (A):** In only his third varsity game as a Spartan, six-foot-five Ralph Simpson connected on 19 of 25 field goal attempts leading to 42 points, nearly one-half of his team's total effort, in the 86-71 victory over Western Michigan. Proving to be more than a perpetual scoring machine, the super sophomore pulled down 16 rebounds. With the game comfortably in hand and two minutes remaining, Coach Ganakas pulled Simpson from the game. The appreciative Western crowd gave him a wild ovation when he left the floor.

Fencing—**January 31, 1970 (H):** Coach Charlie Schmitter's team opened its season by slashing Indiana University, 18-9. The epee team was particularly impressive as Bob Tyler, Dana Day and freshman Paul Herring each went 2-0, and Jeff Tully contributed one point to finish the event 7-2. In foil, Ira Schwartz led, scoring 2-0, while Kent Nietzert and freshman Chris Held each went 2-1 to finish the event at 6-3. The toughest competition came in the sabre, as captain Doug McGaw struggled against the Hoosiers' conference champion, yet as a team, the sabremen managed a 5-4 advantage.

Wrestling—**February 14, 1970 (H):** It was a sweet Valentine's Day for Grady Peninger and his wrestlers. They defeated the always strong Oklahoma Sooners, 26-6. The turning point for the landslide victory was sophomore

Rick Radman's buzzer-beating victory at 158 pounds. State was only up 9-6 at the time, and Radman was down 0-4 after the first period, having just avoided a pin. In the ensuing periods he managed to come back to tie the match at 7-7. Finally, when everyone thought it would be a draw, he scored a take down with one second remaining for the 9-7 win. Another exciting match came from Jack Zindel at 190 pounds. Rebounding from a three week absence due to a rib injury, he managed the only pin of the day in a little more than six minutes. At 167 pounds, Pat Karslake retained his undefeated record, edging out his opponent, 3-2. Other Spartan winners included Greg Johnson at 118 pounds, freshman Tom Milkovich at 134, Keith Lowrance at 142, Dave Ciolek at 177 and heavyweight Vic Mittelberg.

Swimming and Diving—**February 14, 1970 (H):** 1,050 fans showed up to watch Dick Fetters's squad run their season record to 8-1 with a fairly easy 71-52 victory over Ohio State. Two varsity records were broken along the way. Sophomore John Thuerer bettered the team mark with his 10:05.57 winning time in the 1000-yard freestyle, and Ken Winfield set a new mark for the 200-yard butterfly at 1:55.63. Other winners were Mike Kalmbach, Dick Crittenden, Bruce Richards, diver Jim Henderson and the medley relay team of Alan Dilley, Jeff Lanini, Winfield and Mark Holdridge.

Hockey—**February 21, 1970 (A):** Scoring a team record-tying five goals, Don Thompson led the Spartans to an easy 7-1 victory over the University of Michigan. It was a welcomed win following a string of seven straight losses. The State offense didn't waste time, scoring four times in the opening period. Thompson first turned the light on at 1:19, Dave Roberts followed at 3:57, Pat Russo scored next, and it was Thompson again at 16:05. That early assault provoked the Wolverine coach into switching goalies after the opening 20 minutes, but the scoring continued. At 10:16 in the second period, Thompson once more found the back of the net, which prompted the partisan U of M crowd of 3,400 to give the Toronto sophomore a standing ovation. He opened the third period with goal number four at the 1:15 mark and shortly thereafter stole the puck at mid-ice and skated in for an unassisted fifth goal that resulted in yet another standing ovation. Goalie Rick Duffet finished with 28 saves, but had his shutout effort ruined at 14:56 of the third period.

Gymnastics—**February 21, 1970 (A):** Led by the all-around duo of Randy Balhorn and Mickey Uram, MSU swept all but one event in a 155.95-147.40 easy win over Ohio State. Freshman Balhorn took first outright on both the parallel bars and rings and tied for first with teammate Charlie Morse on the side horse. Uram was a double winner with firsts in the all-around competition and floor exercise. The Spartans had established their lead early in a sweep of the vault event, with Richard Murahata, Uram and Pet Sorg finishing one-two-three.

Wrestling—**February 21, 1970 (H):** A highlight of the 25-8 defeat of Michigan came in the match at 177 pounds. This was State's 15th dual meet of the season, and for the first time Gerald Malecek had earned a starting spot in that weight class. As nervous as the fledgling sophomore likely was, he handled himself with acumen, out-pointing his more experienced opponent, 7-4. In other standout matches, 134-pound freshman Tom Milkovich continued unbeaten with a 7-2 win; Pat Karslake saved his undefeated record with a 6-6 tie, and senior Jack Zindel earned his seventh pin and 13th victory of the year. Other Spartan winners were Greg Johnson, Keith Lowrance, Rick Radman and Vic Mittelberg.

Don Thompson led the Spartans to victory over Michigan with his five goals scored on February 21, 1970.

Basketball—**February 28, 1970 (A):** With just seconds remaining and the game with Ohio State tied at 80-80, rookie Ralph Simpson, now playing in his 22nd varsity game, was at the free-throw stripe. Being an 83 percent shooter from the line, a Michigan State victory seemed relatively certain, but it happens to the best of them. One by one, the pair of free throws clanked off the rim. Fortunately, the second miscue ended in the hands of Bob Gale, a senior reserve forward, and he immediately tossed it back up for the buzzer-beating victory. It was a TV game that had been an emotional trip from the beginning. The Spartans led at halftime, 46-40, but OSU climbed back to open a 67-61 advantage. Just when it seemed to be slipping away, MSU came fighting back to knot the score and gain the ultimate victory. Simpson led the team with 29 points and 14 rebounds. Sophomore Ron Gutkowski had 13 points, Rudy Benjamin posted 12 and Pat Miller scored 10.

Basketball—**March 7, 1970 (A):** With their scoring leader rookie Ralph Simpson sidelined with a knee injury, State closed the season with a dazzling 81-76 defeat of Illinois in Champaign. Filling in offensively for the missing star, Rudy Benjamin hit his season-high 28, followed by Pat Miller with 18, Ron Gutkowski with 13 and Tim Bograkos with 12. Deadlocked at intermission, 36-36, the Illini broke out to a 10-point advantage in the second half, but Coach Ganakas's stubborn crew came fighting back to catch and surpass them, eventually holding a 67-64 lead with four minutes remaining. Depending on an effective 3-2 zone defense and the rebounding of Miller and Gutkowski, the Spartans never relinquished the lead thereafter.

Track and Field—**April 18, 1970 (H):** With the temperature at 38 degrees accompanied by gusty winds, there were likely questions of, "Why aren't we still running indoors?" Uninviting conditions or not, State went to work capturing 12 of 18 events, including both relays, to defeat Northwestern, 91-62. The only double winner of the meet was Herb Washington, who sprinted to first place in both the 100- and 220-yard dashes. Other firsts were credited to Al Henderson, who upset teammate Bill Wehwein in the 440, John Mock in the 880, Ken Popejoy in the mile run and Ken Leonowicz, who captured the steeplechase and also finished second to Chuck Starkey in the three-mile run which saw a Spartan slam with Ralph Zoppa in third place.

Lacrosse—**April 25, 1970 (A):** Coach Turf Kaufman was pleased as his MSU lacrosse team conquered Notre Dame 9-8 for the first, and only, victory in the inaugural season. The Spartans came from behind and scored five of their nine goals in the final period, with the winning goal, by sophomore Doug Kalvelage, coming with 4:54 remaining. From then on, it was up to goalie Billy Hermann, who had some critical saves to preserve the win. Co-captain Rick Bays continued to lead the team in scoring, adding two points on the day. Joe McLain also scored twice, and Bill Wasinski, Bob Stevenson and John Beach each found the back of the net for single goals.

Baseball—**May 1, 1970 (H):** Pitcher Phil Fulton, supported by nine hits from the offense and four double plays from the defense, earned a 6-3 victory over Michigan. The Alma senior yielded only four hits through eight innings before tiring in the ninth, when the Wolverines scored all three runs on four additional hits. State opened the game with three runs in the first and one in the third. The remaining runs came in the bottom of the eighth when Fulton aided his own cause with a two-run single. Catcher Phil Rashead managed two hits, which produced three of the six runs.

Tennis—**May 2, 1970 (H):** The highlight of the 6-3 defeat of Minnesota was the two-hour match in which Tom Gray emerged the winner, 10-8, 1-6, 10-8. The tiebreaker, of course, had not yet been introduced. By the time Tom's third set was underway, foul weather had engulfed the area and the match was moved indoors to the gymnasium floor of the IM Arena. Both men initially had trouble serving on the slippery hardwood floor, but Gray eventually emerged with the win. With additional singles successes by Mike Madura, Rick Ferman, Rick Vetter and freshmen DeArmond Briggs, enough team points were put away to gain the eighth victory of the spring. The only doubles win came from Briggs and Jim Symington.

Golf—**May 9, 1970 (H):** After 18 holes of the Spartan Invitational at Forest Akers, Central Michigan's Dick Horgan headed the leader board with a three-under 68, followed two strokes back by John VanderMeiden, who played for the MSU "B" team. Upon conclusion of the 36 holes, it was Ron English of Bruce Fossum's "A" team that eventually caught the CMU star as they both finished five-over-par at 147. In a sudden death play-off to determine the tournament's medalist, English prevailed

on the first hole. In team competition, State's "A" and "B" teams finished one-two atop the heap of 24 visiting teams.

Baseball—May 30, 1970 (H): Playing the role of spoiler in a season-ending doubleheader before a Memorial Day crowd of 2,000, MSU twice scored winning runs in the final inning to defeat Ohio State, 2-1 and 5-3. The two losses dropped the Buckeyes from the top spot in the conference standings, and the wins assured Michigan State of a third-place finish. In the opening game, Rob Ellis homered in the sixth to tie the score at 1-1 and then doubled home Larry Rettenmund in the seventh for the clincher. Highlighted by Steve Cerez's three-run round-tripper, the Spartans scored all five runs in the last inning of game number two. The winning pitchers were Phil Fulton (8-3) and Bob Clancy (2-2).

IN THE SPARTLITE

Baseball: The baseball team concluded their spring trip having compiled an impressive 10-2-2 record, including one win against always strong Florida State and two victories over Miami. Leading hitters on the trip were Rob Ellis, a Grand Rapids sophomore who batted .431, followed closely by Gary Boyce of St. John's with a .428 average. Two pitchers returned north undefeated. Both were from Grand Rapids, Dick Krueger at 3-0 and Larry Ike at 4-0.

Upon completing the season, three Spartans signed professional contracts and were off to minor league affiliates. The three were pitcher Phil Fulton, who went with the Milwaukee Brewers; third baseman Dick Vary, who joined the Chicago Cubs; and first baseman-outfielder Tim Bograkos, who left one year early to become a New York Met minor leaguer.

ATHLETE OF THE YEAR

Michigan State cannot boast of too many world-record holders, but track and field sprint star Herb Washington carried such a title. His exploits in outdoor competition were legendary, with 100-yard dash wins in such glamorous meets as the Ohio relays and Drake relays, three Big Ten titles (1970-1972), and a personal-best time of 9.2. Yet the Flint speedster gained his most national attention during the indoor season in which he also claimed a trio of Big Ten titles plus an NCAA crown in the 60-yard dash. It was in that national meet at Detroit's Cobo Arena that Herb shattered the world mark with a clocking of 5.9. His speed, especially for the shorter distance, caught the eye of Charles O. Finley, the controversial owner of the world champion Oakland Athletics baseball team. In March of 1974, it was announced that Washington had signed a contract as an innovative pinch-runner specialist. Inserted into this role 105 times in two seasons (1974-1975), Washington managed to steal 31 bases and score 33 runs.

Herb Washington

Basketball: In his first game on the bench as the Spartans' head coach, Gus Ganakas directed the team to a season-opening 89-85 victory over Eastern Kentucky. The much-publicized Ralph Simpson, also in his first game as a varsity player, scored a game-high 36 points.

One man (Ralph Simpson) doesn't make a team. The overworked axiom held true for the Spartans as they concluded the 1969-1970 season with a 9-15 record. Oddly, of those scant nine victories, five were on the road.

Cross Country: Sophomore Tom Silvia and junior Kim Hartman were lost to the team due to injuries suffered from being struck by a motorist while returning home from practice on October 23. Silvia ended up in a leg cast and Hartman, one of team's top performers in 1968, underwent surgery to repair a torn ligament.

The loss of Silvia and Hartman was instrumental in State's tumble from first to fourth at the conference meet in Bloomington, Ind. Randy Kilpatrick was the top Spartan finisher, crossing the line in 11th place. Freshmen Warren Kreuger and Ralph Zoppa finished in 13th and 17th, with junior Chuck Starkey next in the 18th spot. Sophomore Dave Dieters completed the scoring with a 47th place finish.

Fencing: The team finished the dual-meet season with a 6-7 record and then placed fourth in the Big Ten championships, scoring 22 points. Sophomore Ira Schwartz and freshman Paul Herring were the only Spartans to reach the finals of that tournament. Schwartz overcame a pulled muscle in his right leg to finish second in foil. Herring tied with OSU's John Rice for first place in the epee before losing in a fence-off, five touches to three.

Football: This was college football's centennial year. MSU acknowledged the fact with a specially-designed "100" logo affixed to either side of the helmet.

Referring to the offensive line, Coach Daugherty labeled them, "the best I have ever had here at MSU." That crew consisted of Frank Foreman, Dave VanElst, Don Baird, Tom Beard, Ron Saul, Craig Wycinsky and Bruce Kulesza.

When a "home" game-clock malfunctions, somehow it is not expected that the visiting team will be the recipients of any advantage, but that's what happened when MSU lost to Iowa, 19-18, on October 25. The Spartan Stadium clock accidentally added one minute of playing time during the fourth quarter, and in the excitement of the game the matter was never attended to. The additional time was instrumental to the Hawkeyes, as they mounted an 80-yard drive to score the game-winning touchdown in the final 3:55.

To accommodate fans without tickets for any of the three straight sellouts—at Ohio State, at Notre Dame and Michigan at home—arrangements were initiated to offer closed-circuit television on a 34' x 22' screen set up in Jenison Fieldhouse. Ticket prices were set at $3.00, with students admitted for $2.00.

Attempting to revive a team that had lost four of five games, Coach Daugherty replaced quarterback Bill Triplett with Steve Piro for the Purdue game of November 8. It was no favor to Piro, as he left the game suffering season-ending ligament damage to his knee.

Golf: In the role of defending champions at the Big Ten meet in Champaign, Ill., Michigan State was tied with Minnesota for the lead following the opening 36 holes. Thereafter, in the final two rounds, the Indiana Hoosiers posted scores that surged them to the front and the team title. Their final total was 1,542, followed by the Gophers with 1,555, and third-place MSU at 1,561. Lynn Janson was the top Spartan, as he carded a score of 306 that placed him fourth, four strokes behind the medalist.

At the NCAA championships in Columbus, Ohio, the MSU five-man team of Rick Woulfe, Ron English, John VanderMelden, Lee Edmundson and Janson shot a combined score of 603, two strokes from the last team qualifier. Edmundson and Janson did qualify for the four-round individual honors. Edmundson shot 72-75-74-74—295 for a 17th place tie, while Janson was three strokes back at 298.

Failure to make that NCAA traveling squad was the greatest thing that could have happened to Denny Vass. Forced to remain home, he opted to enter the 50th Annual Michigan Amateur Championships played that same weekend. The junior from Jackson proceeded to work his way through the match-play brackets and emerged as the 1970 champion.

Gymnastics: At the conference championships in Minneapolis, Minn., Charlie Morse finished fourth in the parallel bars and seventh in the side horse, while teammates Rich Murahata took a fourth in the floor exercise and fourth in the vault. Tom Kuhlman, of East Lansing, added a pair of sixths in the floor exercise and the parallel bars. In the team competition, State finished third with a total of 152 points.

Hockey: Don Thompson led the team with 14 goals and 18 assists for the year, with Gilles Gagnon contributing 14 goals and eight assists. Goalie Rick Duffett accumulated 715 saves in the 13-16-0 overall team record.

The Spartans placed seventh in the WCHA and lost to Denver in the first round of the playoffs.

Lacrosse: After existing as a club sport since 1963, the school's Athletic Council approved the request to adopt lacrosse as the school's 14th varsity sport beginning in 1970. That initial team posted a 1-11 record under the guidance of coach Turf Kaufman.

Soccer: Once more St. Louis University proved to be unconquerable, as they shutout the Spartans of Gene Kenney, 2-0. This brought the overall record against the Billikens to 1-8-5.

During a routine practice session on October 27, Ernie Tuchscherer re-injured a knee that had kept him sidelined for the entire 1968 season. He was lost for the closing game of the season and the playoffs.

Playing without the two top scorers, Tuchscherer and Trevor Harris, and a revamped line-up imposed by sundry other injuries, the NCAA tournament trail was a short one, as Cleveland State topped the defending co-champion Spartans, 3-0.

Swimming and Diving: U of M handed State their only dual meet loss in an otherwise impressive 10-1 season. A meet with the eventual Big Ten champions from Indiana had to be cancelled because of restricted travel conditions precipitated by winter weather.

State finished third behind the Hoosiers and Michigan at the Big Ten championship meet in Bloomington. Dick Crittenden was the sole Spartan titleist, setting a new varsity record with a 21.5 in the 50-yard freestyle. Teammate Mike Kalmbach finished second in the same event. Other top Spartans were Alan Dilley, with a third and fourth in the backstroke events; Bruce Richard with a third in the 400-yard individual medley and a fifth in the 200 IM in a team record time of 1:57.97; Jeff Lanini, with a third in the 100-yard breaststroke; and Ken Winfield, who placed second in both the 100- and 200-yard butterfly events behind the renown Mark Spitz of Indiana. Winfield actually led the champion for seven lengths in the eight-length race before being caught from behind.

The Spartans did not fare too well at the NCAAs in Salt Lake City. Co-captain Kalmbach was the top finisher with a fifth in the 100-yard freestyle, while Jim

Henderson was State's top diver, claiming seventh on the three-meter board and eighth on the one-meter. Managing 43 team points, MSU completed the weekend in 14th place.

Prior to opening the NCAA meet, former head coach Charles "Mac" McCaffree was honored by fellow coaches with a special citation for 33 years of service to the sport.

Tennis: Led by captain "Dusty" Rhoads, the season was successful for the Spartans, as they closed the dual-meet schedule with an 11-8 record.

At the Big Ten championships in Minneapolis, both Tom Gray, at the number two slot and Rick Ferman at number six reached the finals, only to lose. Gray went down in straight sets, 5-3, 6-3, while Ferman lost in three, 6-2, 4-6, 6-4. In the team scoring, State finished with 74 points, good enough for third place.

Track and Field: In addition to individual record-setting performances by Herb Washington, Bill Wehrwein and Eric Allen at the Big Ten indoor championships, the quartet of Al Henderson, Mike Murphy, John Mock and Wehrwein won the meet's final event, the mile relay, in 3:15.5, a new Jenison Fieldhouse record. Other point-winners for MSU were: Ken Popejoy, third in the mile run; Al Henderson and Mike Murphy, third and fifth in the 440; Charles Pollard, third in the high hurdles and John Mock, second in the 880.

At Cobo Hall in Detroit, State managed 12 points for a seventh place finish at the sixth annual NCAA meet. Sprinter Herb Washington led the way, as he topped a classy field in the 60-yard dash with a world record-tying time of 5.9. Other finalists were John Mock, third in the 880, and defending champion Bill Wehrwein, who dropped to third in the 600-yard run.

Outdoors, State scored 68 points to manage a third spot behind Indiana and Wisconsin at the Big Ten championships held in Bloomington, Ind.

For the first time in nearly a decade, MSU failed to score at the NCAA championships that were held at the site of the annual Drake Relays in Des Moines, Iowa. Herb Washington reached the finals of the 100-yard dash but finished a disappointing seventh, and Wayne Hartwick finished eighth after reaching the finals of the intermediate hurdle event.

Wrestling: Greg Johnson led the way for the Spartans, winning the crown in the 118-pound class. In the finals, Johnson wrestled Oklahoma State's Ray Stapp, who had given him his only loss of the regular season. The

two were tied 1-1 at the end of regulation and neither was able to score a point in the three-minute overtime. Stapp, however, did receive a stalling warning, and Johnson's aggressiveness gave him the referee's decision victory. Teammates Jack Zindel, Keith Lowrance and Pat Karslake won consolation victories for third place, while Vic Mittelberg, Gerald Malecek and Tom Milkovich each had to settle for fourth. This team effort was enough to take second place behind Iowa State, the defending champions.

Seven Spartans gained All-American recognition: Greg Johnson, Tom Milkovich, Keith Lowrance, Pat Karslake, Gerry Malecek, Jack Zindel and Jeff Smith.

EXTRA! SEVEN BIG TEN WRESTLING TITLES IN A ROW

(#5) 1970—**Ann Arbor, Mich:** In winning their fifth conference team title in a row, the Michigan State wrestlers outdid even their impressive performances of 1969 as they collected 96 points and laid claim to five of the 10 individual championships. Both seniors Keith

Keith Lowrance

Lowrance and Jack Zindel successfully defended their titles at 142 pounds and 190 pounds respectively. Greg Johnson opened MSU's successful evening with a 10-6 decision at 118 pounds followed by Tom Milkovich's dominant 12-4 decision at 134 pounds and Lowrance's win. Zindel and heavyweight Vic Mittelberg closed the run of gold medal performances. Mittelberg, the heavyweight from Skokie, Ill., secured the solitary pin of the championship round when he put his Northwestern opponent to the mat at 2:49. At 177 pounds, Gerald Malecek was the only Spartan finalist who had to settle for the runner-up spot. Notching thirds were Gary Bissell at 126 and Pat Karslake at 167. Ron Ouellet was a fourth-place finisher at 150 pounds.

Jack Zindel

TALES TO TELL

One of the outstanding early lacrosse players was Val Washington (LA 1971-1974). He shares memories of those pioneer years:

"Very few members of the 1971-1974 teams had ever played organized lacrosse before coming to MSU. However, with backgrounds in football, basketball, track or cross country, they were all excellent athletes eager to master this alien sport. The determination of those early laxers was admirable as they struggled through bitter Michigan spring weather, sometimes impossible field conditions, equipment shortcomings and opposing teams that drew their talent directly from the eastern prep schools where the sport flourished.

As for weather conditions, consider the 'spring' of 1972 as we played the Wayne State Club in an exhibition game. By the noon face-off the temperature was zero degrees with a minus-17 degree windchill index and blowing snow. It was so cold that the parents who came to watch pulled their cars onto the sidelines so that when players came off of the field, they climbed in to warm up. The game was called off at halftime.

Grounds on which we played were not always ideal. At Oberlin in 1973, their field had just begun to thaw and drain the week before the game in late March. The mud was so thick that it literally sucked the shoes from our feet. Shots that were supposed to bounce up from the ground stuck in the mud, creating a shark-like feeding frenzy for those determined to retrieve them.

Many times team members and their families financed the purchase of equipment and supplies, as the school's fiscal support was limited at best. For example, the 1972 budget of $843.30 had to be stretched a long way. It was times like this that provided for camaraderie and bonding between teammates, making them more determined than ever to prevail.

The mismatch in talent was often apparent. In 1973 Kenyon College, a talented squad, humiliated us down in Gambier, Ohio, 23-7. We didn't forget.

HEADLINES of 1971

- Cigarette ads are banned from television and TV networks lose $200 million in annual advertising.
- The Supreme Court rules unanimously that busing of students may be ordered to achieve racial integration.
- Prices of the time included: bread—25 cents/loaf, milk—$1.17/gallon, and gasoline—40 cents/gallon. A new automobile could be purchased for $3,560, and the average annual income was $10,622.
- CBS's controversial All in the Family is introduced, featuring the bigoted Archie Bunker.

SCOREBOARD

	W	L	T	Avg.
Baseball	36	10	0	.783
Track and Field	4	2	0	.667
Football	4	6	0	.400
Basketball	10	14	0	.417
Tennis	10	6	0	.625
Cross Country	3	2	0	.600
Swimming and Diving	9	3	0	.750
Wrestling	7	3	2	.667
Hockey	19	12	0	.612
Fencing	9	6	0	.600
Golf	tournament play only			
Gymnastics	5	5	0	.500
Soccer	5	1	3	.611
Lacrosse	6	8	0	.429

One year later it was a revenge win 7-5, which led to a post-game cheer reminding Kenyon that we had not forgotten them with a resounding chorus of 'Rah Kenyon, 23 to 7.'

Learning more than how to win, those early laxers learned a lifetime lesson that by pulling together they could overcome any obstacle. Indeed they provided the foundation upon which later MSU lacrosse teams would be built, all the while having fun, learning lessons, sharing and maturing."

TEAM OF THE YEAR

With a season record of 36-10-1, the 1971 Big Ten champion baseball team was, at that time, the most productive in MSU history. The total of 36 wins included an impressive sweep of nine doubleheaders, and was the best ever for a State team. They also achieved new team standards for most runs scored (317), most runs batted in (271), and most three-baggers (26). Averaging 10 hits per game, as a team they batted .307 for the season. The starting infield (with overall batting average) included 1B John Dace (.304), 2B Ron DeLong (.352), SS Whitey Rettenmund (.290) and 3B Phil Rashead (.255). The outfield was patrolled by LF Ron Pruitt (.350), CF Gary Boyce (.356) and RF Rob Ellis (.407). Bailey Oliver (.288) was behind the plate. It was more than a team of hitters. The mound duties were primarily shouldered by Rob Clancy, who finished with a 10-1 record (still atop the team record list); basketballer Larry Ike who won eight games; Kirk Maas with seven victories (including a no-hitter); and Dave Leisman, who registered six wins.

The season ended abruptly and sadly when the Spartans were defeated by Cincinnati and Ohio University in the double elimination NCAA District Four tournament hosted on John Kobs Field.

The 1971 baseball team. Letter Winners were K. Maas, P. Rashead, L. Rettenmund, R. Ellis, J. Dace, S. Howitt, L. Ike, R. Pruitt, S. Cerez, D. Bewley, D. Leisman, B. Lieckfelt, J. Turner, B. Oliver, J. Rohde and R. DeLonge.

MAKING HISTORY

Herb Washington tied a world record, again. On February 13th at the 48th annual Michigan State relays, he became only the second man to run a 5.9 on a dirt track in the 60-yard dash. In March 1970, he had won the NCAA title in the event and become one of several men to run a 5.9 on a board track. Though others have run the same time, Washington is the only one to do it on both types of running surface.

In winning the mile relay at the Big Ten indoor track and field championships, the quartet of Mike Holt (49.3), Mike Murphy (48.5), John Mock (48.4) and Bob Cassleman (46.7) combined for 3:12.9, a new world record on a 220-yard dirt track. The previous record of 3:13.1 was set by an Iowa Hawkeye foursome in 1967.

The outdoor track at Ralph Young Field was upgraded with the installation of a Tartan surface over the one-quarter mile oval as well as at the various infield venues.

GREAT STATE DATES

Soccer—**October 7, 1970 (H):** The Spartans scored at ease in defeating the Ball State Cardinals, 13-1. Ray Korkiala led the attack with five goals, all of which came in the second half. Senior John Houska started the scoring two minutes into the match and finished with three goals. Others on the scoring sheet were Jerry Murray with a pair, and one apiece for Rudy Mayer, Sandy Moffat and Nigel Goodison. State made 35 shots on goal, while BSU managed only five.

Football—**October 24, 1970 (H):** Dominating Iowa, 37-0, in front of a Homecoming crowd of 63,482, State came up with the first shutout since beating Wisconsin 39-0 in 1968. The offense racked up 539 yards, while the defense held the Hawkeyes to 109 yards. The first touchdown was set up when Brad VanPelt deflected a pass that Doug Halliday picked off and ran to the one-yard line. Eric Allen then dove over easily for the score. On their third possession, quarterback Mike Rasmussen found halfback Henry Matthews in the end zone. Borys Shlapak finished the opening-half scoring with a 25-yard field goal with just one second of playing time remaining. To start the second-half scoring, Rasmussen handed the ball to flanker Bill Triplett, who connected with Gordie Bowdell for a 10-yard TD, and on their next pos-

session Rasmussen threw 23 yards to Billy Joe DuPree, bringing the count to 31-0. Third-string quarterback Frank Kolch finished the scoring with a 78-yard pass-run to flanker Randy Davis.

Cross Country—**November 6, 1970 (H):** Led by sophomore Randy Kilpatrick over the rain-soaked Forest Akers course, the Spartans comfortably defeated Notre Dame, 19-41. Finishing third through seventh were sophomore Ralph Zoppa, sophomore Ken Popejoy and junior Dave Dieters, followed by seniors Chuck Starkey and Kim Hartman.

Hockey—**January 8 (H) & 9 (A), 1971:** State opened the crucial weekend series with a home ice 5-4 WCHA victory over archrival Michigan before a turn-away crowd of 3,943. In a post-game comment, Coach Bessone prophesied, "It sure would have been nice to have played this game in that 6,000-seat arena they're talking about building. I believe we could have filled the place." They then moved on to Ann Arbor for the Saturday night encounter, and once more the two teams were tied entering the final period, this time at 3-3. Don Thompson put the guys in Green back in front, 4-3, on a penalty shot at the 16:56 mark. Less than one minute later, Frank DeMarco gave MSU a 5-3 edge, and then Michel Chaurest boosted the lead edge to 6-3 at 11:40. The Wolves battled back, but the valiant Spartans held on for a satisfying 6-5 win and two-game sweep.

Wrestling—**January 9, 1971 (H):** After Iowa opened with a tie and a decision, Tom Milkovich inspired an MSU run with a 4-2 win on a reversal in the final 30 seconds of his match. Victories followed from Mike Ellis at 142-pounds, John Abajace at 150, Tom Muir at 158 and Gerald Malecek at 167. The balance of the 22-12 winning margin came on a Dave Ciolek tie and a concluding 9-3 decision by heavyweight Ben Lewis.

Swimming and Diving—**January 15 (A) & 16 (H), 1971:** Committing to a tight travel schedule, The Spartans defeated Purdue, 77-46, at West Lafayette on Friday night and then bused back to East Lansing, arriving at 2:00 A.M. Twelve hours later they were in the process of a 68-55 victory over the Minnesota Gophers to run their season record to 5-0. Coach Fetters did some switching and experimenting with his lineup. Backstroker Gary Dilley won in the first meet and then turned over to take the 200-yard freestyle on Saturday. John Thuerer, Jeff Lanini, Ken Winfield and Steve Mitchell also moved to different events from one meet to the other.

Gymnastics—**February 1, 1971 (H):** On the strength of their top three performers, Mickey Uram, Randy Balhorn and Charley Morse, Michigan State outscored the University of Wisconsin, 156.00-143.50. Uram finished first in the floor exercise and vault and had a tie score for top spot on the still rings. Balhorm won the high bar and Morse the parallel bars. Ken Factor, Tom Kuhlman and Don Waybright also contributed to the scoring.

Fencing—**February 17, 1971 (H):** The fencers held an 11-4 lead at one point, but a late comeback by Wayne State brought the score to 13-10. Doug McGaw then took the meet-winning bout 5-2 with the sabre, enabling the Spartans to edge out their tough opponents, 14-13. Bill Mathers led the team through the day with a record of 3-0 in epee, with fellow epeeists Paul Herring and Bob Rosenberg going 2-0 and 2-1. Ira Schwartz set the pace in foil.

Track and Field—**February 20, 1971 (A):** Having met U of M without success 10 times in indoor meets through the years, on this, the 11th meeting, Michigan State finally endured. But it couldn't have been closer. With one event, the mile relay, remaining, the score sheet read Michigan State 67 1/2, Michigan 67 1/2. The relay lead-off man, Henderson, who had won the quarter-mile in 49.0, immediately forged to the front as he ran a 48.5. Carrying the baton over the remainder of the race were Mike Murphy, Mike Holt and Castleman, all running sub-49.0 legs. It proved to be an easy win as the quartet was clocked in 3:14.4 to establish a new collegiate record on a 220-yard track. The final score was Michigan State 72 1/2, Michigan 67 1/2.

Hockey—**March 6, 1971 (H):** Before a record-setting home crowd of 4,134 crammed-in fans, State defeated Michigan in overtime, 5-4, for the third win of the season over the Wolverines. The Spartans jumped to an early lead on goals by Michael Chaurest and Gilles Gagnon, but U of M battled back to gain a 4-2 advantage after two periods. In the third stanza, Gagnon sent the game into overtime as he completed the hat trick with a pair of goals. At 3:07 in the OT, senior captain Randy Sokoll had the great pleasure of scoring the winning goal against the arch-rival in his final appearance at Dem Hall.

Basketball—**March 9, 1971 (H):** Bill Kilgore paced the MSU 73-71 squeaker over Minnesota with an impressive 18 rebounds. His final carom came on the defensive glass when a Gopher player missed a game-tying attempt from the corner with three seconds remaining. During the opening half, the score flip-flopped 10 times, with the visitors leading at intermission 39-37. Minnesota built a 10 point lead following the break, but the incessant Spartans fought back to tie and then take the lead on a Kilgore driving hook shot with three minutes remaining. They never lost the lead thereafter.

Tennis—**April 16, 1971 (H):** Featuring a slam in the doubles matches, the Spartans defeated Wisconsin, 7-2, on the home courts. All three pairs won in straight sets: number one Tom Gray and DeArmond Briggs, number two Mike Madura and Rick Vetter and number three Jim Symington and Rick Ferman. In singles, number one Gray won in three sets, 6-2, 7-5 and 6-3. Briggs and Madura completed two-set victories, while Vetter also needed three sets to subdue his opponent at the number four position.

Baseball—**April 16, 1971 (H):** Behind the four-hit shutout pitching of Rob Clancy, the Spartans opened their Big Ten season with a 2-0 victory over the University of Minnnesota. The Spartan runs, both unearned, came in the bottom of the fifth when Ron Pruitt and Ron DeLonge were issued back-to-back walks. Phil Rashed, the senior third baseman, followed with a hard hit down the right field line that the first baseman could not handle. Pruitt scored on the error and DeLonge crossed the plate moments later on a wild pitch.

Baseball—**April 30 (A) & May 1 (H), 1971:** Key pitching performances by Rob Clancy and Larry Ike led to wins over the University of Michigan, 7-2, on Friday in Ann Arbor, and then 2-0 on Saturday at Kobs Field. Clancy received plenty of support in the first game. Ron Pruitt led off the fourth with a home run over the left field fence. Two errors, a walk and a single followed and suddenly the score was 4-0. Rob Ellis added a sixth-inning home run, and his ninth-inning triple, along with singles by Gary Boyce and Steve Cerez, accounted for the final two runs. Ike threw a masterful game on the next afternoon in East Lansing as he permitted only two hits. The Spartans' two runs were manufactured on a single by Ellis, a triple by Pruitt and a wild pitch.

Golf—**May 3, 1971 (A):** After placing second over the weekend in the Northern Invitational at Boyne Mountain's Alpine Golf Course, Coach Fossum took his squad to Kalamazoo, where they won a four-team 18-hole match hosted by Western Michigan. The Spartans edged the University of Michigan, 379-380, with Western third at 386 and Notre Dame fourth with 395. Shoot-

ing a one-over par 73, Graham Cooke tied for medalist honors.

Golf—**May 7-8, 1971 (H):** A total of 178 golfers representing 28 schools found their way around the Forest Akers west course during the two-day sixth annual Spartan Invitation. When all of the cards were in, two teams were tied for first place with a total of 747 strokes. As in 1970, those teams were the MSU "A" and the MSU "B." The University of Michigan placed third with 761 strokes, followed by Ohio State and Kent State, who tied for fourth at 762.

Baseball—**May 8, 1971 (A):** In defeating Indiana, 2-1 and 5-3, State won their third straight doubleheader in Big Ten play. After the Hoosiers scored first in the opener, the Spartans retaliated in their next at-bat with doubles by Gary Boyce and Ron Pruitt and a single by Ronald DeLonge. The two runs produced were enough for pitcher Larry Ike, who shut the door the rest of the way. In the nightcap, State broke a 3-3 tie with a pair of runs in the sixth inning as Gary Boyce doubled home both Whitey Rettenmund and John Rohde. That ended the scoring for the afternoon. Starting pitcher Dave Leisman was given the win and Kirk Maas was awarded the save.

Track and Field—**May 8, 1971 (H):** With Purdue winning five of the six field events, the burden of defeating the Boilermakers rested on the legs of State's runners. They responded by taking 10 of the 12 track events, leading to an 87-67 victory. As expected, Herb Washington won the 100-yard dash; LaRue Butchee bettered an 11-year-old track record in winning the 220 in 21.3; John Mock broke the tape in two events, the 660 and 880; Ken Popejoy won the mile, and Randy Kilpatrick finished first in the three mile. Spartan hurdlers John Morrison and Wayne Hartwick captured the highs and intermediate events respectively. The remaining firsts came from Eric Allen in the triple jump, the 440-yard sprint relay, and the final event, the mile relay.

Lacrosse—**May 8, 1971 (H):** Tied at 6-6 with just seconds remaining in the contest, Emery Freeman had a shot blocked by the Notre Dame goalie, but he picked up his own rebound and this time found the back of the net, giving State the victory at the buzzer. It was only Freeman's second goal of the year. Freshman star Val Washington scored three times, and the team's leading scorer, Douglas Kalvelage, scored twice.

ATHLETE OF THE YEAR

Although he departed for the professional ranks after only two seasons of Spartan baseball, Rob Ellis led the team in hitting both years, with a .380 average in 1970 and a robust .407 in 1971. His career average of .393 ranks second on the all-time Spartan list. Rob's 59 base hits in 1971 included 14 home runs and six triples, leading to a school record slugging percentage of .848. He began his career at MSU as a second baseman and was switched to the outfield, where he became a first team 1971 All-American as designated by the American Association of College Baseball Coaches. Drafted and signed by the Milwaukee Brewers, Ellis played three seasons of major league baseball.

Rob Ellis

IN THE SPARTLITE

Baseball: Centering their southern trip at Coral Gables, Fla., Danny Litwhiler's squad went undefeated in the first six games to win the first half of the University of Miami Hurricanes twin tournament. The team then went 5-1 to tie for first in the second half. Overall, it was a successful southern trip in which the batters posted impressive numbers. Leading the hit parade were Ron Delonge .458, Rob Ellis .420, Gary Boyce .408 and John Dace .408, and the total team average was .333.

The five pitchers that emerged as the likely strength of the staff included: lefty Rob Clancy, Kirk Maas, Larry Ike, Dave Leisman and Brian Leickfelt.

Basketball: Coach Gus Ganakas opened the season with the following lineup: Pat Miller and Ron Gutkowski at the forwards, Rudy Benjamin and Paul Dean playing at the guard positions, and center Bill Kilgore.

Students were admitted to home varsity games upon showing their student ID. Otherwise, reserved seats were available for $2.00 each.

Between a noon workout and tip-off time of the Saturday, January 30 game at Ohio State, someone broke into the MSU locker room and stole seven of the Spartans' green uniforms. When game time rolled around, the only viable option was to take the floor in borrowed OSU road uniforms. The strange circumstance apparently didn't disturb Gus Ganakas's crew, as they broke a two-game losing streak with an 82-70 defeat of the Buckeyes.

Cross Country: The Spartan harriers captured the school's 13th Big Ten team title in 22 seasons. Furthermore, it was Jim Gibbard's second conference crown in three years as head coach. Leading the winners with a fourth place finish was Ken Popejoy (pictured far left, next page). It was a remarkable comeback for the Glen Ellyn, Ill., sophomore who had suffered a season-ending knee injury in 1969. He was followed by Randy Kilpatrick in seventh, Ralph Zoppa in eighth, Kim Hartman in 11th, and Chuck Starkey in 12th. Run over the familiar Forest Akers West layout, MSU's winning total of 42 points, was followed by the pre-meet favorite Minnesota with 66 and Indiana with 67. It was a particularly gratifying victory, as both the Gophers and Hoosiers had defeated State in regular season dual-meet competition.

Fencing: After a mediocre 9-6 regular season, the Spartan fencers rose to the occasion in March as they captured the team title for only the second time in the school's history. It was a closely contested match with a meager two points separating State from the defending champions, the Wisconsin Badgers. The epee squad won 17 bouts, led by Detroit sophomore Bill Mathers, who took first place and qualified for the nationals. His teammate Paul Herring placed third. The sabremen took 13 bouts, led by Doug McGaw, who finished in a tie for second place. Foilist Ira Schwartz contributed seven wins to qualify for the NCAA championships.

Of the three MSU entrants in the national collegiate meet in Colorado Springs, Colo., only Schwartz reached the finals, where he dualed to a 7-16 record for the 20th spot. Mathers and McGaw failed to progress beyond the preliminary rounds.

Football: The disappointing 4-6 season of 1970 was severely impacted by an incredibly long list of injuries that grew game by game. A total of 13 players missed the entire season because of a debilitating injury of one type or another. Third-string quarterback Frank Kolch was elevated to the starting role when George Mihaiu followed Dan Werner to the sideline with season-ending cartilage damage to his knee in the sixth game of the season.

With varsity eligibility for freshmen two seasons off, once more a frosh team was organized. In the final contest of their limited three-game schedule, they defeated the Michigan yearlings, 20-6, to finish with a 2-1 record.

"Buck" Nystrom and Denny Stolz, the latter having been head coach at Alma College, joined the coaching staff in replacement of the departed Al Dorow and George Paterno.

An off-season tragedy hit the football team on March 1, 1971, when Tommy Love, a 22-year-old halfback from Sylva, N.C., died of a massive heart attack after being rushed to the Olin Health Center. He had been engaged in a pick-up basketball game at the Men's IM Building.

Golf: With nine holes of play remaining in the Big Ten championships, the five-man team of Denny Vass, Rick Woulfe, Graham Cooke, John Peterson and John VanderMeiden held a three-stroke advantage over the Purdue team. Unfortunately, that lead would not hold up, as the Boilermakers overtook Bruce Fossum's crew and won by nine strokes, 1,501-1,510. John VanderMeiden finished second overall in the tournament with a four-round total of 72-78-70-79—299. His 70 in the third round was the lowest of the weekend. John Peterson was one stroke back, tying for third with a 74-74-75-77—300. Other Spartan scores were Rick Woulfe 73-78-78-73—302, Dick Bradow 76-76-74-79—305, Graham Cooke 76-75-75-82—308 and Denny Vass 78-85-78-68—319.

Gymnastics: In their lowest finish since joining the conference competition in 1951, State placed fifth in the Big Ten meet in Columbus. Gaining the Spartan points were sophomore Randy Balhorn, who was fourth in the all-around competition; Charlie Morse, who earned a fifth on the side horse and Mickey Uram, who contributed a third place on the parallel bars and fourth in floor exercise.

The 1970 Big Ten cross country champions

Hockey: The January 29-30 double win over Notre Dame was marked with major brawls. A total of 51 penalties were dealt out to both teams and six players were ejected from the games.

The final four games on the regular schedule were all concluded in overtime, with the Spartans breaking even, two wins and two losses.

Among the Big Ten hockey schools (MSU, Michigan, Minnesota, Ohio State and Wisconsin) Michigan State completed the best record, 10-4, and consequently clinched the unofficial title of conference champions.

The Spartan's post-season run was short lived, losing to Minnesota-Duluth in the opening round, 4-3 in overtime.

Don "Zippy" Thompson was the only Spartan to be recognized with a spot on the All-WCHA team. The 5' 5" and 155-pound lineman was the team scoring leader with 57 points, including a team-record 38 assists.

Lacrosse: The Spartans reflected a marked improvement in defense from the inaugural 1969-1970 season. Within the span of two seasons, the goals against average dropped from 13.7 to 8.2. Posting four wins also demonstrated progress, but it would be another eight years before a Spartan team would record a winning season. Obviously, initiating a new sport with an extremely limited budget proved to be a severe challenge.

Soccer: After State completed their 5-1-3 season record, two team members gained postseason honors. Buzz Demling was selected as a first team All-American and John Houska was selected to the second team.

Swimming and Diving: Compiling 207 points under the 12-man per event scoring system, State ended up in fourth place at the Big Ten championship meet. Jeff Lanini was MSU's only gold medalist as he won his specialty, the 100-yard breaststroke. He also placed sixth in the 200-yard event. Adding to the team scoring total were Alan Dilley, John Thuerer, Ken Winfield, Steve Mitchell, Tony Bazant, Paul Virtue, Larry O'Neil, Mike Boyle and George Gonzales. The diving trio of Tom Cramer, Jud Alward and Dave Coward scored, and Cramer's fourth place in the one-meter was the Spartan's top finish.

Registering only 19 points, the Spartans finished tied for 18th place in the NCAA championships in Ames, Iowa, the lowest spot since going scoreless in 1964. Leading the way were divers Cramer and Alward, who finished fifth and eighth in the one-meter event. Ken Winfield was the top swimmer with an 11th place in the 200-yard butterfly.

Tragedy struck the Spartan football team and the MSU campus in 1971 when 22-year-old Tommy Love succumbed to a heart attack.

Tennis: After just four matches (3-1), the seven-man team of Tom Gray, Mike Madura, Jim Symington, Rick Ferman, Jim Pitrula, Rick Vetter and DeArmond Briggs found itself home from the southern spring trip earlier than expected. There had apparently been a miscommunication regarding a self-imposed 11:00 P.M. curfew, as the men were out beyond midnight on March 27. Coach Drobac reacted by aborting the remaining schedule and returning the squad to East Lansing.

Four singles players and two doubles teams reached the semi-finals of the Big Ten tournament, but only Mike Madura, playing at the number three position, made it all the way to become the Spartans' first conference champion since 1968. As a team, MSU placed fourth.

Track and Field: Clocked in 56.7, an MSU quartet, running at the Florida Relays in Gainesville, tied a national record in the shuttle hurdle relay event. The foursome and their split times were: Wayne Hartwick 14.2, Rich Jacques 14.6, Dave Martin 14.2 and John Morrison 13.7. One week later they would win the same event at the Kentucky Relays.

Scoring 46 points, State finished a close second behind host Wisconsin's winning total of 57 at the Big Ten Indoor meet. Leading the way for the Spartans was the record-setting mile relay quartet (see "Making History" section). Two other Spartans were crowned champions, Herb Washington, who ran a 6.1 in the 60-yard dash, and Bob Cassleman, who was clocked at 1:10.2 in the 600. Dave Dieters was second in the mile; Wayne Hartwick and John Morrison went 2-3 in the high hurdles; LaRue Butchee placed third in the 300; Mike Holt third in the 440; and Hartwick came back for a third in the low hurdles.

Going outdoors, the mile-relay team, Washington, and Cassleman were each winners again; but this time State had to settle for fourth place in the team standings. Other finalists were Hartwick, Morrison, Butchee, Kim Hartman, Eric Allen, Randy Kilpatrick and John Mock.

Wrestling: Following the football season and stating simply that he was "tired," heavyweight Vic Mittleberg, the 1970 Big Ten champion, opted to forego his senior year of wrestling.

Coach Peninger's most frequent line up was as follows: Greg Johnson at 118, Lon Hicks at 126, Tom Milkovich at 134, Mike Ellis at 142, John Abajace at 150, Tom Muir at 156, Gerald Malicek at 167, Tim Maxim at 177, Dave Ciolek at 190 and Ben Lewis filled the heavyweight slot.

The annual battle against Michigan went to the final match with the team score tied 16-16. An exciting conclusion was anticipated as the heavyweights squared off. Instead, a listless 1-1 draw left the meet still tied at 18-18.

Winning a close 6-5 final match, Greg Johnson successfully defended his 118-pound title at the NCAA championships in Auburn, Ala. Dave Ciolek placed fourth in the 190-pound division and Ben Lewis settled for fifth with the heavyweights. MSU finished third in the team standing with 44 points.

EXTRA! SEVEN BIG TEN WRESTLING TITLES IN A ROW

(#6) 1971—West Lafayette, Ind.: Winning five individual titles and finishing no lower than third in the remaining five weight classifications, Michigan State scored a record 101 team points to easily win an unprecedented sixth straight conference championship. Greg Johnson at 118 pounds and Tom Milkovich at 134 successfully defended their titles. Johnson, a junior from Lansing Everett, scored a 7-2 decision win, while Milkovich, a junior from Maple Heights, Ohio, earned a 6-2 decision. They shared the victory podium with 167-pound Gerald Malecek and 190-pound Dave Ciolek, both of whom won by decision. Heavyweight Ben Lewis was credited with the only pin of the finals, doing so at 3:52 of his match. Both John Abajace at 150-pounds and Mike Ellis at 142 reached the championship match before losing and thus settling for a runner-up position. In the consolation bouts for third place, 126-pound Lon Hicks, 158-pound Rick Radman, and 177-pound Bruce Zindel emerged as winners.

EXTRA! MICHIGAN STATE RELAYS (1970s)

Four Spartans were featured at the 1971 Michigan State relays; but none more noteworthy than Herb Washington (no relation to Gene) who tied the world record of 5.9 for the 60-yard dash. He became only the second person ever to make that mark on a dirt track and the *only one* to do it both on dirt and board tracks. Adding to this excitement, Bob Cassleman, Dave Dieters, and John Morrison took firsts of their own. Cassleman, a freshman, won the 600-yard race, setting a meet record at 1:08.8. Junior Dieters set a personal best, finishing the mile in 4:09.5. Sophomore Morrison took the honors in the 70-yard low hurdles with a 7.8.

Perhaps the most memorable Michigan State relays were those run at the 50th anniversary of the event on February 12, 1972, when two Spartans sprinters bettered world records. First, it was freshman Marshall Dill who brought the 3,000 spectators to their feet when he blazed his way through 300 yards with a clocking of 29.5, one-half second better than the American and world records. Next came Washington, 35 minutes later, running his favorite race over 60 yards, an event in which he held the world record of 5.9 along with 12 others. After that evening he would stand alone. When Herb's time of 5.8 was announced, the uproar of the 3,000 fans could be heard from across the river in the Kellogg Center. Dill and Washington had overshadowed some other remarkable performances by MSU runners. Bob Cassleman went home pleased after setting a new American mark of 1:08.2 in the 600-yard dash and while Ken Popejoy ran a 4:03.2 mile to better Jim Ryan's fieldhouse record set four years earlier. Finally, before the lights of Jenison were dimmed, the foursome of Cassleman, Mike Holt, Mike Murphy and Dill had set a meet and fieldhouse record of 3:14.4 in the mile relay.

Herb Lindsay was the star of the 1976 relays. He opened the evening by blazing to a two-mile victory in the meet and fieldhouse record time of 8:39.2. (He had set the previous record in this same meet during 1975). Only 30 minutes later after breaking the tape in the two-mile, he ran a 4:04.8 to anchor the winning medley relay team which included Dane Fortney, Steve Young and Stan Mavis.

At the 1977 meet, MSU featured a new star sprinter in freshman Randy Smith who raced to a 6.1 win the 60-yard dash. Sophomore Dan King also took a first, leaping 6'10" in the high jump, and the distance medley team of Keith Moore, Steve Young, Stan Mavis, and Herb Lindsay ran a 9:49.1 to repeat their victory of the preceding year.

The 1971 Big Ten championship wrestling team

MSU
1971-1972

TALES TO TELL

It is suggested that records are made to be broken. Could be, but when Eric "The Flea" Allen racked up a national and team record 350 yards rushing against Purdue on October 30, 1971, that was 30 years ago, and although the mark has been surpassed nationally, the standard remains atop the Spartan record book. Perhaps the longevity of this achievement speaks to the magnitude of what Allen accomplished on that afternoon in West Layfayette, Ind. There have been legitimate challengers to the mark: Lorenzo White, Blake Ezor, Sedrick Irvin, Tico Duckett and more recently, T.J. Duckett.

In his book *The Spartans,* Fred Stabley recalls the Allen record and how the gang in the press box contributed to the event. After three quarters of play, the Georgetown, S.C., speedster had already accumulated 282 yards. Fred tells it from there:

"Purdue scored early in the final period and kicked off to State. Allen started going again—up the middle for four, off right tackle for 28 and around right end for 11—and ran his total to 325. Then, to the consternation of the frantically calculating Spartan sports information people, Jim Bond was substituted for Allen. 'The Flea' took a seat on the bench and undoubtedly was through for the day.

Then the Spartan press box people really got to work. Official statisticians confirmed that the total of 325 yards for Allen was correct. Spartan coaches working the press box phones to the bench were asked to relay the word quickly that Eric was just 23 yards short of breaking the all-time NCAA rushing record. Offensive line coach Gordie Serr took the message at the other end, nodded, and immediately said something to Duffy. Duffy turned, called Allen, threw an arm around his shoulder, and said: 'They tell me in the press box you need just 23 yards to break the collegiate rushing record. You're going back and are going to carry the ball on every play until you get it.'

It did not take long. Allen tried the right tackle spot first and was dumped for no gain by giant Dave

---

HEADLINES of 1972

- At the Summer Olympics in Munich, 11 Israeli competitors are killed by Arab terrorists, and the games are temporarily suspended for the first time in history.
- Pong, the first commercial computer game, is created by Atari.
- President Nixon makes an eight-day "journey of peace" to China and three months later becomes the first USA president to visit Moscow, where he engages in a week of summit talks with the Kremlin.
- The Supreme Court rules the death penalty unconstitutional.

SCOREBOARD

	W	L	T	Avg.
Baseball	28	10	1	.731
Track and Field	5	1	0	.833
Football	6	5	0	.545
Basketball	13	11	0	.542
Tennis	6	15	0	.285
Cross Country	4	2	0	.667
Swimming and Diving	7	4	0	.636
Wrestling	11	1	0	.977
Hockey	20	16	0	.556
Fencing	9	6	0	.600
Golf	tournament play only			
Gymnastics	5	4	0	.555
Soccer	7	2	0	.777
Lacrosse	5	8	0	.385

Butz. On the next try he went almost the same route, found an open door, and sprinted into the end zone and the MSU, Big Ten and NCAA record books. His clinching foray was for 25 yards."

TEAM OF THE YEAR

The 1972 track and field team was a star-studded aggregation that won both the indoor and outdoor Big Ten team titles in 1972 and came within one point of sharing the NCAA indoor title with Southern California.

At the indoor conference meet at Ohio State's Frence Fieldhouse, six Spartans captured titles, rolling up 65 points to runner-up Illinois' 42. Those gold medal winners were Herb Washington in the 60-yard dash; freshman Marshall Dill in the 300-yard dash; Bob Cassleman in the 600-yard run; John Morrison in the low hurdles; Ken Popejoy in the mile, and the mile relay team. In all six winning performances, Big Ten championship records were established.

One week following the Big Ten meet, the best in the nation had collected at Detroit's Cobo Hall for the eighth running of the NCAA indoor championships. With victories from Herb Washington in the 60-yard dash and Ken Popejoy in the mile, and thirds from Bob Cassleman in the 600-yard dash and the mile relay, State amassed 18 points, just one shy of USC's winning total of 19.

Projections were for a close meet when the Big Ten teams gathered 11 weeks later in Champaign, Ill., for the outdoor championships. Capping off their two-day effort with a second in the mile relay, the Spartans led the University of Illinois by four points, 105-101. However, the reality of the moment was tenuous. State was through for the weekend, but Illinois had competitors in the high jump and pole vault, events still being contested. As green-and-white clad athletes stood by the two venues cheering for anyone not wearing blue and orange, the challenging Illini managed a fifth and a sixth—worth three points. Michigan State had held on for a one-point win, 105-104. Much like indoors, the same names surfaced as heroes: Herb Washington won the 100-yard dash; Marshall Dill finished first in the 220; and Bob Cassleman was the winner of the 440-yard intermediate hurdle event. There were other supporting contributors; LaRue Butchee, Del Gregory, Ron Kool, John Morrison, Mike Hurd, Marv Roberts, Eric Allen and Bill Nance.

The 1972 track and field team. Letter Winners were D. Martin, H. Washington, J. Morrison, M. Murphy, K. Popejoy, A. Henderson, R. Castleman, D. Gregory, W. Nance, J. Ross, M. Dill and manager M. Groszko.

MAKING HISTORY

There had been many noteworthy performances in the 48 previous runnings, of the Michigan State relays, but the meet of Feb. 12, 1972, remains as the most memorable, before or since. On that evening, both Marshall Dill, the freshman all-purpose sprinter, and Herb Washington, the junior short-distance ace, shattered long-standing world records. First it was Dill who gained the spotlight, as he negotiated the 300-yard sprint, looping beyond the limited one-eighth mile Jenison oval in a swift time of 29.5. When it was announced that this bettered the world record, the 3,000 fans that filled the balcony bleachers responded with a standing ovation. Perhaps Dill's mark was the inspiration Herb Washington needed. On two previous occasions, he had equaled the world record 5.9 over the 60-yard indoor sprint. This time he would break through that barrier and record a world record 5.8. Once more the appreciative fans stood with an erupting applause. The pair of Spartans had made it a night to remember.

Few entertainers gained the applause that Al Hirt, king of trumpeters, and his band did following their Iowa game halftime performance on October 23.

Former Spartan coach Ben Van Alstyne died at age 72. He had coached basketball from 1927 to 1949 and golf from 1932 to 1961.

The NCAA ruled that college basketball teams could start their seasons the last Friday in November, rather than waiting until December 1. This change would translate to having the schedule open one week earlier.

GREAT STATE DATES

Football—**September 12, 1971 (H):** The Spartan defense was outstanding in this season-opening 10-0 defeat of the University of Illinois. Granted, the visitors hadn't helped their cause any, as they fumbled the ball away seven times; but the Spartans, led by Ernie Hamilton, Ron Curl, Gail Clark, Ken Alderson and Mark Niesen, kept the Illini from ever penetrating offensively beyond midfield. State led at halftime, 3-0, on a Borys Shlapak 48-yard field goal. The only touchdown of the afternoon followed the sixth Illinois give-away at their 25-yard line in the final quarter. Eric Allen, who tied a team record with 37 carries on the afternoon, completed the five-play drive, scoring from the six-yard line. It was a frustrating afternoon for MSU as well. On seven other occasions the offense was inside the Illini 25-yard line yet failed to score.

Cross Country—**October 2, 1971 (H):** Ken Popejoy won his first race as a Spartan, and his team placed seven in the top ten to easily defeat Tennessee, 19-39. Popejoy finished the five-mile course in 25:22. Randy Kilpatrick finished third, followed by Rob Cool, Dave Dieters and Ron Cool.

Soccer—**October 2, 1971 (H):** It looked like MSU would be defeated on their home turf, as they trailed 1-0 going into the fourth quarter against Wooster. At the 4:02 mark, however, Lennox Robinson kicked in a goal, assisted by Gerry Murray, and regulation time ended with a 1-1 tie. The coaches agreed to play two overtime periods of five minutes each, which gave the Spartans more than ample time. Junior Higgins scored after just 1:57 into the extra time and Murray shot another past the Scot goalie in the second OT period to finish the game at 3-1.

Football—**November 6, 1971 (A):** Defeating eighth ranked Ohio State, 17-10, in the celebrated horseshoe stadium in Columbus was reason enough for the victorious Spartans to carry Coach Daugherty from the field on their shoulders. It was OSU's first home loss since 1967. Borys Shlapac opened the scoring with an impressive 47-yard field goal with 14:12 remaining in the first half, but the undaunted Bucks drove back for seven points and the lead. An ensuing Buckeye pass attempt from their 37-yard line was picked off by Brad VanPelt and returned to the seven-yard line. Two plays later Eric Allen carried the ball into the end zone. The Buckeyes countered with a 3-pointer to tie the score 10-10. Then with time running out in the third quarter, "The Flea" scored the winning touchdown and with it set a team season record with 13 touchdowns and 80 points.

Swimming and Diving—**January 15, 1972 (A):** As the scoring lead flip-flopped several times during the afternoon, the Spartans eventually prevailed with a 63-60 victory over the Minnesota Gophers. The medley relay quartet of Alan Dilley, Jeff Lanini, Ken Winfield and Jack Martin opened on a positive note. As the meet progressed, veteran performers stepped up, senior co-captain John Thuerer won his specialties, the 500 and 1,000-yard freestyle events; junior Winfield was a double win-

ner in the 50-yard freestyle and 200-yard butterfly; and Dilley, another junior, easily won the backstroke. With two events remaining, the score sheet revealed that MSU needed one victory to prevail, and senior co-captain Jeff Lanini provided the margin with a first-place finish in the breaststroke.

Hockey—**January 19, 1972 (H):** The 3,264 fans that jammed Demonstration Hall knew this MSU-Michigan game would be traditionally rough after watching a first period full of hard checks and 12 penalties. The U of M scored first, knocking one behind the Spartan star goalie Jim Watt, whom the St. Louis Blues had selected in the preceding spring's NHL draft. Don Thompson tied the game on a power play and Mark Calder followed with a score during a four-on-four situation. A melee broke out during the final minute of the opening period. By the time order was restored the game officials sent the teams to their dressing rooms prematurely and used an extended break time to clear the playing surface of debris and equipment, resurface the ice and cool the tempers. Michel Chaurest scored the only goal in the second period, giving State a 3-1 lead, but the Wolverines opened the final 20-minutes with their second marker. This only stimulated the Spartans. Chaurest pulled off the "hat trick" with two more goals consecutively, followed by another Thompson score, with Bob Boyd wrapping up the scoring for an easy 7-2 MSU win.

Michel Chaurest scored a hat trick against Michigan on Jan. 19, 1972.

Wrestling—**January 22, 1972 (H):** The fieldhouse was packed with excited wrestling fans that sensed this might be the time. It was the sixth straight year the Spartans had lined up against always-strong Oklahoma State, and until now, only a 14-14 tie in 1967 was worthy of mention. As could be expected, every match on this afternoon was exciting. With the score tied at 6-6, MSU gained the lead on an 8-4 victory by Tom Milkovich, the Big Ten champion. Rick Radman followed with a 7-3 come-from-behind victory, as did Gerald Malecek with a 5-3 win. Down 2-0 after two periods, Dave Ciolek, the conference 190-pound champion, scored nine points for a resounding 9-2 decision. The final score read MSU 20, OSU 15. Grady Peninger had finally put a team on the mat that could defeat his alma mater.

Swimming and Diving—**January 28, 1972 (H):** The score in the Purdue meet was tied at 24-24 when the State swimmers and divers took control. Jeff Lanini swam a personal best of 2:01.39 in the individual medley for first place and the lead. Mike Cook and Kim Ridinger followed with first and second places in the three-meter diving. This idea of a one-two sweep became contagious. Ken Winfield and Pat Burke followed the routine in the butterfly; backstrokers Alan Dilley and Paul Fetters repeated with a slam, and Larry O'Neill and Tony Bazant did the same in the 200-breaststroke. Meanwhile, other first place finishes were recorded by Paul Virtue, Winfield (a double winner) and diver Tom Benson on the one-meter board. What began as a 24-24 tie ended in a 79-44 rout with seven Spartan swimmers recording personal best times.

Hockey—**February 11, 1972 (A):** Don "Zippy" Thompson stole the show in leading the icers to a 7-2 decision over Minnesota and becoming the new MSU record holder for total career points. The new record was set in the second period, as Thompson assisted Mark Calder's goal to bring his total to 132 career points. By that time, State had already put the game away with an early scoring streak. Thompson scored the first goal, and Calder, Gilles Gagnon and Bill Sipola followed with one each to build a 4-0 lead after just 7:26 of the opening period. In the second stanza, the Gophers managed to slip two shots past the Spartan goalie, but State added two more, one by Bob Micheletti, along with the Thompson-Calder record-setter. Micheletti turned the light on one more time during the final 20 minutes.

Wrestling—**February 12, 1972 (H):** This time the result of the annual MSU-Michigan match was never in doubt, as State built a 13-0 lead before the Wolverines managed to win a match. Those early wins featured two-time NCAA champion Greg Johnson and freshman Pat Milkovich, who won his 10th match of the season. His brother Tom was one of four who managed to shut out his opponent. The other three were Gerald Malecek, Dave Ciolek and heavyweight Ben Lewis. The final score read 25-6, thus suggesting MSU's continued dominance in the conference.

Fencing—**February 12, 1972 (A):** Charlie Schmitter and his squad traveled to Madison, Wis., where they met and defeated the host Badgers and the Wisconsin-Parkside branch by identical 15-12 scores. State lost only in the sabre to the Badgers, 3-6, while stopping them in both epee and foil by identical 6-3 scores. Against Parkside, the Spartans gained 5-4 winning scores in all three weapons. Ira Schwartz (4-0) and Paul Herring (5-0) were both undefeated during the afternoon.

Gymnastics—**February 19, 1972 (A):** The Spartans surprisingly dominated Ohio State, 154.15 to 148.65, in a meet in Columbus. Randy Balhorn led the way and placed in five of six events, finishing first on the horizontal bars and in the all-around competition. Charlie Morse was also a significant supporter, placing first in three events. Also contributing were Don Waybright, Larry Lad and Al Beaudet.

Track and Field—**February 19, 1972 (H):** The Spartan squad took nine of 15 events to easily defeat Michigan, 83-57. World-record holder Herb Washington set a meet record with a 6.0 in the 60-yard dash and was followed by LaRue Butchee and Marshill Dill to give State a sweep in the event and to spark the victory. Dill won the 300-yard dash with a time of 32.5 seconds. Ken Popejoy and Del Gregory were both double winners, while Ron Cool and Randy Kilpatrick took top honors in their events. The final first place finish came from the mile relay team of Popejoy, Bob Cassleman, Mike Murphy and Tom Spuller, who combined for a time of 3:16.5.

Basketball—**March 4, 1972 (H):** Playing before a crowd of 11,813 in Jenison Fieldhouse, Gus Ganakas's Spartans rallied late in the game for an exciting 96-92 victory over the University of Michigan. Sophomore guard Mike Robinson, who completed the season as the conference scoring leader with a 27.2 average, hit for a game-high 37 points. Senior co-captain Pat Miller, with a 19-point outburst in the first half, finished the afternoon with 26 points. After State had gained a 47-44 advantage at intermission, the two teams alternately led throughout the second half until Bill Kilgore made a lay-up to put MSU in charge for good with a little more than two minutes to play. As usual, Gary Ganakas played a stellar defensive game, as well as pumped in two vital free throws in the final minute of play.

Lacrosse—**March 26, 1972 (H):** Oberlin College led most of the game, but MSU came from behind and tied the score 9-9, sending it into overtime. Suddenly it was a game of defense, and it wasn't until the sixth overtime period that Val Washington scored, giving State the sudden death 10-9 victory.

Tennis—**April 8, 1972 (H):** Five of six regulars were in their first year of play at MSU, but the team did manage to win six meets, including a 6-3 defeat of Minnesota. Junior Dave Williams started the action with a 6-2, 6-2, singles match victory. Joe Fodell, Scott Rosen and Al Jacoby followed with additional wins, giving the Spartans a 4-2 lead. The doubles team of Williams and Rick Vetter sealed the meet with the team of Rosen-Jacoby adding an insurance point.

Track and Field—**April 15, 1972 (A):** After an undefeated indoor season, the Spartan track team began the outdoor season by topping Purdue, 78-76, in a meet that came down to the final event. Junior Marvin Roberts scored crucial points for MSU with firsts in the shot put and discus, but the team was still down three points going into the final event. Bill Nance, Ron Cool, Mike Murphy and Bob Cassleman then combined in the mile relay for 3:15.1 to finish off the Boilermakers. Other individual winners for State were John Morrison, Randy Kilpatrick, Ken Popejoy, Delbert Gregory and Cassleman.

Lacrosse—**April 12, 1972 (A):** Coach Ted Swoboda and his team took revenge and won their first victory over Michigan in the fourth year of MSU varsity lacrosse. The U of M took a 6-2 lead when Jim Walters and Fred Hartman were the only Spartans to score in the first half, but tremendous play by goalie Ron Hebert, who tallied 25 saves, kept the Wolverines scoreless in the last two stanzas. Team leader Val Washington started the comeback with two third-quarter goals. In the fourth, Don Gray scored an unassisted marker, and Washington tied the game before Bob Stevenson slipped the winning goal past the Wolverines' goalie.

Baseball—**May 13, 1972 (H):** Hosting Ohio State in the final home weekend doubleheader of the spring, MSU was hoping to maintain their remarkable undefeated home record (14-0). In the opening game, that streak was in jeopardy, as the Spartans trailed 5-2 in the bottom of the seventh. Pinch-hitter Rob Dilday opened with a walk and was followed by a single from Rick Carrow. Ron DeLonge failed to bring in a run, flying out to center, but senior Ron Pruitt followed with a two-base hit that scored pinch-runner Jesse Turner. Not to be outdone, senior Shaun Howitt tied the score with a two-run single, taking second on the play at the plate. Howitt then dashed to third on a wild pitch and crossed home plate for what would prove to be the winning run on yet another errant pitch. State went on to bury the Buckeyes, 10-5, with relief pitcher Brian Lieckfelt earning the win. The unblemished home stand prevailed as they also won the nightcap, 6-3.

Golf—**May 13, 1972 (H):** The Seventh Annual Spartan Invitational golf tournament was again dominated by the host entries. The MSU "A" and MSU "B" teams took first and second with team scores of 583 and 597, respectively, finishing seven strokes ahead of the third place Michigan "A" team. Senior Dick Bradow led the way through the weekend, shooting a 142 to gain medalist honors by four strokes. Mark Timyan, Bill Dickens and Tom Murphy were tied for the third spot, five strokes back at 147.

ATHLETE OF THE YEAR

The highly touted Greg Johnson impressed everyone when he became the first Big Ten wrestler to win three straight NCAA crowns to go alongside his three conference crowns. When the 5' 3" Lansing Everett High School graduate came to MSU, coach Grady Peninger knew he could win, but no one knew the adversity he would have to overcome. In his first year of eligibility, Johnson was sidelined with an ankle fracture he sustained in practice. In his second year, he suffered a broken leg and was forced to start the season late. Finally, he made his college debut against Oklahoma State but lost to their 118-pounder. This was his only loss of the year, and he found revenge when he defeated the same Sooner wrestler in the NCAA finals to win his first national title. Johnson later overcame a knee injury in his final year on

his way to becoming a three-time All-American with a career record of 54-5-2, having been given an extra year of eligibility due to his injuries. In addition, he was a two-time winner of the East-West college All-Star meet. After his collegiate career, he coached wrestling for many years, including six (1978-1983) as the head man at the University of Illinois.

Greg Johnson

IN THE SPARTLITE

Baseball: Even after completing an impressive 28-10-1 overall record, including a 10-4 conference season, State had to settle for second place behind the 13-3 Big Ten champions from the University of Iowa. Ron Pruitt and Shaun Howitt were named first team All-Big Ten. Pruitt led the offense with a .392 batting average, and Howitt finished the season with 12 home runs. Also, Larry Ike set a new career victory record with 23.

Frank Pellerin, varsity letter winner in baseball (1941-1943) and long-time assistant baseball coach under both John Kobs and Danny Litwhiler, shares this story:

"In 1972 we were in Evanston to play Northwestern in a two-game series. Some of our players looked a little tired, and Danny [Litwhiler] and I were discussing the possibility that they were not getting their proper rest. So, we decided to have a bed check that evening to be certain everyone would be where they were supposed to be.

Our curfew that night was 12:00. So at about 12:15, we went to the desk of the hotel and picked up a passkey. I had the rooming list and a pencil, and Danny had the key. We started down the hall, Danny opened doors and I checked off the rooms. We were having great success until we approached the last room. Everyone was tucked in and getting his rest. When Danny opened the last room, we were shocked as we stared at two empty beds. Danny said, 'Now we have a problem. Whose room is this?' I looked at the list and started to laugh. Danny said, 'What's so funny? This is serious!' I said, 'This room belongs to Litwhiler and Pellerin!' That was our last bed check."

Frank Pellerin served as assistant baseball coach under both John Kobs and Danny Litwhiler.

Basketball: Mike Robinson was named Big Ten scoring champion with an average of 27.2 points per game in conference play and was voted First Team All-Big Ten. Center Bill Kilgore was also a statistic leader, averaging a double-double with 16.7 points per game and 11.1 rebounds. Despite these outstanding numbers, the Spartans ended the year in a fifth place tie with a 13-11 overall and 6-8 Big Ten record.

Cross Country: In 1971, the Spartans won one more Big Ten cross country title, the school's 14th in a span of 22 years. In the subsequent 30 years, the most impressive State finishes have been runner-up performances in both 1988 and 1998. The 1971 championship team totaled 74 points, followed closely by previously undefeated Indiana with 82. Dating back to 1908, this was only the second time the meet included team entries from all conference schools. Furthermore, run on a layout at Minneapolis, this was the first time the race was conducted over a six-mile course. Ken Popejoy was the first Spartan across the line, as in 1970 he was a fourth place finisher completing the distance in 30:25. Randy Kilpatrick, five seconds back in fifth, was followed by Dave Dieters and Rob Cool in the 13th and 14th positions. In the final scoring slot, Steve Rockey finished 38th.

In the largest NCAA cross country tournament in history, hosted by the University of Tennessee, the Spartans placed 13th out of 92 entries. Run in unseasonable 36-degree weather, State's top finishers were Ken Popejoy, Randy Kilpatrick, Rob Cool, Dave Dieters and Ron Cool.

Fencing: At the Big Ten Championship in Champaign, Ill., the epee competition came down to a three-way tie among Paul Herring and Bill Mathers, both of MSU, and a swordsman from Ohio State. In projecting the team scores, if the Buckeye won the ensuing fence-off, the team trophy would belong to OSU and conversely so if either of the Spartans emerged as the winner. As it unfolded, Mathers, who finished with a 7-4 mark, including a 4-1 tally in the finals, defeated the challenger from Columbus, and the final score read: Michigan State 37, Ohio State 35, Wisconsin 33, and Illinois 28. In other action, Doug McGaw tied for second in sabre but was later bumped to third based on the number of touches. Ira Swartz was seventh in the foil.

Football: A 6-5 overall record was good enough for a third place Big Ten tie, the team's best finish since the 1966 national championship year. Eric Allen sparked the offense and topped the school's rushing records, running

for more than 100 yards seven times and totaling 1,494 yards and 18 touchdowns for the season. Meanwhile, quarterback Mike Rassmussen finished his career with 1,986 passing yards, the third most for a Spartan ever. Borys Shlapak also made a mark, twice tying his own 1970 record with a 54-yard field goal. Defensively, Ron Curl set records, ending his career with 12 QB sacks and 25 tackles. To top it off, as a team they tied an old Spartan record by holding Georgia Tech to zero completed passes.

Golf: Coach Bruce Fossum's squad consisted of nine: Richard Bradow, Willim Brafford, Steve Broadwell, Bill Dickens, Brad Hyland, Bill Marx, Tom Murphy, Robert Timyan and John VanderMeiden.

Excellent team scoring gave the Spartans a comfortable six-stroke lead after the two rounds of the Big Ten tournament hosted by the University of Minnesota. The final rounds on Saturday were a different story, as the team, man for man, played poorly and ultimately fell all the way to fifth place, thus failing to qualify for the NCAA tournament.

Gymnastics: Although settling for fifth place in the team standings, two Spartan gymnasts performed admirably at the Big Ten championships. Randy Balhorn finished fifth on the vault and scored more than 100 points in the all-around competition, good enough for second place. This qualified him for both the NCAA Championships and the Olympic trials. Charlie Morse was also among the leaders with his second place finish on the parallel bars.

Hockey: An injury-plagued team was not able to manage Denver in the WCHA playoff finals. Left-winger Bob Michelutti was already out for the season with a broken leg, and defenseman Bob Boyd and right-winger Mark Calder were both playing through serious injuries. As if that was not enough, early in the first game against the Pioneers, center and co-captain Gilles Gagnon was hit by a stick just below his right eye and was out for the series. Despite ending the season with those two losses (2-1and 9-3) to the Pioneers, Spartan net minder Jim Watt was voted first-team all-WCHA and first-team All-American, while Boyd and Don Thompson were both voted to the WCHA second team.

Lacrosse: Val Washington's 22 goals and goalie Ron Hebert's 254 saves paced the lacrosse squad, which was 5-8 overall and 2-7 in the Midwest Lacrosse Association.

Soccer: The MSU booters finished with a respectable 7-2-0 mark, giving up just ten goals in nine games. Nick Dujon was the top scorer, with nine goals and two assists for 20 total points. Gerry Murray was not far behind, with 19 points off six goals and seven assists.

Swimming and Diving: Led by Junior Ken Winfield with a second in the 200-yard butterfly and a third at the 100-yard distance, State finished fourth at the Big Ten championships. Later, teamed with Alan Dilley, Jeff Lanini and Tony Bazant, Winfield led MSU to a 19th place finish at the NCAA meet.

Tennis: Playing at the number two slot all season, Dave Williams was unfortunately injured in a bicycle accident and unable to play in the Big Ten tournament. Coach Drobak filled the spot, and the team performed admirably, yet they were unable to finish higher than seventh place. Rick Vetter, with the number one slot, led the way for the Spartans and was voted to the six-man all-Big Ten team.

Track and Field: Letter winners as members of the championship team of 1972 were LaRue Butchee, Bob Cassleman, Rob Cool, Ron Cool, Dave Dieters, Marshall Dill, Delbert Gregory, Alwin Henderson, Mike Holt, Mike Hurd, Randy Kilpatrick, David Martin, John Morrison, Michael Murphy, Bill Nance, Ken Popejoy, Marvin Roberts, John Ross and the famed Herb Washington.

Popejoy, Dill, Gregory and Washington set Spartan indoor records, while Dill, Roberts and the 440-yard relay team set school outdoor records.

Wrestling: Setting a record attendance for a U.S. amateur wrestling meet, approximately 12,300 people gathered at Cole Fieldhouse in College Park, Md., to watch number two MSU battle with number one Iowa State in the NCAA tournament. State captured three individual titles, but Iowa State's three firsts and two seconds left the Spartans in second place overall. Lightweight Greg Johnson was seeded first going into the tournament and he proved his merit by defeating his opponent 9-5 in the finals. Tom Milkovich was almost beaten in the semifinals of his 142-pound match, but a takedown with 12 seconds left put him in the finals, where he won by decision, 8-4. Earlier, following his brother's path to a title, 126-pound Pat Milkovich also emerged from a fifth seed to become the first freshman in 25 years to be crowned a champion.

EXTRA! SEVEN BIG TEN WRESTLING TITLES IN A ROW

(#7) 1972—Bloomington, Ind.: MSU demonstrated its supremacy on the mat, coming up with its seventh consecutive Big Ten title. Greg Johnson (118), Pat Milkovich (126), Tom Milkovich (142), Gerald Malecek (167) and heavyweight Ben Lewis all won Big Ten championships, while Rock Radman (158) and Dave Ciolek (190) lost in the finals. Both Tom and Pat Milkovich held their opponents scoreless in the championship bouts. Tom, who had never lost to a Big Ten opponent, won his third-straight Big Ten title by overcoming Bill Willets of Indiana, who had also been undefeated for the season. Johnson also won his third straight Big Ten title, and he was named the tournament's most outstanding wrestler. Eight Spartans qualified for the NCAA tournament.

The 1972 Big Ten championship wrestling team. (Front row, left to right) G. Johnson, T. Milkovich, M. Malley, J. Bissell, L. Hicks, P. Milkovich, C. Calender, L. Bates, E. Baty, M. Bender, D. Nemeckay T. McDaniels and Mike Ellis. (Back row, left to right) assistant coach D. Blubaugh, trainer D. Kiger, J. Riggs, J. Abajace, G. Malecek, M. Cronin, L. Avery, B. Parimutter, J. Zindel, D. Ciolek, G. Zindel, B. Zindel G, King, S. Morey, R. Flaherty, R. Radman, coach G. Peninger. Individual conference champions included G. Johnson (118 pounds), P. Milkovich (126 pounds), T. Milkovich (142 pounds), G. Malecek (167 pounds), B. Lewis (heavyweight).

MSU
1972-1973

Duffy Daugherty said goodbye to coaching after the 1972 season.

TALES TO TELL

Following a mediocre 5-5-1 record and perhaps pressured from within the University administration, Duffy Daugherty chose to retire from coaching following the 1972 season. In a career that spanned 19 seasons, his teams won 109 games with 69 losses and five ties. In addition to winning two outright Big Ten titles, seven times his teams finished in the nation's Top Ten in wire service balloting. His 1965 team was number one and his 1955 and 1966 teams finished as number two. Above all this, he will be best remembered by many for his "Duffy-isms," those spontaneous witticisms that revealed his persona.

Upon appraising his squad one year he remarked, "We may be small, but we're slow." He defined the game: "Football is not a contact sport, it's a collision sport. Dancing is a good example of a contact sport."

At the opening of one season Duffy was asked, "Whom are you happiest to see returning this year?" Without hesitation he replied, "Me." The defense another year stopped both Notre Dame and Indiana just inches short of touchdowns. Duffy said, "I like those goal-line stands, but I wish they'd make them up around the 50-yard line where I could see them better." His favorite explanation for the disappointing 3-7 season of

---

HEADLINES of 1973

- Roe vs. Wade is upheld by the Supreme Court, legalizing unrestricted abortion in the first trimester of pregnancy.
- A cease-fire agreement is signed that essentially ends the Vietnam War.
- Five of seven defendants in the Watergate break-in trial plead guilty and the other two are convicted.
- Billie Jean King trounces male chauvinist and former champion Bobby Riggs in tennis's much ballyhooed "Battle of the Sexes."

SCOREBOARD

	W	L	T	Avg.
Baseball	27	20	0	.574
Track and Field	1	2	0	.333
Football	5	5	1	.500
Basketball	13	11	0	.542
Tennis	8	9	0	.470
Cross Country	6	0	0	1.000
Swimming and Diving	9	3	0	.750
Wrestling	6	4	1	.590
Hockey	23	12	1	.653
Fencing	11	6	0	.647
Golf	1	0		1.000
Gymnastics	8	5	0	.615
Soccer	4	2	3	.611
Lacrosse	3	9	0	.250

1967, "We won three games, lost none and were upset in seven."

Commenting on the triple option play his team used in the 1969 season, "It's really a quadruple option the way we play it. We can hand the ball off, pitch it out, pass it or just let it lie there on the ground where we dropped it." Said the "Old Coach" as he knocked over a cup of coffee on a table full of play diagrams during a staff meeting, "Well, we've got to learn to play on a wet field anyway."

Defining his All-American halfback in 1963, he said, "Sherm Lewis is a great football player, but he has

one weakness—he's a senior." Finally, perhaps the Duffy-ism that has been most frequently quoted through the years pertains to his evaluation of a tie game. He compared the excitement of a stand-off to that of "kissing your sister."

TEAM OF THE YEAR

The 1972-1973 MSU hockey team was stacked with emerging stars. Tom Ross, Steve Colp, John Sturges, Brendon Moroney and Daryl Rice were all freshman that would leave their marks in the MSU hockey record book. Through the season, the team went 23-12-1 overall, accumulating the most wins ever by a Spartan hockey team. Their 16-9-1 WCHA record, including four wins over arch-rival Michigan, was good only for fourth place, but the standard had been raised as a foreshadow of the hockey powerhouse MSU would become in time. The team beat Colorado College at home in the first round of the WCHA playoffs, but lost in the second round in the total goal series versus Michigan Tech. Colp led the team through the year and set a then school single-season record with 35 goals on his way to 60 points. Meanwhile, first-team All-American junior Bob Boyd set the record for assists with 41 and goalie Ron Clark snagged 867 saves, the second most ever. Mark Calder added 22 goals and 33 assists for 55 points, while Michel Chaurest had 22 goals and 18 assists for 40 points. Ross, Sturges, Rice, and Moroney finished their freshman year with 34, 32, 26 and 18 points, respectively. Other major contributors were Norm Barnes with 26 assists, Bill Sipola with 19 goals and Gilles Gagnon with 19 assists.

The 1972-1973 hockey team

MAKING HISTORY

The Big Ten approved the use of freshmen for varsity football and basketball games beginning with the 1972-1973 academic year. Consequently, freshmen henceforth were eligible to compete in all sports.

The Big Ten tentatively adopted the redshirt rule, giving athletes five years of university attendance to use their four years of eligibility.

Following a recommendation of the school's Board of Trustees, the tradition of an all-men's marching band was broken. Three women tried out and two were accepted into the ranks.

Thanks to a $65,000 gift from the Coca-Cola Bottling Company, new scoreboards were installed in Spartan stadium replacing those that had been in place since 1948.

The Green-White intra-squad basketball game was canceled when members of a group called Coalition of Black Athletes refused to leave the Jenison floor, protesting alleged racism toward black athletes.

MSU weightlifter Gary Hunter had lifts of 240 and 310 pounds to win the NCAA championship for the 148-pound class. His combined total of 550 pounds earned him the best lifter trophy for the 114 to 165 pound classes. While at the AAU senior national championship, Fred Lowe, an MSU graduate, lifted an American record 694 pounds.

The Fellowship of Christian Athletes established a chapter at MSU. As a part of their regular activities, they were interested in following the example of former Spartan quarterback Mike Rassmussen, who held chapel services before all football games.

The WCHA voted to adopt the conventional point system of awarding two points for a win and one point for a tie. In addition, all teams would play 28 games, with 14 away and 14 at home. Formerly, eight points would be at stake with every opponent. Teams that met four times during the season would play for two points per game, while teams that met only twice would play for four points per game.

GREAT STATE DATES

Cross Country—September 29, 1972 (H): MSU leader Randy Kilpatrick finished just one-tenth of a second behind his opponent, with a time of 31:27.5. The next runners to come in during the following minute and a half, however, were Spartans Rob Cool, Fred Teddy, Ron Cool and Ken Popejoy, who together gave the team plenty of points and a 20-35 victory over Notre Dame. Popejoy was suffering from shin splints throughout the race and had to stop at one point to remove his wrap but still finished before a second opponent could cross the finish line.

Soccer—October 4, 1972 (H): Kelly Deneher scored an unassisted goal at the 14:04 mark of the second period to enable MSU to open their season with a 2-1 victory over Hope College. Earlier, a score by Nick Dujon at 3:14 of the first half was matched by the Dutch at 17:26, resulting in a 1-1 deadlock at the intermission.

Soccer—October 25, 1972 (H): Coach Payton Fuller's squad upped their season record to 3-1-1 with a 5-1 victory over Western Michigan. Jay Nesbit led the scoring with goals, while Gary Murray was credited with a pair of assists.

Cross Country—October 28, 1972 (A): Even though running over an unfamiliar layout in Iowa City, Iowa, senior co-captain Randy Kilpatrick won the race in 30:38.5 to establish a new course record. Fred Teddy finished third, Rob Cool took fifth, his brother Ron placed seventh and Ken Popejoy took 10th. The scoring total edged the Hawkeyes, 26-29, and most importantly, the team had a look at the spot where the conference championships would be held one week later.

Football—November 11, 1972 (H): Kicker Dirk Kryt made his first varsity appearance a good one, hitting his fourth field goal with four seconds left in the first half and sending the Spartans to the locker room tied 12-12 with Ohio State. Fortunately, the Buckeyes had run dry after scoring all their points within six minutes on a 44-yard field goal, a 59-yard passing play, and a safety off a blocked punt. The game was won in the third quarter when Mark Niesen scored on a six-yard run after teammate Elmer Lippert had forced an OSU fumble. Kryt converted to make the final score read 19-12. Without even knowing what a football looked like, the 6' 3", 170-pound junior from the Netherlands, had reported for practice one day and asked to try out. He was good enough to stick with the JVs until he was given the chance against OSU.

Football—November 24, 1972 (H): Coach Hugh "Duffy" Daugherty finished his career with a solid 24-14 victory over Northwestern in front of 46,140 enthusiastic fans. The Spartan players came out ready to win, and

on the second play of the game, quarterback Mark Niesen connected with Mark Grua for a 62-yard touchdown. After a fumble recovery two plays later, Niesen threw to Mike Jones for another touchdown on the same pattern. With their third possession, Niesen ran into the end zone on a bootleg around the left end to finish off the Wildcats before the end of the first quarter. Dirk Kryt added three points on a 24-yard field goal in the third quarter. Defensively, the MSU squad held the Cats to a cumulative minus-30 yards rushing. In an effort to overcome this rush defense, opposing quarterback Mitch Anderson threw for a Big Ten record 351 total yards and Jim Lash set a Big Ten record of 226 receiving yards. Niesen finished with 167 passing yards on just eight attempts, throwing for two touchdowns and running one in for the third.

Hockey—**January 5 & 6, 1973 (H):** Amo's crew topped Minnesota in both games of the weekend series, 6-2 and 3-1. The Friday win was highlighted by four goals within six minutes during the second period. Those scores came from Michael Chaurest, Bill Sipola, John Sturges and Brendon Moroney. The Saturday game was far more exciting, with Sipola opening the scoring midway through the second period and the Gophers responding in kind halfway into the final period. Then, with only 2:31 remaining, Chaurest bounced what would prove to be the winning goal off the goalie's pads and into the net. Sturges brought the final count to 3-1 on an empty-netter with State's goalie Ron Clark gaining an assist. The double-win brought the MSU record to eight in a row and to the top of the conference standings. In that week's coaches poll, MSU was ranked third behind Harvard and Wisconsin.

Wrestling—**January 12, 1973 (H):** The Hoosiers came to town under the leadership of a new coach, Doug Blubaugh, former assistant to Grady Peninger. The visitor's strength obviously came in the lower weights, as they jumped to an 8-2 lead, only to loose the meet, 30-8. The turn around began with a pin by Tom Milkovich. Freshman Steve Rodriguez followed Tom by collecting a record 37 points on his opponent, without a pin. Other winners were Rick Greene, Bruce and Jeff Zindel, Scott Wickard and Larry Avery.

Gymnastics—**January 13, 1973 (A):** In a double-dual meet, Coach Szypula saw his squad defeat Wisconsin with ease, 151.35-131.70, and then edge the defending Big Ten champion Iowa Hawkeyes, 152.60-152.50. Junior Don Waybright gave the Spartans an early lead by winning the side horse, but Iowa's depth kept it close the entire meet and the victor was not decided until the final event. It was then that Randy Balhorn, Glenn Hime and Ken Factor performed excellent floor routines to clinch the upset.

Swimming and Diving—**January 13, 1973 (H):** Two Badger swimmers were ineligible for the meet, but it would have made little difference in the Spartans 73-50 victory. Alan Dilley, Kip Bennett and Bruce Wright were all double winners in individual events. Mike Cook, Glen Disosway and Ken Holmes added one win each.

Fencing—**January 19 & 20, 1973 (A):** The Spartan fencers started their season by topping three teams in one weekend. They opened with an upset win over the Air Force Academy, 16-11, and then moved on to Wisconsin, where they defeated Milwaukee Tech, 21-6, and Lake Superior, 22-5. The Spartan swordsmen were led by Robin Luce and Chris Held who controlled the foil, going 6-0 and 7-1, respectively. Paul Herring dominated the epee with a 6-0 record, and Fred Royce and Ed Haugn wielded the sabre to 6-0 and 6-1 scores.

Wrestling—**January 26, 1973 (A):** Randy Miller started MSU off with a pin in the 118-pound class to gain a quick lead over the Illini, a school that had not defeated a Michigan State wrestling team since 1955. Nevertheless, they fought back with three wins and a draw to make it interesting. From there, the Spartans shut the door with straight wins by Rick Greene, Scott Wickard, Bruce Zindel, Jeff Zindel and heavyweight Larry Avery for a final winning score of 23-11.

Gymnastics—**February 9, 1973 (H):** Oklahoma controlled the lead most of the way, but seniors Randy Balhorn and Ken Factor came through in the end to win another close meet for the Spartans, 157.75-156.55. The seniors each scored 9.0 on the parallel bars to bring MSU within one point with one event to go. Balhorn then scored 9.25 in his final routine to clinch the victory.

Basketball—**February 12, 1972 (A):** The Spartans broke the century mark for the first time since 1966 and upset Iowa 100-91. MSU held a 21-point lead early in the second half, but suffered an 18-4 run from the Hawkeyes, who edged in front, 72-71. Sophomore Mike Robinson then hit a field goal to become the Big Ten scoring leader, accruing a career-high 38 points before the end of the game. Bill Kilgore added 21 and Brian Breslin helped out in the stretch, scoring seven of his nine points in the last five minutes.

Track and Field—**February 24, 1973 (H):** In a meet that would go down to the final event, the mile relay, State upset the eventual conference champions, Indiana University, 68-62. In all, MSU captured 10 of the events with a clutch win in the pole vault a key, as Tom Wilson and Jim Stevenson went one-two after the favored Hoosier was forced to withdraw because of a leg injury. Ken Popejoy opened the afternoon by cruising to a victory in the mile with a 4:09.3 clocking and later added a first in the 880. Other victories came from Marshall Dill, the Detroit sophomore who set an MSU varsity record in winning the 440 in 48 seconds flat; freshman Dane Fortney in the 1,000-yard run; John Morrison in his specialty, the 70-yard high hurdles; Bob Casselman, who was seven-tenths of a second off his own American record of 1:08.3 in the 600; and Del Gregory, a double winner in the long jump and triple jump. Rob Cool set a team record 8:49.3 in the two mile yet had to settle for a second, as the IU runner blazed to a 8:45.6, setting a Jenison Fieldhouse record.

Basketball—**March 10, 1973 (H):** MSU trailed most of the way but managed to take the lead 65-63 with just seconds to go. The Badgers, however, sent the game into overtime and regained a six-point lead with just two minutes remaining. State never gave up, though, and after two baskets, a free throw and a tremendous defensive effort by Gary Ganakas, they found themselves with the ball behind by one in the last seconds of the game. Hairston missed the field goal, but freshman Cedric Milton was fouled in the scuffle for the ball and went to the line with the bonus on. He made both and the Spartan season ended with a 79-78 win.

Baseball—**April 7, 1973 (A):** Returning from the annual southern trip where they had posted a 9-6 record, State opened the regular schedule with a pair of wins from Ball State, 6-4 and 5-1. Most of the excitement came in the opener. Elliott Moore pitched well, but was pulled for a pinch hitter after giving up three runs in the 5th inning. With the score tied 4-4 following the regulation seven innings, reliever senior Rick Deller continued on the mound with an impressive six hitless innings. Meanwhile, sophomore second baseman Craig Gerard came through in the 11th with a two run double to seal the victory.

Lacrosse—**April 28, 1973 (H):** In Bob Stevenson's only year as head coach, the Spartans achieved the first ever lacrosse victory over an Ohio State team, 9-7. It was a close contest from beginning to end with neither team leading by more than two points at any one time and the lead changing back and forth. The Spartan scoring leaders were Steve Urban with five goals and Val Washington with two. Tom Hardenbergh contributed four assists.

Tennis—**April 28, 1973 (A):** Senior Rick Vetter increased his winning streak to 6-0, defeating his opponent in straight sets as the Spartans edged Notre Dame 5-4. Dave Williams and Brian Smith finalized the close victory with a win in doubles.

Track and Field—**May 5, 1973 (H):** In their only home meet of the spring, the Spartans won 12 of 15 events to easily defeat the Notre Dame Fighting Irish, 99-44. In an otherwise lack-luster afternoon at the oval, Ken Popejoy, the pint-sized senior from Glen Elyn, Ill., uncorked an amazing 3:57.0 mile to shatter his own Ralph Young Field record of 3:59.0. In doing so, he became the fastest miler in Big Ten history.

Golf—**May 9, 1973 (H):** To boast of a 366-393 victory over the Detroit College of Business seems a bit nonsensical, however, the match is a benchmark of sorts. It was the final time an MSU team engaged in a dual meet format. All competition since that date has been in tournament play. Leading the way against the Detroit school were: Steve Cole 71, Mark Timyan and Bill Marx 72, Mark Weston 74 and Bill Zylstra 77.

Tennis—**May 11 & 12, 1973 (H):** The MSU tennis squad closed out its Big Ten schedule on a positive note by defeating Northwestern on Friday, 6-3, and upending Wisconsin, 7-2, on Saturday. The two victories enabled the Spartans to close out the Big Ten schedule with a 5-4 record and upped their overall slate to 7-4. Winners in both meets were Rick Vetter, Brian Smith, Joe Fodell and the doubles team of Smith-Dave Williams.

One of Michigan State's outstanding early lacrosse players, Val Washington.

ATHLETE OF THE YEAR

As a successful letter winner in three sports—football, baseball and basketball—Brad VanPelt is an easy choice for athlete of the year. The six-foot-five, 225-pound native of Owosso turned down a $50,000 offer from the Detroit Tigers and a $100,000 offer from the California Angels in order to attend college. Football was his forte, and in both 1971 and 1972 he was named first team All-American and first team All-Big Ten. As co-captain of the 1972 team, he became the first defensive back to receive the Maxwell Award as the nation's top collegiate player. When he had finished his career as a safety, he had made 256 tackles and made the school's record books as first for tackles in a single game with 21, first for interceptions in a single game with 3, third for interceptions in a single season with 6, second in career interceptions with 14, and second in career interception yards with 268. He was a first-round draft pick by the New York Giants in 1973, and he played in the NFL for 14 years. In the shadow of football, VanPelt became the number two pitcher for Danny Litwhiler, and was named second team All-American for collegiate baseball in 1972. He led the Big Ten with 55 strike outs in 1972 and remains in the MSU record books with 84 career Ks, the eighth most ever. During the winter, he also contributed to Gus Ganakas's basketball team. Having turned pro before he finished his degree, VanPelt returned to State in 1998 to graduate with a degree in health and physical education. In 2001 he was inducted into the college football Hall of Fame.

Brad VanPelt

IN THE SPARTLITE

Baseball: A decision by Larry Ike to forego his final year of eligibility and sign a professional contract with the Detroit Tigers was a devastating blow to the Spartans' chances for 1973. He had been a mainstay in the MSU pitching rotation.

The Spartans ended the season 9-9 in conference play with a 27-20 record. This tied them with the Wildcats and Badgers for fourth place.

Basketball: Mike Robinson was voted First Team All-Big Ten after earning the conference scoring championship for the second straight year, this time with 26.7 points per game. Bill Kilgore finished the season with 16.7 points per game and ended his career with 814 rebounds, second in school history behind John Green's 1,036.

During Christmas break the team took first place in both the Kodak Classic and the Senior Bowl Classic, but they closed the schedule with a 13-11 overall and 6-8 conference record, identical to the previous year but only good for a sixth place tie in the conference standings.

At one point in the schedule, the team won seven games in a row, the longest winning streak since the 1956-57 season.

Cross Country: The harriers had a long drive home from the Big Ten meet; they finished sixth and did not qualify for the nationals. Still, senior Randy Kilpatrick and freshman Fred Teddy finished in the top 15, Randy in fifth and Fred in 14th. Kilpatrick became the only Spartan to ever finish in the top 15 in each of his four years of eligibility.

Fencing: The team finished with an 11-5 dual-meet record, amassing the most wins in 33 years and reaching the second highest mark in the 47-year history of the sport at MSU. State hosted the Big Ten tournament, but finished a disappointing fourth, 20 points behind defending champion Illinois. Three Spartans reached the final round. Fred Royce took second in the sabre, while Ed Haughn finished in a tie for fifth with the same weapon and Paul Herring was sixth in the epee.

Football: Dirk Kryt, the field-goal kicking import from the Netherlands, admitted to knowing nothing about the game before his first practice in September. Furthermore, knowing nothing about expected training rules, he was observed smoking a cigarette following the

exciting defeat of Ohio State. Duffy would later jokingly suggest, "We've just changed our training rules. Any player who kicks four field goals in the first half of a game can smoke a cigarette after the game." Upon closing out his distinguished career as head coach, Duffy ended on a winning note, a 24-14 home victory over Northwestern.

Bill Simpson was a major contributor for the defensive and special teams. During the season he booted 73 punts, returned 21 punts for 286 yards and came up with six interceptions.

Defensively, Ernie Hamilton also ended his college play and tied a Spartan career record with 25 tackles for losses, totaling 168 yards. He also led a record for quarterback sacks with 10.

Professional football scouts apparently have long memories. As a freshman back in 1969, Dan Werner came off the bench to complete 16 of 35 passes for a school single-game record of 314 yards in a 41-13 loss to Purdue. Since then he had primarily played a back-up role. Regardless, the Dallas Cowboys selected him in the eighth round of the 1973 NFL draft.

Golf: MSU relinquished hold of their Spartan Invitational tournament title for the first time in four years. Stepping up were the Buckeyes of Ohio State, who shot a composite 775 to outscore the MSU "A" team by six strokes. Scores for the host runner-ups were: Mark Timyan 148, Bill Brafford and Steve Cole 152 each, Brad Hyland 153, Steve Broadwell 156 and Bill Marx 159.

For the second straight year, the MSU golfers placed fifth in the conference tournament. Sophomore Hyland and freshman Cole topped the Spartans with four-round scores of 297. The remaining Spartans and their cards were: Timyan 300, Broadwell 311, Brafford 316 and Marx 317.

Gymnastics: The Spartans finished fifth in the Big Ten Championships held in Bloomington, Ind. Randy Balhorn finished sixth in the all-around competition and tied for fourth on the horizontal bar. Freshman Jim Tuerk was sixth on the vault.

Hockey: The icers faced Michigan Tech in the semi-finals of the WCHA playoffs, a series in which the winner was determined by total goals scored in two games. Thus, a 3-1 victory in the second game was not enough for the Spartans to overcome a 7-2 loss in the opening game. Still Amo Bessone's team finished with a 23-12-1 season record, posting the most single-season victories ever for an MSU team.

Lacrosse: Bob Stevenson contributed his only year as head coach of the Spartan stickmen but only could manage a tally of 3-9 at the end of the schedule. Junior Val Washington continued to lead the team and was voted to the second team All-Midwest Lacrosse Association.

Soccer: The Spartans traveled to Akron but played for only 20 minutes before the game was called with the score 0-0. After many penalties, coach protests and several fights, more than one player had been ejected. Finally the officials had enough as they left the pitch and walked away without even giving a ruling.

On October 13, the Spartans played an exhibition game against a touring team from Germany, the University of Munich. There is no media record as to the outcome. However, the match was videotaped and shown on Friday night, October 13 by WKAR-TV.

Swimming and Diving: Glen Disosway and Bruce Wright led the team during the Big Ten tournament in Ann Arbor, taking top honors in the 50 and 100-yard freestyle events. Indiana placed first for the 13th straight year. Alan Dilley set a school record in the 200-yard backstroke, which was good enough for second place.

In the 1972-73 season, Alan Dilley set an MSU record in the 200-yard backstroke.

At the NCAA championships in Knoxville, MSU scored 25 points to finish 14th out of 90 schools. Alan Dilley had the best finish for the Spartans, finishing third in the 200-yard backstroke in yet another varsity record time of 1:52.7.

Tennis: For the first time ever, the team was led by co-captains. Dave Williams and Rick Vetter shared the position rather than having to have the team choose between one or the other of the two seniors.

Five Spartans reached the semi-finals of the Big Ten championships in Madison, Wis., but only the number two doubles team of Williams and Brian Smith made it to the finals where they settled for second place. The other MSU semi-finalists were Vetter, Larry Stark and Joe Fodell. In team scoring, State totaled 69 points to tie Illinois and Wisconsin for fourth place.

Track and Field: The 1973 team, unable to successfully defend their conference championships, settled for third place at both the indoor and outdoor meets. In the winter meet at the Purdue fieldhouse, Marshall Dill won the 300-yard sprint and tied for first in the 60-yard dash. Hurdlers John Morrison and Mike Hurd placed third and fifth respectively.

Four team members won individual titles at the outdoor meet in Minneapolis, Minn. Senior Ken Popejoy posted a 3:59.2 in the mile run, a new record for the Big Ten championships. Junior Bill Cassleman also set a new record with 50.7 in the 440-yard hurdles. Marshall Dill defended his championship, running the 220-yard dash in 21.1, and Rob Cool took the 3,000-meter steeplechase, setting a new varsity standard at 8:49.7.

State rebounded from a third-place Big Ten finish to take it all at Ralph Young Field in the Central Collegiate championships. Sophomore double-winner Marshall Dill was awarded the John. P. Nicholson trophy as the outstanding meet competitor after proving dominance in the 100- and 220-yard dashes and anchoring the 440-relay team for second place. As in the Big Ten meet, Rob Cool won the 3,000 meter steeplechase and Bob Cassleman took the 440-yard hurdles.

Wrestling: After seven consecutive Big Ten team titles, the 1973 Spartans, strapped with a lengthy list of injuries, dropped all the way to fifth place at the championship meet in Minneapolis, Minn. Senior Mark Malley's career ended when he suffered an early-season head injury. Knee injuries hobbled Greg Zindel, Scott Wickard and the 1972 national champion Pat Milkovich, who underwent surgery and was thus lost for the season. Carrying the colors for the defending champions were Captain Tom Milkovich, who won the 142-pound title despite being hampered by a shoulder separation; Randy Miller at 118 pounds and Conrad Calander at 134-pounds settled for second place; and the two other Zindel brothers, 167-pound Bruce and 177-pound Jeff, both won consolation matches to finish in third place.

MSU
1973-1974

TALES TO TELL

It has become a matter of fact that Michigan State hockey plays first-round CCHA tournament action in Munn Arena. Many local fans have become so accustomed to having MSU host these postseason games that they have forgotten this home-ice advantage is earned by finishing the regular schedule lodged in one of the top four slots in the conference standings. Only once since the 1980-1981 season has a Ron Mason team had to pack their gear and head elsewhere during that opening series.

For the Amo Bessone teams of the 1960s and 1970s, even participating in the Western Collegiate Hockey Association (WCHA) playoff was a cherished reward, regardless of whether they played home or away. Until the 1973-1974 season (1973-74), only twice had the Spartans welcomed an opponent to East Lansing for an opening tournament game. So now it was the final weekend of the regular season, 1973-74 and with a conference record of 13-12-1, a two-game sweep of Michigan on March 3-4 was needed to ensure that cherished home-ice advantage in this final season at Demonstration Hall.

Facing the University of Michigan always brings out a level of intensity and excitement, but the Friday sellout crowd of 4,174 fans was in for a particularly bruising game to remember. Fights inevitably broke out throughout the game, culminating in the final minutes when Spartan John Garvey sent Don Dufek, a starting full-

The Spartan hockey team in action at the Munn Ice Arena

HEADLINES of 1974

- President Richard Nixon resigns over the Watergate affair and Vice President Gerald Ford is sworn in as the 38th President of the United States.
- Patricia Hearst, 19-year-old daughter of publisher Randolph Hearst, is kidnapped by the Symbionese Liberation Army, a radical terrorist group.
- People magazine, featuring Mia Farrow on the cover, is launched by Time Inc.
- Streaking becomes a momentary fad, primarily on college campuses, with the madness eventually extending to the telecasts of the Academy Awards and *The Tonight Show*.

SCOREBOARD

	W	L	T	Avg.
Baseball	23	16	1	.588
Track and Field	2	1	0	.667
Football	5	6	0	.455
Basketball	13	11	0	.542
Tennis	7	11	0	.388
Cross Country	2	5	0	.286
Swimming and Diving	7	4	0	.636
Wrestling	12	3	1	.781
Hockey	23	14	1	.647
Fencing	8	8	0	.500
Golf	tournament play only			
Gymnastics	2	9	0	.182
Soccer	4	3	3	.550
Lacrosse	5	7	0	.417

back on the Wolverine football team, into the locker room with a bloodied mouth. A total of 41 penalties were called, amounting to 106 minutes, including three 10-minute misconducts. With the abundance of penalties, State scored all of its goals on power plays and two when they were skating five-on-three. Daryl Rice and Tom Ross each had two goals, while freshman Jeff Addley scored the first goal of his career. Steve Colp contributed one goal and four assists in the 6-2 victory.

It was then off to Ann Arbor for the regular season closer before the usually hostile crowd, which totaled 8,101, the most in U of M hockey history. Those fans were screaming with excitement when the Wolverines tied the game 3-3 in the second period. Thereafter, the intensity of this vocal support slowly diminished to silence as the Spartans finished the game with six unanswered goals. Steve Colp and John Sturges each scored a hat trick in the game, while Tom Ross, Denny Olmstead and Norm Barnes each tallied one.

These two victories over the Wolverines gave State the home advantage to open the WCHA playoffs, an advantage that paid off as they topped Wisconsin in a two-game total-goal series, 7-5. On the next weekend at Houghton, they again split the two games, but this time lost in total goals, 12-10.

TEAM OF THE YEAR

Led by senior All-American Bob Cassleman and junior Marshall Dill, the 1974 track and field team tied for second with Illinois at the Big Ten Indoor Championships. Cassleman won his fourth straight 600-yard run with a time of 1:10.0, while Dill won his third straight 300-yard dash in 30.2 seconds. Mike Hurd added a first in the 70-yard high hurdles with an 8.2, while the mile relay team of Bill Nance, Mike Holt, Cassleman, and Dill set a Big Ten record and won in 3:12.6. At the outdoor conference meet, the team took fourth place with three firsts. Dill won the 220-yard dash for the third time with a 20.9 and the 100-yard dash for first time with a 9.5. Cassleman tied a Big Ten record in gaining his third straight title in the 440 intermediate hurdles in 50.7 seconds.

The 1974 track and field team

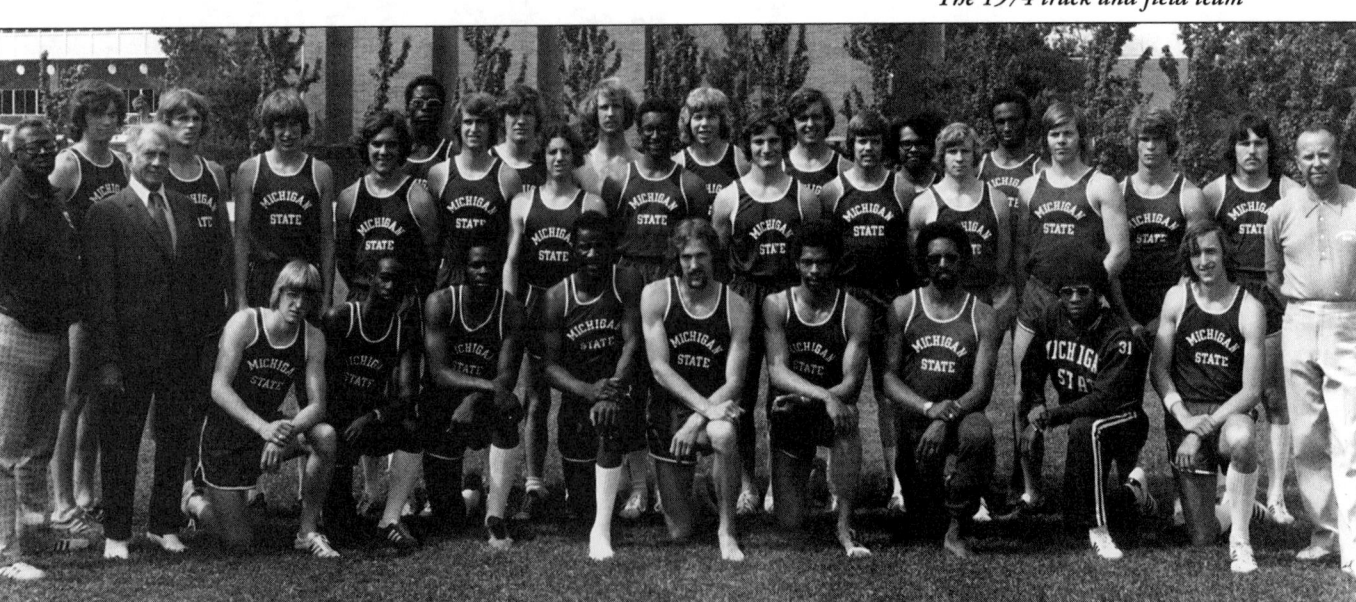

MAKING HISTORY

On April 19, 1974, it was announced that Terry Braverman, associate sports editor for WKAR radio and television, had been appointed director of the Ralph Young Fund. He would succeed Frank Palamara, who had died from cancer on March 27.

In December, the hockey team won the school's first Great Lakes Invitational, first defeating Boston College, 12-5, and then outscoring Michigan Tech, 5-4, in the finals.

A *State Journal* story in the March 10, 1974 issue reported the talents of a six-foot-five lad who was the star basketball player of the Dwight Rich Junior High School team. It noted the junior high student had scored 227 points in 10 games, including a 48-point effort on February 28. The high-scoring youngster was identified as Earvin Johnson.

A new rule in football required all players to wear mouth protectors.

Perhaps out of necessity, coach Gus Ganakas was ready to implement a fast-paced running game with his basketball team. In height, his team averaged a shrunken 6' 2".

The Polish national gymnastics team, ranked fourth worldwide, defeated the U.S. all-star team at a meet held in Jenison Fieldhouse.

On March 25, 1974, Bruce Fossum's golfers, along with all the competition, were snowed out of the final round of the Duke Invitational in Durham, N.C. This was the final stop in the squad's southern trip.

Economic difficulties resulted in 15 to 20 percent budget cuts for many non-revenue sports. While coaches were disappointed, they understood the necessity. Priorities began to shift back to revenue sports as a way to sustain the athletic program.

GREAT STATE DATES

Cross Country—**September 28, 1973 (A):** The Notre Dame top runner broke the tape, but, as usual, depth is the winning factor in cross country, as State defeated the Irish for the sixth year in a row, 23-33. Sophomore Fred Teddy was a mere four seconds behind the leader with his time of 24:56, and he was immediately followed by three Spartans, Herb Lindsay, Stan Mavis and Paul Sewell. Gary Santti completed the MSU scoring with a ninth place finish.

Soccer—**October 6, 1973 (H):** As in 1973 when the Spartans defeated the upstart Eastern Michigan team 8-0, once more they shut out the Hurons, 7-0. In a game played under ideal weather conditions, Mike Kenney scored four goals, three of which were in the first half. Mark Karrer contributed two goals and Ed Randel and Zdravko Rom each had one. Netminder Dave Goldman was not overly challenged in gaining the shutout victory.

Football—**October 27, 1973 (A):** The Spartans defeated the Purdue Boilermakers for the fourth year in a row, 10-7. Deftly running the option series for the first time all season, quarterback Charlie Baggett gained a total of 133 yards on the day, including a game-winning 69-yard touchdown run down the right sideline. Earlier, in the third quarter, he had run for another touchdwon, but the officials called it back on an unusual penalty, saying he had assisted the blocker. The opening score, a 23-yard field goal in the second quarter by Dirk Kryt, was set up by senior safety Bill Simpson, who intercepted a pass and ran it back 54 yards. The Boilers scored their lone touchdown to briefly lead before Baggett's clinching score. Purdue had time to make things interesting, but a second interception from Simpson and two fumble recoveries from defensive end Tom Kronner kept the ball in State's hands.

Football—**November 17, 1973 (H):** Denny Stolz's 1973 team was a low-scoring aggregation, averaging slightly more than 10 points throughout the 11-game schedule. In this game against Indiana, that average was just enough, as Michigan State posted its sixth win of the season, 10-9. Tailback Mike Holt scored State's only touchdown, coming in the first half on a thrilling 54-yard run. The only other Spartan points were on a Dirk Kryt field goal early in the fourth quarter. Thereafter, the Hoosiers came alive. With 10 minutes to play, their field goal specialist boomed a 52-yarder, and then MSU turned the ball over on their next possession at the 22-yard line. From there it took the visitors only four plays to cross the goal line. At this point the courageous IU coach, Lee Corso, was not willing to settle for a tie. Fortunately, the two-point effort failed and State escaped with the victory.

Hockey—**November 17, 1973 (H):** This early season MSU-U of M game had to have been an emotional roller coaster for the hometown fans. First, Tom Ross and Michel Chaurest put State on top 2-0. The Wolverines quickly surged to a 4-2 second period lead when Steve Colp and Mark Calder followed with goals to once

more tie the score. Michigan again pulled ahead, 6-4, with another pair of scores. Late in the final period, two Wolverines were thrown in the penalty box and the MSU icers found themselves with a two-man advantage. It was Daryl Rice who beat the Michigan goalie to bring State within one with just 45 seconds to go; the goal had been scored after coach Amo Bessone had pulled the Spartan net minder to increase the odds. Still playing with an empty net and a two-man advantage, Tom Ross won the ensuing face off, and in confusion around the Wolverine net, Calder slapped in the tying goal with 34 seconds remaining. Both teams had opportunities to win during the 10-minute overtime period, but with just 20 seconds left, Rice finished the game, collecting a rebound off his own shot and knocking it back for the victory.

Wrestling—**January 12, 1974 (A):** After MSU had won the first four matches of the afternoon, Minnesota climbed back to a 15-15 tie, setting up the heavyweights to decide the meet. The Spartans' Larry Avery was up to the challenge, as he managed a 5-2 decision for the 18-15 victory.

Gymnastics—**January 16, 1974 (A):** State won its opener of the dual-meet season, topping Eastern Michigan University, 144.75-137.25. Senior Don Waybright started his final season by winning the side horse, his specialty, with an 8.1. Sophomores Bernie Van Wie and Jim Tuerk also took top honors in the meet, Van Wie on horizontal bar with an 8.85, and Tuerk on the vault with a 9.1

Fencing—**January 19, 1974 (H):** MSU had an easy time with Milwaukee Tech, winning 21-6, but trailed 12-13 against Tri-State with senior fencers Ed Haughn and Fred Royce each having one bout to go. Both triumphed easily to clinch the team victory, 14-13. Haughn, Royce and Mike Bradley each went 3-0 with the sabre.

Swimming and Diving—**January 25 & 26, 1974 (H):** Spartan swimmers surprised coach Richard Fetters and pleased the fans by taking three convincing wins in a single weekend. Northwestern was the first victim, going down 76-47, as MSU posted firsts in 11 of 13 events on Friday evening. Saturday's double dual meet was won early, as the swimmers won five of the first six events. The winning scores were 84-49 over Purdue and 86-37 over Iowa State.

Wrestling—**February 2, 1974 (H):** 3,450 fans saw MSU prove its strength as they took down highly rated Oklahoma, 27-10. Jeff Zindel and Larry Avery topped the afternoon off with pins. Other victors, all by decision, were Pat Milkovich, Conrad Calander, Steve Rodriguez and Scott Wickard. The win elevated the season record to an impressive 11-0.

Basketball—**February 2, 1974 (H):** Hosting and defeating the Purdue Boilermakers, 76-74, State gained revenge for an earlier season 77-75 buzzer-beater loss at West Lafayette. Tied at 74 with 2:32 remaining, the undefeated Boilermakers tried the stalling tactics only to give up the ball at 1:11 when Lindsay Hairston blocked a layup and the Spartans gained possession. MSU then stalled for more than a minute, when Mike Robinson came off Hairston's screen and sank an incredible 20-foot jump shot with three seconds left to win the upset and erupt the 9,831 fans. Hairston finished with 26 points and 23 rebounds. Robinson scored 25 and Terry Furlow contributed 17.

Basketball—**February 23, 1974 (H):** MSU trailed by as many as 10 points before making a comeback run to tie Northwestern at 70 with 1:15 remaining. Then with 0:20 left, Benny White stripped the ball from his opponent for the final possession. With nine seconds remaining, Terry Furlow unleashed a 30-foot jump shot that bounced off the rim and Mike Robinson scored off the offensive rebound and went to the line for the extra point to make the final score read 73-70. Robinson scored 27 points after coming into the game with a 20.1 average. Lindsay Hairston pulled down 10 rebounds and scored 23, while Furlow pulled down a dominating 16 rebounds.

Lacrosse—**April 6, 1974 (H):** The Spartans led until the middle of the fourth quarter when the Fighting Irish came up with two quick goals to take command, 4-3. A quick response by Mike Richard tied the score. Just when overtime began to look inevitable, Steve Wilson threw in the winning goal with five minutes to go.

Baseball—**April 26-28, 1974 (H):** MSU baseball shone bright, gaining six straight wins in a weekend of three double-headers. They defeated Wayne State, 7-2, 4-3; Detroit, 5-4, 8-5; and Notre Dame, 3-0, 5-2. The Spartans came from behind late in three of the games. Rick Seid came through with a bases-loaded single in the bottom of the seventh inning during the second game against WSU to achieve the victory. In imitation, Al Westen batted home the winning run with a bases-loaded infield single in the final frame of the first University of

Detroit game. In the nightcap, Howard Schryer hit a grand-slam home run in the fifth to trigger a seven-run inning and secure the win.

Golf—**April 27, 1974 (A):** The Spartan golf team gave their best performance of the year, as they took first place in the Iowa Invitational with a 36-hole score of 773. Only Big Ten teams were there, where gusts of wind up to 50 miles an hour challenged the golfers. Steve Broadwell led the team with 148, second in individual competition. He was followed by Bill Brafford with 152 and Chris Moore at 156.

Track and Field—**May 3, 1974 (A):** The Spartans took care of business in South Bend, taking first in 13 of 17 events for a 97-48 victory. Two of Notre Dame's firsts were in events that MSU did not even enter, and a third came when the Spartan relay team was disqualified. State definitely put forth a team effort, with Junior Marshall Dill being the only double winner. Other individual firsts came from John Ross, Bob Cassleman, Herb Lindsay, Stan Mavis, Todd Murphy, Charles Davis, Fred Teddy, Steve Kemp, Ralph Simpson and Tom Wilson. The mile relay was won by Davis, Murphy, and the brothers, Chris and Bob Cassleman.

Tennis—**May 6, 1974 (H):** For the second year in a row, the Michigan State netters shutout the Purdue Boilermakers, 9-0. From his number one position, Larry Stark led it off with a 6-4, 6-4 two-set win. He was followed by Joe Fodell at number two with a 6-1, 6-1 win; Dave Williams needed three sets, 3-6, 6-3, 6-3; Brian Smith won in straight sets, 6-3, 6-3; as did Rick Zabor, 6-2, 6-0; and Tom Gudelsky, 6-0, 6-4. Winners in doubles were Stark-Fodell in two sets, 6-2, 6-4; Williams-Smith, 4-6, 6-2, 6-1; and Zabob-Gudesky, 7-5, 6-2.

Baseball—**May 19, 1974 (A):** Coach Danny Litwhiler's team finished the season strong, defeating the Northwestern Wildcats 5-4 and 21-2 in Evanston. First baseman Howard Schryer was instrumental in the second game trouncing, as he batted in eight runs with a three-run homer, a double and two singles. That performance allowed him to tie a Big Ten RBI record and end the season with 29 RBIs to tie teammate Al Weston. Senior Bill Simpson finished the final game of his MSU career with four hits.

ATHLETE OF THE YEAR

In his first year at Michigan State, Pat Milkovich surprised the world by claiming a Big Ten crown and becoming the first freshman since 1947 to win an NCAA championship. He was then redshirted in his second year with a knee injury, but this did not ruin his talent. In his four years of competition, he had claimed three Big Ten and two NCAA titles and become the only four-time NCAA finalist and the youngest champion ever. He accumulated 18 NCAA victories, the most by any Spartan, and his 90 career wins surpassed everyone in school history except his brother, Tom, who had 93. Pat was voted freshman, sophomore and senior wrestler of the nation by the National Wrestling Coaches Association and was voted first-team All-American all four years. In addition, he was a two-time team captain and a three-time member of the national All-Star wrestling team. His graduation marked the end of coach Grady Peninger's Golden Era of MSU wrestling, but he continued to work with Peninger as an assistant coach at State from 1976 to 1986. With sustained training, he made Team U.S.A. in preparation for the 1980 Olympics in the Soviet Union, but he was unable to compete in the games due to the national boycott announced by President Carter.

Pat Milkovich (left) with his brother, Tom

IN THE SPARTLITE

Baseball: MSU ended its season by winning its last four games and finishing sixth in the Big Ten.

Catcher Dale Frietch finished the season with a .425 batting average, the sixth highest ever recorded by a Michigan State player. Frietch and teammate Al Weston were voted to the all-Big Ten first team.

Jim Knivila pitched three shutouts in his first year on the team, placing him third on the Spartan all-time single-season record in that category.

Basketball: All-American and All-Big Ten selection Mike Robinson continued to lead the pack offensively, scoring an average of 22.4 points per game to end his career with an MSU record of 1,717 points. Lindsay Hairston controlled many games from underneath, as he averaged 13.6 rebounds per game, which still stands today as fourth in the school's all-time season records. In addition, Hairston scored 16.5 points per game and Terry Furlow added 14.1.

Cross Country: Fred Teddy paced the Spartan harriers but could do no better than 13th place in the Big Ten championship meet with a time of 29:43. The team avenged an earlier loss to Minnesota and finished fifth in the conference. Craig Virgin of Illinois broke the Big Ten meet record for the six-mile course, running it in 28:30.5.

Fred Royce captured the 1974 Big Ten title in the sabre event.

Fencing: Fred Royce, team captain, won the Big Ten title in the sabre event by defeating the defending champion from Illinois. Teammate Ed Haughn finished fourth in the same event. Collecting 14 points, the Spartans were fourth behind Illinois, Ohio State and Wisconsin.

Football: Dennis Stolz started his three-year career as head coach with a 5-6 record and a tie for fourth place in the Big Ten.

Bill Simpson finished his college career with 12 interceptions, and as the team punter, booted a total of 196 with an average of 39.8 yards.

In other noteworthy statistics, Ray Nester came down with an MSU single season record of 129 tackles, and Mike Holt ran 95 yards to become the second Spartan ever to return a kickoff for a touchdown.

A team highlight for the year came in an away game against Purdue in which the offense moved the ball 573 yards to set a record that remains on the books today.

Golf: At the Big Ten championships, State's five-man crew came back from a disappointed first day of play to place third behind Indiana and Ohio State. Steve Cole finished with rounds of 78-75-73-72—298 good enough for sixth place. Other Spartan scores were Brad Hyland 77-77-73-74—301 for ninth; Steve Broadwell was 15th with cards of 80-74-72-78—305; Gary Domagalski tied for 18th with 78-77-73-78—306; Bill Marx shot rounds of 75-75-82-79—311 and Bill Brafford contributed scores of 81-74-78-78—311.

Gymnastics: The Spartans struggled through the season and managed only a 2-9 dual-meet record going into the Big Ten meet in Iowa City. With 281.60 points, the team placed seventh in the conference. Letter winners were: Glenn Hime, Craig MacLean, Steve Murdock, Joe Shepherd, Richard Stout, James Tuerk, Bernie VanWie, Don Waybright and Steve Welton.

Hockey: Upon conclusion of the season, Steve Colp became an MSU record holder with 43 goals in a single-season and placed second in assists with 54, being outdone only by teammate Norm Barnes, who had 56. Today Colp's total stands in a sixth-place tie for the team's season best, and Barnes's assist total now ranks tied for third place.

In his second year as a Spartan, Tom Ross scored 37 goals and 51 assists on his way to all-time MSU career records.

Lacrosse: Fred Hartman took over the team as head coach and led them to a 5-7 record that included victories of pride against Michigan and Notre Dame. Senior Val Washington continued to lead the team and was named to the first team All-Midwest Lacrosse Association.

Soccer: Coach Payton Fuller struggled in his final year as head coach, posting a 4-3-3 season record. Mike Kenney led the team with seven goals, and Rom Zdravko followed with five.

On May 10, it was announced that veteran athletic staff member Ed Rutherford would assume new responsibilities including the role of soccer coach beginning in the fall of 1974.

Swimming and Diving: Coach Dick Fetters's two top sprinters were the chief performers at the conference meet in Madison, Wis. Glen Disosway finished second in the 50-yard freestyle and eighth in the 100, while Bruce Wright managed a third in both events. Co-captains Paul Fetters and Bill Hall each captured a sixth place.

At the NCAA championships, the team garnered two points to tie for 27th place.

Tennis: At the Big Ten championships in Madison, Wis., Stan Drobak's squad duplicated its efforts of 1973 with a sixth-place finish. Freshman Tom Gudelsky, at number six singles, placed the highest for MSU as he worked his way to the finals before being eliminated. In the singles positions number one through number three, Larry Stark, Joe Fodell and Dave Williams, along with the doubles team of Williams-Brian Smith, all lost in their consolation final matches. Smith at number four singles made it to the semi-finals before being eliminated, as did the remaining doubles teams of Stark-Fodell and Gudelsky-Rick Zabor.

Track and Field: Featuring an impressive four firsts, State finished tied with Illinois in second place at the conference indoor championships held in Jenison Fieldhouse. Marshall Dill led the way with his third straight championship in the 300-yard dash. He also finished second in the 60. The other Spartan titlists were Mike Hurd, who equaled the MSU varsity time of 8.2 in the 70-yard high hurdles; Bob Cassleman, who ran 1:10.0 in the 600-yard run; and the mile relay team of Bill Nance, Mike Holt, Cassleman and Dill, which set a new American record of 3:11.7.

At the NCAA indoor championships in Detroit's Cobo Arena, State managed only two finalists, Bob Cassleman, who placed third in the 600-yard race, and the mile relay team that finished fourth. The resulting five team points put State in a 27th place tie with Indiana and Kansas.

In the most impressive MSU showing ever at the annual Ohio State relays, the Spartans came away with four firsts. Dill sped away to a meet record 9.2 in the 100-yard dash and Cassleman won the 440-yard intermediate hurdles in 51.6. The quarter-mile sprint quartet of Charles Byrd, Hurd, Cassleman and Dill posted a winning time of 41.6, and the shuttle hurdle relay team of Todd Murphy, Hurd, Dave Howard and Howard Neeley ran to a win in 58.6.

At the prestigious Drake Relays, Dill captured first in the 100 with a time of 9.3. Cassleman finished second in the 440-yard hurdle event, as did the shuttle hurdle relay team.

In the outdoor Big Ten meet in Ann Arbor, Dill and Cassleman were again the Spartan stars as MSU finished fourth with 61 points.

Dill was a double winner with firsts in both the 100- and 220-yard sprint events, while Cassleman once more captured first in the intermediate hurdles. It was a fitting end to an illustrious career that saw Bob collect 13 individual and relay Big Ten titles. Other point gatherers were John Ross, fourth in the long jump; Paul Sewell, a fourth in the steeplechase; Stan Mavis, fourth in the mile run; Chris Cassleman and Howard Neeley, fourth and fifth in the intermediate hurdles; and Fred Teddy, sixth in the three-mile run. The 440-yard relay team placed second behind Iowa.

Wrestling: Despite disappointing losses by Grady Peninger's two big guys, Jeff Zindel at 190 pounds and heavyweight Larry Avery, State managed 86 points, good enough for a third place finish in the Big Ten Championships. Randy Miller placed second at 118 pounds; Pat Milkovich cruised to a title at 126; Scott Wickard placed third; and freshman Don Rodgers finished fourth. At the NCAA meet in Ames, Iowa, it was a one-man show for Michigan State. For Pat Milkovich it was a pleasant return to the victory stand. Crowned champion in 1972 as a freshman, he was crippled by an injury that prevented him from defending his title in 1973. Collecting 24 team points, MSU placed 14th.

MSU
1974-1975

TALES TO TELL

There are some games, meets or matches that remain forever in the minds of those who bore witness to them. One such case was the Ohio State football game of November 9, 1974, remembered by some simply as the "Levi Jackson game." Craig Murray, student manager of that team, recalls:

"We were a very young Michigan State team—mostly freshmen and sophomores, a lot more green than white. We were going up against the big, bad Buckeyes of Ohio State—undefeated, defending champions, and ranked number one in the country.

It was us against the world. Outside of Spartan Stadium, the local, national, and campus media, and even our friends and families made MSU 25-point underdogs. But

inside the stadium, coach Denny Stolz preached only one thing, 'Hey, baby, this is our chance, be confident in yourselves.' As team manager, I spent most of game week looking for some small way to help

Levi Jackson's 88-yard touchdown run gave the Spartans a 16-13 victory over the number-one-ranked Buckeyes.

HEADLINES of 1975

- U.S. spacecraft Apollo 18 links in space with Russian craft Soyuz 19.
- The film *Jaws* breaks box office records across the nation, and the musical "A Chorus Line" begins a record run on Broadway.
- Teamster union leader James Hoffa mysteriously disappears.
- "Live from New York City," *Saturday Night Live* first hits the television airways.

SCOREBOARD

	W	L	T	Avg.
Baseball	28	16	0	.636
Track and Field	1	3	0	.250
Football	7	3	1	.682
Basketball	17	9	0	.654
Tennis	6	11	0	.352
Cross Country	4	1	0	.800
Swimming and Diving	6	3	0	.667
Wrestling	10	6	0	.625
Hockey	22	17	1	.609
Fencing	10	6	0	.625
Golf	tournament play only			
Gymnastics	3	7	0	.300
Soccer	8	1	2	.818
Lacrosse	6	8	0	.429

the cause. On Thursday I found it: the *Detroit News* had picked the Spartans to upset the Buckeyes. I clipped out the article, inscribed it with the words, 'you gotta believe,' made 100 copies, and prominently posted one on every player's and coach's locker on game day. (My little contribution to posterity.)

On the field for warm ups, I heard someone call, 'Hey, manager!' It was Woody Hayes [the Ohio State coach]. 'Send your coach over, would ya?' I dutifully and quite rapidly summoned. Woody's words were brief: 'Good luck to you . . . up to a point.' Then the war began and the young Spartans hung in. At halftime it was 3-3, and the coaches were calm and confident. From the visitor's locker room across the way the sounds indicated that Woody was anything but calm.

Trailing by 10 in the fourth quarter, quarterback Charlie Baggett fired a touchdown pass into the end zone. Ohio State still led, 13-9. In the ensuing possession, OSU was forced to punt, downing the ball on State's 12-yard line. The sideline, as I recall, was still in a state of flux, with the kicking team coming in and the defense getting ready (after all, wouldn't we be punting soon ourselves?), when a roar

went up from the tunnel end of the stadium. Levi Jackson had already neared midfield, right in front of our bench, before most of the team even realized what was happening. He kept going and going, and the sideline started screaming and jumping and eventually leaning into the field to catch a glimpse of the miracle. The impossible had happened…Michigan State was ahead.

The ending is well-documented. Ohio State drove 70 yards to our one-yard line with 26 seconds left and no timeouts remaining. They tried a run with no gain, followed by absolute pandemonium with the clock ticking, crowd chanting and players not unpiling. Usually the coaches are in firm control of the sideline, but for once all that they and the team, could do was scream and watch the drama play out…two seconds…one second…the ball was snapped, dropped, picked up and run in, followed by a flurry of signals…game over…maybe…maybe not.

We ran to the tunnel victorious. Then someone yelled to go back onto the field and then the coaches yelled to get in the locker room. Then before the rejoicing could begin, we learned the Big Ten Commissioner was reviewing the outcome of the game…please stand by.

It was the biggest upset of the decade and the biggest (apparently) victory in recent MSU history, yet the team couldn't celebrate. Denny [Coach Stolz] asked me to send a manager up to the commissioner's box to find out what was happening. Were they going to take this moment of glory away? Assistant coach Charlie Butler told me his worst fear, 'That blankety-blank Woody was up there demanding the blankety-blank victory go to blankety-blank OSU.' What should have been one of the civilized world's rowdiest postgame celebrations became a waiting game. All anyone could do was wander around and try to assure one another that something unthinkable wasn't going to happen.

Finally, word drifted down from above, the game was history…the goal posts were history…and 45 minutes after the clock struck 00.00, the final score was official: MSU 16, OSU 13. The good guys had, at long last, won."

TEAM OF THE YEAR

It would be a challenge for any school to demonstrate a success story for a fledgling sport to equal that posted by the Michigan State soccer program under the leadership of coach Gene Kenney from 1956-1969. During that span, his squads completed a composite record of 113-13-11, which included a record of 19-0-3 in the opening three seasons. Comparatively, to stamp the 1974-1975 soccer team, with its "ho-hum" 8-1-2 record, as Team of the Year seems inconsequential. Yet, this was likewise a successful team. Completing a .818 winning percentage, it out-performed each of the remaining 13 Michigan State varsity sports teams of 1974-1975.

Although names of the lettermen associated with this team would never become legendary like "Magic" Johnson and Kirk Gibson, they remain a tribute to the great soccer teams of the 1950s, 1960s and 1970s: Kamran Asdigha, Robert Beck, Doug Bigford, David Camp, James Doby, Mark Gembarowski, Ed McSweeney, James Nugent, Fraser Pahad, Ed Randel, Zdravko Rom, James Stelter, Krien Verberkmoes and Gary Wilkinson.

Under the direction of first-year coach Ed Rutherford, the record included victories over Ohio State and Michigan before the only loss of the campaign, a 3-0 setback to Indiana in the final contest on the schedule.

The 1974 soccer team

MAKING HISTORY

The Munn Ice Arena opened with the first hockey game, an exhibition between the St. Louis Blues and Detroit Red Wings played on September 25, 1974. The facility was formally dedicated five weeks later on Friday, November 1, prior to the MSU-Minnesota game. Although showing the effects of the debilitating stroke, Biggie Munn was on hand for the ceremony accompanied by his wife Vera. It would be his final public appearance. Clarence "Biggie" Munn died on March 18, 1975.

The NCAA basketball tournament was expanded from 16 to 32 teams, and at the same time the Big Ten voted to amend selection policies of more than one conference team.

Astroturf was installed in Spartan Stadium for $150,000. It replaced the synthetic grass field installed in 1969.

Jenison Fieldhouse was renovated to meet the requirements of the state fire marshal. Larger and additional exits were installed and the seating was decreased from 12,500 to 10,000 for easier exiting. Until the changes were made, seating was temporarily reduced to 6,500.

Season hockey tickets were available to students— $20 for 20 games. Regular single game tickets sold for $3 or $4.

The MSU video workshop began taping the Spartans' Friday night hockey games and replaying them Monday evenings.

The Big Ten changed its procedure for the selection of a Rose Bowl team. Previously, the selection was always made by a vote from the athletic directors. Under the new policy, the conference champion would automatically receive the bid, and in the case of a co-championship, the winner of the game between the tied teams would go to the bowl. If the teams did not play each other that year, the team with the best winning percentage would go, and if there was still a tie, the team that most recently competed in the bowl would be eliminated.

Don Coleman, the first unanimous Spartan All-American football player and the first to have his jersey retired, was named to the National Football Foundation Hall of Fame.

GREAT STATE DATES

Cross Country—September 27, 1974 (H): Sophomore Herb Lindsay set a new course record of 24:33.5 for the five-mile run at Forest Akers, and helping MSU soundly defeat Notre Dame, 21-35, in the season opener. Freshman Jeff Pullen, junior Fred Teddy and sophomore Stan Mavis finished from 30 to 45 seconds behind Lindsay but still completed the race before any Irish runners reached the finish line.

Soccer—October 19, 1974 (H): The undefeated Buckeyes went home discouraged as the MSU defense controlled the entire match for a very strong 1-0 victory. Senior forward Jim Nugent scored the only goal on a direct free kick in the first half. Shots-on-goal can describe the game, as the Spartans dominated this statistic, 16-7.

Cross Country—October 24, 1974 (A): Herb Lindsay and Jeff Pullen took a wrong turn two miles into the race and ran 400 yards out of their way following the EMU leader through the first ever race on the course. The two Spartans, however, then left their opponent behind as they overtook the pack and finished in a three-way tie with teammate Stan Mavis. It was a sight to both surprise and impress coach Jim Gibbard, as the three finished the six mile run with a time of 30:23.7.

Football—November 2, 1974 (A): The Spartans moved the ball 80 yards in 11 plays to open the game in Madison, finishing the drive with an 11-yard touchdown run from sophomore Levi Jackson. Wisconsin also scored on their first possession but missed the extra point. In the second period, quarterback Charlie Baggett tossed a three-yard pass to freshman tight-end Larry Bethea to lead at halftime, 14-6. The Badgers opened the second half by tying the score with a touchdown and two-point conversion. State then picked up a Wisconsin fumble and two plays later scored on a 22-yard run by Rich Baes. But once again, the Big Red matched the score and the game stood at 21-21. A second Badger turnover would then decide the game. After the fumble recovery by John Breslin, MSU marched 65 yards in only seven plays when Baggett scored on a rollout around the right end. Hans Nielsen kicked the final point to end the game, 28-21. With an even 100 yards on 22 carries, Baes was the team's leading ball carrier.

Football—November 23, 1974 (H): Some 51,000 fans were thrilled to see MSU finish its season by setting records in a 60-21 thrashing of Iowa. Quarterback Charlie Baggett started the scoring with a 47-yard run and kicker Hans Nielsen knocked a 28-yard field goal between the posts to gain a 10-0 lead. Nevertheless, the Hawkeyes had not yet lost heart, scoring two touchdowns to take a 14-10 lead and responding to Baggett's second touchdown with another one of their own for a 21-17 lead. A pass to Mike Hurd and another field goal, however, gave State a 27-21 lead and silenced the Hawks. Scoring runs by Baggett and Rich Baes in the third period, along with a missed two-point conversion, brought the tally to 40-21. As if that was not enough, a 53-yard pass to Hurd and 5-yard and 53-yard runs from Claude Geiger brought the fans onto the field, preventing MSU from kicking the extra point after the final touchdown. Still, this was the highest Spartan total ever in a Big Ten game.

Wrestling—December 6, 1974 (H): In their second meet of the season, State squeezed past the University of Michigan, 19-16, before over 4,000 fans in Jenison Fieldhouse. The Spartans were behind, 10-16, with only two matches to go when 190 pound Scott Wickard executed a convincing 12-3 victory to put the win within reach. Then senior Larry Avery made it happen with a pin after 4:41 minutes of action in his heavyweight match.

Larry Avery's pin on Dec. 6, 1974, helped the Spartans beat the Wolverines.

Hockey—**December 13 (H) & 14 (A), 1974:** A record-setting crowd of 6,562 came to Munn Arena to see State defeat the University of Michigan rather easily, 6-1. Having been red-shirted in the previous season, fifth-year senior goalie Ron Clark made his first appearance in more than a year by recording 54 saves. Robbie Harris and Brenden Moroney each came up with a goal in the second period, while Steve Colp, Daryl Rice, Pat Betterly and John Sturges put the game away in the final stanza as each scored once. The victory put the Spartans into third place in the WCHA. The next day's game in Ann Arbor, before another record crowd (8,185), featured fights and Spartan scoring. Along with 56 penalty minutes administered in the opening 20 minutes, six players were ejected stemming from fights that broke out at the conclusion of the period with State leading, 3-2. Tom Ross added another early in the second, but the Wolverines responded quickly, keeping the score close at 4-3. This was followed by what was becoming known as MSU's "third period magic." On this occasion, Harris, Paul Pavelich, Dave Kelly and Moroney all found the back of the net, while the MSU goalie, Ron Clark, shutdown the Wolves with no further scoring. The game ended with the score, 8-3. This brought the Spartans to a 39-11 third period scoring dominance for the season. Steve Colp did not score, but he chipped in six assists to tie the record for most assists in a game. He ended his four years with a team record 168 assists.

Basketball—**January 1, 1975 (H):** Junior Terry Furlow, being guarded by former high school teammate Wayman Britt, scored a career-high 33 points, as MSU controlled the Michigan Wolverines for an 86-78 victory. Fouls plagued both teams, but especially the U of M, as two starters sat out a good portion of the opening half with four each. Both eventually fouled out in the second half, along with yet a third starter. The Spartans were a hot-shooting squad, sinking 64 percent of their field goal attempts.

Swimming and Diving—**January 24, 1975 (A):** Personal bests from MSU swimmers Jim Dauw and Mark Outwater were only good enough for second place, but the Spartans would control the rest of the meet and defeat a solid Illinois team, 85 1/2-37 1/2. First place finishes in individual events came from Jesse Griffin, Marc Stiner, Dave Dale, John Apsley, Bruce Wright, Ken Holmes and diver Jesse Griffin. The quartet of Outwater, Holmes, Apsley and Wright combined for a first place tie in the medley relay.

Fencing—**February 1, 1975 (A):** Charlie Schmitter's squad performed well, defeating Chicago, 24-3, and Milwaukee Tech, 23-4. Jack Tintera controlled the sabre with a record of 7-1. Steve Krause dominated the foil at 7-2, while Bill Peterman and Jon Moss wielded the epee, scoring 6-1 and 6-2 respectively.

Gymnastics—**February 10, 1975 (H):** In what was the most one-sided MSU victory since the current scoring system was adopted in 1966, the Spartans defeated Eastern Michigan, 192.45-143.15. State racked up seven first places finishes in the convincing win. Contributors to this total were John Short, Steve Murdock, Glenn Hime, Dan Waterstone, Joe Shepherd, Al Burchi and Jeff Rudolph.

Wrestling—**February 21, 1975 (H):** MSU defending NCAA champion Pat Milkovich was up against a challenge in the former Olympian Jim Carr of Kentucky. Surprisingly, Carr, who had recently been featured in *Sports Illustrated*, fell easily to the Spartan star, scoring only two points and giving up nine. State finished off the Wildcats, 25-9.

Lacrosse—**April 6, 1975 (A):** Notre Dame fell subject to an improving lacrosse team, as Dave Sorrick led the Spartans with three goals. Steve Wilson added one goal and picked up 14 ground balls. The team set a school record of 81 ground balls, while the Irish had only 31. State conquered the Fighting Irish, 7-5.

Baseball—**April 18, 1975 (H):** President Wharton threw the opening pitches in a 13-11 offensive triumph over Minnesota to give MSU first place in the Big Ten. The Gophers started the scoring with three runs in the top of the third inning. After an hour rain delay, catcher Rick Seid nailed a grand slam, and on the next pitch, right-fielder Al Weston soloed for another run, giving the Spartans a 4-3 lead. The Gophers returned with three runs in the fourth, only to be countered by a six-run MSU rally in the same inning. Trying again, the visitors added five more in the fifth, but Spartan Howie Schryer quickly responded by knocking in Pat Simpson and Amos Hewitt with a two-run double. The game was called due to rain after just five and a half innings. In the truncated game, Hewitt had three hits and Schryer two doubles.

Tennis—**April 18 & 19, 1975 (H):** The Badgers tried to blame their 5-4 loss on the East Lansing courts recognized for their poor playing surface, as they were coming from a $3 million dollar facility. The Wildcats, however, had no such excuse, as the next day's matches were moved to the Lansing Tennis Club in Okemos.

Outstanding MSU victors for the weekend were transfer senior Dick Callow, juniors Larry Stark and Rick Zabor, and sophomore Tom Gudelsky.

Baseball—May 3, 1975 (A): Winning their 11th game in the last 14 and running the conference record to 6-0, State looked like a legitimate title contender as they shut out the University of Michigan, 6-0, in Ann Arbor. The winning pitcher was George Mahan, a relatively unheralded six-foot, 190-pound transfer from Genesee Community College, who yielded only three hits in nine innings. The loser was much-heralded Chuck Rogers, who suffered his first Big Ten loss in three years. He had won eight straight and took the mound with a 1.67 ERA in the conference. State picked up one run in the opening inning, another in the sixth and two in the seventh. Of the nine MSU hits, all singles, Joe Palamara, Amos Hewitt and Howard Schryer each connected for two. A sideline to the afternoon featured George Mahan pitching against his brother Ted Mahan, the Michigan catcher. The Spartan Mahan prevailed, as he twice set his brother down on strikes. If the name Ted Mahan sounds familiar, there is reason. He, of couse, is the current Michigan State coach.

Track and Field—May 3, 1975 (H): The Spartans inched by the Boilermakers in the final home meet of coach Fran Dittrich's coaching career with MSU track teams. Senior Marshall Dill led the way with firsts in the 100- and 220-yard dashes, but the victory was not ensured until sophomore Herb Lindsay won in the three mile and tied in the mile with teammate Stan Mavis to defeat Purdue, 72-69. Other first place performers were Chris Cassleman, Tom Wilson and Greg Brewton.

yard and a 440-yard title. By the time he graduated four years later, the two-time All-American sprinter had won five indoor Big Ten titles in two different events and seven outdoor Big Ten titles in three events. In addition, he had won the 1973 NCAA indoor 300-yard championship with a time of 20.9 seconds. He is still listed at the top of the school's all-time charts for four events and is second behind Washington in a fifth.

Marshall Dill

ATHLETE OF THE YEAR

On February 12, 1972, as a freshman, Marshall Dill set a world record in the 300-yard dash at the MSU relays with a time of 29.5. Two years later, as a junior at the same meet, he broke his own record with a 29.3. Now he is remembered as one of the world's greatest runners of all time. In his first year, Dill combined with Herb Washington to lead his team to win both the indoor and outdoor Big Ten championships and to take second place at the NCAA indoor meet. Individually, at the indoor conference meet, he won the first of three straight 300-yard titles and contributed to the first of a pair of mile-relay titles. Outdoors, he won the first of four straight 220-

IN THE SPARTLITE

Baseball: Entering the final weekend of Big Ten play, the Spartans had a decent shot at finishing first. They took both ends of the Friday doubleheader against Wisconsin, 5-4, 3-2, to put their conference mark at 10-3. Next, Northwestern came in for two games on Saturday, and the Cats, sporting a not-to-impressive 5-11 record, came to life and upset Litwhiler's gang, 8-3. That did it. Even though State returned the favor in the second game, 9-2, the damage had been done. That one loss dropped MSU to fourth place.

Second baseman Joe Palamara, the team's leading hitter with a .342 average, was chosen as a Big Ten first-

team selection. Outfielder Mike Fricke and pitcher George Mahan were among the second team choices.

Basketball: In a home game against Indiana, the Spartans suffered their worst defeat in history, 106-55. The lopsided loss was due to the fact that Coach Gus Ganakas was forced to use JV players after suspending ten varsity players who had walked out on the team. One varsity player, Jeff Tropf, a 6-7 freshman from Holt, resisted the boycott and did play against the Hoosiers. The embarrassing situation was the result of accusations regarding racial discrimination.

A 17-9 overall record gave Michigan State the most victories since the championship team of 1958-1959, which went 19-4. A 10-8 conference record, however, left the 1974-1975 Spartans in a disappointing fifth place. Nevertheless, the Associated Press All-Big Ten first team included senior center Lindsay Hairston, who had led the conference in rebounding (11.3 per game), and junior forward Terry Furlow, who led the Big Ten in scoring (21.4 points per game).

Cross Country: Coach Jim Gibbard's runners totaled 84 points and settled for fourth place in the 60th edition of the Big Ten Cross Country Championships. Sophomore Herb Lindsay led the squad by placing third over the six-mile course in Ann Arbor. Other Spartan finishers were freshman Jeff Pullen in 11th; junior Fred Teddy who was 15th, sophomore Stan Mavis in 26th and freshman Amos Brown 28th.

1975 Associated Press All-Big Ten first team member, Lindsay Hairston.

Fencing: On January 25, the varsity crossed blades with a group of alumni, and George "Ted" Willis of Euclid, Ohio, stole the show. The slightly built 54-year old captain of the 1941 and 1942 MSC teams took all three of his matches in the foil competition against the varsity. A squad of six men represented MSU at the Big Ten championships held in Champaign, Ill. The six and their season-long record were: Steve Krause (23-18), and Jim Scieszka (21-13) in foil, Jon Moss (28-13) and Bill Peterman (23-13) in epee, and Jack Tinterra (27-10) and Mike Bradley (26-12) in the sabre.

Football: Overall, it was a strange season of short streaks as they opened with two wins, then had a streatch of three losses and a tie before concluding with five straight wins.

Defensive stalwarts, linebacker Terry McClowry and end Otto Smith, were consensus first-team All-Big Ten selections. Running back Levi Jackson was a selection by the coaches' poll.

Quarterback Charlie Baggett still holds a team record of 7.08 yards for total offense yards per attempt, which he established in 1974.

Golf: State placed second in their own Spartan Invitational, as a surprising member of the host "B" squad emerged with the low score of the weekend. Mark Weston, a 5' 6" Junior, who hadn't played in a tournament since his freshman year, shot a 74-73—147. He hit 16 greens during his second round, so that even three-putting three times still made him the winner by two strokes.

The MSU team shot a composite 1,533 in the 72-hole Big Ten championships held on the Indiana University course. The Spartans were led by Steve Broadwell, a senior from Midland, who finished fourth in the individual standings, just three shy of medalist honors with rounds of 77-75-72-73 for a 297. Bill Brafford shot a 73-76-79-75—303 good for 10th place; Brad Hyland shot 77-73-81-77—308; Gary Domagalski 76-76-80-79—311; Kurt Hassberger 322; and Weston 319.

Gymnastics: Totaling 344.30 points, MSU only finished above Ohio State among the eight teams competing in the Big Ten championship meet in Ann Arbor. Amidst a legion of disappointing Spartan performances, Coach Szypula expressed pleasure with Glenn Hime's fourth on the high bar and Steve Murdock's eighth on the pommel horse.

Hockey: The first sellout crowd in Munn Arena history saw the Spartans down North Dakota, 6-2. MSU goalie Ron Clark set a record with 30 saves in the first period.

With All-American Tom Ross scoring in all 40 of MSU's games, it was an exciting season to watch, but an overall record of 22-17-1 and a WCHA record of 19-12-1 was only good enough for fifth place in the conference. Six of the skaters were given all-WCHA team honorable mentions, including goalie Ron Clark, defenseman Paul Pavelich, and forwards John Sturges, Steve Colp, Daryl Rice and Dave Kelley.

Lacrosse: A season record of 6-8 does not seem a great reason to celebrate, but the 1975 edition of Spartan lacrosse had progressed measurably, and those six wins had only been surpassed by the 1971 edition that went 7-8. The season record was highlighted by a 7-5 victory over Notre Dame and a 12-8 triumph over Ohio State.

Soccer: Eddie Rutherford enjoyed an extremely fruitful premiere as head coach for the Spartans. He opened his career with a 7-0 destruction of Eastern Michigan and by the end of the season had an 8-1-2 record. State outscored their opponents, 21-7, and tied for the third most single season shutouts by an MSU team with seven. Peter Brunnschweiler and Mike Kenney each gained five goals in the year.

Swimming and Diving: John Apsley was the hero of the year, becoming the Big Ten champion in the 100-yard butterfly with a time of 50.69. Paul Fetters captained the team that rallied for 6-3 on the season and fourth place in the conference meet.

Tennis: Tallying only 17 points, the 1975 tennis squad settled for a seventh place finish at the Big Ten championships held in Madison, Wis. Freshman Kevin McNulty played his way into the number six finals before bowing out, while Junior Larry Stark won the consolation round at the number one position.

Track and Field: For sundry reasons, only two Michigan State runners managed to score at the indoor Big Tens held at Indiana University. Herb Lindsay won the two-mile in 8:44.8 and Dane Fortney finished second in the 1,000. The 10 points earned placed State in a tie with Ohio State for eighth place.

Coach Dittrich's charges moved up in the standings outdoors. Led by double winner and sprint star Marshall Dill, the Spartans earned 61 points and managed a third-place finish behind Illinois and Indiana. Dill, the Detroit senior, ran away from the field, posting a 9.4 win in the 100-yard dash and then came back to capture the 220 and also anchor the second place 440-yard sprint relay team. Other finalists were Tim Kline with a second place in the 440-yard intermediate hurdles, followed by Chris Cassleman and Howard Neeley in third and fifth spots respectively. Herb Lindsay took third in the three mile; Fred Teddy finished sixth in the six-mile; and Steve Kemp, who leaped 23' 10" to finished in the long jump.

Wrestling: Scoring 72 1/2 team points, MSU finished third at the Big Ten championships behind Iowa and Wisconsin. In one disappointment, defending champion senior Pat Milkovich was stopped, 3-2, in the finals of his 126-pound match. Balancing this out, Larry Avery won the heavyweight title with a 6-1 revenge decision over his Iowa opponent, who had won a dual-meet match earlier in the season.

Pat Milkovich also missed his bid for a third NCAA wrestling championship when he lost an overtime match in the 126-pound division. He completed his season with an impressive 14-1-4 record. Heavyweight Larry Avery finished the championships in sixth place. Between the two, they accounted for 23 1/2 points, placing MSU in the 15th position out of the 70 schools participating in the championships in Princeton, N.J.

MSU
1975-1976

TALES TO TELL

Initiated by a profuse list of alleged recruitment improprieties (many of them insignificant), NCAA officials began an extensive investigation of the Michigan State football program in April of 1975. The resultant nine-month probe proved frustrating for Spartan officials. Legal representation was not welcomed by the NCAA, for it seemed due process was not within their structure. In summary, it was a case of being guilty until proven innocent. The findings were made public in January of 1976, and the news was not good. The NCAA, followed by the Big Ten, slapped MSU with a three-year probation. The consequences were immense. Holding proof that many of the accused transgressions were unfounded, initially the school president, Clifton R. Wharton, was contentious and threatened to retaliate, but cooler heads prevailed. Although the indecorum had been traced to assistant coaches and not directly to the head coach, Denny Stolz accepted the responsibility of their deeds and was compelled to tender his resignation. In other retrogressions, Athletic Director Burt Smith was forced into early retirement. Jack Breslin stepped down

as overseer of Michigan State athletics. One assistant coach, Howard Weyers, was let go, and six other assistants were censured. The University Board of Trustees, in a purge mode, even reached innocent basketball coach Gus Ganakas and forced his resignation. One football player lost a year of eligibility and six others were hit with various minor penalties. In addition, during the three-year period, extending until Sept. 1, 1979, the football team was banned from bowl games and TV appearances, and scholarships for the sport were reduced by 15.

With empty offices to fill, MSU hired Joe Kearney from the University of Washington as athletic director. He, in turn, hired Darryl Rogers and Jud Heathcote as head coaches for football and basketball respectively. One thing became immediately apparent: Joe Kearney knew how to hire winners. For further proof, consider his decision of 1979 to bring Ron Mason aboard as hockey coach.

The tagline to this story answers the question of who initiated the investigation that pried open this embarrassing situation. From the very beginning many fingered Woody Hayes at Ohio State as the culprit. In his book, *The Spartans,* Fred Stabley relates that in August of 1976, the Buckeye coach indirectly admitted his involvement.

HEADLINES of 1976

- The U.S. celebrates the bicentennial of its independence. Six million people view a parade of tall ships from 31 countries on the Hudson River.
- A mysterious illness kills 29 people and affects 182 others, most of whom attended an American Legion convention in Philadelphia, hence the illness is called the "Legionnaire's Disease."
- *Rocky*, a film starring Sylvester Stallone, wins the Oscar for best picture.
- Viking 1 and Viking 2 land on Mars and begin sending back information about the planet's surface.

SCOREBOARD

	W	L	T	Avg.
Baseball	15	23	1	.397
Track and Field	0	4	0	.000
Football	7	4	0	.636
Basketball	14	13	0	.518
Tennis	7	14	0	.333
Cross Country	3	3	0	.500
Swimming and Diving	7	3	0	.700
Wrestling	7	7	0	.500
Hockey	23	15	2	.600
Fencing	15	5	0	.750
Golf	tournament play only			
Gymnastics	9	6	0	.600
Soccer	10	2	0	.833
Lacrosse	3	10	0	.231

At the Big Ten's annual football kickoff luncheon in Chicago, Woody directed his remarks to fellow coaches while blaring out:

"If I catch any of you cheating, I'll turn you in. Did I turn in the team that cheated in our league? You're damn right I did, and I'll do it again."

TEAM OF THE YEAR

The senior line-up that included Tom Ross, Steve Colp, Daryl Rice and John Sturges led the 1975-1976 hockey team to a 23-win season which tied a team record. They finished 20-12-0 in the WCHA, taking second place, and during the conference playoff finals eventually lost in triple overtime, 7-6, to Minnesota, the eventual NCAA champions. By the end of their careers, this productive foursome had rewritten the Spartan record books. Ross led the way, setting MSU single-season records with 105 points and 51 goals. Ross and Colp each had 54 assists for the year, third on the all-time list behind Ross's 59-goal performance from the previous year and former teammate Norm Barnes's 56 from two years earlier. Goalie Dave Versical snagged an unbelievable 1,410 saves for another season record. As for career records, the senior team held the top four slots for points and assists and the top three for goals. Ross still ranks number one in multiple career records with 324 points, 138 goals and 186 assists. Colp still holds second place in each of those categories with 300 points, 132 goals, and 168 assists. Rice finished his career in third place with 225 points, third place with 96 goals, and fourth place with 129 assists. Sturges finished in third place for total assists with 132 and fourth place for total points with 209. Coach Amo Bessone had reached the pinnacle of his career with MSU hockey and brought some of the attention that years later would result in championships under coach Ron Mason.

The 1975-76 hockey team

MAKING HISTORY

Conference athletic directors voted to use three-man officiating crews for basketball games beginning with the 1975-1976 season.

Big Ten faculty representatives voted that even if a student-athlete became a professional in one sport, he would be eligible for competition in all others.

The longest hockey game in the school's history was played on March 14, 1976, when Minnesota defeated the Spartans, 7-6, at 6:33 of the third overtime in a WCHA playoff game.

With the NCAA outdoor track championships of 1976, races began to be conducted in metric distances and have continued in that manner ever since. The indoor championships remained in yardage distances until 1984.

Spartan cyclist Roger Young won the gold medal at the Pan-American Games in preparation for competition in the 1976 Olympics.

Forest Akers East golf course was expanded to 18 holes.

With the Big Ten champion still in line to receive the automatic bid to the Rose Bowl, a new conference policy stipulated that as many as four other schools could accept bowl bid offers.

The NCAA rejected a proposal to institute a national collegiate football playoff, arguing that it would be too much of a physical and academic burden on the players. The NCAA rescinded a basketball rule that allowed only ten players to travel to road games. Without a Big Ten restriction on the size of the roster while on the road, teams could take an unlimited number from their squad.

Frank Kler, a 29-year-old sophomore, suited up as one of two backup goalies to hockey starter Dave Versical.

Sponsored by the Greater Lansing Tennis Patrons, professional tennis stars Arthur Ashe and Dennis Ralston played an exhibition game in Jenison Fieldhouse with proceeds going to fund youth tennis programs.

GREAT STATE DATES

Football—**October 4, 1975 (A):** Entering the game with a 2-1 record, the Spartans truly upset the previously undefeated Fighting Irish, 10-3. For both sides it was a story of strong defense and an offense plagued with turnovers. Example: on the first possession for the Fighting Irish, sophomore quarterback Joe Montana coughed the ball up on a vicious tackle by junior Kim Rowekamp. Both sides missed a second-quarter field goal and the teams headed for their locker rooms with "goose eggs" glaring from the scoreboard. The third quarter ended as Hans Nielsen, the Denmark import via Manistee, broke the drought with a 37-yard field goal, but the Irish would match this three-pointer with slightly more than four minutes of playing time remaining. The Spartans didn't give the fans much time to linger on the possibility of a 3-3 tie. Just 18 seconds following the ND equalizer, Tyrone Wilson, the Wilkinsburg, Pa., senior, broke through the line and raced 76 yards before being pushed out of bounds at the four-yard line. Levi Jackson carried it the rest of the way on the ensuing play, and State supporters began celebrating a victory over the eighth-ranked team in the nation. MSU had achieved the momentous victory with a rather paltry offensive show: 241 yards rushing and zero yards passing.

Cross Country—**October 11, 1975 (A):** For the sixth year in a row, a Jim Gibbard squad defeated Ohio State, this time by a score of 25-32. Herb Lindsay led all the way and finished first in a time of 24.06. The Buckeye's top runner finished second, but Stan Mavis, Jeff Pullen and co-captain Fred Teddy wrapped up the decision with third, fourth and fifth places, respectively. Ron Smeitzer finished the scoring with his 12th place finish, followed immediately by teammate Walt Malkewitz in 13th.

Soccer—**October 24, 1975:** Ed Rutherford, enjoying his second year as the Spartans' head coach, saw his squad defeat Michigan, 6-1, for the tenth victory in 12 matches. Center-forward Erdal Tekisalp led the attack with three goals, his first scores of the season. The remaining three goals came from Fraser Pahad, Kamy Asdigha and Ed McSweeney.

Hockey—**November 10 & 11, 1975 (A):** Converting on six power play opportunities, State twice defeated Wisconsin, 5-4 on Friday, and 6-5 in overtime on Saturday. Tom Ross completed a hat trick in the first game,

with goals also coming from Steve Colp and Daryl Rice; but it was the second game that was packed with excitement. First, Ross gave the Spartans an early lead, scoring at 2:14 of the opening period on a power play; but the score had reached a 2-2 tie by the end of the first 20 minutes, and the Badgers led 4-3 following period number two. The outlook seemed even more grim when the deficit grew to 5-3 at 11:05 of the third period. Then the homestretch magic began, as Ross scored an unassisted goal at 13:56 and Colp quickly followed with another power play goal to tie the score at 5-5. Unbelievably, with less than two minutes remaining in regulation, two Badgers were sent into the penalty box. The first offender left the ice at 18:29 and the second at 19:11. As the game reached overtime, Amo's crew was determined to capitalize on the advantage, and at the 32-second mark Colp slapped home the winner.

Football—**November 15, 1975 (H):** Ted Bell scored the only first-half touchdown against the Wildcats, and after the extra point was missed on a bad snap, State was behind 14-6 at the half. A different team emerged from the locker room after the intermission, and the Spartans scored on six of seven possessions in the second half, the seventh coming with just five seconds left in the game. These touchdowns came on drives of 80, 80, 79, 45, 80, and 19 yards, giving the team 401 yards rushing and 121 passing for 522 total and setting a new school record of 26 first downs rushing. Eugene Byrd finished the first drive with a 59-yard touchdown, though a missed two-point conversion left state still behind 14-12. Nevertheless, Richard Baes subsequently ran in two touchdowns, Kirk Gibson scored on a 39-yard play, and both Leon Williams and Jim Earley ran one into the end zone to complete the scoring, MSU 47, Northwestern 14.

Gymnastics—**January 17, 1976 (H):** More than 3,000 fans were entertained as the Spartan schedule was opened with a 187.95-186.85 win over the Fighting Illini. After the first two events, the Spartans had less than a one-point lead, which they promptly lost. With his first place performance on the parallel bars, Sophomore Jeffrey Rudolph was able to tie the score going into the final event, the horizontal bar. An Illinois performer finished first, but he was outscored in team points, as Rudolph finished second with two Spartans, Glenn Hime and Brian Sturrock tied for third place.

Wrestling—**February 7, 1976 (H):** Sensing a tight meet, more than 3,500 spectators crowded into Jenison for the 76th meet between Michigan State and the University of Michigan. Early winners for Grady Peninger's team were Randy Smith, Pat Milkovich, Doug Siegert, Wad Nadhir and Shawn Whitcomb. Then, as is often the situation with the score knotted 18-18, the outcome of the meet rested squarely with the heavyweights. The Spartans' Dan Evans, who would letter only one year, was up to the challenge. Down 1-0 after the opening period, he scored a takedown and finished the second tied, 2-2. With 30 seconds remaining, the Michigan opponent was on top and had gained riding time, assuring him of a one-point lead. Consequently, he was simply forcing Evans to remain below until the clock ran out. The Spartan heavyweight later described those final 30 seconds: "I heard the fans coming alive. They started clapping in rhythm and then, suddenly I just found a surge of energy. Luckily I found a knee." Evans grabbed that knee, swung out from under and completed a quick reversal, a maneuver which earned two points and a 4-3 decision. The final score read MSU 21, Michigan 18.

Fencing—**February 7, 1976 (H):** Coach Charlie Schmitter's crew found reason to celebrate upon completing double-dual meet victories over the University of Chicago (24-3) and the University of Illinois (15-12). Defeating the maroon was no reason to revel, they had not lost to a Windy City squad since 1949; but the upset of the defending Big Ten champions from Champaign-Urbana was fulfilling. A State team had not defeated the Illini since 1968. A big reason for the MSU success this time around was Steve Krause at foil, who finished 6-0 for the day, including a match that secured the big win over Illinois. Three other team members were undefeated on the day: epeeist Jon Moss (4-0), epeeist Bill Peterman (4-0) and sabre man Mike Bradley (5-0).

Basketball—**February 7, 1976 (A):** Terry Furlow, the 6' 5" senior from Flint, hit a 10-foot jumper with one second remaining in overtime to top Ohio State, 83-82. Held to only four points in the opening 20 minutes, Furlow, the Big Ten's leading scorer, added 16 in the second half and six more in the extra period for a game high 26. Three additional Spartans scored in double figures: guard Bob Chapman added 17, center Greg Kelser 16 and forward Edgar Wilson 14.

Swimming and Diving—**February 7, 1976 (H):** The Spartans more than doubled the Buckeyes' score in an impressive 83-40 victory. Senior Dave Burgering dominated the one- and three-meter boards once again, while sophomores Shawn Elkins, Dave Seibold, John Apsley, Greg Forman and freshman Steve Poussard all swam for first place finishes.

Swimming and Diving—**February 14, 1976 (H):** MSU was able to close out its home season with a 89-34 landslide victory over Kent State. First place finishes came in droves, as State won every event except the breaststroke. Jim Dauw was the only double winner for the day, but single winners included Steve Ploussard, Barry VanAmberg, Bruce Wright, Mike Rado, Dave Seibold, Don Lindsay, Dave Burgering, and John Apsley. Wright, Shawn Elkins, Rado and Bob Terry combined to win the 400-yard freestyle relay in a respectable 3:13.9.

Basketball—**February 21, 1976 (H):** With four games remaining on the schedule, State topped Illinois, 69-59, for their eighth Big Ten victory of the season. The most memorable moment of the game came at 13:53 of the opening half when Terry Furlow hit a 17-foot jumper to surpass Spartan All-American Ralph Simpson's season scoring record of 667 points set in 1969-1970. With four games remaining on the schedule, Furlow, the six-foot-five senior, would complete the season with 793 points, a record that stood until 1985-1986, when Scott Skiles pumped in 850.

Fencing—**February 28, 1976 (A):** The swordsmen finished their season as the first MSU fencing team to win 15 dual meets in one season. Swords clashed as the Spartans easily defeated Tri-State College 23-4, and the University of Detroit, 17-10. Jack Tintera dominated the sabre with a 5-0 record. The senior captain wielded his epee with a 5-1 record, and Bert Starr performed well with a 4-1 record in the foil.

Hockey—**March 5, 1976 (H):** A record-tying sell-out crowd of 6,605 showed up at Munn Arena to see the Spartans defeat the University of Michigan, 6-3, and clinch first place in the Big Ten and second in the WCHA, their best finishes ever. Fewer penalties than normal were whistled during the night. Apparently, with a team title on the line, players were forced to play good hockey and forget the rough play. State took a 1-0 lead early in the first period on a goal from Tom Ross. From then on, there was no looking back, as Ross, Daryl Rice, Steve Colp and Brendon Moroney worked together and never relinquished the lead.

Tennis—**April 20, 1976 (H):** The Spartans shut out Wayne State for only their second win of the season, 9-0. Playing at the number one position, junior Tom Gudelsky opened the scoring with a three-set victory, 3-6, 6-0 and 6-2. The remaining singles matches, number two through number six, were won by Rick Zabor, 6-3, 6-3; Larry Stark, 6-2, 6-1; Kevin McNulty, 6-1, 6-4; Dick

Callow, 6-2, 6-1 and Lee Woyhan, 6-0, 6-1. The doubles winners were Gudelsky-Callow, 6-3, 6-1, with the remaining pairs of McNulty-Mark Smith and Joe Taylor-Steve Klem also winning easy two-set matches.

Tennis—**April 27, 1976 (H):** Posting a 6-3 win over Notre Dame, State evened its dual-meet record at 4-4. The winning total was achieved by taking five of the six singles matches and one of the three doubles. After number one Tom Gudelsky dropped a two-setter, the remaining Spartan singles players stepped forward. From number two through number six, winners were Rick Zobor, 6-1, 0-6, 6-1; Larry Stark, 6-4, 6-1; Harlan Woyahn, 6-2, 6-2; Kevin McNulty, 6-4, 3-6, 6-0; and Dick Callow, 6-3, 6-0. The team of Woyahn and Callow was the only MSU doubles team to win, and they did so in two sets, 6-4, 6-4.

Lacrosse—**April 27, 1976 (A):** Kevin Willitts led the way for MSU once again with four goals and three assists in a 13-12 nail biter over Albion. The Britons led 5-1 after the first quarter, but the Spartans lit up the net in the second, taking a 9-7 lead at halftime. Nevertheless, the scoring margin stayed within two for the reminder of the game, but Albion scored their last goal with 25 seconds left on the clock and State held on to the ball to seal the victory. Dave Surdam and Harley Liplow added three goals and an assist each, while Tim Topalian and Doug Peterson had one goal and one assist each.

Track and Field—**May 1, 1976 (H):** In winning 12 events and finishing one-two-three in four of them, MSU easily handled Notre Dame for their only dual win of the spring, 100-44. Steve Fox, Charles Byrd and Herb Lindsay were all double winners, with other first-place performances coming from Dan King, Todd Murphy, Steve Young, and Tim Klein. This was Jim Bibbs's first win as State's head coach.

Baseball—**May 22, 1976 (H):** Going against Lary Sorensen, the ace of the U of M pitching staff, the Spartan hitters were not intimidated as they sent him to the bench after a six-run outburst in the fifth inning. Three of those runs came on a four-bagger by the catcher, Ron Seid. His blast was self-satisfying in that he had lettered in Ann Arbor as a freshman, before transferring to MSU. The Spartans picked up three more runs in the bottom of the sixth as Tyrone Willingham lashed a two-run double to highlight the productive frame. Sherm Johnson went the full nine innings for Danny Litwhiler. Yielding one earned run on six hits, the final score read, MSU 10, Michigan 2.

ATHLETE OF THE YEAR

At five foot six and 155 pounds, Tom Ross (HO 1973-76) was not an imposing figure on a pair of skates, but he was a performer. Upon concluding a record-filled four-years, he became the school's career leader in goals scored (138), assists (186) and point total (324). Those marks still remain atop the Michigan State record lists. He was not alone as a scorer. During those same four seasons, Steve Colp registered 300 points with 132 goals to rank second, while fifth-ranked Daryl Rice accounted for 225 points, including 96 goals. Ross also leads the team in career power-play goals (72). In his senior season of 1975-76, the Dearborn, Mich., native totaled 105 points with 29 power-play goals, both team records for a single season. Tom put his name in the book as a freshman on Nov. 10, 1973, when he tied a team record with five goals in a 9-5 win over Notre Dame at Munn Ice Arena. In both his junior season of 1975 and his senior year in 1976, Tom Ross was selected as a first team All-American.

Tom Ross

IN THE SPARTLITE

Baseball: MSU placed fourth with a 7-5 conference record. Al Weston led the team with a .345 batting average, while Weston and Rick Seid were both voted to the All-Big Ten first team. Weston was also selected to the NCAA District All-America first team.

Basketball: In the preseason media poll, State was picked to finish ninth in the conference standings, but they fooled more than sportswriters as they finished fourth with an overall record of 14-13, 10-8 in the conference.

Senior Terry Furlow led the team in scoring throughout the year with an incredible average of 29.4 points per game. His 50-point game against Iowa still stands as the most points scored by a Spartan in a single game. Three days later he connected for 48 points against Northwestern, which remains the second highest total by a Spartan in a single game.

In May of 1976, through a press conference, Joe Kearney, the new athletic director, introduced Jud Heathcote to the East Lansing community. He then escorted Heathcote to the Pretzel Bell restaurant, where the Varsity Alumni "S" Club was holding its annual spring golf outing dinner. On that occasion, alumni were first exposed to the wit that would soon capture Spartan fans. Obviously, doing his homework and realizing the impact of MSU hockey, the new coach predicted: "Next season our guys will outscore the hockey team on any given weekend." Following laughter, he tempered his prediction with, "well . . . considering who we have coming back next season . . . on MOST weekends we'll outscore the hockey team."

Thus, this poker-faced man from Montana gained immediate acceptance into the Michigan State family with his self-deprecating humor that became his stock-and-trade over the next 19 seasons.

Cross Country: Herb Lindsay led the way for the Spartans and finished in second place with a 23:35 in the five-mile Big Ten Championships in Madison, Wis., with the MSU team placing fifth. Lindsay's arch-nemesis, Craig Virgin of Illinois, won the individual crown for the third straight year with a time of 23:04.5. Both Lindsay and teammate Stan Mavis, who finished 13th in the conference meet, qualified as individuals for the NCAA meet.

Fencing: The champion of the Big Ten epee title came down to a tiebreaker duel between MSU's Jon Moss and Wisconson's Joe Crawford. Crawford had won the

title in 1974 and Moss had taken it from him in 1975. Thus, this became champion versus champion, as each man had lost but one bout during that championship weekend of 1976. Fortunately, the Spartan prevailed under the pressure to edge out the Badger, 5-4, and keep his title. In the sabre competition, Jack Tintera finished in a three-way tie for second place, each fencer with two losses. Unfortunately, the tie was broken by counting the total number of touches, and Tintera finished fourth. As a team, MSU was awarded third place, but Moss was the only member of the team to travel to the NCAA tournament.

Football: Dennis Stolz closed his last year of coaching with a win over Iowa, a 7-4 season tally, and a third-place Big Ten finish.

Charlie Baggett ended his collegiate career in second place in the all-time school record books with 287 pass attempts, 128 completions and 2,335 passing yards. Defensively, Larry Bethea set a single-season record in tackles for losses, accumulating 13 tackles for a loss of 60 yards.

Golf: Playing in five tournaments during the spring, the most impressive showings for State came at the Illinois Intercollegiate where they were third among 15 teams, and three weeks later at the Purdue Invitational, where they placed fourth out of another 15 teams.

In his personal best tournaments of the spring, shooting a pair of 72s, Gary Domagalski topped the leader board among those of the 15-team field at the Northern Invitational in Columbus, Ohio. After being hit by the flu bug, Gary faded in the final rounds, scoring a 74 and 80 and slipping to the third spot.

At the conference championships in Ann Arbor, Bruce Fossum's squad finished in sixth place. Domagalski led the way with a four round score of 312, 14 shoots from the lead. Other Spartans and their scores were: Paul Kruzel 315, Scott Broadwell 316, Joe Marx 321, Mark Brooks 322 and Mark Weston 328.

Gymnastics: The men had a successful dual-meet season, finishing 9-6, one win away from becoming only the second team Spartan history to post ten wins. Regardless, dropping to fifth place at the conference meet was a big disappointment. Glenn Hime was the only qualifier for the NCAA meet, scoring 9.35 on the horizontal bar in the finals competition, but he was unable to place in the national tournament.

Hockey: The Spartans finished the season first in the Big Ten and second in the WCHA, with the playoffs on the horizon. In the opening round, they knocked Wisconsin off the ice rather easily. In a total score two-game playoff, the Spartans took both games at Munn by identical scores, 6-4, 6-4. Next in line came the Minnesota Golden Gophers.

Tom Ross led all vote-getters in the *Denver Post* WCHA All-Star balloting.

Lacrosse: Freshman Kevin Willitts set two new Spartan records, scoring 24 goals and 38 points in a single season, surpassing marks set by Val Washington and Ron Hebert, respectively. Despite his efforts, the team went just 3-10 for the year, defeating Albion, Hope and East Lansing C.C.

Soccer: Coach Eddie Rutherford's second year was a very successful one, as the Spartans tallied a 10-2-0 record with six shutouts. They played for the first time in the Big Ten Classic, defeating OSU, 3-1, in the first game and losing to Indiana in the finals. Rom Zdravko sparked the scoring with 12 goals and seven assists, and Mike Price contributed 10 goals and two assists as the team outscored their opponents, 51-17.

Swimming and Diving: The Spartan swimmers amassed 365 points to finish fourth in the Big Tens. Indiana took top honors for the 16th straight year with 765 points. Mark Stiner was named an All-American on the one-meter board, while Dave Burgering and Jesse Grif-

Gary Domagalski started strong at the Northern Invitational but faded in the final rounds.

fin were named All-Americans on the three-meter board. In the NCAA tournament, MSU scored eight points for 24th place.

During a ceremony in April, Charles "Mac" McCaffree, head coach from 1941-1969, was inducted into the International Swimming Hall of Fame at Ft. Lauderdale, Fla.

Tennis: Completing a disappointing 7-14 dual-meet season, Coach Drobac's squad scored 27 team points and finished in fourth place at the Big Ten Conference Championships. Harlan Woyahn reached the finals at number six singles and at number three doubles with teammate Dick Callow before meeting setbacks and settling for second place.

Track and Field: By the 1976 season, the NCAA switched to the internationally accepted metric system for running their meets.

In accumulating 46 points, MSU finished the outdoor championships in sixth place. Herb Lindsay managed the only first, winning the 1,500 meters in 3:43.8. The big event for State was the intermediate hurdles, in which Tim Klein was second, Chris Cassleman placed third, Todd Murphy took fourth and Howard Neeley placed sixth. Murphy also managed a fifth in the high hurdles, and Stan Mavis finished sixth, two seconds behind Lindsay in the 1,500.

Wrestling: As Coach Peninger bemoaned, "I don't remember something like this ever happening to a team, ever!" Grady was referring to the fact that four of his regulars were sidelined with debilitating injuries, thus making a run for the Big Ten team title only a dream. Three other Spartans did, however, earn their way into the conference championship round that year. At 177 pounds, Jeff Hersha won the consolation round to gain a third-place finish. Randy Miller was edged in the finals of the 118-pound division, while Pat Milkovich went all the way to claim his third conference championship. With a total of 35.25 team points, the Spartans finished in fourth place.

At the NCAA championships in Tempe, Ariz., for the second year in a row, Milkovich finished in second place, and accounted for 17 points, MSU tied for 19th place in the team standings.

EXTRA! 1976 WCHA PLAYOFFS
(Second Place)

No, Michigan State did not compete in the NCAA hockey tournament in 1976; yet, no team ever came closer without joining that elite group. The elimination game that season was both memorable and historic; consequently a report of it is included below.

It was the WCHA finals. The first game against the Gophers finished with a 2-2 tie, intensifying the pressure for the second game at the Munn which would decide who would receive the NCAA tournament bid. The 6,605 screaming fans were packed into the sold-out arena, and dozens were watching from outside the glass doors. The visitors started the match-up with an early 2-0 lead when Tom Ross knocked in his 50th goal and 101st point of the season, the first collegiate player ever to reach this milestone. Nevertheless, a third Minnesota goal closed the first period at 3-1. Goals were exchanged early in the second, with Daryl Rice scoring his first, before the Gophers scored two power-play goals to earn a 6-2 advantage. MSU had the next power play, however, when an opposing icer broke Joseph Campbell's nose and received five minutes for high sticking. During this time Rice and Ross both scored, making it 6-4 going into the third. Pat Betterly then knocked one in at 6:55 to put the Spartans within reach, and Rice earned his hat trick goal at 16:26, scoring the eighth straight power play goal of the game and tying it at the end of regulation. State threatened to finish the game quickly, controlling the puck throughout the first overtime, but by the second it was clearly a face off between the goalies, and both sides were making defensive plays. In the third overtime the referees called the only two penalties since regulation, clearing the ice for a four on four battle. It was then, at 6:33 of the period, that the Gophers hit a rebound shot off the top of Dave Versical's pads and into the net for the 7-6 victory. The game, believed to be the longest WCHA playoff in history, had lasted four hours and fifteen minutes. Versical finished with 64 saves in the game and 1,410 for the year, an MSU record. State stayed home and Minnesota went on to win the NCAA championship.

MSU
1976-1977

TALES TO TELL

On April 8, 1976, three days after accepting a five-year contract at $34,000 annually, Michigan State's new football coach, Darryl Rogers, was in town holding forth at a press conference. At that time, the response to a given question offered a clue as to what was in store for the 1976 football season. Rogers said, "I like to pass the ball, but I think that you have to have someone to pass to. I haven't seen what our players can do yet, so I don't know how much we'll pass."

By the second week of the month-long spring practice (April 26-May 29), it was becoming clear; Michigan State, a team that averaged seven passes a game in the preceding season, was definitely going to air it out come fall. It also seemed likely that the receivers could be tight end Mike Cobb, a six-foot-five, 255-pound senior, and the two freshmen starters from 1975, Eugene Byrd and Kirk Gibson (who caught a total of only nine passes in 1976), along with a product of East Lansing High School, Dave Radelet. As for the quarterback position, during four major scrimmages of the spring drills, Eddie Smith had completed 60 percent of his passes, Marshall Lawson

and Kenny Robinson 50 percent and John Vielhaver 40 percent. Consequently, Smith lined up with the Green Team, the number one unit, for the annual spring wrap-up game from which he emerged with the MVP trophy following two touchdown strikes to the speedy Gibson. The die was cast—under Darryl Rogers Michigan State would become a passing team featuring Smith and Gibson.

It would take time. The 1976 season (4-6-1) actually turned out to be a disappointment, with a three-game winning streak against Illinois, Purdue and Indiana the only bright spot. However, by 1978, the Rogers-led Spartans were an 8-3 team with a 7-1 Big Ten record equating to a first place tie in the standings. The eight wins that season included an alumni-satisfying 24-15 defeat of Michigan, the first over the maize and blue since 1969. Even to the most veteran Spartan fan, reviewing some of the massive offensive productions of 1978 seems unbelievable today: Syracuse 49-21, Indiana 49-14, Wisconsin 55-2, Illinois 59-19, Northwestern 52-3, and Iowa 42-7. Unfortunately, the continuing NCAA sanctions kept Michigan State from the Rose Bowl.

HEADLINES of 1977

- Elvis Presley, 42, dies at Graceland, his palatial estate in Memphis, Tenn.
- George Lucas releases *Star Wars*, which becomes the highest grossing movie of all time until it is dethroned by *E.T.* five years later.
- President Jimmy Carter signs an act creating a new cabinet-level Energy Department.
- Alex Haley's novel *Roots*, a story of his quest for his ancestors in Africa and America, is made into the most successful TV miniseries in history.

SCOREBOARD

	W	L	T	Avg.
Baseball	28	26	0	.519
Track and Field	3	1	0	.750
Football	4	6	1	.409
Basketball	12	15	0	.444
Tennis	7	12	0	.368
Cross Country	4	3	0	.571
Swimming and Diving	7	2	0	.777
Wrestling	9	9	0	.500
Hockey	14	21	1	.403
Fencing	11	5	0	.688
Golf	tournament play only			
Gymnastics	6	8	0	.429
Soccer	7	4	1	.625
Lacrosse	6	8	0	.429

Coach Rogers had proven a point. Spinning the ball in the air would result in spinning the numbers on the scoreboard. The following totals compare MSU's three years immediately prior to Rogers's arrival (1973-1975) with his first three years as head coach (1976-1978):

Year	PA	PC	Yards	Pct.	TD
1973-1975	287	128	2,335	.446	14
1976-1978	*789	418	5,706	.530	43

*(PA=passes attempted; PC=passes completed; TD= touchdowns by passing; *an ongoing team record)*

The Rogers's aerial show would also spin some heads in the Big Ten Conference. The unimaginative "three yards and a cloud of dust" offense of Woody Hayes at Ohio State would soon become passe.

The 1977 swimming and diving team. (Front row, left to right) Diving coach J. Narcy, M. Paglia, G. Disosway, M. Stiner, D. Burgering and coach D. Fetters. (Second row, left to right) S. Ploussard, M. Rado, J. Dauw, J. Griffin, J. Apsley, J. VandeBunte, S. Elkins and manager A. Miller. (Third row, left to right) manager T. Morton, G. Moran, R. Maher, P. Saggau, D. Seibold, D. Warnshuis, K. Machemer, R. Terry and M. Johnson. (Fourth row, left to right) D. Fritsch and B. Griffiths.

TEAM OF THE YEAR

No, the MSU swimming and diving team had not suddenly overtaken the Indiana Hoosiers, who would successfully pursue an unprecedented 17th straight conference championship on the way to 20 in a row. Coach Dick Fetters had, however, managed to marshal a competitive squad in 1977 that would complete a 7-2 dual-meet record; place third in that year's conference championships and include four individual titles in the process (Shawn Elkins, 200 butterfly; Mike Rado, 200 individual medley; and Dave Burgering in both the one- and three-meter diving events). Those dual-meet victories include Big Ten wins over Northwestern, Illinois, Purdue and a rare win over the University of Michigan, only the fourth since the schools first met in 1923.

MAKING HISTORY

After an absence of several years, the Spartan Spirit Block, was reintroduced as a feature at home football games. Seated near the center of the lower east stands and using large cards of different colors, 1,200 students formed massive messages from "MSU," a Sparty portrait and Beaumont Tower, to humorous stunts such as characters from the comic strip, "Peanuts."

The Spartan Spirit Block displays its school pride.

The intermission between football halves had been 15 minutes; however, a new rule provided a host school the ability to extend that break to 20 minutes without mutual agreement.

The NCAA added team competition to their championship tennis format which previously included only individual competition.

Tyrone Willingham, a senior who lettered in both football and baseball, was given the Big Ten Conference Medal of Honor as the athlete who best represented the top values of intercollegiate athletics.

Fendley Collins, former Spartan wrestling coach for 33 years, died April 16 from injuries sustained after a seizure caused him to fall from his bicycle.

MSU changed its policy for hockey ticket sales. First, they doubled the student rate from $1 to $2 per game, then they divided the season passes so that a student could buy them for either the Friday series or the Saturday series but not both.

The six-year-old junior varsity hockey program was eliminated due to a lack of coaches, money and players.

GREAT STATE DATES

Cross Country— **September 24, 1976 (H):** The State harriers opened the season with an impressive 20-35 victory over Notre Dame. The first four Spartans to finish the five-mile course all bettered the previous record. Herb Lindsey broke the tape in a course- and meet-record time of 24:06.5. The senior captain was followed by junior Jeff Pullen in 24:32, and freshman Paul Morrison in 24:57. Senior Stan Mavis rounded out the scoring five with a 25:92.

*Football—***October 23, 1976 (A):** Upon defeating Illinois, 31-23, Darryl Rogers earned his first Big Ten victory as head coach. The offense was balanced, with 207 rushing yards and 224 passing yards split almost equally between Eddie Smith and Marshall Lawson, who came in after Smith suffered a bruised shoulder. Kirk Gibson ran off a short pass for a 30-yard touchdown in the first quarter, but the Fighting Illini held a 20-7 lead at the half with each touchdown originating from a fumble recovery. The second half, however, was led by Richard Baes, who ran for two touchdowns and finished with 108 yards. In addition, Hans Nielsen scored a field goal and Eugene Byrd caught one touchdown.

*Soccer—***October 29, 1976 (A):** Coach Eddie Rutherford moved junior Robbie Back to a new spot from fullback to halfback, and it seemed to have paid off as

the Spartans totally dominated the Michigan Wolverines, 8-0. Back had one assist and two goals, both from corner kicks, one by Ed Randel and another from Mike Price. The remaining goals were scored by John Haidler, Tom Coleman, Zdavko Rom, Kamy Asdigha, Randel and Price.

Football—**October 30, 1976 (H):** MSU racked up 553 total offensive yards and held Purdue to just 193 in a 45-10 trouncing. Seven different backs ran for the green and white. Rich Baes ran for 101 yards and Leon Williams followed him with 100. Baes, Williams and Alonzo Middleton each ran for a touchdown, while Levi Jackson, Eugene Byrd and Mike Cobb each scored off passes from quarterback Eddie Smith. A single field goal from Hans Nielsen rounded out the scoring. State had 29 first downs during the game and never had to punt.

Cross Country—**October 30, 1976 (A):** Herb Lindsay broke another course record, this time by almost 20 seconds, running the five-mile layout in Oxford, Ohio, in 24:28, in the 23-33 triumph over Miami of Ohio. Jeff Pullen ran through the rain to finish second, though almost one minute back at 25:26. Stan Mavis and Paul Morrison wrapped up the victory at fourth and fifth place, respectively, and Mike Solis finished 11th.

Football—**November 6, 1976 (H):** The MSU defense controlled the Indiana offense, allowing a total of only 185 rushing yards in a 23-0 shutout. Even more effectively, they squelched two serious scoring threats, first on a fumble recovery at State's 25-yard line and the second on a pass interception at the two-yard line. Meanwhile, the Spartans were setting some team records. Quarterback Eddie Smith tossed his 11th touchdown pass, the most ever in a season. His primary receiver, Kirk Gibson, made 15 receptions for a total of 200 yards, both new stadards. Hans Neilsen kicked three field goals and Nick Rollick added a touchdown run.

Hockey—**November 19, 1976 (H):** This early season 5-2 victory over number one-ranked Wisconsin would prove to be one of the highlights of the season. Just 59 seconds into the first period Joey Campbell scored the team's first goal, and after the first intermission, goals from Russ Welch, Marty McLaughlin and Jim Cunningham put MSU up 4-0 before the third period. Ken Brothers widened the gap with the team's fifth marker before the Badgers ruined goalie Dave Versical's shutout with two goals of their own. The frustrated visitors initiated some fighting after their coach had come onto the

ice to argue with the officials. Numerous penalties and game ejections were administered; consequently, a total of 30 minutes transpired before completing the final three minutes of the period.

Hockey—**December 10 & 11 (H & A) 1976:** Before 6,483 excited fans at Munn Arena, MSU flourished in the final period to defeat Michigan, 7-5. The Wolverines led until 18:04 of the second period, when freshman right winger Russ Welch scored his second goal of the night to set the tie at 3-3. To follow this, the Spartans amazingly scored four goals within the first six minutes of the third period, with Welch completing his first career hat trick, and Paul Klasinski, Ron Heaslip and Robbie Harris each adding one. Two more goals from the Wolves could not close that gap, and Dave Versical's 41 saves sealed the Spartan triumph. It would take overtime to win in Ann Arbor on the next night, but the Spartans prevailed once more, 6-5. With the U of M matching goals by Jim Johnson and Jim Cunningham, the third period began tied 2-2. Russ Welch regained the lead just 14 seconds into the period, but U of M scored the next three for a 5-3 lead with just 11 minutes remaining. In those final minutes Paul Klasinski and Eddie Lubanski each scored to send the game into overtime. In OT, it was junior Tim McDonald who slapped his first score of the season past the net minder for the sudden-death victory.

Basketball—**December 11, 1976 (H):** Jud Heathcote's first victory as head coach at Michigan State was a 54-52 overtime game against Eastern Michigan. State took an 8-0 lead after five minutes, led by four at the half, and opened it up to 36-26 during the second half of a defensive battle. Nevertheless, EMU was not to be taken too lightly, as they climbed back to actually take a 46-44 lead with 4:42 to go. Freshman Terry Donnelly then scored two of his six points to tie, and another Huron field goal at 2:50 was answered by a pair of free throws from junior center Jim Coutre at the 1:36 mark to send the game into overtime. Eastern led at the start of the period, but Edgar Wilson's 25-foot jumper and Bob Chapman's buzzer-beating shot from the corner were the difference. Sophomore Greg Kelser led the team with 20 points and 14 rebounds, while Chapman had 13 points.

Gymnastics—**January 28, 1977 (H):** Indiana was scheduled to come to East Lansing for a double dual meet but found themselves snowed in, while Northern Michigan pushed through from Marquette only to lose, 203.80-

187.60. Jeff Rudolph led the way with a career-high winning score of 52.40 in the all-around competition. Other Spartan firsts came from Al Burchi's 8.90 in free exercise, Paul Hammond's 8.80 on the pommel horse, Brian Sturrock's 9.30 on the vault, and Doug Campbell's 9.20 on the high bar.

Fencing—**February 5, 1977 (A):** The State squad was able to win three of four match ups in the five-team square-off hosted by the University of Illinois-Chicago. Increasing its season record to 6-1, they defeated the host Illinois-Chicago team 18-9, Indiana State 22-5, and Purdue 21-6. The Peterman brothers, Bryan and Bill, led the way as each won in epee with identical scores of 8-2. Mike Bradley and Chris Thomas scored 9-1 and 8-2 in sabre, while the foil team added two winning bouts.

Swimming and Diving—**February 19, 1977 (H):** Coach Dick Fetters was all smiles when the Spartans upset Michigan, 63-60, for the first time since 1967 and handed them their first loss of the season. Leading the way were John Narcy's divers, Dave Burgering and Jesse Griffin. The pair twice finished one-two, Dave winning the one-meter and Jesse the three-meter. Although losing both relays, the "S" swimmers did their part, winning five of the individual events. A particular boost came from the one-two finish of Shawn Elkins and John Apsley in the 200-yard butterfly. Other State winners were Jim Dauw, Glenn Disosway, Michael Rado and Mark Outwater.

Basketball—**February 19, 1977 (H):** Down by 10 points at the half and by a 55-41 score early in the second half, the Spartans finally took charge and outscored the Iowa Hawkeyes, 26-10, to take the lead, 67-65. Thereafter, the two teams battled down the stretch, with the Spartans prevailing at the end, 81-79, as Bob Chapman secured the win by nailing a pair of free throws with 12 seconds of time remaining. While Jud Heathcote applauded the usual solid play of Greg Kelser and Chapman, the performance of 6' 9" junior center Jim Coutre was the key to State's victory. The 212-pound transfer student from DuPage Junior College (Ill.) scored an MSU career-high 18 points on eight-of-11 shots from the floor and was two-for-two at the free-throw line. He also contributed nine rebounds.

Track and Field—**February 26, 1977 (H):** A one-two finish by Jeff Pullen and Herb Lindsay in the two-mile race and an easy victory in the mile relay, led Michigan State to a 69-62 win over a solid Indiana squad. MSU also won six other events, with freshmen accounting for four of them. Randy Smith took the 60-yard dash in a noteworthy time of 6.l and doubled with a 30.7 winning time in the 300. Two other frosh, Ricky Flowers and Keith Moore, took the quarter and the half-mile respectively in 49.2 and 1:53.5. Seniors Herb Lindsay and Stan Mavis were winners in the mile and 1,000-yard run. Linsday was clocked in 4:10 and Mavis in 2:14.4

Wrestling—**February 26, 1977 (A):** The Sigma Chi fraternity sent some fans down to Columbus to cheer MSU on to win its final meet of the season, 22-14. Tim Harrington and Doug Helmink, both on the wrestling reserve list, had brought their fraternity brothers down with them to see the closing meet of the year. Mike Walsh (126 pounds) led the way for the Spartans with a 15-6 decision, while Bob Pollitt (150 pounds) won, 18-5. Dennis Brighton (134 pounds) and Doug Siegert (158 pounds) each shutout their opponents, 9-0, and Rick Warner (167 pounds) took the final Spartan decision, 6-5, while heavyweight Jim Ellis closed the meet with a 2-2 tie.

Lacrosse—**April 9, 1977 (A):** MSU edged out Oberlin to pick up its first win of the season, 8-6. The attack was led by Mike Waring, who scored four goals. Still, the triumph would not have been possible without goalie Chuck Molla, who snagged 25 saves during the afternoon.

Tennis—**April 15, 1977 (H):** Coach Stan Drobac was pleased with his team, as they played solid tennis and downed the Northwestern Wildcats, 7-2. Captain Tom Gudelsky continued to improve, as he won his singles match along with Tighe Keating, Dee McCaffery, and Jon Boukamp. The Spartans then finished the meet with a sweep of the doubles competition: Gudelsky-Kevin McNulty, Keating-Steve Carter and McCaffery-Steve Klemm.

Lacrosse—**April 23, 1977 (A):** In what would be their only shutout of the season, State's laxers completely dominated the Dutchmen of Hope College, 10-0. Co-captain Kevin Willits starred with two goals and two assists, and Bill Chait also scored twice. With the outcome of the game never seeming to be in doubt, Chuck Molla and Bill McGinniss shared the goal-keeping responsibilities, making 11 and 10 saves, respectively.

Track and Field—**May 14, 1977 (H):** In defeating Eastern Michigan, 80-65, State took seven of nine individual track events, plus two field events and both relays. The Hurons managed firsts in four field events

but captured only two races on the oval: the steeplechase and the high hurdles. The only double-winner was Herb Lindsay, who won the mile in 4:05.1 and then led the three-milers to the tape in 13:57.1. Other Spartan winners were Paul Schneider, with a toss of 55' 6" in the shot put; Charles Byrd, 47.4 in the 440; Erwin Homann, 47' 2 1/4" in the triple jump; Tim Klein, 50.8 in the intermediate hurdle event; Keith Moore, 1:53.3 half-mile; freshman Ricky Flowers, 21.2 for the 220; and yet another first-year man, Randy Smith, tied the Ralph Young Field mark with a winning time of 9.4 in the 100-yard dash.

***Baseball*—May 22, 1977 (H):** Michigan State closed its season with an exciting win over arch-rival Michigan, thanks to junior relief pitcher Larry Pashnick. In the second inning, Tony Spada hit a bases-loaded double that brought in three runs and gave the Spartans the lead; but the Wolverines closed the gap with a two-run home run in their very next at-bat. In the sixth, State's starting pitcher Sherm Johnson left the game with a knee injury. Brian Wolcott took over, only to give up a tying home run. Randy Hop responded with a solo homer of his own to reclaim the lead until the eighth inning, when the Wolves pulled in two runs and had the bases loaded with only one out. It was then that Pashnick stepped to the mound. He forced a ground ball to third baseman Dave Radke, who stepped on the bag for out number two and then threw home for the tag to end the inning, but the U of M led, 5-4. MSU wasted little time in reclaiming the lead, this time for good, as first baseman Jerry Weller lined a two-run homer over the fence in the bottom of the eighth inning. Pashnick struck out the last of the opposing batters in the ninth to gain the victory, 6-5.

ATHLETE OF THE YEAR

In 1977, co-captain Dave Burgering made history when he became the only Spartan to win a Big Ten diving championship, and he did it on both the one-meter and three-meter boards. He was voted an All-American in each of his last two years and finished fifth at the national meet in his final year of collegiate competition. His winning ways began in 1974 when he defeated OSU defending national champion Tim Moore in a dual meet; he had been competing behind Moore since age 13. After college, Burgering continued diving and made the second spot on the 1980 Olympic team, although he was unable to compete due to the boycott of the Moscow Games.

Dave Burgering

IN THE SPARTLITE

Baseball: Al Weston joined the MSU ".400 Club," batting .409 on the season and setting MSU records for hits, with 70, and runs batted in, with 49. The 5' 9", 175-pound senior was voted for the second straight year to both the All-Big Ten first team and the NCAA District All-American first team. Despite his efforts, the team could never present a challenge for the conference title during his four years. They finished sixth when Weston was a freshman, were fourth the following season, and fourth in 1976. In this, his final season, State slipped to fifth with a 10-8 Big Ten record and 28-26 overall.

During his sophomore season, Greg Kelser led the Spartans with an average of 21.7 points and 10.8 rebounds per game.

Basketball: Before the season started, new coach Jud Heathcote went into the dormitories to visit with student groups, promote and answer questions about MSU basketball. For attending, students were able to purchase a packet of 14 season tickets for $10.

Senior Edgar Wilson nailed a jump shot with one second to go in his career to end it with a 62-61 victory at Illinois. It was just the beginning of Jud Heathcote's career, however, as he finished his first year as head coach with a fifth place finish in the Big Ten, holding a 9-9 record in the conference and 12-15 overall. Gregory Kelser led the team with an average of 21.7 points and 10.8 rebounds per game, and senior captain Bob Chapman added an average of 19.6.

Cross Country: Four harriers finished in the top 16, as State gave its best team effort of the year to finish in a fourth-place tie at the conference meet. Herb Lindsay finished second overall on the five-mile course with a 23:39, losing for the third straight year to Illinois' Craig Virgin. Jeff Pullen ran one of the best meets of his career, finishing seventh with a time of 24:10. Other Spartan runners included Stan Mavis in 14th place with a 24:27 and Paul Morrison in 16th place with 24:44. For the NCAA meet, the team did not qualify, but Lindsay placed fourth.

Fencing: Junior Chris Thomas followed his father's footsteps to win the Big Ten sabre title and become MSU's 13th Big Ten fencing champion. Bill Peterman was the only other Spartan medal winner, placing fourth in the epee, resulting in a fourth-place team finish in the five-team tournament.

Thomas was the only MSU representative at the NCAA tournament, making the final round and placing in the top 24.

Football: Darryl Rogers put the Spartans on a passing rampage, and quarterback Ed Smith flew by all the old school records, completing 132 passes for 1,749 yards and 13 touchdowns. In obtaining these marks, he threw for more than 200 yards three times, once for a record-setting 324 yards against N.C. State. At the other end of the ball was Kirk Gibson, who set MSU single-season records with 748 receiving yards and seven touchdowns, including 173 yards in the game against N.C. State.

Larry Bethea continued to pace the defensive squad, setting a single-season record of nine quarterback sacks for 63 yards in losses. On the special teams, Hans Nielsen made 11 field goals, tying the Spartan single-season record.

Golf: Hosting the Big Ten championships on the 6,854-yard Forest Akers West Course, coach Bruce Fossum selected the following six-man team for the competition: Gary Domagalski, Joe Marx, Mark Egly, Mark Brooks, Tom Baker and Rick Glover. Despite the advantage of playing on the home course, the Spartans were unable to finish higher that seventh, as Domalgalski and Egly led the team in scoring with 298s. Ohio State took the team competition easily, finishing 28 strokes ahead of second place Indiana.

Hockey: It was a rough way to end the year: being swept by Michigan put MSU in a tie for eighth place in the WCHA and left them out of the playoffs for the first time in more than 10 years. Eight teams advanced to postseason play, but the Spartans were tied with Colorado College and based upon goals for and against, the Tigers were given the final playoff slot. Through the year it was freshman Russ Welch who sparked the team, accumulating 22 goals and as many assists. Jon Cunningham added 11 goals and 25 assists.

In 1977, the varsity hockey team played the first broom ball game against the Legal Eagles, a team of area attorneys. It was a charity fund-raiser that has been played annually ever since.

Lacrosse: Nevin Kanner took over as head coach and led the team to a 6-8 season mark. Included among their wins was a 10-0 demolition of Hope College, the team's fourth shutout in its eight years as a varsity sport. Chuck Molla took the net for the Spartans and gathered 290 saves, a school record.

Soccer: Senior goalie Gary Wilkinson finished the season with six more shutouts, bringing his career number to a team record 19. He had first played organized soccer as a junior in high school and initially had extensive doubts about even trying to play at the collegiate level.

After a brief mid-season slump, the Spartans shutout their last three opponents to finish with a 7-4-1 overall record.

Season-ending statistics show that Rom Zdravko led the team with 11 goals and four assists, while Mike Price contributed with four goals and five assists.

Swimming and Diving: With MSU hosting the Big Ten meet, Dave Burgering won both the one- and three-meter diving events; Shawn Elkins took the 200-yard butterfly with a time of 1:50.26, and Mike Rado swam a winning time of 1:53.90, which also set an MSU pool record.

At the NCAA meet in Cleveland, State placed 18th with 23 points. Divers Dave Burgering and Jesse Griffin led the way with fifth- and seventh-place finishes on the three-meter board that gained them All-American recognition.

Tennis: MSU finished eighth at the Big Ten meet in Ann Arbor, with Tom Gudelsky flashing a slight sign of achievement. He was successful in winning the consolation round at number one singles.

In addition to Captain Gudelsky, the squad included John Boukamp, Steve Carter, Tighe Keating, Steve Klemm, Dee McCaffrey and Dave Tien.

Track and Field: Freshman Randy Smith and senior captain Herb Lindsay were the ones to watch

throughout the year, and this did not change when it came time for championships. At the Big Ten indoor meet, the team took fifth, but Smith ran the 60-yard dash in 6.17 seconds for an individual first. Lindsay just missed becoming a double winner, taking the two mile with a time of 8:42.97 and running the fastest time of his career to lose the mile by .24 seconds with a 4:01.63. Senior Stan Mavis pulled in third with the best time of his career at 4:02.4. Smith and Lindsay went on to the NCAA indoor meet and earned All-American status by each taking fifth place in their events.

At the Big Ten outdoor meet, an excellent team showing put MSU in third place. Smith took second in the 100-meter and first in the 200-meter with a time of 21.68 seconds followed by teammate Ricky Flowers's 21.83, good enough for second place. Meanwhile, Lindsay took his second straight 1,500-meter title in 3:45.3 but just lost to Illinois rival Craig Virgin in the 5,000-meter, finishing in 13:55.65. Charles Byrd, Tim Klein and Howard Neely also placed in their events, while the 1,600-meter relay team of Neely, Flowers, Klein and Byrd finished second.

Wrestling: The last of MSU's Golden Era of wrestling had graduated in 1976 with Pat Milkovich, but 1977 offered moments to cheer. The dual-meet season record of 9-9 featured wins over Indiana, Illinois, Purdue and Ohio State.

At the Big Ten meet in Madison, Wis., State could do no better than seventh place, as 126-pound Mike Walsh and 136-pound Dennis Brighton each finished in third place. Both Spartans thus gained a trip to the NCAAs in Norman, Okla.

At that national meet Walsh was eliminated in the second round, but Brighton continued. After winning his first two matches, 6-2, 9-7, he pinned his third opponent and then downed the second seed, 7-2. The next stop was in the semi-finals, where Brighton avenged an earlier defeat of the season with a 2-1 overtime decision of an Oklahoma State contender. It was Minnesota's Pat Neu who finally ended the dream weekend for Dennis, as the Gopher managed a 4-2 win on a disputed referee's decision. Brighton's run gained 19 points, good enough for a 17th place finish for MSU.

Zeke the Wonderdog, the golden Labrador retriever, entertained MSU sports fans for seven years with his frisbee-catching routine. The 75-pound Zeke made his first appearance at Spartan Stadium in 1977. Football coach Darryl Rogers awarded Zeke with an honorary varsity letter after that season.

TALES TO TELL

If Michigan State fans were ever challenged to select the greatest Spartan ever, very likely the "Magic Man" would win the ballot in a landslide victory. Few, if any, athletes have ever provided, or continued to provide, the impact that basketball star Earvin Johnson has left on the Michigan State campus and Greater Lansing area. The story of how and when the 6' 8" local hero made the decision to attend MSU is documented in his book *My Life,* told to William Novak and published by Ballantine Books in 1992.

Early in his senior year at Lansing Everett High School, Earvin was considering North Carolina, Notre Dame, Maryland, Michigan and Michigan State, with the list soon shortened to include only the two local schools with a slight lean toward Ann Arbor. Thereafter, three encounters refocused Johnson's thinking toward MSU.

From his book:

"In April of my senior year, when I returned from a basketball tour of Germany with other high school all-stars, a huge crowd was waiting for me at the Lan-

Spartan fans were thrilled when Earvin Johnson announced his intention to attend MSU.

sing airport. Most of them were cheering and carrying Michigan State signs. They presented me with a petition signed by five thousand kids in the Lansing school system, urging me to stay in Lansing."

HEADLINES of 1978

- Sony invents the revolutionary Walkman, the first portable cassette player.
- Jim Jones leads his followers to a mass death in Jonestown, Guyana.
- The U.S. Senate approves the Panama Treaty, which will turn the canal over to Panama by the year 2000.
- Pope Paul VI, dead at 80, is replaced by Pope John Paul I, who dies unexpectedly after 34 days in office. He is succeeded by Cardinal Wojtyla of Poland as John Paul II.

SCOREBOARD

	W	L	T	Avg.
Baseball	32	21	0	.604
Track and Field	1	0	0	1.000
Football	7	3	1	.682
Basketball	25	5	0	.833
Tennis	6	15	0	.285
Cross Country	1	5	0	.166
Swimming and Diving	6	2	0	.750
Wrestling	6	6	1	.500
Hockey	7	27	2	.222
Fencing	7	7	0	.500
Golf	tournament play only			
Gymnastics	7	5	0	.583
Soccer	6	7	0	.462
Lacrosse	10	12	0	.455

Next came a home visit from Jud Heathcote, a man that Earvin had reservations about:

> "He [Coach Heathcote] said, 'It seems to me that your head is saying Michigan, but your heart is saying State. Michigan is a great school, no question about that. And they have an outstanding team. But if you go there, you'll be one of several great players. And with your height, they'll probably have you playing center. You're not a center, Earvin. I've seen you play, and you're definitely a point guard. I want you to run our offense.'"

Jud had made a positive impression on Johnson and then, on the very next morning, Vern Payne, Jud's assistant, made a house visit and in great detail dispelled some negative concerns about the Spartan's head coach. Again from Magic's own words:

> "[Payne:] 'If I didn't like him, or I thought he was a bad coach, I would tell you. But he is good, Earvin. Really good. I think you should play for him. I know you have seen him yelling at the guys. But that's because he is intense, and he wants to win so badly. Behind all that screaming and yelling, Jud Heathcote is a terrific coach and an excellent teacher. I've known

you for years, and I have seen how committed you are to improving your game. This is the guy who can help you do this. Besides, if you come to MSU it'll be a great team. We've got Greg Kelser and all the other guys from last year. And you know we have signed Jay Vincent.'"

After listening to Vernon Payne's description of Heathcote, I shocked myself and him too . . . 'Let's do It,' I said. 'Give me the papers and I'll sign.'"

A telephone call to Jud, and he was soon at the house with the papers in hand.

The decision was kept a secret for a couple of days until a press conference was called in the high school auditorium, whereupon Earvin sat at a large table, looked at a dozen microphones staring him in the face and calmly opened with, "Are there any questions?" After the laughter subsided, he wasted little time in making one of the most momentous statements in MSU sports history "Next year I will be attending Michigan State Un—" as the auditorium erupted in applause and drowned out anything that might have followed. Later, in response to questions, the future All-American explained, "I've always wanted to go to Michigan State. Ever since sixth or seventh grade, I've been going to all of their games. Once you get the Spartan in you, you never lose it."

TEAM OF THE YEAR

Coming off a losing season the previous year, Jud Heathcote could not have been more pleased than to win the 1978 Big Ten championship in his second year as head coach at Michigan State. The team went 22-5 overall and 15-3 in the conference to win the title. Their only home loss came in the form of a 65-63 nail-biter against archrival Michigan. State went on to play in the NCAA tournament but lost, 52-49, to Kentucky in the Mideast regional championship in Dayton, Ohio. Junior co-captain Gregory Kelser led the team through the year with 17.7 points and 9.1 rebounds per game, while senior co-captain Bob Chapman contributed 12.3 and shot .802 from the line. Meanwhile, true freshman Earvin Johnson was setting all the freshman records. He registered 17.0

points, 7.3 rebounds and 7.4 assists per game, and he shot .785 from the line, making 161 out of 205 free-throw attempts. Today, Johnson still ranks first in 10 freshman records and second behind Kelser in two others. Other letter winners for the team, shown above, were Mike Brkovich, Alfred Brown, Ron Charles, James Coutre, Terry Donnelly, Stan Feldreich, Don Flowers, Michael Longaker, Nate Phillips, Dan Riewald and Jay Vincent.

The 1978 basketball team

MAKING HISTORY

No other canine, before or since, gained the notoriety and fame around Spartan Stadium that "Zeke, the Wonder Dog" did in the fall of 1977. The three-year old labrador, owned and trained by MSU senior Gary Eisenberg of Haslett, caught Frisbees and put on a unique act in pregame and halftime periods at all home football games. He remains a legend in the memory of veteran Spartan football fans.

On June 20, it was announced that Dr. Gwen Norrell would succeed Dr. John Fuzak as MSU's faculty representative to the Big Ten conference. Fuzak retired after holding the position for 19 years. The appointment, which was announced by President Edgar Harden, took take effect on Jan. 1, 1979. Gwen became the first woman to hold the position at a conference school. She remained in the position for 11 years before stepping aside in 1988.

A 1976 NCAA ruling provided for a college athlete to become a professional in one sport yet remain eligible

to compete in other sports. In June of 1978, Kirk Gibson signed a reported $200,000 contract with the Detroit Tigers. Following a season of minor league baseball play, he returned for a final season of Spartan football. Kirk thus became Michigan State's first amateur-professional.

Shot putter Paul Schneider won the National Collegiate Powerlifting championship in the 242-275 weight division.

GREAT STATE DATES

Soccer—**September 28, 1977 (A):** After missing the opening two games, the return of starting goalie Mark Gembarowski, along with defensive backs Rob Back and Tom Coleman, improved the team performance significantly. In a defensive struggle, State and Calvin were scoreless after regulation. With just 17 seconds remaining in overtime, freshman Scott Campbell scored on a throw-in pass from co-captain Back to win the game, 1-0.

Cross Country—**October 1, 1977 (H):** It was a down year for Michigan State cross country, as the Spartans managed only one victory over their six-meet schedule. This win came at the expense of the Kent State Golden Flashes, 21-39. Scoring the points for MSU were Jeff Pullen, who won the race in 25:00 flat. Following him over the five-mile Forest Akers layout were Steve Carlson in third, Tim Kerr in fourth, Tom Wright, who finished sixth, and Ted Unold in seventh.

Football—**October 22, 1977 (A):** By holding the Badger offense to 54-yards rushing and harassing their passing game with eight quarterback sacks, the MSU defense proved to be a primary factor in the 9-7 victory over the University of Wisconsin. It would be the first of five straight victories to close out the season on a positive note. Hans Nielsen's 51-yard field goal provided a slim 3-0 halftime lead. In the third quarter, a pitiful 13-yard punt put the Spartans in business at the Badger 39-yard line. On the very next play from scrimmage, Jim Earley

rambled all the way to the one-yard line, and from there, Leroy McGee, the California junior, scored to make it 9-0. The conversion attempt was blocked. Wisconsin managed to score in the last two minutes, but time ran out before they could once more gain possession. Punter Ray Stachowitz excelled for the Spartans with a punting average of 43-yards, downing two within the six-yard line. Earley finished with 101 rushing yards.

Football—**November 5, 1977 (A):** The Spartans were scoreless and trailed Minnesota, 10-0, until Hans Nielsen kicked a 34-yard field goal with 1:05 remaining in the half. It was his 39th three-pointer, breaking a Big Ten career record. The second half belonged to MSU. The Gophers collected just three first downs, as Larry Bethea, Mel Land, Paul Rudzinski, Dan Bass, Mike Dean and Craig Fedore dominated the line of scrimmage. Meanwhile, Kirk Gibson, after being sidelined for three games with an injured foot, returned to the lineup with a pair of touchdown catches. His first score came on a short crossing pass from Eddie Smith, whereupon he cut upfield and sprinted 51 yards into the end zone. State took its first lead with 14:43 to play on another Nielsen field goal, this time from 52 yards. From there it was all MSU. Eddie Smith once more found Gibson, this time on a fly pattern, for an 86-yard scoring play. The game was sealed with Nielsen's third three-pointer and a 15-yard touchdown run by freshman Steve Smith to make the final count, 29-10.

Hockey—**November 12, 1977 (H):** It was the 9-4 domination of Michigan that thrilled the soldout crowd at Munn. Ronald Heaslip started the scoring at 9:17 of the first period, though U of M quickly answered with a tying goal. Leo Lynett knocked one in at the 13:33 mark, and thereafter the Wolverines never came close. Tony Jelacie added two more for the Spartans, while Lynett had a second and Russ Welch added his goal before the second intermission. In the third period, the momentum continued with Marty McLaughlin scoring two and Heaslip getting his second to finish off the visitors. Netminder Mark Mazzoleni had 24 saves on the night.

Football—**November 19, 1977 (A):** It was predicted that the strong wind that swept down Kinnick Stadium would impact the Iowa-MSU game. Indeed it did. With the wind at their backs, State scored on their first three possessions to take a 17-0 lead. First, Steve Smith crossed the goal line on a 10-yard rush, then Jim Earley ran on four straight downs before catching a two-yard scoring pass. Finally, Hans Nielsen completed the quarter with a 45-yard field goal. In the second period, the Hawkeyes utilized the wind at their backs, and the result was a 10-point outburst before halftime, making the score 17-10. In the second half, the game continued on the toes of the kickers with the gusting wind at their backs. Nielsen booted one field goal and the Iowa kicker accounted for two three-pointers, cutting the State lead to four points. A fourth-quarter safety accounted for the remaining MSU points and the final score of 22-16. Alonzo Middleton, the Orangeburg, S.C., junior, led the team in rushing with 71 yards, followed by Smith with 44 and Earley with 42.

Wrestling—**November 27, 1977 (A):** In a Sunday afternoon match in Ann Arbor, the 17th ranked Spartans opened the dual-meet season with a 24-18 upset of 10th ranked Michigan. State won five of the matches and most importantly managed to draw on two other square-offs. In the 126-pound division, Jeff Thomas won with ease, 13-3. His win initiated a streak of four decisions for MSU: 134-pound Mike Walsh, 20-6; 142-pound Don Rodgers, 10-2; and 150-pound Dennis Brighton with a 16-8 verdict. Following a Steve Foley loss at 158, Jim Ellis returned the Green-and-White team to the winner's column with an 8-2 decision at 167. This was followed by the two tie scores, Waad Nadhir with a 5-5 score at 177 pounds and Bill Salisbury 1-1 at 190 pounds. By then the meet was secured for the Spartans.

Track and Field—**January 13, 1978 (H):** In the season opener against Northwestern, sophomore Randy Smith even surprised coach Jim Bibbs, as he ran a personal best 6.0 in the 60-yard dash. To follow it up, he became a double winner, by taking the 300-yard dash in 31.3. Keith Moore, another double winner, finished first in the 880 and later captured the 1,000-yard run. The Cats were never in it, as State took 12 of 15 events and piled up an easy 95-35 victory. Other individual winners were Paul Schneider, Dan King, Ricky Flowers, Tim Klein, freshman Ted Unold and Jeff Pullen. The mile relay was easily won by the combination of Tony Taylor, Tyrone Williams, Flowers and Klein.

Fencing—**January 14, 1978 (H):** The fencing team slashed Purdue, 16-11, with four competitors posting perfect records. The sabremen led the way, as brothers Jon and Chris Thomas were each undefeated at 3-0 and Derk Wray scored 2-0. Epeest Bryan Peterman was the fourth to go undefeated, with a 3-0 score.

Gymnastics—**January 22, 1978 (H):** Michigan scored an impressive 200.70 points, but Michigan State scored 206.65 and topped the Wolverines for the first time since 1967. It was an impressive team win, with Doug Campbell and Dan Miller sitting out with injuries. Senior captain Jeff Rudolph led the way, winning the all-around with a 52.45. Freshman Marvin Gibbs took honors in the floor exercise with a 9.25 and third in the all-around with 49.05. Tom Tomkow won the still rings with a 9.10, while Charlie Jenkins (9.20) and Brian Sturrock (9.10) claimed second and third in the vault. Senior Sturrock also took second on the high bar with 9.10.

Swimming and Diving—**February 4, 1978 (H):** The Spartans trailed OSU, 55-51, with only the freestyle relay remaining. The winner of that concluding event would secure seven points and win the meet. Coach Fetters lined up a talented foursome. First came Jeff Gaekle, followed by John Vandebunte, but even with their best efforts, the Buckeyes held a slight lead. The number three man, Mike Rado, closed the gap and handed the chore to anchorman Jim Dauw. The final score tells the story, MSU 58, OSU 55. It was fitting that Dauw was the eventual hero; he had preceded that relay with victories in both the 100- and 200-yard freestyle events. Other winners for State were Shawn Elkins in the 100 freestyle, Gaekle in the 200-yard butterfly, and in a surprise, Jesse Griffin and Greg Moran finished one-two in the three-meter diving event.

Wrestling—**February 10, 1978 (H):** The Wolverines were denied revenge for their loss in November, losing even worse the second time around, 29-15. The Spartans opened with a fabulous start, winning the first five matches. At 118 pounds, Shawn White won 13-7; Jeff Thomas followed with an easy 16-5 decision in the 126-pound division; Mike Walsh was awarded a forfeit win at 134, followed by yet another one-sided decision, this time by Jeff Therrian at 142 pounds. Dennis Brighton topped them all by pinning his 150-pound opponent. Behind 23-0, the Wolves managed to gain some respect, winning three of the remaining events. The closing Spartan wins came from Ron Cramer at 167 and Jim Ellis at 177.

Basketball—**February 11, 1978 (A):** MSU had only 46 shots compared to U of M's 70, but a 60.8 field goal percentage and a little "Magic" was ample enough to put the Wolves down in their own arena, 73-62. State led just 31-28 with less than a minute to go in the first half, when Earvin Johnson did his trick, hitting a jumper, gaining an assist to Gregory Kelser, and sinking another at the buzzer, increasing the lead to nine points. Michigan drew within three points on several occasions during the second half, the last time at 45-42. It was then that Bob Chapman and Ron Charles hit consecutive jumpers, and Kelser and Johnson each shoved down a fast-break jam to increase their lead to 11 points. The U of M did not threaten thereafter. Johnson finished the game with 25 points, while Kelser added 21 points and 12 rebounds.

Gymnastics—**February 17, 1978 (H):** Led by Marv Gibbs, the North Carolina freshman and senior Jeff Rudolph, the Spartan gymnasts defeated the University of Illinois, 203.05-198.70. Gibbs won the floor exercise with a 9.20 score and added third-place finishes in the parallel bars, high bar and all-around. Rudolph was a double winner in the parallel bars and high bar, finishing second in the all-around. Tom Meagher and Tom Tomkow took first and second on the still rings, respectively, while Charlie Jenkins was second in the vault.

Basketball—**February 18, 1978 (H):** This 79-74 victory over Ohio State took on a look that would become all too familiar, the Greg Kelser-Magic Johnson show. In the opening half, Greg gathered in 12 of his career-high 16 rebounds and "Magic" scored 16 of his career-high 32 points. By the break, it looked like a Spartan landslide, as they led, 42-24. Two new teams came out of the locker room for the second half as the Buckeyes lit up the scoreboard and MSU did what it could to keep the lead. Still, Ohio had too far to comeback and the closest they could come was the five-point deficit they suffered at the buzzer. Kelser had 17 points in the win and Bob Chapman scored 11.

Basketball—**March 4, 1978 (A):** An estimated 6,300 fans turned out at Lansing's Capital City Airport to welcome back the Spartans following their conference championship-cinching 71-70 victory at Minnesota. The highlight of the impromptu celebration was a short ceremony in which Lansing mayor Gerald W. Graves presented each player and coach with the traditional key to the city. That final win over the Golden Gophers did not come easily, as Mychal Thompson became the new Big Ten career-scoring leader, racking up 20 for the hosts. State was down, 38-34, at the half, but Johnson, the freshman sensation, never quit. With just minutes to go he knocked down key field goals and free throws to gain a

68-60 lead, only to see the lead melt to a 68-68 tie. Magic then sank two more free throws, but Gopher Kevin McHale matched them with an alley-oop two-pointer to match the score once more. State held out for the final shot in which Johnson was fouled and proceeded to sink the first of two free throws. Racing down the court in hopes of a final desperation shot, one of the overeager Gophers was called for charging into Terry Donnelly and the game ended. Magic finished with 22 points, while freshman Jay Vincent, who hit four crucial shots in the second half, added 12.

Lacrosse—**April 4, 1978 (H):** Injuries could not keep the lacrosse team down as they topped Indiana, 21-2, setting a new team record for the most goals ever scored in a single game. Second on MSU's all-time scoring list, junior Kevin Willitts suffered a broken leg and was lost for the season, while Joe Berlin missed the game due to an injury before the weekend. Nevertheless, the team scored three goals in the first five minutes of play and finished the first period up, 7-0. The Hoosiers managed a point with 7:26 to go in the half, but trailed 10-1 going into the locker room. IU scored another in the third, but the rest of the game belonged to the green and white. Tim Flanagan led the team with five goals and one assist, while co-captain Ken Davis also had six points, with two goals and four assists. Mark Purcell added three goals, while Shawn Grady, Gary Gilde and Joe Politowicz each scored twice. The previous school record of 16 goals in a single game was surpassed with 8:15 remaining in the final period.

Tennis—**April 22, 1978 (H):** Captain Kevin McNulty returned to the courts after missing four meets due to injuries. Perhaps his return was the necessary catalyst for a team that was 2-11, as the Spartans upset Notre Dame, 6-3. McNulty lost the opening set of his match and was down 0-3 in the second set before rallying to win, 5-7, 6-4, 6-3. Other MSU winners at singles were Steve Klein 6-1, 6-4; Matt Sandler 6-3, 6-0, and Steve Heitzner 7-5, 7-5. In doubles competition, the number one pair of Tighe Keating and McNulty went the full three sets, 6-3, 2-6 and 6-4, for the win, and the duo of Sandler-Heitzner won a two-setter to gain the sixth team point.

Baseball—**April 29, 1978 (H):** Tony Spada was an offensive powerhouse in the 8-2 victory over Purdue, as coach Danny Litwhiler looked to keep pace with Michigan in the race for the Big Ten title. Spada hammered a

double, a triple and his seventh home run of the year, raising his season average to an incredible .500 overall and .607 in Big Ten play. For their share in the offensive show, Jerry Weller and Kenny Robinson each hit a homer of their own.

Baseball—**April 30, 1978 (H):** State swept Illinois in a double header, 5-0, 7-6, to remain neck-and-neck with the Wolverines in the Big Ten race. In the opener, pitcher Brian Wolcott was given the win in his four-hit shutout performance, while Jerry Weller took the offensive, hitting three-for-three with a two-run triple in the third inning. Kirk Gibson and Tony Spada each added two hits in the win. In the second game, Gibson led the way, hitting three-for-three with three runs batted in. State took a quick lead of 7-2 and held on from there during the failed Illini comeback. Rodger Bastien and Spada each added two hits, and hurler Chuck Baker was given the win with the support of relief pitcher Mark Sutherland.

ATHLETE OF THE YEAR

It is legendary how Kirk Gibson came to Michigan State out of Waterford Kettering High School as a 1975 football recruit, with baseball coming as a late addendum to his great collegiate athletic credentials. Kirk was one of those specimens classified as a natural athlete, able to compete in nearly any sport he might set his mind to. During preseason fall football practices his freshman year, he flashed evidence of his patented speed and toughness and quickly earned a starting position as a flanker. His career flourished in 1976 with the arrival of head coach Darryl Rogers and his emphatic passing offense. Teamed with quarterback Eddie Smith, Gibson led the Big Ten in receptions in both his sophomore and senior seasons. He still holds the team career record for yards per catch (21.0) and touchdown catches (24). Becoming a scoring threat every time he had his hands on the ball, Kirk became an instant favorite with MSU fans. Although lettering only one year in baseball (1978), his frequent demonstrations of power hitting elicited the attention of major league scouts. Eventually signing a contract with the Detroit Tigers, Kirk spent that summer honing his diamond talents in the minor leagues. Availing himself of a 1976 NCAA policy change that permitted a student-ath-

lete to become a professional in one sport and be eligible to compete in other sports, Gibson returned for his final year of Spartan football in 1978. Eventually returning to professional baseball, mostly with the Tigers and Los Angeles Dodgers, he enjoyed a 17-year major league career highlighted by heroic performances in two World Series.

Kirk Gibson

IN THE SPARTLITE

Baseball: Danny Litwhiler coached the Spartans to an overall 33-21 season record (the second most ever wins for a Spartan team), a solid second-place conference finish and an NCAA tournament bid.

During the season, the offense batted in a total of 275 runs, the most ever posted by an MSU team.

In the NCAA tournament, State was eliminated following the double loss, 7-2, to Southern Illinois and then 7-6 to Oklahoma State on a ninth-inning home run.

All-American Kirk Gibson led the Spartan attack by setting school batting records with 52 RBIs, 16 home runs, and 21 stolen bases. He placed third all-time with a .766 slugging average and batted .390 for the season.

Tony Spada was named a District IV All-American when he joined the ".400 club" with a .421 batting average. Brian Wolcott led the pitching squad with eight complete games and three shutouts for a 9-3 record, just one win away from a first-place tie for the most earned wins in a season by a Spartan.

Basketball: Does anyone remember who Sten Feldreich was? The answer is: he was Michigan State's first seven-foot basketball player. Feldreich had been a member of the Swedish national team that had competed in the pre-Olympic competition in Hamilton, Ontario. Through international acquaintances, Jud Heathcote made contact with the 21-year old from Bromma, Sweden, and suddenly Feldreich had signed a national letter of intent to play basketball for the Spartans. Would he have made a difference in MSU's drive for an NCAA championship that fell short in a regional final game in Dayton, Ohio, against Kentucky? The question could never be answered. By term break in January of that season, the lanky center prospect had returned to his home in Europe.

Cross Country: Although completing an unimpressive 1-5 dual-meet record, the State team was stunned by their 10th place finish at the conference meet in West Lafayette, Ind. It was an unaccustomed spot for a Michigan State team. Over the span of the preceding 27 seasons, MSU had won the event 14 times and finished second six times. Senior captain Jeff Pullen was the first finisher for the Spartans, placing 27th in 25:33.

Fencing: Chris Thomas went undefeated in all nine of his bouts at the Big Ten championships in Columbus, Ohio, to successfully defend his sabre title. Overall, the team collected only 23 points and thus settled for fourth place out of five teams. The remaining five members of the tournament team placed as follows: Bryan Peterman third in epee, Mark Krusac sixth in foil, Ernie Price 10th in foil, freshman Jon Thomas (brother to Chris) seventh in sabre and Scott Ray eighth in epee.

Led by Peterman, who finished 12th in epee, and Chris Thomas, who ended 13th in sabre, State placed 22nd in the NCAA championships held at Wisconsin-Parkside.

Football: Challenging his team record of 257 passes attempted in 1976, quarterback Eddie Smith launched another 240 aerials in 1977 to continue the new look in

Spartan football. Many of his completions were for impressive gains, as his favorite target, Kirk Gibson, averaged 24 yards per catch throughout the 11-game season.

Kicker Hans Nielsen bettered his 1976 team season record of 11 successful field goals by booting 17 through the uprights in 1977. His mark was not bettered until 1988.

Tyrone Willingham returned 23 kickoffs for 454 yards, second on the all-time Spartan lists.

Despite the green-and-white success, the team was unable to go to a bowl game because they were still suffering the sanctions imposed by the NCAA in 1976.

Golf: MSU finished ninth in the Big Ten golf championships in Columbus. Ohio State hit for a landslide victory, finishing 59 strokes ahead of second-place Indiana.

A total of 10 team members earned varsity awards: Tom Baker, Mark Brooks, Jim Christ, Eric Gersonde, Richard Grover, Hillary Herrick, Marty Holda, Ed Kelbel, Doug Lemanski and Steve Lubbers.

Gymnastics: After a successful 7-5 dual-meet season, MSU traveled to Champaign for the conference meet and scored 397.40 points, only to finish fifth. The Spartans fell behind Illinois and Wisconsin, both of whom they had beaten during the regular season. Minnesota won its third consecutive Big Ten championship.

Hockey: The Spartans struggled through a difficult season, being tossed the most single-season losses in school history with a 7-27-2 overall record. Despite this, Russ Welch accumulated 40 points from 17 goals and 23 assists, and Leo Lynett contributed 33 points from 18 goals and 15 assists. Dave Versical made 757 saves on the year, but even this could not keep State from a disappointing last-place finish in the conference.

Lacrosse: The team finished 10-12, earning the most wins ever by an MSU varsity lacrosse team. Joe Politowicz set a school record with 59 goals on the season, assisted mostly by Tim Flanagan, who amassed a school record of 78 points. Yet another school record was set when the Spartans passed for 14 assists in a 21-2 triumph over Indiana.

Soccer: Joe Baum finished his first year as head coach with a respectable 6-7 record. In the Big Ten Classic, the Spartans managed third place, defeating OSU after losing to nationally ranked Indiana. Through the season, freshman Scott Campbell led the team with five goals and five assists for a total of fifteen points. Mike Price was also a major contributor with four goals and two assists.

Swimming and Diving: Shawn Elkins and Jesse Griffin continued to lead the way for the Spartans and performed well despite a sixth-place team finish. Indiana won the meet for the 18th consecutive year. Elkins took the 200-yard butterfly for the second straight year and Griffin won the three-meter diving competition. Kevin Machemer placed third in one-meter diving to qualify with Elkins and Griffin for NCAA competition, while seniors Dan Warnshuis and Dave Seibold broke school and personal records but did not place in their events.

At the NCAA championship meet in Long Beach, Calif., MSU finished 14th with 31 points. Griffin was the team's top performer, as he finished third in both the one- and three-meter diving events. Teammate Machemer was seventh on the high board and 16th on the one meter.

Tennis: Moving up two notches from 1977, the Spartans scored 15 points to tie for sixth place at the conference meet in West Lafayette, Ind. Matt Sandler won the consolation final match at number five singles to finish in the third spot. In doubles action, the teams of Steve Klemm-Frank Willard and Sandler-Steve Carter reached the consolation finals but met defeat.

Track and Field: The results of the conference indoor championships were disappointing, as the Spartans garnered 46 points, which placed them in a fifth-place tie with Illinois. The highlight of the weekend was when sophomore Randy Smith won his second straight 60-yard indoor title with a 6.31. Ricky Flowers also ran well and would have won the 300-yard dash, but he was disqualified for stepping out of his lane.

Freshman high jumper Dennis Lewis finished second at the NCAA Indoor championships at Detroit Cobo Hall with a leap of 7' 3". It was his best jump ever. Smith failed to reach the finals after placing fifth in the 60-yard dash in 1977.

With 29 points, the lowest point total since 1969, the Spartans managed a seventh-place finish at the Big Ten outdoor championships held in Evanston, Ill. Both Smith and Tim Klein were fighting illnesses and consequently faired no better than fourth in their respective specialties, the 100-meter dash and the 400-intermediate hurdles.

At the NCAA outdoor meet in Eugene, Ore., only Klein advanced beyond the preliminaries, and he lost out in the semi-final round while running a 51.3 in his hurdling event.

Throughout the year, Paul Schneider also contributed, setting MSU records in the shot put both indoor and outdoor, though he was unable to win a title or qualify for the NCAA meets.

Wrestling: Michigan State rose to the occasion as a team to prove the predictions wrong and finish in third place at the Big Ten meet. Mike Walsh (134 pounds) and Jim Ellis (177 pounds) each took second place behind a Hawkeye opponent, as Iowa won the title for the fifth straight year. Spartan Dennis Brighton added a third place finish in the 142-pound weight class. At the NCAA meet, the three qualifiers combined for three and a half points and 36th place.

EXTRA! 1978 NCAA BASKETBALL TOURNAMENT

Michigan State reached the regional finals in the 1978 NCAA tournament. The following are the Spartans' box scores for those games.

MICHIGAN STATE 77–PROVIDENCE 63
March 11, 1978, Indianapolis, Ind.

	FG-FGA	FT-FTA	REB	A	PF	TP
Kelser	9-10	5-7	11	3	2	23
Johnson	5-9	4-6	7	7	3	14
Vincent	2-3	2-3	4	1	1	6
Donnelly	6-9	0-0	3	3	2	12
Chapman	7-12	0-0	1	1	2	14
Brkovich	0-0	0-0	0	0	1	0
Charles	3-4	0-2	3	1	4	6
Flowers	0-0	0-0	0	0	0	0
Phillips	0-1	0-0	0	0	1	0
Longaker	0-0	0-0	0	0	0	0
Williams	0-0	0-0	0	0	0	0
Brown	0-2	0-0	1	0	0	0
Riewald	0-0	0-0	0	0	0	0
Kaye	0-0	0-0	1	0	0	0
Feldrich	1-2	0-0	2	0	0	2
Team			2			
TOTALS	33-52	11-18	35	17	17	77

Halftime: Michigan State 38-26; **Officials:** Overhy, Kelley; **Attendance:** 16,519.

MICHIGAN STATE 90–W. KENTUCKY 69
March 16, 1978, Dayton, Ohio

	FG-FGA	FT-FTA	REB	A	PF	TP
Johnson	3-17	7-11	9	14	2	13
Kelser	11-18	1-2	13	1	5	23
Vincent	6-8	0-0	6	1	4	12
Chapman	10-12	3-6	3	2	3	23
Donnelly	0-1	0-0	0	4	0	0
Charles	4-4	5-6	8	0	3	13
Brkovich	1-1	0-0	1	1	3	2
Feldreich	0-0	0-0	1	0	3	0
Brown	1-1	0-0	1	1	0	2
Riewald	0-0	0-0	0	0	0	0
Flowers	1-1	0-0	0	1	0	2
Team			2			
TOTALS	37-63	16-25	47	25	21	90

Halftime: Michigan State 39-29; **Officials:** McCarthur, Clymer; **Attendance:** 13,458.

KENTUCKY 52–MICHIGAN STATE 49
March 18, 1978, Dayton, Ohio

	FG-FGA	FT-FTA	REB	A	PF	TP
Johnson	2-10	2-2	4	5	4	6
Kelser	9-12	1-3	13	1	3	19
Vincent	4-7	0-0	1	2	1	8
Donnelly	0-0	2-2	0	5	5	2
Chapman	5-9	0-0	1	1	5	10
Charles	2-3	0-0	0	0	0	4
Brkovich	0-0	0-0	0	0	0	0
TOTALS	22-41	5-7	20	14	18	49

Halftime: Michigan State 27-22; **Officials:** Clymer, Bishop; **Attendance:** 13,458.

MSU
1978-1979

TALES TO TELL

Baseball coach emeritus Danny Litwhiler defined the May 19, 1979 home game against Michigan as a circumstance that was the "right place, right situation and right time." As he recalled:

"Through the years I have discovered that only truly great thrills come when the right place, situation, timing and personal involvement all come together. In 1979, the place was right, we were playing at John Kobs Field, giving us the home field advantage. The situation was right, we were leading the Big Ten with a 10-3 record and our opponent, Michigan, was right behind in second place. It was a two-game series, with the second game scheduled for Ann Arbor the next day. We needed one victory for the title and, of course, wisdom suggested it would be best to get that win on our home field. The U of M opened with Steve Howe on the mound, a future major leaguer who, with a record of 15-0, had not lost a conference game in four years. We started Brian Wolcott, who had a successful season and was a fine pitcher, but he had a tender arm. He wanted to pitch, so I

told him to go as far as he could and we would have a relief pitcher ready.

As expected, Steve Howe opened strong and sat down the first six hitters that he faced. Meanwhile, two more future major leaguers, Rick Leach and Jim Paciorek, hit solo home runs to put us behind, 2-0. By now the fans were overflowing the field as an estimated 10,000 people were on hand. They were in the trees and on top of the batting cages in left field. Fans spilled out onto the right field grass and they had to be taken as part of the ground rules. In left field, fans seeking a better view of the action knocked down a portion of the fence.

Being down 2-0, those same fans didn't have much to cheer for. The time was right. The MSU pep band that had been performing in Spartan Stadium for the spring football game suddenly appeared at Kobs Field and began playing the school fight song. Much to the delight of the overflow crowd, our players rose to the occasion. Five successive singles, capped off with a three-run homer by Rodger Bastien, and the scoreboard in centerfield read Michigan State six, visitors two. Furthermore, with this abrupt deluge of runs, Steve Howe left the game, shaking his head.

HEADLINES of 1979

- An accident at the Three Mile Island nuclear power station in Pennsylvania causes a nuclear crisis.
- The new cabinet-level Department of Education is established.
- The U.S. suspends Iranian oil imports and Iranian assets in retaliation for the holding of 50 U.S. hostages in Tehran.
- Margaret Thatcher, Conservative Party leader, becomes Britain's first female Prime Minister.

SCOREBOARD

	W	L	T	Avg.
Baseball	28	27	0	.509
Track and Field	3	3	0	.500
Football	8	3	0	.727
Basketball	26	6	0	.813
Tennis	6	15	0	.285
Cross Country	2	6	0	.250
Swimming and Diving	6	7	0	.462
Wrestling	13	7	0	.650
Hockey	15	21	0	.417
Fencing	3	7	0	.300
Golf	tournament play only			
Gymnastics	8	6	0	.571
Soccer	6	6	2	.500
Lacrosse	9	7	0	.563

Rodger Bastien circles the bases following his three-run homer against Michigan.

For the first time in four years, he had been knocked out of the box and would eventually be charged with his first Big Ten loss.

Brian Wolcott pitched four and two-thirds innings before that sore arm forced him to the bench. Mark Pamorski and Mark Sutherland did a fine job in relief to save the game, and Tom Schultz hit a powerful home run to add icing to the cake. With the support of the fans and that impromptu pep band, we had won the Big Ten title in 1979."

In winning the baseball title, MSU athletes could boast of a rare achievement in Big Ten competition. It marked only the fifth time in conference history that during the same year, one school had won or shared titles in football, basketball and baseball.

TEAM OF THE YEAR

Spartan fans will never forget the Magic season. Although they were unbeaten at home, several buzzer-beating losses on the road left the team with a 26-6 overall record and forced them to share the conference crown with Purdue and Iowa. Soon, however, they would have the spotlight to themselves. The NCAA final game between Michigan State with Earvin Johnson and the undefeated Indiana State with Larry Bird still ranks as the highest-rated college basketball game in television history. Johnson registered 24 points and seven rebounds, and Gregory Kelser contributed 19 points and eight rebounds to lead the team to a 75-64 championship victory. All-American Kelser paced the team through the year with 18.8 points and 8.7 rebounds per game, while All-American Johnson provided the court Magic, earning 17.1 points, 7.3 rebounds, 8.4 assists and 2.3 steals per game. He also made 202 out of 240 free throws for 84 percent. Under the shadow of Kelser and Johnson, Jay Vincent scored 12.7 points per game and Ron Charles pulled down 5.1 rebounds. Other letter winners on the team were Terry Donnelly, Mike Longaker, Greg Lloyd, Rick Kaye, Jaimie Huffman, Mike Brkovich, Rob Gonzales, Don Brkovich, Gerald Gilkie and managers Randy Bishop and Darwin Payton.

The 1979 basketball team. (Front row, left to right) manager R. Bishop, manager Ed Belloli, assistant coach F. Paulsen, assistant coach B. Berry, head coach J. Heathcote, assistant coach D. Harshman, trainer C. Thompson and manager D. Payton. (Back row, left to right) T. Donnelly, G. Lloyd, G. Gilkie, D. Brkovich, R. Kaye, R. Charles, E. Johnson, G. Kelser, J. Vincent, R. Gonzalez, M. Brkovich, J. Huffman and M. Longaker.

Darryl Rogers led the football team to an 8-3 record and a share of the Big Ten title, but they were ineligible to compete in a bowl game because of the sustained NCAA probation. The school could celebrate when the probation ended at midnight on January 18th.

MSU earned its first Big Ten triple crown, winning conference championships in three major sports: football, basketball and baseball.

MAKING HISTORY

Although Title IX, a part of the Education Act of 1972, covered all aspects of education, intercollegiate sports received the most publicity. The act proposed regulations for conformity with federal law banning sex discrimination in the nation's schools. As for sports, the expectation was that colleges and universities would provide equity in all phases of men's and women's programs. On Dec. 11, 1978, the federal government's Department of Health, Education and Welfare published proposed guidelines for compliance and set a date of March 4, 1979 for comments from interested parties. One of the "interested" parties was, of course, the NCAA, representing 726 member schools. Among the many points of emphasis in its 49-page response, NCAA officials said it could cost its members $250 million a year to comply with the proposed federal regulation. It was the opening volley in what ultimately would be a losing battle for the NCAA.

Charlie Schmitter entered his 40th year as head coach of the Spartan fencing squad.

MSU implemented a student lottery system for the sale of season football tickets in order to eliminate the need to camp overnight and wait in long lines to get tickets.

GREAT STATE DATES

Soccer—**September 21, 1978 (H):** Coach Joe Baum's squad opened the season with a long but exciting game, scoring the only goal of the game in the second overtime to defeat Ferris State, 1-0. Both teams ran a rigorous defense throughout the game and failed to convert key scoring opportunities. It was Hans Nielsen, after three years with the football team, who came through for State as he took a centering pass from Scott Campbell and headed in the shot from 12 yards out for the winner.

Golf—**September 29, 1978 (A):** Playing in two fall tournaments gave Coach Fossum an opportunity to gauge his squad for the regular spring season. Playing in the Badger Fall Invitational hosted by the University of Wisconsin, the Spartan golfers carded a composite 293 to top four other teams, including the host Wisconsin team that scored a runner-up 296. Freshman Dave Belen fired a one-under par 71 to capture the medalist honors. Both Hilliard Herrick and Steve Lubbers were two strokes back at 73. Following the meet, the team traveled to LaGrange, Ill., for the Playboy Invitational on the next day. It was here, amidst a 12-team entry, that the squad finished in an impressive second place.

Cross Country—**October 7, 1978 (H):** The Spartans completed a 15-50 perfect score against Northwestern, as seven runners finished before a single Wildcat crossed the line. Martin Schulist led the way, finishing on the soggy Forest Akers course in 31:19.7, followed by Mark Mesler, Harold Rutila, Michael White, Keith Moore, Steve Carlson and Tim Kerr.

Football—**October 14, 1978 (A):** In only his third year at the helm, Darryl Rogers succeeded in putting a team on the field that defeated highly-ranked Michigan, 24-15, before 105,132 fans in Ann Arbor. Quarterback Eddie Smith completed 20 of 36 passes to eight different receivers during the game, while his counterpart tossed up six aerials, only to have three picked off by Spartan defenders. After a missed field goal on its first possession, State scored on its next three possessions: a 38-yard field goal from Morten Anderson; a 10-yard pass play; and a dive play from one-yard out by Lonnie Middleton. The second half opened with the Wolverines sticking exclusively to the ground as they ran 17 consecutive plays to score, but Michigan State fans were not daunted. Smith responded by five of six passes, capped with an 11-yard TD toss to Mark Brammer. One more touchdown run by the Wolves was not enough, and the Spartans were in possession at the Michigan 19-yard line as the game clock ticked down.

Soccer—**October 25, 1978 (H):** State's tenacious defense controlled the Central Michigan rushes, while at the other end of the pitch, Joe Baum's crew managed two goals. At this point in the season it was declared that Hans Nielsen no longer had eligibility remaining after his stint with the football team. Therefore, to add to his weakened offense, Coach Baum pulled a rather unique shift in personnel, as he switched goalie Peer Brunnschweiler to a striker position. After 30 scoreless minutes, it was the converted goalie that banged home the first score after taking a centering pass from Kurt Easton. At 7:13 of the second half, Brunnschweiler connected again, this time off a pass from Mike Price. Building the two-goal advantage, the Spartans were content to play a possession game as they continually kept play in the Chippewas' end of the field. Final statistics revealed MSU had a 28-6 shots-on-goal advantage.

Football—**November 4, 1978 (A):** Illinois fans might have been happier if they left for home after three quarters of play. A quick touchdown to start the game and another following a fumble recovery on the immedi-ate kickoff return gave the Fighting Illini a 12-0 lead before the Spartan offense had taken one snap from scrimmage. Quarterback Eddie Smith, who completed 20 of 31 passes, then took command and found the end zone on the next two possessions. The first score came on a 25-yard run from Steve Smith, followed by a one-yard dive for a score by Lonnie Middleton, an Orangeburg, S.C., junior. MSU opened the second half with a third touchdown, which was quickly answered to make it 21-19. This was as close as it would get. Morten Anderson kicked a field goal and Middleton scored his third touchdown with another short dive over the line. This brought the score to 31-19 at the end of the third period. After that, what initially appeared to be a close battle turned into a rout. During the final 15 minutes of play, Bruce Reeves, Mike Hans and Derek Hughes each scored to end the game at, 59-19.

Hockey—**January 13, 1979 (H):** Establishing a team record that likely may never be broken, State jumped to a 3-0 first-period lead over Notre Dame with all three goals coming within a span of 54 seconds. Dan Sutton, Frank Finn and Joe Omiccioli were the sharp-shooters. Penalties plagued the icers in the second period and the Fighting Irish stormed back with two goals of their own. To close the period Leo Lynett nailed one between the net minder's legs from just above the face-off circle. The Irish continued their fight with a marker just 22 seconds into the third period, but goals from Finn and Lynett kept the Spartans out of reach as they came up with a 6-3 victory.

Gymnastics—**January 13, 1979 (A):** Coach George Szypula took his team to Ann Arbor for the early season Big Ten Invitational, in which there would be no team scoring. However, Marvin Gibbs, a talented sophomore, scored and scored big. He entered and won the all-around event with an incredible score of 105.20, one of the highest marks ever recorded in the tournament. Junior Charlie Jenkins, still recovering from a knee injury, also captured a first place in his specialty event, the vault.

Basketball—**January 20, 1979 (H):** In retrospect, this 83-72 overtime defeat of Iowa was a must win, or the eventual NCAA champions may never have reached tournament play. With 25 seconds of time remaining, Iowa canned two free throws to take the lead, 65-63. On State's next possession, Mike Brkovich launched one at the buzzer. The shot bounced off the rim, but the 6' 4" guard was fouled on the play by Hawkeye shooting star

Ronnie Lester. Calling timeout, Jud Heathcote mapped strategy for the ensuing overtime period; after all, wasn't Mike Brkovich shooting 100 percent at the charity line? Sure enough, the Windsor, Ontario, sophomore, dropped both free throws, sending the contest into the extra frame. With Iowa's Lester having fouled out, the Spartans dominated play during the fresh five-minute period, outscoring the Hawks, 18-9. Some were surprised that more players did not foul out, as 53 personal fouls were called, along with five technical fouls. As usual, Earvin "Magic" Johnson led the way with 25 points, and Gregory Kelser hit 22. Jay Vincent had 12, and Brkovich scored 10, including those clutch free throws after regulation time had expired.

Basketball—**February 1, 1979 (H):** For many MSU fans, the 1979 overtime win against Ohio State was the most memorable of the 51 victories during Earvin "Magic" Johnson's colorful two-year Michigan State career. It was a "must" win in which the Spartans were forced to battle during a 13-minute stretch without the "Magic Man." With the Green and White leading, 32-23, and 2:23 remaining in the opening half, Johnson went up for a rebound under the Buckeye basket and came down in a heap, writhing in pain. He had severely sprained his ankle. After being assisted to the training room, the prognosis was that he was through for the afternoon. As the game reconvened following intermission, Johnson remained in the training room, and as might be expected, the Buckeyes crept back from the 34-27 halftime deficit. Listening on the radio and visualizing the game slipping away, Earvin had heard enough. Lacing his shoe back onto the swollen ankle he hobbled his way back to the court amidst a deafening greeting from the 10,004 fans. There was 8:42 left in regulation. Magic's return not only stimulated his teammates, but he managed 15 points (11 from the free-throw line) during the remainder of regulation and the five-minute overtime in which State managed to outscore the Bucks by five points. The final score read MSU 84, OSU 79. The win kept them in the race for a Big Ten title and a trip to the NCAA tournament.

Wrestling—**February 2, 1979 (H):** The MSU wrestlers only held a 20-16 lead over Minnesota going into the final match, but they were soon to be surprisingly delighted. Shawn Whitcomb had a heroic match and pinned Jim Becker, the fourth-ranked heavyweight in the nation, in just 54 seconds. The pin gave the Spartans a 25-16 upset over the Gophers and a team full of smiles.

To bring the team to that point, wins were also produced by Jim Ellis, Mike Walsh, Jeff Thomas and Steve Foley.

Wrestling—**February 8, 1979 (A):** For the second time in the season and the fourth time in a row, the Spartans defeated the Wolverines, this time by a score of 23-17. Yet, the meet was not as close as that final score suggests. Early on, State was in complete command. Led by Mike Walsh, Jeff Therrian and Jim Ellis, they opened with five wins and a draw to build a 20-2 lead and later led 23-7 before a final surge by the U of M made the final score respectable. Another timely win came from Dave Rodregiuz, who edged his opponent, 3-2.

Fencing—**February 10, 1979 (H):** Coach Charlie Schmitter's team won its final home game of the season, defeating Wisconsin-Parkside, 19-8. The Peterman brothers, Bryan, Barry and Brad, controlled the epee once again, as the team downed their opponents, 6-3, in the event. In the foil, senior Mark Krusac went undefeated and Dominic Marazita followed at 2-1 to win the event, also at 6-3. The sabre was won at 7-2 with Paul Ponger going undefeated and sophomores Jonathan Thomas and John Chambers each scoring 2-1.

Swimming and Diving—**February 10, 1979 (H):** Central Michigan was no match for Dick Fetters's squad, as the Spartans soundly defeated the Chippewas, 85-28. Some races were close, but the Spartans dominated their MAC opponent, especially in the freestyle events. Senior Jeff Gaeckle posted a 1:44.7 in winning the 200-yard freesyle, while freshman Mark Lancaster took top honors in both the 50- and 100-yard freestyle races. The meet opened with a win in the medley relay and closed with Lancaster, Gaeckle, Steve Ploussard and Richard Legault capturing the final event, the 400-yard freestyle relay.

Hockey—**February 24, 1979 (A):** The Spartan icers came through on the road, upsetting league-leading North Dakota, 6-5. The win gave State a final chance to enter the playoffs and left the Fighting Sioux with a title-deciding weekend against second-place Minnesota to close out their schedule. Russ Welch led the scoring for MSU with two goals, but it was senior Darryl DiPace who broke a 5-5 tie after 6:06 in the third period to secure the win.

Gymnastics—**March 2, 1979 (H):** The gymnastics team sweated out a close one to end its season with a 200.05-197.65 win over Indiana. It came down to the final events, as MSU won four of six to take the meet. Despite illness, Marvin Gibbs once again paced the team by winning the all-around competition. State's strongest

performance came in a sweep of the floor exercise. Charlie Jenkins won first 9.3, followed by Gibbs, Bruce Unkefer and Dan Miller, who tied for fourth. Seniors Paul Hammonds and Charlie Fanta finished their Spartan careers well, with Hammonds taking second in the pommel horse and Fanta placing second behind Gibbs in the parallel bars. Rich Licats took first in the high bar, and Tom Tomkow placed second on the rings.

Tennis—**April 6 & 7, 1979 (A):** The tennis team opened on the road without a coach, with three rookies in the lineup and faced with the usual misery weather of early spring. Regardless, the Spartans found the way to win two meets, 7-2 over Purdue and 6-3 over Illinois. For the first time in 20 years coach Stan Drobac was not on the sidelines, as he remained home nursing the flu bug. Playing at number two, Matt Sandler was the only winner in both matches, as he won 6-4, 6-2 at West Lafayette.

Lacrosse—**April 8, 1979 (A):** State raised its record to 4-0 in their best start ever by thrashing Indiana on their home turf, 18-1. The only disappointment was that it was not a shutout. Co-captain Kevin Willitts led the team once again with seven goals and one assist. Mark Piavis and Joe Politowicz also played well, each adding three goals and one assist. Greg Brinkman, Shawn Grady, Duane Anderson, Charles Hewitt and Bill Lecos each scored one goal. By the end of the season, Willitts set an MSU record with 97 goals scored in a single season.

Track and Field—**April 24, 1979 (H):** State surpassed CMU, 79-65, in its outdoor opener. Ricky Flowers was the only double winner, with firsts in the 200- and 400-meter dashes. Andre Williams, Ken Eaton and Tom Estes swept the 100-meter dash, as Dan King and Andy Wells finished one-two in the high jump. Other first place winners included Wells, Paul Schneider, Barry Harris and Michael White.

Lacrosse—**April 25, 1979 (A):** Notre Dame might have been a bit overconfident, boasting an 8-0 record before MSU traveled to South Bend, but by the end of the day they had been humbled 12-9. State opened up the game with its best quarter of the year, earning a 6-0 lead. The Irish fought back but could only come within three, and the Spartans successfully stalled to finish the game.

Baseball—**May 13, 1979 (H):** MSU stayed above U of M by just a half game by sweeping Northwestern 3-2, 12-6. With one inning to play in the opener, the score

was tied 2-2 when Joe Lopez singled and advanced to second on a wild pitch. Second baseman Randy Hop followed with a single to center, knocking Lopez home with the winning run. In the second game, State was in trouble when the Wildcats scored four runs in the third for a 4-2 advantage. They kept working, however, and came up with seven runs in the bottom half of the fourth, sparked by a three-run triple from Tom Schultz. In the fifth, a Schultz RBI single and a Lopez two-run double brought in three more for the Spartans and put it out of reach for the Cats. The win for both games was given to pitcher Brian Wolcott.

ATHLETE OF THE YEAR

Earvin "Magic" Johnson may well be the most remembered athlete in MSU history. Although his collegiate career lasted only two years, he left an everlasting mark on the hearts of the fans and changed the face of Michigan State basketball. Before the Magic seasons, MSU had only been to the NCAA tournament three times and the Final Four once. Under Johnson's leadership, the school won its first NCAA basketball championship in 1979 and started down the road to maintaining a nationally competitive basketball program.

Earvin "Magic" Johnson

There are two Magic games that will forever be etched into the minds of Spartan fans. The first came on Feb. 1, 1979, when Johnson suffered an ankle injury and exited the game against undefeated OSU. After Gregory Kelser had fouled out, he re-entered the game and led his team to overcome the undefeated OSU squad in overtime 84-79 (see

"Great State Dates"). The second was Johnson's last game as a Spartan, the 1979 NCAA final four. He led the team with 24 points and seven rebounds and entertained 15,410 fans while convincingly defeating Larry Bird and the previously undefeated Indiana State Sycamores, 75-64.

A two-time All-American and All-Big Ten selection, Magic had no trouble making the record books, despite only competing for two years at the collegiate level. Until Charlie Bell did it in 2000, Johnson was the only Spartan ever to record a triple-double, and he accomplished that feat eight times. In his first year, he racked up 17.0 points and 7.9 rebounds per game and set new freshman records in ten categories, ranking second in two others. All but two of those freshman records have never been surpassed. In just two years, he also set several career records. He ranked first in total assists with 491 and second in steals with 146, just two behind teammate Gregory Kelser. Anyone who has surpassed either of these records needed four seasons to do what Johnson did in two. In addition, Magic ranked fourth in career free throws with 363, seventh in scoring average with 17.1, and 12th in total points with 1,059. As for single season records, he set four marks that still stand today. In his sophomore year he made 202 free throws off 240 attempts, dished out 174 assists and ripped away 75 steals.

IN THE SPARTLITE

Baseball: State hosted the NCAA District IV play-offs, first losing to Pepperdine, 15-0, then defeating Miami (Ohio), 6-4, before being eliminated by San Diego State, 5-4.

Rodger Bastien finished the year with a .357 batting average and was named an NCAA District IV first team All-American along with teammate Ken Mehall. The Spartan squad went on to the NCAA tournament but was eliminated in the regionals.

Basketball: By the time the Spartans had reached Madison, Wis., for the concluding game on the regular season's schedule, they had won 26 games, and a bid to the NCAA tournament was a lock. A win against the Badgers would mean a coveted outright conference championship. The fact that it didn't happen was one matter, but how it didn't happen was exasperating. With the game

tied at 81-81 and three seconds remaining, Wisconsin's Wes Matthews raced the ball up the court and launched a two-handed 55-footer that caromed off the glass and through the hoop with no time remaining. It was the team's fourth Big Ten loss on a buzzer-beater and forced a share of the title with Purdue and Iowa.

Cross Country: A young harrier team made improvement to finish sixth in the Big Ten with a 2-6 dual-meet record. They just missed qualifying for the NCAA meet, though three freshman did reach the District Four meet. Mark Mesler placed 18th with a time of 25:16, Martin Schulist was 25th at 25:29 and Michael White was 29th with 25:39.

Fencing: Junior Bryan Peterman won a Big Ten epee championship to earn some fame for himself, his school and his family. Bryan's twin brothers, Bradley and Barry, freshman at MSU, were also epeeists on the team, and they had all followed in the footsteps of their older brother Bill, who had fenced in East Lansing from 1974 to 1977. The brothers had begun fencing at their New Jersey high school and were two of the few with experience prior to college. With his 1979 crown, Bryan became the most successful of the four. When defending his title in 1980, he would be forced to withdraw from the conference tournament after suffering a knee injury from an opponent's weapon, but he would enter the NCAA tournament and finish sixth, a feat for which he was named second team All-American.

Football: Those who came through the turnstiles to watch the 1978 Spartans play, by many categories, witnessed the most explosive offensive unit ever to represent the Green and White. Over the 11-game schedule, they gained 5,294 yards of offense (passing and rushing), the highest total ever registered by a State team. That averaged to 481.2 yards per contest, another team record. The total points rung up, 411, is tops for any Michigan State team. Likewise for four additional categories: average points per game (37.4), total touchdowns (56), total first downs (265) and average first downs per game (24.1).

The defense wasn't too shabby either, allowing an average of only 15.4 points per game. Only three teams since can boast of more impressive numbers (1987, 1988 and 1989).

Consensus first team All-Big Ten selections included end Eugene Bird, offensive tackle Jim Hinesly, defensive tackle Melvin Land, defensive back Tommy Graves, tight end Mark Brammer and flanker Kirk Gibson. The latter two, Brammer and Gibson, were chosen to select All-American teams.

Tight end Mark Brammer started every game from his sophomore through senior years (1977-79). The 1978 All-American displayed his talent with this magnificent catch over Michigan defenders.

Golf: Continuing to schedule spring invitational meets (the last dual meet was in 1973), the Spartans participated in seven such multi-team meets in 1979, including their own Spartan Invitational. Their best efforts were third place finishes at both the Illinois Invitational and the Michigan Invitational.

At the Big Ten meet in Savoy, Ill., State finished third behind the two best conference teams since 1973, Ohio State and Indiana.

Gymnastics: George Szypula's team finished a disappointing sixth place at the Big Ten meet. Spartan all-arounder Marvin Gibbs was the top scorer, placing fifth. The NCAA regional tournament was a little brighter, however, as MSU placed eighth overall. Charlie Jenkins finished fifth on the parallel bars and third on the vault, qualifying for the national championships in both events.

Hockey: On March 3, just prior to the opening face-off in the final game of the 1978-1979 season, it was announced that 62-year old Amo Bessone would be coaching his final Spartan game. Following a brief ceremony at center ice, which included the presentation of a hockey stick signed by members of the opposing team,

the University of Michigan, the Munn Arena crowd of 5,685 gave the veteran coach a standing ovation. The evening was made complete when his team topped the Wolverines, 5-3.

Lacrosse: The most successful season ever by an MSU lacrosse team ended with a 9-7 overall record. Kevin Willitts scored 70 goals and 98 points for Spartan records that still stand far above the rest. Willitts was voted MVP at the honors banquet, while former lacrosse superstar Val Washington was awarded the first Distinguished Alumni Award.

Soccer: Joe Baum's soccer team had it hard at the Big Ten Classic. The first game went down in the record books as a 1-1 tie with Wisconsin, and indeed it was so at the end of regulation time. A winner must be decided in tournaments, however, so the game actually continued in play that is not reflected by the books. After a ten-minute overtime period, the game was still tied and a shoot-out ensued in which each team would take five shots on goal. Mike Price scored one for MSU, but the Badgers retaliated with one of their own. The teams were finally launched into a second overtime period during which Wisconsin managed to score once to end the game, 3-2, and advance to the finals. This long battle exhausted the Spartans before their consolation game in which OSU defeated them 5-2.

Swimming and Diving: A predominantly freshman team finished ninth in the conference meet, the lowest place ever for an MSU swim team. Senior Jeff Gaeckle took fifth in the 200-yard butterfly and 13th in the 100-yard butterfly, while sophomore Jeff Prange placed ninth on the one-meter board and 10th on the three-meter. Three new varsity records were set during the competition. Freshman Chris Rock set a new standard with a 4:10.85 in the 400-yard individual medley, while Rob Lundquist swam 59.21 and 2:09.02 to better times in both breaststroke events.

Tennis: It was not a very successful Big Ten tournament for the youthful a young team that went to Columbus and finished eighth in Big Ten tournament. The number two doubles team of Matt Sandler and Jeff

Wickman, each having lost in the singles semi-finals, performed well for the Spartans, losing to U of M in the finals. The Wolverines won their 12th consecutive conference title. Sandler made the All-Conference team.

Track and Field: Junior Randy Smith became a Big Ten indoor three-time champion in the 60-yard dash, running a respectable 6.28. Competing in the conference's inaugural running of the 1,000 meters, Keith Moore captured first place with a time of 2:10.2. As a team, MSU scored 57 points, good enough for a fourth-place finish.

At the NCAA indoor meet, Moore and Smith each earned All-American status, placing fourth and sixth in their events, respectively. Tyrone Williams also finished sixth in the finals. Earning five points, the Spartans were only topped by two other Big Ten schools.

In the Big Ten Outdoor Championships conducted in Ann Arbor, State dropped to a sixth-place finish, but Ricky Flowers continued to star as he qualified for the NCAAs by winning the 400 meters in a conference record time of 46.13. He later returned to the track for a gold-medal performance in the 200-meter race.

Wrestling: At the Big Ten championships in Iowa City, State placed fourth behind Iowa, Wisconsin and Minnesota. Mike Walsh, at 134 pounds, took second place for the second year in a row; 177-pound Jim Ellis settled for third place; Charlie Schoen managed a fourth at 190 pounds; and Shawn Whitcomb was a surprise winner in the heavyweight division. All four traveled to Ames, Iowa, for the NCAA meet, but they combined for only six and one fourth points and a 31st place team finish.

EXTRA! 1979 NCAA BASKETBALL TOURNAMENT

The 1979 Michigan State team won the NCAA championship that year. The following are the Spartans' box scores for those games.

MICHIGAN STATE 95–LAMAR 64

	FG-FGA	FT-FTA	REB	A	PF	TP
Kelser	12-21	7-10	14	3	3	31
Johnson	6-14	1-1	17	10	1	13
Vincent	5-10	1-2	3	1	2	11
Donnelly	3-5	0-0	0	2	3	6
M. Brkovich	6-7	0-0	2	3	1	12
Lloyd	0-0	0-1	1	0	0	0
Charles	6-9	0-2	3	0	2	12
Longaker	0-1	1-2	1	0	0	1
Huffman	1-1	0-1	1	0	0	2
Gonzalez	1-2	0-0	2	0	3	2
Kaye	2-2	0-0	1	0	1	4
Gilkie	0-0	1-2	1	0	0	1
D. Brkovich	0-0	0-0	0	0	0	0
Team			4			
TOTALS	42-72	11-21	50	19	16	95

Halftime: Michigan State 46-27; **Officials:** not available; **Attendance:** 10,928.

Randy Smith, three-time champion in the Big Ten indoor 60-yard dash

MICHIGAN STATE 87–LOUISIANA STATE 71

	FG-FGA	FT-FTA	REB	A	PF	TP
M. Brkovich	4-7	3-4	3	3	0	11
Kelser	6-15	3-5	9	1	5	15
Charles	6-10	6-10	14	1	1	18
Donnelly	2-5	0-0	1	2	2	4
Johnson	5-16	14-15	5	12	2	24
Gonzalez	4-7	1-2	1	0	1	9
Longaker	1-3	0-0	0	0	1	2
Kaye	1-1	0-0	1	0	1	2
Lloyd	0-0	0-0	0	1	2	0
D. Brkovich	1-1	0-0	1	1	0	2
Gilkie	0-1	0-0	0	0	0	0
Team			4			
TOTALS	30-66	27-36	39	21	15	87

Halftime: Michigan State 36-19; **Officials:** Herrold, Pavia, Buckiewicz; **Attendance:** 16,823.

MICHIGAN STATE 80–NOTRE DAME 68

	FG-FGA	FT-FTA	REB	A	PF	TP
M. Brkovich	5-10	3-4	4	1	3	13
Kelser	12-25	4-8	13	1	4	34
Charles	2-4	2-2	4	0	4	6
Donnelly	1-1	2-2	2	0	3	4
Johnson	6-10	7-8	5	13	2	19
Gonzalez	1-2	0-0	3	0	0	2
Vincent	1-2	0-0	0	0	0	2
Longaker	0-0	0-0	0	0	0	0
Team			3			
TOTALS	31-54	18-24	33	15	16	80

Halftime: Michigan State 34-23; **Officials:** Buckiewicz, Herrold, Turner; **Attendance:** 17,423.

MICHIGAN STATE 101–PENN 67

	FG-FGA	FT-FTA	REB	A	PF	TP
M. Brkovich	6-10	0-0	1	3	4	12
Kelser	12-19	4-6	9	3	2	28
Charles	2-2	0-0	6	0	0	4
Donnelly	3-5	0-0	3	3	0	6
Johnson	9-10	11-12	10	10	2	29
Vincent	0-1	3-4	1	0	2	3
Gonzalez	1-5	0-0	3	1	2	2
Longaker	2-2	0-0	2	1	0	4
Lloyd	0-2	6-7	1	1	1	6
Kaye	2-2	1-3	2	1	1	5
Huffman	0-0	0-1	2	1	2	0
Gilkie	0-1	0-0	1	0	1	0
D. Brkovich	1-1	0-1	1	0	1	2
Team			3			
TOTALS	38-60	25-34	44	24	22	101

Halftime: Michigan State 50-17; **Officials:** Buckiewicz, Weiler, Silvester; **Attendance:** not available.

MICHIGAN STATE 75–INDIANA STATE 64

	FG-FGA	FT-FTA	REB	A	PF	TP
M. Brkovich	1-2	3-7	4	1	1	5
Kelser	7-13	5-6	8	9	4	19
Charles	3-3	1-2	7	0	5	7
Donnelly	5-5	5-6	4	0	2	15
Johnson	8-15	8-10	7	5	3	24
Vincent	2-5	1-2	2	0	4	5
Gonzalez	0-0	0-0	0	0	0	0
Longaker	0-0	0-0	0	0	0	0
Team			2			
TOTALS	26-43	23-33	34	15	19	75

Halftime: Michigan State 37-28; **Officials:** Nichols, Muncy, Wirtz; **Attendance:** 15,410.

TALES TO TELL

When athletic director Joe Kearney opted to leave Michigan State for Arizona State there were some hurt feelings in East Lansing and, initially, some lashing out of "How could he?" At the time there was speculation that Kearney had discovered that working with MSU's newly appointed president, Cecil Mackey (1979-1985), was not bearable. Although Kearney, now retired, is too much a gentleman to outwardly confess to such theory, a reader might deduct such thinking from the following telephone interview conducted in 2003 to his winter home in Arizona. Kearney:

"While at the 1980 NCAA convention [January 7-9] in New Orleans, I was approached by Arizona State University personnel and eventually met with their president and vice-president. As you recall, ASU was recoiling from the turmoil of an NCAA investigation pertaining to irregularities in their athletic program. The fact that I had faced a similar situation upon arrival at Michigan State in 1976 may have

Coach Rogers (left) talks with Joe Kearney (right).

HEADLINES of 1980

- The U.S. hockey team beat the Soviet Union during the Winter Olympics at Lake Placid, N.Y., on their way to winning the gold medal..."Do you believe in miracles?"
- Post-it notes enter the market, revolutionizing the office and the refrigerator door.
- Mt. St. Helens, a volcano in Washington state, erupts and continues to erupt intermittently throughout the year.
- Ted Koppel's *Nightline* is first aired on ABC and TV's first all-news service begins with Ted Turner's Cable News Network (CNN).

SCOREBOARD

	W	L	T	Avg.
Baseball	15	35	0	.300
Track and Field	1	3	0	.250
Football	5	6	0	.455
Basketball	12	15	0	.444
Tennis	4	16	0	.200
Cross Country	5	1	0	.833
Swimming and Diving	6	5	0	.545
Wrestling	11	8	1	.575
Hockey	14	24	0	.368
Fencing	9	7	0	.563
Golf	tournament play only			
Gymnastics	6	6	0	.500
Soccer	9	6	2	.588
Lacrosse	8	10	0	.444

made me a more viable candidate for the people at Arizona State, but I don't recall that being an expressed factor. I did, however, have suspicions that I was their number one candidate. They talked more money, [than earnings at MSU], but not astronomically so. At that time I was not looking for a move, but, the offer and possibility of returning to the West immediately intrigued me. After all, both my wife and I had spent a good deal of our lives out here. I don't recall exactly how much time it took to make the decision to move, but a fairly quick resolution seemed desirable.

Was the change of presidency at Michigan State a factor in my decision? Only to the extent that the new president [Cecil Mackey] presented an unknown. I had had a wonderful working relationship with Edgar Harden [MSU's president, 1978-1979]…he was a 'dream president' for an athletic director. He was a 'people person' with a strong identity and deep loyalty to the athletic program. Every administrator has his style and that is one's prerogative, but in the case of President Mackey…he presented an unknown.

My first charge upon arriving in Tempe was to hire a football coach. Naturally, I thought of Darryl [Rogers], but had no idea of whether he was interested in making the move. It didn't take long. I made the call. He came out for an interview and that was all that it took.

The decision to leave Michigan State was not an easy one. We had a great experience there and we still have many fond memories of those four years. It is an outstanding institution with many pros and I liked the land-grant philosophy with the commitment to service.

The feeling of being appreciated at State was most vividly expressed when I was back on campus to wrap things up shortly after we had moved. While walking through the lobby of Kellogg Center, John Hannah spotted me and motioned me over to him. Putting his hand on my shoulder he said: 'Young man, first, I want to thank you for what you have done for the athletic program here at Michigan State. You will be missed. Secondly, you should know that if I was still president you would still be here as athletic director.'"

Joe Kearney remained at Arizona State for only 18 weeks whereupon he became commissioner of the Western Athletic Conference (WAC). As he would later paraphrase, "They made me an offer I couldn't refuse."

The 1980 wrestling squad, including Jeff Thomas (second row, second from the left) Fred Worthem (ninth from the left), Jeff Therrian (third row, third from the left) and Shawn Whitcomb, (sixth from the right).

TEAM OF THE YEAR

The 50-3 win over Pittsburgh was the highest score ever achieved by a Spartan team in a dual meet. After going through the conference season with a 6-2-1 record, Michigan State hosted the Big Ten championships in Jenison. Collecting 41.25 points, the Spartans finished fourth behind Iowa, Wisconsin and Minnesota. Senior Jeff Thomas, a number three seed at 126 pounds, dominated his first two opponents 22-5 and 12-6 and then gained the title by upsetting the number one seed from Minnesota, 15-5. Also reaching the finals was sophomore Fred Worthem (158 pounds), who eventually lost to the Gophers' defending champion and 1980 meet MVP. Jeff Therrian finished third at 142 pounds and the defending heavyweight champion, Shawn Whitcomb, settled for fourth place.

Jeff Thomas went on to earn All-American honors with an eighth-place finish at the NCAA championships in Eugene, Ore. MSU as a team placed in a three-way tie for 25th with 11.5 points. Three other qualifiers, Therrian, Worthem and Whitcomb, won two matches apiece but failed to place.

MAKING HISTORY

In late November, the National Cable Company, which served more than 9,000 TV subscribers in East Lansing and Meridian Township, joined up with Entertainment and Sports Programming Network (ESPN) bringing selected sports shows to home viewers. Running 24 hours on Saturday and Sunday and about 10 hours on weekdays, it was suggested that ESPN would soon be a 24-hour per day programming source.

Terry Furlow, scoring star of the 1973-1976 MSU basketball teams, was killed in a one-car accident in Cleveland, where he had been a member of that city's NBA team.

Fred Stabley, serving MSU as sports information director for 33 years, retired from his position in the spring of 1980 and was replaced by his longtime assistant, Nick Vista. Mike Pearson, a 1975 graduate of MSU and coordinator of athletic promotions at Western Michigan, became the new assistant SID.

Stabley was one of seven media experts selected to serve on the USA Olympic Committee's staff for the XIII Winter Games at Lake Placid, N.Y.

With the USA boycott of the XIX Summer Olympics in Moscow, Russia, three Spartans—diver Dave Burgering, diver Kevin Machemer and rower Mark O'Brien—were denied the opportunity to compete for the United States.

A rare 125-meter portable "velodrome" track was temporarily installed in Demonstration Hall and six-days of bicycle racing were conducted featuring riders from Australia, Canada, California, Arizona, Indiana, Pennsylvania and Michigan. The MSU pair of Detroiter Cristoff Meingast and James Ochowicz from Lake Placid, N.Y., were the eventual winners.

Four former Spartans were on the rosters of four major league baseball teams, Steve Garvey with the Los Angeles Dodgers, Ron Pruitt with the Cleveland Indians, Rick Miller of the California Angels and Kirk Gibson with the Tigers.

GREAT STATE DATES

Football—**September 15, 1979 (H):** Filling in for the injured Bruce Reeves, Derek Hughes scored three touchdowns as State cruised to a 41-17 victory over the University of Oregon. Along with Hughes' first score and two Morten Anderson field goals, a 41-yard Bert Vaughn to Eugene Byrd scoring pass-play gave the Spartans a 20-10 halftime lead. After the Ducks closed the margin with a third quarter touchdown, MSU responded with three unanswered TDs, including Derek Hughes' team record-setting 100-yard kickoff return. A Dan Bass interception and 18-yard return to the visitor's 19 set Hughes up for his third score and Rick Milhizer's fumble recovery at the Oregon 36-yard line gave Steve Smith the opportunity to close out the scoring with a one-yard dive into the end zone. Smith, who was celebrating his 20th birthday, was the leading ground gainer with 154 yards on 23 carries. Bass and Steve Otis spearheaded the defense.

Cross Country—**September 29, 1979 (H):** Michigan State registered a perfect 15-48 score in defeating Kent State on a Saturday morning run over the hilly Forest Akers course. Team captain Mark Mesler led the field as he broke the tape in 24:54.6. He was followed (second place through fifth place) by Thad Unold, Keith Moore, Mike White and Martin Schulist. Four additional Spartans completed the race before the fifth and final Golden Flash had reached the finish line. It was the second MSU victory on the way to a 5-1 dual-meet season.

Soccer—**October 13, 1979 (A):** After winning five of the first six games, the soccer team followed with a 0-2-1 record in the next three contests. In a pivotal match to get the season back on track, the Spartans traveled to Bloomington, Ind., for the first round of the Big Ten East Division Classic. MSU responded with a 2-0 shutout win over Ohio State. Mark Neterer scored in the first half, while Steve Schad provided the final goal in the second. It was the fifth shutout of the season for Spartan goalie Rob Grinter.

Hockey—**October 19, 1979 (A):** MSU 7, Western Michigan 6. The season-opening win over the Broncos would be coach Ron Mason's first as Michigan State's head coach and the beginning of a lengthy 23-year career behind the Spartan bench. State jumped to an early 4-0 lead on goals by Paul Gottwald, Conrad Wiggam, Arron Rucks and Joe Omiccioli. Ken Paraskevin and Leo Lynett added scores in the second. Ted Huesing's marker at 5:08 of the final stanza actually proved to be the winner as Western kept in the game with one goal in the first, two in the second and three in the third as they outshot the Green and White, 52-28.

Football—**November 10, 1979 (H):** Contrary to coach Darryl Rogers's style, the offense in the season finale against Minnesota was totally a running show, void of one single-pass completion. On a pair of Derek Hughes's touchdowns and a Morten Anderson 53-yard field goal with only two seconds remaining before intermission, State led at the half 17-3. The energized Gophers returned to the game and quickly tied the score, but Hughes responded with two more TDs to complete the scoring and secure MSU's fifth win of the season, 31-17. It had been a busy afternoon for Derek as he accounted for 213 of State's 385 rushing yards and his four-touchdown performance equaled a team record. Unknown at the time, this would be Rogers's final home game as head coach, two months later he would leave for Tempe, Ariz., to become the new coach at Arizona State.

Hockey—**December 1, 1979 (H):** Before a sellout crowd of 6,549 at Munn Ice Arena, State scored four power play goals en route to a 6-3 win over Michigan. The victory marked the first time a Ron Mason-coached Spartan team would defeat the U of M, a feat that would be duplicated 55 times before his retirement in 2002. MSU led 2-1 after the opening 20 minutes on a rebound tip-in by Frank Finn plus Mark Hamway's 45-foot wrist shoot. The Spartans added three goals (Ken Paraskevin, Mike Stoltzner and Finn) in the second period, two with a one-man advantage. The final tally also came with the Wolverines short-handed as Hamway deflected in a Leo Lynett slap shot with 5:45 remaining in the contest.

Wrestling—**January 14, 1980 (H):** In the first-ever dual meet against Penn State, Grady Peninger's squad totally dominated the afternoon by capturing the first seven matches and eight overall for a 32-9 victory. The parade of Spartan winners included Harrell Milhouse (118 pounds), Chuck Joseph (126 pounds), Jeff Thomas (134 pounds), Jeff Therrian (142 pounds), Greg Sargis with a pin at 150 pounds, Fred Worthem (158 pounds) and Steve Foley (167 pounds). After losses by Jeff Layer (177 pounds) and Scott Shepard (190 pounds), Dan Dudley (heavyweight) completed the scoring by pinning his opponent at 6:41.

Basketball—**January 17, 1980 (H):** With 18 seconds of playing time remaining, the University of Wisconsin upped their advantage to 61-58 on a converted free throw. However, the Spartans were not yet ready to

concede as Terry Donnelly hurried down court and hit a five-foot jumper to cut the deficit to one point with now six seconds remaining on the game clock. Being pressed all over the court, the beleaguered Badger fired the ensuing inbound pass out of bounds and MSU made the best of this final "gift" opportunity. With the time still frozen at six seconds, Jay Vincent fed a perfect pass into Kevin Smith under the basket for a reverse lay-up and suddenly State was leading 62-61. Wisconsin still had an opportunity for a full court desperation shot which was picked off by Smith and the Jenison floor became an immediate mob scene as students flooded the playing surface.

Swimming and Diving—**January 18, 1980 (H):** State lost both relays but did manage to take seven of the 11 individual events and edge the University of Illinois, 59-54, for the fourth win of the season. Sprinter Mark Lancaster was the meet's only double winner as he swam a 22.01 50-yard freestyle and a 47.63 in the 100-yard freestyle. Other winners were Matt Fetters in the 1,000-yard freestyle (9:52.48); Mike Borre, in the individual medley (1:58.54); George Kruggel in the 200-yard butterfly (1:54.88); Rob Lundquist in the 200-yard breaststroke (2:11.36) and diver Matt Johnson on the three-meter board. Scoring valuable team points with second-place finishes were: Terry Inch, Peter Saggau, Dan Mejer along with Johnson, Lundquist and Fetters.

Basketball—**January 24, 1980 (A):** Trailing by 11 points at intermission, MSU came back to outscore Michigan 31-20 during the second half, sending the game into overtime. With the score knotted at 58-58 and two minutes remaining in the extra session, Jay Vincent missed the front end of a one-and-one. Following a Wolverine turnover, Vincent was once more fouled, this time while shooting. With merely three seconds remaining the Lansing senior again failed on the opening attempt but did connect on a second try. Thereafter, Michigan was unable to get a shot off, sealing the MSU victory, 59-58. In the game Ron Charles shot a perfect 12-for-12 from the floor, setting a standard which remains in the Spartan record book.

Basketball—**January 31, 1980 (H):** Urged on by a sellout crowd at Jenison, the Spartans upset Ohio State, the nation's sixth-ranked team, 74-54. With a string of victories that reached back to 1973, it was Michigan State's 14th straight win over OSU. Scoring eight of the first 10 points after intermission, MSU built on its 31-24 lead at the break and established total control. The game became a foul-shooting exhibition over the final ten min-

utes and Jud Heathcote's squad responded by connecting on 26 of 31 from the line. Jay Vincent led all scorers with 21 points and a game-high 14 rebounds. Others scoring in double figures were Mike Brkovich with 13 points and Terry Donnelly with 12. Donnelly, the senior co-captain from St. Louis, Mo., played a remarkable defensive game as he held the Buckeyes' high-scoring ace Kelvin Ransey to one field goal and six total points. Ransey, an All-Big Ten selection had scored in double figures in his preceding 80 games.

Wrestling—**February 8, 1980 (H):** Capturing the first eight matches by decisions, Grady Peninger's squad totally dominated the U of M and coasted to a 26-7 victory before an appreciative packed house in the IM Sports Arena. The winning Spartans were Harrell Milhouse, Chuck Joseph, Jeff Thomas, Greg Sargis, Fred Worthem and Steve Foley with Jeff Therrian and Jim Ellis gaining additional team points on major decisions. The evening streak of wins came to an end when freshman Scott Shepard suffered a loss at 190 pounds and heavyweight Shawn Whitcomb dropped a 6-1 decision in the final match.

Fencing—**February 16, 1980 (A):** In a five-team meet at Notre Dame, the Spartans defeated Purdue 17-10 and the University of Illinois-Chicago, 22-5. Senior Bryan Peterman was a perfect 11-0 for the day in epee, increasing his season record to 33-4. His sophomore brother Barry posted a 7-4 mark in epee. In foil, senior Chris Young was 7-4, while juniors John Chambers and Jon Thomas led the sabre group with 8-4 and 6-6 records respectively.

Gymnastics—**February 16, 1980 (A):** In a triple-dual meet at Madison, Wis., State defeated the host Badgers 255.05-252.85 and Western Michigan 255.05-239.80. Marvin Gibbs placed first on the parallel bars against both Wisconsin and the Broncos, while Rich Licata took top honors on the horizontal bars. Ivan Merritt captured first place in floor exercise against both opponents and Pete Roberts was the top vaulter in the meet against WMU.

Basketball—**February 16, 1980 (H):** Trailing by 10 with 9:30 remaining in the contest, MSU poured it on the Michigan Wolverines throughout the remainder of the game, outscoring the visitors 29-11 for an 82-74 win and a sweep of the season series. Jay Vincent was once again a dominating force as he scored a game-high 36 points on 13 of 21 shots from the floor and 10 of 15 from the free throw line. Two U of M players fouled out

All for one: (left to right) fencers and brothers Barry, Bryan and Brad Peterman

attempting to contain Vincent and a third finished with four fouls. Mike Brkovich added 14 points, Terry Donnelly contributed 13 and Ron Charles finished with 11.

Fencing—**February 23, 1980 (H):** In their final home appearance of the season, a four-team match, the fencers managed to top Detroit 17-10, Tri-State 21-6, and Illinois-Chicago, 22-5. Brad Peterman led the epee group with a 5-1 mark followed by Ward Best and brother Barry Peterman at 4-1 and brother Bryan at 2-0. Jon Thomas posted a 5-1 record in sabre with Brian Morrow at 4-2 and John Chambers at 3-3. In foil, Dominic Marazita was 5-1 while Chris Young finished at 2-2.

Gymnastics—**February 28, 1980 (H):** Punctuated by wins in the final two events on the evening program, State defeated Michigan in a battle of fractional points, 262.60 to 262.10. Juniors Marvin Gibbs, Greg Bosscawen, Terry Olsen and Pedro Sanches finished first-through-fourth on the parallel bars and Rick Lakata scored an impressive 9.55 for first place on the high bar to clinch the team victory. Gibbs tied for first with teammate Hubert Streep on the pommel horse and along with first on the vault, third in floor exercise, fourth on the high bar and fifth on the rings he scored a career-high 54.85 points to gain the all-around honors.

Hockey—**February 29, 1980 (H):** With a 5-4 defeat of Michigan on the final weekend of the regular season, Ron Mason's crew edged Wisconsin by .005 percentage points for eighth place and the final spot in the Western Collegiate Hockey Association playoffs. It would be the Spartans' first post-season appearance in four years. The game-winner against the Wolverines came from freshman Bob Martin at the 16:54 mark in the third period much to the delight of the 6,483 fans. With a one-man advantage, Leo Lynett, the team's leading scorer, opened the game on a power-play goal with less than two minutes to play in the opening period.

Tennis—**April 4, 1980 (H):** Forced indoors to the Lansing Racquet Club by the weather conditions, State defeated the Boilermakers of Purdue, 6-3. Five of MSU's six points were recorded in singles competition by: number one Steve Yorimoto's 6-4, 6-1; number two Matt Sandler 1-6, 7-6, 7-6; number three Scott King 3-6, 7-5, 6-3; number four Jeff Wickman 7-5, 6-2 and number five Dino Demare 6-2, 1-6, 6-3. The final team point was credited to the number two doubles team of Yorimoto-King, 6-4, 6-4.

Lacrosse—**April 19, 1980 (H):** The laxers evened their Midwest Lacrosse Association record at 2-2 with a 6-5 win over Wooster College. It was a game in which the defense was most impressive as goal tender Jim Sanford stopped 15 shots. Also singled out by co-coach Kanner for their "D" were Mark Purcell, Ken Horan, Greg Purcell, and Mike Morgan. Art Barry's goal at 11:25 of the fourth quarter proved to be the game-winner as it gave State a 6-4 lead. At 14:20 the Fighting Scots closed the margin to one before time ran out on them. The Spartan goals were spread among six different players: Kevin Willitts, Duane Andersen, Shawn Grady, Greg Helgemoe, Dan McNulty and Barry.

Track and Field—May 3, 1980 (H): The Spartans collected 70 points to win a triangular meet over Purdue with 58 and Ohio State at 53. The sprint quartet of Randy Smith, Don Muhammad, Ken Eaton and Ricky Flowers opened the afternoon with a first place in the 440-yard relay in the time of 40.76 and the foursome of Andre Williams, Tim Kenney, Calvin Thomas and Flowers closed the afternoon with a winning 3:14.55 in the mile relay. MSU displayed particular strength in sprints. Smith won the 100-meter dash in 10.49 and was followed by teammates Muhammad in second (10.84) with sophomore Andre Williams in fourth (10.98). Smith also finished first in the 200-meters (20.8) with Eaton in third (21.4). Other Michigan State winners were Thad Unold, who ran 3:52.9 in the 1,500-meters; Paul Piwinski with a 6' 10" leap in the high jump; intermediate hurdler Williams in 52.76 and Martin Schulist, who finished the 5,000-meter run in 14.51.9.

Track and Field—May 10, 1980 (H): The Spartans won only four of the nine individual running races but did capture both relay races and four of the six field events in a 82-63 dual-meet win over Eastern Michigan. In addition to leading off the victorious 440-meter relay, Randy Smith was a double winner as he captured the 200-meter dash in 21.2 and the 100-meters in a school record time of 10.1. Jerome Judd also registered two wins as he finished first in both the long jump (22' 9 1/2") and triple jump (46' 1/4"). Other winners for MSU were Randy Smith with a win in the 400 meter (47.2), David Prieskorn in the discus (146' 10"), pole vaulter Mark Zuverink (15') and Andre Williams on the intermediate hurdles (53.1).

Baseball—May 11, 1980 (H): The Spartans defeated Ohio State, 12-4, as Kirk Haines blasted a pair of home runs which produced five runs, enough to give senior right-hander Brian Wolcott his 23rd career win, which tied him with Larry Ike (1970-1972) for MSU's all-time record. Outhitting the Buckeyes 11-5, Coach Litwhiler saw his squad use two productive innings to dominate the game. In the opening frame Jim Buterakos scored ahead of Haines's first homer and Tim Barnes singled home another pair for a total of four. Barnes added another run-scoring base hit in the third before MSU sent nine men to the plate and tallied six runs in the fourth. Haines's three-run round-tripper highlighted that inning and shortstop Al Dankovich drove in two more with his bases-loaded single.

Lacrosse—May 17, 1980 (H): The Spartans scored the most goals of their season in a 17-3 drubbing of the Detroit Lacrosse Club in the final game of the year. Jay Hungerford led the offensive charge, scoring five goals and one assist for six points. Senior Kevin Willitts, MSU's all-time leading scorer, had another outstanding game. He scored two goals and passed off four assists to close out a remarkable collegiate career. It was the final game for co-coaches Nevin Kanner and Boku Hendrickson.

ATHLETE OF THE YEAR

A four-year starter, punter Ray Stachowicz earned All-America honors as a junior in 1979 by the *Football News* and as a senior in 1980 by the Walter Camp Foundation, *Football News* and the Newspaper Enterprise Association. Kicking for a 43.8-yard average in 1979, Ray led the Big Ten and was fifth nationally. In the senior season of 1980 he increased his average to a Big Ten record 46.2 yards which was second-best nationally. Stachowicz's career average of 43.3 yards ranks him as the conference all-time leader and he holds claim to the honor of being the first player ever to earn first-team All-Big Ten honors four consecutive seasons. The team record book reveals that four times during his Spartan career he lofted punts for 72 or more yards. The Brecksville, Ohio, punting specialist was picked by the Green Bay Packers in the third round of the 1981 National Football League draft and he would spend four years in the NFL.

Ray Stachowicz

IN THE SPARTLITE

Baseball: State opened the regular season with an infield consisting of three sophomores and a freshman. All-Big Ten selection sophomore Chris Dorr was at first base, second base was handled by switch-hitting freshman Tom Dieters, sophomore Al Dankovich, moved from third to shortstop and sophomore Frank Gunder won the third base position with his defensive play.

Senior outfielder Ken Robinson led the team in hitting with a .314 batting average. Robinson also was the team leader in hits (48), home runs (six), RBI (27) and runs (30).

Freshman southpaw Terry Johnson was the team's top pitcher. Johnson won five games and posted a 2.53 ERA in 60.1 innings of work. He was also used as a designated hitter and finished with a .333 average.

Basketball: Just one year removed from the NCAA champions of 1979, the 12-15 overall record of the 1979-1980 team was a total letdown for MSU's loyal supporters. Epitomizing the weird season of 1979-1980 was the 75-73 triple-overtime loss to Northwestern in the final home game of the season. State had numerous opportunities for the win before the Cats hit the clincher with three seconds remaining in the third OT. It was one of the seven losses in the final eight games on the schedule.

Jay Vincent won the Big Ten scoring crown with a 22.1 ppg average and also earned first-team All-Big Ten honors and third team All-American. In addition, Vincent was named MSU's Most Valuable Player.

Ron Charles was named most improved, while Terry Donnelly took home Defensive Player of the Year honors. Charles set a new MSU record for best field-goal percentage in a single season with a .676 mark, eclipsing his own record of .665 set during the 1978-1979 season. Charles's 51 blocked shots was second-best in an MSU season.

Michael Longaker was the first men's basketball player to be awarded the Dr. James Feurig Achievement and Service Award, which is presented to a graduating senior for athletic and academic success and who demonstrates involvement in school/campus and community activities. Only two other basketball players have been awarded this honor since.

Donnelly is one of four Spartans in MSU basketball history to be awarded the Chester Brewer Leadership Award, which is presented to a graduating senior for athletic and academic achievement and for possessing a high degree of character, leadership qualities and skill.

Cross Country: While Mark Mesler claimed three first-place finishes during the dual-meet season, as a team MSU went 5-1, including a 20-35 win over Michigan.

Martin Schulist was the top Spartan in the 8K Big Ten championship meet at Columbus, Ohio, with a seventh-place finish (23:57). Mark Mesler was 26th (24:28); Michael White 32nd (24:36); Keith Moore 36th (24:37) and Tim Kerr 40th (25:05). MSU finished in sixth place, ahead of Ohio State, Purdue, Iowa and Northwestern.

In what Coach Jim Gibbard called "our best race of the year," Michigan State hosted and finished fifth out of 20 teams in the 10K District IV championships. Schulist was again the top finisher for State as he placed fifth (32:21).

Fencing: It was a disappointing Big Ten championship meet for Charlie Schmitter's fencers as they collected only 17 points to finish fourth in the five-team field. Bryan Peterman, the defending epee champion, suffered an accidental slash on his knee in his second bout that necessitated seven stitches to close. He was forced to withdraw from competition and finished in tenth place. Top finishers in that conference meet were brother Barry Peterman with a fifth in epee, and senior Chris Young's fifth in foil while juniors Jon Thomas and John Chambers placed seventh and eighth, respectively, in sabre.

Bryan Peterman would later place sixth at the NCAA championships and be named as second team All-American. His final season record was 60-14 leading to his selection as the team's MVP.

Football: Dan Bass, a linebacker from little Bath, Mich., set an MSU record 32 tackles in a 42-0 loss to Ohio State. He concluded his four-year Spartan football career (1976-1979) having been credited with 541 tackles. This total remains as a team record.

Morten Andersen kicked a 54-yard field goal against Iowa, which at the time tied for the longest field goal in MSU history. He would later better that mark in 1980 and again in 1981.

Derek Hughes returned a kickoff 100 yards for a touchdown in the second game of the season, a 41-17 win over Oregon. It was the first time a Spartan had run for a 100-yard touchdown return. It has been done three other times since. Hughes followed his record-breaking performance with a 98-yard kickoff return for a touchdown in the sixth game of the season at Wisconsin.

In the Purdue game, quarterback John Leister attempted a team-record 54 passes only 18 of which were completed.

Punter Ray Stachowicz, tight end Mark Brammer and Bass were first-team All-Big Ten selections with Stachowicz also gaining All-American status.

Golf: In the first tournament of the spring, State finished tied for fourth place at the Marshall Invitational in Huntington, W.Va. Mike Thompson led the team with a three-round score of 225 and was followed by Tom Mase 226, Rick Grover 226, Monty James 231 and Rob Haidler 234.

MSU was second to Ohio State in the 25-team field of the annual Spartan Invitational at Forest Akers West. It was Michigan State's highest finish since 1975.

With a score of 1,535, MSU tied Ball State for third place in the 72-hole Northern Intercollegiate tournament hosted by the University of Michigan. Freshman Rob Haidler tied for fourth in the individual scoring with a 302. Other Spartans scored as follows: James 310, Belen 311, Mase 312, Lubbers 312 and Grover 318.

After the first round of the Big Ten Championships, Michigan State was in second place and only four strokes behind leader Ohio State. However, the Spartans slipped to fifth when the championships were completed. MSU's highest individual finisher was Grover, who placed third with a score of 74-74-71-73—292, only four shots away from a Big Ten individual title. Other scorers for MSU were Lubbers 299, James 302, Haidler 310, Hill Herrick 311 and Belen 312.

Gymnastics: At the early season Wisconsin Classic in Waukesha, Wis., with no team scoring, State was one of 12 schools that had gymnasts compete on an individual basis, but as Coach Szypula described his team's performance, "overall, it was a pretty weak showing." The top finishers were junior Marvin Gibbs who tied for fourth in floor exercise and senior captain Charlie Jenkins with a fifth place in the vault competition. Other finishers in the vault were freshman Pete Roberts, in seventh and junior Ivan Merritt, ninth.

MSU placed second in the four-team Buckeye Invitational at Columbus, Ohio. Gibbs was the star for State as he finished second in the all-around with a score of 50.45. Terry Olsen, a freshman from Alpena, scored a 9.2 to finish first on the parallel bars.

Michigan State hosted Ohio State, Michigan, Indiana, Eastern and Western Michigan at the Big Ten Invitational, which featured only individual scores. Gibbs was a top performer as he finished first in floor exercise and the parallel bars.

Michigan State finished sixth out of eight teams competing in the Big Ten championships at Bloomington, Ind. Gibbs was the top Spartan as he was runner-up in the all-around competition. Roberts added a third in vaulting, Rich Licata a third on the horizontal bar and Pedro Sanchez a fourth on the parallel bars.

Hockey: For the first time in 28 years, Amo Bessone was not behind the MSU bench. Former Bowling Green coach Ron Mason took over and led the Spartans into the Western Collegiate Hockey Association playoffs for the first time in three seasons.

MSU defeated the Polish National Team, 5-4, in an exhibition February 8 at Munn Ice Arena. The Polish team was preparing for the Olympic Winter Games in Lake Placid, N.Y.

MSU returned to the WCHA playoffs after a three-year absence but were dismissed in the opening round with back-to-back losses to North Dakota, 8-1 and 5-3.

Mark Hamway was accorded Spartan Rookie-of-the-Year honors after finishing third in team scoring with 16 goals and 28 assists for 44 points. Center Leo Lynett led the team with 27 goals and 61 points while Russ Welch, team-leader in assists with 37, was named MSU's Most Valuable Player.

Lacrosse: MSU recorded a forfeit victory over Northwestern, which resulted in a 1-0 win.

The Spartans played Hope twice in the 1980 season, beating the Flying Dutchmen by a combined score of 20-2.

Kevin Willits broke his leg in the first game of 1978 and was lost for the season. Awarded an extra year of eligibility by the NCAA, he completed his record-setting Spartan career in 1980. He remains MSU's career leading scorer with 175 goals and 252 points. In a game against Northwestern in 1979 he scored nine goals which tied a school record and his 70 goals that same year set a Michigan State season record.

Soccer: State outscored their opponents 29-16 en route to a 9-6-2 season record. Seven of those nine victories were by shutouts, the most by an MSU team since 1968.

At the mid-season Big Ten Classic hosted by Indiana University, MSU defeated Ohio State 2-0 and then bowed to the number one-ranked Hoosiers in the finale, 5-0.

Mark Neterer led the team through the year with 10 goals for 20 points, and Vancho Cirovski added four goals and five assists for 13 points.

Swimming and Diving: Who do you think would turn in the more impressive performance, a diver by the name (Eric) Best or a swimmer by the name of (Chris) Rock?

Rob Lundquist was the highest Spartan finisher at the Big Ten championships in Ann Arbor. The sophomore placed fifth in the 200-yard breaststroke (2:07.34) and also scored with a 10th at 100-yard distance (59.16). Mark Lancaster placed 11th in the 100-yard freestyle (46.55). The three relays teams and their places were: 800-yard freestyle (eighth), 400-yard medley (ninth) and 400-yard freestyle (ninth). For the team, the 139 points left the Spartans in ninth place.

During the season, first-year distance star Matt Fetters set school records in the 1,000-yard freestyle (9:38.50) and in the 1,650-yard freestyle (9:38.50).

Tennis: Coach Drobac's squad scored only six points which placed them ahead of only Illinois in ninth place at the conference meet in Minneapolis. At the number one singles position, Steve Yorimoto made it to second round, 6-4, 6-3, before being eliminated and then lost in the first match of the playback. All other singles players, number two Matt Sandler, number three Scott King, number four Jeff Wickman, number five Dino Demare and number six John Lapari lost opening matches with Wickman the only winner in the playback. The doubles team of Sandler-Wickman reached the finals of the playback bracket and then lost in the semifinals.

Track and Field: For the fourth consecutive year and with a time of 6.24, Randy Smith won the 60-yard dash at the Big Ten indoor championships. He also joined with Tim Kennedy, Tyrone Williams and Calvin Thomas to capture the mile relay in 3:16.47. Other top performers for State were Keith Moore who placed second in the 1,000-yard run and a third in the mile; Tony Gilbert, a recent transfer from San Jose State, who finished third in the 60-yard high hurdles and fourth in the triple jump; Thomas with a second in the 600-yard run; Michael White, third in the 880 and Daryl Dismond fourth in the high jump. During the two days of competition the team generated 73 2/3 points to finish in fourth place.

Paul Piwinski earned All-America honors during the indoor season after placing sixth at the NCAA championships. His highest jump was 7' 1 1/2" at the Central Collegiate championships in the spring at the first annual MSU track invitational at Ralph Young Field, the

Spartans collected seven first places. Senior Randy Smith captured the 100-meter dash in 10.47, the 200-meter in 20.8 and teamed with Ken Eaton, Andre Williams and Ricky Flowers to capture the 440-yard sprint relay in 40.73. Others winners were Calvin Thomas who ran a 47.6 in the 400-meters; Tim Kenney with a 1:53.4 in the 800-meters; Keith Moore, who ran a 3:49.2 in the 1,500-meters and Piwinski who leaped 6' 10" in the high jump. The winning mile-relay team of Tyrone Williams, Kenney, Flowers and Thomas was clocked in 3:11.99.

Hampered by a strained leg muscle, Smith was limited to one race, the 100-meter dash, at the outdoor Big Ten meet hosted by the University of Illinois, but he did win that event in a time of 10.44. Adding to MSU's 53 points and fourth-place team finish were: Flowers who placed third in the 200- and 400-meter dashes; Tyrone Williams with a third in the 400-meter hurdles; Martin Schulist, fourth in the 5,000; Eaton, fifth in the high hurdles; Don Muhammed, fifth in the 100-meters with Daryl Dismond and Piwinski third and fourth in the high jump. The quartet of Muhammad, Andre Williams, Eaton and Flowers finished third in the 400-meter relay and fourth in the 1,600-meter relay.

Wrestling: MSU wrestlers competed in six of the 10 championship matches at the third annual Spartan Invitational. Three Spartans emerged as champions: Jeff Therrian (142 pounds), Jim Ellis (177 pounds), who pinned his opponent and heavyweight Shawn Whitcomb.

Michigan State also hosted the Big Ten conference championships and finished in fourth place. Two Spartans, Jeff Thomas (126 pounds) and Fred Worthem (158 pounds), reached the finals in their divisions. Worthem lost to the Wisconsin entry who was picked as the meet's MVP. Meanwhile, Thomas was a real surprise. He entered the competition seeded number three and eventually defeated the number one seed from Minnesota, 15-5. In addition, senior Jeff Therrian (142 pounds) finished in third place and defending heavyweight champion Shawn Whitcomb settled for fourth place.

Moving on to the NCAA tournament at Corvallis, Ore., Thomas reached the quarterfinals before being eliminated. His performance would gain him All-American honors. Three other qualifiers, Therrian, Worthem and Whitcomb, won two matches each but failed to place.

MSU
1980-1981

TALES TO TELL

Herb Lindsay, a native of Reed City, Mich., enrolled at Michigan State in the fall of 1973 and immediately became a significant contributor to the school's cross country team and later the track and field team. In four years of competition, the long distance star would be awarded eight varsity "S" awards, four in each sport. While representing MSU, Herb earned four Big Ten titles, indoor and outdoor, ranging from 1,500 meters to two miles. Furthermore, he possessed no less than three varsity records upon completing his collegiate career while gaining All-American status as a long-distance runner. Yet, it would be two years later, after having graduated and moved to Boulder, Colo., that the muscular star would surface as the nation's best in a special branch of the sport identified as "road racing." The monthly publication *Track and Field News* tagged the former Spartan with the title of "Road Racer of the Year" in 1979 and again in 1980.

Displaying his talent across the United States and many other nations in races from 5,000 to 10,000 meters, Lindsay would out-dual world-class and Olympic competitors such as Lasse Viren, Bill Rodgers, Frank Shorter, Dick Quax and his nemesis from college days, Craig Virgin of Illinois. During one stretch from 1979-1980, Lindsay finished second in the 10,000-meter race at the Pan-American Games, set American records at the 10-mile and 10-kilometer distances, won the Diet Pepsi 10-kilometer national championship, and ran away from an international field at the New Year's Eve Sao Sylvestre half-marathon in Brazil.

Upon returning to Michigan in October of 1980 to compete in the East Lansing State Bank 10,000-meter run (which he won), Herb was interviewed by *The State News* writer Brad Ritter. The subsequent article demonstrated the deep affection the former Spartan runner holds for his alma mater when he volunteered:

"I realize how excited I am about coming back to East Lansing and MSU, and having the chance to run this race again [The East Lansing Bank 10,000]. I've been coming back [to Michigan] about every month-and-a-half to race and I've enjoyed it each time."

HEADLINES of 1981

- On March 30, John Hinckley attempts to assassinate president Ronald Reagan as he leaves a Washington, D.C., hotel.
- The video game "Pac Man" devours the market as young people everywhere are seized with acute Pac-mania.
- Private satellite dishes sprout in neighborhoods after the FCC gives them the okay. There are two million by the end of the year.
- The first reusable spacecraft, space shuttle Columbia, completes a successful mission.

SCOREBOARD

	W	L	T	Avg.
Baseball	23	28	0	.451
Track and Field	0	1	0	.000
Football	3	8	0	.273
Basketball	13	14	0	.481
Tennis	5	14	0	.263
Cross Country	1	2	0	.333
Swimming and Diving	6	4	0	.600
Wrestling	7	7	0	.500
Hockey	12	22	2	.361
Fencing	5	10	0	.333
Golf	tournament play only			
Gymnastics	6	5	0	.545
Soccer	10	6	1	.588
Lacrosse	1	14	0	.067

Herb's trips to his native state were successful as well, in 1981 he won races at Clare in March, Ionia in August and the Bobby Crim 10-mile, also in March.

TEAM OF THE YEAR

The 1981 edition of the Michigan State track and field team boasted Big Ten champions in two events and four school records that still stand today. As a double-winner in the Big Ten indoor championships at Columbus, Ohio, Tony Gilbert spearheaded MSU to a third-place, the highest finish in seven years. He first won the triple jump with a school-record leap of 15.56 meters (51' 4-1/2") and then, with a winning time of 7.4, led MSU to a spectacular one-two-three sweep in the 55-meter hurdles. Followed by Andy Wells and Ken Eaton, it was the Spartans' first sweep in any Big Ten event since 1966. Three individuals and a relay placed second at Columbus: Michael White in the 1,000 meters (2:23.99); Ty Williams in the 500 meters (1:03.8); Paul Piwinski with a leap of 2.14 meters in the high jump and the quartet of Gerald Cain, Larry Murphy, Cal Thomas and Williams in the 1600-meter relay (3:14.4).

State hosted the outdoor Big Ten meet and dropped to fifth place with 55 1/2 points, one-half point behind fourth-place Ohio State. Top performers for the Spartans were Jouka Niva who placed second in the triple jump (15.46 meters); Gilbert, who finished second in the high hurdles (14.01); Don Muhammad, who was runner-up in the 100 meters (10:37) and third in the 200 (21.70); Tyrone Williams, third in the 400-meter intermediate hurdles (50.85) and Piwinski who placed third in the high jump (2.14 meters).

At the Central Collegiate championships, State finished third indoors and second outdoors.

MAKING HISTORY

Nell Jackson, assistant athletic director, left the university after eight years to become athletic director at State University of New York at Binghamton.

The delegates to the annual NCAA convention did not vote to revoke the freshmen eligibility rule as it was strongly feared might happen.

MSU lost a pair of legendary coaches in the winter of 1980. Charles McCaffree, swimming coach from 1942-

The 1981 track and field team

1969, died on December 18 while in Austin, Texas, where he was undergoing therapy following a stroke. Mac was 73. Karl Schlademan, track coach from 1941-1958 and cross country coach from 1947-1958, died at the age of 90 on December 22 in Ft. Wayne, Ind.

In April, approximately 7,000 fans turned out to be entertained by the world-famous Harlem Globetrotters in their first-ever appearance at Jenison Field House.

GREAT STATE DATES

Soccer—**October 1, 1980 (A):** MSU managed two first-half goals and held off a pesky Michigan squad 2-1 in Ann Arbor for their fifth win of the season. Mark Neterer opened the scoring 18 minutes into the game. After stealing a Wolverine throw-in, the talented sophomore booted the ball past two defenders and the goalie. Seven minutes later Vancho Cirovski hit the game winner on a free kick after he had been brought down in the penalty area. The game was memorable for the mon-

Vancho Cirovski kicked the game-winning goal in the Spartans' victory over the Wolverines on a rainy October day in 1980.

soon-like rain that began seconds into the second half and drenched the area for 45 minutes. In a postseason comment pertaining to the downpour, Coach Baum said, "I couldn't even see my left wing out there. I sure hope he had a good game."

Cross Country—**October 4, 1980 (H):** With Spartan runners finishing in nine of the first ten slots, State easily defeated Northwestern 15-48 in the season opener at the Forest Akers West course. Michael White paced MSU with a time of 25:02, while Tim Kerr (25.10), Martin Schulist (25:11), Tom Unold and Tom Irmen finished second through fifth to complete the perfect score. Rounding out the remaining field for MSU were Scott Brasington, Harold Rutila, Dave Meyer and Ken Robinson, who took the seventh through 10th spots.

Soccer—**October 3, 1980 (H):** In their biggest win of the season, the Spartans defeated a solid Notre Dame squad, 4-1. Following a scoreless first half, State went up 2-0 on Vancho Cirovski's sixth and seventh goals of the season. After the Irish made it 2-1, freshman Steve Erdman came off the bench and headed in a Steve Schad corner kick with seven minutes of play remaining. Schad would later close out the scoring on a penalty kick. This win was the first ever over ND.

Golf—**October 4, 1980 (A):** Playing in an autumn tournament, Bruce Fossum's squad defeated four other conference teams while winning the 54-hole Gopher Fall Invitational hosted by the University of Minnesota. The team scoring was as follows: MSU 1,100, Minnesota 1,109, Iowa 1,115, Wisconsin 1,153 and Illinois 1,154. Individual cards included Monty James, 72-72-71—215; Steve Lubers, 75-75-69—219; Mike Thompson 77-74-71—222; David Belen 72-76-74—222; Hill Herrick 79-76-69—224 and Wayne Benson 75-76-75—226. The medalist was Minnesota's Tom Lehman, a future professional star.

Football—**November 8, 1980 (H):** Senior tailback Steve Smith totaled 229 rushing yards on 30 carries and scored a team record-tying four touchdowns as he led MSU to a resounding 42-10 victory over winless Northwestern. The Wildcats opened the scoring before the game was four minutes old and then the Spartans came back, distributed their touchdowns evenly with two in the first quarter, two in the second and the remaining pair in the third. Smith was credited with both TDs of the opening period, capping drives of 51 yards and 53 yards. The senior captain from Louisville swept left end and raced 64 yards for his third score. The half ended

28-10 when quarterback John Leister found freshman split end Daryl Turner with a 27-yard scoring pass. The remaining touchdowns were from a Leister-Otis Grant 32-yard hook-up and a nine-yard run by Smith which followed a James Neely interception. Morten Anderson connected on all six PATs and strong safety freshman Tim Cunningham of Lansing Everett, in his first start, led all defenders with seven tackles.

Football—**November 15, 1980 (A):** Aided by six Gopher turnovers, sophomore quarterback John Leister completed 14 of 28 passes for 209 yards and threw for three touchdowns to lead MSU in an upset of the University of Minnesota, 30-12. State was on top 14-12 at halftime on a 32-yard toss from Leister to Ted Jones and another scoring strike, this time a 36-yarder to Tony Gilbert with 6:59 remaining before the break. The only points of the third quarter were credited to Morten Anderson's 24-yard field goal. He would later close the scoring with two more three-pointers in the final 15 minutes, one from 41 yards and another from 30 yards. Leister's third scoring pass, another to Jones, came from ten yards out and was set-up by a 13-yard reception by tight end Alan Kimichik followed by a Steve Smith 22-yard run.

Wrestling—**November 25, 1980 (H):** Dan Holt stunned his heavyweight opponent, who was the defending Big Ten champion, to lead Michigan State to an 18-16 win over Michigan at IM West. Holt, a 6' 9", 333-pound junior, won a decision by a score of 7-2. The Spartans were trailing by one point going into the heavyweight round and needed Holt's triumph to capture the victory. Steve Foley, at 177 pounds, and 190-pounder Mike Potts scored decision wins to set up Holt's dramatic performance. Other MSU winners included Chuck Joseph (126 pounds), Ron Cantini (134 pounds) and Shawn White (142 pounds).

Hockey—**December 12, 1980 (A):** In defeating Notre Dame 1-0, Coach Mason's skaters gained MSU's first shutout since 1975. The winning tally came at 10:22 of the final period during a Michigan State power play. Winning a face-off in the Irish end, senior center Leo Lynett passed the puck to Bob Martin in the right corner. The sophomore forward then sent a pass to sophomore right winger Mark Hamway who was standing in the middle of the circle to the right of the ND goalie. The Detroit sophomore responded with a low slapshot that found the back of the net. Spartan goaltender Ron Scott included many dazzling saves as he kicked out 34 shots during the 60 minutes.

Wrestling—**January 7, 1981 (H):** In the dual meet against Indiana, Jim Mason (118 pounds), Ron Cantini (134 pounds) and Shawn White (142 pounds) gained wins. Regardless, the Spartans trailed after the opening seven matches, 15-9. Steve Foley (177 pounds), the senior captain, put the Spartans back on track with a 18-5 major decision and Mike Potts followed with an injury default that sealed the win, 20-18.

Hockey—**January 17, 1981 (H):** Seldom does one player dominate a contest the way MSU's Ken Paraskevin did in the 4-3 victory over Michigan before a standing-room-only crowd of 6,555. The Detroit native scored once in each period to complete the three-goal hat trick. In addition he played a harassing defensive game and as a member of the Spartans' penalty-killing unit held the Wolverines scoreless in four man-advantage situations. While sophomore right winger Bob Martin accounted for the Spartans' other tally, goalie Ron Scott made 30 saves, five of them in the final three minutes of action.

Swimming and Diving—**January 23, 1981 (A):** Capturing seven of the 11 individual events and one relay, Michigan State defeated Illinois, 70-43. Double winners were Mike Brown, the top scorer in both the one-meter and three-meter diving events along with Mike Borre, in the 200-yard individual medley (2:00.3) and 200-yard breaststroke (2:13.6). Other Spartan winners were Terry Inch in the 1,000-yard freestyle (9:48.8); Greg Sluke in the 200-yard backstroke (2:00.8) and Dan Mejer in the 200-yard freestyle (1:44.1). The winning medley relay of Scott Wilson, Rob Lundquist, George Kruggel and Mark Lancaster swam a 3:38.5.

Gymnastics—**January 30, 1981 (H):** In a double-dual meet, the Spartans finished one-two-three in three events to easily defeat Wisconsin 261.75-244.05 and Illinois State 260.35-253.65. Ivan Merritt, Charles Jenkins and Bart Acino slammed the floor exercise event. Acino, Greg Bosscawen and Merritt were the top finishers on the parallel bars and Acino, Merritt and Pedro Sanchez concluded the evening as the top three scorers in all around. In addition, Tom Tomkow scored a 9.20 to capture the rings event.

Fencing—**February 7, 1981 (A):** Michigan State's fencers won two matches in a quadrangular meet at the University of Chicago. The Spartans beat Purdue, 18-9, and Chicago, 15-12. For the tournament, John Chambers was 7-2 for the sabre competition and Brian Morrow was 5-3. Barry Peterman posted a 6-3 epee record and Mike Dority was 5-3 in foil.

Basketball—**February 14, 1981 (H):** Kevin Smith, who was thrust into a starring role when leading scorer Jay Vincent fell into foul trouble, scored an impressive 28 points in a 70-66 victory over Michigan. Coach Jud Heathcote also singled out Rick Kaye for special merit as he connected on three-for-three from the field in a substitution role. Other contributors were sophomores Derek Perry and Herb Bostic along with freshmen Tim Gore and Ben Tower. When Vincent was whistled for his fifth personal with 4:35 to play, MSU led by 10. The Spartans withstood the pressure during those final minutes and hung on for the four-point victory. State had its best shooting game of the season, sinking 25 baskets in 40 tries for a .625 average.

Hockey—**February 27-28, 1981 (H):** MSU closed out its season schedule with a pair of exciting overtime wins, defeating Colorado College, 6-5 and 5-4. With 1:16 remaining in the Friday affair State trailed 5-3 when Ken Paraskevin tallied a goal and 23 seconds later Frank Finn stickhandled in on the Tiger goalie to tie the game 5-5. Newell Brown's game-winner came at the 52-second mark of OT on a perfect pass from Mark Hamway. At the time, the teams were playing three aside due to a flurry of penalties that followed Finn's tying score. On the next night Brown did it again. With the score knotted at 4-4, the Ontario freshman's overtime game-winner came at 3:23 on a pass from sophomore defenseman Ken Leiter. Brown had opened the State scoring in period number one with Gary Harpell, Dan Sutton and Nigel Thomas each credited with a goal in the second period.

Gymnastics—**February 28, 1981 (H):** MSU picked up a big victory to end the regular season with a 260.60-241.75 win over Indiana. The Spartans put it away early, as four broke the 9.0 mark in the floor exercise. Bryan Walsh took the pommel horse with an 8.95 and Pete Roberts lead the way on the floor (9.40) and the vault (9.65).

Basketball—**March 5, 1981 (H):** For the third time in the 1980-1981 conference schedule Michigan State was faced with a five-minute overtime and on this occasion they prevailed with a 71-70 win over the conference leader and nationally sixth-ranked University of Iowa. In the end it was a free throw by Herb Bostic with 22 seconds remaining that provided the victory margin. The Hawks then had the final possession and a 15-foot jump shot by their leading scorer with five seconds remaining luckily bounced off long. The scoring in regulation ended at 60-60 with 5:15 remaining as determined defense and cold shooting stunted both offenses. The Spartans held the ball for the final three minutes (no shot clock) before Kevin Smith's 25-foot jumper missed the target at the buzzer. The Detroit junior was the game's high scorer with 25 points, six coming in the OT. Jay Vincent contributed 24 points and a team-high 10 rebounds.

Tennis—**April 22, 1981 (A):** After number one Matt Sandler dropped his three-set match, Stan Drobac's squad swept the remaining points to defeat Eastern Michigan, 8-1. Winners at singles were number two Scott King, 6-2, 6-1; number three Steve Yorimoto 6-3, 6-0; number four Jordy Asher 7-6, 4-6, 7-6; number five Francisco Amaya 3-6, 6-4, 6-1 and number six Jeff Wickman 6-2, 6-3. Gaining wins at doubles were number one Sandler-King 6-4, 6-3; number two Yorimoto-Asher 6-2, 6-1 and number three Amaya-Wickman 6-3, 6-2.

Baseball—**May 3, 1981 (H):** MSU scored a pair of exciting Sunday afternoon victories in defeating Ohio State, 8-6 and 7-6. In the opener of the two seven-inning games, Litwhiler's gang trailed 4-0 but came back to tie the Buckeyes with three runs in the third and another in the fourth. After once more relinquishing the lead, an explosive four-run sixth clinched the win. In that game-winning rally Mark Russ and Chris Dorr singled, Mike Cudnohufsky and Jim Buterakos walked and sophomore shortstop Tom Dieters cleared the bases with a three-run double. After three innings of the second game, Michigan State led 6-1, only to have the Bucks knot the score with two in the fourth and three in fifth. The Spartans again pushed across the eventual winning marker in the sixth inning as Al Dankovich scored on an RBI bloop single to right by Russ. Gaining the win was senior righthanded reliever Phil Magsig, who struck out four and allowed no hits in the final two and two-thirds innings.

Baseball—**May 5, 1981 (A):** In a rare road doubleheader sweep of Western Michigan, State defeated the Broncos at Kalamazoo, 7-6 and 3-0. In the opener, the Spartans rallied from a 3-0 deficit as Mark Russ's seventh inning lead-off homer proved to be the winning run. Pitcher Mike Patterson allowed only three hits in four innings of relief to post the victory. In the second contest Ty Schultz tossed a one-hit shutout as Ron Curcio provided a timely bases loaded double in the fourth inning which accounted for all three of MSU's runs. Returning to East Lansing, MSU kept the streak going on the next afternoon with two more wins, 15-1 and 4-2.

Baseball—**May 9, 1981 (H):** MSU scored four runs in the opening inning and never trailed in posting an 8-6 victory over Michigan. Chris Dorr knocked in two with a double and Ken Mehall and Tom Dieters produced run-scoring singles. Dorr later accounted for three more runs with a bases loaded double in the fourth inning. Phil Magsig relieved Tim Birtsas in the fourth and completed the game to gain his third win of the season.

Lacrosse—**May 10, 1981 (H):** Dan McNulty fired the winning marker as State concluded the season with a 12-11 overtime victory against the Chicago Lacrosse Club. With goals by Greg Helgemoe, McNulty, Shawn Grady and Jim Stevens, the game was tied at 4-4 after the opening period. Pat Smith, McNulty, Kirk Lewis and Helgemoe added scores in the second to gain an 8-7 Spartan advantage at intermission. Relinquishing the lead and trailing 11-9 with slightly more than two-and-a-half minutes of regulation time remaining, Helgemoe and Lewis scored to send the contest into the OT. McNulty's winning tally came with a minute and a half left in the first four-minute sudden-death period.

ATHLETE OF THE YEAR

Jay Vincent, a four-year varsity performer, ranks as MSU's fifth all-time leading scorer with 1,914 points. He was named the Big Ten Player of the Year in 1981 after he captured his second-straight Big Ten scoring title with a 24.1 ppg average. Vincent, a two-time first-team All-Big Ten selection, won the scoring title in 1980 with a 22.1 ppg average, and was named MSU's MVP in 1980 and 1981. His biggest disappointment came during the NCAA championships of 1979. Although able to play in four of the five games during that successful run, a stress fracture in his foot limited Jay to minimal playing time and consequentially sub-par performances. Jay Vincent's name appears in the top 10 of four scoring categories in MSU history, and his number 31 jersey is retired in the rafters of the Breslin Center.

IN THE SPARTLITE

Baseball: Conference divisional play began with the 1981 baseball schedule. In the east were Indiana, Michigan, Michigan State, Ohio State and Purdue while Iowa, Illinois, Iowa, Minnesota, Northwestern and Wisconsin comprised the west division. This split conference format would last until 1988.

The Spartans' longest winning streak of the season was six games. MSU outscored opponents 42-21 during that stretch.

Chris Dorr and Terry Johnson were each named to the All-Big Ten team.

At the team's post-season honors banquet, Ken Mehall, with a .317 batting average, nine homers and 43 RBI, was named the team's most valuable player as well as being recipient of the Steve Garvey Sportsmanship Award. The Most Improved Player award went to Dorr.

Pitcher-designated hitter Terry Johnson, was the team's top hitter with a .380 average and Mark Pomorski was the leading pitcher with a 5-1 won-loss record.

Basketball: In what would be the first of an annual early season four-team tournament, MSU hosted the first Cutlass Classic, losing in the finals to Central Michigan, 89-66.

Jay Vincent

Jay Vincent and Kevin Smith each earned first-team All-Big Ten honors. As in 1980, with an average of 24.1, Jay would lead the Big Ten in scoring and be voted media Big Ten Player of the Year.

Vincent netted 36 points and hit 16-of-25 field goals in a January 10 contest at Iowa. Later, in the Minnesota game of February 28, he connected for 17 field goals. During the season, Jay topped the 30-point barrier on three additional occasions and for the second straight year he would be selected the team MVP.

Freshman forward Ben Tower won most improved player honors, while senior forward Rick Kaye was the team's top defender.

Cross Country: Michigan State hosted the annual Big Ten meet and finished tied for sixth with Purdue at 159 points. Crossing the line in 15th place, Ted Unold was the top State runner in a time of 25:00, the best of the season for any Spartan on the Forest Akers West course. Scott Brasington finished 24th (25:19); Michael White was 30th (25:29), Tim Kerr 43rd (25:56) and Tom Irmen rounded out the scoring in 47th spot (26:02). Other finishers for State were Dave Meyer in 54th and Harold Rutila, 55th.

Two weeks later at the NCAA District IV meet in Champaign, Ill., Unold was 51st, White 65th and Brasington 79th.

Fencing: With 16 team points, MSU placed last (fifth) at the Big Ten Championships in Evanston, Ill. In the epee weapon Barry Peterman placed seventh and teammate John Samalik finished in 10th. John Chambers was fifth in sabre with Brian Morrow 10th. In foil, Keith Defever was eighth and Mike Dority tenth.

Chambers and Peterman earned the right to compete in the NCAA championships at Kenosha, Wis.

Football: The 1980 season would be the first for Frank "Muddy" Waters as State's head coach.

In the 36-25 loss to Purdue, John Leister set a team record with 54 pass attempts (18 completions). This topped Eddie Smith's record of 42 set in the Minnesota game during the 1978 season.

In defeating MSU 48-16, Ohio State rolled up 603 rushing and passing yards, the fourth highest total ever accumulated on a Spartan defense.

Senior halfback Steve Smith compiled a four-year total of 2,676 yards to become MSU's newest all-time career leading rusher. Eric Allen had previously held the record at 2,654 yards accumulated during a three-year

career. At the postseason team banquet, Smith would be honored as recipient of three prestigious awards: the Governor of Michigan Award, the President's Award and the Downtown Coaches Club Offense Award.

Steve Smith rushed for 2,676 yards during his four years at MSU.

Punter Ray Stachowicz was a first-team All-Big Ten selection for the fourth consecutive year, marking the first time this feat had ever been accomplished by a conference player. Junior place kicker Morten Andersen and guard Rod Strata were second-team picks.

Golf: Finishing behind Ohio State and Indiana, the MSU golfers took third in the 12-team field at the 17th annual Spartan Invitational. With a two-round score of 69-75—144, Steve Lubbers won medalist honors thus becoming the first Spartan since 1975 to profess the title.

Junior Monty James led the team to a fifth place finish at the Big Ten tournament in Minneapolis. Shooting a 72-71-68-73—286, James finished with the tenth lowest card of the weekend. Other Spartans contributed as follows: Dave Belen 67-69-79-80—295; Hill Herrick 74-77-74-70—295; Rob Haidler 73-74-76-73—296; Mike Thomsen 73-74-77-73—297 and Steve Lubbers 73-75-77-75—300.

Gymnastics: In the all-around competition at the Wisconsin Classic held in early November, Marvin Gibbs was second in compulsory and third in the optional. Also competing in Waukesha, Wis., were Pete Roberts, Charlie Jenkins, Greg Bossawen, Bart Ancino, Ivan Merritt, Pedro Sanches and Tom Tomkow.

In a specially scheduled exhibition match, MSU lost by 19 points to a powerful Japanese national team, 280.4-261.4, in front of a large, enthusiastic crowd at Jenison Fieldhouse.

The Big Ten Invitational was a meet first held in 1970 and continued until 1984. With no team score compiled, it gave coaches an opportunity to evaluate their athletes it competitive conditions. For the second consecutive year, MSU hosted the meet in Jenison and four Spartans, Acino, Jenkins, Roberts and Rick Lacata, emerged as winners of individual events. Coach Szypula was particularly pleased with the performance of Acino, who finished first in the all-around.

Averaging a score of 54.55 in the all-around event over the entire season, Acino proved to be the team's outstanding competitor.

Although none of them placed, five members of the team participated in the NCAA individual championships. They were: seniors Tomkow (still rings) and Merritt (floor exercise), junior Rich Licata (horizontal bars and sophomores Acino (parallel bars) and Roberts (vault).

Hockey: Ron Mason, in his second year as MSU's head coach, saw his squad suffer two winless streaks through the 1980-1981 schedule. From October 31 through November 22, the Spartans went 0-8 and two months later, January 23 through February 14, they suffered an 0-8-1 run. During the next 21 seasons, Ron Mason teams would never suffer such a dismal streak.

Mark Hamway led the team with 18 goals and 33 points, including 13 goals in WCHA play and Gary Haight was the team leader in assists with 17.

In what would be the first of three such honors, goalie Ron Scott was named the team's most valuable player. He would also be voted the team's outstanding rookie as well as being named to the all-WCHA first team. The Guelph, Ontario freshman was the primary reason the Spartans reduced their goals-against average of 5.97 in 1979-1980 to 3.88 in 1980-1981.

Kelly Miller participated in the World Junior Championships.

Lacrosse: The 1981 season was the first under the reign of coach Rich Kimball.

The disastrous 1-16 season was predictable. For the first time MSU played a major college schedule with several top-ranked national powers. Gone were the automatic wins against teams like Lake Forest, Hope, Northwestern, Oberlin and Albion. Replacing the weaker teams were the likes of Ohio Wesleyan, Ohio State and Denison. In addition, the team lost the top four scorers after the 1980 season as Coach Kimball fielded a team that included six members who had never played the game before.

Dan McNulty and Greg Helgemoe combined for 34 goals and 11 assists.

McNulty was selected to the All-Midwest Lacrosse Association second-team.

Soccer: After falling to Indiana in the first round of the mid-season Big Ten east division championship, the Spartans bounced back with a 6-0 shutout win over Purdue. Tom Saxton, who would later become coach of the women's team, scored two of the six goals.

For the second straight year, Mark Neterer led the team in scoring with 13 goals. Along with seven assists, he also led the team with 33 points.

State's offense scored 52 goals, which was more than any other Spartan team since the NCAA championship team of 1968, which netted a team-record 77.

With the 1-0 season-closing win over Bowling Green, MSU completed the schedule with 12 wins, tying a team record.

Steve Erdman, the Brazilian-born striker, completed an impressive seven-goal freshman year.

Swimming and Diving: Scoring 149 points, Dick Fetter's squad placed seventh at the Big Ten championships in Milwaukee. Rob Lundquist led the Spartan swimmers, placing fourth in the 200-yard breaststroke in a time of 2:05.03; seventh in the 100-yard breaststroke with 57.96 and 13th in the 200-yard individual medley in 1:55.14. Diver Mike Brown was sixth in both the three-meter (483.81 points) and one-meter (452.88 points) events. Others who swam to spots in the consolation finals were Mike Borre, George Kruggel, Dick Legault, Greg Sluke and Terry Inch.

Brown was the only Michigan State finalist in the NCAA meet at Austin, Texas, finishing 10th on the three-meter board. Lundquist swam a 2:05.2 in the 200-yard breaststroke but failed to make the finals.

Brown and Lundquist were co-recipients of the team's MVP award.

Tennis: Scott King recorded the most victories at number one singles with seven wins while Francisco Amaya led the team overall with 13 wins.

The squad closed the season on a bitter note by claiming just four points while finishing last in the Big Ten championships. Playing in the number one through number six slots for Coach Drobac were Steve Yorimoto, Matt Sandler, Scott King, Jordy Asher, Francisco Amaya and John LaParl.

Track and Field: As a double-winner in the Big Ten indoor championships at Columbus, Ohio, Tony Gilbert spearheaded Michigan State to a third place, the highest finish in seven years. He first won the triple jump with a leap of 15.56 meters (51' 4-1/2") and then, with a winning time of 7.4, led MSU to a spectacular one-two-three sweep in the 55-meter hurdles. Followed by Andy Wells and Ken Eaton, it was the Spartans' first sweep in any Big Ten event since 1966. Three individuals and a relay placed second, Michael White ran a 2:23.99 in the 1,000-meters; Ty Williams ran a 1:03.8 in the 500-meters; Paul Piwinski managed 2.14 meters in the high jump and the quartet of Gerald Cain, Larry Murphy, Cal Thomas and Williams finished the 1,600-meter relay in 3:14.4.

Six Spartans represented MSU at the indoor NCAA meet in Detroit's Joe Louis Arena: Piwinski, sprinter Corky Wilkins, and the 1,600-meter relay team of Thomas, Kelvin Scott, Elliott Tabron and Marcus Sanders. It would be the final year for the championships in Detroit. In 1982 the meet would move to the Silverdome in Pontiac.

Competing in the prestigious Drake relays, Gilbert was third in the 110-meter high hurdles; Jouka Niva placed fifth in the triple jump with a school record 50' 9"; Piwinski cleared 7' to finish fifth in the high jump and the 400-meter relay of Andre Williams, Don Muhammad, Ken Eaton and Gilbert took sixth place.

Michigan State hosted the outdoor Big Ten meet and finished in fifth place with 55 1/2 points, one-half point behind fourth-place Ohio State. MSU's top performers were Niva who placed second in the triple jump with a leap of 15.46 meters (50' 8-3/4"); Gilbert, who finished second in the high hurdles with a time of 14.01;

Muhammad, who ran a 10:37 for a second in the 100-meter dash and a 21.70 for a third in the 200; Tyrone Williams, a third in the 400-meter intermediate hurdles in 50.85 and Piwinski who placed third in the high jump at 2.14 meters (7' 1/4").

For the second consecutive weekend, MSU hosted a conference championship at Ralph Young Field, this time it was the Central Collegiates. Totaling 88 points, Coach Bibbs's squad finished second to Michigan. The most exciting race of the afternoon was the mile relay led off by Thomas and Cain with Scott third. It was Scott that made up ground and put State in the race for anchorman Tyrone Williams, who burst down the last straight and passed the U of M runner to capture first place. Other winners for MSU were Tony Gilbert in the high hurdles, Paul Piwinski in the high jump and Jouka Niva in the triple jump.

Wrestling: It was an injury-plagued year in which the team lost five starters at various stages of the season.

With 115 points, MSU claimed first place in the early season Lock Haven Tournament.

Hosting the fourth annual MSU-Takedown Club Invitational, State wrestlers claimed two titles as the team garnered 116 points to finish second behind Indiana State in the nine-team field. Those winners were Shawn White (142 pounds) and Steve Foley (177 pounds).

Although he would wrestle for only one year, Dan Holt of Spring Lake, Mich., was the largest wrestler to ever represent Michigan State. He stood six foot nine and weighed in at 330 pounds. Dan came to Coach Peninger after a less-than totally successful two-year career at Muskegon Junior College.

At the Big Ten championship meet in Madison, Wis., State finished in a disappointing seventh place. The bright spots for the Spartans were Shawn White (142 pounds), a walk-on from Warwick, N.Y., who was runner-up and Steve Foley (167 pounds) of Worthington, Ohio, who was consolation champion.

Jim Mason led the team with 10 pins, which still ranks as 13th best in an MSU season.

White (30-8) earned All-America honors with a fourth-place finish at the NCAA championships at 142 pounds and Foley, who posted a 29-6 season record, was named the team's most outstanding wrestler.

EXTRA! MICHIGAN STATE RELAYS (1980s)

The 1980 MSU relays included 475 participants from 24 schools and featured a pair of Michigan State grads in feature races. Posting a 1:10.6 in the 600-yard run, MSU sophomore Calvin Thomas edged Bob Cassleman (1971-1974) by one-tenth of a second. It marked the first loss ever in Jenison Fieldhouse for the former Spartan great. In the other special race, the two-mile invitational, Herb Lindsay (1974-1977) ran eight straight 33-second laps to win in a time of 8:41.6. Although a credible run, the time was shy of his school record of 8:39.2 set in 1976. Current Spartans captured three of the meet's traditional events that evening. Ted Unold was a winner in the mile run with a 4:10.1; Paul Piwinski won the high jump when he cleared 6' 10-3/4" and the quartet of Thomas, Tim Kenney, Mike White and Keith Moore were winners of the distance medley relay in a time of 9:52.5. The meet included a big disappointment for MSU. Senior All-American Randy Smith, who had never lost the 60-yard dash at the MSU Relays, was edged at the finish line by a sprinter from Tennessee.

A strong showing in the sprints and hurdle events highlighted MSU's performances in the 1981 MSU Relays which featured athletes from 14 schools. Senior co-captain Tyrone Williams won the 600-yard dash in a respectable time of 1:12.1. Don Mohammad won the 60-yard dash in 6.39, Tony Gilbert finished first in the high hurdle with a 7.40 while the distance medley relay of Eric Teusche, Cal Thomas, Ted Unold and Michael White cruised to a win in 9:52.1.

In 1982 MSU athletes registered two firsts. Lansing freshman Marcus Sanders won the 600-yard dash in 1:11.78 and the spring medley relay team of Calvin Thomas, Corky Wilkens, Andre Williams and Mike White edged a Michigan quartet in a time of 3:27.78. Competing against stars from 12 other teams, Jim Bibbs's 1983 crew led the parade to the top of the award stand with four individuals titles and one relay. Senior Paul Piwinski jumped higher than any Big Ten performer ever had indoors when he cleared the bar at 7' 5" on his final attempt. In doing so he set a meet and fieldhouse record. On the running oval three other green-clad stars earned gold medals. Marcus Sanders repeated as the 600-yard champion in a time of 1:09.24, less than 1.5 seconds from the world record. Corky Wilkins captured the 300-yard dash in 30.6 and Eliot Tabron set a meet and

fieldhouse record while winning the 440 in 47.41. Sanders, Tabron and Wilkins then joined Kelvin Scott to run away with the final event of the evening, the mile relay, in a meet record time of 3:12.0.

By 1984, the Relays had once against returned to what might be called a gathering of local track and field athletes. Other than a scattering of entries from Marquette, Drake and Toledo, the competitors represented Michigan schools: Saginaw Valley, Hillsdale, Ferris, Central, Eastern, Northwood, Western and the U of M. Top Spartan performers were Larry Jackson, who won the 60-yard dash in 6.2 and Todd Hoover who put the shot 56' 4-1/2".

A sparse crowd was on hand to witness the 11 teams competing in the 19 events at the Relays of 1985. The Spartans captured five of the events as follows: Derrick Leonard with a time of 6.39 in the 60-yard dash; Larry Jackson narrowly won the 300 in 31 seconds flat; Rodney Benson claimed a first in the 440-yard dash in a respectable 48.48; Mark Williamson captured the 1,000-yard run with a time of 2:14.9 and pole vaulter Jon Bartos was a winner with a vault of 15 feet.

The next year (1986) marked the first time the MSU Relays combined events for both men and women. The infusion of female athletes instilled a temporary resurgence of the Relays. Nearly 500 competitors were in venerable Jenison representing 18 men's teams and 16 women's teams. Coach Jim Bibbs was all smiles as his men captured an impressive five gold medals as follows: Derrick Leonard who sprinted to a 6.32 in the 60-yard dash; Anthony Mahone with a 30.5 in the 300-yard dash; Rodney Benson who won the 440 in a time of 47.2 plus the two-mile relay team in 9:02.46 and the Spartan sprint relay team that raced to a first place in 3:27.9.

Winners of 1987 included Leonard, a repeat winner in the 60 (6.23); Rodney Benson, who ran a 48.42 to take the 440; junior Keith Hanson, the three-mile champion in a time of 14:13.8 and the foursome of Marvin Parnell, Dennis Felton, Guy Scott and Benson the winners of the mile relay in 3:14.0. Corey Pryor was a solitary star for State in the 1988 Relays as he won the 200-meters in 22.01 and placed second in the 55-meter sprint with a clocking of 6.35. Amidst a sprinkling of seconds through sixths, one Spartan managed to claim a championship at the 65th annual MSU Relays. Sophomore Daryl Stallworth won the 400-meters in a personal-best time of 48.55.

MSU
1981-1982

TALES TO TELL

In any sport, going against the University of Michigan is most frequently a serious test. In his 24 years as MSU's head wrestling coach, Grady Peninger found no exception to this axiom. It took him only four years to jump from an eighth-place Big Ten team to his conference championship team of 1965-1966 (the first of seven straight titles—a record unchallenged by any other Spartan athletic team). Yet, it took *six* years to register his first victory over the Wolverines, but by 1982 his teams were in complete command, defeating them twice.

On November 24 at Ann Arbor, in the first dual meet of the season, State easily handled the U of M, 33-10. After Harrell Milhouse settled for a tie at 118 pounds, State registered five straight victories: 126-pound Jim Mason's pin at 5:57; Ron Cantini, 5-2 win at 134 pounds; Jeff Felice, 10-5 decision at 142 pounds; 150-pound Greg Sargis's pin in two minutes and Fred Worthem a 10-7 winner at 158 pounds. Following a Phil Welch draw at 167 pounds, Keith Foxx (177 pounds) and Mike Potts (190 pounds) completed the Spartans' afternoon of scoring by posting identical 9-1 decisions.

Before a noisy crowd of 653 in the IM West Sports Arena on January 29, Grady Peninger's wrestlers defeated the U of M , 19-15. After Harrell Milhouse dropped his 118-pound match, Jim Mason, Ron Cantini and Shawn White responded with consecutive wins. In the surprise setback of the evening, Greg Sargis, MSU's top pinner with 15 for the season, was himself put to the mat at 1:17 in his 150-pound match. The Spartans bounced back with victories by Fred Worthem (158 pounds), Keith Foxx (177 pounds) and Mike Potts (190 pounds). Foxx scored an 11-2 major decision and Potts won 7-2 to give MSU an insurmountable advantage.

Seventeen years following his retirement as head coach, Grady Peninger consented to the tough task of compiling an All-Peninger team from the many champions he coached from 1963-1986. His selections were as follows:

• Greg Johnson,115 pounds (1970-1972)—NCAA champion, "unlimited stamina"
• Pat Milkovich, 126 pounds (1972, 1974-1976)—NCAA champion, "real slick"
• Don Behm, 130 pounds (1965-1967)—Big Ten Champion, NCAA and Olympic runner-up, "good as anyone"

HEADLINES of 1982

- On April 2, Argentine forces invade England's Falkland Islands, and by June 14 British forces reclaim the area.
- At the University of Utah Medical Center, a permanent artificial heart is implanted in a human for the first time.
- Halley's Comet is sighted for the first time since 1911.
- The Watchman, Sony's portable micro television, is invented.

SCOREBOARD

	W	L	T	Avg.
Baseball	25	29	0	.463
Track and Field	1	2	1	.375
Football	5	6	0	.455
Basketball	12	16	0	.429
Tennis	7	14	0	.333
Cross Country	1	2	0	.600
Swimming and Diving	6	6	0	.500
Wrestling	10	4	0	.714
Hockey	26	14	2	.643
Fencing	6	5	0	.545
Golf	tournament play only			
Gymnastics	2	7	0	.222
Soccer	12	5	0	.706
Lacrosse	4	13	0	.235

• Dale Anderson, 133 pounds (1966-1968)—Big Ten and NCAA champion, "dogged"

• Tom Milkovich, 141 pounds (1970-1973)—Big Ten and NCAA champion, "also real slick;" or Norm Young, 141 pounds (1959-1961)—Big Ten and NCAA champion, "the quiet man"

• Dale Carr, 149 pounds (1966-1968)—Big Ten champion and NCAA runner-up, "master of grandby roll"

• Dick Cook, 152 pounds (1965-1966)—NCAA champion, "leg man"

• George Radman, 167 pounds (1966-1967)—NCAA and Big Ten champion, "strongest ever"

• Mike Bradley, 174 pounds (1966-1968)—Big Ten champion and NCAA runner-up, "steady winner, no flash, just a winner"

• Jack Zindel, 197 pounds (1968-1970)—Big Ten champion and NCAA runner-up, "would fight a buzz saw"

• Jeff Smith, heavyweight (1968-1969)—Big Ten champion, "key win over U of M's NCAA champion"

TEAM OF THE YEAR

Joe Baum, in his fifth year as a head coach, guided the Spartan soccer team to a 12-5 finish in 1981, which tied the 1967 co-national champion team for most wins in a season. They opened the schedule with an unimpressive 3-4 record, but steam-rolled through the end of the year by winning nine of their last 10 games. In the 12 wins, MSU shut out its opponent seven times. Tom King led the team with 15 goals, which still stands at 10th best in an MSU season. For the third year in a row, Vancho Cirovski was the team leader in assists with seven.

Coach Peninger (left) and NCAA champion Pat Milkovich

The 1981 soccer team. Included in picture are coach Joe Baum (back row, first from left); Tom Saxton (back row, fourth from left); Steven Swanson (fourth from left front row); Tom King, Mark Neterer and Vancho Cirovski (side-by-side back row, fifth, sixth and seventh from the right).

MAKING HISTORY

Having already "pulled the plug" on broadcasts of home baseball games, WKAR radio terminated the airing of live Spartan football and basketball contests beginning in the fall of 1981. Thus, the Michigan State station dropped what had become an ongoing tradition since first broadcasting the school's varsity sports events in 1924. Jim Adams, the 20-year veteran sports director and play-by-play man, would handle the final basketball game, a 69-48 loss to Indiana on March 7, 1981. Meanwhile, Detroit's WXYZ had picked up MSU's football and basketball package with a three-year contract.

In June of 1980 it was announced that MSU would follow the University of Michigan and Notre Dame in withdrawing from the Western Collegiate Hockey Association in favor of the Central Collegiate Hockey Association (CCHA). State played its first game as a member of the CCHA by defeating Lake Superior State, 4-3, on Oct. 23, 1981.

In January, shortly before the case was to go before a magistrate in Grand Rapids, former athletic director, Burt Smith, reached an out-of-court settlement of his suit against the university. He charged that MSU had violated his rights when school officials forced him to resign in October of 1975. The settlement awarded Smith $30,800 and full retirement benefits.

John Narcy, the veteran diving coach, was selected to coach the U.S. men's and women's team that would travel to Sweden and Italy in July to compete in meets against the world's best.

After 19 years of serving as head coach, Danny Litwhiler stepped aside following the 1982 season. He deserved a more pleasant send-off as his Spartans dropped four of four to the Michigan Wolverines.

GREAT STATE DATES

Soccer—**September 28, 1981 (H):** State topped Michigan 2-1 for the third win of the young season. After playing most of the opening half with little emotion, State stole the ball deep inside the U of M area and Mark Neterer scored at 23:38 on an assist from Steve Swanson, but by intermission the Wolverines had tied the game. As time was winding down in the second half and the game still at 1-1, it was obvious the Spartans needed a spark. It was then Coach Baum reluctantly inserted the hobbled Tom King into the line-up. King, the team's top scorer, had been sidelined with a sore leg muscle. The move paid off as the junior transfer student from England booted home the winning goal at 38:50.

Cross Country—**October 3, 1981 (A):** The MSU harriers ran away from Northwestern, placing six of the first seven finishers for a 18-41 win in Kenosha, Wis. Michael White was the top finisher for MSU with a time of 25.41. Also scoring for the Spartans were Tom Irmen in second, Martin Schulist fourth, Keith Harris fifth and David Schoener in sixth.

Football—**October 17, 1981 (H):** Quarterback Bryan Clark completed 18 of 30 passes accounting for 291 total yards as Michigan State beat fourteenth-ranked University of Wisconsin, 33-14. The Spartans opened by scoring in all ways possible. Using a no-huddle offense, the offense drove deep into Badger territory before settling for a 32-yard Morten Anderson field goal. Wisconsin contributed two more points when a snap from center sailed out of the end zone. After the ensuing free kick, Clark's 49-yard touchdown pass to Daryl Turner and Anderson's conversion made it 12-0. James Burroughs recovered a fumble to thwart a drive of the visitors at the State 18-yard line. From there MSU put together a nine-play 82-yard march, featuring a disguised 44-yard run by Clark. His six-yard pass to Turner and Anderson's PAT made it 19-0. After Ralf Mojsiejenko had a punt blocked into the end zone for a TD, the Green and White stormed back as Clark found Otis Grant in the end zone to put the game out of reach. Aaron Roberts added an insurance touchdown on a one-yard run.

Football—**November 7, 1981 (H):** Racking up the school's highest point total since the 75-0 victory of Arizona in 1949, State humbled the Northwestern Wildcats, 61-14. The Spartans scored the first seven times they had the ball as follows: Lance Hawkins on a six-yard run; Otis Grant, a six-yard pass reception from Bryan Clark; a four-yard pass Clark to Al Kimichik; Morten Andersen's 46-yard field goal; another Clark-to-Grant pass, 26 yards; a 10-yard Dick Kolb to Kimichik pass and a second Andersen field goal, for 43 yards. This ended the first half with MSU in full command, 41-0. In the second half a 31-yard TD pass from Kolb-to-Aaron Roberts was sandwiched between the two Cat touchdowns. In the final period Carl Williams ran back an interception 83 yards for a score and fullback Marcus Toney, in his first run of the season, scored from the 21-yard-line. Led by Carl Banks, Tim Cunningham, Lonnie Young, Greg Lauble, Ron Mitchem and Terry Bailey, the defense held Northwestern to minus-60 yards rushing.

Soccer—**November 7, 1981 (H):** It took Tommy King, the team's top scorer, only three minutes and 44 seconds to find the back of the net, but Vancho Cirovski's winning marker came late in the second half for a 2-1 victory over Western Michigan. It was a frustrating afternoon for the Spartans as they had many opportunities to score but were continually turned away. Coach Joe Baum singled out the play of both Matt Davis and Bruce Wilden for special plaudits.

Hockey—**November 13-14, 1981 (H & A):** State completed a weekend two-game sweep of Notre Dame, 4-2 and 8-4, and as a result moved into first place of the Central Collegiate Hockey Association standings. With 25 total penalties called during the first 40 minutes on Friday, five-on-four, four-on-three, five-on-three situations prevailed during the first two periods. Scoring for MSU was as follows: freshman Gord Flegel at 2:50 of period number one; Lyle Phair at 1:12 and Tom Anastos at 15:30 in the second period and Dave Taylor at 15:40 of the final period. On the next night junior captain and right wing Mark Hamway scored a three-goal hat trick and junior winger Nigel Thomas added a pair of tallies to lead the Spartans. Junior Bob Martin, freshmen Lyle Phair and Tom Anastos completed the scoring. Goalie Ron Scott made 29 saves in the opening game and 32 on the next evening.

Football—**November 14, 1981 (H):** MSU jumped out of the gates and led at halftime, 28-6, but Minnesota came back to score 30 unanswered points in the third quarter to take a 36-28 lead. The Spartans bounced back in the fourth as quarterback Bryan Clark threw for one touchdown and ran for another to retake the lead for a 43-36 win. Clark finished the game with 318 yards passing and three touchdowns and halfback Aaron Carter ran for 91 yards on 19 carries.

Hockey—**November 21, 1981 (H):** Defensemen Gary Haight and Ken Leiter netted first-period tallies and freshman Lyle Phair added an insurance goal with less than five minutes to play to lead MSU to a 3-0 shutout win over Michigan. Sophomore goaltender Ron Scott kicked out 27 Wolverine shots for his second shutout of the season.

Basketball—**January 7, 1982 (H):** The Spartan cagers upset defending national champion Indiana, 65-58, in front of a sellout crowd of 10,004 at Jenison Field House. Kevin Smith scored 29 points, including a Big Ten record 19-for-19 from the foul line, and Sam Vincent

added 16 points. Indiana led 43-40 with 11:40 left, but MSU outscored the Hoosiers 21-5 in the next 8:38 to take a 61-48 lead with 3:02 left. Ten of MSU's final points came on Smith free throws.

Gymnastics—**January 17, 1982 (H):** The MSU men's gymnastics team came up with its finest effort of the season by edging defending Big Ten champion Illinois, 257.35-257.25. It was a win attributed to team depth as the Illini took four events to the Spartans' two. With Pete Roberts topping all competitors with a 9.2 score, State jumped to an early four-point lead while taking the floor exercise 44.8 to 40.7. Following that opening event things tightened up considerably and although they were beaten in four of the final five events, Szypula's stalwarts never trailed in the meet. In addition to Roberts first place, Marvin Gibbs grabbed individual honors in the vault with a 9.5 and Greg Bosscawen tied for top honors on the parallel bars with a 9.25.

Basketball—**January 21, 1982 (A):** After trailing throughout the opening half, State ran off a 29-9 rush after intermission to take a 15-point lead, but then held off the U of M for a 64-62 win before 12,202 fans at Crisler Arena. Senior guard Kevin Smith hit for a team-high 23 points while junior forward Derek Perry chipped in 19 points with nine rebounds. Contributing from off the bench were Cleveland Bibbens and Kurt James, who combined for a total of 10 points and 12 rebounds. Smith, who earlier in the season set a Big Ten record by making 19 of 19 free throws against Indiana, missed four in five tries in the final 20 seconds to keep the Wolverines' hope alive. It was MSU's fifth win over Michigan in the past six games.

Wrestling—**January 22, 1982 (H):** For the third time in a span of five meets, State shutout an opponent. With previous wins over Indiana (42-0) and Western Michigan (47-0), this time the victim was the University of Illinois, 33-0, coached by the Spartans' three-time NCAA champion, Greg Johnson. All of the wins against the Illini were by decision: Harrell Milhouse (118 pounds) 8-5: James Mason (126 pounds) 10-2; Ron Cantini (134 pounds) 11-6; Shawn White (142 pounds) 13-4; Greg Sargis (150 pounds) 5-0; Fred Worthem (158 pounds) 10-2; Phil Welch (167 pounds) 4-1; Keith Foxx (177 pounds); Mike Potts (190 pounds) and Dan Dudley (heavyweight) 11-7.

Swimming and Diving—**January 22, 1982 (H):** With two swimmers winning a pair of races, the Spar-

tans took 11 of 13 events and totally dominated the University of Illinois, 72-41. Kevin Hook finished first in the 200-yard freestyle (1:43.72) and a first in the 100-yard freestyle (47.64) while Rob Lundquist captured the individual medley (1:57.49) and 200-yard breaststroke (2:11.89). Other winners for MSU were C.J. Winkel, in the 1,000-yard freestyle (9:42.61); George Kruggel in the 200-yard butterfly (1:54.63); Greg Sluke, the 200-yard backstroke (2:00.63); Matt Fetters, 500-yard freestyle (4:43.25) and diver Mike Brown who scored 309.6 points in the three-meter competition. Both relays were winners. The medley foursome of Sluke, Lundquist, Kruggel and Mark Lancaster swam a 3:33.9 and the freestyle four of Hook, Winkle, Willam Eisenstein and John Kasley finished in 3:11.59.

Wrestling—**January 23, 1982 (H):** Led by pins from Greg Sargis and Mike Potts, State easily defeated Purdue, 34-7. Sargis, at 150 pounds, registered his fall at 4:29 and 190-pound Mike Potts put his opponent to the mat in 1:31. Gaining decisions were Harrell Millhouse (118 pounds) 6-3; Shawn White (142 pounds) 10-2; Fred Worthem (158 pounds) 11-6; Phil Welch (167 pounds) 14-4; Keith Foxx (177 pounds) 4-1 and heavyweight Dan Dudley 8-1. Jim Mason gained a draw in his 126-pound match.

Fencing—**January 23, 1982 (H):** The fencers topped Chicago, 15-12, as foil competitor senior Keith DeFever turned in the most noteworthy performance of the meet. Down 4-0 and one point away from losing his bout, he came back to win 5-4. With records of 3-2 and 4-2 respectively, Jeff Herzbach and John Chambers registered wins in the sabre competition. Senior Barry Peterman won three-of-five epee bouts and senior Kevin White won two-of-three foil bouts.

Fencing—**February 6, 1982 (H):** In a marathon seven-hour five-team meet that was held in the Dem Hall ballroom and ice arena, State defeated Wisconsin-Parkside 20-7 and the U of M-Dearborn, 15-12. In sabre competition, John Chambers was 10-2 on the day and Jeff Herzbach 6-5. The foil attack was led by Keith DeFever at 7-5 and Kevin White, who wound up 6-6. Epeeist Brad Peterman went 7-1, while brother Barry turned in an impressive 6-3 record.

Basketball—**February 11, 1982 (A):** Freshman Sam Vincent stepped it up against Michigan, scoring 24 points on 9-of-14 shooting from the field and six-of-six from the free-throw line. The Wolverines, who hadn't

won at Jenison since 1978, never led in the contest and trailed by as many as 13 before the break. They did, however, close the gap and tie the score in the second half, but MSU made 12-of-17 free throws down the stretch to seal the game. In addition to Vincent's scoring effort, Ben Tower and Kevin Smith scored nine points each.

Hockey—**February 16, 1982 (A):** MSU clinched home ice in the first round of the CCHA Playoffs with a 7-1 thrashing of Michigan before a near-capacity crowd of 6,144. The offensive stars of the evening were Mark Hamway with a two-goal, three-assist performance and Newell Brown who scored one goal and assisted on four other markers. Yet, the defining segment of the game came in the second period with State holding a 2-1 lead. From 5:14 until the 11:15 mark of that middle session, while skating one and/or two men short, Ron Mason's squad successfully thwarted the Wolverines' offense. Led by Frank Finn, Dan McFall, Kelly Miller and Dave Taylor, the U of M was limited to a mere three shots on goaltender Ron Scott during those six minutes of power-play hockey. Other Spartan goal-scorers during the evening were Gord Flegel, Dan Beaty, Craig Larkin and Miller. The win sealed MSU's best record since the 1975-1976 campaign.

Wrestling—**February 20, 1982 (H):** MSU squeaked by Wisconsin, 20-17, in the last regular-season meet of the year at IM West. The Spartans jumped out to a quick 9-0 lead after the first two matches and were ahead 12-3 after four. MSU faltered a bit in the next few matches, but Keith Foxx (177) and Mike Potts (190) once again put together back-to-back victories to lead the Spartans to victory.

Lacrosse—**April 3, 1982 (H):** The Spartans fought off snow, cold weather and gale force winds to crush Kenyon, 9-3, giving second-year coach Coach Rick Kimball his first-ever Midwest Lacrosse Association win. Junior Rick Dobreff single-handedly kept the Spartans in the contest during the opening half as three times he scored to match goals by the visitors, making the halftime score read 3-3. After the intermission, the Spartans took control with four goals in the first six minutes of play, three by freshman star Riney Wilke. Simultaneously, the defense, led by Greg Walker, Craig Purcell and Mike McCarthy stiffened while goalie Jimmy Sanford turned aside 22 shots with a number of acrobatic saves.

Baseball—**April 24, 1982 (H):** With a pair of home victories over Indiana, 2-0 and 5-3, the Spartans ran their winning streak to seven in a row and 12 out of 14. The opener was a beautifully pitched two-hit, 12-strikeout gem by southpaw Tim Birtsas. State scored in the first inning when Ed Grochowalski singled, took second on a wild pick-off throw and came home on Chris Dorr's single. The final run came in the bottom of the sixth as freshman Dave Corey doubled home Andy Krause from second. In the nightcap, IU led 3-0 after five innings. Responding to the rhythmic applause of the 1,069 fans in the bottom of the sixth, State batters parlayed five walks, an error, a sacrifice fly and singles by Steve Barnes and Dorr to register five runs. That was the game as the rally made a winner of pitcher Terry Johnson who gave up just four hits.

Lacrosse—**April 24, 1982 (H):** Featuring a balanced attack that saw seven Spartans register goals, Rich Kimball's squad scored the school's first-ever win over Ohio State, 10-6. Stretching back to 1970, the Buckeye dominance had reached 12 straight victories. Goals by Rick Dobreff, Greg Helgemoe, Greg Sutherland and Dan McNulty gave the Spartans a 4-2 halftime lead. Another four-goal surge (Helgemoe, Mike Behrman and two by Dobreff) put the game out of reach in the third period. MSU's junior netminder, Jimmy Sanford, had particular reason to revel in the win. He hailed from Columbus, Ohio.

Tennis—**April 27, 1982 (H):** Registering their first win over Notre Dame since 1978, Stan Drobac's squad edged the Irish 5-4. It took a pair of three-set victories in the doubles competition to gain the needed points. Spartan winners at singles were number two Jeff Wickman (6-4, 5-0), number four captain Scott King (6-2, 6-4) and number six Marc Cohen (3-6, 7-5, 6-1). The duo of Steve Yorimoto-Joe O'Brien came from behind to capture the team point at number one pairs, 3-6, 7-5, 6-3 and then the number two team of Ross Smith-Wickman also rebounded to salvage the winning team point 2-6, 6-3, 7-5.

Track and Field—**May 1, 1982 (A):** Capturing only two field events, (Paul Piwinski in the high jump and Greg Turner in the long jump), the Spartans ran to eight of 10 first place finishes on the track which led to a rather easy dual-meet victory over Ohio State, 86-59. Those runners who raced to wins were: Don Muhammad with a 10.3 in the 100-meter dash; Eliot

Tabron who ran a 21.2 in the 200-meters; Marcus Sanders, the winner at 400 meters in 47.8; co-captain Michael White, who out-ran the field with a 15:05.5 clocking in the 5,000 meters. Michael Boyd with a 15.1 to prevail in the high hurdles and Robert Murphy, who broke the tape in the 400-meter intermediate hurdle race in a time of 53.5. In addition, MSU quartets managed to win both the 400- and 1,600-meter relay events.

Baseball—May 8, 1982 (A): Blanking Ohio State through the opening five innings, Brian James, a junior right-hander, stretched his record to 7-0 as he held on to defeat the Bucks 7-3. Meanwhile, the Spartans managed 11 hits while scoring twice in the second inning before putting the game away with four more runs in the third. Tom Dieters went four-for-four at the plate, including a home run and two runs scored. Darryl Dixon also lofted a long-ball over the outfield fence.

ATHLETE OF THE YEAR

Like many of the soccer-style kickers that began flooding the collegiate football scene in the 1960s and 1970s, Morten Andersen had a European background, having spent the first 17 years of his life in Struer, Denmark. He came to the United States as an exchange student. Until he began kicking at Ben Davis High School in Indianapolis, Ind., his senior year, he had never seen a football. As he would later describe it, he first thought the pigskin resembled " a funny-looking pumpkin."

Andersen went on to become the greatest kicker in MSU history. He was an All-America honoree his senior year in 1981 as chosen by *The Sporting News*, United Press and the Walter Camp Foundation. He was MSU's leading scorer with 73 points on 28 PATs and 15 field goals. In addition, opponents returned just 17 of his 56 kickoffs. Andersen closed out his career ranked number one on the MSU and Big Ten lists in field goals with 45 while holding down the top spot on the school's all-time chart in PATs (126) and total points (261). He recorded seven field goals of 50 or more yards and three others of 49 yards. Picked by the New Orleans Saints in the fourth round of the 1982 NFL draft, Anderson's professional career spanned three decades during which he became only the third player to ever score more than 2,000 points.

IN THE SPARTLITE

Baseball: The team returned from Texas with a note of optimism. Although the won-loss record had been a 7-7, the pitching corps had registered a 3.29 ERA, significantly better than the 6.31 of the entire 1981 season.

With eight games remaining in the schedule, State's overall record stood at a respectable 25-21 and 6-4 in conference play. Unfortunately, they completed the season 0-8 to end up 25-29 and 6-10 in the Big Ten.

Tim Birtsas pitched eight complete games during the season, which is tied for second-best for an MSU pitcher. Birtsas would become a second-team All-Big Ten selection. Another big contributor to the pitching ranks was junior Brian James who recorded an impressive 7-1 record over the season.

Chris Dorr led the team in hitting with a .365 batting average.

Basketball: Derek Perry had the distinction of being the team's top rebounder, but his season average of 5.4 was the lowest ever to lead a Spartan team since records were first kept in 1956.

Morten Andersen

Senior guard Kevin Smith was named first-team All-Big Ten for the second consecutive year. It marked the fifth-straight year that MSU had been represented among the top five players in the league. Smith, who was the team's top scorer with a 15.6 ppg average, was also named the team's most valuable player.

Freshman Sam Vincent averaged 11.7 ppg, which still ranks as fourth-best for a rookie at MSU.

This was one of the most disappointing seasons of Spartan basketball. Posting a season record of 12-16, the average of .429 was the lowest since the 1970-1971 team went 10-14 for an average .417. The loss column included an unusual six home games.

Cross Country: MSU placed third out of 24 teams at the Purdue Invitational. Michael White was the top Spartan finisher, placing 7th in a time of 24:40.

At the Big Ten championships in Minneapolis, State totaled 197 points and finished in seventh place. White was the top Spartan finisher, placing 20th with a time of 24:46.6. He would also place 20th at the NCAA district IV meet, completing the course in 31:02.

Fencing: Michigan State hosted the 54th Annual Big Ten Fencing Championships at Jenison Field House and compiling 15 points to finish a disappointing fifth out of five competing teams. The only bright spot for Coach Schmitter was the work of senior John Chambers who placed second in sabre and qualified to compete in the NCAA meet at South Bend, Ind. No other Spartan placed in a top-four spot.

For the first time, a conference women's championship was simultaneously conducted with three schools competing: Ohio State, Wisconsin and Northwestern.

Football: In the 27-13 loss to Ohio State, Morten Andersen kicked a Big Ten conference and MSU record 63-yard field goal.

Ted Jones caught 44 passes during the season, which at the time set a new school record. His name is still listed among the team's top 15 receivers.

James Burroughs closed his career with 28 broken passes. Although it set a new standard in 1981, it now stands at fifth on the all-time chart. He had 13 in 1981 alone.

In a 26-3 win over Indiana, MSU tied a school record with 34 first downs.

The defense swarmed all over Northwestern in the 61-14 win at Evanston, Ill., as they held the Wildcats to a net of minus-60 yards rushing. That defensive performance remains as the second most stingy in Spartan his-

tory. The 1950 team dominated Pittsburgh as the Panthers had to settle for a minus-63 yards rushing.

Four Spartans gained All-Big Ten first team recognition: place kicker Morten Andersen, center Tom Piette, linebacker Carl Banks and defensive back James Burroughs.

Golf: With a team composite card of 304, State led the 16-team field at the Michigan Invitational in Ann Arbor after the opening round. As the four-man score soared to 313 on the second day, the Spartans settled for fourth place, six strokes behind the winning-team from Miami of Ohio. With a two-day total of 149, Dave Belen finished one stroke shy of medalist honors.

Michigan State once again yielded the championship of the annual Spartan Invitational to Ohio State, but the Spartans came off the course smiling. In the race for second place, they had overcome a two-shot deficit in the final 18 holes and edged Indiana by one stroke, 738-739. Junior Rob Haidler led the charge with a team-best score of 71-72—143. Other cards turned in by the Spartans were: Todd Hartle 70-75—145; Dave Belen 73-75—148; Mike Thomsen 74-74—148; Bob Fossum 79-75—154 and captain Monty James 79-76—155. Hartle was the top finisher for the Spartans at the Big Ten championships in West Lafayette, Ind., as he shot a 70-75-74-72—291 to tie for eighth place. The team total of 1,499 placed MSU in the seventh spot. Beyond Hartle's success, Coach Fossum would later note that his team's performance was the most disappointing in his coaching career. Other members of that Big Ten tournament team were Fossum, Haidler, James and Belen.

Gymnastics: Marvin Gibbs closed out his career as one of the top gymnasts in Michigan State history. He averaged a 52.77 in the all-around his senior year, with his highest score at 55.60.

State scored 264.50 points to place seventh at the conference meet in Madison, Wis.

Pete Roberts's season average score of 9.62 in the vault competition was good enough for fourth place in the Midwest region and qualified to compete in the NCAAs at Lincoln, Neb.

Hockey: Equipment manager Tom Magee joined the staff in October.

In an odd injury during the 4-2 win over Notre Dame, Mark Hamway was struck by a puck while on the bench with his helmet off. The cut required 20 stitches to close.

One of MSU's finest gymnasts, Marvin Gibbs

With the change in affiliation from the WCHA to the CCHA along with Michigan, Notre Dame and Michigan Tech, the Spartans finished the regular season in second place while later winning the league playoff by defeating the Fighting Irish, 4-1, at Joe Louis Arena in Detroit. With that tournament win, Coach Mason, having completed his third year at MSU, stated:

"That Sunday in Detroit was just fantastic. With the band and the 8,000 people that came out to cheer us on, we made Joe Louis Arena the Munn Arena of Detroit. Certainly, we're a legitimate team now."

The run for the NCAA title was short-lived by losing to New Hampshire, 3-2 and 6-2, in two games at Durham, N.H.

The team's 26 wins and 42 games played were both school records at the time.

Goalie Ron Scott collected a myriad of post-season awards: first-team All-American, first-team Academic All-American, first team All-CCHA selection and CCHA tournament MVP. In addition, Scott finished runner-up in voting for the prestigious Hobey Baker Award.

Forward Newell Brown was MSU's other first-team CCHA All-League selection.

Lacrosse: State returned from a trip East during the term break with a less-than-impressive 1-3 record. Leading the attack had been freshman Riney Wilkie and veteran Dan McNulty, each with eight goals.

Greg Helgmore closed out his Spartan career as the 13th leading scorer in school history with 49 goals, 36 assists for a total of 85 points.

McNulty once more gained All-Midwest Lacrosse second team honors with Helgmore and goalkeeper Jim Sanford gaining honorable mention.

Soccer: After defeating Ohio State 2-1 in the opening round of the mid-season Big Ten East Division tournament, Michigan State proved to be no match for the number two-ranked Indiana University squad, losing to the Hoosiers on the next afternoon, 5-1. Steve Erdman had the solitary goal for MSU when he knocked in a corner kick from Steve Swanson. From that game the Spartans would have an impressive second half of the season, posting an 8-1 record.

During the season State outscored the opposition 38-21 and had seven shutouts compared to the opponents' two.

Only the 1967 NCAA championship team could boast of 12 wins until the 1981 squad posted their 12-5 record. This season-tying mark stood until the 1986 team won 13 games.

Tom King scored a team-high 15 goals, the most productive season since Tony Keyes team-record 28 set in 1968.

Swimming and Diving: The team scored 184 points at the conference championships in Iowa City, Iowa, which resulted in a seventh place finish. Rob Lundquist completed an outstanding season by winning the 200-yard breaststroke (2:05.04), placing second in the 100-yard breaststroke (57.05) and finishing fourth in the 200-yard individual medley (1:53.76). Freshman C.J. Winkel was fourth in both the 500- and 1,650-yard freestyle, posting times of 4:29.48 and 15:36.33. Others who gained team points in consolation heats were Greg Sluke, 14th in both the 100- and 200-yard backstroke; George Kruggel, ninth in the 100-yard butterfly and Kevin Hook in the 200-yard freestyle. Diver Mike Brown placed ninth in the three-meter event.

Brown was the team's solitary representative at the NCAA meet in Milwaukee, Wis., and he scored 510.25 points to place 12th on the three-meter board.

Rob Lundquist capped off a spectacular season at the 1982 conference championships.

Tennis: With a minimal amount of money available to lure the top talent, coach Stan Drobac opened the season with four freshmen walk-ons: Mark Cohen, Ross Smith, Joe O'Brien and Curtis Wright.

In the final meet on the schedule, the Spartans met and defeated the University of Iowa, 7-2, for the first win over the Big Ten team in two years.

Gaining strength from their doubles teams, State surprised many by gaining 16 points and finishing seventh at the conference championships at Madison, Wis. The number two pair of Jeff Wickman and Smith advanced to the third round before elimination and the number three duo of Scott King and Francisco Amaya reached the semifinals before losing to their Minnesota competitors. In singles, Smith worked to the final round of the consolation bracket where he lost 6-2, 6-2.

Although not having an impressive conference showing, Steve Yorimoto, State's number one singles player, earned All-Big Ten honors, the first Spartan to do so since 1979.

Track and Field: The Spartan runners were only able to boast second place finishes upon completion of the indoor Central Collegiate meet at Madison, Wis. Mike Boyd was second in the 50-yard hurdles (.07.49) and Corky Wilkins posted a 30.54 in the 300-yard dash.

Sanders, the Lansing freshman, won a Big Ten indoor title by running the 600-yard race in 1:10.79. He then teamed with Murphy, Calvin Thomas and Scott to capture the mile relay (3:13.77). Wilkins was runner-up in the 300-yard sprint; Daryl Dismond and Piwinski placed fourth and sixth in the high jump; Don Mohammad and Andre Williams finished fourth and fifth in the 60-yard dash; Scott was sixth in the 440 and Terry Ross completed the 880 in sixth.

Moving outdoors, in their own invitational meet at Ralph Young Field, MSU track men paced a 10-team field by winning eight of the 15 events. Elliott Tabron won the 100 meter (10.4), the 200 meter (21.2) and then anchored the 440-yard and mile relays. Shot putter Todd Hoover threw the shot 56' 1" and qualified for the Drake relays. Tom Irman won the 3,000-meter steeplechase (9:09.8).

Paul Piwinski established a team outdoor record when he cleared the high jump bar at 7' 2-1/4" at the Drake Relays in Des Moines, Iowa. The performance also qualified him for the NCAA Championships in Provo, Utah. In that same meet, Sanders placed third in the 400-meters with a time of 47.62.

As a transfer from Wayne State, Elliott Tabron would sit out the first portion of the academic year and therefore miss the indoor season. In the Big Ten outdoor championships at Minneapolis, he ran a 45.32 to set a new meet record in winning the 400-meter dash. In addition, he placed second in the 200-meter dash with a 21.09. Also finishing in second place was Muhammad with a 10:68 in the 100-meters and the 400-meter relay of Williams, Wilkins, Muhammad and Tabron (40.47). Piwinski was sixth in the high jump at 6' 10" as the 1,600-meter relay team of Thomas, Sanders, Scott and Tabron concluded the weekend with a gold-medal performance (3:08.75).

Running in the Central Collegiates at South Bend and with Corky Wilkins filling in for the absent Marcus Sanders, the 1,600-meter relay team posted a (3:07.84) to qualify for the NCAA championships.

Wrestling: Riding the strength of five individual titles, MSU opened the season by wrapping up first-place in their Spartan Invitational, narrowly edged defending champion Indiana State, 52 1/2-50 1/2. The MSU winners were: Jim Mason (126 pounds), Greg Sargis (150 pounds), Fred Worthem (158 pounds), Phil Welch (167 pounds) and Mike Potts (190 pounds).

Later in the schedule the Spartans would win two additional team trophies, at the Michigan Open and in the Bowling Green Tournament.

At the Big Ten tournament in Ann Arbor, MSU wrestlers scored 40 points to finish in fourth place. Sargis and Worthem each placed second; Shawn White (142 pounds), Keith Foxx (177 pounds) and Potts were third-place finishers and gaining fourths were Mason and Ron Cantini (134 pounds).

Mason, Cantini, Sargis, Foxx and Potts competed in the NCAA championship meet at Ames, Iowa. With early round wins by Cantini and Potts, State gained 10 points and finished 25th out of 64 teams that scored.

On the season, Sargis would lead the team with 17 pins and be recipient of the team's Outstanding Wrestler Award. Meanwhile, Mike Potts would earn All-American honors.

EXTRA! 1982 NCAA HOCKEY TOURNAMENT (Regionals)

In the first year of the CCHA, Ron Mason's team easily won the playoff championship, defeating Lake Superior State, Michigan Tech and Notre Dame. This sent them to the NCAA tournament where they faced New Hampshire. The first game was a close 3-2 loss, but the Wildcats outdid the Spartans in the second game 6-2. It was the first and only time all year that MSU lost two consecutive games.

March 19, 1982—Durham, N.H.
New Hampshire 3, MSU 2
1st Pd.: No Scoring.
2nd Pd.: 1. NH, Byrnes (Barton, Potter), 14:47.
3rd Pd.: 2. MSU, Hamway (Haight), 6:40; 3. NH, Potter (unasst.), 7:39; 4. MSU, Hamway (Phair, Flegel), 12:40; 5. NH, Robinson (Doherty, White), 16:20.

March 20, 1982—Durham, N.H.
New Hampshire 6, MSU 2
1st Pd.: 1. NH, Barton (Brickley), 17:03; 2. MSU, Phair (Kl. Miller, Martin), 18:58.
2nd Pd.: 3. NH, Muse (Ellison, Chisholm), 8:05; 4. NH, White (R. Robinson, Doherty), 10:03; 5. NH, Yantzi (Forget, R. Robinson), 15:12.
3rd Pd.: 6. NH, Lacombe (Forget, Lee), 7:14; 7. NH, Chisholm (Muse, Ellison), 12:10; 8. MSU, Brown (Taylor, Phair), 17:49.

Mark Hamway was injured when a puck hit him in the head during the regular season, but he was able to recover in time to contribute during the 1982 regional playoffs.

MSU
1982-1983

TALES TO TELL

Ron Scott, who tended goal for the Spartans' hockey teams of 1981-1983 reminisces about the 1983 playoffs and particularly the CCHA playoff game of March 12:

"After the 1982-1983 regular season in which we had spent time ranked number one in the country, the CCHA playoff championship game came down to MSU and number two-ranked Bowling Green. The Falcons had a potent offense and our strength was an excellent defense and balanced offense.

Playing on an injured ankle sustained in the 8-3 victory over Ohio State on the previous day, I had no intention of sitting this one out. As expected, the game was closely fought and at the end of regulation it was tied 3-3. The championship and a berth in the NCAA tournament had come down to sudden death overtime. Midway through the overtime period Brian Hills of BG broke in alone but our defenseman Gary Haight intervened by instinctively throwing his stick at Hills. Having done so, the rule called for an automatic penalty shot. So there we were, Brian Hills, the nation's leading scorer versus me, the hobbled goalie. I knew that if I let Hills use his great shooting

ability he would have the advantage, but if I was able to force him to try to fake me out of position my quickness and mobility would give me the edge. My strategy was to move far out of the net as soon as Hills touched the puck at center ice, taking away any open net at which to shoot and then to retreat quickly as he got closer. Fortunately, Hills did exactly as I had hoped and tried to fake me out of position, but I was able to move with him and stop the shot. To the relief of the Spartan faithful we were still in it and in less than a minute later, Mark Hamway scored the winner to give us our second straight CCHA playoff championship.

While this game was a great personal moment for me and is remembered for the overtime penalty shot, the quarterfinal series the week before against Ferris State truly signified MSU's transformation into a championship caliber program. Those of us who came to MSU in the early years of the Ron Mason era had two goals: one was to reestablish Michigan State as a hockey power after many years of under-performance and two was to win a national championship. The 1981-1982 and 1982-1983 seasons showed that we were back on the national scene and the Ferris State series showed the championship char-

HEADLINES of 1983

- The first cell phone is introduced to the world.
- *M*A*S*H* ends its 11-year run with the largest audience ever to watch a single TV show.
- Cabbage Patch dolls, introduced by Coleco Industries, is the top-selling Christmas toy.
- U.S. Marines and Rangers, along with small forces from six Caribbean nations, invade the island of Grenada to free citizens from a Marxist regime.

SCOREBOARD

	W	L	T	Avg.
Baseball	22	32	0	.407
Track and Field	1	2	0	.333
Football	2	9	0	.182
Basketball	17	13	0	.566
Tennis	4	15	0	.263
Cross Country	1	5	0	.166
Swimming and Diving	3	8	0	.273
Wrestling	10	4	0	.714
Hockey	30	11	1	.726
Fencing	6	7	0	.461
Golf	tournament play only			
Gymnastics	7	8	0	.467
Soccer	11	5	1	.676
Lacrosse	8	8	0	.500

acter, which would result three years later in the national championship.

That quarterfinal was a two-game total goal series with the winner advancing to Joe Louis Arena. The first night Ferris State upset us 4-2, but we were confident that we could come back in game two. The second game was what I feel was the greatest night of my MSU career. We completely dominated the game right from the start but were frustrated by a hot Ferris State goaltender. With only ten minutes left in the game we found ourselves with a two-goal deficit. Lesser teams would have succumbed to the frustration we were feeling, but we showed the character from which championship teams are born. Rallying for four goals in the last ten minutes we turned seemingly certain defeat into a great victory and sent us on to Joe Louis Arena for those championship victories and a slot in the NCAA tournament. With goal after goal being scored, Munn Arena had been transformed from a subdued atmosphere to complete frenzy. The players who took charge in those last 10 minutes were

the true heroes who by their hard work and determination provided the framework for championships down the road. Players like Mark Hamway, Newell Brown, Ken Leiter, Gary Haight, Dave Taylor, Kelly Miller, Tom Anostos, Dan McFall and Lyle Phair provided standards by which future players were judged. While we may not have had the pure skills of the players who followed us, we provided the foundation upon which Ron Mason built a hockey power."

TEAM OF THE YEAR

The 1983 edition of the Michigan State wrestling team was an impressive crew reminiscent of MSU's glory days in the late 1960s and early 1970s. The Spartans took first as a team in their first four multi-team tournaments of the season and won seven of their first nine dual matches. They finished second in the Big Ten championships, the highest of any MSU team since the 1972 team capped an incredible run of seven straight Big Ten titles. Five Spartans qualified for the NCAA tournament. Those five were Harrell Milhouse, Greg Sargis, Mike Potts, Fred Worthem and Eli Blazeff. Worthem (158 pounds), who reached the semifinals before elimination and Blazeff (190 pounds), a quarterfinalist, both gained recognition as All-Americans. Overall, MSU finished 12th, the best showing for a Spartan team since 1972.

The 1983 wrestling team. (First row) H. Milhouse, ninth from left, and J. Mason, 12th. (Second row) R. Cantini, second from left. (Third row) T. White, fourth from left, M. Potts 10th, Eli Blazeff, 12th, and F. Worthem, 16th.

MAKING HISTORY

A football rule stipulated that the 25 seconds between the ready-for-play and the ball being put in play shall be timed with a watch operated by the appropriate official or with 25-second clocks at each end of the field operated by an assistant.

By a vote of 9-0 with the Wisconsin athletic director abstaining, the Big Ten voted to introduce the three-point shot into basketball games beginning with the 1982-1983 season on a trial basis. The arch line would be established 21 feet from the basket. Later, in May of 1983, the same conference officials voted to rescind the rule; so after one year, the bonus shot had been eliminated.

Demonstration Hall was converted into a recreational facility. The old ice arena had been used by the MSU department of military science since the completion of Munn Ice Arena.

For the first time in history, alumni returned for homecoming to watch a winless football team.

Following the 24-18 loss to Purdue to close the season at 2-9, Muddy Waters was carried off the field in heroic fashion. It was his last game as coach of the MSU Spartans. George Perles was hired as his replacement.

After three tries, the cagers won their own tournament for the first time, the annual Cutlass Classic.

The NCAA passed Proposition 48, a ruling that required athletes to complete a prescribed core of high school courses (math, English, social science and physical-biological sciences) to be eligible for competition as freshmen. They would also have to score a minimum of 700 on the Scholastic Aptitude Test (SAT) or 15 on the American College Test (ACT). A student falling short of the criteria could still be awarded a scholarship but would be ineligible to play or practice until he achieved a 2.0 grade point average at the start of his sophomore year. The rule would not go into effect until 1986.

Eli Blazeff, the standout 177-pound wrestler from Stow, Ohio, who set a season pin record of 19, added to his laurels by winning the national judo title in championships hosted by MSU.

The NCAA approved changes to the basketball rules. All fouls committed in the last two minutes of a game would result in two free throws if the team was in the bonus, and timeouts would be reduced from five to three for games that are broadcast on radio or TV.

Heretofore a part-time basketball coach, Tom Izzo was elevated to the position of assistant coach.

The MSU Board of Trustees approved the extension of basketball coach Jud Heathcote's annual contract of $54,249 two years through 1987. The same extension was made for hockey coach Ron Mason who earned $44,000 a year.

GREAT STATE DATES

Cross Country—**October 2, 1982 (H):** In their first dual meet of the season, the MSU runners downed Northwestern 25-32 at Forest Akers West Golf Course. The Spartans placed six of their runners in the top 10. Junior Tom Irmen was the overall victor in the five-mile race. Running with a chest cold, he broke the tape with a time of 25:08. Also placing for State were fourth-place Eric Stuber in 25:42; Rick Pietras who finished fifth in 25:55; Mike Kavulich was seventh in 26:19 and Tim Simpson finished eighth with a time of 26:37. Other finishers for MSU were Mike Kosnar, Craig Shatney, Kwith Harris and Mark Williamson.

Soccer—**October 6, 1982 (H):** It took overtime to do it, but freshman midfielder Tom Doherty booted in the winning goal to earn MSU a 2-1 victory over a respected Oakland University team. Ranked seventh nationally in division II, the Pioneers had tallied eight consecutive shutouts until forward Vancho Cirovski opened the second half by feeding the ball to Tommy King who scored the game's first goal. Coach Baum offered special praise for goalkeeper Paul Zimmerman.

Football—**October 30, 1982 (A):** In his first collegiate start, freshman quarterback Dave Yarema led MSU to a 22-14 victory over Indiana University, 22-14, before 38,571 fans in Bloomington. Ralf Mojsiejenko climaxed the opening drive with a 34-yard field goal and he connected again in the second quarter with yet another 34-yarder to pull State within one at the intermission. The Spartans turned that 7-6 halftime deficit into a 19-7 lead with a 13-point surge in the third quarter. The first TD followed a Hoosier turnover at their 20-yard line. A pair of Tony Ellis runs covered the distance with the big fullback from Arizona scoring from the 11-yard line. A two-point conversion attempt failed. On the next series, IU was only able to punt out to their 36-yard line and, two plays later, Yarema connected with senior flanker Otis Grant on a crossing pattern for 35 yards and a touchdown. With 1:08 remaining in the game, Mojsiejenko

closed the scoring with his third field goal of the afternoon, a 28-yarder, giving State an eight-point victory margin. Defensive back Phil Parker closed it out when he intercepted a desperation pass in the closing seconds. Yarema finished the day with 10 of 18 completions and two interceptions. Heading the defensive side was Jim Neely who was credited with 10 tackles.

Hockey—**November 5 (A) & 6 (H), 1982:** The undefeated and number one-ranked MSU hockey team swept the weekend series with the University of Michigan, 5-2 and 4-3. In the opener at Ann Arbor, junior Newell Brown scored three of the winners' goals to register his second hat trick of the season and fifth of his career. Lyle Phair broke a 1-1 tie during a power play in the second period when he tipped in yet another Brown shot. Thereafter, State outscored the hosts 3-1. On Saturday night, before a record Munn crowd of 6,793, Ron Mason's offense ran into a "hot" goalie that turned away 50 shots. Trailing 2-1 after two periods, the Spartans exploded for a pair of goals in the opening minute of the third to take the lead for good. First, Ken Leiter assisted Dale Krentz at the 20-second mark, and then at the one-minute mark Dan McFall set up Brown for a second breakaway goal. Kelly Miller added an insurance marker at 11:25.

Soccer—**November 13, 1982 (A):** MSU conquered the cold and a stubborn Northwestern defense for a 3-2 overtime win in the final game of the regular season at Old College Field. Appropriately, playing his final game as a Spartan, Tommy King, scored both goals in regulation. Yet it was a freshman Eric Weissand who knocked in the game-winner at the 10:40 mark of OT.

Football—**November 13, 1983 (H):** After yielding an opening touchdown, State came back with 26 unanswered points to defeat the University of Minnesota, 26-7 in a night game before 57,146 at the Humphrey Metrodome. Dave Yarema completed two touchdown passes to Daryl Turner and Ralf Mojsiejenko tied a school record with four field goals of 26, 44, 30 and 52 yards. The first Yarema-to-Turner TD came in the second quarter as the junior split end fought off two defenders in the end zone to gather in a 40-yard aerial. The second Yarema-Turner score came on a 25-yard pass over the middle on the first play of the fourth quarter. The game was much closer than the score would indicate as the Gophers were plagued by mistakes, committing three turnovers on fumbles, two inside the MSU five-yard line in the opening half, and throwing three interceptions, two pilfered

by sophomore linebacker Jim Morrissey.

Swimming and Diving—**January 8, 1983 (A):** In a triple dual meet hosted by Cleveland State, MSU defeated the Vikings 67-46 and Western Michigan, 100-13. Two Spartans registered double wins. Jim Mathieson won the 200-yard freestyle in 1:44.7 and later captured the 500 in 4:45.6. Diver Mike Brown, coach John Narcy's All-American, scored 276.7 points to win the one-meter event and then came back to post 279.5 points as winner in the three-meter competition. Other Spartan firsts came from T.J. Winkel with a 9:38.9 in the 1,00-yard freestyle; Rafel Segarra, 1:58.4 in the 200-yard butterfly; Greg Sluke, who was timed in 2:04.0 for the backstroke; and Tom Christel, with a winning time of 2:16.1 in the breaststroke. Also scoring points with second-place finishes were Matt Fetters, Kevin Hook and diver Kirk Harrington.

Hockey—**January 28 (H) & 29 (A) 1983:** For the second time of the season, MSU swept a weekend series against the University of Michigan. This time the scores were 3-1 and 2-1 with both games punctuated by pushing, shoving, stick wielding, verbal abuse and fist-swinging exchanges. Friday's encounter, played before a Munn Arena record-tying crowd of 6,703, featured 22 penalties with 32 infractions called during play on the following night. At one point during the opening period on Saturday there were five players in each penalty box. It was either three-on-three or four-on-four from the 2:29 mark of period number one until the 12:38 mark of period number two. Goals in the first game were netted by Rick Fernandez, Mark Hamway and Gord Flegel while Dan McFall and Rob Martin scored in the second victory. Goalie Ron Scott stopped a combined 45 shots during the two contests.

Wrestling—**January 28, 1983 (H):** Coach Grady Peninger would later share the pre-meet instructions he had offered Harrell Milhouse: "We told him take the kid, beat up on him, score on him, then try to pin him, and that's exactly what he did." Indeed, the 118-pounder put his Wolverine opponent's shoulders to the mat after 2:47. It was his fifth straight win in Big Ten competition and his third pin of the season. More importantly, it set the tone for the remainder of the meet as State lost only two matches while registering the school's largest victory margin ever over the University of Michigan, 31-7. Furthermore, it posted MSU's fifth win over the Wolverines during a six-year span. Following Milhouse to the mat was junior Jim Mason (the team's win leader with 21), who

won 9-4 and the route was underway. The Spartans were only stopped twice, at 142 pounds and in the final match at heavyweight. Senior Greg Sargis registered his 12th pin of the season after only 53 seconds at 150 pounds. Winners by decision were Ron Cantini (134 pounds), Fred Worthem (158 pounds), Tony White (167 pounds), Eli Blazeff (177 pounds) and Mike Potts (190 pounds).

Basketball—**February 5, 1983 (A):** Led by sophomore Sam Vincent with 25 points and senior co-captain Derek Perry with 16, Michigan State held on for a 70-65 victory over the University of Michigan before a sellout crowd of 13,609 at Crisler Arena. A 13-point Spartan advantage late in the first half was frittered away until the U of M led by five with nine minutes of playing time remaining. From there State quickly came back to tie the game 51-51 at 6:22 on a Vincent lay-up and free throw. Perry followed with a short jumper to once more put MSU ahead as they slowly pulled away. The win was secured in the final three minutes at the free-throw line, with Perry making four straight, Scott Skiles a pair and Vincent three. The win was the seventh over the Wolverines in the last eight meetings.

Wrestling—**February 6, 1983 (H):** It was a battle of two ranked teams as number seven MSU upset number four Nebraska. Each squad registered five wins with the difference being a pair of Spartan pins (six team points each). Jim Mason (126 pounds), registered the first at 4:13 after Harrell Milhouse (118-pounds) had won 11-6. Following "S" losses in the 134 and 142 pound divisions, Greg Sargis (150 pounds) registered a fall upping the Spartan led to 15-8. MSU took the lead for good after Fred Worthem's (158 pounds) 12-6 victory and the 10-8 win by Eli Blazeff (177 pounds). With one match remaining and State leading 21-15, a Husker pin in the final match would have resulted in a tie meet. State's Heavyweight John Wojciechowski, a defensive tackle on the football team and wrestling in his first collegiate match, hung tough and although losing, 3-2, avoided the tying pin and the final score read Michigan State 21, Nebraska 18.

Hockey—**February 12, 1983 (A):** Captain Mark Hamway had it "his way" in a Saturday night contest at Houghton. The senior right winger scored four goals in regulation to tie the Michigan Tech total and send the game into overtime where Dale Krentz quickly unknotted the score with an unassisted goal at 1:35. Hamway found the back of the net twice in the first period, once in the second and then tied the game with 2:09 remaining in regulation. The Tech goalie faced a barrage of 43 shots during the evening.

Gymnastics—**February 12, 1983 (A):** Relying on the team's star in addition to team depth, the MSU gymnastic team defeated the University of Michigan, 260.15–235.80. Team co-captains Bart Acino and Greg Bosscawen tied for first in the parallel bars while Acino added a first-place tie in floor exercise plus a second in rings, third on the horizontal bar and a second in the all-around. Matt Neurock and Bruce Trevor added valuable team points with seconds and thirds in their specialties.

Basketball—**February 24, 1983 (H):** In what could be considered the most memorable performance ever by an MSU freshman, Scott Skiles pumped in 35 points to lead his team to a triple overtime win over the 15th-ranked Ohio State Buckeyes, 101-94. Described by the *State News* sports editor as the "alley kid from Plymouth, Ind.," Skiles hit on 12 of 19 from the field and 10 for 10 at the free-throw line. That total included: a three-pointer with 13 seconds remaining in regulation to tie the game at 74-74; the only points in the second overtime on a 15-footer with two ticks showing on the clock to knot the score at 89-89; and, finally, eight points in the third extra stanza to seal the victory. Sophomore Sam Vincent contributed 23 points, including a perfect 17 of 17 from the charity strip, before fouling out with 1:00 minute remaining in the first OT.

Fencing—**February 26, 1983 (H):** In what would be 75-year-old Charlie Schmitter's final home meet as the MSU coach, the Spartans defeated the University of Detroit 18-9, Case Western 16-11 and with a 5-4 decision in his final bout of the afternoon, Pete Haeussler vaulted MSU past Tri-State, 14-13. Other top scorers were Tim Russell, Rob Beatty, Jeff Herzbach, Tom Howorth and captain Mike Dority.

Tennis—**April 13, 1983 (H):** Featuring a clean sweep in the singles matches, Coach Drobac's squad easily defeated Eastern Michigan 8-1. Stroking those wins were Joe O'Brien, 6-2, 6-2; Steve Yorimoto, 6-2, 4-6, 6-4; Ross Smith 6-4, 6-1; Joe Webster, 6-3, 6-3; Curtis Wright 6-1, 7-5 and Andy Salski 6-3, 1-6, 6-1. Adding team points in doubles were the pairs of Smith-Webster, 6-3, 6-2 and Wright-Steve Hooley, 6-3, 7-6.

Track and Field—**April 23, 1983 (H):** Finishing first in 10 of the 17 events, the Spartans defeated Ohio State, 78-65, in the only outdoor dual meet of the spring.

Field events winners were Mark Lytle, who heaved the discus 42.5 meters; Todd Hoover with a shot put toss of 55' 3-3/4"; Greg Turner's triple jump leap of 40' 2" and Daryl Dismond who cleared 7' to better his teammate Paul Piwinski. In addition to taking both relays, four runners broke the tape to help seal the victory. Eliot Tabron ran a 10.3 in the 100 meters; Corky Wilkins a 20.9 in the 200 meters; Marcus Sanders circled the oval to win the 400 meters in 46.4 and Tom Irmen negotiated the 5,000-meter run in 14:59.4.

Lacrosse—**April 30, 1983 (A):** The team traveled to Gauthier, Ohio, where they defeated Kenyon College, 13-9, and up their Midwest Lacrosse Association record to 5-2. The Spartans jumped out early and gained a 4-0 lead after the opening period and a 5-0 advantage midway through the second. From there they let up, and by halftime, the Lords were within one, 6-5. MSU quickly regained the initiative and grabbed a 10-6 edge in the third quarter but once more the Kenyon offense closed to within one, 10-9 with nine minutes to play. From there State pulled away to secure the win. As was becoming a repetitious pattern, Riney Wilke and Marc Berman were the big scorers for State.

Baseball—**April 29-30, 1983 (A):** Using some late-inning heroics, State completed the school's first-ever four-game sweep of a Big Ten rival when they defeated Purdue 7-4 and 8-7 on Friday and 8-7 and 6-5 in the Saturday doubleheader. The opening game was tied 4-4 entering the final inning when senior right fielder Andy Krause lashed out a long triple that scored a pair of runs. Bob Goodheart followed with a sacrifice fly to complete the scoring and assure pitcher Mike Patterson of a complete-game victory. In the second game, the Spartans once more waited until the final inning. Training 5-2, Krause hit a two-run homer, closing the margin. This was followed by a two-run single from Bruno Petrella, an RBI single by Mike Whitman and a run-producing infield out by Tom Dieters. Pitcher Brian James choked off a Boiler-maker rally in the bottom of the seventh and the game concluded with an 8-7 victory. On the next afternoon it was more of the same. A three-run, two-out seventh-inning double by sophomore third baseman Dave Corey in the opener provided yet another 8-7 triumph. In the fourth game of the series senior left fielder Steve Barnes slammed a three-run seventh-inning four-bagger over the fence as the Spartans held on for another one-run win, 6-5.

Lacrosse—**May 14, 1983 (H):** State wrapped up the season with a 14-9 victory over Northwestern and an 8-8 season to be assured of a .500 season. They wasted little time by running up a 5-1 lead through the initial 15 minutes. Although things broke down from there, MSU managed to maintain a 6-3 halftime margin and 12-6 after three periods before letting the Wildcats close in a bit in the final quarter. Marc Berman and Riney Wilke led the attack as each contributed four goals. Tom Marchin, Blaine Harrison, Kirk Lewis, Rich Johnson, Mike Behrmann and Al Ferland were each credited with one goal toward the winning total.

ATHLETE OF THE YEAR

Ron Scott was one of the greatest goalies in the history of the storied Michigan State hockey program. Scott is in the top 10 at MSU in nine statistical categories for goalies, including career wins (fifth—64), games played (fourth—112) and saves (third—2,884). His 29 wins in the 1982-83 campaign rank fourth in a season at Michigan State and he led the Spartans to their second consecutive CCHA playoff championship in the spring of 1983. Scott was a two-time first-team All-American and a two-time first-team CCHA All-League selection. The team MVP for three straight years,

Ron Scott

Scott also excelled in the classroom as he was named an Academic All-American in 1982 and 1983. Scott was also respected on the national scene, as he was a Hobey Baker finalist his final two seasons including a runner-up finish in 1982. Selected as the school's Male Athlete of the Year in 1982 and 1983, he would forego his senior year by signing a guaranteed, multi-year contract with the New York Rangers.

IN THE SPARTLITE

Baseball: The annual battle against non-spring-like conditions in Michigan prevailed in mid-April. The Spartans managed to split a doubleheader with Ohio State on Saturday and then an overnight snowstorm covered Kobs Field canceling the scheduled Sunday games.

With a conference record of 8-7, State finished second in the East Division and earned a slot in the four-team tournament at Ann Arbor. The Spartans' appearance was short-lived. In the double-elimination playoff, they were first defeated by Minnesota 14-1 and then 6-2 by Iowa.

Andy Krause was the team's batting champion with a .344 average. He also earned first-team All-Big Ten and Academic All-Big Ten honors.

Mike Patterson won a team-best five games on the mound.

Basketball: Kevin Willis, a third-team All-Big Ten and All-America honorable mention selection, led the Big Ten in rebounding (10.2 per game) and in field-goal percentage (.600) and was 15th in the league in scoring (14.3 per game).

Sam Vincent, named to the All-Big Ten second-team and honorable mention All-America team, led the team in scoring with a 16.6 average and ranked 11th in Big Ten scoring at 16.7.

Freshman Scott Skiles finished third among Big Ten players in assists (5.1) and free-throw percentage (.839). He was named Big Ten freshman of the year.

Cross Country: With a score of 15-50 and for the only time ever, University of Michigan runners shut out the Michigan State entrants in a dual meet.

Tom Irmen of Maumee, Ohio, was the highest Spartan finisher at the Big Ten meet at Iowa City. Also running for State and contributing to the fifth-place score of 214 were Eric Stuber of Williamston, Craig Shantey of Grand Rapids, Rick Pietras of Ann Arbor and Mike Kavulich of Berkeley.

Fencing: Hosting the opening meet of the season, State suffered overwhelming losses, 20-1 to Notre Dame and 4-23 to Northwestern. The one winning bout against Notre Dame was turned in by foilsman Mike Dority.

Sadly, this was not an auspicious career-closing season for 75-year-old Charles Schmitter, who had earlier announced his retirement following the 1983 season. In 45 years, his teams had compiled a record of 272-235-2.

The 1983 edition would post a 6-7 record.

With Schmitter stepping aside, rumors began to circulate that fencing would lose its varsity status at Michigan State. The sport would actually survive another 14 years under the coaching-eye of Fred Freiheit, a 1951-1952 competitor for MSU.

Representing State at the Big Ten championships were Charles Wright and Dority in foil, Peter Heussler and Tim Russell in epee with Beatty and Herzbach in sabre.

Football: John Leister opened the season as the starting quarterback; but, after suffering seven straight losses, he was replaced by freshman Dave Yarema.

In the fifth game of the season, Leister completed a team-record 32 passes (42 attempts) in a 31-17 loss to Michigan. Four weeks later, Yarema, in his first start, threw for a .917 passing percentage (11-for-12) against Northwestern, an average that ranks fourth best in Big Ten history.

Punter Ralf Mojsiejenko set a team-record season average of 44.6 yards per kick. His 3,434 punting yards is still a Big Ten record. He also booted a 61-yard field goal against Illinois.

On Sunday, November 14, with one game remaining on the schedule, coach "Muddy" Waters received an official letter of dismissal during a meeting with AD Doug Weaver. Waters's original contract in 1980 would have expired after the 1982 season; however a two-year extension had been tacked on following that 1980 season.

Linebacker Carl Banks was MSU's lone first-team All-Big Ten selection.

Golf: At the Wolverine Invitational in Ann Arbor, Todd Hartle shot a 75-72—147 to finish second and lead MSU to a fourth-place finish in the 18-team field.

MSU took second-place at the Spartan Invitational over the Forest Akers West Course. The Spartans were in ninth-place after a disappointing day-one, but bounced back to finish with a score of 755. Haidler paced MSU with a 72-74—146.

For the second straight year, Hartle was MSU's top golfer at the Big Ten championships with a score of 72-73-75-74—294, which placed him sixth. The team shot a composite 1,522 over the University of Iowa course to tie Purdue for eighth place.

Gymnastics: Senior Greg Bosscawen entered the NCAA meet with the second highest average in the nation for the parallel bars, but unfortunately, he scored his

lowest marks of the year at the championships. The controversial scoring caused a minor uproar among the meet's 12 judges, but in the end, Bosscawen watched the final round from the sidelines. Pete Roberts also competed at the NCAA meet on the vault.

Hockey: The Spartans defeated Michigan, 6-3, in the first round of the Great Lakes Invitational (GLI) at Detroit's Joe Louis Arena. This would set up a showdown with Michigan Tech in the championship game the next night. With a record collegiate hockey crowd of 21,247 looking on and the game tied at 2-2, State scored three goals in the final 20 minutes for the tournament title.

MSU either tied or established 20 team and individual marks during the season while skating to a 30-11-1 record, the best in school history at the time.

MSU won its first eight games on the schedule, tying a school-winning streak, and earned a number one ranking in the media polls, which was a first for the Spartan hockey program.

All-American goalie Ron Scott surrendered his final year of eligibility to sign a professional contract with the NHL's New York Rangers.

Five members of the team were selected to participate in the 1983 National Sports Festival in Colorado, Colo. They included Gary Haight, Ken Leiter, Dan McFall, Mark Hamway and Kelly Miller.

Lacrosse: While one often conjures a vision of first-class splendor when thinking of the lifestyle for college athletes, consider this message from Blane Harrison of the 1983 lacrosse team:

"One cannot mention 'The Mountain' without instantaneously using coach Rich Kimball's name in vain. Each spring break during the early 1980s, the Michigan State lacrosse team would travel to the East Coast (almost by pack mule) actually by car pool. Following our 12-15 hour ride, we would be taken to where we would stay for the week. At the top of the steepest, most desolate mountaintop in the furthest corner of Pennsylvania stood our base camp. In actuality it was a YMCA children's camp. After strenuous games, which pushed human endurance, we would retire to our quaint quarters through which March winds would whip and the smell of musty mattresses would linger. Each morning Coach Kimball gave us the option of running 'The Mountain'— option?!? There was no alternative. 'The Mountain' was so steep, the pavement was literally inches from your nose as you negotiated the four miles of 'hell.' This was life on 'The Mountain' during our spring break. It was miserable, it was back breaking, it was cold. It was also a blast. The memories that I have of 'The Mountain' are special and I thank Coach Kimball for the experience."

Selected as co-winner of the team's MVP award, the aforementioned Blane Harrison shared the honor with goaltender Jimmy Sanford. The rookie of the year award went to Marc Berman of Long Island, N.Y., who scored an impressive 56 goals during the season. In addition, Harrison was selected to the All-League first team as a midfielder.

Soccer: In what would be the third and final mid-season Big Ten Classic, State defeated Purdue 6-0 in the first game but were then defeated by Indiana University 7-0 in the finals.

Vancho Cirovski closed out his fine Spartan career with 27 assists, which is good for second on the all-time charts at MSU. His 75 points stand at 10th best.

MSU outscored opponents for the fourth consecutive season, 48-22.

Swimming and Diving: For only the third time since joining the Big Ten, MSU could not rise above a ninth-place finish at the championship meet, held in Indianapolis for the first time. Other than relays, only three individuals made the scoring sheet: C. J. Winkel, Greg Sluke and Mike Brown. Winkel, a sophomore from England, placed sixth in the 500 freestyle in a time of 4:27.66; seventh in the 1,650 freestyle with a 15:37.07 and with a 1:39.88 finished tenth in the 200-yard freestyle. Co-captain Sluke, a senior backstroker from Grand Ledge, garnered a 13th and a 14th in consolation finals. Brown, the diver from Grosse Pointe Woods, scored 469.59 for ninth on the one-meter board and 505.68 to place eighth in the three-meter competition.

At the NCAA championship, Brown finished 10th in the one-meter competition, earning three team points to put MSU on the scoreboard. He would later gain All-American recognition in both the one- and three-meter competition as well as being distinguished as an academic All-American.

Tennis: Upon scoring a meager 2.5 points, State finished last in the Big Ten championships at Madison, Wis.

Even as the team struggled, senior captain Steve Yorimoto ended his Spartan career with another solid spring as the team's number one player.

Track and Field: MSU hosted the Big Ten indoor championships at Jenison and scored 63 points to place fourth. In the process they claimed three titles. Marcus Sanders set a conference mark with a time of 1:08.86 in winning the 600-yard run and later teamed with Eliot Tabron, Kelvin Scott and Corky Wilkins to better the Big Ten mark with a 3:10.20. Paul Piwinski took the high jump with a mark of 7' 1 1/2".

Competing in the Dogwood Relays in Knoxville, junior Tom Irman won the 3,000-meter steeplechase with a time of 9:01.84. High jumper Paul Piwinski leaped an impressive 7' 3" to gain a second-place finish. The 800-meter relay team of Corky Wilkins, Demetrius Hallums, Kelvin Scott and Eliot Tabron set a new MSU record while running a 1:27.36 which placed them sixth in this very challenging competition.

Again, Coach Bibbs's squad reaped success at their own MSU Invitational at Ralph Young Field. Demetrius Hallums won the 100-meter dash; Wilkins took the 200-

The Spartan mile relay team: (left to right) Eliot Tabron, Marcus Sanders, Kelvin Scott and Corky Wilkins

meter dash; Greg Turner the long jump and Irman the 3,000-meter steeplechase with a personal best time of 8:55.37. Wilkins, Hallums, Scott and Marcus Sanders teamed up to win the 400-meter relay in 41.79 and the 1,600-meter foursome of Wilkins, Terry Ross, Scott and Sanders edged Michigan at the tape in 3:15.92.

With Tabron replacing both Hallums and Ross in the 74th Drake relays, State finished third in both the 800-meter event with a time of 1:22.53 and the 1,600-meter in 3:03.68.

At the inaugural running of the Jesse Owen Invitational in Columbus, Ohio, the Sanders, Wilkins, Scott and Tabron team won the 1,600-meter event in a time of 3:09.32.

The Spartans managed 53 points in the outdoor conference meet at West Lafayette, Ind., placing them in sixth place. Leading the way was the high jump duo of Daryl Dismond and Paul Piwinski. Dismond won the event with a 7' 3" and Piwinski settled for second after clearing 7' 1-3/4". Also, the 1,600-meter relay team finished first in 3:09.28.

With an impressive time of 45.17 in the Central Collegiates at Toledo, Tabron broke the meet record and tied with the world-record time of 1983.

Within a fraction of a second of winning the 1,600-meter relay, the team of Wilkins, Scott, Sanders and Tabron ran a 3:02.51 to place third at the NCAA outdoor championships in Houston, Texas. Tabron also placed 10th with a 46.41 in the 400-meter dash and Piwinski closed out his great jumping career with a leap of 7' 3" to place seventh. Scoring 19 team points, MSU finished in 26th among the 92 competing schools.

Wrestling: In the early season MSU Invitational, nine Michigan State wrestlers reached the finals in the 10 weight classes with five being crowned champions. Those winners were Jim Mason (126 pounds), Ron Cantini (134 pounds), Fred Worthem (158 pounds), Tony White (167 pounds) and Michael Potts (190 pounds).

As the University of Iowa wrestlers were amassing 200 points to set a Big Ten Conference record in winning a 10th straight team title, MSU was scoring 81 1/2 points to settle for the runner-up trophy. Two Spartans, Worthem and Eli Blazeff (177 pounds) reached the finals before losing to Hawkeye entrants. In addition, three other State wrestlers were consolation finalists: Harrell Milhouse (118 pounds), Jim Mason (126 pounds) and Mike Potts (190 pounds).

Over the entire season, Blazeff had a school-record 19 pins and was named the team's outstanding wrestler in his first season as a Spartan. His 36 wins rank 13th-best for a single MSU season.

EXTRA! 1983 NIT TOURNAMENT

Michigan State reached the second round of the 1983 NIT tournament. The following are the Spartans' box scores for those games.

MICHIGAN STATE 72–BOWLING GREEN 71

	FG-FGA	FT-FTA	REB	A	PF	TP
Tower	4-8	0-0	7	3	3	8
Ford	8-14	1-2	3	4	1	17
Willis	7-11	2-4	12	1	3	16
Skiles	5-8	0-0	0	5	5	10
Vincent	3-8	6-7	2	3	3	12
Polec	4-6	1-2	2	5	5	9
Perry	0-3	0-0	2	0	2	0
Mudd	0-3	0-1	2	0	0	0
Walker	0-0	0-0	0	0	0	0
Cawood	0-0	0-1	0	0	1	0
Gore	0-0	0-0	0	0	0	0
Team			3			
TOTALS	31-61	10-17	33	21	23	72

Halftime: Michigan State 37-36; **Officials:** Murray, Stoudt, Rife; **Attendance:** 10,004.

FRESNO STATE 72–MICHIGAN STATE 58

	FG-FGA	FT-FTA	REB	A	PF	TP
Tower	3-8	0-2	5	3	4	6
Ford	1-4	0-0	3	0	4	2
Willis	7-12	0-1	16	0	3	14
Skiles	7-16	3-4	0	7	3	17
Vincent	6-14	5-8	3	7	4	17
Polec	0-2	2-2	2	0	5	2
Perry	0-0	0-0	0	0	0	0
Walker	0-0	0-0	0	0	0	0
Gore	0-0	0-0	0	0	1	0
Cawood	0-0	0-0	0	0	0	0
Team			3			
TOTALS	24-56	10-17	29	17	24	58

Halftime: Michigan State 35-32; **Officials:** Clougherty, Barnett, Bosone; **Attendance:** 8,000.

EXTRA! 1983 NCAA HOCKEY TOURNAMENT (Regionals)

MSU won its second straight CCHA crown by defeating Ferris State in a total-goals series and Ohio State and Bowling Green in single games. Despite these victories, they were seeded fourth and were forced to face Harvard. The first game was a close 6-5 loss, and with a 3-3 tie the Spartans fell just short in the total-goals series.

March 18, 1983—Cambridge, Mass.
Harvard 6, MSU 5
1st Pd.: 1. MSU, Kl. Miller (Hamway, Beck), 6:51; 2. MSU, Brown (Donnelly, Smyl), 8:53; 3. HU, M. Fusco (Code, Wheeler), 12:27; 4. HU, Kukulowicz (Turner, S. Fusco), 15:53.
2nd Pd.: 5. MSU, Phair (Martin, Krentz), 5:29; 6. MSU, Eisley (Martin, Haight), 13:43; 7. HU, Busconi (Kwong), 15:41.
3rd Pd.: 8. HU, Britz (Wheeler, M. Fusco), 5:05; 9. HU, Falcone (North, Connors), 14:16; 10. MSU, McFall (Hamway, Flegel), 15:09; 11. HU, Chalmers (Britz, Visone), 18:31.

March 19, 1983—Cambridge, Mass.
Harvard 3, MSU 3
1st Pd.: 1. HU, Kukulowicz (Turner, M. Fusco), 5:24.
2nd Pd.: 2. HU, Britz (Chalmers, Sheehy), 1:36; 3. MS, Hamway (Haight), 5:03; 4. MSU, Krentz (Brown, Taylor), 11:19.
3rd Pd.: 5. HU, Wheeler (Burke, Smith), 6:54, 6. MSU, Phair (Brown, Krentz), 12:56.

MSU
1983-1984

TALES TO TELL

Inheriting a team that went 2-9 in 1982, George Perles's first Michigan State team opened with a 23-17 home win over Colorado and then it was off to South Bend where little was expected of his Spartans. After all, ND was ranked number four and MSU had defeated them only once since 1968. However, the 1983 game would have a surprise ending as the scoreboards in Notre Dame Stadium would read: "Mich St 28, Notre Dame 23" and George J. Perles was an instant hero in Spartanland. By the following Monday, the Irish had dropped to 16th in the polls and State was in 19th place, cracking the top 20 for the first time since 1978.

Discussing the game 20 years later, George Perles recalled:

"That win helped us turn the corner. It was a game in which Notre Dame dominated statistically [25-9 in first downs, 283-60 yards rushing, 36:53 minutes-23:07 minutes in possession time and 4-1 in turnovers]. They seldom had good field position, thanks to our punter Ralf Mojsiejenko. His kicks [nine boots

that averaged 48.8 yards, including a personal-best 71-yarder] forced them to continually begin drives deep in their own area. I also remember that Notre Dame was just one play away from pulling it out as they methodically came down the field one last time until we finally stopped them and took over inside of our 20-yard line with less than a minute to play. Dave Yarema tried to run the clock out, but eventually surrendered a safety and again it was up to Ralf (who also kicked-off). We elected to squib-kick expecting to run the final .04 seconds off the clock. Somehow they salvaged one final second and from midfield they tossed up a 'hail Mary' pass. Tim Cunningham went up between two potential receivers and took the ball away to end it.

We had some great kids on that team. There was Carl Butler, our fullback, who could only see out of one eye. He was a transfer student...there was Daryl Turner who caught two touchdown passes that afternoon. He may not have been in the same category as Andre Rison or Mark Ingram, but he was a good one...Butch Rolle was a quality tight end, who also scored a touchdown in that game...there was little

HEADLINES of 1984

- Following the 1982 settlement of a 13-year-old lawsuit against American Telephone & Telegraph, the 22 companies within the Bell System break up.
- The State theatre, which opened on Abbott Road in 1948, shows its final film and closes its doors.
- Congresswomen Geraldine Ferraro of New York is selected as the vice-presidential candidate on the Democratic ticket and becomes the first woman to run for a nationwide major office.
- Federal researchers isolate a virus thought to cause the acquired immune deficiency syndrome (AIDS).

SCOREBOARD

	W	L	T	Avg.
Baseball	34	24	0	.586
Track and Field	0	1	0	.000
Football	4	6	1	.409
Basketball	16	12	0	.571
Tennis	3	17	0	.150
Cross Country	0	4	0	.000
Swimming and Diving	3	8	0	.273
Wrestling	10	5	0	.667
Hockey	34	12	0	.739
Fencing	12	12	0	.500
Golf	tournament play only			
Gymnastics	8	6	0	.571
Soccer	9	7	1	.559
Lacrosse	9	7	0	.562

Phil Parker (five foot 10, 180 pounds) our defensive back who had a great day (two interceptions). Pound-for-pound he was as tough a player as I ever had…linebacker Carl Banks, who would have a great and long professional career…Then, of course, we had Dave Yarema, a class guy. He was less mobile than most quarterbacks, but he had a strong arm and was an intelligent player. Unfortunately, on the very next week after Notre Dame, against Illinois, he was injured [shoulder] and lost for the season. As a result, our season was lost (4-6-1)."

That 1983 victory over Notre Dame became more cherished as the years went by. As successful as George Perles would be during his 12 years as head coach at Michigan State, on only one other occasion would his Spartans defeat the Fighting Irish (20-15 in 1986).

TEAM OF THE YEAR

The 1984 baseball team brought the winning ways back to Kobs Field with a 32-26 record, which at the time was tied for the second-most season wins in school history. The Spartans finished second in the Big Ten east division and ended the season with a six-game winning streak. Mike Eddington, a third-team All-America and first-team All-Big Ten selection, had a record breaking year, breaking school records in home runs (20), RBI (66), runs (59) and total bases (145). Cordell Ross claimed MSU's first Big Ten batting crown in 14 years with a .462 batting average in league play, while Dave Corey was the team's leading hitter in overall games with a .384 average. The Spartans also set team records for hits (563), runs (432), RBIs (377) and home runs (59).

The 1984 baseball team. (Front row, left to right) number four Mike Whitman, number 38 Chris Hayner, number one Cordell Ross, number 34 Mike Eddington, number 22 Tom Shook and number six Ed Grochowalski. At far left in second row is Peggy Frimodig (Brown) student equipment manager, (and, later, assistant athletic director for Budget and Finance), and number 14 Dave Corey.

MAKING HISTORY

A seven-man officiating crew became operable with the 1983 football season. Also, 25-second field clocks were required in stadiums.

Beginning with the first NCAA indoor track championships in 1965 and for the next 18 years, all races were conducted in yardage distances. In 1984 and henceforth, the metric system has been the scale for measure.

The conference experimentation with a three-point shot in basketball during the 1982-1983 season proved to be a one-year anomaly. The idea was dropped in 1983-1984.

MSU assistant athletic director Clarence Underwood was named assistant commissioner of the Big Ten. Returning to MSU in 1990 he became the assistant athletic director for compliance and four years later was elevated to senior associate director. With the departure of Merritt Norvell in 1998, Underwood was appointed interim director while given the full title a year later.

The Spartan icers hosted Team USA in pre-Olympic play. State played close during 40 minutes, but a four-goal second period gave the nation's best a 6-2 victory.

On Feb. 8, 1984 Duffy Daugherty, Spartan football coach for 19 years, was named to the National Football Hall of Fame.

The Michigan State dance group, first identified as the "MSU Motion," was first formed to perform at football and basketball games.

The Olympic torch passed through East Lansing during the afternoon of May 22, 1984. Michigan State was the only university on the longest torch relay in history. The relay began in New York City and finished in Los Angeles after reaching 33 states during an 82-day period.

In the spring, Shawn Walsh, the assistant hockey coach, resigned to become head coach at the University of Maine where he carved a very successful career until his untimely death from cancer in September 2001. George Gwozdecky replaced Walsh as Ron Mason's assistant.

After 25 years of association with the MSU track and cross country programs, Jim Gibbard retried from the staff in the spring of 1984.

GREAT STATE DATES

Soccer—**September 27, 1983 (A):** State trailed the University of Michigan 1-0 at the half on a fluke goal in the first minute of play that rolled past goalkeeper Paul Zimmerman. The Spartans then took control during the second half when they scored three times leading to a 3-1 victory. Sophomore Tom Doherty led the way with two goals as Steve Swanson assisted on all three of MSU's markers.

Soccer—**October 26, 1983 (H):** Sophomore Eric Weissend scored the winning goal in his first collegiate game at the center striker position in the team's 3-0 victory over Western Michigan. The Spartans increased that 1-0 halftime lead just 35 seconds into the second half on Tom Doherty's ninth goal of the season. It was his first as a midfielder.

Football—**November 5, 1983 (A):** State overcame four turnovers (three fumbles and one pass interception) to defeat Northwestern, 9-3. Meanwhile, the MSU secondary was picking off three passes, one each by Phil Parker, Nate Hannah and Tim Cunningham. The only touchdown of the game came with 2:47 remaining in the first quarter following the Parker 12-yard interception return to the Wildcat 23-yard line. With fourth-and-goal at the one-yard line, halfback Aaron Roberts scored on a sweep of right end. Ralf Mojsiejenko's PAT was blocked but he did manage a 31-yard field goal with 5:49 remaining in the second period after cornerback Lonnie Young had recovered a fumble at the Cat's 36-yard line. Led by Jim Morrissey, Kelly Quinn, captain Carl Banks, Tom Tyree and Young, the defense held NW to a minus-56 yards rushing, 103 yards passing and a solitary field goal in the third quarter.

Hockey—**November 18, 1983 (A):** Led by junior right wing Tom Anastos's ninth and 10th goals of the season, State made it eight wins in a row over the University of Michigan, 6-3, in front of 7,833 fans at Yost Ice Arena. The large maize-and-blue crowd was quieted very quickly as MSU soared to a 3-0 lead by 6:05 of the first period. Senior center Newell Brown opened the scoring at 4:42; Anastos scored his first on an easy tip-in at 5:10 and freshman center Bill Shibicky broke in alone and found the back of the net on a wrist shot 55 seconds later. After the Wolverines got back into the game with a pair of scores in the opening period, Anastos netted his second in the middle stanza while Mike Donnelly and Norm Parker sealed the victory with scores in the third.

Basketball—**January 4, 1984 (H):** Freshman Darryl Johnson hit a jump shot to put MSU ahead 73-72 with only seven seconds remaining in the game to give the Spartans a one-point victory over Iowa. A massive midcourt celebration by the MSU players and fans followed after a desperation shot by Iowa flew wide of the basket from 25 feet out. Ken Johnson made hits debut as a Spartan with a double-double performance (17 points, 10 rebounds), and helped MSU out-rebound the Hawkeyes, 39-23.

Fencing—**January 7, 1984 (H):** In his first year as MSU's head coach, Fred Freihert's squad opened with a convincing 22-10 victory over Michigan. The Spartans' strongest event was in the sabre where junior Rob Beatty and senior Jim Gosler went undefeated, sweeping the U of M, 9-0. Senior Mike Dority was dominant in foil competition as he posted a 6-1 record.

Swimming and Diving—**January 20, 1984 (H):** Led by triple-winner C.J. Winkel and a pair of double-winners, the Spartans captured 10 of the 13 events to defeat the University of Illinois, 62-51. Winkle won the 1,000-yard freestyle in 9:47.73, the 200-yard butterfly in 1:55.09 and the 500-yard freestyle in 4:37.60. Freshman butterflyer Jeff Butler was used in the freestyle events where he won the 100-yard event with a 47.82 and the 200-yard race in 1:45.68. Senior Mike Brown scored 301.00 to place first in the one-meter diving event and totaled 599.78 to win the three-meter competition. Other firsts were registered by Rafael Segarra in the 200-yard individual medley (2:00.98) and Tom Christel in the 200-yard breaststroke (2:15.56). The medley relay quartet of John Bodine, Christel, Butler and John Kasley opened the afternoon with a first-place finish in 3:37.92

Wrestling—**January 24, 1984 (A):** Down 16-3 in a hostile environment, MSU battled back to defeat Michigan, 23-16 in Ann Arbor. Junior Ernie Blazeff started the comeback with a 6-6 draw at 158 pounds, and then Greg Sargis really got things going with a pin. Freshman Dave Doppler cut the deficit to 16-14 with a 2-1 decision at 177 pounds. The Spartans then secured the victory with senior Eli Blazeff's 13th pin of the season and Mike Potts's decision at heavyweight.

Hockey—**January 27 (H) & 28 (A) 1983:** State continued its dominance of Michigan, first with an easy 12-1 win before a standing-room crowd at Munn Ice Arena and then in a much closer 3-1 victory at Ann Arbor on Saturday. The 12 goals on Friday were the most ever tallied against the U of M by a Spartan team. Eight different players found the target: Jeff Parker, Gord Flegel, Mike Donnelly and Kelly Miller each scored twice as Craig Simpson, Tom Anastos, Dan Beaty and Newell Brown completed the romp with one goal apiece. Only five players who suited up for the game failed to pick up points. Even Bob Essensa, the freshman goalie, was credited with an assist. In the return game at Yost Ice Arena, the Wolverines led after 20 minutes of play but State overcame the U of M strategy of constant high-sticking and late jabs to prevail, 3-1. Flegel and Miller scored in the second period and junior left winger Lyle Phair added an insurance effort at 15:29 of the final period. MSU's freshman goal tender Norm Foster played brilliantly as he kicked out 24 shots.

Basketball—**February 2, 1984 (H):** MSU defeated Michigan, 72-67, before a sold-out crowd of 10,004 at Jenison Field House. Building on a 12-0 spurt in the opening half, the Spartans led at intermission, 36-30, and never trailed in the final 20 minutes. Outscored 52-42 on field goals, State won the game at the free-throw line where they hit 30 of 39 while the Wolverines settled for 15 of 24. Leading the way at the charity strip were 7-0 center Kevin Willis sinking seven-for-seven; Scott Skiles eight of 11; with Larry Polec, Richard Mudd and Ken Johnson connecting with four each. The game ended with a combined 11 players having four or more fouls with a total of 57 being called.

Gymnastics—**February 12, 1984 (H):** In their final regular home meet of the season, MSU defeated the University of Michigan, 264.25-262.85. After the floor exercise and pommel horse events, State led by less than three points at which time Coach Szypula juggled his line-up to insert seldom used Bill Jenkins. The gamble paid off as Jenkins won the event followed closely by teammates Marty Baerny and Jay Oestriech. Other winners for the Spartans were senior Bruce Trevor who scored a career-high 9.8 on the pommel horse and freshman Allan Powers with a 9.4 on the still rings.

Wrestling—**February 14, 1984 (H):** In winning nine of the 10 matches, MSU totally dominated Ohio State, 42-3. Two premier bouts highlighted the afternoon. At 134 pounds, Jim Mason set a team record with his 56th career pin and in the heavyweight division, Mike Potts also established a team career record with his 106th victory. Other Spartan winners were Wayne Jackson (118 pounds) 9-4; Dan Matauch (125 pounds) 17-1; John

Beaudoin (142 pounds) with a pin at 4:13; Charles Root (150 pounds) 11-4; Ernie Blazeff (158 pounds) 5-0; Greg Sargis (167 pounds) 5-2 and Eli Blazeff (190 pounds) with a pin at 3:46.

Hockey—**February 18, 1984 (A):** First-year center Craig Simpson's second goal of the game at 7:17 of overtime lifted the Spartans past Northern Michigan, 4-3. The London, Ontario, freshman's first marker had tied the game 1-1 on a power play at 16:29 of the opening period. Early in the second stanza State jumped to a 3-1 lead on scores by junior left wing Kelly Miller and defenseman Dan McFall while the clubs were skating three-aside. The Wildcats tied the contest with goals in the second and third periods, leading to Simpson's winning goal.

Basketball—**February 26, 1984 (A):** In a Sunday afternoon regionally televised game at Bloomington, State defeated Indiana University, 57-54. The MSU defense sparkled, holding the Hoosiers to 35.4 percent marksmanship and 28.6 percent after intermission. Those figures would have been even more dismal if it had not been for IU's sophomore sharpshooter Steve Alford, who accounted for 30 of the losers' total. Meanwhile, Jud Heathcote's squad was hitting at a 58.3 percent field-goal accuracy as four Spartans scored in double figures: Sam Vincent with 14, Larry Polec 12, Ken Johnson 12 and Scott Skiles 10. After connecting on only four of their first 17 free-throw attempts, the visitors came through with nine points on the final 11 tries.

Golf—**April 1, 1984 (H):** Tom Rose and Bob Fossum both fired final round 75s to lead MSU to victory in the 12-team, 54-hole Miami (Ohio) Invitational Tournament. Rose's three round total of 75-74-75—224 was good enough for runner-up medalist honors, three strokes from the leader. The remaining Spartans finished as follows: Fossum 231; Bill Kost 232; Steve McKalko 236; Tom Ross 238 and Bob Redford 242. The Michigan State aggregate score of 1,154 was five strokes better than second-place Kent State.

Baseball—**April 11, 1984 (H):** Featuring a pair of well-pitched games, State took both ends of a double-header from Notre Dame, 7-1 and 7-2. In the opener, football kicker-baseball pitcher Ralf Mojsiejenko scattered three hits in six innings to pick-up his second victory of the young season while freshman Dave Mammel yielded five hits in five innings of the nightcap raising his season record to 3-1. Freshman Eric Sandenburg hurled the fi-

nal inning of the first game and senior Bill Archer worked the last two innings of the second game. Third baseman Dave Corey, who entered the weekend with a robust .463 average, picked up four more base hits, two in each game. Mike Eddington opened the MSU scoring of the second contest when he slugged a two-run home run in a four-run second-inning rally.

Tennis—**April 11, 1984 (H):** Taking five of the six singles matches plus all three in doubles State easily defeated Central Michigan, 8-1. From his number two position, freshman Craig Schembri dominated his opponent 6-2, 6-1. Joe Webster fought off five set points and came away with a 7-6, 6-2 victory. Other winners were Curtis Wright 6-4, 6-2; Ross Smith 6-2, 6-0 and Steven Hooley 6-4, 6-2. Gaining team points in doubles were the pairs of Joe O'Brien-Smith, 6-0, 6-2; Schembri-Wright, 8-2, 6-0 and Webster-Hooley, 6-3, 6-4.

Lacrosse—**May 2, 1984 (H):** Playing from behind throughout the contest, State upset previously unbeaten and nationally eighth-ranked Ohio Wesleyan, 7-6. The only time MSU led was with 4:50 remaining when attackman Marc Berman scored the game-winner, his fourth goal of the game. Attackman Andy Kurowski was credited with two goals and midfielder Steve Garcia scored once. The chances for a Spartan victory seemed bleak early as Wesleyan scored just 13 seconds into the match and then scored 38 seconds later to take a quick 2-0 lead. Berman followed with his first two markers to put the Green and White back in contention. The victory sparked a post-game team celebration. After all it was the first win over the small-school power following 10 losses that spanned 13 seasons.

Baseball—**May 5 (A) & 6 (H), 1984:** Chris Hayner tossed a six-hit complete game as MSU defeated Michigan, 7-2, at Ray Fisher Stadium in Ann Arbor. The Spartans pounded out 10 hits and were led by All-American Mike Eddington, who scored two runs and nailed his 15th homer of the year. Ed Grochowalski went three-for-four and had three RBIs. Back home on Saturday, State exploded for 11 runs in the bottom of the eighth as MSU came back to beat Michigan at Kobs Field, 14-5. Eddington had another solid day at the plate, going three-for-three with three RBIs, while Mike Whitman went three-for-four to account for four RBIs. Mark Piazza threw two innings of scoreless relief to pick up the victory.

Lacrosse—**May 12-13, 1984 (H):** The Spartans set a one-game team scoring record while beating their Mid-

west Lacrosse Association (MLA) foe Wittenberg College 21-4 on Saturday and then came back to defeat the Chicago Lacrosse Club, 13-4 on a cold and rainy Sunday afternoon at Old College Field. With the two wins, MSU closed out the MLA season in third place for the second straight year. With six goals and five goals respectively, Marc Berman and Riney Wilke led the scoring parade on Saturday. It was pretty much the same story against the Chicago club as State jumped to a 9-1 lead by the half and then coasted to victory. The highlight of that second win of the weekend came in the fourth quarter as senior defenseman John Rometty brought the ball down the field and dumped in a shot for his only collegiate career goal. The team celebrated the 9-7 season by throwing coach Rick Kimball into the Red Cedar River.

ATHLETE OF THE YEAR

Carl Banks earned All-America honors as a senior in 1983 from the Associated Press, United Press and *The Sporting News*. Named the Spartans' MVP for the 1983 season, he recorded 86 tackles, despite opponents rarely running to his side of the field, while closing out his career with 279 tackles. Named as college football's linebacker of the year by the Columbus Touchdown Club, he was named first-team All-Big Ten three times and was MSU's first non-kicker to be named to the all-league team

Carl Banks

more than twice. Banks was taken in the first round (third player overall) by the New York Giants in the 1984 NFL Draft. In 1996, he was selected as a member of the MSU Centennial Super Squad as picked in a poll conducted by the *Lansing State Journal.*

IN THE SPARTLITE

Baseball: Finishing the Big Ten season with an 8-7 record, State managed a runner-up spot in the loop's East Division and another trip to the conference playoffs. Unfortunately, as in 1983, it was an early exit. In the tournament's opening game, MSU surrendered three errors giving the host Minnesota Gophers an 8-7 come-from-behind victory. On the next afternoon, a ninth-inning grand slam home run led Northwestern to a 9-4 win.

First team All-Big Ten selection and third-team All-American, Mike Eddington became one of 18 Spartans to have completed a season without committing an error. He did so by cleanly handling 161 chances in the outfield, more putouts and assists than any of the other 17 Spartans. Mike also left an impressive offensive record. At the plate he was credited with 66 runs batted in, 20 home runs and 145 total bases, all three on-going school records.

MSU led the Big Ten in hitting with a .318 composite team batting average.

Cordell Ross and Dave Corey were second-team All-Big Ten selections, while Tom Shook earned third-team honors.

Bill Harris and Chris Bucceri were named Academic All-Americans.

Basketball: MSU won 8 of its last 11 games, including the last five in a row, to earn a berth in the National Invitation Tournament.

Three Spartans concluded the season with double-figure scoring averages, paced by Sam Vincent at 15.6, Scott Skiles at 14.5 and Kevin Willis at 11.0. All three were picked for honorable mention on the All-Big Ten team as selected by the Associated Press.

Vincent was named team MVP for the second consecutive year.

Cross Country: Senior Tom Irmen paced the MSU harriers to a second-place finish at the 8,000-meter Purdue Invitational. Irmen, in only his second race of the season, cruised the course in 24:23 to shatter the meet record.

For the second consecutive year, Irmen was the top Spartan at the Big Ten championships, run in Champaign, Ill. With a time of 24:04 he finished 10th and the team finished eighth. Other State finishers were Richard Pietras 46th, Tom Clark 47th, Tim Simpson 56th and Mike Kavulich 57th.

At the NCAA district IV meet run over the snow-covered Forest Akers Course, Irmen ran a 30:52.8, placing him 14th out of 150 runners and qualifying for the national championships. State's only other runner, Pietras finished 94th.

Fencing: Fred Freiheit, a 1952 Big Ten champion at MSU, succeeded MSU legendary coach Charlie Schmitter, who retired after an incredible 45-year stint as head coach. In his first year, Freiheit's team compiled a 12-12 season.

In one of the six multi-team meets during the season, State dropped matches to Cornell and host Cleveland State, but did manage to out-duel Purdue, Case Western, Bowling Green and Oberlin. Rob Beatty took 15 of 16 bouts in sabre; Mike Dority was the winner in 12 of 15 and captain Pete Haeussler went 15-3.

On the season, the top performers and their won-loss records were: Beatty 41-18 for a .700 average in sabre; Dority 40-20 and a .666 average in foil and Haeussler 30-21 and a .588 average in epee. Other contributors during the year were Jim Gosler, Mike Gabocy, Bob Barkley, Tom Howarth, Mike Lang, Ken VanGolen, Monte Falcoff and John Peddie.

Football: Daryl Turner closed out his Spartan career as one the greatest receivers in school history. He currently ranks 12th all-time in receiving yards (1,577) and ninth in touchdown receptions (13).

Phil Parker had 203 interception yards in 1983, which is still a school record.

Ralf Mojseijneko booted a 59-yard field goal against Purdue, which is the third-longest in school history. He also led the Big Ten in league games with a 42.9 punting average.

Keith Gates ran for 168 yards on 38 carries against Minnesota. He rushed for 100 yards three times in 1983.

Linebacker Carl Banks once more earned the honor of first team All-Big Ten along with free safety Parker.

Two from the squad were first team All-American picks, Banks and Ralf Mojsiejenko, the latter having been only a second team conference selection.

Golf: As Ohio State won the Spartan Invitational for the eight consecutive time, the MSU squad finished tied for second. Rob Haidler led the Spartans with a 72-74—146 followed by Mike Kaye at 76-74—150 and Tom Rose 79-73—152.

MSU finished sixth at the Big Ten championships in Bloomington, Ind. Freshman Jon Kosier was the lead-ing player for the Spartans, shooting a 75-78-73-78—304. Other finishers for State were Bob Fossum 77-81-73-74—305; Bill Kost 84-75-75-75—309; Tom Ross 81-73-80-77—311; Rose 76-75-84-78—313 and Kaye 75-80-78-80—313.

Gymnastics: Michigan State hosted the 1984 Big Ten championships at Jenison Fieldhouse and finished sixth in the seven-team field. Three Spartans placed in the top six individually. Bruce Trevor, the team's co-captain scored a 9.7 on the pommel horse, good enough for a second-place tie. John Spellis, a sophomore registered a 9.35 and placed sixth in floor exercise and he also placed 13th in the all-around event. Allan Powers ended a brilliant freshman year with a fourth-place finish on the still rings. His 9.5 score was just a point shy of second place. The only other MSU entrant to compete in the finals was Jay Oestriech with a ninth place on the vault.

Hockey: In the fifth Great Lakes Invitational, State easily disposed of Northern Michigan, 5-1 and for the second consecutive year defeated Michigan Tech, 6-2, in the finals. Five different Spartans scored in the championship game, including a two-goal effort by Dan McFall.

Norm Foster notched his first career shutout and Newell Brown scored two goals and an assist as MSU cooled down red-hot Western Michigan, 5-0, to win its third consecutive CCHA playoff championship. Gord Flegel, Dale Krentz and Jeff Eisley also netted goals for the Spartans.

State hosted and defeated Boston College 6-2 and 7-6 in the NCAA regionals.

Dan McFall was named a second-team All-American. He was also a first-team All-CCHA selection, while Norm Foster was named to the second team.

Lyle Phair earned NCAA All-Tournament team honors.

Bill Shibicky was the first Spartan ever to be named CCHA Rookie of the Year.

Kelly Miller was awarded the Big Ten Medal of Honor.

Lacrosse: The laxers scored 25 goals against Ashland, which was the second-most in MSU single-game history.

Riney Wilke broke the school record for most assists in one season with 32. Wilke was a second-team Midwest Lacrosse Association selection along with Marc Berman, Steve Garcia and Mike McCarthy. Paul Riley earned honorable mention.

Soccer: Radwan Mandily, a native of Saudi Arabia and Master's graduate of Michigan State, joined Joe Baum as a volunteer assistant.

After opening the season with a 1-3 record, senior Steve "Swannie" Swanson suddenly led the team on a 5-1 run. The transforming spark provided by the diminutive midfielder from West Bloomfield was evident. As Coach Baum noted:

"Swannie used to be such an unselfish player. He used to always pass the ball off to his teammates. Now he's taking more of the offense on his shoulders. In critical situations he wants the ball."

Swanson closed out his Spartan career with 17 assists, which is still ranked ninth-best in MSU history.

During the season, sophomore Tom Doherty would lead the team in scoring with 12 goals and 28 points.

After falling to number three-ranked Indiana in the Big Ten eastern tournament by a close score of 4-2, State ended the year on a positive note with a 7-2 defeat of Purdue in the consolation bracket. They finished the season with a 9-7-1 record.

Swimming and Diving: In one of the most complete Big Ten schedules ever encountered, in successive meets the 1984 Spartans took on Wisconsin, Illinois, Purdue, Indiana, Ohio State, Iowa and Michigan. Unfortunately, the results (1-6) weren't as glamorous.

Scoring 133 points, State finished ninth at the Big Ten championship meet in Indianapolis. Junior C.J. Winkel led the way with a sixth in the 500-yard freestyle, ninth in the 1,650 and 16th in the 200-yard freestyle. Jeff Butler was 7th and 9th in the 100- and 200-yard butterfly events, and was also a member of the eighth-place 800-yard freestyle relay team along with Winkel, Rafael Segarra and Juan Tavares. Diver Mike Brown placed the highest for State with a third on the one-meter board and a fourth on the three-meter.

For the fourth-consecutive year, Mike Brown earned All-America honors in the three-meter diving event. He also repeated as an Academic All-American. He was also a recipient of the Dr. James Feurig Achievement and Service Award. Today, Dr. Brown is a practicing physician in Grand Rapids.

Tennis: Eric Sahlin, a 26-year-old freshman and MSU's number one singles player on the spring trip, walked off the court during a doubles match in South Carolina against Landers College. As a result, Coach Drobac dismissed him from the team.

As in 1983, MSU players won a total of only three matches during the Big Ten championships in Evanston, Ill. Freshman Craig Schembri won his opener against his Iowa opponent, 6-4, 7-6, but faced the defending conference champion in the second round and was defeated. At number four singles, Ross Smith won a two-set victory from the Hoosier entrant, 7-5, 7-5. The only other Spartan to win a match was Joe Webster in the consolation round when he defeated the Ohio State number five singles opponent, 7-6, 6-1.

Track and Field: Scoring an unimpressive nine points, MSU dropped from fourth in 1983 to ninth at the 1984 Big Ten indoor meet in Ann Arbor. The one-mile relay team finished third in a time of 3:13.07. Kelvin Scott placed fifth in the 440-yard dash with a time of :48.28 and Terry Lewis was sixth in the long jump with a mark of 23' 2 1/2".

Only 10 men represented MSU in the Central Collegiate meet in Evanston, Ill. Senior Kelvin Scott and freshman Rodney Benson ran third and fifth respectively in the 400 meters and the sprint relay team of Benson, Scott, Dennis Felton and Terry Lewis took fifth in 42.09.

Four individuals and two relays scored 17 points, resulting in a ninth-place finish at the Big Ten Outdoor meet in Columbus, Ohio. Tom Irmen was sixth in the 3,000-meter steeplechase (9:12.36); Tim Simpson sixth in the 1,500-meters (3:48.44); Kelvin Scott fourth in the 400-meter dash (46.78) and Dee Hallums sixth in the 200-meter dash (21.44). The 400-meter sprint relay was fifth (40.87) while the highpoint came when the 1,600-meter relay of senior Scott, freshmen Rodney Benson, Dennis Felton and Hallums completed the weekend with a second place in 3:09.72.

Wrestling: The two outstanding wrestlers of the 1984 team were seniors Eli Blazeff at 190 pounds and heavyweight Mike Potts. Blazeff won 40 matches during the season, which at the time established a new school record. In addition, both he and Potts tied for a team record as each pinned 21 opponents in 1983-1984.

Michigan State hosted the 1984 Big Ten championships at Jenison Field House and finished second to the University of Iowa, a team that would later be crowned national champions. Potts, an NCAA qualifier for the fourth consecutive year, highlighted the Spartans' showing in that meet by winning the heavyweight crown with

a 43-second pin, the fastest in Big Ten tournament history. With the win he became the Spartans' first Big Ten champion since 1980. Jim Mason at 134 pounds and 190 pound Eli Blazeff would both place second.

State sent six competitors to the NCAA championships and each of them made it to the second round or beyond. Wayne Jackson wrestled at 118 pounds, Jim Mason who finished in seventh place at 134, Charles Root 150, Greg Sargis 167, Blazeff, the third-place finisher at 190 and Potts who finished eighth in the heavyweight division. Overall, MSU would garner a total of 29 1/4 points, leading to a ninth place in the team standings. It was the program's 22nd top-10 finish at the NCAAs, and the highest finish since the 1972 team placed second.

EXTRA! 1984 NCAA HOCKEY TOURNAMENT (Fourth Place)

The Spartans lost the CCHA regular season championship to Bowling Green State University but won the CCHA playoff championship with wins over Michigan Tech, Ohio State and Western Michigan. They went on to defeat Boston College in a total-goal series to open the NCAA tournament, but rival BGSU, the eventual crown winner, gave MSU their first loss in 10 games. The Spartans lost again to North Dakota 6-5 in overtime of the consolation game. Lyle Phair was named to the tournament's all-star team with two goals and two assists during the games.

March 17, 1984—East Lansing
MSU 6, Boston College 2

1st Pd.: 1. BC, Sweeney (unasst.), 0:39; 2. BC, Mitchell (unasst.), 9:54; 3. MSU, McFall (Krentz, Simpson), 16:09.
2nd Pd.: 4. MSU, Krentz (Simpson, Anastos), 2:27; 5. MSU, Phair (Eisley, Simpson), 13:57.
3rd Pd.: 6. MSU, Eisley (Flegel, Simpson), 9:16; 7. MSU, Donnelly (Flegel, Smyl), 11:01; 8. MSU, Simpson (Krentz, Anastos), 16:30.

March 18, 1984—East Lansing
MSU 7, Boston College 6

1st Pd.: 1. BC, Campedelli (Rauseo, Chisholm), 2:03; 2. MSU, Krentz (McSween), 11:38; 3. MSU, Donnelly (Taylor), 12:52.
2nd Pd.: 4. MSU, Brown (Shibicky, Taylor), 1:34; 5. BC, Sweeney (Rauseo, Harlow), 6:25; 6. MSU, Smyl (Kl. Miller, McFall), 6:37; 7. MSU, Schibicky (Phair, Brown), 8:01; 8. BC, Harlow (Sweeney, Rauseo), 13:17; 9. BC, Herlihy (Chisholm, McDonough), 18:37.
3rd Pd.: 10. MSU, M. Messier (Taylor, Phair), 5:26; 11. MSU, Kl. Miller (Brown), 8:00; 12. BC, McDonough (Herlihy, Griffin), 14:19; 13. BC, Herlihy (Chisholm, McDonough), 18:37.

March 23, 1984—Lake Placid, N.Y.
Bowling Green 2, MSU 1

1st Pd.: 1. BG, Wansbrough (Kane, Cavallini), 13:25.
2nd Pd.: 2. MSU, Shibicky (Phair), 13:20.
3rd Pd.: 3. BG, Samanski (Randerson, Pikul), 7:13.

March 24, 1984—Lake Placid, N.Y.
North Dakota 6, MSU 5 (OT)

1st Pd.: 1. ND Barsness (unasst.), 6:53; 2. ND, Williams (Zombo), 11:37; 3. MSU, Brown (Phair, Shibicky), 12:38.
2nd Pd.: 4. ND, Jensen (Whitsitt), 4:36; 5. ND, Sherven (Zombo, Jensen), 5:28; 6. MSU, Eisley (Simpson, Flegel), 8:25.
3rd Pd.: 7. MSU, Phair (Brown, Shibicky), 5:23; 8. MSU, Phair (Eisley, Simpson), 6:54; 9. ND, Barsness (Williams, Palmiscno), 16:02; 10. MSU, Donnelly (Phair, Eisley), 19:31.
Overtime: 11. ND, Barsness (Sandelin), 5:57.

MSU 1984-1985

TALES TO TELL

MSU 19, U-M 7—some fans remember it as an upset in which a 1-3 team would turn its season around; others recall it as a long-awaited (since 1978) W against Michigan; but nearly all recall it as the game in which Bobby Morse, a sophomore from Muskegon, returned a punt 87 yards for a touchdown with 12:41 remaining in the second quarter. As reported by Dave Matthews in the *Lansing State Journal:*

"Morse had one surprise for the Wolverines, one no one really expected. Early in the second quarter he gathered in a punt at his own 13, found a wall of blockers along the MSU sideline and scampered 87 yards to provide a two-touchdown lead. Morse's big play created a gap the Wolverines never overcame."

Two decades later, now in business back in Muskegon, Morse reminisces:

"I realize that punt-return represents a special moment in MSU football and in the folklore of Michigan State sports. But to me, simply winning the game was more important. It was also important that I performed well offensively and that I caught some significant passes. That punt return was just icing on the cake and I did receive the game ball, which I gave to my father. His birthday was the next day. My older sister Patty was a member of the cheerleading squad. She escorted me along the sideline for the last few yards and then joined others in the end-zone pile-up [no excessive celebration penalty in 1984]. I remember Norm Parker [assistant coach] yelling to those celebrators: 'Get up! Get up! He's gotta breathe!'

Why didn't I follow in my father's footsteps and attend Notre Dame? First of all, Jerry Faust never offered me a scholarship. Also, as I realized during my recruiting visit to South Bend, they were recruiting track athletes, guys who could run a 4.4 in the 40 or a 45-second 440, not football players. Also, I kept hearing that I was Jim Morse's [Irish captain, 1956] son. Certainly, I am proud of that, but somehow I thought I was going to get lost in the shuffle. Furthermore, Notre Dame was recruiting me as a defensive back and I wanted to play offense. As for MSU, George Perles impressed me and I considered myself his type, a 'blue collar' player. What I eventu-

SCOREBOARD

	W	L	T	Avg.
Baseball	22	35	0	.386
Track and Field	1	0	0	1.000
Football	6	6	0	.500
Basketball	19	10	0	.655
Tennis	4	20	0	.166
Cross Country	0	4	0	.000
Swimming and Diving	5	7	0	.417
Wrestling	8	6	0	.571
Hockey	38	6	0	.864
Fencing	7	13	0	.350
Golf	tournament play only			
Gymnastics	14	10	0	.583
Soccer	12	6	1	.658
Lacrosse	11	6	0	.647

ally lacked in speed I made up in versatility. I could run the ball when called upon, catch passes if needed and, perhaps most important, I became an effective blocker for Carl Butler and Lorenzo White. Often used as a 'man-in-motion,' I would come out of the backfield and defenders weren't certain what to expect of me, a five-foot-nine and a half, 195 pounder. I loved to play 'mind games.' Was I going to race by them as a pass receiver or cut them down with a cutback block, which I had eventually mastered?"

Morse was also instrumental in the Spartans' opening 14-play drive that covered 85-yards and led to the first score. Five straight Dave Yarema passes, three to tight end Veno Belk and two to Morse, accounted for 63 of the yards. Butler eventually scored from the one-yard-line. Ralf Mojsiejenko converted a PAT and completed the scoring with a pair of second-half field goals, one from 49 yards out and the second from 30 yards.

TEAM OF THE YEAR

The 1984-1985 hockey team set an NCAA record for most wins in a season with 38 and a school record for most CCHA wins with 27. Perhaps even more impressive, after opening the schedule with a 10-3 record, the Spartans went on an unprecedented 22-game winning-streak that lasted from November 29 to February 15.

The 1984-1985 Spartans set a number of other team records: most points in a season (76), highest winning percentage (.864), most goals per game (5.95) and biggest scoring differential (162). Defensively, Coach Mason could turn the goal-tending over to either Bob Essensa, who set a new school record with a 1.64 goals against average or Norm Foster, who was named the CCHA tournament's most valuable player. It was a team that ran deep in talent with four All-Americans and two finalists for the Hobey Baker Award. Eighteen members of the team went on to sign professional contracts. After securing the CCHA playoff championship, it all came crashing down in the first round of the NCAA tournament. In a two-game total score series at Munn Ice Arena against Providence, the heavily-favored Spartans were outscored, 6-5 as they faced a "hot" goalie in the tournament's MVP, Chris Terreri, who stopped a total of 83 shots. It was a disappointing and abrupt end to a record-filled season.

The 1984-85 hockey team. (Front row, left to right) asst. coach T. Christensen, T. Anastos, L. Phair, G. Haight, K. Miller, head coach R. Mason, D. McFall, D. Beaty, D. Rizzo, G. Flegel, asst. coach G. Gwozdecky. (Middle row) team physician Dr. J. Downs, trainer D. Carrier, N. Foster, T. Nowland, H. Smyl, D. Krentz, B. Shibicky, D. McSween, R. Fernandez, M. Donnelly, B. Beck, B. Essensa, mgr. S. Allan, equipment mgr. T. Magee. (Back row) T. Budnick, D. Arkeilpane, J. Hamway, S. Clement, J. Parker, M. Messier, C. Simpson, T. Tilley, D. Chiappelli, K. Miller, mgr. Steve Brown

MAKING HISTORY

NCAA rules provided that football in-stadium television replay equipment be permitted.

The Big Ten sent six teams to bowl games, the most ever.

A 45-second shot clock was instituted for Big Ten basketball games on a one-year experimental basis.

The NCAA basketball championship bracket was expanded to 64 teams.

The Harlem Globetrotters made an appearance at Jenison Fieldhouse in a fundraising effort that brought the MSU intramural program $5,129.

In the IM world, the Spartan water-skiing team swept the regional competition and placed sixth at nationals. This was the best finish for a northern school.

A hackey-sack club was started in the fall and grew to well more than 50 members before the end of the academic year. Nineteen seventy-six graduate Rob Werner organized the first competition outside Demonstration Hall, where Andy Linder of Trinity College set a world record with 28,239 consecutive kicks over the course of four and a half hours.

GREAT STATE DATES

Football—September 9, 1984 (A): It was a strange game in which Michigan State led the University of Colorado 24-0 after 45 minutes of play and then surrendered 21 points in the final quarter and hung on for a season-opening victory. The first MSU score came with less than four minutes remaining in the opening quarter when fullback Carl Butler went in from the one-yard line after Lonnie Young had fallen on a loose ball at the three-yard line on a botched Buffalo center snap. The half ended following a Ralf Mojsiejenko 47-yard field goal and a 35-yard scoring pass from Dave Yarema to Mark Ingram. The final Spartan score came early in the second half when Yarema hit Butler on a quick screen pass that covered 56 yards. All three Colorado TDs came on aerials, the third coming with 1:33 remaining and 23 seconds later they recovered a Butler fumble at the State 22-yard line. It was nail-biting time. Fortunately, the Buff's field-goal kicker, who had missed on three previous tries during the afternoon, booted a fourth attempt wide to the right from the 32-yard line with 18 seconds remaining. Co-captain Jim Morrissey was credited with 12 tackles on the afternoon, but end Kelly Quinn was the defensive star with four tackles for losses.

Soccer—September 25, 1984 (A): Pouring rains and windy conditions did not stop the MSU kickers from defeating Michigan, 2-1, at Old College Field. The U of M got on the board first, but MSU tied it up just prior to intermission on a goal by junior fullback Niki Gogri, who took a perfect pass from Mike Maichen. Gorgi then set up the winning score for Tom Doherty, who scored the game-winning goal in the second half. With just seconds remaining, the Wolverines had a good opportunity to tie the game, but Spartan goalie Paul Zimmerman "made one of the best saves in MSU history," according to Coach Joe Baum, to seal the victory.

Football—October 6, 1984 (A): Michigan State 19, the University of Michigan 7—no better way to end a three-game losing streak, and before 105,612 fans in Ann Arbor, as well. The Spartans scored on their first possession, an 85-yard touchdown drive consuming 14 plays and nearly seven minutes from the game clock. Five straight David Yarema pass completions, three to tight end Veno Belk and two to fullback-turned-slotback Bobby Morse, ate up 63 of those yards. Carl Butler carried the ball in from the one-yard line. The most memorable play of the game was when Morse, the Muskegon sophomore, gathered in a Wolverine punt at his 13-yard line, swung left behind a cadre of blockers and sprinted down the sideline 87-yards into the south end zone. Ralf Mojsiejenko's conversion attempt was wide right. The Wolverines' only score came with 4:56 remaining in the half and State led 13-7 at the break. After that TD, Michigan never advanced beyond the MSU 37, leaving their own territory just twice more in 13 possessions. Mojsiejenko accounted for the remaining points of the game, a 49-yard field goal, against the wind, in the third period after an interception by Lonnie Young and a 30-yarder with 8:24 remaining in the game. The U of M suffered a serious loss midway through the third quarter when quarterback Jim Harbaugh left the game with a broken left arm.

Hockey—October 12, 1984 (A): In the first game of the year, Michigan State's Mike Donnelly knocked in the tie-breaker at 1:32 of overtime to give MSU a 5-4 season-opening win over Ohio State. Gordon Flegel started the play by winning a face-off in the Buckeyes' end and then fed the puck to Tom Tilley at the point. The freshman defenseman's shot was blocked, but

Donnelly was in front where he fired a second rebound shot into the back of the cage. After OSU held the initial lead 1-0 at 1:06 of the opening period, Don McSween and Kelly Miller scored ten seconds apart midway through the first period. The score stood at 4-2 after two periods with goals of Craig Simpson and Flegel. Although Norm Foster played well in the net, stopping 26 shots, the Bucks did manage to score twice in period three to send the game into the OT.

Hockey—**November 9 (A) & 10 (H), 1984:** Playing before sell-out crowds both nights, it was another double win over Michigan, 4-1 in Ann Arbor and 8-2 back at Munn on Saturday. Friday's victory featured power play goals by senior defenseman Gary Haight and freshman defenseman Tom Tilley, plus a shorthanded score by junior winger Dale Krentz and a goal at even strength by Rick Fernandez. In the second contest State held a 3-1 lead after two periods and then outscored the U of M 5-1 in the final stanza on goals by senior left winger Lyle Phair, sophomore center Craig Simpson and senior defenseman Dan McFall and two by left winger Mike Donnelly. Tallying earlier were Haight, senior right wing Tom Anastos, sophomore center Bill Shibicky. Led by the Spartan penalty killing unit of Kelly Miller-Phair and Anastos-Krentz, Michigan was held scoreless on all 13 of its power play chances over the weekend.

Football—**November 10, 1984 (A):** MSU gained the sixth win of the season by jumping to a 17-3 lead over the University of Iowa and then hanging on for a thrilling 17-16 victory. Both Spartan touchdowns came after botched Iowa punts. With less than two minutes remaining in the opening quarter and trailing 3-0, State moved 35 yards in six plays following a hurried 25-yard Hawkeye kick. Lorenzo White went over from the two-yard line. Later, in the second period, Kelly Quinn blocked a punt at the 30-yard line and the ball was eventually recovered at the two-yard line. Quarterback Dave Yarema hit Butch Rolle for the score. The Spartans ended their scoring with 2:33 remaining in the third quarter when Ralf Mojsiejenko booted what proved to be a game-winning 24-yard field goal. With 9:18 left in the game, the Hawkeyes culminated an 82-yard drive for one touchdown and then drove 68 yards and crossed the goal line a second time with 44 seconds remaining. Coach Hayden Fry opted for the win on a two-point conversion attempt. Quarterback Chuck Long kept the ball on an option to the right and was met inches short of the goal line by linebackers Jim Morrissey and Shane Bullough.

Basketball—**January 5, 1985 (H):** Led by Larry Polec's 10-for-17 shooting, the 17-rebound total for forward Richard Mudd and center Ken Johnson and eight crucial points from substitutes Carlton Valentine and Greg Pedero, the Spartans upset 12th-ranked Indiana University, 68-61. State first opened a 20-10 lead and then suddenly followed without a basket in an eight minute stretch. Thereafter, the lead changed hands 16 times as MSU led 33-32 at the intermission. The Hoosier defense was keyed on stopping guards Sam Vincent and Scott Skiles and doubling up on Johnson inside and the strategy partially succeeded as Johnson scored 14, Vincent 12 and Skiles 10. It was Sam that broke a 54-54 tie with a jumper and two free throws. Mudd, Johnson, Polec and Pedro hit eight straight shots from the line to ice the victory.

Basketball—**January 10, 1985 (A):** Senior Sam Vincent stole the show at Mackey Arena, scoring a career-high 39 points on 15-of-20 shooting to lead the Spartans past Purdue in overtime, 81-72. Vincent scored 25 points, including seven in the last 57 seconds to force a tie at 64. Down 63-57 with a 1:04 to play, Vincent sparked the comeback, hitting the game-tying shot with 15 seconds left to play in regulation. MSU rode the momentum in overtime, scoring the first 11 points of the extra session. Steve Reid paced Purdue with 26 points, but Vincent outscored him 15-0 in the last six minutes of play.

Wrestling—**January 24, 1985 (H):** Led by pins from Ron Cantini (142 pounds), Ernie Blazeff (158 pounds) and heavyweight John Wojciechowski, State defeated the University of Toledo, 39-5. Cantini's fall came at 7:17, Blazeff pinned his opponent at 1:55 and Wojciechowski used only 1:15 to put the Rockets' heavyweight to the mat. Other wins came from Dan Matauch (134 pounds) 4-1; Charley Root (150 pounds) 16-6; David Mariola (167 pounds) 5-4 and David Dopler (190 pounds) 6-1. Bruce Catanzarite (118 pounds) opened the meet with a forfeit win and John Przybyla (177 pounds) wrestled to a draw.

Hockey—**January 25 (H) & 26 (A), 1985:** Expanding on Michigan State's double defeat of Michigan back in November, *The Lansing State Journal* eluded to the 11-2 and 9-4 victories in January as "Massacre: Part II." In the Friday game, sophomore sensation Craig Simpson scored his fourth three-goal hat trick of the season and junior left wings Dale Krentz and Mike Donnelly each scored twice. Rounding out the total were goals by se-

nior right wing Tom Anastos, freshman center Kevin Miller, senior center Gord Flegel and senior left wing Kelly Miller. The fine play of of the five-man MSU defensive unit of Gary Haight, Dan McFall, Mitch Messier, Brad Beck and Sean Clement made it a fairly easy evening for goalie Bob Essensa who made but one save in the first period, three in the second and 13 in the third. Saturday's 9-4 win at Ann Arbor was played before 8,239 fans, the second-largest crowd in U of M history. Senior left wing Lyle Phair scored twice, Anastos, Kevin Miller, Flegel, Simpson, Kelley Miller and Krentz netted one goal each. Between the pipes for State was Norm Foster, who finished with but nine saves, the second lowest total in the school's record book. The wins upped the Spartan league record to 23-3 and assured them of their first-even regular-season Central Collegiate Hockey Association title.

Swimming and Diving—February 2, 1985 (H): The Spartans placed first in 8 of the 11 individual events and the closing freestyle relay to totally dominate Northwestern, 72-37, at the Charles McCaffree Pool. Diver Todd Ovenhouse scored 324.25 to win the one-meter event and then earned 320.62 points to finish first in the three-meter competition. C.J. Winkel, team co-captain from the Hague, Netherlands, posted his second-best time of the year in winning the 200-yard freestyle in 1:41.85.

Wrestling—February 2, 1985 (H): In a close, competitive match, MSU trailed Minnesota 14-13 with two bouts remaining. With the pressure mounting, MSU won the final two matches at 190 pounds and at heavyweight to beat the Gophers, 22-14. David Dopler pinned his opponent at the 5:58 mark in the 190-pound match, and John Wojciechowski finished the Gophers off with a 7-2 decision. Earlier winners were Tom Mahaney (126 pounds), Dan Matauch (134 pounds) 9-0, Ron Cantini (142 pounds) 12-6 and Ernie Blazeff (158 pounds) 4-3.

Fencing—February 16, 1985 (A): The Spartan fencers defeated Purdue, 16-11, and Oklahoma City, 25-2. Monte Falcoff and Pete Colovas turned in 6-3 and 5-4 records, respectively, in the foil competition. In the sabre, Rob Beatty paced MSU with a 4-2 mark and in the epee, Ken Vangolen posted a 3-3 record.

Gymnastics—February 17, 1985 (H): Posting the highest mark recorded by a Michigan State squad in more than a decade, 20th-ranked MSU defeated the 19th-ranked Wisconsin Badgers, 274.90-271.85. Leading the way was Keith Pettit who won the pommel horse with a 9.30, the high bar by scoring a 9.70 while tying teammate Marty Boerny in the vault, both scoring 9.55. John

Spellis finished first in floor exercise (9.65) and second in all-around (55.80). Other Spartans who contributed toward the scoring by finishing second or third were Andy Ladwig, Al Powers and Ed Malec.

Basketball—March 7, 1985 (A): Needing a big win to keep its NCAA Tournament hopes alive, MSU ousted Indiana on the Hoosiers' home court, 68-58. Sam Vincent once again led the Spartans, scoring 31 points on 11 free throws and 10-of-20 shooting from the field. The game featured Bobby Knight in his first coaching appearance after the famous "chair throwing" incident against Purdue, but the General couldn't rally his troops against a motivated Spartan squad.

Baseball—April 4, 1985 (A): In the middle of a six-game winning streak, MSU took two games from baseball power Notre Dame, 3-1 and 6-5 in a road doubleheader. Pitcher Chris Hayner surrendered six hits, two walks and only one run to gain the win in the opener. The game was tied 1-1 entering the final inning when Bill Hanis banged out a single, was sacrificed to second by Brad Arnold and Steve Marod walked to put runners on first and second. Bob Goodheart, who was two-for-four, doubled home both base runners for the victory. In the nightcap, Todd Krumm was credited with the victory with Eric Sandebergh getting the save. State scored two in the first, one in the second and three in the third and then held off the Irish for the two-game sweep. The big blow of the game was Jim Sepanek's home run in the third inning.

Lacrosse—April 10, 1985 (H): By defeating the University of Michigan 9-8, Michigan State won a school-record six consecutive games and raised the season count to 7-2 overall. The U of M scored the first two markers before State countered with three goals, two by junior attackman Marc Berman and one by freshman midfielder John Giampetroni. The Wolverines regained the lead at 4-3 followed by a four-goal Spartan barrage in the second quarter. Dan Christ tied the game just 1:08 into the second period and Berman put them ahead for good 1:48 later. Freshman attackman Mark O'Brien scored the next two goals before intermission. Senior Rich Johnson and freshman Adam Mueller scored the only two MSU goals of the second half. Although Michigan closed the margin to one with their eighth goal with 2:01 remaining, the defense and sophomore goalie Paul Sullivan made the big plays for the win.

Tennis—April 28, 1985 (H): For only the second time in a span of seven years, the Spartans defeated Notre

Dame, 5-4. Three points came in the singles competition with number one Fernando Belmar winning in three sets, 6-3, 4-6, 6-4; Joe O'Brien came back to win at number four, 3-6, 6-2, 6-0 and number five Ross Smith also needing three sets, 6-2, 4-6, 6-3. The outcome of the meet carried into the doubles competition with State gaining the needed points on tie-breakers. At number one, Paul Mesaros and Craig Schembri won 6-3, 7-6 and the number three pair of Curtis Wright-Smith gained the clincher, 6-4, 7-6.

Baseball—May 24, 1985 (H): MSU swept Cleveland State in two extra-inning games at Kobs Field. The Spartans won their opener against CSU, 7-6, on designated hitter Bob Goodheart's RBI triple in the bottom of the 11th inning. In the second extra-inning game, junior shortstop Bill Gavin belted his second home run of the game with no outs in the bottom of the eighth to give the Spartans a 5-4 victory that completed the sweep.

ATHLETE OF THE YEAR

Sam Vincent, MSU's fifth all-time leading scorer with 1,851 points, scored 23.7 points per game in 1984-85 to win the conference scoring title. Vincent, a starter in all 29 games, averaged 23.0 points overall and was a unanimous choice for the UPI and AP All-Big Ten teams. *The Sporting News* named him a first-team All-American while the Associated Press picked him as a third-team All-America selection. He ranks among the top-10 in eight statistical categories all-time at Michigan State, and is MSU's school record holder for made free throws with

Sam Vincent

476. On Jan. 10, 1985, Vincent scored a career-high 39 points in MSU's 81-72 overtime win against Purdue. A three-time All-Big Ten selection and team MVP, he was awarded the George Alderton Male Athlete of the Year Award at MSU in 1985.

IN THE SPARTLITE

Baseball: The 15-game Southern trip of 1985 resulted in a disappointing 2-13 record. Even more devastating, Coach Smith's pitchers allowed a massive total of 147 runs which was an average of nearly 10 runs per game. Perhaps they could have used sophomore Todd Krumm who was back in East Lansing with a broken bone in his left hand.

Six seniors closed out their collegiate careers, pitchers Bill Archer and Chris Hayner, infielders Dave Corey and Bob Goodheart along with outfielders Jim Sepanek and Steve Marod.

Corey set a new career hit record with 193, one better than the previous mark set by Al Weston (1974-1977). He also became the career leader in doubles with 37, three more than Weston.

In his four-year career, Marod connected for 13 triples, bettering Ray Collard's mark of 11 set in 1954-1956.

Jim Sepanek led the conference in home runs with 10 and was a second-team All-Big Ten selection. In the overall season he batted .353 with 13 homers and 40 RBIs.

Bob Goodheart led the team with a .363 batting average.

Basketball: MSU won 19 games, which, at the time, equaled the third highest in school history and the best since the 1979 NCAA championship team.

Scott Skiles, a second-team All-Big Ten selection, was second on the team in scoring with an average of 17.7 points per games. He was fifth in the Big Ten in assists in league play.

Ken Johnson was the MSU's most dominant player underneath the basket. He was second in the Big Ten in rebounding and third in blocked shots. Johnson set an MSU school record with eight blocked shots against San Diego on December 29.

The Spartans were fans of the road, as they won 10 of 14 away contests.

During the season, State shot a team-record .537 from the field.

Cross Country: Jim Stintzi, a former running great for the University of Wisconsin, replaced Jim Gibbard, who retired after 16 years as head coach.

For only the third time since Michigan State first fielded a cross country team in 1910, the 1984 team was winless in dual-meet competition.

MSU was third out of 11 teams at the Purdue Invitational with 67 points. The top Spartan was junior Mike Kavulich who came in fourth place with a time of 25:09. Other top runners for State were Joe Mihalic in 10th and freshman Jeff Neal in 16th.

Three weeks later it was back to West Lafayette, Ind., for the Big Ten championships where State's runners compiled 173 points for an eighth-place finish. Rick Pietras was 23rd in a time of 32:43. He was followed by Jeff Neal 29th in 33:05; Mark Williamson 36th in 33:26; Dave Schoener, 40th in 33:32 and Mihalic 45th in 33:54.

Fencing: With an impressive season record of 38-19, sabreman Rob Beatty led the team in wins. In foil, Pete Colovas was the team-leader with 20 victories and Ken Van Golen's 17 wins in epee was a team-best.

In the Big Tens at Evanston, Ill., State scored nine points and finished in fifth place out of five teams. With a 4-5 record, Beatty ended up seventh in sabre and Van Golden was eighth in epee with a 2-7 record. Others and their records: Steve Holden (1-8) 10th in sabre; John Peddie (1-8) 10th in epee; Mark Hengen (1-8) ninth in foil and John Gabocy (0-9) 10th in epee.

Football: The Spartans compiled a 6-5 record and earned a berth in the Cherry Bowl. It was MSU's first bowl appearance since the 1966 Rose Bowl.

Kelly Quinn racked up 15 tackles for loss, which is tied for sixth-best in an MSU season. He also had four quarterback sacks against Northwestern, which is good for second in MSU single-game history.

Ralf Mojsiejenko closed out his career as one of the greatest kickers and punters in MSU history. He is MSU's all-time leader in punts (279), second in punting average (43.8) and sixth in field goals (35). In addition, Ralf is the Big Ten's all-time leader in punts and punting yards (12,200).

Larry Jackson set a new school record with 168 kick-off return yards against Ohio State.

Freshman Lorenzo White rushed for 100 yards or more in three games during the season.

Gaining post-season honors as first team All-Big Ten picks were linebacker James Morrissey and a repeat from 1983, safety Phil Parker.

Golf: Sophomore Jon Kosier fired a final-round 78 for a three-round total of 225 to help Michigan State to a third-place finish at the par-72 Scarlet Course in Columbus at the Kepler Invitational. MSU's Dean Holland had the second-best score of the day with a 74 to finish at 232. Bob Fossum and Brad Virkus shot 79 and 83, respectively, to each close the tournament at 233.

Jeff Harding shot a total score of 293 for a third-place finish at the Big Ten championships. It was the highest individual finish for a Spartan since 1980.

Holland earned Academic All-American honors.

Kosier, the only Spartan to qualify for the NCAA championships at Haines City, Fla., missed the cut after three days of play in which he shot rounds of 88-79-79.

Gymnastics: MSU hosted Wisconsin, Western Michigan, Eastern Michigan and Michigan at the Spartan Invitational on January 5-6. Spartan performers captured four of six individual titles. Freshman Keith Pettit finished first on both pommel horse and the vault. Junior John Spellis took top honors on the parallel bars, while senior Marty Baerny was high man on the floor exercise.

Sophomore Al Powers won the Big Ten title in the rings competition with a score of 9.60. His performance, along with strong showing by Spellis and Pettit enabled State to earn 269.65 points. Unfortunately, the score was only good enough for fifth, one spot ahead of Wisconsin and behind Ohio State, Minnesota, Iowa and Illinois.

The team closed out the season with a 14-10 record and a number 20 national ranking.

The season's top performers in the various events were: Ed Malec with a 9.65 on the pommel horse; Powers with his conference-winning 9.60 on the still rings; Pettit, who scored a 9.70 on the high bar and a 9.6 on the vault and Spellis with a 9.45 on the parallel bars, 9.65 in floor exercise and 56.40 in the all-around.

Hockey: Topping the North American hockey record crowd set at the Great Lakes Invitational two year earlier, 21,576 fans watched State once more win the GLI by defeating Michigan Tech in the finals, 7-0.

MSU tallied a team-record 28 assists and 43 points in a 15-1 bombing of defending NCAA champion Bowling Green at Munn Arena. Craig Simpson, Gord Flegel, Dale Krentz, Mike Donnelly and Bill Shibicky scored two goals each for MSU. Simpson also scored four assists in leading to BGSU's worst loss in school history.

During the year, Dale Krentz scored seven shorthanded goals, which is still tied as a team record.

Of the goalies, Essensa's 1.64 goals against average set a new school record, while Norm Foster was named the CCHA tournament's most valuable player. He was also a member of the medal-winning World Junior Championship team.

For the fourth time in his career, Ron Mason was named CCHA coach of the year. It was an honor he would win three more times, in 1989, 1990 and 1999.

The Spartans had seven players receive CCHA All-League recognition.

Co-team MVP Kelly Miller was an Academic All-American. He was also named the recipient of MSU's Chester Brewer Leadership Award.

Simpson and Kelly Miller were among five finalists for the Hobey Baker Award.

In post season honors, defensemen senior Gary Haight, sophomore Don McSween, sophomore goalie Bob Essena, forwards senior Kelly Miller and sophomore Craig Simpson collected five of the six spots on the all-CCHA team for 1985.

Dan McFall, Kelly Miller and Simpson all earned first-team All-America honors, while Haight was named to the second team

Lacrosse: The 1985 team won a school record 11 games, and eight of the first 10 on the schedule.

With a goal and an assist in the 11-4 victory over Ohio State, sophomore Dan Christ was named the first-ever Midwest Lacrosse Association Player of the Week, and at season's end he was chosen as the conference's most valuable player. Upon completing his collegiate career in 1987, Christ would be the school's all-time leader in assists with 84 and MSU's second-time all-time leading scorer with 217 points (133 G, 84 A).

Eight Spartans were named to the All-Great Lakes Conference first and second teams, while five received All-Midwest Lacrosse Association recognition. All-conference first-team choices were Riney Wilke, Christ, Greg Walker and Carlton Evans. Named to the second team were Marc Berman, John Giampetroni, Rex Lynne and Rich Johnson.

John Giampetroni set a new school record with six assists in one game against Wooster on March 30.

Soccer: MSU shutout Ohio State, 1-0, in the first round of the Big Ten East Division Tournament as Tom Froman scored the game-winner. In the championship game, the Indiana Hoosiers turned that score around and ended the Michigan State season, 1-0.

On the season, goalie Paul Zimmerman posted nine shutouts, a team record, which is tied for the most in one season in MSU history. He would duplicate that feat in the following season.

For the second straight year, Tom Doherty led the team in scoring with nine goals and 19 points. Jim Gallina was right behind with eight goals and 17 points.

Swimming and Diving: At the Big Ten champion-ships, junior Jeff Butler of High Point, N.C., was the gold medal winner in the 100-yard butterfly in a time of 49.27. He later swam a 1:51.64 to place eighth in the 200-yard butterfly. Also, in support of MSU's eighth-place finish, C.J. Winkel placed seventh in the grueling 1,650-yard freestyle and 11th in the 200-yard freestyle. Other contributors to the team's 136-point total were: John Bodine, Brad Zylman, John Kasley, Kirk Goins and Richard Grimshaw.

Winkel, of The Hague, Netherlands, completed his Spartan career in 1985 as holder of four school records: the 200-yard freestyle (1:39.88), 500-yard freestyle (4:27.66), 1,000 yard freestyle (9:21.03) and 1,650-yard freestyle (15:36.33).

Tennis: The combo of Ross Smith and Curtis Wright led all doubles teams with eight wins. Wright also had the most wins at singles with 14.

In what would prove to be a one-year-only experi-ment, a team dual-match tournament was held at Champaign, Ill., to determine the conference team cham-pion. In the opening square-off, Wisconsin defeated State 5-1, while Northwestern and Iowa each needed the en-tire format to closeout Stan Drobac's squad, 5-4. The end result was a 10th place finish.

Track and Field: Three Spartans finished in run-ner-up positions at the Central Collegiate indoor cham-pionships. Tim Simpson with a 3:46.77 in the 1,500, Leonard who ran a 6.34 in the 60-yard dash and Jackson

MSU lacrosse superstar Dan Christ

with a 30.60 in the 300-yard dash.

Scoring only 10 points to tie Northwestern for last place, Coach Bibbs had little to cheer about at the Big Ten indoor championships in Madison, Wis. Rodney Benson ran a 48.36 to place third in the 440 while Ron Simpson placed fourth in the 1,000 (2:11.05) and sixth in the mile (4:04.68). No Spartans scored in the remaining 11 events.

Simpson would later set a new school indoor record with a 3:46.77 in the 1,500-meters.

Benson was the lone Spartan gold medal winner at the Central Collegiate meet hosted by Eastern Michigan. He blazed to a season-best and track-record time of 46.43 in the 400 meters.

Alumnus Marcus Sanders, competing for the Atlantic Coast Track Club, returned to Ralph Young Field to run in the sixth annual MSU Track Invitational. He won both the 200-meter and 400-meter races. Jeff Neal captured the 3,000-meter steeplechase with a time of 9:06.1; Marvin Parnell the 400-meter intermediate hurdles with a time of 54.4 and freshman Derrick Leonard the 100-meter dash in 10.4. Leonard joined Demetrius Hallums, Anthony Mahone and Larry Jackson to win the 400-meter relay in 40.9. The MSU quartet of Rodney Benson, Damon Brown, Parnell and Dennis Felton combined to win the mile relay in 3:17.43.

Managing only 24 points, State finished eighth in the Big Ten outdoor championships at Evanston. With a 3:46.41, Simpson placed third in the 1,500 meters; Tony Smith was fourth in the 110 hurdles (14:54); Jackson ran fifth in the 400 (45.98) and Mahone fourth in the 200 (21.37). The four-by-400 relay placed fifth in a time of 3:11.31.

Two school relay records were broken in outdoor competition. In the 400-meter relay, the foursome of Leonard, Mahone, Jackson and Hallums set a new standard with a time of 40.16 and the 1,600-meter foursome of Neal, Mark Williamson, Mike Kaulich and Simpson ran to a new standard of 16:21.24.

Wrestling: As Iowa won its 12th consecutive Big Ten team championship, Michigan State finished in fifth place with 60 points. Charles Root (150 pounds) and Ernie Blazeff (158 pounds), brother of Eli, reached the finals before losing. Ron Cantini (142 pounds) and Tony White (177 pounds) were consolation finalists and Dan Matauch (134 pounds) finished sixth.

Four Spartans, Cantini, Root, Ernie Blazeff and

White advanced to the NCAA tournament in Oklahoma City. Root made it to the second round while Blazeff gained All-American recognition as he reached the semifinals before being eliminated. The efforts of the two earned MSU 11 team points and placed MSU 30th out of 67 teams.

Root, who posted 10 pins during the season, was chosen for the team's Outstanding Wrestler Award. He and Cantini tied with 32 for the most wins over the season.

EXTRA! 1985 NCAA BASKETBALL TOURNAMENT

Michigan State reached the first round of the 1985 NCAA tournament. The following is the Spartans' box score from that game.

ALABAMA-BIRMINGHAM 70—MSU 68

	FG-FGA	FT-FTA	REB	A	PF	TP
Mudd	1-4	0-0	8	0	5	2
Polec	4-7	0-0	3	0	5	8
K. Johnson	4-8	1-1	11	1	4	9
Skiles	6-13	3-4	4	8	4	15
Vincent	13-23	6-6	6	2	3	32
D. Johnson	1-5	0-0	1	4	2	2
Walker	0-0	0-0	0	0	2	0
Pedro	0-0	0-0	0	0	0	0
Team			2			
TOTALS	29-60	10-11	35	15	25	68

Halftime: Michigan State 35-32; **Officials:** Clougherty, Barnett, Bosone; **Attendance:** 8,000.

EXTRA! 1984 CHERRY BOWL

December 22, 1984
Pontiac, Mich.

	1	2	3	4	F
MSU	0	0	0	6	6
Army	0	7	0	3	10

Starting lineup (offense)		*Starting lineup (defense)*	
Bob Wasczenski	SE	Kelly Quinn	LE
Doug Rogers	LT	Jim Rinella	LT
Jeff Stump	LG	Dave Wolff	RT
Mark Napolitan	C	Tom Allan	RE
John Wojciechowski	RG	Anthony Bell	LOLB
Steve Bogdalek	RT	Jim Morrissey (C)	ILB
Don "Butch" Rolle	TE	Jim Tyree	ROLB
Dave Yarema	QB	Lonnie Young	LCB
Lorenzo White	LH	Paul Bobbitt	SS
Keith Gates	FB	Phil Parker	FS
Mark Ingram	FL	Terry Lewis	RCB

The crowd may have been entertained during this bowl game, but it was not from offensive production. Five fumbles and four interceptions led to the only scoring of the game. Michigan State did produce an early threat when Phil Parker intercepted an Army pass and returned it 18 yards to the Cadet 43. Unable to get a first down, however, they were forced to kick, and Ralf Mojsiejenko's 52-yard field-goal attempt was wide left. A second quarter drive ended when Dave Yarema's pass from the Army five-yard line was intercepted in the end zone. Soon after, an MSU fumble near midfield allowed the Cadets to gain their only touchdown. Another MSU fumble in the final quarter set the West Pointers up for a field goal to take a 10-0 advantage with 8:40 remaining. State's only break came when Tom Allan recovered a fumble at the MSU 49 and three plays later Yarema hit Bob Wasczenski with a 36-yard pass in the left corner of the end zone. The two-point conversion failed and that ended the scoring. Lorenzo White ran for 103 yards; but after six sacks the team netted only six yards rushing compared to the oppositions' 256. The one bright spot was pass defense, which held the Cadets to only 10 passing yards compared to Yarema's 155.

EXTRA! 1985 NCAA HOCKEY TOURNAMENT (Regionals)

State won the CCHA regular-season crown and downed Miami (Ohio), Ohio State and Lake Superior State for the conference playoff championship. They were favored to win the NCAA tournament, but after defeating Providence College 3-2 in the first game, MSU lost to them 4-2 in the second. This put MSU one goal short in the total-goals series and gave Providence the upset and the semi-final slot.

March 23, 1985—East Lansing
MSU 3, Providence College 2
1st Pd.: 1. MSU, KL. Miller (McSween), 3:29; 2. PC, Taglianetti (Yeomelakis), 16:43.
2nd Pd.: No Scoring.
3rd Pd.: 3. MSU, Smyl (Kv. Miller), 5:16; 4. PC, Rooney (Army, Cavallini), 15:34; 5. MSU, Beck (unasst.), 17:12.

March 24, 1985—East Lansing
Providence College 4, MSU 2
1st Pd.: 1. PC, Deasey (DeVoe, Bianchi), 2:26; 2. PC, Cruickshank (Boudreault, Sullivan), 3:49; 3. PC, Wilkie (Taglianetti, Catteral), 5:30; 4. MSU, Clement (Shibicky, Beck), 15:17.
2nd Pd.: 5. PC, Boudreault (unasst.), 13:20.
3rd Pd.: 6. MSU, Phair (Beck, Flegel), 10:07.

TALES TO TELL

Early in Scott Skiles's collegiate career (1983-1986), coach Jud Heathcote described the Plymouth, Ind., sharpshooter as "not very big (a shade over six feet), not very fast and not quick. But he's a competitor and makes up for those things with great intensity and intelligence."

Of his 120 games as a Spartan, Scott's 1986 back-to-back scoring outbursts on January18 and January 25 will likely be long-remembered by veteran Spartan fans. In the first game, Skiles accounted for 45 of his team's 76 points in a loss to Minnesota. Then, one week later, at Jenison, he scored 40 points to lead his Spartans to a 91-79 defeat of Michigan. Observers of that earlier game, in Minneapolis, suggest Scott would have likely broken the 50-point mark had the three-point rule been in effect, as it was during his freshman year.

From his first game in green and white, Skiles became the team's "quarterback," directing traffic and barking out instructions to his more experienced teammates. He was a "take charge" leader and played with great confidence, never more obvious than in that January 25 victory over sixth-ranked Michigan. As Jack Ebling would lead in his *Lansing State Journal* story:

"The 'experts' who expected a Big Ten blowout weren't entirely wrong. They were only one team off. Skiles kept pumping, the Wolverines kept bumping and the joint kept jumping, as only sold-out Jenison can.

MSU seized a 44-31 halftime lead, behind 22 of Skiles's 40 points and built the bulge to 17 points with .09 to play. But the game was over long before that, perhaps with 11:49 to play when Michigan's All-American center Roy Tarpley fouled out.

That 40-point performance was reached through 15 of 20 field goals and 10 of 11 at the free-throw line, augmented by eight assists and four rebounds."

Also from the Ebling article:

"When guard Gary Grant, Skiles's alleged shadow, fouled out with 4:16, the only highlights left were a technical foul on Michigan's Antoine Joubert for firing his wristband [into the bleachers] and a Skiles-to-Carr alley-oop slam that sent Wolverine fans to the exit."

HEADLINES of 1986

- Space shuttle Challenger explodes after launch at Cape Canaveral killing, all seven aboard, including schoolteacher Christa McAuliffe, the first private citizen scheduled to go into space.
- A major nuclear accident at the Soviet Union's Chernobyl power station alarms the world.
- The Martin Luther King Jr. holiday is celebrated for the first time.
- Utilizing a new process of "colorizing," Turner Broadcasting begins televising former classic black-and-white movies in color format.

SCOREBOARD

	W	L	T	Avg.
Baseball	28	26	1	.518
Track and Field	0	1	0	.000
Football	7	5	0	.583
Basketball	23	8	0	.742
Tennis	2	21	0	.087
Cross Country	no dual meets			
Swimming and Diving	9	4	0	.692
Wrestling	6	12	1	.342
Hockey	34	9	2	.777
Fencing	12	14	0	.462
Golf	tournament play only			
Gymnastics	5	8	0	.385
Soccer	13	5	2	.700
Lacrosse	7	8	0	.467

Scott could dish it out (verbally), but he could also live up to it. Readers may recall his pregame comments to Michigan's Antoine Joubert that evening when he said something to the effect of "O.K. fatboy, you're going to lose some weight trying to keep up with me tonight."

Skiles later admitted, "Antoine is a competitor just like I am. He likes to talk a little bit, and so do I." Joubert finished the game with 12 points.

The two-game scoring binge earned Scott Skiles the *Sports Illustrated* Player of the Week award.

Time out! Scott Skiles gives "instructions" to coach Heathcote and assistant Mike Dean.

TEAM OF THE YEAR

While many thought the 1985 team had the best chance of bringing a hockey title back to East Lansing, it was the 1986 team that became the NCAA champions. They struggled at the beginning of the year (11-7-1), but after winning the Great Lakes Invitational at Detroit's Joe Louis Arena, they finished 17-2-1 to win a second consecutive Central Collegiate Hockey Association (CCHA) regular-season championship. Opening the NCAA tournament at home, they defeated Boston College, 6-4, 4-2 to advance to the Final Four at Providence, R.I. Their opponent in the semi-final was the best from the West, the Minnesota Golden Gophers, and Ron Mason's crew prevailed, 6-4 with goalie Norm Foster making 42 saves. Then, it all came down to one more game, this time against the best from the East, Harvard. Tied at 5-5, senior Mike Donnelly scored his second goal of the game and 59th of the season with only 2:51 remaining on the clock. Although the Spartans played shorthanded for most of the remaining time, they held the Crimson, for an exciting 6-5 well-earned victory.

MAKING HISTORY

John DiBiaggio started on July 1, 1985 as the new university president.

The 25 yard-line tiebreaker was added to the football rules.

Providing schools a possible opportunity to enhance their football records and improve the likelihood of bowl offers, beginning in 1985-1986 the nine-game round-robin schedule was changed to include only eight conference games.

For the second straight year, the Big Ten sent six football teams to bowl games, the most of any conference in the nation.

While starring on the gridiron, Andre Rison also lettered one time each, in basketball and track and field, a rare multi-sport performer of contemporary times.

The NCAA banned a wide range of stimulants, steroids and street drugs, while instituting a random testing method for all intercollegiate athletics.

Another NCAA ruling required incoming student athletes to have a minimum of a 2.0 GPA in 11 core courses and score at least 13 on the ACT or 660 on the

The 1985-86 hockey team. (Front row, left to right) N. Foster, assistant coach G. Gwozdecky, B. Shibicky, M. Messier, R. Fernandez, D. Rizzo, head coach R. Mason, M. Donnelly, B. Beck, D. McSween, J. Parker, assistant coach T. Christensen, B. Essensa. (Second row) team physician Dr. J. Downs, T. Tilley, D. Cole, R. Tosto, C. Luongo, S. Clement, D. Chiappelli, B. Reynolds, K. Miller, D. Arkeilpane, student manager T. Tuggle.(Third row) equipment manager T. Magee, trainer D. Carrier, G. Hoff, J. Lycett, M. Dyer, B. Rendall, B. McReynolds, J. Murphy, B. Hamilton, student manager S. Brown

SAT in order to compete in Division I sports their freshman year. These marks were lowered from those set two years earlier.

The NCAA interpreter of basketball rules admitted that the controversial "frozen clock" problem leading to the Kansas 76-72 overtime victory over Michigan State in the regional semi-final game at Kemper Arena in Kansas City, Mo., was improperly handled. As play continued during a stretch of about 21 seconds of untimed play, the Jayhawks managed to close the margin and eventually tie the Spartans, forcing the OT. The post-mortem interpretation was that game officials should have determined how much time had elapsed and reset the clock. This was never done. The gross error eventually led to the use of television replay to determine correctable errors.

After 36 years of coaching and 24 years at MSU Grady Peninger announced his retirement. For 35 straight seasons he had posted a winning season in wrestling, and he finished at State with a phenomenal 213-113-10 record for a .649 winning percentage.

GREAT STATE DATES

Football—September 14, 1985 (A): Parlaying one touchdown with two field goals, Michigan State opened the season with a 12-3 victory over Arizona State. At the 12:24 mark of the opening quarter sophomore tailback Lorenzo White took a pitchout, swept left end and raced down the sideline for a 42-yard touchdown. Chris Caudell missed the PAT, but five minutes later he split the uprights with 31-yard field goal for a 9-0 lead at intermission. With MSU leading 9-3 and five minutes remaining in the game, the Sun Devils had a 60-yard punt return to the Spartan 19-yard line nullified by a clipping call. On ASU's very next possession, they lost the ball on a fumble with Rob Stradley recovering. The turnover led to a 49-yard field goal by Caudell to closeout the scoring. Shane Bullough led the defense with 14 tackles.

Cross Country—September 21, 1985 (H): Michigan State hosted the Michigan intercollegiate meet at Forest Akers West Golf Course, and then proceeded to win the team trophy with a total of 41 points. The remaining teams scored as follows: Eastern Michigan 52, Central Michigan 75, University of Michigan 77 and Western Michigan 86. Senior Tim Simpson placed third in a time of 24:50.1 to become MSU's top finisher. Mike Kavulich

(25:09.9), Joe Mihalic (25:17.5) and Jeff Neal (25:18.1) took sixth, seventh and eighth place, respectively, for the Spartans. The final scorer for State was 17-year-old freshman Rick Prince who placed 17th at 25:40.3.

Soccer—**September 25, 1985 (A):** Joe Baum's team ran its record to 5-0-1 with a 4-1 victory over the University of Michigan. The first goal came when senior Silvio Iung took a corner kick from junior Jim Galina and beat the Wolverine goal keeper at the 20-minute mark of the opening half. MSU scored again one minute before intermission as sweeper senior Niki Gorgi booted an unusually long 70-yard pass that senior halfback Tom Doherty took in stride and buried into the Wolverine net. Doherty notched his second goal early in the second half on a pass from Galina and then Galina closed out the Michigan State scoring with an assist from Iung. The Spartans held a commanding four-goal lead before the U of M finally made their solitary marker.

Soccer—**October 11, 1985 (A):** MSU shut out the Wisconsin Badgers, 1-0, in Madison. Junior Pete Crawley scored the game's only goal 25 minutes into the second half on a 20-yard free-kick inside the right post. The Spartan defense then took over and helped goalie Paul Zimmerman to his fourth shutout of the season.

Football—**October 26, 1985 (A):** Michigan State came from a 24-14 deficit after three quarters to score 14 points and upset the Purdue Boilermakers 28-24 on homecoming day at Ross Ade Stadium. Featuring a 42-yard Dave Yarema-to-Mark Ingram pass play, the Spartans drove 83 yards on seven plays with 9:47 remaining in the game as Bobby Morse vaulted in from the one-yard line. It then took 22 plays, including two successful fourth and one gambles, to negotiate a 22-play drive that ended on a Yarema to Butch Rolle five-yard scoring pass with eight seconds showing on the game clock. It was Yarema's first game in six weeks after having been sidelined with a broken thumb. The first two touchdowns, one in the second quarter and another following the second half kickoff, both covered 75 yards and featured the running of Lorenzo White. From behind the lead blocks of Morse, White carried 13 times for 50 yards in a 19-play drive with Morse scoring from the one. The Ft. Lauderdale workhorse then rambled 61 yards and the final one yard to put State temporarily ahead, 14-10. The Boilers followed with two more TDs leading to the MSU resurgence. In total, Lorenzo rushing for 244 yards on a team record 53 carries, which put him over the 1,000-yard barrier in only the seventh game of the year.

Football—**November 2, 1985 (H):** It was a game of two halves. State won the first 31-10 and the University of Minnesota won the second 16-0. Scoring twice in the opening quarter, State first moved the ball 67 yards on 11 plays and then five minutes later culminated a 39-yard drive to gain a 14-0 lead. On both occasions Lorenzo White went over from the one-yard line. Meshed between a Golden Gopher TD and field goal in the second quarter, Chris Caudell booted a 37-yard field goal and quarterback Dave Yarema manged a pair of touchdown passes, first a 31-yard score to Andre Rison at 6:14 and then a 15-yard scoring connection to White with 4:47 remaining before halftime. That final touchdown was set-up after Todd Krumm recovered a fumble at the U of M 20-yard line. Even though Greg Montgomery's towering punts of 49, 52 and 56 yards forced the Gophers to cover extensive grounds to mange the end zone, they did make a game of it with two touchdowns and a field goal during the final 30 minutes. White, the sophomore running back from Ft. Lauderdale, Fla., gained 172 yards on 49 carries. It was his 10th 100-plus yardage game as a Spartan. Leading tacklers for MSU were Tim Moore with 15, Phil Parker 13 and Dean Altobelli 10.

Hockey—**November 22, 1985 (H):** It was an exciting evening of hockey for the standing-room only crowd of 6,682 at Munn Ice Arena. Trailing Bowling Green 3-1 after two periods, MSU came to life with goals by Mike Donnelly and Brian McReynolds in the third to tie the game at 3-3 and force overtime. Then, with just 34 seconds remaining in sudden-death OT, freshman winger Bruce Rendall took a McReynolds pass in the offensive zone and blasted a low slapshot from the left side that beat the Falcon goalie who had made 47 saves on the evening. Donnelly's goal had been on a re-direction of a shot from freshman Geir Hoff at 2:26 of the final period and McReynold's game-tier came at 14:23 from a scramble in front of the BG net. Spartan goalie Norm Foster played a superb game as he turned away 39 shots, including five breakaways.

Basketball—**January 5, 1986 (A):** Senior forward Larry Polec hit four free throws in the final 23 seconds and sophomore Carlton Valentine took control underneath the basket and scored a career-high 21 points in MSU's 77-74 win over Indiana University. Valentine was eight-of-nine from the field and five-of-six from the free throw line. The Spartans led 39-37 at halftime and built that margin to 15 points at 57-42 in the opening 5:16 of the second half. The Hoosiers came back in a 22-9 scor-

ing spree and then knotted the totals at 70-70. It was then State outscored IU 7-4, featuring the Polec free throws and one by the junior guard, Darryl Johnson.

Gymnastics—**January 11, 1985 (H):** In a contest scored and decided by fractional points, State invited five teams to Jenison and then proceeded to compile a 253.10 score, good enough for first place, with the University of Wisconsin at 251.50, Western Michigan 249.50, Georgia 249.20, Michigan 244.45 and Wisconsin-Oshgosh 192.70. The winner was undetermined until the final event when the Spartan squad edged the Badgers by .15 point. Senior Andy Ludwig won the high bar competition with a 9.35 score. Sophomore Keith Pettit scored an 8.90 to win the pommel horse and then became the meet's top performer with a 53.35 all-around total score. Freshman Greg Jung finished second in both floor exercise (9.20) and on the still rings (9.05). Junior Ed Malec finished third in the all-around with a score of 51.45.

Wrestling—**January 16, 1986 (H):** Opening the meet with four straight wins, including 118-pound Dan Nagagan's pin at 4:41, State easily handled Indiana for the 21st straight year, 30-7. Winning by decision were freshman Brian Smith (126 pounds) 13-8, junior Dan Matauch (134 pounds) 7-1 and freshman Stacy Richmond (142 pounds) 9-2. Following Erick Jensen's loss at 150 pounds, Grady's gang gained another four consecutive decisions to seal the victory. Charles Root, the senior captain, squeezed out a close 4-3 verdict at 158 pounds. He was followed by verdicts from senior Mark Beaudoin (167 pounds) 6-1, sophomore Dave Mariola (177 pounds) 21-6 and junior John Przybyla (190 pounds) 2-0.

Swimming and Diving—**January 18, 1986 (H):** The swimmers and divers took seven of the opening nine events against Purdue University and then saw the Boilermakers capture the 200-yard backstroke, 500-yard freestyle and 200-yard breaststroke. The outcome of the meet was then dependent on the result of the closing race, the 400-yard freestyle relay and the Spartan quartet of Frank Deeter, Kirk Goins, Brian Goins and Mike Green met the challenge in a time of 3:07.84. The final score read MSU 57, Purdue 56. The team of Brian Goins, Brad Zylman, Kirk Goins and Green opened the meet by touching first in the 400-yard medley relay with a time of 3:30.10. Deeter, the sophomore sprint ace, was a double-winner with a 21.78 in the 50-yard freestyle and 47.16 in the 100-yard freestyle. Other State firsts were credited to Green with a 1:41.67 in the 200-yard freestyle, Kirk Goins in the 200-yard butterfly (1:54.60), Todd

Ovenhouse with a score of 294.65 in the one-meter diving event and Roland McDonald who scored 310.575 at three meters.

Fencing—**January 25, 1986 (A):** Fred Freihert's squad traveled to Angola, Ind., where they out-dueled the University of Michigan, 21-6. The scoring was fairly well-balanced across the three weapons with a 7-2 win foil, 6-3 in epee and 8-1 in saber competition. Led by Peter Colovas, Mike Gobacy, Ken VanGolen, Steve Holden and Monte Falcoff, the Spartans also defeated the host Tri-State team, 19-8.

Swimming and Diving—**February 8, 1986 (H):** MSU surprised Ohio State, 66-47, at Charles McCaffrec Pool in the IM West Building. MSU struck early, winning the 400-medley relay come-from-behind fashion, thanks to a strong finish by sophomore Mike Green. The other members of the relay team were Brad Zylman, Brian Goins and Kirk Goins. Green went on to finish second in both the 200- and 500-freestyle events.

Fencing—**February 12, 1986 (H):** MSU defeated Detroit, 15-12, in its first home match of the season. In a feature math-up in foil, Mike Gobacy beat Detroit's Bill Kendall, 5-3. With the win the Spartans avenged their earlier season loss to the Titans.

Basketball—**February 20, 1986 (A):** By a convincing score of 74-59 and for the second time of the season, MSU upset the University of Michigan, this time before a sellout crowd of 13,609 at Crisler Arena. Trailing 37-36 at intermission, the smaller Spartans outscored the Wolverines 24-12 in the opening 14 minutes of the second half and used a seven-minute U of M scoring drought to build a 60-49 lead. They did it with a pair of 8-0 runs as Darryl Johnson hit eight of his game-high 26 points in that first spurt with three field goals coming on fast-break passes from Scott Skiles, who rallied to conclude with 20 points and six assists. Johnson's total came on 12-of-19 and two free throws. Assisting in the victory were Vernor Carr and Larry Polec who combined for 19 rebounds. In field-goal percentage Jud Heathcote's squad outshot Michigan .543-.430 overall and .600-.333 after the break.

Hockey—**February 21 & 22, 1986 (H):** In defeating Lake Superior 8-5 on Friday night, Michigan State earned a share of the CCHA title and then topping the Lakers 5-4 in overtime on the next evening the Spartans were able to claim the championship outright. Mike Donnelly, the nation's leading scorer, paced the offense in the opening game with his 50th and 51st goals of the

season. In addition, the Livonia senior picked up assists on goals by Bill Shibicky in the first period along with Kevin Miller and Tom Tilley in the second. Also scoring for State were junior right winger Jeff Parker, freshman center Brian McReynolds and freshman defenseman Brad Hamilton. The game had a weird opening. At the regularly scheduled face-off time of 7:30 p.m. there were no on-ice officials in the building. The referee had been delayed by an automobile accident on I-96 and consequently the game did not get underway until 8:20 p.m. The contracted linesmen never did show-up, meaning fill-ins were recruited in relief. On Saturday night the "Senior Night" crowd of 6,897, the largest turnout in school history, had to wait only 16 seconds to watch Donnelly strike once more. This, his 52nd goal, made him MSU's all-time single-season scoring leader, surpassing Tom Ross's former record of 51 set in 1975-1976. Also scoring in regulation were Shibicky, McReynolds and Bruce Rendall. It was Rendall, the freshman winger, who won it at 5:05 of OT.

Hockey—February 28 & 29, 1986 (H): The icers swept Michigan, 4-3 and 5-2, to advance to the CCHA Final Four at Joe Louis Arena. Down 3-2 after the first period in game one, Tom Tilley and Bill Shibicky notched goals for MSU in the second to put the Spartans up for good. After the tough one-goal game, MSU took it to the Wolverines in the second game, winning 5-2 on the strength of two goals from Bruce Rendall. Mike Donnelly, Jeff Parker and Kevin Milller also netted goals for the Spartans.

Baseball—March 27, 1986 (A): During their annual training trip south, the Spartans stunned defending national champion and second-ranked Miami, 3-2. MSU scored three runs off Hurricane pitcher Kevin Sheary, who had won three games in the 1985 College World Series, and led 3-0 after six innings. Miami tried to rally late, but MSU retaliated by turning in double plays in both the seventh and eighth innings to finish off the nationally-ranked number two team.

Tennis—April 1, 1986 (H): The Spartans were blanked in all three doubles matches, but fortunately, five of the six singles players were able to win and defeat Western Michigan, 5-4. Fernando Belmar, playing in the number two slot, won in two sets, 6-3, 6-1. Other Spartan winners were number three Santiago Cash, 6-2, 6-2; number four Craig Schembri, 5-7, 6-3, 7-6; number five Kurt Streng, 5-7, 6-2, 7-6 and number six Chris Ignas, 6-2, 6-2.

Baseball—April 26, 1986 (A): MSU took two games from Ohio State, 7-2 and 6-5. Tom Kurczewski picked up his fourth victory in game one. In game two, Todd Krumm doubled home two runs in the top of the 12th inning to give MSU a 6-5 win. Dave Mammel pitched four and one-third innings of relief to earn the victory. He struck out three, walked one and allowed two hits.

Lacrosse—May 3, 1986 (A): On a goal from junior midfielder Dan Christ with five seconds of playing time on the game clock, State was able to edge Notre Dame, 12-11. That winning marker came after the Irish goalie had rejected four point-blank efforts during a stretch in which ND had a man in the penalty box. The Spartans were led by sophomore attackman Adam Mueller's four goals and junior Dave Levan's three tallies. Christ and Jon Giampetroni who each connected for a pair while junior Rex Lynne scored once. The turning point of the game came in the third quarter with an MSU two-goal outburst while trailing 9-3 and playing short-handed. Before that period was concluded, MSU had tied the game 9-9. The game would later hold at 11-11 for the final five minutes of play before Christ's tie-breaker found the mark.

Baseball—May 4, 1986 (H): Michigan State trailed the U of M, 4-0 with two outs in the bottom of the sixth inning and then struck back to gain a 7-4 victory. Third baseman Bill Gavin started the comeback with a single to right field and in no time State had seven runs, enough for the win. Davidson added a single and Mark Sayad a double. There were two errors, a hit batsman, a balk and a single by Steve Preston. Pitcher Rick Rozman went the distance to pick up his third victory without a loss, as he scattered seven hits.

Lacrosse—May 7, 1986 (H): The Spartans ended their season by pounding Wittenberg, 16-4, at Old College Field, earning a share of the Midwest Lacrosse Association Great Lakes Conference championship. MSU, which tied Notre Dame for the division title, took a 10-1 lead at the half and never looked back. Jon Giampetroni scored four times and finished the season with a team leading 31 goals and 45 points. Kevin Rice added three goals and Rex Lynne and Doug Brooks netted two each. Dan Christ, Phil Preston, Paul Greenfield, Jeff Halderson and Keith Wadle each tallied one goal for the Spartans. Senior Mike Gabor was the winning goalie.

Baseball—May 11, 1986 (H): In the final Big Ten games of the year, State defeated Indiana University in a doubleheader, 2-1 and 6-4. Todd Krumm pitched a com-

plete-game five-hitter with five strikeouts in the opener with Bill Gavin batted in Bill Hanis with the winning run. With another single in the second game, Gavin's season base hit total reached 71 to top the team record of 70 set by Al Weston in 1977. State opened the second game with a pair of unearned runs on passed balls and wild pitches. Designated hitter John Judge and second baseman Mark Sayad accounted for two runs in the second inning and the Spartans finished off the scoring with two more runs in the fifth inning for the victory. Rick Rozman continued his string of victories, winning his fourth consecutive game on the mound.

ATHLETES OF THE YEAR

The 1985-86 season was one of the greatest in Michigan State athletics history. Along with great teams, there were great athletes. Three Spartans from three different sports distinguished themselves during the year. All three becoming All-Americans in their respective sports: Mike Donnelly in hockey, Scott Skiles in basketball and Lorenzo White in football. Consequently, all three were awarded the George Alderton MSU male athlete of the year award for 1986.

Mike Donnelly wrapped up his brilliant Spartan career with a national championship in 1986. Donnelly was the star on the team as he scored an NCAA record 59 goals—including two in the NCAA championship game. Donnelly was the NCAA tournament MVP along with earning first-team All-America and All-CCHA honors. Donnelly broke the school record for most goals in a series with eight and tied the record for most goals in a game with five against Ohio State in December. The forward also holds the record for most hat tricks in a season with six. He remains the 15th all-time leading scorer in school history with 196 points (110 G, 86 A).

Scott Skiles, the third-leading scorer in MSU history with 2,145 points, earned first-team All-America and Big Ten Player of the Year honors after averaging 27.4 ppg his senior season. Skiles led MSU to its first Sweet Sixteen appearance since 1979 and was designated as player of the year by the *Basketball Times*. He ranks among the top 10 in nine statistical categories all-time at Michigan State, including second in assists (645), field goals (837) and steals (175). His 850 points and 331 field goals in 1985-1986 are still single-season records at MSU, and his 20 field goals (48 points, 20-of-28 shooting) against Minnesota is tied for an MSU single-game record. Skiles's 29.1 conference scoring average in 1985-1986 led the Big Ten, and his 27.4 overall average was second in the nation.

Mike Donnelly (left), Lorenzo White (center) and Scott Skiles (right).

Lorenzo White shattered the Spartan record books in his only second season at tailback for MSU. He captured All-America honors in 1985 as chosen by the Associated Press, United Press, Football Writers, *The Sporting News*, American Football Coaches and the Walter Camp Foundation. He finished fourth in the voting for Heisman Trophy after rushing for a school and Big Ten seasonal record 2,066 yards. At the time, his 1,908 yards during the regular season (173.5 yards per game led the nation) was the fourth-best single-season rushing total in the history of college football and the highest ever by a sophomore. He rushed for 200 or more yards on four occasions, including a 286-yard effort versus Indiana. During the 1987 season, White helped MSU to its first bowl game since the 1966 Rose Bowl by rushing for 1,572 yards. His 132.6 rushing yards per game ranked him number six nationally. In his career, he posted 23 games of 100-plus yards on the ground and finished with school records in rushing yardage (4,887, then number two in Big Ten history) and attempts with 1,082.

IN THE SPARTLITE

Baseball: Bill Gavin led the team with a .417 batting average. Gavin, a third-team All-Big Ten selection, is only one of 22 Spartans in MSU history to bat .400. His 76 hits in 1986 are still fourth-best in an MSU season.

Outfielder Mike Davidson and catcher Bill Hanis earned second-team All-Big Ten honors. Davidson had six home runs and 43 RBIs along with a .368 batting average. Hanis hit .331 with 27 RBIs.

Basketball: The 1985-86 team set three school records which still stand today: field goals (1.043), field-goal percentage (.561) and free-throw percentage (.799).

On January 12 against Michigan, MSU shot a team record 18-for-18 at the free-throw line.

MSU finished 12th in the final *USA Today* poll.

The end of MSU's 1986 tournament trail came abruptly after overtime of the quarter-final game against the University of Kansas at Kemper Arena in Kansas City. It will always be remembered as the game of the malfunctioned clock. With 2:21 remaining in the game and State leading 76-72, play continued for an estimated 21 seconds with the clock stopped and Kansas in posses-

sion. Game officials finally realized the problem, stopped play, deliberated the issue, but did not compensate by removing time from the game clock, as the rules provided. Play continued and with nine seconds remaining in regulation (the game should have been over). The Jayhawks tied the score at 80-80 resulting in overtime where UK outscored State by 10 points and won with ease, 96-86. The incident precipitated the introduction of an NCAA rule to provide a TV review of game-ending controversial incidents that might effect game outcome.

Daryl Johnson, who was the team's second leading scorer with a 16.6 ppg average, was a second-team All-Big Ten selection.

Head coach Jud Heathcote was named the Big Ten coach of the year by both the Associated Press and UPI.

Cross Country: Twice during the fall MSU hosted invitational meets identified as the MSU Open. On September 28, runners from the Tillsonburg (Ontario) Track Club, Wayne State, Macomb Community College and Wurtsmith Air Force Base ran with the Spartans over the five-mile Forest Akers course. Three weeks later teams representing Western Ontario, Waterloo (Ontario) and Macomb toed the line with the MSU runners.

At the Big Ten meet in Ann Arbor, State finished in ninth place, placing ahead of only Iowa. With a time of 25:42 and in 17th place, Tim Simpson was the first Spartan across the line. He was followed by Joe Mihalic in 23rd with a time of 25:55; Jeff Neal, 50th in 26:59; Mike Kavulich, 53rd in 27:08; Waddie Freeman, 54th in 27:11; Keith Hanson, 57th in 27:20 and Dennis Topolinski 62nd in 27:47.

Fencing: The 58th annual Big Ten championships were hosted by the University of Wisconsin and drew entrants from five schools, Illinois, Northwestern, Ohio State, Wisconsin and Michigan State. The Illini scored 40 points for the title while MSU managed only 14 points to place fifth. In the foil competition Pete Colovas finished fifth with a 5-4 record and Monte Faycoff was 10th. In epee, Ken Frazee and Ken VanGolen placed eighth and ninth while Steve Holden and Joe Rivet were eighth and 10th in the sabre.

Football: Shane Bullough recorded 156 tackles during the season, which at the time was second most in the MSU record book. He was credited with 21 of them against Indiana University.

Greg Montgomery led the Big Ten with a 45.1 punting average.

Lorenzo White was a busy running back as he established two MSU season records with 419 carries for 2,066 yards. While gaining more than 100 yards rushing in every game, his 266 yards in the Indiana game ranks second only to Eric Allen's record 350 yards against Purdue in 1971.

White became the first Michigan State running back to gain All-American status since 1971 when Eric Allen was so honored. White joined Phil Parker, John Wojciechowski and Montgomery as first team All-Big Ten selections.

Golf: Following his squad's disappointing 12th place finish at the Marshall Invitational, the usual mild-mannered Bruce Fossum offered: "It appears that we have overrated the team. Unless we can find some players who have the determination and drive to excel, our season could very well be one of mediocrity." Jon Kosier, the junior from Mason, had certainly done his part as he shot 78-80-73—231. Other scores were Steve McKalko 71-77-73—221; Brad Virkus 79-80-81—240 and Tom Harding 81-80-80—241.

State hosted the 1986 Big Ten championships on the Forest Akers West course and finished in fifth place with a score of 1,198. Todd Marston posted the low four-round score of 290 for State, good enough for fifth place. Other Spartan finishers were Kosier 295 for 11th; Chris O'Conner, 31st with a 308; Harding 38th with a 311 and McKalko who shot a 312 to place in 41st.

Gymnastics: Keith Pettit and Allan Powers represented MSU at the NCAA championships. Pettit competed in the high bar event and Powers competed on the rings. Pettit qualified for the high bar with a top score of 9.65 against Minnesota, just lower than his 1985 best of 9.70. He was a team leader and consistently scored high in the pommel horse, vault, parallel bars and floor exercise. Powers placed ninth at the NCAAs with a score of 9.05.

Hockey: The December 19 game against Northern Michigan at Munn Ice Arena was a sellout. This began the lengthy string of consecutive regular-season home sellouts that still continues.

In only his seventh season as MSU's head coach, Ron Mason directed the Spartans to the CCHA and NCAA titles. The key to the season was 16-1-1 run from December 27 until the end of the regular schedule on February 22.

In a two-game series sweep of Ohio State, 6-5 and 8-0, Mike Donnelly scored eight goals, including the overtime winner in the first game.

State defeated Rensselaer, 8-3, to win its fourth straight Great Lakes Invitational title. Boastful fans were facetiously calling Detroit's Joe Louis Arena "Munn Arena-East."

Don McSween was named a second-team All-American and was a recipient of the Big Ten Medal of Honor. He was also a first-team All-CCHA and Academic All-America selection.

Joe Murphy was the second Spartan ever to be named CCHA Rookie of the Year. He also went to the World Junior Championships and won a medal.

In addition to being named the NCAA tournament MVP, Mike Donnelly was named to the all-tournament team along with goalie Norm Foster, Don McSween and Jeff Parker.

What more could he have done? Mike Donnelly, who set an NCAA West record with 57 goals while leading the Spartans to an NCAA title, was a finalist but not the winner of the coveted Hobey Baker Memorial Award which designates college hockey's top player.

Lacrosse: The pre season training trip sent the team east into Pennsylvania and then south into Virginia and North Carolina where they completed a 2-3 record. The most memorable game was the devastating 26-3 loss to Duke University in Durham.

Even though they posted a less-than-impressive 7-8 overall season, the 1986 Spartans claimed a share of the Midwest Lacrosse Association league title with a 4-1 record.

At the conclusion of the season, five team members were selected to the Great Lakes Conference mythical first-team: Riney Wilke, Dan Christ, Rich Johnson, Greg Walker and Carlton Evans.

Soccer: With the 1-0 shutout of Bowling Green on October 30, the 1985 team set the school record for most wins in a season with 13. The season scoring total of 49 goals was the most productive year since the 77 scored during the record year of 1968.

Jim Gallina had 10 assists, which is the fifth-highest season total in MSU history. He also led the team with 26 points. Peter Crawley was the team-leader in goals with 11.

Paul Zimmerman closed out his career as one of the greatest goalies in MSU history. He held nine opponents

scoreless, which tied a team single-season mark and he closed out his career as the school's all-time leader with 29 shutouts.

Tom Doherty left MSU as one of the top scorers in school history. Finishing with a career 78 points (goals and assists), he stands as the eighth all-time scorer.

Swimming and Diving: By 1986, the MSU roster was equally international. Sidney Appelboom was a freshman from Antwerp, Belgium, Mike Green, a sophomore from Romford, England, and Richard Grimshaw, a sophomore from London, England.

The swimmers and divers totaled 242 points leaving MSU sixth in the Big Ten meet at Indianapolis. Frank Deeter of Dearborn swam a 1:38.32, placing him fourth in the 200-yard freestyle and with a 44.92 finished fifth in the 100-yard freestyle, both team records. Todd Overhouse placed fifth and eighth in the two diving events. Others who scored points were Barry Hibbard, Roland McDonald, Brad Zylman, Peter Lundquist, Kirk and Brian Goins, Appelboom, Green and Grimshaw.

Overhouse qualified for the NCAA championships and finished 13th on the one-meter board to earn MSU four points in the team standings.

Tennis: The new $1.9 million MSU Indoor Tennis Facility on Mount Hope Road was opened January 18-19 with a four-team tournament featuring men and women from MSU, Michigan, Texas A&M and the NCAA defending champions, the University of Georgia.

Leaders for the Spartans in 1986 were Fernando Belmar at number one singles (eight wins), Paul Mesaros at number two singles (seven wins) and Chris Ignas (10 wins).

Mesaros and Craig Schembri were the top doubles team.

Winning only four singles matches, State was defeated by the University of Iowa in the battle for ninth spot at the Big Ten meet on the Indiana University courts. The four winners for State were Santiago Cash 6-3, 6-3; Belmar 7-5, 6-4; Mesaros 4-6, 6-3, 6-3 and Steve Hooley 6-4, 6-4.

Track and Field: State totaled 56 points to claim fifth place at the indoor conference championships held in West Lafayette, Ind. Heading the way were Andre Rison who leaped 24' 6" for a second-place finish in the long jump; Tim Simpson ran a 3:51.88 to capture second in the 1,500 meters and later ran a 2:26.68 for sixth in the 1,000-meter run in which Jeff Neal placed fourth. Rodney Benson finished second with a 1:02.36 in the 500-meters,

Guy Scott (47.32) and Marvin Parnell (48.04) were third and fourth respectively in the 400-meter dash and fourth-place finishes went to sprinter Derrick Leonard (6.79) in the 55-meter dash and Dennis Felton (34.64) in the 30-meters. In the 800-meter run, Joe Mihalic was fourth in 1:52.51 and Guy Pace sixth in 1:54.99.

Freshman middle-distance runner Guy Scott ran an impressive 1:49.85 to take fourth place in the half-mile at the Drake relays.

In the seventh running of the MSU invitational meet at Ralph Young Field, Spartan runners captured six individual events. Derrick Leonard won both the 100 meters in 10.5 and the 200 meters in 21.8. Other firsts were registered by Dennis Felton in the 400 meters (48.2); Mark Williamson in the steeplechase (9:13.6); Mike Urynowicz in the 110-meter high hurdles (15.4) and Joe Mihalic in the 1,500 meters (3:57.19).

With a time of 4:02.83, Tim Simpson finished third in the mile run at the Jesse Owens Track and Field Classic in Columbus, Ohio.

MSU placed sixth at the Big Ten outdoor championships, as Guy Scott claimed an individual title in the 800-meter run with a time of 1:48.80. Parnell finished second in the 400-meter hurdles with a time of 51.27 and Williamson ran a 8:55.94 to place second in the 3,000-meter steeplechase.

Wrestling: Winning only two individual titles, the Spartans had to settle for third place among the nine schools represented at the MSU invitational. Dan Matauch (134 pounds) and Dave Mariola (177 pounds) managed to win in the championship round while John Przybyla (190 pounds) lost to the top seed in the finals.

Mariola placed second and Przybyla third to lead State to a six-place finish at the Big Ten championships in Minneapolis. Other contributors to the 55 1/2 team points were Matauch with a fourth place; Erick Jensen (150 pounds) and John Beaudoin (167 pounds), both finishing fifth and Charles Root (158 pounds) sixth.

Three Spartans competed in the NCAA tournament hosted by the University of Iowa: Matauch, Przybyla and Mariola, the latter placing fifth at 177 pounds and gaining All-American status. It marked the eighth consecutive year MSU had at least one All-American wrestler.

Mariola was the season leader in wins with 28 followed by Przybyla with 22 and Matauch 19.

EXTRA! 1986 NCAA BASKETBALL TOURNAMENT

Michigan State reached the regional semifinals in the 1986 NCAA tournament. The following are the Spartans' box scores for those games.

MICHIGAN STATE 72—WASHINGTON 70

	FG-FGA	FT-FTA	REB	A	PF	TP
Polec	2-5	0-0	3	0	4	4
Carr	6-10	3-5	5	2	2	15
Fordham	0-2	0-0	5	0	2	0
Johnson	11-13	0-0	4	3	3	22
Skiles	12-21	7-7	0	7	2	31
Walker	0-0	0-0	5	0	4	0
Valentine	0-1	0-0	1	0	0	0
Izzo	0-0	0-0	1	0	0	0
Team			1			
TOTALS	31-52	10-12	25	12	17	72

Halftime: Washington 36-26; **Officials:** Silvester, Howell, Herring; **Attendance:** 13,260.

MICHGIAN STATE 80—GEORGETOWN 68

	FG-FGA	FT-FTA	REB	A	PF	TP
Polec	4-7	8-8	10	0	4	16
Carr	3-6	7-8	6	1	2	13
Fordham	4-6	0-2	4	0	2	8
Johnson	6-12	0-0	2	6	2	12
Skiles	7-12	10-11	2	5	2	24
Walker	0-0	2-2	3	0	1	2
Valentine	2-3	1-2	4	1	0	5
Team			3			
TOTALS	26-48	28-33	34	13	13	80

Halftime: Michigan State 32-30; **Officials:** McJunkin, Moreau, Crowley; **Attendance:** 13,260.

KANSAS 96—MICHIGAN STATE 86 (OT)

	FG-FGA	FT-FTA	REB	A	PF	TP
Carr	7-13	3-6	4	3	3	17
Polec	6-7	4-5	11	2	5	16
Fordham	7-9	1-3	5	0	3	15
Skiles	6-14	8-10	2	7	3	20
Johnson	4-11	2-2	4	9	4	10
Walker	0-1	2-2	3	0	1	2
Brown	1-2	0-1	2	0	1	2
Valentine	2-4	0-0	1	0	0	4
Team			5			
TOTALS	33-61	20-29	37	21	20	86

Halftime: Kansas 46-37; **Regulation:** not available; **Officials:** Dibler, Armstrong, Pavia; **Attendance:** 16,800.

EXTRA! 1985 ALL-AMERICAN BOWL

December 31, 1985
Birmingham, Alabama

	1	2	3	4	F
MSU	0	7	7	0	14
Georgia Tech	0	0	7	10	17

Starting line-up (offense)		*Starting line-up (defense)*	
Andre Rison	SE	Mark Beaudoin	DE
Tony Mandarich	LT	Mark Nichols	DT
Doug Rogers	LG	Joe Curran	DT
Pat Shurmur	C	John Jones	DE
John Wojciechowski	RG	Anthony Bell(C)	OLB
Steve Bogdalek	RT	Shane Bullough	MLB
Don "Butch" Rolle	TE	Tim Moore	OLB
Dave Yarema	QB	Todd Krumm	CB
Lorenzo White	LH	Dean Altobelli	SS
Bobby Morse	FB	Phil Parker	FS
Mark Ingram	FL	Paul Bobbitt	CB

George Perles's team controlled the game until the fourth quarter, when Georgia Tech came from behind to win 14-17. The first points went up on the scoreboard after Tim Moore's second quarter interception set up State's first scoring drive. In just four plays, Dave Yarema moved the ball 48 yards, finishing with a six-yard TD pass to Ingram with 2:03 left in the first half. It was not

until midway through the third quarter that the Yellow Jackets knotted the score. Forcing Georgia Tech to punt out of their own end zone on their next possession, MSU started their next scoring drive 37 yards from the goal line. Lorenzo White gained 11 yards around the left end on the first play, and on the second Yarema connected again with Ingram for a 27-yard touchdown and a 14-7 lead with 4:41 left in the third quarter. Unfortunately, that was the end of the Spartan scoring. With just 7:08 to play, Georgia Tech managed a 40-yard field goal, and when State fumbled away their next possession, the Yellow Jackets were able to reach the end zone one more time to secure the come-from-behind victory. Lorenzo White had a game-high 158 yards on 33 rushes, while Ingram gained 70 yards on just three catches.

EXTRA! 1986 NCAA HOCKEY TOURNA-MENT (National Champions)

They were behind most of the season, but the Spartans came back to win a regular season CCHA championship and a fourth straight Great Lakes Invitational crown. At the conference playoffs they took second, disposing of Michigan and Lake Superior State but losing to Western Michigan in the finals. In the NCAA tournament they were victorious over Boston College 10-6 in a two-game, total-goals series before defeating conference rival Minnesota 6-5 for a place in the finals. In the championship game, MSU demonstrated its usual third-period magic, scoring three goals after the second intermission to triumph 6-5 over the Crimson and bring East Lansing its second-ever NCAA title.

March 22, 1986—East Lansing
MSU 6, Boston College 4
1st Pd.: 1. BC, Stevens (Janney), 1:45; 2. MSU, McSween (Kv. Miller, M. Messier), 8:17; 3. MSU, Donnelly (Kv. Miller, M. Messier) 9:30; 4. MSU, Messier (Donnelly, Shibicky), 16:35.
2nd Pd.: 5. BC, Stapleton (T. Sweeney), 7:58; 6. MSU, Donnelly (Kv. Miller, M. Messier), 13:07; 7. BC, Brown (Harlow, Hodge), 15:39; 8. MSU, M. Messier (Kv. Miller, Donnelly), 16:34.
3rd Pd.: 9. MSU, Donnelly (Kv. Miller),); 0:15; 10. BC, Sweeney (Stapleton), 12:07.

March 23, 1986—East Lansing
MSU 4, Boston College 2
1st Pd.: No Scoring
2nd Pd.: 1. BC, Stevens (Marshall, Stapleton), 4:57; 2. MSU, Messier (Shibicky, Murphy), 8:43; 3. MSU, Hamilton (M. Messier, Donnelly), 9:11; 4. MSU, Parker (Donnelly), 13:42.
3rd Pd.: 5. BC, Brown (Harlow, Marshall), 2:28; 6. MSU, Kv. Miller (unasst.), 13:22.

March 27, 1986—Providence, R.I.
MSU 6, Minnesota 4
1st Pd.: 1. UM, Orth (Nanne), 3:13; 2. MSU, M. Messier (Hoff, Shibicky), 4:44; 3. MSU, Rendall (McReynolds, Parker), 5:22.
2nd Pd.: 4. MSU, McReynolds (Foster), 5:07; 5. MSU, Kv. Miller (unasst.), 12:03; 6. UM, Broten (Micheletti, Snuggerud), 13:33; 7. MSU, McSween (unasst.), 14:16; 8. UM, Micheletti (Millen, Cates), 15:15.
3rd Pd.: 9. UM, Kellin (Okerlund, MacSwain), 18:17; 10. MSU, Parker (Tilley), 19:24.

March 29, 1986—Providence R.I.
MSU 6, Harvard 5
1st Pd.: 1. HU, Armstrong (Follows, Ohno), 2:15; 2. HU, Bourbeau (MacDonald, Smith), 8:10; 3. MSU, M. Messier (Shibicky), 17:55.
2nd Pd.: 4. HU, Bourbeau (Barakett, Pawloski), 0:53; 5. MSU, Parker (Kv. Miller, Tilley), 6:48; 6. HU, Bourbeau (Krayer, Benning), 16:09; 7. MSU, Donnelly (Kv. Miller, M. Messier), 18:30.
3rd Pd.: 8. MSU, Hamilton (M. Messier, Shibicky), 1:06; 9. MSU, McReynolds (Rendall, Parker), 2:15; 10. HU, Janfaza (Carone, Chiarelli), 6:46; 11. MSU, Donnelly (Murphy), 17:09.

MSU 1986-1987

TALES TO TELL

Few long-standing MSU hockey fans would debate a suggestion that the dynamic duo of Bobby Essensa and Norm Foster formed the greatest pair to ever defend the Spartan cage. The fact that Ron Mason brought them to the campus at the same time and that their egos would tolerate the responsibility of sharing the goal-tending chore for four seasons speaks highly of the Canadian pair. Essensa from Toronto and Foster from Vancouver had never met before that first practice in Munn back in September of 1983. Thereafter they became good friends and lived together during their final three years in East Lansing.

On those frequent two-game weekends, it would often be number 33 Essensa on the ice for the opener and 24 hours later number 41 Foster would be on patrol, or visa versa. Win or lose, teammates and fans never seemed to vocalize a preference. How could they? Either man offered that necessary stability to win more often than lose. The 1986 NCAA championship run in Providence, R.I., was no different. Making 42 saves, Norm Foster was the 6-4 winner in the semi-final game against Minnesota while Bob Essensa needed only 15 stops in the 6-5 title game with Harvard.

Each would later recall those playoff games as their most memorable.

Foster: "That game was one of the toughest I played all year. Everyone figured on Denver and Minnesota being in the finals. It was supposed to be an all-West final. I was just glad to get the win and give Bobby a chance to win it all."

Essensa: "There was a lot of pressure on during that championship game. I didn't think I had my best game, it's hard to be relaxed when it's the last game. You start playing a lot of mind games with yourself. But, without a doubt, it was the most exciting moment, ever, when we won it."

Of even greater importance, the two Spartans

HEADLINES of 1987

- Garrison Keillor broadcasts his final radio show, *A Prairie Home Companion*, from Lake Woebegon and moves to New York City.
- The Reverend Jim Bakker resigns as leader of his religious empire, "Heritage USA," after admitting he had committed adultery.
- Dubbed "Black Monday," on October 20, the New York Stock Exchange suffered a frenzy of selling as the Dow Jones index plummeted 22.6 percent.
- A Northwest Airlines jet crashes on takeoff from Detroit Metropolitan Airport, killing 156 of 157 passengers.

SCOREBOARD

	W	L	T	Avg.
Baseball	34	20	0	.630
Track and Field	0	4	0	.000
Football	6	5	0	.545
Basketball	11	17	0	.393
Tennis	4	16	0	.200
Cross Country	0	3	0	.000
Swimming and Diving	7	5	0	.583
Wrestling	7	8	0	.467
Hockey	33	10	2	.756
Fencing	10	11	0	.477
Golf	tournament play only			
Gymnastics	7	4	0	.636
Soccer	13	7	1	.643
Lacrosse	11	5	0	.668

(W-L-T)	1983-84	1984-85	1985-86	1986-87
Foster	23-6-0	22-4-0	17-5-1	14-7-1
Essensa	11-4-0	15-2-0	17-4-1	19-3-1

Goals Against Average (Save Percentage)
Foster
2.74 (.898) 2.63 (.883) 3.69 (.877) 3.90 (.858)
Essensa
2.79 (.891) 1.64 (.921) 3.33 (.881) 2.78 (.884)

In those four years, the pair would share winning two regular-season CCHA titles, three CCHA playoff titles, three Great Lakes Invitationals, reach the NCAA Final Four three times and play for the title twice.

Both Bobby and Norm would experience long, if not distinguished, professional careers.

TEAM OF THE YEAR

With a regular season won-loss record of 11-4, the 1987 lacrosse team finished with the school's best record to date and were crowned champions of the Great Lakes Lacrosse Conference. They would also become the first Division I school in the Midwest to receive a bid to the NCAA tournament. The record-setting season, which included wins over Ohio State, Michigan and Notre Dame, was truly a surprise as it was virtually the same squad that had gone 7-8 in the preceding year. Coach Rich Kimball commented on the turn-around: "I think the difference is that last year we didn't have that team feeling. This year the seniors have provided us with great leadership."

Throughout the season, the offense managed an amazing 277 goals, 91 more than in 1986. That averaged out to 18.4 per game while defensively holding opponents to seven points per outing. The NCAA tournament trail would be a short one, bowing 21-5 to the defending championship North Carolina Tar Heels in the opening round. Regardless, the 1987 lacrosse team had reached a plateau never before dreamed of in East Lansing. The five goals were scored by John Giampetroni (two), Jim Gallina (two) and Dan Christ (one).

complemented each other as needed. When Bobby injured his hand late in the 1984-1985 campaign, Norm was there to take full command. When Foster experienced an a-typical slump early in their senior year, Essensa was there to pick up the slack.

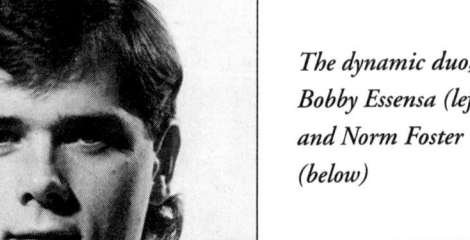

The dynamic duo, Bobby Essensa (left) and Norm Foster (below)

The 1987 lacrosse featured Jim Gallina (number 22), Dan Christ (number 16), Adam Mueller (number 28), John Giampetroni (number 36), Chris Heide (number seven), Dave Levan (number 26), Rex Lynn (number 29) and Mark O'Brien (number 19).

MAKING HISTORY

Quarterback Dave Yarema established a school passing record for one season by connecting on 200 of 297 attempts for a .673 average.

A new NCAA football rule provided that kickoffs would be moved from the 40-yard line to the 35-yard line.

Fencing coach Fred Freiheit won five first-place medals and one third-place medal with the epee, foil, and sabre in the 55-60 age class of the Senior Olympics.

On his way to becoming the winningest collegiate hockey coach ever, during the 1986-1987 season Ron Mason earned his 500th victory.

In their preparation for the 1988 Olympic Games, Team Canada included MSU on their list of exhibition games. They defeated the Spartans in a weekend series in East Lansing, 5-3 and 6-3.

New insurance requirements mandated the installation of nets in Munn Ice Arena behind each end from the top of the glass to the ceiling. The nets, intended to protect spectators from being hit by pucks, would remain until being removed in 2001 and then being reinstalled for the opening of the 2002-2003 season.

Big Ten athletic directors accepted the ABC proposal to televise basketball games through the 1990-1991 season.

Dave Carrier, MSU's assistant trainer, was selected as the official Olympic trainer for the USA hockey team.

Recognizing his 40 years of service to the sport, George Szypula was honored as 1987 Midwest Coach of the Year by fellow NCAA gymnastics coaches.

GREAT STATE DATES

Football—**September 20, 1986 (H):** Entering always-hostile South Bend, the 18th-ranked Spartans received a boost from an unlikely source as they topped Notre Dame, 20-15. In his second season as the starting right cornerback, Todd Krumm was instrumental in shutting down the Fighting Irish passing attack as he intercepted two passes from Irish quarterback Steve Beuerlein. Trailing 3-0 in the first quarter, Krumm returned his first pick 44 yards to put MSU on the board 7-3. Following three field goals from Chris Caudell and a touchdown pass from Dave Yarema, the Spartans led 20-15 in the fourth quarter. With 1:31 remaining in the game, the Irish were threatening at the MSU 18-yard line when Krumm again rose to the occasion. Stepping in front of yet another Beuerlein pass, the West Bloomfield junior pilfered the ball ending all hopes for an Irish victory and preserved the 20-15 Spartan win.

Soccer—September 24, 1986 (A): Helping the Spartans open the season with a 5-1 record, sophomore goalkeeper John Spink earned his third-straight shutout with a 4-0 win against archrival Michigan. Complimenting Spink was a well-balanced attack that scored two goals in the first and second half. Doug Landefeld tallied the first goal of the game, followed by a 30-foot shot from Jim Gallina. In the second half, Carl Hopfinger and Andy Wowk each scored less than a minute apart to kill any dreams the Wolverines had of making a comeback.

Cross Country—October 14, 1986 (A): Competing against four other schools (Indiana State, Rose-Hulman Institute of Technology, Vincennes Junior College and Purdue), the Spartan runners claimed first place at the Purdue invitational with a score of 22. Indiana State finished second, with 69 points. MSU runners claimed seven of the top 10 spots. Senior Keith Hanson took first with a time of 25:27, sophomore Dennis Topolinski finished second with a time of 25:32 and senior Mark Williamson was third in 25:47.

Football—October 18, 1986 (A): Lighting-up the scoreboard in every quarter, Michigan State defeated the University of Illinois, 29-21, before a capacity homecoming crowd of 75,038 in Champaign. Playing without star Lorenzo White for the second week in a row, MSU needed a pair of comeback TDs, once with a 7-0 deficit and later when trailing 14-10. Bobby Morse twice found the end zone from the one-yard line. The first culminated a 72-yard 13-play drive in the opening quarter and the second came on the fifth play following John Miller's third period pass interception at the Illini 28-yard line. The most spectacular play of the season came with 6:50 remaining in the contest, as wingback Mark Ingram took a handoff and raced 72 yards down the sideline for the Spartans' final score of the game. Craig Johnson had put State ahead 16-14 in the second quarter after Chris Caudell had closed the gap at 14-10 with his 29-yard field goal. Johnson's score came with 27 seconds remaining in the opening half as he swept left end and sped 29 yards for the score. A high center snap foiled the PAT attempt.

Football—October 25, 1986 (H): In what would be the easiest Big Ten win of the season, as State topped Purdue 37-3, to spoil another homecoming celebration. Trailing by a field goal midway through the opening quarter, Michigan State moved the ball 76 yards in nine plays to take a 7-3 lead on a Bobby Morse 13-yard run. Lorenzo White, bouncing back from a two-week absence due to injury, scored the next two second-quarter touchdowns, both from short distances, three yards and one yard. The most dramatic score of the afternoon came at 7:59 of the third period when Dave Yarema fired deep down the left-sideline to split end Willie Boyer, who made a twisting, sprawling grab for a 40-yard TD. Another long pass, a 53-yarder from Yarema to Mark Ingram ended at the Boilermaker six-yard line. Tight end Mike Sergent later scored on a fourth-down catch. Chris Caudell booted four of five PATs and a 37-yard field goal.

Soccer—November 6, 1986 (A): Joe Baum's squad wrapped up the season with a 3-1 victory over Purdue, giving the Spartans an overall record of 13-7-1. This victory total tied the school record set in 1985. The game proved to be much closer than had been anticipated as senior forward Jim Gallina scored twice in the opening half, giving State a slim 2-0 lead at intermission. A third goal, a penalty kick by Peter Crawley, was disallowed when the referee ruled that Silvio Iung was in the goal crease. Iung would later make amends by scoring an insurance goal during the second half.

Hockey—November 14 (A) & 15 (H) 1986: The Spartans defeated Michigan 7-6 Friday night in Ann Arbor, then returned home to top the Wolverines, 9-3. In front of 8,105 screaming fans at Yost Ice Arena, the Spartans found themselves in a 6-6 tie after goalie Norm Foster accidentally knocked in the tying goal. With 31 seconds remaining, Geir Hoff found Mitch Messier for the game-winning goal. Back home on Saturday, the Spartan special teams turned a close game into a rout. Trailing 3-2 midway through the second period, MSU struck for three goals, including two shorthanded, within four minutes to jump into a 5-3 lead. Four third-period power-play goals made it a runaway. Messier again shined as he tallied two goals and one assist to win the number one honors for the second-straight night. Also scoring for State were Brad Hamilton, Don McSween, Don Gibson and Tom Tilley. Completing the scoring sheet with one goal each were Bill Shibicky, Kip Miller and Bobby Reynolds. Kevin Miller added three assists, putting him in a tie for the CCHA points lead with Messier at 28 points. Goalie Bob Essensa turned back 19 shots.

Basketball—January 10, 1987 (H): Behind a stellar performance from Darryl Johnson, the Spartans defeated Ohio State 90-80. D.J. finished with a game-high 29 points, eight steals, five rebounds and 11-of-11 from the charity stripe. MSU led 44-39 at the intermission, but the Buckeyes came back to capture a three-point lead

with 13.48 remaining in the second half. The Spartans then answered with a 12-2 run to regain the lead, 65-56 and never trailed thereafter. Carlton Valentine chipped in 21 points to help secure the win. Featuring the patient defensive skills of Todd Wolfe, coach Jud Heathcote's 2-3 matchup zone caused problems for the Buckeyes all night, forcing 16 OSU turnovers.

Swimming and Diving—**January 16, 1987 (A):** The meet with Illinois came down to the final race, the 400-yard freestyle relay, and coach Dick Fetters had saved the right quartet for the challenge. Frank Deeter, Paul Sheff, Brian Goins and Mike Green joined to complete the 16 lengths in an impressive time of 3:08.06 and close the meet with a 58-55 victory. Sid Appelboom was a double-winner with a 1:56.07 in the 200-yard individual medley and a 2:07.19 in the breaststroke. Green finished first in the 200-yard freestyle in 1:42.11; Goins won the butterfly with a time of 1:55.21 and sprint star Deeter took the 100-yard freestyle in 47.17. Diver Todd Ovenhouse was a key performer with victories in both the one-meter (288.90 points) and three-meter (295.20) events.

Hockey—**January 24, 1987 (A):** With a 2-1 win over Michigan, MSU goalie Bobby Essensa improved his personal record to 16-0 as a Spartan. Defenseman Don McSween opened the scoring at 3:31 of the opening period on a rebound slapped high on the glove side of the Wolverine goalie. Mitch Messier took credit for the game-winning goal at the 14:47 mark of the same period as he deflected in a Neil Wilkinson shot.

Hockey—**February 6, 1987 (H):** Bowling Green came to town riding a 16-game winning streak and holding a one-point lead over MSU for the top spot in the Central Collegiate Hockey Association standings. They left town with a 6-3 loss, having surrendered their CCHA front-runner status before a record Munn Arena crowd of 6,902. Selecting the star of the game was simple as senior center Bill Shibicky scored four goals and added one assist. MSU carried a 4-3 lead into the final period and immediately survived a couple of great Falcon scoring opportunities. Soon thereafter State wrapped it up on goals by Mitch Messier at 13:24 and Shibicky at 14:53. Kevin Miller was the other Spartan scorer. Led by goalie Norm Foster with 23 saves, Coach Mason got a solid performance from the defense including Don McSween, Sean Clement and Tom Tilley.

Wrestling—**February 7, 1987 (H):** Spearheaded by the return to the mat of Dave Mariola, the Spartan wrestlers gained a big win over the Minnesota Gophers, 21-13. Recuperated from a knee injury which had sidelined him for six weeks, the 177-pound All-American gained a 9-3 victory and delivered the spark to inspire his teammates. John Przybyla pulled off a dramatic 6-5 win in his 190-pound match to bring MSU ahead, 15-13. With the meet outcome dependent on the heavyweights, big Dave Dopler did more than was needed as he pinned his opponent 11 seconds into the second period, adding six points to the Michigan State total to preserve the win. In earlier match-ups, Brian Smith (126 pounds) and Jeff Mustari (134 pounds) gained draws and Stacy Richmond was a winner at 142 pounds. Dan Matauch, moving up to the 150-pound division from his usual 134-pound bracket, pulled off a last-second reversal to gain an exciting 6-5 decision, putting his team ahead for the first time in the meet.

Basketball—**February 15, 1987 (H):** In front of a sellout crowd and a national television audience, the Spartans defeated Michigan 90-81 at Jenison Fieldhouse. At one point the Wolverines led 30-26, but Todd Wolfe, who scored 11 of his 13 points in the first half, hit a three-pointer with 44 seconds before intermission to give MSU a 43-42 lead they would not relinquish. In the second half, Darryl Johnson and Vernon Carr took over as the seniors refused to lose in their final game against Michigan. Johnson finished with 26 points and Carr with 20.

Gymnastics—**February 21, 1987 (A):** After edging the University of Pittsburgh by a fraction of a point in the preceding season, defeating the Panthers, 272.20-245.85 one year later in 1987, would have been unforeseen. Yet that's exactly what happened. The dominating Spartan performers were Keith Pettit, Eddie Malec and Greg Jung. Pettit won the vault with a score of 9.65; was second with a 9.40 on floor exercise; tied Jung with a 9.5 on the still rings and scored 9.75 to tie Malec on the high bar. Malec won the parallel bars with a 9.60 and scored a 9.40 to win the pommel horse event. He also placed third on the still rings and a third on the vault. In addition to his first-place tie on the still rings, Jung scored a 9.15, good for second place on the parallel bars and a 9.35 to finish third on the high bar. The Spartan trio finished one-two-three in the all-around totals: Pettit (56.40), Malec (56.35) and Jung (53.85).

Wrestling—**February 28, 1987 (A):** With four matches remaining, MSU trailed Ohio State, 12-9, when 167-pound senior Mike Bunce executed a takedown at the buzzer to gain a 6-6 tie. Then the closing trio of Dave Mariola at 177-pounds, John Przybyla at 190 pounds

and heavyweight Dave Dopler all came through with victories to turn the meet back to the Spartans 20-14. Other winners for Michigan State were Brian Smith at 126 pounds, 142-pound Stacy Richmond and Erick Jensen at 142.

Gymnastics—**March 21, 1987 (A):** The Spartan gymnasts defeated both Michigan and the Air Force Academy in a three-team meet at Ann Arbor. George Szypula's team scored 272.50, the U of M 269.80 and the Academy 252.35. Spartans won two events, Ed Malec with a 9.50 on the pommel horse and Keith Pettit with the same score on the vault. Malec added a second on the parallel bars, third on the vault and second in the all-round. Seconds and thirds by Pettit, Andy Ladwig, Greg Jung and Steve Hirsch added to the winning total.

Lacrosse—**April 4, 1987 (H):** MSU opened the Great Lakes Lacrosse Conference season with a convincing 17-8 victory over Ohio State. Led by junior attackman Adam Mueller's 17th goal of the season, Michigan State scored first and often as they led 11-2 at halftime, and for all intents and purposes, the game was over. Senior Rex Lynne quickly opened the second half with a goal and the third period ended with MSU holding a 14-4 advantage. The fourth quarter play became a little sloppy as coach Rich Kimball began clearing his bench. Nine players eventually scored for the Spartans as Mueller led the way with five goals.

Lacrosse—**April 8, 1987 (H):** Winning their fourth game in a row, State defeated the University of Michigan 9-5, but the Wolverines did not submit easily. With the game less than 15 seconds old, Dan Christ found the back of net for the first goal. With scores by Mark O'Brien, Dave Levan and two from Aaron Caruso, the Spartans led at halftime, 5-0. The U of M was on the board early in the third quarter before Christ and Caruso made it 7-1. From that point the game took on a new twist as the Wolves finished that quarter with three unanswered goals and opened the fourth period with yet another score, closing the gap to 7-5. O'Brien then put the game out of reach with a pair of insurance goals in the late stages of the contest.

Tennis—**April 21, 1987 (A):** Playing outdoors for the first time of the season, Coach Drobac's squad easily handled the Eastern Michigan Hurons, 7-2. Excepting Fernando Cash's loss at number one singles and the loss of Cash and Fernando Belmar at number one doubles, the Spartans captured all other matches of the afternoon: number two Richard Applegate 6-4, 6-3; number three

Fernando Belmar 6-2, 6-3; number four Paul Mesaros 6-0, 6-1; number five Tony Florenco 6-4, 2-6, 6-4; number six Eric Kovan 3-6, 6-0, 6-4 in singles. The doubles winning teams included Applegate-Mesaros 6-3, 7-5 and Richard Kynast-Alec Green 6-4, 6-1.

Golf—**April 27, 1987 (A):** Playing without his top two players, seniors Jon Kosier and Tom Harding, coach Bruce Fossum chose to go with a youthful line-up at the nine-team Badger Spring Invitational played on the Cherokee Country Club course in Madison, Wis. The result was gratifying as the Spartans posted a composite score of 929 on the 54-holes to capture the team championship. In addition, sophomore Dave VanLoozen took medalist honors with rounds of 72-75-78—225. Teammate sophomore Todd Marston was one stroke back with 70-78-78—226; Jerome Abood scored 80-76-83—239; freshmen David Kleckner 79-82-79—240 and Mike Heisierkamp 80-81-83—244.

Golf—**May 3, 1987 (H):** Michigan State finished in first place out of nine teams in the 54-hole Spartan Invitational. The MSU fivesome teamed for a score of 886, which was nine better than runner-up Miami of Ohio. Starting the final round in the second slot, senior Jon Kosier shot a 75 to move ahead and capture the medalist honor by three strokes, 72-69-75—216. Scores for the remaining members of Coach Fossum's squad were: Jerome Abood 74-75-73—222; Tom Harding 74-72-78—224; Dave VanLoozen 77-73-76—226 and Todd Marston 81-75-76—232.

Baseball—**May 9 (H) & May 10 (A), 1987:** Racking up the most runs a Green-and-White team had scored against a Michigan team since 1969, State defeated the Wolverines, 17-8 at Kobs Field and then topped the Maize-and-Blue in Ann Arbor, 8-2. MSU hitters broke the Saturday game open early with five runs in the first inning on a three-run homer by Dan Masteller followed by a two-run round-tripper off the bat of Mike Davidson. The attack continued with three runs in the second and six in the third, which featured another three-run four-bagger, this time by Scott Makarewicz. That made it 14-0 and the hometown fans were needling the guests about a mercy ruling. The Sunday win was orchestrated a bit differently. Trailing 2-1 after five innings, the Spartan hitters eventually solved the slants of the Wolves future major leaguer, Jim Abbott, with four runs in the sixth inning, including Todd Irwin's three-run home run and three in the seventh when Dave Metevier doubled home the final three runs.

ATHLETE OF THE YEAR

Six-foot-two, 180-pound Darryl Johnson, or "DJ," played in the shadow of Scott Skiles and Sam Vincent for most of his collegiate career, but in his senior year he took the leadership of the team and made second team All-Big Ten for the second time, scoring 22.1 points per game to finish the season as the second-highest scorer in the conference and finish his career as the seventh-highest scorer in MSU history with 1,383 points. In the same season he shot a remarkable 91 percent from the free-throw line to lead the Big Ten, rank third in the nation, and reach the top of the Spartan single-season record list. He also finished the year behind no one but another Johnson (by the name of Earvin) in single-season steals and set a Big Ten record for steals in a single game with eight. He was drafted by the Golden State Warriors and experienced a short professional career after his graduation.

Darryl Johnson

IN THE SPARTLITE

Baseball: State closed the season by defeating Central Michigan, 7-6, in a night game before 1,604 fans at Lansing's Municipal Park. With the victory, State ended the season with a 34-20 record, the second most wins in school history.

In post season honors, pitcher Mike Erickson and catcher Scott Makarewicz shared rookie of the year honors. Rick Rozman won the Leading pitcher award, Doug Gogolewski the most improved player award, Mike Davidson the offensive player award and the leading hitter award went to senior Pete Przbysz who batted .400, the 14th best average in school history.

As is always a problem, two of MSU's premier pitchers concluded their collegiate careers prematurely by becoming professionals at the end of the season. Tom Kurczewski signed with the Cleveland Indians and Gogolewski went to the New York Yankees.

Basketball: Setting the arch at 19' 9", the NCAA approved the three-point shot in basketball beginning with the 1986-1987 season. The rule would forever change the game.

After two overtimes before 8,755 fans in Jenison, State dropped the season-opener to the touring USSR National team, 116-107. Darryl Johnson led the Michigan State offense with 36 points, followed by Vernon Carr with 25. Featuring their seven-foot-two giant Vladimir Tkachenko, this was the Russian team that would shock the basketball world with a gold-medal performance in the 1988 Olympic Games.

Playing in the opening round of the yearly season Cable Car Classic at Santa Clara, the Spartans were humbled by the host Broncos, 96-88. The loss came despite a career-high 42-point performance by Johnson and 19-point night by freshman guard Kirk Manns.

Cross Country: Scoring a record team high 259 points, as in 1985, MSU was deeply entrenched in the ninth spot at the conference championships hosted by Ohio State University. Finishing for MSU were: Keith Hanson, 25th in 25:19; Rick Prince, 50th in 26:17; Dennis Toplinski, 60th in 26:57; Greg Psihas, 61st in 27.03 and Mark Williamson, 63rd in 27:08.

Although MSU did not qualify as a team to run in the NCAA District IV meet, Hanson did compete as an individual and finished in the 46th spot.

Fencing: Billed as the Michigan intercollegiate meet, in early December, fencers from six schools faced-off in Jenison for individual honors with no team scoring computed. Senior Pete Colovas finished first in foil, Ken VanGolen was second in epee and Joe Rivet and Dale Walter were fourth and fifth in sabre.

This was the first season fencing was not considered an official Big Ten sport because only five schools competed as a varsity status; consequently, a substitute season-ending meet, the Midwestern intercollegiate fencing championships, were held in Jenison Fieldhouse. Competing teams were Illinois, Wisconsin, Northwestern, Ohio State, Michigan State and two teams competing in club status (Michigan and Purdue). Senior Pete Colovas placed third in foil, leading his team to a fifth-place finish. The 5' 5" senior had rattled off 10 straight victories before losing two of his final three matches to miss the opportunity for the individual championship. Other Spartan finishers were Pat Dirker, 4-9 for a 12th place in foil; Joe Rivet, 8-4 for a fourth in the sabre competition; Steve Holden, 4-8 and a 10th in sabre; John Rosetko, 5-7, and ninth in epee and Ken VanGolen who completed a 4-8 record in epee to finish 10th.

In the NCAAs, held at Penn State, Jae Son finished 72nd out of 81 competitors in foil.

Football: The 1986 season produced a modest 6-5 record; regardless, quarterback David Yarema had a busy fall. While setting a team-record completion percentage of .673, he successfully connected on 200 of 297 aerial attempts for 2,561 yards and 16 touchdowns. The primary receiver was Andre Rison with 54 receptions for 966 yards and five touchdowns.

Although losing the 1986 Indiana game 17-14, Rison corralled a single-game, team-record 11 tosses for 196 yards.

Aided by the roll on the artificial surface at Michigan Stadium, kicker Greg Montgomery lofted a team-record 86-yard punt in the annual battle against the Wolverines.

In post-season honors, Shane Bullough, Montgomery and Rison were first team All-Big Ten selections. In addition, the Football Writers Association recognized Montgomery as an All-American.

Golf: The State team shot a composite total of 886 strokes to defeat Miami of Ohio and six other teams competing in the Spartan invitational. It was the first time since 1972 an MSU squad would finish first in this meet.

Furthermore, captain Jon Kosier took medalist honors with three rounds of 72-69-75,—216. Teammate scores included Jerome Abood 74-75-73—222, Tom Harding 74-72-78—224, Dave VanLoozen 77-73-76—226 and Todd Marston 81-75-76—232.

Finishing second among 20 teams at the Moors Golf Club in Kalamazoo, the MSU golfers shot a total of 888 at the Mid-American invitational, seven strokes behind the winning team from Ohio State. Jerome Abood bettered the course record with an opening round of 67. He closed the weekend with 67-80-82 for a 229 total. Jon Kosier played consistently carding 75-70-76—221; Todd Marston shot 72-70-80—222 in route to a fifth-place finish; Tom Harding scored 72-76-76—224 and Dave VanLoozen a 74-79-76—229.

Shooting a four-round 72-72-74-77—295, Kosier tied for fourth at the Big Ten championships. As a team, State finished with a composite score of 1,217, good enough for fifth place, two strokes out of third. The other Spartan cards were as follows, Abood 76-75-76-77—304, Harding, 74-76-75-83—308, VanLoozen 82-79-776-79—316 and Marston 76-79-80-86—321.

Gymnastics: In the Big Ten championships conducted at the U of M's Crisler Arena, the gymnastics squad scored 271.40 points to finish fifth among the seven-team field. Keith Pettit was Coach Szypula's top performer, placing seventh in the all-around. Later, in the individual competition, he scored a 9.45 to tie for second on the vault and a 9.45 for a third on the still rings. His best exhibition of the evening came in his specialty, the high bar, where he placed second with a score of 9.70.

Pettit, Greg Jung and Eddie Malec all competed in the NCAA championships at Los Angeles. Pettit, the Cincinnati junior, scored a 9.40 to tie for seventh in the vault. To exemplify the fractional scoring of the sport, his seventh-place 9.40 was .07 from third place. Jung, a sophomore from Plainfield, N.J., registered a 9.50 on the still rings but could do no better than 17th among the competitors.

Hockey: It has to be some kind of record. At 1:36 of the opening period in the home game against Western Michigan on Jan. 9, 1987, Neil Wilkinson, a 19-year-old freshman, scored from the right point on a power play. The note of interest is that it was the first time the Selkirk, Manitoba, native had ever touched the puck as a Spartan. He had missed the first portion of the season awaiting NCAA clearance based on his SAT scores. Neil

would play but one year before leaving for an extended and successful professional career in the National Hockey League.

With the 5-4 overtime loss to Illinois-Chicago on November 7, State snapped a record 18-game home winning streak that had extended two seasons.

By defeating Illinois-Chicago 5-3 on January 17, Ron Mason reached a milestone by winning his 500th game as a college coach.

During the 45-game season, a record 11 games were extended into overtime.

MSU settled for the runner-up spot in the NCAA tournament as they were defeated by North Dakota 5-3 in the title game at Joe Louis Arena in Detroit.

Defenseman Don McSween was the big winner at the season-ending banquet as he garnered in five of the 10 trophies including the MVP award.

Lacrosse: The 1987 team was a quick-striking edition. In the last home game of the schedule, a 16-5 victory over Notre Dame, MSU exploded for three goals in the first minute of play. In the season closer against Wittenberg four days later, State scored 15 seconds into the contest. Before it was over, the Spartans had overwhelmed the Tigers, 27-3, the largest scoring total in school history.

In the 16-game season, the offense accounted for 220 goals, the greatest output ever for an MSU team.

In their NCAA championship opening-round 21-5 loss to North Carolina, State was scored upon just 30 seconds into the game. After 10 minutes had been played, they were down 5-0 and the score read 9-1 at halftime. Following the break, the Tar Heels found the net for three more quick goals and the rout was on. MSU scoring came from junior Jon Giampetroni and senior Jim Gallina with two goals each and senior Dan Christ with one.

On the season, Adam Mueller led the team with 37 goals and 27 assists for 64 points. He gained first-team All-Conference and first-team All-Midwest Lacrosse Association as well as being voted the team's MVP.

Soccer: Joe Baum coached the 100th victory of his career when the Spartans closed out the home season on November 4 with a 5-0 shutout of Calvin College.

In one of the longest games ever by an MSU soccer team, playing two extra periods could not resolve what would be recorded as a 1-1 tie against the always challenging St. Louis Billikens. With sudden-death OTs not a part of the soccer scene, both teams registered their

score in the first extra session and that was it.

With women's soccer gaining varsity status in 1986, Joe Baum was suddenly doing double-duty as head coach for both programs. Tom Saxton joined the staff as an assistant and in 1991 would relieve Baum as head of the women's program.

Swimming and Diving: In what would be Dick Fetters's final season before retiring as head coach, MSU finished in ninth place at the Big Ten meet held in Indianapolis. Sid Appelboom, the sophomore from Antwerp, Belgium, was the only bright spot for the Spartans as he finished third in the 200-yard breaststroke with an NCAA-qualifying time of 2:03.49. At those NCAA championships in Austin, Texas, Sid could do no better than 38th, but still finished as the third best entry from the Big Ten.

Tennis: As in the preceding year, the Spartans were seeded 10th in the Big Tournament at Minneapolis and that's exactly where they ended up. In the opener against seventh-seeded Wisconsin, the Badgers defeated State, 5-4. The next opponent was fifth-seeded Purdue and again it was a 5-4 loss. In the battle for ninth, Northwestern had a commanding advantage 5-2 after seven matches and that was the final score. Playing for Coach Drobac were Fernando Cash, Fernando Belmar, Richard Applegate, Paul Mesaros, Tony Florenco, Eric Kovan, Richard Kynos and Alec Green.

Track and Field: Derrick Leonard performed admirably in the 78-53 indoor loss to Notre Dame as he ran the 60-meter dash in 6.18, a new MSU varsity record.

At the indoor conference championships in Champaign, Ill., three individuals and a third-place mile relay accounted for 20 points and a ninth-place team finish. Marvin Parnell placed third in the 600 with a time of 1:09.05; Rodney Benson ran a 47.84 in the 440 to take third and Leonard placed third in the 60-yard dash with a 6.33.

State opened the outdoor season at Knoxville, Tenn., where Derrick Coleman, Guy Scott, Keith Hanson and Mark Williamson competed in their specialties with Tim Simpson finishing third in the 5,000 meters in 14:06.0.

At the Big Ten outdoor championships in Iowa City, State managed 25 points and a ninth-place finish. Running a 51.31, Marvin Parnell was a winner in the 400-meter intermediate hurdle event. Others who placed were Simpson, who ran a 14:08.08 to place fourth in the 5,000; Tony Norris, who was fifth in the high hurdles with a

time of 14.39 and Benson with a sixth-place time of 47.36 in the 400-meters. The 1,600-meter relay team completed the scoring by placing third in 3:10.27.

Simpson set a school record with a 3:41.06 clocking in the 1,500-meter run to finish fourth at the national invitational track meet in Indianapolis. He bettered the record of 3:41.90 set by Ken Popejoy in 1972. Simpson's time qualified him for the NCAA meet in Baton Rouge, La., but he did not place.

Wrestling: Seven Spartan wrestlers reached the finals of their own MSU invitational and four emerged as winners: Dan Matauch (134 pounds), Dave Mariola (177 pounds), John Przybyla (190 pounds) and heavyweight Dave Dopler.

For only the second time since joining the Big Ten competition in 1951, Michigan State finished last at the annual conference championships, which were held in Madison, Wis. Gaining only 30 points, a pair of fourth-place finishes was all the Spartans could boast of. Matauch and Stacy Richmond (142 pounds) both reached that level.

At the NCAA meet, hosted by the University of Maryland, Matauch and Richmond won opening matches before elimination.

In postseason honors, Matauch was selected as recipient of the team's Outstanding Wrestler Award.

EXTRA! 1987 NCAA HOCKEY TOURNAMENT (Finals)

Ron Mason led his defending national champions to a second-place, regular-season finish in the conference. They then took their competition up a notch to win the CCHA playoff championship with victories over Michigan, Western Michigan and Bowling Green. From there they proceeded to the national tournament where they finished off Maine easily to enter the Frozen Four to face Minnesota in the semi-finals for the second straight year. The Spartans topped the Gophers 5-3, but in the finals the next day, North Dakota overcame the Green-and-White to win 5-3 after taking a 3-0 first period lead.

March 20, 1987—East Lansing
MSU 6, Maine 2
1st Pd.: 1. UMO, Perron (McHugh), 13:15.
2nd Pd.: 2. MSU, McSween (Cole, Foster), 10:05; 3. MSU, Tilley (unasst.) 16:41; 4. MSU, Rendall (Kv. Miller, Hamilton), 18:07.
3rd. Pd.: 5. UMO, Perron (Beers, Nonis), 2:38; 6. MSU, Messier (Luongo, Shibicky), 7:31; 7. MSU, McReynolds (Gibson, Hoff), 15:00; 8. MSU, Kv. Miller (Tilley, Ki. Miller), 15:33.

March 21, 1987—East Lansing
MSU 5, Maine 3
1st Pd.: 1. MSU, Messier (Kv. Miller), 19:15.
2nd Pd.: 2. UMO, Santini (D. Capuano, Baker), 9:32; 3. MSU, Ki. Miller (Kv. Miller, Rendall), 9:55; 4. MSU, Messier (Rendall, Shibicky), 15:12
3rd Pd.: 5. UMO, Jenkins (Nonis), 1:57; 6. UMO, Jenkins (Nonis), 12:10; 7. MSU, Arkeilpane (Messier, McSween), 15:36; 8. MSU, Reynolds (Cole, Luongo), 19:28.

Marcy 27, 1987—Detroit
MSU 5, Minnesota 3
1st Pd.: 1. MSU, M. Messier (Kv. Miller, Hamilton), 1:39; 2. MSU, Cole (Reynolds, Luongo), 4:16.
2nd Pd.: 3. UM, Millen (Blue), 1:08; 4. UM, Cates (Chorske, Millen), 6:27; 5. MSU, Wilkinson (O'Toole, Cole), 12:39; 6. UM, Chorske (unasst.), 17:18.
3rd Pd.: 7. MSU, Arkeilpane (unasst.), 9:28; 8. MSU, Shibicky (Luongo), 19:04.

March 28, 1987—Detroit
North Dakota 5, MSU 3
1st Pd.: ND, Kidd (Joyce), 15:07; 2. ND, Baron (Bowen, Kidd), 16:44; 3. ND, Joyce (Kidd, Hrkac), 17:02.
2nd Pd.: 4. MSU, Tilley (McReynolds, M. Messier), 8:30; 5. ND, Parks (Koberinski), 15:05; 6. MSU, Kv. Miller (unasst.), 16:56.
3rd Pd.: 7. UN, Bobyck (Parent), 7:54; 8. MSU, Ki. Miller (Kv. Miller), 18:34.

TALES TO TELL

Pat Shurmur, football co-captain of the 1987 Big Ten championship team, reminisces about the regular season-ending November 14 game against Indiana University, with the winner headed for the Rose Bowl:

"The day began with several hundred gathered at St. John's Student Parish for a morning memorial service for Duffy Daugherty, who had died from kidney and heart problems in Santa Barbara, Calif., on Sept. 26, 1987. The day ended when roughly 77,000 gathered at Spartan Stadium for a late afternoon nationally-televised football game. The stakes were high as the winner would be crowned Big Ten champions and win a trip to Pasadena, Calif., to represent the Big Ten at the New Year's Day game in the Rose Bowl.

It was a warm day for November and as the afternoon turned to darkness in the first half of the game, the atmosphere in the lighted Spartan Stadium became unforgettable. We took control of the game near the end of the first quarter and the fans started to really roll. I'll never forget sitting on the bench

after our first touchdown and watching the crowd behind us. As far back as I could see, the fans were on their feet. They had already pushed beyond the short wall onto the field. The first row of people seemed to be holding back the rest of the crowd from falling onto the sideline. Each fan was yelling louder than the next. Spartan Stadium was louder than any place I have ever been.

When we went into the locker room at halftime the score was 17-3. The coaches made their usual adjustment, but most of their instructions centered around scoring on the opening drive of the second half. It was felt a quick strike would kill any hope Indiana had of making a comeback and we could then run the clock out with Lorenzo (White) and Blake (Ezor).

Indiana kicked deep to Blake and he raced 90 yards down the left sideline, setting up John Langeloh's second field goal of the game. Just as we had talked about at halftime, it was the beginning of the end for the Hoosiers. As the game itself was winding down I will never forget how the Indiana players reacted. After each play they would help us up off

---

HEADLINES of 1988

- The very last Playboy Club in America closes in Lansing, Mich.
- A missile, fired from the U.S. warship *Vincennes*, mistakenly shoots down an Iranian civilian airliner in the Persian Gulf with a loss of 290 lives.
- The Stealth bomber, invisible to radar and heat-seeking missiles, makes its first public appearance.
- Pan Am flight 103 explodes over Lockerbie, Scotland, killing all 259 passengers, along with 11 people on the ground.

SCOREBOARD

	W	L	T	Avg.
Baseball	41	20	0	.672
Track and Field	no dual meets			
Football	9	2	1	.792
Basketball	10	18	0	.357
Tennis	10	14	0	.416
Cross Country	no dual meets			
Swimming and Diving	9	4	0	.692
Wrestling	1	12	0	.076
Hockey	27	16	3	.620
Fencing	10	12	0	.455
Golf	tournament play only			
Gymnastics	6	10	0	.375
Soccer	12	8	1	.595
Lacrosse	6	9	0	.400

the surface. I have to admit they were handling defeat better than we might have.

Late in the fourth quarter what was happening began to sink in. We had accomplished something that hadn't been done in East Lansing for a long time. It was as if a long period of struggle and frustration had come to an end with a trip to the Rose Bowl. As a senior and a member of Coach Perles's first recruiting class at MSU, I was proud to have helped restore a football program so rich on tradition. Four long years of close losses, boos, tough off-seasons and injuries were behind us. It was time to enjoy what hard work can bring.

As the game ended and the crowd rushed onto the field, we all fought to get to the locker room. By the time my brother Joe [student manager] and I have reached there, Coach Mallory of Indiana was addressing our team. His speech was talked about a great deal thereafter. It was truly a class display of sportsmanship. As a young coach, I can appreciate how hard it must have been to come into our locker room after his team was defeated.

I wish I could have bottled up that day and saved it forever, but nonetheless I will never forget the sights, the sounds and the emotions of that day in November. Twenty years from now the memories will be as vivid as they are today."

The 1987 football team included an offensive starting line-up of A. Rison (no. 1), T. Mandarich (no. 79), B. Kula (no. 63), P. Shurmur (no. 60), V. Tata (no. 61), D. Houle (no. 74), M. Sargent (no. 49), B. McAllister (no. 8), L. White (no. 34), J. Moore (no. 33) and W. Bouyer (no. 17) and a defensive starting line-up of J. Bergin (no. 45), M. Nichols (83), T. Davis (no. 75), J. Budde (no. 87), T. Moore (no. 42), P. Snow (no. 48), K. Larson (no. 3), D. Reed (no. 6), J. Miller (no. 44), T. Krumm (no. 35) and H. Barnett (no. 36).

TEAM OF THE YEAR

One of the best football teams MSU has ever fielded was the 1988 Rose Bowl squad. The team accumulated a 9-2-1 overall and 7-0-1 conference record that won the Big Ten title and the automatic bid to the bowl, which John Langeloh won when he kicked a 36-yard field goal with 4:14 remaining in a 20-17 victory. Many MSU season records were approached or broken during the year. Lorenzo White rushed for 1,572 yards, second only to his 1985 mark, and he placed third on the touchdown list with 16. Similarly, Andre Rison totaled 785 receiving yards, third behind his previous season and a mark set by Kirk Gibson. Langeloh became the leader in field goals, making 17 on 24 attempts, and Todd Krumm placed second in punt returns, racing for 322 yards on 36 attempts. Defensively, Krumm set a record with nine interceptions, and Travis Davis placed second in tackles for losses with 16 for 113 yards lost, including 12 sacks. The defensive squads pulled in seven interceptions in a 17-11 win over Michigan to rank second in the school's single game records, and they set a new mark when they held Purdue to just one first down rushing. At the end of the year, White was named the Big Ten MVP and Tony Mandarich was named the Big Ten lineman of the year. There were three first-team All-America selections and seven first-team All-Big Ten selections. Five players were drafted into the National Football League in the first eight rounds, with White going to Houston in the first round. All having been said, George Perles had put together a team of many stars that would brighten the eyes of Spartan fans for years to come.

MAKING HISTORY

Lorenzo White, the most prolific runner in MSU football history concluded a four-year career (1984-1987) in which he racked up a team-record 1,082 carries and a likewise team-record 4,887 yards rushing from scrimmage. As could be expected, the Ft. Lauderdale All-American also holds the team one-season record for carries (419 in 1985) and rushing yards (2,066 in 1985).

Prior to the Michigan football game of October 10, Charlie Wedemeyer, a Spartan quarterback-flanker from 1966-1968, was awarded the Varsity Alumni Club's Jack Breslin Lifetime Achievement Award. Wedemeyer of Los Gatos, Calif., and native of Hawaii, suffers from amyotrophic lateral sclerosis (Lou Gehrig's Disease).

In January, after ten years of service, Gwen Norrell retired from the post as MSU's Big Ten faculty representative. She was replaced by Michael Kasavana, effective May 1, 1988.

Nick Vista, director of sports information, announced his retirement effective June 30, 1988. He and his wife Connie would move to Atlanta, Ga., where she had accepted a position as associate vice-president at her alma mater, Emory University.

In the fall of 1987, coach Grady Peninger was inducted into the National Wrestling Hall of Fame.

Father Jerome "Mac" MacEachin, a loyal Spartan fan, founder of St. John's Student Parish and teacher of theology at MSU for 23 years, died on December 2, 1987 at the age of 82.

After serving as an assistant on George Perles's staff from 1983-1987, Nick Saban left to take up a position as defensive backfield coach with the Houston Oilers of the National Football League. Anthony "Dino" Falino would replace the departed Saban.

Nell Jackson, who served as assistant athletic director from 1973-1981, died unexpectedly in Binghampton, N.Y., where she was serving as director of athletics at the State University of New York.

GREAT STATE DATES

Football—**September 7, 1987 (H):** Billed as the "Great American Football Celebration," it was more than a normal season-opener. Played on Monday evening of Labor Day before a capacity crowd of 77,922 and an ABC-TV national audience, State met and defeated Southern California, 27-13. It was the first-ever night game at Spartan Stadium. The holiday festivities included a halftime show, that featured singing star Lee Greenwood, who rendered his signature song, "Proud to Be an American." Featuring the running of Lorenzo White, who gained 111 yards on 22 carries, State opened with an eight-play 65-yard scoring drive after Craig Johnson almost broke loose on the opening kickoff. White accounted for 48 of the yards on five carries including the final three yards and the score. Following three field goals, including John Langeloh's first as a Spartan, MSU led 10-6 at intermission. The Spartans pulled away in the third quarter on two touchdowns. The first, scored by

quarterback Bobby McAllister, came on a three-play drive following John Budde's fumble recovery at the Trojan 25. The second TD covered 84 yards in seven plays with White once more scoring, this time from the one-yard line. Langeloh completed the 27-point winning total with his second field goal, a 43-yard kick with 7:08 remaining in the contest. Leading the defense were Percy Snow with 13 tackles, Tim Moore 11 and John Miller 10. Few fans that evening would have envisioned the likelihood these two teams would conclude the season facing each other in the Rose Bowl on New Year's Day.

Soccer—**September 8, 1987 (H):** Offensively, Jim Blanchard accounted for the game's total output as Michigan State opened the season with a 3-0 victory over Eastern Michigan. The junior forward from Webster, N.Y., broke a scoreless tie with his first goal midway through the second half, then added two more scores to close out the game. In addition to praise for the scoring star, Coach Baum singled out Erik Harsh, Eric Pence, Todd Goodwin and Carl Hopfinger for their defensive efforts.

Cross Country—**September 11, 1987 (H):** Led by a second-place finish from Keith Hanson, MSU scored 28 points to defeat Ohio State with 38 points and the University of Windsor with 67 in a triangular meet at Forest Akers East Golf Course. Other Spartan scorers were Anthony Hamm in fourth, Dennis Topolinski fifth, Greg Psihas eighth and Rick Prince ninth.

Soccer—**September 23, 1987 (A):** With the grass in Ann Arbor more than four inches tall, the Spartans were forced to chance their plan of attack; however, they prevailed, 1-0 over Michigan. John Spink was flawless in the net and Jim Blanchard's fourth goal of the season in the 20th minute was all MSU needed.

Football—**October 10, 1987 (H):** The Spartan defense intercepted a conference record-tying seven passes en route to a satisfying 17-11 victory over the 12th-ranked University of Michigan. The visitors' ground game was likewise stifled as the "Gang Green" held the U of M to a paltry 2.07 yards per-try on 45 carries. Of the seven aerial thefts, John Miller set a team record with four, Todd Krumm grabbed two and Harlon Barnett the other. Choking the Michigan running attempts was a team effort featuring Percy Snow, Tim Moore, John Budde, Kurt Larson, Travis Davis, Derrick Reed and Mark Nichols. On the Tuesday before the game, Coach Perles interjected a wishbone attack as a surprise element to the annual clash. The new wrinkle featured the usual Lorenzo White

who scored both touchdowns on short bursts, one in the opening quarter and the second with 2:16 remaining in the first half. The senior All-American gained a game-high 185 yards on 34 carries for an average of 5.44 yards per run. White's second TD made him the team career leader with 32, surpassing Lynn Chandnois. John Langeloh completed the scoring for the afternoon with a 43-yard field goal. The Wolverines threatened late in the game as they drove to the MSU 31, but the Barnett interception thwarted that final attempt.

Soccer—**October 25, 1987 (A):** Managing their eighth win and sixth shutout of the fall, State topped Purdue 5-0. Jim Blanchard scored his seventh goal of the season just three minutes into the game, Gus Panos made it 2-0 at the 20-minute mark and Tom Busch tallied 30 seconds later. Todd Goodwin booted in his fifth of the year on a corner kick and Dave Hart closed the scoring with his first goal of the campaign midway through the second half. John Spink handled the net-minding duties in the opening half before Chris Heide took over to finish the game.

Football—**October 31, 1987 (A):** Led by tackles Travis Davis and Mark Nichols and linebacker Percy Snow, the MSU defense shutdown the Ohio State running game, leading to a 13-7 victory. The final statistics revealed that OSU: (a) gained only two yards rushing; (b) made only six first downs; (3) gained only 68 yards after scoring on a 79-yard pass on the game's first play from scrimmage; (4) had its quarterbacks sacked seven times for 50 yards in losses and (5) had two passes intercepted (Todd Krumm and Kurt Larson), leading to John Langeloh field goals of 40 yards and 20 yards. The sole Michigan State touchdown came with 4:37 remaining in the opening quarter following three plays that covered 54 yards and took just 50 seconds. Krumm opened the drive by returning a punt 27 yards to the Spartan 46-yard line. Lorenzo White ran through left guard and then cut to the right sideline for a 38-yard gain to the Buckeye 16-yard line. After White rushed for one yard, quarterback Bobby McAllister raced around left end, broke three tackles and lunged into the end zone for a 15-yard touchdown run.

Hockey—**November 13, 1987 (H):** The combination of three power-play goals in the first two periods and a tough defense in the third carried MSU to a 6-3 victory over Michigan at Munn Ice Arena. The final margin was misleading as the Spartans held only a 4-3

lead until Bruce Rendall hit an empty-netter with 32 seconds remaining and Bobby Reynolds scored his second goal of the game with nine seconds to go. The freshmen line of Shawn Heaphy, Kerry Russell and Pat Murray played well with Murray getting a goal and Heaphy scoring with a one-man advantage. Jeff Harding's power-play goal with 18 seconds remaining in the second period proved to be the winner.

Fencing—**January 9, 1988 (H):** Fred Freiheit's fencers defeated Eastern Michigan 17-10 and U of M-Dearborn, 15-12 in action at Jenison Fieldhouse. In addition, the Spartans posted a 5-4 victory over the University of Michigan in a contest that included only foil competition. MSU was led by Steve Holden in sabre and Pete Colovas of the foil squad. Colovas recorded nine wins without a loss on the day.

Basketball—**January 16, 1988 (H):** Playing before a screaming 10,004 fans in Jenison, State defeated the defending NCAA champion Indiana Hoosiers, 75-74 in overtime. With 25 seconds remaining in regulation and IU leading 66-63, the patented Bobby Knight man-to-man defense was blanketing Kirk Manns, MSU's top three-point shooter as well as the other options, Scott Sekal and Todd Wolfe. As the clock ticked down the mission fell to Ed Wright and the senior co-captain responded with the needed triple…all net. A similar scenario prevailed in OT. With 46 seconds of playing time left and trailing 74-73, the Spartans, in possession, were struggling to find an open shot. While Coach Heathcote was screaming for a timeout, the seven-foot center George Papadakos was in possession underneath. He pivoted to his left and tossed up an awkward shot that sat on the rim before dropping threw for the winner. Steve Smith led all scores with 18 points. He also tallied seven assists and six rebounds. Others in double figures were Ken Redfield and Papadakos, 15 each; Wright 11; and Carlton Valentine with 10.

Swimming and Diving—**January 16, 1988 (H):** Bill Wadley, in his first year as MSU's head coach, saw his team improve to a 7-1 record with a 66-47 win over Purdue and 65-48 defeat of Ohio State in a double dual meet at the IM West Pool. With a 20.95 in the 50-yard freestyle and 45.20 in the 100-yard freestyle, Frank Deeters captured both sprint events. Distance ace Mike Green wrapped up the 200- and 500-yard freestyle races with times of 1:41.24 and 4:38.04. The pair joined Brian Goins and Barry Hibbard to set a Spartan team record of 3:04.31 in taking the closing event, the 400-yard freestyle relay. Other Spartan winners were Chris Clarke with a 9:38.89 in the 1,000-yard freestyle and Sid Appelboom, the Belgium Olympian, who finished the 200-yard breaststroke in 2:04.64.

Swimming and Diving—**February 5, 1988 (H):** Although the 58-51 winning score over Northwestern was not overwhelming, the Spartans captured the first 10 events and the outcome was never really in doubt. After finishing first in the opening event, the 400-yard medley relay, seven different individuals led the way with first place finishes: Kurt Johnson with a 9:53.54 in the 1,000 freestyle; Frank Deeter, 1:43.22, 200-yard freestyle; Chris Brundage, 22.69, 50-yard freestyle; Brad Zylman, 2:01.37, 200-yard individual medley, Chris Clarke, 2:00.62, 200-yard butterfly; Mike Green, 46.74, 100-yard freestyle and Sid Appleboom, 1:58.3, 200-yard breaststroke. Diver Bill Cole was the only double-winner as he finished first in both the one-meter and three-meter events.

Wrestling—**February 13, 1988 (H):** Winning six of the 10 matches, State's wrestlers defeated nationally 17th-ranked Indiana University, 21-18. Robert Flanders opened the scoring by pinning his 118-pound opponent at 2:48. Soon Thackthay (126 pounds) gained an 8-0 decision and Stacy Richmond (142 pounds) outpointed his opponent 6-4. After James Richardson tied at 177 pounds Dave Mariola remained undefeated in seven Big Ten matches with his 11-5 decision at 190 pounds and then heavyweight Mark Zenas finished the afternoon with a 7-3 decision to gain the needed team points.

Basketball—**February 27, 1988 (A):** Michigan State 78, Ohio State 77—it doesn't get any closer, and the conclusion could not have been more dramatic. With one second remaining on the clock and MSU trailing 77-76, Steve Smith was fouled on an attempted fall-away jumper and the Detroit freshman dramatically made both free throws to secure the victory as the capacity crowd of 13,320 made every effort to distract him. Smith would later admit: "my legs were real wobbly." Overall, it was an impressive shooting night for the Spartans as they outshot the Bucks 61 percent to 44 percent from the field and 78 percent to 62 percent at the line. Smith was the Spartans leading scorer with 22 points while Carlton Valentine sunk 10 of 12 field goals for a total of 20. The remainder of the total came from George Papadakos 13, Ken Redfield 11, Ed Wright eight and Todd Wolfe four.

Gymnastics—**March 17, 1988 (H):** George Szypula would close out his illustrious 41-year career as MSU's head coach with a satisfying 272.45-271.20 victory over the University of Michigan. Keith Pettit, the senior co-captain, was the hero in his final home appearance as he won the horizontal bar competition with an impressive 9.95 score, the floor exercise with a 9.8, the parallel bars with a 9.50 and the all-around with a total of 56.85. Greg Jung captured the only other Spartan first with a score of 9.85 on the still rings. Bert Vescolani, Allan Powers and Steve Hirsch gained valuable team points with seconds and thirds.

Baseball—**March 25 & 26, 1988 (A):** Michigan State took two from the always-dangerous Miami Hurricanes 7-6 and 5-4. The Spartans used four different pitchers in the 7-6 opener. Rick Rozman (1-0) earned the win after seven and one-third innings of work. MSU led 7-3 entering the eighth, where Rozman allowed two runs before being replaced by Brad Lamont. Lamont, Jim Stros and Mike Ericson strung together the final one and two-thirds to secure the win. Right fielder Mike Davidson took care of the offensive duties with his first two home runs of the season. He finished the game three-for-five with four RBIs and two runs scored. The Spartans squeaked out another close one the following night in Coral Gables, Fla. Instead of fighting off a late Hurricanes rally, it was the Spartans who rallied in the ninth to win 5-4. After scoring the go-ahead run in the top of the inning, Ericson picked up the win by slamming the door on Miami. He pitched the final two and one-third innings with three strikeouts and just one hit.

Tennis—**April 6, 1988 (H):** Playing at the MSU Indoor Tennis Facility, the Spartans won three singles matches and two at doubles to defeat Notre Dame, 5-4. At the number one position junior Santiago Cash won is straight sets, 6-4, 6-1 as did senior Fernando Belmar at number two, 6-2, 6-3. The other singles point came at number six as Andrew Heidenreich topped his Irish opponent, 6-3, 4-6, 6-3. Cash and Belmar were winners at the number one doubles match, 7-5, 6-2, while the outcome of the meet was decided at the number two doubles

with Paul Mesaros and Damon Valentino taking a close three-match encounter, 6-2, 2-6, 7-5.

Lacrosse—**April 13, 1988 (A):** Playing under the lights, the Spartans led at halftime 5-1 and then outscored the University of Michigan 4-3 in the second half for an easy 14-5 victory. Leading the scoring for State were Mickey Redding who tallied two goals and one assist; senior midfielder John Giampetroni with one goal while assisting on three others, plus sophomore Chris Heide, who scored twice on one-man advantage situations. His first marker lengthened the score to 8-1 and his second came in the fourth quarter making the score 11-3. Junior goalie Fred Saintamour played well in his first start of the season as he made eight saves and ignited several fast break opportunities.

Baseball—**April 23, 1988 (H):** For the fourth time in five seasons State swept the two-game series against Notre Dame. The scores were 13-1 and 6-5. In the opener Mike Davidson went four-for-four, scored three times and drove in one run, highlighting a 17-hit attack off of five Irish pitchers. Catcher Scott Markarewicz and Dan Masteller each had three hits with Masteller hitting his second home run of the season. The Spartans broke the game open with four runs in the fifth and five in the sixth. Sophomore pitcher Don Lindsey went six innings for the win. In the nightcap, the Spartans, down 4-0, rallied in the third for two runs on Todd Krumm's eighth home run of the season and two more runs in the fifth on hits by Masteller and Mike Koceski. After trading runs in the seventh, pinch-hitter Jeff Bonchek singled home Koceski for the winning run in the extra eighth inning. Mike Ericson gained credit for the victory in relief.

Baseball—**May 21, 1988 (A):** Michigan State defeated Michigan 4-2 at Fisher Stadium in Ann Arbor on the arm of Todd Krumm who pitched a masterful complete-game four-hitter for the win. In nine innings of work he allowed just one earned run and three walks, while striking out 15 Wolverines. Shortstop Kevin Dalson finished the game three-for-four with two RBIs and one run scored.

ATHLETE OF THE YEAR

Todd Krumm was an outstanding two-sport athlete and the first person since Kirk Gibson to have such leading roles in both the Spartan baseball and football programs. Krumm started the last 35 football games of his collegiate career at free safety. In his senior year he was a primary factor in State's Big Ten title and Rose Bowl championship, leading the conference with nine interceptions to bring his career total to 18, second on the all-time MSU list. For his achievement he was named a second team All-American and first team All-Big Ten selection. In the spring Krumm doubled as an outfielder and pitcher. In the field he was a third team All-Big Ten selection and batted .256 with eight home runs, 30 RBI, and six game winning hits. From the mound, he was voted to the Big Ten all-championship team for leading State to the conference title game. On the year he pitched six complete games for a 4-2 record with one shutout and 78 strikeouts in 69 innings. In 1986 he was drafted by the MLB's New York Mets, and in 1988 he was a selection of the NFL's Seattle Mariners.

Todd Krumm

IN THE SPARTLITE

Baseball: In one of the best efforts in school history, Tom Smith's squad returned from its Southern trip with an impressive 11-3 record which included two wins over always strong Miami of Florida.

During the season, the Spartans registered a total of 41 wins, a new team record.

At the postseason double-elimination conference tournament in Ann Arbor, MSU opened with a convincing 10-5 victory over the University of Minnesota and followed with Todd Krumm's four-hit 4-2 win over Michigan. The Gophers then returned from the losers bracket to defeat Tom Smith's squad 17-4, setting up the showdown battle on Sunday afternoon. In that finale State opened with a 2-0 lead, which held until the fourth inning when Minnesota came up with four runs on four hits and a costly throwing error. That was more than enough as the Spartans went down, 5-2. MSU closed out their schedule with a team record-setting 41 victories but shy of the opportunity to take part in the NCAA tournament.

Mike Davidson completed his collegiate career by becoming the Big Ten batting champion with his lusty .440 average (.415 overall). The Clio, Mich., native holds the team career records for runs scored, hits, runs batted in, home runs and triples. Latter day Spartan players have subsequently topped all but the career triples title (14). For the third straight season, Davidson was selected to the All-Big Ten first team.

Basketball: Although never a prolific scorer (10.1 ppg), George Papadakos, a transfer from Syracuse, was a steady player for Jud Heathcote during the seasons of 1986-1987 and 1987-1988. He had a career game on December 22, 1987, in the 82-68 victory over San Jose State. Before a slim Jenison crowd of 7,081, the seven-footer scored 21 points and matched that with 21 rebounds. That spring he would forego his collegiate career as he signed a four-year contract to play professionally in Greece.

Scoring an average 13.3 per game, Carlton Valentine was the team's top scorer followed by Ken Redfield with an 11.7 average.

Cross Country: In their best conference finish since winning the title in 1972, the Spartan runners placed fourth in the annual Big Ten championships run, held this year over the Indiana University course. Freshman Anthony Hamm of Flint was the top State runner, com-

pleting the eight-kilometer course in 14th place with a time of 25:19. The remaining MSU finishers were Keith Hanson, 22nd 25:48; Ian Smith 27th 26.05.6; Dennis Topolinski 28th in 26:05.9 and Joe Schmidt 31st in 26:14.1. Added runners were Dave Homann in 32nd, Rick Prince in 37th and Joe Mihalic in the 57th slot.

Rewarded for his team's improved performance from ninth spot in 1986, Jim Stintzi was voted Big Ten coach of the year.

Fencing: Michigan State finished in fifth place at the season's ending championship meet. Leading the way was Peter Covolas of Dearborn who placed seventh in foil competition while his teammate in the weapon, Jae Son of Okemos, was 13th. Steve Holden from South Haven was eighth in sabre and Erik Shinn of Haslett 14th. Ken Frazee was 10th in epee and Ralph Hindo 14th.

Football: In the Purdue game of November 7, both Blake Ezor and Lorenzo White had a 100-yard rushing game. Blake ran for 151 yards and Lorenzo 144 yards. On the very next Saturday against Indiana, White had his biggest and busiest game as a Spartan. Carrying the ball for a team-record 56 times, he managed 292 yards, second only to Eric Allen's record 350 yards set in 1971 against Purdue.

Twice, first in 1985 and again in 1987, White finished fourth in the Heisman Trophy balloting. The running back from Ft. Lauderdale was designated as the 1987 Big Ten Most Valuable Player by both the *Chicago Tribune* and the United Press International wire service.

Travis Davis set a team record 12 quarterback sacks during the season.

George Perles was honored as Big Ten coach of the year.

Seven members of the 1987 team were voted as first team All-Big Ten selections. From the defense were Todd Krumm, John Miller and Percy Snow and from the offense were Tony Mandarich, Lorenzo White and Pat Shurmur. In addition, punter Greg Montgomery was selected for the second year. Mandarich, White and Montgomery were picks on sundry All-American teams.

In the National Football League draft, the Houston Oilers chose White as their number one pick and Montgomery their number three choice.

Golf: State finished second to Kentucky, 899 to 893, at the Mid-American Invitational hosted by Kent State. Freshman Mike Anderson carded a three round score of 68-69-72—209 to capture the medalist honor. Speaking specifically to Anderson's opening round, Coach Bruce

Fossum volunteered it was the best 18-holes he had ever witnessed from an MSU player.

With rounds of 78-74-74-72—298, Phil Marston led the Spartans to a fourth-place finish at the Big Ten championships in Champaign, Ill.

Gymnastics: It seems strange that a tiny school with such a non-descript athletic heritage as Houston Baptist could quite easily defeat the MSU gymnastic team in a dual meet. That is until one comes to the realization the Baptist squad included four members of the Spanish Olympic team.

In a schedule-ending four-team meet at Minneapolis, the Spartans tallied 269.60 points, just shy of their season-long goal of 270.00. The score, which was the highest output of 1988, was good enough to defeat Michigan while being defeated by Wisconsin and the host Gophers. Freshman Rich Pulsfort scored team season-highs in the all-around (54.20) and floor exercise (9.4). Freshman Chris Spinosa won the vault in 9.4 while senior Greg Jung tied for second on the rings with a 9.5.

Scoring 272.55 points, the squad placed sixth out of seven teams at the Big Ten championships hosted by Ohio State University. Jung scored a creditable 9.75 in the still rings and finished second for the Spartan's top performance. Senior Keith Pettit had a disappointing weekend placing eighth in the all-around event, with a third in floor exercise his best effort.

Hockey: With 524 penalties, the 1987-1988 team was the most penalized Spartan team ever. Jeff Harding went to the penalty box 62 times which also set a team season record. Don Gilbert would better that mark two seasons later.

State played their NCAA tournament games on enemy ice. First they succeeded in defeating Harvard, 6-5 and 5-3 in the first round at Cambridge, Mass. One week later they traveled to Minneapolis where the University of Minnesota ended the Spartan season with two losses, 4-2 and 4-3.

With 46 season goals, Bobby Reynolds and Danton Cole tied for the team lead.

In postseason honors, Tom Tilley, the team's MVP, was a CCHA first-team all-league selection.

Lacrosse: Dropping all five games during the Eastern spring training trip was bad enough, but losing senior Adam Mueller was an even more severe blow. The team's leading scorer with 37 goals and 64 points in 1987, Mueller was sidelined for the year when he suffered a broken sternum in the season-opener against Penn State.

He would later be awarded an added year of eligibility to complete his Spartan career in 1989.

After wins over Michigan 14-5 and the Stroh's Lacrosse Club 13-6, for the third straight game, State scored in double figures while defeating Lake Forest, 12-8, during a driving rain at Old College Field. Yet, Rich Kimball's squad completed the most productive game of the season in their final home appearance, a 16-4 victory over Wittenberg College. Mike Moss and John Giampetroni led the attack as each scored three goals.

Soccer: The season opened with a 2-4 record, the slowest start since Joe Baum took over the program in 1977. The healing began with a 1-0 victory over Michigan and ended with seven wins in a row, duplicating a streak by the NCAA co-championship team of 1968.

The 1988 roster included four from Sarnia, Ontario: sophomore Paul Phillips, junior Simon Mayo and the Stewart brothers, senior John and junior Alan. Other international players included Earl Parrish of Trinidad-Tobago and two more Ontario, Canadians: Ralph Torre of Mississauga and Sel Eren from Windsor.

With seven goals, five assists and 19 total points, Goodwin and Tim Busch tied as the team's scoring leaders.

Swimming and Diving: A pair of seniors led the way as Dick Fetters's 1988 squad compiled 252 points and placed sixth in the Big Ten championships. Frank Deeter set two team records in freestyle with a third-place 20.35 in the 50 and a 44.67 in the 100. Likewise, Mike Green set a team record, finished second in the 200-yard freestyle with a time of 1:36.79. Also placing in the finals were Brian Goins seventh in the 100-yard butterfly in 50.06; Brad Zylman seventh in the 100-breaststroke in 56.56 and Anthony Higgins eighth in the 100-yard backstroke in 51.41. The 400-yard freestyle relay team of Deeter, Damon Whitfield, Goins and Green finished third in an impressive time of 2:59.64. Other scorers were Sid Appelboom, Anthony Higgins, Brad Zylman and Barry Hibbard.

Appelboom finished seventh in the 200-yard breaststroke at the NCAA championships in Indianapolis to automatically qualify as An All-American. He was the first Spartan to gain such recognition in 16 years. He would later represent his country, Belgium, at the XXII Olympic Games in Seoul, Korea.

Tennis: In the second round of the conference tournament held in West Lafayette, Ind., Stan Drobac's Spartans defeated the University of Iowa squad, 5-1. It was the first victory over a Big Ten team in a span of five seasons, which included 65 straight losses. Paul Mesaros opened the scoring with a 6-4, 6-3 win and Fernando Belmar of Alicante, Spain garnered the important fifth team point with his 3-6, 6-4, 6-4 victory in the number one singles pairing. Other winners were Santiago Cash at number three, Damon Valentino at number four and number six Anthony Florino.

Track and Field: At the conference indoor championship hosted by Ohio State, MSU garnered 26 points and finished tied for seventh place with Minnesota. Leading the way with second-place finishes were Guy Scott who ran a 48.25 in the 400 meters and Marvin Parnell with a 1:03.06 in the 500-meter race. Also placing for State were Tony Norris with a fifth-place time of 7.48 in the hurdles and mile runners Dennis Topolinski who finished fifth in 4:10.60 and Kerry Fly in sixth with a time of 4:13.35.

Spartans who excelled at the annual Drake Relays in Des Moines, Iowa, were gold medal performers Philmore Morris in the long jump and intermediate hurdler Parnell. Morris's leap of 25' 4 1/2" broke Fred Johnson's 40 year-old team record by a scant 1/8". Parnell's winning time of 50.63 qualified him for the NCAA championship. In yet another impressive run, Tony Norris skimmed the high hurdles in 14.16 for a second place finish, just .01 behind the winner.

Managing only 18 team points, as in 1987, Michigan State ended up in ninth place at the outdoor conference championships. Morris was the sole champion as he managed a first place in his specialty, the long jump, with a more convincing school record of 25' 7 1/2". Topolinski finished fourth in the 1,500 meters with a time of 3:45.20; Norris took sixth in the 110-meter high hurdles with a time of 14:30 and Scott was fifth in the 400-meter dash with a mark of 46.95. As defending champion, Parnell had been a favorite in the 400-meter hurdle event. Unfortunately, his weekend ended early when he suffered a groin injury while running his leg on the 400-meter sprint relay team.

Wrestling: For the second straight year, the wrestling team finished last in the conference championship meet. Senior 190-pound Dave Mariola and sophomore Stacy Richmond, at 142-pounds, were both favored to make a run for a title, but both failed in their bids. Mariola placed third and Richmond settled for a fourth place finish. Heavyweight Mark Zenas also finished the weekend with a third place. The remainder of the Spartan line-up,

Erick Jensen, Soon Thackthay, Robert Flanders, Jeff Mustari, Randi Miniard and James Richardson were all eliminated early in the tournament.

EXTRA! 1988 ROSE BOWL

January 1, 1988
Pasadena, California

	1	2	3	4	F
MSU	7	7	0	6	20
Southern California	3	0	7	7	17

Starting line-up (defense)   *Starting line-up (offense)*

Andre Rison	SE	Jim Szymanski	DE
Tony Mandarich	LT	Mark Nichols (C)	DT
Bob Kula	LG	Travis Davis	DT
Pat Shurmur (C)	C	John Budde	DE
Vince Tata	RG	Tim Moore	OLB
David Houle	RT	Percy Snow	MLB
Mike Sargent	TE	Kurt Larson	OLB
Bobby McAllister	QB	Derrick Reed	CB
Lorenzo White (C)	LH	John Miller	SS
James Moore	FB	Todd Krumm	FS
Willie Bouyer	FL	Harlon Barnett	CB

Michigan State was pleased to be the team to break the Big Ten's six-game loosing streak in Pasadena, and without a doubt, John Langeloh was thrilled to be the hero in a game that Spartan fans would forever hold in high esteem. MSU, ranked number eight nationally, had reached the Rose Bowl for the first time in 22 years, and they were matched against 16th-ranked Southern California. The Trojans scored first on a 34-yard field goal, but State responded with a 15-play, 76-yard drive to take a 7-3 lead on Lorenzo White's five-yard touchdown run near the end of the first quarter. Early in the second Bobby McAllister produced a 55-yard completion to Andre Rison to set up White's second TD run from three yards out. The Trojans scored their first six-pointer and made the PAT to close the gap to 14-10 early in the third. Langeloh was called upon just after the start of the fourth quarter when he kicked a 40-yard field goal to increase the lead to 17-10. USC tied the game at 17 with 8:33 remaining, and on the Spartans' next possession they found themselves in a critical position at midfield on third down with eight yards to go. After the snap, McAllister eluded a heavy rush to complete a 36-yard toss to Rison for a first down at the opposition's 18 as both passer and receiver tip-toes the sideline. Then, with 4:14 left in the game, Langeloh appeared once again, this time to boot what proved to be the winning margin from 36-yards away. USC fumbled their next possession away to Todd Krumm, and later John Miller intercepted a Southern Cal "Hail Mary" at the MSU 13 with three seconds remaining. White accumulated a game-high 113 yards rushing with two TDs, but Southern California actually outgained MSU in total yards, 410-276. It was Southern Cal's five turnovers that were costly.

Quarterback Bobby McAllister

EXTRA! 1988 NCAA HOCKEY TOURNAMENT (Quarterfinals)

After overpowering Illinois-Chicago in the first round of the CCHA playoffs, MSU lost to Bowling Green in the semi-finals. A consolation victory over Western Michigan, however, earned them a place at nationals, so they visited Cambridge to face Harvard in a first-round, total-goal series. There, they gave the Crimson their first-ever home NCAA tournament losses, 6-5 and 5-3. Unfortunately, the Minnesota Gophers topped the Spartans twice in the next round to knock them out of the play-offs.

March 18, 1988—Cambridge, Mass.
MSU 6, Harvard 5

1st Pd.: 1. MSU, McReynolds (Gibson), 0:57; 2. MSU, Kv. Miller (Marshall, Ki. Miller), 1:26; 3. HU, Janfanza (Armstrong, Sweeney), 4:43; 4. MSU, Reynolds (Tilley, Cole), 7:54; 5. MSU, Harding (Cole, Beadle), 14:45.
2nd Pd.: 6. MSU, Tilley (unasst.), 0:40; 7. HU, Janfaza (Hartje, Sweeney), 11:35; 8. HU, Vukonich (Weisbrod, Murphy), 18:08.
3rd Pd.: 9. MSU, Kv. Miller (Luongo, Hamilton), 9:56; 10. HU, Pawloski (Donato, Armstrong), 17:23; 11. HU, Ciavaglia (unasst.), 19:20.

Kicker John Langeloh

March 19, 1988—Cambridge, Mass.
MSU 5, Harvard 3

1st Pd.: 1. MSU, Cole (Murray, Reynolds), 3:33; 2. MSU, O'Toole (Cole, Reynolds), 15:46.
2nd Pd.: 3. HU, Weisbrod (Vukonich, Pawloski), 5:08; 4. MSU, Rendall (Luongo, McReynolds), 6:03.
3rd Pd.: 5. MSU, Kv. Miller (Reynolds, Hamilton), 0:19; 6. HU, Pawloski (Hartje), 9:39; 7. HU, Caplan (unasst.), 18:18; 8. MSU, O'Toole (unasst.), 19:56.

March 25, 1988—Minneapolis, Minn.
Minnesota 4, MSU 2

1st Pd.: 1. MSU Reynolds (Russell, Cole), 3:15; 2. UM, Broten (Miller), 7:03; 3. UM, Richards (Broten, Grannis), 19:42.
2nd Pd.: 4. UM, Bloom (Hankinson, Orth), 10:54.
3rd Pd.: 5. MSU, Rendall (unasst.) 14:12; 6. UM, Grannis (Broten), 18:38.

March 26, 1988—Minneapolis, Minn.
Minnesota 4, MSU 3

1st Pd.: 1. MSU, Ki. Miller (Murray, Beadle), 5:42; 2. MSU, Ki. Miller (Murray, Beadle), 10:02; 3. MSU, Ki. Miller (Kv. Miller, Hamilton), 15:35.
2nd Pd.: 4. UM, Cates (Werness, Skarda), 17:14.
3rd Pd.: 5. UM, Bischoff (Cates), 7:44; 6. UM, Richards (unasst.), 13:10; 7. UM, J. Miller (Skarda), 19:56.

TALES TO TELL

The financial report for the Department of Intercollegiate Athletics released in November of 1988 showed a total revenue of $9,357,594 for 1987-1988. Although as impressive as this figure may seem, in reality it proved to be a decline of $269,463 from the earnings of the preceding academic year. Also eating away at the profit was an ever-increasing expenditure of funds as disclosed in the table on the right.

Although there may have been sundry reasons for this growth in disbursements, the primary reason was related to an increase in scholarship funding for the tendered student-athletes.

The financial report also exposed the myth that football bowl games reap a bonanza of revenue for a school. Although the 1988 Rose Bowl appearance meant a paycheck of one million dollars, it took all of that, and more, to pay for the travel, lodging and feeding of the student-athletes, coaches, members of the marching band and other school officials. All post-season appearances are computed as a separate budget and consequently not included in the aforementioned financial report.

SPORT	1987	1988
Football	$2,487,358	$2,631,532
Basketball	$582,911	$640,441
Hockey	$509,304	$550,006
Baseball	$160,378	$170,412
Cross Country	$18,339	$21,000
Fencing	$13,465	$14,292
Golf	$52,437	$55,773
Gymnastics	$97,218	$99,582
Lacrosse	$24,629	$32,322
Soccer	$48,394	$53,461
Swimming and Diving	$114,453	$120,069
Tennis	$52,007	$59,414
Track and Field	$149,678	$163,885
Wrestling	$162,089	$155,742
TOTAL	**$4,472,661**	**$4,767,931**

HEADLINES of 1989

- Thousands killed in Beijing's Tiananmen Square as Chinese leaders take hard line toward student demonstrators.
- The ruptured tanker Exxon Valdez sends 11 million gallons of crude oil into Alaska's Prince William Sound.
- Pete Rose, one of the greatest players in the history of baseball, is banned from the game for life for gambling.
- After 28 years, the Berlin Wall comes down, which one year later leads to the reunification of East and West Germany.

SCOREBOARD

	W	L	T	Avg.
Baseball	25	26	0	.490
Track and Field	no dual meets			
Football	6	5	1	.542
Basketball	18	15	0	.545
Tennis	4	19	0	.174
Cross Country	2	1	0	.667
Swimming and Diving	10	2	0	.833
Wrestling	6	12	0	.333
Hockey	37	9	1	.798
Fencing	12	10	0	.545
Golf	tournament play only			
Gymnastics	9	4	0	.692
Soccer	9	11	1	.452
Lacrosse	8	7	0	.533

TEAM OF THE YEAR

When looking in the record books, it is clear the 1988-89 Spartan hockey team was offensively, one of the school's best. That season's squad continues to hold all-time team season records in five categories (goals 277, assists 439, points 716, power-play goals 91 and most 20-goal scorers seven). After wining the regular season conference title, MSU took home its sixth CCHA play-off crown in eight years on a 4-1 victory over Lake Superior State. Goalie Jason Muzzatti was named the tourna-ment MVP. This finish earned State its eighth straight NCAA appearance. There they defeated Boston College to enter the NCAA Frozen Four for the third time in four years. After suffering a 6-3 loss to Harvard in the semi-finals, they defeated Maine 7-4 to secure third place. Bobby Reynolds and Kip Miller combined to lead the offense through the year, and both were named first team All-American. Reynolds finished with 36 goals and 41 assists for 77 points, while Miller gained 32 goals and 45 assists for the same point total. In addition, the team had many contributors, as a record seven players scored twenty or more goals. The other five were Danton Cole, Pat Murray, Rod Brind'Amour, Peter White, and Shawn Heaphy. Behind this offensive attack, Muzzatti gained the most wins ever by a Spartan goalie.

The 1989 hockey team. (Front row, left to right) J. Stewart, B. Hamilton, D. Cole, asst. coach N. Brown, asst. coach T. Christensen, head coach R. Mason, asst. coach G. Gwozdecky, C. Luongo, B. Reynolds, J. Muzzatti. (Middle row) team physician Dr. J. Downs, K. Miller, W. Bartels, D. Gibson, M. O'Toole, C. Shepard, P. Murray, L. Gustafson, D. McAuliffe, S. Beadle, K. Russell, C. Marshall, S. Heaphy, student manager Jim Preston. (Back row) trainer D. Carrier, student trainer B. Downie, D. Collins, J. Woolley, R. Brind'Amour, J. Messier, M. Hirth, J. Cummins, P. White, D. Norris, M. Gilmore, student manager R. Guzall, equipment manager T. Magee

MAKING HISTORY

Jack Breslin, most recently serving as senior consultant to the school's president, died August 2, 1988, at Ingham Medical Center following a three-year battle with cancer.

Apparently oblivious to any possible sanctions for doing so, massive lineman Tony Mandarich (6' 7", 305 pounds) made an informal inquiry into his possibilities of playing professionally within the National Football League. The initial reaction of the NCAA was the penalty of a one-year suspension, which was later reduced to sitting out the first three games of the 1988 schedule.

After opening the season with four losses and one tie, the football team finally managed their first win, 36-3 over Northwestern at home. As a sarcastic gesture, the students poured onto the field and tore down the goal post in the north end.

Despite snow and chilling winds, on November 6 the MSU rugby club won the Big Ten tournament and conference championship by defeating the University of Michigan, 24-6.

Los Angeles Dodger baseball star Kirk Gibson was recipient of the 1988 National League MVP Award. The last Dodger to win the coveted title was another Spartan great, Steve Garvey, who earned the honor in 1974.

In a timely jester that may have saved the famed Spartan statue from irrevocable damage, the Varsity Alumni "S" Club spearheaded a successful campaign which raised the needed $75,000 to engage a restoration specialist, Robert Pringle of New York City. A rededication ceremony was held on September 16, 1989, prior to the football season opener against Miami (OH) University.

Bob Carey (1949-52), one of only 10 MSU athletes to win nine varsity letters, died of cancer on October 25 in Cincinnati. He was 58.

On March 11, 1989, the final MSU basketball game was played on the renowned Jenison Fieldhouse floor, home to Spartan basketball for 50 years. More than 150 former varsity players were honored at halftime of the game in which State defeated Wisconsin, 70-61.

The Big Ten office announced on April 5 that Jim Delaney would be the new commissioner, replacing Wayne Duke who was on the job for 18 years.

After spending 30 years as a member of the MSU coaching staff, including 24 as head golf coach, Bruce Fossum retired following the spring season of 1989. Later, on April 5, tennis coach Stan Drobac announced that 1989 would also be his final season.

GREAT STATE DATES

Soccer—**September 28, 1988 (H):** It took double overtime, but the Spartans were tenacious as they blanked the University of Michigan 1-0 at Old College Field. After sophomore Matt Hartker sailed a shot just over the crossbar in the first overtime and sophomore Michael Rawlins drilled one off the left crossbar, the Spartans appeared to be a team destined for close calls. Then, just 3:57 into the second overtime, senior Jim Blanchard ended the suspense with his first goal of the season. The defense was forced to repel the Wolverine's continued attempts to even the count and on one occasion goalie Chris Heide had to come way out of his net to thwart a breakaway scoring opportunity.

Cross Country—**October 4, 1988 (H):** In their fifth run of the season, over the four-mile Forest Akers course, Michigan State defeated Eastern Michigan 29-59. Eric Huff led the Spartans with a first place finish in 21:12. Dave Wickens finished fourth, Mark Reinardy sixth, Alex Tomiach eighth and Rob Wood 10th.

Cross Country—**October 8, 1988 (A):** The cross country team traveled to Lawrence, Kan., where they defeated the Kansas University team, 22-35. Anthony Hamm led all runners to the finish line as he covered the course in 24:36. Rick Prince finished third; David Smith placed fifth, Ken Wolters and Kerry Fly completed the team scoring in sixth and seventh spots, respectively. Adam Norman crossed the line in ninth place.

Football—**October 29, 1988 (H):** Michigan State pounded out a 20-10 victory over Ohio State with 372 rushing yards. MSU ran the ball 72 times, which eventually wore down the Buckeye defense. Hyland Hickson, who broke Lorenzo White's high school record in Ft. Lauderdale, Fla., gained 179 yards rushing on 37 carries. Blake Ezor had his number called 29 times and managed 155 yards. The Buckeyes scored early for a 7-0 lead, but the game was knotted 10-10 by halftime. On their second possession of the second half, the Spartans managed 61 yards on nine plays for the winning touchdown. The

score came courtesy of a one-yard naked bootleg from quarterback Bobby McAllister.

Football—**November 19, 1988 (H):** State soundly defeated the University of Wisconsin, 36-0, which guaranteed a second-place finish in the conference and led to an invitation to meet Georgia in the Mazda Gator Bowl at Jacksonville, Fla., on Jan. 1, 1989. To the delight of a sellout home crowd totaling 76,372, the Spartans scored in every quarter and racking up 372 combined yards rushing and passing. Quarterback Bobby McAllister passed for a season-high 186 yards, while split end Andre Rison caught four passes for 128 yards and rushed for 46 more on two reverses. Badger miscues helped the cause as three interceptions (two by Kurt Larson and one by Ventson Donelson) led to the opening touchdown by Blake Ezor and two of John Langeloh's team record-setting five field goals from 47 yards, 31 yards, 27 yards, 48 yards and 30 yards. The only extended scoring drive came in the final period when the Spartans took over on their own 12-yard line and drove 88 yards on 15 plays which included four passes for 54 yards

Hockey—**December 9 (A) & 11 (H) 1988:** The Spartans won their 16th and 17th straight as they shutout Michigan at Ann Arbor, 3-0, and then defeated the Wolverines 5-3 on home ice. In the opening game, goalie Jason Mussatti was especially sharp with some clutch saves in the third period. Bobby Reynolds scored the first two goals, one on a power play in the first period and the second on a four-on-four situation in the second. Defenseman Steve Beadle, with Reynolds assisting, also connected in the second, on a power play. Meanwhile, the U of M failed to connect on six opportunities with a one-man advantage. Back home on Sunday, Danton Cole keyed the victory with a pair of timely second-period goals. The first came 21 seconds into the middle stanza and the second with 1:18 remaining in that same period, giving State a 3-1 lead. Dwayne Norris had opened the Michigan State scoring in the first period on a deflection of Brad Hamilton's shot from the point. The Wolverines pulled within one before Peter White and Pat Murray closed out the scoring in the third period.

Swimming and Diving—**January 14, 1989 (A):** Coach Bill Wadley's Spartans defeated Ohio State with the greatest victory margin ever over the Buckeyes, 76-37. Freshman Steve Leissner won three events, the 100-yard freestyle with a time of 46.8, the 200-yard breaststroke in 2:09.8 and a pool record-setting 4:02.0 in the

400-yard individual medley. Damon Whitfield was a double-winner taking the 50-yard freestyle (21.82) and 500-yard freestyle (4:44.3). Other first places were registered by Kent Johnson in the 1,650-yard freestyle (16:32.2); Kevin Zielinski, 200-yard freestyle (1:41.7); Brian Goins, 200-yard butterfly (1:54.0) and Anthony Higgins, 200-yard backstroke (1:54.1). The quartet of Steve Shipps, Goins, Todd Mercer and Whitfield won the 400-yard freestyle relay in a time of 3:12.5. Bill Cole captured both diving events, winning the one-meter event with 208.1 points and the three-meter with a total of 319.6.

Wrestling—**January 20, 1989 (A):** Winning seven of the 10 matches, State defeated Illinois 26-13. Leading the way were Brian Smith, who pinned his opponent at 126 pounds and nationally third-ranked Stacy Richmond, who easily handled his 142-pound opponent, 12-3. Winning by decisions were Soon Thackthay (118-pounds), 10-7; Erick Jensen (158 pounds), 6-0; Tom Petitto (167 pounds) 8-0; James Richardson (177-pounds), 4-1 and Eric Givens (190-pounds), 15-10.

Basketball—**January 25, 1989 (H):** Junior guard Kirk Manns scored a career-high 40 points, including a Big Ten record-tying eight three-pointers out of 10, in a 106-83 victory over Purdue. His compiled scoring-total included three two-pointers and 10-for-10 at the free throw line. Heathcote's squad shot an impressive .644 from the field (38 out of 59) as three other Spartans scored in double figures: Ken Redfield, 15; Steve Smith, 14 and Todd Wolfe, who hit a perfect five-for-five in field goals with two beyond the three-point arc and a total of 13. At one point in the second half the Spartans hit 13 consecutive shots.

Swimming and Diving—**January 30, 1989 (A):** Heading an impressive array of freshmen talent, Steve Leissner won three events as MSU defeated Purdue, 65-50. Leissner set pool records with a 9:29 in the 1,000-yard freestyle and a 1:55.22 to the 200-yard butterfly. He also won the 500-yard freestyle in 4:35.67. Other freshmen winners were Gregg Mihalik who won both the 50-yard freestyle in 21.81 and the 100-yard freestyle in 46.97 and Kevin Zielinski who captured the 200-yard freestyle in 1:44.62. Additional double winners were senior co-captain Sidney Appelboom with a 1:54.71 in the 200-yard individual medley and 2:06.16 in the 200-yard breaststroke along with Bill Cole who won both diving events, scoring 188.40 on the one-meter and 178.40 at

three-meter. In addition, State took both relay events as the foursome of Anthony Higgins, Appelboom, Brian Goins and Damon Whitfield swam a 3:27.99 in the 400-yard medley relay and the freestyle quartet of Mihalik, Whitfield, Zielinski and Goins combined for a 3:09.66 in the 400.

Gymnastics—**February 18, 1989 (A):** Rick Atkinson's gymnasts battled back from a four-point deficit after two events to win a four-team meet hosted by the University of Michigan. State scored 259.85 points, the U of M 258.70, the Air Force Academy 252.25 and Western Michigan 245.95. The Spartans initiated their winning rally with a stellar performance on the high bar. Nick Westermeyer won the event with a 9.45 and was followed by teammates Terry Gillespie and Bobby Switzer who placed second and fourth with scores of 9.35 and 9.10. Rich Pulsfort won the all-around competition with a score of 52.35.

Fencing—**February 25, 1989 (H):** Hosting the MSU Open, State fencers defeated the University of Michigan 20-7; Purdue 16-12 and Eastern Michigan 15-12. The Spartans were led by junior Mike Kimball who went 7-5 in sabre while senior Chris Karl was 8-7 in foil and Ralph Hindo completed the afternoon with a 6-9 record in epee.

Tennis—**February 18, 1989 (H):** Taking five of six singles matches and two doubles matches, all in straight sets, State defeated Toledo, 7-2, at the Indoor Tennis Facility. Winners at singles were number one Grant Asher, 7-5, 6-4; number two Santiago Cash, 6-3, 6-2; number three Damon Valentino, 7-5, 6-1; number four Brad Rosenbaum, 6-3, 6-2 and number six Jason Volk, 6-3, 6-2. Doubles winners were number two Cash-Rosenbaum, 6-2, 6-1 and Volk-Jason Stanislaw, 7-5, 6-4.

Basketball—**March 2, 1989 (A):** With four players hitting in double figures, Michigan State squeezed out an upset victory over the 11th-ranked University of Iowa, 83-81. Although forced to occasional turnovers, the Spartans did manage to frequently slice through the patented Hawkeye full-court pressure and wound up with several three-on-one breaks. Falling behind 11-2, it was a game of spurts in which the Spartans registered a seven-point run and a nine-point run to settle for a 42-42 tie at the intermission. State scored the first six points after the break, then fell behind, 49-48. By the 7:25 mark they had come back to lead 75-65 and then, starting at 4:41, failed to score for nearly three minutes. Trailing 80-79 with two minutes to play the game was won at the foul line when Steve Smith sank two and Mark Montgomery a pair. Including five-of-seven from three-point range, Kirk Manns led all scorers with 22 points, Smith had 21 and both Matt Steigenga and Parish Hickman scored 10 each.

Lacrosse—**April 12, 1989 (N):** In a game played on the grounds of the Detroit Country Day School in Birmingham, State handed Michigan its first defeat of the spring. Leading by a mere one-goal margin at intermission, 4-3, the Spartans came alive in the second half to win with relative ease, 11-4. Adam Mueller accounted for three goals and one assist while Mike Siegenthaler contributed two goals and three assists. Goaltender Jeff Horowitz thwarted 17 shots on the MSU net.

Baseball—**April 19, 1989 (H):** With the hitting of senior catcher Scott Markarewicz and the pitching of Don Lindsey, Michigan State shut out Michigan for the first time since 1975, 5-0. Markarewicz drove in all five runs, the first in the opening inning as he singled in Kevin Dalson. He added two on a double in the third inning and two more with a single in the fifth. both times after the Michigan coach had ordered his right-handed pitcher to walk left-handed hitter Dan Masteller in order to reach right-hander Markarewicz. Both two-run hits were misplayed, wind-blown fly balls. Meanwhile, Lindsay, a junior, threw a five-hitter complete game with eight strike outs, including three in the first inning with the bases loaded.

Baseball—**April 29, 1989 (H):** First winning with ease and then winning with a four-run rally in the final inning, State swept the doubleheader from the conference-leading Iowa Hawkeyes, 9-1 and 6-4. In the opening game, pitcher Eric Methner allowed four hits while yielding only three base on balls. Offensively, the Spartan 12-hit attack included a three-run home run by Scott Makarewicz and solo four-baggers by Rich Juday and Dan Masteller. In the second game MSU trailed 4-2 entering the bottom of the seventh when singles by Kevin Dalson, Keith Dutkiewicz and Sean Bruce loaded the bases. Pinch-hitter Greg Green hit a sacrifice fly to center to score Dalson. Alexi Gagin, freshman second baseman, was the eventual hero as he cleared the bases and ended the game with his first home run as a Spartan. Derek Darkowski pitched the entire game, giving up only four hits and walking none to extend his perfect record to 4-0.

ATHLETE OF THE YEAR

At just five foot 10, 195 pounds some may have thought Andre Rison, the Flint native, would have difficulty in proving himself, but he had no trouble once he topped the MSU football receiving charts. In his sophomore year he was named first team All-Big Ten after setting new school single season records with 54 receptions and 966 receiving yards. In his junior year he pulled in 34 receptions for 785 yards and five touchdowns to be named second team All-Big Ten and help lead his team to the Rose Bowl, where he caught two passes for an incredible 91 yards. After the completion of his senior year, Rison was named first team All-American and All-Big Ten and held the Spartan records for career receptions with 146 and reception yardage with 2,992. Many State fans remember his final collegiate game, in which he totaled a then MSU single game record 252 reception yards in a loss to Georgia in the Gator Bowl. While he made most of his noise on the football field, Rison also lettered in track and field as a high jumper in 1986 and in basketball as a guard in 1988. After being drafted in the first round by the Indianapolis Colts he went on to have a very successful career in the NFL.

Andre Rison

IN THE SPARTLITE

Baseball: The Spartans finished the season on a sad note as they dropped all four games to Ohio State. Even a split against the Buckeyes would have likely insured them of a berth in the Big Ten playoffs.

Senior catcher Scott Markarewicz, the MSU career record holder with 28 home runs, was named to the All-Big Ten first team and first baseman Dan Masteller was selected to the second honor team.

Shortstop Kevin Dalson broke two team career records, doubles with 38 and total hits with 206.

Committing only 39 errors during the season, the 1989 baseball team led the NCAA in fielding percentage with a .975 mark.

Basketball: Matt Steigenga, the Grand Rapids freshman and designated "Mr. Basketball" of Michigan as a high school senior, was tabbed as the Big Ten's preseason Freshman of the Year. He was also a preseason pick to *Sports Illustrated's* second team Freshmen All-American squad.

State won 12 games and lost only one in the non-conference portion of the schedule. The Big Ten season proved far more challenging as they managed only a 6-12 record.

The final season in Jenison opened with an exhibition game against the Yugoslavia National team on November 14. Imagine the courtside announcer's challenge with such names as: Zdravko Radulovic, Slavisa Koprivica, Predrag Danilovic, Dzevad Alihodzic and Nebojsa Razic.

Junior Kirk Manns was named *Sports Illustrated* Player of the Week after scoring 64 points in back-to-back home wins over Purdue and Minnesota on January 25 and 28. He totaled a career high 40 points in the PU game and followed with 24 points against the Gophers.

Sophomore Steve Smith was the team's leading scorer in 15 of the 28 regular season games. This also equated to a season average of 17.7, also tops for the team. Smith was the only Spartan to gain individual postseason honors, being designated as a third team All-Big Ten selection.

Cross Country: Running to an impressive low score of 30 points, the favored Wisconsin Badgers captured the Big Ten title with the Spartans a distant second with 72, one point better than third place Michigan. Sophomore Anthony Hamm from Flint was MSU's top finisher, placing sixth (24:32) over the 8K course at Iowa

City, Iowa. Senior Rick Prince finished ninth (24:47) and senior teammate Dennis Topolinski finished one second later in 10th (24:48). Sophomore David Smith was 15th (24:58) and senior Greg Psihas finished 32nd (25:34).

For the second year in a row, fellow conference coaches tapped MSU's Jim Stintzi as Coach of the Year.

Fencing: As a substitute for the Big Tens, which were last competed in 1986, the Midwest Invitational championships were conducted in Columbus, OH. The competition, which included teams from eight conference schools, found Michigan State in sixth place at conclusion of the weekend. Juniors Jae Son and Chris Karl placed fifth and sixth respectively in foil while Mike Kimball placed 10th in sabre. Senior Ralph Hindo was eighth and senior Ken Frazee 12th in epee.

Son qualified for the NCAA championships where he placed 23rd in the foil competition.

Football: John Langeloh set a team record of five field goals against the University of Wisconsin. Those completed kicks were of 47, 31, 27, 49 and 30 yards. Later in that same game he missed a 44-yard attempt which, if completed, would have set a Big Ten record for most field goals in one game.

Blake Ezor had the biggest game of his Spartan career against Indiana when he carried the ball 44 times for 250 yards.

President of Washington and Lee University in Lexington, Va., and former MSU defensive back (1950-1952) John Wilson was inducted into the Academic All-American Hall of Fame.

Four Spartans were postseason selections as first team All-Big Ten: Andre Rison, Tony Mandarich, Percy Snow and John Miller.

Mandarich gained further accolades as college offensive lineman of the year by both the Columbus Touchdown Club and the Washington, D.C., Touchdown Club as well as finishing sixth on the Heisman Trophy ballot.

In the National Football League annual draft of collegiate talent, Mandarich was selected second overall by the Green Bay Packers while Rison was the number 22 overall pick by the Baltimore Colts.

Golf: The Michigan State golf team posted a composite score of 1,222 on the 72 holes in the conference meet at Madison, Wis., and ended up 11 strokes behind the University of Minnesota in the battle for ninth place. Individually, the five Spartans and their scores were Brent Kish 301, Mike Spencer 301, Mike Anderson 304, Kevin Collier 322 and Ian Peakes 328. It was a disappointing

finish for the retiring coach Bruce Fossum in his final meet as MSU's head coach.

Gymnastics: Three Spartans placed in the top 12 in the floor exercise event at Chicago's Windy City Invitational in January. Richard Pulsfort tied for second with a 9.45 while Chris Spinosa and Gregory Jung placed fifth and 12th respectively. Scoring 256.90 points, State was able to beat out the University of Michigan for seventh place in the team standings.

Hockey: After losing the season-opener against Lake Superior, the Spartans ran off 19 straight victories, the best early conference season record since the CCHA began playing a 32-game schedule in 1984.

Senior Bobby Reynolds scored the 100th goal of his Spartan career 1:45 into the final regular season game, an overtime 5-4 loss to Lake Superior State. Later in the game he would net yet another, and then adding six scores during the playoffs. His total of 107 would place him fifth on the school's record list for career goals: Tom Ross (138), Steve Culp (132), Kip Miller (116) and Mike Donnelly (110).

Coach Mason moved into second place on the all-time NCAA Division I hockey coaches' total win list with 556 when the Spartans defeated Ferris State on December 16. For the fifth time in his career, he would be selected Coach of the Year.

Jason Woolley scored 37 points to tie Pat Betterly's record of 1974-1975 for the most points by a rookie defenseman.

Brind'Amor was honored by the NCAA as freshman of the year in college hockey. He would leave the Spartans to sign a professional contract with the NHL's St. Louis Blues.

Lacrosse: Finishing the season with an overall record of 8-6 and a perfect 5-0 in the Great Lakes Lacrosse Conference, MSU gained one of the 12 bids to compete in the national collegiate tournament. Playing on the field of Northeastern University in Boston, the Spartans were defeated by Adelphi College of Garden City N.Y., 16-10, in the opening round. Scoring for State were Mike Siegenthaler with three goals, Wayne Sansiviero two goals and one each by Adam Mueller, Mike Ferguson, Rich Montalbano, Brad Smaha and Dave Stein. Junior goalie Chris Barber had a season-high 29 saves.

Mueller, a senior from North Brunswick, N.J., had 37 goals and 28 assists for 65 points on the season and wound-up his collegiate career as the third-leading scorer in Spartan history with 207 points.

Chris Heide and Mueller were first-team All-Midwest Lacrosse Association selections while Heide, Jon Lantzy and goalie Chris Barber gained similiar honors by the Great Lakes Lacrosse Conference.

Soccer: Among their nine wins and for the third time in the season, State edged their opponent, 1-0. In this game, against Central Michigan, Mike Foster, who played mostly in a reserve capacity, booted in the telling score. His goal came with 12 minutes remaining in the game as goaltender John Spink and the MSU defense held the Chippewas scoreless.

The two leading scorers for 1988 were Todd Goodwin with eight goals and seven assists followed by Jim Blanchard with seven goals and four assists. It was Goodwin's second straight year as the team leader.

Swimming and Diving: Following an impressive 10-2 dual-meet season, Coach Wadley's squad managed 216 points and a sixth-place finish at the Big Ten championships in Indianapolis. The most impressive event of the weekend for State was the 200-yard individual medley in which senior Sidney Appelboom finished sixth, Kevin Zielinski was ninth and Steve Leissner 11th. Other MSU finishers were Leissner third in the 400-yard individual medley; Appelboom fifth in the 200-yard breaststroke; Anthony Higgins ninth in the 100-yard backstroke; Damon Whitfield 11th in the 50-yard freestyle and Bill Cole's 13th and 14th in the diving events. All four relays finished in sixth place or higher.

After only two years as MSU's head coach, Bill Wadley resigned to accept a similar post at Ohio State University.

Tennis: The MSU tennis squad finished a disappointing 10th place at the conference championships in Iowa City, Iowa. They were shut out by both Iowa and Indiana and then lost the match for ninth place against Purdue, 5-2. Freshman Brad Rosenbaum and senior Santiago Cash gained the two lone points for the Spartans.

This was Stan Drobac's final season as State's head coach. He had previously announced his retirement following the 1989 season. He would retain his positions of assistant professor and manager of MSU's Indoor Tennis Facility.

Track and Field: At the conference indoor championships in Iowa City, Iowa, coach Jim Bibbs's squad managed 27 points, placing them in eighth place. Cory Pryor, the Jackson sophomore, captured the 55-meter dash in 6.25 seconds for the only MSU victory. Freshman Tony

Nelson finished third in the 600 meters in a time of 1:20.71; Guy Scott was fourth in the 400 with a clocking of 49.09 and Daryl Stallworth's time of 22.18 was good enough for a sixth place in the 200 meters.

Hosting the MSU Open at Ralph Young Field, State's trackmen gained some experience heading into the outdoor season. Senior Dennis Topolinski was a double winner, 800 meters (1:52.9) and the 1,500 meters (3:47.6). Scott, another senior, won the 400 meters (48.4) and freshman Marcelle Richardson was the top long jumper (24' 3").

Prepping for the conference championship two weeks hence, a contingency of the team was at the Eastern Michigan invitational where they turned in respectable performances. Pryor, having completed spring football, turned to track and finished first in the 100 meters. Philmore Morris finished second in the long jump (23' 5"), freshman John Collins was second in the discus (154' 9") and Anthony Hamm placed third in the 5,000 meters (14:18.73).

Gaining only 36 points at the Big Ten outdoor championships, MSU settled for a ninth-place finish. Topolinski was the top finisher as he ran to a second place in the 1,500-meters with a respectable time of 3:46.73. Other Spartan finishers were Scott, fifth in the 400-meters; Tico Duckett and Pryor, the freshmen sprint pair, who were sixth and seventh respectively in the 100-meter dash; Rick Prince with a fourth in the 10,000-meter run; Chuck Cullen, a fourth in the high jump with a leap of 6' 10" and Gary Voss with a fourth-place toss of 157.6' in the discus.

Wrestling: MSU had to settle for a fourth-place finish at their own Spartan 'nvitational; however, two Spartans did win individual titles: Stacy Richmond in the 142-pound division and heavyweight Mark Zenas.

Five straight days of front page *State News* stories in February pursued allegations of questionable conduct by head coach Phil Parker. Although eventually cleared of the charges, he was later removed from the coaching position in 1991 following yet another incident.

Continuing the team's downward spiral since falling from the top echelon in 1985, MSU wrestlers scored only 30.25 points and finished ninth in the Big Ten tournament at West Lafayette, Ind. Richmond, who lost 10-2 in the finals, was the only Spartan to reach the championship round. He would later be the only Spartan to compete in that year's NCAA meet in Oklahoma City where he won the first two matches before being eliminated in the quarterfinals.

EXTRA! 1989 NIT TOURNAMENT

Michigan State placed fourth in the 1989 NIT tournament. The following are the Spartans' box scores for those games.

MICHIGAN STATE 83—KENT STATE 69

	FG-FGA	FT-FTA	REB	A	PF	TP
Redfield	4-7	2-3	3	5	4	11
Wolfe	1-3	2-2	2	0	2	4
Steigenga	4-6	0-0	3	2	0	8
Manns	3-6	0-0	0	0	0	7
Smith	10-17	7-8	7	5	2	28
Montgomery	4-5	2-2	1	4	4	14
Hickman	2-5	4-5	11	0	1	8
Hall	0-1	0-0	2	1	2	0
Casler	1-1	0-0	0	5	3	3
Mueller	0-0	0-0	0	0	0	0
Sekal	0-1	0-0	1	0	0	0
Sarkine	0-0	0-0	0	0	0	0
Team			1			
TOTALS	29-52	17-20	30	22	16	83

Halftime: Kent State 39-37; **Three-point field goals:** 8 (Redfield 1, Manns 1, Smith 1, Montgomery 4, Casler 1); **Officials:** Watts, Boxcroft, Evans; **Attendance:** 7,325.

MICHIGAN STATE 79—WICHITA STATE 67

	FG-FGA	FT-FTA	REB	A	PF	TP
Redfield	5-7	2-3	4	5	4	12
Smith	7-15	2-3	11	5	3	16
Steigenga	5-8	0-0	3	1	4	10
Manns	6-13	0-0	1	2	0	13
Montgomery	2-3	4-4	2	4	3	8
Hickman	1-2	0-0	2	1	2	2
Hall	0-0	0-0	0	0	0	0
Casler	0-1	0-0	0	1	1	0
Wolfe	7-9	0-0	4	1	3	18
Sekal	0-1	0-0	0	0	0	0
TOTALS	33-59	8-10	27	20	20	79

Halftime: Michigan State 33-30; **Three-point field goals:** 5 (Manns 1, Wolfe 4); **Officials:** Kouri, Reynolds, Harvey; **Attendance:** 9,860.

MICHIGAN STATE 70—VILLANOVA 63

	FG-FGA	FT-FTA	REB	A	PF	TP
Redfield	2-9	6-8	12	5	2	10
Smith	11-15	10-10	3	1	3	34
Steigenga	0-2	1-2	8	1	3	1
Wolfe	4-6	0-0	1	0	1	10
Montgomery	1-2	2-2	1	1	5	4
Manns	1-6	0-0	0	1	0	3
Hall	0-1	0-0	0	0	0	0
Casler	0-0	0-0	1	1	0	0
Hickman	2-3	4-4	6	1	4	8
Sekal	0-0	0-0	0	0	0	0
TOTALS	21-54	23-26	32	11	18	70

Halftime: Michigan State 37-30; **Three-point field goals:** 5 (Smith 2, Wolfe 2, Manns 1); **Officials:** McGrath, Markem, Shea; **Attendance:** 5,561.

SAINT LOUIS 74—MICHIGAN STATE 64

	FG-FGA	FT-FTA	REB	A	PF	TP
Redfield	9-16	3-6	14	2	4	21
Wolfe	4-8	0-0	3	4	3	9
Steigenga	1-6	3-4	5	1	3	5
Montgomery	0-4	0-0	1	1	2	0
Smith	1-13	0-1	3	3	4	2
Sekal	0-1	0-0	0	1	0	0
Manns	7-11	5-6	0	1	3	20
Hall	1-3	0-0	1	0	3	3
Casler	0-0	0-0	1	2	0	0
Hickman	1-1	0-0	0	0	0	2
Sarkine	0-0	0-0	0	1	0	0
Mueller	1-1	0-0	3	0	0	2
Team			5			
TOTALS	25-64	11-17	36		16	22
						64

Halftime: Saint Louis 34-23; **Three-point field goals:** 3 (Wolfe 1, Manns 1, Hall 1); **Officials:** Lopes, Barnett, Crowley; **Attendance:** 8,440.

ALA.-BIRMINGHAM 78—MSU 76 (OT)

	FG-FGA	FT-FTA	REB	A	PF	TP
Redfield	1-8	3-7	7	2	2	5
Wolfe	0-0	0-0	2	0	1	0
Steigenga	4-6	2-2	1	0	4	10
Montgomery	2-6	0-1	4	10	1	4
Smith	9-18	2-4	4	7	2	20
Hickman	1-3	2-2	7	1	2	4
Manns	11-12	2-3	3	1	4	29
Casler	1-1	0-0	0	0	1	2
Sekal	0-0	2-2	0	0	0	2
Team			7			
TOTALS	29-54	13-21	35	21	17	76

Halftime: Alabama-Birmingham 37-29;
Regulation: 68-68; **Three-point field goals:** 5
(Manns 5); **Officials:** Mingle, Corio, Donato;
Attendance: 12,511.

EXTRA! 1989 GATOR BOWL

January 1, 1989
Jacksonville, Florida

	1	2	3	4	F
MSU	0	7	6	14	27
Georgia	7	10	10	7	34

Starting line-up (offense)		*Starting line-up (defense)*	
Andre Rison	SE	Matt Vanderbeek	DE
Tony Mandarich (C)	LT	Jason Ridgeway	DT
Bob Kula	LG	Travis Davis	DT
Dave Martin	C	Chris Willertz	DE
Vince Tata	RG	Carlos Jenkins	OLB
Kevin Robbins	RT	Percy Snow	MLB
Rich Gicewicz	TE	Kurt Larson (C)	OLB
Bobby McAllister (C)	QB	Alan Haller	CB
Blake Ezor	LH	John Miller (C)	SS
Steve Montgomery	FB	Derrick Reed	FS
Willie Bouyer	FL	Ventson Donelson	CB

Fans in East Lansing were optimistic, as their beloved Spartans entered the Gator Bowl with a six-game winning streak. Despite a great show by Andre Rison, they were to be disappointed, as head coach Vince Dooley closed his 25-year career at Georgia with a 34-27 win over the Green and White. The Bulldogs earned a 17-0 lead before MSU got on the scoreboard. With just 2:55 left in the first half, Bobby McAllister drove the ball 80 yards on 10 plays and finished with a four-yard TD pass to Rison. Midway through the third quarter, Georgia scored again to increase its lead to 24-7. McAllister responded by finding Rison, this time for a 55-yard bomb to cap off an eight-play, 78-yard drive, but the Bulldogs were not finished as they made a 36-yard field goal near the end of the quarter. Early in the fourth, McAllister hit Rison once again with a 51-yard pass that set up Blake Ezor's three-yard TD run to bring team within striking distance at 27-20. Georgia gained its final touchdown with 11:58 remaining to set the score at 34-20. Attempting to stage a comeback, Rison scored on a 50-yard pass from McAllister late in the quarter but the opposition controlled the ball in the final minutes of the game and the Spartans' rally had fallen short. Rison finished with three touchdowns and a school single-game record of 252 receiving yards on nine catches. The two teams combined for 855 total yards in the offensive battle with the Spartans outgaining the Bulldogs, 446-409. McAllister hit 14-of-24 throws for 288 yards and three TDs while Ezor rushed 33 times for 146 yards.

EXTRA! 1989 NCAA HOCKEY TOURNAMENT (Third Place)

After defeating Ohio State, Bowling Green and Lake Superior State, the Spartans added a CCHA playoff championship to their regular season crown and earned a bye in the first round of the national tournament. The second round was a best-of-three series against Boston College. After the Eagles won the first game 3-6, State came back to win the second 7-2, and a Mark Hirth goal that won the third game 5-4 in overtime sent the Spartans to the NCAA Frozen Four. Harvard topped them 6-3 in the semi-finals, but MSU disposed of Maine 7-4 to win the consolation game.

March 24, 1989—East Lansing
Boston College 6, MSU 3

1st Pd.: BC, McInnis (Franzosa), 10:41; 2. BC, Scheifele (Franzosa, Buckley), 12:41; 3. MSU, Beadle (Reynolds, Murray), 19:55.
2nd Pd.: 4. BC, Kennedy (O'Neill, Sweeney), 1:11.
3rd Pd.: 5. BC, Emma (Muilowney), 6:42; 6. BC, Sweeney (Heinze, McInnis), 8:09; 7. MSU, Heaphy (Hamilton, Brind'Amour), 11:53; 8. BC, Kennedy (Braccia), 12:34; 9. MSU, Hamilton (Cole, Reynolds), 19:16.

March 25, 1989—East Lansing
MSU 7, Boston College 2

1st Pd.: 1. MSU, Cole (Reynolds), 17:59.
2nd Pd.: 2. BC, Marshall (Franzosa), 5:07; 3. MSU, Heaphy (White, Woolley), 7:22; 4. MSU, Hirth (Bartels, Beadle), 9:18; 5. MSU, Heaphy (White, Brind'Amour), 10:34; 6. BC, Heinze (McInnis), 10:49; 7. MSU, Murray (Luongo, Norris), 13:41.
3rd Pd.: 8. MSU, White (Luongo), 12:16; 9. MSU, Ki. Miller (Murray, Brind'Amour), 14:29.

March 26, 1989—East Lansing
MSU 5, Boston College 4 (OT)

1st Pd.: 1. BC, Emma (Heinze, Brown), 3:35 SHG; 2. MSU, Ki. Miller (Brind'Amour, Woolley), 5:22.
2nd Pd.: 3. BC, O'Neill (Brown, Mullowney), 0:34; 4. MSU, White (Brind'Amour), 1:49.
3rd Pd.: 5. MSU, Reynolds (Murray, Beadle), 1:42; 6. BC, Marshall (Emma, Heinze), 3:57; 7. BC, Cleary (Braccia, Buckley), 4:22; 8. MSU Brind'Amour (Heaphy), 5:23.
Overtime: 9. MSU, Hirth (Gibson, Russell), 5:57.

March 30, 1989—St. Paul, Minn.
Harvard 6, MSU 3.

1st Pd.: 1. HU, Ciavaglia (Weisbrod, Krayer), 3:58; 2. HU, Young (Donato, Ciavaglia), 6:54.
2nd Pd.: 3. HU, MacDonald (Ciavaglia, Donato), 10:24; 4. MSU, Cole (Woolley, Ki. Miller), 15:25; 5. HU, Donato (Vukonich), 16:01; 6. HU, Krayer (Hartje, Caplan), 16:24.
3rd Pd.: 7. HU, Krayer (Ciavaglia, Weisbrod), 5:10; 8. MSU, Heaphy (White, Hamilton), 6:37; 9. MSU, Cole (unasst.), 14:16.

April 1, 1989—St. Paul, Minn.
MSU 7, Maine 4

1st Pd.: 1. UM, Corkum (Vitale, Scremin), 2:08; 2. MSU, Heaphy (unasst.), 7:17, 3. MSU, Heaphy (Brind'Amour), 13;17.
2nd Pd.: 4. UM, Cambio (Barkley, Jenkins), 3:06; 5. UM, Pellerin (Burke, Guidotti), 4:16; 6. MSU, Beadle (Norris, Ki. Miller), 8:26; 7. MSU, Russell (Bartels), 11:10; 8. MSU, Cole (Cummins, Reynolds), 12:50; 9. MSU, Brind'Amour (Heaphy, Beadle), 13:07; 10. MSU, Heaphy (White, Brind'Amour), 19:49.
3rd Pd.: 11. UM, Thyer (Perron, Robitaille), 4:09.

MSU
1989-1990

TALES TO TELL

More than 15,000 fans jumped from their seats at Breslin and poured onto the floor as if attracted by a magnet. Hundreds of students swarmed from their dorm rooms onto the streets of East Lansing to celebrate after the final buzzer had sounded to end the game. Jud Heathcote's Spartans had "stolen" one from Purdue, 72-70, and with it captured the conference crown. It was bedlam reminiscent of the "magic" season of 1979, the last time MSU had won a Big Ten basketball championship. The Purdue Boilermakers had come to the new arena for the first time looking to defeat the home team and earn a title share, but instead they returned home disappointed after a game that had slipped away from them in the waning moments.

It opened with the partisan crowd jubilant. Ken Redfield had dunked off the opening tip and forward Matt Steigenga led an offensive attack that resulted in a quick 10-0 lead. Then, less than five minutes into the game, six-foot-10, 270-pound freshman Mike Peplowski went to the bench with two fouls. With Pep gone, Purdue staged a comeback on a 0-13 run to go up 33-25, a lead that was cut to 33-27 after two Steigenga free throws just before the break.

Spartan fans pour onto the floor as Steve Smith cuts down the net after defeating Purdue 72-70 to secure the Big Ten title.

HEADLINES of 1990

- Nelson Mandela is released from prison after 27 years of incarceration for leading a campaign against the South African government.
- The Hubble Space Telescope is launched.
- Prices of the time included: bread 70 cents/loaf, milk $2.78 a gallon and gasoline $1.34 a gallon. A new automobile could be purchased for $16,012 and the average annual income was $28,906.
- Sony creates the first portable compact disc player, the Discman.

SCOREBOARD

	W	L	T	Avg.
Baseball	26	24	0	.520
Track and Field	3	0	0	1.000
Football	8	4	0	.667
Basketball	28	6	0	.824
Tennis	12	13	0	.480
Cross Country	no dual meets			
Swimming and Diving	9	1	0	.900
Wrestling	6	7	2	.433
Hockey	35	7	3	.811
Fencing	13	5	0	.722
Golf	tournament play only			
Gymnastics	6	3	0	.667
Soccer	8	12	1	.405
Lacrosse	9	6	0	.600

In the second half Peplowski was back on the floor and guard Kirk Manns checked in for the first time since sustaining a stress fracture in his right foot six weeks earlier. Manns threw in seven points in ten minutes, including a 10-foot baseline jumper to bring the Spartans to within one, 70-69, with just 35-seconds remaining. Purdue had the lead and a throw-in from the sideline across from the State bench. During the Spartan timeout it was obvious Coach Heathcote had instructed his team to foul intentionally; but the tenacious defense proved more than effective. The Boilermakers tried three times to put the ball into play, calling a time out and having a pass deflected out of bounds before finally getting it into play. Once they did, Redfield knocked the ball loose for a moment and Dwayne Stephens stole it in a scramble. Stephens charged down the court looking to pass but found himself alone to lay-up what would prove to be the winning basket. A missed Boilermaker 21-footer and an insurance free throw from Steve Smith, who led all scorers with 22 points, sealed the victory. Redfield finished an incredible game with 16 points. The Spartans had won ten straight to tie a school record for the winningest year in history with a 26-5 record. In the meantime, they were left with an outright conference championship and a number-one berth in the southeast region of the NCAA tournament.

It was a game that Michigan State fans will long remember, as will Stephens. He's back on campus, having been hired on May 7, 2003, as a Tom Izzo assistant.

TEAM OF THE YEAR

Led by junior All-American and co-captain Steve Smith, the 1989-1990 basketball team brought the Big Ten championship trophy to East Lansing for the first time since 1979. This successful finish also earned them their first NCAA tournament berth since 1986. Unfortunately, after defeating Murray State and UC-Santa Barbara in the first two rounds, they were eliminated in the Sweet Sixteen during an 81-80 controversial overtime loss to Georgia Tech, despite Smith's game-high 32 points. The Yellowjackets scored the winning shot as time expired, but postgame replays proved that the ball was actually released after time had expired. On the year, Smith averaged 7.0 rebounds, 4.8 assists, and 20.2 points per game and finished fifth on the school's all-time single-season scoring list with 627 points. Kirk Manns also had much to contribute, scoring 15.3 points per game and shooting 86 percent from the line while becoming MSU's single-season three-point leader with 81. Manns and Smith were both named first team All-Big Ten. At the other end of the court, co-captain Ken Redfield was named Big Ten defensive player of the year, in addition to grabbing 6.8 rebounds and scoring 11.6 points per game.

MAKING HISTORY

The NCAA Football Rules Committee voted to reduce the width of goal-post uprights from 23' 4" to 18' 6", eliminate the use of tees for field goals and point-after-touchdown and allowed the defense to advance a fumble that happens in or beyond the neutral zone.

After more than 24 years of planning and three years of construction, the Jack Breslin Student Events Center was dedicated with proper ceremony and opened for public viewing on the evening of Nov. 9, 1989. The dedication basketball game, an exhibition against the Russian Soviet National Team, was played on November 21.

In a timely jester that may have saved the famed Spartan statue from irrevocable permanent damage, the

The 1989-90 basketball team. (First row, left to right): assistant coach Herb Williams, Jon Zulauf, Todd Wolfe, Kirk Manns, head coach Jud Heathcote, Mark Montgomery, Jeff Casler, Jesse Casler, manager Eric Spiller, assistant coach Tom Izzo. (Back row, left to right) trainer Tom Mackowiak, assistant coach Jim Boylen, Ken Redfield, Parish Hickman, Matt Hofkamp, Mike Peplowski, David Mueller, Matt Steigenga, Steve Smith, Dwayne Stephens, graduate assistant coach Tom Crean

Varsity Alumni "S" Club spearheaded a successful campaign which raised the needed $75,000 to engage a restoration specialist, Robert Pringle of New York City. A rededication ceremony was held on Sept. 16, 1989, prior to the football season opener against Miami (Ohio) University.

In a dual meet against Cortland State of New York, gymnast Steve Dackerman hit a 9.85 floor exercise score to break a team record of 9.8 made by Keith Pettit.

The 10-meter platform diving event was introduced into the NCAA swimming and diving championship meet.

In December of 1989 it was announced that an invitation had been extended to Pennsylvania State University to join the Big Ten athletic conference. Membership was confirmed in early June.

GREAT STATE DATES

Soccer—**September 11, 1989 (H):** During the pregame warm-ups, Coach Baum alerted his team that their opponent for the day, the University of Detroit, played a very physical game. His players were good listeners. The Spartans got the best of the Titans physically and on the scoreboard, 2-1. State was whistled for 21 fouls and the U of D 24 times. MSU scored first when Carl Hopfinger beat the goalie on a penalty kick with 18:50 remaining in the opening half. Chris Koppi padded that lead in the second half after gaining possession on a header from Chris Larson. Redshirt freshman goalie Mark West lost his bid for a shutout with 16:48 remaining in the game.

Soccer—**October 3, 1989 (H):** It was the inspired play of three first-year players that pushed Michigan State to a 2-1 victory over Michigan at Old College Field. Just five minutes into the game freshman forward Steve McCaul of Livonia booted a beautiful shot into the upper left corner for a 1-0 lead. It was in the 24th minute of play the Spartans put the Wolverines away as Trent Grens, a freshman midfielder from Palatine, Ill., headed in a corner kick to give MSU a 2-0 lead. Freshman goalie Pat Trese of Birmingham Brother Rice did the rest, as he was beaten only once by the Wolverines.

Football—**October 7, 1989 (A):** Iowa's coach, Hayden Frye, opted to pass up a near certain tie with a 27-yard field goal attempt and 35 seconds remaining; thus, the result was a wild 17-14 victory for Michigan State. Under extensive pressure from the defense, the Hawkeyes' fourth-down pass attempt for the win from the nine-yard line fell incomplete. Offensive stars for State

were running back Tico Duckett and quarterback Dan Enos. Duckett, in his first start as a Spartan while filling in for the injured Blake Ezor and Hyland Hickson, rushed for 175 yards in 30 carries and Enos hit on 20 of 25 throws for 217 yards, including two stretches of eight completions in a row. Duckett scored the first touchdown midway through the opening quarter as he topped a 60-yard five-play drive with a 35-yard sprint into the end zone. The next MSU drive stalled at the nine-yard line resulting in a John Langeloh 26-yard field goal. The winning score climaxed a 59-yard drive of 12 plays with 7:30 remaining in the third quarter. Fullback Rob Roy scored the TD as he plowed in from the one-yard line.

Football—**October 28, 1989 (A):** State led Purdue 28-0 with 5:54 remaining in the game and then, in a bizarre finish, the Boilermakers scored 21 unanswered points and even threatened to tie the game before time ran out. After the first half ended 0-0, quarterback Dan Enos received 12 stitches during intermission to close a wound on his chin and then came out to run for two touchdowns and throw for two more. Flanker Courtney Hawkins had a highlight afternoon with seven catches for 193 yards, including an 80-yard pass-run touchdown, the second of three Spartan TDs in the third quarter. The opening score had come one-possession earlier, as Enos led an eight-play sequence with a one-yard option-keeper into the end zone. He would also complete a 12-play, 84-yard drive by going in from the nine with 16 seconds left in the third period. The deciding TD featured three picturesque passes, a leaping 40-yard grab by Jim Bradley, a one-handed 35-yarder by Hawkins and a scoring five-yard payoff to Duckett in the right flat. The final score: MSU 28, Purdue 21.

Hockey—**December 9 (A) & 10 (H) 1989:** Featuring back-to-back hat tricks, first by Shawn Heaphy on Saturday and then Craig Shepherd on Sunday, MSU defeated Michigan 5-3 and 11-4. The first game, in Ann Arbor, was tied 3-3 in the third period when Heaphy directed a pass from defenseman Steve Beadle into the net, completing a three-on-one break. He wrapped up the game on his third goal with 2:22 remaining in the game. Pat Murray, Heaphy and Dwayne Norris had opened the scoring with individual goals in the first period. On the next day at Munn Ice Arena, State scored five straight goals over the first 24 minutes of play. The U of M responded with four straight goals during an eight-minute stretch of the second period to make it a

game and then the Spartans put it away with a six-goal outburst, two in the second and four in the third. Goalie Jason Muzzatti made a two-game total of 43 saves, 19 in the opening game and 24 in the second. The victories moved Michigan State into first place in the CCHA standings.

Basketball—**January 13, 1990 (H):** Leading 49-36 at halftime, State squandered a 13-point lead and then came back to top Iowa 87-80 and improve their overall mark at 14-2, the third best start in school history. With the score tied 70-70, the Spartans outscored the Hawks, 17-10 over the final 4:16 to secure the victory. Guard Kirk Manns led the way with 33 points, including six three-pointers in a school record 13 tries and .625 field-goal shooting. Overall, the team shot an impressive 12 of 22 from the arch. Forward Ken Redfield had 16 points, Matt Steigenga 12 and Steve Smith added 11 points, including a trio of three-pointers with the last one erasing the only second-half lead for the Hawkeyes.

Wrestling—**January 13, 1990 (H):** In an exciting meet that went to the final pairing, State upset 13th-ranked Notre Dame, 21-15. State opened by taking four of the first six matches. Soon Thackthay (118 pounds) won on a forfeit when his scheduled eighth-ranked opponent could not make weight. Pete Schulte (134 pounds) was a 7-1 winner and was followed by Greg Jackson (150 pounds) winning 6-3 and Roy Hall (158 pounds) in a 7-4 decision. With the team score favoring MSU 14-11, the next two matches were draws: Jamie Richardson (177 pounds) and co-captain senior Mark Zenas (190 pounds). With the score at 18-15 still favoring the Spartans, freshman heavyweight Don Whipp needed to win to maintain the lead. In an inspiring match, he completed his assignment by the narrowest of margins, 4-3.

Fencing—**January 20, 1990 (A):** With all respect to the two Motor City schools, only in fencing competition would it be exciting to revel in victories over the University of Detroit and Wayne State University. Both universities had long been considered topflight competitors in this historic sport. Not only did Fred Freihert's squad top the Titans, 14-13 and Tartars 20-7, but they also defeated U of M Dearborn 16-11, Oakland 18-9, Case-Western 18-9 and the University of Michigan 16-11 in a seven-team meet held in Ann Arbor. The foil team went 37-17 with captain Chris Karl 15-3, Jae Son 14-4 and Jason Katowich 8-10. The sabre team was 37-14, led by Timo Kurvi 13-4 and both Nelson Grimes and Mike Kim recording 12-5 won-loss totals.

Tennis—**January 20, 1990 (H):** The Spartans found little opposition in their second meet of the season as they downed the University of Cincinnati, 8-1 by winning all six singles matches and two of the three at doubles. Playing as number one in singles, sophomore Grant Asher was the only Spartan to drop a set in singles action as he won 5-7, 6-3, 6-4. Winning in straight sets in positions number two through number six were Brad Rosenbaum 6-1, 6-2; Damon Valentino 6-3, 6-1; Brad Dancer 6-2, 6-1; Tony Floreno 7-5, 6-3 and Wade Martin 6-2, 7-5. The victorious doubles pairs were number one Asher-Valentino 6-3, 6-4 and Rosenbaum-Dancer 7-6, 6-3.

Track and Field—**January 27, 1990 (H):** State won 10 of the 13 events, including a sweep in the 800-meters (Rick Gledhill, Sam Blumke and Chris Rugh), to defeat Ball State, 74-44. Junior distance runner Kerry Fly was a double-winner with a first in the mile run (4:11.79) and then taking the 3,000-meter run (8:23.91). Junior Corey Pryor outleaned both the Cardinals' top sprinter and teammate Fred Kyles to win the 55-meter (6.15). Freshman triple jumper Chauncey Williams leaped 46' 6" for a win and then placed second in the 55-meter hurdles. Other first-place Spartans were shotputter Mike Edwards (45' 2"), Daryl Stallworth, 400 meters (48.87); Marcel Richardson, long jump (22' 1") and both relays, Tony Nelson, Williams, Richardson, Stallworth with a 3:19.55 in the 1,600-meter event and Rugh, Dave Smith, Blumke, Gledhill with a 7:59.58 in the 3,200-meters.

Swimming and Diving—**February 9, 1990 (H):** For the first time in 33 years, the Michigan State swimmers and divers defeated the Indiana Hoosiers, 65-47. The Spartans reached the impressive point total displaying great team depth with six individual wins including three 1-2 finishes and five 2-3 finishes. Winning the opening event, the 400-yard medley relay and the closing event, the 400-yard freestyle relay were instrumental in the win. IU was leading 31-29 when the versatile Steve Leissner won the 200-yard butterfly (1:51.74). Greg Mahalik followed with a 46.47 to win the 100-yard freestyle and Anthony Higgins took the 200-yard backstroke (1:53.10) followed by teammate Tim Shanley. This built the MSU lead to a 50-37 advantage and Kevin Zielinski and Chris Brundage later cinched the victory with their 2-3 finish in the 200-yard breaststroke.

Hockey—**February 17, 1990 (A):** Michigan State secured its second consecutive CCHA title with a 5-2 win over the University of Michigan. Furthermore, the victory extended the Spartans' unbeaten streak to 26 games (23 wins and three ties). Jim Cummins opened the scoring at 3:06 of the opening period and Kerry Russell made it 2-0 10 minutes later. Junior right winger Shawn Heaphy scored his 24th goal of the season to break a 2-2 deadlock at 10:18 of the second period. Cummins knocked in his second goal in the third period and Walt Bartels closed out the scoring on an empty-netter with 18 seconds remaining. Kip Miller was credited with three assists to increase his nation-leading totals to 38 goals and 42 assists for a career-high 80 points. Goalie Jason Muzzatti was credited with 26 saves.

Gymnastics—**February 23, 1990 (H):** Led by Nick Westermeyer, MSU swept every event in downing Western Michigan, 275.90-247.80. Westermeyer captured three individual events: the rings (9.75), pommel horse (9.40) and parallel bars (9.35) as well as finishing first in the all-around with a 55.75 total. Bob Switzer was a surprise winner in floor exercise (9.55) and Paul Dackerman finished first in the vault (9.35). Featuring a strong dismount that impressed the panel of judges, Brad Marshall scored a 9.55 in winning the horizontal bar competition and finished second in the all-around competition with his score of 53.05. Dan Dellert, Terry Gillespie and Phil Ideson were contributors to the season-high winning total score.

Basketball—**March 1, 1990 (H):** With the team's leading scorer Kirk Manns still sidelined by a stress fracture of the right foot, Steve Smith stepped forward to contribute 36 points, including five-of-seven three-pointers plus nine rebounds, leading MSU to a 78-70 victory over the University of Michigan. The 14th-ranked Spartans displayed championship quality over the final 2:40 after their 14-point, 67-53 lead had been whittled down to three at 69-66. Free throws and a pair of Matt Steigenga field goals accounted for the nine-to-four scoring margin in the closing moments. Many of the 15,138 Breslin Center fans burst onto the court after Matt's two-handed dunk shot had closed out the scoring at the buzzer.

Basketball—**March 3, 1990 (A):** It took overtime, but Steve Smith swished a 19-footer from the left corner with 29 seconds left in the extra session to give him a game-high 39 points and the Spartans a 75-73 victory over the University of Minnesota. The Golden Gophers had ample time to tie the game but failed from 21 feet away. The win gave State a 13-3 Big Ten record and an

eventual showdown one week later with Purdue for the conference title. Smith hit 15 of 28 field goals, four of six three-pointers and all five free-throw attempts. MSU led at halftime 34-28 and 62-60 with three seconds of regulation remaining when the hosts tied it to force the extended five-minute period. The top supporting player was big Mike Peplowski, who had nine points and a game-high 11 rebounds.

Lacrosse—**March 28, 1990 (A):** With a relentless attack in their home-opener, Michigan State defeated the University of Michigan 20-8. Junior Marc Saracene led the scoring with four goals and one assist. Wayne Sansiviero chipped in with three goals and three assists, while Jon Lantzy also tallied three goals. Goalie Jeff Horowitz stopped 18 of 26 shots.

Baseball—**April 21 & 22 1990 (H):** Michigan State swept a four-game series against the Wisconsin Badgers 5-2, 6-2 on Saturday, and 11-8 and 10-2 on Sunday. In the opening doubleheader Badger hitters must have thought they were seeing double as the identical Hirschman twins, Steve (4-3) and Stu (4-0) pitched the wins. Brad Lamont was credited with a save in the opener and Mike Ericson used his blazing fastball to record a save in the second game. The Spartans used three hits, including a two-run single by Rich Juday, to score four of their five runs in the third inning of the first game. Jeff Vogel (3-2) and Derek Darkowski (4-2) were pitchers of record in the high-scoring Sunday victories. In the third inning of game one, catcher Craig Hendricks put MSU ahead in the third with a three-run home run. Rich Juday triggered the six-run fourth inning with yet another three-run blast. Hendricks continued his hitting prowess in game two, heading the 14-hit attack with a two-run homer in the fourth and a two-run double off the left-center field fence in the sixth.

Lacrosse—**May 12, 1990 (A):** Both Wayne Sansiviero and Fritz Killian scored four goals each as State closed out the 1980 season with a surprisingly easy 17-7 win over Ohio State. The Spartans opened the scoring 41 seconds into the match on a goal by Joel Edell and never looked back. It was 6-2 at the end of the opening period, 11-3 at the half and 15-3 after three periods. John Lantzy and Aaron Caruso added to the winning total with two goals each while MSU goalie Chris Barber, in his final collegiate game, made 15 saves.

ATHLETE OF THE YEAR

Even before he received the high honor as the first MSU recipient of the 1990 Hobey Baker Memorial Award and was named the 1990 CCHA player of the year, Kip Miller had proved himself to be one of MSU's all-time great hockey players. He was a member of a team that won three CCHA playoff championships and two CCHA regular season championships. After his freshman year he was drafted by the Quebec Nordiques and chosen as a member of the U.S. Junior National Team at the world championships. In 1988-1989 he tied with teammate Bobby Reynolds to lead the nation in scoring with 77 points, and he led the team in assists with 45. In the same year he was named first team All-CCHA and first team All-American. In his senior year, 1989-1990, Kip was once more a first team All-American and team scoring leader. Upon graduation, Kip Miller ranked third in school history for points with 261 and third for career goals with 116. He had twice scored the second most goals for a Spartan in a game with four, had five hat tricks, and twice tied for most goals scored in a period with three. After finishing his collegiate career he went on to play successfully in the NHL.

Kip Miller

IN THE SPARTLITE

Baseball: The 1990 Spartan baseball team was a family affair. The Juday brothers, sons of MSU two-sport star, Steve, were sophomore Rich, an outfielder, and freshman Bob, who played second base. Rich was the team leader in hits (70), home runs (12) and hitting average (.405). Brother Bob's hitting average was .290 and defensively handled 241 putouts and assists with only six errors for a .976 fielding average. The 1990 team included another pair of brothers, the freshmen Hirschman twins, Stu and Steve from Howell. They were two of the mainstays on the pitching staff with Stu going 5-0 for the season and Steve 4-5.

Basketball: Prior to the Big Ten season, State completed an 11-2 non-conference preseason. It began by defeating Auburn, Texas A&M and Kansas State to win the Great Alaska shootout and later won their own Oldsmobile Spartan Classic.

As in 1988-89, Steve Smith (20.2 ppg), Kirk Manns (15.3 ppg) and Ken Redfield (11.6) were the team's leading scorers over the season. The strength of this team was that a new supporting star seemed to step forward at each game. It could be Matt Steigenga, Mark Montgomery, Mike Peplowski or fellow freshman Dwayne Stephens.

In its fourth year as an offensive weapon, the three-point shot became an ally of the Big Ten champion Spartans. Connecting on 47 of 97 for a .490 average, Manns finished second in the league and Smith third with 28 of 59 for a .475 average. In only four conference games was MSU outshot from behind the arc. In fact, the opponents' overall field-goal accuracy was less than State's three-point shooting accuracy.

Depending on which post season poll was being watched: State was ranked seventh in *USA Today*, fifth by the UPI and fourth by Associated Press.

Jud Heathcote was selected as the Division I Kodak coach of the year by the National Association of Basketball Coaches.

Junior guard Steve Smith was chosen as a first-team All-American by *The Sporting News.*

Cross Country: After a one-year lapse, Coach Stintzi resurrected the MSU Invitational meet and his squad went against runners from Kansas, Ohio State and Michigan in the first competition of the fall. When the places were accounted for, the score read Kansas 28, Michigan State 57, Ohio State 64 and Michigan 96. Scoring for Michigan State were Kerry Fly, fourth place (24:53), Chad Findley 11th (25:24), Dave Wickens, 12th (25:29), Rick Gledhill 14th (25:35) and Jim Huff 15th (25:45).

Competing in the University of Wisconsin Classic against 11 teams, including the likes of Iowa State, Tennessee, Alabama, North Carolina State and Wyoming, State runners settled for a 10th-place finish.

At the conference championship run over the Yahara Hills Golf Course in Madison, Wis., State runners placed sixth, scoring ahead of Indiana, Michigan and Purdue. Individual placing were Fly 15th (25:09), Findley 25th (25:30), Wickens 30th (25:40), Huff 37th (26:03), Gledhill 44th (26:13) and David Couch 47th (26.25).

Fencing: MSU finished fifth out of eight teams at the Midwest Invitational held at Northwestern University. No MSU fencer made the top six finishers, an agreed-upon plateau to qualify for the NCAA tournament. Chris Karl finished seventh out of 22 in the foil competition. Senior Jae Son, a tournament qualifier in 1989, fell short with a 10th place finish in foil. Karl Neumaier, who tore ligaments in his leg and, unable to compete, was replaced by Jason Katowich, who finished 14th in foil.

Football: It was a record-setting year for running back Blake Ezor. In the Northwestern game, the Las Vegas, Nev., senior scored six touchdowns for a total of 36 points. Both marks remain atop the Big Ten Conference record book. Throughout the entire 1989 season, he would score a team-record 19 touchdowns. Completing his four-year career, Ezor would carry the ball over 100 yards from scrimmage in 16 games. That team mark was exceeded only by Lorenzo White's record of 23.

By scoring 76 points in the Northwestern game, the 1989 Spartans topped the team record of 75 set against Arizona in 1949.

Quarterback Dan Enos completed passes for more than 200 yards in six of the 11 games of 1989.

In the eight conference games of 1989, the stingy Spartan defense yielded a meager average of 86 yards rushing per contest, which averaged to 2.5 yards per carry.

For the third year in a row, a Spartan was selected as Big Ten Offensive Lineman of the Year. In 1987 and 1988 it had been Tony Mandarich and in 1989 Bob Kula was selected.

Kula, Travis Davis, Percy Snow, Harlon Barnett and Courtney Hawkins were all designated as first team All-Big Ten. Barnett, Kula and Snow gained further recognition as first team All-American picks.

Snow became the first college player to win both the Butkus Award and the Lombardi Award in the same season. He was also a candidate for the Heisman Trophy as he finished eighth on the balloting.

Golf: Ken Horvath's golfers shot a composite 1,182 at the 72-hole Spartan Invitational to finish fourth in the 16-team field. Senior Brent Kish, one stroke down after two rounds, shot a record-tying 66 over the final 18 holes to capture medallist honors with 71-70-74-66—281. Other Spartan scores were Ian Peakes, 75-73-79-73—300; Mike Anderson, 75-75-74-77—301; Brian Bach, 71-74-79-79—303 and Jon Hartman, 75-77-76-79—307.

At the Big Ten championships, the MSU golfers shot a composite 1,178 over the University of Minnesota course and finished in fifth place. Kish led the way for MSU with rounds of 79-70-71-75—295. Other Spartans and their scores were Anderson 73-72-76-75—296; Peakes, 74-75-73-74—296; Bach, 69-76-77-78—298 and Hartman, 78-72-77-74—301.

Gymnastics: Scoring 266 points, MSU placed fourth at the 12-team Windy City Invitational in Chicago, two places higher than in the preceding season. The Spartans were sparked by the performances of sophomore Nick Westermeyer along with freshmen Paul Dackerman. Westermeyer scored a 9.55 to win the horizontal bar event while Dackermann finished first in the vault with a score of 9.50.

In State's 289.50 to 272.15 dual-meet loss to the University of Michigan, the Spartans earned their share of individual honors. Westermeyer captured first in both the parallel bars and horizontal bar, Dackerman won the vault and Phil Ideson was tops on the still rings.

With a total team score of 270.05, State finished in a disappointing fifth place at the Big Ten meet in Iowa City, topping only Wisconsin and Michigan. Regardless, a bright spot came in the vault competition where Dackerman, the first-year star, registered two 9.60 scores to capture the title. Westermeyer finished eighth on the horizontal bar and 19th in the all-around and Ideson ended up 10th on the rings.

Hockey: The 1989-1990 team would win 20 road games, a Spartan team record.

Reaching one of his many coaching milestones with a 4-2 win over Ohio State on February 3, Ron Mason became only the second NCAA hockey coach to gain 600 career victories.

Upon defeating Michigan 5-2 on February 17, State won a fourth CCHA regular-season title in six years and then four weeks later parlayed the seventh Central Collegiate playoff championship in nine years by topping Lake Superior State, 4-3.

The 4-3 win at Lake Superior State on February 23 extended MSU's unbeaten string to 27 games (24-0-3).

Kip Miller led the team in goals made with 48 and total points with 101. The latter mark was four shy of Tom Ross's team record 105 set in the 1975-1976 season.

Pat Murray, the Dublin, Ontario, senior, was credited with 60 assists, an MSU record which still stands.

Setting a pair of infamous records in 1989-90 was Don Gibson. The senior defenseman from Hartney, Manitoba, was whistled for 71 penalties totaling 167 minutes.

Lacrosse: The 1990 team completed an impressive 9-6 season record, but a late-season 12-6 loss to Notre Dame cost them a berth in the NCAA tournament field. That slot was awarded to the Irish.

At the postseason team banquet, goalie Chris Barber was voted the team's MVP. Midfielder Fritz Kilian and Wayne Sansiviero were selected to captain the 1981 squad. Also receiving awards were sophomore defenseman John Pace, most improved player, and junior attacker Marc Saracene, rookie of the year.

Soccer: The 1989 roster included two freshmen from Okemos, bearing names familiar to the Michigan State soccer program. Steve Belloli, son of Tom Belloli, a member of the NCAA championship team of 1967, and Guy Busch, son of Guy Busch, Sr, the school's career scoring leader and co-captain of the 1967 team.

A rare bench-clearing incident took place in the second half of the 3-1 home win over DePaul. It started when Carl Hopfinger was wiped out from behind by a Blue Demon defender. Captain Chris Larson ran over to protect his teammate and was punched in the back of the head, leading to the melee. By the time matters were settled the referees had handed out five yellow cards to each team and a red card (ejection) to the DePaul player identified as the instigator.

Hopfinger, senior midfielder of Rochester, N.Y., who missed most of the 1987 and 1988 seasons with shoulder injuries, had his most productive game as a Spartan in the 2-0 win over Purdue. He drew an assist on Steve McCaul's goal with 33:47 remaining in the second half.

Less than two minutes later, his header bounced off a Boilermaker defender into the net.

The season-end statistics revealed McCaul as the individual scoring leader with eight goals and 17 points. Both Chris Koppi and Hopfinger were tied in second place with 14 points.

Swimming and Diving: In Richard Bader's first year as head coach, Michigan State's swimmers and divers amassed 395 points and ended up in fourth-place at the Big Ten championships in Ann Arbor. It was MSU's highest finish since 1977. By winning the 200-yard individual medley (IM) in a time of 1:48.97, Steve Leissner became the first Spartan Big Ten swimming champion in five years. He also finished runner-up in the 400-yard IM in an NCAA qualifying time of 3:51.84. Two teammates also qualified for individual events at the national meet: Anthony Higgins with a second-place finish in the 100-yard backstroke and Jon Cohen who finished fourth behind Leissner in the 400-yard IM. With two thirds and a fourth, all four relays also advanced to the NCAA meet and included, in addition to Leissner and Higgins, Kevin Zielinski, Mark Lisenby, Gregg Mihallik, Chris Sholl and Steve Shipps.

Tennis: In late January, MSU hosted the all-singles Spartan Invitational at the Indoor Facilities. The meet featured 64 players from all conference schools. Junior Damon Valentino was the only Spartan to survive the first round, 6-1, 6-1, but then bowed out in the championship bracket, 6-3, 6-3. Sophomore Grant Asher won three matches in the consolation bracket finally meeting defeat in the quarterfinals, 6-4, 6-3. Northwestern's Todd Martin, the East Lansing native, was the tournament winner.

Track and Field: In the Big Ten indoor championships at Bloomington, Ind., State could do no better than ninth with 24 points. The only Spartan to score in the top three was Rick Gledhill who was timed in 1:51.51 and finished second in the 800 meter.

Scoring 64 points, MSU beat out 15 other squads, including four other Big Ten teams, to place fourth at the Central Collegiate indoor championships held in Madison, Wis. State performed without three significant team members who were ailing. Sophomore Fred Kyles paced the Spartans by winning the 55-meter dash and placing second in the 200. Daryl Stallworth ran a 34.49 to finish second in the 300, while Ian Smith took third in the 3,000 with a time of 8:17.75, only three-tenths

from the school record. Kerry Fly finished fourth in the 3,000 and also fourth in the mile run with a personal-best 4:08.84. Anthony Hamm placed fourth in the 5,000 with a 14:26 and sophomore Bill Sheldon leaped to fourth in the high jump, just missing seven foot with 6' 11 3/4", his best ever. Anchored by an impressive 4:04 mile leg from sophomore Gledhill, the distance medley relay quartet was runner-up.

State managed only 40 points and ended-up tied with Iowa for ninth place in the outdoor conference championships at Champaign, Ill. Finishing fifth through eighth in their specialties were Corey Pryor, Ian Smith, Kerry Fly, Anthony Hamm, Chris Brown, Stalworth, Chauncy Williams, Roger Marks, Chuck Cullen and Sheldon.

Wrestling: Upon conclusion of the Big Ten championships, MSU had earned 42 points and an eighth-place team finish. Also, three MSU wrestlers had qualified for the NCAA tournament at College Park, Md. The three were: Brian Smith (126 pounds), who was runner-up in the conference meet; Mark Zenas (190 pounds), who placed fourth and freshman Roy Hall (158 pounds), who finished in fifth place. In addition, Jeff Mustari (142 pounds) also ended the competition in fifth place.

Smith, competing in his first National Collegiate Tournament, won his first two matches before being eliminated in the quarterfinals on an 8-7 decision. Hall won his preliminary match but was sidelined in the next round and Zenas was defeated in the opening round.

EXTRA! 1990 NCAA BASKETBALL TOURNAMENT

Michigan State reached the regional semifinals in the 1990 NCAA tournament. The following are the Spartans' box scores for those games.

MICHIGAN STATE 75—MURRAY STATE 71 (OT)

	FG-FGA	FT-FTA	REB	A	PF	TP
Redfield	5-11	1-2	11	1	3	11
Steigenga	0-2	2-2	3	1	3	2
Peplowski	1-3	0-0	6	1	3	2
Smith	10-16	0-0	11	4	2	22
Montgomery	2-5	0-1	4	9	0	5
Manns	9-18	0-0	3	1	1	21
Hickman	0-3	0-0	2	1	1	0
Stephens	6-9	0-0	5	2	4	12
Wolfe	0-0	0-0	0	0	0	0
TOTALS	**33-67**	**3-5**	**51**	**20**	**17**	**75**

Halftime: Michigan State 33-31; **Regulation:** 65-65; **Three-point field goals:** 6-19 (Redfield 0-1, Smith 2-5, Montgomery 1-2, Manns 3-11); **Officials:** Lembo, McDonald, Clark; **Attendance:** 11,287.

MICHIGAN STATE 62—UC-SANTA BARBARA 58

	FG-FGA	FT-FTA	REB	A	PF	TP
Redfield	2-5	3-8	7	2	1	7
Steigenga	3-4	2-2	4	2	3	8
Peplowski	3-6	2-4	11	0	3	8
Smith	6-15	9-10	6	4	2	21
Montgomery	1-4	0-1	3	2	3	2
Manns	1-5	1-1	2	0	1	3
Hickman	2-2	1-1	2	0	0	5
Stephens	2-3	4-5	3	1	1	8
TOTALS	20-44	22-32	41	11	14	62

Halftime: Michigan State 25-20; **Three-point field goals:** 0-5 (Smith 0-2, Montgomery 0-1, Manns 0-2); **Officials:** Lembo, Stupin, Corio; **Attendance:** 14,153.

GEORGIA TECH 81 (OT)—MICHIGAN STATE 80

	FG-FGA	FT-FTA	REB	A	PF	TP
Redfield	3-6	1-2	5	2	4	7
Steigenga	2-9	0-0	4	3	4	4
Peplowski	4-5	1-1	4	1	1	9
Smith	13-22	3-4	5	6	0	32
Montgomery	2-5	0-0	1	2	5	5
Manns	0-3	0-0	1	0	1	0
Hickman	6-9	1-1	10	0	2	13
Stephens	3-6	4-4	5	2	0	10
TOTALS	33-65	10-12	39	16	17	80

Halftime: Georgia Tech 39-35; **Regulation:** 75-75; **Three-point field goals:** 4-8 (Smith 3-5, Montgomery 1-1, Manns 0-1, Redfield 0-1); **Officials:** Clougherty, Tanco, Range; **Attendance:** 18,172.

EXTRA! 1989 ALOHA BOWL

December 25, 1989
Honolulu, Hawaii

	1	2	3	4	F
MSU	6	13	0	14	33
Hawaii	0	0	6	7	13

Starting line-up (offense)		Starting line-up (defense)	
James Bradley	SE	Matt Vanderbeek	DE
Bob Kula (C)	LT	Tim Ridinger	DT
Eric Moten	LG	Travis Davis	DT
Jeff Pearson	C	Chris Willertz	DE
Mark Keller	RG	Carlos Jenkins	OLB
Jim Johnson	RT	Percy Snow	MLB
Duane Young	TE	Dixon Edwards	OLB
Dan Enos	QB	Alan Haller	CB
Blake Ezor	LH	Harlon Barnett (C)	SS
SteveMontgomery(C)	FB	Mike Iaquaniella	FS
Courtney Hawkins	FL	Ventson Donelson	CB

Kirk Manns finished second in the league with a .490 average in three-point shots.

Blake Ezor was the top ball carrier for the Spartans, rushing for 179 yards and three touchdowns to lead No. 22 Michigan State to a 33-13 triumph over No. 25 Hawaii. Mistakes proved to be crucial, as MSU scored its first 26 points off Rainbow Warrior turnovers. By halftime the Spartans held a comfortable 19-0 lead off TD runs of three and two yards by Ezor and field goals of 30 and 34 yards by John Langeloh. By that point, State had forced six turnovers and outgained Hawaii in total yards, 205-102. After the second-half kickoff, the Warriors orchestrated their first scoring drive but missed the extra-point-conversion to make the score 19-6. Midway through the fourth quarter Mike Iaquaniello picked-off his second interception to set up Hyland Hickson's one-yard dive which increased the difference to 26-6. On the next possession, Hawaii found the end zone for their final seven points, but the Spartans were still not finished. Ezor earned his final TD and the last points of the game on a 26-yard run around the right end with 5:36 to go. In the second half alone, Ezor carried the ball 18 times for 101 yards. At the final buzzer State had outgained the Rainbow Warriors in total yards 341-280.

EXTRA! 1990 NCAA HOCKEY TOURNAMENT (Quarterfinals)

MSU won its second straight CCHA title with victories over Ferris State, Michigan, and Lake Superior State in the playoffs. This earned them a place in the NCAA tournament for the ninth straight year. As conference champions they were given a bye in the first round, and they hosted Boston University in a best-of-three quarterfinal at Munn Arena. After an exchange of games, the Spartans held a 3-1 advantage halfway through the second period, but the Terriers scored the last four goals to win the game 5-3 and advance to the Frozen Four.

March 23, 1990—East Lansing
MSU 6, Boston University 3

1st Pd.: 1. BU, McEachern (Sacco, Krys), 5:09; 2. MSU, Heaphy (Smolinski, Norris), 9:03; 3. BU, Tomlinson (Koskimaki), 10:51; 4. MSU, Murray (Beadle, Ki. Miller), 11:46.
2nd Pd.: 5. MSU, Murray (Ki. Miller), 10:04; 6. MSU, Cummins (Ki. Miller, Murray), 13:31; 7. MSU, Ki. Miller (Cummins, Murray), 14:18.
3rd Pd.: 8. MSU, Ki. Miller (Murray, McCauley), 3:58; 9. BU, Amonte (McEachern), 12:00.

March 24, 1990—East Lansing
Boston University 5, MSU 3

1st Pd.: 1. MSU, Smolinski (White), 1:02.
2nd Pd.: 2. BU, von Stefenelli (Legault, Amonte), 0:23; 3. BU, Ronan (Legault, von Stefenelli), 11:46; 4. MSU, Heaphy (Woolley, Muzzatti), 14:00; 5. BU, McEachern (Amonte), 19:30.
3rd Pd.: 6. BU, Sullivan (McEachern, Amonte), 2:03; 7. MSU, Beadle (Murray, White), 10:54; 8. BU, Amonte (Legault, McEachern), 15:38.

March 25, 1990—East Lansing
Boston University 5, MSU 3

1st Pd.: 1. BU, Mark Bavis (Ahola, Mi. Bavis), 11:14; 2. MSU, Beadle (Murray, Ki. Miller), 19:17 PPG.
2nd Pd.: 3. MSU, Woolley (Ki. Miller, Russell), 2:58 PPG; 4. MSU, Murray (Woolley, Ki. Miller), 7:28; 5. BU, Koskimaki (Ronan), 11:33.
3rd Pd.: 6. BU, Ronan (Sacco, Ahola), 5:36; 7. BU, Amonte (Cashman), 7:02 PPG; 8. BU, Regan (Sullivan, von Stefenelli), 18:03.

TALES TO TELL

Joining the Michigan State staff in 1959 as an assistant basketball coach under Forddy Anderson, Bruce Fossum remained in that capacity until he became head golf coach in 1966, a position he held until retiring from coaching in 1989. In celebration of 25 years since that head coaching assignment, the former coach was asked to select an All-Fossum golf team from the list of over 100 golfers who lettered during his tenure. After much deliberation he completed the task of selecting the top six Spartan golfers. In submitting his slate, he acknowledged that the task was a tough job:

"...Because there are so many good players that I have had the pleasure to work with. I have chosen six players who all have the characteristics that I looked for when I recruited them (in addition to golfing talent), mental toughness, solid work ethics, highly competitive, gentlemen and loyalty to Michigan State University."

Bruce further noted there were other All-Americans who could have qualified: Steve Benson, Richard Bradow,

Graham Cooke, Brad Hyland and Rick Woulfe. as head coach. The six-man team (with Fossum commentary) includes:

• *Lynn Janson* (1968-1970): Three times an All-American, captain of the 1970 team, the best player that Michigan State has ever had, based on the records.
• *Larry Murphy* (1968-1969): Captain of the 1969 Big Ten champion team, scratched and clawed for a good score at all times, fierce competitor.
• *John VanderMeiden* (1970-1972): Had an unorthodox style, he competed extremely hard and was a winner, an All-American.
• *Jon Koiser* (1984-1987): Worked harder than any player to build his game to a higher level, captain in 1986 and 1987.
• *Gary Domagalski* (1974-1977): One of the best shot-makers to ever play for MSU, was the captain in 1976 and 1977.
• *Richard Grover* (1977-1980): Small in stature, big in heart and game, fierce competitor, co-captain of 1980 team.

HEADLINES of 1991

• Operation Desert Shield turns into Desert Storm as in four days the Allied forces defeat Saddam Hussein's Iraqi troops and liberate Kuwait.
• Magic Johnson announces his retirement from NBA because he has tested positive for the HIV virus.
• The U.S. Senate approved the nomination of Clarence Thomas to the Supreme Court after investigating an allegation of sexual harassment that had been leveled against him.
• Boris Yeltsin is inaugurated as the first freely elected president of the Russian Republic.

SCOREBOARD

	W	L	T	Avg.
Baseball	28	25	1	.528
Track and Field	0	1	0	.000
Football	8	3	1	.708
Basketball	19	11	0	.633
Tennis	12	14	0	.462
Cross Country	no dual meets			
Swimming and Diving	9	2	0	.818
Wrestling	6	8	0	.429
Hockey	17	18	5	.488
Fencing	11	12	0	.478
Golf	tournament play only			
Gymnastics	9	3	0	.750
Soccer	9	6	5	.575
Lacrosse	11	5	0	.688

The author has taken the privilege of adding one more member to the All-Fossum team:

• *Bobby Fossum* (1982-1985): Co-captain in 1985, a natural athlete who could have excelled in many sports, and, in fact, also lettered as a Spartan basketball player.

TEAM OF THE YEAR

The 1990 football squad, off to a slow start, won the final five games on the schedule to finish with a 6-2 conference record and end up tied with Iowa, Michigan, and Illinois for the title. Iowa received the Rose Bowl bid, Michigan went to the Gator Bowl, and Illinois was sent to the Hall of Fame Bowl. MSU's destination was the John Hancock Sun Bowl in El Paso, Texas. There, they defeated Southern California 17-16 to finish their season ranked 15th in the *USA Today*/ESPN polls. The keys to the Spartan offense were sophomore Tico Duckett and junior Hyland Hickson. Duckett led the team with 1,394 yards and 11 touchdowns off 257 attempts, while Hickson was not far behind, rushing 234 times for 1,196 yards and 14 touchdowns. Quarterback Dan Enos controlled the passing game, connecting on 137 passes for 1,677 yards and three TDs. On the defensive squad, Chuck Bullough led the way, finishing second on the school's all-time single-season records for tackles with 164, including 86 unassisted.

The 1990 football team featured an offensive starting line-up of M. MacFarland (no. 17), S. Hannah (no. 63), T. Heaton (no. 67), C. Piwowarczyk (no. 56), R. Wagner (no. 50), J. Johnson (no. 69), M. Lyons (no. 85), J. Miller (no. 16), T. Duckett (no. 35), B. Abrams (no. 49), C. Hawkins (no. 5) and J. Delverne (no. 7) and a defensive starting line-up of J. MacNeill (no. 84), A. Jackson (no. 75), B. Reese (no. 74), E. White (no. 94), R. Fredrickson (no. 83), C. Bullough (no 41), M. Christensen (no. 45), B. Winters (no. 18), A. Haller (no. 23), M. Bell (no. 24), S. Callender (no. 32) and J. Butland (no. 88).

MAKING HISTORY

At the 1991 NCAA Convention held in Memphis, Tenn., three significant changes were legislated: (1) athletic dormitories were abolished; (2) football coaching staffs were reduced by one and the number who could recruit on the road was reduced from 10 to seven. Also, (3) schools would be permitted to sign no more than 25 student-athletes to football tenders in a given year. Furthermore, there could be no more than 95 on the football roster at any one time. That number would be further cut to 92 by 1992-1993, to 88 during the following year and to 85 by the fall of 1994.

In a football rule interpretation, a pass immediately thrown to the ground to conserve time was accepted as legal.

The Big Ten office tussled with the issue of basketball scheduling. The game schedules were devised within the parameters dictated by three television contracts, which had to be honored: ESPN, ABC and Raycom. As a result, each conference team had junctures in their schedule which gave them either long layoffs or playing as many as four games in a span of eight days. As usual, when in discord, Coach Heathcote could be pretty blunt:

> "Whoever has devised the second half of the Big Ten schedules is either the town drunk or the village idiot, because there is no rhyme or reason to all of this."

The 1991 National Archery Association U.S. indoor and northern regional championships were held in Jenison Fieldhouse on March 2-3.

GREAT STATE DATES

Soccer—September 21, 1990 (H): Playing on a rain-soaked Old College Field, MSU edged Notre Dame for the first time since 1986 by a score of 1-0. This was the fifth straight win of the season and kept the Spartans undefeated at 5-0-1. The solitary goal of the game was credited to midfielder Carl Hopfinger on a first-half penalty kick. That winning marker was set-up after Doug Consigny's header was illegally hand-slapped at the goalmouth by an ND defender. Returning to the field in the second half, the Irish maintained offensive pressure for more than 10 minutes. State eventually regained the ini-

tiative and preserved the shutout. Frustrated by his team's inability to score, the Notre Dame coach, as well as his assistant, were ejected for unsportsmanlike behavior.

Soccer—October 3, 1990 (H): The Michigan Wolverines scored early in the opening period on a disputed goal. They then hung on until Dan Kennedy booted in the equalizer with 25:21 remaining in the contest. The senior defender wasn't through, as shortly thereafter he drove home the game-winner on a pass from senior midfielder Carl Hopfinger. It was an annoying afternoon for Joe Baum's squad as time after time they missed seemingly "golden" opportunities to score.

Hockey—October 12-13, 1990 (A): The hockey team opened the season successfully with a two-game sweep of Illinois-Chicago, 8-3, 9-1. Fifteen different Spartans were included on the scoring sheet for the weekend. The leaders were Rob Woodward and Shawn Heaphy. Woodward, a freshman from nearby Deerfield, Ill., contributed four assists on Friday and chipped in a goal and another assist on the next evening. Heaphy was busy on Saturday as he scored three goals and added a pair of assists. MSU struck early on Friday as Jim Cummins and Dwayne Norris opened with back-to-back goals at 2:24 and 3:04 of the opening period. The game was actually tied at 3-3 early in the second stanza before the State offense erupted with five unanswered goals. Game number two was put away even earlier and more securely as Heaphy opened the scoring 34 seconds in, followed by scores from Peter White, Jason Woolley and Michael Stewart before the first intermission.

Football—October 13, 1990 (A): In one of the biggest games in MSU history, George Perles's team prevailed in a controversial win over number one-ranked Michigan 28-27. Wolverine fans will forever claim that Spartan Eddie Brown interfered on a two-point conversion attempt in the closing moments of the game, but officials made no such call and the record books will always show a Michigan State victory. The U of M scored first, but State tied the score with an eight-yard run by quarterback Dan Enos. To close that opening quarter the Wolverines drove to the three-yard line, but the stubborn MSU defense held for four downs. Fifteen minutes later the U of M missed a 28-yard field goal; thus, the half ended 7-7. In the third quarter, Michigan took the lead on a one-yard run; however, Enos countered by leading his team on a 15-play, 80-yard TD drive with Hyland Hickson scoring on a four-yard pass. The next "S" touch-

down, a 26-yard run by Hickson, was setup by Michael Iaquaniello's interception at the Wolves' 31-yard line. The small band of Spartan loyalists had little time to gloat as the ensuing kickoff was returned 95 yards to even the score at 21-21. State responded once more, on a 70-yard drive as Tico Duckett raced into the end zone from the nine-yard line. What would eventually prove to be the difference was John Langeloh's fourth successful point after touchdown. The U of M was not through yet. Displaying great clock management, they went the distance, scoring on an eight-yard pass play with six seconds remaining on the game clock. Trailing, 28-27, a decision from the coaching staff was to go for two points and the win. The effort was a quick slant-in pass to a flanker on the left side, the play in which Brown was accused of interfering. The potential receiver managed to get his hands on the ball, but it popped out as he came down and the officials ruled it incomplete. Thousands of Spartan faithful streamed onto the field, but they had to be ushered back into the stands, for time had not yet expired. Then, another heart-stopper...Michigan successfully gained possession with an on-side kick. A "hail Mary" pass was picked off by that same Mr. Brown at the two-yard line and State had won the game.

Football—**October 27, 1990 (H):** Led by Tico Duckett with 34 carries for 210 yards and four touchdowns along with Hyland Hickson's 103 yards and two touchdowns on 16 tries, State amassed 27 first half points and 28 points in the second half en route to a 55-33 defeat of Purdue. With the score 41-10 after three quarters, the Boilermakers were never really a threat. It wasn't until the final period, when it was too late, that they scored three touchdowns, one on a turnover at the State one-yard line and two on desperation passes. Some statistics, all favoring MSU, help tell the story: rushing yards, 423-6, firsts downs by rushing, 23-0 and total first downs, 34-18. In addition, the Boilers committed four turnovers, two leading to MSU scores. Starring for the defense were Cliff Confer. Bobby Wilson, Chuck Bullough, John Dignan and Carlos Jenkins.

Football—**November 24, 1990 (H):** With the 14-9 victory over the University of Wisconsin, MSU could boast of an 8-3-1 season record, a Big Ten co-championship and a December 31 date with Southern California in the John Hancock Bowl at El Paso, Texas. Both Michigan State touchdowns came in the opening quarter, giving the lean crowd of 60,517 a false expectation that another high-scoring day would unfold. Not only did it *not*

happen, but the result of the game was in doubt until the end when a Badger pass fell incomplete on fourth down at the Wisconsin 24-yard line with 1:07 remaining. Regardless, the running duo of Hyland Hickson, the senior from Ft. Lauderdale, Fla., and Tico Duckett, the sophomore from Kalamazoo, shared a productive afternoon. As a result they became only the third backfield pair in Big Ten history to both rush for more than 1,000 yards in a season. Hickson gained 134 yards in 22 attempts, giving him 1,128 for the year and Duckett finished with 82 yards in 19 carries, giving him 1,376. Hickson contributed both touchdowns. The first one followed a Carlos Jenkins pass interception, and the second one capped a 73-yard drive.

Basketball—**January 3, 1991 (H):** The 25th-ranked Spartans opened the conference portion of the schedule with a convincing 85-70 defeat of Michigan before a capacity crowd of 15,138 in the Breslin Student Event Center. All-American guard Steve Smith led the way with 24 points and seven rebounds followed by 20 points from Matt Steigenga; 10 points and nine rebounds from Dwayne Stevens; eight points and seven rebounds from center Mike Peplowski and 10 points off the bench from freshman Andy Penick. With six seconds gone, Steigenga opened the scoring on a crowd-pleasing flying put-back slam and State never looked back. It was 43-33 at halftime and 70-47 midway through the second half before the Wolverines made the score look respectable in the closing minutes. The shooting percentages told the story with MSU firing at a .540 clip and the U of M at .380.

Hockey—**January 4 & 5, 1991 (H):** Recording 43 saves on the weekend (21 in game one and 22 in game two), goalie Mike Gilmore was the star of the two wins over Ohio State, 5-0 and 3-1. The Farmington Hills junior came within four seconds of a weekend double shutout as the lone Buckeyes score came at 19:56 of the final period on Saturday. The Friday night scoring parade included goals by Dwayne Norris, Joby Messier, freshman Bart Turner and a pair from Kerry Russell. Shawn Heaphy opened the second-game scoring with an assist from Messier. Jason Woolley made it 2-0 at 15:00 of the second period extending his point-scoring streak to 17 games and Heaphy put the game out of reach at 15:29 of the third period when he fired a long slapshot into the net.

Swimming and Diving—**January 11 & 12, 1991 (A):** On the road for the weekend, the Spartans first defeated Illinois 139.5–97.5 and then easily handled Purdue

on the next afternoon by a score of 146-97. The busy Alex Mull was a double-winner both days, taking the 100-yard (47.39) and 1,000-yard (9:32.92) freestyle events on Friday and then the 200-yard (1:41.04) and 500-yard (4:37.43) freestyle events on Saturday. Steve Leissner won both the 400-yard individual medley (3:59.28) and the 500-yard (4:39.92) freestyle against the Illini and the 200-yard butterfly (1:52.46) in the Boilermaker meet. Kevin Zielinski was a two-time winner in the breaststroke, swimming a 2:05.79 on the second attempt. Other winners in Champaign were Mark Lisenby with a 21.39 in the 50-yard freestyle and Scott Carl with a 1:51.47 in the butterfly. In West Lafayette, Gregg Mihallik won the 100-yard freestyle (45.87) and Jon Cohen the 1,000-yard freestyle (9:29.66).

Track and Field—**January 12, 1991 (H):** Michigan State hosted an invitational meet in Jenison Fieldhouse and the team point-distribution was as follows: MSU 53, Toledo 48, Central Michigan 28 and Lansing Community College 11. Four Spartan winners were Todd Koning in the 800-meter run (1:58.4); Anthony Hamm, 3,000-meter run (8:20.7), Marcel Richardson, long jump (24' 3") and Chauncey Williams in the triple jump (47' 1"). The meet exhibited the MSU depth with numerous team members placing second and third in their specialty: Jim Huff second in the mile; Richardson second in the 55-meter dash; Mike Edwards, third in the shot put; Roger Marks third in the high jump; Rick Gledhill, second in the 800-meter run; Tony Nelson, third in the 400-meter run; Tim Topolinski, third in the 3,00-meter run and second in the 3,200-meter relay.

Fencing—**January 12, 1991 (A):** With identical winning scores of 17-10, Fred Freiheit fencers defeated Purdue, Miami (Ohio) and Michigan at the Ohio State Invitational in Columbus. The epee and sabre squads were 3-0 while the foil squad was only able to defeat the University of Michigan. Top individuals for MSU were Timo Kurvu and Nelson Grimes, both in sabre and Gary Cooper in epee.

Wrestling—**January 16, 1991 (A):** On the heels of the 22-14 victory over Notre Dame two days earlier, the wrestlers chalked up their second "W" of the week, defeating the University of Illinois, 20-16. Soon Thackthay (118 pounds), the senior co-captain, opened with an easy 12-4 decision. After losses by Demond Betts (126 pounds) and Casey Krause (134 pounds), the next four Spartans turned the meet in MSU's favor: Mike Krause (142 pounds), freshman Dan Wirnsberger (150 pounds), co-

captain Roy Hill (158 pounds) and Brian Woods at 167 pounds. Emilio Collins (177 pounds) settled for a 1-1 tie, but those two team points would serve to ensure Michigan State's third in a row over the Illini. Although Jim Richardson's 4-2 loss at 190 pounds was somewhat unexpected, Don Whipp's 13-0 loss was not. He was up against the defending and eventual two-time conference champion.

Tennis—**January 19, 1991 (H):** Taking four singles and all three doubles matches, the Spartans totally dominated the Cincinnati Bearcats in a dual meet, 7-2. Winning in straight sets were Grant Asher at number one, 6-4, 6-1, Brad Rosenbaum at number two, 6-4, 6-2, number three Brad Dancer, 6-4, 6-2 and number five Kevin Seckel, 6-2, 6-2. The doubles teams and their scores were: number one Asher-Wade Martin, 6-2, 6-1; number two Dancer-James Westfall, 6-4, 6-2 and number three Rosenbaum-Gus Giltner, 6-1. 6-2.

Tennis—**February 1, 1991 (H):** The Spartans surrendered only one loss, at the number five singles position, in defeating Bowling Green, 8-1. Grant Asher, a winner at number one singles, 7-5, 6-0 was followed by number two Brad Dancer, 6-4, 1-6, 6-3; number three Kevin Seckel, 6-4, 6-1; number four Dan Rosenbaum 6-2, 6-2 and number six Jim Westfall, 6-4, 6-7, 6-4. In the final year in which each doubles match would count for a single team point, all three pairs were winners: Seckel-Wade Martin, 6-3, 6-4; Dancer-Westfall, 6-2, 6-3 and Rosenbaum-Chris Trumball, 6-2, 6-7, 6-2.

Gymnastics—**February 2, 1991 (H):** Nipping a school record for total points scored in a dual meet by .35, State defeated Michigan 279.25-270.00. Sophomore Paul Dackerman had a busy afternoon, winning the vault with a 9.60; placing second on floor exercise with a 9.65; scoring a 9.40 to share third place on the rings with teammate Phil Ideson scoring a 9.20 to share third place on the parallel bars with Chris Spinosa. Chris Miller took top honors on the parallel bars with a 9.3, Dave Adams won the high bar with a 9.65, Nick Westermeyer finished first on the pommel horse with a 9.80 and Spinosa was the winner on floor exercise with a 9.75. Scoring a 54.95, freshman Heath Trial won the all-around event.

Wrestling—**February 8, 1991 (H):** Pushing the all-time record against Central Michigan to 4-1, State battled to a closely fought 22-17 victory in the IM West Arena. The difference in the scoring came at both ends of the line-up when Soon Thackthay (118 pounds) and heavyweight Don Whipp were each awarded forfeits. The only

legitimate Spartan wins came from Demond Betts (126 pounds) at 6-5 and 190-pound Jim Richardson in a closely fought 2-1 decision. Back-to-back draws by Tom Neu (158 pounds) and Brian Woods (167 pounds) completed the scoring.

Hockey—**February 16, 1991 (N):** Playing before a CCHA record-crowd of 15,684 at Joe Louis Arena in Detroit, Michigan State defeated the University of Michigan, 6-2. Defenseman Jason Woolley was a key to the win with two power-play goals and three assists. A bench-clearing brawl at the end of the first period sent five Spartans and six Wolverines to early showers. Once the 30-minute melee was cleared up, Jim Cummins, Bryan Smolinski, Kelly Harper, Joby Messier and even goalie Jason Muzzatti were through for the evening. Woolley opened the second period with two crucial goals and suddenly it was 3-0. Michigan never recovered. Shawn Heaphy, freshman Steve Norton and Bill Shalawylo concluded the scoring while replacement goalie Mike Gilmore made 32 saves, including several brilliant stops.

Swimming and Diving—**February 16, 1991 (A):** State captured all but two events in soundly defeating Northwestern, 135-86. Steve Leissner was the only double-winner, first taking the 1,000-yard freestyle (9:19.18) and then the 100-yard freestyle (46.49). Other freestyle winners were Tim Shanley in the 200 (1:42.52) and Alec Mull in the 500 (4:31.52). Freshman Ron Orris won the 200-yard individual medley (1:56.56); Anthony Higgins, the 200-yard backstroke (1:54.57); Jon Moore, the 200-yard breaststroke (2:09.04) and Matt Greimel the one-meter diving (181.80). The foursome of Tim Shanley, Chris Brundage, Alec Mull and Gerg Mihallik won the 200-yard medley relay (1:33.60) while Mark Lisenby, Mull, Orris and Mihallik closed the afternoon by taking the 200-yard freestyle relay (1:23.46).

Gymnastics—**February 22, 1991 (H):** MSU gymnasts closed out the home season on a winning note as they defeated both Wisconsin 277.35-276.00 and Western Michigan 277-35-263.80. Nick Westermeyer was a standout, winning the high bar with a 9.75 and taking first in the all-around (55.55). He also placed second on the still rings with a 9.45 and tied for second with teammate Heath Trial on the pommel horse (9.20). Scoring a 9.65, junior Phil Ideson shared first place on the rings with a Badger while Paul Dackerman tied for first on the vault (9.50), placed second on floor exercise (9.70) and tied for third on the parallel bars (9.30).

Basketball—**February 25, 1991 (A):** Led by six-foot-seven senior Steve Smith, who scored 27 points, State edged Minnesota 74-72 before 15,408 at Williams Arena in Minneapolis. MSU led 62-43 with 8:06 remaining in the game and just before Smith broke Scott Skiles's career total of 2,145 points with a pair of free throws. At that point Jud Heathcote attempted to play a ball-control game, but it backfired. After a 24-7 surge, the Gophers missed a chance to tie the game on a three-pointer with 16 seconds remaining. The Spartans concluded the game by connecting on four of six free throws. State outshot Minnesota .500-.444 for the night and .556-.395 after the intermission.

Basketball—**March 9, 1991 (A):** One of the University of Michigan players said, "While we were putting the pressure on Steve Smith, we left Montgomery wide-open for a lot of shots. He made us pay." Indeed, although Smith led all scorers with 24 points, "Monty" hit a career-high 17 points, including a perfect six-for-six from the field, with one being a three-pointer. Meanwhile, Smith, although defensively double-teamed and sometime triple-teamed, hit 10 of 21 shots from the floor, consistent with his season-wide 474 shooting average. Michigan actually led early as State committed eight turnovers in the first 10 minutes. Once the errors were controlled, the Spartans jumped to a 25-21 advantage at halftime from which they built a 41-29 lead over the first seven minutes of the second half. The Wolverines would not submit easily. With a 19-8 run, suddenly the game was tied at 48-48. MSU countered as Mike Peplowski hit a pair of free throws and Smith took charge, scoring 10 consecutive points. Thereafter, the U of M came no closer than four points and the final score read Michigan State 66, Michigan 59.

Lacrosse—**March 9, 1991 (H):** Amidst flurries of snow, Rich Kimball's squad scored a flurry of goals as the Spartans dominated the University of Michigan, 19-4, in a game played at Spartan Stadium. Led by three markers from senior attacker and team co-captain Wayne Sansiviero and one each from Chris Heide, Andy Hilgartner, Rob Dameron, Chris Stutler and Mark Saracene, State led 8-0 after the opening quarter. Sansiviero scored two more times in the second period along with single scores by Jon Lantzy, Rama Malone, Fritz Kilian and the halftime with MSU leading 13-1. By the second half, reserves had taken the field, but the scoring blitz continued. Along with Dameron's second goal

of the game, five others joined in: Rich Schraff, Mark Shamam, Steve Daray, Matt Hermes and Mike Ferguson.

Baseball—**May 4, 1991 (H):** In an exciting afternoon at Kobs Field, Michigan State swept a Saturday doubleheader from the league-leading Buckeyes of OSU, 3-2 and 4-3, as catcher Craig Mayes delivered the game-winning RBI in both contests. In the opener, State managed the victory with only three hits, but two were home runs. Eric Sumpter's round-tripper tied the game at 1-1 and then later, trailing 2-1, Mayes launched a two-run homer over the right-field fence for the win. Senior Larry Wendt (3-3) was the winning pitcher, although he needed help from Stuart Hirschman and Jeff Vogel. The winning blow of the second game came in the final inning. With the Spartans once more trailing, this time 3-2, Mayes came to the plate with the bases filled and slashed a double by the center fielder to score the tying and winning runs. Vogel (4-0), in relief of Hirschman, retired only two batters but was credited with the victory.

Lacrosse—**May 4, 1991 (H):** Michigan State defeated Notre Dame, 10-8, to up its overall season won-loss record to 10-4 and raise hopes of an NCAA tournament bid. The Irish struck for an early lead but Chris Heide, Fritz Kilian and Chris Stutler retaliated with goals and MSU trailed by only one, 4-3, after the opening period. After dropping back even further to 6-3 in the second quarter, Rick Kimball's crew once more came alive with scores by Jon Lantzy, Wayne Sansiviero and Joe Edell to knot the count at intermission. State took the lead in the third period on another Sansiviero shot. ND answered on an equalizer with 14:17 remaining. Then Jerry Rioux became the hero with two big goals, giving the Spartans a 9-7 lead, one they would not relinquish.

Baseball—**May 10, 1991 (H):** With Larry Wendt playing a key role in both games, State closed out the season with a doubleheader win over the playoff-bound Northwestern Wildcats, 6-1 and 9-6. In the opener he pitched a three-hit complete game, retiring 12 of the first 13 batters he faced. After solitary MSU runs in the third and fourth innings, the Spartans secured the victory with a four-run eruption in the sixth, which featured a three-run home run by Eric Sumpter and a solo blast by Steve Johnson. In the second game, Wendt, the hitter, slashed a three-run double into right-center field to cap a four-run outburst building a 6-0 lead in the third inning. Rich Juday's two-run single had opened the scoring in the first inning. Never trailing, the Spartans closed with one run

in each of the final three innings on RBIs by Alex Gagin, Bob Juday and again by Gagin. Stuart Hirschman was the winning pitcher but needed help from Jeff Vogel in relief.

ATHLETE OF THE YEAR

From Steve Smith's freshman year in which he had started in 26 of 28 games, coach Jud Heathcote exhibited great confidence in his future All-American. By the time Steve had completed his collegiate career (he did stay a full four seasons) he had led his team in scoring for three straight years (1989-1990-1991) and was the Big Ten Conference scoring champion in 1991 with 23.2 points per game average. Smith would also become the all-time MSU scoring leader with 2,263 career points, which ranked him fifth on the all-time Big Ten list. He had both played and started in more games than any other Spartan and finished in the top three in 12 career statistical categories.

Steve Smith

He was named first team All-Big Ten and All-American in his junior and senior years. In 1991, he set a conference record by hitting 45 consecutive free throws. Smith's contribution was not limited to scoring. As a guard, he led the team in assists his junior year, finishing third on the Michigan State all-time list for that category. He also led in rebounding both his sophomore and junior years, being outdone only by center Mike Peplowski in his final year. Originally drafted in the first round by the National Basketball Association's Miami Heat, Smith went on to have a long and successful professional career. Thanks to his generous contribution of $2.5 million, the student-athlete academic center was opened in 1998 and bears the name of his mother, Clara Bell Smith.

IN THE SPARTLITE

Baseball: With an average of .362 and for the third successive season, Rich Juday led the team in hitting.

On a sad note, after going through a week of chemotherapy for cancer, Craig Hendricks, a 21-year-old catcher from Portage, died at his home on Dec. 9, 1990 from a pulmonary embolism (a blood clot to the lung). In 1990, his final season as a Spartan, Hendricks batted .285 and ranked second for the Spartans in home runs (nine) and runs batted in (33).

Jeff Vogel made 22 appearances on the mound for the Spartans, among which he was credited with six saves.

Basketball: With four games remaining on the regular schedule, senior and co-captain Steve Smith became MSU's all-time leading scorer during a 74-72 win at Minnesota. Smith, whose retired number 21 jersey hangs from the rafters at Breslin Arena, hit his 2,146 career point on a free throw to pass Scott Skiles as the Spartans' all-time scoring producer. His eventual total of 2,263 points still ranks as the team's second highest, behind only Shawn Respert's 2,531 (1992-1995).

With an overall season record of 19-11, State earned their way into the NCAA's tournament of 64 teams. It was a short stay. After opening with a thrilling win over Wisconsin-Green Bay, 60-58, they fell by the wayside on a disappointing double-overtime loss to Utah, 85-84.

Cross Country: In the four-team Scarlet and Gray Invitational at Columbus, Spartan runners defeated the host Buckeyes. Nailing down four of the top ten finishing spots were Steve Charlebois (sixth), Rick Gledhill (eighth), Ken Wolters (ninth) and Tim Topolinski (10th).

Traveling to Minneapolis for the 83rd running of the Big Ten cross country championships, State placed third behind Wisconsin and Michigan. Co-captain Anthony Hamm took fourth with a time of 24:55.7 and Dave Smith finished seventh with a time of 25:12.6. The remaining members of the team were Ian Smith ninth (25:18.3), Tim Topolinski 26th (25:55.1) and Adam Norman 30th, (26:14.5).

In the NCAA region IV championships at Purdue, Hamm finished second to qualify for the national championship meet for the second time in three years. Unfortunately, a fourth-place tie with Illinois would not be enough for the Spartans to compete for the NCAA team title. Only the top three teams and the five individuals with the next best times from each region would earn the

opportunity to run. If MSU had been graced with the complete services of its top two runners (Dave Smith and Kerry Fly) things might have been different. Fly suffered a stress fracture in his foot and was sidelined after racing only twice in the season. Smith, the team's number two man, came down with a chest virus two days after the Big Ten meet and ran to a sub-par 74th at Purdue.

At the NCAA championships in Knoxville, Tenn., Hamm finished the 10K race in a time of 29:55 for 18th place and All-American recognition.

Fencing: Originally expecting to field an experienced team, illness and non-returning student-athletes left coach Freiheit with a squad he identified as "loaded with inexperience." At the opening of the season, the squad shaped up as follows: representing the Spartans in epee were three beginners, juniors Gary Cooper and Mike Noller along with sophomore Joe Gruber. Competing in sabre were senior captain Timo Kurvi, junior Nelson Grimes with sophomores Steve Sellepack and Carl Lutzer. Foil competitors were senior Karl Neumaier, junior Dave Koerkel and sophomore Pat Zann.

Upon completion of the season, the top performers with their winning records were: Kurvi (39), Grimes (33), Neumaier (31) and Noller (23).

Football: One of the most bitter setbacks in the long Michigan State-Notre Dame rivalry was the 20-19 loss in 1990 at Spartan Stadium. Leading 19-14 in the waning moments of the game, the dream of an upset seemed real when Irish's Rick Mirer lofted a pass to his potential receiver at the State two-yard line. The defensive back, Todd Murray, stepped in front of the receiver for the apparent interception. The ball bounced off the Spartan's shoulder pad and directly into the hands of the Irish flanker who took three strides into the end zone and ND remained the nation's number one team. A stadium record crowd of 80,401 watched the sad ending unfold.

Field-goal kicking specialist John Langeloh concluded his four-year Spartan football career (1987-1990) with a team scoring record of 308 points.

Running back Hyland Hickson closed out his Spartan career with 1,906 yards rushing and 19 touchdowns, with his 1990 statistics alone including 1,196 of those yards and 14 rushing touchdowns.

Sophomore Tico Duckett ran for 1,394 yards, which ranks sixth in the MSU record book for a season. In the Purdue game he scored four touchdowns, which tied him with 14 others for second place.

Chuck Bullough made 164 tackles to rank second in team totals for one season.

Golf: With composite three-day rounds of 301-288-297, the Spartans wound up in a tie for seventh with Wright State at the University of Michigan Wolverine Invitational. Freshman Heath Feld carded a three-round total of 73-70-73—216 to finish seventh.

At the 25th Annual Spartan Invitational Ken Horvath's squad finished in fifth place. Anderson shot a score of 69-72-76—217 to take sixth place.

Scoring 292-293-303—888 after the first three rounds of the Big Ten championship at West Lafayette, Ind., Michigan State rested in last place. A final round of 285, one of the best during the entire tournament, pushed MSU by Iowa and Purdue in the final standings. Individual scores for State were: Spencer 73-75-73-71—292, Anderson 71-71-73-79—294, Collier 73-73-70-79—295, Angel 75-80-77-73—305 and Feld 77-74-82-72—305.

Gymnastics: At the annual season-opening Windy City invitational in Chicago, State totaled 267.85 points to finish sixth in the field of 15 teams. Paul Dackermann a sophomore from New Jersey, won the floor exercise with a 9.65 and also captured top honors on the vault with a 9.45. Phil Ideson added two fourth-place finishes with a 9.35 in both the still rings and the vault. Chris Miller was sixth on the pommel horse and Chris Tobias sixth on the parallel bars.

In their best showing since 1970, the 1991 gymnasts scored 277.15 points and finished fourth at the Big Ten championships. For the second consecutive year, Dackermann was crowned vault champion. He also placed seventh on the parallel bars and fifth on the horizontal bar.

In April, team captain Nick Westermeyer fell from a mini-trampoline during a training session and landed on his head, causing paralysis and an end to his competitive career. He would return to the Jenison gymnasium in 1992 in the capacity of a volunteer coach.

Hockey: The Spartans suffered their first losing season since 1980-1981, as they finished with a 17-18-5 record. MSU also failed to advance to the CCHA Playoffs for the first time since joining the league in 1981-1982.

State managed to win a second-straight Great Western Freeze-Out Tournament in Inglewood, first defeating Toronto College 4-3 and then Boston College 3-2 in the title game.

In the aftermath of that February 16 Michigan game at Joe Louis Arena in which a bench-clearing brawl resulted in the ejection of 11 players (six Wolverines and five Spartans), coach Ron Mason and his U of M counterpart were suspended for one game by the CCHA commissioner for "failing to control his players."

Defenseman Jason Woolley was named to the West All-American first team, becoming the 11th Spartan to achieve the honor in Coach Mason's 12 years at MSU.

Lacrosse: The 1991 season was one of two halves. In the opening eight games on the schedule, MSU posted a record of 4-4, they then closed in a rush, going 7-0, including wins over Notre Dame and Ohio State in the final two games. The turnaround caught the attention of the NCAA selection committee and Michigan State received a bid to the tournament. Paired in the opening round against Syracuse University in the Orange's Carrier Dome, the hosts and defending NCAA champions totally dominated, 28-7.

Soccer: The top scorer for the season was Carl Hopfinger with nine goals and three assists. Next in line was Mike Rawlins who accounted for six goals and seven assists. Goalkeeper Pat Trese had a goals-against average of 1.21.

The 7-1 loss to Wisconsin-Milwaukee ties for the largest number of goals ever surrendered by a Spartan defense. The 1977 team lost to Indiana 7-0 as did the 1982 squad.

Swimming and Diving: Before a supportive crowd at the Charles McCaffree pool, the Michigan State squad took the University of Michigan team to the wire in their annual dual meet. The Wolverines quieted a rowdy MSU crowd by taking the opening two events, but freshman Alec Mull reactivated the wave of emotion by capturing the 200-yard freestyle, followed by a 1-2-3 slam in the 50-yard freestyle by sprinters Gregg Mihallik, Mark Lisenby and Steve Shipps. In the next event, Steve Leissner set a new pool record of 1:50.58 in winning the 200-yard individual medley. Unfortunately, the Spartan assault was not continuous and they ultimately submitted to a 134-109 loss.

Upon losing the dual meet to Indiana 143-98 on February 8 it seemed strange to refer to it as an upset. Granted, State had defeated the Hoosiers in the preceding season, but IU had handled MSU 33 times in a row prior to that. They were still considered a championship

caliber team. There were not many high spots for Coach Bader to dwell on as his squad registered only four wins: freshman Ron Orris in the 200-yard individual medley; Steve Leissner in the 200-yard butterfly; Anthony Higgins in the 200-yard backstroke and Kevin Zielinski in the 200-yard breaststroke.

Led by Leissner who swam a 1:49.07 to place fourth in the 200 individual medley (IM), a third in the 400-yard IM (3:53.28) and a third in the 1,650-yard freestyle (15:11.29), State completed the three days of Big Ten championship competition in sixth place with 399 points. Breaststroker Kevin Zylinski had an outstanding meet placing second in the 100-yard race with a new MSU varsity record time of 55.23 and third in the 200 (1:59.55). Mull, of Lansing, finished ninth in the 500-yard freestyle with a team record 4:25.03 and seventh in the 200-yard freestyle. Of the five relay events, State was best in the 800-yard freestyle, placing fourth in 6:35.96.

Tennis: In January, MSU hosted the AT&T Invitational, unofficially referred to as the Big Ten singles championship. Sophomore Brad Dancer advanced to the third round, the highest of any MSU player. Freshman Kevin Seckel was the winner on the consolation side of the bracket. Along the way he met and defeated his teammate Grant Asher.

After losing to Northwestern 5-2 in the first round of the Big Ten championships, State came back to defeat Illinois in the consolation round, 5-3, for a ninth-place finish. This also avenging a regular season lost to the Illini. Combined with wins at number one and number three doubles, the Spartans gained the points from singles victories by number three Dancer, number five Damon Valentino and number six Wade Martin.

Track and Field: While many of the Spartans remained home to rest for the upcoming conference meet, others performed well at the Western Michigan Invitational. Alan Haller grabbed first place in the 55-meter dash with a time of 6.46 while teammate Larry Harden won the 55-meter high hurdles in 7.42. In the 800-meter run, Chris Brown placed first in 1:54.67.

Despite the fact State was outscored quite sizably in a triangular meet at Bloomington, Ind., against the Hoosiers and Tennessee, the Spartans were able to grab several top three performances, including Sam Blumke's first-place finish in the 1,000-meter run (2:29.15). Runner-ups were Rick Gledhill in the 600 meters (1:19.99) and Chris Brown in the 800 meters (1:52.93). Finishing third were Larry Harden in the 55-meter hurdles (07.47), Todd Koening in the 800 meters (1:58.22), Anthony Hamm in the 3,000-meter run (8:14.04), Chauncey Williams the triple jump (36' 9") and Bill Sheldon the high jump (6' 9-1/2").

At the indoor Big Ten championships in West Lafayette, Ind., State scored 35 points which tied them with Purdue for sixth place in the team standings. The relay foursome of Blumke, Koning, Brown and Gledhill finished second in the 3,200-meter relay with a time of 7:30.97. In addition, senior distance runner Hamm ran a 14:11.98 for third place in the 5,000-meters and a 8:11.06 for a fourth in the 3,000-meter run.

In the outdoor conference meet at Columbus, Ohio, Spartan runners scored 40.50 points, but could do no better than ninth place in the team standings. Three runners placed in the 10,000-meter run: Hamm was the winner in a new track record time of 29:11.83, Ian Smith was fourth in 29:48.82 and Ken Wolters sixth with a 30:43.74. The Spartans also picked up a pair of third-place finishes by Chris Brown and Rick Gledhill. Marcel Richardson was eighth in the long jump with a leap of 23' 4-3/4".

Wrestling: In a dual meet against Indiana one month before the Big Ten meet, sophomore co-captain Roy Hall (158 pounds) suffered rib damage and was lost to the team for three weeks. More than that, his performance in the Big Tens were affected dramatically by the layoff.

Scoring 56.50 points, State finished sixth at the conference finals held in Champaign, Ill. Although no Spartan made it to the championship round, five wrestlers were third through sixth. Unseeded Soon Thackthay (118 pounds) finished fourth and Demond Betts (126 pounds), also unseeded, placed sixth. Hall (158 pounds) who was seeded number two, settled for a fourth-place finish as did Jamie Richardson (190 pounds). Don Whipp, the heavyweight, finished the highest of any MSU entry with a third-place.

Five MSU wrestlers qualified for the NCAA championships at Iowa City: Thackthay, Woods and Richardson all drew difficult opponents and were winless. Hall (158-pounds), ranked 10th in the nation, won his opening square-off before being stopped in his second match. Whipp was the most successful Spartan with a win, a loss and two more wins before being eliminated.

EXTRA! 1991 NCAA BASKETBALL TOURNAMENT

Michigan State reached the second round in the 1991 NCAA tournament. The following are the Spartans' box scores.

MICHIGAN STATE 60—WISCONSIN-GREEN BAY 58

	FG-FGA	FT-FTA	REB	A	PF	TP
Stephens	3-6	0-0	1	3	3	6
Steigenga	5-9	2-2	2	0	0	12
Peplowski	5-8	2-2	12	1	1	12
Montgomery	0-3	0-0	1	4	5	0
Smith	7-15	2-3	5	1	1	19
Zulauf	2-2	0-0	2	0	0	4
Hickman	2-4	0-0	1	0	0	4
Penick	1-2	0-0	0	4	0	13
Weshinskey	0-0	0-0	0	0	0	0
TOTALS	25-49	6-7	26	13	10	60

Halftime: Wisconsin-Green Bay 35-30; **Three-point field goals:** 4-10 (Montgomery 0-2, Smith 3-7, Penick 1-1); **Officials:** Rutledge, Dodge, Foxcraft; **Attendance:** 13,367.

UTAH 85—MICHIGAN STATE 84 (2OT)

	FG-FGA	FT-FTA	REB	A	PF	TP
Steigenga	7-14	2-2	6	2	5	17
Stephens	2-3	2-2	5	2	3	6
Peplowski	7-11	0-2	11	2	4	14
Montgomery	4-9	0-0	7	7	5	9
Smith	10-21	5-6	5	4	4	28
Hickman	1-3	0-0	2	0	1	2
Zulauf	1-4	0-0	3	2	2	2
Penick	1-7	4-5	2	0	2	6
Weshinskey	0-0	0-0	0	0	0	0
TOTALS	33-72	13-17	43	19	28	84

Halftime: Michigan State 33-29; **Regulation:** 64-64; **First overtime:** 75-75; **Three-point field goals:** 5-14 (Steigenga 1-2, Montgomery 1-2, Smith 3-8, Penick 0-2); **Officials:** Donata, Kaster, Croft; **Attendance:** 13,497.

EXTRA! 1990 SUN BOWL

December 31, 1990
El Paso, Texas

	1	2	3	4	F
MSU	0	7	10	0	17
Southern California	7	0	3	6	16

Starting line-up (offense)		*Starting line-up (defense)*	
James Bradley	SE	Skip Confer	DE
Roosevelt Wagner	LT	Bobby Wilson	DT
Eric Moten	LG	William Reese	DT
Jeff Pearson	C	Bill Johnson	DE
Mark Keller	RG	Carlos Jenkins	OLB
Jim Johnson	RT	Chuck Bullough	MLB
Duane Young	TE	Dixon Edwards	OLB
Dan Enos (C)	QB	Eddie Brown	CB
Tico Duckett	LH	Freddie Wilson	SS
Rob Roy	FB	Mike Iaquaniello (C)	FS
Courtney Hawkins	FL	Alan Haller	CB

The 1990 Sun Bowl was a rematch of the 1988 Rose Bowl teams. This time 21st-ranked University of Southern California was matched against 22nd-ranked Michigan State. The Spartans were in continual trouble in the opening half. The first USC drive was halted when Mike Iaquaniello intercepted a pass in the end zone. Later the Trojans put together an eight-play, 60-yard drive to take an early 7-0 lead. Yet a third threat was thwarted at the one-yard line when the Southern Cal quarterback mishandled a snap and Alan Haller recovered the fumble in the end zone. Then, taking possession on the 20-yard line, MSU's offense finally came alive as Hyland Hickson capped a 10-play drive on an 18-yard scoring run with 2:22 remaining before intermission. Following John Langeloh's successful conversion, the teams left the field tied at 7-7. On the opening drive of the second half the Trojans burned nine minutes but gained only a field goal. After receiving the kickoff the Spartans came back with a purpose. On a crucial third-and-13 play from the MSU 26, Dan Enos connected with Hawkins on a post pattern for a 41-yard gain and a first down. Four plays later, Hawkins pulled in a 21-yard pass in the end zone giving State its first lead at 14-10. A quick interception by Freddie Wilson put the ball in State hands again just sec-

onds later and soon resulted in a 52-yard field goal by Langeloh to establish a 17-10 edge as the quarter wound down. As in the Rose Bowl two years earlier, it was Langeloh's final field goal that would prove to be the winning points. In the fourth quarter USC put two field goals between the post, but with 0:00 showing on the scoreboard MSU was up by one. Hawkins gained 106 passing yards on six receptions with one touchdown to be named the Sun Bowl MVP. Enos connected on nine-of-17 passes for 131 yards, including one run of eight consecutive completions.

EXTRA! MICHIGAN STATE RELAYS (1990s)

Of the five Spartan firsts at the 1991 Spartan Relays, Anthony Hamm's victory in the 5,000-meter run in 14:08.95 was the most impressive as he shattered his own school record of 14:26.35 in the process. Other individual firsts came from Ian Smith, who won the 3,000-meter run with ease in 8:19.64 and Chauncey Williams, who took honors in the triple jump with a leap of 14.3 meters (45'10 3/4"). The remaining MSU firsts came with relays. The distance medley team of Sam Blumke, Rick Gladhill, Chris Pugh and Dave Smith finished first with a time of 10:02.4 and the foursome of Chris Brown, Todd Koning, Blumke and Gladhill were winners of the 3,200-meter relay in 7:34.13. Larry Harden led the Spartans in the 1992 Relays as he broke the school record in winning the 55-meter hurdles in a time of 7.30 seconds.

Facing competition from 15 colleges and clubs, the Spartans of 1993 won six events: Mark Davis in the 55-meter hurdles (7.38), Todd Koning in the 800 meters (1:52.95), Dave Smith the 3,000-meter run (8:15.42), David Couch in the 5,000-meter run, Matt Beard in the shot put (51' 6-1/2") and the 800 relay of Koning, Darian Dew, Cobb, Mark Tonello (7:50.0).

The number of teams competing in the relays of 1994 was down to eight with MSU runners capturing five events: freshman Octavius Long finished first in the 55-meters (6.36); sophomore Brad Fields won the 200-meter dash (21.43), junior Chris Lett captured the mile run (4:14.78), sophomore Bill Crosby broke the tape in the 3,000-meter race (8:34.17) and the sprint relay team was a winner in a time of 3:35.86.

The 1995 competition was drawn from Central Michigan, Eastern Michigan, Grand Valley, Saginaw Valley, Southwest Michigan College and Lansing Community College. Top finishers for State were Jarion Bradley who took first in the 55-meter hurdles (7.58), Damon Heard in the 55-meter dash (6.46); Brad Fields who won the 400 meters (49.39); Eric Eichinger took first in the 800-meter run in 1:54.94; Mark Goodfellow, winner of the mile (4:23.26); Ryan Hawley took the 3,000-meter run (8:46.09); Matt Beard won the shot put and the 1,600-meter relay team was a winner.

MSU
1991-1992

TALES TO TELL

In the fall of 1991, athletic director/football coach George Perles was finding it difficult to avoid the headlines. His newsworthiness did not pertain to the 3-8 football team, but instead it was the ongoing breach that continued to widen between him and the university's president, John DiBiaggio, regarding the issue of George jointly serving Michigan State as both AD and coach. The issue originally surfaced in February of 1990 just after Perles won an initial battle when the school's governing body, the Board of Trustees, voted 5-3 in favor of the dual appointment commencing on July 1, 1990, the date of Doug Weaver's retirement. It was suggested the trustees were reacting to reports that Perles was about to accept a $5 million coaching offer from the NFL's New York Jets. Regardless, approval was forthcoming with the understanding he would receive no additional pay and the arrangement was subject to a one-year review. From the beginning, John DiBiaggio was in total disagreement.

During that one-year period from July 1990 to July 1991 matters seemed to have run smoothly. The athletic staff was apparently content. In fact, there were reports

Former MSU AD and head football coach George Perles

that coaches of non-revenue sports were receiving support from the athletic director's office never before experienced. Then, on Nov. 14, 1991, the school's governing board released to the public a summation of the generally positive evaluation the university had compiled. Yet a closing statement spoke loudly that, "The positions of

HEADLINES of 1992

- Johnny Carson ends his reign over late-night talk shows when he makes his final appearance as host of *The Tonight Show.*
- Rioting, looting and arson sweep Los Angeles after a jury acquits four policemen in the beating of a black man, Rodney King. The death toll in the violence reaches 52.
- Portions of Florida are declared disaster areas in the wake of Hurricane Andrew.

SCOREBOARD

	W	L	T	Avg.
Baseball	36	19	0	.655
Track and Field	2	1	0	.667
Football	3	8	0	.273
Basketball	22	8	0	.733
Tennis	12	11	0	.521
Cross Country	no dual meets			
Swimming and Diving	9	3	0	.750
Wrestling	6	12	0	.333
Hockey	26	10	8	.682
Fencing	4	13	0	.235
Golf	tournament play only			
Gymnastics	12	2	0	.857
Soccer	9	11	1	.452
Lacrosse	10	5	0	.667

director of intercollegiate athletics and head football coach be separated." In his directive to Perles, the president further commented with: "I have considered such a dual appointment inappropriate from the start. The jobs are separate and distinct, and a mistake was made when they were joined over my objections." DiBiaggio was firm and confident, for time had worked against the AD/coach. Since the original vote in 1990, makeup of the board had changed. Three Perles supporters had left office and were replaced by trustees vowing to return power to the president.

Perles had been handed an ultimatum, either accept an offer to become athletic director for three and a half years beginning Jan. 1, 1992, with salary and benefits similar to that of other Big Ten ADs *or* continue as football coach until completion of the current contract through 1997. The issue was a debated topic in the community. On November 22, *The State Journal* ran a poll for its readers questioning the president's decision to split the two positions of athletic director and coach. Perles was supported by 53 percent of those who responded.

Regardless, foregoing a rumored legal battle, one week later George Perles settled for where his heart was—coaching football. On April 3, 1992, Merrily Dean-Baker became the school's 12th athletic director.

Although Coach Perles made overtures to heal the wounds between the two, the president was not conciliatory. On May 19, 1992, DiBiaggio announced his resignation in favor of the presidency at Tufts University in Massachusetts. Upon leaving, he denied the rift with Perles was a factor in his decision.

TEAM OF THE YEAR

The golf team won three of the nine tournaments in which they competed in the spring of 1992. They also placed second in the 35-team Firestone Invitational at Akron, Ohio, and fourth at the 18-team Kepler Invitational in Columbus, Ohio. In winning their own Spartan Invitational, the team shot a composite 868, the lowest winning score since going to a three-round format in 1987. In the Big Ten meet at Iowa City, Iowa, Ken Horvath's squad could do no better than a fourth-place finish with a composite score of 868. It was, however, MSU's best conference performance since the 1979 team placed third. Carding a four-round total of 284, (two shots short of medalist honor), Heath Feld led the State squad. Ian Peakes tied in 16th with 292, freshman Brian Bartolec shot a 297, captain Mike Spencer had a 301 and Eric Spencer completed the scoring with a 304.

The 1991-92 golf team. (Front row, left to right) J. Mleczko, D. Donaldson, C. Lemmon, S. Slazinski, J Barton. (Back row) C. Lane, E. Spencer, E. Eckenrode, H. Feld, B. Bartolec, head coach K. Horvath. (not pictured) M. Spencer and I. Peakes

MAKING HISTORY

Penn State, officially accepted into the Big Ten Conference in June of 1990, began competing in conference play in the fall of 1991.

On Oct. 21, 1991, MSU signed a broadcasting agreement with the Champaign-Urbana, Ill.-based Tieman Broadcasting Company to cover Spartan football and basketball games starting in 1992. The four-year deal was reported to be worth $1.75 million. George Blaha, the Detroit Pistons' play-by-play man, was named the lead announcer with former athletic director Doug Weaver as the color analyst.

The football goalposts were widened to 18 feet, six-inches.

In the spring of 1992 during a black tie banquet at the Kellogg Center, the 30-member charter class was inducted into the MSU Athletic Hall of Fame.

The MSU Sailing Club, braving ice and chilly weather, took second place at the Midwest Collegiate Sailing Association regatta hosted by Northwestern University in Evanston, Ill.

Burt Smith, who served as athletic director from 1972-1975, died on September 17 at the age of 74. Nearly 200 people gathered at the St. John's Student Center for a memorial service on November 23.

Ron Mason accepts the Spencer Penrose Award as 1991-1992 American Hockey Coaches Association Division I coach of the year.

The men's club volleyball team won its second consecutive Big Ten title in Minneapolis. The Spartans were 12-1 in the three-day club championship weekend.

In November, Earvin Johnson shocked the sports world by announcing at a press conference that he was retiring from professional basketball. More thoroughly, he dropped the bombshell:

"Because of the HIV virus I have obtained, I will have to retire from the [Los Angeles] Lakers today. I do not have the AIDS disease, I have the HIV virus. I plan on going on living for a long time. I now get to enjoy some of the other sides of living."

GREAT STATE DATES

Soccer—**October 2, 1991 (A):** Fatigue is never a factor when you're up against the University of Michigan. Playing their fifth game of an eight-game road swing, State struggled but defeated the Wolverines, 2-0, as Doug Consigny was credited with both goals. The sophomore forward booted the ball into the right corner of the net at the 61-minute mark of the game and 18 minutes later added his second. Brett Christensen assisted on Consighy's first score and Jon Petoskey assisted on the insurance goal. The Spartans' goalkeeper, Pat Trese, was only called upon to make four saves during the afternoon.

Cross Country—**October 5, 1991 (H):** In what was scored as a triple-dual meet, Michigan State's runners raced over the Forest Akers West Course layout and managed to defeat Michigan 28-29 and Ohio State 16-45. Anthony Hamm, the senior co-captain, broke the tape in 25:25 and was followed by David M. Smith, who finished fourth. David Ian Smith placed fifth; Adam Norman sixth; Chad Findley 14th; Ken Wolters 16th and Dave Wickens 17th.

Football—**October 19, 1991 (H):** It took long enough. After five straight setbacks to open the season, the Spartans finally earned a "W" by defeating the University of Minnesota, 20-12, in front of a Homecoming Day crowd of 75,097. Offensively, Tico Duckett keyed the victory with a career-high 241 yards on 30 carries, including his first two touchdowns of the fall. His first score came on an eight-yard run capping a 12-play, 67-yard opening drive after Minnesota had taken the lead, 6-0. Junior kicker Jim DelVerne added the PAT with 5:37 remaining in the opening quarter. A DelVerne 32-yard field goal midway through the second period extended the lead to 10-6, but with 1:36 remaining in the opening half, the Gophers struck with a 24-yard touchdown pass and suddenly they led 12-10. In the third quarter once more DelVerne who was called upon and he delivered with an 18-yard chip-shot to regain the lead by one point. The Gophers threatened to score with 13 minutes remaining in the game. On a second-and-seven play at the State 15-yard line the visitors completed a screen pass. As the receiver headed for the end zone, middle linebacker Chuck Bullough wrapped him up and forced a fumble that Damian Manson recovered at the five-yard line. Two plays later, Duckett exploded off right tackle, received a key block from fullback Tony Rollin and raced 88 yards down the sideline for the final score.

Hockey—**October 25, 1991 (H):** By turning back 35 of 38 shots on goal, senior netminder Mike Gilmore was the star of the 5-3 win over Michigan in the season opener. The first period was scoreless, but only 27 seconds into the second stanza right winger Bill Shalawylo gave MSU a 1-0 lead and less than two minutes later junior center Bryan Smolinski added another goal. Dwayne Norris put State up 3-0, but the Wolverines weren't about to go away. Before reaching the second intermission, the U of M had scored twice and the scene was set for the exciting final 20 minutes while the game was being viewed as PASS-Cable TV's CCHA game of the week. The U of M put one more past Gilmore, but sophomore defenseman Nicholas Perreault and freshman center Steve Suk more than matched that effort with the team's fourth and fifth goals.

Swimming and Diving—**November 2, 1991 (A):** On the day before competing in the Northwestern Relays at Evanston, the Spartans pulled off a rare triple win, defeating Indiana 72-41, Penn State 70-43 and the host Wildcats, 91-22. Steve Leissner finished first in three events, the 1,000-yard freestyle (9:22.49), the 200-yard individual medley (1:52.73) and the 500-yard freestyle (4:27.68). Greg Mihallik was a double winner, taking the two freestyle sprint events, the 50 in 20.76 and the 100 in 45.74. Other winners were Alex Mull in the 200-yard freestyle (1:40.46), Scott Carl in the 200-yard butterfly (1:53.19) and Jon Moore in the 200-yard breaststroke (2:08.96). The team of Tim Shanley, Chris Sholl, Andy Faberlle and Mihallik opened the meet with a victory in the 400-yard medley relay (3.25.88).

Soccer—**November 3, 1991 (H):** In their final home game of the season, MSU defeated Ohio State, 6-2. The Spartans overwhelmed the Buckeyes in the opening half as freshman Curt Weiermiller, junior Tim Richey, junior Trent Grens, senior Jeff Petosky and freshman Andrew Roff all managed a goal. The effective Michigan State defense kept the visitors from the scoreboard until midway through the second half and by then sophomore forward Bret Christensen had added his team's sixth and final score.

Swimming and Diving—**November 9, 1991 (A):** The Spartans extended their winning streak to four by finishing first in all but two events to defeat Wisconsin, 137.5-102.5. Jon Cohen was particularly busy with winning performances in three events: the 1,000-yard freestyle, 200-yard individual medley and 200-yard breaststroke. In those latter two events, State swam first-sec-ond-third to garner a bundle of team points. Steve Liessner set a Badger pool record in the 500-yard freestyle with a time of 4:26.48. Gregg Mihallik turned in first-place performances in both the 50-yard and 100-yard freestyle events as did Tim Shanley, who won the 200-yard backstroke.

Hockey—**November 15, 1991 (H):** With the final score reading, Michigan State 1, Lake Superior 0, this MSU-LSSU game was obviously a defensive struggle featuring outstanding goal-tending. The Laker net-minder was credited with 23 saves, including stopping six State breakaways, three by senior right wing, Dwayne Norris. At the other end of the ice, Spartan goalie Mike Gilmore stopped 27 shots, including 13 in the tense third period to earn his third career shutout. Interestingly, the only goal of the game came three minutes and 22 seconds following the opening face-off. Bryan Smolinski, the Genoa, Ohio, sophomore, one-timed Kelly Harper's pass out from behind the cage. The victory extended the MSU unbeaten streak to six games and the defeat saw Superior's 24-game CCHA unbeaten streak come to a halt. The Lakers would, of course, eventually become the NCAA champions.

Football—**November 23, 1991 (H):** The Spartans transformed four of seven University of Illinois turnovers into 24 points, leading to a 27-24 victory in the season finale at Spartan Stadium. Even though the win may have salvaged some pride after a disappointing 3-8 season, a crowd of only 38,739 turned out on a dreary, drizzly afternoon. With a first half touchdown by Tico Duckett and a Jim DelVerne 42-yard field goal following a fumble recovery, the game was tied at intermission, 10-10. A 17-point MSU output in the third quarter would provide the winning margin. The first score came following a jarring tackle by Ty Hallock on an Illini punt return effort. Darrin Eaton picked up the resultant fumble and raced 24 yards into the end zone. Another Illinois fumble, recovered by defensive end Juan Hammonds, set up a second DelVerne field goal, this time a 49-yarder, the longest of his career. The final touchdown drive needed only 17 yards after defensive end John MacNeill picked off a pass attempt that had been deflected by tackle Aaron Jackson. Fullback Tony Rollin negotiated a one-yard dive into the end zone. That score came with 12:24 remaining, thus providing the visitors ample time for two more scoring opportunities, one squelched by a Chuck Bullough interception and the other expiring with the game clock.

Swimming and Diving—**January 12, 1992 (H):** In the season home finale, nine seniors raced for the last

time in the McCaffree pool, as the Spartans defeated Purdue 144-97. The graduating group of Steve Bargwell, Mike Darbee, Jason Dick, Steve Leissner, Mark Lisenby, Gregg Mihalik, Steve Shipps, Matt Simcik and Kevin Zielinski combined for 67 of the team's winning total. The Spartans won the first six events and never looked back. Both Leissner and Mihallik were double-winners as State went one-two in the 1,650-yard freestyle, 200-yard freestyle, 50-yard freestyle, 200-yard individual medley and one-meter dive while taking the first three spots in the 100-yard freestyle.

Wrestling—**January 17, 1992 (H):** In an anomaly that was fairly consistent during a period from 1989-1996, two opponents were scheduled on the same day, this time at the IM West Arena. First, it was the University of Illinois in which the heavyweights would decide the outcome of the meet and reliable Don Whipp settled it all when he pinned his opponent at 1:22 into the match. The final team score read Michigan State 20, the Illini 19. The Spartans then found Ferris State a somewhat easier opponent, 25-16, providing Coach Minkel the opportunity to use some of his less-experienced wrestlers. There were, however, some double winners including Whipp, Jed Kramer (118 pounds), Jay Helm (142 pounds) Troy Hall (158 pounds) and captain Brian Woods (167 pounds).

Gymnastics—**January 25, 1992 (A):** Rick Atkinson's gymnasts won five of six events en route to 275.25 points and a double win over the University of Illinois with 272.15 and University of Michigan with 264.90. Chris Miller was a winner in the all-around. Along the way he won the pommel horse and took second on the parallel bars. Paul Dackerman won two events, the floor exercise with a career-high score of 9.85 and the rings with a 9.50. Completing the list of Spartan winners, Chris Spinosa finished first on the vault with a 9.35 and Chip Downton took first on the horizontal bar.

Basketball—**February 1, 1992 (H):** The 13th-ranked Spartans held a 35-28 lead at the break and never trailed in handing fourth-ranked Indiana their first conference loss of the season, 76-60. With particular efforts from Dwayne Stephens and Mark Montgomery, State demonstrated a typical "Heathcote-type" stifling defense as State out-shot the visitors 59 percent to 39 percent. A key moment in the game came with roughly 13 minutes to play and MSU leading by only five, 46-41, when Shawn Respert and Montgomery had back-to-back breakaways. The Hoosiers never recovered. Mike Peplowski, who

paced the inside attack with 16 points and helped provide a 46-24 rebounding edge with 11. His game drew praise from IU coach Bobby Knight:

> "I thought Peplowski did a very, very good job for them. He's a tremendously improved player. From a coaching standpoint, you've got to admire someone who has had the knee problems he has had and who has worked as hard as he has. Today, he was a dominant player."

In addition to Mike, three others scored in double figures: Montgomery 15, Stephens 15 and Respert 14.

Fencing—**February 1, 1992 (N):** The Spartan fencers defeated Purdue University, 16-11, in a dual meet at the Wayne State Invitational. The victory was achieved on the strength of the epee team of Kyle Glasgow, Gary Cooper and Tom Stempky. Together they won eight of nine matches. Senior captain Nelson Grimes was a winner in the sabre division.

Track and Field—**February 1, 1992 (A):** In an extremely close track meet hosted by the University of Minnesota, Michigan State score 57-1/3 to edge the Gophers, 47-1/3, Purdue, 46-1/3 and Iowa State, 12. Exemplifying the depth of the MSU squad, the Spartans won only three individual events during the afternoon: Chris Brown in the 400-meters (48.70), Richard Gledhill the mile run and Kerry Fly the 3,000-meter run (8:27.58). Other firsts were registered in relays: the quartet of Mark Davis, Ashley Nelson, Larry Harden and Brown won the four- by-400 relay in 3:15.78 and the four-by-800 relay was won by Sam Blumke, Chris Rugh, Fred Koning and Gledhill in a time of 7:40.91. Adding to the winning score with runner-up finishes were: 55 meters, Fred Kyles (6.38), Harden in the 55-meter hurdles (7.47) and 200-meter dash (21.70), Blumke in the 600 meters (1:21.31), Rugh in the mile (4:13.15) and Tim Topolinski in the 3,000 (8:29.19).

Gymnastics—**February 1, 1992 (H):** Although individually winning only three events, the Spartan gymnasts set a team record for total points, defeating the University of Michigan, 280.20-273.45. Phil Ideson won the still rings (9.55), Paul Dackermann the vault (9.55) and Chip Downton the horizontal bars (9.75). The top Spartan finishers in other events were Chris Spinosa, third in floor exercise (9.50); Mark Garny second on the pommel horse (9.45) and Chris Miller second on the parallel bars (9.45).

Basketball—**February 8, 1992 (A):** In what Coach Heathcote would call Mike Peplowski's "best game of the year," the junior center scored 19 points and gathered 16 rebounds in a 79-64 road victory over Wisconsin. The win brought the season record to 15-4 in the Spartans' quest for an NCAA tournament bid. Peplowski had excellent support from the backcourt with Shawn Respert contributing 17 points, 14 points on six-for-seven shooting from Mark Montgomery and three steals by freshman Eric Snow. The team shot 48 percent from the floor and with a halftime lead of 47-28 and second-half margin of no less than 10 points, Jud was provided an opportunity to not be hitting himself in the head. However, the seemingly always-hyper coach was his usual self. When Matt Steigenga missed a lay-up with the score at 35-25, he punted his folding chair four feet to the rear.

Basketball—**February 15, 1992 (A):** What would the odds be of pulling off a road win in Ann Arbor when you shoot nine-for-31 in the first half against a team being called the Freshmen Fab Five? Fortunately, the Wolverines weren't playing much better and MSU trailed by only six, 36-30, at intermission. Turning things around, Jud's crew improved their shooting to .448 in the second half, 13-for-29, while their aggressive defense was limiting the U of M to a meager .360 shooting percentage, nine-for-25. Michigan State did not lead until Mike Peplowski canned a pair of free throws to make it 47-46 with 13:56 remaining in the game. The lead changed hands two times before the Spartans took command for good and won by 11, 70-59. A key statistic revealed that Michigan led in turnovers, 21-9. Of ten who saw action for the winners, only six were scorers: Peplowski 18, Shawn Respert 15, "Pig" Miller 13, Matt Steigenga nine, Mark Montgomery eight and Dwayne Stephens seven.

Wrestling—**February 16, 1992 (H):** In a Sunday afternoon match against Notre Dame at the IM Sports-West Arena, State edged Notre Dame 18-15. After a slow start with losses by freshmen Jed Kramer (118 pounds) and Matt Becker (126 pounds), Demond Betts (134 pounds) won an 8-5 decision followed by Jay Helm (142 pounds) an 11-2 winner. First-year man Todd Garris (158 pounds) kept the streak going, as he won 9-5. From there the team scoring momentum swung back and forth until the final two matches. Everett Simmons's 6-5 win at 190 pounds gave the Spartans a slight edge leaving the outcome up to the heavyweights. Cheered on by the home crowd, including a group of wrestling alumni back for the weekend, Don Whipp gained a last-minute take-

down, salvaged a tie and preserved the team's three-point advantage.

Tennis—**March 7, 1992 (H):** Michigan State downed the Fighting Illini early en route to a 6-3 victory. Grant Asher, Brad Rosenbaum, Brad Dancer, Kevin Seckel and Wade Martin won the first five singles matches for the Spartans. The 5-0 lead guaranteed an MSU win and Asher and Rosenbaum then teamed up to win the number one doubles match for the Spartans' final point.

Lacrosse—**March 7, 1992 (A):** The Spartan laxers added to an 11-2 halftime lead and soundly defeated the University of Michigan, 18-5. Rob Dameron scored all four of his points in the opening half. Mark Shamam and Tim Kaiser each scored three points. Andy Hilgartner contributed two as did Robby Robertson, the junior transfer from Hobart. All 40 members of the MSU squad eventually saw action with two seniors, Stan Zajdel and Jerry Rioux and two sophomores, Jay Ledinsky and Steve Daray adding one goal each toward the winning total.

Gymnastics—**March 13, 1992 (H):** In one of the school's biggest wins ever in gymnastics, Michigan State defeated perennial Big Ten powerhouse Penn State, 281.60-281.05. Capturing firsts in only three of the seven events, they built the winning total on team depth. Junior Paul Dackerman was a double-winner, taking first in the vault with a 9.60 and the parallel bars with a 9.65. Trailing 234.90-234.15 heading to the horizontal bar, the final event, Chip Downton took over, topping the event individually with a 9.85 score and a winning squad score of 47.45-46.15 which was enough to overtake the Nittany Lions' lead and win the meet by the .55 point differential. Also of note, sophomore Mark Grany, a transfer student from the University of Wisconsin, scored a career-high 9.50 on the pommel horse, helping MSU win that event 47.00-46.55.

Lacrosse—**April 4, 1992 (A):** With two goals and two assists, junior midfielder Bobby Robertson, a transfer from John Hopkins, was instrumental in leading Michigan State to an 8-1 halftime lead over the Air Force Academy. From there the Falcons came alive and by 5:08 of the fourth quarter the Spartan advantage had dwindled to one point at 8-7. Tim Kaiser's second goal of the game halted the Falcon's surge and MSU hung on for a 10-9 well-earned victory. Other scoring contributors were Joe Edell, Jerry Rioux, Jay Ledinsky, Andy Hilgartner and two by Rob Dameron. Playing a hunch, Coach Kimball started sophomore Chris McCrady in goal, replacing senior Jeff Horowitz, and the move paid off as McCrady made save after save on 48 shots.

Golf—**April 4, 1992 (A):** With snow on the ground and a strong, chilly wind blowing in Lexington, Ky., the annual Johnny Owens Invitational was shortened to 36-holes. The two-round tournament seemed to satisfy the Spartans as they combined to capture the team trophy with an overall score of 605. This total would lead the field of 19 teams, including Michigan and Indiana, and be eight strokes better than second-place Kent State. Individual scores were as follows: Mike Spencer 77-72—149; Heath Feld 75-76—151; Ian Peakes 75-77—152; Brian Bartolec 76-77—153 and Chris Lemmon 83-78—161. Spencer tied for medalist honors, but lost on the first hole of a playoff.

Tennis—**April 19, 1992 (H):** After splitting the singles matches, the Spartans swept the three doubles matches to gain a 6-3 verdict over Penn State in a dual meet at the MSU Indoor Tennis Facility. Individual winners were number two Brad Rosenbaum, 6-1, 6-2; number four Chad Skorupka, 6-2, 6-1 and number five Wade Martin, 6-3, 6-2. Grant Asher and Rosenbaum teamed for a three-set win, 7-5, 4-6, 6-3; Brad Dancer and Wade Martin teamed for a 6-2, 6-2 win and the James Westfall-Jayson Bedford duo was a 6-3, 1-6, 6-1 winner.

Baseball—**April 26, 1992 (A):** In the second game of a double-header at Ray Fisher Stadium in Ann Arbor, Michigan State used a six-run seventh inning to win 8-4. After giving up two runs in the first inning, Tim Crabtree settled down to throw seven innings for the complete-game victory. He gave up four runs on six hits and struck out four. Third baseman Alex Gain, right fielder Steve Johnson and pinch hitter Eric Sumter each tallied two RBIs in the win.

Lacrosse—**May 1, 1992 (A):** It was likely the most exciting lacrosse game a Michigan State team ever played; but, somehow the expected end-reward never materialized. Playing before 1,000 fans in a season-ending night game at South Bend, State trailed Notre Dame 13-10 with 6:03 remaining on the game clock. Suddenly, the Spartans were only two down as sophomore midfielder Jim Wolfe scored from a face-off which generated this post-game comment from Coach Kimball:

"Jim Wolfe might have been the hero of the night. That was probably the biggest goal. We knew we were coming back once he scored like that. The lift it gave to everyone on the field and the bench was tremendous. You could feel the whole team believing."

Still down two with only 1:30 remaining, junior Robby Robertson scored and then assisted on Joe Edell's tying score 41 seconds later. Suddenly, this was a team destined and with 10 seconds remaining, freshman Tim Kaiser's desperation shot trickled over the goal line and State had completed an incredible comeback, 14-13. They soon went from ecstasy to disbelief. It had been falsely expected the winner of this game would be selected as the area's representative in the pending NCAA tournament. It didn't happen. On the next day it was learned that the vanquished Notre Dame Fighting Irish would be the 12th and final selection.

Track and Field—**May 2, 1992 (A):** As competitors lined up for the final event at the Central Collegiate championships in South Bend, the 10,000-meter run, MSU trailed EMU by six points in the team standings. Perhaps this was a motivating factor in the outcome as a pair of Spartans, Ken Wolters and Adam Norman finished first and sixth. When the final computations were made, including points for the Huron runner who placed third, the scores read: Michigan State 134.5, Eastern Michigan 132, Central Michigan 113.5, Michigan 101, Western Michigan 100 and Notre Dame 90. Other than John Collins's second place in the discus, all of the points were earned on the oval. Fred Kyles won both dashes, the 100-meters in 10.5 and the 200-meters in 21.45. Larry Harden captured two hurdle events with a 13.90 in the 110-meter highs and a 21.50 in the 200-meter lows. Anthony Hamm was a gold medalist, running a 14:07.54 in the 5,000 meters. Other contributors were Tony Nelson (48.40) and Joel Finks (48.60) who ran two-three in the 400-meters; Mark Davis (54.13) who placed second in the 400-meter intermediate hurdles and Todd Koening (1:51.69) who was runner-up in the 800-meter run. Both the sprint relay team of Davis, Harden, Kyles and Howard Triplett and the mile relay quartet of Harden, Nelson, Finks and Rick Gledhill finished in third place.

Golf—**May 3, 1992 (H):** For the first time since 1987, the State team won the team trophy at the Spartan Invitational Tournament. With their composite three-round winning total of 384-289-295—868, the Spartans bettered the tournament scoring record of 871 set by Minnesota in 1991. Freshman golfer Brian Bartolec took top honors for the home team, scoring a 215 over the 54 holes which placed him second overall. Also teeing it up for the winning team was sophomore Heath Feld who finished fourth with a 217; senior Ian Peakes was seventh with a 220; junior captain Mike Spencer fin-

ished eighth with a score of 221 and Eric Spencer carded a 224, good enough for 11th place. Finishing in order behind MSU were Toledo 873, Minnesota 877, Northwestern 881, Illinois 885, Wisconsin 894 and Michigan 898.

Baseball—**May 2 & 3, 1992 (H):** Michigan State took three from Iowa and as a result retained their hold on first place in the conference over Ohio State by a few percentage points. On Saturday Tim Crabtree pitched a brilliant game as the junior right-hander allowed only one base hit, yielded four base-on-balls and struck out seven in gaining a 10-0 decision. Most of the offense was generated by senior catcher Craig Mayes, who went four-for-four with four RBIs, including a home run and two doubles. With the shutout, Crabtree (6-1) lowered his team-leading ERA to 2.14 in the Big Ten. Sunday's first game was a comedy of errors as nine miscues were committed by both teams in State's 5-3 victory. A second-inning home run by sophomore Eric Sumpter put MSU in front 2-0 and then the Hawkeye left fielder dropped two fly balls to give the Spartans the balance of runs. Senior starter left-hander Scott Wolffis upped his record to 4-1. In the second game a bases-loaded single by sophomore shortstop Bob Juday gave State and right-hander Stuart Hirschman the 3-2 win. Hirschman had relieved junior left-hander Keith Davenport in the fourth and allowed just one hit the rest of the way.

Baseball—**May 6, 1992 (H):** The Spartans used two complete-game pitching performances to win both ends of a doubleheader against Michigan at Kobs Field, 8-0 and 3-1. First, it was Stuart Hirschman who threw an eight-hit shutout, pushing his three-year collegiate record to an impressive 21-4. In that opener, State scored single runs in the first and second innings and, featuring Alex Gagin's home run, added two runs in the fourth. In the sixth, two walks and a single loaded the bases for Gagin who lined a single to bring home two runs. A fielder's choice by Craig Mayes and single by Dave Veres drove in the final two runs of the game. In the sixth inning of game two, consecutive singles by Steve Johnson, Mayes, Eric Sumpter and Childers accounted for two runs while Steve Money added a sacrifice fly for the third and final run. Tim Crabtree, the winning pitcher, yielded only two hits while retiring 16 of the final 17 batters he faced.

ATHLETE OF THE YEAR

Six-foot-one, 180-pound Howell native Stuart Hirschman was an exceptional leader both on and off the baseball field. Not to be confused with his twin brother, Steve, who was also a successful Spartan pitcher, Stuart pitched a 7-0 complete game shutout over Providence in 1993 that brought him up to 24 career wins, the most by any Spartan pitcher. Upon completion of his collegiate career, he had accumulated MSU records with 28 wins and 267.1 innings pitched. In the classroom, he held a 3.81 GPA in mechanical engineering, making the Dean's List in eight terms and posting a 4.0 in three of those terms. For his athletic abilities Hirschman was named second team All-Big Ten in 1992. He tied State's single-season record for wins with 10 and ranked second in complete games pitched in a season with eight. For his academic abilities he was named a two-time Academic All-Big Ten, a 1992 Academic All-American, and a two time recipient of the conference Medal of Honor for academic and athletic excellence.

Stuart Hirschman

IN THE SPARTLITE

Baseball: Doug Cossey and Ted Mahan, the future head coach, joined the staff as assistants to Tom Smith.

In sweeping Northwestern at Evanston, Ill., on April 19, Bob Juday connected for three home runs.

Posting a regular-season conference record of 17-11, MSU qualified for the Big Ten four-team playoff joining Minnesota, Ohio State and Illinois for a double elimination tournament in Columbus. Tom Smith's squad was shut out in the opener against Minnesota 5-0, but surprised the defending champion Buckeyes, 10-7, to remain alive. The most exciting game of the weekend came next with a match-up in the loser's bracket against the University of Illinois. The MSU bats were silenced until the eighth inning when Eric Sumpter led off with a pinch-hit home run to tie the game at 1-1. In the bottom half of that frame, Illinois responded with their own four-bagger to regain the lead. The State hitters would not be outdone. With two out in the ninth and facing a 0-2 count, senior catcher Craig Mayes lined the next pitch off the pitcher's glove for a single. Sophomore second baseman Dave Veres reached first on an error and designated hitter Matt Lockwood followed with a double down the right field line scoring both base runners. They would go on to add one additional run to make the final score read 4-2. Now with a record of 2-1, it was "bring on the Golden Gophers" and the pesky Spartans actually led 4-3 in the seventh inning when the Minnesota batters knocked out starter Steve Hirschman. They would go on to score seven runs off four relievers and close the MSU season record at 36-19, tying a team record for second-most wins over a season.

As a team, State completed the year with a Big Ten conference-leading .968 fielding percentage.

Outfielder Steve Johnson was the team's leading hitter with a .398 average. He also starred defensively with 98 putouts and four assists resulting in a perfect 1.000 fielding average.

Stuart Hirschman, Johnson and third baseman Alex Gagin were all selected as third-team All-Big Ten. Catcher Craig Mayes was recognized as the first-team All-Big Ten catcher and Tom Smith was selected as Big Ten Coach of the Year.

Basketball: The team opened with an impressive record of 10-0 in the pre-Big Ten portion of the schedule. The streak included wins over Cincinnati and Stanford.

With the 86-71 defeat of number two Arkansas, Michigan State captured the Maui Invitational title on November 27. The win brought attention to redshirt-freshman Shawn Respert. He averaged 19 points in the tournament and was named to the Maui All-Tournament Team. He continued to lead the team in scoring, averaging 15.8 points per game. Senior guard Mark Montgomery, with an 11.3 scoring average, finished second in tournament MVP voting.

For the third straight season, Matt Steigenga led the team in blocked shots with 23. In his four-year collegiate career, he rejected a total of 74 field goal attempts.

Finishing the conference race tied for third place and with an overall record of 22-8, the Spartans gained a bid to the 64-team NCAA tournament.

Cross Country: In the Wolverine Invitational, a three-team race in Ann Arbor, State and Michigan tied for first place with 29 points each. Scoring 78 points, Ohio State was a distant third. Senior Anthony Hamm took first place with a time of 25:25. David Ian Smith, Dave Smith and Adam Norman placed fourth, fifth and sixth respectively while Chad Findley completed the team scoring 14th place.

One week later, In the State Intercollegiate meet at Ypsilanti, Hamm was not available. This contributed to a fourth-place finish among the 17 in-state schools completing. Tim Topolinski was the Spartans' top finisher in seventh place.

Traveling to Tucson to compete against runners from 20 other schools, State finished fourth behind Arizona, South Florida and the Air Force Academy. Hamm, back in action, was the lead Spartan in third place (26:54.7). He was followed by David Ian Smith in eighth, Norman in 18th, Kerry Fly in 63rd and Dave Smith, who finished in 69th position. Topolinski was the 76th runner across the finish line.

At the Big Ten championships hosted by Purdue, MSU totaled 83 points to finish in third place. David Ian Smith was the top Spartan in fourth place (25:08.3) and was followed by Hamm in sixth (25:11.8), David Smith 24th (25:51.9), Norman 25th (25:53.1) and Findley in 30th (25:57.6).

Once more running at the El Conquistador Country Club in Tucson, Ariz., this time for the NCAA Championships, State's runners finished ninth in a field of 22 teams. Hamm was the leader for MSU, completed the 10K course in 30:42.6 for sixth place. Other Spartan scor-

ers were David Ian Smith (23rd), Toby Lefere (94th), Norman (114th) and Findley (119th).

Fencing: Karl Neumaier, who fenced under Fred Freiheit from 1987-1991, began his first year as an assistant coach.

Upon reviewing the credentials of 1992 team members, only one, captain Nelson Grimes of Louisville, Ky., possessed any significant experience prior to competing for MSU. As was often the case, Spartan fencers most frequently evolved from coach Fred Freiheit's physical education fencing class.

Representatives from ten schools comprised the competition at the midwest regional fencing championships conducted at the IM Sports West in early March. MSU's sole entry, sabre senior Nelson Grimes, fenced to a 2-3 mark, short of advancing to the second round.

Football: In post-season action, five Spartan seniors and their coach were busy. George Perles was selected as one of the two coaches for the Japan Bowl in Tokyo. Joining him for the game were flanker Courtney Hawkins, defensive end Bill Johnson and free safety Alan Haller. Joining Hawkins and Johnson at the Senior Bowl one week later in Mobile, Ala., was linebacker Chuck Bullough and offensive tackle Jim Johnson.

Middle linebacker Bullough, and flanker Hawkins were named to the 1991 first team, All-Big Ten team.

In March it was reported that the former Spartan offensive coordinator Morris Watts, who left the collegiate ranks to coach in the NFL, would return to MSU as quarterback coach and assistant head coach.

Hawkins concluded his career with a four-year total of 138 pass receptions (second only to Andre Rison) and 2,210 reception yards (third in the team record book).

Golf: This would be the final year of the Spartan Invitational in name. Beginning in 1993, the 27-year-old tournament would honor the former coach by taking on a new identity, the Bruce Fossum/Spartan Invitational Tournament.

With a composite score of 1,165, State finished fourth in the Big Ten tournament at the Finkbine Field Golf Course in Iowa City. The host Hawkeyes scored a 1,139 to win the title. Top scorer for State and two shots from medalist honors was Heath Feld with a 69-73-68-74—284. Other Spartans and their scores were: Ian Peakes 73-71-75-73—292; Brian Bartolec 72-76-76-73—297; Mike Spencer 72-77-70-82—301 and Eric Spencer 74-76-80-74—304.

Gymnastics: The gymnasts opened the season by hosting the Spartan invitational. Totaling 275.10 points, they outscored Minnesota with 269.20, Illinois 270.35 and Illinois-Chicago 259.40, while losing to Ohio State at 280.55. Paul Dackermann scored a 9.65 to finish first in the floor exercise and a 9.55 in win the vault event.

In the Windy City Invitational the Spartans finished in fifth place. Junior Paul Dackermann won the floor exercise with a score of 9.70 and also the vault with a 9.60. Sophomore Chip Downton finished third in floor exercise and fifth on the high bar. In the pommel horse, junior Chris Tobias placed fourth with a career-high mark of 9.50.

In the all-around competition at the NCAAs in Lincoln, Neb., sophomore Heath Trial placed 41st out of 72 in the competition.

Hockey: Following the losing season (17-18-5) of 1990-1991, MSU returned to the more expected role of a winner in 1991-1992 (26-10-8).

Of the 34 regular season games, 10 necessitated overtime in which the Spartans registered a record of 2-1-7.

Backed by goalie Mike Gilmore's 36 saves, State edged Maine, 2-1, and for the second time in four years advanced to the NCAA Frozen Four in Albany, N.Y.

Coach Ron Mason was named the American Hockey Coaches Association's coach of the year for the first time in his career.

After three years as a Spartan (1989-1991), Jason Woolley left school during the 1991-1992 seasons to join the Canadian Olympic team that eventually won the silver medal. It was originally anticipated the North York, Ontario, native would return to complete his senior season in 1992-1993. Instead, he signed a professional contract with the Washington Capitals of the NHL.

Lacrosse: An unfortunate twist of fate in the final week of the season may have cost MSU an appearance in the spring's NCAA tournament. Holding an 8-5 season record going into Columbus, Ohio, State dropped a game to Ohio State. Rebounding with a 14-13 win over Notre Dame, the season ended at 9-6. Two weeks following the close of the regular season and after the NCAA tournament brackets had been set, OSU officials confessed that they had played Michigan State with an ineligible player and consequently forfeited the game, 1-0. This corrected the Spartan record to read 10-5 and a likely tournament team, but the change in team record came too late.

Soccer: Brent McCaul had led the team in scoring as a freshman and then slacked off in his second year. The 1991 season held promise as the team scored in the season-opener against Eastern Michigan. Then fate stepped in. One month later, McCaul was in the hospital with a broken leg sustained in 4-0 loss to Wisconsin.

At the Big Ten tournament in Bloomington, Ind., MSU shutout the Ohio State Buckeyes in the opening round, 1-0, on Jon Petrosky's lone goal. They were then defeated by top-seeded Wisconsin 3-0 in the championship game.

Brett Christensen was the top scorer on the season with four goals and four assists for 12 points. Tom Consigny and Jon Petosky had nine points each.

Swimming and Diving: In an early season meet at Minneapolis, Spartan swimmers competed in hopes of qualifying for the upcoming USA Olympic Trials. Four of those who competed, Greg Mihallik, Steve Leissner, Kevin Zielinski and Jon Moore had already met the prescribed qualifying standards. Two other teammates, Ron Orris and Mull swam but failed to advance. Later, in early March, the four qualifiers competed in their specialties at the Trials in Indianapolis with none of the four reaching the ultimate goal.

Senior co-captains Gregg Mihallik and Steve Leissner both placed in the top eight in three individual events to led the team to a sixth-place finish at the Big Tens in Minneapolis. Mihallik was fifth in both the 100-yard freestyle (4.51) and 100-yard butterfly (48.76) along with an eighth place in the 50-yard freestyle (.20.69). Swimming both versions of the individual medley (IM), Leissner was fifth in the 200 (1:50.84) and seventh in the 400 (3:57.34). He concluded his busy weekend with an eighth place in the 1,650-yard freestyle (15:32.95). Tim Shanley and Orris also added to the 290 team points. Shanley was eighth in the 100-yard backstroke (50.56) and seventh in the 200-IM (1:51.69) while Orris swam fifth-place in the 100-yard butterfly (49:05). With all five relays finishing eighth or higher, the 200-yard freestyle quartet placed the highest in fourth (1:21.25).

Leissner would swim in his last NCAA championship meet, winning the consolation finals of the 400-yard individual medley (3:50.79). With 34 team points, State ended up in 22nd place.

Tennis: Following the abbreviated fall schedule, coach Jim Frederick would resign as head coach. His wife, an investment broker, had pursued a career in Knoxville,

Tenn. This, of course, necessitated his departure, as well. Shortly thereafter, Gene Orlando, the 26-year-old Bowling Green head coach, was hired as his replacement.

Although not impressive, the team's seventh place in the Big Ten championships at Madison Wis., was the highest Michigan State finish since 1978. After being blanked by Indiana 6-0, the Spartans dropped a close one to Wisconsin, 5-3, with Brad Rosenbaum losing a deciding match on a tie-breaker. This put Gene Orlando's crew against Michigan in a battle for seventh place and it turned out to be no contest. Rosenbaum was a winner (7-6, 7-5); Kevin Seckel won in three sets (5-7, 6-1, 6-3); Wade Martin in two (6-3, 6-3) and Jim Westfall also in two (6-4, 6-4). Brad Dancer won by default and MSU shut out the U of M, 5-0, for the first win over the Wolverines in 25 years.

Track and Field: In the Big Ten indoor championships held at Jenison Fieldhouse, State scored 50 points and finished in fifth place, the highest spot since 1986. Chris Brown captured the 600-meter run in a conference record time of 1:18.85. Other top finishers for MSU were Fred Kyles, fourth in the 55 meters (6.35) and sixth in the 200 meters (21.59); Todd Koning, fourth in the 800-meter run (1:54.10); Larry Harden, second in the 200-meter dash (21.49) and fourth in the 55-meter hurdles (7.55) plus the 400-meter relay team, comprised totally of freshman (Mark Davis, Ashley Nelson, Harden and Brown) which finished fifth (3:19.52). The most exciting event of the meet was the 3,200-meter relay, won by the Spartans but strongly challenged by Indiana and Wisconsin. The team (Sam Blumke, Koning, Chris Rugh and Rick Gledhill) trailed for much of the race and then anchorman Gledhill, energized by the roar of the home crowd, breezed by the Badger runner on the final turn and broke the tape in a time of 7:37.30.

Hosting a non-scoring meet against competitors from Western Michigan, Eastern Michigan and the University of Michigan, the Spartans placed first in seven events as well as winning the mile relay in 3:12.40 with the quartet of Brown, Koning, Harden and Nelson. The individual winners were Fred Kyles in the 100 meters (10.65), Davis in the 110-meter hurdles (14.6), Dave Smith in the 1500-meters (3:53.87), John Collins, the discus (156' 6"), Anthony Hamm, the 5,000 meters (14:11.75), Nelson, 400 meters (48.15) and Brown in the 800 meters (1:49.99).

Flashing strength in the distance races, State man-

aged 68 points and a sixth-place finish in the Big Ten outdoor championships held at the University of Minnesota. In the 800-meter run, Brown was third (1:49.38) and Koning fifth (1:50.31). In the 5,000-meter run the trio of Dave Smith (14:26.63), Hamm (14:35.34) and Ian Smith (14:36.10) finished fourth, sixth and seventh respectively. Hamm (30:02.38) and Ian Smith (30:05.07) went one-two in the 10,000-meter run. Fred Kyles was fourth in the 100 meters (10:39) and eighth in the 200 meters (21.26). Harden and Davis went two (14.10) and four (14:37) in the 110-meter hurdles while Howard Triplett ran a 53.38 to finish fifth in the 400-meter hurdle event. The Spartans were scoreless in the field events.

With a fifth-place finish in the 10,000-meters (30:07.11) Hamm put Michigan State on the scoreboard at the NCAA championships in Austin, Texas.

Wrestling: At the Eastern Michigan Open in November, not only did Roy Hall, a junior, win the 158-pound title, but he was also voted the outstanding wrestler of the meet. Also earning first-place honors in the early season competition were junior Brian Woods (167 pounds) and freshman Emilio Collins (177 pounds).

The Spartans managed only 31 points in the Big Ten championships at Madison, Wis., which translated to a ninth-place finish. Roy Hall (167 pounds) and heavyweight Don Whipp reached the semifinals before being sidelined. Six others were eliminated in the quarterfinals: Jed Kramer (118 pounds), Demond Betts (126 pounds), Andy Hector (134 pounds), Jeremy Helm (142 pounds), Tom Neu (150 pounds) and Everett Simmons (190 pounds).

EXTRA! 1992 NCAA BASKETBALL TOURNAMENT

Michigan State reached the second round of the 1992 NCAA tournament. The following are the Spartans' box scores for those games.

MICHIGAN STATE 61—SW MISSOURI STATE 54

	FG-FGA	FT-FTA	REB	A	PF	TP
Stephens	6-10	5-7	8	1	0	17
Steigenga	3-5	5-8	8	1	3	11
Miller	0-2	0-0	3	1	2	0
Montgomery	2-8	3-5	5	4	3	7
Respert	1-4	1-1	1	1	3	3
Zulauf	2-2	1-2	3	0	2	5
Peplowski	4-6	1-2	5	2	3	9
Weshinskey	4-9	1-1	3	1	1	9
Snow	0-0	0-0	0	0	0	0
TOTALS	22-46	17-26	39	11	17	61

Halftime: SW Missouri State 24-23; **Three-point field goals:** 0-7 (Montgomery 0-3, Weshinskey 0-2, Stephens 0-1, Respert 0-1); **Officials:** Lembo, Howell, Rote; **Attendance:** 13,007.

CINCINNATI 72—MICHIGAN STATE 65

	FG-FGA	FT-FTA	REB	A	PF	TP
Steigenga	0-4	0-0	2	0	3	0
Stephens	5-11	3-3	6	1	3	15
Peplowski	1-4	0-0	3	1	3	2
Montgomery	3-6	0-0	4	9	4	7
Respert	9-17	5-6	2	1	2	27
Zulauf	0-1	4-4	3	1	1	4
Miller	1-4	5-5	3	1	3	7
Weshinskey	1-5	0-0	2	1	4	3
TOTALS	20-52	17-18	28	15	22	65

Halftime: Cincinnati 42-35; **Three-point field goals:** 8-21 (Stephens 2-6, Steigenga 0-2, Montgomery 1-4, Respert 4-6, Weshinskey 1-3); **Officials:** Lembo, Thomley, Rote; **Attendance:** 13,007.

EXTRA! 1992 NCAA HOCKEY TOURNAMENT (Frozen Four)

In 1991 the team had to sit out the NCAA tournament for the first time in ten years, but in 1992 they came back with a vengeance. First they put away Ferris State in the first round of the CCHA playoffs. In the second round they lost to Lake Superior State University (LSSU) 5-3, but they were able to top Miami (Ohio) in the consolation round to secure a trip to the national tournament. Seeded fifth in the west, they faced Boston University and surprised them with three third-period goals to win 4-2 and give Ron Mason his 650th career goal. Next MSU took on top-ranked Maine and upset them 3-2 to enter the Frozen Four for the second time in four years. Rival LSSU was next in the bracket and they scored two goals in the final period of the semifinals to put away the Spartans 4-2 en route to their NCAA championship.

March 26, 1992—Providence, R.I.
MSU 4, Boston University 2
1st Pd.: No Scoring.
2nd Pd.: 1. MSU, Murray (Smolinski, Thompson), 5:18; 2. BU, Prendergast (Mark Bavis, Sacco), 5:50; 3. BU, Sacco (Mike Bavis), 19:04.
3rd Pd.: 4. MSU Turner (Woodward, Worden), 1:39; 5. MSU, Norris (unasst.), 7:25; 6. MSU, Smolinski (Murray, J. Messier), 12:55.

March 28, 1992—Providence, R.I.
MSU 3, Maine 2
1st Pd.: UMO, Montgomery (Tardiff), 5:39; 2. MSU, Norris (White), 9:53.
2nd Pd.: 3. MSU Norris (White Suk), 1:54; 4. MSU, Smolinski (Norris, Suk), 11:22; 5. UMO, Imes (Tardiff, Montgomery), 17:12.
3rd Pd.: No Scoring

April 2, 1992—Albany, N.Y.
Lake Superior State 4, MSU 2
1st Pd.: 1. LSSU Constantin (Smith, Hanley), 1:27; 2. MSU Perreault (Harper, Garbarz), 5:28.
2nd Pd.: 3. LSSU, Constantin (Hanley, Hendry), 6:32; 4. MSU, Norris (Smolinski, Murray), 17:22.
3rd Pd.: 5. LSSU, Astley (Hendry, Hulett), 10:58; 6. LSSU, Moger (Strachan, Faucher), 12:22.

EXTRA! ATHLETICS HALL OF FAME

The idea of a Michigan State Athletics Hall of Fame had been discussed for a number of years, but it took the support and initiative of athletic director (1990-1992) George Perles, to make the idea a reality.

As noted below, the original class, whose induction ceremony highlighted a black-tie banquet in the Kellogg Center during the spring of 1992, included a whopping 30 former athletes, coaches and administrators. With each inductee presented by a chosen friend, former teammate or coach, this called for no less than 60 mini-speeches. It was a long evening. The program was still underway when the Westminster chimes of Beaumont Tower had struck beyond midnight. Regardless, the evening had served its purpose. The University community had initiated an opportunity to recognize its "heroes of the past."

During a period of 1997-1999 when the athletic department was undergoing some administrative changes, the annual activity of selecting and presenting an honored class was shelved. Otherwise, each year another six or seven former Spartans are singled out for the honor with the induction ceremonies now being held in the fall. Anyone is eligible to nominate a former Spartan great, but to qualify as a viable candidate for the Hall the nominee must have been out of the MSU system for at least 10 years.

In those first few years a frequent concern often surfaced: "We are continuing to initiate men and women into a Hall of Fame that doesn't exist." Buffering such criticism, those early custodians of the Hall of Fame plan remained patient and finally the perfect setting was made available. Located behind the glassed area on the north side of the Clara Bell Smith Student-Athlete Academic Center and visible from Shaw Lane, the hall was born and dedicated during Homecoming weekend on October 1, 1999. Displaying key moments in Spartan athletic history, the facility, of course, includes 70 glass plaques featuring the inductees listed below.

Charter Class of 1992

Fred Alderman	Track and Field	1925-27
Gloria Becksford	Softball	1975-76
Amo Bessone	Hockey coach	1951-79
Jack Breslin	Baseball	1944-46
	Football	1944-45
Bob Carey	Basketball	1950-52

	Football	1949-51
	Track and Field	1950-52
Lynn Chandnois	Basketball	1947
	Football	1946-49
Don Coleman	Football	1949-51
Duffy Daugherty	Football coach	1954-72
Chuck Davey	Boxing	1943, '47-49
Lyman Frimodig	Baseball	1914-17
	Basketball	1914-17
	Football	1915-16
Johnny Green	Basketball	1957-59
John Hannah	MSU president	1941-69
Earvin "Magic" Johnson	Basketball	1978-79
Crawford "Forddy" Kennedy	Track and Field	1957-59
	Cross Country	1957-59
Henry Kennedy	Track and Field	1956-58
	Cross Country	1955-57
Bonnie Lauer	Golf	1970-73
Jane Manchester-Meyers	Swimming and Diving	
		1972-74, '76
Gale Mikles	Wrestling	1945-48
Earl Morrall	Baseball	1954-56
	Football	1953-55
Clarence "Biggie" Munn	Football Coach	1947-53
	Athletic Director	1954-72
Carlton Rintz	Gymnastics	1952-55
Robin Roberts	Baseball	1946-47
	Basketball	1945-47
Ernestine Russell Weaver	Gymnastics	1957-60
Clarke Scholes	Swimming and Diving	
		1950-52
Charles "Bubba" Smith	Football	1954-56
Fred Stabley	Sports information director	
		1948-80
Doug Volmar	Hockey	1965-67
Gene Washington	Football	1964-66
	Track and Field	1965-67
George Webster	Football	1964-66
Ralph Young	Football Coach	1923-27
	Track and Field coach	
		1924-40
	Athletic director	1923-54

Class of 1993

Molly Brennan	Track and Field	1979-82
George Alderton	Sports editor	1923-62
Fred Johnson	Track and Field	1947-50
John Kobs	Baseball coach	1925-63
	Hockey coach	1925-31

	Basketball coach	1925-26
Robert "Buck" McCurry	Football	1946-48
Johnny Pingel	Football	1936-38

Class of 1994

Art Brandstatter Sr.	Football	1934-35
Kirk Gibson	Baseball	1978
	Football	1975-78
Jack Heppinstall	Athletic trainer	1914-59
Joyce Kazmierski	Golf	1964-67
Danny Litwhiler	Baseball coach	1964-82
Gideon Smith	Football	1913-15

Class of 1995

Judi Brown	Track and Field	1980-83
Leander Burnett	Baseball	1889-92
	Track and Field	1888-92
Gary Dilley	Swimming and Diving	
		1965-67
Everett "Sonny" Grandelius	Football	1948-50
Burl Jennings	Wrestling	1941-43
Merle Jennings	Wrestling	1941-43
Karl Schlademan	Cross Country coach	
		1947-57
	Track and Field coach	
		1941-58

Class of 1996

Chet Aubuchon	Basketball	1939-40, '42
Ed Bagdon	Football	1946-49
Fendley Collins	Wrestling Coach	1930-62
John Horne	Boxing	1958-59
Greg Kelser	Basketball	1976-79
William Mack	Cross Country	1948-49
	Track and Field	1949-50
Deanne Moore	Softball	1981-84

No selections were made from 1997-1999

Class of 2000

Richard Berry	Fencing	1952-53
Chester Brewer	Athletic director/coach	
		1903-10, 1917, 1919-20
Dr. James Feurig	Team Physician	1953-75
Roger Grove	Basketball	1929-31
	Football	1928-30
Frank Kush	Football	1950-52
Gwen Norrell	Faculty athletic representative	
		1979-87
George Saimes	Football	1959-62

Brad VanPelt	Baseball	1971-72
	Basketball	1971-72
	Football	1970-72
Herb Washington	Track and Field	1969-72

Class of 2001

Jerry DaPrato	Football	1912, 1914-15
	Basketball	1915
Sue Ertl	Golf	1977-80
George "Jud" Heathcote	Basketball coach	1976-95
Sherman Lewis	Football	1961-63
	Track and Field	1962-63
Weldon Olson	Hockey	1952-55
Steve Smith	Basketball	1988-91
John Wilson	Football	1950-52

(No selections were made for 2002)

Class of 2003

Lauren Brown	Cross Country	1928-30
	Track and Field	1929-31
Joe DeLamiellieure	Football	1970-72
Tom Yewcic	Football	1951-53
	Baseball	1952-54
Cheryl Gilliam	Track and Field	1978-81
Mary Fossum	Womens Golf Coach	1973-97

MSU
1992-1993

TALES TO TELL

In November of 1992 the author paid a visit to 95-year-old George Alderton at his home in Traverse City for what could have been the retired writer's final interview. By then George's eyesight was gone, but his mind was as keen as when he was sports editor of *The Lansing State Journal*. He died three months later on Feb. 19, 1993.

George offered insight into some interpersonal relationships within the Spartan family. Pertaining to Ralph Young (the Spartan AD from 1923-1954), he offered:

"Neither John Hannah nor Biggie Munn demonstrated much respect for Ralph Young. Let me relate a couple of experiences.

First, I recall sitting in the baseball dugout next to Dr. Hannah, just the two us, talking about Michigan State sports. We both looked up and spotted Ralph Young strolling across the field toward us. Analyzing the likelihood that Young would be join-

ing us, the president turned to me and described his athletic director in a very unsavory way. I was shocked. It was so unlike John Hannah, but it was obvious he had little respect for Mr. Young.

At another time during football practice Biggie strolled away from his team and came up the middle of the field. He would stop at about every third step and kick the ground and raise small clods of sod into the air. After seeing him continue to do this I walked out and asked him, 'What's wrong? What's the matter with you?' Biggie answered, 'Let me tell you this, and I mean it. If I ever leave this place [MSU] it will be because of Ralph H. Young.' And he went on kicking the sod down the field. I never asked what precipitated his comments, but I do know this, he did not get along very well with Mr. Young."

When quizzed about the legendary deterioration of friendship between Biggie Munn and Duffy Daugherty, George was somewhat reassuring:

HEADLINES of 1993

- A powerful bomb explodes in an underground parking garage beneath the World Trade Center in New York City, killing six people.
- A government raid on the Branch Davidian compound in Waco, Texas, results in a destructive fire which takes the lives of 80 cult members.
- Vincent Foster, the deputy White House counsel and long-time friend of Bill and Hillary Clinton is found dead in a park in northern Virginia. An autopsy indicates suicide.
- A flood that was the worst ever in the Midwest surged down the Mississippi River and its tributaries leaving 50 people dead, 70,000 homeless and $12 billion in damages.

SCOREBOARD

	W	L	T	Avg.
Baseball	31	23	0	.574
Track and Field	0	0	0	.000
Football	5	6	0	.455
Basketball	15	13	0	.536
Tennis	12	14	0	.462
Cross Country	no dual meets			
Swimming and Diving	8	2	0	.800
Wrestling	5	9	0	.357
Hockey	24	14	2	.625
Fencing	13	10	0	.565
Golf	tournament play only			
Gymnastics	5	5	0	.500
Soccer	9	9	2	.500
Lacrosse	8	6	0	.571

"At times there was some animosity between the two of them, as you probably know. He [Biggie] was a good coach and Duffy wanted to also be a good coach, but he wanted to do it his own way. I think that Biggie sometimes just couldn't hold back."

George Alderton was not physically able to attend the inaugural Hall of Fame induction at the Kellogg Center on Sept. 11, 1992. In his absence, a message was read that he had prepared. It reveals the ongoing loyalty to "his" Michigan State Spartans:

"Hail, Spartans all. Tonight a new chapter is being added to the rich history of intercollegiate athletes at Michigan State University. Pages of history may be lost or shredded, but this ultimate honor you are about to receive as a charter member of the Michigan State University Athletics Hall of Fame for your contribution to this history will remain forever. It is richly deserved. Receive it with Spartan Spirit. I was fortunate to stand on the sidelines of practice fields and to observe the long hours of training and practice, the sacrifices of precious time and the efforts to gain perfection of some of you being honored tonight. You gave of yourself so freely. Somewhere in my 40 years of writing about Michigan State athletes and their games, I worded this phrase:

'Once you have stood on the banks of the tawny tide of the Red Cedar River, played your games and scored your triumph, you are a Spartan forever. And so you are.'"

One year later, George Alderton, himself, was inducted into the MSU Hall of Fame, in absentia.

TEAM OF THE YEAR

Including victories over Wisconsin, Purdue and Indiana, the 1992-1993 varsity swimming and diving squad completed the dual-meet season with an 8-2 won-loss record. The team included championship caliber athletes led by Chris-Carol Bremer, a German Olympian who doubled as a long-distance freestyler and butterflyer. Other consistent performers were freestyler Alex Mull and butterfly-individual medley ace Ron Orris, both of whom swam to team-record times. Other significant contributors included Jon Cohen, Tim Shanley, Chris Sholl. freshman Tom Munley and diver John Maxson, who finished fourth in the always competitive Big Ten championships.

MAKING HISTORY

In the fall of 1992, the university switched calendars from term to semester. No longer would students report to school in later September, often after the Spartans had played two or three football games. On the negative side, gone would be a spring term in which winter term athletes (basketball, hockey, etc.) could concentrate on studies, and studies alone.

In football, 25-second clocks at each end of the field were required.

CKLW of Windsor Canada joined the Spartan Radio Network, bringing the total number of member stations to 40 for football and 36 for basketball, up from 28 and 19 in the preceding year.

In June, the *Detroit News* released a story with accusations that two former basketball players, Parish Hickman (1988-1990) and Jessie Hall (1987-1989) had received improper financial incentives during their playing days at MSU. With fingers pointing particular at two alumni, the story expanded into a short-term media blitz, but with the allegations lacking proven support, in time the Hickman-Hall story died.

The 1992-93 swimming and diving team. (Top row, left to right) S. Carl, J. Cohen, T. Shanley, C. Sholl, K. Zielinski, A. Mull, R. Orris. (Middle row) J. Thurston, A. Faberlle, T. Giannoulis, D. Klaviter, R. Koonce, S. Lang, J. Maxson. (Bottom row) K. Purdy, R. O'Donnell, T. Munley, C. Bremer, C. Harris and C. Wyatt.

John Sheldon of Spring Lake, that's the guy who paints himself green with a large painted white "S" on his bare chest and shows up at every imaginable MSU sporting event, began attending State as a freshman in 1992-1993. From that first year, he has continued as a self-appointed and self-styled MSU cheerleader at home games and often on the road. He described himself: "I'm not a fan, I'm a Spartan."

In April, at a gathering of MSU coaches and nearly 800 athletes at the Wharton Center, the Department of Intercollegiate Athletics sponsored the first-ever Spartan Salute. Various awards were presented and graduating seniors were recognized.

In Big Ten baseball, although the postseason four-team playoff would continue to determine the NCAA automatic qualifier, the regular season winner would once more be declared the conference champion.

GREAT STATE DATES

Soccer—**September 20, 1992 (H):** The Spartans raised their record to 4-1-1 with a 2-0 victory over the University of Cincinnati. Dan Radke opened the scoring at the 14:18 mark from a perfectly placed corner kick by defenseman Rich Goldman. At about 15 minutes into the second half, Coach Baum made substitutions, inserting Roy Otani and Brett Christensen. The move paid off 2:52 later when Otani took a great pass from Christensen and knocked it into the net. Goaltender Curtis Payment made some great saves for MSU to preserve his third shutout of the campaign.

Soccer—**October 14, 1992 (H):** Goalies Curtis Payment and Pat Trese combined for the shutout in Michigan State's 4-0 win over Central Michigan. Jon Petoskey, Doug Consigny, Andrew Roff and Roy Otani each scored in the victory. Four yellow cards were handed out during the game, all to CMU players.

Football—**October 17, 1992 (A):** When starting quarterback John Miller was sidelined with a crunched left shoulder late in the fourth quarter of the University of Minnesota game, back-up signal caller Bret Johnson

faced an appalling, seemingly impossible task. State trailed 15-13, the game clock had wound its way down to the 2:50 mark and the cheers of 35,594 Golden Gopher fans were echoing throughout the Hubert Humphrey Metrodome. Yet it was not like an untested freshman was taking over the offense. The UCLA transfer from Mission Viejo, Calif., had actually started the first three games of 1991. His first eight plays of this crucial drive included a short four-yard pass to Craig Thomas but the fifth play was a 41-yarder to tight end Mitch Lyons, putting the Spartans in business at the Minnesota 17-yard line. It took four more carries by Thomas, but that fourth play was a dive into the end zone with 11 seconds of play showing on the scoreboard clock. The back-up quarterback had led his team to an exciting 20-15 victory.

Football—**October 31, 1992 (A):** The Spartans barely escaped Dyche Stadium in Evanston, Ill., with a 27-26 win over Northwestern University in a game that saw another Michigan State quarterback sidelined with injury. The number one signal caller, Jim Miller, was dressed but benched with a shoulder injury sustained two weeks earlier. One week later, his replacement, number two Bret Johnson, left the Ohio State game with a knee injury. This opened the position to quarterback number three, John Gieselman, who started against the Wildcats, only to exit in the third quarter with a broken right collarbone. Coach Perles had little choice but to call upon Miller, still recovering from his injury, to lead the team over final minutes of a 20-20 tie-game. From then the drama would unfold. The Spartans moved the ball 66 yards in nine plays with Craig Thomas negotiating the final seven yards at 6:59 making the score 26-20. Ross Ivey's center snap for the PAT attempt went behind the anticipated holder, Milt Coleman. A scrambling pass attempt failed, but luckily a defensive-penalty call gave kicker Bill Stoyenovich a second attempt and he succeeded, making it 27-20. The game wasn't over yet. Northwestern countered with a four-play scoring drive of 68 yards and Gary Barnett, the Wildcats' coach, would not settle for the tie but instead opted for the win with a two-point conversion attempt. Fortunately, the pass was broken up by free safety Damian Manson and it fell harmlessly into the end zone. Following a Spartan three-and-out series, the Cats were again on the prowl. Using clock-killing sideline tosses, NU dented the "bend-but-don't-break" pass defense for 54-yards, all the way to the "S" 24-yard line. With two seconds remaining, in came their field goal kicker, who had already made a 37-yarder and

a 28-yarder. On this try, his effort of 34 yards slid inches left as time expired.

Football—**November 7, 1992 (H):** Injuries had so decimated the courageous Michigan State offensive line that only one opening day starter, guard Toby Heaton, remained in the trenches by the time they lined up against the University of Wisconsin for the ninth game of the season. Yet, this patched-up wall of blockers performed well enough to lead the "Green Shirts" to their fourth win of the fall, 26-10. Yielding a scant 108.1 yards per contest, the Badger defense came into the contest ranked second in the conference. Such statistics did not intimidate the Spartans as the running duo of Craig Thomas and the hobbled Tico Duckett accounted for 274 yards and three touchdowns. Thomas carried 17 times for 168 yards, a 9.9 average, and two long scores. Duckett, who became the sixth Big Ten back to crack the career 4,000-yard barrier, added 108 yards and one TD on 21 attempts. Quarterback John Miller had a 7-for-12 passing day, including a 34-yard scoring toss to Mill Coleman. After Miller went down for the second time during the year with a shoulder injury, the versatile Coleman moved to the QB spot where he added a vital nine-yard keeper and a pair of completions to his three catches, which totaled 68 yards.

Hockey—**November 27, 1992 (A):** In this, the first meeting with Notre Dame in 10 years, Michigan State skated to an easy 8-4 victory. The Spartans' top line of Bryan Smolinski, Rem Murray and Brian Clifford accounted for six of the goals, as Murray led the way with his first hat trick (three goals) as a collegian. Smolinski added two goals and two assists while Clifford had a goal and an assist. Kelly Harper had opened the scoring after 1:43 of play on a pass from Steve Guolla while Nicolas Perreault contributed one of the five goals made during the middle stanza.

After gaining their commanding lead, State's defense broke down, leading to a pair of Irish goals in the second and two more in the third.

Hockey—**December 5, 1992 (H):** This Michigan State-Michigan battle progressed for more than 35 scoreless minutes before Rem Murray and Bryan Smolinski collaborated on the opening goal while playing shorthanded. Skating two-on-one, Smolinski's shot was stopped, but Murray picked up the rebound and tucked it back into an open net. There was little time to rejoice as the Wolverines tied the score barely more than a minute later. The game then remained at 1-1 until there were

less than five minutes to play, at which time Smolinski sent a 40-foot drive past the goalie's glove for the winner. The Genoa, Ohio, senior would also score into an empty net with one second remaining on the game clock....the final score: MSU 3, U of M 1. Mike Buzak made 23 saves including a possible game-saver on a breakaway early in the third period.

Swimming and Diving—January 15, 1993 (H): After losing the opening relay and two of the first three individual events to the University of Illinois, the Spartans came back to win five of the next six races and eventually build a 129-114 winning score. Chris Bremer, the German Olympian, captured the 1,000-yard freestyle in 9:38.20 and the 200-yard butterfly with a 1:51.49. Other winners for MSU were Ron Orris in the 200-yard individual medley (1:55.37), Alex Mull in the 100-yard freestyle (47.10) and Jon Cohen in the 500-yard freestyle (4:34.13). Adding crucial team points in diving, John Maxson and Steve Lang went one-two on both the one-meter and three-meter boards.

Wrestling—January 23, 1993 (H): After losing the opening match at 118 pounds, MSU won four of the next five bouts and built a 15-6 lead en route to their first win of the season, a 22-15 victory over Ferris State. Brian Bolton (126 pounds) was a 12-3 winner, Phil Judge (134 pounds) a 5-3 winner, Tom Neu won his match at 150 pounds followed by Dan Wirnsberger's total dominance, 24-8, at 158 pounds. After Joel Morissette's loss at 167, Jason Howell countered with a 6-3 decision at 177 pounds. With a commanding lead, coach Tom Minkel felt comfortable in holding back the hobbled Emilio Collins and forfeiting the 190-pound match. Don Whipp closed out the meet by shutting out his heavyweight opponent, 5-0.

Basketball—February 6, 1993 (H): Shooting 52.1 percent from the field, including 87.5 percent from beyond the arc, efficiency was the key as Michigan State defeated the University of Minnesota 75-63 in front of 15,138 fans at the Breslin Center. Following a 26-26 tie at halftime, the Gophers jumped to a 31-28 lead whereupon the Spartans rallied for 10 straight points, including consecutive three's by Shawn Respert and Chris Weshinskey. A short while later Heathcote's guys went on a 7-0 run followed by three-pointers from Dwayne Stephens and Daimon Beathea. With that, MSU enjoyed its largest lead, 63-49, and was never seriously threatened thereafter. Including a perfect four-for-four from beyond the arc, sophomore guard Shawn Respert scored 28 points to lead all scorers.

Fencing—February 6, 1993 (H): Fred Freihert's swordsmen faced and defeated Purdue 24-3, Detroit-Mercy 20-7 and Michigan 17-10 in a multi-team match at Jenison. The Spartans beat the Boilermakers and the Titans in all three weapons (epee, foil and sabre) while losing only in epee to the Wolverines. Leading the way for State were Kyle Glasgow in foil with William Flynn and Scott Wright in sabre. Although injuries are rare in the sport, Brian Holmes twisted his ankle early in the day and was removed from competition and Shawn Smith needed minor medical attention when cut on the hand by a blade.

Basketball—February 13, 1993 (H): In a Saturday afternoon game televised by Raycom, Michigan State saw a 38-34 halftime advantage disappear as the Ohio State Buckeyes came out of the locker room and stuck a 20-13 run into the scorebook for a 54-51 lead with 12:01 to play. Beginning with a Shawn Respert triple, the Spartans returned the favor with an 11-0 run of their own, resulting in a 62-54 turnabout. The visitors eventually did cut the deficit to 64-59, but Respert took charge, scoring 11 points in the closing 2:21 and 28 overall as the final score read MSU 81, OSU 66. The Buckeyes were outshot .411-.571 from the field and outrebounded 35-25. Mike Peplowski was a big contributor with 19 points and 10 rebounds. Although only scoring five points, Chris Weshinskey likewise collect 10 caroms. Dwayne Stephens contributed 13 points, Quinton Brooks eight, Eric Snow six and Daimon Beathea two.

Swimming and Diving—January 30, 1993 (H): Winning 11 of the 13 events and led by the German Olympian, Chris-Carol Bremer, State defeated Eastern Michigan, 151-90. The versatile Bremer opened by swimming the butterfly leg of the winning medley relay team (3:28.30) that included Tim Shanley, Chris Sholl and Bryan Morrison. He then came back to set a pool record with a winning time of 9:17.01 in the 1,000-yard freestyle followed by a first place in the 200-yard backstroke (1:56.67). Diver Jon Maxon won both the one-meter event (279.45) and the three-meter (285.98). Another double-winner was Ron Orris who took the 200-yard freestyle (1:42.41) and the 200-yard breaststroke (2:13.46). Other winners for MSU were Jon Cohen in the 400-yard individual medley (4:08.45), Andy Faberlle in the 200-yard butterfly (1:54.20), Morrison in the 100-yard freestyle (47.97) and Mark D'Errico in the 500-yard freestyle (4:46.68).

Swimming and Diving—**February 13, 1993 (A):** Michigan State won nine events and defeated Indiana, 130-114, for only their third victory in 36 years over always-powerful Hoosiers. Seniors Tim Shanley and Chris Sholl, along with juniors Ron Orris and Alec Mull opened with a victory in the 400-yard medley relay (3:24.42). Jon Cohen kept the momentum going, winning the 1,000-yard freestyle (9:43.11) and was followed by Chris-Carol Bremer, the German Olympian, who won the 200-yard freestyle (1:41.27). After losing the 50-yard freestyle and diving events, State came back with Orris winning the individual medley, Bremer the butterfly, Mull the 100-yard freestyle (46.37), Shanley in the backstroke (1:52.80) and Bremer once more, his third first of the afternoon, the 500-yard freestyle (4:30.44). Even with all this success, State needed at least a second in the final event, the 400-yard freestyle relay. They did better than that, finishing one-two with the winning foursome of Orris, Shanley, freshman Tom Munley and sophomore David Klaviter posting a time of 3:07.24.

Gymnastics—**February 19, 1993 (H):** Hosting Illinois-Chicago, once more Coach Atkinson depended on the team depth, this time defeating the Flames, 275.85-272.15. Paul Dackerman won the vault (9.30) and placed second in floor exercise (9.65) and was tied for second with teammates Mark Garny on the parallel bars (9.60) and Kevin Brown on the high bar (9.30). John Orlando was the high bar winner (9.50) while finishing second in the all-around (54.70). Dave Adams was second on the pommel horse (9.25). Others scorers for State were Chip Downton, Erik Montgomery, Todd Caufman and Norm Stulz.

Hockey—**March 6, 1993 (H):** It was senior right wing Rob Woodward who netted the game winner as Michigan State defeated Notre Dame 5-2 on senior night. Woodward's goal gave MSU a 3-1 lead. Sophomore left wing Steve Guolla, who also scored the game's first goal, gave MSU a 4-1 advantage on a power play early in the third. Freshman right wing Brian Clifford and freshman center Anson Carter each scored a goal in the win. The victory gave head coach Ron Mason 673 career NCAA victories, tying him with former Boston College coach Len Ceglarski.

Gymnastics—**March 7, 1993 (H):** With a score of 277.50-270.75, the Spartans defeated Michigan in a Sunday afternoon meet at Jenison Fieldhouse. State captured every event: 47.20-46.55 on floor exercise, 45.95-44.45 on the pommel horse, 46.00-45.15 on the still rings,

45.80-44.60 on the vault, 46.55-45.35 on the parallel bars and 46.00-44.65 on the high bar. Despite a recent shoulder injury, junior Mark Garny turned in particularly impressive individual performances by winning the pommel horse (9.75) and high bar (9.50). Both Paul Dackermann and Chip Downton were also double-winners. The impressive win came with some of the MSU starters missing, including pommel horse and high bar specialist senior David Adams.

Lacrosse—**March 17, 1993 (H):** Senior midfielder Stan Zajdel scored an unassisted goal with 1:39 left in double-overtime to lift the team to a 15-14 victory over previously unbeaten University of Maryland-Baltimore County at the Duffy Daugherty Football Building. The Spartans had almost given the game away in the fourth quarter when Baltimore County scored four unanswered goals to erase a 13-10 MSU lead. Midfielder David Kieffer scored the last of his three goals with just 18 seconds remaining to send the game into overtime. In the first OT, Zajdel, the eventual hero, was twice stymied, necessitating the second extra session. Kieffer led the Spartans with four points on three goals and an assist. Andy Hilgartner scored a goal and two assists. Rob Dameron scored three goals, Jeff Jelus had two goals and an assist while Jay Ledinsky and Scott Cebul each had a goal and two assists.

Lacrosse—**March 19, 1993 (H):** Freshman Chris Clark scored four goals to lead Michigan State to a 17-10 win over Canisius. Also standing out for MSU were David Kieffer, who was credited with three goals, and the trio of Dan Edell, Scott Cebul and Jeff Jelus each of whom scored two goals.

Baseball—**March 28, 1993 (H):** In a Sunday afternoon game at Kobs Field, the Spartans swept a doubleheader from Purdue, 1-0 and 5-4. MSU freshman pitcher Dan Garman pitched a seven-inning no-hitter in the opener, striking out eight. Infielder Jon Merchant scored the only run in the fifth inning, knocked in by shortstop Dave Veres, who went two-for-three in the game. Eric Sumpter also connected for two hits in three times at bat. In the second game, Randy Vanderbush gave up three runs on three hits in five and one-third innings while Steve Hirschman picked up his third save of the season, shutting down the Boilermakers in the last two innings. Steve Johnson, who would eventually win his second team-batting title, led the State offense with a two-run single. Merchant went two-for-four with one RBI and also scored a run himself.

Tennis—**April 3, 1993 (H):** With 8-5 one-set wins by both the Brad Dancer-Wade Martin and Jayson Bedford-Gus Giltner pairs, State was awarded the one team point afforded the winner of the doubles competition. From there, four Spartans won their singles matches. At number two, Dancer was a winner 4-6, 6-3, 6-2; number three Kevin Seckel won 6-2, 6-3; number four Martin was a winner in straight sets 6-1, 7-5 and Bedford a 7-6, 6-1 winner. With only number one Masheska Washington and number six Giltner losing in singles, the final score was MSU 5, OSU 2.

Tennis—**April 4, 1993 (H):** With the meet against Indiana tied at 3-3, all eyes turned to the number five singles match where sophomore Jayson Bedford had lost the opening set 2-6. With the pressure on, he proved to be a competitor as he came back 6-4, 7-5 to earn the remaining team point for a 4-3 Big Ten win over the Hoosiers. A key to the successful afternoon came early when all three of Coach Orlando's doubles teams were winners, thus gaining that opening point. The remaining points came from straight set victories by number three junior Kevin Seckel, 6-2, 7-6 and number four Wade Martin, 6-1, 6-2. It was the first time MSU had defeated IU since 1977.

Tennis—**April 11, 1993 (A):** After sweeping the doubles matches and thus earning the first point against the University of Iowa, the Spartans prevailed in singles competition. Brad Dancer returned to the number one spot for the first time in a month and gained a three-set victory. After freshman Mashiska Washington's loss at number two, Kevin Seckel bounced back for a 2-6, 6-0, 7-6 tie-breaker win at number three. Wade Martin won in three sets at number four, 6-4, 5-7, 7-5 and then number five Jayson Bedford, the Canadian, came back from a second-set loss to win a 7-6 tie-breaker in the third. The final team score was Michigan State 5, Iowa 2.

Lacrosse—**April 16, 1993 (H):** Michigan State scored early and often in the first half against the Air Force Academy, then withstood a second half surge by the visitors to gain their fifth win of the spring, 14-11. After clanging three shots off the post in the first two minutes, freshman Doug Jolly broke through at the 9:44 mark on an unassisted goal. Rob Dameron scored the first of his four goals followed by a Jeff Jelus score and another by Dameron before the Cadets found the target and MSU led 4-1 at the end of the quarter. After leading 7-2 at the half and 9-3 midway through the third quar-

ter, the Falcons closed the margin to 9-6. State regained the initiative on scores by Dameron and David Kieffer, making it 11-6 after three periods. In the fourth, the Spartans were outscored 5-3 but prevailed as time ran out. In addition to Dameron's four goals, Mark Shamam had three, Jolly and Andy Hilgarner had two each while Scott Cebul, Jelus and Kieffer had one each.

Baseball—**April 17, 1993 (H):** Michigan State swept a doubleheader from Penn State, 6-3 and 4-3. In the opener, freshman Dan Garman pitched a complete game while winning his fifth of the season without a defeat. State scored four runs in the opening inning, with the key hit a triple by Matt Lockwood, which scored Steve Johnson and Jon Merchant. Trailing 2-0 through five innings of the second game, the Spartans finally came to life in the sixth when they scored all four runs. After Johnson singled and scored an unearned run, Brad Dobin and Jake Rindle walked. Then Eric Sumpter, called upon as a pinch hitter, became an instant hero. Connecting on a fast ball over the middle of the plate, his blast carried over the right field fence at the 352-marker to score three runs. The Spartans hung on as Steve Hirschman, most frequently used as a reliever, started and finished on the mound while striking out eight.

Lacrosse—**May 8, 1993 (H):** With support from a vocal home crowd at Old College Field, Michigan State defeated Ohio State 13-8. Ten different Spartans scored in the victory. Freshman Scott Cebul, sophomore Jeff Jelus and seniors Andy Hilgartner and Mark Shamam each netted two goals. Hilgartner and Shamam added three assists and two assists, respectively.

Baseball—**May 15 (H) & 16 (A), 1993:** The Spartans came up with two convincing wins over the University of Michigan, 10-1 before 1,348 fans at Kobs Field on Saturday and 12-8 in Ann Arbor on the next afternoon. In the home game, State took command early with three runs in the first inning, featuring Eric Sumpter's three-run homer, and six runs in the second, highlighted by consecutive home runs from Scott Ayotte, Jason Rambo and Jake Rindle. Pitcher Stuart Hirschman was the winner, completing his senior year as the team's career leader with 28 victories. Michigan State's big bats remained loaded on Sunday. Trailing 6-5, State regained the lead with four runs in the fifth inning. Dave Veres opened with a base hit and scored on a three-base error. Matt Riggins walked, Ayotte singled before Todd Menard finished it off with a home run. Michigan closed the gap

to 9-8 in their half of the fifth inning, but MSU put the game out of reach in the sixth with three insurance runs, including Sumpter's second round tripper of the weekend.

ATHLETE OF THE YEAR

Although he made Genoa, Ohio, his home, Bryan Smolinski sought a more competitive level of hockey and found it by moving to Detroit during his teen years. It was there he played on two national championship squads as a member of the Little Caesar's team. After six years in Detroit, he played in the Midwestern Junior B League in Ontario with the Stratford Cullitons. The very next year he headed to East Lansing where he was a four-year standout for the Spartans. As a freshman in 1989-1990 Smolinski was a part of the CCHA regular season and playoff championship team, in addition to being a part of the USA Junior National Team. By the time he was in his junior season, Bryan was the second-leading scorer on the team in two categories, with 30 goals and 65 points. From there he worked to become the 1992-1993 offen-

Bryan Smolinski

sive leader. In that year he led the CCHA in scoring with 25 goals and 26 assists for 51 points. He also led the team in scoring with 31 goals and 37 assists for 68 points over the entire schedule. His excellent performance caused him to be voted first team All-American and first team All-CCHA. At two stations in his life he almost never became a Spartan. First, baseball's Chicago Cubs wanted to draft him as a catcher out of high school, but by then he had made the choice of a future in hockey. Secondly, the Boston Bruins of the NHL selected him in the first round of the 1990 draft as the 21st pick overall. Fortunately for the MSU hockey program, Bryan put his professional career on hold as he chose to initially try the college scene. Subsequently, he went on to become a standout in the National Hockey League (NHL).

IN THE SPARTLITE

Baseball: The 1993 team completed an impressive spring trip posting a record of 10-4. Upon returning home, initially they continued their winning ways with a 5-1 record.

For the second consecutive season, Steve Johnson led the team in hitting with a .345 average.

Compared with previous past Spartan teams, the 1993 squad ranked sixth in runs scored (352), sixth in runs batted in (310), fourth with most two-base hits (97) and seventh in home runs (45).

Holding a conference record of 10-10 with only two weeks remaining on the schedule, there was slight hope for a Big Ten playoff spot. The team then finished 2-6 to dash the hope.

Basketball: With the addition of Penn State to the Big Ten, the basketball schedule format would be changed. Rather than a double-round-robin which had been used since 1975, each team would henceforth face eight conference teams twice and a rotating two others only once each year.

By defeating Morehead State 121-53 in the season-opener, MSU set two team records (total team score and 50 field goals).

Occasionally a disappointing loss is as memorable as an exciting victory. Such was the case in the Wisconsin game played at Breslin on January 23. Leading by 11, the Spartans went cold as they managed only eight points,

all from the free-throw line, in the final 11 minutes of play. Meanwhile, the Badgers had drawn within two, 66-64. With 2.5 seconds remaining, their sophomore guard, who had missed all four previous field goal attempts, let a three-pointer go from the southeast corner of the floor that caught the target and stunned the sellout crowd of 15,138.

For the third consecutive year, Mike Peplowski led the team in rebounds with 279 (10.0 per game). His total led the Big Ten for 1992-1993. In addition, making 192 of 399 field goals, Peplowski's shooting percentage of .639 would lead the conference.

Following completion of the 1992-1993 schedule, athletic director Merrily Dean-Baker announced that head coach Jud Heathcote had been granted a one-year extension on his contract, keeping him at the helm through the 1994-1995 season. At the same time, the AD announced that Tom Izzo, associate head coach, would be recommended to the Board of Trustees as the next head man.

Cross Country: During the 1992 season David Smith, team co-captain, was the first Spartan to finish in every meet in which he competed. David was a consistent performer. His times in the first three 8K races of the fall were 25:05, 25:04 and 25:06.

As usual, hosting the annual MSU Invitational provided coach Stintzi the opportunity to put his entire squad onto the course. A total of 15 Spartans negotiated the 8K course at Forest Akers.

At the Big Ten championships, hosted by the University of Illinois, State's runners collected 161 points for a sixth-place finish. Smith completed the course in fifth place (24:15). He was followed by Tim Topolinski in 19th (25:06); Toby Lefere who was 27th (25:13); Todd Koning, 59th (26:20) and Ryan Kennedy, 62nd (26:24).

As a team, MSU did not qualify for the NCAA championships; however, Smith ran independently in the meet at Bloomington, Ind., finishing the 10K race in 32:07 for 51st place.

Fencing: At the midwest championships in February, the team placed eighth.

For the first time since the sport began at State in 1926, all three squads (foil, epee and sabre) qualified to compete in the NCAA regionals where they finished in sixth place.

Leading the squad was senior captain Joe Gruber, who competed in epee and finished the season with a 24-33 record. Other contributors were freshman Shawn Smith who finished 56-17 in foil; sophomore Brian Holmes, 33-27 in foil; junior Kyle Glasgow, 14-10 in foil; senior Carl Lutzer, 42-26 in sabre and freshman William Flynn, 34-31 in sabre.

Smith was a rare recruit. Unlike most Spartan fencers who first became acquainted with the sport as a freshman in a PE class, Smith began fencing while in sixth grade. In his senior year of high school he placed second in the foil weapon at the competitive midwest championships. Smith would be the only Spartan to compete in the U.S. Fencing Association Junior Olympics at Colorado Spring, Colo.

Football: In a highly embarrassing afternoon, for the second year in a row Central Michigan University came down to East Lansing and defeated the Spartans, this time by a score of 24-20. It will forever remain a high point in CMU football history.

Tico Duckett would conclude his four-year career with 4,212 total rushing yards, ranking second only to Lorenzo White's 4,887.

Season leaders included Duckett (1,021 rushing yards), Jim Miller (1,368 passing yards), Mill Coleman (13 receptions for 586 yards), Craig Thomas (90 points scored) and Ty Hallock (87 unassisted tackles).

In planning future football schedules, the Big Ten athletic directors set aside eight rivalries that would not be interrupted. They included two MSU games: Michigan State-Michigan, Michigan State-Penn State, Michigan-Ohio State, Indiana-Purdue, Illinois-Northwestern, Iowa-Minnesota, Minnesota-Wisconsin and Iowa-Wisconsin.

Golf: At the Bruce Fossum Spartan Invitational in May, State's golfers scored a composite 888 to place fourth in the field of 20 teams. Heath Feld led the way with a three-round score of 72-74-72—218 to tie for second place honors. Other Spartan and their scores were Brian Bartolec 72-75-73—220; Mike Spencer 75-73-77—225; Chris Lemmon 79-74-75—228; Eric Spencer 79-73-76—228, Earl Eckenrode 78-77-77—232 and Greg Bartolec 74-82-79—235.

Playing against 17 other teams at the Wolverine Invitational in Ann Arbor, MSU placed fourth. Feld was the top Spartan with 74-71-67—212 and followed by Brian Bartolec with 217, Lemmon 221, Mike Spencer 222 and Eric Spencer 240.

Ken Horvath's squad could do no better than ninth at the Big Ten championships in Bloomington, Ind. As was the case all season long, Feld was the top Spartan, as he shot a 70-71-73-73—287 to tie for second in the individual scoring. Other team members and their scores were Mike Spencer 71-73-76-72—292; Brian Bartolec 72-79-76-74—301; Eric Spencer 75-81-78-73—307 and Lemmon 79-80-76-75—310.

With a composite team score of 895 and eighth-place finish, MSU qualified for the NCAA championships at the central regionals. More significantly, Heath Feld carded a three-round total of 214 to win the medallist honors, one shot under the runner-up from Kent State. He became the first Spartan to finish first in this prestigious event. Both Brian Bartolec and Mike Spencer carded 222s, Eric Spencer a 243 and Lemmon 245.

The NCAA championship team of Feld, Mike Spencer, Lemmon and the Bartolec brothers could not make the cut after the opening two rounds. Officially, they finished tied for 27th out of the field of 30.

Gymnastics: Scoring 276.55 points, State finished third behind Ohio State and Minnesota, at the Big Ten championships in Minneapolis, Minn. The Spartans were especially strong in the floor exercise event where senior Chris Spinosa tied for first, Paul Dackerman was fourth, Chip Downton 12th and Erik Montgomery 14th. Finishing 20th, John Orlando was State's top finisher in the all-around.

For the fourth straight year, State qualified for the NCAA regionals where senior Dave Adams advanced to the championships on the horizontal bar and where coach Rick Atkinson was named the regional coach of the year.

Hockey: In an early season 6-2 victory over Illinois-Chicago, Coach Mason gained his 368th win, passing Amo Bessone as MSU's winningest hockey coach. Then on March 12, Mason made college hockey history with a 6-5 victory over Kent State in the opening round of the CCHA playoff. This would be the 674th win in his total coaching career, surpassing the record for hockey coaches of the USA.

In a holiday special, State traveled to Anchorage, Alaska, to compete in the four-team Nissan-Jeep Classic. After an easy 7-1 opening win over British Columbia, the Spartans were upset by Kent State, 2-1 in the final.

Confronted with a myriad of player illnesses and injuries, Coach Mason guided his young squad to a 24-14-2 record and fourth-place finish in the CCHA regular-season.

Disappointment awaited at season's end. Falling to Ferris 3-2 in the semi-finals of the CCHA playoffs, State failed to qualify for the NCAA tournament for only the second time in 12 seasons.

After a preponderance of ties in the preceding season (eight), the Spartans played to only two draws in 1992-1993.

Lacrosse: The team opened the season with a one-week trip East where they would play three games: Lehigh at the University of Pennsylvania's Franklin Field in Philadelphia, Stony Brook at Long Island, N.Y., and Rutgers at New Brunswick, N.J.

Coach Kimball received a blow upon learning that the 1992 leading scorer with 32 goals, midfielder Robby Robertson, opted to not return to school for his senior year.

Coach Kimball described it best: "They never gave us a chance to breathe defensively. Their second 13 players would still be a top-10 team." He was referring to number one-ranked Syracuse, a team that had just dominated his Spartans, 27-7. In a unique setting, the game was played on the turf of the Duffy Daugherty football building after a driving snowstorm had forced them inside.

Posting a season record of 8-6, two wins were in overtime, 15-14 over Maryland BC and 11-10 at Boston College.

The team's leading scorers were Andy Hilgartner with 45 points and Rob Dameron, who connected for 25 goals.

Soccer: In early October the MSU squad traveled to California to compete in the Santa Clara Cup Tournament. After winning a 2-1 overtime game from the host school, State was shut out by San Diego State 4-0.

Michigan State's young offense was sparked by Andrew Roff (five goals and six assists), Dan Radke (five and six), Brett Christensen (five and two) and Sean Nemnich (four and one).

Swimming and Diving: In a 142-88 dual meet win against Cleveland State, diver John Maxon recorded a three-meter diving score of 359.88 for six dives. In so doing, he broke the team record of 353.30 set in 1977 by former Olympian Dave Burgering.

At the conference championships, freshman Chris-Carol Bremer, the 1992 German national champion and Olympic finalist, was a key contributor. He placed fifth in the 500-yard freestyle (4:23.4), broke a school record and placed third in the 200-yard butterfly (1:46.15) and

qualified for the NCAAs with a 15:21.31 in the 1,650-yard freestyle. Bremer would later better that butterfly time in 1:45.77 while placing seventh in the national meet. Other contributors to the Big Ten team that totaled 214 points were Alex Mull, Tim Shanley, Chris Sholl, David Klaviter, Tom Munley, Kevin Zielinski, divers John Maxson and Ryan Koonce and Ron Orris, who set a new school record (48.740) while placing third in the 100-yard butterfly.

Tennis: Although he remained in school only one year, Mashiska "Mo" Washington from Swartz Creek, Mich., proved to be one of the very best players to ever wear the Green and White. He began play as a Spartan in the fall of 1992 as the top-ranked player in the Midwest after winning the Western Closed Tournament.

Hosting the Spartan Invitational in January, Washington won his four matches before losing in the finals to player of the year in the conference, Rick Naumoff of Minnesota, 2-6, 6-2, 6-3.

State was one of eight teams invited to compete in the Tennessee Vol Tennis Classic in Knoxville, Tenn., and they completed the tournament in third place. Severe weather conditions hampered play significantly, consequently, early meets were shortened to four singles matches and one double. MSU defeated Tulsa and Wake Forest while losing to the eventual winner, Virginia Commonwealth, 4-3.

At the Big Ten matches in Iowa City, MSU lost the opener meet to Penn State, 4-3, as Washington, Kevin Seckel and Wade Martin were the only Spartan winners. After losing the doubles point to Ohio State in the second challenge of the tournament, the singles competitors came alive as number one Brad Dancer won (6-4, 6-3), as did number three Seckel (7-5, 6-3), number four Martin (6-2, 2-6, 6-3) as Gus Giltner closed out the 4-2 win (6-3, 6-2). On the next afternoon the battle for fifth place against the host Hawkeyes stood at 3-3 with Washington, Seckel and Martin registering victories. The team result would fall upon Dancer, who led in his opening set 5-3; but his scrappy competitor fought back for a 7-5, 5-7, 6-1 win, pushing State into sixth place in the final standings.

Track and Field: Competing on the home turf of Jenison, the Spartans scored 54 points but could finish no better than fifth in the assortment of 13 teams at the 67th annual central collegiate indoor championships. In particular, Dave Smith had a busy afternoon. He was a member of the winning distance medley relay team (9:32.99), helped the 800-meter relay place second (7:37.88) and finished third in the 3,000-meter run (8:25.40).

From fifth place in 1992, the Spartans dropped all the way to 10th at the 83rd Big Ten indoor championships run at Madison, Wis. Three runners accounted for the scant 13 points. Dave Couch placed third in the 3,000-meter run (8:19.41) and fifth in the 5,000-meter event (14:41.96). Todd Koning ran fourth in the 800 meters (1:54.01) and Mark Davis was sixth in the 55-meter hurdles (07.58).

In the first outdoor competition of the year, at the Dogwood Relays in Knoxville, Tenn., three Spartans in particular ran impressive races. Senior Dave Smith placed second and surpassed the NCAA provisional qualifying time in the 1,500-meter run with a time of 3:44.0. Junior hurdler Larry Harden finished fourth in the 110-meter hurdles with a time of 14.35, while senior Tim Topolinski finished third in the 10,000-meter race with a 30.17.

With a time of 47.86, Ashley Nelson was the winner of the 400-meter dash at the central collegiate outdoor championships. State runners collected 67 points, good enough for sixth place.

Distance ace Smith was a star performer in the Big Ten outdoor championships at Ralph Young Field. In a challenging triple, he was fourth in the 5,000-meter run (14:37.93), second in the 1,500 meters (3:48.71) and was crowned champion at 10,000 meters (30:09.71). Others who reached the finals were Brad Fields, ninth in the 200-meters (21.71); Koning, ninth, running the 800-meters (1:59.78); Dave Couch, placing fifth at the 3,000-meter steeplechase (9:05.33); Chris Lett, seventh, also in the steeplechase (9:13.67); Toby Lefere, a fifth place finish at 10,000-meters (30:37.06); Davis second in the 110-meter hurdles (14.08) and sixth in the 400-meter hurdles (53.36); Harden, who placed third in the same high hurdle event (14.22). With a fifth-place discus toss of 163' 5" Brett Organek was the only Spartan to place in a field event. Jarion Bradley and Steve Morozovich finished eighth and 11th in the decathlon. Totaling 62.5 points, the team was sixth.

Wrestling: The team placed eighth at the annual early season Midlands Invitational at Evanston, Ill. The invitational is open to collegiate and post-collegiate wrestlers. Freshman Phil Judge (134 pounds) finished with a 5-3 record and sixth place. Another first-year man, Brian

Bolton (126 pounds) finished eighth with a 3-3 record. Emilio Collins (190 pounds) was sixth with a 3-1 mark, Dan Wirnsberger (158 pounds) fifth with a 4-2 record while heavyweight Don Whipp gained third-place honors.

Michigan State finished a disappointing 10th at the Big Ten tournament in Columbus, Ohio. Scoring only 18.75 points, the Spartans were led by Wirnsberger who was fifth, Collins in fourth place, and heavyweight Whipp, a seventh-place finisher.

Following a 5-9 dual-meet record and that 10th-place finish in the Big Tens, MSU had a remarkable showing in the NCAA championship meet at Iowa State, scoring 29.5 points and finishing 12th out of 81 teams. Leading the way were Whipp, the senior, who placed a remarkable second place and Wirnsberger who placed fourth. It was the highest Michigan State team finish since 1984. Placing as top eight competitors, the two automatically gained All-American recognition.

EXTRA! 1993 NIT TOURNAMENT

Michigan State reached the first round of the 1993 NIT tournament. The following is the Spartans' box score for that game.

OKLAHOMA 88—MICHIGAN STATE 86

	FG-FGA	FT-FTA	REB	A	PF	TP
Stephens	5-10	0-0	5	1	4	12
Miller	3-3	2-2	8	1	4	8
Peplowski	9-14	6-6	12	1	4	24
Snow	3-4	0-0	5	9	2	6
Respert	9-19	0-0	4	4	2	20
Weshinskey	6-13	0-0	1	4	4	12
Brooks	0-0	0-0	2	0	1	0
Beathea	1-1	0-0	0	0	0	2
Zulauf	1-2	0-0	2	0	1	2
TOTALS	37-66	8-8	44	20	23	86

Halftime: Michigan State 50-44; **Three-point field goals:** 4-13 (Stephens 2-3, Respert 2-5, Weshinskey 0-5); **Officials:** Olah, McDaniel, Foxx; **Attendance:** 5,483.

In 1992-93, Mike Peplowski led the Big Ten in rebounds (279) and shooting percentage (.639).

MSU
1993-1994

TALES TO TELL

It's comforting to know that on each and every home football Saturday in the fall, 72,027 spectators are assured of a winning performance by a Spartan team. Few experiences can match the surge of adrenaline within a Michigan State loyalist as the marching band takes the field. From the trademark kickstep run-on routine to the kaleidoscopic forming of the moving block "S" while playing refrains of the beloved fight song, it is a patented routine scripted with tradition and perfection. How can such impeccability be assured? The answer is in three words—practice, practice, practice! To be exact, a total of 90 minutes each night, Monday through Friday, 4:30-6:00 p.m. during the season. As band director John Madden himself states, "Membership is granted into the Spartan Marching Band (SMB) through musicianship. Preparation is the most important part of the audition process." Such readiness extends beyond the audition stage. It is ongoing.

Today's edition of SMB comes with a history. Founded in 1870 as a 10-member student musical group, it evolved into a military unit connected with the school's ROTC installation. In fact, until 1952, band members were replete with military khaki uniforms. Slowly, through the remainder of the 20th century the MAC-MSC-MSU band grew in stature, reputation and certainty in numbers. Today a total of 275 members will take the field on a given Saturday afternoon.

John Madden leads the Spartan marching band.

HEADLINES of 1994

- Major league baseball season is shortened and the World Series cancelled by a players' strike.
- A predawn earthquake hits Los Angeles leaving 51 dead and $20 billion damage.
- An ongoing investigation of the Whitewater affair, a real estate venture in Arkansas, involves President Bill Clinton, Hillary Clinton and former business associates.
- Jacqueline Kennedy Onassis dies of cancer.

SCOREBOARD

	W	L	T	Avg.
Baseball	26	29	0	.473
Track and Field	0	1	0	.000
Football	6	6	0	.500
Basketball	20	12	0	.625
Tennis	8	14	0	.364
Cross Country	no dual meets			
Swimming and Diving	7	4	0	.636
Wrestling	11	4	0	.733
Hockey	23	13	5	.622
Fencing	10	12	0	.455
Golf	tournament play only			
Gymnastics	6	11	0	.353
Soccer	7	10	2	.421
Lacrosse	7	6	0	.538

Among the many loyal Spartans there are some real "band fans." Like clockwork, on game day they arrive on Walter Adams Memorial Field (Landon Field) before or at 10:30 a.m., the exact time band members muster for a final rehearsal. These fans seat themselves in the bleachers adjacent to the practice field and proceed to listen and watch those final 60 minutes of preparation. Then at 11:30, as the musicians and color guard begin their march across the bridge toward Sparty Plaza and on to the stadium, the SMB gurus fall in behind the 34th or final row of musicians and join the parade with vicarious pleasure. For some their day is complete, as they would consider staying to watch the football game as extraneous, an event between marching band performances.

The ingredients to professor John Madden's recipe for award-winning performances include 32 alto saxophones, 24 mellophones, 16 tenor saxophones, 48 B-flat trumpets, eight E-flat cornets, 32 trombones, 16 baritones, 16 sousaphones, 10 snare drums, six tenor drums, seven base drums, 12 symbols, 11 Big Ten flag bearers, 32 color guards, two feature twirlers and one limber drum major capable of bending backwards enough to touch the ground with the plume on top of his head piece.

Oh yes, for the record, the MSU athletic department picks up the tab for activities of the SMB and they do so willingly. No group of students better represents the university.

TEAM OF THE YEAR

The "Fire and Ice" combination of Shawn Respert and Eric Snow kept East Lansing fans excited and led MSU to its fourth NCAA appearance in five years, a feat never before accomplished in East Lansing. After closing the regular season with a 20-12 record, the Spartans knocked out Seton Hall 84-73 in the first round of the tournament before losing 85-74 to Duke, the eventual tournament runner-up. In addition to Respert's All-American season (24.3 ppg), Snow stood behind only Magic Johnson for single season assists with 213, and he stood behind Magic and Darryl Johnson for single-season steals with 57. Anthony Miller was another major contributor, averaging nine rebounds and 12.6 ppg.

MAKING HISTORY

The Michigan State Rugby Club won the Michigan Cup Tournament by defeating Cooley Law School, Central Michigan and Ferris State.

In October, as part of the Stars and Stripes volleyball tour, the USA 1992 men's Olympic team met the Japanese national team for a game in the Breslin Student Events Center.

The MSU water skiing team won the Midwest regionals at Camelot Lake near Syracuse, Ind.

In a shift in responsibilities announced by athletic director Merrily Dean-Baker on January 24, everyday duties of football, basketball and hockey would become the responsibility of Clarence Underwood with new title, senior associate AD. The announcement included news on an added, yet unfilled, staff position, director of student-athlete support services. The moves did not affect Baker's $118,000 salary or Underwood's $85,304 salary. Although the message which justified the move noted that the athletic department would become more efficient and responsive, speculation arose that the move was made in an attempt to transfer authority from Baker to MSU President McPherson.

A February 17 confidential memo from Clarence Underwood to President McPherson was intercepted by *The State News* and made public. It seems that Underwood was requesting the authority to seek basketball coach Jud Heathcote's resignation. If Jud refused to retire, then he would be terminated March 31, 1994. The president never

The 1993-94 basketball team. Front row (left to right): trainer T. Mackowiak, manager M. Zimmerman, manager M. Franklin, K. Weshinskey, D. Hart, E. Snow, S. Respert, S. Nicodemus, E. Qualman and manager L. Johnson; back row (left to right): asst. coach S. Joplin, head coach J. Heathcote, Q. Brooks, J. Garavaglia, J. Feick, A. Miller, S. Polonowski, D. Beathea, assoc. head coach T. Izzo and asst. coach B. Gregory

bought into the plan and, to the contrary, public support for Heathcote was overwhelming.

Money is a driving force. During MSU's 1993 football season in which the Spartans finished 6-6, nearly 90,000 tickets were not purchased. This amounted to $1.35 million in lost revenue and precipitated a "perform or else" communiqué from MSU President Peter McPherson to football coach George Perles. In it, a threatening message outlined that the coach was expected to produce "an outstanding 1994 season."

GREAT STATE DATES

Football—**September 11, 1993 (H):** In the first season opening victory since 1989, State defeated Kansas University, 31-14. If outgaining KU 431-265 in total yardage wasn't enough, the Jayhawks turned the ball over five times, three times halting potential scoring drives in the opening half. The first giveaway was an interception by junior cornerback Stan Callender on the game's opening possession, setting up a 16-play, 94-yard drive with Scott Greene scoring on a one-yard pass from Jim Miller. After surrendering a safety, the Spartans raised the halftime score to 14-2 on a 10-play, 80-yard drive concluded on a Jim Miller-to-Napoleon Outlaw seven-yard pass play.

Between two Kansas field goals in the third quarter, State marshaled another 80-yard scoring drive. Featuring the thrusts of Craig Thomas and Duane Goulbourne, Thomas reached the end zone on a 12-yard run. In the final period, Bill Stoyanovich split the uprights on a 50-yard field goal and with 3:05 remaining in the game, Damian Manson intercepted a desperation pass and returned it five-yards for the final touchdown.

Cross Country—**September 11, 1993 (H):** Scoring 37 points, Michigan State managed to win the MSU Invitational by defeating Eastern Michigan with 41 and Arizona, 42. It was the season-opener on the 8,000-meter layout at Forest Akers. Senior Toby Lefere finished in second place with a time of 24:14.35. Sophomore Bill Crosby was fourth (25:20.86) and Chris Lett fifth (25:22.34). The next Spartans to finish were Pat Hoard in 12th (25:55.88) and Kevin Sweeney 14th (26:07.51).

Football—**October 9, 1993 (H):** Before a sell-out crowd of 78,311 fans and an ABC-TV regional audience, State scored on its first three possessions to defeat the University of Michigan 17-7. The opening score came at 9:36 in the first quarter when fullback Brice Abrams topped an 11-play, 65-yard drive by scoring from the one-yard line. On the ensuing kick-off Scott Greene jarred the ball from the U of M's Tyrone Wheatley on a vicious tackle and Pete Drzal recovered at the Michigan 30-yard

line. Failing to gain adequate yardage, field goal kicker Bill Stoyanovich was called upon and he delivered a 47-yarder. State's scoring was complete for the day at 11:23 of the second quarter. Following a 70-yard drive featuring a Jim Miller-Mill Coleman 17-yard pass play and a Duane Goulbourne 17-yard run, Greene scored on a three-yard pass play. Quarterback Miller would finish the game 18-of-24 for 187 yards. From that point and through the entire second half, the Spartan defense took charge. Led by Myron Bell, Stan Callendar, Steve Wasyik, Juan Hammonds, Reggie Garnett and Rob Fredrickson, the Wolverines were held to 33 yards rushing and they succeeded on only four-of-12 third-down conversion attempts.

Soccer—**October 20, 1993 (H):** Playing under a steady drizzle, MSU dominated as they played on the Ohio State end of the field during the opening 55 minutes. With 34:50 to play, forward Sean Nemnich cleanly handled a pass from Andrew Roffand and beat the Buckeye net minder from 15 feet in front. Seven minutes later, Curt Weiermiller squeezed a pass through the defense to Doug Consigny, who was all alone in from of the net. Consigny converted and the Spartans had defeated OSU, 2-0. The Michigan State defense was led by sophomore Chad O'Kulich while keeper Curtis Payment was required to make just four saves during the afternoon.

Soccer—**October 24, 1993 (H):** MSU shocked 16th-ranked Penn State, 1-0, before nearly 600 fans who packed the bleachers of Old College Field. The solitary goal came with 33:52 remaining in the opening half as Dan Radke broke free from the defense and clanged a shot off the post. Alert teammate Sean Nemnich was there for the rebound, which he redirected back into the net. The unheralded defensive line of Scot Schlesinger, Chad O'Kulich, Brent Agin, Andy Stewart and Cullen Brown shut down the usually potent Nittany Lion offense. This only frustrated the PSU players as with one minute of playing time remaining, they initiated a brawl that eventually involved all 22 players on the field. Punches and kicks were exchanged before the three officials restored order.

Football—**November 13, 1993 (A):** The scoreboard at Ross-Ade Stadium in West Lafayette read: Michigan State 27, Purdue 24, and the game was just as close as those numbers would indicate as the lead changed sides five times. Held to a meager 109 yards rushing, the State offense fell dependent on the passing arm of Jim Miller

and the Waterford, Mich., senior responded. Linking up with six different receivers during the afternoon, he connected on 21 of 27 passes for 200 yards. Trailing 24-20 with 7:52 remaining, offensive co-ordinator Morris Watts orchestrated an 11-play, 93-yard drive that finally reached the end zone on a Miller-Scott Greene five-yard pass with 2:19 remaining in the game. Bill Stoyanovich converted. Two plays were prominent in that final series. First, a Miller-to-Napoleon Outlaw toss which netted 39 yards and secondly, a 15-yard flare pass on third-and-six to Duane Goulbourne, a connection that kept the drive alive at the PU 24-yard line. The Boilermakers had two more chances to score, only to see cornerback Stan Callender intercept at the Spartan 30 and then to have a 49-yard field goal attempt sail wide right of the upright with 23 seconds left.

Gymnastics—**January 8, 1994 (H):** Michigan State squeaked out a 269.85 to 268.50 victory against Minnesota. The Spartans won the pommel horse, vault and parallel bars to outperform the Golden Gophers. Kevin Brown finished in first place on the high bar and Stephen Bello took first place on the parallel bars.

Basketball—**January 8, 1994 (H):** Michigan State upset number 21 Illinois, 79-74, for their first conference win of the young season. The game came down to the final 2:38 with MSU leading 67-66 and Shawn Respert at the free-throw line for two shots emanating from an intentional foul. The Illini coach, Lou Henson, protested vehemently, claiming that the less accurate Anthony "Pig" Miller should be at line, not the more accurate Respert. The coach's complaint became so heated that he was charged with one technical foul, followed by a second technical and an automatic game ejection. As it turned out, Henson had a legitimate "beef." As Respert would later confess:

> "I think the refs just got caught up in the confusion. Anthony was the one that was fouled, but I went to the line, figuring it couldn't hurt. All they could do was take me off and put Anthony up there."

The result was six foul shots for Shawn. He sank five, providing State a 72-66 lead. The visitors never recovered.

Swimming and Diving—**January 14, 1994 (H):** State won every event in defeating the University of Toledo, 145-96. The medley relay team of Lars Kalenka, Al

Goecke, Andy Faberlle and Tom Munley opened the evening with a first in a time of 3:27.22. From there, Spartan firsts kept coming with three double-winners: Ron Orris in the, 1,000-yard freestyle (9:29.83) and 200-yard butterfly (1:53.61); Uwe Volk who finished first in the 200-yard freestyle ((1:40.51) and 200-yard backstroke (2:22.44) and diver John Maxson, the winner on both boards 303.60 points on the one-meter and 310.28 on the three-meter. Other winners for MSU were David Klaviter in the 50-yard freestyle (22.57); Kalenka, 200-yard individual medley (1:58.15); Alec Mull in the 100-yard freestyle (46.23); Tom Munley, winner of the 500-yard freestyle (4:37.49) and finally, seldom used Clinton Wyatt was the winner of the 200-yard breaststrokc (2:22.44). The 400-yard freestyle relay team of Volk, Munley, Mull and Orris closed out the meet with a win in the time of 3:04.74.

Hockey—**January 15, 1994 (A):** In a scoreless first period, Anson Carter was one of seven Spartans who had a shot blocked by the alert Bowling Green goalie; however, Carter the Scarborough, Ontario, sophomore found the mark at 11:23 of the second period. He picked up a Steve Guolla pass on a three-on-two rush and after being initially denied, pushed the rebound into the net. Rem Murray made it 2-0 at 14:24 as he scored MSU's first short-handed goal of the season. State widened their lead at the 13:31 mark of the third period as Bart Turner threaded a pass through the Falcon defense to Matt Albers who slapped home the insurance goal. From there the team went into a defensive posture as they succeeded in preserving goalie Mike Buzak's second shutout of the season, 3-0.

Tennis—**January 16, 1994 (N):** In the backdraw of the Volunteer Classic sponsored by the University of Tennessee, State was matched against the University of Michigan and opened by securing the doubles team point on identical winning-set scores of 6-4 by Mishiska Washington-Richard Watson and Jim Madrigal-Jayson Bedford. In singles competition, Washington was a winner at number one, 7-6, 6-2; at number three Madrigal won, 6-1, 6-1; Mark Schwagel won at number four, 6-4, 6-3 as did Jayson Bedford at number five. The 5-2 Michigan State victory over the Wolverines was the first since 1967. Too bad Coach Orlando and his team were 585 miles from home when it happened.

Wrestling—**January 18, 1994 (A):** In the unfriendly confines of Cliff Keen Arena in Ann Arbor, State defeated the favored Michigan Wolverines, 21-15. Tom Minkel's squad put the pressure on early as they won the opening four matches to open a 14-0 lead. Two of the victories were by decision: Kelvin Jackson (118 pounds) and Jud Kramer (134 pounds) while the other two were technical falls, Demond Betts (126 pounds) at 22-8 and Phil Judge (142 pounds) at 10-0. Following losses in the next three weight classes, the Spartans finished with significant wins from Erich Harvey (177 pounds) and Emilio Collins (190 pounds) to seal the first win over the U of M since 1984.

Hockey—**January 21, 1994 (A):** Michigan State upset number one Michigan 6-3 at Crisler Arena for its first win in Ann Arbor since 1990. Following goals from Rem Murray, Kelly Harper and Stcve Guolla, the Spartans led 3-1 in the second period. However, before the next intermission, the Wolverines had responded with another pair of goals and the game was tied 3-3 entering the final 20-minutes of play. Harper quieted the U of M fans as he put the Spartans back on track just 20 seconds into the final stanza with his second goal of the evening. From there the defense, led by Ryan Fleming, Nicholas Perreault, Chris Slater, Chris Sullivan, Steve Norton, Bart Vanstaalduinen, assisted goalie Mike Buzak, in keeping the Blue off the scoreboard. At the opposite end of ice, freshman right wing Tony Tuzzolini made it 5-3 before Murray notched an empty-netter to end the scoring.

Fencing—**January 22, 1994 (A):** Competing in the Wayne State Invitational, the State fencers defeated Tri-State (21-6), Case Western (14-13) and Cleveland State (19-8). The freshmen duo of Jeff Conover and Kevin Ruben led the attack by going 12-3 and 10-5, respectively. Finishing with 9-6 records for the afternoon were sophomores Ben Greenberg, John Flynn and Shawn Smith along with junior Ben Ibach.

Swimming and Diving—**January 28, 1994 (H):** The Indiana swimmers made a statement early as they won the opening event, the 200-yard medley relay, in a new pool record time of 1:33.81. From there, Richard Bader's crew began to make it interesting, winning the next four events. Uwe Volk won the 1,000-yard freestyle in 9:15.20 (also a McCaffree Pool record) and then came back three events later to take the individual medley in 1:53.10. Tom Munley finished first in the 200-yard freestyle (1:41.15) as did Alec Mull in the 50-yard freestyle (21.31) and 100-yard freestyle (45.81). Other Spartans first were swum by Andy Faberlle in the 100-yard butter-

fly (50.96) and Lars Kalenka in the 100-yard backstroke (51.84). Diver John Maxson was a surprise winner on the high board with 320.63 points. When the team points were subtotaled it became evident, the winner of the final event, the 400-yard freestyle relay would win the meet and the quartet of Mull, Faberlle, Kamp Purdy and Ron Orris held of the Hoosiers to win in an impressive time of 3:05.73. The final score read Michigan State 124, Indiana 119.

Basketball—**January 29, 1994 (H):** MSU led 85-84 with 50 seconds remaining, but the University of Iowa was in possession. At this point, Eric Snow altered the plot by slapping the ball away from his man, and suddenly the Spartans were in a position to control their own destiny. Following a timeout, Kris Weshinskey found himself in possession but was smothered by a defender. As the shot clock was on the verge of running out, he forced up a three-point attempt that caromed from the rim to Quinton Brooks, who scored off the glass to seal the victory. The visitors had 8.5 seconds for two desperation three-point attempts that failed. In statistical support of their victory, State won the battle of the rebounds, 42-36 and, as a result, dominated in second-chance points, 37-16. Regardless, it was a nail-biter all the way as the Hawkeyes hung on, leading 71-70 with 6:18 to play. Using their relentless full-court press throughout the game, Iowa led in steals with 12 and prompted Coach Heathcote to comment, "Every out-of-bounds play was an adventure. We just could not get the ball in play (at times)." As usual, Shawn Respert was the leading scorer with 29, he was followed by Jamie Feick and Brooks with 13 each and Weshinskey with 11.

Wrestling—**January 29, 1994 (A):** With Michigan State defeating Northwestern 22-13, the final score is misleading inasmuch as the result was in doubt until the final two matches when Emilio Collins (190 pounds) won by forfeit and Rob Train edged his heavyweight opponent 1-0. Other winners for State were junior college transfer Kelvin Jackson (118 pounds) 16-5; Demond Betts (126 pounds) 7-5; Phil Judge (142 pounds) 7-2 and Dan Wirnsberger (158 pounds) 7-3.

Wrestling—**January 30, 1994 (H):** In a doubleheader, the second of four scheduled for the season, State defeated the University of Illinois 30-10 and then, using many backups, topped Ferris State 28-12. Moving into the national rankings for the first time in three years, the number 13 Spartans were led from the very beginning by Kelvin Jackson (118 pounds) who overwhelmed his Illini opponent 27-11 while later defeating his Bulldog counterpart, 6-2. MSU never trailed in either meet after that. Other impressive performances against Illinois were turned in by Dan Wirnsberger (158 pounds), 9-4. Sophomore Joel Morissette improved to 23-7 at 167 pounds with a 15-7 victory and he was followed by a pair of pins, redshirt freshman Erich Harvey (177 pounds) at 4:02 and junior Emilio Collins (190 pounds), who needed only 2:08. Retired coach, Grady Peninger, returned to the Spartan sideline, being recognized as honorary coach for the day.

Fencing—**January 29, 1994 (H):** In the final home competition of the season, State defeated Michigan 16-11, Cleveland State 17-10, Detroit-Mercy 21-6 and Tri-State 19-8. Leading the way for Coach Freihert were Kevin Reuben and Shawn Smith, each of whom scored perfect 15-0 scores during the afternoon.

Hockey—**February 19, 1994 (A):** Junior goalie Mike Buzak blocked eight shots in the opening minutes and 27 shots throughout the game, leading State to a 5-1 victory over the University of Michigan before 18,398 fans in Detroit's Joe Louis Arena. Following 20 minutes of scoreless hockey, Mike Burkett found the back of the net on a power-play goal at 10:39 of the second period. Anson Carter made it 2-0 on a deflection and freshman defenseman Chris Slater let fly with a slap shot that whizzed by the U of M goalie at 9:25. With the Wolverines registering their only goal on a power play, the middle stanza closed with the Spartans in front 3-1. The final margin expanded from two to four with third-period goals by Scott Worden and Matt Albers, a native of Ann Arbor.

Basketball—**February 23, 1994 (H):** It wasn't "Shawn Respert Appreciation Night," but maybe it should have been. In defeating 20th-ranked Minnesota, 85-68, the six-foot-three junior scored one-half of his team's winning total. Connecting on 16-of-24 field goals, including eight-of-12 three-pointers plus three-of-three free throws, his 43-point total bettered Steve Smith's Breslin Center record of 38 points set in 1990. Even more impressive was his output during the final 20 minutes: 10-of-12 from the field and both tries from the free-throw line for a 27-point second half. As for the game itself, after State built a 21-12 lead in the first half, little question remained as to the eventual winner. Overall, the team outshot the Gophers .517-.414 in field goals and .667-

.333 from beyond the arc. Anthony "Pig" Miller was the only other Spartan in double figures with 11 points on five-of-nine from the field and one free throw.

Basketball—**March 9, 1994 (H):** In their only encounter against Indiana during the season, State met and defeated the Hoosiers in the home-season closer, 94-78. After the 15,138 fans had saluted Erik Qualman, Kris Weshinskey and Anthony Miller as the graduating seniors, junior Shawn Respert began his own night of recognition. As the Hoosier coach Bobby Knight would later say, "The thing I really like about him (Respert) is he plays under control; he's a very, very difficult player to play against." On this night, Respert exploded for 40 points, hitting 13-for-21 from the floor with four-of-six three-pointers. Weshinskey added 20 points and 11 rebounds. Miller tallied 13 points and brought down eight rebounds. Eric Snow contributed 12 assists and his usual smothering defense. The turning point in the contest came after IU had hit eight of its first 10 second-half shots to aid in turning a 48-40 halftime deficit into a 61-59 lead, MSU retaliated with a nine-zero run that once more put them in front, this time for good. The Spartans shot a sizzling .655 (19 of 29) the first half and .567 (34 of 60) for the full 40 minutes.

Lacrosse—**March 17, 1994 (H):** They don't come any closer. David Kieffer muscled his way through a defender and with only 12 seconds remaining in the 8-8 tie with New Hampshire, he blasted the winning goal into the net from 10 yards out. The first quarter was all Michigan State as the offense unleashed five goals while senior goalie Chris McCady held the visitors scoreless. Finally, the Wildcats' offense came alive with their first goal of the game at 4:44 of the second period and before intermission had been reached, the Spartan advantage had shrunk to 5-3. The New Hampshire offense continued after the break as they outscored State 4-3 in the third period narrowing the gap to one. They knotted the score only 11 seconds into the fourth quarter and the game remained tied until Kieffer's game-winner. Kieffer and Stan Ungechauer were credited with two goals each and Jay Ledinski, Eric Huss, Scott Cebul, Dan Edell and Doug Jolly one each.

Baseball—**April 3, 1994 (A):** Thanks to six well-pitched innings by Daron Beitel, State defeated Michigan, 4-3. The right-hander from Midland yielded only two runs and earned his first collegiate win to pace the Spartans. After giving up a double to open the seventh,

he was relieved by Derek Landis, who allowed the final Wolverine run but still earned his second save of the season. State scored twice in the second inning, first on Scott Ayotte's single and the second on a wild pitch. In the third inning, shortstop Dave Veres singled home outfielder Steve Money to score the third run and Ayotte scored MSU's final run on a ground out.

Lacrosse—**April 9, 1994 (H):** In defeating Butler University 14-11, Michigan State improved its record to 6-2 and extended the winning streak to five games, the longest since winning six in 1992. The Bulldogs opened the scoring with two goals within the first three minutes, but MSU bounced back on a goal by co-captain Jay Ledinsky and the Spartans went on to score the next five and later lead 9-5 at halftime. Butler came on strong in the second half, closing to within 11-10 with 9:44 left in the game, and apparently tied on a goal that was called back on a penalty. State then took charge. Scoring the next three goals, including one by junior David Kieffer, who led the team with three goals, they never looked back. Sophomore Scott Cebul and freshman Stan Ungechauer each scored twice, as goalkeeper Chris McCrady stopped 16 shots.

Tennis—**April 23, 1994 (H):** With the Gus Giltner-Masheska Washington pair the only winner for State in the doubles competitions, Illinois was awarded the first team point. The meet then became a battle of the singles matches. Washington continued his winning ways with a 6-4, 6-2 victory from the number one spot. Then, suddenly things looked rather bleak as both number two Kevin Sekal and number three Richard Watson met defeat and State trailed 3-1. It was up to the bottom half of the line-up and amazingly the remaining Spartans turned in straight set wins for a 4-3 victory over the Illini. James Madrigal was a 7-6, 6-3 winner at number four; number five Jayson Bedford managed a 6-4, 6-4 win at the number five spot and Giltner then sealed MSU's first Big Ten "W" of the season, with a 7-5, 7-5 victory at number six.

Tennis—**April 24, 1994 (H):** Led by the #1 doubles pair of Gus Giltner and Masheska Washington who won an 8-6 set, the doubles-team point went to Michigan State. Also adding points in the 6-1 victory over Purdue were Washington with a 7-6, 6-1 win in the number one singles match; both number two Kevin Seckel and number four James Madrigal with identical 6-3, 6-3 straight set wins; number five Jayson Bedford, who coasted through his first set 6-2 and rallied in the second 7-5,

after being down 5-2 and finally number six Giltner, who won a tie-breaker 7-6 set and then crushed his opponent 6-0 in the second set.

Lacrosse—**April 16, 1994 (A):** Michigan State easily defeated Ohio State 16-6, maintaining a perfect 6-0 record in the Great Western Lacrosse League. The Spartans opened the scoring 45 seconds into the game on a goal from sophomore midfielder Scott Cebul. Thirty seconds later junior midfielder Jeff Jelus gave MSU a 2-0 lead. Nine different Spartans scored, including five goals and two assists from freshman midfielder Stan Ungechauer.

Baseball—**May 15-16, 1994 (H):** The Spartans needed three victories in the final weekend against the University of Iowa to guarantee a spot in the Big Ten four-team playoff and that's exactly what they delivered. On Sunday the bats were booming and the results were wins at 6-5 and 13-10. Led by first baseman Todd Menard, who hit two monster home runs in the opener, State scored three times in the sixth inning to break a 3-3 tie. The win in the second game seems remarkable upon realizing the Green and White trailed 10-3 after three and a half innings. From there they began to chip away with two runs in the fourth, four in the fifth and finally, four in the sixth. Suddenly the 10-9 Iowa lead had become a 13-10 Michigan State advantage. Scott Ayotte, Andy Johnson and Coby Garner hit home runs during the comeback and tight relief pitching by Jim Antonangeli aided the cause. Coach Tom Smith called upon Trevor Harvey to pitch on the next afternoon and the big lefthander proceeded to scatter eight hits in a complete-game 7-1 victory. Dave Veres broke a 0-0 game with a two-run homer in the third. From there MSU put the game away with four runs in the bottom of the fourth on four hits, two Hawkeye errors and a balk.

ATHLETE OF THE YEAR

After red-shirting in 1990-1991, Shawn Respert was a four-year basketball starter and led the team in scoring in each of those four seasons (1992-1995). Upon completion of his collegiate career, his 2,531 points ranks him as the all-time leading Spartan scorer. He was a All-Big Ten second-team pick as a sophomore and first-team selection in both his junior and senior years, while earning

All-American recognition in those final two years as well. Shawn was three times voted the team's Most Valuable Player and in his senior season, as the conference scoring leader (25.5 ppg), was selected as the Big Ten player of the year. He holds the school record with 331 three-pointers and ranks second in shooting percentage from beyond the arc (45.4 percent). In the MSU record books, he was listed in the top two in *10* MSU career statistical categories. His highest scoring game came in 1994 when he accounted for 43 points in an 85-68 victory over Minnesota, but he scored 35 points or more on six occasions. Also, in 1994 he tied a Big Ten record with eight three-point baskets in a single-game. After graduation he went on to play in the NBA, being drafted in the first round by the Portland Trailblazers.

Shawn Respert

IN THE SPARTLITE

Baseball: Following a disappointing 3-7 record during the spring trip to Florida, the team performed more impressively upon a return trip south one week later, this time to Tuscaloosa, Ala. Playing on the home field of the University of Alabama, they defeated the U of A at Birmingham, 13-8, and then took two of three from the Crimson Tide, 12-9 and 3-1.

Finishing the regular season with three wins against Iowa, Michigan State qualified for the Big Ten playoffs at C.O. Brown Stadium in Battle Creek. Unfortunately, they were quickly sidelined with back-to-back losses in the double elimination tournament. First it was Ohio State, the nation's fourth-ranked team, that dispensed with the Spartans, 12-5. A devastating nine-run eighth inning is what did the Spartans in after they had led 5-3 through seven innings. The season ended on the next evening when State again came up on the short end, 5-1, this time against Michigan.

Coby Garner led the team in hitting with a .431 average and a slugging percentage of .819.

With 84 hits during the season and 238 hits during his four-year career, Steve Money became the team leader in both categories. He was also a .400 hitter in 1994, finishing with a .414 average, while also leading in runs scored (52) and stolen bases (23).

With 51 runs-batted-in during the year, shortstop Dave Veres ranks seventh on the list of top Spartans. Along with Money he was selected as a member of the first-team All-Big Ten team.

It was a productive season offensively. In the team record book, the 1994 edition ranks second in most hits (566), fourth in most runs scored (380), fourth in most runs-batted-in (334), first in two-base hits (110) and tied with the 1984 team for first in home runs (59).

Basketball: For a team that was predicted to be a ninth to last-place conference finisher, the 1993-1994 team was a pleasant surprise as they concluded the season with a 20-12 overall record and a fourth-place tie in the final Big Ten standings. From there they advanced to the second round of the NCAA tournament before falling to the eventual runner-up Duke Blue Devils.

A significantly improved player in 1993-1994 was Anthony "Pig" Miller of Benton Harbor. Slimmed down by 20 pounds in the off-season, he led the conference in field goal percentage (162 out of 249) at .651. He would be honored as a Big Ten honorable mention selection.

The play of junior point guard Eric Snow was noteworthy as he became the conference assist king with an average of 6.7 feeds per game. He also played with pride at the "other end" of the court and was twice (1994 and 1995) named the team's best defensive player.

Shawn Respert was easily the team's scoring leader as he accounted for 778 points which translated to a 24.3 per game average.

The guy at the end of the bench in 1994 was senior Erik Qualman, who had served as team manager for three years before lacing them up. Fittingly, the six-foot-six forward from Rochester, Mich. scored his team's final bucket in the 94-78 defeat of Indiana on Senior Night.

Cross Country: Two weeks following the MSU Invitational, Michigan State hosted the Spartan Invitational run over the 8K Forest Akers East Course. In somewhat of a surprise, Coach Stintzi's squad had to settle for second place behind the University of Iowa, 42 points to 49. Eastern Michigan was third with 75. Ohio State scored 89, Purdue 101 and Toledo 157. The State runners finished as follows: Bill Crosby, fourth (25:31.13); Toby Lefere, sixth (25:39.13); Chris Lett, 10th (25:58.25); Pat Hoard, 12th (26:04.62) and Kevin Sweeney 17th (26:10.15).

Michigan State also hosted that fall's 79th annual Big Ten championships, but could do no better than sixth with 145 points. Lefere finished 11th (25:06.80); Crosby, 26th (25:32.93); Hoard 29th (25:35.12); Ryan Kennedy 37th, (25:50.43) and Brant Lutz 42nd (26:00.06).

MSU concluded the season at Bloomington, Ind., with the 10K running of the NCAA district IV championships. Scoring 218 points, the Green and White finished seventh among the 29 teams in the competition. Once more Lefere was the first Spartan to finish, placing 16th (32:59.9), followed by Crosby in 25th (33:13.4), Lett 39th (33:42.4), Lutz 63rd (34:07.0) and Hoard 88th (34:36.3).

Fencing: On November 6, the team competed in the preseason seven-team Fall Fencing Festival at Notre Dame. Led by sophomore Joe Flynn in sabre (11-7) and freshman Jeff Conover (9-9), the team racked up two wins, 19-8 over Cleveland State and 18-9 over the University of Chicago.

During the season, State won 12 matches and lost 12. The team members and their individual won-loss record were: Kevin Reuben (foil 60-12), Shawn Smith (foil 52-20), Jeff Conover (epee 50-22), Kyle Glasgow

(epee 36-36), Ben Greenberg (epee 28-44), William Flynn (sabre 42-30) and Ben Ibach (sabre 37-35).

At the NCAA regional championships hosted by Notre Dame University, Reuben and Flynn finished fourth, Smith was sixth and Glasgow eighth. The foil team of Reuben and Smith finished third and qualified for the NCAA championships at Brandeis University in Waltham, Mass., where they scored 250 points and finished 18th out of 29 teams. It was the first time in eight years that Michigan State was represented at the national championships.

Football: With just seven seconds remaining in the 31-29 home victory over Northwestern, a scuffle broke out between the players that spilled over into the stands and reportedly included a chair-throwing incident. While Coach Perles and his staff were able to restrain their players on the sideline, many Wildcat players left the bench area which escalated the incident. After order was restored, NU was penalized 15 yards and the final ticks of the game clock were run off.

Sometimes there is a defeat that lingers in memory as vividly as a cherished victory. Such was the case in the home game of November 27. After holding what seemed to be a commanding 37-17 lead against Penn State for nearly three quarters, the Nittany Lions ran off 21 unanswered points to shock the Spartans and their supporters as they stole a 38-37 victory. The winners walked off with the Land Grant Trophy, an award introduced for the first time which recognized the two schools as the pioneer land grant colleges.

The game following the Penn State fiasco was the season closer against Wisconsin in Tokyo, Japan, where the Badgers made sushi out of MSU, 41-20. The game was originally a home game for Wisconsin, but it was moved overseas and billed as the Coca-Cola Bowl. This, of course, conjures up a future trivia question, "Has Michigan State ever played a football game outside of the United States?" The Badgers' win sent them to the Rose Bowl on New Year's Day. MSU settled for the vastly less-prestigious Liberty Bowl in Memphis, Tenn., against Louisville.

Quarterback Jim Miller concluded his Spartan football career (1990-1993) as the school's most accurate passer, connecting on 467 of 746 throws for a .629 percentage. In addition, season leaders included receiver Mill Coleman (48 catches for 671yards) and Rob Fredrickson (74 unassisted tackles).

Steve Wasylk, a senior free safety who carries a 3.95 GPA in civil engineering, was one of 18 nationwide recipients of an $18,000 scholarship award offered by the National Football Foundation.

Golf: In the opening meet of the fall season, the Spartans finished fifth in the 12-team seventh annual NIU/Sharp's midwestern invitational hosted by Northern Illinois University. Shooting a two-under par for the weekend, Heath Feld carded the low score for MSU.

State finished the Big Ten championship weekend with a significant turnaround from Saturday to Sunday. After carding the highest score of any team on Saturday (307), Ken Horvath's fivesome came back for the lowest Sunday score at 286. The improvement moved State ahead of Iowa and Penn Sate for a fifth-place team finish with a four round total of 1183. Senior Heath Feld, who had been the 1993 player of the year, paced MSU with rounds of 77-72-76-65—290. That 65 tied for the lowest round of the tournament and pushed him into a tie for seventh place individually. Other Spartan scores were Chris Lemmon 295, Greg Bartolec 299, Brian Bartolec 301 and sophomore Earl Eckenrode 308.

Finishing 20th at the NCAA regional tournament in Oklahoma City, the Spartans were 28 strokes shy of the 10th-place finish needed to qualify for the national finals. The three-round scores were Brian Bartolec 218, Feld 224, Greg Bartolec 228, Lemmon 230 and Eckenrode 239.

Gymnastics: Even with a loss to Penn State in the triangular meet which included Western Michigan, Coach Atkinson was pleased to see the return of two stars that had been out with injuries, Mark Garny (shoulder) and John Orlando (ankle).

With a total team score of 272.50, MSU placed no better than sixth at the eight-team Michigan Invitational in Ann Arbor. Strong Spartan performances included sophomore Norm Stulz who scored a 9.6 on floor exorcise; junior Mark Garny with a 9.65 on the pommel horse and senior Kevin Brown with a 9.60 on the horizontal bar.

Hockey: Led by junior Steve Guolla, State defeated Bowling Green in overtime, 3-2, in the quarterfinals of the CCHA playoffs at Joe Louis Arena. The win marked Ron Mason's 698th victory making him the winningest coach in all of college hockey history (this time *including* Canada).

Carter missed two games in mid-season when he traveled with the Canadian Junior National Team to Europe for the World Junior Championships. There he posted three goals and added two assists, helping his country win the gold medal.

Buzak posted an outstanding .903 save percentage as he was at the net during 38 of the 41 games during the season.

The top scoring line consisted of junior Steve Guolla, sophomore Carter and senior Kelly Harper. Carter led the team with 30 goals, and Guolla scored a team-leading 69 total points. Junior Rem Murray and Steve Suk also turned in outstanding years, scoring 55 and 40 points, respectively.

Whistled 148 times for a total of 308 minutes, defenseman Nicolas Perreault would finish his four-year Spartan career as the third most-penalized player in school history.

In postseason honors, Carter was named to the All-Central Collegiate Hockey Association first team

Lacrosse: During the spring-break trip to the East, the Spartans won one of three games. After losing to a University of Maryland-Baltimore County, 12-5, the team traveled into Virginia where they defeated Radford 20-8. David Keiffer was top scorer with four goals and four assists. On the final leg of their trip, they traveled to Hempstead, N.Y., where they were defeated by always strong Hofstra, 14-5.

In a contest that featured eight ties and five lead-changes, the Notre Dame game ended 11-11 in regulation. This called for a sudden-death overtime and unfortunately, it was the Irish that prevailed and with the loss, MSU lost any hope of a berth in the NCAA tournament.

Two of the top scorers of all-time would complete their Spartan careers in 1994: Andy Hilgartner (41 goals, 64 assists) and Rob Dameron (63 goals, 14 assists).

Soccer: Participating in the four-team Soccer Bowl II at Quincy (Ill.) College, the Spartans were winless, losing the opener 2-1 to Northern Illinois and then being shut out in the consolation game by Arkansas-Little Rock, 1-0.

Matched against Ohio State in the first round of the Big Ten tournament at Madison, Wis., the Spartans found themselves down 3-0 early in the second half, but made it competitive with goals by Jon Petoskey and Sean Nemnich. The Buckeyes came back to score once more and win the game, 4-2.

Swimming and Diving: Bryan Morrison, a 1993 letter-winner from Livonia, was lost to the team upon suffering a near-fatal, partially-paralyzing diving incident while in Europe during the summer of 1993.

At the 84th annual Big Ten championships Ron Orris, Alec Mull and Andy Faberelle linked with the German contingent of Chris-Carol Bremer, Uwe Volk and Lars Kalenka to earn 334 points and place MSU in fifth place, the highest finish for a Spartan team since 1990. Bremer was runner-up in the 200-yard butterfly (1:45.71) and placed fifth in the 500-yard freestyle (4:21.69); Volk scored with a third in the 200-yard individual medley-IM (1:48.86), fourth in the 400 IM (3:50.26) and eighth in the 1,650-yard freestyle (15:31.21). Kalanka was a finalist in two events, placed sixth in the 100-yard backstroke (49.70) and seventh in the 500-yard freestyle (4:23.01). Likewise, Orris placed in two events, third in the 100-yard butterfly (48.06) and fifth in the 200-yard IM (1:49.16). Mull placed seventh in the 100-yard freestyle and Faberelle eighth in the 100-yard butterfly (49.30).

Led by Bremer, MSU scored 38 points and tied for 20th at the NCAA championships in Minneapolis, Minn. The German Olympian placed seventh in the 200-yard butterfly (1:46.12), ninth in the 500-meter freestyle (4:21.17) and was a member of the 13th-place 800-yard freestyle relay team along with Orris, Kalenka and Volk (6:33.30) and also a member of the 15th-place 400-yard medley relay which finished in 3:23.54.

Tennis: The team managed to win one of four meets that were scheduled during their trip South. They opened with a 4-3 loss to 29th-ranked Arizona, followed by a 6-1 victory over Nebraska, a 4-3 loss to 33rd-ranked Clemson and a 6-1 loss to third-ranked Texas. Included in his 3-1 individual record, sophomore Mashiska Washington defeated the fifth-ranked collegiate player in the nation from the University of Texas. Senior co-captain Kevin Seckel was 2-1 and junior Richard Watson posted a 3-1 record during the preseason action.

With only number one Masheska Washington, number three Jayson Bedford and number five Gus Giltner able to score victories, the Spartans dropped the opening challenge 4-3 to Illinois in the Big Ten tournament at Minneapolis. They eventually finished in ninth place as they topped Purdue in round two, 4-3. Gaining the points against the Boilermakers were Washington, number two Seckel, Bedford and number four Jim Madrigal, the latter winning a close three-set match 6-7, 7-6, 6-3.

Track and Field: When five members of the football team closed out their season at the Liberty Bowl in December, they immediately turned to Jenison Fieldhouse for yet another adventure in college sports. Joining Jim Bibbs's team for at least an initial try at track and field were Craig Thomas, Tyrone Garland, Octavis Long, Robert Shurelds and Mill Coleman. By the first dual meet of the year, a 59-45 loss to Central Michigan, they were contributing. Long won the 55-meter dash in 6.40 while Garland threw the shot put the furthest at 54' 4 1/4".

At Ypsilanti, in the Eastern Michigan Invitational, Brad Fields set a meet record in winning the 200-meters with a 21.61. He also placed third in the 55-meter race. Jarion Bradley was second in the pentathlon with 3,374 points and Joel Franks second in the 400 meters in 50:35.

At the conference indoor meet in Ann Arbor, Fields ran a 21.40 to finish second in the 200-meter race. Long placed fourth in the 55-meter sprint (06.36) and Chris Lett was sixth in the mile run (4:11.78). The 15 team points were only good enough for ninth place, just ahead of Iowa.

With injuries sidelining sprinters sophomore Brad Fields and junior Ashley Nelson, the Spartans could gather no more than 25 points, not enough to elude a 10th-place at the Big Ten outdoor championships in Madison, Wis. There were few bright spots for MSU. Junior distance runner Chris Lett placed third in the 3,000-meter steeplechase with senior Toby Lefere and sophomore Bill Cosby finishing fourth and fifth, respectively, in the 10,000-meter run.

Wrestling: At the Big Ten championships in Iowa City, Iowa, MSU scored 64.5 points for sixth place, but were just one point shy of fourth place. Both Kevin Jackson (118 pounds) and Emilio Collins (190 pounds) reached the finals where they had to settle for second place. They joined three others who finished in the top six and thus qualified for the NCAA championships. The other three were Demond Betts (126), Dan Wirnsberger (158 pounds) and Erich Harvey (177 pounds).

At the NCAA championships in Chapel Hill, N.C., Emilio Collins reached the semifinal round before losing on an 8-3 decision. Dan Wirnsberger was stopped from advancing through the quarterfinals on a 3-2 decision.

EXTRA! 1994 NCAA BASKETBALL TOURNAMENT

Michigan State reached the second round of the 1994 NCAA tournament. The following are the Spartans' box scores for those games.

MICHIGAN STATE 84—SETON HALL 73

	FG-FGA	FT-FTA	REB	A	PF	TP
Beathea	3-6	2-2	5	1	4	9
Brooks	2-7	0-0	1	1	4	4
Miller	5-7	3-6	7	0	3	13
Snow	5-5	4-5	0	6	3	15
Respert	5-15	13-14	4	3	2	25
Weshinskey	5-8	2-2	2	1	3	12
Garavaglia	3-4	0-0	6	1	0	6
Feick	0-0	0-0	0	1	1	0
TOTALS	28-52	24-29	27	14	20	84

Halftime: Michigan State 32-31; **Three-point field goals:** 4-10 (Beathea 1-1, Snow 1-1, Respert 2-8); **Officials:** Range, Marcum, Cahill; **Attendance:** 24,719.

DUKE 85—MICHIGAN STATE 74

	FG-FGA	FT-FTA	REB	A	PF	TP
Beathea	2-5	0-0	2	1	4	4
Brooks	4-5	8-9	2	0	5	17
Miller	4-5	2-3	10	0	3	10
Snow	4-6	2-5	5	6	4	10
Respert	8-14	5-5	3	4	3	22
Weshinskey	3-7	0-0	1	2	3	7
Garavaglia	0-1	0-0	0	0	2	0
Feick	2-2	0-0	3	1	1	4
Hart	0-0	0-0	0	0	0	0
Prylow	0-0	0-0	0	0	0	0
Nicodemus	0-0	0-0	0	0	0	0
Polonowski	0-1	0-0	0	0	0	0
Qualman	0-0	0-0	0	0	0	0
TOTALS	27-46	17-22	27	14	25	74

Halftime: Duke 35-31; **Three-point field goals:** 3-11 (Brooks 1-1, Snow 0-1, Respert 1-5, Weshinskey 1-2, Garavaglia 0-1, Polonowski 0-1); **Officials:** Hall, Marcum, Range; **Attendance:** 26,102.

EXTRA! 1993 Liberty Bowl

December 28, 1993
Memphis, Tennessee

	1	2	3	4	F
MSU	7	0	0	0	7
Louisville	3	0	0	15	18

Starting line-up (offense)		*Starting line-up (defense)*	
Napoleon Outlaw	SE	Juan Hammonds	DE
Shane Hannah	LT	Aaron Jackson	DT
Colin Cronin	LG	Yakini Allen	DT
Mark Birchmeier	C	Rich Glover	DE
Brett Lorius	RG	Matt Christensen	OLB
Brian DeMarco	RT	Reggie Garnett	MLB
Bob Organ	TE	Rob Frederickson (C)	OLB
Jim Miller	QB	Stan Callender	CB
Craig Thomas	LH	Myron Bell	SS
Brice Abrams (C)	FB	Aldi Henry	FS
Mill Coleman	FL	Demetrice Martin	CB

George Perles took his team to Memphis, Tenn., where they came out with a bang but were shut down quickly by Louisville, eventually losing 18-7 in the Liberty Bowl. The Spartans produced their only touchdown on the opening drive. Quarterback Jim Miller completed all four passes in a 79-yard, 11-play attack that ended with Duane Goulbourne finding the end zone on a one-yard run over left guard. The Cardinals took the ensuing kickoff to score a field goal. MSU had one other scoring opportunity in the second quarter, but Bill Stoyanovich misfired on his 31-yard field-goal attempt. Both teams had entered a scoring drought that lasted until the 12:05 mark of the fourth quarter, when Louisville completed a pass in the end zone for the go-ahead touchdown. Spartan quarterback Jim Miller threw an interception on the next possession, but the Green and White defense stopped the opposition on a fourth-and-one goal line stand to regain control. Unfortunately, recovering the ball on the one-yard line did more damage than good, as Miller was sacked in the end zone for a safety. Louisville added seven more points with 4:57 left in the game. The final totals show that Goulbourne gained a total of 63 yards on 19 carries and Craig Thomas 57 yards on 10 carries. Mil Coleman was the top receiver with an even 100 yards on six receptions.

EXTRA! 1994 NCAA HOCKEY TOURNAMENT (Regionals)

The Spartans finished third in the CCHA regular season and lost in the playoffs to Lake Superior State after beating Illinois-Chicago and Bowling Green. The first round of the NCAA West Regional was held at Munn Arena, but being seeded sixth they sat on the visiting bench against third-seeded Massachusetts-Lowell. The Chiefs came out with a 3-1 lead in the first period, and at the final buzzer the Spartans were defeated 4-3 to close the season.

March 26, 1994—East Lansing
Massachusetts-Lowell 4, MSU 3

1st Pd.: 1. UML, Sbrocca (unasst.), 6:54; 2. MSU, Guolla (Carter), 13:08; 3. UML, Hebert (Angus, Bullock), 14:33; 4. UML, Bazin (Bullock, Henry), 17:08.
2nd Pd.: 5. MSU, Suk (Murray, Guolla), 0:58; 6. UML, Murray (Hebert), 5:19; 7. MSU, Carter (Guolla, Sullivan), 16:09.
3rd Pd.: No scoring.

MSU
1994-1995

TALES TO TELL

The year 1995 marked the 10-year anniversary for Jeff Monroe as head trainer of MSU's athletic teams. Today, with a full title of assistant athletics director for sports medicine, athletic training and strength and conditioning, Monroe heads a staff of nine full-time associates including Sally Nogle, Tom Mackowiak and Dave Carrier, along with a student group of 45 interns who are studying kinesiology through the College of Education.

Starting in 1914 with Jack Heppinstall, who first came on the scene to serve as combined trainer and groundskeeper, there have been only four head trainers at MAC-MSC-MSU: Heppinstall (1914-1959), Gayle Robinson (1959-1972), Clint Thompson (1973-1985) and Monroe. During that span of nearly a century, care of Spartan athletes has been elevated from one room in the Gymnasium Building characterized by heat lamps, rubbing oil and rolls of tape to five centers featuring sophisticated high-tech equipment valued at $400,000. Also evolving from a potential clientele of 50-60 men representing six sports to today's 700-800 men and women, who annually consume $150,000 in expendable supplies, while representing 25 sports.

The Michigan State agenda and its physical facilities are nationally recognized. The program has spawned head trainers at numerous locations including the University of Minnesota, Northwestern University and the Detroit Lions of the NFL. *Sports Illustrated,* in its 2002 preseason football issue, featured a two-page photo spread of the Duffy Daugherty Building's extended training room layout.

Jeff Monroe and his staff are not miracle workers. Yet with the added support of the university's medical staff, sundry professional specialists and today's less debilitating surgical procedures, numerous cases can be sited whereupon a given athlete has returned to action following a surprisingly short convalescing period, particularly in football. Take Amp Campbell who suffered a fractured, dislocated cervic-spinal injury in the second game of the 1998 season against the University of Oregon. Rather than submitting to a seemingly career-ending injury, Campbell followed the rehab regimentation outlined by Monroe and his crew and he returned as a starter in 1999.

Tyrell Dortch represents another comeback story. In 2001, during action as a defensive back against Wisconsin, he broke both bones of his right lower leg (tibia and

SCOREBOARD

	W	L	T	Avg.
Baseball	24	27	0	.470
Track and Field	1	1	0	.500
Football	5	6	0	.455
Basketball	22	6	0	.785
Tennis	13	12	0	.520
Cross Country	no dual meets			
Swimming and Diving	2	6	0	.250
Wrestling	13	4	0	.765
Hockey	25	12	3	.662
Fencing	15	10	0	.600
Golf	tournament play only			
Gymnastics	4	6	0	.400
Soccer	9	8	1	.528
Lacrosse	8	6	0	.571

fibula). The prognosis suggested this would also likely be a career-ending injury. After sitting out the 2002 season and through an extended period of recuperation, the New Jersey native worked his way back into the line-up for the 2003 season.

Then there was Kurt Larson (1985-1988). He suffered a dreaded ACL injury to a knee in the Northwestern game of 1987. Back on his feet following arthroscopic surgery he was downed once more during drills the following spring with a ruptured Achilles tendon. Undaunted, the mended co-captain returned in 1988 to lead the nation in pass interceptions by a linebacker.

No, Michigan State trainers are not miracle workers, but sometimes it seems so.

TEAM OF THE YEAR

In Tom Minkel's fourth year as head coach, the 1994-1995 wrestlers completed a 13-4 dual-meet season including impressive victories over Iowa State, Penn State, Minnesota, Wisconsin and Oklahoma. At the Big Ten championships in Bloomington, Ind., the Spartans accumulated 109.5 points to finish second behind perennial power Iowa, which captured an unprecedented 22nd straight title. At that conference meet, Spartans placed in every weight class except heavyweight. In overtime, Dan Wirnsberger (158 pounds) was champion in his division; Kelvin Jackson lost the 118-pound title on a tie-breaker formula while Emilio Collins (190 pounds) also gained a second place; Chad Bailey (150 pounds) was third; Brian Bolton (126 pounds), Phil Judge (142 pounds) Joel Morissette (167 pounds) and Erich Harvey contributed points as fourth-place finishers and Jed Kramer (134 pounds) finished sixth.

The Spartans closed out the season by earning 69.5 points, good for a third-place finish at the NCAA championships hosted by the University of Iowa. It was the highest finish by MSU since the 1972 team was runner-up to Iowa State. Jackson, a senior from Anderson, Ind., worked his way through the bracket to be crowned champion. Senior Wirnsberger finished second and Collins was third for the second straight year. Both Bolton and Chad Bailey settled for seventh-place finishes.

The 1994-1995 wrestling squad. (First row, left to right) H. Meckl, S. Huff, J. Videto, M. Becker, B. Kerr, D. Morgan, S. Davis, B. Bolton, J. Testeman, I. Miller and head coach T. Minkle. (Second row) M. Burgess, J. Morissette, M. Reeves, R. Porco, B. Meert, D. Kosofsky, L. Tibal, K. Jackson, L. Lisik, J. Kramer and asst. coach J. Pantaaleo. (Third row) J. Asher, unknown, M. Postelli, M. Tonello, R. Kovicak, M. Gowans, P. Judge, S. White, T. Hakim, J. Lara and trainer V. Romano. (Fourth row) B. Picklo, C. Bailey, G. Williamson, E. Harvey, E. Collins, D. VanWyck, R. Train, B. Gilliam, assistant coach D. Dean and D. Chapman. (Fifth row) J. Howell, unknown, J. Peterson, B. Maxwell, R. Smothers and R. Giuliani

MAKING HISTORY

On November 8, with two games remaining on the football schedule, MSU president, Peter McPherson, called a press conference in the Duffy Daugherty Building to announce that George Perles "will not coach next season." It had already been apparent to the president that the 1994 Spartans would not realize an "outstanding season," his imposed expectancy which had been spelled out to Coach Perles at the conclusion of the 6-6 1993 season. Although his mandate may have resulted in unfair pressure, George lived by his own maxim: "work hard and keep your mouth shut."

Spartan Stadium was refurbished, dropping the field eight feet from the first row of seats and a new layer of Astroturf was installed.

Upon defeating Ohio State in basketball, 67-58, on February 4, the Spartans had opened the season with a 16-2 record, the best in Michigan State history.

Three years prior to the reality of the Clara Bell Smith Academic Center, there was discussion and debate as to the merits of such a structure and whether funding would be available. Then along came the generous NBA professional basketball hero, alumnus Steve Smith.

At a hurriedly arranged press conference on Feb. 8, 1995, athletic director Merrily Dean-Baker unexpectedly announced her resignation. The departure came after nearly three years of a somewhat turbulent tenor; yet president Peter McPherson insisted that the move was a mutual decision. It was further noted that Baker's contract would be recognized, thus calling for an annual payment of $130,000 in the remaining two years.

Dr. Doug McKeag, team physician for football and basketball since 1976, resigned to head the Family Practice and Sports Medicine program at the University of Pittsburgh.

Alumnus Tyrone Willingham, who had been on the staff of the Minnesota Vikings, resigned to become head coach at Stanford University.

GREAT STATE DATES

Cross Country—**September 24, 1994 (H):** Defeating Ohio State, Toledo and Detroit, Michigan State claimed the Spartan Invitational title with a score of 24. The Buckeyes totaled 39 points to capture second place. Seven different Spartans finished in the top 10, the five scoring Spartan runners, their places and times were: Chris Lett second in 25:49.52, Jim Jurcevich fourth in 26:08.22, Brant Lutz fifth in 26:10.21, Bill Crosby sixth in 26:16.66 and Jim Marcero seventh in 26:19.60. Not scoring but finishing eighth and 10th were Dean Rugh and Kevin Sweeney.

Soccer—**October 5, 1994 (H):** In a Wednesday afternoon game, State managed only one goal but that was enough to defeat the University of Cincinnati, 1-0. Senior forward Andrew Roff scored the game winner at the 80:17 mark off an assist from sophomore Josh Landefeld. MSU outshot the Bearcats 20-13. Cincinnati kept the game close through physical play. They were whistled for 19 fouls, four on yellow cards, while the Spartans were called for 16 fouls, one off a yellow card.

Soccer—**October 9, 1994 (A):** The Spartans defeated Ohio State 2-1 in overtime for their third win in a row. MSU broke a scoreless tie with 11:30 remaining in the first OT on a goal by junior Dan Radke. Andrew Roff added the game-winner just 45 seconds later to secure the victory. Midfielder Marcus Cudnik assisted on Radke's goal while Landefeld drew an assist on Roff's. OSU scored its only goal with 2:57 left in overtime. Goalkeeper Reid Friedrichs made seven saves.

Soccer—**October 11, 1994 (H):** Michigan State shut out Central Michigan to the tune of 2-0 at Old College Field. Keeper Reid Friedrichs was the star of the day, making 10 saves to keep Central scoreless. Midfielder Curt Weiermiller scored the game winner in the 16th minute and defenseman Chad O'Kulich added the insurance marker in the 48th minute. Forward Andrew Roff recorded assists on both goals.

Football—**October 29, 1994 (H):** Michigan State rallied with 17 straight points in the second half and then held off Indiana University 27-21 in an error-filled struggle. The offense featured Marc Renaud, who gained 181 yards on 36 carries and quarterback Tony Banks, who hit 15 of 23 passes for 248 yards, including a 93-yarder to wideout Nigea Carter. The defense set up 17 points with three takeaways while holding IU to 267 yards. The first score of the game came on a six-yard Renaud run which climaxed a 65-yard, 11-play drive. Chris Garner increased the lead to 10-0 on a 26-yard field goal before the Hoosiers responded with a pair of TDs to lead 14-10 at halftime. The record-setting Carter catch pushed MSU back into the lead for good at 10:22 of the third quarter followed by another Garner field goal.

A Renaud one-yard scoring run and Gardner PAT on the first play of the fourth quarter made it 27-14 while a final Indiana touchdown at 3:50 in that same period closed the scoring for the afternoon. In a post-game interview, Renaud, the freshman running back who filled in for the injured Duane Goulbourne and Antwain Patrick, jokingly noted, "I had to have a great game. My mom was here from Deerfield, Fla. She told me to run the ball hard or she'd come out of the stands and run it for me."

Football—**November 4, 1994 (A):** Featuring the running of tailback Duane Goulbourne, who carried 36 times for 181 yards and Scott Greene, who totaled 142 yards on 13 carries, State outscored Northwestern, 35-17, on a rain-soaked afternoon braved by a mere 22,548 fans at Evanston, Ill. Goulbourne opened the scoring on a 13-yard run that culminated a 10-play, 70-yard drive in the opening quarter. Chris Gardner converted. A second quarter thrust which started at the MSU 26-yard line, ended with quarterback Tony Banks scoring from the five-yard line. Four minutes later a Spartan center-snap sailed over punter Chris Salani's head and was downed at the five-yard line, a 40-yard loss. From there the 'Cats scored, making it 13-7. On State's next possession Greene raced 47-yards into the end zone, but shortly thereafter the visitors went 56 yards on five plays and the score at halftime was 21-14. The second half matched a Wildcat field goal against a pair of Michigan State touchdowns, one by Goulborne and another by Greene.

Hockey—**November 9, 1994 (H):** In an early season battle for first place in the CCHA, Michigan State defeated Bowling Green 7-4 before 6,652 fans on a rare Wednesday evening game at Munn Arena. The win put MSU three points ahead of the Falcons in the CCHA standings. The Spartans wasted little time as they jumped to a 3-0 first-period lead on goals by Dean Sylvester, Matt Albers and Brian Crane while missing on several other opportunities. Anson Carter scored twice in the second period but BG equaled his efforts cutting the MSU lead to 5-2 after 40 minutes. Tensions mounted when the visitors notched two early markers in the final period to make it 5-4. Steve Guolla, the senior from Scarborough, Ontario, then took over and put the game away with a power-play shot at 15:21 and an empty net goal while playing six-on-five with less than a minute remaining.

Football—**November 12, 1994 (H):** Trailing 21-3 midway through the second quarter, State outscored Purdue 39-9 the rest of the way toward their 42-30 vic-

tory. As indicated, it was a game of big numbers for MSU: 347 yards rushing, 176 yards passing, 28 first downs and 34:54 minutes of possession. It was also a game of big plays: a 46-yard Tony Banks-Nigea Carter pass play in the closing moments of the first half to set-up a score; a 24-yard Banks keeper that led to the tying touchdown; Ike Reese's 38-yard dash with a fumble recovery to put the Green and White ahead, 28-21 and an 81-yard fourth quarter kick-off return by Derrick Mason which led to the sixth Spartan score. It would also be George Perles's last game in Spartan Stadium as head coach. Two weeks later against Penn State in University Park, Pa., he would close out his 12 years on the Michigan State sideline.

Hockey—**November 26, 1994 (N):** In the second game of the College Hockey Showcase at St. Paul, State defeated the number 10 University of Wisconsin, 3-2. Following a scoreless opening period, the Badgers took a 2-0 lead in the middle stanza , but the Spartans quickly evened the score 44 seconds apart on goals by Richard Keyes and Anson Carter. Dean Sylvester netted the game-winner 56 seconds into the third period when he stole the puck in front of the Wisconsin net-minder and beat him high on the glove side. The Spartan goalie, Chad Alban, had a busy evening as he finished with 30 saves for State was outshot, 32-21.

Hockey—**January 13, 1995 (H):** Michigan State, ranked sixth, defeated Notre Dame 4-1 in a contest that was described as a tough, physical battle. The line of freshman center Richard Keyes, sophomore right wing Tony Tuzzolino and junior left wing Taylor Clarke accounted for three of MSU's goals. Keyes scored first but the Irish tied it with their only goal of the game at 13:31 of the opening period. Tuzzolino's back-hander on a pass from Clarke gave State the lead for good at 4:23 of the second period. This was followed by Steve Suk's power-play goal, making it 3-1. The victory was finally secured on Tuzzolino's second goal with 1:36 remaining in the game. The Spartans and their fans got a big scare when standout center Anson Carter crashed into the boards during the second period and injured his knee. He was helped to the locker room but returned for action in the final period. Goalie Mike Buzak played a strong game as he turned away 23 ND shots.

Wrestling—**January 15, 1995 (H):** In a meet that featured Dan Wirnsberger's (158 pounds) 100th career win, Michigan State upset fourth-ranked Penn State, 21-13. The meet opened with the eventual NCAA champion, Kelvin Jackson (118 pounds), scoring a 20-5 tech-

nical fall. After losses by Brian Bolton (126 pounds) and Jed Kramer (134 pounds), Phil Judge (142 pounds) won an exciting match in which a two-minute overtime period and 30-seond sudden-death were needed to determine the winner. The Eaton Rapids junior prevailed with a one-point escape 10 seconds in the sudden-death for an 8-7 victory. Both Brian Bailey (150 pounds) and Wirnsberger (158 pounds) shut out their opponents, 13-0 and 4-0 respectively, giving the Spartans a 13-6 lead. Erich Harvey (177 pounds) was a 9-2 winner and Emilio Collins kept his perfect season in tact with a 15-0 technical fall to assure the team victory.

Track and Field—**January 21, 1995 (A):** In a meet hosted by Penn State and also involving the University of Michigan, State edged the Nittany Lions, 46-40. Leading the way for the Spartans were Brad Fields, who set a new Greensberg Sports Complex record in winning the 200 meters (21.71); Chris Lett, who won the mile run in 4:11.74 and Todd Koning, who took 800 meters (1:55.8). Finishing second in their specialties were Damon Heard, 55-meter dash (06.45) and 200 meters (22.73); Ramsey Watkins, 55-meter hurdles (07.61); Ashley Nelson, 400 meters (50.1); Darian Dew, 600 meters (1:21.1); Todd Richmond, 800 meters (1:56.3) and Glen Carlson, triple jump (44' 6").

Basketball—**January 22, 1995 (A):** Shawn Respert would leave MSU as the school's career all-time scorer and in the second half of a nationally televised Sunday afternoon game at Crisler Arena in Ann Arbor and he gave the Michigan Wolverines a sample of that scoring prowess. With 1:26 remaining in the opening half the two-time All-American had connected for a meager three points on three tries. More importantly, he had limped to the bench with a sprained right ankle. With the U of M leading 35-30 at the break, the question prevailed: "Would the senior co-captain return?" Not only did he return but also became the expected scoring threat. As he would later say (from *The Detroit News)*:

"Knowing that I was hurt, I knew that my shot was going to be limited more than it was in the first half. I just tried to stay focused and to get more comfortable in a zone, not just in shooting, but where my shot was going to come from. I felt I could have gotten a shot at any time, but it came down to whether it was going to be a 70-percent shot. That's what you question, and today I think I took a lot of high-percentage shots."

Limping visibly during the closing 20-minutes, Shawn still finished with 33 points, sinking 10-of-14 field goal attempts, including four-of-six three-point tries, to lift the number 12 Spartans to a 73-71 victory. The turnabout came after trailing 48-46 with 12:04 remaining when State went on a 15-4 run to lead 61-52 with 7:49 remaining. Respert would account for the first 13 points in that run.

Fencing—**January 28, 1995 (H):** The Spartans picked up a pair of victories, each by a 15-12 score, against the University of Michigan and the University of Detroit at the IM-West. Kevin Reuben went undefeated, Shawn Smith was 8-1 and Jeff Conover was 5-4 for the squad.

Swimming and Diving—**February 10, 1995 (H):** Winning six of the 11 individual races and the opening event, the 400-yard medley relay, the MSU swimmers and divers defeated Eastern Michigan, 126-117. Sophomore Andres Jensen of Hjorring, Denmark, and Tom Munley of Portage, Mich., were double winners. Jensen took the 1,000-yard freestyle (9:31.86) and the 500-yard freestyle (4:32.99). The versatile Munley finished first in the 200-yard freestyle (1:41.31) and the 200-yard breaststroke (2:08.36). The other Spartan winners were Ned Delozier in the 200-yard backstroke (1:55.03) and senior John Maxson, who scored 299.10 points to lead a one-two-three slam in the one-meter diving which included Chad Hepner and Steve Lang, second and third. The first-place medley relay team of Greg Beer, Munley, David Klaviter and Adam Pawlick swam a 3:29.44.

Gymnastics—**February 11, 1995 (H):** Led by Joe Duda's winning 56.10 in the all-around event, State captured an easy 229.85-221.25 victory over Western Michigan. Duda would also win the parallel bars (9.75) and place second on the pommel horse (9.65). Norm Stulz was also busy as he racked up three thirds and a pair of second-place ties. Chris Skidmore won the pommel horse competition with a score of 9.80 and was top Spartan on the rings with a third place (9.40). Keith Douglas won the floor exercise (9.80 and Sam Smith scored a 9.35 to tie for first in the vault event.

Basketball—**February 21, 1995 (H):** A national television audience joined the 15,138 in attendance at the Breslin Center to view the number 12 Spartans defeat of Michigan 67-64. As the tight score would suggest, the local fans had an anxious moment when the U of M's last-second three-point shot bounced off the rim. Senior guard Shawn Respert hit two free throws on the previous possession to give Michigan State the three-point

edge. Respert hit three three-pointers en route to a game-high 21 points, while junior forward Quinton Brooks also tallied 21 points. The Spartans made 11 of their first 17 shots to open to a 27-19 lead. But a one-for-14 drought allowed the Wolverines to tie the game at 36-36 by half-time. State took an early lead in the second half and, although they never built a commanding lead, they proved to be a tough opponent as they completed the season sweep of the Wolverines in head coach Jud Heathcote's final season.

Wrestling—**February 25, 1995 (H):** For the first time since 1974 and only the fifth time since the Oklahoma-Michigan State series began in 1963, MSU defeated the Sooners 16-10. In their final home appearance, seniors Kelvin Jackson, Dan Wirnsberger and Emilio Collins led the way. Jackson (118 pounds) opened with an 11-3 win and after Brian Bolton's loss at 126 pounds, the Spartans rattled off five successive wins: Jed Kramer (134 pounds) with a close 7-6 score; Phil Judge (142 pounds) a 7-3 winner; Chad Bailey (150 pounds), who pinned his opponent at 2:22; Wirnsberger (158 pounds) with a 16-6 major decision and Joel Morissette (167 pounds) a 6-4 winner. With a 23-3 lead, the outcome of the meet was secure when the 190-pound Collins began his match. Regardless, the 4-1 victory in his final match at Jenison Fieldhouse was cheered by coaches, teammates and fans.

Fencing—**February 25-26, 1995 (A):** In a massive display of fencing talent, teams representing 13 schools gathered on the Notre Dame campus in what was billed as the Midwest championships. It proved to be a successful two days for Fred Freihert swordsmen, as they defeated the University of Chicago 14-13, Lawrence (Wis.) 15-12, Case Western 19-8, University of Detroit 19-8, Purdue 22-5, Michigan 15-12, Tri-State 23-4 and Cleveland State 15-12. In the foil competition sophomore Kevin Reuben compiled a 29-6 record and senior Shawn Smith dueled to a 28-7 winning weekend. Junior John Flynn finished with a 24-12 record in sabre and sophomore Jeff Conover was 20-13 in epee.

Hockey—**March 3, 1995 (A):** The last-place Ohio State Buckeyes were hanging to a 3-2 lead with 18 seconds remaining in the final period. With goalie Mike Buzak pulled for a sixth attacker, Steve Suk won a crucial face-off on the left circle in the OSU zone. Rem Murray tapped the puck back to Chris Smith at the left point and he passed it to Mike Watt who was just inside the blue line in front. Watt fired a shot through a cluster of players and the red light went on at 19:46 to tie the game at 3-3. In overtime, Suk became the ultimate hero when he found the back of the net after 2:06 of play. The victory assured MSU of third-place in the CCHA standings. Smith and Sean Berens had scored the first two goals.

Gymnastics—**March 3, 1995 (H):** For the 11th time since 1987, the Spartan gymnasts once more defeated the University of Michigan, but this time it was by the narrowest of margins, 225.75-225.50. Joe Duda recorded career bests in three events en route to a school-record 57.30 winning score in the all-around event. The New Jersey sophomore took first on the high bar (9.80), tied for first on the parallel bars (9.75), was second on still rings (9.70) and tied for third on floor exercise (9.50). Sam Smith finished first on the pommel horse (9.55), was second on floor exercise (9.60) and tied for third on the high bar (9.55). Also contributing a first-place tie was Chris Skidmore with a career-high 9.60 on the rings. Norm Stulz and Stephen Bello also added to the team score with personal-best performances.

Lacrosse—**March 22, 1995 (A):** Traveling to Buffalo, N.Y., MSU met and defeated Canisius College in a high-scoring game, 25-18. State scored three goals within a minute at the end of the first and into the second quarter on goals by Scott Cebul, Luke Griemsman and Chris Clark. After the Spartans took a 14-7 lead at halftime, the Golden Griffs closed to within two, 15-13; whereupon Rich Kimball's crew again took charge outscoring the hosts the rest of the way, 10-5.

Tennis—**March 25, 1995 (H):** In what would be the second of six regular-season victories over Big Ten opponents, Gene Orlando's tennis squad squeezed out a 4-3 win over Wisconsin. The two teams split the six singles matches but State captured the deciding doubles point. In the number one singles match, co-captain Jayson Bedford was a 7-6, 6-2 winner. From the number five spot, Eric Adams won a hard fought match in three sets, 7-6, 5-7, 7-6 and number six Benjamin Hetzler also needed three sets to defeat his Badger opponent, 7-6, 5-7, 6-1.

Baseball—**March 25-26, 1995 (A):** Traveling to Bloomington, the Spartans defeated Indiana University three times, 5-3 on Saturday and then swept the Sunday doubleheader, 5-1 and 8-4. Trailing in the first game 3-0 after the opening inning, State bounced back with three runs in the third and two in the fourth as Trevor Harvey shut out the Hoosiers the rest of the way. Matt Riggins and Chad Marshall led State with two hits each. Pitcher

Tom Olejnik went the distance in the opener on the next day, yielding one run while scattering nine hits in the seven innings. Brian Murphy surrendered four runs on six hits and gained the win in the second game of the afternoon. Scott Ayotte led the offense during the day as he lashed out seven hits in 15 plate appearances, scored six runs and batted in seven. Four of his hits were for extra bases, including a home run in each game.

Baseball—**April 15 (A) & 16 (H), 1995:** Pitcher Tom Olejnik scattered nine hits and struck out four in gaining his fourth win of the spring. Trailing 4-2, State scored twice in the fifth inning, three times in the sixth and twice in the seventh to turn the deficit into a 9-4 advantage. The final score was 9-6. Coby Garner led the offense with a four-for-four, three-RBI performance. Both sophomore catcher Marty Patterson and freshman short-stop Tom Grigg went three-for-four and the team's leading hitter, Scott Ayotte, contributed an RBI double in the fifth and an RBI single in the sixth. Back at Kobs Field on Sunday, Ayotte blasted a two-run home run in the sixth inning to give the Spartans a 2-0 lead. But the game was tied at two when MSU went to the plate in the ninth. With one out and a runner on second, the Wolverines walked junior designated hitter Mike Andry to set up the double play for sophomore catcher Marty Patterson. Patterson was 0-for-two in the game, belted a one-two curve ball over the left-center field wall for the victory.

Lacrosse—**April 19, 1995 (A):** State defeated Ohio Wesleyan for the first time since 1984, 11-10 in overtime. After trailing 10-7 late in the fourth quarter, the Spartans rallied to score three goals in the final 1:47. Including the tying goal by senior Chris Krause with eight seconds remaining in the contest. Midfielder Scott Cebul then scored the winning marker with 2:41 remaining in the four-minute overtime period. Stan Ungechauer and Eric Huss each scored a pair of goals, while Doug Jolly tallied one goal and assisted on two others.

Tennis—**April 23, 1995 (A):** In the last regular meet of the spring, State defeated the University of Iowa by winning five of the six singles matches. It was the sixth win of the season over a conference school. Leading the way for Coach Orlando were number one Jayson Bedford of Mississauga, Ontario, 6-3, 6-4; number three Danny Wallihan of Indianapolis, IN, 6-1, 6-0; number four Aaron Murray of Traverse City, 6-4, 6-4; number five Eric Adams of Jackson, 6-4, 6-4 and freshman Benjamin Hetzler of Lund, Sweden, 6-1, 7-5.

ATHLETE OF THE YEAR

Wrestler Kelvin Jackson, from Anderson, Ind., transferred to MSU as a junior after winning the junior college national championship for the 118-pound class in 1993. In his first year at State he posted a 27-5 overall record and 10-2 in the Big Ten. He went into the conference tournament seeded first but lost in the finals 3-2, to place second. He was a qualifier for the NCAA tournament but did not advance beyond the opening match. As co-captain his senior year, he set an MSU record for wins in a season with a 42-4 overall record, but he again lost in the finals of the Big Ten tournament. Overcoming that disappointment, however, he went on to capture the first Spartan NCAA individual championship since Pat Milkovich in 1974, a feat for which he was named first-team All-American.

Kelvin Jackson

IN THE SPARTLITE

Baseball: Playing in all 51 games, senior right fielder Scott Ayotte led the team in numerous hitting categories including average (.397), runs batted in (60), total hits (71), doubles (18), triples (7), home runs (13), total bases (140), slugging percentage (.782) and runs scored. In the latter classification, his 65 runs scored remains a team record.

In addition to Ayotte, three other seniors closed out their Spartan careers in 1995, Andy Johnson, Coby Garner and Trevor Harvey. Johnson finished second in team batting average, Garner had a perfect fielding average and Harvey won three games to boost his career pitching victory total to 11.

On Aug. 25, 1995, after 28 years with the program and 13 seasons as head coach, Tom Smith announced his retirement. He stepped aside after his teams had compiled a record of 377-332-2. He remained as an assistant professor in the physical education department and events manager for home football and basketball games.

Basketball: The Spartans opened the pre-conference portion of the schedule with a near-perfect 8-1 record, including victories over Louisville and Tennessee.

In an unprecedented achievement, Respert was the team scoring leader for the *fourth* consecutive year. His 25.6 ppg also led the Big Ten. In addition, his four-year scoring total of 2,531 points established an MSU all-time career record which still stands.

Eric Snow, the six-foot-three senior point guard, set a new conference record with 141 assists. Among his many post-season honors, Eric was chosen Big Ten defensive player of the year.

Coach Jud Heathcote ended his outstanding coaching career on a sad note as his team was upset by Weber State, 79-72, in the opening round of the NCAA tournament in Tallahassee, Fla.

Cross Country: In the Big Ten meet hosted by the University of Iowa, State amassed 189 points and finished seventh on the 8,000-meter layout. Chris Lett lead the Spartan runners, finishing 12th (25:15). He was followed by Bill Crosby, 28th (25:48), Kevin Sweeney 48th (26:22), Jim Marcero 51st (26:24) and Brant Lutz 59th (26:39).

Competing in the NCAA region IV championships at West Lafayette, Ind., MSU finished 15th out of 32 teams with a total of 411 points. The team was once more led by Lett who finished the 8K event in 32nd place out of 216 runners with a time of 31:57. Crosby was 74th (32:49), Marcero 88th (33:02), Lutz 95th (33:11) and Sweeney 122nd (33:36).

Fencing: During the dual-meet season, Kevin Reuben, the Irvington, N.J., sophomore, had an impressive 29-6 record in foil competition and junior Shawn Smith of Northfield, Ill., posted a nearly equal 28-7 record, also in foil.

Nine members of the fencing team competed in the Midwest Regionals hosted by Lawrence University at Appleton, Wis. In the foil weapon, Smith finished in eighth place, Reuben was 10th and Neal Mercado 22nd. The epee event had Jeff Conover place 15th, Brian Maston 24th and Bob Greenberg 25th. Competing in sabre were Ben Ibach who placed 11th, John Flynn was 25th and Matthew Stentz 29th. Of the Spartan contingent, only Smith and Reuben qualified to compete in the NCAA tournament three weeks later at St. Mary's College in South Bend, Ind., where Reuben placed 25th and Smith 28th.

Football: With the graduation of Jim Miller, the job of quarterback for 1994 was turned over to Tony Banks, a transfer from two-year San Diego Mesa College, where he had completed 143 out of 312 passes good 2,094 yards of 14 touchdowns. Banks's route to East Lansing was an unusual one. Upon leaving Mesa, he signed a professional baseball contract with the Minnesota Twins and then spent two years with the Ft. Myers team in Florida. After rotator cuff surgery, Tony had a change of heart back to football and he was off to East Lansing.

The 27-21 victory over Indiana on October 29 was George Perles's 71st victory as Michigan State's head coach, putting him second all-time behind Duffy Daugherty's team-record 109.

Through the years, the Purdue Boilermakers ("Spoilermakers") had been a nemesis to Michigan State football fortunes. Not with George Perles at the helm. Upon defeating PU in 1994 by a score 42-30, it marked nine victories in a span of ten years over the conference rival.

In the 59-31 loss to Penn State, Derrick Mason returned a kickoff 100 yards for a touchdown. This tied a Big Ten record.

Mil Coleman, the quarterback-turned receiver, finished his four-year career with 126 receptions, third only to Andre Rison and Courtney Hawkins.

Offensive tackle Brian DeMarco and defensive back Demetrice Martin were first-team All-Big Ten selections.

For the second consecutive season, Duane Goulborne was the team's leading rusher (930 yards on 214 carries). Other team leaders included kicker Chris Gardner with 72 points on 30 PATs and 14 field goals along with freshman Ike Reese who would lead the defense with 92 tackles.

Golf: Twice during the season coach Ken Horvath's squad placed fifth in tournament action, their best finishes in 11 outings. In opening the fall schedule with a composite three-round total of 897, the team was fifth among 18 teams at the Geneva National Invitational. Chris Lemmon led the way with a three-round score of 73-70-75—218. He was followed by John Ehrgott 225, Greg Bartolec 228, Mike Kramer 228 and Rob Schlissberg 237.

In March, competing in the Fripp Island Intercollegiate the Spartans finished tied for fifth, this time among 24 teams. Low Spartan scorer was Greg Bartolec who carded a three round total of 72-78-74—224. Others and their final scores were Mark Gaynor 233, Brian Bartolec 234, Lemmon 235 and Kramer 237.

At the Big Ten championships in Madison, Wis., Brian Bartolec fired a 73-72-80-74—299 to finish tied for 12th with Lemmon one stroke back at 74-76-76-74—300.

Gymnastics: Chris Skidmore set an MSU all-time record when he scored a 9.90 in the pommel horse event during the Western Michigan dual meet.

State closed the season with a seventh-place finish at the Big Ten meet in Champaign, Ill. Joe Duda was 14th in the all-around; Skidmore finished 14th on the pommel horse with a 9.50; Sam Smith scored 9.20 to place 13th in the vault. In addition, Smith, the Edina, Minn., sophomore scored a 9.4 to place 16th on the pommel horse and was 18th in the all-around with a total score of 54.45. Norm Stulz was 15th on the high bar and 20th all-around. Others competing for Coach Szypula were juniors Alex Wisniewski and Chris Schmitt, sophomores Aaron Byrne and Stephen Bello along with freshman Keith Douglas.

Hockey: In analyzing why it makes sense to play some hockey games at neutral sites such as Joe Louis Arena in Detroit, it all comes down to attendance and revenue. Attendance figures for 1994-1995 reveal:

	Games	Attendance	Average
Home	20	129,259	6,463
Road	13	52,119	4,009
Neutral*	7	105,077	15,011

*Includes five at Joe Louis Arena and two at St. Paul, Minn.

From these figures it doesn't take long to calculate the advantage of occasionally playing where as much as three times as many fans can be accommodated.

Goal-tending duties during the year were shared by Mike Buzak (30 games) and Chad Alban (10 games). Buzak's goals-against average was 3.14 and Alban's, 2.73.

Offensively, the top scorers for State were Anson Carter with 34 goals and Rem Murray with 20.

Lacrosse: On April 8-9, Rich Kimball took his squad to Durham, N.H., to compete in the University of New Hampshire's Wildcat Lacrosse Shootout. It was a successful trip as the Spartans won the four-team affair by first defeating Boston College 13-8 and then the host New Hampshire team, 10-9. Ten members of the team contributed to the scoring with goal distribution as follows: Marc Sullivan four, Stan Ungechauer four, David Kieffer three, Scott Cebul three, Chris Clark three, Doug Jolly two and one each by David Kieffer, Chris Krause, Eric Huss and Dan Edell.

During the 14-game season, Jolly, a junior, led the team in scoring with 35 points on 18 goals and 17 assists. Sullivan, a freshman, scored the most goals (23) but recorded only two assists for a total of 25 points. Rounding out the top five scorers were Cebut, a junior and sophomore Ungechauer with 23 each, along with Kieffer, a senior, with 21 points.

Soccer: On September 29, the team flew to Las Vegas to compete in the four-team Coors Light Classic hosted by the University of Nevada at Las Vegas. MSU lost the opener on Friday to San Diego 2-1, but then came back to shut out host UNLV 2-0 on Sunday. In that second game the defense held UNLV to only 16 shots and very few good scoring opportunities. Craig Abraham scored the first goal just two minutes into the game off a pass from Andrew Roff. Damon Rensing added the second goal midway through the first half off a feed from Marcus Cudnik. Goalie Reid Friedrichs stopped 12 shots in the first game against the Aztecs and had nine saves against the Rebels.

Swimming and Diving: The Spartan swimmers combined for season-best times in 19 events at the Big Ten championships and managed 138 team points, but their efforts still buried them in 10th place when the final team standings were posted. Tom Munley was particularly busy with ninth place in the 200-yard freestyle (1:38.70), 14th in the 200-yard breaststroke (2:05.55) as well as swimming the 500-yard freestyle (4:27.42) and competing on three different relay teams. Other individual point gatherers were Chris Harris, 15th in the 400-yard individual medley (4:01.33) and Francisco Peta 16th in the 200 breaststroke (2:05.91). Other team members who contributed as relay swimmers were Anders Jensen, Kamp Purdy, Greg Beer, David Klaviter, Adam Pawlick, Ned Delozier and Harris. The divers contributed with John Maxson eighth, Steve Lang 12th and Chad Hepner 16th on the three-meter board.

Tennis: In February, three Spartans preformed well at the Big Ten indoor singles championship hosted by the University of Illinois in January. Aaron Murray advanced to the quarterfinals of the consolation before being sidelined and both Luke Linder and Steve Schubert won twice before being eliminated.

At the Big Ten championships in Bloomington, Ind., State opened by shutting out Illinois, 4-0 as the two pairs, Jim Madrigal-Jayson Bedford and Danny Wallingham-Richard Watson won the doubles point. Watson followed by winning at the number four singles position (6-4, 6-2) as did number five Murray (6-3, 6-4) and number six Ben Hetzler (6-3,7-5). After losing to Michigan in the semi-finals, The Spartans took on the Northwestern Wildcats to determine the third-place team. Needing four victories in the singles competition, Bedford at number one was a winner (7-6, 6-4), as were number three Watson (7-6, 4-6, 7-5) and number six Eric Adams (6-7, 7-5, 6-4). The crucial match came at number two where Wallihan lost two tie-breaker sets and the meet (6-7, 6-4, 6-7). Regardless, the fourth-place finish equaled the best placing for State since 1976.

Bedford, the ace of the team, saw his college career come to an end in Athens, Ga., as he was bounced from the NCAA men's singles championship in the opening round, 6-1, 6-2. As the team's number one player, the Canadian senior had posted a 23-15 season record to help the team to its first winning season in 19 years.

Track and Field: In the first meet of the year, the Eastern Michigan Open on January 13, Brad Fields ran a 20.88, the world's fastest 200-meter indoor time of the year.

Scoring 41 points at the Big Ten indoor meet at Champaign, Ill., Michigan State settled for a sixth place. Fields placed first in the 200-meter dash in a time of 21.30 and third in the 55-meter dash, running a 6.35. Chris Lett ran the 3,000 meters in 8:26.24 to finish eighth and then placed fifth in the 5,000-meter run with 14:26.70. Jarion Bradley took fourth in the 55-meter hurdles with a 7.45 and freshman Jason Coulter finished fifth in the 600 meters with a time of 1:20.27.

Competing in the non-scoring Western Michigan Open, Bradley was the only winner for MSU as he topped the 400-meter hurdles in 52.64. Teammate Ramsey Watkins finished third in the 110-meter hurdles in 14.71 and sophomore Cecil Flanigan was fifth in the 100-meter dash with a time of 11.15.

In the first outdoor meet of the season, the team traveled to Houston for the Texas Southern relays where they compiled 56 points to finish in a second-place tie with Houston. Sophomore Jim Marcero captured first in the 5,000-meter run with a time of 15:20.37, just edging teammate Brant Lutz who finished second in 15:20.76. Fields was State's other gold medallist, capturing the 100-meter dash in 10.1.

MSU had two winners at the UNLV invitational in Las Vegas. Sophomore Jim Marcero captured the 5,000-meter run with a time of 15:13.2 and Lett ran to a first place in the 1,500 meters with a time of 3:55.77.

Hosting a non-scoring invitational that attracted athletes from six other schools, State captured three events. The 400-yard relay team of Ashley Nelson, Benny Benford, Bradley and Flanigan ran a first-place time of 41.39. Chris Crosby took the 3,000-meter steeplechase with a season-best time of 9:28.19 and Watkins raced to a first in the 110-meter hurdles with a time of 15.08.

With 34 points, State finished seventh out of 11 teams at the annual Central Collegiate championships held in South Bend, Ind. Bradley was MSU's highest finisher with a second-place in the 400-meter hurdle event in 52.3. Fifth-place runners were Lett in the 5,000 meters (14:16.01), Lutz in the 10,000 meters (31:16.60) and Todd Koning in the 800 meters (52.31).

At the Big Ten outdoor championships in Minneapolis, State managed only 14 points which left then buried in 10th place. The only scoring came from Bradley with a fourth in the 400-meter hurdles (52.13) and

Ramsey Watkins's fifth in the 110-meter hurdles (14.53).The strength of the team suffered significantly with a rash of injuries that sidelined All-American Brad Fields, Damon Heard and Ashley Nelson, the heart of the sprint corps.

In July it was announced that Jim Bibbs would retire as head coach. He had served in the capacity since 1986 and in those 20 years his teams had accumulated a dual-meet record of 16-30-1.

Wrestling: MSU competed in the first-ever national team dual championships held in Omaha, Neb. The team opened with an easy 38-6 win over Western Montana and then defeated third-ranked Iowa State, 16-15. They lost to the number one-ranked and eventual NCAA champions from Iowa, 33-6 amd then defeated Penn State 24-12. In the final match-up they lost to Nebraska 21-15 in the battle for third place.

Hosting the first annual Michigan Open, the Spartans captured three of 10 championships and three more runner-up spots en route to placing 14 wrestlers in the top six of their respective weight classes. Spartan winners were Kelvin Jackson (118 pounds), Joel Morissette (167 pounds) and Emilio Collins (190 pounds).

At the Big Ten championships hosted by Indiana University, State's wrestlers finished in second place with 109.5 points. This was impressive until noting that Iowa scored 185 points to win their 22nd title in a row. Leading the way for MSU was gold medalist Dan Wirnsberger (158 pounds) who won his final two matches in overtime, while Jackson lost in the finals on a tiebreaker. Other contributors were Brian Bolton (126 pounds), fourth place; Jed Kramer (134 pounds) sixth place; Phil Judge (142 pounds), fourth place; Chad Bailey (150 pounds), third place; Morissette (167 pounds), fourth place; Erich Harvey (177 pounds), fourth place and Collins (190 pounds), second place.

Erich Harvey (177 pounds) led the team in pins with 12.

Five members of the 1995 team gained All-American status. They were: Jackson, Bolton, Bailey, Wirnsberger and Collins.

With 120 and 115 wins respectively, graduating seniors Wirnsberger and Collins rank third and sixth on MSU's most career wins list.

EXTRA! 1995 NCAA BASKETBALL TOURNAMENT

Michigan State reached the first round of the 1995 NCAA tournament. The following is the Spartans' box score for that game.

WEBER STATE 79—MICHIGAN STATE 72

	FG-FGA	FT-FTA	REB	A	PF	TP
Garavaglia	1-2	0-0	6	0	2	2
Brooks	4-6	2-4	5	1	4	10
Feick	5-5	1-4	4	0	4	11
Snow	4-7	1-3	6	8	5	9
Respert	10-23	1-1	4	3	5	28
Weathers	1-3	0-0	1	1	1	2
Penick	2-3	0-0	0	0	1	6
Prylow	0-0	0-0	0	0	0	0
Beathea	2-4	0-2	2	1	1	4
TOTALS	29-53	5-14	29	14	21	72

Halftime: Michigan State 46-37; **Three-point field goals:** 9-22 (Respert 7-17, Penick 2-3, Garavaglia 0-1, Weathers 0-1); **Officials:** Hall, Haney, Hendricks; **Attendance:** 13,000.

EXTRA! 1995 NCAA HOCKEY TOURNAMENT (Regionals)

The brackets looked much the same as the previous year. Finishing third in the regular season again, the Spartans mirrored playoff victories over Illinois-Chicago and Bowling Green before losing to Lake Superior State for the second straight year. Their second place playoff finish was good for a fifth seed in the NCAA west regionals, and they were slated to face host Wisconsin in the first round. The score was tied after two periods, but the Badgers scored twice in the final stanza to put MSU away 5-3.

March 24, 1995—Madison, Wis.
Wisconsin 5, MSU 3
1st Pd.: 1. UW, Mark Strobel (Mike Strobel, Spencer), 1:36; 2. MSU Guolla (Slater, A. Carter), 4:22; 3. MSU, Slater (Murray), 6:10.
2nd Pd.: 4. MSU, A. Carter (Guolla), 4:09; 5. UW, Mike Strobel (Rafalski, Balkovec), 10:25 PPG; 6. UW, S. Carter (Rafalski), 15:29.
3rd Pd.: 7. UW, Mike Strobel (Ellick), 3:05; 8. UW, Tok (Spencer, Rafalski), 9:27.

MSU
1995-1996

TALES TO TELL

In a poll of fans conducted by the MSU Sports Information Department (see Tales to Tell, 1998), the Michigan State-Michigan game of Nov. 11, 1995 was voted the most memorable ever played in the 75-year history of Spartan Stadium. On that evening, quarterback Tony Banks capped an 11-play, 88-yard drive with a 25-yard touchdown pass to Nigea Carter with 1:24 remaining, thus giving Michigan State's its 28-25 win over seventh-ranked Michigan.

The game was replete with interesting footnotes: (a) The game was played without a turnover from either team; (b) During the recent span of 27 years of the rivalry, it was first time the team with the most rushing yards lost and (c) Nick Saban became the only Michigan State head coach to defeat the Wolverines in his first year.

Derrick Mason provided the first Spartan lead with a 70-yard punt-return for a touchdown; ironically, State's last punt-return touchdown was also against U of M (1984). Scott Greene scored MSU's other second period TD, but the Wolverines kept up a tremendous ground attack and held a 14-18 advantage when State started the first possession of a decisive fourth quarter.

Beginning on his own 23-yard line, quarterback Tony Banks orchestrated a 77-yard touchdown drive in 11 plays. The key was his 42-yard pass to Muhsin Muhammad as Greene scored from the one-yard line with 6:20 remaining. The visitors kept the fans in suspense as they marched back quickly and went up 25-21.

State's final possession then began 88 yards from the Wolverine goal line with 3:38 remaining on the clock. Banks knew what he had to do, and he started with a seven-yard pass to Greene and a 14-yard shot to Mason for a first down. Then came the critical moment when two unsuccessful passes and one suffocated run left MSU at fourth-and-11. Up for the challenge, Banks took the snap, rolled out to the right and hit Mason on the sidelines in front of the Michigan bench. After game officials had given State a somewhat generous spot, a first-down measurement confirmed the Spartans would retain possession. With that, Banks quickly hit Greene three more times, giving him the school record for single-game receptions for a running back with seven. Continuing the march, the hot-handed QB reached Mason once more, but not before the ball had bounced off a defender's fingertips. Then, to finish the miracle, he completed a final 25-yard touchdown pass to Nigea Carter on a toss that would sail more diagonally than forward with the junior flanker making the reception at the goal-line at the northeast corner.

HEADLINES of 1996

- A bomb mars the Summer Olympic Games in Atlanta.
- England's Prince Charles and Princess Diana agree to divorce.
- The FBI arrests Theodore Kaczynski, 53, suspected of being the Unabomber.
- Madeleine Albright becomes the first female U.S. Secretary of State.

SCOREBOARD

	W	L	T	Avg.
Baseball	14	41	0	.254
Track and Field	no dual meets			
Football	6	5	1	.542
Basketball	16	16	0	.500
Tennis	14	13	0	.519
Cross Country	no dual meets			
Swimming and Diving	5	4	0	.556
Wrestling	13	6	1	.675
Hockey	28	13	1	.679
Fencing	13	13	1	.500
Golf	tournament play only			
Gymnastics	5	4	0	.556
Soccer	12	3	3	.750
Lacrosse	8	1	0	.889

The defense was on the field in the waning moments as they stifled every effort the Wolverines made to counter with their own version of a miraculous finish.

Interviewed by MSU's Sports Information Department in 1998, Carter reminisced about the game and the play:

> "During that game-winning drive, Tony kept telling us in the huddle to execute…no mistakes. All the receivers wanted to do was catch the ball and get out of bounds. The play I scored on was designed to get us down close to the goal line. Tony got flushed out of the pocket and Michigan's cornerback hesitated because he thought Tony was going to take off running the ball. Tony underthrew the ball but I was able to catch it because the defender had no time to react to the ball.
>
> Coming to Michigan State from Florida, I didn't fully understand or appreciate the rivalry with Michigan. But after that game, I understood and the importance of the rivalry finally sunk in. It was a great thrill to catch the game-winning pass."

TEAM OF THE YEAR

The 1995 soccer team completed an impressive regular season record of 11-2-3 including victories over Ohio State and Wisconsin with shutouts in seven games as they outscored the opposition 33-13. The Spartans built their record on a solid defense centered around Reid Friedrichs, the Ann Arbor junior who finished the season ranked as the nation's number one net minder with a goals-against average of 0.41. Offensively, Brad Dennis led all scorers over the season with nine goals and two assists for 20 points. The next four scorers were Brad Snyder with 16 points, Cullen Brown and Marcus Cudnik with nine each and Dan Radke, eight.

In the opening round of the postseason Big Ten tournament played on Old College Field, the Spartans defeated OSU 3-2 as Marcus Curnik scored two overtime goals. Two days later they came up scoreless in a 2-0 semifinal loss to Wisconsin, a team they had defeated two weeks earlier in Madison. Commenting on that season-ending game played amidst cold temperatures on a wet, snow-covered surface, coach Joe Baum noted, "We never found a real good rhythm. Wisconsin moved the ball better in these weather conditions than we did." By the next day the field was declared unplayable; consequently the Badger-Hoosier championship game was never contested leaving the two teams to share the title.

MAKING HISTORY

Under the provisions of a five-year contract, new football coach Nick Saban would earn a base salary of $135,000 a year and would also be eligible for bonus compensation on July 1, 2000. He would reap another $150,000, plus $100,000 to be divided among his assistant coaches if three criteria were met: (a.) the academic GPA of his squad be a minimum of 2.55 for the 1999-2000 year; (b.) there be no major NCAA rules infractions during the five years; and (c.) the Spartans win at least two-thirds of their regular season and bowl games during the preceding four years. New head basketball coach, Tom Izzo, signed a five-year contract which would pay $108,000 per year and hockey coach Ron Mason was awarded a one-year contract extension which carried through June 30, 1999 at a salary of $104,164 per year.

The 1995 soccer team. (Front row, left to right) M. Phillips, D. Rensing, J. Guenther, Hesse, M. Shumlas, R. Friedrichs, J. Sharpe, S. Smith, D. Radke, B. Snyder and S. Shebuski. (Middle row) R. Wells, S. Noble, J. Fliss, M. Cudnik, J. Jaroch, C. Brown, B. Dennis, C. Abraham, J. Landefeld, C. Slosar, H. Howell, C. Myers. (Back row) asst. coach S. Schad, mgr. C. Hanger, mgr. D. Warnke, J. Wolff, R. Townsend, B. Hensley, B. Fisch, C. O'Kulich, S. Schlesinger, J. VanHuysen, asst. coach Mike Rahn and head coach Joe Baum

Although many fans watched the Spartan marching band throughout the 1995 football season, few likely were aware the musicians were led for the first time by a female drum major, Mary Houhanisin.

Lansing's Oldsmobile Park, home of the newly-formed Lugnuts baseball team, was dedicated on April 3, 1996. After appropriate ceremonies, Michigan State hosted Michigan in the first game to be played there.

The 1995-1996 fencing roster listed 13 potential swordsmen. Make that *12* swordsmen and *1* "swordswoman." Like so many others, potential Spartan fencers, Audrey Sorokin would learn the sport while growing with it as a collegian. It took time; but by 1997, she had become a contributing member of the Spartan's epee team and, excluding honoraries and managers, would become the first female athlete to earn a *men's* varsity letter as a competitor.

GREAT STATE DATES

Soccer—**October 8, 1995 (H):** MSU won the eighth game of the season and the second in Big Ten play upon defeating Ohio State 2-1 on Old College Field. Marcus Cudnik first put the Spartans on the scoreboard

16 minutes into the opening half, but the Buckeyes evened the count four minutes later. The game remained tied until the 78:04 mark when Brad Snyder scored the game-winning goal off an indirect kick by Jim VanHuysen. The OSU goalie was forced to make five saves during the afternoon, while Reid Friedrichs, the Green and White net minder, had a lonesome afternoon at the other end of the pitch as he was never forced to make a save.

Football—**October 14, 1995 (A):** In this 27-21 victory over the University of Illinois, Todd Schultz completed 10-of-14 passes for 74 yards while filling in at quarterback for the injured Tony Banks. However, Coach Saban turned to the running game on this afternoon as Scott Greene was credited with four touchdowns and a two-point conversion to personally account for 26 of the winning total. Of the team's 236 yards rushing, Marc Renaud gained 127 and Greene 79. The five-foot-11, 227-pound fullback from Canadaigua, N.Y., opened the scoring on a 15-yard run with 11:21 left in the opening quarter. After the Illini had tied the score, State regained the lead in the second quarter on a 50-yard drive capped by Greene's three-yard run. His number was called on the other two TDs, once on a three-yard run to finish a 10-play, 71-yard drive in the third quarter and finally from the one-yard drive on the fifth-play of a 47-yard

drive early in the final period. With MSU leading 27-14 and only 2:11 remaining in the game, Illinois closed the margin with their third touchdown. Marvin Wright was a key defender with eight solo tackles and Yakini Allen was credited with six.

Football—**October 21, 1995 (H):** After sitting out three straight games with a severe ankle sprain, Tony Banks returned to action and completed 15 of 26 passes for a career-best 309 yards and two touchdowns, leading his team to a 34-31 victory over the University of Minnesota. Tailback Marc Renaud also responded with a career-high 229 yards rushing in 35 carries, two of them for touchdowns. Then Banks's TD tosses went 33 yards to Nigea Carter and 65 yards to Derrick Mason, but the game-winning points were delivered by Chris Gardner who kicked his second field goal of the contest, a 24-yarder with 3:56 to play. The game also featured some scores "that didn't happen." A 48-yard touchdown pass from Banks to Muhsin Muhammad was cancelled by a holding penalty. Renaud lost the ball on a fumble at the Gopher two-yard line. On the visitor's side, a potential game-winning pass with 1:46 remaining was dropped in the end zone. Finally, with State killing the clock in the final minute a Minnesota defender picked-up an apparent turnover and headed for the winning score only to find an official had blown the ball dead before the fumble. Scott Greens, the conference's leading scorer, was unavailable for action having strained a hamstring in practice.

Soccer—**October 29, 1995 (A):** Trailing number six Wisconsin 1-0 at intermission, State bounced back to tie the game 17 minutes into the second half on a goal by Brad Dennis. That 1-1 score held during the remainder of regulation time and through one overtime period. Finally, in the 108th minute of play, Jeremy Guenther, with an assist from Cullen Brown, booted in the game winner. Goalkeeper Reid Friedrichs once more performed admirably, recording 11 saves while facing 24 Badger shooting attempts.

Hockey—**October 31, 1995 (H):** In the 170th consecutive sellout at Munn Ice Arena, Michigan State defeated Notre Dame 6-2. The 6,287 fans watched MSU take a 2-0 lead into the first intermission on goals by Mike Watt and Brian Crane. Another marker came just 39 seconds into the middle period as freshman Mike York made it 3-0. The Irish managed to add some excitement to the game with one goal just before the second break and another during the third period. That ND burst seemed to ignite the Spartans as they responded with a third period flurry resulting in goals by Sean Berens, Steve Ferranti and Tony Tuzzolino.

Basketball—**November 28, 1995 (A):** In an early-season made-for-television match-up of teams called the Great Eight Tournament, MSU faced 25th-ranked Arkansas at the Palace of Auburn Hills. In a remarkable comeback, State scored 14 of the final 17 points to eventually defeat the Razorbacks, 75-72. Still trailing 70-69 with 2:02 left to play, junior forward Jon Garavaglia hit a jumper and then moments later his put-back extended the lead to 73-70. The Spartans hung on from there. The victory came without the top returning scorer who was ill and unable to play. Canter Jamie Feick and forwards Garavaglia, Antonio Smith and Damion Beathea more than picked up the slack, combining for 57 points and 38 rebounds. As new head coach Tom Izzo would later say, "It was probably the most exciting win of my short career as a head coach. Unfortunately, in my four games, there's not much to compare it with."

Hockey—**November 28, 1995 (H):** Anson Carter lead the way with a pair of goals in the opening period, only to be matched by the Wolverines before the first intermission. Taylor Clarke regained the advantage at 14:06 of the second period on a power-play goal but Michigan responded once more, this time at 13:13 of the third period. Just 1:34 later Steve Ferranti tapped in the winner following a scrum 10 feet in front of the U of M net. MSU's goalie Chad Alban had a strong game with 27 saves, including 12 in the first period in which the Spartans were outshot, 13-5.

Basketball—**January 4, 1996 (H):** After Michigan State had wrapped-up a disappointing 6-6 non-conference schedule, they opened Big Ten play with a 65-60 win over Indiana University. It was Tom Izzo's first conference victory as head coach, something his teams would later make a staple. With Izzo out-dueling the famous Bobby Knight from the Breslin sideline, his team outshot (.470-.420) and out-rebounded (37-27) the Hoosiers on the court. When an early 16-6 MSU lead became a 22-22 tie with 3:43 remaining in the opening half, a sudden 11-2 run by State made it 33-27 at intermission. A second-half spurt, this time 11-0, raised the score to 53-36. The Spartans then hung on as IU came alive with a too-late 36-12 scoring drive. Four of the winners reached double-digit totals: Quinton Brooks 22, Jamie Feick 12, Thomas Kelley 10 and Ray Weathers 10.

Swimming and Diving—**January 13, 1996 (H):** Ian Mull, the Lansing native and transfer from Auburn University, captured three firsts to lead the Spartans to a 126-111 victory over Purdue. Mull's winning time of 9:11.14 in the 1,000-yard freestyle set a new Charles McCaffree Pool record. He also captured first-place honors in the 200-yard individual medley (1:52.48) and 200-yard backstroke (1:50.02). State surged ahead on the scoreboard when Tom Munley, Tim Jogan and Chris Harris went one-two-three in the 500-yard freestyle. Munley's winning time in the event was 4:41.07. In addition, the Portage, Mich., senior swam to first place in the 100-yard freestyle (46.29) and 200-yard freestyle (1:39.58). Diver Chad Hepner won both the one-meter (304.88) and three-meter (336.45) competition. Competing in their final home meet were seniors Harris, Mull, Munley, Ryan O'Donnell, Kamp Pyurdy and Clinton Wyatt.

Swimming and Diving—**January 20, 1996 (A):** The swimmers and divers evened their Big Ten record while earning a fifth straight victory, defeating Northwestern, 131-106. Ian Mull won three individual events, taking the 1,000-yard freestyle (9:21.04), the 200-yard individual medley (1:54.21) and the 200-yard backstroke (1:50.08). Senior co-captain Tom Munley won the 200-yard freestyle (1:39.90) and the 100-yard freestyle (46.58). Diver Chad Hepner captured both the one-meter (311.10) and the three-meter (295.35) diving events. Other firsts came from senior Tim Jogan in the 500-yard freestyle (4:38.79) and freshman Mike Mulshine with a season-best (1:53.36) in the 200-yard butterfly.

Basketball—**January 21, 1996 (H):** Still chaffing from back-to-back Big Ten losses, State managed a return to the victory trail by edging 16th-ranked Iowa, 62-60, but it wasn't easy. The visitors quickly jumped to an early 24-12 lead. Then, in the next five minutes, a span in what Coach Izzo would label as "critical to the game's outcome," the Spartans managed a 12-0 run and eventually reached intermission leading, 29-28. The closeness of the second half was exemplified by what happened in the final 41 seconds of play. With State leading 60-57, a sharp-shooting Hawkeye nailed a three-pointer and suddenly the game was tied. With the shot clock running down, Ray Weathers took the fate of his team in his hands, drove the lane and tossed up a 15-foot jump shot that clanged off the rim. Quinton Brooks was in a fortuitous position under the basket as the rebound came to him

for a game-winning tip-in with 5.6 seconds remaining. It was a particularly satisfying evening for Thomas Kelley. After being booed by the home fans one week earlier, he excited the crowd with 13 points and seven assists. The Grand Rapids sophomore committed no turnovers and was instrumental in beating the Hawks' famed full-court press.

Wrestling—**January 31, 1996 (A):** Although the two teams split the 10 matches, coach Tom Minkel and his Spartans left Ann Arbor with a 20-18 victory. The difference in number four Michigan State and number 17 Michigan was Phil Judge's fall at 142 pounds. The fifth-year senior from Eaton Rapids pinned his freshman opponent in 1:51 to earn a valuable six team points rather than three or four for a decision. David Morgan (118 pounds) opened the evening by easily defeating his 118-pound opponent, 13-2. After Brian Bolton's loss (126 pounds), Jed Kramer (134 pounds) scored a one-point escape eight seconds into double overtime for a 2-1 win. The other winners for MSU were senior Joel Morissette (167 pounds), 14-4, and Brian Picklo (190 pounds), 5-2. The latter win gave State a 20-14 lead with only the heavyweight match remaining. Jason Peterson only had to avoid a pin to avoid a 20-20 team tie and this he managed to do, losing 10-1.

Hockey—**February 3, 1996 (H):** Putting a total of 40 shots on goal, Michigan State won its most one-sided game of the year in defeating Notre Dame 7-1. The Spartan line of freshman right winger Mike York, sophomore left wing Mike Watt and senior center Anson Carter would account for four of the goals. The Fighting Irish were never in the game as MSU flexed its muscle and proved to be superior. Sophomore center Sean Berens, senior defenseman Chris Smith and sophomore right wing Richard Keyes finished the scoring for Michigan State.

Fencing—**February 24, 1996 (A):** At the Midwest Team championships hosted by Notre Dame, State fencers defeated six teams: Cleveland State 14-13, Detroit-Mercy 18-9, Purdue 20-7, Tri-State 23-4, Lawrence (Wis.) 20-7 and Michigan 15-12. Leading the scoring for MSU were three seniors, Shawn Smith in foil (20-7), John Flynn in sabre (19-8) and Neal Mercado in epee (19-8).

Gymnastics—**February 24, 1996 (A):** Michigan State won all six events to totally dominate Michigan, 221.40 to 209.75 for their first win of the season. Joe Duda, the New Jersey junior, led the way as he captured

both the still rings (9.65) and parallel bars (9.60). Ethan Sterk finished first on the horizontal bars (9.60) and earned the all-around title with a score of 54.45. Chris Skidmore was first on the pommel horse, Keith Douglas earned a first place in floor exercise and Sam Smith took first on the vault.

Wrestling—**February 24, 1996 (A):** State won the first three matches and the final three matches to defeat Minnesota 21-14 for only the second time in nine years. David Morgan (118 pounds), who would later win the conference title, pinned his opponent at 4:01. The co-captains, Brian Bolton (126 pounds) and Jed Kramer (134 pounds), were both winners, Bolton in a 4-0 shut-out and Kramer with an 8-3 decision. Following losses by Phil Judge (142 pounds), Greg DeGrand (158 pounds) and Joel Morissette (167 pounds), Erich Harvey (177 pounds), the Allegan junior, completed his 101st career victory, 5-4. Jason Howell (190 pounds), filling in for Brian Picklo, maintained the Spartan lead, 7-4, and heavyweight Jason Peterson cemented the team victory with a 3-1 decision.

Lacrosse—**March 16, 1996 (A):** Eric Huss's goal with 2:38 remaining in overtime gave Michigan State a 13-12 thrilling victory over 22nd nationally ranked Rutgers. The Spartans entered the fourth period leading 12-6, but six unanswered goals in the last 8:30 of regulation by the Scarlet Knights sent the game into OT. After a game-winning save by senior defenseman Ryan Thomson, Huss blasted the winning marker into the top corner of net.

Gymnastics—**March 23, 1996 (A):** At the Michigan Invitational in Ann Arbor, State took first among the eight teams with a score of 224.70. The other competing teams were Brigham Young, finishing second with a score of 224.45, Temple, Illinois-Chicago, Illinois, Syracuse, Western Michigan and Michigan. Senior Joe Duda took first on the parallel bars (9.70), fourth on the still rings (9.60) and fifth in the all-around. Ethan Sterk, a sophomore, finished second on the pommel horse with a career-best (9.80), while finishing third in the all-around.

Lacrosse—**March 30, 1996 (A):** The Spartans traveled to Bethlehem, Pa., where they met and defeated Lehigh University, 9-7, for their fourth straight victory. Stan Ungechauer scored the eventual winning goal with 2:30 remaining in the game. Chris Clark and Eric Huss were each credited with two goals, Doug Jolly had a goal and two assists and Luke Griemsman found the back of the net one time.

Tennis—**March 31, 1996 (A):** After failing to win the doubles team point, State won singles positions number one through number four to defeat Northwestern, 4-3. Alberto Brause, the sophomore from Montevideo, Uruguay, began the victory run in a straight set, 6-3, 6-3 wins at the number one spot. Playing in the number two position, Danny Wallihan was victorous 6-3, 6-7, 6-3; number three Trey Eubanks won 6-4, 6-4 and number four Ben Hetzler won the deciding point in a three-set match, 4-6, 6-3, 6-4.

Tennis—**April 13, 1996 (A):** Although the number three pair of Chris Belcy and Trey Eubanks scored an 8-5 one-set victory, that was the only win in the three doubles matches, thus that single team point went to Ohio State. Once more, the chore fell on the racquets of the singles players and for the fourth time in Big Ten play they came through. It wasn't easy. After Albert Brause's loss at the number one position, number two Danny Wallihan, number three Trey Eubanks, number five Ben Hetzler and number six Aaron Murray each needed three sets to earn their individual points and a 4-3 victory.

Baseball—**April 13 & 14, 1996 (H):** In defeating Purdue 5-0, Brian Murphy pitched a remarkable game as he went the distance, allowing only one hit and striking out eight batters. The Spartans scored one run in the opening inning when Marty Patterson lined a double down the right field line bringing home Tom Grigg, who had singled. The drama of the day came in the bottom of the fifth after the Boilers' pitcher had loaded the bases on two hit-batsmen and a walk. First baseman Matt Riggins, the senior from Berrien Springs, proceeded to unload the bases with a grand slam homer over the right-center field fence's 357-foot marker. The 6-2 victory on Sunday featured freshman Jason Rice's first collegiate home run in the third inning. State scored one run in both the first and second innings and its final three runs in the fourth. The MSU defense was outstanding with several diving stops and throws made by freshman second baseman Bryan Page.

Baseball—**April 17, 1996 (H):** In defeating Eastern Michigan 13-6, the Spartans connected for a matching 13 hits, which included four home runs and three triples. None of the hits was more significant than the four-bagger by senior first baseman Matt Riggins. His clout, in the bottom of the eighth inning, was his 28th as a Spartan, tying a school record for home runs in a career. Scott Markarewicz had set the original record in 1987-

1989. By season's end Matt would add another six to establish a new record of 34. The distribution of runs was two in the third, four in the fifth, six in the sixth and Riggins's homer in the eighth. The barrage of extra base hits included home-runs by senior right fielder Mike Stephenson and junior catcher Marty Patterson plus triples by Stephenson and freshman left fielder Jason Rice.

Baseball—**April 13, 1996 (H):** In defeating Purdue, 5-0, sophomore Brian Murphy struck out eight batters and allowed only one hit while pitching his fourth complete game of the season. The Spartans scored one run in the first inning when junior catcher Marty Patterson lined a double down the right field line to bring in Tom Grigg who had singled. MSU struck once more in the bottom of the fifth when the Boiler pitcher hit two batsmen and walked the third, bringing Matt Riggins to the plate. The powerful first baseman wasted little time as he smacked a grand slam home run over the right-center field fence at the 357-foot marker.

Lacrosse—**May 4, 1996 (H):** With the January 1997 announcement of the pending dissolvent of lacrosse as a varsity program at Michigan State that season's schedule was aborted. Consequently, the closing game of 1996, a 14-12 victory over Cornell in Spartan Stadium, would ultimately be the final varsity lacrosse game ever at State. Rich Kimball's crew jumped to a 6-1 lead after the first quarter, as Mike Nicolosi opened the scoring just 56 seconds into the contest, but the Big Red came back with four goals to MSU's three in the second period and then tied the game at 9-9 with four unanswered markers in the third. Stan Ungehauer put State back on track with a goal as the Green outscored the visitors 5-3 for the remainder of the game. Eric Huss and Marc Sullivan led the way with three goals each while senior Doug Jolly and Chris Clark added two each with Luke Griemsman and Jared Miller adding to the total with one each. Goaltender Steve Roge kept busy as he turned aside 20 shots during the afternoon.

ATHLETE OF THE YEAR

Anson Carter led the MSU hockey team in goals for three straight years and in total points his senior year to etch his name into sixth place in school history for career goals with 106. He tied for second for the most goals scored in a single game by a Spartan with four and recorded six career hat tricks (three goals). In 1994-1995 his 22 goals led the CCHA, and he led Division I in

short-handed goals with seven. Carter was a member of the 1993-94 Gold Medal Canadian Junior National Team and in the same year was voted first team All-CCHA. In 1995 he was again named first-team All-CCHA in addition to being second team All-America. To close his collegiate career in 1996 he was voted second team All-CCHA and went to play in the NHL, having been drafted by the Quebec Nordiques in 1992.

Anson Carter

IN THE SPARTLITE

Baseball: This was Ted Mahan's first year as head coach and it is also one he would probably like to forget. The season record of 14-41 for a paltry .269 was not much fun. It was the fewest victories since the 11-17 record of 1953 and the lowest winning percentage since the 1902 team finished 1-9-1 for a .136 average. After posting a 5-12 record from the annual southern trip and a weekend in South Carolina, the Spartans opened the regular season 1-14.

During the Big Ten season Brian Murphy pitched seven complete games, tying him for the conference lead.

Busy with 138 putouts and 26 assists, Carlos Fernandez completed the season with a perfect 1.000 fielding percentage.

During the season, Matt Riggens was the team's leading hitter with a .375 average on 72 hits, which included 17 doubles and 16 home runs. Closing out his MSU career, Matt left some impressive career numbers, ranking first in RBIs (156), first in home runs (34), second in doubles (42) and seventh in runs scored (203).

Basketball: In this, the first year without Heathcote as MSU's head coach, Tom Izzo's squad turned in a respectable 16-16 overall record and 9-9 in the Big Ten, yet had to settle for seventh in the conference standings.

The season opened in somewhat auspicious style with a big win over Arkansas in the Great Eight Shootout and a 6-2 record in the conference schedule.

In a record-low shooting performance, MSU converted only 15 of 57 field goal attempts (.263 percentage) in a 61-48 loss to Wisconsin on January 17.

The Spartans held Ohio State to a total of nine points in the first half while defeating the Buckeyes 55-41 on February 7.

In the postseason NIT, State opened at home with a 64-50 victory over Washington, but then fell 80-70 to a quick Fresno State team in a hostile environment.

The team leaders were Quinton Brooks in scoring (505 points), Jamie Feick in rebounding (303), Thomas Kelley in both free-throw percentage (.790) and assists (114).

Cross Country: Totaling 88 points, State finished fourth out of 22 teams at the Michigan Intercollegiates hosted by Eastern Michigan. Chris Lett finished third with a time 25:31. He was followed by Brant Lutz (15th), Dean Rugh (20th), Pat Hoard (23rd) and Chris Wehrman (27th).

Led by Lett, the senior, who was timed in 25:15.0 for 10th place, State totaled 91 points, finishing third at the Big Ten championships in Minneapolis. Wehrman, a freshman, was 16th in 25:31, Hoard 17th in 25:32.3, Ryan Kennedy 21st in 25:40.5 and Jim Marcero, who ran a season best time of 25:54.7, finished in 27th place.

Finishing third at the NCAA region IV meet held in West Lafayette, Ind., State's runners qualified for the national championships. Lett, the Houghton senior, again was the leading Spartan with a fifth-place time of 31:24

over the 10K course. Hoard was sixth, Kennedy 22nd, Rugh 32nd and Lutz 34th.

In the first appearance of a Michigan State team at the NCAA championships since 1991, Green and White runners combined for 474 points and 19th place in the field of 22 squads. Again, as he had done in all but one meet during the fall, Lett was the first Spartan across the finish line. In the 113th spot, his time on the 10,000-meter course at Ames, Iowa, was 33:06. He was followed by Marcero in 117th, Rugh in 125th, Lutz in 126th, Hoard in 127 and Wehrman in 151st place.

Fencing: Even as fencing was one season away from extinction as a varsity sport at MSU, once again the statistics detail on how much competition can be produced with so little with the multi-team meets. Over a total of only five weekends, Michigan State swordsmen competed against 27 teams. No other sport could come close to "getting their money's worth."

Football: With the tie-breaker rule subsequently in place, The 35-35 game with Purdue was likely the last time MSU would have to settle for a tie.

Scott Greene scored 17 touchdowns during the season, including all four against the University of Illinois. This season TD total ranks third in the team record book, while his total of 112 points scored places him two shy of the top rung in MSU history.

Quarterback Tony Banks, the transfer from Mesa (Calif.) Junior College, concluded his abbreviated two-year Spartan career being listed among the top seven Michigan State QBs in five different categories. The most impressive of these is his pass completion percentage of .607, ranking behind only Jim Miller, Dan Enos and Todd Schultz.

Banks had two effective receivers to throw to, Derrick Mason, who made 53 receptions and Muhsin Muhammad with 50.

Quarterback Tony Banks was named the team's player of the year at the annual football bust awards banquet. Running back Scott Greene won the Governor's Award given to the most valuable player. He also won the Biggie Munn Award for the most inspirational player. Punter Chris Salani was given the Potsy Ross Award for the senior-scholar athlete.

Golf: Of the four tournaments in the fall, Ken Horvath's golfers had their best showing at the D.A. Weibring intercollegiate where they were fifth out of 17 teams. John Ehrgott lead the Spartans with a three-round

total of 222, followed by Greg Bartolec (228), Will Borowski (228), Rich Strozewski (233) and Earl Eckenrode (234).

State finished 14th among the 19 teams playing in the Bruce Fossum/Spartan Invitational. MSU shot a three-round score of 922, led by freshman Ryan Rieckhoff's 73-74-75—222, which tied for sixth place out of 99 golfers. Other Spartans scored as follows: Ehrgott 77-75-79—231, Bartolec 79-77-78—234, Borowski 81-79-79—239 and Rob Schlissberg 80-76-94—240.

After starting in second place at the Big Ten Championships with an opening round total of 294, the Spartans slipped further back each day with scores of 297, 305 and 320 to eventually finish in ninth place. Ehrgott was low man with 79-75-73-77—304 followed by Schlissberg's 75-76-75-79; Borowski's 72-73-80-83—308; Rieckhoff with 74-77-78-81—310; and Bartolec's 73-73-79-86—311.

Gymnastics: As in 1995, State opened the season at the Windy City invitational in Chicago where they placed seventh in the 12-team field. Joe Duda, Norm Stulz and Keith Douglas performed well as Douglas won the vault event with a score of 9.5.

In March the team traveled West to compete in the Brigham Young University Invitational at Provo, Utah, and then continuing on to Albuquerque, N.M., for the Lobo Invitational. The Spartans finished third in both meets.

Scoring 222.45 points, the Spartans placed fifth in the Big Ten championships at Columbus, Ohio. Joe Duda was fourth on the parallel bars (9.60) and ninth in the all-around (55.85). Ethan Sterk finished fifth on the pommel horse (9.65) and eighth on the high bar (9.525). Jon Becker, originally an alternate, filled a vacated spot in the finals and scored a 9.40 in the vault to become a third place finisher.

At the regional qualifying meet, MSU finished sixth out of 10 teams, but more important, three team members qualified to compete in the NCAA championships at Palo Alto, Calif. They were juniors Sam Smith and Stephen Bello along with sophomore Ethan Sterk. Duda, sidelined with an injured thumb, was unable to compete.

Hockey: The Spartan line of senior center Anson Carter, sophomore left wing Mike Watt and freshman right wing Mike York were the top three scorers of the team. Carter was credited with 23 goals and 20 assists for 43 points; Watt made 17 goals and contributed 22 assists for 39 points while York also totaled 39 points, based on 12 goals and 27 assists.

Three Spartan hockey players were selected by their respective national teams to compete in the world junior championships during the Christmas vacation break. Sophomore Mike Watt was a member of the winning Canadian team while freshman Mike York and Chris Bogas played for Team USA.

Lacrosse: When Canisius came on the schedule in 1990 they annually provided the MSU offense an opportunity to pad their statistics. Including the 22-9 victory in 1996, the Spartans totaled 139 goals in the span of seven victories.

Doug Jolly would lead the team with 28 goals and 44 points.

Unknowing at the time, the season closing 14-12 victory over Cornell would be the final lacrosse game as a varsity sport at MSU. In a move designed for gender equity, on Jan. 16, 1997 university officials announced that the men's sports of fencing and lacrosse would be dropped from varsity status following the 1996-1997 seasons. Shortly thereafter team members had a meeting and voted to not support completion of the 1997 schedule. This action would preserve a year of eligibility for any athlete desiring to transfer and continue his playing career.

Fortunately for the seven seniors, they would complete their Spartan careers concurrently with the disbanding of the sport at MSU. They were Luke Griemsman, Brian Hubbard, Doug Jolly, Steven Roge, Rich Rund, Scott Cebul and Jon Raym.

Soccer: Playing in the four-team Florida Atlantic-Puma Tournament at Boca Raton, Fla., on September 30-October 1, State shutout Southern Illinois at Edwardsville 4-0 and then defeated the host Florida Atlantic team 3-1. Brad Dennis, a junior from Brighton, scored four of the seven goals and was named the tournament MVP.

The top goal scorers for the year were Brad Dennis with nine followed by Brad Snyder six and the trio of Cullen Brown, Marcus Cudnik and Dan Radke with three each.

Swimming and Diving: After two seasons with the Spartans (1993-94), Chris-Carol Bremer returned to his native Germany to begin his studies as a medical student. In May of 1996 he once more qualified as a mem-

ber of his nation's Olympic team by finishing first in their trials with a time of 1:59.33 in the 200-meter butterfly.

The foursome of Ian Mull (transfer from Auburn University), Tim Jogan, Chris Harris and Tom Munley won the 800-yard freestyle relay (6:52.09) at the Northwestern Relays as the Spartans finished third in the team scoring.

Mounting 216 points, the swimmers and divers finished ninth at the conference championships in Ann Arbor. Mull was second in the 400-yard individual medley (3:49.75), sixth in the 200-individual medley (1:51.30) and anchored the sixth-place 800-freestyle relay which included Munley, Adam Pawlick and Jogan (6:38.28). Munley was second in the 200-yard freestyle (1:37.55), sixth in the 100-yard freestyle (45.45) and anchored the seventh-place 400-yard medley relay, which included Greg Beer, John Bruesch and Michael Mulshine (3:21.11). In addition, Mulshine, the butterflyer, finished sixth in the 100 (49.39) and 10th in the 200 (1:50.11). In diving competition, Chad Hepner was fourth on the one-meter (486.27) and 10th in the three-meter event (446.59).

At the NCAA championships in Austin, Texas, Mull would place third in the 400-yard individual medley (IM) with a time of 3:45.89, setting a new varsity record. Steve Leissner had set the previous standard of 3:48.89 in 1991. Mull would later swim the 400-meter IM at the Olympic trials in Indianapolis and once more place third, in a time of 4:22.16, and just missed making the team.

Tennis: Alberto Brause, the number 17 seed, advanced to the semi-finals of the ITA Rolex Regional in Madison, Wis., before losing to the eventual champion. Along the way, the sophomore from Montevideo, Uruguay, defeated four opponents, including the number one seed from Notre Dame.

Freshman tennis player Trey Eubanks finished sixth in the USTA 18-and-under national indoor championships held in Dallas in late November. Eubanks, from Louisville, Ky., won five of seven matches and reached the quarterfinals before losing to the number one seed.

State opened the Big Ten tournament by dropping a hard-fought 4-3 decision to Minnesota, the reigning champions. From there the Spartans defeated sixth-seeded Penn State, 5-4, and advanced to defeat the host Purdue Boilermakers, 4-1, for a fourth-place finish. Brause was 3-0 in the tournament and freshman Eubanks finished 2-1 with all of his matches going three sets.

Track and Field: Placing third to sixth in their specialties at the Kentucky Invitational in Lexington were Dean Rugh, Jim Jurcevich, Chris Lett, Pat Hoard, Brant Lutz, Ramsey Watkins and Eric Eichinger. Ryan Kennedy was the top finisher as he ran to a second place with a 4:09.90 in the 1,500 meters.

At the Big Ten indoor championships in Columbus, Ohio, the Spartans collected only 27 points which placed them ninth, two points better than Penn State. The 55-meter dash was one big event for the Spartans with sophomore Jermaine Stafford finishing second (6.25), Brad Fields third (6.35) and Octavis Long sixth (6.42). After that there wasn't much to get excited about. Fields finished second in the 200 meters (21.68) and Kennedy was fourth in the mile run (4:13.16).

Fields, the Kentwood senior, gained his third consecutive All-American honor by running a 21.17 and placing fifth in the 200 meters at the NCAA indoor championships.

Scoring 63 points, State finished fifth in the six-team field at the Michigan intercollegiates at Ann Arbor. Without a gold medalist, four members of the team ran to runner-up spots: Khary Burnley in the 55-meter hurdles (7.44), Damon Heard in the 55-meter dash (6.43), Rugh in the 800 meters (1:53.95) and Mark Goodfellow in the 3,000 meters (8:39.27).

State was third in Central Collegiate conference outdoor meet at Western Michigan. Jarion Bradley captured the 400-meter hurdle title in 51.60 and Lett finished first in the 3,000-meter steeplechase in 8:54.83.

After placing 10th in 1994 and 1995, MSU scored 50 points to move up one notch at the conference outdoor meet hosted by Penn State. Fields was second in the 200 (20.61) and third at 100 meters (10:24). Lett placed fourth in the 3,000-meter steeplechase (9.14.52) and fifth in the 1,500-meters (3:52.09). Others finalists were Jason Bradley, fifth in the 110-meter hurdles (13.93); Hoard, sixth in the 10,000-meter race (31:30.92); Jurcevich, seventh at 5,000 (15:01.69) and Ryan Kennedy with a seventh in the 1,500 (3:53.29). Both relays placed for points, the sprint team ran a 42.23 for sixth place and the 1,600-meter foursome finished seventh in 3:15.27.

Wrestling: As in 1995, Tom Minkel took his Spartans to Nebraska for the national team duals where they defeated Pittsburgh, Central Oklahoma and Penn State, tied North Carolina and were twice defeated by Oklahoma State. Both David Morgan (118 pounds) and Erich Harvey (177 pounds) were undefeated during the competition.

As long as Dan Gable continued to yield championship caliber teams at the University of Iowa, other Big Ten coaches could only gain solace by producing an individual winner now and then. In 1996, before a home crowd at the Breslin, not one but *two* Spartans ascended to the top of the award stand at the conference championships. Sophomore Morgan won his final match 2-0 and the title without one point being scored against him. Brian Picklo (190 pounds) was tied after regulation in his battle for first place but managed a 3-1 win just 16 seconds into OT. Others who added to MSU's third-place total of 81 points were Harvey, who lost a close 9-8 decision in the finals; Brian Bolton (126 pounds), fourth place; Jed Kramer (134 pounds) and Joel Morissette (167 pounds) fifth place and Phil Judge (142 pounds) sixth.

At the NCAAs in Minnesota five Spartans earned All-American status: Morgan, who finished third; both Harvey and Picklo, fourth-place finishers; Morissette, sixth and Judge eighth.

FRESNO STATE 80—MICHIGAN STATE 70

	FG-FGA	FT-FTA	REB	A	PF	TP
Garavaglia	3-11	2-2	9	2	2	8
Brooks	8-14	3-5	4	0	3	19
Feick	5-12	0-0	10	1	4	10
Weathers	5-14	0-0	2	3	1	11
Beathea	3-7	1-5	7	2	2	8
Kelley	2-10	0-1	1	2	4	4
Mull	0-0	0-0	1	0	3	0
Klein	1-1	0-0	1	0	0	2
Smith	2-3	4-4	6	0	0	8
Nicodemus	0-0	0-0	0	0	0	0
TOTALS	29-72	10-17	41	10	19	70

Halftime: Fresno State 35-23; **Three-point field goals:** 2-11 (Garavaglia 0-2, Feick 0-3, Weathers 1-3, Beathea 1-2, Kelley 0-1); **Officials:** Ballesteros, Cartmel, Scott; **Attendance:** 10,138.

EXTRA! 1996 NIT TOURNAMENT

Michigan State reached the second round of the 1996 NIT tournament. The following are the Spartans' box scores for those games.

MICHIGAN STATE 64—WASHINGTON 50

	FG-FGA	FT-FTA	REB	A	PF	TP
Smith	1-1	0-1	8	0	5	2
Brooks	6-8	4-4	5	1	3	16
Feick	6-11	4-5	6	2	3	16
Weathers	3-8	0-1	5	3	0	6
Beathea	3-6	0-0	4	0	2	6
Kelley	1-3	6-6	3	4	3	8
Mull	0-0	0-0	0	0	0	0
Klein	0-2	0-0	1	0	2	0
Garavaglia	4-9	2-2	6	1	0	10
TOTALS	24-68	16-19	38	11	18	64

Halftime: Michigan State 28-21; **Three-point field goals:** Michigan State 0-8 (Weathers 0-2, Beathea 0-3, Klein 0-2, Garavaglia 0-1); **Officials:** Faulkner, Crawford, Primave; **Attendance:** 6,611.

EXTRA! 1995 INDEPENDENCE BOWL

December 29, 1995
Shreveport, Louisiana

	1	2	3	4	F
MSU	7	17	0	2	26
Louisiana State	7	14	21	3	45

Starting line-up (offense)

Muhsin Muhammad	SE
Dave Mudge	LT
Tony Popovski	LG
Matt Beard	C
Brian Mosallam	RG
Flozell Adams	RT
John Kehr	TE
Tony Banks (C)	QB
Marc Renaud	LH
Scott Greene (C)	FB
Derrick Mason	FL

Starting line-up (defense)

Robert McBride	DE
Chris Smith	DT
Yakini Allen (C)	DT
Jabbar Treats	DE
Carl Reeves	OLB
Reggie Garnett	MLB
Ike Reese	OLB
Demetrice Martin	CB
Dan Hackenbracht	SS
Sori Kanu	FS
Ray Hill	CB

Nick Saban closed out his first year as head coach at Michigan State in Shreveport, La., facing Louisiana State University in the Independence Bowl. Ironically, four years later this same school would lure Coach Saban to Baton Rouge to become their own head coach. The first half of the contest was a scoring whirlwind that left the Spartans leading 24-21, but Louisiana State controlled the second half to dominate the final score, 45-26. The early scoring came as follows:

First quarter:
• Muhsin Muhammad scored with a 78-yard pass play from Tony Banks on the second play from scrimmage (Chris Gardner kick was good). MSU 7, LSU 0.
• LSU scored on a seven-play 80-yard drive to tie the game (kick was good). MSU 7, LSU 7.

Second quarter:
• Carl Reeves set up the TD with an interception. Scott Greene scored on a three-yard run (kick was blocked). MSU 13, LSU 7.
• The Tigers returned the ensuing kickoff 78 yards for a touchdown (kick was good). LSU 14, MSU 13.
• Derrick Mason returned the next kickoff 100 yards for a touchdown (Greene's two-pointer was good). MSU 21, LSU 14.
• One minute later, the Tigers scored on a 51-yard run. MSU 21, LSU 21.
• With one second remaining in the first half, Chris Gardner connected on a 37-yard field goal to make it MSU 24, LSU 21.

LSU would rack up 24 unanswered points in the second half before the Tiger punter yielded a safety by stepping out of the end zone with 5:57 remaining in the game.

Despite the loss, Banks completed 22-of-44 passes for a Spartan bowl-record 348 yards, fourth on the school's all-time single-game list, while Muhammad gained 171 yards on nine receptions. Although MSU dominated the passing game, Louisiana won the rushing war to level the total yards tally, in which the Spartans edged out the victors, 448-436.

EXTRA! 1996 NCAA HOCKEY TOURNAMENT (Regionals)

MSU finished third in the conference, and after defeating Ferris State in the opening round of the CCHA playoffs, they suffered a loss to archrival Michigan. They had still earned a berth in the national tournament, and for the second time in three years they sat on the visiting bench in Munn Arena against higher-seeded Massachusetts-Lowell. As before, the Chiefs never trailed, topping the Spartans 6-2.

March 23, 1996—East Lansing
Massachusetts-Lowell 6, MSU 2
1st Pd.: 1. UML, Daw (Donovan, Sbrocca), 7:12; 2. UML, Barrozino (Concannon, Donovan), 16:57.
2nd Pd.: 3. UML, Salsman (Dartsch), 6:52; 4. UML, Concannon (Sbrocca), 11:30; 5. MSU, Berens (York, Watt), 18:52.
3rd Pd.: 6. UML, Barozzino (Concannon), 0:34; 7. MSU, Loeding (Adams, Ford), 2:28; 8. UML, Barozzino (Mahoney, Sandholm), 17:42.

MSU 1996-1997

TALES TO TELL

It all started on Sept. 13, 1994, when a spiteful former player telephoned the NCAA office with claims of impropriety in the Spartan football program. Upon reviewing the list of 68 avowed irregularities, president Peter McPherson weighed the options and on October 31 began an internal investigation by engaging a law firm out of Overland Park, Kan. Three days later the president received a letter of preliminary inquiry from the NCAA enforcement staff into the operation of the football program.

While the inquiry continued amidst rumors and accusations, little public disclosure was forthcoming. Finally, in August of 1995, nearly one year from first opening the investigation, the initial hint of any transgressions came forth. Although none of the former athlete's charges were ever confirmed, other concerns had been uncovered. It seems that two academic advisors attached to the intercollegiate athletic office had taken liberties in asking professors to change grades and postdate records. Also revealed were the activities of two particular overzealous boosters, one in Florida and one in Missouri, who provided improper inducement to athletes.

By April of 1996, the completion of the internal examination was announced detailing three self-imposed sanctions: (a) five football games in 1994 were forfeited when an apparent ineligible player had been used; (b) one less coach was used to recruit off-campus in December-January of 1995-1996 and (c) football scholarships for 1996 were cut by two and the total players on scholarship by six to a maximum of 79. In addition, the liable support staff personnel and one professor were eventually terminated and three people were told to cut their ties with the university.

In an extensive exercise on June 1-3, 1996, President McPherson, accompanied by selected staff persons and the contracted attorneys, presented the case to the NCAA Infraction Committee in Overland Park, Kan. On Sept. 17, 1996, the NCAA responded, via a teleconference call in which the infractions and resultant sanctions were made public. As for the transgressions committed from 1991-1994, grade tampering seemed to be the central issue. As for sanctions, the self-imposed package was added to and altered: (a) the period in which one less coach could recruit off-campus was extended through January of 1997; (b) available scholarships for the incoming class was dropped from 25 to 18; and (c) the institution was placed on probation for four years.

HEADLINES of 1997

- The world mourns the death of Princess Diana of England, victim of a car crash in Paris.
- "Cats" becomes the longest-running show in Broadway history.
- Timothy McVeigh sentenced to death for Oklahoma City bombing.
- A U.S. spacecraft lands on Mars and the robot Sojourner Rover sends back thousands of pictures.

SCOREBOARD

	W	L	T	Avg.
Baseball	26	28	0	.481
Track and Field	5	0	0	1.000
Football	6	6	0	.500
Basketball	17	12	0	.586
Tennis	10	17	0	.370
Cross Country		no dual meets		
Swimming and Diving	1	5	0	.166
Wrestling	9	12	0	.429
Hockey	23	13	4	.625
Fencing	8	12	0	.400
Golf		tournament play only		
Gymnastics	6	4	0	.600
Soccer	12	5	2	.684

TEAM OF THE YEAR

The 1996 soccer team opened by winning their first five games and closed the regular season with six straight wins to post a regular season record of 12-5-1. In the Big Ten tournament they reached the finals before losing to the defending champions from the University of Indiana, 4-0. With All-American Reid Friedrichs as goalkeeper, Coach Baum described both his 1995 and 1996 teams as great defensive squads. During four years in the Spartan net, Friedrichs registered 23 shutouts and a total of 363 saves, the latter a Big Ten record. During his senior season of 1996 he led the conference with 123 saves and a goals-against average of 0.86 while ranking second in shutouts with 10. Offensively, four Spartans reached double-digits. Cullen Brown scored six goals and had three assists for 15 points. Damon Rensing contributed five goals and four assists for 14 points. Both Chris Slosar and Jason Wolff finished the season with 10 points.

In answer to a question from a press conference arranged for that afternoon in the Kellogg Center, President McPherson commented that the $800,000 price tag attached to MSU's internal investigation, conducted by the outside law firm was "worth every penny."

Note: This publication has taken the liberty to disregard the forfeiture of the five football games of 1994. Whatever the circumstances, it seems totally improper to expunge the record established by the overwhelming majority of sincere and loyal student-athletes who sacrificed time and energy.

The 1996 soccer team. (Front row, left to right) S. Shebuski, B. McBride, B. Demling, T. Lieckfelt, M. Shumlas, R. Friedrichs, C. Myers, B. Snyder, D. Rensing, J. Landefeld. (Middle row) M. Phillips, J. Jaroch, C. Brown, C. Abraham, B. Dennis, C. Slosar, J. Fliss, H. Howell, S. Williford, J. Benoist and J. Guenther. (Back row) head coach J. Baum, trainer F. Burnett, K. Gordon, mgr. C. Hanger, R. Wells, S. Noble, B. Hensley, N. Oshio, J. Whitmore, J. Wolff, J. Van Huysen, asst. coach S. Schad and asst. trainer L. Bundt

MAKING HISTORY

In a landmark decision countering a long-standing position, the NCAA voted to allow Division I student-athletes to hold part-time jobs during the school year. There was one restriction to the measure: students could only earn the difference between the value of their athletic scholarship and the full cost of attending the particular school.

Former Spartan basketball star Steve Smith returned to campus for the ground-breaking ceremony of MSU's new student athletic academic center. Smith had donated $2.5 million to put the project over the top of its $6 million goal. It was the largest known contribution by a professional athlete to his alma mater. Appropriately, the new structure would be named honoring his mother, Clara Bell Smith.

In January it was revealed the university intended to scuttle the men's fencing and lacrosse programs in an effort to achieve more acceptable gender equity numbers. Countering the issue, the lacrosse team, which had hired an outside consultant, devised two alternate plans. One plan reduced the lacrosse roster from 37 players to 33 and fencing from 10 to nine. The second proposal kept men's lacrosse and fencing at varsity level while elevating women's lacrosse, water polo and cheerleading from club to varsity status. The alternate plans fell on deafened ears. University officials had made up their minds. Both men's lacrosse and men's fencing would be terminated as varsity sports following 1997 schedules.

In June of 1997, the NCAA announced that it would move its national office from Overland Park, Kan., to Indianapolis in 1999.

GREAT STATE DATES

Cross Country—September 21, 1996 (H): Competing against runners from four others teams, MSU's entries finished with 28 points, well ahead of Eastern Michigan (62), Purdue (97), Central Michigan (101) and Western Michigan (136). Leading the Green and White pack was Pat Hoard in third (25:10.21), Kyle Baker finished fourth (25:10.55), Steve Schell sixth (25:15.65), Jim Jurcevich seventh (25:17.36) and Joe Leo eighth (25:18.32). Preliminary events included races for high school girls, high school boys and a 5K for the women.

Football—October 19, 1996 (A): Before 45,434 Minnesota homecoming fans in the Humphrey Metrodome, the Spartans spotted the Gophers an early field goals and then scored 27 straight points to gain the fourth win of the fall, 27-9. In the second quarter Chris Gardner kicked two field goals, from 37 yards and 25 yards and Duane Goulbourne scored from the two-yard line, climaxing a seven-play 54-yard drive. Early in the second half, quarterback Todd Schultz fired a quick strike 63-yard pass to Octavis Long, who outran the defensive backfield and into the end zone. Freshman Sedrick Irvin, who rushed for 154 yards on the day, scored the final touchdown midway through the third quarter. Tyrone Garland, Sorie Kanu, Lemar Marshall, Ray Hill and Robert Newkirk led the defense in holding the Gophers to 91 yards rushing.

Golf—October 21 & 22, 1996 (A): Michigan State defeated a field of 18 teams while winning the weather-shortened 36-hole Persimmon Ridge Intercollegiate championship in Louisville, Ky. Down two strokes to Marshall University heading into what would be the final round, the Spartans fired a 292 for a six-stroke victory. Two under par for the tournament, MSU junior John Ehrgott emerged as the medalist with 72-70—142. The remainder of the team included Will Borowski, who finished eighth with a 77-71—148; Ryan Reickhoff shot a 76-74—150; Rob Schlissberg was at 76-77—153 and Chad Quinn 77-77—154.

Football—October 26, 1996 (H): Featuring three Chris Gardner field goals (34, 43 and 26 yards) and a pair of Todd Schultz scoring passes (26 yards to Duane Goulbourne and 25 yards to Sedrick Irvin), State defeated the University of Wisconsin, 30-13, for the third consecutive conference victory. Irvin also scored the game's final touchdown on a short carry after opening the seven-play drive on a 38-yard run. The 210-pound freshman from Miami, Fla., was weekly achieving the admiration of Spartan fans with his power and elusive running style. Against the Badgers he rushed for 125 yards, which gave him 734 for the year, setting a new MSU freshman record, beating Lorenzo White's 616 yards set in 1984. The defensive front four of Dimitrius Underwood, Courtney Ledyard, Chris Smith and Robert Newkirk harassed the visitor's offense, shutting them out in the second half. Smith blocked a field goal attempt for the third time in four games.

Soccer—**October 26, 1996 (A):** In one of their most satisfying victories of the season, State defeated Penn State 2-0. State went up 1-0 at the 75:23 mark on a goal by midfielder Cullen Brown who knocked in a rebound off a shot by Damon Rensing. The second goal came shortly thereafter at 79:46 when senior Brad Snyder set-up freshman forward Steve Williford who had penetrated to within eight yards of the Lion's crease.

Hockey—**November 2, 1996 (H):** In a thriller for the fans at Munn, State scored the winning goal with less than one minute remaining, to defeat Michigan 5-4. The Spartans took a 1-0 lead on a goal from junior left wing Mike Watt, from Richard Keyes and Jon Gaskins, at the 4:10 mark of the first period. Tony Tuzzolino and Kevin O'Keefe scored in the second, but the U of M was keeping pace, tying the count 3-3 and then taking the lead for the first time on a power-play goal at 7:54 of the third period. The Spartan skaters kept the pressure on until freshman center Shawn Horcoff netted the equalizer at 9:18. As the game clock ticked down under a minute, the crowd of 6,731 anticipated overtime. On one final rush, sophomore Bryan Adams, who was trailing Mike York and Tuzzolino down the ice, suddenly found the puck on his stick. He let it fly toward the top-right corner of the goal and it eluded the goalie. Bryan had scored the game-winner with 52 seconds remaining.

Football—**November 9, 1996 (H):** With season highs in first downs (30) and rushing yards (257), the Spartan offense struck for three first-quarter touchdowns and went on to dominate the Indiana Hoosiers, 38-15. As was becoming a custom. the offense was once more the Sedrick Irvin-Todd Schultz show. Irvin, the freshman tailback, ran for 158 yards and four touchdowns while quarterback Schultz, the junior from Morris, Ill., connected on 13 of 17 passes for 243 yards. Nigea Carter was particularly busy as a receiver, accounting for 108 of those yards on five receptions. The MSU defense was stingy, allowing 96 yards on the ground and only 35 in the air. The three IU scores (two touchdowns and a field goal) were triggered by a blocked punt and a pair of fumble recoveries. Defensive end Courtney Ledyard recorded his team-leading ninth sack of the season late in the first half. Other standouts on defense were Ike Reese, Reggie Garnett, Sorie Kanu, Mike Austin and Tony Campbell.

Soccer—**November 2, 1996 (H):** The soccer team upset the NCAA defending champion Wisconsin 3-0 at Old College Field. It was the fifth consecutive shutout

for the Spartans. James Whitmore scored first for MSU in the first half while Chris Slosar scored the final two goals in the second half. Damon Rensing assisted on Slosar's first goal at 44:32 of the second half. Reid Friedrichs, State's goalkeeper, made five saves during the afternoon.

Soccer—**November 10, 1996 (H):** In defeating Oral Roberts University, 3-0, senior goaltender Reid Friedrichs set a Michigan State single-season team record for shutouts with 10. The Spartans opened the scoring at the 44:25 mark of the first half on a goal by junior Chris Slosar with assists from a pair of seniors, Brad Dennis and Cullen Brown. Senior midfielder Damon Rensing put State up 2-0 at 85:08 on a pass from freshman Steve Williford. Slosar closed the scoring with his second goal of the day at 87:06 on an assist from senior forward Josh Landefeld. MSU outshot the visitors 25-5, while Friedrichs was called upon to make only two saves.

Hockey—**November 29, 1996 (N):** By a score of 3-1, State defeated Wisconsin for the fourth-straight season in what was becoming an annual Thanksgiving weekend series, the College Hockey Showcase, played this year at Joe Louis Arena in Detroit. Junior defenseman Tyler Harlton and junior center Sean Berens each scored first-period goals in the Spartan victory with Bryan Adams and Mike York assisted on the Harlton marker while Berens scored a backhander on a rebound off a Jeff Kozakowski shot. Mike Watt gave the team a 3-0 edge at 8:34 of the second period when he stole the puck in the Badger zone and quickly beat the goalie for an unassisted score. Goalie Chad Alban lost his shutout bid when he was scored upon at 9:33 of the third period.

Hockey—**December 6, 1996 (H):** MSU looked to be in control, leading 3-1 against Notre Dame entering the final period, but the Fighting Irish refused to go down without a fight. Halfway through the third period they would tie the game at 3-3. With less than a minute to play, the game appeared destined for overtime, but sophomore left wing Mark Loeding rose to the challenge and scored the winning goal with 54 seconds remaining. The Michigan State defense did the rest as the Spartans downed the Irish 4-3.

Wrestling—**January 3, 1997 (H):** State opened the regular dual-meet season against Central Michigan before 610 fans in Jenison Fieldhouse. After David Morgan's (118 pounds) 10-2 major decision, the Chips ran off four consecutive wins, including a pin at 142-pounds, to hold

a 15-4 lead at the break. The team was in a position where they likely needed to win every match thereafter, and that's exactly what they did. Beginning at 158 pounds, Greg DeGrand put his opponent away, 6-3. Next came Ralph Conte (167 pounds) with a close 8-7 decision. With two All-Americans waiting for Coach Minkel, things were looking up and, as was expected, Erich Harvey (177 pounds) was a winner, 10-4, as was Brian Picklo (190 pounds), 8-2. Then it came down to winner-take-all as the heavyweights took to the mat, and MSU's Brooklyn, N.Y., junior won fairly easily, 13-8 and, in the process sealed the victory.

Wrestling—January 5, 1997 (A): In the first Big Ten match of the season, seventh-ranked Michigan State defeated Ohio State for the fourth straight time, 23-12. David Morgan opened the meet with an easy 17-1 major decision, but at that point the MSU scoring production was abruptly halted. Jason Nusbaum (126 pounds), Isaac Miller (134 pounds), Tim Hakim (142 pounds) and Adam Elderkind (150 pounds) all lost their matches by decision and MSU trailed 12-5. Greg DeGrand (158 pounds) put the Green and White back on track by using an overtime takedown to edge his opponent, 4-2. From there the Spartans could not be stopped. Ralph Conte (167 pounds) was a 6-1 winner; nationally ranked number one Erich Harvey (177 pounds) pinned his opponent at 2:57; Brian Picklo (190 pounds) ensured the team victory with an easy 11-4 win and heavyweight Marco Sanchez finished the afternoon on a 6-4 overtime decision.

Basketball—January 11, 1997 (H): Michigan State went to a three-guard line-up to "take care of the basketball" as explained by second-year coach Tom Izzo. At least on this occasion the ploy worked as the Spartans defeated Ohio State, 69-66. Those three backcourt starters were the only Spartans to reach double figures: freshman Mateen Cleaves led the way with 18, Thomas Kelley scored 14 and Ray Weathers chipped in 13. Twelve of Cleaves's points were from the free-throw line and that's where the game was won. State's 27-6 dominance at the charity strip more than compensated for OSU's 60-42 scoring advantage on field goals. The Buckeyes last lead was 49-48 with 6:25 left, whereupon Antonio Smith hit a pair of free throws to put MSU back on top to stay. The front line of Smith, Morris Peterson and Jon Garavaglia was limited to a combined 19 points while yielding a 32-25 rebounding advantage.

Gymnastics—January 25, 1997 (A): The gymnastics team set a school record for team points as it defeated Illinois, 227.75-224.50. Sam Smith finished first on both the pommel horse (9.80) and parallel bars (9.75). Victor Prisk captured first on the rings (9.70) and Ethan Sterk placed first on high bar (9.80). The Spartans also broke a pommel horse team record with a score of 38.35.

Gymnastics—February 8, 1997 (A): In a triangular meet hosted by the University of Minnesota, Michigan State defeated Michigan 218.80-214.70. Ethan Sterk led the Spartans with a first-place on the horizontal bars (9.65). Other scorers for State were Keith Douglas, second in floor exercise (9.35) followed by teammate Mike Quarress in third place (9.30). Sam Smith (9.55) and Ken Baker (9.30) were second and third on the pommel horse while Mike Phipps captured third on the still rings (9.50).

Hockey—February 8, 1997 (A): In the annual Joe Louis Arena game against the U of M, Michigan State prevailed in a low-scoring contest, 2-1. With five key MSU players back in the line-up after being suspended one game for fighting, the Green held a 24-13 edge on shots after 40 minutes of scoreless hockey. Maintaining their poise, the Spartans eventually found the range at the 5:18 mark of the final period as Michael York scored to cap a two-on-one breakaway with Tony Tuzzolino. It quickly became a 2-0 game on a power-play goal by Tuzzolino, who deflected in a Chris Bogus shot from the top of the left circle at 6:08. With time winding down the Wolverines finally beat goalie Chad Alban on a power play marker at 16:49. Pulling their goaltender for a sixth attacker in the final minute, Michigan was thwarted in their effort to tie the game.

Wrestling—February 9, 1997 (A): This was one of two doubleheaders scheduled in 1997. In the afternoon, State had wrestled Nebraska at Jenison before heading to Ypsilanti and going against the Eagles of Eastern Michigan. Winning eight of the 10 matches and gaining a 35-9 victory, coach Minkel was able to use some second-line team members. David Morgan (118 pounds) opened in his usual impressive style with a 14-2 major decision. Following a loss at 126 pounds, the Spartans took command with seven consecutive victories: Isaac Miller (134 pounds) gained a 15-4 major decision followed by Sam Hakim's (142 pounds) pin at 1:48. Adam Elderkin (150 pounds) won in overtime, 8-6, while both Greg DeGrand (158 pounds) and William Hill (167 pounds) followed

with major decisions, 15-2 and 10-2 respectively. Erich Harvey (177 pounds) pinned his opponent at 4:19 and Nick Muzashvili (190 pounds) gained the team's fifth major decision of the evening, 9-1. Jason Peterson, heavyweight back-up, lost a 7-3 decision.

Fencing—**February 22, 1997 (N):** In competing during a six-team match at Northwestern University, Michigan State University would bid farewell to fencing. It had been predetermined that the intercollegiate athletic department would no longer support the sport of fencing as a varsity sport upon completion of the 1996-1997 season. Appropriately, in this finale, the Spartans were matched against the University of Michigan, just as they were in that first meet during the spring of 1926. In this meet at Evanston, the State threesome of Jerden Thompson, Mark Roman and Mike Ammon lost the sabre competition 7-2; but, by that same 7-2 score the team of Josh Sivey, Jeremy Robbins and Daniel Cantillon defeated the U of M's epee trio. The difference in the meet and giving State a 16-11 victory was a 7-2 win in the foil weapon. The MSU winning three were Ysuke Murakami, Paul Steiner and Audrey Sorokin. Yes, that was *Audrey* Sorokin. In fact she won three of those crucial seven points.

Basketball—**March 8, 1997 (H):** Looking ahead to playing in the National Invitational Tournament (NIT), MSU closed out the regular season with a 63-60 victory over Bobby Knight's Hoosiers. Trailing 49-47 with 5:43 to play, State went on a 16-11 run to lead 63-60. With 23.7 seconds remaining, a forced foul sent Thomas Kelley to the line and he missed both free throws. Indiana rebounded and was provided one final opportunity to send the game into overtime with a three-pointer. The try came with a split-second to go and it missed, but just barely as it bounced off the backboard and the rim. In the game Antonio Smith grabbed a career-high 19 rebounds, 17 of which were defensive, an MSU single-game record. Overcoming 10 second-half turnovers, the Spartans shot a remarkable 75 percent with 12-of-16 field goals. Ray Weathers scored a team-high 13 points, Mateen Cleaves added 12 and Smith 10. Honored on this senior night were Weathers, Jon Garavaglia, Steve Polonowski, Anthony Mull and Monte Evans.

Tennis—**March 23, 1997 (A):** Michigan State upset number 16 Illinois 4-3 at Atkins Tennis Center in Champaign, Ill. The game looked to be in the Fighting Illinis' control after taking all three doubles matches and claiming the doubles point, but Trey Eubanks notched the team's first points with an upset at the number one singles slot, 2-6, 6-2, 6-2. The Illini responded with wins in the next two matches. Down 3-1 and needing the final three singles points, the Spartans responded. Ivica Primorac won in two sets, 6-3, 7-6, at number four, Mark Jacobson was a 6-4, 6-4 winner at number five and number six Matt Linder rounded out the scoring in a three-set win, 6-3, 0-6 and 7-6.

Tennis—**April 6, 1997 (A):** State opened by having all three doubles teams win their set against Iowa, which resulted in taking the opening team point. From there, four of six singles points were secured for MSU, resulting in a 5-2 victory. Playing in the number one spot, Trey Eubanks was a winner in straight sets, 6-3, 6-4. The other Michigan State points came from the number four slot with Ben Hetzler at 6-1, 6-4; Ivica Primorac, 6-4, 6-1 at number five and Mark Jacobson at number six, 6-4, 6-2. The doubles pairings and their one-set scores were number one Chris Struck-Eubanks, 8-4, number two, Ken Kigongo-Priormac, 8-2 and no. 3 Francisco Trinidad-Heltzer, 8-6.

Baseball—**April 17, 1997 (A):** Scoring two runs each in the first, fifth, sixth and three in the seventh, MSU easily defeated Western Michigan, 9-0. Spartan lead-off hitter Zack Casey opened the game with a triple and scored the first run. He would later collect two more base hits and score another run. Left fielder Chad Marshall had two RBIs, scored a run, went two-for-three and stole two bases. Second baseman Ted Demetral had two walks, walked once and scored a run, while right fielder Thomas Hartley went three-for-five, scored a run, doubled and batted in three runs. The pitching shutout was a three-man effort. Mark Mulder started and pitched seven innings, striking out four and yielding only five hits.

Baseball—**April 26 & 27, 1997 (A):** In their first doubleheader win of the season, State defeated the Indiana Hoosiers 3-2 and 14-3. In the opener, sophomore left-hander Mark Mulder pitched like a future major leaguer. He threw a complete game for a 3-2 victory and raised his record to 5-1 for the year. This ace of the staff allowed just two hits and one earned run in the seven-inning game while striking out seven. Freshman left fielder Joe Albaugh knocked in all three runs as MSU held on to win the game despite a two-run rally by the visitors in the seventh inning. In the second game, senior right-hander Josh Weeks also threw a complete game as the offense came alive, scoring in every inning, except the sixth. Junior shortstop Tom Grigg had four hits in the

blowout, while senior catcher Marty Patterson went three-for-five with five runs batted in. Mike Pisani was three-for-five with a double and five RBIs and Tom Grigg was four-for-five and scored three runs. The Spartans finished the weekend with a nine-inning 4-1 victory over IU on Sunday. This was also a completely pitched game, thrown by senior Tom Olejnik. The senior right-hander permitted six hits and two walks while striking out seven. Patterson and senior leftfielder Chad Marshall both hit home runs.

Baseball—**May 4, 1997 (H):** Playing at Oldsmobile Park in Lansing, Mich., led 4-0 until State came back with three runs in the third and one in the fourth. The teams exchanged runs in the fifth to knot the score at 5-5. In the bottom of the sixth, Joe Kalczynski led off with a single and ended up on third after the U of M pitcher's pick-off attempt sailed past the first baseball into right field. Shortstop Tom Grigg, who led the Spartans with two hits, slapped a single past the drawn-in infield, bringing Kalczynski home with the go-ahead run. Tom Olejnik, who pitched the entire game, retired the Wolverines in order during the final inning, the seventh, to preserve the victory. Other RBIs were credited to third baseman Mike Pisani, catcher Marty Patterson and second baseman Ted Demetral.

ATHLETE OF THE YEAR

Star wrestler David Morgan transferred from Morgan State after winning the 118-pound Eastern Regional title and qualifying for the NCAA tournament as a true freshman. He was red-shirted for the 1994-1995 academic year before beginning his legacy at MSU. In his first year he posted a 44-3 overall record, collecting the most single-season wins in school history, was voted as outstanding wrestler of the Big Ten tournament for not giving up a single point in the run for his first conference crown, and placed third in the NCAA meet. After his second year he became the first Spartan since Tom Milkovich to repeat as a Big Ten champion, the only Spartan to have more than one season with more than 40 wins, and he placed fifth in the NCAA meet. As captain, Morgan began his senior year ranked number two in the nation, and when he finished the regular season undefeated and had won his third straight Big Ten title, he set his sights on an NCAA championship. Unfortunately, this was not to be, as he was defeated in the final match and was forced to settle for second in the nation. Morgan finished as a three-time All-American and three time All-Big Ten selection. He had the school records for second-most career wins, the highest winning percentage of those with more than 100 matches, and was undefeated on home territory.

Athlete of the Year David Morgan goes for the pin.

IN THE SPARTLITE

Baseball: With an average of 354, Tom Hartley was the team's leading hitter for the year.

Freshman Mark Mulder from South Holland, Ill., was a 55-round draft choice of the Detroit Tigers. The pitcher-first baseman opted to return for his sophomore season in 1998.

Basketball: The pre-conference schedule was not loaded with impressive opponents, but the outcome (7-1) *was* impressive as was the average winning differential (23.4). The Big Ten season followed with an erratic start: two losses followed by four straight wins and then followed by five consecutive losses. This was Tom Izzo's second season as head coach, perhaps it was a learning experience as he would opt to open succeeding years with two or more ranked teams in the early schedule, thus providing more serious early-season experience.

This 1996-1997 edition of Spartan basketball would be the final team before the emergence of the championship seasons leading to the NCAA title in 1999-2000. The roster included some names that would be forgotten by many with the impending success that followed: Ray Weathers, Jon Garavaglia, Monte Evans, Thomas Kelley, Anthony Mull, Steve Polonowski or how about this one…Jason Webber. At the same time there were cornerstones to titles and Final Fours: Mateen Cleaves, Morris Peterson, A.J. Granger, Jason Klein, David Thomas and Antonio Smith.

Cross Country: Running an 8.6K race on a University of Arizona layout in Tucson and billed as the Pre-NCAA Invitational, State runners totaled 172 points and finished fifth out of 32 competing teams. Kyle Baker was 30th with a time of 27:36.23, followed by Dean Rugh, 58th (28:08.39); Ryan Kennedy 65th (28:19.05), Pat Hoard 75th (28:28.80) and Chis Wehrman 83 (28:38.65).

MSU placed third in the conference championship run hosted by Indiana University. Leading the MSU contingent was Baker who finished in 11th place (25:23) and was followed by Rugh in 12th (25:24), Joe Leo at 19th (25:34), Hoard 20th (25:35) and Steve Schell 21st (25:36).

At the NCAA district IV championships run on the 10K course in Champaign, Ill., State's team finished fifth among the 32 competing schools. In the 25th spot, Baker was once more the top Spartan with a time of 31:44. Shell was 28th (31:47), Wehrman 30th (31:51), Leo 44th (32:04) and Miller 45th (32:04).

Fencing: As Michigan State relegated the sport of fencing from varsity to club sport status following the 1996-1997 season, the Spartans' Dan Cantillon had one last hooray. As MSU's final NCAA entrant, he finished in 24th position in the epee event.

Football: Sedrick Irvin, the first-year running back from Miami, Fla., set two freshman team season records that remain in the books: total rushing yards (1,067) and touchdowns (16). Twice he scored four touchdowns in a game, the 52-14 season-opening win over Purdue and the 38-15 victory over Indiana. Each of those performances tied him for second in team statistics with 13 other four-touchdown performances by Spartan runners.

Quarterback Todd Schultz of Morris, Ill., was an effective passer for the 1996 team, completing 130 tosses for 1,693 yards. His primary target was Derrick Mason who made a team-leading 53 catches good for 865 yards. Todd was particularly busy in the 45-29 loss to Michigan when he connected on 24 of 45.

Although yielding to Irvin as the primary runner for most of the season, Duane Goulbourne was *the* man against Illinois on Homecoming Day. The senior and team captain led the team to a 42-14 win as he gained 144 yards on 31 carries. At season's end he would be awarded the coveted Governor of Michigan Award given annually to the player voted most valuable by his teammates.

Linebacker Courtney Ledyard was the team's top defender with 13 tackles for losses on the season, including nine quarterback sacks.

Golf: At the Fossum/Spartan Invitational the Spartans shot a two-day total of 905, placing them sixth behind Northwestern, Ohio State, Kent State, Miami and Indiana among the field of 21 teams. Junior John Ehrgott was the top Spartan as he shot an eight-over par, 74-78-72—224 to tie for 16th.

With a composite of 1,243, MSU was one stroke behind Penn State while settling for 11th at the Big Ten championships hosted by Ohio State. Matt Pumford was the team's low scorer with a 74-77-75-83—309. Ehrgott carded a 80-77-74-81—312; Reigel was next with 77-77-79-81—314 and Quinn with a 81-82-79-75 and Borowski with 75-83-79-80 tied at 317.

Gymnastics: Although Rick Atkinson's squad lost a dual meet to Penn State, the Spartans won four of the six events. Keith Douglas and Mike Quarress tied for first place in floor exercise with a score of 9.55. Ethan Sterk won the pommel horse (9.725) and high bar (9.60) while Prisk won the rings (9.825).

In the Big Ten championships at Minneapolis, four Spartans scored points leading to a sixth-place team finish. Prisk was second on the still rings (9.875), Douglas fifth on the vault (9.975), Sterk tied for fifth on the horizontal bars.

Four members of the gymnastics team qualified for the NCAA championships by placing at the east regionals. Prisk won the still ring event with a 9.82 while Mike Phipps finishing third (9.675). On floor exercise Douglas placed second with a 9.70 and Sterk finished third on floor exercise.

Hockey: It was a season of inconsistency as Ron Mason's 1996-1997 crew split the two games of the College Hockey Showcase series, suffered a loss and then rebounded with a win in the Great Lakes Invitational and after the first of the year played 17 regular-season games while *never* winning two in a row. Finally putting things together for the CCHA playoffs, they defeated Western Michigan 4-1 and 3-1 and Miami 4-3 in overtime before losing to Michigan in the championship game, 3-1. Chosen as an at-large team into the NCAA tournament, it didn't last long. For the fourth year in a row, MSU saw its season end in the first game. This time it was Minnesota that dispensed the Spartans by a score of 6-3 in a game played at VanAndel Arena in Grand Rapids. In a postgame interview, Coach Mason would say: "We were chasing the puck all night. That is not our style of game."

Postseason statistics featured the following leaders: junior goalie Chad Alban with a goals-against average of 2.72, senior Mike Watt with 24 goals and sophomore Mike York with 29 assists and 47 points.

Soccer: In the fourth straight extra-session contest of the season and playing before 1,433 at Old College Field, State dropped a 2-1 double overtime game to perennially tough Indiana 2-1. State scored first on a powerful blast by Jeff Fliss at 32:42 from about 30 feet in front of the net. The Spartans continued to apply pressure throughout the first half as Fliss hit the crossbar on one occasion and Damon Rensing just missed putting in a header from a corner kick. The Hoosiers struck quickly in the second half at 54:29 and then won it with 9:23 remaining in the second OT.

State closed the regular season in grand fashion by stringing together six straight shutouts.

Paired against the defending NCAA champions from Wisconsin in the opening round of the Big Ten tournament, the two teams were scoreless after regulation time. Then, 5:07 into overtime, MSU freshman Scott Williford

put State ahead 1-0 on a quick tap in off a shot by Fliss, but that wouldn't be enough as the Badgers tied it 1-1 at 108.02. That sent the game into a shootout where the Spartans prevailed 5-3. The five scorers were Rensing, Brad Dennis, Craig Abraham, James Whitmore and Cullen Brown. The excitement of the melodrama was short lived as on the next day Indiana University dominated State 4-0 in the championship game.

In postseason balloting, senior midfielder Rensing was named to the All-Big Ten first team. Senior defender Abraham and junior defender Jason Wolff were chosen for the second team. The three joined Big Ten player of the year Friedrichs and coach of the year Joe Baum in corralling well-deserved honors.

Swimming and Diving: In an impressive performance during the 135-98 dual-meet loss to Northwestern, Andreas Siemes won the 200-yard breaststroke in 2:00.89. He would later place fifth in the conference championships with a 2:00.96. Other Spartan finalists were scarce that weekend in Bloomington, Ind. Diver Chad Hebner placed sixth on the three-meter board (467.65) and eighth on the one-meter (496.55); Mike Mulshine was ninth in the 100-yard butterfly (49.31) and Siemes finished 10th in the 100-yard breaststroke (56.31). The 200-yard freestyle relay was disqualified and the other four relays placed 10th.

Tennis: Coach Orlando's 10-man squad presented an international flavor. Ben Hetzler was from Lund Sweden, Ivica Primorac hailed from Mosthar, Bosnia and Francisco Trinidad called Mexico City his hometown.

Although MSU did not complete an impressive dual meet season (7-15), they hosted the 88th annual conference championships and played well enough to finish in seventh place. Upon taking the doubles point followed by singles wins from Trey Eubank (6-2, 6-0), Aaron Murray (6-3, 6-3) and Hetzler (6-0, 6-4), they opened the weekend by defeating Ohio State, 4-1. After another 4-1 win, this time over Wisconsin, the Spartans earned their way into the field of eight, but the trail ended abruptly with losses to Northwestern and Michigan. The tournament closed with a forfeit win over Penn State for the seventh spot. It seems the Lions had to put their rackets away because they had reached the NCAA maximum number of competitive dates for a season. This begs the question, had PSU won rather than lost their opening two meets, would they have likewise forfeited their final round, which in that scenario would have been for championship?

Track and Field: The team opened the season with a triple-dual meet in Ann Arbor where State defeated Indiana 69-52 and lost to Michigan 76-41. Leading the way for State with first-place finishes were freshman Okoineme Giwa-Agbomeirele in both the long jump and triple jump, Jason Coulter in the 400 meters and Kyle Baker in the 3,000-meter run.

Finishing behind Eastern Michigan and Michigan, State was third at the indoor Michigan intercollegiates held in Ypsilanti. The Spartans had two first-place finishes. Tyrone Garland won the shot put and distance specialist Baker won the 3,000 meters. Other finishers were Jim Jurcevich and Steve Schell, second and third in the 5,000-meter run; Ryan Kennedy second in the mile, Jason Coulter third in the 600 meters while both the 1,600-meter and the distance medley relays finished second.

Competing in the non-scoring Spartan invitational at Jenison, freshman Giwa-Agbomeirele tied his career best in the long jump at 23' 6.75". He also took second place in the triple jump with a leap of 46' 5.5".

Winning both the 3,000-meter and 5,000-meter events (14:23.80), Baker was a double-winner at the Big Ten indoor championships in Iowa City, Iowa. In so doing, he became the first Spartan since 1981 to win two individual Big Ten titles. Other MSU standouts were sophomore Coulter, who finished fourth in the 600-meter event (1:19.08) and senior Kennedy, who finished fourth in the mile (4:20.57). The distance medley relay team also finished fourth in a time of 10:01.79. Compiling 41 points, the team finished eighth.

At the indoor NCAAs in Indianapolis, Baker placed fifth in the 3,000-meter run and, as a result, earned All-American status.

Running in the Drake relays, senior Brad Fields placed second in the 100-meter dash with a 10.64, .01 behind the winner. In addition, he ran an impressive 20.88 in the 200 meters, fourth behind the winner, Olympian and world-record holder Ben Johnson. In the distance events, Baker was third in the 1,500 meters (3:48.11), Chris Wehrman, ninth in the 3,000 meters and Pat Hoard, 10th in the 5,000-meter run at 14:29.47.

At the conference outdoor championships run in the Ohio State horseshoe, MSU managed 27 points and once more finished the weekend in last place (fifth time in eight years). Regardless, Baker duplicated his indoor 5,000-meter title with a clocking of (14:06.24). Other contributors were Jurcevich with a fifth place in the 10,000 meters (31:08.18); Wehrman, sixth in the 3,000-meter steeplechase (9:15.19) and Eric Eichinger, sixth in the 1,500 meters (3:50.27). Fields was a disappointing third in the 200-meter dash (20.75).

Wrestling: Competing in the national duals at Lincoln, Neb., State defeated the University of Pittsburgh-Johnstown, 28-9 in the opening round. Following a 36-3 loss to the eventual champions of Oklahoma State, the Spartans entered the consolation round where they defeated Clarion State 26-13 and Oklahoma 28-10. In the consolation semifinals they lost to Minnesota, 28-9, and then defeated Iowa State, 19-16, to gain fifth place in the tournament.

At the Big Tens in Minneapolis the team's top three wrestlers came through as could be expected but the remainder of the team was unable to offer much support. Consequently, State's 48.5 points placed them no higher than eighth at the close of competition. David Morgan (118 pounds) successfully defended his title by defeating the number three-seed from Illinois in overtime. Brian Picklo (190 pounds), also a champion in 1996, settled for the runner-up spot in 1997, and Erich Harvey won the consolation match for third place at 177 pounds after losing his semifinal match in overtime.

Struggling through the most disappointing season in four years, MSU wrapped up the schedule at the NCAA championships in Cedar Falls, Iowa. Both Morgan and Picklo finished fifth, carrying State to 21st place, one spot above Michigan.

EXTRA! 1997 NIT TOURNAMENT

Michigan State reached the second round of the 1997 NIT tournament. The following are the Spartans' box scores for those games.

MICHIGAN STATE 65—GEORGE WASHINGTON 50

	FG-FGA	FT-FTA	REB	A	PF	TP
Peterson	1-5	1-3	5	1	0	3
Granger	2-4	0-0	5	0	2	4
Smith	2-4	3-9	14	2	2	7
Weathers	6-8	3-4	5	1	1	18
Cleaves	4-8	2-2	5	7	2	11
Kelley	3-3	6-6	2	1	0	12
Mull	0-2	0-0	2	0	1	0
Thomas	0-0	0-0	1	0	0	0
Webber	1-2	0-0	0	0	0	0
Garavaglia	1-2	0-0	1	0	2	2
Polonowski	1-3	0-0	2	2	2	2
Klein	2-6	0-0	1	0	0	4
Wiley	0-0	0-0	0	0	2	0
Evans	0-0	0-0	0	0	0	0
TOTALS	23-47	15-24	46	14	14	65

Halftime: Michigan State 36-16; **Three-point field goals:** 4-14 (Peterson 0-2, Granger 0-1, Weathers 3-5, Cleaves 1-1, Mull 0-1, Garavaglia 0-1, Klein 0-3); **Officials:** Gryzwinski, Secrest, Griffith; **Attendance:** 7,066.

FLORIDA STATE 68—MICHIGAN STATE 63

	FG-FGA	FT-FTA	REB	A	PF	TP
Weathers	4-12	3-5	0	1	3	15
Cleaves	5-15	4-4	4	3	5	14
Smith	2-5	1-4	8	1	4	5
Granger	0-1	0-0	3	1	2	0
Klein	1-2	0-0	4	0	1	2
Kelley	4-8	3-3	2	0	3	12
Mull	0-0	0-0	0	0	0	0
Thomas	0-0	0-0	1	0	0	0
Garavaglia	3-7	1-3	7	1	4	7
Polonowski	0-1	0-0	0	0	0	0
Peterson	3-6	2-2	3	1	0	8
TOTALS	22-57	14-21	33	8	22	63

Halftime: Michigan State 39-38; **Three-point field goals:** 5-16 (Weathers 4-9, Cleaves 0-3, Kelley 1-4); **Officials:** Jones, Poole, Stuart; **Attendance:** 6,362.

EXTRA! 1996 SUN BOWL

December 31, 1996
El Paso, Texas

	1	2	3	4	F
MSU	0	0	0	0	0
Stanford	7	14	10	7	38

Starting line-up (offense)		*Starting line-up (defense)*	
Nigea Carter	SE	Dimitrius Underwood	DE
Dave Mudge	LT	Chris Smith (C)	DT
Scott Shaw	LG	Robert Newkirk	DT
Matt Beard	C	Courtney Ledyard	DE
Brian Mosallam	RG	Dwayne Hawkins	OLB
Flozell Adams	RT	Reggie Garnett	MLB
John Kehr	TE	Ike Reese (C)	OLB
Todd Schultz	QB	Amp Campbell	CB
Duane Gouldbourne(C)	TB	Lemar Marshall	SS
Garett Gould	FB	Sori Kanu	FS
Derrick Mason	FL	Ray Hill	CB

MSU traveled to El Paso, Texas, for the Sun Bowl on New Year's Eve, but they were blanked by Stanford, who increased its winning streak to five games and recorded its first shutout since 1974. The Cardinals scored in the first quarter off an interception and a lateral pass that was carried 50 yards into the end zone. In the second quarter they manufactured scoring drives of 75 yards and 50 yards to take a 21-0 halftime lead. Midway through the third they put a field goal through the posts, and on their next possession they ran a double reverse 27 yards for seven more points. Their only fourth quarter TD was a six-yard return off a blocked punt. The Cardinals held the Spartans to a season-low 219 total yards and forced five turnovers. Head coach Nick Saban had four players attempting to pass, but they totaled only 151 yards on 13 of 33 completions.

EXTRA! 1997 NCAA
HOCKEY TOURNAMENT (Regionals)

For the fourth-straight year the Spartans placed third in the CCHA regular season and earned a berth in the national tournament. In the conference playoffs, they defeated Western Michigan easily and topped Miami (Ohio) in overtime before being stopped by Michigan. In the NCAA regionals, fifth-seeded MSU was matched with conference rival and fourth-seeded Minnesota. The score was tied 1-1 midway through the first period, but the Gophers scored the next four goals and won easily 6-3.

March 23, 1997—Grand Rapids, Mich.
Minnesota 6, MSU 3
1st Pd.: 1. UM, Woog (Anderson, Godbout), 3:01; 2. MSU, York (Weaver, Tuzzolino), 9:05; 3. UM, Hendrickson (Miller, Checco), 10:33; 4. UM, Hankinson (LaFleur, Crowley), 18:46.
2nd Pd.: 5. UM, Hankinson (Berg, Clymer), 4:37; 6. UM, Spehar (Hankinson, Berg), 7:19; 7. MSU, Ferranti (Horcroff, Loeding), 14:31.
3rd Pd.: 8. UM, Crowley (Hankinson), 7:44; 9. MSU, Horcoff (Harlton), 17:19.

TALES TO TELL

In recognition of the 50th anniversary of gymnastics as a varsity sport at Michigan State, long-time head coach George Szypula consented to select an All-Szypula team from the many stars he coached during his tenure (1948-1988). During those 40 seasons, "Szyp" saw his Spartans step to the top of the award stand 43 times during Big Ten championships and 18 times as NCAA champions. The pinnacle of his coaching career came when State hosted and shared the national title with the University of Illinois in 1958. His selections from those many gold medallists are as follows:

Trampoline—Steve Johnson (1960-1962): won both the Big Ten and NCAA trampoline crown in 1962.

Pommel Horse—Carlton Rintz (1952-1954): was MSU's most prolific champion with three conference titles in 1953 (still rings, horizontal bar and pommel horse), three in 1954 (still rings, horizontal bar and all-around) and three in 1955 (still rings, pommel horse and all-around). He was the NCAA pommel horse champion in both 1953 and 1955 as

well as winning the 1995 national titles in both horizontal bar and parallel bars.

Vault—Dave Thor (1966-1968): as winner of the 1968 NCAA all-around title, Thor was honored as 1968 recipient of the Nissen Award, emblematic of the top senior collegiate gymnast. He won three Big Ten titles in 1966 (floor exercise, pommel horse and all-around) and the vault in 1968 on the way to another all-around title.

Parallel Bars—Mel Stout (1949-1951): the first Spartan to win an NCAA championship, Stout did so on the parallel bars in the school's second year of competition (1949).

Horizontal Bar—Stan Tarshis (1958-1960) and Jim Curzi (1964-1966): this one was too close to call. Tarshis won five titles on the horizontal bars, three times in the conference championships and twice in the NCAA tournament (1959 and 1960). Curzi actually excelled on both the p-bars and the high bar, winning the gold medal in both events at the 1965 national collegiates. In conference competition he was

---

HEADLINES of 1998

- *Seinfeld*, the hit TV sitcom of the decade, signs off the air.
- President Clinton first denies allegations of a sexual affair with White House intern, Monica Lewinsky. He is later impeached on charges of perjury and obstruction of justice.
- St. Louis Cardinal Mark McGwire breaks Roger Maris's record for most home runs in a season, finishing with 70.
- Unabomber Theodore Kaczynski is sentenced to four life terms.

SCOREBOARD

	W	L	T	Avg.
Baseball	25	27	0	.481
Track and Field	no dual meets			
Football	7	5	0	.583
Basketball	22	8	0	.733
Tennis	15	13	0	.536
Cross Country	no dual meets			
Swimming and Diving	0	7	0	.000
Wrestling	9	10	0	.474
Hockey	33	6	5	.807
Golf	tournament play only			
Gymnastics	3	5	0	.375
Soccer	7	12	0	.368

three times the all-around champion and, in addition, placed first on the horizontal bar in both 1964 and 1966 and the parallel bar in 1965. At an even more prestigious level, Thor was the highest-placed American gymnast at the 1968 Olympic Games ands was also the second Spartan to win the Nissen award.

Floor Exercise—Toby Towson (1967-1969): he was the winner of two NCAA (1968 and 1969) and three Big Ten championships (1967-1969) in floor exercise.

Still Rings—Dale Cooper (1962-1964): in addition to twice becoming a Big Ten champion on the trampoline (1963 and 1964), the versatile Cooper won the still rings title at the NCAAs of both 1962 and 1963.

All Around: This one is a toss-up—consider *Mel Stout*, MSU's first Big Ten titlist in 1951 and a trio who each won the conference all-around title two times, *Carl Rintz* (1954 and 1955), *Jim Curzi* (1964 and 1966) and *Dave Thor* (1966 and 1968), the latter being State's only NCAA champion in the event (1968).

TEAM OF THE YEAR

The 1997-98 season was another stellar one for Ron Mason's team. MSU won the CCHA regular season and playoff championships for the first time since 1989-90, and was the only team in the nation to win both its regular-season and playoff conference championships. The Spartans won 33 games for a winning percentage of .807, which was the third best in school history. The defensive unit was the stingiest in MSU's history—it allowed just 1.73 goals per game and had a 90.2 percent penalty killing rate, both of which led the nation and topped the school record books. MSU also had two Hobey Baker finalists in forward Mike York and goalie Chad Alban. On their march toward the CCHA championship, head coach Ron Mason picked up his 800th career win with a 5-1 victory over Michigan February 20. In the CCHA title game, two Mike York goals—both from behind the goal line—led Michigan State into overtime against Ohio State. After a scoreless first OT, Shawn Horcoff's centering pass to Bryan Adams deflected past OSU's Jeff Maund and ended the longest CCHA title game after 82:30 of play. MSU's dream season ended with a 4-3 overtime loss to Ohio State in the NCAA Tournament.

MAKING HISTORY

The Big Ten and PAC-10 had been matching their football champions in the Rose Bowl since 1947. Henceforth that would not be a guarantee as the Rose Bowl entered into the Bowl Alliance (BA). Under agreement of a seven-year BA contract, the championship game would be played in Pasadena every fourth year, beginning in 2002.

The first Big Ten basketball tournament was held at the Chicago United Center.

ESPN-TV selected to cover the MSU-Michigan football game of October 25. It was the network's first visit to East Lansing and included their *College Gameday* show, which emanated live from a riser set-up on the field in front of Dem Hall.

During the Michigan State Invitational in January, freshman pole vaulter Paul Terek sailed over the bar at 16' 9-1/4" to better a 31-year-old team record. Then, less than two weeks later at the Michigan Intercollegiate championships, Terek successfully upped that mark to 17' 3/4".

The 1997-98 hockey team. Front row (left to right): M.Gresl, asst. coach T. Newton, S. Berens, M. York, T. Harlton, head coach R. Mason, J. Kozakowski, K. O'Keefe, J. Gaskins, asst. coach D. McAuliffe, C. Alban; second row (left to right): trainer D. Carrier, team physician Dr. J. Downs, M. Jalaba, C. Gemmel, B. Adams, M. Ford, M. Loeding, C. Bogas, S. Horcoff, B. Brandstatter, B. Hodgins, M. Weaver, D. Zaluski, equipment manager T. Magee, asst. coach W. Mitchell; third row (left to right): team physician Dr. J. Dunlap, strength coach B. Wilt, manager J. Ostrofsky, A. Bogle, D. Whitten, S. Patchell, R. Dolyny, J Nail, M. Kruzich, J. Blackburn, trainer Brian Chaplin, video coordinator Joe Ford and video coordinator Dan Singleton

In January the NCAA ruled that wrestlers' weight-loss methods, including wearing rubber suits while working out in saunas and artificial methods, including intravenous procedures were immediately banned. Among the new guidelines, wrestlers would be permitted to compete at as many as eight pounds over their weight class. The new guidelines were adopted after the death of three college wrestlers, including a University of Michigan athlete, trying to lose large amounts of weight.

In national competition held during early January at Orlando, Fla., MSU's cheerleading team finished 14th and the dance team, MSU Motion, tied the University of Alabama for 10th.

In season-ending negotiations, Tom Izzo was handed an annual salary increase from $130,000 to $175,000. Endorsements, money from camps and other outside income would raise his total package from $440,000 to nearly $600,000. Football coach Nick Saban's salary was reported to be slightly below $200,000 with sundry perks raising the annual package to $650,000.

Ever wonder who that young man is that steps before the Spartan Brass Band and becomes a pseudo-director during musical numbers during a basketball game? Meet Barry Greer, who was born with Down syndrome in 1986. With no coaxing, he first stepped to "the po-dium" at the age of four and has been a Breslin Center fixture ever since. He accompanies his father who has been a season-ticket holder since 1982.

GREAT STATE DATES

Soccer—**September 6, 1997 (A):** Michigan State remained unbeaten as freshman Ryan Ferguson connected on his third goal of the season with just 3:31 left in overtime gave the Spartans a 1-0 win over Northwestern. That winning marker came on a one-timer after taking a pass from junior Jeff Fliss. The victory continued MSU's dominance over the Wildcats. In the past 17 games they have played against each other, State has won 16 times. The win also marked the 199th career triumph for Spartan head coach Joe Baum.

Football—**September 20, 1997 (A):** Michigan State struck early at South Bend as Marc Renaud tucked away the opening kickoff on the five-yard line and raced to the Notre Dame 44. Seven plays late, with 11:28 showing on the stadium clock, quarterback Todd Schultz flipped a five-yard scoring pass to tight end Josh Keur. Chris Gardner converted. Seven minutes later, Schultz

climaxed a 73-yard drive as he scored from the one-yard line. In the second quarter, Gardner kicked a 31-yard field goal and with the Irish scoring just before intermission, the halftime score showed State leading, 17-7. While totally shutting down ND in the second half, Gardner added two more field goals, from the 32 and from the 31. The Spartan offensive line of Flozell Adams, Scott Shaw, Jason Strayhorn, Shaun Mason and Dave Mudge pushed the Fighting Irish around during the afternoon, allowing the "S" runners to gain 222 yards on the ground. Senior tailback Renaud rushed for 112 yards on 22 carries and Sedrick Irvin 106 yards on 26 carries. Meanwhile, the defense, led by Ike Reese, Ray Hill, Aric Morris and Robaire Smith, stopped the ND rushing game at 61 yards. The final score read 23-7 and it was MSU's first defeat of the Irish since 1986.

Cross Country—**September 20, 1997 (H):** State put five runners in the top eight to win their own Playmakers Niki Spartan Invitational with 21 points. Eastern Michigan had 35, Ohio State 80, Ball State 116 and Macomb Community College 143. Kyle Baker and Jim Jurcevich led the 8,000-meter race from the start with Baker breaking away from the pack with about one mile remaining. He crossed the finish line in 24:47.60. Jurcevich was second (24:50.50), Chris Wehrman fourth (24:56.30), Joe Leo sixth (25:11.40) and Steve Schell eighth (25:28.60).

Hockey—**October 25, 1997 (A):** Michigan State lived up to their number two national ranking by defeating the U of M 4-2 in what would be the first of four wins during the season over their archrival. Mike York opened the scoring with a power-play goal at 10:37 of the opening period. The Wolves equaled the score early in the second period on a fluke shot that hit a defender's skate and slid into the net. From there the Spartans displayed their poise and experience as they regained the lead on Shawn Horcoff's goal at 12:53. Shawn Berens scored on a power-play goal at 19:16 and freshman Rusty Dolyny completed the evening with his first goal as a collegian three minutes into the third. The MSU special teams were instrumental in the victory, scoring two five-on-four goals and skating off eight Michigan power plays, including a five-on-three for 53 seconds in the second period.

Soccer—**October 26, 1997 (H):** Fending off driving snow and 35-degree weather, the Michigan State men's soccer team defeated Penn State in a 3-2 thriller on senior day at Old College Field. Jason Wolff scored first, on an assist from Jeff Fliss, with less that two minutes into the game. MSU held the lead until 13:34 remaining in the first half when the Lions knotted the score and then scored at 35:46 to take the lead and looked to contain Michigan State until the final horn. The Spartans had ideas of their own. With 2:24 left in the game, junior Chris Slosar found his way to the goal and once more the score was tied, 2-2, with sophomore Steve Williford picking up the assist. Barely a minute later, with 1:17 left, Slosar again found an opening, scoring from the left side of the goal off a shot by senior Jeremy Guenther. Michigan State was then able to fend off the visitors until the final horn. Goalie T.J. Lieckfelt had 11 saves.

Football—**November 29, 1997 (H):** Sedrick Irvin and Marc Renaud combined for 441 yards rushing and four touchdowns as Michigan State upset number four Penn State in dramatic fashion, 49-14. Irvin ran for a career-high 238 yards on 28 carries while Renaud picked up a season-best 203 yards on 21 attempts. Their efforts set an NCAA record for combined rushing yards, shattering the previous mark of 420. They led at halftime, 14-7 on a Todd Schultz-Gari Scott 19-yard pass play followed by Renaud's 42-yard scamper around left end. After the break, the Lions came out and tied the game at the 11:15 mark of the third quarter. Just when it appeared it would be a close encounter, the Spartans struck back with five unanswered touchdowns to rack up an impressive 49-14 victory. It was the greatest number of points ever scored by a Big Ten school against Penn State. Irvin, the sophomore, scored four of those final TDs. It was the third time in his two-year collegiate career he had scored four times in one game.

Wrestling—**January 2, 1998 (H):** MSU won the first seven matches to build a 22-0 lead as the Spartans started the dual-meet season with a 22-13 win over Ohio State. The number one-ranked David Morgan (118 pounds) opened by shutting out his opponent 3-0 and was followed by freshman Pat McNamara (126 pounds) with a 12-2 victory. Isaac Miller (134 pounds) won 5-2 on a third-period reversal and riding time. Trailing 3-2 with two seconds remaining in the third period, another freshman, Nick Curry (142 pounds), came from behind with a takedown to register a 4-3 upset. David Hughes (150 pounds) and Greg DeGrand (158 pounds) built a 19-0 team lead with both winning in a 30-second overtime period. Finally, Will Hill (167 pound) guaranteed it for Michigan State by dominating his Buckeye opponent, 6-3.

Basketball—**January 17, 1998 (H):** Mateen Cleaves scored a career-high 27 points, as State defeated the University of Illinois 68-64. The win was not without a few anxious moments, as the Spartans trailed by as many as 16 in the first half and 35-27 at the intermission. Coming out strong in the second half, they outscored the Illini 19-10 to take their first lead of the game, 46-45, on Cleaves's three-pointer. There were six other lead changes before Jason Klein's three-pointer broke a 60-60 tie with 2:32 remaining. Illinois closed the margin to one, 63-62, on two free throws with 1:04 left, but Klein hit the first of two charity tosses with 28.7 remaining. His missed second attempt was rebounded by Morris Peterson. Corralling the outlet pass, Cleaves was fouled and made both free throws to gain an insurmountable four-point lead with 24.9 seconds remaining. Klein finished with 13 points and Peterson added 12.

Wrestling—**January 24, 1998 (A):** Michigan State, ranked eighth by the National Wrestling Coaches Association poll, defeated number 25 Northwestern 23-12. David Morgan, the nation's top-ranked 118-pounder, opened the match with a 6-1 win. Pat McNamara followed with a 15-0 technical fall at 126 pounds. After the Wildcats won the next two matches, consecutive wins by Corey Posey (150 pounds), Greg DeGrand (158 pounds) and Will Hill (167 pounds) sealed the victory for MSU. Heavyweight Matt Lamb closed out the scoring when he won by forfeit.

Wrestling—**February 4, 1998 (H):** James Brimm, the 177-pound freshman, knew how to win when it counted the most. Going into this meet against Michigan, he had won only once in 12 previous dual meets during the season. Now he trailed his U of M foe, 1-0. With 1:20 remaining in the final period, Brimm gained a takedown and an escape for a 3-2 win and suddenly MSU led 15-12 with two matches left on the program. Nick Muzashvili (190 pounds) clinched at least a tie with his 8-2 win putting the Spartans up, 18-12. Freshman heavyweight Matt Lamb lost 10-1, but avoided a pin to protect his team's lead. Winners in the early matches were David Morgan (118 pounds), who remained undefeated by pinning his opponent at 1:59. Pat McNamara (126 pounds) followed with an 8-3 victory. The Wolverines came back to tie the meet 9-9 with decisions at 134, 142 and 150. Greg DeGrand (158 pounds) was an 8-2 winner and following Will Hill's loss at 167 pounds, the meet was knotted at 12-12 going into Brimm's crucial match. The biased crowd of 2,137 cheered in approval as the final score read, 18-16 in MSU's favor.

Basketball—**February 7, 1998 (H):** With 6' 8" Antonio Smith achieving a double-double (17 points and 12 rebounds), Michigan State defeated Iowa, 75-64, and remained atop the Big Ten standing with a 10-1 record. The game had been billed as a "battle of the boards""with the Green ranked number one and the Hawkeyes number two among the conference schools. On this Sunday afternoon, State won the battle convincingly, leading rebounds 45-22. As for the score, the Spartans opened with a 9-0 lead, but by halftime the lead was down to three, 34-31. Early in the second half, MSU went on a 19-7 run and then after the Hawks once more closed within three, 63-60, the Spartans regrouped and reeled off eight unanswered points, including crowd-pleasing dunks by Morris Peterson and DuJuan Wiley. Peterson finished with 14 points, with Wiley and freshman Charlie Bell adding eight each.

Gymnastics—**February 13, 1998 (H):** The gymnasts shattered the school's all-time record in a 228.425-221.750 victory over Minnesota at Jenison. The Spartans took top individual honors in every event and also set a school record in the floor exercise with a score of 38.90. Junior Kenny Baker led with first-place finishes and career-bests in both the pommel horse (9.775) and parallel bars (9.700). Senior Keith Douglas posted a career-high and team season best with a 9.825 in the floor exercise, and also won the vault with a score of 9.70 to tie a career-best. Captain Ethan Sterk clinched the top spot on the high bar (9.700), while sophomores Troy Takagishi and Chris Weedon tied for first on the rings (9.450).

Basketball—**February 17, 1998 (H):** With five players scoring in double figures, number 14 Michigan State defeated number 22 University of Michigan, 80-75. To the chagrin of the Wolverines, "Magic" Johnson, who was in attendance, gave the team a pregame pep talk and, along with Greg Kelser, "fired up" the Breslin crowd of 15,138, who were armed with signs and green-and-white pom-poms. The home team responded, burying the U of M by 13 at the 10-minute mark and eventually owning an impressive 44-29 lead at halftime. However, while the Spartans seemed to lose some of their intensity during the second half, Michigan slowly cut into the lead and with 30 seconds remaining in the game, they trailed by only two, 75-73. From there, Mateen Cleaves connected on two free throws, Charlie Bell added one and Jason Klein clinched the win as he sank two from the line with 6.4 seconds left. When the final buzzer

sounded, MSU fans swarmed the court in celebration. Klein led the team in scoring with 17, followed by Cleaves with 14, Antonio Smith 12, Andre Hutson and Morris Peterson 10 each.

Hockey—**February 20 (H) & 21 (N), 1998:** Number two-ranked Michigan State vaulted past fifth-ranked Michigan with a two-game series sweep, putting Michigan State atop the CCHA standings. The Spartans dominated the U of M on Friday night at Munn Arena, 5-1. The win marked the 800th of Ron Mason's coaching career. Bryan Adams scored MSU's first goal of the game, and Sean Berens added two more in the first to give the Spartans a 3-0 lead. With the game in hand, Rusty Dolyny added one more goal in the second period. Leading 4-1 in the third, Sean Berens completed a hat trick at the 6:25 mark, closing out the scoring for a 5-1 win. Meeting at Joe Louis Arena the next night, MSU once again took it to the Wolverines, 4-1. Mike York and Behrens each accounted for a goal in the opening stanza and that 2-0 score held until 8:03 of the final period when the U of M scored on a deflection. It took only 17 seconds for Damon Whitten to regain the two-goal lead when he scored on a deflection shot. York, the Waterford, Mich., junior, concluded the scoring on an empty-netter with 61 seconds of playing time remaining in the game.

Gymnastics—**March 12, 1998 (A):** In front of a packed crowd at Jenison Field House, MSU defeated number eight Michigan, 229.225-229.150. The score was MSU's second-highest of the season as the Spartans surpassed the Wolverines on the vault (38.775), floor exercise (38.450) and high bar (38.050). The team was led by freshman Chris Weedon, who had a career-best 9.80 on the high bar. Sophomore Brady Grimm was the top MSU performer on the vault, scoring a second-place finish with a 9.80. Freshman Tommy Housley and senior Keith Douglas each clinched a career best on vault (9.700 and 9.725, respectively). Housley also took top honors in the floor exercise event.

Tennis—**March 21, 1998 (A):** The team improved to 9-4 overall and 1-0 in the conference when it opened the dual-meet season with a 5-2 victory over Ohio State. Opening the doubles competition, all three pairs contributed with wins: Chris Struck-Ken Kigongo, Ben Hetzler-Trey Eubanks and Ivica Primorac-Francisco Trinidad. Strength at the lower end of the singles line-up was a primary factor in the victory. After number one Eubanks and number two Primorac dropped their

matches, Struck was a winner at number three in three sets, 6-7, 6-4, 6-0; number four Hetzler won in straight sets, 7-6, 6-3; number five Kigongo took three sets to win, 6-4, 7-6, 6-3 while Trinidad seemingly had the easiest afternoon in the number six slot, winning 6-1, 6-2.

Tennis—**April 11, 1998 (H):** The Spartans won their 10th meet of the year in defeating Penn State, 5-2. MSU opened by taking two sets in the pairs and thus jumped to a 1-0 lead by gaining the doubles point. Chris Struck and Ken Kilgongo won at number one and Trey Eubanks-Ben Hetzler were winners at number two. In the singles competition, Eubanks was the winner at number one, 6-2, 7-5; Hetzler the winner at number four, 6-4, 6-0. The remaining team points were earned by no. 5 Kilgibgo, 6-4, 6-4 and number six Francisco Trinadad, 6-1, 6-2.

Baseball—**April 17, 1998 (A):** En route to his fourth consecutive complete game, senior Brian Murphy pitched out of jams in the second and third innings and then faced the minimum 19 batters over the final six and one-third innings, leading Michigan State to a 10-1 victory over Michigan. Connecting on 15 hits, all nine starters for State either scored or drove in a run. Tied 1-1 in the fourth, MSU sent 11 hitters to the plate and scored six times on six hits with three more runs in the ninth. Sophomore Gary Zsigo led the Spartan offense with a four-for-four afternoon. Tom Hartley was three-for-five with three RBIs and Mark Mulder also contributed three hits.

Baseball—**April 18, 1998 (H):** MSU picked up a 7-2 victory over Michigan at Oldsmobile Park with a solid outing by starter Mark Mulder, who fanned eight in a complete game effort. The Spartan offense delivered as well, banging out 11 hits while scoring in each of its last five at-bats. Junior Mike Wagner went three-for-four with two RBIs, including a long lead-off home run to left-center in the third inning. Sophomore Joe Albaugh also contributed a pair of RBI, as he went two-for-four with two doubles.

Baseball—**April 19, 1998 (A):** Outfielder Tom Hartley, who would be the team's leading hitter at season's end, was three-for-five in this Sunday afternoon game, including a two-run home run in the top of the ninth giving State an 11-10 victory over the University of Michigan. The Wolverines threatened to counter in their ninth, but reliever Josh Axelson secured the final out with runners on first and third. It was a wild afternoon with the

teams combining for five errors, 23 hits, 21 runs, 13 walks and five wild pitches in rainy conditions. Mark Mulder and Mike Pisani each had a pair of hits for the Spartans.

Baseball—April 23, 1998 (A): Michigan State hitters connected for seven home runs as they swept Central Michigan in a doubleheader, 7-5 and 16-5. Trailing 5-4 in the opener and faced with their final time at-bat, Carlos Fernandez knotted the score with a home run to right-center. The next batter, Tom Grigg, also found the range and blasted the ball over the left-field fence, giving State the lead. The Spartans then picked up an insurance run and the victory. Yielding three earned runs, pitcher Brian Murphy received the win with assistance from reliever Chris Yens. The second game was a slugfest, as MSU banged out 15 hits and posted 16 runs. Fernandez, Tom Hartley and Joe Albaugh all homered for the Spartans, as MSU jumped out to a 9-0 lead in the third inning. That was all Spartan starter Mark Mulder would need, as he didn't allow an earned run in six innings while registering nine strikeouts.

ATHLETE OF THE YEAR

Mark Mulder, the number two overall pick in the 1998 Major League Baseball Amateur Draft, was a third-team All-America selection in 1998. Mulder struck out more batters in the 1998 season (113) than any other Spartan in history. Although he pitched at MSU for only two years (turning professional in the fall of 1998), he still ranks as ninth-best in school history in strikeouts with 169. Mulder earned first-team All-Big Ten honors in 1997 and 1998, and is only one of six Spartans to be elected to the first team more than once. He threw five complete games and 89.1 innings in his last year, which is the ninth-most in an MSU season. Mulder also shined at the plate, as he led the 1998 team in hitting with a .335 batting average. He also had five home runs, 30 RBIs and an on-base percentage of .447. He currently pitches for the Oakland Athletics, and was an All-Star selection in 2001.

Mark Mulder

IN THE SPARTLITE

Baseball: Five Michigan State players earned Academic All-Big Ten honors (Joe Kalczynski, Scott Colvin, Carlos Fernandez, Kimya Massey and Mike Pisani). Kalczynski also earned Academic All-District honors.

As a pitcher-first baseman, Mark Mulder completed an impressive sophomore season. On the mound he recorded 113 strikeouts (a team record) and at the plate he batted a team-leading .335 average. For the second consecutive year Mark was chosen as a first team All-Big Ten selection, one of only six Spartans to ever be honored two times. He also gained third-team All-American honors in 1998. As a first-round draft pick by the Detroit Tigers, Mulder would sign professionally and later, in 2002, become a member of the starting pitching rotation for the Oakland Athletics.

Tom Hartley posted a perfect 1.000 fielding percentage.

Tom Grigg closed out his career at MSU as one of the top hitters in school history. He ranks sixth all-time in hits (205), 10th in runs (127) and ninth in doubles (33).

Pitcher Brian Murphy, a second-team All-Big Ten selection, finished his career with 194 strikeouts, which ranks second in school history. He is the all-time leader at MSU in innings pitched with 300.1.

Chris Yens was a third-team All-Big Ten selection. He had seven saves in 1998, tied for second most in an MSU season.

Basketball: For the first time, Coach Izzo orchestrated a Midnight Madness night to open the first basketball practice on Friday, October 17. Approximately 7,500 Spartan fans showed up and filled the lower bowl of Breslin.

Sophomore forward Morris Peterson sustained a fractured scaphoid in his right wrist during a home victory against Gonzaga in the Coca-Cola Spartan Classic. Fortunately, the Flint sophomore is left-handed, thus he could play effectively with a cast on the damaged wrist and he did so over a good portion of the season.

Mateen Cleaves set a school record with nine steals against Minnesota on February 14.

On a stretch from December 17 to February 17, the Spartans won 13 of 14 games.

Although the regular-season finale was a 99-96 overtime loss to Purdue at the Breslin, it was a game with a dramatic touch. Trailing 90-88 with 18 seconds remain-

ing in regulation, the Spartans worked the ball to Jason Klein who took a jumper from just inside the three-point line. His shot was wide and caromed toward the baseline. Freshman Andre Hutson dove for the ball and instinctively flipped it back underneath the basket, a spot where Morris Peterson had raced to seek the original rebound. The Flint sophomore grabbed the frantic pass and laid it in to tie the score with two seconds remaining. Unfortunately, the perfect finish was not to be, forcing the Spartans to share the conference title.

At the end of the season, Coach Izzo was recipient of the *Basketball News* Coach of the Year award. The publication's representative stated that Izzo was honored for getting the most out of his squad. Indeed, MSU claimed a shared of the Big Ten championship for the first time since 1990 and would go on to reach the Sweet Sixteen level of the NCAA championship bracket.

Cleaves, who averaged 7.2 assists per game, was named an All-American, received the Chicago Tribune Silver Basketball and was named Big Ten Player of the Year.

Cross Country: During the season, MSU finished in first place at the Spartan Invitational, the Windsor Open, the Paul Short Invitational and the Tiger Classic.

Led by Kyle Baker, who completed the Ohio State course in third place (24:30), State finished third at the Big Tens with a total of 79 points.

In the NCAA regional championships, MSU placed seventh out of 22 squads, their best effort since 1970. Once more it was Baker leading the way as he finished the 10K layout in ninth place (32.01).The team's effort qualified them for the NCAA championships held at Furman University in Greenville, S.C. This was the third time in the last six years that the team had qualified for the event out of the 300 teams in Division I.

In postseason recognition, Baker and Jurcevich earned All-Big Ten honors, while Baker and Schell were designated as Academic All-Americans.

Football: Offensive tackle Flozell Adams and offensive guard Scott Shaw were named first-team All-Americans. Adams was also a first-team All-Big Ten selection while Shaw made the second-team.

Linebacker Ike Reese was the other Spartan to earn first-team All-Big Ten honors. Reese finished his career third on MSU's all-time tackles list with 420.

Todd Schulz closed out his career as one of the best quarterbacks in MSU history. Schulz is third all-time at

MSU in completion percentage (.607), fourth in touchdown passes (27) and fifth in passing yards (4,273) and pass completions (360). His 177 pass completions in 1997 rank fourth in an MSU season…Josh Keur caught 11 passes against Northwestern, third-best in an MSU game…kicker Chris Gardner left MSU second in school history in points (281) and field goals (52)…Robaire Smith had 12 quarterback sacks, tied for third-best in an MSU season…Ray Hill broke up 16 passes, which is also tied for third best in a Spartan season.

Golf: Heading to Florida in March, the golf team competed in the 18-team Golden Ocala Intercollegiate where they finished tied with Miami (Ohio) for second, just three strokes behind the winning Rollins College team. Matt Pumford, one shot from medalist honors, carded a three-round total of 74-71-73—218. His teammates scored as follows: John Ehrgott, 75-70-76—221, Alberto Quevedo, an international student from Canary Islands, Spain, 76-78-70—224, Matt Riegel, 77-78-73—228, Chad Quinn, 81-76-79—236 and Brent Goik, 73-85-78—236.

For the first time since 1986, there was no Fossum/Spartan Invitational because the Spartans hosted the Big Ten championships at Forest Akers West. For playing on their home course, the sixth-place finish was disappointing. Furthermore, they had led the tournament after 39 holes and stood fourth after 54. Freshman Goik was the top Spartan with a 72-70-77-73—292 scorecard, good for a fifth place tie.

Gymnastics: Scoring 227.975 points, MSU finished fourth at the Big Ten championships in Ann Arbor, its best showing since 1991, and qualified as a team for the NCAA Eastern Regional for only the second time in five years. Top individual finishers in the six individual events and all-around were Tommy Housley, second in floor exercise (9.8); and a sixth-place tie on the parallel bars (9.65); Brady Grimm tied for second in the vault (9.8); Ethan Sterk third on the horizontal bar with a 9.7; Mike Phipps tied for fourth on the rings (9.65); Kenny Baker fifth on the pommel horse (9.725) and Sterk's 19th, the top Spartan in the all-around with a score of 54.55. Another top-five finisher was Ryan Trumpinski with a fifth in the vault (9.775) and a fifth in floor exercise (9.7).

Senior Keith Douglas finished sixth in the vault at the NCAA championships with a score of 9.45 to earn All-America honors. Ethan Sterk and Mike Quarress were alternates for the NCAA championships.

Dave Barron, Ethan Sterk and Troy Takagishi all earned Academic All-Big Ten honors.

Brady Grimm tied a school record on the vault with a score of 9.800 March 12. He then posted the same score March 20 at the Big Ten championship.

Hockey: It had been a long wait, 12 years to be exact. That was the last time MSU wore the Great Lakes Invitational (GLI) crown. The Spartans gained the 1997 title by defeating Michigan Tech 3-1 and the U of M 5-3. As is often the case, teams played in the GLI minus one or more feature players who opt to compete in the World Junior Championships. This year it was State's Michael York who played for the USA team.

At 2:30 of the second overtime, Shawn Horcoff scored the winning goal to defeat Ohio State 3-2 and end the longest CCHA championship game in league history. Junior Mike York had scored the two goals leading to the extra sessions. The victory marked the eighth time MSU had captured the CCHA playoff title.

Chad Alban became just the third Spartan to be named CCHA Player of the Year. He also accomplished another feat that has never been done in MSU history. On February 28, he capped a memorable Senior Night with an empty-net goal, becoming just the fourth college goalie to be credited with a goal. Alban shot the puck from behind and to the right of his net and it went in with 13 seconds remaining in the 6-3 win over Ferris State.

Postseason honors were a-plenty. For the second consecutive year, Tyler Harlton was named the CCHA best defensive defenseman. Mike York was named the CCHA tournament MVP and also played in the world junior championships where he earned a medal. Three players were selected to the CCHA first team: Alban, Sean Berens and Tyler Harlton. Alban and York were selected as first team All-American while Berens and Harlton earned second team honors.

Soccer: Despite holding an 18-4 advantage in shots and 10-2 in corner kicks, State had to settle for 0-0 tie against Duquesne in the opening game of the MSU/Quality Suites Soccer Classic on Old College Field. On the following day, the MSU offense came alive as six different players contributed points in a 6-2 victory of Canisius. In what is likely a record, Steve Wolliford tallied the first point just 14 seconds into the contest. Chris Slosar scored next at 13:56 and MSU led at halftime, 2-0. Four second-half goals put the game out of reach. Scores came from Jeff Fliss, Keith Gordon, Ryan Townsend and senior captain Jeremy Guenther. Michigan State was declared the winner of the tournament on the basis of a goal differential (plus four) in the two games. Duquesne was runner-up with a differential of plus two.

Coach Joe Baum and his team found a pair of teams from the West highly competitive as they were winless in the Snickers/Fila Rebel Classic in Las Vegas. Rick Smith came up with a goal in the first-game loss to Fresno State. On the next afternoon, Nevada-Las Vegas (UNLV) defeated the Spartans 4-2.

Chad Alban, the first Spartan goalie to shoot a goal

Rick Smith scored with 40 seconds remaining in the opening half to tie the game at 1-1. The Rebels then blew the game open with three consecutive goals in the second half. Chris Slosar closed out the scoring at 77:25.

Jason Wolff was a first-team All-Big Ten selection while Chris Slosar earned second-team honors. Slosar led the team in scoring with 14 points.

Swimming and Diving: In the third day of competition at the Big Ten championships, MSU had several top performances. MSU freshman John Munley led the Spartans, advancing to the finals where he finished in 14th place in the 1650 freestyle with a time of 15:41.54. Also finishing in 13th place was freshman Michael Tingley, with a time of 1:49.34 in the 200 backstroke. In the 400 freestyle relay, the MSU team of Munley, senior Adam Pawlick, senior Michael Orris, and sophomore Chad Ganden came in ninth with a time of 3:05.41. John Munley posted the top times for the Spartans in the 100 freestyle (45.77), the 200 freestyle (1:38.50), the 500 freestyle (4:28.29).

Tennis: Drawing players from 30 schools, the 1997 Rolex Regional Championships were held in Champaign,

Ill., in November. The Spartans played well in first-round action, winning all five matches: Trey Eubank, Ken Kigongo, Francisco Trinidad, Ivica Primorac and Chris Struck. However, Eubanks is the only Spartan who advanced into the third round before being sidelined.

Hosting the Big Ten indoor singles championships in January, Eubanks make an impressive showing, as he defeated opponents from Wisconsin, Ohio State and Minnesota before losing in the quarterfinals to a member of the Northwestern team, 6-4, 7-6(3). Ben Hetsler and Francisco Trinidad were both winners in the opening round, but did not advance further.

Trey Eubanks was recipient of both the Big Ten Sportsmanship Award and the Arthur Ashe Regional Sportsman of the Year awarded by *Tennis Magazine.* He was also named the team MVP and earned All-Big Ten honors as well.

At the Big Ten championships in Champaign, Ill., Michigan State upset higher-seeded Indiana to take seventh place. secure crucial points with victories by juniors Chris Struck and Trey Eubanks in the number one match and the sophomore team of Ivica Primorac and Francisco Trinidad in the number three contest. Struck and Eubanks defeated Gabriel Montilla and Derrick Pope by the score of 8-2, while Primorac and Trinidad downed George McGill and Steve Jordan 8-5.

Track and Field: Senior Octavis Long ran a 6.31 to capture the 55 meters at the indoor Red Simmons Invitational in Ann Arbor. Other strong performances came from freshmen pole vaulters Jake Diner and Paul Terek, both clearing 16' 6" and finishing second and third respectively. Matt Deering, yet another freshman, was seventh with a 15' 0" vault.

Scoring 76 points, the track and field team finished fourth at the indoor central collegiate championships in Ann Arbor. Octavis Long won the 55-meter dash in 6.37; Terek prevailed in the pole vault with a mark of 16' 4-3/4" and freshman Joe Leo won the 3,000-meter run with a time of 8:22.24.

At the Big Ten indoor championships hosted by Purdue University, Jim Jurcevich was the only Spartan to place higher than fourth as he was a bronze medallist in the 5,000 meters with an NCAA-qualifying time of 14:14.85. He would later earn All-American honors with an eighth-place finish (14:12.44) at those nationals. Other finalists in the conference meet were Octavius Long, fifth in the 55-meter dash (06.41); Jeff Ferrell and Steve Schell,

sixth and seventh at 3,000 meters (8:26.56 and 8:27.31) with Schell also placing sixth in the 5,000 meters (14:23.62); Ryan Taylor and Chris Wehrman ran fifth and sixth in the mile (4:10.67 and 4:11,45); Okie Giwa-Agbomeirele was fourth best in the long jump (23' 11-3/4"); Jeff Kus leaped 6' 9" for a seventh in the high jump and the pole vaulting duo of Terek and Yakov placed fifth (16' 11") and sixth (16' 07-1/4"). Terek also placed fifth (4,954 points) in the grueling heptathlon event with teammate Matt Ingram placing eighth (4,366).

Only a few Spartans traveled to the Mt. Sac Relays in California, but the trip was well worth it. All-American Jim Jurcevich won the 10,000-meter run with a time of 29:12.49, while junior Schell took seventh in 29:31.32. In the 3,000-meter steeplechase, junior Wehrman finished seventh with an NCAA provisional qualifying time of 8:51.60. Sophomore Ryan Taylor also set a provisional mark with a time of 14:09.22 in the 5,000. He finished ninth.

At the outdoor conference championships in Columbus, Ohio, State could do no better than 36.5 points and 10th place. Nine different team members were contributors. With 7,206 points, Terek placed second in the decathlon and Okie Giwa-Agbomeirele was third in the long jump (24'-8-1/2"). Other contributors in placed four through eight were Jurcevich, Diner, Wehrman, Joe Leo, Ryan Taylor, Eric Eichinger and Matt Ingram.

During the outdoor season, Terek set a school records in the javelin (189'-9"), pole vault (17' 3 1/4") and decathlon (7,206) with Justin Seldon setting varsity records in the discus (166' 6") and hammer throw (130' 1").

Wrestling: With the 1997-1998 season, State began hosting their meets on the raised platform in Jenison Fieldhouse, giving a championship flair to the dual meets.

At the Midlands championship in January, Dave Morgan (118 pounds) went all the way to the title. Pat McNamara (126 pounds) was the only other Spartan to finish in the top eight as he placed fourth. With 59 team points, State finished ninth out of 53 teams.

Scoring 57.5 points, MSU finished seventh at the Big Ten championships held on the Penn State campus. David Morgan (118 pounds) lived up to his number one-ranking by winning his third consecutive title.

Six members of the squad qualified for the NCAA championships at the Convocation Center in Cleveland. Morgan concluded an outstanding collegiate career, going to the finals where he settled for the runner-up spot.

During the year he tied his own team season record of 44 victories and his 129 career-winning matches ranks second in the school record book. McNamara reached the semifinals before losing and capped one of the most outstanding freshman seasons at MSU with a fifth-place finish. Miller, DeGrand, Hill and Muzashvili each opened with wins before bowing out in the second round. Totaling 39 team points, State finished 13 out of the field of 84 competing teams.

EXTRA! 1998 NCAA BASKETBALL TOURNAMENT

Michigan State reached the regional semifinals in the 1998 NCAA tournament. The following are the Spartans' box scores for those games.

MICHIGAN STATE 83—EASTERN MICHIGAN 71

	FG-FGA	FT-FTA	REB	A	PF	TP
Smith	1-5	4-6	9	3	1	6
Klein	2-8	1-2	0	1	2	7
Hutson	3-7	7-8	10	0	1	13
Cleaves	7-14	4-4	2	3	3	20
Bell	7-12	7-8	9	0	2	22
Guess	0-0	0-0	0	0	0	0
Thomas	0-0	0-0	0	0	0	0
Davis	2-2	0-0	1	0	0	4
Peterson	4-6	0-0	4	0	2	9
Granger	0-0	0-0	1	1	0	0
Wiley	1-5	0-2	3	2	1	2
TOTALS	27-59	23-30	43	10	12	83

Halftime: Michigan State 43-35; **Three-point field goals:** 6-15 (Klein 2-5, Cleaves 2-7, Bell 1-1, Peterson 1-2); **Officials:** Clougherty, Hall, Richards; **Attendance:** 16,105.

MICHIGAN STATE 63—PRINCETON 56

	FG-FGA	FT-FTA	REB	A	PF	TP
Smith	2-2	2-2	5	1	3	6
Klein	2-3	0-0	5	0	1	4
Hutson	4-5	0-0	4	1	3	8
Cleaves	9-13	6-9	9	5	2	27
Bell	2-7	1-2	3	1	2	6
Thomas	0-1	0-0	3	0	2	0
Davis	0-0	0-0	1	0	0	0
Peterson	0-1	4-4	4	0	3	4
Granger	0-1	2-2	3	3	2	2
Wiley	3-6	0-0	1	0	2	6
TOTALS	22-39	15-19	39	11	20	63

Halftime: Michigan State 33-31; **Three-point field goals:** 4-8 (Klein 0-1, Cleaves 3-5, Bell 1-1, Peterson 0-1); **Officials:** Clougherty, Valentine, Reischling; **Attendance:** 16,105.

NORTH CAROLINA 73—MICHIGAN STATE 58

	FG-FGA	FT-FTA	REB	A	PF	TP
Smith	0-4	4-4	7	0	4	4
Klein	2-11	0-0	2	1	2	6
Hutson	2-6	0-0	3	1	4	4
Cleaves	7-21	2-3	4	5	4	18
Bell	5-7	1-1	4	2	2	13
Peterson	3-11	3-4	3	1	3	9
Wiley	2-6	0-0	3	0	2	4
Thomas	0-0	0-0	1	0	0	0
Granger	0-2	0-0	2	0	1	0
Cherry	0-0	0-0	0	0	0	0
Davis	0-0	0-0	0	0	0	0
Guess	0-0	0-0	0	0	0	0
Miller	0-0	0-0	0	0	0	0
TOTALS	21-68	10-12	33	10	22	58

Halftime: North Carolina 38-24; **Three-point field goals:** 6-25 (Klein 2-8, Cleaves 2-9, Bell 2-3, Peterson 0-3, Granger 0-2); **Officials:** Higgins, Haney, Greenwood; **Attendance:** 23,235.

EXTRA! 1997 ALOHA BOWL

December 25, 1997
Honolulu, Hawaii

	1	2	3	4	F
MSU	7	3	7	6	23
Washington	14	17	13	7	51

Starting line-up (offense)		*Starting line-up (defense)*	
Octavious Long	SE	Dimitrius Underwood	DE
Flozell Adams	LT	Chris Smith (C)	DT
Scott Shaw (C)	LG	Robert Newkirk	DT
Jayson Strayhorn	C	Rob	DE
Shaun Mason	RG	Dwayne Hawkins	OLB
Dave Mudge	RT	Mike Austin	MLB
Kyle Rance	TE	Ike Reese (C)	OLB
Todd Schultz	QB	Amp Campbell	CB
Sedrick Irvin	TB	Lemar Marshall	SS
Travis Reece	FB	Sori Kanu	FS
Gari Scott	FL	Ray Hill	CB

Nick Saban became the first Spartan coach to lead his team to three bowl games in his first three years as head coach, but unfortunately the team lost all three by at least 19 points. This time, number 21 Washington would take home a 51-23 victory over number 25 Michigan State with the most points ever allowed in a bowl game by the Spartans. The Huskies started the game with a 14-0 lead off two quick scoring drives. Todd Schultz then engineered a six-play, 73-yard drive that ended with a 12-yard pass to Gari Scott to set the score at 14-7. In the second quarter Washington came up with a touchdown and a field goal to increase its lead to 28-7 before MSU could score again. When they did, it was only for three points, as Paul Edinger kicked a 43-yarder through the posts. The Spartans were pushing for another touchdown before the close of the half but gave up an interception that was returned 56 yards for a TD and put Washington up 31-10. After the Huskies started the second half with yet another seven points, Leroy McFadden returned the kickoff 59 yards to set up MSU's second touchdown. It came on a 28-yard strike from Schultz to Scott with 8:11 left in the third quarter. The Huskies had two more uncanny touchdowns, running a fake punt 64 yards and returning another interception 66 yards for their final points. With just two seconds left in the game Bill Burke hit Lavaile Richardson on a 21-yard TD pass to cement the final score. Washington produced 477 total yards, including 298 on the ground, while limiting Michigan State to 296 passing yards and a season-low 47 yards rushing.

EXTRA! 1998 NCAA HOCKEY TOURNAMENT (Quarterfinals)

Ohio State was to be MSU's nemesis for the year. After winning the CCHA regular season crown, the Spartans went into the conference playoffs a favorite. They defeated Ferris State easily before edging out the Buckeyes 3-2 for the title in a grueling double overtime game. MSU was the only team in the country to win both conference championships. Seeded first, they were given a bye in the opening round of the NCAA tournament, and as fate had it, they were paired with Ohio State once again for the quarterfinals. The Spartans scored three power-play goals during the game, but the Bucks tallied three of their own to knot the score at the end of regulation. After 8:47 of the overtime period OSU got its revenge with a goal that sent their opponents back to East Lansing for the rest of the year.

March 28, 1998—Ann Arbor, Mich.
Ohio State 4, MSU 3 (OT)
1st Pd.: 1. MSU, Hodgins (York, Kozakowski), 18:34 PPG.
2nd Pd.: 2. MSU Horcoff (Weaver, York), 6:10 PPG; 3. OSU, Signoretti (Richards), 6:51; 4. OSU, Meloche (Boisevert, Maund), 11:25; 5. MSU Dolyny (Berens, York), 17:23 PPG.
3rd Pd.: 6. OSU, Rech (McMillan), 5:43.
Overtime: 7. OSU, Signoretti (Meloche, Boisvert), 8:47.

MSU 1998-1999

TALES TO TELL

In the fall of 1998, Michigan State's Sports Information Department (SID) conducted an Internet poll among Spartan fans to select the most memorable home football game played in the 75-year history of Spartan Stadium. A ranking of the top 10 was published on October 31. There were ties in the balloting at 5-6 and 8-9. Heading the list was the 1995 game against Michigan (see page 755). Reaching back the furthest in time, the fans remembered the 1966 10-10 tie with Notre Dame, at the time defined as the "Game of the Century." One can only editorialize as to how this list might stack up if fans were polled today. The defeat of Michigan in 1999 and the last-second victory over the Wolverines of 2001 would certainly challenge for a spot on this list today. The top 10 as revealed by the SID poll was as follows:

The crowd enjoys another memorable moment at Spartan Stadium.

1. November 11, 1995: Michigan State 28, Michigan 25. Tony Banks throws a 25-yard touchdown pass to Nigea Carter for the game-winner with 1:24 remaining.

2. November 9, 1974: Michigan State 16, number one Ohio State 13. Levi Jackson races 88 yards for the game-winning touchdown late in the fourth quarter.

3. November 14, 1987: Michigan State 27, Indiana 3. Lorenzo White gains 292 yards and scores twice as Spartans clinch the Big Ten title and a trip to the Rose Bowl.

4. November 29, 1997: Michigan State 49, Penn

HEADLINES of 1999

- The U.S. Senate acquits President Clinton of impeachment charges.
- Two Colorado students go on shooting spree in Columbine High School killing 15, including themselves.
- John F. Kennedy Jr., his wife and his sister-in-law are killed in an airplane crash near Martha's Vineyard.
- Dr. Jack Kevorkian is convicted of second-degree murder in an assisted-suicide case.

SCOREBOARD

	W	L	T	Avg.
Baseball	28	25	0	.528
Track and Field	no dual meets			
Football	6	6	0	.500
Basketball	33	5	0	.868
Tennis	10	13	0	.435
Cross Country	no dual meets			
Swimming and Diving	3	5	0	.375
Wrestling	6	11	1	.361
Hockey	29	6	7	.774
Golf	tournament play only			
Gymnastics	3	6	0	.333
Soccer	7	12	0	.368

State 14. Sedrick Irvin and Mark Renaud combine for 441 yards and four rushing touchdowns.

5. November 19, 1966: Number two Michigan State 10, number one Notre Dame 10. Regis Cavender scores MSU's only touchdown in the second quarter and the defense holds the Irish to 91 yards rushing and 219 total yards.

6. September 12, 1998: Michigan State 45, Notre Dame 23. Spartans jump out to 42-3 halftime lead in the stadium's second-ever night game.

7. October 10, 1987: Michigan State 17, Michigan 11. Lorenzo White picks up 185 yards and scores twice while John Miller intercepts four passes.

8. September 7, 1987: Michigan State 27, Southern Cal 13. Lorenzo White rushes for 111 yards and two scores, as the season opens with the first night game in the stadium's history. The two opponents would also finish the season against each other, in the Rose Bowl.

9. October 10, 1998: Michigan State 38. Indiana 31 (2 OT). Sedrick Irvin's 25-yard touchdown run and Lamar Marshall's pass breakup give the Spartans a come-from-behind victory in the first-ever MSU overtime game.

10. October 26, 1968: Michigan State 21, Notre Dame 17. Tommy Love rushes for 100 yards and two touchdowns, including a game-winning one-yard run in the third quarter."

TEAM OF THE YEAR

Scoring 107 team points to runner-up Illinois' 89, Michigan State captured the Big Ten indoor track and field championships held in Madison, Wis. It was the school's third such title, having finished first in 1966 and 1972. MSU scored in only five of 11 track events and were shut out in all but one field event. Yet when the Spartans scored, they scored big.

Successfully turning to the abundant and talented distance runners, Coach Gatson found the winning formula at the Big Ten indoor championships. In the 3,000 meters Steve Schell was the winner (8:09.45), followed by Jurcevich in second (8:12.10), Kyle Baker fourth (8:13.66) and Taylor fifth (8:17.30. In the 5,000, Jurcevich (14:07.23) and Schell (14:08.81) flip-flopped the top two slots with Baker third (14:13.26). Taylor (4:07.09) and Wehrman. (4:11.12) ran two-three in the mile with E.J. Martin (08.08) and Okoi Giwa-Agbomierie (08.41) finishing four-eight in the 60-meter hurdles. Paul Terek was runner-up in the pole vault (17' 3/4") and third in the seven-event heptathlon (5,462 points). Other contributors toward the title were Matt Deering, third in the pole vault (16' 8-3/4") and Matt Ingram fifth in the heptathlon (5,058 points).

Unfortunately, the charm of February did not carry over to May. In fact, the 1999 indoor champions could muster only 75 points and a fifth-place finish when activities moved outdoors. Kyle Baker was the lone State winner with a 29:26.68 in the 10,000-meter run.

MAKING HISTORY

Baseball star Mark Mulder, a 1998 third-team All-American and two-time All-Big Ten selection, was the number two overall pick in the 1998 Major League Amateur draft by the Oakland Athletics. In October he signed with the A's and became the first drafted baseball player to receive a $3.2 million signing bonus.

On Sept. 8, 1998, 76-year-old Walter Adams, succumbed to cancer at his home in East Lansing. The distinguished economics professor and one-time fill-in as president of the school (1969-1970) was, in addition, a loyal fan of Spartan sports and the marching band, of which he was an honorary member. In the spring he would

The 1998-99 track and field team. (Front row, left to right) S. Weeks, E.J. Martin, S. Schell, J. Jurcevich, R. Taylor, J. Hanson, C. Wehrman, M. Ingram. (Second row) A. Luxey, Lawrence Jones, Larry Jones, J. Ferrell, J. Leo, T. Boring, M. LaFave, M. Jackson, asst. coach W. Wabaunsee. (Third row) M. Chambers, B. Dieffenbacher, N. Ajaeio, W. Howell, P. Terek, L. Mays, M. Deering, K. Baker. (Fourth row) asst. coach J. Stintzi, J. Selden, J. Keller, S. Schultze, J. Kus, O. Giwa-Agbomeirele, Y. Dinere, B. Chapin and head coach D. Gatson.

For the second time in five years, the Big Ten Conference extended a query to Notre Dame officials regarding membership and once again officials at the South Bend, Ind., school (55 board of trustee members) voted unanimously to remain independent. Although most observers suggested that money was the issue, the Irish football coach, Bob Davie, said the decision was probably bigger than just football and it involved a reinforcement of the heritage and culture of the institution.

It was one of the strangest episodes ever perpetrated by the university; yet it was educational, proving that to "resign" from a job can be profitable. In April it was reported that Merritt Norvell had resigned his position as athletic director to take a job with an executive search firm. Regardless, he would continue to receive his $143,500 annual salary for the position until July of 2000. Furthermore, he would receive another $100,000 to be disbursed until July of 2001 during which time he would act as a consultant to strengthen an MSU program designed "to help student-athletes adjust to life after athletics and college."

exhibit his loyalty to the baseball team by sitting behind the first base dugout and heckling the opposition. During basketball season he would take up a spot behind the visitors and "fill their ear." One of his favorite targets was coach Bobby Knight of Indiana. Soon, antagonism turned to friendship and beginning in 1982, just prior to the annual game in East Lansing, the pair would greet each other and exchange appropriate mementos (school wearing apparel, etc.).

Scott Skiles (BK 1983-1986) was honored during halftime of the season-opener on Nov. 13, 1998. Upon officially retiring his number four jersey, a banner was raised into the rafters of Breslin where it joined previously acknowledged Spartan cage heroes Johnny Green, Earvin Johnson, Greg Kelser and Jud Heathcote.

On the weekend of February 19-21, the athletic department hosted a centennial of Michigan State basketball. With players from as far back as the early 1930s, more than 100 alums returned for the festivities, with about 50 of them participating in a Legends Fun Game on Saturday Night that drew over 4,000 spectators. On the next afternoon, Tom Izzo's 1999 squad defeated Wisconsin 56-51 for their 14th win in a row.

Walter Adams heckles the opposition from his familiar spot behind the first base dugout at Kobs Field.

GREAT STATE DATES

Soccer—September 5 & 6, 1998 (H): Hosting the four-team Quality Suites Soccer Classic, State first defeated Northwestern 3-1 and then defeated Wisconsin-Green Bay, 2-1. In the opener against the Wildcats, sophomore midfielder Rick Smith and senior midfielder Jeff Fliss scored during the game's first eight minutes and then senior midfielder Matt Phillips knocked in a corner kick to seal the victory and send MSU into the winners' bracket. The 'Cats' only score came at 88.09 on a penalty kick. Against the Green Bay Phoenix on Sunday, once more Rick Smith opened the scoring, while the Spartans' eventual winning score did not come until the 87.02 mark on a boot by senior James Whitmore. T.J. Lieckfelt, the sophomore goalkeeper, was not totally challenged, making one save on Saturday and two in the second game.

Soccer—September 9, 1998 (A): In a 0-0 defensive struggle that went into two overtime periods, State eventually scored to defeat Eastern Michigan 1-0. Rick Smith scored the game's lone goal at the 106.21 mark. Freshman forward Brett Konley kicked the ball off the post and Smith was there to put the rebound behind the goalkeeper.

Football—September 12, 1998 (H): In the second night game ever scheduled at Spartan Stadium, Michigan State scored early and often to stun the 10th-ranked Fighting Irish of Notre Dame, 45-23. The first MSU touchdown came after only 2:44 had elapsed in the opening quarter on a blocked punt by linebacker Sean Banks which was picked up and taken 25 yards into the end zone by Richard Newsome. Less than six minutes later, quarterback Bill Burke climaxed a 13-play drive with a 16-yard scoring pass to Gari Scott. Before reaching intermission, Sedrick Irvin would score from the three-yard line; Burke would hook up with two TD passes, the first, an 86-yarder to sophomore Plaxico Burress and the second, a 17-yard toss to fullback Leroy McFadden. Defensive star Julian Peterson made it 42-3 at intermission with a 23-yard touchdown run after an interception. State settled into a defensive posture during the final 30-minutes of play as The Spartans limited the Irish option offense to 40 yards on 20 plays, with a paltry four yards in the first half; yet, the Irish countered with 20 second-half points, making the final score more respectable. Defensive backs Aric Morris and Sorie Kanu recorded 11 and 10 tackles, respectively.

Soccer—September 14, 1998 (H): State downed the University of Cincinnati 2-1 in the Sunday afternoon game for their fourth straight win of the season. Rick Smith opened the scoring by heading in an indirect kick at 11:49 for his fourth goal of the young season. The Bearcats evened the count late in the first half. Jeff Fliss put MSU back in front to stay by knocking in a pass from freshman midfielder Steve Arce at 81:49 of the second half.

Golf—September 14, 1998 (A): In the opening tournament of the fall season, Michigan State took first place in the 13-team field at the Detroit Titans Invitational played over the Arbor Hills Course in Jackson. The Spartans shot an impressive 280 on the first day, the lowest round ever produced by a Ken Horvath coached team. The winning two-round score of 570 was 17 strokes better than second-place Eastern Michigan. Sophomore Brent Goik captured his first career overall title with a card of 140. Senior Alberto Quevedo finished just three strokes back at 143 for second place. Senior Matt Pumford and freshman Adam Walicki tied for fourth with a score of 144.

Cross Country—September 19, 1998 (A): The Michigan State cross country team, ranked ninth nationally in the coach's panel, placed first in the Mel Brodt Invitational at Bowling Green with 27 points. Ryan Taylor, the Australian, finished first with a time of 24:58. Jim Jurcevich was second (25:00), Steve Schell seventh (25:40), Joe Leo eighth (25:51) and Matt Lafave ninth (25:52).

Cross Country—September 26, 1998 (H): Coach Stinzi's squad totally dominated their third straight Spartan Invitational as they swept the top five spots to post a perfect score of 15. Senior Jim Jurcevich was the individual winner, completing the 5K layout on the Forest Akers West Course in 24:59. He was followed across the line by junior Joe Leo (24:55). Ryan Taylor placed third (25:04), Steve Schell fourth (25:33) and Matt LaFave fifth (25:53). Competing teams were Western Michigan, Siena Heights, Northwood, Oakland Community College and Rochester College.

Football—October 10, 1998 (H): This was a back and forth game in which State led at halftime 16-3, saw an Indiana comeback turn the game around 24-16 only to have the Spartans tie it up in regulation and win in double overtime, 38-31. It was MSU's first experience with the tiebreaker rule. The initial lead came from a

Cedrick Irvin nine-yard run and three Paul Edinger field goals (48, 47 and 22 yards) after he had sat out a game due to ankle and quadriceps injuries. The third quarter was "Hoosier time" and suddenly MSU trailed 17-16. The IU comeback effort continued into the fourth period and finally State responded with a Bill Burke-to-Gari Scott 12-yard touchdown pass accompanied by an all-important Burke two-point conversion to tie the score with 5:28 of regulation time remaining. The scoreboard stayed at 24-24 as the clock ticked down to force OT. The teams exchanged seven-point possessions as the visitors scored on a 15-yard pass play followed by a pass-run of 25 yards by a new "hero in Green," Plaxico Buress, This necessitated a second extra session featuring a four-and-out stand by the "S" defense in which Lemar Marshall's jarring tackle separated the ball from a potential receiver's TD catch on fourth down. Appropriately, Irvin would emerge with the game-winning score. In the fourth quarter the Miami junior had fumbled in the open field on what would have likely been a game-winning run. This time, leaving no doubt, he sent the Homecoming Day crowd to the exits with a 25-yard patented high-stepping, swerving run into the end zone. State had evened their season record at 3-3.

Cross Country—**October 17, 1998 (A):** The MSU runners closed out their four-meet dual schedule undefeated as they topped a field of 22 teams at the Texas A&M Invitational in College Station, Texas. The Spartan quintet totaled 76 points to place ahead of runner-up University of Texas with 79. Jim Jurcevich crossed the finish line in second place (25:22), just four seconds behind the winner. Ryan Taylor was seventh (26:02), Steve Schell eighth (26:04), Brian Wardlow 17th (26:35) and Brendon Banyon 43rd (27.35).

Football—**November 7, 1998 (A):** Throughout its football history, Michigan State had faced a number one-ranked team 15 times prior to the 1998 season. On four of those match-ups the Spartans looked across the line at the Buckeyes of Ohio State and only once did the David slay the Goliath. That was in 1974 on the historic run of Levi Jackson. Twenty-five years had passed and there they stood once more, the Scarlet and Gray, with an 8-0 record, again ranked number one and favored by 28 points. As the game unfolded, initially the 93,595 fans that packed the Horseshoe and the added thousands viewing on ABC-TV were seeing a game as predicted. While their opponents focused on shutting down star running back Sedrick

Irvin, quarterback Bill Burke led the way in an air attack, throwing for 323 yards. Meanwhile, Paul Edinger shook off a missed extra point and booted five field goals to become the only Spartan kicker to make 10 straight (over a two-game stretch). Except for the play of junior defensive end Julian Peterson, the Buckeyes owned the first half. Peterson was forced to play the entire game after teammate Robaire Smith went out with broken fibula on the seventh play. He responded by gaining ten tackles with four sacks, three of which were in the first half. In addition, he forced the Ohio quarterback into two fumbles to set up MSU field goals. In the third quarter, Burke gave up his only interception which was returned 73 yards for a touchdown to put OSU up by 13. Thankfully, these were the last points for the overconfident home team, and Burke started a 19-point streak immediately with a drive that ended in a 23-yard pass to Lavaile Richardson for a touchdown. The final points came in the form of two Edinger field goals and a three-yard Irvin run.

Hockey—**December 27, 1998 (A):** In front of 18,129 fans at Joe Louis Arena, Michigan State defeated Michigan 3-1. In the first period the Spartans took a 1-0 lead on Jeff Kozakowski's goal just over a minute after the opening face off. MSU tallied the game winner off the stick of Damon Whitten at the 11:41 mark of the first period. Bryan Adams added salt to the Wolverines' wounds two minutes into the third for a 3-0 lead. Mike Gresl's shutout ended on a five-on-five U-M goal at the 8:52 mark of the third period.

Basketball—**January 2, 1999 (H):** In a Saturday afternoon game made for television (CBS), a nation of viewers saw a brilliant performance by a rising star, Morris "Mo Pete" Peterson, who led his team to a 69-57 defeat of the Louisville Cardinals. The junior forward, starting only his second game of the young season, made eight of 12 field goals, including three-of-four from beyond the arc. His repertoire embodied crowd-pleasing dunks, catapulting rebounds, a steal, a block, and the Izzo-style suffocating defense. "Mo Pete" left the image of "someone to watch in the future." The Spartans made 46.9 percent of their shots and held one of nation's top-shooting teams to 43.4 percent. They also outrebounded the Cards, 38-26. State opened with a 10-0 lead, but Louisville battled back to make it 20-17 with 9:38 remaining in the first half, which is as close as the game would be. MSU led 34-24 at the half and as many as 14 in the final

20 minutes. In addition to Peterson's 23 points, Jason Klein chipped in 13, Mateen Cleaves had nine and Charlie Bell eight. Hampered by fouls, Antonio Smith and Andre Hutson spent much of the second half on the sidelines.

Basketball—**January 9, 1999 (H):** After 15 games of mediocre play, Mateen Cleaves finally stepped up when it counted as he led his team to a convincing 81-67 win over the University of Michigan in an ESPN-TV Saturday game. He was seven-for-10 from the field, 10-for-11 at the line, while dishing off two more assists than the entire Michigan team. Among others, Cleaves, Jason Klein and Charlie Bell would later credit the "legend," Earvin "Magic" Johnson, for the team's success on this afternoon. Back for the weekend to be honored along with his 1979 NCAA championship teammates, Johnson gave a pregame speech to the squad in which he encouraged them to stop playing so tight and just relax. However, the U of M did not capitulate willingly. After State led 38-27 at the break, the Wolverines came out and cut that margin to six. Thereafter, the Spartans regrouped and built the lead back to double digits. The victory was actually sealed with a stingy stretch of defense midway through the second half when Michigan went for more than seven minutes without scoring a field goal. In addition to Cleaves's game-high 25 points, Peterson had 16, Jason Klein 12, Antonio Smith 10 and Andre Hutson nine.

Swimming and Diving—**January 15, 1999 (H):** Michigan State earned its third-straight victory with a 138-99 win over Notre Dame. John Munley had a pair of first-place finishes, winning the 200-yard freestyle (1:41.39) and 500-yard freestyle (4:37.57). Munley also was a member of the first place 400-yard freestyle relay team. Chad Ganden also captured two first-place finishes, winning the 50-freestyle in 21.88 and 100-yard freestyle in 47.49.

Gymnastics—**February 6, 1999 (H):** Topping their season-best scoring record, the Spartans defeated Illinois-Chicago 227.025-222.10. Senior Kenny Baker was the standout performer as he won three events after having sat out the previous two meets with ankle and wrist sprains. His firsts were in the pommel horse (9.7), parallel bars (9.65) and high bar (9.75).

Hockey—**February 12, 1999 (H):** Number three MSU defeated number seven Notre Dame 1-0. Sophomore goalie Joe Blackburn made 21 saves for his second career shutout. The only goal of the game came with less than five minutes remaining in the second period, when senior left winger Bryan Adams redirected a Mike York pass over the shoulder of the Irish goalie. It was the Fort St. James, British Columbia, native's 17th goal of the season.

Basketball—**February 18, 1999 (A):** When the fourth-ranked Spartans took the floor at Crisler Arena in Ann Arbor, the cheers that greeted them made it sound more like Breslin Arena in East Lansing. With Wolverine fans staying away in droves from their 10-15 team, ample tickets were available for an estimated 4,000 Spartan fans to follow their 24-4 team on the road, including nearly 500 from the student "Izzone" who chartered buses for the trip. As State's 35-28 halftime lead grew to a more comfortable double-digit margin in the second half, cheers from the upper deck that began with "Go Green-Go White" confidently grew to more cutting cheers like "We own Cris-ler." As for the game, with Mateen Cleaves scoring 19 and Jason Klein 11, the starters performed as expected, but the big difference in the game was from the two benches. Led by Mo Peterson and A.J. Granger, each with 10 points, the Michigan State bench outscored the U of M reserves, 30-0. Other telling figures were significant: State out-rebounded them 36-24, shot with greater accuracy, 51.9 percent to 39.1 percent and hit six, as opposed to two, three-pointers. Most important, it was State's 13th win in a row and guaranteed them at least a share of the conference title.

Gymnastics—**January 31, 1999 (H):** The sixth-ranked Spartans swept all events except the horizontal bar and defeated the seventh-ranked University of Illinois, 226.900-225.475. Those first-place finishers were freshman Jonathon Plante who scored a 9.825 on the pommel horse, sophomore Chris Weedon with a 9.65 on the still rings, junior Jeff Moomaw's 9.55 on the vault and sophomore Tommy Housley with a 9.65 on the parallel bars.

Hockey—**February 19, 1999 (H):** Sophomore goalie Joe Blackburn came just one minute and 14 seconds shy getting the shutout as number three Michigan State defeated number eight Notre Dame 3-1. Senior left wing Bryan Adams netted the Spartans' first two goals, and junior center Shawn Horcoff tallied both assists. Hall had a chance for the hat trick in the third as he led a two-on-one breakaway with defenseman Jeff Kozakowski. But Hall wasn't selfish, feeding Kozakowski to give MSU a 3-0 lead. The Wolverines later scored a desperation goal to salvage some dignity.

Wrestling—**February 19, 1999 (H):** With fans at Jenison Fieldhouse behind them, the number 23 Michigan State narrowly defeated Ohio State 18-17. At one point the situation seemed unrelenting as the Buckeyes won four of the five opening matches and led on the score sheet, 14-3. MSU managed to turn the meet around in the second half of competition featuring sixth-ranked Nick Muzashvili's first collegiate pin and freshman Nik Fekete's (184 pounds) first Big Ten win. It was a satisfying evening for Coach Minkel and his squad, especially for Fekete, because his parents had driven out from New Jersey to see their son in action.

Hockey—**February 20, 1999 (A):** Number three Michigan State defeated number seven Michigan 3-1 in front of 19,983 fans at Joe Louis Arena. Combined with Ohio State's 3-2 overtime loss to Alaska-Fairbanks, the Spartans secured the CCHA title. Sophomore goalie Joe Blackburn made 26 saves in the win, but it was the sharp-shooting of freshman right wing Adam Hall that proved the difference. Hall's first goal beat UM goalie Josh Blackburn's glove side and knocked the water bottle off the net for a 2-0 MSU lead. After the Wolverines pulled within one goal, Hall tallied an empty netter for security.

Basketball—**February 28, 1999 (A):** The number three Spartans defeated 23rd-ranked Purdue 60-46 in front of 14,123 at Mackey Arena. Purdue scored the first seven points of the game, but MSU fought back to tie the game at 13 and take a 24-21 edge at halftime. The game was again tied at 30, but Morris Peterson sparked a 12-2 run with his only eight points of the game. MSU never trailed the remained of the game, as they won a school-record 15th consecutive Big Ten game. Antonio Smith added game-high 12 points and eight rebounds as the Spartans won their 22nd game in 23 contests.

Gymnastics—**March 9, 1999 (A):** Michigan State won all six events as it defeated Minnesota 225.65 to 217.60. The Spartans were led by Mike Querress who finished first on both the parallel bars and still rings. Jon Plante was first place on the pommel horse and second in the all-around with a score of 54.

Tennis—**April 4, 1999 (H):** Forced indoors by the weather, MSU opened the meet against Ohio State by winning all three doubles matches by scores of 8-2 and eventually defeating the Buckeyes, 4-3. The winning pairs were Trey Eubank-Chris Struck, Francisco Trinidad-Ivica Primorac and Ken Kigongo-Mark Findling. That one team point earned through the doubles proved to be the difference as the two schools split the six singles matches. Eubanks was a winner at number one in three sets, 4-6, 6-1, 6-4, along with Trinidad and Mark Jacobson.

Baseball—**April 10, 1999 (H):** The Spartans rallied to defeat Penn State, 4-3, in extra innings. First baseman Kyle Geswein tied the game in the bottom of the seventh with a home run. He was then credited with scoring the winning run on Joe Albaugh's double in the bottom of the ninth, the second extra inning. Geswein finished three-for-four with two home runs and three runs-batted-in. Scott Brandell pitched the complete game, raising his season record to 3-2.

Baseball—**April 17 & 18, 1999 (A):** Traveling to Bloomington, Ind., Michigan State relied on stellar pitching and timely hitting to take three games from the Hoosiers, 3-0, 5-4 on Saturday and 8-4 on Sunday. In the opener, sophomore Scott Brandell threw a masterful one-hit shutout, raising his season record to 4-2. Facing a minimum of 21 batters, he struck out seven. The Spartans' three runs came on a bases-loaded double by Tom Hartley. State completed the afternoon by taking their 11th one-run victory of the spring as outfielder Mike Wagner went two-for-four including a two-run homer and Carlos Fernandez went three-for-four with one RBI. On Sunday, Wagner opened the game with a first-pitch home run, his sixth of the season, but that would be all of MSU's scoring until the top of the seventh. Meanwhile, the Hoosiers managed to generate four runs before two Spartan relievers, Kimya Massey and Chris Yens, combined to shut them down with five scoreless innings. Trailing 4-2, Ted Demetral opened the top of the seventh with a base on balls and then once more it was Wagner to the rescue with a game-tying round tripper to force extra innings. State then put the game away with a four-run eighth inning.

Tennis—**April 24, 1999 (A):** Michigan State defeated Ohio State 5-2 with a late surge. The Spartans looked strong early, taking all three doubles matches for the doubles point. The Buckeyes came alive to win the number one and number two singles point for a 2-1 edge. Chris Struck put MSU back on track with a 6-7, 6-4, 6-0 win at number three followed by wins from number four Ben Hetzler, number five Ken Kigongo and number six Francisco Trinidad.

ATHLETE OF THE YEAR

Mike York was a scoring machine, leading the Spartans in assists for four years, in points for three years, and in goals his senior year. With York's leadership, MSU won the 1997-98 regular season and playoff championships, the 1998-1999 CCHA regular season championship, and advanced to the 1999 NCAA Frozen Four, in which he

Mike York

had two assists in his final collegiate game to bring his career point total to 201, 12th on the school all-time list. In both 1997 and 1998 he was a member of Team USA at the World Junior championships, which won a silver medal in his first year. York was voted first team All-America in 1998 and 1999, second team All-CCHA in 1998, and first team All-CCHA in 1999. He made the CCHA All-Tournament team in both 1998 and 1999 and was named the 1999 CCHA tournament MVP and player of the year. Having been drafted by the New York Rangers in 1997 York moved into a successful career in the NHL and was a member of the 2002 U.S. Olympic team.

IN THE SPARTLITE

Baseball: In the embarrassing 34-4 loss to Ohio State at Oldsmobile Park, State suffered the most one-sided defeat ever in Big Ten play.

A pair of Spartan outfielders, Mike Wagner and Tom Hartley (the team's leading hitter in 1997 with a .354 average) were selected as third-team All-Big Ten. Upon completion of the season, Wagner signed a free-agent contract with the San Diego Padres.

Joe Kalczynski had been drafted by the Arizona Diamondbacks in the 31st round of the 1999 First-Year Player Draft. He signed with the National League affiliate following the Spartan season.

Ted Demetral was the team's leading batter with a .348 average.

Basketball: The 1979 NCAA championship team, including coaches, trainers and managers, was reunited and honored at halftime of the MSU-Michigan game on Saturday, January 9. Each was introduced, one by one with the loudest cheers reserved for Coach Heathcote, Jay Vincent, Greg Kelser and Earvin Johnson. Vincent was singled out during the ceremony as his number was retired while a banner was raised into the rafters.

Of the many memories that Spartan fans have retained from the "Mateen Cleaves years," none is any more unforgettable than his final shot at Minneapolis on February 13, two weeks after his last-second game-winner at Penn State. Trailing the Minnesota Gophers 73-63 with 7:01 remaining, State closed the game to 82-82 on a 19-9 run. With ball possession and seven seconds remaining, Cleaves, the future All-American, assumed sole responsibility for the game's outcome. Taking the inbound pass, he drove the length of the Williams Arena floor and, even though facing a legitimate defender, released a successful lay-up shot from the right side as 1.2 seconds showed on the game clock. That proved to be it, as State registered its 11th consecutive conference victory.

The 2000 championship season was one year away, but the 1999 team actually had a more impressive overall record, posting a 33-5 mark compared to 32-7 during the NCAA trophy year of 2000. Also, the 1999 squad had a remarkable 22-game winning streak that did not end until the 68-62 loss to Duke in the Final Four at St. Petersburg, Fla.

As in 1996-1997, Antonio Smith was the team's leading rebounder this time with 319 caroms. This total ranks fifth in the team record for one season.

Cross Country: With 64 points, State's runners finished second at the Big Ten championships held in Ann Arbor, the best MSU showing since 1988. Ryan Taylor, the junior from Melbourne, Australia, was the top Spartan, placing second with a time of 24:23. Two other MSU runners finished in the top 10. Steve Shell ran a 24:52 in seventh while Jim Jurcevich placed eighth with a time of 24:55. Joe Leo was 13th in 25:11.2 and Brian Wardlow completed the scoring in 34th position.

Led by Taylor's third-place finish over the 10K course at Indiana State (30:41), MSU won the Great Lakes Regional qualifying meet which put them in the NCAA championships at Lawrence, Kan. Placement and times of team members were as follows: Jurcevich, seventh (30:53), Schell, eighth (30:58), Leo, 17th (31:43), Wardlow, 23rd (31:54) and Brendan Banyon, 66th (33:04).

Moving on to the NCAA championships, Michigan State runners registered 352 points, which placed them 12th among the 20 scoring teams. Finishing in the 26th spot with a time of 31:01.6 over the 10K distance, Jurcevich was the leading Spartan. Others who scored were Taylor, 55th (31:30.3); Wardlow, 111th (32:15.4); Schell, 125th (32:26.0 and Leo, 129th (32:28.6). In postrace comments, Jurcevich noted: "[This was] by far the toughest course of the year. It had many steep hills, which takes a lot out of you as a runner."

Football: Running back Sedrick Irvin had his play called 272 times (fifth highest in the MSU record book) for a total of 1,167 yards. At the close of the season he announced a decision to forego a senior year of eligibility and enter the NFL draft. Consequently, Irvin's career totals were set at 755 carries for 3,504 yards, both fourth highest among MSU players. Impressive statistics for a three-year player.

A pair of one-point losses had great impact on the 1998 season. Had the 19-18 loss at Minnesota and the 25-24 loss to Purdue both been turned around, then State would have had a string of six Big Ten wins in a row and a conference mark of 6-2, which would have equaled the championship season of 1990.

Freshman Craig Jarrett had a marvelous first year as State's punter. Ranked second in the Big Ten and number 12 nationally. The six-foot-two, 215 pounder from Martinsville, Ind., completed the season with an 43.8-yard average. He, along with Josh Thornhill, was selected as a freshman All-American.

Golf: In the final meet of the fall season, the squad placed fourth in the 18-team Deep South Intercollegiate played at Abita, La. Finishing tied for seventh, Carlos Foulquie was the top Spartan with a three-round score of 75-72-70—217. Matt Pumford was in a five-way tie for 14th with a consistent 73-73-73—219. The remaining scorers for State were Brent Goik 73-72-79—224; Adam Walicki 73-76-77—226 and Alberto Quevedo 72-77-78—227.

After coaching the men through the fall season of the schedule, Keith Horvath resigned his position as head coach effective December 31. Former coach Bruce Fossum was recruited to fill the position on a temporary basis. After 24 years at the helm (1965-1989) Fossum had retired but volunteered to fill the spot for the remainder of the 1998-1999 season. In May it was announced that former University of Texas at Arlington head coach, Mark Hankins would become the new head coach beginning in the fall of 1999.

Led by Foulquie and Goik, who tied for 12th with scores of 219, the Spartans completed the Dr. Pepper Intercollegiate at Dallas, Texas, in fourth place among 19 competing teams.

Competing at the Big Tens in Minneapolis and shooting a combined score of 1,164, the Spartans finished in seventh place with Foulquie, the top Spartan in 16th place, 74-70-72-72—288. The remaining contributors were Pumford (291), Quevedo (293), Clark (298) and Goik (299), who shot a sub-par 69 on the final day.

Gymnastics: In a triangular meet in Provo, Utah, against eighth-ranked Nebraska and 10th-ranked Utah, State scored 225.675 points, but settled for third place. The host BYU Cougars finished first with 226.00 and the Huskers second with 225.950. Individually, the Spartans faired well as Dave Ruiz won the floor exercise (9.75), senior Kenny Baker the pommel horse (9.70) and sophomore Tommy Housley the vault (9.65). Freshman Jonathan Plante took second on the pommel horse (9.65).

Competing in the Big Ten championships at Iowa City, State finished fifth out of seven teams with a total score of 226.7. The two-day tournament was divided into team and individual competition. Sophomore Tommy Housley was MSU's highest scorer in the team events with a 9.6 and fourth place in the vault. In the individual events, senior Mike Phipps finished third in the still rings with a score of 9.762.

At the NCAA east regional in Champaign, Ill., the MSU team finished sixth out of seven teams and thus did not qualify for the national competition. However, junior Jeff Moomaw and freshman Ruiz qualified to continue on as individuals. Moomaw was second on the vault (9.675) and Ruiz was seventh on the high bar (9.65).

Hockey: State captured its sixth Central Collegiate Hockey Conference (CCHA) regular-season title, its seventh Great Lakes Invitational and made its ninth NCAA Frozen Four appearance during the 1998-1999 season.

In league play, MSU exhibited the best defense in CCHA history as they yielded a mere 1.33 goals per outing. The record performance bettered the 1.88 mark established by the Spartans just one year earlier. Other conference records were set by goalie Joe Blackburn, goals against average, 1.34 (breaking Chad Alban's record of 1.63 set in 1997-1998). Blackburn also set a new save percentage mark at .935. A new team record was set with a penalty-killing percentage of .931.

Including five ties, from the 2-0 win over Nebraska-Omaha on December 4 through the 4-1 win over Ferris State on March 5, the Spartans set a team-record unbeaten streak of 29 games.

Senior center and team captain Mike York was the standout player of the year. He led the team in goals (22), assists (32) and points (54) while becoming the first player in 20 years to lead the team in scoring three times. He was the Hobey Baker Award runner-up, a first team All-American, first team All-CCHA selection and CCHA Player of the Year.

In concluding his 33rd year of head coaching and his 20th season at Michigan State, Ron Mason continued as the all-time winningest college coach ever with 837 career victories of which 548 had been with the Spartans. He was selected as CCHA Coach of the Year.

By the end of the college season, a total of 16 former MSU players had reached the NHL: Rod Brind'Amour, Mike Buuzak, Anson Carter, Jim Cummings, Bob Essensa, Steve Guolla, Kelly Miller, Kevin Miller, Kip Miller, Joe Murphy, Rem Murray, Bryan Smolinski, Mike Watt, Peter White, Neil Wilkinson and Jason Woolley, more than any other college.

Soccer: State's overtime victory in the first game of the four-team Met-Life Tournament in San Diego against Cal State-Northridge ended in a strange way. With the game tied 1-1 and just 2:54 into the extra time, a Matador player, standing just six yards in front of his own net accidentally headed a ball over the top of his own goalie's head and into the net, giving State a 2-1 victory. Senior defender and captain James Whitmore scored the initial MSU goal at the 50:45 mark on a penalty kick. In the second game, Cal State-Fullerton took advantage of two defensive letdowns by the Spartans and scored twice in the opening 20 minutes. Although able to get off 11 shots, the Spartans were unable to match the Titans' scores.

Swimming and Diving: Led by co-captains Mike Mulshine and John Bruesch, the Spartans completed a not-too lustrous 3-5 dual-meet record and 10th place in the conference meet with 133 points. Other varsity lettermen from the squad were Tom Goniea, Casey Guntziller, Chad Gander, Mike Tingley, Tim Gendler, John Munley, Trevor Asti, Chris Koerner, Shawn Holland, Jason Owens, Phil Hillary, Aaron Mahaney, Mike Robbins and Scott Shafer.

Tennis: In the season's first tournament, the Ball State University Fall Classic, the doubles team of senior Mark Jacobson and junior Francisco Trinidad captured the doubles championship in their flight. Jacobson also had the most success for the Spartans in the singles competition as he finished first in the consolation bracket. Others competing were Mark Findling, Todd Kosta, Ken Kigongo, Sean Lasko and Chris Struck. Overall, MSU went 10-11 in singles 6-4 in doubles.

The doubles team of Kigongo and Francisco Trinidad finished the abbreviated fall season in grand style by capturing the ITA region IV championship. This improved their record to 8-0 and at the time, they were voted as the number two doubles team in the nation.

At the outdoor Big Ten championships in Ann Arbor, the sixth-seeded Spartans opened by defeating 11th-seeded Ohio State, 4-2. After taking the doubles point with wins by Kigongo-Struck and Eubanks-Findling, MSU singles wins were registered by number three Struck (0-6, 6-2, 6-2), number four Ivica Primorac (3-6, 6-1, 6-3) and number six Mike Jacobson (6-4, 6-2). The next round had State against Purdue, a team they had defeated 4-3 during the dual-meet season. Having upset Michigan in the opening round, the Boilers were on a roll and this time Orlando's squad never gained a point and was eliminated from the tournament.

Track and Field: With only a handful of entries, State scored 80 points and finished fourth at the Michigan Intercollegiates in Ann Arbor. Senior Jim Jurcevich took first place in the 3,000-meter run with a time of 8:14.18, setting a new meet record. Clocked in 8:16.45, senior Chris Wehrman placed second in the same event. Freshman Andy Lixey ran a 1:55.01 to place second in the 800 meters and junior Ryan Taylor finished third in the mile run with a time of 4:09.97. Sophomore Matt Deering was the top Spartan in the field events, vaulting to 17 feet, just 3/4" from the MSU indoor varsity record.

Three distance runners were named All-American based on their placing at the NCAA indoor championships. In the 5,000-meter run Jurcevich was eighth (14:10.67) and Schell 10th (14:11.21) while Baker placed 11th (8:03.0) in the 3,000.

Competing at the Tom Botts Invitational in Columbia, Mo., with a partial line-up, State scored 135 points to finish third behind Missouri with 195 and Illinois State, 153. MSU swept the 110-meter hurdles as Martin, Giwa-Agbomeirele and Jeff Krus finished one-two-three while Jake Diner, Terek and Deering tied for second in the pole vault at 15' 11".

Wrestling: State placed 11 individuals among the top six in their weight class at the Penn State Open on December 5 in State College, Pa. Senior 197-pound Nick Muzashvili, the Russian via Unadilla, N.Y., was named outstanding wrestler of the tournament after going 5-0, including a pin in the championship match and outscoring his opponents 56-16.

On February 8, Michigan State hosted the 2000 National Wrestling Coaches Association All-Star Classic featuring the nation's top competitors. Perhaps the most exciting match of the evening came in the 133-pound division where MSU's third-ranked Pat McNamara, trailing 2-1, grabbed a single-leg takedown with 45 seconds remaining and held on for a 3-2 victory. The disappointing match of the evening came at 197-pounds when number one Muzashvili found more than he could handle in his second-ranked opponent from Nebraska, 17-4.

Combining a conference champion and a runner-up with strong contributions from a pair of freshmen, MSU scored 87.5 points and finished fourth in the Big Ten championships at West Lafayette, Ind. Senior Muzashvili, who finished the season with a perfect record against Big Ten opponents, controlled his final match throughout and was never in trouble, winning 8-3. McNamara, the junior from Jordan Minn., settled for second at 133 pounds, losing a 4-2 decision to the top-seed representing the University of Iowa. Redshirt freshman Gray Maynard (157 pounds) finished third and fellow redshirt freshman Karl Nadolsky (149 pounds) settled for fourth place. Other contributors were heavyweight Matt Lamb, also fourth; Greg DeGrand (165 pounds), who finished in fifth; Will Hill (174 pounds) and Mike Castillo (141 pounds), both ending in seventh place.

Garnering 36.5 points, State placed 14th at the NCAA tournament held in the Kiel Center in St. Louis, Mo. McNamara finished sixth and Muzashvili fourth while gaining All-American recognition.

EXTRA! 1999 NCAA BASKETBALL TOURNAMENT

Michigan State reached the national semifinals in the 1999 NCAA tournament. The following are the Spartans' box scores for those games.

MICHIGAN STATE 76—MOUNT ST. MARY'S 53

	FG-FGA	FT-FTA	REB	A	PF	TP
A. Smith	5-8	4-4	12	0	3	14
Klein	4-9	0-0	8	4	1	9
Hutson	3-3	5-6	2	1	5	11
Cleaves	3-8	1-1	1	8	3	8
Bell	3-6	0-0	3	0	1	6
Kelley	1-5	0-0	1	1	0	3
Guess	1-2	0-0	1	0	0	2
Cherry	0-1	0-0	1	0	0	0
Davis	0-1	0-0	0	2	1	0
B. Smith	0-0	0-0	0	0	0	0
Peterson	4-8	0-0	12	1	4	8
Granger	5-7	4-4	5	2	1	15
TOTALS	29-58	14-15	46	19	19	76

Halftime: Michigan State 38-24; **Three-point field goals:** 4-16 (Klein 1-5, Cleaves 1-4, Bell 0-1, Kelley 1-2, Guess 0-1, Peterson 0-1, Granger 1-1); **Officials:** Rose, Sanfillipo, Wood; **Attendance:** 18,525.

MICHIGAN STATE 74—MISSISSIPPI 66

	FG-FGA	FT-FTA	REB	A	PF	TP
A. Smith	4-6	1-3	8	0	2	9
Peterson	4-9	3-5	8	3	2	11
Hutson	4-7	5-5	4	0	3	13
Cleaves	7-14	3-4	1	7	1	18
Klein	1-5	4-4	5	0	2	6
Kelley	0-3	1-2	3	0	0	1
Bell	2-2	0-0	0	1	3	5
Davis	0-1	2-2	0	0	0	2
Granger	3-6	2-2	3	0	4	9
TOTALS	25-53	21-27	36	11	17	74

Halftime: Michigan State 74-66; **Three-point field goals:** 3-8 (Cleaves 1-4, Klein 0-1, Bell 1-1, Granger 1-2); **Officials:** Paparo, Range, Reynolds; **Attendance:** 18,525.

MICHIGAN STATE 54—OKLAHOMA 46

	FG-FGA	FT-FTA	REB	A	PF	TP
A. Smith	0-1	0-0	7	0	4	0
Hutson	3-3	6-10	5	0	1	12
Klein	1-5	0-0	0	2	1	3
Cleaves	3-14	3-4	2	2	4	9
Bell	3-3	0-0	2	1	1	9
Kelley	0-4	0-0	1	1	0	0
Davis	0-2	0-0	0	4	2	0
Peterson	4-8	3-4	7	0	1	11
Granger	4-5	0-0	7	0	4	10
TOTALS	18-45	12-18	36	10	18	54

Halftime: Michigan State 26-25; **Three-point field goals:** 6-15 (Klein 1-3, Cleaves 0-4, Bell 3-3, Kelley 0-2, Peterson 0-1, Granger 2-2); **Officials:** Cahill, Corbett, Kitts; **Attendance:** 42,400.

MICHIGAN STATE 73—KENTUCKY 66

	FG-FGA	FT-FTA	REB	A	PF	TP
A. Smith	1-2	2-2	7	0	2	4
Hutson	6-10	2-4	5	1	3	14
Klein	1-6	0-0	1	0	3	3
Cleaves	4-11	0-0	4	11	0	10
Bell	3-5	0-0	3	2	3	7
Kelley	1-1	0-0	0	0	0	2
Davis	0-0	0-0	0	2	0	0
Peterson	6-13	7-8	10	1	3	19
Granger	4-5	3-3	2	0	2	14
TOTALS	26-53	14-17	33	17	16	73

Halftime: Kentucky 36-35; **Three-point field goals:** 7-17 (Klein 1-5, Cleaves 2-5, Bell 1-2, Peterson 0-2, Granger 3-3); **Officials:** Burr, Donato, Greenwood; **Attendance:** 42,519.

DUKE 68—MICHIGAN STATE 62

	FG-FGA	FT-FTA	REB	A	PF	TP
A. Smith	3-7	0-0	10	0	5	6
Klein	2-6	0-0	2	0	2	5
Hutson	6-8	1-1	5	1	2	13
Cleaves	5-16	0-2	3	10	3	12
Bell	0-2	2-4	3	1	3	2
Peterson	6-17	3-4	8	1	5	15
Kelley	2-8	0-0	4	0	2	4
Granger	2-6	0-0	4	0	2	5
Davis	0-0	0-0	0	0	0	0
TOTALS	26-70	6-11	40	13	24	62

Halftime: Duke 32-20; **Three-point field goals:** 4-18 (Klein 1-3, Cleaves 2-9, Peterson 0-2, Kelley 0-1, Granger 1-3); **Officials:** Libbey, Shaw, Cahill; **Attendance:** 41,340.

EXTRA! 1999 NCAA HOCKEY TOURNAMENT (Frozen Four)

A second consecutive regular season conference title helped earn a first-round bye at the NCAA regionals, but the Spartans were unable to take home another CCHA playoff championship, topping Lake Superior State but being defeated by Northern Michigan. At the national quarterfinals the Spartans faced Colorado College in a thrilling win. MSU was down 3-2 with less than two minutes to play when freshmen Andrew Hutchinson and Adam Hall scored two goals 32 seconds apart to gain the victory. The Frozen Four was held in sunny California, where New Hampshire overcame the Green and White squad 3-5.

March 28, 1999—Madison, Wis.
MSU 4, Colorado College 3
1st Pd.: MSU, Goodenow (Dolyny, Horcoff), 1:56; 2. CC, Voorhees (Heerema, Austin), 14:43.
2nd Pd.: 3. CC, Kryway (Heerema, B. Swanson), 5:41.
3rd Pd.: MSU, Hall (Adams, Kozakowski), 9:14, 5. CC, Clark (Manning, Hartsburg), 11:21; 6. MSU, Hutchinson (Adams, Bogas), 18:20; 7. MSU, Hall (York, Adams), 18:52.

April 1, 1999—Anaheim, Calif.
New Hampshire 5, MSU 3
1st Pd.: 1. NH, Krog (Ficek, Filipowicz), 18:49; 2. MSU, Dolyny (Horcoff, Hodgins), 19:27.
2nd Pd.: 3. NH, Souza (Haydar, Walsh), 2:44; 4. MSU, Patchell (Loeding, York), 6:49; 5. NH, Souza (unasst.), 18:17.
3rd Pd.: 6. MSU, Hall (York), 3:44; 7. NH, Shipulski (Krog, Souza), 10:52; 8. NH, Krog (Haydar, Souza), 14:40.

MSU
1999-2000

TALES TO TELL

Much has been written and continues to be written about the 1999-2000 Michigan State NCAA championship basketball season. This chapter features the box scores of the six-game drive to the title.

Of the 32 victories during that season, many recall the regular-season finale, a multi-record-setting 114-63 win over Michigan on March 4. The 114 points were the most scored by Michigan State in a Big Ten game, with the 51-point margin the school's largest in conference play, 14 more than the win over Northwestern in 1995. The 44 field goals, a season-high, included a likewise season-high 16 three-pointers.

As the score built during the afternoon, 51-24 at halftime, a 24-8 run to open the second half and a game-high 57 point lead with 7:14 remaining, the attention of the 14,659 sellout crowd and thousands watching via ESPN-TV, switched from the outcome of the game to focusing on a seldom followed statistic…assists. Pregame hype had alerted fans that senior Mateen Cleaves held a total of 749 career assists entering the game, 16 shy of the conference record. As the game progressed, fans re-

Mateen Cleaves (right) is congratulated by teammate Morris Peterson (left) upon setting the Big Ten career assist record.

acted with anticipation on every Cleaves pass. He would later say:

> "I'm not big on individual things, but assists are special. The guys wanted me to get it [the record]. They were saying, 'Get me the ball, I'll get you the next assist.'"

Continuing to build on the number, his record-setting "helper" came with 6:04 to play on a basket by A.J. Granger. When pulled from the game two minutes later,

HEADLINES of 2000

- 17 U.S. sailors on the navy destroyer *Cole* are killed in a Yemen terrorist attack.
- Federal agents raid the home of Cuban boy Elián González's relatives in Miami and take him into custody. Four weeks later he returns to Cuba with his father.
- The Summer Olympic Games are held in Sydney, Australia.
- In an incredibly close presidential election, the U.S. Supreme Court dispenses with the voter recount in Florida and declares George W. Bush the winner, four weeks after Election Day.

SCOREBOARD

	W	L	T	Avg.
Baseball	20	36	0	.358
Track and Field	no dual meets			
Football	10	2	0	.833
Basketball	32	7	0	.821
Tennis	8	20	0	.286
Cross Country	no dual meets			
Swimming and Diving	2	7	0	.222
Wrestling	9	5	1	.633
Hockey	27	11	4	.690
Golf	tournament play only			
Gymnastics	3	6	0	.333
Soccer	9	9	1	.474

Mateen was greeted by a spontaneous standing ovation. It was an emotional moment as Cleaves, the senior, and Coach Izzo hugged in front of the bench. Over four years, an overwhelming player-coach chemistry had been established between the two. When Tom and his wife Lupe adopted a son one year later, he would be named Steven Mateen. Not only had Cleaves established a new Big Ten career assist record that afternoon (769), but he did so with a total of 20, a single-game conference record.

Other impressive numbers were posted on that Saturday at Breslin. With the win, (a) State would become only the sixth team to win or share three consecutive Big Ten titles; (b) The school-record home-winning streak was extended to 28; (c) A total of 11 players contributed to the scoring, as Charlie Bell led them all, hitting on 13 of 19 attempts, for a career-high 31 points; (d) Four others reached double figures, Granger with 18, Andre Hutson 15, Jason Richardson 13 and Morris Peterson 12.

It was a memorable afternoon, but it would soon diminish in importance as there were nine more games to be played, including three wins to take the conference playoff trophy and stops in Cleveland, Auburn Heights, Mich., and Indianapolis, during a six-game run to the 2000 NCAA title.

TEAM OF THE YEAR

In his fifth year as head coach, Tom Izzo led the Spartans to the school's second-ever NCAA championship with an 89-76 decisive victory over the University of Florida in the RCA Dome at Indianapolis. On the way, the team won its third straight Big Ten regular-season title and its second-straight conference tournament title to fill in the Breslin Center rafters with championship banners. At the end of the season, the Spartans had set seven new team records. They shot 600-816 from the line and 253-669 from behind the arc while totaling 2,889 points, racking up 602 assists, and pulling down 1,521 rebounds. Both Mateen Cleaves and Morris Peterson were named first-team All-America and All-Big Ten, with Peterson also being voted the conference player of the year by the coaches. In addition, Charlie Bell was named third team All-Big Ten. It was clearly a team effort, but Peterson led the Spartans with 16.8 points and 6.0 rebounds per game. Cleaves and Bell backed him up with an average of 12.2 and 11.5 points per game, respectively. Also, Andre Hutson tallied 10.2 points and a team high of 6.2 rebounds per game.

The 1999-2000 basketball team. (Front row, left to right) A.J. Granger, B. Smith, M. Cleaves, head coach T. Izzo, C. Bell, M. Ishbia, M. Peterson. (Middle row) asst. coach B. Gregory, asst. coach M. Garland, M. Chappell, A. Wolfe, A. Hutson, D. Thomas, J. Richardson, asst. coach S. Heath, asst. to coach D. Owens. (Back row) trainer T. Mackowiak, strength and conditioning coach M. Vorkapich, A. Anagonye, A. Ballinger, J. Andreas, S. Cherry, equipment manager D. Pruder and manager M. Armstrong

MAKING HISTORY

On October 25, former MSU basketball coach Forrest "Forddy" Anderson died from complications of pneumonia. He had served as head coach from 1954-1964 and led the Spartans to their first Final Four appearance in 1957.

Following two days of speculation, on November 30 it became official. Football coach Nick Saban would be leaving MSU to assume a similar post at Louisiana State University. Whereas he was reportedly making $697,330 at Michigan State, his contract at LSU called for $6.25 million over five years. Bobby Williams, associate head coach, was named to serve as interim head coach through the upcoming Citrus Bowl in Orlando, Fla.

Having been under the watchful eye of the NCAA since 1996 for violations in the football program, the probationary period to MSU was to have been lifted in December of 1999. Instead, the period was extended until Dec. 2, 2001 to compensate for improprieties self-disclosed in the wrestling and women's track programs.

Since 1992 Michigan State had been inducting former Spartan athletic honorees into a Hall of Fame that didn't exist. Finally, on the weekend of Oct. 1-2, 1999, a "real" hall opened inside the Clara Bell Smith Student-Athlete Academic Center. Featuring 56 etched glass plaques of the hall's inductees, a reading rail highlighting Michigan State's athletic heritage and 11 wall murals that are 10 feet tall, the entire project cost $250,000 which was appropriated through a variety of fund-raisers.

In the 11th home game of the 1999-2000 hockey season, against Michigan, the new Munn Ice Arena spectator area opened for the first time. The added luxury suites and club seating raised the capacity of the arena to 7,117.

With a unanimous vote of the coaches and athletic directors representing the Central Collegiate Hockey Association, the playoff championship trophy was named the Mason Trophy in honor of the long-standing MSU coach, Ron Mason.

The University of Nebraska-Omaha hockey team completed its third season in existence and first as a member of the CCHA and they performed admirably. In the postseason playoffs they became the first team to reach the CCHA semifinals in its first season in the conference.

To the victors go the spoils. The NCAA basketball champions signed a deal with the sports apparel giant, Nike, which would outfit the player with shoes and gear. The school's five-year affiliation with Reebok expired on April 30 and that supplier had expressed no desire to renew the contract.

The MSU club roller hockey team worked its way through the bracket of 32 college teams and emerged as national champions with a 5-4 victory over Colorado State. The tournament was held in Tampa, Fla.

The Athletic Hall of Fame at the Clara Bell Smith Student-Athlete Academic Center

GREAT STATE DATES

Football—**September 18, 1999 (A):** It was an exciting game, as most Michigan State-Notre Dame games are. The defenses prevailed for three quarters with the score tied 7-7. Both TDs came on short passes in the second quarter. In the fourth quarter, the game became a battle of field goals. First, it was the Fighting Irish with a 33-yarder on the first play of the period. State's kicker, Paul Edinger, was called upon for the equalizer from 24-yards at 9:42 and then from 33-yards at 7:44 to give the Green and White a 13-10 lead. It didn't take ND long to once more knot the score, as their second field goal split the uprights at 5:44. It was then that quarterback Bill Burke took center stage. On the afternoon he would connect on 22-of-37 passes for 291 yards, most frequently tossing to tight ends Chris Baker and Ivory McCoy. But his next completion, this time to Gari Scott, would prove to be the most productive. With the game tied at 13 and little more than five minutes remaining State faced a third-and-10 from its own 20-yard line. Burke found the Lake Park, Fla., senior wide open on the left flat. Scott made the reception, shook off a would-be tackler and raced 80 yards for what would be the winning score. In case there was any doubt as to the outcome, Edinger sealed it with his third field goal of the game, from 31 yards with 15 seconds of playing time remaining. The final score: MSU 23, Notre Dame 13. The Spartan defense had its day too, as it forced three costly fumbles along with an end zone interception by Amp Campbell. The Irish quarterback was frequently rushed by Aric Morris, Hubert "Boo Boo" Thompson and Julian Peterson, in particular. Junior linebacker T.J. Turner made a team-high 11 tackles.

Soccer—**September 29, 1999 (H):** Sophomores Jeremy Seney and Brett Konley led the Spartans to victory over Loyola-Chicago, 2-0. Seney scored his first collegiate goal at the 70:09 mark on a pass from Konley. Less than four minutes later, Konley was the scorer as he blasted a foul kick into the right corner of the net. Spartan goalkeeper Tim Lieckfelt recorded four saves while picking up his second shutout of the season.

Football—**October 9, 1999 (H):** It was the type of game that a Spartan fan would say every MSU-U of M football match-up is supposed to be. First, both teams began the contest unbeaten (5-0) and nationally ranked, Michigan State at number 11 and Michigan number

three. Secondly, and most important, the game ended with the score in favor of the team in green, 34-31. State would prevail by combining a record-setting passing offense with a stingy running defense. As for the aerial game, Bill Burke, the six-foot-five senior from Warren, Ohio, completed 21-of-36 passes for a team-record 400 yards and two touchdowns. His primary target was Plaxico Burress, the six-foot-six junior from Virginia Beach, Va., who caught 10 throws for a team-record 255 yards and one touchdown. The Michigan head coach would later say, "He is so hard to match up against, there really isn't anything you can do to stop him." As for that stingy defense, although Michigan was able to complete 36 passes, the vaunted Wolverines running game managed a meager six yards. State's first score, a one-yard TD run by freshman T.J. Duckett, was set up on a 68-yard Burke-Burgess completion. With Paul Edinger kicking two second-quarter field goals, MSU held a 13-10 halftime lead. Burke hooked up with Gari Scott for a 19-yard score at 6:15 of the third quarter. Following an Aric Morris interception, the rangy quarterback found Burress alone in the end zone for a 15-yard score to make it 27-10 after three quarters. The final State touchdown was on a 14-yard run by Dawan Moss at 12:19 of the final period. Meanwhile, the Wolverines were making it interesting with 21 points and an on-side kick with 2:47 remaining. Burress handled the on-side kick and the game ended with the Spartans in possession at the U of M 17-yard line.

Soccer—**October 10, 1999 (H):** MSU upset Ohio State, 2-0, at Old College Field. Sophomore Brett Konley scored two goals for the Spartans, both coming in the second half. He headed in a pass from junior Rick Smith at the 68:46 mark, and provided an insurance goal on a kick from about 30 yards out with only seven seconds remaining in the game. Junior goalie Tim Lieckfelt recorded five saves for the Spartans, en route to his third complete shutout of the season.

Hockey—**October 22-23, 1999 (H):** MSU swept Ohio State in an early CCHA series at Munn Ice Arena, 1-0 and 6-0. In Friday's match-up, Joe Blackburn posted his fourth career shutout and posted 20 saves. Adam Hall scored the game's only goal on a power play in the first period. Game two was dominated by MSU, as the Spartans again shut out the Buckeyes, 6-0. MSU posted back-to-back shutouts for the first time since Nov. 11 and 17, 1995, and for the same time in one weekend

since Nov. 24-25, 1990. Adam Hall and Rustyn Dolyny each scored two goals, while John Michael Liles and Brad Hodgins also notched goals.

Football—**November 6, 1999 (H):** Bill Burke threw for 174 yards and two touchdowns while Michigan State's defense held number 20 Ohio State to 0 yards rushing in MSU's 23-7 win at Spartan Stadium. The victory marked the first time since 1987-88 that MSU had recorded back-to-back wins over the Buckeyes. The Spartans jumped out to a 17-0 lead in the second quarter on a Paul Edinger field goal and two Burke touchdowns. Richard Newsome's first career interception led to Edinger's third field goal. MSU's defense allowed just one first down in the second half and limited Ohio State to 18 total yards.

Football—**November 20, 1999 (H):** In the season-closer, freshman T.J. Duckett scored an impressive four touchdowns and punished the Penn State defense for 159 yards on 22 carries as MSU won a thriller, 35-28. Coming off the bench for starter Lloyd Clemons, Duckett scored the Spartans' first touchdown on a 20-yard carry. His next score came from nine yards out on the first play of the second quarter, and then posted a personal 57-yard drive two possessions later. Bouncing outside for 55 yards, T.J. plunged for two yards and a score to provide a 28-7 halftime lead. The 255-pounder's final TD, the game winner from 11 yards, came off right tackle as he went in backwards with one defender hanging on. It hadn't come easily for the Spartans as they saw the Nittany Lions score on drives of 86, 43, 48 and 48 yards to knot the game, leading to Duckett's game winner with 2:30 remaining in the game. There were other heroes, Gari Scott, who returned a punt 64 yards for Michigan State's second touchdown; punter Craig Jarrett, who averaged 40.5 yards on 10 kicks, with three of 47, 48 and 67 yards that pinned PSU inside its own 15-yard line three times; Amp Campbell, whose vicious tackle caused a fumble and turnover to set up the winning drive at the visitors' 39-yard line and linebacker T.J. Turner, who had two interceptions, including a pick on Penn State's final possession.

Hockey—**November 27, 1999 (H):** In the seventh year of the College Hockey Showcase, State defeated the University of Minnesota on the second night, 6-2. Rusty Dolyny scored the key first goal, putting in a rebound at 6:43 of the first period on assists from Damon Whitten and Brad Hodgins. At 12:43 the roles were reversed when Hodgins scored a short-handed goal with an assist to Dolyny. State continued to dominate

during the middle period, scoring three times. Sophomore winger Adam Hall had his team-leading 12th goal at 1:14 with Dolyny adding his second of the game on a one-timer from the point during power play action. Following a change of goalies in the Gopher net, Shawn Horcoff scored on his own rebound to make it 5-0 at 9:05. Minnesota scored the next two goals, both on power plays, one in the closing two minutes of the second period and the second in the first two minutes of the third period. Jon Insana, the sophomore defenseman, closed out the scoring in the final minute of play with his first collegiate goal.

Basketball—**December 1, 1999 (A):** In this, the second year of the ACC-Big Ten Challenge, eighth-ranked Michigan State was matched against the second-ranked North Carolina Tar Heels. Playing in Chapel Hill and without their star point guard, Mateen Cleaves, the Spartans managed to display the confidence of a champion in gained an 86-76 victory. Cleaves was sidelined with a stress fracture in his right foot. As NC coach Bill Guthridge observed, "When they get Mateen Cleaves back I can't imagine how good they will be." It was a bitter setback for the perennial national power, the first loss of a home opener since 1928. Morris "Mo Pete" Peterson was the scoring star as he hit for a career-high 31 points on 12-of-18 shots from the floor as well as pilfering five of his team's 15 steals. MSU got a pair of three-pointers from "Mo Pete" and one from former Duke starter Mike Chappell during a 15-4 run to grab a 44-36 lead at intermission. Maintaining the scoring touch after the break, Izzo's crew built a 65-48 lead, including three consecutive three-pointers, with 11:52 remaining. Although the Heels closed to 71-65 at the 4:18 mark, Andre Hutson and Peterson answered with consecutive field goals to quiet the crowd and regain the initiative. Others in double-figures were Chappell with 13, A.J. Granger 11, Hutson 10 and Jason Richardson 10.

Basketball—**December 7, 1999 (N):** Playing before 13,127 in Chicago's United Center, Coach Izzo's squad withstood a 19-2 surge after the break to win this pre-conference Great Eight match-up against Kansas University, 66-54. Charlie Bell, who filled the role of the sidelined Mateen Cleaves, was too quick for the Jayhawks to contain in the first half. His 13 points on six-for-eight shooting along with the usual sticky Spartan defense that limited KU to just eight points in the first 10 minutes, resulted in a 39-23 halftime lead. Fol-

lowing the second-half Kansas outburst, the Michigan State lead had diminished to 53-41 with 8:18 to go. After a timeout, Morris Peterson dropped in two free throws, fed Bell for a lay-up and drove to the basket for a field goal and suddenly MSU was back on top by 12. That double-digit lead was fairly consistent until the buzzer. Bell led all scorers with 21, followed by A.J. Granger with 13, Andre Hutson and Peterson with 10 each. Granger connected for three of five three-pointers, all in the first half. Neither team had an impressive evening, offensively. KU shot 21-of-53 for .396, while State was 25-of-64 for .390.

Basketball—**January 11, 2000 (H):** After being sidelined for 10 weeks from a foot injury, Mateen Cleaves "quarterbacked" his team to an overtime win, defeating ninth-ranked Indiana University, 77-71. The victory was the 100th for Coach Izzo and left MSU in sole possession of first place with a 3-0 conference record. The scoring in the game was a series of bursts as Michigan State held the advantage at halftime, 31-28. Each team led once by seven points in the second half, the Hoosiers holding such a edge, 58-51, with 2:45 showing on the game clock. Outscoring IU 11-3 during the remainder of regulation, Morris Peterson's three-pointer with 11.3 seconds to go tied the game at 62-62. Cleaves heaved up a long shot from just inside mid-court at the buzzer, but the ball spun out of the rim, sending the contest into OT. The Spartans proved to be the better team during the extra five-minute period, outscoring Indiana 11-3. With 22 points, Charlie Bell was top scorer for the winners. Cleaves had eight assists for the evening to claim a school career-record with 653, eclipsing the old mark of 645 by Scott Skiles.

Wrestling—**January 16, 2000 (H):** After dropping the first match to Penn State in the 174-pound division, MSU wrestlers regrouped and won the next three square-offs beginning with James Brimm's (184 pounds) 20-9 major decision. The next win came at 197-pounds where State's Nick Muzashvili, the Russian via Unadillla, N.Y., gained a takedown with 36 seconds remaining for a 3-1 verdict. Heavyweight Matt Lamb put the Spartans up 10-3 with his close 2-1 decision. After Chris Williams's disappointing loss at 125 pounds, Pat McNamara (133 pounds) made a successful return to the lineup after having preseason shoulder surgery, with a 14-7 decision. From there it was all Michigan State with Mike Castillo (141 pounds) winning a major decision, 15-5, Cory Posey (149 pounds) a 4-3 winner, seventh-ranked Gray Maynard an

easy winner at 10-3 and Greg DeGrand (165 pounds) finished the evening by posting the fourth major decision of the matches, 11-2. The final score read Michigan State 27, Penn State 7.

Wrestling—**January 29, 2000 (H):** After Chris Williams (125 pounds) lost the evening's opening bout in overtime, the Spartans went on a rampage, winning six matches in succession on the way to posting an overwhelming 27-6 defeat on sixteenth-ranked Purdue. Following the Boilermakers' only other win, at 184 pounds, State finished with two more winning decisions. Pat McNamara (133 pounds), ranked third, opened MSU's scoring by edging his 20th-ranked opponent, 4-2, and was followed by teammate Mike Castillo (141 pounds), who posted a rather easy 11-4 victory. With scores of 11-3 and 15-6, Keith Nadolsky (149 pounds) and Gray Maynard (157 pounds) contributed a total of eight team points as each was credited with a major decision. Greg DeGrand (165 pounds) was a winner at 2-0 followed by Will Hill (174 pounds), who improved the team score to 20-3 with his 7-2 decision. After Joe Cotant's (184 pounds) overtime loss, Nick Muzashvili, ranked number one at 197, won a 16-3 major decision and heavyweight Matt Lamb sneaked in a two-point takedown with four seconds remaining in overtime to upset his ninth-ranked opponent.

Basketball—**February 1, 2000 (A):** Just 25 minutes before tip-off, the University of Michigan's top scorer, a freshman, was declared temporarily ineligible by the NCAA who questioned his pre-college living arrangements. Regardless, Michigan State was favored to win, and they did, 82-62. The Spartans were simply bigger, faster and stronger. Morris Peterson had a remarkable evening, scoring a career-high 32 points, including five-of-eight from beyond the three-point arc, while also pulling down 10 rebounds. Mateen Cleaves, playing his eighth game since recovering from his stress fracture, had 19 points, and Andre Hutson added 10 and 10 rebounds. After leading 38-32 at halftime, State built the margin to 52-34 with 14:30 remaining. For the next three minutes the Wolverines closed to 52-41, but State regained the initiative and by 1:57 possessed an 80-60 lead which prompted Coach Izzo to clear the team bench.

Hockey—**February 4, 2000 (H):** Scoring once in each period, MSU won its 10th game in a row against Lake Superior, 3-0. It was also the fifth shutout of the year for freshman goalie Ryan Miller, one shy of Chad

Alban's school record of six set in 1997-98. With assists from Shawn Horcoff and John-Michael Liles, Junior Rustyn Dolyny accounted for the first goal during a power play at 11:24 of the opening period. Horcoff's assist was a nation-leading 34 for the year. Approximately 15 minutes later, sophomore Joe Goodenow made it 2-0. After a few head fakes to distract the defense, he fired a wrist shot that found an opening in the right top corner of the net. Horcoff finished the scoring on an empty-net goal at 19:49 of the third. Rightfully credited with a scoreless performance in the net, Miller was not all that busy, as he stopped only 22 shots, with a low of four during the final 20 minutes.

Hockey—**February 11, 2000 (H):** With two wins over Northern Michigan, 3-2 and 2-0, State hurdled over NMU into second place in the CCHA standings with 31 points. The two-game total attendance of 13,834 was the largest series crowd in Munn history, breaking the old mark of 13,780 set in 1987 against Lake Superior. The Friday night game was won in overtime on a backhand shot by Adam Hall that went high, hit the post and eventually found the top far corner. Mike Weaver and Shawn Horcoff received assists. Second period goals by Brad Hodgins and Andew Bogle had made it 2-1 until a tying shot found its mark behind goalie Joe Blackburn with 3:35 remaining, thus sending the game into OT. On Saturday, the Spartans scored two first-period goals and then successfully held off the Wildcats for a 2-0 win and a weekend sweep. Meanwhile, freshman goalie Ryan Miller was posting his sixth shutout of the season, tying Chad Alban's school record, and his fifth in CCHA games, tying the conference record. The first goal on Saturday was scored by sophomore defenseman Andrew Hutchinson, who picked up the freely sliding puck just as he was leaving the penalty box. Skating in alone, he scored at 14:39. Five minutes later, Hall took a Rustyn Dolyny rebound and put it in the back of the net.

Wrestling—**February 20, 2000 (H):** For the first time since 1973, the MSU grapplers beat number four Oklahoma State, 21-10. The win marked the 100th of head coach Tom Minkel in his career at MSU. Heavyweight Matt Lamb, 125-pound Chris Williams and 141-pound Mike Castillo all had upset wins over ranked opponents to spark the victory. Pat McNamara and Nick Muzashvili also posted big wins for the Spartans.

Gymnastics—**February 20, 2000 (H):** The MSU gymnasts toppled number 12 Illinois-Chicago, 224.225-217.800. It was a gratifying afternoon as many of Coach Atkinson's performers reached season-high scores: Brady Grimm in both the floor exercise (9.40) and the vault (9.60); Tom Housley, also on floor exercise (9.40); David Ruiz with a 9.65 and Jeff Moomaw with a 9.35, both on the vault and freshman Jamie Shepard on the pommel horse (9.35). Freshman Brad Golden was the only all-around competitor of the meet (55.350) and reached a season-high on the parallel bars with a 9.500.

Baseball—**March 8, 2000 (A):** The Spartans shocked defending national champion and 10th-ranked Miami Hurricanes, 13-11, on its home field in Coral Gables, Fla. In a night game that featured five lead changes and three ties, State was down 11-6 after six innings. From there MSU put three runs on the board in the seventh and four in the eighth to recapture the lead and steal the win. Among Michigan State's 15 hits were five home runs. Bob Malek's blast in the first inning accounted for the opening two runs. Designated hitter Joe Albaugh's third inning homer scored three runs. A Kyle Geswein four-bagger ignited the seventh and his second round-tripper, a two-run smash in the eighth, tied the game at 11-11. Domanick Squires, who tossed three innings of scoreless relief and allowed only one hit, picked up the win.

Tennis—**April 8, 2000 (H):** The Spartans started down 1-0 after losing all three doubles matches to Purdue and thus surrendering that opening point for doubles. Matters brightened thereafter as number two Robert Topalo was a straight set winner, 6-2, 6-2 and was followed by Jimmy McGuire's victory at number six, 6-4, 6-4. The outcome of the meet then came down to number three Ivica Primorac who won in three sets 5-7, 6-4, 6-2 and Francisco Trinidad, who earned that clinching fourth team point with a 6-3, 2-6, 6-1 victory at number four.

Tennis—**April 16, 2000 (H):** Play was originally scheduled to take place outdoors, but the cold temperature moved the matches to the MSU Indoor Tennis Facility where the Spartans defeated Iowa, 4-3. For five seniors it was their final home appearance. Three of them were victorious. The Hawkeyes won the doubles point as the senior pair of Ivica Primorac and Francisco Trinidad were the only winners, playing at the number three spot. State was then forced to take four of the singles matches and they succeeded in their mission. Primorac

won at number three, 4-6, 6-2, 6-3; Robert Topalo was a winner at number two, 6-4, 6-2 and also number six Todd Townsend, 6-3, 6-3. The match then came down to the number four contest. After dropping the first set, Trinidad came back, with the vocal help of the crowd, including his teammates, to win 4-6, 6-4, 6-4.

Baseball—**May 6, 2000 (H):** In a Saturday afternoon doubleheader at Oldsmobile Park, State swept both games from Michigan, 4-1 and 9-7. In the opener, pitcher Gary Zsigo pitched a complete game, allowing only one run on seven hits. Brett Wattles leadoff triple, two walks and Rick Court's single accounted for two runs in the third. Mike Pisani accounted for the third run with a single in the fourth, while the final run was scored on a sixth-inning sacrifice fly. In the second game, the U of M scored four runs in the top of the sixth to build a 7-3 lead. In State's half of the sixth inning, Court slammed a three-run home run onto the grass in right-center and suddenly it was a one-run game. After the Wolverines threatened but did not score in the seventh, MSU put two on in their half of the inning and Bob Malek ended it all as he crushed a home run over the left field wall.

ATHLETE OF THE YEAR

During a 114-63 destruction of U of M on March 4, 2000, Mateen Cleaves simultaneously set a new school record for assists in a game with 20 and surpassed Scott Skiles as the Spartan career assist leader. The Flint native may have come to MSU somewhat green, but as a three-time co-captain he was a leader on a team that won or shared four straight Big Ten titles and claimed the 2000 NCAA championship, a feat for which he overcame multiple injuries to achieve. In each of his four years Cleaves averaged double digits, bringing him to a total of 1,541 points, 10th in all-time Spartan scoring. His forte, however, was making others look good, as he set the school's assist records for a single-season in his junior year with 274 and for a career with an incredible 816. In addition, he broke the record for career steals with 195 and fell second in single-season steals with 73, just two short of Magic Johnson. Cleaves was given All-America and All-Big Ten recognition in his final three years at

State, in addition to being named Big Ten player of the year in 1999. In 2000, the Detroit Pistons drafted him in the first round, and he went on to play NBA basketball.

Mateen Cleaves

IN THE SPARTLITE

Baseball: First playing five games in Las Vegas followed by seven in Florida, the Spartans opened the season by posting an horrendous record of 2-10.

In one of the highlights of the season, State upset the Big Ten champions of Minnesota, 9-7, in a game played at Lansing's Oldsmobile Park. The Spartans struck early, taking a commanding 8-0 lead after three innings while scoring once more in the sixth. They then hung on as the Gophers managed seven runs in the final four innings.

Freshman Bob Malek led the 2000 squad in several categories including: slugging percentage (.545), home runs (nine) and RBIs (58). His .345 average on the season was second on the team, while he finished second in hits (69), doubles (nine) and triples (two). The rookie hit safely in 43 of the 56 games. His outstanding freshman year earned a second team All-Big Ten selection as well as being picked as a Louisville Slugger First Team Freshman All-America.

Mike Pisani ended his collegiate career with 237 hits, one shy of MSU's all-time record of 238 set by Steve Money in 1994. However, the senior did put his name in the Michigan State record book when he broke the career doubles record with 53.

Coming out of the bullpen, Domanick Squires was the top pitcher for the 2000 Spartans. His ERA was 3.12 and he registered five wins over the season.

Josh Axelson, the junior pitcher from Brooklyn, Mich., was selected by the St. Louis Cardinals in the fifth round of the 2000 first year player draft. He was the highest Spartan selected in the draft since Mark Mulder was the second player selected in the 1998 draft by the Oakland Athletics.

Basketball: It is suggested that failure is a wise and prudent teacher. Therefore, if scheduling and losing in preconference games to the likes of Arizona and Kentucky could provide learning experiences that might assist a team in reaching the ultimate goal of a national championship, then "bring them on."

Then there was the case of Wright State. Anyone scrutinizing the 1999-2000 Spartan schedule would have circled the date of December 30 if they had been seeking the "surest possible win." As the world was anticipating an end to the 20th century, MSU faithful instead thought they were seeing an end to the world. The final score:

Wright State 53, the eventual NCAA champions 49.

Every game on the front-end of the 1999-2000 schedule was approached with certain apprehension; for, on October 25 it was disclosed that point guard Mateen Cleaves had a stress facture of the right foot and would likely not be available until after the first of year.

There was no repeat of the 1999 migration of 4,000 Spartan fans to Crisler Arena for the State-Michigan game. This time the U of M ticket office controlled the sale of ducats to only their students and faculty.

While on the tournament trail, the 1999-2000 Spartans made it rather easy for their supporters. Granted there were moments of anxiety as the team made it through the brackets on the way to the 2000 NCAA championship, especially against Syracuse and Iowa State, but there was no key turnover or last-second shot to fidget about. Actually, the pursuit was rather smooth as the Spartans became the first team to defeat all six tournament opponents by double digit figures since the field was expanded to 64 teams in 1985. The road to glory included Valparaiso 65-38, Utah 73-61, Syracuse 75-58, Iowa State 75-64, Wisconsin 53-41 and Florida 89-76.

"Let the good times roll"—and they continued to roll on Wednesday, April 5, less than 48 hours after Michigan State's NCAA championship victory inside the RCA dome of Indianapolis. This day of festivity, proclaimed "MSU Spartan Day" by the Lansing City Council, opened on the steps of the State Capitol where thousands had gathered. Among the revelers were Michigan State administrators, trustees, coaches, players, state legislators, the Michigan Supreme Court justices wearing green wigs and a special Spartan alumnus, governor John Engler. It was he that suggested, "It seems appropriate to propose a new symbol for the state—out with the wolverine and in with Sparty." Among other speakers were the school's president, Peter McPherson, athletic director Clarence Underwood, team captain Mateen Cleaves and coach Tom Izzo, who reminded the assembly, "We've always talked about building a tradition. Our goal was to leave our footprints in the sand. Winning a national championship leaves more than just a footprint." From the capitol steps the champions were paraded down Michigan Avenue, lined with fans of all descriptions, and into Spartan Stadium where a crowd estimated at 25,000 had gathered to greet them. It was a day to be long-remembered by both heroes and hero-worshipers.

Cross Country: MSU finished sixth at the Big Ten championships and several Spartans ran top times. Matt LaFave was the top Spartan runner for the first time this season. He ran a time of 26:13 to finish 21st overall. Jason Mueller was close behind, as the freshman finished 24th running for a time of 26:19. Joe Leo finished at 26:25 to end up in 26th place. Rounding out the Spartans' times were Ben Evans (31st, 26:32), Brian Wardlow (45th, 26:55), Jared Aldrich (59th, 27:14), and Jeff Mulder (69th, 27:39).

Football: Adding to his junior year (1988), quarterback Bill Burke threw for more than 200 yards on 12 occasions. This tied the team record set by Eddie Smith (1976-1978). Burke's most prolific afternoon came on Oct. 9, 1999, when he set an MSU record of 400 yards against Michigan.

T.J. Duckett, the outstanding sophomore runner from Kalamazoo, gained 1,353 yards over the season, as he fell 22 yards shy of passing his brother Tico's mark of 1,394 set in 1990 as fifth highest in the MSU record book. T.J. recorded seven 100-yard plus games, including 149 yards in the season finale against Missouri.

Plaxico Burress (6' 6", 222), a second-team All-America selection by *The Football News*, set Spartan single-season records for receptions (66), receiving yards (1,142) and touchdown receptions (12). He earned Florida Citrus Bowl MVP honors after catching 13 passes for 185 yards and three TDs in the 37-34 victory over Florida. A first-team All-Big Ten pick, he had a school single-game record 255 yards receiving (10 catches) in MSU's 34-31 win over Michigan. He became the first Spartan player ever to record two 1,000-yard receiving seasons. Plaxico also ranks among MSU's all-time leaders in receptions (fourth at 131), receiving yards (fourth at 2,155) and TD catches (tied for second at 20). He would forgo a senior year and declare for the NFL draft where he would be a first-round choice of Pittsburgh Steelers.

Julian Peterson (6' 4", 237), a first-team All-America pick as a defensive end by the *Football News*, produced a school single-season record 30 tackles for losses (140 yards) in 1999, including 15 sacks (104 yards). He earned Defensive MVP honors in the Florida Citrus Bowl after recording eight tackles, including five for losses (32 yards), against the Gators. Despite playing only two seasons, the Hillcrest, Md., native set a Spartan career record with 48 tackles for losses (215 yards). His 25 career sacks (161 yards) rank second on MSU's all-time list. Julian would

become a first-round draft pick of the San Francisco 49ers.

At season's end, Michigan State would be ranked as the seventh team in the *USA Today*/ESPN poll.

Golf: MSU tied for third in the 18-team Fossum Invitational field held at Forest Akers West Golf Course. MSU's Dennis Riedel finished fourth individually and fired a 69-71-76—216 for the tournament. Riedel was in first after day one. Brent Goik tied for 11th-place and fired a 72 on the final day which gave him a total of 77-72-72—221. Eric Jorgensen finished tied for 19th and shot 72-72-80—224 for the tournament. Nathan Clark shot 76-71-77—224 and also tied for 19th place. Lorne Don fired a 79-78-82—239.

The four-day MSU composite score during the Big Ten tournament played on Purdue's Kampen Course was 296-306-300-313—1,215. In the process State dropped from fourth to sixth and finally ended up eighth in the team standings. Riedle, the St. Claire junior, shot a 73-72-76-77—298 to finish tied for 12th place. Other scores were Goik, the Bay City junior, 73-80-74-79—306; freshman Jorgensen of Big Rapids 75-79-72-82—308; Carlos Foulquie, the Spanish senior, 80-75-78-79—312 and sophomore Clark of Mason, 75-83-82-78—318.

Gymnastics: Sophomore Jonathan Plante of Easton, Pa., proved to be the best pommel horse performer in the school's history. Against Ohio State he was rewarded with a team-record score of 9.95 and twice tied the mark in subsequent meets. Plante also led the team on both the parallel bars (9.530 season average) and horizontal bar (9.308 average). In the Michigan meet, freshman Brad Golden from Orlando, Fla., tied Paul Dackerman's 1992 school record on floor exercise with a 9.90.

Totaling 226.1 points, MSU placed fifth in the conference championship held in Jenison Fieldhouse. Plante placed third on the pommel horse (9.80) and fifth on the high bar (9.80). Golden finished sixth on the horizontal bars (9.65) and 11th on the vault (9.55) while Marc Chiappetta was seventh on the still rings (9.55). The sad note of the day came when MSU's David Ruiz broke his right arm on a fall during his horizontal bar routine.

Led by the same duo of Plante and Golden, State finished in sixth position at the NCAA championship qualifying meet in Iowa City, falling short of the necessary slot to compete for the national collegiate team title.

The various rumors pertaining to State dropping the sport of men's gymnastics became a reality on April 24, 2000 when AD Clarence Underwood met with team members and their coaches. First indicating the sport would close-down immediately, a compromise position was agreed upon in which 2001 would be the final year for MSU men's varsity gymnastics.

Hockey: Opening with 10 straight CCHA victories, the 1999-2000 season-start was MSU's best-ever.

Michigan State beat Michigan 3-1 and Michigan Tech, 6-3, to win its third consecutive Great Lakes Invitational title and eighth overall. In the championship game against the Huskies, MSU scored two goals in the first and four in the second, which was MSU's highest scoring period of the year. Six different Spartans accounted for the total: Damon Whitten, Troy Ferguson, Shawn Horcoff, Scan Patchell, Brian Maloney and Andrew Bogle. Against Michigan in the opening round, Joe Blackburn made a career-high 37 saves, including 20 in the third period. With the game tied at one in the third, Kris Koski scored his first-career point, which turned out to be the game-winner. Brian Maloney added an insurance goal six minutes later. Shawn Horcoff was named the tournament MVP, while Joe Blackburn and Mike Weaver joined him on the all-tournament team.

The 2000 Spartans won the school's ninth CCHA Tournament championship by defeating Notre Dame 4-0 in the opening round and Nebraska-Omaha, 6-0, in the championship game. Thus, freshman Ryan Miller became the first goaltender to record two shutouts in the two final games. It was the largest victory margin ever for a championship game as Shawn Horcoff, Rusty Dolyny, Damon Whitten and Adam Hall all found the back of the net in the middle period after a scoreless opening period. In the final 20 minutes, Andrew Bogle scored on a beautiful assist from John Nail while Brad Fast closed out the evening by scoring the final goal with nine seconds remaining in the game.

Horcoff, the senior forward, won an unprecedented five individual CCHA awards (player of the year, best defensive forward, scoring champion, first-team All-CCHA and CCHA All-Academic team).

Soccer: Damon Rensing, a four-time letter-winner and three-year starter for Michigan State (1993-1996) joined the athletic staff as an assistant to Coach Baum. Rensing had spent the 1998 season as an assistant coach with the Nevada-Las Vegas women's team.

The October 13 win over Detroit was costly as two of the team's leading scorers, senior defender Keith Gordon and sophomore forward Brett Konley, sustained season-ending injuries.

Top goal-scorer for the 1999 team was John Benoist, junior defenseman, who connected for six of 12 shots on goal during the 9-9-1 season.

Tim Lieckfelt, the primary goalkeeper during the season, yielded 26 goals. Accompanied with 73 saves, he had a .737 percentage and goals-against average of 1.38.

The postseason action for MSU was short-lived. As the sixth-seeded team in the Big Ten Tournament they met Penn State, the number three-seeded team, on the grounds of Old College Field. After a scoreless first half, Brian Spitzkeit slid a shot past the visitor's goalkeeper five minutes into the second half giving the Spartans the lead. As the game continued and some envisioned an upset, PSU answered by tying the score with less than 10 minutes of regulation time remaining, ultimately forcing overtime. The end came at the 14.51 mark in the second sudden-death overtime, sending the Nittany Lions into the tournament's final game against Ohio State. It was the circumstances that surrounded the winning goal that marred the contest as a Penn State player seemingly committed what most observers considered a foul against defender John Benoist during the closing action.

Swimming and Diving: Top performances turned in during the dual-meet season and prior to the conference championships were: Chad Ganden, 50-yard freestyle (21.54) and 100-yard butterfly (51:47); John Munley, 100-yard freestyle (45.83), 200-yard freestyle (1:39.33) and 500-yard freestyle (4:34.56); Joe Brennan, 1,000-yard freestyle (9:27.95) and 1,650-yard freestyle (15:55.70); Aaron Mahaney, 200-yard butterfly (1:54.56) and 400-yard individual medley (4:12.09); Scott Shafer, 100-yard backstroke (53.08); Michael Tingley, 200-yard backstroke (1:51.04); Chris Koerner, 100-yard breaststroke (1:00.68) and 200-yard breaststroke 2:10.95; Dave Sloan, 200-individual medley (1:55.55).

MSU finished 10th at the Big Ten championships, but several Spartans swam top times. Munley captured fourth in the 200 freestyle with a time of 1:37.52 and took ninth in the 500 freestyle (4:28.35). Freshman Joe Brennan produced four points for the Spartans with a 13th-place finish in the 1,650-yard freestyle (15:49.48). He also took 13th in the 500 freestyle (4:28.25). Junior Tim Gendler was 16th in the 200 backstroke with a time

of 1:49.29 and senior Casey Guntzviller finished 15th in the three-meter dive with a score of 420.75.

Tennis: The Spartans picked up a big win in the first round of the Big Ten Tournament, edging Wisconsin, 4-3. Just like the first meeting between the two schools, Michigan State was able to pick up the doubles point by winning two of the three contests. Four seniors combined to make up the two victorious doubles tandems. Ken Kigongo teamed with Mark Findling to win 8-5 at number one doubles, while Ivica Primorac and Francisco Trinidad won 8-5 at number three. Primorac and Trinidad also claimed victories at number three and number four singles. Senior Robert Topalo was the other Spartan to collect a singles victory to result in the final 4-3 outcome. R. Topalo defeated Wisconsin's David Chang at number two singles.

Track and Field: State finished seventh at the indoor Central Collegiates held on the Central Michigan campus. The Spartans were led by pole vaulters Jack Diner who finished second with a mark of 16' 6"and Matt Deering who tied for third at 16'. In the high jump Brad Dieffenbacher tied for eighth (6' 6") and Jasmin Alverson placed sixth in the high hurdle event (8.28).

Okie Giwa-Agbomeirele leaped 23' 2" to win the long jump at the Michigan Intercollegiate indoor championships in Mt. Pleasant. Dieffenbacher placed fourth in the high jump at 6' 6" and Justin Shelden finished seventh in the weight throw with a toss of 52' 9-1/2".

At the NCAA indoor championships in Fayetteville, Ark., Steve Schell placed 12th in the 5,000-meter run. Later, at the outdoor nationals hosted by Duke University, the Dearborn senior ran a 30:49.45 to place sixth in the 10,000-meter run.

Competing in the Eastern Michigan Twilight Meet the Spartans were performing at their best in the field events. Justin Selden lofted the discus 46.96 meters for a first-place finish and also placed sixth in the hammer throw (166' 3-1/2"). Joe Keller finished second in the shot put (14.20 meters), fourth in the hammer (168' 6") and sixth in the discus (45.20m)while Dieffenbacher took fourth in the javelin (160' 3").

Coach Darroll Gatson had little to cheer about at the Big Ten outdoor championships held in Ann Arbor. Managing only 21 points, MSU ended up in 10th place. Schell placed third in the 5,000-meter run (14:12.78); E.J. Martin was fourth in the high hurdles (14.15), Giwa-Agbomeirele was sixth in the long jump (24'-1/4") while in the decathlon event, Jeff Kus placed third (6,859 points) with Matt Ingram eighth (6,521).

Wrestling: At the Penn State Open in early December, 11 Spartans finished among the top six in their weight classes. Leading the way was senior Nick Muzashvili (197 pounds) who was named outstanding wrestler of the tournament after going 5-0 including a win by a fall in the championship match and outscoring his opponents 56-16. Chris Williams (125 pounds was second; Coret Posey (149 pounds), Gray Maynard (157 pounds), Greg DeGrand (165 pounds) and heavyweight Matt Lamp all finished third. Three members of the squad, Karl Nadolsky (149 pounds), Will Hill (174 pounds) and Joe Cotant (184 pounds), each placed fourth. Mike Castillo (141 pounds) in fifth and Charlie Sageman (141 pounds) in sixth rounds out the MSU place-winners.

In February MSU hosted the National Wrestling Coaches Association (NWCA) All-Star Classic. Two of Tom Minkel's best were chosen to compete, Pat McNamara (133 pounds) who was a 3-2 winner and nationally ranked number-one Muzashvili, who lost to the nation's second-ranked wrestler.

In their best Big Ten Conference showing since 1996, State scored 87 1/2 points, good enough for fourth place. Muzashvili, the senior from the Republic of Georgia, won the title in his division. McNamara was second; Maynard won the consolation match for third place; both Nadolsky and Lamb finished fourth; DeGrand was fifth while Hill and Mike Castillo (141 pounds) both placed seventh and thus qualified for the NCAAs.

Led by Muzashvili and McNamara, Michigan State earned 36 1/2 points which placed them 14th in the final standings at the national collegiate championships held a the Kiel Center in St. Louis. Both Spartans lost at the semifinal level and from there, Muzashvili managed a fourth place while McNamara settled for sixth.

EXTRA! 2000 NCAA TOURNAMENT

The Spartans were crowned the national champions in 2000. The following are the box scores for Michigan State's games in the tournament.

MICHIGAN STATE 65–VALPARAISO 38

	FG-FGA	FT-FTA	REB	A	PF	TP
Peterson	5-9	1-1	4	0	0	12
Granger	3-5	0-0	3	1	1	7
Hutson	1-3	2-2	4	2	4	4
Cleaves	5-11	3-3	2	8	0	15
Bell	0-3	0-0	4	1	3	0
Smith	0-1	0-0	1	0	0	0
Thomas	0-1	1-2	2	1	0	1
Chappell	2-5	4-6	4	0	3	9
Cherry	0-0	0-0	0	1	0	0
Richardson	3-6	2-3	10	0	0	9
Anagonye	0-0	0-0	0	0	1	0
Ballinger	3-6	2-2	3	0	3	8
Team			2			
TOTALS	22-50	15-19	39	14	15	65

Halftime: Michigan State 29-15; **Three-point field goals:** 6-17 (Peterson 1-3, Granger 1-2, Cleaves 2-6, Bell 0-2, Chappell 1-3, Richardson 1-1); **Officials:** Shaw, Lopes, Pool; **Attendance:** 13,374.

MICHIGAN STATE 73–UTAH 61

	FG-FGA	FT-FTA	REB	A	PF	TP
Hutson	7-9	5-10	8	2	1	19
Peterson	5-11	0-0	3	0	2	13
Granger	3-5	0-0	3	2	2	7
Cleaves	7-14	3-4	2	5	1	21
Bell	2-5	5-6	5	3	1	9
Thomas	0-0	0-0	1	0	1	0
Chappell	0-0	0-0	0	0	0	0
Richardson	1-2	0-0	4	0	4	2
Anagonye	1-1	0-0	0	1	2	2
Ballinger	0-0	0-0	0	0	1	0
Team			4			
TOTALS	26-47	13-20	30	13	15	73

Halftime: Utah 35-32; **Three-point field goals:** 8-15 (Peterson 3-4, Granger 1-3, Cleaves 4-7, Bell 0-1); **Officials:** Boudreaux, Thibodeaux, Lopes; **Attendance:** 13,374.

MICHIGAN STATE 75–SYRACUSE 58

	FG-FGA	FT-FTA	REB	A	PF	TP
Hutson	5-7	1-4	5	1	2	11
Peterson	6-10	4-4	3	2	2	21
Granger	7-11	3-3	4	3	1	19
Cleaves	4-12	0-0	1	7	1	10
Bell	3-7	4-4	6	4	1	12
Thomas	0-0	0-0	1	0	0	0
Chappell	0-1	1-2	4	0	2	1
Richardson	0-1	0-0	3	0	0	0
Anagonye	0-0	1-2	1	0	4	1
Team			2			
TOTALS	25-49	14-19	30	17	13	75

Halftime: Syracuse 34-21; **Three-point field goals:** 11-23 (Peterson 5-9, Granger 2-4, Cleaves 2-6, Bell 2-4); **Officials:** Thornley, Sitov, Hartzell; **Attendance:** 21,214.

MICHIGAN STATE 75–IOWA STATE 64

	FG-FGA	FT-FTA	REB	A	PF	TP
Hutson	6-9	5-5	11	2	4	17
Peterson	5-13	7-7	7	0	3	18
Granger	5-8	6-6	0	2	2	18
Cleaves	4-12	1-2	1	2	4	10
Bell	3-11	2-2	5	2	4	9
Smith	0-0	0-0	0	0	0	0
Thomas	0-0	0-0	0	0	1	0
Ishbia	0-0	0-0	0	0	0	0
Chappell	1-2	0-0	0	0	1	2
Richardson	0-1	0-0	2	0	1	0
Anagonye	0-0	1-2	1	0	4	1
Ballinger	0-0	0-0	0	0	0	0
Team			1		1	
TOTALS	24-56	22-24	27	9	24	75

Halftime: Iowa State 34-31; **Three-point field goals:** 5-19 (Peterson 1-3, Granger 2-4, Cleaves 1-4, Bell 1-6, Chappell 0-1, Richardson 0-1); **Officials:** Shaw, Basone, Dixon; **Attendance:** 21,214.

MICHIGAN STATE 53–WISCONSIN 41

	FG-FGA	FT-FTA	REB	A	PF	TP
Hutson	3-7	4-5	10	0	2	10
Peterson	7-15	4-4	7	0	3	20
Granger	0-3	1-2	7	1	4	1
Cleaves	1-7	9-11	4	1	3	11
Bell	2-9	0-0	8	2	2	4
Richardson	0-0	0-0	0	0	1	0
Thomas	0-0	0-0	0	0	0	0
Chappell	2-4	1-1	0	0	1	5
Anagonye	1-1	0-0	2	0	2	2
Ballinger	0-0	0-0	1	0	0	0
Team			3			
TOTALS	16-46	19-23	42	4	18	53

Halftime: Michigan State 19-17; **Three-point field goals:** 2-14 (Peterson 2-8, Granger 0-1, Bell 0-3, Chappell 0-2); **Officials:** Clougherty, Patillo, Higgins; **Attendance:** 43,116.

MICHIGAN STATE 89–FLORIDA 76

	FG-FGA	FT-FTA	REB	A	PF	TP
Hutson	2-4	2-2	1	3	4	6
Peterson	7-14	4-6	2	5	3	21
Granger	7-11	2-2	9	1	2	19
Cleaves	7-11	1-1	2	4	1	18
Bell	3-6	2-3	8	5	2	9
Richardson	4-7	1-2	2	0	1	9
Anagonye	0-0	0-0	2	0	4	0
Chappell	2-4	0-0	1	0	0	5
Ballinger	1-1	0-0	0	0	2	2
Thomas	0-0	0-0	1	1	1	0
Smith	0-0	0-0	0	0	0	0
Cherry	0-0	0-0	0	0	0	0
Ishbia	0-1	0-0	0	0	0	0
Team			3			
TOTALS	33-59	12-16	32	19	20	89

Halftime: Michigan State 43-32; **Three-point field goals:** 11-22 (Peterson 3-8, Granger 3-5, Cleaves 3-4, Bell 1-2, Chappell 1-3); **Officials:** Burr, Boudreaux, Hall; **Attendance:** 43,116.

TALES TO TELL

Michigan State trailed number 16 Notre Dame 21-20 and stood at fourth-and-10 on their own 32-yard line with less than two minutes to play. It was collectively "hold your breath time" in Spartan Stadium as the offense was under the direction of freshman quarterback Jeff Smoker, filling in for the injured senior, Ryan VanDyke. The home crowd realized their heroes needed a first down to maintain possession and keep the desperate drive alive. Time out!

The game reached this juncture after ND had opened the scoring with a touchdown in the first quarter. State then tied it up in the second stanza with a 65-yard, 10-play drive that ended in a six-yard scoring run by T.J. Duckett, and then took a lead into the locker room on David Schaefer's career-long 50-yard field goal. At half-

time, MSU's 2000 NCAA championship basketball team was introduced on the field carrying their tournament trophy. Coach Izzo completed a message over the PA microphone with a bold prediction: "Now let's watch the Spartans beat Notre Dame."

State upped its lead in the third quarter to a seemingly comfortable 20-7, tallying on Smoker's 10-yard TD pass to Travis Wilson and another Schaefer field goal. However, the Irish would prove to be "Fighting" Irish as they opened the fourth quarter with a 43-yard pass to the MSU two-yard line, and after the next play the lead was suddenly cut to 20-14. Smoker fumbled on the next Spartan possession, and ND recovered the ball at MSU's 12-yard line with 12:38 to go. They pressed down to the MSU three, but a momentous goal-line stand culminated when junior defensive lineman Josh Shaw tackled the opposing quarterback for no gain on a fourth-and-one

---

HEADLINES of 2001

- FBI agent Robert Hanssen is accused of spying for Russia during a 15-year period. Found guilty, he is sentenced to a lengthy prison sentence.
- Two hijacked jetliners, controlled by foreign terrorist suicide squads, ram and totally destroy the twin towers of the World Trade Center in New York City. A third plane flies into the side of the Pentagon Building, while a fourth crashes in rural Pennsylvania. Nearly 3,000 people die in the attacks.
- In retaliation for harboring terrorists (especially Osama bin Laden) and supporting Al Qaeda terrorist camps, the United States launches a relentless bombing campaign on Afghanistan. Eventually using ground forces and linking up with Northern Alliance troops, the Taliban regime collapses after two months of conflict.
- The anthrax scare rivets the nation as anthrax-laced letters are sent to various media and government officials. Several die after handling the letters.

SCOREBOARD

	W	L	T	Avg.
Baseball	29	27	0	.518
Track and Field	0	1	0	.000
Football	5	6	0	.455
Basketball	28	5	0	.879
Tennis	7	18	0	.280
Cross Country	no dual meets			
Swimming and Diving	3	4	0	.429
Wrestling	7	8	0	.467
Hockey	33	5	4	.833
Golf	tournament play only			
Gymnastics	6	5	0	.545
Soccer	11	6	2	.579

situation. On the ensuing possession, once more the first-year QB turned the ball over, this time on a screen pass interception which was returned four yards to the MSU two-yard line. Before the murmur of catcalls would subside, Notre Dame had capitalized, retaking the lead, 21-20. Fortunately, as time would tell, this comeback would only serve as an additive to the drama, which would eventually unfold.

Time in! The ball was snapped and the Notre Dame defense was on a blitz, hoping to harass the rookie quarterback and force a quick pass release. Unfazed and seeking redemption, Smoker stepped back, hit junior wide receiver Herb Haygood who caught the pass in stride on a slant pattern. It was immediately obvious the Florida speedster was not going to settle for just 10 yards and a first down. Flashing his 4.4 speed, Herb split the defensive secondary and up the middle he went, headed for the student section more than 50 yards away. It was a play that not only would win the game but also establish Smoker as a Big Ten-caliber quarterback.

Bobby Williams increased his coaching record to 4-0 and MSU had become the first team to defeat Notre Dame four times in a row since Miami (Fla.) accomplished the feat from 1983-1987.

TEAM OF THE YEAR

As the defending national basketball champions, MSU wore a target everywhere they went and were never ranked worse than fifth in the country. They finished with a 13-3 Big Ten record to tie for first, although they suffered a 65-63 loss to Penn State that kept them from winning another conference tournament. Shaking off the loss, they breezed through the south region of the NCAA tournament as a number-one seed before Arizona finally defeated them in the semifinals at Minneapolis, 80-61. At the conclusion of the year, Michigan State had accumulated an impressive four-year Big Ten won-loss record of 115-25. This accompanied an incredible four conference crowns, two Big Ten tournament titles, three final four appearances, and one national championship. The 2000-01 squad was a well-balanced team, with five or more players scoring double digits in eight games and four or more in 18 games. Jason Richardson led in scoring with 14.7 points per game, while Andre Hutson tallied 13.8 points with his team-high 7.6 rebounds. Charlie Bell dished out 5.1 assists while contributing 13.5 points per game, and freshman Zach Randolph made a strong impression during his only year of collegiate play by grabbing 6.7 rebounds and putting up 10.8 points per game. Bell and Richardson were named All-America and All-Big Ten first team, while Hutson was named second team All-Big Ten.

MAKING HISTORY

Larry Nassar, the gymnastics team physician, once more assumed a similar role for the U.S. Olympic team in Sydney Australia. He had also served the 1996 team in Atlanta.

Ryan Miller, record-setting goalie of the hockey team, earned All-American honors and, more impressively, was recipient of the Hobey Baker Award, symbolic of college hockey's supreme player each year. In the 2000-2001 season he led a team to most wins, winning percentage, goals against average, saves percentage and an NCAA record-setting career shutout record of 17.

Approximately 4,700 Spartan followers turned up to share watching the Final Four basketball game on the giant screen at the Breslin Student Event Center.

After five seasons on the Michigan State basketball sideline, coaching assistant Stan Heath accepted the head

The 2000-01 basketball team. (Front row, left to right) B. Smith, M. Chappell, A. Hutson, head coach T. Izzo, C. Bell, D. Thomas, M. Taylor. (Middle row) asst. coach D. Owens, asst. coach S. Heath, T. Bograkos, A. Anagonye, J. Richardson, M. Ishbia, asst. coach M. Garland, asst. coach B. Gregory, mgr. L. Brown. (Back row) manager P. Lalley, equipment manager D. Pruder, strength coach M. Vorkapich, J. Andreas, A. Ballinger, A. Wolfe, Z. Randolph, asst. to the head coach R. Bader, trainer T. Mackowiak and mgr. S. Finamore

coaching job at Kent State. After two years at that school he would move on as head man at the University of Arkansas.

In April of 2001 it was announced that football ticket prices would be increased six dollars per game, from $28 to $34 to the general public with commensurate increases for students and faculty/staff as well. The rationale was publicized as to be fulfilling a need to finance improvements to the athletic facilities which included $15.5 million for revitalizing the stadium (including new natural grass) and $7 to $8 million to renovate the lockers and office areas of Jenison (a structure that cost $1 million to build in 1940).

In July, both head coaches Tom Izzo and Ron Mason were approved for salary increases. Izzo, the basketball coach, saw an annual increase from $195,000 to $267,000 while Mason, the hockey coach, received a $9,315 increase to $153,215.

The entire Michigan State community was shocked when on April 30, 2001, swimmer John Munley, twice the team's MVP, died after collapsing during a morning jog near the campus. A four-year letter-winner, John was a team record holder, a qualifier for the NCAA championships and an alternate on the USA World University Games team. An autopsy would reveal that John had an enlarged heart that contributed to his death.

GREAT STATE DATES

Cross Country—September 16, 2000 (H): Scoring 20 points, all five Michigan State runners finished within the top seven slots to easily capture their own Spartan Invitational, finishing ahead of Edinboro, Loyola-Chicago, Hillsdale and Roberts Wesleyan. Sophomore Jason Mueller and freshman Steve Padgett finished second and third with times of 24:36 and 24:40. They were followed by sophomore Jared Aldrich in fourth (24:50), sophomore Ben Evans in fifth (24:56) and freshman Andy Marsh in seventh (24:56). Another group of 10 MSU hopefuls, led by Brian Wilson in seventh, completed the course.

Cross Country—October 7, 2000 (A): The 14th-ranked MSU squad traveled to Bethlehem, Pa., where they scored 65 points to finish first among 36 schools competing in the 8K Paul Short invitational. Finishing immediately behind State were: Cornell (105), Navy (117), Army (124) and St. Joseph's (171). Spartan finishers and their times were: Ben Evans in eighth (24:47.27), Steve Padgett, ninth (24:47.79), Andy Marsh, 10th (24:48.94), Jared Aldrich, 11th (24:54.13) and Brian Wilson, 27th (25:19.25). It was Michigan State's third title at this invitational hosted by Lehigh University. The teams of 1997 and 1998 had previously finished first.

Soccer—October 15, 2000 (A): A total of 90 minutes of regulation and one overtime period were not enough to settle this annual Michigan State-Michigan soccer battle. Then, just 1:49 into the second OT, Steve Williford, a Livonia senior, notched an unassisted goal to give the Spartans a 2-1 win. Michigan scored first to take 1-0 lead at the 10:41 mark, but senior John Benoist tied the game on a penalty kick in the 35th minute. MSU out-shot the Wolverines 9-2 in the second half, and 22-16 on the day. The intense play resulted in six yellow cards, five being imposed on U-M players. Spartan goalkeeper T.J. Lieckfelt made four saves for the win.

Hockey—October 26 & 27, 2000 (A): With five power-play goals and 65 saves from goalie Ryan Miller, the Spartans took both games of the weekend against Notre Dame, 5-1 and 3-2. The double victory provided Michigan State its first back-to-back wins in South Bend since 1996-1997. The Friday victory featured three power-play goals, the first was scored by Steve Jackson at 14:01 of the opening period on a feed from John Nail. Playing five-on-three in the middle stanza, Jeremy Jackson netted the second goal at 6:00 on a rebound of John-Michael Liles's shot. Shortly after, at 8:32, Steve Clark scored a third power-play goal on a pass-out from behind the cage by Rustyn Dolyny. The Irish finally got on the board, also on a power play, 15 seconds into the third period. Responding, John Insana scored the fourth goal into an empty net and Aaron Hundt broke in alone to complete the scoring at 19:52. With 1:19 remaining in the Saturday night game and overtime nearly assured, Sean Padgett picked-up a pass-out from Nail, who was stationed behind the cage, and fired it into the net for the winning score. MSU scored two power-play goals in the opening period, the first by Dolyny at 5:49 and the second by Adam Hall at 19:24.

Soccer—October 29, 2000 (H): State closed out its Big Ten and home schedule by shutting out the University of Wisconsin, 2-0. It was the Spartans' fifth-straight victory, their longest winning streak since 1998. Following a scoreless first half, Craig Hear, a freshman from Farmington Hills, scored at 52:05 on an assist from John Minagawa-Webster and then in the 75th minute, another first-year man, Thomas Trivelloni of Mt. Clemens, made it 2-0 with an assist to Scott Babinski.

Hockey—November 4, 2000 (A): It was a great night for those who enjoy watching defensive hockey as Ryan Miller shut out the University of Michigan, 1-0, in front of a boisterous standing-room only crowd of 6,521 in Yost Ice Arena. With three minutes remaining in the first period, the team captain, Rustyn Dolyny, scored the game's only goal on a power play. The Fort Frances, Ontario senior, blasted the shot over the right shoulder of the goalie and into the upper right corner of the net. While Miller was sharp in stopping 31 shots, the blue line corp of Brad Fast, John-Michael Liles, Andrew Hutchinson, Joe Markusen, Jon Insana and Jeremy Jackson was equally strong in clogging the passing lanes and limiting odd-man rushes.

Hockey—November 4, 2000 (A): Making his first career start at Yost Ice Arena in Ann Arbor, Spartan goalie Ryan Miller wasn't intimidated. In front of 6,521 hostile Michigan fans, Miller made 31 saves as he shut out the number one Wolverines on their home ice, 1-0. U-M goalie Josh Blackburn only faced 13 shots on the night, but one managed to elude him. It was Rustyn Dolyny who scored the winning goal with three minutes to go in the first period. John-Michael Liles and Brian Maloney picked up assists on the power-play. After the goal, Miller did the rest, making the one goal lead stand up the entire night.

Football—November 11, 2000 (H): Michigan State's 30-10 defeat of the ninth-ranked and Rose Bowl-bound Purdue Boilermakers added to the list of upsets these two schools have spawned throughout their Big Ten rivalry. The victory featured the running of T.J. Duckett, who rushed for 174 yards on 32 carries, as well as the passing of Jeff Smoker, who completed 12 of 23 aerials for 195 yards. After Smoker directed a 10-play first-quarter 80-yard scoring drive, MSU never trailed. Add a second-quarter David Schaefer 32-yard field goal and an 18-yard TD toss from Smoker to tight end Chris Baker, the half ended with State leading, 15-3. The Boilers scored

their only touchdown in the third quarter; however, the Spartans responded by crossing the goal line twice during the final period. Duckett finished off a 62-yard drive with a one-yard touchdown run to the outside and then his back-up, little John Flowers, added to the winning total on a 48-yard run into the end zone. Heading the State defense were Josh Thornhill, Thomas Wright, Renaldo Hill and Richard Newsome.

Swimming and Diving—**November 10, 2000 (H):** Placing first in every swimming event, except the 50-yard freestyle, State defeated Eastern Michigan, 131.5 to 106.5. Junior Aaron Mahaney and sophomore Joe Brennan were each double-winners. Mahaney opened by capturing the 1,000-yard freestyle (9:35.84) and four events later swam to a win in the 200-yard butterfly (1:54.15). Brennan captured the 200-yard individual medley (1:55.80) and then came back to take the 500-yard freestyle (4:41.16). Other Spartan winners were John Munley in the 200-yard freestyle (1:41.73); Scott Shafer, the 100-yard freestyle (46:87); Mike Tingley in the 200-yard backstroke (1:51.93) and Lars Neubauer, the 200-yard breaststroke (2:07. 15). Chad Ganden was touched out in the 50-yard freestyle by .06 seconds, 21.29 to 21.23.

Basketball—**November 29, 2000 (H):** In the ACC/Big Ten Challenge, third-ranked Michigan State defeated sixth-ranked North Carolina, 77-64. Jason Richardson led MSU with 16 points, Charlie Bell had 15, while Andre Hutson had 14 with nine rebounds. The Spartans went on a 14-2 run in the first half and thereafter never relinquished the momentum. During that stretch the high-soaring Richardson brought a roar of appreciation from the partisan fans when he caught a pass with his left hand then glided across the lane for a reverse lay-up with his right. State led by 13 at halftime and during the remainder of the game the Tar Heels were never able to come closer than seven points. The game was really won at the free-throw line with the Green scoring 21 of 29 and Carolina converting only eight of 19.

Basketball—**December 6, 2000 (H):** In a rematch of the 2000 NCAA national championship game, second-ranked Michigan State defeated the eighth-ranked University of Florida 99-83. The game statistics reveal the two teams were comparable regarding three-pointers and free throws. The big difference came in field goals with the Gators hitting 25-of-52 while MSU hit 36-of-65. Related to this disparage was the fact the Spartans out-rebounded Florida 37-26. The visitors led for the

first five minutes of the contest, but State was in control for the remainder of the game, leading by double digits over the final eight minutes. Five Spartans scored in double figures: Zach Randolph 27, Charlie Bell 20, Marcus Taylor 15, Jason Richardson 13 and Andre Hutson 12.

High-soaring Spartan Jason Richardson gets the dunk.

Basketball—**December 16, 2000 (H):** With time running out and trailing the University of Kentucky by one point, Charlie Bell drove into the paint and attracted two defenders. Elevating for a shot, he then dropped a pass to Andre Hutson, who laid it in with 26.4 seconds remaining, to regain the lead, 46-45. The Wildcats came back down the court and their top scorer, while being closely guarded by two defenders, missed a five-foot shot with five seconds left. Thus, State had stretched the nation's longest winning streak to 19 games overall and 35 at home. Kentucky was in front for much of the first half and enjoyed a 27-18 lead at intermission. The Spartans finally found the scoring touch as they opened the second half with a 13-0 run to take a 31-27 lead with 13:48 left. The U of K wasn't through as they led twice

down the stretch, including that moment before Hutson's clutch lay-up. Overall, the 'Cats hit a paltry 18-of-46 on field goals (.391), but outdid the winners, 18 to 51 (.353). With a total of 16 points, Hutson was the only MSU player to reach double digits. It was the lowest point total in an MSU victory since 1951.

Swimming and Diving—**January 20, 2001 (H):** winning the opening relay, six of the nine individual swimming races and both diving events, the Spartans defeated Oakland University, 137-106. The 200-yard medley relay team of Tim Gendler, Lars Neubauer, Alex Ebner, and Nick DeFauw swam a 1:35.11. Aaron Mahaney was the only double-winner, taking the 1,000-yard freestyle (9:40.32) and later capturing the 200-yard butterfly (1:54.59). Other first-place finishers were Joe Brennan with a 1:40.82 in the 200-yard freestyle; John Munley in the 50-yard freestyle (21.63); David Sloan, the 200-yard individual medley (1:55.48) and Scott Shafer with a 46.68 in the 100-yard freestyle. Diver Mike McKee scored 258.375 to place first in the one-meet competition while teammate Nick Visscher won on the three-meter board with a score of 292.425.

Basketball—**January 30, 2001 (A):** Continuing their complete dominance over the U of M, fifth-ranked Michigan State came into Crisler Arena, accompanied by several thousand fans, and won in a rout, 91-64. The Spartans gave an indication of what type of game it was going to be when they jumped out to a 12-3 lead within the first few minutes. They extended a 26-18 advantage to 50-18 in a span of six minutes and settled for a half-time lead of 56-27. State then opened the second half with a 16-3 run to further widen the gap, 74-30, and the multitude of Green and White fans were taunting their hosts from the back row seats with cheers and singing of the fight song. The score became more respectable as Coach Izzo displayed mercy by playing many of his reserves, such as Jason Andreas, Adam Ballinger, Matt Ishbia, and Brandon Smith, in the last several minutes of the game. Jason Richardson led the scoring with 17 and was followed by Andre Hutson with 15, Charlie Bell 13, Zach Randolph 13 and Mike Chappell with 12.

Hockey—**February 10, 2001 (H):** In this game against Alaska-Fairbanks, the usual bulging crowd of 6,701 was on hand at Munn Arena and on this evening they would be concentrating on play at the defensive end of the ice. Leading 3-0, victory seemed assured for State, but the issue was whether sophomore goalie Ryan Miller would gain that one additional shutout. Three

weeks earlier he had accounted for a 16th career shutout against Lake Superior State, 3-0. That feat tied a 70-year-old collegiate record set by Clarkston College's Wally Easton from 1927-1931. Miller, Coach Mason, his teammates and the sold-out crowd hoped this would be the night…a record-setting night. The first two periods were played out…no score by Fairbanks. Then it came time counting down the minutes and then counting down the seconds during the final minute of play. With eyes peering at the huge scoreboard over center ice, the scene was reminiscent of Times Square in New York City on New Year's Eve. Finally, the game-ending horn sounded to a new record. His teammates rushed to the crease and mobbed Ryan Miller as the fans rose in unison to applaud the achievement. Not only had he set a new record, but the Lansing sophomore had done it in slightly less than two seasons.

Hockey—**February 17, 2001 (N):** In front of 19,995 fans at Joe Louis Arena, Michigan State clinched at least a share of the CCHA title with a 4-2 defeat of the University of Michigan. The victory also marked head coach Ron Mason's 600th win at MSU. His NCAA career victory mark of 889 (at Lake Superior, Bowling Green and Michigan State) is tops all-time. Andrew Bogle scored the only goal of the first period on a backhand shot at the two-minute mark. Michigan tied the score at 4:26 of the second period, but Adam Hall regained the lead at 18:41 on a power play with an assist from Brian Maloney. Hall, the Kalamazoo junior, wasted little time before he put MSU up 3-1 on a short-handed goal just more than four minutes into the third period, with assists from Maloney and John-Michael Liles. Maloney added the Spartans final goal at 11:14 when on a 5-3 man-advantage with an assist from Rusty Dolyny. Opting for a sixth skater, the U of M scored their second goal at 19:39.

Wrestling—**February 16, 2001 (H):** The 14th-ranked Michigan State wrestling team defeated 20th-ranked Indiana University, 20-12, in the arena of Jenison Fieldhouse. The matches began at the 165-pound division in which State's Corey Posey lost a hard-fought 1-0 decision. Freshman Nate Mesyn (174 pounds) evened the team score with a 3-1 decision, scoring a takedown as time expired in the third period. After John Wechter's loss at 184 pounds, Nik Fekete (197 pounds) scored a 25-11 major decision to put State ahead for good, 7-6. In the next match, heavyweight Mike Keenan recorded a last-second 3-1 sudden victory decision. With 0.1 seconds remaining in the first extra period, Keenann scored

a takedown. Chris Williams (125 pounds) lost his match, 10-4 and ranked Pat McNamara (133 pounds) followed with his 104th career victory, 7-2. Mike Castillo (141 pounds), tied at 2-2 with 35 seconds remaining, scored a takedown and then hung on for a 4-3 win. Karl Nadolsky (149 pounds) won a 14-5 major decision, followed by the closing square-off in which Charlie Sageman lost a close one, 2-1.

Wrestling—**February 18, 2001 (H):** State's top-ranked competitor, number four Pat McNamara (133 pounds) opened the Sunday afternoon matches against Penn State with a 5-1 decision. He was followed by Mike Castillo (141), who gained a 22-9 major decision. After Karl Nadolsky's loss at 149 pounds, MSU scored two more decisions, putting the team score at 13-3. Charlie Sageman (157 pounds) was a 5-3 winner and Cory Posey (165 pounds) an 11-7 winner. After another setback, (Nate Mesyn at 174 pounds), John Wechter (184 pounds) registered a 14-4 major decision and 12th-ranked Nick Fekete (197 pounds) was a 9-4 winner. Heavyweight Mike Keenan was pinned at 5:37, but by then the meet had been recorded as an MSU victory. Chris Williams (125 pounds) concluded the meet with a 2-0 decision and the final score read 20-12 in favor of Michigan State.

Tennis—**February 26, 2001 (N):** Defeating Valparaiso 7-0, Gene Orlando's youthful squad won their fourth shutout of the season in a match on the courts at Western Michigan. Freshman Eric Simonton opened the meet with a 6-4, 6-2 win at number one singles. Chris Mitchell, also in his first season, won 6-3, 6-3 at number two. Other freshmen earning wins were Mike Jonckheere, 7-5, 6-3, at the number five spot and number six Josh Efros, 7-8 (4), 6-1. The remaining singles slots were filled by sophomores, Adam Hourani, a 2-6, 6-1, 7-5 winner at number three and Rodrigo a 6-3, 6-3 winner as the number four player. Taking two of the doubles matches secured the shutout. The duo of Abucham-Hourani won their set at number two, 8-5 and Efros teamed with Mike Hodge to take the set at number three, 8-4.

Basketball—**March 3, 2001 (H):** For an unprecedented seventh straight time, Michigan State defeated the University of Michigan, 78-57, to gain a share of their fourth Big Ten title in as many years. It was senior night and appropriately, the five seniors started the game, Andre Hutson, Charlie Bell, Mike Chappell, David Thomas and Brandon Smith. This quintet had been a part of two conference tournament championships, been to two consecutive Final Fours and set a Big Ten record with 111 victo-

ries and a 56-3 record at Breslin Arena. Leading 42-27 at the break, State opened the second half with a 10-2 run, highlighted by Jason Richardson's reverse lay-in and a dunk off an inbound pass. As the buzzer signaled an end to the game and assured the Spartans of at least a tie for the conference title, the student section (the Izzone), left their seats and flooded the floor to celebrate with the players. Andre Hutson led the scoring with 19 followed by Richardson with 15, Zach Randolph with 11 and Aloysius Anagonye with nine.

Gymnastics—**March 9, 2001 (A):** The Spartans took first place in a triangular meet at the Air Force Academy in Colorado Springs, Colo. Michigan State's score of 210.500 was enough to defeat both Stanford (205.150) and the Air Force (203.700). Junior Jonathan Plante led MSU with the all-around title (52.850) and a first-place finish in the pommel horse (9.65). Sophomore Brad Golden won the floor exercise (9.20) for the Spartans.

Gymnastics—**March 10, 2001 (H):** In the last ever men's meet at Jenison, State went out as a winner, scoring a season high 214.450 to defeat both Iowa (211.20) and Michigan (177.75). Leading the way for Coach Rick Atkinson was junior Jon Plante with firsts in the all-around competition (53.70), the pommel horse (9.70) and on the high bar (8.85). He also tied for first on the parallel bars with senior Tommy Housley with a score of 8.85. Sophomore Brad Golden finished first on floor exercise (9.35) and the vault (9.20) as well as taking third on the parallel bars.

Baseball—**March 24, 2001 (A):** By nearly identical scores, Michigan State defeated the University of Illinois in a doubleheader, 13-7 and 13-8, and in each game one big inning was instrumental. In the opener, State trailed 5-2 prior to the productive fourth in which they combined five hits with generous pitching to score seven runs and gain a 9-5 lead. Although that proved to be quite enough, they did manage one more run in the fifth and three in the seventh. The big hitters were Brett Wattles, who went three-for-four, and Rick Court who was two-for-five with four runs-batted-in. Kyle Geswein pitched six innings and was credited with the victory. In the second game, the teams were tied 2-2 until the third when MSU broke it open with yet another seven-run inning, this time on five hits and two costly Illini errors. Bob Malek and the pitcher turned hitter, Geswein, each hit a home run. The 9-2 Spartan lead slowly dwindled to 9-7 after six innings, but any fears of an Illinois comeback were dashed in the top of the seventh. Three of the

first four batters reached base and Chris McCuiston drove them all in on a dramatic, two-out grand-slam home run to right field to put State ahead for good. 13-8. Malek went three-for-three in the second game with two RBIs while Geswein went three-for-four with four runs-batted-in. Brian Gale, the Decatur freshman, picked-up the win after relieving starter Nick Bates in the third.

Tennis—**April 8, 2001 (H):** In a meet that played out as close as could be imagined, Michigan State went to the final singles match before securing a 4-3 win over Penn State. The Spartans recorded their first point in doubles. The number two men of Jimmy McGuire and Adam Hourani won their set, 8-6, and Goran Topalo with freshman Mike Jonckheere followed with an exciting win at number one in a tie-breaker, 9-8(4). In singles competition, MSU winners included freshman Eric Simonton at number two (7-5, 6-2) and Jonckheere at number six (7-5, 6-1). With losses at number one Topalo, number three Hourani and Rodrigo Abucham at number five, the meet would be decided at number four where McGuire lost the opening set 4-6. He bounced back to win 6-2 and force a third set which he settled on a tie-breaker, 7-6 (5).

Baseball—**May 4 (H), 5 (A) & 6 (H), 2001:** Michigan State opened the weekend with a 9-7 win over the University of Michigan at Kobs Field on Friday. State wasted little time as they sent 11 batters to the plate while combining four singles with two errors to produce six runs in the opening inning. Thereafter, Kyle Geswein singled home one run in the second and Brady Burrill doubled home two more in the sixth. Jon Huizinga picked-up his fifth win of the spring. On Saturday, MSU traveled to Ann Arbor to claim a 10-2 victory with freshman starter Bryan Gale notching his ninth win. Scattering just five hits, he surrendered two runs and struck out five. Chris McQuiston went two-for-five, including a three-run home run in the sixth inning. The rivals returned to Kobs on Sunday, but the result was the same as the Spartans won 8-5. Without benefit of one base hit, they scored three of the runs in the first inning on four walks and three Wolverine errors. In the next inning they added four more runs in more exciting fashion as Scott Koerber, the Harper Woods freshman, blasted a grand-slam home run over the scoreboard in left field. Scoring one more run in the fourth, they hung on as the Wolverines scored five times in the latter half of the game. Although starting pitcher Geswein was relieved in the seventh inning, he gained his third win of the season.

ATHLETE OF THE YEAR

Goaltender Ryan Miller concluded a remarkable sophomore season by being voted recipient of college hockey's most coveted prize, the Hobey Baker Award. Following in the footsteps of his cousin Kip, Ryan became the second Spartan to be so honored. Over the season he led the team to a 31-5-4 record and led the nation with a 1.32 goal against average, a .950 saves percentage (the best in NCAA history) and 10 shutouts in 40 starts. Adding to eight shutouts his freshman season, the total of 18 career shutouts also constituted an NCAA record which was expanded to 26 upon completion of the 2001-2002 season. In addition to the Baker Award, Goalie Miller would also be tabbed College Hockey Player of the Year by the *Hockey News*. He would also become the first hockey player to be named Big Ten Male Athlete of the Year. CCHA Conference citations included Player of the Year, Best Goaltender, Tournament MVP, All-Conference and All-Tournament First Team selections. A third-generation Spartan hockey player, Ryan was born in East Lansing but spent his high school years in Sault Ste. Marie, Mich., where he played two seasons with the Soo Indians of the NAHL. Following lengthy deliberation, Miller opted to forgo his final season of college hockey as he signed with the Buffalo Sabers of the NHL.

Ryan Miller

IN THE SPARTLITE

Baseball: State concluded its abbreviated fall practices easily, defeating a Canadian amateur team, the Ontario Blue Jays, 21-2 in an exhibition game. The Spartans recorded 19 hits off six different pitchers, scoring eight runs in the first three innings and were never threatened thereafter.

The training trips to the South (February 23-25 to Alabama and March 2-10 to Florida) were an about-face as they opened with five straight losses followed by six straight wins.

On March 28, for the first time since 1995, State would take both games of the season from Eastern Michigan, 14-2 and 8-2. Thus raising the won-loss record to 12-4, this would prove to be the pinnacle point of the season.

The most successful Big Ten weekend was the first as MSU took two out of three at Illinois. The Spartans never won a conference series through the remainder of the schedule, going 6-16. The most devastating weekend was the final one. Needing to take three-of-four at Penn State to earn a conference playoff spot, MSU never came close, losing all four games.

In the 9-4 mid-April win over Western Michigan junior outfielder Chris McCuiston blasted a bases-loaded home run over the left field fence at Kobs Field. It was his second grand slam of the year.

Bob Malek, the sophomore outfielder, was a first team All-Big Ten selection. He concluded the season as the conference leader in batting average (.427) and 88 hits, bettering Steve Money's team record of 84, established in 1994. He also led the team in runs scored (53), doubles (15) and three other significant categories. Second team honors went to a pair of Spartan pitchers, Bryan Gale and Domanick Squires.

Gale was also selected by the *Collegiate Baseball* newsletter as a Louisville Slugger Freshman All-American. The 6' 3", 160-pounder posted a team-leading 9-1 record for the season. Brady Burrill was the RBI leader with 44 while Kyle Geswein led the team in home runs with eight.

Along with 300 other college student-athletes from 22 different sports, Kevin Crews, a junior infielder from Hinckley, Ohio, was selected to attend the four-day NCAA Foundation Leadership Conference at Lake Buena Vista, Fla.

Basketball: The preseason poll one year following the successful run for the NCAA title had Michigan State ranked fifth.

Sophomore Jason Richardson spent the summer of 2000 as a member of a select college all-star team that played in Brazil and Hawaii.

On October 13, before a raucous crowd that nearly filled Breslin, State opened the season with their unique version of "Midnight Madness." Scripted to a boxing theme, team members entered the arena from the concourse as prizefighters. Accompanied to the music from "Rocky," Coach Izzo, dressed in a tuxedo, was driven onto the floor in a white stretch limousine.

In a season-opening exhibition game, the fun-loving Harlem Globetrotters took on an unfamiliar serious role and the Spartans held off a late rally for a 72-68 victory. For the Trottters it ended a 1,270-game winning streak.

In the 97-61 victory over Oakland, Charlie Bell scored 13 points, pulled down 11 rebounds and dished out 10 assists to become only the second Spartan to complete the rare triple-double. Earvin Johnson pulled it off a remarkable eight times during his two years at MSU.

In winning their own Spartan Classic with victories over Cornell (89-56) and then Eastern Washington (83-61), State extended the home court winning streak to 31 straight. In the championship game, Bell hit on 12-of-13 field goals attempts while matching a career high 31 points.

In what would become the "Izzo style," State scheduled some traditionally "top flight" teams during the "pre-conference" schedule and they succeeded with wins over North Carolina (77-64), Florida (99-83) and Kentucky (46-45). As a result, in the AP poll released on Christmas Day, MSU had climbed to the top for the first time during the regular season since 1979. They would conclude the season ranked number three.

Once more the Spartans shared the conference title and once more they gained a spot in the NCAA tournament's Final Four along with Arizona, Duke and Maryland. The Wildcats of Arizona would eventually short circuit the run, 80-61. In support of the team, 4,700 fans gathered to watch the Final Four game on the large screen of Breslin Arena.

In postseason honors both Bell and Jason Richardson gained All-American recognition. This was followed by separate announcements that sophomore Richardson, the

team scoring leader (14.7 ppg) and freshman Zach Randolph would leave early for professional careers in the NBA. Both would become first-round draft picks, Richardson by the Golden State Warriors and Randolph by the Portland Trailblazers.

Cross Country: Coach Stintzi's 16th-ranked squad finished fourth in the Big Ten championships which was run over the Yahara Golf Course at Madison, Wis. Steve Padgett was the first Spartan across the finish line, placing sixth (24:23). He was followed by Ben Evans in 15th (24:26), Andy Marsh, 16th (24:50), Brian Wilson, 31st (25:10) and Jared Aldrich, 35th (25:19). Other MSU runners were Jeff Mulder, 61st (25:57) and Aaron Usher 79th (25:57).

At the NCAA Great Lakes regional 10K race in Ypsilanti, Evans finished 14th (31:33.9) with teammate Padgett 20th (31:52.9). Completing the scoring with 190 points and a sixth-place team finish were Jared Aldrich 51st, Jeff Mulder 52nd and Brian Wilson 53rd.

Football: After starting the season 3-0, including the 27-21 win over Notre Dame (the fourth in a row over the Irish), Michigan State opened the Big Ten schedule with high hopes only to sustain a four-game losing streak. The fourth loss was the most frustrating of them all as the Spartans were held scoreless by Michigan 14-0. It wasn't lack of opportunities, as State outgained the Wolverines in yardage, 355-326. Twice the offense failed to score after sustained long drives (72 yards to the two-yard line and 70 yards to the nine-yard line). Adding to the lack of fulfillment, a conference representative would later apologize for game officials who had made some gross errors during the contest which had major impact on the outcome.

With a final Big Ten record of 2-6, MSU finished tied for ninth-place, a significant slip from the 1999 record of 6-2 and tie for second place.

The following individual statistics for the 2000 season were worthy enough to be included in the appropriate lists of the school record book: T.J. Duckett, 1,299 yards rushing; Thomas Wright, 12 passes broken up; Cedric Henry, 118 yards returned from interceptions; Craig Jarrett, 62 total punts and David Schaefer, 11 successful field goals.

Defensive end Greg Taplin was named a true Freshman All-American by Rivals.com. Jeff Smoker, the first true freshman to start at quarterback for the Spartans since 1982, earned honorable mention.

Golf: MSU wrapped up the fall portion of its schedule by placing seventh out of 15 teams at the Purina Classic held in St. Charles, Mo. Senior Dennis Riedel led the Spartans, shooting a 69-72-74—215. John Koskinen carded a 73-74-72—219, Brent Goik a 72-71-78—221 and Nathan Clark a 80-74-68—222. State was 17 strokes from the winning team of Baylor.

With a three-round total score of 863, State finished third behind Northwestern (851) and Minnesota (861) in the 2001 Bruce Fossum/Teamgear invitational. Shooting a three-round score of 72-71-71—214, Goik was in a fourth-place tie for medalist honors. Other Spartans and their scores were Koskinen, tied for seventh, 70-73-72—215; Eric Jorgensen, tied for 14th, 73-71-73—217; Clark, tied for 27th, 69-73-79—221 and Riedel, tied for 70th, 80-80-75—235.

Jeff Smoker quickly established himself as a Big Ten-caliber quarterback his freshman year.

At the Big Tens played on the Stone Creek course in Urbana, Ill., the Michigan State fivesome shot a composite four-round score of 1,161 (285-294-292-290) to finish in sixth place. Tied for 11th on the leader board was Goik, who, in four rounds, scored 71-74-69-73—287. Koskinen finished tied for 14th with 73-74-71-70—288 and Jorgensen was tied at 70-73-75-73—291 for the 24th spot. Completing the team score were J.J. Beckstrom at 72-75-77-74—298 and Clark with a 72-73-78-77—300.

Gymnastics: One year earlier, on April 24, 2000, dubbed "Black Monday" by members of the squad, MSU athletic director Clarence Underwood had revealed that the men's gymnastic program was being eliminated as a varsity sport because of Title IX, the gender equity policy outlined in the Federal Education Amendments of 1972. Successfully bargaining for one more season, the program was given a reprieve and 2001 would prove to be the final year with the NCAA championships, held at Columbus, Ohio, becoming the last hooray. It was an impressive "last stand" as the Spartans finished in sixth place. Junior Jonathan Plante finished fifth on the pommel horse (8.825) and sophomore Brad Golden placed second on the vault with a season-high score of (9.375) and third in floor exercise (9.287). Two weeks earlier MSU was fifth in the seven-team Big Ten c

hampionships hosted by Penn State. Golden won the floor exercise event, was second in the vault and sixth on the parallel bars. Plante finished first on the pommel horse and senior Tom Housley was sixth on the vault.

Although team members demonstrated and pleaded for preservation of their sport during the school's Board of Trustees meeting on April 20, 2001, the die had been cast. Following 54 years of competition accompanied by countless individual and team victories, the sport was extinguished forever from the men's varsity agenda.

Hockey: In honoring MSU's legendary coach of 22 years, the CCHA's coaches and athletic directors voted unanimously to name the trophy presented to the winning team of the postseason tournament the Ron Mason Trophy.

In a move that seemed strange at the time, the Spartans' All-American senior goalie, Joe Blackburn, was replaced in the nets by sophomore Ryan Miller, who would soon display the talent which earned him the starting position.

After a six-game winning streak and having opened the season with a record of 10-1-2, MSU found itself

atop both the *USA Today/American Hockey* Magazine and U.S. College Hockey Online polls.

State dealt Michigan Tech a 3-2 overtime loss to win their fourth straight Great Lakes Invitational crown before 18,363 fans at Detroit's Joe Louis Arena. John Nail scored the winning goal with 56 seconds remaining in OT. Combined with the 4-1 first-round win over second-ranked Boston College, goalie Miller stopped 68 of 71 shots he faced on the weekend and was appropriately named the most valuable player of the tournament.

The record attendance for a game at Munn was achieved on March 1, 2001, when 7,121 packed into the arena to watch State defeat Michigan 3-1. Reported game-by-game attendance figures for sellout games vary based on how many "standing-room-only" tickets are sold.

Posting won-lost-tie totals of 33-5-4, the 2000-2001 Spartans set a team record for the fewest losses in a season. The team also established a new defensive mark for fewest goals against per game (1.36).

Soccer: Michigan State opened the season by taking their own MSU Soccer Classic with Friday-Saturday victories over Quinnipiac 3-1 and Niagra 5-0. In the opening game Nick DeGraw scored the only goal of the first half when he made a header off a corner kick. Michigan State's second goal came at 52:27 when freshman John Minagawa-Webster made it a 2-0 game and then redshirt freshman Craig Hearn scored the third marker. In the final game against the Purple Eagles five different Spartans scored: Pat Mahoney, Minagwa-Webster, Steve Arce, John Benoist and Tom Trivelloni.

In the opening round of the season-ending Big Ten tournament at Columbus, the Spartans eliminated Northwestern, 6-0. Minagawa-Webster and Tom Trivelloni each scored twice with Tom's brother Mike and Jeff Krass each gaining one goal. On the next afternoon, in a mild upset, the third seeded team, Penn State, put an end to MSU's season, 2-1. Trailing 2-0 with 14:30 remaining, senior forward and co-captain John Benoist was awarded a penalty kick which he put into the upper right corner of the net. Although that would end the scoring, State had other opportunities including one boot by Benoist at the game-ending whistle.

In the season-ending totals the top scorers were (two points for a goal and one point for an assist) Minagawa 16, Benoist 11, Hearn 11, Arce 11, Tom Trvelloni 10 and Nick DeGraw 10.

Swimming and Diving: Former University of Illinois women's coach James Lutz was tabbed as coach for

the combined State men's and women's teams. He replaced Richard Bader who left to become an administrative assistant in the basketball office. Lutz, the winningest swimming coach in Illini history, compiled a 59-37 record in seven seasons in Champaign.

Season-best times leading up to the conference championships were as follows: Joel Hageman, 50-yard freestyle (21.06); Scott Shafer, 100-yard freestyle (45.43) and 100-yard backstroke (52.21; John Munley, 200-yard freestyle (1:36.74), 500-yard freestyle (4:22.04); Aaron Mahaney, 1,000-yard freestyle (9:35.84), 200-yard butterfly (1:49.70) and 400 individual medley (3:55.70); Joe Brennan, 1,650-yrad freestyle (15:31.07); David Sloan, 100-yard butterfly (39.24); Michael Tingley, 200-yard backstroke (1:49.32); Lars Neubauer, 100 breaststroke (55.37); Joe Baicy, 200-yard breaststroke (2:04.16) and Tim Gendler, 200-yard individual medley (1:52.53).

At the conference championships, hosted by the University of Minnesota, State managed 143 points which translated to a 10th-place finish. The primary contributor was John Munley, the Kalamazoo senior. He placed third in the 200-yard freestyle (1:36.74, a new MSU record)), ninth in the 500 (4:22.04) and 10th in the 1,650 (15:27.52). In that same metric mile, Sophomore Joe Brennan placed 12th (15:31.07). Other Spartan finalists were freshman Neubauer, who took eighth place in the 100-yard breaststroke (55.76); Mahaney, 14th in the 400-yard individual medley (3:59.29) and diver Nick Visscher, who was 14th on the three-meter board (439.75). The team of Munley, Shaeffer, Rick Nichols and Brennan finished sixth in the 800-yard freestyle relay (6:35.38).

Tennis: The roster of players who represented Michigan State for the 2001 season included Jason Chem, Goran Topalo, Adam Hourani, Jimmy McGuire, Tank Enustun, Todd Townsend, Mike Hodge, Rodrigo Abucham, Mike Jonckheere, Chris Mitchell and Eric Simonton.

It was a long, struggling season for coach Gene Orlando. For the third season in a row his Spartans finished with a losing rcord, 7-18, and 1-9 in Big Ten dual meets.

Track and Field: The MSU track and field season centered on three athletes: senior Paul Terek, sophomore Andy Lixey and freshman Steve Manz. All three earned All-American status (an honor recognizing only U.S. citizens) based on their performances at the NCAA indoor championships in Fayetteville, Ark. Manz was 10th in the shot put (59' 10-1/4"); Lixey managed to finish 13th

overall and sixth among Americans in the 800-meter run (1:51.62) and Terek cleared 17' 7-3/4" for eighth place in the pole vault.

Three weeks earlier at the Big Ten meet in University Station, Pa., Terek, the multi-event star, captured two firsts, the pole vault in a winning height of 17' 8-1/2" and then by amassing 5,685 points to lead all competitors in the grueling heptathlon event. Lixey, the middle-distance star, was nosed out at the wire and settled for second in the 800-meter race.

Moving outdoors, at the Len Paddock Invitational in Ann Arbor, Manz was the winner with a shot put toss of 59' 8 1/2" while Lixey placed first in the 800-meter run in 1:51.11.

Senior Paul Terek was named the athlete of the meet at the Big Ten outdoor championships held in Bloomington, Ind. He set a team and conference record in winning the decathlon event with 7,695 points as well as setting an outdoor team record in the pole vault (17' 7"). Also at the conference meet, decathlete sophomore Jeff Kus finished fourth with 6,901; Lixey was fourth in the 800-meter run (1:49.30) and Manz placed fifth in the shot put with a throw of 58' 4-1/2". Collecting 43 team points, MSU tied Michigan for eighth place.

Two weeks later, at the NCAAs in Eugene, Ore., Terek would score 7,645 points to finish the decathlon in fourth place.

Wrestling: Coach Tom Minkel called his team's seventh-place performance at the Big Ten championships in Evanston, Ill., as "disappointing." Nevertheless, six members of his squad qualified to compete at the national collegiate meet in Iowa City, Iowa. Chris Williams (125 pounds) and Pat McNamara (133 pounds) were the top MSU finishers, each in third place. Other Spartans moving on and their conference placings were: Mike Castillo, fifth (141 pounds), Gray Maynard, fourth (157 pounds), Karl Nadolsky, sixth (149 pounds) and Nik Fekete, although finishing eighth was extended an at-large spot (197 pounds).

Four of State's six competitors in the NCAAs emerged with the tag of All-American. Although hampered by a nagging knee injury, McNamara, competing in his final collegiate meet, repeated as a sixth-place finisher; Williams, a junior, was seventh; and the pair of sophomores, Maynard and Fekete ended the competition in eighth place. The foursome also garnered enough team points to put MSU in 15th place for the weekend.

EXTRA! 2001 NCAA BASKETBALL TOURNAMENT

Michigan State reached the national semifinals in the 2001 NCAA tournament. The following are the Spartans' box scores for those games.

MICHIGAN STATE 69—ALABAMA STATE 35

	FG-FGA	FT-FTA	REB	A	PF	TP
Thomas	3-6	0-0	2	1	2	6
Bell	3-8	1-2	3	5	0	7
Richardson	6-10	0-0	7	3	1	14
Anagonye	1-2	1-4	4	0	3	3
Hutson	7-7	1-1	11	0	2	15
Taylor	2-5	2-2	1	3	0	6
Wolfe	0-2	0-0	0	0	0	0
Smith	0-1	0-0	1	0	0	0
Ishbia	0-2	0-0	2	0	0	0
Chappell	1-5	0-0	7	0	0	2
Andreas	0-1	0-0	1	0	1	0
Randolph	2-4	8-8	5	0	2	12
Ballinger	2-3	0-0	3	0	2	4
Team			1			
TOTALS	27-56	13-17	48	12	13	69

Halftime: Michigan State 29-25; **Three-point field goals:** 2-15 (Thomas 0-1, Bell 0-4, Richardson 2-4, Wolfe 0-1, Smith 0-1 Ishbia 0-1, Chappell 0-3); **Officials:** Hughes, Hess, Sanfillipo; **Attendance:** 8,602.

MICHIGAN STATE 81—FRESNO STATE 65

	FG-FGA	FT-FTA	REB	A	PF	TP
Thomas	5-8	0-0	14	2	2	10
Bell	6-16	0-0	6	3	1	13
Richardson	3-11	3-3	6	1	3	9
Anagonye	5-7	3-4	6	1	3	13
Hutson	5-7	2-3	8	5	2	12
Taylor	4-8	2-2	1	1	3	11
Chappell	3-4	0-0	1	0	3	7
Randolph	3-6	0-1	2	2	2	6
Ballinger	0-0	0-0	0	0	0	0
Team			3			
TOTALS	34-67	10-13	48	15	19	81

Halftime: Michigan State 37-30; **Three-point field goals:** 3-10 (Bell 1-4, Richardson 0-3, Taylor 1-2, Chappell 1-1); **Officials:** Lopes, Hess, Hartzell; **Attendance:** 10,719.

MICHIGAN STATE 77—GONZAGA 62

	FG-FGA	FT-FTA	REB	A	PF	TP
Richardson	5-13	0-1	7	3	2	12
Anagonye	0-2	0-0	3	0	4	0
Hutson	8-11	3-4	10	3	2	19
Thomas	0-4	0-0	5	3	3	0
Bell	5-12	8-10	10	3	1	21
Taylor	3-9	0-0	0	5	1	6
Chappell	2-3	0-0	6	2	2	5
Andreas	0-1	0-0	1	0	0	0
Randolph	4-8	2-4	5	0	1	10
Ballinger	2-2	0-0	0	0	1	4
Team			2			
TOTALS	29-65	13-15	49	19	17	77

Halftime: Michigan State 37-32; **Three-point field goals:** 6-20 (Richardson 2-6, Bell 3-8, Taylor 0-4, Chappell 1-2); **Officials:** Lopes, Rose, Poole; **Attendance:** 26,873.

MICHIGAN STATE 69—TEMPLE 62

	FG-FGA	FT-FTA	REB	A	PF	TP
Thomas	8-10	2-3	7	2	1	19
Anagonye	1-1	0-0	1	2	5	2
Hutson	2-5	7-10	10	4	3	11
Bell	6-14	0-0	4	3	2	14
Richardson	4-11	2-3	2	2	1	11
Taylor	2-5	0-0	1	3	1	4
Chappell	0-3	0-0	0	0	0	0
Randolph	3-5	2-6	14	3	2	8
Team			4			
TOTALS	26-54	13-22	43	19	15	69

Halftime: Michigan State 30-27; **Three-point field goals:** 4-15 (Thomas 1-2, Bell 2-7, Richardson 1-3, Chappell 0-3); **Officials:** Burr, Patillo, Whitehead; **Attendance:** 25,995.

ARIZONA 80—MICHIGAN STATE 61

	FG-FGA	FT-FTA	REB	A	PF	TP
Thomas	4-6	0-0	5	2	1	8
Anagonye	0-1	0-0	2	0	4	0
Hutson	9-14	2-2	5	0	2	20
Bell	1-10	1-1	10	3	1	3
Richardson	2-11	1-2	7	2	2	6
Taylor	3-9	1-2	1	2	3	8
Ballinger	1-1	0-1	2	0	0	2
Randolph	5-8	2-4	5	0	3	12
Chappell	0-0	2-2	0	2	1	2
Smith	0-0	0-0	0	0	1	0
Wolfe	0-0	0-0	0	0	0	0
Andreas	0-0	0-0	0	0	0	0
Ishbia	0-1	0-0	0	0	0	0
Team			3			
TOTALS	26-61	9-14	40	11	18	61

Halftime: Arizona 32-30; **Three-point field goals:** 2-14 (Bell 0-6, Richardson 1-4, Taylor 1-4); **Officials:** Higgins, Greene, Donato; **Attendance:** 45,406.

EXTRA! 2001 NCAA HOCKEY TOURNAMENT (Frozen Four)

The Spartans earned their third regular season and third playoff conference championship in four years. In the CCHA playoffs they disposed of Alaska Fairbanks and Bowling Green before blanking arch-rival 2-0 in the finals. They entered the NCAA tournament as the top seed and after a bye defeated Wisconsin easily, 5-1 for a bid to the Frozen Four. This paired the nation's best offensive team with the nation's best defensive team and defending champion, North Dakota. The game's only goals were scored in the first period by the Fighting Sioux and MSU was sent home disappointed.

March 25, 2001—Grand Rapids, Mich.
MSU 5, Wisconsin 1

1st Pd.: MSU, Insana (unasst.), 7:45; 2. MSU, Patchell (Fast, Ferguson), 19:02.
2nd Pd.: 3. UW, Hussey (Wheeler, Bourque), 8:52; 4. MSU, Nail (Patchell), 9:04; 5. MSU, Goodenow (Maloney, Dolyny), 11:50.
3rd Pd.: 6. MSU, Dolyny (Goodenow, Maloney), 5:42.

April 5, 2001—Albany, N.Y.
North Dakota 2, MSU 0

1st Pd.: ND, Spiewak (Notermann, B. Lundbohm), 1:15; 2. ND, Bayda (B. Lundbohm, Roche), 19:27.
2nd Pd.: No scoring.
3rd Pd.: No scoring.

EXTRA! MICHIGAN STATE RELAYS (The 21st Century)

By the year 2000, the once famed and respected Michigan State relays had degenerated to an event now identified as the Michigan State Open. Held on Friday, February 4, in the 60-year-old fieldhouse, only one other team was in competition, Central Michigan University. MSU won two events: Jake Diner in the pole vault (16' 8") and Justin Selden in the weight throw (52' 6-3/4"). Other State competitors finished from second to sixth in the following running events: 200-meter dash, 400 meters, 800 meters, the mile run, 60-meter high hurdles and the 1,600-meter relay. Other Spartans competed in the shot put and high jump. There is no record of what other schools, if any, may have been invited and declined an invitation to participate.

This was it. The artificial surface that had replaced the dirt floor many years earlier remains in serious disrepair. The south end of the facility has been commandeered to construct a platform for wrestling matches while the north end has become the home for women's volleyball. All that remains of the Michigan State relays is what continues to linger in the memories of those who participated as competitors or those who viewed those great athletes from the balcony of Jenison.

TALES TO TELL

Any time Michigan State plays Michigan it is a special event and the fans pack the arena. Yes! But who would have ever thought fans would pack Spartan Stadium to watch a hockey game? Dave McAuliffe, a 10-year assistant to Coach Mason, did. He had that vision for a number of years before Mason stopped laughing at the idea and began listening. McAuliffe's persistence paid off. With the University committed to returning the football playing surface to natural grass for the 2002 season, this would be the final opportunity to install a temporary rink over the impermeable artificial surface. At a press conference on June 18, 2001, news was released that the season would open in Spartan Stadium against the University of Michigan on the evening of Saturday, October 7, with the prices for tickets set at $10 to $18. The announced goal was to surpass a hockey attendance record of 55,000 that had gathered for the 1957 world championship game at Lenin Stadium in Moscow between the Soviet Union and Sweden.

MSU prepares to battle with Michigan in the "Cold War."

HEADLINES of 2002

- In his "State of the Union" address, President Bush labels Iran, Iraq and North Korea as an "axis of evil" and declares the United States will wage war against states that develop weapons of mass destruction.
- John Walker Lindh, the American Taliban soldier captured in Afghanistan, was tried, convicted and sentenced 20 years to life for aiding a terrorist nation.
- President Bush proposes and Congress approves a major reorganization of government that would combine 22 federal agencies into a Department of Homeland Security.
- During a month of terror throughout the suburbs of Washington, D.C., 10 innocent people are killed by random sniper shootings. Two prime suspects are apprehended in Rockville, Md.

SCOREBOARD

	W	L	T	Avg.
Baseball	38	18	0	.679
Track and Field	0	1	0	.000
Football	7	5	0	.583
Basketball	19	12	0	.612
Tennis	14	12	0	.538
Cross Country	no dual meets			
Swimming and Diving	3	6	0	.333
Wrestling	5	12	0	.294
Hockey	27	9	5	.720
Golf	tournament play only			
Soccer	13	6	1	.675

Associate athletic director Mark Hollis was appointed coordinator of the event (dubbed the "Cold War") and he engaged Tres Papagayos out of Los Angeles, to set up the makeshift rink. Accompanied by portable lights, it all came together during that first week of October. The only remaining concern was the challenge of the weather as either rain or unpredictably warm weather would have been devastating. By Wednesday anxiety levels rose high as the local afternoon temperature registered 80 degrees, but cooler conditions fortunately prevailed by Friday when the sheet of ice was laid. Soon after, a slight problem arose when the 6,500-pound Zamboni machine forced a small crack in the ice but, without missing a beat a smaller version of the surface-cleaning vehicle was brought in for the chore.

As game-day unfolded it seemed more like a football Saturday as tailgaters sprang forth replete with flags, banners and music. By the 7:05 game time the sellout record-setting crowd of 74,554 was bundled-up amidst temperature readings of the mid-70s. The legendary 73-year-old Gordie Howe, wearing a USA hockey jersey, dropped the ceremonial puck and the war began.

Early in the first period, MSU had a two-man advantage and Adam Hall took a pass from freshman Jim Slater and wasted little time in firing the puck past the U of M goalie at 3:25. Before the first intermission, however, U of M knotted the score, 1-1 and early in the second they took a 2-1 lead. At the 5:43 mark into the final period, State took advantage of another five-on-three situation when freshman Duncan Keith hit a shot from between the circles to make it 2-2, but the Wolves regained their lead at the 8:47 mark. With less than a minute to play and trailing 3-2, the Spartans pulled goalie Ryan Miller for an extra skater and it worked as Slater, the rookie, once more made his presence felt. From below the right circle he slapped the puck by the U of M goalie with 47 seconds of regulation time remaining.

The overtime period proved to be a defensive battle, and after the extra session, both of the Cold War rivals were waving the white flag. A 3-3 tie, perhaps it was fitting.

TEAM OF THE YEAR

The 2002 baseball team shattered records en route to 38 wins, the second most victories ever by a Spartan squad. They set new single-season team record for hits (685), runs (500), RBIs (456), doubles (126), and home runs (95). In addition, they ranked fourth in the nation for batting average with .344 and tenth for runs scored with 8.8 per game. In 28 of the season's 38 victories, the offense produced double-digit numbers in run totals. These outstanding statistics earned them third place in the Big Ten and an appearance in the conference tournament. While batting .402, outfielder Bob Malek, ranked first in the conference for total bases (163) and tied for home runs (16). He was a first team Louisville Slugger All-American as selected by the staff of *Collegiate Baseball*, becoming the first Spartan to be so honored since Kirk Gibson in 1978. There were other stars. Although lacking the times at bat to be considered for the title, Brady Burrill batted .414 while Chris McCuiston hit for a .404 average. Top performers on the pitching mound were freshman Tim Day (11-3), Nick Bates (9-3) and Bryan Gale (8-4).

MAKING HISTORY

Tom Izzo was an assistant coach for the USA Goodwilll Games team that competed in Brisbane, Australia.

Former MSU assistant hockey coach Shawn Walsh, who led the University of Maine to two national championships died on Sept. 24, 2001 after a 15-month battle with a rare form of cancer. He was 46 years old.

The 2002 baseball team. Front Row (left to right): manager M. Lewis, M. Bly, K. Crews, C. Braun, N. Anderson, B. Wattles, T. Gulick, R. Kuntz, A. White and trainer J. Hunt. Middle row (left to right): assistant coach C. Mee, head coach T. Mahan, J. Huizinga, D. Miller, D. Putnam, C. McCuiston, J. Deliz, R. Ortiz, J. Duffy, J. Moreno, E. Morris, B. Malek and assistant coach J. Fletcher. Back row (left to right): J. Koutnik , D. Squires, B. Gale, R. Golem, K. Geswein, P. Gill, S. Koerber, T. Day, N, Bates and B. Burrill.

The National Basketball Association (NBA) announced that Steve Smith, former Spartan All-American, was the winner of the 2001-2002 sportsmanship award. Another former Spartan, Eric Snow, was the winner in 2000.

Earvin "Magic" Johnson was among five others elected to the Naismith Memorial Basketball Hall of Fame in Springfield, Mass.

Brad VanPelt, a former MSU two-time All-American as a defensive back, was inducted into the College Football Hall of Fame.

Ron Mason, hockey coach, was introduced at a January 28 press conference as the school's new director of athletics. He assumed his new role in July 2002, upon the retirement of Clarence Underwood. Two months later, on March 24, Mason introduced his replacement as head hockey coach, Rick Comley, a personal friend and coach at Northern Michigan for 26 years.

Does anyone recall when you forked over $2.50 or $3.00 to see a football game at Macklin Field? Okay! so that was in the 1940s. In April of 2001 it was announced that the price of an individual game ticket would jump to $38-$42, a $2.50 to $6.00 increase depending on the particular ticket package and the opponent.

Out of respect for the lives lost during the terrorist attacks in New York and Washington on September 11, the slate of college football games for Saturday, September 15, were either canceled or rescheduled. The MSU-Missouri game was played at the end of the schedule, December 1.

Eric Jorgensen, a junior from Big Rapids, shot a four-round score of 70-72-69-69—280 at the Finkbine Course in Iowa City to become Michigan State's first-ever medallist at a Big Ten championship.

On June 26th it was announced that Danton Cole, MSU hockey player from 1986-1089, would become the head coach of the Grand Rapids Griffins of the American Hockey League.

GREAT STATE DATES

Football—September 22, 2001 (A): Following a nationwide cancellation of games out of respect for the lives lost from the terrorists attacks of September 11, fall activities resumed with the regularly scheduled Michigan State-Notre Dame game at South Bend. For the fifth consecutive year, MSU defeated the 23rd-ranked Fighting Irish, 17-10, as the entire afternoon of football came down to a 47-yard Ryan VanDyke to Charles Rogers pass play with 7:51 remaining in the game. With the score knotted at 10-10 and ND blitzing on a third-and-six,

Rogers raced across the middle, caught the pass, spun away from a would-be tackler, sprinted down the sideline and hurled himself into the end zone for what would be the winning score. The Irish had two final chances to retaliate. One was a run on a fake field goal the "S" defense smelled out and stopped immediately and the other was snuffed on a pass interception by Broderick Nelson. David Schaefer opened the Spartan scoring with a 29-yard field goal midway through the first quarter and the first touchdown was a VanDyke-Chris Baker six-yard pass play that completed a 79-yard scoring drive in the second quarter.

Soccer—October 7, 2001 (H): After both teams played to a 0-0 first half, the Spartans found the range for three goals after the intermission to defeat 15th-ranked Ohio State, 3-0. John Mingagawa-Webster opened the scoring in the 54th minute, scoring off a header from Steve Arce. A three-on-one break resulted in Bret Konley's goal in the 79th minute with assists to Ryan McMahon and once more, Arce. Jordan Gruber, a Beverly Hills freshman, was credited with the final marker, scoring at 89.43 on an assist from Paul Vance. Goalkeeper Mike Robinson was credited with seven saves.

Football—October 13, 2001 (H): Herb Haygood caught nine passes for 119 yards and scored two touchdowns as Michigan State defeated the University of Iowa, 31-28. State cashed in on their opening two possessions of the game. The first score was set-up when defensive lineman Josh Shaw intercepted a pass and returned it 15 yards to the visitor's 48-yard line. Quarterback Jeff Smoker connected with Haygood for a 47-yard catch-and-run that went to the one-yard line. After a five-yard penalty, T.J. Duckett ran it in from the six. The second touchdown, a 13-yard Smoker-Charles Rogers pass, completed an eight-play 68-yard drive that featured a 25-yard third-down toss to tight end Chris Baker. The second quarter featured a five-touchdown blitz, three by Iowa and two by Haygood. His first was on a 15-yard pass from Smoker and his second was a record 100-yard kickoff return following the second Hawkeye touchdown. Scoring subsided significantly in the second half as the winning margin would eventually prove to be Dave Rayner's 22-yard field goal with 10:39 remaining in the game. The Hawks then made it close with their fourth touchdown of the game with six seconds remaining on the game clock.

Soccer—October 14, 2001 (H): In what Coach Baum described as a fantastic, exciting college soccer game, Michigan State defeated the University of Michigan 4-2 at Old College Field. Nick DeGraw opened the scoring on a penalty kick just under eight minutes into the game, giving MSU a 1-0 lead. Anders Kelto made it two-for-two on penalty kicks as he scored after a handball call at 20:10. The Wolverines got on the board at 36:55, but Jeffrey Krass answered just two minutes later on a pass from Steve Arce. The visitors scored first in the second half at 38:58, narrowing the margin to just one goal and inspiring them into an attack mode which kept the MSU goalkeeper, Mike Robinson, busy, as he handled six saves on the day. Looking for improved defense, the U of M replaced their goalkeeper; but Thomas Trivelloni, on a pass from Craig Heam, beat the replacement for the insurance goal at 79:32.

Football—November 3, 2001 (H): Most of the 75,262 fans who packed Spartan Stadium or the millions who watched on television will likely not recall the first 57:51 minutes of the 2001 Michigan game played in Spartan Stadium. Yet those same fans probably recall the final 2:09. Trailing 24-20 and having just fumbled away the first opportunity to regain the lead, quarterback Jeff Smoker and his offense, with one timeout remaining, began the winning drive at the U of M 43-yard line. On fourth-and-16 from the 49 an incomplete pass turned into a first down when a defensive back grabbed the facemask of Charles Rogers, the Spartan offensive threat who had been mugged all afternoon. Later, the Wolverines were flagged for having too many players on the field, which gave the Spartans a second-and-four at the 12. Smoker threw an eight-yard pass to T.J. Duckett on fourth-and-four and then hurriedly aligned his team and spiked the ball to preserve the final 17 seconds. On the next play, quarterback Smoker couldn't find a receiver and running to his right was stopped at the one-yard line. Once more it was "beat the clock" time as he managed to spike the ball with less than one second remaining to salvage one more play. That final play will be long remembered in the annals of this rivalry. The plan was to forget the number one choice of many, Duckett the runner, who had rushed for 211 yards on 27 carries during the game. Instead, Smoker, forced out of the pocket to the right, lofted a ball toward the southeast corner of the end zone and over a leaping defender and into the arms of Duckett the receiver, who was free in the end zone. There was no need for a point-after-touchdown try, State had pulled it off, 26-24.

Swimming and Diving—**November 13, 2001 (A):** The Spartans escaped with a six-point victory over Toledo, 153-147. Senior Aaron Mahoney captured first in the 200-yard butterfly (1:55.34) as well as third in the 1,000-yard freestyle (9:39.73). Junior Dave Sloan took first in the 100-yard breaststroke (59.69), third in the 200-yard breaststroke (2:11.67) and third in the 200-yard individual medley (1:57.95). Freshman Justin Laskowski took first in the one-meter diving event.

Hockey—**November 23, 2001 (H):** Senior defenseman Andrew Hutchinson scored with 5:17 remaining in the game to give MSU a 2-1 win over Wisconsin in the annual College Hockey Showcase. With the game tied at 1-1, he centered a pass from behind the net, which deflected off both the Badger goalie and a defender and into the net. State had taken the lead just 3:03 into the contest on Jim Slater's tip-in on a John-Michael Liles shot from the point. The visitors had evened the score with 7:45 remaining in the second period. Goalie Ryan Miller, the 2000-01 recipient of the coveted Hobey Baker Award, made 22 saves during the evening.

Hockey—**December 8, 2001 (A):** Michigan State's junior goaltender Ryan Miller made a season-high 41 saves and registered his sixth shutout of the young season and 24th of his career (an NCAA record) while defeating Northern Michigan, 3-0. The Spartans scored early. Freshman winger Mike Lelonde picked-up the rebound of a Kris Koski shot and put it in the net at 3:38. Less than four minutes later, senior defenseman Jon Insana picked up his first goal of the season on a 40-foot shot from just outside the near face-off circle. Brian Maloney was credited with the final goal when he picked-up a loose puck in the neutral zone, skated it in and fired it in from the middle of the near face-off circle.

Basketball—**December 15, 2001 (H):** In a rematch of last year's Final Four loss, number six Arizona took the floor in front of 14,759 Spartan fans at Breslin Center. Much to the fans' delight, the Wildcats were never in the game. Sophomore guard Marcus Taylor led the Spartans with a team-high 19 points, six assists and six rebounds. Junior forward Adam Ballinger contributed a career-high 18 points in the victory; however, it was MSU's defense that shined brightest, holding the visitors to 17.9 percent shooting in the opening 20 minutes leading to a 38-22 Spartans halftime lead. Arizona opened the second with a 10-0 run, but State answered with an 11-2 run of their own to quickly close the door on any threat of a comeback. The win extended the nation's longest home-winning streak to 50 games, which tied a Big Ten record shared by Ohio State (1959-63) and Indiana (1991-95).

Swimming and Diving—**January 18, 2002 (A):** In a Friday night meet, Michigan State traveled to Rochester, Mich., to defeat Oakland University 136-105. Senior Aaron Mahaney and junior Joe Brennan proved to be the Spartan standouts. Mahaney edged Brennan in the 1,000-yard freestyle by 0.49 seconds (9:43.20 to 9:43.69) while Brennan returned the favor in the 500-yard freestyle, squeaking by Mahaney by 0.19 seconds (4:37.71 to 4:37.90). Rounding out the day for the MSU swimmers was senior Scott Shafer with a first-place finish in the 200-yard freestyle and junior Aaron Benore with a first-place finish in the 200-yard individual medley. Not wanting to be outdone by the swimmers, junior Nick Visscher captured first place on both the one-meter (328.72 points) and three-meter (299.75 points) boards. Visscher's score on the low board broke the Oakland pool record.

Basketball—**January 30, 2002 (H):** This 71-44 victory over Michigan, the eighth in a row, looked a great deal like the previous seven in which MSU won by an average of 21.9 points. The Wolverines played very well for the first few minutes, but were outscored 15-4 over the final 6:12 of the opening half and trailed 37-19 at the break. State outplayed the U of M in all facets of the game as they outshot the visitors 52.1 percent to 29.6 percent and out-rebounded them 41-25. Junior forward Adam Ballinger led four Spartans in double figures with 14, he was followed by Alan Anderson with 12 with Marcus Taylor and Aloysius Anagonye, 10 each.

Wrestling—**February 3, 2002 (A):** The 17th-ranked Michigan State wrestling team traveled to Bloomington, Ind., and defeated the Hoosiers 21-16. The Spartans started strong as Anton Hall (165 pounds) recorded a 13-3 major decision followed by Rashad Evans's (174 pounds) convincing 8-1 decision, giving the Spartans a 7-0 lead. After losses by Nathaniel Mesyn (184 pounds) and John Wechter (197 pounds), heavyweight Michael Keenan put State back on the winning track with a 16-5 major decision. At 125 pounds 19th-ranked Chris Williams won a 3-2 overtime decision. The score was tied at 2-2 after three periods, but Williams scored the victory with 1:01 in riding time. Scott Pushman (133 pounds) and Eric Keith (141 pounds) lost bouts to the Hoosiers and MSU trailed 16-14 with two matches re-

maining. Karl Nadolsky, ranked 11th at 149 pounds, won a 15-6 major decision and eighth-ranked Gray Maynard, the Las Vegas, Nev., junior, finished the afternoon with a much-needed decision at 157 pounds.

Hockey—**February 8, 2002 (H):** Michigan State's power play and Ryan Miller's 39 saves translated to a 2-0 victory over Notre Dame. The first goal came with 36 seconds remaining in the second period as freshman forward Ash Goldie intercepted an Irish attempt to clear their defensive zone. He immediately found junior John-Michael Liles in the high slot. From there, Liles unleashed a 50-footer that beat the ND goalie to the upper-right corner of the net. Senior captain Adam Hall added an empty net goal with 12 seconds remaining in regulation time for insurance.

Wrestling—**February 12, 2002 (H):** Even though the evening opened with two straight setbacks, at 141-pounds and 149 pounds, Tom Minkel's crew came back for a relatively easy 23-12 defeat of Northwestern. Karl Nadolsky (157 pounds) got the Spartans on track with a 17-6 major decision. Following another Wildcat win at 165 pounds, 10th-ranked Rashad Evans, the Niagara Falls, N.Y., transfer, began a string of six MSU victories with his 7-2 decision at 174 pounds. Nathaniel Mesyn's (184 pounds) 2-0 win put State ahead for the first time, 10-9. John Wechter (197 pounds) won a 10-4 major decision and heavyweight Mike Keenan gained the only fall of the meet at 2:52. From there, it was back to the top of the line-up where Chris Williams (125 pounds) registered his team's third major decision of the meet, 17-5. The 'Cats would close the evening with a decision at 133 pounds.

Hockey—**February 16, 2002 (N):** Michigan State extended its unbeaten streak against the University of Michigan to six games with a 3-1 victory in a non-conference match in front of 20,587 at Joe Louis Arena in Detroit. State's first two goals, both unusual, were scored by senior winger Joe Goodenow. His first, at 1:36 of the opening period, actually bounced off teammate John-Michael Liles following a scrum in front of the U of M net. After Michigan scored the equalized at 3:50, Goodenow regained the lead at 4:49 on a blue-line shot that hit a rut in the ice and glanced off the goalie's glove and into the net. With three goals in less than five minutes, the fans were then geared for offensive hockey, but they would wait more than 46 minutes for the fourth and final score of the evening when freshman Mike

Lelonde added an insurance goal with 9:41 remaining. Ryan Miller made 27 saves in defending the Spartan goal.

Tennis—**March 22, 2002 (A):** Michigan State opened the match against Wisconsin by taking the doubles point as co-captains Adam Hourani and Jimmy McGuire teamed for the first time and won a 9-7 set at number one, while Goran Topalo and Mike Jonckheere won at number three, 8-5. MSU quickly picked up their second point when number four McGuire won his singles match, 6-2, 6-0. Freshman Cameron Marshall was a 6-4, 6-4 winner at number six. Winning the deciding team point would not come easily as number one Chris Mitchell and number five Eric Simonton lost close matches. With only two matches remaining, Topalo provided the victory with a two-set victory 7-5 and 7-6, the latter on a tiebreaker. With the meet win secure, freshman Andrew Formanczyk won in three sets, 6-7, 7-6 and 10-8 in a tiebreaker. The final winning team score was 5-2.

Golf—**March 24, 2002 (A):** In their third tournament of the spring, the MSU golfers totally dominated the 13-team field in the Pepsi-Cola Invitational at the Tanglewood Golf Course in Pottsboro, Texas. Firing a three-round team score of 873, State finished 23 strokes ahead of both Minnesota and Illinois, teams that tied for the runner-up spot. Co-captain Eric Jorgensen captured medallist honors as he carded a four-under par 74-70-68—212. Other Spartan scores and their finishing position were: sophomore J.J. Beckdtrom (sixth) 73-72-74—219; senior Nathan Clark (t10th) 73-74-73—220; junior John Koskinen (t13th) 75-76-72—223; Casey Lubahn, who competed unattached, (15th) 72-73-79—224 and freshman Andrew Ruthkoski 75-75-82—232. Teams finishing in slots four through 13 were Rollins, Penn State, Wichita State, Notre Dame, Iowa, Florida Gulf Coast, Bowling Green, Princeton, DePaul and Northern Illinois.

Baseball—**March 30, 2002 (H):** For the first time since 1965, Michigan State won both ends of a doubleheader against the University of Minnesota, 5-3 and 14-4. In the first game, Scott Koerber broke a three-all tie and gave MSU the lead for good in the sixth inning with a two-run homer to center field. Brett Wattles accounted for the first three runs when he doubled home a pair of runs in the second and then hit a solo home run into the Red Cedar River in the fifth. Pitcher Nick Bates fanned a career-high 10 batters en route to gaining his sixth win

of the season. Spartan batters were in rare form during the second game, making it easy for Tim Day, the starter and winning pitcher. After opening with two runs in the first, the home run came into play. In the third, Brady Burill accounted for all three runs with a shot over the right field fence. Chris McCuiston provided a three-run base-clearing blast in the fifth and Koerber added a solo shot to account for four of the five runs. In the sixth, McCuiston, the Birmingham senior, repeated with another three-run home run and Jared Koutnik accounted for the final run with the fifth homer of the game.

Golf—**April 8, 2002 (A):** To gain some experience on Iowa City's Finkbine Golf Course, site of the 2002 Big Ten matches, Coach Hankins scheduled a dual meet with the Hawkeyes. It was the first pure dual meet undertaken by Michigan State since 1973. Shooting a team total of 282 strokes, State defeated Iowa by eight strokes. Junior co-captain Eric Jorgensen led the team with a 70, sophomore J.J. Beckstrom and freshman Andrew Ruthkoski each shot 73. Senior co-captain Nathan Clark carded a 75 while junior John Koskinen finished with a 79. Sophomore Ben Fox completed the 18 holes in 82.

Tennis—**April 13, 2002 (H):** With the number one doubles pair of Adam Hourani-Jimmy McGuire winning their set, 8-5 and the number three duo of Andrew Formanczyk-Chris Mitchell likewise winning, 8-2, Michigan State opened the meet with Iowa having secured the first team point. Then State quickly fell behind 2-1 as number one Formanczyk and number four Cameron Marshall lost singles matches. McGuire, replacing the injured Goran Topalo at number three, won in straight sets 6-4, 6-1. It then became a matter of which team could win two out of the three remaining matches. MSU prevailed with number two Mitchell and Eric Simonton, at number five, both victorious in three sets, with one a tiebreaker win. With the outcome of the meet already decided, Mike Hodge, playing at number six, managed to take the opening set 6-3, but then lost 4-6, 4-6. The Spartans had pulled off a dramatic 4-3 upset win over the Iowa Hawkeyes.

Baseball—**April 19, 2002 (A):** Striking out six and allowing just six hits, sophomore Bryan Gale threw his first career complete-game shutout as the Spartans defeated Michigan 11-0. Meanwhile, State opened with two runs in the second, batted around in the fourth for five runs, and added one run in the seventh and three more

in the ninth. Chris McCuiston, the senior from Birmingham, connected for three of the 14 MSU hits. Six different batters drove in runs with two of the longest blasts coming in the ninth. Junior Bob Malek from Canton led off that final inning with a home run over the left field fence and Charlie Braun of Grosse Pointe, another junior, drove in the final two runs with a long triple between the outfielders.

Baseball—**April 20 (H) & 21 (A), 2002 (H):** With another impressive performance from the Spartan pitching corps, Nick Bates, the Blissfield senior, went the distance, allowed Michigan batters only five hits, struck out 11 and earned his eighth win of the season, 4-3. Chris McCuiston accounted for three of the runs with a single in the third and a double in the fifth, he would later score the winning run on a single by James Moreno in that same fifth inning. Back in Ann Arbor on Sunday, State trailed 3-0 after eight innings, but took advantage of what could have been a record *seven* wild pitched in the final at-bat to score five runs and go on for a 5-3 victory. That ninth inning also featured singles by Travis Gulick, Bob Malek and Moreno. Freshman Tim Day was the starting pitcher and went six and one-third innings before giving way to reliever Kyle Geswein, who was credited with the win.

Baseball—**May 18, 2002 (A):** In sweeping the four-game weekend series against Penn State, the Spartans proved most totally dominant in the Saturday doubleheader 16-0, 14-0. It was the first time State pitchers tossed two shutouts in one afternoon since the Toledo games in 1981. In the opener, Tim Day, the Ohio freshman, improved his record to 10-3, which tied him for the school's single-season win record. Jon Hulzinger surrendered five hits in five innings of the second game while Ryan Golem pitched hitless ball over the final two innings. On the day, MSU batters amassed 33 hits, including home runs by Jared Koutnik, James Moreno, Bob Malek, Jim Duffy, David Miller and a grand-slammer by Travis Gulick. Of the 20 hits in the opening game, Scott Koerber led the way with four, while Charlie Braun and Malek had three apiece. In game two, three of the 13 hits were credited to Braun, while four teammates had two each. Both games featured big innings. In game one, they scored six runs in both the second and fifth innings and in game two, six runs crossed the plate in the third inning and five more in the sixth. The double win guaranteed Michigan State a spot in the Big Ten tournament.

ATHLETE OF THE YEAR

Paul Terek of Livonia, Mich., concluded his four-year record-setting Spartan track and field career by being named the Big Ten Track and Field Athlete of the Year for the second straight season after taking first-place honors in the pole vault and decathlon at the conference outdoor championships in Madison, Wis. He became only the second person in Big Ten history to earn the honor in back-to-back seasons. Terek had earlier set a school record in both events during the regular season, 18' 1/2" in the pole vault and 7,926 in the grueling 10-event program. He bettered that latter mark when scoring 8,041 points for a second-place finish in the 2002 NCAA championships at Baton Rouge, La. His score was just 53 points shy of the winning total. Paul would also earn All-American recognition for the second straight year.

Paul Terek

IN THE SPARTLITE

Baseball: Joe Fletcher was hired as an assistant coach to replace Greg Gunderson, who resigned to pursue other career opportunities. Fletcher played five years of minor league professional baseball before beginning a 10-year collegiate coaching career. He had coached at St. Joseph's in Indiana and at Jacksonville State.

With 38 wins on the season, only the 1988 team registered more victories (41).

MSU made its sixth appearance in the Big Ten Tournament and the first since 1994. After dropping the opening game to Northwestern, 4-2, the Spartan bats exploded for a 13-9 win over Iowa and a 14-1 win over Indiana. Playing its fourth game in three days, MSU lost to Minnesota 6-0, in its final game.

Bob Malek and Kyle Geswein were both selected to the first-team All-Big Ten team.

Chris McCuiston set new MSU single season marks in hits (93), RBIs (71), and doubles (22) and led the conference in these statistics as well as in batting average (.414).

Malek finished his collegiate career as team leader in hits with 245 and RBI with 162. For all these accomplishments he was voted in a three-way tie as Big Ten player of the year and named first-team All-America.

Pitcher Nick Bates finished the year with 100 strikeouts, while freshman pitcher Tim Day set a new school record for wins in a season, earning an 11-3 record with a 3.21 ERA and five complete games.

Five members of the team were selected in that spring's major league draft: Brady Burrill, Jared Koutnik, Malek, Bates and McCuiston.

During the off season, the historic cement dugouts were replaced by a larger edition. The team would also benefit from a new locker room, featuring a team room and oak lockers.

Basketball: In August, it was announced that assistant head coach Brian Gregory was promoted to associate head coach. At the same time, Richard Bader, formerly head swimming coach, moved into the Breslin Center as head of basketball operations. After opening the season with preseason NIT wins over Detroit (80-70) and Oklahoma (767-55), State was off to New York City as a Final Four team in the tournament. It was there, at Madison Square Garden, they were defeated by Syracuse in the semi-finals, 69-58 and then dropped the consolation game to Fresno State two nights later, 63-58.

The close of the 2001-2002 season was likewise a disappointment. Entering the Big Ten tournament on a five-game winning streak, they lost in the opening round to Indiana, 67-56. One week later, the favored Spartans dropped the NCAA tournament opener to North Carolina State, 69-58.

Marcus Taylor, a first-team All-Big Ten selection, would end the season as only the second player in Big Ten history to lead the conference in both scoring and assists (17.7 and five per game). At the team's season-ending banquet it was announced that Taylor was the team's MVP. A few weeks later, Taylor announced his intentions to leave the team and enter the National Basketball Association (NBA) draft. He was a late second-round pick (52nd overall) by the Minnesota Timberwolves, but he never made the cut and spent the 2001-02 season playing at the minor-league level.

Sophomore guard Chris Hill, was selected to travel with the Big Ten foreign tour team that played in Europe during August.

Cross Country: The Spartans performed well at the 12th annual Spartan Invitational run over the familiar course at Forest Akers East Golf Course. The non-scoring meet is open to competitors from clubs, schools, as well as to those competing unattached. MSU's Ben Evans (24:37.8) finished fourth, but was the top collegiate runner. Andy Marsh (24:43.8) was the fourth collegian and Chris Toloff (24.47.0) the fifth.

Placing behind first-place Wisconsin and Michigan, MSU scored 94 points and settled for third place at the Big Ten meet in Savoy, Ill. Chris Toloff, a freshman, finished ninth (24:15.4), Ben Evans 11th (24:18.8), Andy Marsh 12th (24:19.7), Jason Mueller 24th (24:36.1), Andrew Alley 38th (24:50.8) and Brian Wilson 39th (24:52.5).

This time finishing third behind Notre Dame and Michigan in the Great Lakes Regional Meet at Terre Haute, Ind., the State runners qualified for the nationals. Ben Evans paced the team with a ninth-place finish in the 10K run (30:58.8). Andrew Alley was 14th (31:10.0), Jason Mueller 20th (31:23.0), Andrew Marsh 21st (31:26.4) and Chris Toloff 22nd (31:31.5).

Advancing on to the 10K NCAA championships in Greenville, S.C., the Spartans were paced by Toloff, the Novi, Mich., freshman, who placed 64th with a time of 30:33. The remaining runners for State were Mueller in 93rd (30:55), Evans 104th (31:02), Marsh in 112th (31:07), Alley 184th (31:53), Nathan Usher 217th (32:35) and Cleve Thorson 218th (32:37).

Football: During the summer of 2001, between his freshman and sophomore seasons, running back T.J. Duckett trimmed his playing weight down from 275-pounds to a "svelte" 252 and it seemed to pay dividends. In the 12 games of 2001, he averaged 118.3 yards and scored a total of 12 touchdowns.

The passing game was enhanced in 2001 with the rise in stature of quarterback Jeff Smoker and the arrival of first-year man Charles Rogers. At season's end, Smoker's statistics had pushed his name among the top 10 in nine team-passing categories, including the number one slot for touchdowns in a season (21). Meanwhile, the productive Rogers zoomed to the top of five categories for receivers, including the career yards per catch (21.9). Three impressive figures for season records stood out: receptions (67), receiving yards (1,470) and touchdown receptions (14).

For the second consecutive season, Josh Thornhill led the team in total tackles (128), while Mike Labinjo became yet another Spartan menace on defense. The Toronto linebacker made 17 tackles for losses (64 yards) to rank fourth on the MSU charts.

In postseason honors, Thornhill was a first team All-Big Ten selection and was then listed as third team on the *Football News* All-American team. Tight end Chris Baker was chosen to the *News* second team.

On Jan. 10, 2002, Duckett, State's star junior running back, announced a decision to forgo his senior year of MSU football in favor of turning to the professional game. Three months later, on April 20, the NFL's Atlanta Falcons would draft Duckett as the 18th overall choice in the first round. Also on that day, Baker, State's career record-holder for receptions by a tight end with 133, was selected by the New York Jets in the third round.

Golf: In one of their five fall tournaments, the Spartans rallied to finish second out of 17 teams in the Adams Cup at Newport, R.I. After two days, MSU was 15 strokes behind the eventual winning team from New Mexico University and five behind Minnesota. Shooting a combined 285 on the final day they moved ahead of the Gophers to claim the runner-up spot. John Koskinen shot a 74-70-70—214, J.J.Beckstrom a 74-71-69=214, Andy Ruthkoski 74-67-77—218, Eric Jorgensen 73-73-73—219 and Nathan Clark 74-83-73—230.

State opened the spring season by finishing second out of 16 teams at the Big Red Classic in Ocala, Fla. Their 54-hole team score of 865 was only three strokes back of the tournament champion Lamar (Texas) University. Koskinen, who entered the final round tied for first, settled for third place with a score of 68-74-73—215. Co-captain Jorgensen was ninth after carding rounds of 70-74-73—217. Ruthkoski finished tied for 12th after recording a 72-74-73—219. Ben Fox shot a 70-73-79—222, Casey Lubahn a 75-78-71—224 and Beckstrom finished with 75-76-77—228.

In the Big Ten championships at Iowa City, State's four-round total score of 1,166 placed them in fifth. As the meet's medalist, Eric Jorgensen led the way with a 70-72-69-69—280. Koskinen shot a four-round total of 293 to tie for 18th, Beckstrom carded a 296 for a 27th-place tie and both Clark and Lubahn posted 305s to tie for 47th.

Jorgensen qualified to compete in NCAAs by finishing 16th in the East Regionals at Roswell, Ga. At the championships on the Ohio State course, he shot a four-day score of one under par, 72-69-69-73—283, to conclude the tournament in 17th place.

Ruthkowski, a 12th seed, went all the way to the finals of the match-play Michigan amateur before bowing out.

Hockey: Using a stingy defense, superior special teams play and the goaltending of Ryan Miller, State handed Ferris State a 2-0 defeat in front of 6,732 fans. It was a special night as Ron Mason notched his 900th career win as a collegiate head coach. Congratulating the legendary coach on the ice after the game was nearly every MSU head coach.

The offense ran into a "hot" Notre Dame goalie and State suffered a 3-2 loss on February 9. The defeat snapped a school-record 33-game home unbeaten record.

Junior goaltender Ryan Miller was named to the Men's National Team that represented the United States at the International Ice Hockey Federation World Championship in Sweden.

Losing in the CCHA playoff finals to Michigan, 3-2, State had an 11-game conference postseason winning streak snapped and kept MSU from winning its third straight conference title.

Losing to Colorado College 2-1 in the first round of the NCAA Tournament was a bitter loss as it marked the end of retiring Ron Mason's legendary coaching career. His 36 years closed with a record of 924-380-83 that included 23 seasons behind the MSU bench during which his Spartans went 635-270-69. Ron would leave his coaching post to become the school's athletic director on July 1, 2002.

At the NHL 2002 draft held in Toronto on June 22-23, four members of the Spartan team were drafted. Going to the Atlanta Thrashers on the final pick of the first round, 30th overall, was freshman center Jim Slater. The others drafted in 2002 were center Lee Falardeau (New York Rangers, second round, 33rd overall; defenseman Duncan Keith (Chicago Blackhawks, second round, 54th overall) and left wing Brock Radunske third round, 79th overall). In addition, incoming freshman, Colton Fretter from Harrow, Ontario, was selected by the Thrashers in the eighth round.

Soccer: In the Big Ten soccer tournament hosted by the University of Wisconsin, State topped Ohio State in the quarterfinals, 2-1, and then defeated 11th-ranked Penn State by an identical 2-1 score. The Nittany Lions score first on a penalty kick 15:16 into the game and carried that 1-0 lead for the remainder of the first half. The Spartans did gain some momentum when the PSU goalie was given a red card in the 40th minute for playing a ball outside the box. This gave Michigan State a man advantage for the remainder of the game. Steve Arce scored for the Green just two minutes into the second frame at 46:55. The game would remain tied until MSU struck again in the 69th minute. Thomas Trivelloni kicked in the winning goal with an assist from Jeff Krass, who had scored both goals in the win over the Buckeyes.

In the conference final, State withstood a high-powered Indiana offense in the first half and into the second. Finally, the favored Hoosiers broke the stalemate at the 68th minute and then scored the clincher eight minutes later for a 2-0 victory.

Senior Steve Arce was MSU's only first team selection on the All-Big Ten team. It was the Windsor, Ontario native's second consecutive year of receiving the honor.

State's soccer team earned its first win in the NCAA Tournament since 1969 by defeating Butler, 2-1. With the win, the Spartans advanced to the second round where the hosts and fifth-ranked Indiana Hoosiers edged the Joe Baum squad, 1-0.

Swimming and Diving: Finishing second at the 19-team Miami (Ohio) Invitational, the Spartans were led by Joe Baicy who placed second in the 200-yard breast-stroke (2:04.99) as teammate Scott Shafer was fourth in the 100-yard freestyle (45.70).

Concluding 36 years of service, John Narcy announced his retirement as the Spartan's head diving coach. During his tenure at MSU, his divers (men and women) earned All-American honors on 50 occasions and he coached an NCAA champion, six Big Ten champions and three U.S. Olympians. Narcy was a four-time Big Ten coach of the year and national coach of the year in 1990. In the summer of 2001, he was honored as recipient of the Fred Cady Award for lifetime achievement in his sport. He was honored on January 30 at halftime of the Michigan State-Michigan basketball game.

Longtime MSU head diving coach John Narcy

Top performances turned in during the dual-meet season and prior to the conference championships were: Joel Hageman, 50-yard freestyle (21.00); Scott Shafer, 100-yard freestyle (45.31); Joe Brennan, 200-yard freestyle (1:39.92) and 500-yard freestyle (4:33.33); Aaron Mahaney, 1,000-yard freestyle (9:25.37) and 200-yard butterfly (1:51.74); Alex Ebner, 100-yard butterfly, (50.36); Karl Sunyrd, 100-yard backstroke (50.91); Aaron Benore, 200-yard backstroke (1:54.08) and 400-yard individual medley (4:09.81); Joe Baicy, 100-yard breaststroke (57.63), 200-yard breaststroke (2:04.38) and 200-individual medley (1:53.01); Nick Visscher one-meter diving-six dives (328.72) and three-meter diving-six dives (299.75).

MSU concluded the Big Ten championships at Bloomington, Ind., with 122 points but had to settle for 10th place. Sunryd, the Swedish junior, finished seventh in the 100-yard backstroke with a school-record time of 49.43. Brennan, a California junior, placed ninth in the 200-yard freestyle and Mahaney, the Pennsylvania senior, placed 10th in the 1,650-yard freestyle with a time of 15:30.31.

Tennis: Opening with five 7-0 shutouts, State concluded their dual-meet season with a 15-10 record, their first winning season since 1997-1998. Individually, the most impressive records came from Cameron Marshall, playing primarily at number six (25-14) and Andy Formanczyk at number two (24-145).

On the spring break trip to Louisiana, the Spartans opened with a 6-1 victory over Southeastern Louisiana. Winning singles points were number one Chris Mitchell, number two Formanczyk, number three Goran Topalo, number five Eric Simonton and number six Marshall. By the next afternoon they were 85 miles west where they defeated Louisiana–Lafayette, 4-3, on singles wins by Formanczyk, number four Jimmy McGuire, Simonton and Marshall. In their third and final stop, Tulane ended the otherwise successful trip, 4-3. Again, the Spartans failed to capture the doubles point which proved to be the difference as singles wins were credited to Topalo, Simonton and Marshall.

Entering the Big Ten championships as the number nine seed, the Spartans had high hopes of upending Penn State, but it wasn't to be. The Nittany Lions, a team that defeated Michigan State 4-3 during the regular season, took advantage of a reshuffled MSU lineup necessitated by Goran Topalo being unable to play. Falling 4-2, the only bright spots for Coach Orlando came on wins from Fornanczyk's (6-3,6-3) and Mike Hodge (5-7, 6-3, 6-4) filling in at number six.

Track and Field: Pole vaulter Paul Terek opened the indoor season with a modest second-place at the Missouri Invitational and then climaxed that senior season four months later by being selected the NCAA region IV track and field athlete of the year. In between, at the Indoor Big Ten championships, the Livonia senior won the pole vault and pentathlon event and then followed with outdoor titles in the vault and decathlon.

At the national-level, Terek came ever so close to winning an NCAA title. At the indoor championships in Fayetteville, Ark., he actually tied the height of the eventual winner in the pole vault (17' 11-3/4"), but settled for second based on more misses during the competition. Turning to the laborious decathlon event at the outdoor championships in Baton Rouge, La., Paul once more came close to NCAA gold, finishing in the runner-up spot.

Additional impressive performances during the indoor season included Andy Lixey's victory in the 1,000-meter run (2:30.1) at the Missouri Invitational; Fresh-

man Julien Williams's first-place in the long jump (23' 0") at Notre Dame's Meyo Invitational and Steve Sherer's winning 1,500-meter time of 4:03.26, also in the Meyo meet and his 8:10.48 for the 3,000-meter run, which placed his 15th in the NCAA championships.

Moving outdoors, Terek and Matt Deering placed one-two at the central collegiates with vaults of 17' 0" and 16' 5 1/2", respectively. Also at that meet in Mt. Pleasant, sophomore Steve Manz recorded a third-place showing in the shot put (56' 5 3/4") and discus (165' 7"). Lixey was the only other Spartan to earn a top-three finish as he finished second in the 800-meter run (1:51.37).

With 47.5 points, State completed the outdoor Big Tens in Madison, Wis., in seventh place. In addition to Terek's double win (17' 10.25" in the pole vault and a Big Ten record 7,829 points in the decathlon), there were other contributors. Deering was third in the pole vault (17' 3.5"); Lixey placed fourth in the 800-meters (1:48.77); Manz was fifth in the shot put (58' 1") and Jeff Kuz tied for fourth in the high jump (6' 10 1/2").

Wrestling: Four Spartans placed at the 39th Annual Midlands championships in December. Both Ryan L'Amoreaux (133 pounds) and Karl Nadolsky (149 pounds) captured third places while Gray Maynard (157 pounds) was fourth and Chris Williams (125 pounds) eighth.

At the national duals meet in January, hosted by Ohio State University, MSU was sent packing after day one. Opening with a 56-5 loss to Oklahoma State, Tom Minkel's squad bounced back to defeat Lock Haven 17-11 before being eliminated by eighth-ranked Pennsylvania, 25-9. Three Spartans finished the day with 2-1 records, L'Amoreaux, Charles Sageman (141 pounds) and John Wechter (197 pounds).

With minor success at the Big Tens in Champaign, Ill., State collected 54.5 points and managed to finish in eighth place. Maynard, the Las Vegas, Nev., junior, ended in fourth place, as did Rashad Evans (174 pounds) of Niagara Falls, N.Y. Three others placed in the top seven and as such advanced to the nationals. They were Nadolsky from Holland, Mich., who finished in fifth place; Wechter of Saginaw was sixth and Williams of Perry, Mich., finished in seventh.

At the NCAAs held in the Pepsi Arena of Albany, N.Y., number nine-seed Maynard was the only Spartan to place in the top eight as he won the seventh-place match 5-1.

EXTRA! 2002 NCAA BASKETBALL TOURNAMENT

Michigan State reached the first round of the 2002 NCAA tournament. The following is the Spartans' box scores for that game.

NORTH CAROLINA STATE 69—MICHIGAN STATE 58

	FG-FGA	FT-FTA	REB	A	PF	TP
Taylor	5-22	5-5	3	6	4	18
Anderson	1-1	3-3	2	0	5	5
Torbert	1-5	0-0	7	1	3	2
Anagonye	1-2	0-0	7	0	2	2
Ballinger	2-6	2-2	1	0	4	6
Hill	5-11	7-8	1	0	4	21
Ishbia	0-0	0-0	0	0	1	0
Bograkos	1-4	0-0	4	0	4	2
Andreas	1-2	0-0	3	0	1	2
Team			5			
TOTALS	17-53	17-18	33	8	28	58

Halftime: Michigan State 30-18; **Three-point field goals:** 7-23 (Taylor 3-13, Ballinger 0-1, Hill 4-9); **Officials:** Greene, Harry, Haney; **Attendance:** 17,725.

EXTRA! 2001 SILICON VALLEY CLASSIC

December 31, 2001
San Jose, California

	1	2	3	4	F
MSU	17	20	0	7	44
Fresno State	14	7	7	7	35

Starting line-up (offense)

Charles Rogers	SE
Ulish Booker	LT
Joe Tate	LG
Brian Ottney	C
William Whitticker	RG
Steven Stewart	RT
Chris Baker	TE
Jeff Smoker	QB
T.J. Dukett	TB
Dawan Moss	FB
Herb Haygood	FL

Starting line-up (defense)

Greg Taplin	LE
Kyle Rassmussen	LT
Kevin Vickerson	RT
Nick Myers	RE
Mike Labinjo	LOLB
Josh Thornhill	ILB
Ron Stanley	ROLB
Broderick Nelson	LCB
Duron Bryan	SS
Lorenzo Guess	FS
Thomas Wright	RCB

Sophomore Charles Rogers set a new Spartan record with 270 reception yards and two touchdowns to help lead the Spartans to a 44-35 victory and snap Fresno State's five-game winning streak. The Bulldogs put the first points on the board with a touchdown 59 seconds into the game, but MSU would soon go on a first half scoring frenzy that would put them up 37-21 at the half. On the first play of their third possession, fellow sophomore Jeff Smoker connected with Rogers for a 72-yard TD. Then the defense took over, forcing a fumble at the goal line that Monquiz Wedlow recovered in the end zone for a seven-point lead. The lead, however, lasted only one possession, as Fresno State came back quickly to tie. T.J. Duckett opened MSU's next drive with a 54-yard gain that led to a 51-yard field goal and a 17-14 advantage with five seconds remaining in the first quarter. On their next possession, the Spartans produced an 82-yard, 10-play drive, capped with Duckett's five-yard burst into the end zone. Fresno kept up the heat, moving the ball 83 yards in three plays to set the score at 24-21, but Duckett came back again, finishing a six-play, 62-yard effort with a 39-yard scoring run that continued the offensive battle. With his next opportunity, Smoker hit Rogers once again

for a 69-yard, one-play TD drive to round out the first half, MSU 37, Fresno 21. By the intermission, MSU had already gained 405 yards. The show slowed in the second half but did not stop. In a comeback attempt, the Bulldogs scored the next two touchdowns to come within reach at 37-35, but Smoker brought the team down the field once more, this time hitting Ivory McCoy in the end zone with 1:59 to go in the game. The two teams combined for an incredible 1,146 total yards. Smoker passed for 376 yards, while Duckett gained two touchdowns and 184 of the team's 227 rushing yards. Bobby Williams became the first Spartan coach to win his first two bowl games.

EXTRA! 2002 NCAA HOCKEY TOURNAMENT (Regionals)

After a second place regular season finish, MSU defeated Bowling Green and Northern Michigan to reach the conference playoff finals, where they lost to Michigan, 2-3. Nevertheless, as runner up they were awarded a third seed in the NCAA West Regional, only to be blanked by sixth seed Colorado College in a 2-0 upset. The loss marked not only the end of the Spartan season, but also the end of an era, as it was Ron Mason's last game as head coach. Mason finished his coaching career with a college-hockey record of 924 wins and a mark of 635-270-69 at Michigan State. On July 1, 2002 he started as the new Spartan athletic director.

March 22, 2002—Ann Arbor, Mich.
Colorado College 2, MSU 0
1st Pd.: 1. CC, Clark (Petoit), 10:05.
2nd Pd.: No scoring.
3rd Pd.: 2. CC, Kim (Clarke, Polaski), 5:43.

TALES TO TELL

MSU varsity soccer coach Joe Baum was a three-year letterman at Michigan State from 1966-1968 when he served as goalkeeper on teams that went 33-1-7, including a 33-game unbeaten streak. He was in goal for two NCAA co-champion squads and was named to the 1968 All-Midwestern team by the National Soccer Coaches of America. Baum began his coaching career in 1969 as an assistant at Southern Illinois-Edwardsville. Following a brief stop at Wisconsin-Green Bay, he returning to his alma mater as an assistant in 1974 and was appointed head coach in 1977. The year 2002 marked

Head soccer coach Joe Baum also played for the 1966-68 Spartan soccer squads.

his 26th year in the position. During that span of years, the record for his teams has been 255 wins, 192 losses and 38 ties for a percentage of .564.

The veteran coach was asked to identify an All-Baum team from the nearly 200 letter winners he has worked with from 1977-2002. As this feature story focuses on the rosters of those more recent 26 years, the players who represented MSU prior to 1977 cannot be ignored. There were some great ones: Cecil Herron, Mabricio Ventura, Guy Busch, Trevor Harris, Tony Keyes, Tommy Kreff, Bill Schwarz, Charlie Dedich, Kevin O'Connell, Jean Lohri and Joe Baum himself.

Accepting the chore, the coach could not break a tie for his all-time goalie. Consequently, he was extended the courtesy of naming two:

Tom King, forward (1980-1981): ranks 10th in goals for a season (10) and also 10th for goals in a career (30).

Tom Doherty, forward (1982-1985): ranks fifth for goals in a career (34).

HEADLINES of 2003

- At a Rhode Island nightclub, a rock band's accompanying pyrotechnics ignite a foam ceiling and engulf the entire structure within three minutes. A total of 96 patrons perish in the blaze.
- Upon re-entry after a 17-day flight, the space shuttle Columbia disintegrates over Texas. All seven astronauts are lost.
- In a 30-day war, U.S.-British air and ground forces destroy and dislodge Saddam Hussein's regime in oil-rich Iraq and commence the construction of a free and democratic form of government.
- With no known cure yet, a deadly respiratory virus (SARS) spreads through Hong Kong and the mainland of south China.

SCOREBOARD

	W	L	T	Avg.
Baseball	21	34	0	.382
Track and Field	0	1	0	.000
Football	4	8	0	.333
Basketball	22	13	0	.629
Tennis	14	13	0	.519
Cross Country		no dual meets		
Swimming and Diving	4	9	0	.308
Wrestling	10	7	0	.588
Hockey	23	14	2	.615
Golf		tournament play only		
Soccer	12	7	0	.666

Vancho Cirovski, midfielder (1979-1982): ranks second in career assists (27) and 10th in career total points (75).

Steve Arce, midfielder (1989-2001): co-captain of 2001 team; ranks seventh in career assists (20); twice selected to first team All-Big Ten.

Steve Swanson, midfielder (1981-1983): co-captain of 1983 team; ranks 10th in all-time.

Peter Crawley, midfielder (1983-1986): captain of the 1986 team; team's MVP in both 1985 and 1986.

John Benoist, defender (1997-2000): team captain in 1999 and 2000; two times selected to NCAA All-Region team in both junior and senior years.

Craig Abraham, defender (1994-1996): captain of 1996 team; selected to NCAA All-Region team in 1996.

Doug Landefeld, defender (1984-1987): co-captain in 1987; the team's defensive MVP in 1986 and 1987.

Dick Huff, defender (1978-1981): selected as the team's defensive MVP in 1980 and 1981; team co-captain in 1981.

Reid Friedrichs, goalkeeper (1993-1996): selected as the 1996 Big Ten Conference player of the year.

Paul Zimmerman, goalkeeper (1982-1985): team's career leader in shutouts in a career (29) and most shutouts for a season (nine).

TEAM OF THE YEAR

Selecting the wrestlers as 2002-03 team of the year was not based on their fourth-place finish in the Big Ten championships at Madison, Wis., or certainly not the distant 18th at the NCAA tournament held in the Kemper Arena of Kansas City, Mo. What focused this team into the limelight is what was achieved during a three-week reach during the dual-meet season in which they arose from an 18th-ranked team to seventh in the nation. Until the Wisconsin Badgers came to town on January 31, the Spartans were no better than 3-5 in the won-loss columns. Then from that date, Tom Minkel's team came alive and rattled off seven straight victories. More impressively, it is whom they defeated: the 21st-ranked Badgers 22-13; fifth-ranked Oklahoma; second-ranked Iowa on a tie-breaker; seventh-ranked Michigan, 16-15; North Carolina, 22-15; 12th-ranked Penn State, 19-18 and 16th-ranked Purdue, 23-9.

The line-up over this impressive run consisted of Nick Simmons (125 pounds), Shane Martin (133 pounds), Ryan L'Amoreaux (141) pounds), Karl Nodolsky (149 pounds), Gray Maynard (157 pounds), Arsen Aleksanyan (165 pounds), Rashad Evans (174 pounds), Jeff Clemens or Nate Mesyn (184 pounds), Nicholas Fekete (197 pounds) and either Mike Keenan or John Wechter at heavyweight.

MAKING HISTORY

For the first time since 1968, Michigan State played its home football games on natural grass. Growth of the turf began in March of 2001and was cultivated on 4,800 46-inch squad plastic modules at the Turfgrass Center south of campus. Once the old artificial turf was removed, a new asphalt floor was laid in the stadium accompanied by an underground irrigation system and heating ducts to provide favorable growing conditions. In June of 2002

The 2002-2003 wrestling team

the 1,000-pound trays were transported to Spartan Stadium where the jigsaw-like surface was interlocked and following a summer of nurturing, it was ready for the opening game on August 31,2002.

In *Sports Illustrated*'s ranking of "America's Best Sports Colleges," Michigan State was listed 29th in the top 200 with the following endorsement: "No. 8 hockey team drew record 74,554 for game in FB stadium; hoops made NCAAs; Izzone hoops cheering section good 'n' rowdy." MSU ranked ahead of such schools as Florida State, Washington, Auburn, California, Wisconsin, Penn State, Kansas and Iowa.

On May 28 it was announced that Michigan State would play Kentucky at Ford Field, the home of football's Detroit Lions, on Dec. 13, 2003. With the possibility of playing before more than 75,000 spectators and national coverage by CBS-TV, immediate thoughts turned to the possibility of setting attendance records. The Harlem Globetrotters set the world record of 75,000 at the Berlin Olympic Stadium in 1951 while the collegiate record of 68,112 was established in 1990 with Notre Dame facing LSU at the Superdome. Plans were made to play the game on the portable MSU floor, which would be relocated to the site, and ticket prices were set, ranging from $125 to $8.

One month later, the entire pre-conference basketball schedule was announced and proved to be one of the most challenging ever undertaken by any school. In addition to Kentucky, Tom Izzo's squad would go on the road to play UCLA and the 2003 NCAA finalists Kansas and Syracuse. Home encounters would include Duke at Breslin and Oklahoma at the Palace in Auburn Hills, Mich. Also, in a nostalgic mode, the 1979 Final Four (DePaul, Pennsylvania and Indiana State) would be reunited for the Coca-Cola Classic at Breslin.

GREAT STATE DATES

Football—**September 28, 2002 (H):** Charles Rogers set an NCAA record by catching a touchdown pass in his 13th straight regular-season game as Michigan State defeated Northwestern, 39-24. That scoring catch, from Jeff Smoker, came with 6:10 remaining in the first half and broke a 10-10 tie. Dave Rayner followed with his second field goal, this one from 37 yards with 24 seconds remaining before halftime. The teams traded touchdowns in the third quarter as Ziehl Kavanaght reeled off an exciting 88-yard punt return with 1:24 left in the period. In the final 15 minutes, Rayner connected for two more field goals, the last being a personal best 53-yarder. In between the Rayner kicks, a 31-yard Smoker-to-Jason Randall touchdown pass ended State's scoring for the day. With the game well in hand, 39-17, the "S" defense yielded a final Wildcat touchdown with 4:28 remaining. Dawan Moss, who caught the game's first touchdown seven minutes before the Rogers TD, ran for a career-high 191 yards on 26 carries. Jason

Harmon, Thomas Wright, Demario Suggs, Clifford Dukes and Mike Labinjo led the State defense.

Golf—**October 9, 2002 (N):** Three days following their first-place tie at the Wolverine Invitational in Ann Arbor, coach Mark Hankins and his squad traveled to Rhode Island, where they finished first out of 17 teams to win the Adams Cup at the Newport Country Club. The team's composite score of 873 was three strokes lower than runner-up Texas A&M. The Spartans were led by co-captain John Koskinen, who tied for 10th overall with a tournament score of 74-73-70—217. Eric Jorgensen scored 72-74-72—218, as did Casey Lubahn, 75-72-71—218, tying for 12th place. Ben Fox tied for 19th with 75-76-69—220 and Andrew Ruthkoski was nine strokes back in 50th place, 79-78-72—229.

Soccer—**October 13, 2002 (A):** Two second-half goals, which came less than three minutes apart, was all that coach Joe Baum's Spartans needed to defeat the University of Michigan, 2-1. The two teams played an evenly matched first half, each with six shots on goal. Then, at the 66:36 mark, Brett Konley, the Plymouth senior, broke the scoreless game as he fielded a pass from Jordan Gruber and chipped the ball over the goalie's head. Less than three minutes later, Jeffrey Krass, a junior from Brighton, beat the U of M goalie with a classic header off a cross from John Kaczmarek. The Wolverines were on the board in the 82nd minute, but State's senior goalie, Tyler Robinson, rebuked all further attempts to tie the score as he finished with a total of seven saves.

Soccer—**October 20, 2002 (H):** Recording four shots to MSU's one, Penn State controlled play during the first half of this conference game played on Old College Field. Eventually, the Spartans took charge in the second half and at 75:25, Nick DeGraw, the junior from Clinton Twp., connected on a header for the game's only score. Kevin Wittig recorded an assist on the play. Tyler Robinson, the State goalkeeper, made three saves in the opening half and one more in the second half to secure his fifth shutout of the season.

Hockey—**October 24 & 25, 2002 (H):** In his first CCHA home games as the Spartan's head coach, Rick Comley couldn't have been more pleased. Although the weekend games were diametrically different in many ways, the outcome was pleasant as both were etched into the win column. The Friday game could be succinctly summarized as a 7-0 blowout or more accurately defined as a mismatch, at least on this night. Sophomore Duncan Keith and senior captain Brad Fast accounted for goals in the opening period and then the offense exploded in the second session with goals by sophomore Tim Hearon, another from Keith, one by freshmen Nenad Gajic and two by yet another first-year man Corey Potter. Meanwhile the MSU defense was strong and sophomore Matt Migliaccio provided solid goaltending. The next night hinged on a far different scenario. With State leading 2-0 on goals by Fast and Lee Falardeau, there was little more than two minutes of playing time remaining and fans were beginning to leave the arena. It was then the Lakers finally broke Migliaccio's second shutout bid on a tip-in at 2:05. About one minute later and with an added attacker on the ice, an LSSU shot from the blue line was deflected into the net and suddenly the game was 2-2. The Green and White fans had little time to grumble and overtime seemed certain when sophomore forward Brock Radunske took a cross-ice feed from junior defenseman Joe Markusen and slid it past the goalie with 2.7 seconds remaining on the game clock. The Spartans would not be denied.

Football—**November 9, 2002 (A):** Following a disappointing 3-6 record in the books and three games remaining on the schedule, Bobby Williams was relieved of his position as head coach on November 4 following the dismal showing in Ann Arbor. Offensive co-ordinator Morris Watts would finish the season as interim head coach. The shake-up at the top filtered down to the team as they overpowered Indiana on that next Saturday in Bloomington, 56-21. It was the largest offensive output since the 1989 team defeated Northwestern 76-19. Damon Dowdell started at quarterback for the third straight game since replacing the suspended Jeff Smoker and connected on 17-of-26 passes for 203 yards. David Richard replaced Dawan Moss, who was released from the squad following an incident after that Michigan game. David Richard gained 142 yards rushing on 20 carries. Charles Rogers continued to set records with his 24th and 25th career touchdown receptions. He also set up two other scores with end-around runs of 41 and 25 yards during a 35-point second quarter that blew the game open. Other than Rogers's two TDs, the scoring was fairly well distributed: Dowdell on an eight-yard run, Eric Knott with a one-yard pass, Jaren Hayes on a six-yard run, Jason Randall a three-yard pass and David Raynor with eight successful conversions. Thomas Wright, Ronald Stanley, Monquiz Wedlow and Mike Labinjo led the defense.

Basketball—**December 4, 2002 (H):** Chris Hill scored 22 points and Aloysius Anagonye added 10 points and nine rebounds as number 21 Michigan State defeated number 22 University of Virginia 82-75 as part of the Big Ten-Atlantic Coast Conference Challenge. Holding the Cavaliers scoreless for more than six minutes, the Spartans took control of the game with a 17-0 run, making the score, 33-19 with 4:19 remaining before intermission. Thereafter, State led by 11 points at halftime and was up 59-41 midway through the second half. The closest that Virginia came was within seven points during the final minute of play. In addition to Hill and Anagonye, Alan Anderson scored 15, Kelvin Torbert 11, Paul Davis nine and Adam Ballinger seven.

Basketball—**December 14, 2002 (A):** Tim Bograkos, a defensive specialist, was the surprise hero in the 71-67 victory over number 12 Kentucky. As Coach Izzo would later joke, "He [Bograkos] was the sixth option out of our five guys." Left alone when the Wildcat defense opted to double-team Chris Hill, Bograkos, the sophomore guard, sank one from beyond the arc to take the lead 69-67 with 49.2 seconds remaining. After the Wildcats failed to answer on a three-pointer with 21 seconds remaining, Hill was fouled seven seconds later and made both free throws to seal the victory. The Indianapolis sophomore would lead the team in scoring with 16 points, freshman Paul Davis had 13 and Alan Anderson 10.

Swimming and Diving—**December 19, 2002 (A):** As part of the team's extensive training trip to California during the holiday break, the Spartans met and defeated the University of California-Irvine in a dual meet, 130-94. Six swimmers won eight events. Joe Brennan, whose home is in nearby Poway, Calif., captured the 200-yard freestyle (1:43.37) and the 500-yard freestyle (4:39.92); Ian Clutten, the freshman from Capetown, South Africa, won the 200-yard individual medley (1:55.80) and the 100-yard breaststroke (57.65). David Sloan captured the 100-yard butterfly (51.40) and Rudolf Wagenaar, also from South Africa, finished first in the 100-yard backstroke (53.00). Both divers, Nick Visscher and Justin Laskowski, achieved scores in the competition that qualified them for the NCAA regional championship.

Swimming and Diving—**January 18, 2003 (H):** Led by 1-2-3 sweeps in both diving events, MSU defeated the 16th-ranked Purdue Boilermakers, 131-112. The winners at the diving end of the natatorium were Justin Laskowski, who scored 299.32 points to win the one-meter, followed by Nick Visscher in second and

Patrick Sheahan-Stahl in third. The trio teamed up the same way in the three-meter event with Laskowski scoring 259.05. Senior Joe Brennan won two swimming events, the 200-yard freestyle (1:40.78) and the 500-yard freestyle (4:32.47). Other Spartan winners were Patrick Saucedo in the 50-yard freestyle (21.72) and Nick DeFauw in the 100-yard freestyle (46.99). In addition to the divers' grand slam, wins in both relays also contributed to the victory. In the opening event, the 200-yard medley relay team of Karl Sunryd, Ian Clutten, David Sloan and DeFauw won in a time of 1:31.85. In the final event, the 200-yard freestyle relay, the foursome of Joel Hageman, Mike Rigali, Saucedo and DeFauw touched out the Boilermakers, 1:24.70 to 1:24.77.

Basketball—**February 2, 2003 (H):** Although Michigan State eventually prevailed 68-65, if statistics were kept on how slow a team gets started, this could have been a team record. The University of Illinois led 15-2 six minutes into the game as the Spartans missed five of their first six shots and committed six turnovers. Finally awakening, they went on a 11-3 run to close the gap, but still trailed by 14 with two minutes left in the first half. From there, another spurt, including Alan Anderson's buzzer beating three-pointer cut the deficit to 40-34. This made the possibility of a second-half comeback much more manageable. MSU took its first lead at 45-44 on Maurice Ager's three-pointer with 14.27 remaining. Five lead changes and two ties were included over the next eight-plus minutes. Chris Hill's three-pointer with 59 seconds left put State ahead 68-64 and essentially sealed the victory. Assisting in the comeback was the fact that Illinois shot only 33.3 percent in the second half, after making 53.6 percent in the opening 20 minutes. Scoring leaders were freshman Paul Davis with 15, Anderson with 15 and Kelvin Torbert 11.

Wrestling—**February 7, 2003 (H):** The 14th-ranked Spartans shocked the wrestling world by defeating second-ranked Iowa on a tie-breaker. After wrestling to a 19-19 team score, State was declared the winner on what is defined as criteria B, which awards victory to the team with the most falls. It so happened that Arsen Aleksanyan (165 pounds) had recorded the only pin of the meet at 6:17 in the sixth match of the evening. Nick Simmons (125 pounds) began the meet by shutting out the 2002 NCAA runner-up by a major decision, 11-0. Ryan L'Amoreaux (141 pounds) held off the nation's 15th-ranked and Big Ten champion by a 9-3 count. Following Karl Nadosky's (149 pounds) disappointing loss in over-

time, fifth-ranked Gray Maynard (157 pounds) defeated the eighth-ranked Hawkeye, 15-11. State pushed the team lead to 16-7 on Aleksanyan's surprising fall. From there State held on as Nik Fekete (197 pounds) managed the only MSU win (8-6) in the final four matches.

Wrestling—February 9, 2003 (H): Before a crowd of more than 3,100 in a jam-packed Jenison Fieldhouse, the Spartans responded by nipping seventh-ranked Michigan, 16-15 in an exciting finish. State was leading 13-12 with two matches remaining when the sixth-ranked Gray Maynard (157 pounds), the Las Vegas, Nev., senior, took on the Wolverine, who had been a high school teammate of Gray. With the match forced into overtime and urged on by the partisan crowd, Maynard escaped with 14 seconds remaining in the last OT for a 5-4 win. With the Spartans then leading 16-12, it was up to Arsen Aleksanyan (165 pounds) to hang on and avoid a pin or major decision. In what other sport can a full house wildly cheer a loss (without a pin)? That's exactly what happened when the Santa Ana, Calif., senior hung on for a manageable 5-0 loss, thus surrendering only three team points as the final score continued to favor of MSU, 16-15. There were four other winners for Michigan State. Rashad Evans (174 pounds) opened the afternoon with a 6-1 victory and two matches later Nicholas Fekete (197 pounds) won a key match 7-3 over an opponent who had defeated him six weeks earlier at the Midlands championships. MSU stretched its lead to 10-3 as heavyweight Mike Keenan upset his ninth-ranked opponent in a major decision, 11-3. After losses at 125 pounds and 133 pounds, Ryan L'Amoreaux (141 pounds) put State back on track with a close 9-8 win, while a loss at 157 pounds set up the thrilling finish.

Hockey—February 15, 2003 (H): John-Michael Liles had two goals as Corey Potter, Jim Slater and Brian Mahoney scored one each to defeat the eighth-ranked University of Michigan, 5-3. Liles was the first to score and he did so after only 48 seconds of the second period on a long flip shot from the right point. At 3:25, on his very next shift, Liles made it 2-0, beating the goalie on the glove side. Four minutes later, the U of M got on the board and the period concluded with Michigan State leading 2-1. Slater opened the final stanza by scoring on a deflection of Liles's shot from the left point at 2:20 and Potter made it 4-1 on a shot from the blue line with 11:33 remaining. The "S" fans among the 7,113 had little time to rejoice as the Wolverines finally came alive, scoring

back-to-back goals within 20 seconds of each other. From there, every rush down the ice became a heart-thumping experience for players, coaches and fans, especially during the final two minutes when Michigan pulled their goalie for an added attacker. The suspense ended when State won a face-off and Brian Maloney raced down the ice and scored an empty-netter from the offensive blue line.

Baseball—February 28, 2003 (N): Bryan Gale pitched a one-run complete game, while striking out seven, as the Spartans upset number 20 North Carolina, 3-1, in the Baseball at the Beach Tournament at Myrtle Beach, S.C. State scored all of their runs in the second inning when Travis Gulick opened with a single. He advanced to second when James Moreno was hit by a pitch. The next batter, Brett Wattles followed with a single to score Gulick. Jim Deliz's sacrifice fly scored Moreno and then Charlie Braun drove in Wattles with the final run of the inning. The Tar Heels scored their one run in the fourth and then continued to threaten thereafter. Finally, in the ninth, with the tying runners on base with one out, Gale got a pop out and a fly out for the win.

Hockey—February 28, 2003 (A): Coach Comley's team connected with what he called some "funky" goals as MSU gained a rare shutout at the Yost Ice Arena in Ann Arbor, 4-0. Joe Markusen opened the scoring on a wrist shot at 8:02 of the first period with assists from Corey Potter and Mike Lelonde. The next goal, at 11:33, was initiated on a shot by Brian Maloney that handcuffed the Michigan goalie. The puck dropped to the ice and was sitting in the goal crease where Lee Falardeau tipped it in. The Wolverines had several scoring opportunities in the middle period, but goalie Matt Migliaccio responded with big saves. Meanwhile, Maloney made it 3-0 during a power-play when he poked in a rebound of John-Michael Liles's original shot at 8:46. The Spartans closed the scoring just 17 seconds into the third period on yet another power-play goal by Maloney with assists to Colton Fretter and Liles. Stopping 37 shots during the evening, Migliaccio registered his fourth career shutout, but none of the others were any bigger.

Basketball—March 8, 2003 (A): Michigan State closed the regular season on a high note, defeating Ohio State at Columbus, 72-58, for the fourth consecutive win. After leading at halftime, 36-29, the Spartans saw the Buckeyes close to within two, 45-43, with 10:12 remaining in the game. After trading baskets, the Spartans reeled

off the next eight points to gain a double-digit lead, 55-45 with 5:43 remaining. OSU was scoreless for more than four minutes, missing four shots from the field and the front end of a bonus situation; consequently, the lead never dropped below seven points again. Shooting 45 percent from the field for the season, MSU hit 63 percent (24 out of 38) against the Bucks for their best shooting performance of the season. Chris Hill was the leading scorer with 20 points, while Paul Davis added 12, Kelvin Torbert 11 and Adam Ballinger 11.

Golf—**March 24, 2002 (A):** Led by junior co-captain Eric Jorgenson, who captured the individual championship with a three-round score of 212 (74-70-68), Michigan State shot a combined score of 873 to capture the 13-team field Pepsi-Cola invitational at the Tanglewood Golf Course in Pottsboro, Texas. J.J. Beckstrom, the North Muskegon junior, finished in sixth place (73-72-74—219); senior co-captain Nathan Clark of Mason was tied for 10th (73-74-73—220); tied for 13th was junior John Koskinen of Baraga (75-76-72—223) and rounding out the squad was the Muskegon freshman Andy Ruthkowski who placed 31st (75-75-82—232). Competing unattached, Casey Lubahn was in 15th place (72-73-79—224). The MSU winning score was 23 strokes better than runners-up Minnesota and Illinois.

Tennis—**March 28, 2003 (A):** With only the Chris Mitchell-Andrew Formanczyk pair winning a set (8-5), State opened with the loss of the doubles team point, but did go on to prevail in four singles matches and defeat the University of Iowa, 4-3. The Hawkeyes did not go down easily as Mitchell lost at number two singles, 6-2, 6-1 and Cameron Marshall at number three, 5-7, 6-3, 6-2. Formanczyk finally started the Spartans down the road to victory at number one, 6-4, 6-3. He was followed by wins from Goran Topalo (Prague, Czech Republic) at number four, with a tie-breaker 7-6 and 6-4; number six Jimmy McGuire, who won in straight sets, 7-5, 6-2. The meet then hinged on the most exciting match of the afternoon. At number five, Jimmy McGuire lost the first set 6-4 and then pushed his opponent to a tie-breaker before winning 8-6 and forcing a third set. Matters looked bleak when the Columbus, Ohio, senior trailed 5-2 in the meet-deciding match, but he managed to come back, knot the score at 6-6 and then breezed through the tie-breaker to win the match as his teammates looked on in support.

Tennis—**April 2, 2003 (H):** Perhaps this would prove to be one of Michigan State's best-ever teams or perhaps time would find this to be one of the University of Michigan's least-talented teams ever. Whichever the case, nothing could temper the reality, State had defeated the U of M 5-2, for the first time since the 1994 victory during the Volunteer Tennis Classic in Knoxville, Tenn. Furthermore, it was the first home victory in the rivalry since 1967, this one played at the Indoor Tennis Facility. The drama of the afternoon unfolded early in the successful pursuit of the valued team point from the doubles matches. The number one pair of Eric Simonton and Cameron Marshall staved off numerous break points on the final service to win 8-4. At number three, Chris Mitchell and Andrew Formanczyk trailed 7-8, but forced the set to a tie-breaker and a 9-8 win. This, of course, secured the doubles team point. For good measure, the number two pair of Adam Hourani-Jimmy McGuire battled back from a 7-5 deficit to win 9-8, also on a tiebreaker. In singles competition, number two Mitchell of Ann Arbor, won in straight sets, 6-1, 6-3; however, Marshall's 6-4, 6-1 loss at number three raised the anxiety level for Coach Orlando. The team's then exchanged victories, number six Simonton winning, 6-4, 6-4 while number one Formanczyk would drop a close match, 7-6, 6-4. That was as close as the visitors would come as Goran Topalo won at number four, 7-5, 7-5 to put the team score at 4-2, guaranteeing a Spartan victory. McGuire would contribute an additional point with a hard earned 7-6, 6-4 victory at number five.

Baseball—**April 13, 2003 (A):** On six consecutive hits, capped by a bases-clearing double off the bat of Brady Burrill, the senior catcher from Newhall, Calif., Michigan State scored all of its runs in the top of the seventh to defeat Indiana 8-5. The Spartans made 10 hits in the game with Scott Koerber and Charlie Braun each collecting two. Freshman starting pitcher Jeff Gerbe earned his first collegiate win but needed help from reliever Ryan Golem who threw one and two-thirds innings to secure a save.

Baseball—**April 18, 2003 (H):** In a Friday night game at Oldsmobile Park in Lansing, junior Bryan Gale pitched the Spartans to a 12-3 victory over Michigan. With the win he raised his lifetime record against the U of M to 3-0 as he threw the complete game, scattering seven hits and striking out seven. Opening an 8-0 lead after four innings, State's eventual total of 12 runs on 13

hits was the most for MSU against the Wolverines since 1993. Every Michigan State starter notched a hit, including Scott Koerber, who went three-for-four. State scored two runs in the second, three in both the third and fourth, one in the sixth and three in the seventh. The most productive hits of the evening were the two-run single in the third by Erik Morris and Brady Burrill's double to center that scored all three runs in the fourth.

Baseball—May 2, 2003 (A): Junior right-hander Bryan Gale retired the first 16 batters he faced and only allowed two hits in seven innings as Michigan State defeated the University of Illinois, 9-3. Gale was credited with his 23rd collegiate win and moved into a three-way tie for second place on the all-time MSU win list. MSU broke the game wide open with five runs in the fourth and two in the fifth to build an 8-0 lead. Three Spartans in particular had an impressive day at the plate. Scott Koerber, the Harper Woods junior, collected three doubles; sophomore Erik Morris of Orchard Lake went three-for-five while junior James Moreno of Holt produced two hits, including his third home run of the season.

ATHLETE OF THE YEAR

Although he only performed two years as a Spartan football player before departing for the professional ranks, Charles Rogers proved to be a standout wide receiver, gaining school records and becoming Michigan State's first consensus All-American since 1989. In addition, the six-foot-four, 202-pound Saginaw native, who caught a school-record 68 passes for 1,351 yards and 13 touchdowns in 2002, was named recipient of the Bilenikoff Award, which is presented annually to college football's top receiver by the Tallahassee Quarterback Club Foundation. He was also selected as the Receiver of the Year by the Columbus (Ohio) Touchdown Club. Charles was only the second receiver in MSU history to record back-to-back 1,000-yard seasons. In 2002, Rogers led the Big Ten in receiving yards (112.6 per game) and touchdowns. He finished his career ranked among the school's all-time leaders in touchdown receptions (first with 27), receiving yards (second with 2,821), yards per catch (second at 20.9) and receptions (third with 135). He produced a school-record 12 career 100-yard receiving games, including a Spartan single-game record 270 yards versus Fresno State (10 receptions) in the 2001 Silicon Valley Football Classic.

IN THE SPARTLITE

Baseball: After opening the season at Shreveport, La., with two out of three wins against Centenary College, the Spartans went on an horrendous 3-13 pre-conference stretch reminiscent of Coach Mahan's first year as head coach in which his 1996 team began at 5-17.

Michigan State finished the season under .500, but frequently outplayed the opposition. Posting better numbers in batting average (.295-.290) and home runs (38-27), MSU produced a frustrating 3-12 record in one-run games.

Senior catcher Brady Burrill, who was selected first-team All-Big Ten, led the team in hitting with a .381 average and a .461 on-base percentage, which ranked second and fourth in the conference, respectively. Sidelined by injuries much of his career, including the final nine games of the 2003 season, the Cal State-Northridge transfer still managed to collect 172 hits, including 40 doubles. On the fielding side, Burrill was selected as the team's defensive player of the year while compiling a near-perfect .992 average. Also, he led the Big Ten with five pick-offs and gunned down 20 base runners.

Charles Rogers

Junior Bryan Gale was named the team's most valuable player and also earned All-Big Ten honors. With seven wins, an ERA of 3.48 and 95 2/3 innings pitched he led the team in all three statistical categories.

Offensively, Travis Gulick led the team in nearly every statistical category and landed himself in the top 10 in MSU single-season history for runs (60), total bases (136) and home runs (13). First baseman Scott Koerber batted .315 and accounted for 27 RBIs, even though he missed a month of action due to a broken right hand.

Before the Penn State game on May 18 two Spartan baseball numbers were retired. Honored were number one coach Danny Litwhiler, the winningest baseball coach in Michigan State history and number 36 Robin Roberts, a major league Hall of Famer who was an outstanding basketball and baseball player while a student at MSC (1945-1947).

After serving as an interim coach during the 2003 season, it was announced that Dylan Putnam (BS 2000-2002) would be hired full-time with special assignment to work with the pitchers.

Basketball: Ever since Tom Izzo directed the 2000 team to the national title, lofty goals have become a normal expectation of Spartan basketball fans. Suddenly, the less-than-Spartanlike 18-11 regular season of 2002-2003 came along. Playing without a true point guard, more losses were recorded (11) than in the preceding two seasons combined (nine). Included in that loss column were opening back-to-back setbacks at the Great Alaska Shootout; a true upset of major proportions (Toledo 76-81); a Big Ten season-opening record of 0-3 and the end of an eight-game winning streak over Michigan. This was followed by a second-round ouster from the conference postseason tournament in Chicago and actual fears of some that an invitation to the NCAA field of 64 was in jeopardy. Consequently, the eventual mini-run to the Elite Eight round at San Antonio, Texas, was an unexpected pleasure. Aided by sudden full-blossoming performances from first-year players, Maurice Ager and Erazem Lorbek, a march down the tournament trail commenced with victories over Colorado (79-76), Florida (68-46) and defending champion Maryland (60-58). Even though Texas would eventually block a trip to the Final Four (85-76), it seemed the team had been vindicated.

It is a compliment when an assistant coach is hired away from a program. In the spring of 2003, Tom Izzo's program was twice complimented. First, Brian Gregory left Breslin after four years to become the head coach at the University of Dayton. Next, it was Mike Garland who departed as he accepted the position of head coach at Cleveland State. Within two weeks after their departure, Doug Wojcik came aboard following three-years in a similar capacity at North Carolina. Two weeks after that, Dwayne Stephens, former Spartan and member of the Marquette coaching staff, returned to East Lansing as an assistant.

Once more the future seemed unsettled as a prime team member announced early departure for the professional game. This time the defector was Lorbek, the six-foot-10 freshman from Ljubljana, Slovenia.

Cross Country: The cross country team opened the season by hosting the 8K Spartan invitational, an unscored meet. Three of the top five finishers were sophomores wearing the Green and White. Chris Toloff of Novi, Mich., was second with a time of 24.45, followed by Jason Mueller of Shelby, Ohio, in fourth (25:00), and fifth place Steve Sherer from Saline, Mich. (25:13) Andrew Alley, the Canadian senior who was 17th (25:51), led 16 other Spartans to the finish line.

Collecting 239 points, the Michigan State fivesome finished seventh in the 36-team field at the pre-NCAA meet held at the Wabash Valley Sports Center in Terre Haute, Ind. Out of the 244 competitors Toloff placed fifth (24.08), Sherer was 24th (2:35.4), Mueller 47th (24:48.4), junior Andy Marsh of Grand Ledge 57th (24:51.1) and Nathan Usher of Gregory, Mich., 106th (25:19.5).

At the Big Ten championships hosted by Purdue University, Toloff was again the first Spartan to finish, placing 17th in 24:44.6. Marsh was 20th (24:47.4), Sherer, 28th (24:54.1), Mueller, 33rd (25:04.6) and Krueger, 33rd (25:04.6).

Returning to West Lafayette, Ind., for the Great Lakes regional championships, this time to an extended 10K, the squad registered 208 points for eighth out of 31 teams. The Spartans finished as follows: Toloff 13th (30:55.8), Marsh 17th (31.00.6), Mueller 45th (31:46.7), Sherer 40th (31:54.4) and Mike Thorson of Port Elgin, Ontario, 83rd (32:49.6).

The season closed back at Terre Haute, this time with the running of the 10K NCAA championships. Slipping from the 18th spot of 2001, State's runners finished in 30th spot led by Marsh for the first time. With a time of 30:40.1, he was the 41st runner across the finish line.

The remaining scorers for MSU were Toloff in 74th (31:06.6), Mueller, 149th (31:45.7), Thorson, 182nd (32:40.0) and Brian Wilson of North Branch, Mich., 200th (33:17.2).

Football: Being ranked 16th in the ESPN/*USA Today* coaches' preseason poll, few MSU seasons have ever opened with greater expectation. Supporting such positive outlook was the anticipated Jeff Smoker-Charles Rogers passing combination. Also, there was the continual reminder of the favorable schedule in which the Spartans opened with five straight home games. Reality arrived early in the campaign as that seemingly cushy schedule produced a less-than-impressive 4-2 start followed by four straight losses in which opponents racked up a total of 163 points (40.7 average per game). The final setback during that negative run, a 49-3 humiliation at Ann Arbor, contributed heavily to the eventual demise of head coach, Bobby Williams. Also chipping in to his demise was the suspension of quarterback Smoker two weeks earlier and the dismissal of senior tailback Dawan Moss after the Michigan game. Also on the Monday after that humiliating defeat in Ann Arbor, athletic director Ron Mason announced that Williams had been relieved of his coaching position and offensive coordination, Morris Watts would serve as interim head coach for the three remaining games. The season ended with an impressive 56-21 win over Indiana followed by two more losses, 45-42 to Purdue and a 61-7 thrashing by Penn State.

The 4-8 season record did not diminish the focus of attention on Charles Rogers. On the evening of the team banquet at which time he was chosen as the team's most valuable player, Rogers announced his intention to forgo his senior year and opt for a professional career in the NFL. He would eventually be selected in the draft by the Detroit Lions and as the number two overall pick.

Following the usual rumor and speculation which accompanies a coaching change, on December 19 54-year-old John L. Smith was introduced as Michigan State's 23rd head football coach. Ranking 14th among active NCAA Division I football coaches with 110 career wins, Smith's most recent stand had been five years at Louisville where he tacked a 41-21 won-loss record only to his resume.

Golf: In the U.S. Amateur Open Sectional at the Country Club of Boyne, Mich., during July 2002, Eric Jorgensen earned medalist honors by shooting a seven-under-par 137 (66-71).

The Spartans rallied on the final day of the Adams Cup in Newport, R.I., to finish second behind the University of New Mexico squad. With a composite score of 861, State was runner up and ahead of 12 other teams including the eventual Big Ten champions from Minnesota. The MSU fivesome consisted of John Koskinen (74-70-70—214) and J.J. Beckstrom (74-71-69—214), tied for fifth; Andrew Ruthkowski, tied for 19th (74-67-77—218); Eric Jorgensen, tied for 23rd (73-73-73—219) and Nathan Clark, who finished tied at 64th (74-83-73—230).

In November, Eric Jorgensen was selected to be among the elite 24 golfers to tee it up in the Western Refining College All-American Classic at the El Paso (Texas) Country Club. Although he did not finish in the top echelon, to have competed was a distinguished honor. Past winners included David Duval, Davis Love III, Jerry Pate and Tiger Woods.

In early spring action, the team finished second out of 16 at the Big Red Classic in Ocala, Fla. Koskinen, the Baraga junior who was tied for first after two rounds, settled for third (68-74-73—215). The remaining Spartan finishers were Jorgensen, ninth (70-74-73—217); freshman Andrew Ruthkowski, in a tie for 12th (72-74-73—219); Ben Fox, who tied for 18th (70-73-79—222) and Casey Lubahn, tied for 27 (75-78-71—224). Nathan Clark, who was entered unattached, shot a 218 (74-69-75).

Hosting the 36th annual Bruce Fossum/TaylorMade Invitational, the Spartans topped the leader board after two rounds, but eventually ended in fourth place with an 874 (289-286-299). Co-champions Kent State and Illinois shot scores of 864. Two strokes under par with a 214 (70-72-72), Lubahn paced the MSU team while sharing eighth place. Ruthkowski finished 12th (71-70-75—216; senior All-American Jorgensen tied for 21st place with a 222 (74-73-75); Fox tied for 45th (82-71-77—230) and Koskinen completed the team scoring (74-82-89—245).

The 2003 Big Ten championships were played on the par 71, 6,942-yard Indiana University course. The Spartans, who entered the final round in fifth place, shot a 299 and dropped back to seventh (286-290-293-299). Jorgensen (73-70-72-74) and Lubahn (68-74-70-77) tied for 13th with 289s. They were followed by Fox who tied for 18th (71-75-75-71—292); Ruthkowski in a tie for 37th (74-72-76-77—299) and Beckstrom who shot a 325 (81-74-76-84).

Moving on to the more competitive NCAA regional at Manhattan, Kan., Jorgenesen completed a rather mediocre senior year with a career-best final round of 66 which landed him in a four-way tie for eighth place. He had begun the last day in 33rd place with rounds of 73 and 72. The remainder of the MSU entries scored as follows: Lubahn 222 for a tie at 67th, Ruthkowski 223, tying for 77th, Fox 226, tied for 102nd and Koskinen, who played three atypical rounds of 86-84-82 for a 252 finished at 140th.

Hockey: It was not easy to get used to. After 23 years, Ron Mason was missing from behind the Michigan State bench. During the season the new athletic director could be seen entering Munn Arena through one of the concourse doors minutes before game time like any regular paying customer.

In both preseason polls, the CCHA Media Poll and the CCHA Coaches Poll, Rick Comley's Michigan State team was selected to finish in second place.

In the annual College Showcase weekend, State settled for a 5-5 overtime tie at Minneapolis against the Gophers, eventual NCAA champions. Moving on to Madison for yet another OT game on Saturday night, senior defenseman John-Michael Liles was the hero as he scored at the 3:50 mark of the extra stanza to give the Spartans a 2-1 victory over the Badgers of Wisconsin.

Sophomore defenseman Duncan Keith naively made a horrendous blunder during the Christmas break. While home in British Columbia for the holidays, he signed what proved to be a professional contract to play with a major junior team. Having a change of heart he decided to return to school, but it was too late. NCAA regulations stipulate that a student-athlete cannot sign a contract with a team defined as professional.

Although the overall record for the 2002-03 team was a respectable 23-14-2, the usual anticipated highlight wins were missing. With an opening 6-2 loss to Boston University at the Great Lakes Invitational, a 6-2 win in the consolation game was little comfort. In the CCHA playoffs, the Spartans did dispense with Alaska-Fairbanks in the first round, Northern Michigan ended the Michigan State season five days later in the quarterfinals, 7-5. For the first time since 1993, MSU would not be a participant in the NCAA tournament.

In postseason honors, three Spartans were voted to the CCHA All-Conference first team: sophomore forward Jim Slater and senior defensemen Brad Fast and John-Michael Liles.

In late March, a coaching change was announced. David McAuliffe, an assistant for 11 years, was not resigned as an assistant. He was replaced by Brian Renfrew, former Western Michigan goalie who had been Coach Comley's assistant at Northern for two years.

Soccer: Two of the most poignant wins of the fall came in the Indiana-Purdue Ft. Wayne Showcase, classified as prseason exhibition games. In the weekend opener 22nd-ranked Michigan State defeated fourth-ranked University of Virginia 4-3 as Thomas Trivelloni scored the eventual game-winner at 37:00. On the next afternoon, MSU topped 27th-ranked Kentucky, 3-1 with a pair of goals by Craig Hearn and one from John Minagawa-Webster.

The first loss of the season, 3-2, was administered by California-Santa Barbara. After Kellen Kalso tied the game 2-2 on a penalty kick in the 79th minute, the Gauchos scored the winning goal 27 minutes later in the second overtime.

Play became rough in the final 15 minutes of the 2-1 loss to Wisconsin as six yellow cards were handed out and two players ejected, one Badger and one Spartan (Scott Babinski).

In the opening game of the Big Ten postseason playoff at State College, Pa., Michigan State was matched against Ohio State. With the score knotted at 2-2 and just under four minutes of regulation time remaining, Jordan Gruber would score the winning goal as he beat the Buckeye goalkeeper with a shot that sailed into the upper corner at the 86.39 mark. Derek Ornekian and Jeff Krass were credited with assists. The first half had ended 1-1 as each team scored into their own goal on misdirected clearing shots. MSU would regain the lead in the 57th minute when Brett Konley scored his ninth goal of the season, unassisted. The victory put the Spartans into the semi-final game against Michigan where they couldn't find the scoring touch and the season ended 1-0.

Swimming and Diving: The Spartans joined teams representing Texas A&M, Connecticut, Buffalo and host Pittsburgh for a three-day early season tournament format and, while collecting 564 points, they placed third behind the Panthers and Aggies. Some of the more impressive Spartan performances were from: breaststroker Ian Clutten who finished second in both the 100 (55.48) and 200 (2:01.41); backstroker Rudolf Wagenaar, fifth in the 100 (52.49) and freestyler Joe Brennan, who was second in both the 200 (1:39.45) and 500 (4:32.57).

At the Big Ten championships, the 400-yard medley relay of Karl Sunryd, Clutten, David Sloan and Patrick Saucedo set a team record with a time of 3:17.57. Top individual performer was Clutten who placed fourth in 100-yard breaststroke (54.43) and eighth in the 200 (2:01.67). Also earning points for MSU were Sunryd, 10th in the 100-yard backstroke (50.04); backstroker Wagenaar, 13th in the 200 (1:49.00); Brennan 15th in the 200-yard freestyle (1:39.33) and 14th in the 500 (4:28.07). Diver Justin Laskowski placed 16th on the three-meter board.

Continuing on to the NCAA championships in Austin, Texas, Clutten swam a respectable 55.61 which placed him no higher than 31st.

Tennis: Coach Orlando had members of his squad competing in five different special tournaments during the fall. They were the Ball State Invitational at Muncie, Ind.; the ITA All-American championship; the Minnesota Invitational, the Omni Hotels ITA region IV championships and the Big Ten indoor singles championship. In the Ball State meet, no Spartan was able to reach the finals of the "A" division; but Adam Hourani emerged as winner of the consolation bracket.

Completing the spring portion of the schedule with an overall won-loss record of 15-12 and 5-2 in Big Ten play, Michigan State ended up fifth in the conference and earned a first-round bye against Purdue in the post-season tournament at Evanston, Ill. Trailing the Boilermakers 3-1, State came back to win four straight singles matches and advance to the semi-finals. Andrew Formanczyk had gained that first team point with a 6-2, 6-3 victory at number one. From there it became exciting as number four Cameron Marshall won in three sets 6-3, 1-6, 6-4 as did Goran Topalo at number three, 6-2, 5-7, 6-4. Now with the team score tied at 3-3 it all came down to the number six match. After splitting sets (6-4, 4-6) and the entire crowd watching, Eric Simonton won the deciding third match 6-3 sending the Spartans into the semifinals against Illinois. It didn't take the Illini long as they dispensed with the Spartans in four quick matches. From a ballot of coaches, Formanczyk, the Rochester Hills sophomore, was named to a spot on the 2003 All-Big Ten team.

Track and Field: Steve Manz, the junior from West Branch, Mich., was throwing his weight around during the entire indoor and outdoor seasons of 2003. Weekend after weekend he was a primary, and often solitary, representative for Michigan State in meets across the midwest. Although he would occasionally pick up a discus or the 35-pound weight, he primarily focused on the shot put. During the indoor season Steve entered five invitational meets, winning four and placing second once. With tosses ranging from 57 to 60 feet, his best throw was a third place and team record 61' 8-1/4" at the Big Ten championships in Champaign, Ill. With a 61' 2-1/4", he placed 12th at the NCAA championships in Fayetteville, Ark. Moving outdoors, Manz was third at the Sea Ray Relays in Knoxville, Tenn. (60' 11-1/2"); first in the Bronco Open at Kalamazoo (56' 9-3/4"), eighth at the legendary Drake relay in Des Moines, Iowa, (58' 6 1/2") and second in the Jesse Owens meet at Columbus, Ohio (59' 9-1/2"). He would conclude the season with a fourth in the Big Tens (56' 5-3/4") and sixth at the NCAA regionals (59' 4").

Another impressive performer was freshman pole vaulter Brad Gebauer from Bad Axe who won four meets during the year and placed fifth at the conference indoor championships. His highest vault was a winning 16' 5" at the Meyo invitational in South Bend.

Other performers of note through the season were Chris Hohn, Mark Langlois, Rob Lowe, Julien Williams, Ricco Roby, Brian Sherwood, Cleve Thorson, Jon Wojcik, Andrew Alley, Jeff Mulder, Eric Chase, Andy Lixey, Derek Strittmatter and Chris Toloff.

Managing only 11 points, State finished 10th at the Big Ten indoor meet and with nine points outdoors, another 10th place was unavoidable.

Wrestling: Gray Maynard (157 pounds) placed second and Nick Simmons (125 pounds) took third, leading MSU to a 14th-place finish at the 40th Annual Midlands Wrestling championships in Evanston, Ill.. Other Spartans who competed in this early-

Steve Manz hurled the shot put, discus and hammer for the Spartans.

season competition were Charles Sageman (157 pounds) along with heavyweights John Wechter and Henry Lossen.

At the Big Ten championships in Madison, Wis., Michigan State finished in fourth with 92.5 points. Both Maynard and Nik Fekete (197 pounds) were runners-up in their divisions as Simmons and Rashad Evans (174 pounds) each placed third. Karl Nadolsky (149 pounds) was fourth and Ryan L'Amoreaux sixth (141 pounds) with all six gaining automatic entry into the NCAA tournament. Three others lost their seven-place matches and thus just missed qualifying for the NCAAs. They were Shane Martin (133 pounds), Nathan Mesyn (174 pounds) and Wechter.

Maynard and Simmons closed the year out with seventh-place spots and All-American selections at the NCAA championships. Maynard, the Las Vegas, Nev., senior won his last career match by a 12-2 major decision. Simmons, the Williamston freshman, came back from an opening round upset and finished the weekend by pinning his Minnesota opponent in just 2:38. With 32 team points, State finished in 18th place.

Simmons, the highly-touted freshman who recorded an undefeated prep record at nearby Williamston High School and then sat out 2001-2002 as a redshirt, finished his first collegiate season with an impressive 29-12 record. He was named the Big Ten Freshman of the Year.

EXTRA! 2003 NCAA TOURNAMENT
(Regional Finals)

Michigan State reached the regional finals in the 2003 NCAA tournament. The following are the Spartans' box scores for those games.

MICHIGAN STATE 79–COLORADO 64

	FG-FGA	FT-FTA	REB	A	PF	TP
Anderson	4-9	6-6	4	7	1	14
Lorbek	8-15	0-0	5	0	3	17
Anagonye	1-3	4-4	7	1	2	6
Hill	4-10	3-4	4	2	0	15
Torbert	2-6	0-2	4	3	4	4
Johnson	0-0	2-2	2	1	0	2
Ager	2-4	1-1	4	0	2	6
Davis	3-7	4-6	3	1	4	10
Andreas	0-0	0-0	0	0	0	0
Ballinger	2-2	0-0	2	1	2	5
TOTALS	26-56	20-25	35	16	18	79

Halftime: Tie 35-35; **Three-point field goals:** 7-13 (Hill 4-9, Ballinger 1-1, Lorbek 1-1, Ager 1-2); **Officials:** Greene, Harry, Lindsay.

MICHIGAN STATE 69–FLORIDA 46

	FG-FGA	FT-FTA	REB	A	PF	PTS
Anderson	1-3	5-7	4	5	2	7
Lorbek	4-7	2-4	7	1	4	12
Anagonye	3-3	0-0	1	0	5	6
Hill	5-8	0-0	3	3	2	12
Torbert	2-8	3-4	2	4	2	7
Wolfe	0-0	0-0	0	0	0	0
Johnson	0-0	0-0	1	0	0	0
Ager	6-9	2-2	1	1	0	16
Bograkos	0-0	0-0	0	0	1	0
Davis	4-5	0-1	5	0	1	8
Andreas	0-0	0-0	0	0	1	0
Westrick	0-1	0-0	0	0	0	0
Ballinger	0-1	0-0	3	1	0	0
TOTALS	25-45	12-18	27	15	18	68

Halftime: Michigan State 31-19; **Three-point field goals:** 6-16 (Ager 2-5, Hill 2-5, Lorbek 2-5, Torbert 0-1); **Officials:** Haney, Shaw, Lindsay; **Attendance:** 21,304.

MICHIGAN STATE 60–MARYLAND 58

	FG-FGA	FT-FTA	REB	A	PF	PTS
Hill	3-14	0-0	3	5	3	8
Anderson	4-8	2-2	5	2	2	10
Torbert	1-6	0-0	2	0	1	2
Anagonye	2-4	0-0	8	0	2	4
Lorbek	1-3	2-4	1	0	5	5
Johnson	0-1	0-0	1	1	0	0
Ager	4-8	0-0	4	1	3	10
Bograkos	0-0	0-0	0	0	1	0
Davis	5-7	3-3	5	0	2	13
Andreas	0-0	0-0	1	0	0	0
Ballinger	2-5	3-3	1	1	1	8
TOTALS	22-56	10-12	31	10	20	60

Halftime: Maryland 34-31; **Three-point field goals:** 6-17 (Hill 2-7, Torbert 0-1, Lorbek 1-2, Johnson 0-1, Ager 2-4, Ballinger 1-2); **Officials:** Kitts, Edsall, Corbett; **Attendance:** 33,009.

TEXAS 85 – MICHIGAN STATE 76

	FG-FGA	FT-FTA	REB	A	PF	PTS
Chris Hill	3-7	1-2	2	3	4	10
Anderson	3-6	3-3	4	3	5	9
Torbert	3-6	0-0	3	0	4	8
Anagonye	2-3	4-5	4	2	2	8
Lorbek	6-11	1-2	9	1	3	14
Wolfe	0-0	0-0	0	0	0	0
Johnson	0-2	0-0	0	0	2	0
Ager	3-7	2-2	2	0	4	10
Bograkos	0-0	0-0	1	0	1	0
Davis	4-9	7-12	7	1	2	15
Ballinger	1-3	0-0	2	1	1	2
TOTALS	25-54	18-26	34	11	28	76

Halftime: Texas 43-38; **Three-point field goals:** 8-16 (Hill 3-6, Ager 2-3, Torbert 2-3, Lorbek 1-2, Ballinger 0-1, Johnson 0-1); **Officials:** Boudreaux, Hicks, Stuart; **Attendance:** 30,169.

ATHLETIC VENUES

Below is a comparison of costs for buildings that have served the intercollegiate athletic program, current and past:

Structure	Year Opened	Total Cost	Per Sq. Ft.
The Armory	1886	$6,197	$1.15
Circle IM	1916	$229,000	$2.91
Dem Hall	1928	$355,000	$4.09
Jenison	1940	$1,025,000	$5.09
Circle IM (add.)	1958	$2,305,076	$22.74
IM West	1958	$3,212,508	$13.78
Munn Ice Arena	1974	$3,581,700	$28.27
Daugherty Bldg.	1980	$1,429,925	$57.77
Daugherty (add.)	1985	$2,807,141	$29.23
Tennis Center	1985	$1,711,894	$24.48
Breslin Center	1989	$37,475,716	$142.54
C. Smith Center	1999	$6,200,000	$200.00

As established earlier, baseball was the first organized sport on the campus of the Agricultural College of Michigan. With that, the question arises: where did these nearly forgotten pioneers of sport play their games? Recalling from his youth, Frank S. Kedzie offered an answer in William Beal's 1915 publication, *History of the Michigan Agricultural College:*

> "The home plate has traveled a good deal, being located back in the 1870s just north of Williams, then east to where the library stands, then north to Howard Terrace, thence westward to the drill ground."

A 21st century translation would read:

> "The home plate has traveled a good deal, being located back in the 1870s just north of the museum, then east to where Linton Hall stands, then north to the parking lot between the Human Ecology Building and Morrill Hall, thence westward to Walter Adams Field between the Circle IM Building and Landon Hall."

As recognized in the opening chapter, it was at that final site, initially known as the parade grounds, where MSU's athletic program was really born in 1884. Few of today's students or faculty, scurrying to the demands of their daily schedules, will cross that plat between the Spartan statue and the Union Building knowing of the historic ground on which they tread. This patch of ground was officially named Walter Adams Field in the fall of 1999 to honor the venerable economics professor, MSU's 13th president and the marching band's number one fan.

Although it is not certain which baseball game could be identified as the inaugural game on the parade grounds layout, it seems certain the games of the first "official" school team in 1884 were played there. For historic note, likely from overuse, the diamond infield was "skinned" prior to the 1890 season.

In August of 1891, a quarter-mile running track was planned to circumscribe that baseball-football ground. This addition to the multi-complex layout on the parade grounds was a necessity for MAC to host the MIAA Field

The Armory

Days of 1892. The estimated cost for the undertaking was to be $95 with this expense incurred by the students. Grading the layout would take place in the fall of 1891 and in the following spring a coating of cinders would be laid down. Upon completion, there was a 140-yard straightaway on the east side, but the oval would end up being one-fifth rather than one-quarter of a mile in distance. Space limitation likely necessitated this alteration.

A plan to erect a permanent grandstand along the east side of the running track was originally rejected by the school's governing board. At a follow-up meeting they did somewhat relent by authorizing the placement of temporary bleachers to accommodate spectators for the pending Field Day.

Located at the site of today's Music Building, the Assembly Hall (The Armory's original name) was built for a cost of $6,197.85 and opened in early 1886. Although by today's standards this was an indisputable "bargain," the Armory was truly an example of basic construction. The floor space, 60 feet by 90 feet, was bare ground dressed with a composition of coal tar and gravel that created a nasty odor. To no surprise, when ladies would attend lectures, orations, commencements or athletic events, those stylish long dresses of the period would become badly soiled. However, this would not be a problem at the 1892 field day, for in the preceding year a beautiful maple floor had been installed over the gravel. Temporary electrical lighting was also in place for the occasion, as 35 incandescent lamps were arranged in a large circle over the center of the room.

From Madison Kuhn's *The First Hundred Years:*

"In the armory, students found the opportunities for physical training for which they had long asked. Another change for the better, Lt. W.L. Simpson, who had been a student here before entering West Point, began in 1888 to equip the rooms with parallel and horizontal bars, a trapeze, rings, ladders, dumb bells, and Indian clubs. He conducted voluntary classes in physical culture along with his ROTC duties."

Ray Stannard Baker wrote for *The Speculum:*

"On the afternoon of any day large classes of students in flannel jackets, white knickerbockers, and long black stockings may be seen tumbling, jumping, climbing, or wildly swinging on bars or rings in the pursuit of athletic renown."

By 1902 the apparatus inventory included a leather horse, mats, high jump standards, and an outfit for measuring and examining.

The Armory was also the original site for the intercollegiate basketball program. The sport was introduced there in 1899 and home games continued in that building until the opening of the gymnasium (Circle IM) in the winter of 1918. The layout held a truly "home court" advantage. The baskets and backboards were attached flush to the brick walls and the overhead steel girders were so low that visiting marksmen were baffled at shooting through or around the obstacles. Accustomed to these obstructions, clever MAC players became adept at arching long shots between the beams. Robert "Red" Dickson, (BK '06-09) also perfected a trick shot that was the joy of the home crowd and a headache for the enemy. As reported in *The M.S.C. Record,* he overcame his lack of stature by being able to scramble up the steam pipes, beneath the basket at each end, and dump the ball into the basket. Dickson could therefore be considered the school's first "dunk-shot" artist.

In the Armory's last season of use for basketball (1918), the baskets were moved from the sides to the ends of the room. With this layout, the interfering girders paralleled the base lines; thus, being less of a hindrance when making close-up carom shots off the backboard. Of course, with this new configuration, making long shots became a real challenge.

As for spectator space, beyond a fire marshal's worst nightmare, as many as 850 could be packed inside the Armory in amphitheater style when a function called for no more than a 30-foot square.

In his year-end summary dated June 30, 1902, president Jonathan Snyder reported that with 275 young men living on campus, in addition to 100 others living near the college grounds, a new bathhouse was urgently needed.

At an expense of $600, the original bathhouse had been erected in 1889 between the river and the future

The Bathhouse

site of Olds Hall. Consisting of a mere 10 zinc tubs, the structure was proven to be inadequate. Conceivably, the line of waiting men on a Saturday evening likely grew long enough that late bathers often settled for the old-fashioned way, a plunge in the Red Cedar River.

Within 30 days of President Snyder's 1902 year-end fiscal report, construction was underway on a $11,181.84 attachment to the north end of the Armory. This structure would house a Liliputian 11 2/3 yards by 5 1/3 yards swimming pool with 14 showers on the deck. Also included was a rubbing room, lounging room, a locker room (an added expense of $264.50 for the 278 lockers) and the area's first barber shop. The new addition opened in November of 1903 and served the continually burgeoning enrollment for the next 15 years.

With the space limitations of the parade grounds, coupled with the administration's resistance to installing bleachers there, it is understandable why the sports aficionados of the time likely gazed longingly across the Red Cedar and had visions for the spacious grounds we now call Old College Field. There were two major problems though. At that time the College did not own the 13 acres along the south edge of the river; secondly, there was not a bridge near this location yet.

MAC did, however, hold title to a 13-acre piece of property referred to as the Delta. This triangular parcel across from the current campus ran west from the Abbott Street entrance between Michigan and Grand River Avenues. Not fitting into the projected plan for the school's growth, it became available and was consequently sold in 1900 to a developer. Money gained in the transaction was immediately put to use for purchase of the land south of the river at a price of $1,137.50 ($87.50 per acre).

Having completed this acquisition, another $516.50 was appropriated for the construction of a bridge to cross the Red Cedar. Located in approximately the same spot as today's bridge at the Spartan statue, the crossing rested on six timbers sunk 14 feet below the river bottom. The wooden structure was 14 feet wide and 85 feet long. With the opening of the bridge in April of 1902, the package was complete and it would serve admirably until the spring of 1926 when it was dynamited to release ice that was backing up a major flood. By then, the concrete structure of today was in place.

Even with what seemed to be an unlimited space for development on the newly purchased acreage, the planners of the sprouting athletic field were again content to weave three venues (track and field, football, and baseball) into one. Thus, the problems of multiple use at the old field would be inherent once more.

The baseball diamond was established at the very site where the sport was played for the next century. Clay was put on the base paths in sufficient quantity to make it fast and the outfield area was well seeded. The football field would run north and south, the south end covering the diamond and the north end the outfield. The quarter-mile cinder running track enclosed both the baseball diamond and the football field and featured a 120-yard straightaway.

The covered stands at College Field

No immediate funds were available to construct seating for spectators at the new field. In fact, the home football games of 1902 (Detroit, Hillsdale, Michigan freshmen, DePauw, and Alma) were played with only a few temporary bleachers along the sideline. The Board of Agriculture offered $200 toward a quoted need of $815 for the construction of a permanent section along the third base line. At a meeting of student leaders on April 16, 1903, a yearlong campaign was a success as more than $600 had been raised. Within three weeks, covered stands measuring 60 feet by 40 feet were made ready to accommodate 600 spectators. The stands were first put to use on May 7 for the DePauw baseball game, the fifth home game of that season.

Erection of additional seating at the field was as follows:

The football bleachers on the south sideline (partially shown adjacent to the covered stands in the picture

above) added 600 seats to the capacity when completed in 1908, at a total expense of $600.

The stands facing the first base line, adding another 600 seats for $600, were constructed during the spring break of 1910 and made available that March.

An additional 1,400 bleacher seats on the north side of the football field were in use in the fall of 1914. With temporary bleachers in the west end zone, the capacity for football reached 7,000.

––––––––––––

From 1907, and in relentless convention thereafter, Chester Brewer and those who succeeded him would appeal for the need of a new gymnasium in their annual reports. Finally, in 1915, approval was secured and bids were taken for the construction of a new building to be erected across from the Armory to be known as (based on one's generation) the Gymnasium, the Women's Gymnasium, or Sports Circle IM.

On November 8, 1915, a Grand Rapids firm was awarded the contract. The original bid was $150,000 (final cost: $229,000) with a projected completion date of May 25, 1917. As is often the case, there would be construction delays and added costs. First, the architects had to contend with the problem of laying a solid foundation upon the ground, which bordered along the Red Cedar River. The original plan for a foundation of the ordinary type was abandoned and bedrock was sought. Secondly, the timing was unfortunate. Europe was at war and the United States would enter the fracas in April of 1917. Shortages of material and predictable periodic lags became commonplace.

The cornerstone was eventually laid with accompanying speeches on the afternoon of Tuesday, October 10, 1916. Sixteen months later on Thursday, February 21, 1918, the first official function, the junior prom, was held. The inaugural athletic event, a 35-20 basketball win over Oberlin, would take place two days later, with the formal dedication taking place on May 22, 1918, three days short of a one-year delay from the contracted date for completion. As for spectators, four rows of chairs lined each sideline with temporary bleachers erected along both baselines. By the 1920-1921 season, a short tier of bleachers replaced the folding chairs along the sidelines. These additional seats raised the spectator capacity for basketball to 3,200.

The new facilities answered every concern expressed in the preceding years. The gymnasium floor measured 165 feet by 75 feet with an open girder ceiling that rose two stories (no more basketball trick shots through the rafters). Circling the room from above was a 110-yard cork-surfaced running track that would provide facilities for hosting indoor meets.

There was a trophy room and other special rooms set-aside for boxing, wrestling, fencing, the varsity club, and the band along with 1,000 lockers and 20 showers in the basement area. The swimming pool, at 90 feet by 30 feet, was reputed to be the largest in the Midwest. The fact that it had been constructed 15 feet longer than a standard competitive pool didn't seem to matter, it would serve the campus community for 65 years. A defective filtering system led to closing the pool in 1983, and today the empty shell remains waiting to serve the university in perhaps a different role.

The new structure welcomed three additional intercollegiate sports onto the scene: fencing, swimming, and wrestling. Also, women would take a more active role with an extensive intramural program to include basketball, tennis, field hockey, track and field and swimming and diving. A separate shower room, dressing room, and lounging room had been installed for the needs of the co-eds. The 1921 year-end report recorded that the women had use of the gymnasium and swimming pool from 8:00 to 12:00 in the morning, leaving the entire afternoon and evening free for activities of the men.

With the opening of the Gymnasium Building, the armory and bathhouse began falling into disuse. By 1938, the faculty-staff directory identified the school photographer, W.E. Laycock, and his assistant as the sole tenants in the nearly abandoned facility. In that year, plans were formalized for constructing the new Music Building, and the site that was selected doomed the armory and bathhouse. The story of its demolition was chronicled in the *M.S.C. Record* of February, 1939:

> "On Monday, December 13, 1938, wreckers razed the structure that for many decades had been a pivotal point for men on the campus. Walls toppled over, floors were ripped out, pillars which once adorned the swimming pool pointed to the open sky."

In the immediate years following the opening of the Gymnasium there were complaints of it being overcrowded. There were good reasons: enrollment was increasing; physical education had become required for freshmen and sophomores, a four-year athletic coaching course was begun in 1927, an increasing number of students were taking part in an expanded intramural pro-

gram, and, in lieu of an auditorium, the gymnasium was being used for more and more non-athletic functions.

In 1926 the State Legislature was solicited for appropriations of $500,000 to expand the facilities of the building. For the next 10 years this request would annually surface, with little sympathy procreated. When an expansion was finally deemed necessary and funds had been secured it was 1958 and the cost would be a whopping $2,305,076.

Macklin Field

As new structures were incorporated into the athletic program, (Demonstration Hall and Jenison Fieldhouse), the women inherited the men's portion of the Gymnasium and it took on a new name: the Women's Intramural Building. Then in 1978, amidst a penchant for a co-recreational environment, it was *déjà vu* as once again the old building served both men and women. In this capacity it would be renamed one more time with the title of today, IM Sports Circle.

———————————

Prior to becoming Michigan State's ninth president (1921-1923), David Friday had served as a budget expert to Michigan's governor Alex J. Groesbeck. Perhaps it was this contact that ensured the support of the governor when in 1923 a push was made for a new football stadium. In that year, on Governor Groesbeck's recommendation, the legislature approved a grant of $160,000 for the project with repayment to be made from game receipts for a 10-year period. The proposal was predicated on the expecta-

tion that a new stadium would result in a more impressive home football schedule and enhanced revenue possibilities.

Three locations were initially considered for the structure, two south of the river and a third facing Grand River at the site of today's Berkey Hall and environs. The eventual choice was on a portion of the 325-acre Woodbury farm (south of the river and east of College Field) that had been purchased in 1914.

As described by Madison Kuhn in his *The First Hundred Years:*

> "A fifteen thousand seat, open-end, concrete structure with an excellent running track circling the gridiron, rose on the dry sandy ridge where Gunson had planted pine trees and the faculty had played golf. It was the scene of the 1923 home games (Lake Forest, Albion, Ohio Wesleyan, and Creighton), although it was not dedicated until Michigan came in 1924 for its only football visit between 1914 and 1948."

Also, in 1924, in anticipation of increased football traffic, a new concrete bridge was opened, connecting the athletic facilities to West Circle Drive.

A series of expansions eventually enlarged the stadium to a listed capacity of 76,000. The first came in 1935, the year the stadium was officially named for the former coach, (John F.) Macklin Field. The project was contracted through the Works Progress Administration (WPA), a federal agency propagated by the Great Depression and contrived to create jobs for the thousands of unemployed workers. By design, steam-powered, earth-moving equipment sat idly by as a swarm of men were put to work with hand shovels, lowering the field eight feet. Eleven new rows of seats were inserted completely around the stadium where the quarter-mile running track had been. With this, the seating capacity rose to 22,674 (29,000 with temporary end zone bleachers). Dirt from the excavation was transported across the bridge and used to raise the riverbank beyond Beal Gardens. Thanks to the generous funding ($126,000) of the WPA, the school's financial outlay was a mere $4,000, or three percent of the total cost. The project included the press box and scoreboard.

At a cost of $1,432,574, an enlargement in 1948 boosted the seating to 51,000. This expansion involved enclosing the end zones as they are today and raising the sideline stands from 34 rows to the present 66 rows. Another $397,347 was disbursed in 1956 to add 9,000 seats

for a capacity of 60,000. One year and $1,805,317 later, the upper decks were attached to the east and west stands, bringing the capacity to 76,000.

The original switch from natural grass to artificial turf came in time for the 1969 football season and it lasted until 1973. The second carpet was in use from 1974 through the 1982 season. A third synthetic surface, Astroturf, was installed in the summer of 1983 at a cost of $548,000. Its replacement, also Astroturf, was included in the $4,400,000 major refurbishing of 1994.

Analogous to the original expansion move of 1935, the playing surface was again lowered by six feet in the 1994 renovation. But unlike one-half century earlier, the seating capacity would be decreased (by 4,000 seats), not increased. The rationale for this second excavation was to enhance the viewing from the lower area. Additionally, between the 20-yard lines, the first 10 rows were compacted into seven rows creating a choice area, labeled the "stadium club." This VIP section of 1,200 would have wider aisles, more legroom, and seats with contoured backs and armrests. Following this 1994 refurbishing, the new capacity was reported at 72,027.

The project of returning the stadium to natural grass began on May 25, 2001 when seed was planted into 4,800 separate modules at the Hancock Turfgrass Research Center on the campus south of Jolly Road. Meanwhile, the Hausman Company of Lansing was contracted at a cost of $650,000 to prepare the stadium floor. In the spring of 2002 they removed the artificial surface, installed drainage and irrigation systems, laid a new foundation of asphalt and placed a rubber walkway around the perimeter of the field. In early summer of 2002, the modules were hauled to the stadium and like a jigsaw puzzle slid into place. Within one week the transformation was complete. The total cost for this unique field would be $2,000,000.

Although still in the planning stage, the future possibility of club seats and luxury suites in a high-rise west of the stadium seemed a definite possibility when, in February of 2003, the MSU Board of Trustees voted unanimously to appoint a construction manager for the project. Plans called that the accommodations would be fully pledged before construction began. With completion charted in time for the 2005 football season, first estimates suggest donations would range from $4,000 to $5,000 annually for a club seat, and $45,000 to $80,000 annually for a suite.

When football and track and field moved into the concrete stadium in 1923, baseball became "king of the scene" at College Field. By then all of the bleachers were worn and in disrepair. Those parallel to the first base line were removed in the spring of 1926. In that same year pranksters following the May 24 baseball victory over Michigan incinerated the north sideline football bleachers that protruded into center field and were a hindrance to baseball. Finally, the landmark covered stands on the third base line were completely dismantled during the spring of 1930.

New seating replaced the old seats, a permanent fence surrounded the outfield in 1949, and in 1965, at a cost of $13,608, the MSU physical plant constructed the restroom and storage behind the backstop. At a meeting of the school's Board of Trustees on Friday, March 21, 1969, the diamond was named in honor of the veteran coach, John Kobs, who had died on January 26, 1968.

Today, while it continues as the home grounds for baseball, the entire Old College Field plot remains flexible as it also serves men's and women's soccer, and women's softball. Three new scoreboards, serving all of these sports, were installed in 1995. Lost and almost forgotten is the golf chipping green that once proudly adorned the west point at the turn of the river.

Since the opening of Lansing's Oldsmobile Park in the spring of 1996, the Michigan State varsity has been a part-time tenant. Home of the Lansing Lugnuts of the Class A professional Midwest League, each subsequent year MSU has managed to schedule from 10 to 12 of their spring games at this state-of-the-art facility located on Michigan Avenue in Lansing. Actually, the Spartans inaugurated the park in a game against the University of Michigan on April 3, 1996, before a sellout crowd of 7,000. The first win at Olds Park for State came in the finals series of the 1997 season when they took three out of four from the Iowa Hawkeyes on May 9 through May 11.

In 1924 the State Legislature approved funds for the construction of a new armory. Although work did not begin immediately after approval, erection of Demonstration (Dem) Hall, the first major enclosed building south of the river, eventually commenced and proceeded with little delay. It was dedicated and first used on Friday, May 13, 1927, during a weekend celebrating the 70th birthday of the college (Founders' Day). Soon thereafter, the R.O.T.C. units moved into the offices, classrooms, and cavalry-riding arena.

The riding hall portion of the structure had interior dimensions of 215 feet by 100 feet, which was boasted to be five feet longer than the famed Madison Square Garden of New York City. The capacity of the permanent seats was 4,500 and when the arena was used for special purposes it could be made to accommodate nearly 9,500 by arranging seats on the dirt floor. A separate gymnasium on the north side was largely designed for social functions and a basement shooting gallery would motivate the organization of a school rifle team.

The state legislature bill that provided appropriations for the new armory read: "to be used for the demonstration of agricultural stock and implements, for college athletics, and the housing of the military department." Consequently, the athletic department was legitimately in the picture when the doors opened in the spring of 1927. Nonetheless, there was no immediate thrust for basketball to leave the confines of the Gymnasium, since they had just completed only their ninth season there.

Perhaps it was the winning ways of the Spartan cagers over the next two years that gave impetus to moving across the river. In Ben VanAlstyne's second year as head coach, the 1927-1928 squad went 11-4 to post the best MSC record since 1912. This was followed by an 11-5 season and suddenly spectators were "hanging from the rafters" in the Gymnasium. Furthermore, the playing surface was supposedly not a regulation size, providing many nationally prominent teams an excuse for rejecting offers to play MSC in East Lansing.

Demonstration (Dem) Hall would hold the answer, but a portable floor would be needed. Construction began only after careful study of five other college fieldhouse floors: the University of Michigan, Xavier in Cincinnati, Notre Dame, Hillsdale, and Northwestern at Evanston, Ill.

The H.G. Christman Company of Lansing installed the floor at a cost of $8,500. The court was 60 feet by 110 feet in size and made up of 96 removable sections, 80 pieces 7 1/2 feet by 10 feet and 16 pieces 7 1/2 feet by 5 feet. A three-foot high netting circumscribed the entire surface that sat on 120 concrete footings and rose two feet above the tan bark floor of the riding hall. End to end it was positioned in the middle of the hall and about five feet from the north wall. The facility included a large scoreboard, a press box, and a band platform. The lights, wired for an expense of $300, gave the playing area the appearance of a modern boxing ring.

As for basketball seating, to the 15 rows of permanent stands on the south side and west end another 1,500 could be accommodated on bleachers set up on the south side of the arena floor. The total capacity was then listed as 6,000, nearly doubling the Gymnasium space.

Although the first basketball game played in Demonstration Hall was against Syracuse on January 1, 1930, the dedication game was played six weeks later on February 15, a thrilling 27-26 win over Michigan before 5,667 fans.

A sharing agreement with the military department permitted use of the arena only through February 15 of each year. Thereafter the floor was disassembled and stored, the ROTC cadets marched in, and Ben VanAlstyne's squad hit the road.

It eventually became clear, even as basketball and occasionally football, baseball, and tennis gained use of the arena, intercollegiate athletics were mere tenants in this facility. A new athletic fieldhouse would be needed.

Plans for a new running track were necessitated when the oval was removed from the stadium during the expansion of 1935. Although revised federal guidelines for federally funded projects would now expect recipients to shoulder 40 percent of construction costs, the college again looked to Washington for the benevolent offerings of the Works Progress Administration (WPA).

Work began the following spring (1936) on what is today labeled Ralph Young Field and the formal dedication came one year later, April 17, 1937, with a track meet against the University of Chicago. Adequate funds also made it possible to construct the tennis courts that were laid out between Dem Hall and the stadium.

In December of 2001 the MSU Board of Trustees approved the $2,800,000 renovation of this outdoor track layout. Demolition of the old facility was completed in February of 2002. Upon reconstruction, the layout was moved south toward Shaw Lane to maximize the available space. Furthermore, the replacement would serve in a dual role: track and field and field hockey. Completed in late summer of 2002, the facility features an artificial surface infield (AstroTurf 12), a scoreboard, small press box, field lighting, bleacher seating to accommodate 1,000 and a storage building.

If, in 1914, a need for a gymnasium proved to be warranted for 1,991 enrolled students, perhaps a bigger and better gymnasium-fieldhouse could be justified for 5,212 students in 1937. The foresighted team of presi-

dent Robert S. Shaw and secretary of the board John Hannah thought so. Again, it was time to turn to Washington. By now Franklin D. Roosevelt's New Deal Administration had reshuffled the alphabet. The WPA had given way to the PWA (Public Works Administration) who was providing 45 percent of funding for approved buildings erected by public agencies. President Shaw made a politically prudent move by soliciting Michigan's Democratic governor Frank Murphy to become the broker at the Capitol. Murphy made the pitch and the PWA responded. Meanwhile, Secretary Hannah had lined up private investors eager to supply the college's obligation of 55 percent.

The *State News* reported the results:

"Thursday, September 29, 1938: Approval of a $337,500 PWA grant for construction of a $750,000 men's gymnasium and fieldhouse was announced yesterday in Washington by Governor Frank Murphy.

Notice of the action is expected to be sent to the Board of Agriculture by PWA officials in the next two or three days Secretary John A. Hannah said last night. Approval of the gymnasium grants were requested. Every request made by the Board of Agriculture was approved Secretary Hannah said."

Figures for the gymnasium-fieldhouse grant had been increased to a total of $460,750 when the final papers were drawn. The balance of funds were made available through the sale of revenue bonds bearing an average interest rate of three percent to be retired for a 20-year period out of revenues of the building, including receipts and the portion of student fee charged all students for admission to athletic events. The final total cost would be approximately $1,025,000. (In 1992, a replacement value of $14,107,635 was placed on the structure.)

All of these financial moves were pushed forward void of any renderings for the planned building. Now with funding available, expediency became a factor. Athletic director Ralph Young immediately dispatched King J. McCristal, the respected professor of health and physical education, and wrestling coach, Fendley Collins, to West Lafayette, Ind. In seems that Purdue University had recently completed a structure similar to that envisioned for MSC. The two emissaries returned with notes, ideas, and the actual blueprints of the Boilermakers' Lambert Fieldhouse. Bruce McCristal, King's son, remembers that of 16 design changes of the West Lafayette structure that

were suggested by Fendley and his father, 13 were eventually incorporated into the Michigan State adoption, including the balcony-like rooms above the east side of the gymnasium. Even with these enhancements, strong "twin-like" similarities do exist between Lambert and Jenison.

Dimensions of the front portion of the structure were 120 feet wide by 200 feet long and the fieldhouse was 170 feet wide by 300 feet long. The plans called for the new building to house complete facilities for men's physical education and intramural athletics. The first level was to house offices on the north end and classrooms on the south end. Initially, the spectator capacity of the dirt-floor fieldhouse was announced to be 8,500 for basketball.

The Board of Agriculture settled on the name Fredrick Cowles Jenison Gymnasium and Fieldhouse with the simplified name of "Jenison" identifying the building to thousands who came to know it. Mr. Jenison was a former student and loyal supporter who came to the football field every afternoon to watch practice during his collegiate days. At his death, he left the college a half-million-dollar estate that included a Washington Avenue business building. His will read: "All that I have in the way of possessions and money I give to my dear friends at Michigan State College to do with as they will." Somehow entrapped in the benefactor's total package of giving was a stipulation that no women would compete in the projected gymnasium-fieldhouse. For many years this condition was honored, with exceptions needing approval from the school's governing arm, the State Board of Agriculture; however, time eventually eroded away this chauvinistic provision.

With the portable floor moved over from Demonstration Hall and put in place, the first basketball game in Jenison was played on January 6, 1940, a win over the previously unbeaten University of Tennessee. Other sports followed: wrestling against Northwestern on January 22, a track meet with Notre Dame two weeks later, a boxing match with Syracuse on February 25, with the first swimming meet swum the next season, January 25, 1941, against Ohio State. Coaches and administrators took possession of their respective offices during the second week of March in 1940. Perhaps because Jenison opened up like this, one event at a time, no traditional dedication ceremony was ever held.

The fieldhouse with its homey dirt floor finally gave way to modern technology after more than 30 years. In 1971, a Tartan Track surface was installed, and, to the veteran fans, things would never be the same.

Michigan State's magnificent swimming pool.

Although the fieldhouse and most of the main level of Jenison have changed very little during the recent renovation, veteran Spartans would need guides to find their way around the remaining portions of today's 63-year-old facility. At a cost of $8,200,000 and nearly two years in renovation (2001-2003), other segments of the landmark have been partially or totally refurbished. Primary changes are visible on the ground level, formerly dominated by the swimming pool and two large locker areas. Although the pool remains intact, the remainder of that level was gutted and redone to include an equipment room, an extensive area for trainers and eight private locker rooms to accommodate the men's track and field, baseball and soccer teams, along with women's teams in track and field, softball, soccer, field hockey and crew. Using a newly installed elevator at the front of the building and moving to the third level, it is readily noted that a gymnastic apparatus for women now covers two-thirds of the old floor. A significant portion of the northeast corner is where two private locker rooms for women have been built in, one for gymnasts and another for volleyball. Offices and a meeting room dominate much of the remainder of the third level and a portion of the fourth. The latter level features a strength and conditioning room that was doubled in size and had $100,000 in new equipment added. Other than central-air conditioning compressors conspicuously housed on the roof, the exterior of Jenison remains the same.

One of the brick and mortar legacies from the Biggie Munn "era" as athletic director is the Intramural West building, which was first named the Men's Intramural building, for whom it originally served. A small, attractively designed town that Biggie had seen while flying over Germany in 1951 presumably inspired the structure's layout. He envisioned this new $3,200,000 building around an open courtyard, with corridors leading to rooms, courts, arenas, and pools. That's basically what was built in 1958-59 at the site of the 15 tennis courts between the football stadium and Demonstration Hall.

At the building's opening in 1959, Munn emphasized, "This facility was built by the students for the students." True, but student-*athletes* would also use it. Initially, four intercollegiate sports would make their home there: fencing, wrestling, swimming and diving, and gymnastics. The AD further noted, "There were just three of us who planned and supervised the entire project. Frank Beeman [intramural director], Charles McCaffree [swimming coach], and myself. We figured it would be best that way so that there wouldn't be a lot of people tripping over each other."

The structure was built with few frills. The two largest areas for spectator sports (each seating 2,000) were the indoor pool and the sports arena in the northwest corner which, when the building opened, was the competitive home for gymnastics and wrestling. As for a dressing area, one huge room (80 feet by 30 feet), lighted through frosted windows from the court, would include 6,000 individual locker spaces and adjacent showers that could accommodate 140 men at once.

Although there have been numerous alterations in the IM Building over the years, the original plans included seven handball and squash courts, six for badminton, two for tennis, and two for volleyball. Along with four lecture classrooms, the layout included separate practice and conditioning rooms assigned to fencing, wrestling, and weight lifting.

The two pools remain as the showpieces of the building. They were designed by the gentleman whose name they now bear, coach Charles McCaffree, and constructed by National Pools of Florence, Ala. The outdoor tank is 65 feet wide and was originally 165 feet long, with a 50-

foot by 60-foot diving well and a 10-meter tower. The indoor unit is 50 feet by 121 feet split by a moveable bulkhead built on a bridge capable of opening to a maximum swimming length of 33 1/3 meters.

On May 18, 1978, it was announced that major changes in the Men's Intramural Building would provide more than 2,300 new locker spaces for women. Jack Breslin, then executive vice-president, reported the work would cost $97,000. Due to architectural holdups, construction would be delayed until that fall. "This work will go a long way toward providing greater equality for women students, and it will help the University to meet its obligation under Title IX," Breslin said. The Men's IM would soon become IM West with facilities open for both men and women.

During 1995 and 1996 the outdoor pool underwent profound remodeling. Precipitated by poorly compacted soil at the time of construction, the deck had sunken significantly in 36 years. In addition, the outside wall of the utility tunnel that surrounded the tank had crumpled. Along with completing these repairs, the pool received a new gutter curb while the north end of the swimming area was shortened approximately 11 inches to reach the precise competitive 50-meter dimension. In the original construction, plans had called for a 55-yard measurement from which metal plates were to be extended to reach the required 50-meter size.

Simultaneous to ground being broken south of the Red Cedar for the new IM building, construction on a significant new addition to the old Gymnasium (Women's IM) would also begin in 1958. Space in the 40-year-old building would be doubled and include a 90-foot by 120-foot gymnasium, a 45-foot by 75-foot swimming pool with seating for 500, a 52-foot by 90-foot activities room, new locker space, and a terrace extending toward the river. Total cost would exceed $2,300,000, nearly 10 times the bill for the original structure of 1916.

In *The M.A.C. Record* of October 8, 1920, it was noted that a nine-hole golf course had been laid out in the pasture across the river from the Gymnasium. The layout encompassed the land now mostly occupied by Demonstration Hall, IM West, Spartan Stadium, and Munn Arena. At that time the field had been assigned to the use of the cavalry, but arrangements had been made for dual operation of the grounds without interference. The course was designed and built by a group of faculty members who later organized the Saturday golf club. This group reportedly continued to play every Saturday through the winter from November until early April. It apparently never got so very cold or the snow so deep that they couldn't play. With the first hole stretching east along the river, the course was plotted around the cavalry area in circular fashion, leaving the center for military maneuvers. Writing from memory in 1969, Lyman Frimodig recalled that occasionally the cavalry would ride onto the area and raise havoc with the greens.

Those links were short-lived when, in 1923, they were sacrificed in favor of the new stadium and contiguous area for parking.

The sport of golf was embraced into the Spartan family of intercollegiate athletics in 1928. At that time an agreement was reached with members of nearby Walnut Hills Country Club to use their facilities for practice and matches. Although there would be occasional use of the Lansing Country Club course, State teams of the next 30 years would call Walnut Hills their home course.

Following two years of moving soil and planting seed, Forest Akers West Golf Course opened on the campus in 1958 as a par 70, 18-hole layout. Beginning that season, for the first time the Spartans would have their own links for hosting matches. The East Course, which initially opened as nine holes in 1966, was expanded to 18 holes in 1978. With the provision that the course also would serve as an arboretum, the project was primarily funded by the distinguished alumnus and automobile executive Forest Akers (BS '06, '07) of Detroit. Most of Michigan's native trees and a wide variety of shrubs are grown throughout the course and are arranged to create a unique setting for the game.

The West Course underwent a one million dollar renovation in 1992-1993 that added 300 yards, all new bunkers, 18 new tees, and seven new greens. The remade layout would hereafter play as a par-72 championship course of 7,012 yards. The architect of the newly designed course was MSU's own Arthur W. Hills (GO '50, '51, '53). Ten years later, in the spring of 2002, the configuration of that layout was altered when the starter house was moved to the new Candlewood Hotel located next to the University Club on Forest Road. From there the former 15th hole became the opening hole.

Upon re-introducing ice hockey onto the scene in 1949, following a 29-year hiatus, versatile and solid Demonstration Hall was made available for conversion into an ice arena. By then the ROTC horse cavalry had given

way to mechanized cavalry and the tan bark arena no longer was needed for equine drills and polo. Within a year the renovation to ice was complete and hockey resumed at the very location basketball departed 10 years prior. No longer would the hockey program depend on the weather, as it did in the '20s and '30s when rinks were laid out on the Red Cedar River and later the tennis courts.

The locker rooms in Dem Hall were dingy, seating was limited to a maximum of just over 4,000, lighting was bad, sight lines were hindered by vertical I-beam supports, but hockey was back…to stay.

Munn Ice Arena, built in 1974 at a cost of $3,500,000, would eliminate all of the negatives and be recognized as one of the finest collegiate hockey facilities in the country. In hindsight, the one lament is that the seating capacity of 6,170 is inadequate. Every regular-season home game has been sold out since the 1989-1990 schedule.

Built into the natural slope of the rolling terrain, the structure gives the impression of being underground, since no external walls are visible. Clear span roof trusses form an angular roof profile and help provide acoustic control within the arena. The lower level contains service areas for building maintenance, coaches' offices, an equipment room, locker rooms, a hospitality room, and a physical therapy area.

The four-sided scoreboard that hung over center ice was installed for the 1991-92 season as part of a package that included new scoreboards for Spartan Stadium and the Breslin Center.

Munn's ice surface is maintained by a direct refrigerant system, rather than by the old heat-exchange method. Due to freon leaks in the pipes that developed early in the 1984-85 season, the entire network of heating and cooling pipes was replaced in the summer of 1985. The new system allows the Arena to maintain ice all year.

The first major event in the new arena was an exhibition game in September of 1974 between two professional hockey teams, the Detroit Red Wings and the St. Louis Blues. This was followed by the Spartans' season opener, October 25, a 3-4 loss to Laurentian College of Sudbury, Ontario. The official dedication, a simple ceremony, was conducted one week later, Friday, November 1, prior to a 4-3 overtime loss to the NCAA defending champions, the Minnesota Golden Gophers. With president Clifton R. Wharton presiding, a large portrait of Biggie was unveiled. Standing on the ice sheet and with tears in his eyes, the former athletic director, acknowl-

edged the standing ovation by waving his cane up to the record crowd of 5,419. This would be his final public appearance. A debilitating stroke suffered in 1971 would take his life in 1975.

In 1999 the Munn Arena underwent a four million dollar renovation that added 14 luxury boxes above the north concourse and 146 club seats above the south side. Eight 12-seat boxes sold for $20,000 and the price of 12 season tickets, while the four eight-seat suites went for $15,000 and eight season tickets. Added perks for the suite owners included food and beverages along with use of a newly added washroom. The club seats carry a price tag of $1,700 along with the price of a season ticket. With these added seats, a record crowd of 7,117 jammed into Munn for the Michigan game of January 7, 2000. Also included in the remodeling were new scoreboards at both ends, which accompanied giant TV monitors.

With this expanded source, gross revenue from the home hockey season increased by $500,000. However, it was predicted the athletic department would not experience large profits for another seven to eight years until the construction costs were paid off.

A significant addition to the intercollegiate athletic plant, planned and undertaken during the Joe Kearney years as athletic director (1976-1980), was the Duffy Daugherty football training facility. The total structure, as it stands today, was actually unveiled in two installments, plus a major renovation in 1997. Construction of the initial phase, the single-story masonry building of approximately 22,000 square feet, was approved by the Board of Trustees in February of 1978. Bids were received nine months later on November 20, with Charles Featherly Construction Company selected as the general contractor.

Highlights of the building would be the 3,888 square foot weight room and the large carpeted locker room. Also included: an athletic training room, coaches' offices, conference and film rooms, and a reception center for visitors. By official dedication time, Saturday, October 4, 1980, (the morning of that fall's Notre Dame game), Doug Weaver and Muddy Waters had respectively replaced Joe Kearney and football coach Darryl Rogers, both having departed for Arizona State University.

The second phase, the 420-foot by 205-foot indoor practice facility, was opened on October 28, 1985, amidst George Perles's third season as head coach. For the first time, everything that had to do with MSU football would now be under one roof, with the obvious exception of the stadium. Prior to this centralization, the football of-

fices were in Jenison, the locker rooms in the stadium and the weight rooms in yet another part of the stadium. Funds for the construction were included in the Breslin Student Events Center appropriations.

The major renovations of 1997 included an extensive expansion of the weight room (9,000 square feet and $160,000 in new equipment), an enlarged and updated training facility, expanded locker room, with new classrooms and meeting rooms.

Three times campus planners have found seemingly ideal locations to install a cluster of tennis courts, only to have those sites proven too valuable to play tennis. First, it was the original white clay tennis courts behind the Women's Building (Morrill Hall) which were displaced when Grand River Avenue became a boulevard and encroached on the area in the early 1930s. Next it was the battery of six clay and nine hard-surface courts located between the stadium and Demonstration Hall that were demolished to make room for the IM Building in 1957. Then in the summer of 1996 it was time to move once more. The area south of Spartan Stadium that had accommodated 40 courts and also functioned as a parking lot for football gave way to being a full-time parking lot.

The current outdoor facilities, located south of the Duffy Daugherty Football Building, include 20 courts (12 competitive and eight recreational), a restroom and storage building, portable spectator seating (with future plans for installing permanent seating for approximately 400), shade shelters and an observation tower. In addition, eight other recreational courts were added on the east side of campus. The project totaled $1,800,000 and was overseen by Sheldon Westervelt, an internationally known designer who created such courts as the USTA National Tennis Center (home of the U.S. Open) and college facilities at Connecticut, Harvard, Yale, and Virginia.

As like the indoor football practice field, funding for the $1,900,000 MSU Tennis Indoor Facility, which opened on January 17, 1986, was included with the package that paved the way for the Breslin Student Events Center. The 69,000 square-foot structure houses eight indoor courts, permanent seating for 1,200 spectators, men's and women's locker rooms, showers, and a pro shop. The walls and ceiling are made with fiberglass tiles that strongly resist punctures and the court surface is asphalt covered with latex filler and color coats.

It is most appropriate that the magnificent structure on Harrison Road, the student events center, bears the name of Jack Breslin. It was he who labored so long for its fruition. Talk of the project began back in 1965 when President Hannah met with student leaders to discuss the proposal. At that time an all-university referendum was established to create a fund for improving athletic facilities. Approximately $200,000 was being added to the fund each year through student football ticket sales.

Things heated up in 1969 when Breslin succeeded in gaining support of the state legislature with a resolution supporting construction of a $7.5 million all-events sports building. The proposed structure was to be financed with private funds and no extra drain on state appropriations.

An architectural firm, Kenneth C. Black Associates Inc., was engaged in March of 1969 and by January of the following year drawings had been submitted and were made public. The new arena was to seat 15,049 while it closely simulated Purdue University's Mackey Arena that had opened in 1967. It was to be located where the Duffy Daugherty Building and football practice field now stand. The groundbreaking was tentatively scheduled for October of 1970.

Although things appeared to be going smoothly, two issues remained unsolved. The university community seemed to be philosophically split on the issue of which should come first, the all-events building or a performing arts center. A second and more realistic issue was the one of financing. A tentative scheme called for an increase in student fees to provide the remaining 10 million dollars that now was the projected need. "We've got to get the students to accept this building," Breslin said. "If we could get the students to put up ten dollars a year, we could pay for it. But the students will have to come out publicly and say they want it and will pay for it." Unfortunately, this never happened. As Jack accurately predicted, "This project will be tough to sell if student government comes out against it." That is exactly what happened in February of 1970. The negative position of the student leaders was interpreted as reflecting the sentiment of the entire student body. Consequently the proposal died an immediate and bitter defeat.

By the time the idea of an arena again received serious attention it was October 1984, and the estimated cost had been inflated to a shattering $30 million. Six months later the athletic department gambled with an "all or nothing" stand. The proposal sought $38.5 million for a "triple dip:" the student events center, the in-

door tennis facility, and the addition to the Daugherty Building. Funding for the package again included an increase in student fees along with $800,000 made available from the department's own coffers. Also tapped was: interest on three million dollars' worth of funds borrowed during construction, one million dollars from the Forest Akers Trust Fund and $1.1 million from the sale of a 397-acre farm in Oakland County which had been bequeathed to the university.

For fall term 1985, student fees would be increased 2.4 percent, or one dollar per credit hour, with yet another dollar added in the following year. Again, as in 1970, student government leaders took a stand. A survey disclosed that 49 percent of those enrolled supported the construction of the sports facility but 80 percent opposed a tuition hike to assist in the funding. School officials had learned their lesson—there would be no further student input to the subject. At their meeting on Thursday, April 4, 1985, the university Board of Trustees approved the plan for underwriting the expenditure.

Following a suggestion via a petition from the state legislature, the official name, the Jack Breslin Student Events Center, was confirmed in December of 1985. On the afternoon of July 24, 1986, a groundbreaking ceremony took place. Serious construction started in November of that fall with a goal to be completed for the start of the 1989-1990 basketball season. This projection date fell into jeopardy when a roof truss fell on February 18, 1988, crumbling concrete and delaying further work for three months. Ultimately, the schedule survived the setback and on November 9, 1989, the building opened with an impressive dedication ceremony.

Many loyal Spartans were in attendance on that open-house night, including 87-year-old John Hannah, in what would be one of his final public appearances. Missing was "Mr. MSU." Following a three-year battle with cancer, Jack Breslin had died on August 2, 1988, at the age of 68, when the arena was still a concrete shell.

In January of 2002, the Alfred Berkowitz Basketball Complex, was opened as an addition to the east side of the Breslin Center. Along with new offices for the coaching staff, the facilities included a large theatre, a video workroom, an expanded training room, a conference room and a second auxiliary gymnasium. In the process, the original auxiliary gym became a practice area for the women's team. The Alfred Berkowitz Foundation pledged two million dollars toward the $7,500,000 project as the entire cost of construction was covered by private funds.

In 1996-1997 a fund-raising campaign succeeded in raising $6,200,000 to finance an academic center for the school's intercollegiate athlete program. Steve Smith, former Spartan basketball All-American and outstanding NBA player, proved to be a record-setting benefactor as he contributed $2,500,000 toward the goal. It was the largest gift ever by a professional athlete to any college or university. Consequently, the center bears the name Clara Bell Smith Student-Athletic Academic Center, honoring Steve's mother, his greatest role model.

On March 1, 1997 ground was broken on the addendum to the north end of the Duffy Daugherty Football Building. Opened in 1999, this 31,000 square-foot facility features computer laboratories with 62 workstations, a 210-seat auditorium, five classrooms, 10 tutorial rooms and a conference room. In addition, the MSU Athletic Hall of Fame, visible from Shaw Lane, was dedicated on Friday, October 1, 1999, homecoming weekend. Plaques of inductees into the hall are displayed on the north-windowed wall of the structure.

ATHLETIC DIRECTORS

When the Reverend Charles Bemies was hired as "coach of sports" at MAC in 1899, it was a given expectation that he would be responsible for all issues pertaining to athletics. Although without a title at the time, it now seems historically appropriate to label Bemies as the school's first athletic director (1899-1900). As late as 1920, Chester Brewer filled the post defined as director of physical education and then, one year later, in 1921, the title was changed to director of athletics. During those years subsequent to 1941, a primary varsity coach would double into the AD's role. The following list therefore includes those who filled the position dually as coach-administrator:

1899-1900 .... Charles Bemies
1901-1902 .... George Denman
1903-1910 .... Chester L. Brewer
1911-1915 .... John F. Macklin
1916 .... George Gauthier (acting)
1917 .... Chester L. Brewer
1918 .... George Gauthier (acting)
1919-1921 .... Chester L. Brewer
1922 .... Albert M. Barron
1923-1940 .... Ralph Young

Ralph Young (1941-1954):

Upon leaving his post as track and field coach following the 1940 season, Ralph Young became the school's first fulltime director of athletics. He would hold the position until stepping aside in favor of Clarence "Biggie" Munn following the Rose Bowl victory of 1954.

During Young's 32 years in the position (1923-1954) State would rise to national prominence in athletics with a multi-faceted program endorsing 13 varsity sports. As for facilities, Young would oversee construction of durable Jenison Fieldhouse-Gymnasium in addition to the first football stadium with latter-day improvements and expansions.

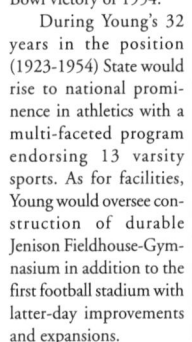

Ralph Young

After leaving the university, Ralph Young would conclude his life of public service with a short stint as an elected official by representing the East Lansing district in the Lower House of the state legislature.

(See track and field season records for a full bio-sketch on Ralph Young.)

Clarence "Biggie" Munn (1954-1971):

Biggie Munn had been John Hannah's handpicked coach back in 1947 and the two maintained an ongoing admiration for one another. Conversely, the president had little respect for Ralph Young, his veteran athletic director. Thus, when Munn expressed a desire to move up to the AD position following the Rose Bowl victory on January 1, 1954, there was little resistance from the top. Ready or not, it seemed that Young had two choices: be asked to leave unwillingly or retire willingly. He judiciously chose the latter.

Munn served as athletic director over an 18-year period in which the stadium was increased in seating capacity from 51,000 to 76,000. In addition, the Men's IM Building (later renamed IM West) was completed and ground was broken on the ice arena which would later bare his name.

Munn's tenure would be suddenly disrupted on October 7, 1971, when he suffered a stroke that led to a health leave and eventually to retirement on September 1, 1973. A second stroke took his life at the age of 66 on March 18, 1975.

Clarence "Biggie" Munn

(See football season records for a full bio-sketch on Biggie Munn.)

Burt Smith (1971-1975):

A native of Detroit, MI, Smith was born March 18, 1917. He attended Redford High School, graduated in 1933 and secured a B.S. degree in education from the University of Michigan in 1938. While an undergraduate, Bert competed three years in varsity hockey and varsity baseball while also playing football as a freshman. He would later earn his Master's degree at MSC in 1954. Smith was a highly successful prep coach in Flint before accepting a position on Duffy Daugherty's original football staff that same year. He became offensive line coach in 1955, switching to defensive line coach in 1959 and in 1965 moved from the football field when he was appointed assistant athletic director. When Biggie Munn was incapacitated with a stroke in early October of 1971, Bert filled the void, carrying the title of "acting" director. By that next spring it was obvious Munn would not be physically capable of returning to his position and at the May 19 meeting of the school's Board of Trustees, Burt Smith was appointed MSU's eighth director of athletics. Among the highlights of his administration was the creation of the Summer Sports School and the development of a program for advisement, counseling and tutoring the student-athletes.

Unfortunately for Burt Smith, he was an innocent casualty of the improprieties that surfaced within the football office in 1975. As the subsequent investigation led to NCAA sanctions, the university administration became engrossed in a "house cleaning" mode. Along with others directly associated with the affair, the innocent director of athletics was forced into

Burt Smith

early retirement. For a few years following his dismissal, Smith remained in the area while serving as Commissioner of the Central Collegiate Hockey Association.

John (Jack) Shingleton (1975-1976):

Although he has never been historically recognized as a "former" athletic director, this publication acknowledges Jack Shingleton for his role as acting director of athletics during a difficult period from October 1975-February 1976. It was an interval in which the university attempted to "weather the storm" following the NCAA sanctions steaming from the football recruiting investigation. Jack, an MSC graduate and varsity tennis player, had served his alma mater in various administrative capacities since 1949, including

John (Jack) Shingleton

his role as director of placement services since 1963, a position he would return to, full time, in February of 1976, and retire from in 1985.

Although Shingleton was among those considered for the permanent AD position, it was President Wharton's feeling that the school would best benefit from an "outside" source. Upon retirement, Shingleton continued to serve the university as a member of its Board of Trustees from 1991-1999.

Joe Kearney (1976-1979):

A native of Pittsburgh, PA, Joe Kearney moved to the west coast with his family and it was there he graduated from El Monte (CA) Union High School in 1945. After serving in the United States Naval Air Force, he entered college at Seattle Pacific and earned a B.A. degree in 1952. While an undergraduate, he played four years of basketball and one year of football.

He began a teaching and coaching career at Paradise (CA) High School in 1951-1953. This preceded stints as assistant basketball coach at the University of Washington (1953-1954); teacher, counselor and coach in three

Joe Kearney

sports at Sunnyside (WA) Senior High School (1954-1957); principal as well as coach of football, basketball and baseball at Onalaska (WA) High School (1957-1961); principal of Tumwater (WA) High School (1961-1963) and assistant executive secretary for the Washington Interscholastic Activities Association (1963-1964).

Joe completed his M.A. degree at San Jose State in 1953 and earned a Ph.D. from the University of Washington in 1970. Prior to making the move to East Lansing in the spring of 1976, Kearney served the U of W from 1965-1976, first as an assistant athletic director for operations before being elevated to director of sports programs in 1969.

Although he would serve Michigan State for only three and one-half academic years and depart suddenly for a simi-

lar post at Arizona State University in November of 1979, Joe Kearney had been the right man at the right place at the right time. Foremost, he was a healer for a program that had suffered through the NCAA investigation. Furthermore, he was a man of vision who hired three winning coaches: Darryl Rogers in football, Ron Mason in hockey and Jud Heathcote in basketball.

Doug Weaver (1980-1990):

When Joe Kearney left in November of 1979, the University turned to former Spartan Doug Weaver who assumed the athletic director's post in January of 1980. Doug's association with MSU began in 1949, when he enrolled as a student after a brief stay at Yale University. He was a three-time football letterwinner as a linebacker for the teams of 1950-1952, which posted an incomparable composite record of 26-1. In addition to his Michigan State diploma, the Goshen, IN, native would later earn a law degree from Kansas University in 1970.

In 1980, Weaver brought a solid athletic administrative background with him to MSU. He had held the position of head football coach at Kansas State (1960-1966) and Southern Illinois (1974-1975)

Doug Weaver

as well as being athletic director at SIU (1973-1976) and Georgia Tech (1976-1980).

During his 11 years as Michigan State's AD, Weaver saw the approval of a nearly $40 million package which facilitated the construction of the indoor football practice facility (Duffy Daugherty Football Building), the indoor tennis facility, IM East and the Jack Breslin Student Events Center. Even as this record-breaking construction program burst forth, the Weaver-era legacy also managed to build an impressive cash surplus.

George Perles (1990-1992):

When Doug Weaver abruptly announced in early December of 1989 that he would retire from the athletic director's post on July 1, 1990, football coach George Perles quickly let it be known he was a candidate for the job. Reminiscent of the Ralph Young era and earlier, Perles proposed tenure in a dual-functionary role as coach *and* administrator. The university's president, John DiBiaggio, met with the self-expressed candidate shortly thereafter to note that he strongly felt the role of athletic director and coach should be separate and distinct. Suddenly, the matter grew beyond a discussion of who should run the $12 million athletic program and into a public power struggle pitting Perles against DiBiaggio. Anti-Perles forces suggested he was holding the school hostage when it was revealed the professional New York Jets were simultaneously offering the Spartan coach a $6 million dollar contract over five years. Just coming off the Rose Bowl victory, pro-Perles forces were confident he could successfully perform the double-duty.

George Perles

Duffy Daugherty once joked that the Board of Trustees had given him

a vote of confidence by a 5-3 measure. It was by that identical vote the school's governing body voted on February 2, 1990, in favor of George Perles and confirmed the coach as the school's 11th director of athletics. Although he had won the battle with the president, the scars were permanent. By August 31, 1992, George had been forced out and returned to his solitary job on the sidelines; John DiBiaggio had moved on as president of Tufts University in Massachusetts and newly appointed Merrily Dean Baker had moved into the Jenison office as director.

(See football season records for a full bio-sketch on George Perles.)

Merrily Dean Baker (1992-1995):

Upon becoming MSU's 12th athletic director on April 3, 1992, Merrily Dean Baker became the first woman to be named to a similar post at a Big Ten university, and only the second at a Division I football-playing institution. She began her career in 1964 as a multi-sport coach at Abington High School in Pennsylvania. This was immediately after receiving her B.S. degree from East Stroudsburg (PA) University. Pushing on to the collegiate scene, Baker became field hockey coach at St. Lawrence University in 1965 and three years later moved to Temple University where she was gymnastics coach while earning her master's degree.

In 1969 Merrily accepted her first administrative position upon being appointed women's director of athletics at Franklin &

Merrily Dean Baker

Marshall. By the following year she had moved on to Princeton University as associate director of athletics. During her 12-year stay at Princeton, Baker initiated and directed women's athletics and also administered physical education and intramural programs for both men and women.

Adding to her dossier, in 1982 she became director of women's intercollegiate athletics at the University of Minnesota. Serving in that capacity for seven years, she successfully focused attention on the Gophers' nine-sport $3 million program. Her responsibilities also extended into facility management as she co-directed the $85 million athletic plant in Minneapolis.

Immediately prior to her arrival at Michigan State, Baker served as the assistant executive director at the National Collegiate Athletic Association in Mission, KS from 1988-1992.

Merritt Norvell (1995-1998):

Merritt Norvell began as MSU's 13th athletic director on July 24, 1995. A native of Jacksonville, IL, he had attended the University of Wisconsin, lettering in both football and baseball and graduating with a bachelor's degree in 1963. Staying on at Madison, he earned both a Master's and doctorate while gaining invaluable administrative experience, first as an assistant to the vice chancellor for student affairs from 1969-1973, and later as assistant dean for graduate school administration from 1973-1977.

Merritt Norvell

Entering the private world of business, Norvell worked 14 years for IBM, concluding his career there as manager of collegiate merchandising. From 1993 until coming to East Lansing in 1995, he ran a successful business as president and chairman of Norvell Group Inc., a marketing and national distributing firm.

During his tenure at MSU, the first-ever athletics capital fund drive was completed, raising $7.8 million to build the Clara Bell Smith Student-Athlete Academic Center. To the tune of $5 million, the Duffy Daugherty Football Building was expanded to make the facility one of the nation's elite. A gender equity program was instituted which would lead to the elimination of two men's sports: lacrosse and fencing.

Clarence Underwood (1998-2002):

Born on October 10, 1933 and raised in Gadsden, AL, Clarence Underwood served in the United States Army 82nd airborne division in Ft. Bragg, NC, for two years following high school. Watching the 1956 Rose Bowl game on television, Underwood saw how many African-American players were featured on the MSU squad and was impressed enough that to head north for his college education seemed like a comfortable decision. In 1951, he received a Bachelor of Science degree in physical education from Michigan State and immediately began a teaching career, serving as a physical education teacher for elementary and junior high schools in the East Lansing School District.

Clarence Underwood

Returning to the college scene in 1972, Underwood served his alma mater as assistant athletic director for academics. His responsibilities included the implementation of an expanded academic support program and coordinating all issues of eligibility, financial aid, athletic certification and rules interpretation. After 10 years in this capacity Underwood moved into the school's Alumni Office where he served one year as associate director before being lured to the Big Ten Office in Chicago as deputy commissioner. Returning to MSU in 1990 he became the assistant athletic director for compliance and four years later was elevated to senior associate director. With the departure of Merritt Norvell in 1998, Underwood was appointed interim director while given the full title a year later. During the academic year 2001-2002, Underwood announced his retirement effective July 1, 2002.

Ron Mason (2002-):

As a member of the search team to replace the retiring Clarence Underwood, Ron Mason, the highly successful hockey coach, suddenly realized, "Hey, I hold the credentials necessary to succeed as the new athletic director." Eventually declaring himself a candidate, it didn't take the committee long to agree. On January 28, 2002, university president Peter McPherson held a press conference to introduce Mason as his man.

"We were looking for an athletic director and we got a legend," McPherson said. "It came clear to us all that the candidate who best fit the requirements—and even more—was Ron Mason. The fact that he is the winningest coach in the history of his sport was a further verification of his superb leadership and management abilities."

Signing a five-year contract at an annual salary of $270,000, Ron Mason took command on Monday, July 1, 2002. The university also included an additional $89,100 a year in deferred compensation if Mason serves until 2007.

Ron Mason

GLOSSARY

The following symbols and abbreviations are used in conjunction with the summary of each sport's year by year season records as noted in the appendix of this publication. An explanation of the various symbols and abbreviations used to tell the story are defined below:

@   MIAA Field Days
*   Big Ten tournament or championship
**   NCAA tournament or championship
+   Central Collegiate Championships
~   Central Collegiate Hockey Association
^   Western Collegiate Hockey Assoc.
GLI Great Lakes Invitational (hockey)
$ National Invit. Tour. (basketball)
>   miscellaneous tournament
<   miscellaneous tournament
__ spring training trip
%   special footnote
ex   exhibition
F   forfeit
NTS no team score

AA .... Ann Arbor, MI	CH .... Chicago, IL	FL .... Ft. Lee, VA	LN .... Lansing, MI
AB .... Auburn Hills, MI	CI .... Cincinnati, OH	FM .... Ft. Meyers, FL	LO .... Louisville, KY
AD .... Addison, IL	CK .... Carrollton, GA	FO .... Fowlerville, MI	LV .... Las Vegas, NV
AE .... Ada, OH	CL .... Camp LeJeune, NC	FP .... Ft. Pierce, FL	LX .... Lexington, KY
AG .... Angola, IN	CM .... College Park, MD	FR .... Franklin, IN	MA .... Madison, WI
AH .... Athens, OH	CN .... Clemson, SC	FT .... Flint, MI	MB .... Murfreesboro, TN
AI .... Ames, IA	CO .... Columbus, OH	GA .... Galesburg, IL	MC .... Montclair, NJ
AK .... Akron, OH	CP .... Chapel Hill, NC	GB .... Greensboro, NC	ME .... Memphis, TN
AL .... Albuquerque, NM	CQ .... Colorado Springs, CO	GC .... Garden City, NY	MF .... Miami, FL
AM .... Annapolis, MD	CR .... Culver, IN	GR .... Greenville, SC	MH .... Manchester, NH
AN .... Anchorage, AK	CS .... College Station, TX	HA .... Hammond, IN	MI .... Milwaukee, WI
AP .... Appleton, WI	CT .... Clairmont, CA	HF .... Hartford, CT	MK .... Manhattan, Kansas
AR .... Auburn, AL	CU .... Champaign-Urbana, IL	HG .... Harrogate, TN	ML .... Mobile, AL
AS .... Athens, GA	CV .... Cleveland, OH	HH .... Highland Heights, KY	MN .... Minneapolis, MN
AT .... Atlanta, GA	CW .... Clearwater, FL	HL .... Hammond, LA	MO .... Montclair, NJ
AU .... Augusta, GA	CX .... Clemson, SC	HO .... Honolulu, HI	MP .... Mt. Pleasant, MI
AX .... Austin, TX	CY .... Columbus, GA	HU .... Houston, TX	MS .... Munising, MI
BA .... Baltimore, MD	CZ .... Charlotte, NC	HW .... Howell, MI	MT .... Morgantown, WV
BC .... Battle Creek, MI	DA .... Dayton, OH	IA .... Ionia, MI	MU .... Maui, HI
BE .... Bethlehem, PA	DC .... Washington, DC	IC .... Iowa City, IA	MY .... Myrtle Beach, SC
BG .... Bowling Green, OH	DB .... Dearborn, MI	IN .... Indianapolis, IN	NA .... Naperville, IL
BH .... Burnt Hills, NY	DE .... Detroit, MI	IS .... Ishpeming, MI	ND .... Notre Dame, IN
BI .... Birmingham, MI	DK .... DeKalb, IL	IT .... Ithaca, MI	NK .... Norfolk, VA
BK .... Bules Creek, NC	DL .... Dallas, TX	JA .... Jamaica, NY	NM .... Normal, IL
BL .... Bloomington, IN	DO .... Dowagiac, MI	JE .... Jenison, MI	NO .... New Orleans, LA
BN .... Boca Raton, FL	DR .... Durand, MI	JX .... Jacksonville, FL	NP .... Newport, RI
BO .... Boston, MA	DU .... Durham, NC	KC .... Kansas City, MO	NR .... Norman, OK
BP .... Brockport, NY	DV .... Denver, CO	KE .... Kenosha, WI	NS .... Nashville, TN
BR .... Birmingham, AL	DW .... Delaware, OH	KT .... Kent, OH	NY .... New York City, NY
BS .... Baseball City, FL	ED .... Edenburg, TX	KX .... Knoxville, TN	OB .... Oberlin, OH
BU .... Buffalo, NY	EL .... East Lansing, MI	KZ .... Kalamazoo, MI	OK .... Oklahoma, City, OK
BY .... Berkeley, CA	EP .... El Paso, TX	LA .... Los Angeles, CA	OK .... Okemos, MI
CA .... Carbondale, IL	ER .... East Rutherford, NJ	LB .... Long Beach, CA	OL .... Ocala, FL
CB .... Columbus, IN	ES .... Evansville, IN	LC .... Las Cruces, NM	OM .... Omaha, NB
CC .... Corpus Christi, TX	EU .... Eugene, OR	LD .... Loredo, TX	OP .... Oak Park, IL
CD .... Colorado Springs, CO	EV .... Evanston, IL	LH .... Lake Charles, LA	OR .... Orlando, FL
CE .... Charlotte, MI	FB .... Ft. Benning, GA	LI .... Lincoln, NE	OS .... Oskosh, WI
CF .... Cedar Falls, IA	FD .... Ft. Lauderdale, FL	LK .... Lakeland, FL	OX .... Oxford, OH
CG .... Coral Gables, FL	FI .... Fripp Island, SC	LL .... Lake Linden, MI	PA .... Palo Alto, CA

PG .... Pittsburgh, PA
PH .... Philadelphia, PA
PI .... Parris Island, SC
PN .... Pontiac, MI
PO .... Portland, OR
PR .... Park Ridge, IL
PS .... Pasadena, CA
PT .... Palatine, IL
PU .... Provo, UT
PV .... Providence, RI
RA .... Raleigh, NC
RC .... Rochester, MI
RE .... Reno, NV
RI .... Richmond, VA
RM .... Richmond, KY
RO .... Rochester, NY
RV .... Ravenna, OH
SA........... St. Louis, MO
SB .... Stateboro, GA
SC .... Santa Clara, CA
SD .... San Diego, CA
SE........... San Jose, CA
SF .... San Francisco, CA
SG .... Spartansburg, SC
SH .... Shreveport, LA
SI .... St. Leo, FL
SJ .... San Juan, Puerto Rico
SL .... Salt Lake City, UT
SN .... St. Joseph, MI
SO .... Savoy, IL
SP .... St. Paul, MN
SR .... Springfield, OH
ST .... St. Petersburg, FL
SU .... Sault Ste. Marie, MI
SV .... Starksville, MS
SW .... Stillwater, OK
SX .... San Antonio, TX
SY........... Syracuse, NY
SZ .... St. Charles, MO
TA .... Tallahassee, FL
TE .... Tempe, AZ
TH .... Thomasville, GA
TI .... Terra Haute, IN
TK........... Tokyo, Japan
TL .... Tulsa, OK
TO .... Toledo, OH
TP .... Tampa, FL
TR.......... Tryon, NC
TS .... Tuscaloosa, AL
TU .... Tucson, AZ
TY .... Troy, NY
UP .... University Park, PA
WA .... Waukesha, WI
WH .... Wheaton, IL
WI .... Winter Haven, FL
WL .... West Lafayette, IN
WP .... Winter Park, FL
WS .... Winston-Salem, NC
YP .... Ypsilanti, MI

This publication has attempted to accurately portray institutions by their proper names at each point in history. It is thought this would add to its authenticity. Conversely, not knowing the exact chronology of school nicknames, current monikers were used throughout the publication. We do know that in the early years Notre Dame was known as the Ramblers, and into the 1930s Central Michigan was identified as the Bearcats.

Until 1956 Eastern Michigan held the name Michigan Normal and also was often referred to as Ypsi Normal.

Until 1923 Wayne State was identified as Detroit Junior College. From 1923 until 1934 it was known as the Detroit City College. From 1934 until 1956 it was Wayne University, whereupon it became Wayne State University.

From 1892 until 1927 Central Michigan University was Central Michigan Normal. It was Central State Teachers from 1927 until 1955, when it became Central Michigan College. It gained University status in 1959.

Western Michigan University was Western State Normal from 1903 until 1927, when the name was changed to Western State Teachers. Beginning in 1955 it was Western State College, becoming WMU in 1957.

Other name changes: Buchtel College became the University of Akron. Armour Tech out of Chicago is today known as Illinois Tech. Michigan Military at Orchard Lake became St. Mary's College; and St. Ignatius College of University Heights, OH, became John Carroll College in 1924, and later John Carroll University.

North Central College of Naperville, IL, founded in 1861, was originally known as Northwestern College, but changed its name in 1926 to avoid confusion with Northwestern University.

BASEBALL
LEADERS, RECORDS and HONORS

ALL-TIME COACHING RECORDS

Coach	Years	W	L	T	Avg.
No Head Coach	1884-98	73	50	1	.593
Max Beutner	1899	5	4	0	.556
Charles Bemies	1900-01	4	11	0	.267
George Denman	1902-03	10	14	0	.417
Chester Brewer	1904-10	64	39	1	.620
John Macklin	1911-15	53	26	0	.671
John Morrissey	1916-17	17	9	0	.654
Chester Brewer	1918-20	18	23	0	.439
George "Potsy" Clark	1921	7	8	0	.467
John Morrissey	1922	8	10	0	.444
Fred Walker	1923-24	20	11	0	.645
John Kobs	1925-63	576	384	18	.599
Danny Litwhiler	1964-82	488	362	8	.573
Tom Smith	1983-95	370	330	2	.533
Ted Mahan	1996-03	201	236	0	.480
Totals		**1923**	**1517**	**30**	**.559**

SEASON RECORDS

See page 874 for explanation of abbreviations.

1884 (4-1)
Coach: No Coach
5-19	H	Olivet	20-9	W
	H	Michigan	4-3	W
6-14	H	Michigan	@3-13	L
7-4	A$_{IA}$	Greenville	26-13	W
7-4	A$_{IA}$	Flint	17-7	W

1885 (3-1)
Coach: No coach
From the *College Speculum*, 6-15-1885, the team has already won three victories from the Lansing nine and expects to play as many more games as the short season and opportunities permit. They expect now to play at Webberville, July 4:

7-4	A	Greenville	5-7	L

1886 (12-4)
Coach: No coach
The Holcad of April 14, 1910 reported that the 1886 team won 12 games out of 16 played. The games lost were one with Cass High School of Detroit, one with Ionia and two with Owossso High School. Known scores are:

5-14	H	Olivet	11-3	W
5-15	H	Albion	16-1	W
5-15	H	Olivet	12-1	W
6-5	H	Albion	8-9	L
6-10	H	Capital City (Lansing)	53-0	W
		Greenville	10-14	L
10-9	A	Bath	22-1	W

Coach: Rollo Carpenter (1887-1888)
In October of 1886 a student-run athletic association was formed with the popular mathematics professor, Rolla Carpenter, as manager. Under the advice and consent of the faculty, this organization was to have control of all college athletics. Born near Orion, MI, in 1852, Carpenter received a B.S. degree from MAC in 1873 and a degree in civil engineering from the U of M in 1875. Returning to MAC as an instructor, he did graduate work and received the degree of masters of science in 1876.

1887 (6-3)
Coach: Rollo Carpenter
4-29	A	Michigan	10-8	W
5-7	H	Lansing	13-6	W
5-14	H	Olivet	8-2	W
5-27	A	Albion	7-9	L
6-3	A	Olivet	8-0	W
6-4	H	Albion	21-8	W
6-11	H	Michigan	11-9	W
6-18		Cass	6-9	L
6-25		Ionia	12-18	L

1888 (6-1)
Coach: Rollo Carpenter
9-17	H	Aurelius	24-6	W
9-27	H	Northville	17-6	W
6-1	H	Olivet	@12-2	W
6-2	H	Albion	@10-8	W
6-23	A	Michigan	5-13	L
		Hillsdale		W
7-4	A$_{HW}$	Owosso	23-3	W

1889 (5-2)
Coach: No coach
4-20	H	Olivet	17-6	W
6-6	A	Albion	@8-6	W
6-11	H	Michigan	12-10	W
		Michigan	5-17	L
9-14	A	Albion City	4-5	L
10-19	A	Lansing	14-10	W
10-26	H	Lansing	15-8	W

1890 (3-2)
Coach: No coach
5-30		Charlotte	unknown result	
		Michigan	5-19	L
6-5	A	Albion	@5-6	L
6-21	H	Jaxon Mutuals	12-4	W
7-4		Albion	11-3	W
	H	Albion	11-3	W

1891 (5-3)
Coach: No coach
4-18	H	Michigan	0-10	L
4-25	A	Michigan	4-26	L
6-2	A	Lansing Athletics	23-3	W
6-5	A	Albion	@11-8	W
6-6	A	Olivet	@10-9	W
6-27	H	Sparta	1-9	L
7-22	H	Battle Creek YMCA	23-2	W
9-19	H	Ionia	9-8	W

1892 (3-2)
Coach: No coach
5-14	A	Albion	9-11	L
5-17	A	Olivet	0-1	L
6-2	H	Albion	@15-4	W
6-4	H	Olivet	@2-1	W
7-29	H	Lansing	7-2	W

1893 (6-3#)
Coach: No coach
4-15	H	Albion	14-13	W
4-29	H	Olivet	10-9	W
6-2	A	Albion	@15-8	W
6-3	A	Olivet	@3-14	L
7-22	H	State Auditors	3-16	L
		#-stats show 9 games completed at season's end.		

1894 (3-2-1)
Coach: No coach
4-14	A	Albion	14-10	W
4-28	H	Albion	6-6	T
4-30	H	Olivet	4-3	W
5-14	A	Olivet	9-1	W
5-15	A	Jackson	10-11	L
6-7	A	Albion	@3-6	L

1895 (5-5)
Coach: No coach
4-20	H	Albion	12-8	W
4-27	A	Kalamazoo	7-21	L
4-29	H	Olivet	6-21	L
5-10	A	Lansing League	2-5	L
5-25	H	Kalamazoo	12-11	W
6-1	A	Olivet	21-13	W
6-6	A	Olivet	@18-15	W
6-7	A	Albion	@0-3	L
7-26	H	Lansing Ath. Club	23-13	W
9-21	H	Wacousta	10-13	L

1896 (3-10)
Coach: No coach
4-4	A	Michigan	6-20	L
4-11	A	Hillsdale	1-4	L
4-18	H	Albion	5-31	L
4-25	H	Mich. Military Acad.	10-15	L
4-27	H	Olivet	15-8	W
5-2	H	Kalamazoo	16-18	L
5-9	AL	Kalamazoo	9-10	L
5-16	A	Albion	1-12	L
5-18	A	Olivet	16-13	W
5-20	A	Mich. Military Acad	7-9	L
6-5	A	Michigan Normal	@11-12	L
6-27	H	Lansing Orients	7-11	L
7-25	H	Holt	13-5	W

1897 (3-6)
Coach: No coach
4-17	A	Albion	2-5	L
4-24	H	Albion	7-2	W
5-1	A	Kalamazoo	5-19	L
5-3	H	Hillsdale	37-5	W
5-8	A	Olivet	7-10	L
5-15	H	Kalamazoo	5-9	L
5-22	A	Hillsdale	11-4	W
5-31	H	Olivet	12-13	L
6-4	AF	Albion	0-2	L

1898 (6-5-1)
Coach: No coach

4-16	A	Kalamazoo	13-26	L
4-18	A	Hillsdale	13-9	W
4-23	A	Olivet	6-7	L
4-30	H	Michigan Normal	10-6	W
5-7	A	Albion	23-14	W
5-13	H	Michigan	5-5	T
5-14	A	Michigan Normal	20-8	W
5-14	A	Michigan	1-20	L
5-16	H	Hillsdale	5-10	L
5-20	H	Albion	14-12	W
5-23	H	Olivet	3-8	L
5-28	H	Kalamazoo	9-4	W

Coach: Max Beutner (1899)
Max Beutner had been on hand to train the field day squad of 1899, and he voluntarily stepped in to coach the baseball team in that same spring. His efforts were recognized by members of both the baseball and field days team as they presented him with a silver smoking set. The tray was engraved with "Max Beutner, from M.A.C. Athletes, 1899." Upon concluding his obligations to the college, Beutner departed for his home in Chicago.

1899 (5-4)
Coach: Max Beutner

4-29	H	Michigan Normal	19-6	W
5-1	A	Albion	10-6	W
5-5	A	Michigan Normal	13-6	W
5-6	A	Olivet	5-6	L
5-8	A	Hillsdale	11-6	W
5-13	H	Olivet	7-6	W
5-15	H	Hillsdale	5-10	L
5-20	H	Kalamazoo	11-16	L
6-2	H	Michigan Normal	@1-2	L

Charles Bemies (1900-1901)
Born in Northfield, VT, in 1867, Charles Bemies' family moved to Springfield, MA, in 1872, where he remained until he was 20 years old. After working three years as physical director in Springfield and Burlington, IA, he attended Geneva College in Beaver Falls, PA,'where he also had charge of the gymnasium. Bemies then entered seminary, graduated in 1897, became ordained an a Presbyterian minister, and served as pastor at Sewickley, PA, for two years. He eventually accepted the MAC position as director of physical culture, thus becoming coach of baseball, football and the emerging sport of basketball. He resigned and returned to the ministry in 1902.

1900 (3-6)
Coach: Charles Bemies

4-21	A	Hillsdale	6-5	W
4-28	H	Detroit A.C.	9-21	L
4-30	H	Olivet	11-17	L
5-5	H	Michigan Normal	5-9	L
5-12	H	Alma	11-6	W
5-14	A	Kalamazoo	0-4	L
5-19	A	Michigan Normal	1-8	L
5-21	H	Hillsdale	34-7	W
5-26	H	Kalamazoo	7-8	L

1901 (1-5)
Coach: Charles Bemies

4-27	H	Albion	3-19	L
5-4	A	Michigan Normal	11-14	L
5-11	H	Alma	8-10	L
5-13	A	Olivet	7-14	L
5-18	H	Michigan Normal	8-10	L
5-27	A	Albion	9-6	W

George Denman (1902-1903)
George Edward Denman, a native of Massachusetts, was the successor to Charles Bemies, coaching all sports for two academic years. An 1898 graduate of Williams College, he was a halfback on the football team and was on the track team two years. For two years following graduation, Denman taught history and English at Riverview Academy in Poughkeepsie, NY, where he was also in charge of athletics. In the following school year he returned to college, this time at Columbia University in New York City. Not restrained by modern-day transfer rules, he immediately took up football again. His next stop prior to accepting the MAC offer was at Central University in Kentucky where he was director of athletics while teaching French and Latin.

1902 (2-8)
Coach: George Denman

4-12	H	Lansing H.S. (ex)	20-23	L
4-18	H	Michigan	2-20	L
4-25	H	Beloit	3-11	L
4-28	H	Michigan Normal	10-12	L
5 3	H	Olivet	22-6	W
5-14	A	Albion	5-15	L
5-17	A	Michigan Normal	4-8	L
5-22	H	Detroit College	8-11	L
5-24	A	Olivet	forfeit	W
5-31	H	Albion	0-2	L
5-31	H	Alma	3-5	L

1903 (8-6)
Coach: George Denman

4-8	H	Lansing H.S (ex)	26-4	W
4-18	H	Michigan	10-9	W
4-23	H	Albion	7-8	L
4-25	H	Michigan Normal	27-22	W
5-2	A	Alma	5-0	W
5-7	H	DePauw	3-4	L
5-12	H	Olivet	7-3	W
5-14	A	Hillsdale	2-5	L
5-16	H	Alma	11-10	W
5-20	H	Hillsdale	4-5	L
5-23	A	Kalamazoo	5-6	L
5-27	A	Albion	0-15	L
5-28	H	Detroit College	19-1	W
5-30	H	Walpole Indians	10-4	W

Chester Brewer (1904-1910 and 1918-1920)
Chester Brewer, a native of Michigan, was born in Owosso, but moved to Evansville, WI, in his youth. He attended the University of Wisconsin where he was a member of the football, baseball and track teams, earning All-Western football honors in 1897. Upon graduation, Brewer became the head football coach at Whitewater (WI) State Normal College where he remained for two years, 1897 and 1898. It was then he returned to Michigan as professor of physical education and director of athletics at Albion College where he stayed until accepting a similar position at MAC in 1904. Following seven highly successful years, Brewer departed for Columbia, MO, where he had accepted an offer to be director of athletics at the University of Missouri. With the opening of the Gymnasium and the offer of an annual salary of $4,500 (a 50 percent increase from the $3,000 earned as the University of Missouri), Brewer was lured into returning to East Lansing in 1918. Assuming the new title of professor of physical education and director of athletics, he would remain until the summer of 1922, moving on to a similar position at the University of California in Davis. His stay on the coast was short, as one year later he was back as AD at the University of Missouri, where he closed out his career. The Brewer Fieldhouse, opened in 1930, stands on the Missouri campus as a tribute to his service.

1904 (13-4)
Coach: Chester Brewer

4-9	H	Howell H.S (ex).	10-5	W
4-14	A	Detroit College	12-2	W
4-22	A	Michigan	3-7	L
4-26	A	Albion	1-3	L
4-27	A	Kalamazoo	5-8	L
4-30	H	Detroit College	4-5	L
5-4	H	Hillsdale	11-1	W
5-7	H	Alma	10-2	W
5-9	A	Olivet	16-7	W
5-14	H	Kalamazoo	3-0	W
5-20	H	Wisconsin	3-2	W
5-21	H	Olivet	15-6	W
5-26	H	Albion	9-0 forfeit	W
5-28	H	Alma	11-0	W
5-30	A	Lansing Oldsmobile	3-2	W
6-4	A	Albion	@2-1	W
6-8	H	Univ. of Toronto	8-7	W

1905 (11-4)
Coach: Chester Brewer

4-15	H	Mich. Sch. for Deaf (ex)	13-1	W
4-21	H	Michigan	6-9	L
4-22	H	Michigan	2-11	L
4-26	H	Hillsdale	14-5	W
4-29	A	Alma	2-1	W
5-8	H	Olivet	7-1	W
5-13	A	Kalamazoo	20-4	W
5-18	H	Albion	6-2	W
5-20	H	Hillsdale	5-2	W
5-24	A	Albion	0-1	L
5-26	A	Detroit College	11-10	W
5-27	H	Kalamazoo	3-2	W
5-30	H	Detroit Business Univ.	2-1	W
6-2	H	Hillsdale	@6-2	W
6-3	H	Albion	@2-12	L

1906 (10-9)
Coach: Chester Brewer

4-11	H	Lansing H.S. (ex)	11-2	W
4-14	H	Olivet	4-7	L
		Olivet	5-2	W
4-20	A	Albion	4-0	W
4-21	H	Olivet	5-0	W
4-28	H	Michigan Military Acad.	2-7	L
4-30	H	DePauw	3-1	W
5-1	H	DePauw	2-5	L
5-2	A	Hillsdale	5-2	W
5-5	A	Alma	19-1	W
5-7	A	Kalamazoo	9-8	W
5-12	H	Kalamazoo	1-0	W
5-18	H	Michigan Normal	0-7	L
5-19	A	Michigan	1-8	L
5-24	A	Albion	1-4	L
5-26	H	Olivet	3-4	L
5-28	H	Hillsdale	8-1	W
5-30	A	Armour Tech.	4-9	L
6-1	H	Olivet	@3-0	W
6-2	H	Albion	@0-2	L

1907 (4-8)
Coach: Chester Brewer

4-18	H	Michigan	2-7	L
4-19	H	Michigan	0-8	L
4-20	H	Michigan	2-7	L
4-27	H	U of D Prep School	13-5	W
5-7	A	Notre Dame	0-1	L
5-8	A	Kalamazoo	16-10	W
5-11	A	Alma	2-3	L
5-15	H	Hillsdale	15-0	W
5-17	A	Michigan Normal	2-5	L
5-18	H	Kalamazoo	13-1	W
5-29	A	Michigan	0-2	L
6-7	A	Albion	@2-4	L

1908 (7-5-1)

Coach: Chester Brewer

4-20	H	Olivet	5-0	W
4-23	A	DePaul	6-5	W
4-24	A	Culver Military Acad.	2-3	L
4-25	A	Notre Dame	2-4	L
5-2	H	Alma	4-0	W
5-9	H	U of D Prep School	1-1	T
5-15	H	Wabash	0-5	L
5-20	H	Lake Forest	5-1	W
5-21	H	Lake Forest	6-3	W
5-23	H	Michigan Normal	10-2	W
5-29	H	Syracuse	2-4	L
6-3	A	Olivet	4-1	W
6-5	H	Detroit A.C.	2-4	L

1909 (10-3)

Coach: Chester Brewer

4-17	H	Olivet	1-0	W
4-20	A	Culver Military Acad.	8-3	W
4-24	H	Michigan	3-8	L
5-5	A	Michigan	3-9	L
5-8	H	U of D Prep School	8-2	W
5-11	H	Lansing Senators (ex)	9-3	W
5-19	H	Wabash	5-4	W
5-20	A	Wabash	10-9	W
5-21	A	St. Viator's	0-7	L
5-26	H	DePaul	5-4	W
5-27	H	DePaul	10-1	W
5-29	A	Olivet	7-4	W
5-31	H$_{LN}$	DePaul	4-2	W

1910 (8-6)

Coach: Chester Brewer

4-16	H	Olivet	1-5	L
4-21	A	Notre Dame	1-3	L
4-23	A	Culver Military Acad.	9-1	W
4-29	H	Ohio Wesleyan	12-1	W
4-30	H	Western Reserve	4-0	W
5-7	A	Michigan	2-4	L
5-11	A	Alma	4-5	L
5-13	H	Western State Normal	12-7	W
5-14	H	Syracuse	1-5	L
5-21	H	Alma	3-1	W
5-28	H	Wabash	6-0	W
5-30	H	Wabash	4-1	W
6-4	H	Michigan Normal	5-1	W
6-11	A	Olivet	2-11	L

John F. Macklin (1911-1915)

Wasting little time, Initially, President Snyder selected the coach from the University of Arkansas, 37-year-old Hugo Bezdek, as Brewer's replacement. As it turned out, there proved to be one slight problem—Bezdek could not be released from his contract at Arkansas. The next candidate to be offered the Aggie job was Jesse Harper, the Wabash College coach; however, the State Board of Agriculture would not approve the deal. The proposed annual salary of $2,200 ($200 over Brewer's final year) seemed exorbitant. Instead, Harper would sign on with Notre Dame in the following year. Heeding the advice of one of the top coaches of the day, Mike Murphy of Pennsylvania, President Jonathan Snyder eventually hired John Macklin, a star of football, baseball, and track at Penn in 1906 and 1907. Macklin had spent three years (1908-1910) developing teams at a private prep school in Pawling, NY. With the title of professor of physical culture and athletic director, he would be paid $2,000 per year. In addition to proving himself as a coach, Macklin demonstrated he was also a manager of funds. Upon his arrival in 1911, the athletic association had a fistful of outstanding debts accompanied by a trifling $6.30 in its treasury. When his tenure was complete in 1916 the account was debt-free and had grown to $14,994. More than belt-tightening, the professor drove a hard bargain. While in past years MAC received $200 for the annual fall football trip to Ann Arbor from which expenses would be

wrested, by 1915 the U of M had agreed to fork over $5,000 for the Aggies' game share. In March of 1916, John Farrell Macklin left the scene as rapidly as he had arrived five years earlier. Retiring from coaching, in March of 1916 he moved to Colver, PA, where he commenced a career of managing a multi million-dollar coal mining business owned by his in-laws.

1911 (11-5)

Coach: John Macklin

4-15	H	Olivet	2-6	L
4-18	H	DePauw	14-1	W
4-22	A	Michigan	1-3	L
4-28	H	Western Reserve	5-0	W
5-5	H	Ohio State	6-1	W
5-6	A	Michigan Normal	2-1	W
5-11	H	Wabash	3-2	W
5-12	H	Syracuse	6-4	W
5-13	H	Alma	6-2	W
5-18	A	Culver Military Acad.	7-3	W
5-19	A	Wabash	0-4	L
5-25	H	Lake Forest	2-1	W
5-27	H	St. John's (Toledo)	15-2	W
5-30	H	Michigan	2-8	L
6-3	H	Central Mich. Normal	5-0	W
6-10	A	Olivet	2-3	L

1912 (11-3)

Coach: John F. Macklin

4-13	H	Olivet	3-0	W
4-20	H	Lansing Senators	7-1	W
4-22	H	Ohio State	8-11	L
4-26	H	Western Reserve	5-1	W
5-1	H	Ohio Wesleyan	1-2	L
5-4	H	Michigan	7-6	W
5-10	H	Syracuse	2-1	W
5-17	H	Wabash	8-4	W
5-18	A	Michigan	5-1	W
5-22	A	Ohio Wesleyan	5-2	W
5-23	A	Western Reserve	2-1	W
5-30	A	Michigan	8-3	W
6-1	H	Olivet	0-2	L
6-8	H	Michigan Normal	8-0	W

1913 (11-7)

Coach: John F. Macklin

4-18	H	Western Reserve	3-2	W
4-19	A	Olivet	8-2	W
4-24	H	Georgia	3-9	L
4-25	H	Georgia	0-4	L
4-26	H	Alma	7-6	W
4-30	H	Kentucky	8-1	W
5-2	H	Case Tech	4-11	L
5-7	H	Washington & Jefferson	7-5	W
5-9	H	Syracuse	5-1	W
5-14	H	Olivet	9-8	W
5-17	H	Michigan	2-9	L
5-22	A	Western Reserve	1-0	W
5-23	A	Ohio Northern	2-3	L
5-24	A	Buchtel	6-3	W
5-28	A	Michigan	4-5	L
5-31	A	Michigan	2-7	L
6-5	H	Lake Forest	4-3	W
6-6	H	Ohio State	5-4	W

1914 (12-5)

Coach: John F. Macklin

4-18	H	Olivet	14-12	W
4-23	H	Ohio Wesleyan	5-4	W
4-24	H	Western Reserve	7-1	W
4-25	H	Bethany (WV)	8-3	W
5-1	H	Case Tech	2-1	W
5-2	A	Notre Dame	3-6	L
5-5	H	Alma	4-1	W
5-6	H	Akron	7-6	W

5-8	H	Syracuse	5-4	W
5-16	H$_{LN}$	Michigan	0-6	L
5-19	A	Oberlin	4-2	W
5-20	A	Western Reserve	13-3	W
5-21	A	Ohio State	5-3	W
5-27	H	Lake Forest	3-8	L
5-29	A	Michigan	3-10	L
5-30	A	Michigan	8-1	W
6-4	H	Notre Dame	4-12	L

1915 (8-6)

Coach: John F. Macklin

4-14	H	Albion	19-5	W
4-19	H	Olivet	9-3	W
4-23	H	Western Reserve	6-1	W
4-24	H	Bethany (WV)	4-0	W
4-29	H	Detroit	3-1	W
5-1	A	Notre Dame	2-3	L
5-7	H	Syracuse	3-4	L
5-12	A	Michigan	3-1	W
5-15	H	Alma	7-1	W
5-18	A	Ohio Wesleyan	1-2	L
5-19	A	Marshall (WV)	2-3	L
5-28	H	Michigan	1-8	L
5-29	H	Michigan	4-2	W
6-3	H	Notre Dame	2-4	L

John Morrissey (1916-1917 and 1922)

With Macklin's departure, it was revealed that a local hero, John "King" Morrissey, manager of Lansing's professional Southern Michigan League team for several years, would take charge of *only* the baseball team. "King" was born in Lansing on May 2, 1876, and began playing professional baseball as far back as 1895 in the Three I League. Moving on to the American Association he would advance to the big league playing in two partial seasons (1902 and 1903) as second baseman with the Cincinnati Reds. Although his major league "career" would total only 41 games, his baseball knowledge was highly respected in the Lansing community. Morrissey coached two Aggie teams (1916 and 1917) and was then called back as interim head coach of the 1922 team with Potsy Clark's sudden departure.

1916 (11-4)

Coach: John Morrissey

4-16	H	Olivet	13-1	W
4-21	H	Marshall (WV)	8-2	W
4-26	H	Western State Normal	1-2	L
4-29	A	Notre Dame	0-2	L
5-3	H	Kalamazoo	5-1	W
5-5	H	Syracuse	3-0	W
5-12	H	Wabash	4-1	W
5-13	H	Wabash	6-1	W
5-18	A	Buffalo	4-0	W
5-19	A	Rochester	6-5	W
5-20	A	Syracuse	2-3	L
5-23	A	Niagara	4-3	W
5-27	H	Michigan	3-5	L
6-1	H	Notre Dame	5-2	W
6-3	H	Michigan Normal	9-1	W

1917 (6-5)

Coach: John Morrissey

4-14	H	Olivet	19-2	W
4-20	H	Marshall (WV)	2-6	L
4-21	H	Marshall	2-1	W
4-27	H	Western State Normal	3-5	L
4-28	H	Western Reserve	9-1	W
5-5	H	Alma	12-1	W
5-12	A	Notre Dame	0-12	L
5-18	H	Niagara	5-4	W
5-19	H	St. Mary's (MI)	8-9	L
5-31	H	Notre Dame	5-0	W
6-1	H	Notre Dame	2-4	L

1918 (7-5)
Coach: Chester Brewer

4-13	H	Alma	16-7	W
4-19	H	Olivet	9-3	W
4-20	H	Kalamazoo	6-4	W
4-24	H	Michigan	2-12	L
4-26	H	St. Mary's (MI)	11-9	W
4-27	A	Michigan Normal	1-4	L
5-4	H	Notre Dame	8-11	L
5-7	H	Indiana	3-8	L
5-9	A	Kalamazoo	10-6	W
5-10	A	Western State Normal	10-3	W
5-11	A	Notre Dame	4-0	W
5-15	A	Michigan	2-5	L

1919 (5-9)
Coach: Chester Brewer

4-19	H	Alma	11-3	W
4-23	H	Kalamazoo	3-6	L
4-28	H	Indiana	0-6	L
4-30	A	Notre Dame	2-1	W
5-2	H	Indiana	0-1	L
5-10	H	Western State Normal	20-12	W
5-14	A	Michigan	0-4	L
5-15	H	Michigan Normal	2-10	L
5-22	H	Michigan	2-5	L
5-31	H	Notre Dame	5-12	L
6-6	H	Central State	10-1	W
6-7	A	Western State Normal	2-0	W
6-9	H	Wabash	5-2	W
6-10	H	Wabash	20-4	W

1920 (6-9)
Coach: Chester Brewer

4-12	A	Rochester	7-0	W
4-14	A	Penn State	5-14	L
4-24	H	Albion	12-2	W
5-1	H	Michigan Normal	5-1	W
5-3	H	Armour Tech	13-4	W
5-5	H	Michigan	3-5	L
5-6	A	Armour Tech	6-4	W
5-7	A	Valparaiso	1-3	L
5-8	A	Notre Dame	10-11	L
5-12	A	Michigan	8-9	L
5-14	H	Oberlin	2-7	L
5-20	H	Valparaiso	2-6	L
5-25	H	Notre Dame	11-12	L
5-26	A	Oberlin	1-0	W
5-29	A	Detroit	4-5	L

George E. "Potsy" Clark (1921)

In August of 1920 it was announced that a University of Illinois great, George E. "Potsy" Clark, would become the next hope for Aggie followers. Clark, stamped as one of the greatest leaders and natural athletes ever produced in the Western Conference, was a popular choice as the new football-baseball coach. He was a quarterback on the Illini football teams of 1913-15 and captained his senior team to the school's first conference championship. Although Clark gained greatest recognition on the gridiron, he was a collegiate three-sport star being a second baseman in baseball and forward on the basketball team. Upon graduation, Potsy signed on at Kansas University as head football coach and assistant in baseball and basketball. His 1916 grid squad finished runner-up to Missouri in the Missouri Valley Conference. It was then that Athletic Director Brewer came to know and appreciate the coaching talent of the former Illini star. In the spring of 1917, Clark enlisted in the U.S. Army and was sent to Europe with one of the country's earliest detachments into World War I. While there he captained the 89th Division teams that won both the A.E.F. football and baseball championships. At war's end, Clark returned to Champaign as an assistant to the legendary Bob Zuppke. Although staying but one year (1919), he would once again bask in the glory of yet another conference football championship team from the University of Illinois, this time as a

coach. Much like his other coaching stops, Potsy Clark would remain in East Lansing for a single season. Following the spring sports banquet in June of 1921, Clark said good-bye and departed for his home in Illinois. He would remain there until time to report for fall practice at Lawrence, KS, where he would resume his pre-war position as the Jayhawk head coach.

1921 (7-8)
Coach: George E. "Potsy" Clark

4-20	H	Albion	11-1	W
4-27	H	Western State Normal	12-6	W
4-30	H	DePauw	6-0	W
5-5	H	Valparaiso	5-6	L
5-6	A	St. Mary's (MI)	12-9	W
5-7	A	Oberlin	9-6	W
5-11	H	Michigan	6-7	L
5-13	H	Iowa	3-5	L
5-19	H	Notre Dame	4-7	L
5-20	H	Oberlin	10-2	W
5-21	H	Oberlin	1-3	L
5-25	A	Western State Normal	3-2	W
5-26	A	Notre Dame	4-8	L
5-27	H	Valaraiso	3-6	L
6-1	H	Michigan	5-8	L

1922 (8-10)
Coach: John Morrissey

4-22	H	Western State Normal	3-4	L
4-25	H	Albion	9-5	W
4-26	A	Kalamazoo	8-4	W
4-27	A	Wabash	2-3	L
4-28	A	Armour Tech	31-7	W
4-29	A	Notre Dame	6-12	L
5-6	H	Notre Dame	1-3	L
5-9	H	DePauw	4-10	L
5-10	H	DePauw	2-1	W
5-13	H	Michigan Normal	5-4	W
5-20	H	Western State Normal	10-11	L
5-27	H	Wisconsin	1-10	L
5-30	H	YMCA Coll. (Chicago)	16-1	W
6-10	H	Kalamazoo	6-2	W
6-15	A	Bethany	3-6	L
6-16	A	Bethany	7-8	L
6-17	A	Oberlin	0-8	L

Fred Walker (1923-1924)

In the fall of 1922, Fred M. Walker was engaged to coach freshmen football, varsity basketball, and varsity baseball. He was a graduate of the University of Chicago in 1908 where he was a three-sport star. After graduation, he played five years of professional baseball, three seasons with New Haven of the Eastern League, and then two years with the Chicago Cubs. In 1920, Walker returned to the University of Chicago where he assisted A.A. Stagg and then spent 1921 as head football coach at DePauw University. The new coach was hailed as possessing a wealth of talent for handling all varieties of athletic teams. John Caruso (BS '27-28) described Walker as a powerful man. All of the players seemed to like him and they obeyed him; but, he was tough and had a strong-willed temper. Caruso noted, "he would smash more bats than the school could buy." Walker would last two academic years, resigning on May 8, 1924, to take effect on September 1.

1923 (14-4)
Coach: Fred Walker

4-6	H	St. Mary's (MI)	7-6	W
4-13	H	Michigan Normal	6-5	W
4-16	A	Valparaiso	5-6	L
4-17	A	Chicago	9-0	W
4-18	A	Notre Dame	9-16	L
4-19	A	Kalamazoo	8-0	W
4-24	H	Michigan	0-21	L
4-28	H	Albion	13-1	W

5-2	A	Michigan	2-16	L
5-4	H	Notre Dame	6-5	W
5-11	H	DePaul	7-6	W
5-12	H	Valparaiso	10-5	W
5-15	H	Beloit	10-2	W
5-19	H	Hope	3-1	W
5-22	H	Kalamazoo	14-1	W
5-24	H	St. Viator's	5-3	W
5-30	A	Michigan Normal	12-8	W
6-7	H	Alma	8-1	W

1924 (6-7)
Coach: Fred Walker

4-11	H	Hope	8-2	W
4-18	H	Western State Normal	1-6	L
4-23	A	Michigan	0-1	L
4-29	H	St. Mary's (MI)	8-0	W
5-3	H	Chicago	4-8	L
5-9	A	Western State Normal	1-2	L
5-16	H	Lake Forest	4-2	W
5-21	H	Michigan	1-3	L
5-26	H	St. Viator's	10-7	W
5-30	H	Wisconsin	8-4	W
5-31	H	Butler	8-4	W
6-6	H	Notre Dame	3-4	L
6-14	A	Notre Dame	2-8	L

John H. Kobs (1925-1963)

Fred Walker's departure was not totally unexpected; consequently, the athletic board had already reviewed a long list of applicants. It took only two days for the announcement that John H. Kobs of Hamline College (MN) would be the successor. By spending nearly four decades in and out of dugouts, John Kobs is most appropriately identified with the sport of baseball; however, he was initially and foremost a multi-sports coach. Upon reporting in the fall of 1924, the 26-year-old's assignments included head coach for basketball, head coach for baseball, and freshmen football coach. One year later, hockey would be added to his duties. Finally, in 1930 Kobs focused his head coaching chores solely at the diamond which now bears his name. Reflecting his love of the gridiron, John did continue to assist with freshmen football well into the Biggie Munn era. John Kobs's diverse athletic background prepared him well for being a multi-sport coach. He entered Hamline in 1916 and over the next four years became a four-year letterman in football, basketball, and baseball. He also performed as a weight man for the track team and won considerable reputation as a hockey player. Upon graduating with an B.A. degree, Kobs joined the staff of his alma mater in the capacity of assistant athletic director and coaching assistant in football, basketball, baseball, and track. He would also take a short fling at professional baseball in the North-South Dakota League. Following 39 years as the Spartans head man on the diamond, John Kobs retired following the 1963 season. He died on January 26, 1968.

1925 (8-5-1)
Coach: John H. Kobs

4-16	A	Armour Tech	9-0	W
4-17	A	St. Viator's	5-5	T
4-18	A	Wisconsin	4-13	L
4-21	H	Olivet	17-4	W
4-25	A	Western State Normal	2-3	L
4-29	A	Michigan	4-10	L
5-4	H	St. Mary's (MI)	7-5	W
5-9	H	Hope	13-1	W
5-14	H	Minnesota	5-2	W
5-20	H	Michigan	6-13	L
5-23	A	Notre Dame	7-11	L
5-28	A	St. Viator's	5-4	W
5-30	H	Butler	8-6	W
6-6	H	Notre Dame	5-4	W

1926 (13-7)

* - Spring trip games
Coach: John H. Kobs

4-1	*	Ft. Benning	5-7	L
4-2	*	Ft. Benning	4-1	W
4-3	*	Mercer	1-0	W
4-5	*	Alabama Institute	5-8	L
4-6	*	Oglethorpe	8-6	W
4-14	H	Albion	7-2	W
4-17	H	Bradley	18-3	W
4-21	A	Michigan	1-6	L
4-29	H	Syracuse	4-3	W
5-1	H	Lake Forest	27-5	W
5-4	H	Olivet	11-0	W
5-8	H	Butler	4-7	L
5-13	H	Hope	6-2	W
5-15	H	St. Viator's	2-3	L
5-24	H	Michigan	8-5	W
5-27	H	Western State Normal	7-4	W
5-29	H	Armour Tech	9-1	W
6-2	A	Western State Normal	0-7	L
6-5	H	Notre Dame	5-3	W
6-12	A	Notre Dame	0-6	L

1927 (13-8)

Coach: John H. Kobs

3-26	*	Western Kentucky	3-4	L
3-28	*	Ft. Benning	11-19	L
3-29	*	Ft. Benning	12-8	W
3-30	*	Ft. Benning	3-5	L
3-31	*	Mercer	0-7	L
4-1	*	Marysville	4-7	L
4-2	*	Marysville	0-17	L
4-4	*	Xavier	1-0	W
4-13	H	Albion	17-0	W
4-22	H	Adrian	13-2	W
4-23	H	Olivet	16-0	W
4-26	A	Michigan	4-6	L
4-28	H	West Virginia	9-3	W
5-5	H	Hope	7-5	W
5-7	A	Notre Dame	4-1	W
5-13	H	Bradley	9-5	W
5-20	H	St. Viator's	5-1	W
5-25	H	Notre Dame	0-5	L
5-28	H	Armour Tech	7-3	W
6-1	H	Michigan	4-1	W
6-11	H	Xavier	11-7	W

1928 (10-8)

Coach: John H. Kobs

3-24	*	Cumberland	5-3	W
3-26	*	Ft. Benning	0-5	L
3-27	*	Ft. Benning	2-21	L
3-28	*	Ft. Benning	9-7	W
3-29	*	Marysville	0-7	L
3-31	*	Tech Trade School (TN)	4-7	L
4-11	H	Adrian	12-0	W
4-19	H	Kalamazoo	10-4	W
4-26	H	Syracuse	2-1	W
5-1	A	Ohio State	5-12	L
5-4	H	Armour Tech	5-2	W
5-9	H	West Virginia	1-21	L
5-15	H	Bradley	8-7	W
5-30	H	Chicago YMCA Coll.	5-2	W
6-2	A	Notre Dame	0-8	L
6-7	H	Hope	11-0	W
6-15	A	Michigan	6-7	L
6-16	H	Michigan	9-4	W

1929 (12-11-1)

Coach: John H. Kobs

4-1	*	Cumberland	5-2	W
4-2	*	Cumberland	4-4	T
4-3	*	Vanderbilt	2-7	L
4-4	*	Vanderbilt	1-12	L
4-6	*	Xavier	2-14	L

4-8	*	Cincinnati	13-4	W
4-18	H	Kalamazoo	20-2	W
4-23	H	Adrian	4-1	W
4-27	H	Luther	2-17	L
5-4	H	Colgate	0-4	L
5-7	H	Hope	8-1	W
5-10	H	Notre Dame	1-9	L
5-13	H	Albion	9-1	W
5-16	A	Notre Dame	5-12	L
5-17	H	Coe	4-3	W
5-21	H	Michigan	4-3	W
5-23	H	Defiance	4-3	W
5-25	H	St. Mary's (MI)	10-5	W
5-29	A	Oberlin	1-5	L
5-31	H	Ohio State	2-5	L
6-6	H	Hillsdale	3-2	W
6-14	A	Michigan	2-6	L
6-15	A	Michigan	6-15	L
6-22	H	Auto Owners Insurance	6-5	W

1930 (18-6)

Coach: John H. Kobs

3-31	*	Marysville	2-11	L
4-1	*	Marysville	3-0	W
4-3	*	Vanderbilt	4-5	L
4-5	*	Xavier	9-2	W
4-7	*	Cincinnati	13-3	W
4-8	*	Miami (OH)	3-5	L
4-12	H	Chicago	12-4	W
4-19	A	Michigan Normal	4-1	W
4-24	H	Syracuse	4-3	W
4-26	H	Central State Teachers	11-1	W
4-30	H	Iowa State Teachers	4-5	L
5-3	H	Notre Dame	3-2	W
5-10	H	Western State Teachers	7-4	W
5-13	H	Hope	13-5	W
5-17	A	Western State Teachers	7-4	W
5-19	A	Chicago	3-4	L
5-22	H	Miami (OH)	11-3	W
5-24	H	Oberlin	3-0	W
5-26	A	Notre Dame	5-3	W
5-27	H	Cincinnati	5-3	W
5-30	H	Michigan	3-1	W
6-7	H	Michigan Normal	9-3	W
6-20	A	Michigan	3-6	L
6-21	H	Michigan	8-4	W

1931 (13-9-1)

Coach: John H. Kobs

3-30	*	Mississippi State	4-3	W
4-1	*	Mississippi	4-5	L
4-2	*	Mississippi	1-10	L
4-3	*	Vanderbilt	3-2	W
4-4	*	Vanderbilt	3-5	L
4-6	*	Xavier	8-4	W
4-18	H	Michigan Normal	3-2	W
4-23	H	Hope	10-2	W
4-25	H	Central State Teachers	6-0	W
5-2	H	Western State Teachers	2-1	W
5-8	H	Iowa State Teachers	17-2	W
5-11	H	Hosei Univ. (Japan)	3-5	L
5-13	H	Hosei Univ. (Japan)	1-4	L
5-14	A	Central State Teachers	16-5	W
5-23	H	Michigan	8-4	W
5-26	A	Chicago	9-10	L
5-27	A	Northwestern	4-5	L
6-1	H	Indiana	10-9	W
6-2	H	Indiana	3-6	L
6-10	H	Western State Teachers	5-3	W
6-13	H	Michigan Normal	5-5	T
6-19	A	Michigan	2-3	L
6-20	H	Michigan	5-0	W

1932 (10-12-2)

Coach: John H. Kobs

3-28	*	Ft. Benning	6-8	L
3-29	*	Ft. Benning	4-5	L
3-30	*	Ft. Benning	6-3	W
3-31	*	Georgia Tech	4-4	T
4-1	*	Vanderbilt	1-2	L
4-2	*	Vanderbilt	8-4	W
4-7	*	Xavier	7-6	W
4-16	A	St. Viator's	6-1	W
4-21	H	Central State Teachers	19-2	W
4-25	H	Luther	1-3	L
4-29	H	Iowa	12-4	W
4-30	H	Iowa	4-3	W
5-3	A	Michigan	3-3	T
5-7	H	Michigan Normal	3-7	L
5-11	H	Hillsdale	8-5	W
5-14	H	Notre Dame	5-2	W
5-19	H	Ohio	8-10	L
5-25	H	Michigan	3-4	L
5-27	A	Central State Teachers	5-6	L
5-28	A	Western State Teachers	2-5	L
5-30	H	Chicago	7 6	W
6-2	A	Michigan Normal	0-1	L
6-4	A	Notre Dame	3-6	L
6-8	A	Western State Teachers	4-6	L

1933 (13-7)

Coach: John H. Kobs

3-28	*	Elon	6-5	W
3-29	*	Wake Forest	6-8	L
3-30	*	North Carolina	6-5	W
3-31	*	North Carolina	5-3	W
4-1	*	Duke	7-8	L
4-13	H	Iowa	4-0	W
4-15	H	Northwestern	5-4	W
4-20	H	Hillsdale	12-0	W
4-22	A	Northwestern	7-3	W
4-29	A	Michigan	5-1	W
5-3	H	Notre Dame	5-3	W
5-13	H	Western State Teachers	0-1	L
5-18	H	Oberlin	14-3	W
5-20	A	Michigan Normal	1-5	L
5-24	H	Michigan	3-4	L
5-27	H	Indiana	3-10	L
5-30	H	Chicago	9-2	W
6-3	A	Notre Dame	14-5	W
6-7	H	Western State Teachers	5-8	L
6-10	H	Michigan Normal	8-3	W

1934 (10-11-1)

Coach: John H. Kobs

3-26	*	Davidson	16-6	W
3-27	*	Duke	4-14	L
3-28	*	Elon	11-10	W
3-29	*	Wake Forest	4-9	L
3-30	*	North Carolina	4-5	L
3-31	*	Rocky Mound Amateurs	8-8	T
4-18	H	Hillsdale	3-2	W
4-21	H	Michigan Normal	5-2	W
4-24	H	Northwestern	9-3	W
5-1	A	Michigan	3-13	L
5-5	A	Western State Teachers	1-4	L
5-9	H	Notre Dame	8-1	W
5-12	H	Western State Teachers	4-9	L
5-18	H	Ohio State	4-6	L
4-19	H	Ohio State	13-4	W
4-22	A	Michigan Normal	0-3	L
5-25	H	Indiana	2-5	L
5-30	H	Michigan	1-5	L
6-2	A	Notre Dame	13-9	W
6-4	H	Cleveland Indians	4-14	L
6-8	H	Iowa	6-0	W
6-9	H	Iowa	6-1	W

1935 (11-9-1)
Coach: John H. Kobs

3-25	*	Clemson	0-5	L
3-26	*	Furman	17-1	W
3-27	*	Newberry	7-7	T
3-28	*	South Carolina	5-1	W
3-29	*	Davidson	1-3	L
3-30	*	Wake Forest	3-4	L
4-13	H	Hillsdale	10-9	W
4-20	H	Northwestern	8-7	W
4-25	H	Wisconsin	4-3	W
4-26	H	Wisconsin	7-6	W
5-2	H	Notre Dame	5-4	W
5-4	A	Western State Teachers	4-6	L
5-10	H	Michigan Normal	4-3	W
5-17	A	Ohio State	7-8	L
5-18	A	Ohio State	2-5	L
5-21	A	Michigan Normal	5-4	W
5-25	H	Western State Teachers	2-5	L
5-30	H	Michigan	4-1	W
6-1	A	Notre Dame	1-2	L
6-7	H	Iowa	2-5	L
6-8	H	Iowa	5-4	W

1936 (13-7)
Coach: John H. Kobs

3-30	*	Clemson	18-0	W
3-31	*	Newberry	5-0	W
4-3	*	North Carolina State	13-5	W
4-4	*	Wake Forest	4-1	W
4-18	H	Toledo	7-0	W
4-23	H	Wisconsin	5-7	L
4-24	H	Wisconsin	7-5	W
4-30	H	Notre Dame	3-12	L
5-7	H	Michigan Normal	19-0	W
5-9	A	Western State Teachers	11-0	W
5-14	A	Cornell	7-2	W
5-16	A	Michigan Normal	19-5	W
5-22	H	Ohio State	6-5	W
5-23	H	Ohio State	6-9	L
5-29	A	Michigan	1-2	L
5-30	H	Michigan	2-5	L
6-4	H	Iowa	4-3	W
6-5	H	Iowa	3-0	W
6-6	A	Notre Dame	4-6	L
6-13	H	Western State Teachers	1-11	L

1937 (15-11)
Coach: John H. Kobs

3-27	*	Eastern Kentucky	12-8	W
3-29	*	Newberry	8-2	W
3-30	*	Oakridge Military Acad.	8-6	W
3-31	*	Duke	5-12	L
4-1	*	North Carolina	5-8	L
4-2	*	Elon	4-6	L
4-3	*	Wake Forest	1-6	L
4-5	*	Ohio	4-3	W
4-22	H	Wisconsin	3-5	L
4-23	H	Wisconsin	3-5	L
4-29	A	Western State Teachers	2-11	L
5-1	H	Notre Dame	7-1	W
5-6	H	Western State Teachers	1-3	L
5-8	H	Indiana	6-5	W
5-12	H	Northwestern	4-1	W
5-13	A	Toledo	8-3	W
5-14	A	Ohio State	0-9	L
5-15	A	Ohio State	12-2	W
5-19	H	Toledo	4-3	W
5-26	A	Notre Dame	10-3	W
5-29	H	Michigan	4-1	W
5-31	A	Michigan	0-1	L
6-5	H	Michigan Normal	18-0	W
6-7	H	Iowa	3-1	W
6-8	H	Iowa	5-7	L
6-12	H	Nebraska	6-0	W

1938 (15-9)
Coach: John H. Kobs

3-26	*	Eastern Kentucky	2-1	W
3-28	*	Georgia	8-5	W
3-29	*	Georgia	12-6	W
3-30	*	Newberry	6-4	W
3-31	*	South Carolina	10-4	W
4-4	*	West Virginia	4-2	W
4-5	*	Ohio	4-1	W
4-20	H	Wisconsin	1-2	L
4-21	H	Wisconsin	0-1	L
4-23	H	Michigan Normal	5-3	W
4-26	A	Michigan	9-3	W
4-29	A	Iowa	5-2	W
4-30	A	Iowa	3-5	L
5-6	H	Indiana	7-4	W
5-7	H	Notre Dame	5-4	W
5-14	H	Armour Tech	5-4	W
5-21	A	Michigan Normal	7-10	L
5-24	H	Notre Dame	1-9	L
5-26	H	California	2-6	L
5-28	H	Toledo	1-2	L
5-30	H	Michigan	0-3	L
6-3	A	Ohio State	2-0	W
6-4	A	Ohio State	2-7	L
6-7	A	Western State Teachers	5-1	W

1939 (13-10)
Coach: John H. Kobs

3-27	*	Georgia	2-3	L
3-28	*	Georgia	5-4	W
3-29	*	South Carolina	10-5	W
3-31	*	Duke	0-3	L
4-1	*	Wake Forest	0-1	L
4-3	*	West Virginia	7-5	W
4-4	*	West Virginia	6-4	W
4-22	H	Michigan Normal	11-13	L
4-28	A	Michigan	6-3	W
5-5	H	Ohio Wesleyan	17-7	W
5-6	H	Notre Dame	14-9	W
5-11	H	Indiana	0-7	L
5-13	H	Ohio	7-8	L
5-18	H	Hillsdale	7-4	W
5-20	H	Minnesota	8-3	W
5-24	H	Toledo	5-0	W
5-26	A	Wisconsin	5-7	L
5-27	A	Armour Tech	5-2	W
5-30	H	Michigan	5-13	L
6-1	A	Michigan Normal	1-7	L
6-4	A	Notre Dame	4-3	W
6-6	A	Western State Teachers	1-2	L
6-10	H	Western State Teachers	1-0	W

1940 (12-8-2)
Coach: John H. Kobs

3-22	*	Georgia	3-2	W
3-23	*	Georgia	4-5	L
3-25	*	Clemson	3-3	T
3-26	*	Presbyterian	11-5	W
3-27	*	South Carolina	14-12	W
4-17	H	Wisconsin	6-6	T
4-18	H	Wisconsin	7-6	W
4-27	H	Western State Teachers	6-19	L
4-30	A	Michigan	5-4	W
5-4	H	Notre Dame	2-1	W
5-11	A	Western State Teachers	7-5	W
5-17	A	Iowa	4-8	L
5-18	A	Iowa	0-4	L
5-22	H	Toledo	8-3	W
5-24	H	Michigan Normal	7-1	W
5-25	A	Hillsdale	16-2	W
5-28	H	Hillsdale	17-4	W
5-30	H	Michigan	4-5	L
6-1	A	Notre Dame	4-2	W
6-4	H	Illinois Wesleyan	8-10	L
6-7	H	Ohio State	3-4	L
6-8	H	Ohio State	3-7	L

1941 (13-10)
Coach: John H. Kobs

3-24	*	South Carolina	14-4	W
3-25	*	Clemson	5-4	W
3-26	*	Georgia	6-4	W
3-28	*	Ft. Benning	12-9	W
3-29	*	Ft. Benning	10-7	W
3-31	*	Alabama Poly (Auburn)	8-9	L
4-2	*	Vanderbilt	10-11	L
4-11	A	Ohio State	4-5	L
4-12	A	Ohio State	5-3	W
4-26	H	Michigan Normal	10-3	W
4-29	A	Michigan	3-4	L
5-2	A	Wisconsin	2-1	W
5-3	A	Wisconsin	2-3	L
5-7	A	Notre Dame	5-14	L
5-10	H	Notre Dame	10-2	W
5-15	H	Indiana	4-3	W
5-17	A	Michigan Normal	4-0	W
5-23	H	Western Michigan	3-2	W
5-31	H	Michigan	4-6	L
6-2	H	Iowa	2-3	L
6-3	H	Iowa	2-6	L
6-6	H	California	7-0	W
6-7	H	California	5-8	L

1942 (13-11-1)
Coach: John H. Kobs

3-23	*	Pensacola NAB	2-5	L
3-24	*	Pensacola NAB	4-1	W
3-25	*	Pensacola NAB	6-3	W
3-28	*	Ft. Benning	6-6	T
3-30	*	Georgia	4-18	L
3-31	*	Georgia	9-20	L
4-1	*	Clemson	11-5	W
4-15	A	Wayne	2-1	W
4-17	H	Ohio State	3-5	L
4-18	H	Ohio State	2-3	L
4-22	A	Detroit	5-3	W
4-24	H	Wisconsin	9-6	W
4-25	H	Wisconsin	8-7	W
4-28	A	Michigan	1-2	L
5-1	H	Wayne	14-7	W
5-4	A	Iowa	2-9	L
5-9	H	Ft. Custer	2-4	L
5-14	H	Detroit	8-7	W
5-20	A	Western Michigan	1-3	L
5-23	A	Michigan Normal	4-2	W
5-25	H	Great Lakes NTS	3-4	L
5-28	H	Michigan	12-1	W
5-30	H	Ft. Custer	2-8	L
6-3	H	Western Michigan	3-1	W
6-6	H	Michigan Normal	10-5	W

1943 (9-7)
Coach: John H. Kobs

4-17	A	Michigan	1-7	L
4-23	A	Ohio State	0-3	L
4-24	A	Ohio State	10-6	W
4-27	A	Notre Dame	2-12	L
4-29	H	Notre Dame	0-8	L
5-1	H	Detroit	9-3	W
5-10	A	Wisconsin	6-7	L
5-11	A	Wisconsin	5-9	L
5-15	H	Hillsdale	12-2	W
5-20	A	Detroit	10-1	W
5-22	A	Michigan Normal	7-1	W
5-25	A	Western Michigan	0-5	L
5-28	H	Michigan Normal	6-4	W
6-5	H	Western Michigan	2-1	W
6-8	A	Selfridge AFB	4-2	W
6-10	H	Selfridge AFB	10-1	W

1944 (4-6-1)
Coach: John H. Kobs

4-29	H	Wayne	12-3	W
5-4	A	Detroit Coast Guard	17-11	W
5-6	H	Grosse Ile Navy Air	4-12	L
5-9	A	Ionia Prison	0-0	T
5-12	A	Wayne	11-8	W
5-13	A	Detroit	6-1	L
5-21	A	Grosse Ile Navy Air	2-14	L
5-24	A	Romulus AFB	6-9	L
5-29	H	Ft. Custer	12-28	L
6-3	H	Romulus AFB	8-3	W
6-7	A	Ft. Custer	2-6	L

1945 (12-4)
Coach: John H. Kobs

4-6	A	Indiana	3-15	L
4-7	A	Indiana	5-7	L
4-25	H	Reformatory at Ionia	4-3	W
4-28	H	Southern Mich. Prison	7-0	W
5-2	H	Wayne	6-2	W
5-9	A	Michigan Normal	7-4	W
5-11	H	Ohio State	1-2	L
5-12	H	Ohio State	3-0	W
5-19	HLN	Ohio	4-11	L
		Ohio	8-7	W
5-23	H	Wayne	10-6	W
5-24	A	Detroit	2-0	W
5-25	A	Detroit	6-5	W
5-29	H	Detroit	9-2	W
5-30	H	Detroit	15-3	W
6-7	H	Percy Jones Hospital	3-2	W

1946 (21-5)
Coach: John H. Kobs

3-20	*	Georgia	6-4	W
3-21	*	Georgia	16-1	W
3-22	*	South Carolina	9-4	W
3-23	*	South Carolina	9-6	W
3-24	*	Ft. Jackson	9-6	W
3-25	*	North Carolina	5-3	W
3-26	*	North Carolina	3-2	W
3-27	*	Duke	5-3	W
3-28	*	North Carolina State	3-1	W
4-19	H	Wisconsin	11-3	W
4-20	H	Wisconsin	12-2	W
4-23	A	Michigan	2-4	L
4-24	A	Wayne	7-8	L
4-27	A	Western Michigan	1-9	L
5-10	A	Michigan Normal	10-3	W
5-11	H	Notre Dame	4-5	L
5-13	A	Detroit	3-1	W
5-15	H	Wayne	3-0	W
5-21	H	Detroit	7-2	W
5-24	H	Michigan Normal	11-0	W
5-26	A	Great Lakes NTS	8-0	W
5-30	H	Ohio State	4-3	W
		Ohio State	7-3	W
6-1	H	Western Michigan	7-0	W
6-5	H	Michigan	0-2	L
6-6	H	Great Lakes NTS	6-3	W

1947 (16-8)
Coach: John H. Kobs

3-22	*	Maryville	10-1	W
3-24	*	Georgia	18-7	W
3-25	*	Georgia	8-4	W
3-27	*	Newberry	9-0	W
3-28	*	South Carolina	12-2	W
3-29	*	South Carolina	13-7	W
3-31	*	North Carolina	3-4	L
4-1	*	Duke	4-2	W
4-12	A	Northwestern	9-0	W
		Northwestern	0-4	L
4-19	H	Detroit	9-0	W
4-26	H	Notre Dame	7-4	W
4-30	A	Western Michigan	1-9	L
5-3	H	Michigan Normal	12-0	W
5-6	A	Michigan	2-1	W
5-10	H	Western Michigan	1-4	L
5-12	A	Wisconsin	8-9	L
5-13	A	Wisconsin	8-5	W
5-19	H	Wayne	6-0	W
5-23	A	Notre Dame	2-10	L
5-27	H	Michigan	8-1	W
5-30	H	Wisconsin	9-5	W
5-31	H	Wisconsin	4-14	L
6-6	H	Ohio State	1-2	L

1948 (10-14-1)
Coach: John H. Kobs

3-22	*	South Carolina	3-4	L
3-24	*	Newberry	14-15	L
3-25	*	Newberry	6-1	W
3-26	*	Presbyterian	5-3	W
3-29	*	North Carolina	2-5	L
3-30	*	Wake Forest	3-2	W
4-9	A	Ohio State	11-12	L
4-10	A	Ohio State	3-4	L
4-16	A	Northwestern	9-9	T
4-17	A	Northwestern	5-7	L
4-21	H	Wisconsin	11-9	W
4-22	H	Wisconsin	6-5	W
4-30	A	Ohio	3-5	L
5-1	A	Ohio	4-5	L
5-4	A	Detroit	7-5	W
5-8	H	Michigan Normal	3-1	W
5-12	A	Michigan	7-3	W
5-15	A	Western Michigan	3-4	L
5-18	H	Detroit	4-2	W
5-22	H	Notre Dame	4-5	L
5-26	H	Michigan	2-9	L
5-29	H	Notre Dame	1-10	L
6-1	H	Western Michigan	5-6	L
6-4	H	Ohio	3-6	L
6-5	H	Ohio	5-4	W

1949 (19-8-1)
Coach: John H. Kobs

3-24	*	Tennessee	5-0	W
3-25	*	Georgia Tech	9-5	W
3-26	*	Georgia Tech	7-2	W
3-28	*	South Carolina	3-7	L
3-29	*	South Carolina	5-3	W
3-30	*	North Carolina	5-5	T
3-31	*	North Carolina	2-4	L
4-1	*	North Carolina State	13-10	W
4-22	H	Northwestern	5-1	W
4-23	H	Northwestern	6-4	W
4-26	H	Michigan	0-5	L
4-28	H	Wayne	22-2	W
4-30	A	Western Michigan	6-7	L
5-4	H	Notre Dame	7-5	W
5-6	H	Ohio State	5-4	W
5-7	H	Ohio State	14-0	W
5-11	A	Eastern Michigan	13-10	W
5-13	A	Purdue	3-6	L
5-14	A	Purdue	7-3	W
5-16	A	Wisconsin	6-5	W
5-17	A	Wisconsin	10-5	W
5-21	H	Michigan	9-10	L
5-28	A	Notre Dame	10-8	W
5-30	H	Detroit	8-3	W
5-31	H	Wayne	11-1	W
6-3	H	Bradley	9-11	L
6-4	H	Bradley	11-3	W
6-6	H	Western Michigan	0-5	L

1950 (19-9)
Coach: John H. Kobs

3-24	*	Clemson	12-14	L
3-25	*	Clemson	18-5	W
3-27	*	South Carolina	6-3	W
3-28	*	South Carolina	5-6	L
3-29	*	Wake Forest	8-11	L
3-30	*	North Carolina	1-8	L
3-31	*	North Carolina	6-7	L
4-1	*	Richmond	7-2	W
4-18	A	Michigan	6-5	W
4-21	H	Purdue	8-5	W
4-22	H	Purdue	9-3	W
4-28	A	Ohio State	1-4	L
4-29	A	Ohio State	6-3	W
5-4	A	Notre Dame	11-10	W
5-5	A	Iowa	3-5	L
5-6	A	Iowa	7-6	W
5-10	H	Michigan	7-6	W
5-13	H	Wayne	11-7	W
5-16	A	Wayne	15-7	W
5-18	H	Eastern Michigan	11-3	W
5-20	H	Detroit	5-0	W
5-24	H	Notre Dame	7-1	W
5-26	H	Western Michigan	3-7	L
5-27	A	Western Michigan	5-1	W
5-29	A	Detroit	4-3	W
6-3	H	Bradley	6-3	W
		Bradley	4-3	W
6-9	H_{MA}	Wisconsin	**6-13	L

1951 (17-9; 4-6 in Big Ten: 7th)
Coach: John H. Kobs

3-23	*	Duke	6-7	L
3-24	*	Duke	8-5	W
3-26	*	Clemson	8-7	W
3-27	*	Clemson	16-6	W
3-28	*	South Carolina	4-3	W
3-30	*	North Carolina	6-7	L
3-31	*	Virginia Tech	17-4	W
4-21	H	Wayne	25-1	W
4-25	A	Notre Dame	9-1	W
4-28	A	Wayne	3-0	W
5-2	H	Western Michigan	5-12	L
5-4	H	Iowa	8-5	W
5-5	H	Iowa	12-9	W
5-9	H	Notre Dame	3-2	W
5-12	H	Michigan	1-15	L
5-15	A	Western Michigan	12-2	W
5-16	H	Michigan Normal	3-1	W
5-18	A	Indiana	7-5	W
5-19	A	Indiana	1-6	L
5-23	A	Detroit	15-3	W
5-25	A	Minnesota	2-9	L
5-26	A	Minnesota	4-5	L
5-29	A	Michigan	10-5	W
5-30	A	Detroit	13-4	W
6-1	H	Ohio State	0-8	L
6-2	H	Ohio State	8-9	L

1952 (18-14; 7-6 in Big Ten: 5th)
Coach: John H. Kobs

3-24	*	Clemson	13-3	W
3-25	*	Clemson	5-1	W
3-26	*	Camp Gordon	2-8	L
3-27	*	South Carolina	4-1	W
3-28	*	South Carolina	1-4	L
3-29	*	North Carolina	3-0	W
3-31	*CZ	Yale	6-3	W
4-1	*CZ	Yale	6-0	W
	*	North Carolina	5-9	L
4-2	*	North Carolina	5-9	L
4-3	*	North Carolina State	7-3	W
4-4	*	Duke	9-10	L
4-25	H	Ohio State	1-4	L
4-26	H	Illinois	1-12	L
		Illinois	1-0	W

(continued)

Date		Opponent	Score	
5-2	A	Minnesota	7-4	W
5-3	A	Iowa	1-4	L
		Iowa	1-0	W
5-7	H	Notre Dame	2-4	L
5-9	H	Michigan	6-5	W
5-10	A	Michigan	2-10	L
		Michigan	4-0	W
5-16	H	Purdue	5-7	L
5-17	H	Indiana	5-3	W
		Indiana	8-2	W
5-19	A	Detroit	4-5	L
5-23	A	Wisconsin	4-5	L
5-28	A	Notre Dame	4-5	L
5-30	H	Detroit	3-1	W
5-31	H	Wayne	10-3	W
6-6	A	Western Michigan	1-8	L
6-7	H	Western Michigan	11-2	W

1953 (11-17; 6-7 in Big Ten: 7th)
Coach: John H. Kobs

Date		Opponent	Score	
3-27	*CL	North Carolina	4-11	L
3-28	*	Camp LeJeune	3-6	L
	*CL	North Carolina	9-11	L
3-30	*	Cherry Point Marines	2-16	L
3-31	*	Cherry Point Marines	7-8	L
4-1	*	North Carolina State	8-7	W
4-2	*	Duke	0-1	L
4-3	*	Duke	3-7	L
4-4	*	Ft. Lee	1-5	L
4-18	H	Wayne	15-0	W
4-24	A	Illinois	1-2	L
4-25	A	Ohio State	1-4	L
		Ohio State	1-2	L
5-1	H	Iowa	3-2	W
5-2	H	Minnesota	1-4	L
		Minnesota	3-2	W
5-6	H	Notre Dame	8-5	W
5-8	A	Michigan	1-9	L
5-9	H	Michigan	6-5	W
		Michigan	2-20	L
5-15	A	Indiana	6-1	W
5-22	H	Northwestern	2-0	W
5-23	H	Wisconsin	3-10	L
		Wisconsin	5-1	W
5-27	A	Notre Dame	4-2	W
5-30	H	Detroit	8-0	W
6-3	A	Western Michigan	5-8	L
6-6	H	Western Michigan	3-9	L

1954 (25-10-1; 11-2 in Big Ten: 1st)
Coach: John H. Kobs

Date		Opponent	Score	
3-26	*	Duke	3-6	L
3-27	*	Duke	8-2	W
3-29	*	North Carolina	2-6	L
3-30	*	North Carolina State	5-3	W
4-2	*	Ft. Eustis	4-12	L
4-3	*	Ft. Eustis	4-5	L
	*	Ft. Eustis	4-0	W
4-17	H	Wayne	4-2	W
4-21	H	Detroit	9-3	W
4-23	A	Northwestern	4-0	W
4-24	A	Wisconsin	3-3	T
4-30	H	Illinois	17-3	W
5-1	H	Purdue	12-0	W
		Purdue	2-5	L
5-5	H	Notre Dame	8-1	W
5-7	A	Iowa	6-3	W
5-8	A	Minnesota	8-5	W
		Minnesota	6-2	W
5-14	H	Michigan	8-4	W
5-15	A	Michigan	8-4	W
		Michigan	8-9	L
5-19	A	Wayne	6-2	W
5-21	H	Indiana	5-2	W
5-22	H	Ohio State	6-4	W
		Ohio State	6-5	W
5-26	A	Notre Dame	6-4	W
5-29	A	Detroit	6-3	W
5-31	H	Ohio	**14-10	W
		Ohio	**0-7	L
6-1	H	Ohio	**5-3	W
6-5	H	Western Michigan	4-5	L
6-10	A[OM]	Massachusetts	**16-5	W
6-11	A[OM]	Arizona	**2-1	W
6-12	A[OM]	Rollins	**4-5	L
6-13	A[OM]	Rollins	**3-2	W
6-14	A[OM]	Missouri	**3-4	L

1955 (21-11; 10-5 in Big Ten: 2nd)
Coach: John H. Kobs

Date		Opponent	Score	
3-25	*	South Carolina	6-3	W
3-26	*	South Carolina	19-11	W
3-28	*	Ft. Jackson	5-9	L
	*	Ft. Jackson	11-1	W
3-29	*	Ft. Jackson	11-5	W
3-30	*	North Carolina State	11-9	W
3-31	*	Wake Forest	4-5	L
4-1	*	Camp LeJeune	5-7	L
	*	Camp LeJeune	9-18	L
4-2	*	North Carolina	1-4	L
4-16	H	Detroit	16-6	W
4-22	H	Wisconsin	14-8	W
4-23	H	Northwestern	6-17	L
		Northwestern	6-1	W
4-29	A	Purdue	2-8	L
4-30	A	Illinois	1-7	L
		Illinois	7-1	W
5-4	A	Western Michigan	14-1	W
5-6	H	Minnesota	0-3	L
5-7	H	Iowa	9-6	W
		Iowa	2-1	W
5-10	A	Detroit	8-9	L
5-13	A	Michigan	3-0	W
5-14	H	Michigan	8-5	W
		Michigan	4-3	W
5-18	H	Notre Dame	5-4	W
5-20	A	Ohio State	1-5	L
5-21	A	Indiana	7-3	W
		Indiana	7-2	W
5-23	A	Notre Dame	4-3	W
6-1	A	Wayne	13-5	W
6-4	A	Wayne	13-1	W

1956 (16-13; 4-7 in Big Ten: 8th)
Coach: John H. Kobs

Date		Opponent	Score	
3-24	*	South Carolina	5-7	L
3-26	*	Parris Island Marines	2-11	L
	*PI	Virginia Military	6-3	W
3-27	*	Parris Island Marines	5-6	L
3-28	*	Camp LeJeune	4-0	W
3-30	*	North Carolina State	10-15	L
3-31	*	Wake Forest	5-6	L
4-3	*	Duke	4-3	W
4-4	*	North Carolina	2-1	W
4-11	H	Detroit	19-3	W
4-21	H	Wayne	17-3	W
		Wayne	8-2	W
4-27	H	Ohio State	7-8	L
5-1	A	Western Michigan	4-2	W
5-4	A	Wisconsin	11-6	W
5-11	H[BC]	Purdue	3-4	L
5-12	H[BC]	Illinois	2-0	W
		Illinois	2-1	W
5-14	H	Detroit	7-3	W
5-16	A	Notre Dame	2-8	L
5-18	A	Minnesota	3-7	L
5-19	A	Iowa	3-5	L
		Iowa	3-8	L
5-23	H	Notre Dame	5-4	W
5-25	H	Michigan	10-4	W
5-26	A	Michigan	3-7	L
		Michigan	1-2	L
5-29	A	Wayne	9-1	W
6-2	H	Western Michigan	12-9	W

1957 (18-13-1; 5-5 in Big Ten: 7th)
Coach: John H. Kobs

Date		Opponent	Score	
3-25	*	Florida State	8-3	W
3-26	*TA	Duke	5-21	L
3-27	*TA	Yale	19-9	W
3-28	*	Florida State	4-7	L
3-29	*TA	Duke	3-2	W
3-30	*TA	Yale	17-8	W
4-1	*WP	Alabama	6-12	L
4-2	*WP	Alabama	9-4	W
4-3	*WP	Amherst	7-7	T
4-4	*	Rollins	3-9	L
4-5	*	Rollins	8-3	W
4-6	*	Rollins	2-3	L
4-13	H	Detroit	8-2	W
4-18	H	Wayne	21-2	W
4-20	H	Albion	8-3	W
		Albion	7-0	W
4-26	A	Indiana	4-2	W
4-27	A	Ohio State	2-6	L
		Ohio State	1-2	L
4-30	A	Notre Dame	4-3	W
5-3	H	Northwestern	2-4	L
5-4	H	Wisconsin	6-7	L
		Wisconsin	11-4	W
5-7	A	Wayne	8-0	W
5-8	H	Western Michigan	12-6	W
5-10	A	Illinois	8-7	W
5-13	H	Notre Dame	1-3	L
5-17	H	Iowa	6-5	W
5-18	H	Minnesota	2-4	L
		Minnesota	2-3	L
5-21	A	Detroit	3-4	L
5-24	A	Michigan	3-0	W

1958 (22-12; 10-5 in Big Ten: 2nd)
Coach: John H. Kobs

Date		Opponent	Score	
3-24	*	Clemson	5-7	L
3-26	*	Parris Island Marines	5-3	W
3-27	*	Parris Island Marines	3-5	L
3-28	*	Parris Island Marines	0-8	L
3-29	*	Parris Island Marines	2-0	W
3-30	*	Hunter Air Force Base	7-0	W
3-31	*	South Carolina	12-0	W
4-1	*	Georgia	8-9	L
4-2	*	Georgia	5-2	W
4-3	*	Clemson	3-2	W
4-19	H	Albion	16-0	W
		Albion	14-1	W
4-25	H	Michigan	4-2	W
4-26	A	Michigan	1-10	L
		Michigan	1-2	L
4-30	A	Western Michigan	5-7	L
5-2	H	Indiana	10-3	W
5-3	H	Ohio State	14-0	W
		Ohio State	7-1	W
5-6	A	Wayne	13-2	W
5-7	H	Notre Dame	0-7	L
5-9	A	Northwestern	9-6	W
5-10	A	Wisconsin	8-3	W
		Wisconsin	5-9	L
5-13	A	Detroit	4-2	W
5-16	H	Illinois	3-0	W
5-17	H	Purdue	8-5	W
		Purdue	3-1	W
5-21	H	Wayne	8-0	W
5-23	A	Iowa	5-2	W
5-24	A	Minnesota	2-3	L
		Minnesota	1-2	L
5-30	H	Detroit	11-5	W
6-7	H	Western Michigan	4-5	L

1959 (21-14; 8-7 in Big Ten: 4th)

Coach: John H. Kobs

3-26	*	Ft. Knox	10-0	W
3-27	*	Ft. Knox	2-0	W
3-28	*	Ft. Knox	8-0	W
3-30	*	Florida State	2-5	L
3-31	*TA	Illinois	3-8	L
4-1	*TA	Western Michigan	1-9	L
4-2	*TA	Duke	7-2	W
	*	Duke	8-13	L
4-4	*TA	Michigan	1-0	W
4-4	*	Florida State	8-2	W
4-11	H	Albion	1-0	W
		Albion	11-5	W
4-15	H	Wayne	26-6	W
4-18	H	Detroit	5-7	L
4-21	H	Western Michigan	1-6	L
4-24	A	Michigan	3-2	W
4-25	H	Michigan	17-12	W
		Michigan	1-2	L
5-1	A	Ohio State	5-3	W
5-2	A	Indiana	1-6	L
		Indiana	3-4	L
5-5	A	Notre Dame	1-3	L
5-8	H	Wisconsin	5-3	W
5-9	H	Northwestern	8-6	W
		Northwestern	3-8	L
5-12	A	Wayne	6-1	W
5-13	H	Notre Dame	5-4	W
5-15	A	Purdue	6-3	W
5-16	A	Illinois	2-8	L
		Illinois	4-1	W
5-20	A	Detroit	8-0	W
5-22	H	Minnesota	6-4	W
5-23	H	Iowa	0-2	L
		Iowa	1-4	L
6-6	H	Western Michigan	8-0	W

1960 (17-13; 4-7 in Big Ten: 8th)

Coach: John H. Kobs

3-25	*	Virginia Tech	17-2	W
3-26	*CL	Springfield	1-2	L
3-27	*CL	Yale	5-7	L
3-27	*	Camp LeJeune	4-9	L
3-28	*	Camp LeJeune	10-9	W
	*	Camp LeJeune	5-1	W
3-29	*	North Carolina State	2-1	W
3-31	*	Wake Forest	1-4	L
4-2	*	Ohio	10-7	W
4-18	H	Albion	6-0	W
4-19	H	Alma	5-1	W
		Alma	7-0	W
4-22	H	Purdue	9-2	W
4-23	H	Illinois	1-2	L
		Illinois	1-15	L
4-29	A	Minnesota	6-13	L
5-3	A	Western Michigan	6-1	W
5-7	A	Michigan	2-1	W
		Michigan	5-6	L
5-10	A	Notre Dame	5-3	W
5-13	H	Ohio State	4-2	W
5-14	H	Indiana	0-3	L
		Indiana	2-0	W
5-18	H	Notre Dame	1-8	L
5-20	A	Wisconsin	0-1	L
5-21	A	Northwestern	2-3	L
5-23	A	Detroit	5-14	L
5-25	H	Central Michigan	3-2	W
5-28	H	Detroit	4-2	W
6-6	H	Western Michigan	6-5	W

1961 (21-11-1; 6-8 in Big Ten: 5th)

Coach: John H. Kobs

3-23	*CL	Wilmington JC	6-8	L
3-24	*	Camp LeJeune	8-2	W
3-25	*	Camp LeJeune	0-7	L
	*CL	Wilmington JC	5-2	W

3-26	*	Camp LeJeune	5-4	W
	*CL	Farleigh Dickinson	4-4	T
3-27	*CL	Farleigh Dickinson	8-2	W
3-28	*FL	Newport News Tech	10-2	W
3-29	*	Ft. Lee	7-2	W
3-30	*FL	Rhode Island	3-2	W
3-30	*	Ft. Lee	4-0	W
4-8	H	Alma	7-1	W
		Alma	7-2	W
4-15	H	Albion	16-1	W
		Albion	1-0	W
4-21	H	Iowa	3-2	W
4-22	H	Minnesota	3-5	L
		Minnesota	0-3	L
4-29	H	Michigan	1-5	L
		Michigan	4-6	L
		Michigan	3-4	L
5-4	A	Notre Dame	6-3	W
5-6	A	Ohio State	6-7	L
		Ohio State	9-3	W
5-12	H	Northwestern	11-8	W
5-13	H	Wisconsin	4-6	L
		Wisconsin	8-4	W
5-17	H	Central Michigan	11-0	W
5-19	A	Illinois	3-6	L
5-20	A	Purdue	4-0	W
		Purdue	4-1	W
5-24	H	Notre Dame	5-4	W
5-27	H	Detroit	11-13	L

1962 (17-13; 6-8 in Big Ten: 5th)

Coach: John H. Kobs

3-22	*	Camp LeJeune	4-0	W
3-23	*	Camp LeJeune	9-5	W
3-24	*	Camp LeJeune	3-8	L
3-25	*	Camp LeJeune	2-6	L
3-27	*	Ft. Lee	7-3	W
3-28	*	Ft. Lee	13-0	W
	*	Ft. Lee	0-4	L
3-29	*FL	Massachusetts	0-6	L
3-30	*	Ft. Belvoir	13-9	W
3-31	*	Ft. Belvoir	6-4	W
4-20	H	Purdue	11-5	W
4-21	H	Illinois	3-11	L
		Illinois	4-5	L
4-25	H	Alma	23-5	W
		Alma	14-2	W
4-28	A	Iowa	10-13	L
		Iowa	7-5	W
5-4	H	Michigan	13-16	L
5-5	A	Michigan	0-4	L
		Michigan	1-14	L
5-8	A	Detroit	7-3	W
5-11	H	Ohio State	3-6	L
5-12	H	Indiana	4-3	W
		Indiana	7-4	W
5-14	A	Central Michigan	16-4	W
5-16	H	Notre Dame	4-0	W
5-18	A	Wisconsin	0-4	L
5-19	A	Northwestern	12-4	W
		Northwestern	20-3	W
5-23	H	Detroit	11-16	L

1963 (18-14-1; 5-9 in Big Ten: 8th)

Coach: John H. Kobs

3-22	*	Camp LeJeune	2-0	W
3-23	*	Camp LeJeune	9-2	W
3-24	*	Camp LeJeune	1-5	L
3-25	*CL	Ithaca	5-10	L
3-25	*	Ft. Lee	25-5	W
3-26	*	Ft. Lee	5-4	W
3-27	*	Ft. Lee	16-5	W
3-28	*	Virginia	9-5	W
3-29	*	Richmond	6-6	T
3-30	*	George Washington	10-2	W
4-13	H	Albion	9-1	W
		Albion	2-1	W

4-20	H	Wayne	13-1	W
		Wayne	10-3	W
4-24	H	Central Michigan	2-1	W
4-26	A	Purdue	3-11	L
4-27	A	Illinois	4-8	L
		Illinois	6-4	W
5-3	H	Minnesota	2-3	L
5-4	H	Iowa	16-8	W
5-6	A	Detroit	3-4	L
5-7	H	Western Michigan	5-9	L
5-10	A	Michigan	3-4	L
5-11	H	Michigan	3-1	W
		Michigan	2-4	L
5-15	H	Detroit	6-0	W
5-17	A	Ohio State	2-5	L
5-18	A	Indiana	8-5	W
		Indiana	3-4	L
5-21	A	Western Michigan	3-13	L
5-24	H	Wisconsin	7-12	L
5-25	H	Northwestern	3-5	L
		Northwestern	7-3	W

Danny Litwhiler (1964-1982)

When athletic director Biggie Munn sought a replacement for the veteran John Kobs in 1963, he vowed to find the "best college baseball coach in the country." With that pledge, Biggie brought the obvious question to his good friend, Dr. Robert Jones, "*Who* is the best baseball coach in the country?" Doc brought the puzzle to his son Robert Jr. (SW '69-70) and the teenager's answer was relayed back to the AD, "Danny Litwhiler of Florida State." Munn accepted the answer and telephoned Litwhiler in Tallahassee. Although flattered, Danny initially conceded no interest in the move. With assistant professorial rank and an annual $9,000 salary, he avowed to be content in the Sunshine State. Yet, through the coaching fraternity, Danny had worked with John Kobs and was thus familiar with the Big Ten Conference. He had second thoughts. At least a trip to East Lansing seemed appropriate and so in early July of 1963, Danny flew into the Capitol City airport. His visit proved to be a pleasant experience and he was favorably impressed as President Hannah proposed a full professorship and Biggie offered a salary of $13,500. Upon returning to Florida, Litwhiler confided in Gordon Blackwell, his school's president, and a counter offer of $11,000 was extended. This was the maximum proposition available at Florida State for faculty members not holding a doctorate. However, the tenacious Munn wasn't through and he telephoned an improved proposition of $15,000. Litwhiler didn't hesitate, this was an offer he couldn't refuse. The Spartans signed "the best college baseball coach in the country." Danny Litwhiler was born and raised in Ringtown, PA, and completed his collegiate degree at Bloomsburg State (PA), where the baseball diamond now bears his name. He spent 12 years as an outfielder in the major leagues before ending his playing career in 1951. During that time he had played with the Philadelphia Phillies, St. Louis Cardinals, Boston Braves, and Cincinnati Reds. Danny was a member of the Cardinals' 1943 league championship team and the world championship club of 1944. Following a three-year stint as a minor league manager, Litwhiler entered the collegiate coaching field, spending nine seasons at Florida State prior to his MSU years. He would spend an impressive 19 years in the Spartan uniform before retiring following the spring of 1982.

1964 (22-12; 8-7 in Big Ten: 4th)

Coach: Danny Litwhiler

3-22	*	Virginia	4-3	W
3-25	*	Virginia Tech	10-6	W
3-26	*	North Carolina State	9-2	W
3-27	*	Camp LeJeune	6-3	W
	*	Camp LeJeune	22-1	W
3-28	*CL	Massachusetts	12-2	W
3-30	*	Georgia Southern	9-0	W
3-31	*	Florida State	5-10	L
4-1	*	Florida State	6-7	L

Date	Site	Opponent	Score	Result
4-2	*TA	Wake Forest	10-16	L
4-9	H	Albion	11-3	W
4-11	H	Hillsdale	22-5	W
		Hillsdale	5-4	W
4-18	H	Central Michigan	1-0	W
		Central Michigan	5-1	W
4-24	A	Northwestern	13-7	W
4-25	A	Wisconsin	8-9	L
		Wisconsin	2-1	W
4-28	H	Detroit	5-4	W
5-1	H	Illinois	5-2	W
5-2	H	Purdue	5-4	W
		Purdue	3-0	W
5-5	A	Notre Dame	8-9	L
5-8	A	Iowa	4-5	L
5-9	A	Minnesota	1-4	L
		Minnesota	4-7	L
5-16	A	Michigan	3-6	L
		Michigan	1-4	L
5-18	H	Michigan	3-2	W
5-22	H	Indiana	14-6	W
5-23	H	Ohio State	7-8	L
		Ohio State	3-1	W
5-25	H_LA	Western Michigan	8-7	W
5-26	A	Western Michigan	2-6	L

1965 (28-11; 9-6 in Big Ten: 3rd)

Coach: Danny Litwhiler

Date	Site	Opponent	Score	Result
3-23	*	Miami	2-1	W
		Miami	1-2	L
3-24	*	Miami	13-3	W
3-25	*CG	Florida	8-3	W
3-26	*CG	Army	12-5	W
3-27	*CG	Florida	2-7	L
3-29	*	Florida State	8-11	L
3-30	*TA	Wake Forest	2-0	W
	*TH	Balt. Orioles- Rookies	11-3	W
4-1	*TA	Duke	4-0	W
4-2	*TA	Duke	4-2	W
	*	Wake Forest	4-2	W
4-3	*TA	Wake Forest	6-0	W
4-10	H	Central Michigan	7-2	W
		Central Michigan	3-5	L
4-20	A	Detroit	8-2	W
4-21	H	Spring Arbor	12-0	W
		Spring Arbor	5-4	W
4-23	H	Northwestern	10-1	W
4-24	H	Wisconsin	4-5	L
		Wisconsin	5-1	W
4-27	H	Detroit	1-0	W
4-30	A	Illinois	4-5	L
5-1	A	Purdue	8-4	W
		Purdue	0-1	L
5-7	H	Iowa	4-3	W
5-8	H	Minnesota	7-2	W
		Minnesota	3-2	W
5-10	H	Notre Dame	3-0	W
5-11	H	Albion	20-1	W
5-14	A	Michigan	6-3	W
5-15	H	Michigan	1-6	L
		Michigan	5-4	W
5-17	A	Notre Dame	8-6	W
5-18	H_LN	Western Michigan	3-2	W
5-21	A	Indiana	6-1	W
5-22	A	Ohio State	10-13	L
		Ohio State	0-2	L
5-25	A	Western Michigan	1-3	L

1966 (24-13-1; 8-5 in Big Ten: 4th)

Coach: Danny Litwhiler

Date	Site	Opponent	Score	Result
3-21	*CG	Ohio State	3-0	W
3-22	*CG	Ohio State	3-7	L
3-23	*	Miami	2-6	L
3-24	*	Miami	6-6	T
3-25	*CG	Army	4-7	L
3-26	*CG	New York University	4-3	W
3-26	*CG	New York University	7-2	W
3-28	*TA	Wake Forest	3-7	L
	*	Florida State	4-5	L
3-29	*TA	Wake Forest	1-7	L
	*	Florida State	7-6	W
3-30	*TA	Rutgers	7-6	W
	*	Florida State	4-5	L
3-31	*TA	Wake Forest	9-8	W
4-8	H	Ball State	15-4	W
4-9	H	Ball State	5-9	L
		Ball State	5-1	W
4-16	H	Detroit	12-8	W
		Detroit	7-1	W
4-19	H	Albion	8-4	W
4-22	H	Ohio State	0-2	L
4-23	H	Indiana	1-2	L
4-29	A	Wisconsin	4-2	W
4-30	A	Northwestern	20-4	W
		Northwestern	4-6	L
5-3	A	Central Michigan	10-4	W
		Central Michigan	4-0	W
5-6	A	Purdue	5-0	W
5-7	A	Illinois	15-6	W
		Illinois	6-5	W
5-9	H_SN	Notre Dame	5-0	W
5-14	A	Iowa	4-2	W
		Iowa	1-0	W
5-16	H_LN	Notre Dame	7-3	W
5-20	H	Michigan	6-5	W
5-21	A	Michigan	1-2	L
		Michigan	3-5	L
5-24	A	Western Michigan	3-0	W

1967 (22-23-1; 8-10 in Big Ten: 6th)

Coach: Danny Litwhiler

(*-Spring trip games at Coral Gables, FL)

Date	Site	Opponent	Score	Result
3-20	*	Rutgers	5-8	L
	*	Miami	11-3	W
3-21	*	Rutgers	5-2	W
3-22	*	Miami	1-5	L
3-23	*	Army	9-4	W
3-24	*	Italian Nationals	8-0	W
3-25	*	Miami	1-2	L
3-26	*	Army	3-3	T
3-27	*	Duke	10-1	W
3-28	*	Duke	3-5	L
3-29	*	Furman	8-0	W
3-30	*	Duke	3-4	L
3-31	*	Duke	4-12	L
4-1	*	Wesleyan	6-0	W
	*	Miami	1-4	L
4-8	A	Ball State	4-6	L
		Ball State	3-1	W
4-11	H	Eastern Michigan	1-5	L
		Eastern Michigan	2-0	W
4-14	A	Ohio State	9-10	L
		Ohio State	2-3	L
4-15	A	Indiana	6-10	L
		Indiana	8-6	W
4-18	H	Albion	7-0	W
		Albion	7-2	W
4-25	A	Detroit	4-1	W
		Detroit	0-1	L
4-28	H	Wisconsin	0-1	L
		Wisconsin	10-0	W
4-29	A	Northwestern	11-4	W
		Northwestern	8-4	W
5-1	H	Detroit	4-5	L
5-5	A	Purdue	2-0	W
		Purdue	1-2	L
5-7	A	Illinois	7-2	W
		Illinoise	5-4	W
5-8	H	Central Michigan	4-3	W
		Central Michigan	2-6	L
5-9	A	Notre Dame	4-5	L
5-12	H	Minnesota	0-7	L
		Minnesota	4-2	W
5-13	H	Iowa	0-3	L
		Iowa	3-4	L

Date	Site	Opponent	Score	Result
5-16	H	Western Michigan	7-1	W
5-19	A	Michigan	4-5	L
5-20	H	Michigan	4-6	L

1968 (32-9-1; 13-4-1 in Big Ten: 2nd)

Coach: Danny Litwhiler

(*- Spring trip games at Coral Gables, FL) ....

Date	Site	Opponent	Score	Result
3-18	*	Ohio State	9-4	W
3-19	*	Miami	1-5	L
3-20	*	Rutgers	17-3	W
3-21	*	Ohio State	6-2	W
3-22	*	Army	11-3	W
3-23	*	Miami	4-7	L
3-25	*	Ohio State	9-7	W
3-26	*	Western Michigan	1-2	L
3-26	*	Miami	3-4	L
3-27	*	Western Michigan	5-1	W
3-28	*	Wesleyan	12-1	W
3-29	*	Western Michigan	6-0	W
3-30	*	Miami	1-2	L
4-6	H	Ball State	2-1	W
		Ball State	6-1	W
4-13	H	Detroit	5-1	W
		Detroit	13-1	W
4-17	H	Albion	6-2	W
		Albion	3-1	W
4-23	A	Notre Dame	15-2	W
4-26	A	Michigan	2-4	L
		Michigan	1-4	L
4-30	H	Eastern Michigan	5-1	W
		Eastern Michigan	5-0	W
5-3	H	Indiana	4-1	W
		Indiana	2-1	W
5-4	H	Ohio State	4-0	W
		Ohio State	8-2	W
5-7	H	Notre Dame	6-2	W
5-10	A	Northwestern	6-0	W
		Northwestern	12-0	W
5-11	A	Wisconsin	3-1	W
		Wisconsin	7-3	W
5-17	H	Illinois	9-0	W
		Illinois	3-2	W
5-18	H	Purdue	9-0	W
		Purdue	1-0	W
5-21	H	Western Michigan	9-11	L
5-24	A	Iowa	5-2	W
		Iowa	4-4	T
5-25	A	Minnesota	2-3	L
		Minnesota	4-10	L
5-28	A	Western Michigan	7-4	W

1969 (24-17; 8-8 in Big Ten: 5th)

Coach: Danny Litwhiler

(*-Spring trip games at Coral Gables, FL)

Date	Site	Opponent	Score	Result
3-17	*	Miami	0-11	L
3-18	*	Miami	7-8	L
3-19	*	Cincinnati	10-5	W
3-20	*	Cincinnati	9-7	W
3-21	*	Army	1-0	W
3-22	*	Miami	0-3	L
3-23	*	Cincinnati	6-2	W
3-24	*	Pittsburgh	13-2	W
3-25	*	Cincinnati	6-9	L
3-27	*	Florida A&M	16-1	W
3-28	*	Pittsburgh	5-7	L
	*	Miami	4-3	W
3-29	*	Pittsburgh	5-3	W
4-12	A	Detroit	10-2	W
		Detroit	2-1	W
4-16	H	Albion	6-0	W
		Albion	4-0	W
4-19	H	Michigan	5-4	W
		Michigan	18-3	W
4-24	H	Eastern Michigan	2-3	L
4-26	A	Eastern Michigan	7-5	W
		Eastern Michigan	8-1	W
4-29	H	Western Michigan	5-6	L
5-2	A	Indiana	1-5	L

		Indiana	2-3	L
5-3	A	Ohio State	1-2	L
		Ohio State	6-7	L
5-6	A	Notre Dame	17-12	W
5-10	H	Wisconsin	1-0	W
		Wisconsin	5-2	W
5-13	H	Central Michigan	0-11	L
		Central Michigan	7-5	W
5-16	A	Illinois	0-1	L
		Illinois	0-1	L
5-17	A	Purdue	2-6	L
		Purdue	6-1	W
5-20	A	Western Michigan	3-4	L
5-23	H	Iowa	5-0	W
		Iowa	14-5	W
5-24	H	Minnesota	5-2	W
		Minnesota	0-9	L

1970 (28-15-2; 9-7 in Big Ten: 3rd)
Coach: Danny Litwhiler
(*-Spring trip games at Coral Gables, FL)

3-22	*	Florida State	6-5	W
3-23	*	Ohio State	3-3	T
3-24	*	Connecticut	10-6	W
3-25	*	Rutgers	10-1	W
3-26	*	Miami	3-1	W
3-27	*	Penn State	4-0	W
3-28	*	Ohio State	0-8	L
3-30	*	Colgate	3-2	W
3-31	*	Notre Dame	11-3	W
4-1	*	Miami	6-6	T
4-2	*	Notre Dame	12-11	W
4-3	*	Miami	11-6	W
4-4	*	Colgate	4-5	L
4-4	*	Miami	5-3	W
4-11	A	Ball State	9-1	W
		Ball State	7-5	W
4-15	H	Eastern Michigan	8-2	W
		Eastern Michigan	0-3	L
4-18	A	Central Michigan	2-4	L
		Central Michigan	0-4	L
4-22	H	Detroit	6-1	W
		Detroit	5-1	W
4-25	A	Minnesota	2-3	L
		Minnesota	8-13	L
4-26	A	Iowa	7-1	W
		Iowa	3-4	L
4-28	H	Western Michigan	3-12	L
5-1	H	Michigan	6-3	W
5-2	A	Michigan	2-3	L
		Michigan	8-1	W
5-5	A	Notre Dame	8-9	L
5-9	H	Indiana	3-0	W
		Indiana	7-9	L
5-12	A	Notre Dame	4-1	W
5-16	A	Northwestern	4-0	W
		Northwestern	4-0	W
5-19	A	Western Michigan	3-2	W
5-22	H	Purdue	1-5	L
		Purdue	1-2	L
5-23	H	Illinois	6-0	W
		Illinois	5-1	W
5-26	A	Albion	2-0	W
		Albion	1-3	L
5-30	H	Ohio State	2-1	W
		Ohio State	5-3	W

1971 (36-10; 13-3 in Big Ten: 1st)
Coach: Danny Litwhiler
(*-Spring trip games at Coral Gables, FL)

3-22	*	Miami	10-2	W
3-23	*	Rutgers	7-2	W
	*	Florida State	5-9	L
3-24	*	Miami	5-2	W
3-25	*	Ohio State	11-1	W
3-26	*	Rutgers	12-5	W
3-27	*	Miami	4-0	W
3-29	*	Cornell	17-8	W
3-30	*	Penn State	9-1	W
3-31	*	Miami	6-0	W
4-1	*	Cornell	12-3	W
4-2	*	Miami	2-4	L
4-3	*	Penn State	12-8	W
4-10	A	Ball State	19-1	W
		Ball State	20-1	W
4-14	H	Albion	8-0	W
		Albion	5-0	W
4-16	H	Minnesota	2-0	W
		Minnesota	3-4	L
4-17	H	Iowa	7-6	W
		Iowa	2-0	W
4-20	H	Central Michigan	5-2	W
		Central Michigan	1-2	L
4-23	A	Detroit	1-0	W
		Detroit	11-11	T
4-26	A	Eastern Michigan	5-1	W
		Eastern Michigan	5-1	W
4-27	A	Western Michigan	3-5	L
4-30	A	Michigan	7-2	W
5-1	H	Michigan	2-0	W
		Michigan	5-6	L
5-4	H	Western Michigan	16-15	W
5-8	A	Indiana	2-1	W
		Indiana	5-3	W
5-11	A	Notre Dame	5-2	W
		Notre Dame	6-4	W
5-14	H	Wisconsin	6-3	W
		Wisconsin	5-7	L
5-15	H	Northwestern	16-6	W
		Northwestern	14-5	W
5-21	A	Purdue	8-2	W
		Purdue	7-2	W
5-22	A	Illinois	2-1	W
		Illinois	2-5	L
5-27	A$_{EL}$	Cincinnati	**7-8	L
5-28	A$_{EL}$	Ohio	**1-7	L

1972 (28-10-1; 10-4 in Big Ten: 2nd)
Coach: Danny Litwhiler
(*-Spring trip games at Coral Gables, FL)

3-20	*	Southern Illinois	2-3	L
3-21	*	Miami	5-6	L
3-22	*	Ohio State	14-4	W
3-23	*	Southern Illinois	2-2	T
3-24	*	Miami	2-3	L
3-25	*	Ohio State	13-5	W
3-27	*	Lafayette	5-8	L
3-28	*	Bernard Baruch	21-3	W
3-29	*	Miami	6-1	W
3-30	*	Lafayette	14-7	W
3-31	*	Bernard Baruch	11-1	W
	*	Miami	8-6	W
4-1	*	Miami	0-6	L
4-11	H	Albion	12-3	W
		Albion	11-1	W
4-14	H	Illinois	5-1	W
		Illinois	1-0	W
4-18	A	Western Michigan	3-1	W
4-22	A	Minnesota	0-5	L
		Minnesota	1-3	L
4-25	H	Notre Dame	16-1	W
		Notre Dame	4-3	W
4-28	H	Eastern Michigan	6-1	W
		Eastern Michigan	4-3	W
4-29	A	Central Michigan	3-7	L
		Central Michigan	11-2	W
5-2	H	Western Michigan	6-3	W
5-5	H	Michigan	8-0	W
5-6	A	Michigan	0-7	L
5-9	H	Detroit	3-1	W
		Detroit	2-0	W
5-12	H	Indiana	11-3	W
		Indiana	9-2	W
5-13	H	Ohio State	10-5	W
		Ohio State	6-3	W

5-19	A	Northwestern	5-1	W
		Northwestern	4-3	W
5-20	A	Wisconsin	5-7	L
		Wisconsin	12-5	W

1973 (27-20; 9-9 in Big Ten: 5th)
Coach: Danny Litwhiler
(*-Spring trip games at Coral Gables, FL)

3-19	*	Cornell	0-2	L
3-20	*	Ohio State	12-23	L
3-21	*	Miami	2-15	L
3-22	*	Miami	1-8	L
3-23	*	Cornell	5-4	W
3-24	*	Ohio State	1-0	W
		Ohio State	12-2	W
3-26	*	Northern Iowa	11-1	W
3-27	*	Army	9-6	W
		Army	6-4	W
3-28	*	Miami	2-1	W
3-29	*	Northern Iowa	3-4	L
		Northern Iowa	5-6	L
3-30	*	Army	15-1	W
3-31	*	Miami	13-6	W
4-7	A	Ball State	6-4	W
		Ball State	5-1	W
4-13	A	Illinois	1-4	L
		Illinois	3-2	W
4-14	A	Purdue	7-2	W
		Purdue	12-4	W
4-17	H	Albion	5-4	W
		Albion	15-1	W
4-20	H	Iowa	5-1	W
		Iowa	2-1	W
4-21	H	Minnesota	5-1	W
		Minnesota	1-7	L
4-24	H	Wayne State	7-1	W
		Wayne State	2-0	W
4-27	A	Detroit	11-4	W
		Detroit	4-5	L
5-1	A	Eastern Michigan	7-8	L
		Eastern Michigan	4-1	W
5-5	H	Michigan	0-7	L
		Michigan	0-2	L
5-8	H	Western Michigan	2-9	L
		Western Michigan	0-4	L
5-11	A	Indiana	2-1	W
		Indiana	3-7	L
5-12	A	Ohio State	2-10	L
		Ohio State	2-8	L
5-15	H	Central Michigan	1-0	W
		Central Michigan	4-8	L
5-18	H	Northwestern	3-5	L
		Northwestern	7-2	W
5-19	H	Wisconsin	6-7	L
		Wisconsin	4-1	W

1974 (23-16-1; 7-8 in Big Ten: 6th)
Coach: Danny Litwhiler
(*-Spring trip games at Coral Gables, FL)

3-18	*	Ohio State	5-3	W
3-19	*	Buffalo	10-2	W
3-20	*	Seton Hall	6-10	L
3-21	*	Ohio State	7-4	W
3-22	*	Seton Hall	20-6	W
3-23	*	Buffalo	7-7	T
3-24	*	Miami	1-4	L
3-25	*	Southern Illinois	1-3	L
3-26	*	Montclair State	10-7	W
3-27	*	Miami	3-10	L
3-28	*	Southern Illinois	14-6	W
3-29	*	Montclair State	7-12	L
3-30	*	Miami	3-13	L
4-9	H	Albion	8-3	W
		Albion	8-0	W
4-12	H	Purdue	9-0	W
		Purdue	5-1	W
4-13	H	Illinois	6-1	W
		Illinois	3-10	L

Date		Opponent	Score	Result
4-19	A	Minnesota	1-6	L
		Minnesota	3-2	W
4-20	A	Iowa	8-9	L
		Iowa	4-10	L
4-26	H	Wayne State	7-2	W
		Wayne State	4-3	W
4-27	H	Detroit	5-4	W
		Detroit	8-5	W
4-28	H	Notre Dame	3-0	W
		Notre Dame	5-2	W
5-30	A	Central Michigan	0-1	L
		Central Michigan	3-4	L
5-4	A	Michigan	1-2	L
		Michigan	4-5	L
5-10	H	Ohio State	10-7	W
		Ohio State	1-2	L
5-11	H	Indiana	4-5	L
5-14	H	Eastern Michigan	9-2	W
		Eastern Michigan	3-2	W
5-19	A	Northwestern	5-4	W
		Northwestern	21-2	W

1975 (28-16; 11-4 in Big Ten: 4th)

Coach: Danny Litwhiler
(*-Spring trip games at Coral Gables, FL)

Date		Opponent	Score	Result
3-15	*	Miami	2-4	L
3-16	*	Mercer	8-4	W
3-17	*	Mercer	2-4	L
3-18	*	Buffalo	13-12	W
3-18	*	Miami	1-14	L
3-19	*	Buffalo	6-3	W
3-20	*	Buffalo	7-3	W
3-20	*	Miami	1-6	L
3-21	*	Louisiana State	6-9	L
3-22	*	Lousiiana State	18-4	W
3-23	*	Florida State	4-3	W
3-24	*	Florida State	3-11	L
3-25	*	Army	10-15	L
	*	Army	13-2	W
3-26	*	Army	5-2	W
4-5	H	Ball State	10-8	W
		Ball State	2-13	L
4-11	A	Purdue	10-4	W
		Purdue	7-5	W
4-12	A	Illinois	9-5	W
		Illinois	5-3	W
4-15	H	Western Michigan	1-10	L
		Western Michigan	2-3	L
4-18	H	Minnesota	13-11	W
4-25	A	Wayne State	7-2	W
		Wayne State	7-2	W
4-26	A	Detroit	2-1	W
		Detroit	4-5	L
4-29	A	Notre Dame	9-0	W
		Notre Dame	2-1	W
5-3	A	Michigan	4-0	W
5-4	H	Michigan	1-4	L
5-6	H	Central Michigan	5-4	W
		Central Michigan	3-2	W
5-9	A	Ohio State	1-0	W
		Ohio State	0-1	L
5-10	A	Indiana	7-2	W
		Indiana	1-7	L
5-13	A	Eastern Michigan	2-4	L
		Eastern Micihigan	3-2	W
5-16	H	Wisconsin	5-4	W
		Wisconsin	3-2	W
5-17	H	Northwestern	3-8	L
		Northwestern	9-2	W

1976 (15-23-1; 7-5 in Big Ten: 4th)

Coach: Danny Litwhiler
(*-Spring trip games at Coral Gables, FL)

Date		Opponent	Score	Result
3-20	*	Miami	2-6	L
3-21	*	Mercer	9-8	W
3-22	*	Seton Hall	7-7	T
3-23	*	Massachusetts	5-2	W
3-24	*	Miami	5-6	L
3-25	*	Seton Hall	13-11	W
3-26	*	Massachusetts	8-9	L
3-27	*	Miami	3-13	L
3-28	*	Maine	1-7	L
3-29	*	Miami	0-10	L
	*	Miami	3-9	L
3-30	*	Maine	9-14	L
3-30	*	Miami	3-13	L
3-31	*	Maine	19-9	W
4-9	A	Eastern Michigan	0-5	L
		Eastern Michigan	2-9	L
4-13	H	Albion	5-12	L
		Albion	4-3	W
4-16	A	Iowa	1-5	L
		Iowa	11-12	L
4-17	A	Minnesota	1-0	W
		Minnesota	0-5	L
4-20	H	Detroit	6-2	W
		Detroit	0-3	L
4-23	H	Wayne State	5-3	W
		Wayne State	4-2	W
5-1	H	Illinois	5-0	W
		Illinois	3-1	W
5-4	H	Eastern Michigan	7-12	L
		Eastern Michigan	6-7	L
5-5	A	Central Michigan	5-6	L
5-8	H	Indiana	3-5	L
		Indiana	14-5	W
5-9	H	Ohio State	4-2	W
		Ohio State	4-3	W
5-11	A	Western Michigan	2-4	L
		Western Michigan	4-12	L
5-22	H	Michigan	10-2	W
5-23	A	Michigan	3-11	L

1977 (28-26; 10-8 in Big Ten: 5th)

Coach: Danny Litwhiler
(*-Spring trip games at Edinburg, TX)

Date		Opponent	Score	Result
3-19	*	Pan American	4-8	L
3-20	*	Wright State	5-4	W
3-21	*	Lubbock Chrsitian	3-9	L
3-22	*	Indiana	0-2	L
3-23	*	Wright State	4-2	W
3-23	*	S.E. Oklahoma State.	0-1	L
3-24	*	Wright State	3-8	L
3-25	*	Lubbock Christian	8-6	W
3-25	*	Pan American	9-5	W
3-26	*	S.E. Oklahoma State	11-2	W
3-27	*	Pan American	12-10	W
3-28	*	Pan American	1-3	L
3-29	*	Pan American	5-9	L
	*	Pan American	8-5	W
4-9	H	Eastern Michigan	14-5	W
		Eastern Michigan	7-8	L
4-12	H	Albion	12-2	W
		Albion	12-3	W
4-13	H	Aquinas	7-6	W
		Aquinas	1-3	L
4-16	H	Iowa	5-4	W
		Iowa	4-3	W
4-17	H	Minnesota	4-5	L
		Minnesota	2-6	L
4-19	A	Central Michigan	3-4	L
		Central Michigan	2-7	L
4-23	H	Detroit	0-3	L
		Detroit	1-2	L
4-26	H	Central Michigan	7-6	W
		Central Michigan	3-5	L
4-27	A	Western Michigan	4-11	L
		Western Michigan	4-5	L
4-30	A	Illinois	1-6	L
		Illinois	2-3	L
5-1	A	Purdue	12-1	W
		Purdue	6-3	W
5-3	H	Eastern Michigan	1-11	L
		Eastern Michigan	7-2	W
5-4	H	Wayne State	4-0	W
		Wayne State	7-2	W
5-7	A	Indiana	0-2	L
		Indiana	4-5	L
5-8	A	Ohio State	2-5	L
		Ohio State	8-4	W
5-10	H	Western Michigan	4-3	W
		Western Michigan	6-2	W
5-14	H	Northwestern	1-0	W
		Northwestern	6-5	W
5-15	H	Wisconsin	11-5	W
		Wisconsin	9-7	W
5-18	H	Oakland	1-5	L
		Oakland	6-2	W
5-21	A	Michigan	2-3	L
5-22	H	Michigan	6-5	W

1978 (33-21; 11-5 in Big Ten: 2nd)

Coach: Danny Litwhiler
(*-Spring trip games at Edinburg, TX)

Date		Opponent	Score	Result
3 18	*	Arkansas	4-7	L
3-18	*	Pan American	1-16	L
3-20	*	Texas-Arlington	2-4	L
3-20	*	Morningside	5-2	W
3-21	*	Indiana	7-3	W
3-21	*	Pan American	5-6	L
3-22	*	Morningside	10-4	W
3-23	*	Indiana	12-4	W
3-24	*	Texas-Arlington	1-0	W
3-25	*	Indiana	10-4	W
3-25	*	Morningside	4-2	W
3-27	*	Pan American	5-9	L
	*	Pan American	6-4	W
3-28	*	Pan American	2-3	L
	*	Pan American	3-9	L
4-8	A	Eastern Michigan	3-2	W
		Eastern Michigan	2-1	W
4-11	H	Albion	7-10	L
		Albion	7-0	W
4-12	H	Aquinas	6-12	L
		Aquinas	3-1	W
4-15	A	Minnesota	7-8	L
		Minnesota	6-3	W
4-16	A	Wisconsin	5-1	W
		Wisconsin	1-4	L
4-19	H	Ferris State	11-3	W
		Ferris State	7-1	W
4-21	H	Wayne State	8-5	W
		Wayne State	13-3	W
4-22	H	Detroit	5-6	L
		Detroit	1-7	L
4-25	A	Central Michigan	4-2	W
		Central Michigan	4-6	L
4-29	H	Purdue	8-2	W
		Purdue	3-4	L
4-30	H	Illinois	5-0	W
		Illinois	7-6	W
5-2	A	Western Michigan	4-3	W
		Western Michigan	15-7	W
5-6	H	Ohio State	3-7	L
		Ohio State	6-5	W
5-7	H	Indiana	3-2	W
		Indiana	5-1	W
5-9	H	Western Michigan	5-6	L
		Western Michigan	2-0	W
5-15	A	Northwestern	3-0	W
		Northwestern	19-4	W
5-16	H	Eastern Michigan	12-2	W
		Eastern Michigan	7-8	L
5-17	H	Oakland	12-2	W
5-20	H	Michigan	10-5	W
5-21	A	Michigan	0-3	L
5-26	A^TL	Southern Illinois	**2-7	L
	A^TL	Oklahoma State	**6-7	L

1979 (28-27; 11-4 in Big Ten: 1st)

Coach: Danny Litwhiler
(*-Spring trip games at Edinburg, TX)

Date	Site	Opponent	Score	W/L
3-17	*	Pan American	3-4	L
3-18	*	Central Michigan	5-9	L
	*	Central Michigan	1-2	L
3-19	*	Morningside (IA)	1-4	L
	*	Oklahoma City	2-12	L
3-20	*	Pan American	1-2	L
3-21	*	Morningside (IA)	12-0	W
	*	Morningside (IA)	12-0	W
3-22	*	Pan American	5-8	L
3-23	*	Morningside	6-0	W
	*	Oklahoma City	9-2	W
3-24	*	Pan American	2-6	L
3-26	*	Pan American	0-6	L
	*	Pan American	3-9	L
3-27	*	Pan American	2-8	L
	*	Pan American	5-7	L
4-10	H	Albion	4-0	W
		Albion	7-0	W
4-11	H	Aquinas	3-0	W
4-14	H	Minnesota	7-6	W
		Minnesota	3-4	L
4-15	H	Wisconsin	5-3	W
		Wisconsin	5-0	W
4-17	H	Western Michigan	5-6	L
		Western Michigan	8-3	W
4-18	A	Eastern Michigan	2-3	L
		Eastern Michigan	8-5	W
4-23	A	Western Michigan	2-14	L
		Western Michigan	7-8	L
4-24	H	Ferris State	4-3	W
		Ferris State	3-4	L
4-25	H	Wayne State	14-5	W
		Wayne State	3-4	L
4-28	A	Purdue	0-3	L
		Purdue	7-6	W
4-29	A	Illinois	9-5	W
		Illinois	1-0	W
5-1	H	Central Michigan	0-1	L
		Central Michigan	3-5	L
5-4	A	Ohio State	0-5	L
5-5	A	Indiana	8-2	W
		Indiana	7-1	W
5-8	A	Central Michigan	13-4	W
		Central Michigan	10-9	W
5-9	H	Oakland	8-5	W
		Oakland	3-2	W
5-13	H	Northwestern	3-2	W
		Northwestern	12-6	W
5-15	H	Eastern Michigan	2-10	L
		Eastern Michigan	2-0	W
5-19	H	Michigan	8-5	W
5-20	A	Michigan	0-6	L
	H	Pepperdine	**0-15	L
5-25	H	Miami (OH)	**6-4	W
	H	San Diego State	**4-5	L

1980 (15-35; 3-13 in Big Ten: 10th)

Coach: Danny Litwhiler
(*-Spring trip games at Edenburg, TX)

Date	Site	Opponent	Score	W/L
3-15	*	Pan American	0-5	L
	*	Maine	3-2	W
3-17	*	Maine	3-4	L
3-18	*	Iowa State	4-10	L
3-19	*	Lubbock Christian	10-11	L
	*	Morningside (IA)	7-3	W
3-20	*	Lubbock Christian	3-4	L
3-21	*	Maine	3-12	L
3-22	*	Lubbock Christian	11-8	W
	*	Pan American	1-7	L
3-23	*	Northwestern	2-6	L
3-24	*	Northern Iowa	0-2	L
	*	Northwestern	1-2	L
3-25	*	Pan American	4-8	L
4-5	H	Eastern Michigan	0-5	L
		Eastern Michigan	1-0	W

Date	Site	Opponent	Score	W/L
4-7	H	Central Michigan	5-6	L
		Central Michigan	0-7	L
4-8	H	Albion	3-0	W
		Albion	1-2	L
4-12	A	Michigan	0-7	L
4-13	H	Michigan	1-4	L
4-19	A	Wisconsin	2-3	L
		Wisconsin	1-3	L
4-20	A	Minnesota	2-6	L
		Minnesota	1-5	L
4-23	H	Ferris State	2-1	W
		Ferris State	0-6	L
4-26	H	Detroit	2-1	W
		Detroit	0-2	L
4-29	A	Central Michigan	3-6	L
4-30	H	Oakland	4-0	W
		Oakland	2-1	W
5-2	H	Illinois	4-1	W
		Illinois	2-6	L
5-3	H	Purdue	8-5	W
		Purdue	1-7	L
5-6	A	Western Michigan	15-8	W
		Western Michigan	1-6	L
5-7	H	Western Michigan	2-0	W
		Western Michigan	3-5	L
5-10	H	Indiana	4-7	L
		Indiana	10-12	L
5-11	H	Ohio State	12-4	W
		Ohio State	3-9	L
5-13	A	Eastern Michigan	4-14	L
5-14	H	Wayne State	5-4	W
		Wayne State	4-11	L
5-18	A	Iowa	2-5	L
		Iowa	0-1	L

1981 (23-28; 6-8 in Big Ten: 4th in East)

Coach: Danny Litwhiler
(*-Spring trip games at Edenburg, TX)

Date	Site	Opponent	Score	W/L
3-22	*	Northwestern	6-12	L
	*	Northwestern	15-12	W
3-23	*	Seton Hall	4-3	W
3-24	*	Pan American	3-6	L
3-25	*	Seton Hall	5-7	L
	*	Missouri	1-9	L
3-26	*	Oklahoma City	2-3	L
3-27	*	Northwestern	8-0	W
3-28	*	Seton Hall	6-9	L
	*	Pan American	4-9	L
03-30	*	Pan American	5-3	W
	*	Pan American	5-12	L
3-31	*	Pan American	3-4	L
	*	Pan American	2-1	W
4-4	H	Eastern Michigan	6-7	L
		Eastern Michigan	3-14	L
4-7	H	Albion	2-21	L
		Albion	7-4	W
4-11	H	Detroit	2-1	W
		Detroit	4-2	W
4-12	H	Toledo	13-0	W
		Toledo	1-0	W
4-14	H	Central Michigan	3-8	L
		Central Michigan	3-7	L
4-15	A	Central Michigan	7-5	W
		Central Michigan	5-10	L
4-18	A	Purdue	4-5	L
		Purdue	4-1	W
4-20	A	Purdue	8-16	L
		Purdue	1-3	L
4-22	A	Ferris State	5-8	L
4-23	H	Wayne State	5-8	L
		Wayne State	9-1	W
4-25	A	Indiana	6-2	W
		Indiana	2-15	L
4-26	A	Indiana	10-5	W
		Indiana	10-11	L
4-29	H	Aquinas	12-5	W
		Aquinas	0-7	L
5-2	H	Ohio State	0-6	L

Date	Site	Opponent	Score	W/L
		Ohio State	5-11	L
5-3	H	Ohio State	8-6	W
		Ohio State	7-6	W
5-5	A	Western Michigan	7-6	W
		Western Michigan	3-0	W
5-6	H	Western Michigan	15-1	W
		Western Michigan	4-2	W
5-9	H	Michigan	2-7	L
		Michigan	8-6	W
5-12	A	Eastern Michigan	3-15	L
		Eastern Michigan	1-10	L

1982 (25-29; 6-10 in Big Ten: 4th in East)

Coach: Danny Litwhiler
(*-Spring trip games at Edinburg, TX)

Date	Site	Opponent	Score	W/L
3-21	*	Nebraska	5-12	L
	*	Nebraska	1-7	L
3-22	*	Oklahoma City	1-2	L
3-24	*	Pan American	1-2	L
	*	Oklahoma City	9-1	W
3-25	*	Pan American	1-3	L
3-26	*	Oklahoma City	6-5	W
	*	Pan American	0-1	L
3-27	*	Oklahoma City	5-0	W
	*	Pan American	3-1	W
3-29	*	Pan American	7-5	W
	*	Pan American	6-4	W
3-30	*	Pan American	7-6	W
	*	Pan American	1-2	L
4-10	A	Central Michigan	5-11	L
		Central Michigan	3-0	W
4-13	H	Eastern Michigan	7-8	L
		Eastern Michigan	6-8	L
4-15	H	Albion	8-7	W
		Albion	9-5	W
4-16	H	Detroit	5-2	W
		Detroit	3-4	L
4-17	H	Detroit	8-2	W
		Detroit	6-5	W
4-19	H	Aquinas	2-1	W
		Aquinas	10-9	W
4-20	H	Central Michigan	6-8	L
		Central Michigan	9-1	W
4-21	H	Ferris State	4-3	W
		Ferris State	8-1	W
4-24	H	Indiana	2-0	W
		Indiana	5-3	W
4-25	H	Indiana	4-12	L
		Indiana	5-3	W
4-27	A	Western Michigan	4-7	L
		Western Michigan	2-6	L
4-30	H	Purdue	3-1	W
		Purdue	0-6	L
5-1	H	Purdue	1-0	W
		Purdue	7-14	L
5-3	H	Wayne State	0-2	L
		Wayne State	5-2	W
5-5	H	Western Michigan	2-6	L
		Western Michigan	0-2	L
5-8	A	Ohio State	5-12	L
		Ohio State	7-3	W
5-9	A	Ohio State	1-7	L
		Ohio State	2-3	L
5-11	A	Eastern Michigan	2-7	L
		Eastern Michigan	0-2	L
5-15	A	Michigan	0-6	L
		Michigan	6-9	L
5-16	H	Michigan	0-4	L
		Michigan	0-4	L

Coach: Tom Smith (1983-1995)

Tom Smith, Litwhiler's assistant for 15 years, was appointed head coach in September of 1982. A native of Coldwater, MI, Smith was a high school standout in baseball, football, and basketball, earning 11 varsity letters. He signed as a switch hitting catcher in the Milwaukee Braves organization following high school graduation in 1961. A severe injury sustained in a home plate collision with Cincinnati's Pete Rose ended his playing career. Smith enrolled at Michigan State in 1963 and graduated in 1967 with a baccalaureate in physical education. He was immediately hired that fall as an assistant baseball coach and instructor in physical education, continuing in those positions until being selected to head the program following Litwhiler's retirement in 1982. In the fall of 1995, without apparent provocation, Smith left his coaching position and turned full time to teaching in the physical education department. After 12 years at the helm, he expressed the desire to do "something else" with his life. Then, three years later, following the 1997 1998 academic year, he retired from the university.

1983 (22-32; 8-6 in Big Ten: 2nd in East)

Coach: Tom Smith
(*-Spring training trip to Edinburg, Texas)

Date		Opponent	Score	
3-21	*	South Dakota State	5-4	W
	*	Pan American	1-10	L
3-22	*	South Dakota State	7-5	W
3-23	*	Pan American	5-6	L
3-24	*	South Dakota State	15-3	W
3-25	*	South Dakota State	7-6	W
	*	Pan American	5-6	L
3-26	*	Pan American	5-7	L
	*	Pan American	4-5	L
3-28	*	Pan American	2-5	L
	*	Pan American	2-4	L
3-29	*	Pan American	5-9	L
	*	Pan American	3-1	W
4-5	H	Albion	2-1	W
		Albion	3-2	W
4-11	H	Central Michigan	4-6	L
		Central Michigan	2-10	L
4-12	A	Central Michigan	4-7	L
		Central Michigan	4-5	L
4-16	H	Ohio State	4-0	W
		Ohio State	1-3	L
4-20	A	Aquinas	1-2	L
		Aquinas	0-1	L
4-23	A	Indiana	0-1	L
		Indiana	4-3	W
4-24	A	Indiana	12-2	W
		Indiana	3-2	W
4-27	H	Western Michigan	7-12	L
		Western Michigan	3-8	L
4-29	A	Purdue	7-4	W
		Purdue	8-7	W
4-30	A	Purdue	8-7	W
		Purdue	6-5	W
5-3	A	Eastern Michigan	15-11	W
5-5	H	Detroit	7-14	L
		Detroit	5-4	W
5-7	H	Michigan	9-11	L
		Michigan	5-13	L
5-8	A	Michigan	0-10	L
		Michigan	3-6	L
5-10	H	Ferris State	10-9	W
		Ferris State	4-6	L
5-11	A	Western Michigan	0-7	L
		Western Michigan	8-13	L
5-13	A	Notre Dame	5-7	L
		Notre Dame	1-2	L
5-14	H	Cleveland State	4-5	L
		Cleveland State	9-8	W
5-15	H	Cleveland State	9-1	W
		Cleveland State	5-4	W
5-16	A	Detroit	5-9	L
		Detroit	4-2	W
5-20	A^AA	Minnesota	*1-14	L
5-21	A^AA	Iowa	*2-6	L

1984 (34-24; 8-7 in Big Ten: 2nd in East)

Coach: Tom Smith
(*-Spring training trip to Florida)

Date		Opponent	Score	
3-19	*MF	Fordham	23-0	W
	*MF	Florida International	3-9	L
3-20	*MF	Fordham	25-4	W
3-21	*MF	Miami	7-9	L
3-22	*MF	Tulane	7-8	L
	*MF	Tulane	9-11	L
3-23	*MF	Miami	3-5	L
3-25	*MF	Bowling Green	17-1	W
	*MF	Florida International	2-3	L
3-26	*MF	Florida International	0-3	L
3-27	*MF	Florida International	16-6	W
3-31	A	Central Michigan	3-4	L
		Central Michigan	2-4	L
4-1	H	Detroit	5-0	W
		Detroit	8-3	W
4-3	H	Albion	17-8	W
		Albion	1-5	L
4-7	A	Eastern Michigan	5-6	L
		Eastern Michigan	4-3	W
4-9	A	Western Michigan	6-7	L
		Western Michigan	5-4	W
4-10	H	Aquinas	4-2	W
		Aquinas	10-8	W
4-11	H	Notre Dame	7-1	W
		Notre Dame	7-2	W
4-14	A	Ohio State	3-5	L
		Ohio State	8-7	W
4-15	A	Ohio State	8-11	L
		Ohio State	6-8	L
4-21	H	Indiana	2-0	W
		Indiana	5-2	W
4-22	H	Indiana	8-7	W
4-24	A	Ferris State	19-1	W
		Ferris State	2-1	W
4-27	H	Purdue	13-3	W
		Purdue	2-9	L
4-28	H	Purdue	11-13	L
		Purdue	7-5	W
5-2	H	Saginaw Valley	9-4	W
		Saginaw Valley	8-4	W
5-3	A	Grand Valley	3-6	L
		Grand Valley	12-3	W
5-5	A	Michigan	1-2	L
		Michigan	7-2	W
5-6	H	Michigan	7-11	L
		Michigan	14-5	W
5-8	H	Ferris State	8-9	L
		Ferris State	18-3	W
5-14	A	Detroit	10-7	W
		Detroit	3-4	L
5-18	A_MN	Minnesota	7-8	L
5-19	A_MN	Northwestern	4-9	L
5-22		Detroit	4-0	W
		Detroit	3-2	W
5-25	A	Cleveland State	6-2	W
		Cleveland State	5-0	W
5-26	A	Cleveland State	4-3	W
		Cleveland State	10-2	W

1985 (22-35; 2-14 in Big Ten: 5th in East)

Coach: Tom Smith
(*-Spring training trip to Florida)

Date		Opponent	Score	
3-17	*MF	Creighton	7-20	L
3-18	*MF	Maine	4-9	L
3-19	*MF	Rutgers	6-8	L
	*MF	Miami	3-11	L
3-20	*MF	Mercer	3-8	L
3-21	*MF	Maine	12-18	L
3-22	*MF	Miami	5-18	L
3-24	*MF	Mercer	3-10	L
3-26	*MF	Glassboro State	12-8	W
	*MF	Florida International	2-4	L
3-27	*MF	Florida International	1-3	L
	*MF	Miami	3-6	L
3-28	*MF	Florida International	3-13	L

Date		Opponent	Score	
3-29	*MF	Miami	1-5	L
3-30	*MF	Miami	7-6	W
4-2	H	Albion	11-1	W
		Albion	1-11	L
4-4	A	Notre Dame	3-1	W
		Notre Dame	6-5	W
4-10	A	Western Michigan	11-8	W
		Western Michigan	2-3	L
4-13	A	Purdue	1-8	L
		Purdue	2-8	L
4-14	A	Purdue	5-6	L
		Purdue	7-13	L
4-17	A	Aquinas	8-4	W
		Aquinas	14-10	W
4-20	A	Indiana	6-7	L
		Indiana	7-14	L
4-21	A	Indiana	8-11	L
		Indiana	7-6	W
4-27	H	Ohio State	0-2	L
		Ohio State	1-3	L
4-28	H	Ohio State	5-3	W
		Ohio State	1-5	L
4-30	A	Saginaw Valley	0-5	L
		Saginaw Valley	7-8	L
5-1	H	Siena Heights	9-6	W
		Siena Heights	7-3	W
5-4	H	Michigan	14-15	L
		Michigan	10-12	L
5-5	A	Michigan	0-7	L
		Michigan	1-6	L
5-7	H	Ferris State	5-4	W
		Ferris State	15-3	W
5-10	A	Bowling Green	5-12	L
		Bowling Green	7-8	L
5-11	H	Grand Valley	12-17	L
		Grand Valley	18-2	W
5-12	H	Detroit	6-4	W
		Detroit	5-7	L
5-14	H	Central Michigan	15-0	W
		Central Michigan	1-10	L
5-24	H	Cleveland State	7-6	W
		Cleveland State	5-4	W
5-25	H	Cleveland State	14-2	W
		Cleveland State	13-8	W

1986 (28-26-1; 7-9 in Big Ten: 4th in East)

Coach: Tom Smith
(*-Spring training trip to Florida)

Date		Opponent	Score	
3-16	*MF	Thomas	4-3	W
3-17	*MF	St. Thomas	1-2	L
3-18	*MF	Creighton	3-1	W
3-19	*MF	Florida International	3-8	L
3-20	*MF	Maine	8-10	L
3-22	*MF	Florida International	9-4	W
3-23	*MF	Montana State	9-4	W
	*MF	Bowling Green	4-3	W
3-24	*MF	Boca Raton	4-4	T
3-27	*MF	Florida International	0-1	L
	*MF	Miami	3-2	W
4-2	H	Albion	5-7	L
		Albion	7-1	W
4-3	H	Grand Valley	5-10	L
		Grand Valley	8-6	W
4-4	H	Detroit	2-1	W
		Detroit	9-5	W
4-8	H	Notre Dame	8-7	W
		Notre Dame	11-20	L
4-11	H	Saginaw Valley	22-3	W
		Saginaw Valley	5-0	W
4-12	H	Aquinas	5-7	L
		Aquinas	8-7	W
4-13	H	Siena Heights	6-8	L
		Siena Heights	10-4	W
4-19	H	Purdue	4-11	L
		Purdue	3-9	L
4-21	H	Purdue	6-7	L
		Purdue	8-1	W

Date	Site	Opponent	Score	Result
4-22	A	Western Michigan	1-5	L
		Western Michigan	1-6	L
4-24	A	Grand Valley	8-2	W
		Grand Valley	10-4	W
4-26	A	Ohio State	7-2	W
		Ohio State	6-5	W
4-27	A	Ohio State	4-5	L
		Ohio State	6-7	L
4-30	H	Eastern Michigan	2-3	L
		Eastern Michigan	7-2	W
5-3	A	Michigan	4-8	L
		Michigan	1-4	L
5-4	H	Michigan	8-9	L
		Michigan	7-4	W
5-5	A	Central Michigan	3-19	L
		Central Michigan	7-14	L
5-7	H	Ferris State	4-3	W
		Ferris State	3-1	W
5-10	H	Indiana	2-4	L
		Indiana	6-5	W
5-11	H	Indiana	2-1	W
		Indiana	6-4	W
5-13	A	Detroit	6-7	L
		Detroit	2-5	L
5-24	A	Cleveland State	3-4	L
		Cleveland State	10-0	W

1987 (34-20; 6-10 in Big Ten: 4th in East)

Coach: Tom Smith
(*-Spring training trip to Florida)

Date	Site	Opponent	Score	Result
3-21	*MF	Barry	11-10	W
3-22	*MF	Barry	1-6	L
3-23	*MF	Boca Raton	8-1	W
3-25	*MF	Miami	3-6	L
3-26	*MF	Monclair State	3-2	W
	*MF	Monclair State	11-13	L
3-27	*MF	St. Thomas	5-15	L
3-28	*MF	Ramapo	17-5	W
	*MF	Florida International	1-2	L
3-29	*MF	Florida International	0-4	L
3-30	*MF	Florida International	8-4	W
4-4	H	Detroit	2-1	W
		Detroit	2-7	L
4-6	A	Central Michigan	4-2	W
		Central Michigan	2-5	L
4-7	A	Notre Dame	13-10	W
		Notre Dame	10-8	W
4-9	H	Saginaw Valley	7-6	W
		Saginaw Valley	10-5	W
4-11	A	Indiana	6-7	L
		Indiana	5-6	L
4-12	A	Indiana	9-5	W
		Indiana	8-6	W
4-14	H	Grand Valley	8-1	W
		Grand Valley	20-1	W
4-16	H	Albion	8-7	W
		Albion	11-2	W
4-18	A	Purdue	4-5	L
		Purdue	2-3	L
4-19	A	Purdue	2-3	L
		Purdue	1-2	L
4-21	H	Wayne State	8-7	W
		Wayne State	18-3	W
4-25	H	Ohio State	0-6	L
		Ohio State	3-5	L
4-26	H	Ohio State	5-2	W
		Ohio State	7-4	W
4-29	A	Eastern Michigan	9-2	W
		Eastern Michigan	15-4	W
4-30	H	Western Michigan	13-6	W
		Western Michigan	16-9	W
5-1	H	Siena Heights	10-0	W
		Siena Heights	10-1	W
5-3	H	Valparaiso	2-1	W
		Valparaiso	13-1	W
5-6	A	Detroit	7-2	W
		Detroit	10-6	W
5-7	H	Ferris State	1-7	L
		Ferris State	4-5	L
5-9	H	Michigan	17-8	W
		Michigan	5-11	L
5-10	A	Michigan	8-2	W
		Michigan	0-2	L
5-14	H_{LN}	Central Michigan	7-6	W

1988 (41-20; 16-12 in Big Ten: tie 3rd)

Coach: Tom Smith
(*-Spring training trip to Florida)

Date	Site	Opponent	Score	Result
3-19	*BN	Glassboro State	9-5	W
3-20	*BN	Southern Illinois	3-4	L
	*BN	Florida International	10-4	W
3-21	*BN	St. Thomas	6-3	W
3-22	*BN	Air Force Academy	11-13	L
3-23	*BN	St. Thomas	2-0	W
	*BN	St. Thomas	7-3	W
3-24	*BN	Florida Memorial	11-0	W
3-25	*MF	Miami	7-6	W
3-26	*MF	Miami	5-4	W
3-27	*MF	Miami	8-10	L
3-28	*BN	Boca Raton	7-6	W
	*BN	Niagara	11-0	W
3-29	*BN	Florida International	11-2	W
4-2	H	Purdue	1-3	L
		Purdue	12-4	W
4-3	H	Purdue	6-1	W
		Purdue	4-1	W
4-7	H	Saginaw Valley	14-13	W
		Saginaw Valley	8-3	W
4-9	H	Illinois	3-0	W
		Illinois	6-1	W
4-10	H	Illinois	1-3	L
		Illinois	4-2	W
4-12	H	Siena Heights	14-5	W
		Siena Heights	10-4	W
4-13	A	Central Michigan	0-6	L
		Central Michigan	2-6	L
4-16	A	Northwestern	6-7	L
		Northwestern	4-1	W
4-17	A	Northwestern	14-8	W
		Northwestern	15-9	W
4-20	A	Michigan	0-2	L
		Michigan	1-2	L
4-23	H	Notre Dame	13-1	W
		Notre Dame	6-5	W
4-26	H	Eastern Michigan	10-0	W
		Eastern Michigan	4-3	W
4-30	A	Iowa	2-3	L
		Iowa	2-5	L
5-1	A	Iowa	3-4	L
		Iowa	2-1	W
5-4	H	Michigan	6-4	W
		Michigan	5-6	L
5-7	H	Indiana	5-3	W
		Indiana	11-10	W
5-8	H	Indiana	8-10	L
		Indiana	11-13	L
5-11	A	Western Michigan	2-8	L
		Western Michigan	9-5	W
5-12	H	Grand Valley	6-4	W
		Grand Valley	5-4	W
5-14	A	Ohio State	4-3	W
		Ohio State	2-3	L
5-15	A	Ohio State	18-10	W
		Ohio State	8-7	W
5-17	H	Detroit	7-5	W
5-20	A_{AA}	Minnesota	10-5	W
5-21	A_{AA}	Michigan	4-2	W
5-22	A_{AA}	Minnesota	4-17	L
		Minnesota	3-5	L

1989 (25-26; 13-15 in Big Ten: 7th)

Coach: Tom Smith
(*-Spring training trip to Florida)

Date	Site	Opponent	Score	Result
3-18	*MF	Montclair State	9-10	L
	*MF	Ramapo	26-3	W
3-20	*MF	Montclair State	7-8	L
3-21	*MF	Kean	2-6	L
3-22	*MF	Rutgers	9-8	W
3-23	*MF	Barry	11-8	W
3-24	*MF	Florida International	5-4	W
3-25	*MF	Florida International	6-7	L
3-27	*MF	Miami	5-7	L
3-30	H	Saginaw Valley	15-2	W
		Saginaw Valley	1-3	L
4-1	A	Purdue	1-7	L
		Purdue	3-0	W
4-3	A	Purdue	1-0	W
		Purdue	7-2	W
4-5	H	Grand Valley	4-1	W
		Grand Valley	3-2	W
4-9	A	Illinois	2-3	L
		Illinois	0-13	L
4-10	A	Illinois	0-6	L
		Illinois	3-4	L
4-15	H	Northwestern	3-1	W
		Northwestern	4-10	L
4-16	H	Northwestern	7-5	W
		Northwestern	12-6	W
4-19	H	Michigan	6-0	W
		Michigan	0-12	L
4-21	H	Siena Heights	6-8	L
		Siena Heights	5-1	W
4-25	A	Eastern Michigan	4-5	L
		Eastern Michigan	0-5	L
4-26	H	Ferris State	8-3	W
		Ferris State	3-2	W
4-28	H	Iowa	5-7	L
		Iowa	3-2	W
4-29	H	Iowa	9-1	W
		Iowa	6-4	W
4-30	H	Central Michigan	0-3	L
		Central Michigan	6-5	W
5-3	A	Michigan	0-2	L
		Michigan	1-6	L
5-6	A	Indiana	5-2	W
		Indiana	6-0	W
5-7	A	Indiana	6-3	W
		Indiana	4-10	L
5-9	A	Detroit	7-2	W
		Detroit	0-2	L
5-13	H	Ohio State	3-4	L
		Ohio State	3-5	L
5-14	H	Ohio State	1-3	L
		Ohio State	2-6	L

1990 (26-24; 13-15 in Big Ten: 7th)

Coach: Tom Smith
(*-Spring training trip)

Date	Site	Opponent	Score	Result
3-19	*TS	Alabama	3-10	L
3-20	*TS	Alabama	1-4	L
	*TS	Alabama	3-5	L
3-21	*AR	Auburn	4-5	L
3-22	*CK	West Georgia	12-8	W
3-23	*CK	Ohio	1-3	L
3-24	*CY	Ohio	3-2	W
	*CY	Columbus College	3-19	L
3-25	*CY	Bellarmine	2-0	W
3-26	*CY	West Georgia	3-0	W
	*CY	Columbus College	9-4	W
3-29	H	Siena Heights	4-1	W
		Siena Heights	10-7	W
3-31	A	Northwestern	9-3	W
		Northwestern	4-2	W
4-1	A	Northwestern	7-1	W
		Northwestern	10-2	W
4-4	H	Grand Valley	12-4	W
		Grand Valley	17-0	W
4-7	H	Indiana	3-9	L
		Indiana	7-6	W
4-8	H	Indiana	0-7	L
4-11	H	Eastern Michigan	8-7	W
4-12	H	Saginaw Valley	17-2	W
4-14	H	Purdue	3-5	L

Date	Site	Opponent	Score	Result
4-15	H	Purdue	5-3	W
		Purdue	9-7	W
4-16	H	Purdue	14-5	W
4-18	A	Michigan	2-3	L
		Michigan	1-2	L
4-21	H	Wisconsin	5-2	W
		Wisconsin	6-2	W
4-22	H	Wisconsin	11-8	W
		Wisconsin	10-2	W
4-25	H	Michigan	3-8	L
		Michigan	6-16	L
4-26	H$_{LN}$	Ferris State	9-6	W
		Ferris State	20-4	W
5-3	H	Detroit	1-8	L
5-4	A	Ohio State	3-4	L
5-5	A	Ohio State	2-3	L
		Ohio State	2-3	L
5-6	A	Ohio State	1-8	L
5-9	H	Oakland	9-7	W
5-11	A	Minnesota	1-8	L
5-12	A	Minnesota	1-2	L
		Minnesota	3-4	L
5-13	A	Minnesota	1-4	L
5-16	A	Central Michigan	6-9	L
		Central Michigan	10-12	L

1991 (28-25-1; 12-16 in Big Ten: 8th)

Coach: Tom Smith
(*-Spring training trip to Florida)

Date	Site	Opponent	Score	Result
3-16	*WI	Connecticut	23-3	W
3-17	*WI	Florida Southern	7-7	T
3-19	*WI	Bellamine (KY)	9-1	W
3-20	*	Mercer (GA)	10-0	W
3-21	*TP	Massachusetts	7-8	L
	*TP	Massachusetts	18-8	W
3-22	*TP	St. Leo (FL)	6-7	L
	*TP	South Florida	6-8	L
3-23	*TP	Tampa	7-13	L
	*TP	South Florida	6-15	L
3-24	*TP	South Florida	8-9	L
3-28	H	Siena Heights	26-1	W
3-30	A	Purdue	5-6	L
		Purdue	4-9	L
3-31	A	Purdue	4-5	L
		Purdue	6-5	W
4-3	A	Eastern Michigan	4-5	L
4-6	A	Wisconsin	8-5	W
		Wisconsin	7-0	W
4-7	A	Wisconsin	5-0	W
		Wisconsin	4-8	L
4-10	H	Grand Valley	4-6	L
		Grand Valley	5-4	W
4-13	H	Minnesota	3-10	L
		Minnesota	7-5	W
4-15	H	Minnesota	3-1	W
		Minnesota	3-13	L
4-17	A	Detroit	15-2	W
		Detroit	9-6	W
4-20	A	Indiana	3-1	W
		Indiana	1-2	L
4-21	A	Indiana	2-3	L
		Indiana	8-2	W
4-24	H	Michigan	4-17	L
		Michigan	0-11	L
4-26	H$_{LN}$	Ferris State	3-2	W
		Ferris State	9-1	W
4-27	H	Butler	7-10	L
		Butler	11-6	W
4-28	H	Butler	6-5	W
4-30	H	Saginaw Valley	20-3	W
		Saginaw Valley	10-0	W
5-1	A$_{BC}$	Western Michigan	7-1	W
		Western Michigan	5-4	W
5-4	H	Ohio State	3-2	W
		Ohio State	4-3	W
5-5	H	Ohio State	3-7	L
5-6	H	Ohio State	1-3	L
5-8	A	Michigan	0-4	L
		Michigan	2-4	L
5-11	H	Northwestern	0-8	L
		Northwestern	4-5	L
5-12	H	Northwestern	6-1	W
		Northwestern	9-6	W

1992 (36-19; 17-11 in Big Ten: 3rd)

Coach: Tom Smith
(*-Spring training trip to Florida)

Date	Site	Opponent	Score	Result
2-21	A$_{EP}$	New Mexico State	9-7	W
2-22	A$_{EP}$	Oklahoma	8-7	W
	A$_{EP}$	Washington	13-12	W
2-23	A$_{EP}$	Washington	7-12	L
3-7		Northern Kentucky	7-2	W
3-8	A$_{HH}$	Lincoln Memorial	8-2	W
3-20	*CW	Harvard	3-1	W
3-21	*LK	Fordham	8-5	W
	*BS	Troy State	4-3	W
3-22	*SI	St. Leo	9-10	L
3-23	*BS	Cleveland State	18-3	W
3-24	*TP	Harvard	4-0	W
		Harvard	9-1	W
3-25	*LK	Rider	6-1	W
3-28	H	Indiana	4-3	W
		Indiana	6-10	L
3-29	H	Indiana	9-6	W
		Indiana	5-6	L
4-5	A	Penn State	9-2	W
		Penn State	16-15	W
4-6	A	Penn State	10-9	W
		Penn State	3-1	W
4-8	H	Grand Valley	1-4	L
		Grand Valley	3-8	L
4-9	H	Siena Heights	2-5	L
		Siena Heights	7-1	W
4-11	H	Purdue	1-0	W
		Purdue	6-9	L
4-12	H	Purdue	5-6	L
		Purdue	0-2	L
4-15	H	Detroit Mercy	11-3	W
		Detroit Mercy	1-6	L
4-18	A	Northwestern	8-7	W
		Northwestern	8-4	W
4-19	A	Northwestern	6-4	W
		Northwestern	6-2	W
4-22	H	Bowling Green	9-0	W
		Bowling Green	8-1	W
4-26	A	Michigan	3-4	L
		Michigan	8-4	W
4-28	H	Ferris State	5-3	W
5-2	H	Iowa	6-7	L
		Iowa	10-0	W
5-3	H	Iowa	5-3	W
		Iowa	3-2	W
5-6	H	Michigan	8-0	W
		Michigan	3-1	W
5-9	A	Ohio State	0-1	L
		Ohio State	2-3	L
5-10	A	Ohio State	3-4	L
		Ohio State	5-7	L
5-14	A$_{CO}$	Minnesota	0-5	L
5-15	A$_{CO}$	Ohio State	10-7	W
5-16	A$_{CO}$	Illinois	4-2	W
		Minnesota	5-11	L

1993 (31-23; 12-16 in Big Ten: 8th tie)

Coach: Tom Smith
(*-Spring training trip to Florida)

Date	Site	Opponent	Score	Result
2-28	*BN	Florida Atlantic	10-4	W
3-1	*MF	Providence	3-2	W
	*	Florida International	2-8	L
3-2	*MF	St. Thomas	9-10	L
3-3	*MF	Barry	17-18	L
3-4	*BN	Villanova	14-7	W
	*	Villanova	9-6	W
3-5	*BN	Providence	7-0	W
3-6	*MF	Barry	11-6	W
3-7	*MF	St. Thomas	6-7	L
3-19	A$_{NS}$	Louisville	3-1	W
3-20	A	Vanderbilt	22-17	W
3-21	A	Vanderbilt	5-1	W
		Vanderbilt	17-8	W
3-27	A	Purdue	1-2	L
		Purdue	4-1	W
3-28	A	Purdue	1-0	W
		Purdue	5-4	W
3-31	H	Siena Heights	7-2	W
		Siena Heights	8-2	W
4-4	H	Northwestern	2-4	L
		Northwestern	3-2	W
4-5	H	Northwestern	8-7	W
		Northwestern	4-11	L
4-7	H	Central Michigan	2-6	L
		Central Michigan	12-14	L
4-10	H	Ohio State	5-4	W
		Ohio State	3-4	L
4-12	H	Ohio State	1-6	L
		Ohio State	3-4	L
4-17	H	Penn State	6-3	W
		Penn State	4-3	W
4-18	H	Penn State	11-1	W
		Penn State	4-6	L
4-21	H	Grand Valley State	5-4	W
		Grand Valley State	8-0	W
4-22	H	Detroit Mercy	9-0	W
4-24	A	Iowa	1-15	L
		Iowa	3-7	L
4-25	A	Iowa	10-2	W
		Iowa	6-8	L
4-28	H	Eastern Michigan	6-4	W
4-29	H	Oakland	7-4	W
4-30	A	Ferris State	7-4	W
		Ferris State	8-3	W
5-9	A	Indiana	0-2	L
		Indiana	6-20	L
5-10	A	Indiana	3-4	L
		Indiana	6-14	L
5-12	A	Western Michigan	3-6	L
5-15	H	Michigan	10-1	W
		Michigan	6-7	L
5-16	A	Michigan	2-4	L
		Michigan	12-8	W

1994 (26-29; 14-17 in Big Ten)

Coach: Tom Smith
(*-Spring training trip to Florida)

Date	Site	Opponent	Score	Result
3-4	*BN	Saginaw Valley	6-11	L
3-5	*BN	Mercy (NY)	23-2	W
3-6	*BN	Florida Atlantic	7-11	L
	*BN	Pace	3-7	L
3-7	*BN	Slippery Rock	10-5	W
3-8	*FD	Nova Southeastern	14-15	L
3-9	*MF	Barry	12-0	W
3-12	A$_{LO}$	Murray State	4-8	L
	A	Louisville	1-11	L
3-13	A$_{LO}$	Valparaiso	6-8	L
3-18	A$_{TS}$	Alabama-Birmingham	13-8	W
3-19	A$_{TS}$	Alabama	12-9	W
		Alabama	3-1	W
3-20	A$_{TS}$	Alabama	1-5	L
3-26	A	Illinois	10-6	W
		Illinois	3-1	W
3-27	A	Illinois	6-2	W
		Illinois	5-9	L
3-30	H	Grand Valley	8-3	W
4-2	H	Michigan	6-9	L
		Michigan	5-21	L
4-3	A	Michigan	0-4	L
		Michigan	4-3	W
4-5	H	Western Michigan	5-8	L
4-7	W	Siena Heights	12-6	W
4-9	H	Indiana	7-1	W
		Indiana	6-5	W
4-10	H	Indiana	2-8	L
		Indiana	4-1	W

4-13	W	Ferris State	19-7	W
		Ferris State	10-8	W
4-16	A	Ohio State	4-13	L
		Ohio State	5-14	L
4-17	A	Ohio State	4-6	L
		Ohio State	0-11	L
4-20	A	Central Michigan	7-14	L
		Central Michigan	11-3	W
4-21	H	Detroit Mercy	10-12	L
4-23	H	Minnesota	0-10	L
		Minnesota	5-4	W
4-24	H	Minnesota	6-19	L
		Minnesota	6-17	L
4-26	A	Eastern Michigan	13-11	W
4-29	H$_{LN}$	Detroit Mercy	14-13	W
5-8	A	Penn State	4-2	W
		Penn State	7-5	W
5-9	A	Penn State	4-9	L
		Penn State	8-9	L
5-11	A	Detroit Mercy	7-13	L
5-15	H	Iowa	6-5	W
		Iowa	13-10	W
5-16	H	Iowa	7-1	W
		Iowa	6-15	L
5-19	A$_{BC}$	Ohio State	5-12	L
5-20	A$_{BC}$	Michigan	1-5	L

1995 (24-27; 12-16 Big Ten: 8th tie)

Coach: Tom Smith
(*-Spring training trip)

3-2	*LC	Oregon State	12-2	W
3-3	*LC	New Mexico State	2-9	L
3-4	*LC	Oregon State	10-11	L
3-5	*LC	New Mexico State	4-11	L
3-7	*LV	Southern Utah	10-4	W
3-8	*LV	Southern Utah	7-5	W
3-9	*LV	Nevada-Las Vegas	5-10	L
3-10	*LV	Nevada-Las Vegas	10-7	W
3-17	A	Tulane	4-7	L
3-18	A	Tulane	6-7	L
3-19	A	Tulane	9-2	W
3-22	H	Siena Heights	11-4	W
		Siena Heights	9-2	W
3-25	A	Indiana	5-3	W
		Indiana	6-7	L
3-26	A	Indiana	5-1	W
		Indiana	8-4	W
4-1	H	Penn State	10-2	W
		Penn State	8-7	W
4-2	H	Penn State	1-5	L
		Penn State	7-11	L
4-7	A	Central Michigan	9-6	W
4-8	H	Ohio State	3-4	L
		Ohio State	0-6	L
4-10	H	Ohio State	4-0	W
		Ohio State	8-7	W
4-12	H	Oakland	5-18	L
4-13	A	Western Michigan	11-12	L
4-15	A	Michigan	4-15	L
		Michigan	9-6	W
4-16	A	Michigan	5-2	W
		Michigan	3-4	L
4-19	H	Eastern Michigan	4-1	W
		Eastern Michigan	6-1	W
4-20	H	Detroit Mercy	2-8	L
4-22	A	Iowa	0-4	L
		Iowa	4-6	L
4-23	A	Iowa	3-1	W
		Iowa	2-3	L
4-27	H	Central Michigan	12-15	L
4-28	H	Siena Heights	11-6	W
		Siena Heights	23-4	W
5-6	A	Minnesota	2-16	L
		Minnesota	8-17	L
5-7	A	Minnesota	0-7	L
		Minnesota	2-14	L
5-11	A$_{GLI}$	Dayton	3-4	L
5-13	H	Illinois	10-12	L
		Illinois	10-4	W
5-14	H	Illinois	7-2	W
		Illinois	10-22	L

Ted Mahan (1996-)

Following the interview of a short list of candidates, in October, 1995, the announcement was made that Tom Smith's assistant for four years, Ted Mahan, would become the Spartan's 12th head coach in the sport. A 1977 graduate of the University of Michigan, Mahan joined the MSU staff in September of 1991. He had previously served as a coach at Davison High School from 1983-1987, whereupon he returned to Ann Arbor as a graduate assistant in 1987-1988, and a full-time assistant coach from 1988 through 1991. While earning two degrees from the U of M, Ted won four varsity letters (1974 1977), helping the Wolverines to Big Ten titles in 1975 and 1976, along with NCAA tournament appearances in 1975, 1976, and 1977.

1996 (14-41; 4-25 in Big Ten: 10th)

Coach: Ted Mahan
(*-Spring training trip to Florida)

2-23	A	South Alabama	6-11	L
2-24	A	South Alabama	3-9	L
2-25	A	Auburn	9-10	L
3-1	*BN	Florida Atlantic	4-5	L
3-3	*BN	Lynn (Boca Raton, FL)	5-2	W
3-4	*BN	Saint Joseph's	6-9	L
3-5	*BN	Detroit Mercy	3-6	L
3-6	*MF	Miami	3-10	L
3-7	*BN	William Patterson (NJ)	3-11	L
		William Patterson (NJ)	0-8	L
3-8	*BN	Slippery Rock	14-0	W
3-9	*BN	Florida Atlantic	12-7	W
3-10	*BN	Columbia	10-5	W
3-16	A	Winthrop (SC)	2-6	L
		Winthrop (SC)	1-2	L
3-17	A	Winthrop (SC)	7-6	W
		Winthrop (SC)	2-3	L
3-23	A	Illinois	1-7	L
		Illinois	3-5	L
3-24	A	Illinois	5-6	L
		Illinois	2-11	L
3-27	A	Eastern Michigan	6-7	L
3-30	A	Ohio State	2-5	L
		Ohio State	0-1	L
3-31	A	Ohio State	4-5	L
		Ohio State	0-16	L
4-3	H	Michigan	4-5	L
4-6	H	Northwestern	5-4	W
		Northwestern	1-6	L
4-7	H	Northwestern	0-1	L
		Northwestern	2-4	L
4-10	A	Detroit Mercy	6-7	L
4-13	H	Purdue	5-0	W
		Purdue	1-2	L
4-14	H	Purdue	1-2	L
		Purdue	6-2	L
4-17	H	Eastern Michigan	13-6	W
4-18	H	Detroit Mercy	6-5	W
4-20	A	Iowa	6-7	L
		Iowa	3-11	L
4-21	A	Iowa	6-4	W
		Iowa	2-4	L
4-24	H	Oakland	13-6	W
4-25	H	Western Michigan	16-17	L
4-26	H	Siena Heights	9-2	W
5-4	H	Indiana	4-5	L
		Indiana	3-7	L
5-5	H	Indiana	4-12	L
		Indiana	5-8	L
5-7	H	Detroit Mercy	6-13	L
5-8	A	Detroit Mercy	11-5	W
5-11	H	Michigan	1-2	L
		Michigan	1-4	L
5-12	A	Michigan	3-10	L
		Michigan	10-13	L

1997 (26-28; 12-16 in Big Ten: 7th)

Coach: Ted Mahan
(*-Spring training trip to Florida)

2-21	A	Nevada-Las Vegas	6-7	L
2-22	A$_{LV}$	Portland State	4-5	L
	A	Nevada-Las Vegas	5-12	L
2-23	A$_{LV}$	Portland State	12-10	W
3-2	*BN	Florida Atlantic	6-0	W
3-3	*BN	LaSalle	5-6	L
3-4	*BN	Florida Atlantic	16-9	W
3-5	*MF	Barry	5-9	L
3-6	*BN	Lynn	7-10	L
3-7	*BN	Villanova	16-12	L
3-8	*BN	Ashland	13-0	W
3-9	*BN	Lewis	16-8	W
3-14	A	Charlestown Southern	4-5	L
3-15	A	Charlestown Southern	2-1	W
		Charlestown Southern	1-2	L
3-16	A	Charlestown Southern	2-6	L
3-21	A	Illinois	6-19	L
3-22	A	Illinois	1-4	L
		Illinois	7-6	L
3-23	A	Illinois	5-10	L
3-26	H	Eastern Michigan	7-20	L
3-28	H	Ohio State	7-1	W
3-29	H	Ohio State	1-6	L
		Ohio State	1-7	L
3-30	H	Ohio State	0-4	L
4-2	H	Central Michigan	9-6	W
4-4	A	Northwestern	9-7	W
4-5	A	Northwestern	5-2	W
		Northwestern	0-5	L
4-6	A	Northwestern	7-16	L
4-8	H	Oakland	11-4	W
4-9	H	Grand Valley	7-4	W
4-11	A	Purdue	3-4	L
4-12	A	Purdue	11-0	W
		Purdue	3-22	L
4-13	A	Purdue	4-5	L
4-16	H	Detroit Mercy	6-0	W
4-17	A	Western Michigan	9-0	W
4-18	H	Indiana Tech	5-6	L
4-20	H	Siena Heights	6-5	W
4-25	H	Indiana	1-3	L
4-26	A	Indiana	3-2	W
		Indiana	14-3	W
4-27	A	Indiana	4-1	W
5-2	H	Michigan	1-7	L
5-3	A	Michigan	0-4	L
5-4	A	Michgian	5-7	L
	H	Michigan	6-5	W
5-6	A	Detroit Mercy	5-6	L
5-7	A	Eastern Michigan	6-4	W
5-10	H	Iowa	6-5	W
5-11	H	Iowa	4-3	W
	H	Iowa	1-4	L
	H	Iowa	11-10	W

1998 (25-27; 8-16 in Big Ten: 9th)

Coach: Ted Mahan

2-20	A	Lamar (TX)	5-6	L
2-21	A	Lamar (TX)	1-2	L
	A	Lamar (TX)	4-0	W
2-27	A$_{MG}$	Iowa	2-3	L
2-28	A$_{MG}$	Troy State	8-4	W
3-1	A$_{MG}$	Columbia	1-14	L
3-7	A$_{BK}$	Columbia	8-3	W
3-9	A	Campbell	6-2	W
	A	Campbell	10-3	W
3-10	A	Campbell	2-13	L
3-11	A	Campbell	1-2	L
3-13	A	Ohio	4-5	L
3-14	A	Ohio	2-14	L
	A	Ohio	11-4	W
3-15	A	Ohio	7-5	W
3-24	A	Western Michigan	5-4	W
3-25	H	Wayne State	12-0	W
3-27	A	Iowa	2-7	L

Date	Site	Opponent	Score	
3-28	A	Iowa	4-0	W
		Iowa	5-16	L
3-29	A	Iowa	1-9	L
4-3	A	Penn State	0-8	L
4-4	A	Penn State	3-5	L
		Penn State	13-9	W
4-5	A	Penn State	8-21	L
4-7	H	Oakland	4-0	W
4-8	H	Detroit Mercy	7-11	L
4-10	H	Indiana	8-4	W
4-11	H	Indiana	0-2	L
		Indiana	2-0	W
4-12	H	Indiana	0-3	L
4-14	H	Grand Valley	9-4	W
4-15	A	Eastern Michigan	5-8	L
4-17	A	Michigan	10-1	W
4-18	H	Michigan	7-2	W
		Michigan	0-6	L
4-19	A	Michigan	11-10	W
4-23	A	Central Michigan	7-5	W
		Central Michigan	16-5	W
4-24	H	Indiana Tech	8-1	W
		Indiana Tech	3-2	W
4-26	H	Siena Heights	4-0	W
		Siena Heights	3-6	L
4-28	A	Notre Dame	4-1	W
5-2	H	Minnesota	1-2	L
		Minnesota	1-4	L
5-3	H	Minnesota	3-9	L
		Minnesota	1-5	L
5-9	A	Ohio State	4-3	W
5-10	A	Ohio State	0-3	L
	A	Ohio State	4-5	L
5-11	A	Ohio State	3-11	L

1999 (28-25; 10-17 in Big Ten: 7th)

Coach: Ted Mahan

(*-Spring training trip to Florida)

Date	Site	Opponent	Score	
2-26	A	McNeese State	4-3	W
2-27	A_{LH}	Louisiana Tech	0-17	L
2-28	A_{LH}	Indiana State	14-9	W
3-6	*BN	St. John's	11-10	W
3-7	*BN	Florida Atlantic	2-17	L
3-8	*BN	Illinois State	4-9	L
3-10	*BN	LaSalle	10-4	W
3-11	*BN	Illinois State	7-6	W
3-12	*BN	Pace	5-4	W
3-13	*BN	Lewis	4-0	W
3-14	*BN	Iona	3-2	W
3-19	A	Ball State	1-10	L
3-20	A	Ball State	3-6	L
		Ball State	1-10	L
3-23	A	Eastern Michigan	13-15	L
3-24	H	Eastern Michigan	14-6	W
3-26	A	Illinois	0-6	L
3-27	A	Illinois	4-7	L
		Illinois	5-6	L
3-28	A	Illinois	15-19	L
3-30	H	Grand Valley	8-3	W
4-2	H	Iowa	5-4	W
4-3	H	Iowa	12-11	W
		Iowa	5-15	L
4-4	H	Iowa	1-10	L
4-7	H	Detroit Mercy	15-2	W
4-10	H	Penn State	4-3	W
		Penn State	6-16	L
4-11	H	Penn State	16-9	W
4-13	H	Oakland	3-2	W
4-14	H	Siena Heights	2-1	W
4-17	A	Indiana	3-0	W
		Indiana	5-4	W
4-18	A	Indiana	7-8	L
		Indiana	8-4	W
4-21	H	Ball State	4-1	W
4-24	H	Indiana Tech	8-7	W
		Indiana Tech	11-2	W
4-25	H	Indiana Tech	13-6	W
4-27	H	Western Michigan	2-7	L
4-30	H	Michigan	2-9	L
5-1	A	Michigan	3-12	L
		Michigan	8-9	L
5-2	H	Michigan	7-8	L
5-7	H	Ohio State	4-34	L
5-8	H	Ohio State	1-11	L
	H	Ohio State	10-5	W
5-9	H	Ohio State	4-11	L
5-12	H	Central Michigan	4-2	W
5-14	A	Minnesota	5-3	W
5-15	A	Minnesota	4-12	L
		Minnesota	7-3	W
5-16	A	Minnesota	6-8	L

2000 (20-36-0; 9-18-0 in Big Ten: 9th)

Coach Ted Mahan

(*-Spring training trip to Florida)

Date	Site	Opponent	Score	
2-24	A_{LV}	Cal State Northridge	>6-9	L
2-25	A_{LV}	West Virginia	>6-5	W
2-26	A_{LV}	UNLV	>4-10	L
2-27	A_{LV}	Nevada-Reno	>2-17	L
	A_{LV}	Santa Clara	>5-8	L
3-4	*BN	Ball State	7-9	L
3-5	*BN	Florida Atlantic	1-11	L
3-6	*BN	Lynn	3-4	L
3-8	*MF	Miami	13-11	W
3-9	*BN	Ball State	3-10	L
3-10	*BN	Iona	2-4	L
3-11	*BN	Iona	5-10	L
3-18	A	West Virginia	5-6	L
		West Virginia	2-3	L
3-19	A	West Virginia	6-4	W
3-21	H	Eastern Michigan	7-6	W
3-24	A	Purdue	1-3	L
3-26	A	Purdue	3-4	L
		Purdue	2-5	L
		Purdue	8-3	W
3-28	A	Eastern Michigan	1-3	L
3-30	H	Grand Valley	8-3	W
4-1	H	Indiana Tech	8-3	W
4-2	H	Indiana Tech	8-10	L
4-5	H	Central Michigan	6-2	W
4-7	H	Penn State	4-19	L
4-9	H	Penn State	4-7	L
4-9	H	Penn State	2-1	W
4-12	H	Detroit Mercy	9-0	W
		Detroit Mercy	3-10	L
4-14	H	Illinois	7-9	L
4-15	H	Illinois	2-8	L
4-16	H	Illinois	6-15	L
4-18	H	Siena Heights	16-3	W
4-19	A	Detroit Mercy	16-9	W
4-22	A	Northwestern	4-5	L
		Northwestern	2-3	L
4-23	A	Northwestern	2-7	L
		Northwestern	4-5	L
4-26	H	Central Michigan	4-14	L
		Central Michigan	3-10	L
4-28	H	Minnesota	5-10	L
4-29	H	Minnesota	2-16	L
		Minnesota	5-7	L
4-30	H	Minnesota	9-7	W
5-5	A	Michigan	2-3	L
5-6	H	Michigan	4-1	W
		Michigan		W
5-7	A	Michigan	1-4	L
5-10	H	Oakland	6-5	W
5-11	A	Western Michigan	5-11	L
5-12	A	Ohio State	8-3	W
5-13	A	Ohio State	1-2	L
	A	Ohio State	6-5	W
5-14	A	Ohio State	3-7	L

> UNLV Classic Games

2001 (29-27-0; 9-17-0 in Big Ten: 8th)

Coach Ted Mahan

(*-Spring training trip to Florida)

Date	Site	Opponent	Score	
2-23	A	Troy State (AL)	4-5	L
2-24	A	Troy State (AL)	4-5	L
3-2	*	Florida State	4-7	L
3-3	*	Florida State	5-10	L
3-4	*	Florida State	5-9	L
3-6	*BN	Lynn	23-6	W
3-7	*FD	Nova	5-2	W
3-8	*BN	Monmouth	9-5	W
3-9	*BN	Rhode Island	9-4	W
3-10	*BN	Iona	4-2	W
	*BN	La Salle	5-2	W
3-16	A	Ohio University	3-7	L
3-17	A	Ohio University	2-21	L
3-18	A	Ohio University	14-9	W
		Ohio University	10-4	W
3-23	A	Illinois	1-10	L
3-24	A	Illinois	13-7	W
		Illinois	13-8	W
3-28	A	Eastern Michigan	14-2	W
		Eastern Michigan	8-2	W
3-30	H	Purdue	2-7	L
3-31	H	Purdue	4-5	L
		Purdue	0-4	L
4-3	H	Saginaw Valley State	2-9	L
		Saginaw Valley State	4-1	W
4-8	A	Minnesota	2-14	L
		Minnesota	0-3	L
4-9	A	Minnesota	1-10	L
		Minnesota	5-2	W
4-10	H	Western Michigan	9-4	W
4-11	A	Grand Valley	6-4	W
4-13	H	Ohio State	9-10	L
4-14	H	Ohio State	14-3	W
		Ohio State	0-4	L
4-15	H	Ohio State	3-13	L
4-18	A	Oakland	12-3	W
4-20	H	Northwestern	4-8	L
4-21	H	Northwestern	5-11	L
		Northwestern	7-6	W
4-22	H	Northwestern	6-2	W
4-24	A	Central Michigan	4-5	L
4-25	A	Central Michigan	6-15	L
4-26	H	Grand Valley	8-3	W
4-27	H	I.U.P.U.-Fort Wayne	9-3	W
4-28	H	Indiana Tech	6-5	W
4-29	H	Indiana Tech	4-2	W
5-4	H	Michigan	9-7	W
5-5	A	Michigan	10-2	W
		Michigan	2-21	L
5-6	H	Michigan	8-5	W
5-8	H	Oakland	6-4	W
5-9	A	Western Michigan	9-3	W
5-11	A	Penn State	11-12	L
5-12	A	Penn State	3-6	L
		Penn State	7-8	L
5-13	A	Penn State	1-10	L

2002 (38-18-0; 16-12 in Big Ten: 3rd)

Coach: Ted Mahan

(*-Spring training trip)

Date	Site	Opponent	Score	
2-22	A_{LV}	Cal. Santa Barbara	19-14	W
2-23	A	UNLV	8-3	W
2-24	A_{LV}	Creighton	15-22	L
3-1	*	Charlotte	12-3	W
3-3	*	Charlotte	11-10	W
3-4	*	Charlotte	22-8	W
3-5	*	Furman	6-7	L
3-6	*	Wofford	5-1	W
3-8	*	Charlestown Southern	13-6	W
	*	Charlestown Southern	10-2	W
3-9	*	Charlestown Southern	16-5	W
3-16	A	Eastern Kentucky	9-3	W
3-17	A	Eastern Kentucky	10-5	W
		Eastern Kentucky	10-1	W
3-23	A	Butler	6-2	W
	A_{IN}	I.U.P.U.-Ft. Wayne	5-4	W
3-24	H	Western Michigan	3-4	L
3-27	H	Siena Heights	6-0	W
3-29	H	Minnesota	3-4	L

3-30	H	Minnesota 5-3	W
		Minnesota 14-4	W
3-31	H	Minnesota 6-10	L
4-5	A	Northwestern 3-6	L
4-6	A	Northwestern 3-1	W
		Northwestern 9-1	W
4-10	H	Grand Valley 20-2	W
4-12	H	Indiana 13-6	W
4-13	H	Indiana 0-1	L
		Indiana 4-8	L
4-14	H	Indiana 10-6	W
4-16	H	Wayne State 22-6	W
4-19	A	Michigan 11-0	W
4-20	H	Michigan 4-3	W
		Michigan 4-19	L
4-21	A	Michigan 5-3	W
4-24	H	Central Michigan 14-4	W
4-26	A	Iowa 3-14	L
4-28	A	Iowa 3-4	L
		Iowa 3-0	W
5-3	H	Illinois 2-3	L
5-4	H	Illinois 3-2	W
		Illinois 4-8	L
5-5	H	Illinois 1-9	L
5-7	H	Eastern Michigan 10-12	L
5-8	A	Central Michigan 10-7	W
5-10	H	Ohio State 12-5	W
5-11	H	Ohio State 4-6	L
5-14	A	Western Michigan 12-10	W
5-15	H	Bowling Green 6-7	L
5-17	A	Penn State 16-7	W
5-18	A	Penn State 16-0	W
		Penn State 14-0	W
5-19	A	Penn State 16-3	W
5-22	A$_{MN}$	Northwestern *2-4	L
5-23	A$_{MN}$	Iowa *13-9	W
5-24	A$_{MN}$	Indiana *14-1	W
	A	Minnesota *0-6	L

2003 (21-34; 10-19 in Big Ten: 9th)

Coach: Ted Mahan

2-22	A$_{SH}$	Centenary 7-3	W
		Centenary 16-3	W
2-23	A$_{SH}$	Centenary 10-11	L
2-28	A$_{MY}$	North Carolina 3-1	W
3-3	A$_{MY}$	St. Johns 3-4	L
3-3	A$_{MY}$	Coastal Carolina 1-7	L
3-4	A$_{JX}$	Central Michigan 2-9	L
3-5	A	Jacksonville 5-9	L
3-6	A$_{JX}$	Vanderbilt 4-5	L
3-8	A$_{JX}$	North Florida 5-13	L
3-15	A	Western Kentucky 2-3	L
		Western Kentucky 3-13	L
3-16	A	Western Kentucky 0-5	L
3-21	A	Ohio 2-4	L
3-22	A	Ohio 6-2	W
		Ohio 1-9	L
3-23	A	Ohio 2-4	L
3-25	A	Bowling Green 6-4	W
3-29	A	Minnesota 4-8	L
	A	Minnesota 4-7	L
3-30	A	Minnesota 1-5	L
		Minnesota 10-11	L
4-2	H	I.U.P.U.-Ft. Wayne 10-4	W
4-6	H	Northwestern 3-2	W
		Northwestern 0-2	L
4-11	A	Indiana 2-4	L
4-12	A	Indiana 6-1	W
	A	Indiana 5-6	L
4-13	A	Indiana 8-5	W
4-15	H	Wayne State 13-12	W
4-16	H$_{LN}$	Western Michigan 2-4	L
4-18	H$_{LN}$	Michigan 12-3	W
4-19	A	Michigan 1-2	L
		Michigan 0-12	L
4-20	H	Michigan 2-5	L
4-22	H	Siena Heights 14-5	W

4-23	H$_{LN}$	Central Michigan 3-4	L
4-25	H	Iowa 2-6	L
4-26	H	Iowa 11-3	W
		Iowa 1-4	L
4-27	H	Iowa 11-7	W
5-2	A	Illinois 9-3	W
5-3	A	Illinois 4-5	L
5-4	A	Illinois 5-3	W
5-6	H	Indiana Tech 12-9	W
5-7	H	Eastern Michigan 15-3	W
5-9	A	Ohio State 2-3	L
5-10	A	Ohio State 1-2	L
5-10	A	Ohio State 5-6	L
5-11	A	Ohio State 8-11	L
5-14	A	Central Michigan 10-8	W
5-16	H$_{LN}$	Penn State 13-8	W
5-17	H	Penn State 2-6	L
5-17	H	Penn State 8-7	W
5-18	H	Penn State 3-4	L

Year-by-Year Team Record

Year	W-L-T	Pct.	Big 10 Place	Coach
1884	4-1-0	.800		No Coach
1885	3-1-0	.750		No Coach
1886	12-4-0	.750		No Coach
1887	6-3-0	.667		No Coach
1888	6-1-0	.858		No Coach
1889	5-2-0	.714		No Coach
1890	3-2-0	.600		No Coach
1891	5-3-0	.625		No Coach
1892	3-2-0	.600		No Coach
1893	6-3-0	.667		No Coach
1894	3-2-1	.583		No Coach
1895	5-5-0	.500		No Coach
1896	3-10-0	.230		No Coach
1897	3-6-0	.333		No Coach
1898	6-5-0	.545		No Coach
1899	5-4-0	.556		Max Beutner
1900	3-6-0	.333		Charles Bemies
1901	1-5-0	.167		Charles Bemies
1902	2-8-0	.200		George Denman
1903	8-6-0	.570		George Denman
1904	13-4-0	.760		Chester Brewer
1905	11-4-0	.733		Chester Brewer
1906	11-9-0	.550		Chester Brewer
1907	4-8-0	.333		Chester Brewer
1908	7-5-1	.577		Chester Brewer
1909	10-3-0	.710		Chester Brewer
1910	8-6-0	.571		Chester Brewer
1911	11-5-0	.688		John Macklin
1912	11-3-0	.786		John Macklin
1913	11-7-0	.611		John Macklin
1914	12-5-0	.667		John Macklin
1915	8-6-0	.571		John Macklin
1916	11-4-0	.733		John Morrissey
1917	6-5-0	.545		John Morrissey
1918	7-5-0	.583		Chester Brewer
1919	5-9-0	.360		Chester Brewer
1920	6-9-0	.400		Chester Brewer
1921	7-8-0	.467		George Clark
1922	8-10-0	.440		John Morrissey
1923	14-4-0	.778		Fred Walker
1924	6-7-0	.462		Fred Walker
1925	8-5-1	.633		John Kobs
1926	13-7-0	.650		John Kobs
1927	13-8-0	.619		John Kobs
1928	10-8-0	.555		John Kobs
1929	12-11-1	.521		John Kobs
1930	18-6-0	.750		John Kobs
1931	13-9-1	.587		John Kobs
1932	10-12-2	.458		John Kobs
1933	13-7-0	.650		John Kobs
1934	10-11-1	.477		John Kobs
1935	11-9-1	.548		John Kobs
1936	13-7-0	.650		John Kobs
1937	15-11-0	.577		John Kobs

1938	15-9-0	.625			John Kobs
1939	13-10-0	.565			John Kobs
1940	12-8-2	.591			John Kobs
1941	13-10-0	.565			John Kobs
1942	13-11-1	.540			John Kobs
1943	9-7-0	.563			John Kobs
1944	4-6-1	.333			John Kobs
I945	12-4-0	.750			John Kobs
1946	21-5-0	.808			John Kobs
1947	16-8-0	.667			John Kobs
1948	10-14-1	.420			John Kob
1949	19-8-1	.696			John Kobs
1950	19-9-0	.679			John Kobs
1951	17-9-0	.654	4-6-0	7th	John Kobs
1952	18-14-1	.563	7-6-0	5th	John Kobs
1953	11-17-0	.393	6-7-0	7th	John Kobs
1954	25-10-1	.708	11-2-0	1st	John Kobs
1955	22-11-0	.656	10-5-0	2nd	John Kobs
1956	16-13-0	.552	4-7-0	8th	John Kobs
1957	18-13-1	.578	5-5-0	7th	John Kobs
1958	22 12 0	.647	10-5-0	2nd	John Kobs
1959	21-14-0	.600	8-7-0	4th	John Kobs
1960	17-13-0	.567	4-7-0	8th	John Kobs
1961	21-11-1	.652	6-8-0	5th	John Kobs
1962	17-13-0	.567	6-8-0	5th	John Kobs
1963	18-14-1	.561	5-9-0	8th	John Kobs
1964	22-12-0	.647	8-7-0	4th	DannyLitwhiler
1965	28-11-0	.718	9-6-0	3rd	DannyLitwhiler
1966	24-13-1	.645	8-5-0	4th	DannyLitwhiler
1967	22-23-1	.489	8-10-0	6th	DannyLitwhiler
1968	32-10-1	.756	13-4-1	2nd	DannyLitwhiler
1969	24-17-0	.585	8-8-0	5th	Danny Litwhiler
1970	28-15-2	.644	9-7-0	3rd	Danny Litwhiler
1971	36-10-0	.783	13-3-0	1st	Danny Litwhiler
1972	28-10-1	.731	10-4-0	2nd	Danny Litwhiler
1973	27-20-0	.574	9-9-0	4th	Danny Litwhiler
1974	23-16-1	.588	7-8-0	6th	Danny Litwhiler
1975	28-16-0	.636	11-4-0	4th	Danny Litwhiler
1976	15-23-1	.397	7-5-0	4th	Danny Litwhiler
1977	28-26-0	.519	10-8-0	4th	Danny Litwhiler
1978	32-21-0	.604	11-5-0	2nd	Danny Litwhiler
1979	28-27-0	.509	11-4-0	1st	Danny Litwhiler
1980	15-35-0	.300	3-13-0	10th	Danny Litwhiler
1981	23-28-0	.451	6-8-0	*4th-e	Danny Litwhiler
1982	25-29-0	.463	6-10-0	3rd-e	Danny Litwhiler
1983	22-32-0	.407	8-6-0	2nd-e	Tom Smith
1984	34-24-0	.586	8-7-0	2nd-e	Tom Smith
1985	22-35-0	.386	2-14-0	5th-e	Tom Smith
1986	28-26-1	.518	7-9-0	t3rd-e	Tom Smith
1987	34-20-0	.630	6-10-0	4th-e	Tom Smith
1988	41-20-0	.672	16-12-0	t3rd	Tom Smith
1989	25-26-0	.490	13-15-0	7th	Tom Smith
1990	26-24-0	.520	13-15-0	7th	Tom Smith
1991	28-25-1	.528	12-16-0	8th	Tom Smith
1992	36-19-0	.655	17-11-0	3rd	Tom Smith
1993	31-23-0	.574	12-16-0	t8th	Tom Smith
1994	26-29-0	.473	14-15-0	t3rd	Tom Smith
1995	24-27-0	.470	12-16-0	t8th	Tom Smith
1996	14-41-0	.254	4-25-0	10th	Ted Mahan
1997	26-28-0	.481	12-16-0	7th	Ted Mahan
1998	25-27-0	.480	8-16-0	9th	Ted Mahan
1999	28-25-0	.528	10-17-0	7th	Ted Mahan
2000	20-36-0	.357	9-18-0	9th	Ted Mahan
2001	29-27-0	.517	9-17-0	8th	Ted Mahan
2002	38-18-0	.679	16-12-0	3rd	Ted Mahan
2003	21-34-0	.382	10-19-0	9th	Ted Mahan

Totals1923-1517-30   .559 471-512-1

From 1981 through 1987, the Conference competed in two divisions.
(Ohio State, Indiana, Purdue, Michigan, and Michigan State comprised
the East Division (e).

Team Batting Champion (1925-2002)

1925	Don Fleser- OF	.589
1926	Don Fleser- OF	.667
1927	Delmar Zimmerman- OF	.545
1928	Gerald Bryne- P-OF	.409
1929	Forest Rinehart- OF	.376
1930	Ed Gibbs-OF	.454
1931	Harold Cuthbertson- 2B	.361
1932	John Madona- SS	.349
1933	Alton Kircher- OF	.430
1934	William McCann- 2B	.375
1935	Steve Sebo- C	.342
1936	Steve Sebo- C	.402
1937	Milton Lenhardt- OF	.326
1938	John Kuk- OF	.354
1939	Norman Duncan- SS	.341
1940	Norman Duncan- SS	.398
1941	Howard Ladue- OF	.415
1942	Peter Fornari- C	.303
1943	Athur MaiSchoss- 3B	.333
1944	averages not computed	
1945	Ben Hudenko- C	.370
1946	Jacweir Breslin- 1B	.338
1947	Edward Barbarito- 2B	.347
1948	Dan Urbanik- 3B	.340
1949	George Rutenbar- OF	.377
1950	Al Cummins- 2B	.367
1951	Darrell Lindley- OF	.418
1952	Robert Ciolek- 1B	.364
1953	Charles Mathews- 1B	.326
1954	Charles Mathews- 1B	.352
1955	George Smith- 2B	.408
1956	Jim Sack- 3B	.393
1957	Frank Palamara- 2B	.358
1958	Ted Kearly- RF	.377
1959	John Fleser- OF	.347
1960	Robert Monczka- C	.283
1961	Tom Riley- LF	.359
1962	Jerry Sutton- 1B	.397
1963	John Hines- 3B	.373
1964	Jerry Sutton- 1B	.383
1965	John Biedenbach- 3B	.390
1966	Steve Polisar- SS	.331
1967	Bill Steckley- 3B	.325
1968	Harry Kendrick- C	.392
1969	Richard Miller- OF	.356
1970	Robert Ellis- IF	.380
1971	Robert Ellis- OF	.407
1972	Ronald Pruitt- C-OF	.392
1973	John Rohde- 1B-2B	.316
1974	Dale Frietch C-DH	.425
1975	Joe Palamara- 2B	.342
1976	Al Weston- OF	.345
1977	Al Weston- OF	.409
1978	Tony Spada- 3B	.421
1979	Rodger Bastien	.357
1980	Ken Robinson- OF	.314
1981	Terry Johnson- DH	.380
1982	Chris Dorr- IF	.365
1983	Andy Krause- RF	.344
1984	Dave Corey- 3B	.384
1985	Bill Goodheart	.363
1986	Bill Gavin- 3B	.417
1987	Mark Sayad- 3B	.431
1988	Mike Davidson- OF	.415
1989	Rich Juday- OF	.354
1990	Rich Juday- OF	.405
1991	Rich Juday- OF	.362
1992	Steve Johnson- OF	.398
1993	Steve Johnson- OF	.346
1994	Coby Garner- OF	.431
1995	Scott Ayotte- RF	.397
1996	Matt Riggins- 1B	.375
1997	Thomas Hartley- OF	.354
1998	Mark Mulder- 1B	.335

1999	Ted Demetral- INF	.348
2000	Mike Pisani- OF	.351
2001	Bob Malek- OF	.427
2002	Brady Burrill	.414
2003	Brady Burrill	.381

Career Hitting Leaders

Average

1925-27	Don Fleser	.539
1930-31	Ed Gibbs	.398
1970-71	Rob Ellis	.393
2000-02	Bob Malek	.392
1978	Kirk Gibson	.390
1984	Cordell Ross	.382
1968	Steve Garvey	.376
1962-64	Jerry Sutton	.374
1964-65	John Biedenbach	.372
1985-88	Mike Davidson	.370

Hits

2000-02	Bob Malek	245
1991-94	Steve Money	238
1997-00	Mike Pisani	237
1988-91	Rich Juday	227
1991-94	Dave Veres	216
1986-89	Kevin Dalson	206
1995-98	Tom Grigg	205
1985-88	Mike Davidson	203
1993-96	Matt Riggins	203
1999-02	Kyle Geswein	201

Runs Scored

1991-94	Steve Money	169
2000-02	Bob Malek	152
1985-88	Mike Davidson	150
1991-94	Dave Veres	145
1986-89	Kevin Dalson	143
1986-88	Steve Preston	138
1992-95	Scott Ayotte	137
1999-02	Chris McCuiston	137
2000-03	Brett Wattles	134
1990-92	Bob Juday	133

Runs Batted In

2000-02	Bob Malek	166
1993-96	Matt Riggins	156
1999-02	Kyle Geswein	150
1985-88	Mike Davidson	148
1991-94	Dave Veres	143
1992-95	Scott Ayotte	139
1988-91	Rich Juday	136
1987-89	Dan Masteller	127
1974-77	Al Weston	126
1982-85	Bob Goodheart	125

Doubles

1992-95	Scott Ayotte	47
2000-02	Bob Malek	45
1993-96	Matt Riggins	42
2000-03	Brady Burrill	40
1999-02	Chris McCuiston	40
1994-97	Chad Marshall	38
1986-89	Kevin Dalson	38
1990-93	Steve Johnson	37
1982-85	Dave Corey	36
1989-92	Craig Mayes	36
1991-94	Dave Veres	34

Triples

1985-88	Mike Davidson	14
1982-85	Steve Marod	13
1991-94	Dave Veres	12
1952-55	Chuck Mathews	11
1954-56	Ray Collard	11
1988-91	Rich Juday	11
1992-95	Scott Ayotte	11

1931-33	Abe Eliowitz	10
1989-92	Alex Gagin	10
1930-31	Ed Gibbs	9
1935-37	Milt Lehnhardt	9
1964-66	John Biedenbach	9
1970-72	Ron Pruitt	9
1974-77	Al Weston	9
1985-87	Todd Krumm	9
1987-89	Scott Makarewicz	9
1989-92	Craig Mayes	9

Home Runs

1999-02	Kyle Geswein	36
1993-96	Matt Riggins	34
2000-02	Bob Malek	29
1987-89	Scott Makarewicz	28
1985-88	Mike Davidson	27
1992-95	Scott Ayotte	26
1982-85	Bob Goodheart	24
1987-89	Dan Masteller	24
1991-94	Eric Sumpter	24
1983-84	Mike Eddington	23

Season Hitting Leaders

Average

1925	Don Fleser	.667
1926	Don Fleser	.589
1927	Del Zimmerman	.545
1930	Ed Gibbs	.454
1927	Don Fleser	.450
1987	Mark Sayad	.431
1994	Coby Gardner	.431
1933	Alton Kircher	.430
2001	Bob Malek	.427
1974	Dale Frietch	.425
1978	Tony Spada	.421
1951	Darrell Lindley	.418
1986	Bill Gavin	.417
1988	Mike Davidson	.415
1941	Howard Ladue	.415
1994	Steve Money	.414
2002	Brady Burrill	.414
1977	Al Weston	.409
1928	Gerry Byrne	.409
1955	George Smith	.408
1971	Rob Ellis	.407
1990	Rich Juday	.405
2002	Chris McCuiston	.404
1936	Steve Sebo	.402
2002	Bob Malek	.402
1987	Pete Przybysz	.400

Slugging Percentage

1971	Rob Ellis	.848
1994	Coby Garner	.819
1995	Scott Ayotte	.782
1959	Al Luplow	.776
1984	Mike Eddington	.773
1978	Kirk Gibson	.766
1962	Jerry Sutton	.762
2002	Bob Malek	.744
1988	Dan Masteller	.733
1985	Jim Sepanek	.727

At Bats

2002	Chris McCuiston	230
2002	Bob Malek	219
1988	Kevin Dalson	217
2000	Ted Demetral	213
2000	Mike Pisani	211
2003	Travis Gulick	211
2002	Jared Koutnik	210
1999	Mike Pisani	208
2001	Bob Malek	206
2001	Brian Wattles	205
2003	Alan Cattrysse	205

Hits

2002	Chris McCuiston	93
2001	Bob Malek	88
2002	Bob Malek	88
1994	Steve Money	84
1988	Mike Davidson	81
2002	Jared Koutnik	79
2003	Travis Gulick	78
1986	Bill Gavin	75
2000	Mike Pisani	74
2002	Charlie Braun	74

Walks

1973	Bill Simpson	46
2000	Kyle Geswein	45
1969	Joe Gavel	43
1984	Cordell Ross	41
1992	Bob Juday	39
1973	Amos Hewitt	38
1991	Rich Juday	38
1955	Chuck Mathews	36
1971	Rob Ellis	36
1988	Dan Masteller	36
1988	Steve Preston	36

Runs Scored

2002	Bob Malek	66
1995	Scott Ayotte	65
1988	Mike Davidson	63
2003	Travis Gulick	60
1984	Mike Eddington	59
2002	Chris McCuiston	59
1984	Cordell Ross	55
2002	Charlie Braun	55
2001	Bob Malek	53
1978	Steve Money	52
1984	Andy Krause	52
1991	Bob Juday	52
2002	Jared Koutnik	52

Runs Batted In

2002	Chris McCuiston	71
1984	Mike Eddington	66
2002	Bob Malek	66
1995	Scott Ayotte	60
1988	Dan Masteller	58
2000	Bob Malek	58
1988	Mike Davidson	57
1978	Kirk Gibson	52
1994	Dave Veres	51
1977	Al Weston	49
1985	Bob Goodheart	49
1990	Rich Juday	49
1996	Matt Riggins	49
2002	Kyle Geswein	49

Doubles

2002	Chris McCuiston	22
2002	Bob Malek	21
1992	Steve Johnson	19
1977	Al Weston	18
1994	Scott Ayotte	18
2000	Mike Pisani	18
1997	Tom Hartley	17
1995	Matt Riggins	17
1999	Mike Pisani	17
1995	Scott Ayotte	16

Triples

1971	Ron Pruitt	7
1986	Mike Davidson	7
1995	Scott Ayotte	7
1931	Abe Eliwitz	6
1971	Rob Ellis	6
1974	Terry Hop	6
1985	Steve Marod	6
1987	Steve Preston	6
1991	Rich Juday	6

Home Runs

1984	Mike Eddington	20
1978	Kirk Gibson	16
1996	Matt Riggins	16
2002	Bob Malek	16
2002	Chris McCuiston	15
1971	Rob Ellis	14
2002	Kyle Geswein	14
1985	Jim Sepanek	13
2003	Travis Gulick	13
1995	Scott Ayotte	13
1972	Shaun Howitt	12
1988	Dan Masteller	12
1990	Rich Juday	12
1997	Marty Patterson	12

Total Bases

2002	Bob Malek	163
2002	Chris McCuiston	160
1984	Mike Eddington	145
1995	Scott Ayotte	140
2003	Travis Gulick	136
1996	Matt Riggins	133
1988	Mike Davidson	132
2002	Jared Koutnik	131
1990	Rich Juday	124
1971	Rob Ellis	123
1988	Dan Masteller	121
2001	Bob Malek	121

Stolen Bases

1988	Steve Preston	27
1994	Steve Money	23
1969	Joe Gavel	21
1978	Kirk Gibson	21
1932	Chuck Fawcett	20
1969	Richie Jordan	18
1934	Theron Fager	17
1931	Ed Gibbs	16
2002	Bob Malek	16
1950	Ab Cummins	15
1967	Tom Hummel	15
1987	Kevin Dalson	15
1987	Steve Preston	15
1988	Mike Davidson	15
1989	Kevin Dalson	15
1999	Mike Wagner	15

Career Pitching Leaders

Wins

1990-93	Stuart Hirschman	28
2001-03	Bryan Gale	24
1970-72	Larry Ike	23
1977-80	Brian Wolcott	23
1956-58	Ron Perranoski	21
1957-59	Dick Radatz	17
1959-61	Mickey Sinks	17
1969-71	Kirk Maas	17
1972-75	Duane Bickel	17
1990-93	Steve Hirshman	17
1995-98	Brian Murphy	17

Winning Percentage (minimum of 10 decisions)

1945-47	Keith Steffee	16-2 .889
1967-69	Zana Easton	11-2 .846
1970-73	Elliott Moore	15-3 .833
1965-66	Jim Goodrich	9-2 .818
1990-92	Stuart Hirschman	22-5 815
1957-59	Dick Radatz	17-4 .810
1951-52	Roger Howard	8-2 .800

Innings Pitched

1995-98	Brian Murphy	300.1
1990-93	Stuart Hirschman	267.1

2001-03	Bryan Gale	259.1
1977-80	Brian Wolcott	255.2
1994-97	Tom Olejnik	243.0
1972-75	Duane Bickel	217.0
1956-58	Ron Perranoski	213.2
1959-61	Mickey Sinks	210.1
1970-72	Larry Ike	209.1
1954-56	Ed Hobaugh	206.1

Saves

1987-90	Brad Lamont	14
1987-90	Mike Ericson	12
1999-02	Domanick Squires	12
1997-99	Chris Yens	8
1990-92	Tim Crabtree	7
1990-93	Steve Hirschman	7
1989-91	Jeff Vogel	6
1993-96	Pat Hachenski	6
1984-88	David Mammel	5
1997-98	Mark Mulder	4
1991-93	Thomas Kutcher	4

Strikeouts

1956-58	Ron Perranoski	223
1995-98	Brian Murphy	194
1957-59	Dick Radatz	193
1959-61	Mickey Sinks	180
2001-03	Bryan Gale	184
1965-67	Dick Kenney	178
1977-80	Brian Wolcott	177
1967-69	Mickey Knight	174
1997-98	Mark Mulder	169
2000-02	Nick Bates	157

Season Pitching Leaders

Appearances

1988	Brad Lamont	29
2001	Domanick Squires	27
1999	Kimya Massey	26
1986	Dave Mammel	24
1995	Pat Hachenski	24
1989	Brad Lamont	23
1992	Tim Crabtree	23
1970	Phil Fulton	22
1991	Jeff Vogel	22
2000	Dylan Putnam	22
2000	Kimya Massey	22

Wins

2002	Tim Day	11-3
1959	Dick Radatz	10-1
1971	Rob Clancy	10-1
1992	Stuart Hirschman	10-3
1955	Dick Idzkowski	9-1
1968	Mel Behney	9-4
1978	Brian Wolcott	9-3
2001	Brian Gale	9-1
2002	Nick Bates	9-3

Lowest ERA (30 plus innings)

1965	Dick Holmes	0.47
1967	Jim Goodrich	0.76
1959	Dick Radatz	1.12
1965	Fred Devereaux	1.43
1957	Bill Mansfield	1.48
1972	Larry Ike	1.53
1945	Bill Page	1.60
1968	Zana Easton	1.60
1967	Mickey Sinks	1.62
1960	Mickey Sinks	1.64

Strikeouts

1998	Mark Mulder	113
1968	Mel Behney	107
1959	Dick Radatz	106

2002	Nick Bates	100
1958	Ron Perranoski	89
1967	Dick Kenney	88
1947	Robin Roberts	86
1957	Ron Perranoski	86
1972	Brad VanPelt	84
1958	Dick Raratz	83

Saves (since 1986)

1990	Mike Ericson	11
2001	Domanick Squires	9
1998	Chris Yens	7
1992	Tim Crabtree	7
1988	Brad Lamont	7
1993	Steven Hirschman	6
1991	Jeff Vogel	6
1989	Brad Lamont	6
1997	Mark Mulder	4
1986	Dave Mammel	4

Walks Allowed

1975	Duane Bickel	58
1973	Duane Bickel	50
1974	Rick Moore	49
1972	Rick Deller	48
1978	Mark Pomorski	48
1957	Ron Perranoski	45
1958	Ron Perranoski	45
1977	Larry Pashnick	45
1997	Josh Weeks	44
1968	Mel Behney	44
1973	Elliott Moore	44

Innings Pitched

2002	Bryan Gale	100
1959	Dick Radatz	96.1
1973	Duane Bickel	95.0
2003	Bryan Gale	95.2
1960	Mickey Sinks	92.2
1997	Brian Murphy	89.1
1988	Rick Rozman	88.1
2002	Nick Bates	88.0
1958	Ron Perranoski	86.2
1970	Phil Fulton	86.2
1992	Stuart Hirschman	86.2

Complete Games

1973	Duane Bickel	11
1971	Larry Ike	8
1978	Brian Wolcott	8
1980	Brian Wolcott	8
1982	Tim Birtsas	8
1983	Mike Patterson	8
1992	Stuart Hirschman	8
1996	Brian Murphy	8

Shutouts Pitched

1946	Robin Roberts	6
1971	Larry Ike	4
1967	Dick Kenney	3
1968	Mel Behney	3
1969	Dan Bielski	3
1970	Phil Fulton	3
1974	Jim Knivila	3
1978	Brian Wolcotyt	3
1979	Jay Strother	3

Season Fielding Leaders
Fielding Average (all with 1.000 record; minimum of 48 chances)

Putouts and Assists   PO-A

1946	Pete Fornari	47 -2
1947	Bud Erickson	75-4
1954	Bob Williams	67-6

1965	Bob Speer	67-4
1968	Bill Linne	99-7
1972	Rick Deller	36-13
1973	Howard Schryer	45-10
1978	Kirk Haines	57-5
1984	Steve Marod	48-4
1984	Mike Eddington	143-18
1989	Sean Bruce	72-1
1989	Keith Dutkiewicz	64-1
1990	Craig Mayes	87-8
1990	Mike Ericson	41-9
1992	Steve Johnson	98-4
1995	Coby Garner	66-5
1996	Carlos Fernandez	138-26
1998	Tom Hartley	45-3
2002	Bob Malek	81-7
2003	Tim Day	31-21

Putouts

1996	Matt Riggins	398
2000	Kyle Geswein	373
1988	Dan Masteller	361
1995	Shane Johnson	355
1994	Todd Menard	354
2003	Scott Koerber	344
1997	Mark Mulder	341
1978	Jerry Weller	336
1967	Tom Binkowski	331
1995	Matt Riggins	325
1990	Duane Young	323

Assists

1996	Tom Grigg	151
1991	Bob Juday	147
1988	Steve Preston	145
1997	Tom Grigg	141
1994	Dave Veres	141
1977	Rodger Bastien	138
1992	Dave Veres	138
1998	Tom Grigg	138
1979	Rodger Bastien	136
2000	Ted Demetral	136
1997	Ted Demetral	134
2003	Alan Cattrysse	115

Double Plays (Since 1964; conference games only)

1990	Duane Young	42
1990	Bob Juday	40
1991	Alex Gagin	39
1991	Bob Juday	37
2001	Scott Koerber	37
1994	Todd Menard	36
1988	Dan Masteller	35
1995	Matt Riggins	35
1994	Dave Veres	31
1978	Jerry Weller	30
1988	Steve Preston	30
1992	Jeff Childers	30

Postseason Honors
All-Americans (American Association of College Baseball Coaches)

First Team

1954	Tom Yewcic	C
1971	Rob Ellis	OF
1972	Ron Pruitt	C
1977	Al Weston	OF
1978	Kirk Gibson	OF
2002	Bob Malek	OF

Second Team

1949	Jack Kinney	OF
1950	Albert Cummins	2B
1954	Jack Risch	OF

1955	Bob Powell	OF
1956	Jim Sack	OF
1959	Dick Radatz	P
1961	Tom Riley	OF
1965	John Biedenbach	3B
1968	Steve Garvey	3B
1975	Joe Palamara	2B

Third Team

1949	George Rutenbar	OF
1951	Darrell Lindley	OF
1955	George Smith	2B
1963	Jerry Sutton	1B
1969	Rick Miller	OF
1974	Dale Frietch	DH
1976	Al Weston	OF
1984	Mike Eddington	DH
1988	Mike Davidson	OF
1995	Scott Ayotte	OF
1998	Mark Mulder	P
2001	Bob Malek	OF

NCAA District IV All-American
First Team

1954	Jack Risch	CF
	Tom Yewcic	C
1955	Charles Mathews	1B
	Bob Powell	LF
	Dick Idzkowski	P
1957	Roscoe Davis	1B
1958	Frank Palamara	2B
1967	Bill Steckley	3B
1968	Steve Garvey	3B
	Mel Behney	P
1969	Harry Kendrick	C
	Rick Miller	OF
	Dan Bielski	P
1971	Rob Ellis	RF
	Rob Clancy	P
1975	Joe Palamara	2B
1976	Al Weston	OF
1977	Al Weston	OF
1978	Tony Spada	3B
	Kirk Gibson	OF
1979	Rodger Bastien	SS
	Ken Mehall	DH
1988	Mike Davidson	OF

NCAA District IV All-American
Second Team

1954	Charles Mathews	1B
	Bud Erickson	P
1955	George Smith	2B
1957	Al Luce	C
1958	Ron Perranoski	P
	Dean Look	CF
1968	Harry Kendrick	C
1971	Ron Pruitt	C
1978	Rodger Bastien	SS
1988	Dan Masteller	2B
1992	Steve Johnson	OF

NCAA District IV All-American
Third Team

1954	John Matsock	SS
	Bob Powell	LF
1957	Frank Palamara	2B
1968	Steve Rymal	2B
1971	Gary Boyce	CF
1977	Jerry Weller	DH

All-Big Ten First Team

1951	Darrell Lindley	OF
1954	Chuck Matthews	1B
	Jack Risch	CF
	Tom Yewcic	C
1955	Chuck Matthews	1B

	Bob Powell	LF
	Dick Idzkowski	P
1956	Jim Sack	LF
1957	Roscoe Davis	1B
	Alan Luce	C
1958	Frank Palamara	2B
	Dean Look	CF
	Ron Perranoski	P
1959	John Fleser	1B
	Dick Radatz	P
1961	Tom Riley	RF
1962	Joe Porrevecchio	LF
1963	Jerry Sutton	1B
	Joe Porrevecchio	LF
1964	Joe Porrevecchio	LF
1965	Jerry Walker	2B
	John Biedenbach	3B
1966	John Biedenbach	3B
	Bob Speer	LF
1967	Bill Steckley	3B
1968	Steve Garvey	3B
	Harry Kendrick	C
	Mel Behney	P
1969	Rick Miller	CF
	Harry Kendrick	C
1970	Dick Vary	3B
1971	Rob Ellis	RF
	Ron Pruitt	C
	Rob Clancy	P
1972	Shaun Howitt	OF
	Ron Pruitt	C
1974	Al Weston	OF
	Dale Frietch	DH
1975	Joe Palmara	2B
1976	Al Weston	OF
	Rick Seid	C
1977	Al Weston	OF
1978	Tony Spada	3B
	Rodger Bastien	SS
	Kirk Gibson	OF
1979	Chris Dorr	1B
1983	Andy Krause	OF
1984	Mike Eddington	DH
1988	Mike Davidson	OF
1989	Scott Makarewicz	C
1992	Craig Mayes	C
1994	Steve Money	OF
	Dave Veres	SS
1995	Scott Ayotte	OF
1996	Brian Murphy	P
1997	Mark Mulder	P
1998	Mark Mulder	P
2001	Bob Malek	OF
2002	Bob Malek	OF
	Kyle Geswein	DH

All-Big Ten Second Team

1951	Bob Ciolek	1B
1953	Chuck Mathews	1B
1954	John Matsock	SS
	Bud Erickson	P
1955	George Smith	2B
1957	Frank Palamara	2B
	Ron Perranoski	P
1958	Don Gilbert	C
	Dick Radatz	P
1959	Dean Look	LF
1963	Malcolm Chiljean	SS
1964	Dick Billings	RF
1965	Bob Maniere	LF
1968	Tom Binkowski	1B
	Steve Rymal	2B
	Dan Bielski	P
1970	Gary Boyce	OF
1971	Gary Boyce	RF
1972	Brad VanPelt	P
	Larry Ike	P
1973	John Rohde	1B
1974	Rick Moore	P

1975	Mike Fricke	OF
	George Mahan	P
1976	Ty Willingham	OF
1980	Ken Robinson	OF
1982	Tim Birtsas	P
1984	Cordell Ross	SS
	Dave Corey	3B
1985	Jim Sepanek	OF
1986	Mike Davidson	OF
	Bill Hanis	C
1988	Scott Makarewicz	C
	Dan Masteller	1B
	Rick Rozman	P
1889	Dan Masteller	1B
1990	Rich Juday	RF
1992	Alex Gagin	3B
	Steve Johnson	OF
	Stuart Hirschman	P
1995	Matt Riggins	1B
1998	Brian Murphy	P
2000	Mike Pisani	OF
	Bob Malek	OF
2001	Domanick Squires	P
	Bryan Gale	P
2002	Nick Bates	P
	Chris McCuiston	OF
2003	Brady Burrill	C
	Bryan Gale	P

All-Big Ten Third Team

1954	George Smith	2B
	Bob Powell	LF
	Ed Hobaugh	P
1956	(Francis) Allen Luce	C
1958	John Fleser	CF
1960	Bill Schudlich	1B
	Mickey Sinks	P
1961	Sam Calderone	3B
1962	Dennis Ketcham	2B
	Jeff Abrecht	LF
1963	Jack Nutter	P
1964	Jerry Sutton	1B
	Malcolm Chiljean	SS
1965	Dick Billings	RF
1966	Jim Goodrich	P
	Dick Kenney	P
1967	Tom Binkowski	1B
	John Walters	CF
1968	Tom Hummel	RF
1969	Dan Bielski	P
1970	Rob Ellis	2B
	Phil Fulton	P
1971	Larry Ike	P
1972	Bailey Oliver	1B
1974	Bill Simpson	OF
1975	Rich Seid	DH
	Terry Hop	SS
1977	Ken Robinson	OF
	Jerry Weller	DH

1978	Jerry Weller	1B
1979	Randy Hop	2B
	Tom Schultz	OF
	Joe Lopez	OF
1980	Brian Wolcott	P
	Kirk Haines	DH
1981	Chris Dorr	1B
	Terry Johnson	DH
1982	Darryl Dixon	RF
1983	Bruno Petrella	2B
	Steve Barnes	DH
1984	Tom Shook	P
1986	Bill Gavin	3B
1987	Mike Davidson	OF
	Dave Metevier	DH
	Scott Makarewicz	C
1988	Todd Krumm	OF
1990	Alex Gagin	SS
1992	Steve Money	OF
1993	Steve Johnson	OF
	Dan Garman	P
1994	Scott Ayotte	OF
1996	Tom Grigg	SS
	Matt Riggins	1B
1998	Chris Yens	P
1999	Tom Hartley	OF
	Mike Wagner	OF
2003	Travis Gulick	OF

BASKETBALL
LEADERS, RECORDS and HONORS

ALL-TIME COACHING RECORDS

Coach	Years	W	L	T	Avg.
No head coach	1899	0	2	0	.000
Charles O. Bemies	1900-1901	5	3	0	.625
George E. Denman	1902-03	11	0	0	1.000
Chester L. Brewer	1904-10	70	25	0	.736
John F. Macklin	1911-16	48	38	0	.558
George E. Gauthier	1917-20	47	39	0	.547
Lyman L. Frimodig	1921-22	24	21	0	.533
Fred M. Walker	1923-24	20	19	0	.513
John H. Kobs	1925-26	11	26	0	.297
Ben F. VanAlstyne	1927-49	231	163	0	.586
Alton Kircher	1950	4	18	0	.182
Peter F. Newell	1951-54	45	42	0	.517
Forrest A. Anderson	1955-65	126	124	0	.504
John E. Benington	1966-69	56	38	0	.595
Gus. G. Ganakas	1970-76	89	84	0	.514
George "Jud" Heathcote	1977-95	340	220	0	.607
Tom Izzo	1996-03	189	78	0	.708
Totals	1899-2003	1316	938	0	.584

Season Records
See page 874 for explanation of abbreviations.

1899 (0-2)
Coach: No Coach
3-6	H	Olivet	6-7	L
3-13	A	Olivet	6-15	L

Charles O. Bemies (1900-1901)
(See baseball season records for Charles Bemies sketch)

1900 (2-3)
Coach: Charles O. Bemies
1-20	A	Olivet	5-6	L
1-27	A	Governor's Guard	3-6	L
2-3	H	Olivet	6-8	L
3-3	H	Michigan Normal	25-8	W
3-10	H	Governor's Guard	25-7	W

1901 (3-0)
Coach: Charles O. Bemies
2-16	H	Olivet	18-10	W
3-2	H	Michigan Normal	21-6	W
3-16	A	Michigan Normal	12-7	W

George E. Denman (1902-1903)

(See baseball season records for George Denman sketch)

1902 (5-0)
Coach: George E. Denman
2-1	H	Alma	102-3	W
2-15	A	Governor's Guard	19-0	W
3-1	H	Hillsdale	58-20	W
3-7	A	Alma	29-3	W
3-15	A	Hillsdale	36-17	W

1903 (6-0)
Coach: George E. Denman
1-26	H	Detroit YMCA	43-8	W
1-29	H	Hillsdale	49-2	W
2-13	A	Michigan Normal	23-7	W
2-18	A	Governor's Guard	19-7	W
3-7	H	Michigan Normal	49-5	W
3-14	H	Gr. Rapids YMCA	42-7	W

Chester Brewer (1904-1910)
(See baseball season records for Chester Brewer sketch)

1904 (5-3)
Coach: Chester Brewer
1-9	H	Chicago Westside "Y"	13-44	L
1-23	H	Alma	52-7	W
2-6	A	Michigan Normal	22-2	W
2-12	A	Gr. Rapids YMCA	14-13	W
2-27	H	Alma	14-22	L
3-5	H	Michigan Normal	62-10	W
3-12	H	Gr. Rapids YMCA	41-10	W
3-25	A	Detroit A.C.	8-33	L

1905 (5-3)
Coach: Chester Brewer
1-14	H	Saginaw YMCA	62-12	W
1-21	H	Bay City YMCA	47-20	W
1-27	A	Gr. Rapids YMCA	22-38	L
1-31	A	Hope	30-44	L
2-4	H	Jackson YMCA	47-12	W
2-10	A	Detroit A.C.	30-39	L
2-25	H	B. Creek YMCA	94-4	W
3-3	A	Bay City YMCA	30-14	W

1906 (11-2)
Coach: Chester Brewer
1-18	H	Adrian	43-18	W
1-26	H	Owosso YMCA	76-12	W
2-2	A	Mich. Deaf School	47-16	W
2-3	H	Cent. Mich. Normal	37-12	W
2-10	A	Gr. Rapids YMCA	25-20	W
2-12	H	Ann Arbor YMCA	20-21	L
2-16	A	Cent. Mich. Normal	21-18	W
2-20	A	Adrian	21-20	W
2-23	A	Albion	47-10	W
2-24	H	Ann Arbor YMCA	25-29	L
2-26	H	Olivet	47-9	W
3-3	H	Albion	59-8	W
3-16	H	Alma	52-3	W

1907 (14-2)
Coach: Chester Brewer
1-5	H	Hope	50-30	W
1-12	H	Armour Institute.	51-24	W
1-18	A	Saginaw H.S.	35-17	W
1-19	A	Sag. Bank Clerks	29-19	W
1-25	A	Jackson YMCA	43-30	W
1-26	H	Cent. Mich. Normal	42-18	W
1-28	A	Detroit YMCA	14-31	L
1-29	A	Michigan Normal	50-25	W
2-2	H	Olivet	41-24	W
2-7	H	Adrian	54-24	W
2-16	A	Hope	33-23	W

2-19	H	Detroit YMCA	17-23	L
2-20	A	Adrian	41-20	W
2-22	A	Olivet	38-24	W
3-1	A	Cent. Mich. Normal	33-22	W
3-2	H	Michigan Normal	72-13	W

1908 (15-5)
Coach: Chester Brewer
1-4	A	Cent. Mich. Normal	46-8	W
1-8	H	Oberlin	46-21	W
1-11	H	Saginaw H.S.	67-23	W
1-17	H	Adrian	30-14	W
1-20	A	Detroit YMCA	20-33	L
1-25	H	Gr. Rapids YMCA	74-16	W
1-31	H	Notre Dame	33-20	W
2-1	H$_{IN}$	Notre Dame	16-23	L
2-3	H	Jackson YMCA	42-29	W
2-7	H	Cent. Mich. Normal	38-23	W
2-8	H	Midland YMCA	39-8	W
2-14	H	Detroit YMCA	27-29	L
2-21	A	Jackson YMCA	38-25	W
2-22	A	Adrian	42-31	W
2-24	H	Haskell Indians	33-18	W
2-26	A	B. Creek YMCA	28-14	W
2-27	A	Notre Dame	20-39	L
2-28AM	A	DePaul	26-17	W
2-28 PM	A	Armour Institute	26-29	L
2-29	A	South Haven Indep.	31-18	W

1909 (10-5)
Coach: Chester Brewer
1-9	A	Michigan	24-16	W
1-13	H	DePaul	76-7	W
1-18	H	Detroit Burroughs	24-15	W
1-22	A	Wabash	24-39	L
1-23	A	Notre Dame	10-26	L
1-25	H	Adrian	53-13	W
2-8	H	Notre Dame	18-22	L
2-11	A	Detroit YMCA	18-25	L
2-18	H	B. Creek YMCA	32-25	W
2-20	H	Michigan	45-23	W
2-21	H	Armour Institute	53-7	W
2-22	A	Detroit Burroughs	20-19	W
3-2	H	Roch. (NY) YMCA	30-18	W
3-3	H$_{IN}$	Roch. (NY) YMCA	24-36	L
3-11	H	Detroit YMCA	33-28	W

1910 (10-5)
Coach: Chester Brewer
1-7	H	Jackson YMCA	51-18	W
1-14	H	Detroit Spalding	20-18	W
1-25	A	Jackson YMCA	27-18	W
1-26	A	Purdue	9-35	L
1-27	A	Rose Poly	28-31	L
1-28	A	Wabash	21-23	L
1-29	A	Notre Dame	28-21	W
2-7	H	Bay City YMCA	84-12	W
2-11	A	Armour Institute	26-11	W
2-12	A	Lake Forest	14-13	W
2-19	A	Notre Dame	43-23	W
3-3	H	Hope	40-21	W
3-5	A	Ohio State	13-31	L
3-7	A	Detroit YMCA	27-24	W
3-11	A	Hope	30-38	L

John Macklin (1911-1916)

(See baseball season records for John Macklin sketch)

1911 (5-9)

Coach: John Macklin

1-9	H	Detroit Spalding	9-21	L
1-13	A	Wabash	15-25	L
1-14	A	Rose Poly	20-26	L
1-18	A	Detroit Spalding	25-18	W
1-20	H	Alma	51-24	W
1-21	H	Armour Institute	51-11	W
1-30	H	Detroit YMCA	11-22	L
2-3	A	Armour Institute	21-36	L
2-4	A	Lake Forest	26-28	L
2-10	A	Detroit A.C.	12-54	L
2-11	A	Ohio State	12-42	L
2-17	A	Hope	24-48	L
2-24	A	Alma	23-21	W
3-2	H	Hope	35-32	W

1912 (12-3)

Coach: John Macklin

1-6	H	Cent. Mich. Normal	72-10	W
1-12	A	Armour Institute	39-30	W
1-13	A$_{NA}$	Northwestern Coll.	19-25	L
1-16	H	Alma	53-14	W
1-18	A	Winona	37-21	W
1-19	A	Wabash	26-32	L
1-20	A	Rose Poly	33-31	W
1-23	A	Hope	40-41(2OT)	L
1-27	H	Armour Institute	51-18	W
2-2	H	Albion	60-23	W
2-10	H	Winona	67-4	W
2-16	A	Alma	37-15	W
2-21	H	Hope	55-23	W
2-24	H	Detroit YMCA	42-26	W
3-4	A	Detroit YMCA	20-17	W

1913 (8-5)

Coach: John Macklin

1-11	H	Winona	75-14	W
1-21	H	Detroit Rayls	37-12	W
1-27	H	Alma	48-24	W
1-29	A	Hope	33-26	W
2-6	H	Northwestern Coll.	21-23	L
2-11	A	Detroit YMCA	22-23	L
2-13	H	Notre Dame	40-7	W
2-21	H	Hope	58-25	W
2-26	A	St. John's (Toledo)	39-24	W
2-27	A	Buchtel (Akron)	30-35	L
2-28	A	Denison	18-44	L
3-1	A	St. Mary's (Dayton)	26-28	L
3-8	H	Detroit YMCA	38-9	W

1914 (8-4)

Coach: John Macklin

1-16	H	Toledo Buckeyes	40-24	W
1-22	H	Lake Forest	30-24	W
1-23	A$_{NA}$	Northwestern Coll.	24-44	L
1-24	A	Notre Dame	18-27	L
1-30	H	Detroit Burroughs	29-22	W
2-4	A	Notre Dame	45-22	W
2-14	H	Detroit YMCA	27-29	L
2-19	A	W. Va. Wesleyan	38-21	W
2-25	A	St. John's (Toledo)	50-17	W
2-26	A	Toledo Buckeyes	26-25	W
2-27	A	Buchtel (Akron)	45-30	W
3-3	H	Detroit YMCA	22-27	L

1915 (7-9)

Coach: John Macklin

1-9	H	Toledo Buckeyes	23-33	L
1-13	H	Hope	56-20	W
1-15	H	Illinois A.C..	21-22	L

1-22	H	Detroit YMCA	23-14	W
1-23	H	Defiance	54-12	W
1-28	A	Toledo Buckeyes	27-31	L
1-29	A	Ohio Northern	45-16	W
1-30	A	Defiance	30-19	W
2-2	H	Notre Dame	14-13	W
2-6	H	Northwestern Coll.	17-28	L
2-11	A$_{NA}$	Northwestern Coll	22-41	L
2-12	A$_{CH}$	Mercury A. C.	20-25	L
2-13	A	Notre Dame	19-24	L
2-18	H	W.Va. Wesleyan	31-43	L
2-24	H	Hope	46-28	W
3-2	A	Detroit YMCA	9-21	L

1916 (8-8)

Coach: John Macklin

1-12	H	Western St. Normal	51-21	W
1-14	H	Hope	14-20	L
1-15	H	St. Mary's (MI)	29-19	W
1-19	H	Notre Dame	18-19	L
1-20	A$_{NA}$	Northwestern Coll.	17-29	L
1-22	A	Illinois A.C.	18-50	L
1-29	H	Kalamazoo	34-27	W
2-2	H	Notre Dame	23-24	L
2-4	A	Hope	21-18	W
2-9	H	Muskingum	39-21	W
2-12	H	Detroit YMCA	27-23	W
2-17	H	Tri State	30-13	W
2-19	A	Toledo Buckeyes	23-32	L
2-24	A	Toledo Buckeyes	28-22	W
3-3	H$_{NA}$	Northwestern Coll.	21-28	L
3-7	A	Detroit YMCA	14-35	L

George Gauthier (1917-1920)

See track and field season records for George Gauthier sketch)

1917 (11-5)

Coach: George Gauthier

1-12	H	W.Va. Wesleyan	41-22	W
1-19	H	Hope	34-20	W
1-20	H	Alma	47-7	W
1-26	H	Illinois A.C.	39-27	W
1-27	H	Notre Dame	31-25	W
2-1	H	Buffalo	36-17	W
2-3	H	Detroit YMCA	33-26	W
2-8	H	Ohio Northern	53-9	W
2-10	H	Wabash	20-19	W
2-15	A	Illinois A.C.	23-43	L
2-16	A$_{NA}$	Northwestern Coll.	16-26	L
2-17	A	Notre Dame	19-33	L
2-23	A	Hope	13-18	L
3-2	H	Northwestern Coll.	28-14	W
3-8	H	Marietta	30-20	W
3-10	A	Detroit YMCA	15-30	L

1917-18 (6-10)

Coach: George Gauthier

12-28	A	Detroit YMCA	13-31	L
12-29	A	Detroit	22-32	L
1-5	A	G. Rapids YMCA	21-22	L
1-9	H	Ft. Custer Enlisted	16-27	L
1-11	A	Michigan	13-17	L
1-18	A	Hope	23-33	L
1-19	H	Ft. Custer Officers	24-20	W
1-25	A	St. John's (Toledo)	27-19	W
1-26	A	Detroit YMCA	20-34	L
2-1	H	Notre Dame	27-12	W
2-7	A	Notre Dame	23-25	L
2-8	A	Northwestern Coll.	16-19	L
2-15	H	Hope	35-10	W
2-23	A	Oberlin	35-20	W
3-2	H	Michigan	25-33	L
3-9	H	Detroit YMCA	23-16	W

1918-19 (9-9)

Coach: George Gauthier

1-3	A	Holland YMCA	15-21	L
1-4	A	G. Rapids YMCA	19-17	W
1-8	H	Western St. Normal	19-18	W
1-10	A	Detroit Rayls	16-37	L
1-11	A	Oberlin	14-24	L
1-15	H	Kalamazoo	42-20	W
1-17	A	Western St. Normal	28-23	W
1-24	H	Ft. Custer Officers	31-13	W
1-30	A	Wabash	19-28	L
1-31	A	DePauw	18-17	W
2-1	A	Notre Dame	32-28	W
2-7	H	Wabash	37-26	W
2-8	A	Hope	18-21	L
2-12	H	DePauw	12-21	L
2-15	H	Michigan	17-19	L
2-22	A	Notre Dame	16-17	L
2-28	A	Michigan	33-24	W
3-1	H	Hope	20-26	L

1919-20 (21-15)

Coach: George Gauthier

12-19	A	Detroit A.C.	%11-23	L
12-20	A$_{TO}$	DeVilbis College	%25-37	L
12-26	A$_{TO}$	AC Spark Plug	%29-28	W
12-19	A	Ft. Custer Officers	%53-3	W
12-20	A	Muskegon YMCA	%21-26	L
12-27	A	Holland YMCA	%20-18	W
12-31	H	Chicago	25-32	L
1-2	A	Oberlin	36-8	W
1-3	A	Detroit	29-30	L
1-7	H	Cent. Mich. Normal	29-15	W
1-9	A	Hope	16-21	L
1-10	A	Kalamazoo	39-21	W
1-16	A	Indiana	19-20	L
1-21	A	Kalamazoo	34-15	W
1-24	H	Notre Dame	23-20	W
1-28	H	Chicago "Y" College	33-20	W
1-30	A	Michigan	23-13	W
2-6	H	Wabash	29-27	W
2-9	A	Notre Dame	23-30	L
2-11	A	Creighton	21-22	L
2-12	A	Creighton	18-15	W
2-13	A	Nebraska	28-43	L
2-14	A	Nebraska	20-29	L
2-18	H	DePauw	21-33	L
2-23	A	DePauw	18-31	L
2-24	A	Wabash	16-24	L
2-28	H	Michigan	34-27	W
3-1	H	Creighton	31-24	W
3-6	H	Hope	34-23	W
3-20	A	Alpena Independents.	22-11	W
3-21	A$_{MS}$	Alger Co. Club	17-14	W
3-23	A	Northern Michigan	43-13	W
3-24	A$_{IS}$	American Legion	24-37	L
3-25	A	Gwinn Club	66-12	W
3-26	A$_{LL}$	American Legion	60-24	W
3-27	A	Mich. Coll. of Mines	28-26	W

%The squad was divided into two teams with separate schedules.

Lyman L. Frimodig (1921-1922)

Upon his retirement as Michigan State's athletic business manager on July 1, 1960, Lyman L. Frimodig had been with the athletic department for nearly 42 years. During that span, he served in numerous capacities: assistant athletic director, ticket sales manager, coach of various freshman teams, professor of health and physical education, and being the varsity basketball coach for two seasons. Frim's hometown was Laurium, MI, but the tall son of Norwegian immigrants went to high school at nearby Calumet. He played four years each on five sports teams: football, basketball, baseball, track, and hockey. Upon graduation and before entering MAC in 1913, Frimodig was a Calumet mail carrier at $50 a month. During his Aggie years (1914-17) he won 10 varsity awards in football, basketball and baseball, a Spartan feat never again achieved. Following his

collegiate years in East Lansing, Lyman Frimodig returned to the Upper Peninsula where he coached and was principal of Escanaba High School until he entered the service in 1918. One year later, on January 1, 1919, MAC hired its illustrious alumnus for six months only, to serve as physical education instructor and freshman coach. Frim never left. His tenure would ultimately stretch to the second longest in school's history, surpassed only by Jack Heppinstall. Frim died on May 6, 1972.

1921 (13-8)
Coach: Lyman L. Frimodig

1-8	H	Cent. Mich. Normal	26-21	W
1-11	H	Kalamazoo	30-18	W
1-14	H	Hope	31-17	W
1-15	H	Western St. Normal	22-16	W
1-18	H	Mt. Union	40-26	W
1-21	A	DePauw	19-39	L
1-22	A	Notre Dame	23-36	L
1-25	A	Western St. Normal	29-19	W
1-27	A	St. John's (Toledo)	20-21	L
1-28	A	Mt. Union	30-28	W
1-29	A	Oberlin	21-23	L
2-1	H	Notre Dame	37-25	W
2-5	A	Michigan	24-37	L
2-7	H	DePauw	23-26	L
2-14	H	Mich. Coll. of Mines	26-18	W
2-19	H	Oberlin	29-37	L
2-22	H	Michigan	10-17	L
2-25	H	Hope	27-23	W
2-26	A	Grand Rapids J.C.	20-11	W
3-2	H	Bethany (W.Va.)	41-18	W
3-3	H	Creighton	27-20	W

1921-1922 (11-13)
Coach: Lyman L. Frimodig

12-10	A	Wisconsin	13-27	L
12-29	H	Carnegie Tech	38-17	W
1-2	H	Albion	33-13	W
1-3	H	Detroit School of Law	56-3	W
1-4	H	Alma	43-17	W
1-6	A	Michigan	26-27	L
1-10	H	Western St. Normal	28-20	W
1-14	H	Michigan Normal	28-22	W
1-19	H	Valparaiso	30-21	W
1-21	H	Kalamazoo	28-39	L
1-25	H	Cent. Mich. Normal	27-21	W
1-28	A	Oberlin	25-26	L
1-29	A	Ohio Wesleyan	22-25	L
1-31	A	Notre Dame	22-31	L
2-3	A	Creighton	30-41	L
2-4	A	Creighton	21-25	L
2-6	A$_{GA}$	Lombard (IL)	14-26	L
2-16	H	Notre Dame	30-24	W
2-17	H	Marquette	19-26	L
2-22	H	Michigan	17-19	L
2-24	H	Ohio Wesleyan	17-29	L
2-27	H	Creighton	28-34	L
3-3	H	Hope	29-28	W
3-4	H	Chicago "Y" College	25-21	W

Fred M. Walker (1923-1924)
(See baseball season records for Fred Walker sketch)

1922-1923 (10-9)
Coach: Fred M. Walker

12-9	H	Notre Dame	15-40	L
12-15	H	Western St. Normal	8-17	L
12-22	H	Valparaiso	17-21	L
12-30	H	Carnegie Tech	37-29	W
1-3	A	Michigan	11-33	L
1-6	H	St. Ignatius (OH)	18-27	L
1-11	H	Victoria (Toronto)	33-10	W
1-13	H	Michigan Normal	19-17	W
1-20	H	Michigan	13-29	L
1-27	H	Cent. Mich. Normal	28-13	W
1-30	H	Chicago "Y" College	23-19	W
2-3	H	Kalamazoo	22-24	L
2-9	H	Lake Forest	26-18	W
2-12	H	Armour Tech	27-22	W
2-17	H	Alma	27-21	W
2-21	H	St. Mary's	43-15	W
2-28	A	Notre Dame	22-21	W
3-2CV	A	St. Ignatius (OH)	17-38	L
3-3	A	Oberlin	16-23	L

1923-1924 (10-10)
Coach: Fred M. Walker

12-15	H	Adrian	25-12	W
12-18	H	St. Mary's (MI)	31-26	W
12-22	A	Chicago	17-21	L
12-28	H	Detroit Coll. Law	25-14	W
1-3	H	Hope	22-7	W
1-5	H	Upper Canada Law	33-26	W
1-7	H	Carleton	12-27	L
1-11	A	Michigan	19-23	L
1-18	H	John Carroll	24-17	W
1-25	A	Notre Dame	18-35	L
1-28	A	Western St. Normal	14-29	L
1-29	A	Cent. Mich. Normal	11-20	L
2-1	H	Lombard (IL)	12-13	L
2-6	H	Michigan	20-31	L
2-12	H	Western St. Normal	16-25	L
2-23	H	Detroit	31-17	W
2-26	H	St. Viator's	25-27	L
2-29	H	Notre Dame	21-23	L
3-6	A	Valparaiso	22-12	W
3-8	H	Lake Forest	29-19	W

John Kobs (1925-1926)
(See baseball season records for John Kobs sketch)

1924-1925 (6-13)
Coach: John Kobs

12-10	H	Adrian	42-16	W
12-13	H	Michigan	10-26	L
12-20	A	Chicago	29-15	W
12-22	H	Northwestern	17-26	L
1-10	H	St. Mary's (MI)	13-21	L
1-13	H	St. Viator's	18-23	L
1-16	A	Notre Dame	14-37	L
1-23	H	Western St. Normal	20-21	L
1-30	H	Earlham	24-23	W
1-31	A	Franklin	14-36	L
2-3	H	Hope	19-20	L
2-11	H	Detroit	23-22	W
2-20	H	Franklin	16-28	L
2-25	A	Western St. Normal	15-29	L
2-28	H	Oberlin	29-27	W
3-3	H	Notre Dame	10-42	L
3-6	A	John Carroll	14-30	L
3-7	A	Oberlin	16-25	L
3-14	H	MAC Alumni	43-19	W

1925-1926 (5-13)
Coach: John Kobs

12-8	H	Olivet	36-13	W
12-12	H	Adrian	30-14	W
12-19	A	Chicago	28-21	W
12-21	A	Northwestern	13-42	L
1-1	H	Mercer (GA)	33-37	L
1-9	H	St. Viator's	30-27	W
1-16	H	Michigan	15-38	L
1-22	A	Notre Dame	14-33	L
1-26	A	Detroit	10-16	L
1-30	H	Mich. Normal	23-35	L
2-2	H	Detroit	22-29	L
2-6	A	Western St. Normal	25-30	L
2-11	H	Marquette	25-29	L
2-13	H	Earlham	21-26	L

2-16	H	Notre Dame	25-40	L
2-19	H	Carnegie Tech	27-22	W
2-26	H	Western St. Normal	15-38	L
3-6	H	MSC Alumni	38-40	L

Ben F. VanAlstyne (1927-1949)

In 1926 John Kobs was relieved of his basketball coaching responsibilities, enabling him to focus on his primary sport of baseball. Picked as his successor was Benjamin F. VanAlstyne, who had been assistant athletic director and head coach for basketball and baseball at Ohio Wesleyan. VanAlstyne was born in Marshville, NY, in 1893 and graduated from high school in Canajoharie, NY. He entered Colgate University where he played basketball, baseball, and football, graduating with the class of 1917. Following a brief nine-month hitch in the U.S. Army, VanAlstyne coached high school basketball at Ashville, NC, for one year. He then moved to Delaware, OH, to accept the position at Ohio Wesleyan where he worked with a Spartan hero of the past, George Gauthier. His appointment at MSC was as an associate professor in the physical education department with the additional obligation of assisting the football staff. Although he would soon be released of that gridiron duty, in 1932 VanAlstyne would be further encumbered with the role of head golf coach. He would hold that dual role, basketball and golf, for 17 years. From 1926 to 1949 the team's scoring average had jumped from 28 to 46 points per game. This seems adequate proof that Ben VanAlstyne had led the Spartans into the modern era of the sport. Regardless, the fans of the late 1940's, including hundreds of World War II ex-GI's that burgeoned MSC's enrollments, became increasingly impatient with mediocre seasons in the "W-L" columns. Aware of this discontentment, in December of 1948 the 55-year-old VanAlstyne requested to be relieved of his basketball coaching responsibility upon conclusion of that season. George Alderton once reported that Coach Van faced another reality, he was going blind. His eyes, always weak, were failing him and under night lights he could hardly see across the floor. Few people were totally aware of his handicap. Continuing on the staff as golf coach until retirement in 1959, Ben VanAlstyne died in August of 1972 at a nursing home in Southfield, MI. He was 79 years old.

1926-1927 (7-11)
Coach: Ben. F. VanAlstyne

12-8	H	Adrian	33-29	W
12-11	A	Michigan	13-34	L
12-18	A	Chicago	24-33	L
12-20	A	Northwestern	22-34	L
1-8	H	Marquette	35-33	W
1-12	H	Albion	31-37	L
1-14	A	Butler	16-53	L
1-15	A	Concordia (IN)	45-25	W
1-19	H	Detroit	30-23	W
1-21	H	Lake Forest	39-30	W
1-22	H	Marquette	12-24	L
1-29	A	Notre Dame	15-36	L
1-31	H	Butler	23-29	L
2-9	H	Hope	46-31	W
2-12	H	Detroit	27-30	L
2-18	H	Pittsburgh	34-36	L
2-23	H	Notre Dame	22-34	L
2-25	H	MSC Alumni	36-24	W

1927-1928 (11-4)
Coach: Ben. F. VanAlstyne

12-7	H	Adrian	30-25	W
12-10	A	Michigan	23-43	L
1-3	H	Ohio Northern	39-25	W
1-7	H	Hillsdale	58-24	W
1-13	H	Detroit	27-23	W
1-16	H	Coe	35-25	W
1-20	A	Loyola (Chicago)	21-23	L
1-21	A	Marquette	18-21	L

1-28	A	Notre Dame	25-29	L
1-30	H	Hope	36-21	W
2-3	H	Notre Dame	26-16	W
2-8	H	Albion	52-20	W
2-11	H	Kalamazoo	36-24	W
2-17	H	Detroit	17-13	W
2-25	H	Marquette	30-25	W

1928-1929 (11-5)
Coach: Ben. F. VanAlstyne

12-7	A	Michigan	31-24	W
12-14	H	Hillsdale	47-15	W
1-2	H	Penn State	16-14	W
1-3	H	Cornell	38-24	W
1-7	H	Ohio Wesleyan	28-31	L
1-11	H	Marquette	29-19	W
1-18	A	Detroit	27-13	W
1-23	A	Notre Dame	24-29	L
1-26	H	Kalamazoo	30-22	W
2-1	A	Colgate	35-36	L
2-2	A	Syracuse	17-24	L
2-8	H	Hope	51-18	W
2-15	H	Detroit	40-15	W
2-22	H	Notre Dame	27-28	L
3-1	H	Lake Forest	49-16	W
3-4	A	Marquette	26-15	W

1930 (12-4)
Coach: Ben. F. VanAlstyne

1-1	H	Syracuse	19-21	L
1-4	H	Ohio Wesleyan	30-14	W
1-9	H	Detroit	26-20	W
1-16	A	Bethany	27-36	L
1-17	A	Carnegie Tech	35-23	W
1-22	H	Notre Dame	28-21	W
1-25	A	Detroit	21-18	W
1-28	H	Hope	55-16	W
1-31	H	Marquette	24-17	W
2-7	H	Kalamazoo	33-12	W
2-11	H	Bethany	36-32	W
2-14	H	Oberlin	24-10	W
2-15	H	Michigan	27-26	W
2-18	A	Notre Dame	17-29	L
2-21	H	Hillsdale	34-28	W
3-1	A	Marquette	14-21	L

1930-1931 (16-1)
Coach: Ben. F. VanAlstyne

12-5	H	Cincinnati	22-8	W
12-13	A	Michigan	22-32	L
12-29	H	Brigham Young	29-28	W
1-1	H	Ohio Wesleyan	25-17	W
1-9	H	Marquette	19-16	W
1-13	H	Xavier (OH)	32-19	W
1-16	A	Colgate	41-31	W
1-17	A	Colgate	50-30	W
1-23	H	Kalamazoo	46-10	W
1-27	H	Central State	31-18	W
1-30	A	Western Reserve	25-25	W
1-31	A	Oberlin	33-22	W
2-6	H	Alma	42-20	W
2-10	H	Detroit	34-16	W
2-14	H	Loyola (Chicago)	24-16	W
2-21	H	Detroit	16-11	W
2-28	A	Marquette	24-21 (ot)	W

1931-1932 (12-5)
Coach: Ben. F. VanAlstyne

12-3	H	Alma	39-12	W
12-12	A	Michigan	5-27	L
1-1	H	Ohio	29-15	W
1-2	H	Cornell	29-26	W
1-8	H	Western Reserve	17-15	W
1-9	H	Notre Dame	25-28	L
1-15	H	Xavier (OH)	22-20	W
1-19	H	Detroit	22-13	W
1-29	H	Colgate	30-21	W
1-30	H	Colgate	29-28 (ot)	W
2-6	H	Kalamazoo	17-9	W
2-13	H	Michigan	14-13(2ot)	W
2-15	H	Marquette	25-23(2ot)	W
2-17	A	Detroit	35-34(ot)	W
2-20	A	Xavier (Ohio)	24-31(ot)	L
2-23	A	Notre Dame	20-28	L
2-25	A	Marquette	18-43	L

1932-33 (10-7)
Coach: Ben. F. VanAlstyne

12-3	H	Albion	31-29	W
12-10	A	Michigan	20-17	W
12-30	A	Wisconsin	16-26	L
1-3	H	Syracuse	23-16	W
1-9	H	Notre Dame	19-34	L
1-12	H	Marquette	28-32	L
1-16	H	Buffalo	29-18	W
1-17	A	Colgate	40-26	W
1-21	H	Olivet	35-13	W
1-27	H	Xavier (OH)	19-16	W
1-28	H	Mieje Univ. (Japan)	63-15	W
2-4	H	Kalamazoo	29-12	W
2-11	H	Michigan	16-28	L
2-15	H	Detroit	30-28	W
2-18	A	Detroit	16-27	L
2-24	A	Notre Dame	25-30	L
2-25	A	Marquette	21-28	L

1933-34 (12-5)
Coach: Ben. F. VanAlstyne

12-4	H	Olivet	23-16	W
12-9	A	Michigan	26-25	W
1-2	H	Mississippi State	35-25	W
1-6	H	Notre Dame	33-34	L
1-12	H	Buffalo	37-30	W
1-13	A	Syracuse	21-27	L
1-18	H	Marquette	24-26	L
1-22	H	Michigan Normal	34-27	W
1-26	H	Cent. Mich. Normal	32-27	W
2-3	H	Loyola (Chicago)	36-15	W
2-5	H	Wisconsin	23-22	W
2-10	H	Michigan	33-26	W
2-14	H	Detroit	27-20	W
2-17	A	Detroit	28-22	W
2-21	A	Notre Dame	19-28	L
2-23	A	Marquette	16-40	L
2-24	A	Loyola (Chicago)	22-20	W

1934-35 (14-4)
Coach: Ben. F. VanAlstyne

12-1	H	Cent. Mich. Normal	43-14	W
12-5	H	Kalamazoo	30-25	W
12-15	A	Michigan	25-31	L
12-22	A	Northwestern	26-39	L
12-24	A	Loyola (Chicago)	26-19	W
12-27	H	Stanford	25-18	W
12-31	A	Wisconsin	21-23	L
1-4	H	Wayne	31-17	W
1-8	H	Michigan Normal	35-14	W
1-12	A	Western Reserve	34-33	W
1-17	H	Marquette	30-29	W
1-21	H	Hillsdale	45-24	W
1-24	A	Michigan Normal	53-28	W
1-26	A	Wayne	37-20	W
2-4	H	Western Reserve	36-17	W
2-9	H	Michigan	30-28	W
2-13	H	Kentucky	32-26	W
2-18	A	Marquette	17-20	L

1935-1936 (8-9)
Coach: Ben. F. VanAlstyne

12-2	H	Albion	36-28	W
12-6	A	Wisconsin	21-26	L
12-14	A	Michigan	24-35	L
12-21	A	Northwestern	25-29	L
12-30	H	West Virginia	25-24	W
1-1	A	Syracuse	34-38	L
1-3	A	Temple	24-47	L
1-8	H	Kalamazoo	32-14	W
1-10	H	Loyola (Chicago)	32-20	W
1-17	H	Marquette	20-21	L
1-18	H	Marquette	35-31	W
1-21	A	Kentucky	19-27	L
1-25	A	Michigan Normal	37-24	W
1-29	H	Michigan Normal	18-15	W
2-1	H	Butler	21-24	L
2-15	H	Michigan	23-41	L
2-22	A	Marquette	29-28	W

1936-1937 (5-12)
Coach: Ben. F. VanAlstyne

12-9	H	Albion	32-22	W
12-12	A	Michigan	21-34	L
1-2	A	Kentucky	21-28	L
1-6	H	Kalamazoo	39-18	W
1-8	A	Case	34-38	L
1-9	A	Geneva	42-41	W
1-14	H	Kentucky	24-23	W
1-16	H	Marquette	25-32	L
1-19	H	Syracuse	36-30	W
1-23	H	Northwestern	29-44	L
1-26	H	Hawaiian All Stars	24-25	L
1-29	H	Hope	21-25	L
2-6	A	Wisconsin	17-22	L
2-8	A	Butler	21-27	L
2-13	H	Michigan	31-38	L
2-16	H	DePaul	21-23	L
2-20	A	Marquette	26-31	L

1937-1938 (9-8)
Coach: Ben. F. VanAlstyne

12-9	H	Hope	51-27	W
12-11	A	Michigan	40-43	L
12-22	H	Iowa	52-37	W
12-30	H	Missouri	43-33	W
1-1	H	Case	48-34	W
1-5	H	California	29-31	L
1-8	H	Kentucky	43-38	W
1-11	H	Hawaiian All Stars	55-31	W
1-14	H	Buffalo	65-35	W
1-15	A	Syracuse	46-59	L
1-22	H	Marquette	24-41	L
1-28	H	Butler	21-15	W
2-5	A	Wisconsin	27-30	L
2-7	A	Kentucky	27-44	L
2-12	H	Michigan	41-35	W
2-19	A	Marquette	26-40	L
2-21	A	Notre Dame	32-48	L

1938-1939 (9-8)
Coach: Ben. F. VanAlstyne

12-7	H	Kalamazoo	36-26	W
12-10	A	Michigan	34-41	L
12-17	H	Oberlin	58-23	W
12-28	H	Penn State	35-21	W
12-31	H	Indiana	33-37	L
1-2	A	Loyola (Chicago)	44-46	L
1-7	H	Cent. Mich. Normal	29-24	W
1-14	H	Western Reserve	36-21	W
1-21	A	Butler	33-34	L
1-23	A	Tennessee	35-31	W
1-28	H	Butler	39-29	W
2-4	A	Wisconsin	37-39	L
2-11	A	Michigan	25-30	L
2-13	H	Marquette	35-29	W
2-15	H	Temple	29-25	W
2-20	A	Marquette	36-38	L
2-24	H	Wayne	33-40	L

1939-1940 (14-6)

Coach: Ben. F. VanAlstyne

12-4	H	Kalamazoo	42-22	W
12-9	A	Michigan	27-33	L
12-16	H	Washington State	52-44	W
12-18	A	Creighton	32-30	W
12-19	A	Creighton	38-21	W
12-22	A	California	37-41	L
12-27	A	Oregon State	33-38	L
12-28	A	Oregon State	36-26	W
1-1	A	Loyola (Chicago)	30-22	W
1-6	H	Tennessee	29-20	W
1-8	H	Syracuse	31-29	W
1-15	H	Marquette	48-19	W
1-20	H	Michigan	27-32	L
1-26	A	Long Island	25-34	L
1-27	A	Temple	40-42	L
1-29	A	Univ. of Baltimore	39-28	W
2-3	H	Wisconsin	48-41	W
2-14	H	Wayne	46-29	W
2-24	A	Marquette	21-17	W
3-1	H	Temple	44-28	W

1940-1941 (11-6)

Coach: Ben. F. VanAlstyne

12-2	H	Kalamazoo	48-29	W
12-7	A	Michigan	14-42	L
12-21	H	Ohio State	46-38	W
12-23	H	Iowa	34-40	L
12-30	H	Creighton	29-37	L
12-31	H	Creighton	34-29	W
1-4	A	Long Island	31-26	W
1-6	A	Temple	37-35	W
1-10	H	Marquette	25-18	W
1-13	H	Temple	23-22	W
1-18	H	West Virginia	44-35	W
1-25	A	Notre Dame	39-46	L
2-8	H	West Virginia	31-40	L
2-12	H	Michigan	35-32	W
2-19	H	Long Island	23-24	L
2-22	A	Marquette	37-36	W
3-1	H	Notre Dame	44-35	W

1941-1942 (15-6)

Coach: Ben. F. VanAlstyne

12-2	H	Ft. Custer Officers	50-29	W
12-8	H	Cent. Mich. Normal	29-23	W
12-13	A	Michigan	20-37	L
12-20	H	South Carolina	41-29	W
12-24	H	Harvard	39-28	W
12-27	A	Syracuse	33-31	W
12-29	A	Rochester	27-28	L
1-2	H	Washington State	42-45	L
1-6	H	Great Lakes NTS	33-31	W
1-10	H	Western Reserve	51-22	W
1-16	H	Marquette	51-40	W
1-22	H	Cincinnati	37-30	W
1-24	A	Notre Dame	49-52	L
1-26	H	Butler	40-39	W
1-31	A	Detroit	32-28	W
2-6	A	Cincinnati	36-30	W
2-7	A	Butler	36-38	L
2-11	H	Michigan	57-34	W
2-16	H	Detroit	37-39	W
2-21	A	Marquette	47-45	W
2-28	H	Notre Dame	46-43	W

1942-1943 (2-14)

Coach: Ben F. VanAlstyne

12-7	A	Michigan	31-36	L
12-29	H	Oregon State	29-33	L
1-1	H	Harvard	28-31	L
1-4	H	Michigan	26-29	L
1-9	A	Great Lakes NTS	34-38	L
1-11	A	Marquette	32-41	L
1-13	A	Minnesota	32-46	L

1-19	H	Dearborn NTS	55-24	W
1-23	A	DePaul	37-45	L
1-29	H	Camp Grant	31-39	L
2-4	H	Romulus AAB	69-27	W
2-6	A	Notre Dame	34-45	L
2-11	H	Great Lakes NTS	39-56	L
2-15	H	Marquette	36-47	L
2-20	A	Camp Grant	31-43	L
2-27	H	Notre Dame	42-45	L

1943-1944

(Intercollegiate athletics suspended due to World War II)

1944-1945 (9-7)

Coach: Ben. F. VanAlstyne

12-2	H	Drake	44-36	W
12-9	A	Ohio State	31-58	L
12-28	A	Ohio State	31-67	L
12-30	A	Iowa	29-66	L
1-6	H	Cincinnati	37-39	L
1-8	A	Albion	72-36	W
1-12	A	Cincinnati	50-54	L
1-13	A	Kentucky	35-66	L
1-18	A	Michigan Normal	75-31	W
1-20	H	Wayne	47-38	W
1-22	H	Albion	58-38	W
1-27	A$_{BU}$	Temple	47-64	L
2-5	H	Kentucky	66-50	W
2-14	H	Detroit	53-29	W
2-19	H	Kalamazoo	81-26	W
2-24	A	Detroit	62-38	W

1945-1946 (12-9)

Coach: Ben. F. VanAlstyne

12-1	A	Michigan	39-47	L
12-5	H	Great Lakes NTS	49-53	L
12-24	H	Minnesota	50-48	W
12-27	A	Ohio State	42-62	L
1-2	H	Syracuse	76-48	W
1-5	H	Cincinnati	69-38	W
1-7	H	Michigan	49-36	W
1-12	H	Kentucky	44-55	L
1-15	A	Wayne	43-37	W
1-18	A	DePaul	52-58	L
1-23	H	Detroit	40-38	W
1-31	A	Notre Dame	57-62	L
2-2	H	Kentucky	51-59	L
2-4	A	Cincinnati	69-39	W
2-7	H	Wayne	46-45	W
2-9	H	Detroit	58-46	W
2-11	A	Great Lakes NTS.	58-59	L
2-16	H	Ohio State	64-41	W
2-20	H	Notre Dame	54-56	L
2-23	A	Wisconsin	59-48	W
3-1	H	Wisconsin	56-52	W

1946-1947 (11-10)

Coach: Ben. F. VanAlstyne

12-7	A	Michigan	29-51	L
12-20	H	Stanford	57-45	W
12-28	A	Wayne	52-25	W
12-31	A	Syracuse	61-57(ot)	W
1-2	H	Arizona	43-45	L
1-4	H	Georgia Tech	62-52	W
1-6	H	Marquette	53-51	W
1-11	A	Detroit	52-44	W
1-14	H	Notre Dame	56-74	L
1-18	A	Minnesota	59-73	L
1-20	H	Wisconsin	48-58	L
1-25	A	DePaul	45-52	L
1-27	A	Kentucky	36-86	L
2-1	H	Wayne	49-36	W
2-3	H	Marquette	56-55	W
2-8	A	Notre Dame	54-70	L
2-11	H	Virginia	51-46	W
2-15	H	Ohio State	46-58	L

2-19	H	Detroit	55-48	W
2-22	H	Boston College	70-49	W
3-1	H	Michigan	47-59	L

1947-1948 (12-10)

Coach: Ben. F. VanAlstyne

12-18	H	Michigan	43-38	W
12-20	A	Purdue	48-50	L
12-23	H	Indiana	64-60	W
12-27	A	Wayne	57-55	W
12-29	H	Harvard	53-47(ot)	W
1-3	A	Washington-St. Louis	56-45	W
1-5	A	Missouri	44-46	L
1-10	H	Kentucky	45-47	L
1-13	H	Marquette	57-54	W
1-17	A	Western Reserve	65-57	W
1-20	A	Detroit	52-34	W
1-24	A	DePaul	42-52	L
1-26	H	Detroit	66-31	W
1-31	A	Minnesota	63-69	L
2-3	H	DePaul	49-63	L
2-9	A	Wisconsin	39-51	L
2-14	H	Marquette	53-48	W
2-17	H	Notre Dame	44-51	L
2-21	H	Ohio State	50-72	L
2-24	A	Notre Dame	54-50	W
2-28	H	Wayne	63-49	W
3-6	A	Michigan	28-69	L

1948-1949 (9-12)

Coach: Ben. F. VanAlstyne

11-27	H	Alma	46-33	W
		Hillsdale	53-43	W
12-4	A	Michigan	33-66	L
12-6	A	Indiana	36-48	L
12-18	H	Iowa	49-43	W
12-20	H	Cornell	45-56	L
12-29	H	Miss. College (Clinton)	74-28	W
1-7	H	Marquette	48-68	L
1-10	H	Detroit	66-49	W
1-14	H	Western Reserve	44-43	W
1-17	A	Detroit	34-35	L
1-22	A	Wayne	37-35(2ot)	W
1-27	H	Wayne	63-48	W
1-31	H	Michigan	38-49	L
2-3	A	Notre Dame	47-63	L
2-5	H	Marquette	42-59	L
2-12	H	Purdue	48-66	L
2-19	H	Virginia	62-43	W
2-21	H	Minnesota	47-57	L
2-23	H	Notre Dame	41-43	L
2-28	A	Ohio State	51-70	L

Alton S. Kircher (1949-1950)
1949-1950 (4-18)

Coach: Alton S. Kircher

12-3	H	Michigan	49-52	L
12-5	A	Iowa	53-73	L
12-10	H	Indiana	58-73	L
12-17	H	Missouri	54-73	L
12-22	H	Georgia Tech	60-68	L
12-23	A	Northwestern	46-68	L
12-28	H	Harvard	>57-68	L
12-29	H	Cornell	>61-54	W
1-2	A	Indiana	50-60	L
1-7	H	Notre Dame	65-76	L
1-9	A	Detroit	55-66	L
1-13	H	Marquette	81-64	W
1-18	A	Notre Dame	65-71	L
1-23	H	Minnesota	56-73	L
1-28	A	Western Reserve	54-57	L
2-4	A	Purdue	53-69	L
2-6	H	Wisconsin	47-66	L
2-11	A	Ohio State	43-87	L
2-14	H	Detroit	57-54	W
2-17	H	Wayne	68-44	W

2-20	A	Michigan	53-70	L
2-25	A	Marquette	58-75	L
		> Holiday Tournament		

Peter F. Newell (1951-1954)

Athletic director Ralph Young reached all the way to the Pacific Coast for the school's 11th head basketball coach. Peter Francis (Pete) Newell had just concluded his fourth successful year as the headman at San Francisco University. His 1948-1949 squad, with a season record of 25-5, had been the surprising winner of the National Invitational Tournament (NIT) in Madison Square Garden. The more recent 1949-1950 team had finished with another impressive record, 19-7. Upon accepting the MSC position, Newell stated: "I think the possibilities here are unlimited. It's an ideal spot for a young coach. The physical plant is the finest I've ever seen, and the people I've met have been most gracious." Although born in Vancouver, BC, Canada, on August 31, 1915, Newell was a U.S. citizen. He attended high school in Los Angeles, CA, graduating in 1934. The following year he entered Loyola University of Los Angeles, where he was a star forward in basketball and also a standout in baseball. Upon graduation in 1940 he signed with the Brooklyn Dodgers and played one year of professional baseball with Pine Bluff, AR, in the Cotton State League. In the fall of 1940 he began his coaching career at St. John's Military Academy in Los Angeles as head coach of all sports. His basketball and football teams were undefeated over three years of competition there. In February of 1942 he enlisted into the U.S. Navy, first serving as a physical education instructor at Great Lakes Naval Center, later moving on to active duty in the South Pacific. Following discharge in November of 1945, Newell entered the collegiate coaching ranks as head coach of basketball and baseball at the University of San Francisco. Apparently the lure of the Golden State never left Pete Newell. His years at Michigan State were limited as he coached only four seasons, 1950-1951 through 1953-1954. Following his final game in East Lansing, a satisfying 76-61 win over Michigan, he returned to the coast, this time as head coach at the University of California. In the move he took a cut of $1,000 from his $16,000 salary at MSC. Regardless, the relocation proved to be right for Newell. In the fifth year at Berkeley, his team captured the NCAA championship with a 71-70 win over West Virginia.

1950-1951 (10-11; 5-9 in Big Ten: 7th)

Coach: Peter F. Newell

12-2	A	Wayne	51-50	W
12-5	H	Detroit	45-31	W
12-19	H	Marquette	74-42	W
12-29	H	Penn State	>51-44	W
12-30	H	Princeton	>46-52	L
1-6	A	Northwestern	67-62	W
1-8	H	Wisconsin	52-53	L
1-13	H	Indiana	37-47	L
1-15	A	Iowa	42-46	L
1-20	A	Michigan	49-36	W
1-25	H	Notre Dame	60-43	W
1-27	A	Ohio State	49-58	L
1-29	A	Purdue	55-59	L
2-5	H	Minnesota	50-44	W
2-12	H	Northwestern	52-48	W
2-17	H	Michigan	43-32	W
2-19	A	Notre Dame	46-56	L
2-24	A	Wisconsin	29-35	L
2-26	A	Minnesota	39-46	L
3-3	H	Iowa	52-65	L
3-5	H	Illinois	43-49	L
		> Holiday Tournament		

1951-1952 (13-9; 6-8 in Big Ten: tie 5th)

Coach: Peter F. Newell

12-1	H	Wayne	52-43	W
12-13	H	Denver	50-48	W
12-15	A	Marquette	53-47	W

12-18	A	Detroit	52-47	W
12-28	H	Dartmouth	>47-42	W
12-29	H	Princeton	>52-46	W
1-2	A	Notre Dame	66-52	W
1-5	H	Iowa	60-61	L
1-7	H	Northwestern	82-49	W
1-12	A	Minnesota	49-55	L
1-15	H	Notre Dame	48-56	L
1-19	A	Michigan	36-50	L
1-21	H	Wisconsin	50-39	W
1-26	H	Purdue	56-47	W
2-2	A	Northwestern	76-86	L
2-9	H	Ohio State	70-52	W
2-11	A	Illinois	62-84	L
2-16	H	Wisconsin	57-55	W
2-18	H	Minnesota	58-60	L
2-25	A	Iowa	52-64	L
3-1	H	Michigan	80-59	W
3-3	A	Indiana	67-70	L
		> Holiday Tournament		

1952-1953 (13-9; 11-7 in Big Ten: tie 3rd)

Coach: Peter F. Newell

12-6	H	Marquette	62-51	W
12-19	A	UCLA	>55-60	L
12-20	H	Kansas State	>80-63	W
12-27	A	Northwestern	52-47	W
12-30	A	Minnesota	47-64	L
1-3	A	Ohio State	68-57	W
1-5	H	Indiana	62-69	L
1-10	H	Iowa	68-61	W
1-17	A	Michigan	66-64	W
1-19	H	Illinois	64-76	L
1-24	H	Northwestern	76-63	W
1-31	H	Minnesota	64-60	W
2-7	A	Ohio State	62-73	L
2-9	A	Iowa	60-48	W
2-14	A	Indiana	50-65	L
2-16	H	Notre Dame	64-72	L
2-21	H	Purdue	68-57	W
2-23	H	Wisconsin	53-45	W
2-28	A	Purdue	77-72	W
3-2	A	Illinois	53-66	L
3-7	H	Michigan	55-52	W
3-9	A	Wisconsin	51-58	L
		> Holiday Tournament		

1953-1954 (9-13; 4-10 in Big Ten: 8th)

Coach: Peter F. Newell

12-5	H	Creighton	88-51	W
12-17	H	Marquette	65-60	W
12-19	H	Southern California	81-63	W
12-22	H	Pittsburgh	83-51	W
12-30	A	Southern California	73-75	L
12-31	A	UCLA	57-67	L
1-4	A	Iowa	63-73	L
1-5	A	Kansas State	78-63	W
1-9	H	Illinois	60-59	W
1-16	A	Michigan	62-64	L
1-18	H	Wisconsin	53-57	L
1-23	H	Ohio State	83-76	W
1-30	A	Minnesota	71-79	L
2-1	H	Northwestern	65-62	W
2-6	A	Indiana	74-79	L
2-9	H	Notre Dame	71-74	L
2-13	A	Purdue	50-64	L
2-20	A	Indiana	61-63	L
2-22	A	Northwestern	71-80	L
2-27	H	Iowa	48-60	L
3-1	A	Wisconsin	56-79	L
3-6	H	Michigan	76-61	W

Forrest "Forddy" A. Anderson (1955-1965)

Thirty-five-year-old Forest "Forddy" Anderson, who had most recently been the successful coach at Bradley University, was selected to replace the departed Pete Newell. In his six years at the Peoria (IL) school, his teams had won 142 with 56 losses for an impressive .717 winning percentage. Anderson was born in Gary, IN, on March 17, 1919, where he was a football and basketball star at Emerson High School. After graduation he headed for the West Coast where he began pursuit of his college degree at Stanford. He compiled a fine record with the basketball squad and was named to the All-Pacific Coast Conference team for his play in the 1940-1941 season. During World War II, Anderson saw service with the U.S. Navy and in 1944 wound up, much like Newell two years earlier, at Great Lakes Naval Training Center. That year, Tony Hinkle was detached from his coaching duties at the center and Forddy, a chief petty officer, was handed the coaching duties on a temporary basis even though he had never coached before. The impermanent assignment became solidified for the year and the sailor squad closed with a fine 32-5 record. Eventually, Fordy went to sea duty aboard a destroyer before receiving an honorary discharge. Returning to Palo Alto, CA, Anderson finished work on his Stanford degree. Sacrificing a final year of eligibility, he opted to become coach of the Stanford junior varsity. In the spring of 1946, Anderson accepted the head coaching position at Drake University and after two years in Des Moines moved on to the Bradley post. Forddy's first five years with the Spartans were his most successful, winning 77, losing 38, for a winning percentage of .669. This was followed by a six years total of 48 wins and 86 losses to result in a trifling percentage of .358. That latter plunge, from 1960-1965, was enough to send athletic director Biggie Munn in search of the school's 13th head basketball coach. On October 25, 1999, Forest "Forddy" Anderson died from complications of pneumonia at the age of 80 in Oklahoma City, OK.

1954-1955 (13-9; 8-5 in Big Ten: 4th)

Coach: Forrest "Forddy" A. Anderson

12-1	H	Marquette	91-72	W
12-4	H	Detroit	78-84	L
12-17	A	Princeton	79-67	W
12-18	A	Pennsylvania	67-73	L
12-22	H	DePaul	75-76	L
12-30	H	Penn State	85-74	W
1-3	A	Ohio State	76-83	L
1-8	H	Wisconsin	94-77	W
1-10	A	Iowa	81-94	L
1-15	H	Michigan	84-82	W
1-17	A	Indiana	79-88	L
1-22	H	Minnesota	87-75	W
1-29	A	DePaul	88-72	W
1-31	H	Purdue	79-72	W
2-5	A	Wisconsin	73-70	W
2-7	A	Notre Dame	93-79	W
2-12	A	Northwestern	54-56	L
2-14	A	Illinois	72-90	L
2-19	H	Iowa	69-78	L
2-21	H	Northwestern	71-69	W
2-28	H	Indiana	93-77	W
3-5	A	Michigan	83-68	W

1955-1956 (13-9; 7-7 in Big Ten: 5th)

Coach: Forrest "Forddy" A. Anderson

12-13	H	Southern Illinois	99-71	W
12-17	A	Pittsburgh	82-81	W
12-21	H	Notre Dame	84-78	W
12-23	H	Wyoming	72-62	W
12-29	H	Maryland	>95-75	W
12-30	A	George Washington	>62-65	L
1-2	A	Illinois	65-73	L
1-7	H	Iowa	65-64	W
1-14	H	Purdue	62-66	L
1-16	H	Indiana	70-79	L
1-21	H	Minnesota	80-69	W
1-28	H	Ohio State	94-91	W

2-1	A	Detroit	85-78	W
2-6	H	Michigan	86-76	W
2-8	A	Marquette	81-90	L
2-13	A	Minnesota	73-77	L
2-18	H	Illinois	76-96	L
2-20	H	Northwestern	96-93	W
2-25	A	Purdue	56-63	L
2-27	H	Wisconsin	89-82	W
3-3	A	Ohio State	84-96	L
3-5	A	Michigan	76-75	W

> Tournament at College Park, MD

1956-57 (16-10; 10-4 in Big Ten: tie 1st)
Coach: Forrest "Forddy" A. Anderson

12-1	H	Iowa State	53-60	L
12-8	H	Brigham Young	79-61	W
12-17	A	Butler	79-83	L
12-22	H	Marquette	92-65	W
12-27	A_KC	Nebraska	>79-65	W
12-28	A_KC	Colorado	>87-90	L
12-29	A_KC	Oklahoma	>76-74	W
1-5	H	Purdue	71-72	L
1-7	H	Michigan	69-70	L
1-15	A	Notre Dame	76-86	L
1-19	A	Ohio State	51-70	L
1-26	A	Minnesota	72-59	W
1-28	H	Ohio State	73-64	W
2-2	A	Northwestern	77-63	W
2-9	H	Illinois	70-64	W
2-11	A	Purdue	68-66	W
2-16	H	Iowa	77-67	W
2-18	A	Illinois	89-83	W
2-23	H	Minnesota	70-65	W
2-25	A	Wisconsin	78-62	W
3-2	H	Indiana	76-61	W
3-4	A	Michigan	72-81	L
3-15	A_LX	Notre Dame	**85-83	W
3-16	A_LX	Kentucky	**80-68	W
3-22	A_KC	N Carolina	**70-74(3 OT)	L
3-23	A_KC	San Francisco	**60-67	L

>Holiday Tournament

1957-1958 (16-6; 9-5 in Big Ten: 3rd)
Coach: Forrest "Forddy" A. Anderson

12-2	H	Butler	74-55	W
12-6	A	Detroit	71-59	W
12-14	A	Colorado	84-44	W
12-21	H	Notre Dame	79-72	W
12-23	A	Iowa State	57-51	W
12-27	A_LA	Southern California	>63-61	W
12-28	A_LA	UCLA	>77-67	W
12-30	A	Washington	69-71	L
1-4	A	Ohio State	56-70	L
1-11	H	Purdue	84-75	W
1-18	A	Northwestern	83-78	W
1-20	H	Wisconsin	52-56	L
1-25	H	Northwestern	74-60	W
2-1	H	Minnesota	88-64	W
2-8	A	Indiana	79-82	L
2-10	H	Iowa	90-84	W
2-15	H	Illinois	69-56	W
2-17	A	Michigan	79-69	W
2-22	H	Wisconsin	93-59	W
2-24	A	Purdue	70-72	L
3-1	A	Iowa	83-65	W
3-8	H	Indiana	72-75	L

> Holiday Tournament

1958-1959 (20-4; 12-2 in Big Ten: 1st)
Coach: Forrest "Forddy" A. Anderson

12-6	H	Detroit	88-51	W
12-8	H	Butler	72-46	W
12-17	A	Notre Dame	74-56	W
12-20	H	Nebraska	80-55	W
12-29	A_RA	Duke	>82-57	W
12-30	A_RA	North Carolina	>75-58	W

12-31	A_RA	North Carolina State	>61-70	L
1-3	H	Indiana	79-77	W
1-5	A	Iowa	68-80	L
1-10	A	Illinois	97-96	W
1-17	H	MSU Alumni	63-56	W
1-19	H	Ohio State	92-77	W
1-24	A	Minnesota	82-76	W
1-31	H	Northwestern	81-72	W
2-2	A	Wisconsin	88-57	W
2-7	A	Purdue	81-85	L
2-14	H	Michigan	103-91	W
2-16	A	Northwestern	71-68	W
2-21	H	Purdue	94-87	W
2-28	A	Indiana	86-82	W
3-2	H	Wisconsin	93-73	W
3-7	H	Iowa	84-74	W
3-13	A_EV	Marquette	**74-69	W
3-14	A_EV	Louisville	**81-88	L

> Dixie Classic

1959-1960 (10-11; 5-9 in Big Ten: 8th)
Coach: Forrest "Forddy" A. Anderson

12-3	H	Bowling Green	96-67	W
12-5	H	Notre Dame	61-56	W
12-17	A	Nebraska	82-80	W
12-19	A	Wyoming	82-72	W
12-21	A	Brigham Young	75-79	L
12-23	A	California	60-71	L
12-28	A	Butler	85-80	W
1-2	A	Wisconsin	91-79	W
1-9	H	Michigan	89-58	W
1-11	A	Iowa	79-92	L
1-16	H	Illinois	88-96	L
1-23	H	Iowa	90-80	W
1-30	A	Ohio State	79-111	L
2-1	H	Minnesota	84-63	W
2-6	H	Purdue	65-68	L
2-8	H	Illinois	78-77	W
2-13	A	Minnesota	73-82	L
2-20	H	Ohio State	83-84	L
2-22	A	Northwestern	69-71	L
2-27	A	Michigan	65-72	L
3-5	H	Indiana	80-86	L

1960-1961(7-17; 3-11 in Big Ten: 9th)
Coach: Forrest "Forddy" A. Anderson

12-3	H	Butler	77-71	W
12-5	A	Bowling Green	70-67	W
12-16	A	Kansas	69-93	L
12-17	A	Kansas State	82-104	L
12-22	H	Iowa State	92-81	W
12-28	A_LA	UCLA	>61-98	L
12-29	A_LA	Stanford	>80-81	L
12-30	A_LA	Minnesota	>77-83	L
1-7	H	Wisconsin	71-74	L
1-9	A	Indiana	55-79	L
1-14	A	Iowa	72-86	L
1-16	H	Michigan	81-69	W
1-21	H	Northwestern	62-77	L
1-23	A	Minnesota	70-89	L
1-30	A	Illinois	92-93	L
2-4	A	Northern Michigan	71-79	L
2-5	H	Notre Dame	89-74	W
2-11	H	Ohio State	68-83	L
2-13	A	Michigan	67-78	L
2-18	H	Minnesota	72-75	L
2-20	H	Illinois	90-80	W
2-25	A	Purdue	74-85	L
3-4	A	Ohio State	83-91	L
3-6	H	Iowa	74-64	W

> Holiday Tournament

1961-1962 (8-14; 3-11 in Big Ten: 9th)
Coach: Forrest "Forddy" A. Anderson

12-2	H	Northern Michigan	75-59	W
12-9	H	Tulsa	90-70	W
12-16	H	Notre Dame	72-73	L

12-18	H	South Carolina	99-91	W
12-23	A	Butler	77-72	W
12-28	A_PO	Oregon	>59-71	L
12-29	A_PO	Portland	>74-60	W
12-30	A_PO	California	>72-85	L
1-6	A	Indiana	71-76	L
1-8	H	Wisconsin	78-83	L
1-13	H	Illinois	65-66	L
1-15	H	Purdue	74-89	L
1-20	A	Michigan	80-74	W
1-22	H	Minnesota	84-79	W
1-27	H	Northwestern	70-71	L
2-3	A	Purdue	64-86	L
2-10	A	Wisconsin	72-77	L
2-17	H	Ohio State	72-80	L
2-19	A	Iowa	51-59	L
2-24	H	Indiana	97-85	W
2-26	A	Northwestern	64-71	L
3-3	A	Minnesota	91-98	L

> Holiday Tournament

1962-1963 (4-16; 3-11 in Big Ten: 9th)
Coach: Forrest "Forddy" A. Anderson

12-1	H	Kansas State	56-66	L
12-4	A	Notre Dame	85-92	L
12-8	H	Kansas	81-62	W
12-19	A	Wichita	69-80	L
12-21	A	Utah	79-88	L
12-22	A	Utah State	87-102	L
1-5	H	Indiana	84-96	L
1-12	A	Wisconsin	75-68	W
1-19	H	Northwestern	80-68	W
1-21	H	Iowa	59-60	L
1-26	A	Minnesota	61-59	W
2-2	H	Michigan	71-72	L
2-4	A	Purdue	81-103	L
2-9	A	Illinois	86-91	L
2-16	A	Minnesota	70-75	L
2-18	A	Ohio State	77-87	L
2-23	A	Indiana	94-113	L
3-2	H	Wisconsin	89-92	L
3-4	H	Purdue	93-94	L
3-9	A	Northwestern	83-100	L

1963-1964 (14-10; 8-6 in Big Ten: tie 4th)
Coach: Forrest "Forddy" A. Anderson

11-30	H	Northern Michigan	109-86	W
12-4	H	Western Michigan	101-100	W
12-7	H	Bowling Green	104-81	W
12-14	A	Pennsylvania	87-75	W
12-18	A	Tulsa	88-89	L
12-20	A_TE	California	>68-78	L
12-21	A_TE	Oklahoma	>118-100	W
12-23	A	Brigham Young	90-95	L
12-28	A	Butler	76-65	W
1-4	A	Illinois	66-87	L
1-6	H	Wisconsin	106-90	W
1-11	H	Indiana	107-103	W
1-14	A	Minnesota	82-103	L
1-18	A	Notre Dame	80-95	L
1-25	H	Michigan	77-91	L
1-27	H	Ohio State	102-99	W
2-1	A	Michigan	79-95	L
2-3	A	Purdue	98-101	L
2-8	A	Northwestern	86-93	L
2-15	H	Iowa	107-82	W
2-17	H	Illinois	85-82	W
2-22	A	Iowa	107-89	W
2-29	H	Northwestern	107-97	W
3-7	A	Ohio State	81-80	W

> Holiday Tournament

1964-1965 (5-18; 1-13 in Big Ten: 10th)
Coach: Forrest "Forddy" A. Anderson

12-3	H	Northern Michigan	82-76	W
12-5	H	Western Michigan	89-80	W
12-8	A	Notre Dame	93-100	L

Date	Site	Opponent	Score	Result
12-12	H	Drake	75-91	L
12-19	A	Butler	89-90	L
12-22	H	Loyola (LA)	94-70	W
12-28	A_LA	Utah	>96-98	L
12-29	A_LA	S. California	>69-100	L
12-30	A_LA	Washington	>93-92	W
1-9	H	Iowa	78-85	L
1-16	A	Iowa	68-111	L
1-23	H	Northwestern	75-76	L
1-26	H	Michigan	98-103	L
1-30	A	Northwestern	75-77	L
2-6	H	Minnesota	79-88	L
2-8	H	Indiana	94-112	L
2-13	A	Michigan	83-98	L
2-20	A	Illinois	94-113	L
2-22	A	Ohio State	90-101	L
2-27	A	Wisconsin	89-99	L
3-1	H	Purdue	110-92	W
3-6	H	Ohio State	75-97	L
3-9	A	Illinois	89-121	L

> Holiday Tournament

John E. Benington (1966-1969)

John Benington, 43-year-old head basketball coach and athletic director at St. Louis University, was named the next head basketball coach on April 22, 1965. It was a homecoming of sort, as he had been an assistant for six years at Michigan State from 1951-1956, four under Pete Newell and two with Anderson. John left MSU in 1956 to become head coach at Drake University, where Forddy Anderson had launched his career 10 years earlier. After two years at the Iowa school, in 1958 he moved on to St. Louis. John's eight Billiken teams won 118 and lost 71, with five squads being invited to the NIT. He was born in Findlay, OH, December 31, 1921, and graduated high school from there in 1940. Following a tour of duty in the U.S. armed forces, he enrolled at the University of San Francisco on a football scholarship. Benington once recalled his college football career. "I almost got killed in the first game. I wanted to keep my scholarship, so I didn't tell them I weighed only 170 pounds after my discharge instead of the 190 pounds I was before. I was clobbered on the first play and knocked out. As I was carried off the field on a stretcher, someone suggested I try basketball. This suggestion probably saved my life." John played two years of varsity basketball, topping it off as captain of the 1948-1949 USF team that won the NIT. He passed up a professional cage career to work in the University of San Francisco alumni relations office for a short period before heading off to East Lansing in April, 1950, as Newell's assistant. His tenure as Spartan head coach ended tragically on September 10, 1969, when a second massive heart attack took his life. He was found by his wife, Barbara, and assistant coach Bob Nordmann, lying on the floor of the coaches' locker room in Jenison when he failed to come home that evening. He was 47 years old. An earlier attack, suffered on the handball court the previous April 11, had put the coach on the critical list for 72 hours.

1965-1966 (17-7; 10-4 in Big Ten: 2nd)

Coach: John E. Benington

Date	Site	Opponent	Score	Result
12-4	H	Western Michigan	82-85	L
12-7	A	Bowling Green	84-59	W
12-9	H	Butler	75-56	W
12-11	A	Notre Dame	93-69	W
12-18	H	St. Joseph (PA)	65-82	L
12-20	H	Tulane	80-61	W
12-22	A	Drake	61-50	W
12-27	A_HO	Hawaiian Marines	>84-53	W
12-28	A_HO	Tulsa	>67-78	L
12-30	A_HO	Hawaiian Army	>97-67	W
1-8	H	Minnesota	85-65	W
1-10	A	Purdue	89-78	W
1-15	H	Ohio State	80-64	W
1-22	A	Iowa	76-90	L
1-24	H	Purdue	92-74	W
1-29	A	Northwestern	77-68	W
2-5	H	Wisconsin	79-65	W
2-12	A	Minnesota	71-81	L
2-19	A	Wisconsin	77-78	L
2-22	H	Illinois	68-66	W
2-26	H	Indiana	69-63	W
2-28	A	Ohio State	98-79	W
3-5	A	Indiana	76-86	L
3-7	H	Michigan	86-77	W

> Holiday Tournament

1966-1967 (16-7; 10-4 in Big Ten: 1st)

Coach: John E. Benington

Date	Site	Opponent	Score	Result
12-1	H	Western Michigan	77-55	W
12-3	H	Miami (OH)	63-51	W
12-5	H	South Dakota	81-54	W
12-10	H	Wichita	103-68	W
12-20	A_NO	Loyola (LA)	>70-74	L
12-21	A_NO	Tulane	>76-66	W
12-27	A_PH	Villanova	<63-66	L
12-28	A_PH	Bowling Green	<67-75	L
1-7	H	Illinois	76-74	W
1-14	H	Iowa	79-70	W
1-21	A	Michigan	59-81	L
1-28	H	Wisconsin	68-61	W
2-1	A	Notre Dame	85-80	W
2-6	A	Indiana	77-82	L
2-11	A	Purdue	79-77	W
2-13	H	Indiana	86-77	W
2-18	H	Minnesota	67-66	W
2-20	A	Ohio State	64-80	L
2-25	A	Wisconsin	64-68	L
2-27	H	Ohio State	74-63	W
3-4	H	Purdue	75-71	W
3-6	A	Minnesota	67-59	W
3-11	H	Northwestern	79-66	W

> First Holiday Tournament
< Second Holiday Tournament

1967-1968 (12-12; 6-8 in Big Ten: tie 6th)

Coach: John E. Benington

Date	Site	Opponent	Score	Result
12-1	H	Cal State-Fullerton	80-49	W
12-12	A	Western Michigan	78-67	W
12-14	H	Butler	55-65	L
12-16	H	Harden-Simmons	95-76	W
12-20	H	Nebraska	74-70	W
12-23	A	Wichita	80-90	L
12-29	A_NO	Vanderbilt	>63-73	L
12-30	A_NO	Memphis State	>57-73	L
1-6	A	Illinois	56-66	L
1-13	A	Michigan	86-81	W
1-16	A	Wisconsin	68-70	L
1-20	H	Northwestern	75-62	W
1-23	H	Iowa	71-76	L
1-27	A	Southern Illinois	68-56	W
1-30	H	Notre Dame	89-68	W
2-3	H	Michigan	82-77	W
2-10	H	Ohio State	62-90	L
2-17	A	Northwestern	61-69	L
2-20	H	Indiana	75-70	W
2-24	H	Wisconsin	87-77	W
2-27	A	Iowa	58-76	L
3-2	H	Minnesota	68-75	L
3-5	A	Purdue	75-93	L
3-9	H	Illinois	62-59	W

> Sugar Bowl Tournament

1968-1969 (11-12; 6-8 in Big Ten: tie 5th)

Coach: John E. Benington

Date	Site	Opponent	Score	Result
12-3	H	Southwest Louisiana	90-84	W
12-6	H	Western Michigan	86-71	W
12-7	A	Toledo	81-80	W
12-13	H	Butler	70-60	W
12-14	A_CH	Western Kentucky	63-67	L
12-16	A	Nebraska	59-73	L
12-27	A_NY	St. John's	>51-61	L
12-28	A_NY	Villanova	>66-75	L
1-4	H	Northwestern	71-85	L
1-7	H	Wisconsin	77-67	W
1-14	A	Iowa	76-77	L
1-18	A	Northwestern	89-75	W
1-25	H	Michigan	70-75	L
2-1	H	Indiana	76-79	L
2-8	A	Michigan	86-82	W
2-11	A	Notre Dame	71-59	W
2-15	H	Illinois	75-70	W
2-18	H	Iowa	78-60	W
2-22	A	Wisconsin	64-76	L
2-25	H	Purdue	72-74	L
3-1	H	Ohio State	85-72	W
3-4	A	Illinois	57-71	L
3-8	A	Minnesota	65-78	L

> ECAC Holiday Festival Tourn.

Gus G. Ganakas (1970-1976)

Nine days following the death of Coach Bennington, his assistant, Gus Ganakas, was elevated to the top post. Gus had been appointed to his original position three years earlier on February 24, 1966, succeeding Clarence "Sonny" Means, who left to become head coach at Western Michigan. Previously, from 1964-1966, Gus had been coordinator of the school's Ralph Young Scholarship Fund. A native of Mt. Morris, NY, Ganakas was born July 3, 1926. Prior to enrolling at Michigan State, he served with the U. S. Marine Corps during World War II. Gus received a B.A. degree in physical education in 1949 and an MSC master's degree in the same field one year later. While an undergraduate, Ganakas was a member of the basketball and baseball teams. In 1950 he began a prep coaching career at Olivet High School. After one year, he moved on to East Lansing High School, where his basketball teams won 176 games while losing only 53 over 12 years. His peak season was 1958 when the Trojans captured the Michigan High School Class B championship at Jenison Fieldhouse. With no link whatsoever to the 1975-1976 NCAA football investigation which caused the resignation of Denny Stoltz, the University's governing board was in a "purge" mood following that season's basketball schedule as well. With no apparent justification, Gus Ganakas found that, after seven seasons and a winning record, his one-year contract would not be renewed. He accepted the decision gracefully and moved into the position of assistant director of athletics. After continuing in that post through the incumbency of five AD's, in 1998 Gus returned to the sport he loves as administrative basketball assistant to head coach Tom Izzo. Retiring in 1999, he continues on at the scene as color commentator for the Spartan radio network.

1969-1970 (9-15; 5-9 in Big Ten: tie 6th)

Coach: Gus G. Ganakas

Date	Site	Opponent	Score	Result
12-1	H	Eastern Kentucky	89-85	W
12-6	H	Toledo	80-82	L
12-13	A	Western Michigan	86-71	W
12-17	A	Butler	60-81	L
12-19	A_SL	Bradley	>89-87	W
12-20	A_SL	Utah	>85-105	L
12-27	A_PO	Oregon	<82-87	L
12-29	A_PO	Illinois	<77-86	L
12-30	A_PO	Temple	<51-90	L
1-3	A	Indiana	85-84	W
1-10	H	Northwestern	98-93	W
1-17	A	Minnesota	78-85	L
1-20	H	Notre Dame	85-82	W
1-24	A	Michigan	88-91	L
1-31	H	Minnesota	87-92	L
2-3	A	Purdue	86-105	L
2-7	A	Wisconsin	79-89	L
2-10	H	Ohio State	66-89	L
2-14	A	Iowa	77-103	L
2-21	H	Indiana	78-66	W
2-24	H	Illinois	67-74	L
2-28	A	Ohio State	82-80	W
3-3	H	Purdue	98-101	L
3-7	A	Illinois	81-76	W

> Utah Classic
< Far West Classic

1970-1971 (10-14; 4-10 in Big Ten: tie 7th)
Coach: Gus. G. Ganakas

12-1	H	Northern Illinois	75-76	L
12-5	A	Toledo	72-62(OT)	W
12-12	H	Western Michigan	97-85	W
12-14	H	Butler	99-75	W
12-18	A_AL	New Mexico	>73-69	W
12-19	A_AL	Rutgers	>81-71	W
12-22	H	Central Michigan	85-74	W
12-29	A_LA	Southern California	<63-88	L
12-30	A_LA	Tennessee	<70-81	L
1-9	A	Illinois	61-89	L
1-12	H	Iowa	84-81	W
1-16	H	Illinois	67-69	L
1-26	A	Notre Dame	80-104	L
1-30	A	Ohio State	82-70	W
2-6	H	Ohio State	76-87	L
2-9	H	Indiana	70-71	L
2-13	A	Minnesota	86-97	L
2-16	A	Indiana	76-90	L
2-20	H	Wisconsin	97-78	W
2-27	A	Purdue	70-100	L
3-2	H	Purdue	60-65	L
3-6	H	Michigan	63-88	L
3-9	H	Minnesota	73-71	W
3-13	A	Northwestern	67-85	L

> Lobo Invitational
< Trojan Tournament

1971-1972 (13-11; 6-8 in Big Ten: tie 5th)
Coach: Gus. G. Ganakas

12-1	A	Missouri	67-77	L
12-4	H	South Alabama	87-72	W
12-11	H	Western Michigan	66-65	W
12-13	A	Kentucky	91-85	W
12-17	A_KX	Colorado State	>67-63	W
12-18	A_KX	Tennessee	>61-85	L
12-20	A	Butler	77-71	W
12-27	A_HU	Texas A&M	<67-65	W
12-28	A_HU	Houston	<73-106	L
1-8	A	Michigan	75-83	L
1-11	H	Wisconsin	83-76	W
1-18	A	Northwestern	69-76(OT)	L
1-22	H	Minnesota	57-67	L
1-29	H	Indiana	83-73	W
2-1	H	Notre Dame	98-74	W
2-5	A	Indiana	69-83	L
2-8	H	Illinois	89-79	W
2-12	A	Iowa	100-91	W
2-19	A	Purdue	68-92	L
2-26	H	Iowa	98-102	L
2-29	A	Wisconsin	74-101	L
3-4	H	Michigan	96-92	W
3-7	A	Ohio State	73-92	L
3-11	H	Northwestern	57-54	W

> Volunteer Classic
< Bluebonnet Classic

1972-1973 (13-11; 6-8 in Big Ten: tie 6th)
Coach: Gus. G. Ganakas

11-28	H	Toledo	98-96	W
12-2	H	Kentucky	66-75	L
12-9	A	South Carolina	64-83	L
12-16	A	Western Michigan	76-73	W
12-19	H	Central Michigan	96-74	W
12-29	A_RO	Rochester	>103-61	W
12-30	A_RO	Arizona State	>83-74	W
1-2	A_BR	Mississippi State	<90-82	W
1-3	A_BR	South Alabama	<86-78	W
1-6	H	Northwestern	90-77	W
1-13	H	Michigan	71-78	L
1-15	A	Iowa	76-74	W
1-20	A	Wisconsin	80-93	L
1-22	H	Indiana	89-97	L
1-27	A	Minnesota	77-93	L
2-3	H	Iowa	94-89	W
2-7	A	Notre Dame	72-85	L

2-10	A	Michigan	81-97	L
2-17	H	Purdue	84-88	L
2-19	A	Indiana	65-75	L
2-24	A	Illinois	71-81	L
2-26	H	Ohio State	87-83	W
3-3	A	Northwestern	86-72	W
3-10	H	Wisconsin	79-78(OT)	W

> Kodak Classic
< Senior Bowl Classic

1973-1974 (13-11; 8-6 in Big Ten: 4th)
Coach: Gus. G. Ganakas

12-1	A	Central Michigan	78-70	W
12-8	H	South Carolina	63-74	L
12-10	H	Eastern Michigan	91-69	W
12-12	H	Northern Michigan	91-63	W
12-15	H	Western Michigan	85-76	W
12-18	A	Toledo	51-79	L
12-22	H	Detroit	71-73(OT)	L
12-28	A_CM	Boston College	>81-94	L
12-29	A_CM	Holy Cross	>97-85	W
1-5	A	Purdue	75-77	L
1-12	H	Ohio State	83-75	W
1-14	A	Illinois	90-82	W
1-19	A	Michigan	82-84	L
1-21	H	Iowa	95-86	W
1-26	A	Minnesota	67-66	W
1-28	A	Illinois	93-82	W
2-2	H	Purdue	76-74	W
2-4	H	Notre Dame	89-91	L
2-11	A	Ohio State	75-67(OT)	W
2-16	H	Minnesota	50-56	L
2-23	H	Northwestern	73-70	W
2-25	A	Indiana	85-91	L
3-2	A	Wisconsin	80-87	L
3-9	H	Michigan	87-103	L

> Maryland Invitational

1974-1975 (17-9; 10-8 in Big Ten: 5th)
Coach: Gus. G. Ganakas

12-2	H	Central Michigan	82-78	W
12-7	H	Eastern Michigan	92-60	W
12-14	H	Western Michigan	62-59	W
12-16	A	Northern Michigan	91-59	W
12-20	A_SF	San Francisco	>86-78	W
12-21	A_SF	Long Beach State	>62-74	L
12-23	A	Detroit	72-69	W
1-2	A	Purdue	86-93	L
1-4	H	Indiana	55-107	L
1-6	H	Ohio State	88-84	W
1-11	H	Michigan	86-78	W
1-18	H	Minnesota	71-82	L
1-20	A	Iowa	79-83	L
1-25	H	Wisconsin	105-87	W
1-27	H	Northwestern	54-50	W
2-1	A	Illinois	75-60	W
2-3	A	Ohio State	101-83	W
2-5	A	Notre Dame	76-73	W
2-8	A	Michigan	84-96	L
2-15	H	Minnesota	86-81(OT)	W
2-17	H	Iowa	90-78	W
2-22	A	Wisconsin	96-103	L
2-24	A	Northwestern	66-67	L
3-1	H	Illinois	96-82	W
3-3	H	Purdue	84-82	W
3-8	A	Indiana	79-94	L

> Cable Car Classic

1975-1976 (14-13; 10-8 in Big Ten: 4th)
Coach: Gus. G. Ganakas

12-1	H	Central Michigan	69-61	W
12-6	A	Eastern Michigan	79-85	L
12-8	H	Canisius	83-68	W
12-13	A	Western Michigan	68-78	L
12-16	H	Northern Michigan	81-65	W
12-20	A	North Carolina State	75-95	L

12-22	A	Detroit	82-85	L
12-29	A_RI	Southern Mississippi	>89-77	W
12-30	A_RI	Va. Commonwealth	>75-80	L
1-3	A	Wisconsin	63-70	L
1-5	H	Iowa	105-88	W
1-8	A	Northwestern	89-105	L
1-10	H	Ohio State	92-82	W
1-12	H	Indiana	57-69	L
1-17	H	Michigan	63-66	L
1-24	A	Illinois	74-63	W
1-26	A	Purdue	66-65	W
1-31	H	Minnesota	75-63	W
2-2	H	Northwestern	91-71	W
2-7	A	Ohio State	83-82(OT)	W
2-9	A	Indiana	70-85	L
2-14	H	Michigan	64-81	L
2-21	H	Illinois	69-59	W
2-23	H	Purdue	89-76	W
2-28	A	Minnesota	61-71	L
3-1	A	Iowa	93-88	W
3-6	H	Wisconsin	82-86	L

> Virginia Commonwealth

George "Jud" Heathcote (1977-1995)

On Monday, April 6, 1976, along with the announcement of new football coach Darryl Rogers, George M. "Jud" Heathcote was named as the new head basketball coach. The 48-year-old Heathcote came to MSU after five seasons as head coach at the University of Montana, a period in which basketball fortunes at Missoula rose to an all-time high. The stint at Montana was the first for Jud as head coach of a college varsity unit. Previously, he had coached at West Valley High School in Spokane, WA, for 14 seasons, and at Washington State University for seven seasons as freshmen coach-varsity coordinator. His Cougar yearling teams compiled a record 99 wins and just nine losses in five seasons. The five varsity teams Heathcote directed at Montana posted an overall record of 80 victories and 53 losses, with the 1974-1975 team winning the school's first Big Sky Conference championship. The Grizzlies advanced to the NCAA regional finals before losing to the eventual champions from UCLA by three points. Jud earned a B.S. degree in mathematics and physical education and a B.Ed. degree from Washington State in 1950. As an undergraduate, he competed in varsity basketball and baseball and was inducted into the school's Hall of Fame in September of 1990. In 1960, he earned an M.S. degree from the University of Washington. With a record of 340-220 during his 19 years in East Lansing, Heathcote became the school's winningest coach. In postseason play, Jud directed the Spartans to nine NCAA tournament appearances, including the title run in 1979, along with three trips to the NIT. Seven of his squads registered 20 or more victories in a season with the Big Ten title team of 1989-1990 topping them all at 28 wins. Two other Heathcote teams, the 1977-1978 and 1978-1979 editions, were also accountable for conference title banners in Breslin Arena. On Saturday, March 11, 1995, a sellout crowd was on hand at the Breslin Student Events Center to watch a great Spartan season wind down (MSU 97, Wisconsin 72); but more importantly, they witnessed the end of the Heathcote era. Jud's retirement had been announced one year earlier; consequently, the lengthy post game presentation of scrolls, citations, plaques, tributes and unfurling of the "Heathcote" banner from the rafters of the arena was well orchestrated. He would leave a legacy of wit and wins.

1976-1977 (12-15: 9-9 in Big Ten: 5th)
Coach: George "Jud" Heathcote

11-29	A	Central Michigan	76-81	L
12-4	H	Western Michigan	73-74	L
12-6	H	North Carolina	58-81	L
12-11	H	Eastern Michigan	54-52(OT)	W
12-15	H	Detroit	94-99	L
12-18	A	Canisius	82-59	W
12-20	H	North Carolina State	78-60	W
12-29	A_JX	Holy Cross	>61-70	L
12-30	A_JX	Jacksonville	>63-65	L
1-6	H	Wisconsin	84-61	W

1-8	H	Northwestern	68-70	L
1-15	H	Michigan	70-83	L
1-17	A	Indiana	61-60	W
1-20	H	Illinois	67-58	W
1-22	H	Purdue	70-76	L
1-24	A	Minnesota	70-75	WF
1-27	A	Northwestern	58-66	L
1-29	A	Wisconsin	83-87(3 OT)	L
2-5	H	Indiana	79-81	L
2-7	A	Iowa	79-87	L
2-12	A	Ohio State	71-67	W
2-17	H	Minnesota	77-99	WF
2-19	A	Iowa	81-79	L
2-26	A	Michigan	65-69(OT)	L
2-28	H	Ohio State	80-79	W
3-3	A	Purdue	69-78	L
3-5	A	Illinois	62-61	W

> Gator Bowl Tournament

1977-1978 (25-5; 15-3 in Big Ten: 1st)
Coach: George "Jud" Heathcote

11-28	H	Central Michigan	68-61	W
12-2	A$_{SY}$	Rhode Island	>92-64	W
12-3	A$_{SY}$	Syracuse	>67-75	L
12-8	H	Wichita State	84-57	W
12-10	H	Western Michigan	79-57	W
12-19	H	Middle Tennessee St.	72-51	W
12-21	A	Detroit	103-74	W
12-29	A$_{NK}$	Southern Methodist	<95-69	W
12-30	A$_{NK}$	New Hampshire	<102-65	W
1-5	H	Minnesota	87-83	W
1-7	H	Wisconsin	74-63	W
1-12	H	Illinois	82-70	W
1-14	A	Northwestern	67-63	W
1-19	H	Purdue	60-51	W
1-21	H	Iowa	68-58	W
1-28	A	Ohio State	70-60	W
1-30	A	Indiana	66-71	L
2-2	H	Michigan	63-65	L
2-4	H	Indiana	68-59	W
2-9	A	Iowa	71-70	W
2-11	A	Michigan	73-62	W
2-16	A	Purdue	80-99	L
2-18	H	Ohio State	79-74	W
2-23	H	Northwestern	66-56	W
2-25	H	Illinois	89-67	W
3-2	A	Wisconsin	89-75	W
3-4	A	Minnesota	71-70	W
3-11	A$_{DA}$	Providence	**77-63	W
3-16	A$_{DA}$	Western Kentucky	**90-69	W
3-18	A$_{DA}$	Kentucky	**49-52	L

> Carrier Classic
< Old Dominion Classic

1978-1979 (26-6; 13-5 in Big Ten: tie 1st and NCAA champions)
Coach: George "Jud" Heathcote

11-27	H	Central Michigan	71-54	W
12-9	H	Cal State-Fullerton	92-89	W
12-13	A	Western Michigan	109-69	W
12-16	A	North Carolina	69-70	L
12-19	AP	Cincinnati	>63-52	W
12-28	A$_{PO}$	Washington State	<98-52	W
12-29	A$_{PO}$	Oregon State	<65-57	W
12-30	A$_{PO}$	Indiana	<74-57	W
1-4	H	Wisconsin	84-55	W
1-6	H	Minnesota	69-62	W
1-11	A	Illinois	55-57	L
1-13	A	Purdue	50-52	L
1-18	H	Indiana	82-58	W
1-20	H	Iowa	83-72(OT)	W
1-25	A	Michigan	48-49	L
1-27	A	Northwestern	65-83	W
2-1	H	Ohio State	84-79(OT)	W
2-3	H	Northwestern	61-50	W
2-4	H	Kansas	85-61	W
2-8	A	Iowa	60-57	W

2-10	A	Ohio State	73-57	W
2-15	A	Indiana	59-47	W
2-17	H	Michigan	80-57	W
2-22	H	Purdue	73-67	W
2-24	H	Illinois	76-62	W
3-1	A	Minnesota	76-63	W
3-3	A	Wisconsin	81-83	L
3-11	A$_{MB}$	Lamar	**95-64	W
3-16	A$_{IN}$	Louisiana State	**87-71	W
3-18	A$_{IN}$	Notre Dame	**80-68	W
3-24	A$_{SL}$	Pennsylvania	**101-67	W
3-26	A$_{SL}$	Indiana State	**75-64	W

> Pontiac Silverdome
< Far West Classic

1979-1980 (12-15; 6-12 in Big Ten: 9th)
Coach: George "Jud" Heathcote

11-30	A$_{JA}$	Princeton	>60-46	W
12-1	A$_{JA}$	St. Johns	>73-88	L
12-6	H	Long Beach State	87-73	W
12-10	H	Portland State	88 54	W
12-14	A	Wichita State	54-55	L
12-18	A	Central Michigan	95-76	W
12-20	A	Detroit	63-57	W
12-28	A$_{LV}$	Weber State	<61-63	L
12-29	A$_{LV}$	Loyola Marymount	<82-65	W
1-3	H	Purdue	73-74	L
1-5	H	Minnesota	80-93	L
1-10	A	Northwestern	61-65	L
1-12	A	Indiana	64-72	L
1-17	H	Wisconsin	62-61	W
1-19	H	Iowa	75-67	W
1-24	A	Michigan	59-58(OT)	W
1-26	A	Illinois	65-74	L
1-31	H	Ohio State	74-54	W
2-2	H	Illinois	68-59	W
2-7	A	Iowa	39-44(OT)	L
2-9	A	Ohio State	59-71	L
2-14	A	Wisconsin	66-80	L
2-16	H	Michigan	82-74	W
2-21	H	Indiana	72-75	L
2-23	H	Northwestern	73-75(3 OT)	L
2-28	A	Minnesota	73-87	L
3-1	A	Purdue	73-91	L

> Lapchick Memorial
< Holiday Classic

1980-1981 (13-14; 7-11 in Big Ten: 8th)
Coach: George "Jud" Heathcote

11-28	H	Western Michigan	<89-77	W
11-29	H	Central Michigan	<66-89	L
12-4	A	Long Beach State	71-60	W
12-6	A	Fullerton State	58-42	W
12-12	H	Eastern Michigan	73-63	W
12-16	H	Brigham Young	50-82	L
12-19	A$_{PV}$	Utah State	>70-74	L
12-20	A$_{PV}$	Providence	>77-76	W
12-27	A	St. Joseph	71-67	W
1-8	A	Indiana	43-55	L
1-10	A	Iowa	57-65	L
1-15	H	Minnesota	77-86	L
1-17	H	Northwestern	84-70	W
1-22	A	Wisconsin	62-63	L
1-24	A	Purdue	74-68	W
1-29	H	Illinois	70-71	L
1-31	H	Ohio State	60-54	W
2-5	A	Michigan	77-79(OT)	L
2-7	A	Ohio State	61-73	L
2-12	H	Purdue	48-63	L
2-14	H	Michigan	70-66	W
2-19	H	Wisconsin	74-65	W
2-21	A	Illinois	62-82	L
2-26	A	Northwestern	74-61	W
2-28	A	Minnesota	89-92(OT)	L
3-5	H	Iowa	71-70(OT)	W
3-7	H	Indiana	48-69	L

< Spartan Cutlass Classic
> Industrial National Classic

1981-1982 (12-16; 7-11 in Big Ten: tie 7th)
Coach: George "Jud" Heathcote

11-27	H	Central Michigan	<89-77	W
11-28	H	Western Michigan	<79-83	L
12-2	A	Detroit	65-62(OT)	W
12-5	A	Kansas	56-74	L
12-12	H	Cincinnati	45-56	L
12-15	H	Wis.-Green Bay	49-48(OT)	W
12-19	H	Marshall	101-82	W
12-28	A$_{HO}$	North Carolina State	>46-67	L
12-29	A$_{HO}$	Cal.-Fullerton	>51-50(OT)	W
12-30	A$_{HO}$	Hawaii	>61-62	L
1-7	H	Indiana	65-58	W
1-9	H	Minnesota	58-64	L
1-14	A	Purdue	47-53	L
1-16	A	Illinois	51-55	L
1-21	A	Michigan	64-62	W
1-23	H	Wisconsin	68-58	W
1-28	H	Iowa	56-57	L
1-30	H	Northwestern	64-61	W
2-4	A	Ohio State	49-50(OT)	L
2-6	A	Northwestern	43-48	L
2-11	H	Michigan	66-55	W
2-13	H	Ohio State	46-51	L
2-18	A	Iowa	53-59	L
2-20	A	Wisconsin	60-65	WF
2-25	H	Illinois	56-47	W
2-27	H	Purdue	49-51	L
3-4	A	Minnesota	51-54	L
3-6	A	Indiana	58-74	L

< Spartan Cutlass Classic
> Rainbow Classic

1982-1983 (17-13; 9-9 in Big Ten: tie 6th)
Coach: George "Jud" Heathcote

11-26	H	Western Michigan	<72-65	W
11-27	H	Central Michigan	<62-47	W
11-29	A	Boise State	71-59	W
12-4	H	Brigham Young	63-55	W
12-11	A	North Carolina State	41-45	L
12-13	A	Cincinnati	70-69	W
12-18	H	Detroit	75-72(OT)	W
12-21	H	Cleveland State	95-56	W
12-28	A$_{HO}$	Southwest Louisiana	>66-71	L
12-29	A$_{HO}$	Tulane	>58-81	L
1-5	A	Iowa	61-59	W
1-8	A	Northwestern	51-62	L
1-13	H	Wisconsin	86-66	W
1-15	H	Minnesota	67-69	L
1-20	A	Indiana	85-89	L
1-22	A	Ohio State	69-74	L
1-27	H	Illinois	71-78	L
1-29	H	Purdue	83-67	W
2-5	A	Michigan	70-65	W
2-12	H	Michigan	67-74	L
2-17	A	Purdue	55-61	L
2-19	A	Illinois	61-69	L
2-24	H	Ohio State	101-94(3 OT)	W
2-26	H	Indiana	62-54	W
3-3	A	Minnesota	79-67	W
3-5	A	Wisconsin	91-65	W
3-9	H	Northwestern	63-58	W
3-12	H	Iowa	57-75	L
3-18	H	Bowling Green	$72-71	W
3-21	H	Fresno State	$58-72	L

< Spartan Cutlass Classic
> Sugar Bowl Tournament

1983-1984 (16-12; 9-9 in Big Ten: 5th)
Coach: George "Jud" Heathcote

11-25	H	Central Michigan	<73-52	W
11-26	H	Western Michigan	<81-52	W
12-1	A	St Peter's (PA)	66-73	L
12-3	A	Illinois-Chicago	99-82	W
12-12	A	Cleveland State	71-62	W
12-15	H	Brooklyn	85-72	W
12-22	A	Missouri	66-79	L

12-28	A$_{AT}$	Alabama	>69-81	L
12-29	A$_{AT}$	Nebraska	>58-45	W
1-4	H	Iowa	73-72	W
1-7	H	Northwestern	69-76	L
1-12	A	Wisconsin	74-81	WF
1-14	A	Minnesota	61-69	L
1-19	H	Indiana	62-70	L
1-21	H	Ohio State	68-82	L
1-26	A	Illinois	40-46	L
1-28	A	Purdue	54-72	L
2-2	H	Michigan	72-67	W
2-5	H	Oregon State	56-55	W
2-11	A	Michigan	61-71	L
2-16	H	Purdue	63-53	W
2-19	H	Illinois	53-70	L
2-22	A	Ohio State	70-86	L
2-26	A	Indiana	57-54	W
3-1	H	Minnesota	83-62	W
3-3	H	Wisconsin	78-59	W
3-8	A	Northwestern	63-55	W
3-11	A	Iowa	51-44	W

< Spartan Cutlass Classic
> Cotton States Classic

1984-1985 (19-10; 10-8 in Big Ten: tie 5th)

Coach: George "Jud" Heathcote

11-24	A	Canisius	80-71	W
11-30	H	Western Michigan	<77-61	W
12-1	H	Army	<76-64	W
12-10	H	St. Peter's (PA)	50-38	W
12-12	A	Western Illinois	93-61	W
12-15	H	Missouri	79-61	W
12-18	A	George Washington	68-54	W
12-22	A	Illinois-Chicago	81-60	W
12-28	A$_{SD}$	Boston College	>78-82	L
12-29	A$_{SD}$	San Diego State	>77-61	W
1-3	H	Ohio State	82-79	W
1-5	H	Indiana	68-61	W
1-10	A	Purdue	81-72(OT)	W
1-12	A	Illinois	63-75	L
1-17	H	Iowa	65-79	L
1-19	H	Minnesota	75-81	L
1-24	A	Michigan	75-86	L
1-31	A	Wisconsin	77-68	W
2-2	A	Northwestern	68-54	W
2-7	H	Illinois	64-56	W
2-9	H	Purdue	65-66	L
2-13	A	Minnesota	64-73	L
2-16	A	Iowa	57-55	W
2-23	H	Michigan	73-75	L
2-27	H	Northwestern	61-47	W
3-2	H	Wisconsin	82-63	W
3-7	A	Indiana	68-58	W
3-9	A	Ohio State	79-90	L
3-15	A$_{HU}$	Ala.-Birmingham	**68-70	L

< Spartan Cutlass Classic
> Cabrillo Classic

1985-1986 (23-8; 12-6 in Big Ten: 3rd)

Coach: George "Jud" Heathcote

11-23	H	Western Illinois	98-63	W
11-26	H	Maine-Orono	89-58	W
11-29	H	Central Michigan	<103-60	W
11-30	H	Western Michigan	<84-64	W
12-4	H	George Washington	87-61	W
12-7	H	Canisius	90-61	W
12-14	A	Iowa State	80-82(OT)	L
12-21	H	Illinois-Chicago	99-74	W
12-27	A$_{AL}$	Massachusetts	>93-45	W
12-28	A$_{AL}$	New Mexico	>76-61	W
1-2	A	Ohio State	73-84	L
1-5	A	Indiana	77-74	W
1-9	H	Purdue	83-88(OT)	L
1-12	H	Illinois	58-51	W
1-16	A	Iowa	71-82	L
1-18	A	Minnesota	71-76	L
1-25	H	Michigan	91-79	W
1-30	H	Wisconsin	83-81	W
2-1	H	Northwestern	97-69	W
2-6	A	Illinois	84-80	W
2-8	A	Purdue	82-88	L
2-13	H	Iowa	83-73	W
2-15	H	Minnesota	76-66	W
2-20	A	Michigan	74-59	W
2-27	A	Northwestern	82-46	W
3-2	A	Wisconsin	84-71	W
3-5	H	Indiana	79-97	L
3-8	H	Ohio State	91-81	W
3-13	A$_{DA}$	Washington	**72-70	W
3-15	A$_{DA}$	Georgetown	**80-68	W
3-21	A$_{KC}$	Kansas	**86-96(OT)	L

< Spartan Cutlass Classic
> Lobo Classic

1986-1987 (11-17; 6-12 in Big Ten: 7th)

Coach: George "Jud" Heathcote

11-28	H	Eastern Michigan	<99-83	W
11-29	H	Navy	<90-91(OT)	L
12-2	H	Brooklyn	80-62	W
12-4	A	Maine	81-84	L
12-6	A	George Washington	77-62	W
12-13	H	Iowa State	86-85	W
12-16	A	Illinois-Chicago	65-74	L
12-20	A	Texas Christian	47-66	L
12-29	A$_{SC}$	Brigham Young	>88-96	L
12-30	A$_{SC}$	Wake Forest	>71-62	W
1-3	A	Purdue	72-87	L
1-5	A	Illinois	72-79	L
1-8	H	Indiana	60-79	L
1-10	H	Ohio State	90-80	W
1-15	A	Michigan	70-74	L
1-22	A	Wisconsin	81-78	W
1-26	A	Northwestern	65-67	L
1-29	H	Iowa	75-89	L
1-31	H	Minnesota	72-60	W
2-4	A	Indiana	80-84	L
2-9	A	Ohio State	72-90	L
2-15	H	Michigan	90-81	W
2-19	H	Northwestern	96-71	W
2-21	H	Wisconsin	63-65	L
2-26	A	Iowa	64-93	L
2-28	A	Minnesota	77-67	W
3-4	H	Purdue	59-69	L
3-7	H	Illinois	64-77	L

< Spartan Cutlass Classic
> Cable Car Classic

1987-1988 (10-18; 5-13 in Big Ten: 8th)

Coach: George "Jud" Heathcote

11-27	H	Detroit	65-63(OT)	W
12-2	H	Maine	87-44	W
12-5	H	George Washington	64-65	L
12-12	H	Texas Christian	69-52	W
12-15	H	Illinois-Chicago	78-64	W
12-17	A	Eastern Michigan	80-84(OT)	L
12-19	A	Austin Peay	77-85	L
12-22	A	San Jose State	82-68	W
12-29	A$_{TU}$	Arizona	>58-78	L
12-30	A$_{TU}$	Florida	>59-83	L
1-7	A	Wisconsin	72-78(OT)	L
1-9	A	Illinois	62-77	L
1-14	H	Michigan	72-90	L
1-16	H	Indiana	75-74(OT)	W
1-20	A	Purdue	67-78	L
1-27	H	Minnesota	56-59	L
2-1	H	Ohio State	76-64	W
2-4	A	Northwestern	64-65	L
2-6	A	Iowa	72-101	L
2-10	H	Purdue	70-72	L
2-13	H	Illinois	65-83	L
2-18	A	Indiana	58-95	L
2-22	A	Michigan	67-77	L
2-27	A	Ohio State	78-77(OT)	W
3-3	H	Iowa	87-103	L
3-5	A	Minnesota	61-62	L
3-10	H	Northwestern	55-53	W
3-12	H	Wisconsin	69-71	L

> Fiesta Classic at Tucson

1988-1989 (18-15; 6-12 in Big Ten: tie 8th)

Coach: George "Jud" Heathcote

11-28	H	Furman	98-68	W
11-30	A	Nebraska	77-75	W
12-10	H	Bowling Green	89-72	W
12-13	A	Illinois-Chicago	96-74	W
12-15	A	Detroit	96-91(OT)	W
12-17	H	Austin Peay	70-60	W
12-22	H	Eastern Michigan	91-76	W
12-28	A$_{PO}$	Colorado	>60-57	W
12-29	A$_{PO}$	Oregon State	>58-63	L
12-30	A$_{PO}$	Oregon	>76-61	W
1-5	H	Iowa	82-93	L
1-7	A	Illinois	54-71	L
1-11	A	Northwestern	64-62	W
1-14	H	Ohio State	81-83	L
1-21	H	Indiana	60-75	L
1-25	H	Purdue	106-83	W
1-28	H	Minnesota	73-64	W
2-2	A	Wisconsin	64-69(OT)	L
2-4	A	Michigan	66-82	L
2-11	A	Ohio State	75-81	L
2-16	H	Illinois	56-75	L
2-18	A	Purdue	63-87	L
2-23	H	Indiana	65-76	L
2-25	H	Northwestern	80-65	W
2-27	H	Michigan	52-79	L
3-2	A	Iowa	83-81	W
3-8	A	Minnesota	61-77	L
3-11	H	Wisconsin	70-61	W
3-16	A$_{DE}$	Kent State	83-69	W
3-20	A	Wichita State	79-67	W
3-22	A$_{PH}$	Villanova	70-63	W
3-27	A$_{NY}$	St. Louis	64-74	L
3-29	A$_{NY}$	Ala-Birmingham	76-78(OT)	L

> Far West Classic

1989-1990 (28-6; 15-3 in Big Ten: 1st)

Coach: George "Jud" Heathcote

11-24	A$_{AN}$	Auburn	>92-79	W
11-25	A$_{AN}$	Texas A&M	>87-75	W
11-27	A$_{AN}$	Kansas State	>73-68	W
11-29	H	Nebraska	80-69	W
12-2	A	Furman	84-63	W
12-9	H	Austin Peay	88-76	W
12-12	A	Illinois-Chicago	57-65	L
12-16	H	Detroit	94-65	W
12-18	H	Bowling Green	79-81	L
12-20	A	Evansville	80-66	W
12-23	H	Eastern Michigan	87-73	W
12-29	H	San Jose State	<88-61	W
12-30	H	Princeton	<51-49	W
1-6	A	Wisconsin	64-61	W
1-11	H	Ohio State	78-68	W
1-13	A	Iowa	87-80	W
1-18	A	Illinois	64-73	L
1-20	H	Northwestern	91-80	W
1-24	A	Indiana	75-57	W
1-27	A	Michigan	63-65	L
2-1	H	Minnesota	74-79	L
2-3	A	Purdue	64-53	W
2-8	H	Wisconsin	60-57	W
2-10	A	Ohio State	84-75	W
2-12	A	Iowa	80-70	W
2-17	H	Illinois	70-63	W
2-25	H	Indiana	72-66	W
3-1	H	Michigan	78-70	W
3-3	A	Minnesota	75-73(OT)	W
3-8	A	Northwestern	84-68	W
3-11	H	Purdue	72-70	W

3-15	A$_{KN}$	Murray State	**75-71(OT)	W
3-17	A$_{KN}$	Santa Barbara	**62-58	W
3-23	A$_{NO}$	Georgia Tech	**80-81(OT)	L

\>Great Alaskan Shootout
< Oldsmobile Spartan Classic

1990-1991 (19-11; 11-7 in Big Ten: tie 3rd)
Coach: George "Jud" Heathcote

11-23	H	Furman	78-73	W
11-28	A	Nebraska	69-71	L
12-1	A	Bowling Green	85-98	L
12-8	A	Detroit	83-61	W
12-13	A	Cincinnati	65-63	W
12-15	A$_{AB}$	UNLV	75-95	L
12-18	H	Evansville	81-76	W
12-20	H	Central Michigan	74-61	W
12-28	H	George Mason	<97-72	W
12-29	H	Louisiana Tech	<77-62	W
1-3	H	Michigan	85-70	W
1-5	A	Iowa	66-79	L
1-10	H	Wisconsin	65-60	W
1-12	H	Northwestern	66-59	W
1-17	A	Illinois	71-68	W
1-19	H	Minnesota	73-64	W
1-23	A	Purdue	51-62	L
1-26	A	Indiana	63-97	L
1-31	H	Ohio State	75-61	W
2-7	H	Iowa	67-71	L
2-9	A	Wisconsin	78-84(2 OT)	L
2-14	A	Northwestern	55-53	W
2-16	H	Illinois	62-58	W
2-23	H	Purdue	75-58	W
2-25	A	Minnesota	74-72	W
2-28	H	Indiana	56-62	L
3-3	A	Ohio State	64-65	L
3-9	A	Michigan	60-58	W
3-15	A$_{TU}$	Wis.-Green Bay	**60-58	W
3-17	A$_{TU}$	Utah	**84-85(2 OT)	L

<Oldsmobile Spartan Classic

1991-1992 (22-8; 11-7 in Big Ten: tie 3rd)
Coach: George "Jud" Heathcote

11-25	A$_{MU}$	Lamar	>81-68	W
11-26	A$_{MU}$	Rice	>75-67	W
11-27	A$_{MU}$	Arkansas	>86-71	W
12-4	H	Nebraska	101-78	W
12-7	A	Dayton	83-74	W
12-14	H	Detroit Mercy	91-75	W
12-17	H	Illinois-Chicago	75-51	W
12-21	H	Cincinnati	90-89	W
12-27	H	Austin Peay	<82-71	W
12-28	H	Stanford	<72-62	W
1-7	A	Ohio State	46-62	L
1-11	H	Illinois	77-75	W
1-15	H	Northwestern	78-61	W
1-18	A	Minnesota	66-70	L
1-22	A	Purdue	66-61	W
1-29	H	Michigan	79-89(OT)	L
2-1	H	Indiana	76-60	W
2-6	A	Iowa	63-77	L
2-8	A	Wisconsin	79-64	W
2-12	H	Wisconsin	76-61	W
2-15	A	Michigan	70-59	W
2-19	A	Indiana	73-103	L
2-22	H	Purdue	70-68	W
2-29	H	Ohio State	65-78	L
3-5	H	Northwestern	72-55	W
3-7	A	Illinois	71-80	L
3-11	H	Minnesota	66-57	W
3-15	H	Iowa	64-53	W
3-20	A$_{DA}$	Southwest Missouri	**61-54	W
3-22	A$_{DA}$	Cincinnati	**65-77	L

\> Maui Invitational
< Oldsmobile Spartan Classic

1992-1993 (15-13; 7-11 in Big Ten: tie 8th)
Coach: George "Jud" Heathcote

12-1	H	Morehead State	121-53	W
12-5	A$_{DE}$	Louisville	69-73	L
12-11	A$_{LA}$	Stetson	>78-59	W
12-12	A$_{LA}$	Loyola-Marymount	>73-70	W
12-15	H	Illinois-Chicago	79-75	W
12-19	H	Dayton	65-60	W
12-29	H	New Hampshire	<81-51	W
12-30	H	Washington State	<77-61	W
1-2	A	East Tennessee	80-69	W
1-6	A	Minnesota	57-64	L
1-9	H	Illinois	39-52	L
1-13	A	Ohio State	77-60	W
1-16	A	Northwestern	80-75	W
1-23	H	Wisconsin	66-67	L
1-28	H	Iowa	90-96(OT)	L
1-30	A	Purdue	72-64	W
2-2	H	Michigan	69-73	L
2-6	H	Minnesota	75-63	W
2-10	A	Illinois	80-83	L
2-13	H	Ohio State	81-66	W
2-17	H	Northwestern	81-55	W
2-24	A	Wisconsin	62-65	L
2-27	A	Iowa	64-66	L
3-3	H	Purdue	58-61	L
3-7	A	Michigan	81-87(OT)	L
3-10	A	Indiana	68-99	L
3-13	H	Penn State	70-53	W
3-17	A$_{NR}$	Oklahoma	$86-88	L

\>Los Angeles Classic
< Oldsmobile Spartan Classic

1993-1994 (20-12; 10-8 in Big Ten: tie 4th)
Coach: George "Jud" Heathcote

11-26	A$_{SJ}$	Pacific	>83-64	W
11-27	A$_{SJ}$	Washington State	>71-76	L
11-28	A$_{SJ}$	East Tennessee	>92-69	W
12-4	A	Louisville	68-77	L
12-7	A	Cleveland State	90-76	W
12-9	H	East Tennessee	107-81	W
12-12	H	Detroit Mercy	74-63	W
12-14	H	Illinois-Chicago	90-77	W
12-18	A	Nebraska	81-85	L
12-21	A	Tennessee	69-60	W
12-29	H	Bowling Green	<62-49	W
12-30	H	Cornell	<83-69	W
1-5	A	Michigan	64-75	L
1-8	A	Illinois	79-74	W
1-12	A	Purdue	77-89	L
1-15	H	Northwestern	67-46	W
1-19	A	Wisconsin	70-60	W
1-22	A	Minnesota	66-68	L
1-26	A	Ohio State	77-71	W
1-29	H	Iowa	87-84	W
2-2	A	Wisconsin	62-87	L
2-5	H	Michigan	51-59	L
2-9	A	Illinois	64-72	L
2-12	H	Purdue	70-74	L
2-17	A	Northwestern	60-55	W
2-23	H	Minnesota	85-68	W
2-26	H	Ohio State	75-60	W
3-2	A	Iowa	80-72	W
3-9	H	Indiana	94-78	W
3-12	A	Penn State	70-71	L
3-18	A$_{ST}$	Seton Hall	**84-73	W
3-20	A$_{ST}$	Duke	**74-85	L

\> San Juan Shootout
< Oldsmobile Spartan Classic

1994-1995 (22-6; 14-4 in Big Ten: 2nd)
Coach: George "Jud" Heathcote

11-30	A	Illinois-Chicago	92-78	W
12-3	A	Louisville	85-71	W
12-10	A	Nebraska	91-96 (OT)	L
12-12	H	Cleveland State	111-68	W
12-17	A	Detroit	80-63	W

12-20	H	Tennessee	79-68	W
12-29	H	Ball State	<117-95	W
12-30	H	Long Beach State	<70-60	W
1-4	H	Wisconsin	78-64	W
1-7	H	Iowa	69-68	W
1-11	A	Indiana	82-89	L
1-14	H	Oklahoma State	70-69	W
1-18	H	Northwestern	93-56	W
1-22	A	Michigan	73-71	W
1-25	H	Minnesota	54-53	W
1-28	A	Illinois	75-67	W
2-2	H	Penn State	82-62	W
2-4	A	Ohio State	67-58	W
2-7	A	Purdue	69-78	L
2-11	H	Penn State	68-53	W
2-15	H	Illinois	68-58	W
2-18	A	Minnesota	57-66	L
2-21	H	Michigan	67-64	W
2-25	A	Northwestern	83-60	W
3-5	H	Indiana	67-61	W
3-8	A	Iowa	78-79	L
3-11	H	Wisconsin	97-72	W
3-17	A$_{TA}$	Weber State	**72-79	L

< Oldsmobile Spartan Classic

Tom Izzo (1996-)

At the same time of Heathcote's retirement announcement, Tom Izzo was pre-ordained as his replacement beginning with the 1995-1996 season. As a member of Jud's staff for 12 seasons (five with the title associate head coach), Tom had earned the promotion. A part-time assistant with the Spartans from 1983-1986, Izzo left MSU in May of 1986 to become the top assistant and recruiting coordinator at Tulsa. He was not in Oklahoma very long. On June 10, when Spartan assistant Mike Dean left to become head coach at Siena College, Tom returned to East Lansing to begin full-time duties under Heathcote. Izzo originally came to MSU from Northern Michigan University, where he had been an assistant from 1979-1983. He was named part-time assistant at MSU in September, 1983. Tom played guard for Northern's basketball team, 1973-1977, and was voted the team's MVP as a senior. He also was a third-team Division II All-American pick that year and established the Wildcat record for most minutes played in a season. Following his graduation from NMU in 1977, Izzo took over as head coach at Ishpeming High School and served in that capacity for the 1977-1978 campaign. A native of Iron Mountain, MI, he was born January 30, 1955.

1995-1996 (16-16; 9-9 in Big Ten: 7th)
Coach: Tom Izzo

11-20	A$_{MU}$	Chaminade	>69-66	W
11-21	A$_{MU}$	North Carolina	>70-92	L
11-22	A$_{MU}$	Santa Clara	>71-77	L
11-28	A$_{AB}$	Arkansas	>>75-72	W
12-2	A	Louisville	59-79	L
12-6	H	Evansville	67-63	W
12-10	H	Detroit	61-63	L
12-16	A	Kansas State	67-54	W
12-18	A	Oklahoma State	57-68	L
12-21	H	East Tennessee	63-57	W
12-29	H	Central Michigan	<62-69	L
12-30	H	Idaho State	<68-55	W
1-4	H	Indiana	65-60	W
1-6	A	Illinois	68-58	W
1-13	A	Michigan	54-76	L
1-17	A	Wisconsin	48-61	L
1-20	H	Iowa	62-60	W
1-24	H	Northwestern	68-54	W
1-27	A	Minnesota	68-54	W
1-31	H	Penn State	61-58	W
2-3	A	Purdue	51-56	L
2-7	H	Ohio State	55-41	W
2-10	A	Penn State	50-54	L
2-14	H	Minnesota	63-64(OT)	L
2-17	A	Northwestern	75-57	W
2-21	A	Iowa	47-83	L

Date	Site	Opponent	Score	Result
2-24	H	Wisconsin	52-73	L
2-27	A	Michigan	46-75	L
3-6	H	Illinois	77-67	W
3-10	A	Indiana	53-57	L
3-13	H	Washington	64-50	W
3-19	A	Fresno State	70-80	L

> Maui Invitational
>>Great Eight
< Oldsmobile Spartan Classic

1996-1997 (17-12; 9-9 in Big Ten: tie 6th)
Coach: Tom Izzo

Date	Site	Opponent	Score	Result
11-25	H	East Tennessee State	83-45	W
12-3	H	Cleveland State	83-78	W
12-5	H	Illinois-Chicago	90-60	W
12-14	A	Detroit-Mercy	84-86 (3 OT)	L
12-17	A	Evansville	86-77	W
12-21	H	Kansas State	75-43	W
12-27	H	Kent State	<83-64	W
12-28	H	Weber State	<83-51	W
1-2	A	Indiana	65-77	L
1-4	H	Minnesota	43-68	L
1-9	A	Wisconsin	58-50	W
1-11	H	Ohio State	69-66	W
1-15	A	Penn State	69-58	W
1-18	H	Northwestern	75-62	W
1-22	H	Illinois	63-66	L
1-25	H	Michigan	61-74	L
1-29	A	Purdue	62-72	L
2-1	A	Michigan	65-85	L
2-8	H	Purdue	62-77	L
2-12	H	Iowa	69-67	W
2-15	A	Illinois	68-79	L
2-19	A	Northwestern	58-70	L
2-22	H	Penn State	71-57	W
2-26	H	Ohio State	67-65	W
3-1	H	Wisconsin	68-49	W
3-6	A	Minnesota	74-81	L
3-8	H	Indiana	63-60	W
3-12	H	George Washington	65-50	W
3-17	A	Florida State	63-68	L

< Oldsmobile Spartan Classic

1997-1998 (22-8; 13-3 in Big Ten: tie 1st)
Coach: Tom Izzo

Date	Site	Opponent	Score	Result
11-17	H	E. Tennessee State	82-59	W
11-21	A	Illinois-Chicago	58-70	L
11-28	H	Central Michigan	<89-61	W
11-29	H	Gonzaga	<70-68	W
12-4	H	Temple	54-56	L
12-6	A	Cleveland State	85-54	W
12-13	H	Detroit	65-68	L
12-17	H	Wright State	95-52	W
12-20	A	South Florida	68-53	W
12-27	H	Eastern Illinois	81-69	W
12-30	A	Purdue	74-57	W
1-8	H	Wisconsin	63-40	W
1-10	A	Michigan	69-79	L
1-14	A	Minnesota	74-60	W
1-17	H	Illinois	68-64	W
1-21	A	Iowa	78-57	W
1-24	H	Penn State	71-59	W
1-28	H	Indiana	84-66	W
1-31	A	Northwestern	72-66(OT)	W
2-4	H	Ohio State	84-58	W
2-7	H	Iowa	75-64	W
2-12	A	Illinois	63-84	L
2-14	H	Minnesota	71-59	W
2-17	H	Michigan	80-75	W
2-21	A	Wisconsin	56-47	W
3-1	H	Purdue	96-99(OT)	L
3-6	A_{CH}	Minnesota	*73-76	L
3-12	A_{HF}	Eastern Michigan	**83-71	W
3-14	A_{HF}	Princeton	**63-56	W
3-19	A_{GB}	North Carolina	**58-73	L

< Coca Cola Spartan Classic

1998-1999 (33-5; 15-1 in Big Ten: 1st)
Coach: Tom Izzo

Date	Site	Opponent	Score	Result
11-13	H	NE Louisiana	89-58	W
11-17	A	Oakland	96-66	W
11-20	A	Temple	59-60	L
11-27	H	Central Florida	<87-64	W
11-28	H	Western Michigan	<90-66	W
12-2	A	Duke	67-73	L
12-5	A	Connecticut	68-82	L
12-10	A	East Tennessee State	86-53	W
12-13	H	Illinois-Chicago	77-33	W
12-21	A	Pepperdine	79-67	W
12-22	A	Tulsa	68-58	W
12-23	A	Alabama	75-58	W
12-30	H	N. Carolina-Asheville	64-39	W
1-2	H	Louisville	69-57	W
1-6	A	Wisconsin	51-66	L
1-9	H	Michigan	81-67	W
1-13	H	Minnesota	71-55	W
1-16	H	Illinois	51-49	W
1-21	H	Iowa	80-65	W
1-24	A	Indiana	73-59	W
1-27	H	Ohio State	76-71	W
1-30	H	Northwestern	65-48	W
2-2	A	Penn State	70-68	W
2-6	A	Iowa	95-81	W
2-11	H	Illinois	61-44	W
2-13	A	Minnesota	84-82	W
2-16	H	Purdue	82-69	W
2-18	A	Michigan	73-58	W
2-21	H	Wisconsin	56-51	W
2-28	A	Purdue	60-46	W
3-5	A_{CH}	Northwestern	*61-59	W
3-6	A_{CH}	Wisconsin	*56-41	W
3-7	A_{CH}	Illinois	*67-50	W
3-12	A_{MI}	Mt. St. Mary's	**76-53	W
3-14	A_{MI}	Mississippi	**74-66	W
3-19	A_{SA}	Oklahoma	**54-46	W
3-21	A_{SA}	Kentucky	**73-66	W
3-27	A_{ST}	Duke	**62-68	L

< Coca Cola Spartan Classic

1999-2000 (32-7; 13-3 in Big Ten: tie 1st and NCAA champions)
Coach: Tom Izzo

Date	Site	Opponent	Score	Result
11-22	H	Toledo	78-33	W
11-25	A_{PR}	Providence	>82-58	W
11-26	A_{PR}	South Carolina	>59-56	W
11-27	A_{PR}	Texas	>74-81	L
12-1	A	North Carolina	86-76	W
12-3	H_{CS}	Howard	<75-45	W
12-4	H_{CS}	Eastern Michigan	<74-57	W
12-7	A_{CH}	Kansas	<<66-54	W
12-11	A	Arizona	68-79	L
12-18	H	Oakland	86-51	W
12-23	A	Kentucky	58-60	L
12-28	H	Miss. Valley State	96-63	W
12-30	A	Wright State	49-53	L
1-5	H	Penn State	76-63	W
1-8	A	Iowa	75-53	W
1-11	H	Indiana	77-71(OT)	W
1-20	A	Ohio State	67-78	L
1-22	H	Northwestern	69-45	W
1-27	A	Northwestern	59-29	W
1-30	H	Illinois	91-66	W
2-1	A	Michigan	82-62	W
2-5	H	Connecticut	85-66	W
2-8	A	Purdue	67-70	L
2-12	A	Wisconsin	61-44	W
2-15	H	Ohio State	83-72	W
2-19	H	Wisconsin	59-54	W
2-23	A	Penn State	79-63	W
2-26	A	Indiana	79-81 (OT)	L
3-2	H	Minnesota	79-43	W
3-4	H	Michigan	114-63	W
3-10	A_{CH}	Iowa	*75-65	W
3-11	A_{CH}	Wisconsin	*55-46	W
3-12	A_{CH}	Illinois	*76-61	W
3-16	A_{CV}	Valparaiso	**65-38	W
3-18	A_{CV}	Utah	**73-61	W
3-23	A_{AB}	Syracuse	**75-58	W
3-25	A_{AB}	Iowa State	**75-64	W
4-1	A_{IN}	Wisconsin	**53-41	W
4-3	A_{IN}	Florida	**89-76	W

>Puerto Rico Shootout
< Coca Cola Spartan Classic
<< Great Eight in Chicago

2000-2001 (28-5; 13-3 in Big Ten: tie 1st)
Coach: Tom Izzo

Date	Site	Opponent	Score	Result
11-19	H	Oakland	97-61	W
11-24	H	Cornell	<89-56	W
11-25	H	Eastern Washington	<83-61	W
11-29	H	North Carolina	77-64	W
12-2	H	Illinois-Chicago	97-53	W
12-6	H	Florida	99-83	W
12-9	A	Loyola (Ill)	103-71	W
12-16	H	Kentucky	46-45	W
12-19	A_{ER}	Seton Hall	>72-57	W
12-27	A_{AB}	Bowling Green	>>85-69	W
12-30	H	Wright State	88-61	W
1-3	H	Penn State	98-73	W
1-7	A	Indiana	58-59	L
1-10	H	Northwestern	84-53	W
1-13	H	Wisconsin	69-59 (OT)	W
1-21	H	Ohio State	71-56	W
1-24	A	Northwestern	74-58	W
1-27	A	Ohio State	55-64	L
1-30	A	Michigan	91-64	W
2-4	H	Purdue	72-55	W
2-6	A	Illinois	66-77	L
2-10	A	Minnesota	94-83	W
2-18	H	Iowa	94-70	W
2-20	H	Indiana	66-57	W
2-24	H	Penn State	76-57	W
2-27	A	Wisconsin	51-47	W
3-3	H	Michigan	78-57	W
3-9	A_{CH}	Penn State	*63-65	L
3-16	A_{ME}	Alabama State	**69-35	W
3-18	A_{ME}	Fresno State	**81-65	W
3-25	A_{AT}	Gonzaga	**77-62	W
3-27	A_{AT}	Temple	**69-62	W
3-31	A_{MN}	Arizona	**61-80	L

< Coca Cola Spartan Classic
> Jimmy V Classic
>> Sprite Holiday Classic

2001-2002 (19-12; 10-6 in Big Ten: 4th)
Coach: Tom Izzo

Date	Site	Opponent	Score	Result
11-12	H	Detroit	>80-70	W
11-14	H	Oklahoma	>67-55	W
11-21	A	Syracuse	>58-69	L
11-23	A	Fresno State	>58-63	L
11-30	H	I.U.P.U.-Ft. Wayne	<81-68	W
12-1	H	Lamar	<80-71	W
12-5	A	Florida	70-74	L
12-9	H	Nicholls State	92-38	W
12-15	H	Arizona	74-60	W
12-17	H	UNC-Asheville	76-56	W
12-19	H	Oakland	78-50	W
12-22	H	Seton Hall	68-64	W
12-29	A	Stanford	64-75	L
1-5	A	Minnesota	67-70	L
1-8	A	Indiana	65-83	L
1-12	H	Wisconsin	63-64	L
1-16	H	Purdue	65-56	W
1-19	A	Penn State	77-65	W
1-22	A	Iowa	71-75	L
1-30	H	Michigan	71-44	W
2-3	A	Illinois	67-61	W
2-6	A	Northwestern	49-61	L
2-10	H	Ohio State	67-64	W
2-12	H	Illinois	61-63	L
2-16	A	Purdue	62-59	W
2-21	H	Minnesota	74-55	W

Date		Opponent	Score	W/L
2-24	H	Indiana	57-54	W
2-26	A	Ohio State	81-76	W
3-2	H	Iowa	93-79	W
3-9	A_IN	Indiana	*56-67	L
3-15	A_DC	N. Carolina State	**58-69	L

> Preseason NIT
< Coca Cola Spartan Classic

2002-2003 (22-13; 10-6 in Big Ten)

Coach: Tom Izzo

Date		Opponent	Score	W/L
11-22	H	UNC-Asheville	66-52	W
11-28	A_AN	Montana	<80-60	W
11-29	A_AN	Villanova	<3-81	L
11-30	A_AN	Oklahoma State	<61-64	L
12-4	H	Virginia	82-75	W
12-8	H	Cleveland State	79-47	W
12-14	A	Kentucky	71-67	W
12-17	H	Loyola	80-54	W
12-21	H	South Florida	65-56	W
12-28	H	Jacksonville State	76-52	W
12-30	H	Toledo	76-81	L
1-4	A_OC	Oklahoma	58-60	L
1-9	H	Ohio State	66-55	W
1-11	A	Iowa	64-68	L
1-14	A	Purdue	60-72	L
1-18	A	Minnesota	69-77	L
1-22	H	Penn State	70-36	W
1-26	A	Michigan	58-60	L
1-28	H	Indiana	61-54	W
2-2	H	Illinois	68-65	W
2-8	A	Indiana	67-62	W
2-11	A	Wisconsin	53-64	L
2-15	H	Northwestern	64-51	W
2-18	A	Illinois	40-70	L
2-23	H	Syracuse	75-76	L
2-26	H	Minnesota	71-61	W
3-1	H	Purdue	69-61	W
3-5	H	Iowa	82-54	W
3-8	A	Ohio State	72-58	W
3-14	A_CH	Purdue	*54-42	W
3-15	A_CH	Ohio State	*54-55	L
3-21	A_TP	Colorado	**79-64	W
3-23	A_TP	Florida	**68-46	W
3-28	A_SX	Maryland	**60-58	W
3-30	A_SX	Texas	**76-85	L

<Great Alaska Shootout

Year-By-Year Record

Year	W-L	Pct.	Big 10	Place	Coach
1898-99	0-2	.000			No Coach
1899-00	2-3	.400			Charles Bemies
1900-01	3-0	1.000			Charles Bemies
1901-02	5-0	1.000			George Denman
1902-03	6-0	1.000			George Denman
1903-04	5-3	.625			Chester Brewer
1904-05	5-3	.625			Chester Brewer
1905-06	11-2	.846			Chester Brewer
1906-07	14-2	.875			Chester Brewer
1907-08	15-5	.750			Chester Brewer
1908-09	10-5	.667			Chester Brewer
1909-10	10-5	.667			Chester Brewer
1910-11	5-9	.357			John Macklin
1911-12	12-3	.800			John Macklin
1912-13	8-5	.615			John Macklin
1913-14	8-4	.667			John Macklin
1914-15	7-9	.438			John Macklin
1915-16	8-8	.500			John Macklin
1916-17	11-5	.688			George Gauthier
1917-18	6-10	.375			George Gauthier
1918-19	9-9	.500			George Gauthier
1919-20	21-15	.583			George Gauthier
1920-21	13-8	.619			Lyman Frimodig
1921-22	11-13	.458			Lyman Frimodig
1922-23	10-9	.526			Fred Walker
1923-24	10-10	.500			Fred Walker
1924-25	6-13	.316			John Kobs
1925-26	5-13	.278			John Kobs
1926-27	7-11	.389			Benjamin VanAlstyne
1927-28	11-4	.733			Benjamin VanAlstyne
1928-29	11-5	.688			Benjamin VanAlstyne
1929-30	12-4	.750			Benjamin VanAlstyne
1930-31	16-1	.941			Benjamin VanAlstyne
1931-32	12-5	.706			Benjamin VanAlstyne
1932-33	10-7	.588			Benjamin VanAlstyne
1933-34	12-5	.705			Benjamin VanAlstyne
1934-35	14-4	.778			Benjamin VanAlstyne
1935-36	8-9	.471			Benjamin VanAlstyne
1936-37	5-12	.294			Benjamin VanAlstyne
1937-38	9-8	.529			Benjamin VanAlstyne
1938-39	9-8	.529			Benjamin VanAlstyne
1939-40	14-6	.700			Banjamin VanAlstyne
1940-41	11-6	.647			Benjamin VanAlstyne
1941-42	15-6	.714			Benjamin VanAlstyne
1942-43	2-14	.125			Benjamin VanAlstyne
1943-44 Intercollegiate athletics suspended due to WW II					
1944-45	9-7	.588			Benjamin VanAlstyne
1945-46	12-9	.571			Benjamin VanAlstyne
1946-47	11-10	.524			Benjamin VanAlstyne
1947-48	12-10	.545			Benjamin VanAlstyne
1948-49	9-12	.429			Benjamin VanAlstyne
1949-50	4-18	.182			Alton Kercher
1950-51	10-11	.476	5-9	t7th	Peter Newell
1951-52	13-9	.591	6-8	t5th	Peter Newell
1952-53	13-9	.591	11-7	t3rd	Peter Newell
1953-54	9-13	.409	4-10	8th	Peter Newell
1954-55	13-9	.591	8-6	4th	Forrest Anderson
1955-56	13-9	.591	7-7	5th	Forrest Anderson
1956-57	16-10	.615	10-4	t1st	Forrest Anderson
1957-58	16-6	.727	9-5	3rd	Forrest Anderson
1958-59	20-4	.826	12-2	1st	Forrest Anderson
1959-60	10-11	.476	5-9	8th	Forrest Anderson
1960-61	7-17	.292	3-11	9th	Forrest Anderson
1961-62	8-14	.381	3-11	t9th	Forrest Anderson
1962-63	4-16	.200	3-11	9th	Forrest Anderson
1963-64	14-10	.583	8-6	t4th	Forrest Anderson
1964-65	5-18	.217	1-13	10th	Forrest Anderson
1965-66	17-7	.708	10-4	2nd	John Benington
1966-67	16-7	.696	10-4	t1st	John Benington
1967-68	12-12	.500	6-8	t6th	John Benington
1968-69	11-12	.478	6-8	t5th	John Benington
1969-70	9-15	.375	5-9	t6th	Gus Ganakas
1970-71	10-14	.417	4-10	t7th	Gus Ganakas
1971-72	13-11	.542	6-8	t5th	Gus Ganakas
1972-73	13-11	.542	6-8	t6th	Gus Ganakas
1973-74	13-11	.542	8-6	t4th	Gus Ganakas
1974-75	17-9	.654	10-8	5th	Gus Ganakas
1975-76	14-13	.518	10-8	4th	Gus Ganakas
1976-77	12-15	.444	9-9	5th	Jud Heathcote
1977-78	25-5	.833	15-3	1st	Jud Heathcote
1978-79	26-6	.813	13-5	t1st	Jud Heathcote
1979-80	12-15	.444	6-12	9th	Jud Heathcote
1980-81	13-14	.481	7-11	8th	Jud Heathcote
1981-82	12-16	.429	7-11	t7th	Jud Heathcote
1982-83	17-13	.566	9-9	t6th	Jud Heathcote
1983-84	16-12	.571	9-9	t5th	Jud Heathcote
1984-85	19-10	.655	10-8	t5th	Jud Heathcote
1985-86	23-8	.742	12-6	3rd	Jud Heathcote
1986-87	11-17	.393	6-12	7th	Jud Heathcote
1987-88	10-18	.357	5-13	8th	Jud Heathcote
1988-89	18-15	.545	6-12	t8th	Jud Heathcote
1989-90	28-6	.824	15-3	1st	Jud Heathcote
1990-91	19-11	.633	11-7	t3rd	Jud Heathcote
1991-92	22-8	.733	11-7	t3rd	Jud Heathcote
1992-93	15-13	.536	7-11	t8th	Jud Heathcote
1993-94	20-12	.625	10-8	t4th	Jud Heathcote
1994-95	22-6	.785	14-4	2nd	Jud Heathcote
1995-96	16-16	.500	9-9	t5th	Tom Izzo
1996-97	17-12	.586	9-9	t6th	Tom Izzo
1997-98	22-8	.733	13-3	t1st	Tom Izzo
1998-99	33-5	.868	15-1	1st	Tom Izzo
1999-00	32-7	.821	13-3	t1st	Tom Izzo
2000-01	28-5	.848	13-3	t1st	Tom Izzo
2001-02	19-12	.613	10-6	4th	Tom Izzo
2002-03	22-13	.629	10-6		Tom Izzo
Total	1,316-938	.584	450-400		

Year-By-Year Leaders

SCORING (Since 1927)

(Total points with season game average in parentheses)

Year	Player	Points
1926-27	Vern Dickeson	162
1927-28	Vern Dickeson	100
1928-29	Arthur Haga	99
1929-30	Roger Grove	91
1930-31	Roger Grove	135
1931-32	Randy Boeskool	80
1932-33	Gerald McCaslin	92
1933-34	Maurice Buysse	126
1934-35	Arnold VanFaasen	133
1935-36	Ron Garlock	109
1936-37	Leonard Oesterink	112
1937-38	George Falkowski	173
1938-39	George Falkowski	119
1939-40	Chet Aubuchon	169
1940-41	Max Hindman	144
1941-42	Joe Gerard	239
1942-43	John Cawood	118
1943-44	(Season suspended-WW II)	
1944-45	Sam Fortino	203 (11.9)
1945-46	Sam Fortino	251 (12.0)
1946-47	Bob Geahan	235 (11.2)
1947-48	Bob Brannum	344 (15.6)
1948-49	Bil Rapchak	211 (10.6)
1949-50	Dan Smith	207 (9.4)
1950-51	Ray Steffen	186 (8.9)
1951-52	Keith Stackhouse	236 (11.8)
1952-53	Al Ferrari	351 (20.1)
1953-54	Julius McCoy	409 (18.6)
1954-55	Al Ferrari	442 (20.1)
1955-56	Julius McCoy	600 (27.2)
1956-57	Jack Quiggle	384 (15.3)
1957-58	John Green	397 (18.0)
1958-59	Bob Anderegg	450 (19.5)
1959-60	Horace Walker	473 (22.6)
1960-61	Dck Hall	390 (16.2)
1961-62	Pete Gent	311 (14.1)
1962-63	Pete Gent	329 (16.4)
1963-64	Pete Gent	506 (21.0)
1964-65	Stan Washington	490 (21.3)
1965-66	Stan Washington	397 (18.0)
1966-67	Matthew Aitch	376 (16.3)
1967-68	Lee Lafayette	405 (16.8)
1968-69	Lee Lafayette	430 (18.7)
1969-70	Ralph Simpson	667 (29.0)
1970-71	Rudy Benjamin	520 (21.2)
1971-72	Mike Robinson	594 (24.7)
1972-73	Mike Robinson	608 (25.3)
1973-74	Mike Robinson	515 (22.4)
1974-75	Terry Furlow	509 (20.4)
1975-76	Terry Furlow	793 (29.4)
1976-77	Gregory Kelser	565 (21.7)
1977-78	Gregory Kelser	531 (17.7)
1978-79	Gregory Kelser	602 (18.8)
1979-80	Jay Vincent	582 (21.6)
1980-81	Jay Vincent	609 (22.6)
1981-82	Kevin Smith	436 (15.6)
1982-83	Sam Vincent	498 (16.6)
1983-84	Scott Skiles	405 (14.5)
1984-85	Sam Vincent	666 (23.0)
1985-86	Scott Skiles	850 (27.4)
1986-87	Darryl Johnson	618 (22.1)
1987-88	Carlton Valentine	371 (13.3)
1988-89	Steve Smith	585 (17.7)
1989-90	Steve Smith	627 (20.0)
1990-91	Steve Smith	752 (25.1)
1991-92	Shawn Respert	474 (15.8)
1992-93	Shawn Respert	563 (20.1)
1993-94	Shawn Respert	778 (24.3)
1994-95	Shawn Respert	716 (25.6)
1995-96	Quinton Brooks	505 (16.3)
1996-97	Ray Weathers	395 (13.6)
1997-98	Mateen Cleaves	484 (16.1)
1998-99	Morris Peterson	516 (13.6)
1999-00	Morris Peterson	657 (16.8)

2000-01 Jason Richardson 486 (14.7)
2001-02 Marcus Taylor 488 (16.8)
2002-03 Chris Hill 479 (13.7)

REBOUNDS (Since 1956)
(Total rebounds with season game average in parentheses)
1955-56 Julius McCoy 219 (10.0)
1956-57 Johnny Green 262 (14.6)
1957-58 Johnny Green 392 (17.8)
1958-59 Johnny Green 382 (16.6)
1959-60 Horace Walker 373 (17.7)
1960-61 Ted Williams 288 (12.0)
1961-62 Pete Gent .... (206 (9.3)
1962-63 Bill Berry 184 (9.2)
1963-64 Stan Washington 245 (10.2)
1964-65 Stan Washington 248 (10.7)
1965-66 Stan Washington 234 (10.6)
1966-67 Lee Lafayette 223 (9.7)
1967-68 Lee Lafayette 253 (10.5)
1968-69 Lee Lafayette 237 (10.3)
1969-70 Ralph Simpson 239 (10.3)
1970-71 Bill Kilgore 309 (12.8)
1971-72 Bill Kilgore 266 (11.1)
1972-73 Bill Kilgore 239 (9.9)
1973-74 Lindsay Hairston 326 (13.6)
1974-75 Lindsay Hairston 287 (11.5)
1975-76 Gregory Kelser 260 (9.5)
1976-77 Gregory Kelser 280 (10.8)
1977-78 Gregory Kelser 274 (9.1)
1978-79 Gregory Kelser 278 (8.7)
1979-80 Ron Charles 241 (8.9)
1980-81 Jay Vincent 229 (8.5)
1981-82 Derek Perry 151 (5.4)
1982-83 Kevin Willis 258 (9.6)
1983-84 Kevin Willis 192 (7.7)
1984-85 Ken Johnson 285 (10.2)
1985-86 Larry Polec 178 (5.7)
1986-87 Carlton Valentine 157 (5.6)
1987-88 Geo. Papadakos 142 (5.7)
1988-89 Steve Smith 229 (6.9)
1989-90 Steve Smith 216 (7.0)
1990-91 Mike Peplowski 206 (6.9)
1991-92 Mike Peplowski 259 (8.6)
1992-93 Mike Peplowski 279 (10.0)
1993-94 Anthony Miller 287 (9.0)
1994-95 Jamie Feick 281 (10.1)
1995-96 Jamie Feick 303 (9.5)
1996-97 Antonio Smith 306 (10.6)
1997-98 Antonio Smith 262 (8.7)
1998-99 Antonio Smith 319 (8.4)
1999-00 Andre Hutson 243 (6.2)
2000-01 Andre Hutson 244 (7.6)
2001-02 Aloysius Anagonye 196 (6.3)
2002-03 Aloysius Anagonye 186 (5.3)

FIELD GOAL PERCENTAGE
(Since 1947)
(Minimum of 100 attempts. Field goals made and attempted in parentheses)
1946-47 Robin Roberts .... (81-208) .389
1947-48 Bob Brannum .... (124-319) .389
1948-49 John Granack .... (42-116) .362
1949-50 Bob Carey .... (65-145) .448
1950-51 Sonny Means............. (39-103) .378
1951-52 G. Stauffer .... (77-211) .365
1952-53 B. Armstrong .... (96-253) .379
1953-54 Bob Devenny .... (53-141) .376
1954-55 D. Peterson .... (107-229) .467
1955-56 Julius McCoy .... (228-538) .423
1956-57 G. Ferguson .... 137-320) .428
1957-58 John Green .... (164-320) .512
1958-59 Lance Olson .... (96-224) .428
1959-60 Dave Fahs .... (108-250) .432
1960-61 Jack Lamers .... (84-190) .422
1961-62 Bill Schwarz .... (71-171) .415
1962-63 Bill Schwarz .... (67-160) .419
1963-64 Fred Thoman .... (145-302) .480

1964-65 S. Washington .... (185-390) .474
1965-66 Bill Curtis .... (149-306) .487
1966-67 H. Edwards .... (59-124) .476
1967-68 John Bailey .... (86-186) .462
1968-69 Lee Lafayette .... (155-335) .436
1969-70 Pat Miller .... (83-158) .525
1970-71 Bill Kilgore .... (134-256) .523
1971-72 Bill Kilgore .... (142-244) .581
1972-73 Bill Kilgore .... (163-284) .574
1973-74 Bill Glover .... (69-119) .580
1974-75 Bill Glover .... (124-227) .546
1975-76 Greg Kelser .... (136-264) .517
1976-77 Terry Donnelly .... (87-163) .534
1977-78 Greg Kelser .... (221-362) .610
1978-79 Ron Charles .... (115-173) .665
1979-80 Ron Charles .... (169-250) .676
1980-81 Derek Perry .... (83-138) .601
1981-82 Derek Perry .... (99-200) .495
1982-83 Kevin Willis .... (162-272) .596
1983-84 Ben Tower .... (63-110) .573
1984-85 Ken Johnson .... (128-212) .604
1985-86 C. Valentine .... (80-123) .650
1986-87 C. Valentine .... (135-217) .622
1987-88 G. Papadakos .... (102-157) .650
1988-89 M. Steigenga .... (115-206) .558
1989-90 M. Steigenga .... (138-235) .587
1990-91 M. Peplowski .... (99-158) .627
1991-92 M. Peplowski .... (168-266) .632
1992-93 M. Peplowski .... (161-252) .639
1993-94 Anthony Miller .... (162-249) .651
1994-95 Jamie Feick .... (111-180) .617
1995-96 Q. Brooks .... (195-346) .564
1996-97 Antonio Smith .... (92-163) .564
1997-98 DuJuan Wiley .... (78-125) .624
1998-99 Andre Hutson .... (111-180) .617
1999-00 Andre Hutson .... (147-251) .586
2000-01 Andre Hutson .... (173-278) .622
2001-02 A. Ballinger .... (116-213) .545
2002-03 Aloysius Anagonye ...... (97-157) .618

FREE THROW PERCENTAGE
(Since 1947)
(Minimum of 50 attempts. Free throws made and attempted in parentheses)
1946-47 Bob Geahan .... (61-93) .656
1947-48 Bob Branum .... (96-156) .615
1948-49 John Granack .... (37-60) .617
1949-50 Jim Snodgrass .... (50-72) .694
1950-51 Bob Carey .... (54-79) .683
1951-52 Gordon Stauffer .... (56-69) .810
1952-53 Al Ferrari .... (123-178) .691
1953-54 Bob Armstrong .... (49-65) .754
1954-55 Al Ferrari .... (152-192) .792
1955-56 Geo. Ferguson .... (65-93) .699
1956-57 Jack Quiggle .... (100-140) .714
1957-58 Jack Quiggle .... (75-104) .721
1958-59 Horace Walker .... (69-96) .719
1959-60 Horace Walker .... (119-149) .798
1960-61 Dick Hall .... (104-130) .800
1961-62 Jack Lamers .... (51-67) .761
1962-63 Jack Lamers .... (47-61) .770
1963-64 Bill Schwarz .... (40-51) .784
1964-65 S. Washington .... (120-141) .851
1965-66 S. Washington .... (91-114) .798
1966-67 Steve Rymal .... (49-71) .690
1967-68 Harrison Stepler .... (44-54) .815
1968-69 Jim Gibbons .... (79-98) .714
1969-70 R. Simpson .... (139-169) .822
1970-71 R. Benjamin .... (116-160) .725
1971-72 M. Robinson .... (104-147) .707
1972-73 M. Robinson .... (90-113) .796
1973-74 M. Robinson .... (99-128) .773
1974-75 Terry Furlow .... (99-120) .825
1975-76 Terry Furlow .... (177-202) .876
1976-77 Terry Donnelly .... (40-52) .769
1977-78 Bob Chapman .... (65-81) .802
1978-79 E. Johnson .... (202-240) .842
1979-80 Terry Donnelly .... (60-68) .882

1980-81 Mike Brkovich .... (56-65) .862
1881-82 Sam Vincent .... 68-91) .747
1982-83 Scott Skiles .... (69-83) .831
1983-84 Scott Skiles .... (99-119) .832
1984-85 Sam Vincent .... (176-208) .846
1985-86 Scott Skiles .... (188-209) .900
1986-87 D. Johnson .... (111-122) .910
1987-88 Steve Smith .... (69-91) .758
1988-89 Kirk Manns .... (47-56) .839
1989-90 Kirk Manns .... (70-81) .864
1990-91 Steve Smith .... (150-187) .802
1991-92 Shawn Respert .... (68-78) .872
1992-93 Shawn Respert .... (119-139) .856
1993-94 Shawn Respert .... (142-169) .840
1994-95 Shawn Respert .... (139-160) .869
1995-96 Thomas Kelley .... (45-57) .790
1996-97 Mateen Cleaves .... (57-79) .722
1997-98 Charlie Bell .... (69-87) .793
1998-99 M. Peterson .... (114-140) .814
1999-00 A.J. Granger .... (67-75) .893
2000-01 Charile Bell .... (94-122) .770
2001-02 Adam Ballinger .... (51-59) .864
200-2-03 Alan Anderson .... (128-152) .842

ASSISTS (Since 1976)
19/5-76 Benny White 106
1976-77 Edgar Wilson 93
1977-78 Earvin Johnson 222
1978-79 Earvin Johnson 269
1979-80 Mike Brkovich 96
1980-81 Kevin Smith 130
1981-82 Kevin Smith 126
1982-83 Scott Skiles 146
1983-84 Scott Skiles 128
1984-85 Scott Skiles 168
1985-86 Scott Skiles 203
1986-87 Darryl Johnson 112
1987-88 Ed Wright 91
1988-89 Ken Redfield 131
1989-90 Steve Smith 150
1990-91 Mark Montgomery 169
1991-92 Mark Montgomery 190
1992-93 Eric Snow 145
1993-94 Eric Snow 213
1994-95 Eric Snow 217
1995-96 Thomas Kelley 114
1996-97 Mateen Cleaves 146
1997-98 Mateen Cleaves 217
1998-99 Mateen Cleaves 274
1999-00 Mateen Cleaves 179
2000-01 Charlie Bell 169
2001-02 Marcus Taylor 153
2002-03 Chris Hill 128

STEALS (Since 1978)
1977-78 Earvin Johnson 71
1978-79 Earvin Johnson 75
1979-80 Kevin Smith 46
1980-81 Kevin Smith 38
1981-82 Sam Vincent 41
1982-83 Sam Vincent 44
1983-84 Scott Skiles 40
1984-85 Scott Skiles 48
1985-86 Scott Skiles 54
1986-87 Darryl Johnson 60
1987-88 Ken Redfield 50
1988-89 Ken Redfield 46
1989-90 Ken Redfield 44
1990-91 Mark Montgomery 52
1991-92 Mark Montgomery 48
1992-93 Eric Snow 27
1993-94 Eric Snow 57
1994-95 Eric Snow 52
1995-96 Quinton Brooks 30
1996-97 Antonio Smith 29
1997-98 Mateen Cleaves 73
1998-99 Mateen Cleaves 69
1999-00 Morris Peterson 47

2000-01 Jason Richardson 38
2001-02 Marcus Taylor 31
2002-03 Chris Hill 51

BLOCKED SHOTS (Since 1980)

1979-80 Ron Charles 51
1980-81 Ben Tower 16
1981-82 Richard Mudd 15
1982-83 Kevin Willis 35
1983-84 Ken Johnson 24
1984-85 Ken Johnson 72
1985-86 Barry Fordham 20
1986-87 George Papadakos 12
1987-88 George Papadakos 35
1988-89 Steve Smith 12
1989-90 Matt Steigenga 30
1990-91 Matt Steigenga 32
1991-92 Matt Steigenga 23
1992-93 Mike Peplowski 24
1993-94 Anthony Miller 29
1994-95 Quinton Brooks 16
1995-96 Quinton Brooks 18
1996-97 DeJuan Wiley 19
1997-98 DuJuan Wiley 50
1998-99 Andre Hudson 22
1999-00 A.J. Granger 21
2000-01 Jason Richardson 28
2001-02 Aloysius Anagonye 31
2002-03 Erazem Lorbek 20
          Alaysius Anagonye 20
          Adam Ballinger 20

THREE-POINTERS (Since 1983)

1982-83* Scott Skiles 25
1986-87 Kirk Manns 35
1987-88 Kirk Manns 27
1988-89 Kirk Manns 69
1989-90 Kirk Manns 81
1990-91 Steve Smith 66
1991-92 Shawn Respert 60
1992-93 Shawn Respert 60
1993-94 Shawn Respert 92
1994-95 Shawn Respert 119
1995-96 Ray Weathers 39
1996-97 Ray Weathers 53
1997-98 Jason Klein 69
1998-99 Jason Klein 46
1999-00 Morris Peterson 85
2000-01 Charlie Bell 52
2001-02 Chris Hill 66
2002-03 Chris Hill 95

* During the 1982-83 season, three pointers were used only in Big Ten and NIT tournament games.

Career Leaders

POINTS SCORED

1990-95 Shawn Respert 2,531
1987-91 Steve Smith 2,263
1982-86 Scott Skiles 2,145
1975-79 Greg Kelser 2,014
1977-81 Jay Vincent 1,914
1981-85 Sam Vincent 1,851
1972-76 Terry Furlow 1,777
1971-74 Mike Robinson 1,717
1995-00 Morris Peterson 1,588
1996-00 Mateen Cleaves 1,541
1997-01 Charlie Bell 1,468
1997-01 Andre Hutson 1,393
1983-87 Darryl Johnson 1,383
1974-78 Robert Chapman 1,382
1953-56 Julius McCoy 1,377

SCORING AVERAGE

(number of games played in parentheses)
1971-74 Mike Robinson .... (71) 24.2
1990-95 Shawn Respert .... (119) 21.2
1953-56 Julius McCoy .... (66) 20.9
1987-91 Steve Smith .... (122) 18.5
1982-86 Scott Skiles .... (118) 18.2
1963-66 Stan Washington .... (69) 18.0
1972-76 Terry Furlow .... (100) 17.8
1975-79 Greg Kelser .... (115) 17.5
1961-64 Pete Gent .... (66) 17.4
1977-79 Earvin Johnson .... (62) 17.1

FIELD GOALS ATTEMPTED

1990-95 Shawn Respert 1,791
1987-91 Steve Smith 1,695
1982-86 Scott Skiles 1,623
1977-81 Jay Vincent 1,555
1971-74 Mike Robinson 1,541
1975-79 Greg Kelser 1,517
1972-76 Terry Furlow 1,478
1996-00 Mateen Cleaves 1,331
1981-85 Sam Vincent 1,294
1953-56 Julius McCoy 1,280

FIELD GOALS MADE

1990-95 Shawn Respert 866
1982-86 Scott Skiles 837
1987-91 Steve Smith 826
1975-79 Greg Kelser 820
1977-81 Jay Vincent 799
1972-76 Terry Furlow 721
1971-74 Mike Robinson 712
1981-85 Sam Vincent 685
1983-87 Darryl Johnson 585
1974-78 Robert Chapman 577

FIELD GOAL PERCENTAGE

(minimum of 350 attempts; field goals made and attempted in parentheses)
1977-80 Ron Charles .... (376-588) .639
1990-93 Mike Peplowski .... (488-786) .621
1992-94 Anthony Miller .... (321-527) .609
1984-87 C. Valentine .... (384-639) .601
1999-03 Aloysius Anagonye .... (278-489) .569
1972-75 Bill Glover .... (214-382) .560
1970-73 Bill Kilgore .... (439-784) .559
1993-96 Quinton Brooks .... (521-952) .547
1975-79 Greg Kelser .... (820-1,517) .540
1989-92 Matt Steigenga .... (504-934) .539

THREE POINTERS ATTEMPTED

1990-95 Shawn Respert 728
1996-00 Mateen Cleaves 457
1986-90 Kirk Manns 446
1995-99 Jason Klein 409
2001-03 Chris Hill 383
1997-00 Charlie Bell 364
1987-91 Steve Smith 353
1990-94 Kris Weshinskey 283
1994-97 Ray Weathers 222

THREE POINTERS MADE

1990-95 Shawn Respert 331
1986-90 Kirk Manns 212
2001-03 Chris Hill 161
1995-99 Jason Klein 152
1987-91 Steve Smith 147
1995-00 Morris Peterson 146
1995-00 Mateen Cleaves 143
1997-01 Charlie Bell 125
1994-97 Ray Weathers 99
1990-94 Kris Weshinsky 97

THREE POINTER PERCENTAGE

(minimum of 75 attempts; three pointers made and three pointers attempted in parentheses)
1986-90 Kirk Manns .... (212-446) .475
1990-95 Shawn Respert .... (331-728) .455
1994-97 Ray Weathers .... (99-222) .446
1996-00 A.J. Granger .... (77-175) .444
1986-90 Todd Wolfe .... (53-121) .438
2001-03 Chris Hill .... (221-383) .420
1987-91 Steve Smith .... (147-353) .416
1988-92 Matt Steigenga .... (32-78) .410
1989-93 Dwayne Stephens .... (35-87) .402
1999-01 Jason Richardson .... (57-149) .383

FREE THROWS ATTEMPTED

1987-91 Steve Smith 614
1981-85 Sam Vincent 593
1975-79 Greg Kelser 590
1990-95 Shawn Respert 546
1953-56 Julius McCoy 544
1982-86 Scott Skiles 525
1952-55 Al Ferrari 512
1997-01 Andre Hutson 491
1877-81 Jay Vincent 481
1966-69 Lee Lafayette 474

FREE THROWS MADE

1981-85 Sam Vincent 476
1990-95 Shawn Respert 468
1987-91 Steve Smith 464
1982-86 Scott Skiles 446
1975-79 Greg Kelser 374
1952-55 Al Ferrari 373
1953-56 Julius McCoy 367
1977-79 Earvin Johnson 363
1997-01 Andre Hutson 357
1972-76 Terry Furlow 335

FREE THROW PERCENTAGE

(minimum of 200 attempts; free throws made and attempted in parentheses)
1990-95 Shawn Respert .... (468-546) .857
1982-86 Scott Skiles .... (446-525) .850
1983-87 Darryl Johnson .... (200-241) .830
1977-79 Earvin Johnson .... (363-445) .816
2001-03 Alan Anderson .... (195-239) .816
1963-66 Stan Washington .... (278-391) .815
1972-76 Terry Furlow .... (335-411) .815
1982-86 Lary Polec .... (188-231) .814
1977-81 Mike Brkovich .... (166-206) .805
1981-85 Sam Vincent .... (476-593) .803
1976-80 Terry Donnelly .... (187-233) .802

REBOUNDS

1975-79 Greg Kelser 1,092
1956-59 John Green 1,036
1995-99 Antonio Smith 1,016
1989-93 Mike Peplowski 906
1997-01 Andre Hutson 835
1970-73 Bill Kilgore 814
1972-73 Lindsay Hairston 803
1987-91 Steve Smith 740
1963-66 Stan Washington 727
1957-60 Horace Walker 720
1966-69 Lee Lafayette 713

ASSISTS

1996-00 Mateen Cleaves 816
1982-86 Scott Skiles 645
1991-95 Eric Snow 599
1988-92 Mark Montgomery 561
1977-79 Earvin Johnson 491
1987-91 Steve Smith 453
1997-01 Charlie Bell 371
1979-82 Kevin Smith 349
1976-80 Terry Donnelly 321
1986-90 Ken Redfield 314

STEALS

1996-00 Mateen Cleaves 195
1982-86 Scott Skiles 175
1988-92 Mark Montgomery 168
1981-85 Sam Vincent 159
1986-90 Ken Redfield 150
1975-79 Greg Kelser 148
1977-79 Eavin Johnson 146
1991-95 Eric Snow 142
1990-95 Shawn Respert 139
1983-87 Darryl Johnson 138

BLOCKED SHOTS

1981-85 Matt Steigenga 97
1983-85 Ken Johnson 96
1999-03 Aloysius Anagonye 88
1998-03 Adam Ballinger 73
1981-84 Kevin Willis 71
1996-98 DuJuan Wiley 69
1992-96 Qunton Brooks 69
1989-93 Mike Peplowski 68
1991-94 Anthony Miller 61
1976-80 Ron Charles 51

GAMES PLAYED

1997-01 Charlie Bell 140
1997-01 Andre Hutson 138
1997-00 Morris Peterson 137
1999-03 Aloysius Anagonye 133
1996-00 A.J. Granger 129
1995-99 Antonio Smith 129
1998-03 Adam Ballinger 128
1988-92 Mark Montgomery 126
1995-99 Jason Klein 124
1988-92 Matt Steigenga 124
1996-00 Mateen Cleaves 123
1987-91 Steve Smith 122
1989-93 Dwayne Stephens 122

Season Leaders

POINTS SCORED

1985-86 Scott Skiles 850
1975-76 Terry Furlow 793
1993-94 Shawn Respert 778
1990-91 Steve Smith 752
1994-95 Shawn Respert 716
1969-70 Ralph Simpson 667
1984-85 Sam Vincent 666
1999-00 Morris Peterson 657
1989-90 Steve Smith 627
1986-87 Darryl Johnson 618

SCORING AVERAGE

1975-76 Terry Furlow 29.4
1969-70 Ralph Simpson 29.0
1985-86 Scott Skiles 27.4
1955-56 Julius McCoy 27.2
1994-95 Shawn Respert 25.6
1972-73 Mike Robinson 25.3
1990-91 Steve Smith 25.1
1971-72 Mike Robinson 24.7
1993-94 Shawn Respert 24.3
1984-85 Sam Vincent 23.0

FIELD GOALS ATTEMPTED

1975-76 Terry Furlow 653
1985-86 Scott Skiles 598
1969-70 Ralph Simpson 588
1990-91 Steve Smith 566
1971-72 Mike Robinson 565
1993-94 Shawn Respert 562

1955-56 Julius McCoy 538
1972-73 Mike Robinson 536
1963-64 Pete Gent 526
1980-81 Jay Vincent 522

FIELD GOALS MADE

1985-86 Scott Skiles 331
1975-76 Terry Furlow 308
1993-94 Shawn Respert 272
1990-91 Steve Smith 268
1969-70 Ralph Simpson 264
1980-81 Jay Vincent 259
1972-73 Mike Robinson 259
1986-87 Daryl Johnson 247
1978-79 Greg Kelser 246
1984-85 Sam Vincent 245
1971-72 Mike Robinson 245

FIELD GOAL PERCENTAGE

(field goals made and field goals attempted in parentheses)

1979-80 Ron Charles .... (169-250) .676
1978-79 Ron Charles .... (115-173) .665
1993-94 Anthony Miller .... (162-249) .651
1987-88 Geo. Papadakos .... (102-157) .650
1985-86 Carlton Valentine .... (80-123) .650
1992-93 Mike Peplowski .... (161-252) .639
1991-92 Mike Peplowski .... (168-266) .632
1990-91 Mike Peplowski .... (99-158) .627
1997-98 DuJuan Wiley .... (78-125) .624
1986-87 Carlton Valentine .... (135-217) .622
2000-01 Andre Hutson .... (173-278) .622

THREE POINTERS ATTEMPTED

1994-95 Shawn Respert 251
2002-03 Chris Hill 235
1993-94 Shawn Respert 205
1999-00 Morris Peterson 200
1989-90 Kirk Manns 178
1997-98 Jason Klein 168
1990-91 Steve Smith 162
1997-98 Mateen Cleaves 152
2000-01 Charlie Bell 152
2001-02 Chris Hill 148

THREE POINTERS MADE

1994-95 Shawn Respert 119
2002-03 Chris Hill 95
1993-94 Shawn Respert 92
1999-00 Morris Peterson 85
1989-90 Kirk Manns 81
1997-98 Jason Klein 69
1988-89 Kirk Manns 69
1990-91 Steve Smith 66
2001-02 Chris Hill 66
1992-93 Shawn Respert 60
1991-92 Shawn Respert 60
2001-02 Marcus Taylor 60

THREE POINTER PERCENTAGE

1988-89 Kirk Manns .... (69-136) .507
1988-89 Todd Wolfe .... (26-52) .500
1982-83 Scott Skiles .... (25-50) .500
1987-88 Kirk Manns .... (27-56) .482
1994-95 Shawn Respert .... (119-251) .474
1986-87 Kirk Manns .... (35-76) .461
1989-90 Steve Smith .... (45-98) .459
1991-92 Shawn Respert .... (60-132) .455
1989-90 Kirk Manns .... (81-178) .455
1999-00 A.J. Granger .... (49-109) .450

FREE THROW ATTEMPTS

1978-79 Earvin Johnson 240
1955-56 Julius McCoy 214
1985-86 Scott Skiles 209

1984-85 Sam Vincent 208
1977-78 Earvin Johnson 205
1958-59 Bob Anderegg 203
1975-76 Terry Furlow 202
1976-77 Greg Kelser 196
1954-55 Al Ferrari 192
1990-91 Steve Smith 187
1953-54 Julius McCoy 187

FREE THROWS MADE

1978-79 Earvin Johnson 202
1985-86 Scott Skiles 188
1975-76 Terry Furlow 177
1984-85 Sam Vincent 176
1977-78 Earvin Johnson 161
1954-55 Al Ferrari 152
1990-91 Steve Smith 150
1955-56 Julius McCoy 144
1993-94 Shawn Respert 142
1994-95 Shawn Respert 139
1969-70 Ralph Simpson 139

FREE THROW PERCENTAGE

1986-87 Darryl Johnson .... (111-122) .910
1985-86 Scott Skiles .... (188-209) .900
1999-00 A.J. Granger .... (67-75) .893
1979-80 Terry Donnelly .... (60-68) .882
1975-76 Terry Furlow .... (177-202) .876
1991-92 Shawn Respert .... (68-78) .872
1994-95 Shawn Respert .... (139-160) .869
1989-90 Kirk Manns .... (70-81) .864
2001-02 Adam Ballinger .... (51-58) .864
1980-81 Mike Brkovich .... (56-65) .862

REBOUNDS

1957-58 John Green 392
1958-59 John Green 382
1959-60 Horace Walker 373
1973-74 Lindsay Hairston 326
1998-99 Antonio Smith 319
1958-59 Horace Walker 312
1970-71 Bill Kilgore 309
1996-97 Antonio Smith 306
1995-96 Jamie Feick 303
1960-61 Ted Williams 288

REBOUND AVERAGE

1957-58 John Green 17.8
1959-60 Horace Walker 17.7
1958-59 John Green 16.6
1956-57 John Green 14.6
1973-74 Lindsay Hairston 13.6
1958-59 Horace Walker 13.5
1970-71 Bill Kilgore 12.8
1960-61 Ted Williams 12.0
1959-60 Lance Olson 11.7
1959-60 Art Gowens 11.6

ASSISTS

1998-99 Mateen Cleaves 274
1978-79 Earvin Johnson 269
1977-78 Earvin Johnson 222
1997-98 Mateen Cleaves 217
1994-95 Eric Snow 217
1993-94 Eric Snow 213
1985-86 Scott Skiles 203
1991-92 Mark Montgomery 190
1999-00 Mateen Cleaves 179
1990-91 Mark Montgomery 169

STEALS

1978-79 Earvin Johnson 75
1997-98 Mateen Cleaves 73
1977-78 Earvin Johnson 71

1998-99	Mateen Cleaves	69
1986-87	Darryl Johnson	60
1993-94	Eric Snow	57
1998-99	Antonio Smith	56
1985-86	Scott Skiles	54
1978-79	Greg Kelser	53
1994-95	Eric Snow	52
1990-91	Mark Montgomery	52

BLOCKED SHOTS

1984-85	Ken Johnson	72
1979-80	Ron Charles	51
1997-98	DuJuan Wiley	50
1982-83	Kevin Willis	35
1987-88	George Papadakos	35
1990-91	Matt Steigenga	32
2001-02	Aloysius Anagonye	31
1989-90	Matt Steigenga	30
1993-94	Anthony Miller	29
2000-01	Jason Richardson	28

Single Game Leaders

POINTS SCORED

1-5-76	Terry Furlow	(Iowa)	50
1-8-76	Terry Furlow	(NW)	48
1-18-86	Scott Skiles	(Minnesota)	45
12-21-55	Julius McCoy	(Notre Dame)	45
2-23-94	Shawn Respert	(Minnesota)	43
3-8-86	Scott Skiles	(Ohio State)	43
12-13-69	Ralph Simpson	(W.Michigan)	42
12-29-86	Darryl Johnson	(Brig.Young)	42
1-10-76	Terry Furlow	(Ohio State)	42
12-22-75	Terry Furlow	(Detroit)	41
12-14-70	Rudy Benjamin	(Butler)	41
2-6-56	Julius McCoy	(Michigan)	41
1-11-95	Shawn Respert	(Indiana)	40
3-9-94	Shawn Respert	(Indiana)	40
1-25-89	Kirk Manns	(Purdue)	40
1-25-86	Scott Skiles	(Michigan)	40
2-9-76	Terry Furlow	(Indiana)	40
3-3-73	Mike Robinson	(NW)	40
12-27-69	Ralph Simpson	(Oregon)	40
1-28-56	Julius McCoy	(Ohio State)	40

FIELD GOALS ATTEMPTED

2-27-56	Julius McCoy	(Wisconsin)	36

FIELD GOALS MADE

12-21-55	Julius McCoy	(Notre Dame)	20
1-18-86	Scott Skiles	(Minnesota)	20

FIELD GOAL PERCENTAGE

(minimum of 10 attempts)

1-24-80	Ron Charles	(Michigan)	12-12

FREE THROWS ATTEMPTED

(minimum of 10 attempts)

2-28-55	Al Ferrari	(Indiana)	26

FREE THROWS MADE

2-28-55	Al Ferrari	(Indiana)	21

FREE THROW PERCENTAGE

(minimum of 10 attempts)

1-7-82	Kevin Smith	(Indiana)	19-19
2-24-83	Sam Vincent	(Ohio St.)	17-17
1-19-91	Steve Smith	(Minn.)	15-15
2-1-60	Lance Olson	(Minn.)	14-14
12-30-92	Shawn Respert	(Wash.St.)	13-13
1-11-75	Terry Furlow	(Michigan)	11-11

3-7-85	Sam Vincent	(Indiana)	11-11
2-27-86	Scott Skiles	(NW)	11-11
1-10-87	Darryl Johnson	(Ohio St.)	11-11
2-6-65	Stan Washington	(Minn.)	10-10
2-1-69	Lee Lafayette	(Indiana)	10-10
1-24-70	Ralph Simpson	(Michigan)	10-10
1-5-74	Mike Robinson	(Purdue)	10-10
1-7-78	Earvin Johnson	(Wis.)	10-10
2-18-78	Earvin Johnson	(Ohio St.)	10-10
2-24-83	Scott Skiles	(Ohio St.)	10-10
12-1-83	Sam Vincent	(St. Peters)	10-10
11-23-85	Scott Skiles	(W. Illinois)	10-10
3-7-87	Darryl Johnson	(Illinois)	10-10
1-25-89	Kirk Manns	(Purdue)	10-10
3-22-89	Steve Smith	(Villanova)	10-10

THREE POINTERS ATTEMPTED

2-23-03	Chris Hill	(Syracuse)	18

THREE POINTERS MADE

2-23-03	Chris Hill	(Syracuse)	10

THREE POINTER PECENTAGE

(minimum of 10 attempts)

1-25-89	Kirk Manns	(Purdue)	8-10

REBOUNDS

12-28-59	Horace Walker	(Butker)	29
12-30-57	John Green	(Washington)	29

ASSISTS

3-4-00	Mateen Cleaves	(Michigan)	20

STEALS

2-14-98	Mateen Cleaves	(Minnesota)	9

Team Records

TOP SCORING GAMES WON

3-4-00	Michigan	114-63
12-1-92	Moorhead State	121-53
12-21-63	Oklahoma	118-100
12-29-94	Ball State	117-95
12-12-94	Cleveland State	111-68
3-1-65	Purdue	110-92
11-30-63	Northern Michigan	109-86
12-13-78	Western Michigan	109-69
2-15-64	Iowa	107-82
1-11-64	Indiana	107-103
2-22-64	Iowa	107-89
2-29-64	Northwestern	107-97
12-9-93	E. Tennessee State	107-81
1-6-64	Wisconsin	106-90
1-25-89	Purdue	106-83
1-25-75	Wisconsin	105-87
1-5-76	Iowa	105-88

SEASON RECORDS
(MISCELLANEOUS CATEGORIES)

1998-99	most wins	33
1999-00	total points scored	2,889
1963-64	average score per game	92.1
1998-99	field goals attempted	2,156
1985-86	field goals made	1,043
1985-86	field goal percentage	.561
1999-00	free throw attempts	816
1999-00	free throws made	600
1985-86	free throw percentage	.799
1999-00	three pointers attempted	669
1990-91	three pointers made	253
1989-90	three pointers percentage	.431
1999-00	rebounds	1,521

1958-59	rebound average	65.5
1999-00	assists	602

SINGLE GAME RECORDS
(MISCELLANEOUS CATEGORIES)

points scored

12-1-92	(Morehead State)	121

field goal attempts

12-23-63	(Brigham Young)	101
3-5-60	(Indiana)	101

field goals made

12-21-63	(Oklahoma)	50
12-1-92	(Morehead State)	50

field goal percentage

2-28-87	(Minnesota)	.738 (31-42)

free throw attempts

12-3-83	(Illinois-Chicago)	53

free throws made

12-3-83	(Illinois-Chicago)	44

free throw percentage

1-30-01	(Michigan)	1.000 (18-18)

three pointers tried

1-4-00	(Michigan)	32

three pointers made

1-4-00	(Michigan)	16

rebounds

1-19-59	(Ohio State)	84
2-15-64	(Iowa)	84

assists

1-4-00	(Michigan)	36

fouls

2-2-52	(Northwestern)	41

victory margin

2-1-1902	(Alma)	102-3

defeat margin

1-4-75	(Indiana)	52-107

combined score

12-21-63	(Oklahoma)	218 (118-100)

Postseason Honors

ALL-AMERICA

1940	Chester Aubuchon	G
1956	Julius McCoy	F
1957	Jack Quiggle	G
1959	John Green	C
1960	Horace Walker	C
1970	Ralph Simpson	F
1974	Michael Robinson	G
1976	Terry Furlow	F
1978	Earvin Johnson	F

1979	Earvin Johnson	G
1979	Gregory Kelser	F
1981	Jay Vincent	F
1985	Sam Vincent	G
1986	Scott Skiles	G
1990	Steve Smith	G
1991	Steve Smith	G
1994	Shawn Respert	G
1995	Shawn Respert	G
1998	Mateen Cleaves	G
1999	Mateen Cleaves	G
2000	Mateen Cleaves	G
2000	Morris Peterson	F
2001	Charlie Bell	G
	Jason Richardson	F

CHICAGO TRIBUNE SILVER BASKETBALL

(Annually awarded to player recognized as the outstanding player in the Big Ten Conference)

1959	John Green	C
1979	Earvin Johnson	G
1986	Scott Skiles	G
1990	Steve Smith	G
1995	Shawn Respert	G
1998	Mateen Cleaves	G
1999	Mateen Cleaves	G
2000	Morris Peterson	F

BIG TEN PLAYER OF THE YEAR

(Recipient chosen by a vote of Big Ten coaches since 1990. Sports writers affiliated with AP and UPI voted prior to 1990.)

1981	Jay Vincent	F
1986	Scott Skiles	G
1995	Shawn Respert	G
1998	Mateen Cleaves	G
1999	Mateen Cleaves	G
2000	Morris Peterson	F

ALL-BIG TEN

First Team

1956	Julius McCoy	F
1957	Jack Quiggle	G
1957	John Green	C
1958	John Green	C
1959	John Green	C
1960	Horace Walker	C
1966	Stanley Washington	F
1969	Lee Lafayette	C
1970	Ralph Simpson	F
1972	Michael Robinson	G
1973	Michael Robinson	G
1974	Michael Robinson	G
1974	Lindsay Hairston	C
1975	Lindsay Hairston	C
1975	Terry Furlow	F
1976	Terry Furlow	F
1978	Earvin Johnson	F
1979	Earvin Johnson	G
1979	Gregory Kelser	F
1980	Jay Vincent	F
1981	Jay Vincent	F
1982	Kevin Smith	G
1984	Sam Vincent	G
1985	Sam Vincent	G
1986	Scott Skiles	G
1990	Steve Smith	G
1991	Steve Smith	G
1992	Mike Peplowski	C
1994	Shawn Respert	G
1995	Shawn Respert	G
1998	Mateen Cleaves	G

1999	Mateen Cleaves	G
1999	Morris Peterson	F
2000	Mateen Cleaves	G
2000	Morris Peterson	F
2001	Charlie Bell	G
2001	Jason Richardson	G/F
2002	Marcus Taylor	G

Second Team

1953	Al Ferrari	G
1954	Julius McCoy	F
1955	Al Ferrari	G
1958	Robert Anderegg	F
1958	Jack Quiggle	G
1959	Robert Anderegg	F
1960	Lance Olson	F
1964	G. Pete Gent	F
1965	Stanley Washington	F
1966	William Curtis	C
1967	Matthew Aitch	C
1967	Lee Lafayette	C
1968	Lee Lafayette	C
1977	Gregory Kelser	F
1978	Gregory Kelser	F
1981	Kevin Smith	G
1983	Sam Vincent	G
1985	Scott Skiles	G
1986	Darryl Johnson	G
1987	Darryl Johnson	G
1990	Kirk Manns	G
1993	Shawn Respert	G
1995	Eric Snow	G
1996	Quinton Brooks	F
2001	Charlie Bell	G
2001	Andre Hutson	F
2003	Chris Hill	G

Third Team

1958	Larry Hedden	F
1962	G. Pete Gent	F
1963	G. Pete Gent	F
1964	Stanley Washington	F
1982	Kevin Smith	G
1983	Kevin Willis	C
1984	Sam Vincent	G
1986	Darryl Johnson	G
1989	Steve Smith	G
1992	Shawn Respert	G
1992	Mark Montgomery	G
1993	Mike Peplowski	C
1995	Jamie Feick	C
1997	Antonio Smith	F
1998	Antonio Smith	F
1999	Antonio Smith	F
2000	Charlie Bell	G
2002	Adam Ballinger	F

BIG TEN DEFENSIVE PLAYER OF THE YEAR

1990	Ken Redfield	F
1995	Eric Snow	G

BIG TEN SCORING CHAMPION

1972	Mike Robinson	27.2 ppg
1973	Mike Robinson	26.7 ppg
1975	Terry Furlow	20.2 ppg
1976	Terry Furlow	31.0 ppg
1980	Jay Vincent	22.1 ppg
1981	Jay Vincent	24.1 ppg
1985	Sam Vincent	23.7 ppg
1986	Scott Skiles	29.1 ppg
1991	Steve Smith	23.2 ppg
1995	Shawn Respert	25.5 ppg
2002	Marcus Taylor	17.7 ppg

MOST VALUABLE PLAYER AWARD

(By vote of press and media representatives to receive the Charles S. Phillips Award)

1951	Ray Steffen	C
1952	William Bower	G
1953	Albert Ferrari	G
1954	Albert Ferrari	G
1955	Albert Ferrari	G
1956	Julius McCoy	F
1957	Jack Quiggle	G
1958	John Green	C
1959	John Green	C
1960	Horace Walker	C
1961	Arthur Schwarm	G
1962	G. Pete Gent	F
1963	E. Ted Williams	C
1964	G. Pete Gent	F
1965	William Curtis	C
1966	Stanley Washington	F
1967	Matthew Aitch	C
1968	Lee Lafayette	F
1969	Lee Lafayette	F
1970	Ralph Simpson	G
1971	William Kilgore	C
1972	Michael Robinson	G
1973	Michael Robinson	G
1974	Michael Robinson	G
1975	Lindsay Hairston	C
1976	Terry Furlow	F
1977	Gregory Kelser	F
1978	Earvin Johnson	F
1979	Earvin Johnson	G
	Gregory Kelser	F
1980	Jay Vincent	G
1981	Jay Vincent	G
1982	Kevin Smith	G
1983	Scott Skiles	G
1984	Sam Vincent	G
1985	Sam Vincent	G
1986	Scott Skiles	G
1987	Darryl Johnson	G
1988	Ken Redfield	F
1989	Steve Smith	G
1990	Steve Smith	G
1991	Steve Smith	G
1992	Mike Peplowski	C
1993	Shawn Respert	G
1994	Shawn Respert	G
1995	Shawn Respert	G
	Eric Snow	G
1996	Quinton Brooks	F
1997	Ray Weathers	G
1998	Mateen Cleaves	G
1999	Mateen Cleaves	G
2000	Mateen Cleaves	G
2001	Charlie Bell	G
	Andre Hutson	F
2002	Marcus Taylor	G
2003	Chris Hill	G

MOST VALUABLE PLAYER AWARD

(By vote of team members to be considered as a candidate for the Chicago Tribune)

1951	James Snodgrass	G
1952	William Bower	F
1953	Albert Ferrari	F
1954	Albert Ferrari	F
1955	Albert Ferrari	F
1956	Julius McCoy	F
1957	George Ferguson	F
1958	John Green	C
1959	John Green	C
1960	Horace Walker	F/C
1961	Arthur Schwarm	G
1962	Pete Gent	F
1963	Ted Williams	C
1964	Frederick Thoman	C
1965	Stanley Washington	F

Year	Player	Pos
1966	Stanley Washington	F
1967	Matthew Aitch	C
1968	Lee Lafayette	F
1969	Lee Lafayette	C/F
1970	Ralph Simpson	G
1971	William Kilgore	C
1972	William Kilgore	C
1973	William Kilgore	C
1974	Michael Robinson	G
1975	Lindsay Hairston	C/F
1976	Terry Furlow	F
1977	Robert Chapman	G
1978	Gregory Kelser	F
1979	Earvin Johnson	G/F
1980	Jay Vincent	C/F
1981	Jay Vincent	C/F
1982	Kevin Smith	G
1983	Sam Vincent	G
1984	Sam Vincent	G
1985	Sam Vincent	G
1986	Scott Skiles	G
1987	Darryl Johnson	G
1988	Carlton Valentine	F
1989	Steve Smith	G
1990	Steve Smith	G
1991	Steve Smith	G
1992	Dwayne Stephens	F
1993	Mike Peplowski	C
1994	Shawn Respert	G
1995	Shawn Respert	G
1996	Quinton Brooks	F
1997	Ray Weathers	G
1998	Mateen Cleaves	G
1999	Mateen Cleaves	G
2000	Mateen Cleaves	G
	Morris Peterson	F
2001	Charlie Bell	G
	Andre Hutson	F
2002	Marcus Taylor	G
2003	Chris Hill	G
	Alan Anderson	F

BEST DEFENSIVE PLAYER AWARD

Year	Player	Pos
1977	James Coultre	C
1978	Robert Chapman	G
1979	Earvin Johnson	G
1980	Terry Donnelly	G
1981	Rick Kaye	F
1982	Ben Tower	F
1983	Ben Tower	F
1984	Ben Tower	F
1985	Richard Mudd	C
1986	Barry Fordham	C
1987	Vernon Carr	G/F
1988	Ed Wright	G/F
1989	Ken Redfield	F
1990	Ken Redfield	F
1991	Dwayne Stephens	F
1992	Mark Montgomery	G
1993	Dwayne Stevens	F
1994	Eric Snow	G
1995	Eric Snow	G
1996	Daimon Beathea	F
1997	Ray Weathers	G
1998	Charlie Bell	G
	Mateen Cleaves	G
	Antonio Smith	C
1999	Charlie Bell	G
2000	Charlie Bell	G
2001	Charlie Bell	G
	Andre Hutson	F
2002	Alan Anderson	F
	Kelvin Torbert	F
2003	Kelvin Torbert	F

MOST IMPROVED PLAYER AWARD

Year	Player	Pos
1963	William Berry	F
1964	Stanley Washington	G-F
1965	Edward (Ted) Crary	F
1966	Matthew Aitch	C
1967	Heywood Edwards	F-C
1968	James Gibbons	C
1969	Tom Lick	C
1970	Rudy Benjamin	G
1971	Paul Dean	G
1972	Gary Ganakas	G
1973	Benny White	G
1974	Lindsay Hairston	C
1975	William Glover	G
1976	Dan Riewald	G
1977	Ronald Charles	F
1978	Michael Brkovich	G
1979	Terry Donnelly	G
1980	Ronald Charles	F
1981	Ben Tower	F
1982	Kevin Willis	C
1983	Kevin Willis	C
1984	Larry Polec	F
1985	Sam Vincent	G
1986	Darryl Johnson	G
1987	Carlton Valentine	F
1988	George Papadakos	C
1989	Kirk Manns	G
1990	Kirk Manns	G
1991	Mark Montgomery	G
1992	Dwayne Stephens	F
1993	Eric Snow	G
1994	Anthony Miller	C
1995	Jamie Feick	C
1996	Ray Weathers	G
1997	Antonio Smith	C
	Mateen Cleaves	G
1998	Morris Peterson	f
	Jason Klein	F
1999	Morris Peterson	F
2000	A.J. Granger	F
	Charlie Bell	G
2001	Jason Andreas	C
2002	Jason Andreas	C
	Adam Ballinger	F
2003	Kelvin Torbert	F

INSPIRATION AWARD

(Was the Sportsmanship Award prior to 1995)

1963	William Schwarz
1964	Marcus Sanders
1965	John Schick
1966	Ted Carey
1967	Ted Carey
1968	Jerry Geistler
1969	John Holms
1970	Steve Kirkpatrick
1971	Ron Gutkowski
1972	Ron Gutkowski
1973	Gary Ganakas
1974	Joe Schackleton
1975	Lovelle Rivers
1976	Benny White
1977	Edgar Wilson
1978	Dan Riewald
	Alfred Brwon
1979	Mike Longaker
1980	Mike Longaker
1981	Mike Brkovich
1982	Derek Perry
1983	Derek Perry
1984	Ben Tower
1985	Scott Skiles
1986	Larry Polec

1987	Barry Fordham
1988	Todd Wolfe
1989	Todd Wolfe
1990	Todd Wolfe
1991	Mike Peplowski
1992	Matt Steigenga
1993	Mike Peplowski
1994	Kris Weshinskey
1995	Eric Snow
1996	David Hart
1997	Steve Polonowski
1998	DuJuan Wiley
1999	Antonio Smith
2000	Mateen Cleaves
2001	Brandon Smith
	David Thomas
2002	Mat Ishbia
2003	Adam Wolfe

BOXING
LEADERS, RECORDS and HONORS

ALL-TIME COACHING RECORDS

Coach	Years	W	L	T	Avg.
Leon "Brick" Burhans	1935-41	9	10	5	.480
Al Kawal	1942-43	5	6	1	.458
No Team-World War II	1944-45				
Lou Zarza	1946-47	4	5	1	.450
George Makris	1948-55	35	16	9	.658
John Brotzmann	1956-58	2	9	3	.250
Totals	1935-58	55	46	19	.538

Season Records
See page 874 explanation of abbreviations.

Leon "Brick" Burhans (1935-1941)
(See wrestling team records for Leon "Brick" Burhans sketch)

1935 (0-1)
Coach: Leon "Brick" Burhans

3-8	A	Wisconsin	2-6	L

1936 (0-1)
Coach: Leon "Brick" Burhans

4-3	A	Wisconsin	1-7	L

1937 (2-0-1)
Coach: Leon "Brick" Burhans

2-26	H	Toledo	6 1/2-1 1/2	W
3-8	A	Toledo	5-3	W
3-11	H	St. Norberts (WI)	4-4	T

1938 (0-3)
Coach: Leon "Brick" Burhans

2-28	H	Florida	3 1/2-4 1/2	L
3-10	A	St. Norberts (WI)	3-5	L
4-5	H	Washington State	3-5	L

1939 (2-1-1)
Coach: Leon "Brick" Burhans

2-25	A	Syracuse	3-5	L
3-3	H	West Virginia	7-1	W
3-14	H	Miami (FL)	6-2	W
3-18	H	Penn State	4-4	T

1940 (1-2-3)
Coach: Leon "Brick" Burhans

2-10	H	Syracuse	4-4	T
2-16	A	Wisconsin	1-7	L
2-24	A	Penn State	1 1/2-6 1/2	L
2-26	A	Bucknell	4-4	T
3-4	H	Temple	4-4	T
3-9	A	West Virginia	6-2	W

1941 (4-2)
Coach: Leon "Brick" Burhans

2-8	A	West Virginia	4 1/2-3 1/2	W
2-10	A	Temple	6 1/2-1 1/2	W
2-22	H	Bucknell	5-3	W
2-26	H	West Virginia	5-3	W
3-7	A	Wisconsin	0-8	L
3-15	H	Penn State	3 1/2-4 1/2	L

Al Kawal (1942-1943)
On February 5, 1941, it was announced that Al Kawal, a native of Cicero, IL, had been hired as football line coach and assistant professor in education. During the preceding six years, the 31-year-old Kawal held a similar position at Boston University. A graduate of Northwestern University, he had won three letters in football and was an All-American honorable mention in his senior year. In addition, he lettered three times in basketball and was a three-time intramural boxing champion. He began at MSC in that spring of 1941 at a salary of $3,000 a year and would eventually be assigned the added responsibility of boxing coach, a position he held for only two seasons. Continuing his football coaching duties under Bachman for another four seasons, Kawal resigned in January of 1947 after being hired as head football coach at Drake University in Des Moines, IA.

1942 (3-3)
Coach: Al Kawal

1-30	H	Purdue	6-2	W
2-11	H	Florida	4 1/2-3 1/2	W
2-23	H	West Virginia	5 1/2-2 1/2	W
2-28	A	Penn State	1-7	L
3-2	A	Bucknell	1 1/2-6 1/2	L
3-6	A	Wisconsin	0-8	L

1943 (2-3-1)
Coach: Al Kawal

1-30	H	Penn State	4-4	T
2-4	H	Virginia Tech	5-3	W
2-6	A	Virginia	3 1/2-4 1/2	L
2-9	A	Catholic U.	3 1/2-4 1/2	L
2-19	A	Wisconsin	1 1/2-6 1/2	L
3-6	A	West Virginia	5-3	W

1944 and 1945
Intercollegiate athletics suspended due to World War II

Lou Zarza (1946-1947)
Lou Zarza was a stellar member of the Spartan football teams of 1933-35 and climaxed his career by being selected to the College All-Star squad for the annual classic at Soldier Field in Chicago. At 165 pounds he was also a member of the first MSC boxing team which was matched against Wisconsin in 1935. Following graduation a year later, Zarza went to St. Viator's College in Kankakee, IL, where he was head football and boxing coach for three years. Following a one-year stay at Washington High School in East Chicago, IN, Lou returned to college coaching as an assistant at the University of Arizona. Entering the U.S. Navy in 1942, he coached boxing at a base in Georgia and then headed an athletic program aboard the aircraft carrier, *Salamana*. Discharged from the navy in December of 1945, Zarza accepted the position as MSC's third boxing coach when he assumed the duties on January 22, 1946. After only two seasons in East Lansing, Lou resigned in the spring of 1947 to become football line coach at Santa Clara University in California. He would later return to the state as head football coach at Wayne University.

1946 (0-3-1)
Coach: Lou Zarza

2-9	A	Ottumwa NTS	1-7	L
2-16	H	Syracuse	3 1/2-4 1/2	L
2-22	A	Wisconsin	2-6	L
3-2	H	Ottumwa NTS	4-4	T

1947 (4-2)
Coach: Lou Zarza

2-9	A	Syracuse	2-6	L
2-11	H	Virginia	3 1/2-4 1/2	L
2-17	H	Georgetown	7-1	W
2-24	A	Minnesota	6 1/2-1 1/2	W
3-1	H	Penn State	5-3	W
3-14	H	Wisconsin	5 1/2-2 1/2	W

George Makris (1948-1955)
On August 8, 1947 it was announced that 27-year-old George Makris had been appointed as the new head boxing coach. He brought with him an excellent ring record. As an undergraduate at the University of Wisconsin he had won three varsity letters while capturing the NCAA light-heavyweight titles in 1942 and 1943. Makris graduated in 1943, winning football honors as a tackle in addition to his boxing awards. Following three years in the United States Marine Corps as a lieutenant, including 22 months of active service in the South Pacific, he returned to Madison to complete his work on a master's degree in physical education. During those graduate study years, George served as an assistant coach at his alma mater in both football and boxing. A native of Michigan, Makris was born August 19, 1920, in Ironwood. He later enjoyed an all-around prep sports career at Rhinelander (WI) High School from where he graduated in 1939. On April 15, 1955, three weeks following the NCAA championships and eight years at State, Makris resigned to become athletic director and head football coach at Bolling Air Force Base in Washington, DC.

1947-1948 (2-5-1)
Coach: George Makris

12-29	H_NO	Maryland	3 1/2-4 1/2	L
1-30	H	Minnesota	6-2	W
2-9	H	Maryland	4-4	T
2-16	H	Western Michigan	5 1/2-2 1/2	W
2-21	A	Virginia	2 1/2-5 1/2	L
2-28	A	Penn State	3 1/2-4 1/2	L
3-2	A	Western Michigan	4 1/2-5 1/2	L
3-5	A	LSU	3 1/2-4 1/2	L
		<Sugar Bowl activities		

1948-1949 (4-3-1)
Coach: George Makris

12-28	A_NO	LSU	2 1/2-5 1/2	L
1-22	A	Army	3-5	L
1-25	H	DePaul	6-2	W
2-18	A	Maryland	2 1/2-5 1/2	L
2-26	H	Penn State	5-3	W
3-5	A	Minnesota	4 1/2-3 1/2	W
3-12	H	Wisconsin	4-4	T
4-1	H	John Carroll	7-1	W
		<Sugar Bowl activities		

1950 (6-0)
Coach: George Makris

1-28	A	Penn State	5-3	W
2-13	H	Maryland	5 1/2-2 1/2	W
2-17	A	DePaul	5 1/2-2 1/2	W
2-25	H	Army	6 1/2-1 1/2	W
3-3	H	Minnesota	5-3	W
3-10	A	Wisconsin	4 1/2-3 1/2	W

1951 (2-3-2)
Coach: George Makris

1-6	H	Quantico Marines	6-2	W
1-27	A	Army	3 1/2-4 1/2	L
2-2	A	Minnesota	4-4	T
2-19	H	Gonzaga	4 1/2-3 1/2	W
3-3	A	Maryland	3 1/2-4 1/2	L
3-10	H	San Jose State	3 1/2-4 1/2	L
3-31	H	Wisconsin	4-4	T

1952 (7-1-2)
Coach: George Makris

1-19	H	Army	7-1	W
1-26	A	San Jose State	4 1/2-4 1/2	T
1-28	A	Gonzaga	3-6	L
2-8	H	Fort Custer	8-0	W
2-16	A	Minnesota	6 1/2-2 1/2	W
2-26	A	Minnesota	7-2	W
2-29	H	Maryland	7-1	W
3-8	A	Fort Custer	7-1	W
3-14	H	Quantico Marines	7-1	W
3-28	A	Wisconsin	4-4	T

1953 (5-2)
Coach: George Makris

1-6	H	Minnesota	4 1/2-3 1/2	W
1-24	A	Army	5 1/2-2 1/2	W
2-7	H	Penn State	5 1/2-2 1/2	W
2-20	A	Minnesota	3-5	L
2-28	H	Maryland	5-3	W
3-28	H	Wisconsin	4-3	L
4-4	H	Quantico Marines	5-3	W

1954 (4-1-2)
Coach: George Makris

1-22	H	Quantico Marines	4 1/2-3 1/2	W
1-30	A	Penn State	5-3	W
2-13	A	Idaho State	4-4	T
2-26	H	Maryland	4 1/2-3 1/2	W
3-8	H	Idaho State	6-2	W
3-13	A	Quantico Marines	4-4	T
3-20	A	Wisconsin	2 1/2-5 1/2	L

1955 (5-1-1)
Coach: George Makris

1-29	H	Maryland	6 1/2-1 1/2	W
2-5	H	Wisconsin State	8-0	W
2-12	A	Quantico Marines	4-4	T
2-26	H	Wisconsin	6-2	W
3-5	A	Wisconsin State	2-1	W
3-12	H	Quantico Marines	5 1/2-2 1/2	W
3-26	A	Wisconsin	3-5	L

John Brotzmann (1956-1958)

Following Makris's departure, Chuck Davey, the Spartan's four-time NCAA champion, talked to athletic director Biggie Munn about the position of head coach. Although fully appreciating the talents of Davey, Biggie lost little time in choosing John Brotzmann, Makris's assistant, as the next coach. He would survive in the position until the school saw fit to drop support of the sport following completion of the 1958 season. Brotzmann had come to MSC in 1946 as a physical education instructor and at various times served as an instructor in golf, football, basketball and baseball in additional to assisting Makris with varsity boxing in 1954 and 1955. Prior to his tenure at State, Brotzmann compiled successful high school coaching records at Lake Odessa, Chesaning, Flint Bendle and Birmingham. A native of Chesaning, he received his B.A. degree in 1929 at Central Michigan College and his M.S. degree from Michigan State in 1947.

Year-by-Year Team Performance

Years	Dual Meets			NCAA Championships[1]		Coach
	W	L	T	PtsPlace	Host or Site	
1935	0	1	0			Leon Burhans
1936	0	1	0	DNC		Leon Burhans
1937	2	0	1	DNC		Leon Burhans
1938	0	3	0	DNC		Leon Burhans
1939	2	1	1	1T12th/16	Madison, WI	Leon Burhans
1940	1	2	3	DNC		Leon Burhans
1941	4	2	0	DNC		Leon Burhans
1942	3	3	0	37th/12	Baton Rouge, LA	Al Kawal
1943	2	3	1	112nd/12	Madison, WI	Al Kawal
1944	Intercollegiate competition suspended due to World War II					
1945	Intercollegiate competition suspended due to World War II					
1946	0	3	1	no meet		Lou Zarza
1947	4	2	0	83rd/14	Madison, WI	Lou Zarza
1948	2	5	1	192nd/12[2]	Madison, WI	George Makris
1949	4	3	1	182nd/15	East Lansing, MI	George Makris
1950	6	0	0	133rd/13	University Park, PA	George Makris
1951	2	3	2	211st/14	East Lansing, MI	George Makris
1952	7	1	2	142nd/15	Madison, WI	George Makris
1953	5	2	0	10T3rd/16	Pocatello, ID	George Makris
1954	4	1	2	9T3rd/14	Madison, WI	George Makris
1955	5	1	1	171st/13	Pocatello, ID	George Makris
1956	0	4	1	173rd/13	Davis, CA	John Brotzmann
1957	2	3	0	3T8th/10	Sacramento, CA	John Brotzmann
1958	0	2	2	86th/12	Madison, WI	John Brotzmann
1959	no official team[3]			106th/9	Reno, NV	no coach
1960	no official team			94th/10	Madison, WI	no coach
Totals:	55	46	19			

DNC = did not compete

[1]Boxing was never competed as a Big Ten sport.

[2]Prior to 1948, team points were not officially awarded and team championships were unofficial. The first official team champion was Wisconsin in 1948 and a team champion was officially recognized annually thereafter.

[3]Although Michigan State dropped boxing as an intercollegiate sport in 1958, John Horne continued without a coach or void of any financial assistance through 1960. He garnered three straight 178-pound titles from 1958-1960.

1956 (0-4-1)
Coach: John Brotzmann

1-27	H	Quantico Marines	3-5	L
2-11	A	Syracuse	3 1/2-4 1/2	L
2-18	H	Quantico Marines	5-5	T
3-10	H	Wisconsin	3 1/2-4 1/2	L
3-29	A	Wisconsin	1 1/2-6 1/2	L

1957 (2-3)
Coach: John Brotzmann

2-15	H	Bolling AFB	5-3	W
3-2	A	Idaho State	1-7	L
3-4	A	San Jose State	2 1/2-5 1/2	L
3-11	H	Wisconsin	5-3	W
3-23	H	Wisconsin	3 1/2-4 1/2	L

1958 (0-2-2)
Coach: John Brotzmann

2-14	H	Wisconsin	4-4	T
2-24	H	San Jose State	4-4	T
3-5	A	Wisconsin	3-5	L
3-10	H	Idaho State	3-4	L

M.I.A.A. Field Day Champions

1888	Robert Clelland	featherweight
1890	Edwin Devendorf	featherweight
	Nelson Mayo	lightweight
	Edward Polhemus	middleweight
	Edward Polhemus	heavyweight
1891	Jonathan Tracey	featherweight
	Edward Polhemus	heavyweight
1892	O.H. Pagelson	lightweight
	Edward Polhemus	middleweight
	Edward Polhemus	heavyweight

NCAA Championship Finalists

1943	Bill Zurakowski	1st, 120 lbs.
	Charles Davey	1st, 127 lbs.
1947	Charles Davey	1st, 135 lbs.
1948	Ernie Charboneau	1st, 112 lbs.
	Charles Davey	1st, 136 lbs.
1949	Charles Davey	1st, 145 lbs.
1950	Henry Amos	2nd, 125 lbs.
	Chuck Spieser	2nd, 175 lbs.
1951	Gerald Black	1st, 145 lbs.
	Chuck Spieser	1st, 175 lbs.
1952	Charles Spieser	1st, 178 lbs.
1953	Tom Hickey	1st, 165 lbs.
1954	Herb Odom	1st, 147 lbs.
1955	Robert Boudreaux	2nd, 119 lbs.
	Herb Odom	1st, 147 lbs.
1956	Choken Maekawa	1st, 119 lbs.
	Walter Sabbeth	2nd, 147 lbs.
	George Sisinni	2nd, 165 lbs.
1958	John Horne	1st, 178 lbs.
1959	John Horne	1st, 178 lbs.
1960	John Horne	1st, 178 lbs.

CROSS COUNTRY
LEADERS, RECORDS and HONORS

ALL-TIME COACHING RECORD
(Dual Meets Only)

Coach	Years	W	L	T	Avg.
Chester Brewer	1910	1	0	0	1.000
John F. Macklin	1911-12	1	0	0	1.000
No record of dual meets in seasons of 1913 and 1914					
George Gauthier	1915	0	0	0	.000
Howard Beatty	1916-17	0	0	0	.000
no team	1918				
George Gauthier	1919	0	0	0	.000
Arthur N. Smith	1920	1	0	0	1.000
Floyd A. Rowe	1921	1	0	0	1.000
Albert M. Barron	1922	1	1	0	.500
John G.Heppinstall	1923	0	2	0	.000
Ralph H. Young	1924	1	2	0	.333
Morton Mason	1925-30	11	7	0	.611
Lauren P. Brown	1931-46	30	15	0	.667
Karl A. Schlademan	1947-58	24	11	1	.681
Francis C. Dittrich	1959-67	20	15	0	.588
Jim Gibbard	1968-83	48	44	0	.521
Jim Stintzi	1984-02	2	9	0	.181
TOTALS	1910-2002	141	106	1	.571

Season Records
See page 874 for explanation of abbreviations.

Chester L. Brewer (1910-1911)
(See baseball team season records for Chester Brewer sketch)

1910 (1-0)
Coach: Chester L. Brewer
4-23	A	Olivet	28-54	W
4-30	A	Hope Invitational	1st/4	

1911 (0-0)
Coach: Chester L. Brewer
4-29	A	Hope Invitational	2nd/4	

John F. Macklin (1912)
(See baseball team season records for John F. Macklin sketch)

1912 (1-0)
Coach: John F. Macklin
11-16	H	Alma	25-31	W

1913- 1914
No record of dual meets in 1913 and 1914.

Coach: George Gauthier (1915 and 1919)
George Gauthier, one of the heroes of the undefeated 1913 football team, stayed on following graduation in the spring of 1914 and replaced the departed Ian Cortright as head track and field coach while assisting in basketball and football. He would become the first alumnus to direct an Aggie team. From 1914 until his departure six years later, he assumed various roles on the staff including that of head coach for the 1918 football team, head coach of the 1919 cross country team and head basketball coach from 1917-1920. Gauthier left on April 1, 1920, to accept a position as supervisor of physical training and recreation in Bay City, MI, where his responsibilities included school playgrounds and the community programs. His stay there was only one year, and he accepted a position as athletic director and coach at Ohio Wesleyan in the fall of 1921. In the ensuing 34 years of service, the Aggie great would become a legend at the Delaware, OH, school. He retired from his AD post in 1955 at the age of 65, but continued as cross country and track coach until 1958. He was named to the Helms Athletic Hall of Fame in 1962, two years prior to his death.

1915 (0-0)
Coach: George Gauthier
5-30	A	Detroit "Y" Meet	1st	
11-6	H	Intercollegiate Meet	3rd/3	
11-25	A	Detroit "Y" Meet	1st	

Howard Beatty (1916-1917)
Howard Beatty lettered at MAC in track and field for an unprecedented five times, 1912-1916, being captain of the 1915 squad. He was a versatile performer with primary efforts in the weights, high jump and hurdle events. Beatty also lettered in football during his senior year. He immediately joined the athletic coaching staff upon graduation. While filling various staff roles, he was assigned as head cross country coach for the 1916 and 1917 seasons.

1916 (0-0)
Coach: Howard Beatty
11-18	H	Intercollegiate Meet	3rd/3	

1917 (0-0)
Coach: Howard Beatty
11-3	H	Intercollegiate Meet	1st/3	
11-29	A	Detroit "Y" Meet	2nd	

1918
No team

1919 (0-0)
Coach: George Gauthier (1919)
11-7	H	Intercollegiate Meet	1st/3	

Arthur N. Smith (1920)
Arthur Smith could be classified as the school's first pure track and field man. A pupil of the respected Mike Murphy of Pennsylvania, Smith had produced winning teams at both Tufts and the University of Maine before accepting the position at MAC. Additionally, his credentials included appointments as assistant coach to the USA Olympic team in both 1912 and 1920. In 1922 he departed MAC for a similar position at Iowa State.

1920 (1-0)
Coach: Arthur N. Smith
11-6	H	Intercollegiate Meet	1st/2	
11-25	H	Notre Dame	15-40	W

Floyd Rowe (1921)
In 1921, the school lined up Floyd Rowe to act as head coach. At the time he was the director of state physical training and was conveniently living in East Lansing. Having frequently acted as a starter at home meets, Rowe was no stranger to the scene. As a varsity runner at the University of Michigan in 1905-1907, he was the conference two-mile champion and record holder.

1921 (1-0)
Coach: Floyd Rowe
11-5	H	Intercollegiate Meet	2nd/2	
11-24	H	Notre Dame	15-40	W

Albert Barron (1922)
Athletic director Brewer announced that Barron, a Penn State graduate of 1915, had signed an unprecedented three-year contract to coach both football and track. The selection of Barron was made following a thorough survey of a list of 75 applicants for the position. As a collegian, Barron was a four-year starter on the gridiron for the Nittany Lions, alternating as a halfback and end. He lined up at the latter position when MAC closed out the 1914 season with a 6-3 victory over Penn State at University Park. Barron was also a letterman in both track and baseball. Following graduation, Barron accepted a position of assistant coach at his alma mater for one season. He then continued his coaching career at the Bethlehem (PA) Preparatory School in 1915. He turned out strong teams there until leaving for military service in 1917. While in the army, Barron was appointed athletic director and coach at Camp Upton where he developed successful teams in 1917 and 1918. Upon discharge he moved on to Bordertown Military Academy and then spent the 1920 season at Germantown Academy in Philadelphia. Barron's Aggie football coaching career (1921-1922) was hardly spectacular. For those who reveled in the highly successful Macklin years of 1911-1915, a couple of 3-5 seasons palled by comparison. The school's new president, David Friday, called for a review of the football situation. Following an exhaustive study headed by Jim Hasselman, the school's first public relations man, the finger pointed directly at the athletic director and former hero, Chester Brewer. He was ultimately held responsible for the sub-par seasons and the cry went up for his resignation. It was charged by many alumni that Brewer was "too much a gentleman" and that he did not assist in lining up players for the teams. In the summer of 1922, the beleaguered Brewer submitted his resignation and moved on to a similar position at the University of California in Davis. With Brewer's departure on September 8 it was announced that Bert Barron would assume the dual duty of coach and "acting" director of athletics for the 1922-23 academic year.

1922 (1-1)
Coach: Albert Barron
10-28	H	Notre Dame	21-36	W
11-4	A	Michigan	40-15	L

Jack Heppinstall (1923)
In 1923, meshed between Baron and Young, 31-year-old Jack Heppinstall, the reliable trainer, would "double" as coach. This would be Jack's only official coaching venture during his 45-year career at State. The writer for the 1924 yearbook, *The Wolverine*, cruely attributed the 0-2 record on, "the lack of sufficient coaching."

1923 (0-2)

Coach: Jack Heppinstall

10-27	A	Michigan	40-15	L
11-3	A	Notre Dame	31-25	L
11-29	A$_{MI}$	Marquette	30	
		Michigan State	35	
		Lawrence (WI)	55	

Ralph H. Young (1924)

In March of 1923 it was disclosed that Ralph H. Young, AD at Kalamazoo College, would assume the combined position of athletic director, head coach of major sports, and professor of physical education at MAC. The "acting" AD, Burt Barron, was apparently never seriously considered for the position. On May 11, 1923, the board of control of athletics announced that Barron would not be actively connected with the college after June 9, 1923. Ralph Young was born in Crown Point, IN, in 1889. He was a graduate from the high school of that city while being a member of the football, basketball, and track teams. His collegiate studies would eventually include transcripts from two campuses. He first spent two years at the University of Chicago where he participated in three sports under the renowned Amos Alonzo Stagg. Leaving school in 1911-12 he returned to his hometown and managed a hotel while also coaching at his old high school. In the fall of 1912 Ralph returned to his education, this time at Washington and Jefferson College from where he received his B.S. degree in 1915. At this time, Young focused his athletic skills on two varsity sports, football and track. The W & J football teams of those three years had a combined record of 28-3-2 and whipped the likes of Penn State, Pittsburgh, Yale, Carnage Tech and Rutgers. His first assignment following graduation was as athletic director at DePauw University in Greencastle, IN. One year later, in the fall of 1916 he moved on to Kalamazoo College as joint director and coach. Married in the summer of 1918, the 29-year-old Young enlisted in the U.S. Army and soon found himself at the University of Michigan for training with the signal corps. This provided Young with one last opportunity to perform on the gridiron as he earned a spot at a guard position on Yost's team that fall. His Wolverine career was, however, abbreviated. It seems that Coach Yost caught Young ready to board the interurban one Sunday on the way to Detroit for an afternoon of play for the Detroit Herald, a professional football team of the time. Coach Yost told Ralph: "Turn in your equipment, you're through." That was the end of Young's "amateur-professional" career. He returned to Kalamazoo after his discharge from the service and remained there until accepting the MAC offer in 1923. His football coaching stint concluded in 1927 and 1940 would mark his final season as coach of track and field. He would serve solely as athletic director from 1941-1953.

1924 (1-2)

Coach: Ralph Young

11-1	H	Michigan	48-15	L
11-8	H	Marquette	27-28	W
11-15	H	Notre Dame	39-16	L

Morton F. Mason (1925-1930)

Following his one-year of doubling (football and cross country) in the fall of 1924, Ralph Young found support to hire a "full-time" coach for the sport. In the fall of 1925, the 6'3" and 175 pound Morton F. Mason, came out of the west to take over as head cross country and assistant track coach. The 23-year-old had graduated that spring from Oregon State College with a B.S. degree in agriculture. His home was really in California where he had graduated from high school in Pasadena. As an Oregon State undergraduate Mason was a four-year member of both the track and cross country teams. Along with MSC coaching chores, he would concurrently serve as a graduate assistant in the soils department from where he pursued an advanced degree. After six years of building a foundation from which the rich Michigan State cross country heritage would endure, Ma-

son resigned in the summer of 1931. He was off to Duke University in Durham, NC, where he would continue his studies, this time in chemistry.

1925 (1-2)

Coach: Morton Mason

10-31	A	Michigan	36-19	L
11-7	H	Notre Dame	39-19	L
11-14	A	Marquette	24-31	W

1926 (0-3)

Coach: Morton Mason

11-29	A	Notre Dame	28-27	L
11-30	H	Michigan	32-23	L
11-13	H	Marquette	31-24	L

1927 (3-0)

Coach: Morton Mason

10-29	A	Marquette	20-37	W
11-5	A	Michigan	20-35	W
11-11	H	Notre Dame	21-36	W

1928 (3-0)

Coach: Morton Mason

11-3	A	Notre Dame	27-28	W
11-9	H	Marquette	17-47	W
11-17	A	Michigan	23-32	W

1929 (3-0)

Coach: Morton Mason

10-28	H	Notre Dame	26-29	W
11-2	H	Michigan	15-40	W
11-9	A	Butler	25-30	W

1930 (1-2)

Coach: Morton Mason

10-25	H	Butler	25-30	W
11-1	A	Michigan	33-22	L
11-8	A	Notre Dame	31-25	L

Lauren "Brownie" Brown (1931-1946)

Having been a champion runner for MSC, Lauren Brown was a natural to eventually serve as coach of the Spartan long distance runners. In 1931, one year following his graduation and having become supervisor of the school's mimeograph department, Brownie was assigned head coach for cross country, while assisting in track and field. In pursuit of NCAA titles, Brownie's runners would place no lower than sixth place and the 1939 quintet would win the school's first NCAA title, in any sport. After 16 years at the helm, he found his "moon-lighting" as a coach became too demanding and on July 24, 1947, Lauren resigned his position with the athletic department.

1931 (2-1)

Coach: Lauren "Brownie" Brown

10-24	A	Butler	19-36	W
10-30	H	Michigan	24-31	W
11-7	H	Notre Dame	28-27	L

1932 (3-0)

Coach: Lauren "Brownie" Brown

10-22	H	Butler	23-32	W
10-29	A	Michigan	26-31	W
11-4	A	Notre Dame	19-39	W

1933 (3-0)

Coach: Lauren "Brownie" Brown

10-14	A	Butler	20-35	W
10-28	H	Michigan	17-40	W
11-4	H	Notre Dame	19-37	W

1934 (3-0)

Coach: Lauren "Brownie" Brown

10-20	H	Butler	19-39	W
10-27	A	Notre Dame	15-44	W
11-3	H	Indiana	26-29	W

1935 (2-1)

Coach: Lauren "Brownie" Brown

10-19	A	Butler	24-33	W
10-26	H	Notre Dame	15-44	W
11-2	A	Indiana	30-26	L

1936 (2-1)

Coach: Lauren "Brownie" Brown

10-17	H	Butler	17-38	W
10-24	A	Pittsburgh	18-37	W
10-31	H	Indiana	33-22	L

1937 (1-1)

Coach: Lauren "Brownie" Brown

10-16	H	Butler	15-40	W
10-29	A	Indiana	38-17	L

1938 (3-0)

Coach: Lauren""Brownie" Brown

10-7	ABL	Butler	20-35	W
10-22	H	Pittsburgh	20-35	W
10-29	H	Indiana	27-28	W

1939 (2-1)

Coach: Lauren "Brownie" Brown

10-14	H	Penn State	24-38	W
10-21	A	Pittsburgh	26-29	W
10-27	A	Indiana	32-23	L

1940 (2-1)

Coach: Lauren "Brownie" Brown

10-12	A	Penn State	20-33	W
10-19	H	Pittsburgh	19-38	W
10-25	A	Indiana	35-20	L

1941 (2-1)

Coach: Lauren "Brownie" Brown

10-11	H	Drake	23-34	W
10-18	A	Pittsburgh	21-34	W
10-25	H	Indiana	28-27	L

1942 (1-2)

Coach: Lauren "Brownie" Brown

10-17	A	Drake	15-40	W
10-24	A	Indiana	37-20	L
10-31	H	Penn State	32-24	L

1943

Intercollegiate athletics suspended due to World War II

1944 (2-2)

Coach: Lauren "Brownie" Brown

10-14	A	Ohio State	39-16	L
10-25	A	Drake	39-15	L
11-15	A	Wayne	21-34	W
11-25	H	Wayne	19-38	W

1945 (1-3)

Coach: Lauren "Brownie" Brown

10-13	H	Ohio State	32-23	L
10-20	A	Indiana	32-23	L
11-3	H	Drake	47-16	L
11-9	H	Wayne	19-38	W

1946 (1-1)

Coach: Lauren "Brownie" Brown

10-19	A	Penn State	31-25	L
10-26	A	Notre Dame	27-28	W

Karl L. Schlademan (1947-1958)

In 1940, Ralph Young elected to close his lengthy coaching career, which had includrd 16 years as MSC head track and field coach. Remaining solely as director of athletics, Young would turn the coaching assignment over to a professional friend, Karl Schlademan, who came to East Lansing from Washington State. Schlademan's pre-MSC years (1912-1940) included coaching a variety of other sports at schools like Missouri Wesleyan, University of Arizona, Baker University, and Kansas University. It wasn't until arriving in East Lansing that he positioned himself solely into the sport of his true love: track and field. From 1941 through 1958, the name Schlademan became synonymous with one or both of those sports in East Lansing. He spent 18 years of coaching at Michigan State and a total of 44 years in the profession. At the age of 50 he had accepted the position to coach track and field at Michigan State. Schlademan's son, Karl Jr., a physician in Ft. Wayne, IN, surmised that his father took the MSC job for a combination of reasons: (a) there were close professional ties with Ralph Young; (b) the thought of moving into the new Jenison Fieldhouse was attractive; (c) he was respectful of the track programs in the midwest; and (d) an annual salary increase from $4,000 to $7,500 was most enticing. Schlademan added the responsibilities of cross country in 1947. Before his retirement from coaching in June of 1958, his harriers would chalk up five NCAA titles and a pair of runner-up spots—a remarkable record over a 12-year span. Upon retirement he returned to his home state of Indiana where he lived in Ft. Wayne and spent a short period as a representative for the Adidas Athletic Shoe Company. He died in 1980 at the age of 90.

1947 (2-1)

Coach: Karl L. Schlademan

10-25	A	Notre Dame	36-19	L
	A$_{ND}$	Iowa	21-37	W
11-1	H	Penn State	28-31	W

1948 (2-0-1)

Coach: Karl L. Schlademan

10-23	A	Penn State	21-36	W
10-30	A$_{WL}$	Wisconsin	31-31	T
		Purdue	31-58	W

1949 (2-0)

Coach: Karl L. Schlademan

10-15	A	Purdue	19-44	W
10-29	H	Penn State	22-36	W

1950 (2-1)

Coach: Karl L. Schlademan

10-14	H	Purdue	20-39	W
10-21	H	Ohio State	20-37	W
10-27	A	Penn State	44-19	L
		Big Tens at Chicago	2nd	

1951 (2-2)

Coach: Karl L. Schlademan

10-13	H	Purdue	20-41	W
10-20	A	Penn State	41-19	L
11-3	A	Wisconsin	32-24	L
11-10	H	Notre Dame	26-29	W
		Big Tens at Chicago	1st	

1952 (1-1)

Coach: Karl L. Schlademan

10-11	H	Wisconsin	28-27	L
10-25	H	Michigan State	31	
		Penn State	41	
		Michigan	50	
11-1	A	Notre Dame	19-39	W
		Big Tens at Chicago	1st	

1953 (1-2)

Coach: Karl L. Schlademan

10-10	H	Notre Dame	23-33	W
10-24	A	Wisconsin	36-23	L
10-31	H	Penn State	30-25	L
		Big Tens at Chicago	1st	

1954 (1-2)

Coach: Karl L. Schlademan

10-18	A	Penn State	39-23	L
10-23	H	Wisconsin	27-28	W
10-30	H	Ohio State	30-27	L
		Big Tens at Chicago, IL	2nd	

1955 (3-1)

Coach: Karl L. Schlademan

10-15	H	Notre Dame	29-28	L
10-22	H	Penn State	18-43	W
10-29	A	Wisconsin	16-43	W
11-5	A	Ohio State	19-38	W
		Big Tens at Chicago	1st	

1956 (4-0)

Coach: Karl L. Schlademan

10-13	A	Ohio State	16-47	W
10-27	A	Penn State	15-40	W
11-3	H	Wisconsin	15-50	W
11-5	A	Notre Dame	19-36	W
		Big Tens at Chicago	1st	

1957 (3-0)

Coach: Karl L. Schlademan

10-26	H	Penn State	24-31	W
10-31	H	Notre Dame	21-34	W
11-2	A	Wisconsin	15-44	W
		Big Tens at Chicago	1st	

Francis "Fran" C. Dittrich (1958-1967)

Francis Dittrich ministered to an unusually long apprenticeship prior to inheriting the head coaching reins of both track and field and cross country in the fall of 1958. Appointed assistant coach in 1938, he would work under Ralph Young for three years followed by 17 seasons with Karl Schlademan. His primary responsibility was working with Spartans who specialized in the field events. Fran's coaching career was interrupted by World War II. In that span he served as a lieutenant in the U.S. Navy with duty in the Pacific theater as commander on an LCI vessel. Born in Detroit on June 17, 1911, Dittrich entered MSC out of that city's Eastern High School in 1931. As a collegian he won three track letters, competing in the hurdles, sprints, high jump, broad jump, while placing fifth in the hop-step-

jump event at the 1936 NCAA championships in Chicago. Fran was named All-American in both 1935 and 1936. Other than earning an M.A. degree from the University of Iowa in 1940, his career never really left East Lansing. Dittrich's original head coaching charge included both cross country and track and field. Dittrich opened his head-coaching career in remarkable fashion, winning NCAA cross country titles in 1958 and 1959, with a second-place finish in 1960. Upon surrendering the head cross country spot to Jim Gibbard in 1968, Fran Dittrich would be recorded as the last multi-sport head coach at Michigan State. He would remain in the track and field top spot for another seven years, until retirement in 1975.

1958 (1-1)

Coach: Francis "Fran" C. Dittrich

10-11	H	Western Michigan	30-27	L
10-25	A	Penn State	23-32	W
11-1	H	Michigan State	21	
		Notre Dame	37	
		Wisconsin	82	
		Big Tens at Chicago	1st	

1959 (2-1)

Coach: Francis "Fran" C. Dittrich

10-10	H	Western Michigan	29-28	L
10-23	H	Penn State	21-40	W
11-7	A	Notre Dame	17-42	W
		Big Tens at Chicago	1st	

1960 (1-1)

Coach: Francis "Fran" C. Dittrich

10-15	A	Penn State	34-23	L
10-28	H	Michigan State	18	
		Notre Dame	54	
		Ohio State	56	
11-5	A	Air Force	26-29	W
		Big Tens at Chicago	1st	

1961 (3-1)

Coach: Francis "Fran" C. Dittrich

10-7	A$_{CO}$	Michigan State	35	
		Ohio	42	
		Ohio State	47	
10-14	A	Wisconsin	33-22	L
10-21	H	Penn State	27-28	W
10-28	A	Notre Dame	23-36	W
11-4	H	Air Force	25-30	W
		Big Tens at Chicago	2nd	

1962 (1-2)

Coach: Francis "Fran" C. Dittrich

10-6	A$_{OX}$	Ohio	19	
		Michigan State	51	
		Ohio State	71	
10-13	H	Wisconsin	34-21	L
10-20	A	Penn State	30-25	L
10-27	H	Notre Dame	23-34	W
		Big Tens at Iowa City	1st	

1963 (2-1)

Coach: Francis "Fran" C. Dittrich

10-5	H	Ohio	21	
		Michigan State	39	
		Ohio State	75	
10-12	A	Wisconsin	25-33	W
10-19	H	Penn State	21-40	W
10-25	A	Notre Dame	40-19	L
		Big Tens at Champaign	1st	

1964 (4-1)
Coach: Francis "Fran" C. Dittrich
10-10	H	Wisconsin	22-37	W
10-10	H	Indiana	16-42	W
10-17	A	Minnesota	27-28	W
10-23	H	Notre Dame	38-20	L
10-30	H	Northern Illinois	15-42	W
		Big Tens at Champaign	2nd	

1965 (2-3)
Coach: Francis "Fran" C. Dittrich
10-2	H	Indiana	15-47	W
10-9	A	Wisconsin	27-28	W
10-16	H	Minnesota	30-27	L
10-22	A	Notre Dame	43-17	L
10-30	H	Western Michigan	43-19	L
		Big Tens at Minneapolis	2nd	

1966 (4-1)
Coach: Francis "Fran" C. Dittrich
10-1	A	Indiana	20-38	W
10-8	H	Wisconsin	24-31	W
10-21	H	Notre Dame	27-30	W
10-21	H	Eastern Michigan	20-36	W
10-29	A	Minnesota	34-25	L
		Big Tens at Madison	2nd	

1967 (1-4)
Coach: Francis "Fran" C. Dittrich
10-7	H	Indiana	32-23	L
10-14	A	Wisconsin	31-24	L
10-21	H	Eastern Michigan	26-29	W
10-27	A	Notre Dame	46-16	L
11-11	H	Minnesota	37-20	L
		Big Tens at Chicago	8th	

James R. Gibbard (1968-1983)
Jim Gibbard was born on July 5, 1924, in Royal Oak, MI. Following high school graduation, he entered the U.S. Army and served as a tank gunner for three years during World War II. Enrolling at MSC in 1946, Jim acquired his B.A. degree in 1950. While earning six varsity awards in both cross country and track, Gibbard was a member of Karl Schlademan's first cross country NCAA championship team in 1948. Upon graduation, he embarked on a prep coaching career which included stays at Roseville, Hazel Park and Royal Oak High Schools. During that stretch, Jim entered Wayne University and ultimately earned his master's degree in 1955. He entered the collegiate coaching scene in 1959 when Fran Dittrich tapped him as his assistant in track and field. Gibbard found success early in his MSU head coaching career as three of his first four teams, 1968, 1970 and 1971, posted Big Ten titles. Having served the University 26 years, he would retire following the track and field season of 1984.

1968 (7-0)
Coach: James R. Gibbard
10-5	A	Indiana	28-29	W
10-12	H	Wisconsin	27-28	W
10-19	H	Minnesota	27-29	W
10-19	H	Eastern Michigan	25-30	W
10-26	A	Oakland Univ. Invit.	3rd	
10-30	H	Central Michigan	15-45	W
11-2	H	Miami (OH)	26-31	W
11-8	H	Notre Dame	17-41	W
		Big Tens at Columbus	1st	

1969 (5-1)
Coach: James R. Gibbard
10-4	H	Indiana	21-38	W
10-11	H	Miami (OH)	24-37	W
10-18	A	Minnesota	29-28	L
10-22	H	Central Michigan	15-50	W
10-25	H	Spartan Invit.	1st/4	
10-31	A	Notre Dame	15-49	W
11-7	H	Eastern Michigan	20-41	W
		Big Tens at Bloomington	4th	

1970 (3-3)
Coach: James R. Gibbard
10-3	A	Indiana	46-21	L
10-10	H	Ohio State	17-46	W
10-17	H	Minnesota	29-26	L
10-24	H	Spartan Invit.	2nd/5	
10-31	H	Miami	26-21	W
10-31	A_{OX} Cincinnati	26-29	W	
11-6	H	Notre Dame	19-41	W
		Big Tens at East Lansing	1st	

1971 (4-2)
Coach: James R. Gibbard
9-25	H	Miami	32-24	L
10-2	H	Tennessee	19-39	W
10-9	A	Ohio State	20-36	W
10-16	H	Spartan Invit.	1st/5	
10-23	H	Minnesota	22-35	W
10-30	H	Indiana	27-22	L
11-6	H	Notre Dame	15-44	W
		Big Tens at Minneapolis	1st	

1972 (5-1)
Coach: James R. Gibbard
9-23	A	Miami	20-21	L
9-29	H	Notre Dame	20-35	W
10-7	A	Tennessee	25-30	W
10-7	A_{KX} Ohio State	15-49	W	
10-14	H	Minnesota	25-30	W
10-21	H	Spartan Invit.	3rd/4	
10-28	A	Iowa	26-29	W
		Big Tens at Iowa City	6th	

1973 (2-5)
Coach: James R. Gibbard
9-22	A_{AA} Miami	37-22	L	
	A	Michigan	32-25	L
9-28	A	Notre Dame	23-33	W
10-6	A_{CO} Tennessee	34-23	L	
	A	Ohio State	22-34	W
10-13	A	Minnesota	42-19	L
10-20	H	Spartan Invit.	3rd	
10-27	A	Wisconsin	36-22	L
		Big Tens at Champaign	5th	

1974 (4-1)
Coach: James R. Gibbard
9-27	H	Notre Dame	21-35	W
10-4	H	Michigan	33-22	L
10-12	H	Ohio State	22-33	W
10-19	A_{AA} Mich. Federal Meet	NTS		
10-25	A	Eastern Michigan	22-35	W
11-2	A	Miami	18-37	W
		Big Tens at Ann Arbor	4th	

1975 (3-3)
Coach: James R. Gibbard
9-26	A	Notre Dame	33-24	L
10-4	H	Illinois State	26-31	W
10-11	A	Ohio State	25-32	W
10-17	A	Michigan	36-22	L
10-24	H	Eastern Michigan	28-29	W
11-1	H	Miami	30-29	L
		Big Tens at Madison	5th	

1976 (4-3)
Coach: James R. Gibbard
9-24	H	Notre Dame	20-35	W
10-2	A	Illinois State	21-35	W
10-9	H	Ohio State	33-24	L
10-16	H	Michigan	30-27	L
	H	Minnesota	25-32	W
10-22	A	Eastern Michigan	31-26	L
10-30	A	Miami	23-33	W
		Big Tens at Chicago	T4th	

1977 (1-5)
Coach: James R. Gibbard
9-23	A	Notre Dame	43-20	L
10-1	H	Kent State	21-39	W
10-8	A	Northwestern	39-20	L
10-14	A	Michigan	45-18	L
10-21	H	Eastern Michigan	45-18	L
10-29	H	Miami	42-20	L
		Big Tens at W. Lafayette	10th	

1978 (2-6)
Coach: James R. Gibbard
9-22	H	Notre Dame	40-20	L
9-30	A	Kent State	21-36	W
10-7	H	Northwestern	15-50	W
	H	Illinois State	33-22	L
10-13	H	Michigan	39-20	L
10-20	A	Eastern Michigan	43-18	L
10-28	H	Miami	29-28	L
		Minnesota	34-23	L
		Big Tens at Bloomington	6th	

1979 (5-1)
Coach: James R. Gibbard
9-25	H	Eastern Michigan	18-41	W
9-29	A	Kent State	15-48	W
10-6	A_{KE} Northwestern	15-48	W	
10-13	H	Michigan	35-20	L
10-13	H	Minnesota	20-35	W
10-27	A	Miami	25-31	W
		Big Tens at Columbus	6th	

1980 (1-2)
Coach: James R. Gibbard
10-4	H	Northwestern	15-48	W
10-10	A	Purdue Invitational	3rd	
10-17	A	Michigan	48-15	L
10-25	H	Miami	28-27	L
		Big Tens at E. Lansing	T6th	

1981 (1-2)
Coach: James R. Gibbard
9-26	H	MSU Open	NTS	
10-4	A_{KE} Northwestern	18-41	W	
10-9	A	Purdue Invitational	3rd/8	
10-16	H	Michigan	35-21	L
10-24	A	Miami	37-22	L
		Big Tens at Minneapolis	7th	

1982 (1-5)
Coach: James R. Gibbard
9-25	A	Western Michigan	44-17	L
	A_{KZ} Eastern Michigan	45-18	L	
10-2	H	Northwestern	25-32	W
10-8	A	Purdue Invitational	7th/8	
10-15	A	Michigan	50-15	L
10-23	H	Hillsdale	29-28	L
		Miami	49-15	L
		Big Tens at Iowa City	9th	

1983 (0-4)

Coach: James R. Gibbard

9-24	H	Eastern Michigan	35-23	L
		Western Michigan	29-28	L
10-7	A	Purdue Invitational	2nd/10	
10-14	H	Michigan	48-15	L
10-22	A	Miami	44-19	L
		Big Tens at Champaign	8th	

1984 (0-4)

Coach: James R. Gibbard

9-22	A	Eastern Michigan	37-25	L
	A$_{YP}$	Western Michigan	30-25	L
10-6	A	Purdue Invitational	3rd/10	
10-12	A	Michigan	35-20	L
10-20	H	Miami	40-16	L
		Big Tens at W. Lafayette	8th	

Jim Stintzi (1984-)

On August 12, 1984, it was announced that Mr Jim Stintzi, a seven-time All-America long distance runner and 1981 graduate of the University of Wisconsin, would replace Gibbard. Stintzi, like Gibbard and other predecessors, would also be accountable as an assistant in track and field. Stintzi graduated in 1981 from the University of Wisconsin with a bachelor's degree in art. Following the death of the Badgers' longtime head coach, Dan McClimon, in the spring of 1983, Stintzi filled in as temporary track assistant for one season. He then served one year (1983-84) as cross country and track assistant at Northwestern University. The native of Menominee Falls, WI, was an outstanding athlete at Wisconsin, claiming six different Big Ten championships as a long-distance runner. He was voted the MVP at the 1981 Big Ten track and field championships, placing first in the 10,000-meter race, and second in both the 5,000-meter run and the 3,000-meter steeplechase. He captained both the Badger cross country and track teams during his senior year. Stintzi had also been a consultant for the "Athletics West" track club in Eugene, OR.

1985 (0-0)

Coach: Jim Stintzi

9-13	A	Ohio State Invit.	3rd/4
9-21	H	Mich. Intercollegiate	1st/5
9-28	H	MSU Open	2nd/ 5
10-5	A	Indiana Invitational	4th/13
10-12	A	Michigan Invitational	NTS
10-19	H	MSU Open	3rd/4
		Big Tens at Ann Arbor	9th

1986 (0-4)

Coach: Jim Stintzi

9-12	A	Notre Dame	52-38	L
	A$_{ND}$	Ohio State	52-32	L
9-20	A$_{YP}$	Mich. Intercollegiate	4th/6	
9-27	A	Western Ontario Invit.	3rd/5	
10-11	A	Purdue Invitational	1st/4	
10-18	A	Miami	45-18	L
		Big Tens at Columbus	9th	

1987 (0-0)

Coach: Jim Stintzi

9-11	H	MSU	28
		Ohio State	38
		Windsor Univ.	67
9-19	A$_{MP}$	Mich. Intercollegiate	5th/6
9-26	A	North Carolina Invit.	3rd/7
10-3	H	Spartan Invitational	2nd/6
10-10	A	Indiana Invitational	4th/12
10-17	H	MSU Open	2nd/6
		Big Tens at Bloomington	4th

1988 (2-1)

Coach: Jim Stintzi

9-3	A	E. Michigan Open	NTS	
9-9	A	Ohio State	38-18	L
9-17	A	Dartmouth Invit.	6th/9	
9-23	A$_{AA}$	Mich. Inter	5th/6	
10-4	H	Eastern Michigan	29-59	W
10-8	A	Kansas	22-35	W
10-12	H	Central Mich.	NTS	
10-15	A	Michigan	NTS	
		CCC's at Athens	2nd/11	
		Big Tens at Iowa City	2nd	

1989 (0-0)

Coach: Jim Stintzi

9-16	A	Dartmouth Invit.	NTS
9-23	A$_{KZ}$	Mich. Intercollegiate	NTS
10-7	H	MSU Invitational	2nd/4
10-14	A	Wisconsin Invit.	10th/12
10-20	A	E. Michigan Open	NTS
		Big Tens at Madison	6th

1990 (0-0)

Coach: Jim Stintzi

9-15	H	Spartan Invitational	3rd/4
9-21	A$_{CO}$	Scarlet and Gray Invit.	2nd/4
		CCC's	3rd/9
10-5	A	Notre Dame Invit.	5th/21
10-13	H	Mich. Intercollegiate	2nd/12
		Big Tens at Minneapolis	3rd

1991 (0-0)

Coach: Jim Stintzi

9-20	H	MSU Invitational	2nd/6	
9-28	A	Illinois Invitational	6th/7	
10-5	A	Wolverine Invit		
		Michigan	28-29	W
		Ohio State	16-45	W
10-11		Mich. Intercollegiate	4th/17	
10-21	A	Arizona Invit.	4th/21	
10-25	A	E. Michigan Invit.	NTS	
		Big Tens at W. Lafayette	3rd	

1992 (0-0)

Coach: Jim Stintzi

9-11	A	Michigan	NTS
9-26	H	MSU Invitational	3rd/4
10-3	A	Minnesota Invit.	8th/30
10-18	A$_{AA}$	Michigan Invitational	6th/9
10-23	A$_{YP}$	Huron Open	NTS
		Big Tens at Champaign	6th

1993 (0-0)

Coach: Jim Stintzi

9-11	H	MSU Invitational	1st/3
9-25	H	Spartan Invitational	2nd/6
10-2	A	Stanford Invitational	7th/13
		Big Tens at East Lansing	6th

1994 (0-0)

Coach: Jim Stintzi

9-10	A	Iowa Invitational	5th/5
9-16	A	E. Michigan Invit.	7th/7
9-24	H	Spartan Invitational	1st/4
10-1	A	Kent Fall Classic	4th/4
10-8	A	Maine Invitational	4th/9
		CCC's	3rd/9
		Big Tens at East Lansing	7th

1995 (0-0)

Coach: Jim Stintzi

9-23	H	Spartan Invitational	3rd/3
9-30	A$_{MN}$	Gopher Classic	10th/16
10-6	A	Notre Dame Invit.	15th/27
10-13	A$_{YP}$	Mich. Inter	4th/22
		Big Tens at Minneapolis	3rd

1996 (0-0)

Coach: Jim Stintzi

9-21	H	Spartan Invitational	1st/5
9-28	A	Minnesota Invit.	6th/19
10-11	A$_{DO}$	Mich. Inter	7th/18
10-19	A$_{TU}$	Pre-NCAA Meet	8th/32
10-25	A	W. Michigan Open	NTS
		Big Tens at Bloomington	3rd

1997 (0-0)

Coach: Jim Stintzi

9-20	H	Spartan Invitational	1st/5
9-27	A	Windsor Open	1st/8
10-4	A$_{BE}$	Paul Short Open Race	NTS
10-18	A$_{CX}$	Tiger Classic	1st/10
10-24	A	E. Michigan Open	NTS
		Big Tens at Columbus	3rd
11-15		ABL Great Lakes Reg.	3rd/26

1998 (0-0)

Coach: Jim Stintzi

9-19	A$_{BG}$	Mel Brodt Invit.	1/16
9-26	H	Spartan Invitational	1/8
10-3	A$_{BE}$	Paul Short Invit.	T1/15
10-17	A	Texas A&M Invit.	1/22
10-23	A	E. Michigan Open	NTS
		Big Tens at Ann Arbor	2nd
11-14	A	Great Lakes Reg.	1/26

1999 (0-0)

Coach: Jim Stintzi

9-18	H	Spartan Invitational	2nd/4
10-1	A	Auburn Invitational	6th/33
10-16	A	Pre-NCAA Meet	27th/27
		Big Tens at University Park	6th
11-13	A	Great Lakes Region	7th/28

2000 (0-0)

Coach: Jim Stintzi

9-16	H	Spartan Invitational.	1st
9-23	A	Great Amer. Fest	3rd
10-7	A$_{BE}$	Paul Short Inv.	1st/38
		Big Tens at Madison	4th

2001 (0-0)

Coach: Jim Stintzi

8-31	A	Grand Valley St. Inv.	NTS
9-21	H	Spartan Invitational.	NTS
9-29	A$_{MN}$	Roy Griak Inv.	9th/16
10-18	A	E. Michigan Open	NTS
		Big Tens at Champaign	3rd

2002 (0-0)

Coach: Jim Stintzi

8-30	A$_{MP}$	Jeff Drenth Invit.	NTS
9-20	H	Spartan Invitational	NTS
9-28	A$_{MN}$	Roy Griak Invit.	14/27
10-19	A$_{TI}$	Pre-NCAA Invit.	7/36
11-16	A	NCAA Gr. Lakes Reg	8/31
11-25	A	NCAA Finals	30/31
		Big Tens at West Lafayette	6/11

Year-by-Year Team Performance

Years	Dual Meets			Conference Championships			NCAA Championships			Coach
	W	L	T	Pts	Place	Host or Site	Pts	Place*	Host or Site	
1910	1	0	0		DNC	Madison, WI	no meet			Chester Brewer
1911	1	0	0		DNC	Iowa City, IA	no meet			John Macklin
1912	0	0	0		DNC	Evanston, IL	no meet			John Macklin
1913		no team			DNC	Columbus, OH	no meet		no record of team	
1914		no team			DNC	West Lafayette, IN	no meet		no record of team	
1915	0*	0	0		DNC	Madison, WI	no meet			George Gauthier
1916	0*	0	0		DNC	West Lafayette, IN	no meet			Howard Beatty
1917	0*	0	0			no meet	no meet			Howard Beatty
1918		no team				no meet	no meet		no record of team	
1919	0*	0	0		DNC	Columbus, OH	no meet			George Gauthier
1920	1	0	0	185	8th	Champaign, IL	no meet			Arthur N. Smith
1921	1	0	0	161	7th	Bloomington, IN	no meet			Floyd Rowe
1922	1	1	0	148	6th	West Lafayette, IN	no meet			Bert Barron
1923	0	2	0	180	8th	Columbus, OH	no meet			Jack Heppinstall
1924	1	2	0	288	14th	Ann Arbor, MI	no meet			Ralph Young
1925	1	2	0	245	T10th	Ann Arbor, MI	no meet			Morton F. Mason
1926	0	3	0		DNC	Minneapolis, MN	no meet			Morton F. Mason
1927	3	0	0		DNC	Ann Arbor, MI	no meet			Morton F. Mason
1928	3	0	0		DNC	Madison, WI	no meet			Morton F. Mason
1929	3	0	0		DNC	Columbus, OH	no meet			Morton F. Mason
1930	1	2	0		DNC	Champaign, IL	no meet			Morton F. Mason
1931	2	1	0		DNC	Iowa City, IA	no meet			Lauren P. Brown
1932	3	0	0		DNC	West Lafayette, IN	no meet			Lauren P. Brown
1933	3	0	0			no meet	no meet			Lauren P. Brown
1934	3	0	0			no meet	no meet			Lauren P. Brown
1935	2	1	0			no meet	no meet			Lauren P. Brown
1936	2	1	0			no meet	no meet			Lauren P. Brown
]937	1	1	0			no meet	no meet			Lauren P. Brown
1938	3	0	0		DNC	West Lafayette, IN	70	4/6	East Lansing, MI	Lauren P. Brown
1939	2	1	0		DNC	Chicago, IL	54	1/9	East Lansing, MI	Lauren P. Brown
1940	2	1	0		DNC	Chicago, IL	102	4/10	East Lansing, MI	Lauren P. Brown
1941	2	1	0		DNC	Chicago, IL	122	T4/14	East Lansing, MI	Lauren P. Brown
1942	1	2	0		DNC	Chicago, IL	108	4/9	East Lansing, MI	Lauren P. Brown
1943					No meets, World War II					
1944	2	2	0		DNC	Chicago, IL	109	5/6	East Lansing, MI	Lauren P. Brown
1945	1	3	0		DNC	Chicago, IL	149	6/8	East Lansing, MI	Lauren P. Brown
1946	1	1	0		DNC	Chicago, IL	187	6/20	East Lansing, MI	Lauren P. Brown
1947	2	1	0		DNC	Chicago, IL	152	7/20	East Lansing, MI	Karl A. Schlademan
1948	2	0	1		DNC	Chicago, IL	41	1/18	East Lansing, MI	Karl A. Schlademan
1949	2	0	0		DNC	Chicago, IL	59	1/18	East Lansing, MI	Karl A. Schlademan
1950	2	1	0	61	2nd	Chicago, IL	55	2/9	East Lansing, MI	Karl A. Schlademan
1951	2	2	0	49	1st	Chicago, IL	150	5/18	East Lansing, MI	Karl A. Schlademan
1952	1	1	0	28	1st	Chicago, IL	46	1/23	East Lansing, MI	Karl A. Schlademan
1953	1	2	0	39	1st	Chicago, IL	125	6/11	East Lansing, MI	Karl A. Schlademan
1954	1	2	0	75	2nd	Chicago, IL	231	10/16	East Lansing, MI	Karl A. Schlademan
1955	3	1	0	36	1st	Chicago, IL	46	1/9	East Lansing, MI	Karl A. Schlademan
1956	4	0	0	21	1st	Chicago, IL	28	1/14	East Lansing, MI	Karl A. Schlademan
1957	3	0	0	43	1st	Chicago, IL	127	2/17	East Lansing, MI	Karl A. Schlademan
1958	1	1	0	43	1st	Chicago, IL	79	1/14	East Lansing, MI	Karl A. Schlademan
1959	2	1	0	17	1st	Chicago, IL	44	1/13	East Lansing, MI	Francis C. Dittrich
1960	1	1	0	30	1st	Chicago, IL	80	2/12	East Lansing, MI	Francis C. Dittrich
1961	3	1	0	59	2nd	Chicago, IL	212	9/17	East Lansing, MI	Francis C. Dittrich
1962	1	2	0	39	1st	Iowa City, IA	147	5/14	East Lansing, MI	Francis C. Dittrich
1963	2	1	0	46	1st	Champaign, IL	175	5/21	East Lansing, MI	Francis C. Dittrich
1964	4	1	0	49	2nd	Champaign, IL	365	16/23	East Lansing, MI	Francis C. Dittrich
1965	2	3	0	65	2nd	Minnesota, MN	321	15/18	Lawrence, KS	Francis C. Dittrich
1966	4	1	0	61	2nd	Madison, WI	332	12/25	Lawrence, KS	Francis C. Dittrich
1967	1	4	0	146	8th	Chicago, IL	-	DNQ	Laramie, WY	Francis C. Dittrich
1968	7	0	0	70	1st	Columbus. OH	287	12/24	Riverdale, NY	James R. Gibbard
1969	5	1	0	106	4th	Bloomington, IN	-	DNQ	Riverdale, NY	James R. Gibbard
1970	3	3	0	42	1st	East Lansing, MI	248	7/39	Williamsburg, VA	James R. Gibbard
1971	4	2	0	74	1st	Minneapolis, MN	383	13/30	Knoxville, TN	James R. Gibbard
1972	5	1	0	137	6th	Iowa City, IA	-	DNQ	Houston, TX	James R. Gibbard
1973	2	5	0	108	5th	Champaign, IL	-	DNQ	Pullman, WA	James R. Gibbard
1974	4	1	0	84	4th	Ann Arbor, MI	-	DNQ	Bloomington, IN	James R. Gibbard
1975	3	3	0	133	5th	Madison, WI	-	DNQ	University Park, PA	James R. Gibbard
1976	4	3	0	98	T4th	Chicago, IL	-	DNQ	Denton, TX	James R. Gibbard
1977	1	5	0	257	10th	West Lafayette, IN	-	DNQ	Pullman, WA	James R. Gibbard
1978	2	6	0	142	6th	Bloomington, IN	-	DNQ	Madison, WI	James R. Gibbard
1979	5	1	0	138	6th	Columbus, OH	-	DNQ	Bethlehem, PA	James R. Gibbard
1980	1	2	0	159	T6th	East Lansing, MI	-	DNQ	Witchita, KS	James R. Gibbard
1981	1	2	0	197	7th	Minneapolis, MN	-	DNQ	Witchita, KS	James R. Gibbard
1982	1	5	0	233	9th	Iowa City, IA	-	DNQ	Bloomington, IN	James R. Gibbard
1983	0	4	0	212	8th	Champaign, IL	-	DNQ	Bethlehem, PA	James R. Gibbard
1984	0	4	0	173	8th	West Lafayette, IN	-	DNQ	University Park, PA	James R. Gibbard

Years	Dual Meets			Conference Championships			NCAA Championships			Coach
	W	L	T	Pts	Place	Host or Site	Pts	Place*	Host or Site	
1985	0	0	0	197	9th	Ann Arbor, MI	—	DNQ	Milwaukee, WI	Jim Stintzi
1986	0	4	0	259	9th	Columbus, OH	—	DNQ	Tucson, AZ	Jim Stintzi
1987	0	0	0	123	4th	Bloomington, IN	—	DNQ	Charlottesville, VA	Jim Stintzi
1988	2	1	0	72	2nd	Iowa City, IA	—	DNQ	Ames, IA	Jim Stintzi
1989	0	0	0	150	6th	Madison, WI	—	DNQ	Annapolis, MD	Jim Stintzi
1990	0	0	0	76	3rd	Minneapolis, MN	—	DNQ	Knoxville, TN	Jim Stintzi
1991	0	0	0	83	3rd	West Lafayette, IN	282	9th/22	Tucson, AZ	Jim Stintzi
1992	0	0	0	161	6th	Champaign, IL	—	DNQ	Bloomington, IN	Jim Stintzi
1993	0	0	0	145	6th	East Lansing, MI	—	DNQ	Bethlehem, PA	Jim Stintzi
1994	0	0	0	189	7th	Iowa City, IA	—	DNQ	Fayetteville, AR	Jim Stintzi
1995	0	0	0	91	3rd	Minneapolis, MN	474	19th/22	Ames, IA	Jim Stintzi
1996	0	0	0	108	4th	Bloomington, IN	—	DNQ	Tucson, AZ	Jim Stintzi
1997	0	0	0	162	5th	Columbus, OH	257	7th/22	Greenville, SC	Jim Stintzi
1998	0	0	0	125	5th	Ann Arbor, MI	352	12th/31	Lawrence, KS	Jim Stintzi
1999	0	0	0	106	4th	University Park, PA	—	DNQ	Bloomington, IN	Jim Stintzi
2000	0	0	0	147	6th	Madison, WI	—	DNQ	Ames, IA	Jim Stintzi
2001	0	0	0	94	3rd	Savoy, IL	449	18th/31	Greenville, SC	Jim Stintzi
2002	0	0	0	156	6th	West Lafayette, IN	646	30th/31	Terra Haute, IN	Jim Stintzi

DNC - Did not compete
DNQ - Did not qualify as a team
* - Indicates number of teams competing

NCAA championship teams
(Place of finish is in parentheses following the name.)

1939
Dick Fry (5), Roy Fehr (13), Ed Mills (19), Al Mangan (20), Bill Mansfield (22), *non-scorers*, George Keller (26), Warren Anderson (45)

1948
Warren Druetzler (5), Bill Mack (6), Jack Dianetti (11), Tom Irmen (16), Bob Sewell (20)

1949
Bill Mack (3), Don Makielski (7), Warren Druetzler (10), Jack Dianetti (18), Walter Atcheson (32)

1952
Jim Kepford (3), John Walter (5), Wayne Schutt (13), John Cook (24), Lyle Garbe (35)

1955
Henry Kennedy (2), Gaylord Denslow (6), Sewell Jones (8), Terry Block (11), Ed Townsend (46)

1956
Henry Kennedy (3), Gaylord Denslow (4), Sewell Jones (5), Phil Wheeler (8), Terry Block (18)

1958
Forddy Kennedy (1), Billy Reynolds (6), Robert Lake (14), Jim Horan (34), Dave Lean (49)

1959
Forddy Kennedy (3), Billy Reynolds (4), Jerry Young (11), Robert Lake 21), Clayton Ward (25)

IC4A championship teams
(Place of finish is in parentheses following the name.)

1933
Tom Ottey (1), Otto Pongrace (7), Eddie Bechtold (12), Johnny Hammer(16), Walter Hertzler(18)

1934
Tom Ottey (1), Nelson Gardner (3), Johnny Hammer (22), Eddie Bechtold (28), Charley Dennis (31)

1935
Eddie Becktold (1), Ken Waite (3), Nelson Gardner (6), Gerard Boss (9), Arthur Green (11)

1936
Ken Waite (1), Nelson Gardner (9), Gerard Boss (16), Arthur Green (18), Harold Sparks (25), *non-scorer*, George Grantham (29)

1937
Ken Waite (5), Richard Fry (6), Arthur Green (15), Harold Sparks(16), Gerard Boss (17) *non-scorers* Robert Hills (20), Harold Butler (36)

1948
Warren Druetzler (5), Bill Mack (8), Tom Sewell (11), Tom Irmen (13),Walter Atcheson (18)

1952
Jim Kepford (3), Lyle Garbe (7), John Walter (8), Wayne Scutt (9), Jerry Zerbe (19)

1953
Lyle Garbe (11), John Cook (19), Richard Jarrett (20), Ron Barr (27), Ken Barley (31)

1956
Henry Kennedy (1), Selwyn Jones (4), Gaylord Denslow ((5), Terry Block (12), Phil Wheeler (15), *non-scorers*, Ed Townsend (41), Ken DeFoe (53)

1957
Forddy Kennedy (1), Robert Lake (7), Henry Kennedy (8), Phil Wheeler (16), Dave Lean (60)

1959
Forddy Kennedy (1), Billy Reynolds (6), Jerry Young (9), Ed Graydon (14), Robert Lake (25)

1961
Gerald Young (4), Don Castle (12), Robert Fulcher (15), Pat Stevens (28), Ron Berby (39)

Big Ten championship teams
(Place of finish is in parentheses following the name.)

1951
Jim Kepford (4), Ron Barr (5), Jim Arnold (9), Jerry Zerbe (15), Dick Jarrett (16)

1952
Jim Kepford (2), John Cook (5), John Walter (6), Wayne Scutt (7), Lyle Garbe (8)

1953
John Cook (3), Ron Barr (7), Lyle Garbe (8), Dick Jarrett (12), Ken Barley (17)

1955
Henry Kennedy (1), Selwyn Jones(3), Gaylord Denslow (6), Terry Block (7), Ed Townsend (19)

1956
Henry Kennedy (1), Sewell Jones (4), Gaylord Denslow (5), Terry Block(12), Phil Wheeler (15)

1957
Forddy Kennedy (2), Henry Kennedy (3), Ron Wheeler (8), Robert Lake (9), David Lean (21)

930   CROSS COUNTRY STATISTICS

1958
Forddy Kennedy (2), Billy Reynolds (8), Jim Horan (10), David Lean (11), Robert Lake (12)

1959
Forddy Kennedy (1), Billy Reynolds (2), Ed Graydon (3), Gerald Young (4), Robert Lake (6)

1960
Gerald Young (1), Clayton Ward (3), Billy Reynolds (5), Frank Weaver (11), Roger Humbarger (13)

1962
Jan Bowen (3), Roger Humbarger (5), Don Castle (7), Mike Kaines (8), Bob Fulcher (16)

1963
Dick Sharkey (2), Jan Bowen (10), Rick Zemper (11), Ron Berby (15), Paul McCollam (16)

1968
Kim Hartman (4), Ken Leonowicz (5), Roger Merchant (6), Dan Simeck (27), John Mock (28)

1970
Ken Popejoy (4), Randy Kilpatrick (7), Ralph Zoppa (8), Kim Hartman (11), Chuck Starkey (12)

1971
Ken Popejoy (4), Randy Killpatrick (5), Killpatrick(5), Dave Dieters (13), Rob Cool (14), Steve Rockey (38)

Individual Champions
NCAA
1958   Forddy Kennedy

IC4A
1930	Clark Chamberlain
1933	Tom Ottey
1934	Tom Ottey
1935	J. Edward Bechtold
1936	Kenneth Waite
1955	Henry Kennedy
1956	Henry Kennedy
1957	Forddy Kennedy
1958	Forddy Kennedy
1959	Forddy Kennedy

CENTRAL COLLEGIATE
1927	Lauren Brown
1929	Lauren Brown
1930	Clark Chamberlain
1931	Clark Chamberlain
1932	Tom Ottey
1933	Tom Ottey

BIG TEN
1955	Henry Kennedy
1956	Henry Kennedy
1959	Forddy Kennedy
1960	Gerald Young

STATE INTERCOLLEGIATES
1917	Louis Geireman
1920	Lloyd Thurston
1932	Thomas Ottey
1933	Thomas Ottey
1934	Thomas Ottey
1935	Edward Bechtold
1936	Kenneth Waite
1937	Kenneth Waite
1938	Richard Frey
1939	Roy Fehr
1942	William Scott
1945	William Mack

Top Spartan in NCAA Championship Meet
Year	Name	Time and Place
1938	Richard Frey	20:51 (6th)
1939	Richard Frey	20:58 (5th)
1940	Albert Mangan	(22nd)
1941	Walter Mack	21:24 (14th)
1942	Bill Scott	(11th)
1943	No meet	
1944	DNC	
1945	Walter Mack	22:14 (9th)
1946	Jack Dianetti	(14th)
1947	Jack Dianetti	(28th)
1948	Warren Druetzler	20:09.78 (5th)
1949	William Mack	20:35 (3rd)
1950	Warren Druetzler	20:39 (2nd)
1951	Ronald Barr	20:48 (11th)
1952	James Kepford	19:54 (3rd)
1953	Lyle Garbe	20:31 (15th)
1954	Gaylord Denslow	20:31 (16th)
1955	Henry Kennedy	19:57.5 (2nd)
1956	Henry Kennedy	20:10 (3rd)
1957	Forddy Kennedy	19:44.5 (5th)
1958	Forddy Kennedy	20:07.1 (1st)
1959	Forddy Kennedy	20:58 (3rd)
1960	Gerald Young	20:03 (4th)
1961	Gerald Young	20:41 (18th)
1962	Roger Humbarger	20:12 (19th)
1963	Dick Sharkey	20:08 (10th)
1964	Eric Zemper	21:17.5 (52nd)
1965	Dick Sharkey	31:16 (36th)
1966	Dick Sharkey	30:32 (11th)
1967	DNQ	
1968	Ken Leonowicz	30:02 (16th)
1969	DNQ	
1970	Ken Popejoy	28:55 (20th)
1971	Ken Popejoy	31:09 (70th)
1972	Randy Kilpatrick	29:39 (41st)
1973	DNQ	
1974	Herb Lindsay	30:29.66 (22nd)
1975	Herb Lindsay	29:10.3 (12th)
1976	Herb Lindsay	28:30.69 (4th)
1977	DNQ	
1978	DNQ	
1979	Martin Schulist	NA
1980	DNQ	
1981	DNQ	
1982	DNQ	
1983	Tom Irmen	31:45.8 (112th)
1984	DNQ	
1985	DNQ	
1986	DNQ	
1987	DNQ	
1988	Anthony Hamm	30:03 (27th)
1989	DNQ	
1990	Anthony Hamm	29:55 (18th)
1991	Anthony Hamm	30:42.6 (6th)
1992	Dave Smith	32:07 (51st)
1993	DNQ	
1994	DNQ	
1995	Chris Lett	33:06 (113th)
1996	DNQ	
1997	Kyle Baker	30:17 (31st)
1998	Jim Jurcevich	31:01 (26th)
1999	Joe Leo	33:03 (175th)

2000	DNQ	
2001	Chris Toloff	30:33 (64th)
2002	Andrew Marsh	30:40.1 (41st)

Distance Note-
  4 miles: 1938-64
  6 miles: 1965-73
  10 K: 1974-95

Top Spartan in NCAA Region IV Championship Meet
Year	Name	Time and Place
1972	Randy Kilpatrick	30:10 (7th)
1973	Herb Lindsay	30:14 (17th)
1974	Herb Lindsay	29:34 (7th)
1975	Herb Lindsay	30.06 (2nd)
1976	Herb Lindsay	29:21 (2nd)
1977	DNC	
1978	DNC	
1979	Martin Schulist	32:31 (5th)
1980	Ted Unold	31:35 (51st)
1981	Michael White	31:02 (20th)
1982	DNC	
1983	Tom Irmen	30:52.8 (14th)
1984	Rick Pietras	NA
1985	DNC	
1986	DNC	
1987	Anthony Hamm	31:10.73 (26th)
1988	Anthony Hamm	31:40.1 (11th)
1989	Kerry Fly	32:09 (26th)
1990	Anthony Hamm	30:53.1 (2nd)
1991	Anthony Hamm	31:02 (2nd)
1992	Dave Smith	21:50.1 (13th)
1993	Toby Lefere	32:59.9 (16th)
1994	Chris Lett	31:57 (32nd)
1995	Chris Lett	31:24 (5th)
1996	Kyle Baker	31:44 (25th)
1997	Kyle Baker	32:01 (9th)
1998	Ryan Taylor	30:41 (3rd)
1999	Joe Leo	30:30 (7th)
2000	Ben Evans	31:33.9 (14th)
2001	Ben Evans	30:58.3 (9th)
2002	Chris Toloff	30:55.8 (13th)

Top Spartan in Big Ten Championship Meet
Year	Name	Time and Place
1950	Warren Druetzler	20:14 (4th)
1951	Jim Kepford	21:39 (4th)
1952	Jim Kepford	19:52 (2nd)
1953	John Cook	19:55 (3rd)
1954	Gay Denslow	20:27 (3rd)
1955	Henry Kennedy	19:06 (1st)
1956	Henry Kennedy	20:25.3 (1st)
1957	Forddy Kennedy	21:12 (2nd)
1958	Forddy Kennedy	20:21 (2nd)
1959	Forddy Kennedy	20:12.3 (1st)
1960	Gerald Young	19:35.3 (1st)
1961	Gerald Young	19:52 (2nd)
1962	Joan Bowen	20:09 (3rd)
1963	Dick Sharkey	19:43 (2nd)
1964	Mike Kaines	20:18 (3rd)
1965	Dick Sharkey	20:13 (3rd)
1966	Dick Sharkey	19:10 (2nd)
1967	Roger Merchant	25:08 (11th)
1968	Kim Hartman	25:14 (4th)
1969	Randy Kilpatrick	26:44 (11th)
1970	Ken Popejoy	25:06 (4th)
1971	Ken Popejoy	30:25 (4th)
1972	Randy Kilpatrick	30:26 (4th)
1973	Fred Teddy	29:43 (13th)
1974	Herb Lindsay	30:05.4 (3rd)
1975	Herb Lindsay	23:35 (2nd)
1976	Herb Lindsay	23:39 (2nd)
1977	Jeff Pullen	25:33 (27th)
1978	Mark Mesler	25:16 (18th)

1979	Martin Schulist	23:57 (7th)
1980	Ted Unold	25:00 (15th)
1981	Michael White	24:46.6 (20th)
1982	Tom Irmen	25:20 (16th)
1983	Tom Irmen	24:04 (10th)
1984	Rick Pietras	32:43 (23rd)
1985	Tim Simpson	25:42 (17th)
1986	Keith Hanson	25:19 (25th)
1987	Anthony Hamm	25:19 (14th)
1988	Anthony Hamm	24:32 (6th)
1989	Kerry Fly	25:09 (15th)
1990	Anthony Hamm	24:55.7 (4th)
1991	Ian Smith	25:08.3 (4th)
1992	Dave Smith	24:15 (5th)
1993	Toby Lefere	25:06.80 (11th)
1994	Chris Lett	25:15.1 (12th)
1995	Chris Lett	25:15 (10th)
1996	Kyle Baker	25:23.6 (11th)
1997	Kyle Baker	24:30 (3rd)
1998	Ryan Taylor	24:23 (2nd)
1999	Matt LaFave	26:12 (21st)
2000	Steve Padgett	24:26 (6th)
2001	Chris Toloff	24:15.4 (9th)
2002	Chris Toloff	24:44.6 (17th)

Distance Note-
>4 miles: 1950-66
>5 miles: 1967-70
>6 miles: 1971-74
>5 miles: 1975-76
>8,000 meters: 1977-present

All-American (Begun in 1948)

Year	Name	Place in NCAA
1948	Warren Druetzler	5th
1948	William Mack	6th
1948	Jack Dianetti	11th
1949	William Mack	3rd
1949	Donald Makielski	7th
1949	Warren Druetzler	10th
1950	Warren Druetzler	2nd
1950	James Kepford	12th
1950	Donald Makielski	15th
1951	Ronald Barr	11th
1951	Wayne Scutt	13th
1952	James Kepford	3rd
1952	John Walter	5th
1952	Wayne Scott	13th
1953	Lyle Garbe	15th
1955	Henry Kennedy	2nd
1955	Gaylord Denslow	6th
1955	Selwyn Jones	8th
1955	Terry Block	11th
1956	Henry Kennedy	3rd
1956	Gaylord Denslow	4th
1956	Selwyn Jones	5th
1956	Ron Wheeler	8th
1957	Crawford Kennedy	5th
1958	Crawford Kennedy	1st
1958	William Reynolds	6th
1958	Robert Lake	14th
1959	Crawford Kennedy	3rd
1959	William Reynolds	4th
1959	Gerald Young	11th
1960	Gerald Young	4th
1960	William Reynolds	13th
1963	Richard Sharkey	10th
1968	Ken Leonowicz	16th
1970	Ken Popejoy	20th
1974	Herb Lindsay	22nd
1975	Herb Lindsay	12th
1976	Herb Lindsay	4th
1988	Anthony Hamm	27th
1990	Anthony Hamm	18th
1991	Anthony Hamm	6th
1991	Ian Smith	23rd
1997	Kyle Baker	31st
1998	Jim Jurcevich	26th
2002	Andrew Alley	

All-Big Ten (Begun in 1984)

Year	Name	Place in Big Ten
1988	Anthony Hamm	6th
1990	Anthony Hamm	4th
1990	Dave Smith	7th
1991	Anthony Hamm	6th
1991	Ian Smith	4th
1992	Dave Smith	5th
1997	Kyle Baker	3rd
1998	Ryan Taylor	2nd
1998	Steve Schell	7th
2000	Steve Padgett	6th
2001	Ben Evans	11th

FENCING
LEADERS, RECORDS and HONORS

ALL-TIME COACHING RECORDS

Coach	Years	W	L	T	Avg.
Joseph Waffa	1926-1929	9	8	0	.529
George Kershaw	1930	2	3	0	.400
George Bauer	1931-1937	31	24	0	.564
Thomas L. Caniff	1938	6	2	1	.722
Charles Schmitter	1939-1983	272	235	2	.536
Fred Freiheit	1984-1997	150	159	1	.485
Totals		470	431	4	.522

Season Records

See page 874 for explanation of abbreviations

Joseph Waffa (1926-1929)

In May of 1926 an announcement was released by the athletic department officially recognizing the sport of fencing as the latest sport at MAC and that yet another all-college tournament was called to assist in assembling a team. Josef Waffa, a graduate student from Egypt, volunteered to act as coach. Waffa would hold forth until 1930 when he returned to his homeland where he would later become their Olympic coach.

1926 (1-0)
Coach: Joseph Waffa

5-29	H	Michigan	10-6	W

1927 (2-2)
Coach: Joseph Waffa

1-29	A	Ohio State	1-8	L
2-12	H	Ohio Wesleyan	7-2	W
3-5	A	Michigan	0-9	L
3-19	H	Michigan	5-4	W

1928 (2-3)
Coach: Joseph Waffa

1-28	H	Ohio State	4-13	L
2-11	A	Ohio Wesleyan.	15-0	W
2-18	A	Detroit Fencing Club	5-12	L
3-3	A	Michigan	6-9	L
5-5	H	K'zoo Fencing Club	6-3	W

1929 (4-3)
Coach: Joseph Waffa

2-9	H	Ka'zoo Fencing Club	8-1	W
2-23	H	Michigan	6-11	L
2-26	A	Detroit	6-3	W
3-1	H	Ohio State	8-9	L
3-9	A	Ka'zoo Fencing Club	9-0	W
3-15	H	Wisconsin	6-8	L
3-16	H	Detroit	9-2	W

George Kershaw (1930)

Finding a replacement for the departed Josef Waffa was a formidable task for the athletic department. They finally settled on senior swordsman George Kershaw of Wyandotte who would serve one year as player-coach.

1930 (2-3)
Coach: George Kershaw

1-22	A	Michigan	4-8	L
2-1	A$_{DW}$	Ohio Wesleyan	12-3	W
		Ohio State	4-13	L
3-1	H	Ohio Wesleyan	10-7	W
3-8	H	Chicago	5-7	L

George Bauer (1931-1937)

Assuming the similar capacity of his predecessor and teammate George Kewshaw, senior George Bauer filled the duo roll of swordsman and coach in 1931. Undefeated as a competitor, he proved to be the most accomplished fencer to ever represent the school and upon conclusion of the 1931 season he was awarded a *major* letter, becoming the first-ever fencer to be so honored at MSC. Upon completing his collegiate eligibility, Bauer began a six-year stint as a graduate student-coach. He continued in this role until 1938, whereupon completing an advanced degree in chemistry, he bid farewell to MSC and its fencing program.

1931 (1-3)
Coach: George Bauer

2-18	H	Michigan	5 1/2-11 1/2	L
2-20	A	Northwestern	6-11	L
2-21	A	Chicago	10-11	L
3-6	H	Northwestern	9-8	W

1932 (5-4)
Coach: George Bauer

1-16	A	Michigan	5-12	L
1-22	A	Wittenberg	11-6	W
1-23	A	Ohio State	5-12	L
2-6	A	Cadillac A.C. (Detroit)	7-10	L
2-12	A	Detroit	10-7	W
2-13	A	Detroit Turnverein	9-8	W
2-20	H	Detroit	11-6	W
2-27	H	Cadillac A.C.	8-9	L
3-5	H	Detroit Turnverein	12-5	W

1933 (4-3)
Coach: George Bauer

1-17	H	Michigan	7-10	L
2-17	A	Detroit Turnverein	10-7	W
2-18	A	Detroit	8-9	L
3-1	H	Detroit Fencing Club	13-6	W
3-3	A	Michigan	7-10	L
3-4	H	Detroit Turnverein	9-8	W
3-18	H	Detroit	11-4	W

1934 (5-1)
Coach: George Bauer

2-2	A	Ohio State	7-10	L
2-3	A$_{SR}$	Wittenberg	11-5	W
		Ohio Northern	15-2	W
2-9	A	Notre Dame	11-6	W
2-10	A	Purdue	11-5	W
2-22	H	Notre Dame	11-6	W

1935 (6-2)
Coach: George Bauer

1-19	A	Lawrence Tech	12-5	W
1-26	A$_{DE}$	Ohio State	12-5	W
2-2	H	Wayne	9-8	W
2-8	H	Salle De Tuscan	9 1/2-7 1/2	W
2-16	A	Wayne	9 1/2-7 1/2	W
2-21	A	Illinois	7-10	L
2-22	A	Northwestern	10-7	W
2-23	A	Chicago	5-12	L

1936 (8-4)
Coach: George Bauer

1-11	H	Detroit Turnverein	9-8	W
1-18	H	Lawrence Tech	13-4	W
2-1	H	Chicago	5-12	L
2-8	H	Notre Dame	6-11	L
2-14	A	Wayne	11-6	W
2-15	A	Lawrence Tech	10-7	W
2-21	H	Wayne	10-7	W
2-28	A	Ohio State	4-13	L
2-29	A	Wittenberg	10-7	W
3-16	H	Detroit	12 1/2-4 1/2	W
3-18	H	Detroit	13-4	W
3-21	A	Notre Dame	4 1/2-12 1/2	L

1937 (2-7)
Coach: George Bauer

1-8	H	Wayne	6-11	L
1-20	A$_{CU}$	Illinois	7-10	L
		Chanute AFB	8-9	L
1-22	A	Northwestern	6-11	L
1-23	A	Chicago	4-13	L
2-19	H	Ohio State	4-13	L
2-27	A	Lawrence Tech	11-6	W
3-6	H	Lawrence Tech	11-6	W
3-13	A	Wayne	6-11	L

Thomas L. Caniff (1938)

Replacing Bauer in 1938 was Thomas Caniff, an instructor in chemistry who had previously served as a volunteer freshmen coach. Charles Schmitter, who commuted from Detroit where he worked full-time as a researcher for the Ditzler Color Paint Co, ably assisted Caniff on weekends. Schmitter had gained a significant reputation as a near unbeatable competitor in the Detroit area.

1938 (6-2-1)
Coach: Thomas L. Caniff

1-15	H	Wayne	7 1/2-9 1/2	L
1-27	A	Western Reserve	8-9	L
1-28	A	Ohio State	10-7	W
1-29	A	Cincinnati	11-6	W
2-5	H	Lawrence Tech	10 1/2-6 1/2	W
2-12	H	Cranbrook School	16-11	W
2-19	A	Wayne	9-8	W
2-26	H	Lawrence Tech	9 1/2-7 1/2	W
3-5	A	Chicago	8 1/2-8 1/2	T

Charles R. Schmitter (1939-1983)

After serving as an assistant to Caniff in 1938, Charles Schmitter agreed to become the Spartan varsity coach in 1939, although part-time in nature. Twice each week he would drive to East Lansing and conduct team practices before returning to Detroit on that same evening. In 1940, only his second year as head coach, Coach Schmitter would lead the squad to a 14-1 season, the most impressive record of the school's history. The team had performed admirably with their coach only available two nights a week during the season. Finally, in 1941 he received a full-time appointment and moved to East Lansing. Charlie Schmitter would hold the position for 45 years, from 1939 until his retirement in 1983, the longest tenure of any Spartan coach ever.

1939 (8-4)
Coach: Charles R. Schmitter

1-13	A	Wayne	11-6	W
1-20	H	Wayne	7-9	L
1-28	H	Lawrence Tech	7-10	L
2-10	A_MI	Marquette	13-4	W
2-11	A_MA	Wisconsin	11-6	W
		Purdue	12-5	W
2-18	H	Chanute AFB	11-5	W
2-23	A	Lawrence Tech	6-11	L
2-25	H	Buffalo	13-4	W
3-4	A_DE	Ohio State	8-9	L
3-10	H	Western Reserve	9-8	W
4-6	H	Dartmouth	11-6	W

1940 (14-1)
Coach: Charles R. Schmitter

1-13	H	Lawrence Tech	8-9	L
1-26	A	Wayne State	9-8	W
1-27	A	Lawrence Tech	12-5	W
2-2	H	Western Reserve	14-3	W
2-3	H	Notre Dame	10-7	W
2-8	A	Buffalo	11-6	W
2-9	A	Western Reserve	13-4	W
2-16	A	Case Tech	16-11	W
2-17	A_DE	Case Tech	14-12	W
2-22	A	Northwestern	12-4	W
2-23	A_CU	llinois	18-9	W
		Chanute AFB	19-8	W
2-24	A	Notre Dame	10-7	W
3-8	H	Wayne	10-7	W
3-29	A	Lawrence Tech	9-8	W

1941 (2-7)
Coach: Charles R. Schmitter

1-31	A_CH	Northwestern	8-19	L
		Chicago	10-17	L
2-1	A	Illinois	9-18	L
2-14	A	Ohio State	11-16	L
2-15	A	Case Tech	17-10	W
2-28	H	Wisconsin	13-14	L
3-1	H	Notere Dame	13-14	L
3-8	A_DE	Wayne	6-11	L
		Lawrence Tech	9-8	W

1942 (5-2-1)
Coach: Charles R. Schmitter

1-23	A	Purdue	10-7	W
1-24	A	Notre Dame	13-14	L
1-30	H	Oberlin	15-12	W
2-13	A	Marquette	12 1/2-14 1/2	L
2-14	A	Wisconsin	15-12	W
2-21	A	Cincinnati	13-10	W
2-28	H	Illinois	5 1/2-6 1/2	L
3-7	H	Ohio State	10-7	W

1943 (2-4)
Coach: Charles R. Schmitter

2-13	H	Notre Dame	14-13	W
2-19	A	Ohio State	6 1/2-10 1/2	L
2-20	H_OB	Case Tech	11 1/2-15 1/2	L
	A	Oberlin	14 1/2-12 1/2	W
2-27	A_CH	Wisconsin	13-14	L
		Chicago	13-14	L

1944

Intercollegiate athletics suspended due to World War II

1945 (1-1)
Coach: Charles R. Schmitter

2-17	A	Ohio State	14 1/2-12 1/2	W
3-3	A	Ohio State	13-14	L

1946 (3-5)
Coach: Charles R. Schmitter

1-15	H	Wayne	9 1/2-17 1/2	L
1-26	A	Chicago	13-14	L
2-2	A_CH	Wisconsin	16-12	W
2-9	A_DE	Chicago	14-13	W
		Wayne	10 1/2-16 1/2	L
2-16	A	Ohio State	13-14	L
3-2	H	Ohio State	9 1/2-17 1/2	L
3-9	H	Cincinnati	20 1/2-6 1/2	W

1947 (5-3)
Coach: Charles R. Schmitter

1-25	H	Wayne	10 1/2-16 1/2	L
2-1	H	Notre Dame	17-10	W
2-7	A	Northwestern	18-9	W
2-8	A	Illinois	12-15	L
2-14	A	Ohio State	16 1/2-10 1/2	W
2-15	A	Cincinnati	15 1/2-6 1/2	W
3-1	A_DE	Chicago	7 1/2-19 1/2	L
3-7	H	Wisconsin	15-12	W

1948 (6-3)
Coach: Charles R. Schmitter

1-24	A	Northwestern	11 1/2-15 1/2	L
1-31	H	Ohio State	14-13	W
2-7	A	Notre Dame	12-15	L
2-13	A	Wisconsin	18-9	W
2-14	A	Chicago	11-12	L
2-21	H	Illinois	16-11	W
2-28	H	Cincinnati	20-7	W
3-6	A_DE	Wayne	15-12	W
		Detroit	16-11	W

1949 (3-5)
Coach: Charles R. Schmitter

1-22	A	Ohio State	10 1/2-16 1/2	L
1-29	H	Notre Dame	12-15	L
2-5	H	Chicago	12-15	L
2-18	H	Wisconsin	17-10	W
2-26	H	Detroit	18-9	W
3-3	A	Illinois	9-18	L
3-4	A	Northwestern	17-10	W
3-12	H	Wayne	9-18	L

1950 (7-1-1)
Coach: Charles R. Schmitter

1-21	A	Notre Dame	7-20	L
1-28	H	Ohio State	21-6	W
2-3	H	Buffalo	22 1/2-4 1/2	W
2-4	H	Northwestern	16-11	W
2-13	H	Illinois	13 1/2-13 1/2	T
2-17	A	Chicago	18-9	W
2-18	A	Wisconsin	18-7	W
2-25	A	Wayne	14-13	W
		Detroit	20-7	W

1951 (7-3)
Coach: Charles R. Schmitter

1-20	H	Detroit	16-11	W
1-26	A	Buffalo	17-10	W
1-27	A	Ohio State	15-12	W
2-10	H	Chicago	15-12	W
2-16	A	Illinois	8-19	L
2-17	A_EV	Northwestern	14-13	W
		Iowa	19-8	W
3-2	H	Notre Dame	12-15	L
3-10	H	Wisconsin	13-14	L
		Wayne	16-11	W
		Big Tens at Madison	5th	

1952 (8-1)
Coach: Charles R. Schmitter

1-26	A_DE	Detroit	18-9	W
		Wayne	15-12	W
2-2	A	Notre Dame	14-13	W
2-8	H	Ohio State	18-9	W
2-23	H	Northwestern	18-9	W
2-29	A	Chicago	16-11	W
3-1	A_IC	Iowa	20-7	W
		Wisconsin	15-12	W
3-8	H	Illinois	11-16	L
		Big Tens at Bloomington	2nd	

1953 (5-5)
Coach: Charles R. Schmitter

1-24	H	Detroit	19-8	W
		Wayne	12-15	L
2-7	A_MA	Wisconsin	10-17	L
		Iowa	20-7	W
2-13	H	Notre Dame	10-17	L
2-14	A_CO	Ohio State	9-18	L
		Indiana	16-11	W
2-27	A	Illinois	10-17	L
2-28	A_EV	Northwestern	17-10	W
		Chicago	14-13	W
		Big Tens at East Lansing	3rd	

1954 (2-9)
Coach: Charles R. Schmitter

1-16	A_DE	Detroit	13-14	L
		Wayne	11-16	L
1-23	H	Northwestern	10-17	L
2-5	H	Illinois	6-21	L
2-13	H	Ohio State	7-20	L
		Buffalo	9-18	L
2-20	H	Wisconsin	10-17	L
		Iowa	14-13	W
2-26	A	Notre Dame	10-17	L
2-27	A_CH	Chicago	18-9	W
		Iowa	12-15	L
		Big Tens at Columbus	6th	

1955 (3-9)
Coach: Charles R. Schmitter

1-15	A_IC	Iowa	14-13	W
		Notre Dame	9-18	L
1-22	A	Ohio State	12-15	L
1-29	H	Detroit	10-17	L
		Chicago	15-12	W
2-5	H	Wayne	12-15	L
2-11	H	Ohio State	11-16	L
		Buffalo	13-14	L
2-25	A_EV	Northwestern	13-14	L
		Illinois	10-17	L
2-26	A_MA	Wisconsin	14-13	W
		Iowa	11-16	L
		Big Tens at Minneapolis	3rd	

1956 (3-5)
Coach: Charles R. Schmitter

1-21	A	Detroit	12-15	L
2-4	A_CH	Illinois	8-19	L
		Chicago	19-8	W
2-11	A_IC	Iowa	9-18	L
		Wisconsin	7-20	L
2-18	A	Notre Dame	13-14	L
2-24	H	Buffalo	19-8	W
2-25	H	Wayne	16-11	W
		Big Tens at Champaign	5th	

1957 (7-3)
Coach: Charles R. Schmitter

1-19	H	Detroit	14-13	W
2-1	H	Buffalo	14-13	W
2-2	A	Wayne State	17-10	W
2-9	A_CH	Chicago	16-11	W
		Illinois	15-12	W
2-16	A_MA	Wisconsin	11-16	L
		Iowa	16-11	W
2-23	H	Notre Dame	12-15	L
		Ohio State	10-17	L
3-2	A	Indiana	15-12	W
		Big Tens at Ann Arbor	4th	

1958 (5-5)
Coach: Charles R. Schmitter

1-11	H	Indiana	14-7	W
1-18	H	Wayne State	12-15	L
1-25	A	Detroit	14-13	W
2-1	H	Illinois	15-12	W
		Chicago	18-9	W
2-15	H	Iowa	21-6	W
		Wisconsin	9-18	L
2-20	A	Buffalo	13-14	L
2-22	A_CO	Notre Dame	11-16	L
		Ohio State	13-14	L
		Big Tens at Iowa City	4th	

1959 (3-8)
Coach: Charles R. Schmitter

1-23	H	Detroit	12-15	L
1-30	H	Buffalo	12-15	L
2-7	A_CH	Chicago	16-11	W
		Illinois	7-20	L
2-14	A_IC	Iowa	13-14	L
		Wisconsin	11-16	L
2-21	A_ND	Notre Dame	7-20	L
		Ohio State	9-18	L
2-28	A_DE	Wayne State	10-17	L
		Case Tech	14-13	W
		Indiana	17-10	W
		Big Tens at Bloomington	3rd	

1960 (2-8)
Coach: Charles R. Schmitter

1-23	A	Detroit	13-14	L
1-30	A_ND	Notre Dame	8-19	L
		Air Force	8-19	L
2-6	A_CH	Chicago	19-8	W
		Illinois	12-15	L
2-13	A_MA	Wisconsin	14-13	W
		Iowa	8-19	L
2-20	H	Notre Dame	11-16	L
		Ohio State	13-14	L
2-27	H	Wayne State	11-16	L
		Big Tens at Minneapolis	T4th	

1961 (4-5)
Coach: Charles R. Schmitter

1-21	H	Detroit	13-14	L
2-4	H	Illinois	6-21	L
		Chicago	17-10	W
2-11	H	Iowa	17-10	W
		Wisconsin	12-15	L
2-18	A_CO	Ohio State	12-15	L
		Notre Dame	14-13	W
2-25	A_BL	Indiana	18-9	W
		Wayne State	12-15	L
		Big Tens at Ann Arbor	4th	

1962 (6-6)
Coach: Charles R. Schmitter

1-13	A_DE	Wayne State	10-17	L
		Air Force	4-23	L
2-3	A_CU	Illinois	9-18	L
		Chicago	17-10	W
		Iowa State	18-9	W
2-10	A_IC	Iowa	16-11	W
		Wisconsin	14-13	W
2-17	A_ND	Notre Dame	10-17	L
		Ohio State	14-13	W
2-24	H	Indiana	18-9	W
		Detroit	11-16	L
		Wayne State	12-15	L
		Big Tens at Columbus	2nd	

1963 (7-3)
Coach: Charles R. Schmitter

2-2	A_CH	Chicago	19-8	W
		Illinois	10-17	L
2-9	A_MA	Wisconsin	20-7	W
		Iowa	15-12	W
2-16	H	Ohio State	15-12	W
		Air Force	8-19	L
		Notre Dame	17-10	W
2-23	A_DE	Detroit	13-14	L
		Indiana	19-8	W
		Wayne State	14-13	W
		Big Tens at East Lansing	1st	

1964 (7-4)
Coach: Charles R. Schmitter

2-1	A_CD	Air Force Acad.	%14-13	L
		Wisconsin	%15-12	L
2-8	H	Chicago	15-12	W
		Wayne State	18-9	W
		Illinois	13-14	L
2-15	H	Iowa	15-12	W
		Wisconsin	18-9	W
2-22	A_CO	Ohio State	16-11	W
		Notre Dame	9-18	L
2-29	A_DE	Indiana	16-11	W
		Detroit	14-13	W
		Big Tens at Madison	2nd	

% These two wins were later forfeited when it was disclosed two of the Spartans competitors were ineligible.

1965 (7-5)
Coach: Charles R. Schmitter

1-30	A_DE	Wayne State	16-11	W
		Fenn	19-8	W
2-6	A_CU	Illinois	4-23	L
		Chicago	17-10	W
2-12	A_IC	Kansas	17-10	W
		Air Force	5-22	L
2-13	A_IC	Iowa	13-14	L
		Wisconsin	18-9	W
2-20	A_ND	Notre Dame	11-16	L
		Ohio State	14-13	W
2-27	H	Indiana	19-8	W
		Detroit	13-14	L
		Big Tens at Champaign	6th	

1966 (9-4)
Coach: Charles R. Schmitter

1-20	H	Wayne State	12-15	L
1-22	A	Illinois-Chicago	16-11	W
2-5	A_CH	Chicago	17-10	W
		Illinois	11-16	L
		Air Force	7-20	L
2-12	A_MA	Wisconsin	15-12	W
		Iowa	15-11	W
		Kansas	19-8	W
2-17	A	Wayne State	11-16	L
2-19	H	Ohio State	14-13	W
		Notre Dame	14-13	W
2-26	A_DE	Detroit	16-11	W
		Indiana	24-3	W
		Big Tens at Bloomington	3rd	

1967 (4-8)
Coach: Charles R. Schmitter

1-14	A_CH	Illinois-Chicago	14-13	W
1-19	A_DE	Iowa State	19-8	W
2-4	H	Illinois	12-15	L
2-10	H	Wayne State	10-17	L
		Chicago	16-11	W
2-11	H	Iowa	13-14	L
		Wisconsin	10-17	L
		Air Force	8-19	L
2-18	A_CO	Ohio State	7-20	L
		Notre Dame	6-21	L
2-25	A_BL	Indiana	17-10	W
		Detroit	10-17	L
		Big Tens at Madison	3rd	

1968 (6-8)
Coach: Charles R. Schmitter

1-20	H	Oakland	20-7	W
1-27	A_DV	Air Force	6-21	L
2-3	A_CH	Illinois	10-17	L
		Chicago	18-9	W
2-9	A	Wisconsin	14-13	W
2-10	A_IC	Iowa	12-15	L
		Kansas	17-10	W
2-17	A_ND	Notre Dame	6-21	L
		Duke	14-13	W
		Ohio State	9-18	L
2-22	A	Wayne State	11-16	L
2-24	A_CH	Illinois-Chicago	15-12	W
		Detroit	12-15	L
2-29	H	Wayne State	9-18	L
		Big Tens at Champaign	5th	

1969 (6-8)
Coach: Charles R. Schmitter

1-24	A	Minnesota	18-9	W
1-25	A_MN	St. Thomas	21-6	W
		Iowa State	16-11	W
1-31	A	Chicago	15-12	W
2-1	A_CH	Illinois	10-17	L
		Air Force	9-18	L
2-5	H	Wayne State	10-17	L
2-8	A_MA	Wisconsin	10-16	L
		Iowa	12-15	L
		Indiana Tech	19-8	W
2-15	H	Ohio State	9-18	L
		Notre Dame	4-23	L
2-22	A_DE	Detroit	12-15	L
		Illinois-Chicago	21-6	W
		Big Tens at East Lansing	4th	

1970 (6-7)

Coach: Charles R. Schmitter

1-31	H	Indiana	18-9	W
2-7	H	Illinois	8-19	L
		Chicago	15-12	W
		Lake Superior	24-3	W
2-14	H	Minnesota	21-5	W
		Wisconsin	12-15	L
2-18	A	Wayne State	9-18	L
2-21	A$_{CO}$	Ohio State	10-17	L
		Notre Dame	8-19	L
2-28	A$_{CH}$	Illinois-Chicago	13-14	L
		Detroit	13-14	L
		Milwaukee Tech	19-8	W
		Wisconsin-Parkside	14-13	W
		Big Tens at Columbus	4th	

1971 (9-6)

Coach: Charles R. Schmitter

1-15	A$_{CR}$	Purdue	19-8	W
	A$_{CR}$	Tri-State	18-9	W
1-23	A$_{SU}$	Lake Superior	21-6	W
		Milwaukee Tech	14-13	W
1-30	H	Detroit	11-16	L
2-6	H$_{CU}$	Illinois	12-15	L
		Chicago	21-6	W
2-13	A$_{KE}$	Wisconsin-Parkside	14-13	W
		Wisconsin	7-20	L
2-17	H	Wayne State	14-13	W
2-20	A$_{ND}$	Notre Dame	7-20	L
		Ohio State	10-17	L
		Indiana	18-9	W
2-27	H	Detroit	12-15	L
		Illinois-Chicago	14-13	W
		Big Tens at Champaign	1st	

1972 (9-6)

Coach: Charles R. Schmitter

1-15	A$_{CR}$	Tri-State	20-7	W
		Indiana	19-8	W
		Purdue	21-6	W
1-20	H	Cornell	10-17	L
1-22	H	Lake Superior	19-8	W
		Milwaukee Tech	16-11	W
2-5	A$_{CH}$	Chicago	24-3	W
		Illinois	10-17	L
2-12	A$_{MA}$	Wisconsin	15-12	W
		Wisconsin-Parkside	15-12	W
2-19	H	Notre Dame	9-18	L
		Ohio State	10-17	L
2-26	A$_{DE}$	Detroit	10-17	L
		Wayne State	9-18	L
		Illinois-Chicago	16-11	W
		Big Tens at Madison	4th	

1973 (11-6)

Coach: Charles R. Schmitter

1-19	A$_{MI}$	Air Force	16-11	W
1-20	A$_{MI}$	Milwaukee Tech	21-6	W
		Lake Superior	22-5	W
1-27	A$_{AG}$	Purdue	25-2	W
		Indiana	20-7	W
		Oberlin	17-10	W
2-3	H	Chicago	21-6	W
		Illinois	10-17	L
		Tri-State	16-11	W
2-10	H	Wisconsin	14-13	W
		Wisconsin-Parkside	15-12	W
2-17	A$_{CO}$	Ohio State	5-22	L
		Notre Dame	9-18	L
2-24	H	Wayne State	6-21	L
		Illinois-Chicago	19-8	W
		Wayne State	6-21	L
		Detroit	5-22	L
		Big Tens at East Lansing	4th	

1974 (8-8)

Coach: Charles R. Schmitter

1-15	A$_{DE}$	Wayne State	4-23	L
		Windsor	17-10	W
1-19	H	Tri-State	14-13	W
		Milwaukee Tech	21-6	W
2-2	A$_{CH}$	Chicago	20-7	W
		Illinois	9-18	L
2-9	A$_{KE}$	Wisconsin-Parkside	12-15	L
		Wisconsin	11-16	L
		Purdue	17-10	W
		Minnesota	19-8	W
2-16	A$_{ND}$	Notre Dame	10-17	L
		Ohio State	9-18	L
		Cleveland State	13-14	L
2-23	H	Illinois-Chicago	12-15	L
		Detroit	14-13	W
		Indiana	15-12	W
		Big Tens at Columbus	4th	

1975 (10-6)

Coach: Charles R. Schmitter

1-11	H	Lake Superior	24-3	W
		UM-Dearborn	24-3	W
1-17	A$_{AG}$	Johns Hopkins	8-19	L
1-18	A$_{AG}$	Tri-State	18-9	W
		Indiana	20-7	W
2-1	A$_{CH}$	Chicago	24-3	W
		Illinois	10-17	L
		Milwaukee Tech	23-4	W
2-8	A$_{MA}$	Wisconsin	14-13	W
		Wisconsin-Parkside	20-7	W
		Air Force	10-17	L
2-15	H	Notre Dame	7-20	L
		Ohio State	8-19	L
2-22	A$_{DE}$	Detroit	17-10	W
		Wayne State	9-18	L
		Tri-State	16-11	W
		Big Tens at Champaign	5th	

1976 (15-5)

Coach: Charles R. Schmitter

1-10	H	UM-Dearborn	20-7	W
		Cleveland State	20-7	W
		Lake Superior	25-2	W
1-16	A$_{MI}$	Milwaukee Tech	22-5	W
		Illinois-Chicago	19-8	W
		Northwestern	19-8	W
		Winnipeg (Manitoba)	20-7	W
1-24	A$_{DE}$	Wayne State	5-22	L
		Bowling Green	25-2	W
		Windsor	21-6	W
1-28	A$_{NY}$	Baruch College	15-12	W
		New York University	5-22	L
2-7	H	Chicago	24-3	W
		Illinois	15-12	W
2-14	H	Wisconsin-Parkside	18-9	W
		Wisconsin	9-18	L
2-21	A$_{CO}$	Ohio State	12-15	L
		Notre Dame	6-21	L
2-28	A$_{AG}$	Tri-State	23-4	W
		Detroit	17-10	W
		Big Tens at Madison	3rd	

1977 (11-5)

Coach: Charles R. Schmitter

1-22	H	Lake Superior	21-6	W
		UM-Dearborn	17-10	W
		Milwaukee Tech	16-11	W
2-5	A$_{CH}$	Illinois	12-15	L
		Illinois-Chicago	18-9	W
		Indiana State	22-5	W
		Purdue	21-6	W
2-12	A$_{KE}$	Wisconsin-Parkside	17-10	W
		Wisconsin	3-24	L
		Northwestern	16-11	W
2-19	H	Notre Dame	9-18	L

(1977 continued, right column top)

		Ohio State	13-14	L
		Illinois-Chicago	16-11	W
2-26	H	Detroit	17-10	W
		Wayne State	6-21	L
		Tri-State	19-8	W
		Big Tens at East Lansing	4th	

1978 (7-7)

Coach: Charles R. Schmitter

1-14	H	UM-Dearborn	13-14	L
		Lake Superior	23-4	W
		Purdue	16-11	W
2-3	A	Northwestern	17-10	W
2-4	A$_{CH}$	Chicago	16-11	W
		Illinois	9-18	L
		Winnipeg (Manitoba)	14-13	W
2-11	A$_{MA}$	Wisconsin	9-18	L
		Wisconsin-Parkside	18-9	W
2-18	H	Ohio State	7-20	L
		Notre Dame	3-24	L
2-25	A$_{DE}$	Detroit	13-14	L
		Wayne State	7-20	L
		Tri-State	20-7	W
		Big Tens at Columbus	4th	

1979 (3-7)

Coach: Charles R. Schmitter

1-12	A	UM-Dearborn	11-16	L
2-3	H	Chicago	12-15	L
		Illinois	8-19	L
2-10	H	Wisconsin-Parkside	19-8	W
		Wisconsin	7-20	L
2-17	A$_{CO}$	Ohio State	10-17	L
		Penn State	7-20	L
		Notre Dame	8-19	L
2-24	A$_{AG}$	Tri-State	24-3	W
		Detroit	14-13	W
		Big Tens at Champaign	5th	

1980 (9-7)

Coach: Charles R. Schmitter

1-19	H	Windsor	17-10	W
		UM-Dearborn	13-14	L
1-19	H	Wayne State	8-19	L
2-2	A$_{CH}$	Illinois	9-18	L
		Chicago	16-11	W
		Milwaukee Tech	18-9	W
2-9	A$_{KE}$	Wisconsin-Parkside	18-9	W
		Wisconsin	10-17	L
		Northwestern	14-13	L
		Lawrence (WI)	15-1	W
2-16	A$_{ND}$	Notre Dame	8-19	L
		Ohio State	9-18	L
		Purdue	17-10	W
2-23	H	Detroit	17-10	W
		Tri-State	21-6	W
		Illinois-Chicago	22-5	W
		Big Tens at Madison	4th	

1981 (5-10)

Coach: Charles R. Schmitter

1-17	A$_{DE}$	Wayne State	4-23	L
		UM-Dearborn	13-14	L
		Bowling Green	18-9	W
		Windsor	11-16	L
1-24	A$_{MA}$	Wisconsin	8-19	L
		Wisconsin-Parkside	16-11	W
		Northwestern	6-21	L
		Milwaukee Tech	13-14	L
2-7	A$_{CH}$	Chicago	15-12	W
		Illinois	6-21	L
		Purdue	18-9	W
2-21	H	Ohio State	8-19	L
		Notre Dame	4-23	L
2-28	A$_{DE}$	Detroit	12-15	L
		Tri-State	21-6	W
		Big Tens at Evanston	5th	

1981-1982 (6-5)

Coach: Charles R. Schmitter

12-5	A$_{DE}$	Michigan Inter.	NTS	
1-16	A$_{CO}$	Ohio State	N/A	
		Bowling Green	N/A	
		Clemson	N/A	
		Purdue	N/A	
1-23	H	Chicago	15-12	W
		Illinois	7-20	L
2-6	H	UM-Dearborn	15-12	W
		Wisconsin	8-19	L
		Wisconsin-Parkside	20-7	W
		Northwestern	12-15	L
2-20	A	Notre Dame	5-22	L
2-27	A$_{AG}$	Tri-State	14-13	W
		Detroit	18-9	W
		Case-Western	16-11	W
		UM-Dearborn	13-14	L
		Big Tens at East Lansing	6th/6	

1983 (6-7)

Coach: Charles R. Schmitter

1-22	H	Notre Dame	1-26	L
		Northwestern	4-23	L
2-5	A$_{CH}$	Illinois-Chicago	22-5	W
		Chicago	21-6	W
		Illinois	3-24	L
2-12	A$_{KE}$	Wisconsin-Parkside	18-9	W
		Wisconsin	6-21	L
		Minnesota	12-15	L
2-25	A	Wayne	3-24	L
2-26	H	Detroit	18-9	W
		Tri-State	14-13	W
		Case W. Reserve	16-11	W
		UM-Dearborn	13-14	L
		Big Tens at Columbus	5th	

Fred Freiheit (1984-1997)

In April of 1983, Fred E. Freiheit, a Big Ten fencing champion as an MSU undergraduate, succeeded Charlie Schmitter and became the school's sixth and final fencing coach. Freiheit earned a degree in mechanical engineering in 1952 and continued his fencing beyond college competition until 1959. He was a U.S. National finalist in sabre in 1952 and captured the Midwest foil championship in 1957. He also received an M.A. degree from State in 1958. Fred served the university's physics department as a part-time data base manager and also did some engineering consulting work. Earlier he had been an instructor in the school's mechanical engineering department. Freiheit has also held positions with several Michigan manufacturing firms. He would coach until 1997 when the sport was dropped from the intercollegiate program.

1984 (12-12)

Coach: Fred Freiheit

1-7	H	Ohio State	9-18	L
		Michigan	22-10	W
1-14	A	Wayne	3-24	L
1-21	A$_{EV}$	Northwestern	12-15	L
		Notre Dame	2-25	L
		Wisconsin	7-20	L
		Minnesota	14-13	W
		Illinois	7-20	L
		Chicago	23-4	W
2-4	A$_{CH}$	Chicago	16-11	W
		Illinois	4-23	L
		Purdue	14-13	W
2-11	A$_{MA}$	Wisconsin	3-24	L
		Wisconsin-Parkside	18-9	W
		Minnesota	15-12	W
2-18	A$_{CV}$	Cleveland State	12-15	L
		Purdue	18-9	W
		Case W. Reserve	19-8	W
		Cornell	9-18	L
		Bowling Green	18-9	W

		Oberlin	26-1	W
2-25	A$_{DB}$	UM-Dearborn	17-10	W
		Tri-State	9-18	L
		Detroit	9-18	L
		Big Tens at Madison	5th	

1985 (7-13)

Coach: Fred Freihert

1-5	A$_{CO}$	Ohio State	11-16	L
		Tri-State	18-9	W
1-12	A$_{DB}$	UM-Dearborn	17-10	W
		Detroit	12-15	L
1-19	A$_{RC}$	Oakland	8-19	L
		Wayne State	2-25	L
2-2	H	Illinois	3-24	L
		Chicago	7-20	L
		UM-Dearborn	8-19	L
		Michigan	22-5	W
2-9	H	Wisconsin	3-24	L
		Northwestern	10-17	L
2-16	A$_{CU}$	Illinois	4-23	L
		Purdue	16-11	W
		Oklahoma City	25-2	W
2-22	A	Notre Dame	8-19	L
2-23	A$_{AG}$	Tri-State	13-14	L
		Detroit	11-16	L
		Bowling Green	25-2	W
		UM-Dearborn	14-13	W
		Big Tens at Evanston	5th	

1985-1986 (12-14)

Coach: Fred Freihert

12-7	A$_{DB}$	Michigan Collegiate	NTS	
1-4	A$_{DB}$	UM-Dearborn	15-12	W
		Windsor (Ontario)	11-16	L
		Eastern Michigan	17-10	W
1-11	A$_{CV}$	Cleveland State	10-17	L
		UM-Dearborn	15-12	W
		Eastern Michigan	17-10	W
1-25	A$_{AG}$	Tri-State	19-8	W
		Michigan	21-6	W
		Cleveland State	10-17	L
		Purdue	11-16	L
		Northwestern	9-18	L
1-29	A	Detroit	13-14	L
2-1	A$_{MA}$	Wisconsin	8-19	L
		Ohio State	2-25	L
		Minnesota	14-13	W
		Lawrence (WI)	23-4	W
2-8	A$_{DE}$	Wayne State	8-19	L
		Detroit	13-14	L
		Chicago	13-14	L
2-12	H	Detroit	15-12	W
2-22	H$_{ND}$	Notre Dame	4-23	L
		Illinois	1-26	L
		Michigan	18-9	W
		Eastern Michigan	18-9	W
		Wayne State	8-19	L
		Oakland	15-12	W
		Big Tens at Madison	5th%	

% Beginning in 1986-1987, only five conference schools would still sponsor a varsity-team. Consequently, this would be the final official Big Ten sponsored championship meet.

1986-1987 (10-11)

Coach: Fred Freihert

12-6	H	Michigan Inter.	NTS	
1-24	A$_{EV}$	Northwestern	10-17	L
		Cleveland State	13-14	L
		Tri-State	14-13	W
		Purdue	15-12	W
		Eastern Michigan	14-13	W
		Case W. Reserve	16-11	W
1-31	A$_{CO}$	Ohio State	11-16	L

		Wisconsin	10-17	L
		Air Force	5-22	L
		Bowling Green	22-5	W
2-7	H	Detroit	12-15	L
		Chicago	8-19	L
		Wayne State	7-20	L
		UM-Dearborn	12-15	L
		Eastern Michigan	20-7	W
2-14	A$_{RC}$	Oakland	15-12	W
		Michigan	21-6	W
		Illinois	3-24	L
2-21	A$_{ND}$	Notre Dame	3-24	L
		Case W. Reserve	18-9	W
		Cleveland State	19-8	W
3-7	A$_{DB}$	Midwest Regional	NTS	

1987-1988 (10-12)

Coach: Fred Freihert

1-9	H	Ohio State	13-14	L
		Oakland	15-12	W
		UM-Dearborn	15-12	W
		Michigan	23-4	W
		Eastern Michigan	17-10	W
1-17	A$_{CO}$	U.S. Fencing Assoc.	NTS	
1-23	H	Northwestern	9-18	L
		Cleveland state	17-10	W
		Tri-State	23-4	W
		Michigan	13-14	L
		Eastern Michigan	16-11	W
1-30	A$_{CO}$	Ohio State	11-16	L
		Wisconsin	9-18	L
		Bowling Green	22-5	W
		Air Force	5-22	L
2-6	A$_{CV}$	Cleveland State	12-15	L
		Case Western	15-12	W
		Chicago	11-16	L
2-13	A	Detroit	9-19	L
		Wayne State	11-16	L
2-20	A$_{CU}$	Illinois	4-23	L
		Notre Dame	5-22	L
		Purdue	17-10	W
3-5	A$_{EV}$	Midwest Regional	NTS	

1988-1989 (12-10)

Coach: Fred Freihert

1-14	A$_{DB}$	UM-Dearborn	16-11	W
		Eastern Michigan	20-7	W
		Oakland	15-12	W
		Michigan	14-13	W
		Detroit	10-17	L
1-21	A$_{CV}$	Cleveland State	12-15	L
		Tri-State	15-12	W
		Case W. Reserve	14-13	W
		Northwestern	8-19	L
2-4	A$_{MA}$	Wisconsin	10-17	L
		Ohio State	8-19	L
		Case W. Reserve	19-8	W
		Lawrence	15-12	W
2-11	A$_{YP}$	Wayne State	11-16	L
		Chicago	10-17	L
		Michigan	16-11	W
		Detroit	7-20	L
2-25	H	Purdue	15-12	W
		Michigan	20-7	W
		Eastern Michigan	15-12	W
		Notre Dame	5-22	L
		Illinois	3-24	L
3-4	A$_{CO}$	Midwest Regional	5th/8	

1989-1990 (13-5)
Coach: Fred Freihert

1-13		Vanderbilt	22-5	W
		Tri-State	22-5	W
		Cleveland State	13-14	L
		Purdue	21-6	W
		Northwestern	12-15	L
1-20	A_AA	Michigan	16-11	W
		Case W. Reserve	18-9	W
		Detroit	14-13	W
		UM-Dearborn	16-11	W
		Wayne State	20-7	W
		Oakland	18-9	W
2-3	A_CO	Oberlin	25-2	W
		Miami (OH)	23-4	W
		N. Carolina State	16-11	W
		Ohio State	11-16	L
		Wisconsin	7-20	L
2-10	H	Michigan	18-9	W
		Eastern Michigan	17-10	W
		Oakland	17-10	W
		Wayne State	9-18	L
		Detroit	13-14	L
2-24	A_ND	Notre Dame	7-20	L
		Illinois	1-17	L
		Lawrence (WI)	17-10	W
3-10	A_DE	Midwest Regional	NTS	

1990-1991 (11-12)
Coach: Fred Freihert

10-31	A	Penn State Open	NTS	
11-7	H	Michigan Collegiate Open	NTS	
1-12	A_CO	Ohio State	6-21	L
		Illinois	2-25	L
		Miami (OH)	17-10	W
		Purdue	17-10	W
		Michigan	14-13	W
2-1	A_DE	Detroit	17-10	W
		Wayne State	3-24	L
		Michigan	9-18	L
		Purdue	16-11	W
2-2	A_AG	Tri-State	14-13	W
		Vanderbilt	16-11	W
		Purdue	18-9	W
		Cleveland State	10-17	L
		Eastern Michigan	13-14	L
		Northwestern	7-20	L
2-7	A_DE	Detroit	10-17	L
		Wayne State	6-21	L
		Eastern Michigan	17-10	W
		Michigan	13-14	L
2-23	A_CU	Illinois	3-24	L
		Notre Dame	5-22	L
		Vanderbilt	16-11	W
		Purdue	21-5	W
3-8		Midwest Regional	NTS	

1991-1992 (4-13)
Coach: Fred Freihert

1-25	A_AA	Ohio State	1-26	L
		Tri-State	16-11	W
		Case W. Reserve	19-8	W
		Cleveland State	19-8	W
2-1	A_DE	Wayne State	3-24	L
		Detroit	12-15	L
		Michigan	8-19	L
		Purdue	16-11	W
2-8	A_CU	Illinois	3-24	L
		Chicago	8-19	L
		Notre Dame	2-25	L
		Northwestern	7-20	L
		Lawrence	16-11	W
2-22	H	Illinois	5-22	L
		Cleveland State	11-16	L
		Detroit	13-14	L
		Wayne State	3-24	L
3-7	A	Midwest Regional	NTS	

1992-1993 (13-10)
Coach: Fred Freihert

12-5	H	Mich. Collegiate Open	NTS	
1-16	A_EV	Notre Dame	6-21	L
		Air Force	8-19	L
		Chicago	13-14	L
		Illinois	4-23	L
		Cal-San Diego	16-11	W
		Tri-State	18-9	W
		Lawrence (WI)	21-6	W
1-23	A_CV	Cleveland State	22-5	W
		Case W. Reserve	20-7	W
		Tri-State	20-7	W
		Ohio State	8-19	L
1-30	A_CO	Ohio State	7-20	L
		Illinois	7-20	L
		Tri-State	21-6	W
		Case W. Reserve	18-9	W
2-6	H	Purdue	24-3	W
		Michigan	17-10	W
		Detroit-Mercy	20-7	W
		Wayne State	7-20	L
2-20	A_DE	Detroit-Mercy	17-10	W
		Cleveland State	17-10	W
		Northwestern	7-20	L
		Wayne State	6-21	L
2-27	H	Midwest Regional	8th/13	
3-6		NCAA Regionals	6th	

1993-1994 (10-12)
Coach: Fred Freihert

10-13	A_EV	Remenyik Open	6th/13	
11-6	A_ND	Notre Dame	8-19	L
		Wayne State	9-18	L
		Ohio State	12-15	L
		Northwestern	11-16	L
		Cleveland State	19-8	W
		Chicago	18-9	W
11-20	A_UP	Penn State Open	NTS	
12-4	H	Michigan Open	NTS	
1-16	A_EV	Northwestern	7-20	L
		Air Force	9-18	L
		Cal.-San Diego	12-15	L
		Cal.-Long Beach	12-15	L
1-22	A_DE	Notre Dame	9-18	L
		Ohio State	7-20	L
		Cleveland State	19-8	W
		Case W. Reserve	14-13	W
		Tri-State	21-6	W
1-29	H	Tri-State	19-8	W
		Michigan	16-11	W
		Detroit-Mercy	21-6	W
		Cleveland State	17-10	W
		Wayne	11-16	L
2-12	A_EV	Northwestern	12-15	L
		Chicago	15-12	W
		Lawrence (WI)	19-8	W
		Purdue	19-8	W
3-5		Midwest Regional	NTS	

1994-1995 (15-10)
Coach: Fred Freihert

10-22	A_EV	Remenyik Open	NTS	
11-12	A	Penn State Open	NTS	
12-3	H	Michigan Open	NTS	
1-14	A_EV	Midwest Mega Meet		
		North Carolina	11-16	L
		Cornell	16-11	W
1-21	A_CO	Ohio State	7-20	L
		Tri-State	24-3	W
		Cleveland State	13-14	L
		Case W. Reserve	21-6	W
1-28	H	Detroit	15-12	W
		Michigan	15-12	W
		Wayne	9-18	L
2-11	A_DE	Lawrence (WI)	16-11	W
		Purdue	21-6	W
		Northwestern	11-16	L

		Chicago	11-15	L
2-25	A_ND	Midwest Championships		
		Chicago	14-13	W
		Lawrence (WI)	15-12	W
		Case W. Reserve	19-8	W
		Detroit	19-8	W
		Purdue	22-5	W
		Michigan	15-12	W
		Tri-State	23-4	W
		Cleveland State	15-12	W
		Notre Dame	3-24	L
		Northwestern	11-16	L
		Wayne State	9-18	L
		Ohio State	12-15	L
3-4	A_AP	Midwest Regionals	NTS	

1995-1996 (13-13-1)
Coach: Fred Freihert

1-21	A_CH	Notre Dame	6-21	L
		Cal State-Long Beach	6-11	L
		Cal State-Fullerton	13-14	L
		Chicago	14-13	W
		North Carolina	5-22	L
		Air Force	11-16	L
1-27	A_DE	Detroit-Mercy	11-11	T
		Wayne State	10-17	L
		Michigan	11-16	L
		Case W. Reserve	14-13	W
2-3	H	Cleveland State	12-10	W
		Tri-State	24-3	W
2-11	A_CH	Lawrence (WI)	14-13	W
		Purdue	23-4	W
		Ohio State	18-9	W
		Chicago	18-9	W
		Northwestern	12-15	L
2-24	A_ND	Notre Dame	9-18	L
		Northwestern	9-18	L
		Cleveland State	14-13	W
		Detroit-Mercy	18-9	W
		Purdue	20-7	W
		Ohio State	8-19	L
		Wayne State	12-15	L
		Tri-State	23-4	W
		Michigan	15-12	W
		Lawrence (WI)	20-7	W
3-9	A_CO	Midwest Regional	NTS	

1996-1997 (8-12)
Coach: Fred Freihert

10-19	A_EV	Remenyik Open	NTS	
11-16	A_UP	Penn State Open	NTS	
12-7	H	Michigan Open	NTS	
1-17	A_CV	Cal State-Fullerton	12-15	L
		Cleveland State	14-13	W
		John Hopkins	7-20	L
		North Carolina	9-18	L
1-25	H_DE	Detroit-Mercy	12-15	L
		Wayne State	11-16	L
		Michigan	12-15	L
2-1	A_CV	Cleveland State	15-12	W
		Ohio State	9-18	L
		Case W. Reserve	16-11	W
		Tri-State	24-3	W
		Notre Dame	4-23	L
		Kent State	17-10	W
2-9	A_NW	Purdue	22-5	W
		Michigan	15-12	W
		Northwestern	9-18	L
2-22	A_ND	Northwestern	9-18	L
		Purdue	23-4	W
		Lawrence (WI)	13-14	L
		Notre Dame	8-19	L
		Michigan	16-11	W
3-8	A_ND	Midwest Regional	NTS	

In a move designed for gender equity, on January 16, 1997, University officials announced that men's fencing would be dropped from varsity status following the 1996-97 seasons.

Year-by-Year Record

Year	W-L-T	Pct.	Big Ten	Coach
1926	1-0-0	1.000	—	Joseph Waffa
1927	2-2-0	.500	—	Joseph Waffa
1928	2-3-0	.400	—	Joseph Waffa
1929	4-3-0	.571	—	Joseph Waffa
1930	2-3-0	.400	—	George Kershaw
1931	1-3-0	.250	—	George Bauer
1932	5-4-0	.556	—	George Bauer
1933	4-3-0	.571	—	George Bauer
1934	5-1-0	.833	—	George Bauer
1935	6-2-0	.750	—	George Bauer
1936	8-4-0	.667	—	George Bauer
1937	2-7-0	.222	—	George Bauer
1938	6-2-1	.722	—	Thomas L. Caniff
1939	8-4-0	.667	—	Charles Schmitter
1940	14-1-0	.933	—	Charles Schmitter
1941	2-7-0	.222	—	Charles Schmitter
1942	5-2-1	.688	—	Charles Schmitter
1943	2-4-0	.333	—	Charles Schmitter
1944	Intercollegiate competition suspended due to World War II			
1945	1-1-0	.500	—	Charles Schmitter
1946	3-5-0	.375	—	Charles Schmitter
1947	5-3-0	.625	—	Charles Schmitter
1948	6-3-0	.667	—	Charles Schmitter
1949	3-5-0	.375	—	Charles Schmitter
1950	7-1-1	.833	—	Charles Schmitter
1951	7-3-0	.700	5th	Charles Schmitter
1952	8-1-0	.889	2nd	Charles Schmitter
1953	5-5-0	.500	3rd	Charles Schmitter
1954	2-9-0	.182	6th	Charles Schmitter
1955	3-9-0	.250	3rd	Charles Schmitter
1956	3-5-0	.375	5th	Charles Schmitter
1957	7-3-0	.700	4th	Charles Schmitter
1958	5-5-0	.500	4th	Charles Schmitter
1959	3-8-0	.273	3rd	Charles Schmitter
1960	2-8-0	.200	T4th	Charles Schmitter
1961	4-5-0	.444	4th	Charles Schmitter
1962	6-6-0	.500	2nd	Charles Schmitter
1963	7-3-0	.700	1st	Charles Schmitter
1964	7-4-0	.636	2nd	Charles Schmitter
1965	7-5-0	.583	6th	Charles Schmitter
1966	9-4-0	.692	3rd	Charles Schmitter
1967	4-8-0	.333	3rd	Charles Schmitter
1968	6-8-0	.429	5th	Charles Schmitter
1969	6-8-0	.429	4th	Charles Schmitter
1970	6-7-0	.462	4th	Charles Schmitter
1971	9-6-0	.600	1st	Charles Schmitter
1972	9-6-0	.600	4th	Charles Schmitter
1973	11-6-0	.647	4th	Charles Schmitter
1974	8-8-0	.500	4th	Charles Schmitter
1975	10-6-0	.625	5th	Charles Schmitter
1976	15-5-0	.750	3rd	Charles Schmitter
1977	11-5-0	.688	4th	Charles Schmitter
1978	7-7-0	.500	4th	Charles Schmitter
1979	3-7-0	.300	5th	Charles Schmitter
1980	9-7-0	.563	4th	Charles Schmitter
1981	5-10-0	.333	5th	Charles Schmitter
1982	6-5-0	.545	5th	Charles Schmitter
1983	6-7-0	.462	5th	Charles Schmitter
1984	12-12-0	.500	5th	Fred Freiheit
1985	7-13-0	.350	5th	Fred Freiheit
1986	12-14-0	.462	5th	Fred Freiheit
1987*	10-11-0	.476	—	Fred Freiheit
1988	10-12-0	.455	—	Fred Freiheit
1989	12-10-0	.545	—	Fred Freiheit
1990	13-5-0	.722	—	Fred Freiheit
1991	11-12-0	.917	—	Fred Freiheit
1992	4-13-0	.235	—	Fred Freiheit
1993	13-10-0	.565	—	Fred Freiheit
1994	10-12-0	.455	—	Fred Freiheit
1995	15-10-0	.600	—	Fred Freiheit
1996	13-13-1	.500	—	Fred Freiheit
1997**	8-12-0	.400	—	Fred Freiheit

TOTALS
1926-97 470-431-4 .522

*Beginning in the 1986-87 season, only five Big Ten schools would still sponsor a varsity team. Consequently, the final conference championship meet was held at the end of the 1985-1986 season.

In an effort to gain more acceptable gender equity numbers in the school's intercollegiate athletic program, university officials saw fit to eliminate fencing as a varsity sport with the completion of the 1997 season.

FOOTBALL
LEADERS, RECORDS and HONORS

ALL-TIME COACHING RECORDS

Coach	Years	W	L	T	Avg.
No Head Coach	1896	1	2	1	.375
Henry Keep	1897-98	8	5	1	.607
Charles O. Bemies	1899-90	3	7	1	.318
George E. Denman	1901-02	7	9	1	.441
Chester L. Brewer	1903-10	54	10	6	.814
John F. Macklin	1911-15	29	5	0	.853
Frank Sommers	1916	4	2	1	.642
Chester L. Brewer	1917	0	9	0	.000
George E. Gauthier	1918	4	3	0	.571
Chester L. Brewer	1919	4	4	1	.500
George "Potsy" Clark	1920	4	6	0	.400
Albert M. Barron	1921-22	6	10	2	.389
Ralph H. Young	1923-27	18	22	1	.451
Harry Kipke	1928	3	4	1	.438
James H. Crowley	1929-32	22	8	3	.712
Charles W. Bachman	1933-46	70	34	10	.658
Clarence "Biggie" Munn	1947-53	54	9	2	.846
Hugh "Duffy" Daugherty	1954-72	109	69	5	.609
Dennis E. Stolz	1973-75	19	13	1	.591
Darrell D. Rogers	1976-79	24	18	2	.568
Frank "Muddy" Waters	1980-82	10	23	0	.303
George Perles	1983-94	73	62	4	.540
Nick Saban	1995-99	35	24	1	.592
Bobby Williams	2000-2002	16	19	0	.457
TOTALS	1896-2002	577	377	44	.600

Season Records

1896 (1-2-1)
Coach: No Coach

9-26	H	Lansing H.S.	10-0	W
10-17	A	Kalamazoo	0-24	L
10-25	H	Alma	0-0	T
11-14	A	Alma	16-18	L

Henry Keep (1897-1898)
The manager of field days brought Henry Keep upon the scene in the spring of 1897. He had been referred by Lieutenant Harry H. Bandholtz, professor of military science and tactics, with the purpose of training men for the 1897 field day at Hillsdale. He was described as a good athlete, a good judge of men and able to inspire confidence in themselves. The achievements of that spring gave evidence. Whereas the disappointing '96 field day squad had won a mere three gold medals in track and field, the Farmers of 1897 would garner 10 first-place awards and the plaudits of their fans. With this backdrop of success, football team members were likely pleased to find that Keep had decided to return that fall as a regularly enrolled mechanical student. Upon being approached, he accepted the offer to guide the men of MAC in their second season of football.

1897 (4-2-1)
Coach: Henry Keep

9-25	H	Lansing H.S.	28-0	W
10-2	H	Olivet	26-6	W
10-9	H	Kalamazoo	0-28	L
10-16	A	Olivet	18-18	T
10-30	A	Alma	30-16	W
11-6	H	Alma	38-4	W
11-25	A	Notre Dame	6-34	L

1898 (4-3)
Coach: Henry Keep

10-8	A	Michigan Normal	11-6	W
10-12	A	Michigan	0-39	L
10-15	A	Notre Dame	0-53	L
10-22	H	Albion	62-6	W
10-29	A	Olivet	45-0	W
11-19	H	Michigan Normal	24-6	W
11-24	H	Kalamazoo	0-17	L

(1899-1900)
Coach: Charles O. Bemies
See baseball season records for Charles Bemies sketch)

1899 (2-4-1)
Coach: Charles Bemies

9-29	A	Notre Dame	0-40	L
10-7	A	Detroit Ath. Club	6-16	L
10-14	H	Kalamazoo	6-10	L
10-21	A	Alma	11-11	T
11-11	A	Michigan Normal	18-0	W
11-25	A	Olivet	17-18	L
11-30	H	DePauw	23-6	W

1900 (1-3)
Coach: Charles Bemies

9-29	H	Albion	0-23	L
10-10	H	Adrian	45-0	W
10-20	A	Detroit Ath. Club	6-21	L
10-27	H	Alma	0-23	L

George Denman (1901-1902)
(See baseball season records for George Denman sketch)

1901 (3-4-1)
Coach: George Denman

9-28	A	Alma	5-6	L
10-5	H	Hillsdale	22-0	W
10-12	A	Albion	11-0	W
10-19	A	Detroit Ath. Club	0-33	L
10-26	H	Kalamazoo	42-0	W
11-2	H	Albion	17-17	T
11-16	A	Kalamazoo	5-15	L
11-28	H	Olivet	18-23	L

1902 (4-5)
Coach: George Denman

9-27	A	Notre Dame	0-32	L
10-4	H	Detroit College	11-0	W
10-8	A	Michigan	0-119	L
10-11	H	Hillsdale	35-0	W
10-18	H	Michigan Freshmen	2-0	W
10-25	H	DePauw	12-17	L
11-1	H	Olivet	6-11	L
11-15	A	Albion	22-11	W
11-22	H	Alma	5-16	L

Coach: Chester L. Brewer
(1903-10, 1917 and 1919)
(See baseball season records for Chester Brewer sketch)

1903 (6-1-1)
Coach: Chester L. Brewer

10-3	A	Notre Dame	0-12	L
10-10	A	Alma	11-0	W
10-14	H	Michigan Freshmen	11-0	W
10-17	H	Kalamazoo	11-0	W
10-31	H	Detroit YMCA	51-6	W
11-7	H	Hillsdale	43-0	W
11-14	H	Albion	6-6	T
11-21	H	Olivet	45-0	W

1904 (8-1)
Coach: Chester L. Brewer

10-1	H	Mich. Sch. for Deaf	47-0	W
10-8	H	Ohio Northern	28-6	W
10-15	H	Pt. Huron YMCA	29-0	W
10-22	A	Albion	0-4	L
10-29	H	Hillsdale	104-0	W
11-5	H	Michigan Freshmen	39-0	W
11-12	A	Olivet	35-6	W
11-19	A	Alma	40-0	W
11-26	H	Kalamazoo	58-0	W

1905 (9-2)
Coach: Chester L. Brewer

9-30	H	Mich. Sch. for Deaf	42-0	W
10-3	A	Notre Dame	0-28	L
10-7	H	Pt. Huron YMCA	43-0	W
10-14	H	Michigan Freshmen	24-0	W
10-21	H	Olivet	30-0	W
10-23	H	Hillsdale	18-0	W
10-28	H	Armour Institute	18-0	W
11-4	A	Kalamazoo	30-0	W
11-11	H	Albion	46-10	W
11-18	A	Northwestern	11-37	L
11-25	A	Alma	18-0	W

1906 (7-2-2)
Coach: Chester L. Brewer

9-29	H	Olivet	23-4	W
10-6	A	Alma	0-0	T
10-13	H	Kalamazoo	38-0	W
10-20	H	DePauw	33-0	W
10-27	A	Notre Dame	0-5	L
11-3	H	Albion	37-0	W
11-10	H	Albion	5-0	W
11-12	H	Alma	12-0	W
11-17	A	Hillsdale	35-9	W
11-24	A	Olivet	6-8	L
11-29	A	Detroit Ath. Club	6-6	T

1907 (4-2-1)
Coach: Chester L. Brewer

10-3	H	Detroit Medical Coll.	17-0	W
10-5	H	Mich. Sch. for Deaf	40-0	W
10-12	A	Michigan	0-46	L
10-26	H	Wabash	15-6	W
11-16	H	Olivet	55-4	W
11-23	A	Alma	0-0	T
11-28	A	Detroit Ath. Club	0-4	L

1908 (6-0-2)
Coach: Chester L. Brewer

10-3	H	Michigan 0-0	T
10-10	H	Western State 35-0	W
10-17	H	Mich. Sch. for Deaf 51-0	W
10-24	A	DePauw 0-0	T
10-31	H	Wabash 6-0	W
11-7	A	Olivet 46-2	W
11-21	H	Saginaw Naval Brigade 30-6	W
11-26	A	Detroit Ath. Club 37-14	W

1909 (8-1)
Coach: Chester L. Brewer

10-7	H	Detroit 27-0	W
10-9	H	Alma 34-0	W
10-16	H	Wabash 28-0	W
10-23	A	Notre Dame 0-17	L
10-30	A	Culver Military Acad. 29-0	W
11-6	H	DePauw 51-0	W
11-10	H	Marquette 10-0	W
11-13	H	Olivet 20-0	W
11-25	A	Detroit Ath. Club 34-0	W

1910 (6-1)
Coach: Chester L. Brewer

10-6	H	Detroit College 35-0	W
10-8	H	Alma 11-0	W
10-15	A	Michigan 3-6	L
10-22	H	Lake Forest 37-0	W
10-29	H	Notre Dame 17-0	W
11-5	A	Marquette 3-2	W
11-19	H	Olivet 62-0	W

John F. Macklin (1911-1915)
(See baseball season records for John Macklin sketch)

1911 (5-1)
Coach: John F. Macklin

10-7	H	Alma 12-0	W
10-14	H	Michigan 3-15	L
10-28	H	Olivet 29-3	W
11-4	A	DePauw 6-0	W
11-11	H	Mt. Union 26-6	W
11-30	H	Wabash 17-6	W

1912 (7-1)
Coach: John F. Macklin

10-5	H	Alma 14-3	W
10-12	A	Michigan 7-55	L
10-19	H	Olivet 52-0	W
10-26	H	DePauw 58-0	W
11-2	H	Ohio Wesleyan 46-0	W
11-9	H	Mt. Union 61-20	W
11-16	H	Wabash 24-0	W
11-28	A	Ohio State 35-20	W

1913   (7-0)
Coach: John F. Macklin

10-4	H	Olivet 26-0	W
10-11	H	Alma 57-0	W
10-18	A	Michigan 12-7	W
10-25	A	Wisconsin 12-7	W
11-1	H	Akron 41-0	W
11-8	H	Mt. Union 13-7	W
11-15	H	South Dakota 19-7	W

1914 (5-2)
Coach: John F. Macklin

10-3	H	Olivet 35-7	W
10-10	H	Alma 60-0	W
10-17	H	Michigan 0-3	L
10-24	A	Nebraska 0-24	L

10-31	H	Akron 75-6	W
11-7	H	Mt. Union 21-14	W
11-13	A	Penn State 6-3	W

1915 (5-1)
Coach: John F. Macklin

10-2	H	Olivet 34-0	W
10-9	H	Alma 77-12	W
10-16	H	Carroll (WI) 56-0	W
10-23	A	Michigan 24-0	W
10-30	H	Oregon State 0-20	L
11-6	H	Marquette 68-6	W

Frank Sommer (1916)

Nine days following receipt of the Macklin resignation letter, it was announced that the Villanova head man, Frank Sommers, would handle the 1916 Aggie team at a one-year fixed salary of $2,500. Prior to the 1915 season at Villanova, Sommers, a 1910 graduate of the University of Pennsylvania, had been head coach for three successful years at Colgate and one at Mercersburg Academy. He was signed after being highly recommended by John Macklin. In early preseason drills, Coach Sommers received "good press," but perhaps the early analysis was premature. Even with a respectable 4-2-1 season record in 1916, backing for Sommers rapidly deteriorated. Supposedly fans had taken a disliking to him because of his method of "bawling out" players in front of the grandstand. Also, it was suggested he was not able to marshal his men for the big games, and, furthermore, there appeared to be friction between the coach and his players. Head man for one year, his contract was not renewed and Frank Sommers returned to Pennsylvania.

1916 (4-2-1)
Coach: Frank Sommers

9-30	H	Olivet 40-0	W
10-7	H	Carroll 20-0	W
10-14	H	Alma 33-0	W
10-21	A	Michigan 0-9	L
10-28	H.	North Dakota State 30-0	W
11-4	A	South Dakota 3-3	T
11-18	H	Notre Dame 0-14	L

1917 (0-9)
Coach: Chester Brewer

10-6	H	Alma 7-14	L
10-13	H	Kalamazoo 3-7	L
10-20	A	Michigan 0-27	L
10-27	H	Detroit 0-14	L
11-3	H	Western St. Normal 0-14	L
11-10	A	Northwestern 6-39	L
11-17	A	Notre Dame 0-23	L
11-24	H	Syracuse 7-21	L
11-29	H	Camp McArthur (TX) 0-20	L

George Gauthier (1918)
See cross country season records for George Gauthier sketch)

1918 (4-3)
Coach: George Gauthier

10-5	H	Albion 21-6	W
10-12	H	Hillsdale 66-6	W
11-2	W	Western State 16-7	W
11-9	H	Purdue 6-14	L
11-16	H	Notre Dame 13-7	W
11-23	A	Michigan 6-21	L
11-28	A	Wisconsin 6-7	L

1919 (4-4-1)
Coach: Chester L. Brewer

10-4	H	Albion 14-13	W
10-8	H	Alma 46-6	W
10-11	H	Western State 18-21	L
10-18	A	Michigan 0-26	L
10-25	H	DePauw 27-0	W
11-1	A	Purdue 7-13	L
11-8	H	South Dakota 13-0	W
11-15	A	Notre Dame 0-13	L
11-27	H	Wabash 7-7	T

George "Potsy" Clark (1920)
(See baseball season records for George "Potsy" Clark sketch)

1920 (4-6)
Coach: George "Potsy" Clark

9-25	H	Kalamazoo 2-21	L
10-2	H	Albion 16-0	W
10-6	H	Alma 48-0	W
10-9	A	Wisconsin 0-27	L
10-16	A	Michigan 0-35	L
10-23	H	Marietta 7-23	L
10-30	H	Olivet 109-0	W
11-13	H	Chicago YMCA 81-0	W
11-20	A	Nebraska 7-35	L
11-25	H	Notre Dame 0-25	L

Albert M. Barron (1921-1922)
(See cross country season records for Albert M. Barron sketch)

1921 (3-5)
Coach: Albert M. Barrron

10-1	H	Alma 28-0	W
10-8	H	Albion 7-24	L
10-15	A	Michigan 0-30	L
10-22	H	Western State 17-14	W
10-27	A	Marquette 0-7	L
11-5	A	South Dakota 14-0	W
11-12	A	Butler 2-3	L
11-24	A	Notre Dame 0-48	L

1922 (3-5-2)
Coach: Albert M. Barrron

9-30	H	Alma 33-0	W
10-7	H	Albion 7-7	T
10-14	A	Wabash 0-26	L
10-21	A	South Dakota 7-0	L
10-28	A	Indiana 6-14	L
11-4	A	Michigan 0-63	L
11-11	H	Ohio Wesleyan 6-9	L
11-18	A	Creighton 0-9	L
11-25	H	Massachusetts State 45-0	W
11-30	A	St. Louis 7-7	T

Ralph H. Young (1923-1927)
(See cross country season records for Ralph H. Young sketch)

1923 (3-5)
Coach: Ralph H. Young

9-29	A	Chicago 0-34	L
10-6	H	Lake Forest 21-6	W
10-13	A	Wisconsin 0-21	L
10-20	H	Albion 13-0	W
10-27	A	Michigan 0-37	L
11-3	H	Ohio Wesleyan 14-19	L
11-10	H	Creighton 7-27	L
11-17	A	Detroit 2-0	W

1924 (5-3)
Coach: Ralph H. Young

9-26	H	North Central	59-0	W
10-4	H	Olivet	54-3	W
10-10	H	Michigan	0-7	L
10-17	H	Chicago YMCA	34-3	W
10-25	A	Northwestern	9-13	L
11-1	H	Lake Forest	42-13	W
11-8	A	St. Louis	3-9	L
11-15	H	South Dakota State	9-0	W

1925 (3-5)
Coach: Ralph H. Young

9-26	H	Adrian	16-0	W
10-3	A	Michigan	0-39	L
10-10	H	Lake Forest	0-6	L
10-17	H	Centre (KY)	15-13	W
10-24	A	Penn State	6-13	L
11-3	H	Colgate	0-14	L
11-7	H	Toledo	58-0	W
11-14	A	Wisconsin	10-21	L

1926 (3-4-1)
Coach: Ralph H. Young

9-26	H	Adrian	16-0	W
10-2	H	Kalamazoo	9-0	W
10-9	A	Michigan	3-55	L
10-16	H	Cornell University	14-24	L
10-23	H	Lake Forest	0-0	T
10-30	A	Colgate	6-38	L
11-6	H	Centre (KY)	42-14	W
11-20	H	Haskell Inst.(KS)	7-40	L

1927 (4-5)
Coach: Ralph H. Young

9-24	H	Kalamazoo	12-6	W
10-1	H	Ohio University	27-0	W
10-8	A	Michigan	0-21	L
10-15	A	Cornell College (IA)	13-19	L
10-29	H	Detroit	7-24	L
11-5	A	Indiana	7-33	L
11-11	H	Albion	20-6	W
11-19	H	Butler	25-0	W
12-3	A	North Carolina State	0-19	L

Harry Kipke (1928)

In November of 1927, coach-AD Ralph Young announced his decision to step down as football coach and he promised, "The name of a successor would soon be forthcoming." True to his word, on November 21, it was disclosed that Harry J. Kipke, former Lansing High School and University of Michigan athletic star and most recently backfield coach at the U of M (1925-1927), had signed a three-year contract to be MSC's new football coach. Although terms of the contract were not made public, Kipke was given full say over the gridiron activities and power to appoint his own assistants. As an athlete at Michigan, Kipke won nine letters, three each in football, basketball, and baseball. Highlighting his many honors as an athlete was the selection to Walter Camp's 1922 All-American team as a halfback. Graduating from Michigan in 1923, he became the assistant coach of football, basketball, and head coach of baseball at the University of Missouri for one year (1924). He returned to his alma mater in 1925 as an assistant in football, basketball, and baseball. With ongoing commitments to the U of M through the spring of 1928, Kipke was not available for duties in East Lansing until the beginning of Spartan practice the following fall. There were some who suggested that Kipke was "on loan" to MSC for one year to gain experience, with an eventual return to Michigan an obvious conclusion. Rumors had circulated for several weeks in the spring of 1929 connecting him with the coaching vacancy at Ann Arbor following the ousting of Elton E. "Tad" Weiman by the U of M athletic director, Fielding Yost. It became a reality. At an emergency meeting of the MSC Athletic Council on June 11, Harry G. Kipke offered his resignation effective at the close of the college year, and asked to be released from the remaining two years of his contract. The council immediately acceded to his wishes. The headline in the next day's *Detroit Free Press* sports page read, "Yost names Kipke head coach." Ralph Young's concluding statement was: "We are sorry to lose Harry, naturally, but the council and myself recognized the fact that we would be standing in his way if we did not release him and he goes from us with all the best wishes for his success. There is no ill-feeling toward him or anyone else because of his sudden departure at a time when it is difficult to obtain another coach." Regardless, the closing comment seemed tainted with sarcastic bitterness.

1928 (3-4-1)
Coach: Harry Kipke

9-29	H	Kalamazoo	103-0	W
10-6	H	Albion	0-2	L
10-13	H	Chicago YMCA	37-0	W
10-20	H	Colgate	0-16	L
11-3	H	Mississippi State	6-6	T
11-10	A	Detroit	0-39	L
11-17	A	Michigan	0-3	L
11-24	H	North Carolina State	7-0	W

James H. Crowley (1929-1932)

Kipke's replacement, 27-year-old James H. (Sleepy Jim) Crowley, was offered and accepted the head coaching position on Saturday, June 22, 1929. The occasion of the day coincided with MSC's annual spring Alumni Day. Seizing the opportunity, Athletic Director Young used the evening dinner in Demonstration Hall to introduce the new coach before the assembly of 400-500 alumni and guests. As a member of the legendary Four Horsemen of Notre Dame, the 27-year-old Jim Crowley was a popular choice. Upon introduction that evening, he was greeted with cheer upon cheer from reunion classes that rose en masse from their tables. Alumni Day of 1929 ended on a high note. Crowley had completed four years as an assistant coach to George Woodruff at the University of Georgia. Upon being called by Young, he had just entered the business world as advertising manager in the Pittsburgh district for the Coca-Cola Company. He was born September 10, 1902, in Chicago and later moved to Wisconsin where he attended East Green Bay High School. Entering Notre Dame at 5' 11" and 165 pounds, Crowley won All-American honors after the 1924 season. He graduated from the South Bend school in 1925. Prior to commencing his coaching career, Crowley played in a handful of professional games for the Green Bay Packers and the Providence Steam Rollers. He was paid $500 to $1,000 per game. The higher amount would be in order if he was accompanied by his famous cohorts, the three other Horsemen: Don Miller, Elmer Layden, and Harry Stuhldreher. Crowley remained at MSC for four seasons. One of his greatest victories was the upset win over Fordham at New York's Polo Grounds on October 22, 1932. Unfortunately, the impressive victory would attract the attention of Fordham people who immediately begin a campaign to lure Crowley from East Lansing. It would be the third time that "Sleepy Jim" had received an offer from another school during his tenure at Michigan State. First it was Gonzaga University of Spokane, WA, that tempted him. Then in 1931, officials at the University of Iowa offered him their head coaching position with an increase in salary. In addition to the ultimate Fordham offer, Crowley had been unofficially mentioned as head coach at Princeton University upon conclusion of the 1932 season. Finally, on January 4, 1933, following a trip east for a national meeting of coaches, the relentless Fordham people offered a contract that Coach Crowley couldn't refuse. For three years he would be paid $11,500 annually, an increase from the $8,000 MSC pact, which had one year remaining. Following a quick conference with members of the State Board of Agriculture, President Shaw consented to Crowley's request to be relieved of his commitment to Michigan State. He would leave East Lansing on February 28. Upon departure he said: "I've had a lot of fun coaching football teams here. I shan't soon forget this campus and the friends I have made here." At the New York school, Jim Crowley would coach for many more years and with great success. Of particular recognition was the famed front line later known as the "Seven Blocks of Granite," which included the legendary Vince Lombardi.

1929 (5-3)
Coach: James H. Crowley

9-28	H	Alma	59-6	W
10-5	A	Michigan	0-17	L
10-12	A	Colgate	0-31	L
10-19	H	Adrian	74-0	W
10-26	H	North Carolina State	40-6	W
11-2	H	Case	38-0	W
11-9	A	Mississippi State	33-19	W
11-16	H	Detroit	0-25	L

1930 (5-1-2)
Coach: James H. Crowley

9-27	H	Alma	28-0	W
10-4	A	Michigan	0-0	T
10-11	H	Cincinnati	32-0	W
10-18	H	Colgate	14-7	W
10-25	H	Case	45-0	W
10-31	A	Georgetown	13-14	L
11-8	H	North Dakota State	19-11	W
11-22	H	Detroit	0-0	T

1931 (5-3-1)
Coach: James H. Crowley

9-26	H	Alma	74-0	W
10-3	H	Cornell Coll. (IA)	47-0	W
10-10	A	Army	7-20	L
10-17	H	Illinois Wesleyan	34-6	W
10-24	H	Georgetown	6-0	W
10-31	H	Syracuse	10-15	L
11-7	H	Ripon	100-0	W
11-14	A	Michigan	0-0	T
11-21	A	Detroit	13-20	L

1932 (7-1)
Coach: James H. Crowley

9-24	H	Alma	93-0	W
10-1	A	Michigan	0-26	L
10-8	H	Grinnell	27-6	W
10-15	H	Illinois Wesleyan	27-0	W
10-22	A	Fordham	19-13	W
10-29	A	Syracuse	27-13	W
11-5	H	South Dakota	20-6	W
11-19	H	Detroit	7-0	W

Charles W. Bachman (1933-1946)

Smarting from two broken agreements (Kipke and now Crowley), the Athletic Council met on the evening of January 9, 1933, whereupon agreed to abolish making contracts with coaches, putting them on the same basis as other faculty members. Athletic director Ralph Young revealed that credentials had been received from more than 100 applicants. By the first of March, the suspense was over and a decision had been made to hire the head coach from the University of Florida, Charles W. Bachman, yet another Notre Dame alum. By the ninth of March he was in his office, room nine in the Gymnasium, and making plans for spring practice, scheduled to open April 3. Born December 2, 1893, in Chicago, Bachman attended that city's Inglewood High School where he excelled in football and track. While at Notre Dame, "Bach" won a trio of monograms in both football and track. He was chosen All-Western guard in 1914 and 1916 and briefly held the world distance record for the discus in the spring of 1917. Bachman's coaching career received a quick start, being appointed as an assistant at DePauw University, immediately following graduation in 1917. Also that fall, he allegedly played under an assumed

name for the professional team in Massillon, OH, a precursor to today's NFL. Following a short stint in the U.S. Navy, Charlie returned to coaching. At his next stop, he was labeled "Boy Wonder of the Western Conference" while coaching Northwestern in 1919 at the age of 25. He then moved on to Kansas State where he coached from 1920-1927 and then to the University of Florida for five seasons, 1928-1932. While at MSC, from 1933 until retiring from the head coaching job in 1946, Charlie's most memorable contribution was the string of four consecutive victories over the University of Michigan from 1934-1937. In 1943, when MSC aborted intercollegiate athletics for one year because of World War II, Charlie took a leave and coached the army team at Camp Grant. Returning to East Lansing by the following fall, his squads of 1944-1946 tallied a composite record of 16-8-1. Spartan fans were unimpressed and grew impatient. Particularly intolerant and vocal were the thousands of discharged ex-GI's that dominated undergraduate enrollments in the mid-1940s following the closure of World War II. Bachman, always a man with class, realized it was time to step aside and he did so upon conclusion of that '46 season, at the age of 52. His resignation covered his assignment as professor of physical education, but his contract extended to July 1, 1947. He was earning an annual salary of $8,600. Bachman left a record of solid accomplishment that became more valued with the passage of time. Appropriately, at halftime of the Notre Dame game on October 7, 1978, Charlie was recognized for his 13 years as the Spartan head coach. Seven years later, in December of 1985, Coach Bachman died in Port Charlotte, FL, of heart failure. He had just celebrated his 92nd birthday.

1933 (4-2-2)
Coach: Charles W. Bachman

9-30	H	Grinnell	14-0	W
10-7	A	Michigan	6-20	L
10-14	A	Illinois Wesleyan	20-12	W
10-21	A	Marquette	6-0	W
10-28	H	Syracuse	27-3	W
11-4	H	Kansas State	0-0	T
11-11	H	Carnegie Tech	0-0	T
11-25	A	Detroit	0-14	L

1934 (8-1)
Coach: Charles W. Bachman

9-29	H	Grinnell	33-20	W
10-6	A	Michigan	16-0	W
10-13	H	Carnegie Tech	13-0	W
10-20	A	Manhattan	39-0	W
11-3	H	Marquette	13-7	W
11-10	A	Syracuse	0-10	L
11-17	H	Detroit	7-6	W
11-24	A	Kansas	6-0	W
12-8	A	Texas A&M	26-13	W

1935 (6-2)
Coach: Charles W. Bachman

9-28	H	Grinnell	41-0	W
10-5	A	Michigan	25-6	W
10-12	A	Kansas	42-0	W
10-19	A	Boston College	6-18	L
10-26	H	Washington-St. L.	47-13	W
11-2	A	Temple	12-7	W
11-9	H	Marquette	7-13	L
11-16	A	Loyola of L.A.	27-0	W

1936 (6-1-2)
Coach: Charles W. Bachman

9-26	H	Wayne	27-0	W
10-3	A	Michigan	21-7	W
10-10	A	Carnegie Tech	7-0	W
10-17	H	Missouri	13-0	W
10-24	H	Marquette	7-13	L
10-31	A	Boston College	13-13	T
11-7	A	Temple	7-7	T

| 11-14 | A | Kansas | 41-0 | W |
| 11-21 | H | Arizona | 7-0 | W |

1937 (8-2)
Coach: Charles W. Bachman

9-25	H	Wayne	19-0	W
10-2	A	Michigan	19-14	W
10-9	A	Manhattan	0-3	L
10-16	A	Missouri	2-0	W
10-23	H	Marquette	21-7	W
10-30	H	Kansas	16-0	W
11-6	H	Temple	13-6	W
11-13	H	Carnegie Tech	13-6	W
11-27	A	San Francisco	14-0	W
1-1	A	Auburn	>0-6	L

>Orange Bowl at Miami, FL

1938 (6-3)
Coach: Charles W. Bachman

9-24	H	Wayne	34-6	W
10-1	H	Michigan	0-14	L
10-8	H	Illinois Wesleyan	18-0	W
10-15	A	West Virginia	26-0	W
10-22	H	Syracuse	19-12	W
10-29	H	Santa Clara	6-7	L
11-5	A	Missouri	0-6	L
11-12	A	Marquette	20-14	W
11-19	H	Temple	10-0	W

1939 (4-4-1)
Coach: Charles W. Bachman

9-30	H	Wayne	16-0	W
10-7	A	Michigan	13-26	L
10-14	H	Marquette	14-17	L
10-21	A	Purdue	7-20	L
10-28	H	Illinois Wesleyan	13-6	W
11-4	A	Syracuse	14-3	W
11-11	A	Santa Clara	0-6	L
11-18	H	Indiana	7-7	T
11-25	H	Temple	18-7	W

1940 (3-4-1)
Coach: Charles W. Bachman

10-5	A	Michigan	14-21	L
10-12	H	Purdue	20-7	W
10-18	A	Temple	19-21	L
10-26	H	Santa Clara	0-0	T
11-2	A	Kansas State	32-0	W
11-9	A	Indiana	0-20	L
11-16	A	Marquette	6-7	L
11-23	H	West Virginia	17-0	W

1941 (5-3-1)
Coach: Charles W. Bachman

9-27	A	Michigan	7-19	L
10-11	H	Marquette	13-7	W
10-18	A	Santa Clara	0-7	L
10-25	H	Wayne	39-6	W
11-1	H	Missouri	0-19	L
11-8	A	Purdue	0-0	T
11-15	H	Temple	46-0	W
11-22	H	Ohio Wesleyan	31-7	W
11-29	A	West Virginia	14-12	W

1942 (4-3-2)
Coach: Charles W. Bachman

10-3	A	Michigan	0-20	L
10-10	H	Wayne	46-6	W
10-17	H	Marquette	7-28	L
10-24	H	Great Lakes NTS	14-0	W
10-31	A	Temple	7-7	T
11-7	A	Washington State	13-25	L
11-14	H	Purdue	19-6	W

| 11-21 | H | West Virginia | 7-0 | W |
| 11-28 | H | Oregon State | 7-7 | T |

1943
Intercollegiate athletics suspended due to World War II

1944 (6-1)
Coach: Charles W. Bachman

9-30	H	Scranton	40-12	W
10-7	A	Kentucky	2-0	W
10-14	A	Kansas State	45-6	W
10-20	A	Maryland	8-0	W
10-27	A	Wayne	32-0	W
11-4	A	Missouri	7-13	L
11-11	H	Maryland	33-0	W

1945 (5-3-1)
Coach: Charles W. Bachman

9-29	A	Michigan	0-40	L
10-6	H	Kentucky	7-6	W
10-13	A	Pittsburgh	12-7	W
10-20	H	Wayne	27-7	W
10-27	H	Marquette	13-13	T
11-3	H	Missouri	14-7	W
11-10	H	Great Lakes NTS	7-27	L
11-17	H	Penn State	33-0	W
11-23	A	Miami (FL)	7-21	L

1946 (5-5)
Coach: Charles W. Bachman

9-28	H	Wayne	42-0	W
10-5	H	Boston College	20-34	L
10-12	H	Mississippi State	0-6	L
10-19	A	Penn State	19-16	W
10-26	H	Cincinnati	7-18	L
11-2	A	Kentucky	14-39	L
11-9	A	Michigan	7-55	L
11-16	H	Marquette	20-0	W
11-23	H	Maryland	26-14	W
11-30	H	Washington State	26-20	W

Clarence "Biggie" Munn (1947-1953)
Gossip of Bachman's replacement was flying almost before President Hannah had a chance to accept the coach's resignation proffer. Immediately cited as potentialities were Ed McKeever of Cornell, Frank Leahy at Notre Dame, Earl "Red" Blake of Army, Dana Bible of Texas, Bobby Neyland of Tennessee, Clark Shaughnessy at Maryland, and the former Spartan assistant, Arizona head coach Mike Casteel. The next move was well chronicled in John Hannah's book, *A Memoir*, published in 1980. The trustees selected a committee of three members of the board to advise the president in filling the vacancy. In compiling a list of ablest prospects, three names were listed; none of which were included on that initial "rumored" list. The first name on the list was Clarence "Biggie" Munn, who for many years had been line coach at the University of Michigan under Fritz Crisler and was then head coach at Syracuse University. In Hannah's appraisal: "He had an illustrious record. Everyone who knew him spoke well of him. He got along well with young men, high school coaches, and alumni." Second on the list was Bud Wilkinson, who later carved an impressive record at the University of Oklahoma; and third was Wes Fesler, who became head coach at Ohio State, his alma mater. After first gaining approval from the Syracuse University president, Hannah talked to Munn on the telephone and found that he was interested. A meeting was arranged to take place at the Statler Hotel in Detroit where the two men initially discussed the proposition. Later that day, the trio of trustees joined the pair and before the sun had set, it was agreed that Munn and his three top aides would be headed to East Lansing. Those assistants were Forest Evashevski, Kip Taylor, and Duffy Daugherty. Rumors prevailed that Biggie would be paid $10,000 per year. Biggie Munn was born in

Grow Township, MN, on September 11, 1908. He attended North High School in Minneapolis where he was a standout fullback in football. From there he enrolled at the University of Minnesota where he established a conference track record in the shot put and twice took All-America honors in football. In 1931, his senior year, Biggie was the recipient of the coveted *Chicago Tribune* Award as the Big Ten's most valuable player in football. Following graduation, Munn stayed on at Minnesota where he was track coach for two years and football assistant for three years under the esteemed Bernie Bierman. Moving on to Albright College, Biggie was the AD and "everything" coach for two years, 1935-1936. Following one year as line coach at Syracuse he served in the same capacity at the University of Michigan from 1938-1946. He returned to Syracuse as head coach for one season before accepting the MSC offer. Biggie's impact at State was so great and his overall record (54-9-2) so impressive, it has always been difficult for veteran Spartan followers to digest that he remained as head coach for only seven years (1947-1953). Included in that short span was a Rose Bowl victory, a national championship, a 28-game winning streak, and a conference co-championship in the only year a Munn team competed for the Big Ten title. Moving into the athletic director's office following that Rose Bowl win over UCLA in 1954, Biggie was a productive and popular administrator. Sadly, his tenure was suddenly disrupted on October 7, 1971, when he suffered a stroke, which led to a health leave, and eventually his premature retirement on September 1, 1973. A second stroke took his life on March 18, 1975.

1947 (7-2)

Coach: Clarence "Biggie" Munn

9-27	A	Michigan	0-55	L
10-4	H	Mississippi State	7-0	W
10-11	A	Washington State	21-7	W
10-18	H	Iowa State	20-0	W
10-25	H	Kentucky	6-7	L
11-1	H	Marquette	13-7	W
11-8	H	Santa Clara	28-0	W
11-15	A	Temple	14-6	W
11-29	A	Hawaii	58-19	W

1948 (6-2-2)

Coach: Clarence "Biggie" Munn

9-25	H*	Michigan	7-13	L
10-2	H	Hawaii	68-21	W
10-9	A	Notre Dame	7-26	L
10-16	H	Arizona	61-7	W
10-23	A	Penn State	14-14	T
10-30	A	Oregon State	46-21	W
11-6	H	Marquette	47-0	W
11-13	H	Iowa State	48-7	W
11-20	H	Washington State	40-0	W
11-27	A	Santa Clara	21-21	T

1949 (6-3)

Coach: Clarence "Biggie" Munn

9-24	A	Michigan	3-7	L
10-1	H	Marquette	48-7	W
10-8	A	Maryland	14-7	W
10-15	H	William & Mary	42-13	W
10-22	H	Penn State	24-0	W
10-29	H	Temple	62-14	W
11-5	H	Notre Dame	21-34	L
11-12	A	Oregon State	20-25	L
11-19	A	Arizona	75-0	W

1950 (8-1)

Coach: Clarence "Biggie" Munn

9-23	H	Oregon State	38-13	W
9-30	A	Michigan	14-7	W
10-7	H	Maryland	7-34	L
10-14	H	William & Mary	33-14	W
10-21	H	Marquette	34-6	W
10-28	A	Notre Dame	36-33	W
11-4	H	Indiana	35-0	W
11-11	H	Minnesota	27-0	W
11-18	A	Pittsburgh	19-0	W

1951 (9-0)

Coach: Clarence "Biggie" Munn

9-22	H	Oregon State	6-0	W
9-29	A	Michigan	25-0	W
10-6	A	Ohio State	24-20	W
10-13	H	Marquette	20-14	W
10-20	A	Penn State	32-21	W
10-27	H	Pittsburgh	53-26	W
11-10	H	Notre Dame	35-0	W
11-17	A	Indiana	30-26	W
11-24	H	Colorado	45-7	W

1952 (9-0)

Coach: Clarence "Biggie" Munn

9-27	A	Michigan	27-13	W
10-4	A	Oregon State	17-14	W
10-11	H	Texas A&M	48-6	W
10-18	H	Syracuse	48-7	W
10-25	H	Penn State	34-7	W
11-1	A	Purdue	14-7	W
11-8	A	Indiana	41-14	W
11-15	H	Notre Dame	21-3	W
11-22	H	Marquette	62-14	W

1953 (9-1; 5-1 in Big Ten: tie for 1st)

Coach: Clarence "Biggie" Munn

9-26	A	Iowa	21-7	W
10-3	A	Minnesota	21-0	W
10-10	H	Texas Christian	26-19	W
10-17	H	Indiana	47-18	W
10-24	A	Purdue	0-6	L
10-31	H	Oregon State	34-6	W
11-7	A	Ohio State	28-13	W
11-14	H	Michigan	14-6	W
11-21	H	Marquette	21-15	W
1-1-54	A_{PS}	UCLA	>28-20	W
	>Rose Bowl			

Hugh "Duffy" Daugherty (1954-1972)

Before the roses had hardly wilted from the bowl game of January 1, 1954, it was disclosed that Biggie's line coach, Hugh "Duffy" Daugherty, would replace the legendary Munn as head football coach. The announcement surprised very few. After all, Duffy was the only member of the original Munn coaching staff still aboard. Kip Taylor had left for the head coaching position at Oregon State in 1949 and Forest Evashevski was at Iowa after originally serving as head coach at Washington State in 1950 and 1951. Born September 8, 1915, in Emeigh, PA, Duffy was raised in Barnesboro, PA. Attending Syracuse University, he played three seasons on the Orange line, one of them under Biggie Munn who was then line coach. Daugherty captained his senior-year team of 1939, after sitting out the 1938 season with a broken neck. From Syracuse, Duffy entered the U.S. Army and served four years during World War II, including 30 months of overseas duty in Australia and New Guinea. He participated in three major campaigns, was awarded the Bronze Star, and rose in rank from private to major. His 19 years as the Spartan head coach are replete with proof of success and tales of anguish. He won two outright Big Ten titles, and placed second four times. Seven times his teams finished in the national top 10 in the wire service balloting, with the 1965 team ranked No. 1 and the teams of 1955 and 1966 ranked No. 2. Conversely, eight of his teams finished fifth or lower in the conference standings. In his final six seasons, only the 6-5 team of 1971 finished above the .500 level. Duffy's Irish wit, unfailing good humor, optimism, puckish refusal to succumb to the nerve-wracking pressures of his occupation, genuine modesty, and unmistakable honesty drew him to the hearts of the nation's sports

audience. On the eve of the November 4, 1972, home game against Purdue, with three additional games remaining on the schedule, a news release announced that Duffy would step down from the head position at the end of the season. It was further reported that he would be appointed special assistant to Les Scott, vice-president for development. Daugherty was eventually granted early retirement from the university on September 20, 1974. He was extended a one-year terminal leave with full salary continuing through August 31, 1976. In the summer of 1975, Duffy officially concluded his long association with Michigan State and, with his wife, took up residency in Santa Barbara, CA. On September 25, 1987, 17 days beyond his 72nd birthday, Hugh "Duffy" Daugherty died.

1954 (3-6; 1-5 in Big Ten: tie for 8th)

Coach: Hugh "Duffy" Daugherty

9-25	A	Iowa	10-14	L
10-2	A	Wisconsin	0-6	L
10-9	A	Indiana	21-14	W
10-16	A	Notre Dame	19-20	L
10-23	H	Purdue	13-27	L
10-30	H	Minnesota	13-19	L
11-6	H	Washington State	54-6	W
11-13	A	Michigan	7-33	L
11-20	H	Marquette	40-10	W

1955 (9-1; 5-1 in Big Ten: 2nd)

Coach: Hugh "Duffy" Daugherty

9-24	A	Indiana	20-13	W
10-1	A	Michigan	7-14	L
10-8	H	Stanford	38-14	W
10-15	H	Notre Dame	21-7	W
10-22	H	Illinois	21-7	W
10-29	A	Wisconsin	27-0	W
11-5	A	Purdue	27-0	W
11-12	H	Minnesota	42-14	W
11-19	H	Marquette	33-0	W
1-2-56	A_{PS}	U.C.L.A.	>17-14	W
	>Rose Bowl			

1956 (7-2; 4-2 in Big Ten: tie for 4th)

Coach: Hugh "Duffy" Daugherty

9-29	A	Stanford	21-7	W
10-6	A	Michigan	9-0	W
10-13	H	Indiana	53-6	W
10-20	A	Notre Dame	47-14	W
10-27	A	Illinois	13-20	L
11-3	H	Wisconsin	33-0	W
11-10	H	Purdue	12-9	W
11-17	A	Minnesota	13-14	L
11-24	H	Kansas State	38-17	W

1957 (8-1; 5-1 in Big Ten: 2nd)

Coach: Hugh "Duffy" Daugherty

9-28	H	Indiana	54-0	W
10-5	A	California	19-0	W
10-12	A	Michigan	35-6	W
10-19	H	Purdue	13-20	L
10-26	H	Illinois	19-14	W
11-2	A	Wisconsin	21-7	W
11-9	H	Notre Dame	34-6	W
11-16	H	Minnesota	42-13	W
11-23	H	Kansas State	27-9	W

1958 (3-5-1; 0-5-1 in Big Ten: 10th)

Coach: Hugh "Duffy" Daugherty

9-27	H	California	32-12	W
10-4	H	Michigan	12-12	T
10-11	H	Pittsburgh	22-8	W
10-18	A	Purdue	6-14	L
10-25	A	Illinois	0-16	L
11-1	H	Wisconsin	7-9	L
11-8	A	Indiana	0-6	L

11-15	A	Minnesota 12-39	L
11-22	H	Kansas State 26-7	W

1959 (5-4; 4-2 in Big Ten: 2nd)
Coach: Hugh "Duffy" Daugherty

9-28	H	Texas A&M 7-9	L
10-3	A	Michigan 34-8	W
10-10	A	Iowa 8-37	L
10-17	H	Notre Dame 19-0	W
10-24	H	Indiana 14-6	W
10-31	A	Ohio State 24-30	L
11-7	H	Purdue 15-0	W
11-14	H	Northwestern 15-10	W
11-20	A	Miami (FL) 13-18	L

1960 (6-2-1; 4-2 in Big Ten: 4th)
Coach: Hugh "Duffy" Daugherty

9-24	H	Pittsburgh 7-7	T
10-1	H	Michigan 24-17	W
10-8	H	Iowa 15 27	L
10-15	A	Notre Dame 21-0	W
10-22	A	Indiana 35-0	W
10-29	H	Ohio State 10-21	L
11-5	A	Purdue 17-13	W
11-12	A	Northwestern 21-18	W
11-19	H	Detroit 43-15	W

1961 (7-2; 5-2 in Big Ten: 3rd)
Coach: Hugh "Duffy" Daugherty

9-30	A	Wisconsin 20-0	W
10-7	H	Stanford 31-3	W
10-14	A	Michigan 28-0	W
10-21	H	Notre Dame 17-7	W
10-28	H	Indiana 35-0	W
11-4	A	Minnesota 0-13	L
11-11	A	Purdue 6-7	L
11-18	H	Northwestern 21-13	W
11-25	H	Illinois 34-7	W

1962 (5-4; 3-3 in Big Ten: tie for 5th)
Coach: Hugh "Duffy" Daugherty

9-29	A	Stanford 13-16	L
10-6	H	North Carolina 38-6	W
10-13	H	Michigan 28-0	W
10-20	A	Notre Dame 31-7	W
10-27	A	Indiana 26-8	W
11-3	H	Minnesota 7-28	L
11-10	H	Purdue 9-17	L
11-17	A	Northwestern 31-7	W
11-24	A	Illinois 6-7	L

1963 (6-2-1; 4-1-1 in Big Ten: tie for 2nd)
Coach: Hugh "Duffy" Daugherty

9-28	H	North Carolina 31-0	W
10-4	A	Southern California 10-13	L
10-12	A	Michigan 7-7	T
10-19	H	Indiana 20-3	W
10-26	A	Northwestern 15-7	W
11-2	H	Wisconsin 30-13	W
11-9	H	Purdue 23-0	W
11-16	H	Notre Dame 12-7	W
11-28	H	Illinois 0-13	L

1964 (4-5; 3-3 in Big Ten: 6th)
Coach: Hugh "Duffy" Daugherty

9-26	A	North Carolina 15-21	L
10-3	H	Southern California 17-7	W
10-10	H	Michigan 10-17	L
10-17	A	Indiana 20-27	L
10-24	H	Northwestern 24-6	W
10-31	A	Wisconsin 22-6	W
11-7	H	Purdue 21-7	W
11-14	H	Notre Dame 7-34	L
11-21	A	Illinois 0-16	L

1965 (10-1; 7-0 in Big Ten: 1st)
Coach: Hugh "Duffy" Daugherty

9-18	H	UCLA 13-3	W
9-25	A	Penn State 23-0	W
10-2	H	Illinois 22-12	W
10-9	A	Michigan 24-7	W
10-16	H	Ohio State 32-7	W
10-23	A	Purdue 14-10	W
10-30	H	Northwestern 49-7	W
11-6	A	Iowa 35-0	W
11-13	H	Indiana 27-13	W
11-20	A	Notre Dame 12-3	W
1-1-66	A$_{PS}$	UCLA .... >12-14	L

>Rose Bowl

1966 (9-0-1; 7-0 in Big Ten: 1st)
Coach: Hugh "Duffy" Daugherty

9-17	H	North Carolina State 28-10	W
9-24	H	Penn State 42-8	W
10-1	A	Illinois 26-10	W
10-8	H	Michigan 20-7	W
10-15	A	Ohio State 11-8	W
10-22	H	Purdue 41-20	W
10-29	H	Northwestern 22-0	W
11-5	A	Iowa 56-7	W
11-12	H	Indiana 37-19	W
11-19	H	Notre Dame 10-10	T

1967 (3-7; 3-4 in Big Ten: tie for 5th)
Coach: Hugh "Duffy" Daugherty

9-23	H	Houston 7-37	L
9-30	H	Southern California 17-21	L
10-7	H	Wisconsin 35-7	W
10-14	A	Michigan 34-0	W
10-21	A	Minnesota 0-21	L
10-28	H	Notre Dame 12-24	L
11-4	H	Ohio State 7-21	L
11-11	H	Indiana 13-14	L
11-18	A	Purdue 7-21	L
11-25	H	Northwestern 41-27	W

1968 (5-5; 2-5 in Big Ten: 7th)
Coach: Hugh "Duffy" Daugherty

9-21	H	Syracuse 14-10	W
9-28	H	Baylor 28-10	W
10-5	A	Wisconsin 39-0	W
10-12	H	Michigan 14-28	L
10-19	H	Minnesota 13-14	L
10-26	H	Notre Dame 21-17	W
11-2	A	Ohio State 20-25	L
11-9	H	Indiana 22-24	L
11-16	H	Purdue 0-9	L
11-23	A	Northwestern 31-14	W

1969 (4-6; 2-5 in Big Ten: 9th)
Coach: Hugh "Duffy" Daugherty

9-20	H	Washington 27-11	W
9-27	H	Southern Methodist 23-15	W
10-4	A	Notre Dame 28-42	L
10-11	H	Ohio State 21-54	L
10-18	H	Michigan 23-12	W
10-25	A	Iowa 18-19	L
11-1	H	Indiana 0-16	L
11-8	A	Purdue 13-41	L
11-15	H	Minnesota 10-14	L
11-22	A	Northwestern 39-7	W

1970 (4-6; 3-4 in Big Ten: tie for 5th)
Coach: Hugh "Duffy" Daugherty

9-19	A	Washington 16-42	L
9-26	A	Washington State 28-14	W
10-3	H	Notre Dame 0-29	L
10-10	A	Ohio State 0-29	L
10-17	A	Michigan 20-34	L
10-24	H	Iowa 37-0	W
10-31	A	Indiana 32-7	W
11-7	H	Purdue 24-14	W
11-14	A	Minnesota 13-23	L
11-21	H	Northwestern 20-23	L

1971 (6-5; 5-3 in Big Ten: tie for 3rd)
Coach: Hugh "Duffy" Daugherty

9-11	H	Illinois 10-0	W
9-18	A	Georgia Tech 0-10	L
9-25	H	Oregon State 31-14	W
10-2	H	Notre Dame 2-14	L
10-9	H	Michigan 13-24	L
10-16	A	Wisconsin 28-31	L
10-23	A	Iowa 34-3	W
10-30	A	Purdue 43-10	W
11-6	A	Ohio State 17-10	W
11-13	H	Minnesota 40-25	W
11-20	A	Northwestern 7-28	L

1972 (5-5-1; 5-2-1 in Big Ten: 4th)
Coach: Hugh "Duffy" Daugherty

9-16	A	Illinois 24-0	W
9-23	H	Georgia Tech 16-21	L
9-30	A	Southern California 6-51	L
10-7	H	Notre Dame 0-16	L
10-14	A	Michigan 0-10	L
10-21	H	Wisconsin 31-0	W
10-28	A	Iowa 6-6	T
11-4	H	Purdue 22-12	W
11-11	H	Ohio State 19-12	W
11-18	A	Minnesota 10-14	L
11-24	H	Northwestern 24-14	W

Dennis E. Stolz (1973-1975)

Much in the same manner that put Duffy into the head coaching slot 19 years earlier, the next Spartan head coach, Dennis E. Stolz, was plucked from the immediate staff. He had joined Daugherty in 1971 with duties as defensive coordinator and then on December 12, 1972, the announcement was made elevating him to the top spot. At an arranged press conference on that Tuesday, school president Clifton Wharton stated: "Candidates were interviewed over the weekend and today, with the final interview held this afternoon. Following this, athletic director Burt Smith and executive vice president Jack Breslin recommended Coach Stolz to me. On the basis of their strong endorsement, I am pleased to ask the board to approve his appointment." Among other candidates had been Barry Switzer, Johnny Majors, Lee Corso, and Bill Mallory. In the six years prior to his move to East Lansing, Stolz had been head coach at his alma mater, Alma College. His 1967 and 1968 Scot teams had compiled unbeaten seasons, the only time in that school's history back-to-back perfect campaigns were put together. Immediately following graduation in 1955, Denny's coaching career began as he was named head football coach at Haslett High School. In 1963, following eight successful seasons there, he moved on to Lansing Eastern High School. During this period he took time to earn an M.A. degree from MSU. Two years later, in 1965, he began his collegiate coaching career with his appointment as head coach for football and track back at Alma. Following Stolz's fourth season as MSU's head coach, an NCAA investigation during the winter of 1975-1976 led to the university being placed on three years probation for infractions in recruiting and aid to student-athletes. Although the violations pointed directly to a member of his staff and not himself, on March 16, 1976, Stolz tendered his resignation to President Wharton, saying, in part: "I have concluded that the ultimate responsibility for violations found by the NCAA, during the time I was head coach, while involving no personal fault on my part, either in allegation or finding, must be mine. I have asked nothing less of my staff or football players, and I am unwilling to accept anything less for myself." Denny Stolz resurfaced as head coach at Bowling Green in 1977. Following nine years at the Ohio school, including the unde-

feated season of 1985, he moved on to San Diego State where he concluded his coaching career.

1973 (5-6; 4-4 in Big Ten: tie for 4th)
Coach: Dennis E. Stolz

9-15	A	Northwestern	10-14	L
9-22	A	Syracuse	14-8	W
9-29	H	UCLA	21-34	L
10-6	A	Notre Dame	10-14	L
10-13	H	Michigan	0-31	L
10-20	H	Illinois	3-6	L
10-27	A	Purdue	10-7	W
11-3	H	Wisconsin	21-0	W
11-10	A	Ohio State	0-35	L
11-17	H	Indiana	10-9	W
11-24	A	Iowa	15-6	W

1974 (7-3-1; 6-1-1 in Big Ten: 3rd)
Coach: Dennis E. Stolz

9-14	H	Northwestern	41-7	W
9-21	H	Syracuse	19-0	W
9-28	A	UCLA	14-56	L
10-5	H	Notre Dame	14-19	L
10-12	A	Michigan	7-21	L
10-19	A	Illinois	21-21	T
10-26	H	Purdue	31-7	W
11-2	H	Wisconsin	28-21	W
11-9	H	Ohio State	16-13	W
11-16	A	Indiana	19-10	W
11-23	H	Iowa	60-21	W

1975 (7-4; 4-4 in Big Ten: tie for 3rd)
Coach: Dennis E. Stolz

9-13	H	Ohio State	0-21	L
9-20	H	Miami (OH)	14-13	W
9-27	H	North Carolina State	37-15	W
10-4	A	Notre Dame	10-3	W
10-11	H	Michigan	6-16	L
10-18	A	Minnesota	38-15	W
10-25	H	Illinois	19-21	L
11-1	A	Purdue	10-20	L
11-8	A	Indiana	14-6	W
11-15	H	Northwestern	47-14	W
11-22	A	Iowa	27-23	W

Darrell D. Rogers (1976-1979)
On April 6, 1976, athletic director Joe Kearney, who himself had undertaken his AD duties only five days earlier, called a press conference to announce the names of two new head coaches. Darryl Rogers, the 40-year-old head coach at San Jose State University, would replace Stolz, and Jud Heathcote, head coach at the University of Montana, would become the school's 15th basketball coach. Rogers was a 14-year veteran of collegiate football coaching whose most recent position had been head coach at San Jose State University. His five-year MSU contract called for an annual salary of $34,500. Born May 28, 1935, Rogers was bitten by the football bug early. At 148 pounds, the lanky six-footer earned all-Southern California accolades as an offensive end at Long Beach Jordan High School. Then trying his hand on the collegiate scene at Long Beach City College, he gained all-league honors. Rogers eventually transferred to Fresno State and became the nation's No. 2 small college pass receiver as a junior with 33 receptions and three touchdowns. He also intercepted four passes in two seasons as a defensive back. Upon earning both bachelor's and master's degrees in physical education, he had a brief NFL career (1958-1960) with the Los Angeles Rams and Denver Broncos. Darryl began his coaching career in 1961, handling the defensive backs at Fresno City College. Before signing on with MSU, he would eventually serve as head coach with three different California schools: Hayward State in 1965, Fresno State in 1966 and San Jose State in 1973. The offensive-minded Rogers brought a new dimension of thinking to the stodgy, conservative, grind-it-out Big Ten style of play, but he re-

mained in East Lansing only four years. In early January of 1980, initially denying rumors of his departure, Rogers again answered the call of Joe Kearney, this time from Tempe, AZ. Just days earlier Kearney had quietly left MSU for a similar position as AD at Arizona State University. Amidst cries of "carpetbaggers," "scalawags," "hypocrites" and "liars," the pair headed to the horizons and challenges of the Southwest. In 1985, Rogers would leave Arizona State in similar sudden fashion to become the head coach of the Detroit Lions for four seasons (1985-1988). At one final head coaching stop, Darryl was with the Winnipeg Blue Bombers of the Canadian League in 1991. He later became director of athletics at Southern Connecticut College in New Haven, CT.

1976 (4-6-1; 3-5 in Big Ten: tie for 7th)
Coach: Darryl D. Rogers

9-11	A	Ohio State	21-49	L
9-18	H	Wyoming	21-10	W
9-25	A	North Carolina State	31-31	T
10-2	H	Notre Dame	6-24	L
10-9	A	Michigan	10-42	L
10-16	H	Minnesota	10-14	L
10-23	A	Illinois	31-23	W
10-30	H	Purdue	45-13	W
11-6	H	Indiana	23-0	W
11-13	A	Northwestern	21-42	L
11-20	H	Iowa	17-30	L

1977 (7-3-1; 6-1-1 in Big Ten: 3rd)
Coach: Darryl D. Rogers

9-10	H	Purdue	19-14	W
9-17	H	Washington State	21-23	L
9-24	H	Wyoming	34-16	W
10-1	A	Notre Dame	6-16	L
10-8	H	Michigan	14-24	L
10-15	A	Indiana	13-13	T
10-22	A	Wisconsin	9-7	W
10-29	H	Illinois	49-20	W
11-5	A	Minnesota	29-10	W
11-12	H	Northwestern	44-3	W
11-19	A	Iowa	22-16	W

1978 (8-3; 7-1-0 in Big Ten: tie for 1st)
Coach: Darryl D. Rogers

9-16	A	Purdue	14-21	L
9-23	H	Syracuse	49-21	W
9-29	A	Southern California	9-30	L
10-7	H	Notre Dame	25-29	L
10-14	A	Michigan	24-15	W
10-21	H	Indiana	49-14	W
10-28	H	Wisconsin	55-2	W
11-4	A	Illinois	59-19	W
11-11	H	Minnesota	33-9	W
11-18	A	Northwestern	52-3	W
11-25	H	Iowa	42-7	W

1979 (5-6; 3-5 in Big Ten: tie for 7th)
Coach: Darryl D. Rogers

9-8	H	Illinois	33-16	W
9-15	A	Oregon	41-17	W
9-22	H	Miami (OH)	24-21	W
9-29	A	Notre Dame	3-27	L
10-6	H	Michigan	7-21	L
10-13	A	Wisconsin	29-38	L
10-20	H	Purdue	7-14	L
10-27	A	Ohio State	0-42	L
11-3	A	Northwestern	42-7	W
11-10	H	Minnesota	31-17	W
11-17	A	Iowa	23-33	L

Frank "Muddy" Waters (1980-1982)
Seven days following the departure of Joe Kearney and Darryl Rogers to Tempe, MSU president, Cecil Mackey,

announced the appointment of Doug Weaver as the school's next director of athletics. The former Spartan linebacker (1950-1952) had been serving in a similar capacity at Georgia Tech in Atlanta. Doug's immediate task was the recommendation and hiring of a new football coach. As the list of candidates shortened, two Spartan alums seemed to emerge as favorites: Sherman Lewis, the 1963 All-American who had been on Darryl Rogers's staff, and George Perles, the defensive wizard of the NFL's Pittsburgh Steelers. Neither would be selected. To the surprise of most, on January 29, 1980, a day before his 57th birthday, Franklin Dean "Muddy" Waters, yet another alumnus, would be approved as the next head coach. Waters, a Spartan varsity starter under Charley Bachman and Biggie Munn, had been a highly successful high school and college coach in Michigan. Although spending his longest tenure at Hillsdale College (1954-1973), Muddy's more recent success had been winning the 1979 Great Lakes Conference championship for Saginaw Valley College, where he had been the founding coach five years prior. Waters was born in Chico, CA, on January 30, 1923. He competed in football, basketball, and track at Pawling Prep in New York before spending his final year of secondary schooling at Choate School in Wallingford, CT, from where he graduated in 1943. At that time his family lived in Bridgeport, CT. Immediately out of prep school, Muddy enlisted in the air corps. Spending the first five weeks of training at Greensboro, NC, he was then stationed at MSC for a five month period from August to December of 1943. Upon his military discharge in 1946, Waters returned to East Lansing and completed his bachelor's degree in physical education. After graduation in 1950, he turned down a professional offer from the Green Bay Packers and entered the interscholastic coaching field with two years at Walled Lake and one season at Albion High School. In 1953, Muddy accepted the position of athletic director at Hillsdale College and in the following year assumed the dual role of AD and head football coach. His collegiate coaching record for 27 years, prior to his MSU assignment, was an imposing 166-80-7. Failing to post a winning record over three years in East Lansing, on November 14, 1982, with one game remaining on the schedule and two years remaining on his contract, it was announced that Muddy would step aside at season's end. Waters would later admit that coaching at the Big Ten level had been more demanding than he had previously experienced. Although his three years were less than spectacular, Muddy, in Doug Weaver's words, "has given so much to Michigan State University and the football program. He has conducted himself with dignity."

1980 (3-8; 2-6 in Big Ten: 9th)
Coach: Frank "Muddy" Waters

9-13	A	Illinois	17-20	L
9-20	A	Oregon	7-35	L
9-27	H	Western Michigan	33-7	W
10-4	H	Notre Dame	21-26	L
10-11	A	Michigan	23-27	L
10-18	H	Wisconsin	7-17	L
10-25	A	Purdue	25-36	L
11-1	H	Ohio State	16-48	L
11-8	H	Northwestern	42-10	W
11-15	A	Minnesota	30-12	W
11-22	H	Iowa	0-41	L

1981 (5-6; 4-5 in Big Ten: tie for 6th)
Coach: Frank "Muddy" Waters

9-12	H	Illinois	17-27	L
9-19	A	Ohio State	13-27	L
9-26	H	Bowling Green	10-7	W
10-3	H	Notre Dame	7-20	L
10-10	H	Michigan	20-38	L
10-17	H	Wisconsin	33-14	W
10-24	A	Purdue	26-27	L
10-31	H	Indiana	26-3	W
11-7	A	Northwestern	61-14	W
11-14	H	Minnesota	43-36	W
11-21	A	Iowa	7-36	L

1982 (2-9; 2-7 in Big Ten: tie for 8th)
Coach: Frank "Muddy" Waters

9-11	A	Illinois	16-23	L
9-18	H	Ohio State	10-31	L
9-25	A	Miami (FL)	22-25	L
10-2	H	Notre Dame	3-11	L
10-9	A	Michigan	17-31	L
10-16	A	Wisconsin	23-24	L
10-23	H	Purdue	21-24	L
10-30	A	Indiana	22-14	W
11-6	H	Northwestern	24-28	L
11-13	A	Minnesota	26-7	W
11-20	H	Iowa	18-24	L

George Perles (1983-1994)

George Perles was named to succeed Frank "Muddy" Waters on December 3, 1982, just six months after taking the reigns as head coach of the Philadelphia Stars of the United States Football League. As a sophomore tackle with the Spartans in 1958, he earned a varsity "S," but sustained a knee injury in a game against Wisconsin that ended his playing career. Perles went on to earn a B.S. degree in 1960 and an M.A. degree in 1961, at which time he also worked as a graduate assistant under Duffy Daugherty. From 1961-1964 he was a successful prep coach at two stops, St. Rita in Chicago and St. Ambrose in Detroit. George's college coaching career began as an assistant under John McVay at the University of Dayton for the 1965 and 1966 seasons. Duffy brought him back to the MSU campus as an assistant in 1967, first as the defensive backfield coach and then in 1970 as defensive line coach. Moving into the professional football ranks in 1972, Perles would gain great fame as architect of the National Football League's Pittsburgh Steelers' famed "Steel Curtain" defense. In 10 years as an assistant under head coach Chuck Noll, including the last three as assistant head coach, George played a significant role in winning four Super Bowl championships (1974, 1975, 1978, 1979) and recognition as "The Team of the Decade" in the 1970s. As the Spartans' head man from 1983-1994 his teams recorded a composite 73-62-4 record with seven teams making bowl appearances. Two squads (1987 and 1990) won conference titles with the No. 8 nationally ranked 1987 edition winning the Rose Bowl and vaulting Coach Perles into the limelight as the *Football News* Coach of the Year.

1983 (4-6-1; 2-6-1 in Big Ten: 7th)
Coach: George Perles

9-10	H	Colorado	23-17	W
9-17	A	Notre Dame	28-23	W
9-24	H	Illinois	10-20	L
10-1	A	Purdue	29-29	T
10-8	H	Michigan	0-42	L
10-15	A	Indiana	12-24	L
10-22	A	Ohio State	11-21	L
10-29	H	Minnesota	34-10	W
11-5	A	Northwestern	9-3	W
11-12	H	Iowa	6-12	L
11-19	A	Wisconsin	0-32	L

1984 (6-6; 2-6-1 in Big Ten: tie for 6th)
Coach: George Perles

9-8	A	Colorado	24-21	W
9-15	H	Notre Dame	20-24	L
9-22	A	Illinois	7-40	L
9-29	H	Purdue	10-13	L
10-6	A	Michigan	19-7	W
10-13	H	Indiana	13-6	W
10-20	H	Ohio State	20-23	L
10-27	A	Minnesota	20-13	W
11-3	H	Northwestern	27-10	W
11-10	A	Iowa	17-16	W
11-17	A	Wisconsin	10-20	L
12-22	A_PN	Army	>6-10	L
		>Cherry Bowl		

1985 (7-5; 5-3 in Big Ten: tie for 4th)
Coach: George Perles

9-14	H	Arizona State	12-3	W
9-21	A	Notre Dame	10-27	L
9-28	H	Western Michigan	7-3	W
10-5	A	Iowa	31-35	L
10-12	H	Michigan	0-31	L
10-19	H	Illinois	17-30	L
10-26	A	Purdue	28-24	W
11-2	H	Minnesota	31-26	W
11-9	A	Indiana	35-16	W
11-16	H	Northwestern	32-0	W
11-23	A	Wisconsin	41-7	W
12-31	A_BR	Georgia Tech	>14-17	L
		>All American Bowl		

1986 (6-5; 4-4 in Big Ten: tie for 5th)
Coach: George Perles

9-13	A	Arizona State	17-20	L
9-20	H	Notre Dame	20-15	W
9-27	H	Western Michigan	45-10	W
10-4	H	Iowa	21-24	L
10-11	A	Michigan	6-27	L
10-18	H	Illinois	29-21	W
10-25	H	Purdue	37-3	W
11-1	A	Minnesota	52-23	W
11-8	H	Indiana	14-17	L
11-15	A	Northwestern	21-24	L
11-22	H	Wisconsin	23-13	W

1987 (9-2-1; 7-0-1 in Big Ten: 1st)
Coach: George Perles

9-7	H	Southern California	27-13	W
9-19	A	Notre Dame	8-31	L
9-26	H	Florida State	3-31	L
10-3	A	Iowa	19-14	W
10-10	H	Michigan	17-11	W
10-17	H	Northwestern	38-0	W
10-24	A	Illinois	14-14	T
10-31	A	Ohio State	13-7	W
11-7	H	Purdue	45-3	W
11-14	H	Indiana	27-3	W
11-21	A	Wisconsin	30-9	W
1-1-88	A_PS	Southern California	>20-17	W
		>Rose Bowl		

1988 (6-5-1; 6-1-1 in Big Ten: 2nd)
Coach: George Perles

9-10	H	Rutgers	13-17	L
9-17	H	Notre Dame	3-20	L
9-24	A	Florida State	7-30	L
10-1	A	Iowa	10-10	T
10-8	A	Michigan	3-17	L
10-15	H	Northwestern	36-3	W
10-22	A	Illinois	28-21	W
10-29	H	Ohio State	20-10	W
11-5	H	Purdue	48-3	W
11-12	A	Indiana	38-12	W
11-19	H	Wisconsin	36-0	W
1-1-89	A_JX	Georgia	>27-34	L
		>Gator Bowl		

1989 (8-4; 6-2 in Big Ten: tie for 3rd)
Coach: George Perles

9-16	H	Miami (OH)	49-0	W
9-23	A	Notre Dame	13-21	L
9-30	H	Miami (FL)	20-26	L
10-7	A	Iowa	17-14	W
10-14	H	Michigan	7-10	L
10-21	H	Illinois	10-14	L
10-28	A	Purdue	28-21	W
11-4	A	Indiana	51-20	W
11-11	H	Minnesota	21-7	W
11-18	H	Northwestern	76-14	W
11-25	A	Wisconsin	31-3	W
12-25	A_HO	Hawaii	>33-13	W
		> Aloha Bowl		

1990 (8-3-1; 6-2 in Big Ten: tie for 1st)
Coach: George Perles

9-15	A	Syracuse	23-23	T
9-22	H	Notre Dame	19-20	L
9-29	H	Rutgers	34-10	W
10-6	H	Iowa	7-12	L
10-13	A	Michigan	28-27	W
10-20	A	Illinois	13-15	L
10-27	H	Purdue	55-33	W
11-3	H	Indiana	45-20	W
11-10	A	Minnesota	28-16	W
11-17	H	Northwestern	29-22	W
11-24	H	Wisconsin	14-9	W
12-31	A_EP	Southern California	>17-16	W
		>John Hancock Bowl		

1991 (3-8; 3-5 in Big Ten: tie for 6th)
Coach: George Perles

9-14	H	Central Michigan	3-20	L
9-21	A	Notre Dame	10-49	L
9-28	H	Rutgers	7-14	L
10-5	A	Indiana	0-31	L
10-12	H	Michigan	28-45	L
10-19	H	Minnesota	20-12	W
10-26	A	Ohio State	17-27	L
11-2	H	Northwestern	13-16	L
11-9	A	Wisconsin	20-7	W
11-16	A	Purdue	17-27	L
11-23	H	Illinois	27-24	W

1992 (5-6; 5-3 in Big Ten: 3rd)
Coach: George Perles

9-12	H	Central Michigan	20-24	L
9-19	H	Notre Dame	31-52	L
9-26	A	Boston College	0-14	L
10-3	H	Indiana	42-31	W
10-10	A	Michigan	10-35	L
10-17	A	Minnesota	20-15	W
10-24	A	Ohio State	17-27	L
10-31	A	Northwestern	27-26	W
11-7	H	Wisconsin	26-10	W
11-14	H	Purdue	35-13	W
11-21	A	Illinois	10-14	L

1993 (6-6; 4-4 in Big Ten: 7th)
Coach: George Perles

9-11	H	Kansas	31-14	W
9-18	A	Notre Dame	14-36	L
9-25	H	Central Michigan	48-34	W
10-9	H	Michigan	17-7	W
10-16	A	Ohio State	21-28	L
10-23	A	Iowa	24-10	W
10-30	H	Indiana	0-10	L
11-6	H	Northwestern	31-29	W
11-13	A	Purdue	27-24	W
11-27	H	Penn State	37-38	L
12-4	A_TY	Wisconsin	>20-41	L
12-28	A_ME	Louisville	<7-18	L
		> Coca Cola Bowl		
		< Liberty Bowl		

1994 (5-6; 4-4 in Big Ten: tie for 5th)
Coach: George Perles

9-10	A	Kansas	10-17	L
9-17	H	Notre Dame	20-21	L
9-24	H	Miami (OH)	45-10	W
10-1	H	Wisconsin	29-10	W
10-8	A	Michigan	20-40	L
10-15	H	Ohio State	7-23	L
10-22	A	Iowa	14-19	L
10-29	H	Indiana	27-21	W
11-5	A	Northwestern	35-17	W
11-12	H	Purdue	42-30	W
11-26	A	Penn State	31-59	L

Nick L. Saban (1995-1999)

In replacing George Perles, President McPherson took command of the search committee. Through the interview process, the front runners appeared to be Frank Kantner, offensive coordinator at Penn State, and Rick Neuheisel, the top assistant at the University of Colorado. Meanwhile, Jack Ebling, feature sports writer for *The State Journal*, wrote in support of a former Spartan assistant, the defensive coordinator for the Cleveland Browns, Nick Saban. Although never publicly revealed, rumors insisted that Kantner was offered and turned down the position. Saban was then offered and accepted with the comment: "Michigan State is a great school. I would like to be here as long as Michigan State wants me to be." The 43-year-old Saban, a native of Fairmont, WV, earned bachelor's (1973) and master's (1975) degrees at Kent State, where he was a standout defensive back from 1970-1972 and a letterman as a shortstop in baseball. The path along Nick Saban's 25-year coaching career has many turns. He began as a graduate assistant at his alma mater while later becoming an official staff member as Kent's linebacker coach in 1975-1976. He moved on as an assistant at Syracuse for one year, followed by two years at West Virginia, two years at Ohio State, and the 1982 season at the U.S. Naval Academy. Nick then joined the George Perles's MSU staff from 1983-1987, rising to the position of defensive coordinator. He left East Lansing to become the secondary coach for the Houston Oilers in 1988-1989. In a lone season as head coach at Toledo University (1990), Saban led the Rockets to a 9-2 record and a co-championship of the Mid-American Conference. He returning to the professional ranks in 1991 as defensive coordinator with the Cleveland Browns, a position he held for four years prior to returning to MSU in 1995. Nick Saban's head coaching career at MSU would last just five years, from 1995-1999. Although his legacy would only be a mildly impressive composite record of 34-24-1, some imposing wins were included in that victory column. Furthermore, it was generally agreed that Nick had achieved a sense of stability for the Spartan program. During the week following the 1999 team banquet, behind-the-scene negotiations were being played out as Saban was being actively pursued by officials from Louisiana State University (LSU). Then on November 29, the 48-year-old coach informed his players he had been offered the head coaching position at LSU. Even though he had twice flirted with NFL head coaching positions during his MSU tenure (Giants in 1995 and Colts in 1998), this announcement came as a shock to the Michigan State community. It seemed incredulous. After all his team had just finished an impressive 10-2 season and was headed for the Citrus Bowl, just weeks away. On the next morning, after just one evening of deliberation, Saban again met with the assembled team and in a brief 10-minute speech disclosed he was *taking* the LSU job. Shortly thereafter he was aboard a private jet headed for a press conference in Baton Rouge, LA. The Saban era had quickly ended. He had been lured by a five-year contract at $6.25 million making him the third-highest paid collegiate coach in the country. The MSU administration had been in no mood to engage in a bidding war.

1995 (6-5-1; 4-3-1 in Big Ten: 5th)
Coach: Nick L. Saban

9-9	H	Nebraska	10-50	L
9-16	A	Louisville	30-7	W
9-23	A	Purdue	35-35	T
9-30	H	Boston College	25-21	W
10-7	H	Iowa	7-21	L
10-14	A	Illinois	27-21	W
10-21	H	Minnesota	34-31	W
10-28	H	Wisconsin	14-45	L
11-4	H	Michigan	28-25	W
11-11	A	Indiana	31-13	W
11-25	H	Penn State	20-24	L
12-29	A_SH	Louisiana State	>26-45	L
	> Independence Bowl			

1996 (6-6; 5-3 in Big Ten, tie for 5th)
Coach: Nick L. Saban

8-31	H	Purdue	52-14	W
9-7	A	Nebraska	14-55	L
9-21	H	Louisville	20-30	L
9-28	H	Eastern Michigan	47-0	W
10-5	A	Iowa	30-37	L
10-12	H	Illinois	42-14	W
10-19	A	Minnesota	27-9	W
10-26	H	Wisconsin	30-13	W
11-2	A	Michigan	29-45	L
11-9	H	Indiana	38-15	W
11-23	A	Penn State	29-32	L
12-31	A_TU	Stanford	>0-38	L
	> Sun Bowl			

1997 (7-5; 4-4 in Big Ten: tie for 6th)
Coach: Nick L. Saban

9-6	H	Western Michigan	42-10	W
9-13	H	Memphis	51-21	W
9-20	A	Notre Dame	23-7	W
10-4	H	Minnesota	31-10	W
10-11	A	Indiana	38-6	W
10-18	A	Northwestern	17-19	L
10-25	H	Michigan	7-23	L
11-1	H	Ohio State	13-37	L
11-8	A	Purdue	21-22	L
11-22	A	Illinois	27-17	W
11-29	H	Penn State	49-14	W
12-25	A_HO	Washington	>23-51	L
	> Aloha Bowl			

1998 (6-6; 4-4 in Big Ten: 6th)
Coach: Nick L. Saban

8-29	H	Colorado State	16-23	L
9-5	A	Oregon	14-48	L
9-12	H	Notre Dame	45-23	W
9-26	A	Michigan	17-29	L
10-3	H	Central Michigan	38-7	W
10-10	H	Indiana	38-31	W
10-24	A	Minnesota	18-19	L
10-31	H	Northwestern	29-5	W
11-7	A	Ohio State	28-24	W
11-14	H	Purdue	24-25	L
11-21	H	Illinois	41-9	W
11-28	A	Penn State	28-51	L

1999 (10-2; 6-2 in Big Ten: tie for 2nd)
Coach: Nick L. Saban

9-2	H	Oregon	27-20	W
9-11	H	Eastern Michigan	51-7	W
9-18	A	Notre Dame	23-13	W
9-25	A	Illinois	27-10	W
10-2	H	Iowa	49-3	W
10-9	H	Michigan	34-31	W
10-16	A	Purdue	28-52	L
10-23	A	Wisconsin	10-40	L
11-6	H	Ohio State	23-7	W
11-13	A	Northwestern	34-0	W
11-20	H	Penn State	35-28	W
1-1	A_OR	Florida	>37-34	W
	> Citrus Bowl			

Bobby Williams (2000-2002)

President Peter McPherson immediately appointed associate head coach Bobby Williams, as the interim head coach and the search for a permanent man was underway. Initially, two names surfaced: Stanford head coach and Spartan alum Tyrone Willingham, along with Tom Izzo's college roommate Steve Marriucci, who was head coach of the NFL's San Francisco 49'ers. After neither of the two expressed interest, the search turned to Minneapolis where McPherson interviewed the Golden Gophers' head coach, Glen Mason, a man who had earlier turned down the LSU job. When it appeared Mason would be loyal to the Minnesota post, the president became impressed by impromptu, yet organized, appeals on behalf of Bobby Williams, first from a contingency of players and then from the cadre of assistant coaches. On Sunday, December 5, a press conference was quickly arranged to announce that the 41-year-old Bobby Williams would be handed the head coaching position. No more "interim" in the title and it all took place in less than a week. Williams, a St. Louis native, was an all-state running back at Summer High School in 1976. He then became a four-year letterman at Purdue, serving as tri-captain during the senior year of 1981. After beginning his college career as a running back, Bobby became a three-year starter at defensive back, being selected honorable mention All-Big Ten as a senior. Prior to joining George Perles's staff on May 31, 1990, he gained nine years of experience at four different stops. Williams first spent one season (1982) at his alma mater as a graduate assistant. His first full-time position (1983-1984) was at Ball State where he coached both running backs and defensive backs. From 1985 to 1989, he was the offensive backfield coach at Eastern Michigan. His final stop, before coming to East Lansing, was one year (1990) as receiver coach at Kansas University under that same Glen Mason, now at Minnesota.

2000 (5-6; 2-6 in Big Ten: tie for 9th)
Coach: Bobby Williams

9-9	H	Marshall	34-24	W
9-16	A	Missouri	13-10	W
9-23	H	Notre Dame	27-21	W
9-30	H	Northwestern	17-37	L
10-7	A	Iowa	16-21	L
10-14	H	Wisconsin	10-17	L
10-21	A	Michigan	0-14	L
10-28	H	Illinois	14-10	W
11-4	A	Ohio State	13-27	L
11-11	H	Purdue	30-10	W
11-18	A	Penn State	23-42	L

2001 (7-5; 3-5 in Big Ten: tie for 8th)
Coach: Bobby Williams

9-8	H	Central Michigan	35-21	W
9-22	A	Notre Dame	17-10	W
9-29	A	Northwestern	26-27	L
10-13	H	Iowa	31-28	W
10-20	A	Minnesota	19-28	L
10-27	A	Wisconsin	42-28	W
11-3	H	Michigan	26-24	W
11-10	H	Indiana	28-37	L
11-17	A	Purdue	14-24	L
11-24	H	Penn State	37-42	L
12-1	H	Missouri	55-7	W
12-31	A_SE	Fresno State	>44-35	W
	> Silicon Valley Bowl			

2002 (4-8; 2-6 in Big Ten: 9th)
Coach: Bobby Williams

8-30	H	Eastern Michigan	56-7	W
9-7	H	Rice	27-10	W
9-14	H	California	22-46	L
9-21	H	Notre Dame	17-21	L
9-28	H	Northwestern	39-24	W
10-12	A	Iowa	16-44	L
10-19	H	Minnesota	7-28	L
10-26	H	Wisconsin	24-42	L
11-2	A	Michigan	3-49	L
11-9	A	Indiana	56-21	W
11-16	H	Purdue	42-45	L
11-23	A	Penn State	7-61	L

John L. Smith (2003-)

On November 4, 2002 after almost 3 years of service, Bobby Williams was relieved of his position as head football coach. Player discipline problems on top of unexpected loses forced Athletic Director Ron Mason to make the move mid-season. Offensive Coordinator and Assistant Head Coach Morris Watts too command of the team for six weeks while

a search was conducted for a permanent replacement. On December 19, 2002 John L. Smith, ranked 14th nationally in wins among active NCAA 1-A football coaches, was named MSU's 23rd head coach. Coming from Louisville and having taken eleven of his fourteen teams into postseason play, he had built an impressive 110-60 career record (.647), including 71-25 (.740) in conference games. A key to Smith's success was willingness to work his way up through the ranks. He began by earning a B.S. in physical education from Weber State while lettering three years as a quarterback and linebacker (1969-71). He started his coaching career as a graduate assistant for his alma mater in 1971 before moving on to assist Montana (1972-76), where simultaneously he earned an M.S. in physical education. From there he moved to Nevada to become a defensive coordinator (1977-81), before serving as both an assistant head coach and defensive coordinator at Nevada (1977-81), Idaho (1982-85), Wyoming (1986) and Washington State (1987). His first chance to take the helm came as he returned to Idaho from 1989-1994 and became the school's winningest head coach ever, compiling a total of 53-21 (.716), with five postseason showings and three straight trips to the NCAA 1-AA play-offs from 1992-94. Utah State was the next to prosper from his leadership, as there Smith earned a 16-18 mark in three seasons with consecutive Big West Conference titles in 1996-97. Next, he inherited a Louisville Cardinal team that had gone 1-10 in 1997. He proceeded to construct an unprecedented turn around and reach a 41-21 (.661) mark in five seasons (1998-2002), including five straight bowl appearances and back to back Conference USA titles in 2000-01. The bowl trips equaled the number of postseason appearances in Louisville's history prior to his arrival and the five consecutive winning seasons marked a first for the school. With a resume of turning losing programs into winning ones and working at success from the bottom up, MSU was confident that Smith, though not the most well known candidate for the job, would be the right man to serve as the next Spartan head coach.

Year-by-Year Results

Year	W-L-T	Pct.	Pts.	Op. Pts.	Coach
1896	1-2-1	.375	26	42	No Coach
1897	4-2-1	.643	146	106	Henry Keep
1898	4-3-0	.571	142	127	Henry Keep
1899	2-4-1	.357	81	101	Charles O. Bemies
1900	1-3-0	.250	51	67	Charles O. Bemies
1901	3-4-1	.437	120	94	George Denman
1902	4-5-0	.444	93	206	George Denman
1903	6-1-1	.813	178	24	Chester L. Brewer
1904	8-1-0	.888	380	16	Chester L. Brewer
1905	9-2-0	.818	280	75	Chester L. Brewer
1906	7-2-2	.727	195	28	Chester L. Brewer
1907	4-2-1	.643	127	60	Chester L. Brewer
1908	6-0-2	.875	205	22	Chester L. Brewer
1909	8-1-0	.888	233	17	Chester L. Brewer
1910	6-1-0	.857	168	8	Chester L. Brewer
1911	5-1-0	.833	93	30	John F. Macklin
1912	7-1-0	.875	297	98	John F. Macklin
1913	7-0-0	1.000	180	28	John F. Macklin
1914	5-2-0	.714	197	57	John F. Macklin
1915	5-1-0	.833	259	38	John F. Macklin
1916	4-2-1	.643	126	26	Frank Sommers
1917	0-9-0	.000	23	179	Chester L. Brewer
1918	4-3-0	.571	134	68	George E. Gauthier
1919	4-4-1	.500	132	99	Chester L. Brewer
1920	4-6-0	.400	270	166	George "Potsy" Clark
1921	3-5-0	.375	68	126	Albert M. Barron
1922	3-5-2	.350	111	135	Albert M. Barron
1923	3-5-0	.375	57	144	Ralph H. Young
1924	5-3-0	.625	210	48	Ralph H. Young
1925	3-5-0	.375	105	106	Ralph H. Young
1926	3-4-1	.438	97	171	Ralph H. Young
1927	4-5-0	.444	111	128	Ralph H. Young
1928	3-4-1	.438	153	66	Harry G. Kipke
1929	5-3-0	.625	244	104	James H. Crowley
1930	5-1-2	.750	151	32	James H. Crowley
1931	5-3-1	.611	291	61	James H. Crowley
1932	7-1-0	.937	220	64	James H. Crowley
1933	4-2-2	.625	73	49	Charles W. Bachman
1934	8-1-0	.888	153	56	Charles W. Bachman
1935	6-2-0	.750	207	57	Charles W. Bachman
1936	6-1-2	.777	143	40	Charles W. Bachman
1937	8-2-0	.800	117	42	Charles W. Bachman
1938	6-3-0	.666	133	59	Charles W. Bachman
1939	4-4-1	.500	102	92	Charles W. Bachman
1940	3-4-1	.438	108	76	Charles W. Bachman
1941	5-3-1	.611	150	77	Charles W. Bachman
1942	4-3-2	.555	120	99	Charles W. Bachman
1943			no varsity team due to World War II		
1944	6-1-0	.857	167	31	Charles W. Bachman
1945	5-3-1	.611	120	128	Charles W. Bachman
1946	5-5-0	.500	181	202	Charles W. Bachman
1947	7-2-0	.777	167	101	Clarence L. Munn
1948	6-2-2	.700	359	130	Clarence L. Munn
1949	6-3-0	.666	309	107	Clarence L. Munn
1950	8-1-0	.888	243	107	Clarence L. Munn
1951	9-0-0	1.000	270	114	Clarence L. Munn
1952	9-0-0	1.000	312	84	Clarence L. Munn
1953	9-1-0	.900	240	110	Clarence L. Munn
1954	3-6-0	.333	177	149	Duffy Daugherty
1955	9-1-0	.900	.253	83	Duffy Daugherty
1956	7-2-0	.777	239	87	Duffy Daugherty
1957	8-1-0	.888	264	75	Duffy Daugherty
1958	3-5-1	.388	117	123	Duffy Daugherty
1959	5-4-0	.555	149	118	Duffy Daugherty
1960	6-2-1	.722	193	118	Duffy Daugherty
1961	7-2-0	.777	192	50	Duffy Daugherty
1962	5-4-0	.555	189	96	Duffy Daugherty
1963	6-2-1	.722	148	63	Duffy Daugherty
1964	4-5-0	.444	136	141	Duffy Daugherty
1965	10-1-0	.909	263	76	Duffy Daugherty
1966	9-0-1	.950	293	99	Duffy Daugherty
1967	3-7-0	.300	173	193	Duffy Daugherty
1968	5-5-0	.500	202	151	Duffy Daugherty
1969	4-6-0	.400	202	231	Duffy Daugherty
1970	4-6-0	.400	190	215	Duffy Daugherty
1971	6-5-0	.545	225	169	Duffy Daugherty
1972	5-5-1	.500	158	156	Duffy Daugherty
1973	5-6-0	.455	114	164	Dennis Stolz
1974	7-3-1	.682	270	196	Dennis Stolz
1975	7-4-0	.636	222	167	Dennis Stolz
1976	4-6-1	.409	236	278	Darryl Rogers
1977	7-3-1	.682	260	162	Darryl Rogers
1978	8-3-0	.727	411	170	Darryl Rogers
1979	5-6-0	.455	240	253	Darryl Rogers
1980	3-8-0	.273	221	279	Frank Waters
1981	5-6-0	.455	263	249	Frank Waters
1982	2-9-0	.181	202	242	Frank Waters
1983	4-6-1	.409	162	233	George Perles
1984	6-6-0	.500	193	203	George Perles
1985	7-5-0	.583	258	219	George Perles
1986	6-5-0	.545	285	197	George Perles
1987	9-2-1	.792	261	153	George Perles
1988	6-5-1	.542	269	177	George Perles
1989	8-4-0	.667	356	163	George Perles
1990	8-3-1	.708	312	223	George Perles
1991	3-8-0	.273	162	272	George Perles
1992	5-6-0	.455	238	261	George Perles
1993	6-6-0	.500	277	289	George Perles
1994	5-6-0	.455	280	267	George Perles
1995	6-5-1	.542	287	338	Nick Saban
1996	6-6-0	.500	358	302	Nick Saban
1997	7-5-0	.583	342	237	Nick Saban
1998	6-6-0	.500	336	294	Nick Saban
1999	10-2-0	.833	378	245	Nick Saban*
2000	5-6-0	.455	197	223	Bobby Williams
2001	7-5-0	.583	374	311	Bobby Williams
2002	4-8-0	.333	316	398	Bobby Williams

TOTALS

* Nick Saban left the head coaching position on November 30 to accept a similar position at Louisiana State University. Associate head coach Bobby Williams took over the head position on December 5, 1999 and coached the team to a 37-34 victory over the University of Florida on January 1, 2000, in the Citrus Bowl in Orlando, Florida.

Rushing Leaders (Since 1944)

CAREER RUSHING ATTEMPTS

84-87	Lorenzo White	1,082
89-92	Tico Duckett	836
86-89	Blake Ezor	800
96-98	Sedrick Irvin	755
92-96	Duane Goulbourne	627
99-01	T.J. Duckett	621
77-80	Steve Smith	574
69-71	Eric Allen	521
73-76	Rich Baes	507
73-76	Levi Jackson	474
94-97	Marc Renaud	451
73-75	Charlie Baggett	406
64-66	Clinton Jones	396
88-90	Hyland Hickson	384
90-93	Craig Thomas	362

CAREER RUSHING YARDAGE

84-87	Lorenzo White	4,887
89-92	Tico Duckett	4,212
86-89	Blake Ezor	3,749
96-98	Sedrick Irvin	3,504
99-01	T.J. Duckett	3,379
92-96	Duane Goulbourne	2,848
77-80	Steve Smith	2,676
69-71	Eric Allen	2,654
94-97	Marc Renaud	2,331
73-76	Levi Jackson	2,287
73-76	Rich Baes	2,234
46-49	Lynn Chadnois	2,093
64-66	Clinton Jones	1,921
88-90	Hyland Hickson	1,906
90-93	Craig Thomas	1,823
46-48	George Guerre	1,721
73-75	Charlie Baggett	1,706

CAREER RUSHING AVERAGE

(yards per attempt, minimum of 150 attempts)

46-48	George Guerre	6.75
46-49	Lynn Chadnois	6.52
61-63	Sherman Lewis	6.21
48-50	Sonny Grandelius	6.09
78-81	Derek Hughes	6.04
74-77	Jim Earley	5.78
52-54	Leroy Bolden	5.75
55-57	Walt Kowalczyk	5.58
50-52	Dick Panin	5.45
99-00	T. J. Duckett	5.44

CAREER RUSHING TOUCHDOWNS

84-87	Lorenzo White	43
96-98	Sedrick Irvin	35
86-89	Blake Ezor	34
99-01	T.J. Duckett	29
46-49	Lynn Chadnois	29
69-71	Eric Allen	28
89-92	Tico Duckett	26
90-93	Craig Thomas	25
51-54	Leroy Bolden	23
92-96	Duane Goulbourne	23
77-80	Steve Smith	21
73-75	Charlie Baggett	21

64-66	Clinton Jones	20
73-76	Rich Baes	20
48-50	Sonny Grandelius	19
88-90	Hyland Hickson	19
92-95	Scott Greene	19

SEASON RUSHING ATTEMPTS

1985	Lorenzo White	419
1987	Lorenzo White	357
1988	Blake Ezor	322
1995	Marc Renaud	312
1998	Sedrick Irvin	272
1991	Tico Duckett	272
1989	Blake Ezor	267
2001	T.J. Duckett	263
1971	Eric Allen	259
1990	Tico Duckett	257
1997	Sedrick Irvin	246
2000	T.J. Duckett	240
1996	Sedrick Irvin	237
1990	Hyland Hickson	234
1975	Levi Jackson	230

SEASON RUSHING YARDS

1985	Lorenzo White	2,066
1987	Lorenzo White	1,572
1988	Blake Ezor	1,496
1971	Eric Allen	1,494
2001	T.J. Duckett	1,420
1990	Tico Duckett	1,394
2000	T.J. Duckett	1,353
1989	Blake Ezor	1,299
1997	Sedrick Irvin	1,270
1991	Tico Duckett	1,204
1990	Hyland Hickson	1,196
1998	Sedrick Irvin	1,167
1996	Sedrick Irvin	1,067
1975	Levi Jackson	1,063
1995	Marc Renaud	1,057

SEASON RUSHING AVERAGE

(yards per attempt, minimum of 90 attempts)

1948	Lynn Chandnois	7.48
1946	George Guerre	7.03
1949	Lynn Chandnois	6.86
1978	Steve Smith	6.71
1963	Sherman Lewis	6.41
1950	Sonny Grandelius	6.27
1948	George Guerre	6.22
1974	Levi Jackson	6.16
1977	Jim Early	6.12
1964	Dick Gordon	6.02

SEASON RUSHING TOUCHDOWNS

1989	Blake Ezor	19
1971	Eric Allen	18
1995	Scott Greene	17
1985	Lorenzo White	17
1996	Sedrick Irvin	16
1987	Lorenzo White	16
1992	Craig Thomas	15
1990	Hyland Hickman	14
2001	T.J. Duckett	12
1950	Sonny Grandelius	11
1988	Blake Ezor	11
1974	Charlie Baggett	11
1998	Sedrick Irvin	10
1965	Clinton Jones	10
1948	Lynn Chandnois	10
1990	Tico Duckett	10
1949	Lynn Chandnois	10
1999	T.J. Duckett	10

SINGLE GAME RUSHING ATTEMPTS

1987	Lorenzo White, Ind	56
1985	Lorenzo White, Pur	53
1985	Lorenzo White, Minn	49
1988	Blake Ezor, Ind	44
1991	Tico Duckett, Wis	42
1985	Lorenzo White, Wis	42
1986	Lorenzo White, ND	41
1989	Blake Ezor, NW	41
1989	Blake Ezor, Hawaii	41

SINGLE GAME RUSHING YARDAGE

1971	Eric Allen, Pur (29 carries)	350
1987	Lorenzo White, Ind (56 carries)	292
1985	Lorenzo White, Ind (25 carries)	286
1966	Clinton Jones, Iowa (21 carries)	268
1988	Blake Ezor, Ind (44 carries)	250
2000	T.J. Duckett, Iowa (30 carries)	248
1971	Eric Allen, Wis (21 carries)	247
1985	Lorenzo White, Pur (53 carries)	244
1991	Tico Duckett, Minn (30 carries)	241
1997	Sedrick Irvin Penn St (28 carries)	238
1995	Marc Renaud, Minn (35 carries)	229
1990	Tico Duckett, Rutgers (33 carries)	229
1980	Steve Smith, NW (30 carries)	229
1989	Blake Ezor, Minn (41 carries)	228
1985	Lorenzo White, Iowa (39 carries)	226
1985	Lorenzo White, Wis (42 carries)	223
2000	T.J. Duckett (26 carries)	219
1991	Tico Duckett, Wis (42 carries)	216
1993	Duane Goulborne, Iowa (29 car.)	213
1979	Derek Hughes, Minn (31 carries)	213

SINGLE GAME RUSHING TOUCHDOWNS

1989	Blake Ezor, NW	6
1995	Scott Greene, Ill	4
1993	Craig Thomas, CMU	4
1992	Craig Thomas, Ind	4
1990	Tico Duckett, Pur	4
1989	Blake Ezor, Ind	4
1965	Clinton Jones, Iowa	4
1971	Eric Allen, Pur	4
1971	Eric Allen, Minn	4
1979	Derec Hughes, Minn	4
1980	Steve Smith, NW	4
1999	T.J. Duckett	4
1996	Sedrick Irvin, Ind.	4

Passing Leaders (Since 1944)

CAREER PASS ATTEMPTS

76-78	Ed Smith	789
82-86	Dave Yarema	767
96-99	Bill Burke	766
90-93	Jim Miller	746
79-82	John Leister	686
00-02	Jeff Smoker	662
94-97	Todd Schultz	593
94-95	Tony Banks	496
87-90	Dan Enos	478
78-81	Bryan Clark	409
85-88	Bobby McAllister	386
63-65	Steve Juday	384
98-01	Ryan VanDyke	288
73-75	Charlie Baggett	287
70-71	Mike Rasmussen	287

CAREER PASS COMPLETIONS

90-93	Jim Miller	467
82 86	Dave Yarema	464
76-78	Ed Smith	418
96-99	Bill Burke	416

00-02	Jeff Smoker	383
94-97	Todd Schultz	360
79-82	John Leister	313
94-95	Tony Banks	301
87-90	Dan Enos	297
78-81	Bryan Clark	204
63-65	Steve Juday	198
85-88	Bobby McAllister	194
98-01	Ryan Van Dyke	161
73-75	Charlie Baggett	128
49-51	Al Dorow	125

CAREER PASS COMPLETION PERCENTAGE

(minimum of 100 attempts)

90-93	Jim Miller	.629
87-90	Dan Enos	.621
94-97	Todd Schultz	.607
94-95	Tony Banks	.607
82-86	Dave Yarema	.605
83	Clark Brown	.582
00-02	Jeff Smoker	.579
98-01	Ryan Van Dyke	.561
96-99	Bill Burke	.543
76-78	Ed Smith	.530
63-65	Steve Juday	.516
55-57	Jim Ninowski	.508
85-88	Bobby McAllister	.503
78-81	Bryan Clark	.499
53-55	Earl Morrill	.495

CAREER PASSING YARDAGE

82-86	Dave Yarema	5,809
76-78	Ed Smith	5,706
00-02	Jeff Smoker	5,537
96-99	Bill Burke	5,463
90-93	Jim Miller	5,037
94-97	Todd Schultz	4,273
94-95	Tony Banks	4,129
79-82	John Leister	3,999
87-90	Dan Enos	3,837
85-88	Bobby McAllister	3,194
78-81	Bryan Clark	2,725
63-65	Steve Juday	2,576
73-75	Charlie Baggett	2,335
98-01	Ryan VanDyke	2,111
53-55	Earl Morrall	2,015

CAREER TOUCHDOWN PASSES THROWN

96-99	Bill Burke	46
82-86	Dave Yarema	43
76-78	Ed Smith	43
00-02	Jeff Smoker	40
94-97	Todd Schultz	27
63-65	Steve Juday	21
94-95	Tony Banks	20
79-82	John Leister	20
78-81	Bryan Clark	20
49-51	Al Dorow	19
46-49	Gene Glick	18
51-53	Tom Yewcic	18
85-88	Bobby McAllister	17
90-93	Jim Miller	17

SEASON PASSES ATTEMPTED

1998	Bill Burke	358
1993	Jim Miller	336
1999	Bill Burke	312
1997	Todd Schultz	299
1986	Dave Yarema	297
1978	Ed Smith	292
2001	Jeff Smoker	262
1995	Tony Banks	258
1976	Ed Smith	257

1982	John Leister	251
1980	John Leister	247
1989	Dan Enos	240
1977	Ed Smith	240
1994	Tony Banks	238
1984	Dave Yarema	222
1990	Dan Enos	220
1991	Jim Miller	218

SEASON PASS COMPLETIONS

1993	Jim Miller	215
1986	Dave Yarema	200
1998	Bill Burke	195
1997	Todd Schultz	177
1999	Bill Burke	173
1978	Ed Smith	169
2001	Jeff Smoker	166
1995	Tony Banks	156
1989	Dan Enos	153
1994	Tony Banks	145
1990	Dan Enos	137
1976	Ed Smith	132
1991	Jim Miller	130
1996	Todd Schultz	130
1992	Jim Miller	122

PASS COMPLETION PERCENTAGE

(minimum of 75 attempts)

1986	Dave Yarema (297-200)	.673
1993	Jim Miller (336-215)	.640
1992	Jim Miller (191-122)	.639
1989	Dan Enos (240-153)	.638
1995	Todd Schultz (83-52)	.627
2001	Jeff Smoker (262-166)	.634
1990	Dan Enos (220-137)	.623
1996	Todd Schultz (209-130)	.622
1994	Tony Banks (238-145)	.609
1995	Tony Banks (258-156)	.605
1991	Jim Miller (218-130)	.596
1997	Todd Schultz (299-177)	.592
1983	Clark Brown (141-82)	.582
1978	Ed Smith (292-169)	.579
1982	Dave Yarema (80-46)	.575

SEASON PASSING YARDS

1998	Bill Burke	2,595
1986	Dave Yarema	2,581
2001	Jeff Smoker	2,579
1993	Jim Miller	2,269
1978	Ed Smith	2,226
1999	Bill Burke	2,214
1995	Tony Banks	2,089
1989	Dan Enos	2,066
1994	Tony Banks	2,040
1997	Todd Schultz	2,003
1976	Ed Smith	1,749
1977	Ed Smith	1,731
1996	Todd Schultz	1,693
1990	Dan Enos	1,677
2002	Jeff Smoker	1,593

SEASON TOUCHDOWN PASSES THROWN

2001	Jeff Smoker	21
1999	Bill Burke	20
1978	Ed Smith	20
1998	Bill Burke	19
1997	Todd Schultz	18
1986	Dave Yarema	16
1981	Bryan Clark	14
1976	Ed Smith	13
1994	Tony Banks	11

1948	Gene Glick	11
1984	Dave Yarema	11
1977	Ed Smith	10
1980	John Leister	10
1974	Charlie Baggett	10
1966	Jimmy Raye	10
1952	Tom Yewcic	10
1985	Dave Yarema	10

SINGLE GAME PASS ATTEMPTS

1980	John Leister, Pur	54
1998	Bill Burke, OSU	46
1982	John Leister, Mich	46
2001	Damon Dowell, Pur	45
1996	Todd Schultz, Mich	45
1982	John Leister, Wis	45
1986	Dave Yarema, NW	45
1995	Tony Banks, LSU	44
1998	Bill Burke, Penn St.	44
1981	Bryan Clark, Minn	43
1993	Jim Miller, OSU	42
1978	Ed Smith, Minn	42
1992	Jim Miller, ND	41
1978	Ed Smith, ND	41
1998	Bill Burke, Pur	40

SINGLE GAME PASS COMPLETIONS

1982	John Leister, Mich	32
1993	Jim Miller, OSU	31
1991	Jim Miller, Mich	30
1986	Dave Yarema, NW	30
1998	Bill Burke, Pur	28
1978	Ed Smith, ND	27
1978	Ed Smith, Minn	26
1986	Dave Yarema, Ariz. St.	26
2000	Ryan Van Dyke, Mich	26
1986	Dave Yarema, Minn	25
1982	John Leister, Wis	25
2001	Jeff Smoker, Penn St.	24
2001	Damon Dowell, Pur	24
2998	Bill Burke, Ind	24
1997	Todd Schultz, NW	24
1996	Todd Schultz, Mich.	24

SINGLE GAME PASSING YARDS

1999	Bill Burke, Mich	400
2001	Jeff Smoker, Fresno St.	376
1978	Ed Smith, Ind	369
1993	Jim MIller, OSU	360
2001	Jeff Smoker, Penn St.	356
1986	Dave Yarema, NW	352
1995	Tony Banks, LSU	348
1998	Bill Burke, Pur	345
2001	Jeff Smoker, Wis	326
1976	Ed Smith, N.C. State	324
1998	Bill Burke, Ind	324
1998	Bill Burke, OSU	323
1986	Dave Yarema, Minn	321
1978	Ed Smith, Wis	320
1985	Tony Banks, Mich	318
1981	Bryan Clark, Minn	318

SINGLE GAME TOUCHDOWN PASSES THROWN

1948	Gene Glick, Iowa State	4
1970	Mike Rasmussen, Ind	4
1978	Ed Smith, Wis	4
1998	Bill Burke, Central Mich.	4
1999	Bill Burke, Iowa	4
	13 players on 25 occasions	3

Receiving Leaders (Since 1944)

CAREER RECEPTIONS

85-88	Andre Rison	146
88-91	Courtrney Hawkins	138
01-02	Charles Rogers	135
96-99	Gari Scott	134
98-01	Chris Baker	133
98-99	Plaxico Burress	131
91-94	Mill Coleman	126
93-96	Derrick Mason	120
80-82	Herb Haygood	115
80-82	Ted Jones	118
75-79	Eugene Byrd	114
75-78	Kirk Gibson	112
92-95	Scott Greene	110
96-98	Sedrick Irvin	108
76-79	Mark Brammer	107

CAREER RECEIVING YARDS

85-88	Andre Rison	2,992
01-02	Charles Rogers	2,821
75-78	Kirk Gibson	2,347
88-91	Courtney Hawkins	2,210
98-99	Plaxico Burress	2,155
96-99	Gari Scott	2,095
75-79	Eugene Byrd	2,082
83-86	Mark Ingram	1,944
93-96	Derrick Mason	1,914
64-66	Gene Washington	1,857
91-94	Mill Coleman	1,813
98-01	Chris Baker	1,705
80-82	Ted Jones	1,678
98-01	Herb Haygood	1,640
80-83	Daryl Turner	1,577
2001	Charles Rogers	1,470

CAREER YARDS PER CATCH

(minimum 30 receptions)

75-78	Kirk Gibson	21.0
01-02	Charles Rogers	20.9
85-88	Andre Rison	20.5
83-86	Mark Ingram	20.5
80-83	Daryl Turner	20.2
55-57	Dave Kaiser	19.5
67-69	Frank Foreman	18.5
75-79	Eugene Byrd	18.3
64-66	Gene Washington	18.2
71-74	Mike Hurd	18.2
70-72	Billy Joe DuPree	17.7
89-90	James Bradley	17.7
93-96	Nigea Carter	17.4

CAREER TOUCHDOWN RECEPTIONS

01-02	Charles Rogers	27
75-78	Kirk Gibson	24
85-88	Andre Rison	20
98-99	Plaxico Burress	20
96-99	Gari Scott	18
64-66	Gene Washington	16
75-79	Eugene Byrd	15
83-86	Mark Ingram	14
49-51	Bob Carey	14
98-01	Chris Baker	13
80-83	Daryl Turner	13
88-91	Courtney Hawkins	12
80-82	Otis Grant	12
51-54	Ellis Duckett	10
93-96	Nigea Carter	10

SEASON RECEPTIONS

2002	Charles Rogers	68
2001	Charles Rogers	67
1999	Plaxico Burress	66
1998	Plaxico Burress	65
1989	Courtney Hawkins	60
1998	Gari Scott	58
2001	Herb Haygood	57
1986	Andre Rison	54
1995	Derrick Mason	53
1996	Derrick Mason	53
1995	Muhsin Muhammad	50
1993	Mill Coleman	48
1991	Courtney Hawkins	47
1981	Ted Jones	44
1978	Eugene Byrd	43

SEASON RECEIVING YARDS

2001	Charles Rogers	1,470
2002	Charles Rogers	1,351
1999	Plaxico Burress	1,142
1989	Courtney Hawkins	1,080
1998	Plaxico Burress	1,013
1986	Andre Rison	966
1988	Andre Rison	961
1995	Muhsin Muhsammad	867
1996	Derrick Mason	865
1998	Gari Scott	843
2001	Herb Haygood	808
1978	Kirk Gibson	806
1995	Derrick Mason	787
1987	Andre Rison	785
1976	Kirk Gibson	748

SEASON YARDS PER CATCH

(minimum 20 receptions)

1966	Gene Washington	25.0
1988	Andre Rison	24.6
1969	Frank Foreman	24.4
1977	Kirk Gibson	24.1
1996	Octavis Long	23.4
1987	Andre Rison	23.1
1984	Mark Ingram	22.7
1985	Mark Ingram	21.9
2001	Charles Rogers	21.9
1981	Daryl Turner	21.1
1949	Bob Carey	20.1
2002	Charles Rogers	19.9
1983	Daryl Turner	19.6
1986	Mark Ingram	19.2
1978	Kirk Gibson	19.2

SEASON TOUCHDOWN RECEPTIONS

2001	Charles Rogers	14
2002	Charles Rogers	13
1999	Plaxico Burress	12
1949	Bob Carey	8
1988	Andre Rison	8
1998	Plaxico Burress	8
1978	Eugene Byrd	7
1976	Kirk Gibson	7
1978	Kirk Gibson	7
1966	Gene Washington	7
1997	Gari Scott	7
1999	Gari Scott	6
1977	Kirk Gibson	6
1989	Courtney Hawkins	6
1991	Courtney Hawkins	6
1981	Ted Jones	5
1964	Gene Washington	5
1981	Otis Grant	5
1983	Daryl Turner	5
1985	Mark Ingram	5
1986	Mark Ingram	5
1986	Andre Rison	5
1987	Andre Rison	5
1996	Nigea Carter	5

SINGLE GAME RECEPTIONS

2000	Plaxico Burress, Fla	13
1992	Mitch Lyons, Mich	12
1986	Andre Rison, Ind	11
1997	Josh Keur, NW	11
1998	Plaxico Burress, Pur	10
2001	Charles Rogers, Fresno St.	10
1999	Plaxico Burress, Mich	10
1982	Darrin McClelland, Mich	10
1996	Derrick Mason, Mich	10
1980	Ted Jones, Ill	10
2001	Herb Haygood, Iowa	9
1998	Gari Scott, Penn St	9
1997	Sedrick Irvin, Mich	9
1995	Muhsin Muhammad, LSU	9
1989	Andre Rison, Georgia	9
1964	Gene Washington, ND	9
1982	Darrin McClelland, Wis	9
1982	Ted Jones, Mich	9
1986	Andre Rison, Wis	9
1989	Courtney Hawkins, Minn	9

SINGLE GAME RECEIVING YARDS

2001	Charles Rogers, Fresno State	270
1989	Andre Rison, Georgia	252
1999	Plaxico Burress, Mich	255
2001	Charles Rogers, Wisconsin	206
1989	Courtney Hawkins, Minn	197
1986	Andre Rison, Ind	196
1989	Courtney Hawkins, Pur	193
2001	Charles Rogers, Penn St.	191
2000	Plaxico Burress, Fla	185
1976	Kirk Gibson, NC State	173
1995	Muhsin Muhammad, LSU	171
2001	Charles Rogers, Missouri	168
1999	Plaxico Burress, NW	164
1987	Andre Rison, Wis	162
1979	Eugene Byrd, Iowa	159

SINGLE GAME TOUCHDOWN RECEPTIONS

2000	Plaxico Burress, Fla	3
1999	Plaxico Burress, NW	3
1999	Plaxico Burress, Iowa	3
1989	Andre Rison, Georgia	3
1986	Mark Ingram, Iowa	3
1965	Gene Washington, Ind	3

Scoring/Total Offense Leaders (Since 1944)

CAREER POINTS SCORED

87-90	John Langeloh	308
94-97	Chris Gardner	281
78-81	Morten Andersen	261
84-87	Lorenzo White	258
96-98	Sedrick Irvin	252
74-77	Hans Nielsen	230
96-99	Paul Edinger	213
86-89	Blake Ezor	204
46-49	Lynn Chandnois	186
99-01	T.J. Duckett	182
69-71	Eric Allen	182
89-92	Tico Duckett	168
92-95	Scott Greene	166
75-78	Kirk Gibson	156
51-54	Leroy Bolden	156

CAREER ALL-PURPOSE YARDS

(rushing, receiving and returns)

84-87	Lorenzo White	5,152
93-96	Derrick Mason	5,114
96-98	Sedrick Irvin	4,833
89-92	Tico Duckett	4,511

86-89	Blake Ezor	4,475
69-71	Eric Allen	4,446
77-80	Steve Smith	4,060
96-99	Gari Scott	3,979
88-91	Courtney Hawkins	3,946
99-01	T.J. Duckett	3,539
98-01	Herb Haygood	3,452
94-97	Marc Renaud	3,402
92-96	Duane Goulbourne	3,332
85-88	Andre Rison	3,270
46-49	Lynn Chandnois	3,205

CAREER TOTAL TOUCHDOWNS

84-87	Lorenzo White	43
96-98	Sedrick Irvin	42
86-89	Blake Ezor	34
46-49	Lynn Chadnois	31
99-01	T.J. Duckett	30
69-71	Eric Allen	30
01-02	Charles Rogers	29
89-92	Tico Duckett	28
92-95	Scott Greene	27
75-78	Kirk Gibson	26
51-54	Leroy Bolden	26
77-80	Steve Smith	25
90-93	Craig Thomas	25
92-96	Duane Goulbourne	24
64-66	Clinton Jones	23
61-63	Sherman Lewis	23

CAREER TOTAL OFFENSE ATTEMPTS

(rushing and passing attempts)

84-87	Lorenzo White	1,083
82-86	Dave Yarema	960
96-99	Bill Burke	909
90-93	Jim Miller	875
76-78	Ed Smith	875
89-92	Tico Duckett	863
00-02	Jeff Smoker	854
79-82	John Leister	830
86-89	Blake Ezor	802
96-98	Sedrick Irvin	762
87-90	Dan Enos	723
73-75	Charlie Baggett	693
85-88	Bobby McAllister	683
94-97	Todd Schultz	648
94-95	Tony Banks	635
63-65	Steve Juday	536

CAREER TOTAL OFFENSE YARDS

76-78	Ed Smith	5,556
00-02	Jeff Smoker	5,433
82-86	Dave Yarema	5,269
96-99	Bill Burke	4,934
84-87	Lorenzo White	4,887
90-93	Jim Miller	4,748
87-90	Dan Enos	4,301
89-92	Tico Duckett	4,212
94-97	Todd Schultz	4,112
94-95	Tony Banks	4,105
79-82	John Leister	4,073
73-75	Charlie Baggett	4,041
85-88	Bobby McAlliser	3,871
86-89	Blake Ezor	3,749
96-98	Sedrick Irvin	3,621

CAREER TOTAL OFFENSE YARDS PER ATTEMPT

(minimum 200 attempts)

53-55	Earl Morrall	7.41
51-53	Tom Yewcic	6.64
46-48	George Guerre	6.57
94-95	Tony Banks	6.46
01-02	Jeff Smoker	6.36

94-97	Todd Schultz	6.35
76-78	Ed Smith	6.35
46-49	Lynn Chandnois	6.35
48-50	Sonny Grandelius	6.17
61-63	Sherman Lewis	6.16
87-90	Dan Enos	5.95
73-75	Charlie Baggett	5.83

SEASON POINTS SCORED

1989	Blake Ezor	114
1995	Scott Greene	112
1971	Eric Allen	110
1996	Sedrick Irvin	108
1999	Paul Edinger	103
1985	Lorenzo White	102
1987	Lorenzo White	96
2001	Charles Rogers	96
1998	Paul Edinger	94
1992	Craig Thomas	90
1990	Hyland Hickson	90
1996	Chris Gardner	86
1997	Sedrick Irvin	84
1988	John Langeloh	83
1987	John Langeloh	79

SEASON TOTAL TOUCHDOWNS

1989	Blake Ezor	19
1996	Sedrick Irvin	18
1995	Scott Greene	18
1971	Eric Allen	18
1985	Lorenzo White	17
1987	Lorenzo White	16
2001	Charles Rogers	16
1992	Craig Thomas	15
1990	Hyland Hickson	15
1997	Sedrick Irvin	14
2001	T.J. Duckett	13
2002	Charles Rogers	13
1999	Plaxico Burress	12
1965	Clinton Jones	12
1950	Sonny Grandelius	12
1948	Lynn Chandnois	12

SEASON TOTAL OFFENSE ATTEMPTS

1998	Bill Burke	423
1985	Lorenzo White	420
1993	Jim Miller	377
1999	Bill Burke	361
1987	Lorenzo White	357
1989	Dan Enos	350
2001	Jeff Smoker	343
1986	Dave Yarema	339
1997	Todd Schultz	329
1994	Tony Banks	325
1988	Blake Ezor	323
1978	Ed Smith	321
1990	Dan Enos	311
1995	Tony Banks	310
1980	John Leister	301
1984	Dave Yarema	301

SEASON TOTAL OFFENSE YARDS

2001	Jeff Smoker	2,521
1986	Dave Yarema	2,359
1998	Bill Burke	2,342
1978	Ed Smith	2,247
1989	Dan Enos	2,219
1993	Jim Miller	2,109
1994	Tony Banks	2,100
1985	Lorenzo White	2,066
1999	Bill Burke	2,014
1995	Tony Banks	2,005
1997	Todd Schultz	1,925
1990	Dan Enos	1,810
1988	Bobby McAllister	1,757
1976	Ed Smith	1,738
1974	Charlie Baggett	1,713

SEASON TOTAL OFFENSE YARDS PER ATTEMPT

(minimum 100 attempts)

2001	Jeff Smoker	7.35
1974	Charlie Baggett	7.08
1996	Todd Schultz	7.07
1978	Eddie Smith	7.00
1986	Dave Yarema	6.96
1988	Bobby McAllister	6.78
1946	George Guerre	6.72
1978	Steve Smith	6.71
1949	Lynn Chandnois	6.66
1981	Bryan Clark	6.51
1995	Tony Banks	6.47
1994	Tony Banks	6.46
1989	Dan Enos	6.34
1966	Jimmy Raye	6.31
1950	Sonny Grandelius	6.28

SINGLE GAME TOTAL TOUCHDOWNS

1989	Blake Ezor, NW	6
1997	Sedrick Irvin, Penn St	4
1996	Sedrick Irvin, Ind	4
1996	Sedrick Irvin, Pur	4
1995	Scott Greene, Ill	4
1993	Craig Thomas, Central Mich	4
1992	Craig Thomas, Ind	4
1990	Tico Duckett, Pur	4
1989	Blake Ezor, Ind	4
1980	Steve Smith, NW	4
1979	Derek Hughes, Minn	4
1971	Eric Allen, Pur	4
1971	Eric Allen, Minn.	4
1965	Clinton Jones, Iowa	4
1947	Bub Crane, Hawaii	4
1999	T.J. Duckett, Penn St	4

SINGLE GAME POINTS SCORED

1989	Blake Ezor, NW	36
1995	Scott Greene, Ill	26
1997	Sedrick Irvin, Penn St	24
1996	Sedrick Irvin, Ind	24
1996	Sedrick Irvin, Pur	24
1993	Craig Thomas, Central Mich	24
1992	Craig Thomas, Ind	24
1990	Tico Duckett, Pur	24
1989	Blake Ezor, Ind	24
1965	Clinton Jones, Iowa	24
1947	Bud Crane, Hawaii	24
1971	Eric Allen, Pur	24
1971	Eric Allen, Minn	24
1979	Derek Hughes, Minn	24
1980	Steve Smith, NW	24
1999	T.J. Duckett, Penn St.	24

SINGLE GAME TOTAL OFFENSIVE YARDS

2001	Jeff Smoker, Fresno St.	393
1999	Bill Burke, Mich	383
1981	Bryan Clark, Minn	372
1978	Ed Smith, Ind	369
1971	Eric Allen, Pur	350
2001	Jeff Smoker, Wis	347
2001	Jeff Smoker, Penn St.	345
1981	Bryan Clark, Wis	343
1986	Dave Yarema, NW	342
1998	Bill Burke, Pur	332
1989	Dan Enos, Pur	330
1976	Ed Smith, NC State	324
1995	Tony Banks, LSU	320
1986	Dave Yarema, Minn	318
1998	Bill Burke, OSU	316

Defense Leaders (Since 1944)

CAREER TACKLES

76-79	Dan Bass	541
86-89	Percy Snow	473
94-97	Ike Reese	420
98-01	Josh Thornhill	395
88-91	Chuck Bullough	391
95-98	Sori Kanu	365
96-99	Aric Morris	350
99-02	Thomas Wright	346
84-87	Tim Moore	332
81-84	Jim Morrissey	329
93-96	Reggie Garnett	327
87-90	Carlos Jenkins	314
83-86	Shane Bullough	311
74-77	Paul Rudzinski	298
91-94	Matt Christensen	289

CAREER TACKLES FOR LOSSES

98-99	Julian Peterson	48
75-77	Larry Bethea	43
86-89	Travis Davis	39
97-99	Robaire Smith	38
98-01	Josh Thornhill	33
91-94	Juan Hammonds	33
82-84	Kelly Quinn	31
83-87	Mark Nichols	29
75-78	Mel Land	29
95-98	Courtney Ledyard	27
88-91	Bill Johnson	27
84-87	Tim Moore	27
94-97	Ike Reese	26
70-72	Ernie Hamilton	25
68-71	Ron Curl	25
80-83	Carl Banks	25
91-94	Matt Christensen	25

CAREER QUARTERBACK SACKS

75-77	Larry Bethea	33
98-99	Julian Peterson	25
82-85	Kelly Quinn	24
86-89	Travis Davis	24
97-99	Robaire Smith	22
83-87	Mark Nichols	15
75-78	Mel Land	15
80-83	Carl Banks	14
68-71	Ron Curl	14
95-97	Dimitrius Underwood	13
95-98	Courtney Ledyard	12
76-79	Larry Savage	12
70-73	John Shinsky	11
93-96	Chris Smith	10.5

CAREER PASS INTERCEPTIONS

46-49	Lynn Chandnois	20
84-87	Todd Krumm	18
82-85	Phil Parker	16
70-72	Brad VanPelt	14
85-88	John Miller	14
85-88	Kurt Larson	14
76-79	Mark Anderson	12
71-73	Bill Simpson	12
48-50	Jesse Thomas	12
92-95	Demetrice Martin	10
47-49	John Polonchek	10

CAREER INTERCEPTION YARDS

46-49	Lynn Chandnois	384
70-72	Brad VanPelt	268
82-85	Phil Parker	217
48-50	Jesse Thomas	212
84-87	Todd Krumm	198
47-49	John Polonchek	189

59-61	Bob Suci	152
85-88	John Miller	145
69-70	Brad McLee	145
76-79	Dan Bass	138
53-55	Earl Morrall	132

CAREER FUMBLE RECOVERIES

76-79	Dan Bass	12
76-79	Larry Savage	8
87-90	Carlos Jenkins	7
80-82	Smiley Creswell	7
77-80	John McCormick	7
75-78	Mel Land	7
66-67	George Chatlos	7
86-89	Matt Vanderbeek	6
94-97	Ike Reese	5
90-93	Myron Bell	5
75-77	Larry Bethea	5
73-77	Kim Rowekamp	5
73-75	Tom Standal	5
71-73	Ray Nester	5
71-73	Bill Simpson	5
70 72	Ernie Hamilton	5
71-73	Tom Kronner	5
81-84	Lonnie Young	5

CAREER PASSES BROKEN UP

96-99	Amp Campbell	56
98-00	Cedric Henry	41
98-00	Renaldo Hill	36
95-97	Ray Hill	30
77-81	James Burroughs	28
95-98	Sori Kanu	27
95-98	Lemar Marshall	27
99-02	Thomas Wright	30
98-01	Josh Thornhill	24
96-99	Aric Morris	23
84-87	Todd Krumm	21
80-83	Nate Hannah	21
98-01	Broderick Nelson	20
82-85	Phil Parker	20
91-94	Stan Callender	18
81-84	Lonnie Young	18

SEASON TACKLES

1991	Chuck Bullough	175
1989	Percy Snow	172
1990	Chuck Bullough	164
1988	Percy Snow	164
1979	Dan Bass	160
1985	Shane Bullough	156
1992	Ty Hallock	144
1997	Ike Reese	137
1984	Jim Morrissey	137
1978	Dan Bass	136
1977	Dan Bass	134
1999	Aric Morris	132
1983	Jim Morrissey	130
1982	James Neeley	130

SEASON TACKLES FOR LOSSES

1999	Julian Peterson (140 yds.)	30
1998	Julian Peterson (75 yds.)	18
1977	Larry Bethea (93 yds.)	18
2001	Mike Labinjo (64 yds.)	17
1997	Robaire Smith (66 yds.)	16
1987	Travis Davis (113 yds.)	16
1990	Bill Johnson (33 yds.)	15
1987	Tim Moore (73 yds.)	15
1984	Kelly Quinn (96 yds.)	15
2001	Josh Thornhill (29 yds.)	15
1999	Robaire Smith (81 yds.)	14
1993	Juan Hammonds (61 yds.)	14
1978	Mel Land (57 yds.)	14
1996	Courtney Ledyard (78 yards.)	13

1990	Bobby Wilson (48 yds.)	13
1983	Kelly Quinn (101 yds.)	13
1975	Larry Bethea (60 yds.)	13
1982	Howard McAdoo (40 yds.)	13

SEASON QUARTERBACK SACKS

1977	Larry Bethea (90 yds.)	16
1999	Julian Peterson (104 yds.)	15
1997	Robaire Smith (58 yds.)	12
1987	Travis Davis (105 yds.)	12
1984	Kelly Quinn (84 yds.)	12
1998	Julian Peterson (57 yds.)	10
1983	Kelly Quinn (84 yds.)	10
1996	Courtney Ledyard (63 yds.)	9
1976	Larry Bethea (61 yds.)	9
1999	Robaire Smith (71 yds.)	8
1997	Dimitrius Underwood (56 yds.)	8
1975	Larry Bethea (57 yds.)	8
1999	Hubert Thompson (44 yds.)	7
1993	Juan Hammonds (43 yds.)	7
1978	Mel Land (32 yds.)	7

SEASON INTERCEPTIONS

1987	Todd Krumm	9
1988	Kurt Larson	8
1987	John Miller	8
1950	Jesse Thomas	8
1994	Demetrice Martin	7
1949	Lynn Chandnois	7
1983	Phil Parker	7
1977	Mark Anderson	6
1973	Bill Simpson	6
1972	Paul Hayner	6
1970	Brad VanPelt	6
1951	Jim Ellis	6
1947	Lynn Chandnois	6

SEASON PASS INTERCEPTION YARDS

1983	Phil Parker	203
1949	Lynn Chandnois	183
1987	Todd Krumm	129
1971	Brad VanPelt	129
2000	Cedric Henry	118
1955	Earl Morrall	109
1949	John Polonchek	108
1948	George Guerre	106
1970	Brad McLee	106
1999	T.J. Turner	105
1988	John Miller	101
1978	Dan Bass	101
1970	Brad VanPelt	100

SEASON FUMBLE RECOVERIES

1966	George Chatlos	7
1973	Tom Kronner	5
1975	Tom Standal	5
1989	Matt Vanderbeek	5
1993	Myron Bell	4
1979	Dan Bass	4
1977	Dan Bass	4
1978	Larry Savage	4
1976	Larry Savage	4
	25 players on 25 occasions	3

SEASON PASSES BROKEN UP

1999	Amp Campbell	26
2000	Cedric Henry	24
2001	Broderick Nelson	20
1998	Lemar Marshall	16
1997	Ray Hill	16
1997	Amp Campbell	15
1996	Amp Campbell	14
2001	Thomas Wright	13
2001	Duron Bryan	13
1999	Renaldo Hill	13
1998	Cedric Henry	13
1981	James Burroughs	13

SINGLE GAME TACKLES

1979	Dan Bass, OSU	32
1969	Don Law, OSU	28
1979	Dan Bass, ND	24
1989	Percy Snow, Ill	23
1992	Ty Hallock, Minn	21
1985	Shane Bullough, Ind	21
1971	Brad VanPelt, ND	21
1969	Doug Barr, OSU	21
1967	Don Law, Ind	21

SINGLE GAME TACKLES FOR LOSSES

1998	Julian Peterson, OSU	7
1999	Julian Peterson, Oregon	6
2000	Julian Perterson, Fla	5
1987	Travis Davis, OSU	5
1968	Rich Saul, Iowa	5
2000	Josh Shaw, Wis	5

SINGLE GAME QUARTERBACK SACKS

1987	Travis Davis, OSU	5
1998	Julian Peterson, OSU	4
1984	Kelly Quinn, NW	4
1969	Rich Saul, Iowa	4
2001	Mike Labinjo, Wis	3
2000	Julian Peterson, Fla	3
1999	Julian Peterson, Illinois	3
1996	Courtney Ledyard, EMU	3
1984	Kelly Quinn, Colorado	3
1983	Kelly Quinn, Ill	3

SINGLE GAME PASS INTERCEPTIONS

1987	John Miller, Mich	4
1950	Jim Ellis, Oregon St	3
1950	Jesse Thomas, Ind	3
1950	Jesse Thomas, Mich	3
1949	John Polonchek, Wm & Mary	3
1970	Brad VanPelt, Wash St	3
1977	Mark Anderson, ND	3

SINGLE GAME FUMBLE RECOVERIES

1966	Phil Hoag, Ill	3
1961	Ernie Clark, Ill	3
1989	Matt Vanderbeek, Hawaii	3
	Several players tied	2

SINGLE GAME PASSES BROKEN UP

2001	Broderick Nelson, Wis	5
1999	Amp Campbell, NW	5
1998	Renaldo Hill, Minn	5
2000	Cedric Henry, Marshall	5
1998	Aric Morris, Minn	4
1999	Amp Campbell, Mich	4
1999	Amp Campbell, EMU	4
1996	Sorie Kanu, Penn St	4
1979	James Burroughs, Pur	4
2000	Thomas Wright, Pur	4
2000	Cedric Henry, Mich	4

Special Teams Leaders (Since 1944)

CAREER PUNTS

81-84	Ralf Mojsiejenko	279
98-01	Craig Jarett	239
77-80	Ray Stachowicz	230
92-95	Chris Salani	224
88-91	Josh Butland	220

71-73	Bill Simpson	196
85-87	Greg Montgomery	184
37-38	John Pingel	150
51-53	Tom Yewcic	123
96-98	Paul Edinger	114
62-64	Lou Bobich	107
67-68	Dick Berlinski	99
65-66	Dick Kenney	85

CAREER PUNTING AVERAGE

(minimum of 50 attempts)

85-87	Greg Montgomery	45.2
81-84	Ralf Mojsiejenko	43.8
77-80	Ray Stachowicz	43.3
98-01	Craig Jarett	42.9
37-38	John Pingel	42.1
88-91	Josh Butland	40.7
96-98	Paul Edinger	40.0
71-73	Bill Simpson	39.8
53-55	Earl Morrall	39.2
62-64	Lou Bobich	39.0
51-53	Tom Yewcic	38.7
74-76	Tom Birney	37.8

CAREER PUNT RETURN YARDS

96-99	Gari Scott (84 rets.)	1,088
93-96	Derrick Mason (61 rets.)	620
51-53	Jim Ellis (55 rets.)	619
83-86	Bobby Morse (70 rets.)	584
84-87	Todd Krumm (64 rets.)	561
46-48	George Guerre (35 rets.)	513
48-50	Jesse Thomas (27 rets.)	490
67-68	Frank Waters Jr. (44 rets.)	434
91-94	Mill Coleman (39 rets.)	411
96-98	Sedrick Irvin (27 rets.)	355
61-63	Sherman Lewis (32 rets.)	355
57-59	Dean Look (20 rets.)	349
74-76	Tom Hannon (41 rets.)	332
46-49	Horace Smith (21 rets.)	329

CAREER KICKOFF RETURN YARDS

93-96	Derrick Mason (106 rets.)	2,575
98-01	Herb Haygood (76 rest.)	1,770
88-91	Courtney Hawkins (65 rets.)	1,571
69-71	Eric Allen (62 rets.)	1,340
83-84	Larry Jackson (43 rets.)	1,022
79-81	Derek Hughes (36 rets.)	898
77-80	Bruce Reeves (45 rets.)	863
96-99	Gari Scott (37 rest.)	796
94-97	Marc Renaud (33 rets.)	661
96-98	Gari Scott (30 rets.)	659
92-93	Steve Holman (29 rets.)	625
83-86	Mark Ingram (27 ret.)	585
77-80	Steve Smith (30 rets.)	563
80-82	Otis Grant (27 rets.)	554
85-88	Craig Johnson (34 rets.)	541

CAREER POINTS AFTER TOUCHDOWNS

(made/attempted)

87-90	John Langeloh	137/140
78-81	Morten Andersen	126/129
94-97	Chris Gardner	125/132
74-77	Hans Nielsen	98/105
47-49	George Smith	94/116
96-99	Paul Edinger	75/81
01-01	Dave Rayner	70/72
85-86	Chris Caudell	60/69
51-53	Evan Slonac	55/63
65-66	Dick Kenney	50/58
92-93	Bill Stoyanovich	49/52
49-51	Bob Carey	47/68
82-84	Ralf Mojsiejenko	44/53
70-71	Borys Shlapak	43/47

CAREER FIELD GOALS

(made/attempted)

87-90	John Langeloh	57/79
94-97	Chris Gardner	52/75
96-99	Paul Edinger	46/58
78-81	Morten Andersen	45/72
74-77	Hans Nielsen	44/70
82-84	Ralf Mojsiejenko	35/53
92-93	Bill Stoyanovich	22/35
64-66	Dick Kenney	19/36
85-96	Chris Caudell	16/35
72-73	Dirk Kryt	15/27
91-92	Jim DelVerne	13/21
70-71	Borys Shlapak	13/34
01-02	Dave Rayner	18/30

SEASON PUNTS

1938	John Pingel	99
1982	Ralf Mojsiejenko	77
1984	Ralf Mojsiejenko	76
1985	Greg Montgomery	75
1983	Ralf Mojsiejenko	74
1991	Josh Butland	73
1972	Bill Simpson	73
1980	Ray Stachowicz	71
1987	Greg Montgomery	70
1973	Bill Simpson	67
2002	Jason Daily	66
1998	Craig Jarrett	64
1979	Ray Stachowicz	62
1999	Craig Jarrett	62
2000	Craig Jarrett	62

SEASON PUNTING AVERAGE

(minimum 20 attempts)

1986	Greg Montgomery	47.8
1980	Ray Stachowicz	46.2
1987	Greg Montgomery	45.0
1984	Ralf Mojsiejenko	44.7
1982	Ralf Mojsiejenko	44.6
1979	Ray Stachowicz	44.3
1985	Greg Montgomery	44.1
1983	Ralf Mojsiejenko	43.9
1998	Craig Jarrett	43.8
2001	Craig Jarrett	43.6
1999	Craig Jarrett	43.5
1978	Ray Stachowicz	43.1
1989	Josh Butland	43.1
1955	Earl Morrall	42.9
1937	John Pingel	42.6

SEASON PUNT RETURN YARDS

1999	Gari Scott (37 rets.)	488
1998	Gari Scott (32 rets.)	440
1950	Jesse Thomas (18 rets.)	358
1987	Todd Krumm (36 rets.)	322
1997	Sedrick Irvin (23 rets.)	313
1996	Derrick Mason (31 rets.)	312
1951	Jim Ellis (24 rets.)	305
2002	Ziehl Kavanaght (33 rets.)	287
1972	Bill Simpson (21 rets.)	286
1967	Frank Waters Jr. (24 rets.)	264
1995	Derrick Mason (24 rets.)	260
1966	Allen Brenner (22 rets.)	256
1946	George Guerre (16 rets.)	253
1978	Steve Smith (22 rets.)	224
1984	Bobby Morse (20 rets.)	218

SEASON KICKOFF RETURN YARDS

1994	Derrick Mason (36 rets.)	966
1995	Derrick Mason (35 rets.)	947
2001	Herb Haygood (24 rets.)	632
1969	Eric Allen (20 rets.)	598
2002	Jaren Hayes (31 rets.)	585
1997	Mark Renaud (27 rets.)	552
1970	Eric Allen (24 rets.)	549

1999	Herb Haygood (26 rets.)	534
1996	Derrick Mason (28 rets.)	524
1984	Larry Jackson (20 rets.)	522
1983	Larry Jackson (23 rets.)	500
1979	Derek Hughes (16 rets.)	497
1989	Courtney Hawkins (18 rets.)	454
1976	Tyrone Willingham (23 rets.)	454
1967	LaMarr Thomas (17 rets.)	392
1977	Bruce Reeves (19 rets.)	387
1986	Mark Ingram (17 rets.)	359

SEASON POINTS AFTER TOUCHDOWNS

(made/attempted)

1978	Morten Andersen	52/54
1989	John Langeloh	42/44
1999	Paul Edinger	40/41
1948	George Smith	39/50
1990	John Langeloh	38/38
1949	George Smith	38/41
1952	Evan Slonac	37/43
2001	Dave Rayner	36/37
1997	Chris Gardner	35/35
1996	Chris Gardner	35/39
2002	Dave Rayner	34/35
1993	Bill Stoyanovich	32/34
1986	Chris Caudell	31/36
1994	Chris Gardner	30/30
1966	Dick Kenney	30/35
1988	John Langeloh	29/30
1985	Chris Caudell	29/33

SEASON FIELD GOALS

(made/attempted)

1998	Paul Edinger	22/26
1999	Paul Edinger	21/26
1988	John Langeloh	18/27
1996	Chris Gardner	17/22
1987	John Langeloh	17/24
1977	Hans Nielsen	17/28
1981	Morten Andersen	15/20
1994	Chris Gardner	14/21
1982	Ralf Mojsiejenko	14/20
1995	Chris Gardner	12/16
1991	Jim DelVerne	12/17
1990	John Langloh	12/15
1980	Morten Andersen	12/18
1993	Bill Stoyanovich	11/21
1992	Bill Stoyanovich	11/14
1979	Morten Andersen	11/18
1965	Dick Kenney	11/17
1983	Ralf Mojsiejenko	11/17
1976	Hans Nielsen	11/20
2000	David Schaefer	11/17

SINGLE GAME PUNT RETURN YARDS

1996	Derrick Mason, EMU (6 rets.)	137
1997	Sedrick Irvin, Ind (4 rets.)	117
1966	Allen Brenner, Ill (3 rets.)	117
1950	Jesse Thomas, Minn (4 rets.)	113
1999	Gari Scott, Penn St. (5 rets.)	107
1995	Derrick Mason, Mich (3 rets.)	106
1950	Jesse Thomas, Wm & Mary (3 rt.)	105
1954	John Matsock, Ill (4 rets.)	104
1963	Sherman Lewis, NW (4 rets.)	103

SINGLE GAME KICKOFF RETURN YARDS

1994	Derrick Mason, Penn St (5 rets.)	186
1984	Larry Jackson, OSU (4 rets.)	168
1994	Derrick Mason, Mich (7 rets.)	156
1995	Derrick Mason, Ind (7 rets.)	148
1970	Eric Allen, Wash (5 rets.)	136
1998	Gari Scott, Oregon (5 rets.)	132
1995	Derrick Mason, LSU (4 rets.)	132

2000	Herb Haygood, Florida (6 rets.)	.. 132
1991	Courtney Hawkins, CMU (3 rt.)	131
1995	Derrick Mason, Minn (5 rets.)	 129
1994	Derrick Mason, Pur (4 rets.)	 125
1996	Derrick Mason, Penn St. (6 rets.)	122
1945	Russ Reader, Miami (5 rets.)	 122
1969	Eric Allen, OSU (7 rets.)	 119
1997	Mark Renaud, OSU (6 rets.)	 116

SINGLE GAME POINTS AFTER TOUCHDOWNS

1989	John Langeloh, NW	... 10
1948	George Smith, Hawaii	 8
1949	George Smith, Temple	 8
1949	George Smith, Arizona	 8
1952	Evan Slonac, Marquette	 8
1978	Morten Andersen, Ill	 8
2001	David Rayner, Missouri	 7
1999	Paul Edinger, Iowa	 7
1981	Morten Andersen, NW	 7
1989	John Langeloh, Miami (OH)	 7
1990	John Langeloh, Pur	 7

SINGLE GAME FIELD GOALS SCORED

1998	Paul Edinger, NW	 5
1998	Paul Edinger, OSU	 5
1988	John Langeloh, Wis	 5
1982	Ralf Mojsiejenko, Minn	 4
1981	Morten Andersen, Ind	 4
1979	Morten Andersen, Ill	 4
1977	Hans Nielsen, Pur	 4
1972	Dirk Kryt, OSU	 4
2002	Dave Rayner, NW	 4
	24 games tied with	 3

Longest Individual Plays (Since 1944)

RUNS FROM SCRIMMAGE

1949	Lynn Chandnois, Arizona	.... *90
1991	Tico Duckett, Minn	.... *88
1974	Levi Jackson, OSU	.... *88
1951	Dick Panin, ND	.... *88
1963	Sherman Lewis, NW	.... *87
1947	George Guerre, Iowa St	.... *87
1963	Sherman Lewis, ND	.... *85
1992	Craig Thomas, Pur	 82
1965	Clinton Jones, OSU	.... *80

* good for touchdown

PASS PLAYS

1994	T. Banks-N. Carter, Ind	.... *93
1963	S. Juday-S. Lewis, USC	.... *88
2001	J. Smoker-C. Rogers, Wis	.... *87
1963	S. Juday-S. Lewis, Wis	.... *87
1998	B. Burke-P. Burress, ND	.... *86
1978	E. Smith-K. Gibson, Ind	.... *86
1977	E. Smith-K. Gibson, Minn	.... *85
1999	R. Van Dyke-P. Burress, NW	.... *84
1968	B. Feraco-A. Brenner, Baylor	.... *83
1949	G. Glick-L. Chandnois, ND	.... *83

* good for touchdown

FIELD GOAL YARDAGE

1981	Morten Andersen, OSU	 63
1982	Ralf Mojsiejenko, Ill	 61
1983	Ralf Mojsiejenko, Pur	 59
1980	Morten Andersen, Mich	 57
1999	Paul Edinger, Wis	 55
1999	Paul Edinger, Ill	 54
1971	Borys Shlpak, Iowa	 54
1970	Borys Shlpak, NW	 54
1971	Borys Shlpak, Minn	 54

1979	Morten Andersen, Iowa	 54
1984	Ralf Mojsiejenko, Pur	 54

INTERCEPTION/FUMBLE YARDAGE RETURNS

1978	Dan Bass, Wis	.... *99
1959	Bob Suci, Mich	.... *93
1955	Earl Morrall, Pur	.... (f)*90
1999	T.J. Turner, Pur	 88
1999	Amp Campbell, Oregon	.... (f)*85
1968	Allen Brenner, Minn	.... *84
1981	Carl Williams, NW	.... *83
1970	Brad McLee, Washington	.... *80
1957	Dave Kaiser, Minn	.... (f)*77
1999	Aric Morris, Pur	.... *76

(f) *fumble recovery*
* *good for touchdown*

PUNT YARDAGE RETURNS

1966	Allen Brenner, Ill	.... *95
1958	Dean Look, Mich	.... *92
1950	Jesse Thomas, Wm & Mary	.... *90
1984	Bobby Morse, Mich	.... *87
1957	Blanche Martin, Ill	.... *86
1947	Horace Smith, Santa Clara	.... *85
1963	Sherman Lewis, NW	 84
1997	Sedrick Irvin, Ind	.... *80
1995	Scott Greene, Ind	.... *76

* *good for touchdown*

PUNT YARDAGE

1986	Greg Montgomery, Mich	 86
1995	Chris Salani, Neb	 83
1998	Craig Jarrett, Penn St	 81
1985	Greg Montgomery, Ind	 80
1985	Greg Montgomery, Mich	 75
1978	Ray Stachowicz, ND	 75
1980	Ray Stachowicz, Pur	 73
1979	Ray Stachowicz, Pur	 73
1978	Ray Stachowicz, Iowa	 72
1984	Ralf Mojsiejenko, ND	 72

KICKOFF RETURN YARDS

2001	Herb Haygood, Iowa	.... *100
1995	Derrick Mason, LSU	.... *100
1994	Derrick Mason, Penn State	.... *100
1979	Derek Hughes, Oregon	.... *100
1979	Derek Hughes, Wis	.... *98
1946	Russ Reader, Wayne	.... *98
1973	Mike Holy, UCLA	.... *95
1967	Dwight Lee, NW	.... *93
1984	Larry Jackson, OSU	.... *93
1987	Blake Ezor, Ind	 90

* *good for touchdown*

Offensive Team Game Records (Since 1944)

RUSHING ATTEMPTS

1950	Indiana	 80
1987	Purdue	 77
1975	North Carolina State	... 77
1975	Indiana	 75
1988	Indiana	 74

NET YARDS RUSHING

1971	Purdue	 573
1974	Iowa	 489
1962	North Carolina	 472
1948	Washington State	 465
1988	Purdue	 460

FIRST DOWNS BY RUSHING

1975	Northwestern	 26
1952	Marquette	 25
1971	Purdue	 24
1962	North Carolina	 24
1957	Indiana	 24

RUSHING TOUCHDOWNS

1948	Hawaii	 9
1978	Illinois	 8
1990	Purdue	 7
1948	Arizona	 7
1947	Hawaii	 7

PASSES ATTEMPTED

1980	Purdue	 56
1982	Michigan	 50
1998	Purdue	 48
1998	Ohio State	 47
2001	Minnesota	 47

PASSES COMPLETED

1982	Michigan	 33
1998	Purdue	 32
1993	Ohio State	 31
1991	Michigan	 31
1986	Northwestern	 30

YARDS GAINED PASSING

1999	Michigan	 400
1998	Purdue	 396
2001	Fresno State	 376
2001	Missouri	 375
1978	Indiana	 369

FIRST DOWNS BY PASSING

1998	Purdue	 23
1978	Minnesota	 19
2001	Minnesota	 18
1993	Ohio State	 17
1986	Minnesota	 17

PASSING TOUCHDOWNS

1999	Iowa	 6
1981	Northwestern	 5

TOTAL YARDS GAINED

1971	Purdue	 698
1974	Iowa	 660
1978	Wisconsin	 645
1978	Indiana	 644
2001	Missouri	 639

TOTAL FIRST DOWNS

1990	Purdue	 34
1981	Indiana	 34
1978	Northwestern	 34
1981	Northwestern	 33
1953	Marquette	 33

TOTAL TOUCHDOWNS SCORED

1989	Northwestern	 11
1949	Arizona	 11
1948	Hawaii	 10
1952	Marquette	 9
1949	Temple	 9
1948	Arizona	 9
1947	Hawaii	 9

POINTS AFTER TOUCHDOWN SCORED

1989	Northwestern	10
1949	Arizona	9
1978	Illinois	8
1952	Marquette	8
1949	Temple	8
1948	Hawaii	8

TOTAL POINTS SCORED

1989	Northwestern	76
1949	Arizona	75
1952	Marquette	62
1949	Temple	62
1948	Arizona	61

YARDS PENALIZED

1957	Indiana	155
1981	Northwestern	149
1967	Northwestern	142
1964	Northwestern	142
1956	Indiana	137

MOST PUNTS

1987	Florida State	12
1996	Nebraska	11
1973	Ohio State	11
1945	Great Lakes	11
1944	Maryland	11

Defensive Team Game Records (Since 1944)

RUSHING ATTEMPTS

1993	by Iowa	12
1987	by Purdue	14
1899	by Purdue	15
1965	by Ohio State	17
1987	by Indiana	18
1985	by Purdue	18

NET YARDS RUSHING

1950	by Pittsburgh	-63
1981	by Northwestern	-60
1983	by Northwesetrn	-48
1965	by Michigan	-39
1946	by Wayne State	-34

FIRST DOWNS BY RUSHING

1999	by Ohio State	0
1990	by Purdue	0
1965	by Ohio State	0
1946	by Wayne State	0
1945	by Wayne State	0

PASSES ATTEMPTED

1944	by Maryland	1
1984	by Army	2
1976	by Ohio State	2
1958	by Indiana	2
1955	by Michigan	2

PASSES COMPLETED

1971	by Georgia Tech	0
1944	by Maryland	0
1944	by Kansas State	0

PASSES INTERCEPTED

1970	vs. Washington State	8
1987	vs. Michigan	7
1949	vs. Arizona	6

1979	vs. Northwestern	5
1956	vs. Kansas State	5
1952	vs. Marquette	5
1949	vs. Penn State	5
1948	vs. Hawaii	5

YARDS GAINED PASSING

1971	by Georgia Tech	0
1944	by Maryland	0
1944	by Kansas State	0
1949	by Maryland	5
1969	by Michigan	7
1963	by Notre Dame	7
1946	by Cincinnati	7

FIRST DOWNS BY PASSING

	13 times by 12 teams	0
	most recently in:	
1977	by Wyoming	
1971	by Georgia Tech	
1971	by Ohio State	

TOTAL YARDS GAINED

1950	by Pittsburgh	-11
1951	by Michigan	6
1944	by Maryland	16
1944	by Wayne State	30
1947	by Iowa State	46

TOTAL FIRST DOWNS

1944	by Maryland	1
1945	by Wayne	3
1944	by Wayne	3
1951	by Michigan	4
1999	by Ohio State	4
1957	by Indiana	4

FUMBLES RECOVERED

1945	vs. Great Lakes	8
1971	vs. Illinois	7
1958	vs. Purdue	7
1952	vs. Notre Dame	7

Assistant Coaches (Since 1910)

Chester Brewer (1903-1910)
Head Coach

William Frazer	1909
Halligan (Amherst)	1909
Ward "Tiny" Parker	1909
H.B. McDermid	1909-10
Parnell McKenna	1910
Amos Ashley	1910

John Macklin (1911-1915)
Head Coach

Ion Cortright	1912-13
Joe Cox	1914-15
George Gauthier	1914-15
Oscar Miller	1915
Chester Gifford	1915
J.E. McWilliams	1915

Frank Sommers (1916)
Head Coach

George Gauthier	1916
Chester Gifford	1916
R.C. "Doc" Huston	1916
Joe Cox	1916
Howard Beatty	1916

Chester Brewer (1917)
Head Coach

George Gauthier	1917
Chester Gifford	1917
George "Carp" Julian	1917
Howard Beatty	1917

George Gauthier (1918)
Head Coach

Ion Cortright	1918

Chester Brewer (1919)
Head Coach

George Gauthier	1919
Lyman Frimodig	1919
Blake Miller	1919

George "Potsy" Clark (1920)
Head Coach

Chester Brewer	1920
Swede Rundquist	1920

Albert Barron (1921-22)
Head Coach

Chester Brewer	1921
Lyman Frimodig	1921
Richard Rauch	1922
Fred Walker	1922
Blake Miller	1922

Ralph Young (1923-27)
Head Coach

John "Tarz" Taylor	1923-25
Fred Walker	1923
Miles "Mike" Casteel	1924, 1926-27
Ben VanAlstyne	1926
John Kobs	1924-26
Barney Traynor	1926-27

Harry Kipke (1928)
Head Coach

Miles "Mike" Casteel	1928
Edward Vandervoort	1928
Hugh "Gob" Wilson	1928

James Crowley (1929-32)
Head Coach

Miles "Mike" Casteel	1929-32
Glenn "Judge" Carberry	1929-32
Hugh "Gob" Wilson	1929
Frank Leahy	1932

Charles Bachman (1933-45, no team in 1943)
Head Coach

Miles "Mike" Casteel	1933-38
Tom King	1933-40
Robert Terlaak	1935-37
Myron Vandermere	1935-38
Al Agett	1937, 1939
Henry Johnson	1934-37
Richard Colina	1938
Gordon Dahlgren	1938-41, 1945
Joe Holsinger	1939-1944
Al Kircher	1940
Don Rossi	1940
Al Kawal	1942-1945
Karl Schlademan	1942, 1944-45
John Kobs	1944-45

Clarence "Biggie" Munn (1947-53)
Head Coach

Forest Evashevski 1947-49
Hugh Daugherty 1947-53
Kip Taylor 1947-48
John Kobs 1947-53
Alton Kircher 1947-49
Robert Flora 1949
Earle Edwards 1949-53
Lowell Dawson 1950-51
Steve Sebo 1950-58
Harold Vogler 1950-51
Dan Devine 1950-53
Donald Mason 1952-53
Dewey King 1952-53
Robert Devaney 1953

Hugh "Duffy" Daugherty (1954-72)
Head Coach

John Kobs 1954
Donald Mason 1954-55
Robert Devaney 1954-56
Dan Devine 1954
Burth Smith 1954-64
William Yeoman 1954-61
Everett Grandelius 1954-58
Lou Agase 1955-59
Doug Weaver 1956-57
Gordon Serr 1957-72
John Polonchek 1957-58
Carl "Buck" Nystrom 1958, 1971
George Perles 1967-71
Don Coleman 1968
Joseph Carruthers 1969-72
George Paterno 1969-70
Sherman Lewis 1969-72
Denny Stolz 1971-72
Ed Youngs 1971-72
Dan Boisture 1959-66
Henry Bullough 1959-69
Cal Stoll 1959-68
Vince Carillot 1960-68
John McVay 1962-64
Edwin Rutherford 1965-72
Al Dorow 1965-70
Dave Smith 1967-70
Woody Widenhofer 1969-70
Jimmy Raye 1972
Herb Paterra 1972

Denny Stolz (1973-75)
Head Coach

Edwin Rutherford 1973
Sherman Lewis 1973-75
Ed Youngs 1973-75
Jimmy Raye 1973-75
Charles Butler 1973-75
Daniel Underwood 1973-75
William Davis 1973-75
Andy MacDonald 1973-75
Howard Weyers 1973-75
Ronald Chismar 1974-75

Darryl Rogers (1976-79)
Head Coach

Marv Braden 1976
Ron Chismar 1976-79
Ray Greene 1976-77
C.T. Hewgley 1976-79
Robert Padilla 1976-77
Leon Burnett 1976
Sherman Lewis 1976-79
Robert Baker 1977-79
George Dyer 1977-79
Mo Forte 1973-79
Walt Harris 1978-79

Frank "Muddy Waters (1980-82)
Head Coach

Dick Comar 1980-82
Dave Driscoll 1980-82
Ted Guthard 1980-82
Sherman Lewis 1980-82
Matt Means 1980-82
Joe Pendry 1980-81
Kurt Schottenheimer 1980-82
Tyrone Willingham 1980-82
Steve Schottel 1982

George Perles (1983-1994)
Head Coach

Charles Baggett 1983-92
Steve Beckholt 1983-89
Larry Bielat 1983-89
Henry Bullough 1994
Anthony Folino 1988-94
Steve Furness 1983-90
Ted Guthard 1983-85
Pat Morris 1987-94
Carl "Buck" Nystrom 1983-86
Willie "Skip" Peete 1993-94
Norm Parker 1983-94
Bill Rademacher 1983-91
Nick Saban 1983-87
Pat Shurmur 1990-94
Kip Waddell 1991-94
Morris Watts .... 1986-90 and 1992-94
Bobby Williams 1990-94
Ed Zaunbrecher 1991-93

Nick Saban (1995-1999)
Head Coach

Charlie Baggett 1995-98
Dean Pees 1995-97
Gary Tranquill 1995-98
Jim Bollman 1995-97
Greg Colby 1995-97
Mark Dantonio 1995-99
Glenn Pires 1995
Pat Shurmur 1995-97
Bobby Williams 1995-99
Todd Grantham 1996-98
Mike Vollmar 1996-99
Chris Cosh 1998
Golden Pat Ruel 1998-99
Bill Sheridan 1998-99
Mike Cummings 1998
Morris Watts 1999
Bill Miller 1999
Brad Lawing 1999
Bob Casullo 1999
Reggie Mitchell 1999

Bobby Williams (2000-2002)
Head Coach

Mark Dantonio 2000
Golden Pat Ruhl 2000
Bill Sheridan 2000
Morris Watts 2000-2002
Bill Miller 2000-2001
Brad Lawing 2000-2002
Bob Casullo 2000
Reggie Mitchell 2000-2002
Don Treadwell 2000-2002
Mike Vollmar 2000-2002
Jeff Stoutland 2000-2002
Pat Perles 2000-2002
Sal Sunseri 2001
Troy Douglas 2001-02
Danny Crossman 2002

John L. Smith (2003-)
Head Coach

Dave Baldwin 2003
Mike Cox 2003
Pail Haynes 2003
Jim McElwain 2003
Reggie Mitchell 2003
Doug Nussmeier 2003
Chris Smeland 2003
Jeff Stoutland 2003
Steve Stripling 2003
Mike Vollmar 2003

All-American
(First Team Selections)

Year, Name, Position and Honoring Organization

1915 Neno J. DePrato–HB (*INS, Detroit Times)
      Blake Miller–E (Atlanta Constitution)
1930 Roger Grove–QB (B)
1935 Sidney Wagner–G (*UP, INS, NYS, Liberty Magazine)
1936 Art Brandstatter–FB (B)
1938 John Pingel–HB (*AP)
1949 Lynn Chandnois–HB (*INS, UP, CP, FN, Collier's)
      Don Mason–G (PN, FN)
      Ed Bagdon–G* (Look, UP, SN, NYN, CP NEA, Tele-News)
1950 Dorne Dibble–E (*Look)
      Everett Grandelius–HB* (AP, INS, CP)
1951 Robert Carey–E (*UP, AP, SN, NEA, NYN, B)
      Don Coleman–T (*AP, UP, Collier's, Look, B, SN, NYN, FN, NEA, CP, Tele-News, INS, CTP)
      Al Dorow–QB (*INS)
      James Ellis–DB (CTP)
1952 Frank Kush–G (*AP, Look, NYN, Fox Movietone, Athletic Publications, All-Catholic)
      Don McAuliffe–HB (*UP, Collier's, FD, PN, All-Catholic)
      Dick Tamburo–C (*AP, CP, NEA, INS, NYN, FD, PN, Athletic Publication)
      Ellis Duckett–E (NBC-TV)
      Thomas Yewcic–QB (NBC-TV)
      Jim Ellis–DB (CTP)
1953 Don Dohoney–E (*AP, UP, Collier's, Look, SN, FN, NEA, CP, NBC-TV)
      LeRoy Bolden–HB (NBC-TV)
      Larry Fowler–G (NBC-TV)
1955 Earl Morrall–QB (*AP, Collier's, Look, INS, SN, PN, NBC-TV, Hearst, Frank)
      Norm Masters–T (*UP, Look, INS, NEA, NBC-TV, CP, Fox Movietone)
      Carl Nystrom–G (Radio-TV Guide, Frank Leahy)
      Gerald Planutis–FB (Jet)
1957 Walter Kowalczyk–HB (*FWA, SN, NEA, UP, CP, FCAK, NBC-TV, FD)
      Dan Currie–C (*FWA, AP, INS, FCA, NBC-TV)
1958 Samuel Williams–E (*UPI, FCA, NYN, Time)
1959 Dean Look–QB (*FWA, FN)
1961 David Behrman–G (AP, FWA)
1962 David Behrman–G (CBS-TV)
      George Saimes–FB (*AP, UPI, FWA, FCA, NYN, SN, CBS-TV, Look)
      Ed Budde–G (Time)
1963 Sherman Lewis–HB (*AP, UPI, CP, FWA, NYN)
      Earl Lattimer–G (NYN)
1965 Robert Apisa–FB (FN)
      Ronald Goovert–LB (*FWA)
      Clinton Jones–HB (*FWA)
      Steve Juday–QB (*AP)
      Harold Lucas–MG (*NEA)
      Charles "Bubba" Smith–DE (*AFC, UPI)
      Eugene Washington–E (*CP, FN, FD)
      George Webster–LB (*AP, NEA, AFC, UPI,

FN, NYN)

1966　Robert Apisa–FB (FN, NYN)
　　　Clinton Jones–HB (*AP, CP, NEA, SN)
　　　Charles "Bubba" Smith–DE (*AP, UPI, FWA, AFC, NEA, SN, CP, FN, NYN)
　　　Eugene Washington–E (*UPI, AFC, SN)
　　　George Webster–LB (*AP, UPI, AFC, FWA, NEA, SN, CP, FN, NYN)
　　　Jerry West–T (*NEA)
1968　Allen Brenner–DB (*AFC, NEA)
1969　Ronald Saul–G (*NEA, Time, SN)
1971　Eric Allen–HB (*AFC)
　　　Brad VanPelt–DB (*UPI, FN)
　　　Ron Curl–T (AFC)
1972　Brad VanPelt–DB (*AP, UPI, AFC, FWA, Time, SN, US, WC, Gridiron)
　　　Joseph DeLamielleure–G (*SN)
　　　Billy Joe Dupree–E (Time)
1973　William Simpson–DB (*UPI,US)
1978　Kirk Gibson–FL (*UPI, SN, FN, NEA)
　　　Mark Brammer–TE (*FWA)
1979　Ray Stachowicz–P (FN)
1980　Ray Stachowicz–P (FN, NEA, WC, MSN)
1981　Morten Andersen–PK (*SN, UPI, WC)
　　　James Burroughs–DB (*SN)
1983　Carl Bank–LB (*AP, UPI, SN)
　　　Ralf Mojsiejenko–P (*SN)
1985　Lorenso White–TB (*AP, UPI, FWA, WC, AFC, SN)
1986　Greg Montgomrey–P (*FWA)
1987　Tony Mandarich–OT (FN)
　　　Greg Montgomrey–P (FN, GNS, MTS)
　　　Lorenzo White–TB (*FN, WC, FWA, GNS, UPI, FCAK, MTS)
1988　Tony Mandarich–OT (*AP, UPI, FCAK, WC, FWA, SN, GNS, FN, MTS)
　　　Andre Rison–SE (GNS)
　　　Percy Snow–LB (*SN)
1989　Harlon Barnett–DB (SN, MTS)
　　　Bob Kula–OT (*FCAK, AP)
　　　Percy Snow–LB (*FCAK, AP, UPI, FWA, FN, SN, WC, MTS)
1997　Flozell Adams–OT (*WC)
　　　Scott Shaw–OG (GNS)
1998　Robaire Smith–DE (*WC)
　　　Paul Edinger–PK (AAFF)
1999　Julian Peterson–LB (FN)
2001　Herb Haygood–KR (*WC/CNNSI)
2002　Charles Rogers–WR (FWA, CNNSI, AFC)

Glossary

AFC	Amercian Football Coaches
AP	Associated Press
B	All-American Board
CBS-TV	CBS Television Sports
CP	Central Press
CTP	Chicago Tribune Players
FCAK	Football Coaches Association Kodak
FD	*Football Digest*
FN	*Football News*
FWA	Football Writers Association
GNS	Gannett News Service
INS	International News Service
MSN	Medalist Sports News
MTV	Mizlou TV Sports (Seniors)
NEA	Newspaper Enterprise Association
NYN	*New York News*
NYS	*New York Sun*
PN	Paramount News
SN	*Sporting News*
UP	United Press
UPI	United Press International
US	Universal Sports WC
WC	Walter Camp
CNNSI	CNN/*Sports Illustrated*
AAFF	All-American Football Foundation
MTS	Mizlou TV Sports (seniors)
NBC-TV	NBC Television Sports
*	Major team selections recognized by NCAB

All-Big Ten Selections
(First Team Selections)

(Each year two selection committees offer their versions of an All-Big Ten team, the media vote on a team and the coaches do likewise. Of the following All-Big Ten picks, those identified with an asterisk (*) were chosen by both committees and thus identified as consensus selections.)

1953	Don Dohoney*	end
	LeRoy Bolden*	halfback
1955	Norm Masters*	tackle
	Earl Morrall*	quarterback
1957	Sam Williams*	end
	Pat Burke*	tackle
	Ellison Kelly*	guard
	Dan Currie*	center
	Jim Ninowski*	quarterback
	Walt Kowalczyk*	halfback
1958	Sam Williams*	end
	Ellison Kelly*	guard
1959	Dean Look	quarterback
1960	Herb Adderley	halfback
1961	George Saimes*	fullback
	David Behrman	center
1962	George Saimes*	fullback
	David Behrman	tackle
1963	Sherman Lewis*	halfback
	Dan Underwood	end
1964	Dick Gordon*	halfback
	Jerry Rush	tackle
	Charles Migyanka	linebacker
1965	Gene Washington*	end
	Clint Jones*	halfback
	Charles "Bubba" Smith*	end
	George Webster*	linebacker
	Steve Juday	quarterback
	Ron Goovert	linebacker
	Don Japinga	defensive back
	Harold Lucas	guard
1966	Gene Washington*	end
	Clint Jones*	halfback
	Charles "Bubba" Smith*	tackle
	George Webster*	linebacker
	Jerry West*	tackle
	Charles Thornhill*	linebacker
	Richard Kenney*	place kicker
	Bob Apisa	fullback
	Nick Jordan	defensive back
	Tony Conti	offensive guard
	Jesse Phillips	defensive back
1967	George Chatlos	defensive end
1968	Allen Brenner*	safety
	Charles Bailey	defensive back
1969	Ronald Saul*	offensive guard
	Richard Saul*	defensive end
	Ronald Curl	defensive tackle
1971	Joe DeLamielleure*	offensive guard
	Eric Allen*	halfback
	Ronald Curl*	defensive tackle
	Brad VanPelt*	defensive back
1972	Joe DeLamielleure*	offensive guard
	Gail Clark*	linebacker
	Brad VanPelt*	defensive back
	Bill Simpson*	defensive back
	Billy Joe DuPree	tight end
1973	Bill Simpson	defensive back
1974	Otto Smith*	defensive end
	Terry McClowry*	linebacker
	Levi Jackson	halfback
	James Taulbert	defensive tackle
1975	Tom Hannon*	defensive back
	Mike Cobb	tight end
1976	Mike Cobb*	tight end
	Tom Hannon	defensive back
1977	Larry Bethea*	defensive tackle
	Ray Stachowicz	punter
	Alfred Pitts	center
1978	Eugene Byrd*	end
	Jim Hinesly*	offensive tackle

	Mark Brammer*	tight end
	Kirk Gibson*	flanker
	Melvin Land*	defensive tackle
	Thomas Graves	defensive back
	Ray Stachowicz	punter
1979	Ray Stachowicz*	punter
	Dan Bass*	linebacker
	Mak Brammer	tight end
1980	Ray Stachowicz*	punter
1981	Morten Andersen*	place kicker
	Thomas Piette	center
	Carl Banks	linebacker
	James Burroughs	defensive back
1982	Carl Banks*	linebacker
1983	Carl Banks*	linebacker
	Phil Parker	safety
1984	Phil Parker	safety
	James Morrissey	linebacker
1985	Lorenzo White*	halfback
	Phil Parker	safety
	John Wojciechowski	offensive guard
	Greg Montgomery	punter
1986	Greg Montgomery*	punter
	Andre Rison*	wide receiver
	Shane Bullough	linebacker
1987	Todd Krumm*	safety
	Tony Mandarich*	offensive tackle
	Lorenzo White*	halfback
	John Miller	safety
	Greg Montgomery	punter
	Pat Shurmur	center
	Percy Snow	linebacker
1988	Andre Rison*	wide receiver
	Tony Mandarich*	offensive tackle
	Percy Snow*	linebacker
	John Miller*	safety
1989	Bob Kula*	offensive tackle
	Travis Davis*	defensive tackle
	Percy Snow*	linebacker
	Harlon Barnett*	defensive back
	Courtney Hawkins	wide receiver
1990	Eric Moten*	offensive guard
	Tico Duckett	tailback
	Jim Johnson	offensive tackle
	Duane Young	tight end
	John Langeloh	place kicker
	Carlos Jenkins	linebacker
1991	Courtney Hawkins	flanker
	Chuck Bullough	linebacker
1992	Tico Duckett*	tailback
1994	Brian DeMarco	offensive tackle
	Demetrice Mortin	defensive back
1997	Flozell Adams*	offensive tackle
	Ike Reese	linebacker
1998	Jason Strayhorn*	center
1999	Plaxico Burress*	wide receiver
	Amp Campbell*	corner back
	Robaire Smith*	defensive tackle
	Craig Jarrett	punter
	Julian Peterson	linebacker
2000	Josh Thornhill	linebacker
	Renaldo Hill	center
2001	Josh Thornhill	linebacker
2002	Charles Rogers	receiver

Postseason Honors

GOVERNOR'S AWARD

(Given annually to the player voted the most valuable by his teammates.)

1931	Abe Eliowitz	fullback
1932	Robert Monnett	halfback
1933	Arthur Buss	tackle
1934	Ed Klewicki	end
1935	Sid Wagner	guard
1936	Sam Ketchman	center
1937	Harry Speelman	tackle

1938	John Pingel	halfback
1939	Lyle Rockenbach	guard
1940	Jack Amon	fullback
1941	Anthony Arena	center
1942	Richard Kieppe	halfback
1943	no team World War II	
1944	Jack Breslin	halfback
1945	Steve Contos	halfback
1946	George Guerre	halfback
1947	Warren Huey	end
1948	Lynn Chandnois	halfback
1949	Eugene Glick	quarterback
1950	Everett Grandelius	halfback
1951	Don Coleman	tackle
1952	Richard Tamburo	linebacker
1953	LeRoy Bolden	halfback
1954	John Matsock	halfback
1955	Carl Nystrom	guard
1956	James Hinesly	end
1957	Dan Currie	center
1958	Sam Williams	end
1959	Dean Look	quarterback
1960	Thomas Wilson	quarterback
1961	George Saimes	fullback
1962	George Saimes	fullback
1963	Sherman Lewis	halfback
1964	Richard Gordon	halfback
1965	Steve Juday	quarterback
1966	George Webster	linebacker
1967	Dwight Lee	halfback
1968	Allen Brenner	end-safety
1969	Ronard Saul	guard
1970	Eric Allen	tailback
1971	Eric Allen	tailback
1972	Gail Clark	linebacker
1973	Ray Nester	linebacker
1974	Charles Baggett	quarterback
1975	Levi Jackson	fullback
1976	Richard Baes	tailback
1977	Larry Bethea	tackle
1978	Edward Smith	quarterback
1979	Dan Bass	linebacker
1980	Steve Smith	halfback
1981	Bryan Clark	quarterback
1982	James Neeley	linebacker
1983	Carl Banks	linebacker
1984	Jim Morrissey	linebacker
1985	Lorenzo White	tailback
1986	Dave Yarema	quarterback
	Mark Ingram	flanker
1987	Lorenzo White	tailback
1988	Kurt Larson	linebacker
1989	Percy Snow	linebacker
1990	Dan Enos	quarterback
	Hyland Hickson	tailback
1991	Chuch Bullough	linebacker
	Courtney Hawkins	wide receiver
1992	Mill Coleman	flanker/quarterback
1993	Brice Abrams	fullback
	Jim Miller	quarterback
1994	Scott Greene	fullback
1995	Scott Greene	fullback
1996	Duane Goulbourne	tailback
1997	Ike Reese	linebacker
1998	Sori Kanu	free safety
1999	Aric Moris	safety
2000	Richards Newsome	free safety
2001	Josh Thornhill	linebacker
2002	Charles Rogers	reciver

Nationally Recognized Postseason Awards

HEISMAN TROPHY BALLOTING

1952	Don McAuliffe	8th
1955	Earl Morrall	4th
1957	Walt Kowalczyk	3rd
	Dan Currie	8th
1959	Dean Look	6th
1962	George Saimes	7th
1963	Sherman Lewis	3rd
1965	Steve Juday	6th
	Clinton Jones	13th
1966	Clinton Jones	6th
1971	Eric Allen	10th
1972	Brad VanPelt	13th
1985	Lorenzo White	4th
1987	Lorenzo White	4th
1988	Tony Mandarich	6th
1989	Percy Snow	8th

OTHER AWARDS

1949 Ed Bagdon
(Outland Trophy)

1952 Don McAuliffe
(Walter Camp Trophy)

1952 Clarence "Biggie" Munn
(AFCA National Coach of the Year)

1955 Hugh "Duffy" Daugherty
(AFCA National Coach of the Year)

1955 Hugh "Duffy" Daugherty
(FWAA National Coach of the Year)

1959 Clarence "Biggie" Munn—coach
(College Football Hall of Fame)

1965 Hugh "Duffy" Daugherty
(FWAA National Coach of the Year)

1966 Charles "Bubba" Smith
(UPI Lineman of the Year)

1968 John Pingel
(College Football Hall of Fame)

1971 Eric Allen
(Chicago Tribune Big Ten MVP)

1972 Brad VanPelt
(Robert W. Maxwell Award)

1975 Don Coleman
(College Football Hall of Fame)

1977 Larry Bethea
(Chicago Tribune Big Ten MVP)

1978 Charles Bachman—coach
(College Football Hall of Fame)

1978 Darryl Rogers
(Sporting News Coach of the Year)

1984 Hugh "Duffy" Daugherty—coach
(College Football Hall of Fame)

1985 Lorenzo White
(UPI Big Ten MVP)

1987 George Webster
(College Football Hall of Fame)

1987 Lorenzo White
(UPI BigTen MVP)

1987 Lorenzo White
(Chicago Tribune Big Ten MVP)

1988 Charles "Bubba" Smith
(College Football Hall of Fame)

1989 Percy Snow
(Butkus Award)

1989 Percy Snow
(Lombardi Award)

1981 Bob Devaney—coach
(College Football Hall of Fame)

1985 Dan Devine—coach
(College Football Hall of Fame)

1995 Frank Kush—coach
(College Football Hall of Fame)

2001 Brad VanPelt
(College Football Hall of Fame)

2002 Charles Rogers
(Biletnikoff Award)

GOLF
LEADERS, RECORDS and HONORS

ALL-TIME COACHING RECORDS

Coach	Years	W	L	T	Avg.
No Head Coach	1928	6	2	0	.750
Harry G. Kipke	1929	4	1	0	.800
James H. Crowley	1930-31	13	6	0	.684
Ben F. VanAlstyne	1932-59	139	118	7	.540
John Brotzmann	1960-65	51	32	3	.610
Bruce Fossum	1966-89	16	9	0	.640
Ken Horvath	1990-99	0	0	0	0
Mark Hankins	1999-2003	1	0	0	1.000
TOTALS	1928-2003	230	168	10	.575

Season Records
See page 874 for further explanation of abbreviations.

1928 (6-2)
Coach: no coach

5-9	A	Flint JC 3-0	W
5-11	A	Grand Rapids JC 3-1	W
5-12	A	Detroit 2 1/2-12 1/2	L
5-17	A	Detroit Law 13-5	W
5-21	H	Grand Rapids JC ... 16 1/2-1 1/2	W
5-22	H	Flint JC 9-0	W
5-25	H	Detroit 1/2-14 1/2	L
5-29	H	Detroit Law 8-4	W

Harry G. Kipke (1929)
(See football season records for Harry Kipke sketch)

1929 (4-1)
Coach: Harry Kipke

5-8	A	Grand Rapids JC 9-6	W
5-16	A	Detroit City Coll ... 10 1/2-4 1/2	W
5-17	A	Detroit 3-12	L
5-22	H	Grand Rapids JC 12-3	W
5-29	H	Detroit City Coll. 7-5	W

Coach: James H. Crowley (1930-1931)
(See football season records for James Crowley sketch)

1930 (7-2)
Coach: James Crowley

5-2	H	Grand Rapids JC 9 1/2-8 1/2	W
5-3	H	St. Johns-Toledo 13 1/2-4 1/2	W
5-7	A	Michigan 1-17	L
5-8	A	Detroit 8-10	L
5-9	A	St. Johns-Toledo 12-6	W
5-17	A	Detroit City Coll ... 11 1/2-6 1/2	W
5-24	A	Grand Rapids JC 15-3	W
5-29	H	Detroit 12-9	W
5-31	H	Detroit City Coll 9 1/2-8 1/2	W

1931 (6-4)
Coach: James Crowley

4-17	H	Notre Dame 1/2-17 1/2	L
4-25	H	Michigan 3-15	L
5-1	H	Grand Rapids JC 12-6	W
5-2	H	Detroit City Coll 14-4	W
5-8	H	Detroit 15 1/2-2 1/2	W

5-9	A	Notre Dame 3 1/2-17 1/2	L
5-15	A	Grand Rapids JC ... 15 1/2-2 1/2	W
5-29	A	Detroit City Coll 10-8	W
5-30	A	Detroit 6 1/2-11 1/2	L
6-3	H	Michigan Normal 12-6	W

Ben VanAlstyne (1932-1959)
(See basketball season records for Ben VanAlstyne sketch)

1932 (5-4)
Coach: Ben VanAlstyne

4-23	A	Michigan 2 1/2-24 1/2	L
4-30	H	Notre Dame 5-13	L
5-7	A	Grand Rapids JC ... 3 1/2-14 1/2	L
5-14	H	Detroit City Coll ... 7 1/2-10 1/2	L
5-16	H	Detroit 11 1/2-6 1/2	W
5-20	H	Grand Rapids JC 11-10	W
5-27	A	Detroit City Coll 9 1/2-8 1/2	W
5-28	A	Detroit 9 1/2-8 1/2	W
6-4	A	Michigan Normal 11-7	W

1933 (5-4-1)
Coach: Ben VanAlstyne

4-29	A	Michigan 3-24	L
5-5	H	Detroit 9-9	T
5-6	A	Notre Dame 1-17	L
5-12	A	Grand Rapids JC 12-0	W
5-16	A	Michigan 2-25	L
5-19	A	Michigan Normal 9 1/2-8 1/2	W
5-20	A	Detroit 13 1/2-4 1/2	W
5-25	H	Michigan Normal 10-8	W
5-26	H	Grand Rapids JC ... 12 1/2-5 1/2	W
6-2	H	Detroit City Coll ... 6 1/2-11 1/2	L

1934 (2-8)
Coach: Ben VanAlstyne

4-21	A	Michigan 0-27	L
4-24	H	Grand Rapids JC 3-15	L
5-5	H	Detroit 14 1/2-3 1/2	W
5-12	H	Wayne 4 1/2-13 1/2	L
5-18	A	Detroit 3 1/2-11 1/2	L
5-19	A	Wayne 1-17	L
5-22	A	Grand Rapids JC ... 7 1/2-10 1/2	L
5-26	H	Michigan 1/2-26 1/2	L
5-29	A	Michigan Normal 8 1/2-9 1/2	L
6-4	H	Michigan Normal .. 13 1/2-4 1/2	W

1935 (4-4-1)
Coach: Ben VanAlstyne

4-20	H	Michigan 3 1/2-32 1/2	L
5-4	H	Wayne 12 1/2-5 1/2	W
5-6	H	Grand Rapids JC 9 1/2-8 1/2	W
5-10	A	Grand Rapids JC 7-11	L
5-17	H	Notre Dame 4 1/2-7 1/2	L
5-18	A	Michigan 1-26	L
5-22	H	Michigan Normal 12-6	W
5-25	H	Wayne 11 1/2-6 1/2	W
6-1	H	Michigan Normal 9-9	T

1936 (6-4)
Coach: Ben VanAlstyne

4-25	A	Michigan 5-19	L
5-2	A	West. St. Tchrs 5 1/2-6 1/2	L

5-8	H	West. St. Tchrs 10 1/2-1 1/2	W
5-9	H	Wayne 14-4	W
5-16	H	Mich. Normal ...... 12 1/2 -5 1/2	W
5-18	A	Notre Dame 3 1/2-8 1/2	L
5-23	A	Ohio State 9-3	W
5-29	H	Michigan 10-10 1/2	L
6-5	A	Michigan Normal 14-4	W
6-6	A	Wayne 11-7	W

1937 (5-4)
Coach: Ben VanAlstyne

4-30	A	Marquette 18-0	W
5-1	A	Northwestern 8-10	L
5-5	A	Michigan 6-12	L
5-7	A	Wayne 9 1/2-8 1/2	W
5-8	A	Toledo 15 1/2-2 1/2	W
5-15	H	Marquette 12 1/2-5 1/2	W
5-17	A	Notre Dame 4-14	L
5-24	H	Michigan 7 1/2-10 1/2	L
5-29	H	Wayne 16 1/2-1 1/2	W

1938 (7-1)
Coach: Ben VanAlstyne

4-23	A	Michigan 11 1/2-6 1/2	W
4-30	A	Wayne 13 1/2-4 1/2	W
5-2	A	Western Reserve 16 1/2-1 1/2	W
5-7	H	Northwestern 9 1/2-8 1/2	W
5-13	H	Wayne 18-0	W
5-14	H	Michigan 14 1/2-3 1/2	W
5-21	H	Notre Dame 11-7	W
5-30	A	Ohio State 8 1/2-9 1/2	L

1939 (5-3)
Coach: Ben VanAlstyne

4-24	A	Northwestern 6 1/2-11 1/2	L
4-28	A	Toledo 4 1/2-13 1/2	L
4-29	A	Wayne 14 1/2-3 1/2	W
5-3	A	Michigan 10-8	W
5-5	H	Ohio State 8-10	L
5-12	H	Toledo 18-0	W
5-13	H	Wayne 10-8	W
5-22	H	Michigan 11 1/2-6 1/2	W

1940 (5-3-1)
Coach: Ben VanAlstyne

4-20	A	Michigan 3-15	L
4-27	A	Ohio State 12 1/2-5 1/2	W
4-29	A	Wayne 16 1/2-1 1/2	W
5-4	H	Northwestern 16 1/2-1 1/2	W
5-10	A	Indiana 8 1/2-9 1/2	L
5-11	A	Purdue 14-4	W
5-13	H	Notre Dame 7 1/2-10 1/2	L
5-17	H	Michigan 9-9	T
5-20	H	Wayne 18-0	W

1941 (5-3)
Coach: Ben VanAlstyne

4-19	A	Ohio State 5-13	L
4-26	A	Michigan 6-12	L
5-3	H	Detroit 26-1	W
5-9	A	Notre Dame 10 1/2-16 1/2	L
5-10	A	Northwestern 15 1/2-11 1/2	W
5-12	A	Marquette 14 1/2-12 1/2	W
5-17	A	Detroit 24-3	W
5-23	H	Michigan 19-8	W

1942 (3-4-1)

Coach: Ben VanAlstyne

4-25	H	Michigan 7-17	L
5-5	H	Detroit 13-8	W
5-9	H	Ohio State 13 1/2-22 1/2	L
5-13	A	Michigan 7 1/2-7 1/2	T
5-16	A$_{AA}$	Northwestern 5 1/2-15 1/2	L
		Indiana 13-5	W
5-23	A	Detroit 13 1/2-7 1/2	W
6-5	H	Notre Dame 12-15	L

1943 (3-4-1)

Coach: Ben VanAlstyne

4-24	A$_{AA}$	Michigan 2 1/2-12 1/2	L
		Notre Dame 7-8	L
5-1	A	Notre Dame 3-18	L
5-10	A	Northwestern 4 1/2-13 1/2	L
5-15	A	Detroit 10 1/2-7 1/2	W
5-22	H	Detroit 9-9	T
5-29	H	Michigan Normal 17-1	W
6-5	A	Michigan Normal 12-6	W

1944

Intercollegiate athletics suspended due to World War II

1945 (0-6)

Coach: Ben VanAlstyne

5-4	A	Wayne 5-16	L
5-5	A	Detroit 6 1/2-11 1/2	L
5-12	A$_{CO}$	Ohio State 0-12	L
		Detroit 5 1/2-6 1/2	L
5-16	H	Wayne 6 1/2-11 1/2	L
5-19	H	Detroit 6-12	L

1946 (7-5)

Coach: Ben VanAlstyne

4-20	A	Michigan 3-24	L
4-27	A	Detroit 23 1/2-3 1/2	W
4-29	H	Marquette 20-4	W
5-6	H	Northwestern 6-21	L
5-8	H	Michigan 20-7	W
5-10	A	Detroit 21-6	W
5-13	A	Wayne 15-12	W
5-18	H	Ohio State 2-25	L
5-27	A$_{WL}$	Purdue 9-18	L
		Detroit 14 1/2- 1/2	W
5-31	H	Notre Dame 8-10	L
		Wayne 10-8	W

1947 (4-6)

Coach: Ben VanAlstyne

4-19	A	Ohio State 8-22	L
4-25	A	Wayne 21-15	W
4-30	A	Michigan 13-23	L
5-3	A	Notre Dame 6 1/2-20 1/2	L
5-5	A	Northwestern 12 1/2-14 1/2	L
5-10	H	Purdue 8-19	L
		Detroit 15-3	W
5-14	H	Michigan 10 1/2-16 1/2	L
5-17	A	Detroit 22 1/2-10 1/2	W
5-28	H	Wayne 19-8	W

1948 (6-6)

Coach: Ben VanAlstyne

4-26	H	Western Mich 18 1/2-26 1/2	L
5-1	H	Detroit 23 1/2-3 1/2	W
5-3	A	Michigan 7-23	L
5-5	A	Western Mich 23 1/2-21 1/2	W
5-8	H	Ohio State 14-13	W
5-15	A	Marquette 20 1/2-6 1/2	W
5-17	A	Wisconsin 7-11	L
5-20	H	Michigan 14-16	L
5-22	A	Detroit 25-2	W

5-24	H	Notre Dame 10 1/2-19 1/2	L
5-26	A	Wayne 7 1/2-19 1/2	L
5-28	H	Wayne 22 1/2-4 1/2	W

1949 (3-5)

Coach: Ben VanAlstyne

4-16	A	Ohio State 4-32	L
4-19	H	Wisconsin 18-15	W
4-30	A	Detroit 4-23	L
5-2	H	Michigan 5 1/2-19 1/2	L
5-7	H	Detroit 16-11	W
5-13	H	Illinois 14 1/2-12 1/2	W
5-16	A	Notre Dame 5-22	L
5-24	A	Michigan 0-18	L

1950 (4-6)

Coach: Ben VanAlstyne

4-22	A	Western Mich. 35 1/2-3 1/2	W
4-24	A	Western Mich. 36 1/2-2 1/2	W
4-26	A	Detroit 10-17	L
4-29	A	Illinois 9 1/2-20 1/2	L
5-3	A	Michigan 11 1/2-15 1/2	L
5-5	A	Wisconsin 20-7	W
5-13	H	Purdue 9-18	L
5-18	H	Michigan 11 1/2-15 1/2	L
5-22	H	Notre Dame 11-16	L
5-27	H	Detroit 18 1/2-8 1/2	W

1951 (10-3)

Coach: Ben VanAlstyne

4-21	A$_{KZ}$	Western Michigan 35-4	W
		Marquette 21-6	W
4-28	H	Western Michigan 37-2	W
5-1	A	Detroit 15-12	W
5-5	H	Michigan 11 1/2-24 1/2	L
		Illinois 26-10	W
5-7	H	Detroit 17-10	W
5-12	A$_{AA}$	Michigan 6 1/2-29 1/2	L
		Ohio State 5 1/2-30 1/2	L
5-14	H	Wisconsin 19-8	W
4-18	A	Notre Dame 15-12	W
4-19	A$_{EV}$	Northwestern 462-465	W
		Minnesota 462-470	W
		Big Tens at Evanston 6th	

1952 (5-5)

Coach: Ben VanAlstyne

4-19	H	Western Mich. 23 1/2-3 1/2	W
4-26	A	Western Mich. 14 1/2-12 1/2	W
5-3	A	Detroit 17-10	W
5-5	A	Detroit 17-10	W
5-7	H	Michigan 11-16	L
5-16	A	Wisconsin 12 1/2-14 1/2	L
5-16	A$_{MA}$	Illinois 11-16	L
5-17	A	Marquette 21 1/2-5 1/2	W
5-24	A	Michigan 2 1/2-16 1/2	L
4-26	H	Notre Dame 13 1/2-16 1/2	L
		Big Tens at Champaign 10th	

1953 (5-5-1)

Coach: Ben VanAlstyne

4-18	H	Western Michigan 23-13	W
4-25	A	Detroit 12 1/2-14 1/2	L
4-27	H	Detroit 19-8	W
5-2	A	Northwestern 13 1/2-13 1/2	T
5-4	A	Notre Dame 14-13	W
5-9	H	Marquette 32 1/2-3 1/2	W
5-9	H	Michigan 16 1/2-19 1/2	L
5-16	A$_{AA}$	Michigan 6 1/2-29 1/2	L
		Purdue 6-30	L
		Ohio State 3 1/2-32 1/2	L
5-18	A	Wisconsin 15 1/2-11 1/2	W
		Big Tens at Madison 10th	

1954 (7-4)

Coach: Ben VanAlstyne

4-16	A	Western Mich. 17 1/2-9 1/2	W
4-19	H	Detroit 15 1/2-11 1/2	W
5-3	A	Notre Dame 15 1/2-11 1/2	W
5-7	A	Wisconsin 16-11	W
5-8	A	Marquette 25-2	W
5-10	H	Northwestern 12 1/2-14 1/2	L
5-13	H	Western Mich. 20 1/2-6 1/2	W
5-15	A	Michigan 15-21	L
5-15	A$_{AA}$	Ohio State 5 1/2-30 1/2	L
5-17	H	Michigan 17-19	L
5-22	A	Detroit 16-11	W
		Big Tens at Minneapolis 8th	

1955 (4-7)

Coach: Ben VanAlstyne

4-16	A$_{WL}$	Purdue 7 1/2-28 1/2	L
		Wisconsin 10 1/2-25 1/2	L
		Detroit 15 1/2-20 1/2	L
4-20	A	Michigan 10-26	L
4-26	H	Michigan 14 1/2-21 1/2	L
4-30	H	Detroit 15 1/2-2 1/2	W
5-2	H	Detroit 21 1/2-5 1/2	W
5-9	H	Wisconsin 20-16	W
5-14	H	Northwestern 5-31	L
		Illinois 17 1/2-18 1/2	L
5-16	A	Notre Dame 20 1/2-15 1/2	W
		Big Tens at W. Lafayette 7th	

1956 (4-5)

Coach: Ben VanAlstyne

4-14	A$_{WL}$	Purdue 12-24	L
		Illinois 22 1/2-13 1/2	W
		Detroit 27 1/2-8 1/2	W
4-21	A	Michigan 12-24	L
4-28	H	Detroit 17 1/2-9 1/2	W
5-7	A	Wisconsin 20-7	W
5-14	H	Northwestern 13 1/2-14 1/2	L
5-19	A	Michigan 8 1/2-20 1/2	L
5-21	H	Notre Dame 9 1/2-13 1/2	L
		Big Tens at Willmette 6th	

1957 (8-6)

Coach: Ben VanAlstyne

4-26	H	Wisconsin 13 1/2-22 1/2	L
		Detroit 26 1/2-9 1/2	W
5-4	A$_{BL}$	Notre Dame 16-20	L
		Iowa 22 1/2-13 1/2	W
		Detroit 26-10	W
5-6	A$_{EV}$	Northwestern 21 1/2-14 1/2	W
		Notre Dame 16 1/2-19 1/2	L
		Iowa 18 1/2-17 1/2	W
5-11	A$_{AA}$	Michigan 11 1/2-24 1/2	L
		Purdue 9 1/2-26 1/2	L
		Ohio State 9-27	L
5-13	A	Michigan 26 1/2-9 1/2	W
5-18	H	Detroit 30-6	W
		Michigan 19 1/2-16 1/2	W
		Big Tens at Iowa City 7th	

1958 (6-2-1)

Coach: Ben VanAlstyne

4-26	H	Northwestern 18-6	W
5-3	H	Detroit 31-5	W
		Notre Dame 23-13	W
5-10	A$_{BL}$	Indiana 6-30	L
		Illinois 18-18	T
5-12	A$_{MA}$	Wisconsin 15 1/2-20 1/2	L
		Northwestern 25-10	W
5-17	A$_{DE}$	Detroit 32-4	W
		Michigan 28 1/2-7 1/2	W
		Big Tens at Columbus 6th	

1959 (11-1)

Coach: Ben VanAlstyne

4-25	H	Western Michigan 12-9	W
		Central Michigan 14-4	W
5-2	A$_{EV}$	Northwestern 21-15	W
		Wisconsin 18 1/2-17 1/2	W
		Notre Dame 20-16	W
5-4	A$_{ND}$	Notre Dame 39-18	W
		Iowa 27 1/2-8 1/2	W
5-9	H	Indiana 15 1/2-20 1/2	L
		Detroit 27-9	W
5-16	A$_{AA}$	Michigan 19 1/2-16 1/2	W
		Wisconsin 23-13	W
		Detroit 32-4	W
		Big Tens at Ann Arbor 7th	

John Brotzmann (1960-1965)

(See boxing season records for John Brotzmann sketch)

1960 (9-1)

Coach: John Brotzmann

4-15	A	W. Michigan 18 1/2-5 1/2	W
4-23	H	Detroit 16 1/2-4 1/2	W
4-30	H	Hillsdale 15-3	W
5-2	H	Northwestern 26 1/2-9 1/2	W
		Wisconsin 27-15	W
5-7	H	Illinois 26 1/2-9 1/2	W
		Purdue 14-22	L
5-14	H	Michigan 29 1/2-12 1/2	W
		Iowa 22-14	W
5-16	H	Notre Dame 18 1/2-17 1/2	W
		Big Tens at East Lansing 2nd	

1961 (10-3-1)

Coach: John Brotzmann

4-8	H	Detroit 16-2	W
4-22	H	Hillsdale 13-5	W
4-29	A$_{EV}$	Northwestern 904-904	T
		Wisconsin 904-953	W
5-1	A$_{MA}$	Wisconsin 962-979	W
		Northwestern 962-988	W
		Notre Dame 962-974	W
5-6	A$_{WL}$	Purdue 920-912	L
		Ohio State 920-946	W
		Indiana 920-960	W
5-8	H	N. Illinois 925-994	W
5-13	A$_{AA}$	Michigan 949-925	L
		Ohio State 949-927	L
5-15	H	Illinois 928-982	W
		Big Tens at Bloomington 3rd	

1962 (12-0-1)

Coach: John Brotzmann

4-14	A$_{CU}$	Illinois 23 1/2-12 1/2	W
		Illinois State 29-7	W
4-21	H	Hillsdale 30-6	W
		Aquinas 22-14	W
		Detroit 18-0	W
4-30	A$_{ND}$	Notre Dame 21 1/2-14 1/2	W
		Tri-State 17-1	W
		S. Illinois 27 1/2-8 1/2	W
5-5	H	Wisconsin 30-24	W
5-7	H	Northwestern 22 1/2-13 1/2	W
5-12	A$_{AA}$	Michigan 11 1/2-11 1/2	T
		Purdue 24-12	W
		Ohio State 21-15	W
		Big Tens at Champaign 7th	

1963 (8-4-1)

Coach: John Brotzmann

4-13	A	Indiana Invit. 5th/10	
4-20	H	Hillsdale 45-3	W
4-27	H	Ohio State 15 1/2-20 1/2	L
		N. Illinois 16-14	W

		Notre Dame 20 1/2-15 1/2	W
5-4	H	Michigan 14 1/2-17 1/2	L
5-10	A$_{MA}$	Wisconsin 15-15	T
		Indiana 14-16	L
		Purdue 16-14	W
5-11	A$_{EV}$	Northwestern 770-779	W
		Indiana 770-775	W
		Illinois 770-804	W
		Purdue 770-775	W
5-14	A	Michigan 6-21	L
		Big Tens at Madison .... (t)7th	

1964 (7-12)

Coach: John Brotzmann

3-28	A	Miami (FL) Invit. 8th	
4-11	A$_{CO}$	Ohio State 20-16	W
		Ohio 16-20	L
4-13	A$_{ND}$	Notre Dame 11 1/2-24 1/2	L
		W. Michigan. 31 1/2-5 1/2	W
		W. Illinois 12 1/2-23 1/2	L
4-25	A	Purdue 16-32	L
5-2	H	Northwestern 912-926	W
		Wisconsin 912-950	W
		Indiana 1072-1067	L
		Michigan 1390-1407	W
5-9	A$_{IC}$	Iowa 807-793	L
		Notre Dame 807-779	L
		Indiana 807-784	L
		Northwestern 807-791	L
		Wisconsin 807-802	L
		Illinois 807-812	W
		Minnesota 807-815	W
5-16	H	N. Illinois 17 1/2-18 1/2	L
5-18	A	Michigan 711-706	L
		Big Tens at Minneapolis 7th	

1965 (5-12)

Coach: John Brotzmann

4-17	A$_{CO}$	Ohio State 10 1/2-25 1/2	L
		Indiana 10 1/2-25 1/2	L
		Purdue 11 1/2-24 1/2	L
4-26	A$_{MA}$	Wisconsin 17 1/2-18 1/2	L
		S. Illinois 20-16	W
5-8	H	Purdue 775-763	L
		Ohio State 775-756	L
		Michigan 775-772	L
		Notre Dame 775-762	L
		Indiana 775-762	L
5-15	A$_{WL}$	Purdue 771-738	L
		Wisconsin 771-783	W
		Minnesota 771-804	W
		Indiana 771-752	L
		Illinois 771-804	W
		Northwestern 771-784	W
5-17	A	Michigan 557-530	L
		Big Tens at W. Lafayette 7th	

Bruce Fossum (1966-1989)

Bruce Fossum joined the Michigan State staff in 1959 as assistant basketball coach under Forddy Anderson. He held that position until 1965, when he took over the golf position from the retired John Brotzmann. A native of Ashland, WI, Fossum was born January 16, 1928. He was an all-around star in sports at Ashland High School where he participated in football, basketball and track and went on to become a top-flight cager at the University of Wisconsin. His career with the Badgers was interrupted by a stint with the U.S. Navy, but he graduated with a bachelor's degree in 1950. After coaching the Wisconsin freshmen basketball team one year, Fossum became head cage coach at West Bend (WI) High School for three years. In 1953 he began a six-year coaching stint of golf and basketball at Green Bay West High School. During that period he produced the school's first conference basketball championship team. His six-year record was 74-55. He then joined Forddy Anderson at MSC in 1959. Following his 24-year career as varsity golf coach, Bruce Fossum retired in 1989.

1966 (6-7)

Coach: Bruce Fossum

3-26	A	Miami (FL) Invit.. .... 9th/35	
4-16	A$_{WL}$	Purdue 772-744	L
		Ohio State 772-757	L
		Indiana 772-765	L
4-23	A$_{IC}$	Iowa 913-932	W
		Indiana 913-906	L
		Notre Dame 762-756	L
4-30	H	Wisconsin 763-774	W
		Bowling Green 763-787	W
		Western Mich. 763-838	W
5-3	H	Spartan Invitational 1st/8	
5-7	A$_{WL}$	Northern Inter 4th/13	
5-9	A$_{ND}$	Notre Dame 777-748	L
		Northwestern 777-783	W
		Illinois State 777-786	W
5-12	A	Michigan 623-620	L
		Big Tens at Iowa City .... (t)4th	

1967 (4-0)

Coach: Bruce Fossum

3-23	A$_{TR}$	Red Fox Invit. 1st/7	
3-24	A$_{SG}$	Furman 11-1	W
		Wofford Coll. 12 1/2-11 1/2	W
		New Haven Coll. 15-9	W
		Mars Hill Coll. 15-3	W
3-23	A	Iowa Invit. 3rd/4	
4-13	A	Purdue Invit. 2nd/5	
4-15	A	Ohio State Invit. 4th/6	
5-1	A	Wisconsin Invit. .... (t)1st/3	
5-3	A	Michigan 654-627	L
5-6	A$_{AA}$	Northern Inter. 5th/15	
5-10	H	Michigan 620-627	W
5-13	H	Spartan Invit. 1st/11	
		Big Tens at Ann Arbor 3rd	

1968 (2-0)

Coach: Bruce Fossum

3-24	A$_{TR}$	Red Fox Invit. .... (t)8th/13	
4-13	A$_{BL}$	Indiana 1065	
		MSU 1085	
		Purdue 1099	
4-20	A$_{CO}$	Ohio State 758	
		Indiana 765	
		Purdue 778	
		MSU 784	
		Marshall 793	
		Illinois 816	
4-24	A	Michigan 719-730	W
4-27	H	Notre Dame 767-770	W
4-27	H	Purdue 915-928	W
4-27	H	Ohio State 1234-1227	L
5-4	H	Northern Inter. 3rd/13	
5-8	H	Michigan 618-638	W
5-11	H	Spartan Invit. 2nd/10	
		Big Tens at Bloomington 2nd	

1969

Coach: Bruce Fossum

3-21	A$_{TR}$	Red Fox Invit. 5th/12	
3-29	A$_{GR}$	Palmetto Invit. 6th/17	
4-19	A	Illinois Invit. 4th/13	
4-21	A	Wisconsin Invit. 1st/4	
4-26	A	Purdue Cent. Tour. 1st/6	
5-3	A$_{CO}$	Northern Inter. 3rd/15	
5-10	H	Spartan Invit. 4th/25	
		Big Tens at East Lansing 1st	

1970

Coach: Bruce Fossum

3-27	A$_{TR}$	Red Fox Invit. 6th/12	
4-3	A$_{FM}$	Cape Coral Invit. 8th/40	
4-12	A	Ohio State Invit. 4th/14	
4-18	A	Illinois Invit. 1st/15	

4-20	A	Mid-Amer. Invit.	2nd/12
4-25	A	Indiana Invit.	1st/12
5-2	A$_{CH}$	Northern Inter.	4th/15
5-9	H	Spartan Invit.	1st/25
		Big Tens at Savoy	3rd

1971
Coach: Bruce Fossum

3-26	A$_{TR}$	Red Fox Invit.	4th/12
4-4	A$_{FM}$	Cape Coral Invit.	8th/40
4-10	A$_{CO}$	Kepler Invit.	2nd/16
4-19	A$_{OX}$	Mid-Amer. Invit.	5th/16
4-24	A	Indiana Invit.	4th/9
5-1	A	Northern Inter.	4th/16
5-8	H	Spartan Invit.	1st/30
		Big Tens at Columbus	2nd

1972
Coach: Bruce Fossum

3-24	A$_{TR}$	Red Fox Invit.	6th/9
4-15	A$_{CO}$	Kepler Invit.	10th/18
4-22	A	Michigan Invit.	3rd/6
4-24	A$_{OX}$	Mid-Amer. Invit.	2nd/16
4-29	A	Illinois Inter.	6th/11
5-5	A	Northern Inter.	9th/16
5-13	H	Spartan Invit.	1st/30
		Big Tens at Minneapolis	5th

1973 (1-0)
Coach: Bruce Fossum

3-23	A$_{TR}$	Red Fox Invit.	9th/12
4-22	A$_{CO}$	Kepler Invit.	5th/18
4-28	A	Purdue Invit.	(t)4th/14
4-30	A$_{OX}$	Mid-Amer. Invit.	8th/15
5-6	A$_{BL}$	Northern Intercoll.	8th/15
5-9	H	Det. Coll. Bus.	366-393
5-12	H	Spartan Invit.	2nd/20
		Big Tens at W. Lafayette	5th

1974
Coach: Bruce Fossum

3-22	A$_{TR}$	Red Fox CC Invit..	5th/13
3-25	A$_{DU}$	Iron Duke Invit.	6th/10
4-6	A$_{WV}$	Big Green Invit.	4th/10
4-21	A$_{CO}$	Kepler Invit.	3rd/19
4-27	A	Iowa Invit.	1st/9
5-5	A$_{WL}$	Northern Inter.	3rd/15
5-11	H	Spartan Invit.	2nd/17
		Big Tens at Iowa City	3rd

1975
Coach: Bruce Fossum

3-21	A$_{TR}$	Red Fox CC Invit.	8th/14
3-24	A$_{DU}$	Iron Duke Invit.	7th/15
4-20	A$_{CO}$	Kepler Invit.	13th/24
4-26	A	Purdue Invit.	4th/12
5-3	A$_{AA}$	Northern Inter.	5th/14
5-5	A$_{KZ}$	Bronco Invit.	7th/10
5-10	H	Spartan Invit.	2nd/13
		Big Tens at Bloomington	3rd

1976
Coach: Bruce Fossum

4-9	A	Illinois Inter.	3rd/15
4-18	A$_{CO}$	Kepler Invit.	13th/22
4-24	A	Purdue Invit.	4th/15
5-1	A$_{CO}$	Northern Inter.	5th/15
5-8	H	Spartan Invit.	11th/22
		Big Tens at Ann Arbor	6th

1977
Coach: Bruce Fossum

4-9	A	Illinois Inter.	3rd/15
4-17	A$_{CO}$	Kepler Invit.	10th/23
4-23	A	Purdue Invit.	8th/15
4-30	A$_{BL}$	Northern Inter.	8th/16
5-7	H	Spartan Invit.	9th/22
5-9	A$_{KZ}$	Bronco Invit.	9th/13
		Big Tens at East Lansing	7th

1978
Coach: Bruce Fossum

3-20	A$_{DU}$	Iron Duke Invit.	18th/20
3-24	A$_{TR}$	Red Fox Invit.	13th/18
4-8	A	Illinois Inter.	8th/13
4-16	A$_{CO}$	Kepler Invit.	21st/26
4-22	A	Purdue Invit.	12th/17
4-30	A$_{WL}$	Northern Inter.	12th/16
5-7	H	Spartan Invit.	7th/25
5-8	A$_{KZ}$	Bronco Invit.	6th/12
		Big Tens at Columbus	9th

1978-1979
Coach: Bruce Fossum

10-12	A$_{LG}$	Playboy Inter.	2nd/12
???	A$_{MA}$	Badger Fall Invit.	1st/5
4-7	A	Illinois Invit.	3rd/15
4-15	A$_{CO}$	Kepler Invit.	16th/22
4-22	A$_{CO}$	Northern Inter.	10th/15
4-28	A	Purdue Invit.	6th/16
5-2	A	Michigan Invit.	3rd/12
5-5	H	Spartan Invit.	8th/25
5-7	A$_{KZ}$	Bronco Invit.	4th/11
		Big Tens at Savoy	3rd

1980
Coach: Bruce Fossum

10-4		Gopher Fall Invit.	1st/5
4-5	A	Marshall Inter.	(t)4th/18
4-12	A	Illinois Inter.	2nd/11
4-20	A$_{CO}$	Kepler Invit.	6th/24
4-26	A	Purdue Invit.	9th/16
5-3	H	Spartan Invit.	2nd/25
5-5	A$_{MA}$	Badger Invit.	2nd/12
5-11	A$_{AA}$	Northern Inter.	3rd/16
		Big Tens at Madison	5th

1981
Coach: Bruce Fossum

4-4	A	Marshall Inter.	6th/18
4-19	A$_{CO}$	Kepler Invit.	3rd/24
4-25	A	Michigan Invit.	7th/8
4-27	A$_{KZ}$	Mid-Amer. Invit.	8th/16
5-3	A$_{WL}$	Northern Inter.	4th/18
5-9	H	Spartan Invit.	3rd/15
		Big Tens at Minneapolis	5th

1982
Coach: Bruce Fossum

4-4	A$_{RM}$	Colonel Classic	8th/22
4-10	A	Marshall Inter.	4th/18
4-18	A$_{CO}$	Kepler Invit.	6th/24
4-24	A$_{AA}$	Michigan Invit.	4th/9
5-1	A$_{IC}$	Northern Inter.	4th/18
5-8	H	Spartan Invit.	2nd/15
		Big Tens W. Lafayette	7th

1982-1983
Coach: Bruce Fossum

9-26	A$_{CO}$	Buckeye Classic	(t)9th/18
3-21	A	Central Florida Classic	8th/24
3-21	A	Miami (OH) Invit.	Canceled-DNC
4-3	A$_{RM}$	Colonel Classic	3rd/20

1984
Coach: Bruce Fossum

3-25	A	S. Florida Invit.	10th/18
4-1	A	Miami (OH) Invit.	1st/12
4-7	A	Marshall Inter.	12th/18
4-15	A$_{CO}$	Kepler Invit.	3rd/20
4-22	A$_{DK}$	Mid-Amer. Invit.	9th/9
4-29	A$_{AA}$	Northern Inter.	11th/15
5-5	H	Spartan Invit.	9th/21
5-7	A	Badger Invit.	5th/10
		Big Tens at Bloomington	6th

1985
Coach: Bruce Fossum

3-19	A$_{OR}$	Cent. Fla. Inter.	6th/15
3-23	A	South Fla. Invit.	10th/15
3-30	A	Duke Invit.	24th/24
4-7	A	Purdue Invit.	11th/15
4-13	A	Marshall Inter.	(t)5th/18
4-20	A$_{DK}$	Mid-Amer. Invit.	10th/21
4-28	A$_{CO}$	Kepler Invit.	3rd/24
5-5	H	Northern Inter.	10th/24
		Big Tens at Ann Arbor	9th

1986
Coach: Bruce Fossum

3-23	A	South Fla. Invit.	12th/14
3-30	A	Duke Invit.	20th/24
4-12	A	Marshall Inter.	12th/18
4-19	A$_{CO}$	Kepler Invit.	10th/21
4-27	A	C. Schenkel Invit.	17th/18
5-4	A$_{DK}$	Mid-Amer. Invit.	19th/21
		Butler Inter.	15th/18
5-11	A$_{CO}$	Northern Inter.	21th/21
		Big Tens at East Lansing	5th

1987
Coach: Bruce Fossum

1-27	A	Tampa Invit.	17th/24
3-20	A$_{DU}$	Iron Duke Invit.	(t)16th/24
4-5	A	Purdue Invit.	5th/16
4-11	A	Marshall Inter.	9th/18
4-19	A$_{CO}$	Kepler Invit.	12th/23
4-27	A$_{MA}$	Badger Spring Invit.	1st/9
5-3	H	Spartan Invit.	1st/8
5-10	A$_{KZ}$	Mid-Amer. Invit.	2nd/20
5-17	A$_{CH}$	Northern Inter.	7th/11
		Big Tens at Columbus	5th

1988
Coach: Bruce Fossum

2-2	A$_{DU}$	Tampa Invit.	8th/19
		Iron Duke Invit.	18th/24
4-4	A$_{AU}$	Coll. Masters	3rd/15
4-9	A	Marshall Inter.	5th/18
4-17	A$_{CO}$	Kepler Invit.	8th/23
4-23	A	Illinois Inter.	(t)5th/13
4-30	A$_{RV}$	Mid-Amer. Invit.	2nd/12
5-7	A$_{MA}$	Northern Inter.	6th/15
		Big Tens at Champaign	4th

1988-1989
Coach: Bruce Fossum

9-24	A	Badger Invit.	7th/16
10-16	A	N. Mex. St. Invit.	10th/19

2-17	A	John Burns Invit.	24th/26
3-26	A$_{DU}$	Iron Duke Invit.	19th/23
4-2	A	Forest Hills Invit.	12th/15
4-16	A	Bradley Invit.	7th/16
4-23	H	Spartan Invit.	(t)6th/16
4-30	A	Mid-Amer. Invit.	7th/15
5-7	A	Northern Inter.	10th/11
		Big Tens at Madison	10th

Ken Horvath (1989-1999)

Following a successful interscholastic golfing career at Bridgeport (OH) High School, Ken Horvath attended college at Ferris State College in Big Rapids, MI, where he graduated in 1981 with a bachelor's degree in marketing/professional golf management. He was appointed varsity coach in 1989, replacing the legendary Bruce Fossum. In addition to his head coaching duties, Horvath has served as course manager and golf professional at MSU's Forest Akers Golf Course, serving in the latter capacities since 1984. He earned his Professional Golfers Association card in 1982 and played on the PGA mini-tour for two years. During that time he also served as an assistant pro at the Country Club of Lansing.

1989-1990

Coach: Ken Horvath

10-8	A$_{LO}$	Colonel Classic	3rd/18
10-15	A$_{CO}$	Buckeye Classic	(t)13th/17
10-24	A$_{SG}$	Fall Festival	7th/10
2-19	A$_{HL}$	Mardi Gras Invit.	11th/14
3-23	A	Fla. Internat. Invit.	3rd/13
3-31	A$_{LX}$	J. Owens Invit.	17th/25
4-8	A	Purdue Invit.	3rd/12
4-14	A	Marshall Inter.	(t)13/21
4-22	A$_{AK}$	Firestone Invit.	(t)14/36
4-29	A$_{CO}$	Kepler Invit.	(t)17/23
5-6	A$_{DK}$	Midwestern Invit.	15th/19
5-13	H	Spartan Invit.	4th/16
		Big Tens at Minneapolis	5th

1990-1991

Coach: Ken Horvath

9-30	A$_{WL}$	Northern Inter.	(t)14/22
10-7	A$_{LO}$	Fall Colonel Classic	7th/20
11-3	A$_{NK}$	Seascape Coll	12th/18
2-19	A$_{HL}$	Mardi Gras Invit.	12th/15
3-24	A$_{SG}$	Wofford Invit.	10th/15
3-30	A$_{LX}$	Kentucky Invit.	(t)4/25
4-6	A$_{EV}$	Oak Meadow Invit.	3rd/13
4-14	A	Indiana Invit.	2nd/14
4-21	A$_{AK}$	Firestone Invit.	3rd/18
4-28	A$_{CO}$	Kepler Invit.	11th/23
5-5	H	Spartan Invit.	5th/14
5-12	A$_{AA}$	Wolverine Classic	7th/14
		Big Tens at W. Lafayette	8th

1991-1992

Coach: Ken Horvath

9-24	A$_{IC}$	Northern Inter.	7th/17
10-6	A$_{LO}$	Fall Colonel Classic	4th/18
11-2	A$_{NK}$	Seascape Coll.	15th/17
2-25	A$_{HL}$	Mardi Gras Invit.	6th/15
3-7	A$_{FI}$	Fripp Is. Inter.	13th/16
3-27	A	Pinehurst Classic	1st/3
4-4	A$_{LX}$	J. Owens Invit.	1st/19
4-12	A	Indiana Invit.	7th/14
4-19	A$_{AK}$	Firestone Invit.	2nd/35
4-26	A$_{CO}$	Kepler Invit.	4th/18
5-3	H	Spartan Invit.	1st/18
5-10	A$_{AA}$	Wolverine Invit.	(t)9th/19
		Big Tens at Iowa City	4th

1992-1993

Coach: Ken Horvath

9-26	A	N. Ill. Midwest	2nd/11
10-4	A$_{BL}$	Northern Inter.	15/20
10-20	A$_{LO}$	Persim'n Ridge	6th/18
2-16	A$_{HL}$	Mardi Gras Invit.	13th/16
2-28	A$_{CS}$	Border Olympics	9th/15
3-11	A$_{FI}$	Fripp Is. Inter.	7th/20
3-28	A$_{LX}$	John Owens Invit.	5th/22
4-11	A$_{FR}$	Indiana Invit.	7th/13
4-18	A$_{AK}$	Firestone Invit.	3rd/20
4-25	A$_{CO}$	Kepler Invit.	4th/20
5-2	H	Spartan Invit.	4th/20
5-9	A$_{AA}$	Wolverine Invit.	4th/18
		Big Tens at Bloomington	9th

1993-1994

Coach: Ken Horvath

9-25	A$_{DK}$	Midwest Invit.	5th/12
10-10	A$_{AA}$	Northern Inter.	4th/24
10-19	A$_{LO}$	Persim'n Ridge	5th/18
3-12	A$_{FI}$	Fripp Is. Inter.	6th/17
3-27	A$_{LD}$	Border Olympics.	11/15
4-2	A$_{LX}$	John Owens Invit.	(t)3rd/14
4-9	A	Marshall Invit.	(t)11/18
4-18	A$_{IN}$	Indiana Inter.coll	5th/18
4-23	A	Kent State Invit.	6th/19
5-1	A$_{CO}$	Kepler Inter.coll	8th/16
5-7	H	Fossum Spart. Invit.	3rd/20
		Big Tens at Ann Arbor	5th

1994-1995

Coach: Ken Horvath

9-24	A$_{MI}$	Geneva Nat. Invit.	5th/18
10-1	H	Northern Inter.	(t)7th/19
10-10	A$_{EV}$	Windon Classic	8th/12
2-20	A$_{FI}$	Fripp Is. Inter.	(t)5th/24
4-1	A$_{DL}$	Dr. Pepper Inter.	10th/16
4-7	A	Marshall Invit.	13th/18
4-21	A$_{CO}$	Kepler Invit.	(t)15/23
4-28	A	Kent Invit.	(t)9th/19
5-6	H	Fossum Spart.Invit.	12th/17
		Big Tens at Verona	10th

1995-1996

Coach: Ken Horvath

9-24	A	Wolverine Classic	14th/21
10-1	A	D.A. Weibring Inter.	5th/17
10-14	A	Northern Inter.	(t)9th/18
10-23	A	Persimmon Ridge	8th/17
3-8	A	Fripp Island Inter.	7th/24
3-30	A	Dr. Pepper Inter.	10th/18
4-12	A	The Legends Invit.	3rd/18
4-20	A	Kepler Invit.	(t)15th/18
4-26	A	King Cobra/Kent Inter. ..	6th/19
5-4	H	Fossum/Spartan Invit.	14th/19
		Big Tens at Univ. Park	9th/11

1996-1997

Coach: Ken Horvath

9-13	A	Yale Fall Inter.	10th/36
9-27	A	Northern Invit.	15th/15
10-5	A	Wolverine Classic	(t)11th/18
10-21	A	Persimmon Ridge Invit. ...	1st/18
3-7	A	Fripp Island Inter.	9th/19
3-21	A	Pepsi/East Car. Inter.	19th/24
3-28	A	Murray State Invit.	6th/8
4-4	A	Johnny Owens Invit.	14th/18
4-11	A	Marshall Invit.	12th/18
4-18	A	The Legends Invit.	16th/18
4-26	H	Fossum Invit.	6th/21
		Big Tens at Columbus	11th/11

1997-1998

Coach: Ken Horvath

9-12	A	Yale Fall Inter.	5th/37
9-27	H	Northern Inter.	11th/17
10-6	A	Legends of In. Inter.	16th/18
10-13	A	Kroger Inter.	11th/18
2-23	A	UTSA Invit.	10th/18
3-12	A	Golden Ocala Invit.	2nd/18
3-30	A	SLU/Mardi Gras Invit. ...	6th/18
4-4	A	Johnny Owens Invit.	5th/20
4-10	A	Marshall Invit.	15th/20
4-18	A	Kepler Invit.	9th/16
5-2	A	Wolverine Invit.	12th/14
		Big Tens at East Lansing	6th/11

1998-1999

Coach: Ken Horvath

9-14	A	Detroit Titans Invit.	1st/13
9-18	A	Northern Inter.	7th/12
9-28	A	Co. St. Ram Inter.	10th/14
10-12	A	Xavier Invit.	(t)6th/19
10-26	A	Tu. Green Wave Inter.	4th/18
2-15	A	Southwest Cl. Invit.	18th/19
3-20	A	Border Olympics	11th/18
3-27	A	Dr. Pepper Inter.	4th/19
4-9	A	Marshall Invit.	19th/20
4-17	A	Kepler Invit.	8th/15
5-1	H	Fossum Invit.	5th/17
5-8	A	Wolverine Invit.	7th/18
		Big Tens at Minnesota	7th/11

Mark Hankins (1999-)

Mark Hankins, a native of Mt. Pleasant, Iowa, was a member of the Iowa State golf team from 1988-93. In 1993, he earned first-team All-American honors while also being named first-team All-Big Eight Conference. He was also a three-time Academic All-Big Eight selection (1988, 1991 and 1993) and his personal-best round of 66 still stands as the Cyclone team record. Following his graduation from Iowa State in 1993 with a degree in psychology, he successfully pursued a master's program in business administration with an emphasis on sports administration and marketing at ISU. His first collegiate coaching experience came when he was appointed as an assistant to the Iowa State men's and women's programs in 1994. From there he moved on to the University of Texas at Arlington where in two seasons his teams won eight tournament titles including the Southland Conference championship in 1998-1999. Outside of college coaching, Hankins has served as a teaching professional at numerous country clubs and camps.

1999-2000

Coach: Mark Hankins

9-20	A	Kansas Invit.	9th/17
9-27	A	Colorado State Inter.	4th/15
10-1	A	Northern Inter.	4th/13
10-13	A	Adams Cup of Newp.	2nd/14
3-10	A	Birkdale Coll. Classic	16th/18
3-25	A	Dr. Pepper Inter.	5th/19
3-31	A	Border Olympics	8th/14
4-7	A	Marshall Invit.	(t)8th/19
4-14	A	Kepler Invit.	(t)14th/17
4-29	H	Fossum Invit.	(t)3rd/19
		Big Tens at W. Lafayette	8th/11

2000-2001

Coach: Mark Hankins

9-11	A	Ne. Fair. Club Invit. ...	(t)6th/12
9-18	A	PSINET Coll. Invit.	8th/12
9-25	A	Colorado State Inter.	5th/15
9-30	A	Northern Inter.	(t)13th/28
10-9	A	Bluffs/Purina Inter.	7th/15
3-10	A	Big Red Classic	7th/17
3-24	A	Dr. Pepper Inter.	3rd/17
4-14	A	Kepler Invit.	5th/17

4-20	A	Kent St. First En. Coll. 2/19
4-28	H	Fossum Invit. 3rd/15
		Big Tens at Champaign 6th/11

2001-2002 (1-0)

Coach: Mark Hankins

9-16	A$_{TA}$	Northern Inter. .... NTS
9-30	A$_{AA}$	Wolverine Invit. .... NTS
10-3	A$_{NP}$	Adams Cup 2nd/17
10-9	A$_{SZ}$	Purina Classic 8th/15
10-14	A$_{DU}$	Duke Invitational 11th/18
3-10	A$_{OC}$	Big Red Classic 2nd/16
3-17	A$_{TS}$	District Challenge 5th/14
3-24	A$_{DL}$	Tanglewood/Pepsi 1st/13
4-6	A	Iowa 282-290	W
4-14	A$_{CO}$	Robert Kepler Invit. 5th/17
4-28	H	Fossum/Spartan Invit. 3rd/15
		Big Tens at Iowa City 9th

2002-2003 (0-0)

Coach: Mark Hankins

9-17	A$_{TO}$	Inverness Intercoll. 3/15
9-29	A$_{BL}$	Northern Intercoll 3/16
10-6	A$_{AA}$	Wolverine Invit .... (t)1st/17
10-9	A$_{NP}$	Adams Cup 1/17
10-22	A$_{DU}$	Duke Golf Classic 6/14
3-9	A$_{OL}$	Big Red Classic 9/18
3-16	A$_{TS}$	Alabama Invitational 7/13
3-25	A$_{EU}$	Duck Invitational 14/16
4-13	A$_{CO}$	Kepler Invitational 10/18
4-27	H	Fossum/Taylor Invit 4/14
5-17	A$_{MK}$	NCAA Central Reg. ...... (t)20/27
		Big Tens at Bloomington 7/11

NCAA Championships

Year	Place	Score	Top Spartan	Score/Place
1938	12th	627	Ed Flowers	
1939	21st	657	Stan Kowal	
1940	9th	620	Bill Zylstra, Stan Kowal	
1941	(t)7th	615	Bill Zylstra, Stan Kowal	
1942	11th	625	Joe Watson	
1944	5th	344	Bob Bowen	
1946	10th	644	Jim Funston	
1956	17th	623		
1960	(t)19th	631		
1961	6th	603	Gen Hunt*	
1967	(t)6th	598	John Bailey	299
1968	9th	1,175	Larry Murphy	291/26th
1969	13th	1,260	Lee Edmundson	311/11th
1970	17th	N/A	Lee Edmundson	295/t7th
1971	16th	1,191	Graham Cooke	288/10
1972			Dick Bradow, John Vandemeiden**	
1975			Bill Bradford, John Domagalski**	
1980			Rick Grover**	300/t31
1985			Jon Kosier**	
1993	(t)27th	616	Heath Feld	151
2002			Eric Jorgensen**	283/t17th

* lost in semi-finals to Jack Nicklaus
** competed as individuals

Big Ten Championships

Year	Place	Score	Top Spartan	Score/Place
1951	6th	1,567	Carl Mosacck	304/t10th
1952	10th	1,661	Harold Ware	318/t18th
1953	10th	1,586	Don Stevens	311/t22nd
1954	8th	1,576	Ken Rodewald	307/t11th
1955	7th	1,204	Jim Sullivan	234/t17th
1956	(t)6th	1,549	Ken Rodewald	297/t4th
1957	7th	1,564	Ken Rodewald	308/t17th
1958	6th	1,572	Arlin Dell	308/t16th
1959	7th	1,615	Tad Schmidt	314/t12th
1960	2nd	1,531	C.A. Smith	296/3rd
1961	3rd	1,539	C.A. Smith	305/6th
1962	7th	1,541	Albert Badger	302/t12th
1963	(t)7th	1,562	Phil Marston	310/t21st
1964	7th	1,534	Phil Marston	298/t6th
1965	7th	1,540	Ken Benson	301/t17th
1966	(t)4th	1,519	John Bailey	301/14th
1967	3rd	1,583	Larry Murphy	310/t6th
1968	2nd	1,523	Steve Benson	297/4th
1969	1st	1,501	Lynn Janson	298/3rd
1970	3rd	1,561	Lynn Janson	306/t4th
1971	2nd	1,510	John VanderMeiden	299/2nd
1972	5th	1,483	Dick Bradow	295/t18th
			Mark Timyan	295/t18th
1973	5th	1,517	Steve Cole	297t9th
			Brad Hyland	297/t9th
1974	3rd	1,513	Steve Cole	298/6th
1975	3rd	1,533	Seve Broadwell	297/t4th
1976	6th	1,573	Gary Domagalski	312/t14th
1977	7th	1,506	Gary Domagalski	298/t15th
			Mike Egly	298/t15th
1978	9th	1,604	Rick Grover	312/24th
1979	3rd	1,503	Rick Grover	297/t8th
1980	5th	1,506	Rick Grover	292/t3rd
1981	5th	1,456	Monty James	286/t10th
1982	7th	1,497	Todd Hartle	291/t8th
1983	(t)8th	1,522	Todd Hartle	294/t6th
1984	6th	1,526	John Kosier	304/t24th
1985	9th	1,533	Tom Harding	293/3rd
1986	5th	1,198	Todd Marston	290/5th
1987	5th	1,217	Jon Kosier	295/t4th
1988	4th	1,204	Todd Marston	298/t4th
1989	10th	1,222	Brent Kish	301/t24th
			Mike Spencer	301/t24th
1990	5th	1,178	Brent Kish	295/t14th
1991	8th	1,173	Mike Spencer	292/t21st
1992	4th	1,165	Heath Feld	284/2nd
1993	9th	1,184	Heath Feld	287/t2nd
1994	5th	1,183	Heath Feld	290/t7th
1995	11th	1,226	Brian Bartolec	299/t12th
1996	9th	1,216	John Ehrgott	304/t24th
1997	11th	1,243	Matt Pumford	309/28th
1998	6th	1,203	Brent Goik	292/t5th
1999	7th	1,164	Carlos Foulquie	288/t16th
2000	8th	1,215	Dennis Riedel	298/t12th
2001	6th	1,161	Brent Goik	287/t11th
2002	5th	1,166	Eric Jorgensen	280/1st
2003	7th	1,168	Eric Jorgensen	289/t13st

All American

Year	Name	Honor
1968	Steve Benson	third team
	Lynn Janson	honorable mention
1969	Lynn Janson	third team
1970	Lynn Janson	second team
	Lee Edmondson	honorable mention
1971	Rick Woulfe	third team
	Graham Cook	honorable mention
1972	John VanderMeiden	honorable mention
1973	Steve Cole	honorable mention
1974	Brad Hyland	honorable mention

All Big Ten

1968	Steve Benson
1969	Lynn Janson
1970	Lynn Janson and Lee Edmundson
1971	John VanderMeiden and Rick Woulfe
1974	Brad Hyland
1982	Mike Thompsen
1988	Todd Marston
1990	Brent Kish
1992	Heath Feld
1993	Heath Feld
1994	Heath Feld
2002	Eric Jorgensen
	John Koskinen
2003	Eric Jorgensen

Year-by-Year Team Performance

Years	Dual Meets			Conference Championships			NCAA Championships			Coach
	W	L	T	Score	Place	Host or Site	Pts	Place	Host or Site	
1928	6	2	0		DNC	Columbus, OH			no meet	no coach
1929	4	1	0		DNC	Minneapolis, MN			no meet	Harry Kipke
1930	7	2	0		DNC	Wilmette, IL			no meet	James Crowley
1931	6	4	0		DNC	Ann Arbor, MI			no meet	James Crowley
1932	5	4	0		DNC	Minneapolis, MN			no meet	Ben VanAlstyne
1933	5	4	1		DNC	Prairie View, IL			no meet	Ben VanAlstyne
1934	2	8	0		DNC	Prairie View, IL			no meet	Ben VanAlstyne
1935	4	4	1		DNC	Prairie View, IL			no meet	Ben VanAlstyne
1936	6	4	0		DNC	Prairie View, IL			no meet	Ben VanAlstyne
1937	5	4	0		DNC	Prairie View, IL			no meet	Ben VanAlstyne
1938	7	1	0		DNC	Minneapolis, MN			no meet	Ben VanAlstyne
1939	5	3	0		DNC	Prairie View, IL		21st/23	Wakanda	Ben VanAlstyne
1940	5	3	1		DNC	Columbus, OH		DNC	Ekwanak	Ben VanAlstyne
1941	5	3	0		DNC	Lake Forest, IL		(t)7th/19	Ohio State	Ben VanAlstyne
1942	3	4	1		DNC	Ann Arbor, MI		11th/13	Notre Dame	Ben VanAlstyne
1943	3	4	1		DNC	Wilmette, IL		DNC	Olympia Fields, IL	Ben VanAlstyne
1944	Intercollegiate competition suspended due to World War II							5th/5	Inverness	Ben VanAlstyne
1945	0	6	0		DNC	Evanston, IL		DNC	Ohio State	Ben VanAlstyne
1946	7	5	0		DNC	Minneapolis, MN		10th/18	Princeton	Ben VanAlstyne
1947	4	6	0		DNC	Lafayette, IN		DNC	Michigan	Ben VanAlstyne
1948	6	6	0		DNC	Evanston, IL		DNC	Stanford	Ban VanAlstyne
1949	3	5	0		DNC	Ann Arbor, MI		DNC	Iowa State	Ben VanAlstyne
1950	4	6	0		DNC	Columbus, OH		DNC	New Mexico	Ben VanAlstyne
1951	10	3	0	1,567	6th	Evanston, IL		DNC	Ohio State	Ben VanAlstyne
1952	5	5	0	1,661	10th	Champaign, IL		DNC	Pudue	Ben VanAlstyne
1953	5	5	1	1,586	10th	Madison, WI		DNC	Broadmoor	Ben VanAlstyne
1954	7	4	0	1,576	8th	Minneapolis, MN		DNC	Houston/Rice	Ben VanAlstyne
1955	4	7	0	1,204	7th	Lafayette, IN		DNC	Tennessee	Ben VanAlstyne
1956	4	5	0	1,549	(t)6th	Willmette, IL		DNC	Ohio State	Ben VanAlstyne
1957	8	6	0	1,564	7th	Iowa City, IA		DNC	Broadmoor	Ben VanAlstyne
1958	6	2	1	1,572	6th	Columbus, OH		DNC	Williams	Ben VanAlstyne
1959	11	1	0	1,615	7th	Ann Arbor, MI		DNC	Oregon	Ben VanAlstyne
1960	9	1	0	1,531	2nd	East Lansing, MI		(t)19th/34	Broadmoor	John Brotzmann
1961	10	3	1	1,539	3rd	Bloomington, IN		6th/28	Lafayette	John Brotzmann
1962	12	0	1	1,541	7th	Savoy (Champaign), IL		DNC	Duke	John Brotzmann
1963	8	4	1	1,582	(t)7th	Madison, WI		DNC	Wichita State	John Brotzmann
1964	7	12	0	1,534	7th	Minneapolis, MN		DNC	Broadmore	John Brotzmann
1965	5	12	0	1,540	7th	West Lafayette, IN		DNC	Tennessee	John Brotzmann
1966	6	7	0	1,580	(t)4th	Iowa City, IA		DNC	Stanford	Bruce Fossum
1967	5	1	0	1,583	3rd	Ann Arbor, MI		(t)6th/39	Shawnee, PA	Bruce Fossum
1968	4	1	0	1,523	3rd	Bloomington, IN		9th/15	New Mexico State	Bruce Fossum
1969	tournaments			1,501	1st	East Lansing, MI		13th/16	Broadmoor	Bruce Fossum
1970	tournaments			1,561	3rd	Savoy (Champaign), IL		DNC	Ohio State	Bruce Fossum
1971	tournaments			1,510	2nd	Columbus, OH		16th/16	Arizona	Bruce Fossum
1972	tournaments			1,483	5th	Mineapolis, MN		DNC	Cape Coral	Bruce Fossum
1973	tournaments			1,517	5th	West Lafayette, IN		DNC	Oklahoma State	Bruce Fossum
1974	tournaments			1,513	3rd	Iowa City, IA		DNC	San Diego State	Bruce Fossum
1975	tournaments			1,533	3rd	Bloomington, IN		DNC	Ohio State	Bruce Fossum
1976	tournaments			1,573	6th	Ann Arbor, MI		DNC	New Mexico	Bruce Fossum
1977	tournaments			1,506	7th	East Lansing		DNC	Colgate	Bruce Fossum
1978	tournaments			1,604	9th	Columbus, OH		DNC	Oregon	Bruce Fossum
1979	tournaments			1,503	3rd	Savoy (Champaign), IL		DNC	Wake Forest	Bruce Fossum
1980	tournaments			1,506	5th	Madison, WI		DNC	Ohio State	Bruce Fossum
1981	tournaments			1,456	5th	Minneasapolis, MN		DNC	Stanford	Bruce Fossum
1982	tournaments			1,499	7th	West Lafayette, IN		DNC	Pinehurst	Bruce Fossum
1983	tournaments			1,522	(t)8th	Iowa City, IA		DNC	Fresno State	Bruce Fossum
1984	tournaments			1,526	6th	Bloomington, IN		DNC	Houston	Bruce Fossum
1985	tournaments			1,533	9th	Ann Arbor, MI		DNC	Florida	Bruce Fossum
1986	tournaments			*1,198	5th	East Lansing, MI		DNC	Wake Forest	Bruce Fossum
1987	tournaments			1,217	5th	Columbus, OH		DNC	Ohio State	Bruce Fossum
1988	tournaments			1,204	5th	Champaign, IL		DNC	Southern California	Bruce Fossum
1989	tournaments			1,222	10th	Madison, WI		DNC	Oklahom & Okla. St.	Bruce Fossum
1990	tournaments			1,178	5th	Minneapolis, MN		DNC	Florida	Bruce Fossum
1991	tournaments			1,173	8th	West Lafayette, IN		DNC	San Jose State	Ken Horvath
1992	tournaments			1,165	4th	Iowa City, IA		DNC	New Mexico	Ken Horvath
1993	tournaments			1,184	9th	Bloomington, IN		DNC	Kentucky	Ken Horvath
1994	tournaments			1,183	5th	Ann Arbor, MI		DNC	Southern Methodist	Ken Horvath
1995	tournaments			1,226	11th	Verona, IL		DNC	Ohio State	Ken Horvath
1996	tournaments			1,216	9th	University Park, PA		DNC	Chattanooga, TN	Ken Horvath
1997	tournaments			1,243	11th	Columbus, OH		DNC	Northwestern	Ken Horvath
1998	tournaments			1,203	6th	East Lansing, MI		DNC	New Mexico	Ken Horvath
1999	tournaments			1,164	7th	Minneapolis, MN		DNC	Minnesota	Ken Horvath
2000	tournaments			1,215	8th	West Lafayette, IN		DNC	Auburn	Mark Hankins
2001	tournaments			1,161	6th	Champaign, IL		DNC	Duke	Mark Hankins
2002	tournaments			1,166	5th	Iowa City, IA		DNC	Ohio State	Mark Hankins
2003	tournaments			1,168	7th	Bloomington, IN		DNC	Oklahoma State	Mark Hankins

* Began using top four individual scores

GYMNASTICS
LEADERS, RECORDS and HONORS

ALL-TIME COACHING RECORDS

Coach	Years	W	L	T	Avg.
George Szypula	1948-88	228	183	5	.551
Rick Atkinson	1989-2001	75	61	0	.559
Totals		303	247	5	.554

Season Records
See page 874 for explanation of abbreviations.

George Szypula (1948-1987)
From the sport's first year at Michigan State through the next 40 seasons, George Szypula would coach 252 dual meet victories against 186 losses. The 1958 squad achieved the most impressive honors, achieving a first place tie with Illinois at that season's NCAA championships. Szypula was born in Pottstown, PA, on June 24, 1921, and attended Northeast High School in Philadelphia. As a prep student, he competed in baseball and gymnastics. Szypula earned both bachelor's and master's degrees at Temple University where he gained numerous honors as a four-year member of the gymnastics squad. He captured the National AAU tumbling crown four straight years and the NCAA title as a junior in 1942. George also won the Middle Atlantic States Senior AA tumbling title 10 times and the Senior AAU horizontal and parallel bar championship five times. Szypula entered the Army Signal Corps after graduation from Temple and during World War II served in North Africa and Italy. He was discharged from the service in 1945 and one year later was coaching gymnastics and teaching physical education at Fitzsimons High School in Philadelphia. Just prior to coming to East Lansing, Szypula served as an assistant coach while completing his M.A. degree at Temple.

1947-1948 (1-5-1)
Coach: George Szypula

1-10	H	Central Michigan	42-42	T
1-19	H	Minnesota	23-73	L
1-24	A	Illinois	28.5-67.5	L
1-30	A	Michigan	30-66	L
2-17	H	Michigan	32.5-62.5	L
2-21	H	Central Michigan	38-26	W
4-3	H	Illinois	34.5-60.5	L

1948-1949 (1-5-1)
Coach: George Szypula

1-22	A	Ohio State	48-48	T
2-7	H	Penn State	51-61	L
2-11	A	Wisconsin	65.5-29.5	W
2-12	A	Minnesota	38-58	L
2-19	H	Illinois	46-50	L
2-25	A	Illinois-Chicago	45.5-50.5	L
3-7	H	Michigan	41.5-54.5	L

1949-1950 (4-4)
Coach: George Szypula

1-18	A	Kent State	51.5-44.5	W
1-28	A	Penn State	52.5-59.5	L
2-6	H	Wisconsin	62.5-33.5	W
2-13	H	Minnesota	47-49	L
2-18	A_{LU}	Illinois	45-52	L
		Wisconsin	59-35	W
3-2	H	Ohio State	60-35	W
3-10	A	Michigan	45-51	L

1950-1951 (6-3)
Coach: George Szypula

1-20	H	Kent State		W
2-3	A	Ohio State	43.5-52.5	L
2-17	H	Wisconsin	64-32	W
		Illinois-Chicago	67-29	W
2-19	A	Minnesota	45-51	L
2-24	H	Notre Dame	77-19	W
		Indiana	62-34	W
3-2	H	Illinois	42-54	L
3-5	H	Michigan	56-40	W
		Big Tens at Madison	2nd/9	

1951-1952 (6-0)
Coach: George Szypula

1-11	A	Illinois-Chicago	56-40	W
1-19	H	Ohio State	61-35	W
2-9	H	Indiana	60-36	W
2-16	H	Illinois	53-43	W
2-23	H	Minnesota	55.5-40.5	W
3-1	A	Michigan	57-39	W
		Big Tens at Bloomington	2nd/9	

1952-1953 (2-6)
Coach: George Szypula

1-10	H	Wisconsin	52-44	W
1-17	A	Indiana	41.5-54.5	L
1-24	H	Ohio State	46-50	L
		Iowa	40-56	L
1-30	H	Penn State	42-70	L
2-7	A	Minnesota	40-56	L
2-13	H	Illinois	43.5-52.5	L
2-28	H	Michigan	48.5-47.5	W
		Big Tens at East Lansing	3rd/8	

1953-1954 (3-4)
Coach: George Szypula

1-23	A	Iowa	41-55	L
1-30	A	Penn State	40-72	L
2-6	H	Ohio State	49-47	W
2-11	H	Minnesota	49-47	W
2-20	A	Illinois	38-58	L
2-27	A	Wisconsin	59-37	W
3-3	A	Michigan	40-56	L
		Big Tens at Columbus	4th/8	

1954-1955 (5-1)
Coach: George Szypula

1-15	H	Michigan	59-37	W
1-22	H	Iowa	51.5-44.5	W
2-5	A	Ohio Stte	54-42	W
2-18	H	Indiana	69-26	W
2-19	H	Illinois	43-53	L
2-25	A	Minnesota	55-41	W
		Big Tens at Minneapolis	2nd/9	

1955-1956 (3-3-1)
Coach: George Szypula

1-7	A	Illinois-Chicago	56-56	T
1-9	A	Michigan	47-65	L
1-20	H	Minnesota	49-63	L
2-4	H	Ohio State	70-42	W
2-17	A	Illinois	44-68	L
2-25	H	Iowa	60-52	W
		Illinois-Chicago	67-45	W
		Big Tens at Champaign	3rd/9	

1956-1957 (7-1)
Coach: George Szypula

1-11	H	Illinois-Chicago	70.5-41.5	W
1-19	H	Ohio State	69-43	W
1-26	H	Minnesota	78-33	W
2-9	H	Illinois	47-65	L
2-16	H	Iowa	66.5-42.5	W
2-18	H	Michigan	58.5-53.5	W
2-23	H	Wisconsin	74-36	W
3-2	A	Indiana	62.5-49.5	W
		Big Tens at Ann Arbor	3rd/9	

1957-1958 (7-3)
Coach: George Szypula

1-10	H	Minnesota	56.5-55.5	W
1-18	A	Ohio State	71-41	W
1-25	A	Illinois	52-60	L
2-1	H	Indiana	72-40	W
2-15	A_{MA}	Wisconsin	77-35	W
		Illinois-Chicago	65-47	W
2-22	H	Northwestern	81-30	W
2-28	A	Michigan	50.5-61.5	L
3-8	A	Iowa	43.5-68.5	L
3-11	A	Central Michigan	88-40	W
		Big Tens at Iowa City	3rd/9	

1958-1959 (7-2)
Coach: George Szypula

1-10	H	Wisconsin	79-33	W
		Central Michigan	84.5-27.5	W
1-17	H	Southern Illinois	64-48	W
1-31	A	Ohio State	63-49	W
2-7	A	Indiana	60-52	W
2-16	H	Michigan	38.5-73.5	L
2-21	H	Illinois-Chicago	73-39	W
		Minnesota	59-53	W
2-28	H	Illinois	48-64	L
		Big Tens at Bloomington	3rd/8	

1959-1960 (10-0-1)
Coach: George Szypula

1-9	A	Central Michigan	87-25	W
1-16	H	Ohio State	85-27	W
1-23	H	Minnesota	65.5-46.5	W
1-29	A	Illinois-Chicago	80-32	W
1-30	A	Wisconsin	90.5-21.5	W
2-5	A_{CA}	Southern Illinois	60-52	W
		Minnesota	72-40	W
2-6	A	Illinois	65.5-46.5	W
2-12	H	Iowa	56-56	T
2-20	H	Indiana	85-27	W
2-26	A	Michigan	60-52	W
		Big Tens at Minneapolis	3rd/8	

1960-1961 (8-2)
Coach: George Szypula

1-14	A_{IC}	Iowa	77-35	W
		Minnesota	78-34	W
1-21	A	Ohio State	73-38	W
1-28	A	Indiana	73.5-38.5	W
2-4	A	Wisconsin	69-41	W
2-10	H	Illinois	49-63	L
2-14	H	Southern Illinois	57.5-54.5	W
2-18	H	Minnesota	72.5-39.5	W
2-21	H	Michigan	54.5-57.5	L
2-25	H	Illinois-Chicago	74-38	W
		Big Tens at Ann Arbor	3rd/8	

1961-1962 (8-4)

Coach: George Szypula

1-12	A	Ball State	72-39	W
1-13	A	Indiana	64.5-47.5	W
1-20	H	Michigan	49-63	L
		Iowa	72.5-38.5	W
1-27	H	Wisconsin	84-27	W
2-3	A	Minnesota	71-41	W
2-10	A	Illinois-Chicago	71-40	W
2-16	A	S. Illinois	43-69	L
2-17	H	Illinois	38-73	L
		Iowa	62-44	W
2-23	A	Michigan	50.5-61.5	L
2-24	H	Ohio State	79-32	W

Big Tens at Columbus 2nd/8

1962-1963 (7-3)

Coach: George Szypula

1-19	A	Ohio State	73.5-38.5	W
1-26	H	Central Michigan	78-32	W
		Indiana	73.5-37.5	W
2-2	A	Iowa	46-66	L
2-9	A	Wisconsin	57-55	W
2-15	H	Illinois	79-21	W
2-20	H	Michigan	39-70	L
2-23	H	Minnesota	63-48	W
2-25	H	S. Illinois	43-69	L
3-2	H	Ill.-Chicago	66.5-45.5	W

Big Tens at East Lansing 4th/8

1963-1964 (5-3-1)

Coach: George Szypula

1-11	H	Wisconsin	62-50	W
		Iowa	54-58	L
1-18	H	Ohio State	60.5-51.5	W
2-1	A	Minnesota	55.5-56.5	L
2-9	A	Illinois-Chicago	64-47	W
2-15	A	Indiana	75-37	W
2-22	A	Michigan	56-56	T
2-28	A	S. Illinois	47-65	L
2-29	A	Illinois	64.5-46.5	W

Big Tens at Madison 3rd/8

1964-1965 (6-4)

Coach: George Szypula

1-16	A	Iowa	54-64	L
1-23	A	Minnesota	75-45	W
1-23	A$_{MN}$	Iowa	42.5-74.5	L
1-30	H	Ohio State	75-37	W
2-6	H	Indiana	80.5-31.5	W
2-12	A	Michigan	52-66	L
2-15	H	Southern Illinois	47-73	L
2-20	H	Wisconsin	63-57	W
2-26	A	Illinois-Chicago	66-54	W
2-27	A	Illinois	71-49	W

Big Tens at Champaign 3rd/8

1965-1966 (8-0)

Coach: George Szypula

12-3	A$_{CH}$	Midwest Open	NTS	
1-8	H	Illinois-Chicago	187.6-156.05	W
1-15	A	Ohio State	181.85-134.4	W
1-22	H	Iowa	188.10-177.20	W
1-29	A	Indiana	153.45-137.6	W
2-12	A	Wisconsin	188.25-174.6	W
2-18	H	Minnesota	178.55-165.0	W
2-19	H	Illinois	192.45-184.0	W
2-26	H	Michigan	190.45-188.35	W

Big Tens at Bloomington 2nd/8

1966-1967 (5-3)

Coach: George Szypula

12-2	A$_{OP}$	Midwest Open	NTS	
12-3	A	Minnesota	178.83-169.93	W
1-14	H	Ohio State	178.47-138.63	W

1-20	A	Southern Illinois ..	190.25-190.9	L
1-28	H	Indiana	178.07-171.8	W
2-4	H	Wisconsin	180.5-163.85	W
2-11	A	Illinois	184.52-189.17	L
2-15	A	Michigan	190.8-190.42	W
2-18	H	Iowa	186.7-189.2	L

Big Tens at Iowa City 3rd/8

1967-1968 (6-3)

Coach: George Szypula

12-1	A$_{AD}$	Midwest Open	NTS	
1-6	A	Ohio State	186.1-165.75	W
1-13	A	Indiana	181.65-160.25	W
1-19	A	S. Illinois	187.45-188.9	L
1-27	H	Illinois	188.3-183.5	W
2-2	H	Minnesota	185.4-177.2	W
2-8	H	Michigan	187.05-188.6	L
2-10	A	Wisconsin	182.95-168.5	W
2-17	H	Ill.-Chicago	176.35-164.85	W
2-24	A	Iowa	187.25-188.75	L

Big Tens at East Lansing .... (t)1st/8

1968-1969 (7-3)

Coach: George Szypula

11-30	A$_{PR}$	Midwest Open	NTS	
1-17	A	S. Illinois	153.35-157.07	L
1-25	A$_{MN}$	Minnesota	180.07-173.82	W
		Indiana St.	154.57-153.8	W
2-1	A	Illinois	179.97-179.75	W
2-8	A	Iowa	181.37-184.75	L
2-15	A$_{AA}$	Michigan	184.87-190.82	L
		Indiana	182.22-167.0	W
2-22	H	Ohio State	181.45-173.67	W
		Wisconsin	178.75-162.35	W
3-1	H	Ill.-Chicago	154.85-150.37	W

Big Tens at Ann Arbor 4th/8

1969-1970 (4-7)

Coach: George Szypula

11-28	A$_{CH}$	Midwest Open	NT	
12-5	A	Big Ten Invitational	NTS	
1-10	A	Ill.-Chicago	155.25-156.55	L
1-24	H	Michigan	150.4-161.9	L
1-28	H	New Mexico	155.8-155.4	W
1-30	H	Minnesota	157.05-146.35	W
1-31	H	Illinois	157.45-158.3	L
2-7	H	Iowa	157.05-157.20	L
2-14	A	S. Illinois	152.6-159.15	L
2-16	A	Wisconsin	157.95-148.50	W
2-21	A	Ohio State	155.95-147.4	W
2-27	A	Indiana St.	151.85-158.25	L
2-28	A	Indiana	151.85-153.60	L

Big Tens at Minneapolis 4th/8

1970-1971 (5-5)

Coach: George Szypula

12-5	H	Big Ten Invitational	NTS	
1-16	A	Illinois	151.35-157.50	L
1-21	H	S. Illinois	153.70-161.80	L
1-23	A	Minnesota	154.95-158.40	L
1-29	H	Indiana St.	159.60-159.40	W
2-1	A	Wisconsin	156.00-143.50	W
2-6	H	Iowa	160.60-160.90	L
2-13	H	Indiana	158.65-155.50	W
		E. Michigan	155.40-143.95	W
2-20	H	Ohio State	158.55-140.40	W
2-26	A	Michigan	158.90-165.00	L

Big Tens at Columbus 5th/8

1971-1972 (5-4)

Coach: George Szypula

12-4	A$_{CH}$	Big Ten Invitational	NTS	
1-8	H	N. Carolina	152.00-120.40	W
1-22	A	S. Illinois	158.35-163.15	L
1-29	A	E. Michigan	154.55-144.75	W

2-4	H	Minnesota	156.00-154.65	W
2-5	H	Iowa	154.95-155.75	L
2-11	A	Indiana St.	152.30-155.90	L
2-12	H	Indiana	157.70-157.60	W
2-19	A	Ohio State	154.15-148.65	W
2-25	H	Michigan	160.65-161.90	L

Big Tens at Champaign 5th/8

1972-1973 (8-5)

Coach: George Szypula

11-24	A$_{CH}$	Midwest Open	NTS	
12-2	A$_{CH}$	Big Ten Invitational	NTS	
1-5	H	E. Michigan	151.10-139.15	W
		Ohio State	150.00-142.05	W
1-13	A$_{MA}$	Wisconsin	151.35-131.70	W
		Iowa	152.60-152.50	W
1-19	H	S. Illinois	156.75-162.35	L
1-27	H	Indiana	157.40-159.15	W
2-2	A$_{KZ}$	W. Michigan	156.30-142.50	W
		Illinois St.	156.00-155.45	W
2-3	H	Indiana St.	158.15-163.30	L
2-9	A	Oklahoma	157.75-156.55	W
2-17	A	Minnesota	156.10-158.45	L
2-19	A	Michigan	154.40-161.50	L
2-24	H	Illinois	158.65-140.30	W

Big Tens at Bloomington 5th/8

1973-1974 (2-9)

Coach: George Szypula

11-30	A$_{CH}$	Windy City Invitational	NTS	
1-11	A$_{CO}$	Big Ten Invitational	NTS	
1-16	A	E. Michigan	144.75-137.25	W
1-19	H	Iowa	150.70-160.15	L
		Illinois St.	150-70-157.90	L
1-25	H	Minnesota	153.95-157.05	L
1-29	H	W. Michigan	150.10-145.10	W
2-8	A	Indiana St.	148.15-163.90	L
2-9	A$_{BL}$	Indiana	155.75-157.25	L
		N. Illinois	156.15-158.05	L
2-12	H	Michigan	149.00-159.30	L
2-16	A	Ohio State	145.96-153.20	L
2-23	A	S. Illinois	144.65-160.10	L

Big Tens at Iowa City 7th/8

1974-1975 (3-7)

Coach: George Szypula

1-10	A$_{AA}$	Big Ten Invitational	NTS	
1-18	H	Penn State	187.05-206.60	L
1-24	H	Wisconsin	192.35-194.45	L
		Ohio State	192.40-188.25	W
1-31	A	Illinois	196.35-199.45	L
2-1	A	Illinois St.	189.95-211.40	L
2-10	H	E. Michigan	192.45-143.15	W
2-15	A	Michigan	184.60-206.00	L
2-21	H	Indiana	196.95-202.50	L
2-25	A	W. Michigan	197.70-189.90	W
3-1	A	N. Illinois	198.60-205.90	L

Big Tens at Ann Arbor 7th/8

1975-1976 (9-6)

Coach: George Szypula

1-10	A$_{CO}$	Big Ten Invitational	NTS	
1-17	H	Illinois	187.95-186.85	W
1-19	A$_{YP}$	E. Michigan	187.05-165.10	W
		Schoolcraft	187.05-121.35	W
1-24	A	Wisconsin	181.10-181.95	L
1-30	A	Indiana	185.30-186.90	L
2-7	A$_{CO}$	Ohio State	189.35-190.10	L
		GA Southern	189.35-169.00	W
		Slippery Rock	189.35-159.65	W
2-9	H	W. Michigan	195.40-182.05	W
2-14	A$_{WH}$	Wheaton	198.35-164.10	W
		N. Michigan	198.35-157.85	W
2-17	H	Kent State	196.95-181.55	W
2-20	A	Michigan	205.45-213.60	L
2-21	H	S. Illinois	199.50-205.05	L
2-28	H	Illinois St.	200.50-2202.05	L

Big Tens at Ann Arbor 5th/8

1976-1977 (6-8)
Coach: George Szypula

12-4	A	Ball State Invitational	NTS	
1-9	A	Kent State	178.35-163.00	W
1-14	A_{AA}	Big Ten Invitational	NTS	
1-22	H	Wisconsin	196.50-185.50	W
1-28	H	N. Michigan	203.80-187.60	W
1-29	A	Michigan	194.30-203.35	L
2-5	H	Ohio State	194.05-183.10	W
		E. Michigan	194.05-184.90	W
2-10	A_{KZ}	W. Michigan	187.05-192.20	L
		N. Illinois	187.05-209.05	L
2-18	A	Illinois St.	201.45-209.55	L
2-19	A_{CH}	Ill.-Chicago	195.05-199.15	L
		W. Illinois	192.85-171.15	W
2-26	A_{CU}	Illinois	182.45-209.05	L
		Iowa	182.45-190.10	L
		Minnesota	182.45-208.45	L
		Big Tens at Minneapolis	7th/8	

1977-1978 (7-5)
Coach: George Szypula

11-4	A_{IN}	Indiana Classic	NTS	
12-2	A	Ball State Invitational	10th	
12-16	A	Penn State	196.80-200.00	L
1-8	H	Illinois State	196.90-198.05	L
1-13	A_{AA}	Big Ten Invitational	NTS	
1-20	A_{KZ}	W. Michigan	201.50-193.15	W
		Wis.-Oshkosh	201.50-199.30	W
1-22	H	Michigan	206.65-200.70	W
1-25	A	E. Michigan	197.15-192.35	W
2-3	H	Ill.-Chicago	384.80-411.95	L
2-6	A_{MA}	Wisconsin	197.45-189.70	W
		St. Cloud St.	197.45-189.70	W
2-11	A	Ohio State	201.10-206.80	L
2-17	H	Illinois	203.05-198.70	W
2-24	A	Illinois State	381.55-410.55	L
		Big Tens at Champaign	5th/8	

1978-1979 (6-6)
Coach: George Szypula

11-10	A_{CB}	Indiana Classic	NTS	
11-25	A_{CH}	Midwest Open	NTS	
12-1	A	Ball State Invitational	NTS	
1-13	A_{AA}	Big Ten Invitational	NTS	
1-22	A	Michigan	198.80-206.50	L
1-26	H	Ohio State	202.25-207.05	L
		Wisconsin	198.50-188.45	W
2-2	A	Ill.-Chicago.	197.35-211.50	L
2-7	H	E. Michigan	200.40-187.90	W
2-11	H	Illinois State	204.15-203.95	W
		W. Michigan	204.15-198.64	W
2-16	A_{CU}	Illinois	202.30-207.00	L
		Iowa	202.30-196.50	L
2-23	A_{MN}	Minnesota	202.00-217.55	L
		St. Cloud State	202.00-192.10	W
3-2	H	Indiana	200.05-197.65	W
		Big Tens at Ann Arbor	6th/8	

1979-1980 (8-6)
Coach: George Szypula

11-10	A_{WA}	Wisconsin Open	NTS	
11-16	A_{CO}	Buckeye Open	NTS	
11-23	A_{CH}	Midwest Open	NTS	
1-12	H	Big Ten Invitational	NTS	
1-18	H	Illinois	243.35-250.95	L
1-21	A	E. Michigan	239.05-199.55	W
1-25	H	Minnesota	254.35-261.95	L
2-1	A	Indiana	251.05-254.70	L
2-6	A	W. Michigan	251.10-244.85	W
2-8	A_{CO}	Ohio State	253.30-263.20	L
		Ball State	253.30-250.50	W
2-16	A_{MA}	Wisconsin	255.05-252.85	W
		W. Michigan	255.05-239.80	W
2-22	A_{NM}	Illinois State	259.60-263.55	L
		Indiana State	259.60-265.60	L
2-28	H	Michigan	262.60-262.10	W
		Big Tens at Bloomington	6th/8	

1980-1981 (6-5)
Coach: George Szypula

11-7	A_{WA}	Wisconsin Classic	NTS	
11-28	A_{CH}	Midwest Open	NTS	
12-3	H	Japan Univ. Games Team	NTS	
12-13	A_{AA}	Wolverine Invitational	NTS	
1-10	H	Big Ten Invitational	NTS	
1-17	H	Iowa	261.10-265.15	L
		Ill.-Chicago	264.20-254.00	W
1-21	H	E. Michigan	254.95-143.05	W
		W. Michigan	257.00-247.80	W
1-30	H	Wisconsin	261.75-244.05	W
		Illinois St.	260.35-253.65	W
1-31	A	Michigan	262.10-264.00	L
2-7	A	Indiana St.	252.85-255.15	L
2-14	A	Minnesota	257.30-268.90	L
2-20	A	Illinois	255.75-267.20	L
2-28	H	Indiana	261.60-241.75	W
		Big Tens at Columbus	7th/8	

1981-1982 (2-7)
Coach: George Szypula

11-7	A	Wisconsin Classic	NTS	
11-13	A_{KZ}	Bronco Classic	NTS	
12-12	A_{AA}	Wolverine Invitational	NTS	
1-8	H	Big Ten Invitational	NTS	
1-17	H	Illinois	257.35-257.25	W
1-20	A	E.Michigan	209.35-175.35	W
1-23	H	Minnesota	257.10-268.45	L
1-29	A	Illinois State	258.40-264.30	L
1-29	A_{NM}	S. Illinois	258.40-262.10	L
2-3	A	W. Michigan	246.40-250.25	L
2-5	A	Iowa	260.20-270-55	L
2-19	A	Wisconsin	259.20-261.05	L
2-28	H	Michigan	264.55-273.15	L
		Big Tens at Madison	7th/8	

1982-1983 (7-8)
Coach: George Szypula

11-12	A_{MA}	Wisconsin Open	NTS	
11-26	A_{CH}	Midwest Open	NTS	
1-7	H	Big Ten Invitational	NTS	
1-12	A_{AA}	Wolverine Invitational	NTS	
1-22	H	Wisconsin	257.05-259.50	L
		S. Illinois	257.05-270.00	L
1-28	H	Ohio State	262.15-274.00	L
1-30	H	Kent State	264.10-249.20	W
2-4	H	Iowa	262.10-267.00	L
		W. Michigan	262.10-248.05	W
2-6	A	Ill.-Chicago	248.45-260.75	L
2-12	A	Michigan	260.15-235.80	W
2-20	A	Illinois	256.75-270-30	L
2-26	A_{MN}	Minnesota	263.85-276.00	L
		E. Montana	263.85-244.15	W
3-19	A	Chicagoland Classic	NTS	
		Big Tens at Iowa City	7th/7	

1983-1984 (8-6)
Coach: George Szypula

11-12	A_{MA}	Wisconsin Classic	NTS	
11-26	A_{CH}	Midwest Open	NTS	
12-11	A_{AA}	Wolverine Classic	NTS	
1-7	H	Spartan Invitational	NTS	
1-13	H	Illinois	262.20-273.90	L
1-15	A	E. Michigan	246.35-210.50	W
1-21	H	Minnesota	264.55-270.10	L
1-28	A	Ohio State	265.60-278.60	L
1-29	A_{KT}	Kent State	267.30-265.85	W
		Towson State.	267.30-163.70	W
2-4	H	Ill.-Chicago	263.80-269.05	L
2-12	H	Michigan	262.85-264.25	W
2-18	A_{MA}	Wisconsin	262.80-265.05	L
		Stout State	262.80-227.25	W
2-24	A_{KZ}	W. Michigan	260.55-252.45	W
		Indiana State.	260.55-259.90	W
		E. Michigan	260.55-197.85	W
2-26	A	Iowa	262.70-274.60	L
		Big Tens at East Lansing	6th/7	

1984-1985 (2-5)
Coach: George Szypula

2-8	A_{AA}	Wolverine Invitational	2nd	
1-16		E. Michigan	262.30-167.85	W
1-19		Minnesota	265.62-269.15	L
1-25		Ohio State	266.65-275.00	L
2-2		Iowa	266.15-271.35	L
2-10	A_{AA}	Michigan State	266.35	
		Kent State	255.30	
		Michigan	243.60	
2-17		Wisconsin	274.90-271.85	W
2-22		S. Illinois	268.50-278.05	L
3-2		Illinois	274.25-274.50	L
3-8		Illinois Open	5th	
		Big Tens at Minneapolis	5th/7	

1985-1986 (5-8)
Coach: George Szypula

11-16	A_{AM}	Navy Metro Invit.	2nd/6	
		Penn State	270.60	
		Michigan State	255.00	
		Pittsburgh	252.60	
		Navy	252.30	
		William & Mary	220.85	
		James Madison	208.10	
11-30	A_{CH}	Midwest Open	NTS	
12-6	A_{MA}	Wisconsin Invitational	NTS	
1-11	H	Spartan Invitational	1st/6	
		Michigan State	253.10	
		Wisconsin	251.50	
		Western Michigan	249.95	
		Georgia	249.20	
		Michigan	244.40	
		Wisconsin-Oshkosh	192.70	
1-17	H	Illinois	256.35-265.35	L
1-19	H	Minnesota	257.90-266.85	L
1-26	H	Kent State	250.50-238.95	W
1-31	A_{KZ}	W. Michigan	254.15-254.35	L
		Indiana State	254.15-254.05	W
2-9	H	Michigan	263.45-264.20	L
2-14	A_{YP}	E. Michigan	254.80-208.50	W
		Pittsburgh	254.80-254.45	W
2-22	A	Wisconsin	265.50-269.00	L
3-1	A_{DK}	N.Illinois	265.50-262.20	W
		Iowa State	265.50-273.15	L
3-7	A_{IC}	Iowa	258.80-281.60	L
		Houston Baptist	258.80-268.00	L
		Big Tens at Champaign	7th/7	

1986-1987 (7-4)
Coach: George Szypula

1-9	A_{CH}	Windy City Invit.	6th/11	
1-14	A_{KZ}	Bronco Invitational	1st	
1-17	A	Minnesota	261.50-268.10	L
1-23	A	Illinois	270.15-273.80	L
2-1	H	Ill.-Chicago	268.90-248.05	W
2-8	H	Wisconsin	267.40-260.45	W
2-13	H	Iowa	269.90-271.20	L
		W. Michigan	269.90-262.15	W
2-21	A	Pittsburgh	272.20-245.85	W
3-7	A	Ohio State	274.80-280.90	L
3-14	A	Kent State	278.10-261.30	W
3-21	A_{IC}	Michigan	272.50-269.80	W
	A_{AA}	Air Force	272.50-252.35	W
3-28	A_{KZ}	Bronco Invitational	1st/5	
		Big Tens at Ann Arbor	5th/7	

1987-1988 (6-10)
Coach: George Szypula

1-9	A_{DK}	Midwest Open	NTS	
1-15	A_{CH}	Windy City Invit.	9th/12	
1-24	H	Illinois	270.50-280.65	L
1-29	H	Minnesota	268.65-276.10	L
		Kent State	268.65-258.90	W
2-6	A_{KZ}	W. Michigan	270.60-261.95	W
		S. Illinois	270.60-264.90	W
2-12	A	Houston Baptist	270.60-276.50	L

2-19	A$_{IC}$	Iowa 267.20-278.80	L
		Wisconsin 267.20-268.70	L
		W. Michigan 267.20-263.75	W
2-27	A	Ill.-Chicago 269.60-272.15	L
	A$_{CH}$	N. Illinois 269.60-272.05	L
3-5	A$_{MA}$	Wisconsin 275.80-276.05	L
		N. Illinois 275.80-278.00	L
		Wisconsin-Oshkosh 275.80-245.80	W
3-11	H	Ohio State 271.35-279.80	L
3-17	H	Michigan 272.45-271.20	W
		Big Tens at Columbus 6th/7	

Rick Atkinson (1988-2001)

After 42 years as head coach, George Szypula stepped aside following the 1987-88 season. Rick Atkinson, who served as a Spartan assistant for two years, became only Michigan State's second head coach of the sport ever. Born February 20, 1963, in Waterloo, IA, Atkinson attended Iowa State University, graduating in 1985 with a bachelor's degree in business administration. He became the Cardinals' first freshman to earn All-American honors, accomplishing that feat in 1982 in floor exercise. In his most successful year, 1985, he won the Big Eight floor exercise championship and was runner-up at the NCAAs. He served as head coach until the MSU administration saw fit to drop the program at the completion of the 2000-2001 season.

1988-1989 (9-4)

Coach: Rick Atkinson

1-20	A$_{CH}$	Windy City Invitational .... NTS	
1-27	A	Illinois 251.45-273.80	L
2-4	H	Iowa 261.50-265.00	L
		Wisconsin 261.50-256.35	W
2-12	H	Ill.-Chicago 263.55-258.45	W
2-18	A$_{AA}$	Michigan 259.85-258.70	W
		W. Michigan 259.85-244.50	W
		Air Force 259.85-252.25	W
2-22	H	W. Michigan 264.85-246.15	W
2-24	A	Kent State 258.50-253.20	W
2-24	A$_{KT}$	S. Illinois 258.50-250.20	W
3-4	A$_{MN}$	Minnesota 269.60-284.30	L
		Wisconsin 269.60-271.40	L
		Michigan 269.60-262.80	W
		Big Tens at Madison 7th/7	

1989-1990 (6-3)

Coach: Rick Atkinson

1-12	H	Ohio State 266.45-274.50	L
		Minnesota 266.45-272.90	L
1-19	A	Windy City Invit. 4th/11	
2-2	A	Michigan 272.15-289.50	L
2-9	A$_{CH}$	Ill.-Chicago 268.70-272.15	L
		Wisconsin-Oshkosh 268.70-247.85	W
2-23	H	W. Michigan 275.90-247.80	W
3-16	A	W. Michigan 258.25-250.05	W
3-17	H	Penn State 274.85-277.00	L
		Wisconsin-Oshkosh 274.85-257.80	W
3-20	A	Syracuse 274.00-271.50	W
3-22	A	Cortland State ... 272.30-270.05	W
		Big Tens at Bloomington 5th/7	
		NCAA Regionals at Penn State 8th	

1990-1991 (9-3)

Coach: Rick Atkinson

1-11	A	Ohio State 267.60-275.10	L
1-18	A$_{CH}$	Windy City Invit. 5th/12	
1-25	H	Illinois 271.55-266.00	W
2-2	H	Michigan 279.25-270.00	W
2-9	H	Ill.-Chicago 277.00-271.15	W
2-15	A	Air Force 276.15-263.80	W
2-22	H	W. Michigan 277.35-263.80	W
		Wisconsin 277.35-276.00	W
2-23	A$_{MN}$	Minnesota 272.70-278.65	L
		Wisconsin-Oshkosh 272.70-239.15	W
3-2	A$_{IC}$	Iowa State 276.65-261.70	W
		Iowa 276.65-275.35	W

3-16	A	Penn State 274.80-283.55	L
		Big Tens at Columbus 4th/7	
		NCAA Regionals at Ohio State 6th/10	

1991-1992 (12-2)

Coach: Rick Atkinson

1-10	H	Minnesota 275.10-269.20	W
		Illinois 275.10-270.35	W
		Ill.-Chicago 275.10-259-40	W
		Ohio State 275.10-280.55	L
1-17	A$_{CH}$	Windy City Invit 5th/12	
1-25	A$_{CU}$	Illinois 275.25-272.15	W
		Michigan 275.25-264.90	W
2-1	H	Michigan 280.20-273.45	W
2-7	H	W. Michigan 274.00-265.45	W
2-14	A	Brigham Young .. 278.30-283.55	L
2-22	H	Ill.-Chicago 280.35-272.65	W
3-1	H	Air Force 280.95-268.95	W
		Iowa 280.95-280.15	W
3-13	H	Penn State 281.60-281.05	W
3-21	A	Michigan 284.35-281.65	W
		Big Tens at Champaign 7th/7	
		NCAA Regionals at Iowa City 6th/10	

1992-1993 (5-5)

Coach: Rick Atkinson

1-15	A$_{CH}$	Windy City Invit. 5th/12	
1-22	A	W. Michigan 261.70-250.00	W
1-29	H	Illinois 273.05-273.10	L
1-31	A	Kent State 275.40-270.40	W
2-13	A	Penn State 275.65-277.65	L
2-19	H	Ill.-Chicago 275.85-272.15	W
2-20	A	Ohio State 275.45-283.25	L
2-26	A	Iowa 276.00-276.20	L
3-1	A	Minnesota 274.85-281.85	L
3-7	H	Michigan 277.50-270.75	W
3-12	H	Brigham Young .. 281.55-280.00	W
		Big Tens at Minneapolis 3rd/7	
		NCAA Regional at Champaign 5th/6	

1993-1994 (4-6)

Coach: Rick Atkinson

1-8	H	Minnesota 269.85-268.50	W
1-14	A$_{CH}$	Windy City Invit. 7th/12	
1-21	A	Illinois 262.45-274.90	L
2-11	H	Penn State 272.45-275.55	L
		W. Michigan 272.45-251.80	W
2-18	A	Iowa 272.20-279.50	L
		Ohio State 272.20-281.85	L
2-26	H	Kent State 271.00-263.80	W
3-4	A$_{PU}$	Brigham Young .. 272.15-270.65	W
		Penn State 272.15-276.90	L
3-12	A$_{AA}$	Michigan Invitational 6th/8	
4-2	H	Michigan 276.90-279.70	L
		Big Tens at University Park 7th/7	

1994-1995 (4-6)

Coach: Rick Atkinson

1-13	A$_{CH}$	Windy City Invit. 8th/10	
1-28	A$_{CQ}$	Winter Cup .... NTS	
2-3	H	Illinois 222.20-222.65	L
2-11	H	W. Michigan 226.85-221.25	W
2-18	A$_{KZ}$	W. Michigan 220.80-221.50	L
		Ill.-Chicago 220.80-225.65	L
2-25	A	Penn State 218.65-228.95	L
3-3	H	Michigan 225.75-225.50	W
3-8	A	Minnesota 220.45-227.85	L
3-10	A	Iowa 219.75-229.175	L
3-18	H	Ill.-Chicago 226.85-223.75	W
		W. Michigan 226.85-223.75	W
		Big Tens at Champaign 7th/7	

1995-1996 (5-4)

Coach: Rick Atkinson

1-19	A$_{CH}$	Windy City Invit. 7th/12	
1-27	A	Illinois 220.50-221.85	L
2-2	A$_{CQ}$	Winter Cup .... NTS	
2-16	H	Minnesota 223.10-223.40	L
2-24	A	Michigan 221.40-209.75	W
3-1	H	Iowa 227.70-224.25	W
		Ohio State 227-70-228.10	L
3-3	A	Ill.-Chicago 225.675-227.55	L
3-7	A	Brigham Young Invitational 3rd/4	
3-9	A$_{AL}$	Lobo Invitational 3rd/6	
3-17	A	W. Michigan 225.25-222.35	W
3-23	A	Michigan Invitational 1st/8	
4-6	H	W. Michigan 226.90-211.95	W
		W. Michigan 226.90-220-35	W
		Big Tens at Columbus 5th/7	
		NCAA Regionals at Iowa City 6th	

1996-1997 (6-4)

Coach: Rick Atkinson

1-11	A	Ohio State 218.40-224.00	L
1-18	A$_{CH}$	Windy City Invit. 5th/9	
1-25	H	Illinois 227.75-224.50	W
2-1	H	Penn State 225.133-189.60	W
2-8	A$_{MN}$	Minnesota 218.80-222.10	L
		Michigan 218.80-214.70	W
2-22	H	Ill.-Chicago 228.10-225-70	W
2-28	A$_{PU}$	Brigham Young 224.475-226.86	L
		Air Force 224.475-212.75	W
3-8	A	Iowa 223.025-228.05	L
3-15	H	Brigham Young .. 228.20-225.85	W
		Big Tens at Minneapolis 6th/7	

1997-1998 (3-5)

Coach: Rick Atkinson

1-10	H	Iowa 221.150-226.850	L
1-17	A$_{CH}$	Windy City Invit. 6th/7	
		Iowa 228.050	
		Illinois 223.800	
		Ohio State 222.850	
		Michigan 220.800	
		Ill.-Chicago 217.900	
		Michigan State 217.300	
		Minnesota 213.850	
1-25	A	Ill.-Chicago ... 225.750-222.575	W
2-7	A	Penn State 225.00-227.125	L
2-13	A	Minnesota ... 228.425-221.750	W
2-21	A	Illinois 226.050-229.175	L
2-27	H	Ohio State ... 228.700-229.875	L
3-6	A	Brigham Young 225.550-228.750	L
3-12	A	Michigan 229.475-229.150	W
		Big Tens at Ann Arbor 4th/7	
		NCAA Regionals at Amherst, MA 6th	

1998-1999 (3-6)

Coach: Rick Atkinson

1-16	A$_{CH}$	Windy City Invit. 5th/7	
		Iowa 226.675	
		Ohio State 225.00	
		Michigan 224.050	
		Illinois 223.40	
		Michigan State 223.20	
		Ill.-Chicago 221-050	
		Minnesota 216.550	
1-23	A	Ohio State 223.600-226.250	L
1-31	H	Illinois 226.900-225.475	W
2-6	H	Ill.-Chicago ... 227.025-222.100	W
2-19	A	Iowa 221.950-227.525	L
2-27	A	Ill.-Chicago ... 224.200-224.550	L
3-6	A$_{PU}$	Brigham Young 225.675-226.000	L
		Nebraska 225.675-225.950	L
3-9	A	Minnesota 225.650-217.600	W
3-20	H	Michigan 229.925-231.850	L
		Big Tens at Iowa City 5th/7	
		NCAA Regionals at Champaign .. 6th	

1999-2000 (3-6)
Coach: Rick Atkinson

1-15	A$_{CH}$	Windy City Invitational ... 6th/7		
1-22	H	Ohio State 221.925-228.275		L
1-29	A	Illinois 220.825-225.285		L
2-5	H	Minnesota 227.550-222.900		W
2-13	A$_{LV}$	Winter Cup .... NTS		
2-20	H	Ill.-Chicago ... 224.225-217.800		W
2-24	A	Michigan 226.500-230.025		L
2-26	A	Ill.-Chicago ... 229.075-222.475		W
3-4	A$_{IC}$	Iowa 223.900-230.10		L
		Illinois 223.90-225.20		L
3-10	H	Michigan 229.250-229.500		L
		Big Tens at East Lansing 5th/7		

2000-2001 (6-5)
Coach: Rick Atkinson

1-13	A$_{CH}$	Windy City Invitational ... 6th/7		
		Michigan 207.550		
		Illinois 207.200		
		Ohio State 205.400		
		Iowa 205.150		
		Minnesota 202.250		
		Michigan State 201.350		
		Ill.-Chicago 196.250		
1-22	A$_{CH}$	Ill.-Chicago ... 208.000-195.200		W
		Illinois 208.000-209.300		L
2-3	A	Minnesota 208.825-209.875		L
2-9	A	Ohio State 212.950-216.450		L
2-24	A	Il.-Chicago 211.250-202.250		W
3-3	A	Southwest Cup 2nd/6		
		University of Oklahoma 215.250		
		Michigan State 210.400		
		Penn State 208.925		
		Stanford 205.425		
		Arizona State 198.325		
		New Mexico 191.500		
3-8	A	Air Force Acad.210-500-203.700		W
		Stanford 210.500-205.150		W
3-10	H	Iowa 214.450-211.200		W
		Michigan 214.450-177.750		W
3-16	A	Michigan 215.000-215.525		L
3-18	A	Penn State 187.550-213.200		L
		Big Tens at University Park 5th/7		

University officials saw fit to eliminate gymnastics as a varsity sport in 2000 with the understanding the sport would conclude upon completion of the 2000-2001 schedule.

Nissen Award
Awarded annually to the outstanding senior collegiate gymnast in the nation.
1966 Jim Curzi
1968 Dave Thor

Glossary
AA–all-around
FR–flying rings
FX–floor exercise
HB–horizontal or high bar
PB–parallel bars
PH–pommel horse
SR–still rings
TR–trampoline
VA–vault

NCAA Champions
1949 Mel Stout . (tie) AA, FR, FX, HB, PB
1951 Mel Stout .... AA, FR, FX, HB, FR
1953 Carl Rintz .... FX, HB, PH

1955	Carl Rintz .... HB, PB, PH
1958	Ted Muzyczko .... PB
1959	Stan Tarshis .... HB
1960	Stan Tarshis .... HB
1962	Dale Cooper .... SR
1962	Steve Johnson .... TR
1963	Dale Cooper .... SR
1965	Jim Curzi .... HB, PB
1966	Ed Gunny .... SR
1968	Dave Thor .... AA
1968	Toby Towson .... (tie) FX
1969	Toby Towson .... FX

Members of the 1958 NCAA championship team:
Richard Becker, Ray James Cook, Cal Girard, George Hopely, Ted Muzyczko, Angelo Festa, Stan Tarshis, Tom Temple, Roger Tuomi, Tom Werthmann, manager Robert Sass.

Big Ten Champions
1951	Mel Stout .... AA, FX, SR, PB, HB
1952	Bob Feldmeier .... HB
1953	Carl Rintz .... FX, SR, HB, PH
1954	Carl Rintz .... FR, AA, HB
1954	Ken Cook .... SR
1955	Carl Rintz .... AA, SR, PH
1956	Roland Brown .... FX
1956	Don Leas .... SR
1958	Stan Tarshis .... HB
1959	Stan Tarshis .... HB
1960	Stan Tarshis .... HB
1961	Larry Bassett .... (tie) PB
1962	Gani Browsh .... FX
1962	Dale Cooper .... SR
1962	Steve Johnson .... TR
1963	Dale Cooper .... TR
1964	Dale Cooper .... TR
1964	Jim Curzi .... PB, HB
1965	Jim Curzi .... PB
1965	Tom Hurt .... VA
1966	Jim Curzi .... AA, HB
1966	Dave Croft .... SR
1966	Dave Thor .... AA, FX, PH
1967	Dave Croft .... SR
1967	Dave Thor .... AA
1967	Toby Towson .... FX
1968	Dave Thor .... AA, VA
1968	Toby Towson .... FX
1969	Toby Towson .... FX
1969	Norn Haynie .... HB
1979	Charlie Jenkins .... VA
1981	Petet Roberts .... VA
1985	Allan Powers .... SR
1990	Paul Dackermann .... VA
1991	Paul Dackermann .... VA

Members of the 1968 Big Ten championship team:
Haynie, Dan Kinsey, Larry Goldberg, Cliff Diehl, Craig Kinsey, Dave Thor, Randy Campbell, Toby Towson, Ed Witzke, Ed Gunny, Norm Jolin, Dave Croft, and Richard Murahata.

All-Big Ten
(Initiated following the 1984 season)
1984	Bruce Trevor
1985	Al Powers
1987	Keith Pettit
1988	Greg Jung
1990	Paul Dackerman
1991	Paul Dackerman

1996	Joe Duda .... 57.50 AA
1992	Paul Dackerman .... 9.90 FX
1995	Chris Skidmore .... 9.90 PH

Team Scoring Record (by event)
1999	Jonathan Plante .... 9.90 PH
1962	Dale Cooper .... 9.95 SR
1995	Joe Duda .... 9.95 SR
1997	Victor Prisk .... 9.95 SR
1983	Pete Roberts .... 9.80 VA
1998	Brady Grimm .... 9.80 VA
1996	Joe Duda .... 9.90 PB
1988	Keith Pettit .... 9.95 HB
1998	Team vs. Michigan 229.475

Year-by-Year Team Performance

Years	Dual Meets			Big Ten Championships			NCAA Championships			Coach
	W	L	T	Pts	Place	Host or Site	Pts	Place	Host or Site	
1948	1	5	1		DNC	Chicago, IL		DNC	Chicago, IL	George Szypula
1949	1	5	1		DNC	Ann Arbor, MI	15	6/12	Berkeley, CA	George Szypula
1950	4	4	0		DNC	Iowa City, IA	17.5	5/14	West Point, NY	George Szypula
1951	6	3	0	49	2nd	Madison, WI	13.5	7/13	Ann Arbor, MI	George Szypula
1952	6	0	0	85.5	2nd	Bloomington, IN	26	6/17	Boulder, CO	George Szypula
1953	2	6	0	72	3rd	East Lansing, MI	38	7/13	Syracuse, NY	George Szypula
1954	3	4	0	71	4th	Columbus, OH	37	5/17	Champaign, IL	George Szypula
1955	5	1	0	91.5	2nd	Minneapolis, MN	55	5/17	Los Angeles, CA	George Szypula
1956	3	3	1	66.5	3rd	Champaign, IL	25	6/21	Chapel Hill, NC	George Szypula
1957	7	1	0	68.5	3rd	Ann Arbor, MI	32.5	12/20	Annapolis, MD	George Szypula
1958	7	3	0	63.5	3rd	Iowa City, IA	79	(t)1st	East Lansing, MI	George Szypula
1959	7	2	0	72	3rd	Bloomington, IN	39	4th	Berkeley, CA	George Szypula
1960	10	0	1	104	3rd	Minneapolis, MN	37.5	5th	University Park, PA	George Szypula
1961	8	2	0	91	2nd	Ann Arbor, MI	38.5	5th	Champaign, IL	George Szypula
1962	8	4	0	106.5	3rd	Columbus, OH	52.5	5th	Albuquerque, NM	George Szypula
1963	7	3	0	51	4th	East Lansing, MI	11	(t)11th	Pittsburgh, PA	George Szypula
1964	5	3	1	93	3rd	Madison, WI	23.5	8th	Los Angeles, CA	George Szypula
1965	6	4	0	—*	3rd	Champaign, IL		DNC	Carbondale, IL	George Szypula
1966	8	0	0	21*	2nd	Bloomington, IN	184.75	3rd	University Park, PA	George Szypula
1967	5	3	0	11*	3rd	Iowa City, IA		DNC	Carbondale, IL	George Szypula
1968	6	3	0	13*	(t)1st	East Lansing, MI		DNC	Tucson, AZ	George Szypula
1969	7	3	0	172.35	4th	Ann Arbor, MI		DNC	Seattle, WA	George Szypula
1970	4	7	0	9*	4th	Minneapolis, MN		DNC	Philadelphia, PA	George Szypula
1971	5	5	0	147.075	5th	Columbus, OH		DNC	Ann Arbor, MI	George Szypula
1972	5	4	0	148.225	5th	Champaign, IL		DNC	Ames, IA	George Szypula
1973	8	5	0	293.25	5th	Bloomington, IN		DNC	Eugene, OR	George Szypula
1974	2	9	0	281.60	7th	Iowa City, IA		DNC	University Park, PA	George Szypula
1975	3	7	0	344.50	7th	Ann Arbor, MI		DNC	Terre Haute, IN	George Szypula
1976	9	6	0	375.90	5th	Ann Arbor, MI		DNC	Philadelphia, PA	George Szypula
1977	6	8	0	365.95	7th	Minneapolis, MN		DNC	Tempe, AZ	George Szypula
1978	7	5	0	397.40	5th	Champaign, IL		DNC	Eugene, OR	George Szypula
1979	8	6	0	403.45	6th	Ann Arbor, MI		DNC	Baton Rouge, LA	George Szypula
1980	6	6	0	258.65	6th	Bloomington, IN		DNC	Lincoln, NE	George Szypula
1981	6	5	0	483.45	7th	Columbus, OH		DNC	Lincoln, NE	George Szypula
1982	2	7	0	264.50	7th	Madison, WI		DNC	Lincoln, NE	George Szypula
1983	7	8	0	261.40	7th	Iowa City, IA		DNC	University Park, PA	George Szypula
1984	8	6	0	264.55	6th	East Lansing, MI		DNC	Los Angeles, CA	George Szypula
1985	2	5	0	269.65	5th	Minneapolis, MN		DNC	Lincoln, NE	George Szypula
1986	5	8	0	260.05	7th	Champaign, IL		DNC	Lincoln, NE	George Szypula
1987	7	4	0	271.40	5th	Ann Arbor, MI		16th	Los Angeles, CA	George Szypula
1988	6	10	0	272.55	6th	Columbus, OH		16th	Lincoln, NE	George Szypula
1989	9	4	0	263.95	7th	Madison, WI		24th	Lincoln, NE	Rick Atkinson
1990	6	3	0	270.05	5th	Iowa City, IA		13th	Minneapolis, MN	Rick Atkinson
1991	9	3	0	277.15	4th	East Lansing, MI		12th	University Park, PA	Rick Atkinson
1992	12	2	0	277.75	7th	Champaign, IL		DNC	Lincoln, NE	Rick Atkinson
1993	5	5	0	276.55	3rd	Minneapolis, MN		DNC	Albuquerque, NM	Rick Atkinson
1994	4	6	0	270.60	7th	University Park, PA		DNC	Lincoln, NE	Rick Atkinson
1995	4	6	0	219.15	7th	Champaign, IL		DNC	Columbus, OH	Rick Atkinson
1996	5	4	0	222.45	5th	Columbus, OH		9th	Palo Alto, CA	Rick Atkinson
1997	6	4	0	227.00	6th	Minneapolis, MN		DNC	Iowa City, IA	Rick Atkinson
1998	3	5	0	227.98	4th	Ann Arbor, MI		DNC	University Park, PA	Rick Atkinson
1999	3	6	0	226.70	5th	Iowa City, IA		DNC	Lincoln, NE	Rick Atkinson
2000	3	6	0	226.10	5th	East Lansing, MI		DNC	Iowa City, IA	Rick Atkinson
2001**	6	5	0	211.95	5th	State College, PA	211.875	6th	Columbus, OH	Rick Atkinson
TOTALS	303	244	5							

* Champion determined on point system combining results of dual meet season and season-ending championship meet.

**In an effort to gain more acceptable gender equity numbers in the school's intercollegiate athletic program, university officials saw fit to eliminate gymnastics as a varsity sport with the completion of the 2001 season.

HOCKEY
LEADERS, RECORDS and HONORS

ALL-TIME COACHING RECORDS

Coach	Years	W	L	T	Avg.
No Head Coach	1922-23	2	7	0	.222
No Team	1924				
John Kobs	1925-31	9	19	1	.328
Harold Paulson	1950-51	6	25	0	.194
Amo Bessone	1951-79	367	427	20	.463
Ron Mason	1980-2002	635	270	69	.687
Rick Comley	2002-	23	14	2	.603
Totals	1922-2003	1,042	762	92	.574

Season Records

Glossary:

GLI–Great Lakes Invitational at Detroit
GWF–Great Western Freezeout at LosAngeles
NJC–Nissan-Jeep Classic Alaska
SPC–St. Paul Classic
BOS–Boston Invitational
BRT–Brown Tournament
CHT–Cleveland Holiday Tournament
SPC–St. Paul (MN) Classic
CHS–College Hockey Showcase
IMA–Flint IMA Tournament

See page 874 for further explanation of abbreviations.

1922 (0-3)
Coach: no coach
1-11	A	Michigan	1-5	L
1-18	H	Notre Dame	1-3	L
1-23	H	Michigan	0-9	L

1923 (2-4)
Coach: no coach
1-11	H	Michigan	1-5	L
1-18	H	Notre Dame	1-3	L
1-26	A	Notre Dame	0-11	L
2-11	H	Lansing Club	6-1	W
2-17	A	Michigan	0-9	L
2-25	H	Lansing Club	9-1	W

1924
No team organized

John H. Kobs (1925-1931)
(See baseball season records for John H. Kobs sketch)

1925 (0-1)
Coach: John H. Kobs
1-24	A	Michigan	3-6	L

1926 (0-4)
Coach: John H. Kobs
1-23	A	Michigan	0-4	L
2-5	H	Michigan	1-4	L
2-10	H	B. Creek Fisher Body	4-5	L
2-19	H	Minnesota	0-2	L

1927 (2-3)
Coach: John H. Kobs
1-15	H	Notre Dame	1-3	L
1-19	H	Battle Creek Civic Club	4-2	W
2-5	A	Michigan	5-2	W
2-12	H	Michigan	0-2	L
2-14	H	Michigan	1-2	L

1928 (3-3)
Coach: John H. Kobs
1-25	H	B. Creek Independents	1-0	W
1-28	H	B. Creek Independents	1-0	W
2-1	H	Michigan	2-1	W
2-2	H	Marquette	1-5	L
2-7	A	Michigan	1-3	L
2-15	H	Michigan Tech	0-5	L

1929 (3-3-1)
Coach: John H. Kobs
1-12	A	Ralph's Sport Shop B.C.	0-1	L
1-14	A	Michigan	1-9	L
2-2	H	Univ. of Detroit	8-0	W
2-5	H	Battle Creek Civic Club	4-1	W
2-8	H	Michigan	2-8	L
2-15	H	Univ. of Detroit	8-0	W
2-26	A	Ralph's Sport Shop B.C.T	0-0	

1930 (1-4)
Coach: John H. Kobs
1-23	A	Univ. of Detroit	1-2	L
1-25	H	Michigan	0-7	L
2-1	H	Ralph's Sport Shop B.C.	1-2	L
2-6	H	Univ. of Detroit	2-0	W
2-17	A	Michigan	1-7	L

1931 (0-1-0)
Coach: John H. Kobs
1-17	H	Haley's AC of Detroit	1-4	L
1-21	A	Detroit City College	%	
1-24	H	Detroit City College	%	
1-27	H	Michigan	%	
1-31	H	Marquette	%	
2-5	H	Univ. of Detroit	%	
2-10	A	Univ. of Detroit	%	
2-16	A	Michigan	%	

% Unseasonably warm weather caused cancellation of the remaining schedule following the game on 1-17.

1932-1949
No team organized

Harold Paulson (1950-1951)
Born March 3, 1919 in Virginia, MN, Harold Paulson graduated from that city's Roosevelt High School in 1937. Entering the University of Minnesota, Paulsen became a three-time All-American as a wingman for the Gopher teams of 1939, 1940 and 1941. During those years he established an all-time school scoring record and captained the squad in his senior season. The Gopher team of 1940 captured the Western Conference and National AAU titles. Upon graduating with the bachelor of science degree in physical education, Paulsen spent three years of service in the U.S.

Navy. Following discharge as a lieutenant (j.g.) he served as athletic director or health director in three Minnesota high schools. Paulsen received a masters of education from the University of Minnesota in 1947 and a Ph.D. in 1956 from the University of Michigan. After two futile seasons, Paulson moved on to become athletic director and chairman of physical education at Slippery Rock State Teachers College in Pennsylvania. He would eventually return to Minnesota as a professor in physical education at Mankato State from where he retired in 1987.

1950 (0-14)
Coach: Harold Paulson
1-12	H	Michigan Tech	2-6	L
1-13	H	Michigan Tech	2-15	L
1-20	H	Minnesota	2-8	L
1-21	H	Minnesota	1-11	L
2-3	A	Michigan Tech	3-13	L
2-4	A	Michigan Tech	0-10	L
2-10	H	North Dakota	1-14	L
2-11	H	North Dakota	3-12	L
2-17	A	Minnesota	1-12	L
2-18	A	Minnesota	0-8	L
2-22	H	Michigan	4-10	L
2-28	H	Western Ontario	5-9	L
3-2	A	Western Ontario	2-12	L
3-9	A	Michigan	1-17	L

1950-1951 (6-11)
Coach: Harold Paulson
12-1	H	Ontario Ag. College	9-5	W
2-2	H	Ontario Ag. College	12-3	W
1-4	A	North Dakota	4-5	L
1-5	A	North Dakota	3-7	L
1-12	H	Ontario Ag. College	3-1	W
1-26	A	Minnesota	3-9	L
1-27	A	Minnesota	2-6	L
2-2	A	Michigan Tech	4-3	W
2-3	A	Michigan Tech	2-4	L
2-9	H	Minnesota	3-7	L
2-10	H	Minnesota	1-7	L
2-15	H	Michigan Tech	3-2	W
2-16	H	Michigan Tech	5-3	W
2-21	H	Michigan	1-10	L
2-27	H	Denver	2-7	L
2-28	H	Denver	2-7	L
3-3	A	Michigan	6-9	L

Amo Bessone (1951-1979)
The Spartans' third coach, the amiable Amo Bessone, graduated from West Springfield (MA) High School in 1934 and gained further schooling at Kents Hill Academy, and later at Hebron Academy, in Maine. He received the B.A. degree in 1943 from the University of Illinois. Amo was a member of the varsity hockey and baseball squads while at Champaign, lettering in both sports. His professional experience came with the Providence Reds of the American Hockey League. Bessone spent three years in the U.S. Navy before beginning a long and rewarding coaching career. He started at Westfield (MA) High School in 1946, moved to the head spot at Michigan Tech two years later and came to State to stay in 1951. Amo spent 28 seasons, encompassing 814 games, behind the bench as Spartan head coach.

1951-1952 (7-13; 3-9-0 in MIHL)
Coach: Amo Bessone

11-29	H	Ontario Ag. College	8-2	W
11-30	H	Ontario Ag. College	7-4	W
12-5	H	Michigan	1-11	L
1-7	A	Denver	2-8	L
1-8	A	Denver	4-7	L
1-11	H	North Dakota	2-7	L
1-12	H	North Dakota	4-3	W
1-16	H	Michigan	1-7	L
1-25	A	Michigan Tech	9-4	W
1-26	A	Michigan Tech	6-4	W
2-8	A	Minnesota	2-9	L
2-9	A	Minnesota	4-6	L
2-12	H	Colorado College	0-3	L
2-13	H	Colorado College	3-6	L
2-15	H	Michigan Tech	3-2	W
2-16	H	Michigan Tech	5-3	W
2-22	H	Minnesota	4-5	L
2-23	H	Minnesota	3-5	L
2-29	H	Michigan	2-8	L
3-1	A	Michigan	2-6	L

1952-1953 (5-16-1; 2-16 in MIHL)
Coach: Amo Bessone

12-5	H	Lawrence	3-2	W
12-12	H	Toronto	6-6	T
12-26	A	North Dakota	4-5	L
12-27	A	North Dakota	4-5	L
12-30	A	Denver	1-2	L
12-31	A	Denver	4-5	L
1-2	A	Colorado College	4-6	L
1-3	A	Colorado College	3-5	L
1-7	H	Michigan	0-6	L
1-9	A	Minnesota	1-3	L
1-10	A	Minnesota	0-5	L
1-14	A	Michigan	2-10	L
1-22	H	Ontario Ag. College	13-1	W
1-23	H	Ontario Ag. College	7-1	W
2-6	A	Michigan Tech	2-1	W
2-7	A	Michigan Tech	2-5	L
2-11	A	Michigan	0-4	L
2-20	H	Michigan Tech	6-5(OT)	W
2-21	H	Michigan Tech	3-5	L
3-4	H	Michigan	4-8	L
3-5	H	Minnesota	3-7	L
3-6	H	Minnesota	2-7	L

1953-1954 (8-14-1; 4-13-1 in WIHL)
Coach: Amo Bessone

11-27	A	St. Lawrence	3-5	L
11-28	A	Clarkston	9-1	W
11-30	A	St. Lawrence	5-1	W
12-4	H	Ontario Ag. College	13-4	W
12-5	H	Ontario Ag. College	6-1	W
1-8	H	Michigan	4-7	L
1-9	A	Michigan	1-3	L
1-22	A	Minnesota	4-5	L
1-23	A	Minnesota	3-8	L
1-29	H	Minnesota	2-7	L
1-30	H	Minnesota	3-5	L
2-5	H	Denver	2-3(OT)	L
2-6	H	Denver	4-5	L
2-9	H	Colorado College	2-3(OT)	L
2-10	H	Colorado College	8-4	W
2-19	H	Michigan	0-0(OT)	T
2-20	A	Michigan	2-3	L
2-26	A	Michigan Tech	4-1	W
2-27	A	Michigan Tech	1-2	L
3-5	H	North Dakota	5-6	L
3-6	W	North Dakota	2-1(OT)	W
3-8	H	Michigan Tech	3-5	L
3-9	H	Michigan Tech	6-1	W

1954-1955 (9-17-1; 5-14-1 in WIHL)
Coach: Amo Bessone

11-16	A	Rensselaer	0-3	L
11-27	A	Clarkston	5-10	L
11-29	A	St. Lawrence	5-4	W
12-3	H	North Dakota	6-2	W
12-4	H	North Dakota	3-4	L
12-17	A	Denver	3-8	L
12-18	A	Denver	5-4	W
12-21	A	Colorado College	4-5	L
12-22	A	Colorado College	4-2	W
12-31	H	Michigan Tech	1-5	L
1-1	H	Michigan Tech	5-3	W
1-7	H	Michigan	0-7	L
1-8	A	Michigan	1-3	L
1-21	A	Michigan Tech	4-9	L
1-22	A	Michigan Tech	2-5	L
1-28	H	Western Ontario	1-8	L
1-29	H	Western Ontario	4-2	W
2-4	A	Minnesota	0-7	L
2-5	A	Minnesota	2-3	L
2-11	H	Michigan	4-7	L
2-12	A	Michigan	3-4	L
2-18	A	North Dakota	2-3(OT)	L
2-19	A	North Dakota	2-1	W
2-25	H	Minnesota	5-5(OT)	T
2-26	H	Minnesota	6-7	L
3-4	H	Ontario Ag. College	9-2	W
3-5	H	Ontario Ag. College	3-2	W

1955-1956 (5-18;1-17 in WIHL)
Coach: Amo Bessone

11-24	A	St. Lawrence	2-0	W
11-25	A	Clarkston	1-6	L
11-26	A	Middlebury	6-2	W
12-2	A	North Dakota	1-3	L
12-3	A	North Dakota	4-5	L
12-16	H	Denver	1-7	L
12-17	H	Denver	4-3	W
12-22	A	Minnesota	1-7	L
12-23	A	Minnesota	3-4	L
1-6	H	Michigan	2-5	L
1-7	A	Michigan	1-3	L
1-20	H	Michigan	2-3(OT)	L
1-21	A	Michigan	1-3	L
1-27	A	Michigan Tech	1-8	L
1-28	A	Michigan Tech	5-6(OT)	L
2-3	H	Colorado College	2-4	L
2-4	H	Colorado College	1-6	L
2-13	H	Minnesota	1-2	L
2-14	H	Minnesota	1-2(OT)	L
2-24	H	Michigan Tech	3-4	L
2-25	H	Michigan Tech	1-3	L
3-2	H	Ontario Ag. College	4-2	W
3-3	H	Ontario Ag. College	7-4	W

1956-1957 (7-15; 5-15 in WCHA)
Coach: Amo Bessone

11-30	A	North Dakota	1-4	L
12-1	A	North Dakota	0-1	L
12-18	A	Denver	3-2	W
12-19	A	Denver	1-3	L
12-22	A	Colorado College	2-8	L
12-23	A	Colorado College	1-7	L
1-8	H	Michigan	3-4	L
1-11	H	Ontario Ag. College	14-2	W
1-12	H	Ontario Ag. College	6-1	W
1-15	A	Michigan	2-3	L
1-25	H	Michigan Tech	1-3	L
1-26	H	Michigan Tech	2-4	L
2-1	H	Minnesota	2-1	W
2-2	H	Minnesota	4-0	W
2-8	A	Michigan Tech	3-5	L
2-9	A	Michigan Tech	2-6	L
2-22	H	Michigan	4-5	L
2-23	A	Michigan	1-2	L
3-1	A	Minnesota	4-2	W
3-2	A	Minnesota	2-3	L
3-8	H	North Dakota	4-2	W
3-9	H	North Dakota	0-3	L

1957-1958 (12-11; 9-11 in WIHL)
Coach: Amo Bessone

12-7	A	Ohio State	18-0	W
12-17	H	Colorado College	2-7	L
12-18	H	Colorado College	6-4	W
12-20	H	Denver	1-5	L
12-21	H	Denver	2-4	L
1-4	H	Harvard	6-2	W
1-8	H	Michigan	4-2	W
1-10	A	Minnesota	3-4	L
1-11	A	Minnesota	3-2	W
1-15	A	Michigan	2-4	L
1-17	H	Michigan Tech	4-3	W
1-18	H	Michigan Tech	6-1	W
1-24	A	North Dakota	2-5	L
1-25	A	North Dakota	3-6	L
1-31	H	Ohio State	17-3	W
2-7	A	Michigan Tech	5-2	W
2-8	A	Michigan Tech	1-3	L
2-14	H	Michigan	3-1	W
2-15	H	Michigan	2-1(OT)	W
2-21	H	North Dakota	1-3	L
2-22	H	North Dakota	2-3(OT)	L
2-28	H	Minnesota	4-3	W
3-1	H	Minnesota	1-5	L

1958-1959 (17-6-1; no WIHL play; runner-up in NCAA)
Coach: Amo Bessone

12-5	H	North Dakota	6-0	W
12-6	H	North Dakota	4-5	L
12-26	A	Northeastern	7-1	W
12-28	A	Boston College	6-0	W
12-30	A	Boston University	3-2	W
1-1	A	Brown	11-3	W
1-2	A	Princeton	7-4	W
1-3	A	Rensselaer	10-3	W
1-9	A	Minnesota	3-7	L
1-10	A	Minnesota	3-3(OT)	T
1-23	H	Minnesota	5-4	W
1-24	H	Minnesota	5-4	W
1-30	A	Michigan Tech	7-0	W
1-31	A	Michigan Tech	4-5(OT)	L
2-6	H	Michigan	3-1	W
2-7	A	Michigan	5-2	W
2-13	A	North Dakota	3-2	W
2-14	A	North Dakota	2-4	L
2-27	H	Michigan Tech	3-0	W
2-28	H	Michigan Tech	5-2	W
3-6	H	Michigan	2-4	L
3-7	A	Michigan	4-1	W
3-13	A	Boston College	**4-3	W
3-14	A	North Dakota	**3-4(OT)	L

1959-1960 (4-18-2; 4-18-2 in WCHA)
Coach: Amo Bessone

11-27	A	North Dakota	2-2(OT)	T
11-28	A	North Dakota	1-5	L
12-7	H	Colorado College	3-4	L
12-8	H	Colorado College	1-5	L
12-18	A	Colorado College	3-5	L
12-19	A	Colorado College	3-6	L
12-21	A	Denver	1-10	L
12-22	A	Denver	0-11	L
1-8	H	North Dakota	5-6	L
1-9	H	North Dakota	4-3	W
1-15	A	Michigan	1-6	L
1-16	A	Michigan	4-5	L
1-22	A	Michigan Tech	3-3(OT)	T
1-23	A	Michigan Tech	1-9	L
2-5	H	Michigan Tech	3-5	L
2-6	H	Michigan Tech	0-7	L

2-9	H	Michigan 4-3	W
2-16	A	Michigan 3-5	L
2-19	A	Minnesota 0-5	L
2-20	A	Minnesota 3-10	L
2-26	H	Denver 0-5	L
2-27	H	Denver 1-5	L
3-4	H	Minnesota 4-5	L
3-5	H	Minnesota 4-3	W

1960-1961 (11-16; 5-15 in WCHA)
Coach: Amo Bessone

11-24	A	St. Lawrence 8-5	W
11-25	A	Clarkston 8-4	W
11-26	A	St. Lawrence 2-6	L
12-2	H	Minnesota 3-6	L
12-3	H	Minnesota .... 5-6(OT)	L
12-16	A	Colorado College 5-2	W
12-17	A	Colorado College ..... 5-6(OT)	L
12-19	A	Denver 2-10	L
12-20	A	Denver 0-9	L
1-6	H	Ohio 12-0	W
1-7	H	Ohio 8-1	W
1-13	A	Michigan Tech 1-0	W
1-14	A	Michigan Tech 3-7	L
1-20	H	Michigan Tech 4-3	W
1-21	H	Michigan Tech 1-3	L
1-27	A	Minnesota 2-5	L
1-28	A	Minnesota 3-7	L
2-3	H	Michigan 3-2	W
2-4	A	Michigan .... 2-3(OT)	L
2-10	A	North Dakota 3-6	L
2-11	A	North Dakota 3-4	L
2-17	A_{CO}	Ohio 14-1	W
2-18	A_{CO}	Ohio 12-4	W
2-24	A	North Dakota 2-4	L
2-25	H	North Dakota 6-1	W
3-3	H	Michigan 1-6	L
3-4	A	Michigan 3-4	L

1961-1962 (13-11-1; 6-9-1 in WCHA)
Coach: Amo Bessone

11-23	A	St. Lawrence 3-2	W
11-24	A	Clarkston 0-3	L
11-25	A	St. Lawrence .... 3-2(OT)	W
12-1	A	North Dakota 5-3	W
12-2	A	North Dakota 4-6	L
12-22	H	Minnesota-Duluth 5-2	W
12-23	H	Minnesota-Duluth 6-1	W
12-26	A	Northeastern 13-4	W
12-28	A	Queens 6-1	W
1-5	H	Minnesota 5-3	W
1-6	H	Minnesota 5-2	W
1-11	H	Colorado College 5-4	W
1-12	H	Colorado College 8-2	W
1-26	A	Minnesota .... 1-1(OT)	T
1-27	A	Minnesota 5-3	W
2-2	H	Michigan 3-5	L
2-3	A	Michigan 1-5	L
2-9	A	Michigan Tech 2-8	L
2-10	A	Michigan Tech .... 2-3(OT)	L
2-15	H	Denver 4-6	L
2-16	H	Denver 3-6	L
2-23	H	Michigan 2-4	L
2-24	A	Michigan 2-10	L
3-1	A	Michigan Tech .... ^1-5	L
3-2	A	Denver .... ^4-3(OT)	W

1962-1963 (11-12; 6-10 in WCHA)
Coach: Amo Bessone

11-22	A	St. Lawrence 7-3	W
11-23	A	Clarkston 2-1	W
11-24	A	St. Lawrence 4-5	L
11-30	A	Michigan 2-1	W
12-1	A	Michigan 4-3	W
12-7	H	North Dakota 4-11	L
12-8	H	North Dakota 6-5	W

1-4	A	Denver 2-6	L
1-5	A	Colorado College .... 7-8(OT)	L
1-7	A	Denver 4-6	L
1-8	A	Colorado College 7-8	L
1-11	H	Minnesota-Duluth 5-4	W
1-12	H	Minnesota-Duluth 3-4	L
1-25	H	Michigan Tech 2-6	L
1-26	H	Michigan Tech 2-6	L
2-1	A	Minnesota-Duluth 5-4	W
2-2	A	Minnesota-Duluth 4-1	W
2-15	A	Minnesota 4-7	L
2-16	A	Minnesota 1-6	L
2-22	H	Michigan 6-2	W
2-23	H	Michigan 2-1	W
3-1	H	Minnesota 1-7	L
3-2	H	Minnesota 6-3	W

1963-1964 (8-17-1; 6-10 in WCHA)
Coach: Amo Bessone

11-28	A	St. Lawrence 5-1	W
11-29	A	Clarkston 1-7	L
11-30	A	St. Lawrence 3-5	L
12-13	H	Ohio 6-4	W
12-14	H	Ohio 7-1	W
12-20	A	Colorado College 2-6	L
12-21	A	Colorado College .... 5-4(OT)	W
1-10	A	Minnesota-Duluth 2-5	L
1-11	A	Minnesota-Duluth 1-6	L
1-16	A	Ohio State 10-2	W
1-17	A	Ohio 11-1	W
1-18	A	Ohio 7-4	W
1-24	A	Minnesota 2-6	L
1-25	A	Minnesota 2-4	L
1-31	H	Minnesota 6-7	L
2-1	H	Minnesota 2-4	L
2-7	H	Minnesota-Duluth 1-6	L
2-8	H	Minnesota-Duluth 4-2	W
2-14	A	Michigan 0-2	L
2-15	A	Michigan 2-7	L
2-21	A	Michigan Tech 3-7	L
2-22	A	Michigan Tech 1-11	L
2-28	H	Colorado College 4-5	L
2-29	H	Colorado College .... 5-5(OT)	T
3-6	A	Michigan 4-9	L
3-7	A	Michigan 4-13	L

1964-1965 (17-12; 8-8 in WCHA)
Coach: Amo Bessone

11-26	A	St. Lawrence 6-5	W
11-27	A	Clarkston 2-3	L
11-28	A	St. Lawrence 8-5	W
12-4	H	Ohio 12-0	W
12-5	H	Ohio 13-1	W
12-11	H	Wisconsin 9-2	W
12-12	H	Wisconsin 9-0	W
1-1	A_{BRT}	Brown 2-6	L
1-2	A_{BRT}	Providence .... 5-6(OT)	L
1-8	A	Minnesota 4-3	W
1-9	A	Minnesota 2-5	L
1-15	A	Colorado College 1-3	L
1-16	A	Colorado College 10-3	W
1-22	A	Minnesota 7-5	W
1-23	A	Minnesota 5-6	L
1-27	H	Michigan 3-6	L
1-29	A	Minnesota-Duluth 5-4	W
1-30	A	Minnesota-Duluth 1-7	L
2-5	A	Michigan 7-4	W
2-6	H	Michigan 6-2	W
2-12	A	Wisconsin 8-4	W
2-13	A	Wisconsin 9-3	W
2-17	A	Michigan 2-7	L
2-19	A	Michigan Tech 3-4	L
2-20	A	Michigan Tech 4-5	L
2-26	H	Colorado College 8-2	W
2-27	H	Colorado College .... 7-6(OT)	W
3-5	A	North Dakota 1-7	L
3-6	A	North Dakota 6-4	W

1965-1966 (16-13; 9-11 in WCHA and NCAA Champions)
Coach: Amo Bessone

11-19	A	Colorado College 0-4	L
11-20	A	Colorado College .... 3-4(OT)	L
11-25	A	St. Lawrence 3-5	L
11-26	A	Clarkston 3-6	L
11-27	A	St. Lawrence 6-4	W
12-3	H	North Dakota 11-5	W
12-4	H	North Dakota 3-5	L
12-10	H	Denver 6-8	L
12-11	H	Denver 4-1	W
1-7	H	Colorado College .... 4-5(OT)	L
1-8	H	Colorado College 6-2	W
1-14	H	Minnesota 5-7	L
1-15	H	Minnesota 5-1	L
1-21	H	Minnesota-Duluth .... 6-5(OT)	W
1-22	H	Minnesota-Duluth 5-2	W
1-28	A	Minnesota .... 5-6(OT)	L
1-29	A	Minnesota 4-3	W
2-4	H	Michigan 8-7	W
2-5	H	Michigan 4-2	W
2-11	A	Wisconsin 3-1	W
2-12	A	Wisconsin 5-3	W
2-18	A	Michigan Tech 4-8	L
2-19	A	Michigan Tech 2-4	L
2-25	A	Michigan 7-1	W
2-26	A	Michigan .... 0-1(OT)	L
3-3	A	Michigan .... ^3-2	W
3-5	H	Michigan Tech .... ^4-3	W
3-8	A	Boston University **2-1	W
3-19	A	Clarkston **6-1	W

1966-1967 (16-15-1; 8-11-1 in WCHA; third place in NCAA)
Coach: Amo Bessone

12-2	A	Minnesota .... 4-5(OT)	L
12-3	A	Minnesota .... 3-2(OT)	W
12-9	H	Michigan 4-10	L
12-10	A	Michigan 2-3	L
12-16	A_{BOS}	Boston College 5-3	W
12-17	A_{BOS}	Cornell .... 2-3(OT)	L
12-22	A_{GLI}	Western Ontario .... 5-4(OT)	W
12-23	A_{GLI}	Michigan 3-5	L
12-27	A_{SPC}	North Dakota 4-2	W
12-28	A_{SPC}	Minnesota 3-9	L
1-6	H	Colorado College 6-0	W
1-7	A	Colorado College 4-5	L
1-13	A	Denver 2-8	L
1-14	A	Colorado College 2-1	W
1-16	A	Colorado College 3-4	L
1-17	A	Denver 2-4	L
1-20	H	Michigan Tech 4-3	W
1-21	A	Michigan Tech .... 3-3(OT)	T
1-27	A	Minnesota-Duluth .... 5-6(OT)	L
1-28	A	Minnesota-Duluth 3-7	L
2-3	H	Minnesota 6-4	W
2-4	H	Minnesota 6-3	W
2-10	A	Michigan 4-3	W
2-11	H	Michigan 5-1	W
2-17	A	North Dakota .... 3-4(OT)	L
2-18	A	North Dakota 1-5	L
3-3	H	Wisconsin 7-3	W
3-4	H	Wisconsin 3-1	W
3-9	A	Michigan .... ^4-2	W
3-16	H	Michigan Tech .... ^2-1	W
3-17	A	Boston Univ. **2-4	L
3-18	A	North Dakota **6-1	W

1967-1968 (11-16-2; 6-13-1 in WCHA)
Coach: Amo Bessone

11-23	A	St. Lawrence 7-4	W
11-24	A	Clarkston 3-3	T
11-25	A	St. Lawrence 3-2	W
12-1	H	Minnesota-Duluth 3-5	L
12-2	H	Minnesota-Duluth 6-2	W
12-8	H	North Dakota .... 2-2(OT)	T

Date		Opponent	Score	Result
12-9	H	North Dakota	2-6	L
12-28	A_{B10}	Minnesota	3-6	L
12-29	A_{B10}	Ohio State	7-0	W
12-30	A_{B10}	Wisconsin	4-3	W
1-5	H	Michigan	1-7	L
1-6	A	Michigan	4-3(OT)	W
1-12	H	Denver	2-3	L
1-13	H	Denver	1-3	L
1-19	A	Minnesota	2-3	L
1-20	A	Minnesota	3-8	L
2-2	A	Michigan Tech	1-4	L
2-3	A	Michigan Tech	2-6	L
2-9	A	Michigan	3-4(OT)	L
2-10	A	Michigan	0-9	L
2-16	A	Colorado College	7-3	W
2-17	A	Colorado College	3-0	W
2-23	H	Minnesota	5-2	W
2 24	H	Minnesota	2-6	L
2-27	H	Colorado College	6-2	W
2-28	H	Colorado College	2-4	L
3-1	A	Wisconsin	3-5	L
3-2	A	Wisconsin	3-1	W
3-5	A	North Dakota	^2-5	L

1968-1969 (11-16-1; 7-10-1 in WCHA)
Coach: Amo Bessone

Date		Opponent	Score	Result
11-22	A	North Dakota	3-4	L
11-23	A	North Dakota	4-7	L
11-28	A	St. Lawrence	5-1	W
11-29	A	Clarkston	1-3	L
11-30	A	St. Lawrence	0-3	L
12-6	A	Michigan	1-2	L
12—7	H	Michigan	1-2	L
12-20	A_{GLI}	Wisconsin	4-6	L
12-21	A_{GLI}	Michigan	4-2	W
12-26	A_{B10}	Wisconsin	3-2	W
12-28	A_{B10}	Michigan	3-8	L
1-10	H	Colorado College	2-3(OT)	L
1-11	H	Colorado College	5-1	W
1-17	A	Minnesota	2-2(OT)	T
1-18	A	Minnesota	2-1(OT)	W
1-24	H	Michigan	7-3	W
1-25	H	Michigan	5-1	W
1-31	A	Minnesota-Duluth	6-3	W
2-1	A	Minnesota-Duluth	1-6	L
2-7	H	Wisconsin	1-2	L
2-8	H	Wisconsin	4-3	W
2-14	A	Denver	4-9	L
2-15	A	Denver	2-1	W
2-21	H	Minnesota	2-1	W
2-22	H	Minnesota	0-1	L
2-28	H	Michigan Tech	3-4	L
3-1	H	Michigan Tech	1-6	L
3-7	A	Michigan Tech	^2-4	L

1969-1970 (13-16; 10-12 in WCHA)
Coach: Amo Bessone

Date		Opponent	Score	Result
11-28	A	North Dakota	8-3	W
11-29	A	North Dakota	2-4	L
12-5	A	Michigan	3-2	W
12-6	H	Michigan	6-8	L
12-19	A_{GLI}	Princeton	2-1	W
12-20	A_{GLI}	New Hampshire	3-4	L
12-22	A_{B10}	Michigan	5-4	W
12-23	A_{B10}	Wisconsin	3-6	L
12-29	A_{BOS}	New Hampshire	5-6	L
12-30	A_{BOS}	Northeastern	6-5	W
1-2	H	Wisconsin	4-3	W
1-3	H	Wisconsin	6-4	W
1-16	H	Minnesota	2-3(OT)	L
1-17	H	Minnesota	4-1	W
1-23	A	Colorado College	6-2	L
1-24	A	Colorado College	6-4	W
1-30	H	Denver	4-6	L
1-31	H	Denver	4-5	L
2-6	A	Michigan Tech	1-8	L
2-7	A	Michigan Tech	4-5(OT)	L
2-13	A	Minnesota	0-8	L
2-14	A	Minnesota	2-4	L
2-20	H	Michigan	3-6	L
2-21	A	Michigan	7-1	W
2-27	H	Minnesota-Duluth	8-5	W
2-28	H	Minnesota-Duluth	3-1	W
3-6	A	Wisconsin	0-5	L
3-7	A	Wisconsin	3-4	L
3-12	A	Denver	^2-6	L

1970-1971 (19-12 & 12-10 in WCHA)
Coach: Amo Bessone

Date		Opponent	Score	Result
11-13	A	North Dakota	3-4(OT)	L
11-14	A	North Dakota	5-7	L
11-20	A	Minnesota	3-4	L
11-21	A	Minnesota	2-1	W
11-27	H	Ohio State	4-2	W
11-28	H	Ohio State	6-1	W
12-4	H	Michigan Tech	8-6	W
12-5	H	Michigan Tech	2-4	L
12-11	A	Notre Dame	10-5	W
12-12	A	Notre Dame	3-4	L
1-2	H	Bowling Green	7-2	W
1-3	H	Bowling Green	6-2	W
1-8	A	Michigan	5-4	W
1-9	A	Michigan	6-5	W
1-15	A	Wisconsin	5-3	W
1-16	A	Wisconsin	2-3	L
1-22	H	Minnesota	8-4	W
1-23	H	Minnesota	3-4	L
1-29	H	Notre Dame	6-3	W
1-30	H	Notre Dame	6-4	W
2-5	A	Minnesota-Duluth	5-4	W
2-6	A	Minnesota-Duluth	4-8	L
2-12	A	Denver	4-3	W
2-13	A	Denver	4-5(OT)	L
2-19	H	Colorado College	4-5	L
2-20	H	Colorado College	6-4	W
2-26	H	Wisconsin	4-2	W
2-27	H	Wisconsin	6-5(OT)	W
3-5	H	Michigan	7-8(OT)	L
3-6	H	Michigan	5-4(OT)	W
3-12	A	Minnesota-Duluth	^3-4(OT)	L

1971-1972 (20-16; 15-13 in WCHA)
Coach: Amo Bessone

Date		Opponent	Score	Result
11-12	A	Bowling Green	5-2	W
11-13	A	Bowling Green	8-3	W
11-19	H	Minnesota	3-2	W
11-20	H	Minnesota	1-3	L
11-26	A	Michigan	1-5	L
11-27	A	Michigan	4-2	W
12-3	A	Wisconsin	1-4	L
12-4	A	Wisconsin	3-4	L
12-10	H	Denver	6-7(OT)	L
12-11	H	Denver	6-3	W
12-15	A	Denver	3-6	L
12-17	A	Denver	^1-7	L
12-18	A	Colorado College	5-6(OT)	L
12-19	A	Colorado College	4-5	L
12-28	A_{GLI}	Dartmouth	8-3	W
12-29	A_{GLI}	Michigan Tech	2-3	L
1-7	H	North Dakota	7-1	W
1-8	H	North Dakota	4-1	W
1-14	H	Notre Dame	8-2	W
1-15	H	Notre Dame	4-1	W
1-19	H	Michigan	7-2	W
2-4	A	Michigan Tech	5-3	W
2-5	A	Michigan Tech	5-3	W
2-9	A	Michigan	2-6	L
2-11	A	Minnesota	7-2	W
2-12	A	Minnesota	6-3	W
2-18	H	Minnesota-Duluth	6-1	W
2-19	H	Minnesota-Duluth	5-1	W
2-25	H	Wisconsin	0-5	L
2-27	H	Wisconsin	4-6	L
3-3	A	Notre Dame	9-8(OT)	W
3-4	A	Notre Dame	2-6	L
3-7	H	Minnesota-Duluth	^4-2	W
3-8	H	Minnesota-Duluth	^4-2	W
3-10	H	Denver	^1-2	L
3-11	H	Denver	^3-9	L

1972-1973 (23-12-1;16-9-1 in WCHA)
Coach: Amo Bessone

Date		Opponent	Score	Result
11-3	A	Ohio State	6-7	L
11-4	A	Ohio State	4-6	L
11-10	A	Minnesota-Duluth	5-4	W
11-11	A	Minnesota-Duluth	6-3	W
11-17	A	Minnesota	5-3	W
11-18	A	Minnesota	3-3(OT)	T
11-24	A	North Dakota	4-2	W
11-25	A	North Dakota	1-7	L
12-1	H	Michigan Tech	6-2	W
12-2	H	Michigan Tech	7-3	W
12-18	A_{CHT}	Ohio State	7-2	W
12-19	A_{CHT}	Brown	8-3	W
12-27	A_{IMA}	Western Ontario	7-2	W
12-28	A_{IMA}	Air Force Academy	4-1	W
1-5	H	Minnesota	6-2	W
1-6	H	Minnesota	3-1	W
1-12	H	Wisconsin	3-4	L
1-13	H	Wisconsin	7-5	W
1-17	A	Michigan	5-2	W
1-19	A	Air Force Academy	10-1	W
1-20	A	Air Force Academy	11-5	W
1-26	A	Notre Dame	5-8	L
1-27	A	Notre Dame	5-13	L
2-2	A	Michigan	6-5	W
2-3	A	Michigan	8-5	W
2-9	A	Wisconsin	2-5	L
2-10	H	Wisconsin	4-6	L
2-16	H	Notre Dame	10-2	W
2-17	H	Notre Dame	5-6	L
2-23	A	Denver	0-5	L
2-24	A	Denver	3-9	L
2-28	H	Michigan	8-3	W
3-2	H	Colorado College	9-4	W
3-3	H	Colorado College	6-2	W
3-5	H	Michigan Tech	^2-7	L
3-6	H	Michigan Tech	^3-1	W

1973-1974 (23-14-1; 15-12-1 in WCHA)
Coach: Amo Bessone

Date		Opponent	Score	Result
11-2	H	Western Ontario	6-1	W
11-3	H	Western Ontario	4-3	W
11-9	H	Notre Dame	8-5	W
11-10	H	Notre Dame	9-5	W
11-16	H	Michigan	6-7	L
11-17	A	Michigan	7-6(OT)	W
11-23	H	Minnesota	3-6	L
11-24	H	Minnesota	3-4	L
1-30	A	Wisconsin	6-6(OT)	T
12-1	A	Wisconsin	5-4	W
12-7	A	Air Force Academy	7-3	W
12-8	A	Air Force Academy	6-4	W
12-14	A	Colorado College	5-4	W
12-15	A	Colorado College	4-3(OT)	W
12-19	A	Denver	7-9	L
12-21	A	Denver	5-7	L
12-27	A_{GLI}	Boston College	12-5	W
12-28	A_{GLI}	Michigan Tech	5-4	W
1-4	H	Wisconsin	5-4	W
1-5	H	Wisconsin	5-4	W
1-11	H	Colorado College	4-5(OT)	L
1-12	H	Colorado College	6-4	W
1-18	A	Minnesota	4-9	L
1-19	A	Minnesota	3-6	L
1-25	H	North Dakota	7-4	W
1-26	H	North Dakota	6-5	W
2-1	A	Michigan Tech	4-5	L
2-2	A	Michigan Tech	6-8	L
2-8	A	Notre Dame	3-8	L
2-9	A	Notre Dame	4-2	W

2-15	H	Minnesota-Duluth	6-2	W
2-16	H	Minnesota-Duluth	5-1	W
3-1	H	Michigan	6-2	W
3-2	A	Michigan	9-3	W
3-5	H	Wisconsin	^4-1	W
3-6	H	Wisconsin	^3-4	L
3-9	A	Michigan Tech	^8-6	W
3-10	A	Michigan Tech	^2-6	L

1974-1975 (22-17-1; 19-12-1 in WCHA)

Coach: Amo Bessone

10-25	H	Laurentian	3-4	L
10-26	H	Laurentian	4-1	W
11-1	H	Minnesota	3-4(OT)	L
11-2	H	Minnesota	4-3	W
11-8	A	Michigan Tech	4-2	W
11-9	A	Michigan Tech	5-4	W
11-15	H	North Dakota	7-4	W
11-16	H	North Dakota	6-2	W
11-22	A	Wisconsin	3-4	L
11-23	A	Wisconsin	4-5	L
11-29	H	Notre Dame	5-3	W
11-30	H	Notre Dame	4-4(OT)	T
12-7	H	Bowling Green	4-7	L
12-8	H	Bowling Green	4-3	W
12-13	H	Michigan	6-1	W
12-14	A	Michigan	8-3	W
12-20	A	Minnesota-Duluth	4-3	W
12-21	A	Minnesota-Duluth	6-5(OT)	W
1-3	A	North Dakota	5-4	W
1-4	A	North Dakota	5-4	W
1-10	A	Coloado College	1-8	L
1-11	A	Coloado College	6-5	W
1-17	H	Denver	7-2	W
1-18	H	Denver	7-4	W
1-24	H	Minnesota-Duluth	6-3	W
1-25	H	Minnesota-Duluth	5-8	L
1-31	H	Michigan Tech	2-5	L
2-1	H	Michigan Tech	4-5(OT)	L
2-7	A	Notre Dame	7-3	W
2-8	A	Notre Dame	7-0	W
2-14	H	Wisconsin	3-1	W
2-15	H	Wisconsin	5-7	L
2-21	A	Minnesota	3-8	L
2-22	A	Minnesota	2-4	L
2-28	A	Michigan	8-11	L
3-1	H	Michigan	5-7	L
3-4	A	Wisconsin	^4-5	L
3-5	A	Wisconsin	^7-4	W
3-8	A	Michigan Tech	^4-6	L
3-9	A	Michigan Tech	^4-9	L

1975-1976 (23-15-2; 20-12-0 in WCHA)

Coach: Amo Bessone

10-24	H	Ohio State	4-2	W
10-25	H	Ohio State	6-6(OT)	T
10-29	H_x	U.S. Olympic Team	6-13	L
10-31	H	Notre Dame	6-2	W
11-1	H	Notre Dame	3-2	W
11-7	H	Wisconsin	5-4	W
11-8	H	Wisconsin	6-5(OT)	W
11-14	A	Michigan Tech	1-5	L
11-15	A	Michigan Tech	4-2	W
11-21	H	Minnesota	3-1	W
11-22	H	Minnesota	2-4	L
11-28	A	North Dakota	6-4	W
11-29	A	North Dakota	8-3	W
12-5	A	Michigan	4-4	W
12-6	H	Michigan	4-8	L
12-12	A	Minnesota-Duluth	2-5	L
12-13	A	Minnesota-Duluth	8-5	W
1-2	H	Harvard	6-8	L
1-3	H	Harvard	3-4	L
1-9	H	Denver	4-5(OT)	L
1-10	H	Denver	3-4	L
1-16	H	Michigan Tech	7-8	L
1-17	H	Michigan Tech	6-9	L

1-23	A	Colorado College	6-4	W
1-24	A	Colorado College	4-6	L
1-30	H	Wisconsin	5-4(OT)	W
1-31	H	Wisconsin	5-3	W
2-6	A	Minnesota	4-2	W
2-7	A	Minnesota	5-4(OT)	W
2-13	H	North Dakota	2-6	L
2-14	H	North Dakota	7-1	W
2-20	A	Notre Dame	7-6	W
2-21	A	Notre Dame	2-5	L
2-27	H	Colorado College	5-4	W
2-28	H	Colorado College	6-4	W
3-5	H	Michigan	6-3	W
3-6	A	Michigan	6-7	L
3-10	H	Wisconsin	^6-4	W
3-11	H	Wisconsin	^6-4	W
3-13	H	Minnesota	^2-2	T
3-14	H	Minnesota	^6-7(3OT)	L

1976-1977 (14-21-1; 11-20-1 in WCHA)

Coach: Amo Bessone

10-22	H	Ohio State	8-1	W
10-23	H	Ohio State	8-4	W
10-29	A	Notre Dame	3-7	L
10-30	A	Notre Dame	7-5	W
11-5	H	Michigan Tech	4-3	W
11-6	H	Michigan Tech	5-6(OT)	L
11-12	A	Minnesota	3-6	L
11-13	A	Minnesota	2-6	L
11-19	H	Wisconsin	5-2	W
11-20	H	Wisconsin	0-8	L
11-26	A	North Dakota	2-6	L
11-27	A	North Dakota	4-5	L
12-3	H	Denver	3-2	W
12-4	H	Denver	4-5	L
12-10	H	Michigan	7-5	W
12-11	A	Michigan	6-5(OT)	W
12-17	H	New Hampshire	3-2	W
12-18	H	New Hampshire	4-11	L
12-31	A	Colorado College	4-6	L
1-2	A	Colorado College	3-7	L
1-7	A	Denver	5-4	W
1-8	A	Denver	5-5(OT)	T
1-14	H	Notre Dame	2-5	L
1-15	H	Notre Dame	3-10	L
1-21	H	Minnesota	3-4	L
1-22	H	Minnesota	2-3(OT)	L
1-28	A	Wisconsin	6-10	L
1-29	A	Wisconsin	2-9	L
2-4	H	Minnesota-Duluth	6-3	W
2-5	H	Minnesota-Duluth	8-3	W
2-18	A	Michigan Tech	5-3	W
2-19	A	Michigan Tech	2-9	L
2-25	H	North Dakota	3-6	L
2-26	H	North Dakota	3-2	W
3-4	A	Michigan	3-6	L
3-5	H	Michigan	2-5	L

1977-1978 (7-27-2; 7-23-2 in WCHA)

Coach: Amo Bessone

10-21	H	Toronto	1-3	L
10-22	H	Toronto	3-4(OT)	L
10-28	A	North Dakota	5-3	L
10-29	A	North Dakota	4-8	L
11-4	H	Minnesota	1-4	L
11-5	H	Minnesota	4-3(OT)	W
11-11	A	Michigan	4-8	L
11-12	H	Michigan	9-4	W
11-18	H	Michigan Tech	6-5(OT)	W
11-19	H	Michigan Tech	2-4	L
11-25	A	Notre Dame	3-4	L
11-26	A	Notre Dame	2-10	L
12-2	A	Minnesota-Duluth	5-8	L
12-3	A	Minnesota-Duluth	6-10	L
12-9	H	Wisconsin	2-6	L
12-10	H	Wisconsin	3-7	L
12-29	H	Boston University	5-7	L

12-30	H	Boston University	3-6	L
1-7	H	Minnesota-Duluth	3-2(OT)	W
1-8	H	Minnesota-Duluth	5-7	L
1-13	A	Michigan Tech	4-5	L
1-14	A	Michigan Tech	5-9	L
1-20	A	Wisconsin	5-5(OT)	T
1-21	A	Wisconsin	2-8	L
1-27	H	Colorado College	6-8	L
1-28	H	Colorado College	3-5	L
2-4	A	Minnesota	0-10	L
2-5	A	Minnesota	3-5	L
2-10	H	North Dakota	2-4	L
2-11	H	North Dakota	5-3	W
2-17	A	Denver	5-6	L
2-18	A	Denver	2-6	L
2-24	H	Notre Dame	0-2	L
2-25	H	Notre Dame	3-2	W
3-3	H	Michigan	7-7(OT)	T
3-4	A	Michigan	2-3	L

1978-1979 (15-21; 12-20 in WCHA)

Coach: Amo Bessone

10-20	H	Ohio State	4-1	W
10-21	H	Ohio State	5-1	W
10-27	A	Denver	2-4	L
10-28	A	Denver	1-4	L
11-3	H	Minnesota	4-6	L
11-4	H	Minnesota	5-6(OT)	L
11-10	A	Michigan Tech	6-10	L
11-11	A	Michigan Tech	5-4	W
11-17	A	Notre Dame	1-9	L
11-18	A	Notre Dame	4-5	L
11-24	A	North Dakota	4-2	W
11-25	A	North Dakota	1-6	L
12-1	H	Wisconsin	6-5	W
12-2	H	Wisconsin	1-5	L
12-8	H	Michigan	4-7	L
12-9	H	Michigan	2-5	L
12-15	H	Colorado College	2-9	L
12-16	A	Colorado College	4-10	L
12-29	H	Northeastern	7-5	W
12-30	H	Northeastern	2-5	L
1-5	A	Wisconsin	4-6	L
1-6	A	Wisconsin	3-13	L
1-12	H	Notre Dame	2-3	L
1-13	H	Notre Dame	6-3	W
1-20	H	Denver	5-3	W
1-21	H	Denver	7-3	W
2-2	A	Minnesota	4-7	L
2-3	A	Minnesota	3-11	L
2-9	H	Michigan Tech	4-3	W
2-10	H	Michigan Tech	5-3	W
2-16	H	Minnesota-Duluth	6-5	W
2-17	H	Minnesota-Duluth	3-5	L
2-23	A	North Dakota	2-7	L
2-24	A	North Dakota	6-5	W
3-2	A	Michigan	5-3	W
3-3	H	Michigan	5-3	W

Ron Mason (1980-2002)

In his short tenure as athletic director, Joe Kearney made some impressive decisions pertaining to hiring staff: Darryl Rogers, Jud Heathcote and none more poignant than replacing the retiring Amo Bessone with Ron Mason in 1979. It took Mason only three years, but by 1981 he had laid the groundwork for Michigan State's dominance in the sport throughout the remainder of the 20th century. By 1993, coupled with his 13 seasons at Lake Superior State and Bowling Green, Ron had registered his 674th victory to become college hockey's winningest coach ever. In the many milestones along his illustrious coaching career, the most recent was reached early in the 2001-2002 campaign when he registered win number 900. Munn Ice Arena is festooned with banners that reveal the Mason success story: seven Central Collegiate Hockey Association (CCHA) regular season titles; 10 CCHA tournament titles; seven Frozen Four appearances and the 1986 NCAA title. Ron Mason received his

bachelor's degree from St. Lawrence College in 1964 and his master's from Pittsburgh in 1965. Both degrees were in physical education. He played hockey at St. Lawrence where he lettered for three years while leading the team in scoring his senior year. Prior to attending St. Lawrence, Ron played junior "A" hockey with both the Peterborough Petes and the Ottawa Junior Canadians. Mason's rise to the top of the college coaching ranks began in 1966, when he was appointed head coach at Lake Superior State, where he guided the Lakers to five NAIA Tournament appearances. He moved on to Bowling Green in 1973, and there began to build a national reputation with six highly productive years including a third-place NCAA finish in 1977-1978. Following the 2001-2002 season, Ron's 23rd behind the Spartan bench and 36th of coaching overall, Ron Mason retired from his position as head coach as he accepted the appointment of MSU's director of athletics beginning on July 1, 2002.

1979-1980 (14-24; 12-16 in WCHA)

Coach: Ron Mason

10-19	A	Western Michigan	7-6	W
10-20	H	Western Michigan	6-8	L
10-26	A	Minnesota	8-9	L
10-27	A	Minnesota	5-11	L
11-2	H	Wisconsin	4-6	L
11-3	H	Wisconsin	5-4	W
11-9	A	Michigan Tech	5-4(OT)	W
11-10	A	Michigan Tech	2-6	L
11-16	A	Notre Dame	5-4	W
11-17	A	Notre Dame	3-5	L
11-23	H	North Dakota	2-9	L
11-24	H	North Dakota	5-4	W
11-30	A	Michigan	2-7	L
12-1	H	Michigan	6-3	W
12-7	H	Ferris State	3-6	L
12-8	A	Ferris State	3-4(OT)	L
12-18	A	Colorado College	6-7(OT)	L
12-19	A	Colorado College	1-6	L
12-28	A_GLI	Michigan	4-7	L
12-29	A_GLI	Wisconsin	4-10	L
1-4	H	Princeton	6-1	W
1-5	H	Boston College	3-5	L
1-11	A	Minnesota-Duluth	6-4	W
1-12	A	Minnesota-Duluth	7-8(OT)	L
1-18	H	Michigan Tech	4-3	W
1-19	H	Michigan Tech	0-6	L
1-25	A	Wisconsin	5-4	W
1-26	A	Wisconsin	2-9	L
2-1	H	Minnesota	7-6	W
2-2	H	Minnesota	1-7	L
2-8	H	Polish Nat. Team (ex)	5-4	W
2-15	H	Denver	4-2	W
2-16	H	Denver	5-8	L
2-22	H	Notre Dame	7-6	W
2-23	H	Notre Dame	5-9	L
2-29	H	Michigan	5-4	W
3-1	A	Michigan	1-6	L
3-7	H	North Dakota	^1-8	L
3-8	H	North Dakota	^3-5	L

1980-1981 (12-22-2; 7-20-1 in WCHA)

Coach: Ron Mason

10-24	H	Northern Michigan	2-5	L
10-25	H	Northern Michigan	6-2	W
10-31	H	North Dakota	3-6	L
11-1	H	North Dakota	4-7	L
11-7	H	Michigan	1-2	L
11-8	A	Michigan	2-3	L
11-14	A	Denver	1-7	L
11-15	A	Denver	4-6	L
11-21	A	North Dakota	4-6	L
11-22	A	North Dakota	2-5	L
11-26	H	Michigan Tech	8-2	W
11-27	H	Michigan Tech	2-4	L
12-3	H	Notre Dame	3-4	L
12-5	H	Miami	4-4(OT)	T
12-6	H	Miami	6-3	W

12-12	A	Notre Dame	1-0	W
12-19	A	Lake Superior	5-2	W
12-20	A	Lake Superior	3-2	W
12-27	A_GLI	Michigan	2-3	L
12-28	A_GLI	Harvard	6-4	W
1-9	H	Minnesota-Duluth	4-0	W
1-10	H	Minnesota-Duluth	3-4	L
1-16	A	Michigan	2-9	L
1-17	H	Michigan	4-3	W
1-23	A	Michigan Tech	0-5	L
1-24	A	Michigan Tech	1-4	L
1-30	H	Denver	3-3(OT)	T
1-31	H	Denver	1-2	L
2-6	A	Minnesota	3-8	L
2-7	A	Minnesota	2-4	L
2-13	H	Notre Dame	2-4	L
2-14	H	Notre Dame	2-4	L
2-20	A	Wisconsin	5-3	W
2-21	A	Wisconsin	4-5	L
2-27	H	Colorado College	6-5(OT)	W
2-28	H	Colorado College	5-4(OT)	W

1981-1982 (26-14-2; 21-10-1 in CCHA: 2nd)

Coach: Ron Mason

10-23	H	Lake Superior	4-3	W
10-24	H	Lake Superior	3-2(OT)	W
10-30	A	Bowling Green	4-3	W
10-31	A	Bowling Green	4-0	W
11-7	H	Ferris State	3-3(OT)	T
11-8	H	Ferris State	3-4(OT)	L
11-13	H	Notre Dame	4-2	W
11-14	A	Notre Dame	8-4	W
11-20	A	Michigan	3-4	L
11-21	H	Michigan	3-0	W
12-4	H	Bowling Green	6-5	W
12-5	H	Bowling Green	3-4	L
12-11	H	Michigan Tech	6-1	W
12-12	H	Michigan Tech	3-4	L
12-17	A	Lake Superior	5-2	W
12-18	A	Lake Superior	3-1	W
12-29	A_GLI	Michigan Tech	3-6	L
12-30	A_GLI	Michigan	4-4	T
1-8	H	Western Michigan	2-3	L
1-9	A	Western Michigan	4-3	W
1-15	H	Illinois-Chicago	8-1	W
1-16	H	Illinois-Chicago	7-2	W
1-18	A	Michigan	5-2	W
1-22	A	Ohio State	7-3	W
1-23	A	Ohio State	1-4	L
1-29	H	Miami	6-5	W
1-30	H	Miami	2-3	L
2-5	A	Northern Michigan	4-2	W
2-6	A	Northern Michigan	3-9	L
2-12	H	Western Michigan	6-2	W
2-13	H	Western Michigan	7-3	W
2-16	H	Michigan	7-1	W
2-20	H	Notre Dame	5-2	W
2-22	A	Notre Dame	2-3	L
2-26	H	Ferris State	10-2	W
2-27	A	Ferris State	3-4	L
3-5	H	Lake Superior	-9-1	W
3-6	H	Lake Superior	-3-4	L
3-12	A	Michigan Tech	-3-2	W
3-13	A	Notre Dame	-4-1	W
3-19	A	New Hampshire	**2-3	L
3-20	A	New Hampshire	**2-6	L

1982-1983 (30-11-1; 23-9 in CCHA: tie 2nd)

Coach: Ron Mason

10-15	H	McMaster	9-2	W
10-16	H	McMaster	8-4	W
10-22	H	Illinois-Chicago	4-0	W
10-23	H	Illinois-Chicago	8-0	W
10-29	H	Ohio State	5-2	W

10-30	H	Ohio State	5-1	W
11-5	A	Michigan	5-2	W
11-6	H	Michigan	4-3	W
11-12	H	Northern Michigan	1-2	L
11-13	H	Northern Michigan	1-3	L
11-19	A	Miami	3-2(OT)	W
11-20	A	Miami	3-2	W
11-27	H	Michigan Tech	6-3	W
11-28	H	Michigan Tech	3-2(OT)	W
12-3	A	Notre Dame	2-3	L
12-4	A	Notre Dame	7-3	W
12-17	A	Lake Superior	3-2	W
12-18	A	Lake Superior	5-3	W
12-28	A_GLI	Michigan	6-3	W
12-29	A_GLI	Michigan Tech	5-3	W
1-5	H	USA National Team (ex)	2-9	L
1-7	A	Bowling Green	4-6	L
1-8	A	Bowling Green	2-4	L
1-14	H	Ferris State	1-4	L
1-15	H	Ferris State	4-2	W
1-21	H	Western Michigan	8-0	W
1-22	H	Western Michigan	6-4	W
1-28	H	Michigan	3-1	W
1-29	A	Michigan	2-1	W
2-4	H	Lake Superior	7-3	W
2-5	H	Lake Superior	2-1	W
2-11	A	Michigan Tech	3-6	L
2-12	A	Michigan Tech	5-4(OT)	W
2-18	A	Ferris State	2-5	L
2-19	A	Ferris State	10-2	W
2-25	A	Northern Michigan	7-3	W
2-26	A	Northern Michigan	1-4	L
3-3	H	Ferris State	-2-4	L
3-4	H	Ferris State	-5-1	W
3-11	A	Ohio State	-8-3	W
3-12	A	Bowling Green	-4-3(OT)	W
3-18	A	Harvard	**5-6	L
3-19	A	Harvard	**3-3	T

1983-1984 (34-12; 21-9 in CCHA: tie 2nd; 4th place in NCAA)

Coach: Ron Mason

10-14	H	Northeastern	5-2	W
10-15	H	Northeastern	1-0	W
10-21	A	Western Michigan	5-2	W
10-22	A	Western Michigan	5-2	W
10-28	A	Illinois-Chicago	7-1	W
10-29	A	Illinois-Chicago	5-3	W
11-4	H	Bowling Green	4-7	L
11-5	H	Bowling Green	3-5	L
11-11	A	Northern Michigan	4-2	W
11-12	H	Northern Michigan	9-4	W
11-18	A	Michigan	6-3	W
11-19	H	Michigan	3-5	L
11-25	A	Ferris State	8-2	W
11-26	A	Ferris State	1-2	L
12-2	H	Michigan Tech	7-2	W
12-3	H	Michigan Tech	6-4	W
12-10	H	Toronto	5-2	W
12-11	H	Toronto	1-7	L
12-16	A	Lake Superior	3-4(OT)	L
12-17	A	Lake Superior	7-3	W
12-29	A_GLI	Northern Michigan	5-1	W
12-30	A_GLI	Michigan Tech	6-2	W
1-6	H	Miami	9-1	W
1-7	H	Miami	9-3	W
1-13	A	Ohio State	2-4	L
1-14	A	Ohio State	5-3	W
1-16	H	U.S. Olympic Team(ex)	2-6	L
1-20	H	Lowell	10-4	W
1-21	H	Lowell	6-0	W
1-27	H	Michigan	12-1	W
1-28	A	Michigan	3-1	W
2-3	A	Michigan Tech	4-6	L
2-4	A	Michigan Tech	1-3	L
2-10	H	Lake Superior	6-1	W
2-11	H	Lake Superior	8-1	W
2-17	A	Northern Michigan	1-4	L

2-18	A	Northern Michigan	4-3(OT)	W
2-24	H	Ferris State	8-4	W
2-25	H	Ferris State	7-4	W
3-2	H	Michigan Tech	-5-3	W
3-3	H	Michigan Tech	-3-1	W
3-9	A	Ohio State	-8-1	W
3-10	A	Western Michigan	-5-0	W
3-17	H	Boston College	**6-2	W
3-18	H	Boston College	**7-6	W
3-23	A	Bowling Green	**1-2	L
3-24	A	North Dakota	**5-6	L

1984-1985 (38-6; 27-5 in CCHA: 1st)
Coach: Ron Mason

10-12	A	Ohio State	5-4(OT)	W
10-14	A	Ohio State	6-3	W
10-19	A	Western Michigan	6-4	W
10-20	A	Western Michigan	2-3	L
10-26	A	Miami	9-1	W
10-27	A	Miami	5-1	W
11-2	H	Ferris State	8-2	W
11-3	A	Ferris State	3-4(OT)	L
11-9	A	Michigan	4-1	W
11-10	H	Michigan	8-2	W
11-16	H	Western Ontario	4-3	W
11-23	A	Bowling Green	4-1	W
11-24	H	Bowling Green	3-4	L
11-29	A	Illinois-Chicago	8-2	W
11-30	A	Illinois-Chicago	8-4	W
12-7	H	Lake Superior	7-2	W
12-8	H	Lake Superior	6-3	W
12-14	H	Ohio State	7-0	W
12-15	H	Ohio State	9-1	W
12-28	A(GLI)	Bowling Green	3-1	W
12-29	A(GLI)	Michigan Tech	7-0	W
1-4	H	Western Michigan	4-3(OT)	W
1-6	H	Western Michigan	7-3	W
1-8	H	Alaska-Fairbanks	13-3	W
1-11	H	Miami	3-2(OT)	W
1-12	H	Miami	5-1	W
1-18	A	Ferris State	3-1	W
1-19	A	Ferris State	7-3	W
1-25	H	Michigan	11-2	W
1-26	H	Michigan	9-4	W
2-1	A	Northern Arizona	5-2	W
2-2	A	Northern Arizona	10-2	W
2-8	H	Bowling Green	15-1	W
2-9	A	Bowling Green	3-1	W
2-15	H	Illinois-Chicago	6-2	W
2-16	H	Illinois-Chicago	4-7	L
2-22	A	Lake Superior	2-4	L
2-23	A	Lake Superior	4-2	W
3-1	H	Miami	-4-3	W
3-2	H	Miami	-7-1	W
3-8	H	Ohio State	-8-0	W
3-9	H	Lake Superior	-5-1	W
3-23	H	Providence	**3-2	W
3-24	H	Providence	**2-4	L

1985-1986 (34-9-2; 23-7-2 in CCHA: 1st; NCAA champions)
Coach: Ron Mason

10-11	A	Ohio State	6-2	W
10-12	A	Ohio State	5-2	W
10-18	A	Western Michigan	1-5	L
10-19	H	Western Michigan	4-3	W
10-25	H	Miami	5-2	W
10-26	H	Miami	7-2	W
11-1	H	Ferris State	5-5(OT)	T
11-2	A	Ferris State	5-3	W
11-8	A	Michigan	4-5	L
11-9	H	Michigan	6-2	W
11-15	H	Team Canada (ex)	3-5	L
11-16	H	Team Canada (ex)	5-4	W
11-22	H	Bowling Green	4-3(OT)	W
11-23	A	Bowling Green	5-6(OT)	L
11-29	A	Illinois-Chicago	6-4	W

11-30	A	Illinois-Chicago	2-3	L
12-6	A	Lake Superior	3-7	L
12-7	A	Lake Superior	5-6(OT)	L
12-14	H	Ohio State	6-5	W
12-15	H	Ohio State	8-0	W
12-19	H	Northern Michigan	2-3	L
12-27	A(GLI)	Michigan Tech	2-1(OT)	W
12-29	A(GLI)	RPI	8-3	W
1-4	H	Western Michigan	4-2	W
1-5	A	Western Michigan	8-5	W
1-10	A	Miami	8-3	W
1-11	A	Miami	6-3	W
1-17	A	Ferris State	8-6	W
1-18	H	Ferris State	9-9(OT)	T
1-24	H	Michigan	7-5	W
1-25	A	Michigan	3-5	L
1-31	H	Northern Arizona	12-2	W
2-1	H	Northern Arizona	9-3	W
2-7	A	Bowling Green	7-4	W
2-8	H	Bowling Green	6-4	W
2-14	A	Illinois-Chicago	4-2	W
2-15	A	Illinois-Chicago	7-2	W
2-21	H	Lake Superior	8-5	W
2-22	H	Lake Superior	5-4(OT)	W
2-28	H	Michigan	-4-3	W
3-1	H	Michigan	-5-2	W
3-7	H	Lake Superior	-3-2	W
3-8	H	Western Michigan	-1-3	L
3-21	H	Boston College	**6-4	W
3-22	H	Boston College	**4-2	W
3-27	A	Minnesota	**6-4	W
3-29	A	Harvard	**6-5	W

1986-1987 (33-10-2; 23-8-1 in CCHA: 2nd; second place in NCAA)
Coach: Ron Mason

10-10	H	Ohio State	8-4	W
10-11	H	Ohio State	6-4	W
10-17	A	Ferris State	3-2	W
10-18	A	Ferris State	6-3	W
10-24	H	Miami	10-4	W
10-25	H	Miami	8-1	W
10-31	A	Western Michigan	6-3	W
11-1	H	Western Michigan	7-3	W
11-7	H	Illinois-Chicago	4-5(OT)	L
11-8	H	Illinois-Chicago	5-4	W
11-14	A	Michigan	7-6	W
11-15	H	Michigan	9-3	W
11-21	H	Maine	3-3(OT)	T
11-22	H	Maine	4-0	W
11-26	H	Michigan Tech	6-0	W
11-28	A	Bowling Green	5-4	W
11-30	H	Bowling Green	5-1	W
12-6	A	Lake Superior	4-5(OT)	L
12-7	A	Lake Superior	3-2(OT)	W
12-12	A	Ferris State	4-3(OT)	W
12-14	H	Ferris State	4-2	W
12-27	A(GLI)	Western Michigan	3-7	L
12-28	A(GLI)	Michigan Tech	7-0	W
1-2	A	Miami	4-5(OT)	L
1-3	A	Miami	5-2	W
1-9	H	Western Michigan	8-6	W
1-10	A	Western Michigan	5-4(OT)	W
1-16	A	Illinois-Chicago	2-4	L
1-17	A	Illinois-Chicago	5-2	W
1-23	H	Michigan	2-8	L
1-24	A	Michigan	2-1	W
1-30	H	Team Canada (ex)	3-5	L
1-31	H	Team Canada (ex)	3-6	L
2-6	H	Bowling Green	6-3	W
2-7	A	Bowling Green	3-3(OT)	T
2-13	H	Lake Superior	3-4	L
2-14	H	Lake Superior	1-4	L
2-20	A	Ohio State	8-4	W
2-21	A	Ohio State	5-7	L
2-27	H	Michigan	-8-7	W
2-28	H	Michigan	-6-3	W
3-6	A	Western Michigan	-6-3	W

3-7	A	Bowling Green	-4-3(OT)	W
3-20	H	Maine	-**6-2	W
3-21	H	Maine	**5-3	W
3-27	A	Minnesota	**5-3	W
3-28	A	North Dakota	**3-5	L

1987-1988 (27-16-3; 18-11-3 in CCHA: 1st; NCAA quarterfinalist)
Coach: Ron Mason

10-9	A	Ohio State	9-4	W
10-10	A	Ohio State	6-6(OT)	T
10-16	A	Ferris State	2-4	L
10-17	H	Ferris State	5-2	W
10-23	H	Miami	6-1	W
10-24	H	Miami	2-4	L
10-30	H	Western Michigan	4-2	W
10-31	A	Western Michigan	4-0	W
11-6	A	Illinois-Chicago	5-2	W
11-7	H	Illinois-Chicago	5-2	W
11-13	H	Michigan	6-3	W
11-14	A	Michigan	4-6	L
11-20		U.S. Olympic Team (ex)	3-3	T
11-22		U.S. Olympic Team(ex)	4-10	L
11-27	A	Bowling Green	6-3	W
11-29	H	Bowling Green	7-3	W
12-4	H	Lake Superior	4-2	W
12-5	H	Lake Superior	4-4(OT)	T
12-11	H	Ferris State	4-5	L
12-12	H	Ferris State	1-1(OT)	T
12-18	A(NJ)	Alaska-Anchorage	5-2	W
12-20	A(NJ)	Maine	3-4	L
12-29	A(GLI)	Michigan Tech	5-2	W
12-30	A(GLI)	Wisconsin	3-4	L
1-8	H	Miami	3-4	L
1-9	A	Miami	7-6(OT)	W
1-15	H	Western Michigan	7-6	W
1-16	H	Western Michigan	3-2	W
1-22	H	Illinois-Chicago	5-4(OT)	W
1-23	H	Illinois-Chicago	8-5	W
1-29	A	Michigan	2-5	L
1-30	H	Michigan	3-5	L
2-5	H	U.S. International	5-1	W
2-6	H	U.S. International	6-2	W
2-12	A	Bowling Green	4-5	L
2-13	A	Bowling Green	5-6	L
2-19	A	Lake Superior	3-7	L
2-20	A	Lake Superior	4-5	L
2-26	H	Ohio State	7-4	W
2-27	H	Ohio State	6-5	W
3-4	H	Illinois-Chicago	-9-4	W
3-5	H	Illinois-Chicago	-6-3	W
3-11	A	Bowling Green	-4-6	L
3-12	A	Western Michigan	**9-6	W
3-18	H	Harvard	**6-5	W
3-19	H	Harvard	**5-3	W
3-25	A	Minnesota	**2-4	L
3-26	A	Minnesota	**3-4	L

1988-1989 (37-9-1; 25-6-1 in CCHA: 1st; third place in NCAA)
Coach: Ron Mason

10-14	A	Lake Superior	2-5	L
10-15	A	Lake Superior	6-1	W
10-21	H	Ferris State	7-4	W
10-22	H	Ferris State	9-2	W
10-28	A	Illinois-Chicago	2-0	W
10-29	A	Illinois-Chicago	5-4(OT)	W
11-4	A	Western Michigan	8-1	W
11-5	H	Western Michigan	12-1	W
11-11	A	Bowling Green	12-1	W
11-12	H	Bowling Green	6-2	W
11-18	H	Boston University	6-4	W
11-19	H	Boston University	9-3	W
11-25	A	Ohio State	5-3	W
11-26	A	Ohio State	9-4	W
12-2	A	Miami	12-7	W

12-3	A	Miami	4-3	W
12-9	A	Michigan	3-0	W
12-11	H	Michigan	5-3	W
12-15	H	Ferris State	8-2	W
12-16	A	Ferris State	3-0	W
12-29	A$_{GLI}$	North Dakota	3-7	L
12-30	A$_{GLI}$	Michigan Tech	7-1	W
1-6	H	Illinois-Chicago	2-4	L
1-7	H	Illinois-Chicago	5-1	W
1-13	H	Western Michigan	5-5(OT)	T
1-14	A	Western Michigan	2-4	L
1-20	H	Bowling Green	8-5	W
1-21	A	Bowling Green	2-5	L
1-27	A	Maine	6-3	W
1-28	A	Maine	6-3	W
2-3	H	Ohio State	6-2	W
2-4	H	Ohio State	4-2	W
2-10	H	Miami	9-3	W
2-11	H	Miami	8-4	W
2-17	H	Michigan	7-3	W
2-18	A	Michigan	5-3	W
2 24	H	Lake Superior	3-6	L
2-25	H	Lake Superior	4-5(OT)	L
3-3	H	Ohio State	~9-5	W
3-4	H	Ohio State	~11-4	W
3-11	A	Bowling Green	~3-2	W
3-12	A	Lake Superior	~4-1	W
3-24	H	Boston College	**3-6	L
3-25	H	Boston College	**7-2	W
3-26	H	Boston College	**5-4(OT)	W
3-30	A	Harvard	**3-6	L
4-1	A	Maine	**7-4	W

1989-1990 (35-7-3; 26-3-3 in CCHA: 1st; quarterfinalist in NCAA)

Coach: Ron Mason

10-13	H	Lake Superior	3-4	L
10-14	H	Lake Superior	4-3	W
10-20	H	Ferris State	9-3	W
10-21	A	Ferris State	2-5	L
10-27	H	Illinois-Chicago	6-2	W
10-28	A	Illinois-Chicago	14-1	W
11-3	A	Western Michigan	6-4	W
11-4	H	Western Michigan	5-4(OT)	W
11-10	H	Bowling Green	11-3	W
11-11	A	Bowling Green	5-4(OT)	W
11-17	A	Boston College	5-3	W
11-18	A	Boston University	4-6	L
11-24	H	Ohio State	8-2	W
11-25	H	Ohio State	6-1	W
12-1	H	Miami	4-2	W
12-2	H	Miami	8-2	W
12-9	A	Michigan	5-3	W
12-10	H	Michigan	11-4	W
12-14	A	Ferris State	5-3	W
12-15	A	Ferris State	5-5(OT)	T
12-18	A$_{GWF}$	Denver	2-1	W
12-19	A$_{GWF}$	Alberta	7-4	W
12-29	A$_{GLI}$	Michigan Tech	3-?	W
12-30	A$_{GLI}$	Michigan	3-6	L
1-5	H	Illinois-Chicago	6-3	W
1-6	A	Illinois-Chicago	6-3	W
1-12	H	Western Michigan	11-2	W
1-13	A	Western Michigan	6-3	W
1-19	A	Bowling Green	5-4	W
1-20	H	Bowling Green	4-4(OT)	T
1-27	H	Michigan-Dearborn	5-3	W
2-2	A	Ohio State	9-2	W
2-3	A	Ohio State	4-2	W
2-9	A	Miami	4-2	W
2-10	A	Miami	5-3	W
2-16	H	Michigan	2-2(OT)	T
2-17	H	Michigan	5-2	W
2-23	A	Lake Superior	4-3	W
2-24	A	Lake Superior	2-3	L
3-2	H	Ferris State	~6-4	W
3-3	H	Ferris State	~13-1	W
3-10	A	Michigan	~4-3(OT)	W
3-11	A	Lake Superior	~4-3	W
3-23	H	Boston University	**6-3	W
3-24	H	Boston University	**3-5	L
3-25	H	Boston University	**3-5	L

1990-1991 (17-18-5; 14-13-5 in CCHA: 5th)

Coach: Ron Mason

10-12	A	Illinois-Chicago	8-3	W
10-13	A	Illinois-Chicago	9-1	W
10-19	H	Lake Superior	4-4(OT)	T
10-20	H	Lake Superior	2-5	L
10-26	H	Western Michigan	3-3(OT)	T
10-27	H	Western Michigan	3-2	W
11-2	H	Bowling Green	4-6	L
11-3	A	Bowling Green	4-5	L
11-9	A	Michigan	2-4	L
11-10	H	Michigan	3-3(OT)	T
11-16	H	Boston College	4-2	W
11-17	H	Boston College	4-5	L
11 24	H	Miami	4-0	W
11-25	H	Miami	8-0	W
11-30	A	Ferris State	2-4	L
12-1	A	Ferris State	4-5	L
12-7	A	Ohio State	3-5	L
12-8	A	Ohio State	2-2(OT)	T
12-14	A	Bowling Green	9-3	W
12-15	H	Bowling Green	4-2	W
12-16	H	Dynamo (Russia) (ex)	5-6	L
12-20	A$_{GWF}$	Toronto	4-3	W
12-21	A$_{GWF}$	Boston College	3-2	W
12-28	A$_{GLI}$	Maine	3-6	L
12-29	A$_{GLI}$	Michigan Tech	2-3	L
1-4	H	Ohio State	5-0	W
1-5	H	Ohio State	3-1	W
1-18	A	Lake Superior	3-3(OT)	T
1-19	A	Lake Superior	0-4	L
1-25	A	Western Michigan	2-3	L
1-26	A	Western Michigan	1-8	L
2-1	H	Ferris State	2-3(OT)	L
2-2	A	Ferris State	3-2	W
2-8	A	Miami	3-2	W
2-9	A	Miami	7-2	W
2-15	A$_{DE}$	Michigan	5-6	L
2-16	A$_{DE}$	Michigan	6-2	W
2-22	H	Illinois-Chicago	~4-5	L
2-23	H	Illinois-Chicago	~8-3	W
3-1	A	Western Michigan	~3-4	L
3-2	A	Western Michigan	**2-4	L

1991-1992 (26-10-8; 18-7-8 in CCHA: 3rd; semifinalist in NCAA)

Coach: Ron Mason

10-25	H	Michigan	5-3	W
10-26	A	Michigan	4-4(OT)	T
11-1	A	Boston College	2-2(OT)	T
11-8	A	Bowling Green	6-3	W
11-9	H	Bowling Green	9-6	W
11-15	H	Lake Superior	1-0	W
11-16	H	Lake Superior	1-3	L
11-22	H	Western Michigan	4-3(OT)	W
11-23	A	Western Michigan	2-5	L
12-6	H	Ohio State	12-4	W
12-7	H	Ohio State	6-3	W
12-13	H	Ferris State	3-3(OT)	T
12-14	A	Ferris State	3-3(OT)	T
12-19	A$_{GWF}$	Maine	1-0(%)	W
12-20	A$_{GWF}$	Waterloo	9-4	W
12-27	A$_{GLI}$	Michigan Tech	5-6	L
12-28	A$_{GLI}$	Harvard	3-1	W
1-4	A	Western Michigan	5-2	W
1-6	A	Western Michigan	5-4	W
1-10	A	Ohio State	6-6(OT)	T
1-11	A	Ohio State	5-3	W
1-17	H	Miami	7-2	W
1-18	H	Miami	2-4	L
1-21	H	Ferris State	8-2	W
1-31	A	Illinois-Chicago	6-3	W
2-1	A	Illinois-Chicago	3-6	L
2-7	A	Lake Superior	3-3(OT)	T
2-8	A	Lake Superior	4-1	W
2-14	A	Bowling Green	1-2(OT)	L
2-15	H	Bowling Green	6-6(OT)	T
2-21	A$_{DE}$	Michigan	1-4	L
2-22	A$_{DE}$	Michigan	4-5	L
2-25	A	Ferris State	3-1	W
2-28	H	Illinois-Chicago	4-0	W
2-29	H	Illinois-Chicago	6-2	W
3-6	A	Miami	7-7(OT)	T
3-7	A	Miami	7-2	W
3-13	A	Ferris State	~5-2	W
3-14	H	Ferris State	~4-1	W
3-21	A	Lake Superior	~3-5	L
3-22	A	Miami	~8-5	W
3-26	A	Boston University	**4-2	W
3-28	A	Maine	**3-2	W
4-2	A	Lake Superior	**2-4	L

% Win was awarded to MSU after the game was forfeited.

1992-1993 (24-14-2; 18-10-2 in CCHA: 4th)

Coach: Ron Mason

10-23	H	Western Ontario	7-2	W
10-30	H	Miami	3-4	L
10-31	H	Miami	4-7	L
11-6	A	Western Michigan	3-5	L
11-7	A	Illinois-Chicago	4-3	W
11-13	H	Western Michigan	4-2	W
11-14	H	Kent State	7-1	W
11-20	H	Illinois-Chicago	3-2	W
11-21	H	Illinois-Chicago	6-2	W
11-27	A	Notre Dame	8-4	W
11-28	A	Ferris State	2-2(OT)	T
12-4	A	Michigan	3-4	L
12-5	H	Michigan	3-1	W
12-11	H	Lake Superior	4-7	L
12-12	H	Lake Superior	4-1	W
12-20	A$_{NJC}$	British Columbia	7-1	W
12-22	A$_{NJC}$	Kent State	1-2	L
12-26	A$_{GLI}$	Northern Michigan	1-4	L
12-27	A$_{GLI}$	Michigan Tech	4-3	W
1-11	A	Lake Superior	4-2	W
1-15	H	Alaska-Fairbanks	5-6	L
1-16	H	Alaska-Fairbanks	3-1	W
1-22	A	Miami	1-2	L
1-23	A	Ohio State	8-2	W
1-29	H	Bowling Green	6-2	W
1-30	A$_{DE}$	Michigan	1-11	L
2-5	H	Notre Dame	5-1	W
2-6	A	Western Michigan	0-2	L
2-9	A	Ferris State	7-4	W
2-12	H	Ohio State	7-2	W
2-13	H	Ohio State	7-1	W
2-19	A	Bowling Green	5-5(OT)	T
2-20	A	Ferris State	3-5	L
2-26	A	Kent State	3-2	W
2-27	A	Kent State	6-4	W
3-5	A	Bowling Green	2-6	L
3-6	H	Notre Dame	5-2	W
3-12	H	Kent State	~6-5	W
3-13	H	Kent State	~5-2	W
3-19	A	Ferris State	~2-3	L

1993-1994 (23-13-5; 17-8-5 in CCHA: 3rd)

Coach: Ron Mason

10-22	A	Illinois-Chicago	6-3	W
10-23	A	Illinois-Chicago	4-3	W
10-29	A	Miami	1-5	L
10-30	A	Miami	6-4	W
11-2	H	Ferris State	3-4	L

11-5	H	Notre Dame	3-0	W
11-6	A	Notre Dame	1-1(OT)	T
11-13	H	Guelph	7-4	W
11-19	H	Miami	1-1(OT)	T
11-20	H	Bowling Green	2-2(OT)	T
11-23	H	Lake Superior	6-4	W
11-26	A_CHS	Wisconsin	4-2	W
11-27	A_CHS	Minnesota	5-6	L
12-3	H	Kent State	5-1	W
12-4	H	Kent State	6-3	W
12-10	A	Western Michigan	1-2	L
12-11	H	Western Michigan	0-2	L
12-29	A_GLI	Michigan Tech	3-2	W
12-30	A_GLI	Michigan	2-4	L
1-7	A	Ohio State	7-3	W
1-8	A	Kent state	9-6	W
1-15	H	Bowling Green	3-0	W
1-21	A	Michigan	6-3	W
1-22	A	Michigan	1-3	L
1-28	A	Bowling Green	8-1	W
1-29	A	Ohio State	7-4	W
2-4	H	Ohio State	4-5	L
2-5	H	Illinois-Chicago	4-2	W
2-11	A	Lake Superior	1-11	L
2-12	A	Lake Superior	3-3(OT)	T
2-19	A_DE	Michigan	5-1	W
2-24	A	Notre Dame	1-1(OT)	T
2-25	H	Ferris State	4-6	L
3-3	A	Ferris State	2-1	W
3-4	H	Western Michigan	5-2	W
3-11	H	Illinois-Chicago	~3-4	L
3-12	H	Illinois-Chicago	~2-1	W
3-13	H	Illinois-Chicago	~8-3	W
3-18	A	Bowling Green	~3-2	W
3-19	A	Lake Superior.	~0-4	L
3-26	H	Massachusetts-Lowell	**3-4	L

1994-1995 (25-12-3; 17-7-3 in CCHA: 3rd)

Coach: Ron Mason

10-15	H	Bowling Green	6-3	W
10-21	H	Illinois-Chicago	4-1	W
10-22	H	Illinois-Chicago	8-3	W
10-28	A	Western Michigan	3-2	W
10-29	A	Illinois-Chicago	2-2(OT)	T
11-4	H	Lake Superior	4-1	W
11-5	H	Ohio State	5-3	W
11-9	H	Bowling Green	7-4	W
11-11	A	Michigan	3-7	L
11-18	H	Alaska-Fairbanks	5-1	W
11-19	H	Alaska-Fairbanks	3-6	L
11-26	A_CHS	Minnesota	2-3	L
11-25	A_CHS	Wisconsin	3-2	W
12-2	H	Ohio State	8-2	W
12-3	H	Lake Superior	7-3	W
12-9	A	Bowling Green	2-6	L
12-10	H	Western Ontario	8-2	W
12-29	A_GLI	Cornell	9-4	W
12-30	A_GLI	Michigan	4-5	L
1-6	H	Ferris State	9-2	W
1-9	A	Lake Superior	4-4(OT)	T
1-13	H	Notre Dame	4-1	W
1-20	A	Notre Dame	8-3	W
1-21	A	Bowling Green	4-6	L
1-28	A	Western Michigan	8-1	W
2-3	A	Ferris State	3-3(OT)	T
2-4	H	Michigan	3-5	L
2-10	H	Miami	2-3(OT)	L
2-11	H	Miami	0-1	L
2-17	H	Western Michigan	4-1	W
2-18	A_DE	Michigan	1-7	L
2-24	H	Notre Dame	4-1	W
2-25	A	Ferris State	6-1	W
3-3	A	Ohio State	4-3(OT)	W
3-4	H	Miami	6-3	W
3-10	H	Illinois-Chicago	~6-4	W
3-11	H	Illinois-Chicago	~4-2	W
3-18	A	Bowling Green	~4-3(OT)	W

1995-1996 (28-13-1; 22-7-1 in CCHA: 3rd)

Coach: Ron Mason

10-13	A_GWF	Boston College	5-2	W
10-15	A_GWF	Maine	3-4	L
10-20	A	Miami	6-3	W
10-21	A	Bowling Green	2-6	L
10-26	H	Lake Superior	1-4	L
10-28	A	Ferris State	6-3	W
10-31	H	Notre Dame	6-2	W
11-3	H	Cornell	6-2	W
11-10	H	Ohio State	4-3(OT)	W
11-11	H	Illinois-Chicago	6-0	W
11-17	H	Miami	3-0	W
11-18	H	Miami	6-5(OT)	W
11-24	A_CHS	Minnesota	5-6(OT)	L
11-25	A_CHS	Wisconsin	5-4	W
11-28	H	Michigan	4-3	W
12-1	A	Ohio State	5-2	W
12-2	A	Ohio State	5-1	W
12-8	H	Western Michigan	3-0	W
12-9	H	Lake Superior	0-3	L
12-29	A_GLI	Michigan Tech	3-2(OT)	W
12-30	A_GLI	Michigan	1-3	L
1-4	A	Alaska Fairbanks	4-3	W
1-5	A	Alaska Fairbanks	3-2	W
1-6	A	Alaska Fairbanks	4-2	W
1-19	H	Bowling Green	4-2	W
1-20	H	Ferris State	5-4	W
1-26	A	Illinois-Chicago	7-3	W
1-27	A	Illinois-Chicago	3-0	W
2-2	H	Ferris State	7-2	W
2-3	H	Notre Dame	7-1	W
2-9	A	Western Michigan	1-7	L
2-10	H	Western Michigan	3-2	W
2-16	A_DE	Lake Superior	4-3	W
2-17	A_DE	Michigan	1-8	L
2-20	A	Notre Dame	4-4(OT)	T
2-22	H	Team Canada (ex)	1-7	L
2-29	H	Bowling Green	1-5	L
3-1	A	Michigan	0-3	L
3-8	H	Ferris State	~3-2(OT)	W
3-9	H	Ferris State	~3-5	L
3-10	H	Ferris State	~3-1	W
3-15	A	Michigan	~2-6	L
3-23	A	U. Mass-Lowell	**2-6	L

1996-1997 (23-13-4; 16-7-4 in CCHA: 3rd)

Coach: Ron Mason

10-12	H	Western Ontario	7-2	W
10-19	H	Western Michigan	3-1	W
19-22	H	Ferris State	7-2	W
10-25	A	Boston College	3-4	L
10-27	A	Northeastern	5-6	L
11-1	H	Bowling Green	8-2	W
11-2	H	Michigan	5-4	W
11-8	H	Alaska-Fairbanks	2-5	L
11-9	H	Alaska Fairbanks	5-3	W
11-15	A	Michigan	1-5	L
11-16	A	Ferris State	7-3	W
11-22	A	Miami	4-3	W
11-23	A	Bowling Green	5-3	W
11-29	A_CHS	Wisconsin	3-1	W
11-30	A_CHS	Minnesota	3-5	L
12-6	H	Notre Dame	4-3	W
12-27	A_GLI	Lake Superior	0-5	L
12-28	A_GLI	Michigan Tech	4-3	W
12-31	H	Colorado College	6-2	W
1-10	A	Lake Superior	4-4(OT)	T
1-11	A	Lake Superior	4-4(OT)	T
1-14	H	Alaska-Fairbanks	3-1	W
1-21	A_GR	Ferris State	3-3(OT)	T
1-24	H	Ohio State	3-0	W

1-25	H	Ohio State	2-3	L
1-28	A	Notre Dame	3-0	W
1-31	A	Western Michigan	2-3(OT)	L
2-7	A	Western Michigan	2-5	L
2-8	A_DE	Michigan	2-0	W
2-14	H	Miami	1-2	L
2-15	H	Lake Superior	6-3	W
2-22	A	Miami	7-3	W
2-23	A	Ohio State	3-8	L
2-28	A	Notre Dame	3-2	W
3-1	A	Bowling Green	0-0(OT)	T
3-7	H	Western Michigan	~4-1	W
3-8	H	Western Michigan	~3-1	W
3-14	A	Miami	~4-3(OT)	W
3-15	A	Michigan	~1-3	L
3-22	A	Minnesota	**3-6	L

1997-1998 (33-6-5; 21-5-4 in CCHA: 1st)

Coach: Ron Mason

10-4	H	Guelph	3-3(OT)	T
10-10	A_CIB	Boston University	3-1	W
10-11	A_CIB	Wisconsin	2-1	W
10-17	H	Western Michigan	2-2(OT)	T
10-18	H	Western Michigan	2-0	W
10-25	A	Michigan	4-2	W
10-28	A_GR	Ferris State	6-1	W
10-31	A	Notre Dame	5-1	W
11-1	H	Notre Dame	1-6	L
11-8	H	Notre Dame	3-1	W
11-14	H	Mankato State	5-2	W
11-15	H	Mankato State	4-0	W
11-21	A	Ohio State	2-1	W
11-22	H	Bowling Green	5-2	W
11-28	H_CHS	Wisconsin	2-0	W
11-30	H_CHS	Minnesota	3-2	W
12-6	H	Bowling Green	4-2	W
12-7	H	Bowling Green	0-1	L
12-27	A_GLI	Michigan Tech	3-1	W
12-28	A_GLI	Michigan	5-3	W
1-2	A	Alaska-Fairbanks	4-6	L
1-3	A	Alaska-Fairbanks	6-2	W
1-9	H	Northern Michigan	1-1(OT)	T
1-10	H	Northern Michigan	6-1	W
1-16	H	Alaska-Fairbanks	6-1	W
1-17	A	Ferris State	7-0	W
1-24	H	Lake Superior	4-3	W
1-30	H	Miami	1-1(OT)	T
1-31	H	Miami	7-0	W
2-6	A	Ohio State	2-4	L
2-7	A	Miami	0-0(OT)	T
2-13	H	Western Michigan	4-2	W
2-14	H	Ohio State	4-1	W
2-20	H	Michigan	5-1	W
2-21	A_DE	Michigan	4-1	W
2-27	H	Lake Superior	4-2	W
2-28	H	Ferris State	6-3	W
3-6	A	Lake Superior	4-1	W
3-7	A	Northern Michigan	1-5	L
3-13	H	Ferris State	~3-1	W
3-14	H	Ferris State	~2-1	W
2-20	A	Northern Michigan	~5-1	W
2-21	A	Ohio State	~3-2(OT)	W
2-28	A	Ohio State	**3-4(OT)	L

1998-1999 (29-6-7; 20-3-7 in CCHA: 1st; Frozen Four in NCAAs)

Coach: Ron Mason

10-13	H	Western Ontario	5-0 (ex)	W
10-16	H	Western Michigan	1-1(OT)	T
10-17	H	Massachusetts	3-1	W
10-23	A	Bowling Green	7-1	W
10-24	H	Ohio State	4-4(OT)	T
10-30	H	Northern Michigan	3-1	W
11-6	H	Ohio State	3-1	W
11-7	H	Lake Superior	2-1	W
11-13	A	Ohio State	2-3	L
11-14	A	Miami	5-0	W

Date		Opponent	Score	
11-20	A	Michigan	1-2	L
11-21	A	Western Michigan	4-1	W
11-27	A$_{CHS}$	Wisconsin	3-1	W
11-29	A$_{CHS}$	Minnesota	1-2	L
12-4	H	Nebraska-Omaha	2-0	W
12-5	H	Nebraska-Omaha	3-1	W
12-12	H	Northern Michigan	2-1	W
12-26	A$_{GLI}$	Northern Michigan	5-3	W
12-27	A$_{GLI}$	Michigan	3-1	W
1-1	A	Alaska-Fairbanks	4-1	W
1-2	A	Alaska-Fairbanks	3-1	W
1-3	A	Alaska-Fairbanks	5-0	W
1-8	H	Miami	5-1	W
1-9	H	Bowling Green	3-1	W
1-15	A	Bowling Green	2-2(OT)	T
1-16	A$_{CI}$	Miami	5-1	W
1-22	A	Lake Superior	4-1	W
1-23	A	Northern Michigan	1-1(OT)	T
1-29	H	Michigan	3-3(OT)	T
2-5	A	Notre Dame	2-2(OT)	T
2-6	A$_{DE}$	Lake Superior	3-2	W
2-12	H	Notre Dame	1-0	W
2-19	H	Notre Dame	3-1	W
2-20	A$_{DE}$	Michigan	3-1	W
2-26	A	Ferris State	1-1(OT)	T
2-27	H	Western Michigan	4-2	W
3-5	H	Ferris State	4-1	W
3-6	H	Ferris State	1-2	L
3-12	H	Lake Superior	~3-2	W
3-13	H	Lake Superior	~4-0	W
3-19	A	Northern Michigan	~3-5	L
3-28	A	Colorado College	**4-3	W
4-1	A	New Hampshire	**3-5	L

1999-2000 (27-11-4; 18-8-2 in CCHA: 2nd)
Coach: Ron Mason

Date		Opponent	Score	
10-5	H	Guelph	11-1 (ex)	W
10-9	A	Colorado College	1-4	L
10-15	A	Nebraska-Omaha	5-2	W
10-16	A	Nebraska-Omaha	6-2	W
10-22	H	Ohio State	1-0	W
10-23	H	Ohio State	6-0	W
10-29	H	Ferris State	4-1	W
10-30	A	Ferris State	4-1	W
11-5	A	Alaska Fairbanks	5-1	W
11-6	A	Alaska Fairbanks	3-0	W
11-12	H	Bowling Green	3-1	W
11-13	H	Bowling Green	5-2	W
11-19	A	Miami	2-3	L
11-20	A	Miami	0-3	L
11-26	H$_{CHS}$	Wisconsin	1-5	L
11-27	H$_{CHS}$	Minnesota	6-2	W
12-4	A	Notre Dame	0-1	L
12-5	H	Notre Dame	4-1	W
12-11	H	Alabama-Huntsville	5-0	W
12-29	A$_{GLI}$	Michigan Tech	6-3	W
12-30	A$_{GLI}$	Michigan	3-1	W
1-7	H	Michigan	0-2	L
1-13	H	Nebraska-Omaha	3-4(OT)	L
1-14	H	Nebraska-Omaha	3-1	W
1-21	H	Rensselaer	2-2(OT)	T
1-22	H	Rensselaer	4-1	W
1-28	A	Western Michigan	2-2(OT)	T
1-29	A	Western Michigan	2-3(OT)	L
2-3	A	Lake Superior	3-0	W
2-5	A$_{DE}$	Lake Superior	1-3	L
2-11	H	Northern Michigan	3-2(OT)	W
2-12	H	Northern Michigan	2-0	W
2-18	H	Alaska Fairbanks	3-1	W
2-19	H	Alaska Fairbanks	5-2	W
2-25	A	Michigan	2-4	L
2-26	A$_{DE}$	Michigan	3-3(OT)	T
3-3	A	Notre Dame	4-4(OT)	T
3-4	H	Notre Dame	5-3	W
3-10	H	Miami	~6-2	W
3-11	H	Miami	~5-1	W
3-17	A	Notre Dame	~4-0	W
3-18	A	Nebraska-Omaha	~6-0	W
3-24	A	Boston College	**5-6(OT)	L

2000-2001 (33-5-4; 21-4-3 in CCHA: 1st)
Coach: Ron Mason

Date		Opponent	Score	
9-29	H	USA Under-18 Team	(ex)	L
10-5	H	Western Ontario	6-0 (ex)	W
10-13	A$_{NJC}$	Alaska-Anchorage	5-4	W
10-14	A$_{NJC}$	Merimack	1-1(OT)	T
10-20	H	Nebraska-Omaha	1-2	L
10-21	H	Nebraska-Omaha	4-1	W
10-26	A	Notre Dame	5-1	W
10-27	A	Notre Dame	3-2	W
11-4	A	Michigan	1-0	W
11-9	H	Northern Michigan	3-2	W
11-10	H	Northern Michigan	4-1	W
11-17	H	Western Michigan	2-2(OT)	T
11-21	H	Lake Superior State	5-0	W
11-24	A$_{CHS}$	Minnesota	3-2	W
11-26	A$_{CHS}$	Wisconsin	6-2	W
12-1	A	Bowling Green	3-3(OT)	T
12-2	A	Bowling Green	3-1	W
12-8	A	Ferris State	0-0(OT)	T
12-9	H	Ferris State	4-1	W
12-29	A$_{GLI}$	Boston College	4-1	W
12-30	A$_{GLI}$	Michigan Tech	3-2(OT)	W
1-5	H	Yale	5-0	W
1-6	H	Yale	4-0	W
1-12	A	Lake Superior State	2-0	W
1-14	A	Lake Superior State	2-1(OT)	W
1-19	H	Miami	1-0	W
1-20	H	Miami	5-0	W
1-23	A	Lake Superior State	3-0	W
1-27	A$_{DE}$	Michigan	3-4(OT)	L
2-2	A	Northern Michigan	2-3	L
2-3	A	Northern Michigan	2-1	W
2-9	A	Alaska Fairbanks	4-1	W
2-10	A	Alaska Fairbanks	3-0	W
2-16	A	Western Michigan	2-4	L
2-17	A$_{DE}$	Michigan	4-2	W
2-23	A	Ohio State	5-2	W
2-24	A	Ohio State	7-2	W
3-1	H	Michigan	3-1	W
3-9	H	Alaska Fairbanks	~5-2	W
3-10	H	Alaska Fairbanks	~3-2(OT)	W
3-16	A	Bowling Green	~2-1	W
3-17	A	Michigan	~2-0	W
3-25	A	Wisconsin	**5-1	W
4-4	A	North Dakota	**0-2	L

2001-2002 (27-9-5; 18-6-4 in CCHA: 2nd)
Coach: Ron Mason

Date		Opponent	Score	
9-29	H	Queens University	14-1(ex)	W
10-6	H	Michigan (Cold War)	3-3	T
10-11	H	Lake Superior State	5-0	W
10-12	H	Lake Superior State	6-1	W
10-20	H	Ferris State	2-0	W
10-26	A	Nebraska-Omaha	3-4	L
10-27	A	Nebraska-Omaha	1-5	L
11-1	H	Bowling Green	6-3	W
11-2	H	Bowling Green	4-0	W
11-9	H	Mass.-Amherst	6-1	W
11-16	H	Miami	3-0	W
11-17	H	Miami	2-0	W
11-23	H	Minnesota	3-4	L
11-25	H	Wisconsin	4-4(OT)	T
11-30	A	Alaska-Fairbanks	1-2	L
12-1	A	Alaska-Fairbanks	5-1	W
12-7	A	Northern Michigan	4-2	W
12-8	A	Northern Michigan	3-0	W
12-28	A$_{DE}$	Michigan Tech	4-1	W
12-29	A$_{DE}$	North Dakota	4-5(OT)	L
1-4	H	Quinnipiac	4-1	W
1-5	H	Quinnipiac	3-1	W
1-11	H	Western Michigan	6-3	W
1-12	A	Western Michigan	0-2	L
1-15	A	Ferris State	3-2	W
1-19	A	Michigan	1-1	T
1-25	H	Ohio State	3-1	W
1-26	H	Ohio State	5-1	W
2-1	A	Ohio State	3-3	T
2-2	A	Ohio State	3-3	T
2-8	H	Notre Dame	2-0	W
2-9	H	Notre Dame	2-3	L
2-16	A$_{DE}$	Michigan	3-1	W
2-22	H	Miami	3-1	W
2-23	H	Miami	4-3	W
3-1	A	Ferris State	2-3	L
3-2	H	Ferris State	2-0	W
3-8	H	Bowling Green	~4-3(OT)	W
3-9	H	Bowling Green	~4-2	W
3-16	H	Northern Michigan	~2-1	W
3-17	A	Michigan	~2-3	L
3-22	A	Colorado College	**0-2	L

Rick Comley (2002-2003)

On March 25, 2002, it was announced that Rick Comley would become MSU's fifth head hockey coach, replacing Ron Mason. The former Northern Michigan University mentor and Stratford, Ontario, native began his coaching career as an assistant to Mason at Lake Superior State in 1972, following a four-year Laker playing career. He moved into the top spot when Mason headed for Bowling Green in 1973. Following three seasons at his alma mater (1973-1976), Comley accepted the offer to become Nothern's first varsity coach and it was there he spent 26 seasons (1976-2002). His coaching career mark of 597-475-71 (.553) stands seventh on the NCAA's college hockey all-time win list. His most successful season as coach came in 1990-1991 when his squad posted a 38-5-4 record and an NCAA Division I title.

2002-2003 (23-14-2; 18-11-1 in CCHA)
Coach: Rick Comley

Date		Opponent	Score	
10-11	A	Nebraska-Omaha	0-5	L
10-12	A	Nebraska-Omaha	2-1	W
10-18	A	Northern Michigan	4-10	L
10-19	A	Northern Michigan	3-1	W
10-24	H	Lake Superior	7-0	W
10-25	H	Lake Superior	3-2	W
11-8	H	Niagara	1-2	L
11-9	H	Niagara	5-4(OT)	W
11-15	A	Ohio State	2-5	L
11-16	A	Ohio State	1-4	L
11-22	A	Bowling Green	3-4(OT)	L
11-29	A$_{CHS}$	Minnesota	5-5(OT)	T
11-30	A$_{CHS}$	Wisconsin	2-1(OT)	W
12-6	A	Ferris State	6-2	W
12-7	A	Ferris State	3-5	L
12-28	A$_{GLI}$	Boston University	1-6	L
12-29	A$_{GLI}$	Michigan Tech	6-2	W
1-3	A	Lake Superior	1-7	L
1-4	A	Lake Superior	6-0	W
1-10	H	Alaska-Fairbanks	5-2	W
1-11	H	Alaska-Fairbanks	6-2	W
1-17	H	Nebraska-Omaha	5-2	W
1-18	H	Nebraska-Omaha	7-0	W
1-24	A	Notre Dame	2-1	W
1-25	A	Notre Dame	3-3(OT)	T
1-31	H	Miami	3-5	L
2-1	H	Miami	3-2	W
2-8	A	Bowling Green	6-3	W
2-14	A	Michigan	1-3	L
2-15	H	Michigan	5-3	W
2-21	H	Northern Michigan	7-4	W
2-22	H	Northern Michigan	2-4	L
2-28	A	Michigan	4-0	W
3-1	A	Michigan	1-3	L
3-7	A	Western Michigan	4-0	W
3-8	H	Western Michigan	8-5	W
3-14	H	Alaska-Fairbanks	~11-1	W
3-15	H	Alaska-Fairbanks	~3-1	W
3-2	A	Northern Michigan	~5-7	L

Year-by-Year Leaders

GOALS

Yrs.	Total	
49-50	Don Kauppi	
	Bill McCormick	6
50-51	Bill McCormick	11
51-52	Weldon Olson	13
52-53	Weldon Olson	18
53-54	Weldon Olson	19
54-55	Weldon Olson	21
55-56	Gene Grazia	
	Ross Parke	15
56-57	Ross Parke	12
57-58	Ross Parke	19
58-59	Terry Moroney	23
59-60	Jack Roberts	8
60-61	Art Thomas	17
61-62	Claude Fournel	20
62-63	Bob Doyle	
	Dick Johnstone	15
63-64	Doug Roberts	21
64-65	Mike Jacobson	29
65-66	Doug Volmar	26
66-67	Tom Mikkola	
	Doug Volmar	21
67-68	Nino Crisofoli	16
68-69	Ken Anstey	
	Bill Watt	13
69-70	Gilles Gagnon	
	Don Thompson	14
70-71	Gilles Gagnon	27
71-72	Don Thompson	32
72-73	Steve Colp	35
73-74	Steve Colp	43
74-75	Tom Ross	38
75-76	Tom Ross	51
76-77	Russ Welch	22
77-78	Leo Lynett	18
78-79	Joe Omiccioli	20
79-80	Leo Lynett	27
80-81	Mark Hamway	18
81-82	Mark Hamway	34
82-83	Mark Hamway	30
83-84	Kelly Miller	28
84-85	Craig Simpson	31
85-86	Mike Donnelly	59
86-87	Mitch Messier	44
87-88	Bobby Reynolds	42
88-89	Bobby Reynolds	36
89-90	Kip Miller	48
90-91	Shawn Heaphy	30
91-92	Dwayne Norris	44
92-93	Bryan Smolinski	31
93-94	Anson Carter	30
94-95	Anson Carter	34
95-96	Anson Carter	23
96-97	Mike Watt	24
97-98	Sean Berens	36
98-99	Mike York	22
99-00	Adam Hall	26
00-01	John Nail	20
01-02	Adam Hail	19
02-03	Jim Slater	18

ASSISTS

49-50	Bob Gorman	7
50-51	Neil Brostol	
	Dick Lord	
	Bob Revou	9
51-52	Jak Mayes	18
52-53	Steve Raz	18
53-54	Weldon Olson	22
54-55	Jim Ward	28
55-56	Ross Parke	21
56-57	Ross Parke	13
57-58	Joe Polono	23

58-59	Dick Hamilton	26
59-60	Andre LaCoste	8
60-61	Real Turcotte	28
61-62	Real Turcotte	25
62-63	Dick Johnstone	14
63-64	MacOrme	25
64-65	Doug Roberts	33
65-66	Doug Volmar	28
66-67	Tom Mikkola	
	Sandy McAndrews	25
67-68	Ken Anstey	19
68-69	Ken Anstey	20
69-70	Don Thompson	18
70-71	Don Thompson	38
71-72	Don Thompson	35
72-73	Bob Boyd	41
73-74	Norm Barnes	56
74-75	Tom Ross	59
75-76	Steve Colp	
	Tom Ross	54
76-77	Jim Cunningham	25
77-78	Russ Welch	23
78-79	Russ Welch	30
79-80	Russ Welch	37
80-81	Gary Haight	17
81-82	Newell Brown	51
82-83	Newell Brown	
	Mark Hamway	29
83-84	Craig Simpson	43
84-85	Craig Simpson	53
85-86	Kevin Miller	52
86-87	Kevin Miller	56
87-88	Steve Beadle	37
88-89	Kip Miller	45
89-90	Pat Murray	60
90-91	Jason Woolley	44
91-92	Peter White	51
92-93	Bryan Smolinski	37
93-94	Steve Guolla	46
94-95	Rem Murray	36
95-96	Mike York	27
96-97	Mike York	29
97-98	Mike York	34
98-99	Mike York	32
99-00	Shawn Horcoff	51
00-01	Rustyn Dolyne	26
01-02	John-Michael Liles	22
02-03	John-Michael Liles	32

TOTAL POINTS

49-50	Don Kauppi	11
50-51	Bill McCormick	18
51-52	Jack Mayes	29
52-53	Jack Mayes	30
53-54	Weldon Olson	41
54-55	Jim Ward	43
55-56	Ross Parke	36
56-57	Ross Parke	25
57-58	Ross Parke	36
58-59	Joe Polano	41
59-60	Jack Roberts	14
60-61	Real Turcotte	43
61-62	Claude Fournel	35
62-63	Dick Johnstone	29
63-64	Mac Orme	40
64-65	Doug Roberts	61
65-66	Doug Volmar	54
66-67	Tom Mikkola	46
67-68	Ken Anstey	30
68-69	Ken Anstey	33
69-70	Don Thompson	32
70-71	Don Thompson	57
71-72	Don Thompson	67
72-73	Steve Colp	60
73-74	Steve Colp	97
74-75	Tom Ross	97
75-76	Tom Ross	105
76-77	Russ Welch	44

77-78	Russ Welch	40
78-79	Russ Welch	46
79-80	Leo Lynett	61
80-81	Mark Hamway	33
81-82	Newell Brown	73
82-83	Mark Hamway	59
83-84	Craig Simpson	57
84-85	Craig Simpson	84
85-86	Mike Donnelly	97
86-87	Mitch Messier	92
87-88	Bobby Reynolds	67
88-89	Bobby Reynolds	
	Kip Miller	77
89-90	Kip Miller	101
90-91	Jason Woolley	59
91-92	Dwayne Norris	83
92-93	Bryan Smolinski	68
93-94	Steve Guolla	69
94-95	Rem Murray	56
95-96	Anson Carter	43
96-97	Mike York	47
97-98	Mike York	61
98-99	Mike York	54
99-00	Shawn Horcoff	65
00-01	Rustyn Dolny	39
01-02	John-Michael Liles	35
02-03	John-Michael Liles	50

PENALTIES

49-50	Jim Doyle	10
50-51	Dick Lord	16
51-52	Dick Lord	28
52-53	Dick Lord	29
53-54	Derio Nicoli	31
54-55	Derio Nicoli	26
55-56	Ellwood Miller	20
56-57	Ed Pollesel	29
57-58	Ed Pollesel	22
58-59	Ed Pollesel	33
59-60	Mel Christofferson	20
60-61	Marty Quirk	25
61-62	Jim Jacobson	22
62-63	Jim Jacobson	30
63-64	Jim Jacobson	30
64-65	Bob Brawley	28
65-66	Tom Purdo	
	Doug Volmar	27
66-67	Doug Volmar	38
67-68	Doug French	27
68-69	Bill Watt	21
69-70	Bill Watt	29
70-71	Bob Boyd	40
71-72	Rick Olson	37
72-73	Bob Boyd	50
73-74	Norm Barnes	52
74-75	John Sturges	42
75-76	John Sturges	36
76-77	Ron Heaslip	51
77-78	Jeff Barr	39
78-79	Conrad Wiggin	25
79-80	Ken Leiter	44
80-81	Gary Haight	32
81-82	Newell Brown	33
82-83	Newell Brown	31
83-84	Harvey Smyl	43
84-85	Harvey Smyl	
	Kevin Miller	42
85-86	Kevin Miller	
	Bill Shibicky	52
86-87	Bruce Rendall	52
87-88	Jeff Harding	62
88-89	Don Gibson	52
89-90	Don Gibson	71
90-91	Jim Cummins	37
91-92	Nicolas Perreault	37
92-93	Nicolas Perreault	45
93-94	Nicolas Perreault	50
94-95	Tony Tuzzolino	36

95-96	Tony Tuzzolino	52
96-97	Mike Watt	49
97-98	Chris Bogas	36
98-99	Sean Patchell	37
99-00	Brian Maloney	34
00-01	Brian Maloney	31
01-02	Brian Maloney	34
02-02	Brian Maloney	24

PENALTY MINUTES

49-50	Jim Doyle	20
50-51	Dick Lord	48
51-52	Dick Lord	59
52-53	Derio Nicoli	60
53-54	Derio Nicoli	65
54-55	Derio Nicoli	73
55-56	Ellwood Miller	56
56-57	Ed Pollesel	63
57-58	Fred Devuono	50
58-59	Ed Pollesel	70
59-60	Ed Ozybko	48
60-61	Marty Quirk	50
61-62	Jim Jacobson	44
62-63	Jim Jacobson	79
63-64	Jim Jacobson	79
64-65	Bob Brawley	59
65-66	Tom Purdo	57
66-67	Doug Volmar	100
67-68	Dick Bois	56
68-69	Bill Watt	45
69-70	Bill Watt	72
70-71	Bob Boyd	88
71-72	Rick Olson	85
72-73	Bob Boyd	124
73-74	Norm Barnes	107
74-75	John Sturges	93
75-76	John Sturges	80
76-77	Ron Heaslip	134
77-78	Jeff Barr	85
78-79	Ted Heusing	68
79-80	Ken Leiter	96
80-81	Gary Haight	64
81-82	Gary Haight	75
82-83	Newell Brown	70
83-84	Harvey Smyl	92
84-85	Harvey Smyl	100
85-86	Kevin Miller	112
86-87	Bruce Rendall	113
87-88	Jeff Harding	129
88-89	Don Gibson	107
89-90	Don Gibson	167
90-91	Jim Cummings	110
91-92	Joby Messier	85
92-93	Bryan Smolinski	91
93-94	Nicolas Perreault	109
94-95	Tony Tuzzolino	81
95-96	Tony Tuzzolino	120
96-97	Tony Tuzzolino	120
97-98	Chris Bogas	75
98-99	Chris Bogas	86
99-00	Brian Maloney	87
00-01	Brian Maloney	86
01-02	Brian Maloney	71
02-03	David Booth	51

GOALIE SAVES

49-50	Delmar Reid	453
50-51	Delmar Reid	484
51-52	Delmar Reid	373
52-53	Gerald Bergin	409
53-54	Ed Schiller	597
54-55	Ed Schiller	728
55-56	Ed Schiller	772
56-57	Joe Selinger	525
57-58	Joe Selinger	678
58-59	Joe Selinger	770
59-60	Eldon VanSpybrook	790

60-61	John Chandik	439
61-62	John Chandik	721
62-63	John Chandik	699
63-64	Harry Woolf	560
64-65	Jerry Fisher	517
65-66	Gaye Cooley	521
66-67	Gaye Cooley	823
67-68	Bob Johnson	564
68-69	Rick Duffett	456
69-70	Rick Duffett	715
70-71	Jim Watt	766
71-72	Jim Watt	1,116
72-73	Ron Clark	867
73-74	Gary Carr	989
74-75	Ron Clark	1,400
75-76	Dave Versical	1,410
76-77	Dave Versical	941
77-78	Dave Versical	757
78-79	Mark Mazzoleni	583
79-80	Mark Mazzoleni	763
80-81	Ron Scott	1,003
81-82	Ron Scott	992
82-83	Ron Scott	899
83-84	Norm Foster	734
84-85	Norm Foster	505
85-86	Norm Foster	623
86-87	Norm Foster	545
87-88	Jason Muzzatti	775
88-89	Jason Muzzatti	898
89-90	Jason Muzzatti	795
90-91	Mike Gilmore	492
91-92	Mike Gilmore	736
92-93	Mike Buzak	877
93-94	Mike Buzak	964
94-95	Mike Buzak	856
95-96	Chad Alban	822
96-97	Chad Alban	876
97-98	Chad Alban	869
97-98	Chad Alban	798
98-99	Joe Blackburn	667
99-00	Ryan Miller	537
00-01	Ryan Miller	1,024
01-02	Ryan Miller	1,039
02-03	Matt Migliaccio	892

GOALS AGAINST AVERAGE

49-50	Delmar Reid	11.20/ 10 games
50-51	Delmar Reid	5.80/ 15 games
51-52	Delmar Reid	5.73/ 15 games
52-53	Gerald Bergin	5.28/ 14 games
53-54	Ed Schiller	3.73/ 16 games
54-55	Ed Schiller	4.58/ 24 games
55-56	Ed Schiller	4.28/ 21 games
56-57	Joe Selinger	3.40/ 20 games
57-58	Joe Selinger	3.27/ 23 games
58-59	Joe Selinger	2.67/ 24 games
59-60	Eldon VanSpybrook	5.42/ 24 games
60-61	John Chandik	3.53/ 15 games
61-62	John Chandik	3.79/ 25 games
62-63	John Chandik	4.30/ 21games
63-64	Harry Woolf	4.33/ 20 games
64-65	Alex Terpay	2.54/ 11 games
	Jerry Fisher	4.40/ 18 games
65-66	Gaye Cooley	3.11/ 18 games
66-67	Gaye Cooley	4.00/ 24 games
67-68	Rick Duffett	3.40/ 13 games
	Bob Johnson	4.10/ 17 games
68-69	Rick Duffett	2.74/ 16 games
69-70	Rick Duffett	4.10/ 24 games
70-71	Jim Watt	4.08/ 25 games
71-72	Jim Watt	3.55/ 36 games
72-73	Ron Clark	3.96/ 28 games
73-74	Gary Carr	4.43/ 28 games
74-75	Ron Clark	4.31/ 39 games
75-76	Dave Versical	4.32/ 38 games
76-77	Dave Versical	5.43/ 26 games
77-78	Mark Mazzoleni	5.36/ 14 games
	Dave Versical	5.64/ 14 games

78-79	Doug Belland	5.07/ 18 games
	Mark Mazzoleni	5.51/ 19 games
79-80	Mark Mazzoleni	5.81/ 23 games
80-81	Ron Scott	3.89/ 33 games
81-82	Ron Scott	2.85/ 39 games
82-83	Ron Scott	2.64/ 40 games
83-84	Norm Foster	2.74/ 32 games
84-85	Bob Essensa	1.64/ 18 games
85-86	Bob Essensa	3.33/ 23 games
86-87	Bob Essensa	2.78/ 25 games
87-88	Jason Muzzatti	3.41/ 33 games
88-89	Jason Muzzatti	3.03/ 42 games
89-90	Mike Gilmore	2.73/ 12 games
	Jason Muzzatti	3.01/ 33 games
90-91	Mike Gilmore	2.66/ 22 games
	Jason Muzzatti	3.74/ 22 games
91-92	Mike Gilmore	3.07/ 36 games
92-93	Mike Buzak	2.93/ 38 games
93-94	Mike Buzak	2.72/ 39 games
94-95	Chad Alban	2.73/ 13 games
	Mike Buzak	3.14/ 31 games
95-96	Chad Alban	3.07/ 40 games
96-97	Chad Alban	2.71/ 39 games
97-98	Chad Alban	1.57/ 40 games
98-99	Joe Blackburn	1.55/ 33 games
99-00	Ryan Miller	1.53/ 26 games
00-01	Ryan Miller	1.32/ 40 games
01-02	Ryan Miller	1.77/ 40 games
02-03	Matt Migliaccio	2.48/ 34 games

Career Records

TOTAL POINTS

1. Tom Ross (1972-76) 324
2. Steve Colp (1972-76) 300
3. Kip Miller (1986-90) 261
4. Peter White (1988-92) 230
5. Daryl Rice(1972-76) 225
6. Bill Shibicky (1983-87) 222
7. Dwayne Norris (1988-82) 218
   Rem Murray (1991-95) 218
8. Mitch Messier (1983-87) 210
9. John Sturges (1972-76) 209
10. Newell Brown (1980-84) 202

TOTAL GOALS

1. Tom Ross (1972-76) 138
2. Steve Colp (1972-76) 132
3. Kip Miller (1986-90) 116
4. Mike Donnelly (1982-86) 110
5. Bobby Reynolds (1985-89) 107
6. Anson Carter (1992-96) 106
7. Dwayne Norris (1988-92) 105
8. Shawn Heaphy (1987-91) 103
9. Mark Hamway (1979-83) 98
10 Daryl Rice (1972-76) 96

TOTAL ASSISTS

1. Tom Ross (1972-76) 186
2. Steve Colp (1972-76) 168
3. Peter White (1988-92) 155
4. Rem Murray (1991-95) 147
5. Kip Miller (1984-88) 145
6. Kevin Miller (1984-88) 140
7. Bill Shibicky (1983-87) 135
8. John Sturges (1972-76) 132
9. Steve Suk (1991-95) 130
10. Daryl Rice (1972-75) 129

TOTAL SAVES

1. Dave Versical (1975-78) 3,108
2. Jason Muzzatti (1987-91) 2,928
3. Ron Scott (1980-83) 2,884
4. Mike Buzak (1991-95) 2,836

5. Chad Alban (1994-98) 2,735
6. Ron Clark (1971-75) 2,430
7. Norm Foster (1983-87 2,407
8. Ed Shiller (1953-56) 2,097
9. Mark Mazzoleni (1976-80) 2,094
10. Joe Selinger (1956-59) 1,973

SAVES-PER-GAME AVERAGE
(Minimum of 30 games)
1. Dave Versical (1975-78) 35.4
2. Ron Clark (1971-75) 34.1
3. Ed Shiller (1953-56) 33.1
4. Mark Mazzoleni (1975-80) 32.9
5. Del Reid (1950-52) 32.8

GOALS AGAINST AVERAGE
(Minimum of 30 games)
1. Ryan Miller (1999-02) 1.40
2. Joe Blackburn (1997-01) 1.76
3. Matt Migliaccio (2002-03) 2.22
4. Chad Alban (1994-98) 2.46
5. Bob Essensa (1983-87) 2.68
6. Mike Gilmorer (1988-92) 2.91
7. Mike Buzak (1991-95) 2.98
8. Ron Scott (1980-83) 3.08
9. Joe Selinger (1956-59) 3.09
10. Norm Foster (1983-87) 3.14

TOTAL PENALTIES
1. Don Gibson (1986-90) 218
2. Bill Shibicky (1983-87) 159
3. Tony Tuzzolino (1993-97) 154
4. Nicolas Perreault (1991-94) 148
5. Kip Miller (1986-90) 137
6. Kevin Miller (1984-88) 134
7. Bob Boyd (1970-73) 126
8. Jeff Parker (1983-86) 123
9. John Sturges (1972-75) 123
10. Brian Maloney (2002-03) 123

TOTAL PENALTY MINUTES
1. Don Gibson (1986-90) 466
2. Tony Tuzzolino (1993-97) 371
3. Bill Shibicky (1983-87) 323
4. Nicolas Perreault (1991-94) 308
5. Jim Cummins (1988-91) 304
6. Kip Miller (1986-90) 299
7. Brian Maloney (2002-03) 292
8. John Sturges (1972-76) 287
9. Bob Boyd (1970-73) 286
10. Brad Hodgins (1996-00) 281

Season Records

TOTAL POINTS
1. Tom Ross (1975-76) 105
2. Kip Miller (1989-90) 101
3. Mike Donnelly (1985-86) 97
4. Tom Ross (1974-75) 97
5. Steve Colp (1973-74) 97
6. Steve Colp (1975-76) 94
7. Mitch Messier (1986-87) 92
8. Tom Ross (1973-74) 88
9. Craig Simpson (1984-85) 84
10. Pat Murray (1989-90) 84

TOTAL GOALS
1. Mike Donnelly (1985-86) 59
2. Tom Ross (1975-76) 51
3. Kip Miller (1989-90) 48
4. Dwayne Norris (1991-92) 44

Mitch Messier (1986-87) 44
6. Bill Shibicky (1986-87) 43
Steve Colp (1973-74) 43
8. Bobby Reynolds (1987-88) 42
9. Steve Colp (1975-76) 40
10. Tom Ross (1974-75) 38

TOTAL ASSISTS
1. Pat Murray (1988-89) 60
2. Tom Ross (1974-75) 59
3. Kevin Miller (1986-87) 56
4. Norm Barnes (1973-74) 56
5. Tom Ross (1975-76) 54
6. Steve Colp (1975-76) 54
7. Steve Colp (1973-74) 54
8. Kip Miller (1989-90) 53
9. Craig Simpson (1984-85) 53
10. Kevin Miller (1985-86) 52
11. John Sturgis (1974-75) 52
12. Newell Brown (1981-82) 52

GOALIE SAVES
1. Dave Versical (1974-75) 1,410
2. Ron Clark (1974-75) 1,400
3. Jim Watt (1971-72) 1,116
4. Ryan Miller (2000-01) 1,024
4. Ron Scott (1980-81) 1,003
5. Ron Scott (1981-82) 992
6. Gary Carr (1973-74) 989
7. Dave Versical (1976-77) 941
8. Jason Muzzatti (1988-89) 898
9. Matt Migliaccio (2002-03) 892
10. Ron Scott (1982-83) 889

SAVES-PER-GAME AVERAGE
(Minimum 0f 15 games)
1. Ed Schiller (1953-54) 39.0
2. Dave Versical (1975-76) 37.8
3. Dave Versical (1976-77) 37.0
4. Ed Schiller (1955-56) 36.8
5. Gary Carr (1973-74) 35.3
6. Ron Clark (1974-75) 35.0
7. Gaye Cooley (1966-67) 34.7

GOALS AGAINST AVERAGE
(Minimum of 15 games)
1. Ryan Miller (200-01) 1.32
2. Ryan Miller (1999-00) 1.53
3. Joe Blackburn (1998-99) 1.55
4. Chad Alban (1997-98) 1.57
5. Bob Essensa (1984-85) 1.64
6. Joe Blackburn (199-00) 2.17
7. Matt Migliaccio (2002-03) 2.35
8. Norm Foster (1984-85) 2.63
9. Ron Scott (1982-83) 2.64
10. Mike Gilmore (1990-91) 2.66

TOTAL PENALTIES
1. Don Gibson (1989-90) 71
2. Jeff Harding (1987-88) 62
3. Don Gibson (1987-88) 58
4. Bruce Rendall (1986-87) 52
5. Kevin Miller (1985-86) 52
6. Bill Shibicky (1985-86) 52
7. Norm Barnes (1973-74) 52
8. Don Gibson (1983-84) 52
9. Tony Tuzzolino (1995-960) 52
10. Ron Heaslip (1976-77) 51
11. Bob Boyd (1972-73) 50

TOTAL PENALTY MINUTES
1. Don Gibson (1989-90) 167
2. Ron Heaslip (1976-77) 134
3. Jeff Harding (1987-88) 129
4. Bob Boyd (1972-73) 124
5. Tony Tuzzolino (1996-97) 120
6. Tony Tuzzolino (1995-96) 120
7. Don Gibson (1987-88) 118
8. Bruce Rendall (1986-87) 113
9. Kevin Miller (1985-86) 112
10. Jim Cummins (1990-91) 110
11. Norm Varnes (1973-74) 107
12. Don Gibson (1988-89) 107

All-American

Glossary:
F–Forward
D–Defenseman
G–Goalie
NO–Norway Olympic Team
CA–Canada Olympic Team

FIRST TEAM
1959	Joe Selinger	G
1962	John Chandik	G
1964	Carl Lackey	D
1965	Doug Roberts	F
1966	Doug Volmer	F
1969	Ron Duffett	G
1971	Don Thompson	F
1972	Jim Watt	G
1973	Bob Boyd	D
1974	Norm Barnes	D
	Steve Colp	F
1975	Tom Ross	F
1976	Tom Ross	F
1982	Ron Scott	G
1983	Ron Scott	G
1985	Kelly Miller	F
	Craig Simpson	F
	Dan McFall	D
1986	Mike Donnelly	F
1987	Mitch Messier	F
1989	Kip Miller	F
	Bobby Reynolds	F
1990	Kip Miller	F
1991	Jason Woolley	D
1992	Dwayne Norris	F
	Joby Messier	D
1993	Bryan Smolinski	F
1998	Chad Alban	G
	Mike York	F
1999	Joe Blackburn	G
2000	Shawn Horcoff	F
2001	Ryan Miller	G
2002	Ryan Miller	G
2003	John-Michael Liles	D

SECOND TEAM
1984	Dan McFall	D
1985	Gary Haight	D
1986	Don McSween	D
1987	Don McSween	D
1990	Jason Muzzatti	G
1994	Steve Guolla	F
1995	Anson Carter	F
1998	Sean Berens	F
	Tyler Harlton	D
1999	Mike Weaver	D
2000	Mike Weaver	D
2002	Andrew Hutchinson	D
	John-Michael Liles	D
2003	Brad Fast	D

OLYMPIC COMPETITORS

1956	Weldon Olson	silver medal
1960	Weldon Olson	gold medal
1960	Gene Grazia	gold medal
1968	Doug Volmar	did not medal
1984	Gary Haight	did not medal
1988	Geir Hoff NO	did not medal
1988	Kelly Miller	did not medal
1992	Jason Wooley CA	did not medal
1994	Dwayne Norris CA	gold medal
1994	Geir Hoff NO	did not medal

All-CCHA

FIRST TEAM

1982	Ron Scott	G
	Newell Brown	F
1983	Ron Scott	G
	Ken Lieter	D
1984	Dan McFall	D
1985	Bob Essensa	G
	Gary Haight	D
	Don McSween	D
	Craig Simpson	F
	Kelly Miller	F
1986	Don McSween	D
	Mike Donnelly	F
1987	Don McSween	D
	Mitch Messier	F
1988	Tom Tilley	D
1989	Kip Miller	F
1990	Kip Miller	F
	Jason Muzzatti	G
1991	Jason Woolley	D
1992	Dwayne Norris	D
	Joby Messier	D
1993	Bryan Smolinski	F
1994	Anson Carter	F
1995	Anson Carter	F
1998	Chad Alban	G
	Sean Berens	F
	Tyler Harlton	D
1999	Mke Weaver	D
	Mike York	F
2000	Shawn Horcoff	F
	Mike Weaver	D
2001	Ryan Miller	G
2002	Ryan Miller	G
	John-Michael Liles	D
2003	John-Michael Liles	D
	Bradd Fast	D
	Jim Slater	F

SECOND TEAM

1982	Newell Brown	F
	Mark Hamway	F
1983	Gary Haight	D
1984	Norm Foster	G
1985	Dan McFall	D
	Tom Anastos	F
1986	Bob Essensa	G
1987	Bil Shibicky	F
1988	Jason Muzzatti	G
	Bobby Reynolds	F
1989	Bobby Reynolds	F
	Chris Luongo	D
1990	Don Gibson	D
	Pat Murray	F
1991	Mike Gilmore	G
1994	Mike Buzak	G
	Steve Guolla	F
1995	Mike Buzak	G
	Rem Murray	F
1996	Anson Carter	F
1997	Sean Berens	F
1998	Mike York	F

1999	Joe Blackburn	G
2000	Adam Hall	F
2001	Andrew Hutchinson	D
	John-Michael Liles	D
2002	Andrew Hutchinson	D

MVP AWARD

1952	Jack Mayes	F
1953	Weldon Olson	F
1954	Ed Schiller	G
1955	Jim Ward	F
1956	Ed Schiller	G
1957	Bob Jasson	D
1958	Joe Selinger	G
1959	Joe Selinger	G
1960	Eldon VanSpybrook	G
1961	Frank Silka	D
1962	John Chandik	G
1963	Jim Doyle	D
1964	Carl Lackey	G
1965	Doug Roberts	F
1966	Gaye Cooley G.	F
	Mike Coppo	F
1967	Tom Mikkola	F
1968	Ken Anstey	F
1969	Rick Duffett	G
1970	Rick Duffett	G
1971	Gilles Gagnon	F
1972	Jim Watt	G
1973	Bob Boyd	D
1974	Norm Barnes	D
1975	Tom Ross	F
1976	Tom Ross	F
1977	Dave Versicle	G
1978	Dave Versicle	G
1979	Russ Welch	F
1980	Russ Welch	F
1981	Ron Scott	G
1982	Ron Scott	G
1983	Ron Scott	G
1984	Kelly Miller	F
1985	Kelly Miller	F
	Dale Krentz	F
1986	Mike Donnelly	F
1987	Don McSween	D
1988	Tom Tilley	D
1989	Danton Cole	F
1990	Kip Miller	F
1991	Jason Woolley	D
1992	Joby Messier	D
1993	Bryan Smolinski	F
1994	Mike Buzak	G
1995	Rem Murray	F
1996	Chad Alban	G
1997	Chad Alban	G
1998	Chad Alban	F
1999	Mike York	F
2000	Shawn Horcoff	F
2001	Ryan Miller	G
2002	Ryan Miller	G
2003	John-Michael Liles	D

Year-by-Year Record

Year	Conf. GP	W-L-T	Pct.	Total Conf.	W-L-T	Finish	GF	GA	Coach
1922	3	0-3-0	.000				2	17	no coach
1923	6	2-4-0	.333				17	29	no coach
1924				No team organized					
1925	1	0-1-0	.000				3	6	John Kobs
1926	4	0-4-0	.000				5	15	John Kobs
1927	5	2-3-0	.400				7	9	John Kobs
1928	6	3-3-0	.500				6	14	John Kobs
1929	7	3-3-1	.500				23	19	John Kobs
1930	5	1-4-0	.200				5	18	John Kobs
1931	1	0-1-0	.000				1	4	John Kobs
1950	14	0-14-0	.000				27	157	Harold Paulsen
1950-51	17	6-11-0	.353				65	95	Harold Paulsen
1951-52	20	7-13-0	.350	MIHL	3-9-0	6th of 7	72	110	Amo Bessone
1952-53	22	5-16-1	.227	MIHL	2-16-0	7th of 7	74	104	Amo Bessone
1953-54	23	8-14-1	.370	WIHL	4-13-1	6th of 7	92	81	Amo Bessone
1954-55	27	9-17-1	.352	WIHL	5-14-1	7th of 7	89	125	Amo Bessone
1955-56	23	5-18-0	.217	WIHL	1-17-0	7th of 7	55	96	Amo Bessone
1956-57	22	7-15-0	.318	WIHL	5-15-0	7th of 7	62	71	Amo Bessone
1957-58	23	12-11-0	.522	WIHL	9-11-0	5th of 7	98	73	Amo Bessone
1958-59	24	17-6-1	.728	———			115	64	Amo Bessone
1959-60	24	4-18-2	.208	WCHA	4-18-2	7th of 7	54	130	Amo Bessone
1960-61	27	11-16-0	.407	WCHA	5-15-0	6th of 7	121	115	Amo Bessone
1961-62	25	13-11-1	.540	WCHA	6-9-1	4th of 7	98	94	Amo Bessone
1962-63	23	11-12-0	.478	WCHA	6-10-0	(t)5th of 7	90	108	Amo Bessone
1963-64	26	8-17-1	.327	WCHA	6-10-0	7th of 7	100	134	Amo Bessone
1964-65	29	17-12-0	.586	WCHA	8-8-0	4th of 7	165	118	Amo Bessone
1965-66	29	16-13-0	.552	WCHA	9-11-0	6th of 7	123	111	Amo Bessone
1966-67	32	16-15-1	.516	WCHA	8-11-1	5th of 8	119	121	Amo Bessone
1967-68	29	11-16-2	.414	WCHA	6-13-1	6th of 8	92	111	Amo Bessone
1968-69	28	11-16-1	.411	WCHA	7-10-1	6th of 8	78	91	Amo Bessone
1969-70	29	13-16-0	.413	WCHA	10-12-0	7th of 9	112	124	Amo Bessone
1970-71	31	19-12-0	.612	WCHA	12-10-0	4th of 9	152	124	Amo Bessone
1971-72	36	20-16-0	.556	WCHA	15-13-0	(t)4th of 10	154	129	Amo Bessone
1972-73	36	23-12-1	.653	WCHA	16-9-1	4th of 10	194	149	Amo Bessone
1973-74	38	23-14-1	.647	WCHA	15-12-1	4th of 10	207	177	Amo Bessone
1974-75	40	22-17-1	.609	WCHA	19-12-0	5th of 10	191	173	Amo Bessone
1975-76	40	23-15-2	.600	WCHA	20-12-0	2nd of 10	193	176	Amo Bessone
1976-77	36	14-21-1	.403	WCHA	11-20-1	(t)8th of 10	145	189	Amo Bessone
1977-78	36	7-27-2	.222	WCHA	7-23-2	10th of 10	130	201	Amo Bessone
1978-79	36	15-21-0	.417	WCHA	12-20-0	(t)8th of 10	140	192	Amo Bessone
1979-80	38	14-24-0	.368	WCHA	12-16-0	8th of 10	158	227	Ron Mason
1980-81	36	12-22-2	.361	WCHA	7-20-1	10th of 10	116	144	Ron Mason
1981-82	42	26-14-2	.643	CCHA	21-10-1	2nd of 11	184	123	Ron Mason
1982-83	42	30-11-1	.726	CCHA	23-9-0	2nd of 12	187	115	Ron Mason
1983-84	46	34-12-0	.739	CCHA	21-9-0	(t)2nd of 11	241	129	Ron Mason
1984-85	44	38-6-0	.864	CCHA	27-5-0	1st of 9	262	100	Ron Mason
1985-86	45	34-9-2	.777	CCHA	23-7-2	1st of 9	245	161	Ron Mason
1986-87	45	33-10-2	.756	CCHA	23-8-1	2nd of 9	231	156	Ron Mason
1987-88	46	27-16-3	.620	CCHA	18-11-3	3rd of 9	222	173	Ron Mason
1988-89	47	37-9-1	.798	CCHA	25-6-1	1st of 9	277	150	Ron Mason
1989-90	45	35-7-3	.811	CCHA	26-3-3	1st of 9	251	138	Ron Mason
1990-91	40	17-18-5	.488	CCHA	14-13-5	5th of 9	155	130	Ron Mason
1991-92	44	26-10-8	.682	CCHA	18-7-7	3rd of 9	199	143	Ron Mason
1992-93	40	24-14-2	.625	CCHA	18-10-2	4th of 11	169	127	Ron Mason
1993-94	41	23-13-5	.622	CCHA	17-8-5	3rd of 11	155	123	Ron Mason
1994-95	40	25-12-3	.662	CCHA	17-7-3	3rd of 11	183	124	Ron Mason
1995-96	42	28-13-1	.679	CCHA	22-7-1	3rd of 11	154	129	Ron Mason
1996-97	40	23-13-4	.625	CCHA	16-7-4	3rd of 10	145	118	Ron Mason
1997-98	44	33-6-5	.807	CCHA	21-5-4	1st of 11	156	76	Ron Mason
1998-99	42	29-6-7	.774	CCHA	20-3-7	1st of 11	128	64	Ron Mason
1999-00	42	27-11-4	.690	CCHA	18-8-2	2nd of 12	141	76	Ron Mason
2000-01	42	33-5-4	.833	CCHA	21-4-3	1st of 12	134	57	Ron Mason
2001-02	41	27-9-5	.719	CCHA	18-6-4	2nd of 12	129	73	Ron Mason
2002-03	39	23-14-2	.615	CCHA	18-11-1	4th of 12	155	119	Ron Mason
TOTALS	**1896**	**1042-762-92**	**.574**		**695-533-68**		**7853**	**6849**	

ALL-TIME COACHING RECORDS

Coach	Years	W	L	T	Avg.
Turf Kauffman	1970	1	11	0	.083
Ted Swoboda	1971-72	11	16	0	.407
Bob Stevenson	1973	3	9	0	.250
Fred Hartman	1974-76	14	25	0	.359
Nevin Kanner	1977	6	8	0	.429
Kanner & Henderson*	1978-80	27	29	0	.482
Rich Kimball	1981-96	126	112	0	.529
*Nevin Kanner and Boku Henderson co-coaches					
Totals	1970-1996	188	210	0	.472

Season Records

See page 874 for explanation of abbreviations.

Robert "Turf" Kauffman (1970)

Turf Kauffman, who initially came to MSU as a candidate for the football team, was appointed the first-ever Spartan varsity lacrosse coach in June of 1969 following two seasons as coach of the Michigan State Lacrosse Club. Turf was born on January 13, 1940 in Lancaster, PA, where he lettered in football and wrestling at J.P. McCaskey High School. Following a stint with the U.S. Marines, Turf enrolled at MSU and was graduated in 1966. He taught for a year at Penn Manor High School in Millersville, PA, before returning to East Lansing to complete work on a master's degree, which was awarded in 1968. As to his unique nickname, Kauffman explained: "They started calling me that during junior high football. I guess I had more than a just a nodding acquaintance with the ground."

1970 (1-11)
Coach: Turf Kauffman

3-28	A	Lafayette	5-12	L
3-29	A	Franklin and Marshall	4-8	L
4-4	H	Michigan	8-14	L
4-8	A	Kenyon	2-10	L
4-11	A	Ohio State	0-13	L
4-15	A	Michigan	5-13	L
4-17	A	Denison	2-25	L
4-20	H	Oberlin	7-14	L
4-25	A	Notre Dame	9-8	W
4-29	H	Bowling Green	0-12	L
5-9	H	Chicago L.C.	5-6	L
5-23	H	Wittenberg	5-12	L

Theodore L. Swoboda (1971-1972)

Ted Swoboda replaced Turf Kauffman as head coach and remained in the position for two seasons, 1971-1972, during which his teams completed a 12-16 record. A native of Rochester, MI, he was born on June 2, 1945 and would later attend and graduate from MSU in 1969 with a B.S. degree. As a member of the Michigan State Lacrosse Club, he participated in the sport's pre-varsity years.

1971 (6-8)
Coach: Ted Swoboda

3-21	A	Georgetown	7-2	W
3-23	A	Randolph-Macon	4-14	L
3-24	A	West Virginia	9-3	W
3-31	A	Kenyon	6-5	W
4-3	A	Michigan	3-8	L
4-7	H	Michigan	4-9	L
4-10	H	Ohio Wesleyan	9-12	L
4-17	H	Denison	2-12	L
4-18	H	Ohio State	3-4	L
4-28	A	Bowling Green	2-13	L
5-1	H	Ashland	16-6	W
5-8	H	Notre Dame	7-6	W
5-15	H	Chicago L.C.	9-6	W
5-22	H	Wittenberg	6-9	L

1972 (5-8)
Coach: Ted Swoboda

3-25	A	West Virginia	16-4	W
3-26	H	Oberlin	(6OT) 10-9	W
4-5	H	Michigan	13-15	L
4-8	A	Illinois	11-0	W
4-12	A	Michigan	7-6	W
4-15	A	Ohio Wesleyan	8-13	L
4-22	A	Notre Dame	4-9	L
4-26	H	Bowling Green	4-15	L
4-29	A	Ohio State	3-9	L
5-6	H	Kenyon	1-4	L
5-13	A	Denison	7-19	L
5-14	A	Ashland	6-5	W
5-20	A	Wittenberg	4-10	L

Bob Stevenson (1973)

Upon graduating from Detroit Osborn High School in 1968, Bob Stevenson enrolled at MSU in the following fall. Although playing football, basketball and running track as a prep, he had never been exposed to lacrosse until the spring of 1969 when the sport still flourished as a club activity at MSU. As a member of the ensuing pioneer varsity teams, he would become a Spartan three-time letter winner in 1970-1972. Upon filling the coaching position for the 1973 season, Stevenson would become the youngest man to ever head a State athletic team. He also joined the coaching ranks with the most impressive-ever academic credentials. Bob had come to MSU as a national merit scholar and four years later would graduate Phi Beta Kappa with an overall 3.83 gpa as an English major. He capped his senior year by entering the Rhodes scholarship competition.

1973 (3-9)
Coach: Bob Stevenson

3-24	A	Oberlin	7-5	W
3-31	A	Ashland	2-4	L
4-7	H	Illinois	12-7	W
4-14	H	Ohio Wesleyan	3-14	L
4-18	H	Michigan	9-11	L
4-21	A	Michigan	4-15	L
4-25	A	Bowling Green	5-12	L
4-28	H	Ohio State	9-7	W
5-2	H	Notre Dame	4-11	L
5-5	A	Kenyon	7-23	L
5-12	H	Denison	2-11	L
5-19	H	Wittenberg	6-7	L

Fred Hartman (1974-1976)

If Bob Stevenson was the youngest-ever head coach at Michigan State, Fred Hartman, at 23 years of age, had to be the second youngest. Taking charge over a three-year span, his squads of 1974-1976 compiled an aggregate record of 14-25. Hailing from Birmingham, MI, Hartman graduated from Groves High School in 1968 where he had partici-

pated in football and baseball. Like so many of those early Spartan lacrosse competitors, he had been introduced to the sport upon enrolling as an MSU student. Also like Stevenson, Fred Hartman was a member of that charter team of 1970. He eventually earned varsity awards in 1971-1972, first serving as goalie and then switching to a midfielder as a senior.

1974 (5-7)
Coach: Fred Hartman

3-23	H	Oberlin	10-4	W
3-24	H	Wayne State	4-2	W
3-30	A AA	Ashland	4-10	L
4-3	A	Michigan	9-7	W
4-6	A	Notre Dame	5-4	W
4-13	A	Wittenberg	9-18	L
4-17	H	Michigan	7-8	L
4-20	A	Ohio Wesleyan	7-16	L
4-24	A	Bowling Green	0-8	L
4-27	A	Ohio State	4-10	L
5-4	H	Kenyon	7-5	W
5-11	A	Denison	1-17	L

1975 (6-8)
Coach: Fred Hartman

3-15	H	West Virginia	16-7	W
3-21	A	New York Tech	3-9	L
3-22	A	Oberlin	13-3	W
3-26	H	Hillsdale	9-0	W
3-29	A	Kenyon	4-5	L
4-6	A	Notre Dame	7-5	W
4-10	H	Ohio State	12-8	W
4-19	H	Ohio Wesleyan	8-20	L
4-23	A	Bowling Green	4-12	L
4-26	H	Wittenberg	6-9	L
5-3	A	Ashland	11-12	L
5-4	A	Wooster	6-9	L
5-10	H	Denison	4-6	L
5-11	H	Madison L.C.	F1-0	W

1976 (3-10)
Coach: Fred Hartman

3-20	H	Oberlin	7-9	L
3-24	A	Hillsdale	3-18	L
4-3	A	Denison	2-26	L
4-10	H	Notre Dame	7-12	L
4-13	H	Michigan	4-8	L
4-17	H	Kenyon	4-8	L
4-21	A	Bowling Green	8-23	L
4-24	A	Ohio Wesleyan	2-29	L
4-27	H	Albion	13-12	W
4-28	H	Hope	16-4	W
5-1	H	Ashland	4-10	L
5-9	H	East Lansing L.C.	14-9	W
5-15	H	Ohio State	6-19	L

Nevin Kanner (1977)

Twenty-five-year old Nevin Kanner became the school's fifth lacrosse coach in eight years. Much like three of the coaches who immediately preceded him, Nevin gained his initial experience in the sport as a Michigan State varsity player. He was a three-year performer, earning varsity letters his final two seasons (1975-1976) as a midfielder and defenseman in his final year. He was MSU's lone representative at the Midwest Lacrosse Association All-Star game in

1976, the year he was named the Spartans' outstanding senior player. Kanner would gain both a baccalaureate and masters degree from MSU.

1977 (6-8)
Coach: Nevin Kanner

3-26	H	Lake Forest	4-5	L
4-2	H	Denison	1-17	L
4-6	H	Michigan	2-20	L
4-9	A	Oberlin	8-6	W
4-13	H	Hope	10-3	W
4-15	H	Hillsdale	12-7	W
4-17	A	Notre Dame	1-7	L
4-20	A	Bowling Green	6-17	L
4-23	H	Hope	10-0	W
4-26	H	Albion	10-9	W
4-30	A	Ashland	1-8	L
5-7	A	Kenyon	6-11	L
5-8	H	East Lansing L.C.	10-8	W
5-14	A	Ohio State	3-13	L

Co-Coaches: Nevin Kanner and Boku Henderson (1978-1980)

In a unique arrangement, Nevin Kanner would join forces with Boku Hendrickson as co-coaches from 1978-1980. The teams during this span of three years produced a respectable composite record of 27-29 and the 1979 edition went 9-7 to become the school's first winning team. Henderson was a 1974 graduate of Cortland State College in New York. He had attended high school in the Bronx where he was an all-city wrestler, played football, ran track and cross country. In 1970 he enrolled at Cortland where he picked up the game of lacrosse. He topped his three-year varsity career by being named All-American as a defenseman following his senior season. He received his master's degree in education from Michigan State in 1979. With the appointment of Rich Kimball as head coach in 1981, Hendrickson remained in a capacity of assistant coach, a position he held during the Kimball years.

1978 (10-12)
Coaches: Nevin Kanner and Boku Hendrickson

3-19	A$_{MF}$	Wilkes College	>11-8	W
3-20	A$_{MF}$	RPI	>3-13	L
3-21	A	Miami (FL)	>1-0	W
3-23	A	Florida International	14-10	W
3-29	A	Michigan	3-12	L
4-2	H	Indiana	21-2	W
4-8	H	Oberlin	13-15	L
4-9	A	Albion	6-9	L
4-12	H	Notre Dame	11-12	L
4-15	H	Ashland	6-16	L
4-16	H	Northwestern	17-3	W
4-19	H	Bowling Green	6-18	L
4-22	A	Ohio Wesleyan	0-16	L
4-24	H	Hope	17-5	W
4-26	A	Hillsdale	13-1	W
4-30	A	Ohio State	7-19	L
5-3	A	Hope	11-7	W
5-6	H	Kenyon	10-16	L
5-7	A	Lake Forest	13-10	W
5-10	A	Denison	8-10	L
5-13	A	Wooster	11-16	L
5-20	H	East Lansing L.C	F 1-0	W

> Florida Suncoast Tournament

1979 (9-7)
Coaches: Nevin Kanner and Boku Hendrickson

3-28	H	Hope	16-5	W
4-1	H	Lake Forest	11-6	W
4-7	H	Oberlin	10-3	W
4-8	A	Indiana	18-1	W
4-11	A	Kenyon	8-13	L
4-14	A	Wooster	12-14	L
4-16	H	Albion	21-6	W

4-18	A	Ashland	7-10	L
4-19	A	Hope	14-2	W
4-22	H	Michigan	7-10	L
4-25	A	Notre Dame	12-9	W
4-28	H	Wooster	10-13	L
5-2	A	Oberlin	10-11	L
5-6	A	Northwestern	21-8	W
5-7	H	Ashland	9-8	W
5-12	A	Ohio State	8-19	L

1980 (8-10)
Coaches: Nevin Kanner and Boku Hendrickson

3-27	H	Hope	13-2	W
3-29	A	Chicago L.C.	6-9	L
3-30	A	Lake Forest	10-14	L
4-5	H	Oberlin	12-10	W
4-6	A	Albion	10-5	W
4-10	A	Hope	7-0	W
4-12	H	Ashland	10-12	L
4-16	A	Denison	3-18	L
4-19	H	Wooster	6-5	W
4-22	H	Kenyon	11-6	W
4-23	A	Michigan	6-16	L
4-26	H	Ohio State	10-14	L
4-27	H	Northwestern	1-0	W
4-30	H	Notre Dame	10-14	L
5-3	A	Ashland	6-21	L
5-4	A	Ohio State	7-11	L
5-9	A	Wooster	9-17	L
5-17	H	Detroit L.C.	17-3	W

Rich Kimball (1981-1996)

After serving as an assistant coach at MSU in 1980, 31-year-old Rich Kimball became the school's first solidified lacrosse coach in 1981, a position he held until the university aborted the sport following the 1996 season. Kimball began his coaching in 1973 at Brunswick High School in Maine, where he guided the 1976 squad to the state championship. He earned a bachelor's degree in American Studies from Bowdoin College in 1972 and a master's degree in exercise physiology from Michigan State in 1982. He played lacrosse at Bowdoin, lettering all four years and serving as team captain while leading his team to a school-record 10 wins his senior year. During his tenure as head coach, three Spartan teams (1987, 1989, 1991) made it into the NCAA tournament.

1981 (1-14)
Coach: Rich Kimball

3-25	A	Westchester State	5-10	L
3-26	A	Villanova	3-7	L
3-28	A	Gettysburg	3-20	L
4-3	A	Denison	2-12	L
4-5	H	Ohio Wesleyan	3-23	L
4-8	H	Notre Dame	4-12	L
4-11	A	Kenyon	5-11	L
4-14	H	Michigan	6-11	L
4-16	A	Ashland	6-19	L
4-18	H	Ohio State	4-12	L
4-22	A	Notre Dame	5-8	L
4-25	A	Wooster	5-14	L
4-30	A	Ashland	7-10	L
5-2	A	Ohio State	6-11	L
5-10	H	Chicago L.C.	12-11	W

1982 (4-13)
Coach: Rich Kimball

3-22	A	Villanova	7-9	L
3-24	A	Westchester State	10-11	L
3-25	A	Widner	9-5	W
3-27	A	Bowdoin	3-17	L
3-31	H	Notre Dame	4-9	L
4-3	A	Kenyon	9-3	W
4-8	A	Ohio State	4-6	L
4-10	A	Denison	2-20	L

4-14	A	Ashland	7-9	L
4-17	H	Ohio Wesleyan	3-11	L
4-21	A	Wooster	4-13	L
4-24	H	Ohio State	10-6	W
		Michigan	3-6	L
4-27	H	Ashland	7-10	L
5-1	A	Notre Dame	7-11	L
5-2	A	Chicago L.C.	7-10	L
5-5	H	Oberlin	13-3	W

1983 (8-8)
Coach: Rich Kimball

3-20	A$_{BA}$	Budweiser L.C.	13-14	L
3-23	A	Villanova	8-9	L
3-25	A	Westchester	6-9	L
3-28	A	Lehigh	6-12	L
4-2	H	Wooster	12-6	W
4-6	A	Ashland	17-4	W
4-9	H	Ohio State	8-7	W
4-12	H	Notre Dame	6-7	L
4-16	H	Michigan	6-10	L
4-20	H	Mt. Union	19-3	W
4-23	A	Oberlin	14-3	W
4-27	H	Denison	8-9	L
4-30	A	Kenyon	13-9	W
5-5	A	Ohio Wesleyan	5-12	L
5-7	A	Wittenberg	12-1	W
5-14	H	Northwestern	14-9	W

1984 (9-7)
Coach: Rich Kimball

3-19	A	C.W. Post	6-24	L
3-21	A	Villanova	4-13	L
3-23	A	Westchester State	15-8	W
3-31	A	Wooster	12-10	W
4-4	H	Ashland	25-6	W
4-7	A	Ohio State	7-8	L
4-11	A	Michigan	6-9	L
4-14	A	Denison	6-17	L
4-21	H	Lake Forest	12-4	W
4-28	H	Kenyon	20-4	W
5-2	H	Ohio Wesleyan	7-6	W
5-5	A	Notre Dame	10-11	L
5-6	H	Columbus L.C.	7-10	L
5-9	A	Northwestern	6-3	W
5-12	H	Wittenberg	21-4	W
5-13	H	Chicago L.C.	13-4	W

1985 (11-6)
Coach: Rich Kimball

3-17	H	Columbus (OH) L.C.	15-14	W
3-19	A	Villanova	6-7	L
3-21	A$_{MC}$	Vermont	8-11	L
3-23	A	Georgetown	11-9	W
3-25	A$_{PH}$	Bowdoin	12-8	W
3-30	H	Wooster	16-11	W
4-2	A	Ashland	17-2	W
4-5	H	Ohio State	11-4	W
4-10	H	Michigan	9-8	W
4-13	H	Denison	5-12	L
4-17	H	Mt. Union	19-4	W
4-20	A	Ohio Wesleyan	10-11	L
4-24	A	Lake Forest	10-11	L
4-27	A	Kenyon	11-10	W
5-4	H	Notre Dame	5-15	L
5-8	A	Wittenberg	21-4	W
5-12	A	Grand Rapids	15-9	W

1986 (7-8)
Coach: Rich Kimball

3-15	A	Columbus (OH) L.C.	14-13	W
3-18	A	Villanova	9-11	L
3-20	A	Westchester State	6-5	W
3-22	A	Radford (VA)	5-7	L
3-24	A	Duke	3-26	L
3-29	A	Wooster	10-6	W

4-5	A	Ohio State	7-13	L
4-9	A	Michigan	10-11	L
4-12	A	Denison	7-18	L
4-16	A	Mt. Union	15-5	W
4-19	A	Ohio Wesleyan	5-13	L
4-22	H	Lake Forest	7-6	W
4-26	H	Kenyon	9-18	L
5-3	A	Notre Dame	12-11	W
5-7	H	Wittenberg	16-4	W

1987 (11-5)
Coach: Rich Kimball

3-14	A$_{UP}$	Penn State	>7-16	L
3-15	A$_{UP}$	Bucknell	>15-5	W
3-21	A	Mary Washington	24-2	W
3-22	A	Drexel	F1-0	W
3-24	A	Bowdoin	16-17	L
3-28	H	Wooster	21-8	W
4-4	H	Ohio State	17-8	W
4-6	H	Chicago L.C.	14-11	W
4-8	H	Michigan	9-5	W
4-11	H	Denison	10-12	L
4-18	A	Ohio Wesleyan	4-13	L
4-21	A	Lake Forest	13-3	W
4-25	A	Kenyon	13-9	W
5-2	H	Notre Dame	16-5	W
5-6	A	Wittenberg	27-3	W
5-13	A	North Carolina	**	L

> Penn State Tournament

1988 (6-9)
Coach: Rich Kimball

3-19	A$_{UP}$	Penn State	>9-10	L
3-20	A$_{UP}$	New Hampshire	>4-8	L
3-23	A	Bowdoin	3-10	L
3-25	A	Hofstra	3-10	L
3-29	A	West Point	3-25	L
4-2	A	Ohio State	10-4	W
4-6	A	Denison	7-12	L
4-13	A	Michigan	14-5	W
4-17	H	Stroh's L.C.	13-6	W
4-20	H	Lake Forest	12-8	W
4-23	H	Kenyon	(OT) 6-7	L
4-27	A	Notre Dame	6-7	L
4-30	A	Wooster	14-10	W
5-4	H	Wittenberg	16-4	W
5-7	A	Ohio Wesleyan	4-16	L

> Penn State Tournament

1989 (8-7)
Coach: Rich Kimball

3-18	A$_{BA}$	Maryland	>7-19	L
3-19	A$_{BA}$	Salisbury State	>10-17	L
3-22	A	Maryland B.C.	7-13	L
3-25	A	Vermont	10-3	W
3-29	H	Hartford	18-3	W
4-1	H	Air Force	13-7	W
4-7	H	Denison	7-8	L
4-12	A	Michigan	11-4	W
4-19	A	Lake Forest	14-7	W
4-22	A	Kenyon	7-10	L
4-26	H	Notre Dame	9-7	W
4-29	H	Wooster	23-4	W
5-6	H	Ohio Wesleyan	8-16	L
5-13	H	Ohio State	18-12	W
5-17	A$_{GC}$	Adelphi	**10-16	L

> Loyola (MD) College Tournament

1990 (9-6)
Coach: Rich Kimball

3-10	A$_{PH}$	Towson State	9-20	L
3-19	A$_{BA}$	Vermont	6-10	L
3-22	A	Maryland B.C.	7-10	L
3-28	H	Michigan	20-8	W
3-31	H	Canisius	17-9	W
4-4	A	Wooster	12-6	W
4-7	H	Ohio Wesleyan	8-14	L
4-14	A	Air Force	19-3	W
4-15	A	Denver	12-6	W
4-18	H	Lake Forest	17-3	W
4-21	H	Kenyon	10-6	W
4-28	H	Hobart	7-15	L
5-2	A	Notre Dame	6-12	L
5-5	A	Denison	17-15	W
5-12	A	Ohio State	17-7	W

1991 (11-5)
Coach: Rich Kimball

3-9	A	Michigan	19-4	W
3-17	A$_{BA}$	Dartmouth	14-13	W
3-19	A	Maryland B.C.	13-16	L
3-23	A	Rutgers	2-14	L
3-28	H	Villanova	9-11	L
3-30	H	Air Force	14-8	W
4-6	A	Delaware	(OT) 11-10	W
4-10	A	Ohio Wesleyan	9-15	L
4-13	H	Denison	(OT) 8-7	W
4-17	A	Lake Forest	19-3	W
4-20	A	Canisius	17-11	W
4-27	A	Hobart	11-10	W
4-30	H	Wooster	10-9	W
5-4	H	Notre Dame	10-8	W
5-11	H	Ohio State	17-6	W
5-15	A	Syracuse	**7-28	L

1992 (10-5)
Coach: Rich Kimball

2-29	A	Villanova	2-11	L
3-7	A	Michigan	18-5	W
3-21	H	Rutgers	8-7	W
3-25	H	Lake Forest	20-4	W
3-28	H	Canisius	18-2	W
4-4	A	Air Force	10-9	W
4-5	A	Denver	21-7	W
4-9	H	Ohio Wesleyan	7-8	L
4-11	H	Stony Brook (NY)	9-7	W
4-14	A	Wooster	13-7	W
4-18	A	North Carolina	8-18	L
4-19	A	Duke	5-22	L
4-25	H	Hobart	5-11	L
4-29	A	Ohio State	F1-0	W
5-1	A	Notre Dame	14-13	W

1993 (8-6)
Coach: Rich Kimball

2-28	A$_{PH}$	Lehigh	8-5	W
3-3	A	Stony Brook (NY)	7-9	L
3-6	A	Rutgers	9-13	L
3-10	H	Syracuse	7-27	L
3-16	H	Maryland B.C.	(2OT) 15-14	W
3-27	A$_{SY}$	Boston College	(OT) 11-10	W
4-3	A	Butler	9-8	W
4-11	A	Duke	7-14	L
4-14	A	Ohio Wesleyan	11-13	L
4-17	H	Air Force	14-11	W
4-24	A	Hobart	9-7	W
4-25	A	Canisius	23-4	W
5-1	H	Notre Dame	11-13	L
5-8	H	Ohio State	13-8	W

1994 (7-6)
Coach: Rich Kimball

3-6	A	Maryland B.C.	6-12	L
3-8	A	Radford	20-8	W
3-12	A	Hofstra	5-14	L
3-17	H	New Hampshire	9-8	W
3-19	H	Canisius	17-10	W
3-26	A	Villanova	11-7	W
4-1	A	Air Force	6-5	W
4-9	H	Butler	14-11	W
4-13	H	Ohio Wesleyan	6-9	L
4-16	A	Ohio State	16-6	W
4-23	H	Hobart	10-15	L
4-29	A	Notre Dame	(OT) 11-12	L
5-8	A	Syracuse	10-26	L

1995 (8-6)
Coach: Rich Kimball

3-4	A	Pennsylvania	8-13	L
3-8	A	Loyola (Baltimore)	1-15	L
3-11	H	Bucknell	9-10	L
3-17	H	Villanova	7-6	W
3-22	A	Canisius	25-18	W
3-25	A	Butler	13-8	W
4-1	H	Mount St. Mary's	14-8	W
4-8	A$_{MH}$	Boston College	13-8	W
4-9	A	New Hampshire	10-9	W
4-15	H	Air Force	8-9	L
4-19	A	Ohio Wesleyan	(OT)11-10	W
4-22	H	Ohio State	11-7	W
4-29	H	Notre Dame	6-13	L
5-6	A	Cornell	6-14	L

1996 (8-4)
Coach: Rich Kimball

2-24	H	Penn State	8-13	L
3-2	A	Villanova	8-9	L
3-6	A	Pennsylvania	14-6	W
3-16	A	Rutgers	13-12(OT)	W
3-23	A	Ohio Wesleyan	17-13	W
3-30	H	Lehigh	9-7	W
4-3	H	Canisius	22-9	W
4-6	A	Ohio State	9-8	W
4-13	A	Air Force	7-6	W
4-21	H	Butler	13-14	L
4-26	A	Notre Dame	4-12	L
5-4	H	Cornell	14-12	W

By edict of the university administration, lacrosse was to be dropped as a varsity sport following the 1997 season. On February 14, 1997, one week prior to the season opener, the players met and voted to dissolve the team and cancel the schedule. Thus the 1996 season would be the final year of varsity lacrosse at Michigan State.

Year-by-Year Record

Year	W L	Pct.	Coach
1970	1-11	.083	Turf Kaufman
1971	6-8	.429	Ted Swoboda
1972	5-8	.385	Ted Swoboda
1973	3-9	.250	Bob Stevenson
1974	5-7	.417	Fred Hartman
1975	6-8	.429	Fred Hartman
1976	3-10	.231	Fred Hartman
1977	6-8	.429	Nevil Kanner
1978	10-12	.455	Kanner/Handrickson
1979	9-7	.563	Kanner/Handrickson
1980	8-10	.444	Kanner/Handrickson
1981	1-14	.067	Rich Kimball
1982	4-13	.235	Rich Kimball
1983	8-8	.500	Rich Kimball
1984	9-7	.563	Rich Kimball
1985	11-6	.647	Rich Kimball
1986	7-8	.467	Rich Kimball
1987*	11-5	.688	Rich Kimball
1988	6-9	.400	Rich Kimball
1989*	8-7	.533	Rich Kimball
1990	9-6	.600	Rich Kimball
1991*	11-5	.688	Rich Kimball
1992	10-5	.667	Rich Kimball
1993	8-6	.571	Rich Kimball
1994	7-6	.538	Rich Kimball
1995	8-6	.571	Rich Kimball
1996	8-1	.889	Rich Kimball
Totals	**188-210**	**.472**	

* Includes NCAA tournament appearances

Scoring Leaders (Career)

Name	Years	Position	Goal	Assists	Points
Kevin Willitts	1976-80	attack	175	77	252
Riney Wilke	1982-85	attack	133	84	217
Adam Mueller	1985-89	attack	126	81	205
Marc Berman	1983-85	attack	153	40	193
John Giampetroni	1985-88	midfield	103	57	160
Wayne Sansiviero	1988-91	attack	108	50	158
Doug Jolly	1993-96	attack	67	48	115
Joe Politowicz	1978-79	attack	97	16	113
Andy Hilgartner	1990-93	attack	41	64	105
Mike Siegenthaler	1987-89	attack	45	60	105
Marc Saracene	1990-91	attack	58	40	98
Tim Flanagan	1976-78	midfield	59	36	95
Val Washington	1971-74	midfield	77	11	88
Greg Helgmoe	1979-82	attack	49	36	85
Dan Christ	1984-87	midfield	62	19	81
Rob Dameron	1990-93	attack	63	14	77
Jon Lantzy	1988-91	midfield	53	23	76
David Kieffer	1992-95	attack	58	19	76
Scott Cebul	1993-96	midfield	57	15	72
Stan Ungechauer	1994-96	attack	51	20	71
Jay Ledinsky	1991-94	midfield	33	35	68
Chris Heide	1987-89/91	midfield	54	12	66
Rex Lynne	1984-87	midfield	40	24	64
Fritz Kilian	1988-91	midfield	50	12	62
Mark O'Brien	1985-87	attack	42	19	61
Tom Hardenberg	1972-74	attack	36	21	57
Shawn Grady	1979-81	attack and midfield	30	27	57
Dan McNulty	1979-82	midfield	38	17	55
Steve Urbin	1971-74	attack	29	22	51
Mark Pinto	1977-80	attack and midfield	34	15	49
Kevin Rice	1984-87	midfield	36	12	48
Aaron Caruso	1986-90	attack	29	19	48
Doug Kalveledge	1970-71	attack	26	22	48
Stan Zajdel	89-90/92-93	midfield	36	11	47
Ken Davis	1976-79	midfield	18	28	46
Greg Brinkman	1977-80	midfield	29	16	45
Mark Shamam	1990-93	attack	34	10	44
Blane Harrison	1983	midfield	23	21	44
Robby Robertson	1992	midfield	32	10	42
Joe Edell	1989-92	midfield	28	11	39
Duane Anderson	1978-80	midfield	31	8	39
Jerry Rioux	1989-92	midfield	23	14	37
Jeff Jelus	1992-95	midfield	23	12	35
Chris Stutler	88/90-91	midfield	22	12	34
Dave Sorrick	1974-75	attack	21	13	34
Rich Johnson	1983-87	midfield	14	20	34
Rick Dobreff	1979/82	attack and midfield	27	6	33
Ron Hebert	1972-75	attack and Gard	17	16	33

ALL-CONFERENCE SELECTION

Midwest Lacrosse Association

FIRST TEAM

Year	Name	Position
1972	Val Washington	midfield
1974	Val Washington	midfield
1983	Blane Harrison	midfield
1986	Dan Christ	midfield
1987	Adam Mueller	attack
1989	Chris Heide	midfield
	Adam Mueller	attack
1990	Wayne Sansiviero	attack
	Jon Lantzy	midfield
1991	Fritz Kilian	midfield
1992	John Pace	defense
	Robby Robertson	midfield

SECOND TEAM

Year	Name	Position
1973	Val Washington	midfield
1981/82	Dan McNulty	midfield
1983	Jim Sanford	goalkeeper
	Craig Purcell	defense
1984	Riney Wilke	attack
	Marc Berman	attack
	Steve Garcia	midfield
	Mike McCarthy	defense
1985	Mark Berman	attack
	Rich Johnson	midfield
	Greg Walker	defense
	Mike McCarthy	defense
1986	John Giampetroni	midfield
1987	Dan Christ	midfield
	Tim Mueller	defense
	Terry Monahan	defense
	Chris Barber	goalkeeper
1990	Chris Barber	goalkeeper
	Fritz Kilian	midfield
	John Pace	defense
1991	Jeff Horowitz	goalkeeper
	Jon Lantzy	midfield
	Brian Rice	defense
	Wayne Sansiviero	attack
	Marc Saracene	attack
1992	Rob Dameron	attack
	Jeff Horowitz	goalkeeper
	Tim Kaiser	midfield

Great Western Lacrosse League

Michigan State, Butler, Notre Dame, Ohio State and Air Force combined to form the Great Western Lacrosse League prior to the 1993 season.

FIRST TEAM

Year	Name	Position
1993	Scott Cebul	midfield
1994	Jay Ledinski	midfield
	Jon Raym	defense
	Chris McCrady	goalkeeper
1995	Scott Cebul	midfield
	Jon Raym	defense

SECOND TEAM

Year	Name	Position
1993	Chris McCrady	goalkeeper
	Rob Dameron	attack
	Jason Penoyer	defense
	Stan Zajdel	midfield
1994	Scott Cebul	midfield
	David Kieffer	attack
1995	David Kieffer	attack
	Doug Jolly	attack
	David Schlackman	defense
1996	Kevin Sheedy	midfield

SOCCER
LEADERS, RECORDS and HONORS

ALL-TIME COACHING RECORDS

Coach	Years	W	L	T	Avg.
Gene Kenney	1956-69	120	13	13	.866
Payton Fuller	1970-73	20	8	9	.662
Ed Rutherford	1974-76	25	7	3	.714
Joe Baum	1977-2002	255	192	38	.565
Totals	1956-2002	420	220	63	.642

Season Records

See page 874 for further explanation of abbreviations.

Willard "Gene" Kenney (1956-1969)

Gene Kenney, a native of Urbana, IL, was born on May 15, 1928. He stayed home to attend the University of Illinois where he was a member of the varsity football and wrestling teams. After graduation in 1950, Gene accepted a position at the University of North Carolina as assistant wrestling coach. When the Tar Heels' soccer coach became ill in 1951, Kenney volunteered to fill in. While at Chapel Hill he earned a master's degree in education. He then spent two years as an army officer in Korea where he was coach of several soccer teams. Kenney came to State in 1955 as an assistant wrestling coach and instructor in physical education. He was also advisor to the soccer team that at the time was operating as a club sport in the intramural department. When the sport was put on the varsity level in 1956, Gene Kenney was at the right spot at the right time. He was immediately named head coach and led the team through 14 seasons. With a stretch of eight straight NCAA tournament appearances and a pair of co-championships, Gene stepped down following the 1969 season. He was then named assistant director of athletics in charge of facilities. In addition to planning the use and upkeep of all Spartan athletic plans, Gene managed the highly successful Summer Sports School program. He retired from the staff in 1993.

1956 (5-0-1)
Coach: Gene Kenney

10-13	H	Michigan	3-1	W
10-27	A	Kenyon	3-2	W
11-3	A	Illinois	6-3	W
11-10	A	Wheaton	4-0	W
11-11	A	Illinois-Chicago	2-2	T
11-24	A	Purdue	5-4	W

1957 (6-0-2)
Coach: Gene Kenney

10-5	H	Michigan	3-3	T
10-12	H	Illinois-Chicago	1-1	T
10-19	H	Purdue	3-2	W
10-26	H	Illinois	1-0	W
10-30	H	Wheaton	2-1	W
11-2	A	Ohio State	2-0	W
11-9	H	Kenyon	5-0	W
11-16	A	Indiana	7-0	W

1958 (8-0-0)
Coach: Gene Kenney

10-4	H	Indiana Tech	6-0	W
10-11	H	Pittsburgh	1-0	W
10-18	A	Purdue	4-0	W
10-25	A	Illinois	10-5	W
11-1	H	Ohio State	8-1	W

11-5	A	Wheaton	5-0	W
11-8	A	Slippery Rock	4-0	W
11-15	A	Indiana	11-3	W

1959 (7-2-0)
Coach: Gene Kenney

10-3	A	Indiana Tech	4-3	W
10-7	H	Calvin	9-0	W
10-10	A	Slippery Rock	4-2	W
10-17	H	St. Louis	2-4	L
10-21	A	Calvin	5-0	W
10-24	H	Indiana	5-1	W
10-31	H	Wheaton	3-4	L
11-7	H	Purdue	9-1	W
11-14	A	Pittsburgh	2-1	W

1960 (8-1-0)
Coach: Gene Kenney

10-1	H	Earlham	6-2	W
10-8	H	Pittsburgh	4-0	W
10-15	A	St. Louis	0-4	L
10-22	H	Wheaton	3-1	W
10-26	H	Ohio	10-0	W
10-29	H	Indiana Tech	7-2	W
11-2	H	Calvin	5-0	W
11-5	A	Purdue	17-0	W
11-12	H	Indiana	6-0	W

1961 (8-1-0)
Coach: Gene Kenney

9-30	A	Earlham	7-0	W
10-7	H	Wheaton	5-0	W
10-14	A	Pittsburgh	4-1	W
10-18	A	Calvin	4-0	W
10-21	H	Indiana	10-0	W
10-25	A	Indiana Tech	5-1	W
10-28	H	Purdue	13-2	W
11-4	A	Ohio	4-1	W
11-11	H	St. Louis	0-1	L

1962 (9-2-0)
Coach: Gene Kenney

9-29	A	Purdue	3-1	W
10-6	H	Earlham	10-0	W
10-10	H	Calvin	4-1	W
10-13	A	Wheaton	2-0	W
10-20	H	Akron	6-4	W
10-25	H	Ball State	5-0	W
10-27	H	Ohio	4-0	W
11-3	A	Indiana	12-0	W
11-10	A	St. Louis	1-2	L
11-19	H	Howard	**4-0	W
11-29	A	St. Louis	**0-2	L

1963 (9-1-0)
Coach: Gene Kenney

9-28	A	Earlham	3-1	W
10-5	H	Wheaton	6-0	W
10-9	A	Calvin	4-0	W
10-12	H	Purdue	14-1	W
10-18	A	Akron	3-0	W
10-23	A	Ball State	10-1	W
10-26	H	Indiana	7-0	W
11-2	A	Ohio	11-1	W

11-9	H	St. Louis	4-3	W
11-21	H	St. Louis	**0-2	L

1964 (10-1-2, NCAA—2nd Place)
Coach: Gene Kenney

9-26	H	Earlham	6-1	W
10-3	A	Purdue	15-0	W
10-7	H	Calvin	8-0	W
10-10	A	Wheaton	9-0	W
10-17	H	Akron	5-0	W
10-22	H	Ball State	8-0	W
10-24	A	Indiana	3-3	T
10-31	H	Ohio	4-0	W
11-7	A	St. Louis	1-1	T
11-21	H	Maryland	**1-0	W
11-28	A	East Stroudsburg	**4-0	W
12-3	A_PV	U.S. Military Acad.	**3-2	W
12-5	A_PV	U.S. Naval Acad.	**0-1	L

1965 (10-2-0, NCAA—2nd Place)
Coach: Gene Kenney

9-25	H	Wheaton	9-0	W
10-1	H	Denison	4-3	W
10-6	A	Calvin	7-1	W
10-9	H	Indiana	6-0	W
10-15	A	Akron	5-2	W
10-23	H	Marquette	9-0	W
10-30	A	Ohio	2-0	W
11-6	H	St. Louis	2-3	L
11-20	H	Baltimore	**7-0	W
11-21	H	East Stroudsburg	**2-1	W
11-27	A_SA	U.S. Military Acad.	**3-1	W
11-28	A_SA	St. Louis	**0-1	L

1966 (10-0-2, NCAA semifinalist)
Coach: Gene Kenney

9-24	A	Purdue	10-0	W
10-1	H	Pittsburgh	6-0	W
10-5	H	Calvin	13-0	W
10-8	A	Denison	6-1	W
10-15	H	Akron	4-1	W
10-22	A	Marquette	7-0	W
10-27	H	Ball State	7-0	W
10-29	H	Ohio	5-0	W
11-5	A	St. Louis	1-1	T
12-1	A_BY	Akron	**2-0	W
12-2	A_BY	Temple	**3-1	W
12-3	A_BY	Long Island	%**2-2	T

% Long Island advanced based on more corner kicks

1967 (12-0-2, NCAA co-champion)
Coach: Gene Kenney

9-23	H	Purdue	11-0	W
9-26	H	Calvin	7-1	W
9-30	A	Pittsburgh	1-0	W
10-6	A	Denver	3-1	W
10-8	A	Air Force Acad.	4-0	W
10-14	H	Akron	4-2	W
10-18	A	Ball State	11-0	W
10-21	H	Denison	12-1	W
10-30	H	St. Louis	3-3	T
11-3	A	Ohio	6-1	W
11-18	H	Maryland	**4-1	W
11-25	A	Akron	**3-1	W
11-30	A_SA	Long Island	**4-0	W
12-2	A_SA	St. Louis	**0-0	T

1968 (11-1-3, NCAA co-champion)

xCoach: Gene Kenney

9-20	A	Purdue	13-0	W
9-25	H	Ball State	12-0	W
9-27	A	Toledo	8-0	W
10-4	H	Denver	7-0	W
10-5	H	Illinois-Chicago	4-0	W
10-9	A	Hope	7-0	W
10-12	H	Air Force Acad.	8-0	W
10-18	A	Akron	1-4	L
10-26	A	St. Louis	0-0	T
11-2	H	Ohio	5-0	W
11-18	A	North Carolina	**5-0	W
11-23	A	Akron	**1-0	W
11-30	A_AT	West Chester	%**2-2	T
12-5	A_AT	Brown	**2-0	W
12-7	A_AT	Maryland	**2-2	T

% MSU advanced based on more corner kicks

1969 (7-2-1)

Coach: Gene Kenney

9-19	H	Purdue	8-0	W
9-23	H	Hope	6-0	W
9-26	H	Kent State	12-0	W
10-4	A	Air Force Academy	1-1	T
10-8	A	Ball State	8-0	W
10-11	A	Toledo	8-0	W
10-17	H	Akron	1-0	W
10-25	H	St. Louis	0-2	L
10-31	A	Ohio	3-0	W
11-22	H	Cleveland State	0-3	L

Payton Fuller (1970-1973)

Upon Kenney's departure from the coaching ranks in 1970, the soccer program was turned over to Payton Fuller from Kingston, Jamaica. Fuller, a member of the 1963-65 Spartan teams that recorded a combined record of 29-4-2, gained All-Amercian status as a junior. In his senior year he was recipient of MSU's prestigious Chester L. Brewer Award, which distinguishes performance in both athletics and scholastics. After receiving his master's degree from the California Institute of Technology, Fuller had returned to the MSU campus as a graduate assistant in mechanical engineering while working on a Ph.D. He would be the head coach for only four years. In the spring of 1974, with no public pronouncement other than to say there were problems connected with the team, athletic director Burt Smith relieved Fuller of the head coaching position.

1970 (5-1-3)

Coach: Payton Fuller

10-2	H	Cleveland State	0-0	T
10-7	H	Ball State	13-1	W
10-10	A	Wooster	2-0	W
10-16	H	Wisconsin-Green Bay	3-3	T
10-17	H	Illinois-Chicago	4-1	W
10-24	A	Akron	1-3	L
10-28	A	Bowling Green	4-2	W
10-31	H	Ohio	3-1	W
11-6	H	Western Michigan	0-0	T

1971 (7-2-0)

Coach: Payton Fuller

9-25	H	Cincinnati	4-1	W
10-2	H	Wooster	3-1	W
10-6	H	Michigan.	6-2	W
10-13	H	Spring Arbor	2-1	W
10-16	A	Wisconsin-Green Bay	0-1	L
10-20	A	Western Michigan	3-0	W
10-23	A	Ohio	4-3	W
10-27	H	Bowling Green	3-0	W
10-30	H	Akron	0-1	L

1972 (4-2-3)

Coach: Payton Fuller

10-4	H	Hope	2-1	W
10-7	A	Michigan	2-2	T
10-11	A	Spring Arbor	1-0	W
10-21	A	Southern Illinois	1-4	L
10-25	H	Western Michigan	5-1	W
10-28	A	Ohio	0-2	L
10-31	A	Bowling Green	1-1	T
11-4	A	Akron	0-0	T
11-11	A	Illinois-Chicago	1-0	W

1973 (4-3-3)

Coach: Payton Fuller

9-29	H	Air Force Academy	0-4	L
10-6	H	Eastern Michigan	8-0	W
10-10	H	Albion	2-0	W
10-14	H	U of M-Dearborn	3-0	W
10-17	H	Spring Arbor	1-0	W
10-20	H	S. Illinois-Edwardsville	0-2	L
10-24	A	Western Michigan	1-1	T
10-27	H	Michigan	1-1	T
10-30	H	Bowling Green	1-3	L
11-6	A	Hope	2-2	T

Eddie Rutherford (1974-1976)

The school's third soccer coach, Edwin R. (Eddie) Rutherford, first joined the MSU staff in 1965 as a football assistant. He had replaced John McVay who had resigned to take the head coaching job at the University of Dayton. Rutherford came to East Lansing following a brilliant football coaching record in Detroit prep ranks. A native of Highland Park, MI, Eddie was born on July 27, 1927. He played football at Alma in 1944 while in the Navy V12 program and at the University of Michigan in 1945. Rutherford then went to Wayne University, played football and received the B.S. degree in education in 1947 and the master's in education in 1956. While coaching soccer, he also assisted with the operation of the Summer Sports School.

1974 (8-1-2)

Coach: Eddie Rutherford

9-28	A	Eastern Michigan	7-0	W
10-2	A	Calvin	2-1	W
10-9	A	U of M-Dearborn	4-1	W
10-12	H	Oakland	0-0	T
10-16	A	Spring Arbor	1-0	W
10-19	H	Ohio State	1-0	W
10-23	H	Western Michigan	2-2	T
10-26	A	Albion	1-0	W
10-30	A	Michigan	1-0	W
11-6	H	Hope	2-0	W
11-8	A	Indiana	0-3	L

1975 (10-2-0)

Coach: Eddie Rutherford

9-26	H	Eastern Michigan	9-1	W
10-1	A	Calvin	2-0	W
10-4	H	U of M-Dearborn	10-0	W
10-8	H	Albion	6-0	W
10-11	A	Akron	0-5	L
10-15	A	Oakland	1-0	W
10-18	A_CO	Ohio State	*3-1	W
10-19	A_CO	Indiana	*0-6	L
10-22	H	Spring Arbor	3-0	W
10-24	H	Michigan	6-1	W
10-28	A	Kalamazoo	4-3(OT)	W
11-5	A	Hope	7-0	W

1976 (7-4-1)

Coach: Eddie Rutherford

9-25	H	Hope	4-1	W
9-29	H	Calvin	0-0	T
9-30	A	U of M-Dearborn	1-0	W
10-6	A	Albion	3-0	W

10-10	A	Akron	0-4	L
10-13	H	Oakland	0-1	L
10-16	H	Ohio State	*1-3	L
10-17	H	Wisconsin	*4-1	W
10-20	A	Spring Arbor	1-6	L
10-26	H	Central Michigan	2-0	W
10-29	A	Michigan	8-0	W
11-5	A	Bowling Green	3-0	W

Joe Baum (1977-)

Joe Baum came to MSU in 1974 as Eddie Rutherford's assistant. Baum held that position for three years before being promoted to the head coaching position in 1977 when Rutherford stepped down to serve as a full-time administrative assistant to athletic director Joe Kearney. Baum was a three-year Spartan letterman from 1966-68 when the team recorded an incredible 33-1-7 record. He was in goal for two NCAA co-championship squads and was named to the 1968 All-Midwestern team in the coaches' poll. Baum received the bachelor's degree in communication from MSU in 1969 and a master's degree in counseling from Southern Illinois University at Edwardsville in 1971.

1977 (6-7-0)

Coach: Joe Baum

9-21	A	Ferris State	3-4	L
9-24	A	Hope	1-2	L
9-28	A	Calvin	1-0(OT)	W
10-1	H	U of M-Dearborn	3-1	W
10-5	H	Albion	2-0(OT)	W
10-8	A	Akron	1-5	L
10-12	A	Oakland	2-1	W
10-14	A_BL	Indiana	*0-7	L
10-15	A_BL	Ohio State	*2-1	W
10-19	H	Spring Arbor	0-1	L
10-25	A	Central Michigan	1-2	L
10-29	H	Michigan	4-3(OT)	W
11-4	H	Bowling Green	0-2	L

1978 (6-6-2)

Coach: Joe Baum

9-21	H	Ferris State	1-0(OT)	W
9-23	H	Hope	1-0	W
9-27	H	Calvin	1-2	L
10-3	A	Grand Valley	9-0	W
10-7	H	Notre Dame	2-2(2OT)	T
10-11	H	Oakland	0-1	L
10-14	A_MA	Wisconsin	*1-1	T
10-15	A_MA	Ohio State	*2-5	L
10-18	A	Spring Arbor	4-1	W
10-25	H	Central Michigan	2-0	W
10-28	A	Akron	0-2	L
11-1	A	Michigan	0-1	L
11-3	A	Bowling Green	1-2	L
11-7	A	Albion	6-0	W

1979 (9-6-2)

Coach: Joe Baum

9-17	H	Eastern Michigan	4-0	W
9-19	A	Ferris State	0-1	L
9-22	H	Hope	1-0	W
9-24	H	Albion	7-0	W
9-26	A	Calvin	4-1	W
9-29	A_BA	Maryland	>2-0	W
9-30	A_BA	Duke	>0-2	L
10-3	H	Michigan	1-1	T
10-9	A	Oakland	0-1	L
10-13	A_BL	Ohio State	*2-0	W
10-14	A_BL	Indiana	*0-5	L
10-17	H	Spring Arbor	2-1	W
10-19	A	Notre Dame	0-2	L
10-24	A	Central Michigan	2-0	W
10-27	H	Akron	0-2	L
11-3	H	Bowling Green	0-0	T
11-7	A	Toledo	4-0	W

> Loyola (MD) Invitational

1980 (10-6-1)
Coach: Joe Baum

9-17	A	Eastern Michigan	3-1	W
9-20	H	Hope	3-2	W
9-23	H	Calvin	2-1	W
9-25	H	Ferris State	4-0	W
9-27	A	Wisconsin-Milwaukee	1-4	L
10-1	A	Michigan	2-1	W
10-3	H	Notre Dame	4-1	W
10-7	H	Oakland	2-2	T
10-11	A$_{CO}$	Indiana	*0-5	L
10-12	A$_{CO}$	Purdue	*6-0	W
10-15	A	Alma	6-0	W
10-19	H	Cincinnati	1-2(OT)	L
10-22	H	Central Michigan	6-1	W
10-25	A	Akron	0-4	L
11-1	A	Bowling Green	3-4	L
11-5	H	Toledo	9-1	W
11-8	A	Western Michigan	0-1	L

1981 (12-5-0)
Coach: Joe Baum

9-16	H	Eastern Michigan	3-0	W
9-19	A	Hope	3-1	W
9-25	H	Wisconsin-Milwaukee	1-2	L
9-28	H	Michigan	2-1	W
10-2	A	Notre Dame	1-4	L
10-7	A	Oakland	0-3	L
10-10	A$_{BL}$	Indiana	*1-5	L
10-11	A$_{BL}$	Ohio State	*2-1	W
10-14	A	Alma	5-0	W
10-17	A	Cincinnati	2-0	W
10-19	A	Calvin	2-0	W
10-21	H	Central Michigan	6-1	W
10-24	A	Akron	0-2	L
10-30	A	Northwestern	2-0	W
11-4	A	Toledo	5-0	W
11-7	H	Western Michigan	2-1	W
11-10	H	Bowling Green	1-0	W

1982 (11-5-1)
Coach: Joe Baum

9-15	A	Eastern Michigan	0-1	L
9-17	H	Hope	2-1	W
9-18	A	Ferris State	8-0	W
9-23	H	Calvin	3-1	W
9-29	A	Michigan	4-1	W
10-1	A	Illinois-Chicago	0-2	L
10-6	H	Oakland	2-1(OT)	W
10-9	A	Purdue	6-0	W
10-10	H	Indiana	0-7	L
10-13	A	Alma	5-1	W
10-16	A	Cleveland State	1-1	T
10-20	H	Central Michigan	4-0	W
10-23	A	Akron	1-2	L
10-30	A	Bowling Green	0-2	L
11-3	H	Toledo	6-0	W
11-6	A	Western Michigan	3-0	W
11-13	H	Northwestern	3-2(OT)	W

1983 (9-7-1)
Coach: Joe Baum

9-14	H	Eastern Michigan	2-0	W
9-17	H	Bowling Green	0-2	L
9-19	A	Hope	1-2	L
9-24	A	Northern Illinois	0-1(OT)	L
9-27	H	Michigan	3-1	W
9-29	A	Calvin	3-2	W
10-1	H	Illinois-Chicago	4-0	W
10-5	A	Oakland	0-1	L
10-7	A	Northwestern	5-1	W
10-10	H	Alma	6-0	W
10-15	H	Cleveland State	0-6	L
10-19	A	Central Michigan	1-1	T
10-22	H	Akron	0-3	L
10-26	H	Western Michigan	3-0	W

11-2	A	Toledo	6-0	W
11-5	A$_{BL}$	Indiana	*2-4	L
11-6	A$_{BL}$	Purdue	*7-2	W

1984 (12-6-1)
Coach: Joe Baum

9-12	A	Eastern Michigan	1-0(OT)	W
9-15	H	Notre Dame	2-2	T
9-20	H	Hope	1-0	W
9-22	H	Northern Illinois	1-2	L
9-25	A	Michigan	2-1	W
9-27	H	Calvin	1-0	W
9-30	A	Illinois-Chicago	2-0	W
10-3	H	Oakland	0-2	L
10-7	H	Northwestern	5-0	W
10-9	A	Cleveland State	1-3	L
10-11	A	Alma	8-0	W
10-14	A	St. Louis	3-1	W
10-17	H	Central Michigan	3-0	W
10-20	A	Akron	1-4	L
10-24	A	Western Michigan	3-2	W
10-28	A	Bowling Green	0-1	L
10-31	H	Toledo	6-0	W
11-3	A$_{BL}$	Ohio State	*1-0	W
11-4	A$_{BL}$	Indiana	*0-1	L

1985 (13-5-2)
Coach: Joe Baum

9-11	H	Eastern Michigan	7-2	W
9-13	A	Hope	2-0	W
9-15	A	Ohio State	2-1	W
9-20	A	Notre Dame	1-1	T
9-22	H	Purdue	5-0	W
9-25	A	Michigan	4-1	W
9-29	H	Illinois-Chicago	7-0	W
9-30	H	Alma	7-0	W
10-2	A	Oakland	0-3	L
10-5	A	St. Louis	0-2	L
10-9	H	Cleveland State	1-1	T
10-11	A	Wisconsin	1-0	W
10-13	A	Northwestern	2-0	W
10-16	H	Central Michigan	5-1	W
10-20	H	Akron	0-2	L
10-23	H	Western Michigan	1-0	W
10-25	H	Toledo	2-0	W
10-28	A	Calvin	1-2	L
10-30	H	Bowling Green	1-0	W
11-3	A	Indiana	0-4	L

1986 (13-7-1)
Coach: Joe Baum

9-10	A	Eastern Michigan	2-0	W
9-12	H	Hope	5-1	W
9-14	A	Indiana	1-3	L
9-19	H	Notre Dame	1-0	W
9-21	H	Northwestern	1-0	W
9-24	H	Michigan	4-0	W
9-26	A	St. Louis	1-1	T
9-28	H	Loyola-Chicago	2-1	W
10-1	H	Oakland	0-2	L
10-5	A	Wisconsin-Milwaukee	1-0	W
10-6	A	Alma	9-0	W
10-8	A	Cleveland State	0-3	L
10-12	A	Wisconsin	1-0	W
10-15	H	Central Michigan	3-0	W
10-18	A	Akron	0-1	L
10-22	H	Ohio State	2-1(OT)	W
10-26	H	Cincinnati	2-3	L
10-30	A	Bowling Green	1-2	L
11-2	H	Western Michigan	2-0	W
11-4	H	Calvin	5-0	W
11-6	A	Purdue	3-1	W

1987 (12-8-1)
Coach: Joe Baum

9-8	H	Eastern Michigan	3-0	W
9-11	A	Indiana	0-6	L
9-15	A	Hope	4-1	W
9-16	H	Detroit	1-2	L
9-18	A	Notre Dame	1-3	L
9-20	A	S. Illinois-Edwardsville	2-4	L
9-23	A	Michigan	1-0	W
9-27	A	Cincinnati	1-0	W
9-30	A	Oakland	0-1	L
10-4	H	Wisconsin-Milwaukee	0-1	L
10-7	H	Cleveland State	2-0	W
10-11	A	Wisconsin	1-4	L
10-14	H	Akron	0-1	L
10-17	A	Central Michigan	3-0	W
10-22	H	Wright State	2-1	W
10-25	H	Purdue	5-0	W
10-28	H	Bowling Green	1-0	W
10-31	H	Loyola-Chicago	2-0	W
11-3	A	Calvin	2-1	W
11-5	H	Western Michigan	1-0	W
11-7	A	Northwestern	1-1	T

1988 (9-11-1)
Coach: Joe Baum

9-7	A	Eastern Michigan	4-0	W
9-9	H	Hope	4-1	W
9-11	H	Indiana	0-6	L
9-14	A	Detroit	3-2	W
9-16	H	Notre Dame	0-5	L
9-18	H	Northwestern	1-2	L
9-21	H	Oakland	1-2	L
9-25	H	Cincinnati	1-2(OT)	L
9-28	H	Michigan	1-0v	W
10-2	A	Wisconsin-Milwaukee	1-0	W
10-5	A	Cleveland State	2-4	L
10-9	H	Wisconsin	2-3	L
10-12	H	Central Michigan	1-0	W
10-14	A	Akron	0-2	L
10-19	H	Wright State	0-2	L
10-21	H	DePaul	5-4(OT)	W
10-23	A	Purdue	1-2	L
10-26	A	Bowling Green	0-1(OT)	L
10-29	H	Loyola-Chicago	3-2(OT)	W
11-1	H	Calvin	2-0	W
11-5	A	Western Michigan	0-0	T

1989 (8-12-1)
Coach: Joe Baum

9-7	H	Eastern Michigan	3-1	W
9-11	H	Detroit	2-1	W
9-19	A	Oakland	2-5	L
9-22	A	Notre Dame	1-4	L
9-24	A	Cincinnati	1-4	L
9-27	A	Northwestern	2-1	W
10-1	A	Indiana	0-3	L
10-3	A	Michigan	2-1	W
10-8	A	Wisconsin	1-2	L
10-11	A	Central Michigan	2-1	W
10-13	H	Loyola-Chicago	2-1	W
10-15	H	Akron	1-2(2OT)	L
10-17	H	Hope	4-0	W
10-20	H	DePaul	3-1	W
10-22	H	Purdue	2-0	W
10-25	H	Bowling Green	1-2	L
10-27	H	Ohio State	0-1	L
10-29	A	Wright State	0-4	L
10-31	A	Calvin	0-1	L
11-3	H	Western Michigan	0-0	T
11-5	H	Wisconsin-Milwaukee	1-2	L

1990 (9-6-5)
Coach: Joe Baum

9-5	A	Eastern Michigan	2-1(OT)	W
9-7	A	Detroit	2-0	W

Date		Opponent	Score	Result
9-10	A	Hope	5-1	W
9-14	H	Northwestern	2-1	W
9-18	A	Western Michigan	1-1	T
9-21	H	Notre Dame	1-0	W
9-23	H	Cincinnati	0-0	T
9-26	H	Oakland	1-1	W
9-30	H	Indiana	1-2(OT)	L
10-3	H	Michigan	2-1	W
10-7	H	Wisconsin	1-1	T
10-10	H	DePaul	3-0	W
10-13	A	Wisconsin-Milwaukee	1-7	L
10-16	A	Akron	2-3	L
10-19	A	Loyola-Chicago	2-2	T
10-24	A	Bowling Green	1-0	W
10-27	H	Central Michigan	0-1	L
10-30	H	Calvin	2-0	W
11-2	A	Ohio State	0-2	L
11-6	H	Wright State	0-3	L

1991 (9-11-1)
Coach: Joe Baum

Date		Opponent	Score	Result
9-7	H	Eastern Michigan	3-0	W
9-10	H	Akron	1-4	L
9-11	H	Hope	0-1	L
9-13	A	Northwestern	3-2	W
9-17	A	Western Michigan	2-1	W
9-20	A	Notre Dame	0-1	L
9-22	A	Cincinnati	2-1(OT)	W
9-25	A	DePaul	4-0	W
9-27	A	Indiana	0-4	L
10-2	A	Michigan	2-0	W
10-6	A	Wisconsin	0-4	L
10-9	A	Oakland	0-2(OT)	L
10-13	H	Wisconsin-Milwaukee	0-4	L
10-16	A	Central Michigan	1-5	L
10-20	H	Detroit	1-0	W
10-23	H	Bowling Green	0-0	T
10-27	H	Penn State	1-2	L
11-3	H	Ohio State	6-2	W
11-5	H	Calvin	1-2	L
11-8	A_BL	Ohio State	*1-0	W
11-9	A_BL	Wisconsin	*0-3	L

1992 (9-9-2)
Coach: Joe Baum

Date		Opponent	Score	Result
9-5	H	Northwestern	3-0	W
9-11	H	Loyola-Chicago	3-0	W
9-13	H	Illinois-Chicago	3-2	W
9-15	A	Detroit-Mercy	1-3	L
9-18	H	Notre Dame	2-2(OT)	T
9-20	H	Cincinnati	2-0	W
9-23	A	Western Michigan	3-2(OT))	W
9-27	H	Indiana	0-3	L
10-2	A	Santa Clara	>2-1(OT)	W
10-4	A	San Diego	>0-4	L
10-7	A	Akron	1-2	L
10-11	A	Wisconsin-Milwaukee	3-2	W
10-14	H	Central Michigan	4-0	W
10-18	A	Wisconsin	1-4	L
10-21	A	Ohio State	3-4	L
10-24	A	Penn State	0-1	L
10-28	H	DePaul	1-2(OT)	T
11-1	A	Bowling Green	0-3	L
11-3	H	Eastern Michigan	2-0	W
11-6	A_BL	Penn State	*0-5	L

> Metropolitan Life Tournament at Santa Clara, CA

1993 (7-10-2)
Coach: Joe Baum

Date		Opponent	Score	Result
9-4	A	Northwestern	4-0	W
9-8	A	Cincinnati	1-2	L
9-10	A	Loyola-Chicago	0-1	L
9-12	A	Illinois-Chicago	4-1	W
9-14	H	Eastern Michigan	2-1(OT)	W
9-17	A	Notre Dame	2-3	L
9-22	H	Detroit-Mercy	3-3(OT)	T

Date		Opponent	Score	Result
9-26	A	Indiana	0-2	L
10-1	A	Northern Illinois	>1-2(OT)	L
10-3	A	Arkansas-Little Rock	>0-1	L
10-6	H	Akron	1-2(OT)	L
10-10	H	Western Michigan	0-2	L
10-14	A	Central Michigan	4-0	W
10-17	A	Wisconsin	1-2	L
10-20	H	Ohio State	2-0	W
10-24	H	Penn State	1-0	W
10-27	A	DePaul	0-0(OT)	T
10-31	H	Bowling Green	6-1	W
11-5	A_MA	Ohio State	*2-4	L

>Soccer Bowl II at .... Quincy (IL) College

1994 (9-8-1)
Coach: Joe Baum

Date		Opponent	Score	Result
9-3	H	Northwestern	3-0	W
9-5	A	Louisville	6-1	W
9-9	H	Illinois-Chicago	3-0	W
9-11	H	Wisconsin-Green Bay	2-0	W
9-14	A	Detroit-Mercy	0-2	L
9-21	A	Eastern Michigan	1-1(OT)	T
9 25	H	Indiana	0-2	L
9-30	A	San Diego State	>1-2	L
10-2	A	Nevada-Las Vegas	>2-0	W
10-5	A	Cincinnati	1-0	W
10-9	A	Ohio State	2-1(OT)	W
10-11	H	Central Michigan	2-0	W
10-16	H	Wisconsin	0-3	L
10-19	A	Western Michigan	3-2(OT)	W
10-22	A	Penn State	0-1(OT)	L
10-26	H	DePaul	1-2(OT)	L
10-30	A	Bowling Green	0-3	L
11-11	A_CO	Wisconsin	*0-4	L

> Coors Light Classic at Las Vegas, NV

1995 (12-3-3)
Coach: Joe Baum

Date		Opponent	Score	Result
9-2	A	Northwestern	4-2	W
9-4	H	Louisville	0-0(OT)	T
9-8	A	Illinois-Chicago	1-0	W
9-10	A	Wis.-Green Bay	0-0(OT)	T
9-13	H	Detroit	2-1(OT)	W
9-17	A	Cincinnati	3-0	W
9-20	H	Eastern Michigan	3-0	W
9-24	A	Indiana	0-1(OT)	L
9-30	A	SIU-Edwardsville	>4-0	W
10-1	A	Florida Atlantic	>3-1	W
10-8	A	Ohio State	2-1	W
10-11	A	Bowling Green	1-1(OT)	T
10-18	A	Western Michigan	4-0	W
10-22	A	Penn State	0-1	L
10-25	A	DePaul	1-0	W
10-29	A	Wisconsin	2-1(OT)	W
11-10	A	Ohio State	>3-2(OT)	W
11-12	A	Wisconsin	>0-2	L

> Florida Atlantic Tournament at Boca Raton, FL

1996 (12-5-2)
Coach: Joe Baum

Date		Opponent	Score	Result
8-30	A	Buffalo	2-1	W
8-31	A_BU	Canisius	4-0	W
9-8	H	Northwestern	4-1	W
9-11	A	Eastern Michigan	4-0	W
9-15	H	Wis.-Green Bay	1-0(OT)	W
9-20	A	San Diego	>1-3(OT)	L
9-22	A	San Diego State	>1-1(OT)	T
9-29	H	Indiana	1-2(OT)	L
10-2	H	Illinois-Chicago	3-0	W
10-9	A	Bowling Green	0-3	L
10-13	A	Ohio State	0-1	L
10-16	A	Detroit	2-0	W
10-20	H	Cincinnati	2-1	W
10-26	A	Penn State	2-0	W
10-30	A	Western Michigan	1-0	W
11-2	H	Wisconsin	3-0	W

Date		Opponent	Score	Result
11-10	H	Oral Roberts	3-0	W
11-16	A_UP	Wisconsin	%*1-1	T
11-17	A_UP	Indiana	*0-4	L

% MSU advanced to final game based on 5-3 penalty kick score)

> San Diego Tournament

1997 (6-9-4)
Coach: Joe Baum

Date		Opponent	Score	Result
8-30	H	Duquesne	0-0(OT)	T
9-1	H	Canisius	6-2	W
9-3	H	Eastern Michigan	2-2(OT)	T
9-6	A	Northwestern	1-0	W
9-10	A	Detroit	1-2	L
9-14	A	Cincinnati	0-1(OT)	L
9-19	A_LV	Fresno State	1-3	L
9-21	A	Nevada-Las Vegas	2-4	L
9-28	A	Indiana	0-3	L
10-1	H	Illinois-Chicago	1-2	L
10-7	H	Loyola-Chicago	2-1	W
10-12	H	Ohio State	0-0(OT)	T
10-15	A	Valparaiso	2-1	W
10-19	H	Bowling Green	1-3	L
10-26	H	Penn State	3-2	W
10-29	H	Western Michigan	0-0(OT)	T
11-2	A	Wisconsin	0-3	L
11-14	A_BL	Northwestern	*2-0	W
11-15	A_BL	Ohio State	*0-3	L

1998 (7-12)
Coach: Joe Baum

Date		Opponent	Score	Result
9-1	A	Buffalo	0-1	L
9-5	H	Northwestern	3-1	W
9-6	H	Wis.-Green Bay	2-1	W
9-9	A	Eastern Michigan	1-0(OT)	W
9-13	H	Cincinnati	2-1	W
9-18	A	Cal St.-Northridge	>2-1(OT)	W
9-20	A	Cal State-Fullerton	>0-2	L
9-27	H	Indiana	0-3	L
9-30	A	Loyola-Chicago	2-3	L
10-4	H	Illinois-Chicago	2-3	L
10-7	A	Oakland	1-3	L
10-11	A	Ohio State	0-5	L
10-14	H	Valparaiso	5-1	W
10-18	A	Bowling Green	0-3	L
10-25	A	Penn State	0-1	L
10-28	A	Western Michigan	5-0	W
11-1	A	Wisconsin	0-2	L
11-7	A	Maryland	0-1	L
11-13	A_EV	Wisconsin	*0-2	L

> Met Life Tournament at San Diego, CA

1999 (9-9-1)
Coach: Joe Baum

Date		Opponent	Score	Result
9-1	H	Buffalo	1-1(ex)	T
9-4	H	IUPUI	>0-1	L
9-6	H	Cleveland State	>4-0	W
9-9	H	Eastern Michigan	2-1(OT)	W
9-17	A	St. Mary's	2-1	W
9-19	A	California	1-4	L
9-26	A	Indiana	0-2	L
9-29	H	Loyola	2-0	W
10-3	A	Illinois-Chicago	0-3	L
10-6	H	Oakland	3-0	W
10-10	H	Ohio State	2-0	W
10-13	H	Detroit	4-3(OT)	W
10-20	H	Valparaiso	3-1	W
10-24	H	Penn State	0-1(OT)	L
10-27	H	Western Michigan	3-0	W
10-31	A	Wisconsin	1-2	L
11-4	A	Northwestern	0-1	L
11-6	A	Cincinnati	2-5	L
11-12	H	Penn State	>1-2(2OT)	L

> MSU Soccer Classic

2000 (11-6-2)

Coach: Joe Baum

8-27	H	Kentucky	0-0(ex)	T
9-1	H	Quinnipiac	>3-1	W
9-3	H	Niagara	>5-0	W
9-8	A	Robert Morris	2-0	W
9-10	A	Cleveland State	3-2	W
9-15	A	Loyola Marymount	<0-2	L
9-17	A	Gonzaga	<0-1(OT)	L
9-24	H	Indiana	0-1	L
9-29	H	Valparaiso	1-2	L
10-1	H	Northwestern	6-2	W
10-4	A	Oakland	0-1	L
10-8	A	Ohio State	0-0(OT)	T
10-11	A	Loyola-Chicago	2-1(OT)	W
10-15	A	Michigan	2-1(2OT)	W
10-22	A	Penn State	2-0	W
10-25	A	Western Michigan	3-1	W
10-29	H	Wisconsin	2-0	W
10-31	A	Bowling Green	1-1(OT)	T
11-9	A_CO	Northwestern	*6-0	W
11-10	A_CO	Northwestern	*1-2	L

> MSU Soccer Classic
< LMU Tournament (Los Angeles)

2001 (13-6-1)

Coach: Joe Baum

8-26	H	Western Ontario	2-0(ex)	W
9-1	H	Wisconsin-Green Bay	>6-1	W
9-2	H	Robert Morris	>2-1	W
9-9	H	Cleveland State	2-0	W
9-17	H	Bowling Green	1-3	L
9-21	A	Valparaiso	3-2	W
9-23	A	Indiana	0-3	L
9-30	A	Northwestern	1-0	W
10-3	H	Loyola-Chicago	2-2(2OT)	T
10-7	H	Ohio State	3-0	W
10-10	H	Oakland	4-1	W
10-14	H	Michigan	4-2	W
10-21	H	Penn State	0-1(2OT)	L
10-24	H	Western Michigan	4-0	W
10-28	A	Wisconsin	3-5	L
11-2	A	IUPUI	1-0	W
11-8	A_MA	Ohio State	*2-1	W
11-9	A_MA	Penn State	*2-1	W
11-11	A_MA	Indiana	*0-2	L
11-23	A_BL	Butler	**2-1	W
11-25	A_BL	Indiana	**0-1	L

> MSU Soccer Classic

2002 (12-7)

Coach: Joe Baum

8-23	A	Virginia	4-3(ex)	W
8-25	A	Kentucky	3-1(ex)	W
9-1	H	Wright State	4-0	W
9-2	H	Cal-Santa Barbara	2-3	L
9-8	H	IUPUI	2-1	W
9-13	A	Hartford	3-0	W
9-15	A	Massachusetts	3-0	W
9-20	H	Valparaiso	4-0	W
9-22	H	Indiana	1-6	L
9-29	H	Northwestern	1-0	W
10-2	H	Loyola	4-0	W
10-6	A	Ohio State	1-3	L
10-9	A	Oakland	1-3	L
10-13	A	Michigan	2-1	W
10-16	A	Notre Dame	0-2	L
10-20	A	Penn State	1-0	W
10-23	A	Western Michigan	4-1	W
10-27	H	Wisconsin	1-2	L
11-1	A	Bowling Green	1-0 (OT)	W
11-14	A_UP	Ohio State	*3-2	W
11-15	A_UP	Michigan	*0-1	L

Career Records

Most Goals

Years	Name	Score
66-68	Tony Keyes	56
65-67	Guy Busch	54
67-69	Trevor Harris	48
60-62	Macricio Ventura	46
82-85	Tom Doherty	34
60-62	Jean Lohri	33
59-60	Cecil Heron	32
63-65	George Janes	32
73-76	Al Sarria	31
73-76	Zdravko Rom	30
81-82	Tom King	30

Most Assists

66-68	Tommy Kreft	32
79-82	Vancho Cirovski	27
60-62	Rubens Filizola	23
65-67	Guy Busch	22
65-67	Gary McBrady	22
65-67	Guy Busch	22
83-87	Jim Gallina	21
67-69	Trevor Harris	20
98-01	Steve Arce	20
63-65	Payton Fuller	18
66-68	Tony Keyes	17
80-83	Steve Swanson	17
85-88	Todd Goodwin	17
91-94	Andrew Roff	17

Most Points

65-67	Guy Busch	130
66-68	Tony Keyes	129
67-69	Trevor Harris	116
60-62	Mabricio Ventura	101
60-62	Jean Lohri	82
63-65	George Janes	80
66-68	Tommy Kreft	80
82-85	Tom Doherty	78
60-62	Rubens Filizola	77
79-82	Vancho Cirovski	75

Season Records

Most Goals

1968	Tony Keyes	28
1965	Guy Busch	24
1967	Trevor Harris	23
1961	Mabricio Ventura	22
1966	Tony Keyes	21
1966	Guy Busch	20
1959	Cecil Heron	19
1962	Jean Lohri	15
1964	George Janes	15
1981	Tom King	15
1982	Tom King	15
1968	Trevor Harris	15

Most Assists

1968	Tommy Kreft	15
1968	Trevor Harris	14
1963	George Janes	11
1963	Bill Schwarz	11
1985	Jim Gallina	10
1994	Andrew Roff	10
1965	Gary McBrady	9
1966	Barry Tiermann	9
1967	Tommy Kreft	9
1968	Alex Skotarek	9
1983	Steve Swanson	9

Most Points

1968	Tony Keyes	62
1965	Guy Busch	56
1967	Trevor Harris	50
1961	Mabricio Ventura	49
1966	Guy Busch	49
1966	Tony Keyes	48
1966	Trevor Harris	44
1963	Bill Schwarz	39
1963	George Janes	37
1968	Tommy Kreft	33

Scoring Leaders

Most Points

Year	Name	G	A	Pts
1957	Art Southan	12	–	–
1958	Erich Streder	11	–	–
1959	Ceci Heron	19	–	–
1960	Mabricio Ventura	14	2	30
1961	Mabricio Ventura	22	5	49
1962	Jean Lohri	15	6	36
1963	Bill Schwarz	14	11	39
1964	George Janes	15	5	35
1965	Guy Busch	24	8	56
1966	Guy Busch	20	9	49
1967	Trevor Harris	23	4	50
1968	Tony Keyes	28	6	62
1969	Ernie Tuchscherer	10	5	25
1970	John Houska	9	6	24
1971	Nick Dujon	9	2	20
1972	Jay Nisbet	4	1	9
1973	Mike Kenney	7	0	14
1974	Peer Brunnschweiler	5	2	12
1975	Rom Zdravko	12	7	31
1976	Rom Zdravko	11	4	26
1977	Scott Campbell	5	5	15
1978	Mike Price	7	6	20
1979	Mark Neterer	10	0	20
1980	Mark Neterer	13	7	33
1981	Tom King	15	0	30
1982	Tom King	15	1	31
1983	Tom Doherty	12	4	28
1984	Tom Doherty	9	1	19
1985	Jim Gallina	8	10	26
1986	Peter Crawley	12	1	25
1987	Todd Goodwin	7	5	19
	Tim Busch	7	5	19
1988	Todd Goodwin	8	7	23
1989	Steve McCaul	8	1	17
1990	Carl Hopfinger	9	3	21
1991	Brett Christensen	4	4	12
1992	Dan Radke	5	6	16
	Andrew Roff	5	6	16
1993	Sean Nemnich	8	0	16
1994	Andrew Roff	6	10	22
1995	Brad Dennis	9	2	20
1996	Cullen Brown	6	3	15
1997	Chris Slosar	7	2	16
1998	Chris Slosar	6	2	14
1999	Mike Trivelloni	4	6	14
2000	J. Minagawa-Webster	6	4	16
2001	Jeffrey Krass	7	5	18
2002	Brett Konley	9	4	22

Year-by-Year Team Record

Year	W-L-T	Pct.	Big 10	NCAA	Coach
1956	5-0-1	.917	—	—	Willard "Gene" Kenney
1957	6-0-2	.875	—	—	Willard "Gene" Kenney
1958	8-0-0	1.000	—	—	Willard "Gene" Kenney
1959	7-2-0	.778	—	—	Willard "Gene" Kenney
1960	8-1-0	.889	—	—	Willard "Gene" Kenney
1961	8-1-0	.889	—	—	Willard "Gene" Kenney
1962	9-2-0	.818	—	—	Willard "Gene" Kenney
1963	9-1-0	.900	—	—	Willard "Gene" Kenney
1964	10-1-2	.846	—	2nd	Willard "Gene" Kenney
1965	10-2-0	.833	—	2nd	Willard "Gene" Kenney
1966	10-0-2	.917	—	(t)3rd	Willard "Gene" Kenney
1967	12-0-2	.929	—	(t)1st	Willard "Gene" Kenney
1968	11-1-3	.833	—	(t)1st	Willard "Gene" Kenney
1969	7-2-1	.750	—	—	Willard "Gene" Kenney
1970	5-1-3	.722	—	—	Payton Fuller
1971	7-2-0	.778	—	—	Payton Fuller
1972	4-2-3	.688	—	—	Payton Fuller
1973	4-3-3	.550	—	—	Payton Fuller
1974	8-1-2	.818	—	—	Eddie Rutherford
1975	10-2-0	.833	—	—	Eddie Rutherford
1976	7-4-1	.625	—	—	Eddie Rutherford
1977	6-7-0	.462	—	—	Joe Baum
1978	6-6-2	.500	—	—	Joe Baum
1979	9-6-2	.588	—	—	Joe Baum
1980	10-6-1	.618	—	—	Joe Baum
1981	12-5-0	.706	—	—	Joe Baum
1982	11-5-1	.676	—	—	Joe Baum
1983	9-7-1	.559	—	—	Joe Baum
1984	12-6-1	.658	—	—	Joe Baum
1985	13-5-2	.700	—	—	Joe Baum
1986	13-7-1	.643	—	—	Joe Baum
1987	12-8-1	.595	—	—	Joe Baum
1988	9-11-1	.452	—	—	Joe Baum
1989	8-12-1	.405	—	—	Joe Baum
1990	9-6-5	.575	—	—	Joe Baum
1991	9-11-1	.452	4th	—	Joe Baum
1992	9-9-2	.500	5th	—	Joe Baum
1993	7-10-2	.421	3rd	—	Joe Baum
1994	9-8-1	.528	(t)3rd	—	Joe Baum
1995	12-3-3	.750	(t)3rd	—	Joe Baum
1996	12-5-2	.722	2nd	—	Joe Baum
1997	6-9-4	.421	3rd	—	Joe Baum
1998	7-12-0	.368	(t)4th	—	Joe Baum
1999	9-9-1	.500	(t)5th	—	Joe Baum
2000	11-6-2	.632	2nd	—	Joe Baum
2001	13-6-1	.675	(t)3rd	—	Joe Baum
2002	12-7-0	.632	6th	*	Joe Baum

* Lost in the second round of the NCAA tournament.

All Big Ten

First Team

1995	Reid Friedrichs
1996	Reid Friedrichs
	Damon Rensing
1997	Jason Wolff
2000	John Benoist
	T.J. Lieckfelt
	Steve Arce
2001	Steve Arce
2002	Tyler Robinson

Second Team

1991	Doug Consigny
	Jeff Petoskey
	Brett Christensen
1992	Doug Consigny
	Sean Nemnich
	Dan Radke
1993	Doug Consigny
	Chad O. Kulich
1994	Craig Abraham
	Damon Rensing
	Andrew Roff
1995	Craig Abraham
	Damon Rensing
	Brad Dennis
1996	Craig Abraham
	Jason Wolff
1997	Chris Slosar
1998	Chris Slosar
2000	Steve Williford
	John Minagawa-Webster
	Scott Babinski
2001	Anders Kelto
	Nick DeGraw
2002	Kevin Witig
	Brett Konley
	Nick DeGraw

SWIMMING AND DIVING
LEADERS, RECORDS AND HONORS

ALL-TIME COACHING RECORDS

Coach	Years	W	L	T	Avg.
Southard Flynn	1922	0	3	0	.000
Richard H. Rauch	1923	1	3	0	.250
Wright B. Jones	1924-25	5	8	0	.385
Rollin D. Keifaber	1926	2	4	0	.333
W. Sterry Brown	1927	4	3	0	.571
No season due to pool repair in 1928					
Frank Hoercher	1929	3	3	0	.500
Russell "Jake" Daubert	1930-41	48	38	1	.593
Charles McCaffree Jr.	1942-69	189	57	2	.769
Richard B. Fetters	1970-87	119	79	0	.612
William Wadley	1987-89	19	6	0	.750
Richard Bader	1989-00	55	46	0	.550
Jim Lutz	2000-03	9	22	0	.290
Totals	1922-2003	454	272	3	.623

Season Records
See page 874 for explanation of abbreviations.

Southard F. Flynn (1922)

Southard Flynn came along at the right time. Enrolled in 1921 as a graduate student in entomology, the Californian possessed the aquatic credentials long awaited by the athletic department. He had been an interscholastic competitor during his high school days at Berkeley, CA, at which time he also served as a three-year swimming instructor at the local YMCA. He later competed three years as a member of the varsity team at the University of California and then followed that with two years of experience as a coach while doing graduate work at Cal Berkeley. After a short deliberation he agreed to a one-year assignment as coach and instructor for beginning swimming. Following completion of his Ph.D. he moved to Flint where he had assumed a position with the Department of Health.

1922 (0-5)
Coach: Southard F. Flynn

1-28	H	Detroit J.C.	23-45	L
2-3	H	G. Rapids YMCA	22-46	L
2-18	H	Michigan	16-52	L

Richard H. Rauch (1923)

Richard Rauch joined the staff in 1922 as the football line coach and assistant in the Department of Physical Training. Although his credentials confirm his football prowess as a lineman at Penn State, there is no evidence of swimming or diving experience. His alma mater did not even have a team until 1936.

1923 (1-3)
Coach: Richard H. Rauch

1-19	H	G. Rapids J.C.	44-24	W
1-26	H	Michigan	20-48	L
2-2	A	Indiana	15-50	L
3-3	A	Michigan	20-48	L

Wright B. Jones (1924-25)

Wright B. Jones was likewise a Penn State alumnus. He had initially enrolled at MAC as a graduate student in dairy science and later became an instructor within that department.

1924 (3-4)
Coach: Wright B. Jones

1-12	H	Indiana	18-50	L
2-2	H	G. Rapids J.C	39-29	W
2-13	A	Michigan Normal	38-30	W
2-23	A	G. Rapids YMCA	25-42	L
3-4	H	Michigan	18-50	L
3-10	H	G. Rapids YMCA	36-32	W
3-14	A	Detroit Coll. of Law	31-37	L

1925 (2-4)
Coach: Wright B. Jones

1-24	H	Michigan Normal	49-19	W
1-31	H	Indiana	19-49	L
2-7	H	Ohio Wesleyan	46-22	W
2-26	H	Detroit City College	30-38	L
2-28	A	Notre Dame	19-49	L
3-5	H	Michigan	15-53	L

Rollin D. Keifaber (1926)

In the fall of 1925 it was announced that Rollin Keifaber would become the head coach for the 1926 season. He had been a member of the MAC swimming teams of 1922 and 1923 and would later become an instructor in the physical education department. Kiefaber hailed from Saginaw and attended Blair Academy (Blairstown, NJ) where he was a member of that prep school's swimming team.

1926 (2-4)
Coach: Rollin D. Keifaber

1-16	H	G. Rapids J.C.	34-25	W
2-5	A	Wooster College	23-37	L
2-6	A	Ohio Wesleyan	36-24	W
2-12	H	Cincinnati	19-50	L
2-17	A	Michigan	11-58	L
2-27	A	Notre Dame	22-47	L

W. Sterry Brown (1927)

With four win and three losses, W. Sterry Brown, the fifth coach in six years, would lead the 1927 squad to the school's first winning season. R.H. Baugh, a graduate assistant and former star at Purdue University, joined him as an assistant. Prior to coming to State, Brown had served in a similar capacity for four years at the University of Illinois. Before that, he had been head coach, from 1922-1924, at the University of Michigan. Brown remained only one year, and in May he announced his resignation with plans to go into his own business following a summer of instruction back at Champaign-Urbana. It seems that Sterry had made an extensive study of diving boards, obtained three patents, and would begin a process of manufacturing them.

1927 (4-3)
Coach: W. Sterry Brown

1-22	H	G. Rapids J.C.	43-17	W
2-11	H	Cincinnati	31-38	L
2-19	H	Michigan Normal	51-18	W
2-21	A	Michigan	13-56	L
2-25	A	Notre Dame	31-38	L
2-26	H	DePauw	38-31	W
3-4	H	Wooster College	45-24	W

1928
No schedule—pool under repair

Frank Hoercher (1929)

Following the 1928 season when the team was unable to compete because of pool repairs, Frank R. Hoercher, became yet another one-year coach. He was a member of the physical education faculty. On March 30, 1929, he left the college to accept a position with the American Red Cross as a field representative.

1929 (3-3)
Coach: Frank Hoercher

2-2	H	G. Rapids YMCA	38-20	W
2-9	H	Michigan Normal	51-16	W
2-27	A	Michigan	13-58	L
3-2	H	DePauw	50-17	W
3-6	A	G. Rapids YMCA	34-37	L
3-9	H	Northwestern	15-52	L

Russell "Jake" B. Daubert (1930-41)

Russell Daubert, head coach from 1930-1941, was originally hired to establish and organize MSC's emerging recreation department. In dire need of a replacement for Hoercher, Ralph Young would change those plans. He met Daubert at the railroad station upon his arrival and immediately introduced the idea to Russ of becoming the new aquatic man. After all, Daubert, along with three brothers, had competed in the sport at Iowa State, where his father was head coach. Having just completed his advanced degree at Columbia University and with the nation in the thralls of the Great Depression, the "new man in town" realized it was no time to debate the issue...a job was a job. Having been properly coerced, his career in recreational education would have to wait. Although when at home he insisted on being addressed as Russell, at the work place he would be forever addressed as Jake. Baseball coach John Kobs attached the new moniker, which was the nickname of the former National League first baseman, Jacob "Jake" Ellsworth Daubert. Finally, 13 years after arriving in East Lansing, the mustached Daubert, by now an assistant professor, was able to fulfill his original plans by moving full-time into the classroom to teach such classes as Theory of Play, Tests and Measurements, Playground Supervision, and Scoutcraft. Following the 1941 season, he stepped aside as head coach of swimming and diving.

1930 (4-3)
Coach: Russell "Jake" B. Daubert

12-13	A	Northwestern	22-54	L
2-1	H	G. Rapids YMCA	38-37	W
2-8	H	MSC	45	
		Case Tech	36	
		Western Reserve	21	
2-15	A	Michigan Normal	44-31	W
2-19	H	Michigan	18-57	L
2-21	A	DePauw	52-23	W
2-22	A	Purdue	44-31	W
2-26	A	G. Rapids YMCA	27-48	L

1931 (4-1)
Coach: Russell "Jake" B. Daubert

1-31	H	G. Rapids J.C.	55-20	W
2-6	A	Wooster College	55-20	W
2-7	A	MSC	54	
		Case Tech	32	
		Western Reserve	16	
2-8	A	Michigan	13-62	L
2-20	H	Wooster College	57-18	W
2-27	H	Chicago YMCA Coll.	59-16	W

1932 (1-3)
Coach: Russell "Jake" B. Daubert
1-23	H	G. Rapids J.C. 50-25		W
2-19	A	Ohio State 27-57		L
2-20	A	Western Reserve 43		
		MSC 40		
		Case Tech 19		
2-23	H	Michigan 17-67		L
2-27	H	Cincinnati 31-44		L

1933 (3-4)
Coach: Russell "Jake" B. Daubert
1-28	H	Normal 44-31		W
2-4	H	Illinois Wesleyan 54-21		W
2-10	H	Crane J.C. 39		
		Loyola 38		
		MSC 25		
2-18	A	Michigan Normal 36-39		L
2-11	A	Armour Tech 45-30		W
2-23	A	Michigan 17-58		L
2-24	A	Cincinnati 27-50		L
3-4	H	Northwestern 22-53		L

1934 (1-4)
Coach: Russell "Jake" B. Daubert
1-24	H	Michigan 23 1/2-60 1/2		L
2-9	A	Loyola (Chicago) 37-47		L
2-10	A	Illinois Wesleyan 57-18		W
2-17	H	Ohio State 33-51		L
2-24	H	Iowa 17-67		L

1935 (4-3-1)
Coach: Russell "Jake" B. Daubert
1-23	A	Michigan 22-62		L
2-2	H	Wayne 57-27		W
2-9	H	Western Reserve 42-42		T
2-15	H	Butler 61-22		W
2-18	A	Grinnell 54-30		W
2-19	A	Iowa State 30-54		L
2-23	H	Loyola (Chicago) 41-43		L
3-2	A	Wayne 53-31		W

1936 (5-2)
Coach: Russell "Jake" B. Daubert
1-24	H	Michigan 26-58		L
2-8	H	Cincinnati 62-21		W
2-12	H	Wayne 63-21		W
2-21	A	Case Tech 44-40		W
2-22	A	Western Reserve 38-46		L
2-26	A	Wayne 54-30		W
3-6	A	Wisconsin 53-31		W

1937 (6-3)
Coach: Russell "Jake" B. Daubert
1-27	A	Michigan 22-58		L
2-10	H	Wayne 58-26		W
2-17	A	Cincinnati 58-16		W
2-20	A	Case Tech 57-27		W
2-27	H	Western Reserve .. 33 1/2-41 1/2		L
3-1	H	Wisconsin 39-42		L
3-6	H	Ohio Wesleyan 68-16		W
3-9	A	Wayne 60-24		W
3-12	A	DePauw 70-14		W

1938 (6-3)
Coach: Russell "Jake" B. Daubert
1-26	H	Michigan 17-67		L
2-5	H	Purdue 49-35		W
2-12	H	Cincinnati 64-10		W
2-18	H	Case Tech 52-23		W
2-19	A	Western Reserve 31-44		L
2-21	A	Ohio Wesleyan 44-31		W
3-2	H	Wayne 56-25		W
3-5	A	Wisconsin 22-62		L
3-9	A	Wayne 52-32		W

1939 (1-7)
Coach: Russell "Jake" B. Daubert
1-25	A	Michigan 17-67		L
1-27	A	Kenyon 35-40		L
1-28	A	Cincinnati 32-43		L
2-11	H	Ohio Wesleyan 37-39		L
2-18	H	Western Reserve 42-23		W
2-23	H	Wayne 19-56		L
3-3	A	Purdue 36-48		L
3-4	A	Indiana 18-57		L

1940 (7-2)
Coach: Russell "Jake" B. Daubert
2-3	H	Ohio Wesleyan 52-23		W
2-10	H	Purdue 53-22		W
2-15	H	Wayne 19-56		L
2-17	A	Toronto 55-20		W
2-20	H	Michigan 14-70		L
2-24	H	Indiana 44-31		W
3-2	A	Western Reserve 52-23		W
3-6	H	Kenyon 45-30		W
3-9	H	Cincinnati 58-15		W

1941 (6-3)
Coach: Russell "Jake" B. Daubert
1-25	H	Ohio State 33-42		L
2-1	H	Purdue 36-39		L
2-8	H	Ohio Wesleyan 58-16		W
2-21	A	Cincinnati 54-20		W
2-22	A	Kentucky 58-17		W
2-28	H	Wisconsin 47-28		W
3-10	A	Michigan 34-50		L
3-14	A	Indiana 49-35		W
3-15	A	Ball State Teachers Coll. ... 47-26		W

Charles "Mac" McCaffree (1942-69)

The 33-year-old Charles "Mac" McCaffree replaced Daubert to become the school's eighth head coach of swimming and diving. He found his way from Sioux Falls, SD, to Ann Arbor and the U of M where the nationally respected Matt Mann coached him. Following graduation, he accepted the head swimming coach post in Battle Creek for teams at both the W.K. Kellogg Junior High and Central High School. His success was immediate, notching wins in 53 of 56 dual meets at Central while nabbing six straight high school state championships. Mac returned to the University of Michigan for one year as an assistant and then accepted the assignment as head coach at Iowa State University. In the ensuing years at Ames his teams won 17 of 26 dual meets and captured four successive Big Six championship trophies. Coach McCaffree would establish himself as a highly respected figure in national and world swimming circles during his 28 years as the Spartan head coach. Upon arrival in East Lansing, Mac organized the Central Collegiate Conference (CCC) as a swimming and diving conference and then proceeded to direct his squads to eight straight CCC titles. Thereafter, in 20 years of Big Ten championships. his teams finished first once (1957), runner-up on three occasions and placed third during seven seasons. In the summer of 1945, Mac's fifth season in East Lansing, his team captured the National AAU title at Cayahoga Falls, OH. Eighteen times his teams were in the top 10 of the NCAA championships, with the 1951 team placing second. McCaffree served in various capacities for the NCAA, NAAU, YMCA, and the U.S. Olympic Committee. His legacy to the sport has included numerous innovative procedures in major meet management. In acknowledgment of his contributions, Mac was recognized with every appropriate accolade, including being voted into the Swimming Hall of Fame at Ft. Lauderdale, FL. At Michigan State proper respect was accorded to Charles McCaffree when the competitive swimming pool complex of IM West was named his honor. Coach Mac died on December 13, 1980.

1942 (2-3-2)
Coach: Charles "Mac" McCaffree
1-24	A	Northwestern 42-42		T
1-31	A	Purdue 36-48		L
2-7	H	Ohio Wesleyan 62-18		W
2-9	H	Illinois 51-33		W
2-20	A	Ohio State 27-43		L
3-2	H	Michigan 25-49		L
3-7	A	Pittsburgh 42-42		T

1943 (4-2)
Coach: Charles "Mac" McCaffree
1-25	H	Ohio State 19-62		L
2-10	A	Michigan 21-63		L
2-19	A	Iowa State 62-21		W
2-20	A	Iowa State 57-27		W
3-1	A	Illinois 48-36		W
3-6	H	Bowling Green 62-22		W

1944

Intercollegiate competition suspended due to World War II

1945 (0-1)
Coach: Charles "Mac" McCaffree
2-3	H	Indiana 47		
		MSC 44		
		Detroit Tech 13		
3-3	A	Ohio State 24-60		L

1946 (4-3)
Coach: Charles "Mac" McCaffree
1-5	A	Northwestern 51-33		W
1-19	H	Illinois 48-36		W
1-25	H	Purdue 57-27		W
2-2	H	Michigan 36-48		L
2-9	A	Wisconsin 64-20		W
2-21	A	Ohio State 21-63		L
3-2	H	Great Lakes NTS. 39-45		L

1947 (8-2)
Coach: Charles "Mac" McCaffree
1-6	H	Cincinnati 60-24		W
1-10	A	Michigan 39-45		L
1-17	A	Purdue 54-30		W
1-18	A	Indiana 61-23		W
1-25	A	Illinois 55-29		W
1-31	H	Wisconsin 62-22		W
2-7	H	Wayne 68-16		W
2-14	H	Iowa State 56-28		W
2-22	H	Ohio State 37-47		L
2-28	H	Bowling Green 64-20		W

1948 (8-2)
Coach: Charles "Mac" McCaffree
1-10	A	Purdue 55-29		W
1-14	A	Bowling Green 60-24		W
1-30	H	Wayne 55-28		W
2-6	A	Iowa State 58-26		W
2-7	A	Nebraska 57-26		W
2-14	A	Indiana 63-21		W
2-20	A	Cincinnati 53-30		W
2-21	A	Ohio State 41-43		L
2-27	A	Wisconsin 53-31		W
3-5	H	Michigan 31-53		L

1949 (8-1)
Coach: Charles "Mac" McCaffree
1-8	H	Wisconsin 68-16		W
1-15	H	Toronto YMCA 57-17		W
1-29	H	Cincinnati 60-24		W
2-7	H	LaSalle 56-19		W

2-12	A	Michigan	33-51	L
2-19	H	Iowa State	53-28	W
		Bowling Green	68-16	W
2-26	A	Purdue	44-40	W
3-3	H	Wayne	50-32	W

1950 (10-1)
Coach: Charles "Mac" McCaffree

1-14	A	Minnesota	68-25	W
1-16	A	Indiana	57-27	W
1-21	A	Bowling Green	60-24	W
1-28	H	Ohio State	38-42	L
2-8	H	Michigan	46-38	W
2-11	H	Purdue	54-30	W
2-20	H	Iowa	57-27	W
2-24	A	Iowa State	48-36	W
2-25	A	Iowa State	55-29	W
3-3	A	Wayne	55-29	W
3-4	A	Cincinnati	62-30	W

1951 (9-1)
Coach: Charles "Mac" McCaffree

1-6	H	Northwestern	35-29	W
1-15	H	Michigan	55-29	W
1-20	A	Ohio State	35-49	L
1-27	H	Iowa State	60-24	W
		Bowling Green	55-19	W
2-5	A	Purdue	48-36	W
2-10	H	Minnesota	54-26	W
2-17	A	Iowa	59-33	W
2-24	H	Indiana	56-37	W
2-28	H	Wayne State	66-18	W

1952 (8-2)
Coach: Charles "Mac" McCaffree

1-5	H	Bowling Green	66-27	W
1-12	A	Iowa State	54-39	W
1-19	A	Indiana	61-32	W
2-1	H	Purdue	66-27	W
2-9	H	Ohio State	40-53	L
2-16	A	Michigan	41-52	L
2-20	A	Wayne	68-25	W
2-22	A	Minnesota	68-25	W
2-26	A	Northwestern	56-37	W
3-1	H	Pittsburgh	70-23	W
		Big Tens at East Lansing	2nd	

1953 (7-1)
Coach: Charles "Mac" McCaffree

1-10	H	Bowling Green	75-18	W
1-17	H	Indiana	66-27	W
1-31	A	Ohio State	51-39	W
2-2	H	Illinois	65-28	W
2-7	A	Purdue	58-35	W
2-14	H	Michigan	38-55	L
2-21	H	Minnesota	69-24	W
		Big Tens at Iowa City	3rd	
2-23		Iowa State	59-34	

1954 (6-2)
Coach: Charles "Mac" McCaffree

1-9	A	Illinois	61-32	W
1-16	H	Wisconsin	66-27	W
1-22	A	Iowa State	53-40	W
1-23	A	Iowa	53-40	W
2-5	H	Purdue	58-35	W
2-13	A	Michigan	24-69	L
2-20	H	Ohio State	38-55	L
2-27	A	Indiana	57-36	W
		Big Tens at Ann Arbor	3rd	

1955 (7-3)
Coach: Charles "Mac" McCaffree

1-18	H	Iowa State	48-45	W
1-12	H	Bowling Green	63-30	W
1-15	A	Wisconsin	55-37	W
1-22	A	Iowa State	39-54	L
1-29	A	Ohio State	28-65	L
2-3	H	Illinois	54-39	W
2-5	A	Purdue	59-34	W
2-11	H	Michigan	25-68	L
2-18	H	Iowa	48-44	W
2-26	H	Indiana	49-44	W
		Big Tens at Columbus	5th	

1956 (4-3)
Coach: Charles "Mac" McCaffree

1-7	H	Wisconsin	71-22	W
1-21	A	Michigan	48-45	W
1-28	H	Ohio State	42-51	L
2-4	H	Purdue	66-27	W
2-11	A	Indiana	46-47	L
2-18	A	Iowa	46-47	L
2-19	H	Iowa State	50-43	W
		Big Tens at W. Lafayette	6th	

1957 (7-2)
Coach: Charles "Mac" McCaffree

1-3	H	North Carolina St.	54-30	W
1-12	H	Bowling Green	77-19	W
1-19	H	Indianapolis A.C.	71-34	W
1-26	A	Ohio State	42-59	L
2-2	A	Purdue	72-33	W
2-9	A	Indiana	63-42	W
2-23	H	Northwestern	73-31	W
2-25	H	Michigan	47-58	L
3-2	A	Wisconsin	70-35	W
		Big Tens at Minneapolis	1st	

1958 (8-1)
Coach: Charles "Mac" McCaffree

1-6	A	Iowa State	76-29	W
1-18	H	Iowa	62-43	W
1-25	H	Ohio State	68-37	W
2-1	H	Purdue	59 1/2-33 1/2	W
2-8	A	Indiana	59-42	W
2-14	H	Northwestern	69-35	W
2-15	A	Minnesota	67-38	W
2-22	A	Michigan	30-67	L
3-1	H	Wisconsin	62-43	W
		Big Tens at Iowa City	2nd	

1959 (5-3)
Coach: Charles "Mac" McCaffree

1-8	H	Iowa State	73-23	W
1-17	A	Iowa	63-42	W
1-24	H	Minnesota	70-31	W
1-31	A	Purdue	76-29	W
2-7	H	Indiana	46 1/2-58 1/2	L
2-14	A	Ohio State	38-67	L
2-20	H	Michigan	41-64	L
2-28	A	Wisconsin	59-46	W
		Big Tens at East Lansing	4th	

1960 (7-3)
Coach: Charles "Mac" McCaffree

1-7	H	Iowa State	77-28	W
1-16	H	Iowa	70-31	W
1-23	A	Minnesota	72-33	W
1-29	H	Wisconsin	71-22	W
1-30	A	Northwestern	74-31	W
2-2	H	Purdue	73-32	W
2-6	H	Indiana	33-72	L
2-13	A	Michigan	43-62	L
2-20	H	Ohio State	48-57	L
2-27	H	Illinois	74-31	W
		Big Tens at Madison	4th	

1961 (8-2)
Coach: Charles "Mac" McCaffree

1-13	A	Iowa State	74-27	W
1-14	A	Iowa	71-34	W
1-20	H	Minnesota	72-33	W
1-21	H	Indiana	47-58	L
1-28	A	Purdue	80-21	W
2-4	A	Illinois	68-37	W
2-10	H	Michigan	46-59	L
2-11	H	Northwestern	77-28	W
2-18	A	Ohio State	56 1/2-48 1/2	W
2-25	A	Wisconsin	68-37	W
		Big Tens at Columbus	4th	

1962 (5-4)
Coach: Charles "Mac" McCaffree

1-13	H	Illinois	75-30	W
		Iowa	75-30	W
1-20	A	Indiana	40 1/2-64 1/2	L
1-27	H	Purdue	77-28	W
2-3	H	Minnesota	50-55	L
		Iowa State	71-34	W
2-10	H	Ohio State	46-59	L
2-16	A	Michigan	46-59	L
2-24	H	Wisconsin	81-24	W
		Big Tens at Bloomington	4th	

1963 (8-4)
Coach: Charles "Mac" McCaffree

1-12	A	Iowa	73-32	W
1-19	H	Indiana	44-61	L
1-26	A	Purdue	64-40	W
1-29	H	Wisconsin	74-31	W
		Bowling Green	75 1/2-29 1/2	W
2-2	H	Minnesota	52-53	L
		Iowa State	73-32	W
2-9	H	Northwestern	68-36	W
		Bowling Green	69-36	W
2-16	A	Ohio State	42-63	L
2-23	A	Illinois	63-42	W
3-2	H	Michigan	50-55	L
		Big Tens at W. Lafayette	5th	

1964 (6-2)
Coach: Charles "Mac" McCaffree

1-11	H	Iowa	79-26	W
1-18	A	Iowa State	66-39	W
1-24	H	Purdue	76-29	W
2-1	A	Minnesota	49-56	L
2-8	A	Michigan	44-61	L
2-15	H	Ohio State	61-44	W
2-21	A	Wisconsin	74-31	W
2-22	W	Illinois	66-39	W
		Big Tens at Minneapolis	5th	

1965 (11-1)
Coach: Charles "Mac" McCaffree

1-6	H	Bowling Green	78-27	W
1-15	A	Iowa State	63-42	W
1-16	A	Iowa	62-43	W
1-23	H	Michigan	41 1/2-63 1/2	L
1-29	A	Purdue	66-38	W
1-30	A	Illinois	66-38	W
2-5	H	Minnesota	68-36	W
2-6	H	Ohio	77-28	W
2-13	A	Ohio State	60-45	W
2-20	H	Northwestern	73-31	W
2-27	H	Wisconsin	70-34	W
		Pittsburgh	82-21	W
		Big Tens at Madison	3rd	

1965-1966 (10-2)
Coach: Charles "Mac" McCaffree

12-3	A	Ohio	72-33	W
12-4	A	Pittsburgh	90-33	W
1-15	H	Northwestern	63-42	W
		Iowa State	89-34	W
1-21	A	Michigan	53-70	L
1-22	H	Iowa	86-37	W
1-28	H	Illinois	73-38	W
		Purdue	81-30	W
1-29	A_AA	Michigan	209	
		MSC	159	
		Ohio State	104	
2-5	H	Indiana	53-70	L
2-12	H	Ohio State	75-48	W
2-18	A	Wisconsin	73-50	W
2-19	A	Minnesota	77-46	W
		Big Tens at Iowa City	3rd	

1966-1967 (9-1)
Coach: Charles "Mac" McCaffree

12-10	H	Bowling Green	144 1/2-54 1/2	W
1-13	A	Iowa State	70-44	W
1-14	A	Iowa	88-35	W
1 21	H	Michigan	63-60	W
1-26	H	Wisconsin	79-44	W
		Ohio	102-17	W
1-28	A	Purdue	82-37	W
2-4	A	Indiana	45-78	L
2-11	A	Ohio State	71-52	W
2-18	H	Minnesota	86-37	W
		Big Tens at East Lansing	3rd	

1968 (8-3)
Coach: Charles "Mac" McCaffree

1-6		ABL Big Ten Relays	NTS	
1-13	H	Iowa State	70-42	W
		Bowling Green	90-33	W
1-19	A	Michigan	50-69	L
1-20	H	Iowa	75-43	W
1-26	H	Purdue	76-47	W
1-27	H	Illinois	79-35	W
		Ohio	78-45	W
2-3	A	Indiana	43-80	L
2-10	H	Ohio State	87-40	W
2-16	A	Wisconsin	55-68	L
2-17	A	Minnesota	72-50	W
		Big Tens at Ann Arbor	3rd	

1969 (12-2)
Coach: Charles "Mac" McCaffree

1-4	H	Western Michigan	78-45	W
		Oakland	77-46	W
1-6	A	Illinois	79-35	W
1-11	H	Big Ten Relays	NTS	
1-13	H	Minnesota	84-39	W
1-17	A	Iowa State	83-30	W
1-18	A	Iowa	82-40	W
1-24	A	Miami	83-30	W
1-25	A	Purdue	87-36	W
2-1	H	Michigan	57-66	L
2-7	H	Indiana	44-79	L
2-8	H	Northwestern	77-42	W
		Ohio	85-38	W
2-15	A	Ohio State	64-59	W
2-22	H	Wisconsin	92-31	W
		Big Tens at Madison	3rd	

Richard Fetters (1970-1987)

Dick Fetters joined the MSU staff in September of 1962 as an assistant to Coach McCaffree. Coming from Royal Oak Kimball High School, he replaced Bob Mowerson who had moved on as head coach at the University of Minnesota. Fetters later assumed the head coaching position, replacing the retired McCaffree, in July of 1969. Before initially em-barking on his college studies, Fetters served four and a half years as a navy pilot in the South Pacific during World War II. A native of South Bend, IN, he earned a B.S. degree in 1951 from Notre Dame and three years later completed a master's degree at Indiana University. Preceding the Royal Oak Kimball position, Fetters coached at South Bend Riley High School, where his teams won two state titles in six years. This was followed by two highly successful years at Ft. Lauderdale (FL) High School. He arrived in East Lansing with a wealth of coaching experience and a family of competitors. Three of six sons would earn their varsity "S" under the coaching of their father. Concluding an 18-year career as head coach, Dick Fetters retired following the 1986-87 season whereupon he with his wife moved to Buford, SC.

1970 (10-1)
Coach: Richard Fetters

1-3	H	Western Michigan	83-40	W
		Oakland	77-45	W
1-9	H	Iowa	86-37	W
1-9	H	Illinois	66-48	W
1-10	A_AA	Big Ten Relays	NTS	
1-17	H	Iowa State	83-28	W
		Miami (OH)	71-42	W
1-23	H	Purdue	100-23	W
1-31	A	Michigan	53-70	L
2-14	H	Ohio State	71-52	W
2-20	A	Wisconsin	77-51	W
2-21	A	Minnesota	72-51	W
		Big Tens at Bloomington	3rd	

1971 (9-3)
Coach: Richard Fetters

1-2	A_KZ	Western Michigan	75-38	W
		Oakland	88-25	W
1-8	A	Illinois	76-44	W
1-15	A	Purdue	77-46	W
1-16	A	Minnesota	68-55	W
1-23	H	Michigan	52-71	L
1-30	H	Ohio	83-40	W
2-6	H	Indiana	42-81	L
2-13	A	Ohio State	59-64	L
2-19	A	Iowa State	69-44	W
2-20	A	Iowa	73-50	W
2-23	H	Wisconsin	78-45	W
		Big Tens at Columbus	4th	

1972 (7-4)
Coach: Richard Fetters

12-3	A	Eastern Michigan	60-53	W
1-8	H	Iowa State	80-33	W
1-14	A	Wisconsin	46-77	L
1-15	A	Minnesota	63-60	W
1-22	A	Michigan	41-82	L
1-28	H	Purdue	79-44	W
1-29	H	Iowa	86-37	W
2-5	A	Indiana	38-85	L
2-12	H	Ohio State	48-75	L
2-18	H	Northwestern	77-41	W
2-19	H	Ohio	85-28	W
		Big Tens at East Lansing	4th	

1972-1973 (9-3)
Coach: Richard Fetters

12-1	H	Eastern Michigan	72-41	W
1-6		Illinois	54-69	L
1-13	H	Wisconsin	73-50	W
1-20	H	Michigan	41-82	L
1-26	A	Purdue	69-54	W
1-27	H	Texas	73-50	W
2-3	H	Indiana	40-53	L
2-9	A	Ohio	71-42	W
2-10	A	Ohio State	69-54	W
2-16	A	Iowa State	66-47	W

2-17 section (continued)

2-17	A_IC	Iowa	77-46	W
		Minnesota	74-46	W
		Big Tens at Ann Arbor	4th	

1973-1974 (7-4)
Coach: Richard Fetters

11-30	A	Eastern Michigan	72-41	W
12-1	A_AA	Big Ten Relays	4th/10	
12-8	H	Illinois	59-64	L
1-11	A	Wisconsin	35-88	L
1-19	A	Michigan	57-66	L
1-25	H	Northwestern	76-47	W
1-26	H	Purdue	84-49	W
		Iowa State	86-37	W
2-2	A	Indiana	28-95	L
2-9	H	Ohio State	68-55	W
2-16	H	Iowa	92-31	W
		Minnesota	77-46	W
		Big Tens at Madison	6th	

1974-1975 (6-3)
Coach: Richard Fetters

12-6	H	Eastern Michigan	90-33	W
1-4	A	Northwestern	85-38	W
1-11	H	Wisconsin	54-69	L
1-18	H	Michigan	52-71	L
1-24	A	Illinois	85 1/2-37 1/2	W
1-25	A	Purdue	64-59	W
2-1	H	Indiana	43-80	L
2-8	A	Ohio State	79-44	W
2-15	A	Kent State	89-24	W
		Big Tens at Bloomington	4th	

1975-1976 (7-3)
Coach: Richard Fetters

12-5	A	Eastern Michigan	89-24	W
1-3	H	Oakland	81-42	W
1-10	A	Wisconsin	55 1/2-67 1/2	L
1-16	A	Michigan	52-71	L
1-23	H	Northwestern	81-38	W
1-24	H	Purdue	93-30	W
2-7	H	Ohio State	83-40	W
2-13	H	Illinois	73-47	W
2-14	H	Kent State	89-34	W
2-21	A	Indiana	39-84	L
		Big Tens at Champaign	4th	

1976-1977 (7-2)
Coach: Richard Fetters

12-3	H	Eastern Michigan	89-34	W
12-4	A	Oakland	74-40	W
1-8	A	Northwestern	84-37	W
1-15	H	Central Michigan	81-42	W
1-21	A	Illinois	67-56	W
1-22	A	Purdue	78-45	W
2-5	H	Ohio State	60-63	L
2-12	H	Wisconsin	55-68	L
2-19	H	Michigan	63-60	W
		Big Tens at East Lansing	3rd	

1977-1978 (6-2)
Coach: Richard Fetters

12-2	A	Eastern Michigan	66-47	W
12-3	H	Oakland	83-29	W
1-7	H	Northwestern	79-32	W
		Cleveland State	77-36	W
1-13	A	Wisconsin	42-70	L
2-4	H	Ohio State	58-55	W
2-11	A	Central Michigan	72-41	W
2-18	A	Michigan	32-81	L
		Big Tens at Champaign	6th	

1978-1979 (6-7)

Coach: Richard Fetters

12-1	H	Eastern Michigan	83-30	W
12-2	A	Oakland	62-51	W
1-6	A$_{CV}$	Northwestern	84-27	W
		Cleveland State	77-36	W
1-12	H	Minnesota	55-58	L
1-13	H	Wisconsin	36-77	L
1-19	A	Illinois	47-66	L
1-20	A	Purdue	43-70	L
1-27	H	Indiana	32-81	L
2-3	A	Ohio State	53-60	L
2-9	H	Northern Michigan	92-21	W
2-10	H	Central Michigan	85-28	W
2-17	H	Michigan	36-77	L
		Big Tens at Columbus	9th	

1979-1980 6-5)

Coach: Richard Fetters

11-29	A	Eastern Michigan	53-60	L
12-1	H	Oakland	73-40	W
1-5	H	Northwestern	90-21	W
		Cleveland State	83-31	W
1-12	A	Wisconsin	52-61	L
1-18	H	Illinois	59-54	W
1-19	H	Purdue	70-43	W
1-26	A	Indiana	46-67	L
2-2	H	Ohio State	38-75	L
2-9	A	Central Michigan	77-36	W
2-23	A	Michigan	37-76	L
		Big Tens at Ann Arbor	9th	

1980-1981 (6-4)

Coach: Richard Fetters

11-21	A	Oakland	67-46	W
12-4	H	Eastern Michigan	64-49	W
1-10	A	Cleveland State	68-45	W
1-17	H	Wisconsin	45-68	L
1-23	A	Illinois	70-43	W
1-24	A	Purdue	68-45	W
1-31	H	Indiana	50-63	L
2-7	A	Ohio State	47-66	L
2-14	H	Central Michigan	75-38	W
2-21	H	Michigan	38-75	L
		Big Tens at Milwaukee	7th	

1981-1982 (6-6)

Coach: Richard Fetters

11-20	H	Oakland	66-47	W
11-24	H	Wyoming	50-63	L
12-1	H	Wayne State	81-32	W
1-3	A	Eastern Michigan	44-69	L
1-9	H	Cleveland State	80-33	W
1-16	A	Wisconsin	49-64	L
1-22	H	Illinois	72-41	W
1-23	H	Purdue	70-43	W
1-30	A	Indiana	46-67	L
2-6	H	Ohio State	51-64	L
2-13	A	Central Michigan	82-31	W
2-20	A	Michigan	41-72	L
		Big Tens at Iowa City	7th	

1982-1983 (3-8)

Coach: Richard Fetters

11-19	A	Oakland	54-59	L
11-23	A	Wayne State	72-41	W
1-1	H	Eastern Michigan	45-68	L
1-8	A	Cleveland State	67-46	W
	A$_{CV}$	Western Michigan	100-13	W
1-21	A	Illinois	46-66	L
1-22	A	Purdue	32-87	L
1-29	H	Indiana	52-62	L
2-5	A	Ohio State	46-67	L
2-19	A	Michigan	31-82	L
		Big Tens at Indianapolis	9th	

1983-1984 (3-8)

Coach: Richard Fetters

11-18	H	Oakland	44-69	L
11-22	H	Wayne State	78-43	W
11-30	A	Eastern Michigan	43-70	L
1-7	H	Cleveland State	62-48	W
1-14	A	Wisconsin	47-66	L
1-20	H	Illinois	62-51	W
1-21	H	Purdue	48-65	L
1-28	A	Indiana	50-63	L
2-4	H	Ohio State	53-60	L
		Iowa	50-60	L
2-18	A	Michigan	44-69	L
		Big Tens at Indianapolis	9th	

1984-1985 (5-7)

Coach: Richard Fetters

11-16	A	Oakland	74-39	W
11-20	A	Wayne State	79-27	W
11-28	A	Eastern Michigan	53-60	L
1-12	A	Cleveland State	64-49	W
1-18	A	Purdue	47-66	L
1-19	A	Illinois	48-65	L
1-25	H	Wisconsin	49-66	L
1-26	H	Indiana	53-60	L
2-2	H	Northwestern	72-37	W
2-9	A	Ohio State	42-71	L
2-11	H	Ferris State	79-34	W
2-23	H	Michigan	34-79	L
		Big Tens at Indianapolis	8th	

1985-1986 (9-4)

Coach: Richard Fetters

11-8	H	Waterloo (ONT.)	69-26	W
11-8	H	Etobicoke A.C.	54-40	W
11-22	H	Oakland	65-53	W
11-26	H	Wayne State	68-36	W
12-4	A	Eastern Michigan	46-67	L
1-10	A	Wright State	78-35	W
1-11	H	Cleveland State	64-47	W
1-17	H	Illinois	52-61	L
1-18	H	Purdue	57-56	W
1-25	A$_{IN}$	Purdue Invit.	5th/5	
2-1	H	Northwestern	58-33	W
2-8	H	Ohio State	66-47	W
		Iowa	37-76	L
2-22	A	Michigan	42-70	L
		Big Tens at Indianapolis	6th	

1986-1987 (7-5)

Coach: Richard Fetters

11-7	H	Etobicoke A.C.	50-33	W
11-21	A	Oakland	122-93	W
11-25	A	Wayne State	137-60	W
12-3	A	Eastern Michigan	99-118	L
1-10	A	Cleveland State	75-38	W
1-16	A	Illinois	58-55	W
1-17	A	Purdue	48-65	L
1-24	A	Indianapolis Invit.	5th/5	
1-31	H	Indiana	54-59	L
2-7	A$_{EV}$	Northwestern	75-34	W
		Wisconsin	44-66	L
2-14	H	Ferris State	63-50	W
2-21	H	Michigan	38-74	L
		Big Tens at Indianapolis	9th	

William "Bill" Wadley (1987-1989)

Bill Wadley, originally from Rockford, IL, earned his bachelor's degree in physical education from Austin Peay University. While in school he began coaching the Clarksville (TN) Swim Club. After earning his bachelor's degree, Wadley went on to graduate school at the University of Alabama where he was also the assistant coach of both the men's and women's swimming teams for two years. Leaving Alabama, he began a six-year coaching career in the age-group swim-

ming program. He first spent three years with the Rock Island (IL) YMCA swimming team and another three years (1982-84) as head coach of the Joliet (IL) Jets where his team finished second at the 1984 YMCA nationals. Wadley re-entered the collegiate coaching ranks in 1985 as head assistant at the University of Iowa where he served three years subsequent to becoming the 10th head swimming coach at Michigan State in 1988. After only three years in East Lansing, Wadley accepted the head coaching position at Ohio State University.

1987-1988 (9-4)

Coach: William "Bill" Wadley

11-6	H	Etobicoke A.C.	56-30	W
11-20	H	Oakland	62-51	W
11-23	H	Wayne State	70-43	W
12-2	A	Eastern Michigan	112-103	W
1-9	H	Cleveland State	61-41	W
1-15	H	Stanford	50-62	L
1-16	H	Purdue	66-47	W
		Ohio State	65-48	W
1-22	A	Wisconsin	54-59	L
2-5	H	Northwestern	58-51	W
2-12	A	Michigan	28-85	L
2-13	A	Ferris State	105-90	W
2-20	A	Indiana	53-60	L
		Big Tens at Indianapolis	6th	

1988-1989 (10-2)

Coach: William "Bill" Wadley

11-11	H	Michigan	41-72	L
11-12	H	Bowling Green	145-96	W
11-19	H	Wisconsin	51-62	L
11-22	A	Wayne State	80-13	W
12-26	A	Minnesota	%NTS	
		Northwestern	%NTS	
1-7	A$_{CV}$	Cleveland State	79-34	W
		Toledo	75-33	W
1-13	A	Purdue	65-50	W
1-14	A	Ohio State	76-37	W
1-20	A	E. Michigan Invit.	NTS	
1-28	A	Northwestern	74-31	W
2-11	H	Eastern Michigan	65-47	W
		Ferris State	60-48	W
2-17	A	Oakland	119-118	W
		Big Tens at Indianapolis	6th	
		% Training trip in Florida		

Richard Bader (1989-2000)

Richard Bader, received his bachelor's degree in recreation and park administration from Clemson in 1980. In addition to his collegiate swimming career, Richard spent the summers of 1979 and 1980 as a member of the Mission Viejo (CA) Nadadores USA national championship team. He began his coaching career as an assistant at Virginia Tech in 1981 and then moving on as head coach in 1983 where he remained through 1986. Bader then moved on to become head coach at Indian River Community College in Fort Pierce, FL. There he led his teams to a total of six junior college national championships (three men and three women), establishing 21 national records, and developing 84 individual All-Americans. Bader was named men's and women's NJCAA Coach of the Year in 1988 and 1989. Beginning with the 1993-1994 season, Richard Bader took on the assignment of coaching both the Spartan men's and women's teams. He left the position following the 1999 season to become administrative assistant to Tom Izzo in the basketball office.

1989-1990 (9-1)

Coach: Richard Bader

11-18	H	Illinois	71-39	W
11-21	H	Wayne State	86-28	W
12-21	A	Minnesota	%70-43	W
1-6	H	Cleveland State	73-38	W

1-13	H	Purdue 75-35		W
1-27	A	Eastern Michigan 146-92		W
2-2	A	Michigan 34-79		L
2-3	A	Bowling Green 140-72		W
2-9	A	Indiana 65-47		W
2-10	H	Oakland 78-35		W
		Big Tens at Ann Arbor 4th		
		% Training trip in Florida		

1990-1991 (9-2)
Coach: Richard Bader

11-4	A	Northwestern Relays .... NTS		
11-10	H	Wisconsin 138-105		W
11-17	A	Oakland 141-100		W
11-20	A	Wayne State 134-50		W
12-22	A	Auburn .... %156-106		W
1-5	A	Cleveland State 141-92		W
1-11	A	Illinois 139 1/2-97 1/2		W
1-12	A	Purdue 146-97		W
1-26	H	Eastern Michigan 156-124		W
2-1	H	Michigan 109-134		L
2-8	A	Indiana 98-143		L
2-16	A	Northwestern 135-86		W
		Big Tens at Indianapolis 6th		
		% Training trip in Florida		

1991-1992 (9-3)
Coach: Richard Bader

11-2	A_EV	Northwestern 91-22		W
		Indiana 72-41		W
		Penn State 70-43		W
11-3	A	Northwestern Relays 2nd/7		
11-9	A	Wisconsin 137 1/2-102 1/2		W
11-23	H	Oakland 156-81		W
11-29	A_MN	U.S. Open .... NTS		
12-16	H	Ball State 165-81		W
		Penn State 160-123		W
1-6	A	UCLA .... %39-76		L
		Nebraska .... %47-68		L
1-11	H	Purdue 144-97		W
1-18	A	Eastern Michigan 147-94		W
1-24	A	Michigan 106-137		L
		Big Tens at Minneapolis 7th		
		% Training trip in California		

1992-1993 (8-2)
Coach: Richard Bader

10-31	A	Northwestern Relays 2nd/6		
11-14	H	Wisconsin 127-116		W
11-22	A_UP	Penn State 43-70		L
		St. Bonaventure 93-20		W
12-4	A	Purdue Invit. 4th/7		
1-15	H	Illinois 129-114		W
1-16	A	Purdue 140-96		W
1-23	H	Cleveland State 142-88		W
1-29	H	Northwestern 143 1/2-96 1/2		W
1-30	A	Eastern Michigan 151-90		W
2-5	H	Michigan 111-166		L
2-13	A	Indiana 130-114		W
2-26	A_AA	Michigan Open .... NTS		
		Big Tens at Indianapolis 8th		

1993-1994 (7-4)
Coach: Richard Bader

11-13	A_MA	Wisconsin 111 1/2-130 1/2		L
		Minnesota 74-179		L
12-3	A_LB	U.S. Open 4th/10		
12-10	H	Harvard 121-123		L
1-6	A	Arkansas .... %49-27		W
1-14	H	Toledo 145-96		W
1-15	H	Purdue 139-102		W
1-22	A_EV	Northwestern 130-111		W
		Illinois-Chicago 82-31		W
1-28	H	Indiana 124-119		W
1-29	A	Eastern Michigan 135-103		W

2-4	A	Michigan 91-149		L
		Big Tens at Minneapolis 5th		
		% Training trip in Florida		

1994-1995 (2-6)
Coach: Richard Bader

10-30	A	Northwestern Relays .... 2nd /6		
11-4	A	Toledo 149-94		W
11-11	H	Wisconsin 94-150		L
12-1	A_LB	Speedo Invitational 10th		
1-7	A	Syracuse .... %NTS		
1-14	A	Purdue 86-149		L
1-21	H	Northwestern 118-124		L
1-27	A	Indiana 98-145		L
2-3	H	Michigan 87-148		L
2-4	H	Penn State 107-136		L
2-10	H	Eastern Michigan 126-117		W
		Big Tens at Minneapolis 10th		
		% Training trip in Florida		

1995-1996 (5-4)
Coach: Richard Bader

10-29	A	Northwestern Relays 3rd/6		
11-4	A_MA	Wisconsin 103-133		L
		Minnesota 71-168		L
11-18	A	E. Michigan 127-114		W
11-30	A	Notre Dame Invit. 5th/7		
12-5	A	Amherst .... %NTS		W
1-8	H	Toledo 141-95		W
1-13	H	Purdue 126-111		W
1-20	A	Northwestern 131-106		W
1-26	A_AA	Michigan 31-132		L
		Indiana 49-114		L
		Big Tens at Ann Arbor 9th		
		% Training trip in Florida		

1996-1997 (1-5)
Coach: Richard Bader

10-27	A	Northwestern Relays 2nd/5		
11-22	A	Indiana Invitational 5th/6		
1-3	A	W.Va. Wesleyan .... %121-71		W
1-11	H	E. Michigan 88-154		L
1-18	A	Purdue 67-174		L
1-21	A	Toledo 99.5-137.5		L
1-25	H	Northwestern 98-135		L
2-1	A	Indiana 73.5-165.5		L
2-7	H	Michigan 75-139		L
		Big Tens at Bloomington 10th		
		% Training trip in Florida		

1997-1998 (0-7)
Coach: Richard Bader

11-21	A	N. Carolina Invit. 2nd/2		
12-4	A	IN U. S. Open .... NTS		
12-20	A	Ft. Lauderdale Relays 2nd/5		
1-9	A	E. Michigan 118-125		L
1-16	H	Penn State 104-136		L
1-20	H	Toledo 121-122		L
1-24	A	Northwestern 134-165		L
1-30	H	Indiana 110-133		L
2-6	A	Michigan 95-138		L
		Big Tens at Minneapolis 10th		

1998-1999 (3-5)
Coach: Richard Bader

10-24	A	Penn State 80-160		L
10-30	A	Michigan Open 3rd/4		
11-1	A	Northwestern Relays 3rd/7		
12-3	A	Notre Dame Invit. 4th/8		
1-8	H	E. Michigan 137-106		W
1-9	H	Northwestern 143-100		W
1-15	H	Notre Dame 138-99		W
1-16	A	Purdue 79-164		L
1-23	A	Toledo 118-125		L

1-30	A	Indiana 82.5-160.5		L
2-5	H	Michigan 84-159		L
		Big Tens at Bloomington 10th		

1999-2000 (2-7)
Coach: Richard Bader

10-29	H	Michigan Open 3rd/4		
10-31	A	Northwestern Relays 2nd/5		
11-10	H	Butler 122-72		W
11-13	H	Eastern Michigan 97-146		L
12-2	A	Notre Dame Invit. 4th/9		
1-8	A	Northwestern 112-129		L
1-15	A	Purdue 91.5-147.5		L
1-16	A	State 142-101		W
1-22	A	Oakland 118-119		L
1-30	H	Indiana 95-148		L
2-4	A	Michigan 123-210		L
2-5	A_UM	Ohio State 133-206		L
		Big Tens at Ann Arbor 10th/10		

Jim Lutz (2000-)
In the fall of 2000, Jim Lutz joined the staff as head coach for both the men's and women's swimming and diving teams. A native of Covington, KY, he graduated from the University of Tennessee in 1985. During those years in Knoxville, Jim doubled as an undergraduate student and an assistant coach for both a local age-group club and later with the volunteer swimming and diving program. Upon graduation and from 1985 until 1989, he was head coach of age group programs including stops in Des Moines, IA, and Tucson, AZ. In 1989 Lutz was hired as the assistant swimming coach at the University of Arizona where he also served as recruiting coordinator from 1989-1993. He accepted the position of head coach for women at the University of Illinois in 1993 where over an eight-year span he became the school's winningest coach ever in the sport. He has produced 29 NCAA All-Americans, four Olympic Festival gold medalists and two swimmers of the USA National Team.

2000-2001 (3-4)
Coach: Jim Lutz

10-27	H	Michigan Open 3rd/4		
10-29	A	Northwestern Relays 2nd		
11-10	H	Eastern Michigan .. 131.5-106.5		W
11-30	A	Notre Dame Invit. .... NTS		
12-9	A	Ball State 135-108		W
1-3	A	Texas A&M 102-136		L
1-13	H	Northwestern 81-108		L
1-19	H	Purdue 128-172		L
1-20	H	Oakland 140-98		W
2-3	H	Michigan 95-133		L
		Big Tens 10th/10		

2001-2002 (3-6)
Coach: Jim Lutz

10-26	A	E. Michigan 79.5-163.5		L
11-2	H	Georgia 97-143		L
11-8	A	Ball State 113-130		L
11-13	A	Toledo 153-147		W
12-2	A	Miami (OH) Invitational ... 2nd		
1-5	A_HI	Rainbow Invitational .... NTS		
1-11	A	Northwestern 110-131		L
1-12	A	Purdue 115.5-187.5		L
1-18	A	Oakland 136-105		W
1-19	A	Ohio State 94-149		L
2-8	A	Michigan .... NTS		
2-9	A	Michigan 99-137		L
		Big Tens at Bloomington 10th		

2002-2003 (4-9)
Coach: Jim Lutz

10-25	A	Indiana 104-129		L
10-26	A	Southern Illinois 99-200		L
10-26	A	Missouri 122-177		L

11-8	A	Notre Dame 102.5-140.5		L
11-9	H	Michigan 98-145		L
11-15	H	Eastern Mich. 107.5-135.5		L
11-24	A	Pittsburgh Invit. 3/5		
12-19	A	Cal-Irvine 138-83		W
1-10	H	Northwestern 131-91		W
1-11	H	Ball State 136-104		W
1-17	A	Ohio State 96-147		L
1-18	H	Purdue 131-112		W
1-25	H	Penn State 83-158		L
2-1	A	Oakland 117.5-124.5		L

Big Tens at Ann Arbor 10th

School Records

Event	Name	Time/Mark	Year
50 yard freestyle	Mark Lisenby	20.17	1990
100 yard freestyle	Gregg Mihallik	44.51	1992
200 yard freestyle	John Munley	1:36.60	2001
500 yard freestyle	Steve Leissner	4:20.81	1992
1,000 freestyle	Steve Leissner	9:06.09	1992
1,650 freestyle	Steve Leissner	15:05.49	1992
100 yard butterfly	Ron Orris	48.06	1994
200 yard butterfly	Chris-Carol Bremer	1:45.71	1994
100 yard backstroke	Lars Kalenka	49.47	1994
100 yard backstroke	Karl Sunryd	49.19	2002
200 yard backstroke	Lars Kalenka	1:46.81	1994
100 yard breaststroke	Kevin Zielinski	55.23	1991
200 yard breaststroke	Kevin Zielinski	1:59.19	1991
200 yard indiv. Medley	Iian Mull	1:47.80	1996
400 yard medley relay	Iian Mull	3:45.89	1996
200 yard freestyle relay		1:21.12	1990

Mark Lisenby, Kevin Zielinski, Steve Shipps, Greg Mihalllik

400 yard freestyle relay		2:59.19	1990

Kevin Zielinski, Mark Lisenby, Steve Leissner, Greg Mihallik

800 yard freestyle relay		6:32.35	1989

Steve Leissner, Kevin Zielinski, Steve Leissner, Kevin Zielinski, Greg Mihallik, Damon Whitfield

200 yard medley relay		1:29.38	2003

Karl Sunyrd, Ian Clutten, Joel Hageman, Nick Defauw

400 medley relay		3:17.57	2003

Karl Sunyrd, Ian Clutten, David Sloan, Patrick Saucedo

1 meter diving (6 dives)	John Maxson	345.45	1994
I meter diving (11 dives)	Chad Hepner	496.55	1997
3 meter diving (6 dives)	P.J. Sheahan-Stahl	395.60	2003
3 meter diving (11 dives)	Dave Burgering	564.57	1977

NCAA Champions

Event	Name	Time/Mark	Year
400 yard freestyle relay		3:27.2	1946

Zigmund Indyke, John DeMond, Jim Quigley, Bob Allwardt

1500 yard freestyle	George Hoogerhyde	19:44.2	1947
400 yard freestyle relay		3:31.0	1948

Abel Gilbert, George Hoogerhyde, Bob Allwardt, Jim Duke

100 yard freestyle	Clarke Scholes	50.9	1950
50 yard freestyle	Clarke Scholes	22.9	1951
100 yard freestyle	Clarke Scholes	51.0	1951
400 yard freestyle relay		3:26.7	1951

David Hoffman, Jim Quigley, Clarke Scholes, George Hoogerhyde

100 yard freestyle	Clarke Scholes	49.9	1952
400 yard medley relay		3:50.0	1957

Don Nichols, Paul Reinke, Roger Harmon, Frank Parrish

100 yard breaststroke	Frank Modine	1:05.0	1958
200 yard breaststroke	Frank Modine	2:25.4	1958
100 yard freestyle	Donald Patterson	49.5	1958
440 yard freestyle	Bill Steuart	4:34.3	1958
1500 yard freestyle	Bill Steuart	18:45.8	1958
440 yard freestyle	Bill Steuart	4:31.9	1959
1500 yard freestyle	Bill Steuart	18:26.2	1959
400 yard freestyle relay		3:15.8	1962

Jeff Mattson, Doug Rowe, Bill Wood, Mike Wood

100 yard backstroke	Gary Dilley	52.6	1965
200 yard backstroke	Gary Dilley	1:56.2	1965
100 yard backstroke	Gary Dilley	52.39	1966
200 yard backstroke	Gary Dilley	1:56.41	1966
100 yard freestyle	Ken Walsh	45.67	1967

NAAU Champions (* indoor ** outdoor)

Event	Name	Time/Mark	Year
300 meter medley relay**		3:32.4	1945

Howard Patterson, David Seibold, Jim Quigley

300 meter indiv. medley**	David Seibold	4:18.5	1945
200 meter breaststroke**	David Seibold	2:55.5	1945
100 yard freestyle*	Clarke Scholes	51.3	1950
100 yard freestyle*	Clarke Scholes	50.3	1952
100 meter breaststroke**	John Dudeck	1:08.4	1953
400 meter indiv. medley**	Pete Williams	4:50.8	1967

Olympians

Event	Name	Country	Year
800 meter freestyle relay	George Hoogerhyde	USA	1948
100 meter backstroke	Howard Patterson	USA	1948
100 meter freestyle	Clarke Scholes (gold)	USA	1952
100, 400 meter freestyle	Bill Steuart	South Africa	1956
200 meter backstroke	Gary Dilley (silver)	USA	1964
All freestyle events	George Gonzales	Puerto Rico	1968
100 m. freestyle and relay	Ken Walsh (silver and gold)	USA	1968
400 meter indiv. medley	Pete Williams	USA	1968
1 meter diving	Dave Burgering	USA	1980
1 meter diving	Kevin Machemer	USA	1980
200 meter breaststroke	Sydney Appelboom	Belgium	1988
200 meter freestyle	Mike Green	Great Britian	1988
200 meter butterfly	Chris-Carol Bremer	Germany	1992
200 meter butterfly	Chris-Carol Bremer	Germany	1996

Big Ten Champions

50 yard freestyle	Clarke Scholes	23.0	1951
100 yard freestyle	Clarke Scholes	50.7	1951
220 yard freestyle	Bert McLachlan	2:10.9	1951
440 yard freestyle	Bert McLachlan	4:41.8	1951
100 yard freestyle	Clarke Scholes	49.8	1952
440 yard freestyle	Bert McLachlan	4:43.9	1953
100 yard breaststroke	John Dudeck	1:01.1	1953
100 yard breaststroke	John Dudeck	59.7	1954
100 yard breaststroke	Paul Reinke	1:03.8	1957
400 yard freestyle relay		3:25.0	1957

Jim Clemens, Gordon Fornell, Frank Parrish, Don Patterson

440 yard freestyle	Bill Steuart	4:37.5	1958
1500 yard freestyle	Bill Steuart	18:40.5	1958
220 yard freestyle	Bill Steuart	2:04.2	1959
440 yard freestyle	Bill Steuart	4:30.9	1959
1500 yard freestyle	Bill Steuart	18:36.6	1959
100 yard breaststroke	Frank Modine	1:04.8	1959
220 yard freestyle	Mike Wood	2:01.3	1962
400 yard freestyle relay		3:14.5	1962

Jeff Mattson, Doug Rowe, Mike Wood, Bill Wood

100 yard backstroke	Jeff Mattson	54.6	1963
400 year freestyle relay		3:13.90	1964

Dick Gretzinger, Darryle Kifer, Jim MacMillan, Bob Sherwood

100 yard backstroke	Gary Dilley	53.15	1965
200 yard backstroke	Gary Dilley	1:56.28	1965
400 yard freestyle relay		3:11.54	1965

Gary Dilley, Dick Gretzinger, Darryle Kifer, Jim MacMilllan

100 yard backstroke	Gary Dilley	54.2	1966
200 yard backstroke	Gary Dilley	1:57.4	1966
100 yard freestyle	Ken Walsh	46.17	1967
200 yard freestyle	Ken Walsh	1:43.45	1967
100 yard backstroke	Gary Dilley	53.10	1967
200 yard backstroke	Gary Dilley	1:56.23	1967
400 yard freestyle relay		3:08.68	1967

GaryDilley, Gary Langley, Don Rauch, Ken Walsh

400 yard indiv. medley	Bruce Richards	4:16.09	1969
400 yard freestyle relay		3:10.99	1969

Dick Crittenden, Mark Holdridge, Mike Kalmbach, Don Rauch

50 yard freestyle	Dick Crittenden	21.5	1970
100 yard breaststroke	Jeffrey Lanini	1:00.19	1971
50 yard freestyle	Glen Disoway	21.48	1973
100 yard freestyle	Bruce Wright	46.66	1973
200 yard indiv. medley	Mike Rado	1:53.90	1977
200 yard butterfly	Shawn Elkins	1:50.26	1977
1 meter diving	Dave Burgering	495.06	1977
3 meter diving	Dave Burgering	564.57	1977
200 yard butterfly	Shawn Elkins	1:51.49	1978
3 meter diving	Jesse Griffin	502.83	1978
200 yard breaststroke	Bob Lundquist	2:05.40	1982
200 yard indiv. medley	Steve Leissner	1:48.97	1990

All-Americans

50 yard freestyle
Don Paton 1948
Don Paton 1949
Don Paton 1950
Clarke Scholes 1951
Clarke Scholes 1952
Ken Guest 1956
Don Patterson 1957
Jeff Mattson 1962
Jeff Mattson 1963
Daryle Kifer 1964
Dick Crittenden 1970
Mike Kalmbach 1970

100 yard freestyle
George Hoogerhyde 1948
Clarke Scholes 1950
George Hoogerhyde 1951
Clarke Scholes 1951
Clarke Scholes 1952
Don Patterson 1957
Don Patterson 1958
Don Patterson 1959
Jeff Mattson 1962
Mike Wood 1962
Mike Wood 1963
Bill Wood 1963
Jim MacMillan 1965
Gary Dilley 1965
Ken Walsh 1965
Ken Walsh 1966
Ken Walsh 1967
Mike Kalmbach 1969
Mike Kalmbach 1970

200 yard freestyle
(swum as 220 yards until changed in 1960)
Abel Gilbert 1946
George Hoogerhyde 1947
George Hoogerhyde 1948
George Hoogerhyde 1949
Bert McLachlan 1951
Bert McLachlan 1952
Bert McLachlan 1953
C. James Clemens 1958
Bill Steuart 1959
Dick Brackett 1960
Mike Wood 1962
Mike Wood 1963
Jim MacMillan 1964
Jim MacMillan 1965
Ken Walsh 1965
Jim MacMillan 1966
Ken Walsh 1967

500 yard freestyle
(swum as 440 yards until changed in 1960)
Bert McLachlan 1951
Bert McLachlan 1952
Bert McLachlan 1953
C. James Clemens 1957
Bill Steuart 1958
Bill Steuard 1959
Ken Walsh 1965
Ken Walsh 1966
Ken Walsh 1967
Steve Leissner 1992

1,650 yard freestyle
(swum as 1500 meters until changed in 1963)
George Hoogerhyde 1947
Bert McLachlan 1951
Bert McLachlan 1952
Bert McLachlan 1953

Bill Steuart 1958
Bill Steuart 1959
Dick Brackett 1960
Edgar Glick 1965
Edgar Glick 1966
Dennis Hill 1966
Edgar Glick 1967
Steve Leissner 1991
Steve Leissner 1992
Iian Mull 1996

100 yard butterfly
Roger Harmon 1957
Wally Dobler 1958
Roger Harmon 1958
Bill Steuart 1961
Ken Winfield 1970

200 yard butterfly
John Dudeck 1955
Tom Kwasny 1956
Wally Dobler 1958
Carl Shaar 1960
Carl Shaar 1961
Carl Shaar 1962
Ken Winfield 1970
Chris-Carol Bremer 1993
Chris-Carol Bremer 1994

100 yard backstroke
Howard Patterson 1950
Harold Shoup 1950
Harold Shoup 1951
Don Nichols 1958
Ron Gage 1960
Jeff Mattson 1961
Jeff Mattson 1962
Jeff Mattson 1963
Gary Dilley 1965
Gary Dilley 1966
Gary Dilley 1967
Pete Williams 1967
Pete Williams 1968

200 yard backstroke
(swum as 150 yards until 1951)
Don Korten 1950
Howard Patterson 1950
Harold Shoup 1950
Harold Shoup 1951
Harold Shoup 1952
Bert McLachlan 1953
Jeff Mattson 1963
Gary Dilley 1965
Gary Dilley 1966
Gary Dilley 1967
Pete Williams 1967
Pete Williams 1968

100 yard breaststroke
David Patton 1951
Bruce Aldrich 1952
John Dudeck 1953
Bob Hynes 1953
John Dudeck 1954
Paul Reinke 1957
Frank Modine 1958
Frank Modine 1959
Dennis Ruppart 1960
Bill Singleton 1961
Bill Driver 1963

200 yard breaststroke
David Seibold 1949
David Seibold 1950
Glen Al Omans 1950
Glen Al Omans 1951
John Dudeck 1953
John Dudeck 1954
John Dudeck 1955
Paul Reinke 1956
Paul Reinke 1957
Frank Modine 1958
Frank Modine 1959
Dennis Ruppart 1960
Lee Driver 1966
Bruce Richards 1968
Sidney Appleoom 1989

200 yard individual medley
(swum as 150 yard indiv. medley until 1956)
Don Miller 1950
Bruce Aldrich 1952
Frank Reynolds 1953
Les Lobaugh 1956
Roger Harmon 1958
Bill Wood 1963
Pete Williams 1966
Pete Williams 1967
Pete Williams 1968

400 yard individual medley
Bill Wood 1962
Dick Gretzinger 1963
Pete Williams 1966
Pete Williams 1967
Pete Williams 1968
Bruce Richards 1969
Steve Leissner 1991
Iian Mull 1996

One meter diving
Ray Williams 1949
John Hellewege 1953
Duane Green 1967
Fred Whiteford 1967
Doug Todd 1968
Duane Green 1969
Tom Cramer 1970
Jim Henderson 1970
Tom Cramer 1971
Mike Cook 1973
Marc Stiner 1976
Jesse Griffin 1977
Jesse Griffin 1978
Mike Brown 1983

Three meter diving
John Hellewege 1953
Fred Whiteford 1967
Doug Todd 1968
Doug Todd 1969
Duane Green 1969
Tom Cramer 1970
Jim Henderson 1970
Jud Alward 1971
Tom Cramer 1971
Dave Burgering 1976
Dave Burgering 1977
Jesse Griffin 1977
Dave Burgering 1978
Jesse Griffin 1978
Kevin Machemer 1978
Mike Brown 1981
Mike Brown 1982
Mike Brown 1983
Mike Brown 1984

400 yard freestyle relay

Bob Allwardt, John DeMond, Zigmund Indyke,
Jim Quigley 1946
Jim Duke, Ed Dzioba, Abel Gilbert,
George Hoogerhyde 1947
Bob Allwardt, Jin Duke, Abel Gilbert, George
Hoogerhyde 1948
Don Miller, Jim Quigley, Clarke Scholes,
Gordon Verity 1950
Dave Hoffman, Geo. Hoogerhyde, Jim Quigley,
Clarke Scholes 1951
Chuck Baldwin, Tom Payette, Clarke Scholes,
Bob Schumacher 1952
Bruce Aldrich, Charles Baldwin, Jack Beattie,
Tom Payette 1954
Jim Clemens, Gordon Fornell, Les Lobaugh,
Frank Parrish 1956
Jim Clemens, Gordon Fornell, Frank Parrish,
Don Patterson 1957
Dennis Baker, Dave Diget, Larry Jones,
Don Patterson 1959
Dan Convis, Dave Diget, Larry Jones,
Matt Juergen 1960
Larry Jones, Doug Rowe, Mike Wood,
Bill Wood 1961
Jeff Mattson, Doug Rowe, Mike Wood,
Bill Wood 1962
Dick Gretzinger, Jeff Mattson, Mike Wood,
Bill Wood 1963
Dick Gretzinger, Darryle Kifer, Jim MacMillan,
Bob Sherwood 1964
Gary Dilley, Darryle Kifer, Jim MacMillan,
Ken Walsh 1965
Gary Dilley, Edgar Gkick, Jim MacMillan,
Ken Walsh 1966
Gary Dilley, Gary Langley, Don Rauch,
Ken Walsh 1967
Dick Crittenden, Mark Holdridge,
Mike Kalmbach, Don Rauch 1969

800 yard frestyle relay

(first swum in 1966)
Edgar Glick, Jim MacMillan, Ken Walsh,
Pete Williams 1966
Edgar Glick, Rolf Groseth, Don Rauch,
Pete Williams 1967
Rolf Groseth, Don Rauch,, Bruce Richards,
Pete Williams 1968
Dick Crittenden, Mike Kambach, Don Rauch,
Bruce Richards 1969
Dick Crittenden, Geo. Gonzales,
Bruce Richards, Ken Winfield 1970
Steve Leissner, Gregg Mihalik,
Damon Whitefield, Kevin Zielinski 1989

400 yard medley relay

(swum as 300 yard event until 1957)
Howard Patterson, Paul Seibold,
Jim Quigley 1946
Howard Patterson, Paul Seibold, Jim Duke 1948
Howard Patterson, Glen Al Omans,
Jim Duke 1950
Harold Shoup, David Patton,
George Hoogerhyde 1951
Harold Shoup, Bob Hynes, Chuck Baldwon 1952
Bert McLachlan, John Dudeck,
Chuck Baldwin 1953
Frank Paganini, John Dudeck,
Chuck Baldwin 1954
Frank Paganini, John Dudeck,
Jim Clemens 1955
Al Coxon, Les Lobaugh, Frank Parrish 1956
Roger Harmon, Paul Reinke, Roger Harmon,
Frank Parrish 1957
Al Coxon, Frank Modine, Dave Digit,
Don Patterson 1959
Ron Gage, Dennis Ruppart, Carl Shaar,

Larry Jones 1960
Jeff Mattson, Bill Singleton, Carl Shaar,
Mike Wood 1961
Bill Wood, Bill Driver, Carl Shaar,
Doug Rowe 1962
Jeff Mattson, Bill Driver, Chuck Strong,
Bill Wood 1963
Gary Dilley, Lee Driver, Edgar Glick,
Jim MacMillan 1966
Bob Burke, Jeff Lanini, Van Rockefeller,
Don Rauch 1970
Alan Dilley, Ken Holmes, Ken Winfield,
Bruce Wright 1973

Year-by-Year Team Performance

Years	Dual Meets			Conference Championships			NCAA Championships			Coach
	W	L	T	Pts	Place	Host or Site	Pts	Place	Host or Site	
1922	0	3	0	—	DNC	Chicago, IL			no meet	Southard Flynn
1923	1	3	0	—	DNC	Chicago, IL			no meet	Richard Rauch
1924	3	4	0	—	DNC		—	DNC	Annapolis, MD	Wright Jones
1925	2	4	0	—	DNC		—	DNC	Evanston, IL	Wright Jones
1926	2	4	0	—	DNC	Ann Arbor, MI	—	DNC	Annapolis, MD	Rollin Keifaber
1927	4	3	0	—	DNC	Champaign, IL	0	DNS	Iowa City, IA	W. Sterry Brown
1928					No team or meets, pool under repair					
1929	3	3	0	—	DNC	Chicago, IL	—	DNC	Philadelphia, PA	Frank Hoercher
1930	4	3	0	—	DNC	Evanston, IL	—	DNC	St. Louis, MO	Russell Daubert
1931	4	1	0	—	DNC	Ann Arbor, MI	—	DNC	Cambridge, MA	Russell Daubert
1932	1	3	0	—	DNC	Columbus, OH	—	DNC	Evanston, IL	Russell Daubert
1933	3	4	0	—	DNC	Chicago, IL	—	DNC	Ann Arbor, MI	Russell Daubert
1934	1	4	0	—	DNC	Iowa City, IL	0	DNS	Columbus, OH	Russell Daubert
1935	4	3	1	—	DNC	Champaign, IL	—	DNC	Cambridge, MA	Russell Daubert
1936	5	2	0	—	DNC	Minneapolis, MN	—	DNC	New Haven, CT	Russell Daubert
1937	6	3	0	—	DNC	Bloomington, IN	0	DNS	Minneapolis, MN	Russell Daubert
1938	6	3	0	—	DNC	Winnetka, IL	—	DNC	New Brunswick, NJ	Russell Daubert
1939	1	7	0	—	DNC	West Lafayette, IN	0	DNS	Ann Arbor, MI	Russell Daubert
1940	7	2	0	—	DNC	Columbus, OH	0	DNS	New Haven ,CT	Russell Daubert
1941	6	3	0	—	DNC	Iowa City, IA	0	DNS	East Lansing, MI	Russell Daubert
1942	2	3	2		1st*	East Lansing, MI	0	DNS	Cambridge, MA	Charles McCaffree
1943	4	?	0		1st*	East Lansing, MI	4	12th/15	Columbus, OH	Charles McCaffree
1944					Intercollegiate competition suspended due to World War II					
1945	0	1	0		1st*	East Lansing, MI	12	(t)4th/13	Ann Arbor, MI	Charles McCaffree
1946	4	3	0		1st*	East Lansing, MI	18	3rd/17	New Haven, CT	Charles McCaffree
1947	8	2	0		1st*	East Lansing, MI	18	4th/22	Seattle, WA	Charles McCaffree
1948	8	2	0		1st*	East Lansing, MI	21	4th/37	Ann Arbor, MI	Charles McCafrree
1949	8	1	0		1st*	East Lansing, MI	10	(t)7th/20	Chapel Hill, NC	Charles McCaffree
1950	10	1	0		1st*	East Lansing, MI	17	5th/46	Columbus, OH	Charles McCaffree
1951	9	1	0	68	2nd	Minneapolis, MN	60	2nd/22	Austin, TX	Charles McCaffree
1952	8	2	0	66	2nd	East Lansing, MI	27	4th/20	Princeton, NJ	Charles McCaffree
1953	7	1	0	48	3rd	Iowa City, IA	14	(t)5th/22	Columbus, OH	Charles McCaffree
1954	6	2	0	35	3rd	Ann Arbor, MI	9	(t)8th/26	Syracuse, NY	Charles McCaffree
1955	7	3	0	27.5	5th	Columbus, OH	0	DNS	Oxford, OH	Charles McCaffree
1956	4	3	0	32	6th	West Lafayette, IN	0	DNS	New Haven, CT	Charles McCaffree
1957	7	2	0	87	1st	Minneapolis, MN	52	3rd/22	Chapel Hill, NC	Charles McCaffree
1958	8	1	0	76	2nd	Iowa City, IA	62	3rd/24	Ann Arbor, MI	Charles McCaffree
1959	5	3	0	53.5	4th	East Lansing, MI	35	5th/19	Ithaca, NY	Charles McCaffree
1960	7	3	0	35	4th	Madison, WI	3	16th/18	Dallas, TX	Charles McCaffree
1961	8	2	0	100.5	4th	Columbus, OH	24	5th/27	Seattle, WA	Charles McCaffree
1962	5	4	0	96.8	4th	Bloomington, IN	20	6th/27	Columbus, OH	Charles McCaffree
1963	8	4	0	84.3	5th	West Lafayette, IN	15	8th/22	Chapel Hill, NC	Charles McCaffree
1964	6	2	0	88.3	5th	Minneapolis, MN	0	DNS	New Haven, CT	Charles McCaffree
1965	11	1	0	273	3rd	Madison, WI	90	6th/38	Ames, IA	Charles McCaffree
1966	10	2	0	325	3rd	Iowa City, IA	173	4th/	Colorado Springs, CO	Charles McCaffree
1967	9	1	0	308	3rd	East Lansing, MI	115	8th/35	East Lansing, MI	Charles McCaffree
1968	8	3	0	248	3rd	Ann Arbor, MI	38	13th/37	Hanover, NH	Charles McCaffree
1969	12	2	0	304	3rd	Madison, WI	38	12th	Bloomington, IN	Charles McCaffree
1970	10	1	0	311	3rd	Bloomington, IN	43	14th/28	Salt Lake City, UT	Richard Fetters
1971	9	3	0	207	4th	Columbus, OH	19	18th/32	Ames, IA	Richard Fetters
1972	7	4	0	184	4th	East Lansing, MI	14	19th/29	West Point, NY	Richard Fetters
1973	9	3	0	186	4th	Madison, WI	25	14th/29	Knoxville, TN	Richard Fetters
1974	7	4	0	219	6th	Madison, WI	—	DNC	Long Beach, CA	Richard Fetters
1975	6	3	0	255	4th	Bloomington, IN	—	DNC	Cleveland, OH	Richard Fetters
1976	7	3	0	365	4th	Champaign, IL	8	24//	Providence, RI	Richard Fetters
1977	7	2	0	426	3rd	Champaign, IL	23	19th/35	Cleveland, OH	Richard Fetters
1978	6	2	0	261	6th	Champaign, IL	31	14th/28	Long Beach, CA	Richard Fetters
1979	6	7	0	147	9th	Columbus, OH	—	DNC	Cleveland, OH	Richard Fetters
1980	6	5	0	139	9th	Ann Arbor, MI	—	DNC	Cambridge, MA	Richard Fetters
1981	6	4	0	149	7th	Brown Deer, WI	3	(t)25th	Austin, TX	Richard Fetters
1982	6	6	0	184	7th	Iowa City, IA	1	33rd/33	Madison, WI	Richard Fetters
1983	3	8	0	117	9th	Indianapolis, IN	3	(t)28th/33	Indianapolis, IN	Richard Fetters
1984	3	8	0	133	9th	Indianapolis, IN	4	26th/31	Cleveland, OH	Richard Fetters
1985	5	7	0	136	8th	Indianapolis, IN	—	DNC	Austin, TX	Richard Fetters
1986	9	4	0	242	6th	Indianapolis, IN	—	DNC	Indianapolis, IN	Richard Fetters
1987	7	5	0	150	9th	Indianapolis, IN	4	37th/40	Austin, TX	Richard Fetters
1988	9	4	0	252	6th	Indianapolis, IN	12	(t)28th/43	Indianapolis, IN	Bill Wadley
1989	10	2	0	216	6th	Indianapolis, IN	17	29th/41	Indianapolis, IN	Bill Wadley
1990	9	1	0	395	4th	Ann Arbor, MI	9	(t)37th/46	Indianapolis, IN	Richard Bader
1991	9	2	0	399	6th	Indianapolis, IN	31	(t)24th/42	Austin, TX	Richard Bader
1992	9	3	0	290	7th	Minneapolis, MN	34	22nd/40	Indianapolis, IN	Richard Bader
1993	8	2	0	214	8th	Indianapolis, IN	15	29th/42	Indianapolis, IN	Richard Bader
1994	7	4	0	334	5th	Indianapolis, IN	38	(t)20th/43	Minneapolis, MN	Richard Bader
1995	2	6	0	138	10th	Minneapolis, MN	—	DNS	Indianapolis, IN	Richard Bader
1996	5	4	0	216	9th	Ann Arbor, MI	38	24th	Austin, TX	Richard Bader

1997	1	5	0	110	10th	Bloomington, IN	DNC	Minneapolis, MN	Richard Bader
1998	0	7	0	131	10th	Minneapolis, MN	DNC	Auburn, AL	Richard Bader
1999	3	5	0	133	10th	Bloomington, IN	DNC	Indianapolis, IN	Richard Bader
2000	2	7	0	119	10th	Ann Arbor, MI	DNC	Minneapolis, MN	Jim Lutz
2001	3	4	0	143	10th	Minneapolis, MN	DNC	College Station, TX	Jim Lutz
2002	3	6	0	122	10th	Bloomington, IN	DNC	Athens, GA	Jim Lutz
2003	4	9	0	146.5	10th	Ann Arbor, MI	DNC	Austin, TX	Jim Lutz
TOTALS	455	269	3						

* Prior to joining the Big Ten in 1951, Michigan State competed in the Central Collegiate championships from 1942-1950.
DNC—Did not compete
DNS—Did not score

TENNIS
LEADERS, RECORDS and HONORS

ALL-TIME COACHING RECORDS

Coach	Years	W	L	T	Avg.
No head coach	1913-20	19	12	4	.653
Charles D. Ball	1918-20	8	3	2	.653
Harry C. Young	1921-22	6	6	2	.500
Charles D. Ball	1923-46	143	93	4	.600
Gordon A. Dahlgren	1947	11	6	0	.647
H. Frank Beeman	1948-50	32	20	0	.615
Thomas Martin	1951	12	4	0	.750
John A. Friedrich	1952	12	4	0	.750
H. Frank Beeman	1953-57	49	34	0	.590
Stan Drobac	1958-89	264	360	0	.423
Jim Frederick	1990-91	24	27	0	.471
Gene Orlando	1991-	138	183	0	.430
Totals	1913-2003	710	749	10	.487

Season Records

See page 874 for explanation of abbreviations.

1909 (1-0)
Coach: no coach
5-25	H	Olivet	6-0	W

1910 (1-1-1)
Coach: no coach
5-14	A	Olivet	2-2	T
6-7	A	Michigan Normal	1-5	L
6-13	H	Olivet	4-1	W

1911 (2-2)
Coach: no coach
4-29	H	Olivet	2-3-1	L
5-6	A	Michigan Normal	5-1	W
5-13	A	Alma	3-0	W
6-10	A	Olivet	2-4	L

1912
Coach: no coach
	A	Olivet	unavailable
5-25	H	Olivet	unavailable
	H	Michigan Normal unavailable	

1913 (1-1-1)
Coach: no coach
5-9	A	Michigan Normal	0-6	L
5-17	H	Olivet	6-0	W
5-24	A	Olivet	3-3	T

1914 (1-1-1)
Coach: no coach
	A	Olivet	5-1	W
6-6	H	Michigan Normal	3-3	T
	H	Olivet	2-4	L

1915 (5-0)
Coach: no coach
5-14	A	Olivet	5-1	W
5-15	H	Alma	5-1	W
5-21	A	Michigan Normal	7-2	W
5-29	H	Detroit Law School	6-0	W
6-17	H	Michigan Frosh	5-1	W

1916 (8-2-1)
Coach: no coach
5-11	H	Olivet	6 1	W
5-12	H	Detroit Law School	3-0	W
5-13	A	Albion	3-5	L
5-16	H	Alma	6-0	W
5-17	A	Hillsdale	3-3	T
5-19	A	Albion	6-3	W
5-20	H	Michigan Normal	6-3	W
5-26	A	Alma	9-0	W
5-27	H	Hillsdale	3-4	L
5-31	A	Olivet	5-1	W
6-3	A	Michigan Normal	7-2	W

No team in 1917

Charles D. Ball (1918-1920 and 1923-1946)

Charles Ball, who was the head coach for 27 years, was actually never under the total direction of the athletic department. He held a professorial position in the department of chemistry and, being loyal to his teaching position, seldom joined the team for road matches. This meant that a team captain or manager often shouldered significantly more responsibility than would normally be considered. Other than the fact he was team manager during his undergraduate years at the University of Pennsylvania, little is known of Ball's tennis skills or tennis experience.

1918 (1-1-0)
Coach: Charles D. Ball
5-11	H	Michigan Normal	5-1	W
5-21	A	Michigan Normal	3-3	T

1919 (3-2-1)
Coach: Charles D. Ball
5-15	A	Michigan	0-3	L
5-16	A	Michigan Normal	3-0	W
5-17	H	Central Mich. Normal	3-3	T
5-23	H	Alma	3-2	W
5-30	A	Central Mich. Normal	2-4	L
6-3	H	Michigan Normal	3-0	W

1920 (4-1)
Coach: Charles D. Ball
5-15	H	Kalamazoo	3-1	W
5-20	H	Albion	6-0	W
5-22	H	Michigan Normal	4-0	W
6-5	A	Kalamazoo	1-3	L
6-6	H	Central Mich. Normal	6-0	W

Harry C. Young (1921-1922)

In Coach Ball's absence for two years, Harry Young, an instructor in botany, stepped forward to fill the void. Other than being a fan of the game, little is known about his tennis background. It is surmised, however, that Harry Young is the same "Young" that teamed with Nicholson to win the doubles competition at an open tournament held on the college courts during the summer of 1918.

1921 (3-4)
Coach: Harry C. Young
4-30	A	Pontiac Tennis Club	4-5	L
5-7	H	Kalamazoo	1-5	L
5-11	A	Albion	5-1	W
5-20	H	Michigan Normal	3-0	W
5-21	H	Oberlin	1-2	L
5-30	H	Pontiac Tennis Club	7-2	W
5-31	A	Michigan	0-6	L

1922 (3-2-2)
Coach: Harry C. Young
4-22	A	Pontiac Tennis Club	4-5	L
5-5	H	Oberlin	4-2	W
5-6	H	Oklahoma	0-4	L
5-10	H	Kalamazoo	6-0	W
5-30	H	Pontiac Tennis Club	8-1	W
6-3	H	Detroit Law School	3-3	T
6-10	A	Central Mich. Normal	3-3	T

1923 (2-6-1)
Coach: Charles D. Ball
4-27	H	Michigan	0-6	L
5-2	A	Michigan	0-6	L
5-11	A	Kalamazoo	1-5	L
5-12	A	Valparaiso	4-2	W
5-29	A	Detroit City College	4-0	W
5-30	A	Oberlin	1-3	L
6-1	A	Penn State	1-3	L
6-2	A	Pittsburgh	1-3	L
6-4	A	Alleghany	2-2	T

1924 (1-2)
Coach: Charles D. Ball
5-3	A	Michigan	0-6	L
5-10	H	Detroit City College	3-1	W
5-20	H	Penn State	2-8	L

1925 (4-3)
Coach: Charles D. Ball
4-25	H	Michigan	0-7	L
5-9	H	Central Mich. Normal	6-0	W
5-14	A	Oberlin	1-6	L
5-15	A	Detroit	2-5	L
5-16	A	Detroit City College	4-1	W
5-30	H	Western State Normal	4-3	W
6-3	H	Detroit	5-2	W

1926 (9-5)
Coach: Charles D. Ball

4-23	A	Detroit	5-2	W
4-24	A	Michigan	0-7	L
4-30	H	Detroit City College	6-2	W
5-1	H	Central Mich. Normal	7-0	W
5-4	H	Notre Dame	4-3	W
5-8	H	Western State Normal	4-3	W
5-12	H	Albion	7-0	W
5-14	A	Detroit City College	4-5	L
5-15	H	Michigan Normal	5-1	W
5-17	A	W. Va. Wesleyan	6-1	W
5-19	A	Penn State	3-4	L
5-21	A	Cincinnati	0-7	L
5-22	A	Xavier (OH)	2-5	L
5-29	H	Detroit	5-2	W

1927 (2-7-1)
Coach: Charles D. Ball

4-29	H	Kalamazoo	4-3	W
4-30	H	Grand Rapids J.C.	3-4	L
5-5	A	Michigan	0-7	L
5-6	A	Detroit City College	2-5	L
5-7	H	Hillsdale	3-3	T
5-11	H	Michigan	0-8	L
5-13	H	Armour Tech	1-6	L
5-26	A	Armour Tech	1-6	L
5-27	A	Marquette	5-2	W
5-28	A	Notre Dame	1-6	L

1928 (5-2)
Coach: Charles D. Ball

4-27	H	Detroit City College	5-1	W
4-28	H	Albion	7-0	W
5-3	A	Michigan	0-9	L
5-12	H	Notre Dame	4-3	W
5-15	H	Marquette	4-3	W
5-21	H	Armour Tech	3-4	L
5-31	A	Detroit City College	5-2	W

1929 (3-3)
Coach: Charles D. Ball

4-20	H	Detroit City College	5-2	W
4-27	H	Albion	7-0	W
5-11	H	Western St. Teachers	1-6	L
5-13	A	Notre Dame	0-7	L
5-15	A	Armour Tech	4-3	W
5-16	A	Chicago	0-7	L

1930 (2-9)
Coach: Charles D. Ball

4-25	H	Albion	6-1	W
4-26	H	Michigan Normal	5-2	W
5-2	H	Northwestern	0-9	L
5-3	H	Detroit	2-7	L
5-6	H	Michigan	0-9	L
5-10	H	Oberlin	2-4	L
5-14	A	Western St. Teachers	0-7	L
5-20	H	Notre Dame	1-8	L
5-22	A	Oberlin	3-4	L
5-23	A	Detroit City College	1-4	L
5-24	A	Detroit	1-8	L

1931 (1-6-1)
Coach: Charles D. Ball

4-25	H	Kalamazoo	2-7	L
5-1	A	Michigan	0-9	L
5-3	A	Michigan Normal	3-6	L
5-12	A	Detroit City College	5-2	W
5-18	H	Detroit	4-4	T
5-22	H	Detroit	1-8	L
5-26	H	Western St. Teachers	2-5	L
5-28	H	Michigan Normal.	3-6	L

1932 (9-2)
Coach: Charles D. Ball

4-23	H	Kalamazoo	9-0	W
4-29	H	Detroit	8-1	W
5-3	H	Michigan	3-6	L
5-7	H	Ohio Wesleyan	6-1	W
5-11	H	Loyola (IL)	7-0	W
5-14	H	Oberlin	6-1	W
5-16	A	Michigan Normal	6-3	W
5-20	A	Detroit City College	7-2	W
5-21	H	Notre Dame	7-2	W
5-27	A	Western St. Teachers	4-5	L
5-28	A	Notre Dame	8-1	W

1933 (11-1)
Coach: Charles D. Ball

4-22	H	Kalamazoo	9-0	W
4-28	H	Michigan Normal	7-2	W
4-29	H	Notre Dame	8-1	W
5-6	A	Notre Dame	8-1	W
5-12	H	Ohio State	5-0	W
5-13	H	Oberlin	7-0	W
5-18	H	Western St. Teachers	6-3	W
5-19	A	Michigan	4-5	L
5-23	H	Michigan	7-2	W
5-26	H	Detroit	6-1	W
5-27	H	Detroit City College	6-1	W
5-30	H	Detroit	7-0	W

1934 (13-0)
Coach: Charles D. Ball

4-27	A	Michigan	5-4	W
4-28	A	Kalamazoo	9-0	W
5-3	A	Oberlin	8-1	W
5-4	A	Ohio State	10-0	W
5-5	A	Toledo Tennis Club	7-1	W
5-10	H	Michigan Normal	5-4	W
5-11	H	Oberlin	9-0	W
5-12	H	Notre Dame	7-2	W
5-18	A	Western St. Teachers	5-4	W
5-19	A	Notre Dame	6-3	W
5-25	H	Michigan	7-2	W
5-26	H	Ohio State	5-1	W
5-28	H	Chicago	5-1	W

1935 (4-5-1)
Coach: Charles D. Ball

4-26	H	Michigan	1-8	L
4-29	H	Chicago	1-5	L
5-8	H	Albion	7-0	W
5-10	H	Wayne	9-1	W
5-11	A	Notre Dame	5-3	W
5-17	A	Michigan	1-8	L
5-24	H	Michigan Normal	9-0	W
5-25	H	Western St. Teachers	3-6	L
5-31	A	Toledo Tennis Club	5-5	T
6-1	A	Ohio State	2-8	L

1936 (12-2)
Coach: Charles D. Ball

4-18	H	Kalamazoo	12-3	W
4-21	H	Michigan	6-3	W
4-24	A	Wayne	9-0	W
4-25	H	Michigan Normal	6-1	W
4-30	H	Oberlin	9-0	W
5-1	H	Western St. Teachers	4-5	L
5-8	A	Toledo Tennis Club	8-1	W
5-9	A	Ohio State	3-6	L
5-14	H	Kentucky	5-4	W
5-15	A	Michigan	8-1	W
5-22	A	Oberlin	9-0	W
5-23	A	Western Reserve	6-3	W
5-29	H	Notre Dame	8-1	W
5-30	H	Western St. Teachers	6-3	W

1937 (11-1)
Coach: Charles D. Ball

4-16	H	Wisconsin	4-2	W
4-23	H	Ohio State	7-3	W
4-30	A	Northwestern	2-7	L
5-1	H	Marquette	9-0	W
5-6	A	Indiana	8-1	W
5-7	A	Kentucky	8-1	W
5-8	A	Cincinnati	9-0	W
5-15	A	Notre Dame	8-1	W
5-29	H	Western Reserve	8-1	W
5-31	H	Wayne	5-4	W
6-2	H	Kalamazoo	9-0	W
6-12	H	Alumni	6-3	W

1938 (7-4)
Coach: Charles D. Ball

4-16	H	Kalamazoo	5-4	W
4-22	A	Toledo	9-0	W
4-23	A	Ohio State	5-4	W
4-30	A	Michigan	4-5	L
5-6	H	Indiana	6-3	W
5-7	H	Kentucky	2-7	L
5-10	H	Michigan	6-3	W
5-12	H	Notre Dame	6-3	W
5-21	H	Marquette	6-1	W
5-26	A	Wayne	1-8	L
6-1	H	Wayne	0-9	L

1939 (10-5)
Coach: Charles D. Ball

4-3	*	Richmond	5-1	W
4-4	*	Virginia	0-9	L
4-6	*	Kentucky	8-1	W
4-21	H	Cincinnati	8-1	W
4-22	H	Toledo	9-0	W
4-29	A	Notre Dame	6-3	W
5-4	H	Indiana	8-1	W
5-6	H	Kalamazoo	6-3	W
5-12	A	Michigan	3-6	L
5-13	H	Michigan Normal	9-0	W
5-19	H	Illinois	3-6	L
5-20	H	Ohio State	5-4	W
5-24	H	Michigan	3-6	L
5-26	H	Western St. Teachers	5-4	W
6-2	A	Wayne	3-6	L

1940 (6-7-0)
Coach: Charles D. Ball

3-21	*	Davidson	1-6	L
3-22	*	Duke	1-8	L
3-23	*	North Carolina State	8-1	W
3-25	*	Wake Forest	6-1	W
4-20	H	Kentucky	9-0	W
5-2	A	Illinois	2-7	L
5-3	A	Purdue	8-1	W
5-4	A	Ohio State	3-6	L
5-11	H	Indiana	9-0	W
5-18	A	Michigan	3-6	L
5-20	H	Michigan	3-6	L
5-25	A	Western St. Teachers	4-5	L
5-30	H	Wayne	6-3	W

1941 (7-7)
Coach: Charles D. Ball

3-26	*	Arkansas	4-5	L
3-27	*	Tulsa	2-5	L
3-28	*	Oklahoma A&M	6-3	W
3-29	*	Oklahoma	4-5	L
4-26	H	Ohio State	4-5	L
5-1	H	Michigan	2-7	L
5-2	H	Illinois	8-1	W
5-15	A	Notre Dame	3-6	L
5-16	A	Ball State	9-0	W
5-17	A	Kentucky	6-3	W

5-23	H	Michigan Normal	8-1	W
5-24	A	Michigan	4-5	L
5-28	A	Wayne	8-1	W
5-30	H	Western Michigan	6-3	W

1942 (10-5)
Coach: Charles D. Ball

3-25	*	Arkansas	7-1	W
3-27	*	Oklahoma	3-6	L
3-28	*	Oklahoma	4-5	L
4-16	A	Michigan	2-7	L
4-17	H	Notre Dame	3-6	L
4-24	H	Kentucky	7-2	W
4-25	A	Ohio State	9-0	W
4-29	H	Michigan	1-8	L
5-2	H	Indiana	9-0	W
5-7	A	Illinois	5-4	W
5-8	A	Purdue	7-0	W
5-16	H	Michigan Normal	8-1	W
5-22	H	Wayne	9-0	W
5-23	H	Detroit	8-1	W
5-30	A	Western Michigan	5-4	W

1943 (7-1)
Coach: Charles D. Ball

4-26	H	Michigan	6-3	W
4-30	H	Notre Dame	6-3	W
5-10	A	Michigan	3-6	L
5-20	A	Detroit	8-0	W
5-21	H	Michigan Normal	7-0	W
5-22	A	Western Michigan	7-2	W
5-28	H	Central State	5-1	W
6-4	A	Central State	4-2	W

1944
Intercollegiate athletics suspended due to World War II

1945 (3-1)
Coach: Charles D. Ball

5-19	H	Detroit	5-1	W
5-23	A	Wayne	3-6	L
5-24	A	Detroit	4-2	W
5-28	H	Wayne	5-4	W

1946 (4-10)
Coach: Charles D. Ball

4-20	A	Northwestern	4-5	L
4-24	A	Michigan	2-7	L
4-25	A	Ohio State	2-7	L
4-26	A	Cincinnati	1-8	L
4-27	A	Kentucky	6-3	W
5-3	A	Western Michigan	5-4	W
5-4	A	Indiana	9-0	W
5-10	A	Illinois	4-5	L
5-11	A	Purdue	5-4	W
5-18	H	Notre Dame	4-5	L
5-23	H	Michigan	4-5	L
5-27	H	Wayne	4-5	L
5-29	H	Wayne	4-5	L
5-31	H	Western Michigan	3-6	L

Gordon A. Dahlgren (1947)
After prepping in Lindblom High School in Chicago, IL, Gordon "Jake" Dahlgren enrolled at MSC in the fall of 1933. He would earn three football letters as a lineman for Coach Bachman (1934-1936), serving as captain in his senior season. Upon graduation he joined the staff at nearby Lansing Eastern High School only to return to State in 1939 as an assistant professor of physical education and line coach in football. In 1947 the popular Spartan was diagnosed with incurable cancer. He continued on the job whereupon he accepted the position of coaching the varsity tennis team of 1947, replacing the

retiring veteran Charles Ball. Dahlgren's 1947 squad would post an impressive 11-6 record. By fall of that year he had become bed-ridden with the malady and he succumbed to the illness on February 26, 1948. He was 36 years old.

1947 (11-6)
Coach: Gordon A. Dahlgren

3-22	*	Virginia	5-4	W
3-24	*	Virginia	5-4	W
3-25	*	William & Mary	1-8	L
3-26	*	Georgetown	9-0	W
4-14	H	Cincinnati	7-2	W
4-19	H	Chicago	8-1	W
4-21	H	Wayne	8-1	W
4-25	H	Purdue	6-1	W
4-26	A	Notre Dame	3-6	L
4-30	A	Michigan	3-6	L
5-2	A	Western Michigan	7-2	W
5-3	A	Kalamazoo	3-6	L
5-12	A	Wayne	5-4	W
5-19	A	Illinois	4-5	L
5-22	H	Michigan	4-5	L
5-23	H	Ohio State	8-1	W
5-27	H	Western Michigan	7-2	W

H. Frank Beeman (1948-1950 and 1953-1957)
Entering Michigan State College out of Royal Oak (MI) High School in the fall of 1939, Frank Beeman would later earn three varsity letters as a member of the Spartan tennis teams of 1941, 1942 and 1943. He captained the team during his junior and senior seasons. Following graduation, Beeman served three years in the parachute infantry of the U.S. Army, 16 months of which he spent in Europe. It was while in Europe that Frank added further credence to his tennis background. In addition to serving as tennis instructor in the Army Athletic school in Struttgart, Germany, he found time to win the Army's European Theatre of Operation Invitational championship held in Frankfurt. Following discharge, Frank enrolled at the University of Michigan in 1947 where he received a master's degree in physical education. He joined the PE staff at MSC in the spring of 1947 and by March of 1948 had become the school's tennis coach, succeeding the deceased Gordon A. Dahlgren. After four years in a dual role of coach and director of intramural activities, Beeman elected to leave the coaching position only to be called back once more, this time serving for five years (1953-1957).

1948 (13-4)
Coach: Harris F. Beeman

3-23	*	Lynchburg	9-0	W
3-24	*	William & Mary	1-8	L
3-25	*	William & Mary	0-9	L
3-29	*	North Carolina	0-9	L
4-23	A	Ohio State	9-0	W
4-28	H	Michigan	6-3	W
4-30	A	Purdue	9-0	W
5-1	A	Chicago	9-0	W
5-7	H	Illinois	6-2	W
5-8	H	Kalamazoo	7-2	W
5-15	H	Wayne	9-0	W
5-19	H	Western Michigan	9-0	W
5-21	A	Michigan	4-5	L
5-22	H	Detroit	8-1	W
5-28	H	Wayne	8-1	W
5-29	A	Detroit	9-0	W
6-1	A	Western Michigan	9-0	W

1949 (12-6)
Coach: Harris F. Beeman

3-25	*	North Carolina	1-8	L
3-26	*	North Carolina	0-9	L
3-28	*	East Carolina	9-0	W
3-30	*	Virginia	1-8	L
4-25	H	Detroit	8-0	W
4-26	A	Wayne	9-0	W
4-28	H	Michigan	2-7	L
5-5	A	Illinois	5-4	W
5-6	A	Wisconsin	5-4	W
5-7	A	Marquette	8-0	W
5-11	A	Western Michigan	8-1	W
5-14	A	Notre Dame	7-2	W
5-16	A	Michigan	1-8	L
5-18	A	Purdue	7-2	W
5-20	H	Ohio State	4-5	L
5-21	H	Western Michigan	8-1	W
5-23	H	Wayne	9-0	W
5-28		Detroit	7-2	W

1950 (8-10)
Coach: Harris F. Beeman

3-23	*	Duke	1-8	L
3-24	*	Duke	1-8	L
3-25	*	North Carolina State	9-0	W
3-27	*	North Carolina	0-10	L
3-28	*	North Carolina	1-9	L
3-30	*	Virginia	2-8	L
3-31	*	William & Mary	1-9	L
4-26	H	Detroit	9-0	W
4-28	H	Wisconsin	6-3	W
5-2	H	Notre Dame	5-4	W
5-12	H	Illinois	1-8	L
5-13	H	Purdue	7-2	W
5-15	A	Michigan	1-7	L
5-19	A	Ohio State	9-0	W
5-20	A	Indiana	3-6	L
5-24	A	Wayne	5-0	W
5-27	H	Michigan	4-5	L
5-29	H	Western Michigan	8-1	W

Thomas F. Martin (1951)
As a recent graduate of Mihicgan State, Tom Martin filled in for Coach Beeman on a temporary basis after Frank had been called back into military service. As a four-year member of rhte Ferndale Lincoln High School squad, Martin led squads that were regional champions for three years. By the time he had reached his senior year at Lincoln he was also crowned singles champion in that same regional competition. Tom enrolled at MSC in 1942, leaving shortly thereafter to enter the U.S. Navy from 1943-1946. Re-entering State in 1947, he earned three letters (1947-1949) as a member of the varsity tennis team. The 1948 squad won the Central Collegiate Conference championship.

1951 (12-4)
Coach: Harris F. Beeman and Thomas F. Martin

3-22	*	Duke	4-5	L
3-23	*	Duke	2-7	L
3-24	*	North Carolina State	9-0	W
3-26	*	Virginia	3-6	L
3-27	*	William & Mary	5-4	W
3-29	*	North Carolina	4-5	L
3-30	*	North Carolina	5-4	W
4-23	H	Wayne	9-0	W
4-27	H	Wisconsin	9-0	W
4-28	A	Minnesota	9-0	W
5-4	A	Purdue	9-0	W
5-5	A	Notre Dame	9-0	W
5-12	H	Indiana	7-2	W
5-14	A	Illinois	8-1	W
5-17	H	Michigan	8-1	W
5-18	H	Ohio State	9-0	W
		Big Tens at Evanston	1st	

John A. Friedrich (1952)

A native of Grand Rapids, John Friedrich had been a member of the MSC physical education staff since 1947. He attended Grand Rapids Junior College after high school, then spent three years in the U.S. Army during World War II before arriving in East Lansing. He received a B.S. degree in 1947 and then joined the PE staff as a graduate assistant while working on his master's degree, which he received in 1949. Friedrich then became a full-time instructor at his alma mater, teaching classes in tennis, handball and archery. After only one season as head coach, John left his position to join the staff at Duke University.

1952 (12-4)

Coach: John A. Friedrich

3-25	*	North Carolina	4-5	L
3-26	*	North Carolina	4-5	L
3-27	*	North Carolina State	9-0	W
3-29	*	Davidson	6-3	W
3-30	*	Sedgefield Inn	8-1	W
3-31	*	Duke	4-3	W
4-1	*	Virginia	1-6	L
4-26	H	Western Michigan	8-1	W
4-29	H	Wayne	9-0	W
5-3	A	Indiana	4-5	L
5-6	A	Detroit	9-0	W
5-9	H	Illinois	5-2	W
5-10	H	Wisconsin	9-0	W
5-13	H	Michigan	9-0	W
5-17	A	Ohio State	9-0	W
5-19	H	Notre Dame	7-1	W
		Big Tens at Evanston	2nd	

1953 (12-4)

Coach: Harris F. Beeman

3-27	*	Presbyterian	4-5	L
3-28	*	Presbyterian	3-6	L
3-30	*	Davidson	8-1	W
3-31	*	Duke	1-8	L
4-1	*	North Carolina State	9-0	W
4-4	*	North Carolina	3-6	L
4-25	A	Illinois	9-0	W
5-7	H	Northwestern	9-0	W
5-8	H	Notre Dame	8-1	W
5-11	H	Western Michigan	9-0	W
5-13	A	Michigan	7-2	W
5-15	H	Ohio State	8-1	W
5-16	H	Indiana	6-3	W
5-18	H	Michigan	7-2	W
5-22	A	Iowa	9-0	W
5-23	A	Wisconsin	8-1	W
		Big Tens at Evanston	2nd	

1954 (10-7)

Coach: Harris F. Beeman

3-27	*	Marshall	9-0	W
3-29	*	Davidson	3-6	L
3-30	*	North Carolina State	9-0	W
3-31	*	North Carolina	0-6	L
4-1	*	Virginia	3-7	L
4-2	*	West Virginia	10-0	W
4-27	H	Wayne	9-0	W
4-30	A	Northwestern	6-3	W
5-1	A	Notre Dame	5-4	W
5-6	A	Western Michigan	2-7	L
5-8	A	Indiana	3-6	L
5-11	H	Michigan	8-1	W
5-14	H	Detroit	9-0	W
5-15	H	Wisconsin	7-1	W
5-19	H	Michigan	3-6	L
5-21	H	Illinois	4-5	L
		Iowa	6-3	W
		Big Tens at Champaign	3rd	

1955 (7-8)

Coach: Harris F. Beeman

3-26	*	Marshall	7-2	W
3-28	*	Davidson	0-9	L
3-29	*	North Carolina	0-9	L
3-30	*	North Carolina State	9-0	W
4-22	A	Detroit	9-0	W
4-23	A	Wayne	7-2	W
4-30	H	Indiana	0-9	L
5-2	A	Illinois	3-6	L
5-5	H	Northwestern	2-7	L
5-7	H	Purdue	6-3	W
5-9	H	Western Michigan	2-7	L
5-14	H	Notre Dame	5-4	W
5-16	H	Michigan	0-9	L
5-20	A	Minnesota	0-9	L
5-21	A	Wisconsin	7-2	W
		Big Tens at Evanston	6th	

1956 (13-5)

Coach: Harris F. Beeman

3-26	*	Davidson	8-1	W
3-27	*	WSKenyon	7-2	W
3-28	*	Wake Forest	7-2	W
3-30	*	Fort Belvoir	8-1	W
3-31	*	Andrews AFB	9-0	W
4-2	*	George Washington	5-4	W
4-3	*	Fort Lee	9-0	W
4-5	*	North Carolina State	9-0	W
4-24	H	Detroit	7-2	W
4-27	A	Purdue	4-5	L
4-28	A	Indiana	1-8	L
4-30	H	Wayne State	9-0	W
5-4	A	Western Michigan	1-8	L
5-5	H	Wisconsin	8-1	W
5-8	A	Notre Dame	5-4	W
5-12	H	Illinois	5-4	W
5-14	A	Michigan	0-9	L
5-18	A	Northwestern	2-7	L
		Big Tens at Indianapolis	6th	

1957 (7-10)

Coach: Harris F. Beeman

3-25	*	Pensacola NATS	0-11	L
3-26	*	Florida State	6-3	W
3-27	*	Florida	1-8	L
3-28	*	Rollins	4-5	L
3-30	*	Florida Southern	8-1	W
4-1	*	Miami	0-9	L
4-5	*	Presbyterian	2-7	L
4-20	A	Ohio State	8-1	W
4-27	A	Detroit	9-0	W
4-29	A	Wayne	9-0	W
5-2	H	Northwestern	3-6	L
5-4	A	Illinois	0-9	L
5-7	H	Western Michigan	6-3	W
5-11	H	Notre Dame	1-5	L
5-13	H	Michigan	0-9	L
5-17	A	Iowa	0-9	L
5-18	A	Wisconsin	5-4	W
		Big Tens at Evanston	6th	

Stan Drobac (1958-1989)

Stan Drobac was one of Michigan State's most outstanding players. He teamed with Tom Belton to capture the Big Ten no. 1 doubles title in 1952 and 1953 while also being crowned the conference's no. 1 singles champion in 1952. Drobac graduated from State in 1953 with a B.S. degree and returned to complete a master's degree in 1956. He first joined the MSU staff as an instructor of physcial education at East Lansing High School. Following this short stint into the prep ranks, Drobac served Frank Beeman as an assistant at State for two seasons (1956-57), making him an immediate and viable candidate for the head coaching position when Beeman announced his departure from the courts.

1958 (6-8)

Coach: Stan Drobac

3-25	*	Pensacola NATS	5-1	W
3-27	*	Florida State	4-5	L
3-28	*	Florida	5-4	W
3-29	*	Rollins	2-7	L
3-31	*	Miami	0-9	L
4-3	*	Tennessee	7-2	W
4-24&25	A_EV	quadrangular meet		
		Northwestern	36	
		MSU	22	
		Purdue	22	
		Chicago	10	
4-30	A	Detroit	9-0	W
5-2	A	Notre Dame	1-8	L
5-3	A	Indiana	3-6	L
5-6	H	Wayne	7-2	W
5-7	A	Western Michigan	2-7	L
5-9	H	Wisconsin	7-2	W
5-10	H	Illinois	0-9	L
5-13	A	Michigan	0-9	L
5-16	H	quadrangular meet		
		Iowa	34	
		Minnesota	27	
		MSU	15	
		Ohio State	14	
		Big Tens at Evanston	6th	

1959 (9-7)

Coach: Stan Drobac

3-28	*	Florida State	1-8	L
3-30	*	Troy State Teachers	9-0	W
3-31	*	Auburn	9-0	W
4-2	*	Georgia	2-7	L
4-25	A	Ohio State	5-4	W
5-2	A	Illinois	2-7	L
5-4	H	Detroit	9-0	W
5-6	H	Notre Dame	1-8	L
5-7	H	Northwestern	7-2	W
5-9	H	Purdue	8-1	W
5-12	H	Michigan	2-7	L
5-13	H	Western Michigan	6-3	W
5-15	A	Minnesota	3-6	L
5-16	A_MA	Wisconsin	8-1	W
		Iowa	3-6	L
5-19	A	Indiana	6-3	W
		Big Tens at East Lansing	5th	

1960 (17-3)

Coach: Stan Drobac

3-24	*	Vanderbilt	7-2	W
3-26	*	Howard	8-1	W
3-28	*	Florida State	5-4	W
3-29	*	Florida State	5-4	W
3-31	*	Georgia Tech	5-4	W
4-1	*	Georgia	6-3	W
4-2	*	Tennessee	6-3	W
4-19	A	Detroit	9-0	W
4-22	A	Purdue	9-0	W
4-23	A_BL	Indiana	5-4	W
		Illinois	5-4	W
4-26	H	Wayne State	9-0	W
4-30	A_MN	Northwestern	5-4	W
		Minnesota	6-1	W
		Iowa	7-2	W
5-7	H	Illinois	8-1	W
5-10	A	Michigan	2-7	L
5-12	A	Western Michigan	4-5	L
5-14	A	Notre Dame	4-5	L
5-18	A	Ohio State	8-1	W
		Big Tens at Evanston	3rd	

1961 (16-4)

Coach: Stan Drobac

3-23	*	George Washington	8-1	W
3-24	*	Georgetown	7-2	W

Date		Opponent	Score	
3-25	*	Virginia	3-6	L
3-27	*	North Carolina	4-5	L
3-28	*	North Carolina	5-4	W
3-29	*	North Carolina State	7-1	W
3-30	*	Davidson	9-0	W
4-15	A	Ohio State	8-0	W
4-21	H	Notre Dame	6-3	W
4-22	H	Detroit	9-0	W
5-1	A	Wayne State	9-0	W
5-3	H	Western Michigan	9-0	W
5-5	A	Northwestern	7-2	W
5-6	A_EV	Iowa	8-1	W
		Minnesota	8-1	W
5-9	H	Michigan	4-6	L
5-12	A_MA	Wisconsin	9-0	W
		Purdue	9-0	W
		Illinois	8-1	W
5-17	H	Indiana	4-6	L
		Big Tens at East Lansing	2nd	

1962 (12-5)
Coach: Stan Drobac

Date		Opponent	Score	
3-22	*	Davidson	6-1	W
3-23	*	Duke	3-6	L
3-24	*	North Carolina State	9-0	W
3-26	*	North Carolina State	2-7	L
3-27	*	East Carolina	9-0	W
4-20	H	Northwestern	1-8	L
4-24	H	Detroit	9-0	W
4-27	A_IC	Minnesota	9-0	W
4-28	A_IC	Iowa	4-5	L
		Wisconsin	6-3	W
5-2	A	Notre Dame	9-0	W
5-4	H	Illinois	8-1	W
5-5	H	Indiana	8-1	W
5-8	A	Michigan	2-7	L
5-12	A_AA	Ohio State	8-1	W
5-14	H	Western Michigan	8-1	W
5-28		Detroit	7-2	W
		Big Tens at Minneapolis	3rd	

1963 (16-5)
Coach: Stan Drobac

Date		Opponent	Score	
3-22	*	Davidson	9-0	W
3-23	*	Wake Forest	9-0	W
3-25	*	Ft. Eustis	4-5	L
3-26	*	East Carolina	5-2	W
3-27	*	North Carolina	0-9	L
3-28	*	Virginia	7-2	W
3-29	*	George Washington	5-4	W
3-30	-DC	Dartmouth	7-2	W
-		Georgetown	5-4	W
4-19	A_CU	Wisconsin	5-4	W
4-20	A	Illinois	0-9	L
4-23	A	Northwestern	0-9	L
4-26	A_BL	Indiana	4-5	L
		Purdue	7-0	W
		Minnesota	9-0	W
5-3	H	Notre Dame	5-4	W
5-7	H	Michigan	5-4	W
5-8	A	Western Michigan	6-3	W
5-10	H	Iowa	9-0	W
5-11	H	Minnesota	9-0	W
		Ohio State	9-0	W
		Big Tens at Evanston	4th	

1964 (14-6)
Coach: Stan Drobac

Date		Opponent	Score	
3-24	*	Duke	6-3	W
3-26	*	North Carolina	1-7	L
3-27	*	North Carolina	1-8	L
3-28	*_CP	Williams	7-2	W
3-30	*	George Washington	5-4	W
3-31	*	Georgetown	9-0	W
4-1	*	The Citadel	5-1	W
4-4	*	Virginia	9-0	W
4-10	A	Ohio State	7-2	W
4-11	A	Purdue	8-1	W
4-18	A	Notre Dame	4-5	L
4-22	A	Wayne State	9-0	W
4-28	A	Western Michigan	7-0	W
5-5	A	Michigan	1-8	L
5-8	H	Iowa	7-2	W
5-9	H	Illinois	9-0	W
5-12	H	Northwestern	1-7	L
5-15	A	Minnesota	8-1	W
5-16	A_MN	Indiana	2-5	L
		Wisconsin	6-3	W
		Big Tens at Champaign	4th	

1965 (11-6)
Coach: Stan Drobac

Date		Opponent	Score	
3-23	*	Wake Forest	9-0	W
3-26	*	North Carolina	1-8	L
3-27	*	North Carolina	3-6	L
3-29	*	Presbyterian	5-4	W
3-30	*	VMI	9-0	W
4-20	H	Wayne State	9-0	W
4-23	A_BL	Indiana	2-7	L
		Illinois	5-4	W
4-24	A_BL	Northwestern	3-6	L
4-29	H	Notre Dame	2-7	L
5-1	A	Iowa	8-1	W
5-5	A	Western Michigan	5-4	W
5-7	H	Ohio State	9-0	W
5-8	H	Purdue	8-1	W
5-11	H	Michigan	1-8	L
5-14	A	Minnesota	5-2	W
5-15	A_MN	Wisconsin	8-1	W
		Big Tens at Bloomington	4th	

1966 (11-7)
Coach: Stan Drobac

Date		Opponent	Score	
3-22	*	Houston	4-2	W
3-23	*	Rice	2-5	L
3-28	*	Trinity	1-8	L
3-29	*	Texas A&M	3-6	L
3-30	*	Baylor	3-4	L
3-31	*	Texas Christian	4-3	W
4-15	A	Michigan	1-8	L
4-16	A	Minnesota	8-1	W
4-27	H	Wayne State	9-0	W
4-29	H	Wisconsin	6-3	W
4-30	H	Northwestern	9-0	W
5-3	A	Notre Dame	2-7	L
5-6	A	Ohio State	8-1	W
5-7	A	Illinois	7-2	W
5-10	A	Western Michigan	9-0	W
5-13	A_WL	Indiana	5-4	W
5-13	A_WL	Iowa	9-0	W
5-14	A	Purdue	9-0	W
		Big Tens at East Lansing	2nd	

1967 (15-4)
Coach: Stan Drobac

Date		Opponent	Score	
3-22	*	Florida State	3-6	L
3-23	*	Georgia	5-4	W
3-24	*	Clemson	4-5	L
3-25	*	South Carolina	7-2	W
3-27	*	East Carolina	9-0	W
3-29	*	North Carolina	2-7	L
		North Carolina	1-8	L
3-31	*	George Washington	8-1	W
4-18	A	Wayne State	9-0	W
4-21	H	Northwestern	7-2	W
4-22	H	Wisconsin	8-1	W
4-28	A	Iowa	8-1	W
4-29	A	Minnesota	8-1	W
5-3	A	Western Michigan	7-2	W
5-5	H	Ohio State	9-0	W
5-7	H	Indiana	7-2	W
5-9	H	Michigan	5-4	W
5-12	H	Illinois	9-0	W
5-13	A	Purdue	9-0	W
		Big Tens at Ann Arbor	1st	

1968 (11-10)
Coach: Stan Drobac

Date		Opponent	Score	
3-20	*_NO	Tulane	1-8	L
3-21	*_NO	Tulane	0-5	L
3-22	*	Louisiana State	4-5	L
3-23	*	Louisiana State	3-6	L
3-25	*	Millsaps College	6-0	W
3-26	*	Mississippi College	9-0	W
3-27	*_SV	Mississippi State	0-9	L
3-28	*_SV	Florida State	2-7	L
3-29	*_SV	Oklahoma	2-5	L
4-12	H	Illinois	5-4	W
4-13	H	Purdue	9-0	W
4-19	H	Iowa	8-1	W
4-20	H	Minnesota	4-5	L
4-26	A	Indiana	9-0	W
4-27	A	Ohio State	8-1	W
4-30	A	Wayne State	7-0	W
5-3	A	Wisconsin	8-1	W
5-4	A	Northwestern	7-1	W
5-7	H	Western Michigan	7-2	W
5-11	A	Michigan	0-9	L
5-13	H	Miami (OH)	0-9	L
		Big Tens at Iowa City	2nd	

1969 (6-12)
Coach: Stan Drobac

Date		Opponent	Score	
3-18	*_MF	Yale	2-7	L
3-19	*	Miami (FL)	0-9	L
3-21	*	Florida State	1-8	L
3-24	*	Dartmouth	5-4	W
3-25	*	George Washington	2-6	L
3-26	*	Maryland	3-6	L
3-28	*	North Carolina	0-9	L
4-11	A	Illinois	0-9	L
4-12	A	Purdue	6-3	W
4-28	H	Northwestern	5-4	W
4-19	H	Wisconsin	2-7	L
4-22	A	Wayne State	7-2	W
4-29	A	Western Michigan	6-3	W
5-2	A	Minnesota	1-8	L
5-3	A	Iowa	2-7	L
5-6	H	Michigan	0-9	L
5-9	H	Ohio State	7-2	W
5-10	H	Indiana	2-7	L
		Big Tens at East Lansing	8th	

1970 (11-8)
Coach: Stan Drobac

Date		Opponent	Score	
3-25	*	Oklahoma City	2-6	L
3-27	*	Baylor	7-2	L
3-30	*	Pan American	4-5	L
3-31	*	Corpus Christi	1-8	L
4-1	*	Trinity	0-9	L
4-2	*	Texas	2-7	L
4-3	*	Texas A&M	5-4	W
4-10	A	Ohio State	9-0	W
4-11	A	Indiana	3-6	L
4-17	A	Northwestern	5-4	W
4-18	A	Wisconsin	7-2	W
4-22	A	Notre Dame	3-6	L
4-28	H	Wayne State	9-0	W
5-1	H	Iowa	9-0	W
5-2	H	Minnesota	6-3	W
5-5	A	Michigan	3-6	L
5-6	H	Western Michigan	9-0	W
5-8	H	Purdue	8-1	W
5-9	H	Illinois	6-3	W
		Big Tens at Minneapolis	3rd	

1971 (10-6)
Coach: Stan Drobac

Date		Opponent	Score	
3-23	*	Mississippi State	4-5	L

3-24	*	Alabama	6-3	W
3-26	*	South Alabama	8-1	W
3-27	*	Tulane	5-4	W
4-9	A	Purdue	8-1	W
4-10	A	Illinois	3-6	L
		Western Michigan	8-1	W
4-16	H	Northwestern	9-0	W
4-17	H	Wisconsin	7-2	W
4-20	A	Wayne State	9-0	W
4-28	H	Notre Dame	1-6	L
4-30	A	Iowa	2-7	L
5-1	A	Minnesota	5-1	W
5-5	H	Michigan	4-5	L
5-7	H	Ohio State	9-0	W
5-8	H	Indiana	4-5	L
		Big Tens at Evanston	4th	

1972 (6-15)
Coach: Stan Drobac

3-20	*	Mississippi State	0-9	L
3-21	*	Alabama	0-9	L
3-22	*	Alabama	2-7	L
3-23	*	Georgia	0-9	L
3-25	*	Samford	1-8	L
3-27	*	Georgia Tech	3-6	L
3-28	*	North Carolina	0-9	L
3-30	*	Navy	1-8	L
4-7	H	Iowa	4-5	L
4-8	H	Minnesota	6-3	W
4-11	H	Notre Dame	2-7	L
4-14	A	Wisconsin	2-7	L
4-15	A	Northwestern	3-6	L
4-18	H	Wayne State	9-0	W
4-21	A	Ohio State	5-1	W
4-22	A	Indiana	1-8	L
4-28	H	Western Michigan	7-2	W
4-29	A	Hampton	6-3	W
5-3	A	Michigan	1-8	L
5-5	H	Illinois	4-5	L
5-6	H	Purdue	9-1	W
		Big Tens at Madison	7th	

1973 (8-9)
Coachs: Stan Drobac

3-19	*	Mississippi State	2-7	L
3-20	*	Alabama	1-7	L
3-21	*	Samford	4-5	L
3-22	*	Georgia	0-9	L
3-24	*	North Carolina	0-9	L
4-13	A	Illinois	4-5	L
4-14	A	Purdue	9-0	W
4-17	A	Western Michigan	7-2	W
4-20	H	Indiana	2-7	L
4-21	H	Ohio State	8-1	W
4-28	A	Notre Dame	5-4	W
5-4	A	Iowa	3-6	L
5-5	A	Minnesota	6-3	W
5-9	H	Michigan	0-9	L
5-11	H	Northwestern	6-3	W
5-12	H	Wisconsin	7-2	W
5-15	A	Wayne State	9-0	W
		Big Tens at Madison	6th	

1974 (7-11)
Coach: Stan Drobac

3-18	*	Nicholls State	3-6	L
3-19	*	Southwest Louisiana	4-5	L
3-20	*	Louisiana State	0-9	L
3-23	*sv	Bulldog Classic	2nd/4	
3-25	*	Alabama	2-7	L
4-12	H	Iowa	2-7	L
4-13	H	Minnesota	4-5	L
4-15	A	Michigan	0-9	L
4-19	A	Wisconsin	6-3	W
4-20	A	Northwestern	7-2	W
4-26	H	Notre Dame	4-5	L

4-27	H	Central Michigan	8-1	W
5-1	A	Eastern Michigan	9-0	W
5-4	H	Illinois	4-5	L
5-6	H	Purdue	9-0	W
5-7	H	Wayne State	9-0	W
5-10	A	Ohio State	4-5	L
5-11	A	Indiana	3-6	L
5-13	H	Western Michigan	7-2	W
		Big Tens at Madison	6th	

1975 (6-11)
Coach: Stan Drobac

3-17	*	Hampton	3-6	L
3-18	*	Hampton	2-7	L
3-19	*	Navy	4-5	L
3-20	*	Navy	4-5	L
4-11	A	Iowa	1-8	L
4-12	A	Minnesota	1-8	L
4-18	H	Wisconsin	5-4	W
4-19	H	Northwestern	8-1	W
4-22	A	Wayne State	9-0	W
4-26	A	Notre Dame	3-6	L
4-29	H	Central Michigan	7-2	W
5-2	A	Illinois	1-8	L
5-5	A	Western Michigan	6-3	W
5-7	H	Eastern Michigan	8-1	W
5-9	H	Ohio State	3-6	L
5-10	H	Indiana	3-6	L
5-12	H	Michigan	0-9	L
		Big Tens at Madison	7th	

1976 (7-14)
Coach: Stan Drobac

3-23	*	Texas A&M	2-7	L
3-24	*	Central Texas State	4-5	L
3-25	*	Mary Hardin Baylor	2-7	L
3-27	*	Baylor	5-4	W
3-29	*	Texas	2-7	L
3-30	*	Texas Christian	0-6	L
3-31	*	Southern Methodist	0-9	L
4-9	H	Iowa	4-5	L
4-10	H	Minnesota	4-5	L
4-12	A	Michigan	1-8	L
4-16	A	Wisconsin	3-6	L
4-17	A	Northwestern	5-4	L
4-20	H	Wayne State	9-0	W
4-21	A	Central Michigan	8-1	W
4-27	H	Notre Dame	6-3	W
4-28	A	Eastern Michigan	9-0	W
4-30	H	Illinois	3-6	L
5-1	H	Purdue	7-2	W
5-3	H	Western Michigan	6-3	W
5-7	A	Ohio State	4-5	L
5-8	A	Indiana	4-5	L
		Big Tens at Minneapolis	4th	

1977 (7-12)
Coach: Stan Drobac

3-22	*	Louisiana State	0-9	L
3-23	*	Northeast Louisiana	3-6	L
3-24	*	Northwest Louisiana	2-7	L
3-25	*	Nicholls State	3-6	L
3-27	*	Tulane	2-7	L
4-8	A	Iowa	3-6	L
4-9	A	Minnesota	3-6	L
4-12	H	Michigan	2-7	L
4-15	H	Northwestern	7-2	W
4-16	H	Wisconsin	3-6	L
4-20	A	Wayne State	9-0	W
4-23	A	Notre Dame	8-1	W
4-26	A	Central Michigan	9-0	W
4-29	A	Purdue	8-1	W
4-30	A	Illinois	3-6	L
5-4	A	Western Michigan	4-5	L
5-6	H	Indiana	7-2	W
5-7	H	Ohio State	2-7	L

| 5-11 | H | Eastern Michigan | 8-1 | W |
| | | Big Tens at Ann Arbor | 8th | |

1978 (6-15)
Coach: Stan Drobac

3-20	*	Duke	0-9	L
3-21	*	Davidson	0-9	L
3-22	*	Wake Forest	4-5	L
3-23	*	North Carolina	0-9	L
3-24	*	Navy	2-7	L
3-25	*	Penn State	1-8	L
3-27	*	Washington & Lee	7-2	W
4-7	H	Iowa	1-8	L
4-8	H	Minnesota	2-7	L
4-11	A	Michigan	0-9	L
4-14	A	Wisconsin	0-9	L
4-15	A	Northwestern	3-6	L
4-17	H	Wayne State	8-1	W
4-22	H	Notre Dame	6-3	W
4-25	A	Kalamazoo	2-7	L
4-28	H	Illinois	5-4	W
4-29	H	Purdue	7-2	W
5-2	A	Central Michigan	8-1	W
5-5	A	Indiana	3-6	L
5-6	A	Ohio State	2-7	L
5-9	H	Western Michigan	3-6	L
		Big Tens at W. Lafayette	6th	

1979 (6-15)
Coach: Stan Drobac

3-19	*	Memphis State		L
3-20	*	Mississippi State		L
3-21	*	Arkansas-Little Rock		L
3-22	*	Murray State		L
3-23	*	Middle Tennessee State		L
3-25	*	Mississippi		L
4-6	A	Purdue	7-2	W
4-7	A	Illinois	6-3	W
4-13	A	Iowa	1-5	L
4-14	A	Minnesota	2-7	L
4-17	H	Michigan	0-9	L
4-20	H	Wisconsin	2-7	L
4-21	H	Northwestern	2-7	L
4-25	A	Wayne State	8-1	W
4-27	A	Notre Dame	3-6	L
4-28	H	Kalamazoo	7-2	W
4-29	H	Central Michigan	6-3	W
5-1	H	Eastern Michigan	9-0	W
5-3	A	Western Michigan	3-6	L
5-5	A	Ohio State	3-6	L
5-6	H	Indiana	3-6	L
		Big Tens at Columbus	8th	

1980 (4-16)
Coach: Stan Drobac

3-17	*	Southern California	0-9	L
3-18	*	Cal State-Long Beach	0-9	L
3-19	*	San Diego State	1-8	L
3-20	*	San Diego	1-8	L
3-21	*CT	Yale	4-5	L
	*CT	Washington	4-5	L
3-22	*	Clairmont-H. Mudd	4-5	L
3-24	*	Redlands	0-6	L
4-4	HLN	Purdue	6-3	W
4-5	HLN	Illinois	5-4	W
4-11	HLN	Minnesota	1-8	L
4-12	HLN	Iowa	3-6	L
4-18	A	Northwestern	3-6	L
4-19	A	Wisconsin	1-8	L
4-22	A	Michigan	0-9	L
4-25	H	Notre Dame	3-6	L
4-26	A	Kalamazoo	5-4	W
4-28	H	Western Michigan	5-4	W
5-2	A	Indiana	2-7	L
5-3	A	Ohio State	1-8	L
		Big Tens at Minneapolis	9th	

1981(5-14)
Coach: Stan Drobac

3-23	*	Western Kentucky	6-3	W
3-24	*	Austin Peay	0-9	L
3-25	*	Murray State	1-8	L
3-26	*	Memphis State	2-7	L
3-27	*	Southwest Missouri	8-1	W
3-28	*	Alabama-Birmingham	6-3	W
4-3	A	Illinois	2-7	L
4-4	A	Purdue	3-6	L
4-7	H	Kalamazoo	7-2	W
4-10	H	Wisconsin	4-5	L
4-11	H	Minnesota	0-9	L
4-14	A	Western Michigan	4-5	L
4-16	H	Michigan	0-9	L
4-18	A	Notre Dame	4-5	L
4-21	A	Eastern Michigan	8-1	W
4-24	A	Indiana	0-9	L
4-25	H	Ohio State	0-9	L
5-1	A	Northwestern	0-9	L
5-2	A	Iowa	3-6	L
		Big Tens at Ann Arbor	10th	

1982(7-14)
Coach: Stan Drobac

3-22	*	Murray State	2-7	L
3-23	*	Western Kentucky	5-4	W
3-24	*	Austin Peay	1-3	L
3-25	*	Mississippi	3-6	L
3-26	*	Tennessee-Martin	8-1	W
3-27	*	Alabama-Birmingham	5-4	W
3-29	*	Memphis State	2-7	L
4-2	H	Illinois	2-7	L
4-3	H	Purdue	4-5	L
4-6	H	Western Michigan	4-5	L
4-9	A	Wisconsin	1-8	L
4-10	A	Minnesota	2-7	L
4-13	H	Eastern Michigan	8-1	W
4-14	A	Michigan	1-8	L
4-15	A	Central Michigan	6-3	W
4-19	A	Kalamazoo	1-5	L
4-23	A	Indiana	2-7	L
4-24	A	Ohio State	2-7	L
4-27	H	Notre Dame	5-4	W
4-30	H	Northwestern	1-8	L
5-1	H	Iowa	7-2	W
		Big Tens at Madison	7th	

1983 (4-15)
Coach: Stan Drobac

3-21	*	Trevacca Nazarene	6-3	W
	*	Murray State	1-8	L
	*	Western Michigan	4-5	L
	*	Southeast Missouri	7-2	W
3-28	*	Memphis State	0-9	L
4-1		Minnesota	2-7	L
4-2		Wisconsin	0-9	L
4-5		Kalamazoo	4-5	L
4-8		Illinois	2-7	L
4-9		Purdue	1-8	L
4-12		Eastern Michigan	8-1	W
4-15		Western Michigan	4-5	L
4-16		Notre Dame	1-8	L
4-19		Michigan	1-8	L
4-22		Indiana	1-8	L
4-23		Ohio State	3-6	L
4-26		Central Michigan	7-2	W
4-29		Northwestern	0-9	L
4-30		Iowa	3-6	L
		Big Tens at Madison	10th	

1984 (3-17)
Coach: Stan Drobac

3 19	*	Murray State	0-8	L
3-20	*	Murray State	2-7	L
3-21	*	Vanderbilt	2-7	L
3-23	*	Lander College	2-7	L
3-24	*	Furman	0-9	L
3-27	*	Georgia	0-9	L
3-30	H$_{LN}$	Purdue	2-7	L
3-31	H$_{LN}$	Illinois	1-8	L
4-3	H$_{LN}$	Western Michigan	3-6	L
4-6	H$_{LN}$	Iowa	3-6	L
4-7	H$_{LN}$	Northwestern	1-8	L
4-10	A	Central Michigan	8-1	W
4-13	A	Wisconsin	0-9	L
4-14	A	Minnesota	0-9	L
4-17	A	Michigan	1-8	L
4-20	A	Indiana	3-6	L
4-22	A	Ohio State	2-7	L
4-24	H	Eastern Michigan	8-1	W
4-27	H	Marquette	7-2	W
4-28	H	Notre Dame	2-7	L
		Big Tens at Evanston	10th	

1985 (4-20)
Coach: Stan Drobac

2-9	A	Western Michigan	1-8	L
3-9	H$_{OK}$	Kalamazoo	3-6	L
3-18	*	Murray State	4-5	L
3-19	*	Murray State	2-7	L
3-20	*	Vanderbilt	0-9	L
3-23	*	Furman	9-0	W
3-24	*	Lander College	1-8	L
3-29	A	Illinois	1-8	L
3-30	A	Purdue	2-7	L
4-5	A	Iowa	4-5	L
4-6	A	Northwestern	1-8	L
4-9	A	Western Michigan	4-5	L
4-12	H$_{OK}$	Minnesota	2-7	L
4-13	H$_{OK}$	Wisconsin	1-8	L
4-16	A	Eastern Michigan	7-2	W
4-17	H$_{OK}$	Michigan	3-6	L
4-19	H	Indiana	2-7	L
4-20	H	Ohio State	2-7	L
4-23	A	Kalamazoo	4-5	L
4-28	A	Notre Dame	5-4	W
4-29	H	Central Michigan	9-0	W
		Big Tens at Champaign	10th	
		Wisconsin	*1-5	L
		Northwestern	*4-5	L
		Iowa	*4-5	L

1986 (2-21)
Coach: Stan Drobac

1-18	A	Georgia	0-9	L
1-19	A$_{AS}$	Texas A&M	1-8	L
3-18	*	Murray State	4-5	L
3-19	*	Tennessee-Martin	4-5	L
3-21	*	Furman	2-7	L
3-22	*	Greenville	4-5	L
3-23	*	Lander College	0-9	L
3-29	H	Northern Illinois	3-6	L
4-1	H	Western Michigan	5-4	W
4-4	H	Iowa	2-7	L
4-5	H	Northwestern	4-5	L
4-11	H	Illinois	2-7	L
4-12	H	Purdue	2-7	L
4-18	A	Wisconsin	0-9	L
4-19	A	Minnesota	1-8	L
4-22	A	Michigan	0-9	L
4-26	H	Notre Dame	0-9	L
4-29	H	Eastern Michigan	7-2	W
5-2	A	Indiana	1-8	L
5-3	A	Ohio State	0-9	L
		Big Tens at Bloomington	10th	
		Purdue	*0-6	L
		Northwestern	*2-5	L
		Iowa	*4-5	L

1987 (4-16)
Coach: Stan Drobac

1-29	H	Spartan Invitational		
		Georgia	0-9	L
		Texas A&M	1-8	L
2-21	H	Bowling Green	5-3	W
2-28	H	Ferris State	5-4	W
4-3	H	Wisconsin	3-6	L
4-4	H	Minnesota	2-6	L
4-7	A	Western Michigan	5-4	W
4-10	A	Purdue	0-9	L
4-11	A	Illinois	4-5	L
4-14	H	Michigan	0-9	L
4-17	H	Indiana	4-5	L
4-18	H	Ohio State	1-8	L
4-21	A	Eastern Michigan	7-2	W
4-24	A	Iowa	3-6	L
4-25	A	Northwestern	4-5	L
4-30	A	Kalamazoo	1-8	L
5-2	A	Notre Dame	4-5	L
		Big Tens at Minneapolis	10th	
		Wisconsin	*4-5	L
		Purdue	*3-5	L
		Northwestern	*2-5	L

1988 (10-14)
Coach: Stan Drobac

1-29	H	Spartan Invitational	NTS	
2-6	H	Northern Illinois	6-3	W
2-13	H	Miami (OH)	4-5	L
2-14	H	Western Michigan	8-1	W
2-20	H	Bowling Green	8-1	W
2-27	H	Kalamazoo	7-2	W
2-28	H	Eastern Michigan	8-1	W
4-1	H	Hawaii	4-5	L
4-2	H	Ohio	6-3	W
4-6	H	Notre Dame	5-4	W
4-8	H	Purdue	4-5	L
4-9	H	Illinois	4-5	L
4-12	A	Michigan	0-9	L
4-16	A	Ohio State	2-7	L
4-17	A	Indiana	2-7	L
4-20	H	Eastern Michigan	6-3	W
4-23	H	Northwestern	1-8	L
4-24	H	Iowa	2-7	L
5-3	H	Kalamazoo	8-1	W
5-6	A	Wisconsin	0-9	L
5-7	A	Minnesota	0-9	L
		Big Tens at W. Lafayette	8th	
		Northwestern	*0-5	L
		Iowa	*5-1	W
		Purdue	*3-5	L
		Ohio State	*2-5	L

1989 (4-19)
Coach: Stan Drobac

1-28	H	Spartan Invitational	NTS	
2-4	H	Bowling Green	8-1	W
2-11	H	Cleveland State	8-1	W
2-18	H	Toledo	7-2	W
2-25	H	Eastern Michigan	8-1	W
2-26	H	Kalamazoo	2-7	L
3-4	H	Miami (OH)	0-9	L
4-2	H	Ohio	2-7	L
4-5	H	Western Michigan	3-6	L
4-8	H	Ohio State	2-7	L
4-9	H	Indiana	0-9	L
4-11	H	Michigan	0-9	L
4-15	A	Iowa	0-9	L
4-16	A	Northwestern	*3-6	L
4-21	A	Notre Dame	3-6	L
4-25	A	Eastern Michigan	4-5	L
4-28	H	Wisconsin	0-9	L
4-29	H	Minnesota	2-7	L
5-2	A	Kalamazoo	4-5	L

5-6	A	Illinois	1-8	L
5-7	A	Purdue	2-7	L
		Big Tens at Iowa City	10th	
		Iowa	*0-5	L
		Indiana	*0-5	L
		Purdue	*2-5	L

Jim Frederick (1990-1991)

Upon receiving his bachelor's degree in physical education from East Stroudsburg University in 1968, Jim Frederick began his coaching career at Whitehall (PA) High School in 1969. Following three years on the prep scene, he returned to East Stroudsburg and earned a master's degree in 1972. Frederick then spent six years (1972-1978) as the director of junior development at the Columbus (OH) Indoor Tennis Clubs and one year as director of tennis at Cedar Bluff Racquet Club in Knoxville, TN. Prior to his appointment at Michigan State in 1990, Jim spent 10 years coaching at Miami (OH) University where his teams compiled a composite record of 190-82 while winning four conference crowns. Dictated by his wife's career in the business world, Frederick resigned his position in the fall of 1991 and moved to Knoxville.

1990 (12-13)

Coach: Jim Frederick

1-19	H	Eastern Michigan	7-2	W
1-20	H	Cincinnati	8-1	W
1-23	H	Western Michigan	5-4	W
1-27	H	Spartan Invitational	NTS	
2-9	H	Toledo	9-0	W
2-24	A	Ball State	2-7	L
2-25	A	Miami (OH)	5-4	W
3-2	H	Indiana State	9-0	W
3-3	H	Kalamazoo	9-0	W
3-5	H	Ferris State	5-4	W
3-22	*	South Florida	3-6	L
3-23	*	Florida International	3-6	L
3-31	A	Indiana	0-9	L
4-1	A	Ohio State	1-8	L
4-3	H	Bowling Green	9-0	W
4-7	H	Iowa	6-3	W
4-8	H	Northwestern	2-7	L
4-12	H	Michigan	2-6	L
4-20	A	Wisconsin	1-8	L
4-21	A	Minnesota	2-7	L
4-27	H	Purdue	5-4	W
4-28	H	Illinois	4-5	L
4-29	H	Ohio	1-5	L
		Big Tens at Champaign	9th	
		Illinois	*0-5	L
		Iowa	*5-3	L
		Purdue	*5-4	W

1990-1991 (12-14)

Coach: Jim Frederick

9-21	A	Notre Dame Invit.	NTS	
10-13	A	Bowling Green Invit.	NTS	
10-20	H	Spartan Doubles Classic	NTS	
10-26	A	Volva Fall Qualifying	NTS	
11-9		AMA ITA Rolex Regional	NTS	
11-19	A	Converse Doubles	NTS	
1-18	H	Eastern Michigan	9-0	W
1-19	H	Cincinnati	7-2	W
1-20	H	Toledo	7-2	W
1-26	H	Spartan Invitational	NTS	
2-1	H	Bowling Green	8-1	W
2-16	H	Wisconsin	2-7	L
2-17	H	Western Michigan	7-2	W
2-23	H	Miami (OH)	7-2	W
		Kalamazoo	6-3	W
2-24	H	Northern Illinois	7-2	W
3-1	H	Ferris State	8-1	W
3-8	H	Northwestern	1-8	L
3-19	A$_{HU}$	Cornell	6-3	W
3-22	A$_{HU}$	Arkansas	2-5	L

3-23	A$_{HU}$	W. Texas-El Paso	5-3	W
3-24	A$_{HU}$	Trinity	3-5	L
3-29	H	Ball State	2-7	L
4-1	H	Notre Dame	2-7	L
4-5	A	Illinois	3-6	L
4-6	A	Purdue	4-5	L
4-13	H	Ohio State	2-7	L
4-14	H	Indiana	2-7	L
4-19	A	Iowa	0-9	L
4-20	A	Minnesota	1-8	L
4-26	A	Michigan	1-8	L
		Big Tens at Evanston	9th	
		Northwestern	*2-5	L
		Illinois	*5-3	W

Gene Orlando (1991-)

With the sudden departure of Jim Frederick in the fall of 1991, Gene Orlando took over the reins after having served three seasons as head coach at Bowling Green. He had played college tennis at Ball State University in Muncie, IN, helping the Cardinals to four MAC championships while winning conference championships while winning conference crowns in his final two years at the Indiana school. His overall collegiate record was an impressive 91-40 in singles and 98-24 in doubles and he made an NCAA appearance in his seionr season. Gene spent one year as a graduate assistant at BSU before accepting the position at Bowling Green. In his 12-year tenure in East Lansing, six of Orlando's players qualified for play in the NCAA tournament.

1991-1992 (12-11)

Coach: Gene Orlando

9-27	A	Notre Dame Invit.	NTS	
10-17	A	Ball State Invit.	NTS	
10-25	H	Drobac Classic	NTS	
1-25	H	Spartan Invitational	NTS	
2-1	A	Notre Dame	0-7	L
2-2	A$_{ND}$	Colorado	2-7	L
2-14	A	Ball State	4-5	L
2-16	H	Bowling Green	8-1	W
2-28		Western Michigan	9-0	W
2-29		Ferris State	8-1	W
		Kalamazoo	8-1	W
3-7		Illinois	6-3	W
3-14		Purdue	6-0	W
3-26		Jacksonville	6-3	W
		Cincinnati	6-3	W
3-27	A	Southern Illinois	5-1	W
4-4	A	Ohio State	4-5	L
4-5	A	Indiana	1-8	L
4-10	H	Minnesota	1-8	L
4-11	H	Iowa	5-4	W
4-17	A	Michigan	0-6	L
4-19	H	Penn State	6-3	W
4-25	A	Wisconsin	4-5	L
4-26	A	Northwestern	1-6	L
		Big Tens at Madison	7th	
		Indiana	*0-6	L
		Wisconsin	*3-5	L
		Michigan	*5-0	W

1992-1993 (12-14)

Coach: Gene Orlando

9-18	A	Notre Dame Invit.	NTS	
10-2	A	Ball State Invit.	NTS	
10-23	A	Kentucky Invit.	NTS	
11-6		AMA ITA Rolex Regional	NTS	
1-30	H	Spartan Invit.	NTS	
2-6	H	Cincinnati	9-0	W
		Bowling Green	9-0	W
2-13	H	Kalamazoo	5-4	W
2-20	A	Miami (OH)	3-4	L
3-6	A	Kentucky	2-5	L
3-12	A$_{KX}$	Tennessee Classic	3rd/8	
		Tulsa	4-1	W

		VA Commonwealth	3-4	L
		Wake Forest	6-3	W
3-24	H	Notre Dame	3-4	L
3-28	A$_{CN}$	Clemson	3-4	L
		South Alabama	2-4	L
		Rollins	1-4	L
		Furman	2-4	L
4-3	H	Ohio State	5-2	W
4-4	H	Indiana	4-3	W
4-9	A	Minnesota	1-6	L
4-11	A	Iowa	5-2	W
4-14	H	Michigan	3-4	L
4-17	A	Penn State	3-4	L
4-24	H	Northwestern	2-5	L
4-25	H	Wisconsin	5-2	W
4-30	A	Illinois	5-2	W
5-1	A	Purdue	4-3	W
		Big Tens at Iowa City	6th	
		Penn State	*3-4	L
		Ohio State	*4-2	W
		Iowa	*3-4	L
		>Clemson Invitational	T5th/5	

1993-1994 (8-14)

Coach: Gene Orlando

9-24	A	Notre Dame Invit.	NTS	
10-1	A	Ball State Invit	NTS	
10-14	A$_{AX}$	All-American Tournament	NTS	
10-22	A$_{BL}$	Midwest Collegiate Champ.	NTS	
11-4		AND ITA Rolex Regional	NTS	
1-14	A$_{KX}$	Volunteer Tennis Classic		
1-16		South Alabama	0-7	L
		Southern Methodist	6-1	W
		Michigan	5-2	W
2-15	A	Notre Dame	2-5	L
2-25	A$_{CU}$	Big Ten Singles	NTS	
3-4	A$_{CC}$	H.E.B. Coll. Team Champ.		
		Arizona	3-4	L
		Nebraska	6-1	W
		Clemson	3-4	L
		Texas	1-6	L
3-25	H	Western Michigan	7-0	W
3-26	H	Ball State	4-3	W
4-1	H	Minnesota	2-5	L
4-2	H	Iowa	3-4	L
4-6	A	Michigan	1-6	L
4-9	H	Penn State	3-4	L
4-16	A	Wisconsin	0-7	L
4-17	A	Northwestern	2-5	L
4-23	H	Illinois	4-3	W
4-24	H	Purdue	6-1	W
4-30	A	Indiana	2-5	L
5-1	A	Ohio State	1-6	L
		Big Tens at Minneapolis	10th	
		Illinois	*3-4	L
		Purdue	*4-3	W

1994-1995 (12-10)

Coach: Gene Orlando

9-16	A	Notre Dame Invit	NTS	
10-7	A	Kentucky	NTS	
10-14	A	Ball State Invit	NTS	
11-4		AMA ITA Rolex Regional	NTS	
1-14	H	Western Michigan	5-2	W
		Cincinnati	5-2	W
1-28	A$_{CH}$	Big Ten Singles	NTS	
2-5	H	Northwestern	4-3	W
2-7	H	Notre Dame	1-6	L
2-11	A	Ball State	3-4	L
2-18	H	Bowling Green	6-1	W
		Kalamazoo	5-2	W
3-3	A	Corpus Christi Classic		
		Texas Christian	0-7	L
		Boise State	0-4	L
3-16	A	Boise State Invitational	4th/8	
		Brigham Young	5-2	W
		Kansas	0-7	L

		SW Louisiana	2-5	L
3-25	H	Wisconsin	4-3	W
3-26	H	Miami (OH)	4-3	W
4-1	A	Illinois	2-5	L
4-2	A	Purdue	6-1	W
4-5	H	Michigan	0-7	L
4-9	A	Penn State	4-3	W
4-15	H	Indiana	3-4	L
4-16	H	Ohio State	5-2	W
4-21	A	Minnesota	1-6	L
4-23	A	Iowa	5-2	W
		Big Tens at Bloomington	4th	
		Illinois	*4-0	W
		Michigan	*0-4	L
		Northwestern	*3-4	L

1995-1996 (14-13)
Coach: Gene Orlando

9-29	A	Notre Dame Invit.	NTS	
10-6	A	Ball State Invit	NTS	
10-28	H	Bowling Green	4-3	W
		Northern Illinois	6-1	W
11-6	AMA	ITA Rolex	NTS	
1-14	H	Western Michigan	6-1	W
1-21	A	Penn State	3-4	L
1-29	H	Big Ten Singles	NTS	
2-3	NCH	Vanderbilt	3-4	L
2-4	NCH	Alabama	1-6	L
2-10	H	Ball State	4-3	W
2-17	H	Illinois State	7-0	W
		Kalamazoo	6-1	W
2-23	A	Cincinnati	5-2	W
2-24	A	Miami (OH)	3-4	L
2-28	A	Notre Dame	3-4	L
3-5	A	Baylor	4-3	W
3-6	A	Texas Christian	0-7	L
3-7	A	Texas	2-5	L
3-19	H	Minnesota	1-6	L
3-30	A	Wisconsin	4-3	W
3-31	A	Northwestern	4-3	W
4-5	H	Purdue	3-4	L
4-6	H	Illinois	3-4	L
4-10	A	Michigan	2-5	L
4-13	A	Ohio State	4-3	W
4-14	A	Indiana	3-4	L
4-21	H	Iowa	5-2	W
		Big Tens at W. Lafayette	5th	
		Minnesota	*3-4	L
		Penn State	*4-3	W
		Purdue	*4-1	W

1996-1997 (10-17)
Coach: Gene Orlando

9-22	A	Notre Dame Invit	NTS	
10-6	A	Ball State Invit.	NTS	
10-11	A	Kentucky Fall Invit	NTS	
11-4	A	ITA Rolex Regional	NTS	
1-18	A	Ball State	3-4	L
1-27	A_CU	Big Tens Singles	NTS	
2-1	H	Cincinnati	6-1	W
		Western Michigan	6-1	W
2-8	H	Bowling Green	7-0	W
		Kalamazoo	7-0	W
2-16	H	Miami (OH)	3-4	L
2-21	A	UNLV	2-5	L
2-22	A_LV	Oklahoma	3-4	L
2-26	H	Notre Dame	2-5	L
3-3	A	Southern Methodist	0-7	L
3-4	A	Texas Christian	3-4	L
3-5	A	Texas A&M	3-4	L
3-15	H	Ohio State	5-2	W
3-22	A	Purdue	3-4	L
3-23	A	Illinois	4-3	W
3-29	H	Indiana	1-6	L
4-4	A	Minnesota	2-5	L
4-6	A	Iowa	5-2	W
4-9	H	Michigan	3-4	L

4-13	A	Penn State	2-5	L
4-19	H	Wisconsin	2-5	L
4-20	H	Northwestern	1-6	L
		Big Tens at East Lansing	8th	
		Ohio State	*4-3	W
		Wisconsin	*4-0	W
		Northwestern	*0-4	L
		Michigan	*0-4	L
		Penn State	*W	F

1997-1998 (15-13)
Coach: Gene Orlando

10-4	A	Ball State Invitational	NTS	
10-18	AAX	ITA All-American	NTS	
11-4	ADL	ITA Rolex Regional	NTS	
1-18	H	DePaul	5-2	W
		Cincinnati	5-2	W
1-25	H	Big Ten Singles	NTS	
2-1	A_KX	Tennessee Classic	2nd/4	
		Tennessee	3-4	L
		Indiana	4-3	W
		William & Mary	5-2	W
2-14	A	Miami (OH)	6-1	W
2-21	H	Bowling Green	7-0	W
		Western Michigan	6-1	W
3-4	A	Notre Dame	0-7	L
3-14	A	Boise State Invitational		
		Southern Mississippi	6-1	W
		Boise State	2-5	L
		Virginia Tech	2-5	L
3-21	A	Ohio State	5-2	W
3-24	H	Ball State	5-2	W
3-28	A	Indiana	3-4	L
4-4	H	Minnesota	4-3	W
4-5	H	Iowa	3-4	L
4-8	H	Michigan	1-6	L
4-11	H	Penn State	5-2	W
4-18	A	Wisconsin	2-5	L
4-19	A	Northwestern	1-6	L
4-25	H	Purdue	2-5	L
4-26	H	Illinois	1-6	L
		Big Tens at Champaign	7th	
		Penn State	*4-2	W
		Iowa	*4-2	W
		Illinois	*0-4	L
		Wisconsin	*0-4	L
		Indiana	*4-3	W

1998-1999 (10-13)
Coach: Gene Orlando

9-27	A_BA	Clay Court Champ.	NTS	
9-27	A	Ball State Invit.	NTS	
10-4	A	Western Mich. Invit.	NTS	
10-8	A_AX	All-American Invit.	NTS	
11-9	H	Region IV Champ.	NTS	
1-18	A_MA	Big Tens Indoor	NTS	
2-7	A_DL	Rolex Nat. Inter	NTS	
2-14	A	UNLV Invit.	3rd	
		Northern Arizona	4-3	W
		New Mexico State	4-3	L
		Northeast Louisiana	4-3	W
2-27	A	South Florida	7-0	L
2-28	A	Florida	6-1	L
3-3	H	Notre Dame	4-3	L
3-8	H	LSU	5-2	L
3-10	A	Tulane	6-1	L
3-12	A	SW Louisiana	4-1	L
3-20	A	Ball State	4-3	W
3-24	A	Louisville	4-3	W
3-27	A	Wisconsin	5-2	W
3-28	A	Iowa	5-2	L
4-3	H	Penn State	5-2	W
4-4	H	Ohio State	4-3	W
4-7	H	Michigan	5-2	W
4-10	A	Purdue	4-3	W
4-11	A	Indiana	5-2	L
4-18	H	Minnesota	5-2	L

4-24	H	Northwestern	5-2	W
4-25	H	Illinois	5-2	L
		Big Tens	6th	
		Ohio State	*4-2	W
		Purdue	*0-4	L

1999-2000 (8-20)
Coach: Gene Orlando

9-26	A	Clay Court Champ.	NTS	
9-26	A	Ball State Invit.	NTS	
10-17	A	All-American Invit.	NTS	
10-17	H	Adv. Spartan Invit.	NTS	
11-8	A	ITA Midwest Reg.	NTS	
		Big Tens Indoor	NTS	
1-22	H	Western Michigan	4-3	L
		Dayton	7-0	W
2-1	A	Notre Dame	7-0	L
2-5	H	Toledo	7-0	W
		Eastern Michigan	6-1	W
2-12	H	Ball State	6-1	L
		Valparaiso	7-0	W
2-19	H	Louisville	5-2	L
		Wright State	6-1	W
2-26	A	Virginia Commonwealth	7-0	L
2-27	A	Virginia	6-1	L
3 5	A	H.E.B Coll. Team Champ.		
		TCU	4-0	L
		Minnesota	4-0	L
		Tulane	4-2	L
		New Mexico	4-3	L
3-8	A	Southern Methodist	7-0	L
3-18	A	Minnesota	6-1	L
4-1	A	Northwestern	4-3	L
4-2	A	Illinois	5-2	L
4-5	A	Michigan	5-2	L
4-8	H	Purdue	4-3	W
4-9	H	Indiana	7-0	L
4-15	H	Wisconsin	5-2	L
4-16	H	Iowa	4-3	L
4-22	H	Penn State	5-2	L
4-23	A	Ohio State	7-0	L
		Big Tens at Bloomington		
		Wisconsin	*4-3	W
		Illinois	*4-0	L

2000-2001 (7-18)
Coach: Gene Orlando

10-8	A	Indiana State Invit.	NTS	
10-22	H	Adv. Spartan Invit.	NTS	
10-30	A	ITA Midwest Reg.	NTS	
1-15	A_AA	Big Tens Indoor	NTS	
1-20	H	Toledo	7-0	W
		Wright State	7-0	W
1-26	H	Tulane	6-1	L
2-3	H	Louisiana-Lafayette	4-3	W
2-10	H	Western Illinois	7-0	W
		Xavier	6-1	W
2-15	H	Notre Dame	7-0	L
2-18	H	Northwestern	7-0	L
2-23	H	Minnesota	6-1	L
2-25	A	Western Michigan	7-0	L
		Valparaiso	7-0	W
3-6	A	Jacksonville University	5-2	L
3-7	A	South Florida	7-0	L
3-17	A	Ball State	7-0	L
3-19	A	Louisville	7-0	L
3-24	A	Indiana State	7-0	L
3-25	A	Illinois	7-0	L
3-31	H	Wisconsin	6-1	L
4-7	H	Ohio State	7-0	L
4-8	H	Penn State	4-3	W
4-11	H	Michigan	6-1	L
4-14	A	Iowa	5-2	L
4-21	A	Purdue	6-1	L
4-22	H	Indiana	5-2	L
		Big Tens at Madison		
		Wisconsin	*1-4	L

2001-2002 (14-12)

Coach: Gene Orlando

9-23	A	Ball State Invit.	NTS	
9-30	A	Notre Dame Invit.	NTS	
10-29	H	ITA Region IV	NTS	
11-12	H	Big Ten Indoor	NTS	
1-19	H	Wisconsin-Green Bay	7-0	W
		Wright State	7-0	W
1-26	H	Toledo	7-0	W
		Dayton	7-0	W
2-2	H	Ball State	7-0	W
2-3	H	Tulsa	1-6	L
2-10	H	Louisville	4-3	W
		Valparaiso	6-1	W
2-20	A	Notre Dame	0-7	L
2-23	H	Northwestern	3-4	L
2-24	H	Illinois	0-7	L
3-4	A	SE Louisiana	6-1	W
3-5	A	Louisiana-Lafayette	4-3	W
3-6	A	Tulane	3-4	L
3-16	H	Bowling Green	5-2	W
		Bradley	7-0	W
3-22	A	Wisconsin	5-2	W
3-27	H	Western Michigan	6-1	W
3-29	A	Minnesota	0-7	L
4-3	A	Michigan	2-5	L
4-6	A	Ohio State	0-7	L
4-7	A	Penn State	3-4	L
4-13	H	Iowa	4-3	W
4-20	A	Purdue	2-5	L
4-21	A	Indiana	3-4	L
		Big Tens at Columbus		
		Penn State	*2-4	L

2002-2003 (14-13)

Coach: Gene Orlando

9-29	A	Ball State Invit.	NTS	
10-6	A	ITA All-American	NTS	
10-13	A	Minnesota Invit.	NTS	
10-24	A	ITA Midwest Regional.	NTS	
11-17	A	Big Ten Indoors	NTS	
1-18	H	Butler	4-3	W
1-18	H	Wright State	7-0	W
1-25	H	Toledo	6-1	W
1-25	H	Dayton	7-0	W
2-1	A	Western Michigan	4-3	W
2-1	A	Valparaiso	7-0	W
2-8	H	DePaul	7-0	W
2-8	H	Xavier	7-9	L
2-15	A	Ball State	3-4	L
2-19	H	Notre Dame	3-4	L
2-23	A	Cleveland State	7-0	W
3-4	A	Arkansas	2-5	L
3-6	A	Tulsa	1-6	L

3-8	A	Oklahoma	2-5	L
3-14	H	Ohio State	3-4	L
3-22	H	Penn State	2-5	L
3-24	A	Louisville	2-5	L
3-28	A	Iowa	4-3	W
3-30	A	Minnesota	1-6	L
4-2	H	Michigan	5-2	W
4-6	H	Indiana	6-1	W
4-12	A	Illinois	2-5	L
4-13	A	Purdue	2-5	L
4-18	H	Northwestern	4-3	W
4-19	H	Wisconsin	5-2	W
		Big Tens at Evanston		
		Purdue	*4-3	W
		Illinois	*0-4	L

NCAA Championship Qualifiers

1930	Paul Kane	singles
1934	Stan Weitz	singles
1934	Rex Norris	singles
1935	Will Klunzinger	singles
	Bob Rosa	singles
1938	Herman Struck .... singles, doubles	
	Chester Olson .... singles, doubles	
	Charles Gibbs .... singles, doubles	
	Leonard Kositchek .... singles, doubles	
1951	Leonard Brose	singles
1993	Wade Martin	doubles
1993	Brad Dancer	doubles
1994	Mashiska Washington	singles
1995	Jayson Bedford	singles
1996	Alberto Brause	singles

Big Ten Champions

SINGLES

1951	Leonard Brose	No. 1
	Dick Reiger	No. 6
1953	Stan Drobac	No. 1
	Jim Pore	No. 5
1955	Dana Squire	No. 6
1960	Ron Mescall	No. 5
1961	Dick Hall	No. 2
	Jack Damson	No. 4
1966	Mickey Szilargyi	No. 2
	Vic Dhooge	No. 5
1967	John Good	No. 4
	Jim Phillips	No. 6
1968	Rich Monan	No. 2
	Steve Schafer	No. 5
1971	Mike Madura	No. 3

DOUBLES

1951	Leonard Brose & John Sahratian	No. 1
1952	Stan Drobac & Tom Belton	No. 1
	Dick Roberts & Jim Pore	No. 3
1953	Stan Drobac & Tom Belton	No. 1
	Dick Roberts & John Sahratian	No. 2
1966	Jim Phillips & Vic Dhooge	No. 2
1967	Rich Monan & Chuck Brainard	No. 1
	John Good & Mickey Szilagyi	No. 2
	Jim Phillips & Vic Dhooge	No. 3

TEAM

1951   Leonard Brose, Wally Kau, Keith Kimble, Ken Kimble, Dave Mills, Richard Rieger, and John Sahratian.

1967   Chuck Brainard, John Buse, Vic Dhooge, John Good, Richard Monan, James Phillips, Steve Schafer, and Mickey Szilagyi

Postseason Honors

ALL-AMERICA

1994   Mashiska Washington

ALL-BIG TEN

1972	Rick Vetter
1973	Rick Vetter
1976	Tom Gudelsky
1977	Tom Gudelsky
1978	Kevin McNulty
1979	Matt Sandler
1982	Steve Yorimoto
1992	Grant Asher
1993	Brda Dancer
	Mashiska Washington
1994	Mashiska Washington
1995	Jayson Bedford
1996	Albert Brause
1997	Trey Eubanks
1998	Trey Eubanks
1999	Trey Eubanks
2003	Andrew Formanczyk

Year-by-Year Record

Year	W-L-T	Pct.	Big Ten Place	Coach
1909	1-0	1.0		no coach
1910	1-1-1	.166		no coach
1911	2-2	.500		no coach
1912		record not available		no coach
1913	1-1-1	.500		no coach
1914	1-1-1	.500		no coach
1915	5-0	1.000		no coach
1916	8-2-1	.772		no coach
1917		Did not compete		
1918	1-0-1	.525		Charles D. Ball
1919	3-2-1	.583		Charles D. Ball
1920	4-1	.800		Charles D. Ball
1921	3-4	.428		Harry C. Young
1922	3-2-2	.642		Harry C. Young
1923	2-6-1	.277		Charles D. Ball
1924	1-2	.333		Charles D. Ball

cont.

Year	W-L-T	Pct.	Big Ten	Place	Coach
1925	4-3	.571			Charles D. Ball
1926	9-5	.650			Charles D. Ball
1927	2-7-1	.250			Charles D. Ball
1928	5-2	.714			Charles D. Ball
1929	3-3	.500			Charles D. Ball
1930	2-9	.181			Charles D. Ball
1931	1-6-1	.111			Charles D. Ball
1932	9-2	.818			Charles D. Ball
1933	11-1	.916			Charles D. Ball
1934	13-0	1.000			Charles D. Ball
1935	4-5-1	.450			Charles D. Ball
1936	12-2	.857			Charles D. Ball
1937	11-1	.916			Charles D. Ball
1938	7-4	.636			Charles D. Ball
1939	10-5	.667			Charles D. Ball
1940	6-6-0	.500			Charles D. Ball
1941	7-7	.500			Charles D. Ball
1942	10-5	.667			Charles D. Ball
1943	7-1	.875			Charles D. Ball
1944		Did not compete due to World War II			
1945	3-1	.750			Charles D. Ball
1946	4-10	.285			Charles D. Ball
1947	11-6	.647			Gordon A. Dahlgren
1948	13-4	.770			H. Frank Beeman
1949	12-6	.666			H. Frank Beeman
1950	8-10	.444			H. Frank Beeman
1951	12-4	.750	7-0	1st	Thomas F. Martin
1952	12-4	.750	4-1	2nd	John A. Friedrich
1953	12-4	.750	7-0	2nd	H. Frank Beeman
1954	10-7	.588	3-3	3rd	H. Frank Beeman
1955	7-8	.467	2-5	6th	H. Frank Beeman
1956	13-5	.722	2-4	7th	H. Frank Beeman
1957	7-10	.411	2-4	6th	H. Frank Beeman
1958	6-8	.428	1-3	6th	Stan Drobac
1959	9-7	.562	5-4	5th	Stan Drobac
1960	17-3	.850	8-1	3rd	Stan Drobac
1961	16-4	.800	7-2	2nd	Stan Drobac
1962	12-5	.705	5-3	3rd	Stan Drobac
1963	16-5	.761	7-3	4th	Stan Drobac
1964	14-6	.700	6-3	4th	Stan Drobac
1965	11-6	.647	6-3	4th	Stan Drobac
1966	11-7	.611	8-1	2nd	Stan Drobac
1967	15-4	.789	9-0	1st	Stan Drobac
1968	11-10	.523	7-2	2nd	Stan Drobac
1969	6-12	.333	3-6	8th	Stan Drobac
1970	11-8	.584	7-2	3rd	Stan Drobac
1971	10-6	.625	5-4	4th	Stan Drobac
1972	6-15	.285	3-6	7th	Stan Drobac
1973	8-9	.470	5-4	4th	Stan Drobac
1974	7-11	.388	3-6	5th	Stan Drobac
1975	6-11	.352	2-6	7th	Stan Drobac
1976	7-14	.333	2-7	4th	Stan Drobac
1977	7-12	.368	3-6	8th	Stan Drobac
1978	6-15	.285	2-7	(t)6th	Stan Drobac
1979	6-15	.285	2-7	8th	Stan Drobac
1980	4-16	.200	2-7	9th	Stan Drobac
1981	5-14	.263	0-9	10th	Stan Drobac
1982	7-14	.333	1-8	7th	Stan Drobac
1983	4-15	.263	0-9	10th	Stan Drobac
1984	3-17	.150	0-9	10th	Stan Drobac
1985	4-20	.166	0-9	10th	Stan Drobac
1986	2-21	.087	0-12	10th	Stan Drobac
1987	4-16	.200	0-9	10th	Stan Drobac
1988	10-14	.416	1-12	8th	Stan Drobac
1989	4-19	.174	0-12	8th	Stan Drobac
1990	12-13	.480	3-9	9th	Jim Frederick
1991	12-14	.462	1-10	9th	Jim Frederick
1992	12-11	.521	5-8	7th	Gene Orlando
1993	12-14	.461	7-6	6th	Gene Orlando
1994	8-14	.364	4-9	10th	Gene Orlando
1995	13-12	.520	7-6	4th	Gene Orlando
1996	14-13	.519	6-7	5th	Gene Orlando
1997	10-17	.370	6-9	7th	Gene Oralndo
1998	15-13	.536	6-9	7th	Gene Orlando
1999	10-13	.435	6-6	6th	Gene Orlando
2000	8-20	.286	3-9	9th	Gene Orlando
2001	7-18	.280	1-10	10th	Gene Orlando
2002	14-12	.538	2-9	9th	Gene Orlando
2003	14-13	.519	6-6	5th	Gene Orlando
Totals	710-749-10	.487	198-309		

TRACK AND FIELD
LEADERS, RECORDS AND HONORS

ALL-TIME COACHING RECORDS
(Dual Meets Only)

Coach	Years	W	L	T	Avg.
Henry Keep	1898	0	0	1	.000
George Denman	1902-03	3	0	0	1.000
Chester Brewer	1904-10	16	2	0	.888
John F. Macklin	1912-13	1	4	0	.200
Ion Cortright	1914	1	1	0	.500
George Gauthier	1915-19	3	5	0	.375
Arthur N. Smith	1920-21	5	5	0	.500
Albert Barron	1922-23	5	4	0	.555
Ralph H. Young	1924-40	41	36	0	.532
Karl A. Schlademan	1941-58	69	34	2	.521
Francis Dittrich	1959-75	40	23	1	.633
Jim Bibbs	1976-95	20	29	1	.351
Darroll Gatson	1996-	5	3	0	.625
Totals	1898-2002	191	146	6	.567

Season Records
See page 872 for explanation of abbreviations.

1886 (0-0-1)
Coach: no coach

5-14	H	MAC	19	
		Albion	14	
		Alma	0	
6-4	A	Albion	25-25	T

1887 (0-0)
Coach: no coach

6-2	H	MAC	55	
		Albion	35	
		Hillsdale	20	
		Olivet	10	

Henry Keep (1898)
(See football season records for Henry Keep sketch.)

1898 (2-0-1)
Coach: Henry Keep

2-5	A	Lansing H.S.	10-10	T
3-12	H	Lansing H.S.	11-5	W
5-13	A$_{CE}$	Olivet	77-24	W

1989-1901
There were no dual meets during these three years, yet a team did compete in the annual MIAA Field Days.

George Denman (1902-1903)
George Edward Denman, a native of Massachusetts, was the successor to Charles Bemies, coaching all sports for two academic years. An 1898 graduate of Williams College, he was a member of the track team as well as playing halfback on the football team. For two years following graduation, Denman taught history and English at Riverview Academy in Poughkeepsie, NY, where he was also in charge of athletics. In the following school year he returned to college, this time at Columbia University in New York City. Not being restrained by modern-day transfer rules, he immediately took up football again. His next stop prior to accepting the MAC offer was at Central University in Kentucky where he was director of athletics while teaching French and Latin.

1902 (2-0)
Coach: George Denman

| 5-24 | A$_{TT}$ | Alma | 114-62 | W |
| 5-31 | H | Albion | 74-47 | W |

1903 (1-0)
Coach: George Denman

| 5-23 | H | Albion | 80-31 | W |

Chester L. Brewer (1904-1910)
(See baseball season records for Chester Brewer sketch)

1904 (2-0)
Coach: Chester L. Brewer

| 3-12 | A | Alma | 50-38 | W |
| 5-21 | H | Alma | 56 1/2-28 1/2 | W |

1905 (5-0)
Coach: Chester L. Brewer

2-25	A	Alma	21-3	W
3-4	H	Olivet	38 1/2-31 1/2	W
3-17	H	Albion	49 1/2-22 1/2	W
5-6	A	Notre Dame	75-56	W
5-27	H	Armour Tech	93-38	W

1906 (2-0)
Coach: Chester L. Brewer

2-20	H	Olivet	23-22	W
5-12	A	Armour Tech	66-47	W
6-1	H	MAC	54	
		Olivet	39	
		Alma	15	

1907 (2-1)
Coach: Chester L. Brewer

2-2	H	Olivet	26 1/2-13 1/2	W
2-16	A	Notre Dame	42-71	L
5-25	H	Armour Tech	82-35	W
6-1	H	MAC	54	
		Olivet	39	
		Alma	15	

1908 (3-0)
Coach: Chester L. Brewer

3-2	H	Mich. Normal	43 2/3-33 1/3	W
5-2	H	Alma	77-49	W
5-16	H	Notre Dame	65 5/6-60 1/6	W
5-23	A$_{CH}$	Wabash	53	
		MAC	36	
		Armour Tech	19	

1909 (1-1)
Coach: Chester L. Brewer

| 5-13 | A | Notre Dame | 39-87 | L |

5-22	H	Olivet	77-49	W
6-5	H	Notre Dame	65	
		MAC	38	
		Armour Tech	32	

1910 (1-0)
Coach: Chester L. Brewer

2-25	H	Mich. Normal	43 1/2-28 1/2	W
5-21	H	MAC	77	
		Olivet	42	
		Alma	7	
5-28	A$_{ND}$	Notre Dame	62	
		MAC	43	
		Armour Tech	12	

John F. Macklin (1911-1913)
With the departure of Chester Brewer, President Snyder selected the coach from the University of Arkansas, 37-year-old Hugo Bezdek, as his replacement. As it turned out, there proved to be one slight problem—Bezdek could not be released from his contract at Arkansas. The next candidate to be offered the Aggie job was Jesse Harper, the Wabash College coach; however, the State Board of Agriculture would not approve the deal. The proposed annual salary of $2,200 ($200 over Brewer's final year) seemed exorbitant. Instead, Harper would sign on with Notre Dame in the following year. Heeding the advice of one of the top coaches of the day, Mike Murphy of Pennsylvania, president Jonathan Snyder eventually hired John Macklin, a star of football, baseball, and track at Penn in 1906 and 1907. Macklin had spent three years (1908-1910) developing teams at a private prep school in Pawling, NY. With the title of professor of physical culture and athletic director, he would be paid $2,000 per year. In addition to proving himself as a coach, Macklin demonstrated he was also a manager of funds. Upon his arrival in 1911, the athletic association had a fistful of outstanding debts accompanied by a trifling $6.30 in its treasury. When his tenure was complete in 1916 the account was debt-free and had grown to $14,994. More than belt-tightening, the professor drove a hard bargain. While in past years MAC received $200 for the annual fall football trip to Ann Arbor from which expenses would be wrested, by 1915 the U of M had agreed to fork over $5,000 for the Aggies' game share. In March of 1916, John Farrell Macklin left the scene as rapidly as he had arrived five years earlier. Retiring from coaching, in March of 1916 he moved to Colver, PA, where he commenced a career of managing a multimillion dollar coal-mining business owned by his in-laws.

1911 (0-0)
Coach: John F. Macklin

2-16	A$_{DE}$	Detroit YMCA	43	
		MAC	21	
		Adrian YMCA	13	
		Ann Arbor YMCA	3	
5-21	H	MAC	60	
		Olivet	42	
		Alma	24	

1912 (0-1)
Coach: John F. Macklin

2-15	A	Detroit YMCA	37-40	L
5-25	H	MAC	61	
		Olivet	39	
		Alma	35	

1913 (1-3)
Coach: John F. Macklin
2-27	A	Detroit YMCA	46-49	L
3-15	A	Michigan Frosh	19-63	L
5-5	H	Western Reserve	78-52	W
5-10	H	Michigan Frosh	44-87	L

Ion J. Cortright (1914)
John Macklin saw advantages in employing the services of former athletes. In the fall of 1911 he appointed Ion J. Cortright, a nine letterman, as freshman football coach. The new aide, a native of Mason, MI, had captained Macklin's first MAC baseball team in the preceding spring. Carrying the title of assistant athletic director, Cortright would also assist in basketball and track over the next three years. He was assigned as head track coach in 1914. By that summer he had absorbed enough experience to receive a position as head coach for athletic teams at the University of South Dakota in Vermillion. By the fall of 1916 he had moved on to the University of Cincinnati where he had assumed a similar coaching position.

1914 (1-1)
Coach: Ion Cortright
5-2	H	Western Reserve	81-50	W
5-9	H	MAC	87	
		Alma	25	
		Olivet	19	
5-30	A	Michigan Frosh	49-82	L

George Gauthier (1915-1919)
See cross country season records for George Gauthier sketch.)

1915 (1-1)
Coach: George Gauthier
5-1	H	MAC	90	
		Alma	27	
		Olivet	14	
5-22	H	Notre Dame	51 1/2-78 1/2	L
5-29	A	Michigan Frosh	70 1/2-59 1/2	W

1916 (1-1)
Coach: George Gauthier
5-3	A	Notre Dame	41-90	L
5-27	H	Michigan Frosh	90-41	W

1917 (0-1)
Coach: George Gauthier
5-10	H	Notre Dame	42 1/3-83 2/3	L

1918 (0-1)
Coach: George Gauthier
5-11	A	Notre Dame	35-85	L

1919 (1-1)
Coach: George Gauthier
5-10	H	Detroit Jr. College	101-29	W
5-17	H	Notre Dame	31-95	L

Arthur Smith (1920-1921)
(See cross country season records for Arthur Smith sketch.)

1920 (2-4)
Coach: Arthur N. Smith
2-25	H	Western St. Normal	40-46	L
3-6	H	Kalamazoo	79-25	W
3-13	H	Notre Dame	27-50	L
5-8	H	Detroit J.C.	80-46	W
5-15	A	Notre Dame	31 5/6-85 1/6	L
5-22	H	DePauw	30-96	L

1921 (3-1)
Coach: Arthur N. Smith
3-5	H	Western St. Normal	54-32	W
3-12	H	MAC Carnival	NTS	
5-7	A	W. St. Normal	81-47	W
5-14	H	Notre Dame	40-77	L
5-21	A	DePauw	73-53	W
		Big Tens at Chicago	12th/14	

Albert M. Barron (1922-1923)
(See cross country season records for Albert Barron sketch.)

1922 (4-1)
Coach: Albert M. Barron
2-4	H	W. St. Normal	50 1/2-34 1/2	W
2-18	H	DePauw	64 1/2-30 1/2	W
3-11	H	MAC Relay Carnival	NTS	
5-6	H	DePaul	104-22	W
5-13	H	Oberlin	78 1/2-47 1/2	W
5-20	H	Ohio State	58-68	L
5-30	A_{EV}	MAC	67 1/2	
		Chicago "Y" Coll.	53 1/2	
		Kalamazoo	28	

1923 (1-3)
Coach: Albert M. Barron
2-10	H	Mich. Normal	32 1/2-53 1/2	L
2-25	H	MAC Carnival	NTS	
4-28	A	Drake Relays	NTS	
5-5	A	Ohio State	34 1/2-91 1/2	L
5-12	H	Oberlin	66-65	W
5-19	A	Notre Dame	32 1/2-93 1/2	L
5-26	H	State Intercollegiate	3rd	

Ralph H. Young (1924-1940)
(See cross country season records for Ralph H. Young sketch.)

1924 (2-3)
Coach: Ralph H. Young
2-9	H	Chicago "Y" Coll.	68 1/2-26 1/2	W
2-23	H	Western St. Normal	30-56	L
3-8	H	MAC Carnival	NTS	
5-3	H	Detroit City College	67-64	W
5-10	A	Iowa State	29-102	L
5-17	H	Notre Dame	34 1/6-91 5/6	L
5-24	H	State Intercollegiate	3rd	

1925 (1-3)
Coach: Ralph H. Young
1-31	A_{DE}	Michigan AAU	NTS	
2-21	H	Western St. Normal	48-38	W
2-28	A_{CU}	Illinois Relays	NTS	
3-6	H	MSC Carnival	NTS	
3-13	H	Michigan Normal	31-73	L
5-2	H	Detroit City College	61-70	L
5-8	H	Western St. Normal	50-81	L
		Big Tens at Columbus	11/15	

1926 (2-3)
Coach: Ralph H. Young
2-13	H	Marquette	34 1/2-74 1/2	L
2-20	A	W. St. Normal	47 1/2 -38 1/2	W
2-27	A_{CU}	Illinois Relays	NTS	
3-6	H	MSC Carnival	NTS	
5-1	H	Detroit City Coll.	74 1/2-56 1/2	W
5-8	H	Iowa State	64-67	L
5-15	H	Notre Dame	48-78	L

1927 (4-0)
Coach: Ralph H. Young
2-5	A_{CH}	Illinois AC Meet	NTS	
2-11	A	W. St. Teachers	67 1/2-41 1/2	W
2-19	H	Michigan AAU	1st	
2-26	A_{CU}	Illinois Relays	NTS	
3-5	H	MSC Carnival	NTS	
3-12	H	Marquette	75-34	W
	A	Texas Relays	NTS	
5-5	H	Detroit City Coll.	86 2/3-44 1/3	W
5-13	A	Notre Dame	68-58	W
	H	State Intercollegiate	1st	

1928 (2-2)
Coach: Ralph H. Young
2-18	H	Ohio Wes.	70 1/6-38 5/6	W
2-25	A_{CU}	Illinois Relays	NTS	
3-3	H	MSC Carnival	NTS	
3-10	H	Marquette	52 1/2-56 1/2	L
3-17	A_{SB}	CCC	2nd	
5-5	H	Detroit City College	85-46	W
5-12	H	Notre Dame	62-64	L
	H	State Intercollegiate	1st	

1929 (2-2)
Coach: Ralph H. Young
2-16	A	Ohio Wesleyan	44-65	L
2-23	H	Marquette	67 1/3-41 2/3	W
4-20	H	Detroit City College	85-46	W
5-11	A	Notre Dame	40 2/3-85 1/3	L
	H	State Intercollegiate	1st	

1930 (2-3)
Coach: Ralph H. Young
2-15	A	Marquette	36 1/2-72 1/2	L
2-22	H	Ohio Wesleyan	66-43	W
2-27	A_{AA}	Michigan	63 1/2	
		Michigan Normal	38 1/2	
		MSC	17	
3-1	H	MSC Carnival	NTS	
3-8	A_{ND}	CCC	6th	
3-15		ACUIllinois Relays	NTS	
3-22	A	Chicago	39 1/2-46 1/2	L
4-19	H	Det. City Coll.	78 2/3-52 1/3	W
5-10	H	Notre Dame	37-89	L

1931 (5-0)
Coach: Ralph H. Young
2-7	H	Chicago	58 2/3-36 1/3	W
2-18	H	Marquette	58 1/2-50 1/2	W
2-21	H	Ohio Wesleyan	55-54	W
4-18	H	Detroit City College	78-53	W
5-9	H	Detroit	80-51	W

1932 (4-1)
Coach: Ralph H. Young
2-19	H	Ohio Wesleyan	73 1/2-35 1/2	W
3-1	A	Marquette	44 1/2-64 1/2	L
4-23	H	Detroit City College	110-21	W
5-7	H	Notre Dame	65 3/4-65 1/4	W
5-14	A	Detroit	96 1/2-34 1/2	W

1933 (3-0)
Coach: Ralph H. Young
2-25	W	Ohio Wesleyan	83 3/4-25 1/4	W
3-3	W	Marquette	61 3/5-47 2/5	W
5-6	A	Notre Dame	67-64	W

1934 (1-2)
Coach: Ralph H. Young

2-24	AAA	Michigan 60		
		MSC 30 1/2		
		Michigan Normal 28 1/2		
3-2	A	Marquette 37-72	L	
5-5	H	Detroit 95-34	W	
5-12	A	Notre Dame 50 2/3-80 1/3	L	

1935 (0-2)
Coach: Ralph H. Young

2-22	A_AA	Michigan 72 1/2		
		Michigan Normal 24 1/3		
		MSC 22 1/6		
3-2	H	Marquette 47 3/4-61 1/4	L	
5-11	H	Notre Dame 38 1/2-92 1/2	L	

1936 (1-1)
Coach: Ralph H. Young

2-21	A	Michigan 36-59	L	
2-29	A	Marquette 55 1/2-53 1/2	W	
5-9	A_SB	Notre Dame 71 3/4		
		Ohio State 70 1/2		
		MSC 20 3/4		

1937 (5-1)
Coach: Ralph H. Young

2-17	H	Michigan Normal 63-32	W	
2-20	A	Michigan 28-67	L	
3-1	H	Marquette 84-20	W	
4-17	H	Chicago 88-43	W	
5-1	A	Marquette 84-47	W	
5-21	H	Notre Dame 66 1/2-64 1/2	W	

1938 (5-3)
Coach: Ralph H. Young

2-12	A_AA	Michigan Normal 73-22	W	
2-17	A	Michigan 26 1/2-68 1/2	L	
2-26	H	Marquette 52 1/2-56 1/2	L	
3-26	A	West Virginia Relays 1st/4		
3-30	A	Maryland 83 1/2-47 1/2	W	
4-1	A	Penn State 75-51	W	
4-16	H	Purdue 87-44	W	
5-7	H	Marquette 82 1/6-53 5/6	W	
5-14	A	Notre Dame 45 1/3-85 2/3	L	

1939 (2-5)
Coach: Ralph H. Young

2-11	A	Notre Dame 30-65	L	
2-14	A	Michigan 18-77	L	
2-25	H	Marquette 31-78	L	
4-15	H	Purdue 76 1/6-54 5/6	W	
5-6	H	Marquette 45-91	L	
5-8	H	Penn State 57-74	L	
5-15	H	Notre Dame 70-61	W	

1940 (0-5)
Coach: Ralph H. Young

2-5	H	Notre Dame 37 1/3-57 2/3	L	
2-13	A_AA	Michigan 79		
		MSC 29 1/2		
		Michigan Normal 21 1/2		
2-23	H	Marquette 32-86	L	
4-13	H	Purdue 53-69	L	
5-4	A	Marquette 35 1/2-101 1/2	L	
5-11	A	Notre Dame 52-79	L	

Karl Schlademan (1941-1958)

See cross country season records for Karl L. Schlademan
sketch.)

1941 (0-6)
Coach: Karl A. Schlademan

2-7	A	Notre Dame 20-84	L	
2-21	H	Marquette 49 1/2-68 1/2	L	
2-23	H	Michigan 75 1/5		
		Michigan Normal 39 7/10		
		MSC 15 1/10		
4-12	H	Purdue 62-69	L	
5-3	A	Marquette 53-83	L	
5-10	H	Notre Dame 40 1/2-90 1/2	L	
5-24	A	Penn State 44-87	L	

1942 (3-4)
Coach: Karl A. Schlademan

1-31	H	Ohio State 34-75	L	
2-7	A	Illinois 37-67	L	
2-14	H	Michigan 64 1/2		
		MSC 35 1/2		
		Michigan Normal 30		
2-21	H	Marquette 65 1/2-45 1/2	W	
4-11	H	Purdue 67 2/3-54 1/3	W	
5-2	H	Penn State 58-73	L	
5-9	A	Notre Dame 48-83	L	
5-23	A	Marquette 69-62	W	

1943 (3-2)
Coach: Karl A. Schlademan

1-29	H	Ohio State 36-73	L	
2-9	A	Michigan 39-65	L	
2-20	H	Illinois 62-42	W	
4-17	H	Purdue 81-41	W	
5-1	H	Marquette 77-59	W	
5-7	A_AA	Michigan 82		
		Ohio State 41 1/2		
		MSC 28 1/2		

1944

Intercollegiate athletics suspended due to World War II

1945 (2-2)
Coach: Karl A. Schlademan

1-27	H	Ohio State 31-73	L	
2-7	H	Wayne 66 2/3-37 1/3	W	
2-24	H	Indiana 37 1/3-66 2/3	L	
5-5	A_CO	Great Lakes NTS 74 1/2		
		Ohio State 64		
		MSC 12 1/2		
5-19	A	Indiana 61 1/2-60 1/2	W	

1946 (4-2)
Coach: Karl A. Schlademan

1-26	H	Ohio State 68-50	W	
2-16	A_ND	Notre Dame 78 2/3		
		MSC 44 1/3		
		Marquette 6		
2-23	H	Wayne 86 2/3-17 1/3	W	
3-2	A_AA	Michigan 70 1/6		
		Notre Dame 33 1/6		
		MSC 25 1/2		
4-20	A_CO	Ohio State 74		
		Purdue 45 1/2		
		MSU 35 3/4		
		Miami (OH) 25 3/4		
5-4	A	Ohio State 51-71	L	
5-11	A	Marquette 92-44	W	
5-18	A	Notre Dame 87-44	W	
6-1	H	Penn State 96 1/2-34 1/2	W	

1947 (6-1)
Coach: Karl A. Schlademan

1-25	H	Ohio St 66 7/12-66 5/12	W	
2-15	A	Michigan 53 14/15-60 1/15	L	

(continued, top right)

2-24	H	MSC 106		
		Marquette 24		
		Wayne 22		
3-1	A	Notre Dame 61 1/3-52 2/3	W	
4-19	A_CO	Ohio State 77 1/3		
		MSC 50 2/3		
		Purdue 29		
5-3	H	Notre Dame 76-65	W	
5-10	A	Penn State 71 3/5-59 2/5	W	
5-17	A	Marquette 99 2/3-50 1/3	W	
5-23	H	Michigan 68 1/3-63 2/3	W	

1948 (2-2-1)
Coach: Karl A. Schlademan

1-24	H	Ohio State 57 1/6-56 5/6	W	
2-27	A	Michigan 57-57	T	
4-17	A_CO	Ohio State 94		
		Purdue 34 1/2		
		MSC 32 1/2		
5-8	H	Penn State 54-77	L	
5-15	A	Notre Dame 77-54	W	
5-22	H	Illinois 46-86	L	

1949 (5-0-1)
Coach: Karl A. Schlademan

2-17	H	Ohio State 79 1/2-34 1/2	W	
4-16	A	Southern California 61-61	T	
4-23	H	Notre Dame 86-56	W	
5-7	H	Ohio State 79 1/2-52 1/2	W	
5-14	A	Penn State 83 1/2-47 1/2	W	
5-21	H	Marquette 105-36	W	

1950 (3-0)
Coach: Karl A. Schlademan

2-18	H	Ohio State 67-47	W	
4-22	A_CO	MSC 65 1/2		
		Ohio State 57 1/2		
		Penn State 38		
4-29	A_LA	Southern California 96		
		MSC 34		
		Yale 32		
5-6	H	Penn State 82-59	W	
5-17	H	Notre Dame 78-53	W	

1951 (2-4)
Coach: Karl A. Schlademan

2-10	H	MSC 66 2/3		
		Penn State 47 1/2		
		Northwestern 26 5/6		
2-17	A	Iowa 68-40	W	
2-24	A	Wisconsin 56 1/6-57 5/6	L	
		Big Ten (I) at Champaign 3rd		
4-21	A	Indiana 55-77	L	
5-5	H	Ohio State 74-58	W	
5-12	A	Michigan 47 1/2-84 1/2	L	
5-19	H	Illinois 59 1/2-72 1/2	L	
		Big Ten (O) at Champaign 2nd		

1952 (4-1)
Coach: Karl A. Schlademan

2-2	H	Notre Dame 62 2/3-51 1/3		
2-23	H	Michigan 39 1/3-74 2/3	L	
		Big Ten (I) at Champaign 5th		
5-3	A	Penn State 91-40	W	
5-10	H	Wisconsin 84-48	W	
5-17	H	Syracuse 100-36	W	
		Big Ten (O) at Ann Arbor 5th		

1953 (4-1)
Coach: Karl A. Schlademan

2-20	H	E. Michigan 77 2/3-36 1/3	W	
2-24	A	Notre Dame 73 1/3-40 2/3	W	

Big Ten (I) at Champaign 5th
5-2   A   Illinois 43-89   L
5-9   H   Penn State 89-47   W
5-16 A   Wisconsin .... 84 1/3-47 2/3   W
Big Ten (O) at Champaign 3rd

1954 (1-2)
Coach: Karl A. Schlademan
2-15 H   Illinois 48 1/2
MSC 42
Kansas 39 1/2
2-27 A   Indiana 56-75   L
Big Ten (I) at Champaign 5th
5-1   H   Notre Dame 79-62   W
5-15 A   Penn State 61-70   L
Big Ten (O) at W. Lafayette 3rd

1955 (2-1)
Coach: Karl A. Schlademan
2-5   H   Eastern Michigan 79-48   W
2-12 H_ Missouri 54
Penn State 45 1/2
MSU 37
Ohio State 30 1/2
2-26 H   MSC 92 5/6
Western Michigan 49 5/6
Northwestern 31 1/3
Big Ten (I) at East Lansing 2nd
5-6   H   Indiana .... 71 1/2-60 1/2   W
5-19 A   Illinois .... 63 2/3-68 1/3   L
Big Ten (O) at Columbus 5th

1956 (2-2)
Coach: Karl A. Schlademan
2-17 A   E. Michigan .... 95 1/3-45 2/3   W
Big Ten (I) at East Lansing 4th
5-5   H   Notre Dame 54-86   L
5-12 A   Wisconsin 72-60   W
5-18 H   Michigan 63-84   L
Big Ten (O) at Minneapolis 4th

1957 (3-2)
Coach: Karl A. Schlademan
2-11 H   Kansas 53-88   L
2-18 A   Ohio State .... 74 1/2-66 1/2   W
2-22 H   Western Michigan 108-33   W
Big Ten (I) at Columbus 3rd
5-7   H   Chicago T.C. .... 88 1/2-51 1/2   W
5-11 H   Ohio State 66 1/2
MSC 47 1/2
Penn State 47
5-18 A   Notre Dame 67-74   L
Big Ten (O) at Evanston T5th

1958 (3-3)
Coach: Karl A. Schlademan
2-14 A   Kansas 36-68   L
2-21 H   Western Michigan 78-63   W
3-1   H   Iowa 74-49   W
Big Ten (I) at Champaign 5th
5-3   H   Notre Dame 75-66   W
5-10 A   Nebraska 55-72   L
5-17 H   Ohio State .... 51 1/2-80 1/2   L
Big Ten (O) at W. Lafayette 4th

Francis C. Dittrich (1959-1975)
(See cross country season records for Francis C. Dittrich sketch.)

1959 (1-4)
Coach: Francis C. Dittrich
2-14 A   Ohio State 49-65   L
2-21 A_KZ Western Michigan 92
MSC 45
Marquette 35
2-28 A   Iowa .... 60 1/3-79 2/3   L
Big Ten (I) at Madison 7th
5-2   H   Wisconsin .... 72 1/2-59 1/2   W
5-9   A   Penn State .... 39 1/4-91 3/4   L
5-14 A   Notre Dame 57-74   L
Big Ten (O) at Madison 7th

1960 (2-1)
Coach: Francis C. Dittrich
2-6   A   Ohio State .... 62 2/3-51 1/3   W
2-20 AIC MSC 71 1/2
Iowa 65 1/2
Northwestern 35
2-27 H   Michigan 54-87   L
Big Ten (I) at Columbus 3rd
5-7   A_WL Illinois 84
MSC 40
Purdue 33
5-14 H   Notre Dame 72-69   W
Big Tens (O) at East Lansing 4th

1961 (2-2)
Coach: Francis C. Dittrich
1-28 A   Ohio State .... 64 1/3-61 2/3   W
2-17 A   Michigan .... 44 1/3-96 2/3   L
2-25 H   Cent. Michigan ... 71 1/2-69 1/2   W
Big Ten (I) at Champaign 6th
5-6   H   Penn State 65 1/3
MSC 49 2/3
Ohio State 46
5-13 A   Notre Dame 51-80   L
Big Ten (O) at Iowa City 4th

1962 (2-0)
Coach: Francis C. Dittrich
1-27 H   MSC 90 1/2
Ohio State 60 1/2
Northwestern 22
2-15 A   Central Michigan 97-44   W
2-24 A_BL MSC 58 1/2
Oklahoma 54 1/2
Indiana 45
Big Ten (I) at East Lansing 3rd
5-12 H   MSC 75 1/2
Michigan 65 1/4
Ohio State 31 1/4
5-15 H   Penn State 73-63   W
Big Ten (O) at W. Lafayette 3rd

1963 (2-0)
Coach: Francis C. Dittrich
1-26 A   Ohio State 82-59   W
2-16 A_MP MSC 72 1/2
Central Michigan 55
Bowling Green 24 1/2
2-23 H   Wisconsin 86
MSC 79
Indiana 13
Big Ten (I) at Madison 4th
5-11 H   Notre Dame 72-67   W
Big Ten (O) at Minneapolis 4th

1964 (4-1)
Coach: Francis C. Dittrich
1-25 A   Ohio State 63-78   L
2-22 A_MA Wisconsin 86
MSU 50
Indiana 35

2-29 H   Miami (OH) 66-47   W
Big Ten (I) at Columbus 3rd
5-2   H   Ohio State 81-51   W
5-9   A   Notre Dame 67-55   W
5-16 H   Chicago Track Club 84-53   W
Big Ten (O) at Evanston 4th

1965 (4-0)
Coach: Francis C. Dittrich
1-30 A   Ohio State 87-54   W
2-20 ABL Wisconsin 77
Indiana 51 1/2
MSU 47 1/2
2-27 H   Miami (OH) 87-54   W
Big Ten (I) at Champaign 2nd
5-1   H   Ohio State .... 97 1/2-43 1/2   W
5-8   AKZ Western Michigan 70
MSU 69
Miami (OH) 34
5-15 H   Notre Dame 98-43   W
Big Ten (O) at Iowa City 1st

1966 (4-0)
Coach: Francis C. Dittrich
1-29 ACOMSU 101
Ohio State 53
Kentucky 17
2-19 H   Indiana 98-43   W
2-29 A   Wisconsin 73-68   W
Big Ten (I) at East Lansing 1st
5-7   H   Ohio State 104-37   W
5-14 H   Notre Dame 87-54   W
Big Ten (O) at Bloomington 1st

1967 (4-0)
Coach: Francis C. Dittrich
2-18 A   Indiana 94-47   W
2-25 H   Wisconsin 76-64   W
Big Ten (I) at Madison 2nd
5-6   H   Ohio State 115-58   W
5-10 A   Notre Dame .... 97 1/2-47 1/2   W
Big Ten (O) at Iowa City 2nd

1968 (0-1)
Coach: Francis C. Dittrich
2-17 H   Ohio State 67-83   L
2-24 A_WL MSU 77
Purdue 57
Murray State 37
Big Ten (I) at Columbus 4th
4-13 A_CU MSU 93
Illinois 74
Northwestern 44
5-4   A_DM Indiana 68
Illinois 53
MSU 52
Iowa 47
5-11 H   Wisconsin 104
Notre Dame 64
MSU 40
Big Ten (O) at Minneapolis 7th

1969 (1-3)
Coach: Francis C. Dittrich
2-15 A   Wisconsin 63-86   L
2-19 A   Indiana 65-84   L
2-22 H   Ohio 80-69   W
Big Ten (I) at Champaign 4th
4-12 A_CH Wisconsin 104
Illinois 64
MSU 40
5-3   A   Minnesota 82-91   L
Big Ten (O) at W. Lafayette 4th

1970 (1-3)
Coach: Francis C. Dittrich

2-21	A	Illinois 59-81		L
2-28	A	Michigan 51-89		L
		Big Ten (I) at East Lansing 3rd		
4-11	A$_{WL}$	Purdue 86		
		MSU 84		
		Bradley 21		
4-18	H	Northwestern 91-62		W
5-2	H	Indiana 84		
		Wisconsin 66		
		MSU 41		
5-9	A	Notre Dame 65-80		L
		Big Ten (O) at Bloomington 3rd		
		CCCs at Bloomington 4th		

1971 (4-2)
Coach: Francis C. Dittrich

1-30	A	Michigan Relays .... NTS	
2-6	A	Northwestern 67-70	L
2-13	H	Michigan State Relays .... NTS	
2-20	A	Michigan 72 1/2-67 1/2	W
2-27	H	Iowa 82-54	W
		Big Ten (I) at Madison 2nd	
4-17	A$_{CO}$	Ohio Relays .... NTS	
4-23	A	Drake Relays .... NTS	
5-1	A	Ohio State 83-71	W
5-8	H	Purdue 87-67	W
5-15	A	Indiana 52-101	L
		Big Ten (O) at Iowa City 4th	
		CCCs at Bowling Green 10th	

1972 (5-1)
Coach: Francis C. Dittrich

2-5	H	Northwestern 108-31	W
2-19	H	Michigan 83-57	W
2-26	A	Iowa 95-44	W
		Big Ten (I) at Columbus 1st	
4-15	A	Purdue 78-76	W
		A	Drake Relays .... NTS	
5-6	H	Ohio State 95-58	W
5-13	A	Indiana 72-82	L
		Big Ten (O) at Champaign 1st	

1973 (2-1)
Coach: Francis C. Dittrich

1-27	A	Michigan Relays .... NTS	
2-2	A	W. Michigan Relays .... NTS	
2-10	H	MSU Relays .... NTS	
2-17	A	Michigan 57-74	L
2-24	H	Indiana 68-62	W
		Big Ten (I) at W. Lafayette 3rd	
4-20	A	Kansas Relays .... NTS	
4-27	A	Drake Relays .... NTS	
5-5	H	Notre Dame 99-44	W
		Big Ten (O) at Minneapolis	
		CCCs at East Lansing 1st	

1974 (2-1)
Coach: Francis C. Dittrich

1-26	A	Michigan Relays .... NTS	
2-2	A	W. Michigan Relays .... NTS	
2-9	H	MSU Relays .... NTS	
2-14	H	Michigan 70-61	W
2-23	A	Indiana 42-88	L
		Big Ten (I) at East Lansing 2nd	
4-19	A	Kansas Relays .... NTS	
4-26	A	Drake Relays .... NTS	
5-3	A	Notre Dame 97-48	W
		Big Ten (O) at Ann Arbor 4th	
		CCCs at Bowling Green T11th	

1975 (1-3)
Coach: Francis C. Dittrich

1-25	A	Michigan Relays .... NTS

1-31	A	W. Michigan Relays .... NTS	
2-8	H	MSU Relays .... NTS	
2-15	A	Michigan 55-81	L
2-22	H	Indiana 39-92	L
3-1	A	Wisconsin 44-87	L
		Big Ten (I) at Bloomington 8th	
4-25	A	Drake Relays .... NTS	
5-3	H	Purdue 72-69	W
		Big Ten (O) at Iowa City 3rd	
		CCCs at Ann Arbor 12th	

Jim Bibbs (1976-1995)

Jim Bibbs first joined the MSU staff in 1968 as an assistant, later serving as acting head coach in 1976 and 1977. He was named as Fran Dittrich's permanent replacement on June 1, 1977. Bibbs was born on March 12, 1929 in Ecorse, MI. It was also here that he began his track career at Ecorse High School, where he was an outstanding sprinter and long jumper. He later earned three letters at Eastern Michigan (1949-51) when he led the Hurons to three consecutive conference team titles as the sprint champion. Jim's greatest accomplishment as a sprinter came in 1951 when he posted a fine 06.1 clocking in the 60-yard dash event. After earning a B.A. from EMU, Bibbs went on to achieve a master's degree from Wayne. His first teaching position was as physical education instructor in the Detroit school system. Then in 1964 he became track coach at his prep alma mater, Ecorse High School, and remained there until accepting the appointment at Michigan State. Bibbs's story includes a progression of success while coaching at Ecorse. His 1964 team placed fourth in the state championship followed by a third in '65, second in '66 and the team title in '67. Besides working with the high school boys, Jim tutored the women's Detroit Track Club, directing the ladies to national relay titles in 1964, 1965, 1966, and 1967. In 1995, following 20 years as head coach at Michigan State, Jim Bibbs announced his retirement.

1976 (1-4)
Coach: Jim Bibbs

1-17	H	MSU 67	
		Northwestern 54	
		Wayne State 41	
1-24	A	Michigan Relays .... NTS	
1-31	A	W. Michigan Relays .... NTS	
2-7	H	MSU Relays .... NTS	
2-12	H	Michigan 44-87	L
2-19	H	Wisconsin 60-70	L
		CCCs at Ypsilanti 10th	
2-28	A	Indiana 50-81	L
		Big Ten (I) at Madison 7th	
4-16	A	Ohio State Relays .... NTS	
4-23	A	Drake Relays .... NTS	
5-1	H	Notre Dame 100-44	W
5-8	H	Central Michigan 64-81	L
		Big Ten (O) at Champaign 6th	
		CCCs at Kalamazoo 11th	

1977 (3-1)
Coach: Jim Bibbs

1-15	A	E. Michigan Relays .... NTS	
1-22	A	Michigan Relays .... NTS	
1-29	A	Michigan 54-77	L
2-5	A	W. Michigan Relays .... NTS	
2-12	H	MSU Relays .... NTS	
		CCCs at Ann Arbor 11th/16	
2-26	H	Indiana 69-62	W
		Big Ten (I) at Ann Arbor 5th	
4-16	A$_{KX}$	Dogwood Relays .... NTS	
4-23	A	Ohio State Relays .... NTS	
4-29	A	Drake Relays .... NTS	
5-7	A	Northwestern 90-54	W
5-14	H	E. Michigan 80-65	W
		Big Ten (O) at Bloomington 3rd	
		CCCs at Bloomington 3rd/18	

1978 (3-2)
Coach: Jim Bibbs

1-13	H	Northwestern 95-35	W
2-1	H	Michigan 44-87	L
2-51	A	W. Michigan Relays .... NTS	
2-12	H	MSU Relays .... NTS	
2-15	H	Central Michigan 70-61	L
		CCCs at Ypsilanti T14th	
		Big Ten (I) W. Lafayette T5th	
4-14	A	AKXDogwood Relays .... NTS	
4-22	A	Ohio State Relays .... NTS	
4-28	A	Drake Relays .... NTS	
5-3	A	Central Michigan 105-57	W
5-6	A	Eastern Michigan 37-108	L
		Big Ten (O) at Evanston 7th	
		CCCs at Ann Arbor 7th/16	

1979 (3-3)
Coach: Jim Bibbs

1-13	H	Western Ontario 105-24	W
1-20	A$_{CO}$	MSU 68	
		Ohio State 58	
		Ohio 38	
1-31	H	Michigan 59-72	L
2-3	A	W. Michigan Relays .... NTS	
2-10	H	MSU Relays .... NTS	
		CCCs 4th	
2-21	H	Central Michigan 72-50	W
2-24	A	Wisconsin 56-75	L
		Big Ten (I) at Champaign. 4th	
4-13	A$_{KX}$	Dogwood Relays .... NTS	
4-21	A	Ohio State Relays .... NTS	
4-24	H	Central Michigan 79-65	W
4-27	A	Drake Relays .... NTS	
5-5	H	E. Michigan 69 1/2-75 1/2	L
5-12	A$_{AA}$	Michigan Open .... NTS	
		Big Ten (O) at Ann Arbor 6th	
		CCCs at Notre Dame 10th	

1980 (1-3)
Coach: Jim Bibbs

1-12	H	Wisconsin 61 1/2-69 1/2	L
1-19	A	Eastern Michigan Invit ...... NTS	
1-26	A	Michigan Relays .... NTS	
2-2	A	W. Michigan Relays .... NTS	
2-9	H	Michigan State Relays .... NTS	
2-16	A	Michigan 69-71	L
		CCCs at Ann Arbor 2nd	
		Big Ten (I) at Madison 4th	
3-8	A	Eastern Michigan 39-92	L
4-11	A$_{KX}$	Dogwood Relays .... NTS	
4-19	H	MSU Invitational .... NTS	
4-25	A	Drake Relays .... NTS	
5-3	H	MSU 70	
		Purdue 58	
		Ohio State 53	
5-10	H	Eastern Michigan 82-63	W
		Big Ten (O) at Champaign 4th	
		CCCs at Bowling Green 11th	

1981 (0-1)
Coach: Jim Bibbs

1-17	A	E. Michigan Relays .... NTS	
1-24	A	Michigan Relays .... NTS	
1-31	A	W. Michigan Relays .... NTS	
2-7	H	MSU Relays .... NTS	
2-10	H	Michigan	
	A$_{AA}$	CCC 3rd/7	
2-27	A	Michigan Open .... NTS	
		Big Ten (I) at East Lansing 3rd	
4-10	A$_{KX}$	Dogwood Relays .... NTS	
4-18	H	Michigan State Invit. .... NTS	
4-24	A	Drake Relays .... NTS	
5-9	A	Chicago Relays .... NTS	
5-16	A	Illinois 53-90	L
		Big Ten (O) at East Lansing 5th	
		CCCs at East Lansing 2nd	

1982 (1-2-1)

Coach: Jim Bibbs

1-23	A	Michigan Relays	NTS	
1-30	A	W. Michigan Relays	NTS	
2-6	H	Michigan State Relays	NTS	
2-9	H	Michigan	56-75	L
		CCCs at Madison	10th	
		Big Ten (I) at Bloomington	5th	
4-9	A KX	Dogwood Relays	NTS	
4-17	H	Michigan State Invit.	NTS	
4-23	A	Drake Relays	NTS	
5-1	A	Ohio State	86-59	W
5-8	H	Eastern Michigan	72-72	T
5-15	H	Illinois	60-85	L
		Big Ten (O) at Minneapolis	5th	
		CCCs	3rd	

1983 (1-2)

Coach: Jim Bibbs

1-16	A	Chicago Invit.	NTS	
1-22	A	Michigan Relays	NTS	
1-29	A	W. Michigan Relays	NTS	
2-5	H	MSU Relays	NTS	
2-12	A	Michigan	39-90	L
		CCCs at Kalamazoo	6th/17	
2-26	A AA	Michigan Open	NTS	
		Big Ten (I) at East Lansing	4th	
4-8	A KX	Dogwood Relays	NTS	
4-16	H	MSU Invitational	NTS	
4-23	H	Ohio State	78-65	W
4-29	A	Drake Relays	NTS	
5-7	A	Eastern Michigan	53-87	L
5-8	A	Ohio State Invit.	NTS	
5-14	A AA	Michigan Open	NTS	
		Big Ten (O) at W. Lafayette	6th	
		CCCs at Toledo	6th	

1984 (0-1)

Coach: Jim Bibbs

1-13	A	E. Michigan Relays	NTS	
1-15	A	Chicago Relays	NTS	
1-21	A	Michigan Relays	NTS	
1-28	A	W. Michigan Relays	NTS	
2-4	A	E. Michigan Classic	NTS	
2-11	H	MSU Relays	NTS	
		CCCs at Yipsilanti	7th	
2-25	A	Michigan Open	NTS	
		Big Ten (I) at Ann Arbor	9th	
4-13	A KX	Dogwood Relays	NTS	
4-21	H	MSU Invitational	NTS	
4-27	A	Drake Relays	NTS	
5-4	A CO	Jesse Owens Invit.	NTS	
5-12	A	Eastern Michigan	32-112	L
		Big Ten (O) at Columbus	9th	
		CCCs at Evanston	19th	

1985 (1-0)

Coach: Jim Bibbs

1-5	H	Western Ontario	90-62	W
1-12	A	Eastern Michigan Invit.	NTS	
1-19	A	Michigan Invit.	NTS	
1-25	A	W. Michigan Invit.	NTS	
2-2	H	MSU Relays	NTS	
2-8	A	E. Michigan Invit.	NTS	
		CCCs at Ann Arbor	10th/17	
		Big Ten (I)	T9th	
4-6	A BL	Indiana	98	
		Notre Dame	57	
		MSU	35	
4-12	A KX	Dogwood Relays	NTS	
4-20	H	MSU Invitational	NTS	
4-26	A	Drake Relays	NTS	
5-4	H	MSU Open	NTS	
5-5	A CO	Jesse Owens Invit.	NTS	
5-10	A	E. Michigan Invit.	NTS	
		Big Ten (O) at Evanston	8th	
		CCCs at Yipsilanti	9th/20	

1986 (0-1)

Coach: Jim Bibbs

1-10	A	Eastern Michigan Invit.	NTS	
1-17	A	Western Ontario	1st/4	
1-25	A	W. Michigan Relays	NTS	
2-1	A	Indiana Relays	NTS	
2-8	H	MSU Relays	NTS	
2-16	A CH	Bally Invitational	NTS	
		CCCs at Madison	6th/10	
		Big Ten (I) at Indianapolis	5th	
4-11	A KX	Dogwood Relays	NTS	
4-19	H	MSU Invitational	NTS	
4-25	A	Drake Relays	NTS	
5-3	A KZ	Michigan Intercollegiate	NTS	
5-4	A CO	Jesse Owens Classic	NTS	
5-9	H	Eastern Michigan	43-102	L
		Big Ten (O) at Madison	6th	
		CCCs at Evanston	13/22	

1987 (0-4)

Coach: Jim Bibbs

1-10	A	Ohio State	49-58	L
1-16	A IN	Hoosierdome Invit.	NTS	
1-23	A	Notre Dame	53-78	L
1-31	A	Western Mich. Relays	NTS	
2-7	H	MSU Relays	NTS	
2-14		CCCs at Eastern Mich.	T10/18	
2-21	A	E. Michigan Classic	NTS	
2-27		Big Tens (I) at Champaign	9th	
4-11	A KX	Dogwood Relays	NTS	
4-18	H	MSU Open	NTS	
4-25	A	Drake Relays	NTS	
5-1	A	Eastern Michigan	44-101	L
5-2	A AA	Phil Diamond Invit.	NTS	
5-2	A IN	National Invitational	NTS	
5-3	A CO	Jesse Owens Classic	NTS	
5-9	A YP	Michigan Intercollegiate	NTS	
5-16	A	Central Michigan	58-86	L
		Big Tens (O) at Iowa City	9th	
		CCCs at Evanston	6th	

1988

Coach: Jim Bibbs

1-16	A	Eastern Mich. Relays	NTS	
1-23	A	Michigan Relays	NTS	
1-29	A	Western Mich. Relays	NTS	
2-6	H	MSU Relays	NTS	
		CCCs		
2-19	A	E. Michigan Classic	NTS	
		Big Ten (I) at Columbus	8th	
4-15	A KX	Dogwood Relays	NTS	
4-23	H	MSU Open	NTS	
4-29	A	Drake Relays	NTS	
5-7	H	Mich. Championships	NTS	
5-8	A CO	Jesse Owens Classic	NTS	
5-14	H	Central Michigan	NTS	
		Big Ten (O) at Ann Arbor	9th	
		CCCs at Notre Dame	T4th/21	

1989

Coach: Jim Bibbs

1-13	A	Eastern Michigan Invit.	NTS	
1-23	A	Michigan Relays	NTS	
1-28	A	W. Michigan Invit.	NTS	
2-4	A	Notre Dame Invit.	NTS	
		CCCs at Notre Dame	11th/22	
2-18	A	E. Michigan Classic	NTS	
		Big Ten (I) at Iowa City	8th	
3-14	A KX	Dogwood Relays	NTS	
4-22	H	MSU Open	NTS	
4-28	A	Drake Relays	NTS	
5-6		AAA Michigan Champ.	NTS	
5-13	A CO	Jesse Owens Invit.	NTS	
		Big Ten (O) at Indianapolis	8th	
		CCCs at Champaign	14th/19	

1990 (3-0)

Coach: Jim Bibbs

1-13	H	Central Michigan	64-54	W
1-20	A	Michigan Relays	NTS	
1-27	H	Ball State	74-44	W
		CCCs at Madison	4th/16	
2-16	A	Eastern Mich. Classic	NTS	
		Big Tens (I)	9th/9	
3-1	A	EMU Last Chance.	NTS	
4-13	A	Dogwood Relays	NTS	
4-14	H	Michigan	89-57	W
4-21	A	Kansas Relays	NTS	
4-21	A	MSU Relays	NTS	
4-28	A	Drake Relays	NTS	
4-28	A	Hillsdale Invit.	NTS	
		CCCs at Notre Dame	8th/14	
5-12	A	Jesse Owens Classic	NTS	
5-12	A	Michigan Inter.	NTS	
		Big Tens (O) at Champaign	T8th/9	

1991 (0-1)

Coach: Jim Bibbs

1-11	H	Michigan State	53	
		Toledo	48	
		Central Michigan	28	
		Lansing Comm. Coll.	11	
1-19	A	Illinois Invit.	NTS	
1-26	A	Western Mich. Invit.	NTS	
2-2	H	MSU Relays	NTS	
2-9	A	Indiana (Tennessee)	NTS	
2-16	A	Eastern Mich. Relays	NTS	
		Big Tens (I) at W. Lafayette	T6th	
3-2	A	EMU Last Chance.	NTS	
3-30	A	Inv./Diet Pepsi Chall.	NTS	
4-13	A	Michigan	57-93	L
4-13	A KX	Dogwood Relays	NTS	
4-20	H	MSU Open	NTS	
4-27	A	Drake Relays	NTS	
		CCCs at Notre Dame	6th/12	
5-10	A	Central Mich. Open	NTS	
5-11	A	Len Paddock Invit.	NTS	
		Big Tens (O) at Columbus	T8th	
5-23	A	Michigan Last Chance	NTS	

1992 (2-1)

Coach: Jim Bibbs

1/11	H	Central Michigan	71-69	W
		Toledo	74-57	W
		Illinois	50-83	L
1-25	A AA	Michigan	51	
		Ohio State	50	
		Penn State	32	
		MSU	27	
2-1	A MN	MSU	57 1/3	
		Minnesota	49 1/3	
		Purdue	46 1/3	
		Iowa State	12	
2-8		MSU Relays	NTS	
2-15	A	CCCs at Iowa City, IA	2nd/13	
2-22	A	E. Michigan Open	NTS	
		Big Tens (I) at East Lansing	5th	
4-11	A	Barnett Bank Invit.	5th/6	
4-17	A	Indiana Invitational	4th/4	
4-26	A	Drake Relays	NTS	
5-2		CCCs at Notre Dame	1st/11	
5-9	H	Michigan, Eastern Mich.		
		And Western Mich.	NTS	
5-16	A	Len Paddock Invit.	NTS	
		Big Tens (O) at Minneapolis	6th	

1993

Coach: Jim Bibbs

1-15	A	E. Michigan Invit.	NTS	
1-23	A	Michigan Relays	NTS	
1-30	A CO	Ohio State	77	
		Penn State	48	
		Michigan	46	

Kentucky 37
Michigan State 30

2-6	H	Michigan State Relays	NTS
2-13		CCC at	
2-19	A	E. Michigan Relays	NTS
2-27	A	Notre Dame Invit.	NTS
		Big Tens (I) at Madison	10th
4-10	A$_{KX}$	Dogwood Relays	NTS
4-24	A	Drake Relays	NTS
		CCCs at Notre Dame	6/13
5-9	A$_{CO}$	Jesse Owens Invit.	NTS
5-15	A	Len Paddock Invit.	NTS
		Big Tens (O) at East Lansing	6th

1994 (0-2)
Coach: Jim Bibbs

1-15	A	E. Michigan Invit.	NTS
1-22	H	Michigan	73
		Penn State	51
		Michigan State	35
1-29	A	Michigan Open	NTS
2-5	H	MSU Relays	NTS
		CCCs	5th/14
2-17	H	Central Michigan 45-59	L
		Big Tens (I) at Ann Arbor	9th/10
4-6	A$_{KX}$	Sea Ray Relays	NTS
4-16	H	Iowa 71-75	L
4-23	A	E. Michigan Open	5th/6
4-27	A	Drake Relays	NTS
		CCCs at Kalamazoo	7th/13
5-14	A	Central State Invit.	NTS
		Big Tens (O) at Madison	10th/10

1995 (1-1)
Coach: Jim Bibbs

1-13	A	E. Michigan Open	NTS
1-21	H	Penn State 46-40	W
1-21	H$_{UP}$	Michigan 46-65	L
1-28	H	Mich. Championships	3rd/5
2-4	H	Michigan State Open	NTS
		CCCs at Notre Dame	3rd/15
2-16	H	Central Michigan	NTS
		Big Tens (I) at Champaign	6th/10
3-24	A	Texas Southern Rel.	2ndT/22
4-7	A	UNLV Invitational	NTS
4-22	H	MSU Invitational	NTS
4-28	A	Drake Relays	NTS
		CCCs at Notre Dame	7th/11
5-13	A	W. Michigan Open	NTS
		Big Tens (O) at Minneapolis	10th/10

Darroll Gatson (1996-)

One of the initial responsibilities for Merritt Norvell, the newly appointed athletic director, was the selection of a replacement for Jim Bibbs. In late September of 1995 his choice was announced: Charles Greene, a winner of six NCAA sprint titles as a student-athlete at the University of Nebraska. Greene had also garnered a pair of medals at the 1968 Olympics Games in Mexico City (a relay gold and a bronze in the 100 meters). Although he had never coached in the collegiate ranks, the 51-year-old Greene had served 20 years in the U.S. Army as a track coach until he retired with the rank of major in 1989. Upon discharge, Greene took up residence in Washington, D.C., where he became summer sports director of Special Olympics International. There was one small hitch in the scheme; Greene's wife eventually expressed a desire to remain in Washington, D.C. She would veto the plan and the retired major telephoned Norvell to say he wasn't coming after all. The AD moved rapidly. On Oct 13, 1995, it was revealed that Darroll Gatson would become he new head coach as of October 23. Gatson came to East Lansing from Lincoln University (MO) where he had been the head men's and women's track and field coach for the preceding year and a half. Prior to accepting that position at Liberty, Gatson spent six successful years as the assistant head coach of the men's and women's track

and field program at the University of Missouri. Raised in Detroit, Gatson graduated from East Catholic High School in the Motor City. He later spent two years at Southwestern Michigan College where he was runner-up in the 400 meters at the 1976 NJCAA championships. He then concluded his collegiate career at Alabama where he earned All-American honors with a third-place finish in the 400 meters at the 1978 NCAA championship meet. He was also a member of the mile relay team that captured the national collegiate indoor title in '78.

1996
Coach: Darroll Gatson

1-20	A	Kentucky Invit.	NTS
1-27	A	Michigan Inter.	5th/6
2-3	A	Meyo Invit.	NTS
		CCCs at Purdue	5th/12
2-15	H	Michigan State Invit.	NTS
		Big Tens (I) at Columbus	9th
3-2	A	Silverton Invit.	NTS
3-23	A	Alabama Relays	16th/24
2-30	A	Florida Relays	NTS
3-30	A	Purdue Invit.	NTS
4-13	A	Sea Ray Relays	NTS
4-20	A	Iowa Invit.	5th/9
4-20	H	Spring Sports Festival	NTS
4-27	H	Drake Relays	NTS
		CCCs	3rd/10
5-11	A	Western Mich. Invit.	NTS
		Big Tens (O) at Univ. Park	9th

1997 (4-0)
Coach: Darroll Gatson

1-11	A	Michigan 76-41	W
		Indiana 69-52	W
1-18	H	Michigan State Invit.	2nd/5
1-24	A$_{YP}$	Michigan Inter.	3rd/6
2-1	H	Spartan Invit.	NTS
	H	CCCs at East Lansing	5th/12
2-13	H	Spartan Invit.	NTS
2-23	A	Alabama Relays	6th/27
		Big Tens (I) at Iowa City	8th
3-29	A	Jim Quick Shootout	
		Colorado 95-34	W
		Baylor 72-39	W
		Arizona 119-31	W
4-12	A	SeaRay Relays	NTS
4-19	H	Michigan State Open	NTS
4-26	A	Drake Relays	NTS
		CCCs	T11th/14
5-10	A	Bronco Invit.	NTS
5-17	A	Len Paddock Invit.	NTS
		Big Tens (O) at Champaign	10th

1998
Coach: Darroll Gatson

1-17	H	Michigan State Invit.	NTS
1-24	A$_{AA}$	Red Simmons Invit.	NTS
1-30	H	Michigan Inter.	4th/6
2-7	A$_{ND}$	Meyo Invit.	NTS
		CCCs at Ann Arbor	4th/11
		Big Tens (I) at W. Lafayette	9th
3-7	A$_{AA}$	Silverstone Invit.	NTS
3-21	A	Clemson Relays	NTS
3-28	A	Florida Relays	NTS
4-11	H	Michigan State Invit.	NTS
4-18	A	Mt. Sac Relay	NTS
4-18	H	Spartan Invit.	NTS
4-25	A	Drake Relays	NTS
5-3	A	Jesse Owens	NTS
5-9	A	Bronco Invit.	NTS
5-10	A	Cardinal Invit.	NTS

5-16	A	Len Paddock Invit.	NTS
		Big Tens (O) at Columbus	10th

1999
Coach: Darroll Gatson

1-16	A	Michigan Quadrangular ...	4th/4
1-23	H	Michigan State Quad.	3rd/4
1-30	A	Mich. Indoor Champ.	4th/6
2-6	A	Cyclone Invit.	NTS
		CCCs	4th/7
		Big Tens (I) at Madison	1st
3-12	A	Florida Relays	NTS
3-28	A	US Coll. Series	3rd/4
4-18	A	Mt. Sac Relays	NTS
4-18	A	Long Beach Invit.	NTS
4-25	A	Hillsdale Invit.	NTS
		CCCs	4th/6
5-1	A	Oregon Invit.	NTS
5-7	A	Chippewa Open	NTS
		Big Tens (O) at W. Lafayette	5th

2000
Coach: Darroll Gatson

1-16	A	Michigan State Invit.	NTS
1-22	A	Notre Dame Invit.	4th/4
		CCCs at Mt. Pleasant	7th/9
2-11	A$_{AI}$	Cyclone Invit.	NTS
2-12	A$_{MP}$	Michigan Champ	T5th/5
2-19	A	Silverston Invit.	NTS
		Big Tens (I) Bloomington	10th
4-25	A	Alabama Relays	NTS
4-5	A	Texas Relays	NTS
4-21	A	EMU Relays	NTS
4-29	A	Hillsdale "Gina" Relays	NTS
5-13	A	WMU Bronco Relays	NTS
		Big Tens (O) at Iowa City	10th

2001 (0-1)
Coach: Darroll Gatson

1-13	H	MSU Invit.	NTS
1-20	A	Red Simmons Invit.	NTS
1-26	A	Notre Dame 63-93	L
2-2/3	A	Meyo Invit.	NTS
2-10	A	Cyclone Invit.	NTS
		Big Tens (I) at Univ. Park, PA	8th
3-10	A	NCAA Championships	37th
3-25	A	Alabama Relays	NTS
3-31	A	Stanford Invit.	NTS
4-7	A	Notre Dame Quad.	4th
4-22	A	Mt. Sac Relays	NTS
4-29	A	Hillsdale "Gina" Rel.	NTS
		CCCs at Kalamazoo	5th
5-7	A	Jesse Owens Classic	NTS
5-13	A	Len Paddock Invit.	NTS
		Big Tens (O) at Bloomington	8th

2002 (0-1)
Coach: Darroll Gatson

1-11	A	Chippewa Open	NTS
1-18	A	Missouri Invit.	NTS
1-25	A	Notre Dame 61-96	L
2-1	A$_{ND}$	Meyo Invit.	NTS
2-9	A	Penn State Collegiate	10th
		Big Tens (I) at Minneapolis*	
3-1	A	Alex Wilson Invit.	NTS
3-23	A	Alabama Relays	NTS
3-29	A	Stanford Invit.	NTS
4-6	A	Notre Dame Quad.	NTS
4-20	A	Western Michigan Invit.	4th
4-25	A	Penn Relays	NTS
4-26	A	Hillsdale Relays.	NTS
		CCCs	NTS
		Big Tens (O)	7th

*Meet Cancelled

2003 (0-1)
Coach: Darroll Gatson

1-10	A$_{MP}$	Chippewa Open	NTS

1-17	A$_{RE}$	Pole Vault Summit	NTS
1-18	A$_{AA}$	Indiana	172
		Michigan	157
		Kent State	135
		Michigan State	53
1-25	A$_{AA}$	Red Simmons Invit.	NTS
1-31	A	Notre Dame	54-93 L
2-8	A$_{ND}$	Mayo Invitational	NTS
2-15	A	EMU Classic	NTS
		Big Tens (I) at Champaign	10th
3-8	A$_{ND}$	Alex Wilson Invitational	NTS
4-12	A$_{KX}$	Sea Ray Relays	NTS
4-19	A$_{KZ}$	Bronco Open	NTS
4-26	A	Drake Relays	NTS
4-26	A	Hillsdale Invitational	NTS
5-4	A$_{CO}$	Jesse Owens Invitational	NTS
		Big Tens (O) at Minneapolis	10th

Year-by-Year Team Performance—Indoor

Years	Dual Meets			Conference Championships			NCAA Championships			Coach
	W	L	T	Pts	Place	Host or Site	Pts	Place	Host or Site	
1951 *	1	1	0	28	3rd	Champaign, IL			no meet	Karl Schlademan
1952	1	1	0	11.6	5th	Champaign, IL			no meet	Karl Schlademan
1953	2	0	0	15.42	5th	Champaign, IL			no meet	Karl Schlademan
1954	0	0	0	19.25	5th	Champaign, IL			no meet	Karl Schlademan
1955	1	0	0	46.5	2nd	East Lansing, MI			no meet	Karl Schlademan
1956	1	0	0	33.4	4th	East Lansing, MI			no meet	Karl Schlademan
1957	2	1	0	30.6	3rd	Columbus, OH			no meet	Karl Schlademan
1958	2	1	0	19	5th	Champaign, IL			no meet	Karl Schlademan
1959	0	2	0	13.75	7th	Madison, WI			no meet	Francis Dittrich
1960	1	1	0	31.9	3rd	Columbus, OH			no meet	Francis Dittrich
1961	2	1	0	20	6th	Champaign, IL			no meet	Francis Dittrich
1962	1	0	0	28	3rd	East Lansing, MI			no meet	Francis Dittrich
1963	1	0	0	30	4th	Madison, WI			no meet	Francis Dittrich
1964	1	1	0	32	3rd	Columbus, OH			no meet	Francis Dittrich
1965	2	0	0	45.5	2nd	Champaign, IL	10	4/46	Detroit, MI	Francis Dittrich
1966	2	0	0	50	1st	East Lansing, MI	3	28/44	Detroit, MI	Francis Dittrich
1967	2	0	0	53	2nd	Madison, WI	4	24/41	Detroit, MI	Francis Dittrich
1968	0	1	0	25	4th	Columbus, OH	8	(t)9/43	Detroit, MI	Francis Dittrich
1969	1	2	0	26	4th	Champaign, IL	9	(t)7/39	Detroit, MI	Francis Dittrich
1970	0	2	0	43	3rd	East Lansing, MI	12	7/43	Detroit, MI	Francis Dittrich
1971	2	1	0	46	2nd	Madison, WI	9	(t)8/47	Detroit, MI	Francis Dittrich
1972	3	0	0	65	1st	Columbus, OH	18	(t)2/52	Detroit, MI	Francis Dittrich
1973	1	1	0	35	3rd	West Lafayette, IN	7	(t)13/56	Detroit, MI	Francis Dittrich
1974	1	1	0	36	(t)2nd	East Lansing, MI	5	(t)27/52	Detroit, MI	Francis Dittrich
1975	0	3	0	10	(t)8th	Bloomington, IN	1	(t)45/54	Detroit, MI	Francis Dittrich
1976	0	3	0	12	7th	Madison, WI	1	(t)51/55	Detroit, MI	Jim Bibbs
1977	1	1	0	29	5th	Ann Arbor, MI	2	(t)35/53	Detroit, MI	Jim Bibbs
1978	2	1	0	46	(t)6th	West Lafayette, IN	8	(t)25/55	Detroit, MI	Jim Bibbs
1979	2	2	0	57	4th	Champaign, IL	5	(t)41/60	Detroit, MI	Jim Bibbs
1980	0	2	0	73.67	4th	Madison, WI	1	(t)54/59	Detroit, MI	Jim Bibbs
1981	0	0	0	70.5	3rd	Columbus, OH	-	DNC	Detroit, MI	Jim Bibbs
1982	0	1	0	43	5th	Bloomington, IN	-	DNC	Pontiac, MI	Jim Bibbs
1983	0	1	0	63	4th	East Lansing, MI	4	(t)32/57	Pontiac, MI	Jim Bibbs
1984	0	0	0	9	9th	Ann Arbor, MI	-	DNC	Syracuse, NY	Jim Bibbs
1985	1	0	0	10	(t)9th	Madison, WI	-	DNC	Syracuse, NY	Jim Bibbs
1986	0	0	0	56	5th	West Lafayette, IN	-	DNC	Oklahoma City, OK	Jim Bibbs
1987	0	2	0	20	9th	Champaign, IL	-	DNC	Oklahoma City, OK	Jim Bibbs
1988	0	0	0	26	(t)7th	Columbus, OH	-	DNC	Oklahoma City, OK	Jim Bibbs
1989	0	0	0	27	8th	Iowa City, IA	-	DNC	Indianapolis, IN	Jim Bibbs
1990	2	0	0	24	9th	Bloomington, IN	-	DNC	Indianapolis, IN	Jim Bibbs
1991	0	0	0	35	(t)6th	West Lafayette, IN	-	DNC	Indianapolis, IN	Jim Bibbs
1992	2	1	0	50	5th	East Lansing, MI	-	DNC	Indianapolis, IN	Jim Bibbs
1993	0	0	0	13	10th	Madison, WI	-	DNC	Indianaplois, IN	Jim Bibbs
1994	0	1	0	15	9th	Ann Arbor, MI	2	(t)49/57	Indianapolis, IN	Jim Bibbs
1995	1	1	0	41	6th	Champaign, IL	3	(t)49/57	Indianapolis, IN	Jim Bibbs
1996	0	0	0	27	9th	Columbus, OH	4	(t)44/60	Indianapolis, IN	Darroll Gatson
1997	2	0	0	41	8th	Iowa City, IA	4	(t)43/66	Indianapolis, IN	Darroll Gatson
1998	0	0	0	46.5	9th	West Lafayette, IN	1	(t)60/65	Indianapolis, IN	Darroll Gatson
1999	0	0	0	107	1st	Madison, WI	1	(t)56/59	Indianapolis, IN	Darroll Gatson
2000	0	0	0	19	10th	Bloomington, IN	-	DNC	Fayetteville, AK	Darroll Gatson
2001	0	1	0	53	8th	University Park, PA	1	(t)55/60	Fayetteville, AK	Darroll Gatson
2002	0	1	0			no meet	8	(t)23/64	Fayetteville, AK	Darroll Gatson
2003	0	1	0	11	10th	Champaign, IL	-	DNC	Fayetteville, AK	Darroll Gatson

* Dual meet results prior to 1951 are included with Outdoor totals.

Year-by-Year Team Performance—Outdoor

Years	Dual Meets			Conference Championships			NCAA Championships			Coach
	W	L	T	Pts	Place	Host or Site	Pts	Place*	Host or Site	
1886	0	0	1			no meet			no meet	no coach
1887	0	0	0			no meet			no meet	no coach
1888						no meet			no meet	no coach
1889						no meet			no meet	no coach
1890						no meet			no meet	no coach
1891						no meet			no meet	no coach
1893						no meet			no meet	no coach
1893						no meet			no meet	no coach
1894						no meet			no meet	no coach
1895						no meet			no meet	no coach
1896						no meet			no meet	no coach
1897						no meet			no meet	no coach
1898	2	0	1			no meet			no meet	Henry Keep
1899						no meet			no meet	Henry Keep
1900						no meet			no meet	Charles Bemies
1901					DNC	Chicago, IL			no meet	Charles Bemies
1902	2	0	0		DNC	Chicago, IL			no meet	George Denman
1903	1	0	0		DNC	Chicago, IL			no meet	George Denman
1904	2	0	0		DNC	Chicago, IL			no meet	Chester Brewer
1905	5	0	0		DNC	Chicago, IL			no meet	Chester Brewer
1906	2	0	0		DNC	Chicago, IL			no meet	Chester Brewer
1907	2	1	0		DNC	Chicago, IL			no meet	Chester Brewer
1908	3	0	0	8	7/13**	Chicago, IL			no meet	Chester Brewer
1909	1	1	0	5	(t)7/14**	Chicago, IL			no meet	Chester Brewer
1910	1	0	0		DNC	Champaign, IL			no meet	Chester Brewer
1911		no dual meets			DNC	Minneapolis, MN			no meet	Chester Brewer
1912	0	1	0		DNC	West Lafayette, IN			no meet	John Macklin
1913	1	3	0		DNC	Madison, WI			no meet	John Macklin
1914	1	1	0		DNC	Chicago, IL			no meet	Ion Cortright
1915	1	1	0		DNC	Champaign, IL			no meet	George Gauthier
1916	1	1	0		DNC	Evanston, IL			no meet	George Gauthier
1917	0	1	0		DNC	Chicago, IL			no meet	George Gauthier
1918	0	1	0		DNC	Chicago, IL			no meet	George Gauthier
1919	1	1	0		DNC	Chicago, IL			no meet	George Gauthier
1920	2	4	0		DNC	Ann Arbor, MI			no meet	Arthur Smith
1921	3	1	0	3	(t)12th/14**	Chicago, IL		DNC	Chicago, IL	Arthur Smith
1922	4	1	0		DNC	Iowa City, IA		DNC	Chicago, IL	Albert Barron
1923	1	3	0		DNC	Ann Arbor, MI		DNC	Chicago, IL	Albert Barron
1924	2	3	0		DNC	Chicago, IL		no meet	Chicago, IL	Ralph Young
1925	1	3	0	5	(t)11th/15**	Columbus, OH		no team champion	Chicago, IL	Ralph Young
1926	2	3	0		DNC	Iowa City, IA		no team champion	Chicago, IL	Ralph Young
1927	4	0	0		DNC	Madison, WI		no team champion	Chicago, IL	Ralph Young
1928	2	2	0		DNC	Evanston, IL	7	(t)23/39	Chicago, IL	Ralph Young
1929	2	2	0		DNC	Evanston, IL	1	(t)38/47	Chicago, IL	Ralph Young
1930	2	3	0		DNC	Evanston, IL		DNC	Chicago, IL	Ralph Young
1931	5	0	0		DNC	Evanston, IL	14	10/44	Chicago, IL	Ralph Young
1932	4	1	0		DNC	Evanston, IL	2	35/43	Chicago, IL	Ralph Young
1933	3	0	0		DNC	Evanston, IL	3/7	(t)40/43	Chicago, IL	Ralph Young
1934	1	2	0		DNC	Evanston, IL	2	34/42	Los Angeles, CA	Ralph Young
1935	0	2	0		DNC	Ann Arbor, MI	9	15/41	Berkeley, CA	Ralph Young
1936	1	1	0		DNC	Columbus, OH	8	(t)17/33	Chicago, IL	Ralph Young
1937	5	1	0		DNC	Ann Arbor, MI	7	23/36	Berkeley, CA	Ralph Young
1938	5	3	0		DNC	Columbus, OH	20	(t)7/32	Minneapolis, MN	Ralph Young
1939	2	5	0		DNC	Ann Arbor, MI	1.75	(t)32/40	Los Angeles, CA	Ralph Young
1940	0	5	0		DNC	Evanston, IL	11	(t)15/40	Minneapolis, MN	Ralph Young
1941	0	6	0		DNC	Minneapolis, MN	1/7	(t)35/38	Palo Alto, CA	Karl Schlademan
1942	3	4	0		DNC	Evanston, IL	6	(t)20/35	Lincoln, NE	Karl Schlademan
1943	3	2	0		DNC	Evanston, IL	14	12/32	Evanston, IL	Karl Schlademan
1944		Intercollegiate competition suspended due to World War II					4	22/24	Milwaukee, WI	Karl Schlademan
1945	2	2	0		DNC	Champaign, IL	1	25/26	Milwaukee, WI	Karl Schlademan
1946	4	2	0		DNC	Champaign, IL	5	(t)28/40	Minneapolis, MN	Karl Schlademan
1947	6	1	0		DNC	Evanston, IL	16.5	9/38	Salt Lake City, UT	Karl Schlademan
1948	2	2	1		DNC	Madison, WI	8	(t)26/43	Bethlehem, PA	Karl Schlademan
1949	5	0	1		DNC	Evanston, IL	26	4/41	Fort Collins, CO	Karl Schlademan
1950**	3	0	0		DNC	Evanston, IL	13	(t)11/45	Minneapolis, MN	Karl Schlademan
1951*	1	3	0	49	2nd	Evanston, IL	23	5/42	Seattle, WA	Karl Schlademan
1952	3	0	0	10.85	5th	Ann Arbor, MI	1	(t)50/54	Berkeley, CA	Karl Schlademan
1953	2	1	0	25	3rd	Champaign, IL	-	DNC	Lincoln, NE	Karl Schlademan
1954	1	1	0	37.64	3rd	West Lafayette, IN	6	(t)26/45	Ann Arbor, MI	Karl Schlademan
1955	1	1	0	19.44	5th	Columbus, OH	4	(t)30/43	Los Angeles, CA	Karl Schlademan
1956	1	2	0	28.50	4th	Minneapolis, MN	29	4/54	Berkeley, CA	Karl Schlademan
1957	1	1	0	16	(t)5th	Evanston, IL	0	DNS	Austin, TX	Karl Schlademan
1958	1	2	0	23.50	4th	West Lafayette, IN	5	29/43	Berkeley, CA	Karl Schlademan
1959	1	2	1	11	8th	Ann Arbor, MI	0	DNS	Lincoln, NE	Francis Dittrich

Years	Dual Meets				Conference Championships			NCAA Championships			Coach
	W	L	T	Pts	Place	Host or Site	Pts	Place*	Host or Site		
1960	1	0	1	22	4th	East Lansing, MI	1	(t)44/49	Berkeley, CA		Francis Dittrich
1961	0	1	0	16	6th	Iowa City, IA	2	(t)40/55	Philadelphia, PA		Francis Dittrich
1962	1	0	0	34.40	3rd	West Lafayette, IN	-	DNC	Eugene, OR		Francis Dittrich
1963	1	0	0	31	4th	Minneapolis, MN	-	DNC	Albuquerque, NM		Francis Dittrich
1964	3	0	0	22	4th	Evanston, IL	-	DNC	Eugene, OR		Francis Dittrich
1965	1	0	0	56	1st	Iowa City, IA	11	22/61	Berkeley, CA		Francis Dittrich
1966	2	0	0	52.50	1st	Bloomington, IN	10	17/56	Bloomington, IN		Francis Dittrich
1967	2	0	0	49	2nd	Iowa City, IA	-	DNC	Provo, UT		Francis Dittrich
1968	0	0	0	21	7th	Minneapolis, MN	2	(t)48/65	Berkeley, CA		Francis Dittrich
1969	0	1	0	27	4th	West Lafayette, IN	-	DNC	Knoxville, TN		Francis Dittrich
1970	1	1	0	68	3rd	Bloomington, IN	-	DNC	Des Moines, IA		Francis Dittrich
1971	2	1	0	73	4th	Iowa City, IA	2	(t)50/65	Seattle, WA		Francis Dittrich
1972	2	1	0	105	1st	Champaign, IL	-	DNC	Eugene, OR		Francis Dittrich
1973	1	0	0	79	3rd	Minneapolis, MN	18	11/59	Baton Rouge, LA		Francis Dittrich
1974	1	0	0	61	4th	Ann Arbor, MI	-	DNC	Austin, TX		Francis Dittrich
1975	1	0	0	61	3rd	Iowa City, IA	1	(t)53/61	Provo, UT		Francis Dittrich
1976	1	1	0	46	6th	Champaign, IL	-	DNC	Philadelphia, PA		Jim Bibbs
1977	2	0	0	89	3rd	Bloomington, IN	-	DNC	Champaign, IL		Jim Bibbs
1978	1	1	0	29	7th	Evanston, IL	-	DNC	Eugene, OR		Jim Bibbs
1979	1	1	0	40	6th	Ann Arbor, MI	-	DNC	Champaign, IL		Jim Bibbs
1980	1	1	0	53	4th	Champaign, IL	-	DNC	Austin, TX		Jim Bibbs
1981	0	1	0	55.50	5th	East Lansing, MI	-	DNC	Baton Rouge, LA		Jim Bibbs
1982	1	1	1	57	5th	Minneapolis, MN	16	(t)30/85	Provo, UT		Jim Bibbs
1983	1	1	0	53	6th	West Lafayette, IN	19	26/92	Houston, TX		Jim Bibbs
1984	0	1	0	17	9th	Columbus, OH	-	DNC	Eugene, OR		Jim Bibbs
1985	0	0	0	24	8th	Evanston, IL	-	DNC	Austin, TX		Jim Bibbs
1986	0	1	0	33	(t)6th	Madison, WI	-	DNC	Indianapolis, IN		Jim Bibbs
1987	0	2	0	25	9th	Iowa City, IA	-	DNC	Baton Rouge, LA		Jim Bibbs
1988	0	0	0	18	9th	Ann Arbor, MI	-	DNC	Eugene, OR		Jim Bibbs
1989	0	0	0	36	8th	Indianapolis, IN	-	DNC	Provo, UT		Jim Bibbs
1990	1	0	0	40	(t)8th	Champaign, IL	-	DNC	Durham, NC		Jim Bibbs
1991	0	1	0	40.50	9th	Columbus, OH	-	DNC	Eugene, OR		Jim Bibbs
1992	0	0	0	68	6th	Minneapolis, MN	4	(t)50/69	Austin, TX		Jim Bibbs
1993	0	0	0	62.50	6th	East Lansing, MI	-	DNC	New Orleans, LA		Jim Bibbs
1994	0	1	0	25	10th	Madison, WI	-	DNC	Boise, ID		Jim Bibbs
1995	0	0	0	14	10th	Minneapolis, MN	-	DNC	Knoxville, TN		Jim Bibbs
1996	0	0	0	50	9th	University Park, PA	-	DNC	Eugene, OR		Darroll Gatson
1997	3	0	0	27	10th	Champaign, IL	4	(t)53/76	Bloomington, IN		Darroll Gatson
1998	0	0	0	36.50	10th	Columbus, OH	-	DNC	Buffalo, NY		Darroll Gatson
1999	0	0	0	75	5th	West Lafayette, IN	4	(t)51/77	Boise, ID		Darroll Gatson
2000	0	0	0	21	10th	Iowa City, IA	3	(t)53/75	Durham, NC		Darroll Gatson
2001	0	0	0	43	(t)8th	Bloomington, IN	5	(t)39/74	Eugene, OR		Darroll Gatson
2002	0	0	0	47-5	7th	Madison, WI	8	(t)30/75	Baton Rouge, LA		Darroll Gatson
2003	0	0	0	9	10th	Minneapolis, MN	-	DNC	Minneapolis, MN		Darroll Gatson
Totals	148	107	6								

** The Western Conference (Big Ten) permitted "at large" team entries until 1926

*** Prior to being included in the Big Ten championships of 1951, Michigan State competed in the Central Collegiate championships from 1942-1950

School Records (Indoor)

Event	Name	Time/Mark	Year
55 meters	Herb Washington	6.04	1969
60 meters	Octavis Long	6.89	1998
200 meters	Brad Fields	20.81	1995
300 yards	Marshall Dill	29.54	1972
400 meters	Eliot Tabron	47.05	1983
600 yards	Bob Cassleman	1:08.44	1973
600 meters	Chris Brown	1:18.85	1992
800 meters	Mike White	1:50.14	1980
1,000 yards	Roger Merchant	2:08.94	1969
1,000 meters	Mike White	2:24.14	1981
3,000 meters	Kyle Baker	7:57.09	1999
5,000 meters	Jim Jurcevich	13:57.2	1998
Mile	Ken Popejoy	4:01.14	1972
Two miles	Herb Lindsay	8:39.24	1976
Three miles	Herb Lindsay	13:16.64	1977
55 meter hurdles	Larry Hardon	7:30	1992
60 meter hurdles	E. J. Martin	7.98	1999
Mile relay	Corky Wilkins, Kelvin Scott, Marcus Sanders, Eliot Tabron	3:10.20	1983
4 x 800 meter relay	Rick Gledhill, Chris Rugh, Todd Koning, Chris Brown	7:20.43	1992
Sprint medley relay	Calvin Thomas, Randy Smith, Ricky Flowers, Keith Moore	3:23.84	1980
Distance medley relay	Tim Kenney, Calvin Thomas, Michael White, Keith Moore	9:45.14	1980
Long Jump	Fred Johnson	25' 4 3/4"	1948
Pole Vault	Paul Terek	17' 2 3/4"	1999
Shot Put	Steve Manz	57' 1 1/2"	2003
35-lb. Weight	Joe Keller	55' 3 1/2"	2000
Triple Jump	Tony Gilbert	5' 4"	1981
High Jump	Paul Piwinski	7' 5"	1983
Heptathlon	Paul Terek	5,462	1999

School Records (Outdoor)

Event	Name	Time/Mark	Year
100 yards	Herb Washington	9.2	1974
	Marshall Dill	9.2	1974
100 meters	Marshall Dill	10.28	1972
	Eliot Tabron	10.28	1982
200 meters	Marshall Dill	20.54	1973
	Eliot Tabron	20.54	1982
400 meters	Eliot Tabron	45.00	1982
660 yards	John Spain	1:16.70	1967
800 meters	Ken Popejoy	1:47.44	1973
Mile	Ken Popejoy	3:57.0	1973
1,500 meters	Tim Simpson	3:41.06	1987
5,000 meters	Herb Lindsay	13:55.2	1977
10,000 meters	Steve Schell	28:39.74	1999
3,000 meter steeplechase	Ryan Taylor	8:44.53	1999
110 meter hurdles	Gene Washington	13.82	1966
	Tony Gilbert	13.82	1981
400 meter hurdles	Bob Cassleman	49.64	1972
440 yard relay	Herb Washington, LaRue Butchee, Bob Cassleman, Marshall Dill	40.2	1972
4 x 100 meter relay	Derrick Leonard, Anthony Mahone, Larry Jackson, Demetrius Hallums	40.16	1985
4 x 200 meter relay	Corky Wilkins, Kelvin Scott, Marcus Sanders, Eliot Tabron	1:22.53	1983
Mile Relay	Pat Wilson, John Mock, Roger Merchant, Bill Wehrwein	3:08.3	1969
4 x 400 meter relay	Corky Wilkins, Kelvin Scott, Marcus Sanders, Eliot Tabron	3:02.52	1983
4 x 800 meter relay	Brian Castle, Robert Lake, Dave Lean, Willie Atterbury	7:21.64	1958
4 x 1600 meter relay	Jeff Neal, Mark Williamson, Mike Kavulich, Tim Simpson	16:21.24	1985
Sprint medley relay	Daswell Campbell, Gene Washington, Richard Dunn, John Spain	3:19.74	1967
Distance medley relay	Keith Moore, Charles Byrd, Stan Mavis, Herb Lindsay	9:39.64	1977
Long Jump	Philmore Morris	25' 7"	1988
High Jump	Paul Piwinski	7' 3"	1983
	Daryl Dismond	7' 3"	1983
Triple Jump	Jouka Niva	50' 3"	1981
Shot Put	Paul Schneider	57' 7"	1978
Discus	Justin Selden	166' 6"	1998
Hammer Throw	Joe Keller	181' 4"	2000
Javelin (pre-1984)	Tony Kumiega	213' 10"	1961
Javelin (post-1984)	Paul Terek	189' 9"	1998
Pole Vault	Paul Terek	17' 3 1/4"	1998
Decathlon	Paul Terek	7,225	1999

NCAA Champions (Indoor)

60 yard high hurdles	Gene Washington	7.2	1965
600 yard run	Bill Wehrwein	1:09.8	1969
60 yard dash	Herb Washington	5.9	1970
Mile	Ken Popejoy	4:02.9	1972

NCAA Champions (Outdoor)

100 yard dash	Fred Alderman	9.9	1927
220 yard dash	Fred Alderman	21.1	1927
Two miles	Clark Chamberlain	9:23.0	1931
Two miles	Roy Fehr	9:18.9	1940
Broad Jump	Fred Johnson	25' 2 1/2"	1949
Mile	Warren Druetzler	4:08.0	1951
10, 000 meters	Selwyn Jones	31:15.3	1956
3,000 meter steeplechase	Henry Kennedy	9:16.5	1956
440 yard hurdles	Bob Steele	50.4	1966
440 yard hurdles	Bob Steele	50.2	1967

Big Ten Champions (Indoor)

Event	Name	Time/Mark	Year
High Jump	James Vrooman	6' 4 1/2"	1953
880 yard run	John Cook	1:54.9	1954
440-yard dash	Kevin Gosper	48.2	1955
600 yard run	Kevin Gosper	1:11.3	1955
60 yard dash	Ed Brabham	6.2	1955
60 yard dash	Ed Brabham	6.3	1956
70 yard high hurdles	Joe Savoldi	8.5	1956
440 yard run	Dave Lean	49.4	1957
600 yard run	Dave Lean	1:10.2	1958
Mile run	Bob Lake	4:10.9	1959
1000 yard run	Willie Atterberry	2:11.7	1960
Two mile run	Gerald Young	9:08.1	1961
300 yard dash	Sherman Lewis	31.2	1962
Long Jump	Sherman Lewis	24' 6"	1962
Long Jump	Sherman Lewis	23' 8 1/2"	1963
60 yard dash	Robert Moreland	6.1	1963

Event	Name	Time/Mark	Year
60 yard dash	Robert Moreland	6.1	1964
1000 yard run	Mike Martens	2:10.3	1964
Long Jump	Jim Garrett	24' 7"	1964
Long Jump	Jim Garrett	24' 11"	1965
70 yard low hurdles	Gene Washington	7.7	1965
300 yard dash	Daswell Campbell	30.9	1965
Mile run	Keith Coates	4:09.5	1965
Long Jump	Jim Garrett	24' 1 1/2"	1966
70 yard high hurdles	Gene Washington	8.3	1966
70 yard low hurdles	Gene Washington	7.8	1966
Two Mile Run	Dick Sharkey	9:01.4	1966
600 yard Run	Patrick Wilson	1:11.3	1967
Two Mile Run	Dick Sharkey	9:03.8	1967
High Jump	Mike Bowers	6' 9"	1967
Pole Vault	Roland Carter	15' 0"	1967
Mile Relay	Don Crawford, Rich Stevens, Pat Wilson, Bill Wehrwein	3:14.4	1968
600 yard run	Bill Wehrwein	1:09.4	1969
Mile Relay	James, Bastian, Roger Merchant, Pat Wilson, Bill Wehrwein	3:13.4	1969
600 yard run	Bill Wehrwein	1:09.3	1970
60 yard dash	Herb Washington	6.0	1970
Mile Relay	Al Henderson, Mike Murphy, John Mock, Bill Wehrwein	3:15.5	1970
60 yard dash	Herb Washington	6.1	1971
600 yard run	Bob Cassleman	1:10.2	1971
Mile Relay	Mike Holt, Mike Murphy, John Mock, Bob Cassleman	3:12.9	1971
60 yard dash	Herb Washington	5.9	1972
300 yard dash	Marshall Dill	29.6	1972
600 yard run	Bob Cassleman	1:09.9	1973
Mile Run	Ken Popejoy	4:05.4	1972
70 yard low hurdles	John Morrison	7.8	1972
Mile Relay	Alwyn Henderson, Marshall Dill, Mike Murphy, Bob Cassleman	3:12.6	1972
300 yard dash	Marshall Dill	30.1	1973
600 yard run	Bob Cassleman	1:08.8	1973
300 yard dash	Marshall Dill	30.2	1974
600 yard run	Bob Cassleman	1:10.0	1974
70 yard high hurdles	Mike Hurd	8.2	1974
Mile Relay	Bill Nance, Mike Holt, Bob Cassleman, Marshall Dill	3:11.7	1974
Two Mile Run	Herb Lindsay	8:44.8	1975
60 yard dash	Randy Smith	6.1	1977
Two Mile Run	Herb Lindsay	8:42.9	1977
60 yard dash	Randy Smith	6.31	1978
60 yard dash	Randy Smith	6.28	1979
1000 yard run	Keith Moore	2:10.2	1979
60 yard dash	Randy Smith	6.24	1980
Mile Relay	Randy Smith, Tim Keeney, Chancy Williams, Calvin Thomas	3:16.5	1980
Triple Jump	Tony Gilbert	51' 4 1/2"	1981
55 meter high hurdles	Tony Gilbert	7.40	1981
600 yard run	Marcus Sanders	1:10.19	1982
Mile Relay	Kelvin Scott, Rob Murphy, Calvin Thomas, Marcus Sanders	3:13.77	1982
600 yard run	Marcus Sanders	1:08.86	1983
High Jump	Paul Piwinski	7' 1 3/4"	1983
Mile Relay	Corky Wilkins, Kelvin Scott, Marcus Sanders, Eliot Tabron	3:10.20	1983
55 meter dash	Corey Pryor	6.28	1989
600 meter run	Chris Brown	1:18.85	1992
4 x 800 meter relay	Sam, Blumke, Todd Koning, Chris Rugh, Rick Gledhill	7:37.30	1992
200 meter dash	Brad Fields	21.30	1995
3000 meter run	Kyle Baker	8:16.22	1997
5000 meter run	Kyle Baker	14:23.60	1997
3,000 meter run	Steve Schell	8:09.45	1999
5,000 meter run	Jim Jurcevich	14:07.23	1999

Big Ten Champions (Outdoor)

Event	Name	TimeMark	Year
Two Mile Run	Ralph Carr	9:56.2	1908
Two Mile Run	Fred Tillotson	not available	1909
Shot Put	Robert Carey	53' 0"	1951
880 yard run	Don Makielski	1:56.0	1951
220 yard low hurdles	Jesse Thomas	23.8	1951
100 yard dash	Jesse Thomas	10.0	1951
Mile Run	Jim Kepford	4:18.4	1953
Mile Run	John Cook	4:14.1	1954
Long Jump	Ed Brabham	23' 8"	1955
440 yard run	Kevin Gosper	47.8	1955
Two Mile Run	Henry Kennedy	9:19.1	1956
220 yard dash	Ed Brabham	21.2	1956
100 yard dash	Ed Brabham	9.7	1956
880 yard run	Dave Lean	1:52.9	1957
880 yard run	Dave Lean	1:50.3	1958
Two Mile Run	Forddy Kennedy	9:15.1	1959

Event	Name	Time/Mark	Year
Mile Run	Bob Lake	4:09.0	1959
Pole Vault (tie)	Mike Kleinhans	14' 3-5/8"	1960
Two Mile Run	Gerald Young	9:12	1962
Mile Run	Jan Bowen	4:14.3	1963
High Jump	Mike Bowers	6' 7"	1965
Mile Run	Keith Coates	4:08.2	1965
120 yard high hurdles	Gene Washington	14.2	1965
220 yard dash	Jim Garrett	21.6	1965
Long Jump	Jim Garrett	24' 5 1/2"	1965
440 yard inter. hurdles	Bob Steele	50.7	1966
120 yard high hurdles	Gene Washington	13.8	1966
880 yard run	John Spain	1:48.0	1966
Mile Relay	Mike Martens, Rick Dunn, Daswell Campbell, John Spain	3:10.9	1966
660 yard run	John Spain	1:16.7	1967
Pole Vault	Roland Carter	16' 3/4"	1967
120 yard high hurdles	Gene Washington	13.7	1967
440 yard run	Bill Wehrwein	46.2	1969
100 yard dash	Herb Washington	9.5	1970
100 yard dash	Herb Washington	9.4	1971
660 yard run	Bob Cassleman	1:18.3	1971
Mile Relay	Tom Spuller, Mike Murphy, John Mock, Bob Cassleman	3:11.5	1971
220 yard dash	Marshall Dill	20.7	1972
440 yard inter. hurdles	Bob Cassleman	52.4	1972
440 yard relay	Herb Washington, LaRue Butchee, Bob Cassleman, Marshall Dill	40.2	1972
100 yard dash	Herb Washington	9.4	1972
220 yard dash	Marshall Dill	21.1	1973
Mile Run	Ken Popejoy	3:59.2	1973
3,000 meter steeplechase	Rob Cool	8:49.7	1973
440 yard inter. hurdles	Bob Cassleman	50.7	1973
100 yard dash	Marshall Dill	9.5	1974
220 yard dash	Marshall Dill	20.9	1974
440 yard inter. hurdles	Bob Cassleman	50.7	1974
100 yard dash	Marshall Dill	9.4	1975
220 yard dash	Marshall Dill	21.0	1975
1500 meter run	Herb Lindsay	3:43.8	1976
200 meter dash	Randy Smith	21.68	1977
1500 meter run	Herb Lindsay	3:45.3	1977
200 meter dash	Ricky Flowers	21.20	1979
400 meter dash	Ricky Flowers	46.13	1979
100 meter dash	Randy Smith	10.44	1980
1600 meter relay	Calvin Thomas, Marcus Sanders, Kelvin Scott, Eliot Tabron	3:08.75	1982
400 meter dash	Eliot Tabron	45.32	1982
1600 meter relay	Corky Wilkins, Kelvin Scott, Marcus Sanders, Eliot Tabron	3:09.28	1983
High Jump	Daryl Dismond	7' 3"	1983
800 meter run	Guy Scott	1:48.80	1986
400 meter inter. hurdles	Marvin Parnell	51.31	1987
Long Jump	Philmore Morris	25' 7 1/2"	1988
10,000 meter run	Anthony Hamm	29.11.83	1991
10,000 meter run	Anthony Hamm	30.02.38	1992
10,000 meter run	Dave Smith	30.09.71	1993
5,000 meter run	Kyle Baker	14.06.24	1997
10,000 meter run	Kyle Baker	29.26.68	1999

All Americans (Indoor and Outdoor)

* indoor   ** outdoor

Event	Name	Year
Mile Run *	William Mack	1950
Shot Put **	Bob Carey	1951
3,000 m steeplechase**	Henry Kennedy	1956
5,000 meters**	Selwyn Jones	1956
10,000 meters**	Selwyn Jones	1956
440 yard relay**	Daswell Campbell, Clint Jones, Jim Summers, Gene Washington	1965
440 yard inter. hurdles**	Bob Steele	1966
440 yard inter. hurdles**	Bob Steele	1967
Pole Vault*	Roland Carter	1968
Mile Relay*	Don Crawford, Dick Stevens, Pat Wilson, Bill Wehrwein	1968
600 yard run*	Bill Wehrwein	1969
60 yard dash*	Herb Washington	1969
440 yard dash**	Bill Wehrwein	1969
600 yard run*	Bill Wehrwein	1970
60 yard dash*	Herb Washington	1969
880 yard run*	John Mock	1970
Mile relay*	Alwin Henderson, Marshall Dill, Mike Murphy, Bob Cassleman	1972
600 yard run*	Bob Cassleman	1972
60 yard dash*	Herb Washington	1972
Mile Run*	Ken Popejoy	1972

Event	Name	Year
220 yard dash**	Marshall Dill	1973
600 yard run*	Bob Cassleman	1973
60 yard dash*	Marshall Dill	1973
600 yard run*	Bob Cassleman	1974
60 yard dash*	Randy Smith	1977
High Jump*	Dennis Lewis	1978
1,000 yard run**	Keith Moore	1979
60 yard dash*	Randy Smith	1979
High Jump**	Paul Piwinski	1980
400 meter dash**	Eliot Tabron	1982
Mile relay**	Marcus Sanders, Kelvin Scott, Eliot Tabron, Corky Wilkins	1983
4 x 400 meter relay*	Marcus Sanders, Kelvin Scott, Eliot Tabron, Corky Wilkins	1983
High Jump**	**Paul Piwinski**	**1983**
600 meter run*	Marcus Sanders	1983
440 yard dash*	Eliot Tabron	1983
1500 meter run*	Tim Simpson	1987
10,000 meter run**	Anthony Hamm	1990
4 x 800 meter relay*	Chris Brown, Rick Gledhill, Todd Koning, Chris Rugh	1991
10,000 meter run**	Anthony Hamm	1991
200 meter dash*	Brad Fields	1994
200 meter dash*	Brad Fields	1995
200 meter dash*	Brad Fields	1996
5,000 meter run**	Kyle Baker	1997
3,000 meter run*	Kyle Baker	1997
10,000 meter run**	Jim Jurcevich	1998
5,000 meter run*	Jim Jurcevich	1998
10,000 meter run**	Jim Jurcevich	1999
3,000 meter run*	Kyle Baker	1999
5,000 meter run*	Jim Jurcevich	1999
5,000 meter run*	Steve Schell	1999
10,000 meter run**	Steve Schell	2000

WRESTLING
LEADERS, RECORDS and HONORS

ALL-TIME COACHING RECORDS

Coach	Years	W	L	T	Avg.
James Devers	1922-23	2	6	0	.250
Leon Burhans	1924-26	2	13	0	.133
Ralph Leonard	1927-28	8	5	0	.615
Glenn Ricks	1929	1	3	0	.250
Fendley Collins	1930-62	158	84	11	.646
Grady Peninger	1963-86	214	113	10	.650
Phil Parker	1987-91	26	47	2	.360
Tom Minkel	1992-	103	100	3	.507
Totals	1922-2003	514	371	26	.578

Season Records

See page 874 for explanation of abbreviations.

James "Jimmy" Devers (1922-1923)

Jimmy Devers was once hailed as a strong contender for the world's lightweight boxing championship. Retiring from competition, he remained active as a promoter, referee and coach for numerous athletic clubs and YMCAs. Although he had lived in Jackson, MI, most of his life, Jimmy's boxing contacts could find him anywhere across the country. Hired in the fall of 1920 as an assistant instructor in physical training, Devers was a natural to become the school's first wrestling coach when the sport was adopted in 1922.

1922 (1-3)
Coach: James Devers

1-28	H	Indiana	5-39	L
2-17	A	Iowa State	0-50	L
2-25	A	Michigan	24-20	W
3-7	H	Michigan	18-20	L

1923 (1-3)
Coach: James Devers

2-3	H	Chicago YMCA Coll.	18-13	W
2-15	A	Iowa State	0-27	L
2-17	A	Cornell Coll. (IA)	11-17	L
3-2	A	Ohio State	5-28	L

Leon D. "Brick" Burhans (1924-1926)

(See boxing season records for Leon "Brick" Burhans sketch)

1924 (0-4)
Coach: Leon D. "Brick" Burhans

1-12	A	Indiana	2-24	L
1-19	H	Ohio State	2-18	L
3-1	H	Iowa State	10-22	L
3-4	A	Michigan	9-11	L

1925 (2-4)
Coach: Leon D. "Brick" Burhans

1-17	H	Michigan	20-6	W
1-24	A	Northwestern	15-2	W
1-31	H	Indiana	0-29	L
2-7	A	Ohio State	7-13	L
2-21	A	Iowa State	3-17	L
3-7	H	Purdue	9-11	L

1926 (0-5)
Coach: Leon D. "Brick" Burhans

1-16	A	Indiana	5-18	L
1-23	A	Purdue	2-12	L
2-6	H	Cornell Coll. (IA)	0-17	L
2-20	H	Ohio State	2-15	L
2-27	H	Michigan	0-14	L

Ralph C. Leonard (1927-1928)

At Penn State Ralph Leonard turned out the championship wrestling team of the east in 1925. His coaching experience would later include stops at West Point and Brooklyn Polytechnical Institute. Although his stay in East Lansing was for just two seasons, he was successful in generating both winning teams and local interest in the sport. Then, for seemingly fabricated reason, on April 25, 1928, it was announced that Leonard, along with assistant football and freshmen basketball coach Barney Traynor, would be "cut from the college payroll." In Leonard's case it was stated that two of his (club) sports, lacrosse and soccer, were being dropped and he was therefore no longer needed. He would later take the school's governing board (the State Board of Agriculture) to court over his dismissal, suing for a year's salary ($4,500). His contention was that he was not notified his services were no longer needed until it was too late to secure another position. The matter was settled out of court.

1927 (4-3)
Coach: Ralph C. Leonard

1-8	H	Cincinnati	16-4	W
1-15	H	Chicago	14-11	W
1-22	A	Michigan	8-15	L
1-29	A	Ohio State	6-19	L
2-5	H	Northwestern	9-18	L
2-11	H	Notre Dame	36-0	W
2-26	H	Ohio	17-10	W

1928 (4-2)
Coach: Ralph C. Leonard

1-14	H	Lawrence Tech	36-0	W
1-20	A	Chicago	18-11	W
1-28	A	Ohio State	3-22	L
2-4	A	Michigan	5-22	L
2-14	H	Michigan Normal	30-8	W
2-18	A	Ohio	16-11	W

Glenn L. Ricks (1929)

First enrolled at MSC in the fall of 1927 as a graduate student in physical education, Glenn Ricks accepted an offer to coach the team for only the 1929 season. He had come to East Lansing from Oklahoma. Like his predecessor and his successor, Ricks had earned his undergraduate degree from Oklahoma A&M where he had also been a member of the varsity wrestling team.

1929 (1-3)
Coach: Glenn Ricks

1-12	H	Chicago	9-21	L
1-25	A	Michigan	0-26	L
2-16	A	Ohio	16-18	L
3-2	H	Western Reserve	27-3	W

Fendley Collins (1930-1962)

Fendley Collins was born in Heanrick, OK, on August 27, 1903. He graduated in 1927 from Oklahoma A&M, where he was undefeated in his collegiate mat career. While in college, Collins won the 1926 middleweight amateur championship of Canada and the U.S. National AAU crown in 1927. His first coaching job was at Cushion (OK) High School where he handled the football, wrestling, and track squads. Two years later he became Michigan State's fifth wrestling coach. In 1956, Fendley was elected to the Helms Foundation Wrestling Hall of Fame. During 33 years as head coach, he served as president of the American Wrestling Coaches and Officials Association, and a myriad of positions with the National AAU, U.S. Olympic Committee, and Pan-American Wrestling Confederation. In 1955 Collins coached the U.S. Pan-American team.

1930 (3-3)
Coach: Fendley Collins

1-17	A	Chicago	11-23	L
1-18	A	Northwestern	25-3	W
1-25	H	Michigan	6-24	L
2-8	H	Ohio	12-18	L
2-21	A	Case Tech	28-8	W
2-22	A	Western Reserve	27-3	W

1931 (3-1)
Coach: Fendley Collins

1-24	A	Michigan	5-23	L
2-7	H	Ohio	24-8	W
2-27	A	Mechanics Inst.(NY)	22-10	W
2-28	A	Alfred	25-5	W

1932 (4-1)
Coach: Fendley Collins

1-11	H	Toledo	36-0	W
1-15	H	Michigan	14 1/2-13 1/2	W
1-23	H	Mechanics Inst.(NY).	28-0	W
2-12	H	Syracuse	20-6	W
2-27	A	Indiana	5-25	L

1933 (3-2)
Coach: Fendley Collins

1-21	A	Michigan	14-18	L
2-1	H	Indiana	4 1/2-19 1/2	L
2-4	H	Ohio State	15 1/2-12 1/2	W
2-11	H	Cornell Coll.(IA)	25 1/2 -4 1/2	W
2-25	A	Syracuse	25 1/2-6 1/2	W

1934 (2-4)
Coach: Fendley Collins

1-20	A	Michigan	11 1/2-16 1/2	L
1-27	A	Ohio State	8-22	L
2-16	H	Cornell Coll. (IA)	14-16	L
2-24	H	Chicago	17 1/2-10 1/2	W
3-3	H	Michigan	11-15	L
3-10	H	Kent State	18-14	W

1935 (4-4)
Coach: Fendley Collins

1-12	H	Michigan	20-14	W
1-19	A	Detroit Tech.	36-0	W
1-26	H	Ohio State	10-20	L
2-2	A	Kent State	13-17	L
2-7	H	Cornell Coll. (IA)	13-17	L
2-9	A	Michigan	18-12	W
2-22	H	Indiana	10-22	L
3-1	H	Detroit Tech	28-8	W

1936 (0-6)
Coach: Fendley Collins

1-25	A	Michigan	10 1/2-15 1/2	L
2-1	A	Ohio State	3-27	L
2-8	A	Indiana	10-20	L
2-15	H	Michigan	13-21	L
2-22	H	Washington & Lee	8-20	L
3-6	H	Cornell Coll. (IA)	3-23	L

1937 (1-6)
Coach: Fendley Collins

1-16	H	Dearborn Boys Club	13-19	L
1-23	A	Northwestern	10-26	L
1-30	H	Ohio State	8-20	L
2-6	H	Kent State	10 1/2-15 1/2	L
2-19	H	Wheaton	17-9	W
2-27	A	Dearborn Boys Club	13-17	L
3-5	H	Michigan	0-24	L

1938 (5-4)
Coach: Fendley Collins

1-15	A	Wheaton	25-5	W
1-17	A	Michigan	0-32	L
1-29	H	Ohio State	6-26	L
2-12	H	Northwestern	23-5	W
2-18	A	Case Tech	20-6	W
2-19	A	Kent State	6-24	L
2-25	A	Frank & Marshall	1 1/2-26 1/2	L
2-26	A	Brown	15 1/2-14 1/2	W
2-28	A	MIT	38-0	W

1939 (5-3)
Coach: Fendley Collins

1-14	H	Wheaton	22-8	W
1-21	H	Kent State	9-19	L
1-28	A	Ohio State	8-24	L
2-4	H	Case Tech	20-6	W
2-10	A	Wisconsin	20-8	W
2-11	A	Northwestern	22-8	W
2-18	A	Michigan	3-29	L
3-4	A	West Virginia	20-8	W

1940 (5-2-1)
Coach: Fendley Collins

1-13	A	Wheaton	30-6	W
1-22	H	Northwestern	23-11	W
1-27	A	Ohio State	14-14	T
2-8	H	Nebraska	22-6	W
2-10	L	Michigan	8-26	L
2-17	A	West Virginia	25-5	W
2-23	A	Case Tech	26-6	W
2-24	A	Kent State	6-24	L

1941 (8-1)
Coach: Fendley Collins

1-11	H	Wheaton	33-5	W
1-25	H	Ohio State	21-3	W
1-29	H	Michigan	16-14	W
2-3	H	Case Tech	31-5	W
2-8	H	Wisconsin	27-3	W
2-14	A	Nebraska	27-3	W
2-15	A	Kansas State	28-8	W

2-18	A	Oklahoma A&M	5-25	L
2-22	H	Kent State	20-8	W

1942 (7-1)
Coach: Fendley Collins

1-10	A	Wheaton	24-10	W
1-13	H	Kansas State	17-11	W
1-17	A	Michigan	17-13	W
1-24	A	Ohio State	19-11	W
2-14	H	Oklahoma A&M	15-19	L
2-17	H	Nebraska	21-10	W
2-20	A	Case Tech	20-8	W
2-21	A	Kent State	19-11	W

1943 (5-2-1)
Coach: Fendley Collins

1-18	H	Michigan	16-14	W
1-23	H	Case Tech	28-0	W
2-10	A	Michigan	14-16	L
2-13	H	Ohio State	22-6	W
2-19	A	Iowa State	24-8	W
2-20	A	Iowa Teachers	14-14	T
2-26	A	Purdue	23-11	W
2-27	A	Indiana	11-15	L

1944

Intercollegiate athletics suspended due to World War II

1945 (5-0)
Coach: Fendley Collins

1-13	A	Wheaton	22-8	W
1-20	A	Ohio State	23-11	W
2-2	H	Indiana	14-12	W
2-3	H	Ohio State	18-13	W
2-17	H	Wheaton	24-6	W

1946 (5-2-1)
Coach: Fendley Collins

1-12	H	Wheaton	33-3	W
1-19	A	Illinois	15-11	W
1-25	H	Purdue	11-19	L
2-2	A$_{EV}$	Northwestern	28-0	W
		Minnesota	23-8	W
2-16	H	Ohio State	17-11	W
2-25	A	Michigan	9-15	L
3-1	H	Iowa Teachers	12-12	T

1947 (7-3)
Coach: Fendley Collins

1-18	H	Purdue	20-6	W
1-25	A	Indiana	9-15	L
2-1	A	Ohio State	17-9	W
2-8	A	Purdue	14-12	W
2-14	H	Illinois	14-12	W
2-15	A	Wheaton	24-6	W
2-21	A	Cornell Coll. (IA)	6-24	L
2-22	A	Iowa Teachers	9-15	L
2-28	H	Michigan	18-8	W
3-10	A	Nebraska	25-3	W

1948 (9-0)
Coach: Fendley Collins

1-16	H	Iowa Teachers	14-13	W
1-24	A	Ohio State	24-0	W
2-4	H	Kansas State	27-2	W
2-7	A	Illinois	17-11	W
2-9	H	Indiana	19-8	W
2-14	H	Purdue	18-12	W
2-21	H	Cornell Coll. (IA)	25-3	W
2-23	A	Michigan	19-8	W
2-28	H	Nebraska	17-8	W

1949 (6-1-1)
Coach: Fendley Collins

1-7	H	Illinois	13-13	T
2-14	A	Kansas State	32-0	W
2-22	A	Ohio State	28-0	W
1-24	H	Purdue	20-6	W
1-29	A	Iowa Teachers	9-15	L
2-7	H	Cornell Coll. (IA)	15-13	W
2-12	A	Purdue	15-9	W
2-21	H	Indiana	24-5	W

1950 (5-5)
Coach: Fendley Collins

1-7	A	Bowling Green	28-0	W
1-14	A	Indiana	19-9	W
1-16	H	Iowa Teachers	6-18	L
1-21	A	Illinois	12-16	L
1-28	H	Ohio State	6-18	L
1-30	A	Purdue	16-11	W
2-7	H	Michigan	18-6	W
2-11	H	Purdue	13-14	L
2-18	A	Cornell Coll. (IA)	12-14	L
2-25	H	Bowling Green	21-9	W

1951 (6-3)
Coach: Fendley Collins

1-5	H	Pittsburgh	18-11	W
1-15	H	Indiana	25-8	W
1-19	A	Iowa Teachers	10-21	L
1-27	A	Ohio State	8-19	L
2-1	H	Wisconsin	17-8	W
2-3	A	Purdue	18-11	W
2-9	A	Illinois	15-9	W
2-17	A	Michigan	8-17	L
2-24	A	Northwestern	20-5	W
		Big Tens at Evanston	3rd	

1952 (5-2-2)
Coach: Fendley Collins

1-12	A	Pittsburgh	16-14	W
1-18	H	Iowa Teachers	8-21	L
1-26	H	Ohio State	16-11	W
2-1	H	Purdue	19-8	W
2-9	A	Illinois	15-15	T
2-15	H	Northwestern	26-5	W
2-16	A	Wisconsin	16-11	W
2-23	H	Michigan	13-13	T
3-1	A	Indiana	12-14	L
		Big Tens at Ann Arbor	3rd	

1953 (7-2)
Coach: Fendley Collins

1-3	H	Pittsburgh	9-17	L
1-10	H	Indiana	17-8	W
1-17	A	Ohio State	20-5	W
1-24	A	Iowa	22-5	W
1-31	A	Purdue	23-3	W
2-7	A	Michigan	13-17	L
2-13	H	Illinois	18-6	W
2-21	A	Northwestern	15-9	W
2-28	A	Iowa Teachers	16-13	W
		Big Tens at Bloomington	2nd	

1954 (6-2)
Coach: Fendley Collins

1-16	A	Pittsburgh	9-21	L
1-18	A	Iowa	15-14	W
1-23	A$_{EV}$	quadrangular meet:		
		1st MSC		
		2nd Minnesota		
		3rd Purdue		
		4th Northwestern		
1-30	A	Ohio State	20-6	W
2-5	H	Purdue	18-10	W
2-6	H	Iowa Teachers	24-4	W

2-13	A	Illinois	20-10	W
2-20	H	Michigan	9-15	L
2-27	A	Indiana	26-5	W
		Big Tens at East Lansing	3rd	

1955 (2-7)
Coach: Fendley Collins

1-8	H	Pittsburgh	5-24	L
1-14	H	Indiana	12-14	L
1-22	A_EV	quadrangular meet:		
		1st MSC		
		2nd Purdue		
		3rd Northwestern		
		4th Minnesota		
1-29	A	Ohio State	14-16	L
2-5	A	Purdue	14-15	L
2-8	H	Illinois	10-16	L
2-11	H	Minnesota	21-8	W
2-19	H	Iowa	14-11	W
2-21	A	Michigan	7-19	L
2-26	A	Iowa Teachers	11-16	L
		Big Tens at Minneapolis	6th	

1956 (4-4-1)
Coach: Fendley Collins

1-7	A_EV	quadrangular meet:		
		1st Purdue		
		2nd Minnesota		
		3rd MSU		
		4th Northwestern		
1-16	H	Iowa Teachers	11-15	L
1-21	A	Iowa	14-16	L
1-28	H	Ohio State	29-9	W
2-2	H	Wisconsin	20-5	W
2-4	H	Purdue	20-19	W
2-6	H	Michigan	12-14	L
2-11	A	Illinois	17-17	T
2-18	A	Minnesota	12-24	L
2-25	A	Indiana	20-12	W
		Big Tens at Evanston	4th	

1957 (7-2)
Coach: Fendley Collins

1-5	A_EV	quadrangular meet:		
		1st MSU		
		2nd Minnesota		
		3rd Purdue		
		4th Northwestern		
1-12	H	Indiana	17-9	W
1-19	H	Iowa	9-15	L
1-26	A	Ohio State	24-5	W
2-2	A	Purdue	19-11	W
2-4	H	Illinois	26-5	W
2-9	A	Iowa Teachers	16-14	W
2-16	A	Michigan	16-15	W
2-23	A	Wisconsin	24-5	W
3-1	A	Minnesota	13-14	L
		Big Tens at Evanston	T6th	

1958 (3-5)
Coach: Fendley Collins

1-4	A_EV	quadrangular meet:		
		1st Minnesota		
		2nd Purdue		
		3rd MSU		
		4th Northwestern		
1-11	A	Iowa	9-17	L
1-18	H	Iowa Teachers	11-17	L
1-25	H	Ohio State	22-6	W
2-1	H	Purdue	27-3	W
2-8	A	Indiana	11-17	L
2-15	A	Illinois	19-9	W
2-22	H	Michigan	13-14	L
3-1	A	Minnesota	12-21	L
		Big Tens at Champaign	3rd	

1959 (5-3-1)
Coach: Fendley Collins

1-3	A_EV	quadrangular meet:		
		1st MSU		
		2nd Northwestern		
		3rd Minnesota		
		4th Purdue		
1-10	H	Indiana	7-20	L
1-17	H	Iowa	9-17	L
1-24	H	Iowa Teachers	16-10	W
1-31	A	Purdue	14-12	W
2-6	H	Illinois	24-5	W
2-9	A	Pittsburgh	11-15	L
2-14	A	Ohio State	22-6	W
2-20	H	Minnesota	16-14	W
2-27	A	Michigan	14-14	T
		Big Tens at Iowa City	3rd	

1960 (7-1-1)
Coach: Fendley Collins

1-9	A_EV	quadrangular meet:		
		1st MSU		
		2nd Purdue		
		3rd Minnesota		
		4th Northwestern		
1-16	A	Illinois	22-5	W
1-23	H	Ohio State	26-6	W
1-30	A	Minnesota	18-6	W
2-2	H	Purdue	24-6	W
2-6	A	Indiana	24-6	W
2-12	A	Iowa Teachers	15-15	T
2-15	H	Pittsburgh	11-13	L
2-20	A	Iowa	18-9	W
2-27	H	Michigan	14-11	W
		Big Tens at Ann Arbor	3rd	

1961 (8-1)
Coach: Fendley Collins

1-7	A_EV	quadrangular meet:		
		1st MSU		
		2nd Purdue		
		3rd Minnesota		
		4th Northwestern		
1-9	H	Indiana	24-11	W
1-14	A	Ohio State	30-5	W
1-21	H	Iowa Teachers	20-12	W
1-28	A_WL	Purdue	22-13	W
		Bowling Green	30-7	W
2-2	A	Pittsburgh	8-19	L
2-18	H	Iowa	31-3	W
2-20	A	Michigan	20-16	W
2-25	H	Minnesota	40-0	W
		Big Tens at East Lansing	1st	

1962 (6-1-2)
Coach: Fendley Collins

1-6	A_EV	quadrangular meet:		
		1st Minnesota		
		2nd MSU		
		3rd Purdue		
		4th Northwestern		
1-13	A	Indiana	14-14	T
1-19	A	Iowa Teachers	19-8	W
1-20	A	Iowa	15-13	W
1-27	H	Purdue	22-12	W
2-2	H	Southern Illinois	20-6	W
2-3	H	Illinois	22-8	W
2-10	H	Ohio State	14-14	T
2-17	H	Michigan	11-14	L
2-23	H	Minnesota	14-12	W
		Big Tens at Minneapolis	5th	

Grady Peninger (1963-1986)

Grady Peninger was born in Weletka, OK, on April 28, 1927. While still in high school he captured the National AAU crown at 115 pounds. As a collegian, he was never beaten in four years of dual meet competition at Oklahoma State. While there, in 1947 he again captured the National AAU title and was runner-up in 1948. Grady also placed second in the 1949 NCAA championships. After receiving his B.S. degree in physical education, Grady stayed on in Stillwater to work as the Cowboys' freshmen coach while completing an M.S. degree in school administration. Peninger's interscholastic coaching career was highly successful. His Ponca City High School teams won the state title three times and were second twice in his nine-year stay as head coach. Grady was selected the Sooner State's "Outstanding High School Wrestling Coach" in 1960. In that following fall he came to MSU as an assistant before replacing the venerable Collins.

1963 (7-3)
Coach: Grady Peninger

1-5	A_EV	quadrangular meet:		
		1st Northwestern		
		2nd MSU		
		3rd Minnesota		
		4th Purdue		
1-11	A	Purdue	19-8	W
1-19	A	Ohio State	19-8	W
1-26	H	Oklahoma	11-14	L
2-2	H	Pittsburgh	10-16	L
2-4	H	Iowa State	20-5	W
2-9	A	Illinois	14-11	W
2-15	H	Indiana	17-8	W
2-16	H	Iowa	14-11	W
2-23	A	Michigan	8-19	L
3-2	A	Minnesota	15-9	W
		Big Tens at Evanston	8th	

1964 (5-5-1)
Coach: Grady Peninger

1-4	A_EV	quadrangular meet:		
		1st Northwestern		
		2nd Minnesota		
		3rd Purdue		
		4th MSU		
1-11	H	Mankato State	20-5	W
1-18	A	Oklahoma	8-19	L
1-24	H	Purdue	22-5	W
1-25	H	Illinois	12-12	T
1-31	A	Iowa State	21-7	W
2-8	A	Pittsburgh	5-22	L
2-13	A	Iowa	13-15	L
2-15	A	Indiana	14-11	W
2-22	H	Michigan	5-20	L
2-24	A	Ohio State	14-11	W
2-28	H	Minnesota	9-15	L
		Big Tens at Madison	10th	

1964-1965 (7-3-1)
Coach: Grady Peninger

12-5	H	Air Force	27-3	W
12-11	H	Indiana	14-14	T
1-2	A_EV	quadrangular meet:		
		1st MSU		
		2nd Minnesota		
		3rd Northwestern		
		4th Purdue		
1-9	H	Iowa	18-10	W
1-16	A	Illinois	20-8	W
1-23	H	Pittsburgh	21-8	W
1-30	A	Purdue	18-6	W
2-6	A_MN	Minnesota	11-14	L
2-6	H	Mankato State	14-15	L
2-13	H	Ohio State	23-3	W
2-20	H	Iowa State	20-6	W
2-27	A	Michigan	8-17	L
		Big Tens at Ann Arbor	2nd	

1965-1966 (10-2)

Coach: Grady Peninger

12-4	A_CD	Colorado State	16-14	W
		Air Force	36-3	W
12-11	A	Indiana	15-9	W
1-8	A_EV	quadrangular meet:		
		1st Minnesota		
		2nd MSU		
		3rd Northwestern		
		4th Purdue		
1-15	A	Ohio State	15-11	W
1-22	H	Minnesota	20-8	W
1-28	H	Purdue	25-3	W
1-29	H	Oklahoma	5-27	L
2-5	H	Illinois	25-3	W
2-12	A	Cornell (NY)	27-5	W
2-18	A	Iowa	21-8	W
2-19	A	Iowa State	24-10	W
2-26	H	Michigan	11-16	L
		Big Tens at Champaign	1st	

1966-1967 (8-1-1)

Coach: Grady Peninger

12-3	H	Air Force	40-0	W
12-9	H	Iowa State	25-5	W
12-10	H	Indiana	25-5	W
1-7	A_EV	quadrangular meet:		
		1st MSU		
		2nd Northwestern		
		3rd Minnesota		
		4th Purdue		
1-14	H	Ohio State	37-0	W
1-20	A	Oklahoma State	14-14	T
1-21	A	Oklahoma	15-12	W
2-4	A	Minnesota	17-12	W
2-11	H	Iowa	24-8	W
2-18	A	Illinois	32-3	W
2-25	A	Michigan	14-16	L
		Big Tens at Columbus	1st	

1967-1968 (9-4)

Coach: Grady Peninger

12-1	A	Colorado State	19-20	L
12-2	A	Air Force	25-8	W
12-12	A	Indiana	20-9	W
1-6	H	quadrangular meet:		
		1st MSU		
		2nd Miami (OH)		
		3rd Eastern Michigan		
		4th Central Michigan		
1-13	A	Arizona State	16-13	W
1-20	A	Oklahoma	15-16	L
1-26	H	Purdue	35-0	W
1-27	H	Oklahoma State	6-21	L
2-3	H	Illinois	30-2	W
2-9	A	Northern Iowa	21-6	W
2-10	A	Iowa	12-15	L
2-17	H	Michigan	17-12	W
2-24	A_MN	Minnesota	28-3	W
		Mankato State	20-9	W
		Big Tens at Iowa City	1st	

1968-1969 (9-2)

Coach: Grady Peninger

12-5	A	Maryland	24-11	W
1-4	H	quadrangular meet:		
		1st MSU		
		2nd Central Michigan		
		3rd Miami (OH)		
		4th Eastern Michigan		
1-6	H	Indiana	31-0	W
1-18	H	Southern Illinois	35-4	W
1-24	A	Oklahoma	3-24	L
1-25	A	Oklahoma State	14-15	L
1-29	A	Arizona State	30-2	W
2-1	A	Illinois	32-3	W

2-7	H	Northern Iowa	23-5	W
2-8	H	Iowa	18-9	W
2-15	A	Michigan	20-9	W
2-22	H	Minnesota	27-5	W
		Big Tens at East Lansing	1st	

1969-1970 (16-1)

Coach: Grady Peninger

12-6	H	Maryland	32-0	W
12-29	A	Midlands Tournament	1st	
1-3	H	quadrangular meet:		
		1st MSU		
		2nd Central Michigan		
		3rd Miami (OH)		
		4th Eastern Michigan		
1-7	A	Colorado State	30-6	W
1-9	A	Arizona State	28-5	W
1-10	A	California Poly	18-12	W
1-17	A	Southern Illinois	24-15	W
1-23	H	Purdue	35-2	W
1-24	H	Oklahoma State	16-17	L
1-27	A	Indiana	36-0	W
1-31	H	Illinois	40-0	W
2-6	A	Northern Iowa	31-3	W
2-7	A_IC	Iowa	20-13	W
		Wisconsin	28-6	W
		Southern Illinois	26-5	W
2-14	H	Oklahoma	26-6	W
2-21	H	Michigan	25-8	W
2-28	A_MI	Minnesota	30-5	W
		Mankato State	27-3	W
		Big Tens at Ann Arbor	1st	

1970-1971 (7-3-2)

Coach: Grady Peninger

12-4	A	Ohio	18-18	T
12-29	A_EV	Midlands Tournament	3rd	
1-8	H	Indiana	38-0	W
1-9	H	Iowa	22-12	W
1-16	H	Southern Illinois	28-8	W
1-22	A	Oklahoma State	13-21	L
1-23	A	Oklahoma	14-19	L
1-29	A	Purdue	26-6	W
1-30	A	Illinois	26-11	W
2-5	H	California Poly	14-17	L
2-12	H	Northern Iowa	21-11	W
2-20	A	Michigan	18-18	T
2-26	H	Minnesota	27-5	W
		Big Tens at W. Lafayette	1st	

1971-1972 (11-1)

Coach: Grady Peninger

12-4	A	Indiana	36-6	W
12-17	A	Minnesota	33-6	W
12-29	A_EV	Midlands Tournament	2nd	
1-8	H	Iowa	14-22	L
1-9	H	Northern Iowa	36-6	W
1-14	H	Southern Illinois	32-6	W
1-15	H	Ohio	32-6	W
1-22	H	Oklahoma State	20-15	W
1-28	H	Purdue	27-11	W
1-29	H	Illinois	36-0	W
2-5	H	Oklahoma	24-12	W
2-12	H	Michigan	25-6	W
2-19	H	Wisconsin	24-10	W
		Big Tens at Bloomington	1st	

1972-1973 (6-4-1)

Coach: Grady Peninger

12-2	H	Ohio	36-5	W
12-28	A_EV	Midlands Tournament	3rd	
1-11	H	Southern Illinois	25-6	W
1-12	H	Indiana	30-8	W
1-18	A	Oklahoma	14-26	L
1-19	A	Oklahoma State	6-28	L
1-26	A	Illinois	23-11	W

1-27	A	Purdue	32-6	W
2-2	H	Minnesota	18-15	W
2-3	H	Iowa	19-19	T
2-10	A	Michigan	6-27	L
2-17	A	Wisconsin	6-21	L
		Big Tens at Minneapolis	5th	

1973-1974 (12-3-1)

Coach: Grady Peninger

11-29	A	Ohio	29-12	W
12-9	A_PG	Pittsburgh	33-2	W
		Lehigh	20-16	W
12-21	A_EV	Midlands Tournament	7th	
1-5	A	Indiana	33-5	W
1-10	H	Oklahoma State	21-10	W
1-12	A	Minnesota	18-15	W
1-18	H	Northwestern	26-6	W
1-19	H	Southern Illinois	25-9	W
1-25	H	Illinois	33-2	W
1-26	H	Purdue	23-12	W
2-2	H	Oklahoma	27-10	W
2-9	H	Michigan	10-23	L
2-12	A	Ohio State	30-5	W
2-16	H	Wisconsin	16-18	L
2-22	A	Iowa	16-16	T
2-23	A	Iowa State	12-21	L
		Big Tens at Evanston	3rd	

1974-1975 (10-6)

Coach: Grady Peninger

12-2	H	Penn State	27-16	W
12-6	H	Michigan	19-16	W
12-27	A_EV	Midlands Tournament	13th	
1-10	H	Iowa	9-21	L
1-11	H	Indiana	28-6	W
1-13	H	Rhode Island	28-6	W
1-17	A	Oklahoma	11-27	L
1-18	A	Oklahoma State	15-19	L
1-24	A	Illinois	19-15	W
1-25	A	Purdue	31-8	W
2-1	H	Iowa State	18-19	L
2-7	H	Ohio State	24-12	W
2-8	A	Michigan	12-18	L
2-11	A	Ohio	23-11	W
2-15	A	Wisconsin	14-20	L
2-21	H	Kentucky	25-9	W
2-22	H	Southern Illinois	23-12	W
		Big Tens at Columbus	3rd	

1975-1976 (7-7)

Coach: Grady Peninger

12-1	A	Michigan	12-27	L
12-6	A	Penn State Invitational	2nd	
12-27	A_EV	Midlands Tournament	13th	
1-8	H	Oklahoma State	14-24	L
1-10	A	Indiana	26-13	W
1-12	A	Northwestern	16-19	L
1-17	H	Southern Illinois	24-12	W
1-19	A	Rhode Island	25-17	W
1-20	A	Mass. Maritime	30-17	W
1-23	H	Illinois	30-6	W
1-24	H	Purdue	39-5	W
1-30	A	Iowa State	5-39	L
1-31	A	Iowa	3-34	L
2-7	H	Michigan	21-18	W
2-14	H	Wisconsin	17-19	L
2-21	A	Oklahoma	11-27	L
		Big Tens at Iowa City	5th	

1976-1977 (9-9)

Coach: Grady Peninger

11-30	H	Michigan	15-27	L
12-3	A	Penn State Invitational	6th	
12-17	A_YP	Eastern Michigan	34-10	W
		Ohio Northern	33-6	W
		Chicago State	35-9	W

Date	Loc	Opponent	Score	Result
12-29	A_EV	Midlands Tournament	14th	
1-7	H	Southern Illinois	32-5	W
1-8	H	Indiana	21-12	W
1-13	A	Oklahoma State	0-40	L
1-14	A	Oklahoma	6-30	L
1-21	H	Northwestern	11-24	L
1-22	H	Iowa State	5-37	L
1-28	A	Illinois	24-15	W
1-29	A	Purdue	34-8	W
2-4	H	Brockport St. (NY)	26-9	W
2-5	H	Iowa	6-35	L
2-12	A	Michigan	9-30	L
2-19	A	Wisconsin	2-40	L
2-21	H	Missouri	16-19	L
2-26	A	Ohio State	22-14	W
		Big Tens at Madison	7th	

1977-1978 (6 -6-1)
Coach: Grady Peninger

Date	Loc	Opponent	Score	Result
11-18	H	MSU Invitational	1st	
11-27	A	Michigan	24-18	W
12-2	A	Penn State Invitational	4th	
12-17	A_BH	Brockport St. (NY).	24-12	W
		Syracuse	20-24	L
12-29	A_EV	Midlands Tournament	18th	
1-7	A	Indiana	31-10	W
1-13	H	Southern Illinois	33-10	W
1-14	H	Oklahoma State	10-32	L
1-21	A	Northwestern	17-19	L
2-3	A	Iowa State	3-41	L
2-4	A	Iowa	3-49	L
2-10	H	Michigan	29-15	W
2-17	H	Ohio State	30-8	W
2-18	H	Wisconsin	20-20	T
2-25	H	Oklahoma	16-25	L
		Big Tens at Ann Arbor	3rd	

1978-1979 (13-7)
Coach: Grady Peninger

Date	Loc	Opponent	Score	Result
11-17	H	MSU Invitational	1st	
11-27	H	Michigan	23-14	W
12-1	A	Penn State Invitational	1st	
12-13	A	UCLA	26-12	W
12-14	A	Long Beach State	34-3	W
12-15	A	Cal State-Fullerton	42-3	W
12-16	A	Cal Poly	12-27	L
12-18	A	Cal St.-Bakersfield	12-29	L
12-29	A_EV	Midlands Tournament	18th	
1-6	H	Indiana	33-5	W
1-12	H	Iowa State	16-26	L
1-13	H	Northwestern	37-8	W
1-16	H	Southern Illinois	41-0	W
1-19	A	Oklahoma	15-25	L
1-20	A	Oklahoma State	11-29	L
1-26	A	Illinois	25-14	W
1-27	A_WL	Purdue	40-5	W
		Nebraska	34-6	W
2-2	H	Minnesota	25-16	W
2-3	H	Iowa	9-28	L
2-8	A	Michigan	23-17	W
2-11	A	Ohio State	33-8	W
2-17	A	Wisconsin	7-26	L
		Big Tens at Iowa City	4th	

1979-1980 (11-8-1)
Coach: Grady Peninger

Date	Loc	Opponent	Score	Result
11-16	H	MSU Invitational	1st	
11-27	H	Michigan	18-18	T
12-12	A	Cal St.-Bakersfield	17-25	L
12-13	A	Fresno State	41-4	W
12-14	A	Cal Poly	12-26	L
12-17	A	Cal State-Stanislaus	47-3	W
12-18	A	San Jose State	16-26	L
12-29	A_EV	Midlands Tournament	22nd	
1-5	A	Indiana	31-6	W
1-11	H	Hofstra	35-14	W
1-12	H	Oklahoma State	15-26	L
1-14	H	Penn State	32-9	W
1-19	A	Northwestern	31-11	W
1-25	H	Illinois	36-8	W
1-26	H	Purdue	40-3	W
2-1	A	Iowa State	17-20	L
2-2	A	Iowa	9-35	L
2-8	H	Michigan	26-7	W
2-9	H	Pittsburgh	50-3	W
2-15	H	Ohio State	26-16	W
2-16	H	Wisconsin	11-25	L
2-23	H	Oklahoma	13-34	L
		Big Tens at East Lansing	4th	

1980-1981(7-7)
Coach: Grady Peninger

Date	Loc	Opponent	Score	Result
11-14	H	MSU Invitational	2nd	
11-25	H	Michigan	18-16	W
11-29	A_MP	Michigan Open	1st	
12-13	A	Lock Haven (PA) Invit.	1st	
12-27	A_EV	Midlands Tournament	10th	
1-7	H	Indiana	20-18	W
1-10	H	Northwestern	32-11	W
1-13	H	Indiana State	24-23	W
1-16	A	Oklahoma	6-40	L
1-17	A	Oklahoma State	6-40	L
1-21	H	Western Michigan	33-15	W
1-23	A	Illinois	25-13	W
1-24	A	Purdue	30-13	W
1-30	A	Michigan	10-26	L
2-7	H	Iowa	0-46	L
2-13	A	Ohio State	18-23	L
2-15	H	Iowa State	15-23	L
2-21	A	Wisconsin	14-26	L
		Big Tens at Madison	7th	

1981-1982 (10-4)
Coach: Grady Peninger

Date	Loc	Opponent	Score	Result
11-14	H	MSU Invitational	1st	
11-24	A	Michigan	33-10	W
12-5	A_MP	Michigan Open	1st	
12-11	A	Lock Haven (PA) Invit.	2nd	
12-18	A	Bowling Green Tourn.	1st	
12-29	A_EV	Midlands Tournament	10th	
1-8	A	Indiana State	27-14	W
1-9	A	Indiana	42-0	W
1-13	H	Oklahoma State	9-27	L
1-16	A	Northwestern	33-6	W
1-19	A	Western Michigan	47-0	W
1-22	H	Illinois	33-0	W
1-23	H	Purdue	34-7	W
1-29	H	Michigan	19-15	W
1-31	H	Oklahoma	0-39	L
2-13	A	Iowa	3-43	L
2-14	A	Iowa State	2-44	L
2-16	H	Ohio State	24-17	W
2-20	H	Wisconsin	20-17	W
		Big Tens at Ann Arbor	4th	

1982-1983 (10-4)
Coach: Grady Peninger

Date	Loc	Opponent	Score	Result
11-13	H	MSU Invitational	1st	
11-20	A_DA	Ohio Open	1st	
12-4	A_MP	Michigan Open	1st	
12-11	A	Lock Haven (PA) Invit.	1st	
12-29	A_PT	Midlands Tournament	9th	
1-8	H	Nevada- Las Vegas	36-8	W
1-9	H	Indiana	26-13	W
1-13	A	Oklahoma	12-28	L
1-14	A	Oklahoma State	4-38	L
1-16	H	Northwestern	29-8	W
1-21	A	Illinois	29-11	W
1-22	A	Purdue	38-2	W
1-28	H	Michigan	31-7	W
1-31	H	Ohio State	22-12	W
2-4	H	Iowa	8-38	L
2-6	H	Nebraska	21-18	W
2-12	H	Iowa State	16-27	L
2-13	H	Indiana State	33-8	W
2-19	A	Wisconsin	27-12	W
		Big Tens a Iowa City	2nd	

1983-1984 (10-5)
Coach: Grady Peninger

Date	Loc	Opponent	Score	Result
11-12	H	MSU Invitational	1st	
11-19	A_DA	Ohio Open	1st	
12-3	A_MP	Michigan Open	1st	
12-10	A	Lock Haven (PA) Invit.	3rd	
12-29	A_EV	Midlands Tournament	9th	
1-5	H	Oklahoma	12-25	L
1-7	A	Indiana	46-3	W
1-10	A_TO	Toledo	34-9	W
		Slippery Rock	39-8	W
1-13	A	Indiana State	25-18	W
1-15	A	Northwestern	34-16	W
1-20	H	Illinois	44-0	W
1-21	H	Purdue	32-11	W
1-24	A	Michigan	23-16	W
1-28	A	Minnesota	29-15	W
2-3	H	Oklahoma State	14-27	L
2-11	A	Northern Iowa	19-23	L
2-12	A	Iowa	11-29	L
2-14	A	Ohio State	42-3	W
2-18	H	Wisconsin	15-29	L
		Big Tens at East Lansing	2nd	

1984-1985 (8-6)
Coach: Grady Peninger

Date	Loc	Opponent	Score	Result
11-9	H	MSU Invitational	2nd	
11-17	A_DA	Ohio Open	10th	
12-1	A_MP	Michigan Open	1st	
12-8	A	Lock Haven (PA) Invit.	6th	
12-29	A_EV	Midlands Tournament		
1-4	H	Indiana State	18-33	L
1-5	H	Indiana	28-15	W
1-11	H	Northwestern	37-9	W
1-18	A	Illinois	24-14	W
1-19	A	Purdue	23-15	W
1-24	H	Toledo	39-5	W
1-25	H	Michigan	11-30	L
1-27	H	Iowa	3-40	L
1-31	H	Morgan State	24-15	W
2-2	H	Minnesota	22-14	W
2-8	A	Oklahoma State	3-38	L
2-9	A	Oklahoma	11-33	L
2-16	H	Wisconsin	8-24	L
2-23	A	Ohio State	29-10	W
		Big Tens at Evanston	5th	

1985-1986 (6-12-1)
Coach: Grady Peninger

Date	Loc	Opponent	Score	Result
11-9	H	MSU Invitational	3rd	
11-23	A_DA	Ohio Open	5th	
12-6	H	Ohio State	16-21	L
12-28	A_EV	Midlands Tournament	25th	
1-5	A	Indiana State	18-18	T
1-7	H	Oklahoma	9-33	L
1-10	A_KX	Tennessee	27-14	W
		North Carolina	9-34	L
1-11	A	Ohio State	14-21	L
1-16	A	Indiana	30-7	W
1-17	H	Illinois	16-19	L
1-18	H	Purdue	14-26	L
1-21	A	Michigan	4-42	L
1-23	A	Oklahoma State	9-34	L
1-26	A	Northwestern	17-28	L
2-2	A	Minnesota	9-33	L
2-6	H	Notre Dame	25-12	W
2-8	A	Iowa	5-51	L
2-15	H	Wisconsin	13-28	L
2-16	A	Indiana	18-16	W
2-18pm	A	Central Michigan	24-9	W
2-21	A	Toledo	29-19	W
		Big Tens at Minneapolis	6th	

Phil Parker (1986-1991)

A native of Waukegan, IL, Parker was a 1972 sociology graduate of Iowa State University. He also holds a master's degree in counseling, earned in 1978 from California Lutheran College. While at Iowa State, he was a three-time All-American and member of three Cyclone NCAA championship teams from 1970-1972. He earned a Big Eight Conference championship in 1970 and was an Olympic Trials finalist in 1976. Prior to coming to MSU, Parker completed 11 years of head coaching experience at Ventura (CA) Junior College and Washington State where those combined teams recorded 111 wins against 55 losses. In his final season at Ventura he was selected Metro Conference Coach of the Year and then was named the NCAA Rookie Coach of the Year in his first season at WSU. Following five years at the helm, Phil Parker was released from his position and he left the coaching profession.

1986-1987 (7-8)
Coach: Phil Parker

11-9	H	MSU Invitational	1st/8	
11-16	A	E. Michigan Open	NTS	
11-22	A$_{DA}$	Ohio Open	1st/17	
12-29	A$_{EV}$	Midlands Tournament	31st/51	
1-9	H	Northwestern	15-28	L
1-16	A	Illinois	15-24	L
1-17	A	Purdue	8-26	L
1-23	H	Michigan	8-28	L
1-25	H	Iowa	6-35	L
1-30	A$_{SW}$	Oklahoma State	0-44	L
		Missouri	30-7	W
1-31	A	Oklahoma	6-36	L
2-5	A	Notre Dame	25-17	W
2-7	H	Minnesota	21-13	W
2-9	A	Indiana	24-19	W
2-13	H	Central Michigan	25-16	W
2-14	H	Toledo	26-15	W
2-21	A	Wisconsin	8-34	L
2-28	A	Ohio State	20-14	W
		Big Tens at Madison	10th	

1987-1988 (1-12)
Coach: Phil Parker

11-8	H	MSU Invitational	4th	
11-15	A	E. Michigan Open	NTS	
11-21	A$_{DA}$	Ohio Open	NTS	
12-4	A	Las Vegas Invitational	20th	
12-5	A	Central Michigan Open	NTS	
12-29	A$_{EV}$	Midlands Tournament	24th	
1-2	H	Oklahoma	10-31	L
1-9	A	Northwestern	8-25	L
1-15	H	Illinois	13-27	L
1-16	H	Purdue	19-26	L
1-19	A	Michigan	9-39	L
1-21	H	Eastern Michigan	19-23	L
2-6	A	Minnesota	9-35	L
2-7	A	Iowa	15-32	L
2-12	A	Central Michigan	11-29	L
2-13	H	Indiana	21-18	W
2-19	H	Edinboro	11-25	L
2-20	H	Wisconsin	18-23	L
2-27	H	Ohio State	6-27	L
		Big Tens at Ann Arbor	10th	

1988-1989 (6-12)
Coach: Phil Parker

11-6	H	MSU Invitational	4th	
11-19	A$_{DA}$	Ohio Open	NTS	
12-2	A	Las Vegas Invitational	20th	
12-29	AE$_V$	Midlands Tournament	24th	
1-6	H	Northwestern	10-28	L
		Lake Superior	28-15	W
1-7	H	Morgan State	22-20	W
1-14	H	Michigan	7-30	L
1-20	A	Illinois	26-13	W
1-21	A	Purdue	11-25	L
1-28	A$_{IN}$	Great American Classic:		

		Purdue	16-24	L
		Wisconsin	15-30	L
2-1	A	Notre Dame	12-31	L
2-4	H	Minnesota	10-37	L
		Ferris State	22-24	L
2-9	H	Central Michigan	30-12	W
		Toledo	25-21	W
2-12	H	Ashland	22-26	L
		Grand Valley	21-14	W
2-16	A	Indiana	14-20	L
2-18	A	Wisconsin	15-26	L
2-25	A	Ohio State	14-19	L
		Big Tens at W. Lafayette	9th	

1989-1990 (6-7-2)
Coach: Phil Parker

11-5	H	MSU Invitational	2nd	
11-11	A	E. Michigan Open	NTS	
11-18	A$_{DA}$	Ohio Open	NTS	
12-1	A	Las Vegas Invitational	20th	
12-29	A$_{TA}$	Sunshine Open	3rd	
1-5	A	Northwestern	12-28	L
1-13	H	Notre Dame	21-15	W
1-19	H	Illinois	24-13	W
1-20	H	Purdue	20-20	T
1-23	A	Michigan	12-25	L
1-27	A$_{BA}$	Morgan State	21-18	W
		Drexel	28-13	W
2-3	A$_{NR}$	Oklahoma	15-25	L
		Central State (OK)	15-15	T
2-9	A	Central Michigan	23-15	W
2-10	A	Minnesota	15-24	L
2-16	A	Grand Valley	23-12	W
2-24	H	Wisconsin	13-19	L
2-25	H	Indiana	8-23	L
3-3	H	Ohio State	14-19	L
		Big Tens at Evanston	8th	

1990-1991 (6-8)
Coach: Phil Parker

11-4	H	MSU Invitational	4th	
11-11	A	E. Michigan Open	NTS	
11-17	A$_{DA}$	Ohio Open	NTS	
11-30	A	Las Vegas Invitational	20th	
12-28	A$_{EV}$	Midlands Tournament	22nd	
1-6	H	Oklahoma	11-24	L
1-16	A	Notre Dame	22-14	W
1-18	A	Illinois	20-16	W
1-19	A	Purdue	13-23	L
1-23	H	Michigan	7-29	L
1-25	H	Northwestern	23-20	W
		Ferris State	19-16	W
2-2	A	Indiana	16-19	L
2-8	H	Central Michigan	22-17	W
2-9	H	Minnesota	7-30	L
		Grand Valley	31-5	W
2-15	H	Iowa	6-42	L
2-17	A	Wisconsin	7-34	L
2-24	A	Ohio State	12-28	L
		Big Tens at Champaign	6th	

Tom Minkel (1991-)

Tom Minkel arrived at Michigan from Central Michigan University, where he had been an assistant coach for 12 years followed by two seasons as head coach. As a competitor for CMU, Minkel was a three-time All-American and the only wrestler in that school's history to go through an entire year undefeated in dual meets (35-0). His overall career record was 73-13-1. Particularly knowledgeable and crafted at the Greco-Roman style of wrestling, Minkel was a four-time national champion at 149-pounds. He made seven U.S. teams that competed internationally, and was a member of the 1980 Olympic Team. From 1986 through 1996, Minkel's resume has been highlighted by numerous international coaching experiences. In 1991, he served as head coach of the U.S. World Wrestling Team in Bulgaria and

the U.S. Pan-American Team in Cuba. During that time he also began his tenure as the U.S. Olympic Greco-Roman head coach, culminating with the 1992 Olympic Games in Barcelona, Spain.

1991-1992 (6-12)
Coach: Tom Minkel

11-10	A	E. Michigan Open	NTS	
11-23	A$_{CO}$	Ohio Open	NTS	
12-6	A	Las Vegas Invitational	15th	
12-14	A$_{BO}$	Boston Univ.	15-20	L
		Harvard	20-14	W
12-14	A$_{BO}$	Central Connecticut	21-16	W
12-28	A$_{EV}$	Midlands Tournament		
1-17	H	Illinois	20-19	W
		Ferris State	25-16	W
1-19	H	Purdue	17-22	L
1-21	A	Michigan	3-38	L
1-26	A$_{EV}$	Northwestern	5-32	L
		Illinois State	13-32	L
2-1	H	Ohio State	6-35	L
2-2	H	Indiana	18-23	L
		Grand Valley	32-15	W
2-8	A$_{NR}$	Oklahoma	11-24	L
		Central State (OK)	12-30	L
2-15	A$_{MP}$	Central Michigan	8-32	L
		Kent State	6-30	L
2-16	H	Notre Dame	18-15	W
2-22	H	Wisconsin	8-28	L
		Big Tens at Madison	9th	

1992-1993 (5-9)
Coach: Tom Minkel

11-1	A	E. Michigan Open	NTS	
11-14	A$_{CO}$	Ohio Open	NTS	
12-4	A	Las Vegas Hall of Fame	13th	
12-29	A$_{EV}$	Midlands Tournament	8th	
1-6	H	Oklahoma	13-23	L
1-9	H	MSU Open	NTS	
1-16	H	Northwestern	14-19	L
		Penn State	9-31	L
1-23	H	Ferris State	22-15	W
1-30	A$_{BL}$	Indiana	22-13	W
		Illinois	15-19	L
1-31	A$_{WL}$	Purdue	12-19	L
		Illinois State	22-13	W
2-6	A	Ohio State	4-34	L
2-13	H	Central Michigan	27-7	W
		Carson Newman	40-9	W
		Minnesota	10-28	L
2-17	H	Michigan	12-28	L
2-21	A	Wisconsin	10-28	L
		Big Tens at Columbus	10th	

1993-1994 (11-4)
Coach: Tom Minkel

11-20	A$_{CO}$	Ohio Open	NTS	
12-4	A$_{CF}$	Northern Iowa Open	NTS	
12-29	A$_{EV}$	Midlands Tournament		
1-6	A	Kent State	23-9	W
1-9	H	MSU Open	NTS	
1-15	A$_{UP}$	Penn State	12-31	L
		Clarion	21-15	W
1-18	A	Michigan	21-15	W
1-23	H	Findlay	28-7	W
1-29	A	Northwestern	22-13	W
1-30	H	Illinois	30-10	W
		Ferris State	28-12	W
2-5	H	Purdue	36-9	W
		Ohio State	20-19	W
2-13	A	Minnesota	15-20	L
2-19	H	Wisconsin	16-21	L
2-20	H	Indiana	19-16	W
		Central Michigan	21-13	W
2-26	A	Oklahoma	11-25	L
		Big Tens at Iowa City	6th	

1994-1995 (13-4)
Coach: Tom Minkel

Date	H/A	Opponent	Score	Result
11-5	A	E. Michigan Open	NTS	
11-19	A	Michigan Open	NTS	
12-3	A	Northern Iowa Open	NTS	
12-11	H	Eastern Michigan	32-12	W
12-29	A$_{EV}$	Midlands Tournament	NTS	
1-4	A	Ohio State	22-9	W
1-11	H	Michigan	15-18	L
1-14	H	Kent State	37-3	W
1-15	H	Penn State	21-13	W
1-21	A$_{OM}$	National Team Duals:		
		Western Montana	38-6	W
		Iowa State	16-15	W
		Iowa	6-33	L
1-22	A$_{OM}$	National Team Duals	4th	
		Penn State	24-12	W
		Nebraska	18-21	L
1-29	H	Northwestern	27-7	W
	H	Central Michigan	29-9	W
2-3	A	Illinois	12-19	L
2-4	A	Purdue	35-9	W
2-12	H	Minnesota	19-15	W
2-19	A	Wisconsin	25-16	W
2-25	H	Oklahoma	26-10	W
		Big Tens at Bloomington	2nd	

1995-1996 (13-6-1)
Coach: Tom Minkel

Date	H/A	Opponent	Score	Result
11-5	A	E. Michigan Open	NTS	
11-11	H	Michigan State Open	NTS	
12-1	A	Iowa	13-25	L
12-2	A	Northern Iowa Open	NTS	
12-9	H	E. Michigan	36-3	W
		Cuyahoga C.C.	51-0	W
12-29	A$_{EV}$	Midlands Tournament	NTS	
1-4	H	Ohio State	23-12	W
1-13	A	Penn State	14-23	L
1-14	A	Kent State	28-5	W
1-20	A$_{LI}$	National Team Duals		
		Pittsburgh	19-15	W
		Central Oklahoma	31-6	W
		Penn State	16-15	W
		North Carolina	17-17	T
		Oklahoma State	10-24	L
		Oklahoma	15-17	L
1-31	A	Michigan	20-18	W
2-3	H	Purdue	20-14	W
2-4	H	Illinois	26-11	W
2-10	A	Northwestern	18-17	W
??	A	Central Michigan	24-9	W
2-24	A	Minnesota	21-14	W
2-25	H	Indiana	14-23	L
3-2	A	Oklahoma	14-20	L
		Big Tens at East Lansing	3rd	

1996-1997 (9-12)
Coach: Tom Minkel

Date	H/A	Opponent	Score	Result
11-23	H	Michigan State Open	NTS	
12-7	A	N. Iowa Open	NTS	
12-14	A	Oklahoma State	0-39	L
12-28	A$_{EV}$	Midlands Tournament	8th/48	
1-3	H	Central Michigan	19-15	W
1-5	A	Ohio State	23-12	W
1-11	H	Iowa	10-26	L
1-12	H	Penn State	18-19	L
1-18	A$_{OM}$	National Team Duals:		
		Pitt-Johnstown	28-9	W
		Oklahoma State	3-36	L
		Clarion	26-13	W
		Oklahoma	28-10	W
		Minnesota	9-28	L
		Iowa State	19-16	W
1-26	H	Northwestern	16-17	L
1-29	H	Michigan	15-28	L
2-1AM	A	Purdue	16-19	L
2-1PM	A	Illinois	9-28	L

Date	H/A	Opponent	Score	Result
2-8	H	Oklahoma	18-21	L
2-9AM	H	Nebraska	13-29	L
2-9PM	A	E. Michigan	35-9	W
2-15	H	Minnesota	12-23	L
2-21	A	Indiana	23-12	W
2-23	A	Wisconsin	19-15	W
		Big Tens at Minneapolis	8th	

1997-1998 (9-10)
Coach: Tom Minkel

Date	H/A	Opponent	Score	Result
11-15	H	Michigan State Open	NTS	
11-22	A	Ashland Open	NTS	
12-6	H	Northern Iowa Open	NTS	
12-29	A$_{EV}$	Midlands Tournament	9th/53	
1-2	H	Ohio State	22-13	W
1-4	A	Iowa	12-31	L
1-10	A	Penn State	14-27	L
1-17	A$_{OM}$	National Team Duals	4th/16	
		Oklahoma	19-12	W
		Arizona State	27-9	W
		Minnesota	7-31	L
		Nebraska	23-18	W
		Penn State	10-26	L
1-24	A	Northwestern	23-13	W
2-1	H	Illinois	13-22	L
		E. Michigan	39-0	W
2-4	H	Michigan	18-16	W
2-8AM	H	Purdue	12-21	L
2-8PM	H	Central Michigan	27-11	W
2-13	A	Minnesota	6-39	L
2-15	A	Nebraska	6-28	L
2-20	H	Oklahoma State	10-24	L
2-22	H	Indiana	25-12	W
2-26	A	Oklahoma	9-28	L
		Big Tens at Penn State	7th	

1998-1999 (6-11-1)
Coach: Tom Minkel

Date	H/A	Opponent	Score	Result
11-7	H	Michigan State Open	NTS	
11-21	A	Ashland Open	NTS	
12-5	A	Northern Iowa Open	NTS	
12-11	A	Michigan	9-21	L
12-29	A$_{EV}$	Midlands Tournament	5th/64	
1-8	A	Arizona State	17-16	W
1-10	A$_{JE}$	Central Michigan	13-25	L
1-10	A$_{DR}$	Univ. of Findlay	25-10	W
1-16	A$_{OM}$	National Team Duals		
		Iowa	3-35	L
		Montana St. Northern	30-18	W
		Arizona State	18-30	L
1-22	A	Wisconsin	25-11	W
1-24	A	Minnesota	10-27	L
1-29	H	Northwestern	17-28	L
2-5	H	Michigan	11-22	L
2-8	A	Oklahoma State	4-31	L
2-12	A	Purdue	7-24	L
2-14	A	Indiana	20-20	T
2-19	A	Ohio State	18-17	W
2-21AM	H	Penn State	14-25	L
2-21PM	A	E. Michigan	46-3	W
2-27	H	Oklahoma	10-23	L
		Big Tens at Ann Arbor	8th	

1999-2000 (9-5-1)
Coach: Tom Minkel

Date	H/A	Opponent	Score	Result
11-14	H	Michigan State Open	NTS	
12-5	A	Penn State Open	NTS	
12-10	A	Michigan	15-19	L
12-30	A$_{EV}$	Midlands Tournament	NTS	
1-4	H	Arizona	17-15	W
1-7	A	Central Michigan	28-12	W
1-9	H	Kent State	35-12	W
1-16	A	Penn State	27-7	W
1-23	A	Michigan	18-18	T
1-28	H	Purdue	27-6	W
1-30	A	Iowa	22-13	L
2-4	A	Northwestern	24-13	W
2-6	A	Illinois	25-6	L

Date	H/A	Opponent	Score	Result
2-7	H	NWCA All-Star Meet	NTS	
2-11	H	Wisconsin	24-10	W
2-13AM	H	Minnesota	25-9	L
2-13 PM	A	Eastern Michigan	48-3	W
2-20	A	Oklahoma State	21-10	W
2-24	A	Oklahoma	31-5	L
		Big Tens at Purdue	4th	

2000-2001 (7-8)
Coach: Tom Minkel

Date	H/A	Opponent	Score	Result
11-19	H	Michigan State Open	NTS	
12-2	A	Northern Iowa Open	NTS	
12-8	A	Michigan	22-12	L
12-28	A	Midlands Tournament	8th	
1-5	A	Central Michigan	21-12	W
1-6	H	Missouri	29-3	W
1-14	A	Oklahoma State	31-3	L
1-21	H	Findlay	45-3	W
1-26	A	Illinois	16-15	W
1-28	A	Michigan	20-12	L
2-2	A	Ohio State	28-9	L
2-3	A	Purdue	18-14	L
2-9	A	Minnesota	32-3	L
2-11	A	Iowa	31-9	L
2-16	A	Indiana	20-12	W
2-18AM	H	Penn State	23-12	W
2-18PM	A	Eastern Michigan	39-7	W
2-23	H	Oklahoma	30-6	L
		Big Tens at Northwestern	7th	

2001-2002 (5-12)
Coach: Tom Minkel

Date	H/A	Opponent	Score	Result
11-18	H	Michigan State Open	NTS	
11-28	A	Central Michigan	18-16	W
12-7	H	Michigan	27-6	L
12-30	A$_{EV}$	Midlands Tournament	6th	
1-5	H	Clarion	34-7	W
1-19	A$_{OM}$	National Team Duals		
		Oklahoma State	36-5	L
		Lock Haven	25-10	W
		Penn State	25-9	L
1-26	H	Purdue	24-10	L
1-27	H	Minnesota	37-0	L
2-1	A	Wisconsin	21-19	L
2-3	A	Indiana	21-16	W
2-9	H	Oklahoma State	32-6	L
2-10	A	Missouri	30-6	L
2-15	A	Northwestern	23-12	W
2-17	A	Penn State	17-16	L
2-22	H	Ohio State	20-13	L
2-24	A	Michigan	29-7	L
3-1	A	Oklahoma	38-3	L
		Big Tens at Illinois	8th	

2002-2003 (10 -7)
Coach: Tom Minkel

Date	H/A	Opponent	Score	Result
11-2	A	Eastern Michigan Open	NTS	
11-9	H	Michigan State Open	NTS	
11-24	A	Hofstra	21-16	W
12-3	H	Central Michigan	16-16(tb)	L
12-29	A$_{EV}$	Midlands Championships	NTS	
1-4	H	Kent State	15-18	L
1-18	A	Cornell	<16-16(tb)	W
1-18	A	Ohio State	<15-19	L
1-18	A	Minnesota	<12-24	L
1-24	A	Northwestern	33-7	W
1-25	A	Minnesota	14-22	L
1-31	H	Wisconsin	22-13	W
2-2	A	Oklahoma	24-14	W
2-7	A	Iowa	19-19(tb)	W
2-9	H	Michigan	16-15	W
2-14	H	North Carolina	22-15	W
2-16	H	Penn State	19-18	W
2-21	A	Purdue	23-9	L
2-23	A	Illinois	16-17	L
2-28	A	Oklahoma State	9-27	L
		Big Tens at Madison	4th	
		< National Duals at Columbus		
		(tb) tie-breaker		

Year-by-Year Team Performance

Years	Dual Meets			Conference Championships			NCAA Championships			Coach
	W	L	T	Pts	Place	Host or Site	Pts	Place	Host or Site	
1922	1	3	0			no meet			no meet	James Devers
1923	1	3	0			no meet			no meet	James Devers
1924	0	4	0			no meet			no meet	Leon Burhans
1925	2	4	0			no meet			no meet	Leon Burhans
1926	0	5	0		DNC	West Lafayette, IN			no meet	Leon Burhans
1927	4	3	0		DNC	Chicago, IL			no meet	Ralph Leonard
1928	4	2	0		DNC	Bloomington, IN		no team points	Ames, IA	Ralph Leonard
1929	1	3	0		DNC	West Lafayette, IN	-	DNC	Columbus, OH	Glen Ricks
1930	3	3	0		DNC	Champaign, IL	1	(t)14/18	College Park, PA	Fendley Collins
1931	3	1	0		DNC	Chicago, IL		no team points	Providence, RI	Fendley Collins
1932	4	1	0		DNC	Bloomington, IN	2	(t)13/17	Bloomington, IN	Fendley Collins
1933	3	2	0		DNC	Champaign, IL		no team points	Bethlehem, PA	Fendley Collins
1934	2	4	0		DNC	Bloomington, IN		no team points	Ann Arbor, MI	Fendley Collins
1935	4	4	0		DNC	Chicago, IL	-	DNC	Bethlehem, PA	Fendley Collins
1936	0	6	0		DNC	Iowa City, IA	5	(t)4/11	Lexington, VA	Fendley Collins
1937	1	6	0		DNC	Ann Arbor, MI		no team points	Terre Haute, IN	Fendley Collins
1938	5	4	0		DNC	Evanston, IL	-	DNC	College Park, PA	Fendley Collins
1939	5	3	0		DNC	Chicago, IL		no team points	Lancaster, PA	Fendley Collins
1940	5	2	1		DNC	West Lafayette, IN	1	(t)15/21	Champaign, IL.	Fendley Collins
1941	8	1	0		DNC	Columbus, OH	26	2/24	Bethlehem, PA	Fendley Collins
1942	7	1	0		DNC	Chicago, IL	26	2/14	East Lansing, MI	Fendley Collins
1943	5	2	1		DNC	Evanston, IL		no tournament—World War II		Fendley Collins
1944	Intercollegiate competition suspended due to World War II							no tournament—World War II		Fendley Collins
1945	5	0	0		DNC	Evanston, IL		no tournament—World War II		Fendley Collins
1946	5	2	1		DNC	Champaign, IL	5	8/12	Stillwater, OK	Fendley Collins
1947	7	3	0		DNC	Evanston, IL	11	4/14	Champaign, IL	Fendley Collins
1948	9	0	0		DNC	Champaign, IL	28	2/23	Bethlehem, PA	Fendley Collins
1949	6	1	1		DNC	Bloomington, IN	13	4/19	Fort Collins, CO	Fendley Collins
1950	5	5	0		DNC	Iowa City, IA	2	(t)12/17	Cedar Falls, IA	Fendley Collins
1951	6	3	0	19	3rd	Evanston, IL	7	(t)6/24	Bethlehem, PA	Fendley Collins
1952	5	2	2	19	3rd	Ann Arbor, MI	5	(t)12/26	Fort Collins, CO	Fendley Collins
1953	7	2	0	22	2nd	Bloomington, IN	7	(t)8/28	University Park, PA	Fendley Collins
1954	6	2	0	20	3rd	East Lansing, MI	11	6/26	Norman, OK	Fendley Collins
1955	2	7	0	15	6th	Minneapolis, MN	9	15/38	Ithaca, NY	Fendley Collins
1956	4	4	1	39	4th	Evanston, IL	20	(t)8/36	Stillwater, OK	Fendley Collins
1957	7	2	0	18	(t)6th	Evanston, IL	5	(t)21/38	Pittsburgh, PA	Fendley Collins
1958	3	5	0	44	3rd	Champaign, IL	35	4/50	Laramie, WY	Fendley Collins
1959	5	3	1	45	3rd	Iowa City, IA	17	9/47	Ithaca, NY	Fendley Collins
1960	7	1	1	37	3rd	Ann Arbor, MI	9	(t)18/49	College Park, MD	Fendley Collins
1961	8	1	0	69	1st	East Lansing, MI	19	(t)8/39	Corvallis, OR	Fendley Collins
1962	6	1	2	27	5th	Bloomington, IN	18	(t)9/45	Stillwater, OK	Fendley Collins
1963	7	3	0	16	8th	West Lafayette, IN	10	(t)21/44	Kent, OH	Grady Peninger
1964	5	5	1	1	10th	Minneapolis, MN	-	DNC	Ithaca, NY	Grady Peninger
1965	7	3	1	38	2nd	Ann Arbor, MI	11	(t)15/51	Laramie, WY	Grady Peninger
1966	10	2	0	71	1st	Champaign, IL	32	6/54	Ames, IA	Grady Peninger
1967	9	1	1	92	1st	Columbus, OH	74	1/68	Kent, OH	Grady Peninger
1968	9	4	0	74	1st	Iowa City, IA	55	4/75	University Park, PA	Grady Peninger
1969	9	2	0	93	1st	East Lansing, MI	57	4/72	Provo, UT	Grady Peninger
1970	16	1	0	96	1st	Ann Arbor, MI	84	2/81	Evanston, IL	Grady Peninger
1971	7	3	2	101	1st	West Lafayette, IN	44	3/69	Auburn, AL	Grady Peninger
1972	11	1	0	95	1st	Bloomington, IN	72.50	2/72	College Park, MD	Grady Peninger
1973	6	4	1	76	5th	Minneapolis, MN	14	(t)16/68	Seattle, WA	Grady Peninger
1974	12	3	1	86.5	3rd	Evanston, IL	24	14/70	Ames, IA	Grady Peninger
1975	10	6	0	72.5	3rd	Columbus, OH	23.50	15/70	Princeton, NJ	Grady Peninger
1976	7	7	0	35.25	5th	Iowa City, IA	17	(t)19/72	Tucson, AZ	Grady Peninger
1977	9	9	0	20	7th	Madison, WI	19	17/66	Norman, OK	Grady Penninger
1978	6	6	1	33.75	3rd	Ann Arbor, MI	3.50	(t)36/69	College Park, MD	Grady Penninger
1979	13	7	0	37.25	4th	Iowa City, IA	6.50	(t)31/69	Ames, IA	Grady Penninger
1980	11	8	1	41.25	9th	East Lansing, MI	11.50	(t)23/74	Corvallis, OR	Grady Penninger
1981	7	7	0	24	7th	Madison, WI	6.25	31/69	Princeton, NJ	Grady Penninger
1982	10	4	0	40.75	4th	Ann Arbor, MI	10	26/64	Ames, IA	Grady Penninger
1983	10	4	0	81.50	2nd	Iowa City, IA	24.75	12/56	Oklahoma City, OK	Grady Penninger
1984	10	5	0	103.25	2nd	East Lansing, MI	29.25	8/60	Princeton, NJ	Grady Penninger
1985	8	6	0	60	5th	Evanston, IL	11	30/67	Oklahoma City, OK	Grady Penninger
1986	4	12	1	55.50	6th	Minneapolis, MN	14.25	23/75	Iowa City, IA	Grady Penninger
1987	7	8	0	56	7th	Madison, WI	5.50	(t)40/67	College Park, MD	Phil Parker
1988	1	13	0	26.50	10th	Ann Arbor, MI	-	DNC	Ames, IA	Phil Parker
1989	6	12	0	30.25	9th	West Lafayette, IN	4	(t)44/71	Oklahoma City, OK	Phil Parker
1990	6	7	2	42	8th	Evanston, IL	5.50	42/64	College Park, MD	Phil Parker
1991	6	8	0	56.50	6th	Champaign, IL	3.50	(t)47/66	Iowa City, IA	Phil Parker
1992	6	3	0	31	9th	Madison, WI		60/	Oklahoma City, OK	Tom Minkel
1993	8	12	0	75.50	10th	Columbus, OH	29.50	12/72	Ames, IA	Tom Minkel
1994	11	4	0	64.5	6th	Iowa City, IA	16	28/71	Chapel Hill, NC	Tom Minkel

Years	Dual Meets					Conference Championships			NCAA Championships			Coach
	W	L	T	Pts	Place	Host or Site	Pts	Place	Host or Site			
1995	14	4	0	109.5	2nd	Bloomington, IN	69.50	3/68	Iowa City, IA			Tom Minkel
1996	15	6	0	81	3rd	East Lansing, MI	53.50	7/64	Minneapolis, MN			Tom Minkel
1997	9	12	0	48.50	8th	Minneapolis, MN	25	21/72	Cedar Falls, IA			Tom Minkel
1998	9	10	0	57.50	7th	University Park, PA	39	13/70	Cleveland, OH			Tom Minkel
1999	6	11	1	53.50	8th	Ann Arbor, MI	21.50	22/70	University Park, PA			Tom Minkel
2000	9	5	1	87.50	4th	West Lafayette, IN	36.50	(t)16/70	St. Louis, PA			Tom Minkel
2001	8	8	0	65	7th	Evanston, IL	38	15/71	Iowa City, IA			Tom Minkel
2002	5	12	0	54.5	8th	Champaign, IL	15.50	34/71	Albany, NY			Tom Minkel
2003	10	7	0	92.5	4th	Madison, WI	32	18/73	Kansas City, MO			Tom Minkel
Totals	514	371	26	.578								

Olympic Competitors

Year	Name	Weight & Place
1948	Leland Merrill	(160 1/2) 3rd
	Bob Maldegan	(Hwt) alternate
1968	Don Behm	(126) 2nd
1972	Don Behm	(126) alternate
1976	Tom Muir	(180) alternate

Pan-American Competitors

Year	Name	Weight & Place
1959	Jim Ferguson	(174) 1st
1969	Don Behm	(126) 1st
1972	Jeff Smith	(hwt) 1st

National AAU Champions

Year	Name	Weight
1937	Walter Jacob	160
1938	Walter Jacob	160
1939	Walter Jacob	160
1943	Merle Jennings	134
	Bill Maxwell	145
1945	Gale Mikles	145
1948	Leland Merrill	160
	Bob Maldegan	Hwt
1951	Bob Hoke	145
1953	Jim Sinadinos	136
1954	Norman Gill GRECO-ROMAN	14/
1956	Ken Maidlow GRECO-ROMAN	191
1957	George Woodin	191
1959	Jim Ferguson	174
1960	Jim Ferguson	174

NCAA Champions

Year	Name	Weight
1936	Walter Jacobs	158
1941	Merle Jennings	121
	Burl Jennings	128
1942	Merle Jennings	121
	Burl Jennings	128
	Bill Maxwell	136
1948	Dick Dickenson	136 1/2
1951	Gene Gibbons	167
1954	Bob Hoke	157
1956	Jim Sinadinos	137
1958	Ken Maidlow	191
1961	Norm Young	137
1966	Dick Cook	152
1967	George Radman	167
1967	Dale Anderson	137
1968	Dale Anderson	137
1970	Greg Johnson	118
1971	Greg Johnson	118
1972	Greg Johnson	118
1972	Tom Milkovich	142
1972	Pat Milkovich	126
1974	Pat Milkovich	126
1995	Kelvin Jackson	118

Big Ten Champions

Year	Name	Weight
1951	George Bender	167
	Gene Gibbons	177
1952	Orrris Bender	167
1953	Bob Hoke	157
	Vito Perrone	167
1954	Bob Hoke	157
1956	Don Stroud	137
	Jim Sinadinos	123
1958	Tim Woodin	177
1959	Norm Young	130
	Jim Ferguson	167
	Tim Woodin	Hwt
1961	Okla Johnson	115
	Norman Young	137
1965	Don Behm	130
	Jeff Richardson	Hwt
1966	Dale Anderson	130
	Dale Carr	137
	Mike Bradley	177
1967	Don Behm	130
	Dale Anderson	137
	Dale Carr	145
	George Radman	167
	Mike Bradley	177
1968	Dale Anderson	137
	Mike Bradley	177
	Jeff Smith	Hwt
1969	Gary Bissell	123
	Keith Lowrance	137
	John Abajace	152
	Tom Muir	160
	Jack Zindel	177
	Jeff Smith	Hwt
1970	Greg Johnson	118
	Tom Milkovich	134
	Keith Lowrance	142
	Jack Zindel	190
	Vic Mittelberg	Hwt
1971	Greg Johnson	118
	Tom Milkovich	134
	Gery Malecek	167
	Dave Ciolck	190
	Ben Lewis	Hwt
1972	Greg Johnson	118
	Pat Milkovich	126
	Tom Milkovich	142
	Ben Lewis	Hwt
1973	Tom Milkovich	142
1974	Pat Milkovich	126
1975	Larry Avery	Hwt
1976	Pat Milkovich	134
1979	Shawn Whitcomb	Hwt
1980	Jeff Thomas	126
1984	Mike Potts	Hwt
1995	Dan Wirnsberger	158
1996	David Morgan	118
	Brian Picklo	190
1997	David Morgan	118
1998	David Morgan	118
1999	Pat McNamara	133
2000	Nick Muzashvili	197

All Americans

Year	Name	Weight
1931	Harry Byam	135
1936	Walter Jacobs	158
1939	Dale Ball	123
1941	Merle Jennings	121
	Burl Jennings	128
	Bill Maxwell	136
	Charles Hutson	165
1942	Merle Jennings	121
	Burl Jennings	128
	Bill Maxwell	136
	Leland Merrill	155
1945	Cliff Fletcher	121
1946	Gale Mikles	145
1947	Donald Johnson	136
	Don Anderson	145
	Gale Mikles	155
1948	M. Gene McDonald	115
	Cliff Fletcher	121
	Ignatius Konrad	128
	Richard Dickenson	136.5
	Don Anderson	147
	Gale Mikles	160
	Bob Maldegan	Hwt
1949	Richard Dickenson	136
	Don Anderson	145
	Bob Maldegan	Hwt
1950	Gene Gibbons	165
1951	Gene Gibbons	167
1952	Orris Bender	167
1953	Eddie Casalicchio	130
	Bob Hoke	147
	Vito Perrone	157
1954	Jim Sinadinos	130
	Bob Hoke	157
1955	Jim Sinadinos	137
1956	Jim Sinadinos	137
1958	Don Stroud	130
	Jim Ferguson	167
	Tim Wooden	177
	Ken Maidlow	191
1959	Tim Woodin	191
1961	Norman Young	137
1962	Okla Johnson	115
	John Baum	Hwt
1963	Okla Johnson	115
1965	Don Behm	130
1966	Dale Anderson	130
	Dick Cook	152
	Jeff Richardson	Hwt
1967	Don Behm	130
	Dale Anderson	137
	Dale Carr	145
	George Radman	167
	Mike Bradley	177
	Jack Zindel	191
	Jeff Richardson	Hwt
1968	Dale Anderson	137
	Dale Carr	145
	Rodney Ott	177
	John Schneider	191
	Jeff Smith	Hwt

1969	Keith Lowrance	137
	Tom Muir	160
	Jack Zindel	177
	John Schneider	191
	Jeff Smith	Hwt
1970	Greg Johnson	118
	Tom Milkovich	134
	Keith Lowrance	142
	Pat Karslake	167
	Gerry Malecek	177
	Jack Zindel	190
	Vic Mittelberg	Hwt
1971	Greg Johnson	118
	Dave Ciolek	190
	Ben Lewis	Hwt
1972	Greg Johnson	118
	Pat Milkovich	126
	Tom Milkovich	142
	Richard Radman	158
	Gerry Malecek	167
1973	Tom Milkovich	142
1974	Pat Milkovich	126
1975	Pat Milkovich	126
	Larry Avery	Hwt
1976	Pat Milkovich	134
1977	Dennis Brighton	134
1979	Shawn Whitcomb	Hwt
1980	Jeff Thomas	126
1981	Shawn White	142
1982	Mike Potts	190
1983	Eli Blazeff	177
1984	Jim Mason	134
	Eli Blazeff	190
	Mike Potts	Hwt
1985	Ernie Blazeff	158
1986	Dan Matauch	134
	Dave Mariola	177
1993	Dan Wirnsberger	158
	Don Whipp	Hwt
1994	Dan Wirnsberger	158
	Emilio Collins	190
1995	Kelvin Jackson	118
	Brian Bolton	126
	Chad Bailey	150
	Dan Wirnsberger	158
	Emilio Collins	190
1996	David Morgan	118
	Phil Judge	142
	Joel Morissette	167
	Erich Harvey	177
	Brian Picklo	190
1997	David Morgan	118
	Brian Picklo	190
1998	David Morgan	118
	Pat McNamara	126
1999	Nick Muzashvili	197
2000	Pat McNamara	133
	Nick Muzashvili	197
2001	Chris Williams	125
	Pat McNamara	133
	Gray Maynard	157
	Nik Fekete	197
2002	Gray Maynard	157
2003	Gray Maynard	

Walter Jacobs Award

Awarded (since 1940) to the wrestler who has earned the largest number of team points during the season.

1940	Leland Merrill
1941	J. William Maxwell
	Leland Merrill
1942	Merle Jennings
1943	Merle Jennings
1944	no team—World War II
1945	Gale Mikles
1946	Gale Mikles

1947	Gale Mikles
1948	Gale Mikles
1949	Robert Maldegan
1950	Gene Gibbons
1951	Gene Gibbons
1952	Orris Bender
1953	Bob Hoke
1954	Bob Hoke
1955	Jim Sinadinos
1956	Jim Sinadinos
	Don Stroud
1957	Leroy Fladseth
1958	Ken Maidlow
1959	Tim Woodin
1960	John Baum
1961	George Hobbs
1962	John Baum
1963	Alex Valcanoff
1964	Homer McClure
1965	Don Behm
1966	Dick Cook
1967	Dale Anderson
1968	Jeff Smith
1969	Jeff Smith
1970	Keith Lowrance
1971	Dave Ciolek
1972	Gerry Malecek
1973	Tom Milkovich
1974	Pat Milkovich
1975	Larry Avery
1976	Pat Milkovich
1977	Mike Walsh
1978	Mike Walsh
1979	Shawn Whitcomb
1980	Shawn Whitcomb
1981	Steve Foley
1982	Greg Sargis
1983	Eli Blazeff
1984	Eli Blazeff
1985	Charles Root
1986	Dave Mariola
1987	Dan Matauch
1988	Dave Mariola
1989	Stacy Richmond
1990	Brian Smith
1991	Don Whipp
1992	Don Whipp
1993	Don Whipp
1994	Emilio Collins
1995	Kelvin Jackson
	Dan Wirnsberger
	Emilio Collins
1996	David Morgan
1997	David Morgan
1998	David Morgan
1999	Nick Muzashvili
2000	Nick Muzashvili
2001	Pat McNamara
2002	Gray Maynard
2003	Gray Maynard

Wins and Pins

MOST CAREER WINS

Years	Name	Wins
92-97	Erich Harvey	147
95-98	David Morgan	129
90-95	Dan Wirnsberger	120
81-84	Mike Potts	120
90-93	Don Whipp	119
90-95	Emilio Collins	115
98-01	Pat McNamara	115
96-99	Nick Muzashvili	110
81-84	Jim Mason	107
84-88	Dave Mariola	105

91-96	Joel Morissette	105
94-97	Brian Picklo	99
99-03	Gray Maynard	95
86-89	Stacy Richmond	95
70-73	Tom Milkovich	93
72-76	Pat Milkovich	90
91-96	Phil Judge	89
98-01	Mike Castillo	86
91-96	Brian Bolton	85
79-83	Fredd Worthem	84
86-90	Brian Smith	84

MOST SEASON WINS

95-96	David Morgan	44
97-98	David Morgan	44
94-95	Kelvin Jackson	42
96-97	David Morgan	41
96-97	Brian Picklo	41
83-84	Eli Blazeff	40
95-96	Erich Harvey	40
95-96	Brian Picklo	39
93-94	Mike Potts	38
94-95	Chad Bailey	37
94-95	Erich Harvey	37
96-97	Erich Harvey	37
82-83	Eli Blazeff	36
92-93	Dan Wirnsberger	36
95-96	Joel Morissette	36
98-99	Nick Muzashvili	36

MOST CAREER PINS

80-84	Jim Mason	45
81-84	Greg Sargis	42
80-84	Mike Potts	41
82-84	Eli Blazeff	40
92-97	Erich Harvey	35
89-93	Don Whipp	28
99-03	Gray Maynard	26
68-69	Jeff Smith	23
41-43	Merle Jennings	22
95-98	David Morgan	22
40-42	Leland Merrill	21
45-48	Gale Mikles	21

MOST SEASON PINS

83-84	Eli Blazeff	21
83-84	Mike Potts	21
82-83	Eli Blazeff	19
82-83	Greg Sargis	17
81-82	Greg Sargis	17
82-83	Jim Mason	15
96-97	Erich Harvey	14
68-69	Jeff Smith	13
81-82	Jim Mason	12
94-95	Erich Harvey	12
69-70	Jack Zindel	11
79-80	Shawn Whitcomb	11
02-03	Nick Simmons	11
40-41	Billy Maxwell	10
67-68	Jeff Smith	10
71-72	Gerry Malecek	10
80-81	JimMason	10
1985	Charles Root	10

BEST SEASON RECORDS

Years	Name	W L T
1967	Dale Anderson	25-0-0
1967	George Radman	24-0-0
1972	Tom Milkovich	23-0-0
1951	Gene Gibbons	16-0-0
1948	Richard Dickenson	14-0-0
1942	Merle Jennings	14-0-0

BEST CAREER WINNING
PERCENTAGE

Years	Name	W L T Pct.
41-43	Merle Jennings	37-1-0 .974
68-69	Jeff Smith	50-2-0 .962
45-48	Gale Mikles	44-2-0 .957
66-68	Dale Anderson	61-4-1 .932
95-98	David Morgan	129-10-0 .928
70-73	Tom Milkovich	93-7-1 .926
65-67	Don Behm	66-6-0 .917
58-59	Tim Woodin	22-2-0 .917
41-43	J. Wm. Maxwell	32-3-0 .914
70-72	Greg Johnson	54-5-2 .902

LETTERWINNERS

Abajace, John J. ...... WR 69, 71, 72
Abbott, A.O. ...... TR 1902
Abbott, David ...... SO 77, 78, 79, 80
Abbott, William ...... SO 77, 78, 79, 80
Abdo, Edward S. ...... FB 38, 39, 40
Abood, Andrew ...... GO 87
Abood, Jerome ...... GO 86, 87
Abou-El-Seoud, Easam ...... SO 73
Abraham, Craig ...... SO 94, 95, 96C
Abraham, Mark ...... BS 84, 85
Abraham, Richard J. ...... WR 54, 55
Abraham, Steven R. ...... FB 75
Abrams, Brice ...... FB 90, 91, 92, 93CoC
Abrecht, Jeffrey L. ...... FB 61, 62 / BS 62, 63
Abucham, Rodrigo ...... TN 2000, 01
Acino, Bart ...... GY 80, 81, 82, 83CoC
Ackerman, Holt ...... BX 48M
AcMoody, Samuel ...... BK 2000M, 01M, 02M, 03M
Acosta, Arthur ...... FB 58
Adamo, Vince ...... HO 95M, 96M, 97M
Adams, A. Gordon Jr. ...... FB 41M
Adams, Bryan ...... HO 96, 97, 98, 99CoC
Adams, Charles H. ...... BS 1896C, 97, 98
Adams, Dave ...... GY 90, 91, 92, 93
Adams, Eric ...... TN 95
Adams, Flozell ...... FB 94, 95, 96, 97
Adams, Howard J. ...... FB 52
Adams, Ken ...... BS 82
Adams, Paul ...... TR 80M
Adcock, Robert L. ...... TR 36, 37, 38
Adderley, Herbert A. ...... FB 58, 59 ,60
Addley, Jeffrey ...... HO 74, 75, 76, 77
Adler, Orville ...... TR 32, 33
Adolph, Bryce E. ...... FB 67M
Adolph, Fred P. ...... TR 20, 21, 22
Aenis, James E. ...... SW 60
Ager, Maurice ...... BK 2003
Agett, Albert H. ...... FB 34, 35, 36 / TR 34, 36
Agin, Brent ...... SO 91, 92, 93
Agnew, Thomas G. ...... FB 02
Ahlgren, Robert ...... SW 66
Aitch, Matthew ...... BK 66, 67C
Akana, Alan ...... FB 84, 85
Akers, Forrest H. ...... BS 06, 07
Akers, John ...... TR 84, 85, 86CoC
Akin, Wankeith ...... FB 83
Akpata, Solomon S. ...... TR 60, 61 / WR 61
Alban, Chad ...... HO 95, 96, 97, 98
Albaugh, Joe ...... BS 97, 98, 99, 2000
Albers, Matthew ...... HO 92, 93, 94
Albright, Joseph W. ...... GO 52, 53, 54C
Alcorn, William P. ...... TR 61
Alderman, A. LeRoy ...... TR 13, 14
Alderman, Fred P. ...... TR 25, 26, 27C
Alderson, Kenith O. ...... FB 70, 71, 72
Aldrich, Bruce D. ...... SW 52, 53, 54
Aldrich, Jared ...... TR 2000, 01 / CC 99, 2000CoC
Aldrich, Samuel R. ...... WR 37
Aleksanyan, Arsen ...... WR 2001, 03
Alexander, Aaron ...... BK 2002
Alexanderson, Earl M. ...... CC 51M
Alfsen, Albert H. ...... FB 1899
Allan, E. Thomas ...... FB 82, 83, 84
Allen, Eric B. ...... FB 69, 70, 71C / TR 70, 71
Allen, Gerald ...... TR 06, 07, 08, 09M / FB 07, 08
Allen, Henry R. ...... TR 1892
Allen, Wade W. ...... TR 35, 36
Allen, William C. ...... WR 58
Allen, Yakini ...... FB 92, 93, 94, 95CoC

Alley, Andrew ...... TR 2001 / CC 2000, 01, 02
Alling, Ronald V. ...... FB 37, 38, 39
Allmann, Robert M. ...... FB 34, 35
Allwardt, Robert K. ...... SW 43, 46, 47, 48C
Alozie, Sydney O. ...... SO 64
Alsup, John M. ...... WR 67, 68
Altobelli, Aldo ...... HO 57, 58
Altobelli, Dean ...... FB 83, 84, 85, 86
Alverson, Jasmin ...... TR 2000, 01CoC
Alward, Bradley ...... FB 89M
Alward, George ...... SW 69
Amacker, Matt ...... FB 91, 92
Amaya, Francisco ...... TN 81, 82
Amie, Jack M. ...... CC 64
Ammon, Harry R., Jr. ...... FB 63, 64
Amnon, Mike ...... FC 97
Amon, Jack R. ...... FB 39, 40C
Amori, Chuck ...... FB 78M, 79M, 80M
Amos, Henry C. ...... BX 50, 51C
Anagonye, Aloysius ...... BK 2000, 01, 02, 03CoC
Anastos, Thomas ...... HO 82, 83, 84, 85
Anderegg, Robert H. ...... BK 57, 58, 59C
Andersen, Duane ...... LA 78, 79, 80
Andersen, Morten ...... FB 78, 79, 80, 81
Andersen, Roger W. ...... GY 61M
Anderson, Alan ...... BK 2002, 03
Anderson, Bruce E. ...... LA 71
Anderson, Dale ...... WR 66, 67, 68
Anderson, Don E. ...... WR 45C, 47, 48, 49
Anderson, Earl ...... FB 68, 70
Anderson, Felix A. ...... TR 32M
Anderson, Gregory ...... FB 92, 93, 94
Anderson, John H. ...... FB 26, 27, 28
Anderson, Mark A. ...... FB 76, 77, 78, 79
Anderson, Michael ...... FB 86, 87, 88
Anderson, Michael ...... GO 88, 89, 90, 91C
Anderson, Paul J. ...... FB 24
Anderson, Valda R. ...... BK 29M
Anderson Warren J. ...... CC 39 / TR 40
Andreas, Jason ...... BK 2001, 02, 03
Andreoli, Robert L. ...... BS 42, 43
Andrews, C. Ward ...... BS 18, 19, 20 / FB 19
Andrews, Herbert ...... BS 19
Andrews, Vernon J. ...... FC 50
Andrews, Earl ...... GY 65
Andrie, Norman E. ...... BX 52, 54
Andry, Michael ...... BS 94, 95
Ane, Charles T. ...... FB 72, 73, 74
Angel, Anthony J. ...... FB 65
Angel, Juan ...... GO 91
Angyal, Todd ...... TN 89
Annesi, Genero M. ...... WR 58
Ansorge, William A. ...... BS 1893, 94, 95C
Anstey, Kenneth W. ...... HO 67, 68, 69CoC
Antonangeli, James ...... BS 94
Antonetti, Joseph ...... FC 62
Apisa, Robert ...... FB 65, 66, 67
Appleboom, Sidney ...... SW 86, 87, 88, 89CoC
Applegate, Richard ...... TN 87
Apsley, John ...... SW 75, 76, 77
Aquino, John ...... BS 62, 63
Arbanas, Fredrick V. ...... FB 58, 59, 60C
Arbogast, Arthur ...... TR 31
Arbury, James ...... FB 60M, 61M
Arce, Steve ...... SO 98, 99, 2000, 01CoC
Archbold, Harold K. ...... FB 21
Archer, Larry C. ...... FB 17, 18C, 19 / BK 18
Archer, Nick ...... SO 67, 68, 69
Archer, Robert L. ...... WR 63

Archer, William ...... BS 83, 84, 85
Arena, Anthony G. ...... FB 39, 41 / TR 42
Arend, Donald R. ...... FB 56, 58
Arkeilpane, David ...... HO 86, 87
Armstrong, Andrew ...... BS 03, 04, 05C, 06C
Armstrong, George W. ...... SW 37
Armstrong, Marc ...... SW 87C
Armstrong, Mark ...... BK 97M, 98M, 99M, 2000M
Armstrong, Robert E. ...... FB 32, 33, 34
Armstrong, Robert P. ...... HO 58, 59, 60
Armstrong, Sterling ...... FB 65, 66, 67
Armstrong, Theo. Robert ...... BK 53, 54, 55
Armstrong, William C. ...... BS 1899, 00
Arndt, Mayo L. ...... TR 47, 48, 49, 50
Arnest, Stephen R. ...... FC 59C, 60
Arnold, William Bradley ...... BS 85, 86
Arnold, David ...... GY 65
Arnold, James F. ...... CC 51
Arnott, Scobie I. ...... SW 53M
Arnson, Don ...... FB 44, 45, 46, 47
Arntz, Arthur B. ...... FB 44
Aronson, Fred ...... FB 44, TR 45
Arrington, Walter A. ...... TR 39, 40, 41C
Arteaga, Manuel R. ...... FC 38, 39C
Arthurs, Jeffrey ...... FB 75M, 76M, 77M
Asdigha, Kamran ...... SO 75, 76
Asher, Grant ...... TN 89, 90, 91, 92CoC
Asher, Jordan ...... TN 81, 83
Ashley, Amos H. ...... FB 03, 04
Askew, Matthias ...... FB 2001, 02
Aslin, Richard ...... CC 68
Asmah, John H. ...... SO 57, 58
Asman, Nick ...... LA 96
Asti, R. Trevor ...... SW 98, 99, 2000CoC
Atack, James ...... SO 59, 60, 61
Atcheson, Walter C. .. CC 47, 48, 49 / TR 47, 48, 49, 50
Atkin, Arthur W. ...... TR 16, 17, 19C, 20
Atkins, Hazen S. ...... TR 21, 22, 23C
Atterberry, Willie J. ...... TR 58, 60
Atwood, Michael D. ...... SW 63
Aubuchon, Chester J. ...... BK 39, 40, 42C
Audas, Sedric ...... FB 77, 79
Auer, Scott ...... FB 80, 81, 82, 83
Auffrey, Joe J. ...... TR 69
Auge, Robert L. ...... FC 50
Aurand, Rex H. ...... TR 32, 33
Aure, Ronald ...... GY 65, 66, 67
Austin, Charles O. ...... FB 49M
Austin, David ...... BS 85
Austin, Floyd E. ...... WR 34C
Austin, Matthew ...... FC 89, 90
Austin, Mike ...... FB 96, 97, 98, 99
Avellano, Anthony F. ...... WR 57
Avery, Henry ...... TR 1886, 87
Avery, Kenneth ...... BS 60, 61
Avery, Larry D. ...... WR 73, 74, 75
Axelson, Josh ...... BS 98, 99, 2000
Ayala, Reginald P. ...... BK 52, 53, 54
Ayotte, Scott ...... BS 92, 93, 94, 95CoC
Azar, George ...... FB 60, 61, 62 / BS 61, 62, 63
Azikiwe, Ayo ...... TR 63, 64
Babich, Richard ...... FB 84
Babinski, Scott ...... SO 97, 99, 2000, 01CoC
Bach, Brian ...... GO 88, 89, 90, 91
Bach, Jay D. ...... BS 62, 63, 64
Bacheler, Dan ...... SW 98, 99
Back, Robert ...... SO 75, 76, 77CoC
Bacon, Jeff ...... HO 79
Badaczewski, Joseph D. ...... FB 53, 54, 55

Badger, Albert E. .... GO 60, 61, 62
Baer, Charles .... FC 66, 67, 68C
Baerny, Marty .... GY 82, 83, 84CoC, 85C
Baes, Richard W. .... FB 74, 75, 76CoC
Bagdon, Ed .... FB 46, 47, 48, 49
Bagdon, Frank A. .... BS 47, 48, 49
Baggett, Charles A. .... FB 73, 74, 75CoC
Bagley, Patrick .... LA 85, 86, 87
Baguley, Keith .... TR 22, 23, 24C
Baicy, Joe .... SW 2000, 01, 02CoC
Bailey, Chad .... WR 95
Bailey, Charlie .... FB 66, 67, 68
Bailey, John .... BK 66, 67, 68C / GO 66,67, 68CoC
Bailey, Phillip F. .... FB 17
Bailey, Terry .... FB 80, 81
Baird, Donald, G. .... FB 67, 68, 69
Baird, Quentin .... FC 93
Baker, Albert H. .... FB 34
Baker, Charles .... BS 76, 77, 78
Baker, Chris .... FB 98, 99, 2000, 01
Baker, Corey .... FB 93, 94
Baker, Dennis K. .... SW 57, 59, 60
Baker, Harry D. .... TR 43
Baker, Harry L. .... BS 08, 09, 10C, 11 / TR 08
Baker, Hugh P. .... FB 1897, 98, 99
Baker, J, Fred .... BS 1900
Baker, Kenneth .... GY 96, 97, 98, 99
Baker, Kyle .... CC 96, 97CoC / TR 97CoC, 99CoC
Baker, Park F. .... FB 58, 59
Baker, Thomas .... GO 77, 78
Bakunas, Joseph .... BS 76
Balai, Joseph T. .... HO 56
Balasis, Michael .... FB 86
Balbach, Edward .... BK 1902, 03, 04C / TR 04
Baldino, Louis G. .... SO 74
Baldwin Irving .... TR 50M
Baldwin, Charles C. .... SW 52, 53, 54
Baldwin, Ernest W. .... FB 10
Baldwin, Kirk .... FB 94M
Baldwin, Patrick K. .... HO 61, 62, 63
Baldwin, Russell H. .... TR 1902
Baldwin, Tim L. .... GO 58, 59, 60
Baldwin, William W. .... FB 46
Balge, Kenneth E. .... FB 42, 46CoC, 47
Balhorn, Randall .... GY 70, 71, 72, 73CoC
Ball, B. Dale .... WR 39
Ball, Elton E. .... FB 20
Ball, Stanley .... WR 32, 33C
Ball, Walter J. .... FB 40
Ballard, Clint V. .... FB 11
Ballard, Donald .... BS 73, 74, 75
Ballinger, Adam .... BK 2000, 01, 02CoC, 03CoC
Ballman, Gary .... FB 59, 60, 61
Balogh, Eugene M. .... FC 50
Balthrop, George .... TR 65, 66, 67
Bancroft, H. Lee .... FB 11M
Banks, Carl .... FB 80, 81, 82CoC, 83C
Banks, Sean .... FB 97, 98
Banks, Tony .... FB 94, 95CoC
Banyon, Brendan .... CC 97, 98 / TR 96, 97, 98
Barbarito, Edward R. .... BS 47, 48
Barbas, Constantino J. .... FB 45, TR 46
Barber, Chris .... LA 87, 88, 89, 90CoC
Barber, Thomas K. .... SW 45
Barbour, James M. .... TR 43, 46
Barcroft, Glenn A. .... TR 10
Barcroft, John E. .... TR 09, 10
Bargwell, Steve .... SW 90, 91, 92
Barker, Arthur W. .... HO 56
Barker, Homer L. .... FB 73
Barker, Richard .... FB 57, 58
Barkley, Robert .... FC 84
Barley, Kenneth L. .... CC 53 / TR 53, 54
Barnard, John A. .... BS 29, 30, 31 / BK 32
Barnes, Daron .... BK 86M
Barnes, Norman .... HO 72, 73, 74
Barnes, Steven .... BS 80, 81, 82, 83C
Barnett, Clayton F. .... TR 14, 15, 16
Barnett, Harlon .... FB 86, 87, 88, 89CoC

Barnett, Michael D. .... BS 63
Barnett, William D. .... BK 10, FB 09
Barnum, Thomas E. .... FB 69, 70
Baron, Matt .... HO 98, 99M, 2000M, 01M
Barr, Douglas E. .... FB 69, 70, 71
Barr, Jeffrey H. .... HO 76, 77, 78, 79C
Barr, John H. .... BK 21
Barr, Ronald W. .... CC 51, 53
Barrell, Clark L. .... TR 17
Barratt, Fred W. .... BS 27 / FB 26
Barrett, Gary D. .... GO 59, 61, 62
Barrett, Robert .... HO 81, 82M
Barrie, Joseph H. .... FB 34, 35
Barrington, Gordon L. .... BS 36
Barron, Bruce A. .... SO 79
Barron, David .... GY 96, 97, 98, 99C
Barry, Arthur .... LA 80, 81
Barry, Joseph R. .... HO 52, 53
Barta, Joseph W. .... BS 48, 49 50
Bartels, Walter .... HO 88, 89, 90, 91CoC
Bartling, Irving H. .... BS 34, 35, 36C
Bartmess, Edward A. .... BS 1886
Bartolec, Brian .... GO 92, 93, 94CoC, 95CoC
Bartolec, Gregory .... GO 93, 94, 95, 96CoC
Bartos, Jon .... TR 85
Basich, Peter P. .... BK 40, 41
Bass, Dan E. .... FB 76, 77, 78, 79CoC
Bass, Julian R. .... BX 53
Bassett, Charles F. .... FB 17, 19, 20
Bassett, Donald B. .... WR 51
Bassett, Larry A. .... GY 60, 61, 62
Bastian, James J. .... TR 68, 69
Bastien, Rodger A. .... BS 76, 77, 78, 79
Batchelor, Daniel .... SW 81C
Batchelor, William .... FB 39, 40
Bates, Erving B. .... BS 1886, 87
Bates, Lindsey .... WR 75
Bates, Nick .... BS 2000, 01, 02
Bates, Roy E. .... TR 56
Bates, Steven .... BK 80, 81, 82
Bateson, George F. .... BS 1894, 95 / TR 1895
Bateson, Rueben E. .... BS 1894, 95
Bath, Edwin G. .... TR 31, 32, 33C
Bathrop, George .... CC 66
Battershell, Chris .... FB 2000M
Baty, Earnest, Jr. .... WR 73
Bauer, George T. .... FC 31C
Baum, Joe .... SO 66, 67, 68
Baum, John D. .... WR 58, 60, 62C
Bauman, Paul L. .... BK 45
Baver, Hugh .... BS 83
Baxter, Dave R. .... SW 76
Bayles, Kenneth .... SW 72M
Bayless, Paul A. .... TR 30
Baylor, Art .... BK 66, 67
Baynes, Carl D. .... BS 24, 26, 27
Bays, Richard P. .... LA 70
Bazant, Anthony J. .... SW 71, 72
Bazemore, Michael .... FB 2002
Beach, John J. .... LA 70, 71
Beachum, James C. .... TN 54, 55, 56
Beadle, Steve .... HO 87, 88, 89, 90
Beale, John .... FB 39M
Beam, John P. .... FC 65, 66
Bean, Stephen M. .... TN 60M,61M,62M
Beard, Matt .... FB 95, 96 / TR 93
Beard, Thomas L. Jr. .... FB 69, 70
Beardslee, Walter E. .... CC 41
Beardsley, William .... FB 42
Beathea, Daimon .... BK 93, 94, 95, 96
Beattie, Jack R. .... SW 54, 55, 56
Beatty, Charles .... WR 67M, 68M
Beatty, Howard E. .... TR 12, 13,1 4, 15C, 16 / FB 15
Beatty, Robert A. .... FC 83, 84, 85C
Beaty, Daniel .... HO 82, 83
Beaubien, Paul .... FB 36
Beaudet, Albert F. .... GY 70, 71, 72
Beaudoin, John .... WR 84, 86, 87
Beaudoin, Mark .... FB 82, 83, 84, 85

Beaudry, Eric .... WR 80, 81
Beaumont, Cleo E. .... TR 33, 34
Beauvais, Joseph W. .... BS 1893
Bechard, Joseph E. .... BS 48, 49, 50
Bechtold, J. Edward .... CC 33, 34, 35C
Beck, Brad .... HO 83, 84, 85, 86
Beck, Don M. .... BS 76
Beck, Jordan .... FB 85
Becker, Chris .... SW 90, 92
Becker, Henry L. .... FB 1896, 97
Becker, John T. .... SW 41, 42C
Becker, John .... GO 65
Becker, Jon .... GY 96, 97
Becker, Matt .... WR 93, 94, 95
Becker, Richard J. .... GY 58, 60
Beckley, Arthur K. .... FB 22, 23, 24 / BS 23, 24
Beckord, Raymond .... TR 45, 46
Beckstrom, J. J. .... GO 2001, 02, 03
Bedford, Jayson .... TN 92, 93, 94, 95CoC
Beebe, Channing D. .... BS 1899, 00C
Beechnau, Louis H. .... GY 48C
Beeman, Harris Frank .... TN 41, 42C, 43C
Beer, Greg .... SW 95, 96, 97, 98
Beery, Robert L. .... FB 69M
Beese, Arthur J. .... TR 1892, 93
Begeny, Joseph .... FB 62, 63
Beggs, Wallace J. .... BS 49
Behan, Mike .... TR 85
Behm, Donald .... WR 65, 66, 67
Behney, Melvin .... BS 67, 68
Behnke, Michael .... TN 86
Behrman, David .... FB 60, 61, 62
Behrmann, Michael .... LA 82, 83
Beinlich, Kurt .... WR 80, 81
Beitel, Daron .... BS 94, 95
Belen, David .... GO 79, 80, 81, 82
Beley, Chris .... TE 96
Belk, Veno .... FB 82, 83, 84, 85
Belknap, Leon V. .... BK 09, 89, 09
Belknap, Leslie H. .... BS 09
Bell, Anthony .... FB 82, 83, 84, 85CoC
Bell, Charlie .... BK 98, 99, 2000, 01CoC
Bell, Chris .... FB 81
Bell, Myron .... FB 90, 91, 92, 93
Bell, Preston C. .... SW 37
Bell, Robert Floyd .... FB 02, 03, 04C
Bell, Theodore .... FB 75
Bell, William D. .... SW 36, 37, 38C
Belland, Doug .... HO 79, 80
Bellefeville, Edward .... LA 74
Bello, Stephen .... GY 94, 95, 96
Belloli, Steve .... SO 89, 90, 91
Belloli, Nick .... SO 2002
Belloli, Thomas .... SO 65, 66, 67
Belmar, Fernando .... TN 85, 86, 87, 88
Belt, Thomas A. .... TR 26
Belton, Thomas W. .... TN 52, 53
Beltz, Lester L. .... TR 20
Bencie, Charles J. .... BK 56, 57, 58
Bencie, Luke .... FB 94, 95
Bender, G. Michael .... WR 73
Bender, George A. .... WR 49, 50, 51
Bender, Orris H. .... WR 50, 51, 52C
Bender, Timothy .... LA 71
Benedict, Richard R. .... FB 67, 68
Benford, Benny .... TR 95
Benington, John J. .... BK 72
Benjamin, Harlan L. .... TR 52, 53, 54
Benjamin, S. Rudy .... BK 69, 70, 71C
Bennett, Byron D. .... BK 32M
Bennett, Kemp D. .... SW 73
Bennett, Ralph E. .... FB 38, 39
Bennett, Wilfred P. .... TR 42, 43
Benoist, John .... SO 97, 98, 99C, 2000C
Benore, Aaron .... SW 2001, 02, 03
Benson, Hubert E. .... FB 63
Benson, Ken C. .... GO 64, 65, 66C
Benson, Rodney .... TR 84, 85, 86CoC
Benson, Steve .... GO 66, 67, 68CoC

Benson, Thomas L. .... SW 75, 76
Benson, Wayne E. .... FB 50, 51, 52
Benson, Wayne III .... GO 81
Bentley, S. Rahn .... FB 62, 63, 64
Benton, Chandler .... FC 54
Benus, John A. .... SO 61
Berby, Ronald F. .... CC 61, 62, 63 / TR 63
Bercich, Robert E. .... FB 57, 58, 59
Berens, Sean .... HO 95, 96, 97, 98CoC
Beresford, Bruce .... LA 83
Berg, John C. .... BS 34, 35
Berger, Donald .... FB 55, 56, 57
Berger, Douglas .... TN 75
Bergin, Gerald P. .... HO 52, 53
Bergin, Joseph .... FB 86, 87
Bergman, Troy .... BS 99, 2000, 01CoC
Bergquist, Allerd W. .... WR 27C
Bergstrom, Wayne R. .... GY 61, 62
Berlin, Joseph W. .... LA 77
Berlinski, Richard A. .... FB 66, 67, 68
Berman, Edward .... TR 51
Berman, Marc .... LA 83, 84, 85
Bernard, Lacey .... FB 56
Bernardin, Dave .... GY 97
Bernart, William F. .... TR 1891, 92, 93 / BS 1894
Bernecker, Scott .... BK 90M, 91M, 92M, 93M
Bernitt, Richard O. .... BS 42, 43
Bernstein, Mike .... SW 78
Berry, Richard N. .... FC 52, 53C
Berry, Richard O. .... BS 42, 43
Berry, Robert L. .... FB 69
Berry, William E. .... BK 62, 63, 64 / TR 62, 63
Bertelsen, Phillip E. .... SO 71, 72, 73, 74
Besanceney, Chris .... FB 88, 89, 90, 90M
Bessler, Lawrence .... LA 82
Best, George R. .... TR 55, 56, 57
Best, Ward E. .... FC 80
Bethea, Larry .... FB 74, 75, 76, 77 CoC
Betterley, Patrick M. .... HO 75, 76, 78
Betts, Demond .... WR 91, 92, 94
Beuter, John H. .... BX 55, 56M
BeVan, Geraint .... TR 97
Beverly, Walker .... TR 63, 64
Bewley, David .... BS 71
Beyer, George J. .... BK 45
Beyer, Howard .... FB 42
Bibbens, Cleveland .... BK 82
Bibbins, Arthur Leal .... BS 12, 13, 14, 15C
Bickel, Duane C. .... BS 73, 74, 75
Bickers, John .... LA 96
Bidiak, Terry .... SO 65, 66, 67M
Biedenbach, John C. .... BS 64, 65, 66
Bielat, Lawrence J. .... FB 57, 58, 59
Bielat, Scott .... FB 83M, 84M, 85M, 87M
Bielski, Daniel N. .... BS 68, 69
Bierman, Kim .... LA 80M
Bierowicz, Donald J. .... FB 64, 65
Bierwirth, James .... FC 75, 76
Bigane, Michael .... SW 72
Bigelow, Charles A. .... SW 41, 42
Bigelow, Rolla L. .... FB 1898
Bigford, Douglas .... SO 73, 74, 75, 76CoC
Bigford, Thomas .... SO 71, 72
Bignell, George A. .... TR 06, 07, 08, 09
Bilkey, Robert B. .... BK 24
Billian, Douglas .... TN 82M, 83M
Billig, Robert F. .... GO 47C, 48
Billings, Richard A. .... BS 63, 64, 65C
Binder, Nick .... SO 2001, 02
Binge, Ronald E. .... BK 70
Binkowski, Thomas E. .... BS 66, 67, 68C
Biondo, Michael H. .... FB 60
Birchmeier, Mark .... FB 92, 93, 94CoC
Bird, John C. .... SO 58
Bird, Ralph C. .... BS 06
Birnbaum, Herman A. .... TR 42M
Birney, Thomas F. .... FB 74, 75, 76, 77
Birtsas, Tim .... BS 81, 82
Bisard, William .... TN 56, 57, 58C
Bisgeier, Benjamin .... FC 40
Bishop, Judson E. .... FB 1896
Bishop, Randy .... BK 79M, 80M
Bishop, Richard T. .... GO 52
Bissell, Gary .... WR 67, 69, 70
Bissell, James .... WR 73, 74, 75
Bissell, Warren .... SW 36
Bitner, Gerald .... BS 90
Bitter, Terry .... BS 86, 88, 89
Black, Allan R. .... SW 36, 37, 38
Black, Donald D. .... FB 45
Black, Gerald D. .... BX 51, 52
Black, Steve .... FB 88. 90
Blackburn, Bruce .... FB 38, 39, 40
Blackburn, Joe .... HO 98, 99, 2000, 01
Blacklock, Hugh M. .... FB 13, 14, 15, 16 / TR 15
Blackman, Mark S. .... FB 45, 46, 47, 48
Blair, William B. .... HO 50, 51C
Blalark, Terry .... SO 70, 71, 72
Blanchard, Charles M. .... BK 1901C, 02 / FB 1900, 01 / TR 1902, 03C
Blanchard, James .... SO 85, 86, 87, 88
Blanchard, Richard D. .... BS 50, 51
Blank, Steve .... FB 80, 81
Blase, John .... LA 94, 95
Blazeff, Eli .... WR 83, 84
Blazeff, Ernest .... WR 83, 84, 85
Blazejewski, Richard J. .... SW 60, 61, 62
Blenkhorn, James .... FB 46, 47, 48, 49
Blight, James .... BS 66
Bloch, Louis P. .... BS 48, 49, 50
Block, Terrance J. .... CC 54, 55, 56 / TR 55
Blood, Douglas K. .... WR 62M
Bloom, Dan .... FC 77
Blostein, Jay .... HO 75M, 76M, 77M
Blount, Dale M. .... FC 55
Blount, Harry M. .... FC 54, 55
Blue, William W. .... TR 10, 11, 15
Bluem, Mark .... BK 92, 93
Blumke, Sam .... TR 90, 91, 92
Bly, Mark .... BS 2003
Boak, W. Bryan .... FB 81
Bobbitt, James .... FB 60, 61, 62
Bobbitt, Paul .... FB 83, 84, 85, 86
Bobchick, Gregory .... WR 84
Bobel, Jay .... BS 84, 85, 86
Bobich, Louis L. .... FB 62, 63, 64
Bobo, Douglas M. .... FB 51, 52
Bodary, Charles E. .... BS 53
Bodary, Jeff .... BS 78
Bodine, John .... SW 85, 87
Bodoh, Robert B. .... TR 43
Boehringer, Rudolph E. .... FB 25, 26
Boeskool, Randall D. .... BK 31, 32
Bogart, Robert .... LA 77
Bogas, Christopher .... HO 96, 97, 98, 99
Bogdalek, Steven .... FB 83, 84, 85
Boggs, Chris .... TR 71
Bogle, Andrew .... HO 98, 99, 2000, 01
Bograkos, Timothy .... BK 2002, 03
Bograkos, Timothy G. .... BK 69, 70 / BS 69, 70
Bohn, Ted .... FB 67
Bois, Richard .... HO 66, 67, 68
Boisvert, Harry .... SO 95
Boland, John .... BS 76
Bolden, LeRoy .... FB 51, 52, 53, 54C
Boles, Denis .... SO 67, 68, 69
Boles, Emerson .... WR 64, 65
Boles, Kevin .... SO 68
Bologlu, Ali .... SO 60
Bolster, Maurice W. .... BS 41
Bolte, Gregory .... FB 83
Bolton, Brian .... WR 93, 94, 95, 96CoC
Bolton, Darl .... HO 73, 74, 75, 76
Bolton, George L. .... HO 51, 53, 56
Bonacci, Anthony O. .... HO 57
Bond, James A. .... FB 71, 72
Bond, Robert C. .... TR 62M
Bongiorni, Mario .... FB 90
Bonito, Matt .... FB 98, 99, 2000
Booker, Ulish .... FB 2000, 01
Boomsliter, George P. .... FB 04, 05
Booth, David .... HO 2003
Borgman, Paul G. .... BS 19M
Boring, Burl J. .... WR 46, 47
Boring, Tim .... CC 98
Born, Brandon .... FB 86, 87
Boron, Kevin .... FB 92
Borovich, Jon .... BK 02M, 03M
Borowski, Will .... GO 96, 97
Borre, Michael .... SW 79, 81
Borton, Thomas E. .... WR 58
Bos, John .... FB 18, 19, 20, 21C
Bosma, Al .... TR 85
Boss, Fred .... WR 76
Boss, Gerald H. .... CC 35, 36, 37 / TR 35, 36, 37
Bosscawen, Gregory B. .... GY 80, 81, 82C, 83CoC
Bostic, Herb .... BK 80, 81, 82
Boucher, Thomas .... HO 58, 60, 61
Boudreaux, Robert .... BX 55
Boukamp, John .... TN 77
Bouma, Robert .... BK 67M, 68M / FB 67
Boutell, William H. .... FB 57M
Bouyer, Willie L. .... FB 85, 86, 87, 88
Bowdell, Gordon B. .... FB 68, 69, 70C
Bowditch, John J. .... BS 1903, 04 / FB 06
Bowen, D. Nicholas .... SO 77, 78,79CoC, 80 CoC
Bowen, Jan A. .... TR 63, 64, 65 / CC 62, 63
Bowen, Robert C. .... GO 43
Bowen, Thomas .... HO 73, 74
Bower, William R. .... BS 50, 51, 52C / BK 50, 51, 52
Bowerman, Francis E. .... TR 47, 48, 49, 50
Bowers, Charles P. .... FB 51, 52
Bowers, John E. .... TR 65, 66, 67
Bowers, Michael J. .... TR 65, 66, 67
Bowman, Bradley .... SO 70M
Bowman, Gary R. .... HO 58
Bowman, Thomas Y. .... LA 70
Boyce, Gary C. .... FB 68, 69 / BS 69, 70, 71
Boyd, Leo J. .... FB 51, 52
Boyd, Michael .... TR 82
Boyd, Robert .... HO 71, 72, 73
Boyd, Samuel K. .... TR 1888, 89
Boyer, Shawn .... TR 84
Boyle, Jesse G. .... BS 05, 06 / FB 05, 06
Boyle, Michael .... SW 69, 70, 71
Boylen, Fred J. .... FB 58, 59, 60C
Brabham, Edger C. .... TR 54, 55, 56
Brackett, Richard H. .... SW 66
Bradbury, Debbie .... GY 74M
Braden, Ralph L. .... TN 55
Bradford, Daniel W. .... TR 1888, 91
Bradford, James .... SW 72, 73, 74, 75
Bradley, Charles T. .... BS 12
Bradley, James .... FB 89, 90
Bradley, Jarion .... TR 93, 94, 95, 96
Bradley, Jason .... FB 2001
Bradley, Leon H. .... TR 33
Bradley, Michael B. .... FC 74, 75, 76, 77
Bradley, Michael .... WR 66,67, 68 / FB 66
Bradow, James .... GO 75
Bradow, Richard A. .... GO 70, 71, 72CoC
Bradshaw, Robert .... BS 72M
Brady, Jacob O. .... BS 22, 23 /FB 20, 21, 22 / TR 21
Brafford, William .... GO 72, 73, 74, 75CoC
Bragiel, Jason .... SW 96
Brainard, Charles .... TN 67, 68
Brainard, Walton K. .... BS 1899M /FB 1897C, 01
Brakeman, James R. .... FB 34
Brammer, Mark .... FB 76, 77, 78, 79CoC
Brand, Louis J. .... FB 42
Brand, Thomas H. .... GO 36, 38
Brandell, Scott .... BS 98, 99, 2000, 01CoC
Brandstatter, Arthur F. .... FB 34, 35, 36
Brandstatter, Arthur F., Jr. .... FB 59, 60, 61
Brandstatter, Brody .... HO 98, 99, 2000
Brandt, J.P. .... WR 85M, 86M
Brannum, Robert W. .... BK 48C
Brasington, Scott .... CC 80 / TR81

Braun, Charlie ... BS 2000, 01, 02, 03CoC
Braun, Norwin W. ... BK 49M
Brauning, Dennis W. ... FC 80
Brause, Alberto ... TE 96
Brawley, Robert L. ... FB 65, 66 / HO 65, 66, 67
Brecher, Sidney R. ... TR 41, 42, 43
Breck, Samuel L. ... HO 51M
Breen, Gerald M. ... FC 55,56
Breen, Gerald ... FB 29, 30
Bremer, Chris-Carol ... SW 93, 94
Bremer, Ernest K. TR 37, 38, 39 / FB 36, 37, 38 / BS 37
Bremer, Robert K. ... BS 27
Bremer, William M. ... TN 63
Brendel, Anthony J. ... TR 19, 21, 22
Brendel, William J. ... TR 52, 53, 54
Breniff, Robert G. ... FB 52
Brennan, Joseph ... SW 2000, 01, 02, 03CoC
Brenner, Allen ... FB 66, 67, 68C
Brentar, Jerome A. ... WR 47, 48
Breslin, Brian S. ... BK 71, 72, 74
Breslin, Jacwier ... FB 44, 45C / BS 45C, 46
Breslin, Jacwier Jr. ... FB 68, 69, 70
Breslin, John T. ... FB 74, 75, 76
Brevitz, Bruce R. ... TN 49
Brewer, Eugene S. ... TR 1900
Brewton, Gregory ... FB 74, 75 / TR 75
Breza, James ... GY 55, 56, 57
Brezny, Robert M. ... FC 48
Bricker, Paul ... LA 82
Bridges, Lloyd ... TR 70
Briggs, DeArmond ... TN 70, 71
Brigham, G. Hobart ... BK 18
Brightman, Alan H. ... SW 37, 38C
Brighton, Dennis ... WR 75, 77, 78
Brimm, James ... WR 98, 99, 2000
Brind'Amour, Rod ... HO 89
Briningstool, Anthony ... FB 88, 89, 90, 91
Brinkman, Gregory ... LA 77, 78, 79, 80 CoC
Brinkman, Rick ... LA 75
Brinn, David ... SO 69M
Bristol, Cornelius G. ... HO 50, 51
Bristol, Ralph W. ... FC 34
Bristol, Robert W. ... FC 52, 53
Britton, Dean R. ... TN 54
Brkovich, Donald ... BK 79
Brkovich, Michael ... BK 78, 79, 80, 81 CoC
Broadway, William V. ... FB 75
Broadwell, Scott ... GO 76
Broadwell, Steven ... GO 72, 73, 74, 75CoC
Brodin, Glenn H. ... SO 79, 81
Brogan, David H. ... TN 54, 55, 56C
Brogan, John C. ... TN 54, 55C
Brogan, Timothy ... FB 87
Brogger, Robert H. ... FB 44
Bromley, William ... LA 79
Bronson, Arthur A. ... GY 54
Brookens, Harold A. ... BK 59, 61
Brooks, Doug ... LA 86
Brooks, Mark ... GO 76, 77, 78CoC
Brooks, Quinton ... BK 93, 94, 95, 96CoC
Brooks, Raynard E. ... HO 51, 52, 53
Brooks, Robert A. ... FC 62, 63CoC
Brose, Alfred E. ... BS 32
Brose, Leonard D. ... TN 50, 51C
Brothers, Kenneth ... HO 77
Brown, Alfred ... BK 77, 78
Brown, Amos ... CC 74 / TR 75
Brown, Arthur Lynn BS 15, 16, 21, 22C / FB 16 / BK 22
Brown, C. Dean ... TR 36M
Brown, Charles E. ... FB 61, 62, 63
Brown, Charles M. ... BS 34 / FB 33
Brown, Clark ... FB 83, 84
Brown, Cullen ... SO 93, 94, 95, 96
Brown, Damon ... TR 85M
Brown, Daniel R. ... BS 53, 54
Brown, David E. ... FB 72, 73
Brown, Eddie ... FB 89, 90
Brown, Gavin A. ... BS 26M
Brown, Gregory B. ... SW 67, 68, 69
Brown, Haxen N. ... BS 1896
Brown, Kevin ... GY 90, 92, 93, 94
Brown, Kyle ... FB 2002
Brown, Lauren H. ... BS 30M
Brown, Lauren P. ... CC 27, 28, 29 / TR 28, 29, 30C
Brown, Luke ... BK 98M, 99M, 2000M, 01M
Brown, Mark ... BK 86
Brown, Michael ... SW 81, 82, 83, 84CoC
Brown, Neil P. ... FB 62
Brown, Newell ... HO 81, 82, 83, 84C
Brown, Peg ... BS 82M, 83M, 84M
Brown, Ray L. ... TR 1898, 99
Brown, Richard ... FB 97, 2000
Brown, Robert A. ... TR 13C, 14
Brown, Robert F. ... TR 55
Brown, Roland M. ... GY 57
Brown, Steven ... HO 84M, 85M, 86M, 87M
Brown, Thomas B. ... FB 71, 72
Brown, William L. ... FB 74
Brown., Chris ... TR 89, 90, 91CoC, 92, 93CoC
Browsh, Gani ... GY 60, 61, 62
Brubaker, Jason ... WR 95M
Bruce, Sean ... BS 88, 89
Bubacz, Tony ... BS 97
Bruce-Okine, Emanuel ... SO 58, 59
Bruckner, Leslie C. ... FB 37, 38, 39 / TR 39, 40
Bruesch, John ... SW 96, 98CoC, 99CoC
Bruggenthies, Anthony ... FB 74, 75, 76
Brumm, Lynn S. ... BS 12M
Brundage, Chris ... SW 90, 91
Brundage, Joseph E. ... CC 37M
Brunette, Ralph H. ... FB 30, 31, 32
Brunk, James ... LA 96
Brunnschweiler, Peer ... SO 74, 78
Brusseau, Michael ... HO 96, 97
Brusselbach, Jack ... TR 15, 16C
Bryan, Duron ... FB 99, 2000, 01
Bryan, Paul S. ... CC 65
Bryan, Tim ... FB 90, 91, 92
Bryce, Richard ... FB 2001, 02
Buck, Charles W. ... TR 43M
Buck, Conrad F. ... HO 51, 52C
Buckingham, William J. ... WR 49, 50, 51
Buckridge, Francis P. ... FB 1900
Budde, Donald J. ... BS 49M
Budde, Edward ... FB 60, 61, 62
Budde, John ... FB 85, 86, 87, 88
Burdett, Raymond A. ... SO 57
Budinski, John ... FB 38
Bufe, Noel C. ... FB 55, 56
Buggs, Travis ... FB 54 / TR 54, 55
Bullach, Melville E. ... BS 28, 29 ,30
Bullock, Clarence ... FB 72, 73, 74CoC
Bullock, Robert ... HO 81
Bullough, Charles ... FB 88, 89, 90, 91
Bullough, Henry ... FB 52, 53, 54
Bullough, Shane ... FB 83, 84, 85, 86C
Bulson, Albert E. ... BS 1886, 87, 88
Bunbury, J. Christopher ... FB 77
Bunce, Michael ... WR 85, 86, 87
Bunch, Derek ... FB 80, 83, 84
Bunn, William K. ... WR 64
Burchill, Kenneth Q. ... BK 51M
Burde, John ... BS 67M, 68M
Burge, Fredrick L. ... FB 38M
Burgering, David ... SW 75, 76, 77, 78
Burgess, Jeff ... BK 2002M, 03M
Burgess, William G. ... TR 33
Burgett, Glenn E. ... TR 57, 58
Burk, William R. ... BK 41, 42
Burke, Oliver W ... BS 03, 04, 05C
Burke, Patrick ... SW 70
Burke, Patrick F. ... FB 55, 56, 57C
Burke, Robert ... SW 68, 69, 70
Burke, Tom ... FB 69M
Burke, William ... FB 96, 97, 98,99
Burkett, Michael ... HO 91, 92, 93, 94
Burlingame. Mark V. ... BS 25M
Burnett, Leonder L. ... TR 1888, 89, 90, 91, 92 / BS 1889, 90, 91C, 92
Burnley, Khary ... TR 96
Burns, Brian ... FB 2001
Burrell, Orange B. ... TR 04, 05
Burress, Plaxico ... FB 98, 99
Burrill, Brady ... BS 2000, 01, 02, 03CoC
Burrington, Gray K. ... BS 03 / FB 02
Burroughs, Charles G. ... FB 05, 06, 08 / TR 05, 06, 07
Burroughs, James ... FB 77, 78, 79, 81
Burtch, James E ... CC 55M
Busch, Fred ... BK 10, 11C / BS 09, 10, 11
Busch, George A., Jr. ... GO 42
Busch, Guy ... SO 65, 66, 67CoC
Busch, Timothy ... SO 88
Buschman, Melvin ... TR 41, 42, 43
Buse, John ... TN 67, 68, 69
Bushnell, Elwood P. ... TR 09
Buss, Arthur ... FB 31, 32, 33 / TR 32, 33, 34
Butchee, LaRue ... TR 70, 71, 72
Buterakos, James ... BS 78, 79, 80, 81
Buth, George ... GO 67, 68
Butland, Josh ... FB 88, 89, 90, 91
Butler, Carl ... FB 83, 84
Butler, Charles O. ... FB 15, 16
Butler, Frank A. Jr. ... FB 71
Butler, Frank J. ... FB 32, 33
Butler, Harry L. ... CC 36, 37 / TR 37
Butler, Jeffrey ... SW 84, 85
Butler, John H. ... BX 55, 56, 57
Butler, Neil H. ... SO 57, 58
Butzirus, Gregory ... BS 79, 80
Buys, Joe D. ... SW 65
Buysse, Maurice J. ... BK 34, 36
Buzak, Michael ... HO 92, 93, 94, 95
Buzenberg, Robert J. ... BS 38M
Byam, Harry S. ... WR 31
Byington, Walter M. ... WR 62, 63, 64C
Byram, Jack L. ... WR 58
Byrd, Charles ... TR 74, 75, 76, 77
Byrd, Eugene W. ... FB 75, 76, 78, 79
Byrne, Aaron ... GY 95
Byrne, Gerald ... BS 28, 29
Byrne, Keith M. ... BS 30, 31
Byrnes, Kevin ... SO 71, 72
Byrum, Robert G. ... WR 68
Cady, Earl C. ... TR 41
Cahill, Kelly ... HO 74, 75, 76
Cain, Gerald ... TR 80, 81
Calder, Mark ... HO 71, 72, 73, 74
Calderone, Sam ... BS 61, 62, 63
Calendar, Conrad A. ... WR 72, 73, 74
Calhoun, George H. ... SW 37
Calkins, Charles F. ... BX 43
Callahan, Leo A. ... BK 37, 38, 39C
Callendar, Stan ... FB 91, 92, 93, 94
Callinicos, James D. ... FB 61M
Callow, Richard ... TN 75
Caluory, Francis D. ... TR 36, 38
Calvert, William W. ... HO 50, 51
Cammett, Bryan ... HO 77
Camp, David ... SO 74, 75, 76, 77
Campanini, Henry P. ... HO 53, 54, 55
Campbell, Amp ... FB 96, 97, 98CoC, 99
Campbell, Arthur L. ... FB 06, 07, 08, 09 / BK 09, 10M / TR 09, 10
Campbell, Daswell ... TR 65, 66, 67
Campbell, David J. ... WR 66, 67
Campbell, Douglas ... GY 77, 78
Campbell, James F. ... FB 08, 09, 10
Campbell, Jason ... BS 94
Campbell, Jon ... FB 90
Campbell, Joseph ... HO 76, 77, 78
Campbell, Leroy W. ... FB 11, 12
Campbell, Robert ... HO 71, 72
Campbell, Scott ... SO 77, 78, 79, 80
Campbell, Stuart ... WR 86
Campbell, Thomas Randy ... GY 68, 69
Campbell, Troy ... GO 66, 67CoC, 68
Campion, Robert ... BS 77
Canfield, Birkley K. ... BS 1886, 87, 89C
Canfield, Russell S. ... BS 04, 05, 06, 07C

Cantillon, Daniel	FC 96, 97C	
Cantini, Ron	WR 81, 82, 83, 85	
Cantrell, Daniel	FB 95	
Cantrell, Harmon W.	TR 36, 37	
Caplin, T. Tyler	GO 60	
Cappaert, Carl W.	FB 46, 47, 48, 49	
Cappaert, Francis J.	TR 46	
Carey, Charles L.	FB 40	
Carey, Owen	FB 09	
Carey, Robert W.	FB 49, 50, 51C / BK 50, 51, 52 / TR 50, 51, 52	
Carey, William R.	BK 51, 52 / FB 49, 50, 51	
Carl, Scott	SW 90, 91, 92, 93	
Carleton, Monroe P.	TR 08, 10	
Carlson, Arnold O.	CC 27M	
Carlson, Charles R.	BS 50, 51, 52	
Carlson, Ernest F.	TR 17	
Carlson, Glen	TR 95	
Carlson, Gustaf F.	BS 51, 52, 53 / HO 51	
Carlson, Leif M.	BK 50, 51, 52	
Carlson, Sherman F.	BK 27M	
Carlson, Stephen	CC 77, 78	
Carlstrom, Emil H.	TR 48	
Carmen, Robert E.	GY 61, 63	
Carnahan, Rene P.	GY 48, 49	
Carnaghi, Brian	FB 93M	
Carpenter, Frank G.	TR 1900, 01, 02	
Carpenter, William E.	BK 37, 38 / TR 37, 38, 39	
Carr, Dale	WR 66, 67, 68	
Carr, Gary	HO 74	
Carr, George L.	FC 52	
Carr, Harry F.	SW 37, 38	
Carr, James M.	TR 58, 59, 60	
Carr, Nels R.	BS 19, 20, 21	
Carr, Ralph J.	TR 06, 07, 08C	
Carr, Vernon	BK 86, 87	
Carrier, Lyman	TR 01	
Carrier, Robert	TR 43	
Carrigan, Cornelius R.	FB 47	
Carrington, Matthew	BK 83	
Carrio, Louis	SO 81	
Carrow, Rick	BS 72	
Carruthers, Joseph D.	FB 55, 56, 57	
Carruthers, Robert H.	BK 31M	
Carter, Amien A.	TR 46	
Carter, Anson	HO 93, 94, 95, 96CoC	
Carter, Devarrio	FB 97	
Carter, Fred L.	FB 39, 40, 41	
Carter, John M.	BS 58, 59	
Carter, Nigea	FB 93, 94, 95, 96	
Carter, Roland	TR 65, 66, 67, 68	
Carter, Steve	TN 77, 78	
Cartwright, Paul	LA 79	
Cartwright, Wade R.	BS 59, 60, 61	
Caruso, Aaron	LA 87, 88, 90	
Caruso, John I.	BS 27, 28	
Carver, Francis T.	TR 20, 22	
Casalicchio, Eddie	WR 52, 53, 54	
Casavola, John J.	TR 37, 39	
Case, Albert H.	FB 1899, 00, 01C	
Case, Athol A.	FB 03	
Case, Ralph W.	BS 1899, 01, 02 / FB 1899	
Casey, Zack	BS 94, 95, 96, 97	
Cash, Santiago	TN 86, 87, 88, 89	
Cashard, David	SO 71	
Cashen, Henry	LA 73, 74, 75	
Casler, Jeff	BK 89, 90, 91	
Cassleman, Chris	TR 73, 74, 75, 76	
Cassleman, Robert	TR 71, 72, 73, 74	
Castellani, Rudolph J.	BS 45	
Castillo, Michael	WR 98, 99, 2000, 01CoC	
Castle, Brian F.	TR 58, 59, 60	
Castle, Donnard L.	CC 60, 61, 62C / TR 62, 63	
Catanzarite, Bruce	WR 85	
Cattrysee, Alan	BS 2003	
Caudell, Chris	FB 85, 86	
Caufman, Todd	GY 90, 91, 92, 93	
Caukin, Elmer A.	FB 12	
Cavender, Regis	FB 66, 67, 68	
Cawood, John F.	BK 43, 47	
Cawood, William	BK 80, 81, 82, 83CoC	
Cebul, Scott	LA 93, 94, 95, 96CoC	
Cerez, Steve	BS 70, 71, 72, 73	
Ceskowski, Joseph A.	BX 40	
Cessna, S. Roger	TN 45, 46, 47C	
Chada, William H.	FB 71	
Chaddock, Frank G.	FB 12, 14	
Chadwick, Jerry H.	SW 58, 59, 60	
Chaffin, Mike	WR 78	
Chait, William	LA 76, 77	
Chalmers, David	GO 74	
Chamberlain, Clark S.	CC 29, 30C, 31C / TR 30, 31C, 32	
Chamberlain, Maurice L.	FB 85, 86, 87	
Chamberlain, Ralph	BK 10, 11, 12C, 13M / FB 12M / TR 10	
Chambers, John A.	FC 80, 81C, 82	
Chandik, John	HO 61, 62, 63	
Chandler, Stanley L.	BK 62	
Chandnois, Lynn E.	FB 46, 47, 48, 49 / BK 47	
Chang, Kai	LA 89, 90, 91, 92	
Chapman, Clayton W.	BS 04	
Chapman, Marcus	FB 95	
Chapman, Robert	BK 75, 76, 77C, 78CoC	
Chappell, Mike	BK 2000, 01	
Chappie, Clarence	FC 65	
Charboneau, Ernest R.	BX 47, 48, 49, 50	
Charest, Georges	HO 69	
Charette, Mark S.	FB 70, 71, 72	
Charlebois, Steve	CC 90CoC	
Charles, Ronald	BK 77, 78, 79, 80CoC	
Charon, Carl H.	FB 59, 60, 61 / BS 61	
Charter, Brien	GO 47	
Chartos, William	FB 39	
Chase, Albert B.	BS 1891, 93	
Chase, David W.	FC 53	
Chase, George L.	BS 1886, 87, 89 / TR 1887, 88, 89	
Chastain, James W.	FB 58, 59	
Chatlos, George	FB 65, 66, 67	
Chaurest, Michel	HO 70, 71, 72, 73	
Checco, Albert	HO 60, 61	
Checkett, Chester	SO 62, 63, 64	
Chen, Jason	TN 99, 2000, 01	
Cherocci, James	FB 86	
Cherry, Steve	BK 98, 99, 2000	
Chesney, M. James	FB 60	
Chiappetta, Marc	GY 2000, 01	
Childers, Jeff	BS 90, 91, 92	
Childers, Matthew	GY 2001	
Childs, Dennis	FB 84	
Childs, Donald M.	FB 02	
Childs, Harold A.	TR 1902 / FB 02	
Chiljean, Malcolm	BS 62, 63, 64C	
Chilton, Elmer	BS 14	
Chilton, Leslie	BS 14	
Chlopan, Roy	BS 41, 42, 43C	
Christ, Daniel	LA 84, 85, 86 CoC, 87 CoC	
Christ, James	GO 78	
Christel, Thomas	SW 86	
Christensen, Brett	SO 91, 92, 93	
Christensen, Koester L.	FB 26, 27, 28	
Christensen, Matt	FB 91, 92, 93, 94	
Christiansen, Mike	TR 85	
Christiansen, Paige W.	TR 47, 48, 49, 50	
Christiansen, Paul	BK 70M	
Christie, David	SO 59, 60, 61	
Christoff, Larry	SO 63, 64, 65	
Christofferson, Keith A.	HO 57, 58	
Christofferson, Melvin	HO 58, 59, 60	
Christopher, Clarence W.	TR 1899	
Chuck, Robert T.	TN 47, 48	
Ciolek, David	WR 70, 72	
Ciolek, Edwin W.	BS 42, 43	
Ciolek, Eugene S.	BS 37, 38, 39 / FB 37, 38	
Ciolek, Mark	BK 70M	
Ciolek, Robert W.	BS 50, 51, 52 / FB 49, 51	
Cirovski, Vancho	SO 79, 80, 81, 82	
Ciungan, Gregory	HO 74, 75	
Clabbers, Reiner P.	SO 62	
Clancy, C. Robert	BS 70, 71	
Clark, Alvah B.	BS 1896, 97, 98	
Clark, Beth	LA 80M	
Clark, Chris	LA 94, 95, 96	
Clark, Ernest	FB 60, 61, 62	
Clark, Gail A.	FB 70, 71, 72	
Clark, Geoffrey	SO 73	
Clark, Harold A.	BS 15, 16	
Clark, Howard C.	TR 35, 37	
Clark, Howard K.	SW 31	
Clark, James	WR 77	
Clark, Kenneth	BS 48M	
Clark, M. Bryan	FB 78, 79, 80, 81	
Clark, Meredith G.	TR 27, 28, 29	
Clark, Nathan	GO 99, 2000, 01, 02CoC	
Clark, Ronald	HO 72, 73, 74, 75	
Clark, Steve	HO 2000, 01, 03	
Clark, Thomas	CC 83	
Clarke, Chris	SW 91	
Clarke, Taylor	HO 95, 96	
Clary, James R.	FC 59	
Clary, Kevin	CC 2001	
Cleaves, Mateen	BK 97, 98 CoC, 99 CoC, 2000 CoC	
Cleland, Roland J.	BS 1889	
Clemens, C. James	SW 55, 56, 57	
Clemens, Jeff	WR 2003	
Clement, Sean	HO 85, 86, 87, 88	
Clemons, Lloyd	FB 98, 99	
Clemons, William G.	SW 48, 49	
Cleveland, Andy	BK 95M, 96M, 97M, 98M	
Click, David C.	FC 63, 64	
Clifford, Brian	HO 93, 94, 95, 96	
Clifford, James V.	SO 57	
Clifford, James	HO 78, 79, 80	
Climer, Joseph H.	TN 41M	
Clise, Burton B.	TR 07M	
Clutten, Ian	SW 2003	
Clore, Chris	GY 90, 91	
Clouse, Sean	FB 87	
Clupper, Steve	FB 68M	
Coates, Keith	TR 65, 66 / CC 65	
Cobb, Andrew W.	TR 32, 33, 34	
Cobb, Clifton A.	TR 31	
Cobb, Jeff	SO 88, 89, 90, 92CoC	
Cobb, Leslie A.	FB 14	
Cobb, Michael	FB 73, 74, 75, 76	
Cochran, Donald D.	GO 60, 61	
Coco, Michael	GY 56, 59	
Cofer, Jimel	FB 99	
Cohen, Jon	SW 90, 91, 92, 93CoC	
Cohen, Marc	TN 82, 83	
Cohrs, William	BK 70, 71, 72	
Colby, Richard H.	TN 62	
Cole, Clarence L.	BK 26	
Cole, Danton	HO 86, 87, 88, 89	
Cole, Otis R.	TR 1895	
Cole, Steve	GO 73, 74	
Cole, Thomas C.	FB 74, 75, 76	
Cole, William L.	TR 62	
Cole, William	SW 88, 89, 90	
Coleman, Derrick	TR 86, 88	
Coleman, Don E.	FB 49, 50, 51	
Coleman, Millard	FB 91, 92, 93, 94CoC	
Coleman, Thomas	SO 77, 78, 79CoC	
Colina, Richard W.	FB 33, 34, 35 / TR 34, 35	
Collard, Raymond D.	BS 54, 55, 56	
Collier, Kevin	GO 88, 89, 90, 91	
Collins, Archer	FB 96, 97	
Collins, Dennis J.	SW 62, 63	
Collins, Emilio	WR 91, 93, 94CoC, 95CoC	
Collins, Franklyn M.	TR 47, 48	
Collins, John	TR 89, 90, 91, 92	
Collins, Robert W.	TR 51M	
Collins, William M.	BS 63, 64, 65	
Collinson, William R.	BS 18	
Collison, David	BS 74, 75	
Colovas, Peter	FC 86, 87, 88	
Colp, Steve	HO 73, 74, 75, 76	
Colvin, John C.	BK 27, 28	
Colvin, Scott	BS 98, 99	
Colwell, Fred E., Jr.	FB 40M	

Comerford, Willie .... FB 97
Condit, Thomas .... LA 70
Confer, Cliff .... FB 87, 88, 89, 90
Conigilio, Chris P. .... WR 56
Conklin, Sean .... TR 89
Conley, James M. .... WR 58, 60
Conley, Timothy .... WR 92
Conlin, James L. .... BS 58, 59, 60
Conn, Chris .... SO 94
Connell, John M. .... FC 47C
Connelly, Paul .... LA 89, 90
Conner, Alger V. .... FB 42, 46
Conover, Frank W. .... BS 31M
Conover, Jeffrey .... FC 94, 95
Consigny, Douglas .... SO 90, 91, 92, 93C
Cotant, Joseph .... WR 2000
Conte, Ralph .... WR 97
Conti, Anthony N. .... FB 66, 67
Conti, Dominic F. .... FB 45
Contos, Steve G. .... FB 45
Converse, Craig .... FB 77, 78, 79
Convertini, Fred E. .... FB 65
Convis, Danny .... SW 60
Conway, Lynn V. .... FB 46
Cook, Albert B., Jr. .... TR 23M
Cook, Bernard K. .... SO 58, 59, 60
Cook, Edward F. .... SW 27, 30C
Cook, Harvey J. .... BS 39, 40
Cook, Herbert R. .... CC 50
Cook, John F. .... CC 52, 53 / TR 52, 53, 54
Cook, Kenneth C. .... GY 51, 54
Cook, Michael .... SW 72, 73, 74
Cook, Raymond James .... GY 57, 58
Cook, Richard A. .... WR 65, 66
Cooke, Leonard Graham .... GO 69, 70M, 71
Cooke, Paul .... TR 70
Cool, Robin .... CC 71, 72, 73 / TR 72
Cool, Ronald .... CC 71, 72, 73 / TR 72
Cooley, Charles W. .... TR 39, 40
Cooley, Gaye .... HO 66, 67
Cooley, Harry R. .... SW 43
Cooley, Willard D. .... SW 46, 47C
Coolidge, John K. .... FB 36, 37
Coombs, David L. .... CC 59M, 61M / TR 59M
Cooney, Edward G. .... BS 1887
Cooper, Amy .... LA 96M
Cooper, Dale L. .... GY 62, 63, 64
Cooper, Gary .... FC 91, 92
Cooper, George .... FB 78, 79, 80CoC, 81CoC
Cooper, James A. .... BK 1902C
Cooper, John K. .... TR 63, 65
Cooper, Josh .... BS 95, 96
Cooper, Larry S. .... HO 54, 55
Cooper, Luray .... TR 73
Copeland, Bernard .... BK 68, 69
Coppo, Michael .... HO 64, 65, 66CoC
Corbelli, John P. .... TR 52, 53, 54
Corbelli, Joseph J. .... TR 50, 51
Corbitt, Donald R. .... BK 54
Cordaro, Robert .... GY 66
Cordery, James W. .... FB 73
Cordley, Arthur B. .... BS 1886, 87, 89C, 90
Corey, David .... BS 82, 83, 84, 85CoC
Corgiat, James .... FB 59, 61
Corless, Rex E. .... FB 51, 52
Corrigan, Michael E. .... SW 61, 62, 63
Cortright, Ion J. FB 1907, 08, 09, 10C / BS 1910, 11C / TR 1908, 09, 10
Cortright, Wesley H. .... FB 02
Corwin, Chris .... FB 70M
Coryell, Sherman .... FB 16, 17C, 19
Cosgrove, Paul .... LA 89
Costanzo, Louis P. .... BS 55 / FB 54
Costello, Brad .... FB 94
Costello, Daniel W. .... BS 62, 63
Cotant, Joseph .... WR 2000
Cotter, James .... BS 77, 79C
Cotton, Eddie .... FB 64, 65
Couch, David .... TR 90, 91, 92, 93 / CC 91, 92
Couey, Darrell R. .... BS 45
Coughlin, Kevin .... HO 76, 77, 78
Coulter, Jason .... TR 95, 96, 97
Counter, Douglas .... HO 76, 77, 78CoC
Court, Rick .... BS 2000, 01CoC
Coutre, James .... BK 77, 78
Covey, William .... FB 84
Cowall, Jeffrey .... LA 73, 74
Coward, David .... SW 70, 71
Cowden, David G. .... TR 40
Cowherd, Steven .... SO 83
Cowing, Frank .... FB 38M
Cox, Don .... WR 67, 68
Coxon, Alfred G., Jr. .... SW 56, 58, 59
Coykendall, Charles E. .... TR 53, 54, 55
Coyne, John .... HO 71M, 72M, 73M
Coyne, Kenneth G. .... SW 51, 52, 53
Crabill, Charles J. .... FB 26, 27, 28
Crabtree, Timothy .... BS 90, 91, 92
Craig, Douglas A., Jr. .... TR 33
Craig, Horace S. .... SW 29, 30, 31C
Craig, Robert C. .... TR 41
Crall, Max B. .... BS 28, 29, 30 / FB 29
Cramer, Ronald .... WR 78
Cramer, Thomas .... SW 69, 70, 71
Crane, Alexander A. .... SW 47
Crane, Brian .... HO 94, 95, 96, 97
Crane, Bud C. .... FB 47, 48, 49
Crane, Leroy R. .... FB 48, 49, 50C
Crane, Martin .... BK 82M, 83M
Crary, Edward Ted, Jr. .... BS 65, 66, 67
Crary, John R. .... FB 35M
Crawford, Donald .... TR 67, 68
Crawley, Peter .... SO 83, 84, 85, 86CoC
Creager, Basil J. .... FB 33M
Creamer, James E. .... FB 50, 51
Creamer, Norman R. .... BS 57
Cregg, Richard .... HO 73
Crenshaw, Tyrone .... FB 95
Creswell, Smiley .... FB 80, 81, 82
Crews, Kevin .... BS 99, 2000, 01, 02
Crissey, Chase .... BS 07, 08, 09
Crissman, William I. .... CC 39M
Cristofoli, Nino .... HO 66, 67, 68
Criswell, Elmont E. .... TR 31, 33
Crittenden, Richard .... SW 69, 70
Croft, Dave .... GY 66, 67, 68
Croll, John T. .... TN 24C
Cronin, Colin .... FB 91, 92, 93, 94
Crosby, Chris .... TR 95
Crosby, Dick J. .... BS 1893, 95, 96
Crosby, Matt A. .... FB 1898, 99, 00, 01 / TR 02
Crosby, William .... CC 93, 94CoC / TR 94, 95
Crosthwaite, Duane T. .... FB 39
Crow, Irvin S. .... CC 27
Crowell, Jack L. .... TR 60
Croxton, Gregory .... FB 73, 74, 75
Crump, Gary .... WR 80, 83
Cudney, Cam .... SO 84, 85, 86, 87
Cudnik, Marcus .... SO 93, 94, 95CoC
Cudnohufsky, Michael .... BS 81, 82
Cull, Leo .... SW 51, 52
Cullen, Charles .... TR 87, 88, 89, 90
Culp, Steve .... FB 92, 93M
Culver, Edward G. .... FB 10, 11
Cummins, Albert B. .... BS 49, 50
Cummins, James .... HO 89, 90, 91CoC
Cundiff, Larry L. .... FB 57, 58, 59
Cunningham, James .... HO 77
Cunningham, Timothy .... FB 80, 81, 82, 83
Curl, Ron .... FB 68, 69, 71C
Curley, Douglas G. .... TN 50, 52
Curran, Joseph .... FB 82, 83, 84, 85
Currie, Daniel G. .... FB 56, 57, 58
Currie, Michael J. .... FB 61, 63
Currie, Tim .... FB 89
Currott, Richard .... FC 75, 76
Curry, Edgar .... HO 51M
Curtis, Fred S. .... FB 1898, 99
Curtis, Todd .... GY 86
Curtis, William .... BK 64, 65, 66C
Curzi, James J. .... GY 64, 65, 66
Custer, George A. .... FC 48, 49C
Cuthbertson, Harold G. .... BS 30, 31, 32
Cutler, Donald E. .... FB 52
Cyran, Michael .... BK 96M, 97M
Dace, John .... BS 70, 71, 72
Dackerman, Paul .... GY 90, 91, 92, 93
Dacthler, Harold .... WR 45
Dafoe, Kenneth F. .... TR 55, 56, 57
Daggett, Dean .... FC 68
Dahlgren, Gordon .... FB 34, 35, 36C
Dahlin, Chris .... SO 2002
Dahlke, Craig A. .... FB 72, 73
Dahlstrom, John D. .... BS 09
Dahlstrom, John R. .... BS 38, 39
Daily, Jason .... FB 2002
Dale, David .... SW 75, 76
Dales, Herbert P. .... SW 38
Dales, Oliver O. .... BS 02M
Daley, Daniel .... HO 61, 62, 63
Daley, William B. .... BS 22, 23
Dalponte, Peter L. .... BS 38, 39
Dalrymple, Max E. .... BK 38, 39, 40C
Dalson, Kevin .... BS 86, 87, 88, 89
Dameron, Rob .... LA 90, 91, 92, 93CoC
Damson, Jack E. .... TN 61, 62, 63C
Danaher, Kenneth J. .... SO 72
Dancer, Brad .... TN 90, 91, 92, 93CoC
Dancer, Paul C. .... BS 12, 13
Danciu, George W. .... FB 40, 41
D'Angelo, James .... SO 73
Dangl, Robert W. .... BS 51, 52, 53
Danielewicz, Michael A. .... FB 72, 73
Daniels, John F. .... GY 59, 60, 61
Dankovich, Albert .... BS 79, 80, 81
Dann, Roscoe J. .... GY 63M, 64M
Danziger, Fredrick W. .... FB 26, 28, 29C
DaPrato, N. Jerry .... FB 12, 14, 15
Daray, Steve .... LA 92
Darbee, Michael .... SW 92
Darby, Keith A. .... FB 53M
Dare, Charles W. .... TN 56
Dargush, Bennie J. .... BK 37, 38
Darkowski, Derek .... BS 89, 90, 91, 92
Daubenmeyer, John P. .... FB 75
Dauw, James .... SW 75, 76, 77, 78
Davenport, Charles S. .... GO 52
Davenport, Keith .... BS 92
Davenport, Matt .... LA 96
Davey, Berten E. .... BX 49
Davey, Charles P. .... BX 43, 47C, 48C, 49C
Davey, James .... FC 68
Davey, Neil .... HO 84
Davidson, Michael .... BS 85, 86, 88C
Davidson, Timothy .... BS 89, 90
Davis, Alan .... FB 77, 78, 79
Davis, Andrew .... GY 2001
Davis, Bayley .... FB 89, 90M
Davis, Benjamin .... BS 1894
Davis, Charles E. .... BK 39M
Davis, Charles .... TR 74
Davis, Deland H. .... TR 27, 29
Davis, Doug .... BK 98, 99
Davis, Frank R. .... FB 11
Davis, Hugh G. .... FB 42, 43
Davis, J. Francis .... BS 15
Davis, Jon C. .... BS 56
Davis, Kenneth .... LA 76, 77, 78CoC, 79CoC
Davis, Mark .... TR 92, 93
Davis, Matthew G. .... SO 79, 80, 81CoC
Davis, Paul .... BK 2003
Davis, Peter .... BK 73, 74, 75
Davis, Randolph, Jr. .... FB 70
Davis, Rondle L. .... CC 54
Davis, Roscoe W. .... BS 56, 57
Davis, Russell J. .... BS 27, 28
Davis, Steve .... WR 94, 95
Davis, Travis .... FB 86, 87, 88, 89

Davis, Wilford D. ... FB 39, 40, 41CoC / BS 40, 41, 42
Davis, Wyman Dale ... FB 39, 40, 41 / BS 40, 41, 42
Davison, Paul ... BS 90, 91
Dawa, Justin ... HO 99M
Dawes, Matt ... FB 2000, 01
Dawluk, Bill ... TN 87M
Dawson, Hugh A., Jr. ... BK 47, 48, 49 / TR 47, 51
Dawson, John B. ... BS 11, 12, 13
Dawson, William, Jr. ... FB 68, 69, 71
Day, Arthur E. ... TR 11, 12
Day, Tim ... BS 2002, 03
Deacon, Fredrick E. ... FB 26, 27
Deal, Wade H. ... BS 62, 63, 64
Dean, Michael A. ... FB 74, 75, 76, 77
Dean, Paul ... BK 69, 70, 71
Dean, Scott ... HO 92, 93
Dear, Rawdon E. ... TR 54M
DeBenedet, Flavio Nelson ... HO 67, 68, 69
Debergh, John ... SO 62
DeBoer, Clarence L. ... SO 63, 64
DeBrine, Thomas R. ... FB 63, 64M
DeCenzo, Mark ... HO 75, 76, 77, 78CoC
Decker, Arthur J. ... BS 1899, 00
Decker, Arthur R. ... FB 1900
Decker, John W. ... FB 02, 03
Decker, Michael ... FB 77, 78, 79
Dedich, Charles ... SO 63, 64
Dedich, Peter ... SO 64
Deering, Matt ... TR 98, 99, 2000, 01CoC, 02
Deeter, Frank ... SW 86, 87, 88CoC
DeFauw, Nicholas ... SW 2000, 01, 02, 03CoC
Defever, Keith S. ... FC 80, 81, 82C
Deford, Mark ... CC 86
DeGrand, Greg ... WR 96, 97, 98, 2000CoC
DeGraw, Al ... FB 83M, 84M, 85M
DeGraw, Nick ... SO 2000, 01, 02
Dehenau, Gerald ... TR 60, 61, 62
Dehn, Arthur J. ... TR 42
Deibert, Glenn E. ... FB 41, 42
Deihl, Roy H. ... BK 42, 43
Dekker, James ... BK 33, 34
Dekker, Paul N. ... FB 51, 52
DeLamielleure, Joseph M. ... FB 70, 71, 72
Delellis, Joseph ... HO 61
Delgrosso, Daniel J. ... FB 58
Delia, Kyle ... SW 92
Deliz, Jim ... BS 2002, 03
Dell, Arlin L. ... GO 56, 57, 58
Deller, Rick ... BS 72
Dellert, Daniel J. ... GY 87, 88, 89
DeLonge, Ronald ... BS 71, 72, 73C
Delozier, Ned ... SW 95
DelVerne, Jim ... FB 91, 92
DeMarco, Brian ... FB 91, 92, 93, 94
DeMarco, Frank ... HO 70, 71, 72, 73
DeMarco, Gerald ... HO 69, 70, 71
DeMarco, Michael ... HO 69, 70, 71
DeMarco, Robert J. ... HO 67, 68, 69C
Demare, Dino ... TN 78M, 80M
Demarest, Benjamin H. ... FB 33, 34
Demetral, Ted ... BS 97, 98, 99, 2000
Demling, Art ... SO 68, 69, 70
Demling, Brady ... SO 96, 97, 98, 99
DeMond, John E. ... SW 46, 49, 51
DeMond, Raymond J. ... BS 16, 17, 18C
Demos, Constance S. ... FB 63, 64M
Dendal, Charles T. ... FB 12
Dendrinos, Peter C. ... FB 44
Dendy, Robert F. ... GY 60, 61
DenHerder, Fred J. ... BK 28, 29, 30
Dennis, Brad ... SO 93, 94, 95, 96
Dennis, Charles B. ... TR 34, 35, 36C / CC 34
Denov, Daniel ... LA 70, 71
Densley, Theodore ... BK 69M
Denslow, Gaylord E. ... CC 54, 55, 56 / TR 55, 56, 57
Densmore, Michael ... FB 76, 77, 78, 80
Denton, Robert ... FB 92, 93, 94, 95
Derby, Steven G. ... TN 67, 68, 69
Derkovitz, Mark ... LA 87
DeRose, Daniel ... FB 76
Derrickson, Paul W. ... BS 39, 40, 41 / FB 38, 39
D'Errico, Mark ... SW 93
Dersnah, Bernard E. ... FB 06
DeShelter, Chris ... BS 96
Desmond, Robert G. ... SW 64, 65
Devendorf, Craig ... FC 73
Devenny, Robert H. ... BK 53, 54, 55
Devereaux, Fred A. ... BS 65, 66
DeVries, Tim ... GY 83M
DeVuono, Alfred J. ... HO 57, 58, 59
Dew, Darian ... TR 93, 95
Dewell, Ernest P. ... SW 59
Dewolf, Scott ... SW 93
Dhooge, Vic ... TN 65, 66, 67
Diane, Jean P. ... SC 64
Dianetti, Jack ... TR 47, 48, 49C, 50 / CC 46, 47, 48, 49
Diaz, Carlos ... SO 77
Dibble, Dorne A. ... FB 49, 50
Dibello, Joseph V. ... WR 49, 50, 51
Dick, Jason ... SW 89, 90, 91, 92
Dickens, William D. ... GO 71, 72
Dickenson, Richard C. ... WR 47, 48, 49
Dickeson, Verne C. ... BK 27, 28C, 29 / FB 27, 28, 29
Dickinson, James ... FB 87
Dickson, Robert M. ... BK 06, 07, 08, 09
Diebold, Allen O. ... FB 36, 37, 38C / BS 37, 38, 39C
Diedrich, William B. ... GO 54
Diehl, Clifford C. ... GY 67, 68
Diehl, David D. ... FB 36, 37, 38C
Diehl, Roy ... BK 42, 43
Diener, Carl A. ... FB 53, 54
Dieters, David D. ... CC 70, 71 / TR 71, 72
Dieters, Dick I. ... BS 47, 48
Dieters, Thomas ... BS 80, 81, 82, 83
Dietz, William ... FB 1898
Diget, David K. ... SW 59, 60, 61
Diggins, William ... GY 67
Dignan, John ... FB 90, 91
Dilday, Bobbie D. ... BS 52, 53C
Dilday, Robin ... BS 72, 73
Dill, Marshall ... TR 72, 73, 74, 75C
Dill, Reuben ... FB 28, 29 31 / TR 29, 30, 32
Diller, Burgoyne A. ... TR 27
Dilley, Alan ... SW 70, 71, 72, 73CoC
Dilley, Gary ... SW 65, 66, 67
Dillon, John H. ... BS 43, 46, 48, 49
Dimitroff, Boris N. ... FB 64, 65
Dimitrou, Van ... SO 63, 64
Dimmick, Guerdon L. ... TR 11M
Dinan, Ralph E. ... TR 14
Diner, Yakov ... TR 98, 99
DiPace, Darryl ... HO 78, 79
Dirker, Patrick ... FC 87
Dismond, Daryl ... TR 80, 81, 82, 83CoC
Disosway, Glenn ... SW 73, 74, 75, 77
Distel, David ... HO 80
Dittrich, Francis C., Jr. ... TR 34, 35, 36C
Dittus, Barry ... SW 82
Divjak, Ronald ... BK 62, 63
Dixon, Darryl ... FB 81, 82, 83 / BS 82
Dixon, Kenneth K. ... TN 58M
Dizon, Chris ... LA 89, 92
Dobin, Bradley ... BS 93, 94
Dobler, Wally ... SW 57, 59C
Dobreff, Rick ... LA 79, 82
Dobrei, Douglas M. ... BS 63, 64, 65C
Doby, James ... SO 73, 74, 75
Dodge, Glenn W. ... BK 05
Dodge, Harlan P. ... SW 46
Dodge, Ralph J. ... BS 11, 12, 14 / BK 12, 13
Doerr, Brian ... TN 89
Doerr, Maxwell H. ... BK 30M
Doherty, Thomas ... SO 82, 83, 84, 85
Dohoney, Donald C. ... FB 51, 52, 53C
Doll, Anthony ... BS 89, 90, 91, 92
Dolyny, Rustyn ... HO 98, 99, 2000CoC, 01CoC
Domagalski, Gary ... GO 74, 75, 76C, 77C
Dominguez, Cesar A. ... SO 60, 62
Don, Lorne ... GO 2000
Donelson, Ventson ... FB 87, 88, 89
Donnahoo, Roger J. ... FB 57, 58
Donnelly, Michael ... HO 83, 84, 85, 86
Donnelly, Paul E. ... BS 18, 19, 20
Donnelly, Samuel ... SO 61, 62, 63C
Donnelly, Terry ... BK 77, 78, 79, 80CoC
Dooley, James D. ... FC 56
Doolittle, Stewart I. ... BS 1900
Dopler, David ... WR 84, 85, 87
Doran, George E. ... TR 40, 41
Dority, Michael ... FC 81, 82, 83C, 84
Dorman, Brigham Taft ... GY 2001
Dorow, Albert R. ... FB 49, 50, 51
Dorr, Christopher ... BS 79, 80, 81, 82C
Dorsch, Christian ... CC 97, 98
Dortch, Tyrell ... FB 2000, 01
Doscher, Herman C. ... BS 18, 19
Doster, Steve ... SO 2002
Dotsch, Allan J. ... TR 48
Dotsch, Roland D. ... FB 53, 54
Dotson, Nathan ... GY 2001
Doty, Stephen W. ... FB 03, 04, 05, 06C / BS 07M
Dougherty, Patrick F. ... BS 47, 49, 50
Doughty, Howard ... TR 70, 71
Douglas, Keith ... GY 95, 96, 97, 98
Douglas, Thomas H. ... BK 63, 64
Dow, Jeremy ... BS 2003
Dowd, Arthur B., Jr. ... FC 59, 60
Dowd, Charles E. ... TR 31M
Dowd, Leonard R. ... CC 28
Dowdell, Damon ... FB 2001, 02
Dowell, John K. ... WR 46, 47, 48, 49
Downton III, Chip ... GY 91, 92, 93
Doyle, Eric ... BS 98
Doyle, James W. ... HO 50C, 51C
Doyle, Robert ... HO 61, 62, 63
Dozier, Robert ... FB 93, 94
Drago, Noel ... SO 57, 58, 59
Dragonajtys, Ray ... GY 82
Drake, Gerald A. ... FB 38, 39
Dredge, Bradford ... HO 78
Drew, Franklin F. ... FB 02
Drew, Kenneth L. ... BK 26, 27C / FB 25, 26, 27
Drews, Uve ... HO 71, 72, 73, 74
Drilling, Fredrick M. ... TN 41
Driskel, Harry G. ... TR 1900
Driver, Lee P. ... SW 64, 66
Driver, William F. ... SW 62, 63
Drobac, Stanley ... TN 52, 53
Drobot, Richard T. ... FB 71M
Druckman, Marc ... HO 50
Druetzler, Warren O. CC 48, 49, 50C / TR 49, 50, 51C
Dryden, Marion ... BK 98M, 99
Drynan, Bruce W. ... TR 40, 41, 42C, 46
Drzal, Peter ... FB 92, 93, 94
DuBois, Stanley ... HO 54, 55, 56
Dubpernell, James E. ... TN 55M
Ducker, James ... SO 76, 77
Duckett, Ellis ... FB 52, 53, 54
Duckett, Tico ... FB 89, 90, 91, 92CoC / TR 89, 90, 91
Duckett. T.J. ... FB 99, 2000, 01
Duda, David ... FB 74, 75, 76
Duda, Joseph ... GY 94, 95, 96
Duda, Michael C. ... FB 72, 73, 74
Dudeck, John E. ... SW 53, 54, 55, 56
Dudley, Daniel ... WR 78, 80, 81, 82, 83
Dudley, Darwin C. ... FB 36, 37 / TR 37
Dudley, James D. ... BK 75
Dudley, William C. ... WR 86
Duffett, Richard ... HO 68, 69, 70, 71
Duffett, Wayne ... HO 66, 67, 68
Duffield, Arnold W. ... BK 32
Duffy, Jim ... BS 2002, 03
Dujon, Nicolas V. ... SO 70, 71, 72
Duke, James R. ... SW 47, 48, 50C
Dukes, Clifford ... FB 2001, 02
Dukes, Harold C. ... FB 56, 57
Dunbar, Donald H. ... SW 46

Duncan, Harold A. CC 61
Duncan, Norman J. BS 39, 40, 41C
Dunford, Charles S. BS 34M
Dunford, John A. TR 1902
Dunlap, Charles W. FB 06
Dunn, Ernest C. BX 39
Dunn, Richard G. TR 66, 67, 68
Dunphy, Herbert G. FB 18
Dunsmore, Robert S. SO 59, 60M
DuPree, Billy Joe FB 70, 71, 72CoC
Durkee, James L. GY 60, 61, 62C
Dust, Robert C. SW 54 / TR 53
Duthie, Herbert I. BK 10, 11
Dutkiewicz, Keith BS 89
Dworken, Arthur M. SO 61M, 62, 63
Dykema, Jonathan BK 2000M, 01M, 02M, 03M
Dykstra, Mike TR 93, 94
Dysert, Walter J. TR 33
Earley, James FB 74, 75, 76, 77
Early, Thomas W. GO 62
Easter, Eric FB 2001
Easton, Kurt SO 77, 78, 79
Easton, Zana E. BS 67, 68, 69
Eaton, Darrin FB 88, 89, 90, 91
Eaton, James P. FB 60
Eaton, Kenneth TR 78, 80, 81CoC
Eberhard, Harold FB 84, 85
Ebey, Warren W. FB 59M
Ebner, Alex SW 2001, 02
Echols, Brian FB 93, 94, 95
Eckel, Clifford B. FB 41
Eckenrode, Earl GO 94
Eckerman, Harold FB 22, 23, 24
Eckert, Edward C. FB 22, 23, 24
Eckhardt, Ludwig, Jr. SO 62, 63, 64
Eckstrom, William R. BK 51, 52
Eddington, Michael BS 83, 84CoC
Eddy, Howard J. FB 20
Edell, Dan LA 94, 95, 96
Edell, Joel LA 90, 91, 92
Edgar, Oliver W. FB 1900 / TR 1898
Edgerton, Robert E. TR 34
Edin, Richard J. BS 52, 53
Edinger, Paul FB 96, 97, 98, 99
Edington, Dee W. SW 57, 58
Edmunds, Allen T. FB 23
Edmundson, Lee GO 68, 69, 70
Edwards, Dixon FB 87, 88, 89, 90
Edwards, Heywood BK 67, 68
Edwards, Hulett N. TR 63
Edwards, Mike FB 90, 92
Edwards, Richard A. FB 34, 35 / TR 37
Efrusy, Brian LA 89
Egeler, Charles C. SW 52, 53
Eggenberger, Eric WR 82, 83
Eggert, Marvin A. BS 27, 28, 29C
Eggleston, Raymond C. TR 54, 55, 56
Egly, Mark GO 76, 77
Ehrgott, John GO 96, 97, 98
Eichinger, Eric TR 95, 97, 98
Eisenstein, William SW 81
Eisley, Jeffrey C. HO 81, 82, 83, 84
Eisner, Brian W. TN 60, 61, 62C
Eisner, Jerry FB 80M
Eissler, Walter G. TN 36
Ejups, Gunars FC 54
Ekstrom, Lee K. TR 59
Ekstrom, William BK 51, 52
Elderkind, Adam WR 97
Eldred, Robert R. BK 27
Elias, John BS 61, 62
Eliowitz, Abe FB 30, 31, 32CoC / BS 31, 32, 33
Eliowitz, Samuel TR 57, 58
Elis, Milton BS 50M
Elkins, Shawn SW 75, 76, 77, 78CoC
Ellias, Howard S. TR 52M
Ellinger, Alvin G. SW 27
Elliot, Anthony HO 62, 63, 64
Elliott, Charles HO 92
Elliott, Gordon B. TN 47
Elliott, James E. FB 1896
Elliott, Mark TR 78 / LA 79
Elliott, Maurice F. TR 25
Elliott, Robert C. TR 57
Elliott, Robert H. TR 32, 33 / CC 32
Elliott, Steve SO 75
Ellis, Anthony FB 79, 80, 81, 82
Ellis, Ben C. BS 06, 07, 08C
Ellis, James FB 51, 52, 53
Ellis, James WR 77, 78C, 79C, 80C
Ellis, Larry A. SW 56, 57
Ellis, Michael SW 71
Ellis, Michael WR 69
Ellis, Robert BS 70, 71
Ellis, Thomas BS 67, 68
Ellison, Irene TR 81M
Ellsworth, Bert B. BS 04
Ellward, John E. BS 64
Elsasser, Richard L. TR 68, 69
Elsenheimer, William WR 73, 74
Elwy, Sherin SO 82, 83, 84, 85
Elzinga, Thomas TR 80
Emery, Brian BK 87M, 88M
Emmert, Wesley GY 78
Engelman, Mark GO 71
English, Ronald J. GO 70, 71
Enos, Dan FB 87, 88, 89, 90CoC
Enrico, William HO 67, 68, 69
Ensign, Daron WR 87
Enustun, Orhan SO 65, 67, 68 / TN 68
Enustun, Tarik TN 2001
Enustun, Turgud SO 63, 64, 65
Epolito, James C. FB 73, 74, 76
Epperson, Robert N. BX 58
Erdman, Steven SO 80, 81, 82, 83CoC
Erickson, Dennis J. BS 63
Erickson, Edward Bud M. BS 47, 48C
Erickson, Ernest B., Jr. BS 53, 54
Ericson, Michael BS 87, 88, 89, 90
Ernsberger, Scott FB 95, 96, 97, 98
Ernst, DeGay TR 20, 21C, 22C
Esbaugh, Ernest Kent FB 45, 48, 49
Essensa, Robert HO 84, 85, 86, 87
Estrada, Kevin HO 2002, 03
Etchison, Terry WR 77, 79
Eubanks, Trey TN 96, 97, 98C, 99CoC
Eva, Wesley L. BK 23, 24C
Evans, Ben TR 2000, 01, 02 /CC 99, 2000CoC, 01CoC
Evans, Carlton LA 83, 84, 85
Evans, Daniel WR 76
Evans, James D. BX 52
Evans, Monty BK 97
Evans, Rashad WR 2002, 03CoC
Evans, Scott BS 74, 75
Exelby, Leon C. FB 07, 08, 09 10
Exo, Lester W. FB 29, 30
Ezor, Blake FB 86, 87, 88, 89
Faberlle, Andy SW 92, 93, 94
Factor, Kenneth GY 71, 72, 73CoC
Fagan, Terrance S. BK 72
Fager, Theron C. BS 33, 34, 35
Fager, Willard J. TR 38
Fahs, David BK 59, 60, 61C
Fairbanks, Charles L. FB 54
Fairman, Robert P. GO 49
Fairrow, Jeremy FB 2000
Falardeau, Lee HO 2002, 03
Falcoff, Monte L. FC 86
Fales, Thomas HO 70, 71, 72M
Falinski, Larry LA 96
Falkowski, George BK 38, 39
Fallat, Robert HO 66, 67, 68
Fanning, Lawrence E. BK 60
Fanta, Charles GY 76, 77, 78, 79C
Fantini, Richard LA 74
Farleman, Arthur W. TR 1903
Farley, Horace B. TR 26
Farmer, Donald I. SW 40, 41C
Farrell, Jim FB 84M, 85M
Farris, Harold FB 75M
Fase, Jacob P. FB 29, 30 31
Fast, Brad HO 2000, 01, 02CoC, 03CoC
Fata, Robert FB 87, 89
Faughn, John H. TR 47
Faulman, Duane L. BS 43 / FB 40
Faunce, Eric SO 78
Faunt, William N. HO 65, 66, 67
Faust, Ralph HO 66M, 67M
Fawcett, Charles E. BS 31, 32, 33C
Fayerweather, Bruce L. BS 29M
Feamster, Peter HO 77
Featherstone, James LA 72
Featherstone, Neil CC 77
Featherstone, William FB 80M, 81M, 82M
Fedorchik, Joseph GY 68, 70, 71
Fedore, Craig A. FB 74, 75, 76, 77
Feeney, Todd FB 93, 94, 95
Fehr, Roy B. TR 38, 39, 40C / CC 38, 39
Feick, Jamie BK 93, 94, 95, 96CoC
Fekete, Nicholas WR 99, 2001, 03CoC
Feld, Heath GO 91, 92, 93, 94CoC
Feldman, Chris LA 96
Feldmeier, Robert J. GY 50, 51, 52C
Feldreich, Sten BK 78
Felice, Jeff WR 81, 83
Felt, Carl R. BK 27, 28, 29C
Felt, Derek SO 89, 90, 91
Felton, Dennis TR 84, 85, 86
Fenney, Todd FB 95
Fenton, Jack W. FB 40, 41, 42
Feraco, William A. FB 67, 68, 69
Ferguson, Alan G. BK 61
Ferguson, George H. BK 56, 57C
Ferguson, James T. WR 57, 58, 59
Ferguson, Michael LA 89, 90
Ferguson, Troy HO 2000, 01, 02, 03
Ferguson, Ryan SO 97
Ferland, Al LA 83
Ferman, Richard D. TN 70, 71
Fernandez, Carlos BS 96, 97, 98, 99CoC
Fernandez, Richard HO 83, 85, 86
Ferranti, Steven HO 94, 95, 96, 97
Ferrar, George D. FB 27, 28, 29
Ferrar, Joseph C. FB 32
Ferrari, Albert R. BK 53, 54, 55C
Ferrari, George D. FB 27, 28, 29
Ferrell, Fred I. BK 75M, 76M
Ferrell, Jeff CC 97, 99
Ferrer, Clay LA 77, 78
Ferris, Dean V. FB 18
Ferris, Henry M. FB 47
Fertig, Norman FB 36
Fessenden, Clarence W. BK 21, 22, 23C / TR 21, 22, 23C
Festa, Angelo R. GY 58, 59, 60C
Fetters, Matthew SW 80, 82, 83CoC
Fetters, Paul SW 72, 73, 74, 75CoC
Fick, Hilmar A. BS 14, 15, 16, 17C / FB 15, 16
Fiedler, Edwin BS 33, 34, 35
Fiegelson, Arthur R. FB 46M
Field, Howard W. TR 30
Fields, Angelo FB 76, 77, 78, 79
Fields, Brad TR 93, 94, 95, 96, 97CoC
Fifield, William HO 70
Figueroa, Juan LA 79
Filizola, Rubens SO 60, 61, 62
Finamore, Steve BK 2000M
Fincher, Mark FB 83, 85, 86
Findley, Chad CC 88, 89, 90, 91 / TR 91
Findling, Mark TN 98, 99, 2000
Fine, Todd BS 93, 94
Finegan, Daniel HO 69, 70, 71
Finkbeiner, Wayne TR 45, 46
Finlayson, Gerald LA 79
Finn, Frank HO 79, 80, 81, 82
Finn, John B. BK 50
Finneran, William J. HO 50, 51, 52
Fisch, Brad SO 92, 94, 95

Fischer, Robert H. ... FB 47
Fishbeck, Kenneth B. ... BS 27M
Fisher, Carleton W. ... BS 25
Fisher, Duncan ... GO 46, 47, 48, 49
Fisher, Edward ... LA 71
Fisher, Frank ... SO 71
Fisher, Gerald ... HO 65, 66, 67
Fisher, Keith ... FB 84, 85
Fisher, Royal S. ... BS 1893, 94, 95, 97 / TR 1895
Fisk, James E. ... FB 04, 05
Fitzpatrick, John ... BS 86
Fitzsimmons, James W. ... BS 41, 42C
Fladseth, LeRoy A. ... WR 56, 57, 58
Flaherty, Richard ... WR 73M
Flagg, Robert ... FB 2001, 02
Flake, Rudolf G. ... TR 39
Flanagan, Timothy ... LA 77, 78
Flanders, Walter B. ... HO 50
Flanigan, Cecil ... TR 95
Flegel, Gordon M. ... HO 82, 83, 84, 85
Fleischmann, Donald W. ... BS 41, 42
Fleischmann, Robert C. ... TN 48, 49
Fleming, Ryan ... HO 93, 94, 95, 96
Fleser, Don W. ... BS 25, 26, 27C / TR 25
Fleser, John P. ... BS 58, 59, 60
Fletcher, Clifford H. ... WR 45, 46
Flint, Rodney ... TN 84
Fliss, Jeff ... SO 95, 96, 97, 98
Floreno, Anthony ... TN 87, 88, 89, 90C
Flores, David ... BK 2001M, 02M, 03M
Flowers, Don ... BK 78
Flowers, Edward L. ... GO 37, 38C
Flowers, Little John ... FB 98, 99, 2000, 01CoC
Flowers, Ricky ... TR 77, 78, 79 / 80CoC
Fly, Kerry ... CC 89, 91 / TR 90, 92
Flynn, John J. ... BX 49
Flynn, Richard O. ... FB 62, 63, 64
Flynn, Thomas R. ... TR 55, 56
Flynn, Walter H. ... FB 1898M
Flynn, William III ... FC 93, 94, 95C, 96C
Fodell, Joseph ... TN 72, 73, 74
Foerch, Craig M. ... GY 69M
Foerch, Richard L. ... GY 49, 50C
Fogg, Cecil C. ... FB 28, 29, 30
Foley, Stephen ... WR 78, 79, 80, 81C
Folino, Anthony ... FB 94
Folkening, Ryan ... HO 93
Follis, Daniel ... FB 58
Foltz, Dale E. ... FB 54
Fomenko, Joseph ... FB 57
Fontes, Wayne ... FB 59, 60, 61 / BS 61
Foote, Jack B. ... HO 60
Ford, John A. ... HO 63, 64, 65
Ford, Michael ... HO 96, 97, 98, 99
Ford, Patrick ... BK 83, 84
Ford, Zachary III ... TR 60, 61, 62
Fordham, Barry ... BK 84, 85, 86, 87CoC
Fordyce, James ... FC 65
Foreman, Franklin S. ... FB 67, 68, 69CoC
Forman, Gregory ... SW 75, 76
Forman, Walter H. ... FB 65
Formanczyk, Andrew ... TN 2002, 03
Fornari, Peter A. ... BS 42, 46 / FB 41, 42
Fornell, Gordon E. ... SW 56, 57, 58C
Forrest, Stuart ... HO 65
Forsythe, Pete ... FB 90, 91, 92, 93M
Fortino, M. Samuel ... BK 45, 46
Fortney, Dane E. ... TR 73, 74, 75, 76 / FB 73, 74, 75
Fortson, Damien ... FB 2001, 02
Fossum, Robert B. ... GO 82, 83, 84, 85CoC / BK 81
Foster, Joseph F. ... BS 1890
Foster, Lamont ... TR 84
Foster, Larry L. ... BS 58
Foster, Matthew ... FB 76, 77, 78, 79
Foster, Michael ... SO 88, 89, 90, 91
Foster, Norman ... HO 84, 85, 86, 87
Foster, Shawn ... FB 98, 99, 2000
Foster, Walter J. ... BK 19, 20, 21C, 22
Foulquie, Carlos ... GO 99, 2000

Fournel, Claude A. ... HO 60, 62
Fourre, Joe ... SO 2002
Fouts, Leslie J. ... FB 25
Fowler, Larry D. ... FB 51, 52, 53 / WR 52, 53, 54
Fox, Ben ... GO 2003
Fox, Calvin J. ... FB 68, 69, 70
Fox, Steve ... TR 76
Foxx, Keith ... WR 82
Fracassa, Albert ... FB 54
Fraleigh, Royden G. ... FB 41, 42
Franchi, Frank ... BS 56
Francis, Milton J. ... FB 25M
Francisco, George D. ... BS 1900
Frank, Charles W. ... FB 51, 52, 53
Frankel, Charles M. ... BK 45
Franklin, Donvetis ... FB 98, 99
Franklin, Michael ... BK 92M, 93M, 94M, 95M
Franks, Joel ... TR 92, 93, 94CoC
Franson, Harry E. ... FB 17, 18, 19C
Fraser, Albert M. ... BS 02, 03
Fraser, James M. ... TR 43, 46, 47C
Fraser, John A. ... BS 1900, 02
Fraser, Robert A. ... TR 47, 48, 49
Fraser, William B. ... TR 47, 48, 49
Fratcher, Charles W. ... BS 42M
Frauenheim, Peter ... SO 89, 90, 91, 92
Frazee., Kenneth ... FC 89C
Frazer, William D. ... FB 06, 07, 08 / TR 06M
Frazier, Walter E. ... TR 17
Frederick, Charles C. ... BK 25, 26
Frederick, Charles ... BS 89
Fredrickson, Rob ... FB 90, 91, 92, 93CoC
Freeland, Paul F. ... SW 29
Freeman, Emery ... LA 70, 71
Freeman, Josh ... FB 95
Freeman, Waddie ... CC 85
Freiberger, Clifford H. ... WR 38
Freiheit, Fred E. ... FC 51, 52
Fremont, Perry J. ... BS 24, 25, 26 / FB 24
French, Douglas ... HO 66, 67, 68
Fretter, Colton ... HO 2003
Frey, Mark ... LA 82
Frey, Richard D. ... CC 37, 38, 39C / TR 37, 38, 39
Friar, Edward J. ... TR 10, 11
Fricke, Michael ... BS 74, 75, 76
Friedlund, Robert M. ... FB 39, 40, 41 / TR 40
Friedman, Allan ... HO 60M, 61M, 62M
Friedrich, Michael H. ... CC 62M
Friedrich, Steven ... TR 80, 81, 82
Friedrichs, Reid ... SO 93, 94, 95, 96
Friese, Kurt ... TR 79
Frietch, Dale ... BS 73, 74, 75
Frimodig, Lyman L. . BK 14, 15, 16C, 17 / BS 14, 15, 16, 17 / FB 15, 16
Frizzo, Leo V. ... BK 35
Froman, Thomas ... SO 81, 82, 83, 84CoC
Fruit, Kenneth R. ... TR 69
Fry, Clement C. ... BS 17M
Fry, Robert G. ... WR 62, 63, 64
Frye, John ... BS 66
Frye, John ... LA 89, 90
Fryman, George R. ... BS 04M
Fulcher, Robert S. ... CC 61, 62, 63C / TR 62, 63, 64
Fullen, Noel V. ... BS 21, 22
Fuller, Merrill S. ... BS 13, 14, 15, 16C / FB 15M
Fuller, Payton ... SO 63, 64, 65
Fullerton, Barry A. ... BS 56, 57
Fullerton, Loring V. ... TR 30, 33 / CC 32
Fulton, Philip N. ... BS 68, 69, 70C
Funston, James E. ... GO 41, 46C
Furlow, Terry L. ... BK 73, 74, 75, 76C
Furry, John A. ... GY 53, 54C
Furseth, Eric O. ... BK 51, 52, 53C
Fusi, Peter ... FB 46, 47, 48, 49
Gabocy, Michael ... FC 86
Gabor, Mike ... LA 85, 86CoC
Gabucci, Harold ... LA 72
Gach, Ronald E. ... BX 58M
Gaddini, Rudolph ... FB 55, 56
Gaekle, Jeff ... SW 78, 79 CoC

Gaff, Joel ... TR 2002
Gaffney, Norman M. ... HO 69, 70
Gafner, John ... BS 31, 32, 33
Gage, Ronald W. ... SW 60
Gaggin, Brian ... LA 78, 80
Gagin, Alexander ... BS 89, 90, 91, 92
Gagne, Rob ... HO 90, 91
Gagnon, Giles ... HO 70, 71, 72, 73CoC
Gagnon, Mark ... HO 78
Gaines, Frank, Jr. ... FB 35, 36, 37
Gaines, Nelson ... GY 74
Gajic, Nenad ... HO 2003
Gale, Robert S. ... BK 68, 69, 70
Gale, Bryan ... BS 2001, 02, 03
Gallina, James ... SO 83, 84, 85, 86 / LA 87
Gallinagh, Patrick F. ... FB 65, 66
Galloway, Chris ... BS 89, 90, 91
Ganakas, Gary E. ... BK 71, 72, 73
Ganden, Chad ... SW 98, 99, 2000
Gandini, David ... HO 78, 79
Gang, Robert W. ... WR 47, 49, 50, 51
Ganz, Joseph G. ... WR 64, 65
Garavaglia, Jon ... BK 94, 95, 96, 97
Garbarz, Douglas ... HO 91, 92
Garbe, Lyle E. ... CC 51, 52, 53C / TR 52, 53, 54
Garbus, Jerome J. ... SW 58
Garcia, Steven ... LA 82, 83, 84C
Gardiner, Todd ... HO 81, 82, 83
Gardner, Chris ... FB 94, 95, 96, 97
Gardner, John Nelson .. CC 34, 35, 36C / TR 35, 36, 37
Gardner, Robert D. ... BS 1889, 90
Gardner, Robert M. ... CC 34
Gargett, George G. ... FB 38, 39
Garland, Tyrone ... FB 94, 95, 96, 97 / TR 94, 97, 98
Garlock, Ronald B. ... BK 35, 36, 37C
Garman, Daniel ... BS 93, 94
Garmhausen, Brad ... BS 86
Garner, Coby ... BS 91, 93, 94, 95CoC
Garner, Deane H. ... FB 50, 51
Garnett, Reggie ... FB 93, 94, 95, 96
Garny, Mark ... GY 92, 93, 94
Garrett, Drake ... FB 65, 66, 67
Garrett, George A. ... BK 18, 19, 20C
Garrett, James T. ... TR 64, 65, 66 / FB 65
Garver, John E. ... FB 24, 25, 26
Garvey, C. Ross ... TR 09
Garvey, John ... HO 72, 73, 74
Garvey, Phillip L. ... SW 37M
Garvey, Steven ... FB 67 / BS 68
Gaskins, Jon ... HO 95, 96, 97, 98
Gasser, Harold F. ... FB 47, 48, 49
Gasser, Harold H. ... BS 23
Gates, Keith ... FB 83, 84, 85
Gates, Todd M. ... GY 63, 64
Gaudette, Bryant ... SO 73
Gauthier, George ... FB 12, 13 / BK 11, 12, 13, 14C
Gavel, Joseph A. ... BS 68, 69
Gavin, William ... BS 85, 86
Gay, Franklin ... TR 88, 89
Geahan, Robert R. ... BK 47, 48, 49CoC
Gebauer, Brad ... TR 2003
Gebben, Brad ... BS 79, 80, 81
Geggie, Charles W. ... SW 67, 68, 69
Gehan, John C. ... BX 57, 58
Gehan, Robert R. ... 47, 48, 49C
Geib, Horace V. ... TR 09, 10, 11, 12C
Geiermann, Louis J. ... TR 18
Geiger, Claude ... TR 75
Geiger, Jay ... SW 69M
Geistler, Gerald ... BK 66, 67, 68
Gellis, Benjamin A. ... SO 79
Gelmisi, John ... SO 60
Gelston, Kelby ... LA 92
Gembarowski, Mark ... SO 74, 75, 76, 77
Gemmel, Curtis ... HO 96, 97, 98, 99
Gemmel, Taylor ... HO 96
Gemmell, James S. ... BX 49, 50
Gendler, Tim ... SW 98, 99, 2000, 01CoC
Genova, Kenneth E. ... SW 65, 66

Genson, Wendell E. .... WR 35
Gent, G. D. Pete .... BK 62, 63, 64C
George, Gerald W. .... GY 62
Gerard, Craig .... BS 73, 74, 75
Gerard, Joseph E. .... BK 40, 41, 42
Gerbe, Jeff .... BS 2003
Gerhard, Gerald M. .... TR 60
Gersonde, Eric .... GO 77, 78, 79C
Gest, Kenneth W. .... SW 56, 57
Geswein, Kyle .... BS 99, 2000, 01, 02
Getz, Colin W. .... BS 42, 43
Gezelius, Roy A. .... TR 28M
Ghise, Cornell .... BS 51, 52
Giampetroni, John .... LA 85, 86, 87, 88C
Giannoulis, Thanasis .... SW 95
Gibbard, James R. .... TR 46, 47, 48, 49 / CC 46, 48
Gibbons, Bernie .... BS 96
Gibbons, Eugene .... WR 49, 50, 51
Gibbons, James .... BK 68, 69, 70CoC
Gibbs, Charles V. .... TN 39CoC
Gibbs, Edward H. .... BS 29, 30, 31C
Gibbs, Frank J. .... WR 27
Gibbs, J. Marvin .... GY 78, 79, 80 CoC, 82
Gibbs, Louis C. .... BS 1890, 91
Gibson, Arthur K. .... TR 50
Gibson, Charles C. .... BS 1898
Gibson, Donald .... HO 87, 88, 89, 90C
Gibson, Kirk H. .... FB 75, 76, 77, 78 / BS 78
Gicewicz, E. Richard .... FB 85, 86, 87, 88
Giddings, Rupert J. .... TR 10
Gieche, Adelbert E. .... HO 50
Gieselman, John .... FB 89, 92
Gifford, Chester W. .... FB 11, 12, 13C
Gilbert, Abel O. .... SW 46, 47, 48
Gilbert, Donald D. .... FB 55, 56, 57 / BS 58
Gilbert, George D. .... TR 12
Gilbert, Gregory .... TR 70
Gilbert, Peter .... LA 82
Gilbert, Roy H. .... TR 06, 07, 08
Gilbert, M. Tony .... TR 80, 81 / FB 80
Gilde, Gary .... LA 78
Gildemeister, Gerald L. .... GY 53, 54, 55
Giles, Paul .... TR 81
Giliberto, Richard A. .... GY 62, 63, 64C
Gilkenson, Robert .... SW 90
Gilkey, Edward A. .... BK 20, 21, 22
Gilkie, Gerald .... BK 79
Gill, Norman R. .... WR 55, 56, 57C
Gill, Patrick .... BS 99, 2001, 02, 03
Gill, Ralph A. .... WR 50, 53C
Gill, William .... BK 1904C
Gillergerten, John .... SO 74M, 75M, 76M
Gillespie II, Terry .... GY 89
Gilliland, William O. .... FB 33
Gillis, Henry L. .... TR 52, 53, 54
Gilman, John L. .... FB 47, 48, 49
Gilmore, Michael .... HO 89, 90, 91, 92
Gilpin, Russell L. .... FB 42, 46, 47
Gilson, Kenneth B. .... SO 60, 62
Giltner, Gus .... TN 92, 93, 94CoC
Gimmel, Matt .... SW 91
Gingrass, Morgan J. .... FB 41, 42
Gingrich, Wayne A. .... FB 20, 21 / BS 22M
Ginsburg, Jack .... SO 74
Gipp, John M. .... HO 53, 54, 55
Girard, Calvin J. .... GY 57, 58, 59C
Givens, Eric .... WR 89
Givens, Terry .... FC 65, 66, 67
Giwa-Agbomeirele,Okie .... TR 97, 98, 99, 2000C
Glasgow, Kyle .... FC 90, 92, 93, 94C
Glass, Morris W. .... FC 34C
Glaza, Stephen M. .... BS 36
Gleason, Bobby .... BK 2001M
Gledhill, Richard .... TR 89, 90, 91, 92 / CC 89
Glenn, David .... LA 77
Glick, Edgar .... SW 65, 66, 67CoC
Glick, Gene R. .... FB 46, 47, 48, 49
Glickman, Robert .... TN 74
Glimn, Terrance C. .... FC 59
Glover, Richard .... FB 90, 91, 92, 93
Glover, William J. .... BK 73, 74, 75
Goble, Gary D. .... HO 63, 64, 65
Godfrey, Robert B. .... TR 35, 39
Godfrey, Robert E. .... FB 44, 45
Godfrey, Walter G. .... BK 55, 56C / BS 54, 55, 56
Goebel, Mark .... FB 2000, 01, 02
Goecke, Al .... SW 94
Gogolewski, Doug .... BS 85, 86
Gogri, Niki .... SO 83, 84, 85CoC
Goik, Brent .... GO 98, 99, 2000, 01CoC
Goins, Brian .... SW 86, 87, 88, 89
Goins, Kirk .... SW 85, 86CoC
Gokey, Gary .... SO 77M
Goldberg, Larry .... GY 66, 67, 68
Golden, Bradley .... GY 2000, 02
Golden, Richard J. .... BS 58, 59, 60C
Goldie, Ashley .... HO 2002, 03
Goldman, David .... SO 70, 71, 72, 73
Goldman, Richard .... SO 89, 90, 91, 92
Goldrick, James .... LA 80
Golec, Michael .... SO 83
Golem, Ryan .... BS 2000, 01, 02, 03
Golis, William .... BK 60
Gongwer, J. Verne .... TR 05, 07
Goniea, Tom .... SW 97, 98, 99, 2000
Gonzalez, Jorge .... SW 69, 70, 71
Gonzalez, Robert .... BK 79, 80
Gonzenbach, Max A. .... BK 56, 58
Good, John P. .... TN 67, 68, 69
Goode, Benjamin L. .... FB 24
Goodell, David L. .... TR 54, 55
Goodenough, Walter J. .... BS 1894, 95
Goodenow, Joe .... HO 99, 2000, 01, 02
Goodfellow, MarkCC 94, 95, 96, 97CoC / TR 95, 96, 97
Goodheart, Robert .... BS 82, 83, 84, 85
Goodison, Nigel .... SO 69, 71, 72
Goodrich, James .... BS 65, 66
Goodrich, Jerry .... CC 74
Goodrow, Richard A. .... SW 51M
Goodwin, Marshall B. .... TN 34
Goodwin, Todd .... SO 84, 85, 87CoC, 88CoC
Goovert, Ronald E. .... FB 63, 64, 65
Gordon, Keith .... SO 97, 99
Gordon, Richard F. .... FB 63, 64
Gordon, Samalj .... FB 2000
Gore, Tim .... BK 81, 82, 83, 84
Gorenflo, Elmer F. .... BS 11, 12, 13C / FB 11, 12
Gorenflo, Oscar W. .... BS 1894, 95
Goresch, Jerry .... FB 74M
Gorman, Charles D. .... BS 51, 53, 54
Gorman, John .... BK 66
Gorman, Robert J. .... HO 50, 51
Gorman, Thomas P. .... GO 62
Gortat, Thomas A. .... FB 35, 36, 37
Gosler, James .... FC 84
Gosper, Richard Kevan .... TR 54, 55C
Goss, Robert W. .... BK 11, 12, 13C, 14
Gottwald, Paul .... HO 79, 80
Gough, Geoffrey S. .... SW 39
Goulbourne, Duane .... FB 92, 93, 94. 96 CoC
Gould, Garett .... FB 95, 96, 97, 98CoC
Gould, George N. .... BS 1896, 97, 98, 99
Govens, Pete .... FB 96, 97, 98
Gowans, Mike .... WR 94
Gowens, Arthur L. .... BK 59
Grabenhorst, Ted J. .... FB 77, 78, 79
Grabowski, Todd .... FB 90, 91, 92
Grady, Shawn .... LA 78, 79, 80, 81
Graft, Clare A. .... TR 37, 38, 39
Graham, Ernest R. .... TR 1904
Graham, Jeff .... FB 90, 91, 92
Graham, Douglas Jr. .... TN 73, 74
Graham, Kenneth J. .... SO 60, 61
Graham, Ralph C. .... BK 1905M, 06M / TR 1904, 05, 06C
Grams, James P. .... WR 45
Grams, Milton H. .... BK 28M
Granack, John W. .... BK 46, 49
Grandelius, Everett J. .... FB 48, 49, 50
Granger, A. J. .... BK 97, 98, 99, 2000CoC
Granham, Tony .... BS 97
Grannell, James M. .... FB 74
Grant, Alexander W. .... BS 41M
Grant, Brian .... FB 97
Grant, Howard B. .... BS 37M
Grant, James .... BS 45, 46
Grant, Tom .... BS 2003
Grant, Otis .... FB 80, 81, 82
Grant, Tony .... FB 2000, 01
Grantham, George R. .... TR 36, 37, 38 / CC 36
Grasser, Michael .... SO 76
Grau, James A. .... TR 55M
Graves, Harry C. .... FB 18, 21, 22
Graves, Thomas E. .... FB 74, 75, 77, 78
Gray Andrew D. .... LA 71, 72
Gray, Jacob .... BK 2000M
Gray, Phillip .... GY 84, 85, 87. 88 CoC
Gray, Thomas .... TN 69, 70, 71
Graydon, Edward B. .... CC 59
Grazia, Eugene W. .... HO 55, 56, 57
Green, Alec .... TN 87
Green, Arthur L. .... CC 35, 36, 37 / TR 36, 37, 38
Green, Duane E. .... SW 67, 68, 69CoC
Green, Edward .... LA 73
Green, Gregory .... BS 88, 89
Green, Harry A. .... BK 43M
Green, John Jeff .... TN 58
Green, John M. .... BK 57, 58, 59C
Green, Mike .... SW 86, 88
Green, Patrick .... FB 98M, 99M, 00M, 01M
Green, Shawn .... TR 97
Green, William R. .... TR 61
Greenberg, Benjamin .... FC 94, 95, 96
Greene, Bill .... FB 95, 97, 98
Greene, David G. .... HO 57M, 58M
Greene, Jay .... FB 93, 94
Greene, Richard .... WR 73, 74, 75
Greene, Scott .... FB 92, 93, 94, 95CoC
Greenway, William E. .... BX 53, 54, 55
Greer, Ernest Wilbur .... TR 37, 38, 39C
Gregg, James M. .... GY 63
Gregory, Cuba .... TR 73
Gregory, Delbert .... TR 72, 73
Gregory, J. Nicholas .... BS 45, 46
Gregory, Nick .... FB 98M
Grens, Trent .... SO 89, 90, 91
Grentz, Gerhard .... SO 58, 59, 60
Grenzke, George R. .... FC 40
Gresl, Mike .... HO 97, 98, 99, 2000
Gretzinger, Richard E. .... SW 63, 64, 65C
Griemsman, Luke .... LA 93, 94, 95, 96
Griffeth, Paul L. .... FB 38, 39 40
Griffin, Charles W. .... BS 30, 31, 32
Griffin, Chester A. .... TR 07
Griffin, Curtis D. .... FB 76, 78, 79
Griffin, Isaac .... FB 78, 79, 80, 81
Griffin, Jesse .... SW 75, 77, 78CoC
Griffin, Richard .... BS 57
Griffiths, Barry .... SW 75
Griffiths, Roy, Jr. .... LA 79
Grigg, Thomas .... BS 95, 96, 97, 98CoC
Griggs, Mark K. .... BS 11, 12, 13, 14
Grim, Bohn W. .... TR 25, 26C, 27 / FB 25, 26
Grimes, Nelson .... FC 90, 91, 92C
Grimes, Ogden E. .... FB 26, 27
Grimm, Brady .... GY 97, 98, 99, 2000C
Grimm, Robert A. .... TR 68
Grimmel, Matt .... SW 91
Grimshaw, Richard .... SW 85, 86, 87, 88
Grimsley, Ike R. .... FB 59, 60
Grimson, Richard .... SW 85, 86, 87, 88
Grinter, Robert W. .... SO 78, 79, 80
Grochowalski, Edward .... BS 82, 83, 84
Grommens, George H. .... SW 63
Grondzak, Donald .... FB 44
Groseth, Rolf .... SW 66, 67, 68
Gross, Carl E. .... FC 64, 65, 66
Gross, David .... LA 89, 90

Gross, Dean .... BS 87, 88, 89
Gross, Milton C. .... FB 29, 30, 31
Groszko, Michael .... TR 72M, 73M
Grove, Donald B. .... BK 28, 29, 30
Grove, Roger R. .... FB 28, 29, 30 / BK 29, 30, 31CoC
Grover, Richard .... GO 77, 78, 79, 80CoC
Groves, Robert W. .... BS 46
Grua, R. Mark .... FB 72
Gruber, Jordan .... SO 2001, 02
Gruber, Joseph .... FC 93C
Grys, Michael .... BS 90
Grzibowski, Chester .... FB 87
Gucciardo, Biagio, Jr. .... WR 59, 60, 62
Gudelsky, Thomas .... TN 74, 75, 77C
Guenther, Jeremy .... SO 94, 95, 96, 97C
Guerre, George T. .... FB 46, 47, 48
Guess, Lorenzo .... BK 98, 99 / FB 98, 99, 2000, 01
Guest, James F. .... BS 46
Guinee, Patrick .... LA 84
Gulick, Travis .... BS 2002, 03
Gunderson, Leroy E. .... FB 45 /TR 45
Gunesch, Mike .... WR 66M
Gunn, Frank S. .... BS 1897
Gunner, Richard J. .... WR 52, 53, 56
Gunner, Robert W. .... WR 52, 53, 55
Gunning, Benjamin N. .... GY 54, 55
Gunnison, E. J. .... BS 02, 03, 05
Gunny, Ermund R., III .... GY 66, 67, 68
Guntzviller, Casey .... SW 97, 98, 99, 2000CoC
Guolla, Steve .... HO 92, 93, 94, 95
Gurka, John .... WR 77
Gustafson, Leif .... HO 88
Guthard, Theodore .... FB 62
Gutkowski, Ronald J. .... BK 70, 71, 72CoC
Guzall, Ray .... HO 88, 89, 90, 91, 92, 93, 94M
Gyde, Richard J. .... CC 61
Haas, Chris .... FB 85M
Haas, Greg .... FB 89M, 98M, 91M
Habel, David .... SW 2003
Habrle, Lodo A. .... TR 36, 37, 38
Hach, Charles A. .... TR 1903
Hachenski, Patrick .... BS 93, 94, 95, 96
Hackel, Melvin A. .... SW 61
Hackenbracht, Dan .... FB 95, 96, 97
Hackett, Paul M. .... BK 25, 26C / FB 23, 24, 25
Hackney, Lewis H. .... TR 27, 28, 29
Haeussler, Mark .... FC 82
Haeussler, Peter .... FC 82, 83, 84C
Haftencamp, Joseph . BK 1902, 03C, 04 / FB 1903M, 04M / BS 1903M
Haga, Arthur J. .... BK 29, 30, 31CoC
Hagan, Peter .... SO 77
Hagan, Terry A. .... SW 65
Hagbom, Gregory A. .... FB 75
Hagel, Gerald .... SW 78
Hagemen, Joel .... SW 2001, 02, 03
Hahn, Harvey D. .... FB 04
Hahn, Oscar Charles .... FB 58, 59, 60
Haidler, John .... SO 75, 76, 77CoC, 78CoC
Haidler, Robert .... GO 80, 81, 82, 83C
Haidys, Leo T. .... FB 55
Haight, Gary .... HO 81, 82, 83, 85
Haines, Kirk .... BS 78, 79, 80CoC
Hairston, Lindsay .... BK 73, 74, 75C
Hakim, Sam .... WR 97
Hakim, Timothy .... WR 96
Halbert, Charles .... FB 36, 37
Hale, Elmer B. .... BS 1893
Haley, Ronald .... BK 91, 92
Hall, Adam .... HO 99, 2000, 01CoC, 02CoC
Hall, Andrew .... SO 88
Hall, Anton .... WR 2002
Hall, Clifford C. .... BK 26M
Hall, Harris F. .... BS 1889, 90 / TR 1888
Hall, Jesse .... BK 88, 89, 90
Hall, Marion E. .... TR 06
Hall, Richard D. .... BK 61 / TN 61
Hall, Robert E. .... BS 39, 40
Hall, Roy .... WR 90, 91CoC, 92
Hall, William .... SW 72, 73, 74, 75CoC
Halldorson, Jeff .... LA 87, 88
Haller, Alan .... FB 88, 89, 90, 91CoC / TR 91
Halliday, Douglas G. .... FB 69, 70, 71
Hallmark, Ferris E. .... FB 52, 53, 54
Hallock, Ty .... FB 89, 90, 91, 92
Hallums, Demetrius .... TN 82, 83, 84, 85CoC
Hamann, Kenneth .... SO 67, 68, 69
Hamblin, Stephen .... GO 79
Hamel, David .... LA 73, 74, 75
Hamilton Leon G. .... BX 51, 52
Hamilton, Brad .... HO 86, 87, 88, 89
Hamilton, Colin .... SO 99, 2002
Hamilton, Darrell .... FB 2002
Hamilton, Ernest .... FB 70, 71, 72
Hamilton, Geoffery .... BK 61M, 62M, 63M
Hamilton, Horace F. .... SO 58, 59
Hamilton, Richard C. .... HO 57, 58, 59
Hamm, Anthony .... CC 88, 90CoC, 91CoC / TR 89, 90, 91CoC
Hammer, John M. .... CC 32, 33, 34 / TR 33, 34, 35
Hammes, John H. BS 17, 18, 19C / BK 18, 20 / FB 17, 19, 20
Hammond, Scott .... LA 83, 84, 85
Hammond, William .... FC 40
Hammonds, Juan .... FB 91, 92, 93, 94CoC
Hammonds, Paul .... GY 77, 78, 79
Hamway, Mark .... HO 80, 81, 82C, 83C
Hancock, Jack M. .... WR 48
Hancock, John .... HO 68M, 69M, 70M
Handler, George W. .... TR 39, 40
Handloser, Robert A. .... FB 56, 58
Handy, George B. .... FB 30, 31, 32
Hanes, William N. .... GO 49
Haney, Usif .... FB 36, 37, 38
Hanger, Craig .... SO 94M, 95M, 96M
Hanis, William .... BS 83, 84, 85, 86C
Hanish Claude .... BK 06, 07, 08, 09, 10C, 11
Hankey, Dennis .... GO 67
Hankey, Douglas .... GO 65
Hannah, Nathaniel .... FB 80, 81, 82, 83
Hannah, Shane .... FB 91, 92, 93, 94
Hannas, Allan E. .... GY 50, 51, 52
Hannon, Thomas .... FB 73, 74, 75, 76 CoC
Hans, Michael .... FB 77, 78
Hansen, Dale W. .... SW 40
Hansen, Martin W, ... BS 45, 46, 47C
Hansen, Robert L. .... WR 65
Hansen, Robert .... HO 51, 53
Hanson, Jon .... TR 99
Hanson, Keith .... CC 84, 85, 86 CoC, 87 CoC
Hanson, T. .... TR 07
Harbaugh, Michael .... BS 87, 88, 89
Harden, Larry .... TR 91, 92, 93CoC
Hardenbergh, Thomas .... LA 72, 73, 74
Harding, Jeff .... HO 88
Harding, Larry R. .... FB 56, 57 / TR 56M
Harding, Thomas .... GO 85, 86, 87
Hardy, Clifton .... FB 68, 69, 70
Hardy, Dante .... FB 94
Hare, Bill .... FB 88
Harewicz, Joseph .... FB 81
Hargreaves, Richard .... HO 63, 64, 65
Harker, Paul .... FB 98, 2002
Harley, Nick .... SW 2003
Harlon, Vernon .... TR 85
Harlow, Peter C. .... TR 39, 40
Harlow, Richard .... BS 66, 67, 68
Harlton, Tyler .... HO 95, 96CoC 97CoC, 98CoC
Harmon Glen R. .... TR 64M
Harmon, Jason .... FB 2001, 02
Harmon, Roger N. .... SW 57, 58
Harms, Bruce C. .... FB 72, 73
Harner, F. Daniel .... SW 65, 66
Harness, Jason E. .... FB 58, 59, 60 / TR 59
Harpell, Gary .... HO 79, 80, 81, 82
Harper, Floyd A. .... TR 26
Harper, Kelly .... HO 91, 92, 93, 94
Harper, Matt .... FB 99M
Harriatte, Cheadrick .... FB 72
Harrington, Bruce .... WR 76, 77C, 78
Harrington, Kirk .... SW 84
Harrington, Timothy .... WR 77
Harris, Barry .... FB 77, 78
Harris, Chester .... TR 63
Harris, Chris .... SW 93, 94, 95, 96
Harris, David .... SO 78
Harris, Donald R. .... BS 47
Harris, James P. .... BK 55
Harris, Keith .... CC 81
Harris, Lynn H. .... TR 41
Harris, Michael H. .... FB 62M
Harris, Robert B. .... TR 41, 42
Harris, Robert .... HO 75, 76, 77
Harris, Trevor .... SO 67, 68, 69
Harrison, Blane .... LA 83
Harrison, Howard H. .... BS 07, 08, 09
Harrison, Richard .... SW 66M, 67M, 68M
Harryman, James E. .... SW 35, 36, 37C
Harsch, Erik .... SO 84, 85, 86, 87
Hart, David .... BK 93, 94, 95, 96
Hart, Shon .... FB 94, 95
Hart, William W. .... TR 34
Hart. Edward W. .... TR 34M
Hartker, Matthew .... SO 88
Hartle, Todd .... GO 82, 83
Hartley, Tom .... BS 96, 97, 98, 99CoC
Hartman, Frank .... TN 61M
Hartman, Frederic W. .... LA 71, 72
Hartman, Jon .... GO 89, 90, 91
Hartman, Kim .... CC 68, 70 / TR 69, 71
Hartman, Leonard D. .... BK 52, 53, 54
Hartsig, Lawrence J. .... TR 46
Hartsuch, Paul J. .... TR 22, 23, 24
Hartwick, Norman R. .... TR 52
Hartwick, Wayne .... TR 69, 70
Hartwig, Herbert B. .... BS 19, 20
Harvey, Andrew BK2002
Harvey, Burwell .... BS 10, 11, 12C, 13
Harvey, Erich .... WR 94, 95, 96, 97CoC
Harvey, Terry .... FB 92, 95
Harvey, Trevor .... BS 92, 94, 95CoC
Harvie, William H. .... TR 19
Harwick, Richard .... TR 74
Hasbrook, Matt .... FB 2002
Hashu, Nickolas .... BK 42, 43, 45C
Haskell, Mark L. .... FC 65, 66C
Haskin, Ralph .... TR 1891, 92
Haskins, Donald R. .... FB 23, 24, 25C / BS 26
Hassberger, Kurt .... GO 75
Hatcher, Ronald .... FB 59, 60, 61
Hatfield, Glen J. .... FB 44
Hathaway, James .... WR 82
Hathaway, Leland .... HO 67. 68
Hatland, Clarence M. .... TR 19
Hauck, Thomas .... FB 86
Haughn, Edward W. .... FC 72, 73, 74
Haun, Harold E. .... FB 29 / BK 30
Hauptli, Clifford H. .... FB 26M
Hauser, Fred .... TR 40
Haven, Frank S. .... TR 25
Havens, Glyn D. .... TR 51
Hawkins, Courtney .... FB 88, 89, 90, 91CoC
Hawkins, Dwayne .... FB 95, 96
Hawkins, Terry Lance .... FB 81, 82
Hawn, Louis .... HO 53M
Hawryliciw, Peter C. .... TR 39, 40
Hawthorne, David .... GO 84
Hay, Bernard .... FB 77, 78, 79, 80CoC
Hayden, Douglas .... SW 84CoC
Hayden, James G. .... BS 28, 30 / TR 28, 29 / FB 29
Hayes, George R. .... BS 18
Hayes, Jaren .... FB 2002
Hayes, Kelly .... LA 87, 88, 89, 90M
Hayes, Orion .... FB 94, 95
Haygood, Herb .... FB 98, 99, 2000, 01CoC
Hayner, Chris .... BS 82, 83, 84, 85
Hayner, Paul M. .... FB 71, 72, 73
Haynes, A. Maurice .... FB 66, 67
Haynes, Johnny Lee .... FB 78. 79, 80, 81
Haynes, Matt .... BS 99, 2000, 01

Haynes, Sherald E. ...... BX 57, 58
Haynie, Norman ...... GY 67, 68, 69
Headen, John W. ...... BK 68M
Heaphy, Donald ...... HO 64, 65, 66CoC
Heaphy, Shawn ...... HO 88, 89, 90, 91
Heard, Damon ...... CC 95, 96 / TR 95, 96
Hearn, Craig ...... SO 2000, 01, 02
Hearon, Tim ...... HO 2001, 02, 03
Heasley, Lloyd E. ...... BK 20, 21, 22C
Heaslip, Ronald ...... HO 76, 77
Heaton, Toby ...... FB 89, 90, 91, 92CoC
Hebert, Ronald R. ...... LA 72, 73, 74, 75CoC
Hecker, Paul Gene ...... FB 57
Hector, Andrew ...... WR 92
Hedden, Larry ...... BK 56, 57, 58
Heffernan, Harold J. ...... SW 41, 42, 43C
Heft, Kenneth ...... FB 67, 68
Hefter, Megan ...... TR 2003
Hegre, Arthur B. ...... TR 43
Heide, Chris ...... SO 87, 88, 89, 91 / LA 87, 88
Heisler, Ray ...... WR 89
Heitzner, Steven ...... TN 78, 79
Held, Arthur C. ...... FC 71
Helgemoe, Greg ...... LA 80, 81, 82CoC
Hellwege, John A. ...... SW 52, 53, 54
Helm, Jeremy ...... WR 92
Helmink, Douglas ...... WR 77
Helstowski, Gerald ...... FB 87
Hemphill, Charles M. ...... TR 1886
Hendee, John C. ...... BS 59, 60
Hendershott, Karl J. ...... BS 20
Henderson, Alwin ...... TR 70, 72
Henderson, Harry ...... BS 1902
Henderson, James ...... SW 68, 69, 70
Henderson, Ronald G. ...... BS 61
Hendricks, Craig ...... BS 88, 89, 90, 91
Hendricks, Donald R. ...... FB 45
Hendricks, Jabari ...... FB 2000
Hendrickson, David J. ...... HO 54, 55, 56
Hendrickson, Gustav ...... HO 60, 61, 62
Hendrie, Leland J. ...... FB 58M
Hendriksen, Klass ...... SO 70
Hengchel, David ...... TN 93
Hengen, Mark D. ...... FC 85
Henkel, Blaine M. ...... BS 36, 37
Henn, Phillip L. ...... SW 37M
Henning, Ralph B. ...... FB 13, 14, 15, 16C
Henry, Aldi ...... FB 93, 94, 95, 96
Henry, Cedric ...... FB 98, 99, 2000, 2002
Henry, Charles A. ...... BK 38, 39
Henry, Robert ...... FB 89, 90
Henry, Ronald L. ...... TN 60, 61
Hens, Peter ...... SO 65, 66, 67C
Henschel, Dave ...... TN 93
Henson, H. Lyle ...... TR 27, 28, 29C
Henson, John ...... SW 74, 76
Henson, Richard L. ...... TR 50, 51, 52
Hepler, James ...... FB 93
Hepner, Chad ...... SW 94, 95, 96, 97
Herbert, Fred W. ...... FB 1895M
Herbert, Thomas A. ...... TR 64, 65, 66
Herdell, Mark C. ...... TR 22, 23, 24
Herman, Charles F. ...... BS 1896M
Herman, David J. ...... FB 61, 62, 63
Hermes, Matt ...... LA 91
Herner, Arthur R. ...... SW 35
Heron, Cecil B. ...... SO 59, 60
Heron, Gerald W. ...... SO 60, 61, 62
Herr, Charles R. ...... TR 13, 14
Herrick, K. Hilliard ...... GO 78, 79, 80, 81
Herrick, Robert C. ...... BK 33, 34, 35CoC
Herrick, William M. ...... TR 43M
Herring, Paul L. ...... FC 70, 71, 72CoC, 73C
Herrman, John W. ...... LA 70
Hersha, Jeffrey ...... WR 73, 74, 75, 76C
Hertza, Jeremy ...... SW 98
Hertzler, Walter L. ...... CC 53
Hervey, H. William ...... TR 50, 52
Herzbach, Jeff ...... FC 81, 82, 83

Hess, Leon J. ...... BK 48
Hesse, Robin R. ...... SW 54
Hetzler, Benjamin ...... TN 95, 96, 97, 98
Hewitt, Amos ...... BS 73, 74, 75
Hewitt, Charles ...... LA 80, 81
Hiatt, Daniel ...... HO 81
Hibbard, Barry ...... SW 86, 87, 88CoC
Hickey, Daniel H. ...... BX 47
Hickey, Thomas E. ...... BX 52, 53, 54
Hickman, Parish ...... BK 89, 90, 91
Hicks, Lon G. ...... WR 70, 71, 72
Hickson, Hyland ...... FB 88, 89, 90
Higbie, Charles C. ...... BK 18, 20, 21 / BS 22
Higgins, Anthony ...... SW 88, 89, 90, 91
Higgins, Junior ...... SO 70, 71, 72
Higgins, Kevin P. ...... CC 46, 47
Higgins, Sheldon J. ...... BS 23
Highsmith, Donald C. ...... FB 68, 69
Hilarides, Robert M. ...... TR 48
Hildebrant, Edgar V. ...... FC 57, 58
Hiler, Matthew ...... BS 92
Hilgartner, Andy ...... LA 90, 91, 92, 93CoC
Hill, Brian ...... FB 88, 89
Hill, Christopher ...... BK 2002, 03
Hill, Dennis D. ...... SW 65, 66C
Hill, Douglas W., Jr. ...... GO 52
Hill, George R. ...... BS 35, 36, 37
Hill, Leon J. ...... FB 09, 10, 11 / TR 10, 11
Hill, Mark ...... FB 86, 87, 88
Hill, Raymond ...... FB 95, 96, 97
Hill, Renaldo ...... FB 98, 99, 2000CoC
Hill, Richard B. ...... GO 67
Hill, William ...... WR 97, 98, 99CoC, 2000CoC
Hill, Willie ...... FB 90, 91 / TR 89
Hillary, Phil ...... SW 99, 2000, 01
Hillmer, Donald ...... TR 54, 55, 56
Hills, Arthur W. ...... GO 50, 51, 53
Hills, Robert W. ...... TR 36, 38, 39C / CC 35, 37
Hime, Glenn ...... GY 73, 74, 75, 76
Himmelein, Fred T. ...... SW 40, 41
Hind, Devon ...... CC 73
Hindman, Oren M. ...... BK 39, 40, 41
Hindo, Ralph ...... FC 89
Hines, John ...... BS 63
Hinesly, James A. ...... FB 75, 76, 77, 78
Hinesly, James ...... FB 54, 55, 56
Hinkin, Paul E. ...... BK 54
Hinkle, Olin N. ...... BS 17
Hinkley, Robert ...... HO 50
Hippler, Ralph ...... FC 58
Hiram, Damien ...... FB 95, 96, 97
Hirsch, Steve ...... GY 86, 87, 88
Hirschman, Steve ...... BS 90, 91, 92, 93
Hirschman, Stuart ...... BS 90, 91, 92, 93
Hirth, Mark ...... HO 89
Hitchcock, Lytton B. ...... FB 05M
Hitchings, Glenn E. ...... FB 26, 27, 28
Hjortars, Gordon ...... BS 61, 62
Hoag, Philip M. ...... FB 64, 66
Hoard, Pat ...... TR 94, 95, 96, 97 / CC 93, 95, 96
Hobaugh, Edward R. ...... BS 54, 55, 56C
Hobbs, George W. ...... WR 60, 61, 62
Hoddy, George R. ...... WR 68, 69
Hodge, Mike ...... TN 2001, 02
Hodges, Karl P. ...... BS 1900
Hodgins, Brad ...... HO 97, 98, 99, 2000
Hodgson, Arthur D. ...... SO 59, 61
Hodo, James ...... FB 81
Hoff, Frank W. ...... TR 33, 34
Hoff, Geir ...... HO 86, 87
Hoff, Guy F. ...... BK 11
Hoffman, Arnold G. ...... TN 54
Hoffman, Howard V. ...... TR 19, 20C
Hoffman, Lee S. ...... BK 50M
Hoffman, Michael ...... FB 80
Hoffman, Robert F. ...... TN 57, 58, 59C
Hoffman, Robert L. ...... BX 53
Hoffmann, David ...... SW 49, 50, 51
Hofkamp, Matt ...... BK 90, 91

Hofstetter, John N. ...... BS 51
Hogan, Dennis ...... HO 70, 71, 72
Hogan, Michael P. ...... FB 68, 69, 70
Hohn, Chris ...... TR 2003
Hohs, Larry ...... BS 78
Hoisington, Clark D. ...... BS 27, 28
Hoke, David ...... TR 54, 55, 56 / CC 54
Hoke, Jerry ...... WR 56, 57, 61
Hoke, Richard P. ...... WR 55
Hoke, Robert ...... WR 52, 53, 54C
Holcomb, Monte S. ...... TR 31, 32, 33 / BK 31
Holda, Marty ...... GO 78
Holden, Steve ...... FC 86, 87, 88C
Holdridge, Mark ...... SW 68, 69, 70
Holdsworth, Byron H. ...... TR 1897, 98
Holdsworth, Phillips H. ...... TR 1902C, 03, 04
Holdsworth, Wilbur G. ...... FB 04, 05
Holewinski, Patrick ...... BK 76
Holland, Dean ...... GO 85
Holland, Robert ...... SW 73, 74, 75, 76CoC
Holland, Robert ...... FB 80
Holland, Shawn ...... SW 99
Hollern, Dale F. ...... FB 53, 54, 55
Hollis, Mark ...... BK 82M, 83M, 84M, 85M
Holly, Irving R. ...... FC 63
Holman, Rick ...... BS 94
Holman, Steve ...... FB 92, 93
Holmes, Brian ...... FC 93
Holmes, Cecil C. ...... WR 63, 65
Holmes, Kenneth ...... SW 73, 74, 75, 76CoC
Holmes, Richard ...... BK 64, 65, 66 / BS 65, 66
Holmes, Ronald M. ...... BS 60
Holms, D. John ...... BK 67, 68, 69
Holt, Daniel ...... WR 81
Holt, Michael E. ...... FB 71, 72, 73C / TR 70, 71, 72, 73, 74
Homa, Andrew ...... LA 70
Homann, David ...... CC 86, 87 / TR 88
Homann, Erwin ...... TR 79
Hontvet, Chad ...... HO 2003
Hood, Charles C. ...... BS 14, 15, 17 / BK 15, 16
Hood, Daniel ...... SW 81M
Hood, Oliver Z. ...... BK 26, 27
Hood, Robert L. ...... FB 62M
Hoogerhyde, George A. ...... SW 47, 48, 49, 51C
Hook, Kevin ...... SW 80, 81, 82, 83
Hooley, Steven ...... TN 83, 84, 85, 86C
Hooper, James H. ...... TR 1888
Hooper, John ...... LA 74
Hooth, Douglas W. ...... BX 47
Hoover, Herbert D. ...... TN 42, 46
Hoover, Todd ...... TR 81, 82, 83, 84 CoC
Hop, Randall ...... BS 77, 78, 79
Hop, Terry ...... BS 74, 75, 76
Hopely, George J. ...... GY 57, 58
Hopfinger, Carl ...... SO 86, 87, 89, 90
Hopkins, F. George ...... BS 34, 35
Hopping, William ...... BS 53, 54
Horan, James J. ...... TR 58, 59 / CC 58
Horan, Kenneth ...... LA 79, 80
Horcoff, Shawn ...... HO 97, 98, 99CoC, 2000CoC
Horn, William G. ...... SO 63M
Hornbeck, Lewis A. ...... FB 26, 27, 28C
Horne, John M. ...... BX 58, 59
Horning, Donald L. ...... TR 62, 63, 64C
Horowitz, Jeff ...... LA 89, 90, 91, 92
Horrell, William G. ...... FB 49, 50, 51
Horsch, Mitch ...... HO 78, 79
Horski, Maurice L. ...... CC 41 / TR 42
Horvath, Dan ...... BS 99
Hotchkiss, Harley N. ...... HO 50
Hotchkiss, William G. ...... TN 58, 59, 60
Hough, Walter K. ...... TR 06
Houle, David ...... FB 85, 86, 87
Hourani, Adam ...... TN 01, 02CoC, 03CoC
Hourigan, William ...... HO 74
Houska, John ...... SO 68, 69, 70
Housley, Tommy ...... GY 98, 99, 2000, 01
Houston, Robert E. ...... TR 21, 22
Houtteman, Lee ...... HO 80

Houtteman, Richard	HO 69, 71
Hovanesian, Dan	BS 50
Hovey, Donald D.	TR 32, 33, 34
Howard, Brian	FB 90, 93
Howard, Carroll I.	SW 53
Howard, David	TR 74
Howard, Roger E.	BS 51, 52
Howard, Samson E.	FB 78, 79, 81
Howell, Carl	HO 65
Howell, Charles O.	BS 60M
Howell, Franklin J.	TR 29M
Howell, Hal	SO 96, 97, 98, 99
Howell, Jason	WR 95, 96
Howell, Richard P.	WR 48
Howitt, Dann	BS 83, 84
Howitt, Shaun	BS 70, 71, 72
Howorth, Thomas	FC 84
Hoxie, Herbert E.	WR 47M
Hrisko, Peter A.	FB 85, 86
Hruby, Paul F.	HO 57, 58, 59
Hubbard, Beth	LA 96M
Hubbard, Brian	LA 93, 94, 95, 96
Hubbell, Stephen	LA 73, 74
Hubert, Todd	BS 75, 76, 77
Huck, Christopher D.	BK 72M, 73M
Huckins, Alan R.	WR 64
Hudas, Larry J.	FB 60, 61
Hude, Dan	FB 98M
Hudenko, Benjamin J.	BS 45, 46C
Huebel, Robert	FB 15, 16 / BS 16
Huesing, Theodore	HO 77, 78, 79, 80CoC
Huey, Warren B.	FB 45, 46, 47, 48
Huff, James	CC 89
Huff, Richard	SO 78, 79, 80, 81CoC
Huffman, Jaimie	BK 79
Hughes, Brandon	FB 99
Hughes, David	WR 96
Hughes, Derek	FB 78, 79, 81
Hughes, Harrison W., Jr.	BS 46, 47
Hughes, Hugh E.	TR 46
Hughes, James M.	TN 36M
Hughes, Leslie W.	BS 38
Hughes, Robert B.	TR 57, 58, 59
Hughes, Timothy	FB 91 / TR 91
Hughes, William L.	FB 50, 51
Hughlett, Charles A.	BX 47, 48, 49
Huizinga, Jon	BS 99, 2000, 01, 02
Hulkow, Richard J.	FB 72, 73
Hultman, V. Joseph	FB 22, 23, 24C / BK 23
Humbarger, Roger H.	CC 60, 61, 62C / TR 61
Hume, George J.	TR 1887
Hummel, Thomas	BS 67, 68
Hungerford, Jay	LA 80
Hunt, Eugene A.	GO 61
Hunt, Gilbert A.	CC 48
Hunt, Joseph	FB 74, 75
Hunt, Mark W.	SW 65
Hunter, John R.	GO 63
Hunter, Kam D.	FB 79M, 80M, 81M
Hurd, Martin A.	GO 55
Hurd, Michael H.	FB 71, 73, 74 / TR 72, 73, 74
Hurd, Wesley V.	TR 33, 34, 35C
Hurley, Albert E.	BS 1894
Hurt, John	FB 83, 84
Hurt, Paul Thomas	GY 64, 65
Huss, Eric	LA 94, 95, 96
Hutchinson, Andrew	HO 99, 2000, 01, 02CoC
Hutson, Andre	BK 98, 99, 2000, 01CoC
Hutson, Charles T.	WR 39, 40CoC, 41C
Hutt, Martin C.	BK 38, 39, 40C
Hutton, Kenneth W.	FB 12
Hyatt, George, Jr.	TN 36, 37
Hyde, Carl W.	BS 04
Hyland, Bradley	GO 72, 73, 74, 75CoC
Hynes, Robert W.	SW 52, 53
Iaquaniello, Michael	FB 87, 88, 89, 90 CoC
Ibach, Benjamin	FC 94, 95
Ichesco, Wesley R.	TN 69
Ideson, Phillip	GY 89, 90, 91, 92CoC

Idoni, Matthew	BS 93
Idzkowski, Richard J.	BS 53, 54, 55
Ignas, Chris	TN 86
Ike, Larry	BS 70, 71, 72
Ikens, Kirk	CC 91
Iling, Silvio	SO 84
Imhoff, Michael A.	FB 74, 75, 76, 77
Imlay, Alex	WR 80
Inch, Terry	SW 80, 81, 82CoC
Indyke, Zigmund J.	SW 46
Ingram, Arthur L.	TR 51, 54
Ingram, Mark	FB 83, 84, 85, 86 / TR 83, 84, 85, 86
Ingram, Matt	TR 97, 98, 99, 2000, 01
Insana, Jonathan	HO 99, 2000, 01, 02
Irmen, Thomas	CC 80, 81, 82C, 83C / TR 81, 82, 83, 84CoC
Irmen, Thomas L.	CC 47, 48 / TR 48, 49C
Irvin, Sedrick	FB 96, 97, 98CoC
Irwin, Todd	BS 85, 86
Ishbia, Mat	BK 2000, 01
Iung, Silvio	SO 84, 85, 86
Ivey, Ross	FB 91, 92
Ivy, Joe	SW 73
Izzo, Mario	BK 86, 87, 88
Jackard, Jerald W.	WR 58, 59
Jacks, Fred H.	FB 16
Jackson, Aaron	FB 91, 92, 93, 94
Jackson, Alvin F	TR 33, 34 / FB 33
Jackson, Cleveland L.	FB 75
Jackson, Greg	WR 90
Jackson, Karl F.	HO 54, 55, 56
Jackson, Kelvin	WR 94, 95CoC
Jackson, Larry	FB 73
Jackson, Lawrence	TR 84, 85CoC / FB 83, 84
Jackson, Levi	FB 73, 74, 75, 76
Jackson, Matt	TR 2000, 01, 02 / CC 2000
Jackson, Ricardo	FB 92, 93, 94
Jackson, Steve	HO 2000, 01, 02
Jackson, Wayne	WR 84
Jacob, Walter C.	WR 34, 35, 36C
Jacobs, Allan J.	FC 50
Jacobs, Jeffrey	FB 87
Jacobsen, Bert	SO 65, 66, 67
Jacobson, C. Michael	HO 65, 66, 67
Jacobson, James A.	HO 62, 63, 64
Jacobson, Mark	TN 96, 97, 98, 99
Jacoby, Alan	TN 73
Jacquemain, Joseph	FB 79, 80, 81
Jacques, Richard	TR 71
Jaeger, John	SO 81, 82
Jagger, William	TN 72
Jakinovich, Larry	HO 71, 72
Jakubiec, Jim	TN 66
Jakubowski, Steven A.	BS 40, 41
Jalaba, Mike	HO 98
James, Brian	BS 80, 81, 82, 83
James, David	WR 60, 61, 63
James, Kenneth A.	HO 56, 57
James, Kurt	BK 80, 82 CoC
James, Monty	GO 80, 81, 82C
James, Tim	FB 2001, 02
Jamieson, Daniel K.	SW 61, 62
Jamieson, Thomas K.	TN 62, 63, 64C
Janes, George	SO 63, 64, 65
Janson, Lynn	GO 68, 69, 70C
Janson, Ronald J.	FB 62M
Japinga, Donald	FB 63, 64, 65CoC
Jaroch, Jason	SO 95, 96, 97, 98
Jarrard, Donald S.	GO 48C
Jarrett, Craig	FB 98, 99, 2000, 01
Jarrett, Richard S.	CC 51, 52 / TR 52, 53, 54
Jasson, Robert W.	HO 56, 57, 58C
Jebb, James R.	FB 53
Jedlowski, Rich	LA 92, 93
Jefferson, Thomas G.	TR 60, 61
Jeffrey, LeRoy	BX 52
Jelacie, Tony	HO 78
Jelus, Jeff	LA 93, 94, 95
Jcmilo, Robert F.	BX 56, 57
Jen, Enoch	SO 71, 72

Jenkins, Arthur G.	TR 36, 37, 38
Jenkins, Carlos	FB 87, 88, 89, 90CoC
Jenkins, Charles	GY 77, 78, 79, 80CoC, 81CoC
Jenkins, Norman F.	FB 65
Jenkins, Robert N.	BS 63M, 64M, 65M
Jenkins, Terry	TC 2001
Jenkins, William R.	FB 60M
Jenkins, William	GY 84
Jennings, Brandon	BK 2003M
Jennings, Burl	WR 41, 42, 43CoC
Jennings, Merle	WR 41, 42, 43CoC
Jensen, Anders	SW 95
Jensen, Casey	FB 96, 97, 98, 99
Jensen, Erick	WR 86, 87, 88CoC, 89 CoC
Jewell, Douglas F.	FC 59
Jewett, Robert G.	FB 55, 56, 57
Jiron, Roger K.	FC 58
Joachim, Joseph L.	TR 27
Joba, Edwin L.	SW 47, 48, 49, 50
Joblonski, Charles F.	BS 50, 51
Jogan, Timothy	SW 96
Johengen, George A.	BS 49
Johns, J. Edmond	FB 18
Johns, Lawrence A.	CC 48M
Johnson, Andy	BS 94, 95
Johnson, Arthur L.	FB 56, 57, 58
Johnson, Bret	FB 91, 92
Johnson, Carl V.	FB 51M
Johnson, Chauncey J.	SW 60
Johnson, Craig T.	FB 85, 86, 87 / TR 86
Johnson, Darryl	BK 84, 85, 86, 87CoC
Johnson, David B.	FB 36M
Johnson, Derek	BK 92M
Johnson, Donald E.	FC 61C
Johnson, Donald F.	WR 47C
Johnson, Earvin	BK 78, 79CoC
Johnson, Fred D.	TR 47, 48, 49, 50
Johnson, George	BK 83M, 84M, 85M, 86M, 87M
Johnson, Glenn H.	FB 41, 45
Johnson, Gordon C.	WR 60
Johnson, Gregory	WR 70, 71C, 72C
Johnson, Harold C.	FB 44
Johnson, Herman	FB 61, 62, 64 / TR 62
Johnson, Huntley A.	SW 40
Johnson, Jack	HO 75, 76, 77
Johnson, James	FB 88, 89, 90, 91CoC
Johnson, James	HO 75, 76, 77, 78
Johnson, James	CC 2002
Johnson, Kenneth	BK 84, 85
Johnson, Kent	SW 90
Johnson, Lanny L.	SW 52, 53, 54, 55 / GO 55
Johnson, Leo G	BS 1911M / FB 09M
Johnson, Louis Jr.	BK 92M, 93M, 94M, 95M
Johnson, Marvin K.	SW 43
Johnson, Matthew	SW 80
Johnson, Mike	WR 66
Johnson, Okla	WR 61, 62, 63
Johnson, Paul C.	SW 62, 63
Johnson, Rashi	BK 2003
Johnson, Richard	LA 83, 84, 85
Johnson, Robert B.	BK 53
Johnson, Robert	HO 68, 69, 70
Johnson, Shane	BS 94, 95, 96, 97
Johnson, Sherman	BS 76, 77
Johnson, Stephen	BS 90, 91, 92, 93C
Johnson, Stephen C.	GY 60, 61, 62
Johnson, Terrance	BS 80, 81, 82
Johnson, Thomas A.	FB 40, 41
Johnson, Vernon	BK 67, 68
Johnson, Victor	GY 82
Johnson, Warner A.	FC 57
Johnson, William C.	FB 20, 21, 22C / BS 21, 22, 23
Johnson, William M.	FB 44
Johnson, William	FB 88, 89, 90, 91CoC
Johnson, Wilmer L.	TR 62, 63
Johnson., Andy	BS 94, 95
Johnston, Orlin T.	SW 47
Johnston, Rae	BK 50
Johnston, Stanley	BS 18, 19, 20C

Johnstone, Walter D. .... HO 61, 62, 63C
Jolin, Mike .... GO 95
Jolin, Norman B. .... GY 68, 69
Jolly, Douglas .... LA 93, 94, 95, 96
Jonckheere, Mike .... TN 2001, 02
Jones, Albert E., III .... BS 41, 42 / TR 42
Jones, Allen, Jr. .... FB 51
Jones, B. Lee, Jr. .... TR 50, 51, 52
Jones, Brian .... FB 87, 89
Jones, Bruce M. .... BS 53
Jones, Clinton .... FB 64, 65, 66CoC / TR 65, 66
Jones, Donald F. .... TR 14
Jones, Dudley P. .... BK 41, 42, 46
Jones, Eric .... FB 76, 77, 78, 79
Jones, George L. .... SW 59, 60, 61
Jones, Gerald .... BK 2002
Jones, Gerald R. .... FB 31, 32
Jones, Jeffrey .... FB 89, 90
Jones, Jerald L. .... FB 64, 65, 66
Jones, Joel .... FB 55, 56
Jones, John .... FB 83, 84, 85
Jones, Kenneth .... FB 74, 75, 76
Jones, Mark .... FB 77, 78, 79, 80
Jones, Michael H. .... FB 80, 81
Jones, Michael .... FB 73, 74
Jones, Milford H. .... FB 45 / TR 46
Jones, Robert M. .... SW 69, 70
Jones, Selwyn .... TR 56, 57C / CC 55C, 56
Jones, Stephen A. .... LA 72
Jones, Theodore .... FB 80, 81, 82
Jones, Walter A. .... WR 57
Jones, Zeb .... FB 91, 93
Joranko, Daniel .... LA 80
Jordan, J. Nicholas .... FB 66, 67, 68
Jordan, Richard C. .... BS 67, 68, 69 / BK 67
Jordan, Thomas W. .... FB 61, 62
Jorgensen, Eric .... GO 2000, 01, 02CoC, 03CoC
Joseph, Charles .... WR 80, 81
Joseph, Ronald J. .... FB 68, 69, 71
Joslin, Marion L. .... FB 27, 28, 29 / WR 30C
Joyce Donn .... BK 49
Joyce, Douglas O. .... GY 50M
Jozwiak, Max W. .... BK 53
Jubenville, Mike .... FB 88, 89
Juday, James .... FB 67
Juday, Richard .... BS 88, 89, 90, 91CoC
Juday, Robert .... BS 90, 91, 92
Juday, Steve .... FB 63, 64, 65CoC / BS 64, 65, 66
Judd, Jerome .... TR 78, 80, 81
Judge, John .... BS 84, 85, 86
Judge, Phil .... WR 93, 94, 95, 96CoC
Juengel, Allen V. .... BS 50M
Julian, George E. .... FB 11, 12, 13, 14C / TR 13, 14C
Jung, Gregory .... GY 86, 87, 88, 89C
Junker, Herman J. .... GY 55, 56
Juntikka, John .... HO 67, 68, 69
Juratovac, Robert P. .... LA 72
Jurcevich, Jim .... CC 94, 96, 97, 98CoC / TR 96, 97, 98, 99C
Justice, Morgan A. .... FB 69
Kaae, William K. .... FB 55
Kaczmarek, John .... SO 2002
Kaczmarek, Mark .... FB 82
Kage, Lowell M. .... WR 51
Kahl, Harris A. .... BS 29, 30, 31
Kaines, Michael A .... CC 62, 63, 64 / TR 62, 63, 64C
Kaiser, David M. .... FB 55, 56,57
Kaiser, Timothy .... LA 92
Kakela, Peter J. .... FB 59, 60, 61
Kalakailo, Andrew .... FB 90
Kalczynski, Joe .... BS 97, 98, 99
Kalenka, Lars .... SW 94
Kalman, Kazmer C. .... FB 57M
Kalmar, H. Ralph .... FC 52
Kalmbach, Michael .... SW 68, 69, 70
Kalmbach, Walter A., Jr. .... TR 45, 47, 48 / CC 44
Kalvelage, Douglas .... LA 70, 71
Kaman, Roman J. .... FB 39
Kamana, Carter .... FB 81, 82, 83, 84
Kaminski, Mark .... LA 77
Kamrath, Robert M. .... BS 40, 41
Kane, Paul L. .... TN 30C
Kanicki, James H. .... FB 60, 61, 62
Kanitz, Hugo F. .... FB 26, 27
Kanner, Jan Nevin .... LA 75, 76
Kanu, Sorie .... FB 95, 96, 97, 98CoC
Kapral, Frank S. .... FB 50, 51 / WR 50, 51
Kapsalis, Peter .... SO 80, 81, 82
Karas, Frank .... FB 39, 40, 41
Karfis, Mel .... SO 90
Karfis, Steve .... SO 88, 89
Karll, Christopher .... FC 89, 90C
Karlstrom, Gunnar .... GO 88, 89, 90, 91
Karpinski, John J. .... FB 63, 64, 65
Karr, Robert F. .... TR 70
Karrer, Mark .... SO 73
Karslake, Pat .... WR 68, 69, 70
Kasley, John .... SW 85
Kasten, Jack .... SW 45
Kastner, William R. .... TR 1902
Kathrein, John A. .... BK 52M
Katowich, Jason .... FC 90
Kau, Wallace Y. .... TN 51
Kaufman, Anton, J. .... SW 59
Kauffman, James .... LA 74, 75
Kaulitz, Dale E. .... TR 41, 42, 43
Kauppi, Donald K. .... HO 50
Kauth, Don F. .... FB 52, 53, 54C
Kavanaght, Ziehl .... FB 2000, 01, 02
Kavulich, Michael .... CC 82, 83, 84, 85CoC / TR 85
Kawa, Justimn HO99M
Kaye, Michael .... GO 83, 84
Kaye, Richard .... BK 79, 80, 81
Kazma, Leo J. .... SO 79, 80, 81
Kearly, Ted H. .... BS 57, 58
Kearly, Tim .... BS 80, 81
Keast, Roger .... TR 32, 33, 34 / BK 32 / FB 32
Keating, Tighe .... TN 77, 78
Kebschull, Herbert W. .... CC 46
Keeler, David .... BK 66, 67
Keenan, Mike .... WR 2001, 02, 03
Keene, Jon .... LA 70
Keesler, Starr H. .... TR 39, 40, 41
Kehr, David .... FB 95
Keir, Gerald J. .... BK 64M
Keith, Duncan .... HO 2002
Keith, Eric .... WR 2002, 03
Kelbel, Edward .... GO 78
Keller, George C. .... CC 38, 39 / TR 40
Keller, Mason .... TR 46
Keller, Matthew .... FB 87, 88, 89, 90
Keller, Wayne M. .... BX 53
Kelley, John .... LA 70
Kelley, Thomas .... BK 95, 96, 97, 99 CoC
Kellogg, Orson T. .... FB 17 / BS 18
Kelly, David .... HO 74, 75, 76, 77
Kelly, Ellison L. .... FB 56, 57, 58
Kelly, Martin J. .... FB 48
Kelly, Russell W. .... FB 57
Kelser, Gregory .... BK 76, 77, 78CoC, 79CoC
Kelson, Kellen .... SO 2001
Kelto, Anders .... SO 2001
Kemeling, Reiner .... SO 60, 61, 62C
Kemler, John .... BK 65, 66
Kemp, Edward .... BK 35M
Kemp, Steven .... TR 73, 74, 75
Kempf, Robert .... HO 60, 61, 62
Kendall, Gerald G. .... BX 56
Kendrick, Harry E. .... BS 67, 68, 69C
Kennedy, Crawford .... CC 57, 58, 59C / TR 57, 58, 59
Kennedy, Daniel .... SO 88, 89, 90
Kennedy, Henry .... CC 55, 56, 57C / TR 56, 57, 58
Kennedy, J. Martin .... FB 75
Kennedy, Joseph K. .... TR 43
Kennedy, Paul .... SO 75, 76 77
Kennedy, Robert .... SO 83
Kennedy, Ryan .... CC 92, 93, 95CoC, 96CoC / TR 93, 96, 97
Kennedy, Samuel J. .... BS 1898, 99, 00
Kennedy, William J. .... FB 39, 40, 41
Kenney, Richard K. .... FB 64, 65, 66 / BS 65, 66, 67
Kenney, Timothy .... TR 80
Kent, Bryan D. .... CC 69
Kent,William R. .... GO 46
Kenyon, Pierre M. .... TR 28
Kepford, James R. .... CC 50, 51C, 52C / TR 51, 52, 53
Kepple, Ted .... FB 54
Kern, Sidney A. .... BK 45M
Kernen, Kevin .... BS 95
Kerner, William .... FC 68
Kerr, Timothy .... CC 77, 78, 79, 80
Ketcham, Donald D. .... BS 62, 63, 64
Ketchman, Sam .... FB 36
Ketchum, James P. .... FB 50M
Ketzko, Alexander G. .... FB 38, 39
Keur, Josh .... FB 94, 95, 96, 97
Keyes, Corey .... FB 90, 91
Keyes, Richard .... HO 95, 96, 97CoC
Keyes, Tony .... SO 66, 67, 68C
Keyton, Kerry .... FB 88, 89, 90
Kiczenski, Edward L. .... CC 46
Kidder, Charles A. .... CC 29M
Kidman, James L. .... BK 24
Kiebler, Harold C. .... BS 24, 25, 26C
Kiebler, Sean .... WR 94
Kieffer, David .... LA 93, 94, 95CoC
Kiel, David .... FB 87
Kieppe, Richard N. .... FB 40, 41, 42
Kifer, L. Darryle .... SW 65, 66
Kigongo, Ken .... TN 97, 98, 99, 2000
Kilbourn, Richard .... BS 65, 66
Kilbride, Duane R. .... BK 61
Kilgore, William .... BK 71, 72, 73C
Kilian, Fritz .... LA 89, 90, 91CoC
Kiljan, John J. .... TR 39
Killoran, John L. .... TR 24
Kilpatrick, Randall J. .... CC 69, 70, 71, 72CoC / TR 71, 72
Kimball, Michael .... FC 89, 90
Kimble, Keith D. .... TN 50, 51, 52
Kimble, Kenneth G. .... TN 51
Kimichik, Alan .... FB 79, 80, 81
Kinek, Michael K. .... BK 37, 39C
King, Christopher .... FB 70, 71, 72
King, Daniel .... TR 76, 77, 78, 79
King, Gary .... WR 61
King, Gordon A. .... HO 52, 53, 54, 55
King, James M. .... FB 50
King, LeRoy B. .... BS 1895
King, Scott .... TN 79, 80, 81, 82C
King, Thomas V. .... BS 43
King, Thomas .... SO 81, 82
King, Tom .... GY 68M
Kingsley, Chris .... FB 92M, 93M
Kingston, Kyle .... LA 96
Kinkel, Ted .... GY 65, 66
Kinnan, William A. .... TR 1886
Kinney, Charles E. .... GY 60M
Kinney, John R. .... BS 49, 50C
Kinney, Steven .... BS 80
Kinsey, Craig M. .... GY 68, 69
Kinsey, Daniel B. .... GY 67, 68, 69
Kipke, Ray L. .... FB 23, 24
Kiple, John .... FB 88, 89
Kipp, Steven .... SO 77, 78
Kircher, Alton S. ... BK 32, 33CoC / BS 31, 32, 33 / FB 32, 33
Kircher, Steven .... GO 86
Kirchhausen, Bryce .... SO 99, 2000, 01, 02
Kirchoff, John .... GY 69
Kirkling, Jack .... FB 79, 80, 81, 82
Kirkpatrick, Steve .... BK 70
Kirkpatrick, Thomas .... SW 74M, 75M
Kish, Brent .... GO 87, 88, 89C, 90C
Kitto, Clyde E. .... BK 24
Klaase, Leonard S. .... TR 23
Klasinski, Paul .... HO 77, 78, 79
Klassa, Andrew .... CC 86
Klaviter, David .... SW 92, 93, 94, 95
Kleckner, David .... GO 87
Klein, Jason .... BK 96, 97, 98, 99 CoC

Klein, Joseph A. .... FB 49, 50, 51
Klein, Timothy .... TR 75, 76, 77, 78CoC
Kleinhans, Michael L. .... TR 59, 60
Kleinheksel, John .... TR 31, 32, 33
Klemm, Michael .... TN 79, 80
Klemm, Steven .... TN 77, 78, 79C
Kleva, Marty L. .... GO 61
Klewicki, Casmer J. .... BS 39, 40, 41
Klewicki, Edward L. .... FB 32, 33, 34 / BS 33, 34
Klewicki, Herman A. .... FB 39
Klewicki, Wesley L. .... BS 60, 62
Kling, Fredrick J. .... BS 1896
Klos, Tom .... LA 89
Klose, Gregory .... LA 82, 83, 84, 85
Klott, Scott .... FB 89M, 90M, 91M
Klunzinger, Willard R. .... TN 34, 36
Knapp, William W. .... BS 07
Knecht, John W. .... TR 09, 10C
Knight, Dale W. .... FB 53
Knight, Marvin .... BS 67, 68, 69
Knight, Roger .... SW 86
Knisel, Wendell O. .... BS 29, 30
Knivila, James .... BS 74, 75, 76
Knott, Eric .... FB 2001, 02
Knotts, James D. .... WR 52, 53
Knox, Robert D. .... SW 43
Kobel, Robert J. .... SW 61
Koceski, Michael .... BS 87, 88, 89, 90C
Koehn, Jack I. .... BX 58 / WR 58
Koellhoffer, Dave .... TN 89
Koerber, Scott .... BS 2001. 02, 03
Koerkel, David .... FC 93
Koerner, Chris .... SW 98, 99, 2000CoC, 01CoC
Kohler, Neil .... BS 99M, 00M, 01M
Kolb, Richard .... FB 83
Kolbe, Joseph W. .... SW 62, 64
Kolch, Frank E. .... FB 71
Kolodziej, Anthony M. .... FB 55, 56, 57
Kolodziej, Joseph .... FB 78, 80
Koning, Fred .... TR 91, 92
Koning, Todd .... TR 92, 93, 94C, 95
Konley, Brett .... SO 98, 99, 2001, 02
Konrad, Ignatius J. .... WR 43, 46C, 47
Koonce, Ryan .... SW 93
Koppi, Chris .... SO 86, 87, 88, 89
Kopriva, Donald TR 69M, 70M, 71M / CC 69M, 70M
Korkiala, Raimo .... SO 69, 70
Korman, Bruce .... LA 84, 87
Korten, Donald H. .... SW 47, 48, 49, 50
Kortge, Ralph M. .... GO 42
Korwek, Jerome L. .... BS 57, 58, 59
Kosier, Jon .... GO 84, 85, 86C, 87C
Kositcheck, Leonard .... TN 39
Koski, Kris .... HO 2000, 01, 02
Koskinen, John .... GO 2001, 02, 03CoC
Kost, William .... GO 84
Kosta, Todd .... TN 99
Kostegian, Vanar A. .... BS 45
Kough, Stephen J. .... FB 69, 70, 71
Kouri, John .... FB 81, 82
Koutnik, Jared .... BS 2001, 02
Kovacich, George T. .... BS 37 / FB 36, 37, 38
Kovacs, M. Dan .... FB 72M
Kovan, Eric .... TN 87, 88
Koverly, George T. .... FB 36, 37, 38 / BS 37
Kovicak, Randy .... WR 95
Kowal, Stanley J. .... GO 39, 40C, 41CoC
Kowalczyk, Walter J. .... FB 55, 56, 57
Kowalk, Clayton J. .... BK 43
Kowalewski, Alec .... WR 2001, 02, 03
Kowalski, Jonathon .... BS 2003
Kowalski, Kendall .... FB 89
Kowalski, Stewart .... LA 83
Kowatch, Joseph .... FB 30, 31, 32
Koyl, Matthew .... WR 99, 2001
Kozakowski, Jeff .... HO 96, 97, 98, 99
Kozikowski, Renaldo .... FB 50
Kraft, Howard A. .... BK 36, 37, 38C
Krajczinski, Alex, A. .... SW 47

Krakora, Joseph G. .... BK 45
Krall, William R. .... BK 45, 46
Kramer, Ezra .... WR 98, 99
Kramer, Jedaiah .... WR 92, 94, 95, 96CoC
Kramer, Mike .... GO 95
Krasman, John R. .... BS 65, 66
Krass, Jeff .... SO 2000, 01, 02CoC
Krat, Nickolas .... SO 64, 65
Kratz, Frank J. FB 1901, 02, 03C, 04 / TR 1903, 04, 05
Kratz, Oscar A. .... BS 06, 07 / FB 05
Krause, Andrew .... BS 82, 83, 84
Krause, Casey .... WR 91
Krause, Chris .... LA 95
Krause, Floyd J. .... TN 41
Krause, Michael .... WR 89, 90, 91
Krause, Stephen .... FC 69, 70
Kreft, Thomas W. .... SO 66, 67, 68
Krehl, Edward C. .... BK 05C, 06C, 07C, 08
Kreiner, Jack B. .... WR 47, 48, 49
Kreitsch, Robert .... FC 69, 70
Krental, Adorf B. .... BS 1896, 97
Krental, Alexander ... BS 1895, 96, 97, 98, 99 / TR 1895
Krental, Christian M. .... BS 1897M
Krentz, Dale .... HO 83, 84, 85
Krestel, Robert D. .... BS 48, 49 / FB 47, 48
Kreuger, Richard .... BS 70
Krichevsky, Evan .... FC 73
Kritzer, Robert J. .... TR 48
Kroll, William H. .... TR 27, 28
Kronbach, Allan J. .... BS 34, 35
Kronk, Charles .... LA 70, 71
Kronner, Thomas G. .... FB 71, 72, 73
Kropf, Matt .... FB 2000, 01
Krueger, Jason .... FB 96
Krueger, Warren .... CC 69
Kruggel, George .... SW 79, 80, 81, 82
Krumm, Todd FB 84, 85, 86, 87 / BS 85, 86, 88
Krusac, Mark .... FC 77, 78C, 79C
Kruse, Eric .... HO 92, 93, 94
Kruse, Stephen .... BS 79
Krushak, Donald H. .... FC 43
Kruyer, Timothy .... GY 94, 95
Kruzel, Paul .... GO 76
Kruzich, Matt .... HO 98
Kryt, Dirk .... FB 72, 73
Krzemienski, Thomas C. .... BS 63, 64
Kucab, Jeff .... BK 96M, 97M, 98M, 99M
Kuczerepa, George .... GY 50, 51
Kuester, Fred R. .... WR 55
Kuh, Richard E. .... FB 50, 51
Kuhl, K. Robert .... FB 55M
Kuhlman, John P. .... GY 67M, 68M
Kuhlman, Thomas .... GY 70, 71
Kuhn, Bernard D. .... BS 21, 22, 23C
Kuhn, Gary .... FB 93, 94
Kuhn, George W. .... BS 24, 25, 26
Kuhne, Kurt H. .... BS 36 / FB 35
Kuk, John E. .... BS 37, 38
Kukurba, Ihor .... SO 80, 81
Kula, Robert .... FB 86, 87, 88, 89CoC
Kulesza, Bruce A. .... FB 68, 69
Kulikowski, Dan J. .... FB 70, 71
Kumiega, Anthony L. .... FB 59, 60, 61 / TR 61
Kumiega, Ronald .... FB 71, 72, 73
Kunkel, Thomas .... LA 79
Kuper, George .... GY 50, 51
Kupper, James .... BK 64, 65, 66
Kurczewski, Thomas .... BS 85, 86
Kurowski, Andrew .... LA 84, 85
Kurrle, Harry A. .... FB 26, 27, 28
Kurtis, Douglas .... TR 71 / CC 71
Kurtz, Lawrence D. .... BK 18, 19C, 20 / TR 18C, 19
Kurtz, Lloyd B. .... TR 24, 25C, 26
Kurtz, Raymond L. .... FB 08M
Kurtz, Ryan .... BS 2001, 02, 03
Kurvi, Timo .... FC 89, 90, 91C
Kus, Jeff .... TR 98, 99, 2000, 01, 02
Kush, Frank J. .... FB 50, 51, 52
Kutcher, Thomas .... BS 91, 92, 93

Kutchins, Bryon A. .... FC 63, 64, 65
Kutchins, Henry K. .... FB 34, 35, 36C
Kutchins, Walter S. .... FB 39, 40
Kutchinski, Tom .... FB 68, 69, 70
Kuzma, Theodore R. .... GO 85
Kwasney, Thomas A. .... SW 56, 57, 58
Kyles, Fred .... TR 90, 91, 92
Kynast, Richard .... TN 86, 87, 88
Laackman, Dale .... LA 72
Labinjo, Mike .... FB 2000, 01, 02
Lacey, William H. .... FC 47, 48, 49, 50C
Lackey, Carl K. .... HO 62, 63, 64
Lackey, Thomas W. .... HO 61, 62, 63
Lacoste, Andre .... HO 59, 60, 61
Lacy, Mark .... FB 91
Lad, Lawrence .... GY 72, 73
Ladd, Donald B. .... SW 39, 40C, 41
Ladd, John C. .... SW 65
Ladue, Howard A. .... BS 41, 42, 43
Ladwig, Andrew .... GY 85, 86CoC, 87
LaFave, Matt .... CC 97, 98, 99C / TR 98, 2000
Lafayette, Kenneth F. .... TR 31, 32
Lafayette, Lee .... BK 67, 68, 69C
Lafever, Albert M. .... BS 13
Laforge, Richard W. .... BX 52
LaFrance, Leonard B. .... SW 40
Lagrou, Alfred J., Jr. .... TR 46, 48
Laitner, Cass B. .... TR 1896, 97 / FB 1896
Lake, Robert L. .... CC 57, 58, 59 / TR 58, 59, 60C
Lakian, Craig .... HO 79, 80, 81, 82
Laking, J. Alan .... HO 70, 71, 72
Lalain, Scott .... FB 91
Lalley, Patrick .... BK 98M, 99M, 2000M, 01M
Lalonde, Mike .... HO 2002, 03
Lamarche, Andre .... HO 81, 82, 84
Lamb, Jim Bob .... FB 82, 83
Lamb, Matthew .... WR 98, 99, 2000
Lambert, Jeff .... SW 90, 91
Lambros, James .... HO 92
Lamers, John G. .... BK 61, 62, 63C
Lamont, Brad .... BS 87, 88, 89, 90
L'Amoreaux, Ryan .... WR 2002, 03
Lampel, Thomas R. .... TR 46
Lampke, Louis J. .... FB 03
Lamssies, Robert R. .... FB 44, 45
Lancaster, Mark .... SW 79, 80, 81, 82
Lancour, Harvard L. .... BX 57, 58
Land, Melvin .... FB 75, 76, 77, 78CoC
Lande, Lars O. .... BS 63
Landefeld, Douglas .... SO 84, 85, 86, 87CoC
Landefeld, Josh .... SO 93, 94, 95, 96
Landis, Derek .... BS 91, 92. 93, 94
Landman, Jack E. .... SW 53
Landreth, Tom .... FB 88
Landry, J. Christopher .... FB 81
Landry, Patrick .... FB 87
Landsburg, George .... WR 28C
Lane, Randy .... GY 87, 88
Lane, Ray .... BS 51, 52
Lang, Forrest J. .... TR 27, 28, 29
Lang, Michael J. .... FC 85
Lang, Steve .... SW 93, 94, 95CoC
Lange, Robert .... FB 67
Langeloh, John .... FB 87, 88, 89, 90
Langer, Clarence A. .... BS 31, 32, 33
Langerveld, Todd .... FB 80
Langley, Gary .... SW 67, 68
Lanini, Jeffrey .... SW 70, 71, 72CoC
Lanker, James E. .... SW 56, 57, 58
Lanschwager, Kurt .... HO 78M, 79M, 80M
Lantz, Douglas .... FB 76
Lantzy, Jon .... LA 89, 90, 91
Laparl, John .... TN 80, 81
Lapin, Rob .... SO 86
Lapointe, James .... HO 73
Lark, Randy .... FB 80, 82, 83
Larkin, George T. .... LA 71, 72
LaRose, Clifford E. .... FB 56, 57, 58
Larsen, Thomas H. .... WR 56

Larson, Chris .... SO 88, 89C
Larson, Edward Lee .... BK 34M
Larson, Fran .... WR 66
Larson, Kurt A. .... FB 85, 86, 87, 88 CoC
Larson, Orlin C. .... CC 62
Lartigue, Kevin .... FB 91, 92, 93
Laska, Melvin E. .... FC 65, 66
Laskowski, Justin .... SW 2002, 03
Lassila, Gordon A. .... HO 56
Lattimer, Earl B. .... FB 61, 62, 63
Lau, William F. .... TN 61, 62
Lauble, Gregory .... FB 81, 82
Lautenschlager, Edmund H. .... TR 39
Lavelanet, Garry .... SO 82, 83
Lavelle, Denis .... FB 82
Law, Donald .... FB 67, 68, 69
Lawing, Rhett .... SO 86
Lawless, Richard J. .... FC 59, 60, 61
Lawrence, James G. .... HO 62, 63, 64
Lawrence, Wendell B. .... BS 48, 49, 50
Lawrie, Wayne L. .... BS 51, 52, 53, 54
Lawson, Marshall L. .... FB 75, 76, 77
Lawson, Paul .... FB 66, 67
Lawson, Thomas J. .... BS 50, 51, 52
Lay, Russell, M. .... FB 32, 33
Layer, Jeffrey .... WR 79, 80, 81
Lazar, Dennis .... BS 69
Lean, David F. .... CC 57, 58C / TR 56, 57, 58C
Learned, William L. .... BS 1887
Leas, Donald E. .... GY 55, 56, 57 / SW 55, 56
Lebamoff, Robert .... BS 83
LeClair, Donald D. .... FB 41, 42, 46
Lecos, William .... LA 77, 79
Ledinski, Jay .... LA 92, 93, 94CoC
Ledlow, Ryan .... FB 93M
Ledyard, Courtney .... FB 95, 96, 97, 98CoC
Lee, Alvin R. .... FB 54, 55
Lee, Andre L. .... FC 66
Lee, Dwight .... FB 65, 66, 67
Lee, Martin E. .... FB 08
Lee, Stephen .... LA 70
Lefere, Tobin .... CC 91, 92, 93C / TR 92, 93, 94
LeFevre, Neil .... FB, 41M
Lefler, Martin J. .... FB 17, 19, 20
Legault, Richard .... SW 79, 81
Lehner, Luke .... SW 2002, 03
Lehnhardt, Milton O. .... BS 35, 36, 37CoC / FB 35, 36
Leikert, Howard .... LA 76, 77
Leisman, David .... BS 71
Leissner, Steve .... SW 89, 90, 91, 92CoC
Leister, John .... FB 80, 81CoC, 82CoC / BS 83
Leite, Timothy .... BS 77
Leiter, Kenneth .... HO 80, 81, 82, 83
Lekenta, Eugene E. .... FB 52
Lemanski, Douglas .... GO 75, 76, 77, 78CoC
Lemmon, Charles A. .... FB 08, 09
Lemmon, Chris .... GO 93, 94, 95CoC
Lenardson, Faunt V. .... FB 10, 11, 12, 13
Lennox, Theodore R. .... WR 54, 55
Leo, Joe .... CC 96, 97, 98, 99 / TR 97, 98, 2000
Leonard, Derrick .... TR 85, 86, 88
Leonard, Lewis R. .... FC 64
Leonard, Terry G. .... WR 64, 65
Leonis, Mille .... BS 01M
Leonowicz, Kenneth CC 67, 68C, 69C / TR 68., 69, 70
Lepard, Olin L. .... WR 33
Lesnik, Mike .... SO 65
Leson, Ryan .... BS 97, 98
Lester, Warren .... FB 83, 84, 85
Lett, ChristopherCC 93, 94, 95CoC / TR 93, 94, 95, 96
Levagood, George E. .... BS 38, 39
Levan, Dave .... LA 86, 87
Leventhal, Donald .... SW 83
Levin, Harvey A. .... BK 65M
Levine, Fredrick A. .... TN 55
Lewin, Dennis .... HO 63M, 64M, 65M
Lewis, Ben L. .... WR 70, 72
Lewis, Dennis A. .... TR 78
Lewis, Dwight .... HO 70, 71
Lewis, Floyd W. .... FB 29
Lewis, Jamie .... LA 90M, 91M, 92M
Lewis, Jason .... GY 99, 2001
Lewis, Jeffrey .... TR 80, 82
Lewis, John .... FB 53, 54, 55
Lewis, Kirk .... LA 81, 83
Lewis, Sherman .... FB 61, 62, 63C / TR 62, 63C
Lewis, Terry .... FB 81, 82, 83, 84 / TR 84
Lewis, Tyrone L. .... BK 72
Libbers, Arthur J. .... BS 37, 38, 39
Liberty, Clifford P. .... TR 31, 32, 33
Licata, Richard .... GY 79, 80, 82
Licata, Robert .... GY 83M
Lick, Thomas W. .... BK 67, 68, 69
Lickley, Ralph M. .... FB 1899M
Lickman, Ronald F. .... TN 62
Lieberman, Albert G. .... BK 49M
Lieberman, James K. .... BK 71M, 72M
Lieckfelt, Brian .... BS 71, 72
Lieckfelt, T.J. .... SO 97, 98, 99, 2000
Liggett, John A. .... TR 42, 43
Liles, John-Michael .... HO 2000, 01, 02, 03CoC
Lilly, Richard J. .... FB 72M, 73M
Lillyblad, Robert B. .... TR 57
Limber, Peter E. .... FB 44M
Lincoln, Dewey R. .... FB 61, 62, 63
Lincoln, James E. .... TR 52, 53
Lincoln, John .... BS 75, 76, 77
Lindeman, Edward C. .... FB 10M
Linder, Luke .... TN 94, 95, 96, 97CoC
Lindley, Darrell E. .... BS 51
Lindsay, Donald .... SW 74, 76
Lindsay, Herbert . CC 73, 74, 75, 76 / TR 74, 75, 76, 77
Lindsey, Don .... BS 87, 88, 89
Linebaugh, Timothy .... WR 75M
Link, Arthur B. .... CC 65, 66 / TR 66
Link, Donald .... TN 34
Linne, William V. .... BS 67, 68, 69
Lionas, Mike .... BS 2001, 02
Lioret, Ernest L. .... FB 22, 23, 24
Lipscomb, Timothy .... SO 93, 94
Lische, Charles H. .... TR 29
Lisenby, Mark .... SW 90, 91, 92
List, David .... BS 96
Little, Kenneth E. .... FB 67, 68, 69
Little, Kenneth R. .... BS 33
Little, Stephen H. .... TR 51, 52, 53
Littlejohn, Bradshaw .... FB 2000
Litwhiler, Richard W. .... BS 67
Livensparger, Donald E. .... BS 61
Lixey, Andy .... TR 99, 2000, 01, 02, 03CoC
Lloyd, Gregory .... BK 79
Lobaugh, Leslie L. .... SW 56, 57, 58
Locke, Fred .... SW 97, 98
Lockwood, Matthew .... BS 92, 93
Loeding, Mark .... HO 96, 97, 98, 99
Lofgren, Bruce E. .... FB 56M
Logan, Ben .... TR 2001
Logan, John M. .... CC 53
Logan, Leonard N. .... FB 31M
Lohri, Jean .... SO 60, 61, 62
Lonce, Craig .... FB 76, 77, 78
Loney, Glenn .... TR 67M
Long, John E. .... FC 38C
Long, Octavius .... FB 95, 96, 97 / TR 94, 96, 97, 98
Longaker, Michael .... BK 78, 79, 80
Longstreet, Gregory .... SO 90
Lonigro, Aldo F. .... SO 58
Lonsbury, Pierre B. .... TR 26M
Look, Bruce .... BS 64
Look, Dean Z. .... FB 57, 58, 59 / BS 58, 59
Loomis, Ladd N. .... SW 38, 40
Loose, William S. .... TN 34
Loper, Mark M. .... FB 70, 71
Lopes, Roger .... FB 61, 62, 63
Lopez, Joseph .... BS 78, 79
Lorbek, Erazem .... BK 2003
Lord, Charles S. .... TR 10, 11, 12
Lord, Richard L. .... HO 51, 52, 53
Lord, Russell R. .... TR 26, 27, 28
Lorius, Brett .... FB 90, 91, 92, 93
Lossen, Max .... WR 2003
Lothamer, Edward D. .... FB 62, 63
Loulakis, Nickolas M. .... BS 45
Loutzenhiser, Rodger .... FC 66, 67C
Love, Robert .... FB 86
Love, Thomas E. .... FB 68
Loveland, Clarence W. .... TR 12, 13, 14,15 / FB 14
Loveland, Harold V. .... TR 09
Lovett, B. J. .... FB 2001, 02
Lowe, Gary R. .... FB 54, 55
Lowe, Richard V. .... SW 62, 63, 64
Lowrance, Keith .... WR 68, 69, 70
Lowther, Charles .... FB 66
Lubahn, Casey .... GO 2002, 03
Lubanski, Edward .... HO 77
Lubanski, Paul .... LA 78, 79
Lubbers, Steven .... GO 78, 79, 80, 81C
Lucas, Harold W. .... FB 63, 64, 65
Lucas, Leslie .... SO 68, 69, 70
Luce, Francis Alan .... BS 55, 56, 57C
Luce, Robin .... FC 72, 73
Luchenbill, David .... WR 69M, 70M, 71M
Ludwig, Robert H. .... BS 46 / FB 45
Ludwig, Stanley .... LA 75, 76C, 77CoC
Lueck, Walter H. .... FB 36, 37
Lugar, Chris .... SO 80, 81
Lukasik, Larry .... FB 64, 66
Luke, Edwin B. .... FB 50, 51, 52
Lukins, Darle J. .... TR 16, 17
Lumianski, Jeremy P. .... BS 59, 60, 62C
Lumsden, David H. .... FB 48, 49 / BK 47, 48
Lund, Donald .... FC 65, 66
Lundquist, Peter .... SW 86 CoC
Lundquist, Robert .... SW 79, 80, 81, 82CoC
Lundy, Charles B. .... FB 1898
Luongo, Chris .... HO 86, 87, 88, 89C
Luoto, Larry .... SW 42, 43
Luplow, Alvin D. .... FB 58
Luplow, Harley .... LA 76
Lustik, Donald P. .... TR 57
Lutz, Brantly .... CC 93, 94, 95 / TR 95, 96
Lutz, Harry J. .... FC 35C
Lutzer, Karl .... FC 93
Lux, Harry J. .... BK 56, 57
Lycett, James .... HO 87, 88
Lyke, Wardell H. .... TR 43
Lyman, Richard P., Jr. .... FB 23, 24, 25
Lynett, Leo .... HO 78, 79, 80, 81
Lynn, Geoffrey .... GO 66
Lynne, Rex .... LA 84, 85, 86CoC, 87CoC
Lyons, Michael .... TR 75
Lyons, Mitchell .... FB 89, 90, 91, 92
Lytle, Gary .... BS 65
Lytle, Mark .... TR 83, 84, 85
Maas, Gregory .... HO 76
Maas, Kirk .... BS 69, 70, 71
Mabon, Graham .... LA 93, 95
MacArthur, Duncan C. .... BS 1890
Macauley, William A. .... CC 33M
MacDonald, Glenn H. .... HO 57, 58, 59
MacDonald, Robert B. .... TR 38M
MacDonald, Timothy . BK 85M, 86M 87M, 88M, 89M
MacDonell, Dennis A. .... GO 63
MacDougall, Everett R. .... BK 40M
MacFarland, Mark .... FB 90, 91, 92
MacGrain, Donald .... BS 36, 37
Machemer, Kevin .... SW 77, 78
Macholz, Dennis .... FB 70, 71, 72
Macier, George W. .... BS 28, 29
MacInnes, Donald E. .... TR 39
Mack, Leslie .... HO 51M
Mack, Walter C. .... CC 41, 45C, 46C / TR 42, 46, 47
Mack, William G. .... CC 48, 49C / TR 49, 50
MacKenzie, Thomas W. .... HO 56, 57, 58, 59
Mackey, Frederick .... GO 65, 66
Mackey, Lawrence L. .... FB 64
MacKinnon, Arthur C. .... BS 1893, 94, 95

Mackowiak, Thomas .... GY 80M
MacLean, Craig .... GY 74, 75, 76, 78
MacLean, Jordan D. .... GY 80, 81
MacMaster, Hugh D. .... BK 52
MacMillan, James A. .... SW 65, 66
MacMillan, Roy A. .... BS 21, 23, 24C / BK 23, 25 / FB 20, 22
MacNeill, John .... FB 90, 91
Macomber, Ronald M. .... FC 63
Macon, David C., Jr. .... TR 40
Macuga, Edward J. .... FB 64
Macy, Mark .... LA 73
Mader, Kurt E. .... TR 38, 40, 41
Madonna, John .... BS 30, 31, 32C
Madrigal, James .... TN 94, 95CoC
Madura, Michael .... TN 70, 71
Maedo, Dennis .... BS 64, 66
Maekawa, Choken .... BX 54, 55, 56
Magi, Vincent .... BS 49, 50, 51C
Magsig, Philip .... BS 79, 80, 81
Mahan, George .... BS 74, 75
Mahaney, Aaron .... SW 99, 2000, 01, 02
Mahaney, Robert C. .... BK 51M
Mahaney, Thomas .... WR 85
Mahone, Anthony .... TR 85
Mahoney, Earl L. .... FB 46
Mahoney, Pat .... SO 97, 98, 99, 2000
Mahoney, Thomas .... TR 81
Maichen, Michael .... SO 82, 83, 84
Maichoss, Arthur F. .... BS 42, 43
Maidlow, James .... WR 65, 66
Maidlow, Kenneth A. .... WR 56, 57, 58, 59
Maidlow, Steven .... FB 79, 80, 81, 82
Mailbach, Allan .... TR 67
Maisner, Michael J. .... BK 80M, 81M, 82M
Major, Curt .... SO 78
Maki, Alfred W. .... HO 51
Maki, Edwin C. .... TR 40M
Makielski Donald J. .... TR 49, 50, 51 / CC 49, 50
Makielski, Edward L. .... TR 49
Malaga, Robert S. .... TN 46, 47, 48, 49C
Malaney, Scott .... GO 74, 75
Maldegan, Robert G. .... WR 46, 47, 48, 49C
Malec, Edward .... GY 84, 85, 86, 87
Malecek, Gerald J. .... WR 70, 71, 72
Malek, Bob .... BS 2000, 01, 02
Malinosky, John M. .... FB 75, 76, 77
Malinowski, Joseph S. .... FB 75
Maliskey, Donald C. .... FB 38
Malkewitz, Walter .... CC 75
Malley, Mark .... WR 70, 72, 73
Mallory, William E. .... TR 49
Malone, Rama .... LA 91, 92
Maloney, Brian .... HO 2000, 01, 02, 03CoC
Maloney, Maurice E. .... CC 49
Mammel, David .... BS 84, 85, 86, 88
Mancour, David A. .... GO 53, 54
Mandarich, Tony .... FB 85, 86, 87, 88CoC
Manderino, Paul A. .... FB 71, 73, 74
Manders, David .... FB 59, 60, 61
Mangan, Albert J. .... TR 39, 40, 41 / CC 39, 40
Mangrum, Richard W. .... FB 41, 42C
Maniere, Robert C. .... BS 63, 64, 65
Manion, Edward J. .... BS 40
Manique, Dennis R. .... SW 66
Mankovich, John .... GY 77
Manley, Tony .... FB 84
Mann, William Alfred .... TR 61, 62
Manning, George H. .... TR 04
Manning, Richard .... GY 72, 74
Manning, Sean Peter .... SO 82, 83, 84, 85
Mannor, Richard L. .... CC 57M, 58M / TR 58M
Manns, Kirk .... BK 87, 88, 89, 90
Mansfield, William C. .... BS 54, 57
Mansfield, William H. .... TR 38, 39, 40 / CC 39
Manson, Damian .... FB 91, 92, 93, 94
Mantinelli, Perry .... LA 92
Mantos, Marvin .... FB 79, 80, 81, 82
Manwell, Arthur R. .... SW 59
Manz, Steve .... TR 2001, 02, 03CoC
Maples, Roderick .... FB 2001, 02
Marazita, Dominic .... FC 80
Marcero, James .... CC 94, 95, 96CoC / TR 95
Marchal, Joseph H. .... WR 59
Marchin, Thomas .... LA 82, 83, 84
Marchini, Donald E. .... GY 57
Marek, Anthony .... FB 76
Marek, Gabriel .... BX 49, 50
Marin, Nels V. .... FC 63, 64, 65
Marino, Carlos .... FB 88, 89, 90
Mariola, David .... WR 85, 86, 87CoC, 88CoC
Marion, Louis W. .... FC 45
Mark, Forrest .... FC 58
Markarewicz, Scott .... BS 87, 88, 89C
Markham, Arthur G. .... FB 11
Marks, Cornelius E. .... TR 18
Marks, Roger .... TR 90, 91, 92
Markusen, Joe .... HO 2001, 02, 03
Marlatt, Ronald G. .... BS 60
Marod, Steven .... BS 82, 83, 84, 85CoC
Maronick, Gregory D. .... SW 56
Marr, Richard C. .... GO 64
Marrs, John .... WR 42
Marsa, Lee A. .... WR 33
Marsh, Andrew .... TR 2001 / CC 2000, 01, 02CoC
Marsh, Donald F. .... TR 57, 59
Marsh, Jack D. .... SW 65, 66, 67
Marsh, Robert G. .... GY 55, 56C
Marshall, Brad .... GY 90, 91, 92, 93
Marshall, Cameron .... TN 2002, 03
Marshall, Chad .... BS 94, 95, 96, 97
Marshall, Christopher .... HO 88
Marshall, Donald B. .... SW 40M
Marshall, Eric R. .... FB 67
Marshall, Harvey .... TR 41M
Marshall, Lemar .... FB 95, 96, 97, 98
Marshall, Merrill G. .... WR 30
Marshall, Michael B. .... FB 76, 78, 79, 80
Marshall, Philip T. .... BX 47, 48
Marston, Phillip C. .... GO 63C, 64
Marston, Todd .... GO 86, 87, 88C
Martens, Michael J. .... TR 65, 66
Martin, Arthur D. .... FB 20
Martin, Blanche .... FB 56, 57, 59
Martin, David J. .... TR 70, 71, 72
Martin, David .... FB 86, 87, 88
Martin, Demetrice .... FB 92, 93, 94, 95
Martin, E.J. .... TR 99, 2000
Martin, George E. .... TR 03, 04
Martin, John E. .... BK 33M
Martin, John E. .... FB 72
Martin, Michael L. .... HO 63M
Martin, Robert E, ... TR 51
Martin, Robert .... HO 80, 81, 82, 83
Martin, Shane .... WR 2002, 03
Martin, Stanley A. .... FB 11
Martin, Thomas F. .... TN 49
Martin, Wade .... TN 90, 91, 92, 93CoC
Martin, William P. .... WR 39, 40
Martin, Wilton J. .... FB 68, 69, 70C
Martinek, Julius A. .... FB 48M
Marvin, Quentin .... GY 94
Marvin, Virgil I. .... FB 29M
Marx, Harry B. .... BK 25
Marx, Joseph .... GO 76, 77
Marx, William .... GO 72, 73, 74C
Mascaro, Michael .... GY 72M, 73M, 74M
Mase, G. Thomas .... GO 79, 80CoC
Maskill, William R. .... FB 44 / TR 45, 46
Masny, Myron .... FB 38
Mason, Elwood M. .... BK 25
Mason, Derrick .... FB 93, 94, 95, 96
Mason, Donald L. .... FB 47, 48, 49
Mason, James .... WR 81, 82, 83, 84
Mason, John .... SW 72
Mason, John D. .... SW 56, 57
Mason, Paul .... CC 76
Mason, Shaun .... FB 97, 98, 99, 2000CoC
Massey, Brandon .... FB 2002
Massey, Kimya .... BS 97, 98, 99, 2000
Massuch, Richard C. .... BS 46, 47 / FB 44, 45
Masteller, Dan .... BS 87, 88, 89
Masters, Norman D. .... FB 53, 54, 55
Matalon, Ralph .... TN 80M
Matauch, Daniel .... WR 84, 85, 86, 87CoC
Mather, Richard R. .... TR 63, 64
Mather, Shawn .... HO 99
Mathers, William M. .... FC 71, 72
Mathews, Arnold .... BS 83, 84, 85, 86
Mathews, Charles L. .... BS 52, 53, 54, 55
Mathieson, James .... SW 82, 83, 84
Mathieson, Roderick R. .... BK 12
Matsko, John .... FB 54, 55, 56C
Matsock, John J. .... FB 53, 54 / BS 54, 55C
Matson, Edward I. .... FB 20, 21 / BK 21, 22
Matsos, Archie G. .... FB 55, 56, 58
Matsuda, Yuka .... BS 80M
Matt, Juergen H. .... SW 60, 61, 62
Mattera, James .... BK 2002M
Matthews, Henry .... FB 70, 71
Matthews, Wallace B. .... BK 25M
Mattson, Charles .... BS 83
Mattson, Jeffrey P. .... SW 61, 62, 63C
Maupin, Theodore .... BS 49, 50
Mavis, Stanley .... CC 73, 74, 75, 76 / TR 74, 75, 76,77
Maxson, John .... SW 92, 93, 94, 95
Maxwell, John William .... WR 41, 42, 43 / TN 42, 43
Maxwell, Mark A. .... CC 69
May, Floyd Earl .... TN 42, 43 / BK 43
May, Frank O. .... FB 47M
Mayer, Rudolph .... SO 69, 70, 71
Mayer, Tim .... HO 2003M
Mayes, Craig .... BS 89, 90, 91, 92C
Mayes, John W. .... HO 52, 53, 54, 55
Mayhew, Harold D. .... TR 46, 47
Maynard, Gray .... WR 2000, 01, 02, 03CoC
Maynard, Keith .... GY 95
Mays, Damond .... FB 72, 73
Mays, Lee .... TR 97
Mazza, Matthew A. .... BK 46, 47
Mazza, Orlando J. .... FB 51
Mazzoleni, Mark .... HO 77, 78, 79, 80
McAdoo, Howard .... FB 80, 81, 82
McAllister, Bobby, Jr. .... FB 85, 86, 87, 88CoC
McAndrew, Brian . GO 65, 66, 67CoC / HO 65, 66, 67
McAtee, Harold A. .... TR 27, 28, 29
McAuliffe, David .... HO 90
McAuliffe, Donald F. .... FB 50, 51, 52C
McAuliffe, Thomas .... BK 51
McBrady, Gary .... SO 65, 66, 67
McBride, Dunbar .... TR 24M
McBride, Robert .... FB 92, 93, 94, 95
McCabe, Albert M. .... TR 27
McCaffree, David Lee .... SW 58, 59
McCaffree, Donald C. .... SW 65M, 66M
McCaffrey, Dee .... TN 77
McCall, Thomas .... BK 84M, 85M, 86M, 87M
McCalla, Darold .... FC 57, 58C
McCallum, Albert D. .... FC 61
McCann, William C. .... BS 32, 33, 34
McCarthy, Dan .... LA 86, 87, 88
McCarthy, Jamie .... LA 95, 96
McCarthy, Kevin .... FB 76M, 77M, 80M, 81M
McCarthy, Michael .... LA 82, 83, 84, 85CoC
McCarthy, Robert J. .... TR 41, 42, 43
McCarthy, William E. .... BS 11
McCarty, Matt .... WR 2002, 03
McCaslin, Garold E. BK 31, 32, 33CoC / BS 31, 32, 33
McCaul, Steve .... SO 89, 90, 91
McCauley, Robert H. .... BS 28, 29, 30
McCauley, Wes .... HO 90, 91, 92, 93CoC
McClain, Jack .... TR 45
McClain, Joseph .... LA 70
McCleary, Eugene J. .... BS 40M
McClelland, Albert L. .... BK 15, 16, 17C / FB 16
McClelland, Darrin .... FB 79, 81, 82
McClelland, Robert L. .... TR 51
McClintock, Tim .... LA 81, 82

McClowry, Patrick G. ... FB 73, 74, 75
McClowry, Robert J. ... FB 70, 71, 72
McClowry, Terrence G. ... FB 72, 73, 74
McClure, Homer R. ... WR 63, 64
McCollam, Paul ... TR 65 / CC 65
McComb, J. Robert ... FB 37
McConnell, Brian T. ... FB 70, 71, 72
McConnell, Mike ... FB 2001
McCook, Jack ... BS 61
McCool, Paul F. ... FB 17
McCormick, David M. ... FB 63, 64
McCormick, John ... FB 77, 78, 79, 80
McCormick, Norman F. ... BS 45
McCormick, William E. ... HO 50, 51, 52C
McCosh, James A. ... FB 25, 26, 27
McCoy, Ivory ... FB 98, 99, 2000, 01CoC
McCoy, Julius ... BK 54, 55, 56 / TR 54, 55
McCrady, Chris ... LA 91, 92, 94CoC
McCrary, James L. ... FB 33, 34
McCray, John L. ... WR 59, 61, 62
McCue, Charles ... FB 1898, 99C, 00C, 01M
McCue, Kenneth ... HO 73M, 74M
McCuiston, Chris ... BS 1999, 2000, 01, 02
McCulloch, Robert W. ... BS 1886, 87 / TR 1887
McCulloh, James ... FB 77, 78
McCullum, Albert D. ... FC 61
McCurdy, Russell J. ... FB 12, 13
McCurry, Robert B. ... FB 46CoC, 47C, 48C
McDaniel, Lewis E. ... GO 61, 62
McDermid, H. B. ... FB 04, 05 / TR 04
McDermid, Frank H. ... FB 11
McDonald, Malcolm E. ... WR 47, 48
McDonald, Roland ... SW 86
McDonald, Timothy ... HO 75, 76, 77, 78
McDowell, John ... FB 83, 84, 85
McDurmon, Claire J. ... TR 36, 37, 38
McElroy, Edward M. ... BS 1893
McFadden, Leroy ... FB 97, 98
McFadden, Marvin G. ... FB 50, 51
McFall, Daniel ... HO 82, 83, 84, 85CoC
McFarland, Jerome ... FB 58
McFetters, Douglas ... TR 52
McGaw, Donald D. ... FC 70, 71
McGee, E. Leroy ... FB 77, 78
McGill, Thomas ... BK 73, 74, 75
McGilliaray, Lodowic A. ... FB 08
McGilliard, Michael ... WR 68, 69
McGillicuddy, Robert J. ... BK 28
McGiness, John M. ... FB 79M
McGiness, Joseph D. ... FB 78M, 79M
McGinniss, William ... LA 76, 78, 79
McGohey, Thomas ... LA 73
McGowen, Leon W. ... TR 49
McGrath, John E. ... SW 45
McGuire, Jimmy ... TN 2000, 01, 02CoC, 03CoC
McInnis, Frank G. ... BS 24
McIntyre, Jeff ... SW 94
McIntyre, Malcolm M. ... FB 00
McKalko, Steven ... GO 85, 86
McKay, Raymond F. ... TR 51, 52, 53
McKee, Michael ... SW 2000
McKenna, Edward B. ... FB 03, 04 ,05C, 06 / TR 02, 04, 05C / BS 05M
McKenna, George F. ... TR 36, 37
McKenna, Parnell ... BK 06, 07, 08, 09C, 10 / FB 06, 07, 08, 09C
McKenzie, Richard D. ... BS 57
McKillop, Edward A. ... TR 55
McKinney, Brandon ... FB 2002
McKinnon, Peter A. ... SO 58, 59
McKoy, Fredrick G. ... TR 64, 65, 66
McLachlan, Robert H. ... SW 51, 52, 53C
McLaughlin, Duane J. ... FB 70, 71
McLaughlin, Ernest L. ... TR 36, 37, 38
McLaughlin, Martin ... HO 76, 77, 78
McLaughlin, Thomas ... LA 74
McLaughry, DeArmond ... FB 11
McLaurin, Jeremiah ... FB 2001, 02
McLee, Bradley M. ... FB 69, 70
McLoud, Eddy W. ... FB 67, 68
McLouth, Aldrich L. ... FB 1898, 99
McLouth, John D. ... BS 1896, 97C
McLucas, Edwin ... FB 59
McMahen, Ryan ... SO 2001
McMillen, Larry D. ... GO 61
McNamara, B. Edward ... SW 36, 37C
McNamara, Patrick ... WR 1998, 99, 2000, 01CoC
McNamara, William J. ... FC 61
McNeely, Thomas W. ... BX 58
McNeil, Robert A. ... FB 40, 41, 42
McNulty, Daniel ... LA 79, 80, 81 & 82CoC
McNulty, Kevin ... TN 75, 77, 78
McNutt, Bernard G. ... FB 32, 33C / TR 32, 33
McQuaide, Regis G. ... FB 77, 78, 79
McRae, Robert H. ... BX 48
McRae, Stanley P. ... FB 38, 39
McReynolds, Brian ... HO 86, 87, 88
McShannock, Thomas ... FB 37, 38
McSween, Don ... HO 84, 85, 86, 87CoC
McSweeney, Edward ... SO 73, 74, 75
McWilliams, Jams E. ... FB 10, 11
McWilliams, Robert H. ... BS 15, 16, 17
Meadows, Clinton L. ... FB 67
Meagher, Thomas ... GY 76, 77, 78
Meahan, Don ... LA 86
Means, Clarence T. ... BK 50, 51, 52C
Meckl, Heidi ... WR 97M
Medland, Gary ... LA 74
Medonis, Michael ... GO 79
Meek, Harry C. ... FB 1901, 02 / TR 03
Mehall, Kenneth ... BS 79, 80, 81
Meiers, Francis H. ... FB 30, 31, 32
Mejer, Daniel ... SW 79, 80, 81, 82
Mekules, Frank A. ... BS 40, 41 / BK 41
Melhorn, Wilton N. ... BS 42M
Melkonian, Michael ... WR 78M, 79M, 80M, 81M
Mellencamp, Burton C. ... BS 22
Mellinger, Stephen T. ... FB 61, 62, 64
Menard, Todd ... BS 91, 92, 93, 94
Mencotti, Edo ... BX 43, FB 42
Mendyk, Dennis A ... FB 55, 56 / BS 57
Menoni, Glenn ... HO 73, 74
Menzel, Richard G. ... TN 54, 55, 56
Mercado, Neal ... FC 95, 96
Mercer, Ralph E. ... SW 45
Mercer, Todd ... SW 90
Merchant, Jon ... BS 93
Merchant, Roger T. ... CC 66, 67, 68C / TR 67, 68, 69
Merkel, William J. ... FB 1897M
Merrill, Leland G., Jr. ... WR 40, 41, 42C
Merritt, Ivan L. ... GY 80, 81
Mervin, Clyde E. ... FB 07M
Merz, Elmer H. ... BK 08, 09
Mesaros, Paul ... TN 85, 86, 87, 88
Mescall, Ronald T. ... TN 57, 59, 60
Mesler, Leon L. ... CC 55
Mesler, Mark K. ... CC 78, 79C / TR 79, 80
Messier, Joby ... HO 89, 90, 91, 92C
Messier, Mitchell ... HO 84, 85, 86, 87CoC
Mesyn, Nathaniel ... WR 2001, 02, 03
Metevier, David ... BS 86, 88
Methner, Eric ... BS 88, 89, 90
Meyer, David ... CC 80
Meyer, Donald H. ... FB 54M, 55M
Meyer, Robert F. ... GO 63, 64C
Meyermann, Jay ... SO 73
Michaud, Lewis E. ... SW 52, 53, 54, 55M
Michelutti, Robert ... HO 70, 71, 72
Middleton, Alonzo ... FB 76, 77, 78, 79
Middleton, John L. ... FB 56, 57, 58
Miesel, Mark ... GY 89, 90, 91, 92
Migiaccio, Nicolo ... TR 43
Migliaccio, Matt ... HO 2002, 03
Mignow, Griffin ... SW 99M
Migyanka, Charles, Jr. ... FB 62, 63, 64C
Mihaiu, George M. ... FB 70, 71, 72
Mihalic, Joseph ... CC 84, 85 / TR 85, 86
Mihallik, Gregg ... SW 89, 90, 91, 92CoC
Mikalacki, Daniel ... SO 70, 71, 72, 73
Miketinac, Michael N, ... FB 42
Mikkola, Thomas M. ... HO 65, 66, 67
Mikles, Gale ... WR 45, 46, 47, 48C
Miknavich, Norbert A. ... FB 36, 37
Mikula, Eric ... TR 99
Mikulich, Robert L. ... TR 51M
Mikus, Dennis ... WR 76
Milbourn, John D. ... TR 52
Milhizer, Richard ... FB 79, 80
Milhouse, Harrell ... WR 79, 80, 82, 83CoC
Milkovich, Patrick ... WR 72, 74, 75C, 76
Milkovich, Thomas ... WR 70, 71, 72, 73C
Millar, Wilson F. ... BS 1902, 03, 04C / TR 1902, 03, 04 / FB 03 / BK 1903M, 04M
Millard, Forrest G. ... BS 17, 19
Miller, Alfred ... SW 76M, 77M, 78M
Miller, Anthony ... BK 92, 93, 94
Miller, Art ... SW 71M
Miller, Blake William ... FB 12, 13, 1 4, 15C / BS 13, 14, 15 / BK 13, 15
Miller, Carl F. ... BK 16
Miller, Carl P. ... TR 49, 50
Miller, Charles D. ... FB 23M
Miller, Chris ... GY 90, 91, 92, 93
Miller, Costa ... BK 60M
Miller, Curtis ... TR 83
Miller, Daniel ... GY 77, 79
Miller, David ... BS 2001, 02, 03
Miller, Dean E. ... HO 78, 79
Miller, Donald E. ... SW 48, 49, 50
Miller, Douglas L. ... BS 63
Miller, Ellwood J. ... HO 56, 59
Miller, G. Devere ... FB 1896
Miller, Henry R. ... GY 60
Miller, Hiram H. ... FB 13, 14, 15 / BK 13, 14
Miller, Howard D. ... BS 64, 66
Miller, Issac ... WR 96, 97, 98, 99CoC
Miller, James ... FB 90, 91, 92, 93
Miller, Jared ... LA 95, 96
Miller, John ... FB 85, 86, 87, 88CoC
Miller, Kelly ... HO 82, 83, 84, 85CoC
Miller, Ken ... BK 98
Miller, Kevin ... HO 85, 86, 87CoC, 88
Miller, Kip ... HO 87. 88. 89. 90
Miller, Lyle W. ... HO 64
Miller, Oscar R. ... BK 14, 15C / FB 13, 14
Miller, Patrick F. ... BK 70, 71, 72CoC / FB 69, 70
Miller (Melnitsky), Peter T. ... SW 50M
Miller, Richard R. ... WR 73, 74, 76
Miller, Richard ... BS 68, 69
Miller, Robert E., II ... BK 65, 66
Miller, Robert T. ... SW 50 M
Miller, Roger B. ... SW 47, 48, 49, 50
Miller, Roger L. ... FB 66M
Miller, Ryan ... HO 2000, 01, 02
Miller, Sean ... TR 92
Miller, Stephen H. ... GO 58
Miller, Wilbert E. ... FB 17, 19
Miller, William A. ... CC 55
Miller, William B. ... FB 12, 13, 14, 15C / BS 13, 14, 15
Milliken, William F. ... FB 41, 42
Milliman, Douglas G. ... WR 62
Mills, David B. ... TN 50, 51
Mills, Edward L. ... CC 39, 40C / TR 39, 40
Mills, George H. ... BS 17, 20
Mills, Herbert ... BS 07, 08, 09C, 10 / BK 07, 08, 09
Mills, Robert E. ... FB 71, 72, 73
Mills, William H. ... BS 56, 57
Milne, James A. ... TR 41, 42, 43, 47
Miltenberger, Scott A. ... FB 71
Milton, Cedric L. ... BK 73, 74, 75, 76
Minagawa-Webster, John ... SO 2000, 01
Minahan, Jeffrey M. ... FB 77M, 78M
Minarik, Henry J. ... FB 48, 49, 50
Miner, Elmer F. ... TR 25
Mineweaser, Richard L. ... BS 45, 46, 47, 48 / FB 44
Minier, Howard G. ... GO 31
Mitchell, Brian ... FB 86
Mitchell, Chris ... TN 2001, 02, 03
Mitchell, Dave ... TN 69
Mitchell, Kerry ... FB 89, 90

Mitchell, Robert B. .... FB 58M
Mitchell, Seth .... FB 2002
Mitchell, Steve .... SW 71
Mitchem, Ronald .... FB 79, 80, 81
Mittelberg, Victor .... FB 69, 70 / WR 70
Mitten, Patrick .... FB 79
Mittenberger, Scott A. .... FB 71
Mock, John A. .... TR 69, 70, 71 / CC 68
Mock, John .... FB 65
Modine, Franklin .... SW 59, 60C
Moeller, William .... FB 26, 27, 28
Moen, Steven .... GY 82
Moffat, Alexander .... SO 69, 70
Moffett, John C. .... FC 53, 54
Mogge, Norton W. .... BS 11, 12, 13, 14C
Mojsiejenko, Ralf .... FB 81, 82, 83, 84 / BS 83, 84
Molla, Charles .... LA 76, 77
Monahan, Denis .... LA 71
Monahan, Terry .... LA 85, 86, 87
Monan, Richard .... TN 66, 67, 68
Monczka, Robert M. .... BS 59, 60
Money, Steven .... BS 91, 92, 93, 94CoC
Monnett, Robert C. .... FB 30, 31, 32C
Monroe, DeMarco .... FB 2000, 01
Monroe, George C. .... BS 38, 39, 40C
Monroe, George C. .... TR 1891, 92
Monroe, Ralph. B, Jr. .... CC 40, 41C, 42C / TR 41, 42
Monroe, William R. .... FB 42
Montalbano, Richard .... LA 89
Montalvo, Sergio .... FC 67
Monte, Raymond L. .... FC 53
Montford, Roy M. .... FB 10
Montgomery, Clayton, Jr. .... FB 72
Montgomery, Erik .... GY 92, 93, 94
Montgomery, Gregory H. .... FB 57, 58
Montgomery, Gregory H., Jr. .... FB 85, 86, 87
Montgomery, Mark .... BK 89, 90, 91, 92CoC
Montgomery, Russell F. .... FB 17M
Montgomery, Stephen .... FB 87, 88, 89CoC
Moody, Michael .... LA 70, 71, 72
Moomaw, Jeff .... GY 97, 98, 99, 2000
Moon. Harry E. .... TR 02, 03, 04C, 05C
Moore, Allen .... FB 81, 83, 84
Moore, Chris .... GO 74
Moore, Clyde D. .... FB 06, 07, 08, 09
Moore, Cyril F. .... TR 38
Moore, Donald Dean .... BS 57
Moore, Elliott .... BS 72, 73
Moore, Gerald .... GY 66, 67, 68
Moore, Glenn B. .... FB 45M
Moore, James .... FB 86, 87, 88
Moore, John I. .... BK 50
Moore, John R. .... TR 41
Moore, Jon .... SW 91, 92
Moore, Keith . CC 76, 78C, 79 / TR 77, 78, 79, 80CoC
Moore, Rex W. .... FB 44
Moore, Richardson .... BS 74, 75, 76
Moore, Timothy .... FB 84, 85, 86, 87
Moore, Walter J. .... TN 64M, 65M, 66M
Moore, Wendell .... FB 74
Morabito, Daniel L. .... FB 40
Moran, Gregory .... SW 77, 78
Morant, Frank .... SO 68, 69, 70
Morehouse, Robert B. .... WR 58M, 59M
Moreland, Gary S. .... GY 61
Moreland, Robert L. .... TR 63, 64
Moreno, James .... BS 2001, 02, 03
Morey, Donald E. .... SW 53, 54, 57
Morford, Shannon .... WR 93
Morgado, Arnold, Jr. .... FB 72
Morgan, David .... WR 96, 97CoC, 98
Morgan, Jack .... FB 50, 51, 52
Morgan, Michael .... LA 80, 81
Morgan, Rodney S. .... BS 47
Morgan, William R. .... TR 40
Morissette, Joel .... WR 93, 94, 95, 96CoC
Moroney, Brendon .... HO 73, 74, 75, 76
Moroney, Terrance B. .... HO 58, 59 60
Morrall, Earl E. .... FB 53, 54, 55 / BS 54, 55, 56
Morris, Aric .... FB 96, 97, 98, 99CoC
Morris, Chris .... FB 2002
Morris, Erik .... BS 2003
Morris, Philmore .... TR 89CoC
Morris, Robert M. .... BK 39, 40, 41
Morris, Thomas W. .... SW 34, 35C, 36
Morris, Thomas .... FB 80, 81
Morris, Thomas .... GY 78, 79, 80
Morrison, Bolton .... GO 65
Morrison, Bryan .... SW 93
Morrison, John .... TR 70, 71, 72, 73
Morrison, Paul .... CC 76
Morrison, Randy .... BK 81
Morrison, Robert J. .... FB 32M
Morrison, Russell A. .... FB 20, 21, 22
Morrison, William R. .... BS 40
Morrissey, Harry T. .... FB 53M
Morrissey, James .... FB 81, 82, 83, 84C
Morrow, Brian .... FC 80, 81
Morrow, Robert E. .... BS 1898M
Morse, Charles .... GY 70, 71, 72C
Morse, Floyd .... BS 32, 33, 34C
Morse, Robert .... FB 83, 84, 85, 86
Morton, Thomas .... SW 78M, 79M, 80M
Mosack, Carl L. .... GO 51, 52, 53C
Mosallam, Brian .... FB 93, 95, 96
Moser, Richard J. .... BS 51, 52
Moser, Robert O. .... WR 58, 59, 60C
Moser, Travis .... SO 83, 84, 85
Mosher, Joseph D. .... BS 28M
Mosher, Richard W. .... FB 46M
Moss, Jonathan B. .... FC 72, 74, 75, 76C
Moss, Dawan .... FB 99, 2000, 01, 02
Moss, Todd .... CC 77
Motaghi, Shervin .... SO 98, 99
Moten, Eric .... FB 87, 88, 89, 90CoC
Mouch, Robert .... FB 82
Moulthrop, Maurice J. .... TR 32
Mounteer, Jack E. .... GO 47, 48C
Moyes, Paul L. .... BS 37, 38
Mroz, Vincent P. .... FB 42
Mrozowski, Nick .... SW 2003
Mudd, Richard .... BK 82, 83, 84, 85CoC
Mudge, Dave .... FB 95, 96, 97
Mueller, Adam .... LA 85, 86, 87, 88CoC, 89
Mueller, Carl T. .... TR 35, 36, 37C
Mueller, David .... BK 86, 88, 89, 90
Mueller, Jason . TR 2000, 01, 02 / CC 99, 2001CoC, 02
Mueller, John H. .... TR 47, 48, 49, 50
Mueller, Joseph F. .... SW 45
Mueller, Tim .... LA 85, 86, 87
Mueller, William F. .... FB 28
Muhammad, Don TR 80, 81, 82,83CoC
Muhammad, Muhsin .... FB 92, 94, 95
Muir, Thomas G. .... WR 69, 70, 71
Mulcahy, Matthew .... HO 64, 65, 66
Mulder, Jeff .... TR 2000, 01 / CC 99, 2000
Mulder, Mark .... BS 97, 98
Mulder, Thomas .... WR 62
Mulheron, Hugh M. .... TR 1891, 92
Mull, Alec .... SW 91, 92, 93, 94CoC
Mull, Anthony .... BK 96, 97
Mull, Iian .... SW 96
Mullinder, Luc .... FB 2002
Mullen, John .... FB 64, 66
Mullinneux, Thomas H. .... GY 52M
Mullins, Robert D. .... BX 54, 55
Mulshine, Mike .... SW 96, 97, 98, 99CoC
Munce, Donald C. .... BS 59
Munley, John .... SW 98, 99, 2000, 01CoC
Munley, Thomas .... SW 93, 94, 95, 96CoC
Munn, Arthur H. .... BS 1891
Munn, John S. .... TR 34
Munroe, James .... FC 93, 95, 96
Murahata, Richard .... GY 68, 69, 70
Murakami, Ysuke .... FC 97
Murdock, Steve .... GY 74, 75, 76CoC
Murfey, Christopher .... HO 72, 73, 74
Murphy, Brian T. .... GY 77, 78
Murphy, Brian .... BS 95, 96, 97CoC, 98CoC
Murphy, Edwin .... GO 67
Murphy, Fred M. .... BS 1899, 00
Murphy, John H. .... FC 29, 33
Murphy, Joseph .... HO 86
Murphy, Larry .... GO 68, 69C
Murphy, Michael J. .... TR 68
Murphy, Michael .... TR 70, 71, 72, 73
Murphy, Morley R. .... FB 52, 53, 54
Murphy, Neil .... CC 95
Murphy, Robert .... TR 81, 82, 83
Murphy, Thomas .... GO 70, 72
Murphy, Todd .... TR 73, 74, 75, 76
Murray, Aaron .... TN 94, 95, 96, 97CoC
Murray, Byron M. .... BK 17, 18C
Murray, Craig .... FB 73M, 74M
Murray, Darren .... LA 89, 90, 91
Murray, Gerald H. .... SO 69, 70, 71, 72
Murray, Patrick .... HO 88, 89, 90
Murray, Rem .... HO 92, 93, 94, 95
Murray, Todd .... FB 89, 90, 91, 92
Musat, Nicholaus P. .... HO 62, 63, 64
Muscari, John .... HO 77, 78M
Musetti, Gerald A. .... FB 54, 55
Mustari, Jeff .... WR 87, 88, 89
Muster, Michael .... FB 81
Mustonen, Tom .... HO 59, 60, 61
Musulin, John .... SW 66, 67, 68
Mutchler, David G. .... TR 62, 63, 64
Muth, Charles K. .... BK 33 / FB 33
Muzashvili, Shota .... WR 97, 98, 99CoC, 2000CoC
Muzyczko, Thaddeus .... GY 58
Muzzatti, Jason .... HO 88, 89, 90, 91
Myers, Craig .... SO 98
Myers, Garry .... TN 68
Myers, Nick .... FB 98, 99, 2000, 01
Myles, Reggie H., Jr. .... GO 51
Naab, Leonard G. .... TR 42, 43, 46
Nadhir, Waad .... WR 76, 78
Nadolsky, Karl .... WR 2000, 01, 02, 03CoC
Nagel, Robert F. .... BK 50 / TR 50
Nail, John .... HO 98, 99, 2000, 01
Nance, William .... TR 72, 73, 74
Napolitan, Mark .... FB 83, 84
Naragon, Daniel .... WR 86
Nash, Ricky .... BK 76
Nasitir, Darren .... BS 2003
Nawojczyk, Ron .... HO 77M, 78M, 79M
Nay, Jacob .... TR 97
Ndukwu, Henry .... SO 80, 81
Neal, James E. .... FB 52, 53
Neal, Jeffrey .... CC 84, 85 / TR 85, 86
Neal, Michael .... FB 96, 97, 98, 99
Neaves, Mitchell .... BK 96M, 97M
Needham, George W. .... FB 27
Neely, Howard .... TR 74, 75, 76, 77
Neely, James .... FB 79, 80, 81, 82
Neitzert, Kent D. .... FC 70
Nelke, Richard .... SO 65, 66, 67
Neller, Elton G. .... FB 22, 23, 24
Nelson, Anthony .... TR 89, 90, 91CoC, 92
Nelson, Arnold P. .... GY 48, 49
Nelson, Ashley .... TR 92, 93, 94, 95C
Nelson, Broderick .... FB 2000, 01, 02
Nelson, Carl Walter .... FB 36, 37, 38
Nelson, J, Harold .... BS 06, 07, 08
Nelson, Joseph E. .... BS 42
Nelson, Kirk .... SW 91, 92
Nelson, Roy P. .... GO 38, 39C
Nemer, Guy .... HO 79M, 80M
Nemnich, Sean .... SO 92, 93
Nern, Carl R. .... FB 02
Nester, Raymond .... FB 71, 72, 73
Nestor, Carl .... FB 47
Neterer, Mark E. .... SO 79, 80, 81 & 82CoC
Neu, Thomas .... WR 91, 92, 93
Neubert, Bernard E. .... FB 42
Neumaier, Karl .... FC 90, 91
Neumann, Allan W. .... TR 59

Neumann, Harrison H.	FB 35, 36
Neumann, James R.	GO 62
Neurock, Matthew	GY 82, 83, 84, 86
Nevulis, Kazimer	BS 37
Newkirk, Robert	FB 96, 97, 98
Newman, Harold C.	BK 24M
Newman, Jason	GY 96
Newman, Joseph M.	TR 25M
Newman, Mitchell	FB 61
Newman, Raymond A.	GO 48, 49, 50C
Newsome, Richard	FB 97, 98, 99, 2000
Newton, Ralph J.	SW 41, 42, 43
Ngo, Donald	BK 2002M, 03M
Nichols, Donald H.	SW 57, 58
Nichols, John W.	SW 43
Nichols, Mark E.	FB 85, 86, 87 CoC
Nicholson, Elmer	TR 05
Nicholson, James B.	FB 70, 72
Nicodemus, Steve	BK 93, 94, 95, 96
Nicoli, Derio J.	HO 52, 53, 54, 55C
Nicolosi, Mike	LA 96
Niebylski, Gordon	FB 1902
Nielsen, Hans J.	FB 74, 75, 76, 77
Niemeyer, Roy K.	TR 47
Niemi, John A.	CC 53M
Nies, Eric E.	BS 05, 06, 07
Niesen, Mark W.	FB 71, 72, 73
Nightingale, Jared	HO 2003
Ninowski, James A., Jr.	FB 55, 56, 57
Nisbet, John J.	SO 72
Niswander, James E.	BS 1894M
Niva, Jouka	TR 81
Noack, William M.	BK 64C
Noble, Chester John	GY 63, 64
Noblet, Ubald J.	FB 19, 20, 21
Nodus, Robert J.	GO 55, 56, 57
Ngo, Donald	BK 2002M
Noller, Michael	FC 91
Norcutt, Larry	FC 69
Nordberg, Carl A.	FB 28, 29, 30
Nordwall, David	SO 91
Norman, Adam	CC 88, 90, 91CoC / TR 89, 92
Norman, David A.	SW 51, 52
Norman, Dempsey	FB 84
Norman, Robert F.	HO 58, 59, 60 / SO 57
Norris, Anthony	TR 85, 86, 88
Norris, Dwayne	HO 89, 90, 91, 92
Norris, Rex	TN 33, 34C
Northcross, David C.	FB 57, 58, 59
Northey, Clifford	BS 77
Northey, Richard H.	HO 51, 52, 53
Norton, Roy M.	BS 1898, 99, 00
Norton, Steve	HO 91, 92, 93, 94
Novak, Greg	BS 69M, 70M
Nowak, Gary W.	FB 68, 69, 70
Nower, Arthur	BS 32M
Nowland, Thomas	HO 85
Nowotarski, Mark	HO 75M, 76M, 77M
Nozewski, Jerry	BS 96, 97, 98
Nugent, James W.	SO 70, 71, 72, 74
Nusbaum, Jason	WR 97, 98, 99, 2000
Nutter, Jack W.	BS 61, 62, 63C
Nuttila, Matt E.	BK 23, 24, 25C
Nuznov, Sam	BS 37, 38, 39
Nwabara, Obioha	SO 77, 78
Nyquist, Richard L.	CC 47M
Nystie, Charles V.	FB 48, 49
Nystrom, Carl W.	FB 53, 54, 55C / HO 54
Oas, Reginald G.	BS 17, 20, 21 / FB 17
Obelnicki, Andrew	LA 73, 75
O'Bradovich, Ed	FB 90, 91
O'Brien, Francis J.	FB 56, 57, 58
O'Brien, Joseph	TN 82, 83, 84, 85
O'Brien, Mark	LA 85
O'Brien, Richard W.	GY 55, 56, 57
O'Callaghan, Jack W.	BS 16M
Ocean, Edward J.	SW 38, 39
O'Connell, Kevin	SO 66
O'Conner, Chris	GO 86
O'Connor, Daniel	HO 69
O'Connor, Michael J.	HO 69, 70
O'Connor, Robert L.	TR 29, 31 / CC 29
Odom, Herbert D.	BX 52, 53, 54, 55
O'Donnell, Eugene A.	TN 63, 64
O'Donnell, Ryan	SW 96
O'Donohue, Brenden	WR 86
Odorico, Armando L.	FC 54, 55, 56
Oesetek, Paul	GY 76
Oestriech, Jay	GY 82, 83, 84
Ogar, Robert	TR 80
Ogbeide, Wilson	TR 2002
O'Gara, Francis	FB 06M
O'Keefe, Kevin	FB 86
O'Keefe, Kevin	HO 97, 98, 99
O'Kulich, Chad	SO 92, 93, 94, 95CoC
O'Kulich, Chad	SO 95CoC
O'Leary, Robert	TR 45 / BK 45
Olejnik, Thomas	BS 94, 95, 96, 97
Olexa, Russell E.	TR 52, 53
Olin, Bruff W.	TR 03
Oliver, Bailey	BS 71, 72, 73
Oliver, Thomas W.	TR 60M
Olman, Norman A.	FB 36, 37
Olmstead, Clifford G.	FB 00
Olmstead, Dennis A.	HO 72, 73, 74, 75
Olmstead, James L.	FC 63
Olsen, Robert C.	TR 27, 30, 31
Olsen, Terry A.	GY 80, 83, 84
Olsen, William R.	CC 52M
Olson, Chester M.	TN 38, 39 40C
Olson, Duane E.	BK 54
Olson, Franklin	TR 1899
Olson, Hilding C.	TN 32C
Olson, Lance	BK 58, 59, 60C
Olson, Mark	TN 72
Olson, Michael	HO 68, 69, 70 / BS 69
Olson, Richard	HO 70, 71, 72
Olson, Weldon C.	HO 52, 53, 54, 55C
Omans, Glenn A.	SW 49, 50, 51
Omel, Richard	LA 78
Omerod, Craig	FB 72
Omiccioli, Joseph	HO 79, 80, 81, 82
O'Neil, Scott	GO 89
O'Neill, Lawrence	SW 70, 71, 72
Onopa, William	SO 61, 62
Organ, Bob	FB 91, 92, 93, 94
Organek, Brett	TR 93, 95 / FB 93
Orlando, John	GY 93, 94
Orme, Malcolm L.	HO 62, 63, 64, 65
Orna, Brandon	GY 2001
Ornekian, Derek	SO 99, 2000, 01, 02
Ornstein, Gus	FB 96
Orr, James B.	FB 66M
Orr, John J.	WR 40
Orr, Stephen T.	BS 09, 10
Orr, Wesley B.	TR 35, 36, 37
Orris, Mike	SW 97, 98CoC
Orris, Ron	SW 91, 92, 93CoC, 94CoC
Orth, Rodney	BS 89, 90
Ortiz, Randy	BS 2002, 03
Osborn, George E.	TR 46, 48, 49
Osborn, Ralph H.	BS 1896
Osborn, Raymond L.	TR 37, 39
Osetek, James	FC 73
Osgood, Richard A.	SW 65M
Oshio, Norihiko	SO 96
Osterink, Leonard	BK 37
Ostrofsky, Jason	HO 95, 96M, 97M, 98M
Oswald, Garth B.	FC 40
Oswalt, Ferris H.	TR 30
Oswalt, Stanley M.	TR 31
Oswalt, William L.	TR 58
Otani, Roy	SO 91, 92
Otis, David	TN 75
Otis, Steven	FB 76, 77, 78, 79
O'Toole, Michael	HO 87, 88, 89
Ott, Rodney R.	WR 66, 67, 68
Ottey, Thomas C.	CC 32, 33C, 34C
Otting, Robert W.	FB 42, 46
Ottmar, Dale N.	GO 46
Ottney, Brian	FB 2000, 01, 02CoC
Ouellet, Ron	WR 68, 69, 70
Oulahen, Steven	HO 74
Outlaw, Napoleon	FB 92, 93, 94, 95
Outwater, Mark	SW 74, 75, 76, 77
Ovenhouse, Todd	SW 85, 86, 87
Overgard, Jon T.	GO 62
Oviatt, Charles J.	TR 07, 08, 09C
Oviatt, Clarence R.	FB 15
Owen, Frank M.	BS 1897
Owen, George E.	BS 38, 39 40
Owen, Michael	WR 75
Owen, Robert H.	TR 39M
Owen, Scott	WR 2000
Owens, Alton L.	FB 63, 64, 65
Owens, Forrest F.	SW 39
Owens, Jason	SW 99
Oxendine, Richard C.	FB 60
Ozybko, Edward	HO 59, 60, 61
Pace, Guy	TR 86
Pace, John	LA 89, 90, 91, 92CoC
Pacynski, Stanley L.	BS 21, 22 / BK 22
Padgett, Steve	CC 2000 / TR 2001
Paganini, Frank T.	SW 54, 55, 56
Page, Bryan	BS 96
Page, Jerry M.	TR 41, 42, 43 / CC 42
Page, William W.	BS 45, 46
Pagel, William L.	FB 45
Paglia, Marc	SW 74, 77
Pahad, Fraser	SO 74, 75
Paior, John J.	FB 54
Pajokowski, Joseph A.	FB 45
Palamara, Frank	BS 56, 57, 58C
Palamara, Joseph	BS 74, 75
Palm, Wayne V.	BK 19, 20, 21
Palmateer, Bernard B.	FB 62
Palmer, Jeffrey	FB 87
Palmer Russell E.	SW 54
Palmer, Michael	WR 78
Pangborn, Daniel	SW 66, 67, 68
Panin, Lewis R.	FB 50, 51, 52
Panitch, Michael B.	FB 56, 57, 58
Panks, Gary A.	HO 61 / GO 63
Panos, Gus	SO 88, 89, 90C
Panter, Robert B.	TR 60M
Papachristou, Gerald	SO 60, 61, 62
Papadakos, George	BK 87, 88CoC
Paraskevin, Kenneth	HO 78, 79, 80, 81C
Parke, Ross A.	HO 56, 57, 58
Parker, Arnold P.	BS 33, 34, 35
Parker, Delmer G.	CC 53
Parker, Frederick E.	TR 78
Parker, Frederick	FB 87
Parker, Jack B.	GY 48
Parker, Jeffrey	HO 84, 85, 86
Parker, John D.	TR 62, 63
Parker, Phillip	FB 82, 83, 84, 85
Parker, Rodney D.	LA 78
Parker, Ward H.	FB 06, 07
Parks, Warren A.	FB 21
Parks, William T.	FB 1897, 98, 99
Parmalee, Charles H.	TR 03
Parmentier, Gary	FB 68, 70
Parnell, Marvin	TR 85, 86, 88CoC
Parrish, Frank B.	SW 55, 56, 57
Parrish, Harry R.	BS 1895
Parrott, Roy	FB 61
Parsell, Rex J.	FB 47, 48, 49
Partchenko, Peter	FB 92
Pashnick, Larry	BS 76, 77, 78CoC
Passerini, M. Harold	HO 52
Passink, Clarence	TR 27, 29
Pataconi, Ronald J.	TR 56M
Patchell, Sean	HO 98, 99, 2000, 01
Patchett, Wendell T.	BK 32, 33, 34C
Paterra, Herbert E.	FB 62
Paterra, Jeffery	FB 86

Paton, H. Don, Jr. ... SW 47, 48, 49, 50
Patrick, Antwain ... FB 94, 95
Patrick, J. Cuthbert ... BS 1893
Patrick, Joe ... FB 2000, 01
Patridge, Ernest D. ... TR 1895
Patten, Ronald J. ... TR 56M
Patterson, Donald W. ... SW 57, 58, 59
Patterson, Howard F. ... SW 46, 48, 49, 50
Patterson, Marty ... BS 94, 95, 96, 97
Patterson, Michael ... BS 82, 83
Pattison, Benjamin P. ... BS 09, 10 / FB 09, 10 / BK 11
Patton, David C. ... SW 51
Pattullo, Robert ... HO 68, 69, 70
Pauga, Kevin ... BK 2001M, 02M, 03M
Paul, Russell L. ... GY 57, 58C
Paull, Richard A. ... TR 68, 69
Paulson, Donald H. ... BK 49M
Pauwels, Remi ... LA 94, 95, 96
Pavelich, Paul ... HO 72, 73, 74, 75
Pavlick, George R. ... BS 48
Pawlak, Richard L. ... FB 73
Pawlick, Adam ... SW 95, 96, 97CoC, 98CoC
Pawlik, Eugene P. ... FC 63
Pawlowski, Walter L. ... FB 40, 41, 42C
Paxson, Avery B. ... FB 33
Payette, Thomas M. ... SW 52, 53, 54, 55C / TR 52
Payk, Eric ... BS 80, 81, 82
Payment, Curtis ... SO 91, 92, 93, 94
Payne, Wade ... FB 67
Payton, Darwin ... BK 77M, 78M, 79M
Payton, Gerald L. ... FC 49
Payton, Lenier ... FB 87, 88
Peakes, Ian ... GO 89, 90, 92
Peaks, Clarence E. ... FB 54, 55, 56
Pearce, Edward J. ... FB 37, 38, 39
Pearsall, Gilson P. ... TR 34, 35
Pearsall, Ropha V. ... TR 04, 05, 06, 07
Pearson, Chris ... TN 86M, 87M
Pearson, Helge E. ... FB 37
Pearson, Jeffrey ... FB 89, 90
Peck, Clair B. ... FB 03
Peckham, Thomas J. ... TR 61, 62, 63
Peddie, John H. ... FC 85
Peden, David ... LA 74, 75
Pedro, Gregory ... BK 84, 85
Peirce, Rob ... LA 89, 91, 92
Peko, Siitupe ... FB 1999, 2000
Pellerin, Frank E. ... BS 41, 42, 43
Pelletier, John R. ... FC 62, 63CoC
Pemberton, T. Berwyn ... BS 31, 32, 33
Pence, Eric ... SO 84, 85, 86, 87
Pendell, Tim ... BS 81, 82
Pendergrass, John ... SO 73
Penick, Andy ... BK 91, 95
Penoyer, Jason ... LA 92, 93
Peplowski, Michael ... BK 90, 91, 92, 93CoC
Peppard, David L. ... TR 14, 16, 17C / BK 17
Peppard, David L., Jr. ... TR 48, 49, 50
Peppler, Albert P. ... BS 46, 47, 48 / BK 43, 46, 47
Perez, Evaristo ... BK 82
Perillo, Daniel R. ... TN 49, 50
Perkins, Calvin ... FB 80, 81, 82
Perkins, Charles H. ... TR 09
Perkins, Fred E. ... TN 39, 40, 41C
Perkins, John W. ... BS 35M
Perles, George ... FB 58
Perles, John ... FB 82, 83, 84
Perlin, Dave ... SO 2002
Perne, Donald C. ... GO 49, 50, 51C
Perranowski, Ronald P. ... BS 56, 57, 58
Perreault, Nicolas ... HO 91, 92, 93, 94
Perrin, Arthur C. ... BS 1889
Perrone, Vito ... WR 52, 53C, 54
Perry, Derek ... BK 80, 81, 82, 83CoC
Perry, J. Carleton ... TR 21
Person, Dale ... FB 92, 93, 94
Peta, Francesco ... SW 95
Petela, Stanley F. ... BK 48
Peterman, Barry ... FC 79, 80, 81, 82
Peterman, Bradley ... FC 79, 80, 82
Peterman, Bryan ... FC 77, 78, 79, 80C
Peterman, William T. ... FC 74, 75, 76, 77C
Peters, Arthur D. ... FB 01, 02C, 03
Peters, Dale ... BS 63, 64, 65
Peters, Howard F. ... BS 18
Petersen, Robert ... LA 75, 76, 77
Petersen, Thomas ... SO 70
Peterson, Andrew ... FB 2002
Peterson, Carl H. ... BS 13, 14 / FB 14M
Peterson, Carl ... HO 57
Peterson, Donald L. ... HO 55M, 56M
Peterson, Douglas ... LA 75, 76
Peterson, Duane ... BK 54, 55, 56
Peterson, Ernest E. ... BS 15M
Peterson, Harry S. ... BS 08, 09
Peterson, Jason ... WR 96, 97
Peterson, John ... GO 70, 71
Peterson, John H. ... BK 42M
Peterson, Julian ... FB 98, 99
Peterson, Lorwyn E. ... TR 29
Peterson, Melvin ... BK 40, 41, 42
Peterson, Morris ... BK 97, 98, 99, 2000CoC
Peterson, Robert L. ... BS 66, 67
Peterson, Thomas H. ... FB 75, 76
Petitto, Thomas ... WR 89
Petley, James R. ... TR 1893, 94
Petoskey, Jeff ... SO 88, 89, 90, 91C
Petoskey, Jon ... SO 90, 91, 92, 93
Petrella, Bruno ... BS 81, 82, 83
Petroff, George J. ... BS 69, 70
Petroski, Carl F. ... BK 41, 42, 43
Pettibone, R. Bruce ... BS 64, 65
Pettit, Arvilee W. ... FB 80M, 81M, 82M
Pettit, Keith ... GY 85, 86, 87, 88CoC
Pettit, Nick ... FB 93M
Pettyjohn, Fred M. ... BX 57
Petzinger, Brad ... SO 88
Petzold, Rudolf H. ... FB 54M, 55M
Pevic, Charles Vincent ... BS 28, 29, 30
Pfeffer, Gregg ... BK 83M, 84M, 85M
Pfeffer, Steven R. ... BK 80M, 81M, 82M
Pfeil, Richard J. ... FC 54
Pflug, Melville M. ... TR 30, 31, 32C
Phair, Lyle ... HO 82, 83, 84, 85
Phelps, Brian ... FB 83
Philips, David P. ... TN 41, 45, 46
Phillips, Charles W. ... HO 67, 68, 69
Phillips, David ... TR 84, 85CoC
Phillips, Donald F. ... WR 54
Phillips, Frank G. ... TR 02, 03
Phillips, Harold B. ... FB 68, 69, 70
Phillips, James ... TN 65, 66, 67
Phillips, Jess, Jr. ... FB 65, 66
Phillips, Matt ... SO 96, 97, 98
Phillips, Nate ... BK 77, 78
Phillips, Richard K. ... GY 55, 57M
Phillips, Robert H. ... BK 39, 40, 41C
Phillips, Tony ... SO 86, 87, 88CoC
Phipps, Michael ... GY 96, 97, 98, 99
Piavis, Mark ... LA 79
Piazza, Mark ... BS 84, 85
Picard, Patrick ... SW 80, 81
Picciuto, Nicholas T. ... BS 42
Pickens, Bob ... WR 65
Pickering, H. Lee ... TR 45
Picklo, Brian ... WR 94, 95, 96, 97CoC
Pieh, Lou ... SO 98, 99
Pierson, William R. ... FC 50, 52
Pietras, Richard ... CC 82, 83, 84 / TR 85
Piette, Thomas ... FB 78, 80, 81, 82
Pilarowski, David ... LA 89
Pilitsis, Angelos ... SO 57
Pillinger, Andrew ... LA 95, 96
Pingel, John S. ... FB 36, 37, 38 / TR 37
Pinnance, Edward W. ... BS 2003
Pinneo, Dee W. ... BK 31, 32C
Pinto, Mark ... LA 78, 79, 80CoC
Piro, Steven P. ... FB 69
Pirronello, William G. ... FB 44
Pisani, Mike ... BS 97, 98, 99, 2000
Pisano, Vincent F. ... FB 50, 51, 52
Pitawanakwat, Jefrey ... HO 90, 91
Pitts, Alfred E., Jr. ... FB 74, 75, 76, 77CoC
Pitts, Jack ... FB 67
Piwinski, Paul ... TR 80, 81, 82, 83CoC
Piwowarczyk, Chris ... FB 88, 89, 90, 91
Pjesky, Daniel D. ... BK 43, 46
Plagenhoef, Roger D. ... TN 59, 60, 61
Planchon, Carl ... SO 83, 84, 85
Plante, Jonathan ... GY 99, 2000, 01
Planutis, Gerald R. ... FB 53, 54, 55
Pleiness, Dale ... LA 78
Pletz, John E. ... FB 46
Plotts, James ... BS 67, 68
Ploussard, Stephen ... SW 76, 77, 79CoC
Pobur, Edward ... FB 82
Pogor, Edmund F. ... FB 39
Poirot, James ... SW 90
Poland, Roger ... SO 70, 71
Polano, Joseph ... HO 57, 58, 59
Polec, Lawrence ... BK 83, 84, 85, 86CoC
Polhamus, Edward H. ... TR 1891
Polisar, Steve ... BS 66
Politi, Peter ... SW 2002
Politowicz, Joseph ... LA 78, 79
Pollard, Charles N. ... TR 67, 68, 70
Pollard, Gerald ... BS 77, 78, 79, 80
Pollesel, Bruno ... HO 57, 58, 59
Pollesel, Edward ... HO 57, 58, 59
Pollitt, Robert ... WR 77
Polomsky, John ... BS 54, 55, 56 / HO 54, 55, 56C
Polonchek, John N. ... FB 47, 48, 49
Polonowski, Steve ... BK 94, 95, 96, 97CoC
Pomerleau, Bertrand T. ... HO 54, 55, 56
Pomorski, Mark ... BS 78, 79, 80, 81
Pongrace, Otto W. ... TR 32, 33,3 4C / CC 32, 33
Pontius, Larry ... SW 59
Poole, Sean ... FB 2001, 02
Popejoy, Kenneth L. ... TR 70, 71, 72, 73 / CC 70, 71,72CoC
Popovski, Tony ... FB 95
Popp, Robert T. ... FB 57
Popper, Edward ... FC 47, 48
Pore, James H. ... TN 52, 53, 54C
Porrevecchio, Joseph S. ... BS 62, 63, 64
Porteous, William L. ... TR 40M
Porter, Anthony E. ... FB 75, 76
Posey, Cory ... WR 1998, 99, 2000CoC, 01
Poss, Frank R. ... TR 1891, 92, 93, 94
Postula, Victor A. ... FB 54
Postula, William J. ... FB 53
Potter, Corey ... HO 2003
Potter, James ... FB 84
Potts, Michael ... WR 81, 82, 83, 84
Pougnet, Michael ... SO 76
Pound, Howard E. ... FB 39
Powell, James H. ... BS 49M
Powell, Robert L. ... BS 53, 54, 55
Powers, Allan ... GY 84, 85, 86, 88CoC
Powers, John F., III ... FB 75, 76
Prange, Jeffrey ... SW 79
Prashaw, Milton L. ... FB 44
Pratt, Leon A. ... BS 17
Pratt, Robert M. ... BS 33M
Prebel, Merle L. ... WR 61
Prescott, James ... GY 79
Preston, Phillip ... LA 86
Preston, Ronald J. ... TR 24
Preston, Steven ... BS 86, 88
Price, H. Eugene ... FB 1896, 97
Price, David L. ... GY 63, 64, 65C
Price, Ernest A. ... FC 77, 78
Price, Herbert ... HO 70, 71
Price, James W. ... SO 71, 72
Price, Michael ... SO 75, 76, 77, 78CoC
Price, Robert E. ... CC 44C & TR 45C
Price, Troy ... CC 81
Prieskorn, David ... TR 80, 82

Prieskorn, George W. ... GO 55
Primorac, Ivica ... TN 1997, 98, 99, 2000
Prince, Richard ... CC 85, 87, 88CoC
Prins, Kurt ... FB 89, 90, 91, 92
Prisk, Victor ... GY 97
Pritula, James ... TN 71
Proctor, John E. ... CC 54
Proebstle, James M. ... FB 65
Proebstle, Richard J. ... FB 61, 63, 64 / BS 62, 64
Pruder, Dave ... FB 84M, 85M, 86M
Pruiett, Mitchell ... FB 65, 66, 67
Pruitt, Randy ... BS 75, 76, 77
Pruitt, Ronald ... BS 70, 71, 72
Prutton, Lee ... LA 73, 74, 75
Prylow, Mark ... BK 94, 95
Pryor, Corey ... FB 88, 89, 90 / TR 88, 89, 90
Przybycki, Joseph R. ... FB 65, 66, 67
Przybyla, John ... WR 85, 86, 87CoC
Psihas, Gregory ... CC 86, 88
Pugh, Dean ... CC 95, 96
Pugh, Joseph ... FB 86, 87
Pullen, Jeffrey ... CC 74, 75, 76, 77C / TR 75, 77
Pulsfort, Richard ... GY 89
Pumford, Matt ... GO 97, 98, 99CoC
Purcell, Craig ... LA 80, 81, 82, 83C
Purcell, Mark ... LA 78, 79, 80CoC, 81CoC
Purdo, Thomas ... HO 65, 66
Purdy, Kamp ... SW 93, 94, 95CoC, 96
Pushman, Scott ... WR 2002
Putnam, Dylan ... BS 2000, 01, 02
Pyle, W. Palmer ... FB 57, 58, 59
Qualman, Erik ... BK 91, 92, 93, 94M
Quarress, Mike ... GY 97, 98, 99, 2000
Quayle, Donald E. ... BS 51, 52
Queen, David ... GY 94, 95, 96C
Quevedo, Albereto ... GO 98, 99CoC
Quiggle, Jack E. ... BK 56, 57, 58
Quigley, Arlon B. ... SW 47M
Quigley, Fred K., Jr. ... FB 39
Quigley, James L. ... SW 46, 49, 50, 51
Quigley, John R. ... SW 51, 52
Quinlan, William D. ... FB 52, 53
Quinn, Chad ... GO 97, 98
Quinn, Edward ... SO 76, 77
Quinn, Kelly ... FB 82, 83, 84, 85
Quirk, Martin W. ... HO 61, 62C, 63
Rabias, Robert J. ... BS 57, 58
Radatz, Richard R. ... BS 57, 58, 59C
Radelet, David P. ... FB 75, 76, 77
Radelet, Kevin ... BK 81
Radewald, Carl B. ... FB 20
Radford, Fred ... FB 1900M
Radke, Daniel ... SO 92, 93, 94, 95CoC
Radke, David ... BS 77, 78
Radman, George ... WR 66, 67
Radman, Richard W. ... WR 70, 71, 72
Rado, Michael ... SW 75, 76, 77, 78
Radulescu, George ... FB 42
Radunske, Brock ... HO 2002, 03
Rae, George H. ... TR 02
Raines, Richard C. ... TN 69
Rainko, Brad ... FB 97, 98, 99
Rains, Ralph J. ... BS 10
Rajkovich, Nick J. ... WR 33
Ralph, Donald ... FB 55M
Ralph, William ... SO 80, 81
Ralston, Merle C. ... BK 24
Ralston, Milo J. ... BS 23M
Rambo, Jason ... BS 91, 92, 93
Ramsey, Clarence F. ... FB 16, 17, 19
Ramsey, Kenneth ... FB 76
Rance, Kyle ... FB 96, 97, 98, 99
Rand, Thomas A. ... BK 58, 59 / TR 57
Randall, Clyde J. ... BS 36, 37, 38
Randall, Jason ... FB 2001, 02
Randel, Bradley ... SO 73
Randel, Edward ... SO 73, 74, 754, 76
Randolph, Steve ... TR 71
Randolph, Zach ... BK 2001
Ranieri, Ron ... FB 66, 67
Rankin, Glenn B. ... BS 38
Ranney, Ellis W. ... BS 1897, 98, 99C, 00 / FB 1897, 98C, 99C
Ranney, Frederick ... BS 24
Ransom, Brian ... FB 91, 92, 93M
Ranval, Timothy ... SW 74
Rapchak, William M. ... BK 45, 48, 49, 50
Rapes, Anthony L. ... TR 36, 37
Rashead, Philip ... BS 69, 70, 71
Rasmussen, Gary ... HO 71M, 72M, 73M
Rasmussen, Kyle ... FB 2000, 01, 02
Rasmussen, Michael J. ... FB 70, 71
Rasmussen, Rasmus ... BS 02, 03, 04M, 05C
Rathbun, Michael ... FC 76, 77
Rathke, Richard ... WR 79
Rauch, Donald M. ... SW 67, 68, 69 CoC
Ravenna, William H. ... SO 85, 86, 87
Rawlins, Michael ... SO 88, 89, 90, 92CoC
Ray, Harlan C. ... FB 27M
Ray, Jonathan S. ... FB 74
Ray, Scott ... FC 78, 79
Raye, James ... FB 65, 66, 67
Raym, Jon ... LA 93, 94, 95, 96CoC
Raymond, James A. ... GO 55 & BK 55
Rayner, Dave ... FB 2001, 02
Raz, Steve ... HO 52, 54
Rea, William M., III ... SW 64M, 65M
Reader, Casey ... BS 98
Reader, Russell B. ... FB 45, 46 / TR 46
Reading, Shannon ... BK 66, 67
Reading, Willard L. ... BK 48M
Reavely, Gordon ... FB 32, 33, 34 / WR 32, 33, 35C
Reavely, William H. ... BS 43
Reaves, Carl ... FB 94, 95
Reck, Daniel J. ... BK 34, 35, 36C
Redd, Keith L. ... FB 66
Redding, Mickey ... LA 89
Redfern, Scott J. ... FB 1896M
Redfield, Kenneth ... BK 87, 88, 89C, 90
Redford, Robert ... GO 84, 86
Reece, Travis ... FB 94, 95, 96, 97
Reed, Derrick ... FB 87, 88
Reed, Oswald H. ... BS 1895
Reese, Elroy ... FB 95, 96
Reese, Ike ... FB 94, 95, 96CoC, 97CoC
Reese, Kevin ... BK 88M, 89M, 90M, 91M
Reese, William ... FB 89, 90, 91, 92CoC
Reeves, Bruce ... FB 77, 78, 79, 80
Reeves, Michael ... WR 95, 96
Reid, Delmar Tice ... HO 50, 51, 52
Reid, Earl W. ... BX 43M
Reid, Greg ... FB 95
Reid, John D. ... CC 29
Reid, Michael T. ... TR 39
Reiff, Peter A. ... CC 69
Reinardy, Mark ... CC 89, TR 90
Reinfelder, David ... BS 93, 94, 95
Reinhard, Eric W. ... SO 79
Reinke, Paul G. ... SW 55, 56, 57
Reisig, Timothy ... WR 86
Renaud, Marc ... FB 94, 95, 97
Rendall, Bruce ... HO 86, 87, 88
Rendon, George ... SO 62, 63
Rensing, Damon ... SO 93, 94, 95, 96
Renwick, Howard M. ... BS 20M
Repko, Stephen M. ... FB 73M
Respert, Mike ... BK 95, 96
Respert, Shawn ... BK 92, 93, 94CoC, 95CoC
Rettenmund, Larry ... BS 69, 70, 71
Reuben, Kevin ... FC 94, 95
Revou, Robert C. ... HO 51, 52, 53
Rex, Robert ... SW 74, 75, 76CoC
Reynolds, Albert S., Jr. ... TN 47, 48C
Reynolds, Bobby ... HO 86, 87, 88, 89
Reynolds, Bruce W. ... BK 54M
Reynolds, Frank E. ... SW 53
Reynolds, John C. ... GO 58, 59, 60
Reynolds, Russell H. ... FB 33, 34C
Reynolds, William T. ... CC 58, 59, 60 / TR 60, 61C
Rhoades, Ralph ... TN 70
Rhodes, Eugene N. ... BK 53
Rhodes, Matthew ... GO 84
Rhodes, Tyrone ... FB 83, 84, 85, 86
Riba, Michael ... FB 82
Ribby, Robert ... FB 93
Riblett, William R. ... FB 10, 11, 12C
Ricamore, Wilford W. ... FB 1899, 00, 01
Rice, Brian ... LA 89, 91
Rice, Brian ... LA 96
Rice, Dan ... LA 89, 90, 91, 92
Rice, Daryl ... HO 73, 74, 75, 76
Rice, Jason ... BS 96
Rice, Kevin ... LA 84, 85, 86, 87CoC
Richard, David ... FB 2002
Richard, Michael ... LA 73, 74, 75CoC
Richard, Shepard A. ... GO 63, 64
Richards, Bruce Warren ... SW 68, 69, 70
Richards, James M. ... SW 47, 49
Richards, Roland ... BS 24 / FB 22, 23, 24 / BK 24, 25
Richardson, Brett ... GY 82
Richardson, Gerald C. ... FC 39, 40C
Richardson, James ... WR 89, 90, 91CoC
Richardson, Jason ... BK 2000, 01
Richardson, Jeffrey ... WR 65, 66, 67 / FB 66
Richardson, Kenneth ... LA 70
Richardson, Lavaile ... FB 97, 98, 99, 2000
Richardson, Marcel ... TR 89, 90, 91
Richendollar, Melvin ... FB 86
Richey, Timothy ... SO 89, 90, 91, 92
Richey, William K. ... BX 47
Richman, Todd ... TR 94, 95, 96, 97
Richmond, Ernest A. ... SW 24C
Richmond, Stacy ... WR 86, 87, 88CoC, 89CoC
Richmond, Todd ... TR 94, 95, 96
Richter, Richard R. ... GY 49, 50, 51
Rickens, Ronald F. ... FB 56, 57, 58
Ricker, Fred G. ... BK 15, 16
Ricketts, Neil H. ... BS 48
Ricucci, Robert J. ... FB 59
Ridgeway, Jason E. ... FB 85, 86, 87, 88
Ridgway, Ronald D. ... SW 53
Ridinger, Kim ... SW 72, 73
Ridinger, Tim ... FB 86, 87, 88, 89 / WR 86
Ridler, Donald G. ... FB 28, 29, 30
Ridley, Michael E. ... BK 72
Rieckhoff, Ryan ... GO 96
Riedel, Dennis ... GO 2000, 01CoC
Riedesel, Henry K. ... GY 55M
Riegel, Matt ... GO 97, 98
Rieger, Richard H. ... TN 50, 51, 52C
Riewald, Daniel A. ... BK 76, 77, 78
Riffe, Wade ... SO 73
Rigali, Michael ... SW 2002, 03
Rigby, Cyril P. ... BK 16
Riggins, Matthew ... BS 93, 94, 95, 96CoC
Riggs, Benjamin F. ... WR 39, 40CoC, 41
Rickard, James B. ... SW 54, 55
Riley, Paul ... LA 84
Riley, Thomas E. ... BS 60, 61
Rimler, Cal ... GY 2001
Rindle, Jake ... BS 93
Rinehart, Forrest ... BS 26, 27, 28C
Rinella, James ... FB 82, 83, 84, 85
Rintz, Carlton L. ... GY 52, 53, 54, 55C
Riordan, Edward D. ... BK 33
Riordan, Sidney R. ... TR 41
Rioux, Jerry ... LA 89, 90, 91, 92
Ripmaster, Peter E. ... FB 40, 42
Rippberger, Donald R. ... WR 43
Ripper, Clarence E. ... TR 24, 25, 26
Risch, John I. ... BS 52, 53, 54
Rison, Andre ... FB 85, 86, 87, 88 / BK 88 / TR 86
Ristau, Greg ... LA 96
Rittenger, Charles F. ... BS 1887, 89, 90C, 91
Ritz, Alfred H. ... BK 36
Rivers, David ... LA 92, 93, 94CoC
Rivers, Lovelle ... BK 74, 75, 76
Rivest, Robert N. ... GO 54

Rivet, Joseph .... FC 87
Rivich, Joseph N. .... BS 50, 51, 52
Rizzo, Donald Dee .... HO 82, 83, 86
Roach, Marty E. .... GY 65
Robbins, Alan D. .... SO 72, 73
Robbins, Kevin .... FB 87, 88
Robbins, Mike .... SW 99, 2000, 01, 02CoC
Robbins, Robert D. .... BK 47, 48, 49, 50C
Roberts, Aaron .... FB 81, 82, 83, 84
Roberts, David .... HO 70, 71, 72
Roberts, David .... SW 97
Roberts, Douglas W. .... HO 63, 64, 65C / FB 63, 64
Roberts, Floyd T. .... CC 27, 28
Roberts, Irving M. .... TN 40
Roberts, John A. .... HO 58, 59, 60
Roberts, Marvin E. .... FB 70, 71, 72 / TR 72, 73
Roberts, Peter .... GY 80, 81, 82, 83
Roberts, Richard K. .... TN 53
Roberts, Richard W. .... TN 52 / CC 50
Roberts, Robin .... BK 45, 46, 47C / BS 46, 47
Roberts, Thomas .... BS 81M
Roberts, Timothy .... LA 96
Roberts, Wesley W. .... SW 60
Roberts, William W. .... TR 43
Robertson, Walter .... LA 92
Robie, Richard R. .... SW 52
Robins, Jeremy .... FC 97
Robinson, David K. .... BK 20
Robinson, Embry L. .... FB 54, 55
Robinson, Gayle B. .... TR 37, 38, 39
Robinson, Hugh A. .... FB 22,23, 24 / BK 23, 25
Robinson, Kenneth .... BS 77, 78, 79, 80CoC / FB 77
Robinson, Lennox .... SO 69, 70, 71, 72
Robinson, Michael A. .... BK 72, 73, 74C
Robinson, Mike .... SO 2000, 01, 02
Robinson, Theodore K. .... FB 59M
Robinson, Thomas .... FB 82, 83
Robinson, Tyler .... SO 99, 2000, 01, 02
Robinson-Randall, Greg .... FB 98, 99
Robuck, John .... GY 49, 50
Roche, Thomas .... HO 66
Rochester, Paul G. .... FB 58, 59
Rock, Christopher .... SW 79, 80
Rockefeller, Van .... SW 69
Rockenbach, Lyle J. .... FB 37, 38, 39C
Rockey, Steve .... CC 70, 71
Rockwell, James .... SW 73
Rodbro, Ryan .... GY 78
Rodewald, Kenneth G. .... GO 54, 56, 57
Rodgers, David S. .... WR 74
Rodgers, Donald B. .... WR 74, 75, 77, 78
Rodriguez, David .... WR 76, 77, 79, 80
Rodriguez, Steve .... WR 73, 74, 75, 76
Rody, Fred A. .... FB 53, 54
Roe, James W. .... TR 61
Roeser, John .... LA 90
Roff, Andrew .... SO 91, 92, 93, 94
Roge, Steven .... LA 93, 94, 95, 96
Rogers, Brad .... TR 74
Rogers, Charles .... FB 2001, 02
Rogers, Deb .... LA 79M
Rogers, Douglas .... FB 83, 84, 85, 86
Rogers, Spencer W. .... LA 78
Rogge, Harry E. .... BS 11, 12
Rogula, Michael G. .... TR 48, 49
Rohacz, Stephan .... LA 78
Rohde, John .... BS 71, 72, 73
Rohs, John D. .... GY 63, 66
Roland, Charles B. .... TR 52
Rolen, Edward C. .... BK 35, 36, 37
Rolle, Donald "Butch" .... FB 82, 83, 84, 85
Rollick, Nicholas .... FB 76, 77
Rollin, Anthony .... FB 90, 91, 92
Rollin, Arthur S. .... FC 54C
Rollins, James .... FB 89, 90
Rom, Zdravko .... SO 73, 74, 75, 76
Romaine, Larry .... BS 73, 74
Roman, Mark .... FC 96, 97
Romano, Sam .... WR 85
Rometty, John .... LA 82, 83, 84
Ronan, Arthur P. .... BS 50
Ronan, Kenneth M. .... BS 17
Ronberg, Gary M. .... BS 61, 62
Rone, Kirk W. .... SO 78, 79
Ronie, Andrew M. .... BX 55
Rood, Joe .... BK 2003M
Roossien, Elmer J. .... CC 27, 28, 29 / TR 28, 29
Root, Charles .... WR 82, 84, 85, 86C
Root, Chris .... WR 87
Roper, Dedrick .... FB 2001
Rork, Frank C. .... FB 1899, 01
Rosa, Robert J. .... TN 36C, 37
Rose, Peter .... BS 85
Rose, Phil .... LA 81, 82
Rose, Thomas .... GO 83, 84, 85CoC
Roseboro, Ronald .... FB 84
Rosekrans, Eric .... BS 78, 79
Rosen, Robert .... TR 13
Rosen, Scott .... TN 72, 73
Rosenbaum, Brad .... TN 89, 90, 91, 92 CoC
Rosenbaum, Daniel M. .... TR 39, 40, 41
Rosenberg, Robert C. .... FC 71
Rosenberg, W. Dean .... CC 66, 67 / TR 67
Rosengren, David .... GY 75, 76
Roskopp, Bernard G. .... FB 42, 46, 47
Ross, Archie F. .... FB 34, 35
Ross, Cordell .... BS 84
Ross, Daniel M. .... TR 39, 40, 41
Ross, Donald L. .... FB 63, 64
Ross, Guy .... WR 82M, 83M
Ross, Henry T. .... TR 03M
Ross, John .... TR 72, 73, 74
Ross, Loren S. .... BS 21, 22, 23
Ross, Robert H. .... BS 59, 60, 61
Ross, Robert William .... FB 52, 53
Ross, Ronald R. .... FB 62
Ross, Terry .... TR 82
Ross, Thomas .... GO 82, 83, 84CoC
Ross, Thomas .... HO 73, 74, 75, 76
Ross, Ward F. .... FB 25, 26, 27
Ross, William L. .... FB 52, 53
Rossi, Donald A. .... FB 38, 39 / BX 38
Rossi, Furio .... SW 94
Rossi, Robert A. .... TR 53
Rossman, Victor H. .... TR 27, 28, 29
Rossow, William C. .... SW 63
Roth, Donald .... HO 65, 66
Roth, Lori .... SW 85M
Rouse, Arthur K. .... BS 33, 34, 35C
Rouse, Milo M. .... BK 34, 35C
Rowe, Douglas E. .... SW 61, 62
Rowe, Ronald .... FB 85, 86
Rowekamp, Kim A. .... FB 73, 74, 75, 77
Rowley, Gail A. .... BS 26, 27
Rowley, Glenn .... BS 14
Roy, Errol A. .... FB 69, 70, 71
Roy, Rob .... FB 88, 89, 90
Roy, Robert L. .... HO 53M, 54M, 55M
Royce, Frederick E. .... FC 71, 72, 73, 74
Rozman, Rick .... BS 86, 88
Rubick, Ronald R. .... FB 61, 62, 63
Rucks, Aaron .... HO 79
Rudolph, Jeffrey .... GY 75, 76, 77, 78C
Rudzinski, Paul G. .... FB 74, 75, 76, 77CoC
Ruff, Timothy W. .... FB 74, 75
Rugg, Gary L. .... FB 64
Rugh, Chris .... TR 89, 90, 91, 92
Rugh, Dean .... TR 95, 96, 97 / CC 95
Ruhl, Jack W. .... FB 28
Ruiz, David .... GY 99, 2000
Ruminski, Roger J. .... FB 66
Rummel, Martin F. .... FB 24, 25, 26C
Rund, Rich .... LA 93, 94, 95, 96
Rupp, Vernon W. .... TR 25
Rupp, William, Jr. .... FB 39, 40, 41CoC
Ruppart, Dennis .... SW 60, 61
Ruscheinski, Emanual .... SO 64, 65
Rush, Jerry .... FB 62, 63, 64
Russ, Mark .... BS 78, 79, 80, 81C
Russell, Jack J. .... TR 15, 16C
Russell, John G. .... BS 57, 58, 59C
Russell, Kerry .... HO 88, 89, 90, 91
Russell, Robert K. .... TR 29, 30, 31
Russell, Timothy .... FC 83
Russell, William E. .... FB 1897, 98, 99 / TR 1898, 99C
Russo, Leroy G. .... BK 28, 29
Russo, Patrick .... HO 68, 69 70
Russow, Walter F. .... TR 29, 30
Rutenbar, George H. .... BS 46, 47, 48, 49
Ruthkoski, Andrew .... GO 2002, 03
Rutila, Harold .... CC 78, 80
Rutledge, Leslie E. .... FB 55, 56, 57
Ruzich, John L. .... FB 73
Ryan, Barry A. .... TR 39, 40
Ryan, Edward J. .... FB 60, 61C
Ryan, Sean .... TN 93
Rymal, Steven A. .... BK 66, 67, 68 / BS 66, 67, 68
Ryon, Edgar G. .... TR 30
Sabin, Adam .... SO 2001
Sabo, Ronald J. .... BK 61
Sachs, Albert W. .... BS 28, 29, 30C
Sack, James F. .... BS 54, 55, 56
Sackett, Donald K. .... BS 59, 60
Sackett, Mark .... BS 85M, 86M
Sackman, Jerry .... BS 72, 73
Sackrider, Thomas C. .... BK 55M, 56M
Saffran, William S. .... BS 53
Safran, Paul .... LA 70, 71, 72
Sageman, Charlie .... WR 2000, 01, 02, 03
Sagendorph, William K. .... TR 1892
Saggau, Peter .... SW 79, 80
Sahratian, John .... TN 51, 52, 53
Saidock, Thomas .... FB 55, 56
Saimes, George .... FB 60, 61, 62C
Salamone, Louis P. .... FC 63, 64C
Salani, Chris .... FB 92, 93, 94, 95
Salani, Richard A. .... FB 72
Salisbury, William .... WR 78
Salling, Carl L. .... BS 63
Salling, Mike .... BS 99, 2001
Salmon, David A. .... TR 28, 29, 30
Salski, Andrew .... TN 83, 84M, 85M
Saltzman, Rael J. .... BK 74M
Salvaterra, George .... BS 80M
Samalik, John .... CC 82
Sanabria, Zenon A. .... SO 57
Sanchez, Marco .... WR 97
Sanchez, Pedro P. .... GY 80, 81
Sandenburgh, Eric .... BS 84, 85, 86
Sanders, Lonnie .... FB 60, 61, 62 / BK 62
Sanders, Marcus L. .... BK 63, 64, 65C
Sanders, Marcus .... TR 82, 83
Sanders, Terry A. .... SO 66, 67, 68
Sandler, Matthew .... TN 78, 79, 80, 81C
Sandoval, Rodolfo P. .... SO 74
Sanford, James .... LA 80, 81, 82, 83
Sansiviero, Wayne .... LA 89, 90CoC
Santavicca, Michael .... WR 86
Santti, Gary .... CC 73
Saperstein, Melvin D. .... TN 60
Saracene, Marc .... LA 90, 91
Sarenac, Bosco .... SW 57M
Sargent, Michael .... FB 84, 85, 86, 87 / TR 85
Sargis, Gregory .... WR 80, 81, 82, 83, 84
Sarkine, James .... BK 86, 87, 88, 89
Sarria, Paz Alvaro .... SO 57, 58
Sartorius, Patrick J. .... BS 59, 60, 61
Sasanko, Alvin M. .... SO 58
Sass, Robert C. .... GY 58M
Sassack, Robert S. .... TN 58, 59
Satchell, Donald P. .... FC 68, 69C
Saucedo, Patrick .... SW 2002, 2003
Saul, Richard .... FB 67, 68, 69CoC
Saul, Ronald R. .... FB 67, 68, 69
Saunders, Luther .... SO 60, 61
Sauve, Joseph L. .... HO 54, 55
Savage, Lawrence .... FB 76, 77, 78, 79

Savoldi, Joseph A. .... TR 54, 55, 56
Sawyer, Charles M. .... TN 34M
Saxton, Thomas .... SO 80, 81, 82CoC
Sayad, Mark .... BS 86
Sayler, Jace .... FB 97, 98, 99, 2000
Saylor, Ben .... LA 76
Saylor, Franklin .... FB 47, 48
Scales, John J. .... TR 38, 39, 40
Scales, R. Wilson .... TR 39
Scarlett, Todd .... FB 80, 81
Schad, Steve .... SO 79, 80CoC
Schaefer, David .... FB 98, 2000, 01
Schafer, Steve .... TN 67
Schaffer, John E. .... BK 1903, 04, 05
Schaller, Chris .... LA 96
Schario, Richard .... FB 78, 81, 82
Scharmer, Fred .... SW 98
Schau, Henry W. .... FB 27, 28, 29 / BK 28
Schaubel, Ray C. .... SW 30, 31
Schaum, Gregory J. .... FB 73, 74, 75CoC
Scheff, Paul .... SW 87, 88
Scheid, Charles G. .... SW 30
Scheifler, Lee Roy M. .... BS 37, 38, 39
Schelb, Michael W. .... FB 39, 40, 41 / TR 40, 41
Schell, Steve .... CC 96, 97, 98CoC / TR 96, 97, 98, 99, 2000C
Schembri, Craig .... TN 84, 85
Schenck, Ray M. .... TR 19
Schenk, Robert F. .... SO 72, 73, 74
Schepers, Robert E. .... TR 46, 47, 48
Schiele, Paul .... FB 75M
Schiesel, Richard J. .... BS 58
Schiesswohl, Don .... FB 52, 53 / TR 52
Schiffler, Walter .... BS 39
Schiller, Edward A. .... HO 54, 55, 56C
Schinderle, Jack W. .... FB 64, 65
Schlackman, David .... LA 93, 94, 95CoC
Schlaeger, David P. .... TR 38
Schlatter, G. James .... BK 52, 53, 54
Schlesinger, Scot .... SO 92, 93, 94, 95
Schlissberg, Rob .... GO 95, 96CoC
Schloemer, Richard L. .... FC 61, 62C, 63
Schloss, Harvey J. .... FB 70M
Schluter, Robert C. .... WR 60, 61
Schmidt, Tad B. .... GO 59, 60, 61
Schmitt, Chris .... GY 93, 94, 95
Schmitter, Charles, Jr. .... FC 59, 60C, 61
Schmuckal, Timothy .... BS 89, 90
Schmyser, Verne .... FB 23, 24
Schneider, Bert L. .... BS 19
Schneider, John .... WR 68, 69
Schneider, Michael .... HO 81M, 82M, 83M, 84M
Schneider, Paul .... TR 77, 78, 79CoC
Schneider, Robert .... TN 67
Schoen, Charles .... WR 79
Schoenegge, Walter .... TR 51
Schoener, David .... CC 81, 84
Scholes, Clarke C. .... SW 50, 51, 52C
Scholtz, Harold C. .... BK 35, 36, 37 / TN 36, 37C
Schortreed, Greg .... LA 94, 95
Schrader, Nelson C. .... FB 36, 37
Schraff, Rich .... LA 92
Schrag, Truman F. .... FC 58
Schramm, Andrew J, ... FB 77, 78, 79 80
Schramm, Walter .... FB 81, 82
Schrecengost, Randall P. .... FB 52, 53, 54
Schroeder, Fred A. .... FB 36, 37
Schroeder, Robert E. .... FB 44
Schroeter, Herbert R. .... BS 50, 51
Schryer, Howard .... BS 74, 75
Schubel, Otto .... GO 56, 57, 58
Schubert, Frank A. .... FC 67
Schudlich, Wlliam H. .... BS 59, 60, 61
Schuler, Donald .... BS 45
Schulgen, George F. .... FB 20, 21
Schulist, Martin .... CC 78, 79, 81
Schultz, Carl F. .... FB 23, 24
Schultz, Harry W. .... TR 1900, 01
Schultz, Thomas .... BS 78, 79, 80
Schultz, Todd .... FB 95, 96, 97
Schultz, Tyler .... BS 81, 82
Schulz, Donald C. .... LA 72, 73
Schumacher, Robert G. .... SW 50, 51, 52, 53
Schuster, John H. .... HO 65, 66, 67
Schutt, Bill .... CC 97, 98
Schutz, Mike .... FB 97
Schwarm, Arthur V. .... BK 60, 61, 62C
Schwartz, Ira A. .... FC 70, 71, 72
Schwartz, Mark .... LA 89
Schwartz, Ronald .... SW 61
Schwarz, William R. .... BK 62, 63, 64 / SO 63
Schwei, John J. .... TR 19, 20, 21, 22 / FB 18, 19, 20
Scialli, Vince .... HO 67M, 68M
Sciarini, James M. .... FB 75, 76, 77
Sciarini, Michael P. .... FB 78, 79, 80
Scieszka, James A. .... FC 73, 74, 75
Scott, Bill HO2000M,01M, 02M, 03M
Scott, Chris .... FB 90
Scott, Colvin .... BS 98, 99
Scott, David A. .... BK 57, 60
Scott, Edward W. .... BK 29, 30, 31CoC
Scott, Gari .... FB 96, 97, 98, 99CoC
Scott, Guy .... TR 86, 87, 88, 89CoC
Scott, Harper .... BS 36, 37, 38C
Scott, Kelvin .... TR 81, 82, 83, 84CoC
Scott, Ronald .... HO 81, 82, 83
Scott, William .... SW 70, 71
Scott, William J. .... TR 41, 42, 43C / CC 40, 42
Scott, William W. .... SW 66
Scutt, Wayne E. .... CC 50, 51, 52 / TR 51, 52
Sebo, Stephen .... BS 35, 36, 37CoC / FB 34, 35, 36
Seckel, Kevin .... TN 91, 92, 93, 94CoC
Secura, Dave .... FB 97, 98
Sedelbauer, Norman .... FB 56M
Seelig, Scott .... FB 83M, 84M, 85M
Segarra, Rafael .... SW 83, 84
Seibold, David H. .... SW 46, 47, 48, 49C, 50
Seibold, David K. .... SW 76, 77, 78
Seibold, Jack D. .... SW 47, 50
Seibold, Paul A. .... SW 46, 47, 48
Seid, Richard .... BS 74, 75, 76
Sekal, Scott .... BK 86, 87, 88, 89
Selden, Justin .... TR 98, 99, 2000
Selinger, Joe R. .... HO 57, 58, 59
Sell, Joseph P. .... FB 40M
Sellepack, Steve .... FC 91
Selz, John C. .... BX 56
Selzer, Scott .... FB 88, 89
Seney, Jeremy .... SO 98, 99, 2000, 01
Senkle, David .... TR 89
Senzig, Michael J. .... WR 60, 61
Sepaneck, Jack A. .... BS 22,23, 24C
Sepanek, James .... BS 84, 85
Sepetys, George N. .... SO 57, 58, 59
Sergeant, Dale L. .... HO 54
Serlin, Joel .... FC 63, 64, 65C
Serr, Gordon H. .... FB 50, 51, 52
Servis, Lawrence R. .... FB 12
Sessions, Richard .... GO 74
Severance, Roy W. .... TR 27
Severn, Mark .... WR 80
Sewell, Paul .... CC 73 & TR 74
Sewell, Robert A.CC 46, 47, 48C, 49 / TR 47, 48, 49, 50
Sexsmith, Jim .... HO 99
Seyfarth, Theodore H. .... SO 61, 62
Sgroi, Roy C. .... LA 72, 73
Shaar, Carl J. .... SW 60, 61, 62C
Shabaj, Agim .... FB 2002
Shackelford, John H. .... HO 52, 53
Shackleton, Robert J. .... BK 73, 74
Shafer, Charles .... FB 77, 78
Shafer, Scott .... SW 99, 2000, 01, 02
Shaffer, John R. .... BS 05
Shalawylo, William .... HO 91, 92, 93
Shamam, Mark .... LA 90, 91, 92, 93
Shanahan, Robert E. .... BS 09M
Shanley, Tim .... SW 90, 91, 92, 93
Shannon, Harlow G. .... TR 22
Shapiro, Mark .... FB 89
Shaprow, Mark .... GO 75
Sharkey, Richard .... TR 65, 66, 67 / CC 65, 66
Sharp, John E. .... FB 59, 61 / TR 59, 61
Sharpe, Joel .... SO 93, 95
Shatney, Craig .... CC 82
Shaw, George W. .... TR 10
Shaw, Harold T. .... FB 03
Shaw, Josh .... FB 98, 99, 2000, 01
Shaw, Scott .... FB 95, 96, 97CoC
Shaw, Steven J. .... FB 36, 37, 38
Shea, Chris .... BS 2003
Sheathelm, Russell W. .... BK 30
Sheahan-Stahl, Patrick .... GY 2001 / SW 2002, 2003
Shebuski, Steve .... SO 94, 95, 96, 97
Sheck, Aaron .... GY 2000, 01
Shedd, Bert .... FB 1905, 06, 07, 08C, 09
Shedd, John G. .... FB 39M
Shedd, Robert W. .... FB 42M
Shedd, Ward R. .... FB 00, 01
Sheedy, Kevin .... LA 96
Sheffield, Arthur R. .... BK 16, 17
Shehigian, John .... WR 55
Shehigian, Ruben B. .... WR 51, 52, 53
Shek, Paul P. .... TR 50
Shelden, Michael .... LA 75
Sheldon, Earl B. .... TR 15, 16
Sheldon, William .... TR 89, 90, 92
Shelley, Roger .... SW 70
Shelton, Dwight J. .... TN 63, 64, 65
Shepard, Jamie .... GY 2000, 01
Shepard, Scott .... WR 80
Shepherd, Craig .... HO 88, 90
Shepherd, Joseph .... GY 74, 75, 76, 77C
Shepherd, Leroy .... FB 81, 82, 83
Sheppard, Holly C. .... BS 1887
Shereda, James E. .... BK 71, 73
Sherer, Steve .... TR 2001, 02 / CC 2001, 02
Sherman, Martin J. .... WR 51
Sherman, Robert G. .... FB 39, 40, 41
Sherman, Thomas .... CC 73
Sherwood, Robert O. .... SW 64
Sherwood, Brian .... TR 2003
Shibicky, William .... HO 84, 85, 86, 87
Shick, John .... BK 65
Shidler, Frank J. .... BK 38, 39
Shields, Edmund H. .... TR 47
Shimkos, Jason .... BS 95, 96
Shingleton, John D. .... TN 47, 48
Shingleton, Thomas .... TN 79M, 81M
Shinsky, John E. .... FB 70, 72, 73C
Shipps. Steve .... SW 90, 91, 92CoC
Shlapak, Borys W. .... FB 70, 71
Sholl, Chris .... SW 90, 91, 92, 93
Shomin, George H. .... TR 47, 48
Shook, Thomas .... BS 82, 83, 84CoC
Shopwell, Nathan .... HO 2002
Shore, Jay .... GY 75
Shorr, Harold D. .... GY 59, 60
Short, Jack .... HO 73M, 74M
Short, John .... GY 73, 75, 76
Shortreed, Gregory .... LA 94, 95, 96
Shoup, Harold A. .... SW 50, 51, 52
Shovers, William .... TN 73
Shulak, Frederick B. .... FC 56
Shumay, Guy C. .... FB 19
Shumlas, Matt .... SO 96, 97, 98
Shurelds, Robert .... FB 92, 93, 94, 95
Shurmur, Joe .... FB 89M
Shurmur, Patrick .... FB 83, 85, 86, 87CoC
Shutt, William .... HO 79, 80, 81, 82
Shuttleworth, Earl H. .... FB 11
Sibbald, John H. .... HO 52
Siebert, William N. .... FC 65, 66
Siegel, John .... HO 77
Siegenthaler, Michael .... LA 87, 88, 89
Siegert, Douglas .... WR 76, 77, 78
Siemes, Andreas .... SW 97
Sieminski, Adam C. .... FB 55
Sieradzki, Stephen H. .... FB 46, 47 / BS 47

Sierra, Jeff ... SO 85, 87
Sierra, Lawrence ... SO 58
Siler, William M. ... FB 44
Silka, Frank ... HO 60, 61, 62C
Silverstone, Michael ... FB 83
Silvia, Thomas V. ... CC 69
Simas, Michael ... WR 83
Simcik, Matt ... SW 90, 92
Simcox. Harry ... BS 50
Simeck, Daniel ... CC 68
Simmons, David C. ... FC 63
Simmons, Everett III ... WR 92
Simmons, George E. ... BS 1893, 94C
Simmons, Irving L. ... BS 1896
Simmons, Lonnie ... FB 2001
Simmons, Matt ... BK 96M, 97M, 98M
Simmons, Walter H. ... TR 19
Simon, Chad ... FB 2002
Simon, Michael ... GY 76
Simons, Nick ... WR 2003
Simonds, Harold E. ... FC 58
Simonetti, David ... HO 81
Simons, Delrico ... FB 96
Simonson, Ronald W. ... FB 50M
Simonton, Eric ... TN 2001, 02, 03
Simpson, Craig ... HO 84, 85
Simpson, David ... FB 87
Simpson, J.W. ... SO 98
Simpson, Nathan D. ... BS 13M
Simpson, Patrick ... BS 75, 76, 77
Simpson, Ralph ... BK 70
Simpson, Ralph ... TR 76
Simpson, Timothy ... CC 82, 83, 84, 85CoC / TR 83, 84, 85
Simpson, William Danny ... SW 49, 50
Simpson, William T. ... FB 71, 72, 73 / BS 73, 74C
Sims, Albert G. ... SW 37, 38
Sims, Marion ... TR 69
Sinadinos, James P. ... WR 54, 55C, 56C
Sinadinos, James ... WR 86
Sinclair, Joel ... TR 94
Sinclair, Norman ... TR 65
Sinelli, Jeffery ... LA 87, 88, 89
Singleton, William ... SW 59, 60, 61
Sinks, Michael G. ... BS 59, 60, 61C
Sipola, William ... HO 70, 71, 72, 73
Sirhal, Charles M. ... BX 49
Sisinni, George J. ... BX 54, 55, 56
Sivey, Josh ... FC 97
Skandalaris, Richard ... SO 73
Skidmore, Chris ... GY 93, 94, 95, 96
Skiles, Scott ... BK 83, 84, 85, 86CoC
Skinner, J. Hackley ... FB 1898, 99
Skinner, Ralph ... FB 67
Skokos, Zachery G. ... TR 49
Skotarek, Alex ... SO 67, 68 69
Skotarek, Edward ... SO 66, 67, 68
Skrocki, Joseph ... BS 41, 42, 46
Skuce, Thomas W. ... FB 21M
Slack, Michael ... HO 76
Slamkowski, Barney X. ... SW 39
Slank, Ronald J. ... FB 69, 70
Slater, Chris ... HO 94, 95, 96
Slater, Jim ... HO 2002, 03
Slater, Eugene B. ... FB 34M
Slayton, Philip W. ... FC 62, 63
Sleder, Julius C. ... FB 34, 35, 36
Slezak, Steve M. ... WR 38, 39C
Sloan, David ... SW 2000, 01, 02
Slonac, Evan J. ... FB 51, 52, 53
Slosar, Chris ... SO 96, 97, 98
Sluke, Gregory ... SW 80, 81, 82, 83CoC
Smaha, Brad ... LA 89
Small, Ralph E. ... CC 32 & TR 32
Small, Sebastian ... FB 90, 91
Small, Walter H. ... FB 03, 04, 05, 06, 07C / TR 04, 05, 06, 08
Smead, Harold E. ... FB 28, 29, 30C
Smedley, Ernest Leo ... WR 56
Smeltzer, Ronald ... CC 75

Smieska, Paul ... BS 67
Smiley, Lewis N. ... FB 39, 40, 41 / TR 40
Smith, Patrick ... LA 79, 80, 81
Smith, Allen ... BK 72, 73
Smith, Antonio ... BK 96, 97CoC 98CoC, 99CoC
Smith, Arnold W. ... TR 51, 52
Smith, Benjamin T. ... SW 59M
Smith, Brandon ... BK 99, 2000, 01
Smith, Brian ... WR 86, 87, 89CoC, 90
Smith, C. A., III ... GO 59, 60, 61C
Smith, Charles A. ... FB 64, 65, 66
Smith, Chester ... FB 27
Smith, Chris ... FB 93, 94, 95, 96CoC
Smith, Chris ... HO 93, 94, 95, 96
Smith, Chris ... FB 2002
Smith, Cleon L. ... TR 40, 41, 42
Smith, D. Steve ... FB 77, 78, 79, 80CoC
Smith, Daniel R. ... BK 50
Smith, David A. ... CC 74
Smith, David Ian ... CC 88, 90CoC, 91CoC / TR 89, 90, 91, 92
Smith, David M. ... CC 90, 91, 92CoC / TR 90, 91, 92, 93CoC
Smith, Demont ... FB 98, 99, 2000
Smith, Dennis ... GY 66, 67, 68
Smith, Denton L. ... CC 41M
Smith, Earl I. ... FB 1897, 98
Smith, Edward L. ... FB 76, 77, 78CoC
Smith, Gary ... BS 65, 66
Smith, George B. ... FB 47, 48, 49 / BX 48
Smith, George W. ... BS 54, 55
Smith, Gideon E. ... FB 13, 14, 15
Smith, Gregory ... FB 84, 85
Smith, H. Randal ... TR 77, 78C, 79C, 80 CoC
Smith, Hal Douglas ... TN 57, 58, 59, 60
Smith, Horace ... FB 46, 47, 48, 49 / TR 48, 49C, 50
Smith, Howard B. ... FB 1902
Smith, J. Gary ... WR 63, 64, 65C
Smith, James ... FB 81, 82
Smith, Jeff ... WR 68, 69
Smith, Joseph F. ... BK 35, 36
Smith, Kermit ... FB 67, 68, 69
Smith, Kevin ... BK 80, 81, 82CoC
Smith, Lawrence J. ... FB 37M
Smith, Lawrence J. ... FB 66, 67
Smith, Louis A. ... FB 51
Smith, Louis J. ... BK 26, 27
Smith, Michael R. ... FB 72
Smith, Nicholas ... GY 53 / WR 53
Smith, Nile C. ... BS 1886, 87, 89
Smith, Norman E. ... TR 31, 33
Smith, Otto C. ... FB 73, 74, 76
Smith, Paul M. ... FB 25, 26, 27C / TR 26, 27, 28
Smith, Peter ... FB 61, 62 / BS 62
Smith, Philip R. ... SO 72, 73, 74, 75CoC
Smith, Rick ... SO 97, 98, 99, 2000
Smith, Robaire ... FB 97, 98, 99
Smith, Ross ... TN 82, 83, 84, 85
Smith, Sam ... GY 94, 95, 96, 97C
Smith, Shawn ... FC 93, 94, 95, 96
Smith, Stanley ... SO 71
Smith, Steve ... BK 88, 89, 90, 91CoC
Smith, Steven ... SO 86, 86, 87
Smith, Thomas M., Jr. ... HO 75
Smith, Webb Anthony ... CC 57, 58, 59 / TR 59, 60
Smith, William ... HO 66M, 67M
Smith, William C. ... FB 75, 77
Smith, William E. ... FB 52M
Smith, William H. ... TR 35, 36, 37
Smoker, Jeff ... FB 2000, 01, 02
Smolinski, Brian ... FB 87, 88, 89, 90
Smolinski, Bryan ... HO 90, 91, 92, 93CoC
Smolinski, Philip C. ... FB 73
Smolinski, Theodore C. ... FB 41
Smyl, Harvey ... HO 83, 84, 85
Snider, Irving J. ... BS 18, 19, 20 / FB 17, 18, 19 /BK 18, 19
Snodgrass, James A. ... BK 49, 50, 51C
Snorton, H. Matthew ... FB 61, 62, 63
Snow, Eric ... BK 92, 93, 94, 95CoC
Snow, Percy ... FB 86, 87, 88, 89
Snow, Todd ... CC 79

Snyder, Brad ... SO 93, 94, 95, 96
Snyder, Robert W. ... FB 70M
Soave, John ... FB 57
Sobczak, Edward F. ... BS 46, 47, 48, 49 / FB 46, 48
Sobel, Ronald ... WR 79
Soehnlen, Chris ... FB 87, 88, 89
Sohacki, Edward ... FB 47
Sokoll, Mark R. ... FB 70
Sokoll, Randolph ... HO 69, 70, 71
Solis, Michael ... CC 76
Soltys, Charles ... FB 82, 83
Sommer, Robert ... FB 74M, 76M
Son, Jae ... FC 87, 88, 89, 90
Sorensen, Harry D. ... FC 70, 71C
Sorge, Herbert, Jr. ... GY 69, 70
Sorokin, Andrey ... FC 97
Sorrick, David ... LA 74, 75
Soto, Hank ... BS 94, 95
Southan, Arthur H. ... SO 57, 58
Southan, John R. ... SO 58, 59
Southworth, Fred M. ... TR 41M
Spada, Anthony ... BS 77, 78
Spain, John ... TR 66,67
Spalink, John ... WR 42
Sparks, Harold L. ... CC 35, 36, 37 / TR 36, 37, 38
Sparling, William J. ... TR 27M
Sparvero, Robert P. ... BK 62
Spauling, Donald ... BK 69M
Speare, Almus R. ... TR 1895
Speelman, Harry E. ... FB 35, 36, 37C
Speer, Robert H. ... BS 65, 66
Speers, Mitchell L. ... SO 79M
Speerstra, Herbert A. ... FB 44, 48 / TR 45
Speier, Donald ... CC 86
Spellis, John ... GY 83, 84, 85, 86CoC
Spencer, Eric ... GO 92, 93
Spencer, Michael ... GO 89, 91, 92C
Spencer, Norman M. ... BK 10, 11, 12
Spencer, Raymond ... FB 73, 74, 75
Spiedel, Fred C. ... TR 19
Spiegel, William S., Jr. ... FB 46, 47, 48
Spiekerman, Roy P. ... FB 23, 24, 25 / BS 25, 26
Spieser, Edward ... BX 50, 51, 52
Spiess, Kevin ... WR 99, 2001
Spiller, Eric ... BK 87M, 88M, 89M, 90M
Spink, John ... SO 86, 87, 88
Spinner, Robert W. ... BS 39M
Spinosa, Chris ... GY 89, 91, 92C, 93C
Spitzkeit, Brian ... SO 98, 99, 2000, 01
Sporn, Clifford J. ... SO 73M
Spragg, Clay ... FB 82M, 84M
Springer, Harold A. ... FB 15, 19, 20C / BS 15, 20
Springer, R. Dale ... TR 37, 38
Springer, Ronald K. ... HO 68, 69, 70
Spuller, Thomas ... TR 71
Squier, George G. ... FB 32
Squire, Dana D. ... TN 53, 54
Squires, Domanick ... BS 99, 2000, 01, 02
Squires, Justin ... BK 2001M, 02M, 03M
St. Jean, Donald ... HO 72
Stachelek, Joe ... LA 87, 88, 89
Stachow, Theodore ... SO 62
Stachowicz, Raymond ... FB 77, 78, 79, 80
Stack, J.R. ... BS 1889
Stackhouse, Keith ... BK 52, 53, 54C
Stafford, Jermaine ... FB 95 / TR 96
Stallworth, Daryl ... TR 89, 90
Stamper, James ... SO 91, 92, 93, 94
Standal, Thomas P. ... FB 74, 75
Stanick, Kenneth J. ... BS 53
Stanislaw, Jason ... TN 89, 90
Stanley, Dale E. ... CC 66
Stanley, Ronald ... FB 2001, 02
Stansbery, Kevin ... FB 92, 93
Stanton, Edmund ... FB 77, 78
Stanton, Jerome ... FB 76, 77, 78 / TR 79
Starck, Paul W. ... BS 40
Stark, Elbert J. ... FB 42
Stark, George W. Jr. ... BS 39

Stark, Larry	TN 73, 74, 75
Starkey, Charles W.	TR 69, 70 / CC70
Starr, Nobert	FC 75, 76
Staser, Joe A.	GY 53, 54C
Stauffer, Gordon C.	BK 50, 51, 52
Stead, Ronald S.	BS 54, 55
Steckler, Ben	FB 2002
Steckley, William	BS 65, 66, 67C
Steeh, John R.	LA 78
Steele, Rex B.	TR 31, 33, 34
Steele, Robert	TR 65, 66, 67
Steenken, Thomas A.	GO 68
Steere, Robert	SO 74
Steffee, Donald Keith	BS 45, 46
Steffen, Raymond B.	BK 49, 50, 51
Steffen, William	TR 49, 50
Steigenga, Matt	BK 89, 90, 91CoC, 92CoC
Steiger, John	BS 98, 99
Steimle, David H.	SW 52, 53
Steimle, Earl H.	TR 31
Steimle, John E.	GO 54, 55
Stein, David	LA 86, 87, 88, 89
Stein, Dennis	SO 81, 82, 84CoC, 85CoC
Steiner, Paul	FC 97
Steinmetz, Artie	FB 97
Stelmashenko, Stanley	SO 61, 62, 63
Stelmaszek, Mike	BK 89M, 90M, 91M, 92M
Stelter, James	SO 73, 74CoC 75CoC, 76CoC
Stemm, Merle R.	BS 36, 37
Stempky, Thomas	FC 90
Stentz, Matthew	FC 95, 96
Stepanovic, George	TN 55, 56, 57C
Stephens, Dwayne	BK 90, 91, 92, 93CoC
Stephens, Keith	BK 2001M, 02M, 03M
Stephens, Wallace T.	BS 22. 23
Stephenson, Mark T.	TR 31, 32
Stephenson, Michael	BS 95, 96CoC
Stepter, Harrison	BK 68, 69
Sterk, Ethan	GY 95, 96, 97, 98C
Sterling, Joel Tom	TR 68, 69, 70
Sterner, Keith	GY 66, 67
Steuart, William	SW 58, 59, 61
Stevens, Chad	SO 97M
Stevens, Dewey D.	FB 50
Stevens, Donald E.	GO 52, 53
Stevens, Earl L.	TR 40, 41 / FB 39
Stevens, Frederick D.	TR 02
Stevens, James	LA 81
Stevens, Jerome	LA 71
Stevens, John B., Jr.	TR 43
Stevens, Joseph A.	FB 79, 80, 81, 82
Stevens, Patrick L.	CC 61
Stevens, Richard A.	CC 67 / TR 68
Stevens, Robert L.	BK 48, 49
Stevenson, George A.	FB 60
Stevenson, Robert B.	LA 70, 71, 72
Steward, Ernest	FB 89, 90, 91, 92
Stewart, Andrew	SO 92
Stewart, Donald M.	FB 45
Stewart, Donald W.	FB 59, 60, 61
Stewart, Frank	TR 16
Stewart, Guy L.	BS 1895M
Stewart, James F.	TR 66, 67
Stewart, Jamie	HO 88, 89, 90
Stewart, Jimmy	TR 79, 81
Stewart, John B.	TR 1900, 01C
Stewart, Michael	HO 90, 91, 92
Stewart, Steve	FB 2000, 01, 02
Stifler, Gerald R.	BS 57, 58
Stilling, Marty	SO 70
Stillman, Fred	SW 45C
Stiner, Marc	SW 76, 77
Stobinski, Frank R.	LA 70, 72
Stockwell, Frederick B.	BS 1889
Stockwell, Kenneth	FB 81, 82, 83
Stoll, Paul	BK 76
Stoltzner, Michael	HO 78, 79, 80, 81
Stone, Fred A.	FB 09, 10, 11C
Stone, Fred A., Jr.	BK 42, 43, 47

Stone, James	SO 71
Stonebraker, Guy W.	TN 34
Stonebraker, Louis V.	TN 36, 37
Stoner, Norman H.	WR 28, 30, 32
Story, Brian	SW 78
Stott, Michael	LA 84, 85, 86CoC
Stouffer, James	BK 58, 59
Stout, Melvin L.	GY 49, 50, 51C
Stout, Richard	GY 73, 74, 75C
Stow, Arthur F.	BS 1891
Stoyanovich, Bill	FB 92, 93
Stradley, Robert	FB 84, 85, 86, 87CoC
Straight, Herbert D.	FB 14, 15, 16
Strand, William C.	FB 02
Strata, Rodney	FB 77, 78, 79, 80CoC
Strauch, Clark M.	FB 24M
Strautnieks, Gundars	SO 59, 60
Strayhorn, Jason	FB 96, 97, 98CoC
Streb, Claude R.	FB 29, 30
Streder, Erich	SO 58, 59
Streep, Hubert	GY 78, 79, 80
Street, James	LA 75
Strickland, Kenneth R.	TR 52M
Strobel, Ray	GY 66
Stroia, Eugene J.	FB 50
Strong, Charles E.	SW 62, 63, 64C
Strong, Lawrence F.	BK 58M
Stros, James	BS 88, 89, 90
Strother, James	BS 78, 79, 80
Stroud, Donald E.	WR 56, 57, 58
Strozewski, Rich	GO 96
Strubbe, Scott	BS 94
Struck, Chris	TN 96, 97, 98, 99CoC
Struck, Herman R.	TN 39C, 40
Strunk, Daid	BS 98, 99, 2000, 01
Stuart, James L.	SW 53
Stuber, Eric	CC 82
Stulz, Norman	GY 93, 94, 95, 96
Stump, Jeffrey	FB 84, 85
Stupak, Ken	BK 2000M
Sturges, John	HO 73, 74, 75, 76
Sturgess, Brian	CC 84 / TR 85
Sturrock, Brian	GY 76, 77, 78
Stutler, Chris	LA 90, 91
Stutsman, Richard R.	TR 54
Suarez, Joseph E.	HO 50, 51
Suchara, Michael	SW 82
Suci, Robert L.	FB 59, 60, 61
Sucura, Dave	FB 97, 98, 99, 2000
Sudbay, Steven	BS 82
Suess, Ronald D.	TR 54, 55
Suggs, DeMario	FB 98, 99, 2000, 01, 02
Suk, Steve	HO 92, 93, 94, 95
Sullivan, Charles P.	WR 48, 49
Sullivan, Chris	HO 93, 94, 95
Sullivan, James E.	GO 55, 56, 57
Sullivan, Marc	LA 95, 96
Sullivan, Paul	LA 85, 87
Sullivan, Thomas Brady	FB 44C
Summers, James, III	FB 65, 66 / TR 65, 66
Sumners, Roger K.	TR 62, 63
Sumpter, Eric	BS 91, 92, 93, 94
Sunnen, August	TR 41, 43
Sunryd, Karl	SW 2002, 2003
Super, Robert	FB 66, 67, 68
Surato, Leslie C.	TR 23
Surdam, David	LA 75, 76
Sutherland, Donald M.	BK 53M
Sutherland, Greg	LA 81, 82
Sutherland, Mark	BS 77, 78, 79
Sutilla, Edward D.	FB 58
Sutton, Daniel	HO 78, 79, 80, 81
Sutton, Jerry	BS 62, 63, 64
Sveden, Ronald F.	HO 54, 55
Swaney, Michael A.	SO 72
Swanson, Alan L.	HO 68, 69, 70C
Swanson, David W.	TR 30
Swanson, Hugo T.	FB 20, 21, 22 / BK 22
Swanson, Steven	SO 81, 82, 83CoC

Swanson, Thomas L.	CC 69
Swartz, Douglas	GO 64, 65, 66
Swartz, Howard R.	FB 35, 36, 37
Sweda, Jon	BK 94. 95, 96M, 97M
Sweeney, Kevin	CC 93, 94CoC
Switzer, Robert	GY 89, 90, 91
Sykes, Phil	SO 68M
Sylvester, Dean	HO 95
Sylvia, Richard	HO 53
Symington, James	TN 70, 71
Syria, Ronald L.	SW 61
Szasz, Stephen J.	FB 36, 37, 38
Szilagyi, Mickey	TN 66, 67, 68
Szmanski, James	FB 86, 87
Sztykiel, John	HO 76, 77
Szwast, Robert F.	FB 60, 61
Szymanski, James	FB 86, 87, 89
Szymke, Theodore J.	FC 36C
Szypula, Carl J.	GY 79
Tabron, Eliot	TR 82, 83CoC
Takagishi, Troy	GY 97, 98, 99, 2000
Tallefson, Willard T.	TR 34
Tam, George	FC 75
Tambo, William	WR 54
Tamburo, Richard P.	FB 50, 51, 52
Tanker, Terry	FB 82, 83
Tanner, Kinsey H.	TR 46, 48
Tansey, Robert L.	GO 47, 48, 49
Tansey, Warren E.	GO 38
Taplin, Greg	FB 2000, 01, 02
Tapling, Mark	FB 77, 78, 79
Tarnow, Jason	LA 95, 96
Tarshis, Stanley G.	GY 58, 59, 60
Tata, Vincent P.	FB 85, 86, 87, 88
Tate, Charles G.	FB 1897
Tate, Joe	FB 2000, 01, 02
Tate, Mark T.	FB 58
Tatter, Jordan B.	SO 57, 58
Tatu, George W.	CC 58, 60
Taubert, James	FB 72, 73, 74CoC
Tavares, Juan	SW 84, 85CoC
Tavenner, Rober C.	WR 60
Taylor, Clifford A.	GO 48, 49, 50
Taylor, David	HO 81, 82, 83, 84
Taylor, Dean R.	SW 57, 58
Taylor, Donavan	FB 85
Taylor, Marcus	BK 2001, 02C
Taylor, Maurice R.	FB 22, 23C
Taylor, Neal C.	BK 37M
Taylor, Ryan	CC 98 / TR 98, 99
Teague, Jason	FB 2002
Teale, George W.	GO 46
Techlin, David G.	FB 65, 66
Teddy, Fred	CC 72, 73, 74, 75 / TR 73, 74, 75, 76
Teifer, Gerald E.	TN 49
Tekisalp, Erdal	SO 75
Telder, Robert A.	BS 42
Temby, Bruce	TR 78
Temple, Percy F.	TR 22
Temple, Thomas D.	GY 58, 60
TenEyck, Rex C.	TR 35, 36
Terek, Paul	TR 98, 99, 2001, 02C
Terlaak, Robert T.	FB 32, 33
TeRoller, Henry	BS 10
Terpay, Alexander	HO 64, 65
Terry, Robert	SW 77, 79
Tetzlaff, Ted J.	TR 55, 56, 57
Teufer, Philip H.	FB 22
Teutsch, Eric	TR 82
Thackthay, Soon	WR 89, 90. 91CoC
Thalken, Francis R.	FC 41CoC, 42C
Thatcher, Fent E.	BS 06, 07
Thayer, Robert F.	FB 24
Thedos, Dean	BK 77M, 78M
Therrian, Jeffrey	WR 77, 78, 79, 80
Theuerkauf, Robert	FB 73
Thiele, Earl O.	SO 62, 63, 64
Thierry, Aaron	BK 97M, 98M, 99M
Thiess, Albert A., Jr.	GO 66, 67, 68

Thomann, Frederick J. .... BK 62, 63, 64
Thomas, Arthur .... HO 61, 62, 63
Thomas, Calvin .... TR 79, 80, 81, 82
Thomas, Christopher .... FC 77, 78
Thomas, Craig .... FB 91, 92, 93
Thomas, David W. .... FB 68, 69, 70
Thomas, David .... BK 97, 98, 2000, 01CoC
Thomas, Deane A. .... FB 50
Thomas, Desmond .... FB 96, 97, 98, 99
Thomas, E. James .... FB 74, 75, 76. 77
Thomas, George C. .... TR 30, 31, 32
Thomas, George H. .... FC 55C, 56, 57
Thomas, Gordon G. .... GY 48
Thomas, Horace L. .... TR 26
Thomas, James P. .... SW 43
Thomas, Jeffrey .... WR 77, 78, 79, 80
Thomas, Jesse L. .... FB 48, 49, 50 / TR 49, 50, 51
Thomas, John E. .... HO 52, 53, 54C
Thomas, Jonathan .... FC 78, 79 80
Thomas, LaMarr .... FB 67
Thomas, Marc .... LA 71
Thomas, Nigel .... HO 80, 81, 82, 83
Thomas, Reinhold .... SW 27
Thomas, Richard .... FB 74M
Thomas, Robert C. .... SW 59
Thomas, Steven .... WR 78
Thomas, Walter P. .... BS 15, 16
Thompson, Arthur R. .... SW 53
Thompson, Charles F. .... GY 59, 60, 61
Thompson, Donald .... HO 70, 71, 72CoC
Thompson, Earl C. .... BX 39
Thompson, Herbert J. .... WR 43
Thompson, Hubert .... FB 1999
Thompson, Jeroen .... FC 97
Thompson, Kelly A. .... TR 57
Thompson, Matthew .... WR 82, 84
Thompson, Michael .... HO 90, 91, 92
Thompson, Robert C. .... TR 42 / CC 41
Thomsen, Michael .... GO 80, 81, 82
Thomson, Charles J. .... FB 17, 19, 20
Thomson, Elmer L. .... FB 1896
Thomson, Ryan .... LA 94, 95, 96
Thor, David .... GY 66, 67, 68
Thorburn, Robert .... GY 67M
Thornhill, Charles E. .... FB 64, 65, 66
Thornhill, Josh .... FB 98, 99, 2000CoC, 01CoC
Thornton, Gregory .... FB 84
Thornton, Richard L. .... WR 52
Thorpe, Gustave A. .... FB 20, 21, 22
Thorson, Mike .... CC 2001, 02
Threats, Jabbar .... FB 95
Thrower, Willie L. .... FB 52
Thuerer, John .... SW 70, 71, 72CoC
Thurston, Jim .... SW 94
Thurston, Lloyd M. .... TR 20, 21
Thurtell, Herbert .... BS 1887
Tibai, Louis .... WR 94, 96
Tichnor, Jack R. .... TR 33M
Tiemann, Barry R. .... SO 66, 67, 69
Tien, David .... TN 77
Tierney, Jack .... BX 48, 50
Tilley, Thomas .... HO 85, 86, 87, 88CoC
Tillotson, Ivan G. .... TR 26, 27, 28
Timmerman Edward G. .... FB 50, 51, 52
Timmons, Frank D. .... FB 71, 72
Timyan, Robert M. .... GO 72, 73C
Tingley, Mike .... SW 98, 99, 2000
Tinnick, John F. .... FB 64
Tintera, John .... FC 75, 76
Tipton, Norman E. .... FB 45
Toan, John W. .... TR 1888
Tobe, Justin .... HO 2003
Tobias, Chris .... GY 90, 91, 92, 93
Tobin, John F. .... FB 48, 49, 50
Tobin, Michael G. .... FB 68, 69, 70
Todd, Douglas .... SW 67, 68
Todd, Jerry .... FB 88, 89
Toepper, Chris .... BS 2003
Tolles, Albert R. .... BS 26, 27
Toloff, Chris .... TR 2001, 03 / CC 2001, 02CoC
Tomkow, Thomas .... GY 77, 78, 79, 81CoC
Tompkins, Chandler Z. .... TR 1898
Tompkins, Richard S. .... WR 30, 31
Tonello, Mark .... TR 93
Toney, Marcus .... FB 80, 81, 82
Toombs, Charles .... GY 76, 78
Topalo, Goran .... TN 2000, 01, 02, 03
Topalo, Robert .... TE 2000
Topilian, Timothy .... LA 76, 77
Topolinski, Dennis .... TR 86, 88CoC, 89 CoC / CC 86, 87, 88CoC
Topolinski, Timothy .... TR 92, 93 / CC 90, 91
Topouzian Daron .... LA 81, 82, 83, 84
Torbert, Kelvin .... BK 2002, 03
Tosto, Richard .... HO 86
Toth, Kenneth A. .... FB 85
Totte, Raymond, Jr. .... FC 50, 51, 52
Totten, Edward C. .... BK 28, 29
Tower, Benjamin .... BK 81, 82, 83, 84CoC
Tower, Gordon E. .... FB 1899
Tower, Ray R. .... BS 1902, 03C / BK 1902, 03 / TR 1903M
Towner, John H. .... BK 48M
Towner, Wilford S. .... BS 03, 04, 05
Towns, Ivan A. .... GY 48, 49C
Townsend, Alphonso .... FB 2003
Townsend, Anthony .... FB 79, 80
Townsend, Clinton D. .... GO 62
Townsend, Edward E. .... CC 55, 56
Townsend, Ryan .... SO 95, 96, 97
Towson, Toby W. .... GY 67, 68, 69
Townsend, Todd .... TE 2001
Trace, David R. .... SO 67, 68, 69
Tracy, John E. .... TR 1894
Trahan, John Carroll .... BX 55
Train, Rob .... WR 94, 95
Trapp, Donald G. .... SW 34
Travis, William E. .... FB 1899
Traylor, Frank .... FB 67
Trese, Patrick .... SO 89, 90, 91, 92
Trevor, Bruce .... GY 81, 82, 83, 84CoC
Trial, Heath .... GY 91, 92
Trier, Howard E. .... TN 53
Trinidad, Francisco .... TN 97, 98, 99, 2000
Triplett, Howard .... FB 92, 93
Triplett, William L. .... FB 68, 69, 70
Trivelloni, Mike .... SO 99, 2000, 01, 02
Trivelloni, Thomas .... SO 99, 2000, 01
Trombly, Craig .... WR 2002, 03
Tropf, Jeffrey L. .... BK 75
Troscinski, Robert .... HO 81, 82
Trowbridge, Charles L. .... BS 13
Trueman, John J. .... FB 59
Truesdell, Cory .... SW 96
Truitt, Ralph .... FB 98
Trull, Donald B. .... CC 47M
Trull, Richard T. .... CC 50M / TR 50M
Truman, Merle C. .... LA 72
Trumball, Chris .... TN 91
Trumpinski, Ryan .... GY 97, 98
Tryon, Donald J. .... FB 65M
Tryon, Edward C. .... TR 1892
Tryon, James H. .... TR 05
Tsakiris, Alexander .... BX 52, 53
Tuber, Gary H. .... BS 65M
Tuchscherer, Ernest .... SO 67, 68, 69
Tuerk, James .... GY 73, 74, 75
Tungate, Paul S. .... BS 63
Tuomi, Roger L. .... GY 58
Turchan, Manuel C. .... GY 63
Turcotte, Real J. .... HO 60, 61, 62, 63
Turnas, Jeff .... LA 92
Turnbull, Richard J. .... WR 64
Turner, Bart .... HO 91, 92, 93, 94C
Turner, Daryl .... FB 80, 81, 82, 83
Turner, Gregory .... TR 82, 83, 84, 85
Turner, Jesse .... BS 71, 72
Turner, Joseph E. .... FB 16, 17
Turner, Kenneth F. .... SW 40
Turner, Stanley A. .... BS 53
Turner, T.J. .... FB 97, 98, 99, 2000
Turton, Jason .... GY 2001
Tuttle, H. Foley .... BK 1903, 04, 05C
Tuzzzolino, Anthony .... HO 94, 95, 96, 97CoC
Twellman, Steven .... SO 69, 70, 71
Tyler, Bobby .... FC 69, 70
Tyler, Chris .... WR 98, 99, 2001CoC
Tynan, Scott .... LA 86
Tyree, Thomas .... FB 83, 84 / TR 83
Tyrrell, Milford A. .... FB 22M
Tyson, James .... BS 21M
Uckele, William E. .... TR 35
Uhlmann, Tony M. .... WR 80, 81
Ulmer, Jack D. .... BK 59M, 60M
Ulrich, Rudolph .... TR 37, 38, 39
Underwood, Daniel D. .... FB 61, 62,63C
Underwood, Dimitrius .... FB 95, 96, 97
Ungechauer, Stan .... LA 94, 95. 96
Unkefer, Bruce .... GY 79
Unold, Thaddeus .. TR 78, 79, 80, 81CoC / CC 77, 79, 80, 81
Uram, Michael .... GY 69, 70, 71
Urbanik, Daniel A. .... BS 48, 49C
Urbin, Gregory J. .... LA 74
Urbin, Stephen .... LA 71, 72, 73, 74
Urquhart, Gordon .... SO 75
Usher, Aaron .... TC 2001 / CC 2000
Usher, Nathan .... CC 2001, 02
Valcanoff, Alexander A. .... WR 61, 62, 63 / FB 60
Valentine, Carlton .... BK 85, 86, 87, 88CoC
Valentino, Damon .... TN 89, 90, 91C
Vallier, Donald J. .... FC 53
VanAmberg, Barry .... SW 76
VanAntwerp, Mike .... LA 94
VanArman, John P. .... TR 25, 26
VanAuken, E. W. .... TR 39
VanBuren, Earl .... FB 25
Vance, Paul .... SO 98, 99, 2000, 01
Vance, Walter E. .... BS 08, 09
VanDagens, John L. .... FC 50, 51
Vandebunte, John .... SW 76, 77, 78
Vandenburg, Vincent I. .... FB 34, 35, 36
Vandenbussche, Kevin M. .... BK 76, 77
Vanderbeek, Matthew .... FB 86, 87, 88, 89
Vanderbush, Randy .... BS 92, 93 / FB 89
Vanderhoef, Wilfred R. .... FB 1895C, 96C
VanderHorst, Leo .... SO 57, 58
Vanderjagt, Mark .... BK 65
Vanderlaan, Steve .... BS 72, 73, 74
Vanderlende, Jeff J. .... BK 71
Vandermeer, Myrton L. .... FB 30, 31, 32
Vandermeiden, John .... GO 70, 71, 72
VanderRoest, Nick A. .... BK 32, 33, 34
Vanderstolp, John H. .... FB 1896, 97, 98
Vandervoort, Adelbert D. .... FB 14, 15, 16, 19
VanDyke, Ryan .... FB 98, 99, 2000, 01
Vanek, Gregory .... BK 85
VanElst, G. David .... FB 68, 69
VanElst, Gary L. .... FB 69, 71, 72
VanFaasen, Arnold B. .... BK 33, 34, 35CoC
VanGolen, Ken .... FC 86C, 87C
VanHammen, Stephen J. .... BK 80M, 81M
VanHavel, John J. .... BS 58M
VanHuysen, James .... SO 95, 96, 97
VanLoozen, David .... GO 87
VanMeter, Clfford W. .... HO 58M
VanNoppen, Donald M. .... TR 24, 25, 26
VanOrden, Richard .... FB 18, 19
VanPelt, Brad A. ... FB 70, 71, 72CoC / BK 71, 72 / BS 71, 72
VanPelt, Chris .... FB 79, 80, 81, 82
VanPoppelen, John W. .... BX 51M
VanRavensway, Jamie .... GO 97, 99
Vanrhee, Corey .... BK 96M, 97M, 98M, 99M
VanSciever, Craig W. .... BS 59, 60
VanSpybrook, Eldon .... HO 58, 60
Vanstaalduinen, Bart .... HO 93, 94, 95, 96CoC
Vantine, Donald E. .... GO 47
VanWie, Bernard .... GY 73, 74
VanZylen, James H. .... BK 28, 29, 30C
Vargha, Louis A. .... TR 52, 53, 54

Vargo, Joel .... GY 2001
Varmette, T. Michael .... WR 80
Vary, Richard .... BS 68, 69, 70
Vass, Dennis .... GO 69, 70, 71CoC
Vatz, Abe M. .... BK 12, 13, 14 / BS 13
Vaughn, Bert R. .... FB 77, 78, 79, 80, 81
Vaughn, Ernest .... BS 07, 08 / FB 07 / TR 07
Vaughn, Lawrence F. .... FB 13, 14
Vaydik, Frank J. .... BK 35
Vedejs, Dainis .... HO 64, 65
Vela, Luis F. .... TN 55, 56, 57
Venema, Jacob G. .... FC 47
Venia, James .... LA 70
Ventura, Mabricio .... SO 61, 62
Verberkmoes, Krien, III .... SO 72, 73, 74
Verberkmoes, Robert .... SO 75M
Verburg, Mike .... TR 91, 92, 93, 94
Veres, David .... BS 91, 92, 93, 94CoC
Verity, Gordon L. .... SW 49, 50
Verran, Garfield C. .... TR 1902, 03
Vershinski, Thomas F. .... FB 59
Versical, David .... HO 76, 77, 78 CoC
Vescolani, Bert .... GY 87, 88
Vesikallio, Walter .... TN 91
Vest, Donald S. .... GY 52
Vetter, Frederick J. .... TN 70, 71 , 72 C, 73
Vevia, Paul J. .... BK 16, 17
Vezmar, Walter .... FB 45
Vickerson, Kevin .... FB 2001, 02
Videto, Judd .... WR 95, 96
Vielhaber, John T. .... FB 79
Vincent, Dan .... BK 2003M
Vincent, J. Sam .... BK 82, 83, 84, 85CoC
Vincent, Jason .... BK 2002
Vincent, Jay F. .... BK 78, 79, 80, 81CoC
Vincent, Wendell C. .... CC 56M / TR 57M
Viney, Robert W. .... FB 63, 64, 65
Virkus, Bradley W. .... GO 85, 86, 87
Virtue, Paul .... SW 71, 72, 73
Visscher, Nicholas .... SW 2000, 01, 02, 03
Vissing, Paul R. .... BK 47M
Vissing, William C. .... FB 42M
Voelker, Arthur F. .... TR 29
Vogel, Alfred R. .... FB 24, 25
Vogel, Jeffery .... BS 89, 90, 91
Vogler, Harold .... FB 47, 48, 49C
Vogt, Raymond A. .... FB 50, 51, 52
Volas, Brandon .... BS 2003
Volk, Jason .... TN 89
Volk, Uwe .... SW 94
Vollrath, Mark .... FB 73M
Vollweiler, Andy .... TN 69
Volmar, Douglas .... HO 65, 66, 67
Vondette, Roy W. .... BK 06, 07, 08C
Vondette, William L. .... BK 32, 33
VonEberstein, John A. .... TR 43
Vooletich, Brian .... FB 90, 91CoC
Vore, Stephen .... FC 64, 65, 66
Voorheis, Donald N. .... TR 61, 63
Vorkapich, Mike .... FB 94
Vosburg, Robert L. .... TR 46, 47
Vosper, Richard H. .... TR 10
Voss, Gary .... TR 85, 87, 88, 89
Voss, Tom .... LA 86M
Vrablec, John .... SO 60, 61
Vrooman, James .... TR 52, 53, 54, 55
Wachman, Mitchell .... FB 83, 84, 85
Wadle, Keith .... LA 84, 86
Wagenaar, Rudolf .... SW 2003
Wagner, Matt .... SW 96M, 97M, 98M, 99M
Wagner, Michael .... SW 86, 87
Wagner, Mike .... BS 98, 99
Wagner, Roosevelt .... FB 89, 90, 91
Wagner, Sidney P. .... FB 33, 34, 35C
Wagner, Thomas F. .... TR 56
Wagonlander, Edward .... BK 51
Waha, Carrie .... TR 80M
Waite, Kenneth A. .... CC 35, 36, 37C / TR 36, 37, 38C
Waite, Michael .... LA 75, 76, 77

Waite, Roy H. .... TR 1904, 05, 06, 07C
Wakefield, Harry K. .... BS 24, 25, 26
Waks, Charles A. .... HO 54, 55
Wakulsky, George T. .... GO 56, 57, 58
Walcott, Roland .... BS 65, 66
Waldron, Donald .... BK 46, 47, 48 / FB 46 / TN 48
Walendzik, Tom .... BS 81, 82
Walicki, Adam .... GO 99
Walker, Alan N. .... FC 52
Walker, Don .... FB 94, 95
Walker, George M. .... FB 58, 59, 60
Walker, Gregory .... LA 82, 83, 84, 85
Walker, Horace .... BK 59, 60C
Walker, Jerry .... BS 64, 65, 66
Walker, John .... SW 60
Walker, John C. .... GY 51, 52, 53C
Walker, Ralph .... BK 83, 84, 85, 86
Wallace, Matthew .... SW 2002
Wallberg, Josh .... BS 97M, 98M
Waller, Joel .... FB 83
Wallihan, Danny .... TN 95, 96
Walsh, Brian .... GY 80, 81, 82
Walsh, David .... SO 70
Walsh, Eugene G. .... SW 48
Walsh, Eugene J. .... BS 46, 47
Walsh, John J. .... FB 63, 64
Walsh, Kenneth .... SW 65, 66, 67CoC
Walsh, Michael .... WR 77, 78, 79
Walsh, Robert D. .... GO 58
Walter, John P. .... TR 51, 52, 53 / CC 50, 52
Walter, L. Dale .... FC 87
Walters, James .... LA 71
Walters, John .... BS 66, 67
Walters, Warren P. .... BS 36
Wandeloski, Stan .... SO 81
Waole, Keith .... LA 84, 86
Ward James C. .... HO 52, 53, 54, 55
Ward, George R. .... TR 57, 58, 59
Ward, Joseph .... BS 83, 84
Ward, Lloyd .... BK 68, 69, 70CoC
Ward, Morgan C. .... CC 59, 60 / TR 61
Ward, William .... LA 83
Wardian, Michael .... LA 93, 94
Wardlow, Brian .... CC 98, 99
Ware, Darron .... FB 2002
Ware, Harold W. .... GO 52, 53, 54
Ware, Michael .... HO 93
Ware, William H., Jr. .... FB 67
Wareham, Earl D. .... TR 27
Waring, Michael .... LA 76, 77
Warmbein, Kurt C. .... FB 33, 34, 35
Warner, Arthur E. .... TR 12 , 13
Warner, Frank E. .... TR 41
Warner, Frank T. .... TR 16
Warner, Jeff .... GY 79
Warner, John A. .... TR 46M, 47M
Warner, K. Gary .... BS 57, 58
Warner, Laird .... TN 64, 65, 66
Warner, Rickey N. .... WR 77
Warner, Robert E. .... TR 23
Warner, Roy C. .... BS 29
Warnke, Derek .... SO 95
Warnshuis, Daniel .... SW 77, 78
Warren, Carl L. .... TR 20
Warren, Charles K. .... TR 32, 33, 34
Warren, Frank V. .... BS 1896, 97, 98C
Warren, John L., III .... BK 66M, 67M
Wasczenski, Robert .... FC 48C
Washburne, Chandler .... FC 48C
Washington, Eugene ..... FB 64, 65, 66 / TR 65, 66, 67
Washington, Herb .... TR 70, 71, 72
Washington, Masheska .... TN 93, 94
Washington, Richard .... FB 74, 75
Washington, Stan .... BK 64, 65, 66
Washington, Valdemar ..... LA 71, 72, 73 CoC, 74
Wasinski, William F. .... LA 71, 72
Wasylk, Steve .... FB 90, 91, 92, 93
Watchowski, Don .... BS 99, 2000, 01
Waters, Frank D., III .... FB 66, 67, 68

Waters, Frank D., Jr. .... FB 46, 47, 48, 49
Waters, Marcus .... FB 2000
Watkins, Douglas A. .... BS 28, 29
Watkins, Kevin .... CC 77
Watkins, L. Whitney .... BS 1893M
Watkins, Ramsey .... TR 94, 95, 96, 97
Watkins, Ronald .... FB 62 / TR 62
Watson, Ashton .... FB 2002
Watson, George G. .... TR 49
Watson, Joseph A., Jr. .... GO 42C
Watson, Richard .... TN 94, 95
Watt, James .... HO 70, 71, 72
Watt, John .... HO 95, 96, 97 CoC
Watt, Mark .... BS 94
Watt, Michael .... HO 95, 96
Watt, William .... HO 68, 69, 70
Wattles, Brett .... BS 2000, 01, 02, 03
Watts, Neil S. .... SW 62, 63, 64
Watts, Robert .... BK 52M
Waver, Hal C. .... TR 1903
Wawzysko, John H. .... GO 46
Waybright, Donald .... GY 72, 73, 74
Weamer, Philip E. .... TR 22, 23
Weathers, Ray .... BK 95, 96, 97CoC
Weatherspoon, Donald .... FB 65
Weaver, Dee Lee .... TR 35
Weaver, Douglas W. .... FB 50, 51, 52
Weaver, Frank J. .... CC 60
Weaver, Mike .... HO 97, 98, 99, 2000CoC
Webb, Tanya W. .... BK 76, 77 / FB 78, 79
Webber, Jason .... BK 97
Weber, Joseph A. .... BK 71M, 72M
Webster, Craig .... LA 71
Webster, George .... FB 64, 65, 66CoC
Webster, Joseph .... TN 83, 84
Webster, William R. .... TR 39, 40, 41
Wechter, John .... WR 2000, 01, 02, 03
Weckler, Charles A. .... FB 21
Wedemeyer, Charlie .... FB 66, 68
Wedemeyer, Harry P. .... TR 1899, 00C
Wedgeworth, George H. .... BK 50M
Wedley, Daniel .... BS 76
Wedlow, Monquiz .... FB 2000, 01, 02
Weed, Stanley F. .... BS 28, 29
Weeder, Maurice G. .... BS 14, 15
Weedon, Chris .... GY 98, 99, 2000
Weeks, Fred H. .... BX 51
Weeks, Josh .... BS 94, 95, 96, 97
Weeks, Kenneth B. .... FB 27
Weening, Bertrand T. .... TR 48M
Wehrman, Chris .... CC 95, 96, 97 CoC / TR 96, 97, 98, 99CoC
Wehrwein, William H. .... TR 68, 69, 70
Weideman, Charles H. .... BS 1890, 91
Weiermiller, Curt .... SO 91, 92, 93, 94C
Weil, Norman O. .... FB 60M
Weiland, Jeff .... FB 83
Weimer, L. Austin .... BS 35, 36
Weinacker, Adolph J. .... TR 47, 48, 50
Weiner, Ira .... FC 82
Weinland, Arthur A. .... TR 30
Weisshlum, Herbert .... BX 57
Weissend, Eric .... SO 82, 83, 85
Weissengruber, Max E. .... TR 59
Weitz, Stanley E. .... TN 32, 33, 34C
Weitzmann, James .... SW 51, 52
Welch, Bill .... LA 89
Welch, Daniel .... GO 74
Welch, Harold I. .... BS 34, 35, 36
Welch, Phil .... WR 82
Welch, Russell .... HO 77, 78, 79, 80CoC
Welfare, Ronald E. .... SW 60
Weller, Gerald .... BS 76, 77, 78CoC
Weller, Paul R. .... FB 73M, 75M
Wellman, Jeff .... SO 86, 87
Wells, Andrew .... TR 79, 80, 81CoC
Wells, George B. .... FB 1896, 97 / TR 1897, 98
Wells, Jonathan .... SO 98, 99, 2000, 01CoC
Wells, Stephen .... GY 65
Wells, Willliam P. .... FB 51, 52, 53

Welton, Steve ... GY 74
Wenceslao, Honorato ... FC 93
Wendt, Larry ... BS 88, 89, 90, 91CoC
Wenger, Ralph D. ... FB 45, 48, 49
Wenner, Elywn A. ... FB 26
Wenner, George ... BS 22, 23, 24
Wenner, Jack H. ... BS 54, 55
Wenson, Anthony ... BS 76
Werner, Daniel L. ... FB 69, 72
Werner, Edward R. ... HO 54
Werthmann, Thomas ... GY 57, 58
Weshinskey, Kris ... BK 91, 92, 93, 94CoC
Wesling, Richard M. ... BK 52, 53
Wessells, Phillip H. ... BK 05
West, Jerry ... FB 64, 65, 66
West, Mark ... SO 89, 90, 91
Westerman, Leslie B. ... BK 06, 07
Westermeyer II, Nickolas ... GY 89, 90, 91C
Westfall, James ... TN 91, 92
Weston, Alfred ... BS 74, 75, 76, 77C
Weston, Gerald W. ... BS 10
Weston, James W. ... BS 14M
Weston, Mark ... GO 73, 75, 76
Westrick, Brian ... BK 2002, 2003
Weyland, Robert L. ... BK 43M
Wheeler, Burr ... FB 1902M
Wheeler, John P. Jr. ... FB 46
Wheeler, Joseph R. ... TR 50
Wheeler, Philip R. ... CC 56, 57 / TR 56
Wheeler, Roy S. ... FB 07, 08 / TR 07, 08
Wheeler, Stephon ... FB 2002
Wherley, James R. ... HO 61
Whetter, Lloyd A. ... TR 43, 46
Whipp, Don ... WR 90, 91, 92, 93CoC
Whitcomb, Shawn ... WR 76, 77, 79, 80
White, Adam ... BS 2002, 03
White, Benny A. ... BK 73, 74, 75, 76
White, Curtis W. ... BK 35, 36
White, Eric ... FB 91
White, Grover C. ... TR 08
White, James L. ... SW 62
White, Kevin ... FC 82
White, Lorenzo ... FB 84, 85, 86, 87CoC
White, Mark ... FC 72, 73
White, Michael ... CC 78, 79, 80C, 81C / TR 79, 80, 81CoC, 82C
White, Oliver G. ... BK 43, 46C, 47
White, Peter ... HO 89, 90, 91, 92
White, Shawn ... WR 78, 80, 81, 82
White, Thorpe ... TN 42M
White, Tony ... WR 81, 83, 84, 85
Whiteford, Frederick G. ... SW 66, 67
Whitfield, Damon ... SW 88, 89
Whitinger, Robin ... LA 88, 89, 90M
Whitlock, Stanley C. ... SW 26C
Whitman, Michael S. ... BS 81, 82, 83, 84
Whitmore, James ... SO 96, 97, 98C
Whittemore, Olin S. ... FB 51M
Whitten, Damon ... HO 98, 99, 2000, 01CoC
Whitticker, William ... FB 2001, 02
Whittle, David ... FB 79, 80
Wickard, Scott ... WR 73, 74, 75
Wickens, David ... TR 90, 91, 92 / CC 89
Wickering, Jack ... SW 60
Wickman, Jeffrey ... TN 79, 80, 81, 82
Wiegand, Geary ... HO 94
Wieleba, Ralph C. ... FB 69, 70, 71
Wierman, Thomas H. ... TN 62, 63, 64
Wietecha, Raymond W. ... FB 46
Wiggan, Conrad ... HO 79
Wightman, Robert R. ... SW 53
Wilcox, Ernest A. ... BS 02, 03, 05
Wilcox, Fred E. ... FB 20,21 / BK 22
Wilden, Bruce ... SO 78, 79, 80, 81
Wiley, Carroll E. ... WR 57
Wiley, DuJuan ... BK 97, 98
Wiley, Milton ... BK 76
Wiley, Robert ... SW 94, 95, 96CoC, 97CoC
Wilke, Riney ... LA 82, 83, 84, 85 CoC
Wilkens, Dave ... TR 90, 91, 92

Wilkins, Corky ... TR 82
Wilkinson, Bradley ... HO 78
Wilkinson, Dorian C. ... BK 36, 37
Wilkinson, Gary ... SO 73, 74, 75, 76
Wilkinson, Harry G. ... GY 53
Wilkinson, Harry V. ... BS 43M
Wilkinson, Neil ... HO 87
Wilks, John J. ... FB 57, 59
Willard, Frank ... TN 78, 79
Willard, William D. ... TR 24, 25 / CC 23
Willertz, Chris ... FB 86, 87, 88, 89
Williams, Andre ... TR 79, 80, 81, 82
Williams, Carl ... FB 79, 80, 81, 82
Williams, Chauncy ... TR 90, 91
Williams, Chester I. ... BS 24M
Williams, Chris ... WR 99, 2000, 01, 02C
Williams, David ... TN 72, 73, 74
Williams, David S. ... BS 67, 68, 69
Williams, Dean E. ... BS 15, 16
Williams, Edward L. ... BK 61, 62, 63
Williams, Eugene ... TR 27
Williams, Fred J ... BS 23, 24
Williams, Fred T. ... FB 1897
Williams, Glenn ... FB 68, 69
Williams, J. C. ... FB 48, 49, 50
Williams, James A. ... FB 78, 79, 80
Williams, Jesse D. ... FB 71
Williams, Julien ... TR 2003
Williams, Leon L. ... FB 74, 75, 76 / TR 75, 77
Williams, Leonard ... BK 78
Williams, Mark L. ... HO 63
Williams, Oliver ... WR 75
Williams, Peter E. ... SW 66, 67, 68
Williams, Raymond P. ... SW 47, 48, 49, 50
Williams, Robert C. ... BS 53, 54
Williams, Samuel F. ... FB 56, 57, 58C
Williams, Terence L. ... FB 77, 78
Williams, Tyrone ... TR 78, 79, 80, 81CoC
Williams, P. Van ... FB 79, 80
Williams, William G. ... SW 61
Williams, William ... TR 53
Williamson, Herbert H. ... FB 34
Williamson, Leon M. ... SW 38
Williamson, Mark ... CC 82, 83, 84, 85CoC / TR 84, 85, 86
Williford, Steve ... SO 96, 97, 98, 99, 2000
Willingham, L. Tyrone ... FB 73, 74, 76 / BS 75, 76, 77CoC
Willis George E. ... FC 41CoC, 42
Willis, Kevin ... BK 82, 83, 84CoC
Willits, Kevin S. ... LA 76, 77CoC, 79CoC, 80
Willman, Walter K. ... BS 17, 20, 21C
Willmarth, Theodore ... CC 27, 28, 29C / TR 27, 28, 29
Willoughby, Theodore C. ... TR 22M
Wilson, Adam ... BK 2000M
Wilson, Bernard ... FB 85, 86, 87, 88
Wilson, Bobby ... FB 89, 90
Wilson, Brian ... TR 2001 / CC 2000, 01, 02
Wilson, Chad ... SW 2002, 2003
Wilson, Charles A. ... FB 73, 74
Wilson, Edgar P. ... BK 74, 75, 76, 77 / FB 77
Wilson, Edward B. ... GY 65, 66
Wilson, Freddie ... FB 88, 89, 90
Wilson, Howard D. ... SW 48
Wilson, Howard H. ... TR 20, 22
Wilson, James A. ... BS 1890, 91
Wilson, John B. ... TR 29, 30 / FB 27
Wilson, John D. ... FB 50, 51, 52
Wilson, John ... GY 89, 92
Wilson, Miles M. ... FB 34, 35
Wilson, Patrick J. ... FB 54, 55, 56 / BK 55, 56, 57
Wilson, Patrick ... CC 66 / TR 67
Wilson, Pierre ... FB 99
Wilson, Robert P. ... TR 33
Wilson, Scott ... SW 79, 81, 82
Wilson, Steve ... LA 74, 75CoC
Wilson, Thomas V. ... TR 73, 74, 75
Wilson, Thomas ... BS 76
Wilson, Tom R. ... FB 58, 59, 60

Wilson, Travis ... FB 2000
Wilson, Tyrone C. ... FB 73, 74, 75
Wines, Thomas J. ... SW 55
Winfield, Kenneth J. ... SW 70, 71, 72, 73CoC
Winger, Norman ... FC 55, 57
Winiecki, Thomas ... FB 60, 61
Winkel, C. J. ... SW 82, 83, 84, 85CoC
Winters, Brian ... FB 90, 91
Winther, Paul C. ... SO 58, 59
Wirnsberger, Dan ... WR 91, 93 / 94CoC, 95CoC
Wirs, Nick ... SO 66
Wiseman, Donald R. ... FB 34, 35
Wishart, George ... BK 2001M, 02M
Wiska, Jeffrey ... FB 79, 80, 81
Wisniewski, Alex ... GY 94, 95C
Wisniewski, Matt ... SW 2003
Wissner, Walter F. ... TR 31, 32, 32 / CC 32C
Witherill, Thomas ... GY 62M
Witter, Gordon L. ... BS 27
Wittig, Jeff ... FB 88, 89
Wittig, Kevin ... SO 2000, 01, 02
Witzke, Edward S. ... GY 67, 68, 69
Wohlfert, Duane G. ... WR 59, 61
Wojciechowski, John ... FB 81, 82, 84, 85CoC / WR 85
Wolcott, Brian ... BS 77, 78, 79, 80
Wolcott, Oliver ... BS 2003
Wolf, Charles ... WR 76M, 77M
Wolf, Clyde M. ... FB 1898 / BS 1899
Wolf, David ... LA 73
Wolf, Michael J. ... SW 65, 66, 67
Wolf, Robert H. ... SW 65, 66, 67
Wolfe, Adam ... BK 2001, 02, 03
Wolfe, David A. ... HO 52M
Wolfe, James ... LA 91, 92, 93, 94CoC
Wolfe, Todd ... BK 87, 88, 89CoC, 90
Wolff, Charles R. ... TN 63, 64, 65C
Wolff, David ... FB 83, 84, 85, 86
Wolff, Jason ... SO 94, 95, 96, 97
Wolffis, Scott ... BS 91, 92
Wolkowicz, Leo R. ... BS 40, 41
Wolschlager, Brian ... BS 83, 84
Wolters, Kenneth ... CC 88, 90, 91 / TR 91, 92
Won, Douglas ... FB 72
Wonch, Ted N. ... TR 41, 42, 43, 46C
Wood, J. Edward ... BX 43
Wood, Michael J. ... SW 61, 62, 63C
Wood, Robert ... TR 89, 90
Wood, William L. Jr. ... SW 61, 62, 63
Wood, William W. ... BK 16
Woodin, George B. ... WR 58, 59
Woodruff, Janet ... LA 83M
Woods, Anthony ... FB 81, 82
Woods, Brian ... WR 91, 92C
Woods, Ryan ... FB 2001, 02
Woods, Stanley H. ... TR 25
Woodstra, Harvey P. ... TR 38
Woodward, Mike ... WR 2001
Woodward, Rob ... HO 90, 91, 92, 93
Woodworth, Fred L. ... FB 1897
Woodworth, Thomas L. ... FB 30M
Woody, Troy ... FB 88
Wooley, Billie V., Jr. ... BS 66M, 67M
Woolf, Harry R. ... HO 63, 64, 65C
Woolley, Jason ... HO 89, 90, 91CoC
Worden, Scott ... HO 91, 92, 93, 94
Workman, Robert ... GO 66
Worthem, Fred ... WR 79, 80, 82, 83CoC
Worthington, Robert ... BK 87, 88
Wostl, Eric ... SO 78, 79, 80
Woulfe, Richard T. ... GO 69, 70, 71CoC
Wowk, Andrew ... SO 83, 84, 86
Woyahn, Harlan ... TN 75
Wren, Leon P. ... TR 41
Wright, Bruce ... SW 73, 74, 75, 76
Wright, Charles ... FC 83
Wright, Curtis ... TN 83, 84, 85
Wright, Donald M. ... FB 57, 58, 59C
Wright, Edward ... BK 87, 88CoC
Wright, Harry A. ... FB 05

Wright, James H. .... CC 35 / TR 35, 36, 37
Wright, Marvin .... FB 93, 94, 95, 96
Wright, Scott .... FC 93
Wright, Shawn .... FB 96, 97, 98, 99
Wright, Thomas .... FB 99, 2000, 01, 02CoC
Wulf, John (Jack) V. .... BK 47, 48, 49CoC
Wulff, James F. .... FB 55, 56, 58
Wyatt, Clinton .... SW 96
Wycinsky, Craig .... FB 68, 69
Wylie, Henry .... CC 27C / TR 26, 27, 28C
Yamamoto, Steven M. .... SW 67
Yanik, Gregory L. .... LA 72
Yap, James .... LA 94, 95
Yarema, David .... FB 82, 84, 85, 86CoC
Yarger, Kenneth W. .... TR 29, 30, 31
Yarian, Stephen E. .... FB 64
Yatchman, Michael W. .... TN 49
Yeaster, Greg .... FB 2002
Yee, Dennis .... GY 77
Yee, Wayne .... FC 76, 77
Yengo, Gregory .... LA 83, 84, 85, 86
Yens, Chris .... BS 97, 98, 99
Yerkes, Donald P. .... BS 1886, 87C / TR 1886, 87
Yewcic, Thomas .... FB 51, 52, 53 / BS 53, 54
Yocca, John .... FB 48, 50
Yokom, Donald .... LA 73, 75
Yorimoto, Steven .... TN 80, 81, 82, 83C
York, Eugene A. .... TR 49M
York, Michael .... HO 96, 97, 98CoC, 99CoC
Younes, Soleman .... SO 77, 78
Young, Barney C. .... CC 69
Young, Christopher .... FC 79, 80
Young, Drew 99, 2000
Young, Duane .... FB 88, 89, 90 / BS 87, 90
Young, Edmund C. .... FB 18
Young, Gerald A. .... CC 60, 61 / TR 62
Young, Gregory T. .... FB 75
Young, H. Earl .... FB 1901M
Young, Hendricks M. .... FB 58
Young, John L. .... BK 60
Young, Lawrence .... BS 82
Young, Lonnie .... FB 81, 82, 83, 84 / TR 84
Young, Michael S. .... FB 67, 68

Young, Norman .... WR 59, 60, 61
Young, Robert G. .... BS 41, 42
Young, Russell .... GY 99, 2000, 01
Young, Steve .... TR 75, 76, 77
Youngs, Edward W. .... FB 61, 62, 63
Youngs, Michael .... TN 65, 66C
Yuhse, Frank J. .... FB 13M
Zabor, Rick .... TR 74, 75
Zacks, Kenneth W. .... HO 59M, 60M, 61M
Zafran, Frederick .... GY 71
Zagers, Bert A. .... FB 52, 53, 54
Zahnow, Jake .... LA 93
Zajdel, Stan .... LA 89, 90, 92, 93
Zalar, Edward J. .... FB 55
Zaremba, Michael F. .... TN 57
Zarza, Louis F. .... FB 33, 34, 35
Zbiciak, Edward .... BS 48, 49
Zdrauko, Rom .... SO 73, 74, 75, 76
Zeitler, John W. .... BS 52, 53, 54C
Zemper, Eric .... TR 64, 65, 67 / CC 66
Zenas, Mark .... WR 89
Zensen, John .... SO 68
Zerbe, Jerry A. .... CC 50, 51, 52 / TR 51, 52
Ziegel, Frederick K. .... FB 34, 35, 36 / BS 34, 35, 36 / SW 34, 35,36
Ziegenfus, Gilbert A. .... SW 39C & TR 39
Ziegert, David .... GY 70, 71, 72, 73
Ziegler, Nickolas J. .... FB 45
Zielinski, Kevin .... SW 89, 90, 91, 93CoC
Zielinski, Tom ... CC 77M, 78M, 79M / TR 78M, 79M
Ziemann, Frederick S. .... TN 43
Ziemke, Kirk .... SW 2001
Zienteck, Gabriel .... WR 2000
Zimmer, Mark .... FB 81M, 82M
Zimmer, Michael .... FB 80M, 81M, 82M
Zimmerman, Delmar R. .... BS 25, 26, 27 / TR 25
Zimmerman, Matt .... BK 93M, 95M, 96M, 97M
Zimmerman, Paul .... SO 82, 83, 84, 85
Zindel, Barry L. .... FB 59
Zindel, Bruce .... WR 70, 72
Zindel, Greg .... WR 72
Zindel, Howard C. .... FB 34, 35, 36
Zindel, Jack D. .... WR 68, 69, 70 / FB 68
Zindel, Jeff .... WR 72, 73, 74C

Zinn, Jack .... GO 50, 51, 52C
Zito, James J. .... FB 46, 47 / TR 47, 48, 49
Zobel, Richard J. .... TR 46
Zolynsky, Paul .... TR 73, 74, 75
Zoppa, Ralph M. .... TR 68, 59, 70, 71 / CC 69, 70
Zorn, William .... FB 62
Zsigo, Gary .... BS 98, 99, 2000
Zucco, Victor .... FB 56
Zulauf, Jon .... BK 90, 91, 92, 93
Zurakowski, William .... BX 41, 42, 43C
Zuverink, Mark .... TR 80
Zvoda, Alvin P. .... BS 51
Zylman, Brad .... SW 85, 86. 87, 88
Zylstra, William H. .... GO 40, 41CoC
Zylstra, William .... GO 73
Zysk, Donald H. .... FB 55, 56, 57

Bibliography

Books:

A Memoir by John Hannah, 1980.
Athletic Journal's Encyclopedia of Basketball by Tom Ecker and Don King, 1983.
Anatomy of the Game by David M. Nelson, 1994.
Big Ten Football by John D. McCallum, 1976.
College Basketball USA by John D. McCallum, 1980.
Encyclopedia of Sports by Frank G. Menke, 1945.
Guinness Book of the 20th Century, 2000.
A History of the Michigan Agricultural College and Biographical Sketches of Trustees and Professors by William Beal, 1915.
Michigan State, the First Hundred Years by Madison Kuhn, 1955.
My Life by Earvin Johnson, 1992.
NCAA Championships (The Official National Collegiate Championships Record Book), 2002.
Pictorial History of American Sports by John Durant and Otto Bettmann, 1965.
Spartan Saga (A History of Michigan State's Athletics) by Fred W. Stabley, 1972.
The Annual Record (MAC-MSC annual report), 1914-1988.
The Big Ten Conference Record Book, 2002.
The Illustrated History of the 20th Century edited by Ted Smart, 1993.
The Michigan State University Media Guides (for sundry sports) published by the MSU Sports Information Department, 2002-2003.
The Spartans (Michigan State Football) by Fred W. Stabley, 1988.
The Timetables of American History edited by Laurence Urdang, 1980.
The Wolverine school yearbook (titled the *Heliostat* in—1896, 1907), 1910-1975.
Time Almanac, 2003.

Periodicals:

Chicago Tribune
Detroit Free Press
The Detroit News
The Lansing Republican
The Lansing State Journal
The Record (a student publication 1896-1912, as an alumni journal 1913-1948)
The State News (the *Speculum* in 1883-1895 and the *Holcad* in 1903-1925)

DOUG PENSINGER / GETTY IMAGES

Sparty, the seven-foot walking (but not talking MSU mascot) made his first appearance prior to the football home-opener against Miami (OH) on September 16, 1989. Predecessor student-made papier-mâché headpieces of the affable character were on display as far back as the 1950s. They were crude productions compared to today's $8,000 full-bodied professionally designed costume.